Blue Book of Acoustic Guitars

15th Edition

by Zachary R. Fjestad

$29.95
Publisher's Suggested List Price

15th Edition Blue Book of Acoustic Guitars™

Publisher's Note: This book is the result of continual guitar research accomplished by attending guitar shows, receiving contributing editor's updates, tracking auction results, communicating with guitar dealers and collectors throughout the country each year, and staying on top of trends as they occur. This book represents an analysis of prices and information on currently manufactured, recently manufactured, and vintage/collectible guitars.

Although every reasonable effort has been made to compile an accurate and reliable guide, guitar prices may vary significantly depending on such factors as the locality of the sale, the number of sales we were able to consider, famous musician endorsement of certain makes/models, regional economic conditions, and other critical factors.

Accordingly, no representation can be made that the guitars listed may be bought or sold at prices indicated, nor shall the editor or publisher be responsible for any error made in compiling and recording such prices.

No part of this publication may be reproduced in any form whatsoever, by photograph, mimeograph, PDF files, facsimile (fax) transmission, or any other mechanical or electronic means. Nor can it be broadcast or transmitted, by translation into any language, nor by recording electronically or otherwise, without the express written permission from the publisher - except by a reviewer, who may quote brief passages for critical articles and/or reviews.

The percentage breakdown of a guitar's condition factor with respective values per condition as utilized in the Photo Grading System™ is a trademark of Blue Book Publications, Inc. Any unauthorized usage of this grading system for the evaluation of a guitar's value and photo percentage breakdown is expressly forbidden by the publisher.

Blue Book Publications, Inc.
8009 34th Avenue South, Suite 250
Minneapolis, MN 55425 U.S.A.
Orders Only: 800-877-4867
Phone: 952-854-5229
Fax: 952-853-1486
Email: support@bluebookinc.com
Website: http://bluebookofguitarvalues.com

Published and printed in the United States of America
ISBN: 1-936120-57-7
ISBN 13: 978-1-936120-57-4

15th Edition *Blue Book of Acoustic Guitars* Credits:

Production Manager & Art Director - Clint H. Schmidt
Cover Layout & Design - Clint H. Schmidt & Zachary R. Fjestad
Proofreading/Copyediting – Kelsey Fjestad & Zachary R. Fjestad
Cover Guitar - Front Cover: Taylor 615CE
Printing Representative - Bang Printing, Brainerd, MN

TABLE OF CONTENTS

GENERAL INFORMATION

Many of you have probably purchased products from Blue Book Publications, Inc. over the years, and it may be helpful for you to know more about the company operation and what we are currently publishing, both in books and electronic products. We are also the leaders in online informational services in various fields of collectibles, including guns. As this edition goes to press, the following titles, products, and services are currently available. Please check our website for more information, including pricing, availability, and S/H charges on all products.

Guitar Related Products & Services:

15th Edition *Blue Book of Electric Guitars,* by Zachary R. Fjestad, pub. date 2014

15th Edition *Blue Book of Acoustic Guitars,* by Zachary R. Fjestad, pub. date 2014

15th Edition *Blue Book of Guitars* on DVD, pub. date 2014

4th Edition *Blue Book of Guitar Amplifiers,* by Zachary R. Fjestad, pub. date 2010

4th Edition *Blue Book of Guitar Amplifiers* on CD-ROM, pub. date 2010

The Marshall Bluesbreaker - The Story of Marshall's First Combo, by John R. Wiley, pub. date 2010

Gibson Amplifiers 1933-2008 – 75 Years of the Gold Tone, by Wallace Marx, Jr. pub. date 2009

Gibson Flying V – Second Edition, by Larry Meiners & Zachary R. Fjestad, pub. date 2007

B.B. King's Lucille and the Loves Before Her by Eric E. Dahl, pub. date 2013

Online Subscription Services:

Please visit our website for more information, as well as sample pages for most titles.

Firearms Related Products & Services:

35th Edition *Blue Book of Gun Values,* by S.P. Fjestad, pub. date 2014

5th Edition *Blue Book of Tactical Firearms Values,* by S.P. Fjestad, edited by John B. Allen & David Kosowski, pub. date 2014

11th Edition *Blue Book of Airguns,* by Dr. Robert Beeman & John B. Allen, pub. date 2014

8th Edition *Blue Book of Modern Black Powder Arms,* by John B. Allen, pub. date 2013

The Book of Colt Paper - 1834-2011, by John Ogle, pub. date 2011

The Book of Colt Memorabilia, by John Ogle, pub. date 2014

3rd Edition *The Book of Colt Firearms,* by R.L. Wilson, pub. date 2008

2nd Edition *Blue Book Pocket Guide for Colt Dates of Manufacture,* by R.L. Wilson, pub. date 2012

Firmo & Francesca Fracassi – Master Engravers, by Elena Micheli-Lamboy & Stephen Lamboy, pub. date 2008

Giancarlo & Stefano Pedretti – Master Engravers, by Elena Micheli-Lamboy & Stephen Lamboy, pub. date 2010

Mario Terzi – Master Engraver, by Elena Micheli-Lamboy & Stephen Lamboy, pub. date 2011

American Gunsmiths, 2nd Edition, by Frank Sellers, pub. date 2008

5th Edition *Ammo Encyclopedia,* by Michael Bussard, edited by John B. Allen and David Kosowski, pub. date 2014

John Bianchi - An American Legend - 50 Years of Gunleather, by Dennis Adler, pub. date 2010

Parker Gun Identification & Serialization, compiled by Charlie Price and edited by S.P. Fjestad, pub. date 2002

If you would like to order or get more information about any of the above publications/products, simply contact us at:

Blue Book Publications, Inc.

8009 34th Avenue South, Suite 250

Minneapolis, MN 55425 USA

http://bluebookofguitarvalues.com

800-877-4867 (toll-free domestic), Ext. 3 for operator

952-854-5229 (non-domestic) • Fax: 952-853-1486

CONTACT INFORMATION

Since our phone system has been updated to auto-attendant technology, please follow the prompts and use the following extension numbers when contacting our staff:

Office hours are: 8:30 a.m. - 5:00 p.m. CST, Monday – Friday, except major holidays.

Ext. 1000 - Beth Schreiber	(beths@bluebookinc.com)	Ext. 1700 - Zachary R. Fjestad (zachf@bluebookinc.com)
Ext. 1200 - Karl Stoffels	(karls@bluebookinc.com)	Ext. 1800 - Tom Stock (toms@bluebookinc.com)
Ext. 1300 - S.P. Fjestad	(stevef@bluebookinc.com)	Ext. 1900 - Kate Steffenson (kates@bluebookinc.com)
Ext. 1400 - Kelsey Fjestad	(kelseyf@bluebookinc.com)	Ext. 2000 - Adam Burt (adamb@bluebookinc.com)
Ext. 1500 - Clint H. Schmidt	(clints@bluebookinc.com)	Ext. 2200 - Shauna Ritter (shaunar@bluebookinc.com)
Ext. 1600 - John B. Allen	(johna@bluebookinc.com)	

General Email: support@bluebookinc.com (checked several times daily)

Guitar Website: http://bluebookofguitarvalues.com

Guitar Email: guitars@bluebookinc.com

Facebook: Blue Book of Guitar Values

YouTube: Blue Book of Guitar Values

Customer Service: 800-877-4867 or Phone: 952-854-5229

Additionally, an automated message service is available for both ordering and leaving messages.

Fax: 952-853-1486 (available 24 hours a day)

We would like to thank all of you for your business in the past - you are the reason(s) we are successful. Our goal remains the same - to give you the best products, the most accurate and up-to-date information for the money, and the highest level of customer service available in today's marketplace. When it's right, spread the word. If it's wrong, we want to know about it.

MEET THE STAFF

Many of you may want to know what the person on the other end of the telephone/fax/email looks like, so here are the faces that go with the voices and emails.

S.P. Fjestad
Author/Publisher

Zachary R. Fjestad
Author/Editor Guitar &
Amp Division

Adam Burt
President

John B. Allen
Author & Associate
Editor Arms Division

Tom Stock
CFO

Clint H. Schmidt
Art Director

Karl Stoffels
Lead Developer

Kelsey Fjestad
Web Media Manager/
Proofreader

Kate Steffenson
Executive Editor

Beth Schreiber
Operations Manager

Shauna Ritter
Operations

ACKNOWLEDGEMENTS

Contributing Editors

Contributing Editors are the people who take certain sections of the book and physically revise it. Aside from the author, the contributing editors are the next in line for providing critical information and pricing updates. Without these contributors, many sections of this book would be a lot skinnier and we appreciate the time they take to help us out.

John Beeson, The Music Shoppe
Steve Brown www.vintaxe.com
Walter Carter
Barry Clark
Eric Cummins, Wilcutt Guitars
Chris Emery

Eric Dahl
Teddy Gordon, Make'N Music
Dave Hinson, Killer Vintage
David Johnson
Michael Jones, Michael Jones Vintage Guitars
Larry Meiners, Flying Vintage

Walter Murray, Frankenstein Fretworks
Fred Oster, Vintage Instruments
Jay Pilzer, New Hope Guitar Traders
Edward Pitt

Dave Rogers, Dave's Guitar Shop
Keith Smart, Zemaitis Guitar Owner's Club
Chris Trider, Blue Chip Guitars
Tom Van Hoose
Rick Wilkiewicz
Jay Wolfe, Wolfe Guitars

Friends of Blue Book

The following people don't necessarily have an active role in the actual content of the book, but they are important friends of ours in the industry. Whether seeing these people at shows, talking on the phone, or emailing, they are helpful in their own way and it's a privilege to have such nice friends!

Kent Armstrong
Bob & Cindy Benedetto
Dick Boak, Martin
Larry Briggs
Gurney Brown
John Brown, Brown's Guitar Factory
Dean Campbell, Campbell American Guitars
Zebuelon Cash-Lane - R.I.P.
Dave Crocker
Bill Dixon, Lakewood
Seymour Duncan
Ren Ferguson
S.J. "Frog" Forgey
Thom Fowle, Gibson Custom Shop

Rick Gembar, Gibson Custom Shop
Janet Godin, Godin Guitars
George Gruhn
Norm Harris
Paul Jernigan
Michael Keller
John Kinnemeyer, JK Lutherie
Don & Jeff Lace, Lace Music Products
Joe Lamond, NAMM
William "Grit" Laskin
Henry Lowenstein
Chris F. Martin IV, Martin Guitars
Willie Moseley
Tom Murphy
Joe Naylor, Reverend

Hartley Peavey, Peavey
Kevin Pederson, Pederson Custom Guitars
Brett Petrusek, DBZ Guitars
Mark Pollock
Jerry Reno, G.H. Reno
Greg Rich
Eugene Robertson
Scott Surine, Surine Basses
Paul Reed Smith, PRS Guitars
Chad Speck, Encore Guitars
Robert Steinegger, Steinegger Guitars
Ulrich Teuffel, Teuffel
Michael Tobias, MTD
Jimmy & Ryan Triggs, Triggs Guitars

Rick Turner, Renaissance Guitar Company
Larry Urie, PRS Guitars
Rick Vito
Mike Voltz, Gibson
Pete Wagener
Jimmy Wallace, Jimmy Wallace Guitars/Dallas Guitar Show
Lon Werner, Martin
Nate Westgor, Willie's American Guitars
Edwin Wilson, Gibson Custom Shop
Debra Wolstein, PRS Guitars

Photo Acknowledgements

The images in this book and on our website would not be possible without the following people's contributions. Many photos are taken at shows, and these dealers are nice enough and allow us to photograph them during the often hectic shows. Other people below have welcomed us to their stores/homes, allowed us to set up shop, and photograph their entire inventory/collection.

Dave Rogers, Dave's Guitar Shop
John Beeson, The Music Shoppe
Nate Westgor, Willie's American Guitars

Dale Hanson
Glenn Wetterland
S.P. Fjestad
Zachary R. Fjestad
Jimmy Wallace, Jimmy Wallace Guitars

Rick Wilkiewicz
Chris Emery
Jack Wadsworth
David J. Brass, Fretted Americana, Inc.
Harry Harris, GuitarTracker

Kelly Jones Violin Shop
David Chandler, R & R Guitars
George McGuire
Chad Speck, Encore Music

In Memoriam

Stan Jay, owner of the famous vintage guitar store Mandolin Brothers, passed away in 2014, leaving the guitar world without one of its most witty and knowledgeable personalities. In the pages of his monthly *Vintage News* newsletter, he informed us and entertained us, coining the phrase "wood and steel confection" for the guitars he loved so much. A leader in the vintage guitar industry, Stan will be missed by his many friends and clients.

Jack Wadsworth, a consummate musician from the Fort Worth area, was part of our original "Dallas guitar crew" and will be sorely missed. Jack never had a bad word to say about anyone. What we'll remember the most is sharing the gastronomical delicacies at Uncle Julio's Mexican Restaurant in Fort Worth in addition to Jack taking us to the DFW airport after the shows in Dallas and Arlington in his elongated Lincoln.

INTRODUCTION
by Zachary R. Fjestad

Welcome to the new and improved 15th Edition *Blue Book of Acoustic Guitars*. At 892 pages, no other book or publication comes even close to providing you with up-to-date acoustic guitar information and accurate values. We started this project in 1991 and continue to monitor not only the vintage guitar marketplace, but we strive to be at the forefront of new guitar manufacturers and models. Our goal is encompassing to include all guitars, not just the extremely collectible and valuable ones, but the less expensive and harder to find instruments. I've noticed several changes since our last edition.

MSR PRICING - 86'ED

In 2014, we saw the acceleration of manufacturers dropping MSR pricing and going strictly to MAP. For those unfamiliar with these terms, we use them heavily in this book. MSR (Manufacturer's Suggested Retail) is traditionally what manufacturers used to price their instruments; however, guitar dealers rarely sold them at this price - it was simply a benchmark. MAP (Minimum Advertised Pricing) appeared in the mid-1990s to help level the playing field between brick and mortar stores and the new rising technology called "the Internet." Twenty years later, many manufacturers exclusively use MAP pricing and disregard MSR. Large manufacturers such as Fender, PRS, and Gibson all abandoned MSR pricing in 2014. You'll notice in the book a lot of "N/A" listings in the MSR field, meaning there isn't one anymore.

NEXT YEAR'S MODEL

Also gone is the age of a manufacturer offering the same guitar over the course of several years. To generate interest (and sales), many manufacturers are producing an entirely different line of guitars from year-to-year. This is a challenge for us in the *Blue Book of Acoustic Guitars* because we don't have the physical space to list a different guitar each year (especially when the differences are so minor). Limited Editions are increasingly popular as well. Think of the number of J-45 variations offered over the past five years. During the 1970s, there was one J-45 produced for the entire *decade*. We'll continue to do our best to list as many guitars as possible, but the shift may force us to rely more heavily on our online offerings.

NEXT YEAR'S MODEL

Technology and guitars (once as compatible as oil and water and largely dismissed as unnecessary) are now part of nearly every manufacturer's line-up. The guitars in Martin's Performing Artist Series have become some of their most popular models. Utilizing Fishman electronics, the Performing Artist fills the need that many musicians are looking for in a guitar suitable for both studio and on stage. Gibson offers electronics as standard equipment on all of their acoustic guitars today. Look for technology to become even more important in the future.

VINTAGE PRICING

I believe we have finally hit the bottom of the vintage guitar market, and values overall are inching upward. Most collectible vintage acoustic guitars saw a modest gain since the last edition.

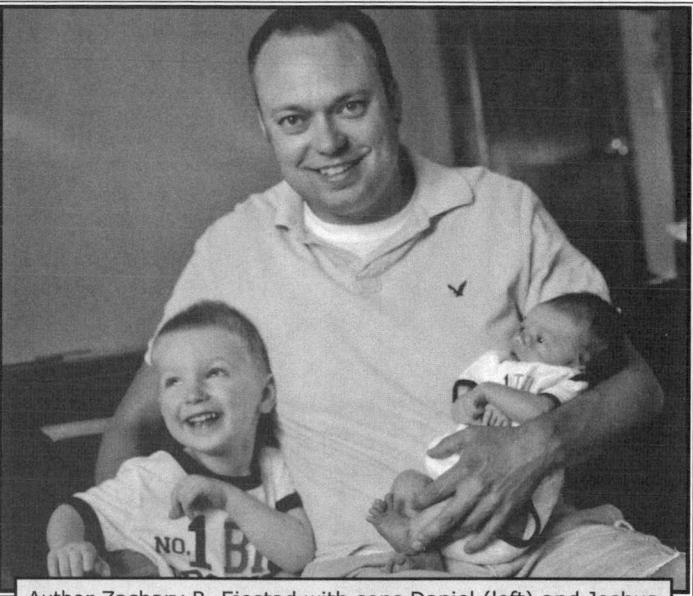

Author Zachary R. Fjestad with sons Daniel (left) and Joshua (right). Hopefully they'll both be playing guitar soon!

The acoustic guitar market was never inflated as much as the electric market (meaning guitar values didn't fall as hard), so many models didn't change at all in value. I hope we see a gradual increase in the future instead of the sharp rise we saw in the mid-2000s. Nobody wants to go through that again!

THANKS

Again, this book is more of a team effort each year. We're always adding models, but nothing gets deleted, which is why page count increases by each edition. This means there is that much more work to do on each edition, and I lean on several key staff members to get this book completed and they should be mentioned. Beth Schreiber, our operations manager, entered her first guitars into the database for this edition. Kelsey Fjestad (who is also my sister) continues to update more sections and joins me annually at the NAMM Show in Anaheim, CA. Clint Schmidt published another book in record time and continues to be one of the easiest guys to work with. I also have to thank my uncle, Steve Fjestad, for the opportunity to work on this project. Who wouldn't love to work with guitars every day?

Lastly, I want to thank all of our faithful readers - without you we wouldn't be publishing a book. I also want to hear feedback from you! There are thousands of guitars that could be added to this book, but we only have so much space and time, so please let me know what is important to see between these covers.

Sincerely,

Zachary R. Fjestad
Author
Blue Book of Acoustic Guitars

FOREWORD

Publisher's Note: I have decided to proxy my ink on this page to longtime friend Henry Lowenstein, who is one of the few people in this industry that's as passionate about fretted instruments as I am. Henry is the leading spokesman in trying to establish some middle ground quickly before some of the finest guitars ever manufactured may be considered illegal, with possible confiscation and criminal prosecution of the owner. S.P. Fjestad

Henry Lowenstein, longtime guitar aficionado, is shown playing (and enjoying) one of George Gruhn's rarer fretted instruments following this year's summer NAMM show in Nashville.

GUITAR COLLECTING AT THE CROSSROADS
BY HENRY LOWENSTEIN

For over 15 years, the *Blue Book of Acoustic Guitars* has been answering what we thought was a pretty straight forward question - "What is it worth?" Answering this question involved a collection of knowledge, a significant amount of elbow grease, and a dedicated staff with a cornucopia of advisors contributing information about sales trends, model styles, serial numbers and often the arcane history of identification. The Blue Books also developed a pictorial grading system for condition of instruments with the first, and as far as I know, only system of evaluation based on percentages of wear and tear, with ranges both buyers and sellers could compare and depend upon. With all these years of work in the music industry, imagine our shock, when just this year, that turned out to not be enough. Now we have to try to predict politics also.

Indeed, with an unprecedented number of Presidential Proclamations and the resultant executive orders concerning the implementation of the CITES (Convention on International Trade in Endangered Species) treaty taking effect this year, we now have no way of knowing what many guitars and other wooden instruments are worth. Worse, within ten years, we may

even be in a situation where the sale of anything with hundreds of common woods and shell material - whether they are endangered or not - will be illegal not only to other countries, but between states in the United States, and even within states themselves. You need only read the Presidential Strategy documents published by the White House concerning the future of environmental enforcement. Will future Blue Books need to add a category for political analysis along with condition and rarity? If something does not drastically change - the answer to that question is most likely yes.

Here's the shortest legal summary I can give you. Effective June 14, 2014, by Executive Order 13648 and Presidential Proclamation (FR Doc. 2013-16387), Brazilian Rosewood, elephant ivory (whether a fretboard dot, nut, bridge saddle, inlay, hundred-year-old tuner button, or even piano key with ivory top) along with over 1,000 other items on the Appendix I list of the CITES Agreement (Convention on International Trade in Endangered Species) became illegal to sell abroad and most likely, within the United States. I say "most likely" because the documents that produced this bizarre set of laws (now found within Volume 50 of the Code of Federal Regulations, Parts 13, 17, and 23) are so vague and contradictory, that no federal agency to date will provide a written ruling to the public on its exact interpretation or enforcement. And that's a pretty strong statement, considering that the very same Presidential Proclamation made no fewer than 14 federal agencies responsible for the implementation and enforcement of this "National Strategy for Combating Wildlife Trafficking," including the Department of Defense, Homeland Security, the NSA and the Office of the Director of National Intelligence! If you thought you had to worry about the government taking your guns, you were mistaken - it's your guitars they're after now.

I've been accused of being an alarmist (the definition of alarmist apparently means that you can read government-issued documents) and I wish I had the space to publish everything in my file. But since the publisher is worried about space, I will tell you a short, sad story. In my recent, unfortunate divorce, I spent approximately ten thousand dollars in legal and accounting fees just on the issue of the value of my guitar collection. I had the *Blue Book of Acoustic Guitars*, which was pretty specific about the values, but that wasn't in contention. The issue was that since this Presidential Proclamation, neither I nor my wife's attorney could find one appraiser or auction house that was willing to provide a written valuation or even an offer on my extensive guitar collection. Why? Because it contained Brazilian Rosewood and tiny little ivory pieces. With a little bit of research on Google, I found that I was not alone. This was happening everywhere. Even worse, while we could estimate the future value of a life insurance policy or annuity, nobody was willing to conjecture on the value of instruments (or antiques), all of which might be illegal to sell within ten years. Needless to say, my former wife and I settled our differences out of court, but if you think for a minute that these new laws, which have never been reviewed by Congress, do not affect you or your guitars, think again.

Henry Lowenstein is an international trade law attorney, a business owner, a guitar collector, and owns the Newport Guitar Festival

HOW TO USE THIS BOOK

When used properly, the 15th Edition *Blue Book of Acoustic Guitars* will provide you with more up-to-date acoustic guitar information and pricing than any other single source. With over 850 pages of specific guitar models and pricing, this publication continues to be more of a complete informational source than strictly a "hold-your-hand" pricing guide. In theory, you should be able to identify the trademark/name off the guitar's headstock (where applicable), and find out the country of origin, date(s) produced, and other company/model-related facts for that guitar. Many smaller, out-of-production trademarks and/or companies which are only infrequently encountered in the secondary marketplace are intentionally not priced in this text, as it is pretty hard to pin the tail on a donkey that is nowhere in sight. Unfortunately, this lack of information can be a disadvantage to sellers, who may find buyers saying, "Would you take any less? After all, nobody seems to know anything about it." In other words, don't confuse rarity with desirability when it comes to these informational voids. As in the past, if you own this current 15th Edition of the *Blue Book of Acoustic Guitars* and still have questions, we will try to assist you in identifying/evaluating your guitar(s). Please refer to page 19 for this service.

The values listed in the 15th Edition *Blue Book of Acoustic Guitars* are based on average national selling prices or "private party" values for both currently manufactured and vintage instruments. This is **NOT** a wholesale pricing guide – prices reflect what you should expect to pay for a guitar. More importantly, do not expect to walk into a music store, guitar shop, or pawn shop, and think that the proprietor should pay you the retail price listed in this text. Dealer offers on most models could be 30%-60% less than the values listed, depending upon desirability, locality, and profitability.

In other words, if you want to receive 100% of the value listed in the book, then you have to do 100% of the work (become the retailer, which also includes assuming 100% of the risk). Business is business, and making regular bank deposits usually means turning a profit every once in a while.

Currently manufactured guitars are typically listed with the manufacturer's suggested retail (MSR), a 100% value (reflecting standard market place discounting if applicable such as MAP - Minimum Advertised Pricing or Street Pricing - the price the guitar sells for in a store), and in most cases, values for both Excellent and Average condition factors are included. Please consult the digital color Photo Grading System (pages 25-39) to learn more about the condition of your guitar(s). The *Blue Book of Acoustic Guitars* will continue using selected photos to illustrate real world condition factors and/or problems. Since condition is the overriding factor in price evaluation, study these photos carefully. As the saying goes, one picture can be worth a thousand words.

For your convenience, an explanation of factors that can affect condition and pricing, guitar grading systems, how to convert them, and descriptions of individual condition factors appear on pages 23-24 to assist you in learning more about guitar grading systems and individual condition factors. Please read these pages carefully, as the values in this publication are based on the grading/condition factors listed. This will be especially helpful when evaluating older vintage instruments. Remember, the price is wrong if the condition factor isn't right.

All values within this text assume original condition. The grading lines within the *Blue Book of Acoustic Guitars* reflect the 100%, Excellent, and Average condition factors only. From the vintage marketplace or (especially) a collector's point of view, any repairs, alterations, modifications, "enhancements," "improvements," "professionally modified to a more desirable configuration," or any other non-factory changes usually detract from an instrument's value. Please refer to page 23 regarding an explanation to finishes, repairs, alterations/modifications, and other elements which have to be factored in before determining the correct condition. Depending on the seriousness of the modification/alteration, you may have to lower the condition factor when re-computing prices for these alterations. Determining values for damaged and/or previously repaired instruments will usually depend on the parts and labor costs necessary to return them to playable and/or original specifications.

We also still have the ability to view all images included in the *Blue Book of Acoustic Guitars* on our website. Within the text, a small guitar icon ⌾ appears whenever a corresponding image(s) is available and you can refer to our website to see a full color guitar image at http://images. bluebookofguitarvalues.com

The 15th Edition *Blue Book of Acoustic Guitars* provides many company histories, notes on influential luthiers and designers, and other bits of knowledge as a supplement to the make/model format. Hopefully, this information will alleviate those "gray areas" of the unknown, and shed light on many new luthiers who have emerged within the past several decades, and produce excellent quality instruments.

Starting with the 12th Edition, we reformatted and redesigned the *Blue Book of Acoustic Guitars* to maximize the value of the book. We utilize as much white space as possible (paper isn't cheap), printed on thinner paper, and instead of including a few select black and white images, we have every image in the *Blue Book of Acoustic Guitars* database (over 4,000 guitar images) accessible for viewing on our website! Simply go to http://images.bluebookofguitarvalues.com to begin browsing our image database. We hope that this is still an easy-to-use (and consistent) text format that will assist you in quickly finding specific information. The following pages detail every component that you will encounter in the 15th Edition *Blue Book of Acoustic Guitars*.

EASTMAN   219 **E**

E SECTION
EASTMAN

6

CONTACT INFORMATION

EASTMAN
2138 Pomona Boulevard
Pomona, CA 91768
Phone No.: 800-624-0270
Fax No.: 800-390-7416
www.eastmanguitars.com
info@eastmanstrings.com

Instruments currently produced in China. Distributed in the U.S. by Eastman Strings.

Eastman Strings was founded by Qian Ni in 1992. Qian came from China to the U.S. to study music, and, at first, started importing violins from his hometown in China. Shortly after this he founded a workshop with several master violinmakers, using old world techniques. Now they produce a wide variety of instruments including guitars, violins, cellos, basses, bows, and other accessories. For models with exposed pickups, refer to the *Blue Book of Electric Guitars*. For more information, visit Eastman's website or contact them directly.

ACOUSTIC ARCHTOP

Eastman produces both flattops and archtops. Archtop models include the Uptown Professional series with models **AR800** (disc. 2006, last MSR was $1,895), **AR804** (disc. 2009, last MSR was $1,995), **AR804C** Cutaway (disc. 2009, last MSR was $2,195), **AR805** (MSR $1,995), **AR805C** Cutaway (disc. 2009, last MSR was $2,195), the **AR810** (disc. 2009, last MSR was $2,095), and the **AR810C** Cutaway (disc. 2009, last MSR was $2,295). The Uptown Luxury series include the **AR900** (disc. 2006, last MSR was $2,895), **AR904** (disc. 2009, last MSR was $2,895), the **AR904C** Cutaway (disc. 2009, last MSR was $3,095), **AR905** (disc. 2009, last MSR was $2,995), the **AR905C** Cutaway (disc. 2009, last MSR was $3,195), the **AR910** (disc. 2006, last MSR was $3,095), and the **AR910C** Cutaway (disc. 2009, last MSR was $3,295). The 800/900 series feature oval soundholes. The 804/904 have a suspended neck over the body. The 805/905 series have f-holes. The 810/910 series have a 17 in. body with f-holes.

In 2004, Jim Fisch started working at Eastman Guitars and after his sudden death in 2006, Eastman introduced a line of guitars named after him in 2007. The Jim Fisch Mahogany Archtop Guitar comes in a variety of configurations. Models include the **AR604** (disc. 2009, last MSR was $1,695), the **AR604C** Cutaway (disc. 2009, last MSR was $1,795), the **AR605** (MSR $1,695), the **AR605C** Cutaway (disc. 2009, last MSR was $1,795), the **AR610** (MSR $1,795), and the **AR610C** Cutaway (disc. 2009, last MSR was $1,895).

ACOUSTIC FLATTOP

Flattop guitars include the Super Jumbo series with models **SJ400** (disc. 2004, last MSR $950), SJ600 (disc. 2004, last MSR $1,250), 2004, last MSR $1,650). Standard flattop and flatback acoustic guitars co... variety of configurations and all ...odels ...ns an...

---

1. Manufacturer/Trademark Name - The manufacturer, trademark, brand name, luthier, company, importer, or distributor is listed in uppercase and bold type. These are centered on each page and listed alphabetically throughout the book

2. Manufacturer/Trademark Status - Any information regarding the production status of the manufacturer is listed directly below the manufacturer name. This includes whether instruments are currently or were previously produced, when they were produced, where they were produced, and any distributor and/or importer information.

3. Manufacturer/Trademark Description - This area typically describes the history of the manufacturer and/or trademark/brand. If the section is small enough, all following information may be included in this area including model descriptions and pricing.

4. Category Name - When a manufacturer/trademark is long enough, the section may be split up into categories. Category names appear in bold uppercase and are centered on each page. Categories are typically broken up into the instruments' primary configuration (Acoustic, Acoustic-Electric, Acoustic Bass, etc.). Categories may also include general information, identification, options, etc.

5. Category Description - Some categories may have a description (some categories may only have a description with no models). This description contains information specific to the category.

6. Contact Information – On most current manufacturers and a select few previous manufacturers who still are accessible, their contact information will appear in a gray box below the manufacturer name and justified to the right. This used to appear in the Trademark Index at the back of the book, but it is included directly in the text now.

7. Model Name and Description - Categories are typically comprised of individual model listings and descriptions. A model name is listed in bold uppercase text, flush left, and they are typically listed alpha-numerically. Manufacturer model designations/codes may appear in parentheses after the model name (i.e. Fender has a number code for every model). A model name is followed by the description, and contains important information specific to the model name. Typically, this includes type of body style/design, wood(s) used, identifying features such as inlays, bridge type, frets (14/20 refers to an instrument with 20 frets, 14 which are clear of the body), tuners, year of mfg., finishes, etc.

8. Price Lines - Price lines are typically located directly under a model description. These are used to evaluate the individual model, and price ranges appear in Excellent and Average condition factors. A grading bar appears on the top of all pages that contain at least one price line. Many price lines in the *Blue Book of Acoustic Guitars* include either an instrument's MSR or Notes line (see Grading Line, #9), 100% price, Excellent price range, Average price range, and last MSR (if known). These five areas make up all pricing for the book:

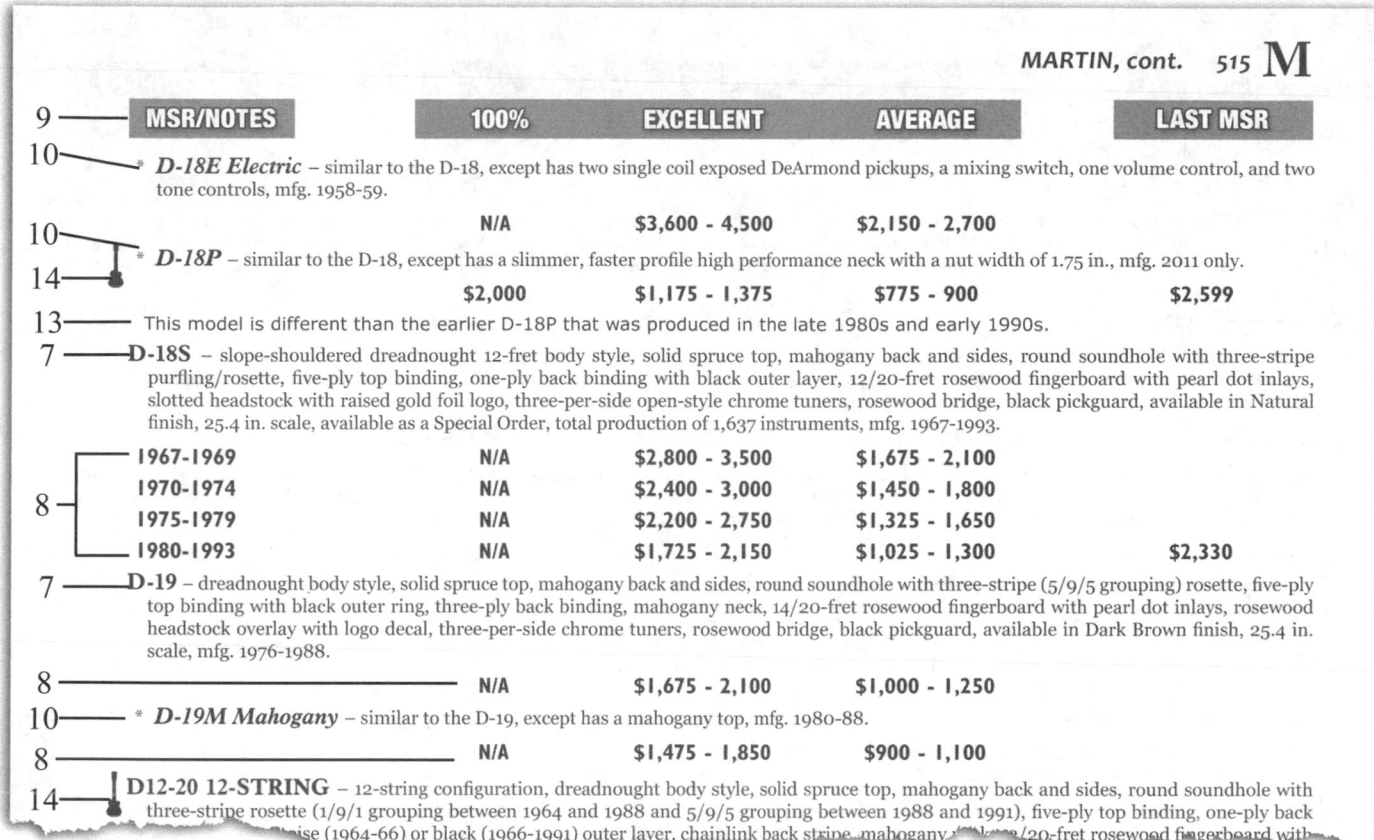

9 — | **MSR/NOTES** | **100%** | **EXCELLENT** | **AVERAGE** | **LAST MSR** |

10 — * **D-18E Electric** – similar to the D-18, except has two single coil exposed DeArmond pickups, a mixing switch, one volume control, and two tone controls, mfg. 1958-59.

| | N/A | $3,600 - 4,500 | $2,150 - 2,700 | |

10 —
14 — * **D-18P** – similar to the D-18, except has a slimmer, faster profile high performance neck with a nut width of 1.75 in., mfg. 2011 only.

| | $2,000 | $1,175 - 1,375 | $775 - 900 | $2,599 |

13 — This model is different than the earlier D-18P that was produced in the late 1980s and early 1990s.

7 — **D-18S** – slope-shouldered dreadnought 12-fret body style, solid spruce top, mahogany back and sides, round soundhole with three-stripe purfling/rosette, five-ply top binding, one-ply back binding with black outer layer, 12/20-fret rosewood fingerboard with pearl dot inlays, slotted headstock with raised gold foil logo, three-per-side open-style chrome tuners, rosewood bridge, black pickguard, available in Natural finish, 25.4 in. scale, available as a Special Order, total production of 1,637 instruments, mfg. 1967-1993.

8 —
1967-1969	N/A	$2,800 - 3,500	$1,675 - 2,100	
1970-1974	N/A	$2,400 - 3,000	$1,450 - 1,800	
1975-1979	N/A	$2,200 - 2,750	$1,325 - 1,650	
1980-1993	N/A	$1,725 - 2,150	$1,025 - 1,300	$2,330

7 — **D-19** – dreadnought body style, solid spruce top, mahogany back and sides, round soundhole with three-stripe (5/9/5 grouping) rosette, five-ply top binding with black outer ring, three-ply back binding, mahogany neck, 14/20-fret rosewood fingerboard with pearl dot inlays, rosewood headstock overlay with logo decal, three-per-side chrome tuners, rosewood bridge, black pickguard, available in Dark Brown finish, 25.4 in. scale, mfg. 1976-1988.

8 — | | N/A | $1,675 - 2,100 | $1,000 - 1,250 | |

10 — * **D-19M Mahogany** – similar to the D-19, except has a mahogany top, mfg. 1980-88.

8 — | | N/A | $1,475 - 1,850 | $900 - 1,100 | |

14 — **D12-20 12-STRING** – 12-string configuration, dreadnought body style, solid spruce top, mahogany back and sides, round soundhole with three-stripe rosette (1/9/1 grouping between 1964 and 1988 and 5/9/5 grouping between 1988 and 1991), five-ply top binding, one-ply back ... ise (1964-66) or black (1966-1991) outer layer, chainlink back stripe, mahogany ... 0/20-fret rosewood fingerboard with ...headstock, si...le chro...ner with...

MSR/Notes: If the model is currently manufactured, and has a factory retail price, the MSR price will appear flush left. If a model justifies more than one price line, the Notes will indicate what features or years of manufacture are represented by the additional price lines. The *Blue Book of Acoustic Guitars* does not display decimal points - all MSR prices that have decimals are rounded to the nearest dollar (i.e. $666.67 = $667).

100%: The 100% condition factor (new), when encountered in a currently manufactured guitar, assumes the guitar has not been previously sold at retail and includes a factory warranty. A currently manufactured new instrument must include EVERYTHING the factory originally provided with the instrument – including the case (if originally included), warranty card, instruction manual (if any), hanging tags (if any), etc. If the model is currently or recently manufactured (2010 or later), the value will appear in this column. This is the price a consumer should expect to pay on an instrument, which includes all standard discounting, and usually takes into consideration factory MAP (Minimum Advertised Pricing). Nearly all manufacturers establish retail pricing, but instruments rarely sell for the MSR, and sell closer to the MAP. If the instrument is 2009 or older, or is currently not available for sale, an N/A (Not Applicable) will appear in this field.

Excellent: If the model is in excellent condition, the value range will be displayed in this column. The lowest value in this range represents Low Excellent condition while the higher one represents High Excellent condition. The High Excellent condition factor represents a slightly used instrument that appears new but no longer qualifies for 100% since it has already sold at retail, and may be worth only 50%-90% of its current MSR, depending on

the overall desirability factor. On currently/recently manufactured instruments, there usually is a fairly large price difference between the 100% and High Excellent condition factors due to used instrument pricing, which typically is affected by dealer replacement costs. Refer to the Photo Grading System on pages 25-39 to determine the condition of your instrument. An N/A may also appear in this condition factor indicating the instrument's rarity precludes accurate pricing.

Average: If the model is in average condition, the value range will be displayed in this column. The lowest value in this range represents Low Average condition while the higher one represents High Average condition. Refer to the Photo Grading System on pages 25-39 to determine the condition of your instrument.

Last MSR: Once a model is discontinued, the MSR will be moved to this column. While the last MSR of a model is generally used for historical purposes, it is also useful for determining used values, especially on run-of-the-mill instruments. Many guitar dealers look at the last MSR and base the used value off of that.

9. Grading Line - This acoustic grading line is the typical page header, and provides three distinct column locations (left to right) including the manufacturer's suggested retail (MSR) on currently manufactured instruments (if published). Important notes may also be part of this column, which include year/period of manufacture, identifying features, options, etc. that may result in multiple price lines per model. The wide middle column includes all pertinent new/used evaluating including the 100%/New value, the Excellent value range, and the Average value range. The last column indicates

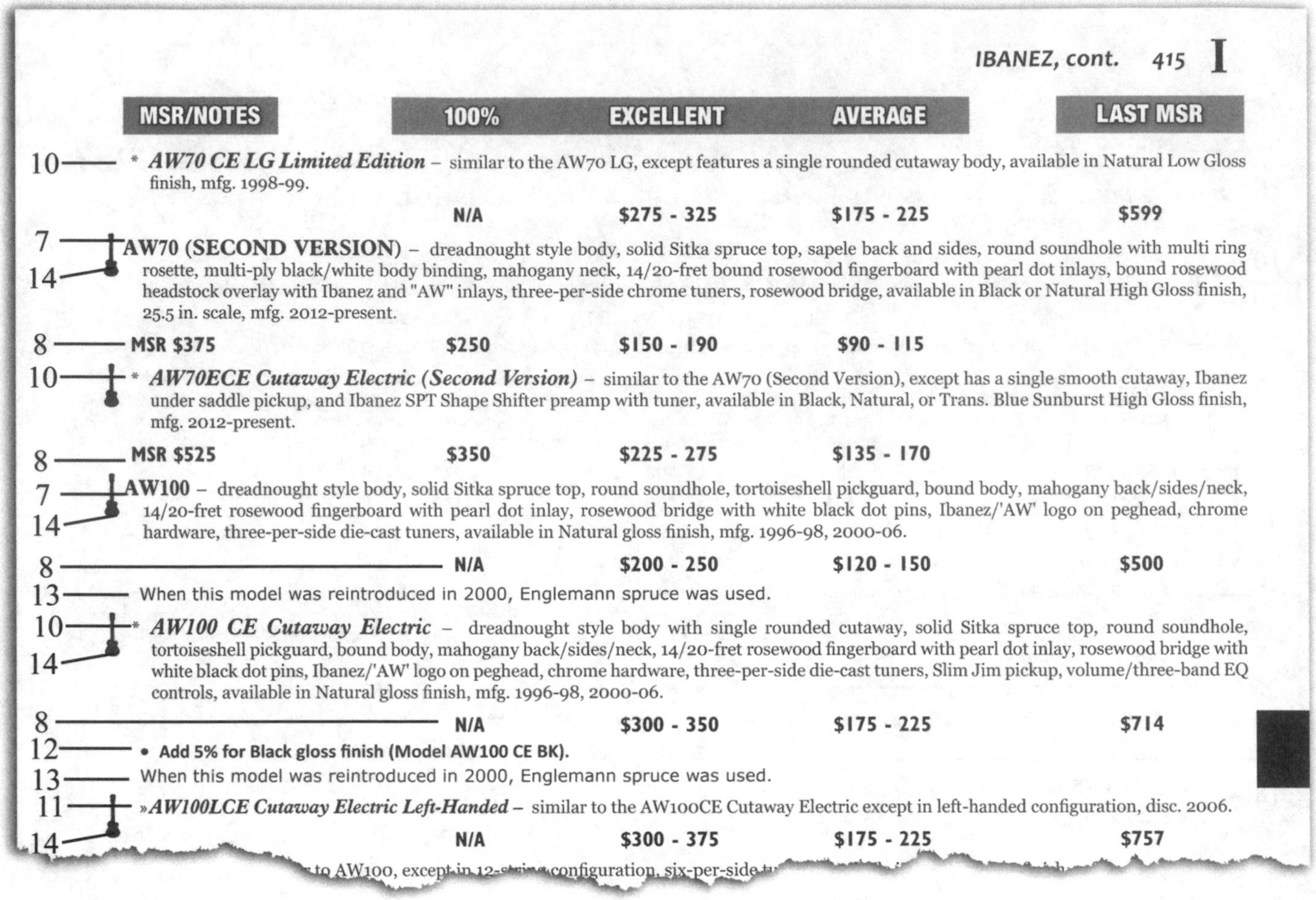

MSR/NOTES	100%	EXCELLENT	AVERAGE	LAST MSR
10 — * **AW70 CE LG Limited Edition** – similar to the AW70 LG, except features a single rounded cutaway body, available in Natural Low Gloss finish, mfg. 1998-99.				
	N/A	$275 - 325	$175 - 225	$599
7 — **AW70 (SECOND VERSION)** – dreadnought style body, solid Sitka spruce top, sapele back and sides, round soundhole with multi ring rosette, multi-ply black/white body binding, mahogany neck, 14/20-fret bound rosewood fingerboard with pearl dot inlays, bound rosewood headstock overlay with Ibanez and "AW" inlays, three-per-side chrome tuners, rosewood bridge, available in Black or Natural High Gloss finish, 25.5 in. scale, mfg. 2012-present.				
8 — MSR $375	$250	$150 - 190	$90 - 115	
10 — * **AW70ECE Cutaway Electric (Second Version)** – similar to the AW70 (Second Version), except has a single smooth cutaway, Ibanez under saddle pickup, and Ibanez SPT Shape Shifter preamp with tuner, available in Black, Natural, or Trans. Blue Sunburst High Gloss finish, mfg. 2012-present.				
8 — MSR $525	$350	$225 - 275	$135 - 170	
7 — **AW100** – dreadnought style body, solid Sitka spruce top, round soundhole, tortoiseshell pickguard, bound body, mahogany back/sides/neck, 14/20-fret rosewood fingerboard with pearl dot inlay, rosewood bridge with white black dot pins, Ibanez/'AW' logo on peghead, chrome hardware, three-per-side die-cast tuners, available in Natural gloss finish, mfg. 1996-98, 2000-06.				
8 —	N/A	$200 - 250	$120 - 150	$500
13 — When this model was reintroduced in 2000, Englemann spruce was used.				
10 — * **AW100 CE Cutaway Electric** – dreadnought style body with single rounded cutaway, solid Sitka spruce top, round soundhole, tortoiseshell pickguard, bound body, mahogany back/sides/neck, 14/20-fret rosewood fingerboard with pearl dot inlay, rosewood bridge with white black dot pins, Ibanez/'AW' logo on peghead, chrome hardware, three-per-side die-cast tuners, Slim Jim pickup, volume/three-band EQ controls, available in Natural gloss finish, mfg. 1996-98, 2000-06.				
8 —	N/A	$300 - 350	$175 - 225	$714
12 — • Add 5% for Black gloss finish (Model AW100 CE BK).				
13 — When this model was reintroduced in 2000, Englemann spruce was used.				
11 — »**AW100LCE Cutaway Electric Left-Handed** – similar to the AW100CE Cutaway Electric except in left-handed configuration, disc. 2006.				
14 —	N/A	$300 - 375	$175 - 225	$757

to AW100, except in 12-string configuration, six-per-side t

the Last MSR whenever applicable. Once a model is discontinued, the MSR will be moved to this column, which is helpful in determining used values.

10. Sub-model Name and Description - Models that have several variations (i.e. 12-string, left-handed, electric, etc.) may be split up into sub-models. In this case, any sub-models would be listed directly below the model. These are displayed in lowercase and italics, are indented more than the model name, and a have an asterisk before the model name. All other listings are the same as the model name.

11. Sub-Sub-model Name and Description - Sub-models that have several variations (i.e. 12-string, left-handed, electric, etc.) may be split up into sub-sub-models. In this case, any sub-sub-models would be listed directly below the submodel. These are displayed in lowercase, and are slightly more indented than the sub-model. All other listings are the same as the model name.

12. Model Price Adjustment - Options, special orders, and other value add/subtract items apply to many models. This may include optional finishes, accessories, parts, etc. These price adjustments will be displayed as an add or subtract value to and an amount or a percentage. Actual dollar amounts are typically added on currently or recently manufactured instruments (mostly referring to the current or last MSR of that option) and percentages are used on many vintage instruments. Percentages may also be used on currently or recently manufactured instruments in certain situations (i.e. A finish option of $250 on a $1,000 guitar only applies the amount to the MSR price because an Average condition guitar is only worth $500 and you can only apply 50% of the finish option to the current value. In other words you can't apply a 100% price to a finish, when the finish devalues along with the entire guitar). There may be several model price adjustments after each model, sub-model, or sub-sub-model.

13. Model Notes - Any additional information pertaining to the model, sub-model, or sub-sub-model description will be displayed last including changes to the model during its production, finish changes, and other information pertinent to the model.

14. Images – The guitar icon ⌯ indicates that there is a guitar image or images available for that manufacturer or model on our website that can be accessed at http://images.bluebookofguitarvalues.com. Our website is formatted exactly like the book where you select the letter of manufacturer, the manufacturer, category, and model. Go to images.bluebookofguitarvalues.com for more information, or scan this QR code.

ANATOMY OF AN ACOUSTIC GUITAR

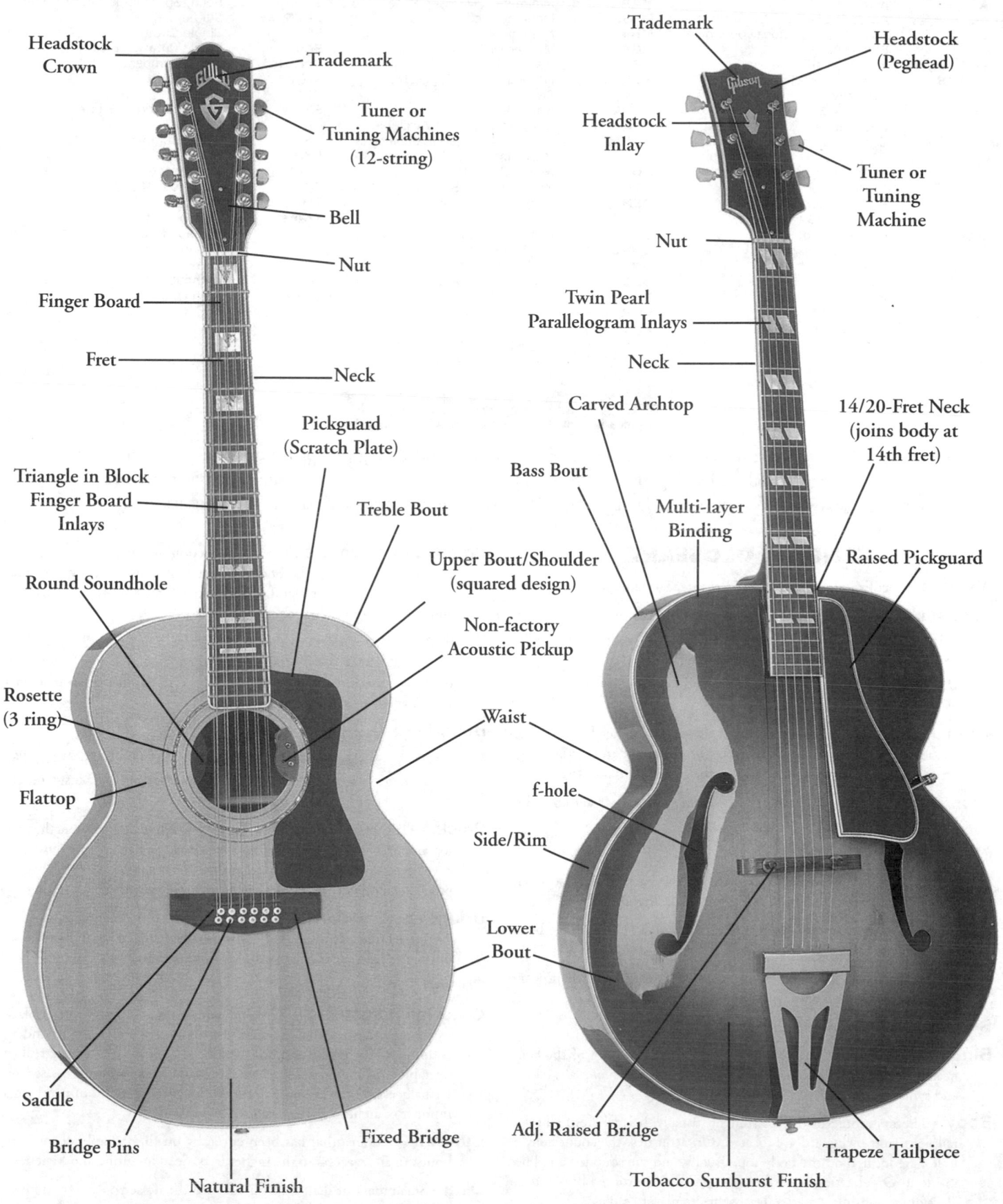

Headstock Crown

Trademark

Tuner or Tuning Machines (12-string)

Bell

Nut

Finger Board

Fret

Neck

Pickguard (Scratch Plate)

Triangle in Block Finger Board Inlays

Treble Bout

Round Soundhole

Rosette (3 ring)

Flattop

Upper Bout/Shoulder (squared design)

Non-factory Acoustic Pickup

Saddle

Bridge Pins

Fixed Bridge

Natural Finish

Trademark

Headstock (Peghead)

Headstock Inlay

Tuner or Tuning Machine

Nut

Twin Pearl Parallelogram Inlays

Neck

Carved Archtop

14/20-Fret Neck (joins body at 14th fret)

Bass Bout

Multi-layer Binding

Raised Pickguard

Waist

f-hole

Side/Rim

Lower Bout

Adj. Raised Bridge

Trapeze Tailpiece

Tobacco Sunburst Finish

ABBREVIATIONS

0	Concert Size	L, LH	Left-Handed	REFIN	Refinished
00	Grand Concert Size	LE	Limited Edition	REFRET	Refretted
000	Auditorium Size	LSH	Large Soundhole	REPRO	Reproduction
0000	Grand Auditorium Size	M	Mahogany or Maple	RSH	Round Soundhole
A	Ash	MAP	Minimum Advertised Price	S	Solid, Spruce Special, or Super
AE	Acoustic Electric	MFG.	Manufactured	SB, S/B	Sunburst
B	Bass, Brazilian Rosewood, or Blue (finish)	MH	Mahogany	SC	Single Cutaway
		MOP	Mother-Of-Pearl	SCE	Single Cutaway Electric
BLK, BK, BL	Black (finish)	MPL	Maple	Ser. No.	Serial Number
B/W/B	Black/White/Black	MSR	Manufacturer's Suggested Retail	SG	Solid Guitar
C	Cutaway			SGL	Single
CE	Cutaway Electric	N/NAT	Natural	SJ	Super Jumbo or Southern Jumbo
Ch.	Channel	N/A	Not Applicable/Not Available		
C.I.T.E.S.	Convention on International Trade in Endangered Species of Wild Fauna and Flora (July 1, 1975)	NAMM	National Association of Musical Merchants	SN	Serial Number
				STD	Standard
		NOS	New Old Stock	SWD	Smartwood
		NTB	Neck Through Body	T	Tremolo or Thinline
D	Dreadnought	OEM	Original Equipment Manufacture	TOB	Tobacco
DC	Double Cutaway			Trans.	Transparent
Disc.	Discontinued	OH	Original Hardshell	V	V shaped Neck, Venetian, Vibrato, or Vintage Series
E	Electric	OHSC	Original Hardshell Case		
EQ	Equalizer	OM	Orchestra Model	W/	With
F	Fretless or Florentine	OSC	Original Soft Case	W/O	Without
FB	Fingerboard	PG	Pickguard	WOB	With Out Binding
Flour.	Fluorescent	POR	Priced on Request		
H	Herringbone	PU (P.U.)	Pickup		
J	Jumbo	R	Reverse (headstock) Red (finish), or Rosewood		
K	Koa				

GLOSSARY

This glossary is divided into four sections: General Glossary; Hardware: Bridges, Pegs, Tailpieces, and Tuners; Pickups/Electronics; and Book Terminology. If you are looking for something and can't find it in one section, please check the others. You may also want to refer to "Anatomy of An Acoustic Guitar" (page 13) for visual identification on many of the terms listed below.

GENERAL GLOSSARY

Abalone - Shellfish material used in instrument ornamentation.

Acoustic - Generic term used for hollow bodied instruments that rely on the body to produce the amplified sound of the instrument, rather than electronic amplification.

Acoustic Electric - A thin hollow bodied instrument that relies on a pickup to further amplify its sound.

Action - Everybody wants a piece of it. It is also the height the strings are off of the fingerboard, stretched between the nut and bridge. High action indicates a large space between the fingerboard and the strings.

Arch/Arched Top - The top of an instrument that has been carved or pressed to have a "rounded" top.

Avoidire - Blonde mahogany.

Back Plate - Refers to the cover plate on the back of an instrument allowing access into the body cavity for repair/alterations.

Bass Bout - Upper left hand part of body (left side of lower fingerboard on right-hand guitars).

Bell - Truss Rod cover located directly above nut. Most are bell shaped, and may have model/make information on the outside.

Belly - Refers to the inside of the soundboard.

Binding (bound) - Trim that goes along the outer edge of the body, neck, or headstock. It is made out of many different materials, natural and synthetic.

Body - The main bulk of the instrument, usually. It is where the bridge, tailpiece, and pickguard are located. On acoustics, the soundhole, or holes, are located on the body top, usually, and the sound is amplified inside it. On electrics, it is where the pickups are routed into and the electronics housing is stored. It is what the player cradles.

Bolt On/Bolt On Neck - Construction technique that involves attaching the neck to the body by means of bolts or screws. Bolt-on necks are generally built and finished separately from the guitar body, and parts are assembled together later.

Bookmatched - Refers to the process where a single block of wood is cut in half lengthwise. Both pieces are then "bookmatched" – glued so that the grain of the two pieces matches. Very popular on instruments with maple backs and a lot of flame.

Bound - See Binding.

Bout/Bouts - Also see Bass Bout, Lower Bout, and Treble Bout. The rounded, generally, side/sides on the top and bottom of an instrument's body.

Bracing - The splayed pattern of supportive wooden struts that strengthen the top and back of a guitar and effect tone; "scalloped" braces are those that have been shaved or carved to lighten the guitar and/or to allow for tone-producing flexibility, especially on the top of the guitar; also "strutting."

Bridge - Component that rests on the top of the instrument and transfers vibrations from string to body. It is usually attached by glue or screws but is also held in place by string tension, the same as a violin.

Carved Top - See Archtop.

Cello Tail Adjuster - The Cello tail adjuster is a 1/8 in. diameter black nylon-type material that attaches to the tailpiece and loops around an endpin jack (or ebony endpin). Nylon, of course, replaced the real (if unstable) gut material several years ago. This tail adjuster is used on virtually every cello tailpiece in the world, and figures prominently in a number of archtop guitar designs.

Cutaway - An area that has been cut away on the treble bout, or both bouts, to allow access to the higher frets. See Florentine and Venetian.

Ding - Small mark or dent on a guitar. Also the noise you swear you hear when your guitar hits another object, thus causing the mark.

Dovetail - Woodworking procedure allowing one piece to be precisely fit with another. This is a standard procedure used on set neck instruments. Also see Mortise.

Dreadnought - A generic term used to describe steel string guitar configuration consisting of a boxy body and solid headstock.

Ebonized - A process by which the wood has been stained dark to appear to be ebony; alternatively, also referring to something black in color (such as bridge adjuster wheels) made to blend in with ebony fittings on an archtop guitar.

Ebonol - A synthetic material that is used as replacement for wood (generally as a fingerboard).

Electric - A generic term referencing the fact that the instrument relies on pickups to amplify its sound.

F-Hole - Stylized f-shaped soundhole that is carved into the top of various instruments, most commonly acoustic. It usually comes in pairs.

Fingerboard - The area on the front of the neck where the string(s) is pressed against to create the desired note (frequency). Another way of saying fingerboard and specifying that it has frets embedded into it. Fingerboards are usually made from extreme hardwoods, including ebony, rosewood, and maple.

Finish - The outer coat of an instrument. The sealant of the wood. The protector of the instrument. Finishes include Gloss, Satin, Nitrocellulose, Matte, Spar, Polyurethane, Tongue Oil, etc.

Flamenco - Refers to a classically-designed Spanish guitar with modifications made for the Flamenco music for which it became famous. Traditional flamenco guitars typically feature a slightly smaller body than a classical guitar, thinner rims made from Spanish cyprus, wooden pegs, and low action fingerboard with high tension strings. Flamenco music and instruments initially centered around Andalucia, a region in Spain, and was well established by the end of the 1800s.

Flattop - Term used to describe an acoustic steel stringed instrument whose top is flat.

Florentine - Sharp point on the treble forward horn of a body cutaway. See also Venetian.

Fret - A strip of metal that is embedded at specific intervals into the fingerboard or fretboard.

Fretboard - Older designation for fingerboard. See Fingerboard.

Fretless Fingerboard - Commonly found on bass instruments, this fingerboard is smooth, with no frets.

Golpeador - Protective (generally clear) plate added to top of flamenco guitars for tapping.

Graphite - Used in various forms of instrument construction because of its rigidity and weight, this type of synthetic material may be used in the body, neck, nut, saddle, etc.

Hardware - Generic term for the bridge, tailpiece, tuners. or vibrato system.

Headless - The instrument has no headstock.

Headstock - Top portion of the neck assembly where the tuning machines are located. Headstock design is a field unto itself, and many makes and models can be instantly identified by simply looking at an instrument's headstock design or configuration. Additional information about the instrument, such as serialization (typically on back side or top), model number, and/or distinctive logo/trademark may also be part of the headstock.

Heel - On the backside of an instrument, the heel is located at the base of the lower neck where the neck meets the body. May be bound, inlaid, or carved as well.

Inlay - Decoration or identifying marks on an instrument that are inlaid into one of the surface areas. They are made of a number of materials, though abalone, pearl, and wood are the most common.

Lining - Typically made from small wooden strips, this lining is traditionally "kerfed" (sawed frequently, but not through, allowing bending), and is glued around the inside of the body, both on the top and back. Both the top and back of the instrument are precisely glued to these body linings.

Locking Tuners - These tuners are manufactured with a locking mechanism built right into them, thus preventing string slippage.

Logo - An identifying feature on an instrument: it could be a symbol or a name; and it could appear as a decal, an inlay, or painted on (and it could be missing).

Lower Bout(s) - Refers to the lower part of an instrument's contour(s). A lower bout measurement is the maximum distance between an instrument's two lower bouts.

Maccaferri Design - Refers to unusual flattop design featuring wide oval soundhole, long/thin bridge, and distinctive body cutaway. This configuration was originally built by the French Selmer company during the early 1930s, and was the design used exclusively by noted guitarist Django Reinhardt.

Mortise - Wood construction procedure where one piece of wood is carefully fitted to join another. Also see Dovetail.

Mother-of-Pearl (MOP) - A shellfish (oyster/clam) material used for inlay.

Nato - A lower grade or quality of mahogany, sometimes referred to as "lumberyard" mahogany.

Neck - The area that the strings of the instrument are stretched along, the headstock sits at the top, and the body lies at the bottom.

Neck Angle/Pitch - The angle at which the neck joins the body (more common on set neck instruments). Different neck angles can affect both tone and volume, especially on acoustic guitars.

Octave - In Western Notation, every 12 frets on a stringed instrument is an octave in the musical scale of things.

Pearl - Short for mother-of-pearl, the inside shell from a shellfish. See Mother-Of-Pearl.

Pearloid - A synthetic material made of plastic and pearl dust.

Peghead - See Headstock. Originally used to describe the pegs/ tuners extruding from the guitar head.

Phenolic - A synthetic material that is used as fingerboard wood replacement.

Pickguard - A piece of material used to protect the instrument's top or finish from gouges that are caused by the pick or your fingers.

Pickup - An electronic device utilizing magnetic induction to transform string vibrations into electronic signals needed for sound amplification. Pickups can either be high (most popular) or low (less output) impedance.

Position Marker - Usually, some form of decorative inlay which is inlaid into the neck to help the player identify fret position.

"Pre-CBS" - Collector's terminology that refers to the CBS purchase of Fender Instruments in 1965. A "Pre-CBS" instrument is one built by Leo Fender's original company.

Purfling - Decorative trim that is found running along the inside of the binding.

Relief - The upward slope of the fingerboard that keeps the strings off the frets.

Resonator - A metal device located in some instruments that is the means of their amplification. Resonator instruments transfer the vibrations of their strings through the bridge to a round metal dish or cone which acts as a resonator within the guitar. Because of this, they are typically louder than conventional acoustic instruments. Preferred by slide guitarists.

Reverse Headstock - On this instrument the headstock has been flipped over from the normal configuration and the tuners are all on the highest note side of the instrument (tuners are all located on one side).

Rims/Ribs - Also referred to as Sides – refers to the sides of an instrument, typically between 1½ -5 inches deep.

Rosette - A decorative design that is inlaid around the soundhole. A three-ring rosette (see page 12) refers to three decorative rings inlaid around the soundhole, with varying widths.

Saddle - A natural or synthetic component generally attached to the bridge on which the strings rest, enabling the strings to resonate properly through the bridge and instrument top, and to assist in intonation. On many currently manufactured acoustic electric instruments, the area between the bottom of the saddle and bridge is where the acoustic pickup (Fishman, L.R. Baggs, etc.) is installed. Usually stepped or slanted.

Scale Length - The area between the nut and bridge over which the strings of the instrument are stretched.

Scalloped - What the area on the fingerboard between the frets is called when it has been scooped out, creating a dip between the frets.

Scratch Plate - Slang for Pickguard. See Pickguard.

Semi-Acoustic - Term used to describe a shallow bodied instrument that is constructed with a solid piece of wood running the length of the center of the body.

Sides - also referred to as Rims – refers to the sides of an instrument, typically between 1½ -5 inches deep.

Slotted Headstock - A headstock design usually associated with classical acoustic guitars, featuring two internal "slotted" areas where the strings are guided and the tuning machine's spindles are placed horizontally.

Soundboard - The top of an acoustic guitar. This top (typically spruce for its tonal quality), resonates from the vibrations coming down from the saddle and bridge. It, in turn, vibrates the rims and backside. This amplified sound typically escapes through a round hole(s) or f-holes.

Soundhole - A hole found in the top of acoustic instruments (mostly), that allows the sound to be projected from the body.

Strings - Typically made from gut (older), nylon, steel, or bronze. Metal strings may or may not be coated also. They range in a variety of sizes, both in diameter and length. The weight of the string is what determines the range of frequencies it will cover.

Sunburst (Sunburst Finish) - Typically, either a two or three color finish that is applied around the outside of the body (may include rims, back, and neck also), leaving the inside a lighter, unstained natural color.

Thinline - Original Gibson terminology referring to a hollowbodied instrument that has a shallow depth of body.

Through Body (Thru Body; Neck Through) - Type of construction that consists of the neck wood extending through the entire length of the instrument and the pieces of wood that make up the body being attached to the sides of the neck wood (called wings).

Tone Bars - Traditional single strip bracing (one for treble, and one for bass) attached to the inside of an archtop to assist with an instrument's harmonics.

Top Block - Wood component that is attached to the inside part of the neck where it joins the body. This "locks" the neck in place with the body.

Treble Bout - Upper right-hand part of body (right side of lower fingerboard on right hand guitars).

Tremolo - An increase or decrease in the frequency of a tone. Tremolo in relation to guitars usually refers to a tremolo unit, or tremolo effects. Please refer to individual listings.

Truss Bar - A square or T-shaped bar fit into the back of the neck, typically non-adjustable.

Truss Rod - Refers to a metal truss rod fitted into the back of an instrument's neck, adding stability, and allowing for a neck adjustment in the case of a warped/curved neck. Gibson invented this solution for neck adjusting in the mid-1920s.

Venetian - Rounded point on the treble forward horn of a body cutaway. See also Florentine.

Vibrato - The act of physically lengthening or shortening the medium (in this case, it will be strings) to produce a fluctuation in frequency. The pitch altering mechanism on your guitar is a vibrato, not a tremolo!

Volute (also Neck Volute) - Additional protruding wood used as a strengthening support where an angled-back headstock is spliced to the end of the neck. This carved (or shaped) piece of the neck is also referred to as a "handstop."

Warpage - Generally refers to a neck that becomes bowed or warped, making playability difficult/impossible. On necks with truss rods, the neck may be adjusted to become straight again. On instruments with set necks, often times the neck must be taken off and repaired, or needs to be replaced.

Wings - The body pieces attached to the sides of a through body neck blank, thus forming a complete body.

X Bracing - A traditional method of internal top bracing which resembles an X pattern.

Zero Fret - The zero fret is a length of fret wire fitted into a fret slot which is cut at the exact location as that of a conventional nut. The fingerboard is generally cut off 1/8" longer than usual, at which point the nut is fitted. When used in conjunction with the zero fret, the nut serves as a string guide. The fret wire used on the zero fret is usually slightly larger than that used on the fingerboard itself – the slightly higher zero fret establishes the open string's height above the fingerboard.

HARDWARE: BRIDGES, PEGS, TAILPIECES, AND TUNERS

Acoustic Bridge - The bridge on an acoustic instrument is usually glued to the top and though pins are usually used there are still numerous ways of holding the strings taut.

Banjo Tuners - Tuners that are perpendicular to the headstock and pass through it, as opposed to being mounted on the side of the headstock, (like classic style headstock tuners).

Bigsby Vibrato - A vibrato system that involves a roller bar with little pegs that run in a perpendicular line, around which you hook the string balls. One end of the bar has an arm coming off of it, a spring is located under the arm, and the entire apparatus is connected to a trapeze tailpiece. The bridge is separate from the vibrato system. This vibrato was designed by Paul Bigsby.

Bridge - Component that connects the strings to the body of the instrument. Bridge materials may be wood, metal, alloy, synthetic, or even a combination. It is usually attached to the top of an instrument's body by glue or screws but can also be held in place by string tension, the same as a violin. Bridge placement is determined by the instrument's scale length.

Bridge Pins - Pins or dowels used to secure string to bridge. These pins usually utilize friction to seat properly, and are typically made from hard wood, synthetic materials (ivoroid is popular), or ivory. Also referred to as Pegs.

Double Locking Vibrato - A vibrato system that locks the strings into place by tightening down screws on each string, thus stopping the string's ability to slip. There is also a clamp at the top of the fingerboard that holds the strings from the tuners. These more modern designs were formulated separately by Floyd Rose and the Kahler company. As guitarist Billy Gibbons (ZZ Top) is fond of saying, the locking vibratos give you the ability to "turn Steel into Rubber, and have 'er bounce back on a dime." See Vibrato.

Fixed Bridge - Body hardware component that typically contains the saddles, bridge, and tailpiece in one integrated unit, and is usually mounted utilizing screws/studs.

Friction Pegs - Wooden dowels that rely on the friction created between itself and the wood of the hole it is put in to keep the tension of the strings constant.

Headless - Term meaning that the instrument's headstock is missing. The top of the neck is capped with a piece of hardware that acts like a regular tailpiece on the instrument body.

Locking Tuners - These tuners are manufactured with a locking mechanism built into them, thus preventing string slippage.

Nut - Device located at the top of the fingerboard (opposite from the bridge) that determines the action and spacing of the strings.

Pegs - See Friction Pegs. Can refer to either the small pegs used to secure the strings in the bridge or older tuners used on some vintage instruments (hence the term peghead).

Pins - Pegs that are used to anchor the strings in place on the bridge.

Roller Bridge - This is a Gretsch trademark feature. It is an adjustable metal bridge that sits on a wooden base, the saddles of this unit sit on a threaded bar and are easily moved back and forth to allow personal string spacing.

Saddle/Saddles - A part of the bridge that holds the string/strings in place, helps transfer vibrations to the instrument body and helps in setting the action.

Set-In Neck - Guitar construction that involves attaching the neck to the body by gluing a joint (such as a dovetail). Set necks cannot be adjusted by shims, as their angle of attachment to the body is pre-set in the design.

Single Locking Vibrato - A vibrato system that locks the strings on the unit to keep them from going out of tune during heavy arm use. This style of vibrato does not employ a clamping system at the top of the fingerboard.

Standard Vibrato - Usually associated with the Fender Stratocaster, this unit has the saddles on top and an arm off to one side. The arm allows you to bend the strings, making the frequencies (notes) rise or drop. All of this sits on a metal plate that rocks back and forth. Strings may have an area to attach to on top or they may pass through the body and have holding cups on the back side. A block of metal, usually called the Inertia Block, is generally located under the saddles to allow for increased sustain. The block travels through the instrument's body and has springs attached to it to create the tension necessary to keep the strings in tune. See Vibrato.

Steinberger Bridge - A bridge designed by Ned Steinberger, it combines the instrument bridge and tuners all in one unit. It is used with headless instruments.

Stop Tailpiece - Machined metal part attached to lower body by screws, which is usually slotted to hold the string balls. Generally used with a tune-o-matic bridge.

Strap Button - Typically refers to oversized metal buttons on the outside of an instrument allowing the player to attach a strap to the instrument.

Strings Through Body (Anchoring) - A tailpiece that involves the strings passing through an instrument's body and the string balls are held in place by recessed cups on the back side.

Stud Tailpiece - See Stop Tailpiece.

Tailpiece - The device that holds and typically positions (along with a possible bridge) the strings at the lower body. It may be all in one unit that contains the saddle/saddles also, or stands alone. Electric tailpieces are mostly metal construction, although metal, wood, alloy, synthetic, or other materials have also been used.

Tied Bridge - Style of bridge usually associated with "classical" style instruments that have the strings secured by tying them around the bridge.

Trapeze Tailpiece - A type of tailpiece that is hinged, has one end attached to the bottom bout of the instrument and the other end has grooves in it to hold the string balls.

Tremolo Unit - Refers to a mechanical device typically incorporated into the bridge of an instrument utilizing a tremolo (whammy) bar to produce changes in frequencies.

Tuner(s)/Tuning Machine(s) - Mechanical device that is used to stretch the strings to the right tension for adjustable tuning. These are typically located on the headstock.

Tunable Stop Tailpiece - A tailpiece that rests on a pair of posts and has small fine tuning machines mounted on top of it.

Tune-o-matic Bridge - A bridge that is attached to the instrument's top by two metal posts and has adjustable saddles on the topside.

Wrapover Bridge - A self contained bridge/tailpiece bar device that is attached to the body, with the strings wrapping over the bar.

Wrapunder Bridge - The same as above except the strings wrap under the bar.

PICKUPS/ELECTRONICS

The following terms are usually associated with acoustic electric guitars and basses. Refer to the *Blue Book of Electric Guitars* for a more complete listing of Pickups/Electronics.

Active Electronics - A form of electronic circuitry that involves some power source, usually a 9-volt battery. Most of the time the circuit is an amplification circuit, though it may also be onboard effects circuitry.

Amplify/Amplification - To increase, in this case to increase the volume of the instrument.

Onboard - Usually referencing effects, it means built into the instrument.

Parametric Equalizer - An equalizer that allows you to specifically choose which range of frequencies you wish to affect.

Passive Electronics - Electronic circuitry that has no power supply. Usually it consists of filter circuitry.

Pickup - An electronic device utilizing magnetic induction to transform string vibrations into electronic signals needed for sound amplification. Pickups can either be high (most popular) or low (less output) impedance. Pickups on most acoustic electric instruments are of the ribbon type, and are placed where the bottom of the saddle and bridge join. Often times, an onboard equalizer is utilized in conjunction with these acoustic pickups, allowing the player to control the tone and volume. Popular brands include Fishman, L.R. Baggs, Rio Grande, etc.

Piezo (Piezoelectric) - A crystalline substance that induces an electrical current caused by pressure or vibrations.

Pot - Short for "potentiometer."

Potentiometer - A variable resistor that is typically used to make tone and volume adjustments on an instrument.

Preamp - An electronic circuit that amplifies the signal from the pickup(s) and preps it for the amplifier.

Transducer/Transducer Pickup - A device that converts energy from one form to another, in this instance it is the vibrations caused by the strings, moving along the wood and being converted into electrical energy for amplification.

BOOK TERMINOLOGY

This glossary section should help you understand the jargon used in the model descriptions of the instruments in this text.

3/2-per-side - This is in reference to a five-string instrument with three tuners on one side of the headstock and two tuners on the other.

335 Style - refers to an instrument that has a semi-hollowbody cutaway body style similar to that of the Gibson 335.

4/1-per-side - On an instrument with five strings this would mean four tuners are on one side of the headstock, and one is on the other.

4/2-per-side - Four tuners on one side and two on the other side of a headstock.

4/3-per-side - This instrument has seven strings with four of the tuners located on one side of the headstock and three on the other side.

6/1-per-side - A seven-string instrument with six tuners on one side and one on the other.

14/20-Fret - Term in which the first number describes the fret at which the neck joins the body and the second number is the total number of frets on the fingerboard.

Classical Style - This term refers to a gut or nylon string instruments fashioned after the original guitar design. Used predominately in classical music, this design features a 12/19 fretboard, round soundhole, slotted (or open) headstock, and a tied-end bridge.

Contoured Body - A body design that features some carved sections that fit easier to the player's body.

Dreadnought Style - This term refers to steel string instruments that are fashioned after the traditional build of a Martin instrument, a boxy type instrument with squared top and bottom bouts, approximately 14 inches across the top bouts, 16 inches across the bottom bouts, there is not much of a waist and the depth of instrument is about 4-5 inches.

Dual Cutaway - Guitar design with two forward horns, both extending forward an equal amount (see Offset Double Cutaway, Single Cutaway).

Five-on-one-side - All the tuners on one side of the headstock on a five-string instrument.

Flamenco Style - The Flamenco style guitar is similar to the Classical style, save for the addition of the (generally clear) 'tap plate.' by the bridge.

Four-on-one-side - Four tuners on one side of the headstock on a four-string instrument.

Four-per-side - Four tuners on each side of the headstock on an eight-string instrument.

Jazz Style - A body shape similar to the traditional jazz archtop or semi-hollowbody design, or affiliated parts of such models.

Jumbo Style - A body shape similar to the traditional jumbo acoustic body, or affiliated parts of such models.

Offset Double Cutaway - Guitar design with two forward horns, the top (bass side) horn more prominent of the two (see Dual Cutaway, Single Cutaway).

Point Fingerboard - A fingerboard that has a "V-ed" section on it at the body end of the fingerboard.

Seven-on-one-side - A term referring to a seven-string instrument with all the tuners on the headstock on one side.

Single Cutaway - Guitar design with a single curve into the body, allowing the player access to the upper frets of the fretboard (see Dual Cutaway, Offset Double Cutaway).

Six-on-one-side - All six tuners on one side of the headstock on a six-string instrument.

Six-per-side - Six tuners on each side of the headstock on a twelve-string instrument.

SJ Style - A body shape similar to the traditional Southern Jumbo (slope-shouldered dreadnought) acoustic body, or affiliated parts of such models.

Sleek - A more modern body style, perhaps having longer forward horns, a more contoured body, or a certain aerodynamic flair (!).

Three-per-side - Three tuners on each side of the headstock on a six-string instrument.

Through Body (Neck-Thru-Construction) - Type of construction that consists of the neck wood extending through the entire length of the instrument and the pieces of wood that make up the body being attached to the sides of the neck wood.

Tune-o-matic Stop Tailpiece - This unit is a combination bridge/tailpiece that has adjustable (tune-o-matic) saddles mounted on a wrap around tailpiece.

Volume/Tone Control - When encountered, refers to an instrument which has a volume and/or tone control. A numerical prefix (2 or 3) preceding the term indicates the amount of volume/tone controls.

INTERESTED IN CONTRIBUTING?

The *Blue Book of Acoustic Guitars* is the result of non-stop, and continual guitar research carried out by obtaining relevant information from both manufacturers and luthiers. Also of major importance is speaking directly with experts (both published and unpublished), reading books, catalogs, and company promo materials, gathering critical and up-to-date manufacturer/luthier information obtained from the biannual NAMM trade shows and the makers themselves, and observing and analyzing market trends by following major vintage dealer and collector pricing and trends.

We also have a great batch of contributing editors and advisory board members that pump out a lot of good information annually - including vintage pricing updates. Going to a lot of guitar and trade shows, in addition to visiting a variety of music stores, guitar shops, pawn shops, and second-hand stores, also hones our chops.

If you feel that you can contribute in any way to the materials published herein, you are encouraged to submit hard copy regarding your potential additions, revisions, corrections, or any other pertinent information that you feel would enhance the benefits this book provides to its readers. Unfortunately, we are unable to take your information over the phone (this protects both of us)! Earn your way into the ranks of the truly twisted, join the motley crew of contributing editors, and see that your information can make a difference! We thank you in advance for taking the time to make this a better publication.

All materials sent in for possible inclusion into upcoming editions of the *Blue Book of Acoustic Guitars* should be mailed, faxed, or emailed to us at the address listed below. Each new edition should be an improvement on the last. Even though you can't do it all in one, ten, or even twenty editions, accumulating new information is an ongoing process, with the results being published in each new edition.

ADDITIONAL SERVICES
(CORRESPONDENCE INQUIRIES, APPRAISALS, AND BUYING/SELLING)

Aside from publishing the *Blue Book of Acoustic Guitars*, Blue Book Publications offers additional services that are helpful in identifying and evaluating guitars. It is literally impossible to list every guitar that has ever been produced in one book – if we continued doing this for 100 years, there would still be information missing. Because of this, and our continued commitment to help the customer, we offer a full guitar correspondence policy. If you own the current *Blue Book of Acoustic Guitars* and either have a question about a guitar in our book or can't find something that you are looking for, contact us via mail, phone, fax, or email, and we'll do our best to answer your questions. Whenever possible, please include pictures of the guitar(s) in question – the results will be a lot more accurate.

For those who don't own an edition of the *Blue Book of Acoustic Guitars*, we can help you out with a value and some information either over the phone or through email for only $10 per guitar. This service is also available on our website through an online submittal form.

We also offer full written guitar appraisals that are extremely useful for insurance purposes and other situations where written documentation is necessary. Appraisals are $25 per instrument and can be submitted via mail or email, and images of the guitar must be included to determine condition and configuration. Turn around time is usually within a week (five business days) unless additional input is needed from outside sources, and appraisals come on official Blue Book letterhead. This service is also available on our website through an online submittal form.

Another service that comes with the purchase of the *Blue Book of Acoustic Guitars* is buying and selling assistance. If you are looking for a specific guitar to buy, or have a guitar you want to sell, we can provide you with trusted guitar dealers in your area. We have a wide network of dealers that we can recommend virtually anywhere in the U.S.A. This is strictly a referral service and no commission is involved on our part in any transaction.

Please submit all guitar contributions, correspondence inquires, appraisals, and other information requests to:

Blue Book Publications, Inc.
Attn: Guitars
8009 34th Ave. S., Ste #250
Minneapolis, MN 55425
1-800-877-4867, ext. 5
Fax: 952-853-1486
http://bluebookofguitarvalues.com
guitars@bluebookinc.com (include "Blue Book" in the subject line)

When submitting images, please send images in .jpg format that are no larger than 1 mb per image in size. Images should include a complete frontal and back shot of the guitar, a picture of the serial number/label, and any other important features of the guitar. Also, please take clear high res pictures of your guitars – if you can't see the guitar clearly in the picture, then we're not going to be either.

REFERENCES & RECOMMENDED READING

The following titles are part of our reference library here at Blue Book Publications and much of the information compiled in this book comes from them. Several of these titles are currently available, while many are out of print and hard to obtain. Visit our website for additional guitar titles that are available.

Achard, Ken
The Fender Guitar, The Bold Strummer, Ltd., Westport, CT, 1990

Achard, Ken
The History and Development of the American Guitar, The Bold Strummer, Ltd., Westport CT, 1990

Achard, Ken
The Peavey Revolution - The Gear, The Company, and the All-American Success Story, Backbeat Books, San Francisco, CA, 2005

Bacon, Tony (Editor), et al
Classic Guitars of the 50s, Miller Freeman, San Francisco, CA, 1996

Bacon, Tony (Editor), et al
Classic Guitars of the 60s, Miller Freeman, San Francisco, CA, 1997

Bacon, Tony
The History of the American Guitar, Friedman/ Fairfax Publishers, New York, NY, 2001

Bacon, Tony, et al
The Classical Guitar - A Complete History, Outline Press Ltd./ Miller Freeman, San Francisco, CA, 1997

Bacon, Tony
The Fender Electric Guitar Book, Backbeat Books, New York, NY, 2007

Bacon, Tony
The Les Paul Guitar Book - A Complete History of Gibson Les Paul Guitars Third Edition, Backbeat Books, San Francisco, CA, 2009

Bacon, Tony
Rickenbacker Electric 12-String, Backbeat Books, Milwaukee, WI, 2010

Bacon, Tony
The Ultimate Guitar Book, Alfred A. Knopf, Inc., New York, NY, 1991

Bacon, Tony
50 Years of Gretsch, Backbeat Books, San Francisco, CA, 2005

Bacon, Tony and Day, Paul, et al (Editors)
Guitar - A Complete Guide for the Player, Thunder Bay Press, San Diego, CA, 2002

Bacon, Tony and Day, Paul
The Fender Book, GPI/Miller Freeman Inc., San Francisco, CA, 1992

Bacon, Tony and Day, Paul
50 Years of Fender, Balafon Books, London, England, 2000

Bacon, Tony and Day, Paul
The Gretsch Book, GPI/Miller Freeman Inc., San Francisco, CA, 1996

Bacon, Tony and Day, Paul
The Guru's Guitar Guide, Track Record Publishing, London, England, 1990

Bacon, Tony and Day, Paul
The Rickenbacker Book, GPI/Miller Freeman Inc., San Francisco, CA, 1994

Bacon, Tony and Moorhouse, Barry
The Bass Book, GPI/Miller Freeman Inc., San Francisco, CA, 1995

Benedetto, Robert
Making an Archtop Guitar - The Definitive Work on the Design and Construction of an Acoustic Archtop Guitar, Centerstream Publishing/Hal Leonard Corp, Anaheim Hills, CA, 1996

Bishop, Ian C.
The Gibson Guitar, The Bold Strummer, Ltd., Westport CT, 1990

Bishop, Ian C.
The Gibson Guitar From 1950 Vol. 2, The Bold Strummer, Ltd., Westport, NY, 1990

Boak, Dick
Martin Guitar Masterpieces A Showcase of Artists' Editions, Limited Editions, and Custom Guitars, Palazzo Editions LTD., Bath England,

Briggs, Brinkman, and Crocker
Guitars, Guitars, Guitars, All American Music Publishers, Neosho, MO, 1988

Brozeman, Bob
The History and Artistry of National Resonator Instruments, Centerstream Publishing, Anaheim Hills, CA, 1993

Burrluck, Dave
The PRS Guitar Book, Backbeat Books, San Francisco, CA, 2002

Carter, Walter
Epiphone, The Complete History, Hal Leonard Corporation, Milwaukee, WI, 1995

Carter, Walter
Gibson Guitars, 100 Years of an American Icon, General Publishing, Inc., New York, NY, 1994

Carter, Walter and Dave Hunter
Interactive Gibson Bible, Jawbone/Outline Press, London, England 2008

Carter, Walter
The History of the Ovation Guitar, Hal Leonard Corporation, Milwaukee, WI, 1996

Carter, Walter
The Martin Book - A Complete History of Martin Guitars, 2nd Edition, Backbeat Books, San Francisco, CA, 2006

Chapman, Richard
The Complete Guitarist, (Foreword by Les Paul), DK Publishing, New York, NY, 1993

Chapman, Richard
Guitar - Music, History, Players (Foreword by Eric Clapton), DK Publishing, New York, NY, 2000

Charle, Francois
The Story of Selmer Maccaferri Guitars, published by the author, Paris, France, 1999

Dahl, Eric E.
B.B. King's Lucille and the Loves Before Her, Blue Book Publications, Inc. Minneapolis, MN, 2013

Day, Paul
The Burns Book, The Bold Strummer, Ltd., Westport, CT, 1990

Denyer, Ralph
The Guitar Handbook, Alfred A. Knopf Inc., New York, NY, 1982

Duchossoir, A.R.
Guitar Identification, Fourth Edition Hal Leonard Publishing Corp., Milwaukee, WI, 2008

Erlewine, Vinolpal and Whitford
Gibson's Fabulous Flat-Top Guitars, Miller Freeman Books, San Francisco, CA, 1994

Evans, Tom and Mary Anne
Guitars from the Renaissance to Rock, Facts on File, New York, NY, 1977

Fellman, John
Meeting the Makers - Minnesota's Finest Guitar Builders, Ground Table Publishing, LLC, Robbinsdale, MN 2010

Fisch, Jim, and Fred, L.B.
Epiphone: The House of Stathopoulo, Amsco Publications (Music Sales Corporation), New York, NY, 1996

Fox, Paul
The Other Brands of Gibson, Centerstream Publishing, LLC, Anaheim Hills, CA, 2011

Freeth, Nick and Alexander, Charles
The Acoustic Guitar, Courage Books, Philadelphia, PA, 1999

Freeth, Nick and Alexander, Charles
The Guitar, Salamander Books, London, England, 2002

Fullerton, George
Guitar Legends, Centerstream Publishing, Fullerton, CA, 1993

Giel, Kate, et al
Ferrington Guitars, HarperCollins, New York, NY, 1992

Giltrap, Gordon and Marten, Neville
The Hofner Guitar - A History, International Music Publications Limited, Essex, England, 1993

Gjörde, Per
Pearls and Crazy Diamonds - Fifty Years of Burns Guitars 1952-2002, Addit Information AB, Göteborg, Sweden, 2001

Goudy, Rob
Electric Guitars, Schiffer Publishing, Atglen, PA, 1999

Green, Frank Wm.
The Custom Guitar Shop and Wayne Richard Charvel (What's In a Name?), Working Musician Publications, Sierra Madre, CA, 1999

Green, Frank Wm.
D'Angelico, Master Guitar Builder - What's in a Name? Centerstream, Milwaukee, WI, 2008

Gruhn, George, and Carter, Walter
Acoustic Guitars and Other Fretted Instruments, Miller Freeman Inc., San Francisco, CA, 1993

Gruhn, George, and Carter, Walter
Gruhn's Guide to Vintage Guitars, 3rd Edition, Backbeat Books, New York, NY, 2010

Hartman, Robert Carl
The Larsons' Creations, Guitars and Mandolins, Centerstream Publishing, Fullerton, CA, 1995

Hembree, Gil
Gibson Guitars - Ted McCarty's Golden Era 1948-1966, GH Books, Austin, TX, 2007

Howe, Steve
The Steve Howe Guitar Collection, GPI/Miller Freeman, Inc., San Francisco, CA, 1993

Huber, John
The Development of the Modern Guitar, The Bold Strummer, Ltd., Westport, CT, 1994

Ingram, Adrian
The Gibson L5, Centerstream Publishing, Anaheim Hills, CA, 1997

Ingram, Adrian
The Gibson ES175, Music Maker Books, Cambs, England, 1994

Johnston, Richard and Dick Boak
Martin Guitars: A History, Hal Leonard Books, New York, NY, 2008

Johnston, Richard and Dick Boak
Martin Guitars: A Technical Reference, Hal Leonard Books, New York, NY, 2009

Kasulen, Mark, and Matt Blackett
The History of Yamaha Guitars, Over Sixty Years of Innovation, Hal Leonard, Milwaukee, WI, 2006

Kellerman, Jonathan
With Strings Attached - The Art and Beauty of Vintage Guitars, Ballantine Books, New York, NY, 2008

Juan, Carlos
Collectables and Vintage, American Guitar Center, Stuttgart, Germany, 1995

Lawrence, Robb
The Early Years of the Les Paul Legacy 1915-1963, Hal Leonard, Milwaukee, WI, 2008

Lawrence, Robb
The Modern Era of the Les Paul Legacy 1968-2009, Hal Leonard, Milwaukee, WI, 2009

Lincoln, William A.
World Woods in Color, Linden Publishing Co. Inc. Fresno, CA, 1986

Longworth, Mike
Martin Guitars, a History, 4 Maples Press Inc., Minisink Hills, PA, 1987

Meiners, Larry
Gibson Shipment Totals 1937-1979, Flying Vintage Publications, 2001

Moseley, Willie G.
Classic Guitars U.S.A., Centerstream Publishing, Fullerton, CA, 1992

Moseley, Willie G.
Stellas and Stratocasters, Vintage Guitar Books, Bismarck, ND, 1994

Moseley, Willie G.
Guitar People, Vintage Guitar Books, Bismarck, ND, 1997

Moust, Hans
The Guild Guitar Book, The Company and the Instruments, 1952-1977, Guitar Archives Publications, The Netherlands, 1995

Pensa, Rudy and Vincent J. Ricardel
Archtop Guitars - The Journey From Cremona to New York, Graphis, Inc. 2010

Pleijsier, Hubert
Washburn Prewar Instrument Styles - Guitars, Mandolins, Banjos and Ukuleles 1883-1840, Centerstream Publishing, Milwaukee, WI, 2008

Production, Maurice
Burst Gang, 1G Inc., Tokyo, Japan, 1999

Rich, Bill and Nielsen, Rick
Guitars of the Stars, Volume 1: Rick Nielsen, Gots Publishing Ltd., A Division of Rich Specialties, Inc., Rockford, IL, 1993

Rothman, Ron
Harmony, The People's Guitar, Rothguitar, Southold, NY, 2006

Sandberg, Larry
The Acoustic Guitar Guide, a cappella books, Pennington, NJ, 1991

Schiller, David
Guitars – A Celebration of Pure Mojo, Workman Publishing, New York, NY, 2008

Schmidt, Paul William
Acquired of the Angels: The lives and works of master guitar makers John D'Angelico and James L. D'Aquisto, The Scarecrow Press, Inc., Metuchen, NJ, 1991

Scott, Jay
'50s Cool: Kay Guitars, Seventh String Press, Hauppauge, NY, 1992

Scott, Jay
The Guitars of the Fred Gretsch Company, Centerstream Publishing, Fullerton, CA, 1992

Scott, Jay and Da Pra, Vic
'Burst 1958-'60 Sunburst Les Paul, Seventh String Press, Hauppauge, NY, 1994

Shaw, Robert
Hand Made, Hand Played – The Art & Craft of Contemporary Guitars, Lark Books, New York, NY, 2008

Smith, Richard R.
Fender - The Sound Heard 'Round the World, Garfish Publishing Company, Fullerton, CA, 1995

Smith, Richard R.
The History of Rickenbacker Guitars, Centerstream Publishing, Fullerton, CA, 1989

Spann, Joseph E.
Spann's Guide to Gibson 1902-1941, Centerstream Publishing, LLC, Anaheim Hills, CA, 2011

Spect, Paul, Michael Wright, et al.
Ibanez The Untold Story, Hoshino (USA) Inc., Bensalem, PA, 2005

Teagle, John
Washburn: Over One Hundred Years of Find Stringed Instruments, Music Sales Corp, New York, NY, 1996

Teeter, Don E.
The Acoustic Guitar, University of Oklahoma Press, Oklahoma City, OK

Tollach, Doug
Neptune Bound - The Ultimate Danelectro Guitar Guide, Centerstream, Milwaukee, WI, 2008

Trynka, Paul (Editor)
The Electric Guitar - An Illustrated History, Chronicle Books, San Francisco, CA, 1993

Van Hoose, Thomas A.
The Gibson Super 400, Miller Freeman, Inc., San Francisco, CA, 1991

Vose, Ken
Blue Guitar, Chronicle Books, San Francisco, CA, 1998

Wade, Graham
A Concise History of the Classic Guitar, Mel Bay Publications, Pacific, MO, 2001

Walker, Aidan
The Encyclopedia of Wood, Facts on File, New York, NY, 1989

Washburn, Jim and Johnston, Richard
Martin Guitars, Rodale Press, Emmaus, PA, 1997

Wheeler, Tom
American Guitars, HarperCollins Publishers, New York, NY, 1990

Wheeler, Tom
The Guitar Book, A Handbook for Electric and Acoustic Guitarists, Harper and Row, New York, NY, 1974

White, Forrest
Fender: The Inside Story, GPI/Miller Freeman Books, San Francisco, CA, 1994

Wood, Ronald Lynn
Moderne - Holy Grail of Vintage Guitars, Centerstream, Milwaukee, WI, 2008

Wright, Michael
Guitar Stories, Volume One, Vintage Guitar Books, Bismarck, ND, 1995

Wright, Michael,
Guitar Stories, Volume Two, Vintage Guitar Books, Bismarck, ND, 2000

PERIODICALS

Acoustic Guitar
String Letter Publishing, Inc.
255 W. End Ave.
San Rafael, CA 94901
Phone: 415-485-6946,
Fax: 415-485-0831
Website: www.acousticguitar.com
Published monthly. A one-year subscription (12 issues) is $29.95 in the USA.

Acoustic Guitar UK
Bass Media Ltd.
Oyster House, Hunter's Lodge
Kentisbeare, Devon, UK EX15 2DY
Phone: 011-44-1884-266100
Website: www.acousticmagazine.com
Published monthly. A one-year subscription (12 issues) is £38.25.

American Lutherie
8222 South Park
Tacoma, WA 98408
Phone: 253-472-7853
Website: www.luth.org
Email: tim@luth.org
Published quarterly, must be a member of the Guild of American Lutherie (GAL). A yearly membership to the GAL is $55 and includes four quarterly issues.

Bass Guitar UK
Bass Media Ltd.
Oyster House, Hunter's Lodge
Kentisbeare, Devon UK EX15 2DY
Phone: 011-44-1884-266100
Website: www.bassguitarmagazine.com
Published monthly. A one-year subscription (12 issues) is £38.25.

Bass Player
NewBay Media LLC
1111 Bayhill Dr., Ste. 125
San Bruno, CA 94006
Phone: 650-238-0300
Fax: 650-238-0261
Website: www.bassplayer.com
Email: bassplayer@pcspublink.com
Published monthly with an extra issue in December. A one-year subscription (13 issues) is $18.99 and a two-year subscription (26 issues) is $26.99 in the USA.

Classical Guitar Magazine
Ashley Mark Publishing
1 & 2 Vance Court
Trans Britannia Enterprise Park
Blaydon on Tyne, NE21 5NH UK
Phone: +44(0) 191 414 9000
Fax: +44(0) 191 414 9001

Website: www.classicalguitarmagazine.com
Published monthly. A one-year subscription (12 issues) is £72.60 in the USA.

Downbeat
102 N. Haven
Elmhurst, IL 60126-2932
Toll Free: 800-554-7470
Phone: 630-941-2030
Fax: 630-941-3210
Website: www.downbeat.com
Email: service@downbeat.com
Published monthly. A one-year subscription (12 issues) is $26.99, a two-year subscription (24 issues) is $48.99, and a three-year subscription (36 issues) is $64.99.

EQ
NewBay Media LLC
1111 Bayhill Dr., Ste. 125
San Bruno, CA 94403
Phone: 650-238-0300
Fax: 650-238-0262
Website: www.eqmag.com
Email: eqmag@musicplayer.com
Published monthly. A one-year subscription (12 issues) is $23.97 in the U.S.

The Fretboard Journal
2221 NW 56th Street, Suite 101
Seattle, WA 98107
Phone: 206-706-3252
Fax: 650-238-0261
Website: www.fretboardjournal.com
Email: subscriptions@fretboardjournal.com
Published quarterly. A one-year subscription (4 issues) is $40 and a two-year subscription (8 issues) is $75 in the U.S.

Gitarre & Bass (Germany)
MM-Musik-Media-Verlag GmbH,
An Der Wachsfabrik 8, Koln, 50996 Germany
Phone: 011-39-2236-96217
Fax: 011-39-2236-96217-5
Website: www1.gitarrebass.de/magazine
Published monthly.

Guitar Aficionado
Future US
149 5th Ave., 9th Floor
New York, NY 10010
Phone: 800-456-6441
Website: www.guitaraficionado.com
Published bi-monthly. A one-year subscription (6 issues) is $24.95 and a two-year subscription (12 issues) is $44.95 in the U.S.

Guitar & Bass UK
Anthem Publishing
Office 6B, Rathbone Square, Tanfield Road
Croydon, Surrey, CR0 1BT UK
Phone: + 44 (0) 20-8240-6627
Website: www.guitarmagazine.co.uk
Email: guitarandbass@anthem-publishing.com
Published monthly. A one-year subscription (12 issues) is $89 in the U.S.

Guitar Digest
PO Box 66
The Plains, Ohio 45780
Phone: 740-797-3351
Website: www.guitardigest.com
Published bi-monthly. A one-year subscription (6 issues) is $10.00 in the USA.

Guitar Player
NewBay Media, LLC
1111 Bayhill Dr., Ste. 125
San Bruno, CA 94403
Phone: 650-238-0300
Fax: 650-238-0261
Website: www.guitarplayer.com
Email: guitarplayer@sfsdayton.com
Published monthly. A one-year subscription (12 issues) is $14.99 and a two-year subscription (24 issues) is $22.99 in the USA.

Guitar World
Future US
149 5th Ave., 9th Floor
New York, NY 10010
Phone: 800-456-6441
Website: www.guitarworld.com
Published monthly. A one-year subscription (12 issues) is $14.95 and a two-year subscription (24 issues) is $24.95 in the USA.

Guitarist UK
Future Publishing
Beaufort Ct., 30 Monmouth Street
Bath, UK BA1 2BW
Website: www.guitarist.co.uk
Published monthly. A one-year subscription (13 issues) is $135 in the USA

JazzTimes
Madavor Media
85 Quincy Ave., Ste. 2,
Quincy, MA 02169
Phone: 617-706-9110
Fax: 617-536-0102
Website: www.jazztimes.com
Email: info@jazztimes.com
Published 10 times per year. A one-year subscription (10 issues) is $29.99 in the USA and a two-year subscription (20 issues) is $55.98.

Just Jazz Guitar
PO Box 76053
Atlanta, Georgia 30358-1053
Phone: 404-250-9298
Fax: 404-250-9298
Website: www.justjazzguitar.com
Published quarterly. A one year subscription (4 issues) is $44 in the USA.

MMR (Musical Merchandise Review)
Symphony Publishing
21 Highland Circle, Ste. 1
Needham, MA 02494
Phone: 781-453-9310
Fax: 781-453-9389
Website: www.mmrmagazine.com
Published monthly. Magazine is free to those who qualify.

The Music and Sound Retailer
Testa Communications
25 Willowdale Ave.
Port Washington, NY 11050-3779
Phone: 516-767-2500
Fax: 516-767-9335
Website: www.msretailer.com
Published monthly. Magazine is free to those who qualify.

Music Inc.
102 N. Haven
Elmhurst, IL 60126-2932
Toll Free: 800-554-7470
Phone: 630-941-2030
Fax: 630-941-3210
Website: www.musicincmag.com
Email: editor@musicincmag.com
Published Monthly except for April. Magazine is free to music retailers.

Music Trades, The
PO Box 432
80 West Street
Englewood, NJ 07631
Toll Free: 800-423-6530
Phone: 201-871-1965
Fax: 201-871-0455
Website: www.musictrades.com
Published monthly. One year subscription (12 issues) is $16.00 and a two year subscription (24 issues) is $23.00.

Premier Guitar
Gearhead Communications, LLC
PO Box 127
Mount Vernon, IA 52314
Toll free: 877-704-4327
Phone: 319-895-0050
Fax: 319-895-0058
Email: info@premierguitar.com
Website: www.premierguitar.com
Published monthly. One year subscription is $24.95, two year subscription is $39.95.

The Tonequest Report
Mountainview Publishing LLC
PO Box 717
Decatur, GA 30030-0717
Toll Free: 1-877-MAX-TONE
Phone: 404-377-0300
Fax: 404-377-0604
Email: tonequest1@aol.com
Website: www.tonequest.com
Published monthly. A one-year subscription (12 issues) is $89, a two-year subscription (24 issues) is $159, and a three-year subscription (36 issues) is $229.

Vintage Guitar Magazine
PO Box 7301
Bismarck, ND 58507
Phone: 701-255-1197
Fax: 701-255-0250
Website: www.vintageguitar.com
Published monthly. A one-year subscription (12 issues) is $24.95 and a two-year subscription (24 issues) is $46.95 in the USA.

Vintage News, The
Mandolin Brothers, Ltd.
629 Forest Ave.
Staten Island, NY 10310-2576
Phone: 718-981-3226
Fax: 718-816-4416
Email: mandolin@mandoweb.com
Website: www.mandoweb.com
Published bi-monthly. A one-year subscription (6 issues) is $20.00 in the USA.

In addition to the regular publications put out by these publishers, most offer Special Edition (i.e., yearly buyers' guides, new product reviews, market overviews, etc.) magazines that are released annually, or bi-annually. Please contact them directly for more information.

UNDERSTANDING CONDITION FACTORS

Rating the condition factor of a guitar is, at best, subjective, while at worst, totally misrepresentative. We've given a few examples of things that may affect the value and desirability of vintage acoustic guitars, but it's almost impossible to accurately ascertain the correct condition factor (especially true on older instruments) without knowing what to look for - which means having the instrument in your hands (or someone else's who has checked it out). Even then, three different experienced sources will probably come up with slightly different grades, not to mention different values based on different reasons. Listed below are major factors to consider when determining both the condition and value of any used acoustic instruments. Also, please study the Photo Grading System color photographs carefully on pages 25-39 to learn more about the factors described below.

Finish - Original finish in good shape is, of course, the most desirable, and is typically the most important factor for collectors when hooked up with a major trademark and desirable model. A light professional overspray will negatively affect the value of a guitar somewhat. Professionally refinished instruments are typically worth 50-60% of the value of an original, and a poor refinish is below than that. A guitar with original finish in average condition is often worth more than a guitar that is refinished in excellent condition.

Major Repairs - Many older acoustic guitars have had repairs, which are expected. A well-done neck reset won't affect the overall value that much. Replaced bridges will have an effect, but the better the work, the better the resale value. A replaced neck, fingerboard, part of a side, top or back will cause the price to drop noticeably. Items that are less visible, but still important include altered bracing, shaved necks, and repaired/replaced/shaved bridges. Repair work at an authorized facility for certain trademarks/manufacturers is the best way to ensure work is done properly and the most value is maintained.

Modifications - Any non-factory modification on an original guitar is going to hurt the value. Electronics are the most common addition to acoustic guitars, and as long as no holes have to be drilled, this modification can actually add value. Think really hard before you make any of these changes on vintage guitars – remember, you don't get a second chance to make it original!

Replacement Tuners and Other Non-Original Parts - Many older guitars have been fitted with new tuners at some point. These days, there are good replacement tuners available that fit the original holes, etc. There are also sleeves that will make an oversized hole into the correct size for original style tuners. Even a good, appropriate replacement set will have a negative effect on value, even though it constitutes a playing improvement over what was available when the instrument was manufactured. Replacement parts that are as close to the original pieces will have the least negative effect on the value.

Cracks - Acoustic instruments susceptible to cracking because the bodies are typically not solid, and the thinner wood may crack due to humidity and/or temperature variations. Many older pre-WWII acoustic guitars have a cracked top. The seriousness of the crack and/or how professionally it has been repaired make all the difference in determining both playability and value. Unfortunately, unattended cracks tend to get bigger and usually do not go back together perfectly. Any crack will affect value, but a small, professionally well repaired crack will take much less of a bite out of the price than a large gaping crack that wouldn't go together properly.

Frets/String - A good analogy for frets and strings would be found in the vintage car market: you rarely find a vintage car with original tires. Guitars were meant to be played and frets and strings do wear out. A good professional fret job using factory spec parts should not affect the value of your instrument. Also, strings are meant to be changed, so don't get too wound up if these two items are not original.

Cosmetics - The cleaner an instrument, the more its worth. Don't ever underestimate the value of eye appeal. A mint, unplayed, original condition guitar with tags will always bring more than the prices for "excellent" condition. On the other hand, an instrument with most of the finish worn off from years of use, but is unaltered with no problems is still more desirable than an instrument with higher condition but with a cracked top, replaced bridge, shaved neck, etc.

General Guitar Maintenance & Tips - Airplanes are meant to be flown, cars are meant to be driven, and guitars are meant to be played. Since instrument construction is typically wood, and wood expands/contracts like many other natural materials, don't allow instruments to go from one extreme temp/humidity factor to another (i.e., don't ship your Stromberg Master 400 from Ft. Meyers, FL to International Falls, MN in January). Try to maintain a stable temp. and humidity level. Also, use good quality, professional products to clean, polish, and maintain your instrument (investment). Remember, maintaining a fine guitar requires some common sense and TLC.

Guitars, even vintage ones, are meant to be played. Enjoy yours, take proper care of it, play it once in awhile, and don't let temperature and/or humidity factors get to extremes.

EXPLANATION & CONVERTING GUITAR GRADING SYSTEMS

Since the 15th Edition *Blue Book of Acoustic Guitars* continues to use the descriptive grading system of Average and Excellent factors to describe condition, please study the digital color acoustic guitar condition photos on the following pages carefully to help understand and identify each acoustic guitar's unique condition factor. These photos, with condition factors, serve as a guideline, not an absolute. Remember, if the condition factor isn't right, the price is wrong!

The Acoustic Guitar Factor chart listed below has been provided to help you understand the Photo Grading System™ and other condition factors that may be used in the industry. All percentage descriptions and/or possible conversions made thereof are based on original condition - alterations, repairs, cracking, refinishing work, and any other non-original alterations that have changed the condition of an instrument must be listed additionally and typically subtracted from the values based on condition throughout this text (please refer to page 23 for an explanation of these critical factors affecting both condition and price).

ACOUSTIC GUITAR CONDITION FACTORS WITH EXPLANATIONS

100%/New - New with all factory materials, including warranty card, owner's manual, case, and other items that were originally included by the manufacturer. On currently manufactured instruments, the 100% value refers to an instrument not previously sold at retail. Even if a new instrument has been played only once and traded in a week later, it no longer qualifies at 100% - no dealer is going to buy the same guitar at the 100%/New price since they can buy it at the wholesale price. Likewise, no independent buyer would buy a used guitar when they could buy one brand new from the same dealer. The 100%/New condition factor only applies to guitars that are currently manufactured or that have been discontinued no later than 2007 since it may take a while for inventory to sell out. It is instinctive to consider the 100%/New condition factor a "mint" category, but the reality on vintage instruments is that if it is truly mint, it needs to be evaluated and appraised individually.

Excellent & Average condition factors are typically represented by a price range that reflects the high and low condition factors in each range. Obviously, an Average acoustic with a lot of body wear (low average) is less desirable than an Average acoustic with little body wear (high average) - and should be priced accordingly.

Excellent - the Excellent condition range is represented by both High Excellent and Low Excellent condition. High Excellent refers to an instrument that is very clean, looks almost new (perhaps a few light scratches/dings only), and has hardly been used. Low Excellent refers to a guitar that has been played/used, and has accumulated some minor wear in the form of light scratches, dings, small chips, etc. The older an instrument, the less likely it will be in High Excellent condition. Even Low Excellent is seldom encountered on instruments over 50 years old, since most acoustic instruments were originally purchased to be played. High Excellent condition also includes currently manufactured instruments that have been previously sold at retail, even though they may have only played a few times. On recently manufactured instruments, there usually is a fairly large price difference between the 100% and High Excellent condition factors due to used instrument pricing which typically is affected by dealer replacements costs. Instruments in this condition may not have the original manufacturer's warranty card, depending on the age of the instrument, but should include the original case if it was included when new.

Average - The Average guitar condition factor indicates an acoustic guitar that has been in a player's hands and has worn due to player use (hopefully, no abuse). High Average condition instruments have normal dents, small chips, and light dings on the body, and/or scratches on the top and back. However, there should be no problems unless indicated separately. Low Average condition instruments may reflect major finish problems, replacement parts, previous repairs (especially on older instruments), alterations, and neck/fret wear is typically visible. No excuses as a player, however. May or may not have case.

Below Average - Finish and or colors are still discernible, some parts possibly missing/replaced/repaired, could be either refinished or repaired, structurally sound, though frequently encountered with non-factory alterations and other problems. Must be playable. This condition factor is not valued in the *Blue Book of Acoustic Guitars*.

Poor - Ending a life sentence of hard labor, must still be playable, most of the licks have left, family members should be notified immediately, normally not worthy unless the ad also mentions pre-war D-45. May have to double as kindling if in a tight spot on a cold night. This condition factor is not valued in the *Blue Book of Acoustic Guitars*.

100% OR NEW CONDITION

GIBSON SJ-200 "TRUE VINTAGE"
Courtesy Gibson Guitar Corporation

Vintage Sunburst, Ser. No. N/A. Gibson's True Vintage Series represent instruments built from Gibson's greatest era of production. In this case, this SJ-200 is based on the original Super Jumbo built in the late 1930s. Not only do Gibson's True Vintage guitars look and sound like a vintage guitar, they also feel like one! Once a guitar has been sold, it can no longer be valued in the 100% or New pricing category.

100% OR NEW CONDITION

2009 PAUL REED SMITH TONARE GRANDE
Courtesy PRS Guitars

Natural Finish, Ser. No. N/A. After nearly 30 years of building electric guitars and a line of prototype models in the early 1990s, PRS finally released a line of acoustic guitars in 2009. The Tonare is a full-bodied acoustic guitar with all the appointments expected from PRS including fifteen elaborate binding, purfling, inlays, and a soundhole rosette. Several options include the tone woods, inlays, and electronics. The 100% or New condition grading factor assumes the guitar has never been bought or sold at a retail level. Once a guitar has been played, it can no longer be evaluated under the 100% or New condition grading factor.

HIGH EXCELLENT CONDITION

2008 IBANEZ EW20AS QUILTED ASH
Courtesy Chad Speck, Encore Music

Natural finish, Ser. No. 08008022. Ibanez is one of the largest guitar manufacturers in the industry offering a wide range of anything guitar related, and in 2005 they introduced their Exotic Wood Series of acoustics. This model features quilted ash top, back, sides, and headstock overlay as well as a rosewood fingerboard and bridge. This guitar is no longer produced, but Ibanez continues to produce the Exotic Wood Series with non-traditional tone woods. There is little to no wear on this Ibanez, so it is considered in the higher end of the Excellent condition range.

HIGH EXCELLENT CONDITION

1937 MARTIN D-28
Courtesy Dave Rogers, Dave's Guitar Shop

Natural finish, Ser. No. 66725. Martin's dreadnought-shaped body has become the most common acoustic guitar in production. 1937 is widely considered to be right in the middle of Martin's "Golden Era" of production. With Brazilian rosewood back and sides, this is one of the most valuable Martin guitars in existence. Notice the second smaller pickguard next to the fingerboard on the upper bass bout. We're not entirely sure why a customer would request a pickguard here, but it appears to be affixed from the factory. This guitar is in great condition considering it was built before World War II. Aside from some minor wear that is hardly visible, this guitar appears in the High Excellent pricing category.

EXCELLENT CONDITION

1990 OVATION ELITE SPECIAL
Courtesy Dave Rogers, Dave's Guitar Shop

Blue Burst finish, Ser. No. 407585, Note the wear around edge and binding – on Ovation instruments; it is difficult to determine condition from looking at the back of the guitar, since it is a fiberglass bowl that is very resistant to scratches, nicks, belt buckle wear, etc. Pay attention to fretwear, potential cracks in the top, and always check the action, making sure that it's not too high. If the bridge and/or saddle has been shaved as low as it can go, and the action is still way off the strings, the neck might have to be reset to ensure playability.

LOW EXCELLENT CONDITION

CIRCA 1938 WARDS ARCHTOP
Courtesy Dave Hull

Sunburst finish, Ser. No. N/A. This original no-name guitar sure looks like a Gibson, doesn't it? It should, because Gibson made it. This guitar is known as a "House Brand" private label instrument. These instruments were typically made by big-name manufacturers for major department stores, in this case, Montgomery Wards. Even though this Wards Archtop is a Gibson-made guitar, it does not command the same amount of money or premium for a Gibson-marked instrument. This guitar shows typical playing wear with scratches, dings, and dents throughout the body. The headstock logo has also fallen off.

LOW EXCELLENT CONDITION

1937 MARTIN 00-18 SUNBURST
Courtesy Dave Rogers, Dave's Guitar Shop

Sunburst finish, Ser. No. 66879. Martin's 00 Grand Concert body shape has been around since the 19th century, but this particular model was produced during Martin's "Golden Era." Martin began building this guitar designed for steel strings in 1924 and it features a rare, but optional Sunburst finish. This acoustic shows honest playing wear with pick marks and scrapes on the upper treble bout and light wear across the rest of the body. For a guitar going on 75 years, it is still in remarkable condition. The light wear puts this guitar in the Low Excellent pricing category.

HIGH AVERAGE CONDITION

CIRCA 1973-1975 GIBSON J-45 "DELUXE"
Courtesy Chad Speck, Encore Music

Sunburst finish, Ser. No. A160237. The label on this Gibson states it is a "J-45 Deluxe" but it is no different than a regular J-45. In fact, Gibson never produced a Deluxe version in addition to a regular version – it was strictly a name change/marketing ploy in the 1970s. By 1970, all of Gibson's jumbos, including the J-45, had adopted the square-shouldered body shape. This J-45 has some general wear on the top and back along with slight weather checking and worn binding around the neck. Based on the amount of wear, this guitar appears in the higher part of the Average range.

HIGH AVERAGE CONDITION

1933 EPIPHONE DE LUXE MASTERBILT
Courtesy Dave Hull

Sunburst finish, Ser. No. 6972. Epiphones from this era are considered to be some of the finest archtops built in the U.S. Considering this guitar is over seventy-five years old, it is in remarkably good shape. The guitar shows typical playing wear and the finish still shows the bookmatched flame maple. The Average condition price ranges (from low to high) in this text refer to the value range of instruments found in between High Average or Low Average condition factors. The only real problem with this guitar is the cracked pickguard. The headstock inlays were also probably a factory-added item that didn't come standard on the guitar. All of these factors place the guitar in High Average condition.

AVERAGE CONDITION

CIRCA 1960S HARMONY H 1213 ARCHTONE
Courtesy Chad Speck, Encore Music

Shaded Brown Sunburst finish, Ser. No. 3714. Harmony is probably the best-known private label manufacturer of all time. Countless retailers came to Harmony and had them build private label guitars – it is unknown how many different trademarks appeared on the same guitar. This H 1213 Archtone is a very simple archtop acoustic with f-holes and white painted lines along the edge. Most vintage Harmonys today are used and abused, and after comparing the front to the back of this guitar, it is evident that the front was exposed to sunlight for quite some time. There is medium wear across the guitar including a worn-down fingerboard, a missing pickguard, and dinged headstock. This guitar appears in the Average range.

AVERAGE CONDITION

LATE 1920S GIBSON L-0

Courtesy Dave Rogers, Dave's Guitar Shop

Natural finish, Ser. No. N/A. The L-0 was introduced in 1926 as the "Robert Johnson" shape, and by 1928 it was produced with a complete mahogany body, which is the variation shown here. Gibson's L Series was much adored by Blues players such as Johnson and Nick Lucas because of its small body shape and tone. This L-0 has been played heavily and if you look close, you can see that the bridge is pulling up on the body. Other than that, this guitar is still structurally intact. With heavy wear like this, the guitar appears in the Average pricing category.

LOW AVERAGE CONDITION

1947 GIBSON J-45
Courtesy Dave Rogers, Dave's Guitar Shop

Sunburst finish, Ser. No. N/A. Gibson's round-shouldered dreadnought "Advanced Jumbo" design was one of their most popular designs. The J-45 in Sunburst finish was a player's guitar and this one is no different. A quick glance at this guitar shows heavy wear across the instrument. Of the remaining finish, it is heavily checked and cracked, and it is outright missing in several places. The neck is especially rough indicating that this guitar was played hard. The good news is that the guitar is all intact and still very collectible. With extreme wear like this, and the fact that the guitar is still playable, this appears in the Low Average pricing category.

LOW AVERAGE CONDITION

1944 MARTIN 00-17
Courtesy Willie Del Mar

Natural finish, Ser. No. 89739. This WWII era Martin is a good example of a well-used guitar. Some wood was whittled off the bass side of the fingerboard, the bridge saddle is tipping, and the original tuners have been replaced with incorrect non-originals. This guitar needs to have the Brazilian rosewood fingerboard replaced, along with repairs to the frets and the bridge. Unfortunately, professional repairs of this nature are expensive, and the costs involved may be more than the additional value after the repairs have been made. The original finish shows tons of wear, but is intact.

BELOW AVERAGE, (REPAIRED CONDITION)

1930S GIBSON L-0
Courtesy Music Go 'Round

Natural finish, Ser. No. N/A. If you could use one word to sum up this guitar's condition, it would be "problems!" The top pulled up behind the bridge, and an oversized bridge and braces were added to make this wonderful old guitar sound like it was made out of cement. A qualified luthier with extensive repair experience is a must for this type of repair. Unfortunately, this instrument was "fixed" by someone who didn't know what they were doing. A lot of wood was also added under the top, effectively dampening the sound while providing no additional structural support. The neck was reset at an incorrect angle, causing a low action that buzzes all up and down the neck. One of the tuners was replaced by a piece of a three-on-a-side, and it turns the wrong way. A very sorry example of a guitar that could and should have been repaired properly, but wasn't - hence the Below Average condition factor. The cost of fixing it correctly at this point probably exceeds the value of the instrument.

NO CONDITION FACTOR, NOT PLAYABLE

1920 MARTIN MODEL 1-28

Courtesy Hoffman Guitars

Natural finish, Ser. No. 15123. This pre-war Martin came into the guitar shop with two bolts in the bridge–right through the tops of the pyramids. This image was taken before any work had been done. Repairman Ron Tracy replaced the pyramid tops without removing the bridge, which was no small feat. The guitar will also be getting a neck reset. Other than one side crack that appears to have been poorly repaired, this instrument with Brazilian rosewood back/sides will be in pretty good shape again once the surgery is carefully and professionally completed. A guitar that is not playable, with major problems requiring extensive repair like this, is worth virtually the wood that makes up the components, unless it is exceedingly rare and collectable (this one is). Once this guitar is reassembled, its value will go up substantially. It won't be worth as much as a no problem original, but a professionally repaired guitar that is playable is always worth more than a broken/parts instrument.

PREVIOUS EDITIONS

1st Edition
1993

2nd Edition
1994

3rd Edition
1996

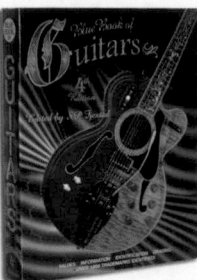

4th Edition
1997

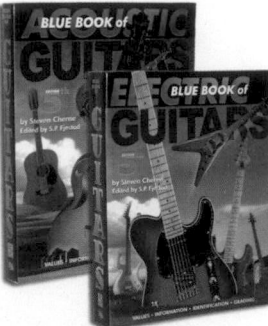

5th Edition
1998

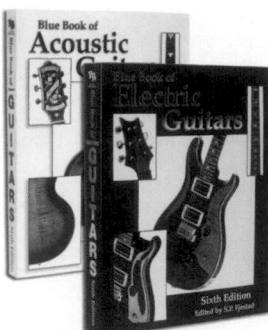

6th Edition
1999

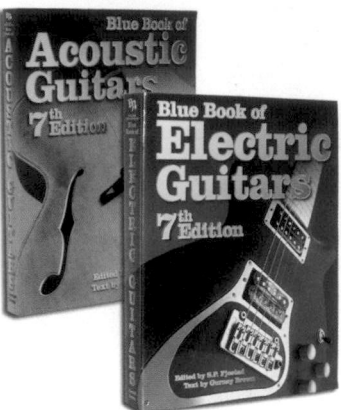

7th Edition
2001

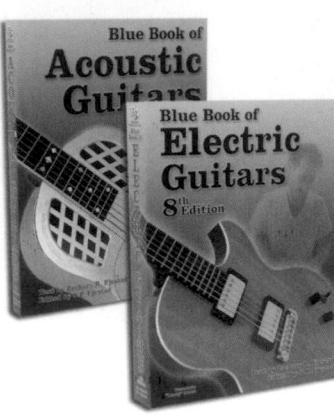

8th Edition
2003

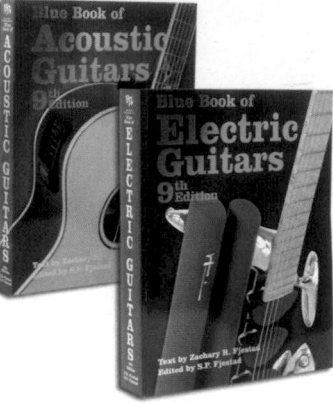

9th Edition
2005

10th Edition
2006

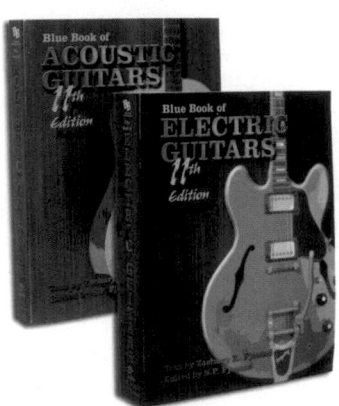

11th Edition
2007

12th Edition
2009

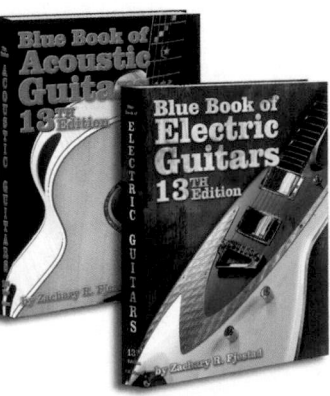

13th Edition
2011

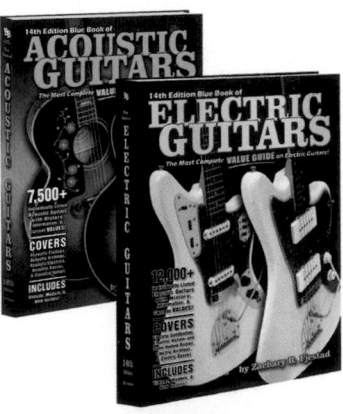

14th Edition
2012

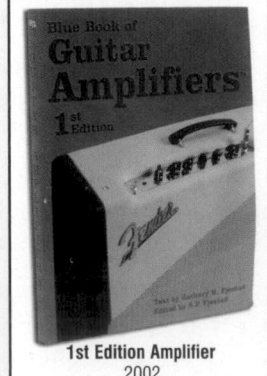

1st Edition Amplifier
2002

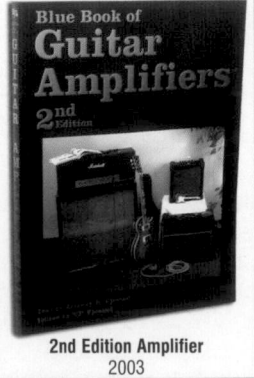

2nd Edition Amplifier
2003

3rd Edition Amplifier
2007

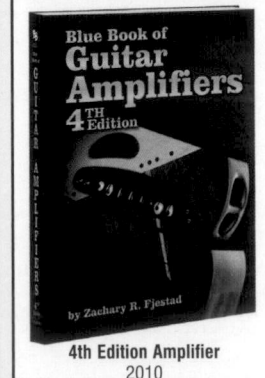

4th Edition Amplifier
2010

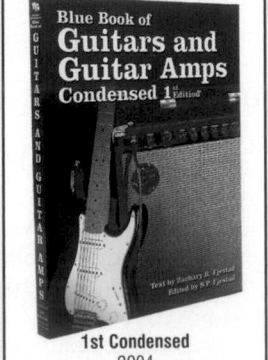

1st Condensed
2004

800.877.4867 • www.BlueBookofGuitarValues.com

A SECTION
A

See chapter on House Brands.

This trademark has been identified as a House Brand of the Alden department store chain. One of the models shares similarities with the Harmony-built Stratotone of the 1960s, while a previously identified model dates back to the 1950s. Source: Willie G. Moseley, *Stellas & Stratocasters*.

ABILENE

Instruments previously produced in Korea by Samick. Previously distributed in the U.S. by Samick.

The Abilene trademark was previously distributed in the U.S. by Samick and Advantage Worldwide. Abilene offered a range of acoustic, acoustic/electric, solid body electric guitars and practice amplifiers. The guitars were built by Samick of Korea, and the acoustic guitar models feature designs based on popular American models.

This company produced a full range of acoustic models, ranging from classical to dreadnought guitars. Also, there were resonator and folk guitars in the line. All guitars have model designations. The first letter (A) stands for Abilene, and the second letter indicates dreadnought (W), classical (C), folk (F), or jumbo (J). The following numbers indicate the size and configuration of the guitar. There may also be numbers following that indicate the finish color and whether it has a satin or a gloss finish. Numbers typically start around 15 and contain many variations. Prices on these guitars are usually very reasonable and used models can typically be purchased for between $50 and $200.

ACADEMY

Instruments previously built in Korea. Previously distributed by Lark in the Morning of Mendocino, CA.

Academy offered nice quality steel string guitars, four-, five-, and six-string banjos, and chord harps. Used prices are unknown on these instruments.

A.C.E. GUITARS

Instruments currently built in Somersworth, NH by the Poly-Tech Company.

A.C.E. Guitars are produced in Somersworth, NH, and are hand-built models designed by the Poly-Tech Company also of Somersworth, NH. Models are acoustic-electric, electric arch-top and nylon string electric which are thin hollowbody construction. For more information, visit A.C.E.'s website or contact them directly.

Acoustic-electric and archtops range in price between $800 and $1,400, including case. Details of construction are found on the A.C.E. Guitar's website. Custom instruments are priced higher.

CONTACT INFORMATION
A.C.E. GUITARS
A division of The Poly-Tech Company
21 Montrose Rd
Stratham, NH 03885
Phone No.: 603-778-9610
www.ace-guitars.com
info@ace-guitars.com

ACEPRO

Instruments currently produced in China since 2004. Headquarters are located in Korea. Distributed in the U.S. by Acepro America in Marion, IL.

Ace Musical Instruments, LTD. was founded March 29, 2004. Mr. Gil Hyo-Park is the president, and he has worked in musical instrument development and construction since the early 1980s. Acepro has five Korean engineers working at their China factory to train Chinese workers and oversee production.

Acepro produces mainly electric guitars and basses, but they also make acoustics, resonators, cases, and amplifiers. Most guitar designs are based on traditional American models, but they do offer their own twist on several instruments. Many guitars are entry level models, but they do offer a few higher-end models. For more information, visit Acepro's website or contact their distributor directly.

CONTACT INFORMATION
ACEPRO
Headquarters
3Ra-508 Ho, 1384-7 Jungwang Dong
Shiheung City, Gyeonggi-Do 429-450
Korea
www.aceguitars.co.kr
ace@aceguitars.co.kr

U.S. Distributor: Acepro America
805 N. McLaren Street
Marion, IL 62959
Phone No.: 618-751-9211
www.aceproguitars.com
aceproamerica@gmail.com

ADAMAS

Instruments currently manufactured since 1975. Distributed by KMC Music in Bloomfield, CT.

Adamas guitars have been produced since 1975. Charlie Kaman, an innovator of the helicopter, took the carbon fiber material used in aviation and applied it to guitars. The top of this guitar is carbon fiber and is remarkably thin. These guitars also have a round back to give a smooth sound. Adamas was a series of Ovation until about 1997, when they were introduced as their own line. Adamas also offers a custom shop on select models. In late 2007, Fender Musical Instrument Corporation (FMIC) acquired Kaman Music, which includes Adamas. In 2008, Kaman Music changed the name of their company to KMC Music. For more information, visit Adamas' website or contact KMC Music directly.

CONTACT INFORMATION
ADAMAS
Distributed by KMC Music
55 Griffin Road South
Bloomfield, CT 06002
Phone No.: 860-243-7105
Fax No.: 860-243-7287
www.ovationguitars.com
askus@ovationguitars.com

MSR/NOTES	100%	EXCELLENT	AVERAGE	LAST MSR

ACOUSTIC

The first production Adamas was introduced in 1976. The model designation is unknown currently, but was available with a Blue, Green, Red, Natural, or a Black finish. Pricing and specs are currently unknown and research is underway. Adamas also made two guitars with center soundholes: the W591, which was part of the CVT series, and the 6591, part of the SMT series. Adamas currently offers custom shop guitars where the customer starts with a base model and select options are available. Currently, Adamas features the following base models for their Custom Shop program: the 1581 (base MSR $3,999), the 1680 (last base MSR was $4,249), the 1687 (base MSR $4,099), the 2080 (base MSR $3,649), and the W2097 (base MSR $3,649).

1581-KK KAKI KING – single cutaway, mid-depth bowl-back body, carbon fiber top, abalone top purfling, multi-soundholes on the bass bout with chrome rosette, five-piece mahogany/maple neck, 14/22-fret diagonal end ebony fingerboard with 12th fret Kaki crown inlay, three-per-side gold tuners, walnut with rosewood stain bridge, Adamas Hi-Output pickup, OP50 electronics, available in Black finish, mfg. 2010-present.

MSR $4,999	$3,500	$2,200 - 2,750	$1,325 - 1,650	

CVT W597 – single cutaway, mid-depth bowl-back body, cross weave carbon fiber top, five-piece mahogany/maple/ebony neck, 14/22-fret diagonal end ebony fingerboard, multi-soundhole, ebony bridge, three-per-side tuners, Adamas Hi-Output pickup, OP50 electronics, gold hardware, available in Graphite (4G), Bronze (BZ), or Cobalt Blue (CB) finish, mfg. 1999-2007.

	N/A	$1,275 - 1,600	$750 - 950	$2,979

* Add 7.5% (Last MSR was $3,199) for VIP preamp.

CVT W598 12-STRING – similar to the W597, except in 12-string configuration and six-per-side tuners, mfg. 1999-2003, 2005-07.

	N/A	$1,325 - 1,650	$800 - 1,000	$3,179

* Add 7.5% (Last MSR was $3,399) for VIP preamp.

CVT W597ME (MELISSA ETHERIDGE) – single cutaway, mid-depth bowl-back body, cross weave carbon fiber top, abalone top purfling, MOP soundhole inlays, five-piece mahogany/maple neck, 14/22-fret diagonal end ebony fingerboard, multi-soundhole, ebony bridge, three-per-side tuners, Adamas Hi-Output pickup, OP50 electronics, black with pearloid hardware, available in White Pearl (WP) finish, hand signed by Melissa Etheridge, mfg. 2002-present.

MSR $4,299	$3,000	$1,875 - 2,350	$1,125 - 1,400	

CVT 1680 – deep body style, woven graphite composite top with multi-hole walnut rosette, 12/20 extended fret ebony fingerboard with MOP Adamas style inlays, three-per-side open-style tuners with ebony buttons, ebony bridge, VIP-5 preamp electronics, gold hardware, available in Natural Weave finish, 25.25 in. scale, mfg. 2006-08.

	N/A	$1,900 - 2,300	$1,200 - 1,450	$4,249

This model was available through Adamas Custom Shop where it could be totally customized. The specs and prices listed above are strictly standard options/features.

CVT 2080 – single cutaway deep body style, woven carbon graphite composite top, aluminum tear drop soundhole, 14/22 extended fret ebony fingerboard with 12th fret contour inlays, three-per-side tuners with black buttons, ebony bridge, Original Patented Pickup, VIP-5 preamp electronics, chrome hardware, available in Natural Weave finish, 25.25 in. scale, mfg. 2006-09.

	N/A	$1,550 - 1,900	$1,050 - 1,250	$3,649

This model was available through Adamas Custom Shop where it could be totally customized. The specs and prices listed above are strictly standard options/features.

CVT W2097 – single cutaway deep contour body style, woven carbon fiber composite top, multi-piece exotic hardwood rosette, 14/22 extended fret ebony fingerboard, three-per-side gold tuners, ebony bridge, Original Patented Pickup, VIP-5 preamp electronics, available in Cobalt Blue Crossweave finish, 25.25 in. scale, mfg. 2008-09.

	N/A	$1,550 - 1,900	$1,050 - 1,250	$3,649

This model was available through Adamas Custom Shop where it could be totally customized. The specs and prices listed above are strictly standard options/features.

SMT 1597 – single cutaway, mid-depth bowl-back body, unidirectional carbon fiber top, five-piece mahogany/maple/ebony neck, 14/22-fret diagonal end ebony fingerboard, multi-soundhole, ebony bridge, three-per-side tuners, Adamas Hi-Output pickup, OP50 electronics, gold hardware, available in Natural Graphite (4G), Graphite Burst (4GB), or Ruby Graphite (RG) finish, mfg. 1997-2005.

	N/A	$1,000 - 1,250	$600 - 750	$2,199

SMT 1598 12-STRING – similar to the SMT 1597, except in 12-string configuration and six-per-side tuners, mfg. 1997-2005.

	N/A	$1,075 - 1,350	$650 - 800	$2,499

SMT 1598ME 12-STRING (MELISSA ETHERIDGE) – similar to the CVT W597ME, except has unidirectional carbon fiber design, has 12-string configuration, and has six-per-side tuners, available in Natural Graphite or Ruby Burst (disc.) finish, mfg. 2002-present.

MSR $3,999	$2,800	$1,750 - 2,200	$1,050 - 1,325	

MILLENIUM – Adamas guitar made specially for the year 2000, features neck inlays of the planets including Earth with Millennium on the 5th fret, 75 total made, abalone body binding, 50 sold in the U.S. market, mfg. 2000 only.

	N/A	$1,875 - 2,350	$1,125 - 1,400	$3,000

MSR/NOTES	100%	EXCELLENT	AVERAGE	LAST MSR

Q597 – single cutaway, mid-depth bowl-back body, carbon fiber top, five-piece mahogany/maple/ebony neck, 14/22-fret diagonal end ebony fingerboard, multi-wavy soundhole, ebony bridge, three-per-side tuners, Adamas Hi-Output pickup, OP50 electronics, gold hardware, available in Natural or Blue finish, mfg. 2003-05.

	N/A	$1,350 - 1,650	$850 - 1,000	$2,599

Q598 – similar to the Q597, except in 12-string configuration, mfg. 2004-05.

	N/A	$1,400 - 1,750	$950 - 1,150	$2,699

STANDARD MODEL 1581 – single cutaway deep bowl body, unidirectional carbon fiber top, Adamas Quinted bracing, one 13 soundhole grouping and one four soundhole grouping with original Adamas II design epaulets, five-piece mahogany/maple neck, walnut fingerboard with Adamas II style inlays, walnut headstock overlay with Ovation profile, three-per-side gold Schaller tuners, carved walnut bridge, OCP-1 pickup, Standard FET electronics, available in Black, Reverse Blue Burst, or Reverse Burst finish, mfg. 2008-2010.

$2,800	$1,800 - 2,150	$1,150 - 1,350	$3,999

This model was available through Adamas Custom Shop where it could be totally customized. The specs and prices listed above are strictly standard options/features.

STANDARD MODEL 1687 – deep bowl non-cutaway body, unidirectional carbon fiber top, Adamas Quinted bracing, two 13-piece soundholes with epaulets, walnut neck, walnut fingerboard with Adamas I style inlays, styled headstock with carved scroll, three-per-side gold Schaller tuners, carved walnut bridge, OCP-1 pickup, Standard FET electronics, available in Black, Reverse Blue Burst, or Reverse Burst finish, mfg. 2008-2010.

$2,880	$1,850 - 2,200	$1,200 - 1,400	$4,099

This model was available through Adamas Custom Shop where it could be totally customized. The specs and prices listed above are strictly standard options/features.

ACOUSTIC: 30TH ANNIVERSARY SERIES

The models in this series were built to commemorate Charlie Kaman's 30th Anniversary of the Adamas model. Each model was built in limited quantities and sold through 2005 and 2006.

1187-247 ADAMAS #47 – reissue of the Model 1187 slot head, deep non-cutaway body, unidirectional carbon fiber top, 13-piece exotic hardwood soundholes, bowl-back body, walnut fingerboard with original Adamas gold inlays, slotted headstock, three-per-side tuners, carved walnut bridge, gold hardware, available in Reverse Red Burst finish, mfg. 2005 only.

	N/A	$3,000 - 3,500	$2,100 - 2,500	$4,999

1581-5 ADAMAS II – reissue of the Adamas II, single cutaway deep bowl body, unidirectional carbon graphite top, seven-piece exotic hardwood soundholes, bowl-back body, resin-impregnated walnut fingerboard with original Adamas II design maple inlays, three-per-side tuners, walnut bridge, original patented pickups, two knobs, gold hardware, available in Black Graphite finish, mfg. 2005 only.

	N/A	$2,100 - 2,500	$1,400 - 1,750	$3,600

1687-8 ADAMAS I – reissue of the Adamas I, non-cutaway deep bowl body, unidirectional carbon graphite top, 13-piece exotic hardwood soundholes, bowl back, resin-impregnated walnut fingerboard with original Adamas I design maple inlays, carved walnut headstock with three-per-side tuners, carved walnut bridge, original patented pickups, two knobs, gold hardware, available in Reverse Blue Burstfinish, mfg. 2005 only.

	N/A	$2,200 - 2,700	$1,550 - 1,900	$3,800

U681-T5 12-FRET ADAMAS – non-cutaway deep bowl body, unidirectional carbon graphite top, five-piece exotic hardwood soundholes, bowl-back body, ebony fingerboard with MOP Adamas I design inlays, slotted headstock with three-per-side tuners, ebony bridge, Ovation original patented pickups, side-mounted electronics, gold hardware, available in Black Graphite finish, mfg. 2005 only.

	N/A	$1,550 - 1,900	$1,000 - 1,250	$2,669

ADMIRA

Instruments currently handcrafted in Spain. Currently there is no U.S. distributor.

Admira guitars are all classical models with female model names. Models include Sofía, Elena, Alicia, Eva, Rosa, Málaga, Sevilla, Solista, Virtuoso, Ávila, Artista, Soledad, Teresa, Crisitina, Paloma, Juanita, María, Capricho, Princesa, Sombra, JK80, and the SK 90. Each model has different kinds of woods available, and Fishman electronics are available on all models. For more information, visit Admira's website.

CONTACT INFORMATION
ADMIRA
20800 Zarautz, Apt. 15
Guipuzcoa, Spain
www.admira.es
contacto@admira.es
keller@zarautz.com

AIRCRAFT

Instruments previously built in Japan.

Guitars carrying the Aircraft logo were actually manufactured by the Morris company, which also builds instruments for their own Morris trademark, and the Hurricane logo.

AIRLINE

See Supro. Instruments previously manufactured by Valco in Chicago, IL during the 1960s. See chapter on House Brands.

This trademark has been identified as a House Brand of the Montgomery Wards department store chain. Author/researcher Willie G. Moseley indicates that the unique body design is proprietary to the Airline brand. Models can be found constructed of both Res-O-Glas (a hollow fiberglass body) and wood. Airline also produced acoustic flattop and archtop models. Although several acoustic and acoustic archtop guitars exist, the electric Airline models are significantly more collectible. Source: Willie G. Moseley, *Stellas & Stratocasters*.

ACOUSTIC

ARCHTOP MODELS – hollow archtop bodies, cutaway or non-cutaway, f-holes, raised pickguards, various appointments, mfg. 1950s-1960s.

	100%	EXCELLENT	AVERAGE
Low Appointments	N/A	$250 - 300	$125 - 175
Mid Appointments	N/A	$325 - 400	$175 - 225
High Appointments	N/A	$400 - 500	$250 - 300

FLATTOP MODELS – flattop acoustic body with various appointments, mfg. 1960s.

	100%	EXCELLENT	AVERAGE
Low Appointments	N/A	$175 - 225	$110 - 140
Mid Appointments	N/A	$250 - 300	$125 - 175
High Appointments	N/A	$350 - 425	$200 - 250

ALBERICO, FABRIZIO

Guitars currently produced in Victoria, British Columbia, Canada since 1998.

Luthier Fabrizio Alberico hand-builds acoustic guitars in his 700 square foot shop approximately twenty miles north of Vancouver. Alberico visited Jeff Traugott's shop looking for an ideal fingerstyle, and he was so inspired he decided to go into guitar building. After this, he took a five-week course from Sergei de Jonge who was an apprentice of Jean Larrivee (Larrivee Guitars). Although Alberico has always been a recreational woodworker, he has learned much in his years and has become a well-known builder. He offers about twelve guitars a year that are available as an OM, Grand Auditorium, and classical shape. Guitars start at $5,900. For more information, visit Alberico's website or contact him directly.

CONTACT INFORMATION
ALBERICO, FABRIZIO
4983 Cordova Bay Road
Victoria, BC V8Y 2K1 Canada
Phone No.: 250-589-1624
www.albericoguitar.com
albericoguitar@gmail.com

ALDEN

Instruments currently produced in China since the early 2000s with their headquarters based in Korea. Distributed in the U.S. by Alden Guitar, USA in Plympton, MA.

Alden guitars is a collaboration between British luthier Alan Entwhistle and the Korean-based guitar company Muse R&D, Inc. Currently, Alden offers a variety of solidbody and semi-hollowbody electric guitars, electric basses, guitar amplifiers, and other guitar related accessories, but they have also offered acoustic guitars and mandolins in the past. For more information, visit Alden's website or contact the distributor directly.

CONTACT INFORMATION
ALDEN
U.S. Distributor: Alden Guitar, USA
221 Main St.
Plympton, MA 02367
Phone No.: 781-588-9282
www.aldenguitarsales.com
info@aldenguitarsales.com

ALEX

See Domino. Instruments previously manufactured in Japan circa mid- to late 1960s. Distributed by Maurice Lipsky Music Company, Inc. of New York, NY.

Alex acoustic guitar models featured laminated mahogany tops, backs, and sides, as well as internal fan bracing. The Alex acoustic was offered in standard size (retail list was $29.95), concert size (retail list was $34.50), grand concert (retail list was $37.50), or in a 12-string configuration (retail list was $80.00) (Domino catalog courtesy John Kinnemeyer, JK Lutherie).

ALHAMBRA

Instruments currently built in Spain. Distributed in the U.S. by Alhambra USA, Inc. located in Asheville, NC. Alhambra has been producing guitars since 1965.

The first Alhambra guitar was manufactured in 1965 in Spain. Alhambra classical guitars are medium to very high quality Spanish instruments. These guitars epitomize the sound and beauty of a traditional Spanish guitar. The more elaborate the wood is, the more the guitar is worth. Rosewood is worth more than mahogany, and Brazilian rosewood comands a premium over all. Models are constructed with either solid cedar, red cedar, or solid spruce tops, and cypress, Brazilian rosewood, laminated rosewood, or laminated sycamore sides. Alhambra is also building a number of steel string guitars. Classical models start at $503. Flamenco guitars start at $916. Steel string guitars start at $925. For a full listing of models and information, contact Alhambra directly or visit their website.

CONTACT INFORMATION
ALHAMBRA
U.S. Distributor: Alhambra USA, Inc.
2002 Riverside Dr., Suite 42-i
Asheville, NC 28804
Phone No.: 828-254-3380
Fax No.: 828-254-3346
www.alhambrausa.com
info@alhambrausa.com

ALLAN

Instruments currently produced in China. Currently, there is no U.S. Distributor.

Allan guitars are all designed and supervised by Mr. Yulong Guo. Guo is a master guitar maker in China who has been building guitars for over twenty years. Allan produces mainly classical acoustic nylon string guitars. The series includes the C, AC, and HC models. Allan released the AF Series, which is a regular acoustic guitar. Allan also produces a line of violins, accordions, and mandolins.

ALLEN GUITARS

Instruments currently built in Colfax, CA. Distributed by Randy Allen Guitars. Allen has been building guitars since 1980.

Luthier Randy Allen builds high quality acoustic instruments in several models: Dreadnought, OM, S-J, and Resonator guitars. All acoustic guitar models have options, including a cutaway body configuration, abalone edging, varied fingerboard inlays, and wood bindings. Allen imports and supplies exotic woods and abalone inlay materials to manufacturers. He also produces cast tailpieces for mandolins and resophonic guitars. All instruments include a custom case. For further information, contact luthier Randy Allen directly.

CONTACT INFORMATION
ALLEN GUITARS
PO Box 1883
Colfax, CA 95713
Phone No.: 530-346-6590
Phone No.: 800-953-3035
Fax No.: 530-346-6590
www.allenguitar.com
ag@allenguitar.com

Standard features on the acoustic guitar models include East Indian rosewood or Honduran mahogany back and sides, a Sitka spruce top; bound ebony fingerboards and bridges. Basic models include the **Dreadnought** ($5,140), **Small Jumbo** ($5,537), the **Parlor** ($5,537), the **OM** ($5,537), the **Resophonic RN** (disc., last MSR was $4,175), and the **Resophonic SN** ($4,837). There are several options available on all guitars. These include different wood types, inlays, and body features.

In 1996, Allen debuted a new series of resophonic guitars. The **Allen Resonator** guitar models are equipped with high quality hardware and a spun resonator cone. The chrome-plated cover-plate is held in position with machine screws (as opposed to wood screws, which may strip out over time). The top, back, and sides are maple (a spruce top is available on request).

ALLEN, RICHARD C.

Instruments currently built in El Monte, CA.

Luthier Richard C. Allen has been playing guitar since his high school days in the late 1940s, and has been collecting, repairing, and building guitars ever since. After working sixteen years as a warehouseman for a paper company, Allen began doing repair work for West Coast guitar wholesalers and distributors like C. Bruno and Pacific Music. In 1972, Allen began building guitars full time.

CONTACT INFORMATION
ALLEN, RICHARD C.
2801 New Deal Ave.
El Monte, CA 91733
Phone No.: 626-442-8806

Allen's designs focus on hollowbody and semi-hollowbody guitars. While he has built some electric guitars, the design was semi-hollow (similar to the Rickenbacker idea) with a flattop/back and f-holes. Currently, Allen focuses on jazz-style archtops. He's been building guitars for over 50 years, and is building 15 in., 16 in., 17 in., and 18 in. wide guitars. He also built a series of commemorative guitars honoring country singer Hank Thompson. For more information, contact Allen directly.

ALMANSA

Please refer to Guitarras Almansa in the G section.

ALMCRANTZ

Instruments previously built in Chicago, IL in the late 1800s and early 1900s.

Gerhard Almcrantz started producing guitars and mandolins around 1895, in Chicago, Illinois. He apparently had a patent for a detachable neck. He joined up with a partner, Gideon Tornquist, to produce some other products, and made guitars until about 1905. An Almcrantz acoustic guitar bearing a label reading "July 1895" was featured in the first edition of Tom Wheeler's reference book *American Guitars* (HarperCollins Publishers, New York). Due to the extreme age and rarity of these guitars, a used price has not been established.

ALOHA

Instruments previously built in San Antonio, TX and Chicago, IL. Distributed by the Aloha Publishing and Musical Instrument Company of Chicago, IL.

The Aloha company was founded in 1935 by J.M. Raleigh. True to the nature of a House Brand distributor, Raleigh's company distributed both Aloha instruments and amplifiers and Raleigh brand instruments through his Chicago office. Acoustic guitars were supplied by Harmony, and initial amplifiers and guitars were supplied by the Alamo company of San Antonio, Texas. By the mid-1950s, Aloha was producing its own amps, but continued using Alamo products. Source: Michael Wright, *Vintage Guitar Magazine*.

ALOSA

See Sandner in the S section.

MSR/NOTES	100%	EXCELLENT	AVERAGE	LAST MSR

ALVAREZ

Instruments currently manufactured in China, Japan, and Korea. Distributed by St. Louis Music Inc., in St. Louis, MO.

CONTACT INFORMATION
ALVAREZ
Distributed by St. Louis Music
1400 Ferguson Avenue
St. Louis, MO 63133
Phone No.: 314-727-1191
www.alvarezguitars.com

The St. Louis Music Supply Company was originally founded in 1922 by Bernard Kornblum as a violin shop. In 1957, Gene Kornblum (Bernard's son) joined the family business.

The Alvarez trademark was established in 1965, and the company was the earliest of Asian producers to feature laminate-body guitars with solid wood tops. Initially, Alvarez guitars were built in Japan during the late 1960s, and distributed through St. Louis Music.

St. Louis Music also distributed the Electra and Westone brands of solid body electrics. St. Louis Music currently manufactures Crate and Ampeg amplifiers in the U.S., while Alvarez instruments are designed in St. Louis and produced overseas. In 2005, LOUD Technologies, Inc. purchased St. Louis Music, Inc. and all of their trademarks. With this acquisition, the headquarters based in St. Louis was moved to Woodinville, WA. However, the guitar repair and set-up shop was still located in St. Louis. In 2009, Mark Ragin moved Alvarez guitars back to St. Louis Music in St. Louis that included management and distribution. For more information, contact Alvarez directly or visit their website.

GENERAL INFORMATION

All Alvarez acoustic steel string guitars (except models 5212, 5214 and 5216), have a stylized double A shell logo inlay and rosewood veneer on their pegheads. Regent series models are the entry level to the Alvarez line, and generally feature laminated tops, backs, and sides. Artist series models feature more exotic woods, and have shell and pearl inlay work. Professional series models have solid tops. The acoustic/electric Fusion series models currently feature the Alvarez System 500 bridge pickup/onboard EQ. Alvarez numbered their guitars with a four-digit designation up until 1998. In 1999, they started using a two-letter and two-number system. Each series can be identified by this system. The first letters are for the series and style (i.e.: AD stands for Artist Dreadnought). The following two numbers are the rank in the series. The higher the number, the higher quality wood and such. Almost all Alvarez acoustic guitars are available with an electronic option. This addition retails for $300 for the System 500 MK II and $400 for the System 600T. As a rule, an additional 20% can be added to instruments that feature this as an option and not standard equipment. Another 10% can be added with the original case that is an option and not standard equipment.

ACOUSTIC: ARTIST SERIES (DISC. MODELS, 4-DIGIT MODELS)

The Professional Series are split up into prior 1999 models with the four-digit models, and post-1999 with two letter and two number model designations

5002 MAHOGANY CLASSIC – classical style, laminated spruce top, round soundhole, bound body, wooden inlay rosette, mahogany back/sides, nato neck, 12/19-fret rosewood fingerboard, rosewood bridge, rosewood veneer on peghead, three-per-side gold tuners, available in Natural finish, disc. 1998.

	N/A	$175 - 225	$95 - 125	$410

5004 ARTIST ROSEWOOD (ROSEWOOD CLASSIC) – similar to 5002, except has rosewood back/sides, available in Natural finish, disc. 1998.

	N/A	$235 - 285	$165 - 195	$579

5014 ARTIST FOLK (MOUNTAIN FOLK) – folk style, laminated spruce top, round soundhole, multi-layer black/white body binding, black/white ring inlay rosette, tortoiseshell pickguard, mahogany back/sides/neck, 14/20-fret rosewood fingerboard with pearl dot inlays, stylized bird wings inlay at 12th fret, rosewood bridge with white black dot pins, blackface peghead with pearl logo inlay, three-per-side chrome die-cast tuners, available in Sunburst finish, mfg. 1995-98.

	N/A	$195 - 240	$120 - 150	$479

5019 MIDNIGHT SPECIAL – dreadnought style, laminated spruce top, round soundhole, multi-layer black/white body binding, abalone shell rosette, black pickguard, mahogany back/sides, nato neck, 14/20-fret rosewood fingerboard with pearl dot inlays, stylized bird wings inlay at 12th fret, rosewood bridge with white pearl dot pins, three-per-side chrome tuners, available in Black finish, disc. 1998.

	N/A	$250 - 300	$150 - 200	$629

* *5019 AV* – similar to the 5019 except has electronics with a bridge pickup system, mfg. 1994 only.

	N/A	$350 - 425	$200 - 250	$825

5020 MOUNTAIN DELUXE (MOUNTAIN) – dreadnought style, laminated spruce top, round soundhole, multi-layer black/white body binding, synthetic shell rosette, black pickguard, mahogany back/sides/neck, 14/20-fret rosewood fingerboard with pearl dot inlay/stylized bird wings inlays at 12th fret, rosewood bridge with black pearl dot pins, rosewood veneer on peghead, three-per-side chrome tuners, available in Natural or Sunburst finish, mfg. 1991-95, reintroduced 1997-98.

	N/A	$225 - 275	$140 - 170	$499

* *5020 M* – similar to 5020 Mountain, except has laminated mahogany top, disc. 1995.

	N/A	$170 - 220	$95 - 125	$400

MSR/NOTES	100%	EXCELLENT	AVERAGE	LAST MSR

* **5020 SB Mountain Deluxe Sunburst** – similar to 5020 Mountain, available in Sunburst finish, disc. 1998.

	N/A	$200 - 250	$120 - 160	$499

* **5020 C Mountain Deluxe** – similar to the 5020 Mountain except has a single cutaway and standard System 500 electronics with bridge pickup system, disc. 1998.

	N/A	$350 - 425	$225 - 275	$879

5021 – similar to 5020, except has a 12-string configuration, six-per-side tuners, disc. 1993.

	N/A	$175 - 225	$95 - 125	$425

5040 KOA – dreadnought style, laminated koa top, round soundhole, three-stripe bound body and rosette, brown pickguard, koa back/sides, nato neck, 14/20-fret rosewood fingerboard with pearl dot inlays, stylized bird wings inlay at 12th fret, rosewood bridge with black pearl dot pins, koa veneer on peghead, three-per-side chrome tuners, available in Natural finish, disc. 1998.

	N/A	$200 - 250	$120 - 160	$500

5043 BURGUNDY (BURGUNDY ARTIST) – dreadnought style, laminated oak top, round soundhole, multi-bound body, abalone rosette, oak back/sides, mahogany neck, 20-fret rosewood fingerboard with pearl cross inlays, rosewood bridge with black white dot pins, oak peghead veneer with pearl logo inlay, three-per-side die-cast tuners, available in Burgundy Stain finish, mfg. 1994-98.

	N/A	$275 - 325	$150 - 200	$629

5055 BLUESMAN – jumbo style, laminated spruce top, two f-holes, multi-bound body, mahogany back/sides/neck, 14/20-fret bound rosewood fingerboard with pearl dot inlays, stylized bird wings inlay at 12th fret, rosewood bridge with white black dot pins, blackface peghead with pearl logo inlay, three-per-side chrome die-cast tuners, available in Sunburst finish, mfg. 1995-98.

	N/A	$250 - 300	$150 - 200	$599

5072 JUMBO (ARTIST JUMBO) – jumbo style, laminated spruce top, round soundhole, tortoiseshell pickguard, abalone bound body/rosette, mahogany back/sides, 14/20-fret rosewood fingerboard with pearl dot inlays, stylized bird wings inlay at 12th fret, rosewood bridge with white black dot pins, rosewood peghead veneer with pearl logo inlay, three-per-side die-cast tuners, available in Natural finish, mfg. 1994-98.

	N/A	$275 - 325	$150 - 200	$619

* **5072 C BK** – similar to the 5072 except has a single cutaway, standard three-band EQ System 500 electronics with piezo bridge pickup, available in Black finish, mfg. 1995-98.

	N/A	$450 - 525	$275 - 325	$979

5088 C (FUSION DELUXE) – dreadnought style, single rounded cutaway, laminated spruce top, round soundhole, tortoiseshell pickguard, three-stripe bound body/rosette, mahogany back/sides/neck, 20-fret rosewood fingerboard with pearl dot inlays, pearl curlicue inlay at 12th fret, rosewood bridge with black white dot pins, pearl logo peghead inlay, three-per-side die-cast tuners, piezo bridge pickups, three-band EQ, System 500 electronics, available in Natural finish, mfg. 1994-98.

	N/A	$425 - 500	$250 - 300	$929

* **5088 C BK (Fusion Deluxe)** – similar to 5088C, except has black pickguard, abalone flake rosette, white black dot bridge pins, available in Black finish, mfg. 1994-98.

	N/A	$475 - 550	$275 - 325	$999

This model was also available in a White finish with no pickguard (Model 5088 C WH). The White finish was disc. in 1996.

* **5088/12 12-String** – similar to 5088 C, except has 12-string configuration, six-per-side tuners, mfg. 1994 only.

	N/A	$400 - 475	$225 - 275	$850

5220 C – single cutaway dreadnought style, spruce top, round soundhole, three-stripe bound body and rosette, black pickguard, mahogany back/sides, nato neck, 20-fret rosewood fingerboard with pearl dot inlays, rosewood bridge with black pearl dot pins, three-per-side chrome tuners, available in Natural finish, disc. 1995.

	N/A	$150 - 195	$80 - 110	$350

5224 – dreadnought style, solid spruce top, round soundhole, five-stripe bound body/rosette, mahogany back/sides, nato neck, 14/20-fret rosewood fingerboard with dot inlay, rosewood bridge with white pearl dot pins, three-per-side chrome tuners, available in Natural finish, disc. 1988.

	N/A	$200 - 250	$110 - 140	$450

5225 ROSEWOOD – similar to the 5224, except features rosewood back/sides, available in Natural finish, mfg. 1981-1992.

	N/A	$200 - 250	$110 - 140	$459

5227 ROSEWOOD SPECIAL – similar to the 5225, except has laminated spruce top, disc. 1985.

	N/A	$150 - 195	$80 - 110	$349

5237 CURLY MAPLE – dreadnought style, laminated spruce top, round soundhole, five-stripe bound body/rosette, curly maple back/sides, nato neck, 14/20-fret rosewood fingerboard with pearl dot inlays/stylized bird wings inlay at 12th fret, rosewood bridge with white pearl dot pins, three-per-side chrome tuners, available in Sunburst finish, disc. 1995.

	N/A	$225 - 275	$120 - 160	$475

MSR/NOTES	100%	EXCELLENT	AVERAGE	LAST MSR

ACOUSTIC: ARTIST (AC, AD, AF, & AJ) SERIES (RECENT MFG.)

AC 40 S – classical style, rounded body, spruce top, round soundhole, multi-layer black body binding, wood mosaic rosette, rosewood back/sides, mahogany neck, 12/19-fret rosewood fingerboard, rosewood bridge, three-per-side gold tuners with plastic buttons, available in Natural gloss finish, mfg. 1998-2001.

	N/A	$240 - 290	$150 - 200	$579

* *AC 40SC* – similar to the AC 40S except has a single cutaway and a standard piezo bridge pickups with three-band EQ System 500 electronics, mfg. 1998-2001.

	N/A	$350 - 425	$200 - 250	$799

AC 60 S – grand concert classical style, rounded body, solid cedar top, round soundhole, multi-layer black body binding, wood mosaic rosette, mahogany back/sides, mahogany neck, 12/19-fret Indian rosewood fingerboard, rosewood bridge, three-per-side gold tuners with plastic buttons, optional System 600T Mk II electronics, available in Natural gloss finish, mfg. 2002-08.

	N/A	$175 - 225	$110 - 140	$430

* *AC 60SC* – similar to the AC 60S except has a single cutaway and standard System 600T Mk II electronics, mfg. 2002-08.

	N/A	$300 - 350	$175 - 225	$700

AC460 – grand concert classical style body, solid cedar top, mahogany back and sides, round soundhole with wood mosaic rosette, multi-layer black body binding, mahogany neck, 12/19-fret Indian rosewood fingerboard, slotted headstock, three-per-side open-style gold tuners with plastic buttons, rosewood bridge, available in Natural gloss finish, mfg. 2009-present.

MSR $450	$320	$200 - 250	$110 - 140	

* *AC460C* – similar to the AC460, except has a single cutaway and System 600TMKII electronics, available in Natural finish, mfg. 2009-present.

MSR $800	$560	$350 - 425	$200 - 250	

AD 60S – dreadnought body style, spruce top, mahogany sides and back, White Pearl soundhole rosette, ivory/black multi-body binding, rosewood fingerboard, rosewood bridge, chrome die-cast tuners, optional System 500 MK II (disc. 2001) or System 600T Mk II (2002-08) electronics, available in Natural finish, disc. 2008.

	N/A	$175 - 225	$110 - 140	$430

• **Add 5% (Last MSR was $450) for Black finish (Model AD 60SBK).**

* *AD 60SC* – similar to AD 60S, except in a single cutaway body style, standard System 500 Mk II (disc. 2001) or System 600T Mk II (2002-08) electronics, available in Natural finish, disc. 2008.

	N/A	$250 - 300	$135 - 175	$600

• **Add 7.5% (Last MSR was $650) for Black finish (Model AD 60SCBK).**

* *AD 60S-12* – similar to the AD 60S except in 12-string configuration, optional System 500 Mk II (2001 only) or System 600T Mk II (2002-08) electronics, mfg. 2001-08.

	N/A	$200 - 250	$120 - 150	$500

* *AD 60SCL* – similar to the AD 60S, except has a cutaway and is in left-hand configuration, standard System 600T Mk II electronics, mfg. 2004-08.

	N/A	$275 - 325	$150 - 200	$650

AD 60 K – dreadnought style, koa top, round soundhole, black pickguard, ivory body, white pearl rosette, koa back/sides, mahogany neck, 14/20-fret bound rosewood fingerboard with stylized Alvarez slash inlay at 12th fret, three-per-side chrome tuners, rosewood bridge with white pearl dot pins, optional System 500 Mk II (1998-2001) or System 600T Mk II (2002-08) electronics, available in Natural gloss finish, mfg. 1998-2008.

	N/A	$175 - 225	$110 - 140	$450

* *AD 60 CK* – similar to AD60K except with a single cutaway dreadnought body and standard System 500 Mk II (disc. 2001) or System 600T Mk II (2002-08) electronics, available in Natural finish, disc. 2008.

	N/A	$275 - 325	$150 - 200	$650

AD 62SC – single cutaway dreadnought style, solid cedar top, burled mahogany back/sides, black pickguard, maple body binding, 14/20-fret rosewood fingerboard with 12th fret diagonal inlay, rosewood bridge, standard System 600T Mk II electronics, gold hardware, available in Natural Satin finish, mfg. 2004-08.

	N/A	$475 - 550	$275 - 325	$1,090

AD 65 BLUESMAN – vintage dreadnought body style, spruce top, mahogany sides and back, ivory/black multi-body binding, rosewood fingerboard and bridge, chrome die-cast tuners, f-holes, available in Sunburst finish, disc. 2001.

	N/A	$275 - 325	$150 - 200	$649

MSR/NOTES	100%	EXCELLENT	AVERAGE	LAST MSR

AD 65CE – cutaway archtop, f-holes, spruce top, maple back and sides, ivory/black multi-ply binding, rosewood fingerboard, diagonal inlay on 12th fret, rosewood bridge, vintage nickel hardware, trapeze bridge, single coil Alnico and Piezo pickup, three control knobs, available in Natural or Sunburst finish (AD 65CESB), mfg. 2001 only.

	N/A	$475 - 550	$250 - 300	$999

AD 70S – dreadnought style, solid spruce top, rosewood back and sides, round soundhole with white pearl rosette, tortoiseshell pickguard, 14/20-fret rosewood fingerboard with 12th fret diagonal inlay, rosewood bridge, three-per-side chrome tuners, optional System 500 Mk II (2001 only) or System 600T Mk II (2002-08) electronics, available in Natural finish, mfg. 2001-08.

	N/A	$175 - 225	$110 - 140	$450

* *AD 70SC* – similar to the AD 70, except has a single cutaway and standard System 600T Mk II electronics, mfg. 2005-08.

	N/A	$275 - 325	$150 - 200	$650

AD 80S – dreadnought style, solid spruce top, Indian rosewood back and sides, round soundhole with white pearl rosette, tortoise pickguard, 14/20-fret rosewood fingerboard with 12th fret diagonal inlay, rosewood bridge, three-per-side chrome tuners, optional System 600T Mk II electronics, available in Natural (disc.) or Sunburst finish, mfg. 2003-08.

	N/A	$300 - 350	$175 - 225	$700

AD 90SCK – dreadnought single cutaway style, solid spruce top, Figured dao back and sides, round soundhole with white pearl rosette, tortoiseshell pickguard, 14/20-fret rosewood fingerboard with 12th fret diagonal inlay, rosewood bridge, three-per-side chrome tuners, standard System 600T Mk II electronics, available in Natural finish, mfg. 2003-07.

	N/A	$325 - 375	$200 - 250	$749

AD222 – dreadnought-style body, dao top, dao back and sides, round soundhole with white pearl rosette, multi-layer ivory body binding, mahogany neck, 12/19-fret rosewood fingerboard with three-piece 12th fret Alvarez inlay, bound headstock with dao overlay and Alvarez logo, three-per-side chrome tuners, rosewood bridge, black pickguard, available in Natural finish, mfg. 2009 only.

	N/A	$175 - 225	$110 - 140	$450

* *AD222C* – similar to the AD222, except has a single smooth cutaway and System 600TMKII electronics, available in Natural finish, mfg. 2009-present.

MSR $650	$460	$275 - 325	$150 - 200	

AD410 – dreadnought-style body, solid spruce top, mahogany back and sides, round soundhole with white pearl rosette, multi-layer white body binding, mahogany neck, 12/19-fret bound rosewood fingerboard with three-piece 12th fret Alvarez inlay, bound headstock with mahogany overlay and Alvarez logo, three-per-side chrome tuners, rosewood bridge, black pickguard, available in Natural finish, mfg. 2009-present.

MSR $450	$320	$175 - 225	$110 - 140	

* *AD410-12 12-String* – similar to the AD410, except in 12-string configuration with six-per-side tuners, available in Natural finish, mfg. 2009-present.

MSR $550	$380	$225 - 275	$120 - 150	

* *AD410C Cutaway Electric* – similar to the AD410, except has a single smooth cutaway and System 600TMKII electronics, available in Natural finish, mfg. 2009-present.

MSR $670	$470	$300 - 350	$225 - 275	

»*AD4104CBK Cutaway Electric Black* – similar to the AD410C Cutaway Electric, except has hexagon fingerboard inlays and available in Black finish with matching headstock overlay, mfg. 2009-present.

MSR $700	$490	$300 - 375	$225 - 275	

»*AD410CL Cutaway Electric Left-Handed* – similar to the AD410C Cutaway Electric, except in left-handed configuration, available in Natural finish, mfg. 2009-present.

MSR $700	$490	$300 - 375	$225 - 275	

AD411 – dreadnought-style body, solid spruce top, rosewood back and sides, round soundhole with white pearl rosette, multi-layer white body binding, mahogany neck, 12/19-fret bound rosewood fingerboard with three-piece 12th fret Alvarez inlay, bound headstock with mahogany overlay and Alvarez logo, three-per-side chrome tuners, rosewood bridge, black pickguard, available in Natural finish, mfg. 2009-present.

MSR $500	$350	$200 - 250	$120 - 150	

* *AD411C Cutaway Electric* – similar to the AD411, except has a single smooth cutaway and System 600TMKII electronics, available in Natural finish, mfg. 2009-present.

MSR $700	$490	$300 - 375	$225 - 275	

AD511SB – dreadnought-style body, solid spruce top, rosewood back and sides, round soundhole with white pearl rosette, multi-layer white pearl body binding, mahogany neck, 12/19-fret bound rosewood fingerboard with three-piece 12th fret Alvarez inlay, bound headstock with mahogany overlay and Alvarez logo, three-per-side chrome tuners, rosewood bridge, black pickguard, available in Sunburst finish, mfg. 2009-present.

MSR $800	$560	$350 - 425	$200 - 250	

MSR/NOTES	100%	EXCELLENT	AVERAGE	LAST MSR

AF 60 CK – single cutaway folk body style, koa top, round soundhole, black pickguard, ivory body, white pearl rosette, koa back/sides, mahogany neck, 14/20-fret bound rosewood fingerboard with stylized Alvarez slash inlay at 12th fret, three-per-side chrome tuners, rosewood bridge with white pearl dot pins, standard System 500 Mk II (disc. 2001) or System 600T Mk II (2002-08) electronics, available in Natural gloss finish, disc. 2008.

	N/A	$275 - 325	$150 - 200	$650

AF 60 S – folk grand concert style, solid spruce top, mahogany back and sides, round soundhole with white pearl rosette, black pickguard, 14/20-fret rosewood fingerboard with 12th fret diagonal inlay, rosewood bridge, three-per-side nickel die-cast tuners, optional System 600T Mk II electronics, available in Natural finish, mfg. 2002-08.

	N/A	$175 - 225	$110 - 140	$450

AF 62SC – single cutaway folk style, solid cedar top, burled mahogany back/sides, black pickguard, maple body binding, 14/20-fret rosewood fingerboard with 12th fret diagonal inlay, rosewood bridge, standard System 600T Mk II electronics, gold hardware, available in Natural Satin finish, mfg. 2007 only.

	N/A	$475 - 550	$275 - 325	$1,049

AF 90 SCK – single cutaway folk body, solid Englemann spruce top, figured dao back and sides, white pearl rosette and B/N/H binding, 14/20-fret rosewood fingerboard with diagonal 12th fret inlay, three-per-side tuners, rosewood bridge, black pickguard, standard System 600T Mk II electronics, nickel hardware, available in Natural finish, mfg. 2005-07.

	N/A	$325 - 375	$200 - 250	$749

AF222C – single cutaway Grand Concert folk-style body, dao top, dao back and sides, round soundhole with white pearl rosette, multi-layer ivory body binding, mahogany neck, 12/19-fret rosewood fingerboard with three-piece 12th fret Alvarez inlay, bound headstock with dao overlay and Alvarez logo, three-per-side chrome tuners, rosewood bridge, black pickguard, System 600T Mk II electronics, available in Natural finish, mfg. 2009-present.

MSR $650	$460	$275 - 325	$150 - 200	

AF410 – Grand Concert folk-style body, solid spruce top, mahogany back and sides, round soundhole with white pearl rosette, multi-layer white body binding, mahogany neck, 12/19-fret bound rosewood fingerboard with three-piece 12th fret Alvarez inlay, bound headstock with mahogany overlay and Alvarez logo, three-per-side chrome tuners, rosewood bridge, black pickguard, available in Natural finish, mfg. 2009-present.

MSR $500	$350	$200 - 250	$120 - 150	

AJ 60-12 ARTIST MAPLE JUMBO 12-STRING – dreadnought style, koa top, round soundhole, black pickguard, ivory body, white pearl rosette, koa back/sides, mahogany neck, 14/20-fret bound rosewood fingerboard with stylized Alvarez slash inlay at 12th fret, rosewood bridge with white pearl dot pins, three-per-side chrome tuners, available in Natural gloss finish, mfg. 1998-99.

	N/A	$275 - 325	$150 - 200	$599

AJ 60 S – jumbo body, maple back and sides, solid spruce top, rosewood fingerboard with 12th fret diagonal position marker, white pearl rosette, white/black multi-ply body binding, gold die-cast tuners, rosewood bridge, optional System 500 Mk II (disc. 2001) or System 600T Mk II (2002-08) electronics, available in Blonde finish, disc. 2008.

	N/A	$275 - 325	$150 - 200	$630

* *AJ 60 S 12* – similar to the AJ60S, except in 12-string configuration with six-per-side tuners, available in Blonde finish, disc. 2008.

	N/A	$300 - 350	$175 - 225	$700

AJ 60 SC – similar to the AJ60S, except has a single cutaway jumbo body, standard System 500 Mk II (disc. 2001) or System 600T Mk II (2002-08) electronics, available in Blonde finish, disc. 2008.

	N/A	$350 - 425	$200 - 250	$800

* *AJ 60 SC 12* – similar to AJ60SC, except in a 12-string configuration, available in Blonde finish, disc. 2008.

	N/A	$400 - 475	$225 - 275	$900

AJ414CBK – single cutaway Jumbo-style body, solid spruce top, maple back and sides, round soundhole with white pearl rosette, multi-layer ivory body binding, mahogany neck, 12/20-fret bound rosewood fingerboard with three-piece 12th fret Alvarez inlay, bound headstock with black overlay and Alvarez logo, three-per-side chrome tuners, rosewood bridge, black pickguard, System 600 T Mk II electronics, available in Black finish, mfg. 2009 only.

	N/A	$300 - 350	$225 - 275	$670

AJ417 – Jumbo-style body, solid spruce top, bubinga back and sides, round soundhole with white pearl rosette, multi-layer ivory body binding, mahogany neck, 14/20-fret bound rosewood fingerboard with three-piece 12th fret Alvarez inlay, bound headstock with mahogany overlay and Alvarez logo, three-per-side chrome tuners, rosewood bridge, black pickguard, available in Natural finish, mfg. 2009 only.

	N/A	$275 - 325	$150 - 200	$650

MSR/NOTES	100%	EXCELLENT	AVERAGE	LAST MSR

* **AJ417-12 12-String** – similar to the AJ417, except in 12-string configuration with six-per-side tuners, available in Natural finish, mfg. 2009 only.

	N/A	$300 - 350	$225 - 275	$700

AJ418C – single cutaway Jumbo-style body, solid spruce top, spalted maple back and sides, round soundhole with white pearl rosette, multi-layer white/black body binding, mahogany neck, 12/19-fret bound rosewood fingerboard with three-piece 12th fret Alvarez inlay, bound headstock with mahogany overlay and Alvarez logo, three-per-side chrome tuners, rosewood bridge, black pickguard, System 600 T Mk II electronics, available in Natural finish, mfg. 2009-present.

MSR $900	$620	$400 - 475	$225 - 275	

* **AJ418C-12 12-String** – similar to the AJ418C, except in 12-string configuration with six-per-side tuners, available in Natural finish, mfg. 2009-present.

MSR $950	$660	$425 - 500	$250 - 300	

ACOUSTIC: FUSION SERIES

FCC7103 – single cutaway chambered classical mahogany body, spruce top, multi-ply body binding, mahogany neck, 12/19-fret bound rosewood fingerboard with no inlays, slotted headstock, three-per-side open-style nickel tuners, rosewood bridge, Fishman Aura IC electronics, available in Natural finish, mfg. 2009-present.

MSR $1,500	$1,040	$650 - 800	$375 - 450	

FCC7603 – single cutaway chambered classical mahogany body, cedar top, multi-ply body binding, mahogany neck, 12/19-fret bound rosewood fingerboard with no inlays, slotted headstock, three-per-side open-style nickel tuners, rosewood bridge, Fishman Aura IC electronics, available in Natural finish, mfg. 2009-present.

MSR $1,500	$1,040	$650 - 800	$375 - 450	

FCF7103 – single cutaway chambered folk mahogany body, spruce top, multi-ply body binding, mahogany neck, 14/20-fret bound rosewood fingerboard with 12th fret three-piece Alvarez inlay, multi-ply bound headstock with rosewood overlay and Alvarez logo, three-per-side nickel tuners, rosewood bridge, Fishman Aura IC electronics, available in Natural finish, mfg. 2009-present.

MSR $1,500	$1,040	$650 - 800	$375 - 450	

* **FCF7103BK Black** – similar to the FCF7103, except has abalone purfling and available in Black finish with a matching black finish headstock overlay, mfg. 2009-present.

MSR $1,550	$1,080	$675 - 825	$400 - 475	

FCF7403 – single cutaway chambered folk mahogany body, quilted maple top, multi-ply body binding, mahogany neck, 14/20-fret bound rosewood fingerboard with 12th fret three-piece Alvarez inlay, multi-ply bound headstock with rosewood overlay and Alvarez logo, three-per-side nickel tuners, rosewood bridge, Fishman Aura IC electronics, available in Natural finish, mfg. 2009-present.

MSR $2,000	$1,350	$900 - 1,050	$500 - 600	

FCF7503 – single cutaway chambered folk mahogany body, koa top, multi-ply body binding, mahogany neck, 14/20-fret bound rosewood fingerboard with 12th fret three-piece Alvarez inlay, multi-ply bound headstock with rosewood overlay and Alvarez logo, three-per-side nickel tuners, rosewood bridge, Fishman Aura IC electronics, available in Natural finish, mfg. 2009 only.

	N/A	$850 - 1,000	$475 - 575	$1,900

FD 60 S – cutaway thin dreadnought body, solid spruce top, maple back and sides, pearl rosette, ivory/black body binding, rosewood fingerboard with 12th fret diagonal position marker, three-per-side gold die cast tuners, rosewood bridge, standard System 600T Mk II electronics, available in Black or Natural finish, mfg. 2007-08.

	N/A	$275 - 325	$150 - 200	$650

* **FD 60 Quilted Maple** – similar to the FD 60S, except has a quilted maple top and standard Alvarez System 500 Mk II (disc. 2001) or System 600T Mk II (2002-08) electronics, available in Cherry Sunburst, Tobacco Sunburst, Trans. Amber, Trans. Black, Trans. Blue, Trans. Purple, or Trans. Red finish, disc. 2008.

	N/A	$300 - 350	$175 - 225	$700

* **FD 60S-12 12-String** – similar to the FD 60S, except in 12-string configuration and six-per-side tuners, available in Natural finish, mfg. 2005-08.

	N/A	$325 - 375	$200 - 250	$750

FF 60 – similar to the FD 60, except has a folk style body, available in Tobacco Sunburst (2004-05) or Wine Red finish, mfg. 2004-08.

	N/A	$300 - 350	$175 - 225	$700

5008 C CLASSIC – classical style, single rounded cutaway, laminated spruce top, round soundhole, bound body, wooden inlay rosette, mahogany back/sides/neck, 19-fret rosewood fingerboard, rosewood wraparound bridge, rosewood peghead veneer with pearl logo inlay, three-per-side gold tuners with plastic buttons, piezo bridge pickups, three-band EQ, available in Natural finish, mfg. 1994 only.

	N/A	$400 - 475	$250 - 300	$900

MSR/NOTES	100%	EXCELLENT	AVERAGE	LAST MSR

5080 N FUSION DELUXE THINLINE (NATURAL) – dreadnought style, thinline rounded cutaway body, spruce top, round soundhole, multi-layer black/white body binding, abalone shell rosette, mahogany back/sides/neck, 20-fret rosewood fingerboard with pearl dot inlays/stylized bird wings inlay at 12th fret, rosewood bridge with black pearl dot pins, abalone logo peghead inlay, three-per-side chrome tuners, piezo bridge pickups, volume/tone controls, System 500 electronics, available in Natural gloss finish, disc. 1998.

	N/A	$350 - 425	$200 - 250	$799

5081 N FUSION DELUXE THINLINE (BLUE) – similar to 5080 N, except has flamed maple top, maple back/sides, available in Trans. Blue gloss finish, disc. 1998.

	N/A	$350 - 425	$200 - 250	$819

5082 N – similar to 5080 N, except has laminated curly maple top, curly maple back and sides, available in Trans. Violin finish, disc. 1995.

	N/A	$350 - 425	$200 - 250	$800

5083 N FUSION DELUXE THINLINE (SUNBURST) – similar to 5080 N, except has flame maple top, maple back and sides, available in Trans. Red gloss finish, disc. 1998.

	N/A	$350 - 425	$200 - 250	$819

In 1996, Sunburst finish replaced Trans. Red finish.

5084 N – similar to 5080 N, available in Black gloss finish, mfg. 1994-96.

	N/A	$325 - 400	$175 - 225	$750

5220 C EQ FUSION STANDARD (5220 C EQ CH, 5220 C EQ VS) – dreadnought style, single rounded cutaway body, spruce top, round soundhole, three-stripe bound body and rosette, black pickguard, mahogany back and sides, nato neck, 20-fret rosewood fingerboard with pearl dot inlays, rosewood bridge with black pearl dot pins, three-per-side chrome tuners, bridge pickup system, three-band EQ, available in Natural finish, disc. 1998.

	N/A	$325 - 375	$175 - 225	$699

- **Add $50 for Cherry (Model 5220 C EQ CH FUSION STANDARD) or Sunburst (Model 5220 C EQ VS FUSION STANDARD) finish.**

This model was similar to the Model 5220 C, with electronics.

ACOUSTIC: MASTERWORKS SERIES

MC 80 – classical style, solid cedar top, solid mahogany back and sides, round soundhole with mosaic rosette, rosewood fingerboard, green abalone inlays, die-cast gold three-per-side tuners, rosewood bridge with white pins, multi-layer white/black binding, optional System 600T Mk II electronics, available in Natural finish, mfg. 2003-04.

	N/A	$350 - 425	$200 - 250	$799

MC 90 – similar to the MC 80, except has solid Indian rosewood back and sides, optional System 600T Mk II electronics, mfg. 2003-08.

	N/A	$450 - 525	$275 - 325	$1,000

* *MC 90C* – similar to the MC 90, except has a single cutaway and standard System 600T Mk II electronics, mfg. 2003-08.

	N/A	$600 - 675	$375 - 450	$1,300

MC761 – classical body style, solid cedar top, solid rosewood back and sides, round soundhole with wood mosaic rosette, black body binding, mahogany neck, 12/19-fret rosewood fingerboard, slotted headstock with rosewood overlay, three-per-side open-style gold tuners, rosewood bridge, available in Natural finish, modern foam core case included, mfg. 2009-present.

MSR $1,100	$770	$500 - 575	$300 - 350	

* *MC761C Cutaway Electric* – similar to the MC761, except has a single cutaway and System 600T Mk II electronics, available in Natural finish, mfg. 2009-present.

MSR $1,400	$980	$625 - 750	$350 - 425	

MC 1000 – classical style, solid western cedar top, solid Indian rosewood back and sides, round soundhole with mosaic rosette, tortoise body binding, ebony fingerboard, slotted headstock with three-per-side open-style tuners, ebony bridge, available in Natural finish, mfg. 2007-08.

	N/A	$1,000 - 1,200	$650 - 750	$2,300

MD 60 – dreadnought style, solid cedar top, mahogany back and sides, round soundhole with abalone shell inlay, 14/20-fret rosewood fingerboard, 12th fret diagonal inlay, die-cast nickel three-per-side tuners, Indian rosewood bridge with white pins, multi-layer white/black binding, optional System 600T Mk II electronics, available in Natural finish, mfg. 2004-08.

	N/A	$450 - 525	$275 - 325	$1,000

* *MD 60C* – similar to the MD 60 except has a single cutaway and standard System 600T Mk II electronics, mfg. 2006-08.

	N/A	$600 - 675	$375 - 450	$1,300

MSR/NOTES	100%	EXCELLENT	AVERAGE	LAST MSR

MD 65 – dreadnought style, solid cedar top, ovangkol back and sides, round soundhole with abalone shell inlay, 14/20-fret rosewood fingerboard, 12th fret diagonal inlay, die-cast nickel three-per-side tuners, Indian rosewood bridge with white pins, multi-layer white/black binding, optional System 600T Mk II electronics, available in Natural finish, mfg. 2004 only.

	N/A	$350 - 425	$200 - 250	$799

MD 70 – dreadnought style, solid cedar top, Indian rosewood back and sides, round soundhole with abalone shell inlay, 14/20-fret rosewood fingerboard, 12th fret diagonal inlay, die-cast nickel three-per-side tuners, Indian rosewood bridge with white pins, multi-layer white/black binding, optional System 600T Mk II electronics, available in Natural finish, mfg. 2004-08.

	N/A	$550 - 625	$300 - 375	$1,200

MD 80 – dreadnought style, solid spruce top, mahogany back and sides, round soundhole with black and white circles, 14/20-fret rosewood fingerboard, green abalone inlays, die-cast nickel three-per-side tuners, rosewood bridge with white pins, multi-layer white/black binding, optional System 500 Mk II (2001 only) or System 600T Mk II (2002-08) electronics, available in Natural finish, mfg. 2001-08.

	N/A	$450 - 525	$275 - 325	$1,000

* *MD 80-12 12-String* – similar to the MD 80 except in 12-string configuration and six-per-side tuners, optional System 600T Mk II electronics, mfg. 2002-08.

	N/A	$500 - 575	$300 - 350	$1,100

* *MD 80C AURA* – similar to the MD 80 except has a single cutaway and custom Aura Fishman electronics, mfg. 2006-08.

	N/A	$850 - 1,000	$550 - 650	$1,930

MD 85 – similar to the MD 80, except has solid ovangkol back and sides, mfg. 2003-04.

	N/A	$375 - 450	$225 - 275	$849

MD 90 – similar to the MD 80 except has rosewood back and sides, optional System 500 Mk II (2001 only) or System 600T Mk II (2002-08) electronics, mfg. 2001-08.

	N/A	$575 - 650	$325 - 400	$1,250

* *MD 90C* – similar to the MD 90, except has a single cutaway and standard System 600T Mk II electronics, mfg. 2005-08.

	N/A	$650 - 775	$425 - 500	$1,500

MD 95 – similar to the MD 90, except has gold hardware, optional System 600T Mk II electronics, mfg. 2003-08.

	N/A	$600 - 700	$375 - 450	$1,350

MD 200C – single cutaway dreadnought body, solid Englemann spruce top, solid flame maple back and sides, abalone rosette, maple body binding, 14/20-fret ebony fingerboard with tree-of-life inlays, three-per-side tuners, ebony bridge, black pickguard, standard System 600T Mk II electronics, gold hardware, available in Natural finish, mfg. 2005-08.

	N/A	$725 - 875	$475 - 550	$1,700

MD 350 – dreadnought style, solid Englemann spruce top, solid Indian rosewood back/sides, tortoise/herringbone body binding, round soundhole with wood rosette, 14/20-fret ebony fingerboard with 12th fret oval inlay, gold three-per-side tuners with ebony buttons, ebony bridge, black pickguard, optional System 600T Mk II electronics, available in Natural finish, mfg. 2006-08.

	N/A	$675 - 800	$450 - 525	$1,550

* *MD 350C* – similar to the MD 350, except has a single smooth cutaway and standard System 600T Mk II electronics, mfg. 2006-08.

	N/A	$850 - 1,000	$550 - 625	$1,900

MD660 – dreadnought body style, solid cedar top, solid mahogany back and sides, round soundhole with abalone rosette, multi-ply body binding, mahogany neck, 14/20-fret bound rosewood fingerboard with 12th fret three-piece Alvarez inlay, bound headstock with rosewood overlay and Alvarez logo, three-per-side nickel tuners, rosewood bridge, available in Natural Satin finish, modern foam core case included, mfg. 2009-present.

MSR $1,100	$770	$500 - 575	$300 - 350	

* *MD660C Cutaway Electric* – similar to the MD660, except has a single cutaway and System 600T Mk II electronics, available in Natural Satin finish, mfg. 2009-present.

MSR $1,400	$980	$625 - 750	$350 - 425	

MD710-12 12-STRING – 12-string configuration, dreadnought body style, solid spruce top, solid mahogany back and sides, round soundhole with combination abalone/brown ring rosette, multi-ply maple body binding, mahogany neck, 14/20-fret rosewood fingerboard with 12th fret three-piece Alvarez inlay, rosewood headstock overlay with Alvarez logo, six-per-side nickel tuners, rosewood bridge, available in Natural finish, modern foam core case included, mfg. 2009-present.

MSR $1,200	$830	$550 - 625	$300 - 375	

MSR/NOTES	100%	EXCELLENT	AVERAGE	LAST MSR

* **MD710BK-12 12-String Black** – similar to the MD710MK-12 12-String, except has an abalone only soundhole rosette and available in Black finish with a matching finish headstock, mfg. 2009 only.

	N/A	$550 - 625	$300 - 375	$1,240

MD711/MD711SB – dreadnought body style, solid spruce top, solid rosewood back and sides, round soundhole with a combination abalone/brown ring rosette, multi-ply maple body binding, mahogany neck, 14/20-fret rosewood fingerboard with 12th fret three-piece Alvarez inlay, rosewood headstock overlay with Alvarez logo, three-per-side nickel tuners, rosewood bridge, available in Natural (MD711) or Sunburst (MD711SB) finish, modern foam core case included, mfg. 2009-present.

MSR $1,350	$940	$600 - 700	$325 - 400	

  • Add 5% (MSR $1,400) for Sunburst finish.

* **MD711C Cutaway Electric** – similar to the MD711, except has a single cutaway and System 600T Mk II electronics, available in Natural finish, mfg. 2009-present.

MSR $1,700	$1,200	$750 - 900	$425 - 500	

MD 1000 – dreadnought style, solid spruce top, solid Indian rosewood back and sides, round soundhole with abalone rosette, ivory multi-ply body binding, ebony fingerboard with 12th fret oval inlay, three-per-side gold tuners, ebony bridge, optional System 600T Mk II electronics, available in Natural finish, mfg. 2007-08.

	N/A	$1,150 - 1,400	$750 - 900	$2,700

* **MD 1000C** – similar to the MD 1000, except has a single cutaway and standard System 600T Mk II electronics, available in Natural finish, mfg. 2007-08.

	N/A	$1,250 - 1,500	$800 - 950	$2,900

MD 5000 – dreadnought style, solid Englemann spruce top, solid Brazilian rosewood back and sides, round soundhole with abalone rosette, maple/herringbone body binding, ebony fingerboard with 12th fret oval inlay, three-per-side gold tuners, ebony bridge, optional System 600T Mk II electronics, available in Natural finish, mfg. 2007 only.

	N/A	$1,550 - 1,850	$1,050 - 1,200	$3,499

MD6104 – dreadnought body style, solid spruce top, solid mahogany back and sides, round soundhole with black two-ring rosette, maple body binding, mahogany neck, 14/20-fret bound ebony fingerboard with 12th fret three-piece Alvarez inlay, rosewood headstock overlay with Alvarez logo, three-per-side black tuners, ebony bridge, available in Natural finish with Vintage Tint, modern foam core case included, mfg. 2009-present.

MSR $900	$630	$400 - 475	$225 - 275	

MF 60C – single cutaway folk body style, solid cedar top, solid mahogany back and sides, round soundhole with abalone shell inlay, 14/20-fret rosewood fingerboard, 12th fret diagonal inlay, die-cast nickel three-per-side tuners, Indian rosewood bridge with white pins, multi-layer white/black binding, standard System 600T Mk II electronics, available in Natural finish, mfg. 2007 only.

	N/A	$550 - 625	$325 - 375	$1,199

MF 80 – folk style, solid spruce top, mahogany back and sides, round soundhole with black and white circles, 14/20-fret rosewood fingerboard, green abalone inlays, die-cast nickel three-per-side tuners, rosewood bridge with white pins, multi-layer white/black binding, optional System 500 Mk II (2001) or System 600T Mk II (2002) electronics, available in Natural finish, mfg. 2001-02.

	N/A	$350 - 425	$175 - 225	$799

* **MF 80C** – similar to the MF 80, except has single cutaway and standard System 600T Mk II electronics, mfg. 2002-04, 2006-08.

	N/A	$550 - 650	$325 - 400	$1,250

* **MF 80C AURA** – similar to the MF 80, except has a single cutaway and custom Aura Fishman electronics, mfg. 2006-08.

	N/A	$850 - 1,000	$550 - 625	$1,930

MF 90 – similar to the MF 80, except has rosewood back and sides, optional System 500 Mk II (2001 only) or System 600T Mk II (2002-05) electronics, mfg. 2001-05.

	N/A	$450 - 525	$250 - 300	$999

MF 350 – folk style, solid Englemann spruce top, solid Indian rosewood back/sides, tortoise/herringbone body binding, round soundhole with wood rosette, 14/20-fret ebony fingerboard with 12th fret oval inlay, gold three-per-side tuners with ebony buttons, ebony bridge, black pickguard, optional System 600T Mk II electronics, available in Natural finish, mfg. 2007 only.

	N/A	$675 - 775	$375 - 450	$1,499

* **MF 350C** – similar to the MF 350, except has a single smooth cutaway and standard System 600T Mk II electronics, mfg. 2007 only.

	N/A	$800 - 925	$500 - 575	$1,799

MF 1000 – folk style, solid spruce top, solid Indian rosewood back and sides, round soundhole with abalone rosette, ivoroid multi-ply body binding, ebony fingerboard with 12th fret oval inlay, three-per-side gold tuners, ebony bridge, optional System 600T Mk II electronics, available in Natural finish, mfg. 2007-08.

	N/A	$1,150 - 1,400	$750 - 900	$2,700

MSR/NOTES	100%	EXCELLENT	AVERAGE	LAST MSR

* MF 1000C – similar to the MD 1000, except has a single cutaway and standard System 600T Mk II electronics, available in Natural finish, mfg. 2007-08.

	N/A	$1,250 - 1,500	$800 - 950	$2,900

MJ 80 – jumbo style, solid Canadian spruce top, mahogany back and sides, round soundhole with black and white circles, 14/20-fret Indian rosewood fingerboard, 12th fret abalone inlay, die-cast nickel three-per-side tuners, rosewood bridge with white pins, multi-layer white/black binding, optional System 600T Mk II electronics, available in Natural finish, mfg. 2002 only.

	N/A	$375 - 450	$200 - 250	$849

MSD1 – small dreadnought style, solid Englemann Spruce top, mahogany back and sides, round soundhole with abalone shell inlay, 14/20-fret rosewood fingerboard, 12th fret diagonal inlay, die-cast nickel three-per-side tuners, Indian rosewood bridge with white pins, multi-layer white/black binding, available in Natural finish, mfg. 2004-08.

	N/A	$225 - 275	$120 - 150	$550

MSD610 – small dreadnought body style, solid spruce top, solid mahogany back and sides, round soundhole with abalone rosette, multi-ply maple body binding, mahogany neck, 14/19-fret rosewood fingerboard with 12th fret three-piece Alvarez inlay, black headstock overlay with Alvarez logo, three-per-side nickel tuners, rosewood bridge, available in Natural finish, gig bag included, mfg. 2009-present.

MSR $600	$400	$275 - 325	$150 - 200	

SLM 80 – dreadnought style, solid grade AAA Canadian spruce top, solid Indian rosewood back and sides, round soundhole with black and white circles, 14/20-fret Indian rosewood fingerboard, tree-of-life abalone inlay, gold vintage style three-per-side tuners, rosewood bridge with white pins, multi-layer white/black binding, available in Natural finish, mfg. 2002 only.

	N/A	$825 - 950	$550 - 650	$1,799

This guitar commemorated the 80th anniversary of St. Louis Music. SLM is the parent company of the Alvarez guitar company.

ACOUSTIC: PROFESSIONAL SERIES (DISC. MODELS 4-DIGIT MODELS)

The Professional Series are split up into pre-1999 models with the four-digit models, and post-1999 with two-letter and two-number model designations.

5009 PROFESSIONAL ROSEWOOD CLASSIC – classical style, solid spruce top, round soundhole, bound body, wooden inlay rosette, rosewood back/sides, nato neck, 19-fret rosewood fingerboard, rosewood bridge, rosewood veneer on peghead, three-per-side gold tuners, available in Natural finish, disc. 1998.

	N/A	$300 - 350	$175 - 225	$679

5022 HERRINGBONE PROFESSIONAL (GLENBROOKE) – dreadnought style, solid spruce top, round soundhole, tortoiseshell pickguard, herringbone bound body/rosette, rosewood back/sides, mahogany neck, 14/20-fret rosewood fingerboard with pearl dot inlays, stylized bird wings inlay at 12th fret, rosewood bridge with white pearl dot pins, rosewood peghead veneer with pearl logo inlay, three-per-side chrome tuners, available in Natural finish, disc. 1998.

	N/A	$300 - 350	$150 - 200	$649

5028 MAHOGANY PRO – dreadnought style, solid spruce top, round soundhole, tortoiseshell pickguard, black/white multi-layer bound body, black/white inlay rosette, mahogany back/sides/neck, 14/20-fret rosewood fingerboard with pearl dot inlays/stylized bird wings inlay at 12th fret, rosewood bridge with white pearl dot pins, three-per-side chrome tuners, available in Natural satin finish, disc. 1998.

	N/A	$200 - 250	$120 - 160	$499

5030 TIMBERLINE SATIN – dreadnought style, solid spruce top, round soundhole, tortoiseshell pickguard, black/white multi-layer bound body, abalone shell inlay rosette, mahogany back/sides/neck, 14/20-fret rosewood fingerboard with stylized diamond inlay at 12th fret, rosewood bridge with white pearl dot pins, three-per-side chrome tuners, available in Natural satin finish, disc. 1998.

	N/A	$275 - 325	$150 - 200	$619

5031 TIMBERLINE – similar to the 5030 Timberline Satin, except has Natural gloss finish, disc. 1998.

	N/A	$300 - 350	$150 - 200	$649

5032 TIMBER RIDGE – dreadnought style, solid spruce top, round soundhole, tortoiseshell pickguard, wood body binding, wood inlay rosette, mahogany back/sides/neck, 14/20-fret rosewood fingerboard with pearl dot inlays, stylized bird wings inlay at 12th fret, rosewood bridge with white pearl dot pins, rosewood peghead veneer with pearl logo inlay, three-per-side chrome tuners, available in Natural finish, mfg. 1994-98.

	N/A	$300 - 350	$175 - 225	$640

5037 WILDWOOD 12-STRING – dreadnought style, solid cedar top, round soundhole, five-stripe bound body/rosette, mahogany back/sides, nato neck, 14/20-fret rosewood fingerboard with pearl dot inlays, 12th fret has stylized bird wings inlay, rosewood bridge with white black dot pins, rosewood veneer on peghead, six-per-side gold tuners with amber buttons, available in Natural finish, disc. 1998.

	N/A	$350 - 425	$200 - 250	$819

In 1995, solid spruce top replaces original part/design.

MSR/NOTES	100%	EXCELLENT	AVERAGE	LAST MSR

5045 MOUNTAIN – dreadnought style, solid spruce top, round soundhole, wood body binding, wood inlay rosette, mahogany back/sides/neck, 14/20-fret rosewood fingerboard with pearl dot inlays, stylized bird wings inlay at 12th fret, rosewood bridge with white pearl dot pins, peghead logo decal, three-per-side chrome tuners, available in Vintage Satin finish, disc. 1995.

	N/A	$225 - 275	$130 - 160	$500

* *5045 G Graphite Pro (5045 G Mountain)* – similar to 5045, except has wood herringbone body binding, graphite bridge, mfg. 1996-98.

	N/A	$275 - 325	$150 - 200	$599

5054 (GOLDEN CHORUS) – dreadnought style, solid spruce top, round soundhole, herringbone bound body and rosette, tortoiseshell pickguard, rosewood back/sides, nato neck, 14/20-fret rosewood fingerboard with pearl dot inlay, 12th fret has stylized bird wings inlay, rosewood bridge with white pearl dot pins, rosewood veneer on peghead, six-per-side chrome tuners, available in Natural finish, disc. 1994.

	N/A	$275 - 325	$150 - 200	$600

5062 WILDWOOD (WILDWOOD NATURAL) – dreadnought style, solid spruce top, round soundhole, five-stripe bound body/rosette, mahogany back/sides, nato neck, 14/20-fret rosewood fingerboard with pearl dot inlays, 12th fret has stylized bird wings inlay, rosewood bridge with white black dot pins, three-per-side chrome tuners, available in Natural finish, disc. 1998.

	N/A	$300 - 350	$175 - 225	$649

* *5063 Wildwood Special* – similar to 5062, except has gold tuners with amber buttons, available in Natural finish, disc. 1993.

	N/A	$300 - 350	$175 - 225	$430

5086 WILDWOOD – single cutaway dreadnought style, solid spruce top, round soundhole, five-stripe bound body/rosette, mahogany back/sides, nato neck, 14/20-fret rosewood fingerboard with pearl dot inlays, 12th fret has stylized bird wings inlay, rosewood bridge with white black dot pins, three-per-side gold tuners with amber buttons, and bi-phonic pickup system and controls, available in Natural finish, disc. 1995.

	N/A	$425 - 500	$225 - 275	$950

This model was similar to the model 5062, with electronics.

5202 MAHOGANY – classical style, solid spruce top, round soundhole, bound body, wooden inlaid rosette, African mahogany back/sides, nato neck, 19-fret rosewood fingerboard, rosewood bridge, rosewood veneer on peghead, three-per-side gold tuners, available in Natural finish, disc. 1997.

	N/A	$225 - 275	$130 - 160	$525

5224 MAHOGANY – dreadnought style, solid spruce top, round soundhole, three-stripe bound body/rosette, black pickguard, mahogany back/sides, nato neck, 14/20-fret rosewood fingerboard with pearl dot inlays, rosewood bridge with black dot pins, rosewood veneer on peghead, three-per-side chrome tuners, available in Natural finish, disc. 1995.

	N/A	$225 - 275	$130 - 160	$450

5225 ROSEWOOD – similar to 5224, except has tiger rosewood back/sides, bound fingerboard, bound peghead, disc. 1994.

	N/A	$225 - 275	$130 - 160	$460

6010 ELEGANCE SIGNATURE – dreadnought style, solid spruce top, round soundhole, multi-layer bound body, abalone rosette, mahogany back/sides/neck, 14/20-fret bound rosewood fingerboard with pearl double A inlaid at 12th fret, rosewood bridge with white pearl dot pins, bound peghead with rosewood veneer/pearl logo inlay, three-per-side gold die-cast tuners, available in Natural finish, mfg. 1995-97.

	N/A	$325 - 400	$175 - 225	$775

6015 ELEGANCE ROSE – similar to the 6010, except features a solid mahogany back, multi-layer maple/rosewood body binding, tortoiseshell pickguard, 14/20-fret rosewood fingerboard with pearl rose inlay at 12th fret, rosewood bridge with black pearl dot pins, available in Natural semi-gloss finish, mfg. 1995-98.

	N/A	$450 - 525	$250 - 300	$999

6020 C ELEGANCE CUTAWAY – similar to the 6010, except features Florentine cutaway body, Honduran mahogany back/sides, abalone shell body binding, 14/20-fret bound rosewood fingerboard with pearl inlay at 12th fret, rosewood bridge with black pearl dot pins, ornate pearl headstock inlay, available in Natural gloss finish, disc. 1998.

	N/A	$625 - 725	$400 - 475	$1,399

ACOUSTIC: PROFESSIONAL (PD, PF, & PC) SERIES (RECENT MFG.)

Alvarez introduced eight new Professional Series models in 2009 that were only produced for a year. They include the **PD311AV**, **PD311CAV**, **PD361**, **PD410C**, **PD511**, **PF411**, **PJ311CDVS**, and **PJ311CDVS-12**. We never received retail pricing for these models, so we were unable to individually list them.

PC 50S – classical style, solid spruce top, rosewood sides and back, rosewood neck with 12/19 fretboard, rosewood bridge, rosette wood mosiac soundhole, open-style gold tuners, optional System 500 Mk II (1998-2001) or System 600T Mk II (2002 only) electronics, available in Natural finish, mfg. 1998-2002.

	N/A	$400 - 475	$200 - 250	$899

* *PC 50SC* – similar to the PC-50S, except has a single cutaway and standard System 500 Mk II (1998-2001) or System 600T Mk II (2002 only) electronics, mfg. 1998-2002.

	N/A	$500 - 575	$275 - 325	$1,099

MSR/NOTES	100%	EXCELLENT	AVERAGE	LAST MSR

PD 80 S – dreadnought body, mahogany back and sides, solid spruce top, rosewood fingerboard with 12th fret diagonal position marker, abalone soundhole rosette, ivory/herringbone body binding, chrome die-cast tuners, rosewood bridge, optional System 500 Mk II (disc. 2001) or System 600T Mk II (2002-08) electronics, available in Natural finish, disc. 2008.

	N/A	$300 - 350	$175 - 225	$680

* **PD 80 SC** – similar to PD80S, except has a single cutaway and standard System 500 Mk II (disc. 2001) or System 600T Mk II (2002-08) electronics, available in Natural finish, disc. 2008.

	N/A	$375 - 450	$250 - 300	$900

* **PD 80 S 12** – similar to PD80S, except in a 12-string configuration, available in Natural finish, disc. 2002.

	N/A	$325 - 400	$200 - 250	$759

PD 85S – dreadnought body, solid cedar top, solid rosewood back and sides, abalone soundhole rosette, maple/herringbone body binding, 14/20-fret rosewood fingerboard with 12th fret diagonal inlay, chrome die-cast tuners, rosewood bridge, optional System 600T Mk II electronics, available in Antique Violin finish, mfg. 2006-08.

	N/A	$375 - 450	$250 - 300	$900

* **PD 85SC** – similar to the PD 85S, except has a single cutaway and standard System 600T Mk II electronics, mfg. 2005-08.

	N/A	$475 - 550	$300 - 350	$1,050

PD 90 S – dreadnought body, rosewood back and sides, solid spruce top, scalloped bracing, rosewood fingerboard with 12th fret diagonal position marker, abalone soundhole rosette, ivory/herringbone body binding, chrome die-cast tuners, rosewood bridge, optional System 500 Mk II (disc. 2001) or System 600T Mk II (2002-08) electronics, available in Natural finish, disc. 2008.

	N/A	$350 - 425	$200 - 250	$830

PD 91S – dreadnought body, solid cedar top, rosewood back and sides, ivory/herringbone body binding, scalloped bracing, abalone soundhole rosette, rosewood fingerboard with 12th fret diagonal position marker, chrome three-per-side tuners, rosewood bridge, optional System 600T Mk II electronics, available in Natural finish, mfg. 2006-08.

	N/A	$350 - 425	$200 - 250	$830

PD 100 S – dreadnought style, solid spruce top, round soundhole, abalone/ivory body binding, abalone rosette, black pickguard, rosewood back/sides, mahogany neck, 14/20-fret bound rosewood fingerboard with fancy pearl leaves/vine inlay, bound peghead, rosewood bridge with black abalone dot pins, three-per-side gold tuners, optional System 500 Mk II (disc. 2001) or System 600T Mk II (2002-08) electronics, available in Natural gloss finish, disc. 2008.

	N/A	$500 - 575	$300 - 375	$1,100

PF 90 S – similar to the PD90S except has a folk body, optional System 500 Mk II (disc. 2001) or System 600T Mk II (2002-present) electronics, available in Natural finish, disc. 2004.

	N/A	$325 - 400	$200 - 250	$749

* **PF 90 SC** – similar to PF90S except has a single cutaway folk body and standard System 500 Mk II (disc. 2001) or System 600T Mk II (2002-08) electronics, available in Natural finish, disc. 2008.

	N/A	$450 - 525	$275 - 325	$1,030

PJ 85SC – single cutaway jumbo body, solid spruce top, solid rosewood back and sides, maple/herringbone body binding, round soundhole with abalone rosette, bound 14/20-fret rosewood fingerboard with 12th fret diagonal inlay, bound headstock with gold three-per-side tuners, rosewood bridge, black pickguard, standard System 600T Mk II electronics, Satin Deep Violin Stain finish, mfg. 2006-08.

	N/A	$475 - 550	$300 - 350	$1,050

* **PJ 85SC12 12-String** – similar to the PJ 85SC, except is in 12-string configuration with six-per-side tuners, mfg. 2006-08.

	N/A	$525 - 600	$325 - 375	$1,190

ACOUSTIC: REGENT SERIES (DISC. 4-DIGIT MODELS)

The Regent series is divided into models made prior to 1999, which feature four-digit models and models after 1999 that have two letters and two numbers.

5003 ARTIST MAHOGANY – classical style, laminated spruce top, round soundhole, multi-layer black body, wood mosaic rosette, mahogany back/sides/neck, 12/19-fret rosewood fingerboard, rosewood bridge, slotted headstock, three-per-side tuners with plastic buttons, available in Antique Natural gloss finish, disc. 1998.

	N/A	$150 - 200	$95 - 125	$379

5201 REGENT CLASSIC (5201 CLASSIC) – classical style, laminated spruce top, round soundhole, black body binding, wood mosaic rosette, mahogany back/sides/neck, 12/19-fret rosewood fingerboard, rosewood bridge, three-per-side tuners with plastic buttons, available in Vintage Stain finish, mfg. 1994-95, 1997-98.

	N/A	$80 - 110	$50 - 70	$199

• Add $100 for Model 5201 VP (last MSR was $299).

MSR/NOTES	100%	EXCELLENT	AVERAGE	LAST MSR

5208 N – dreadnought style, laminated spruce top, round soundhole, bound body, three-stripe rosette, black pickguard, mahogany back/sides/neck, 14/20-fret rosewood fingerboard with pearl dot inlay, rosewood bridge with black pins, three-per-side chrome tuners, available in Natural finish, mfg. 1995-97.

	N/A	$110 - 140	$70 - 90	$250

* **5208 M** – similar to 5208 N, except has laminated mahogany top, mfg. 1995-97.

	N/A	$110 - 140	$70 - 90	$225

5209 REGENT – dreadnought style, laminated spruce top, round soundhole, single layer black body binding, black/white ring rosette, tortoiseshell pickguard, mahogany back/sides/neck, 14/20-fret rosewood fingerboard with dot inlays, rosewood bridge with black pins, three-per-side chrome tuners, available in Natural gloss finish, disc. 1998.

	N/A	$110 - 140	$70 - 90	$219

• Add $90 for Model 5209 VP (last MSR was $309).

5210 SATIN – dreadnought style, laminated spruce top, round soundhole, bound body, three-stripe rosette, tortoise pickguard, mahogany back/sides/neck, 14/20-fret rosewood fingerboard with pearl dot inlays, rosewood bridge with white pins, three-per-side chrome tuners, available in Natural satin finish, mfg. 1994-97.

	N/A	$140 - 180	$80 - 110	$335

5212 REGENT SPECIAL – dreadnought style, laminated spruce top, round soundhole, multi-layer black/white body binding, three-stripe rosette, tortoiseshell pickguard, mahogany back/sides/neck, 14/20-fret rosewood fingerboard with dot inlays, rosewood bridge with white pins, three-per-side chrome tuners, available in Natural gloss or Sunburst finish, disc 1997.

	N/A	$120 - 160	$80 - 100	$279

In 1996, Sunburst finish was discontinued.

* **5212 BK** – similar to the 5212 Regent Special, except has black pickguard, available in Black finish, disc. 1997.

	N/A	$140 - 190	$100 - 120	$380

5214 REGENT DELUXE – dreadnought style, spruce top, round soundhole, multi-layer black/white body binding, black/white ring rosette, black pickguard, mahogany back/sides/neck, 14/20-fret rosewood fingerboard with dot inlay, rosewood bridge with black pins, three-per-side chrome tuners, available in Natural gloss finish, disc. 1998.

	N/A	$180 - 220	$100 - 130	$399

* **5214 12 Regent Deluxe 12-String** – similar to 5214, except has 12-string configuration, six-per-side tuners, disc. 1998.

	N/A	$250 - 300	$140 - 190	$579

5216 FOLK – similar to 5212, except has parlor-style folk body configuration, disc. 1997.

	N/A	$120 - 150	$70 - 90	$265

ACOUSTIC: REGENT (RD, RC, & RF) SERIES (RECENT MFG.)

RC 10 – classical style, spruce top, mahogany back and sides, round soundhole, wood mosiac soundhole, single black binding, 12/19-fret rosewood fretboard, rosewood bridge, acrylic dot inlays, open tuners, available in Natural satin finish, mfg. 2001-08.

	N/A	$80 - 110	$50 - 70	$220

RC 20(S)C – classical style, single cutaway, solid spruce top, mahogany back and sides, round soundhole, wood mosaic soundhole, single black binding, 12/19-fret rosewood fretboard, rosewood bridge, acrylic dot inlays, open tuners, three-per-side tuners, standard System 200T electronics, available in Natural satin finish, mfg. 2001-08.

	N/A	$225 - 275	$135 - 175	$550

In 2006, a solid spruce top replaced a laminated spruce top.

RC 30S – classical style, spruce top, mahogany back and sides, wood mosaic rosette soundhole, 12/19-fret rosewood fingerboard, black multi-layer binding, rosewood bridge, optional System 500 MK II electronics, available in Natural finish, mfg. 2001 only.

	N/A	$175 - 225	$110 - 140	$399

RC210 – classical body style, spruce top, mahogany back and sides, round soundhole with mosaic rosette, black body binding, mahogany neck, 12/19-fret rosewood fingerboard, slotted headstock, three-per-side open-style gold tuners with pearl buttons, rosewood bridge, available in Natural finish, mfg. 2009-present.

MSR $250	$170	$110 - 140	$65 - 80	

RC460C – single sharp cutaway classical body style, solid cedar top, mahogany back and sides, round soundhole with mosaic rosette, black body binding, mahogany neck, 14/22-fret rosewood fingerboard, slotted headstock, three-per-side open-style gold tuners with pearl buttons, rosewood bridge, available in Natural finish, mfg. 2009 only.

	N/A	$225 - 275	$120 - 150	$550

MSR/NOTES	100%	EXCELLENT	AVERAGE	LAST MSR

RD 6 – dreadnought style, select spruce top, mahogany back and sides, round soundhole with acrylic pearl soundhole rings, maple body binding, 14/20-fret rosewood fretboard with acrylic dot inlays, covered three-per-side tuners, rosewood bridge, black pickguard, available in Natural finish, mfg. 2007-08.

	N/A	$95 - 120	$60 - 75	$240

RD 8 – dreadnought style, spruce top, mahogany back and sides, round soundhole, black/white soundhole rings, black pickguard, multi-layer black binding, 14/20-fret rosewood fretboard, rosewood bridge, acrylic dot inlays, covered three-per-side tuners, available in Brown Satin, Natural, Sunburst, or Trans. Black finish, case included, mfg. 2001-08.

	N/A	$130 - 165	$80 - 100	$320

* **Add 10% (Last MSR was $360) for Brown Satin, Sunburst, or Trans. Black finish.**

* *RD 8C* – similar to the RD 8, except is a single cutaway and has standard electronics with a two-band EQ, mfg. 2002-08.

	N/A	$175 - 225	$110 - 140	$440

RD 9VP VALUE PACK – dreadnought style, select spruce top, mahogany back and sides, round soundhole with acrylic pearl soundhole rings, maple body binding, 14/20-fret rosewood fretboard with acrylic dot inlays, covered three-per-side tuners, rosewood bridge, black pickguard, available in Natural finish, includes a gig bag, digital tuner, polish cloth, strings, string winder, strap, and picks, mfg. 2007-08.

	N/A	$120 - 150	$75 - 95	$300

RD 10 – dreadnought style, spruce top, mahogany back and sides, round soundhole, black/white soundhole rings, single black binding, 14/20-fret rosewood fretboard, rosewood bridge, acrylic dot inlays, chrome covered tuners, Natural finish, mfg. 2001-06.

	N/A	$90 - 120	$60 - 80	$219

* **Add 10% for Black finish (Model RD 10BK).**

* *RD10VP* – similar to the RD 10 except comes with a gigbag, strings, winder, strap, picks, tuner, and polish, mfg. 2001, 2004-06.

	N/A	$130 - 170	$90 - 110	$319

RD 20S – dreadnought style, laminated spruce top, round soundhole, multi-layer black/white body binding, three-stripe rosette, tortoise pickguard, mahogany back/sides/neck, 14/20-fret rosewood fingerboard with dot inlays, rosewood bridge with white pins, three-per-side chrome tuners, optional System 200T electronics, available in Black, Natural, or Sunburst finish, disc. 2008.

	N/A	$135 - 175	$85 - 105	$340

* **Add 5% (Last MSR was $350) for Black or Sunburst finish.**

* *RD 20VP* – similar to the RD 20 except comes with a gigbag, strings, winder, strap, picks, tuner, and polish, mfg. 2001 only.

	N/A	$150 - 190	$90 - 120	$369

* *RD 20SL Left-Handed* – similar to the RD 20, except is in left-hand configuration, mfg. 1998-2008.

	N/A	$150 - 190	$95 - 120	$380

* *RD 20S-12 12-String* – similar to the RD 20, except is in 12-string configuration and six-per-side tuners, available in Natural gloss finish, mfg. 1998-2008.

	N/A	$200 - 250	$120 - 150	$500

* *RD 20SC* – similar to the RD 20, except has a single cutaway and standard System 200T electronics, available in Natural, Black, or Sunburst finish, mfg. 1998-2008.

	N/A	$200 - 250	$120 - 150	$500

* **Add 5% (Last MSR was $530) for Black or Sunburst finish.**

» *RD 20SCL Left-Handed* – similar to the RD 20SC, except is in left-hand configuration, mfg. 2006-08.

	N/A	$225 - 275	$135 - 175	$530

* *RD 20SV/SSB* – similar to the RD 20S, except is a slope-shouldered dreadnought body style, available in Vintage Sunburst finish, mfg. 2004-08.

	N/A	$140 - 175	$90 - 115	$350

In 2007, this model was renamed the RD 20SSB (Slope-Shouldered body).

RD 30S – dreadnought style, spruce top, round soundhole, multi-layer black/white body binding, black/white ring rosette, black pickguard, mahogany back/sides/neck, 14/20-fret rosewood fingerboard with dot inlays, rosewood bridge with black pins, three-per-side chrome tuners, optional electronics, available in Natural or Sunburst (SB) finish, mfg. 1998-2001.

	N/A	$150 - 200	$95 - 125	$379

* *RD 30 L* – similar to the RD 30 BK, except in left-handed configuration, available in Natural gloss finish, mfg. 1998-99, 2001.

	N/A	$175 - 225	$110 - 140	$399

MSR/NOTES	100%	EXCELLENT	AVERAGE	LAST MSR

* **RD 30SC** – similar to the RD 30S except has a single cutaway with standard System MK II electronics, mfg 2001 only.

	N/A	$250 - 300	$140 - 180	$549

RD 50 REGENT DELUXE ROSEWOOD – similar to the RD 30 BK, except has rosewood back/sides, available in Natural gloss finish, mfg. 1998-99.

	N/A	$200 - 250	$120 - 160	$449

RD010 – dreadnought body style, spruce top, mahogany back and sides, round soundhole with two-ring black/white rosette, black body binding, mahogany neck, 14/20-fret rosewood fingerboard with dot inlays, mahogany headstock overlay with Alvarez logo, three-per-side nickel tuners, rosewood bridge, available in Natural finish, mfg. 2009-present.

MSR $230	$150	$95 - 120	$50 - 70	

* **RD010BK** – similar to the RD010, except available in Black finish with matching headstock overlay, mfg. 2009 only.

	N/A	$110 - 140	$65 - 80	$250

RD110 – dreadnought body style, spruce top, mahogany back and sides, round soundhole with three-ring black/white rosette, black body binding, mahogany neck, 14/20-fret rosewood fingerboard with dot inlays, mahogany headstock overlay with Alvarez logo, three-per-side nickel tuners, rosewood bridge, black pickguard, available in Natural finish, mfg. 2009-present.

MSR $270	$180	$120 - 150	$70 - 90	

RD210/RD210BR/RD210SB – dreadnought body style, spruce top, mahogany back and sides, round soundhole with multi-ring acrylic pearl rosette, black body binding, mahogany neck, 14/20-fret rosewood fingerboard with dot inlays, mahogany headstock overlay with Alvarez logo, three-per-side nickel tuners, rosewood bridge, black pickguard, available in Brown (RD210BR), Natural (RD210), or Sunburst (RD210SB) finish, hardshell case included, mfg. 2009-present.

MSR $370	$270	$150 - 200	$95 - 120	

   • **Add 7.5% (MSR $400) for Brown or Sunburst finish.**

* **RD210C Cutaway Electric** – similar to the RD210, except has a single cutaway and two-band electronics, available in Natural finish, mfg. 2009-present.

MSR $520	$360	$225 - 275	$120 - 150	

RD410/RD410SB – dreadnought body style, solid spruce top, mahogany back and sides, round soundhole with multi-ring acrylic pearl rosette, multi-ply body binding, mahogany neck, 14/20-fret rosewood fingerboard with dot inlays, mahogany headstock overlay with Alvarez logo, three-per-side chrome tuners, rosewood bridge, black pickguard, available in Natural (RD410) or Sunburst (RD410SB, 2009 only) finish, mfg. 2009-present.

MSR $370	$250	$150 - 200	$95 - 120	

* **RD410BK** – similar to the RD410, except available in Black finish with matching headstock overlay, mfg. 2009-present.

MSR $370	$250	$150 - 200	$95 - 120	

* **RD410L Left-Handed** – similar to the RD410, except in left-handed configuration, mfg. 2009-present.

MSR $410	$285	$175 - 225	$110 - 140	

RD2104VP VALUE PACK – dreadnought body style, spruce top, mahogany back and sides, round soundhole with three-ring black/white rosette, multi-ring body binding, mahogany neck, 14/20-fret rosewood fingerboard with dot inlays, mahogany headstock overlay with Alvarez logo, three-per-side chrome tuners, rosewood bridge, black pickguard, available in Natural finish, includes extra strings, string winder, strap, picks, digital tuner, polish cloth, and gig bag, mfg. 2009-present.

MSR $300	$200	$135 - 175	$80 - 105	

RD4102C/RD4102CSB – single cutaway dreadnought body style, solid spruce top, mahogany back and sides, round soundhole with multi-ring acrylic pearl rosette, multi-ply body binding, mahogany neck, 14/20-fret rosewood fingerboard with dot inlays, mahogany headstock overlay with Alvarez logo, three-per-side chrome tuners, rosewood bridge, black pickguard, Fishman AERO electronics, available in Natural (RD4102C) or Sunburst (RD4102CSB) finish, mfg. 2009-present.

MSR $550	$380	$225 - 275	$150 - 150	

* **RD4102CBK** – similar to the RD4102C, except available in Black finish with matching headstock overlay, mfg. 2009-present.

MSR $550	$380	$225 - 275	$120 - 150	

* **RD4102CL Left-Handed** – similar to the RD4102C, except in left-handed configuration, mfg. 2009-present.

MSR $600	$390	$250 - 300	$135 - 175	

RF 8 – folk style, spruce top, mahogany back and sides, round soundhole, black/white soundhole rings, black pickguard, multi-layer black binding, 14/20-fret rosewood fretboard, rosewood bridge, acrylic dot inlays, covered three-per-side tuners, Natural gloss finish, case included, mfg. 2001-08.

	N/A	$130 - 165	$80 - 100	$320

MSR/NOTES	100%	EXCELLENT	AVERAGE	LAST MSR

* RF 8C – similar to the FD 8 except has a single cutaway and standard electronics with a two-band EQ, mfg. 2008 only.

	N/A	$175 - 225	$110 - 140	$440

RF 10 – folk style, spruce top, mahogany back and sides, round soundhole, black/white soundhole rings, black pickguard, multi-layer black binding, 14/20-fret rosewood fretboard, rosewood bridge, acrylic dot inlays, covered three-per-side tuners, Natural gloss finish, case included, mfg. 2003-06.

	N/A	$90 - 120	$50 - 70	$219

RF 19S – folk body style, solid spruce top, mahogany back/sides, round soundhole with white/black rosette, 12/20-fret rosewood fingerboard with dot inlays, rosewood bridge, tortoise pickguard, slotted headstock with open style banjo tuners, optional electronics, nickel hardware, available in Natural finish, mfg. 2004-05.

	N/A	$140 - 180	$95 - 120	$329

RF 20 – folk style, spruce top, mahogany back and sides, round soundhole, black/white soundhole rings, multi-layer black/white binding, 14/20-fret rosewood fretboard, rosewood bridge, acrylic dot inlays, chrome tuners, three-per-side tuners, optional electronics, Natural finish, mfg. 2001 only.

	N/A	$120 - 150	$80 - 100	$279

* RF 20SC – similar to the RF 20 except has a single cutaway and standard System 200T electronics, mfg. 2001-08.

	N/A	$200 - 250	$120 - 150	$500

* RF 20SM Mahogany – similar to the RF 20 except has a solid mahogany top and optional System 200T electronics, available in Natural Satin finish, mfg. 2006-08.

	N/A	$140 - 175	$85 - 110	$350

RF 22S – folk body style, solid spruce top, mahogany back and sides, multi-ply body binding, round soundhole with acrylic pearl rosette, 14/20-fret rosewood fingerboard with dot inlays, matching headstock with chrome three-per-side tuners with pearl buttons, rosewood bridge, white pickguard, optional System 200T electronics, available in Light Blue, Raspberry, Yellow, or Violet finish, mfg. 2006 only.

	N/A	$150 - 200	$95 - 120	$389

RF 30 – similar to RD 30 BK, except in folk body configuration, available in Natural gloss finish, mfg. 1998-2001.

	N/A	$150 - 200	$95 - 125	$379

RF010 – folk body style, spruce top, mahogany back and sides, round soundhole with two-ring black/white rosette, black body binding, mahogany neck, 14/20-fret rosewood fingerboard with dot inlays, mahogany headstock overlay with Alvarez logo, three-per-side nickel tuners, rosewood bridge, available in Natural finish, mfg. 2009-present.

MSR $230	$150	$95 - 120	$50 - 70	

RF210 – folk body style, spruce top, mahogany back and sides, round soundhole with multi-ring acrylic pearl rosette, black body binding, mahogany neck, 14/20-fret rosewood fingerboard with dot inlays, mahogany headstock overlay with Alvarez logo, three-per-side nickel tuners, rosewood bridge, black pickguard, available in Natural finish, hardshell case included, mfg. 2009-present.

MSR $370	$250	$150 - 200	$95 - 120	

* RF210C – similar to the RF210, except has a single cutaway with two-band electronics, available in Natural finish, mfg. 2009 only.

	N/A	$225 - 275	$125 - 150	$500

RF300 – folk body style, solid mahogany top, mahogany back and sides, round soundhole with multi-ring acrylic pearl rosette, multi-ply body binding, mahogany neck, 14/20-fret rosewood fingerboard with dot inlays, mahogany headstock overlay with Alvarez logo, three-per-side chrome tuners, rosewood bridge, black pickguard, available in Natural finish, mfg. 2009-present.

MSR $400	$280	$175 - 225	$100 - 135	

RF4102C – single cutaway folk body style, solid spruce top, mahogany back and sides, round soundhole with multi-ring acrylic pearl rosette, multi-ply body binding, mahogany neck, 14/20-fret rosewood fingerboard with dot inlays, mahogany headstock overlay with Alvarez logo, three-per-side chrome tuners, rosewood bridge, black pickguard, Fishman AERO electronics, available in Natural finish, mfg. 2009-present.

MSR $550	$380	$225 - 275	$150 - 150	

SILVER ANNIVERSARY & WILLOW RIDGE ACOUSTIC SERIES

2551 ROSEWOOD – dreadnought style, solid spruce top, round soundhole, five-stripe bound body, abalone rosette, rosewood back/sides, mahogany neck, 14/20-fret rosewood fingerboard with pearl diamond inlays, rosewood bridge with white black dot pins, rosewood veneer on bound peghead with Silver Anniversary inlay, three-per-side chrome tuners, available in Natural finish, disc. 1997.

	N/A	$300 - 350	$150 - 200	$650

* 2551/12 12-String – similar to 2551 Rosewood, except in 12-string configuration with six-per-side tuners, disc. 1995.

	N/A	$350 - 425	$200 - 250	$800

MSR/NOTES	100%	EXCELLENT	AVERAGE	LAST MSR

2552 – dreadnought style, spruce top, round soundhole, five-stripe bound body, abalone rosette, mahogany back/sides/neck, 14/20-fret rosewood fingerboard with pearl dot inlays, rosewood bridge with black white dot pins, rosewood veneer on peghead, three-per-side chrome tuners, available in Natural finish, disc. 1993.

	N/A	$175 - 225	$110 - 140	$400

2555 JUMBO – jumbo style, Florentine cutaway, laminated spruce top, round soundhole, five-stripe bound body, abalone flake rosette, mahogany back/sides/neck, 21-fret rosewood fingerboard with abalone offset bar inlays, rosewood bridge with black white pins, rosewood veneer on bound peghead with Silver Anniversary inlay, three-per-side chrome tuners, available in Natural or Sunburst finish, disc. 1995.

	N/A	$475 - 550	$275 - 325	$1,050

This model was available with an Alvarez Bi-Phonic pickup system.

* *2555 BK (Folk)* – similar to the 2555, except has folk body configuration, single Florentine cutaway, abalone body binding, abalone rosette, available in Gloss Black finish, mfg. 1994 only.

	N/A	$400 - 475	$250 - 300	$900

2531 – single round cutaway classical style, spruce top, round soundhole, wooden inlay rosette, bound body, mahogany back/sides/neck, 19-fret rosewood fingerboard, rosewood wraparound bridge, three-per-side chrome tuners with plastic buttons, piezo bridge pickups, three-band EQ, available in Natural finish, mfg. 1994 only.

	N/A	$475 - 550	$275 - 325	$1,050

2532 – single round cutaway dreadnought style, spruce top, black pickguard, three-stripe bound body/rosette, maple back/sides, mahogany neck, 22-fret rosewood fingerboard with pearl dot inlays, rosewood bridge with white black dot pins, three-per-side die-cast tuners, piezo bridge pickups, three-band EQ, available in Natural finish, disc. 1995.

	N/A	$475 - 550	$275 - 325	$1,050

2533 – similar to 2532, except has mahogany back/sides, available in Natural finish, disc. 1995.

	N/A	$475 - 550	$275 - 325	$1,050

ACOUSTIC ELECTRIC BASS

4070 ACOUSTIC BASS – single round jumbo style, laminated spruce top, round soundhole, three-stripe bound body/rosette, mahogany back/sides/neck, 23-fret rosewood fingerboard, rosewood bridge with white black dot pins, bound rosewood peghead with pearl logo inlay, two-per-side die-cast tuners, piezo bridge pickups, three-band EQ, available in Natural gloss finish, mfg. 1994-98.

	N/A	$525 - 600	$325 - 375	$1,149

* Add $50 for Black finish (Model 4070 BK, mfg. 1994-96).

AB4102C – single cutaway bass body, solid spruce top, mahogany back and sides, round soundhole with abalone rosette, multi-layer white body binding, mahogany neck, 16/22-fret bound rosewood fingerboard with three-piece 12th fret Alvarez inlay, bound headstock with mahogany overlay and Alvarez logo, two-per-side chrome tuners, rosewood bridge, Fishman AERO+ or Presys electronics, available in Natural finish, mfg. 2009-present.

MSR $750	$525	$325 - 400	$175 - 225	

* *AB4102CBK* – similar to the AB4102C, except available in a Black finish with a matching finish headstock overlay, mfg. 2009 only.

	N/A	$325 - 400	$175 - 225	$750

MSB 1 TRAVEL BASS – small travel-sized bass body, solid Englemann spruce top, solid mahogany back and sides, round soundhole with abalone rosette, rosewood fingerboard with 12th fret diagonal inlay, two-per-side chrome tuners, rosewood bridge, passive internal pickup, available in Natural finish, mfg. 2007-08.

	N/A	$300 - 350	$175 - 225	$700

MSB6102 – small bass body style, solid spruce top, solid mahogany back and sides, round soundhole with abalone rosette, multi-ply maple body binding, mahogany neck, 17/23-fret rosewood fingerboard with 12th fret three-piece Alvarez inlay, black headstock overlay with Alvarez logo, two-per-side nickel tuners, rosewood bridge, available in Natural finish, gig bag included, mfg. 2009 only.

	N/A	$275 - 325	$150 - 200	$600

RB 30SC (RB 30C) – cutaway Jumbo Bass body, spruce top, mahogany back and sides, 17/23-fret rosewood fingerboard with acrylic dot inlays, round rosette soundhole with black and white rings, white/black multi-layer binding, chrome die-cast tuners, rosewood bridge, standard System 500 MK II (2000-03) or System 200T (2004-07) electronics, Natural finish, mfg. 2000-07.

	N/A	$300 - 350	$175 - 225	$699

ALVAREZ YAIRI

Instruments currently produced in Kani, Japan. Distributed by St. Louis Music, Inc. in St. Louis, MO. Alvarez Yairi instruments have been produced since 1966.

These handcrafted guitars are built by craftsmen under the direction of luthier/designer Kazuo Yairi. Yairi, who learned to construct violins and guitars from his father, started his own company to produce handmade guitars in larger quantities.

Alvarez Yairi acoustics were first imported to the U.S. in 1966, and were exclusively

CONTACT INFORMATION
ALVAREZ YAIRI
Distributed by St. Louis Music
1400 Ferguson Avenue
St. Louis, MO 63133
Phone No.: 314-727-1191
www.alvarezguitars.com

MSR/NOTES	100%	EXCELLENT	AVERAGE	LAST MSR

distributed by St. Louis Music, Inc. These quality acoustic guitars are designed by both luthier Yairi in Japan and the designers at St. Louis Music. Instruments are adjusted at the Alvarez Yairi factory in Japan, and re-inspected after shipping at St. Louis Music before delivery to dealers. In 2005, LOUD Technologies, Inc. purchased St. Louis Music, Inc. and all of their trademarks. With this acquisition, the headquarters of St. Louis Music was moved to Woodinville, WA. However, the guitar repair and set-up shop was still located in St. Louis. In 2009, Mark Ragin moved Alvarez Yairi guitars back to St. Louis Music in St. Louis that included management and distribution. For more information, contact Alvarez directly or visit their website.

ACOUSTIC: MISC. MODELS

All Alvarez Yairi acoustic steel string guitars have an abalone or pearl peghead logo inlay. All Alvarez Yairi models may be purchased with Alvarez Natural Response or System 500 pickups.

- Add $110 for installed BP Natural Response pickup (without volume/tone control).
- Add $135 for installed BT Natural Response pickup (with volume/tone control).
- Add $300 for installed System 500 pickup.

ADY1 ANI DIFRANCO SIGNATURE – single cutaway folk body, solid cedar top, mahogany back and sides, black body binding, 14/20-fret ebony fingerboard with 12th fret diagonal inlay, matching headstock with two diagonal lines and three-per-side tuners, rosewood direct coupled bridge, gray pickguard that covers most of the upper body and extends below, standard System 600T Mk II electronics, gold hardware, available in Gold Satin finish, mfg. 2005-present.

MSR $2,800	$2,150	$1,250 - 1,450	$700 - 800	

DY 1 CK – single cutaway dreadnought body, koa top/back/sides, abalone body binding, round soundhole with abalone rosette, 14/20-fret ebony fingerboard with 12th fret diagonal inlay, black headstock with diagonal lines and three-per-side gold tuners with pearl buttons, ebony direct coupled bridge, standard System 600T Mk II electronics, Natural finish, mfg. 2006-08.

	N/A	$1,300 - 1,550	$800 - 950	$3,000

FY 40 CAROLINA FOLK – dreadnought clinched waist style, solid Canadian spruce top, round soundhole, ivoroid/wood bound top and back, three-stripe rosette, mahogany back/sides/neck, 14/20-fret rosewood fingerboard with snowflake inlays, rosewood bridge, rosewood headstock veneer, three-per-side chrome tuners, available in Natural finish, mfg. circa mid-1970s.

	N/A	$475 - 550	$275 - 325	

JY 10 NASHVILLE JUMBO – jumbo style, solid spruce top, round soundhole, tortoiseshell pickguard, ivoroid bound body, abalone purfling/rosette, maple back/sides, mahogany neck, 14/20-fret rosewood fingerboard with pearl dot inlay, 12th fret pearl curlicue inlay, ebony bridge with white black dot pins, ebony veneered bound peghead, three-per-side gold tuners, available in Sunburst finish, mfg. 1994-98.

	N/A	$675 - 775	$375 - 450	$1,400

MMY1 MONTE MONTGOMERY SIGNATURE – single cutaway dreadnought body style, solid cedar distressed top, burled mahogany back/sides, round soundhole with abalone shell rosette, brown pickguard, 14/20-fret ebony fingerboard with double M and star 12th fret inlays, rosewood bridge, three-per-side tuners, standard System 600T Mk II electronics, gold hardware, available in Aged Satin finish, mfg. 2004-present.

MSR $3,400	$2,500	$1,500 - 1,750	$1,000 - 1,150	

YB 1 BARITONE – jumbo style, solid spruce top, round soundhole, five-stripe body binding, shell rosette, rosewood back/sides, mahogany neck, 14/20-fret ebony fingerboard, ebony bridge with white abalone dot pins, three-per-side gold tuners, piezo bridge pickup, volume/tone controls, standard System 500 Mk II (disc. 2001) or System 600T Mk II (2002-present) electronics, available in Natural gloss finish, current mfg.

MSR $2,200	$1,650	$950 - 1,100	$625 - 750	

ACOUSTIC: CLASSICAL SERIES

All classical guitars have rosewood veneer on their pegheads. All of these models have a CY prefix. Check the Masterwork series for the CY-200 since it is part of the Masterworks series.

CY 110 MAHOGANY CLASSIC – classical style, solid cedar top, round soundhole, black multi-ply body binding, wooden mosaic rosette, Honduran mahogany back/sides, mahogany neck, 12/19-fret rosewood fingerboard, rosewood bridge, slotted headstock, three-per-side gold tuners with pearloid buttons, available in Natural semi-satin finish, disc 2002.

	N/A	$550 - 650	$350 - 425	$1,249

CY 116 BURLED (CY116 LA GRANJA) – classical style, solid cedar top, round soundhole, maple body binding, wooden mosaic rosette, burled mahogany back/sides, mahogany neck, 12/19-fret ebony fingerboard, rosewood bridge, rosewood veneer headstock, slotted headstock, three-per-side gold tuners with pearloid buttons, optional electronics, available in Antique gloss finish, mfg. 1975-present.

1975-1995	N/A	$750 - 900	$500 - 575	
1996-2005	N/A	$725 - 850	$475 - 550	
2006-Present MSR $1,600	$1,280	$700 - 825	$450 - 525	

CY 118 JACARANDA – similar to CY 116, except has jacaranda back/sides, wood multi-layer body binding, optional electronics, current mfg.

MSR $1,600	$1,200	$700 - 825	$450 - 525	

MSR/NOTES	100%	EXCELLENT	AVERAGE	LAST MSR

CY 125 EL LORCA – classical style, solid cedar top, round soundhole, wooden inlaid rosette and stripe on headstock, three-stripe bound body, rosewood sides, rosewood book matched back, mahogany neck, 12/19-fret ebony fingerboard, rosewood bridge and headstock veneer, three-per-side gold tuners with pearloid buttons, available in Natural finish, mfg. circa mid-1970s.

	N/A	$525 - 600	$350 - 400	

CY 127 CE CUTAWAY CLASSIC – shallow depth classical style body, rounded cutaway, solid cedar top, round soundhole, multi-layer wood body binding, wood mosaic rosette, rosewood back/sides, mahogany neck, 12/19-fret ebony fingerboard, rosewood bridge, slotted headstock, three-per-side gold tuners with pearloid buttons, Alvarez Natural Response pickup system and volume/tone control, available in Natural gloss finish, mfg. 1980s-2004.

	N/A	$750 - 875	$475 - 550	$1,699

CY 128 CE – similar to the CY 127 CE except has a deeper body, and standard Alvarez NR electronics, available in Natural Gloss finish, mfg. 2001-present.

MSR $1,900	$1,520	$850 - 1,000	$550 - 625	

CY 130 CONQUISTADOR – classical style, cedar top, round soundhole, wooden inlaid rosette, three-stripe bound body, rosewood sides, two-piece rosewood back, mahogany neck/headstock, 12/19-fret ebony fingerboard, carved headstock design, rosewood bridge, three-per-side gold tuners with pearloid buttons, available in Natural finish, mfg. circa mid-1970s.

	N/A	$650 - 750	$375 - 450	

CY 132 C CONQUISTADOR CUTAWAY – similar to the CY 130 Conquistador, except has single stepped down cutaway, mfg. circa mid-1970s.

	N/A	$550 - 650	$325 - 375	

CY 135 CONCERT MASTER – classical style, Canadian cedar top, round soundhole, wooden inlaid bound body and rosette, jacaranda sides, jacaranda book matched back, mahogany neck/headstock, 12/19-fret ebony fingerboard, ebony bridge, three-per-side gold tuners with pearloid buttons, available in Natural finish, mfg. circa mid-1970s.

	N/A	$650 - 750	$375 - 450	

CY 140 CONCERT MASTER (CY 140 GRAND CONCERT MASTER) – classical style, solid cedar top, round soundhole, multi-layer wood body binding, wood mosaic rosette, jacaranda back/sides, mahogany neck, 12/19-fret ebony fingerboard, rosewood bridge, slotted headstock, three-per-side gold tuners with pearl buttons, optional electronics, available in Antique Natural gloss finish, mfg. circa mid-1970s-present.

MSR $1,900	$1,520	$850 - 1,000	$550 - 625	

YC 1 CUSTOM CUTAWAY (NYLON STRING) – sloped rounded cutaway body, solid spruce top, round soundhole, multi-layer tortoiseshell body binding, turquoise rosette, rosewood back/sides, mahogany neck, 12/20-fret ebony fingerboard with turquoise inlays, rosewood bridge, slotted headstock, three-per-side gold tuners with pearloid buttons, piezo bridge pickup, volume/tone controls, System 500 electronics, available in Natural gloss finish, disc. 1998.

	N/A	$775 - 900	$525 - 625	$1,899

YC 2 CUSTOM CUTAWAY (STEEL STRING) – similar to the YC 1, except features graphite bridge, solid headstock, three-per-side gold tuners, available in Natural gloss finish, disc. 1998.

	N/A	$775 - 900	$525 - 625	$1,899

ACOUSTIC: DREADNOUGHT SERIES (DY PREFIX)

Alvarez Yairi has produced several dreadnoughts over the years. Early models were just known as DY Models, but today they are broken up into series including the Traditional, Fusion, Innovative (disc.), and Signature models.

DY 47 – dreadnought-style body, solid spruce top, laminated mahogany back and sides, round soundhole with three-ring rosette, single-ply body binding, aged nato mahogany neck, 14/20-fret ebony fingerboard with pearl dots and 12th fret decorative inlays, abalone insignia on headstock overlay, three-per-side tuners, ebony bridge, black pickguard, available in Sunburst finish, mfg. early 1980s.

	N/A	$300 - 375	$175 - 225	

DY 48 – dreadnought-style body, solid spruce top, laminated mahogany back and sides, round soundhole with three-ring rosette, single-ply body binding, aged nato mahogany neck, 14/20-fret ebony fingerboard with pearl dots and 12th fret decorative inlays, abalone insignia on headstock overlay, three-per-side tuners, ebony bridge, black pickguard, available in Natural finish, mfg. early 1980s.

	N/A	$300 - 375	$175 - 225	

DY 50 N – dreadnought style, cedar top, round soundhole, three-stripe bound body, abalone rosette, tortoiseshell pickguard, jacaranda back/sides, mahogany neck, 14/20-fret bound rosewood fingerboard with abalone diamond inlays, rosewood bridge with white pearl dot pins, rosewood veneer on bound peghead, three-per-side gold tuners, available in Natural finish, mfg. 1991-95.

	N/A	$550 - 650	$350 - 400	$1,275

* DY 50 NEQ – dreadnought style, cedar top, round soundhole, three-stripe bound body, abalone rosette, tortoiseshell pickguard, jacaranda back/sides, mahogany neck, 14/20-fret bound rosewood fingerboard with abalone diamond inlays, rosewood bridge with white pearl dot pins, rosewood veneer on bound peghead, three-per-side gold tuners, piezo bridge pickup, three-band EQ, available in Natural finish, mfg. 1994 only.

	N/A	$625 - 725	$425 - 500	$1,575

MSR/NOTES	100%	EXCELLENT	AVERAGE	LAST MSR

DY 51 BLUE RIDGE – dreadnought style, solid cedar top, round soundhole, ivoroid bound body, herringbone rosette, burled mahogany back/sides, nato mahogany neck, 14/20-fret ebony fingerboard with snowflake inlay, ebony bridge, burled mahogany headstock veneer, mother-of-pearl headstock inlay, three-per-side chrome tuners, available in Natural finish, mfg. circa mid-1970s.

| | N/A | $550 - 650 | $350 - 400 | |

DY 52 SILVER LARK – dreadnought style, solid Canadian spruce top, round soundhole, white maple bound body, herringbone rosette, walnut pickguard, walnut back/sides, mahogany neck, 14/20-fret ebony fingerboard with snowflake inlay, ebony bridge, MOP headstock inlay, walnut veneer on peghead, three-per-side chrome tuners, available in Natural finish, mfg. circa mid-1970s.

| | N/A | $650 - 750 | $375 - 450 | |

This model had a solid oboncol wood pickguard (adhesive-backed for optional installation) available.

DY 53 SILVER HARP – dreadnought style, solid Canadian spruce top, round soundhole, white maple bound body, herringbone rosette, burled mahogany back/sides, nato mahogany neck, 14/20-fret ebony fingerboard with snowflake inlay, ebony bridge, mother-of-pearl headstock inlay, three-per-side chrome tuners, available in Natural satin finish, mfg. circa mid-1970s.

| | N/A | $650 - 750 | $375 - 450 | |

This model had a solid oboncol wood pickguard (adhesive-backed for optional installation) available.

DY 53 N – orchestra-style body, spruce top, round soundhole, five-stripe bound body and rosette, tortoiseshell pickguard, rosewood back/sides, mahogany neck, 14/20-fret bound rosewood fingerboard with pearl block inlays, rosewood bridge with white pearl dot pins, rosewood veneer on bound peghead, three-per-side chrome tuners, available in Natural finish, mfg. 1990-95.

| | N/A | $500 - 575 | $300 - 350 | $1,100 |

In 1994, coral rosewood back/sides replaced original part/design.

DY 54 SILVER FAWN – dreadnought style, solid Canadian spruce top, round soundhole, maple bound body, turquoise/wood rosette, oboncol back/sides, nato mahogany neck, 14/20-fret black ebony fingerboard with snowflake inlays, ebony bridge, rosewood inlay on lower body bout, MOP headstock inlay, three-per-side chrome tuners, available in Natural finish, mfg. circa mid-1970s.

| | N/A | $550 - 650 | $300 - 350 | |

This model had a solid oboncol wood pickguard (adhesive-backed for optional installation) available.

DY 57 WINCHESTER DREADNOUGHT – dreadnought style, solid Canadian spruce top, round soundhole, ivoroid/wood marquetry bound body, herringbone rosette, mahogany back/sides, nato mahogany neck, 14/20-fret ebony fingerboard with dot inlays, ebony bridge, three-per-side chrome tuners, available in Natural finish, mfg. circa mid-1970s.

| | N/A | $650 - 750 | $375 - 450 | |

DY 58 DREADNOUGHT NINE – dreadnought style, solid Canadian spruce top, round soundhole, ivoroid bound body, wood inlaid rosette, mahogany back/sides/neck, 14/20-fret ebony fingerboard with pearl dot inlays, ebony bridge, mahogany headstock veneer, tortoiseshell pickguard, 3/6-per-side chrome tuners, available in Natural finish, mfg. circa mid-1970s.

| | N/A | $750 - 900 | $475 - 550 | |

This nine-stringed guitar combines three single bass-side strings with three pairs of treble strings. This model will also function as a six-string acoustic.

DY 68 RAMBLING TWELVE – dreadnought style, solid Canadian spruce top, round soundhole, wood inlay bound body, wood inlay rosette, mahogany back/sides/neck, 14/20-fret ebony fingerboard with pearl dot inlay, ebony bridge, mahogany headstock veneer, abalone logo inlay on headstock, tortoiseshell pickguard, six-per-side chrome tuners, abalone inlays on bridge pins, available in Natural finish, mfg. circa mid-1970s.

| | N/A | $600 - 700 | $375 - 450 | |

DY 75 – dreadnought style, spruce top, round soundhole, wooden inlaid bound body/rosette, tortoiseshell pickguard, rosewood back/sides, mahogany neck, 14/20-fret rosewood fingerboard with pearl dot inlays, Direct Coupled rosewood bridge, rosewood veneer on bound peghead, three-per-side chrome tuners, available in Natural finish, mfg. 1991-95.

| | N/A | $600 - 700 | $350 - 425 | $1,300 |

The original design circa mid-1970s featured a bound ebony fingerboard with abalone dot inlays and ebony bridge (DY75 Lexington Dreadnought).

DY 76 HERRINGBONE TWELVE – 12-string configuration, dreadnought style, solid Canadian spruce top, round soundhole, ivoroid bound body, three-stripe wood rosette, rosewood back/sides/neck, 14/20-fret ebony fingerboard with snowflake inlays, ebony bridge, rosewood headstock veneer, abalone logo inlay on headstock, tortoiseshell pickguard, six-per-side chrome tuners, abalone inlays on bridge pins, available in Natural finish, mfg. circa mid-1970s.

| | N/A | $550 - 650 | $350 - 425 | |

DY 77 N – dreadnought style, solid spruce top, round soundhole, herringbone bound body/rosette, tortoiseshell pickguard, rosewood back/sides, mahogany neck, 14/20-fret ebony fingerboard with abalone diamond inlays, rosewood Direct Coupled bridge, rosewood veneer on bound peghead, three-per-side chrome tuners, available in Natural finish, mfg. 1991-95.

| | N/A | $525 - 625 | $325 - 375 | $1,200 |

MSR/NOTES	100%	EXCELLENT	AVERAGE	LAST MSR

* DY 77 NEQ – dreadnought style, solid spruce top, round soundhole, herringbone bound body/rosette, tortoiseshell pickguard, rosewood back/sides, mahogany neck, 14/20-fret ebony fingerboard with abalone diamond inlays, rosewood Direct Coupled bridge, rosewood veneer on bound peghead, three-per-side chrome tuners, piezo bridge pickup, three-band EQ, available in Natural finish, mfg. 1994 only.

	N/A	$625 - 725	$425 - 500	$1,500

DY 78 HERRINGBONE TRI-BACK – dreadnought style, Canadian spruce top, round soundhole, herringbone bound body, herringbone rosette, burled thuya pickguard, rosewood sides, three-piece rosewood/mahogany/rosewood back, mahogany neck, 14/20-fret ebony fingerboard with pearl snowflake inlays, ebony bridge, burled thuya veneer on peghead, three-per-side chrome tuners, available in Natural finish, mfg. circa mid-1970s.

	N/A	$700 - 800	$425 - 500	

DY 85 STANDARD ABALONE – dreadnought style, Canadian spruce top, round soundhole, abalone and celluloid bound body and soundhole, black pickguard, burled mahogany sides, three-piece burled mahogany/rosewood/burled mahogany back, nato mahogany neck, 14/20-fret ebony fingerboard with abalone inlays, ebony bridge, internal lacquering, three-per-side gold Grover tuners, available in Natural finish, mfg. circa mid-1970s.

	N/A	$700 - 825	$425 - 500	

DY 87 JUMBO DOUBLE NECK – double neck configuration, dreadnought style, solid Canadian spruce top, shared oval soundhole, celluloid bound body, wood inlaid rosette, mahogany back/sides, mahogany necks, 14/20-fret ebony fingerboard with snowflake inlays, double ebony bridge, black headstocks, three-per-side headstock (six-string), six-per-side headstock (12-string), chrome tuners, available in Natural finish, mfg. circa mid-1970s.

	N/A	$750 - 875	$425 - 500	

DY 87 – dreadnought style, rounded cutaway body, curly maple top, round soundhole, five-stripe bound body and rosette, maple back/sides, mahogany neck, 21-fret ebony fingerboard with pearl dot inlays, 12th fret has pearl snowflake inlay, ebony bridge with white abalone dot pins, three-per-side chrome tuners, bridge pickup, three-band EQ, available in Trans. Black finish, mfg. 1991-95.

	N/A	$625 - 725	$400 - 475	$1,450

* DY 87/12 – similar to DY 87, except has 12 strings, six-per-side tuners, available in Violin Sunburst finish, mfg. 1991-95.

	N/A	$650 - 750	$450 - 525	$1,575

DY 90 – dreadnought style, solid spruce top, round soundhole, abalone bound body and rosette, black pickguard with Alvarez Yairi logo in abalone, rosewood back/sides, mahogany neck, 14/20-fret bound ebony fingerboard with abalone diamond inlays, abalone bound ebony bridge with black pearl dot pins, rosewood peghead veneer with abalone logo inlay, three-per-side gold tuners, available in Natural finish, mfg. circa mid-1970s-1995.

	N/A	$650 - 750	$400 - 475	$1,475

The original design featured a jacaranda three-piece back, jacaranda sides, Canadian spruce top, and internal lacquering as well as the abalone appointments (DY90 Super abalone).

DY 92 LUTE BACK – dreadnought style, spruce top, round soundhole, herringbone bound body and rosette, 33-piece mahogany/rosewood/maple lute style rounded back, 14/20-fret bound ebony fingerboard with pearl dot inlays, ebony bridge with black pearl dot pins, three-per-side gold tuners, available in Natural finish, mfg. circa 1975-1993.

	N/A	$1,500 - 1,750	$875 - 1,000	$2,775

The DY 92 was produced in limited quantities.

DY 96 ABALONE SUPREME – dreadnought style, Canadian spruce top, round soundhole, abalone bound body and rosette, book matched jacaranda back with inlaid middle strip of marquetry, jacaranda sides, abalone bound jacaranda pickguard, 14/20-fret abalone bound ebony fingerboard with abalone diamond-shaped inlays, ebony bridge with abalone inlay, three-per-side gold tuners, abalone bound headstock, available in Natural finish, mfg. circa mid-1970s.

	N/A	$875 - 1,000	$550 - 650	

ACOUSTIC: DREADNOUGHT INNOVATIVE SERIES (DY52, DY70, DY71, DY80)

DY 52 CANYON CREEK – dreadnought style, solid spruce top, round soundhole, three-stripe body binding, shell rosette, tortoiseshell pickguard, rosewood back/sides, mahogany neck, 14/20-fret rosewood fingerboard with pearl dot inlays/12th fret pearl snowflake inlay, Direct Coupled ebony bridge with black pearl dot pins, rosewood veneer on peghead, three-per-side chrome tuners, available in Natural gloss finish, mfg. 1991-98.

	N/A	$550 - 650	$350 - 425	$1,249

In 1994, coral rosewood back/sides replaced original part/design.

DY 70 MAPLE GRAPHITE – dreadnought style, solid spruce top, round soundhole, tortoiseshell bound body/rosette, flamed maple back/sides, mahogany neck, 14/20-fret rosewood fingerboard with pearl dot inlays/12th fret pearl curlicue inlay, graphite bridge with black abalone dot pins, graphite peghead veneer with pearl logo inlay, three-per-side chrome tuners, available in Natural gloss finish, mfg. 1994-98.

	N/A	$500 - 575	$350 - 400	$1,099

DY 71 KOA GRAPHITE – similar to DY 70, except has tortoiseshell pickguard, tortoiseshell/ivory body binding, koa back/sides, graphite bridge/bridge plate, disc. 1998.

	N/A	$500 - 575	$350 - 400	$1,149

MSR/NOTES	100%	EXCELLENT	AVERAGE	LAST MSR

DY 80 CANYON CREEK 12-STRING – similar to the DY 52, except has 12-string configuration, six-per-side chrome tuners, available in Natural gloss finish, mfg. 1991-98.

	N/A	$550 - 650	$375 - 450	$1,299

ACOUSTIC: FUSION SERIES

The DY 88 Express Pro was renamed the Fusion Series in 1998.

DY 88 BK ADVANCED (DY 88 EXPRESS PRO) – dreadnought style, rounded cutaway Closed Chamber body, spruce top, abalone/ivory body binding, mahogany back/sides/neck, 23-fret ebony fingerboard with pearl dot inlays/pearl snowflake inlay on 12th fret, ebony bridge with white abalone dot pins, three-per-side gold tuners, Hexaphonic piezo bridge pickup, System 500 electronics, available in Gloss Black, Pearl White, Sunburst, or Trans. Blue finish, mfg. 1991-2001.

	N/A	$825 - 950	$550 - 650	$1,949

In 1998, a spruce top and mahogany back and sides replaced the original curly maple top and maple back and sides.

* **DY 88 BK 12 Advanced (DY 88/12 Express Pro)** – similar to DY 88 BK, except has 12-string configuration, six-per-side gold tuners, available in Gloss Black finish, mfg. 1991-2001.

	N/A	$900 - 1,050	$550 - 650	$1,999

* **DY 88K** – similar to DY 88 BK, except has koa top, back and sides, mfg. 1998-2001.

	N/A	$925 - 1,075	$600 - 700	$2,099

* **SY 88 BK Advanced** – similar to DY 88 BK, except features a thinline body, small Closed Chamber body, ivory body binding, available in Gloss Black finish, mfg. 1998-2001.

	N/A	$700 - 825	$475 - 550	$1,599

ACOUSTIC: MASTERWORKS SERIES

The Masterworks Series represents the top-of-the-line Alvarez Guitars. In 2004, the model names received an "M" letter designation. Models CYM 200, DYM 200, DYM 500, and FYM 500V all have a six-month order time, so most dealers will not keep these guitars in stock.

CYM 95 (CY 95) – classical body style, solid spruce top with scalloped bracing, solid Indian rosewood sides and back, abalone shell soundhole rosette, maple body binding, ebony fingerboard and ebony direct coupled bridge, gold die-cast tuners, available in Vintage Natural Lacquer finish, current mfg.

MSR $2,400	$2,000	$1,050 - 1,250	$675 - 800	

* **CYM 95CE (CY 95CE)** – similar to the CY 95, except has a cutaway and Alvarez NR electronics, disc. 2004.

	N/A	$1,150 - 1,300	$650 - 750	$2,499

CYM 200 (CY 200) – classical grand concert body, solid cedar top, solid Indian rosewood back and sides, round soundhole, wood multi-layer binding, 12/20-fret ebony fingerboard, ebony bridge, six-per-side, gold plated tuning machines, available in Vintage Natural Lacquer, mfg. 2001-08.

	N/A	$1,600 - 1,900	$1,100 - 1,250	$3,500

* **CY 200S** – similar to the CY 200 except has a solid spruce top for a lighter color, mfg. 2001 only.

	N/A	$1,600 - 1,850	$1,100 - 1,250	$3,299

DYM 85 – slope shoulder dreadnought body style, solid cedar top with scalloped bracing, solid Kihada sides and back, herringbone shell soundhole rosette, maple body binding, 14/20-fret ebony fingerboard with 12th fret diagonal inlay, ebony direct coupled bridge, wood grain pickguard, nickel tuners, available in Natural Satin finish, mfg. 2005-present.

MSR $2,200	$1,800	$950 - 1,150	$625 - 750	

DYM 90 – slope shoulder dreadnought body style, solid cedar top with scalloped bracing, solid ovangkol sides and back, abalone shell soundhole rosette, maple body binding, ebony fingerboard and ebony direct coupled bridge, gold die-cast tuners, available in Vintage Natural Lacquer finish, mfg. 2004 only.

	N/A	$950 - 1,100	$600 - 700	$2,149

DYM 94 (DY 94) – dreadnought body style, sloped shoulder, solid spruce top with scalloped bracing, solid mahogany sides and back, abalone shell soundhole rosette, maple body binding, ebony fingerboard and ebony direct coupled bridge, gold die-cast tuners, available in Vintage Natural Lacquer finish, current mfg.

MSR $2,300	$1,900	$1,000 - 1,200	$650 - 775	

DYM 95 (DY 95) – dreadnought body style, sloped shoulder, solid spruce top with scalloped bracing, solid Indian rosewood sides and back, abalone shell soundhole rosette, maple body binding, ebony fingerboard and ebony direct coupled bridge, gold die-cast tuners, available in Sunburst or Vintage Natural Lacquer finish, current mfg.

MSR $2,500	$2,100	$1,100 - 1,300	$700 - 825	

• Add 2.5% (MSR $2,600) for Sunburst finish.

MSR/NOTES	100%	EXCELLENT	AVERAGE	LAST MSR

* **DYM 95-12 12-String** – similar to the DYM 95, except in 12-string configuration and six-per-side tuners, available in Natural finish, mfg. 2005-present.

| MSR $2,900 | $2,400 | $1,300 - 1,500 | $850 - 1,000 | |

* **DYM 95C** – similar to the DYM 95, except has a single cutaway and System 600T MK II electronics, available in Natural finish, mfg. 2005-present.

| MSR $3,200 | $2,650 | $1,400 - 1,650 | $900 - 1,050 | |

»**DYM 95 C AURA** – similar to the DYM 95C, except has AURA Fishman custom electronics, mfg. 2006-present.

| MSR $3,700 | $3,000 | $1,700 - 2,000 | $1,000 - 1,200 | |

* **DYM 95V** – similar to the DYM 95, except has a 12/20-fret fingerboard and slotted headstock with open-style tuners, mfg. 2004-05.

| | N/A | $1,350 - 1,600 | $900 - 1,050 | $3,199 |

DYM 96 – dreadnought body style, solid distressed spruce top, solid ovangkol back and sides, tortoiseshell/herringbone body binding, herringbone soundhole rosette, 14/20-fret ebony fingerboard with 12th fret diagonal inlay, three-per-side gold antique die-cast tuners, ebony bridge, available in Natural Satin finish, mfg. 2006-present.

| MSR $2,400 | $2,000 | $1,050 - 1,250 | $675 - 800 | |

DY 100 – dreadnought body style, solid spruce top with scalloped braces, solid mahogany sides and back, abalone shell soundhole rosette, maple body binding, Indian rosewood fingerboard, rosewood direct coupled bridge, gold die-cast tuners, available in Vintage Natural Lacquer finish, disc. 2002.

| | N/A | $1,500 - 1,750 | $975 - 1,125 | $3,299 |

DYM 200 (DY 200) – dreadnought body style, solid spruce top with scalloped bracing, solid Indian rosewood sides and back, abalone shell soundhole rosette, maple body binding, ebony fingerboard and ebony direct coupled bridge, gold die-cast tuners, available in Vintage Natural Lacquer finish, disc. 2008.

| | N/A | $1,700 - 2,000 | $1,000 - 1,200 | $3,600 |

DYM 500 (DY 500) – dreadnought body style, solid spruce top with scalloped bracing, solid Indian rosewood sides and back, abalone shell soundhole rosette, maple/abalone body binding, 14/20-fret ebony fingerboard and ebony direct coupled bridge, gold die-cast tuners, available in Natural Lacquer finish, mfg. 2001-present.

| MSR $5,200 | $4,300 | $2,500 - 3,000 | $1,900 - 2,200 | |

* **DYM 500V/FYM500 V** – similar to the DYM 500, except has a 12/20-fret fingerboard and a slotted style headstock, available in Natural finish, mfg. 2005-present.

| MSR $5,200 | $4,300 | $2,500 - 3,000 | $1,900 - 2,200 | |

FY 94 – OM body style folk, solid spruce top, solid mahogany sides and back, abalone shell soundhole rosette, maple body binding, rosewood fingerboard and direct coupled bridge, gold die-cast tuners, available in Vintage Natural Lacquer finish, disc. 2004.

| | N/A | $825 - 950 | $550 - 650 | $1,799 |

FYM 95 (FY 95) – OM body style folk, solid spruce top, solid Indian rosewood sides and back, abalone shell soundhole rosette, maple body binding, ebony fingerboard and ebony direct coupled bridge, gold die-cast tuners, available in Vintage Natural Lacquer finish, current mfg.

| MSR $2,500 | $2,100 | $1,100 - 1,300 | $700 - 825 | |

* **FY 95C** – similar to the FY 95, except has a single cutaway, mfg. 2003 only.

| | N/A | $1,150 - 1,400 | $750 - 875 | $2,399 |

* **FYM 95 AURA** – similar to the FYM 95, except has a single cutaway and AURA Fishman custom electronics, mfg. 2006-present.

| MSR $3,700 | $3,000 | $1,700 - 2,000 | $1,000 - 1,200 | |

* **FYM 95V** – similar to the FYM 95, except has a 12/20-fret fingerboard and a slotted style headstock, available in Natural finish, mfg. 2005 only.

| | N/A | $1,350 - 1,600 | $900 - 1,050 | $3,199 |

FYM 96C – single cutaway folk body style, solid distressed spruce top, solid ovangkol back and sides, tortoiseshell/herringbone body binding, herringbone soundhole rosette, 14/20-fret ebony fingerboard with 12th fret diagonal inlay, three-per-side gold antique die-cast tuners, ebony bridge, standard System 600T Mk II electronics, available in Natural Open Pore finish, mfg. 2007-present.

| MSR $3,200 | $2,650 | $1,400 - 1,650 | $900 - 1,050 | |

FYM 200 (FY 200) – orchestra body style, solid spruce top with scalloped braces, solid Indian rosewood sides and back, abalone shell soundhole rosette, maple body binding, ebony fingerboard and ebony direct coupled bridge, gold die-cast tuners, available in Vintage Natural Lacquer finish, disc. 2008.

| | N/A | $1,700 - 2,000 | $1,000 - 1,200 | $3,600 |

MSR/NOTES	100%	EXCELLENT	AVERAGE	LAST MSR

* FY 200C – similar to the FY 200, except has a single cutaway body, disc. 2002.

	N/A	$1,800 - 2,100	$1,100 - 1,300	$3,699

JYM 86 – jumbo body style, solid spruce top, solid flame maple back and sides, round soundhole with ring rosette, multi-ply body binding, ebony fingerboard with 12th fret diagonal inlay, three-per-side gold tuners, ebony bridge, available in Natural Gloss finish, mfg. 2007-09.

	N/A	$1,050 - 1,250	$675 - 800	$2,400

* JYM 86C TS – similar to the JYM 86, except has a single cutaway and standard optional System 600T Mk II electronics, available in Sunburst Gloss finish, mfg. 2007-09.

	N/A	$1,400 - 1,650	$900 - 1,050	$3,200

ACOUSTIC: SIGNATURE SERIES

All Signature models have Kazuo Yairi's signature on them.

AY 20 SIGNATURE – concert style, solid cedar top, round soundhole, wood bound body, abalone rosette, walnut back/sides, mahogany neck, 14/20-fret rosewood fingerboard, 12th fret abalone diamond/slash inlays, rosewood bridge with black abalone dot pins, walnut peghead veneer with abalone logo inlay, three-per-side gold tuners, available in Natural finish, mfg. 1994-98.

	N/A	$600 - 700	$375 - 450	$1,250

DY 61 SIGNATURE – dreadnought style, solid cedar top, round soundhole, maple/wood body binding, abalone shell rosette, burled mahogany back/sides, mahogany neck, 14/20-fret ebony fingerboard/12th fret pearl diamond/abalone slash inlay, rosewood bridge with black abalone dot pins, burl mahogany veneer on peghead with abalone/wooden strip inlays, abalone logo peghead inlay, three-per-side gold tuners with amber buttons, available in Natural semi-satin finish, mfg. 1991-98.

	N/A	$650 - 750	$425 - 500	$1,499

In 1994, burled mahogany back/sides replaced original part/design.

DY 69 – similar to DY 61, except has spruce top, tortoiseshell pickguard, wooden inlaid rosette, burled mahogany back/sides, upper belly bridge with white abalone dot pins, mfg. 1994 only.

	N/A	$525 - 625	$375 - 450	$1,350

DY 72 12-STRING – similar to DY 61, except in 12-string configuration with six-per-side tuners and rosewood headstock overlay, disc. 1997.

	N/A	$575 - 675	$350 - 400	$1,275

YM 1 YAIRI MASTER MAHOGANY – dreadnought style, solid cedar top, multi-layer wood body binding, abalone shell rosette, solid mahogany back/sides, mahogany neck, 14/20-fret rosewood fingerboard, 12th fret abalone stripe/pearl cross inlays, rosewood bridge with black pearl dot pins, ebony veneered peghead with pearl logo inlay, three-per-side gold die-cast tuners, available in Natural semi-satin finish, mfg. 1995-98.

	N/A	$625 - 725	$400 - 475	$1,399

YM 2 YAIRI MASTER OVANGKOL – similar to the YM 1, except features solid spruce top, solid ovangkol back/sides, disc. 1998.

	N/A	$650 - 750	$425 - 500	$1,499

AYL 1 LUTHIER CUTAWAY – dreadnought style, rounded cutaway body, solid spruce top, round soundhole, synthetic tortoiseshell body binding, abalone shell rosette, mahogany back/sides/neck, 14/20-fret rosewood fingerboard/12th fret pearl diamond/abalone slash inlays, rosewood bridge with black abalone dot pins, three-per-side gold tuners, piezo bridge pickup, volume/tone controls, System 500 electronics, available in Natural semi-gloss finish, disc. 1998.

	N/A	$650 - 750	$450 - 525	$1,549

ACOUSTIC: TONEWOOD SERIES

DY 84 – dreadnought style, Indian rosewood back and sides, solid spruce top, scalloped braces, ebony fingerboard, 12th fret diagonal fingerboard inlay, abalone shell rosette, ivory multi-layer binding, chrome die-cast tuners, ebony direct coupled bridge, optional System 500 electronics, available in Natural Gloss finish, disc. 2005.

	N/A	$700 - 825	$475 - 550	$1,599

* DY 84BR – similar to DY 84 except has Brazilian rosewood back and sides, available in Natural Gloss finish, disc. 2004.

	N/A	$950 - 1,100	$600 - 700	$2,199

* DY 84C – similar to DY 84 except with a single cutaway dreadnought style body and standard System 600T Mk II electronics, available in Natural Gloss finish, current mfg.

MSR $2,200	$1,775	$950 - 1,150	$625 - 725	

* DY 84K – similar to DY 84 except has koa back and sides, available in Natural Gloss finish, disc. 2004.

	N/A	$650 - 750	$450 - 525	$1,549

* DY 84M – similar to DY 84 except has flamed maple back and sides, available in Vintage Natural Lacquer finish, disc. 2002.

	N/A	$650 - 750	$450 - 525	$1,549

MSR/NOTES	100%	EXCELLENT	AVERAGE	LAST MSR

* DY 84W – similar to DY 84 except has walnut back and sides, available in Vintage Natural Lacquer finish, disc. 2002.

	N/A	$650 - 750	$450 - 525	$1,549

DY 91 – dreadnought style, solid spruce top, round soundhole, abalone bound body and rosette, flamed koa back/sides, black pickguard with Alvarez Yairi logo in abalone, mahogany neck, 14/20-fret bound ebony fingerboard with abalone diamond inlays, abalone bound ebony bridge with black pearl dot pins, koa peghead veneer with abalone logo inlay, three-per-side gold tuners, optional System 500 Mk II (disc. 2001) or System 600T Mk II (2002-present) electronics, available in Natural gloss finish, mfg. 1994-present.

MSR $2,400	$1,800	$1,050 - 1,250	$675 - 800	

* DY 91C – similar to the DY 91, except has a single cutaway and standard System 600T Mk II electronics, mfg. 2005-present.

MSR $3,200	$2,500	$1,350 - 1,650	$900 - 1,050	

FY 84 – orchestra-style body, solid spruce top, Indian rosewood back and sides, round soundhole with abalone shell, 14/20-fret ebony fingerboard with pearl dot/cat's-eye inlays, ebony direct coupled bridge, ivory multi-layer binding, three-per-side chrome die-cast tuners, optional system 600T electronics, available in Natural gloss finish, mfg. 2001 only.

	N/A	$725 - 850	$500 - 575	$1,549

FY 91 – folk style, solid spruce top, round soundhole, abalone bound body and rosette, koa back/sides, black pickguard with Alvarez Yairi logo in abalone, mahogany neck, 14/20-fret bound ebony fingerboard with abalone diamond inlays, abalone bound ebony bridge with black pearl dot pins, koa peghead veneer with abalone logo inlay, three-per-side gold tuners, available in Natural gloss finish, mfg. 2003 only.

	N/A	$850 - 975	$525 - 625	$1,899

JY 84 – jumbo-style body, solid spruce top, coral rosewood back and sides, 14/20 ebony fingerboard, round soundhole, ebony bridge, ivory multi-layer binding, snowflake/cat's-eye fingerboard inlays, three-per-side gold tuners, optional System 600T electronics, Natural gloss finish, mfg. 2002-04.

	N/A	$750 - 875	$525 - 600	$1,699

* JY 84C – similar to the JY 84 except has a single cutaway and standard System 600T electronics, mfg. 2002-04.

	N/A	$925 - 1,075	$650 - 750	$2,099

* JY 84-12 – similar to the JY 84 except is in 12-string configuration, mfg. 2002-04.

	N/A	$850 - 975	$600 - 700	$1,899

ACOUSTIC: TRADITIONAL SERIES

CY 62 CE – single cutaway classical body, round soundhole with abalone shell, solid cedar top, burl mahogany back and sides, 14/20-fret rosewood fingerboard with snowflake/cat's-eye inlays, three-per-side die-cast tuning machines, maple and natural wood binding, rosewood direct coupled bridge, Standard System 600T electronics, available in Natural finish, mfg. 2003-04.

	N/A	$1,000 - 1,150	$650 - 750	$1,949

DY 38 WOOD RIDGE – dreadnought style, solid spruce top, round soundhole, three-stripe body binding, five-stripe rosette, black pickguard, mahogany back/sides/neck, 14/20-fret rosewood fingerboard with pearl dot inlays/12th fret has pearl snowflake inlay, rosewood bridge with black white dot pins, three-per-side chrome tuners, available in Natural gloss finish, mfg. 1991-2004.

	N/A	$525 - 600	$350 - 400	$1,099

In 1996, flamed maple back/sides replaced mahogany back/sides.

DY 38 C CUTAWAY – dreadnought style, sloped rounded cutaway body, solid spruce top, round soundhole, three-stripe body binding, five-stripe rosette, black pickguard, flamed maple back/sides, mahogany neck, 14/20-fret rosewood fingerboard with pearl dot inlays/12th fret has pearl snowflake inlay, rosewood bridge with black white dot pins, three-per-side chrome tuners, available in Natural gloss finish, mfg. 1991-98.

	N/A	$525 - 625	$425 - 500	$1,249

DY 40 – dreadnought body, mahogany back and sides, solid spruce top, scalloped bracing, ebony fingerboard, 12th fret diagonal position marker, abalone shell rosette, ivory multi-layer body binding, chrome die cast tuners, ebony direct coupled bridge, optional System 500 electronics, available in Black, Natural gloss, or Sunburst finish, disc. 2005.

	N/A	$650 - 750	$400 - 475	$1,429

* DY 40C – similar to DY 40 except has a single cutaway dreadnought body, optional System 500 Mk II (disc. 2001) or System 600T Mk II (2002-present) electronics, available in Black (disc. 2009) or Natural Gloss finish, current mfg.

MSR $1,950	$1,450	$850 - 1,000	$550 - 625	

* DY 40-12 – similar to DY 40 except in a 12-string configuration, available in Natural Gloss finish, disc. 2004.

	N/A	$700 - 800	$450 - 525	$1,549

DY 45 WOOD RIDGE – dreadnought style, solid spruce top, round soundhole, three-stripe body binding, five-stripe rosette, black pickguard, mahogany back/sides/neck, 14/20-fret rosewood fingerboard with pearl dot inlays, 12th fret has pearl snowflake inlay, ebony bridge with black white dot pins, three-per-side chrome tuners, available in Dark Satin Antique finish, mfg. 1975-1998.

	N/A	$400 - 475	$250 - 300	$899

In 1996, Sunburst Mahogany finish replaced Dark Satin Antique finish.

MSR/NOTES	100%	EXCELLENT	AVERAGE	LAST MSR

DY 45 AV – dreadnought style, solid spruce top, round soundhole, three-stripe bound body, five-stripe rosette, black pickguard, mahogany back/sides/neck, 14/20-fret rosewood fingerboard with pearl dot inlays, 12th fret has pearl snowflake inlay, ebony bridge with black white dot pins, three-per-side chrome tuners, piezo bridge pickup, three-band EQ, available in Dark Satin Antique finish, mfg. 1994 only.

	N/A	$500 - 575	$300 - 350	$1,075

This model is similar to DY 45, with electronics.

DY 46 DREADNOUGHT – similar to the DY 45 Vintage Dreadnought, except had gloss finish, mfg. circa mid-1970s.

	N/A	$550 - 650	$350 - 400	

DY 62 C – single cutaway dreadnought body, round soundhole with abalone shell, solid cedar top, burl mahogany back and sides, 14/20-fret rosewood fingerboard with snowflake/cat's-eye inlays, three-per-side die-cast tuning machines, maple and natural wood binding, rosewood direct coupled bridge, standard System 500 Mk II (2001 only) or System 600T Mk II (2002-present) electronics, available in Natural finish, mfg. 2001-present.

MSR $2,400	$1,800	$1,050 - 1,250	$675 - 800	

DY 74 WELLINGTON – dreadnought style, solid spruce top, round soundhole, five-stripe bound body and rosette, tortoiseshell pickguard, rosewood back/sides, mahogany neck, 14/20-fret ebony fingerboard with varying pearl inlays, ebony bridge with white pearl dot pins, rosewood veneer on peghead, three-per-side chrome tuners, available in Natural gloss finish, mfg. circa 1975-1998.

	N/A	$525 - 600	$350 - 425	$1,219

The original design circa mid-1970s featured an ebony fingerboard and bridge, and jacaranda veneer peghead (DY74 Wellington rosewood).

* ***DY 74 C Wellington Cutaway*** – similar to DY 74, except has single rounded cutaway, mfg. circa 1975-1998.

	N/A	$550 - 650	$375 - 450	$1,319

* ***DY 74 S Wellington Sunburst*** – similar to DY 74 Wellington, except has Brown Sunburst finish, mfg. circa mid-1970s.

	N/A	$500 - 575	$300 - 350	

DY 74 CEQ (DY 74 CEQ1) – dreadnought style, rounded cutaway body, solid spruce top, round soundhole, five-stripe body binding/rosette, tortoiseshell pickguard, rosewood back/sides, mahogany neck, 14/20-fret ebony fingerboard with varying pearl inlays, ebony bridge with white pearl dot pins, rosewood veneer on peghead, three-per-side chrome tuners, piezo bridge pickups, three-band EQ/System 500 electronics, available in Natural gloss finish, mfg. 1995-98.

	N/A	$625 - 725	$425 - 500	$1,449

FY 40 – orchestra style body, solid spruce top, mahogany back and sides, 14/20-fret rosewood fingerboard with 12th fret diagonal inlays, rosewood direct coupled bridge, ivory multi-layer binding, three-per-side chrome die-cast tuners, optional system 600T electronics, available in Natural gloss finish, mfg. 2001-04.

	N/A	$700 - 800	$475 - 550	$1,349

ACOUSTIC: VIRTUOSO SERIES

DC 1 VIRTUOSO 12-STRING – rounded shoulder dreadnought style, solid spruce top, round soundhole, ivoroid bound body, herringbone purfling/rosette, Indian rosewood back/sides, mahogany neck, 12/19-fret ebony fingerboard with pearl cross/ellipse inlays, ebony bridge with white pearl dot pins, tortoiseshell pickguard, ebony veneered peghead with pearl logo inlay, six-per-side chrome die-cast tuners, available in Natural gloss finish, mfg. 1995-99.

	N/A	$700 - 825	$475 - 550	$1,599

GY 1 – dreadnought style, rounded cutaway body, solid spruce top, round soundhole, five-stripe bound body and rosette, tortoiseshell pickguard, rosewood back/sides, mahogany neck, 20-fret bound ebony fingerboard with varied abalone inlays, rosewood bridge with white abalone dot pins, rosewood veneer on bound peghead with pearl tulip inlay, three-per-side gold tuners, bridge pickup, three-band EQ, available in Natural finish, mfg. 1991-96.

	N/A	$725 - 850	$450 - 525	$1,700

This model was co-designed with Jerry Garcia.

GY 2 (VIRTUOSO DELUXE) – single round cutaway jumbo style, solid spruce top, round soundhole, tortoiseshell pickguard, ivoroid bound body, abalone purfling/rosette, lace wood back/sides, mahogany neck, 20-fret bound ebony fingerboard with pearl dot inlays, 12th fret pearl curlicue inlay, abalone bound ebony bridge, rosewood veneered peghead with pearl logo inlay, three-per-side gold die-cast tuners, available in Natural finish, mfg. 1995-97.

	N/A	$875 - 1,000	$525 - 625	$2,000

This instrument was co-designed with Jerry Garcia.

* ***GY 2E*** – similar to the GY 2E, except has standard System 600T Mk II electronics, available in Natural finish, mfg. 2005-present.

MSR $3,000	$2,400	$1,350 - 1,550	$775 - 900	

MSR/NOTES	100%	EXCELLENT	AVERAGE	LAST MSR

WY 1 – jumbo style, rounded cutaway body, solid cedar top, round soundhole, multi-layer wood body binding, abalone shell rosette, rosewood back/sides, mahogany neck, 14/20-fret ebony fingerboard/12th fret has pearl diamond/abalone slash inlays, Direct Coupled ebony bridge with black abalone dot pins, rosewood veneer on peghead with abalone and wooden strip inlays, three-per-side gold tuners, piezo bridge pickup, three-band EQ/System 500 electronics, available in Black (disc. 2009), Natural, Sunburst, Trans. Purple (disc. 2008), or Trans. Red (disc. 2008) finish, mfg. 1991-present.

MSR $2,699	$2,000	$1,075 - 1,350	$650 - 800	

In 1994, folk style body replaced original part/design. This model was co-designed with Bob Weir. The models finished in Trans. Purple and Trans. Red have Fiddleback Maple wood.

* **WY 112 12-String** – similar to WY 1 Virtuoso (folk style body), except has 12-string configuration, six-per-side tuners, available in Natural Semi-Satin finish, mfg. 1996-2001.

	N/A	$1,000 - 1,200	$675 - 800	$2,149

* **WY 1 M Amber** – similar to the WY 1, except has flamed maple top, back, and sides, available in Amber-Tint finish, mfg. 2007-present.

MSR $2,300	$1,700	$1,000 - 1,200	$675 - 800	

* **WY 1 BR** – similar to the WY 1, except has Brazilian rosewood back and sides, mfg. 2004 only.

	N/A	$1,150 - 1,300	$725 - 850	$2,599

* **WY 1 BW Bob Weir Signature** – similar to the WY 1, except has coral rosewood back and sides, maple/herringbone binding, a 12th fret lightning bolt inlay, fancy headstock inlays, and Custom Dual Transducer with Crossover electronics, mfg. 2006-present.

MSR $2,700	$2,000	$1,200 - 1,400	$750 - 900	

* **WY 1 K Koa** – similar to WY 1 Virtuoso (folk style body), except features koa top/back/sides, abalone rosette, abalone body binding, fingerboard dot inlays, snowflake bridge inlays, available in Natural Gloss finish, mfg. 1998-present.

MSR $2,600	$2,000	$1,150 - 1,350	$700 - 825	

* **WY 1 RR** – similar to WY 1 Virtuoso (folk style body), except features a thin cutaway body with solid spruce top, mahogany back and sides, has Roland GK2 electronics, available in Satin Graphite finish, mfg. 1998-2004.

	N/A	$1,000 - 1,150	$650 - 750	$2,299

* **WY 1 TS Tobacco Sunburst** – similar to the WY 1, except has a solid spruce top and flamed maple back and sides, available in Tobacco Sunburst finish, current mfg.

MSR $2,999	$2,300	$1,200 - 1,500	$725 - 900	

WY 80 LIMITED EDITION ANNIVERSARY – folk style single cutaway body, solid cedar top, round soundhole, multi-layer maple/abalone body binding, abalone shell rosette, Brazilian rosewood back/sides, mahogany neck, 14/20-fret ebony fingerboard, tree-of-life inlay, Direct Coupled ebony bridge with black abalone dot pins, rosewood veneer on peghead with abalone and wooden strip inlays, three-per-side gold tuners, piezo bridge pickup, Standard System 600T electronics, available in Natural finish, mfg. 2002 only.

	N/A	$1,400 - 1,600	N/A	$2,999

AMADA

Instruments previously produced in Luby, Czech Republic and later produced in China. Distributed by Geneva International Corporation in Wheeling, IL.

Amada classical guitars and mandolins (as well as Lidl orchestra instruments) were made by Strunal Manufacture of Luby. These guitars were available in five fractional sizes for the younger, entry-level student. Amada believes that fitting the right size guitar to the physical size of the student aids in the learning curve, as opposed to younger students struggling with a full-sized guitar.

The general fractional scale runs from 1/4, 1/2, 3/4, 7/8, up to full size. The scale lengths range from 17 in. (1/4 size), to 20.25 in. (1/2 size), 24 in. (3/4 size), 24.5 in. (7/8 size), up to 25.5 in. (full size). Corresponding metric measurements run from 440 mm to 650 mm. Some of these measurements will vary depending upon model. Models are offered in oak or mahogany back and sides, and are available in a Natural high gloss or matte finish.

ACOUSTIC: A SERIES

All the models in Amada's Classical Nylon string series have a spruce top, round soundhole, classical style slotted headstock, three-per-side tuners, and tied bridge.

A144 (4/4 SIZE) – spruce top, mahogany back and sides, nato neck with rosewood fingerboard, 25 3/4 in. scale, rosewood bridge, available in Natural Gloss finish, disc. 2000.

	N/A	$60 - 85	$30 - 50	$179

A134 (3/4 SIZE) – similar to A144, except in 23.5 in. scale, disc. 2000.

	N/A	$50 - 75	$30 - 50	$159

MSR/NOTES	100%	EXCELLENT	AVERAGE	LAST MSR

A112 (1/2 SIZE) – similar to A144, except has 22.25 in. scale, disc. 2000.

	N/A	$50 - 75	$30 - 50	$139

A114 (1/4 SIZE) – similar to A144, except has 17.5 in. scale, disc. 2000.

	N/A	$45 - 65	$30 - 50	$129

ACOUSTIC: 4000 SERIES

MODEL 4635 (4/4 SIZE) – spruce top, 25.5 in. scale, oak back/sides, rosewood fingerboard, rosewood bridge, available in Natural high gloss finish, disc. 1998.

	N/A	$90 - 120	$50 - 75	$240

* *Model 4635 PM (4/4 Size)* – similar to the Model 4635, available in Natural Matte finish, disc. 1998.

	N/A	$85 - 115	$45 - 65	$232

MODEL 4655 (4/4 SIZE) – spruce top, 25.5 in. scale, mahogany back/sides, rosewood fingerboard, rosewood bridge, available in Natural high gloss finish, disc. 1998.

	N/A	$90 - 120	$50 - 75	$240

* *Model 4655 PM (4/4 Size)* – similar to the Model 4655, available in Natural Matte finish, disc. 1998.

	N/A	$85 - 115	$45 - 65	$232

MODEL 4735 (4/4 SIZE) – solid cedar top, 25.5 in. scale, oak back/sides, rosewood fingerboard, rosewood bridge, available in Natural high gloss finish, disc. 1998.

	N/A	$135 - 175	$80 - 105	$342

* *Model 4735 PM (4/4 Size)* – similar to the Model 4735, available in Natural Matte finish, disc. 1998.

	N/A	$130 - 165	$70 - 95	$332

MODEL 4755 (4/4 SIZE) – solid cedar top, 25.5 in. scale, mahogany back/sides, rosewood fingerboard, rosewood bridge, available in Natural high gloss finish, disc. 1998.

	N/A	$135 - 175	$80 - 105	$342

* *Model 4755 PM (4/4 Size)* – similar to the Model 4755, available in Natural Matte finish, disc. 1998.

	N/A	$130 - 165	$70 - 95	$332

ACOUSTIC: 5000 SERIES

MODEL 5432 (7/8 SIZE) – spruce top, 24.5 in. scale, oak back/sides, rosewood fingerboard, rosewood bridge, available in Natural high gloss finish, disc. 1998.

	N/A	$75 - 100	$40 - 60	$198

* *Model 5432 PM (7/8 Size)* – similar to the Model 5432, available in Natural matte finish, disc. 1998.

	N/A	$70 - 95	$35 - 55	$190

MODEL 5433 (1/2 SIZE) – spruce top, 21 in. scale, oak back/sides, rosewood fingerboard, rosewood bridge, available in Natural high gloss finish, disc. 1998.

	N/A	$70 - 95	$35 - 55	$190

* *Model 5433 PM (1/2 Size)* – similar to the Model 5433, available in Natural matte finish, disc. 1998.

	N/A	$60 - 90	$30 - 50	$182

MODEL 5434 (1/4 SIZE) – spruce top, 17 in. scale, oak back/sides, rosewood fingerboard, rosewood bridge, available in Natural high gloss finish, disc. 1998.

	N/A	$60 - 90	$30 - 50	$184

MODEL 5437 (3/4 SIZE) – spruce top, 22.5 in. scale, oak back/sides, rosewood fingerboard, rosewood bridge, available in Natural high gloss finish, disc. 1998.

	N/A	$70 - 95	$35 - 55	$192

* *Model 5437 PM (3/4 Size)* – similar to the Model 5437, available in Natural matte finish, disc. 1998.

	N/A	$60 - 90	$30 - 50	$184

MODEL 5452 (7/8 SIZE) – spruce top, 24.5 in. scale, mahogany back/sides, rosewood fingerboard, rosewood bridge, available in Natural high gloss finish, disc. 1998.

	N/A	$75 - 100	$40 - 60	$198

* *Model 5452 PM (7/8 Size)* – similar to the Model 5452, available in Natural matte finish, disc. 1998.

	N/A	$70 - 95	$35 - 55	$190

MSR/NOTES	100%	EXCELLENT	AVERAGE	LAST MSR

MODEL 5453 (1/2 SIZE) – spruce top, 21 in. scale, mahogany back/sides, rosewood fingerboard, rosewood bridge, available in Natural high gloss finish, disc. 1998.

	N/A	$70 - 95	$35 - 55	$190

* *Model 5453 PM (1/2 Size)* – similar to the Model 5453, available in Natural matte finish, disc. 1998.

	N/A	$60 - 90	$30 - 50	$182

MODEL 5457 PM (3/4 SIZE) – spruce top, 22.5 in. scale, mahogany back/sides, rosewood fingerboard, rosewood bridge, available in Natural matte finish, disc. 1998.

	N/A	$60 - 90	$30 - 50	$184

MODEL 5732 (7/8 SIZE) – solid cedar top, 24.5 in. scale, oak back/sides, rosewood fingerboard, rosewood bridge, available in Natural high gloss finish, disc. 1998.

	N/A	$135 - 175	$80 - 105	$342

MODEL 5737 (3/4 SIZE) – solid cedar top, 22.5 in. scale, oak back/sides, rosewood fingerboard, rosewood bridge, available in Natural high gloss finish, disc. 1998.

	N/A	$135 - 175	$80 - 105	$342

MODEL 5752 (7/8 SIZE) – solid cedar top, 24.5 in. scale, mahogany back/sides, rosewood fingerboard, rosewood bridge, available in Natural high gloss finish, disc. 1998.

	N/A	$135 - 175	$80 - 105	$342

MODEL 5757 (3/4 SIZE) – solid cedar top, 22.5 in. scale, mahogany back/sides, rosewood fingerboard, rosewood bridge, available in Natural high gloss finish, disc. 1998.

	N/A	$135 - 175	$80 - 105	$342

ACOUSTIC: 8000 SERIES

MODEL 8010 (4/4 SIZE) – solid spruce top, 25.5 in. scale, beechwood back/sides, available in Natural high gloss finish, disc. 2000.

	N/A	$60 - 90	$30 - 50	$179

MODEL 8011 (3/4 SIZE) – solid spruce top, 24 in. scale, beechwood back/sides, available in Natural high gloss finish, disc. 2000.

	N/A	$55 - 80	$30 - 50	$159

MODEL 8012 (1/2 SIZE) – solid spruce top, 20.5 in. scale, beechwood back/sides, available in Natural high gloss finish, disc. 2000.

	N/A	$50 - 75	$30 - 50	$139

ACOUSTIC STEEL STRING GUITARS

MODEL 8253 (4/4 SIZE) – solid beechwood top, 25.5 in. scale, beechwood back/sides, available in Natural matte finish, disc. 2000.

	$90	$45 - 65	$30 - 50	$129

MODEL 8251 (3/4 SIZE) – solid beechwood top, 24 in. scale, beechwood back/sides, available in Natural matte finish, disc. 2000.

	$70	$30 - 50	$10 - 20	$99

MODEL 8252 (1/2 SIZE) – solid beechwood top, 20.5 in. scale, beechwood back/sides, available in Natural matte finish, disc. 2000.

	$60	$30 - 50	$10 - 20	$89

AMERICAN ACOUSTECH

Instruments previously produced in Rochester, NY between circa 1993 and 2001.

Tom Lockwood, the former plant manager at Guild Guitars and Dave Stutzman of Guitar Center formed a partnership in the early 1990s to build acoustic guitars. Acoustech's guitars combined traditional craftsmanship with the latest technology. Guitars appeared to have sold for between $500 and $1,000 when new.

AMERICAN ARCHTOP

Instruments currently built in Nazareth, PA. American Archtop guitars have been produced since 1996.

Dale Unger, the president and owner of American Archtop Guitars, is the sole craftsman behind each of his custom designed instruments. Unger, a former apprentice to luthier Robert Benedetto for four years, grew up in the Nazareth, Pennsylvania area, and recalls building Martin-style flattop acoustics during the 1970s. His twenty-plus years of guitar building served as a great foundation for the four years working and studying with Benedetto, beginning in 1991. Since that time, Unger has incorporated all of his knowledge and experience into developing his own line of handcrafted archtop guitars. Unger also collaborated with Martin in the early 2000s to produced the Martin Special Edition CF-1 and CF-2 electric archtop guitars. For more information, visit Unger's website or contact him directly. For model specifications, pricing, and options refer to American Archtop in the *Blue Book of Electric Guitars.*

AMIGO

Instruments currently manufactured overseas. Distributed by Musicorp (MBT) in Charleston, SC. Previously distributed by Midco International of Effingham, IL.

Amigo acoustic guitars are designed and priced with students and entry-level players in mind. For more information, contact Musicorp directly.

The **AM 10** steel string (Last MSR $80), and the **AM 15** nylon string ($144) models both feature spruce tops and maple backs and sides. The **AM 10** has a Sunburst finish; the **AM 15** features a solid spruce top. The **AM 12** replaced the AM 10, and does not have Sunburst finish ($144). Here is a listing of Amigo 3/4-sized guitars: The **AM 20** steel string (Last MSR $109) and the **AM 30** nylon string ($165) models again both feature spruce tops and maple backs and sides. The **AM 20** has a Sunburst finish; the **AM 30** has a natural solid spruce top. The **AM 22** replaced the AM 20, and does not have Sunburst finish ($165).These are the full-sized acoustics in the Amigo line: the **AM 40** classical (Last MSR $149) has a natural-amber laminate top, and beech back and sides. The **AM 50** classical ($219) has a solid spruce top and maple back and sides. The **AM 100** dreadnought (disc., last MSR was $175) has a spruce top and mahogany back and sides. The **AM 200S** dreadnought (disc., last MSR was $205) has mahogany back and sides and a solid spruce top. The **AM 112** (disc., last MSR was MSR $185) is a 12-string version of the AM100. The **AMT10** Travel Guitar (MSR $145, MSR $165 with a case) is a small guitar perfect for traveling. The **AMB300** Bass (Last MSR $375) is also available. Most Amigo guitars can be found used between $50 and $150.

CONTACT INFORMATION
AMIGO
Distributed by Musicorp
PO Box 63366
N. Charleston, SC 29419
Phone No.: 843-745-8501
Phone No.: 800-641-6931
Fax No.: 843-745-8502
www.musicorp.com
kmcmcpsales@kmcmusic.com

ANDERSEN STRINGED INSTRUMENTS

Instruments currently built in Seattle, WA beginning 1978. Instruments are available through luthier Steven Andersen, and Pioneer Music (Portland, OR).

Luthier Steven Andersen built his first guitar in 1973, and has earned his living solely as a guitar maker since 1978. Andersen specializes in custom building to meet the player's needs. Working alone, Andersen builds two or three instruments at a time, generally completing sixteen to eighteen a year. Andersen guitars have been sold across the U.S., as well as in a dozen countries around the world. Although Steven Andersen doesn't actively pursue the endorsements of famous musicians, he has been fortunate in having a number of well-known players purchase his instruments (Steve Miller, Bill Frisell, and mandolinist Sam Bush). Andersen introduced a program called "Fresh Fish." Every now and then, he will build a guitar that isn't part of his regular backlog. He does this to build new instruments that may not be to spec and have other features different than his standard models. Andersen keeps a listing of these guitars on his website.

In addition to his guitar models, Andersen also builds mandolins, mandolas, and mandocellos. For more information, contact Andersen directly or visit his website.

CONTACT INFORMATION
ANDERSEN STRINGED INSTRUMENTS
7811 Greenwood Ave. N.
Seattle, WA 98103
Phone No.: 206-782-8630
www.andersenguitars.com
steve@andersenguitars.com

Andersen archtop guitars all share certain specifications. The body depth is 3 in., and the scale lengths available are either 24.9 in. or 25.4 in. The soundboard is crafted of either Engelmann or Sitka spruce. The back, sides, and neck are highly figured maple; and the pickguard, bridge, fingerboard, and headstock overlay are ebony. The instrument's tailpiece is a graphite composite with an ebony veneer. The archtops are finished in Amber Blonde or Clear Blonde. Andersen does offer several options on various models, as well as suggestions for floating pickups. The base price also includes a standard hardshell case. While Andersen is currently backlogged around twenty months, a delivery date will be confirmed when an order is placed. For those who prefer to purchase a guitar without the wait, Andersen occasionally has completed guitars available for sale (call for information). Prior to 2001, left-handed ($200) and seven-string models ($600) were available.

The **Gold Standard** ($18,000), is the flagship archtop of the Andersen line. 14k gold wire is used in place of all regular silver wire. The body is made of German spruce and maple and features the gold wire for binding. This guitar also features the "teardrop" f-holes. This guitar is available in 16, 17, and 18 in. lengths.

The **Emerald City** ($12,000) and **Metropolitan** ($11,000) are the most ornate members of the Andersen family of archtop guitars. The designs are reminiscent of the Art Deco style popular in the 1930s and 1940s. Construction details include hand engraved mother-of-pearl inlays, ivoroid binding around the body, f-holes, neck, and peghead; and the most highly figured maple for the back, sides, and neck. The Emerald City is available in either a 17 in. or 18 in. body width, and the Metropolitan is only available in a 17 in. body width. The Metropolitan was designed in collaboration with vintage guitar enthusiasts John G. Stewart and K.C. Wait. The **Emerald City Reserve** ($14,000) is a limited edition model built with rare woods reserved especially for this model. Wood combinations include a European spruce top and European maple back, or an Adirondack spruce top with a ninety-year-old one-piece American maple back. Further model specifications will be supplied by Andersen. The **Model 16** ($8,000), **Model 17** ($8,000), and the **Model 18** ($8,000) are elegant in their simplicity. The Model 16 has a 16 in. body, the Model 17 has a 17 in. body width, and the Model 18 has an 18 in. body width. By using a minimal amount of inlay and decoration, Andersen is able to build a guitar whose design and materials are first class, yet at a price somewhat less than the more ornate instruments. Body, f-holes, neck, and headstock are bound in ivoroid. The **Oval Hole Archtop** model ($7,200) is designed as an archtop with a warmer sound than a traditional model. Andersen feels that the oval soundhole allows the guitar to sustain more than an f-hole top. The overall design of this model is intended to make the guitar as lightweight and resonant as possible. Andersen's newest model is the **Model 14 "Litte Archie"** Archtop guitar ($7,500). The Model 14 is designed as an option for the guitarist who travel on airplanes. Due to space consideration, and the tightening of regulations regarding "carry-on" luggage, Andersen devised an archtop guitar that is full-sized where it needs to be, and reduced where the designs allows. Thus, the scale length (25.4 in.), neck size and shape, and bridge/soundboard design retain their usual size. The body and peghead size then are reduced: the body width is 14 in., and the depth is 2 in. (or 2.5 in.). Pickup choices range from Armstrong, Bartolini, or EMG. Andersen collaborated with guitarist Bill Frisell on this new electrified archtop model. The **Electric Archie** ($8,000), is a 14 in. like the Litte Archie, except it has two pickups and f-holes.

The **Streamline** ($5,600) is an archtop that was available only through dealers. The **Vanguard** ($8,200) is an archtop that has a mounted pickup and controls. A **Vanguard Laminate** ($5,800) with laminated back and sides is also available. Andersen also offers the **Concert Model** flattop ($6,500).

- Add $300 for stainless steel fretwire.
- Add $700 for Sunburst or Violin finish.
- Add $900 for Adirondack Spruce top.
- Add $500 for an Armstrong or Lollar pickup with volume knob.
- Add $800 for European Spruce top.
- Add $1,000 for European maple back and sides.

ANGELICA

Instruments previously built in Japan from circa 1967 to 1975.

The Angelica trademark is a brand name used by UK importers Boosey & Hawkes on these entry-level guitars and basses based on classic American designs. Some of the original designs produced for Angelica are actually better in quality. Angelica instruments were not distributed to the U.S. market, but some models may be encountered in the U.S. with the average price for these guitars ranging around $100 to $150. Source: Tony Bacon and Paul Day, *The Guru's Guitar Guide*.

ANGELO

Instruments previously produced in Thailand.

The T. Angelo Industrial company built acoustic and electric guitar models based on classic American designs. The prices were in the entry to intermediate players range, with acoustics retailing between $185 and $260, and acoustic/electrics ranging from $499 and $595.

ANGUS GUITARS

Instruments previously built in Laguna Beach, CA between the mid-1970s and the early 2000s.

Luthier Mark Angus built his first guitar in the 1970s, and combined his many years as a player and craftsman to deliver an exceptionally versatile instrument. A Carl Uerheyen (L.A. studio musician) Studio Signature Model was also available. Angus later went on to build custom instruments at The Guitar Shoppe in Laguna Beach, CA.

Angus guitars were handcrafted instruments consisting of Honduran mahogany necks, Englemann, Sitka, or European spruce bodies, Indian rosewood back and sides, and an ebony fretboard. These custom guitars came in many shapes and sizes, including one model with a seven-piece back of maple and rosewood. Prices ran between $2,500 and $4,500 per instrument, on average.

ANTARES

Instruments previously manufactured in Korea during the 1980s and 1990s. Distributed in the U.S. by Vega Musical Instruments (VMI) Industries in Brea, CA.

Antares guitars were designed for entry-level musicians and guitar students. Designs range from a six-string classical model to six-string steel string models of various finishes and even a twelve-string model with advertised prices starting around $100. Antares also offered electric guitars and basses.

ANTONIO APARICIO GUITARS

Instruments currently produced in Valencia, Spain.

Antonio Aparicio has been a guitar maker for over forty years and been partners in several guitar companies. He makes guitars with his name on them in a workshop. All guitars currently produced are classical models and there are four current lines: the Standard Series (priced $656-$929), the Craftman Series (priced $964-$2,590), the Stage Series (priced $1,103-$2,254), and the Signature Series (priced $4,168-$9,979). All models are finished with a traditional finish, and built from the best woods around the world.

CONTACT INFORMATION	CONTACT INFORMATION
ANTONIO APARICIO GUITARS	**ANTONIO APARICIO GUITARS**
Headquarters/Factory	*Antonio Aparicio Guitars, USA: Zeke Guereque*
Villa de Bilbao, 31, Pol. ind. fuente del jarro	13329 Boyd Lake Dr.
Paterna, Valencia 46988 Spain	Bakersfield, CA 93314
Phone No.: +34 96 134 41 22	Phone No.: 661-368-0605
Fax No.: + 34 96 134 16 36	Fax No.: 661-414-7533
	zekeguereque@gmail.com

ANTONIO LORCA

Instruments currently built in Spain.

Antonio Lorca guitars are known as "A Work of Art." They feature solid cedar tops on flamenco-style acoustics. The most current retail list is from 1996 and the prices are as follows: Student models begin at $369, recital models begin at $529, and concert level guitars begin at $599.

MSR/NOTES	100%	EXCELLENT	AVERAGE	LAST MSR

ANTONIO LORIENTE

Instruments currently built in Spain. Distributed in the U.S. by Cordoba Music Group in Santa Monica, CA.

Handmade in Spain, the Loriente Collection guitars are constructed with the finest all-solid tone woods available. The designs adhere to the traditions and techniques of Spain's master luthiers. Select models feature traditional French polish finishes. Cordoba guitars are distributed by Cordoba Music Group. The Loriente collection starts at $2,495 and the highest-priced model is $6,250 retail. For more information, visit Antonio Loriente's website or contact the Cordoba Music Group directly.

CONTACT INFORMATION
ANTONIO LORIENTE
Cordoba Guitars, Loriente Collection
Phone No.: 310-586-1180
www.oordobaguitars.com/loriente
info@lorienteguitars.com

ANTONIO SANCHEZ

Instruments currently built in Spain. Distributed in the U.S. by Concert Guitars, Inc. in Miami, FL, and by California Guitar Works in Huntington Beach, CA. Antonio Sanchez guitars have been produced since 1984.

Luthier Antonio Sanchez founded Concert S.A. in 1984 in Valencia, Spain. Sanchez has several years experience in guitar making. He continues to study the stetic and sonorous instrument quality. Currently, the factory is located in Paterna City and twenty craftsmen work for Sanchez. The factory can produce up to 10,000 instruments a year.

Sanchez produces a full line of classical guitars. There are several different models within four distinct categories. For more information, contact the U.S. distributor or visit Sanchez's website.

CONTACT INFORMATION
ANTONIO SANCHEZ
46988 Pol. Fuente del Jarro-Paterna
Valencia, Spain
Phone No.: +34 96 132 14 97
Fax No.: +34 96 132 09 02
www.antoniosanchezguitars.com
export@antoniosanchezguitars.com

APOLLONIO GUITARS

Instruments currently built in Rockport, ME since 1967.

Luthier Nikos Apollonio, a musician interested in Celtic music, estimates that he has built over six hundred stringed instruments such as lutes, louds, mandolins, mandocellos, citterns, bouzoukis, and guitars. Prices start at $1,800 for six-string acoustics and $1,900 for 12-string acoustics. For more information, contact Apollonio directly.

CONTACT INFORMATION
APOLLONIO GUITARS
15 Blackberry Lane
Rockport, ME 04856
Phone No.: 207-594-0032
www.nikosapollonio.com

APPLAUSE

Instruments currently manufactured in Korea since 1980. Distributed by KMC Music in Bloomfield, CT. Applause guitars were originally produced in New Hartford, CT between 1975 and 1979.

The Applause instruments were originally designed to be the entry level version of the Ovation guitars. In 1975, the new line of guitars was first offered to Ovation dealers as the "Ovation Medallion." A year later, models under the Applause trademark, they were offered to Kaman distributors. The Medallion name ran into some trademark claim problems, and was changed to Matrix. Matrix "Applauses" carried a list price of $249. In 1983, The Ovation Celebrity (also Korean, with U.S. produced synthetic backs) was introduced, again serving as an entry point to Ovation guitars.

CONTACT INFORMATION
APPLAUSE
Distributed by KMC Music
55 Griffin Road South
Bloomfield, CT 06002-0507
Phone No.: 860-509-8888
www.ovationguitars.com/applause
askus@ovationguitars.com

Applause instruments feature the same guitar design and synthetic "bowl back" that the American-built Ovations possess. While engineered and manufactured with the same attention to quality, production of these models overseas is Kaman's key to offering good quality guitars for players on a budget.

Applause guitars are offered in acoustic and acoustic/electric models. The acoustic/electrics offer similar under-the-saddle piezoelectric systems with volume and tone controls as the Ovation guitars. Models encoded with an "AA" are Applause Acoustics, while an "AE" denotes an Applause Electric. The "AN" code indicates an Applause Nylon string model. Beginning in 2013, the "AB" stands for Applause Balladeer and the "AE" stands for Applause Elite, which are both based on Ovation models.

ACOUSTIC: GENERAL INFORMATION

All Applause instruments feature a solid walnut bridge, Sitka spruce top (some models may be laminated tops), Ping tuning machines, a steel reinforced truss rod, solid mahogany neck, and mother-of-pearl inlay dots. All models are available in a Natural finish; some models may also be Black, White, Brownburst, "Barnboard" (enhanced grain), or Purpleburst. On model designations there is a number after the model that indicates the finish (-4 is Natural).

ACOUSTIC: AA/AB/AE SERIES

AA 10 VOYAGER – travel-size body, spruce top, mini-bowl, 12/19-fret fingerboard with pearl dot inlays, three-per-side tuners, available in Natural finish, mfg. 1993-early 2000s.

	N/A	$95 - 125	$65 - 90	$286

MSR/NOTES	100%	EXCELLENT	AVERAGE	LAST MSR

AA 12 – 1/2 size single round cutaway, three-stripe bound body/rosette, mini bowl, 20-fret bound fingerboard with pearl dot inlay, three-per-side tuners, available in Natural finish, disc. 2012.

	$175	$85 - 115	$55 - 80	$249

AA 13 – similar to AA 12, except has 3/4 size body, disc. 2012.

	$150	$95 - 125	$55 - 80	$250

* **AE 13** – similar to AA 13, except has electronics, available in Natural finish, disc. 2012.

	$180	$120 - 150	$75 - 95	$300

AA 21 – Lyrachord deep bowl body, round soundhole, binding, 14/20-fret rosewood fingerboard with pearl dot inlays, three-per-side tuners, available in Natural or Black finish, mfg. 2000-2012.

	$150	$95 - 125	$60 - 80	$270

AA 28 – Lyrachord single cutaway super shallow bowl body, round soundhole, binding, 14/20-fret rosewood fingerboard with pearl dot inlays, three-per-side tuners, DJ-2 electronics, available in Natural, Black, Ruby Red, or Honey Burst finish, mfg. 2000-08.

	N/A	$160 - 210	$100 - 130	$430

AA 31 – dreadnought style, black pickguard, five-stripe bound body/rosette, deep bowl, 14/20-fret fingerboard with pearl dot inlays, body matching peghead, three-per-side tuners, available in Barnboard, Brownburst, or Natural finish, disc.

	N/A	$130 - 160	$70 - 95	$310

AE 32 – dreadnought style, black pickguard, five-stripe bound body/rosette, deep bowl, 14/20-fret bound fingerboard with pearl diamond inlays, three-per-side tuners, available in Natural finish, disc.

	N/A	$150 - 190	$95 - 120	$390

AA 33 – classic style, bound body, decal rosette, deep bowl, 12/19-fret fingerboard, wraparound walnut bridge, three-per-side gold tuners, available in Natural finish, disc.

	N/A	$130 - 160	$95 - 125	$310

AE 34 – single round cutaway classic style, bound body, decal rosette, shallow bowl, 12/19-fret fingerboard, wraparound walnut bridge, three-per-side gold tuners, available in Natural finish, disc.

	N/A	$150 - 200	$95 - 120	$430

AA 35 – dreadnought style, black pickguard, five-stripe bound body/rosette, deep bowl, 14/20-fret fingerboard with pearl dot inlays, six-per-side tuners, optional electronics, available in Black or Natural finish, disc.

	N/A	$150 - 190	$95 - 125	$390

* **AE 35** – similar to the AA 35, except has electronics, available in Black, Honey Burst, or Natural finish, disc. 2012.

	$300	$150 - 200	$95 - 120	$500

AE 36 – dreadnought style, black pickguard, five-stripe bound body/rosette, deep bowl, 14/20-fret bound fingerboard with pearl diamond inlays, three-per-side tuners, available in Barnboard, Brownburst, Natural, or White finish, disc.

	N/A	$155 - 195	$100 - 130	$410

AE 38 – dreadnought style, black pickguard, five-stripe bound body/rosette, shallow bowl, 14/20-fret bound fingerboard with pearl diamond inlays, three-per-side tuners, available in Barnboard, Black, Brownburst, Natural, Purpleburst, or White finish, disc.

	N/A	$160 - 210	$100 - 130	$450

AE 44 – single cutaway mid-depth Elite-style body, spruce top, Lyrachord body, multi soundholes with exotic hardwoods rosette, set nato neck, 23-fret angled rosewood fingerboard with pearloid dot inlays, three-per-side chrome tuners, rosewood bridge, Ovation Slimline pickup and OP-4BT electronics, available in Black, Natural, or Ruby Red finish, 25.5 in. scale, mfg. 2013-present.

MSR $469	$330	$200 - 250	$120 - 150	

AE 128 – single cutaway super shallow body, spruce top, synthetic bowl back, center round soundhole with black/white design rosette, 14/20-fret bound rosewood fingerboard with dot inlays, Ovation-style headstock, three-per-side chrome tuners, rosewood bridge, OP-4B electronics, available in Black, Honey Burst, Natural, or Ruby Red finish, disc. 2012.

	$200	$120 - 150	$75 - 95	$350

AE 148 – single cutaway super shallow body, spruce top, synthetic bowl back, multiple soundholes inlaid in exotic wood epaulets, 14/20-fret bound rosewood fingerboard with dot inlays, Ovation-style headstock, three-per-side chrome tuners, rosewood bridge, OP-4B electronics, available in Black, Natural, or Ruby Red finish, current mfg.

MSR $440	$250	$150 - 190	$90 - 115	

MSR/NOTES	100%	EXCELLENT	AVERAGE	LAST MSR

AB 24 – single cutaway mid-depth Balladeer-style body, spruce top, Lyrachord body, round soundhole with chevron pattern rosette, set nato neck, 20-fret rosewood fingerboard with pearloid dot inlays, three-per-side chrome tuners, rosewood bridge, Ovation Slimline pickup and OP-4BT electronics, available in Black, Honey Burst, Natural, or Ruby Red finish, 25.5 in. scale, mfg. 2013-present.

MSR $359	$250	$145 - 180	$85 - 110	

* *AB 2412 12-String* – similar to the AB 24, except in 12-string configuration with six-per-side tuners, available in Black or Natural finish, 25.5 in. scale, mfg. 2013-present.

MSR $499	$350	$200 - 250	$120 - 150	

* *AB 24A Acoustic* – similar to the AB 24, except has no electronics, available in Black or Natural finish, mfg. 2013-present.

MSR $289	$200	$120 - 150	$70 - 90	

AN 12 – 1/2 size nylon string configuration single round cutaway body, spruce top, bowlback, three-stripe bound body/rosette, mini bowl, 12/18-fret bound fingerboard with no inlays, slotted headstock, three-per-side tuners, rosewood bridge, available in Natural finish, disc 2011.

	$180	$120 - 150	$75 - 95	$260

AN 13 – 3/4-size nylon string configuration single round cutaway body, spruce top, bowlback, three-stripe bound body/rosette, mini bowl, 12/18-fret bound fingerboard with no inlays, slotted headstock, three-per-side tuners, rosewood bridge, available in Natural finish, disc. 2012.

	$180	$120 - 150	$75 - 95	$250

ACOUSTIC ELECTRIC BASS

AE 40 – single round cutaway dreadnought style, Sitka spruce top, round soundhole, five-stripe bound body/rosette, deep bowl, mahogany neck, 19-fret walnut fingerboard with pearl dot inlays, strings through walnut bridge, logo decal on peghead, two-per-side chrome tuners, available in Black or Natural finish, disc.

	N/A	$250 - 300	$150 - 200	$600

AE 40F – similar to AE 40, except features a fretless neck, disc.

	N/A	$200 - 250	$125 - 175	$515

AE 140 – single cutaway mid-depth body, spruce top, synthetic bowl back, center round soundhole with black/white design rosette, 14/20-fret bound rosewood fingerboard with dot inlays, Ovation-style headstock, two-per-side chrome tuners, rosewood bridge, OP-4B electronics, available in Black or Natural finish, 34 in. scale, current mfg.

MSR $600	$300	$175 - 225	$110 - 140	

APPLEGATE GUITARS

Guitars currently produced in Chanhassen, MN since 2001.

Luthier Brian Applegate builds custom acoustic guitars in Chanhassen, MN, which is a suburb of Minneapolis. Applegate offers various body styles including the SJ, Jumbo, Jumbo Baritone, Classical, Jazz Flat-top, and Archtop Jazz. Base price on guitars is $6,000 and Applegate offers an almost infinite list of options. For more information, visit Applegate's website or contact him directly.

CONTACT INFORMATION
APPLEGATE GUITARS
7350 Kurvers Point Road
Chanhassen, MN 55317
Phone No.: 952-250-7063
www.applegateguitars.com
brian@applegateguitars.com

ARBITER

Instruments previously built in Japan during the mid-1960s to late 1970s.

The Arbiter trademark is the brand of a UK importer. Original models are of entry-level quality, later models are good quality copy designs and some original designs. Source: Tony Bacon and Paul Day, *The Guru's Guitar Guide*.

ARBOR

Instruments currently manufactured in Asia. Distributed in the U.S. by Musicorp (MBT) in Charleston, SC. Previously distributed by Midco International in Effingham, IL.

Arbor guitars are aimed at the entry-level student to the intermediate player. The Midco International company has been importing and distributing both acoustic and solid body guitars to the U.S. market for a good number of years, and now offers a five-year warranty on their acoustic guitar line.

Model coding carries an **A** for an acoustic model. The double digits after the prefix (such as A 30) indicate a regular acoustic and triple digits following the prefix (like A 700) for acoustic/electric models. Currently, Arbor only offers electric guitars and basses.

CONTACT INFORMATION
ARBOR
Distributed by Musicorp
PO Box 63366
N. Charleston, SC 29419
Phone No.: 843-745-8501
Phone No.: 800-641-6931
Fax No.: 843-745-8502
www.musicorp.com
kmcmcpsales@kmcmusic.com

ACOUSTIC

Unless specified otherwise, Acoustic models feature a dreadnought body size, mahogany neck, sides, and back, rosewood fingerboard with dot position markers, rosewood bridge, three-per-side tuners, and chrome tuning machines.

MSR/NOTES	100%	EXCELLENT	AVERAGE	LAST MSR

A 12 – spruce top, 12-string configuration, black pickguard, available in Natural finish, disc.

	N/A	$120 - 150	$70 - 95	$300

A 19 – spruce top, black multiple binding on top and back, available in Natural finish, mfg. 1997-2001.

	N/A	$80 - 110	$40 - 60	$230

A 20 – spruce top, mahogany back and sides, black pickguard, available in Natural finish, disc.

	N/A	$100 - 130	$60 - 80	$260

This model was also available in a left-handed configuration (A 20L) for the same retail price.

A 29 – spruce top, mahogany back and sides, bound fingerboard, white multiple binding on top and back, center marquetry stripe on back, available in Natural finish, mfg. 1997-2001.

	N/A	$100 - 130	$60 - 80	$260

A 30 – spruce top, mahogany back and sides, black pickguard, available in gloss Black finish, disc.

	N/A	$105 - 135	$65 - 85	$270

This model was also available in a White finish as the model A 45.

A 39 C – concert size classical body, spruce top, mahogany back and sides, multiple binding on top and back, center marquetry stripe on back, chrome butterfly button tuning machines, available in Natural finish, mfg. 1997-2001.

	N/A	$80 - 110	$40 - 60	$230

A 40 – spruce top, mahogany back and sides, black pickguard, available in Tobacco Burst finish, disc.

	N/A	$105 - 135	$65 - 85	$270

A 60 – jumbo body, spruce top, ovangkol back and sides, black pickguard, available in Natural finish, disc.

	N/A	$180 - 230	$120 - 150	$460

AC 45 – classical style, spruce top, mahogany back/sides, nato neck, rosewood fingerboard/bridge, open-style tuners, gold hardware, Natural finish, disc.

	N/A	$80 - 100	$40 - 60	$190

AD 100 – dreadnought style, spruce top, mahogany back/sides, nato neck, rosewood fingerboard, black pickguard, chrome hardware, Natural finish, disc.

	N/A	$85 - 105	$40 - 60	$200

Was also available as a left-hand model at no additional charge and available as a guitar pack with tuner, strap, and gig bag (last MSR was $239).

AD 200 – dreadnought style, spruce top, mahogany back/sides, nato neck, rosewood fingerboard, black pickguard, chrome hardware, available in Black, Trans. Blue, or Wine Red finish, disc.

	N/A	$90 - 110	$50 - 70	$210

ACOUSTIC: ARBOR BY WASHBURN SERIES

AW 1 N – concert size body, spruce top, mahogany back and sides, rosewood fingerboard and bridge, available in Natural finish, disc.

	N/A	$105 - 135	$65 - 85	$270

AW 2 N – dreadnought body, select spruce top, mahogany back and sides, rosewood fingerboard and bridge, available in Natural finish, disc.

	N/A	$110 - 140	$70 - 90	$300

AW 3 – dreadnought body, select spruce top, mahogany back and sides, rosewood fingerboard and bridge, die cast tuning machines, available in Natural finish, disc.

	N/A	$140 - 180	$95 - 120	$350

AW 5 S – dreadnought body, solid spruce top, scalloped spruce bracing, mahogany back and sides, rosewood fingerboard and bridge, Grover tuning machines, available in Natural finish, disc.

	N/A	$200 - 250	$130 - 170	$480

AW 6 S – dreadnought body, solid spruce top, scalloped spruce bracing, ovangkol back and sides, rosewood fingerboard and bridge, Grover tuning machines, available in Natural finish, disc.

	N/A	$220 - 270	$140 - 180	$520

ACOUSTIC ELECTRIC

All acoustic/electric models have a single rounded cutaway, chromed tuning machines, rosewood fingerboards and bridges, and piezo pickups.

MSR/NOTES	100%	EXCELLENT	AVERAGE	LAST MSR

A 20 E – dreadnought non-cutaway body, spruce top, mahogany back and sides, black pickguard, one volume control, one tone control, available in Natural finish, disc.

	N/A	$110 - 140	$65 - 90	$300

A 600 – spruce top, nato back and sides, hardwood fingerboard with white dot position markers, hardwood bridge, piezo pickup, black pickguard, one volume and one tone control, available in Natural, Tobaccoburst, or Wine Red finish, disc.

	N/A	$120 - 150	$75 - 100	$340

A 800 CS – slim dreadnought body, curly maple top, mahogany back and sides, rosewood fingerboard with white dot and diamond position markers, rosewood bridge, gold hardware, piezo pickup, four-band EQ preamp, volume slider, available in Cherry Burst or Trans. Black finish, disc.

	N/A	$200 - 250	$130 - 170	$520

ACE – single cutaway, mini-dreadnought style, flamed maple top, nato neck, rosewood fingerboard, four-band EQ, chrome hardware, available in Natural, Trans. Black, Trans. Blue, or Trans. Red finish, disc.

	N/A	$90 - 120	$50 - 70	$230

ACOUSTIC ELECTRIC: ARBOR BY WASHBURN SERIES

AW 2 CE – dreadnought body with single cutaway, select spruce top, mahogany back and sides, rosewood fingerboard and bridge, active electronic pickup system, available in Gloss Black or Natural finish, disc.

	N/A	$170 - 220	$110 - 140	$430

AW 3 CE – dreadnought body with single cutaway, select spruce top, mahogany back and sides, rosewood fingerboard and bridge, die-cast tuning machines, active electronic pickup system, available in Natural finish, disc.

	N/A	$200 - 250	$130 - 170	$500

ACOUSTIC ELECTRIC BASS

A 100 – spruce top, mahogany back and sides, multiple binding, piezo pickup, two-per-side headstock, one volume and one tone control, available in Natural finish, disc.

	N/A	$200 - 250	$130 - 170	$500

ARCHER GUITARS

Instruments currently produced overseas. Distributed by Dynamic Music Distributing, Inc. in Milwaukee, WI.

Archer offers a wide range of beginner and intermediate guitars, basses, and other musical instruments. Acoustic models are available in dreadnought, cutaway folk, and classical styles. For more information, visit Archer's website or contact the distributor directly.

CONTACT INFORMATION
ARCHER GUITARS
Distributed by Dynamic Music Distributing, Inc.
PO Box 270655
Milwaukee, WI 53227
Phone No.: 800-343-3003
Fax No.: 800-211-5570
www.archerguitars.com
scicero@dynamicmusicdist.com

ARCH KRAFT

Instruments previously built by the Kay Musical Instrument Company of Chicago, IL, during the early 1930s.

These entry-level acoustic flattop and archtop guitars were built by Kay (one of the three U.S. jobber guitar companies), and distributed through various outlets. Arch Kraft developed a tilt-neck adjustment for the Venetian Kay Kraft models around the 1920s. Arch Kraft produced guitars between the 1920s and the 1960s. Used models in excellent condition can be priced between $200 and $400, depending upon features. Source: Michael Wright, *Vintage Guitar Magazine*.

ARIA/ARIA PRO II

Instruments currently produced in Japan, Korea, China, Indonesia, U.S., and Spain since 1956. Distributed in the U.S. by Dana B. Goods in Ventura, CA. Previously distributed by Hanser Music Group (previously HHI) in Hebron, KY and by Aria USA/NHF in Pennsauken, NJ.

CONTACT INFORMATION
ARIA/ARIA PRO II
Factory/Headquarters
www.ariaguitars.com

U.S. Distributor: Dana B. Goods
4054 Transport St., Unit A
Ventura, CA 93003
Phone No.: 800-741-0109
www.danabgoods.com

Aria is the trademark of the Arai Company of Japan, which began producing guitars in 1956. Prior to 1975, the trademark was either Aria or Aria Diamond. Original designs in the 1960s gave way to a greater emphasis on replicas of American designs in the late 1970s. Ironically, the recognition of these well-produced replicas led to success in later years as the company returned to producing original designs. The Aria trademark has always reflected high production quality, and currently there has been more emphasis on stylish designs (such as the Fullerton guitar series, or in bass designs such as the AVB-SB).

The Aria company has produced instruments under their Aria/Aria Diamond/Aria Pro II trademark for a number of years. They have also built instruments distributed under the Univox and Cameo labels. Aria also offers the Ariana line of acoustic steel-string and nylon-string models.

MSR/NOTES	100%	EXCELLENT	AVERAGE	LAST MSR

ACOUSTIC: GENERAL INFORMATION

Aria began producing guitars in 1956 and they have built guitars for both their own trademark and for many other manufacturers. Aria also hasn't had their own representation/distribution in the U.S. for many years now. While Aria offers a full line of models in their catalogs and on their websites, often times several of these are not available to the U.S. market. Also, U.S. distribution has changed several times since the 2000s, meaning each distributor picked different models to sell in the U.S. All models that are currently available through U.S. distribution are listed with the manufacturer's suggested retail price. Models that are still listed in the catalog, but were offered in the U.S. at least once will still appear as currently manufactured, but a not available (N/A) field will appear next to the MSR. Please be aware that models may not be listed here because of distribution and availability issues.

ACOUSTIC: MISC. MODELS

1 FA 50 BS – all mahogany construction, non-cutaway design with arched top, f-holes, vintage-style tuners, Brown Sunburst finish, disc.

	N/A	$225 - 275	$135 - 175	$549

GYPSIE MM10 – single cutaway Gypsie-style body, solid spruce top, D-shaped soundhole, rosewood back and sides, mahogany neck, 12/24-fret rosewood fingerboard that extends into the soundhole with pearl dot markers, open-style headstock with three-per-side gold banjo-style tuners, long rosewood bridge, gold metal tailpiece, available in Gloss Natural finish, mfg. 2005-present.

MSR $390	$315	$160 - 210	$100 - 125	

* *Gypsie MM10E Electric* – similar to the MM10, except has a piezo pickup available in Gloss Natural finish, mfg. 2005-present.

MSR $520	$420	$225 - 275	$130 - 165	

GYPSIE MM20 – single cutaway Gypsie-style body, solid spruce top, small oval-shaped soundhole, rosewood back and sides, mahogany neck, 12/24-fret rosewood fingerboard that extends into the soundhole with pearl dot markers, open-style headstock with three-per-side gold banjo-style tuners, long rosewood bridge, gold metal tailpiece, available in Semi-Gloss Natural finish, mfg. 2005-present.

MSR $390	$315	$160 - 210	$100 - 125	

* *Gypsie MM20E Electric* – similar to the MM20, except has a piezo pickup available in Gloss Natural finish, mfg. 2005-present.

MSR $520	$420	$225 - 275	$130 - 165	

19th CENTURY A19C-200S – 19th Century parlor-style body, solid spruce top, solid mahogany (Black finish) or solid rosewood (Natural finish) back and sides, round soundhole with decorative rosette, white body binding with decorative purfling, mahogany neck, 14/20-fret ebony fingerboard with decorative inlays, slotted headstock with matching finish overlay, three-per-side open-style gold tuners, ebony mustache bridge, available in Black or Natural finish, 24.8 in. scale, mfg. 2009-present.

MSR $1,500	$1,200	$675 - 800	$375 - 450	

19th CENTURY A19C-200N – nylon-string configuration, 19th Century parlor-style body, solid spruce top, solid mahogany (Black finish) or solid rosewood (Natural finish) back and sides, round soundhole with decorative rosette, white body binding with decorative purfling, mahogany neck, 14/20-fret ebony fingerboard, slotted headstock with matching finish overlay, three-per-side open-style gold tuners, ebony mustache tied bridge, available in Black or Natural finish, 24.8 in. scale, mfg. 2009-present.

MSR $1,500	$1,200	$675 - 800	$375 - 450	

ACOUSTIC: AD SERIES

AD 28 – dreadnought style, solid Sitka spruce top, mahogany back and sides, round soundhole with multi-ring rosette, black body binding, mahogany neck, 14/20-fret rosewood fingerboard with dot inlays, three-per-side chrome tuners, rosewood bridge, black pickguard, available in Brown Sunburst or Natural finish, current mfg.

MSR $550	$440	$225 - 275	$135 - 175	

* *AD 28 CE* – similar to the AD 28 except has single cutaway and electronics, disc. 2006.

	N/A	$250 - 300	$150 - 200	$575

AD 35 – dreadnought style, solid Sitka spruce top, rosewood back and sides, round soundhole with multi-ring rosette, W/B body binding, mahogany neck, 14/20-fret rosewood fingerboard with dot inlays, three-per-side chrome tuners, rosewood bridge, black pickguard, available in Brown Sunburst or Natural finish, current mfg.

MSR $630	$500	$275 - 325	$150 - 200	

* *AD 35 CE* – similar to the AD 35, except has a single cutaway and electronics, disc. 2006.

	N/A	$300 - 350	$175 - 225	$675

AD 50 – dreadnought style, solid Englemann spruce top, solid rosewood back, rosewood sides, round soundhole with multi-ring herringbone rosette, W/B body binding with herringbone purfling, mahogany neck, 14/20-fret rosewood fingerboard with diamond inlays, three-per-side chrome tuners, rosewood bridge, tortoise pickguard, available in Natural finish, current mfg.

MSR $940	$750	$400 - 475	$250 - 300	

* *AD 50 CE* – similar to the AD 50, except has a single cutaway and electronics, disc. 2006.

	N/A	$425 - 500	$275 - 325	$875

MSR/NOTES	100%	EXCELLENT	AVERAGE	LAST MSR

AD 65 – dreadnought style, solid Englemann spruce top, solid mahogany back and sides, round soundhole with multi-ring abalone rosette, W/B body binding with herringbone purfling, mahogany neck, 14/20-fret rosewood fingerboard with diamond/snowflake inlays, three-per-side chrome tuners, rosewood bridge, tortoise pickguard, available in Natural finish, current mfg.

MSR N/A	$875	$475 - 550	$275 - 325	

This model is currently not distributed in the U.S.

* *AD 65 EXF* – similar to the AD 65, except has flamed mahogany back and sides, available in Natural finish, current mfg.

MSR N/A	$875	$475 - 550	$275 - 325	

This model is currently not distributed in the U.S.

AD 80 – dreadnought style, solid Englemann spruce top, solid rosewood back and sides, round soundhole with multi-ring abalone rosette, W/B body binding with abalone purfling, mahogany neck, 14/20-fret bound rosewood fingerboard with diamond/snowflake inlays, bound headstock, three-per-side gold tuners, rosewood bridge with snowflake inlays, tortoise pickguard, available in Natural finish, current mfg.

MSR $1,400	$1,120	$600 - 700	$375 - 450	

* *AD 80 CE* – similar to the AD 80, except has a single cutaway and electronics, disc. 2006.

	N/A	$625 - 750	$400 - 475	$1,225

* *AD 80 CEMB* – similar to the AD 80, except has a single sharp cutaway and Fishman Ellipse Matrix Blend electronics, available in Brown Sunburst or Natural finish, current mfg.

MSR $1,700	$1,375	$725 - 875	$425 - 500	

* *AD 80 EXQ* – similar to the AD 80, except has quilted mahogany back and sides, available in Brown Sunburst or Natural finish, current mfg.

MSR N/A	$1,120	$600 - 700	$375 - 450	

This model is currently not distributed in the U.S.

AD 150 – dreadnought style, solid Englemann spruce top, solid rosewood back and sides, round soundhole with multi-ring abalone rosette, white body binding with abalone purfling, mahogany neck, 14/20-fret ebony fingerboard with hexagon pearl inlays, bound rosewood headstock overlay with pearl design, three-per-side gold tuners, ebony bridge, yellow tortoise pickguard, available in Brown Sunburst or Natural finish, current mfg.

MSR $2,500	$2,000	$1,100 - 1,300	$675 - 800	

AD SH/CST – dreadnought style, solid Sitka spruce top, solid rosewood back, rosewood sides, round soundhole with multi-ring rosette, black body binding, mahogany neck, 14/20-fret bound rosewood fingerboard with dot inlays, three-per-side chrome tuners, rosewood bridge with snowflake inlays, clear pickguard, Shadow Nanoflex pickup and NanoMAG magnet pickup, Sonic Double Play electronics, available in Brown Sunburst or Natural finish, current mfg.

MSR N/A	$850	$450 - 525	$250 - 300	

This model is currently not distributed in the U.S.

ACOUSTIC: AF SERIES

AF 20 – grand concert folk style, spruce top, whitewood (early models) or mahogany back and sides, round soundhole with multi-ring rosette, multi-ply W/B body binding, mahogany neck, 14/20-fret bound rosewood fingerboard with pearl dot inlays, three-per-side chrome tuners, rosewood bridge, black pickguard, available in Brown Sunburst, Cherry Sunburst, or Natural finish, current mfg.

MSR $220	$175	$95 - 120	$50 - 70	

This model is also available as a 3/4-sized body and a 1/2-sized body.

AF 25 – grand concert-style body, solid Sitka spruce top, mahogany back and sides, round soundhole with multi-ring rosette, black body binding, mahogany neck, 14/20-fret bound rosewood fingerboard with pearl dot inlays, three-per-side chrome tuners, rosewood bridge, black pickguard, available in Blue Sunburst, Brown Sunburst, Cherry Sunburst, or Natural finish, current mfg.

MSR $620	$360	$175 - 225	$100 - 130	

AF 28 – grand concert-style body, solid Sitka spruce top, mahogany back and sides, round soundhole with multi-ring rosette, black body binding, mahogany neck, 14/20-fret bound rosewood fingerboard with pearl dot inlays, three-per-side chrome tuners, rosewood bridge, black pickguard, available in Brown Sunburst or Natural finish, current mfg.

MSR N/A	$450	$240 - 290	$140 - 185	

This model is currently not distributed in the U.S.

* *AF 28CE* – similar to the AF 28, except has single smooth cutaway and electronics, current mfg.

MSR N/A	$650	$325 - 400	$190 - 240	

This model is currently not distributed in the U.S.

MSR/NOTES	100%	EXCELLENT	AVERAGE	LAST MSR

AF 35 – grand concert-style body, solid Sitka spruce top, rosewood back and sides, round soundhole with multi-ring rosette, multi-ply W/B body binding, mahogany neck, 14/20-fret bound rosewood fingerboard with pearl dot inlays, three-per-side chrome tuners, rosewood bridge, black pickguard, available in Brown Sunburst or Natural finish, current mfg.

MSR N/A	$500	$275 - 325	$150 - 200	

This model is currently not distributed in the U.S.

AF 36 MINI – grand concert-style mini body, solid Sitka spruce top, mahogany back and sides, round soundhole with two ring rosette, multi-ply B/W body binding, mahogany neck, 14/19-fret sonokelin fingerboard with pearl dot inlays, three-per-side chrome tuners, rosewood bridge, black pickguard, available in Brown Sunburst or Natural finish, 22.7 in. scale, current mfg.

MSR $550	$450	$240 - 290	$140 - 185	

AF 60 – auditorium style, solid Englemann spruce top, solid rosewood back, rosewood sides, fancy body binding, mahogany neck, rosewood fingerboard and bridge, tortoise pickguard, gold hardware, available in Natural finish, disc. 2006.

	N/A	$300 - 375	$175 - 225	$750

AF 65 – auditorium-style body, solid Englemann spruce top, solid mahogany back and sides, round soundhole with multi-ring abalone rosette, white body binding with herringbone purfling, mahogany neck, 14/20-fret bound rosewood fingerboard with diamond/snowflake inlays, three-per-side chrome tuners, rosewood bridge, tortoise pickguard, available in Natural finish, current mfg.

MSR N/A	$880	$500 - 575	$300 - 350	

This model is currently not distributed in the U.S.

AF 75 (AW-75 F) – grand concert folk style, spruce top, round soundhole, black pickguard, bound body, five-stripe rosette, mahogany back/sides/neck, 14/20-fret rosewood fingerboard with pearl dot inlays, rosewood bridge with black pins, three-per-side nickel tuners, available in Natural finish, disc. 2005.

	N/A	$150 - 200	$95 - 120	$390

AF 530 – grand concert folk style, solid spruce top, round soundhole, black pickguard, bound body, five-stripe rosette, maple back/sides, mahogany neck, 14/20-fret rosewood fingerboard with pearl dot inlays, rosewood bridge with black pins, three-per-side deluxe tuners, available in Natural finish, mfg. 1998-2007.

	N/A	$250 - 300	$130 - 170	$600

AF SH – auditorium-style body, solid Sitka spruce top, solid rosewood back, rosewood sides, round soundhole with multi-ring rosette, black body binding, mahogany neck, 14/20-fret rosewood fingerboard with pearl dot inlays, three-per-side chrome tuners, rosewood bridge, clear pickguard, Shadow Nanoflex pickup and NanoMAG magnet pickup, Sonic Double Play electronics, available in Brown Sunburst or Natural finish, current mfg.

MSR $1,050	$850	$450 - 525	$250 - 300	

ACOUSTIC: AK SERIES

AK Series guitars are currently produced in Korea.

AK 20 – classical style, spruce top, whitewood (early models) or mahogany back and sides, round soundhole with wooden inlay rosette, black body binding, hardwood or mahogany neck, 12/19-fret ebonized maple fingerboard, slotted headstock, three-per-side open-style chrome tuners, ebonized maple bridge, available in Natural finish, current mfg.

MSR $180	$140	$70 - 90	$40 - 55	

  * **AK 20 3/4** – similar to the AK 20, except has 3/4 size body, 22.8 in. scale, current mfg.

MSR $180	$140	$70 - 90	$40 - 55	

  * **AK 20 1/2** – similar to the AK 20, except has 1/2 size body, 20.8 in. scale, current mfg.

MSR $180	$140	$70 - 90	$40 - 55	

AK 30 – classical style, spruce top, mahogany back and sides, round soundhole with wooden inlay rosette, W/B body binding, mahogany neck, 12/19-fret rosewood fingerboard, slotted headstock, three-per-side open-style chrome tuners, rosewood bridge, available in Natural finish, mfg. 2001-present.

MSR $240	$190	$100 - 130	$60 - 80	

  * **AK 30 CE** – similar to the AK30, except has a single cutaway and PZP-5 Piezo pickup with four-band EQ, available in Natural finish, current mfg.

MSR $320	$260	$135 - 175	$80 - 100	

AK 35 – classical style, solid cedar top, mahogany back and sides, round soundhole with wooden inlay rosette, W/B body binding, mahogany neck, 12/19-fret rosewood fingerboard, slotted headstock, three-per-side open-style gold tuners, rosewood bridge, available in Natural finish, mfg. 2004-present.

MSR $300	$240	$130 - 165	$75 - 95	

This model is also available in three different scales including 18.9 in. (480 mm), 20.9 in. (530 mm), and 22.8 in. (580 mm).

MSR/NOTES	100%	EXCELLENT	AVERAGE	LAST MSR

* **AK 35 CE** – similar to the AK 35, except has a single cutaway and electronics, available in Natural finish, current mfg.

MSR N/A	$275	$140 - 175	$85 - 110	

This model is currently not distributed in the U.S.

AK 45 – classical style, solid cedar top, rosewood back and sides, round soundhole with wooden inlay rosette, W/B body binding, mahogany neck, 12/19-fret rosewood fingerboard, slotted headstock, three-per-side open-style gold tuners, rosewood bridge, available in Natural finish, mfg. 2004-present.

MSR $350	$280	$150 - 190	$95 - 120	

AK 50 – classic style, spruce top, round soundhole, bound body, wooden inlay rosette, mahogany back/sides/neck, 12/19-fret rosewood fingerboard/bridge, three-per-side chrome tuners, available in Natural finish, disc.

	N/A	$80 - 105	$50 - 70	$200

AK 70 – classic style, mahogany top, round soundhole, bound body, wooden inlay rosette, mahogany back/sides/neck, 12/19-fret rosewood fingerboard/bridge, three-per-side nickel tuners, available in Natural finish, mfg. 1991-93.

	N/A	$80 - 110	$45 - 65	$200

AK 75 – classic style, spruce top, round soundhole, bound body, wooden inlay rosette, mahogany back/sides/neck, 12/19-fret rosewood fingerboard/bridge, three-per-side nickel tuners, available in Natural finish, mfg. 1991-99.

	N/A	$150 - 190	$95 - 125	$379

AK 80 – classic style, spruce top, round soundhole, bound body, wooden inlay rosette, mahogany back/sides/neck, 12/19-fret rosewood fingerboard/bridge, three-per-side chrome tuners, available in Natural finish, disc. 2004.

	N/A	$110 - 140	$65 - 90	$250

* **AK 80CE** – similar to the AK 80, except has a single cutaway with electronics, disc. 2004.

	N/A	$150 - 190	$90 - 120	$350

AK 100 – similar to AK 75, except has different rosette and rosewood veneer on peghead, mfg. 1985-1993.

	N/A	$100 - 130	$60 - 80	$240

AK 200 – similar to AK 75, except has different rosette and rosewood veneer on peghead, mfg. 1985-1993.

	N/A	$95 - 125	$55 - 80	$240

AK 200 3/4 – similar to AK 75, except is three-quarter body size, mfg. 1985-1993.

	N/A	$95 - 125	$60 - 80	$240

AK 210 – classic style, select cedar top, round soundhole, bound body, wooden inlay rosette, mahogany back/sides/neck, 12/19-fret rosewood fingerboard/bridge, three-per-side chrome tuners, available in Natural finish, mfg. 1993-2004.

	N/A	$150 - 200	$95 - 125	$399

AK 310 – similar to AK 210, except has gold tuners, mfg. 1993-95.

	N/A	$175 - 225	$110 - 140	$439

AK 320 – classic style, solid cedar top, round soundhole, multiple bound body, wooden inlay rosette, mahogany back/sides/neck, 12/19-fret rosewood fingerboard/bridge, three-per-side chrome tuners, available in Natural finish, mfg. 1997-2004.

	N/A	$225 - 275	$135 - 175	$549

AK 600 – classic style, solid spruce top, round soundhole, five-stripe bound body, wooden inlay rosette, rosewood back/sides, mahogany neck, 12/19-fret rosewood fingerboard/bridge, rosewood veneer on peghead, three-per-side gold tuners, available in Natural finish, mfg. 1985-1995.

	N/A	$150 - 200	$95 - 125	$400

AK 800 – classical style, solid cedar top, rosewood back/sides, round soundhole, mfg. 1993-95.

	N/A	$160 - 210	$100 - 130	

AK 900 – similar to AK 600, except has solid cedar top, mfg. 1991-96.

	N/A	$225 - 275	$135 - 175	$559

AK 920 – classic style, solid cedar top, round soundhole, bound body, wooden inlay rosette, rosewood back/sides, mahogany neck, 12/19-fret rosewood fingerboard/bridge, rosewood veneer on peghead, three-per-side gold tuners, available in Natural finish, mfg. 1997-2004.

	N/A	$275 - 325	$150 - 200	$659

AK 1000 – classic style, spruce top, round soundhole, bound body, wooden inlay rosette, mahogany back/sides/neck, 12/19-fret rosewood fingerboard/bridge, rosewood peghead veneer, three-per-side nickel tuners, available in Natural finish, mfg. 1991-93.

	N/A	$300 - 350	$150 - 200	$700

MSR/NOTES	100%	EXCELLENT	AVERAGE	LAST MSR

ACOUSTIC: AW SERIES

AW 20 – dreadnought-style body, spruce top, whitewood (early models) or mahogany back and sides, round soundhole with multi-ring rosette, multi-ply W/B body binding, hardwood (early models) mahogany neck, 14/20-fret bound rosewood fingerboard with pearl dot inlays, three-per-side chrome tuners, rosewood bridge, black pickguard, available in Black, Blue Shade, Brown Sunburst, Green Shade, Natural, or Red Shade finish, mfg. 1980-present.

MSR $200	$160	$75 - 100	$40 - 60	

* **AW 20 CE** – similar to the AW 20, except has a single cutaway, pickup, and four-band EQ electronics, current mfg.

MSR $360	$290	$140 - 190	$85 - 110	

* **AW 20 E** – similar to the AW 20, except has electronics, current mfg.

MSR $250	$200	$95 - 120	$50 - 70	

* **AW 20 T 12-String** – similar to the AW 20, except in 12-string configuration with six-per-side tuners, mfg. 2004-present.

MSR N/A	N/A	$95 - 120	$50 - 70	

This model is currently not distributed in the U.S.

AW 30 – dreadnought-style body, spruce top, mahogany back and sides, round soundhole with multi-ring rosette, multi-ply W/B body binding, mahogany neck, 14/20-fret bound rosewood fingerboard with pearl dot inlays, three-per-side chrome tuners, rosewood bridge, black pickguard, available in Natural finish, mfg. 1980-2005.

	N/A	$75 - 100	$40 - 60	$195

* **AW 30 CE** – similar to the AW 30, except has a single cutaway and five-band electronics, disc. 2005.

	N/A	$130 - 165	$80 - 105	$329

AW 35 – dreadnought-style body, solid Sitka spruce top, mahogany back and sides, round soundhole with multi-ring rosette, multi-ply W/B body binding, mahogany neck, 14/20-fret bound rosewood fingerboard with pearl dot inlays, three-per-side chrome tuners, rosewood bridge, black pickguard, available in Black, Blue Shade, Brown Sunburst, Natural, or Red Shade finish, current mfg.

MSR $300	$240	$120 - 150	$75 - 95	

* **AW 35 CE** – similar to the AW 35, except has a single cutaway and electronics, mfg. 2006-present.

MSR $400	$320	$150 - 200	$95 - 120	

* **AW 35T 12-String** – similar to the AW 35, except in 12-string configuration with six-per-side tuners, mfg. 2006-present.

MSR N/A	$280	$135 - 175	$70 - 95	

This model is currently not distributed in the U.S.

AW 45 – dreadnought-style body, solid Sitka spruce top, rosewood back and sides, round soundhole with multi-ring rosette, multi-ply W/B body binding, mahogany neck, 14/20-fret bound rosewood fingerboard with pearl dot inlays, three-per-side chrome tuners, rosewood bridge, black pickguard, available in Natural finish, current mfg.

MSR $360	$290	$140 - 190	$85 - 110	

* **AW 45T 12-String** – similar to the AW 45, except in 12-string configuration with six-per-side tuners, mfg. 2011-present.

MSR $430	$340	$175 - 225	$100 - 135	

AW 50 – dreadnought style, spruce top, round soundhole, black pickguard, bound body, five-stripe rosette, mahogany back/sides/neck, 14/20-fret rosewood fingerboard with white dot inlays, rosewood bridge, three-per-side chrome tuners, available in Black, Blue Shade, Brown Sunburst, Natural, or Red Shade finish, disc. 2004.

	N/A	$95 - 120	$60 - 80	$240

AW 70 – dreadnought style, mahogany top, round soundhole, black pickguard, bound body, five-stripe rosette, mahogany back/sides/neck, 14/20-fret rosewood fingerboard with pearl dot inlays, rosewood bridge with black pins, three-per-side nickel tuners, available in Walnut finish, mfg. 1991-93.

	N/A	$80 - 110	$50 - 70	$200

AW 73 N – dreadnought style, spruce top, round soundhole, black pickguard, bound body, five-stripe rosette, mahogany back/sides/neck, 14/20-fret rosewood fingerboard with white dot inlays, rosewood bridge, three-per-side nickel tuners, available in Natural gloss finish, mfg. 1996-99.

	N/A	$120 - 150	$75 - 100	$299

* **AW 73 C** – similar to the AW 73 N, except has single cutaway, available in Black, Blue Sunburst, Natural, or Red Sunburst finish, mfg. 1996-99.

	N/A	$150 - 200	$105 - 135	$369

AW 75 – dreadnought style, spruce top, round soundhole, black pickguard, bound body, five-stripe rosette, mahogany back/sides/neck, 14/20-fret rosewood fingerboard with pearl dot inlays, rosewood bridge with black pins, three-per-side chrome tuners, available in Black, Black Sunburst, Blue Sunburst, Brown Sunburst, Natural, Red Sunburst, or White finish, disc. 2005.

	N/A	$130 - 160	$75 - 100	$300

MSR/NOTES	100%	EXCELLENT	AVERAGE	LAST MSR

* **AW 75 L Left-Handed** – similar to the AW 75, except in left-handed configuration, available in Natural gloss finish only, mfg. 1995-2005.

	N/A	$150 - 200	$95 - 120	$400

* **AW 75 T 12-String** – similar to the AW 75, except in 12-string configuration, available in Natural gloss finish only, mfg. 1995-2005.

	N/A	$135 - 175	$80 - 105	$330

AW 100 – dreadnought style, spruce top, round soundhole, black pickguard, bound body, three-stripe rosette, black pickguard, mahogany back/sides/neck, 14/20-fret rosewood fingerboard with pearl dot inlays, rosewood bridge with black white dot pins, three-per-side chrome tuners, available in Natural finish, mfg. 1987-1991.

	N/A	$110 - 140	$65 - 90	$275

* **AW 100 C** – similar to AW-100, except has single round cutaway, disc. 1991.

	N/A	$120 - 150	$75 - 100	$300

AW 110 N – dreadnought style, cedar top, round soundhole, black pickguard, bound body, three-stripe rosette, black pickguard, mahogany back/sides/neck, 14/20-fret rosewood fingerboard with pearl dot inlays, rosewood bridge with black white dot pins, three-per-side chrome tuners, available in Natural semi-gloss finish, mfg. 1991-99.

	N/A	$150 - 200	$95 - 125	$399

* **AW 110 C** – similar to AW 110 N, except has single rounded cutaway, mfg. 1991-2002.

	N/A	$180 - 230	$130 - 160	$469

* **AW 110 CT** – similar to AW 110 C, except in a 12-string configuration, mfg. 1991 only.

	N/A	$135 - 175	$85 - 115	$350

* **AW 110 LN** – similar to AW 110 N, except in left-handed configuration, mfg. 1996-99.

	N/A	$175 - 225	$120 - 150	$449

* **AW 110 T** – similar to AW 110 N, except in a 12-string configuration, mfg. 1996-99.

	N/A	$190 - 240	$130 - 160	$479

AW 130 S – dreadnought style, solid spruce top, round soundhole, mahogany back/sides/neck, 14/20-fret rosewood fingerboard with white dot inlays, rosewood bridge, three-per-side chrome die-cast tuners, available in Natural satin finish, mfg. 1997-2002.

	N/A	$145 - 185	$95 - 125	$350

• **Available in Natural gloss finish for an additional $20 (AW 130).**

AW 200 – dreadnought style, spruce top, round soundhole, bound body, three-stripe rosette, black pickguard, ovangkol back/sides/neck, 14/20-fret rosewood fingerboard with pearl dot inlays, rosewood bridge with white black dot pins, three-per-side chrome die-cast tuners, available in Antique Violin, Black, Brown Sunburst, or Natural finish, mfg. 1987-2002.

	N/A	$190 - 240	$130 - 160	$479

In 1993, Brown Sunburst finish was disc. In 1996, Antique Violin finish was disc.

* **AW 200 C** – similar to AW 200, except has single round cutaway, available in Black or Natural finish, mfg. 1991-2002.

	N/A	$200 - 250	$130 - 170	$499

* **AW 200 F** – similar to AW 200, except has folk-style body, disc. 1987-1993.

	N/A	$150 - 190	$95 - 120	$379

* **AW 200 L** – similar to AW 200, except in left-handed configuration, available in Natural gloss finish only, mfg. 1997-2002.

	N/A	$215 - 265	$135 - 175	$529

* **AW 200 T** – similar to AW-200, except has 12 strings, six-per-side tuners, mfg. 1987-2002.

	N/A	$235 - 285	$150 - 190	$579

AW 250 – dreadnought style, figured maple top, round soundhole, black pickguard, three-stripe bound body/rosette, flamed maple back/sides, mahogany neck, 14/20-fret rosewood fingerboard with pearl dot inlays, rosewood bridge with white black dot pins, three-per-side chrome die-cast tuners, available in Black Sunburst or Vintage Sunburst finish, mfg. 1994-96.

	N/A	$175 - 225	$120 - 150	$450

AW 300 N – dreadnought style, spruce top, round soundhole, black pickguard, three-stripe bound body/rosette, rosewood back/sides, mahogany neck, 14/20-fret rosewood fingerboard with pearl dot inlays, rosewood bridge with white black dot pins, three-per-side gold tuners, available in Black Sunburst or Natural finish, mfg. 1997-2002.

	N/A	$280 - 330	$170 - 220	$659

In 1998, the Black Sunburst finish was disc.

MSR/NOTES	100%	EXCELLENT	AVERAGE	LAST MSR

AW 310 N – dreadnought style, cedar top, round soundhole, herringbone bound body/rosette, tortoiseshell pickguard, ovangkol back/sides, mahogany neck, 14/20-fret rosewood fingerboard with pearl dot inlays, rosewood bridge with white black dot pins, three-per-side gold tuners, available in Natural semi-gloss finish, mfg. 1991-92, 1996-99.

	N/A	$280 - 330	$170 - 220	$659

In 1997, rosewood back and sides replaced original part/design.

* *AW 310 C* – similar to AW 310, except has single round cutaway and ovangkol back/sides, mfg. 1991-92.

	N/A	$150 - 200	$100 - 130	$400

* *AW 310 T* – similar to AW 310, except has 12 strings, mfg. 1991-96.

	N/A	$150 - 200	$95 - 125	$400

AW 320 T – similar to AW 310, except has 12 strings, gold hardware, mfg. 1991-96.

	N/A	$175 - 225	$120 - 150	$450

AW 330 – dreadnought style, solid spruce top, solid mahogany back and sides, mahogany neck, 14/20-fret rosewood fingerboard with dot inlay, rosewood bridge, tortoise pickguard, chrome hardware, available in Natural finish, mfg. 2004-06.

	N/A	$240 - 290	$140 - 180	$570

AW 410 – jumbo style, cedar top, round soundhole, herringbone bound body/rosette, black pickguard, ovangkol back/sides, mahogany neck, 14/20-fret rosewood fingerboard with pearl dot inlays, rosewood bridge with white black dot pins, three-per-side chrome die-cast tuners, available in Natural finish, mfg. 1991-92.

	N/A	$140 - 180	$90 - 120	$360

AW 420 N – dreadnought style, solid cedar top, round soundhole, black pickguard, three-stripe bound body, mahogany back/sides, mahogany neck, 14/20-fret bound rosewood fingerboard with pearl dot inlays, rosewood bridge with black pins, three-per-side chrome die-cast tuners, available in Natural gloss finish, mfg. 1997-2002.

	N/A	$275 - 325	$150 - 200	$669

AW 600 – dreadnought style, spruce top, round soundhole, black pickguard, three-stripe bound body/rosette, rosewood back/sides, mahogany neck, 14/20-fret bound rosewood fingerboard with pearl dot inlays, rosewood bridge with white black dot pins, rosewood veneer on bound peghead, three-per-side chrome die-cast tuners, available in Natural finish, mfg. 1987-1996.

	N/A	$190 - 240	$120 - 150	$479

In 1994, gold tuners replaced original parts/design. This model was also available with mahogany back/sides.

AW 620 – dreadnought style, solid cedar top, round soundhole, tortoiseshell pickguard, three-stripe bound body, rosewood back/sides, mahogany neck, 14/20-fret bound rosewood fingerboard with pearl dot inlays, rosewood bridge with white black dot pins, three-per-side gold tuners, available in Natural satin finish, disc. 1994.

	N/A	$200 - 250	$125 - 155	$500

AW 630 – dreadnought style, solid spruce top, round soundhole, tortoiseshell pickguard, three-stripe bound body, ovangkol back/sides, mahogany neck, 14/20-fret bound rosewood fingerboard with pearl dot inlays, rosewood bridge with white black dot pins, three-per-side gold tuners, available in Black or Natural gloss finish, mfg. 1996-2002.

	N/A	$240 - 290	$150 - 190	$550

AW 650 – similar to AW 600, except has solid spruce top, mahogany back/sides, gold tuners, mfg. 1994-96.

	N/A	$175 - 225	$120 - 150	$450

AW 700 – dreadnought style, solid spruce top, round soundhole, black pickguard, three-stripe bound body/rosette, rosewood back/sides, mahogany neck, 14/20-fret rosewood fingerboard with pearl diamond inlays, rosewood bridge with white black dot pins, rosewood veneer peghead, three-per-side gold die-cast tuners, available in Natural finish, mfg. 1991 only.

	N/A	$155 - 195	$95 - 125	$390

AW 800 – dreadnought style, solid spruce top, round soundhole, tortoiseshell pickguard, herringbone bound body/rosette, rosewood back/sides, mahogany neck, 14/20-fret rosewood fingerboard with pearl diamond inlays, rosewood bridge with white black dot pins, rosewood veneer on peghead, three-per-side gold die-cast tuners, available in Natural finish, mfg. 1992-96.

	N/A	$225 - 275	$135 - 175	$559

* *AW 800 T* – similar to AW 800, except in 12-string configuration with six-per-side tuners, mfg. 1994-96.

	N/A	$250 - 300	$150 - 200	$599

AW 830 N – dreadnought style, solid spruce top, round soundhole, tortoiseshell pickguard, herringbone bound body/rosette, rosewood back/sides, mahogany neck, 14/20-fret rosewood fingerboard with pearl diamond inlay, rosewood bridge with white black dot pins, three-per-side gold die-cast tuners, available in Natural gloss finish, mfg. 1996-2000.

	N/A	$300 - 350	$175 - 225	$699

MSR/NOTES	100%	EXCELLENT	AVERAGE	LAST MSR

* **AW 830 T 12-String** – similar to AW 830, except has 12 strings, six-per-side tuners, mfg. 1996-2000.

	N/A	$325 - 375	$200 - 250	$749

AW 920 N – dreadnought style, solid cedar top, round soundhole, tortoiseshell pickguard, abalone bound body/rosette, rosewood back/sides, mahogany neck, 14/20-fret rosewood fingerboard with pearl diamond inlays, rosewood bridge with white black dot pins, three-per-side gold tuners, available in Natural finish, mfg. 1996-99.

	N/A	$500 - 575	$325 - 375	$1,159

AW 930 N – dreadnought style, solid spruce top, round soundhole, tortoiseshell pickguard, abalone bound body/rosette, rosewood back/sides, mahogany neck, 14/20-fret rosewood fingerboard with pearl diamond inlays, rosewood bridge with white black dot pins, three-per-side gold tuners, available in Natural finish, mfg. 1996-2000.

	N/A	$525 - 600	$325 - 375	$1,199

* **AW 930 T** – similar to AW 930, except has 12 strings, six-per-side tuners, mfg. 1996-2000.

	N/A	$575 - 650	$350 - 425	$1,299

ACOUSTIC: LJ SERIES

The LJ series stands for Jumbo models. Other models included the LJ 10B, LJ 11T 12-string, LJ 15, and the LJ 16CE (cutaway, electric).

LJ 8 – jumbo style, cedar top, round soundhole, three-stripe bound body/rosette, black pickguard, bubinga back/sides, mahogany neck, 14/20-fret rosewood fingerboard with pearl dot inlays, ebonized maple bridge with white black dot pins, three-per-side chrome die-cast tuners, available in Natural finish, mfg. 1994-96.

	N/A	$225 - 275	$135 - 175	$530

ACOUSTIC: LW SERIES

LW 8 – dreadnought style, spruce top, ovangkol back/sides, available in Natural finish, mfg. 1994-96.

	N/A	$225 - 275	$135 - 175	$530

LW 10 – dreadnought style, spruce top, round soundhole, three-stripe bound body/rosette, black pickguard, mahogany back/sides/neck, 14/20-fret rosewood fingerboard with pearl dot inlays, ebonized maple bridge with white black dot pins, three-per-side chrome die-cast tuners, available in Black, Natural, Tobacco Brown, or Wine Red finish, mfg. 1984-1992.

	N/A	$230 - 280	$150 - 190	$560

* **LW 10 T** – similar to the LW 10, except in a 12-string configuration, mfg. 1991-92.

	N/A	$245 - 295	$150 - 195	$575

LW 12 – dreadnought style, cedar top, round soundhole, herringbone bound body/rosette, tortoiseshell pickguard, walnut back/sides, mahogany neck, 14/20-fret rosewood fingerboard with pearl dot inlay, ebonized maple bridge with white black dot pins, rosewood veneer on peghead, three-per-side chrome die-cast tuners, available in Black or Natural finish, mfg. 1980-1992.

	N/A	$225 - 275	$130 - 170	$540

* **LW 12 T** – similar to the LW 12, except in a 12-string configuration, mfg. 1991-92.

	N/A	$250 - 300	$135 - 175	$575

LW 14 – dreadnought style, sycamore top, round soundhole, herringbone bound body/rosette, black pickguard, walnut back/sides, mahogany neck, 14/20-fret rosewood fingerboard with pearl dot inlays, ebonized maple bridge with white black dot pins, sycamore veneer on peghead, three-per-side chrome die-cast tuners, available in Tobacco Sunburst finish, disc. 1993.

	N/A	$250 - 300	$150 - 200	$575

LW 18 – dreadnought style, spruce top, round soundhole, five-stripe bound body/rosette, rosewood back/sides, mahogany neck, 14/20-fret rosewood fingerboard with pearl dot inlays, ebonized maple bridge with white black dot pins, rosewood veneer on peghead, three-per-side chrome die-cast tuners, available in Natural finish, mfg. 1980-1993.

	N/A	$250 - 300	$140 - 180	$600

* **LW 18 T** – similar to LW-18, except has 12 strings, six-per-side tuners, mfg. 1980-1993.

	N/A	$275 - 325	$150 - 200	$640

ACOUSTIC: SW SERIES

SW 8 – dreadnought style, solid cedar top, round soundhole, tortoiseshell bound body/rosette/pickguard, mahogany back/sides/neck, 14/20-fret rosewood fingerboard with pearl dot inlays, ebonized maple bridge with white black dot pins, rosewood veneer on peghead, three-per-side chrome die-cast tuners, available in Natural finish, mfg. 1984-1993.

	N/A	$275 - 325	$150 - 200	$640

SW 8 C – similar to SW 8, except has single round cutaway, disc. 1993.

	N/A	$325 - 375	$175 - 225	$715

MSR/NOTES	100%	EXCELLENT	AVERAGE	LAST MSR

SW 8 CT – similar to SW 8, except has single round cutaway, 12 strings, six-per-side tuners, disc. 1993.

	N/A	$325 - 375	$200 - 250	$750

SW 8 T – similar to SW 8, except has 12 strings, six-per-side tuners, mfg. 1989-1993.

	N/A	$300 - 350	$175 - 225	$670

ACOUSTIC: CONCERT CLASSIC SERIES

Instruments are made in Spain to Shiro Arai's specs. All instruments in this series have classical-style bodies, round soundholes, wood inlay rosettes, mahogany necks, 12/19-fret fingerboards, tied rosewood bridges, rosewood veneered slotted pegheads, three-per-side tuners with pearloid buttons, and are available in Natural finish.

AC 25 – solid cedar top, African sapelli back/sides, rosewood fingerboard, nickel hardware, mfg. 1995-present.

MSR $1,189	$900	$500 - 600	$300 - 350	

* **AC 25CE** – similar to the AC 25, except has single cutaway and Fishman Matrix electronics, current mfg.

MSR $1,849	$1,360	$750 - 900	$425 - 500	

AC 35 – solid cedar top, African sapelli back/sides, rosewood fingerboard, gold hardware, mfg. 1995-present.

MSR $1,499	$1,200	$625 - 750	$350 - 425	

* **AC 35CE** – similar to the AC 35, except has single cutaway and Fishman Matrix electronics, current mfg.

MSR N/A	$1,200	$625 - 750	$350 - 425	

This model is currently not distributed in the U.S.

»**AC 35CEO** – similar to the AC 35 CE, except has ovangkol back and sides, current mfg.

MSR N/A	$1,280	$650 - 800	$375 - 450	

This model is currently not distributed in the U.S.

* **AC 35 A** – similar to AC 35, except has alto-style (530 mm scale), solid spruce top, single flat cutaway, disc. 1997.

	N/A	$225 - 275	$135 - 175	$495

AC 50 – solid cedar top, rosewood back/sides/fingerboard, gold hardware, mfg. 1995-present.

MSR $1,749	$1,400	$775 - 925	$450 - 525	

This model was also available with a spruce top (Model AC 50 S). Model AC 50 S was disc. in 1997.

* **AC 50CE** – similar to the AC 50, except has single cutaway and Fishman Matrix electronics, current mfg.

MSR $2,399	$1,920	$1,000 - 1,250	$625 - 750	

* **AC 50 A** – similar to AC 50, except has alto (530mm scale) style, single flat cutaway, disc. 1997, reintroduced 2001-present.

MSR $1,599	$1,280	$725 - 850	$400 - 475	

This model had an optional solid spruce top.

AC 75 CB – contra bass (750 mm scale) style, solid cedar top, African sapelli back/sides, rosewood fingerboard, gold hardware, disc. 1997, reintroduced 2001-present.

MSR $2,899	$2,320	$1,200 - 1,500	$750 - 900	

* **AC 75 B** – similar to AC 75 CB, except in bass (700 mm scale) style, disc. 1997, reintroduced 2001-present.

MSR $2,899	$2,320	$1,200 - 1,500	$750 - 900	

AC 80 – solid spruce top, rosewood back/sides, ebony fingerboard, gold hardware, mfg. 1995-present.

MSR $2,499	$2,000	$1,050 - 1,300	$725 - 850	

* **AC 80CE** – similar to AC 80, except has single cutaway and Fishman Matrix electronics, current mfg.

MSR N/A	$2,100	$1,150 - 1,400	$650 - 800	

This model is currently not distributed in the U.S.

AC 85 A – single flat cutaway alto (530 mm scale) style, solid spruce top, rosewood back/sides, ebony fingerboard, gold hardware, disc. 1997, reintroduced 2001-present.

MSR N/A	$1,750	$900 - 1,100	$550 - 650	

This model is currently not distributed in the U.S.

AC 90 CB – contra bass (750 mm scale) style, solid spruce top, rosewood back/sides, ebony fingerboard, gold hardware, disc.

	N/A	$550 - 650	$350 - 425	$1,255

MSR/NOTES	100%	EXCELLENT	AVERAGE	LAST MSR

AC 90 B – similar to AC 90 CB, except has bass (700 mm scale) style, disc.

	N/A	$550 - 650	$350 - 425	$1,255

AC 150 – handcrafted, traditional Spanish construction, solid spruce or solid red cedar top, solid rosewood sides and back, ebony fingerboard, rosewood bridge, gold hardware, wood purfling, mfg. 2003-present.

MSR N/A	$2,250	$1,200 - 1,500	$675 - 800	

This model is currently not distributed in the U.S.

AC 200 – handcrafted, traditional Spanish construction, solid spruce top, solid rosewood sides and back, ebony fingerboard, rosewood bridge, gold hardware, wood purfling, current mfg.

MSR N/A	$2,600	$1,400 - 1,700	$800 - 925	

This model is currently not distributed in the U.S.

AC 300 – handcrafted, traditional Spanish construction, solid spruce top, solid rosewood sides and back, ebony fingerboard, rosewood bridge, gold hardware, wood purfling, mfg. 2001-present.

MSR N/A	$3,500	$1,800 - 2,200	N/A	

This model is currently not distributed in the U.S.

ACOUSTIC: FLAMENCO SERIES

AC 65FCE – Flamenco guitar, single cutaway, solid spruce top, sycamore back and sides, rosewood fingerboard, 75 mm body depth, mfg. 2001 only.

	N/A	$375 - 450	$225 - 275	$875

AC 70F – Flamenco guitar, traditional Spanish construction, solid spruce top, sycamore back and sides, rosewood fingerboard, 650 mm scale, mfg. 2000-05.

	N/A	$650 - 800	$375 - 450	$1,599

This model was not distributed in the U.S.

AC 70FCE – similar to the AC 70F, except has a single cutaway with onboard pickup and Fishman PRO electronics, mfg. 2001-present.

MSR $2,299	$1,840	$1,000 - 1,200	$625 - 750	

This model is currently not distributed in the U.S.

AC 100F – Flamenco guitar, traditional Spanish construction, solid spruce top, solid cyprus back and sides, ebony fingerboard, 650 mm scale, mfg. 2000-present.

MSR N/A	$1,275	$650 - 800	$375 - 450	

This model is currently not distributed in the U.S.

AC 150F – Flamenco guitar, traditional Spanish construction, solid spruce top, solid cyprus back and sides, ebony fingerboard, 650 mm scale, mfg. 2001-present.

MSR $3,369	$2,700	$1,400 - 1,750	$850 - 1,000	

ACOUSTIC: PEPE SERIES

The Pepe Series models are made in Spain. All instruments in this series have a classical-style body, solid cedar top, round soundhole, wood inlay rosette, African sapelli back/sides, mahogany neck, 12/19-fret rosewood fingerboard, tied rosewood bridge, rosewood veneered slotted peghead, three-per-side gold tuners with pearloid buttons, and are available in Natural finish, mfg. 1995-current. These models are currently not distributed in the U.S.

PS 48 – 480 mm scale.

MSR N/A	$550	$300 - 350	$175 - 225	

PS 53 – 530 mm scale.

MSR N/A	$550	$300 - 350	$175 - 225	

PS 58 – 580 mm scale.

MSR N/A	$550	$300 - 350	$175 - 225	

ACOUSTIC: SANDPIPER SERIES

SANDPIPER ASP-30 – folk-style body, spruce top, mahogany back and sides, round soundhole with multi-ring rosette, multi-ply body binding, mahogany neck, 14/20-fret bound rosewood fingerboard with offset dots and 12th fret design inlays, three-per-side chrome tuners, rosewood bridge, available in Natural finish, current mfg.

MSR N/A	$225	$120 - 150	$70 - 95	

This model is currently not distributed in the U.S.

MSR/NOTES	100%	EXCELLENT	AVERAGE	LAST MSR

SANDPIPER ASP-75 – folk-style body, spruce top, solid mahogany back and sides, mahogany neck, 14/21-fret rosewood fingerboard, round soundhole, rosewood bridge, three-per-side chrome tuners, available in Black or Natural finish, current mfg.

MSR N/A	$210	$120 - 150	$70 - 95	

This model is currently not distributed in the U.S.

SANDPIPER ASP-100 CE – folk-style single cutaway body, solid cedar top, rosewood back and sides, mahogany neck, 14/21-fret rosewood fingerboard, round soundhole, rosewood bridge, three-per-side chrome tuners, X-TN electronics, available in Natural finish, mfg. 2004-present.

MSR N/A	$425	$225 - 275	$120 - 150	

This model is currently not distributed in the U.S.

SANDPIPER ASP-130 – folk-style body, solid spruce top, solid mahogany back and sides, mahogany neck, 14/21-fret rosewood fingerboard, round soundhole, rosewood bridge, three-per-side chrome tuners, available in Natural finish, disc. 2005.

	N/A	$175 - 225	$110 - 140	$450

* *Sandpiper ASP-130T 12-String* – similar to the ASP-130, except in 12-string configuration and six-per-side tuners, disc. 2005.

	N/A	$200 - 250	$120 - 150	$495

SANDPIPER ASP-330 – folk-style body, solid Englemann spruce top, rosewood back and sides, mahogany neck, 14/21-fret rosewood fingerboard, round soundhole, rosewood bridge, three-per-side chrome tuners, available in Natural finish, disc. 2005.

	N/A	$225 - 275	$135 - 175	$550

SANDPIPER ASP-930 – folk-style body, solid spruce top, solid mahogany back and sides, mahogany neck, 14/21-fret rosewood fingerboard, round soundhole, rosewood bridge, three-per-side gold tuners, available in Natural finish, disc. 2005.

	N/A	$275 - 325	$175 - 225	$650

ACOUSTIC ELECTRIC: AMB SERIES

AMB-35 – Fiber Capsule backed single cutaway body, round soundhole with elaborate design, flamed maple top, ABS fiber back and sides, mahogany neck, 14/20-fret rosewood fingerboard with diamond inlays, three-per-side chrome tuners, rosewood bridge, PZP-3 pickup, volume and tone controls, available in Black Shade, Blue Shade, Brown Sunburst, Green Shade, Natural, or Red Shade finish, disc. 2005.

	N/A	$120 - 150	$70 - 95	$295

AMB-40 – similar to the AMB-35, except has an active four-band EQ-7545, disc. 2005.

	N/A	$150 - 200	$95 - 120	$395

AMB-70 – Fiber Capsule backed single cutaway body, round soundhole with elaborate design, quilted maple top, ABS fiber back and sides, mahogany neck, 14/20-fret rosewood fingerboard with pearl dot inlays, three-per-side gold tuners, rosewood bridge, Fishman Sonicore pickup, Fishman SC Deluxe four-band EQ, available in Black Shade, Blue Shade, Brown Sunburst, Green Shade, Natural, or Red Shade finish, disc. 2005.

	N/A	$200 - 250	$120 - 150	$495

ACOUSTIC ELECTRIC: ELECORD SERIES

Elecord series guitars feature Fishman Matrix pickups and electronics, and a single rounded cutaway.

FET 01 – single rounded cutaway large body, spruce top, oval soundhole, bound body, soundhole rosette, daowood back/sides, mahogany neck, 22-fret bound rosewood fingerboard with pearl snowflake inlay, rosewood bridge with white black dot pins, bound peghead, three-per-side gold tuners, Fishman Matrix pickup, four-band EQ, available in Black, Blue Shade, or Natural finish, mfg. 1996-99.

	N/A	$350 - 400	$225 - 275	$789

In 1997, Blue Shade finish was disc.

FET 02 – single rounded cutaway small body, spruce top, oval soundhole, bound body, soundhole rosette, daowood back/sides, mahogany neck, 22-fret bound rosewood fingerboard with pearl snowflake inlays, rosewood bridge with white black dot pins, bound peghead, three-per-side gold tuners, Fishman Matrix pickup, four-band EQ, available in Black, Blue Shade (1996-97), Natural, See-Through Blue (1997-99), Vintage Sunburst (1996-97), or Violin Sunburst (1997-99) finish, mfg. 1996-99.

	N/A	$350 - 400	$225 - 275	$789

FET 03 – similar to the FET 02, except has a silky oak top/back/sides, available in Amber, Blue Shade (1996-97), or See-Through Black (1996-97) finish, mfg. 1996-99.

	N/A	$350 - 425	$225 - 275	$859

FET 85 C – single sharp cutaway jumbo style, arched spruce top, oval soundhole, five-stripe bound body/rosette, chestnut back/sides, mahogany neck, 21-fret bound rosewood fingerboard with pearl diamond inlays, rosewood bridge with black pearl dot pins and pearl diamond inlay, bound peghead with chestnut veneer, three-per-side gold die cast tuners, piezo pickup, three-band EQ, available in Amber Natural or Antique Sunburst finish, mfg. 1991-92.

	N/A	$600 - 700	$375 - 450	$1,400

This model had an optional rosewood back/sides (Model FET 85R).

MSR/NOTES	100%	EXCELLENT	AVERAGE	LAST MSR

FET 100 – cutaway jumbo style, arched chestnut/spruce laminated top, oval soundhole, three-stripe bound body and rosette, chestnut arched back/sides, maple neck, 21-fret bound ebony fingerboard with abalone/pearl split block inlays, rosewood bridge with white pearl dot pins and pearl diamond inlay, bound peghead, three-per-side gold die-cast tuners, piezo pickup, three-band EQ, available in Amber Natural, Blue Shade, or Red Shade finish, mfg. 1991-92.

| | N/A | $650 - 750 | $400 - 475 | $1,500 |

FET 500 (FET SPL) – round cutaway jumbo style, spruce top, oval soundhole, five-stripe bound body and rosette, mahogany arched back/sides/neck, 21-fret rosewood bound fingerboard with pearl dot inlays, rosewood bridge with white pearl dot pins, bound peghead, three-per-side die cast tuners, piezo pickup, volume/tone control, available in Antique Sunburst, Black Sunburst, or Trans. Red finish, mfg. 1991-92, reintroduced 2003-05.

| | N/A | $150 - 200 | $95 - 120 | $350 |

FET 600 (FET DLX) – cutaway jumbo style, arched sycamore top, oval soundhole, five-stripe bound body and rosette, sycamore arched back/sides, mahogany neck, 21-fret bound rosewood fingerboard with pearl diamond inlays, rosewood bridge with white pearl dot pins, bound peghead, three-per-side die-cast tuners, piezo pickup, three-band EQ, available in Amber Natural or Antique Sunburst finish, mfg. 1989-1994.

| | N/A | $350 - 400 | $175 - 225 | $765 |

* **FET 600/12 12-String** – similar to the FET 600, except in a 12-string configuration, mfg. 1991-92.

| | N/A | $350 - 425 | $200 - 250 | $765 |

FET-CTS – single smooth cutaway, quilted maple Gravure grain arched top, mahogany arched back, oval soundhole, B/N/H binding, mahogany neck, 14/22-fret rosewood fingerboard with dot inlays, rosewood bridge, Fishman pickup and electronics, chrome hardware, available in Black Shade, Blue Shade, or Natural finish, mfg. 2004-05.

| | N/A | $300 - 350 | $175 - 225 | $660 |

FET-STD – Elecord small body with spruce top and mahogany back and sides, mahogany neck with rosewood fingerboard, chrome-plated hardware, 22 frets, Fishman System-one pickup, volume control and two-band EQ, available in Black, Brown Sunburst, See-Through Blue, or See-Through Red finish, current mfg.

| MSR $780 | $625 | $325 - 400 | $200 - 250 | |

* **FET-STD-T 12-String** – similar to the FET-STD, except in twelve-string configuration and six-per-side tuners, current mfg.

| MSR N/A | $425 | $250 - 300 | $135 - 175 | |

This model is currently not distributed in the U.S.

* **FET-SPT** – same as FET-STD, except has a Piezo PZP-CG pickup and AEQ-5 four-band EQ, disc. 2005.

| | N/A | $100 - 130 | $60 - 80 | $260 |

FET-DLX – Elecord small body with a flamed maple top, mahogany back, sides, and neck, 22-fret rosewood fingerboard, chrome plated hardware. Fishman System 1 pickup, volume control and two-band EQ, available in See-Through Blue or See-Through Red finish, disc. 2005.

| | N/A | $250 - 300 | $150 - 200 | $595 |

CE-STD – classical body with spruce top and mahogany back and sides, mahogany neck with rosewood fingerboard, gold hardware, 22 frets, Fishman Matrix pickup, volume control and four-band EQ, available in Natural finish, disc. 2005.

| | N/A | $200 - 250 | $120 - 150 | $500 |

ACOUSTIC ELECTRIC: SANDPIPER SERIES

The Sandpiper Series was introduced in 1998. Models feature solid spruce tops, arched backs, fine ornamentation, and Fishman electronics.

SANDPIPER SP-1 (SP-CST) – folk style, single rounded cutaway body, solid spruce top, round soundhole, pearl rosette, pearl/ivory body binding, rosewood back/sides, mahogany neck, 21-fret rosewood ebony with pearl inlays, rosewood bridge with black pins, three-per-side gold tuners, Fishman Matrix Pro pickup, volume/brilliance/three-band EQ, phase switch, available in Natural finish, mfg. 1998-99, 2001-present.

| MSR N/A | $3,600 | $1,800 - 2,250 | $1,050 - 1,250 | |

This model is currently not distributed in the U.S.

SANDPIPER SP-2 – similar to the Sandpiper SP-1, except features inset soundhole mosaic, rosewood fingerboard, PZP-6 piezo pickup, volume/mid contour/three-band EQ, PR-500 electronics, available in Natural finish, mfg. 1998-99.

| | N/A | $950 - 1,100 | $650 - 750 | $1,999 |

* **SANDPIPER SP-3** – similar to the Sandpiper SP-1, except features rosewood fingerboard, Fishman pickup, volume/mid contour/three-band EQ, available in Natural finish, mfg. 1998-99.

| | N/A | $825 - 950 | $500 - 600 | $1,779 |

SANDPIPER SP-4 – similar to the Sandpiper SP-1, except features pau ferro back/sides, rosewood fingerboard, Fishman pickup, volume/mid contour/three-band EQ, available in Blue Sunburst, Natural, or Sunburst finish, mfg. 1998-1999, 2001-02.

| | N/A | $700 - 800 | $450 - 525 | $1,460 |

MSR/NOTES	100%	EXCELLENT	AVERAGE	LAST MSR

SANDPIPER SP STD – folk style, single rounded cutaway body, solid spruce top, round soundhole, pearl rosette, pearl/ivory body binding, mahogany back/sides/neck, 21-fret rosewood fingerboard with pearl inlays, rosewood bridge with black pins, three-per-side gold tuners, Fishman Sonicore pickup, four-band EQ, phase switch, available in Natural finish, current mfg.

MSR $1,050	$850	$450 - 525	$250 - 300	

* *Sandpiper SP STD-T 12-String* – similar to the SP STD, except in 12-string configuration and six-per-side tuners, current mfg.

MSR N/A	$525	$325 - 375	$200 - 250	

This model is currently not distributed in the U.S.

ACOUSTIC ELECTRIC: MISC. MODELS

AW 73 CE – dreadnought style, single cutaway, spruce top, round soundhole, black pickguard, bound body, five-stripe rosette, mahogany back/sides/neck, 14/20-fret rosewood fingerboard with white dot inlays, rosewood bridge, three-per-side nickel tuners, piezo pickups, volume/tone controls, available in Black or Natural finish, mfg. 1996-99.

	N/A	$175 - 225	$120 - 150	$449

AW 200 E – dreadnought style, spruce top, round soundhole, bound body, three-stripe rosette, black pickguard, ovangkol back/sides/neck, 14/20-fret rosewood fingerboard with pearl dot inlays, rosewood bridge with white black dot pins, three-per-side chrome die-cast tuners, piezo pickup, and three-band EQ, available in Black or Natural finish, mfg. 1987-2000.

	N/A	$240 - 290	$150 - 190	$579

* *AW 200 CE* – similar to AW 200 E, except has single round cutaway, piezo pickup, three-band EQ, mfg. 1991-2000.

	N/A	$275 - 325	$175 - 225	$649

* *AW 200 CTE* – similar to AW-200 CE, except has 12 strings, six-per-side tuners, piezo pickup, three-band EQ, available in Natural finish only, disc. 2000.

	N/A	$300 - 350	$175 - 225	$699

AW 310 CE – dreadnought style, single round cutaway, cedar top, round soundhole, herringbone bound body/rosette, ovangkol back/sides, mahogany neck, 14/20-fret rosewood fingerboard with pearl dot inlay, rosewood bridge with white black dot pins, three-per-side chrome die-cast tuners, piezo pickup, three-band EQ, available in Natural finish, mfg. 1991-92.

	N/A	$185 - 235	$125 - 155	$470

CES 50 – single round cutaway classic style, spruce top, bound body, wooden inlay rosette, mahogany body/neck, 22-fret extended rosewood fingerboard, rosewood bridge, three-per-side gold tuners, piezo pickups, volume/tone control, available in Black, Natural, or White finish, mfg. 1992-94.

	N/A	$250 - 300	$155 - 195	$600

This model is a solidbody with a routed out soundhole and installed plastic dish for resonance.

CE 40 N – deep nylon string single round cutaway classical style, spruce top, round soundhole, mahogany neck, bound body, rosewood back/sides/neck, 19-fret rosewood fingerboard/bridge, three-per-side gold tuners, Fishman Matrix pickup with four-band EQ, available in Natural finish, mfg. 1996-99.

	N/A	$325 - 375	$175 - 225	$749

The CE 40 N has a body depth of 100 mm (3.9 inches).

CE 42 N – similar to the CE 40 N, except has a shallow body depth, mfg. 1996-99.

	N/A	$325 - 375	$175 - 225	$749

The CE 42 N has a body depth of 75 mm (2.9 inches).

3 MBA 09 – single cutaway design, molded back, spruce top, volume and tone controls, chrome hardware, PZP - 3 pickup, available in Black, See-Through Black, or See-Through Blue finish, disc. 2000.

	N/A	$130 - 160	$80 - 110	$319

3 MBA 11 – single cutaway design, molded back, spruce top, mahogany neck with rosewood fingerboard, chrome plated hardware, PZP-5 pickup and three-band EQ, available in Black, Natural, See-Through Blue, or Three-Tone Sunburst finish, disc. 2000.

	N/A	$140 - 180	$90 - 120	$369

3 MBA 21 – single cutaway design, molded back, spruce top, mahogany neck with rosewood fingerboard, chrome-plated hardware. Fishman OEM/MAT pickup and Fishman four-band EQ, available in Black, Natural, See-Through Blue, or Three-Tone Sunburst finish, disc. 2000.

	N/A	$210 - 260	$130 - 170	$529

3 MBA 31 FM – single cutaway design, molded back, Flamed Maple top, mahogany neck with rosewood fingerboard, gold-plated hardware, Fishman OEM/MAT pickup and Fishman four-band EQ, available in Amber Natural, See-Through Black, See-Through Blue, or See-Through Red finish, disc. 2000.

	N/A	$230 - 280	$140 - 180	$579

MSR/NOTES	**100%**	**EXCELLENT**	**AVERAGE**	**LAST MSR**

CE 60 – single round cutaway classic style, spruce top, round soundhole, bound body, wooden inlay rosette, mahogany back/sides/neck, 19-fret rosewood fingerboard/bridge, rosewood veneer on peghead, three-per-side gold tuners, piezo pickups with three-band EQ, available in Natural finish, mfg. 1991-94.

	N/A	$300 - 350	$180 - 230	$700

* ***CE 60 S*** – similar to CE 60, except has 22-fret extended fingerboard with pearl dot inlays, steel strings with white black dot bridge pins, disc. 1994.

	N/A	$300 - 350	$180 - 230	$700

* ***CE 60/14*** – similar to CE 60, except has 22-fret extended fingerboard, disc. 1994.

	N/A	$300 - 350	$180 - 230	$700

FEA 10 – single round cutaway dreadnought style, cedar top, round soundhole, bound body, wooden inlay rosette, mahogany back/sides/neck, 22-fret rosewood fingerboard with pearl dot inlays, rosewood bridge with black pearl dot pins, three-per-side die-cast tuners, piezo pickup, three-band EQ, available in Natural or Walnut finish, mfg. 1992-95.

	N/A	$375 - 450	$225 - 275	$900

FEA 15 – similar to FEA 10, except has a spruce top, available in Brown Sunburst, Natural, or Trans. Black finish, mfg. 1992-93.

	N/A	$400 - 475	$275 - 325	$950

FEA 16 N – single round cutaway dreadnought style, figured sycamore top, round soundhole, bound body, wooden inlay rosette, mahogany back/sides/neck, 22-fret rosewood fingerboard with pearl dot inlays, rosewood bridge with black pearl dot pins, three-per-side die-cast tuners, piezo pickup, three-band EQ, available in Natural finish, mfg. 1994 only.

	N/A	$450 - 525	$250 - 300	$1,050

FEA 20 – single round cutaway dreadnought style, sycamore top, round soundhole, bound body, abalone designed rosette, sycamore back/sides, mahogany neck, 22-fret bound rosewood fingerboard with pearl dot inlays, rosewood bridge with black pearl dot pins, three-per-side gold die-cast tuners, piezo pickup, three-band EQ, available in See-Through Black or See-Through Blue finish, mfg. 1991-96.

	N/A	$550 - 650	$300 - 350	$1,300

ACOUSTIC ELECTRIC BASS

AMB-50B – single rounded cutaway body, spruce top, round soundhole, bound body, ABS fiber back/sides, mahogany neck, 22-fret bound rosewood fingerboard with pearl dot inlays, rosewood bridge, bound peghead, two-per-side chrome tuners, PZP-3 Piezo, AEQ-41 Active four-band EQ, available in Black Shade, Blue Shade, Brown Sunburst, Natural, or Red Shade finish, mfg. 1996-2005.

	N/A	$150 - 200	$95 - 120	$395

FEB-SPL – single rounded cutaway body, spruce top, oval soundhole, bound body, mahogany back/sides, maple neck, 24-fret bound rosewood fingerboard with pearl dot inlays, string through rosewood bridge, bound peghead, two-per-side chrome tuners, Fishman Sonicore pickup, four-band EQ, available in Black, Black Shade, or Natural finish, mfg. 1996-2002.

	N/A	$350 - 400	$200 - 250	$790

FEB DLX – single round cutaway dreadnought style, arched flame maple top, f-holes, multi-bound body, figured maple back/sides/neck, 21-fret rosewood fingerboard with pearl snowflake inlays, string-through rosewood bridge, flame maple peghead veneer with pearl flower/logo inlay, two-per-side gold tuners, piezo bridge pickup, four-band EQ, available in Brown Sunburst, Natural, or Violin Sunburst finish, mfg. 1994-97 and 1999.

	N/A	$375 - 450	$200 - 250	$859

FEB-STD – single cutaway body, spruce top, mahogany back and sides, mahogany neck, 24-fret rosewood fingerboard with dot inlay, rosewood bridge, piezo pickup, four-band EQ, chrome hardware, available in Black, Black Shade, Blue Shade, Brown Sunburst, Natural, or Red Shade finish, mfg. 1994-96, 2004-present.

MSR $500	$400	$225 - 275	$120 - 150	

SANDPIPER BASS SPB 04 – single rounded cutaway body, solid spruce top, round soundhole, ivory body binding, ivory rosette, rosewood back/sides, maple neck, 24-fret ebony fingerboard with pearl inlays, rosewood bridge with black pins, two-per-side gold tuners, Fishman pickup, volume/three-band EQ, available in Natural finish, mfg. 1998-2002.

	N/A	$1,050 - 1,200	$725 - 850	$2,200

* ***Sandpiper Bass SPB 05 5-String*** – similar to the Sandpiper Bass SPB 04, except in five-string configuration, 3/2-per-side tuners, available in Natural finish, mfg. 1998-2000.

	N/A	$1,200 - 1,350	$825 - 975	$2,500

» ***Sandpiper Bass SPB 05 FL 5-String Fretless*** – similar to the Sandpiper SPB 05 Five-String, except in fretless configuration, available in Natural finish, mfg. 1998-2000.

	N/A	$1,200 - 1,350	$850 - 975	$2,500

* ***Sandpiper Bass SPB 06 6-String*** – similar to the Sandpiper Bass SPB 04, except in six-string configuration, three-per-side tuners, available in Natural finish, mfg. 1998-2000.

	N/A	$1,250 - 1,400	$850 - 975	$2,600

MSR/NOTES	100%	EXCELLENT	AVERAGE	LAST MSR

ARIANA

Instruments currently built in Asia.

Ariana is the budget line of Aria, which is one of the trademarks of the Aria Company of Japan. These guitars are generally low quality and meant for the student or entry-level guitar player. Most guitars retail for around $100 and sell for considerably less.

ARIRANG

Instruments previously built in Korea during the early 1980s.

This trademark consists of entry-level copies of American designs, and some original designs. Source: Tony Bacon and Paul Day, *The Guru's Guitar Guide*.

ARISTONE

See Framus & Besson. Instruments previously built in West Germany during the late 1950s through the early 1960s.

While Aristone was the brand name for a UK importer, these guitars were made by and identical to certain Framus models. Research also indicates that the trademark Besson was utilized as well. Source: Tony Bacon and Paul Day, *The Guru's Guitar Guide*.

ARITA

Instruments previously manufactured in Japan.

Arita instruments were distributed in the U.S. market by the Newark Musical Merchandise Company of Newark, NJ. Source: Michael Wright, *Guitar Stories*, Volume One.

ARMSTRONG, ROB

Instruments currently produced in Coventry, England since 1971.

Luthier Rob Armstrong is known for his custom guitar building. He makes custom flattop guitars, mandolins, parlor guitars, and other instruments. One of his more famous jobs appears to be a Kellogg's Corn Flakes box-turned-guitar for Simon Nicol (Fairport Convention). Source: Tony Bacon, *The Ultimate Guitar Book*.

ARMY & NAVY SPECIAL

Instruments previously produced by Gibson during the late 1910s. See chapter on House Brands.

This trademark has been identified as a Gibson-built budget line available only at military post exchanges (PXs) toward the end of World War I (1918). They will have a label different from the standard Gibson label of the time, yet still be credited to the Gibson Mandolin - Guitar Co. of Kalamazoo, MI, USA. As a Gibson-built, budget line instrument, these guitars do not possess an adjustable truss rod in the neck, and by now we all know what that means to its value. Source: Walter Carter, *Gibson: 100 Years of an American Icon*.

ART & LUTHERIE

Instruments currently produced in La Patrie, Canada. Distributed by Godin Guitars in Baie D'Urfe Quebec, Canada.

CONTACT INFORMATION
ART & LUTHERIE
A Division of Godin Guitars
19420 Clark Graham Ave.
Baie d'Urfe, Quebec H9X 3R8 Canada
Phone No.: 514-457-7977
Fax No.: 514-457-5774
www.artandlutherieguitars.com

Art & Lutherie models are an affordable line of acoustic guitars by Godin Guitars that complements their higher end models from Godin and Simon & Patrick. Lead by Guitar Luthier Daniel Gervais, Art & Lutherie produces guitars built with Canadian tonewoods such as wild cherry, maple, and walnut (gives those trees from the rain forest a little breathing room!).

In 2000, Art & Lutherie underwent a model number change where all models were changed to a five-number designation from a four-number designation. All efforts have been made to update these changes. For more information, visit Art & Lutherie's website or contact Godin Guitars directly.

ACOUSTIC: DREADNOUGHT & FOLK MODELS

ART & LUTHERIE DREADNOUGHT – three-ply wild cherry laminated top, wild cherry back/sides, round soundhole, big leaf maple neck, walnut fingerboard with a white dot inlay, solid headstock, three-per-side chrome tuners, black pickguard, and walnut bridge with white bridgepins, available in Almond Brown (disc. 2011, 8568/14620/014620), Antique Burst (8582/14644/014309), Black (8605/14668/013876), Burgundy (2007-present, 013982), Chestnut Brown (disc. 8629/14682), Sunrise (2000-present, 15931/016778), Trans. Blue/Blue (9190/14729/013890), or Trans. Red (disc., 9176/14705) satin lacquer finish or Antique Burst (2006-2011, 028474) or Trans. Red/Burgundy (2006-2011, 028498) Gloss Top finish, current mfg.

MSR $419	$350	$190 - 240	$110 - 140	

- **Subtract 5% (Last MSR was $399) for Almond Brown finish (disc. 2011).**
- **Add 5% (Last MSR was $435) for a Natural Cedar top (disc. 2011, 0180/14866/014866).**
- **Add 10% (Last MSR was $439) for a Natural Spruce top (2000-2011, 13043/013043).**
- **Add 15% (Last MSR was $455) for a Gloss Top finish (disc. 2011).**
- **Add 35% (Last MSR was $565) for a Natural Spruce top with a high gloss finish (disc. 2011, 031115).**

MSR/NOTES	100%	EXCELLENT	AVERAGE	LAST MSR

* **Art & Lutherie Dreadnought Electric** – similar to the Art & Lutherie Dreadnought, except has Quantum I or EPM EQ (disc.) electronics, available in Almond Brown (8575/14637/023271), Antique Burst (disc. 2011, 8599/14651/023608), Black (8612/14675/023622), Burgundy (2007-present, 023646), Chestnut Brown (disc., 8636/14699), Sunrise (2000-present, 15948/023615), Trans. Blue/Blue (9206/14736/023653), or Trans. Red (disc., 9183/14712) satin lacquer finish, or Antique Burst (2006-2011, 028481) or Trans. Red/Burgundy (2006-2011, 028504) Gloss Top finish, current mfg.

| MSR $545 | $450 | $250 - 300 | $150 - 190 | |

- Subtract 5% (Last MSR was $525) for Almond Brown finish (disc. 2011).
- Add 5% (Last MSR was $565) for a Natural Cedar top (disc. 2011, 0197/14613/024896).
- Add 7.5% (Last MSR was $579) for a Natural Spruce top (2000-2011, 13050/024902).
- Add 12.5% (Last MSR was $605) for a Gloss Top finish (disc. 2011).
- Add 27.5% (Last MSR was $691) for a Natural Spruce top with a high gloss finish (disc. 2011, 031122).

* **Art & Lutherie Dreadnought Left-Hand** – similar to the Art & Lutherie Dreadnought, except in left-handed configuration, available in Almond Brown (laminated top, disc.) or Antique Burst (solid cedar top, 026364) finish, current mfg.

| MSR $455 | $380 | $200 - 250 | $120 - 150 | |

- Subtract 10% (disc. 2007, last MSR was $309) for Almond finish.
- Add 27.5% (MSR $579) for Quantum I electronics (026371).
- Add 40% for EPM EQ electronics.

* **Art & Lutherie Dreadnought 12-String** – similar to the Art & Lutherie Dreadnought, except in 12-string configuration with six-per-side tuners, available in Antique Burst finish (026548), current mfg.

| MSR $545 | $450 | $250 - 300 | $150 - 190 | |

- Add 22.5% (MSR $669) for Quantum I electronics (026555).

ART & LUTHERIE CUTAWAY – similar to the Art & Lutherie model, except features a single sloped shoulder cutaway body, available in Almond Brown (disc., 9213/14743), Antique Burst (9237/14767/014361), Black (9251/14781/014385), Burgundy (2007-present, 014415), Chestnut Brown (disc., 9275/14804), Natural Cedar (026524), Sunrise (017515), Trans. Blue (9312/14842/014422), or Trans. Red (disc., 9299/14828) satin lacquer finish, disc. 2011.

| | $400 | $215 - 265 | $130 - 160 | $479 |

- Add 5% (Last MSR was $505) for a Natural Cedar top.

* **Art & Lutherie Cutaway Electric** – similar to the Art & Lutherie Cutaway, except has EPM (disc.) or Quantum I electronics, available in Almond Brown (disc., 9220/14750), Antique Burst (9244/14774/023677), Black (9268/14798/023684), Burgundy (2007-present, 023707), Chestnut Brown (disc., 9282/14811), Natural Cedar (disc. 2011, 026531), Sunrise (023721), Trans. Blue/Blue (disc. 2011, 9329/14859/023714), or Trans. Red (disc. 2011, 9305/14835) satin lacquer finish, current mfg.

| MSR $605 | $500 | $275 - 325 | $150 - 200 | |

- Add 5% (Last MSR was $629) for a Natural Cedar top (disc. 2011).

ART & LUTHERIE FOLK – folk body style, solid cedar top, wild cherry back and sides, Silver Leaf maple neck, rosewood fingerboard, rosewood bridge, available in Almond Brown (032921), Antique Burst (032945), Black (032969), Burgundy (032983), Sunrise (disc.), Trans. Blue (disc.), or Trans. Red (disc.) finish, current mfg.

| MSR $419 | $350 | $190 - 240 | $110 - 140 | |

- Subtract 5% (MSR $399) for Almond Brown finish (laminate top).

* **Art & Lutherie Folk Cutaway** – similar to the Art & Lutherie Folk, except has a single cutaway, available in Antique Burst finish (033027), disc. 2011.

| | $400 | $215 - 265 | $130 - 160 | $479 |

- Add 27.5% (MSR $579) for Quantum I electronics (033034).

»**Art & Lutherie Folk Cutaway Electric** – similar to the Art & Lutherie Folk Cutaway, except has Quantum I electronics, available in Antique Burst finish (033034), current mfg.

| MSR $605 | $500 | $275 - 325 | $150 - 200 | |

* **Art & Lutherie Folk Electric** – similar to the Art & Lutherie Folk, except has Quantum I electronics, available in Almond Brown (032938), Antique Burst (032952), Black (032976), Burgundy (032990), Sunrise (disc.), Trans. Blue/Blue (disc.), or Trans. Red (disc.) satin lacquer finish, current mfg.

| MSR $545 | $450 | $250 - 300 | $150 - 190 | |

- Subtract 2.5% (MSR $525) for Almond Brown finish (laminate top).

* **Art & Lutherie Folk Left-Handed** – similar to the Art & Lutherie Folk, except in left-handed configuration, available in Almond Brown (disc.) or Antique Burst finish (033003), current mfg.

| MSR $455 | $380 | $200 - 250 | $120 - 150 | |

- Subtract 10% for Almond Brown finish (laminate top, disc.).
- Add 32.5% (MSR $579) for Quantum I electronics (033010).

MSR/NOTES	100%	EXCELLENT	AVERAGE	LAST MSR

ACOUSTIC: AMI MODELS

Drawing inspiration from those turn-of-the-century parlor guitars, Art & Lutherie also offers the **Ami** model. This model has full-scale fingerboard yet scaled-down body size designed with children in mind.

AMI NYLON STRING – three-ply laminated wild cherry top, wild cherry back/sides, round soundhole, maple neck, walnut fingerboard, classical style tied walnut bridge, slotted headstock, three-per-side tuners, available in Almond Brown lacquer finish (8704/14583/023257), mfg. 1998-present.

MSR $419	$350	$190 - 240	$110 - 140	

- **Add 45% for EPM electronics (disc., 11230/14590).**
- **Add 30% (MSR $545) for Quantum I electronics (2011-present, 023264)**

* *Ami Nylon String Cedar Top* – similar to the Ami Nylon String model, except features a solid cedar top, available in Natural lacquer finish (14606), mfg. 1998-2004.

	N/A	$170 - 220	$110 - 140	$249

- **Add 45% for EPM EQ electronic pickup (14613).**

AMI STEEL STRING – similar to the Ami Nylon String, except features a solid headstock, walnut bridge with white bridgepins, chrome tuners, available in Almond Brown (disc. 2011, 8643/14460/023097), Antique Burst (8667/14507/023509), Black (9404/14569/023561), Burgundy (2007-present, 023523), Chestnut Brown (disc., 8681/14484), Trans. Blue (disc. 2011, 9152/14545/023547), or Trans. Red (disc., 9138/14521) lacquer finish, mfg. 1998-present.

MSR $419	$350	$190 - 240	$110 - 140	

- **Add 40% for EPM EQ electronics (disc.), available in Almond Brown (11179/14477), Antique Burst (11186/14514), Black (11193/14576), Chestnut Brown (11209/14491), Trans. Blue (11216/14552), or Trans. Red (11223/14538) finish.**

* *Ami Steel String Electric* – similar to the Ami Steel String, except has Quantum I electronics, available in Almond Brown (2011 only, 023103), Antique Burst (023516), Black (2011-present, 023578), Blue (2011 only, 023554), or Burgundy (023530) satin lacquer finish, mfg. 2010-present.

MSR $545	$450	$250 - 300	$150 - 190	

ARTESANO

Instruments currently built in Valencia, Spain.

Artesano acoustics are built in Spain and distributed by Juan Orozco. These classical guitars are fine instruments for the money and include the Model 25, Model 30, Model 40, Model 60, and Model 70. It is also reported that he built some higher-end models as well that included the Model 8, Model 10, and Model 15. Retail prices range between $625 and $1,400.

ARTISAN

Instruments previously produced in Japan.

Artisan instruments were distributed in the U.S. market by the Barth-Feinberg company of New York. Source: Michael Wright, *Guitar Stories*, Volume One.

ARTISAN (RECENT MFG.)

Instruments previously manufactured by Eikosha Musical Instrument Co., Inc. of Nagoya, Japan. Distributed in the U.S. by V.J. Rendano in Boardman, OH.

Artisan acoustic instruments included archtops, flattops, classical, a mini-series, and acoustic electric models.

ARTISTA

Instruments previously built in Spain. Previously distributed by Musicorp, a division of MBT, in Charleston, SC.

These reasonably priced handmade guitars were designed for the beginning classical guitar student.

The Artista line featured these models: the **Flamenco** (last MSR was $419) has an Oregon Pine top, sycamore body, and a mahogany neck, the **Granada** (last MSR was $319) has an Oregon pine top, sapelle (mahogany) body and neck, and a rosewood fingerboard; the **Morena** (last MSR was $399) has the same Oregon pine top combined with a rosewood body and mahogany neck; and the **Segovia** (last MSR was $599) features a solid cedar top, rosewood back and sides, and a rosewood fingerboard.

ASAHI

Instruments previously produced in Japan during the 1970s. Distributed by Sam Ash in New York, NY.

Asahi was a trademark of acoustic guitars that Sam Ash distributed in the 1970s. Asahi guitars are mainly Martin acoustic copies including a D-35 copy with a three-piece back.

ASAMA

Instruments previously built in Japan during the early 1980s.

Guitars with this trademark are generally medium to good quality copies of American designs as well as some original designs. Source: Tony Bacon and Paul Day, *The Guru's Guitar Guide*.

ASHLAND

Instruments previously produced in Asia. Distributed by VMI Industries in Brea, CA.

Ashland instruments were manufactured for the entry-level or beginning guitarist. Ashland offered at least three dreadnought-style guitars with a spruce top and mahogany back and sides. Models included the **AD 26** (last MSR was $249), **AD 36** (last MSR was $269), and the **AE 16** (last MSR was $279). The AE 16 was an acoustic/electric that featured a fingerboard-mounted pickup with adjustable pole pieces.

ASHTON

Guitars currently produced overseas. Currently, there is no U.S. Distributor.

Ashton guitars are designed in Australia and produced overseas. These guitars are priced and built for the beginner guitar player and the acoustic guitars include standard dreadnought, folk, classical, and acoustic/electric models. They also produce a wide variety of other musical products including electric guitars, bass guitars, guitar amplifiers, sound reinforcement, keyboards, and accessories. Guitar packs (guitar, amplifier, accessories, etc.) are also available. For more information, visit Ashton's website.

> **CONTACT INFORMATION**
> **ASHTON**
> www.ashtonmusic.com

ASPEN

Instruments previously produced in Korea between 1987 and 1991. Distributed by International Music Corporation (IMC) in Fort Worth, TX.

Aspen was a trademark used by the International Music Corporation on a number of imported acoustic guitars and banjos. The A series featured laminated tops and bodies, and had a retail price range between $200 and $570. Aspen's high end Aspen Luthier (or AL) series had solid wood tops, and a retail new price range between $790 and $1,500. Aspen A-Series guitars carry a used price between $100 and $150, depending on condition; the AL-Series rates a bit higher, between $300 and $500.

ASPRI CREATIVE ACOUSTICS

Instruments currently produced in Brentwood, TN. Distributed by Aspri Creative Acoustics.

The Aspri Creative Acoustics trademark used to be based in Montreal, Canada, but has relocated to Brentwood, TN. Any further information on the Aspri Creative Acoustics trademark can be submitted directly to Blue Book Publications.

ASTURIAS

Instruments currently built on the island of Kyushu, Japan since 1962. Previously distributed in the U.S. market by J.T.G. of Nashville, located in Nashville, TN. Currently, there is no U.S. distributor.

> **CONTACT INFORMATION**
> **ASTURIAS**
> www.asturias.jp

The Asturias Workshops in southern Japan employ seventeen people who have worked at Asturias most of their lives or have a family connection. Guided by chief luthier Wataru Tsuji, these luthiers take great care with their production methods to ensure a quality guitar. There are currently several models available. For more information, visit Asturias' website.

ATHELETE

Instruments previously built in New York, NY.

Luthier Fumi Nozawa created high quality four-, five-, and six-string acoustic basses, as well as acoustic guitars for several years.

ATKIN GUITARS

Guitars currently produced in Canterbury, Kent, England since 1993.

Alister Atkin builds acoustic flattop guitars and custom mandolins. Standard production guitars are available in 0, 00, OM, Small Jumbo, J-45, Dreadnought, and Jumbo configurations. Standard features include a Sitka spruce top and Indian rosewood back and sides, and several options are available. Prices start at £1,695. For more information, visit Atkin's website or contact him directly.

> **CONTACT INFORMATION**
> **ATKIN GUITARS**
> Unit 89, Thomas Way, Lakesview Int.
> Business Park, Hersden
> Canterbury, Kent CT3 4NH United
> Kingdom
> Phone No.: +44 (0)1227 719933
> www.atkinguitars.com
> info@atkinguitars.com

ATLAS

Instruments previously built in East Germany. See chapter on House Brands.

This trademark has been identified as a House Brand of the RCA Victor Records Stores. Source: Willie G. Moseley, *Stellas & Stratocasters*.

AUDITION

See chapter on House Brands.

This trademark has been identified by researcher Willie G. Moseley as a House Brand of the F.W. Woolworth (Woolco) department stores. Further information from authors Tony Bacon and Paul Day indicate that guitars with this trademark originated in Japan (later Korea) during the 1960s and 1970s. Source: Tony Bacon and Paul Day, *The Guru's Guitar Guide*.

AUSTIN

Instruments currently built in Korea and China since 1999. Distributed by St. Louis Music (U.S. Band & Orchestra) in St. Louis, MO since late 2008. Previously distributed by LOUD Technologies, Inc. in Woodinville, WA between 2005 and 2008 and by St. Louis Music Inc., in St. Louis, MO between 1999 and 2005.

St. Louis Music introduced the Austin line of guitars as budget models to complement their other lines. Instead of adding a budget line to Alvarez and Alvarez Yairi, they did like many other brands have done and added an entirely new trademark. Austin has a wide variety of products including acoustic, acoustic electric, banjos, electric guitars, electric basses, mandolins, and amplifiers. In 2005, LOUD Technologies, Inc. purchased St. Louis Music, Inc. and all of their trademarks. With this acquisition, the headquarters of St. Louis Music was moved to Woodinville, WA. However, the guitar repair and set-up shop were still located in St. Louis. In late 2008, Mark Ragin and U.S. Band & Orchestra bought the Austin brand from LOUD Technologies, and Austin is currently a division of St. Louis Music. For more information, visit Austin's website or contact them directly.

CONTACT INFORMATION

AUSTIN

Distribution: St. Louis Music (U.S. Band & Orchestra)
1933 Woodson Road
St. Louis, MO 63114
Phone No.: 314-727-4512
Phone No.: 800-727-4512
Fax No.: 314-727-4710
www.austingtr.com
rich@usbandsupplies.com

Austin offers several different styles of guitars: 3/4-sized, classical, folk, dreadnought, left-handed models, and 12-string models. For acoustic models there are three series and each one is better than the last: Intermediate (low), Deluxe (mid), and Custom (high).

The Intermediate line of guitar models all start with a 3 prefix. The student series are entry level guitars that include the **AU132** and **AU134** models which are of folk and classical designs (disc., last MSR was $55). The **AU334N** is a 3/4-sized nylon guitar (disc., last MSR was $90) and the **AU334S** is a 3/4-sized folk guitar (disc., last MSR was $100). The **AU336N** is a Standard Classic guitar (disc., last MSR was $100) and the **AU336S** is a Standard Folk guitar (disc., last MSR was $110). The **AU 341 S Dreadnought** (MSR $150), which has a spruce top, mahogany back and sides, and a rosewood fingerboard. The **AU 339 N 39 Guitar** (MSR $120) is a classical model with a spruce top, agathis back and sides, nato/mahogany neck, and hardwood fingerboard.

The Deluxe Series of guitar models all start with 5 prefix. The **AU502 Concert Folk** has a spruce top, mahogany back/sides, and a rosewood fingerboard (disc., last MSR was $209). The **AU 506 Ozark** features a rosewood bridge, chrome tuners, and a gloss finish (disc., last MSR was $229, also available in left-handed configuration and black finish last MSR was $239). The 12-string **AU 518 Osage** dreadnought has a laminated spruce top, mahogany back and sides, hardwood bridge and fingerboard, chrome tuners, five-ply body binding, and a pearl inlaid logo (disc., last MSR was $289). The **AU560 Concert Classic** (disc., last MSR was $209) has a laminated spruce top, mahogany back/sides/neck, rosewood bridge and fingerboard, and inlaid marquetry soundhole rosette. The **AU565 Concert Classic Cutaway** is the same as the AU560, except has a single cutaway (disc., last MSR was $329).

The Custom Series was introduced in 2004. These guitars are built with better woods, higher quality construction, and retail for a slightly higher price. The **AU532 Parlor** has a solid spruce top, rosewood back and sides, and white snowflake inlays (disc., last MSR was $299). The **AU536QTS Dreadnought** has a spruce top with a quilted maple veneer, mahogany back and sides, and snowflake inlays (disc., last MSR was $299). The **AU538 Dreadnought** has a solid cedar top, mahogany back and sides, and open hexagaon inlays (disc., last MSR was $329). The **AU541 Dreadnought** has a solid spruce top, rosewood back and sides, and hexagon inlays (disc., last MSR was $399), The **AU550 Dreadnought** is the same as the AU541 except has the tree of life inlay in the neck (disc., last MSR was $449). The **AU570 Custom Rosewood** Classic guitar has a solid spruce top and rosewood back and sides (disc., last MSR was $349). The **AU578 Custom Rosewood** is the same as the AU570 except has a solid cedar top (disc., last MSR was $349).

In 2010, St. Louis Music/Austin Guitars introduced an entirely new line of guitars. All acoustic guitars are numbered starting with an "AA", followed by a two-digit suffix and ending with a combination of letters. The **AA20** Series of guitars are available in dreadnought, jumbo, and 000-sized bodies and have a spruce top and Linden back and sides. The AA20 guitars are available as regular acoustics (MSR $149) or acoustic electrics (MSR $199). The **AA30** Series of guitars are available in dreadnought, jumbo, and 000-sized bodies and have a spruce top and mahogany back and sides. The AA30 guitars are available as regular acoustics (MSR $199) or acoustic electrics (MSR $239). The **AA40** Series of guitars are available in dreadnought, jumbo, and 000-sized bodies and have a solid Sitka spruce top and mahogany back and sides. The AA40 guitars are available as regular acoustics (MSR $259) or acoustic electrics (MSR $299). The **AA50** Series of guitars are available in dreadnought, jumbo, and 000-sized bodies and have a solid Sitka spruce top, mahogany back and sides, and maple body binding. The AA50 guitars are available as regular acoustics (MSR $329) or acoustic electrics (MSR $369).

Classical guitars are also available in either nylon or steel string configurations and have a "AC" prefix. These are available in 1/2 size (AC12S/AC12N, disc. 2010, last MSR was $76), 3/4 size (AC34S/AC34N, disc. 2010, last MSR was $76), or 4/4 size (AC44N/AC440N, MSR $109).

Austin guitars typically sell around 70% of the retail price, and used guitars in excellent condition are valued between 40% and 60% of the retail price.

The **AU 520 Table Rock** (disc., last MSR was $349) has a cutaway dreadnought body with laminated spruce top, mahogany back/sides/neck, diecast tuners, pearl inlaid logo, bridge pickup with volume and three-band EQ controls, and a Natural Gloss or Black finish. The **Branson Series** features 000-sized bodies, spruce tops, mahogany back/sides/neck, and a bridge pickup with volume control and four-band EQ. These models are designated the **AU510** and are available in Natural, Blue Burst, Purple Burst, Tobacco Sunburst, and Wine Red. These guitars last retailed for $349 for all colors. The Bootheel Series were introduced in 2006 and are designed for woman guitar players. The **AU512 Bootheel** features a single cutaway, 000-sized body, spruce top, mahogany back and sides, and are available in Coral, Magenta, or Sienna finish (disc., last MSR was $369). The Meramec Metallic Series have unbound bodies and metallic finishes. The **AU515 Meramec** features a single cutaway, 000-sized body, spruce top, mahogany back and sides, and are available in Metallic Blue, Metallic Red, or Platinum finish (disc., last MSR was $379).

AVALON GUITARS

Instruments currently produced in North Ireland since the 1980s. Previously distributed by Musical Distributors Group of Kinnelon, NJ between 2005 and 2007, and by the Lowden Guitar Co. in Fort Worth, TX between 2002 and 2005.

CONTACT INFORMATION
AVALON GUITARS
8 Glenford Way
Newtownards, N. Ireland BT23 48X
United Kingdom
Phone No.: +44 (0) 2891 820 542
Fax No.: +44 (0) 2891 820 650
www.avalonguitars.com
info@avalonguitars.com

Avalon has been building guitars since the 1980s. In 2002, the Lowden Guitar Company launched Avalon as a new brand of acoustic guitars. This guitar line was established to make guitars that are of the Lowden quality but keep the price range low. Lowden guitars typically sell in the $3,000-$5,000 range while the Avalon guitars start at a retail price of under $2,000, with none going over $2,600. In 2005, Avalon broke away from Lowden and became their own trademark and they currently offer a wide range of acoustic guitars. For more information contact Avalon directly.

Under the direction of Lowden, Avalon featured four levels of guitars: Standard, Premier, Silver, and Gold. The Standard Series were available in jumbo, grand auditorium, and grand concert styles and retail prices started at $3,590. The Premium Series is Avalon's high end models with jumbo, grand auditorium, grand concert, and dreadnought styles available in most configurations and prices start at $4,395. The Gold Series represents Avalon's entry-level models, which are available in most styles and configurations and prices start at $1,899. The Silver Series were designed by Avalon, but produced overseas and prices started at $799.

Today, Avalon offers their Master Series that include the models **Americana** (MSR starts at $5,750), the **Bevel** (MSR starts at $6,590), the **Classical** (MSR starts at $5,950), and limited editions that start at $5,350. The Avalon **Premier Series** feature a wide range of body shapes, styles, and wood types and prices start at $5,250. The **Legacy Series** are genuinely handcrafted guitars made to an exceptionally high standard specification by gifted luthiers. These are available in various body shapes and woods, and prices start at $4,590. Avalon also offers the **Jazz Series** that are crossover guitars (MSR starts at $4,990), and two signature models: the **Roby Duke Signature** (MSR starts at $5,990) and the **Carl Verheyen Signature** (MSR starts at $5,690).

AVON

Instruments previously built in Japan during the early to late 1970s.

The Avon trademark is the brand name of a UK importer. Avons are generally low to medium quality copies of American designs. Source: Tony Bacon and Paul Day, *The Guru's Guitar Guide*.

AXELSON, RANDY

Instruments previously built in Duluth, MN during the 1990s and early 2000s.

Luthier Randy Axelson provided top-notch guitar repair, restoration, and custom guitar building in his shop in Duluth, MN. Axelson left the music business in the early 2000s to pursue other interests.

AXEMAN

Instruments previously built in Japan during the late 1970s.

The Axeman trademark is the brand name of a UK importer. The guitars are generally medium quality copies of American designs. Source: Tony Bacon and Paul Day, *The Guru's Guitar Guide*.

AXION

Guitars currently produced in Korea since 2005. Distributed by SP Musical Co. LTD in Korea. Currently, there is no U.S. distributor.

CONTACT INFORMATION
AXION
www.spaxmusic.com

Axion guitars feature many unique features not found in many other acoustic guitars including a cross-woven spherical alder body, a rolling soundhole, and a body tie strip on the back. At first look, these guitars have a striking resemblence to Ovation, but closer inspection shows their own designs and innovations. Several variations are available in six- and twelve-string configurations. For more information, visit Axion's website.

AXL

Acoustic instruments previously built in China between 2001 and 2005. Distributed by The Music Link in Hayward, CA.

The Axl trademark was introduced in 2001 as a line of electric and acoustic guitars as well as a line of amplifiers. These instruments were produced with modern equipment and the best available material to create a quality line of guitars at affordable prices. In 2005, Axl stopped producing acoustic instruments to focus on electric guitars. Refer to the *Blue Book of Electric Guitars* for model information.

Axl produced the Songwriter and Studio series acoustic guitars. All of these guitars were dreadnought in style. The Songwriter Series was offered as the **AG-700** (last MSR was $199), which had a Canadian Sitka spruce top and mahogany back and sides. The **AG-710** (last MSR was $239) is the same as the AG-700 except has Indian rosewood back and sides. The Studio series is the same as the Songwriter series except features a solid Sitka spruce top. The **AG-705** (last MSR was $229) has mahogany back and sides like the AG-700. The **AG-715** (last MSR was $279) has Indian rosewood back and sides.

AXTECH

Instruments previously built in Korea during the 1990s.

Axtech instruments are generally entry level to medium quality solid body and acoustic guitars based on Classic American designs. Used models can be typically found priced between $75 and $200.

AYERS

Instruments currently produced in Vietnam since 1989. Headquarters are located in Taiwan. Distributed in the U.S. by Ayers Guitar USA in Dallas, TX.

Ayers currently produces a wide variety of acoustic guitars that includes dreadnoughts, classicals, folks, cutaways, archtops, and acoustic basses. In 2006, they released a few 10th Anniversary models that featured unqiue inlay designs. Guitars range in price between $899 and $2,499. For more information, please visit their website.

CONTACT INFORMATION

AYERS
Phone No.: 886-2-2505-8856
Fax No.: 886-2-2501-3934
www.ayersguitar.com
guitars@ayersmusic.com

U.S. Distributor: Ayers Guitar USA
Dallas, TX
Phone No.: 800-289-5810
www.ayersguitarusa.com
sales@ayersguitarusa.com

AZAHAR

Instruments currently produced in Spain since 1971.

Azahar S.L. produces a wide variety of classical guitars that are available for reasonable prices. Models are built out of quality tonewoods and follow mainly traditional construction techniques. For more information, visit Azahar's website or contact them directly.

CONTACT INFORMATION

AZAHAR
www.guitarras-azahar.com
azahar@guitarras-azahar.com

AZALEA

Guitars currently produced in China. Distributed by Great Wall Musical Instruments Manufacturer Co. Ltd. in Jie Yang City, China. Currently, there is no U.S. distributor.

Azalea produces a wide range of acoustic guitars that are mainly modeled after popular U.S. designs. They also produce electric guitars and basses, mandolins, and other accessories. For more information, visit Azalea's website.

CONTACT INFORMATION

AZALEA
www.jyguitars.com

B SECTION
BABICZ, JEFF GUITARS

Instruments currently produced in China and Newburgh, NY since 2003. Distributed and sold direct by Jeff Babicz Guitars. Previously distributed by HSS (a division of Hohner, Inc.) in Glen Allen, VA.

CONTACT INFORMATION
BABICZ, JEFF GUITARS
421 Violet Avenue
Poughkeepsie, NY 12601
Phone No.: 845-790-5250
Phone No.: 877-856-0780
Fax No.: 845-790-5260
www.babiczguitars.com
info@babiczguitars.com

Jeff Babicz used three patented technologies to make his acoustic guitar different than others. These include the Lateral Compression Soundboard, the Continually Adjustable Neck, and a Torque Reducing Split Bridge. A Babicz guitar looks different because the strings are physically attached to the soundboard near the edge of the body which enhances tone. The neck can be adjusted by a provided key without de-tuning the guitar. The bridge can also be adjusted for intonation and little torque is forced on it keeping the soundboard stable.

Babicz produces the Identity series, which were made in Indonesia on a production line and are now made in China. He also makes custom handmade models in his Babicz Signature Series Ltd. that are produced in Newburgh, New York. In late 2004, Babicz signed a deal with Hohner/HSS to exclusively distribute his guitars. The Tribeca line of acoustic guitars was also introduced and are licensed by Babicz Design Ltd. In 2006, Babicz introduced his first electric model, the Octane. Babicz has simplified his line and offers two acoustic models: the Dreadnought Cutaway and the Spider. The Super Jumbo acoustic and Octane electric models were released in late 2011. Now Babicz uses KMC Music as his importer since 2010. Guitars are sold directly through Babicz's website and they will work with you on ordering a guitar. For more information, visit Babicz's website or contact him directly.

MSR/NOTES	100%	EXCELLENT	AVERAGE	LAST MSR

ACOUSTIC

ACUTE – single cutaway folkbody style, solid spruce top, solid mahogany (disc. 2006) or rosewood back and sides, mahogany neck, 14/20-fret rosewood fingerboard with dot inlay, three-per-side tuners, rosewood bridge, clear pickguard, LR Baggs iMix electronics, black hardware, Natural finish, 25.5 in. scale, disc. 2010.

	$1,375	$750 - 900	$475 - 550	$1,695

* Subtract 7.5% (last MSR $1,295) for mahogany back and sides.
* Subtract 20% (last MSR $1,395) for no electronics.

DREADNOUGHT – dreadnought body style, solid spruce top, solid mahogany (disc. 2006) or rosewood back and sides, mahogany neck, 14/20-fret rosewood fingerboard with dot inlay, three-per-side tuners, rosewood bridge, clear pickguard, black hardware, Natural finish, 25.5 in. scale, disc. 2010.

	$800	$475 - 550	$275 - 325	$995

* Subtract 10% for mahogany back and sides (disc.).
* Add 40% for LR Baggs iMix electronics (disc.).

* *Dreadnought Cutaway* – similar to the Dreadnought, except has a single cutaway and LR Baggs iMix electronics, current mfg.

MSR $1,688	$1,400	$750 - 900	$475 - 550	

* Subtract 10% for mahogany back and sides.
* Subtract 30% for no electronics.

JUMBO – jumbo body style, solid spruce top, solid mahogany or rosewood back and sides, mahogany neck, 14/20-fret rosewood fingerboard with dot inlay, three-per-side tuners, rosewood bridge, clear pickguard, black hardware, Natural finish, 25.5 in. scale, disc. 2006.

	N/A	$600 - 700	$350 - 425	$1,295

* Add 10% for rosewood back and sides.
* Add 30% for LR Baggs iMix electronics.

* *Jumbo Cutaway* – similar to the Jumbo, except has a single cutaway and LR Baggs iMix electronics, mfg. 2005-2010.

	$1,450	$800 - 950	$500 - 575	$1,795

* Subtract 5% for mahogany back and sides.
* Subtract 30% for no electronics.

SPIDER – thinline single cutaway folk body style, solid mahogany top (disc. 2010) or solid Englemann spruce top (current mfg.), solid mahogany back and sides, mahogany neck, 14/20-fret rosewood fingerboard with dot inlay, three-per-side tuners, rosewood bridge, clear pickguard, LR Baggs pickup, electronics, chrome hardware, Black finish, 25.5 in. scale, current mfg.

MSR $1,488	$1,200	$675 - 800	$375 - 450	

SMALL JUMBO – single cutaway folkbody style, solid spruce top, solid rosewood back and sides, mahogany neck, 14/20-fret rosewood fingerboard with dot inlay, three-per-side tuners, rosewood bridge, clear pickguard, LR Baggs iMix electronics, black hardware, Natural finish, 25.5 in. scale, mfg. 2007-2010.

	$1,450	$800 - 950	$500 - 575	$1,795

BACHMANN GUITARS

Instruments currently built in Antholz, Italy.

Luthier Rudolf Bachmann builds a number of high quality guitars including acoustic, electric, and electric bass models. Bachmann built his first prototype in 1993, and has been producing ever since. For further information regarding specifications and pricing, visit Bachmann's website or contact him directly.

> **CONTACT INFORMATION**
> **BACHMANN GUITARS**
> Zona artigianale 130
> Antholz, I-39030 Italy
> Phone No.: +39 0474 492 349
> Fax No.: +39 0474 492 349
> www.bachmann-guitars.com
> info@bachmann-tonewood.com

BACKWOODS GUITARS

Instruments previously produced in Columbia Falls, MT by Mark Gasser during the 1980s and 1990s. Previously produced under the name Mark Gasser in Cottonwood, AZ.

Mark Gasser was born and raised on a cattle ranch in eastern Montana. He learned to make things himself at an early age, including a guitar out of a hubcap and two by four. He dreamt of building guitars ever since. He tried his luck in Arizona and Seattle before he returned to Montana. Then he met Drew Johnston in Helena, Montana. Drew had been a student of Bozo Padunavac's guitar creation school in San Diego, CA. Drew purchased the shop from Bozo and was setting up his shop in Helena where Mark became his first student. Mark produced guitars through the 1990s, and his line of guitars included classical and steel string models that are made out of quality woods.

BACON & DAY

Guitars previously produced between the 1920s and the 1940s.

Bacon & Day was a brand name used on guitars during the 1920s and 1940s that came from the two men involved: David L. Day and Frederick J. Bacon. Bacon was a popular banjo artist that set up his own production facility in Connecticut in 1921. Day was the general manager of Vega and prior to his employment there, he built banjos under the A.C. Fairbanks & Company until 1904. In 1922, Bacon wooed Day away from Vega to become vice president of the newly formed Bacon & Day company. While Bacon & Day marketed several models of guitars, banjos, and banjo-mandolins, they had no facility for building them. It is speculated that the Bacon & Day instruments were built by the Regal company of Chicago, IL. Around 1940, Gretsch bought the Bacon & Day trademark.

BACORN CUSTOM GUITARS & MANDOLINS

Instruments currently built in Nichols, NY.

Luthier Roger Bacorn manufactures both acoustic and electric custom instruments, built per individual work order. Almost any configuration or type is possible including acoustic guitars, electric archtop guitars, and mandolins. He specializes in instruments using older vintage aesthetics, with modern construction innovations such as X-bracing, and spring fitted braces on both archtops and mandolins. Each instrument has a hand-rubbed lacquer finish. Master quality restorations are offered as well. Thorough understanding of staining and period correct finishing as well as aging/relicing techniques ensure perfect results. For more information, contact Bacorn directly.

> **CONTACT INFORMATION**
> **BACORN CUSTOM GUITARS & MANDOLINS**
> 2230 East River Rd.
> Nichols, NY 13812
> Phone No.: 607-699-3094
> www.bacornguitars.com
> roger@bacornguitars.com

BADEN GUITARS

Guitars previously produced in Vietnam between 2006 and 2010. Distributed by Baden Guitars in Escondido, CA.

Baden Guitars was founded by luthier T.J. Baden and Errol Antzis with design input from European designers Andreas Pichler and Ulrich Teuffel. Baden is the former vice president of sales and marketing at Taylor Guitars, and Antzis is a former investment banker. In 2004, Baden was contacted by the Ayers factory in Vietnam to help distribute their guitars. After visiting the factory and seeing what they were capable of producing, Baden started putting together the new Baden line. Andreas Pichler of Andreas Guitars worked in conjunction with Baden and Antzis to design the dreadnought and auditorium-style guitars. These guitars were produced in the Ayers factory in Vietnam under the close supervision of six French luthiers. Guitars ranged between $1,348 and $3,000, and they were distributed through a select number of small independent retailers. It appears that Baden closed their doors in mid-2010.

BAGGS, LLOYD R.

Instruments previously produced in the Los Angeles, CA area during the late 1970s and early 1980s.

Lloyd Baggs, who is best known for his acoustic guitar pickups and electronics, began his career building a variety of acoustic guitars. After developing a friendship with musician Ry Cooder, Baggs' convinced him to play his first completed guitar. Takamine made an exact copy of Baggs' guitar with the addition of a pickup and electronics system. Upset by the fact that Takamine copied his guitar, but intrigued by the pickup system, Baggs began spending more time with pickup systems and electronics. He built a few more guitars, but after he developed his LB-6 pickup and began selling it to local guitar stores, Baggs formed his company L.R. Baggs.

BARBERO

Instruments previously built in Spain during the 1940s and 1950s.

Luthier Marcelo Barbero (1904-1955), was considered one of the great flamenco guitar makers. Source: Tony Bacon, *The Ultimate Guitar Book*.

BARON (U.S. MFG.)

See chapter on House Brands.

This trademark has been identified as a House Brand of the RCA Victor Records Store; furthermore, KAY exported guitars bearing this trademark to the Thibouville-Lamy company of France. Source: Willie G. Moseley, *Stellas & Stratocasters*.

BARRINGTON

Instruments previously produced in Japan between circa 1988 and 1991. Distribution in the U.S. by Barrington Guitars in Barrington, IL.

Barrington Guitars offered both solid body electric guitars and basses during the late 1980s, as well as acoustic and acoustic/electric models. The guitar models were produced in Japan by Terada. The company now specializes in brass instruments as the L.A. Sax Company of Barrington, Illinois.

Barrington offered both acoustic and acoustic/electric Barrington Gruhn signature series models as well.

The acoustics were similar to a design prototype produced in collaboration between George Gruhn and Collings guitars in 1988; and the Barrington models carried a new retail list price between $1,225 and $1,325 (a Fishman transducer pickup was optional equipment on the four models). The **AT-1** and **AT-2** f-hole archtops were listed new at $1,650. Used prices on flattops are between $250 and $400 and archtops are between $400 and $600.

BARTOLINI, BILL (U.S. MFG.)

Instruments previously built in 1960s.

Luthier Bill Bartolini used to build classical guitars in California during the 1960s. Bartolini estimates that perhaps only a dozen guitars were built. Research on resonances produced during this time formed the basis for his pickup designs, and his clear, high quality pickups are standard features on numerous luthiers creations. Information courtesy Bill Bartolini.

BATSON GUITARS

Instruments currently produced in Nashville, TN since the late 1990s.

Brothers Cory and Grant Batson build custom acoustic guitars in their Nashville, TN shop. In 1997, they were both working at a custom mill work company and Cory's guitar was stolen. Cory liked the Lowden Grant had, but he was unable to afford it. As he spent time looking for new acoustic guitars, he noticed that while many guitars look similar they can be very tonally different. Cory bought William Cumpiano's book *Guitarmaking: Tradition and Technology* and began using the resources at the mill work company to start building his first guitar. After building his first guitar, Cory looked further into improving the design of the guitar and his results include a sideport soundhole, lightweight bridge, and the ShorTail tailpiece. The Batson brothers continue to expand and evolve their guitar production and they currently offer several designs including a parlor, grand concert, auditorium, jumbo, traditional classic, nylon-string crossover, an SJ model, and a Batson signature. Prices start at $2,800 for the Batson No. 5 and at $6,500 for Custom Shop guitars. In late 2011, Grant Batson resigned as president of Batson Guitars because of health issues and turned over the entire company to Cory. For more information, visit Batson's website or contact them directly.

BAUER

Guitars previously built between the late 1880s and 1910 in Philadelphia, PA. Also see S.S. Stewart.

George Bauer established himself as a guitar and mandolin builder during the late 1880s and early 1890s. Banjo builder S.S. Stewart and Bauer began building instruments under the Bauer & Stewart name. After Stewart died in 1898, Bauer formed a partnership with Stewart's sons to produce instruments under the S.S. Stewart name. Bauer continued to produce instruments under the Bauer & Stewart, S.S. Stewart, and Acme Professional (Sears & Roebuck house brand) names until his death in 1910. The Bauer & Stewart company was sold shortly after Bauer died, and the name was never used again. The Stewart name has been sold several times and used on a variety of instruments ever since. Information courtesy Tom Wheeler, *American Guitars*.

BAY STATE

Instruments previously manufactured in Boston, MA between 1865 and circa 1910.

The Oliver Ditson Company, Inc. was formed in 1835 by music publisher Oliver Ditson (1811-1888). Ditson was a primary force in music merchandising, distribution, and retail sales on the East Coast. He also helped establish two musical instrument manufacturers: The John Church Company of Cincinnati, Oh, and Lyon & Healy (Washburn) in Chicago, IL.

In 1865, Ditson established a manufacturing branch of his company under the supervision of John Haynes, called the John C. Haynes Company. This branch built guitars for a number of trademarks, such as **Bay State, Tilton,** and **Haynes Excelsior**. Source: Tom Wheeler, *American Guitars*.

MSR/NOTES	100%	EXCELLENT	AVERAGE	LAST MSR

B.C. RICH

Acoustic instruments previously produced in Korea during the mid-2000s and the mid-1990s. Electric instruments are still currently produced in the U.S. and overseas. Distributed by Hanser Music Group in Hebron, KY. Previously distributed by B.C. Rich Guitars and HHI.

CONTACT INFORMATION
B.C. RICH
Distributed by Hanser Music Group
3015 Kustom Drive
Hebron, KY 41048
Phone No.: 859-817-7100
Phone No.: 800-999-5558
Fax No.: 859-817-7150
www.bcrich.com
info@bcrich.com

Luthier Bernardo Chavez Rico used to build classical and flamenco guitars at Bernardo's Valencian Guitar Shop, the family's business in Los Angeles. During the mid-1960s folk music boom (and boom in guitar sales), a distributor suggested a name change - and B.C. Rich guitars was born. Between 1966 and 1968, Rico continued to build acoustic guitars, and then changed to solid body electrics. The company began producing custom guitars based on Fender and Gibson designs, but Rico wanted to produce designs that represented his tastes and ideals. The Seagull solid body (first produced in 1971) was sleek, curvy, and made for rock 'n roll. Possessing a fast neck, hot-rodded circuitry and pickups, and a unique body profile, this was (and still is) an eye-catching design.

In 1974, Neal Mosher joined the company. Mosher also had a hand in some of the guitars designed, and further explored other designs with models like the Mockingbird, Eagle, Ironbird, and the provocatively named Bich. The first six-tuners-on-a-side headstocks began to appear in 1981. In the mid-1980s, B.C. Rich moved from Los Angeles to El Monte, California.

The company began to import models in the U.S. Production Series, Korean-produced kits that were assembled in the U.S. between 1984 and 1986. In 1984, the Japanese-built N.J. Series line of B.C. Rich designs were introduced, and were built by the Terada company for two years. Production of the N.J. series was moved to Korea in 1986 (models were built in the Cort factory).

In 1988, Rico licensed the Korean-built, lower-priced Platinum and entry-level Rave Series to the Class Axe company, and later licensed the B.C. Rich name and designs in 1989. Class Axe moved production of the U.S.-built guitars to a facility in Warren, New Jersey, and stepped up importation of the N.J. (named after Nagoya, Japan - not New Jersey), Platinum, and Rave Series models.

Unfortunately, the lower-priced series soon began to show a marked drop in quality. In 1994, Rico came back out of semi-retirement, took control over his trademark again, and began to rebuild the company. Rico became partners with Bill Shapiro, and the two divided up areas of responsibility. Rico once more began building acoustic and high end electrics at his Hesperia facilities, and Shapiro began maintaining quality control over the imported N.J., Platinum, and U.S. series in San Bernadino. In 1998, Davitt & Hanser Music of Cincinnati, Ohio began distributing the import models (NJ, Platinum, and Bronze Series). Additional model commentary courtesy Bernie Rich, President/Founder of B.C. Rich International, May 1997.

ACOUSTIC: EAGLE & THINLINE SERIES

EAGLE – double cutaway, ash body, quilted maple top, mahogany neck, 20-fret rosewood fingerboard with diamond inlay, rosewood bridge, three-per-side chrome tuners, four-band active EQ, available in Natural, Trans. Black, or Trans. Amber finish, mfg. 2003-06.

	N/A	$375 - 450	$225 - 275	$800

THINLINE ACOUSTIC MOCKINGBIRD – double sharp cutaway, milky pine body with tone chambers, flamed top, bolt-on maple neck, 24-fret rosewood fingerboard with dot inlay, rosewood bridge, three-per-side chrome tuners, three-band active EQ, available in Natural, Tobaccoburst (2006 only), Trans. Blue, or Trans. Red finish, mfg. 2003-06.

	N/A	$300 - 350	$175 - 225	$700

THINLINE ACOUSTIC WARLOCK – double sharp "X Style" cutaway, milky pine body with tone chambers, flamed top, bolt-on maple neck, 24-fret rosewood fingerboard with dot inlay, rosewood bridge, Widow style headstock, three-per-side chrome tuners, three-band active EQ, available in Trans. Black or Trans. Red, finish, mfg. 2003-05.

	N/A	$300 - 350	$175 - 225	$700

ACOUSTIC: ELITE SERIES

Elite Series acoustic guitars were imported to the U.S. market.

BR40D – dreadnought style, solid spruce top, round soundhole, mahogany back/sides, mahogany neck, 21-fret rosewood fingerboard with white dot inlay, rosewood bridge, white pearl dot bridge pins, three-per-side chrome tuners, available in Natural or Sunburst high gloss finish, mfg. 1995-97.

	N/A	$200 - 250	$120 - 150	$479

BR60D – dreadnought style, solid cedar top, round soundhole, mahogany back/sides, abalone body binding, mahogany neck, 21-fret rosewood fingerboard with pearl eagle inlay, rosewood bridge, white pearl dot bridge pins, three-per-side gold plated die cast tuners, available in Natural satin finish, mfg. 1995-97.

	N/A	$275 - 325	$150 - 200	$689

• **Add 25% for factory installed Fishman Matrix 4-band EQ system/bridge transducer.**

MSR/NOTES	100%	EXCELLENT	AVERAGE	LAST MSR

BR65DE – dreadnought style, solid spruce top, round soundhole, mahogany back/sides, white body binding, mahogany neck, 21-fret bound rosewood fingerboard with white dot inlay, rosewood bridge, white pearl dot bridge pins, three-per-side chrome tuners, Fishman Matrix EQ system, available in Gloss Black finish, mfg. 1995-97.

	N/A	$350 - 425	$225 - 275	$899

* **BR65DCE** – similar to the BR65DE, except has single rounded cutaway, mfg. 1995-97.

	N/A	$375 - 450	$250 - 300	$899

BR70D – dreadnought style, solid spruce top, round soundhole, rosewood back/sides, abalone/white body binding, abalone rosette, mahogany neck, 21-fret bound rosewood fingerboard with cat's-eye position markers, rosewood bridge, white pearl dot bridge pins, bound headstock, three-per-side tuners, available in Natural Gloss finish, mfg. 1995-97.

	N/A	$250 - 300	$135 - 175	$649

• **Add 25% for factory installed Fishman Matrix 4-band EQ system/bridge transducer.**

ACOUSTIC: SIGNATURE SERIES

The Signature Series acoustics were handcrafted in the U.S.
• **Add $100 for six-on-a-side headstock (acoustic models).**
• **Add $150 for an installed Fishman Matrix four-band EQ.**

B20-D – dreadnought style, solid spruce top, round soundhole, white body binding, solid mahogany back/sides, mahogany neck, 21-fret rosewood fingerboard with white dot inlay, rosewood bridge, white pearl dot bridge pins, three-per-side chrome tuners, available in Stained High Gloss finish, mfg. 1995-96.

	N/A	$550 - 650	$350 - 425	$1,299

All B20 models were available with a solid Black finish with white body binding or solid White finish with black body binding.

* **B20-C Cutaway** – similar to B20-D, except has single rounded cutaway, available in Natural High Gloss finish, mfg. 1995-96.

	N/A	$575 - 675	$375 - 450	$1,399

* **B20-C DS Cutaway** – similar to the B20-D, except has a solid red cedar top, single rounded cutaway, diamond-shaped soundhole with abalone and rosewood inlays, mfg. 1995-96.

	N/A	$625 - 750	$400 - 475	$1,499

B30-D – dreadnought-sized flattop body, select spruce top, round soundhole, rosewood bound body, abalone rosette, solid quilted maple back/sides, mahogany neck, 21-fret rosewood fingerboard with abalone diamond inlay, rosewood bridge, white pearl dot bridge pins, three-per-side chrome tuners, available in Natural, Trans. Blue, Trans. Emerald Green, Trans. Pagan Gold, or Trans. Red finish, mfg. 1995-96.

	N/A	$600 - 700	$375 - 450	$1,499

* **B30-C** – similar to B30-D, except has a single rounded cutaway, mfg. 1995-96.

	N/A	$625 - 750	$400 - 475	$1,499

B35-D – dreadnought style, select spruce top, round soundhole, white body binding, solid rosewood back/sides, mahogany neck, 14/21-fret bound ebony fingerboard with abalone cloud inlay, ebony bridge with pearl cloud inlay, white pearl dot bridge pins, peghead with abalone logo inlay, three-per-side chrome tuners, available in Natural finish, mfg. 1995-96.

	N/A	$675 - 800	$450 - 525	$1,699

* **B35-C** – similar to B35-D, except has a single rounded cutaway, mfg. 1995-96.

	N/A	$700 - 850	$475 - 550	$1,699

B41-C DIAMOND – single round cutaway flattop body, select spruce top, diamond-shaped soundhole, abalone purfling/rosette, rosewood back/sides, mahogany neck, 21-fret bound ebony fingerboard with abalone cloud inlay, ebony bridge with pearl cloud inlay, white pearl dot bridge pins, bound rosewood veneered peghead with abalone logo inlay, three-per-side Grover Imperial gold tuners, available in Natural finish, mfg. 1995-96.

	N/A	$1,100 - 1,350	$700 - 850	$2,699

* **B41-D** – similar to B41-C, except has non-cutaway dreadnought-style body, 14/21-fret rosewood fingerboard, available in Natural finish, mfg. 1995-96.

	N/A	$1,000 - 1,250	$675 - 800	$2,495

BD DEY

Instruments previously built in the Czech Republic during the 1990s. Distributed by BD Dey Musical Instruments of the Czech Republic.

The Czech Republic is the popular place for companies looking for an alternative to Asian guitar production. Various areas in the Czech Republic have a reputation for excellent instrument craftsmanship, evolving from the earlier days of violin and viola production. BD Dey offered five different electric guitar models, and a six- and twelve-string jumbo acoustic guitar model.

The **Rieger-Kloss** jumbo guitar model featured a solid spruce top, mahogany veneer back and sides, maple neck, 14/20-fret ebony fingerboard with pearl dot inlays, ebony bridge, three-per-side (or six-per-side, depending on the configuration) chrome tuners and a plastic pickguard. The acoustics were available in Natural and Sunburst finishes; both configurations were also available with a piezo pickup and on-board equalizer.

BEAR CREEK GUITARS

Instruments currently built in Kula, HI since 1995.

Luthier Bill Hardin builds fine handmade Hawaiian steel guitars in the "Weissenborn" tradition. Instruments are styled after the classic steel guitars of the 1920s but with beautiful craftsmanship and more attention to details than the originals. The price range for the individual models runs from $2,500 to $4,900, plus available options. Bear Creek instruments are played and recommended by noted musician/author Bob Brozman. They were previously located in Monterey, CA. For more information refer to their website or contact them directly.

CONTACT INFORMATION
BEAR CREEK GUITARS
Kula, HI
Phone No.: 808-264-2770
www.bearcreekguitars.com
contact@bearcreekguitars.com

BEARD GUITARS

Resonators currently produced in Hagerstown, MD since 1985.

Luthier Paul Beard built his first resonator guitar in 1985 after he became dissatisfied with the quality of available resonator guitars on the market. Beard guitars are built on the traditional Dopyera-style instrument, but Paul uses modern technologies and techniques. Notable players of Beard Guitars include Mike Auldridge, LeRoy Mack, and Tim Graves. Currently, Beard offers fourteen square and round neck models, as well as a full online parts and accessories store for resonators. Prices start at $3,500. For more information, visit Beard's website or contact them directly.

CONTACT INFORMATION
BEARD GUITARS
21736 Leitersburg Pike
Hagerstown, MD 21742
Phone No.: 301-733-8271
Fax No.: 301-791-7811
www.beardguitars.com
cheth@beardguitars.com

BEDELL GUITARS

Instruments currently produced in China since 2009. Previously produced in Japan during the 1960s. Distributed by Two Old Hippies, LLC in Spirit Lake, IA.

Tom Bedell began importing guitars from Japan in the mid-1960s under the Bedell name when he was just 14 years old. After leaving the music industry and working as a political consultant and for the Pure Fishing Company, Bedell and his wife bought The Great Divide guitar shop in Aspen, Colorado. They renamed it Two Old Hippies, and Bedell began importing guitars again under the Bedell name. Bedell currently offers a full line of acoustic guitars ranging from $900 to $2,300 in price. For more information, visit Bedell's website or contact Two Old Hippies directly.

CONTACT INFORMATION
BEDELL GUITARS
Two Old Hippies Office
PO Box 557
Spirit Lake, IA 51360
Phone No.: 877-264-3356
www.bedellguitars.com
service@twooldhippies.com

Two Old Hippies Store
111 S. Monarch Street
Aspen, CO 81611
Phone No.: 970-925-7492
www.twooldhippies.com

BELTONA

Instruments currently built in Paekakariki, New Zealand since 2010. Previously produced in Whangarei, New Zealand between 1998 and 2010, and the United Kingdom from 1990 to 1998.

Steve Evans, a luthier, and Bill Johnson, an engineer, created Beltona in 1990 that are custom-made resonator instruments. Beltona resonators were originally produced out of metal and in the mid-1990s, they introduced resin and carbon fibre models. These lightweight guitars became so popular that Beltona discontinued their metal models in 2002. All resonators are hand-made and can be individually customized. For more information regarding prices and specifications, visit Beltona's website or contact them directly.

CONTACT INFORMATION
BELTONA
Paekakariki, New Zealand
www.beltona.net
steve@beltona.net

BELTONE

Guitars previously built during the 1920s and the 1930s.

The Beltone trademark was a house brand of sorts used by distributor Perlberg & Halpin of New York City, NY. They offered acoustic guitars, resonators, and mandolins, and these instruments were more than likely built by Harmony and/or Regal of Chicago, IL. Most instruments were entry-level to student models that sold at competitive prices. It is also reported that Martin supplied some instruments with the Beltone name (approx. thirty-six or less instruments total). Source: Walter Murray, Frankenstein Fretworks.

BENEDETTO GUITARS

Instruments currently manufactured in Savannah, GA since 2006. Instruments were previously produced from 1999-2006, under a licensing agreement with Fender Musical Instruments Corporation (FMIC). Instruments were first made in Nashville, TN by the Guild Custom Shop in the early 2000s, and later in Corona, CA, by the Fender Custom Shop till mid-2006. Benedetto also built custom instruments during this period at his shop in Riverview, FL.

CONTACT INFORMATION
BENEDETTO GUITARS
10 Mall Terrace, Ste A
Savannah, GA 31406
Phone No.: 912-692-1400
Fax No.: 912-692-1403
www.benedettoguitars.com
cbenedetto@benedettoguitars.com

Master Luthier Robert Benedetto has been handcrafting fine archtop guitars since 1968. Born in New York in 1946, both his father and grandfather were master cabinetmakers, and Benedetto's uncles were artisans and musicians. While growing up in New Jersey, Benedetto began playing the guitar professionally at age thirteen. Being near the New York/New Jersey jazz music scene, Benedetto had numerous opportunities to perform repair and restoration work on other classic archtops. Benedetto built his first archtop in 1968, and his pre-eminence

MSR/NOTES	100%	EXCELLENT	AVERAGE	LAST MSR

in the field is evidenced by his having made archtop guitars longer than any living makers and a growing list of endorsers. Current endorsers range from Jimmy Bruno and Kenny Burrell to Earl Klugh and Andy Summers.

Benedetto moved to Homosassa, Florida in 1976. Three years later, he relocated to Clearwater, Florida. A veteran innovator, Benedetto began concentrating on the acoustic properties of the guitar designs, and started a movement to strip away unnecessary adornment (inlays, bindings) in 1982. While continuing his regular work on archtop building, Benedetto also built violins between 1983-1987. Violinist extraordinaire Stephane Grappelli purchased one of his violins in 1993. Benedetto even built a small number of electric solid body guitars and basses (which debuted at the 1987 NAMM show) in addition to his regular archtop production schedule. After 10 years in East Stroudsburg, PA (1990-2000), Benedetto relocated back to Florida in 2000. His endorsers span three generations of jazz guitarists. Not since John D'Angelico has anyone made as many archtop guitars nor had as many well-known players endorsing and recording with his guitars. Closer scrutiny reveals nuances found only from a maker of his stature. His minimalist delicate inlay motif has become a trademark as have his novel use of black, rather than gold, tuning machines, black bridge height adjustment wheels, and an ebony nut (versus bone), all of which harmonize with the ebony fittings throughout the guitar. He is the originator of the solid ebony tailpiece, uniquely fastened to the guitar with cello tail adjustor. Likewise, he was the first to use exotic and natural wood veneers on the headstock and pioneered the use of violin pigments to shade his guitars. His Honey Blonde finish is now widely used within the guitar industry. Benedetto is also well-known for refining the seven-string archtop and is that unique model's most prolific maker. Benedetto is the Archtop Guitar Construction Editor and "Guitar Maintenance" columnist for *Just Jazz Guitar* magazine, and is the author of *Making an Archtop Guitar* (Center stream Publishing, 1994). He released his 9 1/2 hour instructional video, *Archtop Guitar Design & Construction*, in November 1996. He also markets the Benedetto "floating" pickup, a standard size humbucking pickup, and solid ebony tailpiece for his (and other) archtop acoustic guitars.

Benedetto has built over 800 musical instruments. While the majority (500) are archtop guitars, he has produced 157 electric solid body guitars, fifty-two electric basses, forty-eight violins, five violas, two mandolins and one cello.

Benedetto pickups were licensed in 2000 to be sold exclusively by Seymour Duncan. In 2006, FMIC (Fender) and Benedetto parted ways, amicably. Benedetto and longtime friend and professional guitarist Howard Paul formed BENEDETTO GUITARS, INC. in Savannah, GA.

During his archtop making career, Benedetto made eight semi-hollowbody electric guitars (six of which were made between 1982 and 1983 and have been dubbed Semi-dettos by author Adrian Ingram). These versatile guitars feature a carved top, double cutaway body design with two separate tone chambers and a solid center block. Each model was crafted to the original owner's needs and specifications, resulting in slight differences between the models. The other two semi-hollowbody electric guitars were prototypes built by Benedetto in 1997 (Biographical information courtesy Cindy Benedetto). For more information, contact Benedetto directly or visit his website.

ACOUSTIC ARCHTOP

Benedetto's current acoustic models (no pickups) include the **Andy Elite** (MSR $12,000), **Cremona** (MSR $30,000), **Gypsy** (MSR $10,000), the **Gypsy Elite** (MSR $20,000), and the top-of-the-line **Sinfonietta** (MSR $40,000).

AMERICANA – 18 in. body width, carved select aged spruce tops, non-cutaway body, carved select flamed maple back with matching sides, black/white binding, three-piece flamed maple neck, large flared headstock, neo-classical (no inlays) fingerboard, narrow Chuck Wayne-style finger rest, gold Schaller tuners with solid ebony buttons, disc. 1999.

	N/A	N/A	N/A	$35,000

Both the Americana and Limelite models offer a tribute to the early days of archtop building and big bands.

CREMONA – hand carved/graduated/tuned European cello wood top and back, matching sides, fine line binding, flamed maple neck, large flared burl-veneered headstock with elegant mother-of-pearl/abalone inlay, gold Schaller tuners with gold (or solid ebony or mother-of-pearl) buttons, disc. 1999.

	N/A	N/A	N/A	$60,000

The Cremona was Benedetto's first standard model. Options included headstock-matching inlay on tailpiece and pickguard, and split block mother-of-pearl fingerboard inlay.

FRANK VIGNOLA MODEL (NO. 395-9905) – single cutaway acoustic archtop, carved hand graduated and tuned select Sitka spruce top, carved two-piece select mahogany back and matching sides, one-piece mahogany neck, 21-fret ebony fingerboard with 12th fret abalone inlay, three-per-side black chrome Schaller mini tuners with ebony buttons, adjustable ebony bridge, black hardware plating, available in Natural, Natural with Bordeaux back and sides, Natural with Espresso back and sides, or Opulent Brown finish, mfg. 2005-07.

	N/A	N/A	N/A	$18,000

* *Frank Vignola Deluxe Model (No. 395-9900)* – similar to the Frank Vignola Model, except has a European spruce top and select European flamed maple back and sides, available in Gypsy Maple, Honey Blonde, Natural, Opulent Brown, or Violin Burst finish, mfg. 2005-07.

	N/A	N/A	N/A	$20,000

LA VENEZIA (NO. 395-9800) – select aged spruce hand graduated and tuned archtop, highly flamed European maple back/sides, ebony fingerrest and fretboard, 25 in. scale, available in Autumn Burst or Honey Blonde finish, mfg. 2000-04.

	N/A	$12,500 - 15,000	$8,000 - 9,500	$17,500

MSR/NOTES	100%	EXCELLENT	AVERAGE	LAST MSR

LIMELITE – carved select aged spruce tops, carved flamed maple back with matching sides, three-piece flamed maple neck, large flared headstock, split fingerboard inlay, traditionally shaped bound pickguard, intricate inlay work on the pickguard/tailpiece, gold Schaller tuners with solid ebony buttons, disc. 1999.

	N/A	N/A	N/A	$45,000

THE 7-STRING – seven-string configuration, carved select aged spruce tops, carved flamed maple back with matching sides, black/white binding, three-piece flamed maple neck, neo-classical fingerboard, narrow Chuck Wayne-style finger rest, gold Schaller tuners with solid ebony buttons, disc.

	N/A	N/A	N/A	$17,500

ACOUSTIC ARCHTOP: RENAISSANCE SERIES

Renaissance Series instruments are very custom, one-of-a-kind archtop guitars. While the features may vary, the most distinct similarity between them are the clustered sound openings (unique to Benedetto) which range in design and location from one instrument to another. To date, only two instruments have been constructed -- the Il Fiorentino, and the Il Palissandro. List price on these models is $50,000. All Renaissance series instruments will have their own name.

The Il Palissandro model has a 16 in. width, non-cutaway body, and features a European spruce top, Indian rosewood back and sides, one-piece Honduran mahogany neck, ebony fingerboard/bridge/tailpiece/endpin, rosewood binding/natural wood purfling, a classical-style tapered neck heel, serpentine-style headstock with flamed curly maple and rosewood border/flamed curly maple truss rod cover, no finger rest and no pickup.

BENETEAU GUITARS

Guitars currently produced in St. Thomas, Ontario, Canada since 1974.

Luthier Marc Beneteau builds custom flattop acoustic guitars in his St. Thomas shop. Beneteau met Jean Larrivee of Larrivee Guitars in 1974 and decided to start building his own acoustic guitars. Currently, Beneteau offers several body styles available in many wood selections and other options. Prices start around $5,000 and he builds about twenty-five guitars a year. For more information, visit Beneteau's website or contact him directly.

CONTACT INFORMATION
BENETEAU GUITARS
109 Forest Ave.
St. Thomas, Ontario N5R 2J8 Canada
Phone No.: 519-633-6994
www.beneteauguitars.com
info@beneteauguitars.com

BENOIT RESONATOR GUITARS

Guitars currently produced in Mauriceville, TX.

Luthier Caroll Benoit builds standard and custom resonator guitars in Mauriceville, TX. Standard resonators start at $2,550 for six-strings and $2,675 for eight-strings. Benoit has also worked with artist Howard Reinlieb in developing the D'Angelico-styled resonator nicknamed the "D'Benoito Archtop" that has a teardrop body style and other high-end appointments reminiscent of a D'Angelico. For more information, visit Benoit's website or contact him directly.

CONTACT INFORMATION
BENOIT RESONATOR GUITARS
PO Box 213
Mauriceville, TX 77626
Phone No.: 409-745-1071
www.benoitguitars.com
ben@benoitguitars.com

BENTLY

Instruments previously manufactured in Asia between circa 1985 and 1998. Distributed in the U.S. by St. Louis Music in St. Louis, MO.

St. Louis Music imported Bently instruments as their entry-level to medium quality solid body guitar and bass line. Most models featured designs based on classic American favorites. In 1998, SLM discontinued the Bently line when they introduced the Austin line. Bently guitars are usually found priced between $50 and $100 on the used market.

BERTONCINI GUITARS

Guitars currently produced in Olympia, WA since 1995.

Dave Bertoncini builds custom-made acoustic, acoustic/electric, and electric guitars as well as mandolins in his one person shop. Each guitar is entirely custom-made by him, which allows the customer to choose what he or she wants. Dave usually has ongoing projects, but he encourages customers to request special orders so he can start from scratch on the instrument of choice. For more information, visit Bertoncini's website or contact him directly.

CONTACT INFORMATION
BERTONCINI GUITARS
3700 14th Avenue S.E. #53
Olympia, WA 98501
Phone No.: 360-491-5051
www.bertonciniguitars.com

BESSON

Instruments previously built in West Germany during the late 1950s through the early 1960s. Also see Framus and Aristone.

While Besson was the brand name for a UK importer, these guitars were made by and identical to certain Framus models. Research also indicates that the trademark Aristone was utilized as well. Source: Tony Bacon and Paul Day, *The Guru's Guitar Guide*.

MSR/NOTES	100%	EXCELLENT	AVERAGE	LAST MSR

BEVERLY

Unknown source of production and/or date of manufacture. See chapter on House Brands.

This trademark has been identified as a House Brand of Selmer U.K. in England. Source: Willie G. Moseley, *Stellas & Stratocasters*.

BIG HEART

Instruments previously built in the U.S. between 1998 and the late 2000s. Distributed by the Big Heart Slide Company in Placentia, CA.

CONTACT INFORMATION
BIG HEART
Distributed by the Big Heart Slide Company
1058 E. 1st St. Studio 003
Santa Ana, CA 92701
Phone No.: 714-547-1974, 714-349-1928
Fax No.: 714-502-9365
www.bigheartslide.com
sales@bigheartslide.com

In 1998, the Big Heart Slide Company debuted their own guitar model, the **Big Heart BrassTop**. They have also since released the **Big Heart Resonator Brass Top**. The Big Heart Slide Company is well-known for their various aluminum, porcelain, and glass slides; the guitar model is an electric hollow body guitar set up for the slide technique, and features a full brass top. Retail prices ranged from $900 to $1,300. Big Heart no longer offers a guitar, but they continue to produce slides. For further information on their slides or guitars, visit the Big Heart Slide Company's website or contact them directly.

BI LEVEL GUITARS

See La Jolla Luthiers in the L section.

B & J

Instruments previously produced during the 1910s and 1920s. See chapter on House Brands.

B & J (Buegeleisen and Jacobson) was a distributor in New York, NY during the 1920s that distributed guitars under their own name. However, B & J never produced their own guitars as they had other companies build guitars for them, including Martin. B & J also distributed guitars under the name S.S. Stewart after 1915. Source: Willie G. Moseley, *Stellas & Stratocasters*.

BLACKBIRD GUITARS

Guitars currently produced in San Francisco, CA since 2006.

CONTACT INFORMATION
BLACKBIRD GUITARS
1736 Grove Street
San Francisco, CA 94117
Phone No.: 415-706-0632
Fax No.: 415-358-6862
www.blackbirdguitars.com
joe@blackbirdguitars.com

Joe Luttwak and Kyle Wolfe started Blackbird Guitars to create a travel-sized guitar that was actually road worthy. Luttwak and Wolfe searched for years to find a truly worthy travel guitar, but they always sounded too thin and were fragile in construction. Along with Troy Stevens, they developed the Blackbird Rider acoustic guitar that is built out of carbon fibre. Other innovations including an entire hollow body, neck, and headstock, Stereo Sound Hole, and Soundscoop all add to the Rider's large sound, and the carbon fibre construction makes the guitar virtually undestructible. The rider also offers a full 24.5 in. scale in a travel-sized body. Blackbird has also introduced the **Super OM** full-sized body, **Lucky 13** parlor-style body, and a ukulele. For more information, visit Blackbird's website or contact them directly.

ACOUSTIC

RIDER STEEL STRING – 2/3-sized offset uniquely-shaped carbon fiber body, soundhole in upper bass bout, carbon fiber neck, 14/18-fret Micarta fingerboard with long red block inlays, carbon fiber headstock overlay with Blackbird logo, three-per-side tuners, Micarta bridge, optional Fishman Matrix electronics, 24.5 in. scale, gig bag included, mfg. 2006-present.

MSR $1,995	$1,600	$925 - 1,150	$600 - 700

* Add 10% (MSR $2,250) for Fishman Matrix electronics.

* *Rider Nylon String* – similar to the Rider Steel String, except in nylon-string configuration with open-style tuners, gig bag included, mfg. 2008-present.

MSR $2,495	$1,900	$1,100 - 1,400	$700 - 850

* Add 12.5% (MSR $2,895) for Fishman Matrix electronics.

BLACK HILLS

Unknown source of production and/or date of manufacture. See chapter on House Brands.

Black Hills has been identified as a House Brand of the Wall Drug stores. Source: Willie G. Moseley, *Stellas & Stratocasters*.

BLACKSHEAR, TOM

Instruments currently built in San Antonio, TX.

CONTACT INFORMATION
BLACKSHEAR, TOM
17303 Springhill
San Antonio, TX 78232
Phone No.: 210-494-1141
tguitars.home.texas.net/index.htm
tguitars@texas.net

Tom Blackshear started building classical guitars in 1975. Blackshear builds high quality classical guitar models based on the Spanish motif; particularly the Miguel Rodriguez style in Cordoba, Spain, and since the dynasty has passed on, he is currently known as the keeper of their tradition. Tom also spends substantial time fine-tuning his guitars and has shared his fine-tuning system with notable luthiers around the world. Blackshear considers guitar building his full-time business, but he only makes about four to six guitars a year. Since starting his building career in 1958, Blackshear is currently known as one of the top flamenco guitar builders in the world. For further information, please contact luthier Blackshear directly.

BLAIR GUITARS LTD.

Instruments previously built in Ellington, CT during the 1990s.

Designer Douglas Blair has over twenty years experience in the music field, and has been building his own guitars since his teens. Blair has recorded three independent EP/LPs, and toured with acts like Run 21 and W.A.S.P. Throughout his professional playing career, Blair found himself constantly switching between his electric guitar and an Ovation acoustic on a stand for live performances. In 1990, Blair conceived of the **Mutant Twin** guitar model as a way to solve the problem, which combined a solid body half with an "acoustic" half (with hollow tuned sound chamber and Fishman preamp). Prototypes were developed with the aid of Ovation R & D designer Don Johnson in 1990, and the guitar debuted in Boston in 1991. Blair Guitars Ltd. debuted at the 1994 NAMM winter show. In 1997, Blair's design was licensed to Guild (FMIC) as the new Slash signature **Crossroads** custom design doubleneck guitar.

Blair produced the **ASIA Acoustic 12** (last MSR was $1,999), which is a Dual Format twelve-string model with six pairs of unison strings and nylon strings. This guitar has a cedar top, mahogany neck, mahogany/koa back and sides, Steinberger tuners, Fishman piezo bridge pickup, active volume/tone/controls, discrete outputs, and a three-way format selector.

BLUEBERRY GUITARS

Guitars currently produced in Bali, Indonesia. Distributed by Blueberry Guitars in Montreal, Canada.

CONTACT INFORMATION
BLUEBERRY GUITARS
4420 Poirier
Ville St. Laurent, Quebec H4R 2C5
Canada
Phone No.: 514-333-3390
Fax No.: 514-745-1758
www.blueberryguitars.com
info@blueberryguitars.com

Businessman Danny Fonfeder founded Blueberry Guitars with master carver Wayan Tuges and guitar luthier George Morris. Fonfeder was in Bali, Indonesia for business and noticed how many shops that specialized in carved woodworking. He also noticed that nobody was applying this art to guitars and that the only guitars available were cheap imports from other Asian countries. Fonfeder went to Tuges' shop in Bali and commissioned him to build six guitars. Tuges had built two by the time Fonfeder returned and was amazed at how beautiful the instruments were but how poor they sounded. Fonfeder then set out to find a luthier to make these pieces of art sound better. Fonfeder found luthier George Morris, who had been teaching guitar making for several years, and brought him on to complete the team.

Every Blueberry guitar is hand built by an experienced team of craftsmen in Bali, Indonesia and every guitar is unique - no two guitars are the same. Guitars are available in classical, dreadnought, and grand concert configurations and only high-quality tonewoods are used. Unique features of Blueberry include extensive carvings, wood selections/combinations, and inlays. Prices on Blueberry guitars range greatly because each instrument is unique, but most guitars range between $2,500 and $3,500. For more information, visit Blueberry's website or contact them directly.

BLUE LION

Instruments currently built in Santa Margarita, CA since 1977.

CONTACT INFORMATION
BLUE LION
10650 Little Quail Lane
Santa Margarita, CA 93453
Phone No.: 805-438-5569
www.bluelioninstruments.com
dulcimers@bluelioninstruments.com

The Blue Lion company of Robert and Janita Baker are more known for the dulcimers they produce, but they also produce acoustic guitars. For more information contact Blue Lion directly.

The Blue Lion Model **B2** retail price starts at $3,800 (with case) and is designed to give players a very well balanced instrument with superior tone, clarity and playability using only light-gauge strings. Smaller than a dreadnought, the B2 size is easier for most people to hold and play yet delivers all the power of the much larger-bodied guitars and with much better balance. It is also available in a cutaway version. The B2 is available in a variety of wood combinations and with custom fretboard inlay if desired. Amplification is available with the L.R. Baggs acoustic pickup and electronics.

BLUERIDGE

Instruments currently produced in China. Distributed by Saga Musical Instruments in San Francisco, CA.

CONTACT INFORMATION
BLUERIDGE
Distributed by Saga Musical Instruments
PO Box 2841
South San Francisco, CA 94080
Phone No.: 650-558-5558
Fax No.: 650-871-7590
www.sagamusic.com
info@sagamusic.com

Blueridge acoustics are dreadnought-style guitars designed in part for the entry-level to intermediate guitar player. These guitars feature a solid spruce top, mahogany neck, bound rosewood fingerboard with mother-of-pearl position dots, rosewood bridge, a concentric circle rosette, black pickguard, Natural Satin or Clear high gloss finish, chrome sealed tuners, and a solid three-per-side headstock. Models feature rosewood or mahogany back and sides and prices start at $495. Visit Saga's website for more information.

MSR/NOTES	100%	EXCELLENT	AVERAGE	LAST MSR

ACOUSTIC

BR-40 – dreadnought style, solid Sitka spruce top, mahogany back and sides, round soundhole with multi-layer rosette, five-ply black/white binding, mahogany neck, 14/20-fret rosewood fingerboard with MOP dot inlays, rosewood headstock overlay with MOP Blueridge logo/design, three-per-side nickel tuners, rosewood bridge, black pickguard, available in Natural finish, 25.5 in. scale, current mfg.

MSR $550	$390	$225 - 275	$130 - 170

BR-160-12 – 12-string configuration, jumbo style, solid Sitka spruce top, solid Indian rosewood back and sides, round soundhole with multi-layer rosette, scalloped X-bracing, white body binding with herringbone purfling, mahogany neck, 14/20-fret rosewood fingerboard with MOP diamond inlays, rosewood headstock overlay with unique MOP Blueridge logo/design, six-per-side chrome tuners, rosewood bridge, Dalmation-style pickguard, available in Natural finish, 25.5 in. scale, mfg. 2010-present.

MSR $1,095	$775	$475 - 550	$275 - 325

BR-343 GOSPEL – grand auditorium 000-style body, solid Sitka spruce top, mahogany back and sides, pre-war, forward-X pattern position bracing, round soundhole with multi-layer rosette, five-ply black/white binding, mahogany neck, 14/20-fret rosewood fingerboard with pearl Trinity inlays, rosewood headstock overlay with pearl and abalone Cross and Chalice headstock inlay design, three-per-side gold tuners with butterbean knobs, rosewood bridge, black pickguard, available in Sunburst finish, 25.5 in. scale, current mfg.

MSR $750	$525	$300 - 375	$175 - 225

* *BR-343CE Gospel Cutaway* – similar to the BR-343 Gospel, except has a single cutaway and Fishman Presys electronics, available in Sunburst finish, current mfg.

MSR $995	$650	$400 - 500	$250 - 300

BLUESOUTH

Instruments previously built in Muscle Shoals, AL between circa 1991 through 2006.

Ronnie Knight began Bluesouth Guitars in 1991 with the idea of building stringed musical instruments which celebrate the musical heritage of the American South. Blues, jazz, country, rock, and spiritual music were all created in the southern American states. This small area from Texas to the Carolinas, from Kentucky to Florida, has been the hotbed of the world's musical culture in the twentieth century. Several small towns within the southeast have had a huge impact on today's popular music: Muscle Shoals, Alabama; Macon, Georgia; and Clarksdale, Mississippi.

The results of this project have been unique, light-bodied guitars with large, comfortable necks. Bluesouth contends that "fierce individualism" is the key ingredient in their guitar-making operation. Starting in a small shop over a record store in early 1992, Bluesouth moved to a much larger industrial facility in the spring of 1995. The company offered seven models, including two electric basses. Bluesouth also built its own cases and pickups in house. Company history courtesy Ronnie Knight, April 17, 1996.

Bluesouth guitars offered two acoustic models, an archtop model and a flattop model. The archtop **Storyville** model has a single cutaway body with hand carved European spruce top, European maple back and sides, five-ply black/ivoroid body binding, hard maple neck, and ivoroid bound ebony fingerboard. The last MSR of $5,300 includes a case. The **Tutweiler** (last MSR $2,195, case included) has a solid spruce top, mahogany back and sides, ivoroid body binding, mahogany neck, and rosewood fingerboard.

BOAZ ELKAYAM GUITARS

Instruments currently built in North Hollywood, CA since 1985.

Boaz Elkayam hand builds commissioned guitars, customized prototypes, classical and flamenco style guitars, mandolins, and his Travel Guitar. Elkayam, the son of a violin builder, was taught building techniques of stringed instruments, and has performed restoration work on museum pieces.

Luthier Elkayam handcrafts his guitars using traditional lutherie techniques, and eschews the use of power tools. Elkayam prefers to build with top-of-the-line woods such as Brazilian and Indian rosewood, Macassar and Gaboon ebony, Honduran mahogany, German and Canadian spruce, and Alaskan red cedar. Pieces are limited to a small yearly output. For more information, visit Boaz's website or contact him directly.

BOGDON MUSIC

Guitar kits currently produced in Dearborn, MI. Distributed by Bogdon Music, which is a division of EdenCompanies.com.

Bogdon Music produces the Bogdon Box Bass, which is basically a do-it-yourself kit that results in a cardboard box bass. The parts are shipped to the customer and the customer assembles all of the components. Unlike most guitar kits, this one uses an odd variety of components including nuts and bolts tuners, nylon weed whacker strings, and a finishing nail for a nut. A three-piece white oak glues to the cardboard box and there is a Piezo pickup mounted inside. Although this is a true hardware store instrument, it actually sounds pretty good! Retail prices range from $120 to $134. For more information, visit Bogdon's website or contact them directly.

BOHMANN, JOSEPH

Guitars previously built in Chicago, IL between 1878 and the late 1920s.

Luthier Joseph H. Bohmann was born in Neumarkt (Bohemia), Czechoslovakia in 1848. He later emigrated to America, and then founded Bohmann's American Musical Industry in 1878. He produced several types of instruments including flattop acoustic guitars, harp guitars, mandolins, banjos, and violins. Bohmann's Perfect Artist violins won a number of international honors, and his American mandolin model was the top of the line in both the Montgomery Ward and Sears catalogs in 1894. Bohmann guitars were available in many different configurations and sizes including 12, 13, 14, and 15 in. bodies. By 1900, Bohmann had thirteen styles of the Concert, Grand Concert, and Standard models. By 1900, Bohmann was offering thirteen grades of guitars. Source: Michael Wright, *Vintage Guitar Magazine*.

Since Bohmann produced many different variations, and very few of them show up on the second hand market, pricing is difficult. Guitars are usually valued between $500 and $1,500 depending on condition and level of ornateness. Harp guitars are worth quite a bit more between $3,500 and $4,500. Each guitar should be valued individually.

BOOM BASSES

See Donnell, Ken.

BOUCHER GUITARS

Instruments currently produced in Berthier-sur-Mer, Quebec, Canada. Distributed in the U.S. by Boucher Guitars. They have been producing guitars as Boucher Guitars since 2003.

CONTACT INFORMATION
BOUCHER GUITARS
40 route St-François
Berthier-sur-Mer, Quebec G0R 1E0
Canada
Phone No.: 418-259-2083
Fax No.: 418-259-2283
www.boucherguitars.com
info@guitareboucher.com

Norman Boucher founded Canada's first acoustic guitar manufacturing company in 1968. Norman's sons, Claude and Richard, worked with him building a Martin D-style body with X bracing. In 1988, Boucher closed the store and sold the company and trademarks. Norman passed away in 1997. In 2000, Claude decided to build high-quality acoustic guitars made out of the finest woods, and they began stocking material. In 2003, Boucher introduced the Adirondack Series of guitars. These instruments featured "resonance aging," which is a process where the top is exposed to music 24 hours a day for three years to mature the acoustic chamber. In 2004, Claude's son Nicolas began working at Boucher guitars, and in 2005, Claude's nephew Robin joined him and Nicolas to start the Boucher Adirondack Collection Company. For more information on Boucher guitars, visit their website or contact them directly.

Until 2004, models included the Adirondack SE (Adirondack Red Spruce, Last MSR was $3,795), Clifton (Adirondack Red Spruce, Last MSR $3,500), Ditton (flamed cherry, Last MSR $2,795), Dudswell (Indian rosewood, Last MSR $3,995), Hatley (flamed maple, Last MSR $3,295), Orford (Brazilian rosewood, Last MSR $5,595), Tingwick (Madagascar rosewood, Last MSR $4,595), and Woburn (walnut, Last MSR $2,995). All models are dreadnoughts and cutaways were available for an additional $300.

In 2005, a new line of guitars was introduced called the Goose Series. These guitars are available as a dreadnought, jumbo, OM, and 000 style. Prices start at $2,795 for the Native Goose.

BOUCHET

Instruments previously built in Paris, France from 1946 to possibly the late 1970s.

Luthier and painter Robert Bouchet (1898-1986) began building guitars in Paris in the mid-1940s. A keen guitarist, he produced very high quality guitars in small numbers. Source: Tony Bacon, *The Ultimate Guitar Book*.

BOULDER CREEK GUITARS

Guitars currently produced. Distributed by Morgan Hill Music in Morgan Hill, CA.

CONTACT INFORMATION
BOULDER CREEK GUITARS
A division of Morgan Hill Music
375 Digital Drive
Morgan Hill, CA 95037
Phone No.: 408-779-3845
Fax No.: 408-465-2117
www.bouldercreekguitars.com
info@morganhillmusic.com

Boulder Creek Guitars are built with a new type of bracing called the Suspended Bracing System (SBS). For over 150 years, guitar builders have been using the standard X pattern bracing style on all acoustics. Mike Shellhammer, who is the designer for Boulder Creek Guitars, wanted to increase sustain and vibration, and his experiments resulted in the SBS. SBS has less points of contact in the guitar and less rigid bracing around the bridge that allows the top to vibrate more. Shellhammer also eliminated the traditional soundhole on the top and replaced it with a side port (standard soundholes on the top that still utilize the SBS are also available in the Stage and Studio series). The Solitaire Series are available in a variety of configurations and tonewoods. For more information, visit Boulder Creek's website or contact them directly.

BOURGEOIS

Instruments currently produced in Lewiston, ME since the early 1990s.

CONTACT INFORMATION
BOURGEOIS
Pantheon Guitars
2 Cedar Street
Lewiston, ME 04240
Phone No.: 410-254-4433
www.pantheonguitars.com
info@pantheonguitars.com

Dana Bourgeois built his first guitar in his dorm room during his college days at Bowdoin College in Maine. In 1978, Dana became a luthier full-time and shortly thereafter was contacted by Eric Schoenburg to build an OM (Orchestra Model) cutaway in a traditional design. This led to a ten-year partnership with Schoenburg and the basis of Bourgeois' first small handcrafted guitars. These first guitars were labeled Schoenburg, but they had the

MSR/NOTES	100%	EXCELLENT	AVERAGE	LAST MSR

sound Dana had created in the tops. In 1990, Dana started as a designer for Paul Reed Smith's acoustic line. Dana was also a consultant for the setup and construction of the Gibson Montana Acoustic plant in Montana. Dana started building guitars under the Bourgeois name in 1993, and he established Bourgeois Guitars as a company in 1995. Due to financial problems, Bourgeois went out of business in 1999, but that was only temporary. In October 2000, Pantheon Guitars was established to "promote and support the lutherie trade" with seven original luthiers, including Bourgeois. Pantheon/Bourgeois currently build their guitars at an 1840 Textile Mill located in Lewiston, Maine. For more information on Bourgeois or Pantheon, visit their website or contact them directly.

ACOUSTIC

Bourgeois offers these features standard on all models except where noted: 25.5 in. scale, bone nut and saddle, one-piece mahogany neck, ebony fingerboard, ebony bell bridge, rosewood headstock veneer, black fingerboard binding, high gloss body and headstock finish, satin neck finish, MOP Bourgeois headstock inlay, Bourgeois premium pickguard, ivoroid bridge and end pins, custom hardshell case, and a limited lifetime warranty.

Keep in mind that it is possible that Bourgeois changed standard specs over the years and not every guitar will contain these. As of 2011, these are the standard specs. Bourgeois also offers several options on all models including some popular package combinations. Even though they offer their guitars through dealers, guitars can still be ordered with several options that make them one of a kind in a sense. A list of pricing options is listed but use this with some caution. Many models already have these options as standard equipment and therefore do not add additional value. Left-handed guitars are available at no additional cost. If you are really confused with what guitar you have or the options, it is best to contact Bourgeois directly.

Bourgeois also produces a small line of archtop guitars. Production models in past years have included the A-350, A-360 (A-350 with gold hardware and Kent Armstrong pickup and controls), and the A-500 (premium wood version). Currently, archtop guitars are built on a limited availability basis. Contact Bourgeois for more information.

- Add $100 for DB HB pack including signature herringbone, rosette, and back strip.
- Add $100 for a gloss finish headstock.
- Add $100 for gold tuners.
- Add $100 for herringbone top border.
- Add $100 for ivoroid fingerboard binding.
- Add $100 for ivoroid headstock binding.
- Add $150 for wood fingerboard binding.
- Add $150 for square/diamond inlays.
- Add $200 for abalone rosette.
- Add $200 for ebony pyramid bridge.

- Add $250 for wood headstock binding.
- Add $400 for hot hide glue.
- Add $450 for Advanced Floral fingerboard inlay.
- Add $450 for DB snowflake fingerboard inlay.
- Add $600 for cutaway.
- Add $600 for wood body binding.
- Add $650 for standard Sunburst finish.
- Add $750 for Pale Burst finish.
- Add $1,200 for Style 41 abalone top border.
- Add $1,600 for varnish finish.

0 STYLE – 0 body style, solid European spruce top, Indian rosewood back and sides, round soundhole with wood rosette, ivoroid body binding with B/W/B maple back and side purfling, one-piece mahogany neck, black-bound ebony fingerboard with squares and diamonds inlays, square headstock, three-per-side gold Waverly tuners with ebony buttons, ebony belly bridge, available in short 25 in. scale, hardshell case included, mfg. 2011-present.

MSR $4,495	$4,050	$2,250 - 2,700	$1,350 - 1,650	

ARTISAN DR-A – dreadnought body, spruce top, rosewood back and sides, mfg. 1999 only.

	N/A	$850 - 1,000	$550 - 650	$1,995

ARTISAN JR-A – jumbo orchestra model body style, spruce top, rosewood back and sides, mfg. 1999 only.

	N/A	$850 - 1,000	$550 - 650	$1,995

COUNTRY BOY 00 – 00 body style, solid Sitka spruce top, mahogany back and sides, wood rosette, tortoise body binding, black line backstrip, tiny dot fingerboard inlay, three-per-side nickel Waverly tuners, ebony belly bridge, available in short 25 in. scale, mfg. 2009-present.

MSR $3,695	$3,325	$1,850 - 2,200	$1,225 - 1,475	

* *Country Boy 00 Adirondack* – similar to the Country Boy 00, except has a figured Adirondack spruce top, mfg. 2009-present.

MSR $4,095	$3,700	$2,050 - 2,500	$1,375 - 1,650	

COUNTRY BOY DREADNOUGHT (RICKY SKAGGS) – dreadnought body style, solid Sitka spruce top, mahogany back and sides, tortoise body binding, black line backstrip, tiny dot fingerboard inlay, mfg. 1998-present.

MSR $3,695	$3,325	$1,850 - 2,200	$1,225 - 1,475	

* *Country Boy Dreadnought Adirondack* – similar to the Country Boy Dreadnought, except has a figured Adirondack spruce top, mfg. 2007-present.

MSR $4,095	$3,700	$2,050 - 2,500	$1,375 - 1,650	

* *Country Boy Dreadnought Deluxe* – similar to the Country Boy Dreadnought, except has figured Adirondack spruce top, figured mahogany back and sides, rosewood body binding with black and white purfling, black fingerboard binding, gold tuners, bone bridge and end pins, and a premium pickguard, mfg. 2003-present.

MSR $4,595	$4,150	$2,300 - 2,750	$1,525 - 1,825	

MSR/NOTES	100%	EXCELLENT	AVERAGE	LAST MSR

* ***Ricky Skaggs Signature Model*** – similar to the Country Boy Dreadnought, except has rosewood back and sides, an abalone rosette, and different binding, mfg. 1997-99.

	N/A	$2,500 - 3,000	$1,500 - 1,800	$4,000

D-150 – dreadnought body style, solid premium Adirondack spruce top, premium Brazilian rosewood back and sides, triple-bound ivoroid B/N/H binding, side pufling, Bourgeois backstrip, abalone rosette, squares and diamonds fingerboard inlay, Brazilian rosewood headstock overlay, bone bridge and end pins, gold tuners, premium pickguard, mfg. 2002-present.

MSR $7,995	$7,200	$4,000 - 5,000	N/A	

SLOPE D – sloped dreadnought body style, solid Adirondack spruce top, mahogany back and sides, ivoroid B/N/H binding, black line backstrip, ivoroid rosette, tiny dot fingerboard inlay, snakehead ebony veneer headstock, ivoroid tuners, available in Natural or Sunburst finish, mfg. 1994-present.

MSR $4,195	$3,775	$2,100 - 2,525	$1,400 - 1,675	

* Add 10% (MSR $4,595) for Sunburst finish.
* Add 10% for Model SD-200 option.
* Add 15% for Model SD-240 option.

In the mid-1990s, Bourgeois offered packages on several models. The Slope D featured the SD-100 (Standard), SD-200 (Indian rosewood back and sides), and the SD-240 (Indian rosewood back and sides, red spruce top, abalone rosette, and nickel tuners).

* ***Advanced Slope D*** – similar to the Slope D, except a fancier version with Indian rosewood back and sides, triple-bound ivoroid B/N/H binding, side purfling, Burgeois backstrip, floral fingerboard inlays, bone bridge and end pins, and a premium pickguard, available in Natural or Sunburst finish, mfg. 2004-present.

MSR $4,795	$4,325	$2,400 - 2,900	$1,600 - 1,925	

* Add 7.5% (MSR $5,195) for Sunburst finish.

* ***BK Slope D*** – similar to the Slope D, except has a Bearclaw spruce top, figured mahogany back and sides, Burgeois backstrip, Brazilian fingerboard with floral inlays, Brazilian headstock veneer, Brazilian bridge, ebony bone bridge and end pins, and a wood rosette, available in Natural finish, mfg. 2006-present.

MSR $4,595	$4,150	$2,300 - 2,750	$1,525 - 1,825	

* ***DS-260 12-Fret Slope D*** – similar to the Slope D, except has a 12-fret fingerboard with a slotted headstock, ivoroid/herringbone body binding, herringbone rosette and backstrip, and squares/diamonds fingerboard inlays, available in Natural finish, mfg. 2004-present.

MSR $4,295	$3,900	$2,150 - 2,550	$1,300 - 1,600	

»***DS-260 12-Fret Slope D Cutaway*** – similar to the DS-260 12-Fret Slope D, except has a single cutaway, available in Natural finish, mfg. 2009-2010.

	$4,050	$2,250 - 2,700	$1,350 - 1,650	$4,495

* ***Slope D Short Scale*** – similar to the Slope D, except has a shorter 24.9 in. scale, available in Natural or Sunburst finish, mfg. 2007-present.

MSR $4,195	$3,775	$2,100 - 2,525	$1,400 - 1,675	

* Add 7.5% (MSR $4,595) for Sunburst finish.

»***Varnish Slope D Short Scale*** – similar to the Slope D Short Scale, except has a mahogany top, standard square headstock with Ziricote overlay and an ivoroid logo, Ziricote fingerboard with tiny dot inlays, Ziricote bridge, and an oil varnish finish, mfg. 2011-present.

MSR $6,195	$5,575	$3,100 - 3,725	$2,075 - 2,475	

VINTAGE D (DREADNOUGHT) – dreadnought body style, solid Adirondack spruce top, Indian rosewood back and sides, herringbone body binding, zig-zag backstrip, vintage rosette, squares and diamonds fingerboard inlay, ivoroid heel cap and butt wedge, nickel tuners, mfg. 2000-present.

MSR $4,195	$3,775	$2,100 - 2,525	$1,400 - 1,675	

* ***Standard D (Dreadnought)*** – similar to the Vintage D, except has a Sitka spruce top, mfg. 2003-present.

MSR $3,795	$3,425	$1,900 - 2,275	$1,250 - 1,525	

* ***Vintage Mahogany Dreadnought (Model VM-D)*** – similar to the Vintage D, except has a mahogany top, wood soundhole rosette, ebony wood body binding, black line backstrip, squares and diamonds fingerboard inlays, and nickel Waverly tuners with vintage oval buttons, mfg. 2009-present.

MSR $4,595	$4,150	$2,300 - 2,750	$1,525 - 1,825	

»***Vintage Varnish Mahogany Dreadnought (Model V2M-D)*** – similar to the Vintage Mahogany Dreadnought, except has an oil varnish finish, mfg. 2009-present.

MSR $6,195	$5,575	$3,100 - 3,725	$2,075 - 2,475	

DB JUMBO – jumbo body style, cedar top, Indian rosewood back and sides, black body binding with white pinstripe, wood rosette, Bourgeois backstrip, tiny dot fingerboard inlays, square headstock with gold tuners, ebony belly bridge, no pickguard, mfg. 2005-06.

	N/A	$1,800 - 2,100	$1,200 - 1,400	$3,295

MSR/NOTES	100%	EXCELLENT	AVERAGE	LAST MSR

* **DB Jumbo Cutaway (Petite Jumbo)** – similar to the DB Jumbo, except has a single cutaway, snakehead headstock, and B/N/H black binding with white pinstripe, mfg. 2005-2010.

	$3,600	$2,000 - 2,400	$1,200 - 1,500	$3,995

DB SIGNATURE DREADNOUGHT – dreadnought body style, Adirondack spruce top, Madagascar rosewood back and sides, round soundhole with DB Signature rosette, curly maple body binding with DB Signature herringbone purfling, one-piece mahogany neck, 14/20-fret black bound ebony fingerboard with ivroy square and diamond inlays, Madagascar rosewood headstock veneer with MOP Bourgeois inlay, three-per-side gold Waverly tuners, ebony bridge, tortoiseshell pickguard, available in Natural high gloss finish, 25.5 in. scale, hardshell case included, mfg. 2006-present.

MSR $5,195	$4,675	$2,600 - 3,150	$1,725 - 2,075	

DB SIGNATURE OM – Orchestra Model body style, Adirondack spruce top, Madagascar rosewood back and sides, round soundhole with DB Signature rosette, curly maple body binding with DB Signature herringbone purfling, one-piece mahogany neck, 14/20-fret black bound ebony fingerboard with ivroy square and diamond inlays, Madagascar rosewood headstock veneer with MOP Bourgeois inlay, three-per-side gold Waverly tuners, ebony bridge, tortoiseshell pickguard, available in Natural high gloss finish, 25.5 in. scale, hardshell case included, mfg. 2008-present.

MSR $5,195	$4,675	$2,600 - 3,150	$1,725 - 2,075	

JOMC STANDARD CUTAWAY – jumbo orchestra model single cutaway body style, solid Sitka spruce top, Indian rosewood back and sides, ivoroid B/N/H binding (disc. 2010) or tortoise body binding (2011-present), Bourgeois backstrip, abalone rosette, no fingerboard inlays (disc. 2010) or squares and diamonds inlays (2011-present), ebony headstock veneer, nickel tuners (disc. 2010) or gold tuners (2011-present), mfg. 1994-present.

MSR $4,695	$4,225	$2,350 - 2,825	$1,575 - 1,875	

* **Subtract 25% for JOMC-100 package.**
* **Add 10% for JOMC-300 package.**

In the mid-1990s, Bourgeois offered packages on several models. The Jumbo OM featured the JOMC-100 (Standard), JOMC-240 (Indian rosewood back and sides and an ebony fingerboard and bridge), and the JOMC-300 (Englemann spruce top, curly maple back and sides, ebony fingerboard and bridge, black/white/black top/back/side purfling, and no fingerboard inlays). In 1999, a cedar top was standard on the JOMC. In 2011, new specs were introduced.

JOMC DELUXE – jumbo orchestra model single cutaway body style, solid Bearclaw Sitka spruce top, Madagascar rosewood back and sides, triple bound curly maple B/N/H binding, side purfling, Bourgeois backstrip, abalone rosette, floral fingerboard inlays, Snakehead ebony headstock veneer, gold tuners, bone bridge and end pins, premium pickguard, mfg. 1994-2006.

	N/A	$3,000 - 3,500	N/A	$5,495

JOM CELTIC STYLE – jumbo orchestra model body style, western red cedar top, figured walnut back and sides, curly maple B/N/H binding, side purfling, Bourgeois backstrip, abalone rosette, Celtic Knot fingerboard inlays designed by Dana Bourgeois (inspired by The Book of Kells), Snakehead ebony headstock veneer, gold tuners, bone bridge and end pins, no pickguard, mfg. 2005-08.

	N/A	$2,500 - 3,000	N/A	$4,995

* **JOMC Celtic Style Cutaway** – similar to the JOM Celtic Style, except has a single cutaway, mfg. 2005-08.

	N/A	$2,800 - 3,350	N/A	$5,595

SMALL JUMBO – Small Jumbo body style, solid European spruce top, Indian rosewood back and sides, round soundhole with wood rosette, ivoroid body binding with B/W/B maple back and side purfling, one-piece mahogany neck, black-bound ebony fingerboard with squares and diamonds inlays, square headstock, three-per-side gold Waverly tuners with ebony buttons, ebony belly bridge, available in short 25 in. scale, hardshell case included, mfg. 2011-present.

MSR $4,495	$4,050	$2,250 - 2,700	$1,350 - 1,650	

VINTAGE JOM (JUMBO ORCHESTRA MODEL) – jumbo orchestra model body style, solid Adirondack spruce top, Indian rosewood back and sides, herringbone body binding, zig-zag backstrip, vintage rosette, squares and diamonds fingerboard inlay, ivoroid heel cap and butt wedge, nickel tuners, mfg. 2004-present.

MSR $4,195	$3,775	$2,100 - 2,525	$1,400 - 1,675	

* **Vintage JOM Cutaway** – similar to the Vintage JOM, except has a single cutaway, available in Natural finish, mfg. 2009-present.

MSR $4,795	$4,325	$2,400 - 2,900	$1,600 - 1,925	

VINTAGE JOM-150 – jumbo orchestra model body style, solid premium Adirondack spruce top, premium Brazilian rosewood back and sides, triple-bound ivoroid B/N/H binding, side pufling, Bourgeois backstrip, abalone rosette, squares and diamonds fingerboard inlay, Brazilian rosewood headstock overlay, bone bridge and end pins, gold tuners, premium pickguard, mfg. 2007-08.

	N/A	$4,000 - 5,000	N/A	$7,795

MARTIN SIMPSON SIGNATURE MODEL – sloped dreadnought single cutaway body style, solid spruce top, rosewood back and sides, ivoroid B/N/H binding, multi-color herringbone backstrip, abalone rosette, leaf fingerboard inlay, standard Bourgeois ebony overlay headstock, ivoroid tuners, mfg. 1997-99.

	N/A	$2,300 - 2,800	$1,400 - 1,700	$4,100

MSR/NOTES	100%	EXCELLENT	AVERAGE	LAST MSR

* **Martin Simpson European Signature Model** – similar to the Martin Simpson Signature Model, except has a cedar top, mahogany back and sides, and Vintage Style Gotoh tuners, mfg. 1998-99.

	N/A	$1,800 - 2,200	$1,100 - 1,300	$3,450

PICCOLO PARLOR – parlor 12-fret body style, solid Adirondack spruce top, mahogany back and sides, round soundhole with wood rosette, Ziricote body binding with half herringbone/maple back and side purfling, one-piece mahogany neck, black-bound ebony fingerboard with short pattern Fossil ivory squares and diamonds inlays, square headstock, three-per-side nickel Waverly tuners with ebony buttons, ebony pyramid bridge, available in short 25 in. scale, hardshell case included, mfg. 2011-present.

MSR $4,695	$4,225	$2,350 - 2,825	$1,575 - 1,875	

OM-150 – orchestra model body style, solid premium Adirondack spruce top, premium Brazilian rosewood back and sides, triple-bound ivoroid B/N/H binding, side purfling, Bourgeois backstrip, abalone rosette, squares and diamonds fingerboard inlay, Brazilian rosewood headstock overlay, bone bridge and end pins, gold tuners, premium pickguard, mfg. 2003-present.

MSR $7,995	$7,200	$4,000 - 5,000	N/A	

OM – orchestra model body style, solid Englemann spruce top, mahogany back and sides, tortoiseshell body binding with black/white purfling, black backstrip, wood rosette, small MOP dot fingerboard inlays, square Indian rosewood headstock overlay with gold tuners, ivoroid heel cap and butt wedge, ebony pyramid bridge, tortoiseshell pickguard, mfg. 1993-99.

	N/A	$2,000 - 2,500	$1,200 - 1,500	$2,850

- Add 10% for the OM-240 package.

In the mid-1990s, Bourgeois offered packages on several models. The OM featured the OM-140 (Standard) and the OM-240 (rosewood back and sides with a pyramid/belly bridge).

OMC – orchestra model single cutaway body style, solid Englemann spruce top, Indian rosewood back and sides, tortoiseshell body binding with black/white/black purfling, multi-color herringbone backstrip, abalone or wood rosette, square and diamonds fingerboard inlays, square Indian rosewood headstock overlay with gold tuners, ivoroid heel cap and butt wedge, ebony pyramid bridge, tortoiseshell pickguard, mfg. 1993-present.

MSR $4,695	$4,225	$2,350 - 2,825	$1,575 - 1,875	

- Subtract 20% for OMC-140 package.

In the mid-1990s, Bourgeois offered packages on several models. The OMC featured the OMC-140 (Mahogany back and sides) and the OMC-240 (rosewood back and sides with a pyramid/belly bridge). In 2006, new specs were introduced on the OMC including a wood rosette, short square fingerboard inlays, and no pickguard.

OMC SOLOIST – orchestra model body style, solid premium European spruce top, premium Brazilian rosewood back and sides, triple-bound rosewood body binding, black/white/black back and side purfling, Bourgeois backstrip, short pattern squares and diamonds fingerboard inlay, Brazilian rosewood headstock overlay, bone bridge and end pins, slotted triangle heel cap inlay, ebony pyramid bridge, gold tuners, no pickguard, mfg. 2003-present.

MSR $8,595	$7,750	$4,250 - 5,250	N/A	

OMS-150 – Orchestra Model-style body, Premium Adirondack spruce top, premium Brazilian rosewood back and sides, round soundhole with abalone rosette, triple-bound ivoroid body binding, side purfling, Bourgeois backstripe, 12/20-fret ebony fingerboard with short pattern squares and diamonds inlays, slotted headstock with Brazilian rosewood overly, three-per-side side-mounted Waverly tuners with ivoroid buttons, ebony bridge, Natural finish with Vintage Toner top, mfg. 2007-08.

	N/A	$4,250 - 5,250	N/A	$8,295

OMS STANDARD – orchestra model body style, 12 frets to the body, Adirondack spruce top, Indian rosewood back and sides, ivoroid/herringbone body binding, vintage rosette, zig-zag backstrip, square/diamond fingerboard inlays, slotted headstock with ivoroid side-mount tuners, ebony pyramid bridge, no pickguard, mfg. 2004-present.

MSR $4,295	$3,900	$2,150 - 2,550	$1,300 - 1,600	

* **OMS Standard Cutaway** – similar to the OMS Standard, except has a single cutaway, available in Natural finish, mfg. 2009-2010.

	$4,350	$2,400 - 2,900	$1,400 - 1,700	$4,795

OMS DELUXE – orchestra model body style, 12 frets to the body, European spruce top, Brazilian rosewood back and sides, ivoroid/Style 42 abalone body binding, ivoroid head and fingerboard binding, side purfling, abalone rosette, Bourgeois backstrip, square/diamond fingerboard inlays, Brazilian slotted headstock with ivoroid side-mount tuners, ebony or Fossil Ivory pyramid bridge, bone bridge and end pins, no pickguard, mfg. 2004-07.

	N/A	N/A	N/A	$10,000

In 2006, new specs were introduced with the Fossil Ivory bridge and different bindings.

COUNTRY BOY OM – orchestra body style, solid Sitka spruce top, mahogany back and sides, wood rosette, tortoise body binding, black line backstrip, tiny dot fingerboard inlay, three-per-side nickel Waverly tuners, ebony belly bridge, available in short 25 in. or long 25.5 in. scale, mfg. 2009-present.

MSR $3,695	$3,325	$1,850 - 2,200	$1,225 - 1,475	

* **Country Boy OM Adirondack** – similar to the Country Boy OM, except has a figured Adirondack spruce top, mfg. 2009-present.

MSR $4,095	$3,700	$2,050 - 2,500	$1,375 - 1,650	

MSR/NOTES	100%	EXCELLENT	AVERAGE	LAST MSR

VINTAGE OM (ORCHESTRA MODEL) – orchestra model body style, solid Adirondack spruce top, Indian rosewood back and sides, herringbone body binding, zig-zag backstrip, vintage rosette, squares and diamonds fingerboard inlay, ivoroid heel cap and butt wedge, ebony pyramid bridge, nickel tuners, available in short 25 in. or long 25.5 in. scale, mfg. 2000-present.

MSR $4,195	$3,775	$2,100 - 2,525	$1,400 - 1,675	

* *Vintage Mahogany OM (Model VM-OM)* – similar to the Vintage OM, except has a mahogany top, wood soundhole rosette, ebony wood body binding, black line backstrip, squares and diamonds fingerboard inlays, and nickel Waverly tuners with vintage oval buttons, mfg. 2009-present.

MSR $4,595	$4,150	$2,300 - 2,750	$1,525 - 1,825	

»*Vintage Varnish Mahogany OM (Model V2M-OM)* – similar to the Vintage Mahogany OM, except has an oil varnish finish, mfg. 2009-present.

MSR $6,195	$5,575	$3,100 - 3,725	$2,075 - 2,475	

BOWN, RALPH S.

Instruments currently built in York, England.

Ralph Bown builds high quality guitars, in a number of variations including six-string, twelve-string, harp, and baritone. Bown has built guitars for many people including Martin Simpson, Henry Kaiser, and Allan Taylor. For more information, contact Bown directly.

> **CONTACT INFORMATION**
> **BOWN, RALPH S.**
> 8 Gillamoor Avenue, Burnholme
> York, YO31 0QE England
> http://www.see.ed.ac.uk/~afm/music/bown

BOZO

Instruments currently built in East Englewood and Port Charlotte, FL since 2005. Previously produced in Lindenhurst, IL.

Bozidar (Bozo) Podunavac was born in Serbia in Eastern Europe and was raised in Belgrade. Bozo was originally apprenticed to luthier Milutin Mladenovicin. Bozo came to the USA in the late 1950s and settled in Chicago, Illinois. In the early 1960s he set up shop as a luthier and began building his own instruments. Bozo moved to Escondido (near San Diego), California in 1972, and to San Diego in 1975. In 1978, Bozo opened a school of lutherie, which he ran for a number of years. Bozo has also called Linderhurst, Illinois and East Englewood, Florida home.

> **CONTACT INFORMATION**
> **BOZO**
> 16866 Toledo Blade Blvd.
> Port Charlotte, FL 33954
> Phone No.: 941-743-9020
> Fax No.: 941-743-9020

His instruments are unique for a variety of reasons. The most notable feature is his "Bell Western" design. This style features an upper bout of a Martin Dreadnought combined with the lower bout of a Gibson J-200. His guitars are typically very ornate with complex and unusal rosettes and wide purfling. The high-quality of craftsmanship is evident in his guitars as well. Many guitars are constructed out of Brazilian rosewood, koa, and Indian rosewood. The sound of his guitars are also unique as they have an original fullness to the notes and sustain that rings for a long time without losing the roundness of the note. His twelve-string guitars are particularly special as Leo Kottke and Peter Lang (among others), used them early in their careers and recorded several songs with them.

In the mid-1970s, Bozo licensed his designs to a Japanese firm, Morris, that manufactured the instruments under the Bozo name. A majority of Bozo guitars consist of the Japanese-made models. Bozo was one of the luthiers contacted by esteemed collector Scott Chinery for a model in the Blue Guitars Collection. Bozo still builds guitars on a limited basis. For more information or to talk to Bozo, contact him directly. Source: Matt Hayden.

ACOUSTIC: CURRENT MODELS

Known for both his flattop and archtop guitar designs, Bozo is currently building archtop models only. Instruments feature very ornate detailing and inlay work, as well as a large distinct headstock. The guitars feature hand-selected European woods, carved tops, elaborate abalone and herringbone inlays, and wood binding (no plastic or celluloid is used on his guitars). The Bell Western model ranges from $5,500-$12,000, the Bell Western XII from $6,000-$14,000, the Requinto from $5,500-$12,000 and Archtops from $8,000-$22,000.

* **Add $800 for cutaway option.**
* **Add $700 for custom abalone inlaid pickguard.**
* **Add $800 for deluxe fingerboard inlays.**
* **Add $500 for left-hand configuration.**

ACOUSTIC: JAPANESE MODELS

Most of Bozo's guitars feature original designs and only resemble traditional shapes. Models B3, B5, B8, B10, and B15 are all traditional classical models. Models B20, B25, and B30 are called grand concerts, but they are more of a combination of a classical guitar and an OM-style Martin. The B35 is based on traditional a dreadnought. The B60, B80, and B100 are all Bozo's Bell Western design, which is a cross between a dreadnought and a Gibson J-200.

B3 – classical style, solid cedar top, laminated rosewood back and sides, round soundhole with rosette, multi-ply body binding, cedro or mahogany neck, 12/19-fret unbound rosewood fingerboard, Bozo open-style unbound headstock with three-per-side open-style gold tuners, rosewood bridge, Natural finish, mfg. mid-1970s.

	N/A	$425 - 500	$250 - 300	

MSR/NOTES	100%	EXCELLENT	AVERAGE	LAST MSR

B5 – classical style, solid cedar top, laminated rosewood back and sides, round soundhole with rosette, multi-ply body binding, cedro neck, 12/19-fret unbound ebony fingerboard, Bozo open-style unbound headstock with three-per-side open-style gold tuners, rosewood bridge, Natural finish, mfg. mid-1970s.

	N/A	$450 - 550	$275 - 325	

B8 – similar to the B5, except has a Spanish foot-style neck, mfg. mid-1970s.

	N/A	$450 - 550	$275 - 325	

B10 – classical style, solid cedar top, solid Indian rosewood back and sides, round soundhole with rosette, multi-ply body binding, cedro neck with Spanish foot construction, 12/19-fret unbound ebony fingerboard, Bozo open-style unbound headstock with three-per-side open-style gold tuners, ebony bridge, Natural finish, mfg. mid-1970s.

	N/A	$500 - 600	$300 - 350	

B15 – classical style, solid German spruce top, solid Indian rosewood back and sides, round soundhole with rosette with matching top, back, and back strip binding, cedro neck with Spanish foot construction, 12/19-fret unbound ebony fingerboard, Bozo open-style unbound headstock with three-per-side open-style gold tuners, ebony bridge, Natural finish, mfg. mid-1970s.

	N/A	$600 - 750	$325 - 400	

B20 – grand concert style, solid spruce top, laminated mahogany back and sides, round soundhole with herringbone rosette, multi-ply body binding, 14/20-fret unbound rosewood fingerboard with dot inlay, Bozo unbound headstock with three-per-side Schaller-style chrome tuners, rosewood bridge, Natural finish, mfg. mid-1970s.

	N/A	$500 - 600	$300 - 350	

B25 – grand concert style, solid spruce top, laminated rosewood back and sides, round soundhole with herringbone rosette, multi-ply body binding, 14/20-fret bound rosewood fingerboard with dot inlay, Bozo unbound headstock with three-per-side Schaller-style chrome tuners, rosewood bridge, Natural finish, mfg. mid-1970s.

	N/A	$550 - 700	$325 - 400	

B30 – grand concert style, solid spruce top, solid rosewood back and sides, round soundhole with pearl rosette, pearl body purfling, white body binding, 14/20-fret bound rosewood fingerboard with pearl hexagon inlays, Bozo unbound headstock with three-per-side Schaller-style chrome tuners, rosewood bridge, Natural finish, mfg. mid-1970s.

	N/A	$750 - 1,000	$425 - 550	

B35 – dreadnought style, solid spruce top, laminated rosewood back and sides, round soundhole with pearloid rosette, pearloid purfling, white body binding, checkerboard back strip, 14/20-fret bound rosewood fingerboard with dot inlay, brown Bozo unbound headstock with three-per-side Schaller-style chrome tuners, rosewood bridge, Natural finish, mfg. mid-1970s.

	N/A	$700 - 900	$400 - 500	

* **B35 12-String** – similar to the B35, except in 12-string configuration and six-per-side tuners, mfg. mid-1970s.

	N/A	$750 - 1,000	$425 - 550	

* **B35 Cutaway** – similar to the B35, except has a single smooth cutaway, mfg. mid-1970s.

	N/A	$750 - 1,000	$425 - 550	

B60 – Bell Western body style, solid spruce top, laminated rosewood back and sides, round soundhole with herringbone rosette, multi-ply body purfling and white body binding, 14/20-fret unbound rosewood fingerboard with dot inlay, black Bozo unbound headstock with three-per-side Schaller-style chrome tuners, rosewood bridge, Natural finish, mfg. mid-1970s.

	N/A	$1,200 - 1,500	$750 - 900	

B80 – Bell Western body style, solid spruce top, laminated rosewood back and sides, round soundhole with herringbone rosette, herringbone body binding and backstrip, 14/20-fret bound rosewood fingerboard with snowflake inlay, black Bozo headstock with inlay and three-per-side Schaller-style gold tuners, rosewood bridge, Natural finish, mfg. mid-1970s.

	N/A	$1,500 - 1,800	$800 - 1,000	

* **B80S** – similar to the B80, except has solid Indian rosewood back and sides, distinctive black and pearl rosette, ebony fingerboard, more elaborate headstock inlay, and an ebony bridge, mfg. mid-1970s.

	N/A	$1,800 - 2,200	$1,000 - 1,250	

»**B80S 12-String** – similar to the B80S, except in 12-string configuration and six-per-side tuners, mfg. mid-1970s.

	N/A	$2,200 - 2,700	$1,300 - 1,600	

B100 – Bell Western body style, solid spruce top, solid Indian rosewood back and sides, round soundhole with pearl and herringbone rosette, herringbone body and side purfling, maple body binding, herringbone backstrip, 14/20-fret bound ebony fingerboard with three bar abalone inlays, black Bozo headstock with ornate inlay and three-per-side Schaller-style gold tuners, ebony bridge with MOP inlays, Natural finish, mfg. mid-1970s.

	N/A	$2,500 - 3,000	$1,500 - 1,800	

MSR/NOTES	100%	EXCELLENT	AVERAGE	LAST MSR

BRADFORD

Instruments previously produced in Japan during the 1960s. See chapter on House Brands.

The Bradford trademark has been identified as a House Brand of the W. T. Grant company, one of the old style Five and Dime retail stores. W. T. Grant offered the Bradford trademarked guitars during the mid-1960s. Many of the instruments have been identified as produced by Guyatone in Japan. Bradford models ranged from flattop acoustics to thinline hollowbody and solidbody electric guitars and basses. Used prices on these guitars are typically between $100 and $200 in excellent condition. Source: Michael Wright, *Vintage Guitar Magazine*.

BRADLEY

Instruments previously produced in Japan.

The American distributor for Bradley was Veneman Music of Bethesda, MD, but little else is known about this trademark. Source: Michael Wright, *Guitar Stories*, Volume One.

BREEDLOVE

Instruments currently built in Bend, OR, Korea, Japan, and China. Distributed by the Breedlove Guitar Company of Bend, OR. Breedlove has been producing guitars since 1990.

CONTACT INFORMATION
BREEDLOVE
2843 Lolo Drive
Bend, OR 97701
Phone No.: 541-385-8339
Phone No.: 877-800-4848
Fax No.: 541-385-8183
www.breedloveguitars.com
info@breedloveguitars.com

Kim Breedlove was inspired to build guitars while on a six-month surfing trip in Mexico during the 1970s. Kim had a strong art background, and he used that with the tools and experience he gathered to build guitars. Breedlove is known for building guitars with beautiful woods and stunning inlay work. Breedlove and Steve Henderson came together in 1990 to form Breedlove Guitars and moved to the Pacific Northwest. They worked as a custom-shop style factory until about 1995, when they started to offer more standard production models. In 2004, they turned their main models into strictly custom shop orders and introduced the Atlas Series. These guitars are hand built in Korea and inspected upon their arrival in the U.S. They also produce a line of mandolins. In 2007, the first chambered electric Breedlove guitars were introduced (see the *Blue Book of Electric Guitars*). In 2008, the Pro/Roots Series was introduced, and these guitars are 60% built in the U.S. and the remaining 40% built between Korea, Japan, and/or China. Currently their president and CEO is Peter Newport, and the vice president is Kim Breedlove. In late 2010, Breedlove joined forces with Two Old Hippies. For more information, visit Breedlove's website or contact them directly.

GENERAL INFORMATION

In 1997, Breedlove developed a new system that designates model description. This system consists of three parts: a letter (or letters) indicates the body shape:

C - Concert	MJ - Jumbo	SD - S Series Dreadnought
CM - Concert Asymmetrical	EG - Gerhard Jumbo	SJ - S Series Jumbo
RD - Dreadnought	SC - S Series Concert	

The first number indicates body depth:
1 - Shallow (4 1/16 in. at tall)   2 - Deep (4 9/26 in. at tall)
The second number indicates body cutaway style:
0 - Non-Cutaway   2 - Sharp (pointed horn) cutaway   5 - Soft (rounded horn) cutaway
An optional "X" following the model designation indicates traditional X-bracing.

Breedlove offers the Extraordinary Experience. This is a once-in-a-lifetime experience where you sign up to tour the Breedlove Guitar Workshop and scenic Oregon area. During this time you spend time with a consultant who will learn about your playing style and they end up building a guitar for you. It is an experience where you tour the workshop and they build a guitar for you while you are touring. Contact Breedlove for more information.

In 2004, the standard models (C20, D20, etc.) became custom shop models. Instead of a standard production model with several options, the customer can order the guitar exactly the way he or she wants it. Most non-cutaway models start at $3,199 and cutaways start at $3,499. Contact Breedlove for a complete listing of options.

- **Add $225 for Fishman Matrix Natural pickup system.**
- **Add $230 for L.R. Baggs Ribbon RTS pickup system.**
- **Add $400 for L.R. Baggs Dual Source pickup system.**
- **Add $350 for 12-string configuration.**
- **Add $350 for left-handed configuration.**
- **Add $300 for single cutaway (where it is not a standard option).**

ACOUSTIC: AMERICAN SERIES

AMERICAN C20/SM – concert-style body, solid Sitka spruce top, solid mahogany back and sides, round soundhole with American abalone ring rosette, black body binding, one-piece bolt-on mahogany neck, 14/20-fret rosewood fingerboard with offset Breedlove dot inlays, rosewood headstock overlay, three-per-side chrome tuners, winged rosewood bridge, available in Natural gloss finish, 25.5 in. scale, hardshell case included, mfg. 2010 only.

	100%	EXCELLENT	AVERAGE	LAST MSR
	$1,000	$600 - 700	$375 - 450	$1,339

* *American C20/SR* – similar to the American C20/SM, except has solid rosewood back and sides, mfg. 2010 only.

	100%	EXCELLENT	AVERAGE	LAST MSR
	$1,300	$800 - 950	$500 - 600	$1,729

MSR/NOTES	100%	EXCELLENT	AVERAGE	LAST MSR

AMERICAN C25/SMe – single soft cutaway concert-style body, solid Sitka spruce top, solid mahogany back and sides, round soundhole with American abalone ring rosette, black body binding, one-piece bolt-on mahogany neck, 14/20-fret rosewood fingerboard with offset Breedlove dot inlays, rosewood headstock overlay, three-per-side chrome tuners, winged rosewood bridge, L.R. Baggs Element Active VTC electronics, available in Natural gloss finish, 25.5 in. scale, hardshell case included, mfg. 2010 only.

	$1,200	$725 - 850	$450 - 525	$1,599

* Subtract 20% for no electronics (Model C25/SM).

AMERICAN C25/SMYe – single soft cutaway concert-style body, solid Sitka spruce top, solid Myrtlewood back and sides, round soundhole with American abalone ring rosette, one-piece bolt-on mahogany neck, 14/20-fret black-bound ebony fingerboard with offset Breedlove dot inlays, ebony headstock overlay, three-per-side gold tuners with black buttons, winged ebony bridge, L.R. Baggs Element active electronics, available in Natural gloss finish, 25.5 in. scale, hardshell case included, mfg. 2011 only.

An example of an American C25/SMYe courtesy Breedlove

	$2,500	$1,400 - 1,750	$900 - 1,050	$3,329

AMERICAN C25/SRe HERRINGBONE – single soft cutaway concert-style body, solid Sitka spruce top, solid rosewood back and sides, round soundhole with American abalone ring rosette, ivoroid body binding with herringbone top purfling, one-piece bolt-on mahogany neck, 14/20-fret ebony fingerboard with offset Breedlove dot inlays, ebony headstock overlay, three-per-side chrome tuners, winged ebony bridge, L.R. Baggs Element Active VTC electronics, available in Natural gloss finish, 25.5 in. scale, hardshell case included, mfg. 2010-present.

MSR $2,669	$2,000	$1,150 - 1,400	$675 - 800	

* *American C25/SRe Herringbone Solo* – similar to the American C25/SRe Herringbone, except has a side Solo-style soundhole, available in Natural gloss finish, hardshell case included, mfg. 2010 only.

	$1,900	$1,150 - 1,400	$675 - 800	$2,539

* *American C25/CRe-12 Herringbone 12-String* – similar to the American C25/CRe Herringbone, except in 12-string configuration with six-per-side tuners, available in Natural gloss finish, hardshell case included, mfg. 2011 only.

	$2,300	$1,350 - 1,650	$850 - 1,000	$3,069

AMERICAN C25/SSe – single soft cutaway concert-style body, solid Sitka spruce top, solid Sapele back and sides, round soundhole with American abalone ring rosette, one-piece bolt-on mahogany neck, 14/20-fret black-bound ebony fingerboard with offset Breedlove dot inlays, ebony headstock overlay, three-per-side chrome tuners, winged ebony bridge, L.R. Baggs Element active electronics, available in Natural gloss finish, 25.5 in. scale, hardshell case included, mfg. 2011-present.

MSR $2,399	$1,800	$1,075 - 1,325	$600 - 725	

* *American C25/SSe-12 12-String* – similar to the American C25/SSe, except in 12-string configuration with six-per-side tuners, available in Natural gloss finish, hardshell case included, mfg. 2011 only.

	$2,000	$1,150 - 1,400	$675 - 800	$2,669

AMERICAN D20/SM – dreadnought-style body, solid Sitka spruce top, solid mahogany back and sides, round soundhole with American abalone ring rosette, black body binding, one-piece bolt-on mahogany neck, 14/20-fret rosewood fingerboard with offset Breedlove dot inlays, rosewood headstock overlay, three-per-side chrome tuners, winged rosewood bridge, available in Natural gloss finish, 25.5 in. scale, hardshell case included, mfg. 2010 only.

	$1,000	$600 - 700	$375 - 450	$1,339

* *American D20/SR* – similar to the American D20/SM, except has solid rosewood back and sides, mfg. 2010 only.

	$1,300	$800 - 950	$500 - 600	$1,729

AMERICAN D25/SMe – single soft cutaway dreadnought-style body, solid Sitka spruce top, solid mahogany back and sides, round soundhole with American abalone ring rosette, black body binding, one-piece bolt-on mahogany neck, 14/20-fret rosewood fingerboard with offset Breedlove dot inlays, rosewood headstock overlay, three-per-side chrome tuners, winged rosewood bridge, L.R. Baggs Element Active VTC electronics, available in Natural gloss finish, 25.5 in. scale, hardshell case included, mfg. 2010 only.

	$1,200	$725 - 850	$450 - 525	$1,599

* Subtract 20% for no electronics (Model D25/SM).

MSR/NOTES	100%	EXCELLENT	AVERAGE	LAST MSR

AMERICAN D25/SRe HERRINGBONE – single soft cutaway dreadnought-style body, solid Sitka spruce top, solid rosewood back and sides, round soundhole with American abalone ring rosette, ivoroid body binding with herringbone top purfling, one-piece bolt-on mahogany neck, 14/20-fret ebony fingerboard with offset Breedlove dot inlays, ebony headstock overlay, three-per-side chrome tuners, winged ebony bridge, L.R. Baggs Element Active VTC electronics, available in Natural gloss finish, 25.5 in. scale, hardshell case included, mfg. 2010 only.

| | $1,800 | $1,075 - 1,325 | $600 - 725 | $2,399 |

AMERICAN REVIVAL 000/SSe – traditional 000-style 12-fret body, solid Sitka spruce top, solid Sapele back and sides, round soundhole with American 000 abalone ring rosette, black body binding, bolt-on one-piece mahogany neck, 12/20-fret black-bound ebony fingerboard with centered dots inlays, slotted headstock with ebony overlay, three-per-side nickel open-style tuners, ebony pyramid bridge, tortoise pickguard, L.R. Baggs Element active electronics, available in Natural deluxe high gloss finish, 25.5 in. scale, hardshell case included, mfg. 2011 only.

| | $2,000 | $1,150 - 1,400 | $675 - 800 | $2,669 |

* *American Revival 000/SRe Herringbone* – similar to the American Revival 000/SSe, except has solid East Indian rosewood back and sides and ivoroid binding with herringbone top purfling, available in Natural deluxe high gloss finish, hardshell case included, mfg. 2010-2011.

| | $2,200 | $1,300 - 1,600 | $800 - 950 | $2,939 |

AMERICAN REVIVAL D/SSe – traditional dreadnought-style body, solid Sitka spruce top, solid Sapele back and sides, round soundhole with American 000 abalone ring rosette, black body binding, bolt-on one-piece mahogany neck, 12/20-fret black-bound ebony fingerboard with centered dots inlays, slotted headstock with ebony overlay, three-per-side nickel open-style tuners, ebony belly bridge, tortoise pickguard, L.R. Baggs Element active electronics, available in Natural deluxe high gloss finish, 25.5 in. scale, hardshell case included, mfg. 2011 only.

| | $1,800 | $1,075 - 1,325 | $600 - 725 | $2,399 |

* *American Revival D/SRe Herringbone* – similar to the American Revival D/SSe, except has solid East Indian rosewood back and sides and ivoroid binding with herringbone top purfling, available in Natural deluxe high gloss finish, hardshell case included, mfg. 2010-present.

| MSR $2,669 | $2,000 | $1,150 - 1,400 | $675 - 800 | |

AMERICAN REVIVAL OM/SSe – traditional orchestra-style body, solid Sitka spruce top, solid Sapele back and sides, round soundhole with American 000 abalone ring rosette, black body binding, bolt-on one-piece mahogany neck, 12/20-fret black-bound ebony fingerboard with centered dots inlays, slotted headstock with ebony overlay, three-per-side nickel open-style tuners, ebony belly bridge, tortoise pickguard, L.R. Baggs Element active electronics, available in Natural deluxe high gloss finish, 25.5 in. scale, hardshell case included, mfg. 2011 only.

| | $1,800 | $1,075 - 1,325 | $600 - 725 | $2,399 |

* *American Revival OM/SRe Herringbone* – similar to the American Revival OM/SSe, except has solid East Indian rosewood back and sides and ivoroid binding with herringbone top purfling, available in Natural deluxe high gloss finish, hardshell case included, mfg. 2010-present.

| MSR $2,669 | $2,000 | $1,150 - 1,400 | $675 - 800 | |

ACOUSTIC: ATLAS FIRST SERIES

The Atlas series was introduced in 2004 as a line of instruments that are produced overseas but use Breedlove's traditional way of designing and building guitars. All guitars are inspected in Bend, Oregon before they are shipped to dealers.

AC25/SM – single cutaway concert style body, solid mahogany back and sides, solid Stika spruce top, Indian rosewood fingerboard, bridge, and peghead overlay, Fishman Classic IV pickup and electronics, gold hardware, Natural finish, mfg. 2004-08.

| | N/A | $475 - 550 | $275 - 325 | $1,069 |

* *AC25/CM Plus "Black Magic"* – similar to the AC25/SM, except has a cedar top, mahogany back and sides, ivoroid body and neck binding, and abalone body accents, available in Black Gloss finish, mfg. 2007-08.

| | N/A | $600 - 700 | $350 - 425 | $1,339 |

* *AC25/SF Plus* – similar to the AC25/SM, except has solid flamed maple back and sides, available in Sunburst finish, mfg. 2007-08.

| | N/A | $650 - 775 | $375 - 450 | $1,469 |

* *AC25/SR* – similar to the AC25/SM, except has solid rosewood back and sides, mfg. 2004-07.

| | N/A | $525 - 625 | $325 - 375 | $1,199 |

»*AC25/SR Plus* – similar to the AC25/SR, except has ivoroid body and neck binding and abalone body accents, mfg. 2004-08.

| | N/A | $600 - 700 | $350 - 425 | $1,339 |

»*AC25/SR Plus 12-String* – similar to the AC25/SR Plus, except in 12-string configuration and six-per-side tuners, mfg. 2007-08.

| | N/A | $650 - 775 | $375 - 450 | $1,469 |

AC200/SM – full body concert style, laminate mahogany back and sides, solid Sitka spruce top, Indian rosewood fingerboard, bridge, and peghead overlay, chrome tuners, Natural finish, mfg. 2004-07.

| | N/A | $300 - 350 | $150 - 200 | $669 |

MSR/NOTES	100%	EXCELLENT	AVERAGE	LAST MSR

AC250/CR – full body concert style, laminate rosewood back and sides, solid Sitka spruce top, Indian rosewood fingerboard, bridge, and peghead overlay, chrome tuners, Natural finish, mfg. 2005-08.

	N/A	$425 - 500	$250 - 300	$929

* *AC250/CR Left-Handed* – similar to the AC250/CR, except in left-handed configuration, mfg. 2005-08.

	N/A	$425 - 500	$250 - 300	$929

* *AC250/SF Plus* – similar to the AC250/CR, except has solid flamed maple back and sides, available in Natural finish, mfg. 2008 only.

	N/A	$600 - 700	$350 - 425	$1,339

AC250/SM-12 STRING – 12-string configuration full body concert style, solid Sitka spruce top, laminate mahogany back and sides, Indian rosewood fingerboard, bridge, and peghead overlay, six-per-side chrome tuners, Natural finish, mfg. 2005-08.

	N/A	$475 - 550	$275 - 325	$1,069

AD20/SM – dreadnought style body, solid mahogany back and sides, solid Sitka spruce top, pickguard, Indian rosewood fingerboard, bridge, and peghead overlay, Natural finish, mfg. 2004-08.

	N/A	$350 - 425	$225 - 275	$799

* *AD20/SR Plus* – similar to the AD20/SM, except has solid rosewood back and sides, ivoroid body and neck binding, and abalone body accents, mfg. 2004-07.

	N/A	$525 - 625	$325 - 375	$1,199

AD25/SM – single cutaway dreadnought style body, solid mahogany back and sides, solid Sitka spruce top, Indian rosewood fingerboard, bridge, and peghead overlay, Fishman Classic IV pickup and electronics, gold hardware, available in Natural or Sunburst (2007-08) finish, mfg. 2004-08.

	N/A	$475 - 550	$275 - 325	$1,069

• Add 20% (Last MSR was $1,269) for Sunburst finish.

* *AD25/SF Plus* – similar to the AD25/SM, except has solid flamed maple back and sides, ivoroid body and neck binding, and abalone body accents, mfg. 2007-08.

	N/A	$650 - 775	$375 - 450	$1,469

* *AD25/SR Plus* – similar to the AD25/SM, except has solid rosewood back and sides, ivoroid body and neck binding, abalone body accents, mfg. 2004-08.

	N/A	$600 - 700	$350 - 425	$1,339

AD200/SM – dreadnought style, laminate mahogany back and sides, solid Sitka spruce top, pickguard, Indian rosewood fingerboard, bridge, and peghead overlay, chrome tuners, Natural finish, mfg. 2004-08.

	N/A	$300 - 350	$150 - 200	$669

AJ200/SF – jumbo-style body, solid Sitka spruce top, laminated flame maple back and sides, pickguard, Indian rosewood fingerboard with dot inlay, bridge, and peghead overlay, Natural finish, mfg. 2005 only.

	N/A	$325 - 400	$175 - 225	$689

* *AJ200/SF-12 String* – similar to the AJ200/SF, except in 12-string configuration and six-per-side tuners, mfg. 2005 only.

	N/A	$425 - 500	$250 - 300	$819

AJ250/SF PLUS – jumbo-style single cutaway body, solid Sitka spruce top, laminated flame maple back and sides, pickguard, 20-fret rosewood fingerboard with ellipse inlays, rosewood peghead overlay, rosewood bridge, Fishman Classic IV electronics, Natural finish, mfg. 2006-08.

	N/A	$600 - 700	$350 - 425	$1,339

* *AJ250/SF Plus 12-String* – similar to the AJ250/SF Plus, except in 12-string configuration and six-per-side tuners, mfg. 2006-08.

	N/A	$625 - 725	$375 - 450	$1,399

AJ250/SM – jumbo style body, solid Sitka spruce top, laminated mahogany back and sides, pickguard, Indian rosewood fingerboard with dot inlay, bridge, and peghead overlay, Natural finish, mfg. 2005-08.

	N/A	$425 - 500	$250 - 300	$929

* *AJ250/SM-12 String* – similar to the AJ250/SM, except in 12-string configuration and six-per-side tuners, mfg. 2005-08.

	N/A	$525 - 625	$325 - 375	$1,199

AN250/CR – full body concert nylon string style, laminate rosewood back and sides, Western Red Cedar top, Indian rosewood fingerboard, bridge, and peghead overlay, chrome tuners, Natural finish, mfg. 2005-08.

	N/A	$425 - 500	$250 - 300	$929

MSR/NOTES	100%	EXCELLENT	AVERAGE	LAST MSR

ACOUSTIC: ATLAS SOLO SERIES

ATLAS SOLO C350/CMe – single smooth cutaway extra deep Grand Concert body, solid Western red cedar top, mahogany back and sides, round soundhole with single ring abalone rosette and "monitor" side soundhole, black binding with multi-ply B/W purfling, 14/20-fret rosewood fingerboard with Breedlove dot inlays, rosewood headstock overlay with B logo, three-per-side chrome Grover mini tuners, rosewood bridge, black pickguard, L.R. Baggs Stage Pro pickup, electronics, and tuner, available in Satin Natural finish, gig bag included, mfg. 2009-present.

MSR $999	$750	$450 - 525	$250 - 300	

ATLAS SOLO C350/CRe – single smooth cutaway extra deep Grand Concert body, solid Western red cedar top, rosewood back and sides, round soundhole with single ring abalone rosette and "monitor" side soundhole, black binding with multi-ply B/W purfling, 14/20-fret rosewood fingerboard with Breedlove dot inlays, rosewood headstock overlay with B logo, three-per-side chrome Grover mini tuners, rosewood bridge, black pickguard, L.R. Baggs Stage Pro pickup, electronics, and tuner, available in Satin Natural finish, gig bag included, mfg. 2009-present.

MSR $1,119	$840	$500 - 575	$300 - 350	

ATLAS SOLO D350/CMe – single smooth cutaway extra deep dreadnought body, solid Western red cedar top, mahogany back and sides, round soundhole with single ring abalone rosette and "monitor" side soundhole, black binding with multi-ply B/W purfling, 14/20-fret rosewood fingerboard with Breedlove dot inlays, rosewood headstock overlay with B logo, three-per-side chrome Grover mini tuners, rosewood bridge, L.R. Baggs Stage Pro pickup, electronics, and tuner, available in Satin Natural finish, gig bag included, mfg. 2009-present.

MSR $1,049	$790	$475 - 550	$275 - 325	

ATLAS SOLO J350/CMe – single smooth cutaway extra deep jumbo body, solid Western red cedar top, mahogany back and sides, round soundhole with single ring abalone rosette and "monitor" side soundhole, black binding with multi-ply B/W purfling, 14/20-fret rosewood fingerboard with Breedlove dot inlays, rosewood headstock overlay with B logo, three-per-side chrome Grover mini tuners, rosewood bridge, L.R. Baggs Stage Pro pickup, electronics, and tuner, available in Satin Natural finish, gig bag included, mfg. 2009-2010.

	$750	$450 - 525	$250 - 300	$999

ACOUSTIC: ATLAS STAGE SERIES

ATLAS STAGE C25/SRe – single smooth cutaway deep Grand Concert body, solid Sitka spruce top, solid Indian rosewood back, Indian rosewood sides, round soundhole with multi ring abalone rosette with black border, multi-ply ivoroid binding with abalone purfling, 14/20-fret bound rosewood fingerboard with Stage inlays, rosewood headstock overlay with B logo, three-per-side chrome Grover mini tuners, rosewood bridge, L.R. Baggs Stage Pro pickup, electronics, and tuner, available in Gloss Natural finish, hardshell case included, mfg. 2009-present.

MSR $1,339	$1,000	$600 - 700	$375 - 450	

* Atlas Stage C25/CM "Black Magic" – similar to the Atlas Stage C25/SR, except has a solid Western red cedar top, solid mahogany back, and mahogany sides, available in Gloss Black finish, mfg. 2009 only.

	N/A	$600 - 700	$375 - 450	$1,339

ATLAS STAGE C250/CK 35th ANNIVERSARY LIMITED EDITION – single smooth cutaway deep Grand Concert body, solid Western red cedar top, koa back and sides, round soundhole with multi ring abalone rosette with black border, multi-ply ivoroid binding with abalone purfling, 14/20-fret bound rosewood fingerboard with limited edition Stage inlays, rosewood headstock overlay with B logo, three-per-side chrome Grover mini tuners, rosewood bridge, L.R. Baggs Stage Pro pickup, electronics, and tuner, available in Gloss Natural finish, hardshell case included, limited edition run of 300 instruments, mfg. 2009 only.

	N/A	$900 - 1,050	$500 - 600	$1,999

ATLAS STAGE C250/EF – single smooth cutaway deep Grand Concert body, solid Englemann spruce top, solid AAAA flamed maple back and sides, round soundhole with multi ring abalone rosette with black border, multi-ply ivoroid binding with abalone purfling, 14/20-fret bound rosewood fingerboard with Stage inlays, rosewood headstock overlay with B logo, three-per-side chrome Grover mini tuners, rosewood bridge, L.R. Baggs Stage Pro pickup, electronics, and tuner, available in Gloss Natural or Gloss Sunburst finish, hardshell case included, mfg. 2009 only.

	N/A	$600 - 700	$375 - 450	$1,339

ATLAS STAGE D25/SRe – single smooth cutaway deep dreadnought body, solid Sitka spruce top, solid Indian rosewood back, Indian rosewood sides, round soundhole with multi ring abalone rosette with black border, multi-ply ivoroid binding with abalone purfling, 14/20-fret bound rosewood fingerboard with Stage inlays, rosewood headstock overlay with B logo, three-per-side chrome Grover mini tuners, rosewood bridge, tortoise pickguard, L.R. Baggs Stage Pro pickup, electronics, and tuner, available in Gloss Natural finish, hardshell case included, mfg. 2009-present.

MSR $1,339	$1,000	$600 - 700	$375 - 450	

* Atlas Stage D25/ER "Black Magic" – similar to the Atlas Stage D25/ER, except has a solid Englemann spruce top, solid rosewood back, and rosewood sides, available in Gloss Black finish, mfg. 2009 only.

	N/A	$600 - 700	$375 - 450	$1,339

MSR/NOTES	100%	EXCELLENT	AVERAGE	LAST MSR

ATLAS STAGE J350/EFe – single smooth cutaway extra deep jumbo body, solid Englemann spruce top, flamed maple back and sides, round soundhole with multi ring abalone rosette with black border, multi-ply ivoroid binding with abalone purfling, 14/20-fret bound rosewood fingerboard with Stage inlays, rosewood headstock overlay with B logo, three-per-side chrome Grover mini tuners, rosewood bridge, tortoise pickguard, L.R. Baggs Stage Pro pickup, electronics, and tuner, available in Gloss Natural finish, hardshell case included, mfg. 2009-present.

MSR $1,539	$1,160	$650 - 775	$425 - 500	

* *Atlas Stage J350/EFe12 12-String* – similar to the Atlas Stage J350/EF, except in 12-string configuration and six-per-side tuners, available in Gloss Natural finish, mfg. 2009-present.

MSR $1,599	$1,200	$675 - 825	$450 - 525	

ACOUSTIC: ATLAS STUDIO SERIES

ATLAS STUDIO C25/SMe – single smooth cutaway deep Grand Concert body, solid Sitka spruce top, solid mahogany back, mahogany sides, round soundhole with single ring abalone rosette, tortoise binding with abalone purfling, 14/20-fret rosewood fingerboard with Studio (dots and 12th fret diamonds) inlays, rosewood headstock overlay with B logo, three-per-side chrome Grover mini tuners, rosewood bridge, L.R. Baggs Stage Pro pickup, electronics, and tuner, available in Gloss Natural finish, gig bag included, mfg. 2009-present.

MSR $1,199	$900	$550 - 625	$325 - 400	

* *Atlas Studio C250/SMe12 12-String* – similar to the Atlas Studio C25/SM, except in 12-string configuration with six-per-side tuners and has a laminated mahogany back, available in Gloss Natural finish, mfg. 2009-present.

MSR $1,199	$900	$550 - 625	$325 - 400	

ATLAS STUDIO C250/EF – single smooth cutaway deep Grand Concert body, solid Englemann spruce top, flame maple back and sides, round soundhole with single ring abalone rosette, ivoroid binding with multi-ply W/B purfling, 14/20-fret ivoroid-bound rosewood fingerboard with Studio (dots and 12th fret diamonds) inlays, black headstock overlay with B logo, three-per-side chrome Grover mini tuners, rosewood bridge, L.R. Baggs Stage Pro pickup, electronics, and tuner, available in Gloss Natural finish, gig bag included, mfg. 2009 only.

	N/A	$525 - 600	$300 - 375	$1,129

ATLAS STUDIO D25/SMe – single smooth cutaway deep dreadnought body, solid Sitka spruce top, solid mahogany back, mahogany sides, round soundhole with single ring abalone rosette, tortoise binding with abalone purfling, 14/20-fret rosewood fingerboard with Studio (dots and 12th fret diamonds) inlays, rosewood headstock overlay with B logo, three-per-side chrome Grover mini tuners, rosewood bridge, tortoise pickguard, L.R. Baggs Stage Pro pickup, electronics, and tuner, available in Gloss Natural finish, gig bag included, mfg. 2009-present.

MSR $1,199	$900	$550 - 625	$325 - 400	

ATLAS STUDIO D250/EF – single smooth cutaway deep dreadnought body, solid Englemann spruce top, flame maple back and sides, round soundhole with single ring abalone rosette, ivoroid binding with multi-ply W/B purfling, 14/20-fret ivoroid-bound rosewood fingerboard with Studio (dots and 12th fret diamonds) inlays, black headstock overlay with B logo, three-per-side chrome Grover mini tuners, rosewood bridge, tortoise pickguard, L.R. Baggs Stage Pro pickup, electronics, and tuner, available in Gloss Natural finish, gig bag included, mfg. 2009 only.

	N/A	$525 - 600	$300 - 375	$1,129

ATLAS STUDIO J350/CRe – single smooth cutaway extra deep jumbo body, solid Western red cedar top, rosewood back and sides, round soundhole with single ring abalone rosette, ivoroid binding with multi-ply W/B purfling, 14/20-fret ivoroid-bound rosewood fingerboard with Studio (dots and 12th fret diamonds) inlays, rosewood headstock overlay with B logo, three-per-side chrome Grover mini tuners, rosewood bridge, L.R. Baggs Stage Pro pickup, electronics, and tuner, available in Gloss Natural finish, gig bag included, mfg. 2009-2010.

	$1,000	$600 - 700	$375 - 450	$1,339

* *Atlas Studio J350/CRe12 12-String* – similar to the Atlas Studio J350/CR, except in 12-string configuration with six-per-side tuners, available in Gloss Natural finish, mfg. 2009-2010.

	$1,050	$625 - 750	$400 - 475	$1,399

ATLAS STUDIO N250/CR – nylon string configuration, single smooth cutaway deep Grand Concert body, solid Western red cedar top, solid rosewood back, rosewood sides, round soundhole with single ring abalone rosette, black binding with multi-ply W/B purfling, 14/20-fret rosewood fingerboard with Studio (dots and 12th fret diamonds) inlays, slotted headstock with rosewood overlay, three-per-side chrome Grover open-style tuners, rosewood tied bridge, L.R. Baggs Stage Pro pickup, electronics, and tuner, available in Gloss Natural finish, gig bag included, mfg. 2009-present.

MSR $1,119	$840	$500 - 575	$300 - 350	

ACOUSTIC: CASCADE SERIES

CASCADE C25/CRe – single soft cutaway Concert-style body, solid Western red cedar top, solid East Indian rosewood back and sides, round soundhole with abalone rosette, rosewood body binding, dovetail two-piece mahogany neck, 14/20-fret rosewood fingerboard with offset dot inlays, rosewood headstock overlay, three-per-side gold tuners with black buttons, rosewood winged bridge, L.R. Baggs Element active system electronics, available in Natural gloss finish, 25.5 in. scale, hardshell case included, mfg. 2011-present.

MSR $1,739	$1,300	$750 - 900	$500 - 575	

MSR/NOTES	100%	EXCELLENT	AVERAGE	LAST MSR

CASCADE D25/CRe – single soft cutaway dreadnought-style body, solid Western red cedar top, solid East Indian rosewood back and sides, round soundhole with abalone rosette, rosewood body binding, dovetail two-piece mahogany neck, 14/20-fret rosewood fingerboard with offset dot inlays, rosewood headstock overlay, three-per-side gold tuners with black buttons, rosewood winged bridge, tortoise pickguard, L.R. Baggs Element active system electronics, available in Natural gloss finish, 25.5 in. scale, hardshell case included, mfg. 2011-present.

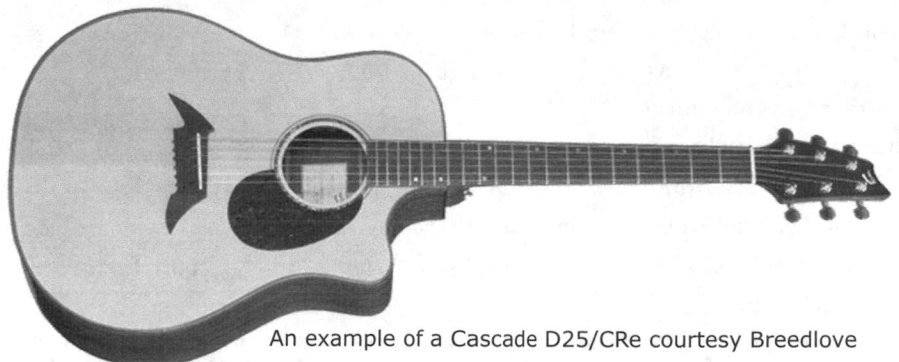

An example of a Cascade D25/CRe courtesy Breedlove

MSR $1,739	$1,300	$750 - 900	$500 - 575	

CASCADE J25/CRe – single soft cutaway jumbo-style body, solid Western red cedar top, solid East Indian rosewood back and sides, round soundhole with abalone rosette, rosewood body binding, dovetail two-piece mahogany neck, 14/20-fret rosewood fingerboard with offset dot inlays, rosewood headstock overlay, three-per-side gold tuners with black buttons, rosewood winged bridge, L.R. Baggs Element active system electronics, available in Natural gloss finish, 25.5 in. scale, hardshell case included, mfg. 2011-present.

MSR $1,739	$1,300	$750 - 900	$500 - 575	

CASCADE REVIVAL 000/CRe – traditional 000 12-fret-style body, solid Western red cedar top, solid East Indian rosewood back and sides, round soundhole with multi-ring abalone rosette, rosewood body binding, dovetail two-piece mahogany neck, 12/20-fret rosewood fingerboard with dot inlays, slotted headstock with rosewood overlay, three-per-side open-style gold tuners, rosewood pyramid bridge, tortoise pickguard, L.R. Baggs Element active system electronics, available in Natural gloss finish, 25.5 in. scale, hardshell case included, mfg. 2011-present.

MSR $1,999	$1,500	$875 - 1,050	$550 - 650	

CASCADE REVIVAL D/CRe – traditional dreadnought-style body, solid Western red cedar top, solid East Indian rosewood back and sides, round soundhole with abalone rosette, rosewood body binding, dovetail two-piece mahogany neck, 14/20-fret rosewood fingerboard with dot inlays, rosewood headstock overlay, three-per-side gold tuners, rosewood belly bridge, tortoise pickguard, L.R. Baggs Element active system electronics, available in Natural gloss finish, 25.5 in. scale, hardshell case included, mfg. 2011-present.

MSR $1,739	$1,300	$750 - 900	$500 - 575	

CASCADE REVIVAL OM/CRe – traditional orchestra-style body, solid Western red cedar top, solid East Indian rosewood back and sides, round soundhole with abalone rosette, rosewood body binding, dovetail two-piece mahogany neck, 14/20-fret rosewood fingerboard with dot inlays, rosewood headstock overlay, three-per-side gold tuners, rosewood belly bridge, tortoise pickguard, L.R. Baggs Element active system electronics, available in Natural gloss finish, 25.5 in. scale, hardshell case included, mfg. 2011-present.

MSR $1,739	$1,300	$750 - 900	$500 - 575	

* *Cascade Revival OM/CRe Cutaway* – similar to the Cascade Revival OM/CRe, except has a single soft cutaway, available in Natural gloss finish, hardshell case included, mfg. 2011-present.

MSR $1,869	$1,400	$800 - 950	$550 - 625	

ACOUSTIC: C, D, J, MJ, N, AND RD SERIES

All Breedlove Premier Line instruments have ivoroid or black plastic binding, top and back purflings, and abalone rosettes. Bridges, fingerboards, and peghead veneers are made of ebony. The following prices are for guitars with Sitka spruce tops and mahogany back and sides (price includes a case).

When Breedlove started building guitars, all models were available with several different options and wood styles (mahogany, walnut, maple, rosewood, koa, striped ebony, etc.). Keep in mind that unless otherwise noted, all guitars are assumed to have mahogany back and sides. Cutaways, twelve-string, and seven-string configurations were all options on all guitars at one point. Even though a certain model may not be listed, it is possible that it was order with some options. The *Blue Book of Acoustic Guitars* lists only the factory cataloged models. The letter prefix indicates what style body the guitar is (C: concert, D: dreadnought, J: jumbo, MJ: jumbo, N: nylon, and RD: dreadnought).

- **Add $495 for Classic Appointments (choice of bloodwood, koa, maple, walnut, or rosewood body/fingerboard and headstock binding, top/side/ back purfling, and a V-shaped tailstrip.)**

C10 (C1) – concert style shallow body, extensive purfling on body/neck/fingerboard, 14/20-fret bound ebony fingerboard with pearl dot inlay, ebony pinless bridge, bound peghead, ebony peghead veneer, three-per-side gold Schaller tuners, available in satin finish, body length: 19.875 in., body width: 15.375 in., body depth: 4 1/16 in., mfg. early 1990s-2004.

	N/A	$1,650 - 2,000	$1,100 - 1,300	$3,099

In 1997, the C1 was renamed the C10.

MSR/NOTES	100%	EXCELLENT	AVERAGE	LAST MSR
* **C12** – similar to the C10 (C1), except has a single sharp cutaway, mfg. early 1990s-2004.				
	N/A	$1,800 - 2,200	$1,200 - 1,400	$3,399
* **C15** – similar to the C10 (C1), except has a single smooth cutaway, mfg. early 1990s-2004.				
	N/A	$1,800 - 2,200	$1,200 - 1,400	$3,399
C20 (C2) – similar to the C10 (C1), except has a deep body depth: 4 9/16 in., mfg. early 1990s-2004.				
	N/A	$1,650 - 2,000	$1,100 - 1,300	$3,099
In 1997, the C2 was renamed the C20.				
* **C22** – similar to the C20 (C2), except has a single sharp cutaway, mfg. early 1990s-2004.				
	N/A	$1,800 - 2,200	$1,200 - 1,400	$3,399
* **C25 (C5)** – similar to the C20 (C2), except has a single smooth cutaway, mfg. early 1990s-2004.				
	N/A	$1,800 - 2,200	$1,200 - 1,400	$3,399
In 1997, the C5 was renamed the C25.				
D20 – dreadnought style, Sitka spruce top, mahogany back and sides, ivoroid, black, or tortoiseshell binding, abalone rosette, ebony bridge, ebony fingerboard with fancy inlays, peghead overlay, three-per-side tuners, available in Natural finish, mfg. 2002-04.				
	N/A	$1,650 - 2,000	$1,100 - 1,300	$3,099
D25 – similar to the D-20, except has a soft-cutaway body, mfg. 2002-04.				
	N/A	$1,800 - 2,200	$1,200 - 1,400	$3,399
J20 – jumbo style body, mahogany back and sides, Sitka spruce top, ivoroid, black, or tortoiseshell binding, spoked abalone rosette, ebony bridge, ebony fingerboard, peghead overlay, three-per-side tuners, available in natural finish, mfg. 2001-04.				
	N/A	$1,650 - 2,000	$1,100 - 1,300	$3,199
* **J22** – similar to the J20, except has a single sharp cutaway, mfg. 2001-04.				
	N/A	$1,800 - 2,200	$1,200 - 1,400	$3,499
* **J25** – similar to the J20, except has a single soft cutaway, mfg. 2001-04.				
	N/A	$1,800 - 2,200	$1,200 - 1,400	$3,499
MJ20 (MJ) – jumbo style deep body, extensive purfling on body/neck/fingerboard, 14/20-fret bound ebony fingerboard with pearl dot inlay, ebony pinless bridge, bound peghead, ebony peghead veneer, three-per-side gold Schaller tuners, available in satin finish, body length: 21 in., body width: 17 in., body depth: 4 9/16 in., mfg. early 1990s-2003.				
	N/A	$1,650 - 1,900	$1,100 - 1,300	$2,695
* **MJ22** – similar to the MJ20, except has a single sharp cutaway, mfg. early 1990s-2003.				
	N/A	$1,750 - 2,050	$1,150 - 1,400	$3,095
N20 (NL/NS 20) – western red cedar top, Indian rosewood back and sides, mahogany neck, 12-fret (NS) or 14-fret (NL) ebony fingerboard, slotted peghead, gold Schaller tuners, ebony bridge and peghead veneer, 12 frets, 25.5 in.scale, mfg. 1999-2004.				
	N/A	$1,600 - 1,900	$1,050 - 1,250	$2,999
* **N25 (NL/NS 25)** – similar to the N20, except has a soft cutaway body, 12-fret (NS) or 14-fret (NL), mfg. 1999-2004.				
	N/A	$1,750 - 2,100	$1,150 - 1,350	$3,299
RD20X (RD) – dreadnought style deep body, standard mahogany back and sides, extensive purfling on body/neck/fingerboard, 14/20-fret bound ebony fingerboard with pearl dot inlay, ebony pinless bridge, bound peghead, ebony peghead veneer, three-per-side gold Schaller tuners, available in Natural satin finish, body length: 20.125 in., body width: 16.125 in., body depth: 4 9/16 in., mfg. early 1990s-2001.				
	N/A	$1,500 - 1,750	$950 - 1,100	$2,595
* **RD22X** – similar to the RD20X (RD), except has a single sharp cutaway, mfg. early 1990s-2001.				
	N/A	$1,650 - 2,000	$1,100 - 1,300	$2,995

ACOUSTIC: MASTER CLASS SERIES

Breedlove also offers the **Kim Breedlove Signature** model that starts at $13,339.

ATLANTIC – orchestra-style body, solid Adirondack spruce top, solid quilted maple back and sides, round soundhole with spoked abalone rosette, rosewood Master Class binding package, one-piece maple neck, 14/20-fret ebony fingerboard with green abalone snowflake inlays, ebony headstock overlay, three-per-side Waverly nickel tuners, ebony belly bridge, tortoise pickguard, available in Natural gloss finish, 25.5 in. scale, hardshell case included, mfg. 2011-present.

MSR $5,999	$4,500	$2,750 - 3,250	$1,650 - 2,000	

MSR/NOTES	100%	EXCELLENT	AVERAGE	LAST MSR

CELTIC CLASSIC – Custom Shop auditorium soft cutaway-style body, solid red spruce top, solid figured walnut back and sides, round soundhole with spoked abalone rosette, figured koa Master Class binding package with five-ply B/W/B/W/B top purfling, one-piece mahogany neck, 14/20-fret ebony fingerboard with Celtic mosaic pin inlays, ebony headstock overlay, three-per-side gold tuners, ebony asymmetrical winged bridge, tortoise pickguard, available in Natural gloss finish, 25.5 in. scale, hardshell case included, mfg. 2011-present.

| MSR $5,999 | $4,500 | $2,750 - 3,250 | $1,650 - 2,000 | |

CLASSIC XII 12-STRING – 12-string configuration, deep jumbo single sharp cutaway body (J22 12-String), Sitka spruce top, select striped ebony back and sides, ivoroid binding, abalone rosette, mfg. 1999-2010.

| | $4,400 | $2,500 - 3,000 | $1,550 - 1,800 | $5,869 |

* *Classic XII Maple 12-String* – similar to the Classic XII, except has flamed maple back and sides, a koa spoked rosette, and koa binding, available in Natural gloss finish, hardshell case included, mfg. 2011-present.

| MSR $5,869 | $4,400 | $2,500 - 3,000 | $1,550 - 1,800 | |

CM CLASSIC – concert-style asymmetrical (similar to the C20, except longer and wider) body, extensive purfling on body/neck/fingerboard, 14/20-fret bound ebony fingerboard with pearl dot inlay, ebony pinless bridge, bound peghead, ebony peghead veneer, three-per-side gold Schaller tuners, available in satin finish, body length: 21.125 in., body width: 16.125 in., body depth: 4 5/16 in., mfg. summer 1998-present.

| MSR $7,329 | $5,500 | $3,500 - 4,200 | $2,000 - 2,500 | |

DESCHUTES (C2 DESCHUTES) – concert-style deep body with sharp cutaway, figured mahogany back and sides, herringbone purfling, striped ebony rosette/peghead veneer, 14/20-fret bound ebony fingerboard with mother-of-pearl trout and trout fly inlays, ivoroid neck binding, ebony pinless bridge, bound peghead, three-per-side gold Schaller tuners, available in satin finish, mfg. 1996-98.

| | N/A | $2,050 - 2,400 | $1,250 - 1,400 | $3,195 |

This model was dedicated to the Deschutes River and the sport of fly fishing.

DIAMOND-B DREADNOUGHT – dreadnought-style deep body (D20), red spruce top, Indian Rosewood back and sides, abalone rosette, 14/20-fret ebony fingerboard with slotted diamond inlays, ebony headstock overlay, ebony bridge, top purfling, three-per-side chrome tuners, Natural finish, mfg. 2004-06.

| | N/A | $2,500 - 3,000 | $1,450 - 1,800 | $5,329 |

ED GERHARD CUSTOM (EG 15) – jumbo-style shallow body with soft cutaway, choice of tone wood on top/back/sides, extensive purfling on body/neck/fingerboard, 14/20-fret bound ebony fingerboard with pearl dot inlay, ebony pinless bridge, bound peghead, ebony peghead veneer, three-per-side gold Schaller tuners, available in satin finish, mfg. 1997-98.

| | N/A | $2,250 - 2,750 | $1,500 - 1,800 | $3,295 |

ED GERHARD SIGNATURE – jumbo style shallow body with soft cutaway (J15), Sitka spruce top, rosewood back/sides, koa binding, wood rosette, 14/20-fret bound ebony fingerboard with pearl dot inlay, ebony pinless bridge, bound peghead, ebony peghead veneer, three-per-side gold mini tuners with oversized buttons, available in satin finish, mfg. 1997-2010.

| | $4,400 | $2,500 - 3,000 | $1,550 - 1,800 | $5,869 |

* *Ed Gerhard Exotic Signature* – similar to the Gerhard, except has a German Spruce top, Brazilian rosewood back and sides, Koa soundhole rosette, and Gerhard's initials on the fingerboard, mfg. 2001-2010.

| | $8,500 | $5,000 - 6,000 | N/A | $10,529 |

EXOTIC VI – concert style deep single soft cutaway body (C25), solid red spruce top, striped ebony back and sides, abalone rosette, wing inlays, top purfling, three-per-side gold tuners, Natural finish, mfg. 2004-07, 2010.

| | $5,200 | $3,500 - 4,000 | $2,000 - 2,500 | $6,799 |

KING KOA – deep concert body style with soft cutaway (C25), Presentation Grade Koa back and sides, Bloodwood body binding, Western Red cedar top, mermaid and dolphin inlay on fingerboard, ebony buttons on gold tuners, natural finish, mfg. 2002-present.

| MSR $8,669 | $6,500 | $4,000 - 5,000 | $2,750 - 3,250 | |

NORTHWEST CLASSIC (C5 NORTHWEST) – concert style deep body with soft cutaway (C25), myrtlewood back/sides, maple neck, walnut binding, 14/20-fret bound ebony fingerboard with hand-engraved abalone and mother-of-pearl reproductions of North West Indian totems (whale and fish motifs), ebony pinless bridge, bound peghead, ebony peghead veneer, three-per-side gold Schaller tuners, available in satin finish, mfg. 1996-present.

| MSR $5,999 | $4,500 | $2,750 - 3,250 | $1,650 - 2,000 | |

In 1997, this model was renamed the Northwest, and in 1999, it was renamed the Northwest Classic.

* *Northwest XII 12-String* – similar to the Northwest Classic, except has a jumbo-style body and in 12-string configuration, mfg. 2004-06.

| | N/A | $3,000 - 3,500 | $1,800 - 2,250 | $5,869 |

MSR/NOTES	100%	EXCELLENT	AVERAGE	LAST MSR

NYLON NOUVEAU – deep concert-style body with soft cutaway, select Myrtlewood back and sides, Port Orford Cedar top, Master Class Appointed with walnut binding, abalone rosette, linear fusion inlay, open-style tuners, natural finish, mfg. 2002-07.

	N/A	$2,400 - 2,800	$1,400 - 1,600	$5,329

PACIFIC – concert-style shallow single cutaway body (C15), Sitka sprucetop, flame mapleback and sides, abalone rosette, 14/20-fret ebony fingerboard with sea leave inlays, ebony headstock overlay, ebony bridge, top purfling, three-per-side chrome tuners, Natural finish, mfg. 2001-07, 2011-present.

MSR $5,999	$4,500	$2,750 - 3,250	$1,650 - 2,000	

PHOENIX – concert-style shallow body (C10), Redwood top, Ziricote back and sides, abalone rosette, 14/20-fret ebony fingerboard with Phoenix inlays, ebony headstock overlay, ebony bridge, top purfling, three-per-side chrome tuners, Natural finish, mfg. 2004-present.

MSR $7,329	$5,500	$3,500 - 4,200	$2,000 - 2,500	

ACOUSTIC: PASSPORT SERIES

Breedlove's Passport Series are designed as travel guitars. Like the Atlas Series, these guitars are produced overseas.

C20 PASSPORT – mini C-20 travel-sized guitar, western red cedar top, laminated mahogany back and sides, abalone ring rosette, 21-fret rosewood fingerboard with dot inlays, chrome tuners, rosewood bridge, Satin Natural finish, mfg. 2005-07.

	N/A	$200 - 250	$120 - 150	$469

C25 PASSPORT – similar to the C20 Passport, except has a single cutaway, mfg. 2005-09.

	N/A	$225 - 275	$130 - 170	$529

C25FS PASSPORT – full-scale C-25 travel-sized single cutaway guitar, western red cedar top, laminated mahogany back and sides, abalone ring rosette, 20-fret rosewood fingerboard with dot inlays, chrome tuners, rosewood bridge, Satin Natural finish, mfg. 2007-09.

	N/A	$300 - 350	$175 - 225	$669

PASSPORT C200/SMP – concert-style body, solid spruce Englemanm or Sitka spruce top, laminated dark stained maple back and sides, round soundhole with single ring B/W/B rosette, black body binding, dovetail three-piece mahogany neck, 14/20-fret rosewood fingerboard with dot inlays, black headstock overlay, three-per-side chrome tuners, rosewood bridge, available in Natural satin finish, 25.5 in. scale, gig bag included, mfg. 2010-present.

An example of a Passport C200/SMP courtesy Breedlove

MSR $429	$320	$175 - 225	$110 - 140	

PASSPORT C250/CMe – single soft concert-style body, solid Western red cedar top, laminated mahogany back and sides, round soundhole with single ring B/W/B rosette, black body binding, dovetail three-piece mahogany neck, 14/20-fret rosewood fingerboard with dot inlays, black headstock overlay, three-per-side chrome tuners, rosewood bridge, Breedlove VTC electronics, available in Natural satin finish, 25.5 in. scale, gig bag included, mfg. 2010-present.

MSR $669	$500	$300 - 350	$175 - 225	

* ***Passport C250/CMe Ensemble/Travel*** – similar to the Passport C250CMe, except is in a smaller ensemble/travel body size with a 19.1 in. scale, available in Natural satin finish, gig bag included, mfg. 2010-present.

MSR $599	$470	$275 - 325	$150 - 200	

* ***Passport C250/COe Ovangkol*** – similar to the Passport C250/CMe, except has laminated ovangkol back and sides, available in Natural satin finish, gig bag included, mfg. 2010-present.

MSR $699	$530	$300 - 375	$175 - 225	

D20 PASSPORT – full-scale 7/8 sized dreadnought-style body, solid Sitka spruce top, laminated mahogany back and sides, ring rosette, 20-fret rosewood fingerboard with dot inlays, chrome tuners, rosewood bridge, Satin Natural finish, 25.5 in. scale, mfg. 2007-09.

	N/A	$225 - 275	$130 - 170	$529

MSR/NOTES	100%	EXCELLENT	AVERAGE	LAST MSR

* **_D20 E Passport_** – similar to the D20 E Passport, except has an active pickup, mfg. 2009 only.

	N/A	$275 - 325	$150 - 200	$619

PASSPORT D200/SM, T – 7/8-sized dreadnought-style body, solid Sitka spruce top, laminated dark mahogany back and sides, round soundhole with single ring B/W/B rosette, black body binding, dovetail three-piece mahogany neck, 14/20-fret rosewood fingerboard with dot inlays, three-per-side chrome tuners, rosewood bridge, available in Natural satin finish, 25.5 in. scale, gig bag included, mfg. 2010 only.

	$400	$225 - 275	$130 - 170	$529

PASSPORT N200/CMP – nylon-string configuration, concert-style body, solid Western red cedar top, laminated dark stained maple back and sides, round soundhole with single ring B/W/B rosette, black body binding, dovetail three-piece mahogany neck, 14/20-fret rosewood fingerboard with dot inlays, slotted headstock with black overlay, three-per-side open-style chrome tuners, rosewood tied bridge, available in Natural satin finish, 25.5 in. scale, gig bag included, mfg. 2010 only.

	$300	$175 - 225	$110 - 140	$399

PASSPORT N250/COe – nylon-string configuration, single soft concert-style body, solid Western red cedar top, laminated ovangkol back and sides, round soundhole with single ring B/W/B rosette, black body binding, dovetail three-piece mahogany neck, 14/20-fret rosewood fingerboard with dot inlays, slotted headstock with black overlay, three-per-side open-style chrome tuners, rosewood tied bridge, Breedlove VTC electronics, available in Natural satin finish, 25.5 in. scale, gig bag included, mfg. 2010-present.

MSR $699	$530	$300 - 375	$175 - 225	

OM FS PASSPORT – full-scale orchestra model-style body, western red cedar top, laminated mahogany back and sides, ring rosette, 20-fret rosewood fingerboard with dot inlays, chrome tuners, rosewood bridge, Satin Natural finish, 25.5 in. scale, mfg. 2007-09.

	N/A	$225 - 275	$130 - 170	$529

* **_OM E Passport_** – similar to the OM FS Passport, except has an active pickup, mfg. 2009 only.

	N/A	$275 - 325	$150 - 200	$619

PASSPORT RETRO D/MMe – traditional dreadnought-style body, solid mahogany top, laminated mahogany back and sides, round soundhole with single ring B/W/B rosette, black body binding, dovetail three-piece mahogany neck, 14/20-fret rosewood fingerboard with dot inlays, rosewood headstock overlay, three-per-side chrome tuners, rosewood belly bridge, Breedlove VTC electronics, available in Natural satin finish, 25.5 in. scale, gig bag included, mfg. 2010-present.

MSR $629	$450	$275 - 325	$150 - 200	

PASSPORT RETRO OM/MMe – traditional orchestra-style body, solid mahogany top, laminated mahogany back and sides, round soundhole with single ring B/W/B rosette, black body binding, dovetail three-piece mahogany neck, 14/20-fret rosewood fingerboard with dot inlays, rosewood headstock overlay, three-per-side chrome tuners, rosewood belly bridge, Breedlove VTC electronics, available in Natural satin finish, 25.5 in. scale, gig bag included, mfg. 2010-present.

MSR $629	$450	$275 - 325	$150 - 200	

ACOUSTIC: PASSPORT PLUS SERIES

PASSPORT PLUS C250/SBe – single soft cutaway concert-style body, solid Sitka spruce top, laminated bubinga back and sides, round soundhole with abalone ring rosette, multi-ply back and top inlay, dovetail three-piece mahogany neck, 14/20-fret rosewood fingerboard with dot inlays, three-per-side chrome tuners, rosewood bridge, tortoise pickguard, VTC electronics, available in Natural finish, 25.5 in. scale, gig bag included, mfg. 2010-present.

MSR $799	$600	$350 - 425	$200 - 250	

* **_Passport Plus C250/SBe-12 12-String_** – similar to the Passport Plus C250/SBe, except in 12-string configuration with six-per-side tuners, available in Natural finish, gig bag included, mfg. 2010-present.

MSR $899	$680	$400 - 475	$225 - 275	

* **_Passport Plus C250/SBe Left-Handed_** – similar to the Passport Plus C250/SBe, except in left-handed configuration, available in Natural finish, gig bag included, mfg. 2010-present.

MSR $799	$600	$350 - 425	$200 - 250	

PASSPORT PLUS C250/SFe – single soft cutaway concert-style body, solid Sitka spruce top, laminated flamed maple back and sides, round soundhole with abalone ring rosette, multi-ply back and top inlay, dovetail three-piece mahogany neck, 14/20-fret rosewood fingerboard with dot inlays, three-per-side chrome tuners, rosewood bridge, tortoise pickguard, VTC electronics, available in Sunburst finish, 25.5 in. scale, gig bag included, mfg. 2010-present.

MSR $979	$740	$425 - 500	$250 - 300	

PASSPORT PLUS D200/SB – dreadnought-style body, solid Sitka spruce top, laminated bubinga back and sides, round soundhole with abalone ring rosette, cream body inlay, dovetail mahogany neck, 14/20-fret rosewood fingerboard with dot inlays, three-per-side chrome tuners, rosewood bridge, tortoise pickguard, available in Natural finish, 25.5 in. scale, gig bag included, mfg. 2010 only.

	$500	$300 - 350	$175 - 225	$669

MSR/NOTES	100%	EXCELLENT	AVERAGE	LAST MSR

* *Passport Plus D250/SBe Cutaway Electric* – similar to the Passport Plus D200/SB, except has a single soft cutaway and VTC electronics, available in Natural finish, gig bag included, mfg. 2010 only.

	$600	$350 - 425	$200 - 250	$799

PASSPORT PLUS RETRO D/CMe HH – traditional dreadnought-style body, solid Western red cedar top, laminated mahogany back and sides, round soundhole with abalone ring rosette, cream back and top inlay with herringbone purfling, dovetail three-piece mahogany neck, 14/20-fret rosewood fingerboard with dot inlays, three-per-side chrome tuners, rosewood bridge, tortoise pickguard, VTC electronics, available in Natural finish, 25.5 in. scale, gig bag included, mfg. 2010-present.

MSR $769	$580	$325 - 450	$175 - 225	

PASSPORT PLUS RETRO OM/CMe HH – traditional orchestra-style body, solid Western red cedar top, laminated mahogany back and sides, round soundhole with abalone ring rosette, cream back and top inlay with herringbone purfling, dovetail three-piece mahogany neck, 14/20-fret rosewood fingerboard with dot inlays, three-per-side chrome tuners, rosewood bridge, VTC electronics, available in Natural finish, 25.5 in. scale, gig bag included, mfg. 2010-present.

MSR $769	$580	$325 - 450	$175 - 225	

ACOUSTIC: PERFORMANCE SERIES

BALANCE – grand concert deep body style (SC25), mahogany back and sides, Sitka spruce top, black body binding, ebony fingerboard and peghead overlay, Natural finish, mfg. 2003-07.

	N/A	$1,750 - 2,050	$1,050 - 1,250	$3,729

* **Add 10% for soft cutaway configuration.**

BOSSA NOVA – concert-style deep single cutaway body (SN25), Western Red Cedar top, Indian Rosewood back and sides, abalone ring with purfling rosette, 14/20-fret ebony fingerboard with Breedlove B inlays, ebony headstock overlay, ebony bridge, top purfling, three-per-side chrome tuners, Baggs Dual Element electronics, Natural finish, mfg. 2000-present.

MSR $3,999	$3,000	$1,900 - 2,200	$1,250 - 1,450	

This model is now part of Breedlove's Master Class Series.

FOCUS – grand concert body (SC25), Sitka spruce top, East Indian rosewood back and sides, ivoroid bound body and neck with purfling, ebony fingerboard with Breedlove Focus inlay, Fishman Prefix Pro Blender system, Natural finish, mfg. 2001-09.

	N/A	$1,900 - 2,200	$1,250 - 1,450	$3,999

* *Focus Special Edition* – similar to the Focus, except has a redwood top, new inlay pattern, and a bound soundhole with abalone rosette, mfg. 2007-present.

MSR $3,999	$3,000	$1,900 - 2,200	$1,250 - 1,450	

This model is now part of Breedlove's Master Class Series.

»*Focus Special Edition Walnut* – similar to the Focus Special Edition, except has figured walnut back and sides, mfg. 2011-present.

MSR $4,999	$3,750	$2,350 - 2,750	$1,400 - 1,750	

This model is part of Breedlove's Master Class Series.

* *Focus Dreadnought* – similar to the Focus, except has a single cutaway dreadnought style body (SD25), mfg. 2001-09.

	N/A	$1,900 - 2,200	$1,250 - 1,450	$3,999

»*Focus Dreadnought Special Edition* – similar to the Focus Dreadnought, except has a red spruce top, koa bound body, new inlay pattern, and a bound soundhole with abalone rosette, mfg. 2007-09.

	N/A	$2,100 - 2,500	$1,350 - 1,600	$4,399

* *Focus 12-String* – similar to the Focus, except in 12-string configuration and has a jumbo style deep body with soft cutaway (SJ25 12-String), mfg. 2001-2010.

	$3,400	$2,100 - 2,500	$1,400 - 1,650	$4,529

FUSION – grand concert deep with sharp cutaway body style (SC22), Sitka spruce top, mahogany back and sides, black body binding, ebony fingerboard and peghead overlay, Natural finish, mfg. 2001-09.

	N/A	$1,750 - 2,050	$1,050 - 1,250	$3,729

* *Fusion Special Edition* – similar to the Fusion, except has a new inlay pattern and L.R. Baggs Custom I-Mix M1 electronics, mfg. 2007-09.

	N/A	$1,900 - 2,200	$1,250 - 1,450	$3,999

ACOUSTIC: PRO/ROOTS SERIES

The Pro/Roots Series of guitars are 60% built in the U.S. with the remaining 40% constructed in Korea, Japan, and/or China.

C25/CR (PRO SERIES) – single soft cutaway deep Grand Concert body, solid Western Red cedar top, solid rosewood back and sides, round soundhole with abalone pearl rosette, ivoroid binding, herringbone purfling, one-piece mahogany neck, 14/20-fret ebony fingerboard with

MSR/NOTES	100%	EXCELLENT	AVERAGE	LAST MSR

small offset dot inlays, asymmetrical headstock with ebony overlay and B logo, three-per-side chrome Gotoh tuners, ebony bridge, L.R. Baggs Element active electronics, Gloss Natural finish, deluxe hardshell case included, mfg. 2008-09.

	N/A	$1,000 - 1,200	$650 - 775	$2,269

C25/KK 35th ANNIVERSARY LIMITED EDITION (PRO SERIES) – single soft cutaway deep Grand Concert body, solid koa top, back, and sides, round soundhole with abalone pearl rosette, ivoroid binding, herringbone purfling, one-piece mahogany neck, 14/20-fret ebnoy fingerboard with small offset dot inlays, asymmetrical headstock with ebony overlay and B logo, three-per-side chrome Gotoh tuners, ebony bridge, Carlos CP1A electronics, Gloss Natural finish, deluxe hardshell case included, mfg. 2009 only.

	N/A	$1,850 - 2,200	$1,000 - 1,200	$3,999

D25/SR (PRO SERIES) – single soft cutaway deep dreadnought body, solid Sitka spruce top, solid rosewood back and sides, round soundhole with abalone pearl rosette, ivoroid binding, herringbone purfling, one-piece mahogany neck, 14/20-fret ebony fingerboard with small offset dot inlays, asymmetrical headstock with ebony overlay and B logo, three-per-side chrome Gotoh tuners, ebony bridge, L.R. Baggs Element active electronics, Gloss Natural finish, deluxe hardshell case included, mfg. 2008-09.

	N/A	$1,000 - 1,200	$650 - 775	$2,269

D/SR (ROOTS SERIES) – dreadnought-style body, soild Sitka spruce top, solid rosewood back and sides, round soundhole with abalone rosette, ivoroid body binding, herringbone top purfling, one-piece mahogany neck, 14/20-fret ebony fingerboard with pearl dot inlays, standard headstock with ebony overlay and B logo, three-per-side Gotoh tuners, ebony bridge, L.R. Baggs Element Active electronics, Gloss Natural finish, deluxe hardshell case included, mfg. 2008-09.

	N/A	$950 - 1,150	$650 - 750	$2,199

OM/SR (ROOTS SERIES) – Vintage Orchestra Model-style body, soild Sitka spruce top, solid rosewood back and sides, round soundhole with abalone rosette, ivoroid body binding, herringbone top purfling, one-piece mahogany neck, 14/20-fret ebony fingerboard with pearl dot inlays, standard headstock with ebony overlay and B logo, three-per-side Gotoh tuners, ebony bridge, tortoise pickguard, L.R. Baggs Element Active electronics, Gloss Natural finish, deluxe hardshell case included, mfg. 2008-09.

	N/A	$950 - 1,150	$650 - 750	$2,199

ACOUSTIC: RETRO SERIES

D/SMe – pre-war dreadnought-style body, solid Sitka spruce top, solid mahogany back, laminated mahogany sides, pre-war X bracing, round soundhole with B/W/B rosette, ivoroid body binding, multi-ply B/W top purfling, 14/20-fret rosewood fingerboard with diamond inlays, square-style headstock, three-per-side chrome Grover Sta-Tite vintage tuners, rosewood belly bridge, L.R. Baggs Stage Pro electronics, Natural gloss finish, case included, mfg. 2008-present.

MSR $1,049	$790	$500 - 575	$275 - 325	

* **D/ERe** – similar to the D/SMe, except has a solid Englemann spruce top and solid rosewood back and sides, mfg. 2008-present.

MSR $1,269	$950	$550 - 650	$325 - 400	

* **D/SMe Left-Handed** – similar to the D/SMe, except in left-handed configuration, mfg. 2011 only.

	$790	$500 - 575	$275 - 325	$1,049

OM/SMe – Orchestra Model-style body, solid Sitka spruce top, solid mahogany back, laminated mahogany sides, pre-war X bracing, round soundhole with B/W/B rosette, ivoroid body binding, multi-ply B/W top purfling, 14/20-fret rosewood fingerboard with diamond inlays, square-style headstock, three-per-side chrome Grover Sta-Tite vintage tuners, rosewood belly bridge, L.R. Baggs Stage Pro electronics, Natural gloss finish, case included, mfg. 2008-present.

MSR $1,049	$790	$500 - 575	$275 - 325	

* **OM/ERe** – similar to the OM/SMe, except has a solid Englemann spruce top and solid rosewood back and sides, mfg. 2008-present.

MSR $1,269	$950	$550 - 650	$325 - 400	

ACOUSTIC: REVIVAL SERIES

The Revival Series is a celebration of popular guitars (mainly Martin styles) that were produced in the 1930s and 40s.

REVIVAL 000-M – 000-style body, solid Sitka spruce top, solid Mahogany back and sides, tortoiseshell binding, decorative black/white/black purfling, Revival Pre-War X Bracing, decorative black/white/black purfling rosette, centered dot inlays, Aged Toner Semi-Gloss finish, mfg. 2006-09.

	N/A	$1,300 - 1,500	$800 - 950	$2,799

* **Revival 000-(A)M Deluxe** – similar to the 000-M, except has a select red spruce top, several embellishments, and a high-gloss finish, mfg. 2006-present.

MSR $3,999	$3,000	$1,900 - 2,200	$1,250 - 1,450	

* **Revival 000-R** – similar to the 000-M, except has solid Indian rosewood back and sides, mfg. 2006-09.

	N/A	$1,350 - 1,550	$850 - 1,000	$2,939

» **Revival 000-(A)R Deluxe** – similar to the 000-R, except has a select red spruce top, several embellishments, and a high-gloss finish, mfg. 2006-present.

MSR $4,269	$3,200	$2,000 - 2,350	$1,300 - 1,500	

MSR/NOTES	100%	EXCELLENT	AVERAGE	LAST MSR

REVIVAL DM – dreadnought body, solid Sitka spruce top, solid Mahogany back and sides, tortoiseshell binding, decorative black/white/black purfling, Revival Pre-War X Bracing, decorative black/white/black purfling rosette, centered dot inlays, Aged Toner Semi-Gloss finish, mfg. 2005-09.

	N/A	$1,200 - 1,400	$700 - 850	$2,529

* *Revival D/(A)M Deluxe* – similar to the DM, except has a select red spruce top, several embellishments, and a high-gloss finish, mfg. 2005-present.

MSR $3,729	$2,800	$1,750 - 2,050	$1,050 - 1,250	

* *Revival DR* – similar to the DM, except has solid Indian rosewood back and sides, mfg. 2005-09.

	N/A	$1,275 - 1,475	$750 - 900	$2,669

»*Revival D/(A)R Deluxe* – similar to the DR, except has a select red spruce top, several embellishments, and a high-gloss finish, mfg. 2005-present.

MSR $3,999	$3,000	$1,900 - 2,200	$1,250 - 1,450	

REVIVAL OM-M – orchestra model body style, solid Sitka spruce top, solid Mahogany back and sides, tortoiseshell binding, decorative black/white/black purfling, Revival Pre-War X Bracing, deocrative black/white/black purfling rosette, centered dot inlays, Aged Toner Semi-Gloss finish, mfg. 2005-09.

	N/A	$1,200 - 1,400	$700 - 850	$2,529

* Add 12.5% (Last MSR was $2,829) for a single cutaway.

* *Revival OM/(A)M Deluxe* – similar to the OM-M, except has a select red spruce top, several embellishments, and a high-gloss finish, mfg. 2005-present.

MSR $3,729	$2,800	$1,750 - 2,050	$1,050 - 1,250	

* Add 7.5% (disc. 2009, last MSR was $4,029) for a single cutaway.

* *Revival OM-R* – similar to the OM-M, except has solid Indian rosewood back and sides, mfg. 2005-09.

	N/A	$1,275 - 1,475	$750 - 900	$2,669

* Add 10% (Last MSR was $2,969) for a single cutaway.

»*Revival OM/(A)R Deluxe* – similar to the OM-R, except has a select red spruce top, several embellishments, and a high-gloss finish, mfg. 2005-present.

MSR $3,999	$3,000	$1,900 - 2,200	$1,250 - 1,450	

* Add 7.5% (disc. 2009, last MSR was $4,299) for a single cutaway.

REVIVAL TENOR – four-string tenor configuration, OM-style body, solid Sitka spruce top, mahogany back and sides, 24 1/16 in. scale, Natural gloss finish, mfg. 2007-09.

	N/A	$1,200 - 1,400	$700 - 850	$2,529

ACOUSTIC: S SERIES

The S Series guitars may not be as ornate as the regular line but are built with the same materials at the Breedlove facility with the same attention to detail. The primary difference is in the appointments, fewer purflings, a simpler bridge, abalone rosette, and a rosewood peghead veneer. However, almost all of Breedlove's custom shop options were available on the S Series.

* Add $100 for western red cedar top.
* Add $100 for myrtlewood back and sides.

SC20 – concert style deep body, Sitka spruce top, walnut back/sides, round soundhole, top purfling, one piece wood rosette, ebony fingerboard/pinless bridge, rosewood peghead veneer, three-per-side asymmetrical headstock with gold Grover tuners, available in satin finish, body length: 19.875 in., body width: 15.375 in., body depth: 4 9/16 in., mfg. 1995-2004.

	N/A	$1,500 - 1,800	$1,000 - 1,200	$2,499

* *SC25* – similar to the SC20, except has a single soft cutaway, mfg. 1995-2004.

	N/A	$1,650 - 2,000	$1,100 - 1,300	$2,799

SD20 – dreadnought style deep body, round soundhole, walnut back/sides, top purfling, one piece wood rosette, ebony fingerboard/pinless bridge, rosewood peghead veneer, three-per-side asymmetrical headstock with gold Grover tuners, available in satin finish, body length: 20.125 in., body width: 16.125 in., body depth: 4 9/16 in., mfg. 1996-2004.

	N/A	$1,500 - 1,800	$1,000 - 1,200	$2,499

* *SD25* – similar to the SD20, except has a single soft cutaway, mfg. 1996-2004.

	N/A	$1,650 - 2,000	$1,100 - 1,300	$2,799

SJ10 – jumbo-style shallow body, round soundhole, walnut back/sides, top purfling, one-piece wood rosette, ebony fingerboard/pinless bridge, rosewood peghead veneer, three-per-side asymmetrical headstock with gold Grover tuners, available in satin finish, mfg. 1997-early 2000s.

	N/A	$1,300 - 1,600	$850 - 1,000	$2,095

MSR/NOTES	100%	EXCELLENT	AVERAGE	LAST MSR

* *SJ15* – similar to the SJ10, except has a single soft cutaway, mfg. 1997-early 2000s.

	N/A	$1,400 - 1,750	$900 - 1,100	$2,395

SJ20 – similar to the SJ10, except has a deep body, mfg. 1997-2004.

	N/A	$1,500 - 1,800	$1,000 - 1,200	$2,599

The SJ 20 model was offered in a 12-string configuration as a separate model 1997-98. Retail list price for Walnut back/sides was $1,995; Rosewood back/sides were $2,145. Models featured similar construction details as the SJ 20, with six-per-side tuners.

* *SJ25* – similar to the SJ20, except has a single soft cutaway, mfg. 1997-2004.

	N/A	$1,650 - 2,000	$1,100 - 1,300	$2,899

SN20 – western red cedar top, East Indian rosewood back and sides, mahogany neck, 12-fret ebony fingerboard, slotted peghead, gold Schaller tuners, ebony bridge and peghead veneer, 25.5 in.scale, mfg. 2001-04.

	N/A	$1,500 - 1,800	$1,000 - 1,200	$2,499

* *SN25* – similar to Model SN20, except has a single soft cutaway, mfg. 2001-04.

	N/A	$1,650 - 2,000	$1,100 - 1,300	$2,799

ACOUSTIC ELECTRIC BASS

All basses are part of the Atlas series, except for a model Breedlove produced in the early 1990s. Retail price was around $2,800.

ABC25/SM 4 BASS – single soft cutaway deep Grand Concert bass-style body, solid Sitka spruce top, solid mahogany back and sides, abalone rosette, ivoroid binding, 22-fret rosewood fingerboard with offset dot inlays, black headstock overlay with two-per-side chrome tuners, rosewood bridge, Fishman Classic IV electronics, Gloss Black finish, 32 in. scale, mfg. 2008 only.

	N/A	$550 - 625	$325 - 400	$1,199

ABJ25/CM4 FRETLESS BASS – single cutaway jumbo bass-style body, solid western red cedar top, solid mahogany back and sides, abalone rosette, fretless rosewood fingerboard with no inlays, rosewood headstock overlay with two-per-side gold tuners, rosewood bridge, Fishman Classic IV electronics, Satin Natural finish, 34 in. scale, mfg. 2005-08.

	N/A	$600 - 700	$350 - 425	$1,339

* *ABJ25/CR5 Plus Five-String Bass* – similar to the ABJ25/CM4 Fretless Bass, except in five-string configuration, has rosewood back and sides, ivoroid body and neck binding, abalone body accents, a fretted fingerboard, and Fishman electronics, mfg. 2007 only.

	N/A	$700 - 825	$450 - 525	$1,599

ABJ250/SM4 BASS – single cutaway jumbo bass-style body, solid Sitka spruce top, laminated mahogany back and sides, abalone rosette, 23-fret rosewood fingerboard with offset pearl inlays, rosewood headstock overlay with two-per-side chrome tuners, rosewood bridge, Fishman Classic IV electronics, Satin Natural finish, 34 in. scale, mfg. 2005-08.

	N/A	$475 - 550	$300 - 350	$1,069

* *ABJ250/SM5 Five-String Bass* – similar to the ABJ250/SM4 Bass, except in five-string configuration and 3/2-per-side tuners, mfg. 2005-08.

	N/A	$550 - 625	$325 - 400	$1,199

ATLAS STAGE BJ350/CR4e BASS – single smooth cutaway extra deep jumbo bass body, solid Western red cedar top, rosewood back and sides, round soundhole with multi ring abalone rosette with black border, multi-ply ivoroid binding with abalone purfling, 14/20-fret bound rosewood fingerboard with Stage inlays, rosewood headstock overlay with B logo, two-per-side chrome Grover bass tuners, rosewood bridge, tortoise pickguard, L.R. Baggs Stage Pro pickup, electronics, and tuner, available in Gloss Natural finish, hardshell case included, mfg. 2009-2010.

	$1,000	$600 - 700	$375 - 450	$1,339

ATLAS STAGE BC25 "BLACK MAGIC" BASS – single smooth cutaway deep Grand Concert bass body, solid Englemann spruce top, mahogany back and sides, round soundhole with multi ring abalone rosette with black border, multi-ply ivoroid binding with abalone purfling, 14/20-fret bound rosewood fingerboard with Stage inlays, black headstock overlay with B logo, two-per-side chrome Grover bass tuners, rosewood bridge, tortoise pickguard, L.R. Baggs Stage Pro pickup, electronics, and tuner, available in Gloss Black finish, hardshell case included, mfg. 2009 only.

	N/A	$600 - 700	$375 - 450	$1,339

ATLAS SOLO BJ350/CMe4 BASS – single smooth cutaway extra deep jumbo bass body, solid Western red cedar top, mahogany back and sides, round soundhole with single ring abalone rosette and "monitor" side soundhole, black binding with multi-ply B/W purfling, 14/20-fret rosewood fingerboard with Breedlove dot inlays or fretless fingerboard, rosewood headstock overlay with B logo, two-per-side chrome Grover bass tuners, rosewood bridge, L.R. Baggs Stage Pro pickup, electronics, and tuner, available in Satin Natural finish, gig bag included, mfg. 2009-present.

MSR $1,049	$790	$500 - 575	$275 - 325	

ATLAS STUDIO BJ350/SMe4 BASS – single smooth cutaway extra deep jumbo bass body, solid Sitka spruce top, mahogany back and sides, round soundhole with single ring abalone rosette, tortoise binding with multi-ply W/B purfling, 14/20-fret ivoroid-bound rosewood fingerboard with Studio (dots and 12th fret diamonds) inlays, rosewood headstock overlay with B logo, two-per-side chrome Grover bass tuners, rosewood bridge, L.R. Baggs Stage Pro pickup, electronics, and tuner, available in Gloss Natural finish, gig bag included, 34 in. scale, mfg. 2009-present.

MSR $1,069	$800	$500 - 575	$275 - 325	

MSR/NOTES	100%	EXCELLENT	AVERAGE	LAST MSR

🎸 * ***Atlas Studio BJ350/SMe5 Five-String Bass*** – similar to the Atlas Studio BJ350/SM4, except in five-string configuration with 2/3-per-side tuners, available in Gloss Natural finish, mfg. 2009-2010.

	$900	$550 - 625	$325 - 400	$1,199

BC35 PASSPORT BASS – single smooth cutaway extra deep Grand Concert bass body, solid Western red cedar top, laminated mahogany back and sides, abalone ring rosette, black binding, 14/20-fret rosewood fingerboard with dot inlays, two-per-side chrome tuners, rosewood bridge, Passport active pickup, available in Satin Natural finish, 32 in. scale, mfg. 2009 only.

	N/A	$325 - 400	$200 - 250	$799

PASSPORT PLUS B350/CBe4 BASS – single smooth cutaway extra deep Grand Concert bass body, solid Western red cedar top, laminated ovangkol or bubinga back and sides, abalone ring rosette, black binding, 14/20-fret rosewood fingerboard with dot inlays, two-per-side chrome tuners, rosewood bridge, VTC electronics, available in Satin Natural finish, 32 in. scale, mfg. 2010-present.

MSR $899	$680	$400 - 475	$225 - 275	

BRIDWELL WORKSHOP

Instruments previously produced in Palatine, IL.

The Bridwell Workshop produced high quality guitars during the late 1990s and possibly into the 2000s. Any further information on Bridwell Workshop can be submitted directly to Blue Book Publications.

BRILEY, CLINT

Instruments previously built in Clearwater, FL during the 1990s.

🎸 Clint Briley Resonator Guitars was founded by Clint Briley in 1989, motivated by his experience of making new parts for his vintage National Duolian Resonator guitar. Briley, a machinist, has a background in dye making. With assistance from local luthier/repairman (and friend) Charlie Jirousek, Briley hand-built necks and steel bodies as he established his company.

Briley offered two models that feature his own spun resonator cones and parts. The **Cutaway Steel Body** (last MSR was $1,500) has a mahogany neck and rosewood fingerboard, and meets the metal body at the twelfth fret. The **Econo-Steel** (last MSR was $800) has no cutaway on its steel body.

BRONSON

Instruments previously produced. See chapter on House Brands.

George Bronson was a guitar teacher in Detroit, MI during the 1930s and 1940s. He specialized in steel guitars and many of the Bronsons are square neck guitars made by the National/Valco company. There are also regular Bronson guitars made by the Harmony company. George ran the "Bronson Music & Sales Company" in the Kerr Building in Detroit, MI, where he sold and distributed sheet music and guitars. There was also a popular model electric lap steel that National/Valco made for Bronson, which was sold under the name "Bronson Singing Electric." Source: Walter Murray, Frankenstein Fretworks.

BRUKO

Instruments currently built in Germany. Previously distributed by Lark in the Morning of Mendocino, CA.

Bruko Instruments consists of solid wood ukuleles and half-size miniature guitars. It is unknown if they are currently available in the U.S.

BURGUET, AMALIO

Instruments currently produced in Spain since 1984.

Amalio Burguet acoustics are offered in the classical and flamenco configurations. Handmade in Spain, these guitars feature a solid cedar or solid spruce top, mahogany neck, rosewood or ebony fingerboard, rosewood bridge, an inlaid marquetry rosette, clear high gloss finish, gold-plated tuners, and a slotted three-per-side headstock. Models feature rosewood, walnut, mahogany, cypress, or sycamore back and sides. Retail prices start at $1,295 and climb over $3,000. For more information, visit Burguet's website or contact them directly.

CONTACT INFORMATION
BURGUET, AMALIO
Calle Senda de les Ánimes s/n
Catarroja, Valencia 46470 Spain
Phone No.: 96 126 34 75
Fax No.: 96 126 75 12
www.burguet.com
burguet@burguet.com

BURRELL GUITARS

Guitars currently produced in Brighton, MI. Previously produced in Huntington, WV.

Luthier Leo Burrell builds guitars and basses by hand in his shop in Brighton, MI. Burrel spent many years in West Virginia building guitars, but now builds guitars in a shop on his daughter's land in Michigan. What makes Burrell's guitars unique is the patented tapered body shape that conforms to the player's body. This twisted body is accompanied by a twisted neck that reduces strain on the player while at the same time pushing sound outward rather than up. Burrell applies his conformed body to acoustic guitars, electric guitars, and bass guitars. Each guitar is individually hand-crafted with solid woods. For more information, visit Burrell's website or contact him directly.

CONTACT INFORMATION
BURRELL GUITARS
10428 Buno Road
Brighton, MI 48114
Phone No.: 517-376-8448
www.burrellguitars.net
leo@burrellguitars.com

BURTON, CYNDY

Instruments currently built in Portland, OR since 1980.

Luthier Cyndy Burton builds high quality acoustic classical guitars. Although she specializes in classical guitars, she has built other acoustic designs as well.

BUSCARINO GUITARS

Instruments currently built in Franklin, NC. Distributed by the Buscarino Guitar Company of Franklin, NC.

CONTACT INFORMATION
BUSCARINO GUITARS
2348 Wide Horizon Dr.
Franklin, NC 28734
Phone No.: 828-349-9867
www.buscarino.com
john@buscarino.com

Luthier John Buscarino apprenticed with Master acoustic guitar builder Augustino LoPrinzi for over a year in 1978, and with Bob Benedetto of archtop lutherie fame from 1979 to 1981. Later that year, Buscarino formed **Nova U.S.A.**, which built high quality solid body electrics, and acoustic/electric instruments. In 1990, Buscarino changed the company name to **Buscarino Guitars** to reflect the change to building acoustic instruments. Buscarino continues to produce limited production custom guitars, and is currently focusing on archtop guitar building. Circa 2002, they relocated to Franklin, NC from Largo, FL. There is typically a twelve-month wait on guitar orders and they all require a deposit when ordering. For more information, visit Buscarino's website or contact him directly.

ACOUSTIC ARCHTOP

The **Artisan** (base price is $9,800) features a carved single-A aged spruce top, carved single-A flamed maple back with matching sides, Venetian cutaway, black/white body binding, three-piece flamed maple neck, 25 in. scale, 22-fret ebony fingerboard, ebony pickguard/tailpiece/truss rod cover, three-per-side gold M6 Schaller tuners with solid ebony buttons, and is available in Natural high gloss lacquer finish.

The **Monarch** (base price is $15,000) features a carved double-A aged spruce top, carved double-A flamed maple back with matching sides, Venetian cutaway, bound f-holes, black/white body binding, three-piece flamed maple neck, 25 in. scale, 22-fret ebony fingerboard, ebony pickguard/tailpiece/truss rod cover, three-per-side gold M6 Schaller tuners with solid ebony buttons, and is available in Honey Blonde, Natural, Traditional Sunburst, or Vintage Natural high gloss lacquer finishes.

The **Vituoso** (base price is $24,000) features a carved master grade aged spruce top, carved master grade flamed maple back with matching sides, Venetian cutaway, bound f-holes, fine line black/white body binding, three-piece flamed maple neck, 25 in. scale, 22-fret ebony fingerboard with block inlay, ebony pickguard/tailpiece/truss rod cover, bound pickguard, three-per-side gold M6 Schaller tuners with solid ebony buttons, and is available in Honey Blonde, Natural, Traditional Sunburst, or Vintage Natural high gloss lacquer finishes.

- Add $300 for a built-in humbucker pickup.
- Add $300 for Honey Blonde, Vintage Natural, or Sunburst finish.
- Add $300 for solid white bound f-holes.
- Add $100 for Schaller gold Tune-Amatic bridge.
- Add $100 for bound fingerboard.
- Add $100 for bound pickguard.
- Add $200 for personalized tailpiece.
- Add $350 for tree-of-life tailpiece inlay.
- Add $350 for block inlays.
- Add $500 for custom colors.
- Add $650 for AAA highly figured wood.
- Add $800 for tree-of-life fingerboard inlay.
- Add $800 for a 7-string configuration.
- Add $800 for an 18 in. body width.
- Add $1,000 for wood binding.
- Add $800 for left-handed configuration.
- Add $1,200 for European cello woods.
- Add $1,500 for the Poly-Drive MIDI system.

ACOUSTIC FLATTOP

The **Cabaret** (base price is $8,500) features an Englemann spruce (or Sitka spruce or Western cedar) top, flame maple (or mahogany or Indian rosewood or Bolivian rosewood) carved back with matching sides, rounded cutaway, round soundhole, black plastic binding with multiple purflings, Honduran mahogany neck, 25.5 in. scale, ebony fingerboard, ebony bridge with abalone inlay, slotted headstock, three-per-side Schaller Deluxe tuners with ebony buttons, available in Natural high gloss lacquer finish, body width 13.875 in., and body depth 3.5 in. The Cabaret model is available with optional lattice bracing or flying braces, Gilbert tuners, or internal (or external) electronics (call for price quote). Price includes a custom double arched five-ply case with crushed velvet lining. This model is also available in a longer body style (Grand Cabaret) with a body width of 14.375 in. and a body depth of 3.75 in.

The **Rhapsody** (base price is $9,850) is a single cutaway body with master-grade Sitka or Adirondack spruce top, rock flame maple, bird's-eye maple, Honduras mahogany, or Bolivian rosewood carved back with matching sides, oval soundhole, matching natural wood binding, three-piece figured rock maple neck, 25 in. scale, 21-fret ebony fingerboard, ebony bridge, regular headstock, three-per-side Gotoh Delta Series tuners with ebony buttons, and Buscarino's proprietary pickup with internal electronics, available in Natural high gloss lacquer finish, body width 16 in., and body depth 3.75 in.

- Add $300 for Snakewood bridge.
- Add $300 for Snakewood binding.
- Add $300 for Flying Braces.
- Add $350 for wood binding.
- Add $350 for RMC Diffu pickup system.
- Add $500 for Snakewood fingerboard.
- Add $500 for RMC Poly-Drive II Outside MIDI electronics.
- Add $800 for left-handed configuration.
- Add $800 for the seven-string configuration.
- Add $1,000 for RMC Poly-Drive IV built-in electronics.

NOTES

C SECTION
CADENZA

Instruments previously produced in Korea. Distributed by the Kimex Company of Seoul, Korea.

Cadenza features a wide range of steel-string, classical, and bass acoustic guitars. Most of these guitars are entry-level instruments and are relatively inexpensive.

CA GUITARS

Instruments currently produced in Lafayette, LA, since 1999. Distributed by Peavey in Meridian, MS since 2010.

CONTACT INFORMATION
CA GUITARS
3403 Moss Street
Lafayette, LA 70507
Phone No.: 337-233-4119
Phone No.: 877-860-5903
www.caguitars.com
customerservice@compositeacoustics.com

CA Guitars stands for Composite Acoustic Guitars, and they are guitars made out of composite and graphite materials instead of wood. This material is stronger and is able to withstand extreme conditions, whereas a regular wood guitar would not. CA started in 1999 and by 2003, they had become very backordered. In 2005, CA stopped building guitars to retool and reorganize their operation. In summer, 2006, CA was at a new facility where they can produce up to twenty guitars a day. The guitars were slightly redesigned as well. In late 2010, Peavey aquired CA Guitars. For more information, refer to their website.

MSR/NOTES	100%	EXCELLENT	AVERAGE	LAST MSR

ACOUSTIC

When CA closed its shop for a year and a half in the mid-2000s, they changed their guitar availability as well. On models built prior to 2005, electronics came as a package option that was added as a premium. Models produced between 2005 and 2010 are divided into two series: the Player Series are strictly acoustic and the Performer Series have built-in electronics. There are also minor structural and cosmetics changes between the two eras, but the body shapes are generally the same. When Peavey bought CA in 2010, they discontinued almost every current model and narrowed the line to just a few guitars. Models available in 2011 include the **Cargo Raw** (MSR $1,350), **Cargo Raw ELE** electric (MSR $1,500), **OX Raw** (MSR $1,600), **OX Raw ELE** electric (MSR $1,750), and the **GX HG CBB ELE** electric (MSR $3,500).

* Add $300 for the Legacy AE option (Fishman Prefix Pro Blend system and on-board preamp, microphone, and piezo pickup, on models produced before 2005).
* Add $400 for the AE option and black top finish (models produced before 2005).
* Add $500 for the AE option and Vintage Burst finish (models produced before 2005).
* Subtract $200 for models without electronics.

5S-CE (X RT) – single sharp cutaway thin carbon fiber body, carbon reveal soundhole rosette, side dots and 12th fret fingerboard inlays, three-per-side Gotoh tuners, Fishman Matrix VT electronics with controls mounted inside the soundhole, available in Blue, Charcoal, Green, Red, or Wine Road Tough Satin finish, 25.5 in. scale, disc. 2010.

	$1,800	$900 - 1,100	$500 - 600	$1,998

5M-CE (GX RT) – single sharp cutaway Grand Auditorium carbon fiber body, carbon reveal soundhole rosette, side dots and 12th fret fingerboard inlays, three-per-side Gotoh tuners, Fishman Matrix VT electronics with controls mounted inside the soundhole, available in Blue, Charcoal, Green, Red, or Wine Road Tough Satin finish, 25.5 in. scale, gig-bag included, disc. 2010.

	$1,800	$900 - 1,100	$500 - 600	$1,998

5i-M-CE (GXi RT) – similar to the 5M-CE, except has intregrated bracing and a treble bout soundhole, disc. 2010.

	$1,800	$900 - 1,100	$500 - 600	$1,998

5L-E (LEGACY RT) – dreadnought carbon fiber body, carbon reveal soundhole rosette, side dots and 12th fret fingerboard inlays, three-per-side Gotoh tuners, Fishman Matrix VT electronics with controls mounted inside the soundhole, available in Blue, Charcoal, Green, Red, or Wine Road Tough Satin finish, 25.5 in. scale, gig-bag included, disc. 2010.

	$1,800	$900 - 1,100	$500 - 600	$1,998

6S-CE (X TRIBAL) – single sharp cutaway thin carbon fiber body, carbon reveal soundhole rosette, side dots and 12th fret fingerboard inlays, three-per-side Gotoh tuners, Fishman Matrix VT electronics with controls mounted inside the soundhole, available in Blue, Charcoal, Green, Red, or Wine Road Tough Satin finish with tribal graphics, 25.5 in. scale, disc. 2010.

	$1,900	$1,000 - 1,200	$550 - 650	$2,098

6M-CE (GX TRIBAL) – single sharp cutaway Grand Auditorium carbon fiber body, carbon reveal soundhole rosette, side dots and 12th fret fingerboard inlays, three-per-side Gotoh tuners, Fishman Matrix VT electronics with controls mounted inside the soundhole, available in Blue, Charcoal, Green, Red, or Wine Road Tough Satin finish with Tribal graphics, 25.5 in. scale, gig-bag included, disc. 2010.

	$1,900	$1,000 - 1,200	$550 - 650	$2,098

6L-E (LEGACY TRIBAL) – dreadnought carbon fiber body, carbon reveal soundhole rosette, side dots and 12th fret fingerboard inlays, three-per-side Gotoh tuners, Fishman Matrix VT electronics with controls mounted inside the soundhole, available in Blue, Charcoal, Green, Red, or Wine Road Tough Satin finish with tribal graphics, 25.5 in. scale, gig-bag included, disc. 2010.

	$1,900	$1,000 - 1,200	$550 - 650	$2,098

MSR/NOTES	100%	EXCELLENT	AVERAGE	LAST MSR

7L-E (LEGACY/LEGACY PLAYER) – dreadnought carbon fiber body, carbon reveal soundhole rosette, side dots and 12th fret fingerboard inlays, three-per-side Gotoh tuners, Fishman Ellipse VT electronics with controls mounted inside the soundhole, available in Acadia Green (disc.), Black Metallic (disc.), Carbon Burst, Dark Red Metallic (disc.), Indi Blue (disc.), or high-gloss finish, 25.5 in. scale, disc. 2008.

	N/A	$1,100 - 1,350	$600 - 725	$2,266

7M-CE (GX PLAYER) – single sharp cutaway Grand Concert carbon fiber body, carbon reveal soundhole rosette, side dots and 12th fret fingerboard inlays, three-per-side Gotoh tuners, Fishman Ellipse VT electronics with controls mounted inside the soundhole, available in Carbon Burst high-gloss finish, 25.5 in. scale, disc. 2008.

	N/A	$1,100 - 1,350	$600 - 725	$2,266

* *7i-M-CE* – similar to the 7M-CE, except has intregrated bracing and a treble bout soundhole, disc. 2008.

	N/A	$1,100 - 1,350	$600 - 725	$2,266

7S-CE (X STANDARD/X PLAYER) – single sharp cutaway thin carbon fiber body, carbon reveal soundhole rosette, side dots and 12th fret fingerboard inlays, three-per-side Gotoh tuners, Fishman Ellipse VT electronics with controls mounted inside the soundhole, available in Carbon Burst high-gloss finish, 25.5 in. scale, disc. 2008.

	N/A	$1,100 - 1,350	$600 - 725	$2,266

8LB BLUEGRASS (BLUEGRASS PERFORMER/BLUEGRASS STANDARD) – dreadnought carbon fiber body, shell soundhole rosette, full dot fingerboard inlays, three-per-side open-back Gotoh tuners, L.R. Baggs i-Mix electronics with controls mounted inside the soundhole, available in Carbon Burst high-gloss finish, 25.5 in. scale, disc. 2008.

	N/A	$1,250 - 1,500	$800 - 950	$2,698

8L-E (LEGACY PERFORMER) – dreadnought carbon fiber body, carbon reveal soundhole rosette, full dot fingerboard inlays, three-per-side Gotoh tuners, Fishman AP-7 pickup and Prefix Premium Blend electronics (early models) or Fishman Ellipse VT electronics with controls mounted inside the soundhole (later models), available in Acadia Green (disc.), Black Metallic (disc.), Carbon Burst, Dark Red Metallic (disc.), Indi Blue (disc.), or high-gloss finish, 25.5 in. scale, mfg. 2006-2010.

	$2,700	$1,350 - 1,650	$900 - 1,050	$2,998

8LV-E VINTAGE (VINTAGE PERFORMER) – dreadnought carbon fiber body, shell soundhole rosette, full dot fingerboard inlays, three-per-side Gotoh tuners, L.R. Baggs i-Mix electronics with controls mounted inside the soundhole, available in Carbon Burst high-gloss finish, 25.5 in. scale, disc. 2008.

	N/A	$1,350 - 1,650	$900 - 1,050	$2,998

8M-CE (GX PERFORMER) – single sharp cutaway Grand Concert carbon fiber body, shell soundhole rosette, full dot fingerboard inlays, three-per-side Gotoh tuners, L.R. Baggs i-Mix electronics with controls mounted inside the soundhole, available in Carbon Burst high-gloss finish, 25.5 in. scale, disc. 2010.

	$2,700	$1,350 - 1,650	$900 - 1,050	$2,998

8S-CE (X PERFORMER) – single sharp cutaway thin carbon fiber body, shell soundhole rosette, full dot fingerboard inlays, three-per-side Gotoh tuners, L.R. Baggs i-Mix electronics with controls mounted inside the soundhole, available in Carbon Burst high-gloss finish, 25.5 in. scale, disc. 2010.

	$2,700	$1,350 - 1,650	$900 - 1,050	$2,998

AT-6 (ALTERNATE TUNING) – composite dreadnought body, longer scale length for alternate and low tunings, two round soundholes in the bouts, composite fingerboard, Acoustically Tailored Composite bridge, three-per-side tuners, available in Black Metallic finish, disc. 2005.

	N/A	$1,150 - 1,350	$700 - 800	$2,600

CARGO XS-C – 3/4-sized single sharp cutaway carbon fiber body, upper bass bout soundhole, side dot inlays, three-per-side Gotoh tuners, available in Charcoal, Green, Red, or Wine Road Tough Satin finish, 22.75 in. scale, disc. 2010.

	$1,000	$575 - 675	$300 - 375	$1,232

* *Cargo XS-CE* – similar to the Cargo XS-C, except has a Fishman Matrix VT electronics with controls mounted inside the soundhole, disc. 2010.

	$1,100	$650 - 750	$350 - 425	$1,332

LEGACY C.O.T./C.O.T. STANDARD – similar to the Legacy, except designed for live performances with two electronic L.R. Baggs systems, Element under saddle transducer, satin finished neck, and available in Black Metallic finish, disc. 2007.

	N/A	$1,450 - 1,750	$950 - 1,100	$3,300

VINTAGE PLAYER – composite dreadnought body, 20-fret ebony fingerboard, Acoustically Tailored Composite bridge, three-per-side black tuners, available in Black Carbon Burst finish, mfg. 2006-07.

	N/A	$1,100 - 1,300	$700 - 800	$2,450

ACOUSTIC BASS

VORTEX F4/FL4 – composite bass body, composite fretted (F4) or fretless fingerboard (FL4), two-per-side tuners, available in Black Metallic finish, disc. 2005.

	N/A	$1,100 - 1,300	$650 - 750	$2,550

CALVIN CRAMER

Instruments previously built in Markneukirchen, Germany. Distributed in the U.S. by Musima North America of Tampa, FL.

Calvin Cramer concert guitars debuted in the United States, Canada, and South American markets in 1996. The guitars were built by Musima, Germany's largest acoustic guitar manufacturer. The company headquarters in Markneukirchen, Germany are near the Czech border. In 1991, Musima was purchased by industry veteran Helmet Stumpf following the German re-unification.

M. CAMPELLONE GUITARS

Instruments currently built in Greenville, RI since 1978.

CONTACT INFORMATION
M. CAMPELLONE GUITARS
5 Mapleville Road
Greenville, RI 02828
Phone No.: 401-949-3716
www.mcampellone.com
mcgtr@verizon.net

Luthier Mark Campellone originally began building solid body guitars in the late 1970s, and turned his attention to archtops around 1987. All of his models are constructed of solid wood, and feature carved tops and backs. For more information and a history on Mark, visit their website or contact him directly.

Campellone currently offers three models of solid wood carved acoustics: each model is available in a 16 in., 17 in., or 18 in. Venetian cutaway body, body depth of 2.75 in., 3 in. or 3.25 in., a fingerboard scales of 24.5 in., 25 in., or 25.5 in., a nut width of 1 11/16 in. or 1.75 in., and an optional floating pickup system. All three models have genuine shell inlays, and gold-plated hardware. Finishes include Natural, Tinted Blonde, and a variety of Transparent Sunbursts.

The **Cameo** (base price $12,500) is a limited production model that uses the finest woods.

The **Standard Series** (base price $4,500) features a hand graduated spruce top, hand graduated figured maple back with matching rims, multi-bound top, single-bound back, fingerboard, peghead, and tortoiseshell style pickguard, maple neck, rosewood fingerboard, bridge, and tailpiece applique.

The **Deluxe Series** (base price $5,995) features a hand graduated select spruce top, hand graduated back of highly figured maple with matching rims, multi-bound top, back, fingerboard, peghead, and tortoiseshell style pickguard, bound f-holes, figured maple neck, ebony fingerboard with three-piece keystone position markers, ebony bridge, Deluxe Series peghead inlay, and a Deluxe series tailpiece.

The **Special Series** (base price $7,595) features a hand graduated select spruce top, hand graduated back of choicest figured maple with matching rims, multi-bound top, back, fingerboard, peghead, f-holes, and tortoiseshell-style pickguard, figured maple neck, ebony fingerboard with five-piece keystone position markers of mother-of-pearl and abalone, ebony bridge, Special Series peghead inlay, rear peghead inlay, bridge bass inlay, shell truss rod cover, Special series tailpiece, and a custom case.

The **EP Series** (base price $3,850) is designed to offer tonal and response characteristics similar to a full size archtop guitar when amplified, but in a more compact, moderately priced package. It has a 15 in. body width with a solid carved top and laminated back and sides.

Since Campellone has been producing guitars for several years, certain models are often seen in the used marketplace. Most guitars that Campellone builds have additional options on top of the base price appointments. Because of this, every Campellone guitar needs to be valued on an individual basis. If the guitar has many of the standard appointments, it will probably sell close to the new price of that model.

- **Subtract $200 for no pickup system.**
- **Add $300 for an 18 in. body width.**

CANVAS GUITARS

Instruments previously produced in China during the mid-2000s. Distributed in the U.S. by America Sejung Corp. in Walnut, CA.

Canvas Guitars produced a line of beginner acoustic guitars. Canvas thinks of guitars as more than skin deep. A painter uses more than just paint and a canvas to create art - the same can be applied to guitars. A guitar is more than how it looks - it all depends upon how the guitar is built and toned. Models include classical, dreadnought, folk, and an acoustic bass design. Prices ranged from $220 to $360.

CAPITAL

Instruments previously produced in Kalamazoo, MI during the 1930s and 1940s. See chapter on House Brands.

This Gibson-built budget line of guitars has been identified as a House Brand of the J.W. Jenkins Company of Kansas City. While built to the same standards as other Gibson guitars, they lack the one true Gibson touch: an adjustable truss rod. House Brand Gibsons were available to musical instrument distributors in the late 1930s and early 1940s. Source: Walter Carter, *Gibson Guitars: 100 Years of an American Icon*.

CARDINAL

Guitars currently produced in China. Distributed by Trio Musical Instruments in China and Hong Kong. Currently, there is no U.S. distributor.

Cardinal produces a wide range of acoustic guitars including classicals, dreadnoughts, jumbos, and concerts. Several models feature ornate inlays and other fancy features. They also produce acoustic basses, mandolins, and bluegrass instruments.

CARELLI

Instruments previously built in Chicago, IL circa mid-1930s.

Carelli archtop guitars were produced in the 1930s by the Harmony Guitar company. Harmony, well-known for producing an estimated fifty-seven "different" brands throughout its history, was the largest jobber production house in the history of guitar production. The Carelli trademark, or distributing company, is yet unidentified. Source: Jim Fisch, author (with L.B. Fred) of Epiphone: *The House of Stathopoulo*; and Gary Sullivan, owner of photographed guitar.

The Carelli **Artist E** that was documented at the 19th Annual Dallas Vintage Guitar show has a number of features similar to Harmony's **Cremona** models. Harmony began producing the Cremona series circa 1934, and these models featured carved solid tops and laminated curly maple backs. The Carelli Artist E bears the same distinct features as the Cremona **model #7**. It is estimated that the model shown in the picture is a 1935 or 1936.

CARL BARNEY GUITARS

Instruments currently built in Southbury, CT since 1968.

Luthier Carl Barney started building classical guitars in 1968, and built his first archtop guitar in 1972. Two years later, Barney built a guitar for jazz legend Sal Salvador and began a long friendship and collaboration with Salvador (Barney later created the Sal Salvador Artist model for Salvador in 1980).

All guitars are handcrafted by Barney in his workshop. Since the mid-1970s, Barney has been searching and stockpiling fine instrument woods. In 1976, Barney purchased a good-sized quantity of Gabon ebony, as well as Brazilian and Indian rosewood. Barney currently uses figured woods for all models, and has a supply of figured maple for special commissions. Barney began using Adirondack (American Red) spruce for guitar tops since 1993, which is whiter in appearance than the Sitka spruce that is also available.

Although archtops have been Barney's focus since 1974, he has also built over one hundred classical, flat-top acoustics, and solid body electrics since the mid-1970s. For more information, visit Barney's website or contact him directly.

Although Barney is best-known for his archtop jazz-style guitars, he started out building classical acoustic guitars that he continues to build today. Classical guitars range in price from $3,500 to $4,300 for Indian or Amazon rosewood back and sides and from $3,900 and $4,700 for Brazilian rosewood back and sides. Barney also imports a line of Brazilian handmade guitars that range in price from $1,200 to $2,000.

CONTACT INFORMATION
CARL BARNEY GUITARS
PO Box 128
Southbury, CT 06488
Phone No.: 203-264-9207
Fax No.: 203-267-5857
http://barneyguitars.com
cbarney@earthlink.net

CARLO ROBELLI

Instruments previously produced in China during the 2000s and in Japan during the 1970s. Previously distributed by Sam Ash in New York, NY.

The Carlo Robelli trademark was initially used on a line of guitars that were produced in Japan during the 1970s. These instruments were mainly copies of popular American designs. In the 2000s, the Carlo Robelli trademark appeared again on a line of acoustic guitars. These later guitars were sold in many big box stores, including Sears. Any more information on Carlo Robelli would be appreciated and can be submitted directly to Blue Book Publications.

CARLOS

Instruments previously produced in Korea between the late 1970s and late 1980s. Distributed by Coast Wholesale Music.

Coast Wholesale Music imported and distributed the Carlos trademark of acoustic guitars between circa 1976 and the late 1980s. Carlos guitars are mainly copies of popular models including Takamine and Ovation instruments. Used values on Carlos guitars range between $50 and $250 depending on configuration and condition.

CARLSON, FRED

Guitars currently produced in Santa Cruz, CA since the early 1970s.

Luthier Fred Carlson builds a variety of instruments that feature wild shapes, odd configurations, and other unique aspects. Carlson is well-known for combining the features of certain instruments into one unique piece; however he does offer more traditional guitars with his own unique touch. Carlson's Dreadnautilus (a portable six-string guitar that has a full sound and a round shape) and the New Dream (a 39-string harp contraption that includes a regular six-string guitar, 12 sitar-style strings, six bass harp strings, and 15 high harp strings) are two of his most unusual/unique designs. Carlson is also the co-founder of Beyond The Trees. For more information, visit Carlson's website or contact him directly.

CONTACT INFORMATION
CARLSON, FRED
2026 Back Ranch Road
Santa Cruz, CA 95060
Phone No.: 831-466-9356
www.beyondthetrees.com
wildsols@beyondthetrees.com

CARMELO CATANIA

Guitars previously produced in Italy between circa 1950 and 1967.

Carmelo Catania guitars were mainly ornate and decorated acoustic guitars that were produced in Italy. Source: Walter Murray, Frankenstein Fretworks.

MSR/NOTES	100%	EXCELLENT	AVERAGE	LAST MSR

CARSON ROBISON

Instruments previously produced during the 1930s. See chapter on House Brands.

Carson J. Robison was a popular country singer and songwriter in the 1930s who endorsed a Recording King flattop model. Recording King was the House Brand for Montgomery Ward, and Gibson built the high end models for the line (cheaper models were built by someone else). Early models had only a white paint stencil of "Carson J. Robison" on the peghead (hence this listing) but later models had the Recording King logo as well. Source: Walter Carter, *Gibson Guitars: 100 Years of an American Icon*.

CARVIN

Instruments currently produced in Escondido, CA and overseas (Cobalt Series). Carvin instruments are sold through direct catalog/online sales, as well as through their five factory stores in CA: Corvina, Hollywood, Sacramento, San Diego, and Santa Ana. Carvin has been producing instruments since 1946. Previous production was located in Covina, CA from 1949 to 1969.

CONTACT INFORMATION
CARVIN
12340 World Trade Drive
San Diego, CA 92128
Phone No.: 858-487-1600
Phone No.: 800-854-2235
www.carvin.com

In 1946, Lowell Kiesel founded Kiesel Electronics in Los Angeles, California. Three years later, the Kiesel family settled in Covina, California and began the original catalog business of manufacturing and distributing lap steel guitars, small tube amps and pickups. The Carvin trademark was derived from Kiesel's two oldest sons, Carson and Gavin. Guitars were originally offered in kit form, or by parts since 1949; Carvin began building complete guitars in 1964. By 1978, the glued set-neck design replaced the bolt-on necks. The majority of the current guitar and bass models currently feature a neck-through design.

Carvin has always been a mail-order-only company, and offers the players a wide range of options on the individual models. Even though they can't be tried out before they're bought, Carvin offers a ten-day money back guarantee. Because Carvin sells factory direct, they are not stocked in music stores; by requesting a catalog the careful shopper will also find a difference between the new list price and the actual sales price. Carvin offers a full range of guitar and bass replacement parts in their full line catalog. The Carvin company also offers mixing boards, power amplifiers, powered mixers, P.A. speakers, monitor speakers, guitar combo amps/heads/cabinets, and bass amps/cabinets as well.

In 2001, Carvin introduced a line of imported guitars called the Cobalt Series. These acoustics are hand-crafted overseas to Carvin's specs, and then they are set up and tuned at the Carvin factory before they are shipped. Lowell Kiesel passed away on December 28, 2009. For more information visit Carvin's website, visit one of their stores, or contact them directly.

CUSTOM INFORMATION

Almost every Carvin guitar is available with an extensive list of options. These options include different types of woods, binding, inlays, hardware, and finishes. Each option has a different price that alters the value of the guitar. The models listed in this section are listed with and valued according to Carvin's standard features. For more information on Carvin guitar options visit their website or contact them directly to request a catalog.

ACOUSTIC: COBALT SERIES

C250/C250S – dreadnought body, AA solid cedar (C250S) or AA solid spruce (C250) top, mahogany back and sides, tortoiseshell pickguard, 14/20-fret fingerboard, binding, three-per-side tuners, chrome hardware, available in Natural finish, mfg. 2001-2012.

	100%	EXCELLENT	AVERAGE	LAST MSR
	$400	$250 - 300	$150 - 200	$979

Also available as a left-handed model (C-250LH).

C350 – dreadnought body, AA solid mahogany top/back/sides, tortoiseshell pickguard, 14/20-fret fingerboard, binding, three-per-side tuners, chrome hardware, available in Natural finish, mfg. 2001-2012.

	100%	EXCELLENT	AVERAGE	LAST MSR
	$425	$275 - 325	$160 - 210	$999

C550 – dreadnought body, AA solid spruce top rosewood back/sides, tortoiseshell pickguard, 14/20-fret fingerboard, binding, three-per-side tuners, chrome hardware, available in Natural finish, mfg. 2001-05.

	100%	EXCELLENT	AVERAGE	LAST MSR
	N/A	$350 - 425	$200 - 250	$1,079

C650 – dreadnought body, AA solid spruce top rosewood back/sides, tortoiseshell pickguard, 14/20-fret fingerboard, binding, three-per-side tuners, chrome hardware, Fishman Matrix pickup and electronics, available in Natural finish, mfg. 2001-05.

	100%	EXCELLENT	AVERAGE	LAST MSR
	N/A	$425 - 500	$275 - 325	$1,319

C750(T)/C750TS – dreadnought single cutaway body, AA solid spruce top, mahogany back/sides, tortoiseshell pickguard, 14/20-fret fingerboard, binding, three-per-side tuners, chrome hardware, Fishman Matrix pickup and electronics, available in Natural Gloss (C750TC) or Satin (C750TS) finish, mfg. 2001-2012.

	100%	EXCELLENT	AVERAGE	LAST MSR
	$600	$375 - 450	$250 - 300	$1,399

C770T/C770TS – single cutaway dreadnought body, AA solid mahogany top, mahogany back and sides, set mahogany neck, 14/20 fret bound rosewood fingerboard, bound headstock with rosewood overlay, three-per-side chrome tuners, rosewood bridge with ebony pins, tortoiseshell pickguard, Fishman Matrix pickup and Prefix Plus electronics with built-in tuner, available in Natural Gloss (C770T) or Satin (C770TS) finish, 25.4 in. scale, mfg. 2010-12.

	100%	EXCELLENT	AVERAGE	LAST MSR
	$600	$375 - 450	$250 - 300	$1,399

MSR/NOTES	100%	EXCELLENT	AVERAGE	LAST MSR

C780(T)/C780TS – Jumbo single cutaway body, AA solid spruce top, mahogany back/sides, tortoiseshell pickguard, 14/20 fret fingerboard, binding, three-per-side tuners, chrome hardware, Fishman Matrix pickup and electronics, available in Natural Gloss (C780TC) or Satin (C780TS) finish, mfg. 2001-09.

	N/A	$425 - 500	$275 - 325	$1,339

C850(T) – dreadnought single cutaway body, AA solid spruce top, rosewood back/sides, tortoiseshell pickguard, 14/20-fret fingerboard, binding, three-per-side tuners, chrome hardware, Fishman Matrix pickup and electronics, available in Natural finish, mfg. 2001-2012.

	$650	$425 - 500	$275 - 325	$1,499

This model is also available in a left-handed configuration.

C980(T) – jumbo single cutaway body, AA solid spruce top, rosewood back/sides, tortoiseshell pickguard, 14/20-fret fingerboard, elaborate binding and inlays, three-per-side tuners, gold hardware, Fishman Matrix pickup and electronics, available in Natural finish, mfg. 2001-2012.

	$750	$500 - 600	$325 - 400	$1,739

* **C980(T)12 12-String** – similar to the C980, except in 12-string configuration, six-per-side tuners, mfg. 2003-2012.

	$800	$525 - 625	$350 - 425	$1,839

* **C980(T)MW (Mark Wills Signature)** – similar to the C980, except has maple back/sides and available in Gloss Black finish, mfg. 2003-2012.

	$750	$500 - 600	$325 - 400	$1,739

ACOUSTIC ELECTRIC

AC175 – single cutaway hollowed-out mahogany body, spruce top, round soundhole, through-body mahogany neck, 24-fret ebony fingerboard with pearl dot inlay, ebony bridge with black pins, blackface peghead with screened logo, three-per-side gold tuners, transducer bridge Fishman pickup, volume/treble/bass controls, active electronics, available in Classic White, Ferrari Red, Jet Black, Natural, Pearl Blue, Pearl Red, or Pearl White finish, mfg. 1994-2011.

	$950	$600 - 700	$400 - 475	$2,099

AC275 – similar to the AC175, except the mahogany body is 1.5 in. wider, and features a F60 acoustic transducer with volume/treble/bass controls and active electronics, mfg. 1996-2009.

	N/A	$650 - 750	$400 - 475	$2,099

* **AC275-12 12-String** – similar to the AC275, except in 12-string configuration with six-per side tuners, mfg. 1996-2009.

	N/A	$675 - 800	$450 - 525	$2,299

AC375 – single rounded cutaway hollowed-out mahogany body, round soundhole, through body neck, 21-fret ebony fingerboard with pearl dot inlay, ebony bridge with black pins, natural peghead with three-per-side tuners, Fishman Acoustic Matrix pickup, active electronics, gold hardware, available in Natural or custom color finish, mfg. 2000-09.

	N/A	$675 - 800	$475 - 550	$2,279

CC275 CRAIG CHAQUCIO SIGNATURE – similar to the AC275 except is the Craig Chaqucio model, which features a flamed maple top, MOP inlaid eagle headstock & fingerboard, body binding gold hardware, "Craig Chaquico" on truss-rod cover, mfg. 2001-present.

MSR $2,499	$1,300	$750 - 900	$475 - 550	

* **CC275-12 Craig Chaqucio Signature 12-String** – similar to the CC275, except in 12-string configuration and six-per-side headstock, mfg. 2002-present.

MSR $2,699	$1,380	$800 - 950	$500 - 575	

CL450 CLASSICAL – single rounded cutaway hollowed-out mahogany body, AAA cedar top, round soundhole, through body neck, 21-fret ebony fingerboard with pearl dot inlay, ebony bridge with black pins, matching finish peghead with three-per-side banjo-style tuners, Fishman Acoustic Matrix pickup, active electronics, gold hardware, available in Natural or custom color finishes, mfg. 2001-present.

MSR $2,379	$1,300	$725 - 875	$450 - 525	

NS1 NYLON SYNTH ACCESS – nylon string configuration, single smooth cutaway chambered mahogany body, AAAA flame maple top with wood binding effetc, mahogany NTB, 21-fret ebony fingerboard, slotted flame maple headstock with three-per-side open-style banjo gold tuners, ebony bridge, piezo and Hexaphonic MIDI pickups, three stacked knobs (v1/v2, mid-boost/mid sweep, t/b), MIDI mini-switch, available in Natural or Custom Color finishes, 25.5 in. scale, mfg. 2007-present.

MSR $2,799	$1,450	$900 - 1,050	$550 - 650	

ACOUSTIC ELECTRIC BASS

All Carvin U.S. acoustic bass models have a 34 in. scale, and are available in these standard colors: Classic White, Ferrari Red, Jet Black, Pearl Blue, Pearl Red, Pearl White, and a Tung Oil finish. Translucent finishes are optional.

AC40 – offset double cutaway semi-hollow mahogany body, AAA Englemann spruce top, through-body mahogany neck, 24-fret ebony fingerboard with pearl dot inlay, fixed acoustic-style bridge, four-per-side tuners, Carvin F40 acoustic bridge transducer, master volume control, bass/treble tone controls, current mfg.

MSR $1,979	$1,000	$625 - 725	$425 - 500	

This model has an optional fretless fingerboard (AC40F).

MSR/NOTES	100%	EXCELLENT	AVERAGE	LAST MSR

AC50 – similar to the AC40, except in a five-string configuration, 3/2-per-side-tuners, current mfg.

MSR $2,099	$1,050	$650 - 750	$450 - 525	

This model has an optional fretless fingerboard (AC50F).

C450T – single cutaway jumbo body, AA solid spruce top, mahogany back and sides, abalone rosette/purfling, 22-fret rosewood fingerboard with dot inlay, two-per-side chrome tuners, rosewood bridge, Fishman Matrix pickup and Prefix Plus T electronics, Natural finish, mfg. 2006-07.

	N/A	$400 - 500	$250 - 300	$1,439

CASA MONTALVO

Instruments currently built in Mexico. Distributed by the Berkeley Musical Instrument Company in Berkeley, CA.

Montalvo guitars are the result of a collaboration between George Katechis-Montalvo (a highly skilled craftsman) and Marc Silber (a noted guitar historian, restorer and designer). Montalvo had already been importing guitars from Mexico since 1987. Silber joined him in 1990 to found the K & S Guitar Company. K & S introduced higher quality woods, glues, finishes and American builders' knowledge to the Mexican luthiers for actual production in Mexico. Casa Montalvo guitars are currently being distributed by Berkeley Music. They were previously distributed by K&S Guitars, Inc. Berkeley took over circa 2001. Casa offers classical, flamenco, Hawaiian, and other stringed instruments. Retail prices range from $650 to $2,050. For more information, contact Berkeley directly.

CONTACT INFORMATION
CASA MONTALVO
Distributed by Berkeley Musical Instrument Company
2923 Adeline St.
Berkeley, CA 94703
Phone No.: 510-548-7538
Phone No.: 866-548-7538
www.berkeleymusic.com
bmie@berkeleymusic.com

CATALINA

Unknown date or location of production. See chapter on House Brands.

The Catalina trademark has been identified as a House Brand of the Abercrombie & Fitch company. Source: Willie G. Moseley, *Stellas & Stratocasters*.

CATALUNA

Instruments currently built in Taiwan, Republic of China. Distributed by Reliance International Corporation of Taiwan, Republic of China.

Reliance International's Cataluna instruments are entry-level to medium-quality acoustic guitars. The Apex series features four traditional-style, Dreadnought-style acoustics, and two classical acoustics. Apex series instruments feature spruce tops, nato backs/sides/necks, and rosewood fingerboards.

C. B. ALYN GUITARWORKS

Instruments currently built in Key West, FL. Previously produced in Pacific Palisades, CA. C.B. Alyn Guitarworks have been building instruments since 1993.

C.B. Alyn Guitarworks offers the Rosebud series that are chambered solidbody acoustic guitars with no soundholes. Retail prices range from $2,599 to $2,899. For more information, visit C.B. Alyn's website.

CONTACT INFORMATION
C. B. ALYN GUITARWORKS
Phone No.: 305-292-6089
www.cbalyn.com
cbalyn@cbalyn.com

C. BRUNO & SONS

Guitars previously produced in Macon, GA during the 1830s and various other locations until the 1920s. See chapter on House Brands.

C. Bruno & Sons was originally formed in Macon, GA in 1834. C. Bruno & Son guitars were built by another manufacturer, and distributed by the company. The company has been in the music distribution business since then and C. Bruno & Son distributors is currently part of Kaman Music Corporation.

In 1838, Charles Bruno and C.F. Martin entered into a partnership to produce and distribute acoustic guitars. These specific guitars are labeled with both names, and were produced in New York. In 1839, Martin moved the company to Nazareth, PA and dissolved the partnership. C.F. Martin did not provide the guitars that bear the "Bruno" or "C. Bruno & Sons" logos on the peghead (source: Mike Longworth, *Martin Guitars*).

Instruments bearing the C. Bruno & Sons logo were available in several variations. The most popular appears to be parlor guitars produced during between the 1880s and the 1920s. They also produced harp guitars. Prices on these guitars generally start around $500 and climb from there depending on the condition and level of ornateness.

CBS MASTERWORKS

Instruments previously produced in Japan during the mid- to late 1960s.

CBS Masterworks was a trademark used on a line of acoustic guitars built in Japan by Kazuo Yairi. Reportedly, these guitars were imported by Fender shortly after they were acquired by CBS in 1965, which is why they chose the CBS Masterworks trademark. Any further information on this brand can be submitted directly to Blue Book Publications.

CELEBRITY

Instruments previously built in Korea, and distributed by the Kaman Music Corporation of Bloomfield, CT during the late 1980s.

The Celebrity line of bowl back guitars was introduced in 1983 as a Korean-built entry level introduction to the American-built Ovation line. Celebrity models offer similar design features, and a variety of options as their overseas production saves money on their retail price. The Celebrity trademark was also applied to a number of solid body electrics based on popular American designs.

CENTURY GUITARS

Instruments currently produced. Distributed by Century Guitars in Northridge, CA.

Century guitars are acoustic guitars that have the new "Stress-A-Way Bridge." This bridge takes the strings of the guitar and moves them outward, away from the center. With the strings anchored farther away from the center and spaced apart, it puts less stress on the bridge itself. It is possible then to use the whole top of the guitar for strength. Century is now taking the bridge that they have used for several years and making their own brand of guitar out of it. Retail prices start at $590 and can climb as high as $2,000 for the very ornate models. For more information, contact Century directly.

CONTACT INFORMATION

CENTURY GUITARS

Main Office
Box 404
Hillsboro, OH 45133
Phone No.: 937-393-4391
Fax No.: 937-393-4391
centuryguitars@yahoo.com

West Coast Office/Warehouse
18657 Parthenia Street
Northridge, CA 91324
Phone No.: 818-886-4673
Fax No.: 818-886-1301

CFOX

Instruments previously produced in Healdsburg, CA between 1997 and 2002. For current production Charles Fox guitars, see Charles Fox Guitars.

CFox Guitars debuted at the 1998 NAMM industry show in January, and introduced the newest line of high quality handcrafted acoustic guitar models. Charles Fox has a worldwide reputation as a luthier, educator, and consultant in the field of guitar building. The CFox guitar line was the product of Fox's thirty years experience as an artist, craftsman, and teacher. In 2002, he stopped production under the CFox trademark and moved to Oregon. He has since started producing guitars as Charles Fox Guitars. For a complete history on Charles Fox see Charles Fox Guitars.

All four of the CFox models (Concert, Dreadnought, Hybrid, and Small Jumbo) are available in three different quality series (Napa, Sonoma, and Frisco). The **Napa Series** of guitars featured a solid AAA Sitka spruce top, carbon-graphite reinforced Honduran mahogany neck, 25.5 in.scale, Honduran mahogany back/sides, black top binding, round soundhole with rosette, 14/21-fret ebony fingerboard, ebony peghead overlay with mother-of-pearl logo, ebony bridge with ebony bridgepins, ebony end pin, three-per-side nickel Grover tuners, and available in Natural finish. Last MSR on this series was $2,800.

The **Sonoma Series** were similar to the Napa Series with the exception of Indian rosewood back/sides, grained ivoroid top binding, grained ivoroid neck/headstock binding, abalone rosette, ebony bridgepins with abalone dots, three-per-side chrome Schaller tuners, and available in Natural finish. Last MSR on this series was $3,200.

The **Frisco Series** were similar to the Napa Series with the exception of a master grade Sitka spruce top, Indian rosewood back/sides, ebony end graft, grained ivoroid body binding, grained ivoroid neck/headstock binding, abalone rosette, ebony bridgepins with abalone dots, and three-per-side gold Schaller tuners with ebony buttons. Last MSR on this series was $3,700. Left-handed configurations were available at no extra charge.

- **Add $100 for Engelmann Spruce soundboard.**
- **Add $150 for Western Red Cedar soundboard.**
- **Add $175 for extended fretboard.**
- **Add $250 for German Spruce soundboard.**
- **Add $350 for cocobola back and sides.**
- **Add $400 for figured maple back and sides.**
- **Add $400 for wood binding.**
- **Add $500 for wood binding, cutaway configuration.**
- **Add $500 for koa back and sides.**
- **Add $500 for standard cutaway.**
- **Add $700 for abalone trim.**
- **Add $750 for compound cutaway.**

CHAPIN

Instruments currently built in San Jose, CA.

Handcrafted Chapin guitars feature carefully thought out designs that provide ergonomic comfort and a wide palette of tones. All Chapin guitars are handcrafted by luthiers Bill Chapin and Fred Campbell; all guitars feature the Campbell/Chapin locking dovetail set-in neck joint. Chapin also offered the Chapin Insight Guitar Inspection Camera that allowed luthiers/repairmen/customers/etc. to view the inside of an acoustic guitar. For current information on Chapin's acoustic electric models, please refer to the *Blue Book of Electric Guitars*. For more information, visit Chapin's website or contact them directly.

CONTACT INFORMATION

CHAPIN

PMB 410, 1477 SE 1st Ave, Suite #108
Canby, OR 97013
Phone No.: 503-651-1625
www.chapinguitars.com
shades@chapinguitars.com

All of Chapin's models are available with additional options such as choice of wood(s), pickups, or hardware (call for price quote). Retail prices listed below reflect the base price.

Chapin's acoustic electric **Eagle** (last MSR $1,850) is available in nylon or steel string configuration. It features semi-solid body design with tuned acoustic chambers, spruce (or maple) top, rosewood acoustic-style bridge or electric-style bridge with piezo pickups (steel string model only), and Gilbert or Sperzel tuners. The **Eagle Custom** model has a figured redwood or master-grade spruce top, interchangeable ebony soundports, figured wood binding, violin-style purfling, acoustic transducer, and Gilbert tuners with abalone inlay (pricing is different for every order). The **Fatline Acoustic** model is a tuned chamber semi-solid version of the Fatline Electric. It features steel strings, and electric guitar bridge with six piezo pickups and a Fishman Rare Earth neck pickup.

CHARIS ACOUSTIC

Guitars currently produced in Bay City, MI since 1996.

CONTACT INFORMATION
CHARIS ACOUSTIC
2356 Delta Rd.
Bay City, MI 48706
Phone No.: 989-686-9775
www.charisacoustic.com
bill@charisacoustic.com

Luthier Bill Wise builds custom high-end flattop acoustic guitars. In 1996, Wise, an automotive engineer, decided he wanted a better guitar than the junker he had from college. Instead of spending a lot of money on the guitars that were out there, he decided to build his own. In circa 2001, he quit his job and started building guitars full time. Currently, Wise offers three basic shapes in the small jumbo, grand concert, and dreadnought body styles. Baritone and 12-String options are available on the Dreadnought model. Prices start at $5,000. Wise builds about thirty to forty guitars a year. For more information, visit Charis' website or contact Wise directly.

CHARLES FOX GUITARS

Instruments currently produced in Portland, OR since 2002. Charles Fox has been a luthier since 1968.

CONTACT INFORMATION
CHARLES FOX GUITARS
2745 SW Scenic Drive
Portland, OR 97225
Phone No.: 503-292-2385
www.charlesfoxguitars.com
cfox@charlesfoxguitars.com

Charles Fox (b. 1943) did his undergraduate work at the Art Institute of Chicago and completed his postgraduate work at Northwestern University in 1966. Fox began building his own guitars in 1968, and since then has worked both as a custom guitar builder and as the head of his own guitar production shop. In the late 1970s and early 1980s, Fox's GRD Guitars (see GRD) were among the first instruments to define the market for high end electric guitars.

In 1973, Fox founded the first school for guitar builders in North America, the Guitar Research and Design Center. In recent years, Fox has founded and directed the American School of Lutherie in Healdsburg, California and has been a founder and educational coordinator of the Healdsburg Guitar Festival. In 2002, he stopped production under the C. Fox trademark and moved to Oregon. He has since started producing guitars under the trademark Charles Fox Guitars. For more information on C. Fox instruments see C. Fox. Charles has also introduced the Ergo line of guitars. For more information about Charles Fox Guitars, ErgoGuitars, or the American School of Lutherie, contact Charles Fox directly or visit his website.

Charles Fox builds traditional steel- and nylon-stringed guitars using fine tonewoods. Steel-string models are available in traditional Martin shapes (00, OM, 12-fret, etc.), Concert, Fingerstyle, and Small Jumbo body sizes. Classical models include Avante, Hauser, and a Hybrid design. Prices on all guitars start at $9,000 with several options available.

CHARVEL

Trademark previously manufactured in Korea until 1999. The Charvel trademark was established in 1978 by the Charvel Manufacturing Company. Previously distributed until 1999 by Jackson/Charvel Guitar Company (Akai Musical Instruments) of Fort Worth, TX. Previously produced in the U.S. between 1978 and 1985; later, (post-1985) production was based in the U.S., Japan, and Korea.

In the late 1970s, Wayne Charvel's Guitar Repair shop in Azusa, California acquired a reputation for making custom high quality bodies and necks. Grover Jackson began working at the shop in 1977, and a year later bought out Charvel and moved the company to San Dimas. Jackson debuted the Charvel custom guitars at the 1979 NAMM show, and the first catalog depicting the bolt-neck beauties and custom options arrived in 1981.

The standard models from Charvel Manufacturing carried a list price between $880 and $955, and the amount of custom options was staggering. In 1983, the Charvel company began offering neck-through models under the Jackson trademark.

Grover Jackson licensed the Charvel trademark to the International Music Corporation (IMC) in 1985; the company was sold to them a year later. In late 1986, production facilities were moved to Ontario, California. Distribution eventually switched from Charvel/Jackson to the Jackson/Charvel Guitar company, currently a branch of the Akai Musical Instruments company. As the years went by and the Charvel line expanded, its upper end models were phased out and moved into the Jackson line (which had been the Charvel/Jackson Company's line of custom-made instruments) and were gaining more popularity. For example, the **Charvel Avenger** (mfg. 1991 to 1992), became the **Jackson Rhoads EX Pro** (mfg. 1992 to date). For further details, see the Jackson guitars section in this edition.

In 1988, Charvel sent a crew of luthiers to Japan for a year or so to cross-train the Japanese builders on building methods for custom built guitars. The resulting custom instruments had a retail list price between $1,000 and $1,300. U.S. custom-built guitars have a four-digit serial number and the Japanese custom-built models have a six-digit serial number. Numbers may be prefaced with a "C," which may stand for custom made (this point has not been completely verified).

By the early 1990s, the only Charvel models left were entry level Strat-style electrics and Dreadnought and jumbo-style (full bodied and cutaways) acoustic guitars. In the late 1990s, even the electrics were phased out in favor of the acoustic and acoustic/electric models. During 1999, instruments with the Charvel trademark had ceased production, and Wayne Charvel began building a new line of instruments utilizing the Wayne Guitars trademark (early Charvel history courtesy Baker Rorick, *Guitar Shop* magazine; additional information courtesy Roland Lozier, Lozier Piano & Music).

MSR/NOTES	100%	EXCELLENT	AVERAGE	LAST MSR

ACOUSTIC/ACOUSTIC ELECTRIC

125S – dreadnought style, solid spruce top, round soundhole, seven-stripe bound body/rosette, mahogany back/sides/neck, 14/20-fret bound rosewood fingerboard with abalone dot inlay, rosewood bridge with white black pins, rosewood veneered peghead with pearl logo inlay, three-per-side chrome tuners, available in Natural or Tobacco Sunburst finish, mfg. 1994-96.

	N/A	$300 - 350	$175 - 225	$595

* *125SE* – similar to 125S, except has transducer bridge pickup, three-band EQ, available in Natural or Tobacco Sunburst finish, mfg. 1994-96.

	N/A	$325 - 400	$200 - 250	$695

150SC – single round cutaway dreadnought style, solid spruce top, round soundhole, seven-stripe bound body/rosette, rosewood back/sides, mahogany neck, 14/20-fret bound rosewood fingerboard with abalone dot inlay, rosewood bridge with white black pins, rosewood veneered peghead with pearl logo inlay, three-per-side chrome tuners, available in Natural or Tobacco Sunburst finish, mfg. 1994-96.

	N/A	$300 - 350	$175 - 225	$595

* *150SEC* – similar to 150SC, except has transducer bridge pickup, three-band EQ, available in Natural or Tobacco Sunburst finish, mfg. 1994-96.

	N/A	$325 - 400	$200 - 250	$695

325SL – double offset cutaway asymmetrical style, spruce top, offset wedge soundhole, bound body and soundhole, nato back/sides/neck, 22-fret rosewood fingerboard with offset abalone dot inlay, rosewood bridge with white pearl dot pins, rosewood veneer with abalone Charvel logo, three-per-side chrome tuners, transducer bridge pickup, three-band EQ, active electronics, available in Black, Bright Red and Turquoise finish, mfg. 1992-94.

	N/A	$325 - 400	$200 - 250	$500

* *325SLX* – similar to 325SL, except has figured maple top, rosewood back/sides, bound fingerboard with shark fin inlay, bound peghead, active electronics with built-in chorus, available in Cherry Sunburst, Tobacco Sunburst, or Trans. Red finish.

	N/A	$375 - 450	$225 - 275	$600

525 – single round cutaway dreadnought style, spruce top, round soundhole, five-stripe bound body and rosette, mahogany arched back/sides/neck, 22-fret bound rosewood fingerboard with pearl dot inlay, rosewood bridge with white black dot pins, bound peghead with abalone Charvel logo inlay, three-per-side chrome tuners, available in Cherry Sunburst, Metallic Black, Natural, or Tobacco Sunburst, disc. 1994.

	N/A	$300 - 350	$175 - 225	$400

* *525D* – similar to 525, except has transducer bridge pickup with three-band EQ, available in Metallic Black, Natural or Tobacco Sunburst finish, disc. 1994.

	N/A	$325 - 400	$200 - 250	$500

550 – dreadnought style, spruce top, round soundhole, black pickguard, three-stripe bound body/rosette, mahogany back/sides/neck, 25.6 in.scale, 14/20-fret rosewood fingerboard with pearl dot inlay, rosewood bridge with black white dot pins, rosewood veneered peghead with pearl logo inlay, three-per-side chrome tuners, available in Mahogany or Natural finish, mfg. 1994-2000.

	N/A	$200 - 250	$120 - 150	$275

* *550C* – similar to the 550, except has a single rounded cutaway, available in Natural finish, mfg. 1994-2000.

	N/A	$175 - 225	$110 - 140	$295

* *550E* – similar to 550, except has transducer bridge pickup, three-band EQ, available in Natural finish, mfg. 1994-2000.

	N/A	$250 - 300	$135 - 175	$450

» *550CE* – similar to the 550C, except has transducer bridge pickup, three-band EQ, available in Natural finish, mfg. 1994-2000.

	N/A	$275 - 325	$175 - 225	$475

625 – single round cutaway jumbo style, spruce top, round soundhole, five-stripe bound body and rosette, nato back/sides, mahogany neck, 25.6 in.scale, 20-fret rosewood fingerboard with abalone dot inlay, rosewood bridge with white black dot pins, rosewood veneer on peghead with abalone Charvel logo inlay, three-per-side gold tuners, available in Cherry Sunburst, Metallic Black, Natural, and Tobacco Sunburst finish, mfg. 1992-2000.

	N/A	$150 - 200	$95 - 120	$365

In 1997, abalone inlay was changed to faux abalone.

* *625C* – similar to 625, except has abalone bound body/rosette, rosewood back/sides, 24-fret bound extended fingerboard, abalone dot pins, bound peghead, transducer bridge pickup, three-band EQ, active electronics, mfg. 1992-2000.

	N/A	$250 - 300	$150 - 200	$645

* *625C-12* – similar to 625, except has 12-string configuration, abalone bound body/rosette, rosewood back/sides, 24-fret bound extended fingerboard, abalone dot pins, bound peghead, six-per-side tuners, transducer bridge pickup, three-band EQ, active electronics, available in Metallic Black, Natural, or Tobacco Sunburst finish, mfg. 1994-2000.

	N/A	$275 - 325	$175 - 225	$795

* *625D* – similar to 625, except has transducer bridge pickup, three-band EQ, active electronics, disc.

	N/A	$200 - 250	$120 - 150	$475

MSR/NOTES	100%	EXCELLENT	AVERAGE	LAST MSR

* *625F* – similar to 625, except has figured maple top, available in Tobacco Sunburst, Trans. Black and Trans. Red, mfg. 1994-95.

| | N/A | $300 - 350 | $175 - 225 | $650 |

725 – jumbo style, solid spruce top, round soundhole, seven-stripe bound body/rosette, mahogany back/sides/neck, 14/20-fret rosewood fingerboard with pearl offset dot inlay, rosewood bridge with white black pins, rosewood veneered peghead with pearl logo inlay, three-per-side chrome tuners, available in Natural finish, mfg. 1994-96.

| | N/A | $250 - 300 | $135 - 175 | $495 |

* *725E* – similar to 725, except has transducer bridge pickup, three-band EQ, available in Natural finish, mfg. 1994-96.

| | N/A | $300 - 350 | $175 - 225 | $595 |

750E – jumbo style, solid spruce top, round soundhole, seven-stripe bound body/rosette, figured maple back/sides, mahogany neck, 14/20-fret rosewood fingerboard with pearl offset dot inlay, rosewood bridge with white black pins, figured maple veneered peghead with pearl logo inlay, three-per-side gold tuners, available in Natural finish, mfg. 1994-96.

| | N/A | $325 - 400 | $200 - 250 | $695 |

ATX – single cutaway hollow mahogany body, bound maple top, maple neck, 24-fret rosewood fingerboard with offset pearl dot inlay, strings through rosewood bridge, six-per-side one chrome tuners, Fishman transducer bridge pickup, volume/three-band EQ controls, available in Black, Deep Metallic Blue, Dark Metallic Red, or Deep Metallic Violet finish, mfg. 1993-96.

| | N/A | $500 - 600 | $325 - 400 | $895 |

* *ATX Trans* – similar to ATX, except has figured maple top, available in Tobacco Sunburst, Trans. Black, or Trans. Violet finish, disc. 1996.

| | N/A | $550 - 650 | $350 - 425 | $995 |

CM-100 – dreadnought style, cedar top, round soundhole, multibound body, three-stripe rosette, figured mahogany back/sides, mahogany neck, 14/20-fret bound rosewood fingerboard with pearl dot inlay, ebony bridge with white black dot pins, bound rosewood veneered peghead with pearl logo inlay, three-per-side chrome tuners, available in Natural finish, mfg. 1994 only.

| | N/A | $425 - 500 | $275 - 325 | $895 |

CM-400 LIMITED EDITION – jumbo style, solid spruce top, round soundhole, maple bound/abalone purfling body, abalone rosette, jacaranda back/sides, mahogany neck, 14/20-fret ebony fingerboard with pearl cloud inlay, ebony bridge with black abalone dot pins, abalone bound rosewood veneered peghead with abalone logo inlay, three-per-side gold tuners, available in Natural finish, mfg. 1994 only.

| | N/A | $1,750 - 2,000 | $1,150 - 1,300 | $3,995 |

ACOUSTIC ELECTRIC BASS

425 SL – offset double rounded cutaway asymmetrical style, spruce top, offset wedge soundhole, bound body and soundhole, nato back/sides/neck, 22-fret rosewood fingerboard with offset abalone inlay, rosewood bridge with abalone dot inlay, abalone Charvel logo peghead inlay, two-per-side chrome tuners, transducer bridge pickup, three-band EQ, active electronics, available in Bright Red, Metallic Black, or Turquoise finish, mfg. 1992-94.

| | N/A | $300 - 350 | $175 - 225 | $550 |

* *425SLX* – similar to 425SL, except has figured maple top, rosewood back/sides, bound fingerboard/peghead, active electronics with built-in chorus, available in Cherry Sunburst, Tobacco Sunburst, or Trans. Red finish, mfg. 1992-94.

| | N/A | $325 - 400 | $200 - 250 | $650 |

ATX BASS – single cutaway hollow mahogany body, bound maple top, maple neck, 22-fret rosewood fingerboard with offset pearl dot inlay, strings through rosewood bridge, four-on-a-side chrome tuners, volume/three-band EQ controls, available in Black, Deep Metallic Blue, or Deep Metallic Violet finish, mfg. 1993-96.

| | N/A | $475 - 550 | $300 - 375 | $995 |

* *ATX Bass Trans* – similar to ATX Bass, except has figured maple top, available in Tobacco Sunburst, Trans. Black, or Trans. Violet finish, disc.

| | N/A | $500 - 600 | $325 - 400 | $1,095 |

CHARVETTE

Instruments previously produced in Korea from 1989 to 1994. Charvette, an entry-level line to Charvel, was distributed by the International Music Corporation of Ft. Worth, TX.

The Charvette trademark was distributed by the Charvel/Jackson company as a good quality entry-level guitar based on their original Jackson USA designs. They also applied this to some acoustic guitars.

ACOUSTIC ELECTRIC

500 – single round cutaway flattop style, maple top, plectrum-shaped soundhole, one stripe bound body/rosette, bolt-on maple neck, 22-fret rosewood fingerboard with pearl dot inlay, rosewood bridge with black pins, six-on-a-side tuners, black hardware, six piezo bridge pickups, volume/treble/bass controls, active electronics, available in Ferrari Red, Midnite Black, or Snow White finish, mfg. 1991-92.

| | N/A | $200 - 250 | $95 - 125 | $495 |

MSR/NOTES	100%	EXCELLENT	AVERAGE	LAST MSR

CHATWORTH

Instruments previously built in England.

Luthier Andy Smith previously built high quality guitars in England.

CHRIS

Unknown production location and date. See chapter on House Brands.

This trademark has been identified as a separate budget line of guitars from the Jackson-Guldan company of Columbus, OH. Source: Willie G. Moseley, *Stellas & Stratocasters*.

CHRIS LARKIN CUSTOM GUITARS

Instruments currently built in Ireland beginning in 1977.

CONTACT INFORMATION
CHRIS LARKIN CUSTOM GUITARS
Castlegregory, County Kerry Ireland
Phone No.: +353861712331
www.chrislarkinguitars.com
chris@chrislarkinguitars.com

Since 1977, Chris Larkin Custom Guitars have been based at Castlegregory, County Kerry, on the west coast of Ireland. Chris Larkin works alone hand building a range of original designs to custom order to a very high level of quality from the finest available materials. The range is wide including acoustic, electric, archtop, semi-acoustic guitars, acoustic, electric, semi-acoustic, and archtop mandolins. One-off designs are also built and Chris admits to having made some very high spec copies when offered enough money. Whenever possible, Chris uses Irish wood in his instruments. Chris is a partner in the Leonardo Guitar Research Project, which is supported by the European Union and is promoting the use of non-tropical woods in the guitar making industry thus helping to save the rain forests and the residents of those forests.

As each instrument is handmade to order, the customer has a wide choice of woods, colors, fret type, fingerboard radius, neck profile, and dimensions within the design to enable the finished instrument to better suit the player often within the standard price range. Every model can be customized further as required. All Larkin instruments from 1980 on have a shamrock as the headstock inlay. Sales are worldwide through distributors in some areas, or direct from the maker. For more information, visit Larkin's website or contact him directly.

SERIALIZATION

Since 1982, a simple six-digit system has been used. The first two digits indicate the year, the next two the month, and the final two the sequence in that month. For example, 970103 was the third instrument in January 1997. Before 1982 the numbers are a bit chaotic. Chris Larkin has full documentation for almost every instrument (about 700) that he has ever built, so he can supply a history from the serial number in most cases.

ACOUSTIC

ASAP acoustic flattop models are lightly built for performances with an emphasis on balanced tone. This model is available in various configurations such as a nylon string, a twelve-string, an acoustic bass model, a longscale for DADGAD tuning, a baritone, a jumbo and most recently a parlour model. Prices start at 2,150 euro. All models feature a Highlander pickup and preamp system, and Schaller tuners.

ASAS archtop guitars are available in two acoustic models and one semi-acoustic (both acoustic models feature fingerboard mounted custom made humbuckers). All models are built from European spruce and highly figured maple, and have multiple binding on body, neck, headstock, and scratchplate. The archtops are available with a Florentine cutaway. The ASAS semi-hollow has a cedar sustain block running from neck to tail, two humbuckers, and a stop tailpiece. Prices on the archtops start at 4,250 euro.

CIGANO

Guitars currently produced in Asia since 2007. Distributed by Saga Musical Instruments in San Francisco, CA.

CONTACT INFORMATION
CIGANO
Distributed by Saga Musical Instruments
PO Box 2841
South San Francisco, CA 94080
Phone No.: 650-558-5558
Fax No.: 650-871-7590
www.sagamusic.com
info@sagamusic.com

Saga introduced the Cigano brand to offer affordable Gypsy Jazz-style guitars. These guitars are styled after the classic Maccaferri guitars of the 1930s. The Cigano brand can also be considered Gitane's (also a Saga brand) budget version. For more information, visit Saga's website or contact them direcetly.

ACOUSTIC

GJ-0 – single horizontal cutaway Gypsy Jazz-style body, spruce top, Asian rosewood back and sides, oval soundhole with multi-ring rosette, black plastic body binding, mahogany neck, 14/21-fret rosewood fingerboard with pearl dot inlays, slotted headstock, three-per-side open-style gold-plated tuners, rosewood moustache bridge with movable center, traditional brass tailpiece with plastic insert, Natural finish, mfg. 2009-present.

MSR $550	$300	$175 - 225	$100 - 135

GJ-5 – single horizontal cutaway Gypsy Jazz-style body, Sitka spruce top, Asian rosewood back and sides, large D-shaped soundhole with multi-ring rosette, black plastic body binding, mahogany neck, 14/21-fret rosewood fingerboard with pearl dot inlays, slotted headstock, three-per-side open-style gold-plated tuners, rosewood moustache bridge with movable center, traditional brass tailpiece with plastic insert, Natural finish, mfg. 2009-present.

MSR $595	$350	$225 - 275	$135 - 175

MSR/NOTES	100%	EXCELLENT	AVERAGE	LAST MSR

GJ-10 – single horizontal cutaway Gypsy Jazz-style body, solid Sitka spruce top, Asian rosewood back and sides, oval soundhole with multi-ring rosette, nato neck, 14/21-fret rosewood fingerboard with pearl dot inlays, slotted headstock, three-per-side open-style gold-plated tuners, ebony moustache bridge with movable center, traditional brass tailpiece with plastic insert, Natural finish, mfg. 2007-present.

MSR $550	$300	$175 - 225	$100 - 135

GJ-15 – single cutaway horizontal Gypsy Jazz-style body, solid Sitka spruce top, Asian rosewood back and sides, large D-shaped soundhole with multi-ring rosette, nato neck, 14/21-fret rosewood fingerboard with pearl dot inlays, slotted headstock, three-per-side open-style gold-plated tuners, ebony moustache bridge with movable center, traditional brass tailpiece with plastic insert, Natural finish, mfg. 2007-present.

MSR $595	$350	$225 - 275	$135 - 175

CIMARRON GUITARS

Instruments currently built in Ridgeway, CO since 1980.

Luthier John Walsh produces acoustic, electric semi-acoustic, and electric guitars. He chose to produce guitars in Ridgeway, Colorado because of the dry and relatively mild climate. Early in his career, it was estimated that Walsh produced twenty-four acoustic guitars a year. Currently he produces about thirty to forty instruments a year. The acoustic guitar models featured Sitka spruce tops, maple or mahogany necks, and ebony fingerboards on standard models to custom configurations. The sides are mahogany (list $2,000) or rosewood (list $2,200). Options and personal requests are encouraged. Contact Walsh for further information.

CITATION

Instruments previously produced in Japan.

The U.S. distributor of Citation guitars was the Grossman company of Cleveland, OH. Source: Michael Wright, *Guitar Stories,* Volume One.

CITRON

Instruments currently built in Woodstock, NY. Distributed by Harvey Citron Enterprises. Harvey Citron has been building Citron guitar and basses since 1994.

Luthier Harvey Citron has been building high quality, innovative, solid body guitars since the early 1970s. Citron, a noted guitarist and singer, co-founded the Veillette-Citron company in 1975. During the partnership's eight years, they were well-known for the quality of their handcrafted electric guitars, basses, and baritone guitars. Citron also designed the **X-92 Breakaway** model for Guild and was a regular contributing writer for several guitar magazines.

Citron instruments are available direct from Harvey Citron, or through a limited number of dealers. Citron maintains a current price list and descriptions of his models at his website. His *Basic Guitar Set-Up and Repair* instructional video is available from Homespun Tapes. For most model listings, refer to the *Blue Book of Electric Guitars.* For more information contact Citron directly or visit their website.

ACOUSTIC ELECTRIC BASS

All acoustic electric bass models are available with or without a headstock or a fretless fingerboard at no additional charge.

AE5 SWALLOW FIVE-STRING – five-string configuration, 3 in. thick Honduras Mahogany body with x-braced Spruce top, offset double cutaway body, oval soundhole, one-piece Honduras Mahogany neck, East Indian Rosewood fingerboard, bridge, tailpiece, sound hole inlay, and headplate, 3/2-per-side tuners, rosewood bridge, wood pickguard on the bass horn, no exposed pickups - piezo only instrument, 6 piezos and with a single volume control on upper horn and bass, treble, and gain controls for piezos located in cavity mfg. 2006-present.

MSR $6,730	$6,730	N/A	N/A

CLIFFORD

Guitars previously produced in Kansas City, MO during the late 1890s and early 1900s.

The Clifford trademark was used on a variety of acoustic guitars and mandolins by J.W. Jenkins & Sons of Kansas City, MO. Around 1895, Jenkins built a factory to start manufacturing guitars and they first used the names Clifford, Washington, and possibly Harwood. It is unknown how long Clifford instruments were produced.

COLE CLARK

Instruments currently produced in Australia since 2001. Distributed in North America by Cole Clark North America in Lockport, NY.

Brad Clark is the director of Cole Clark and he previously worked at Maton as the factory manager and later as CEO. Cole Clark produces acoustic and electric guitars that are built using classic construction techniques with modern principles and technology to make the guitars lighter and stronger. A wide variety of acoustic instruments are available in various configurations including six-strings and twelve-strings. For more information, visit Cole Clark's website or contact them directly.

CONTACT INFORMATION
COLE CLARK
Cole Clark North America
Ulrich City Centre, Suite #2
Lockport, NY 14094
Phone No.: 905-525-0323
Fax No.: 905-525-7943
www.coleclark-america.com
info@coleclark-america.com

Factory/Headquarters
3/7 Clare St.
Bayswater, Vic, 3153 Australia
www.coleclarkguitars.com
info@coleclarkguitars.com

COLLINGS GUITARS

Instruments currently built in Austin, TX beginning in 1986. Distributed by Collings Guitars, Inc. of Austin, TX.

Luthier Bill Collings was born in Michigan, and raised in Ohio. In 1973, Collings moved from Ohio to Houston, Texas, and originally did guitar repair work. Colling's first flattop guitars date from this period. In 1980, Collings relocated his workshop to Austin, Texas. In addition to his flattop guitars, he also began building archtop guitars. Collings Guitars was founded in 1986. Today, the company maintains tight quality control over their production, and consumer demand remains high. In 2005/2006 Collings moved to a new building within Austin, TX. In 2007, Collings released a new electric line of guitars (see *Blue Book of Electric Guitars*). Company information courtesy Collings Guitars, some model and serialization information courtesy George Gruhn and Walter Carter, *Gruhn's Guide to Vintage Guitars*.

CONTACT INFORMATION
COLLINGS GUITARS
11210 W. Hwy 290
Austin, TX 78737
Phone No.: 512-288-7776
Fax No.: 512-288-6045
www.collingsguitars.com
customerservice@collingsguitars.com

LABEL IDENTIFICATION/SERIALIZATION

Label Identification

1975-1979: Models do not have a label; instead, there is a signature in ink on the inside back strip.

1979-1984: Light brown oval label with brown ink marked *Bill Collings, Luthier* and illustrated with logs floating in a river.

1984-1989: Darker brown oval label with brown ink marked *Bill Collings, Luthier* and illustrated with logs and guitars floating in a river.

1989-Present: Light brown oval label with black ink marked *Collings, Austin, Texas*.

Flattop Serialization:

1975-1987: Guitars do not posses a serial number. Most are marked with a handwritten date on the underside of the top. Some guitars from 1987 may have a serial number.

1988-Present: Guitars began a consecutive numbering series that began with number 175. The serial number is stamped on the neck block. Serial numbers had reached 4700 by 1999, and 15500 by 2009.

Archtop Serialization:

Before 1991: Archtops before 1991 had their own separate serialization.

1991-Present: Archtops are numbered with a two-part serial number. The first number indicates the archtop as part of the general company serialization, and the second number indicates the ranking in the archtop series list.

GENERAL INFORMATION/OPTIONS

Collings guitars are offered with a number of options, such as abalone top border inlays, custom inlays, tuning machines, wood binding, and body wood, including Brazilian rosewood (please call for prices and availability). Each custom feature that is on a Collins needs to be assessed separately. Refer to the chart of pricing additions for options.

In 1989, Collings built about 20 guitars that were designed by George Gruhn. They were available as a dreadnought (D) or jumbo (F) body shape with either plain (Style 1) or fancy (Style 2) appointments. A Gruhn logo is on the headstock with a Collings label inside the guitar and are numbered 001-021. These guitars are worth approx. between $3,000 and $3,500.

In 2012, Collings began shipping all their guitars with hardshell cases included in the price.

All instruments available in left-handed configuration at no extra charge.

- Subtract $300 for no original hardshell case.
- Add $100 for herringbone body binding ($175 on cutaway model).
- Add $100 for Adirondack braces.
- Add $150 for nickel Waverly tuners on C10 and SJ models.
- Add $150 for cedar top (disc.).
- Add $175 for headstock binding.
- Add $175 for fingerboard binding.
- Add $200 for short scale on OM, C10, 000, SJ, and CJ models.
- Add $250 for deep body on OM and C10 models.
- Add $250 for abalone rosette.
- Add $250 for gold Waverly tuners on C10 and SJ models.
- Add $300 for a mahogany top.
- Add $300 for Engelmann spruce top.
- Add $300 for a European spruce top.
- Add $300 for wood headstock binding.
- Add $300 for wood fingerboard binding.
- Add $350 for a Western Shaded Top.
- Add $500 for German spruce top (disc.).
- Add $600 for a cutaway ($675 on Herringbone models).

MSR/NOTES	100%	EXCELLENT	AVERAGE	LAST MSR

- Add $600 for flamed koa top.
- Add $600 for sunburst top.
- Add $600 for wood body/rosette binding ($675 on cutaway model).
- Add $750 for flamed maple body and neck.
- Add $900 for an abalone top border (Style 41, $1,050 on cutaway model).

- Add $1,000 for a Red Spruce top.
- Add $1,500 for an abalone top border (Style 42, $1,650 on cutaway model).
- Add $1,500 for a sunburst body.
- Add $1,500 for flamed koa back and sides.
- Add $2,000 for Varnish finish.

ACOUSTIC: 0, 00, & 000 MODELS

01 14-FRET – 0 style, spruce top, mahogany back/sides/neck, round soundhole, tortoise binding, black/white wood strip rosette, 14/20-fret bound ebony fingerboard with pearl dot markers, rosewood veneer on bound open-style peghead with MOP logo inlay, three-per-side nickel Waverly tuners, ebony bridge with white black dot pins, tortoiseshell pickguard, available in Natural finish, total length 38 in., body length: 18 3/16 in., body width: 13 7/16 in., body thickness: 4.125 in., 24.875 in. scale, mfg. 2006-present.

MSR $3,800	$3,420	$2,225 - 2,650	$1,575 - 1,850

* 02H 14-Fret – similar to the 01, except has East Indian rosewood back and sides, grained ivoroid binding, herringbone purfling, crosscut grained ivoroid and wood strip rosette, and traditional diamond and square fingerboard inlays, mfg. 2006-present.

MSR $3,950	$3,550	$2,300 - 2,750	$1,625 - 1,925

* 03 14-Fret – similar to the 01, except has East Indian rosewood back and sides, crosscut grained ivoroid binding, select abalone black/white strip rosette, crosscut grained ivoroiddouble black/white strip purfling, mutli-colored chevron backstrip, black/ivoroid strip purfling on bound headstock and fingerboard, no fingerboard inlays, and gold tuners, mfg. 2006-present.

MSR $4,700	$4,230	$2,750 - 3,250	$1,950 - 2,300

00-1 12-FRET – grand concert style, spruce top, round soundhole, tortoiseshell pickguard, three-stripe bound body/rosette, mahogany back/sides/neck, 12/20-fret bound ebony fingerboard with pearl dot markers, ebony bridge with white black dot pins, rosewood veneer on bound open-style peghead with MOP logo inlay, three-per-side chrome Gotoh tuners, available in Natural finish, total length 38 in., body length: 19.375 in., body width: 14.25 in., body thickness: 4 in., 25.5 in. scale, mfg. 2004-present.

MSR $4,250	$3,825	$2,500 - 2,950	$1,775 - 2,075

* 00-2H 12-Fret – similar to the 00-1 except has East Indian rosewood back/sides, herringbone purfling, and diamond fingerboard inlays, mfg. 1994-present.

MSR $4,350	$3,915	$2,550 - 3,000	$1,800 - 2,125

* 00-3 12-Fret – similar to the 00-2H except has abalone purfling/rosette, no fingerboard, and gold hardware, mfg. 2004-present.

MSR $5,100	$4,600	$3,000 - 3,550	$2,125 - 2,500

000-1 12-FRET – orchestra style, spruce top, ivoroid binding, round soundhole, ivoroid/wood stripe rosette, tortoise style pickguard, mahogany back/sides, mahogany neck, 12/20-fret bound ebony fingerboard with pearl diamond/square inlay, ebony pyramid bridge with white black dot pins, rosewood veneer on bound slotted peghead with MOP logo inlay, three-per-side nickel Waverly slot-head tuners, available in Natural finish, total length: 39.5 in., body length: 20.25 in., body width: 15 in., body thickness: 4.125 in., 25.5 in. scale, mfg. 2004-present.

MSR $4,250	$3,825	$2,500 - 2,950	$1,775 - 2,075

* 000-2H 12-Fret – similar to the 000-1, except has East Indian rosewood back/sides, herringbone purfling, and diamond/square fingerboard inlay, mfg. 1994-present.

MSR $4,350	$3,915	$2,550 - 3,000	$1,800 - 2,125

* 000-3 12-Fret – similar to the 000-2H, except has abalone purfling/rosette, no fingerboard inlays, and gold hardware, mfg. 2004-present.

MSR $5,100	$4,600	$3,000 - 3,550	$2,125 - 2,500

ACOUSTIC: ARCHTOP SERIES

In addition to their well-known flattop acoustic models, the Collings handcrafted **Archtop** model is offered in a 16 in. wide body ($9,700), 17 in. wide body ($16,000) and an 18 in. wide body ($17,000). The 16 in. body was discontinued in 1996, and reintroduced in 2004. These only reflect the base starting price for the archtop. Contact Collings for a personal quote on archtop instruments.

ACOUSTIC: BABY SERIES

BABY 1 – 3/4 size dreadnought style, spruce top, ivoroid binding, round soundhole, ivoroid/wood stripe rosette, tortoiseshell-style pickguard, mahogany back/sides, mahogany neck, 14/20-fret bound ebony fingerboard with pearl diamond/square inlay, ebony bridge with white black dot pins, rosewood veneer on bound peghead with mother-of-pearl logo inlay, three-per-side nickel Waverly tuners, available in Natural finish, total length: 36.5 in., body length: 17.125 in., body width: 12.5 in., body thickness: 3 15/16 in., 24.125 in. scale, mfg. 1997-present.

MSR $3,800	$3,420	$2,225 - 2,650	$1,575 - 1,850

BABY 2H – similar to the Baby 1, except has East Indian rosewood back/sides and herringbone purfling, mfg. 2004-present.

MSR $3,950	$3,550	$2,300 - 2,750	$1,625 - 1,925

BABY 3 – similar to the Baby 2H, except has abalone purfling/rosette, no fingerboard inlays, and gold hardware, mfg. 2004-present.

MSR $4,700	$4,230	$2,750 - 3,250	$1,950 - 2,300

MSR/NOTES	100%	EXCELLENT	AVERAGE	LAST MSR

ACOUSTIC: C & CJ MODELS

C-10 – folk style, spruce top, round soundhole, tortoise style pickguard, ivoroid bound body/rosette, mahogany back/sides/neck, 14/20-fret bound ebony fingerboard, ebony bridge with white black dot pins, rosewood veneer on bound peghead with mother-of-pearl logo, three-per-side gold Kluson tuners, available in Natural finish, total length: 39.5 in., body length: 19.25 in., body width: 14.75 in., body thickness: 4.25 in., 25.5 in. scale, mfg. 1986-present.

MSR $3,850	$3,475	$2,225 - 2,675	$1,600 - 1,875	

In 1992, this model was also available in Blonde, Blue, Midnight Black, and Red finishes with a pearloid pickguard and pearloid headstock veneer. In 1995, nickel Schaller mini-tuners replaced original part/design.

* **C-10 Deluxe** – similar to C-10, except has East Indian rosewood back/sides, pearl dot fingerboard inlay, ebony peghead veneer with pearl logo inlay, gold Schaller mini tuners, available in Natural finish, mfg. 1986-present.

MSR $4,350	$3,915	$2,550 - 3,000	$1,800 - 2,125	

In 1995, nickel Schaller mini-tuners replaced original part/design.

C-100 – similar to C-10, except has larger body dimensions, body length 20.125 in., body width 16 in., body thickness 4.5 in., mfg. 1986-1994.

	N/A	$2,150 - 2,600	$1,500 - 1,750	$2,225

* **C-100 Deluxe** – similar to C-10 Deluxe, except has larger body dimensions, body length: 20.125 in., body width: 16 in., body thickness: 4.5 in., mfg. 1986-94.

	N/A	$2,350 - 2,850	$1,700 - 2,050	$2,725

CJ COLLINGS JUMBO – slope-shouldered dreadnought-style body, select Sitka spruce top, East Indian rosewood back and sides, round soundhole with black/white strip rosette, grained ivoroid binding with double black/white purfling, multi-color mosaic backstrip, mahogany neck, 14/20-fret ivoroid bound ebony fingerboard with pearl dot markers, ebony veneer on ivoroid bound peghead with mother-of-pearl logo, three-per-side nickel Waverly tuners, ebony bridge with white black dot pins, tortoise style pickguard, available in Natural finish, total length: 40.25 in., body length: 20.125 in., body width: 16 in., body thickness: 4.875 in., 25.5 in. scale, mfg. 1995-present.

MSR $4,400	$3,960	$2,575 - 3,050	$1,825 - 2,150	

* **CJ Mh Collings Jumbo Mahogany** – similar to the CJ Collings Jumbo, except has mahogany back and sides, tortoise-style binding and a simple walnut backstrip, mfg. 2009-present.

MSR $4,400	$3,960	$2,575 - 3,050	$1,825 - 2,150	

ACOUSTIC: D, CW, & SJ MODELS

The Collins Winfield (CW) is a reissue of the Collins Clarence White model.

D-1 – dreadnought style, spruce top, round soundhole, tortoise pickguard, three-stripe bound body/rosette, mahogany back/sides/neck, 14/20-fret bound ebony fingerboard, ebony bridge with white black dot pins, rosewood veneer on bound peghead with pearl logo inlay, three-per-side chrome Gotoh tuners, available in Natural finish, total length: 40.25 in., body length: 20 in., body width: 15.625 in., body thickness: 4.875 in., 25.5 in. scale, mfg. 1986-present.

MSR $3,800	$3,420	$2,225 - 2,650	$1,575 - 1,850	

In 1995, nickel Waverly tuners replaced original part/design.

* **DS-1 12-Fret** – similar to the D-1, except has a 12/20-fret fingerboard and open-style headstock, mfg. 2004-present.

MSR $4,250	$3,825	$2,500 - 2,950	$1,775 - 2,075	

D-2 – similar to D-1, except has Indian rosewood back/sides, pearl diamond/square peghead inlay, mfg. 1986-1995.

	N/A	$2,300 - 2,750	$1,500 - 1,850	$2,300

D-2H – dreadnought style, spruce top, ivoroid binding, herringbone purfling, round soundhole, ivoroid/wood stripe rosette, tortoiseshell-style pickguard, East Indian rosewood back/sides, mahogany neck, 14/20-fret bound ebony fingerboard with pearl diamond/square inlay, ebony bridge with white black dot pins, rosewood veneer on bound peghead with mother-of-pearl logo inlay, three-per-side nickel Waverly tuners, available in Natural finish, mfg. 1986-present.

MSR $3,950	$3,550	$2,300 - 2,750	$1,625 - 1,925	

* **DS-2H 12-Fret** – similar to the D-2H, except has a 12/20 fret fingerboard and open-style headstock, total length: 40.125 in., body length: 20.875 in., body width: 15.625 in., body thickness: 4.125 in., mfg. 1995-present.

MSR $4,350	$3,915	$2,550 - 3,000	$1,800 - 2,125	

D-3 – similar to the D-2H, except has grained ivoroid binding with double B/W purfling, an ivoroid-bound fingerboard with no inlays, an ivoroid-bound headstock, and gold Waverly tuners, mfg. 1990-present.

MSR $4,700	$4,230	$2,750 - 3,250	$1,950 - 2,300	

* **DS-3 12-Fret** – similar to the D-3, except has a 12/20-fret fingerboard and open-style headstock, mfg. 2004-present.

MSR $5,100	$4,600	$3,000 - 3,550	$2,125 - 2,500	

MSR/NOTES	100%	EXCELLENT	AVERAGE	LAST MSR

SJ SMALL JUMBO – small jumbo style, spruce top, round soundhole, tortoise pickguard, double black/ivoroid strip purfling, black/white wood and nitrate strip rosette, maple back/sides/neck, 25.5 in.scale, 14/20-fret bound ebony fingerboard with modern pearl diamond inlay, ebony bridge with white black dot pins, ebony veneer on bound peghead with pearl diamond and logo inlay, three-per-side gold Schaller mini tuners, available in Natural finish, total length: 40.25 in., body length: 20.125 in., body width: 16 in., body thickness: 4.5 in., mfg. 1986-present.

| MSR $5,250 | $4,725 | $3,100 - 3,650 | $2,200 - 2,575 | |

* SJ Indian Small Jumbo – similar to the SJ Small Jumbo, except has East Indian rosewood back and sides, a mahogany neck, and nickel Schaller mini tuners, mfg. 2009-present.

| MSR $4,600 | $4,150 | $2,700 - 3,200 | $1,900 - 2,250 | |

* SJ MH Small Jumbo Mahogany – similar to the SJ Small Jumbo, except has mahogany back and sides, tortoise-style binding and rosette, simple walnut back strip, a mahogany neck, and nickel Schaller mini tuners, mfg. 2009-present.

| MSR $4,600 | $4,150 | $2,700 - 3,200 | $1,900 - 2,250 | |

CW MAHOGANY – dreadnought style, red spruce top, enlarged round soundhole, dalmation style pickguard, three-stripe bound body/rosette, mahogany back/sides/neck, no tongue brace extended 14/21-fret ebony fingerboard, ebony bridge with white black dot pins, ebony veneer on bound peghead with pearl logo inlay, three-per-side chrome Gotoh tuners, available in Natural finish, total length: 40.25 in., body length: 20 in., body width: 15.625 in., body thickness: 4.875 in., 25.5 in. scale, mfg. 2004-present.

| MSR $5,425 | $4,900 | $3,200 - 3,800 | $2,275 - 2,675 | |

CW INDIAN – similar to the CW Indian, except has East Indian rosewood sides/back, herringbone purfling, and diamond/square inlays, mfg. 2004-present.

| MSR $5,550 | $5,000 | $3,275 - 3,900 | $2,325 - 2,725 | |

ACOUSTIC: OM MODELS

OM-1 – grand concert style, spruce top, round soundhole, tortoiseshell pickguard, three-stripe bound body/rosette, mahogany back/sides/neck, 14/20-fret bound ebony fingerboard with pearl dot markers, ebony bridge with white black dot pins, rosewood veneer on bound peghead with mother-of-pearl logo inlay, three-per-side chrome Gotoh tuners, available in Natural finish, total length: 39.5 in., body length: 19.25 in., body width: 15 in., body thickness: 4.125 in., 25.5 in. scale, mfg. 1986-present.

| MSR $3,800 | $3,420 | $2,225 - 2,650 | $1,575 - 1,850 | |

In 1995, nickel Waverly tuners replaced original part/design.

OM-2 – similar to OM-1, except has Indian rosewood back and sides, pearl diamond/square peghead inlay, mfg. 1986-1994.

| | N/A | $2,100 - 2,500 | $1,450 - 1,750 | $2,300 |

* OM-2H – grand concert style, spruce top, ivoroid binding, herringbone purfling, round soundhole, ivoroid/wood stripe rosette, tortoise style pickguard, East Indian rosewood back/sides, mahogany neck, 14/20-fret bound ebony fingerboard with pearl diamond/square inlay, ebony bridge with white black dot pins, rosewood veneer on bound peghead with mother-of-pearl logo inlay, three-per-side nickel Waverly tuners, available in Natural finish, mfg. 1986-present.

| MSR $3,950 | $3,550 | $2,300 - 2,750 | $1,625 - 1,925 | |

OM-3 – similar to OM-2H, except has abalone purfling/rosette, no fingerboard inlays, and gold Waverly tuners, mfg. 1986-present.

| MSR $4,700 | $4,230 | $2,750 - 3,250 | $1,950 - 2,300 | |

COLLOPY

Instruments previously built in San Francisco, CA.

Luthier Rich Collopy built and repaired guitars for over twenty-five years. In later years, Collopy opened a retail musical instrument shop in addition to his repairs and building. Collopy passed away in 2009.

COMINS GUITARS

Instruments currently built in Willow Grove, PA since 1991.

Bill Comins began playing guitar at an early age, and later went on to major in Jazz Guitar at Temple University. During this time, along with performing and teaching privately, Comins cultivated an interest in Luthery. Eventually he took a job in a violin shop where he worked for four years while building his own repair/custom shop business. In 1991, Comins met Master Luthier Bob Benedetto whose shared knowledge inspired Comins to develop his own line of archtop guitars. In the time since Comins has carved out a reputation as one of the more highly regarded contemporary archtop guitar builders. He has built over 200 instruments for international clientele consisting of players, educators, and collectors. His work has appeared in numerous books and collections, including the Chinery "Blue Guitar" project. Well versed in both traditional and contemporary approaches, Comins offers personalized collaborations with dedicated attention to design and detail. In 2011, Comins began building D'Angelico replica guitars for GTR. For electric models, refer to the *Blue Book of Electric Guitars*. For more information, contact Comins directly or visit his website.

CONTACT INFORMATION
COMINS GUITARS
PO Box 611
Willow Grove, PA 19090
Phone No.: 215-376-0595
www.cominsguitars.com
bill@cominsguitars.com

MSR/NOTES	100%	EXCELLENT	AVERAGE	LAST MSR

ACOUSTIC

ARBORETUM – nylon string configuration, single cutaway, Sitka spruce, Englemann spruce, or cedar top, rosewood back and sides, flat or carved back, round soundhole with classical style rosette, mahogany neck, ebony fingerboard, slotted headstock, three-per-side open-style tuners, B-Band Undersaddle Transducer pickup system, Natural finish, 15 in. lower bout width, current mfg.

MSR $7,000	$7,000	$4,000 - 5,000	N/A	

PARLOR – single smooth cutaway, Sitka spruce top, figured maple back and sides, three-piece maple neck, sculptured nonbound edges, ebony pickguard, mini tuning black machines with ebony buttons, otherwise similar to the Classic, available in violin-style finish, disc. 2005.

	N/A	$2,750 - 3,500	$1,850 - 2,250	$4,750

WOODLAND – single smooth jumbo style, 16 or 17 in. bout, cutaway or non-cutaway, oval soundhole, master grade Sitka spruce top, figured maple back and sides, fancy wood bindings and purfling around the top and peghead, maple neck with carbon fiber reinforcement, 22-fret bound ebony fingerboard,ebony adjustable bridge and violin-style floating tail piece, gold Schaller mini tuning machines with ebony buttons, floating suspended pickup with volume control, available in various finishes, current mfg.

MSR $7,000	$7,000	$4,000 - 5,000	N/A	

CONCERTONE

Instruments currently produced in Chicago, IL during the 1920s and 1930s. See chapter on House Brands.

This trademark has been identified as a House Brand of Montgomery Wards. Instruments were built by either Kay or Harmony, during the 1920s and 1930s. Source: Michael Wright, *Guitar Stories*, Volume One.

CONDE HERMANOS

Instruments currently produced in Madrid, Spain. Distributed in the U.S. by Guitar Salon International in Santa Monica, CA. Previously distributed by Luthier Music Corporation in New York City, NY and Tornavoz Music Company in Santa Monica, CA.

Conde Hermanos was founded by Domingo Esteso in 1915. Domingo trained his nephews in to the business, where they eventually took over. The business is now operated by Felipe Conde since 2010, which still maintains it as a family business. He offers a wide range of classical, concert-grade classical, flamenco, and concert-grade flamenco acoustic guitars built in Madrid, Spain. These models are constructed with the medium level to professional classical guitarist in mind. Hermanos lists their prices in euros. Since the dollar to euro ratio fluxes, the prices are going to be different in the U.S. Because of this, it is difficult to establish values on these guitars. For more information, visit Conde Hermanos' website or contact them directly.

CONTACT INFORMATION
CONDE HERMANOS
Factory
Calle Felipe V, 2 Corner Arrieta,3
Madrid, 28013 Spain
www.condehermanos.com
fconde.guitarras@felipeconde.es,
condehermanos@condehermanos.com

*U.S. Distributor: Guitar Salon
International*
1455 19th Street
Santa Monica, CA 90404
Phone No.: 310-586-1100
Fax No.: 310-586-1142
www.guitarsalon.com
info@guitarsalon.com

ACOUSTIC: AC/EC CLASSICAL SERIES

AC Series Concert Classical guitars feature German spruce or Canadian red cedar tops, Indian rosewood back and sides, cedar neck, and an ebony fingerboard. Models include the **Model AC 22** (last U.S. MSR was $6,500), **Model AC 23**,the **Model AC 23 R** (last U.S. MSR was $9,000) has Brazilian rosewood (Jacaranda) back and sides. The eight-string **Model AC 23 R.8** also features Brazilian rosewood (Jacaranda) back and sides and is available in a ten-string configuration. The top of the line is the **Felipe V**. A model that is a recreation of the original templates used by **Domingo Esteso** and is named after it.

The **EC** Studio classical guitars, like the Concert classicals, have German Spruce or Canadian red cedar tops, Indian rosewood back and sides, cedar neck, and an ebony fingerboard. Models include the **Model EC 1** (last U.S. MSR was $2,800), **Model EC 2** (last U.S. MSR was $3,300), and **Model EC 3** (last U.S. MSR was $3,700).

ACOUSTIC: AF/EF FLAMENCO SERIES

Conde Hermano's **AF Series** Concert Flamenco guitars have German spruce tops, Indian rosewood back and sides, cedar neck, and an ebony fingerboard. These flamenco models are equipped with a transparent tapping plate ("Golpeador transparente") and choice of machine head or wooden peg tuners. Models include the **Model AF 24**, **Model AF 25** (last U.S. MSR was $8,500),and the **Model AF 25 R** (last U.S. MSR was $8,800), which has Brazilian rosewood (Jacaranda) back and sides. The top of the line is the **Felipe V Flamenco**. Other models include the **Model A 26** (last U.S. MSR was $8,500),**Model A 27** (last U.S. MSR was $3,850), and **Model A 28** (last U.S. MSR was $6,500).

The **EF** Studio Flamenco guitars feature Spanish cypress back and sides, German spruce or Canadian red cedar tops, cedar neck, and an ebony fingerboard. Flamenco models are equipped with a transparent tapping plate and choice of machine head or wooden peg tuners. Models include the **Model EF 4** (last U.S. MSR was $4,200), **Model EF 5** (last U.S. MSR was $5,300), and the **Model EF 5 N** (last U.S. MSR was $5,300), which features Indian rosewood back and sides.

CONN

Instruments previously built in Japan between circa 1968 and 1978.

The U.S. distributor for Conn brand name instruments was Conn/Continental Music Company of Chicago, IL. The Conn trademark is perhaps more recognizable on their brass band instruments. Conn offered both classical models and six-string and

MSR/NOTES	100%	EXCELLENT	AVERAGE	LAST MSR

twelve-string acoustic steel-string models, built by Aria and Company in Japan. Many models of student level to intermediate quality, and some feature a bolt-on neck instead of the usual standard. Source: Michael Wright, *Guitar Stories*, Volume One.

ACOUSTIC

CLASSICAL MODELS – includes C-7, C-9, C-11, C-19, C-21, C-23, C-31, and C-33 models, various wood types and other features, mfg. 1970s.

C-7/C-9/C-11/C-19	N/A	$100 - 150	$50 - 75	
C-21/C-23/C-31/C-33	N/A	$150 - 200	$95 - 120	

DREADNOUGHT MODELS – includes F-5, F-12, F-15, F-15M, F-21, F-27, F-27CH, F-28, F-29, F-31, and F-35 models, various wood types and other features, mfg. 1970s.

F-5/F-12/F-15/F-15M/F-21	N/A	$100 - 150	$50 - 75	
F-27/F-28/F-29/F-31/F-35	N/A	$150 - 200	$95 - 120	

GRAND CONCERT MODELS – includes F-9, F-11, and F-18 models, various wood types and other features, mfg. 1970s.

F-9/F-11	N/A	$100 - 150	$50 - 75	
F-18	N/A	$150 - 200	$95 - 120	

12-STRING MODELS – includes F-1212, F-1512, F-2112, and F-2712 models, 12-string configuration, various wood types and other features, mfg. 1970s.

F-1212/F-1512	N/A	$125 - 175	$75 - 100	
F-2112/F-2712	N/A	$175 - 225	$100 - 130	

CONQUEROR

Instruments previously produced in Japan circa 1970s.

The Conqueror label is found on classical-style acoustic guitars. Source: Walter Murray, Frankenstein Fretworks.

Conqueror models have a spruce top, round soundhole, geometric rosette (black, red, green, yellow pattern), nato back and sides, one-piece nato neck ("steel reinforced"), 12/19-fret laminated fingerboard (perhaps bubinga), nato bridge. The slotted headstock has three-per-side ivory-colored plastic tuners. The soundboard is stained redwood color, the back/sides/neck stained mahogany. They have a distinctive coat of arms and armor plastic ornament on the headstock, with the word "Conqueror" in Old English typeface. A similar crest can be found on the interior paper label inside the body, and a "Made in Japan" label on the back of the headstock. Conqueror acoustics in average condition are valued between $50 and $100.

CONRAD

Instruments previously produced in Japan between circa 1968 and 1977.

The Conrad trademark was a brand name used by U.S. importers David Wexler and Company of Chicago, IL. The Conrad product line consisted of six-string and twelve-string acoustic guitars, thinline hollowbody electrics, solid body electric guitars and basses, mandolins, and banjos. Conrad instruments were produced by Kasuga International (Kasuga and Tokai USA, Inc.), and featured good quality designs specifically based on popular American designs. Used prices on most models are usually between $150 and $250. Source: Michael Wright, *Guitar Stories*, Volume One.

CONTESSA

Instruments previously built in Italy between 1966 and the early 1970s. Distributed in the U.S. by M. Hohner, Inc. of Hicksville, NY.

The Contessa trademark covered a wide range of medium quality guitars and solid state amplifiers. The HG series (that possibly stands for Hohner Guitars) featured acoustic "Folk, Classical, and Country & Western" and original design solid body electrics. Source: Tony Bacon and Paul Day, *The Guru's Guitar Guide*.

ACOUSTIC

HG 01 – dreadnought style, spruce top, round soundhole, mahogany back/sides, 18-fret rosewood fingerboard with white dot inlay, rosewood bridge with white pins, black pickguard, three-per-side Contessa tuners with plastic buttons, available in Natural finish, length 38.5 in., body width 14.5 in., mfg. circa early 1970s.

	N/A	$150 - 200	$95 - 120	$79.95

HG 06 J – dreadnought style, spruce top, round soundhole, mahogany back/sides, 20-fret rosewood fingerboard with white dot inlay, rosewood bridge with white black-dot pins, black pickguard (half covers soundhole rosette), three-per-side Contessa tuners, available in Natural finish, Length 40.25 in., Body Width 14.5 in., mfg. circa early 1970s.

	N/A	$175 - 225	$110 - 140	$99.95

HG 12 J – dreadnought style, spruce top, round soundhole, mahogany back/sides, 21-fret rosewood fingerboard, rosewood bridge, black pickguard, three-per-side Contessa tuners, available in Natural finish, length 42.5 in., body width 14.25 in., mfg. circa early 1970s.

	N/A	$200 - 250	$120 - 150	$139.95

MSR/NOTES	100%	EXCELLENT	AVERAGE	LAST MSR

CONTINENTAL

Instruments previously produced in Japan. See also Conn.

As well as distributing the Conn guitars, the Continental Music Company of Chicago, IL also distributed their own brand name guitars under the Continental logo in the U.S. Source: Michael Wright, *Guitar Stories*, Volume One.

Continental was also used on a brand of National-style resonators in the mid-1990s.

COOG INSTRUMENTS

Instruments previously built in Santa Cruz, CA until the mid-2000s.

Ronald Cook was the luthier and craftsman of Coog Instruments. Cook designed and built early American and early European stringed folk instruments based on historic originals, such as guitars, mountain banjos, and dulcimers. He also crafted several types of medieval instruments, including hurdy-gurdies, harps, and rebecs. Cook was well-known for his intricately carved heads and features, as well as his use of recycled, salvaged, and sustainably harvested woods. Cook also repaired stringed instruments including common styles such as the guitar and dulcimer to the unusual style like zithers and marxophones. Cook stopped producing guitars in the mid-2000s and sold remaining stock through the early 2010s. Cook now runs Ron Cook Studios where he builds finely crafted furniture and other instruments.

COPLEY INSTRUMENTS

Instruments currently produced overseas. Distributed by Simba Products in Nashville, TN.

Copley is a trademark offered by Simba Products. Simba offers various musical instruments including band instruments, guitars, violins, and other related accessories. The Copley Acoustic line features dreadnoughts, classicals, cutaways, resonators, and acoustic basses. Copley also offers electric guitars, electric basses, and mandolins. For more information, visit Copley's website or contact them directly.

CONTACT INFORMATION
COPLEY INSTRUMENTS
Distributor: Simba Products
637 Bluewater Drive
Nashville, TN 37217
Phone No.: 800-811-0109
www.simbaproducts.com
sales@simbaproducts.com

CORDOBA

Instruments currently produced in Spain since 1997 and in China (Iberia and Fusion Series) since 2009. Distributed by Cordoba Music Group (previously Tornavoz Music) in Santa Monica, CA.

Founded in 1997, Cordoba seeks to guide the evolution of the nylon string guitar, blending traditional craftsmanship of the early master luthiers with modern developments. Inspired by the organic beauty and honesty of acoustic instruments, every Cordoba is lightweight, responsive, and a direct descendant of the Spanish tradition. Cordoba continues to challenge the definition of the acoustic guitar without sacrificing the authenticity of its heritage. For more information, visit Cordoba's website or contact the Cordoba Music Group.

CONTACT INFORMATION
CORDOBA
U.S. Distributor: Cordoba Music Group
1455 19th Street
Santa Monica, CA 90404
Phone No.: 310-586-1180
Fax No.: 310-586-1181
www.cordobamusicgroup.com

Factory/Headquarters
Spain
www.cordobaguitars.com
info@cordobaguitars.com

ACOUSTIC: ESPAÑA SERIES

30R – classical style, solid cedar top, round soundhole, laminated mahogany back/sides, mahogany neck, 650 mm scale, 12/19-fret rosewood fingerboard, rosewood tied bridge, slotted headstock, three-per-side nickel plated tuners, available in Natural finish, disc. 2005.

	N/A	$300 - 350	$150 - 200	$725

30F/32EF – flamenco style, spruce top, cypress back and sides, cedar neck, 12/20-fret rosewood fingerboard, open-style gold-plated tuners, 650 mm scale, mfg. 2005-09.

	N/A	$350 - 425	$200 - 250	$800

The 32EF replaced the 30F and they are essentially the same guitar with a few minor cosmetic changes. Early models may have laminated sycamore back and sides.

32E – classical style, spruce top, sapele back and sides, cedar neck, 12/20-fret rosewood fingerboard, open-style gold-plated tuners, 650 mm scale, mfg. 2005-09.

	N/A	$350 - 425	$200 - 250	$800

40R – similar to the 30 R, except features laminated rosewood back/sides, maple purfling, gold plated tuners, available in Natural finish, disc. 2005.

	N/A	$375 - 450	$250 - 300	$925

45F/45FP – flamenco style, spruce top, sycamore back and sides, cedar neck, 12/20-fret ebony fingerboard, open-style deluxe gold-plated (45F) or ebony friction-peg (45FP) tuners, 650 mm scale, mfg. 2005-present.

MSR $1,235	$900	$550 - 625	$325 - 400	

MSR/NOTES	100%	EXCELLENT	AVERAGE	LAST MSR

* 45FCE Cutaway Electric – similar to the 45F/FP, except has a single cutaway and Fishman Classic 4 electronics, mfg. 2005-2010.

	$1,000	$650 - 750	$400 - 475	$1,348

45R – classical style, Canadian spruce top, sapele lined Indian rosewood back and sides, cedar neck, 12/20-fret ebony fingerboard, open-style deluxe gold-plated tuners, 650 mm scale, mfg. 2005-present.

MSR $1,235	$900	$550 - 625	$325 - 400	

* 45MR – similar to the 45R, except has Madagascar rosewood back and sides, available in Natural high gloss finish, mfg. 2009-present.

MSR $1,370	$1,000	$600 - 725	$375 - 450	

50R – similar to the 30 R, except features laminated rosewood back/sides, ebony-reinforced Honduran cedar neck, ebony fingerboard, gold plated tuners, available in Natural finish, disc. 2005.

	N/A	$475 - 550	$300 - 350	$1,175

* 50EC Cutaway Electric – similar to the 50 R, except features a single rounded cutaway body, slightly narrower fingerboard, Fishman transducer, available in Natural finish, disc. 2005.

	N/A	$825 - 950	$475 - 550	$2,075

55FCE CUTAWAY ELECTRIC – flamenco-style single cutaway, European spruce top, flame maple back and sides, cedar neck, 12/20-fret ebony fingerboard, open-style deluxe gold-plated tuners, Fishman Prefix Pro Blend electronics, mfg. 2005-present.

MSR $1,760	$1,300	$800 - 950	$525 - 600	

55R – classical style, European spruce top, Indian rosewood back and sides, cedar neck with ebony reinforcement, 12/20-fret ebony fingerboard, open-style deluxe gold-plated tuners, 650 mm scale, mfg. 2005-09.

	N/A	$650 - 750	$425 - 500	$1,469

* 55RCE Cutaway Electric – similar to the 55R, except has a single cutaway and electronics, mfg. 2005-2010.

	$1,300	$800 - 950	$500 - 600	$1,708

60R – similar to the 50 R, except features rosewood back/sides, maple purfling, available in Natural finish, disc.

	N/A	$425 - 500	$225 - 275	$1,239

70F – similar to the 70 R, except features solid cypress back/sides, translucent tap plate, available in Natural finish, disc.

	N/A	$475 - 550	$275 - 325	$1,459

70R – similar to the 60 R, except features German spruce top, ebony-reinforced Spanish cedar neck, detailed headstock/purfling/rosette, available in Natural finish, disc.

	N/A	$425 - 500	$250 - 300	$1,239

75F – similar to the 75 R, except in Flamenco style, disc. 2005.

	N/A	$525 - 600	$300 - 350	

75R – similar to the 70 R, except features a Honduran Cedar neck, cypress back/sides, available in Natural finish, disc. 2005.

	N/A	$475 - 550	$275 - 325	

90 – similar to the 70 R, except features quartersawn German spruce (or cedar) top, solid Indian rosewood back/sides, available in Natural high gloss lacquer finish, disc. 2005.

	N/A	$950 - 1,100	$525 - 600	$2,349

110 – similar to the 70 R, except features quartersawn German spruce (or cedar) top, solid Indian rosewood back/sides, detailed headstock/purfling/rosette, available in Natural high gloss lacquer finish, disc. 2005.

	N/A	$1,250 - 1,400	$675 - 800	$3,076

FCWE REISSUE – single smooth cutaway classical-style body, solid European spruce top, solid cypress back and sides, round soundhole with wood inlaid rosette, Indian rosewood binding, thinline flamenco-style bracing, cedar neck, 12/19-fret ebony fingerboard, slotted headstock, three-per-side open-style gold deluxe tuners with ebony buttons, Indian rosewood bridge, Fishman Prefix Problend electronics, available in Natural high gloss top with Honey Amber tinted back and sides finish, 25.6 in. scale, case included, mfg. 2009-present.

MSR $2,685	$2,000	$1,200 - 1,450	$800 - 950	

SOLISTA – classical style, Canadian cedar or European spruce top, solid Indian rosewood back and sides, cedar neck with ebony reinforcement, 12/20-fret ebony fingerboard, open-style deluxe black anodized tuners, 650 mm scale, mfg. 2005-present.

MSR $2,080	$1,550	$950 - 1,100	$625 - 725	

* Solista CE – similar to the Solista, except has a single smooth cutaway and BBand A2.2 electronics, mfg. 2009-present.

MSR $2,465	$1,850	$1,050 - 1,350	$700 - 825	

»Solista CE-M – similar to the Solista CE, except has solid flamed maple back and sides, current mfg.

MSR $2,465	$1,850	$1,050 - 1,350	$700 - 825	

MSR/NOTES	100%	EXCELLENT	AVERAGE	LAST MSR

SOLISTA F – flamenco style, European spruce top, solid cypress back and sides, cedar neck with ebony reinforcement, 12/20-fret ebony fingerboard, open-style deluxe black anodized tuners, 650 mm scale, mfg. 2005-present.

| MSR $2,080 | $1,550 | $950 - 1,100 | $625 - 725 | |

ACOUSTIC: FUSION SERIES

FUSION 12 JET/14 JET – single smooth cutaway thinbody classical-style body, solid Canadian cedar top, mahogany back and sides, cutaway electric fan bracing pattern, round soundhole with MOP rosette, ivoroid ABS binding, mahogany neck with truss rod, 12/19-fret (12 Jet) or 14/21-fret (14 Jet) rosewood fingerboard with MOP dot side inlays, slotted headstock, three-per-side open-style silver tuning machines with ebony buttons, rosewood bridge, Fishman Presys electronics, available in Jet Black finish, 25.5 in. scale, gig bag included, mfg. 2007-present.

| MSR $675 | $550 | $300 - 375 | $175 - 225 | |

FUSION 12 MAPLE/14 MAPLE – single smooth cutaway thinbody classical-style body, solid European spruce top, flamed maple back and sides, cutaway electric fan bracing pattern, round soundhole with Fusion multi-ring rosette, Indian rosewood binding, double maple/ebony top purfling, mahogany neck with truss rod, 12/19-fret (12 Maple) or 14/21-fret (14 Maple) ebony fingerboard, slotted headstock, three-per-side open-style silver tuning machines with ebony buttons, rosewood bridge, BBand A6T Blended electronics (disc. 2010) or Fishman Presys Blend electronics (2011-present), available in Natural finish, 25.5 in. scale, case included, mfg. 2009-present.

| MSR $955 | $760 | $450 - 525 | $250 - 300 | |

FUSION 12 NATURAL/14 NATURAL – single smooth cutaway thinbody classical-style body, solid Canadian cedar top, mahogany back and sides, cutaway electric fan bracing pattern, round soundhole with Fusion multi-ring rosette, ivoroid ABS binding, mahogany neck with truss rod, 12/19-fret (12 Natural) or 14/21-fret (14 Natural) rosewood fingerboard with MOP dot side inlays, slotted headstock, three-per-side open-style silver tuning machines with ebony buttons, rosewood bridge, Fishman Presys electronics, available in Natural finish, 25.5 in. scale, gig bag included, mfg. 2011-present.

| MSR $630 | $500 | $300 - 350 | $175 - 225 | |

FUSION 12 OV/14OV – single smooth cutaway thinbody classical-style body, solid ovangkol top, ovangkol back and sides, cutaway electric fan bracing pattern, round soundhole with MOP rosette, ivoroid ABS binding, mahogany neck with truss rod, 12/19-fret (12 OV) or 14/21-fret (14 OV) ebony fingerboard with MOP dot side inlays, slotted headstock, three-per-side open-style silver tuning machines with ebony buttons, rosewood bridge, BBand A6T Blended electronics, available in Natural finish, 25.5 in. scale, gig bag included, disc. 2010.

| | $800 | $450 - 525 | $250 - 300 | $1,000 |

FUSION 12 ROSE/14 ROSE – single smooth cutaway thinbody classical-style body, solid Indian rosewood top, Indian rosewood back and sides, cutaway electric fan bracing pattern, round soundhole with Fusion multi-ring rosette, Indian rosewood binding, mahogany neck with truss rod, 12/19-fret (12 Rose) or 14/21-fret (14 Rose) ebony fingerboard with MOP dot side inlays, slotted headstock, three-per-side open-style silver tuning machines with ebony buttons, rosewood bridge, Fishman Presys electronics, available in Natural finish, 25.5 in. scale, case included, mfg. 2007-present.

| MSR $925 | $750 | $450 - 525 | $250 - 300 | |

FUSION 12 RS/14RS – single smooth cutaway thinbody classical-style body, solid European spruce top, Indian rosewood back and sides, cutaway electric fan bracing pattern, round soundhole with MOP rosette, ivoroid ABS binding, mahogany neck with truss rod, 12/19-fret (12 RS) or 14/21-fret (14 RS) ebony fingerboard with MOP dot side inlays, slotted headstock, three-per-side open-style silver tuning machines with ebony buttons, rosewood bridge, BBand A6T Blended electronics, available in Natural finish, 25.5 in. scale, gig bag included, mfg. 2007-2010.

| | $800 | $450 - 525 | $250 - 300 | $1,000 |

FUSION ORCHESTRA – orchestra-style classical body, solid Canadian cedar or solid European spruce top, Indian rosewood back and sides, Spanish classic fan bracing pattern, round soundhole with wood inlaid rosette, mahogany binding, mahogany neck with truss rod, 12/19-fret rosewood fingerboard, slotted headstock, three-per-side open-style silver tuning machines with ebony buttons, rosewood bridge, available in Natural finish, 25.5 in. scale, gig bag included, current mfg.

| MSR $755 | $600 | $325 - 400 | $200 - 250 | |

Fusion Orchestra CE – similar to the Fusion Orchestra, except has a single smooth cutaway and Fishman Presys Blend electronics, available in Natural finish, gig bag included, current mfg.

| MSR $905 | $730 | $425 - 500 | $225 - 275 | |

FUSION ORCHESTRA PRO – orchestra-style classical body, solid Canadian cedar or solid European spruce top, solid Indian rosewood back and sides, Spanish classic fan bracing pattern, round soundhole with wood inlaid rosette, mahogany binding, double maple/ebony top purfling, mahogany neck with truss rod, 12/19-fret rosewood fingerboard, slotted headstock, three-per-side open-style silver tuning machines with ebony buttons, rosewood bridge, BBand A2.2 electronics, available in Natural finish, 25.5 in. scale, case included, mfg. 2010-present.

| MSR $1,500 | $1,200 | $750 - 900 | $475 - 550 | |

ACOUSTIC: IBERIA SERIES

CADETTE – classical style, solid cedar top, mahogany back and sides, cedar neck, 12/20-fret fingerboard, open-style nickel-plated tuners, 580 mm scale, mfg. 2005-present.

| MSR $340 | $260 | $150 - 190 | $95 - 120 | |

MSR/NOTES	100%	EXCELLENT	AVERAGE	LAST MSR

C3(M) – classical style, solid cedar top, mahogany back and sides, round soundhole with standard rosette, black body binding, nato neck, 12/19-fret rosewood fingerboard slotted headstock, three-per-side open-style nickel banjo tuners with pearl buttons, rosewood tied bridge, available in satin/matte Natural finish, 25.6 in. scale, mfg. 2009-present.

MSR $265	$200	$110 - 140	$65 - 85	

* *C3(M) Cadete* – similar to the C3(M), except in a 3/4-sized Cadete-style body, available in satin/matte Natural finish, 23.25 in. scale, mfg. 2011-present.

MSR $250	$190	$105 - 135	$60 - 80	

C-5 – classical style, solid cedar top, mahogany back and sides, cedar neck, 12/20-fret fingerboard, open-style nickel-plated tuners, 650 mm scale, mfg. 2005-present.

MSR $380	$300	$160 - 210	$105 - 130	

* *C-5CE Cutaway Electric* – similar to the C-5, except has a single cutaway and electronics, available in Black or Natural high gloss finish, mfg. 2005-present.

MSR $515	$400	$250 - 300	$120 - 150	

• **Add 5% for Black finish.**

»*C-5CE(T) Cutaway Electric Thinbody* – similar to the C-5CE Cutaway Electric, except has a thinner body depth, available in Black or Natural high gloss finish, current mfg.

MSR $515	$400	$250 - 300	$120 - 150	

• **Add 5% for Black finish.**

C7 – classical style, solid Canadian cedar or solid European spruce top, Indian rosewood back and sides, round soundhole with wood inlaid rosette, Spanish classic fan bracing, Indian rosewood binding, maple/ebony top purfling, maple back and sides purfling, mahogany neck, 12/19-fret rosewood fingerboard, slotted headstock, three-per-side open-style gold tuners with pearl buttons, rosewood tied bridge, available in high gloss Natural finish, 25.6 in. scale, gig bag included, mfg. 2009-present.

MSR $650	$500	$275 - 325	$150 - 200	

* *C7-CE* – similar to the C7, except has a single cutaway and Fishman Presys Blend electronics, mfg. 2009-present.

MSR $780	$600	$325 - 400	$175 - 225	

C9 – classical style, solid Canadian cedar or solid European spruce top, solid mahogany back and sides, round soundhole with MOP and ebony Esteso weave rosette, Spanish classic fan bracing, Indian rosewood binding, American mahogany neck, 12/19-fret cherry stained mahogany fingerboard with MOP inlays on side of board, slotted headstock, three-per-side open-style gold banjo tuners, Indian rosewood tied bridge, available in high gloss Natural finish, 25.6 in. scale, case included, current mfg.

MSR $885	$700	$450 - 525	$250 - 300	

C10 – classical style, solid Canadian cedar or solid European spruce top, solid Indian rosewood back and sides, round soundhole with MOP and ebony Esteso weave rosette, Spanish classic fan bracing, Indian rosewood binding, maple/ebony top, back, and sides purfling, American mahogany neck, 12/19-fret ebony fingerboard with MOP inlays on side of board, slotted headstock, three-per-side open-style gold floral tuners with ebony buttons, Indian rosewood tied bridge, available in high gloss Natural finish, 25.6 in. scale, case included, mfg. 2009-present.

MSR $1,315	$1,000	$575 - 650	$350 - 425	

CP110 CLASSIC PACK – classical package that includes a classical style guitar with a cedar top, mahogany back and sides, round soundhole with standard rosette, black body binding, nato neck, 12/19-fret rosewood fingerboard slotted headstock, three-per-side open-style nickel banjo tuners with pearl buttons, rosewood tied bridge, available in satin/matte Natural finish, 25.6 in. scale, gig bag, electronic tuner, string winder, and strings included, current mfg.

MSR $265	$200	$110 - 140	$65 - 85	

DOLCE – 7/8-sized classical-style body, solid Canadian cedar top, mahogany back and sides, round soundhole with wood inlaid rosette, Indian rosewood body binding, maple and ebony top purfling, maple back and sides purfling, mahogany neck, 12/19-fret rosewood fingerboard, slotted headstock, three-per-side open-style gold tuners with pearl buttons, rosewood tied bridge, available in high gloss Natural finish, 24.8 in. scale, gig bag included, current mfg.

MSR $350	$280	$150 - 190	$95 - 120	

F7 – flamenco style, solid European spruce top, cypress back and sides, round soundhole with wood inlaid mosaic rosette, Spanish flamenco bracing, Indian rosewood binding, maple/ebony top purfling, mahogany neck, 12/19-fret rosewood fingerboard, slotted headstock, three-per-side open-style gold and black tuners with ebonized buttons, rosewood tied bridge, available in high gloss Natural finish, 25.6 in. scale, gig bag included, mfg. 2009-present.

MSR $650	$500	$275 - 325	$150 - 200	

F10 – flamenco style, solid European spruce top, solid Indian rosewood back and sides, round soundhole with MOP and ebony Esteso weave rosette, lightweight Spanish flamenco bracing, Indian rosewood binding, maple/ebony top purfling, American mahogany neck, 12/19-fret ebony fingerboard with MOP inlays on side of board, slotted headstock, three-per-side open-style gold and black tuners with ebonized buttons, Indian rosewood tied bridge, available in high gloss Natural top wih Honey Amber tinted back and sides finish, 25.6 in. scale, case included, mfg. 2011-present.

MSR $1,315	$1,000	$575 - 650	$350 - 425	

MSR/NOTES	100%	EXCELLENT	AVERAGE	LAST MSR

GK STUDIO – single smooth cutaway classical style, solid European spruce top, cypress back and sides, round soundhole with wood inlaid mosaic rosette, Spanish flamenco fan bracing, Indian rosewood binding, maple/ebony top purfling, mahogany neck, 12/19-fret rosewood fingerboard with MOP dots on side of fingerboard, slotted headstock, three-per-side open-style gold and black tuners with ebonized buttons, rosewood tied bridge, Fishman Presys Blend electronics, available in high gloss Natural finish, 25.6 in. scale, gig bag included, mfg. 2009-present.

| MSR $780 | $600 | $325 - 400 | $175 - 225 | |

* *GK Studio Negra* – similar to the GK Studio, except has Indian rosewood back and sides, available in high gloss Natural finish, gig bag included, mfg. 2011-present.

| MSR $825 | $650 | $350 - 425 | $200 - 250 | |

REQUINTO – 1/2-sized classical style, cedar top, mahogany back and sides, cedar neck, 12/20-fret fingerboard, open-style nickel-plated tuners, mfg. 2007-present.

| MSR $325 | $250 | $140 - 190 | $85 - 110 | |

ACOUSTIC: CUSTOM ARTIST SERIES

CUSTOM ARTIST INDIAN CEDAR – classical style, Canadian cedar top, Indian rosewood back and sides, Spanish cedar neck, round soundhole with rosette, ebony fingerboard, Madagascar rosewood headstock veneer with three-per-side open-style gold tuners, Madagascar rosewood bridge, available in Natural lacquer finish, 650mm scale, mfg. 2007-09.

| | N/A | $1,300 - 1,550 | $900 - 1,050 | $3,000 |

CUSTOM ARTIST MAPLE SPRUCE – classical style, European spruce top, flamed figured maple back and sides, Spanish cedar neck, round soundhole with rosette, ebony fingerboard, Madagascar rosewood headstock veneer with three-per-side open-style gold tuners, Madagascar rosewood bridge, available in Natural lacquer finish, 650mm scale, mfg. 2007-09.

| | N/A | $1,300 - 1,550 | $900 - 1,050 | $3,000 |

CUSTOM ARTIST MADAGASCAR – classical style, Canadian cedar or European spruce top, Madagascar rosewood maple back and sides, Spanish cedar neck, round soundhole with rosette, ebony fingerboard, Madagascar rosewood headstock veneer with three-per-side open-style gold tuners, Madagascar rosewood bridge, available in Natural lacquer finish, 650mm scale, mfg. 2007-09.

| | N/A | $1,650 - 2,000 | $1,100 - 1,350 | $3,975 |

CORONADO

Unknown production date and location. See chapter on House Brands.

The Coronado trademark was used as a House Brand for the store Gambles that had locations in Nebraska, Illinois, and possibly other Midwest states. One known example was an acoustic archtop probably made by Kay as it had the circular medallion that Kay is famous for. Any further information on the Coronado brand can be submitted directly to Blue Book Publications. Information courtesy: Walter Murray, Frankenstein Fretworks.

CORT

Instruments currently produced in Inchon and Taejon, Korea, Surabuya, Indonesia, and China. Distributed in the U.S. by Cort Musical Instrument Company, Ltd. in Northbrook, IL.

CONTACT INFORMATION
CORT
3451 W. Commercial Ave.
Northbrook, IL 60062
Phone No.: 847-498-6491
Fax No.: 847-498-5370
www.cortguitar.com
cortsales@cort.com

Cort was originally a guitar factory in Japan and Jack Westheimer began distributing guitars from them into U.S. during the early 1960s. Some of the trademark/brand names that Westheimer distributed included Cortez, Kingston, Pearl, Teisco, and Silvertone. In 1973, Westheimer along with Yung H. Park founded the Yoo-Ah company in South Korea. Yoo-Ah eventually changed names to Cor-Tez and Park bought the company from Westheimer.

Cort is one of the few brand names that owns its manufacturing facility overseas. They also build guitars for several other trademarks other than Cort including Epiphone, Ibanez, G&L, Parkwood, and Schecter. Cort continues to build guitars in their Korean factory where several other manufacturers have shifted production to China and other Asian companies.

Most early Cort models were copies of popular American models, mainly modeled after the Stratocaster. In recent years, Cort has shifted its product line to include only all-original models. Cort has also endorsed several guitartists with their own model including Larry Coryell, Matt "Guitar" Murphy, Hiram Bullock, Neil Zaza, and Claudio Pagelli. Luthiers Jim Triggs and Gary Curbow have also designed a line of semi-hollowbody guitars and electric basses respectively for the Cort line.

Currently, Cort offers a full line of acoustic, electric, and electric bass guitars. For more information, visit Cort's website or contact them directly.

GENERAL INFORMATION

The Cort instruments listed below are listed alphabetically by series. Cort's left-handed models are generally a special order, and produced in limited quantities. There is an additional $30 charge for left-handed configuration models in the current production line-up.

Cort briefly offered specialty versions of their acoustic models: SJ-DLX (retail list $1,295), the SF-Classic (retail list $995), and the NAT-28 DLX (retail list $795) between 1996 and 1998.

MSR/NOTES	100%	EXCELLENT	AVERAGE	LAST MSR

ACOUSTIC: CJ/SJ SERIES

CJ1F – single smooth cutaway full-sized jumbo body, solid spruce top, mahogany back and sides, ivory binding, mahogany neck, 14/20-fret rosewood fingerboard with dot inlays, three-per-side gold nickel tuners with black buttons, rosewood bridge, Sonicore pickup, Fishman Isys Plus electronics, available in 3 Tone Sunburst, Black, or Natural finish, mfg. 2010-present.

MSR $399	$280	$180 - 220	$100 - 130	

CJ3 (SJ3) – traditional jumbo body, solid spruce top, flamed maple sides/back, maple neck, 14/20-fret rosewood fingerboard with pearl dot inlay, multiple layer binding, abalone rosette soundhole, three-per-side tuners, chrome hardware, available in Natural, Natural Satin, or 3-Tone Sunburst, mfg. 2001-02.

	N/A	$200 - 250	$135 - 175	$499

* **SJ3F** – similar to the SJ3 except has Fishman Classic 4 & Sonicore pickups, not available in the USA.

	N/A	$215 - 265	$135 - 175	$499

* **CJ3-12 (SJ3-12) 12-String** – similar to the SJ3 except is in 12-string configuration, not available in the USA.

	N/A	$250 - 300	$150 - 190	$569

CJ5X (SJ5 X) – similar to the SF1, except has a deeper body, solid spruce top, mahogany back/sides/neck, gold Grover tuners, Fishman acoustic pickup, Fishman Prefix EQ with three-band/contour/volume sliders, available in Natural Satin finish, current mfg.

MSR $679	$475	$300 - 350	$175 - 225	

CJ7X – similar to the CJ5X, except has quilted maple back and sides, and Fishman Prefix Plus T electronics, available in Antique Burst or Natural Satin finish, mfg. 2005-2010.

	$575	$350 - 425	$200 - 250	$799

SJ7 X – similar to SJ5 X, except has quilted maple top, sides, and back, maple neck and rosewood fingerboard, available in Red Burst and Blue Burst, disc. 2001.

	N/A	$300 - 350	$200 - 250	$795

CJ10X (SJ10 X) – similar to the SJ5, except has rosewood back and sides, abalone binding on body/soundhole, abalone position inlays, available in black or Natural Glossy finish, mfg. 1996-present.

MSR $995	$700	$450 - 525	$275 - 325	

* **CJ10 X12 (SJ10X) 12-String** – similar to SJ10 X, except in 12-string configuration, Natural finish, mfg. 1999-2010.

	$800	$525 - 600	$300 - 375	$1,150

CJ CUSTOM – jumbo style, master grade Engelmann solid spruce top, solid rosewood sides/back, abalone soundhole rosette, mahogany neck, 14/20 ebony fingerboard with pearl dot inlay, flamed maple wood binding on body, fretboard, and headstock, Grover three-per-side Super Rotomatic tuners, ebony bridge, gold hardware, Natural finish, made in the Cort Custom Shop, 25.3 in. scale, mfg. 2006-07.

	N/A	$600 - 700	$375 - 450	$1,395

* **CJ Custom CE Cutaway Electric** – similar to the CJ Custom, except has a single cutaway and Fishman Premium blender electronics, mfg. 2006-07.

	N/A	$800 - 950	$525 - 600	$1,895

CJ LE2 LIMITED EDITION – jumbo style, solid Englemann spruce top, solid flame maple back and sides, five-piece maple neck, round soundhole with abalone rosette, abalone body binding, 14/20-fret ebony fingerboard with 12th fret pyramid and other various inlays, bound headstock with three-per-side gold Gotoh tuners, ebony bridge, available in Natural finish, mfg. 2006-07.

	N/A	$1,150 - 1,350	$750 - 850	$2,695

ACOUSTIC: CLASSICAL MODELS

AC-10 – nylon string configuration, classical style body, spruce top, mahogany back and sides, classical rosette, black binding, mahogany neck, 12/19-fret rosewood fingerboard, slotted headstock, three-per-side open style chrome tuners with white buttons, rosewood bridge, available in Natural finish, mfg. 2011-present.

MSR $179	$125	$80 - 95	$45 - 60	

AC-11R – nylon string configuration, classical style body, spruce top, rosewood back and sides, classical rosette, black binding, mahogany neck, 12/19-fret rosewood fingerboard, slotted headstock, three-per-side open style chrome tuners with brown buttons, rosewood bridge, available in Natural finish, mfg. 2011-present.

MSR $229	$160	$95 - 120	$60 - 75	

AC-12 – classical nylon-string style, spruce top, mahogany back/sides/neck, soundhole inlay, 12/19-fret rosewood fingerboard, rosewood bridge, three-per-side open style tuners, available in Natural finish, mfg. 2005-present.

MSR $289	$200	$130 - 160	$70 - 95	

MSR/NOTES	100%	EXCELLENT	AVERAGE	LAST MSR

AC-15 – classical nylon-string style, solid cedar top, rosewood back/sides/neck, soundhole inlay, 12/19-fret rosewood fingerboard, rosewood bridge, three-per-side open style tuners, available in Natural finish, mfg. 2005-present.

MSR $375	$260	$170 - 210	$95 - 120	

* *ACC-15F* – similar to the AC-15, except has a single rounded cutaway, a Sonicore pickup, and Fishman Classic 4 preamp/electronics, available in Natural finish, mfg. 2007-present.

MSR $539	$380	$240 - 285	$135 - 175	

CEC-1 – classical single cutaway, solid cedar top, mahogany back/sides/neck, 14/22-fret fingerboard, nylon-string, three-per-side banjo style tuners, soundhole inlay, Fishman Classic 4 & Sonicore pickup, available in Natural finish, mfg. 2001-06.

	N/A	$325 - 400	$175 - 225	$780

CEC-5 – classical single cutaway, spruce, mahogany back/sides/neck, 14/22-fret fingerboard, nylon-string, three-per-side banjo style tuners, soundhole inlay, Fishman Classic 4 electronics, available in Black (2010-present) or Natural finish, mfg. 2005-present.

MSR $475	$330	$210 - 250	$120 - 155	

• **Add 2.5% (MSR $489) for Black finish.**

CEC-7 – classical nylon-strig configuration, single cutaway, spruce top, rosewood back and sides, mahogany neck, 14/22-fret fingerboard, three-per-side banjo style tuners, soundhole inlay, Fishman Classic 4 electronics, available in Natural finish, mfg. 2007-present.

MSR $650	$450	$300 - 350	$160 - 210	

ACOUSTIC: EARTH SERIES

EARTH 52 – grand concert style, solid spruce top, round soundhole, tortoiseshell pickguard, black body binding, four-ring rosette, mahogany back/sides/neck, 14/20-fret rosewood fingerboard with dot inlay, rosewood bridge with white pins, three-per-side chrome die-cast tuners, available in Natural Satin finish, mfg. 2004 only.

	N/A	$100 - 130	$70 - 95	$260

EARTH 70 – dreadnought style, solid spruce top, round soundhole, tortoiseshell pickguard, ivory body binding, four-ring rosette, mahogany back/sides/neck, 14/20-fret rosewood fingerboard with dot inlay, three-per-side chrome die cast tuners, rosewood bridge with white pins, available in Black (2011-present), Natural Satin, or Natural (2004-07, 2011-present) finish, mfg. 2004-present.

MSR $279	$195	$125 - 150	$70 - 90	

• **Add 7.5% (MSR $299) for Black or Natural Tone finish.**

* *Earth 70-12 12-String* – similar to the Earth 70, except in 12-string configuration, mfg. 2004-present.

MSR $350	$250	$160 - 195	$90 - 115	

»*Earth 70-12E 12-String Electric* – similar to the Earth 70-12 12-String, except has Cort CE series electronics, available in Natural finish, mfg. 2006-present.

MSR $439	$310	$195 - 235	$110 - 145	

* *Earth 70 E Electric* – similar to the Earth 70, except has Cort CE series electronics, available in Natural Satin finish, mfg. 2004-present.

MSR $359	$250	$165 - 200	$90 - 115	

EARTH 72/EARTH 70 GC – similar to the Earth 70, except in grand concert configuration, mfg. 2004-09.

	N/A	$95 - 125	$45 - 65	$249

In 2008, this model was renamed the Earth 70 GC.

* *Earth 72E Electric* – similar to the Earth 72, except has a Slim Jim pickup and Cort CE series electronics, mfg. 2004-05.

	N/A	$120 - 150	$70 - 90	$300

EARTH 100 – dreadnought style, solid spruce top, round soundhole, tortoiseshell pickguard, black body binding, four-ring rosette, maple back/sides/neck, 14/20-fret rosewood fingerboard with dot inlay, rosewood bridge with white pins, three-per-side chrome die cast tuners, available in Black (2011-present), Natural Satin, or Natural Tone finish, mfg. 1998-present.

MSR $359	$250	$165 - 200	$90 - 115	

• **Add 5% (MSR $379) for Natural Tone finish.**
• **Add 12.5% (MSR $399) for Black finish.**

* *Earth 100 DX* – similar to the Earth 100, except has maple wood binding and gold tuners with black buttons, available in Natural Tone finish, disc. 2010.

	$300	$190 - 230	$105 - 140	$425

* *Earth 100 F* – similar to Earth 100, except has Fishman Classic 4 electronics and Sonicore pickup, available in Tone finish, current mfg.

MSR $479	$335	$215 - 260	$120 - 155	

* *Earth 100 LH Left-Handed* – similar to the Earth 100, except in left-handed configuration, available in Natural finish, mfg. 2006 only.

	N/A	$135 - 175	$80 - 105	$349

MSR/NOTES	100%	EXCELLENT	AVERAGE	LAST MSR

* Earth 100 OV/QB/SE – similar to the Earth 100, except has a solid cedar top with ovankol back and sides (OV), bubinga back and sides (QB), or striped ebony back and sides (SE), available in Natural finish, mfg. 2008-2010.

	$300	$190 - 230	$105 - 140	$425

* Earth 100 R – similar to Earth 100, except has rosewood back and sides, available in Natural finish, mfg. 2007-present.

MSR $429	$300	$195 - 235	$105 - 140	

EARTH 150 – similar to the Earth 100 except is available in Natural, Trans. Red, Trans. Blue, or Sunburst finishes, disc. 2004.

	N/A	$120 - 150	$75 - 95	$299

* Earth 150 F – similar to Earth 150, except has Fishman Classic 4 electronics and Sonicore pickup, available in Tone finish, disc 2003.

	N/A	$135 - 175	$105 - 135	$390

EARTH 190 – similar to the 150, Natural finish, disc. 2004.

	N/A	$115 - 145	$80 - 105	$280

EARTH 200 – dreadnought style, solid spruce top, round soundhole, tortoiseshell pickguard, herringbone bound body/rosette, mahogany back/sides/neck, 14/20-fret rosewood fingerboard with dot inlay, stylized inlay at 12th fret, three-per-side chrome Grover tuners, rosewood bridge with white pins, available in Three-Tone Sunburst or Natural Satin finish, current mfg.

MSR $499	$350	$225 - 275	$125 - 165	

* Earth 200-12 12-String – similar to the Earth 200, except in 12-string configuration, six-per-side tuners, mfg. 1998-2003, reintroduced 2005-present.

MSR $499	$350	$225 - 275	$125 - 165	

* Earth 200 GC Grand Concert – similar to the Earth 200, except in a grand concert style body, and featuring a solid cedar top, no pickguard, mfg. 1996-2009.

	N/A	$175 - 225	$110 - 140	$450

* Earth 200 LH Left-Handed – similar to the Earth 200, except in left-handed configuration, disc. 2010.

	$350	$225 - 275	$125 - 165	$499

EARTH 202 – dreadnought style, solid cedar top, round soundhole, herringbone bound body/rosette, solid mahogany back, mahogany sides and neck, 14/20-fret rosewood fingerboard with dot inlay, rosewood bridge with white pins, three-per-side Grover tuners with black knobs, available in Natural Satin finish, mfg. 2005-09.

	N/A	$175 - 225	$110 - 140	$450

EARTH 250 – similar to the Earth 200 except features a solid mahogany top and back, and mahogany sides and neck, gives a darker natural finish, disc. 2003.

	N/A	$145 - 185	$95 - 125	$450

EARTH 500 – similar to the Earth 200, except has gold Grover tuners, available in Natural Glossy finish, disc. 2000.

	N/A	$175 - 225	$125 - 150	$469

EARTH 600 – dreadnought style, solid spruce top, rosewood sides/back, mahogany neck, 14/20 rosewood fingerboard with pearl dot inlay, rosewood bridge, tortoiseshell pickguard, abalone soundhole rosette, three-per-side tuners, chrome hardware, Natural finish, mfg. 2001-05.

	N/A	$225 - 275	$135 - 175	$550

EARTH 700 – dreadnought style, solid spruce top, rosewood sides/back, mahogany neck, 14/20 rosewood fingerboard with pearl dot inlay, rosewood bridge, tortoiseshell pickguard, abalone soundhole rosette, three-per-side tuners, chrome hardware, Natural finish, mfg. 2005-present.

MSR $739	$515	$325 - 400	$185 - 240	

EARTH 900 – parlor-style guitar, solid cedar top, solid mahogany back, mahogany neck, 12/19 fret rosewood fingerboard with abalone inlay, soundhole rosette, three-per-side banjo-style tuners, available in Natural Satin finish, mfg. 1998-2007.

	N/A	$325 - 375	$175 - 225	$750

EARTH 1000 – similar to the Earth 200, except has rosewood sides and back, abalone fingerboard/soundhole inlays, and gold Grover tuners, available in Natural Glossy finish, disc. 1999.

	N/A	$250 - 300	$150 - 190	$595

EARTH 1200 – dreadnought style, solid spruce top, rosewood sides/back, mahogany neck, 14/20-fret rosewood fingerboard with abalone tree-of-life inlay, rosewood bridge, tortoiseshell pickguard, abalone soundhole rosette, three-per-side Grover tuners, gold hardware, Natural finish, mfg. 1999-2005.

	N/A	$325 - 400	$200 - 250	$795

MSR/NOTES	100%	EXCELLENT	AVERAGE	LAST MSR

EARTH 1500 – dreadnought style, solid Englemann spruce top, solid rosewood back, rosewood sides, abalone binding and rosette, mahogany neck, 14/20-fret rosewood fingerboard with abalone inlays, three-per-side Grover tuners, rosewood bridge, tortoiseshell pickguard, gold hardware, Natural finish, mfg. 2005-07.

	N/A	$400 - 475	$250 - 300	$950

EARTH CUSTOM – dreadnought style, master grade Engelmann solid spruce top, solid rosewood sides/back, mahogany neck, 14/20 ebony fingerboard with pearl dot inlay, ebony bridge, flamed maple wood binding on body, fretboard, and headstock, abalone soundhole rosette, Grover three-per-side Super Rotomatic tuners, Fishman Prefix Plus & Matrix pickups, gold hardware, Natural finish, made in the Cort Custom Shop, mfg. 2002-07.

	N/A	$600 - 700	$375 - 450	$1,395

EARTH GRAND – petite dreadnought body, solid spruce top, mahogany back and sides, advanced scalloped bracing, multi-ply red pearl acrylic, mahogany neck, 19-fret fingerboard with small dot inlays, three-per-side tuners with black buttons, Natural finish, gig bag included, mfg. 2010-present.

MSR $299	$210	$135 - 160	$75 - 95	

EARTH LE2 HK LIMITED EDITION – dreadnought style, solid cedar top, solid Hawaiian koa back and sides, round soundhole with abalone rosette, abalone body binding, 14/20-fret ebony fingerboard with flower inlays, bound headstock with three-per-side gold Gotoh tuners, ebony bridge, available in Natural finish, mfg. 2006-07.

	N/A	$1,150 - 1,350	$750 - 850	$2,695

EARTH LE3 IR/QB LIMITED EDITION – dreadnought style, solid Bear Claw spruce top, solid Indian rosewood (Earth LE3 IR) or quilted bubinga (Earth LE3 QB) back and sides, round soundhole with abalone rosette, wood body binding, 14/20-fret ebony fingerboard with dot and 12th-fret flower inlays, bound headstock with three-per-side gold Gotoh tuners, ebony bridge, available in Natural finish, mfg. 2006-07.

	N/A	$900 - 1,050	$600 - 700	$1,995

EARTH MINI – petite dreadnought body, solid spruce top, mahogany back and sides, scalloped bracing, 19-fret fingerboard with small dot inlays, three-per-side tuners with black buttons, Natural finish, gig bag included, mfg. 2008-present.

MSR $299	$210	$135 - 160	$75 - 95	

EARTH PACK – acoustic guitar starter pack that includes a Cort Earth 60, gig bag, capo, tuner, picks, accessory pouch, guitar strap, and an extra set of strings, current mfg.

MSR $329	$230	$180 - 180	$85 - 105	

ACOUSTIC: EVL SERIES

EVL-A6 – single Florentine cutaway body, solid spruce top, arched mahogany back and sides, modern white thinline binding, slim V profile mahogany neck, 14/20-fret ebony fingerboard with star in circle and 11-15th fret cross inlays, EVL-style headstock with black overlay and unique truss rod cover, three-per-side pewter tuners, ebony bridge, black bridge pins, black pickguard, Fishman Classic 4T electronics, available in Black Satin finish, mfg. 2008-present.

MSR $595	$420	$275 - 325	$150 - 195	

ACOUSTIC: JADE SERIES

JADE 2 – single cutaway smaller body style, solid European spruce top, maple back and sides, round soundhole with red pearl acrylic rosette, multi-ply layer ivory binding, slim profile mahogany neck, 14/20-fret bound rosewood fingerboard with 12th fret white acrylic leaves inlay, matching finish headstock overlay with leaves design, three-per-side chrome tuners, rosewood bridge, available in Natural Satin (disc. 2010), Pale Blue Metallic, or Pale Pink Metallic finish, 25.3 in. scale, gig bag and floral sticker included, mfg. 2008-present.

MSR $399	$280	$180 - 220	$100 - 130	

JADE 6 – single cutaway smaller body style, solid European spruce top, flamed maple back and sides, round soundhole with red pearl acrylic rosette, bubinga binding, slim profile mahogany neck, 14/20-fret rosewood fingerboard with 12th fret white acrylic leaves inlay, bubinga headstock overlay with leaves design, three-per-side chrome tuners with black buttons, rosewood bridge, Fishman Classic 4T electronics, available in Natural or Trans. Wine Burst finish, 25.3 in. scale, gig bag and floral sticker included, mfg. 2008-present.

MSR $650	$450	$300 - 350	$160 - 210	

ACOUSTIC: LUCE SERIES

Cort's Luce Series are inspired by the most collectible guitars from the golden age of acoustics.

L100C – concert-style body, solid spruce top, mahogany back and sides, round soundhole with multi-ring rosette, ivory binding, mahogany neck, 14/20-fret rosewood fingerboard with dot inlays, three-per-side nickel tuners with black buttons, rosewood bridge, tortoise pickguard, available in Natural Satin finish, mfg. 2009-present.

MSR $299	$210	$135 - 160	$75 - 95	

MSR/NOTES	100%	EXCELLENT	AVERAGE	LAST MSR

L100F – single cutaway SF-style body, solid spruce top, mahogany back and sides, round soundhole with multi-ring rosette, ivory binding, mahogany neck, 14/20-fret rosewood fingerboard with dot inlays, three-per-side nickel tuners with black buttons, rosewood bridge, tortoise pickguard, Sonicore pickup, Fishman Isys+ electronics, available in Natural Satin finish, mfg. 2009-present.

MSR $425	$300	$195 - 235	$105 - 140	

L450C – concert-style body, solid mahogany top, back, and sides, round soundhole with multi-ring abalone rosette, ivory binding, mahogany neck, 14/20-fret rosewood fingerboard with white snowflake inlays, three-per-side Grover vintage nickel tuners, rosewood bridge, tortoise pickguard, available in Natural Satin finish, mfg. 2009-present.

MSR $399	$280	$180 - 220	$100 - 130	

L900P – parlor Martin 00-style body, solid red cedar top, solid rosewood back and sides, round soundhole with multi-ring abalone rosette, ivoroid binding with herringbone purfling, mahogany neck, 12/19-fret rosewood fingerboard with abalone snowflake inlays, slotted headstock, three-per-side open-style Grover vintage nickel tuners, rosewood bridge, available in Natural Satin finish, mfg. 2009-present.

MSR $699	$490	$300 - 375	$175 - 225	

ACOUSTIC: MR SERIES

MR100 F – dreadnought style, single cutaway body, solid spruce top, round soundhole, black body binding, four-ring rosette, mahogany back/sides/neck, 14/20-fret rosewood fingerboard with dot inlay, three-per-side chrome die cast tuners, rosewood bridge with white pins, Fishman Classic 4 electronics, available in Black or Natural Satin finish, mfg. 2005-09.

	N/A	$165 - 215	$95 - 125	$429

MR710 F – dreadnought style, single cutaway body, spruce top, round soundhole, black body binding, four-ring rosette, maple back/sides/neck, 14/20-fret rosewood fingerboard with offset dot inlay, rosewood bridge with white pins, three-per-side chrome die cast tuners, Fishman acoustic pickup, Fishman Deluxe EQ with three-band sliders and mid-frequency sweep/volume controls, available in Black, Three Tone Sunburst, Natural, or Natural Tone finish, mfg. 1998-present.

MSR $499	$350	$225 - 275	$125 - 165	

* **Add 7.5% (MSR $539) for Black finish.**

* *MR710F-12 12-String* – similar to the MR710 F, except in 12-string configuration and six-per-side tuners, available in Natural finish, mfg. 2006-present.

MSR $579	$400	$260 - 310	$145 - 190	

* *MR710F-AE* – similar to the MR710 F, except has Asian ebony back and sides, available in Natural finish, mfg. 2006-07.

	N/A	$240 - 290	$130 - 170	$569

* *MR710F-DAO/FM/OV/QB/SE* – similar to the MR710F, except has flame maple back and sides (FM), a solid cedar top with dao back and sides (DAO), ovankol back and sides (OV), quilted ash back and sides (QA), bubinga back and sides (QB), or striped ebony back and sides (SE), available in Natural finish, mfg. 2008-present.

MSR $550	$385	$250 - 290	$140 - 180	

* *MR710F-LH Left-Handed* – similar to the MR710 F, except in left-handed configuration, available in Natural finish, mfg. 2009-present.

MSR $539	$380	$245 - 285	$135 - 175	

MR720 F (FIRST VERSION) – single cutaway dreadnought style, spruce top, round soundhole, tortoiseshell pickguard, multiple ivory body binding/rosette, mahogany back/sides/neck, 14/20-fret rosewood fingerboard with offset dot inlay, rosewood bridge with white pins, three-per-side chrome Grover tuners, Fishman acoustic pickup, Fishman Deluxe EQ with three-band sliders and mid frequency sweep/volume controls, available in Natural Glossy, Natural Satin, or See-Through Black finish, disc. 1999.

	N/A	$225 - 275	$135 - 175	$550

MR720 F (SECOND VERSION) – single cutaway dreadnought body style, solid Sitka spruce top, rosewood back and sides, round soundhole with multiple ring rosette, multi-ply ivory body binding, mahogany neck, 14/20-fret rosewood fingerboard with white dot inlays, three-per-side chrome tuners with black buttons, rosewood bridge, tortoiseshell pickguard, Sonicore pickup, Fishman Classic 4T preamp/electronics, available in Natural finish, 25.3 in. scale, mfg. 2007-09.

	N/A	$250 - 300	$150 - 200	$579

MR727 F – dreadnought single cutaway, flamed maple top, maple sides/back, matching headstock, 14/20 fret rosewood fingerboard, three-per-side tuners, rosewood bridge, multiple layer binding and soundhole rosette, Fishman Classic 4 & Sonicore pickup, available in Antique Violin, Natural, Trans. Blue, or Trans. Red finish, mfg. 2003-07.

	N/A	$325 - 375	$175 - 225	$750

MR730 FX (MR730 F) – similar to the MR720 F, except has a solid spruce top, Fishman Prefix EQ system, available in Natural Satin finish only, disc. 2003, 2005-06, 2008-present.

MSR $750	$525	$325 - 400	$190 - 240	

MR740 FX – similar to MR730 FX, except has Grover gold tuning gears. Natural finish, mfg. 1999-2001, reintroduced 2003-present.

MSR $995	$700	$450 - 525	$250 - 300	

MSR/NOTES	100%	EXCELLENT	AVERAGE	LAST MSR

MR750 F (MR750 FX) – similar to the MR720 F, except has a bound flamed maple top, bound neck/headstock, Fishman Prefix EQ system, tortoise pickguard, gold Grover tuners, available in Amber Satin, See-Through Black, See-Through Blue, See-Through Red, and Tobacco Sunburst finish, disc. 1999.

	N/A	$300 - 350	$175 - 225	$695

MR770 F – similar to MR750 F, except has a rounded profile back, disc. 1999.

	N/A	$325 - 275	$175 - 225	$695

MR780 FX – dreadnought single cutaway, flamed maple top, maple sides/back, matching headstock, 14/20-fret rosewood fingerboard with 12th fret inlay, three-per-side tuners, rosewood bridge, multiple layer binding and soundhole rosette, Fishman Prefix Plus & Matrix pickup, chrome hardware, available in Antique Violin, Light Vintage Burst, Red Burst, Blue Burst, or Natural finish, mfg. 1998-2010.

	$675	$425 - 500	$225 - 275	$950

MR-A – dreadnought single cutaway, spruce top, mahogany sides/back, maple or mahogany neck, 14/20-fret rosewood fingerboard with pearl dot inlay, three-per-side tuners, rosewood bridge, black binding and soundhole rosette, tortoiseshell pickguard, CE-300 active EQ & Slim Jim pickup, chrome hardware, available in Sun Burst Satin, Black, or Natural Satin finish, mfg. 2001-04.

	N/A	$135 - 175	$95 - 125	$325

MR CUSTOM – dreadnought single cutaway, master grade solid Engelmann spruce top, solid rosewood back and sides, mahogany neck, 14/20 ebony fingerboard with pearl dot inlay, ebony bridge, flamed maple wood binding on body, fretboard, and headstock, abalone soundhole rosette, Grover three-per-side Super Rotomatic tuners, Fishman Prefix Plus & Matrix pickups, gold hardware, Natural finish, made in the Cort Custom Shop, mfg. 2002-07.

	N/A	$800 - 950	$525 - 600	$1,895

MR-E – single smooth cutaway dreadnought style body, solid spruce top, mahogany back and sides, round soundhole with multi-ring white pearl acrylic rosette, black with white acrylic binding, mahogany neck, 14/20-fret rosewood fingerboard with offset dot inlay, three-per-side nickel die cast tuners with black buttons, rosewood bridge with white pins, Cort electronics, available in Black, Three Tone Sunburst, or Natural finish, mfg. 2011-present.

MSR $349	$250	$160 - 200	$90 - 115	

ACOUSTIC: NATURAL SERIES

NATURAL – dreadnought style, solid cedar top, round soundhole, maple bound body, wood design rosette, mahogany back/sides/neck, 14/20-fret rosewood fingerboard with double dot inlay at 12th fret, rosewood bridge with white pins, three-per-side vintage chrome tuners, available in Natural Satin finish, mfg. 1996-99.

	N/A	$200 - 250	$120 - 150	$479

NATURAL DLX – similar to the Natural, except has solid rosewood back, rosewood sides, stylized inlay at 12th fret, vintage gold tuners, mfg. 1996-98.

	N/A	$350 - 425	$200 - 250	$795

ACOUSTIC: NDX SERIES

NDX 20 – single scooped cutaway NDX-style body, solid Sitka spruce top, mahogany back and sides, round soundhole with double abalone rosette, ivory binding, mahogany neck, 14/20-fret bound rosewood fingerboard with white ring inlays, three-per-side nickel tuners with black buttons, rosewood bridge, Sonicore pickup, Fishman Classic 4T Blend electronics, available in Black or Natural finish, mfg. 2010-present.

MSR $625	$430	$275 - 325	$155 - 200	

  • **Add 5% (MSR $650) for Black finish.**

NDX 50 – single scooped cutaway NDX-style body, solid Sitka spruce top, mahogany back and sides, round soundhole with double abalone rosette, ivory binding, mahogany neck, 14/20-fret bound rosewood fingerboard with white ring inlays, three-per-side gold tuners with black buttons, rosewood bridge, Sonicore pickup, Fishman Classic 4T Blend electronics, available in Natural finish, mfg. summer 2010-present.

MSR $750	$525	$325 - 400	$190 - 240	

ACOUSTIC: NTL SERIES

NTL 20 – similar to NTL 50, except has solid spruce top, mahogany sides and back, Grover Super Rotomatic chrome tuners, available in Natural Satin finish, mfg. 1999-2009.

	N/A	$200 - 250	$120 - 150	$499

  * *NTL 20F* – similar to NTL 20, except has Fishman Classic 4T electronics, mfg. summer 2008-09.

	N/A	$275 - 325	$150 - 200	$650

NTL 50 – similar to NTL Custom, except has solid spruce A grade top, rosewood sides and back, rosewood fingerboard, available in Natural finish, mfg. 1999-2002.

	N/A	$210 - 260	$145 - 185	$595

  * *NTL 50FX* – similar to the NTL 50, except has Fishman Prefix Plus T electronics, mfg. 2005-09.

	N/A	$375 - 450	$225 - 275	$849

MSR/NOTES	100%	EXCELLENT	AVERAGE	LAST MSR

NTL CUSTOM – body slightly larger than Earth Series guitars, Engelmann spruce AA grade top, solid Indian rosewood sides and back, mahogany neck with ebony fingerboard, Grover Super Rotomatic gold tuners, 25.25 in.scale, figured maple bindings, bone nut and bone bridge saddle, produced in the Cort Custom Shop, case included, available in Natural finish, mfg. 1999-2007.

	N/A	$600 - 700	$375 - 450	$1,395

* **NTL Custom CE Cutaway Electric** – similar to the NTL Custom, except has a single cutaway and Fishman Prefix Premium Blender electronics, mfg. 2005-07.

	N/A	$800 - 950	$525 - 600	$1,895

ACOUSTIC: PARKWOOD SERIES

PW310 – dreadnought style, solid spruce top, solid mahogany or rosewood back and sides, 14/20-fret rosewood fingerboard with dot inlays, three-per-side tuners, multi-layer binding, chrome hardware, Natural finish, mfg. 2005 only.

	N/A	$350 - 425	$225 - 275	$950

PW340 – jumbo style, solid spruce top,flamed mapleback and sides, 14/20-fret rosewood fingerboard with dot inlays, three-per-side tuners, multi-layer binding, chrome hardware, Natural finish, mfg. 2005 only.

	N/A	$375 - 450	$250 - 300	$995

PW370 – single cutaway folk style, solid spruce top, solid mahogany back and sides, 14/20-fret rosewood fingerboard with dot inlays, three-per-side tuners, multi-layer binding, Fishman Premium electronics, chrome hardware, Natural finish, mfg. 2005 only.

	N/A	$550 - 650	$325 - 400	$1,250

ACOUSTIC: RESONATOR SERIES

ADR6 – dreadnought-style resonator guitar, spruce top, mahogany back/sides, mahogany rounded neck, multiple ivory body binding, a 14/20-fret rosewood fingerboard with white dot inlays, resonator cone/soundwell, two mesh soundholes, spider bridge, three-on-a-side chrome die cast tuners, available in Natural Glossy or Tobacco Sunburst finish, mfg. 1996-98.

	N/A	$325 - 375	$175 - 225	$699

ADS6 – similar to the ADR6, except has square neck and chrome open tuning machines, mfg. 1996-98.

	N/A	$350 - 400	$175 - 225	$750

ACOUSTIC: SF(X) SERIES

SF models were not available in the USA until 2005.

SFX 1F – single cutaway body, solid spruce top, round soundhole, bound body, rosette, arched back, mahogany back/sides/neck, 14/20-fret rosewood fingerboard with dot inlay, rosewood bridge with white pins, three-per-side chrome die cast tuners, Fishman Classic 4 electronics, available in Arctic White, Black Satin, Natural Glossy, Natural Satin, or Trans. Wine Burst finish, mfg. 2005-present.

MSR $469	$330	$210 - 250	$115 - 150	

• **Add 2.5% (MSR $489) for Arctic White, Black Satin, Natural Glossy, or Trans. Wine Burst finish.**
This model was available overseas in a different configuration.

SF5 X (SF5) – similar to SF1, except has solid cedar top, mahogany back/sides/neck, gold Grover tuners, Fishman acoustic pickup, Fishman Prefix EQ with three-band/contour/volume sliders, available in Black, Light Vintage Burst, or Natural Satin finish, mfg. 1996-97 (as SF5), 1998-2000, 2005-present.

MSR $599	$420	$275 - 325	$150 - 200	

* **SFX5-12 12-String** – similar to the SFX5, except in 12-string configuration with six-per-side tuners, available in Natural Glossy finish, disc. 2010.

	$450	$300 - 350	$175 - 225	$649

SFX 6B/6R – single cutaway thin body, solid spruce top, bubinga (SFX 6B, 2006-07) or rosewood (SFX 6R) arched back and sides, multi-layer top and back body binding, round soundhole with abalone-style rosette, mahogany neck, bound 14/20-fret rosewood fingerboard with small dot and 12th-fret diamond/arrowhead inlays, bound headstock with three-per-side chrome tuners, rosewood bridge, Sonicore pickup, Fishman Classic 4T electronics, available in 3 Tone Sunburst (6R only) or Natural finish, 25.3 in. scale, mfg. 2006-2010.

	$450	$275 - 325	$150 - 200	$659

SFX 6W – single cutaway thin body, solid cedar top, walnut arched back and sides, multi-layer top and back body binding, round soundhole with abalone-style rosette, mahogany neck, bound 14/20-fret rosewood fingerboard with small dot and 12th-fret diamond/arrowhead inlays, bound headstock with three-per-side chrome tuners, rosewood bridge, Sonicore pickup, Fishman Classic 4T electronics, available in Natural or Natural Satin finish, 25.3 in. scale, mfg. 2008-09.

	N/A	$275 - 325	$150 - 200	$630

SF10 X – similar to SF5X, except has solid spruce top, quilted maple back and sides, gold Grover tuners, Fishman acoustic pickup, Fishman Prefix Plus electronics, available in Natural Satin finish, mfg. 2005-present.

MSR $799	$560	$350 - 425	$200 - 250	

MSR/NOTES	100%	EXCELLENT	AVERAGE	LAST MSR

SF-A – folk single cutaway body, solid spruce top, mahogany or maple back/sides, mahogany neck, 14/20 fret rosewood fingerboard with pearl dot inlay, binding, abalone soundhole rosette, CE-300 active EQ & Slim Jim pickup, three-per-side tuners, chrome hardware, available in Natural, Natural Satin, or Sunburst Satin finish, disc.

	N/A	$135 - 175	$95 - 125	$325

SFX CUSTOM – single cutaway thin body, master grade solid Engelmann spruce top, solid rosewood arched back and sides, mahogany neck, 14/20 ebony fingerboard with pearl dot inlay, ebony bridge, flamed maple wood binding on body, fretboard, and headstock, abalone soundhole rosette, Grover three-per-side Super Rotomatic tuners, Fishman Prefix Plus & Matrix pickups, gold hardware, Natural finish, made in the Cort Custom Shop, mfg. 2006-07.

	N/A	$800 - 950	$525 - 600	$1,895

SFX-E – single cutaway SFX-style body, solid spruce top, mahogany back and sides, round soundhole with multi-ply white pearl acrylic rosette, black with white acrylic binding, mahogany neck, 14/20-fret rosewood fingerboard with dot inlays, three-per-side nickel tuners with black knobs, rosewood bridge with white pins, Cort electronics, available in Three Tone Sunburst, Black Satin, or Natural Satin finish, mfg. 2011-present.

MSR $349	$250	$160 - 200	$90 - 115	

SFX LE2 LIMITED EDITION – single cutaway thin body, solid Bear Claw spruce top, solid flame maple back and sides, five-piece maple neck, round soundhole with abalone rosette, abalone body binding, 14/20-fret ebony fingerboard with Eiffel tower and other various inlays, bound headstock with three-per-side gold Gotoh tuners, ebony bridge, Fishman Premium blender electronics, available in Natural finish, mfg. 2006-07.

	N/A	$1,150 - 1,350	$750 - 850	$2,695

ACOUSTIC: STANDARD (AD/AF/AJ) SERIES

The Standard Series was introduced as a budget-line or entry level of Cort acoustic guitars. Circa 2002, the AJ models were changed to AD models.

AD 810 – dreadnought-style body, spruce top, mahogany back and sides, round soundhole with multi-ring rosette, black line binding, mahongany neck, 14/20-fret rosewood fingerboard with dot inlays, three-per-side nickel tuners, rosewood bridge, black pickguard, available in Black or Natural finish, mfg. 2009-present.

MSR $189	$130	$85 - 110	$50 - 65	

* **AD 810E** – similar to the AD 810, except, available in Natural Satin finish, mfg. 2010-present.

MSR $249	$175	$110 - 135	$60 - 80	

AD 850/AJ 850 – dreadnought style, spruce top, mahogany back and sides, mahogany neck, 14/20-fret rosewood fingerboard with dot inlay, three-per-side chrome tuners, rosewood bridge, tortoiseshell pickguard, Natural Satin finish, mfg. 1998-2010.

	$160	$95 - 120	$55 - 75	$229

* **AD 850 CE Cutaway Electric** – similar to the AD 850, except has a single cutaway and Cort CE Series electronics, mfg. 2006-2010.

	$240	$150 - 185	$85 - 110	$339

AJ 860 – dreadnought style, spruce top, round soundhole, black pickguard, multiple black body/rosette binding, mahogany back/sides/neck, 14/20-fret rosewood fingerboard with dot inlay, rosewood bridge with white pins, three-per-side chrome die-cast tuners, available in Natural Satin finish, disc. 1999.

	N/A	$120 - 150	$75 - 95	$299

AD 870/AJ 870 – dreadnought style, spruce top, mahogany back and sides or maple back and sides, mahongany neck, 14/20-fret rosewood fingerboard with dot inlay, three-per-side chrome tuners, rosewood bridge, tortoiseshell pickguard, available in Black, Blue Burst, Natural, or Sunburst finish, disc. 2010.

	$180	$115 - 140	$65 - 85	$259

* **AD 870-12/AJ 870-12 12-String** – similar to the AJ 870, except in 12-string configuration and six-per-side tuners, available in Natural finish, disc. 2010.

	$210	$120 - 150	$70 - 90	$295

* **AD 870-LH Left-Handed** – similar to the AD 870, except in left-handed configuration, available in Natural finish, mfg. 2006-2010.

	$200	$130 - 160	$75 - 95	$289

* **AJ 870 C** – similar to the AJ 870, except has a transducer pickup mounted in the bridge, disc. 1998.

	N/A	$150 - 200	$95 - 120	$399

AD 880 – dreadnought-style body, spruce top, mahogany back and sides, round soundhole with multi-ring tiger pearl acrylic rosette, ivory with tiger acrylic binding, mahongany neck, 14/20-fret rosewood fingerboard with dot inlays, three-per-side nickel tuners with black buttons, rosewood bridge, black pickguard, available in Black, Natural Gloss, Natural Satin, or Sunburst finish, mfg. 2010-present.

MSR $229	$160	$95 - 120	$55 - 75	

* **Add 10% (MSR $249) for Natural Gloss finish.**
* **Add 17.5% (MSR $269) for Black or Sunburst finish.**

MSR/NOTES	100%	EXCELLENT	AVERAGE	LAST MSR

* **AD 880CE Cutaway Electric** – similar to the AD 880, except has a single cutaway and electronics, available in Natural Satin finish, mfg. 2010-present.

MSR $289	$200	$130 - 160	$75 - 95	

* **AD 880LH Left-Handed** – similar to the AD 880, except in left-handed configuration, available in Natural Gloss finish, mfg. 2010-present.

MSR $269	$190	$120 - 150	$65 - 85	

AF 510 – concert-style body, spruce top, mahogany back and sides, round soundhole with multi-ring rosette, black line binding, mahogany neck, 14/20-fret rosewood fingerboard with dot inlays, three-per-side nickel tuners, rosewood bridge, black pickguard, available in Natural Gloss or Natural Satin finish, mfg. 2010-present.

MSR $189	$130	$85 - 110	$50 - 65	

• Add 7.5% (MSR $199) for Natural Gloss finish.

* **AF 510E** – similar to the AF 510, except, available in Natural Satin finish, mfg. 2010-present.

MSR $249	$175	$110 - 135	$60 - 80	

AF 550 – grand concert style, spruce top, mahogany back and sides, mahongany neck, 14/20-fret rosewood fingerboard with dot inlay, three-per-side chrome tuners, rosewood bridge, tortoiseshell pickguard, Natural Satin finish, mfg. 2000-2010.

	$160	$95 - 120	$55 - 75	$229

AF 580 – concert-style body, spruce top, mahogany back and sides, round soundhole with multi-ring tiger pearl acrylic rosette, ivory with tiger acrylic binding, mahongany neck, 14/20-fret rosewood fingerboard with dot inlays, three-per-side nickel tuners with black buttons, rosewood bridge, black pickguard, available in Black, Natural Gloss, Natural Satin, or Sunburst finish, mfg. 2010-present.

MSR $229	$160	$95 - 120	$55 - 75	

• Add 12.5% (MSR $259) for Black or Sunburst finish.

ACOUSTIC ELECTRIC BASS

MR720 BF – single cutaway dreadnought style, spruce top, round soundhole, multiple ivory body binding/rosette, maple back/sides, mahogany neck, 15/20-fret rosewood fingerboard with offset dot inlay, rosewood bridge with white pins, two-per-side chrome die cast tuners, Fishman acoustic pickup, Fishman Deluxe EQ with three-band sliders and mid-frequency sweep/volume controls, available in Natural Glossy and See-Through Black finish, disc. 2000.

	N/A	$325 - 375	$200 - 250	$795

NTL B – classic design with solid spruce top and rosewood sides and back, mahogany neck with rosewood fingerboard, die-cast gold tuning gears. Fishman Prefix EQ and Fishman Sonicore pickup, available in Natural finish, 34 in.scale, mfg. 1999-2001.

	N/A	$375 - 450	$225 - 275	$895

* **NTL FBL** – similar to NTL B, except in fretless configuration, Natural finish, mfg. 1999-2000, 2005-06.

	N/A	$425 - 500	$250 - 300	$1,095

SJB – single cutaway design with solid spruce top, maple sides, back, and neck, rosewood fingerboard, die-cast gold tuning gears, Fishman Prefix EQ and Fishman sonicore pickup, available in Natural Satin finish, 29.75 in.scale, disc. 2000.

	N/A	$350 - 400	$225 - 275	$795

SJB3 – jumbo body bass, solid spruce top, mahogany sides/back, mahogany neck, 15/20 rosewood fingerboard, natural headstock two-per-side tuners, binding, abalone soundhole rosette, CE-300B active EQ, Slim Jim pickup, available in Black, Natural Satin, or Walnut Satin finish, 30 in. scale, mfg. 2002-03, 2005-09.

	N/A	$200 - 250	$120 - 150	$500

SJB5 – single cutaway super jumbo body, solid spruce top, mahogany back and sides, round soundhole with multi-ring rosette, black binding, mahogany neck, 15/20 rosewood fingerboard with dot inlays, mahogany headstock overlay, two-per-side tuners, rosewood bridge, Sonicore pickup, Fishman Isys+ electronics, available in Natural Gloss finish, 34 in. scale, mfg. 2009-present.

MSR $549	$385	$250 - 290	$140 - 175	

SJB6FX – single cutaway jumbo body bass, solid Sitka spruce top, rosewood back and sides, abalone soundhole rosette, multi-ply body binding, mahogany neck, 17/22 bound rosewood fingerboard with dot inlays, natural bound headstock overlay, two-per-side tuners, rosewood bridge, Fishman Prefix Plus T electronics, available in Natural finish, 34 in. scale, mfg. 2008-present.

MSR $795	$560	$350 - 425	$200 - 250	

* **SJB6FX Fretless** – similar to the SJB6FX, except has a fretless fingerboard, mfg. 2008-present.

MSR $795	$560	$350 - 425	$200 - 250	

SJB CE – jumbo body single cutaway bass, solid spruce top, mahogany sides/back, mahogany neck, 19/22 rosewood fingerboard, natural headstock with two-per-side tuners, binding, abalone soundhole rosette, Fishman Classic 4 & Sonicore pickup, available in Natural Satin finish, 34 in. scale, mfg. 2002-07.

	N/A	$400 - 475	$225 - 275	$950

MSR/NOTES	100%	EXCELLENT	AVERAGE	LAST MSR

CORTEZ

Instruments previously built in Japan circa 1969 to 1988. Distributed in the U.S. market by Westheimer Musical Industries of Chicago, IL.

Cortez acoustics were produced in Japan, and imported to the U.S. market as an affordable alternative in the acoustic guitar market. Westheimer's Cortez company and trademark could be viewed as a stepping stone towards his current Cort company (See Cort).

COWBOY LOYE

Unknown production location and date.

Cowboy Loye is actually the stage name of country-western singer Loye Donald Pack who performed between 1920s and early 1940s. At some point in his career, he had a few guitars built with the name "Cowboy Loye" on the label. Very little else is known about the origin of manufacturer, and any further information can be submitted directly to Blue Book Publications. Initial information courtesy: Jeannie Heltsley.

The two known Cowboy Loye examples feature a small grand auditorium body-size with a brown-grained wood, white body binding, fingerboard sparkle dot inlays, open-style headstock, trapeze tailpiece, and a label on the inside that has a picture of Loye Donald Pack. Another example has a picture of a cowboy riding a bucking horse with his name.

CRAFTER

Instruments currently built in Korea. Distributed by Crafter USA in Ashland, VA. Crafter has been building guitars since 1972, and under the Crafter name since 1986.

CONTACT INFORMATION
CRAFTER
319 Business Lane, Suite 500
Ashland, VA 23005
Phone No.: 804-798-2006
Fax No.: 804-798-2116
www.crafterusa.com
info@crafterusa.com

Crafter guitars was founded by HyunKwon Park in April, 1972. He started business in his home, making guitars in a twenty-square-meter area with four employees. Early guitars were classical models that were distributed in Korea. Guitars at this time were branded "Sungeum." In 1978, they moved to a bigger location in Yangju-gun. In 1986, his oldest son, Injae Park, joined forces and decided to change the name to something more user friendly. They came up with the name Crafter, which has been in use ever since. HSS (Honner) distributed Crafter guitars in the U.S. in the late 1990s and early 2000s. In 2000, they opened a new 7,000-square-meter factory with a workforce of 140 people. They currently are distributing guitars in forty different countries.

Keep in mind that all models listed here are strictly the models that are offered in the U.S. market. Crafter produces several more models, but many of them are or never will be available in the U.S. Contact Crafter or visit their website for more information.

ACOUSTIC: AUDITORIUM/GRAND AUDITORIUM MODELS

GA-6 – Grand Auditorium style, solid Sitka spruce top, mahogany back and sides, 14/20-fret rosewood fingerboard with dot inlay, pickguard, chrome hardware, Natural finish, current mfg.

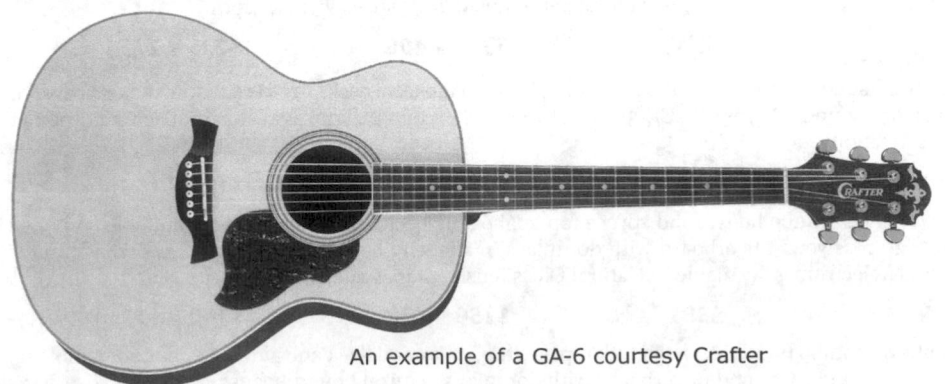

An example of a GA-6 courtesy Crafter

MSR $439	$300	$175 - 225	$110 - 140

GAE-6 – similar to the GA-6, except has a single cutaway, piezo pickup, and electronics, current mfg.

MSR $639	$450	$250 - 300	$150 - 200

GA-7 – Grand Auditorium style, solid cedar top, mahogany back and sides, wood soundhole inlay, 14/20-fret rosewood fingerboard with abalone dot inlay, pickguard, Mushroom buttons, chrome hardware, Natural finish, current mfg.

MSR $489	$340	$190 - 240	$120 - 150

MSR/NOTES	100%	EXCELLENT	AVERAGE	LAST MSR

GA-8 – Grand Auditorium style, solid Englemann spruce top, mahogany back and sides, abalone soundhole inlay, 14/20-fret rosewood fingerboard with abalone dot inlay, pickguard, Mushroom buttons, chrome hardware, Natural Gloss finish, current mfg.

| MSR $539 | $380 | $225 - 275 | $135 - 175 | |

* *GAE-8* – similar to the GA-8, except has a single cutaway, pickup, and electronics, current mfg.

| MSR $769 | $550 | $300 - 375 | $175 - 225 | |

GAE-12 – single cutaway Grand Auditorium style, solid Sitka spruce top, dao back and sides, wood Padouk soundhole inlay, 14/20-fret rosewood fingerboard with abalone dot inlay, Mushroom buttons, pickup, electronics, chrome hardware, Natural Satin finish, disc. 2005.

| | N/A | $240 - 290 | $150 - 190 | $639 |

GAE-15 – single cutaway Grand Auditorium style, solid cedar top, dao back and sides, wood Crafter soundhole inlay, 14/20-fret rosewood fingerboard with wood snowdrop inlays, Mushroom buttons, pickup, electronics, chrome hardware, Natural Satin finish, current mfg.

| MSR $849 | $600 | $350 - 425 | $225 - 275 | |

* Add 2.5% (MSR $869) for left-handed configuration.

GAE-33 – single cutaway Grand Auditorium style, solid Englemann spruce top, quilted maple back and sides, abalone body binding, Crafter soundhole inlay, 14/20-fret rosewood fingerboard with abalone elegant design inlays, Mushroom buttons, pickup, electronics, gold hardware, Natural Gloss finish, current mfg.

| MSR $1,259 | $875 | $500 - 575 | $300 - 375 | |

GAE-36 – single cutaway Grand Auditorium style, solid Englemann spruce top, rosewood back and sides, abalone body binding, Crafter soundhole inlay, 14/20-fret rosewood fingerboard with abalone hexagon inlays, Mushroom buttons, pickup, electronics, gold hardware, Natural Gloss finish, current mfg.

| MSR $1,349 | $950 | $575 - 650 | $350 - 425 | |

GAE-45 – single cutaway Grand Auditorium style, solid Englemann spruce top, rosewood back and sides, abalone body binding, Tree of Life soundhole inlay, 14/20-fret rosewood fingerboard with abalone Tree of Life inlays, Mushroom buttons, pickup, electronics, gold hardware, Natural Gloss finish, current mfg.

| MSR $1,479 | $1,050 | $600 - 700 | $375 - 450 | |

GAE-648 – single cutaway Grand Auditorium style, solid Sitka spruce or cedar top, South American rosewood back and sides, tortoise body binding, abalone soundhole inlay, 14/20-fret rosewood fingerboard with abalone dot inlays, Mushroom buttons, pickup, electronics, chrome hardware, Natural Gloss finish, disc. 2005.

| | N/A | $300 - 350 | $175 - 225 | $799 |

GCL-80 – single cutaway Grand Auditorium style, Tiger maple top, maple back and sides, white body binding, white rosette, 14/20-fret rosewood fingerboard with dot inlays, pickup, electronics, chrome hardware, available in Black Sunburst, Brown Sunburst, Marine Blue Sunburst, Purple Sunburst, Red Sunburst, or Tobacco Sunburst finish, current mfg.

| MSR $759 | $525 | $300 - 350 | $175 - 225 | |

TGAE-06 – single cutaway Grand Auditorium style, solid Englemann spruce top, solid mahogany back, mahogany sides, abalone body binding, wood mosaic soundhole inlay, 14/20-fret rosewood fingerboard with abalone dot inlays, Mushroom buttons, pickup, electronics, chrome hardware, Natural Satin finish, disc. 2005.

| | N/A | $290 - 340 | $175 - 225 | $769 |

TV-200 – auditorium body style, solid Englemann spruce top, scalloped T-bracing, solid mahogany back and sides, herringbone rosette, top and back body binding, 20-fret rosewood fingerboard with MOP dot inlays, three-per-side deluxe chrome tuners with mushroom buttons, rosewood bridge, Satin Natural finish, mfg. 2006-09.

| | N/A | $350 - 425 | $225 - 275 | $849 |

* *TV-200CEQ Cutaway Electric* – similar to the TV-200, except has a single cutaway and L.R. Baggs pickup and electronics, mfg. 2006-09.

| | N/A | $475 - 550 | $275 - 325 | $1,109 |

TV-250 – auditorium body style, solid Englemann spruce top, scalloped T-bracing, solid maple back and sides, herringbone rosette, top and back body binding, 14/20-fret rosewood fingerboard with MOP dot inlays, three-per-side deluxe chrome tuners with mushroom buttons, rosewood bridge, Vintage Sunburst gloss finish, mfg. 2007-09.

| | N/A | $350 - 425 | $220 - 270 | $899 |

* *TV-250CEQ Cutaway Electric* – similar to the TV-250, except has a single cutaway and L.R. Baggs pickup and electronics, mfg. 2007-09.

| | N/A | $500 - 575 | $300 - 350 | $1,159 |

TV-300 – auditorium body style, solid Englemann spruce top, scalloped T-bracing, solid Indian rosewood back and sides, herringbone rosette, top and back body binding, 14/20-fret rosewood fingerboard with MOP dot inlays, three-per-side deluxe chrome tuners with mushroom buttons, rosewood bridge, Natural gloss finish, mfg. 2007-09.

| | N/A | $400 - 475 | $250 - 300 | $979 |

MSR/NOTES	100%	EXCELLENT	AVERAGE	LAST MSR

* **TV-300CEQ Cutaway Electric** – similar to the TV-300, except has a single cutaway and L.R. Baggs pickup and electronics, mfg. 2007-09.

	N/A	$525 - 600	$325 - 400	$1,239

ACOUSTIC: CLASSICAL MODELS

C-6 – classical style, solid Sitka spruce top, mahogany back and sides, slotted headstock, gold hardware, Natural Satin finish, current mfg.

An example of a C-6 courtesy Crafter

MSR $409	$290	$150 - 200	$95 - 120	

C-18 – classical style body, solid cedar top, rosewood back and sides, satin finish, mfg. 2003-present.

MSR $629	$440	$250 - 300	$150 - 190	

CE-15 – single cutaway classical style, solid cedar top, wood soundhole inlays, dao back and sides, slotted headstock, chrome hardware, Mushroom tuner buttons, pickup, electronics, Natural Satin finish, current mfg.

MSR $779	$550	$300 - 350	$190 - 225	

CE-24 – classical body, solid Englemann spruce top, rosewood back and sides, mfg. 2003-05.

	N/A	$250 - 300	$140 - 180	$729

ACOUSTIC: DREADNOUGHT MODELS

D-6 – dreadnought style body, solid Sitka spruce top, mahogany back and sides, die-cast tuners, satin finish, current mfg.

MSR $419	$300	$150 - 200	$95 - 120	

* **DE-6** – similar to the D-6, except has a single cutaway and Timber Plus electronics, current mfg.

MSR $639	$450	$250 - 300	$150 - 185	

D-7 – dreadnought style body, solid cedar top, mahogany back and sides, Mushroom chrome tuners, current mfg.

MSR $469	$330	$160 - 210	$110 - 135	

* **DE-7** – similar to the D-7, except has a single cutaway and electronics, current mfg.

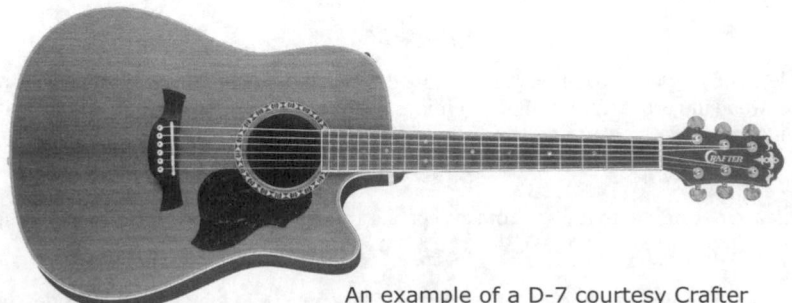

An example of a D-7 courtesy Crafter

MSR $709	$500	$275 - 325	$165 - 200	

D-8 – dreadnought style body, solid Engelmann spruce top, mahogany back and sides, Mushroom chrome tuners, available in Natural or Tobacco Sunburst finish, current mfg.

MSR $529	$370	$190 - 240	$125 - 150	

   • Add 5% (MSR $549) for Tobacco Sunburst finish.
   • Add 5% (MSR $569) for left-handed configuration.

* **D-8-12 12-String** – similar to the D-8, except in 12-string configuration, six-per-side tuners, current mfg.

MSR $639	$450	$240 - 290	$160 - 195	

MSR/NOTES	100%	EXCELLENT	AVERAGE	LAST MSR
* **DE-8** – similar to the D-8, except has a single cutaway and electronics, current mfg.				
MSR $749	$525	$300 - 350	$175 - 225	
»**DE-8-12 12-String** – similar to the D-8-12, except has a pickup and electronics, current mfg.				
MSR $769	$540	$300 - 375	$175 - 225	
D-18 – dreadnought style body, solid cedar top, rosewood back and sides, wood inlay, Grover tuners, disc. 2004.				
	N/A	$215 - 265	$135 - 175	$519
D-30 – dreadnought style body, solid Engelmann spruce top, brown tiger maple back and sides, gold Grover tuners, disc. 2004.				
	N/A	$325 - 375	$200 - 250	$765
* **DE-30** – similar to the D-30, except has a single cutaway and electronics, disc. 2005.				
	N/A	$350 - 425	$225 - 275	$949
D-45 – dreadnought body style, solid Englemann spruce top, rosewood back and sides, abalone body binding, tree-of-life rosette, rosewood fingerboard with tree-of-life inlays, three-per-side Deluxe gold tuners with mushroom buttons, Natural finish, disc. 2009.				
	N/A	$475 - 550	$300 - 375	$1,239
DV-200 – dreadnought body style, solid Englemann spruce top, scalloped T-bracing, solid mahogany back and sides, herringbone rosette, top and back body binding, 20-fret rosewood fingerboard with MOP dot inlays, three-per-side deluxe chrome tuners with mushroom buttons, rosewood bridge, tortoise pickguard, Satin Natural finish, mfg. 2006-09.				
	N/A	$325 - 400	$210 - 250	$849
* **DV-200CEQ Cutaway Electric** – similar to the DV-200, except has a single cutaway and L.R. Baggs pickup and electronics, mfg. 2006-09.				
	N/A	$425 - 500	$275 - 325	$1,099
DV-250 – dreadnought body style, solid Englemann spruce top, scalloped T-bracing, solid maple back and sides, herringbone rosette, top and back body binding, 14/20-fret rosewood fingerboard with MOP dot inlays, three-per-side deluxe chrome tuners with mushroom buttons, rosewood bridge, tortoise pickguard, Vintage Sunburst gloss finish, mfg. 2007-present.				
MSR $899	$630	$340 - 410	$225 - 270	
* **DV-250CEQ Cutaway Electric** – similar to the DV-250, except has a single cutaway and L.R. Baggs pickup and electronics, mfg. 2007-present.				
MSR $1,159	$810	$450 - 525	$275 - 325	
DV-300 – dreadnought body style, solid Englemann spruce top, scalloped T-bracing, solid Indian rosewood back and sides, herringbone rosette, top and back body binding, 14/20-fret rosewood fingerboard with MOP dot inlays, three-per-side deluxe chrome tuners with mushroom buttons, rosewood bridge, tortoise pickguard, Natural gloss finish, mfg. 2007-09.				
	N/A	$375 - 450	$250 - 300	$979
* **DV-300CEQ Cutaway Electric** – similar to the DV-300, except has a single cutaway and L.R. Baggs pickup and electronics, mfg. 2007-09.				
	N/A	$475 - 550	$300 - 350	$1,249
MD-35 – dreadnought body style, spruce top, mahogany back and sides, die-cast tuners, disc. 2004				
	N/A	$125 - 150	$75 - 100	$299
MD-50 – dreadnought-style body, spruce top, bubinga back and sides, die-cast tuners, disc. 2004.				
	N/A	$120 - 160	$70 - 90	$339
* **MD-50-12 12-String** – similar to the MD-50, except in 12-string configuration with six-per-side tuners, disc. 2009.				
	N/A	$150 - 200	$95 - 120	$449
MD-60 – dreadnought body style, tiger maple top, ash back and sides, mahogany neck, rosewood fingerboard with dot position markers, rosewood bridge, disc.				
	N/A	$150 - 190	$105 - 135	$369
MD-80-12 – dreadnought style body, 12-string configuration, solid Sitka spruce top, mahogany back and sides, chrome die-cast tuners, disc. 2004.				
	N/A	$175 - 225	$125 - 150	$429
MD-220-OS – dreadnought-style body, quilted maple top, back and sides, abalone soundhole, gold die-cast tuners, disc. 2004.				
	N/A	$225 - 275	$140 - 180	$529

MSR/NOTES	100%	EXCELLENT	AVERAGE	LAST MSR

SD-008 – dreadnought style, solid Englemann spruce top, solid mahogany back and sides, maple wood body binding, wood Crafter rosette, 14/20-fret rosewood fingerboard with wood inlays, Mushroom buttons, chrome hardware, Natural finish, disc. 2005.

	N/A	$375 - 450	$225 - 275	$979

SD-0038 – dreadnought body, Englemann solid spruce top, solid rosewood back and sides, mfg. 2003-04.

	N/A	$450 - 525	$350 - 400	$1,059

* SDE-0038 – similar to the SD-0038, except has a single cutaway and electronics, disc. 2005.

	N/A	$475 - 550	$300 - 350	$1,279

SGA008N – grand auditorium, Englemann solid spruce top, solid rosewood back and sides, mfg. 2003-05.

	N/A	$450 - 525	$350 - 400	$1,059

TD-06 – dreadnought-style body, Englemann solid spruce top, mahogany solid back, wooden mosaic soundhole and abalone inlay, electronics, disc. 2005.

	N/A	$325 - 375	$200 - 250	$729

ACOUSTIC: JUMBO, SOUTHERN JUMBO, AND FOLK MODELS

FE-12 – single cutaway small jumbo style, solid Sitka spruce top, dao back and sides, white binding, wood Padouck soundhole inlay, 14/20-fret rosewood fingerboard with tiny abalone dot inlays, Mushroom buttons, rosewood bridge, pickup, electronics, chrome hardware, available in Natural Satin finish, disc. 2005.

	N/A	$250 - 300	$140 - 180	$679

FE-27 – single cutaway small jumbo style, solid Sitka spruce top, South African rosewood back and sides, white binding, wood Crafter soundhole inlay, 14/21-fret rosewood fingerboard with wood tree-of-life inlays, Mushroom buttons, rosewood bridge, pickup, electronics, gold hardware, Natural Gloss finish, disc. 2005.

	N/A	$325 - 400	$200 - 250	$879

J-30-12 12-STRING – 12-string configuration jumbo style, solid Sitka spruce top, abalone Crafter soundhole inlay, Tiger maple back and sides, abalone body binding, 14/20-fret rosewood fingerboard with elegant abalone inlays, Mushroom buttons, rosewood bridge, gold hardware, Natural Gloss finish, current mfg.

MSR $1,029	$720	$400 - 475	$250 - 300	

JE-18 – single cutaway jumbo style, solid cedar top, wood Crafter soundhole inlay, rosewood back and sides, 14/20-fret rosewood fingerboard with elegant wood inlays, Mushroom buttons, rosewood bridge, pickup, electronics, chrome hardware, Natural Satin finish, current mfg.

MSR $899	$630	$325 - 400	$220 - 270	

JM-180 – Southern Jumbo style, spruce top, mahogany back and sides, white binding, 14/20-fret rosewood fingerboard with dot inlay, rosewood bridge, pickguard, chrome hardware, Violin Sunburst Vintage Gloss finish, disc. 2005.

	N/A	$135 - 175	$80 - 100	$359

JM-250 – Southern Jumbo style, solid Sitka spruce top, mahogany back and sides, white binding, 14/20-fret rosewood fingerboard with dot inlay, rosewood bridge, pickguard, chrome hardware, available in Natural or Violin Sunburst Vintage Gloss finish, current mfg.

MSR $519	$360	$190 - 240	$125 - 150	

• **Add 2.5% (MSR $509) for Violin Sunburst finish.**

SE-15 – single cutaway small jumbo style, solid cedar top, dao back and sides, white binding, wood Crafter soundhole inlay, 14/20-fret rosewood fingerboard with abalone snowdrop inlays, Mushroom buttons, rosewood bridge, pickup, electronics, chrome hardware, available in Natural Satin finish, disc. 2005.

	N/A	$275 - 325	$150 - 200	$699

T-035 – folk size body, Englemann solid spruce top, mahogany back and sides, mfg. 2003-present.

MSR $519	$370	$190 - 240	$125 - 150	

* TC-035 – similar to the T-035, except has a single cutaway, pickup, and electronics, current mfg.

MSR $729	$510	$300 - 350	$175 - 225	

TA-050 – concert-style body, Englemann solid spruce top, mahogany back and sides, available in Amber Gloss or Natural Gloss finish, mfg. 2003-present.

MSR $769	$540	$300 - 375	$190 - 225	

TA-070 – concert-style body, Englemann solid spruce top, mahogany back and sides, herringbone body and soundhole binding, open-style tuners, available in Natural satin finish, mfg. 2007-09.

	N/A	$300 - 375	$190 - 225	$769

TA-080 – concert-style body, Englemann solid spruce top, rosewood back and sides, abalone purfling and soundhole rosette, MOP diamond and oval fingerboard inlays, bound headstock, open-style tuners, available in Natural gloss finish, mfg. 2007-present.

MSR $809	$570	$325 - 400	$200 - 250	

MSR/NOTES	100%	EXCELLENT	AVERAGE	LAST MSR

TCL-70 – slim single cutaway folk style body, Tiger maple top, maple back and sides, 14/21-fret rosewood fingerboard with dot inlay, matching headstock, rosewood bridge, chrome hardware, available in Black Sunburst, Brown Sunburst, Marine Blue Sunburst, Purple Sunburst, Red Sunburst, or Tobacco Suburst finish, disc. 2005.

	N/A	$225 - 275	$135 - 175	$599

TR-060 – Southern Jumbo style, solid Sitka spruce top, rosewood back and sides, abalone binding, wide neck,12/20-fret rosewood fingerboard with snowdrop inlays, slotted headstock, rosewood bridge, pickguard, chrome hardware, available in Violin Sunburst Vintage Gloss finish, current mfg.

MSR $829	$580	$325 - 400	$200 - 250	

ACOUSTIC: LIMITED EDITION SERIES

ML-BUBINGA – single cutaway body, Englemann solid spruce top, Moon Light soundhole inlay, bubinga back and sides, 14/21-fret rosewood fingerboard with Moon Light inlays, Mushroom buttons, rosewood bridge, pickup, electronics, chrome hardware, Natural Gloss finish, disc. 2010.

	$675	$360 - 430	$240 - 290	$959

* **ML-Rose** – similar to the ML-Bubinga, except has rosewood back and sides, disc. 2010.

	$775	$425 - 500	$275 - 325	$1,099

PK-BUBINGA – single cutaway body, Englemann solid spruce top, scalloped T-bracing, peacock tail wood soundhole inlay, bubinga back and sides, 14/21-fret rosewood fingerboard with peacock inlays, three-per-side deluxe chrome tuners with Mushroom buttons, rosewood bridge, pickup, electronics, clear pickguard, Natural Gloss finish, mfg. 2006-09.

	N/A	$375 - 450	$250 - 300	$999

* **PK-Rose** – similar to the PK-Bubinga, except has rosewood back and sides, mfg. 2006-2010.

	$825	$450 - 525	$300 - 350	$1,199

SM-BUBINGA – single cutaway body, Englemann solid spruce top, wavy soundhole inlay, bubinga back and sides, 14/21-fret rosewood fingerboard with dot and salmon wood inlays, three-per-side deluxe chrome tuners with Mushroom buttons, rosewood bridge, pickup, L.R. Baggs pickup and electronics, Natural Gloss finish, mfg. 2007-09.

	N/A	$375 - 450	$250 - 300	$1,019

* **SM-Rose** – similar to the SM-Bubinga, except has rosewood back and sides and abalone body binding and figerboard inlays, mfg. 2007-present.

MSR $1,199	$840	$450 - 525	$300 - 350	

TB-BUBINGA – single cutaway body, Englemann solid spruce top, bird soundhole inlay, bubinga back and sides, 14/21-fret rosewood fingerboard with bird inlays, Mushroom buttons, rosewood bridge, pickup, electronics, chrome hardware, Natural Satin finish, disc. 2010.

	$700	$375 - 450	$250 - 300	$999

* **TB-Rose** – similar to the TB-Bubinga, except has rosewood back and sides, disc. 2010.

	$825	$450 - 525	$300 - 350	$1,179

WD-BUBINGA – single cutaway Grand Auditorium body, solid Englemann spruce top, bubinga back and sides, wood deer soundhole inlay, 14/21-fret rosewood fingerboard with wood deer inlays, three-per-side deluxe chrome tuners with Mushroom buttons, rosewood bridge, pickup, L.R. Baggs pickup and electronics, Natural Gloss finish, mfg. 2008-09.

	N/A	$375 - 450	$250 - 300	$1,029

* **WD-Rose** – similar to the WD-Bubinga, except has rosewood back and sides, abalone body binding and figerboard inlays, and gold tuners, mfg. 2008-09.

	N/A	$450 - 525	$300 - 350	$1,199

WS-BUBINGA – single cutaway body, Englemann solid spruce top, wind surfer soundhole inlay, bubinga back and sides, 14/21-fret rosewood fingerboard with wind surfer inlays, three-per-side deluxe chrome tuners with Mushroom buttons, rosewood bridge, pickup, electronics, chrome hardware, Natural Gloss finish, mfg. 2006 only.

	N/A	$375 - 450	$200 - 250	$949

* **WS-Rose** – similar to the WS-Bubinga, except has rosewood back and sides, mfg. 2006 only.

	N/A	$425 - 500	$250 - 300	$1,075

ACOUSTIC: LITE SERIES

LITE-C – classical body, solid cedar or spruce top, mahogany back and sides, plain body binding and rosette, 12/19-fret rosewood fingerboard, slotted headstock with three-per-side open-style chrome tuners, rosewood bridge, Open Pore Mat Natural finish, mfg. 2007-2010.

	$280	$140 - 180	$90 - 110	$349

* **Lite-CE Cutaway Electric** – similar to the Lite-C, except has a single cutaway and Crafter pickup and electronics, mfg. 2007-present.

MSR $569	$400	$200 - 250	$120 - 150	

MSR/NOTES	100%	EXCELLENT	AVERAGE	LAST MSR

»*Lite-SCE Cutaway Electric* – similar to the Lite-CE Cutaway Electric, except has a solid spruce top, mfg. 2008-present.

| MSR $569 | $400 | $200 - 250 | $120 - 150 | |

LITE-D – dreadnought body, solid cedar or spruce top, mahogany back and sides, plain body binding and rosette, 14/20-fret rosewood fingerboard with dot inlay, three-per-side chrome tuners, rosewood bridge, black pickguard, Open Pore Mat Natural finish, mfg. summer 2005-present.

| MSR $369 | $260 | $130 - 170 | $90 - 110 | |

* Add 5% (Last MSR was $369) for left-handed configuration (disc. 2007).

* *Lite-DE Cutaway Electric* – similar to the Lite-D, except has a single cutaway and Crafter pickup and electronics, mfg. summer 2005-07, 2009-present.

| MSR $569 | $400 | $200 - 250 | $120 - 150 | |

LITE-T – orchestra body, solid cedar or spruce top, mahogany back and sides, plain body binding and rosette, 14/20-fret rosewood fingerboard with dot inlay, three-per-side chrome tuners, rosewood bridge, black pickguard, Open Pore Mat Natural finish, mfg. summer 2005-present.

| MSR $369 | $260 | $130 - 170 | $90 - 110 | |

* Add 5% (MSR $389) for left-handed configuration.

* *Lite-TE Cutaway Electric* – similar to the Lite-T, except has a single cutaway and Crafter pickup and electronics, mfg. summer 2005-present.

| MSR $539 | $380 | $190 - 240 | $125 - 150 | |

* Add 5% (MSR $569) for left-handed configuration.

LITE-TRV TRAVEL GUITAR – small body, solid Sitka spruce top, mahogany back and sides, plain body binding and rosette, 14/20-fret rosewood fingerboard with dot inlay, three-per-side chrome tuners, rosewood bridge, Open Pore Mat Natural finish, 22.75 in. scale, mfg. summer 2005-present.

| MSR $419 | $300 | $145 - 185 | $100 - 120 | |

ACOUSTIC: SOLID WOOD SERIES

DLX-2500 – dreadnought body style, solid Englemann spruce top, solid mahogany back and sides, tiger maple body binding, abalone rosette, tiger maple bound rosewood fingerboard abalone dot and 12th fret design inlays, three-per-side gold tuners, rosewood bridge, Natural gloss finish, 25.5 in. scale, mfg. 2007-09.

| | N/A | $475 - 550 | $300 - 350 | $1,239 |

DLX-3000 – dreadnought body style, solid Englemann spruce top, solid bubinga, Ovangkol (2008-present), Indonesian SK rosewood, or regular rosewood back and sides, tiger maple body binding, abalone rosette, tiger maple bound rosewood fingerboard abalone dot and 12th fret design inlays, three-per-side gold tuners, rosewood bridge, Natural gloss finish, 25.5 in. scale, mfg. 2007-present.

| MSR $1,459 | $1,025 | $550 - 650 | $325 - 400 | |

DLX-4000 – dreadnought body style, solid German spruce top, solid Indonesian SK rosewood or regular rosewood back and sides, Indonesian SK rosewood body binding, abalone fire rosette, one-piece mahogany neck, 14/20-fret Indonesian SK rosewood bound ebony fingerboard with abalone fire inlays, three-per-side gold tuners, ebony bridge, Natural gloss finish, 25.5 in. scale, mfg. 2008-present.

| MSR $1,579 | $1,100 | $600 - 700 | $400 - 475 | |

GLXE-2500 – single cutaway grand auditorium body style, solid Englemann spruce top, solid mahogany back and sides, tiger maple body binding, abalone rosette, tiger maple bound rosewood fingerboard abalone dot and 12th fret design inlays, three-per-side gold tuners, rosewood bridge, L.R. Baggs Element pickup and electronics, Natural gloss finish, 25.5 in. scale, mfg. 2007-09.

| | N/A | $625 - 725 | $400 - 475 | $1,599 |

GLXE-3000 – single cutaway grand auditorium body style, solid Englemann spruce top, solid bubinga, Ovangkol (2008-present), Indonesian SK rosewood, or regular rosewood back and sides, tiger maple body binding, abalone rosette, tiger maple bound rosewood fingerboard abalone dot and 12th fret design inlays, three-per-side gold tuners, rosewood bridge, L.R. Baggs Element pickup and electronics, Natural gloss finish, 25.5 in. scale, mfg. 2007-present.

| MSR $1,799 | $1,260 | $675 - 800 | $425 - 500 | |

GLXE-4000 – single cutaway grand concert body style, solid German spruce top, solid Indonesian SK rosewood or regular rosewood back and sides, Indonesian SK rosewood body binding, abalone fire rosette, one-piece mahogany neck, 14/20-fret Indonesian SK rosewood bound ebony fingerboard with abalone fire inlays, three-per-side gold tuners, ebony bridge, L.R. Baggs Element pickup and electronics, Natural gloss finish, 25.5 in. scale, mfg. 2008-present.

| MSR $1,869 | $1,310 | $725 - 850 | $475 - 550 | |

ACOUSTIC: VINTAGE CLASSICS

Other Vintage Classic models were produced in 2005: the **Oakland 55** (Last MSR $659), the **Monroe 77** (Last MSR $729), and the **Key West 99** (Last MSR $989).

MSR/NOTES	100%	EXCELLENT	AVERAGE	LAST MSR

RICHMOND 88 – single cutaway dreadnought or grand auditorium body style, solid Sitka spruce top, tiger maple back and sides, abalone binding and rosette, 14/21-fret bound rosewood fingerboard with MOP dot inlays, bound headstock with three-per-side Antique tuners, rosewood bridge, clear pickguard, L.R. Baggs pickup and electronics, available in Gloss Sunburst finish, mfg. summer 2005-06.

	N/A	$300 - 350	$175 - 225	$869

ACOUSTIC: MISC. MODELS

AGE-100MH – single cutaway small jumbo-style body, spruce top, mahogany arched back, mahogany sides, round soundhole with abalone rosette, multi-ply body binding, mahogany neck, 14/21-fret Indonesian rosewood fingerboard with abalone inlays, three-per-side chrome tuners, Indonesian rosewood bridge, CR-T DV electronics, available in Black, Natural, or Three-Tone Sunburst finish, 25.5 in. scale, mfg. 2008-present.

MSR $689	$480	$275 - 325	$150 - 200	

AGE-500TM – single cutaway small jumbo-style body, tiger maple top, tiger maple arched back, tiger maple sides, round soundhole with abalone rosette, multi-ply body binding, mahogany neck, 14/21-fret Indonesian rosewood fingerboard with abalone inlays, matching finish headstock, three-per-side chrome tuners, Indonesian rosewood bridge, CR-T DV electronics, available in Marine Sunburst, Orange Sunburst, or Vintage Sunburst finish, 25.5 in. scale, mfg. 2008-present.

MSR $799	$560	$300 - 375	$175 - 225	

ATE70CEQ – arched top body, tiger maple top, maple back and sides, disc. 2004.

	N/A	$225 - 275	$135 - 175	$559

* **ATE70CEQ-LH** – similar to the ATE70CEQ except is in left-handed configuration, disc. 2004.

	N/A	$225 - 275	$135 - 175	$569

ATE100CEQ – arched top body, tiger maple top, back, and sides, disc. 2004.

	N/A	$300 - 350	$175 - 225	$699

CUTE – single cutaway grand auditorium body style, spruce top with T-bracing, maple back and sides, multi-ply body binding, abalone rosette, 14/20-fret bound rosewood fingerboard with abalone dot and 12th fret design inlays, matching finish headstock with three-per-side chrome tuners, rosewood bridge, L.R. Baggs Element pickup and LR-T Pro preamp, available in Black, Marine Blue Sunburst, Pink, Purple, or Tobacco Sunburst finish, mfg. 2007 only.

	N/A	$265 - 315	$175 - 210	$699

ED155EQ-TB – dreadnought body, quilted maple top, bubinga back and sides, disc. 2004.

	N/A	$225 - 275	$135 - 175	$549

SE33 – Englemann solid spruce top, quilted maple back and sides, gold Grover tuners, EMF preamp, disc. 2004.

	N/A	$450 - 525	$250 - 300	$995

SN285EQ – ultra slim classical body, spruce top, mahogany back and sides, disc. 2004.

	N/A	$200 - 250	$130 - 170	$479

TM-035 – orchestra-style body, solid Englemann spruce top, rosewood back and sides, round soundhole with abalone pearl rosette, multi-ply binding, mahogany neck, 14/21-fret bound Indonesian rosewood fingerboard with MOP snowflake inlays, slotted headstock, three-per-side open-style chrome tuners, Indonesian rosewood bridge, tortoise pickguard, CR-T DV electronics, available in Natural finish, 25.5 in. scale, mfg. 2008-present.

MSR $689	$480	$275 - 325	$150 - 200	

* **TMC-035 Cutaway** – similar to the TM-035, except has a single cutaway, mfg. 2008-present.

MSR $899	$630	$350 - 425	$200 - 250	

TM-045 – orchestra-style body, solid Englemann spruce top, rosewood back and sides, round soundhole with abalone pearl rosette, multi-ply binding, abalone purfling, mahogany neck, 14/21-fret bound Indonesian rosewood fingerboard with abalone hexagon inlays, slotted headstock, three-per-side open-style chrome tuners, Indonesian rosewood bridge, tortoise pickguard, CR-T DV electronics, available in Natural finish, 25.5 in. scale, mfg. 2008-present.

MSR $819	$575	$300 - 375	$175 - 225	

* **TMC-045 Cutaway** – similar to the TM-045, except has a single cutaway, mfg. 2008-present.

MSR $1,039	$725	$400 - 475	$250 - 300	

TRV23 TRAVEL GUITAR – single cutaway small body, solid Sitka spruce or solid cedar top, mahogany back and sides, top binding, rosette, 20-fret fingerboard with dot inlay, three-per-side chrome tuners, available in Gloss Black or Satin Natural finish, 22.75 in. scale, travel bag included, mfg. 2004-present.

MSR $469	$330	$165 - 215	$110 - 130	

• Add 5% (MSR $479) for left-handed configuration.

* **TRV23 Electric Travel Guitar** – similar to the TRV23 Travel Guitar, except has built-in electronics, mfg. 2008-present.

MSR $599	$420	$240 - 290	$150 - 190	

MSR/NOTES	100%	EXCELLENT	AVERAGE	LAST MSR

ACOUSTIC ELECTRIC: FIBERGLASS BACK MODELS

FSG250 – spruce top, single cutaway, shadow pickup, PR-40 Passive Slide controls, available in Natural or Sunburst, disc. 2004.

	N/A	$150 - 200	$95 - 120	$429

FA820-EQ – Ashwood top, single cutaway, shadow pickup, P4 Preamp, Dark Brown Sunburst, disc. 2004.

	N/A	$175 - 225	$105 - 135	$489

FSG260EQ-BK – spruce top, single cutaway, shadow pickup, P4 Preamp, Black finish, disc. 2004.

	N/A	$175 - 225	$105 - 135	$499

FX550 – ashwood top, single cutaway, shadow pickup, P4 Preamp, available in Trans. Blue or Trans. Red finishes, disc. 2004.

	N/A	$175 - 225	$105 - 135	$499

FX560EQ – single cutaway folk-style body, ashwood, bubinga, or spruce top, fiberglass bowl back, abalone rosette, top binding, 21-fret rosewood fingerboard with abalone dot inlays, three-per-side chrome tuners, rosewood bridge, L.R. Baggs pickup and electronics, available in Black, Bubinga, Marine Blue Sunburst, Purple Sunburst, or Red Sunburst finish, mfg. 2005-09.

	N/A	$220 - 265	$150 - 175	$599

* Add 5% (Last MSR was $609) for left-handed configuration (disc. 2007).

FA900EQ-TR – quilted maple top, single cutaway, shadow pickup, P4 Preamp, available in Trans. Red finish, disc. 2004.

	N/A	$180 - 230	$110 - 140	$529

ACOUSTIC ELECTRIC: MINI SERIES

The Crafter Mini Series debuted in 1997. The travel-style **Mini RF 30** had a fiberglass back, full-scale mahogany neck and rosewood fingerboard, and a spruce top. The RF 30 was available in Natural, Blue Stain, and Black Stain finishes (last MSR was $299). The acoustic/electric **RF 40 E** has a similar construction, and includes a piezo bridge pickup with volume and tone controls. The RF 40 E (list $339) is available in Green Stain, Purple Stain, and Tobacco Sunburst finishes.

ACOUSTIC ELECTRIC: SA/SAT SLIM ARCH SERIES

SA SLIM ARCH MODEL – single cutaway slim arch body style, acoustic sound chamber, Andes Rosewood, bubinga, or tiger maple top, solid mahogany back and sides, two split bound S-holes, body and fingerboard binding, mahogany neck, 21-fret rosewood fingerboard with dot and 12th fret special MOP inlays, matching headstock with three-per-side chrome tuners, rosewood bridge, one exposed Kent Armstrong lipstick pickup, and an L.R. Baggs acoustic pickup, L.R. Baggs electronics with acoustic/electric blending, available in Natural, Sunburst, or Trans. Black finish, mfg. 2006-present.

MSR $939	$650	$350 - 425	$235 - 285	

* Add 2.5% (MSR $959) for left-handed configuration.

*** SA Slim Arch Model 12-String** – similar to the SA Slim Arch Model (Tiger Maple), except in 12-string configuration and six-per-side tuners, available in Trans. Black finish, mfg. 2006-09.

	N/A	$380 - 460	$250 - 300	$1,019

*** SAC Slim Arch Model Nylon String** – similar to the SA Slim Arch Model (Tiger Maple), except in nylon-string configuration, no fingerboard inlays, a slotted headstock with three-per-side open-style tuners, no exposed pickup, and an L.R. Baggs Element piezo pickup and electronics, available in Violin Sunburst finish, mfg. 2007-09.

	N/A	$325 - 375	$220 - 270	$869

*** SA Slim Arch Model Quilted Maple** – similar to the SA Slim Arch Model, except has a quilted maple top and quilted maple headstock veneer, available in Marine Blue Sunburst or Orange Sunburst finish, mfg. 2007-present.

MSR $959	$675	$360 - 430	$240 - 290	

*** SA Slim Arch Model Spruce** – similar to the SA Slim Arch Model, except has a spruce top and spruce headstock veneer, available in Black or Ivory finish, mfg. 2007-09.

	N/A	$375 - 450	$250 - 300	$989

SAT-M SLIM ARCH MODEL – single cutaway slim arch body style, acoustic sound chamber, arched spruce top, solid wood back and sides, two split bound S-holes, body and fingerboard binding, mahogany neck, 21-fret rosewood fingerboard with dot and 12th fret special MOP inlays, black headstock overlay, three-per-side chrome tuners, rosewood bridge, one exposed Kent Armstrong P-90 pickup, and an L.R. Baggs acoustic pickup, L.R. Baggs electronics with acoustic/electric blending, four knobs on lower treble bout (two v, two tone), available in Blue, Gold, or Silver finish, 25.5 in. scale, mfg. 2008-present.

MSR $1,039	$725	$400 - 475	$250 - 300	

*** SAT-TM/QM Tiger Maple/Quilted Maple Slim Arch Model** – similar to the SAT-M, except has tiger maple or quilted maple top, available in Marine Sunburst (quilted maple), Trans. Black (tiger maple), or Vintage Sunburst (quilted maple) finish, 25.5 in. scale, mfg. 2008-present.

MSR $1,039	$725	$400 - 475	$250 - 300	

* Add 5% (MSR $1,049) for left-handed configuration.

MSR/NOTES	100%	EXCELLENT	AVERAGE	LAST MSR

»SAT-12 TM 12-String Tiger Maple Slim Arch Model – similar to the SAT-TM/QM Tiger Maple/Quilted Maple Slim Arch Model, except in 12-string configuration, available in Trans. Black finish (tiger maple), 25.5 in. scale, mfg. 2008-present.

MSR $1,099	$775	$425 - 500	$275 - 325	

ACOUSTIC ELECTRIC: SUPER JUMBO SERIES

The **SJC 330 EQ** Super Jumbo had a spruce top, and was available in a Tobacco Sunburst finish (last MSR was $589); the **SJC 390 EQ** (last MSR was $679) had a similar construction design. The **SJ 270** Super Jumbo had a tiger maple top, mahogany back/sides/neck, rosewood fingerboard, and Tobacco Sunburst finish (last MSR was $499).

ACOUSTIC ELECTRIC: THINLINE SERIES

CT-120 – single cutaway thin body, solid Sitka spruce top, CTS brace system, solid wood body, no soundhole, 15/21-fret rosewood fingerboard with dot inlays, rosewood bridge, pickup and electronics, available in Natural Satin or Trans. Blue Gloss finish, current mfg.

MSR $739	$520	$275 - 325	$175 - 210	

* **CT-120-12 12-String** – similar to the CT-120, except in 12-string configuration, six-per-side tuners, disc. 2004.

	N/A	$300 - 350	$175 - 225	$599

CT-125 – single cutaway classical thin body, solid Sitka spruce top, CTS brace system, solid wood body, no soundhole, 15/21-fret rosewood fingerboard with dot inlays, slotted headstock, rosewood bridge, pickup and electronics, available in Black Gloss finish, current mfg.

MSR $749	$525	$275 - 325	$185 - 220	

CTS-150 – single cutaway thin body, solid Sitka spruce top, CTS brace system, solid wood body, wood Crafter soundhole, 15/21-fret rosewood fingerboard with dot inlays, rosewood bridge, pickup and electronics, available in Natural Satin or Trans. Blue Gloss finish, current mfg.

MSR $869	$610	$325 - 400	$210 - 250	

* **CTS-150-12 12-String** – similar to the CTS-150, except in 12-string configuration, six-per-side tuners, available in Natural Satin finish, disc. 2006.

	N/A	$350 - 425	$225 - 275	$769

CTS-155C – single cutaway classical thin body, solid Sitka spruce top, CTS brace system, solid wood body, wood Crafter soundhole, 15/21-fret rosewood fingerboard with dot inlays, rosewood bridge, pickup and electronics, available in Black Gloss finish, current mfg.

MSR $879	$615	$325 - 400	$210 - 250	

ACOUSTIC ELECTRIC BASS

BA-400 EQ – single cutaway bass body, spruce top, white body binding, ashwood back and sides, 15/22-fret rosewood fingerboard with dot inlays, rosewood bridge, pickup, electronics, chrome hardware, Natural Satin finish, current mfg.

MSR $789	$550	$300 - 375	$190 - 225	

- **Add 5% for left-handed configuration.**

Also available in fretless configuration.

BA-550 EQ – single cutaway bass body, quilted maple top, abalone soundhole inlay, white body binding, ashwood back and sides, 15/22-fret rosewood fingerboard with dot inlays, rosewood bridge, pickup, electronics, gold hardware, available in Marine Blue Sunburst Gloss finish, disc. 2007.

	N/A	$340 - 410	$225 - 270	$899

* **BA-580 EQ Five-String** – similar to the BA-550 EQ, except in five-string configuration, 3/2-per-side tuners, available in Trans. Black Sunburst Gloss finish, current mfg.

MSR $949	$675	$350 - 425	$225 - 275	

GAB-24S – single cutaway bass body, solid Sitka spruce top, abalone sunny soundhole inlay, pearloid body binding, rosewood back and sides, 15/22-fret rosewood fingerboard with dot inlays, rosewood bridge, pickup, electronics, gold hardware, Natural Gloss finish, disc. 2005.

	N/A	$300 - 375	$175 - 225	$819

GAB-748 – single cutaway bass body, solid Sitka spruce top, abalone soundhole inlay, tortoise body binding, South American rosewood back and sides, 16/23-fret rosewood fingerboard with abalone dot inlays, two-per-side chrome tuners, rosewood bridge, L.R. Baggs pickup and electronics, Natural Gloss finish, 34 in. scale, mfg. summer 2005-06.

	N/A	$375 - 450	$225 - 275	$949

CRAFTERS OF TENNESSEE

Instruments currently built in Nashville, TN since 1976.

Mark Taylor's company is currently offering a range of high quality acoustic guitars, banjos and resophonic guitars marketed under the Tennessee brand name. These instruments reflect a deep commitment to the players that seek the tone and vibe of the fabled "pre-war" instruments that are so often sought out by players and collectors alike. As the son of internationally acclaimed "flat picking reso man" and collector Tut Taylor, Mark Taylor's Crafters Of Tennessee also offers a premium signature line of Tut Taylor

CONTACT INFORMATION
CRAFTERS OF TENNESSEE
8220 Central Pike
Mt Juliet, TN 37122
Phone No.: 615-553-2459
www.crafterstn.com
mark@crafterstn.com

MSR/NOTES	100%	EXCELLENT	AVERAGE	LAST MSR

Resophonic Guitars. For more information, visit Crafters of Tennessee's website or contact them directly.

ACOUSTICS

Acoustic models are available in three sizes with a dreadnought, 000, and a Studio. All models have standard solid spruce tops. The dreadnought is available with maple (Model TNFMp, MSR $3,649), mahogany (TNFTM, MSR $3,699), or rosewood (TNFTR, MSR $3,899) back and sides. The 000 is available with maple (Model TNMp000, MSR $3,449), mahogany (TNM000, MSR $3,449), or rosewood (TNR000, MSR $3,649) back and sides. The Studio is available with maple (Model TNSMp, MSR $2,999), mahogany (TNSS, MSR $2,899), or rosewood (TNSR, MSR $3,199) back and sides.

RESONATORS

All **Tut Taylor Signature Model** resophonic guitars feature a solid peghead with an ebony overlay, bound ebony fingerboard with intricate abalone inlay, an old-style sound well with parallelogram openings, an aluminum cast and machined spider, and improved design brass cover plate. The 50th Anniversary Tut Taylor (MSR $9,875) was introduced in 2006 and features extremely ornate appointments.

Square neck resophonic guitars include the **Tut Taylor Tennessean** (mahogany, MSR $2,899), the **Tut Taylor Virginian** (AAA curly maple, MSR $3,299), the **Tut Taylor Californian** (walnut, MSR $3,699), the **Tut Taylor Carolina** (spruce top, MSR $3,699) and the **Tennessee Original** (disc., Last MSR was $1,700).

Round neck resophonic models include the **TN-9 Tennessee Blues Resophonic Guitar** (MSR $2,999), the **TN-10M Tennessee Blues Resophonic Guitar** (maple back and sides, MSR $2,999), the **TN-10S Tennessee Blue Resophonic Guitar** (mahogany back and sides, MSR $2,999), and the **TN-10C Custom Tennessee Blues Resophonic Guitar** (MSR $3,495).

- **Add $400 for 24k gold engraving (Deluxe Tut Taylor models).**

CRAFTSMAN

Instruments previously produced in Japan between the late 1970s and mid-1980s.

Craftsman built entry level to medium quality copies of American designs. Source: Tony Bacon and Paul Day, *The Guru's Guitar Guide*.

CRANDALL, TOM

Instruments previously built in Phoenix, AZ, and in Iowa City, IA (circa 1990-2000).

Luthier Tom Crandall built a limited number of flattop and archtop acoustic guitars and also did repairs during the 1990s.

CRESTLINE

Instruments previously built in Japan circa mid- to late 1970s. Distributed by the Grossman Music Corporation in Cleveland, OH.

These entry-level to intermediate solid body guitars featured designs based on classic American favorites. Crestline offered a wide range of stringed instruments, including classical, folk, dreadnought, and twelve-string acoustics; solid body electric guitars and basses; amplifiers; banjos, mandolins, and ukuleles. Considering the amount of instruments available, the Crestline trademark was probably used on guitars built by one of the bigger Japanese guitar producers and rebranded for the U.S. market.

CRESTWOOD

Guitars previously produced in Japan during the 1970s. Distributed by La Playa Distributing Company in Detroit, MI.

The La Playa Distributing Company imported the Crestwood line of acoustic guitars, electric guitars, mandolins, and various other instruments from Japan. Most (if not all) designs were based on popular American designs. The Crestwood trademark is rumored to be in use again on a line of cheap guitars built in China.

For acoustic guitars, Crestwood offered dreadnoughts and classicals and it is possible other variations exist. Today, values are typically between $100 and $250 depending on condition and level of ornateness.

CROMWELL

Instruments previously produced in Kalamazoo, MI by Gibson between circa 1935 and 1939. See chapter on House Brands.

Cromwell was a house brand trademark used on a budget line of guitars that were built by Gibson. These guitars were sold through a few midwestern mail order companies including Grossman, Continental, and Richter & Phillips. These guitars are similar to Gibson standards, but they do lack the truss rod that sets Gibsons with truss rods apart from the brands without. Cromwell branded instruments included acoustic archtops, acoustic flattops, tenor guitars, and mandolins. Source: Walter Carter, *Gibson Guitars: 100 Years of an American Icon*.

ACOUSTIC

ACOUSTIC ARCHTOP MODEL – non-cutaway hollow body, arched spruce top, mahogany back and sides, top and back body binding, two f-holes, mahogany neck with no truss rod, bound fingerboard, three-per-side tuners, bound pickguard, mfg. circa 1935-39.

	100%	EXCELLENT	AVERAGE	
	N/A	$1,200 - 1,500	$850 - 1,000	

CROUCH, JOHN

Guitars currently produced in Mechanicsville, VA.

Luthier John Crouch builds flattop acoustic and archtop guitars in his Mechanicsville, VA shop. Flattops start at $3,000 and archtops start at $4,200. For more information, contact luthier Crouch directly.

CONTACT INFORMATION
CROUCH, JOHN
4539 Market Rd.
Mechanicsville, VA 23113
Phone No.: 804-781-0812

CUMBUS

Instruments currently built in Turkey. Distributed by Lark in the Morning in Fort Bragg, CA.

These instruments are traditional stringed instruments of Turkey, and include the Cumbus twelve-string fretless banjo, twelve-string banjo guitar, Cumbus saz, Cumbus banjo mandolin, and others. See Lark in the Morning for more information.

CONTACT INFORMATION
CUMBUS
Distributed by Lark in the Morning
PO Box 799
Fort Bragg, CA 95437
Phone No.: 877-964-5569
Fax No.: 707-964-1979
www.larkinthemorning.com
support@larkinam.com

CUMPIANO, WILLIAM R.

Instruments currently built in Northampton, MA.

For over twenty-five years, William R. Cumpiano has been making guitars in the North American, European, and Latin American traditions, primarily on a commission basis. Over the years, he has achieved wide recognition in the field for his innovative designs and fine craftsmanship, as well as for having authored the principle textbook (*Guitarmaking: Tradition and Technology*) and for his numerous feature articles in guitar magazines, such as *Acoustic Guitar* and *Guitarmaker*. Cumpiano has supplied custom-made instruments to some of the finest and most prominent guitarists in the United States. Guitars typically sell between $4,500 and $8,500. Cumpiano also has a selection of completed instruments of all kinds in inventory, which he made while he was teaching—an activity which he undertakes several times per year. These completed instruments are unfinished ("in-the-white") and can be tried out before they are finished and delivered. For more information, visit Cumpiano's website or contact him directly. Biographical material courtesy of William R. Cumpiano, September 2014.

CONTACT INFORMATION
CUMPIANO, WILLIAM R.
Factory
8 Easthampton Road
Northampton, MA 01027
Phone No.: 413-586-3730
www.cumpiano.com
william@cumpiano.com

Office
PO Box 854
Easthampton, MA 01027

CUSTOM KRAFT

Guitars previously produced in Chicago, IL during the early 1960s and Japan during the late 1960s. See chapter on House Brands.

This trademark has been identified as a House Brand of St. Louis Music. The St. Louis Music Supply Company was founded in 1922 by Bernard Kornblum, originally as an importer of German violins. The St. Louis, MO-based company has been a distributor, importer, and manufacturer of musical instruments over the past seventy-five years.

In the mid-1950s, St. Louis Music distributed amplifiers and guitars from other producers such as Alamo, Harmony, Kay, Magnatone, Rickenbacker, and Supro. By 1960, the focus was on Harmony, Kay, and Supro: all built "upstream" in Chicago, IL. 1960 was also the year that St. Louis Music began carrying Kay's **Thinline** single cutaway electric guitar.

Custom Kraft was launched in 1961 as St. Louis Music's own House Brand. The first series of semi-hollowbody Custom Kraft **Color Dynamic** Electric guitars were built by Kay, and appear to be Thinline models in Black, Red, and White. In 1963, a line of solid body double cutaway electrics built by Valco were added to the catalog under the Custom Kraft moniker, as well as Kay-built archtop and flattop acoustic.

In 1967, Valco purchased Kay, a deal that managed to sink both companies by 1968. St. Louis Music continued advertising both companies models through 1970, perhaps NOS supplies from their warehouse. St. Louis Music continued to offer Custom Kraft guitars into the early 1970s, but as their sources had dried up so did the trademark name. St. Louis Music's next trademark guitar line was Electra (then followed by Westone, and Alvarez).

Custom Kraft models are generally priced according to the weirdness/coolness factor, so don't be surprised to see the range of prices from $125 up to $450! The uncertainty indicates a buyer-directed market, so if you find one that you like, don't be afraid to haggle over the price. The earlier Kay and Valco built guitars date from the 1960s, while later models were probably built in Japan. Source: Michael Wright, *Vintage Guitar Magazine*.

CYCLONE

Instruments previously produced in Japan.

Cyclone guitars were distributed in the U.S. market by Leban Imports of Baltimore, MD. Source: Michael Wright, *Guitar Stories*, Volume One.

NOTES

D SECTION
D'AGOSTINO

Instruments produced in Italy by the EKO company between 1978 and 1982. After 1982, instruments were produced in Japan (then later Korea). Instrument production was contracted to the EKO custom shop in Milwaukee, WI. Distributed by PMS Music of New York, NY.

Pat D'Agostino (ex-Gibson/Maestro effects) began his own instrument importing company in 1975. The D'Agostino Corporation of New Jersey began importing acoustic dreadnoughts, then introduced the Italian-built Benchmark Series of guitars in 1977. These models featured laminated neck-through designs, two humbuckers and a three-per-side headstock. Production then moved to Korea in the early 1980s, although some better models were built in Japan during the 1990s. Pat, assisted by Steven D'Agostino and Mike Confortti, has always maintained a high quality control level and limited quantities. Used guitars are typically priced between $150 and $250. Source: Michael Wright, *Vintage Guitar Magazine*.

DAIMARU

Instruments previously produced in Japan.

Daimaru guitars were distributed in the U.S. by the Daimaru New York Corporation of New York, NY. Source: Michael Wright, *Guitar Stories*, Volume One.

DAION

Instruments previously built in Nagoya, Japan circa late 1970s through the mid-1980s by Terada Guitars. Some guitars may also carry the trademark of Joodee or Yamaki. Distributed by MCI, Inc. in Waco, TX.

Originally, these Japanese-produced high quality guitars were based on popular U.S. designs in the 1970s, but turned to original designs in the 1980s. The Daion logo was applied to a range of acoustic, semi-hollowbody, and solid body guitars and basses. Some Daion headstocks also feature a stylized lyre.

MSR/NOTES	100%	EXCELLENT	AVERAGE	LAST MSR

ACOUSTIC: HERITAGE SERIES

The Heritage series was Daion's top of the line for acoustic models.

78 DAION HERITAGE – dreadnought style, solid cedar top with hand-stained mahogany finish, hardwood neck, round soundhole, maple binding, mahogany sides/two-piece back, 14/20-fret rosewood fingerboard with brass dot inlay, rosewood bridge with brass saddle, brass nut, rosewood string pins, three-per-side gold plated sealed tuning machines, available in Natural finish, mfg. late 1970s-mid-1980s.

	N/A	$375 - 450	$225 - 275	

* *78/12 Daion Heritage* – similar to the 78 Daion Heritage, except in 12-string configuration, has a slotted headstock and six-per-side tuners, mfg. late 1970s-mid-1980s.

	N/A	$425 - 500	$275 - 325	

79 DAION HERITAGE – similar to the 78 Daion Heritage, except has spruce or solid cedar top and brass binding, available in gloss Black finish, mfg. late 1970s-mid-1980s.

	N/A	$425 - 500	$275 - 325	

80 DAION HERITAGE – dreadnought style, solid spruce top with hand-stained ovangkol facing, nato neck, oval soundhole, maple binding, ovangkol back/sides, 14/20-fret maple bound rosewood fingerboard with brass dot inlay, tortoise pickguard, rosewood bridge with brass saddle, brass nut, maple bound headstock with carved Daion design inlay, rosewood string pins, three-per-side gold plated sealed tuning machines, available in Natural finish, mfg. late 1970s-mid-1980s.

	N/A	$525 - 600	$325 - 400	

ACOUSTIC: MAPLEWOOD SERIES

The Maplewood Series debuted in 1980. The dreadnought-styled MS-100 had a spruce top, maple back/sides/neck/fingerboard, brown dot inlays, sealed tuners, three-on-a-side headstock, and a Natural Blonde finish. The MS-101 was similar, but featured a hand-rubbed Tan finish. A 12-string configuration with slotted headstock and six-on-a-side plate tuners was called the MS-100/12. Reliable market prices for these models are not available.

ACOUSTIC: MARK SERIES

Truss rod access was at the body end of the neck, through the soundhole.

MARK I – dreadnought style, solid cedar top, hardwood neck, round soundhole, black binding, mahogany sides/back, 14/20-fret rosewood fingerboard with white dot inlay, rosewood bridge, rosewood pickguard, three-per-side chrome sealed tuning machines, available in Natural finish, mfg. late 1970s-mid-1980s.

	N/A	$325 - 400	$250 - 300	$255

* *Mark I/12* – similar to the Mark I, except in 12-string configuration, has a slotted headstock, and six-on-a-side tuners, mfg. late 1970s-mid-1980s.

	N/A	$350 - 425	$250 - 300	$290

MSR/NOTES	100%	EXCELLENT	AVERAGE	LAST MSR

MARK II – dreadnought style, solid cedar top, hardwood neck, round soundhole, white binding, redwood sides/two-piece back, 14/20-fret rosewood fingerboard with white dot inlay, rosewood bridge, rosewood pickguard, three-per-side chrome sealed tuning machines, available in Natural finish, mfg. late 1970s-mid-1980s.

	N/A	$325 - 400	$200 - 250	$300

* *Mark II/12* – similar to the Mark II, except in 12-string configuration, has a slotted headstock, and six-on-a-side tuners, mfg. late 1970s-mid-1980s.

	N/A	$350 - 425	$225 - 275	$315

MARK III – dreadnought style, spruce top, maple neck, round soundhole, white binding, maple sides/two-piece back, 14/20-fret maple fingerboard with brown dot inlay, maple bridge, rosewood pickguard, three-per-side chrome sealed tuning machines, available in Natural finish, mfg. late 1970s-mid-1980s.

	N/A	$350 - 425	$225 - 275	$340

* *Mark III/12* – similar to the Mark III, except in 12-string configuration, has a slotted headstock, and six-on-a-side tuners, mfg. late 1970s-mid-1980s.

	N/A	$375 - 450	$250 - 300	$380

MARK IV – dreadnought style, solid cedar top, hardwood neck, round soundhole, black binding, five-layer maple/rosewood soundhole purfling, rosewood sides/two-piece back, 14/20-fret rosewood fingerboard with offset slash inlay, bone nut, rosewood bridge with bone saddle, rosewood pickguard, three-per-side chrome rotomatic tuners, available in Natural finish, mfg. late 1970s-mid-1980s.

	N/A	$375 - 450	$250 - 300	$395

* *Mark IV/12* – similar to the Mark IV, except in 12-string configuration, has a slotted headstock, and six-on-a-side tuners, mfg. late 1970s-mid-1980s.

	N/A	$400 - 475	$275 - 325	$425

MARK V – dreadnought style, solid cedar top, hardwood neck, round soundhole, herringbone binding/soundhole purfling, rosewood sides/two-piece back, 14/20-fret rosewood fingerboard with offset white dot inlay, bone nut, rosewood smile-shaped bridge with bone saddle, rosewood pickguard, three-per-side chrome sealed tuners, available in Natural finish, mfg. late 1970s-mid-1980s.

	N/A	$400 - 475	$275 - 325	$479

* *Mark V/12* – similar to the Mark V, except in 12-string configuration, has a slotted headstock, and six-on-a-side tuners, mfg. late 1970s-mid-1980s.

	N/A	$425 - 500	$300 - 350	$495

DAISY ROCK

Instruments currently produced in China since 2000. Distributed by Alfred Publishing in Van Nuys, CA.

Daisy Rock was founded by Tish Ciravolo in October 2000. Tish created Daisy Rock to make guitars that appealed to girls specifically. In a male-dominated rock 'n roll world, guitars that were sculpted to the female just didn't exist. Being the mother of two girls and playing guitar for many years, she was inspired to create this company. Guitars feature slimmer necks for smaller hands, more light-weight and smaller bodies, and they also have visual features appealing towards women. Originally, Daisy Rock was a division of Schecter Guitar Research, but they are now part of Alfred Publishing who distributes the line exclusively. Hard shell cases and custom guitars are also available. For more information on Daisy Rock and Alfred Publishing, visit their website or contact them directly.

CONTACT INFORMATION
DAISY ROCK
Distributed by Alfred Publishing
16320 Roscoe Blvd Ste #100
Van Nuys, CA 91406
Phone No.: 877-693-2479
Fax No.: 800-632-1928
www.daisyrock.com
info@daisyrock.com

ACOUSTIC: BUTTERFLY SERIES

BUTTERFLY JUMBO ACOUSTIC/ELECTRIC – jumbo-style body, bubinga, spalted maple, zebra wood top, back, and sides, round soundhole with abalone pearl rosette, white binding, multi-layer top purfling, mahogany neck, 14/20-fret bound rosewood fingerboard with 12th fret butterfly inlay, matching finish bubinga or zebra wood headstock overlay with butterfly graphics, three-per-side chrome tuners, butterfly-shaped rosewood bridge, Daisy Rock Custom Piezo System electronics, available in Bubinga Butterfly, Spalted Maple Butterfly, or Zebra Butterfly (all Natural) finish, 25.5 in. scale, gig bag included, mfg. 2008-present.

MSR $480	$350	$200 - 250	$120 - 150

• **Add 7.5% (MSR $500) for Zebra Butterfly or Spalted Maple Butterfly finishes.**

ACOUSTIC: PIXIE SERIES

The Daisy Acoustic is available as the increasingly popular Guitar Pack Set. This includes a gig bag, strap, picks, polishing cloth, string winder, and Girl's Guitar Method book and enhanced CD.

PIXIE ACOUSTIC – composite oval back with spruce top body, mahogany set-neck, 20-fret rosewood fingerboard with pearloid daisy inlay, body binding, matching color headstock with three-per-side tuners, chrome hardware, available in Blue Sparkle (2007-present), Pink Sparkle (2007-present), Pixie Purple, Powder Pink, Silver Sparkle (2007-present), Sky Blue, or Sunny Yellow (2000-07) finish, 24.5 in. scale, mfg. 2000-present.

MSR $260	$200	$110 - 140	$55 - 80

MSR/NOTES	100%	EXCELLENT	AVERAGE	LAST MSR

- Add 10% (MSR $290) for Blue Sparkle, Pink Sparkle, or Silver Sparkle finish.
- Add 5% (MSR $280) for left-handed configuration (Powder Pink finish).
- Add 20% (MSR $310) for Guitar Box Set (fully intact, Pixie Purple, Powder Pink, or Sky Blue finishes).
- Add 20% (MSR $310) for left-handed configuration (Pink Sparkle finish).
- Add 30% (MSR $330) for Guitar Box Starter Set (fully intact, Blue Sparkle, Pink Sparkle, or Silver Sparkle finishes).
- Add 30% (MSR $330) for Guitar Box Starter Set in left-handed configuration (Powder Pink finish).
- Add 35% (MSR $350) for Guitar Box Starter Set in left-handed configuration (Pink Sparkle finish).

Every guitar comes with a gig bag as well as two full pages filled with removable butterfly and daisy decals.

PIXIE ACOUSTIC/ELECTRIC – composite oval back with flamed maple top body, body binding, mahogany neck, 20-fret rosewood fingerboard with pearloid daisy inlays, matching finish headstock, three-per-side chrome tuners, Daisy Custom piezo pickup and electronics, available in Blueberry Burst, Pink Sparkle (2009-present), Pixie Purple (2003-07), Plum Purple Burst, or Raspberry Burst (2009-present) finish, 25.25 in. scale, gig bag/back pack included, mfg. 2003-present.

MSR $320	$250	$135 - 175	$80 - 110	

- Add 5% (MSR $340) for left-handed configuration.
- Add 7.5% (MSR $350) for Pink Sparkle finish.

PIXIE CLASSICAL ACOUSTIC/ELECTRIC – composite oval back, mahogany set-neck, 21-fret rosewood fingerboard with pearloid daisy inlay, body binding, matching color headstock with three-per-side open style tuners, chrome hardware, Daisy Custom piezo pickup and electronics, available in Powder Pink or Sky Blue finish, 25.5 in. scale, mfg. 2004 only.

	N/A	$135 - 175	$75 - 100	$329

- Add 5% (Last MSR $349) for left-handed configuration.

ACOUSTIC: STARDUST SERIES

ACOUSTIC/ELECTRIC SPARKLE GUITAR – double cutaway hollow body, composite oval back, glitter top, two f-holes, mahogany neck, 22-fret rosewood fingerboard with daisy inlays, three-per-side chrome tuners, Custom Piezo electronics, available in Gold Sparkle or Pink Sparkle finish, mfg. 2004-05.

	N/A	$175 - 225	$100 - 135	$469

ACOUSTIC/ELECTRIC FLAMED MAPLE GUITAR – similar to the Acoustic/Electric Sparkle Guitar, except has a flamed maple top, available in Blondie or Vintage Burst finish, mfg. 2004 only.

	N/A	$200 - 250	$120 - 150	$499

ACOUSTIC: WILDWOOD SERIES

WILDWOOD – single cutaway folk-style body, spruce top or flame maple top (Bleach Blonde finish only), maple or mahogany back and sides, round soundhole with multi-ring rosette, multi-ply body binding, mahogany neck, 21-fret bound rosewood fingerboard with daisy inlays, matching finish headstock overlay, three-per-side chrome tuners, rosewood bridge, available in Atomic Pink (2008-present), Bleach Blonde, Pink Burst, Purple Daze (2006-present), or Rainbow Sparkle finish, 22.75 in. scale, gig bag/back pack included, mfg. 2005-present.

MSR $250	$190	$100 - 135	$50 - 75	

- Add 5% (MSR $270) for left-handed configuration (Pink Burst finish only).

WILDWOOD ACOUSTIC/ELECTRIC – single cutaway folk-style body, solid spruce top or optional flame maple top (Bleach Blonde finish only), maple back and sides, set mahogany neck, 20-fret rosewood fingerboard with daisy inlays, matching headstock with three-per-side tuners, rosewood bridge, four-band EQ electronics, chrome hardware, available in Bleach Blonde, Pink Burst, or Purple Daze (2006 only) finish, mfg. 2005-06.

	N/A	$200 - 250	$120 - 150	$499

- Add 5% (Last MSR $519) for left-handed configuration (Pink Burst finish only).

WILDWOOD ARTIST ACOUSTIC/ELECTRIC – single cutaway folk style-body, spruce top, maple back and sides, creme body binding, round soundhole with rosette, mahogany neck, 20-fret bound rosewood fingerboard with daisy inlays, matching finish headstock, three-per-side chrome tuners, rosewood bridge, pickup and two-band electronics with tuner, available in Bleach Blonde (2009-present), Pink Burst, Purple Daze (2007 only), Rainbow Sparkle, or Royal Blue Burst (2010-present) finish, 25.5 in. scale, mfg. 2007-present.

MSR $480	$350	$200 - 250	$120 - 150	

- Add 2.5% (MSR $500) for left-handed configuration (Pink Burst finish only).

* *Wildwood Artist Deluxe Acoustic/Electric* – similar to the Wildwood Artist Acoustic/Electric, except has a solid spruce top, 21-fret fingerboard, and Fishman Aero-201 pickup/electronics with four-band EQ and tuner, available in Atomic Pink, Royal Purple Burst, or Sunset Burst finish, mfg. 2009-present.

MSR $610	$450	$275 - 325	$160 - 210	

- Add 2.5% (MSR $630) for left-handed configuration (Sunset Burst finish only).

ACOUSTIC BASS

PIXIE BASS – composite oval back, spruce top, mahogany neck, 22-fret rosewood fingerboard with daisy inlays, matching finish headstock overlay, two-per-side chrome tuners, Daisy Custom Piezo electronics, available in Powder Pink or Sky Blue finish, mfg. 2003-04.

	N/A	$200 - 250	$125 - 150	$499

- Add 5% (Last MSR was $519) for left-hand configuration.

MSR/NOTES	100%	EXCELLENT	AVERAGE	LAST MSR

STARDUST BASS – double cutaway composite oval back, quilted maple top, mahogany neck, 22-fret rosewood fingerboard with daisy inlays, matching finish headstock overlay, two-per-side tuners, Daisy Custom Piezo electronics, chrome hardware, available in Gold Sparkle or Purple Quilt finish, 34 in. scale, mfg. 2005 only.

	N/A	$200 - 250	$125 - 150	$499

• **Add 5% (Last MSR was $519) for left-hand configuration.**

DAKOTA

Instruments previously built in Asia. Previously distributed by Sound Trek Distributors of Tampa, FL.

Dakota Guitars' acoustic models were constructed with traditional "old world" craftsmanship augmented by high-tech computer designs. Dakota models are named after America's rare wildlife, and are quite recognizable by their abalone bound headstock which features a white pearl "Snow-covered mountain top" inlay. 200 of each model were slated for production to "create an added excitement and collectible factor," but it is unknown how many of each guitar were actually produced.

ACOUSTIC

BH1 BIG HORN – grand concert style, solid Englemann spruce top, round soundhole, abalone binding, Indian rosewood back/sides, 14/20-fret fingerboard with inlay, bone nut, bridge with bone saddle, three-per-side tuners, available in Natural finish, disc.

	N/A	$375 - 450	$225 - 275	$899

B1 BUCK – dreadnought style, solid Englemann spruce top, round soundhole, abalone binding, Indian rosewood back/sides, 14/20-fret fingerboard with inlay, bone nut, bridge with bone saddle, three-per-side tuners, available in Natural finish, disc.

	N/A	$375 - 450	$225 - 275	$915

W1 WOLF – dreadnought style, tiger maple top, round soundhole, tiger maple back/sides, 14/20-fret fingerboard with inlay, bone nut, bridge with bone saddle, three-per-side tuners, available in Gloss See-Through Black finish with matching headstock, disc.

	N/A	$325 - 400	$175 - 225	$749

ACOUSTIC ELECTRIC

C1 COUGAR – dreadnought style, single rounded cutaway, solid Englemann spruce top, round soundhole, abalone and wood rosette, Indian rosewood back/sides, 14/20-fret fingerboard with inlay, bone nut, bridge with bone saddle, three-per-side tuners, Max-Q 1 Deluxe pickup, available in Natural finish, disc.

	N/A	$400 - 475	$250 - 300	$949

E1 EAGLE – grand concert style, single rounded cutaway, solid Englemann spruce top, round soundhole, abalone binding, Indian rosewood back/sides, 14/20-fret fingerboard with inlay, bone nut, bridge with bone saddle, three-per-side tuners, Max-Q 1 Deluxe pickup, available in Natural finish, disc.

	N/A	$400 - 475	$250 - 300	$1,049

G1 GRIZZLY – dreadnought style, single rounded cutaway, solid Englemann spruce top, round soundhole, abalone binding, Indian rosewood back/sides, 14/20-fret fingerboard with inlay, bone nut, bridge with bone saddle, three-per-side tuners, Max-Q 1 Deluxe pickup, available in Natural finish, disc.

	N/A	$425 - 500	$275 - 325	$1,065

DALACK, TED

Instruments currently built in Gainesville, GA.

Luthier Ted Dalack has been handcrafting custom flattop steel string acoustic guitars for a number of years. Prices on Dalack's custom-built instruments start at $10,000. Dalack also offers repairs, restorations, and custom services on all fretted instruments. Dalack's shop is an authorized factory service repair shop for Martin and Taylor. For further information regarding custom built instruments or repairs, contact Ted Dalack directly.

CONTACT INFORMATION
DALACK, TED
8940 Bay Drive
Gainesville, GA 30506
Phone No.: 770-889-1104

DALLAS

Instruments previously built in England, West Germany, and Japan during the early to mid-1960s. Some guitars may also carry the trademark of Tuxedo.

The Dallas and Tuxedo trademarks are the brand names used by a UK importer/distributor. Early solid body guitars were supplied by either Fenton-weill or Vox in Britain, with entry level German and Japanese original design guitars being imported. Source: Tony Bacon and Paul Day, *The Guru's Guitar Guide.*

DANA BOURGEOIS GUITARS

See Bourgeois in the B section.

D'ANGELICO

Instruments previously built in New York City, NY 1932-1964.

Master Luthier John D'Angelico (1905-1964) was born and raised in New York City, NY. In 1914, he apprenticed to his great uncle, and learned the luthier trade of building stringed instruments and repair. After eighteen years of working on stringed instruments, he opened his own shop on Kenmare Street (D'Angelico was twenty-seven). D'Angelico guitars and mandolins were entirely handcrafted by D'Angelico with assistance by shop employees such as Vincent DiSerio (assistant/apprentice from 1932 to 1959). In the early 1950s, D'Angelico's workshop had a bench and counter for guitar work, and a showcase with new United or Favilla guitars, used "trade-ins" and a few amplifiers from Nat Daniel's Danelectro or Everett Hull's Ampeg company. A very young James D'Aquisto became the second assistant to the shop in 1953.

In 1959, the building where D'Angelico worked and lived was condemned by the city due to an unsafe foundation. While scouting out new locations, D'Angelico and DiSerio had a serious argument over finances. DiSerio left and accepted work at the Favilla guitar plant. After a number of months went by, D'Angelico and D'Aquisto finally reopened the guitar shop at its new location. Unfortunately, D'Angelico's health began to take a turn for the worse. John D'Angelico passed away in his sleep in September of 1964. Source: Paul William Schmidt, *Acquired of the Angels*.

D'ANGELICO HISTORY

The publisher wishes to express thanks to Mr. Jim Fisch, co-author of *Epiphone: The House of Stathopoulo*, and senior contributing editor for *20th Century Guitar*, for the following D'Angelico information.

Although D'Angelico maintained a relative amount of consistency in his production, an overview of his instruments shows that the design of his guitars was representative of his evolution as a luthier, the demands of his customers, and the external influences of other, commercial guitar manufacturers. Since he did very little in the way of advertising and publishing catalogs, his ledger books (Reprinted in Paul William Schmidt's *Acquired of the Angels* and Akira Tsumura's *American Guitars*) have become the bible for D'Angelico collectors. In spite of the fact that these are incomplete and often contain puzzling references known only to the maker or his clients, the bulk of his work -1,164 guitars - is represented and accurately dated. However, since some early examples lack any manufacturing dates, the subsequent list of models notes the first date entered for a particular model, but it is not necessarily the first appearance of the model on the consecutive serial number list or the first example to be produced. Reference will be made to earlier undated examples where necessary.

EARLY GUITARS 1932-34

The first documented date for a D'Angelico guitar - 11/28/32 - corresponds to serial #1002. His early guitars were strongly influenced by Gibson's 16 in. L5 model. These examples have the distinctive, bound "snake head" headstock which features a script "D'Angelico" logo engraved upon a mother-of-pearl arch inlaid above a filigree, marquetry torch. The tuners were typically gold-plated, oval-button Grovers. The necks, like those of the L5, consisted of two pieces of maple, bisected with a narrow strip of mahogany. The fingerboards were bound and constructed of ebony, inlaid with pearl blocks at frets 3, 5, 7, 9, 12, and 15. They terminated in a decorative, reverse pendant arch. The book matched, carved spruce top was multiple bound, parallel braced and featured narrow f-holes. The bridge was of ebony, and the bound tortoiseshell, celluloid pickguard was closely copied from that of the L5. Early tailpieces were simple, wire trapeze units, generally with a "reverse" string attachment. Later guitars bore the more substantial and decorative, gold-plated Grover "DeLuxe" tailpiece. The sides and book matched, carved back were of highly figured curly maple. The standard finish was a full Sunburst.

LATER GUITARS 1935-1964

By late 1935, John D'Angelico was developing three distinct models, the "Style A," "Style B," and "Excel." Following Gibson's then-recent example, he increased the width of his new instruments to 17 inches - grand auditorium size. They were likewise priced, so as to be competitive with Gibson's comparable models, with the A, B and Excel - priced at $150.00, $200.00 and $275.00 respectively -- roughly matching up with Gibson's L10, L12, and aforementioned L5.

The New Yorker was D'Angelico's 1936 entry into the 18 in. guitar market. With a $400 price tag, it was a competitor of Gibson's Super 400, Epiphone's Emperor, and Stromberg's Master 400. It - along with the Excel - is considered by connoisseurs to be amongst the finest vintage archtop guitars. Taking its name and aesthetics from the city of its manufacture, the recurrent skyscraper motifs which adorned it represented the epitome of Art Deco design applied to a guitar.

The 17 in. A-1 was introduced by 1938 as D'Angelico's least expensive model, and would have been comparably priced to Gibson's L7 and Epiphone's Triumph. It varied from the Style A, in that, like the L7 of the period, it was sunbursted only on the top, with the sides and back having a monochromatic mahogany finish. Also like certain L7s, it had only single bindings. The luthier, however, still paid close attention to the sound of this economy model, and they can sound every bit as good as his most costly guitars.

The features which were standard to all D'Angelico models were: Carved spruce tops, carved maple backs, maple sides and necks, ebony fingerboards and adjustable bridges, and later, the inlaid pearl, script "D'Angelico" logo on the headstock. It is important to note however, that any instrument could be customized according to a client's wishes. Hence, many deviations from standard specifications exist. These typically include body size, bracing, neck construction, fingerboard and headstock inlays, headstock shape, hardware, bindings, pickguard and finish. D'Angelico would commonly use the designation "Special" in his ledger books to identify many of these guitars. He also made a few guitars with round or oval soundholes, and at least one which measured 19 in. across the lower bout.

Customers would also bring their older instruments back to the maker for refinishing, updated hardware, rebinding and occasionally the installation of an adjustable truss rod (a standard feature by the late '40s) or new fingerboard, resulting in many

MSR/NOTES	100%	EXCELLENT	AVERAGE	LAST MSR

instruments today having features from different periods, but all done by John D'Angelico, himself. One of the most common ailments of D'Angelico guitars is deterioration of the nitrocellulose bindings and pickguards. In order to preserve the integrity of the instrument, it is often necessary to have them completely replaced.

As previously stated, early D'Angelicos featured simple wire or Grover DeLuxe tailpieces, nickel or gold-plated according to the type of instrument. By 1936, tailpieces designed by John D'Angelico and fabricated by the Joseph Schaffner Co. began to appear on his instruments. The earliest was apparently designed for the newly introduced New Yorker, and was used on the Excel, as well. It was hinged, and featured a cutout reminiscent of the Chrysler Building's distinctive spire, although the initials "DA" can also be traced in its combination of curves and angles. The strings were threaded through a broad rectangular, horizontal retainer with the logo "D'Angelico, New York" engraved in script.

It was followed by the first of his "compensated" tailpieces (circa 1937). This consisted of a diagonally positioned, rhomboidal plate through which the strings passed. It was likewise engraved, and affixed to a non-hinged bracket whose face also employed a rectilinear skyscraper inspired motif. This was short-lived. An adaptation, with the diagonal rhomboid replaced by a more conventional horizontal plate, was used on some later acoustic instruments, and many electric guitars of the '50s.

By the late '30s, the compensated "stair step" tailpiece was standard issue on Excels and New Yorkers. This is the unit which most people associate with D'Angelico guitars. It harked back to the original Chrysler building motif, however that was now surmounted by a diagonally positioned, engraved "stair step" plate. This consisted of a series of graduated steps, the center six designed to accommodate a single string anchor apiece. The New Yorker's was a bit fancier than that of the Excel's. Eventually this unique design was utilized throughout the entire D.A. line.

As X-bracing became more popular towards the end of the 1930s, it became the preferred method of bracing the more expensive D'Angelico models, although later examples of parallel braced instruments are not uncommon, and most likely reflect a specific client's desires. Again, it is important to remember that deviations from the norm characterize this master's guitars.

In 1947, he introduced a cutaway option on his Excel and New Yorker models, setting a standard for modern jazz guitars which has seldom been equaled. After 1948, D'Angelico concentrated mainly on the manufacture of New Yorkers and Excels (the bulk of which were cutaway,) and electric models, which he continued to make up until his death.

ACOUSTIC MODELS/STYLES

Most D'Angelicos are in better than average condition. Because each guitar was normally custom built per individual specifications, there is very little standardized pricing structure within the variations. The price range of a D'Angelico guitar can be under $10,000 for a repaired, player's grade instrument; the high range has exceeded $100,000 - specifically depending on the condition, rarity, and even previous owner premium in some cases. It is highly recommended that several professional appraisals be secured before buying/selling/trading any D'Angelico guitar.

With the rise of the "archtop renaissance" in the 1990s and 2000s, a number of current luthiers are offering very high quality archtops in the same price range as the player's grade D'Angelicos (various models that have had professional repair). As a result, the player's grade D'Angelico market is fairly soft these days while challenged by the instruments of such builders as Monteleone, Triggs, Mortoro, De Cava, and a number of others.

EARLY MODELS (1932-34) – various configurations of models produced between 1932 and 1934.

	N/A	$9,500 - 12,000	$6,000 - 7,250	

STYLE A – 17 in. wide, generally parallel braced, carved spruce top, carved maple back and maple sides, f-holes not bound, three-ply bound body (some early models single bound,) adjustable ebony bridge, rounded bound tortoiseshell celluloid pickguard (later models with bound stair step guard,) bound ebony fingerboard with block position markers (some early models with dots,) usually equipped with simpler trapeze and Grover DeLuxe tailpieces, bound three-point or five-point headstock, early models having a block inlays bearing "D'Angelico" logo and model name (later models w/"Style A" engraved on inlaid shield design and inlaid "D'Angelico" script logo), button tuners, originally available only in full Dark Brown Sunburst, some later models in Blonde, all metal parts nickel-plated. Earliest ledger date: 3/10/36. Last ledger date: 9/14/45.

	N/A	$9,500 - 12,000	$6,000 - 7,250	

STYLE A-1 – 17 in. wide, parallel braced, carved spruce top, carved maple back and maple sides, single bound top, f-holes not bound, adjustable ebony bridge, rounded single bound tortoiseshell celluloid pickguard (later examples w/double stairstep pickguard), single bound ebony fingerboard with block position markers (some models w/ dots), usually equipped wtih simpler trapeze or Grover DeLuxe tailpiece (some later models with hinged "A-1" tailpiece - flat plate trapeze with diagonal cross bar and arched string retainer), single bound arched headstock bearing "D'Angelico" pearl script logo and engraved diagonal pearl block with "A-1" name, button tuners, sunburst top only, all metal parts nickel plated. Earliest ledger date: 5/2/38. Last ledger date: 11/20/43.

	N/A	$8,750 - 11,000	$5,500 - 6,750	

STYLE B – 17 in. body width, generally parallel braced, carved spruce top, carved maple back and maple sides, f-holes not bound, three-ply to five-ply bindings on top, adjustable ebony bridge, rounded bound tortoiseshell celluloid pickguard (later models w/ bound double stair step pickguard), bound ebony fingerboard with block position markers and pendant arch, early models with simpler trapeze or Grover DeLuxe tailpieces, later models with stair step tailpiece, triple-bound broken arch pediment headstock (with decorative finial) with "Style B" in banner, oval pearl marquetry inlay (later models with engraved "Style B" on inlaid pearl shield) and inlaid "D'Angelico" script logo, button tuners (later examples with Grover Imperials), originally available only in full reddish brown Sunburst, some later models in Blonde, all metal parts gold-plated. Earliest ledger date: 9/2/33. Last ledger date: 2/17/48.

	N/A	$12,000 - 15,000	$8,000 - 9,500	

EXCEL – 17 in. body width, generally X-braced, carved spruce top, carved maple back and maple sides, one-ply to three-ply bound f-holes, seven-ply binding on top, adjustable ebony bridge, engraved three-ply to five-ply bound double or triple stair step tortoiseshell celluloid pickguard,

MSR/NOTES	100%	EXCELLENT	AVERAGE	LAST MSR

triple bound ebony fingerboard with engraved block position markers and pendant arch, early models with w/ simpler trapeze or Grover DeLuxe tailpieces, (later models see preceding explanation), three-ply to five-ply bound broken arch pediment headstock (with decorative finial - some later with center dip headstock), with script "Excel" logo inlaid in shield (some early examples labeled "Exel") and pearl "D'Angelico" script logo (pearl or aluminum skyscraper truss rod cover by the late '40s), scalloped Grover tuners (later examples with Grover Imperials), originally available only in full reddish Brown Sunburst, Blonde option by late '30s, all metal parts gold-plated. Earliest ledger date: 3/16/36, some earlier undated entries.

	N/A	$17,500 - 22,500	$10,750 - 13,250	

* *Excel Cutaway* – similar to the Excel, except has a single cutaway, earliest ledger date: 05/09/47.

	N/A	$32,000 - 37,500	$20,000 - 25,000	

MEL BAY (SPECIAL) – Earliest ledger date: 05/07/49. A variation of the New Yorker, headstock inlaid with the guitarist's name. Sold through Gravois Music, St. Louis, MO.

	N/A	$20,000 - 25,000	$12,000 - 15,000	

NEW YORKER – 18 in. body width, generally X-braced, carved spruce top, carved maple back and maple sides, seven-ply (or more) binding on top, five-ply bound f-holes, inlaid ebony bridge, engraved seven-ply bound tortoiseshell celluloid triple stairstep pickguard, three-ply bound ebony fingerboard with diagonally segmented pearl block position markers and pendant arch (tailpieces see preceding explanation), center dip headstock with seven-ply binding (some later models with broken arch pediment headstock and decorative finial), inlaid pearl script "D'Angelico" logo, "New Yorker" skyscraper logo (pearl or aluminum skyscraper truss rod cover by the late '40s), Grover Imperial tuners (some with Kluson "Seal-Fast" models), originally available in full reddish brown sunburst, blonde option by late '30s, all metal parts gold-plated. Earliest ledger date: 9/26/36.

	N/A	$25,000 - 30,000	$15,000 - 20,000	

* *New Yorker Cutaway* – similar to the New Yorker, except with a single cutaway, earliest ledger date: 9/18/48.

	N/A	$50,000 - 60,000	$35,000 - 45,000	

* *New Yorker Special* – similar to the New Yorker Cutaway, except with a 17 in. body, earliest ledger date: 11/26/47. Listed as "small NY Cutaway," also later referred to as "Excel New Yorker" or "Excel Cutaway Johnnie (sic) Smith" model. Smith's personal guitar (01/05/55) was listed as an "Excel 1000." All names were applied interchangeably to 17 in. Excel Cutaways with New Yorker appointments.

	N/A	$35,000 - 40,000	$25,000 - 30,000	

D'ANGELICO II

Instruments previously built in the U.S during the 1990s. Distributed by Archtop Enterprises, Inc. in Merrick, NY.

The D'Angelico II company offered high quality reproductions of John D'Angelico's New Yorker and Excel models. Models share similar construction features such as spruce tops, figured maple back and sides, ebony fingerboard with MOP inlays, and gold-plated Grover tuners and tailpiece. All guitars are individually handcrafted and hand engraved.

The 18 in. **New Yorker** was offered in cutaway (last MSR was $12,000) and non-cutaway (last MSR was $11,750) versions, and in a Sunburst or Antique Natural finish. The **Excel** cutaway model (last MSR was $11,500), **Style B** non-cutaway (last MSR was $9,500), and **Jazz Classic** (last MSR was $7,250) share a 17 in. body (measured across the lower bout). A smaller single pickup electric model called the **Jazz Artist** (last MSR was $4,650) has a 16 in. body. A semi-hollowbody electric archtop called the **Fusion** (last MSR was $3,750) is offered in Antique Natural, New Yorker Sunburst, or Flaming Red nitrocellulose lacquer finish.

D'ANGELICO GUITARS OF AMERICA

Trademark of instruments previously manufactured by Vestax in Japan from 1988-2004. Distributed by D'Angelico Guitars of America in Colts Neck, NJ.

CONTACT INFORMATION

D'ANGELICO GUITARS OF AMERICA
264 Route 357 East
East Colts Neck, NJ 07722
Phone No.: 732-380-0995
Fax No.: 732-380-1303
www.dangelicoguitars.com
info@dangelicoguitars.com

In 1988, Mr. Jerry Berberine signed a deal with Mr. Hidesato Shino to re-launch the D'Angelico line of guitars to be made in Japan. These instruments were built with the same quality that the vintage models. Vestax built its last instruments during 2004. Refer to the website for more information.

Almost all D'Angelico guitars come standard with exposed pickups as opposed to the vintage models were most were standard acoustics. For model listings, please refer to the *Blue Book of Electric Guitars*.

D'Angelico produced a line of flattop acoustics in the 2000s, but as of 2004 they were discontinued. The **NYA-2R** has a rounded top and back, 16 in. body, solid spruce top with maple back/sides/neck, 21-fret fingerboard with pearl zig-zag position inlays, black New Yorker style pickguard, and is available in Natural Yellow, V-Blue, Natural, or Transparent Sunburst finish. The **NYA-2** is similar to the NYA-2R except is a flattop and back, features elaborate binding, and last retailed for $3,950.

D'Angelico also offered one archtop that is fully acoustic. This model is the New York Large Body Tear Drop (**NYL-1**). This model is based off the original and last retailed for $12,600.

D'ANGELICO REPLICA

Instruments previously in Grass Valley, CA from 1994 to late 1990s. Distributed by The Working Musician of Arcadia, CA.

Frank W. Green, author of the book, *D'Angelico, What's in a Name*, offered a replica of the D'Angelico Excel (**Deluxe LB-175**). The D'Angelico replicas were officially sanctioned by the current name owner.

Green offered the **Excel Deluxe LB-175**, an instrument with a 17.5 in. lower bout, hand carved Engelmann spruce top, western

MSR/NOTES	100%	EXCELLENT	AVERAGE	LAST MSR

curly maple back and sides, a curly maple neck, bound ebony fingerboard with split block inlays, Grover tuners, and gold plated stairstep tailpiece. Retail list prices ranged from $10,000 to $18,000. An 18.5 in. **New Yorker** had a last retail price between $12,000 and $20,000. The top-of-the-line instruments allowed for personalizing and custom features as long as they fell within the parameters of what the master would've done.

D'AQUISTO

Instruments previously built in Huntington, NY, and Greenport, NY, between 1965 and 1995.

Master Luthier James L. D'Aquisto (1935-1995) met John D'Angelico around 1953. At the early age of seventeen, D'Aquisto became D'Angelico's apprentice, and by 1959 was handling the decorative procedures and other lutherie jobs. When D'Angelico had a falling out with another member of the shop during the move of the business, D'Aquisto began doing actual building and shaping work. This lutherie work continued until the time of D'Angelico's death in 1964. The loss of D'Angelico in 1964 not only affected D'Aquisto personally, but professionally. Although he took over the business and shop with the encouragement of D'Angelico's brother, business under his own trademark started slowly. D'Aquisto continued to work in D'Angelico's shop repairing instruments at the last address - 37 Kenmare Street, New York City, NY. Finally, one year after D'Angelico's death, D'Aquisto summoned the nerve to build a guitar with the D'Aquisto inlay on the headpiece.

In 1965, D'Aquisto moved his shop to Huntington, NY, and sold his first instrument, styled after a D'Angelico New Yorker. Most of D'Aquisto's traditional design instruments are styled after John D'Angelico's Excel and New Yorker, with D'Aquisto adding refinements and improvements. D'Aquisto set up a deal with the Swedish-based Hagstrom company to produce guitars based on his designs in 1968, and the Ampeg company was one of the U.S. distributors. In 1973, D'Aquisto relocated his business once again, this time setting up shop in Farmingdale, NY. He produced his first flattop guitar in 1975, and his first solid body electric one year later. The Fender Musical Instrument Corporation produced a number of D'Aquisto-designed guitars beginning in the 1980s, and two models in the Designer series (D'Aquisto Ultra and Deluxe) are still in production at the Fender USA Custom shop. In the late 1980s, D'Aquisto again moved his shop to Greenport, NY, and continued to produce instruments from that location. In 1987, D'Aquisto broke away from archtop design tradition when he debuted the Avant Garde. The Excel and New Yorker style models were discontinued in 1991, as D'Aquisto concentrated on creating more forward-looking and advanced archtops. In 1994, models such as the Solo with four soundholes (only nine built), and Centura models were introduced. James L. D'Aquisto passed away in April, 1995. Source: Paul William Schmidt, *Acquired of the Angels*.

James D'Aquisto built 325+ instruments, from archtops to flattops to solid body electrics. D'Aquisto prices have gone up considerably in the past several years, and as a result, instruments have to be evaluated individually to ascertain the current market desirability and price. Generally, prices start in the $20,000 range, with the model, configuration (very important), and special order embellishments adding considerably to the base price. Deluxe New Yorkers are currently in the $40,000-$60,000 range. Remember, many of D'Aquisto's finer archtops sold for $15,000+ when new! Like D'Angelico, most of D'Aquisto's instruments were made to order and varied in dimensions and details. When buying/selling/appraising a D'Aquisto, it is the recommendation of the *Blue Book of Acoustic Guitars* that two or three professional appraisals be obtained.

D'AQUISTO (CURRENT MFG.)

Instruments currently produced in Japan since 2002. Distributed in the U.S. by Dana B. Goods in Ventura, CA. Previously distributed by Aria USA in Pennsauken, NJ between 2002 and 2006.

In 2002, D'Aquisto licensed their designs to be built by Aria of Japan. Designs are based off of the popular models that D'Aquisto produced during his lifetime.

CONTACT INFORMATION
D'AQUISTO (CURRENT MFG.)
U.S. Distributor: Dana B. Goods
4054 Transport St., Unit A
Ventura, CA 93003
Phone No.: 800-741-0109
www.danabgoods.com

ACOUSTIC ARCHTOP

For models that have electronics, refer to the *Blue Book of Electric Guitars*.

AVANTE GARDE – non-cutaway full-body archtop, solid Sitka spruce top, flame maple back and sides, two teardrop-style soundholes, one-piece maple neck, 22-fret ebony fingerboard, matching headstock with two slots and three-per-side tuners, ebony Accutone adj. bridge, ebony tailpiece, small ebony fingerboard, gold hardware, available in Natural finish, 17 in. width, 25.5 in. scale, mfg. 2002-present.

MSR $5,500	$4,400	$2,750 - 3,300	$1,850 - 2,200

CENTURA – single cutaway full-body archtop, solid Sitka spruce top, flame maple back and sides, two teardrop soundholes, one-piece maple neck, 22-fret ebony fingerboard, standard headstock with three-per-side tuners, ebony Accutone adj. bridge, ebony tailpiece, small ebony fingerboard, gold hardware, available in Centura Red (Sunburst) or Natural finish, 17 in. width, 25.5 in. scale, mfg. 2002-present.

MSR $5,000	$4,000	$2,500 - 3,000	$1,650 - 2,000

NEW YORKER – single cutaway full-body archtop, solid Sitka spruce top, flame maple back and sides, two bound f-holes, ivory multi-ply B/N/H binding, one-piece maple neck, 22-fret ebony fingerboard with diagonally split pearl block inlays, standard headstock with New Yorker inlay and three-per-side stairstep tuners, ebony Accutone adj. bridge, ebony tailpiece, small bound ebony fingerboard, gold hardware, available in Almond Burst, Natural, or Violin Burst finish, 17 in. width, 25. 5 in. scale, mfg. 2002-present.

MSR $5,100	$4,100	$2,550 - 3,050	$1,700 - 2,050

MSR/NOTES	100%	EXCELLENT	AVERAGE	LAST MSR

SOLO – single cutaway full-body archtop, solid Sitka spruce top, flame maple back and sides, two teardrop split soundholes, one-piece maple neck, 22-fret ebony fingerboard, open-style headstock with three-per-side tuners, ebony Accutone adj. bridge, ebony tailpiece, small ebony fingerboard, gold hardware, available in Natural finish, 17 in. width, 25.5 in. scale, mfg. 2002-08.

	N/A	$2,250 - 2,700	$1,550 - 1,800	

TEAR DROP – single cutaway full-body archtop with a "tear drop" pointed treble bout, solid Sitka spruce top, flame maple back and sides, two teardrop split soundholes, one-piece maple neck, 22-fret ebony fingerboard, open-style headstock with three-per-side tuners, ebony Accutone adj. bridge, ebony tailpiece, small ebony fingerboard, gold hardware, available in Centura Red (Sunburst) or Natural finish, 17 in. width, 25.5 in. scale, mfg. 2002-05.

	N/A	$3,000 - 3,500	$2,100 - 2,500	$5,999

DARLING GUITARS

Instruments currently produced in Washington state since 1976.

> **CONTACT INFORMATION**
> **DARLING GUITARS**
> Phone No.: 253-973-8177
> www.darlingguitars.com
> darlinguitars@yahoo.com

Master builder, designer, and restoration artist Denis Merrill has trained with the finest craftsmen in the world. He builds classical, acoustic and electric guitars, basses, archtops, mandolins, and harp guitars. He specializes in innovation and is able to create instruments for all different body types and physical conditions. He is a classically trained fine artist with work in museums and private collections. He has written numerous articles relating to the art and craft of guitar making.

A Darling Guitar is a thing of inspiration and magic - part science, art, and deft craftsmanship. All instruments convey a unique and individual sonic quality that can be traced to the builder. Superior instruments of all kinds judged as such because their sound mysteriously defies explanation - they are magical. Darling Guitars are strong in tradition, and they are an eco-friendly business with high tech smart designs and advanced ergonomics for special needs. No standard models are offered - just high standards. Prices range from $1,200 to $8,000, and according to Merrill, his used guitars are selling for approximately three times their value in 2002.

Denis offers accurate vintage-voiced heirloom quality at non-vintage prices. He uses 30 to 100-year-old aged materials to create a true vintage sound. He includes a proprietary treatment called "Soul Aging," which adds a distinct vintage-quality sound typically associated with years of playing. All are completed with traditional and custom-made finishes using natural dyes and extracts applied with Old World techniques. Using proprietary build techniques, including many components that are custom-made, he is always open to new suggestions and ideas. For more information, visit Darling's website or contact Merrill directly.

DAVID DAILY GUITARS

Instruments currently built in the U.S. Distributed by Kirkpatrick Guitar Studio of Baltimore, MD.

> **CONTACT INFORMATION**
> **DAVID DAILY GUITARS**
> Phone No.: 775-359-6370
> Fax No.: 775-359-2047
> www.dailyguitars.com
> dsdaily118@cs.com

Luthier David Daily has been building high quality classical model guitars since 1976. His guitars are of classical design inspired by Spanish design. In 1994, Daily traveled to Granda, Spain and worked with Antonio Marin Montero. As of 2007, he had built over 500 instruments. Base prices are $7,000 for Indian rosewood back and sides and $10,000 for Brazilian rosewood. Models come with either cedar or spruce tops and other options are also available (different tuning machines, cases, woods, etc.). The current waiting list is over three years. For further information regarding model specifications and pricing, please contact David Daily Guitars directly or visit his website.

DAVIS, J. THOMAS

Instruments currently built in Columbus, OH.

> **CONTACT INFORMATION**
> **DAVIS, J. THOMAS**
> 3135 N. High Street
> Columbus, OH 43202-1125
> Phone No.: 614-263-0264
> www.jthomasdavis.com
> customerservice@jthomasdavis.com

J. Thomas Davis began building guitars in a basement workshop while working on a music degree in 1975. The shop was moved to a storefront in Grandview Heights, OH in 1977 and relocated to the present location in Columbus, OH in 1993. The shop now employs four people dedicated to the service of fretted instruments (both electric and acoustic) while Tom spends his time building individual hand-made instruments. Tom individually designs and builds acoustic guitars one instrument at a time. He performs all of the work on his handmade guitars himself. Each instrument is built for a specific customer; each designed with a specific set of goals in mind. J. Thomas Davis also does guitar repair and warranty work for several makes. For further information about repair work or custom guitar pricing, please contact J. Thomas Davis directly.

In general, the materials selected, as well as the shape and size of the body, are contingent upon the sound characteristics desired by the customer. Prices are dependent upon the various materials used to as well as the specific work that is required to accomplish the customer's objectives. General prices for steel string flattop guitars are between $4,500 and $6,000, twelve-string guitars are between $5,000 and $7,500, classical guitars are between $5,000 and $9,000, archtop guitars are between $7,000 and $10,000, and harp guitars are between $7,000 and $9,000. Carved top Irish citterns and Irish bouzoukis are also available. The waiting list is currently twelve to sixteen months.

DAVIS, WILLIAM

Instruments currently built in Boxford, MA.

William Davis' hand-built guitars are available through his Boxford, MA lutherie. For up-to-date information concerning models and pricing, please contact William Davis directly.

CONTACT INFORMATION
DAVIS, WILLIAM
57 Main Street
Boxford, MA 01921
Phone No.: 508-887-0282
Fax No.: 508-887-7214

DAWAI

Instruments previously produced in Indonesia during the late 1990s and early 2000s.

Dawai made a number of acoustic guitars in their production facilities overseas. Models are the Primrose and the Rasquedo. These designs are basic folk and dreadnought models that are available in a number of colors. Most of these guitars are entry level guitars at entry level prices, and it is unkown if there was a U.S. distributor.

DBZ GUITARS

Guitars currently produced overseas and in Chicago, IL since 2009. Distributed by DBZ Guitars in Houston, TX.

Dean Zelinsky, founder of Dean Guitars, left the company in 2008 and started a new guitar company called DBZ Guitars. Zelinsky founded Dean Guitars in 1977 and developed a reputation as an innovator building high-quality electric guitars that looked unstoppable on stage. Dean was the first to offer custom appointments like flame maple tops, full binding, block pearl inlays, state of the art electronics and brilliant finishes on radical designs fit for stage. Dean grew into a large company that continues to offer a wide variety of musical instruments. Zelinsky has partnered with Jeff Diamant of Diamond Amplification to aid in the development of his new guitar line. DBZ Guitars embraces the latest in guitar building technology, forward thinking designs, vivid graphics and dimensional body contouring. DBZ offers both radical shapes as well as traditional rounded guitars. A line of acoustic guitars is available as well including the Verona and Tuscan Models. For more information, visit DBZ Guitars' website or contact them directly.

CONTACT INFORMATION
DBZ GUITARS
707 N. Shepherd Dr., Ste 300
Houston, TX 77007
Phone No.: 713-934-0100
Fax No.: 713-934-0155
www.dbzguitars.com
dbz@dbzguitars.com

D.C. HILDER BUILDER

Instruments previously built in Guelph (Ontario), Canada during the 1990s and 2000s.

David Hilder built instruments for over twenty years with his main model being the acoustic stand-up bass. These models include the **Doghouse** and **Cathouse** and they are oversix feet tall. Last retail was $750 for the Cathouse and $1,200 for the Doghouse. Hilder's Garcia's Guitar model features seven laminated layers of hard wood, which are then hand carved for the top and back contouring. These guitars ranged in price between $900 and $2,000 depending upon options.

DEAN

Instruments currently produced in Tampa, FL, Korea, Japan, and China. Distributed by Armadillo Enterprises of Tampa, FL. Previously produced in Evanston, IL 1977-1986, and in Plant City, FL 1990-94, and Clearwater, FL 1995-2005. Instruments have been produced in Tampa, FL since 2005 and overseas since 1985.

CONTACT INFORMATION
DEAN
4924 West Waters Ave.
Tampa, FL 33634
Phone No.: 813-600-3920
Phone No.: 800-793-5273
Fax No.: 813-600-3933
www.deanguitars.com
questions@deanguitars.com

The original Evanston, Illinois-based company was founded by Dean Zelinsky in 1977. Zelinsky, fond of classic Gibson designs, began building high quality electric solid body instruments and eventually started developing his own designs. Originally, there were three models: The **V** (similar to the Flying V), the **Z** (Explorer body shape), and the **ML** (sort of a cross between the V and an Explorer - and named after the initials of Matt Lynn, Zelinsky's best friend growing up). As the company's guitars gained popularity, production facilities were moved to Chicago in 1980.

In 1986, Dean closed the USA Shop, leaving all construction to be completed overseas. The U.S. market had shifted towards the then-popular bolt neck super-strat design, and Zelinsky's personal taste leaned in the opposite direction. Zelinsky sold Dean Guitars in 1990 to Oscar Medros, founder and owner of Tropical Music (based in Miami, Florida). The Dean Guitars facility in Plant City, Florida was run by Tracy Hoeft and Jon Hill, and new guitars were distributed to markets in the U.S., Japan, Korea, and Europe. In 1995, Armadillo Enterprises or Clearwater, FL bought Dean from Tropical Music. In 2000, Zelinsky came back to work for Dean. They currently produce several lines of guitars overseas and they also have a high-end custom shop that builds several original models. Most acoustic models are produced overseas (with the exception of a few custom shop models). Dean did produce a few acoustics in the early 1990s, but the bulk of acoustic guitars were first introduced in 1998. For more information, contact Dean directly or visit their website.

MSR/NOTES	100%	EXCELLENT	AVERAGE	LAST MSR

ACOUSTIC: ARTIST SERIES

ARTIST CE (MODEL ACE) – single cutaway thin body, solid Englemann spruce top, mahogany back/sides/neck, 14/22-fret rosewood fingerboard with pearl dot inlay, multi-ply binding, abalone sound hole inlay, Grover three-per-side tuners, Shadow P7 Electronics, available in Gloss Natural finish, mfg. 1999-2006.

	N/A	$250 - 300	$150 - 190	$590

ARTIST CS (MODEL DGA-ACS) – jumbo style, single rounded cutaway medium thin body, solid spruce top, round soundhole, body binding, mahogany back/sides, 14/20-fret fingerboard with white dot inlay, triangular Dean rosewood bridge, three-per-side Grover tuners, chrome hardware, available in Classic Black or Gloss Natural finish, mfg. 1998-2000.

	N/A	$150 - 200	$95 - 120	$399

ARTIST CSE (MODEL DGA-ACSE) – jumbo style, single rounded cutaway medium thin body, solid spruce top, round soundhole, abalone binding, Dean "Wing" design rosette, solid rosewood sides, rosewood back, 14/24-fret extended fingerboard with block inlays, triangular Dean rosewood bridge, three-per-side Grover tuners, gold hardware, piezo bridge pickup, Shadow five-band EQ, available in Classic Black, Gloss Amber, or Gloss Natural finish, mfg. 1998-2004.

	N/A	$375 - 450	$225 - 275	$875

ARTIST TRIBAL (MODEL TRBL) – single cutaway thin body, solid Sitka spruce top, mahogany back/sides/neck, barb wire rosette, 14/22-fret rosewood fingerboard with pearl barbed wire inlay, multi-ply binding, Grover three-per-side tuners, Fishman Electronics, available in Classic Black finish, mfg. 2004-05.

	N/A	$400 - 475	$250 - 300	$940

ACOUSTIC: CONCERT SERIES (CLASSICAL)

CONCERT (MODEL C) – classical style body, cedar top, mahogany back/sides/neck, 12/18-fret rosewood fingerboard, three-per-side open-gear tuners, multi-ply binding, abalone sound hole inlay, available in Gloss Natural finish, mfg. 1999-2006.

	N/A	$120 - 150	$70 - 90	$300

* *Concert CE (Model CCE)* – similar to the Concert except has a single rounded cutaway and Dean electronics, mfg. 1999-2006.

	N/A	$180 - 230	$100 - 135	$465

CONCERT C (MODEL DGA-CC) – classical style, single rounded cutaway body, select cedar top, round soundhole, multi-ply body binding, mahogany back/sides, 12/19-fret fingerboard, slotted headstock, tied bridge, three-per-side tuning machines, available in Gloss Natural finish, mfg. 1998-2000.

	N/A	$95 - 125	$50 - 70	$249

CONCERT CRSE (CONCERT 24) – single rounded cutaway classical body, solid spruce top, rosewood back and sides, mahogany neck, 12/18-fret rosewood fingerboard, three-per-side open-gear gold tuners, multi-ply binding, abalone soundhole inlay, Shadow P7 Electronics, available in Gloss Natural finish, mfg. 1999-2003.

	N/A	$250 - 300	$150 - 190	$619

ACOUSTIC: CONTOUR & "D" SERIES

CONTOUR – single cutaway hollow mahogany body, solid spruce top, set mahogany neck, 25.25 in. scale, multi-ply binding, extended rosewood fingerboard with dot position markers, 23 frets, Shadow P7 preamp, Grover tuners, chrome hardware, Abalone soundhole inlay, available in Metallic Blue (Calypso), Metallic Red (Del Feugo), Classic Black (Onyx) or Metallic White (Tundra), mfg. 2001-02.

	N/A	$200 - 250	$120 - 150	$599

Each color specifies a different model. In another words there are four different model names, one for each color.

D-1 – dreadnought style, laminated spruce top, round soundhole, maple neck, rosewood fingerboard with dot inlays, mahogany back/sides, enclosed chrome tuning machines, available in Natural finish, mfg. 1991-92.

	N/A	$80 - 100	$45 - 60	$199

ACOUSTIC: EARTH SERIES

EARTH 00CE – 00 size single cutaway body, solid Sitka spruce top, mahogany back and sides, round soundhole with rosette, 14/20-fret fingerboard with offset dot inlays, ebony bridge, bone nut and saddle, Piezo pickup and Fishman preamp, satin Natural finish, mfg. 2005 only.

	N/A	$400 - 475	$250 - 300	$938

EARTH 000 – 000 size body, solid Sitka spruce top, mahogany back and sides, 12/19-fret fingerboard with offset dot inlays, ebony bridge, bone nut and saddle, satin Natural finish, mfg. 2005 only.

	N/A	$300 - 350	$175 - 225	$689

ACOUSTIC: ESPAÑA CLASSICAL

CGP – classical design, spruce top, mahogany back/sides/neck, rosewood fingerboard, slotted style headstock, Mosaic rosette, Gloss Natural finish, plush lined case included, mfg. 2005-present.

MSR $359	$240	$140 - 175	$85 - 105	

MSR/NOTES	100%	EXCELLENT	AVERAGE	LAST MSR

CS – classical design, solid cedar top, mahogany back/sides/neck, rosewood fingerboard, slotted style headstock, Mosaic rosette, Gloss Natural finish, mfg. 2004-present.

MSR $344	$230	$135 - 170	$80 - 100	

CSR – classical design, solid cedar top, rosewood back/sides, rosewood fingerboard, slotted style headstock, Mosaic rosette, mahogany binding, maple purfling, Gloss Natural finish, mfg. 2004-2010.

	$320	$160 - 210	$90 - 120	$469

* CSCR Cutaway – similar to the CSR, except has a single cutaway, electronics, and a pickup, mfg. 2004-present.

MSR $728	$450	$275 - 325	$150 - 200	

CSCM – classical design, single cutaway, solid cedar top, mahogany back/sides, rosewood fingerboard, slotted style headstock, Mosaic rosette, pickup, electronics, Gloss Natural finish, mfg. 2004-present.

MSR $483	$320	$190 - 240	$115 - 145	

* CSCML Left-Handed – similar to the CSCM except is in left-handed configuration, mfg. 2004-2010.

	$305	$160 - 210	$90 - 120	$466

PCPK ESPAÑA PACK – classical guitar pack with a guitar that features a solid cedar top, rosewood back and sides, rosewood fingerboard and pro grade classical tuners, includes a foot stool and pitch pipe, current mfg.

MSR $224	$140	$85 - 110	$50 - 65	

ACOUSTIC: EXOTICA SERIES

EXOTICA FM (MODEL EFM) – single cutaway hollow flame maple body, flame maple top, mahogany set neck, 21-fret rosewood fingerboard with dot position markers, abalone soundhole inlay, multi-ply binding, Dean Electronics, Grover tuners, chrome hardware, available in Trans. Black, Trans. Blue, Trans. Green (disc.), Trans. Red (disc. 2011), or Gloss Natural finish, 25.25 in. scale, mfg. 1999-present.

MSR $567	$370	$225 - 275	$110 - 140	

* Exotica FM Faded (Model EFMFD) – similar to the Exotica FM, except features a faded finish, available in Denim, Tiger Eye, Tiger Eye Satin, or Trans. Green finish, mfg. summer 2004-present.

MSR $636	$400	$250 - 300	$150 - 190	

* Exotica FM Left-Handed – similar to the Exotic FM except in left-handed configuration, mfg. 1999-2007.

	N/A	$275 - 325	$120 - 150	$690

* Exotica FM 12-String (Model EFM12) – similar to the Exotica FM except in 12-string configuration and six-per-side tuners, available in Tiger Eye finish, mfg. summer 2004-present.

MSR $846	$530	$350 - 425	$200 - 250	

EXOTICA ANDES (MODEL EANDES) – similar to the Exotica FM except features East Andes rosewood top/back/sides, available in Gloss Natural finish, mfg. 2001-present.

MSR $652	$400	$225 - 275	$135 - 170	

EXOTICA BB (MODEL EBB) – similar to Exotica FM, except has solid spruce top, bubinga back and sides, available in Gloss Natural finish, mfg. 1999-2007.

	N/A	$225 - 275	$125 - 150	$615

EXOTICA BUBINGA (MODEL EBUBINGA) – single cutaway Exotica-style body, bubinga top, back, and sides, round soundhole with woodcut rosette, celluloid binding, set mahogany neck, 14/20-fret rosewood fingerboard with dot inlays, matching headstock, three-per-side chrome tuners, rosewood bridge, Dean DMT 12EX pickup with Dean DWC-Aphex Aural exciter and Big Bottom circutry, available in Natural finish, mfg. 2010-present.

MSR $672	$430	$275 - 325	$160 - 200	

EXOTICA COCOBOLO (MODEL ECOCO) – single cutaway Exotica-style body, cocobolo top, back, and sides, round soundhole with woodcut rosette, celluloid binding, set mahogany neck, 14/20-fret rosewood fingerboard with dot inlays, matching headstock, three-per-side chrome tuners, rosewood bridge, Dean DMT 12EX pickup with Dean DWC-Aphex Aural exciter and Big Bottom circutry, available in Natural finish, mfg. 2010-present.

MSR $700	$450	$275 - 325	$160 - 200	

EXOTICA CSW SCOTT WEILAND (MODEL ECSW SW) – single cutaway Exotica-style body, solid Sitka spruce top, solid rosewood back and sides, round soundhole with abalone rosette, abalone body binding, set mahogany neck, 14/20-fret bound rosewood fingerboard with split pearl block inlays, black headstock with Dean logo and "SW" inlay, three-per-side chrome stairstep tuners, rosewood bridge, B-Band A3TY electronics, available in Natural or Trans. Brazilia finish, 25.25 in. scale, mfg. 2011-present.

MSR $1,162	$700	$400 - 500	$250 - 300	

EXOTICA DAO (MODEL DAO) – similar to Exotica FM, except has dao top/back/sides, available in Gloss Natural finish, mfg. 2001-07.

	N/A	$225 - 275	$125 - 150	$615

MSR/NOTES	100%	EXCELLENT	AVERAGE	LAST MSR

EXOTICA FREEDOM (MODEL EFMSL) – similar to Exotica FM, except has custom Statue of Liberty inlay on fingerboard, available in Trans. Black finish, mfg. 2003-04.

	N/A	$300 - 350	$150 - 200	$790

EXOTICA KOA (MODEL EKOA) – single cutaway Exotica-style body, koa top/back/sides, round soundhole with rosette, 14/20-fret rosewood fingerboard with dot inlays, matching headstock with three-per-side tuners, rosewood bridge, pickup system with built in tuner, available in Natural finish, mfg. 2007-present.

MSR $661	$400	$225 - 275	$135 - 170	

EXOTICA NOMAD (MODEL ENA) – small auditorium single cutaway body, spruce top, mahogany back and sides, round soundhole with wood and abalone rosette, maple body and neck binding, 14/21-fret rosewood fingerboard, three-per-side tuners, rosewood bridge, Dean electronics, chrome hardware, Natural finish, mfg. summer 2004-2011.

	$240	$160 - 200	$90 - 120	$432

EXOTICA PADAUK (MODEL EPADUK) – single cutaway Exotica-style body, padauk top, back, and sides, round soundhole with woodcut rosette, celluloid binding, set mahogany neck, 14/20-fret rosewood fingerboard with dot inlays, matching headstock, three-per-side chrome tuners, rosewood bridge, Dean DMT 12NR pickup with four-band EQ and tuner, available in Natural finish, mfg. 2009-present.

MSR $595	$400	$250 - 300	$150 - 190	

EXOTICA QUILTED ASH (MODEL EQA) – single cutaway Exotica-style body, quilted ash top/back/sides, round soundhole with rosette, 14/20-fret rosewood fingerboard with dot inlays, matching headstock with three-per-side tuners, rosewood bridge, pickup system with built in tuner, available in Natural, Trans. Amber, Trans. Black, Trans. Black Satin, Trans. Blue Satin, Trans Braziliaburst, or Trans. Cherryburst finish, mfg. 2007-present.

MSR $565	$370	$225 - 275	$135 - 170	

* *Exotica Quilted Ash 12-String (Model EQA12)* – similar to the Exotica Quilted Ash, except in 12-string configuration with six-per-side tuners, available in Natural finish, mfg. 2009-present.

MSR $682	$450	$275 - 325	$160 - 200	

* *Exotica Quilted Ash Aphex (Model EQAA)* – similar to the Exotica Quilted Ash, except has DMT 12EX electronics with DWC Aphex Aural Exciter and Big Bottom circuitry, available in Trans. Blue or Trans. Power Purple finish, mfg. 2009-present.

MSR $621	$400	$250 - 300	$150 - 190	

EXOTICA QUILT SUPREME (MODEL EQSES) – similar to Exotica BB, except has Shadow P7 electronics, solid Engelmann Spruce top, quilt maple back and sides, AB multi-ply binding, available in Gloss Natural, Trans. Blue, Trans. Red, or Trans. Power Purple finish, mfg. 1999-2008.

	N/A	$300 - 350	$150 - 200	$790

* *Exotica Quilt Supreme Left-Handed (Model EQSESL)* – similar to the Exotica Quilt Supreme except in left-handed configuration, available in Gloss Natural finish, mfg. 1999-2006.

	N/A	$375 - 450	$225 - 275	$900

EXOTICA ROSEWOOD SUPREME (MODEL ERSES) – similar to Exotica QSE, except has rosewood back and sides, rosewood EX fingerboard, hexagon position markers, available in Gloss Natural finish, mfg. 1999-2011.

	$615	$375 - 450	$200 - 250	$987

EXOTICA RADIANT (MODEL EX RAD) – similar to Exotica FM, except has solid Englemann spruce top, rosewood back/sides, radiant sun inlays, available in Gloss Natural finish, mfg. 2001-04.

	N/A	$425 - 500	$275 - 325	$1,040

EXOTICA SELECT (MODEL ESEL) – similar to Exotica FM, except has quilted maple top/back/sides, and abalone hourglass inlay, available in Tiger Eye finish, mfg. 2003-present.

MSR $853	$520	$300 - 375	$175 - 225	

EXOTICA SPALT MAPLE (MODEL ESPALT) – single cutaway Exotica-style body, spalt maple top, back, and sides, round soundhole with woodcut rosette, celluloid binding, set mahogany neck, 14/20-fret rosewood fingerboard with dot inlays, matching headstock, three-per-side chrome tuners, rosewood bridge, Dean DMT 12NR pickup with four-band EQ and tuner, available in Natural finish, mfg. 2009-present.

MSR $656	$420	$250 - 300	$150 - 190	

EXOTICA SPRUCE (MODEL ESPRUCE) – single cutaway Exotica-style body, solid spruce top, mahogany back and sides, round soundhole with woodcut rosette, celluloid binding, set mahogany neck, 14/20-fret rosewood fingerboard with dot inlays, black headstock overlay, three-per-side chrome tuners, rosewood bridge, Dean DMT 12NR pickup with four-band EQ and tuner, available in Natural finish, mfg. 2010-present.

MSR $522	$320	$175 - 225	$105 - 130	

EXOTICA WALNUT (MODEL EWAL) – single cutaway Exotica-style body, walnut top/back/sides, round soundhole with rosette, 14/20-fret rosewood fingerboard with dot inlays, matching headstock with three-per-side tuners, rosewood bridge, pickup system with built in tuner, available in Natural finish, mfg. 2007-present.

MSR $572	$370	$225 - 275	$135 - 170	

MSR/NOTES	100%	EXCELLENT	AVERAGE	LAST MSR

EXOTICA ZEBRA (MODEL EZEBRA) – single cutaway Exotica-style body, zebra top, back, and sides, round soundhole with woodcut rosette, celluloid binding, set mahogany neck, 14/20-fret rosewood fingerboard with dot inlays, matching headstock, three-per-side chrome tuners, rosewood bridge, Dean DMT 12NR pickup with four-band EQ and tuner, available in Natural finish, mfg. 2008-present.

MSR $581	$370	$225 - 275	$135 - 170	

MICHAEL SCHENKER EXOTICA – single cutaway Exotica style, select spruce top, maple back/sides mahogany neck, 14/21-fret rosewood fingerboard, round soundhole with custom rosette, matching headstock, three-per-side tuners, Piezo pickup with built-in tuner, chrome hardware, custom black and white finish with alternating patterns, mfg. 2005-06.

	N/A	$375 - 450	$225 - 275	$900

ACOUSTIC: EXOTIGLASS SERIES

EXOTIGLASS – single rounded cutaway body, flame maple top, fiberglass composite back and sides, mahogany neck, 14/20-fret rosewood fingerboard with pearl dot inlay, three-per-side chrome tuners, multi-ply binding, abalone soundhole inlay, Dean Electronics, available in Gloss Natural, Trans. Blue, Trans. Brownburst, or Trans. Red finish, mfg. 2000-06.

	N/A	$170 - 220	$100 - 130	$465

* Add 7.5% (Last MSR $500) for Trans. Brownbust, Blue, or Red finish.

ACOUSTIC: MASTERS SERIES

Masters Series acoustics were produced in Czechoslovakia.

MASTERS SD (MODEL DGA-MSD) – dreadnought style, solid cedar top, round soundhole, wood body binding, mahogany back/sides, 14/20-fret fingerboard with white dot inlay, triangular Dean rosewood bridge, three-per-side Schaller tuners, chrome hardware, available in Satin Natural finish, mfg. 1998-2000.

	N/A	$135 - 175	$70 - 95	$449

MASTERS SS (MODEL DGA-MSS) – similar to the Masters SD, except features a solid spruce top, mahogany neck, available in Gloss Natural finish, mfg. 1998-2000.

	N/A	$135 - 175	$70 - 95	$449

MASTERS SR (MODEL DGA-MSR) – similar to the Masters SD, except features a solid spruce top, rosewood back/sides, mahogany neck, available in Gloss Natural finish, mfg. 1998-2000.

	N/A	$175 - 225	$95 - 125	$569

MASTERS SE (MODEL DGA-MSE) – dreadnought style, solid spruce top, round soundhole, wood body binding, mahogany back/sides, mahogany neck, 14/20-fret fingerboard with white dot inlay, triangular Dean rosewood bridge, three-per-side Schaller tuners, chrome hardware, piezo bridge pickup, Shadow five-band EQ, available in Gloss Natural finish, mfg. 1998-2000.

	N/A	$165 - 215	$95 - 125	$599

ACOUSTIC: NTA (NEW TECHNOLOGY ACOUSTICS) SERIES

NOUVEAU CM – offset double cutaway hollow mahogany body, solid Engelmann spruce top, 25.25 in. scale, mahogany set neck, 22 frets, rosewood fingerboard with dot position markers, Dean electronics, Grover tuners, chrome hardware, abalone sound hole inlay, available in Gloss Natural finish, mfg. 2001-02.

	N/A	$150 - 200	$95 - 125	$529

* *Nouveau CR* – similar to Noveau CM, except has gold hardware, Shadow P7 electronics, rosewood back and sides, AB multi-ply binding, available in Gloss Natural finish, mfg. 2001-02.

	N/A	$200 - 250	$125 - 150	$699

FRANA TM – similar to Nouveau CM, except has 80mm body, available in Gloss Natural finish, mfg. 2001-02.

	N/A	$135 - 175	$75 - 100	$499

* *Frana TR* – similar to Frana TM, except has gold hardware, Shadow P7 electronics, rosewood back and sides, AB multi-ply binding, available in Gloss Natural finish, mfg. 2001-02.

	N/A	$200 - 250	$125 - 150	$699

* *Frana R* – similar to Frana TR, except has solid spruce top, available in Gloss Natural finish, mfg. 2001-02.

	N/A	$185 - 235	$110 - 140	$669

ACOUSTIC: PERFORMER SERIES

PERFORMER E (MODEL PE) – jumbo style single rounded cutaway body, select spruce top, mahogany back and sides, round soundhole, body binding, 14/20-fret fingerboard with dot inlay, triangular Dean rosewood bridge, three-per-side tuners, piezo bridge pickup, volume and tone controls, chrome hardware, available in Blue Burst, Classic Black, Gloss Natural, Tobacco Sunburst, Trans. Power Purple, or Trans. Red finish, mfg. 1998-present.

MSR $452	$280	$160 - 200	$95 - 120	

* *Perfomer EA (Model PATEC)* – similar to the Performer E except has no electronics, available in Brownburst, Classic Black, or Vintage Sunburst finish, mfg. 2003-2010.

	$220	$120 - 150	$70 - 90	$356

MSR/NOTES	100%	EXCELLENT	AVERAGE	LAST MSR

* ***Performer Denim (Model PED)*** – similar to the Performer, except has a flame maple body with tortoiseshell binding, abalone inlays, available in Fade Denim, Fade Tiger Eye, Faded Black Denim, or Faded Pink finish, mfg. 2004-05.

	N/A	$275 - 325	$135 - 175	$750

* ***Performer DSE (Model DGA-PDSE)*** – similar to the Performer E, except features a solid spruce top, solid rosewood sides, rosewood back, abalone binding, 14/24-fret extended fingerboard with block inlays, Dean "Wing" design rosette, three-per-side Grover tuners, gold hardware, Shadow 5-band EQ, available in Classic Black or Gloss Natural finish, mfg. 1998-2005.

	N/A	$275 - 325	$135 - 175	$750

* ***Performer Left-Handed (Model PELH)*** – similar to the Performer E except in left-handed configuration, available in Classic Black finish, mfg. 1998-present.

MSR $525	$330	$190 - 235	$110 - 140	

* ***Performer QSE*** – similar to Performer DSE, except has chrome hardware, quilt maple back and sides, dot position markers, available in Gloss Natural or Gloss Amber finish, mfg. 1998-2003.

	N/A	$175 - 225	$110 - 140	$559

PERFORMER FLAME MAPLE (PEFM) – single smooth cutaway folk-style body, flame maple top, mahogany back and sides, round soundhole with abalone rosette, multi-ply celluloid binding, set mahogany neck, 14/21-fret rosewood fingerboard with split pearl block inlays, flame maple matching finish headstock overlay, three-per-side gold tuners, triangular rosewood bridge, Dean DMT 12NR electronics with Aphex Exciter, available in Gloss Natural, Red Tiger Eye, Tiger Eye, or Trans. Black finish, 25.25 in. scale, mfg. 2010-present.

MSR $541	$350	$200 - 250	$120 - 150	

PERFORMER FLORENTINE QUILT (PEFQA) – single sharp cutaway folk-style quilt ash body, multi-ply top binding, round soundhole with a large ring of abalone pearl rosette, 14/21-fret bound rosewood fingerboard with pearl dot inlays, quilt ash matching finish headstock overlay, three-per-side gold tuners, triangular rosewood bridge, Dean electronics, available in Cherry Sunburst, Trans. Blue, or Trans. Braziliaburst finish, part of the Independent Series, mfg. 2008-present.

MSR $486	$320	$185 - 230	$105 - 135	

PERFORMER FLORENTINE SPALT MAPLE (PEFSM) – single sharp cutaway folk-style spalt maple body, multi-ply top binding, round soundhole with a small ring of abalone pearl rosette, 14/21-fret bound rosewood fingerboard with custom inlays, spalt maple matching finish headstock overlay, three-per-side gold tuners, triangular rosewood bridge, Dean electronics, available in Gloss Natural finish, part of the Independent Series, mfg. 2008-present.

MSR $581	$370	$215 - 265	$130 - 160	

PERFORMER SE (MODEL DGA-PSE) – similar to the Performer E, except features a solid spruce top, abalone binding, extended fingerboard, three-per-side Grover tuners, Shadow five-band EQ, available in Classic Black or Gloss Natural finish, mfg. 1998-2002.

	N/A	$150 - 200	$95 - 125	$529

• **Add $40 for left-handed configuration (Model DGA-PSE-L), available in Gloss Natural finish only.**

* ***Performer SE-7 7-String*** – similar to Performer SE, except in a seven-string configuration, available in Gloss Natural finish, mfg. 1998-2002.

	N/A	$250 - 300	$125 - 150	$619

* ***Performer SE-12 12-String*** – similar to Performer SE, except in a 12-string configuration and six-per-side tuners, available in Gloss Natural or Classic Black finish, mfg. 1998-2007.

	N/A	$300 - 350	$135 - 175	$800

* ***Performer SE Left-Handed (Model DSE-L)*** – similar to the Performer SE, except in left-handed configuration, available in Gloss Natural finish, disc. 2006.

	N/A	$300 - 350	$175 - 225	$740

PERFORMER KOA (PEKOA) – single smooth cutaway folk-style body, koa top, back, and sides, round soundhole with abalone rosette, multi-ply celluloid binding, set mahogany neck, 14/21-fret rosewood fingerboard with split pearl block inlays, koa matching finish headstock overlay, three-per-side gold tuners, triangular rosewood bridge, Dean DMT 12NR electronics with Aphex Exciter, available in Gloss Natural finish, 25.25 in. scale, mfg. 2010-present.

MSR $634	$400	$230 - 285	$135 - 170	

PERFORMER KEY LARGO (MODEL PQSEKL) – similar to the Performer E, except has a Sitka spruce top, quilted maple sides and backs, Florida palm fingerboard inlays, dolphin rosette, available in Trans. Blue finish, mfg. 2003-2010.

	N/A	$375 - 450	$200 - 250	$969

PERFORMER QUILT ASH (PEQA) – single smooth cutaway folk-style body, quilt ash top, back, and sides, round soundhole with abalone rosette, multi-ply celluloid binding, set mahogany neck, 14/21-fret rosewood fingerboard with split pearl block inlays, quilt ash matching finish headstock overlay, three-per-side gold tuners, triangular rosewood bridge, Dean DMT 12NR electronics with Aphex Exciter, available in Gloss Natural, Trans. Blue, or Trans. Brazilia finish, 25.25 in. scale, mfg. 2010-present.

MSR $550	$350	$200 - 250	$120 - 150	

MSR/NOTES	100%	EXCELLENT	AVERAGE	LAST MSR

PERFORMER TRIBAL (MODEL PETRBL) – single rounded cutaway jumbo maple body, multi-ply top binding, round soundhole with barbwire rosette, mahogany neck, 14/21-fret bound rosewood fingerboard with barbwire "tribal" fingerboard inlays, black headstock overlay, three-per-side chrome tuners, triangular rosewood bridge, Dean pickup and electronics, available in Classic Black finish, 24.75 in. scale, mfg. 2008-present.

MSR $512	$330	$190 - 235	$110 - 140	

MICHAEL SCHENKER PERFORMER (MSP) – single cutaway Performer style, select spruce top, mahogany back/sides/neck, 14/21-fret rosewood fingerboard, round soundhole with custom rosette, matching headstock, three-per-side tuners, Piezo pickup with built-in tuner, chrome hardware, custom black and white finish with alternating patterns, mfg. 2005-present.

MSR $544	$340	$195 - 240	$115 - 145	

ACOUSTIC: RESONATOR SERIES

RESONATOR C (MODEL DGA-RC) – single rounded cutaway body, metal resonator plate, multi-ply body binding, mahogany back/sides, biscuit bridge, chrome hardware, three-per-side tuning machines, available in Black Satin or Natural Mahogany finish, mfg. 1998-2000.

	N/A	$125 - 150	$50 - 75	$399

RESONATOR SP (MODEL DGA-RSP) – dreadnought style, metal resonator plate, multi-ply body binding, mahogany back/sides, mahogany neck, spider bridge, chrome hardware, three-per-side tuning machines, available in Cherry Sunburst and Natural Mahogany finish, mfg. 1998-2007.

	N/A	$135 - 175	$70 - 95	$500

* *Resonator SPS* – similar to the Resonator SP except features mahogany back/top/sides, mfg. 1998-2004.

	N/A	$225 - 275	$125 - 150	$625

RESONATOR CE (MODEL DGA-RCE/RCE NM) – single rounded Dean cutaway body, metal resonator plate, multi-ply body binding, mahogany back/sides, biscuit bridge, chrome hardware, three-per-side tuning machines, chrome lipstick pickup, volume/tone controls, available in Black Satin (disc.) or Natural Mahogany finish, mfg. 1998-present.

MSR $624	$400	$225 - 275	$135 - 170	

RESONATOR GCE (MODEL DGA-RGCE) – single rounded Dean cutaway body, metal resonator plate, multi-ply body binding, mahogany back/sides, biscuit bridge, gold hardware, three-per-side tuning machines, humbucker pickup, volume/tone controls, available in Black Satin finish, mfg. 1998-2004.

	N/A	$300 - 350	$150 - 200	$790

RESONATOR CHROME G/S (MODEL RESC) – chrome steel resonator body, mahogany neck, 15/19 rosewood fingerboard with dot inlay, three-per-side chrome tuners, biscuit bridge, mfg. 2001-present.

MSR $942	$600	$350 - 425	$210 - 260	

• **Add 7.5% (MSR $993) for Chrome G version.**

* *Resonator Chrome Engraved* – similar to the Resonator Chrome except features an engraved chrome body, mfg. 2001-04.

	N/A	$350 - 425	$200 - 250	$875

HEIRLOOM RESONATOR (MODEL RESHB/RESHC) – brass or copper body, two f-holes, single cone resonator, mahogany neck, 19-fret rosewood fingerboard with dot inlays, black headstock, three-per-side tuners, Dean logo embossed into bridge cover, mfg. summer 2004-present.

MSR $962	$640	$350 - 450	$225 - 275	

ACOUSTIC: STAGE SERIES

STAGE ACOUSTIC (MODEL DGK-SA) – offset double cutaway hollow basswood body, round soundhole, body binding, set-in neck, 22-fret rosewood fingerboard with dot inlay, rosewood bridge, chrome hardware, small offset V-shaped headstock, three-per-side tuners, available in Classic Black, Cherry Sunburst, Trans. Blue, or Trans. Purple finish, mfg. 1998-2000.

	N/A	$175 - 225	$125 - 150	$499

STAGE ACOUSTIC DELUXE (MODEL DGK-SD) – similar to the Stage Acoustic, except features a flame maple top, gold hardware, Shadow piezo bridge, volume/tone controls, available in Flame Black, Flame Cherry Sunburst, Flame Gloss Natural, or Flame Red finish, mfg. 1998-2000.

	N/A	$225 - 275	$150 - 195	$599

• **Add $20 for left-handed configuration (Model DGK-SD-L), available in Flame Gloss Natural finish only.**

ACOUSTIC: STUDIO SERIES

STUDIO S – classic body style, solid spruce top, mahogany back/sides/neck, 14/20-fret rosewood fingerboard with dot inlay, multi-ply binding, abalone soundhole inlay, three-per-side Grover chrome tuners, available in Gloss Natural or Vintage Sunburst finish, mfg. 2001-06.

	N/A	$130 - 170	$70 - 95	$400

STUDIO S DELUXE – similar to the Studio S except has an extended fingerboard to 23 frets and abalone body binding, available in Gloss Natural finish, mfg. 2001-03.

	N/A	$150 - 195	$95 - 125	$419

MSR/NOTES	100%	EXCELLENT	AVERAGE	LAST MSR

ACOUSTIC: SWEETWOOD SERIES

The Sweetwood series was introduced in 2003. These are a higher end line of acoustic guitars having the highest price tag of any new Dean acoustic guitars.

SWEETWOOD OOR (MODEL SWOOR) – classical style, solid Sitka spruce top, solid rosewood back/sides, 12/20-fret rosewood fingerboard with inlays, slotted style headstock, available in Satin Natural finish, mfg. 2003-04.

	N/A	$500 - 575	$325 - 375	$1,225

SWEETWOOD DM (MODEL SWDM) – dreadnought style, solid Sitka spruce top, solid mahogany back/sides, 14/20-fret rosewood fingerboard with inlays, tortoiseshell binding, herringbone rosette, three-per-side tuners, available in Satin Natural finish, mfg. 2003-04.

	N/A	$350 - 425	$200 - 250	$965

SWEETWOOD DR (MODEL SWDR) – similar to the Sweetwood DM, except has rosewood back/sides, mfg. 2003-04.

	N/A	$500 - 575	$325 - 375	$1,225

SWEETWOOD JCR (MODEL SWJCR) – jumbo style, solid Sitka spruce top, solid mahogany back/sides, 14/20-fret rosewood fingerboard with inlays, tortoise binding, herringbone rosette, three-per-side tuners, available in Satin Natural finish, mfg. 2003-04.

	N/A	$550 - 650	$275 - 325	$1,440

ACOUSTIC: TRADITION SERIES

The **Tradition AK48 Pack** (AK48PK, MSR $199) includes an AK48 guitar, travel bag, pitch pipe, and picks. The **Tradition Guitar/ Amp Pack** (AEP, MSR $320) includes a single cutaway acoustic/electric guitar, DA20 acoustic guitar amp, gig bag, and cord.

TRADITION AK48 (MODEL AK48) – dreadnought style, select spruce top, mahogany sides/back/neck, 14/20-fret rosewood fingerboard with dot inlay, chrome hardware, Gloss Natural, Trans. Black, Trans. Blue, or Trans. Red finish, mfg. 2004-present.

MSR $339	$220	$130 - 160	$75 - 95	

TRADITION AK48 FLORENTINE (MODEL AK48 F) – single sharp cutaway jumbo-style body, select spruce top, quilt ash back and sides, black top binding, round soundhole with three-ring rosette (large middle ring of abalone pearl), 14/20-fret rosewood fingerboard with pearl dot inlays, quilt ash headstock overlay, three-per-side gold tuners, triangular rosewood bridge, black pickguard, Dean electronics, available in Gloss Natural finish, part of the Independent Series, mfg. 2008-present.

MSR $382	$250	$140 - 175	$85 - 105	

TRADITION CUTAWAY (MODEL T100C) – single rounded cutaway dreadnought-style body, spruce top, mahogany back and sides, single-ply black binding, round soundhole with three-ring rosette, 14/20-fret rosewood fingerboard with pearl dot inlays, mahogany headstock overlay, three-per-side chrome tuners, triangular rosewood bridge, Dean electronics, available in Blue Burst, Classic Black, or Gloss Natural finish, part of the Independent Series, mfg. 2008-2011.

	$170	$95 - 120	$55 - 75	$273

TRADITION D24 – dreadnought style body, solid Englemann spruce top, quilted rosewood back and sides, mahogany neck, 14/20 rosewood fingerboard with abalone tree-of-life inlay, three-per-side gold Grover tuners, multi-ply binding, abalone soundhole inlay, available in Gloss Natural finish, mfg. 2001-04.

	N/A	$275 - 325	$135 - 175	$740

TRADITION DAYTONA (MODEL DAYTONA) – dreadnought style, solid spruce top, mahogany sides/back/neck, 14/20-fret rosewood fingerboard with dot inlay, chrome hardware, Gloss Natural finish, mfg. 2003-present.

MSR $338	$220	$130 - 160	$75 - 95	

* *Tradition Daytona Electric* – similar to the Tradition Daytona except has a piezo pickup and electronics, mfg. 2003-2010.

	$240	$125 - 165	$70 - 90	$365

TRADITION EXOTIC (MODEL DGA-TE) – dreadnought style, solid Sitka spruce top, round soundhole, body binding, bird's-eye maple, European MAPA (disc.), Lacewood, Maple Burl, Quilted Ash (2006-2010), or Zebra (2006-2010) back/sides, 14/20-fret fingerboard with white dot inlay, triangular Dean rosewood bridge, three-per-side die-cast tuners, available in Gloss Natural finish, mfg. 2005-2010.

	$280	$150 - 200	$90 - 120	$438

* *Tradition Exotic Cutaway Electric (Model TEC)* – similar to the Tradition Exotica except has a single cutaway, (quilted ash is not available, but all other exotic woods are), and Dean electronics, available in Gloss Natural finish, mfg. 2006-2010.

	$400	$250 - 300	$130 - 170	$626

• Subtract 12.5% (MSR $550) for mahogany back and sides.

TRADITION FLORENTINE (MODEL T77FQM) – single cutaway dreadnought-style quilt maple body, multi-ply binding, round soundhole with abalone pearl rosette, 14/21-fret bound rosewood fingerboard with pearl diamond inlays, quilt maple headstock overlay, three-per-side gold tuners, triangular rosewood bridge, Dean electronics, available in Gloss Amber, Trans. Black, or Trans. Purple finish, part of the Independent Series, mfg. 2008-present.

MSR $454	$270	$150 - 200	$95 - 120	

MSR/NOTES	100%	EXCELLENT	AVERAGE	LAST MSR

TRADITION NOIR – similar to the Tradition One, except has no fingerboard inlay, select spruce top, and available in Powder Black finish, mfg. 2003-04.

	N/A	$125 - 150	$50 - 75	$375

TRADITION ONE (MODEL DGA-T1) – dreadnought style, select spruce top, round soundhole, body binding, mahogany back/sides, 14/20-fret fingerboard with white dot inlay, triangular Dean rosewood bridge, three-per-side die-cast tuners, available in Gloss Natural finish, mfg. 1998-2005.

	N/A	$110 - 140	$50 - 75	$365

* **Add $20 for left-handed configuration (Model DGA-T-L), available in Gloss Natural finish only.**
Left-hand model discontinued in 2000.

TRADITION S (MODEL TS) – dreadnought style, solid spruce top, round soundhole, body binding, mahogany back/sides, 14/20-fret fingerboard with white dot inlay, triangular Dean rosewood bridge, three-per-side Grover tuners, available in Gloss Natural, Classic Black, Satin Natural, Trans. Red, or Vintage Sunburst finish, mfg. 1998-2005.

	N/A	$130 - 170	$70 - 95	$400

* *Tradition S Left-Handed (Model TS LH)* – similar to the Tradition S except in left-handed configuration, mfg. 1998-2006.

	N/A	$150 - 200	$90 - 120	$450

* *Tradition S2 (Model TS2)* – similar to the Tradition S except has tortoiseshell binding, different rosette, and sealed tuners with oyster buttons, available in Classic Black, Gloss Natural, Satin Natural (disc.), Trans. Red (disc.), or Vintage Sunburst finish, mfg. 2006-present.

MSR $365	$240	$135 - 170	$80 - 100	

» *Tradition S2 Left-Handed (Model TS2LH)* – similar to the Tradition S2 except in left-handed configuration, mfg. 2007-08.

	N/A	$140 - 180	$85 - 105	$361

* *Tradition SE Electric* – similar to the Tradition S except features a piezo bridge pickup and Shadow five-band EQ, available in Gloss Natural finish, mfg. 1998-2000.

	N/A	$150 - 200	$85 - 115	$429

* *Tradition S CE Cutaway Electric (Model TSCE)* – similar to the Tradition S except features a single cutaway with Dean electronics, available in Gloss Natural or Blueburst finish, mfg. 2001-07.

	N/A	$200 - 250	$95 - 125	$565

* *Tradition S12 12-String (Model TS12)* – similar to the Tradition S except in 12-string configuration, available in Gloss Natural finish, mfg. 1999-2010.

	$320	$200 - 250	$95 - 125	$525

TRADITION TQS12 – dreadnought style 12-string body, solid spruce top, quilted maple back and sides, mahogany neck, 14/20 rosewood fingerboard with dot inlay, six-per-side gold Grover tuners, multi-ply binding, abalone soundhole inlay, available in Gloss Natural finish, mfg. 2001-03.

	N/A	$190 - 240	$125 - 150	$569

TRADITION TUCSON – similar to the Tradition One, except has a single cutaway, electronics, and lizard inlays, available in Sunburst or Gloss Natural finish, mfg. 2003-06.

	N/A	$275 - 325	$135 - 175	$750

TRADITION WING (T-WING) – dreadnought style, select spruce top, mahogany back and sides, Dean wing custom design soundhole, 20-fret rosewood fingerboard with dot inlay, rosewood bridge, piezo pickup, Buffer preamp with built-in tuner, chrome hardware, available in Black finish, mfg. summer 2005-2010.

	$275	$160 - 210	$90 - 120	$423

ACOUSTIC: MISC. MODELS

12 GAUGE (MODEL 12GAUGE) – dreadnought-style body, solid spruce top, mahogany body, round soundhole with three-ring rosette, multi-ply body binding, set mahogany neck, 14/20-fret rosewood fingerboard with maple open dot and 11-13th fret round shotgun shell end inlays, mahogany headstock overlay, three-per-side distressed chrome tuners, rosewood bridge, mahogany gun stock pickguard, DMT 12EX preamp with tuner and DWC-Aphex Aural Exciter and Big Bottom circuitry, available in Gloss Natural finish, 25.5 in. scale, mfg. 2011-present.

MSR $572	$350	$200 - 250	$120 - 150	

* *12 Gauge Cutaway (Model 12GAUGE CE)* – similar to the 12 Gauge, except has a smooth cutaway, available in Gloss Natural finish, mfg. 2011-present.

MSR $643	$400	$235 - 285	$140 - 175	

AXS FLAME (AX FLAME) – single cutaway body, select spruce top, mahogany body, round soundhole with no rosette, single-ply body binding, set mahogany neck, 14/20-fret rosewood fingerboard with pearl dot inlays, matching finish headstock overlay, three-per-side chrome tuners, rosewood bridge, no pickguard, Dean RD-0904TL preamp with four-band EQ, available in Gloss Natural finish with flame maple graphic, 25.5 in. scale, mfg. 2011-present.

MSR $323	$160	$90 - 115	$55 - 70	

MSR/NOTES	100%	EXCELLENT	AVERAGE	LAST MSR

AXS PERFORMER (AX PE) – single cutaway body, select spruce top, mahogany body, round soundhole with abalone rosette, single-ply body binding, set mahogany neck, 14/20-fret rosewood fingerboard with pearl dot inlays, black headstock overlay, three-per-side chrome tuners, rosewood bridge, no pickguard, Dean FTE-3, available in Silverburst finish, 25.5 in. scale, mfg. 2011-present.

MSR $348	$190	$110 - 135	$70 - 85	

AXS SPALT (AX SPALT) – single cutaway body, select spruce top, mahogany body, round soundhole with no rosette, single-ply body binding, set mahogany neck, 14/20-fret rosewood fingerboard with pearl dot inlays, rosewood headstock overlay, three-per-side chrome tuners, rosewood bridge, no pickguard, Dean RD-0904TL preamp with four-band EQ, available in Gloss Natural finish with spalt maple graphic, 25.5 in. scale, mfg. 2011-present.

MSR $323	$160	$90 - 115	$55 - 70	

DAVE MUSTAINE "MAKO" (MODEL MAKO) – single sharp cutaway folk-style body, solid maple top (Classic Black finish) or flame maple top (Trans. Black finish), mahogany back and sides, Mako-inspired four slot soundhole, multi-ply body binding, set mahogany neck, 14/21-fret ebony fingerboard with pearly Dave Mustaine "Mako" inlays, matching finish headstock overlay with shark inlay, three-per-side chrome tuners, ebony bridge, B-Band A3TY electronics with tuner, available in Classic Black or Trans. Black finish, 25.25 in. scale, mfg. 2010-present.

MSR $793	$500	$275 - 350	$170 - 210	

* Dave Mustaine "Mako Glory" (Model MAKOGLORY) – similar to the Dave Mustaine "Mako", except has sharktooth/dot fingerboard inlays and a USA flag-inspired finish, mfg. 2012-present.

MSR $793	$500	$275 - 350	$170 - 210	

EVOCOUSTIC – EVO-shaped acoustic body, spruce top, mahogany back/sides/neck, offset oval soundhole with rosette, bound top, 22-fret rosewood fingerboard with dot inlay, three-per-side tuners, triangle shaped bridge, Piezo pickup and three-band EQ, chrome hardware, available in Classic Black or Natural finish, mfg. summer 2004-06.

	N/A	$125 - 175	$70 - 90	$340

EXHIBITION THIN BODY (MODEL EX) – single sharp cutaway folk-style body, mahogany top, back, and sides, round soundhole with decorative rosette, single-ply body binding, set mahogany neck, 14/21-fret ebony fingerboard with pearly diamond inlays, matching finish headstock overlay, three-per-side black tuners, ebony bridge, DMT 12EX preamp with tuner and DWC-Aphex Aural Exciter and Big Bottom circuitry, available in Black Satin or Satin Natural finish, 25.25 in. scale, mfg. 2011-present.

MSR $569	$370	$215 - 265	$130 - 160	

* Exhibition Thin Body Flame Maple (Model EXFM) – similar to the Exhibition Thin Body, except has a flame maple body, available in Faded Denim or Trans. Red finish, mfg. 2012-present.

MSR $621	$400	$235 - 285	$140 - 175	

* Exhibition Thin Body Quilt Ash (Model EXQA) – similar to the Exhibition Thin Body, except has a quilt ash body, available in Gloss Natural or Tiger Eye finish, mfg. 2012-present.

MSR $621	$400	$235 - 285	$140 - 175	

GYPSY (MODEL GPS) – small single cutaway body with an arched back, select spruce top, lacewood back and sides, round soundhole, 14/20-fret rosewood fingerboard, three-per-side tuners, rosewood bridge, Piezo pickup system, chrome hardware, Natural finish, 22 in. scale, 34 in. overall length, mfg. 2005-2010.

	$240	$160 - 200	$90 - 120	$401

JUMBO CUTAWAY (MODEL 771J) – single rounded cutaway jumbo body, solid spruce top, spalted maple back and sides, multi-ply B/W top binding, round soundhole with a single ring of abalone pearl rosette, 14/20-fret bound rosewood fingerboard with custom inlays, spalted maple headstock overlay, three-per-side gold tuners, triangular rosewood bridge, Dean electronics, available in Gloss Natural finish, deluxe hardshell case included, part of the Independent Series, mfg. 2008-2010.

	$470	$300 - 350	$175 - 225	$794

MAMBA (MODEL MAMBA) – single rounded cutaway body, solid spruce top, maple back and sides, multi-ply black binding, round soundhole, maple neck, 14/21-fret maple fingerboard with double offset dot inlays and a black snake inlay that extends the length of the fingerboard down around the soundhole, maple headstock overlay, three-per-side chrome tuners, triangular rosewood bridge, Dean pickup and electronics, available in Gloss Natural finish, 24.75 in. scale, mfg. 2008 only.

	N/A	$275 - 325	$150 - 200	$668

MLCOUSTIC (MODEL MLCOUSTIC) – ML-shaped acoustic mahogany body, multi-ply body binding, triangular soundhole, mahogany neck, 23-fret rosewood fingerboard with pearl dot inlays, wing-style headstock with black overlay, three-per-side chrome tuners, triangular rosewood bridge with one pearl dot inlay, Dean Buffer electronics, available in Classic Black finish, 24.75 in. scale, mfg. 2008 only.

	N/A	$150 - 180	$95 - 120	$416

NATURAL SERIES DREADNOUGHT (MODEL NSD) – dreadnought-style body, solid Sitka spruce top, rosewood back and sides, round soundhole with abalone rosette, multi-ply herringbone body binding, set mahogany neck, 14/20-fret rosewood fingerboard with abalone dot inlays, rosewood headstock overlay with abalone logo and wing inlays, three-per-side Grover black tuners, rosewood bridge, DMT 12EX preamp with tuner and DWC-Aphex Aural Exciter and Big Bottom circuitry, available in Gloss Natural finish, 25.25 in. scale, mfg. 2012-present.

MSR $599	$400	$235 - 285	$140 - 175	

MSR/NOTES	100%	EXCELLENT	AVERAGE	LAST MSR

* ***Natural Series Dreadnought 12-String (Model NSD12)*** – similar to the Natural Series Dreadnought, except in 12-string configuration with six-per-side tuners, available in Gloss Natural finish, mfg. 2012-present.

MSR $761	$500	$280 - 350	$170 - 210	

* ***Natural Series Dreadnought Cutaway (Model NSDC)*** – similar to the Natural Series Dreadnought, except has a smooth cutaway, available in Gloss Natural finish, mfg. 2012-present.

MSR $704	$470	$270 - 335	$160 - 200	

NATURAL SERIES NSFC (MODEL NSFC) – single Florentine cutaway NSFC-style body, solid Sitka spruce top, mahogany (Classic Black finish) or rosewood (Gloss Natural finish) back and sides, round soundhole with abalone rosette, multi-ply herringbone body binding, set mahogany neck, 14/20-fret ebony fingerboard with abalone dot inlays, matching finish headstock overlay with abalone logo and wing inlays, three-per-side Grover black tuners, rosewood bridge, DMT 12EX preamp with tuner and DWC-Aphex Aural Exciter and Big Bottom circuitry, available in Classic Black or Gloss Natural finish, 25.25 in. scale, mfg. 2012-present.

MSR $599	$400	$235 - 285	$140 - 175	

* Add 17.5% (MSR $704) for Gloss Natural finish.

VCOUSTIC (MODEL VCO) – V-shaped acoustic body, select spruce top, mahogany back and sides, multiple-layer body binding, triangle-shaped soundhole with Dean T-Wing rosette, mahogany neck, 20-fret rosewood fingerboard with dot inlay, Dean V-shaped headstock with three-per-side chrome tuners, rosewood triangle-shaped bridge, pickup and electronics, available in Gloss Natural finish, mfg. 2006-2010.

	$220	$120 - 150	$70 - 90	$366

V-WING – single cutaway dreadnought-style body, baseball field-shaped soundhole Dean wing logo, 14/20-fret rosewood fingerboard with pearl block inlays, V-shaped black headstock, three-per-side chrome tuners with buttons, rosewood bridge, pickup system with built in tuner, available in Black finish, mfg. 2007-present.

MSR $423	$270	$150 - 200	$95 - 120	

ACOUSTIC ELECTRIC BASS

EAB BASS (MODEL EAB) – jumbo-style mahogany body, multi-ply body binding, round soundhole with multi-ring rosette, mahogany neck, rosewood fingerboard, rosewood headstock overlay, two-per-side chrome tuners, triangular rosewood bridge, Dean electronics, available in Classic Black finish, 34 in. scale, mfg. 2008-present.

MSR $299	$150	$95 - 120	$50 - 70	

* ***EAB Bass Cutaway (Model EABC)*** – similar to the EAB Bass, except has a single cutaway, available in Satin Natural finish, mfg. 2008-present.

MSR $348	$180	$115 - 145	$75 - 95	

»***EAB Bass Cutaway Five-String (Model EABC5)*** – similar to the EAB Bass Cutaway, except in five-string configuration, available in Satin Natural finish, mfg. 2008-present.

MSR $363	$200	$130 - 170	$85 - 105	

* ***EAB Bass Fretless (Model EABF)*** – similar to the EAB Bass, except has a fretless fingerboard with no markings, available in Satin Natural finish, mfg. 2008-present.

MSR $366	$200	$120 - 150	$75 - 95	

EQA BASS (MODEL EQAB) – single cutaway quilted ash body, multi-ply black binding, round soundhole with custom rosette, maple neck, 16/21-fret rosewood fingerboard with MOP dot inlays, quilted ash headstock overlay, two-per-side chrome tuners, triangular rosewood bridge, Dean electronics, available in Gloss Natural, Trans. Black, or Trans. Blue finish, mfg. 2008-present.

MSR $599	$400	$250 - 300	$135 - 175	

PQ (PERFORMER PLUS) BASS – jumbo style, single rounded cutaway body, quilted maple top, round soundhole, multi-ply body binding, mahogany back/sides, 22-fret fingerboard with white dot inlay, triangular Dean rosewood bridge, two-per-side Grover tuners, chrome hardware, Shadow P7 pickup, four-band EQ, available in Trans. Black or Gloss Natural finish, mfg. 1998-2004.

	N/A	$275 - 325	$135 - 175	$740

In 2004, the Performer Plus series was renamed the PQ series.

* ***PQ (Performer Plus) 5 Bass*** – similar to the Performer Plus bass except in five-string configuration, mfg. 1998-2004.

	N/A	$350 - 400	$175 - 225	$875

EXOTICA RADIANT BASS – single rounded cutaway, Sitka spruce top, flame maple top, mahogany neck, 15/22 fret rosewood fingerboard with radiant sun inlays, two-per-side chrome Grover tuners, Shadow pickups, multi-ply binding, abalone soundhole inlay, available in Gloss Natural finish, mfg. 2000-04.

	N/A	$350 - 425	$200 - 250	$875

MAMBA BASS (MODEL MAMB) – single rounded cutaway body, solid spruce top, maple back and sides, multi-ply black binding, round soundhole, maple neck, 16/21-fret maple fingerboard with thumbnail inlays and a black snake inlay that extends the length of the fingerboard down around the soundhole, maple headstock overlay, two-per-side chrome tuners, triangular rosewood bridge, Dean pickup and electronics, available in Gloss Natural finish, mfg. 2008 only.

	N/A	$300 - 375	$175 - 225	$798

MSR/NOTES	100%	EXCELLENT	AVERAGE	LAST MSR

PERFORMER BASS CE (MODEL DGA-PBCE) – jumbo style, single rounded cutaway body, spruce top, round soundhole, multi-ply body binding, mahogany back/sides, 20-fret fingerboard with white dot inlay, triangular Dean rosewood bridge, two-per-side Grover tuners, chrome hardware, piezo bridge pickup, four-band EQ, available in Satin Natural finish, mfg. 1998-2007.

	N/A	$200 - 250	$95 - 125	$525

* *Performer Bass CE Fretless* – similar to the Performer Bass CE except in Fretless configuration, mfg. 2002-07.

	N/A	$225 - 275	$125 - 150	$615

* *Performer Bass CE Left-Handed* – similar to the Performer Bass CE except in left-handed configuration, disc. 2007.

	N/A	$230 - 280	$125 - 150	$625

PERFORMER BASS DAO (MODEL DGA-DAO) – jumbo style, single rounded cutaway body, dao top/back/sides, round soundhole with wood Celtic rosette, multi-ply body binding, mahogany neck, 22-fret rosewood fingerboard with white dot inlay, triangular Dean rosewood bridge, two-per-side tuners, chrome hardware, Dean electronics, available in Natural finish, 32 in. scale, mfg. summer 2004-07.

	N/A	$300 - 375	$175 - 225	$751

PERFORMER BASS QM (MODEL PBQM) – single rounded cutaway jumbo-style body, quilted maple top/back/sides, round soundhole with wood abalone rosette, multi-ply body binding, mahogany neck, 22-fret rosewood fingerboard with white dot inlay, bound headstock with two-per-side chrome tuners, triangular Dean rosewood bridge, Prener dual pickup with microphone and saddle sensor, available in Cherry Sunburst or Natural finish, 34 in. scale, mfg. 2007-08.

	N/A	$300 - 350	$150 - 200	$698

DEAR

Instruments previously produced in Asia. Distributed by L.A. Guitar Works in Reseda, CA.

Dear guitars are medium quality acoustic guitars that feature a wood top mated to a shallow fiberglass back. The Dear design is similar to the design pioneered by Ovation, except instead of a rounded bowl back the Dear design is squared. At the given list price point, it is estimated that the Dear guitar tops are laminated, not solid.

The three Dear acoustic/electric models have a cutaway body, on board preamp and bridge-mounted pickup system. The **DAC-480E** (last MSR was $299) has a round soundhole and spruce top. The **DAC-485E** (last MSR of $319) features similar construction with a highly flamed maple top. Instead of a round soundhole, the **DAC-500E** has a pair of f-holes.

In addition to the acoustic/electrics, Dear also offers two classical style/synthetic back models. The **EL 1500** (last MSR of $439) has a cedar top and matte finish; the **EL 2000** (last MSR of $459) has a spruce top.

DEARSTONE MANDOLIN WORKS

Instruments currently produced in Blountville, TN since 1993.

Luthier Ray Dearstone has been building instruments since the late 1980s and he focuses mainly on archtop guitars and mandolins. Dearstone also produces flattop guitars, acoustic/electric guitars, electric upright basses, and violins. All instruments are carefully built by hand and Dearstone has earned a reputation for his precision, quality, and consistency between instruments. For more information, contact Dearstone directly or visit their website.

Dearstone produces three main archtop guitars: the **Appalachian**, the **Mockingbird**, and the **Iris**. For flattop guitars, Dearstone offers four models: the **HD-18**, the **HD-23**, the **HD-28**, and the **PAR-1**.

DEBUTANTE

Guitars currently produced in China since 2008. Distributed by Alfred Publishing in Van Nuys, CA.

Debutante was introduced in 2008 as a branch of Daisy Rock guitars. While Daisy Rock builds high-quality professional instruments that are designed for women and girl players, the Debutante line offers entry-level instruments that are designed for the beginner guitar player and children. Many of the lower priced guitars that were once produced under the Daisy Rock trademark are now branded Debutante and also feature lower prices. For more information, visit Debutante's website or contact them directly.

ACOUSTIC

JUNIOR MISS ACOUSTIC SHORT-SCALE GUITAR – folk-style agathis body, round soundhole with multi-ring rosette, set mahogany neck, 12/18-fret rosewood fingerboard with pearl dot inlays, matching finish headstock overlay, three-per-side chrome tuners, rosewood bridge with two pearl dot inlays, available in Bubble Gum, Cotton Candy Blue (2009-present), or Popsicle Purple (2009-present) finish, 23.25 in. scale, mfg. 2008-present.

MSR $139	$80	$50 - 65	$30 - 40	

• **Add 12.5% (MSR $159) for left-handed configuration (Bubble Gum finish only).**

This model is also available as part of a guitar package that includes a Junior Miss Acoustic Short-Scale guitar, tuner, picks, and guitar strap (MSR $169).

DECAVA

Instruments currently built in Stratford, CT since 1983.

Luthier James R. DeCava Born was born and raised in Stratford, CT, and he began playing guitar and banjo as a teenager. DeCava began performing repairs on his guitars simply because there were few repair people around at the time. While spending time meeting others with similar interests, DeCava came into contact with Paul Morrisey and Bob Flesher at Liberty Banjo Co. DeCava worked for them between 1975 and the early 1980s cutting and inlaying mother-of-pearl with intricate designs. Through the years DeCava has built many different stringed instruments including banjos, mandolins, flattop guitars, and solid body guitars. DeCava now focuses on archtop guitar building. For more information, visit DeCava's website or contact them directly.

CONTACT INFORMATION
DECAVA
369 Nichols Ave.
Stratford, CT 06614
Phone No.: 203-243-4036
www.decava.com
Admin@DeCava.com

GENERAL INFORMATION

All De Cava archtop guitars share similar features such as a solid hand-carved Sitka or Adirondack spruce top, carved maple back with matching sides, ebony fingerboard, hinged ebony tailpiece, an adjustable bridge, ebony pickguard, ebony peghead overlays, and bound f-holes. De Cava offers his models in either a 16 in. or 17 in. body width, with parallel or X-bracing. Prices include a hard shell case: Banjos, Ukuleles, Mandolin, and Classical guitars are also available.

De Cava briefly offered the Classic model (disc. last MSR was $5,720), which featured a flame or quilted maple top, fancy scroll position markers on the fingerboard, a pearl nut, an engraved pearl truss rod cover, and hand-engraved inlay pieces on the peghead (front and back)/pickguard/tailpiece/heel. An 18 in. body width was available at no extra charge.

- **Add $125 (and up) for special fingerboard inlays.**
- **Add $200 for Blonde finish.**
- **Add $200 (and up) for floating or built-in pick-up.**

ACOUSTIC: ARCHTOP SERIES

De Cava's **Stratford** (list $8,500) is his traditional style guitar model, and features three layer body binding/single layer bound peghead and fingerboard, gold plated trim and tuners, pearl peghead logo, ebony truss rod cover, and gold and ebony tailpiece, available in a traditional Sunburst finish. A seven-string model was also available.

The **Stylist** model, discontinued, (last MSR was $7,450) was the deluxe model, with the highly figured maple back and sides, multi-layer bindings on the body/neck/peghead, five-piece laminated figured maple neck, hand cut and engraved pearl pattern throughout the guitar, hand engraved pearl truss rod cover, and gold plated Schaller tuners with ebony buttons. The Stylist was available in either 16 in., 17 in., or 18 in. body widths; and Antique, Natural, or Sunburst finishes. A seven-string configuration was available at no extra charge.

ACOUSTIC: SIGNATURE SERIES

De Cava has a new model, the **Signature Blues**. The Signature Blues model was designed in conjunction with blues guitarist Debbie Davis. The Signature models are lightweight, contemporary hand-carved hollow body archtops with all the sleek contours of a solid body. Signature Series models have a 15.25 in. body width, 2.25 in. body depth, either a single neck pickup (Jazz model) or double pickups (Blues model), tune-o-matic style bridge/ebony tailpiece, and Neo-Classic fingerboard. The retail price of $5,450 includes a durable gig bag. The Signature models are available with optional customer's signature inlaid in pearl, and fingerboard inlays. This model is available in seven-, eight-, or nine-string.

The **Mark Elf Custom Classic** (list is $10,400) is a guitar designed by and for Mark Elf. It has Grover Imperial tuners, one-piece neck, multi-bound body, neck and peghead, split-block fingerboard inlays, Adirondack spruce and other select woods used throughout, 17 in. body width, floating pickup, jack, voume and tone controls mounted on the pickguard. The **Mark Elf Neo Classic** model was also available (last list was $6,300).

The **Auditorium Model** (disc. last list was $3,000) has Indian rosewood back and sides, Adirondack red spruce top, ebony fingerboard and bridge, gold plated tuners, other wood options. The **L'Artista** (list price is $8,500) is a single cutaway archtop guitar. A Ten String Classical guitar was introduced in 2004, as a signature model for Janet Marlow, which was available in the base **Essence** model (last list was $2,450) or the **NY Concert Model** (last list was $5,650) with higher appointments for $5,650 (disc.).

DECCA

Instruments previously produced in Japan during the 1960s.

The Decca trademark is a brand name used by U.S. importers Decca Records. Used acoustic models are typically found priced between $100 and $200. Source: Michael Wright, *Guitar Stories*, Volume One.

DEERING BANJO COMPANY INC.

Guitars were previously built from 1989 to 1991. Banjos have been manufactured in Spring Valley since 1975. Previously produced in Lemon Grove, CA.

In 1975, Greg and Janet Deering began producing the quality banjos for which the company is known and respected. While continuing to offer innovative banjo designs, the Deerings also offer several models from entry level to professional play. No other company has produced banjos longer than Deering in the U.S.

Deering offers a banjo model that is tuned and played like a guitar. The **MB-6** is designed so the guitar player who doesn't have to learn banjo to play banjo. The MB-6 is

CONTACT INFORMATION
DEERING BANJO COMPANY INC.
3733 Kenora Drive
Spring Valley, CA 91977-1829
Phone No.: 619-464-8252
Fax No.: 619-464-0833
www.deeringbanjos.com
info@deeringbanjos.com

also available in a 12-string configuration.

In the late 1980s, Deering offered four different solid body guitar models in two variations that carried a retail price between $1,498 and $2,850. The guitar models were also offered with some custom options, but were only produced for a little over one year.

For more information on Deering banjos, visit their website or contact the company directly.

DEGENNARO GUITARS

Instruments currently produced in Grand Rapids, MI since 2003.

CONTACT INFORMATION
DEGENNARO GUITARS
Grand Rapids, MI
Phone No.: 616-617-0829
http://degennarocustoms.tripod.com/
degennaroguitars@email.com

Luthier William DeGennaro builds acoustic guitars in Grand Rapids, MI. His Acoustic Bell Guitar is based on the traditional dreadnought design with a bell-shaped soundhole. The basic model starts at $6,000. DeGennaro also builds mandolins, electric guitars, and electric basses. For more information, visit DeGennaro's website or contact him directly.

DELL'ARTE INSTRUMENTS, INC.

Instruments currently built in Fallbrook, CA. Distributed by Dell'Arte Instruments, Inc. Dell'Arte guitars have been produced since 1997.

CONTACT INFORMATION
DELL'ARTE INSTRUMENTS, INC.
852 Pamela Lane
El Cajon, CA 92020
Phone No.: 619-596-7739
www.gypsyjazz.net
info@gypsyjazz.net

Jazz guitarist Alain Cola started Dell'Arte Instruments in 1997, and the first line of Maccaferri style guitars were built in Mexico. Luthier John Kinnard started a small repair/retail store in 1996 called Finegold Guitars and Mandolins, and in 1998, Alain Cola met Kinnard and formed a partnership. Dell'Arte Instruments still specializes in Maccaferri-style guitars that are endorsed by performers worldwide. In 2001, Dell'Arte strings were introduced. For more information, contact Dell'Arte Instruments directly.

The standard models include: **Anouman** (MSR $3,978), **Dark Eyes** (MSR $3,978), **Swing 42 Standard** (MSR $4,104), **Swing 42 Deluxe** (MSR $2,400), **Model 503** (MSR $3,978), **Hommage** (MSR $4,104), **Tenor Maccaferri** (MSR $4,104). They also have some recent models including the **Angelo Debarre Signature** (MSR $4,934), the **Leadbelly 12-String** (MSR $3,904), the **Jimmy Rosenberg** (MSR $4,934), the **Tchavolo Schmitt** (MSR $4,934) and the **Boulou Ferre** (MSR $4,934).

Discontinued models include the **Sweet Chorus** (last MSR was $1,800), **Minor Swing** (last MSR was $1,800), **Finegold OM** (3 variations last MSR was $1,400-$2,200), **Jazz Arch Top** (last MSR was $2,900), the **Studio Dreadnought**, the **Studio OM**, and the **Pigalle**.

DELMUNDO GUITARS

Instruments previously produced in Boulder, CO. Guitars were produced until 2005.

Delmundo guitars were produced under the direction of Bob Alexander. The guitars were dubbed as being "the best sounding, most beautiful guitars in the world." They produced a wide variety of acoustic guitars including classical, flamenco, original, and historic models. Many models had original shapes with sharp points similar to mandolins and tear-drop D'Aquisto models.

DELTA

Guitars previously produced during the mid-2000s. Distributed by Musician's Wholesale American in Nashville, TN.

Musician's Wholesale America distributed the Delta line of acoustic and electric guitars as well as Old Hickory bluegrass instruments, and Romeo violins. Most acoustic guitars retailed between $100 and $150.

DEMARS GUITARS

Acoustic guitars currently produced in Norwich, VT.

CONTACT INFORMATION
DEMARS GUITARS
PO Box 622
Norwich, VT 05055
Phone No.: 802-649-2098
www.demarsguitars.com
info@demarsguitars.com

Luthier Dan DeMars builds hand-crafted acoustic and solidbody acoustic guitars in his Norwich, VT shop as well as a line of electric instruments. DeMars has played guitar since the 1970s, worked for Ned Steinberger and, was the head of marketing, advertising, and artist relations for Ned's company NS Design. DeMars' guitars include the Viridis chambered solidbody acoustic (MSR $3,400) and the Long Trail Bass available in four-string (MSR $3,300) and five-string (MSR $3,600) configurations. For more information, visit DeMars' website or contact him directly.

DEY

See BD Dey in the B section.

DIASONIC

Instruments previously produced in Japan, unknown production dates.

It is estimated that Diasonic instruments were constructed in the 1970s, as their headstock design skirts infringe on Gibson's standard design.

The Diasonic folk style acoustic has a spruce top, geometric pattern rosette, nato back and sides, 14/20-fret rosewood fingerboard with rectangular pearloid inlay, three-per-side chrome tuners, adjustable saddle, white bridge pins, and tortoise pickguard. Diasonic instruments in average condition command between $100 and $150. Source: Walter Murray, Frankenstein Fretworks.

DILLON

Instruments currently built in Taos, NM.

CONTACT INFORMATION
DILLON
PO Box 2913
Taos, NM 87571
Phone No.: 505) 758-1996
www.dillonguitars.com

John Dillon started building guitars in New Mexico in 1975. Dillon moved to Bloomsburg, PA for ten years and produced guitars. Dillon then returned to New Mexico, where he currently builds guitars. He also gives workshops on guitar making and tours part time as part of a folk duo, John & Viv. Prices start at $2,250. For a full listing of prices, options, and other information, visit Dillon's website or contact him directly.

DINOSAUR

Instruments and other products currently produced in China. Distributed by Eleca International Inc. in Chino, CA.

CONTACT INFORMATION
DINOSAUR
Distributed by Eleca International, Inc.
5635 Daniels St.
Chino, CA 91710
Phone No.: 909-287-0500
Phone No.: 888-463-5322
www.dinosauramps.com
info@eleca.com

Dinosaur makes a wide variety of products including guitars, amplifiers, and other accessories in the music industry. They are built in China and sold throughout the United States. Among the products that they produce include combo packs that have a guitar, amp, and other accessories for the starting guitar player. For more information refer to the distributor's website.

Dinosaur's lineup consists mainly of basic acoustic models such as the dreadnought, the folk-style, and the classical. Some models are offered with electronics and have cutaways. These guitars are offered at a competitive price.

DITSON

Instruments previously manufactured in Boston, MA from 1865 to the early 1900s and in Nazareth, PA between the mid-1910s and early 1930s.

The Oliver Ditson Company, Inc. was formed in 1835 by music publisher Oliver Ditson (1811-1888). Ditson was a primary force in music merchandising, distribution, and retail sales on the East Coast. He also helped establish two musical instrument manufacturers: The John Church Company of Cincinnati, Ohio, and Lyon & Healy (Washburn) in Chicago, IL.

In 1865, Ditson established a manufacturing branch of his company under the supervision of John Haynes, called the John C. Haynes Company. This branch built guitars for a number of trademarks, such as Bay State, Tilton, and Haynes Excelsior.

Ditson later had Martin build guitars for them as sort of a House Brand. Martin built guitars for Ditson from circa 1916 to 1930, and Ditson is credited for requesting the first dreadnought-sized guitar. Ditson became Martin's largest client as they produced thousands of instruments over the years. Source: Tom Wheeler, *American Guitars* and Teja Gerken, *Acoustic Guitar Magazine*.

Due to the close assocation with Martin guitars and the influence Ditson had on Martin, their guitars have become quite collectible. Most models will follow Martin's typical size/style chart (Style 1 Size 0, Style 2 Size 3, Style 3 Size 000, etc.). Since almost every guitar is different, all examples should be evaluated on a case by case basis. Prices on these guitars can typically be found between $3,000 and $6,000 in excellent condition. Original dreadnought models have been seen priced between $7,500 and $10,000.

DIXON

Guitars previously produced in Japan, Korea, and/or China between the 1960s and the 1990s.

The Dixon trademark has probably been used on a variety of different guitars and manufacturers. Catalogs exist from the 1960s, 1980s, and 1990s and most indicate that the instruments were built in either Japan or Korea. In the mid-1980s, Dixon guitars were distributed by the Reliance International Corp. in Taiwan. Regardless of where Dixon instruments came from, they are largely copies of popular American designs. Any further information on the Dixon trademark can be submitted directly to Blue Book Publications.

D.J. ARGUS

Instruments previously built in New York, NY during the early 1990s. Distributed by Rudy's Music Shop in New York City, NY.

D.J. Argus archtops featured traditional D'Angelico stylings, solid spruce tops, laminated curly maple back and sides, engraved tailpieces, and Grover Imperial tuners. It is unknown how many guitars were actually produced.

DOBRO

Current trademark of instruments currently built by Original Acoustic Instruments (OAI), located in Nashville, TN. Original Acoustic Instruments is a division of the Gibson Guitar Corporation. Previously manufactured by Original Musical Instruments Company, located in Huntington Beach, CA. In 1997, production was moved to Nashville, TN. Distributed by the Gibson Guitar Corporation of Nashville, TN. The original Dobro company was formed in 1928 in Los Angeles, CA.

CONTACT INFORMATION
DOBRO
A Division of Gibson
161 Opry Mills Drive
Nashville, TN 37214
Phone No.: 615-514-2200
www.gibson.com/products/bluegrass

The Dopyera family emigrated from the Austro-Hungary area to Southern Califonia in 1908 and in the early 1920s, John and Rudy Dopyera began producing banjos. They were approached by guitarist George Beauchamp to help solve his volume (or lack thereof) problem with other instruments in the vaudeville orchestra. In the course

MSR/NOTES	100%	EXCELLENT	AVERAGE	LAST MSR

of their conversation, the idea of placing aluminum resonators in a guitar body for amplification purposes was developed. John Dopyera and his four brothers (plus some associates, like George Beauchamp) formed National in 1925. The initial partnership between Dopyera and Beauchamp lasted for about two years, and then John Dopyera left National to form the Dobro company. The Dobro name was chosen as a contraction of the Dopyera Brothers (and it also means good in Slavic languages).

The Dobro and National companies were later remerged by Louis Dopyera in 1931 or 1932. The company moved to Chicago, IL in 1936, and a year later granted Regal the rights to manufacture Dobros. The revised company changed its name to Valco in 1943, and worked on war materials during World War II. In 1959, Valco transferred the Dobro name and tools to Emil Dopyera. Between 1966 and 1967, the Dobro trademark was sold to Semie Moseley, of Mosrite fame. Moseley constructed the first Dobros out of parts from Emil's California plant, and later built his own necks and bodies. Moseley also built Mobros, a Mosrite-inspired Dobro design. In 1970, Mosrite fell into bankruptcy and Moseley lost the Dobro trademark, however after he started producing Mosrites again he also produced Dobro-inspired guitars under the Mobro brand. In the late 1960s, Emil's company produced resonator guitars under the tradename of Hound Dog and Dopera (note the missing "y") Originals. When the Dobro name finally became available again, Emil and new associates founded the Original Musical Instruments Company, Inc. (OMI) in 1970. In 1985, Chester and Mary Lizak purchased OMI from Gabriela and Ron Lazar; and eight years later in 1993, OMI was purchased by the Gibson Guitar Corporation, and production continued to be centered in California. Gibson changed the name to OAI (Original Acoustic Instruments), and the production of Dobro instruments was moved to Nashville, TN in the Spring of 1997. Gibson continues to produced Dobro resonators under the OAI trademark. Early company history courtesy Bob Brozman, *The History and Artistry of National Resonator Instruments*.

ACOUSTIC: CALIFORNIA MADE MODELS 1929-1939

Not only do Dobro guitars not have a model number, but models were often inconsistent. To determine your model of Dobro, you have to read through the model descriptions in order to match it up with the correct number. Woods and other pieces are known to be inconsistent as well. There are also overlapping models where a California model was made and at the same time a Regal model was introduced with the same number designation.

MODEL 36 – magnolia body, mahogany round neck, macawood fingerboard, silver painted hardware, available in Black finish, mfg. 1932-34.

	N/A	$1,950 - 2,250	$1,300 - 1,500	

MODEL 37 – mahogany body, round neck, bound body and bound 12-fret fingerboard with dot inlay, Light-red finish, mfg. 1932-34.

	N/A	$1,800 - 2,100	$1,300 - 1,500	

MODEL 45 – wood body of unknown woods, square or round-neck, silver metal parts and other painted parts, Dark Walnut finish, mfg. 1929-1934.

	N/A	$1,900 - 2,250	$1,300 - 1,500	

Certain pieces may be painted a mahogany color and serial numbers of this variation run between 1200 and 1300.

MODEL 55/56 – hardwood body, round or square neck, binding on the 12-fret fingerboard only, chrome plated hardware, Walnut finish, mfg. 1929-1934.

	N/A	$2,100 - 2,500	$1,350 - 1,600	

In 1932 the Model 55 was renamed the Model 56 and featured a birch body, mahogany neck, a bound red bean fingerboard, and nickel hardware. This model was also referred to as the Standard.

MODEL 65/66 – wood body with sandblasted French scroll design on the entire body, binding on fingerboard, mfg. 1929-1933.

	N/A	$3,200 - 4,000	$2,100 - 2,500	

In 1932, the Model 66 replaced the Model 65 with a birch body, mahogany neck, and chrome-plated hardware. Some models were available with a sandblasted design on the headstock as well. In 1932 the Model 66 was also available as the 66B with body binding.

* *Model 60* – similar to the Model 66 except features a large D on the back and a bound red bean fingerboard, mfg. 1933-36.

	N/A	$4,000 - 5,000	$2,500 - 3,000	

MODEL 85/86 – mahogany body, engraved coverplate, handrest with fleur-de-lis engraving, triple bound body, mahogany neck, bound fingerboard, available in round or square neck, mfg. 1929-1934.

	N/A	$4,800 - 6,000	$3,000 - 3,500	

This model was also known as the Professional. In 1932 it was renamed from the Model 85 to the Model 86 and features a rosewood fingerboard, chrome plated hardware, engraved tuners, and has a two-tone red/brown finish.

MODEL 125 (DE LUXE) – five-ply black walnut body with matching burl, handrest engraved with "Dobro Deluxe," triple bound body, black walnut round or square neck, ebony fingerboard, celluloid inlay logo, nickel plated hardware, available in Natural finish, mfg. 1929-1934.

	N/A	$8,000 - 10,000	$5,000 - 6,000	

MSR/NOTES	100%	EXCELLENT	AVERAGE	LAST MSR

ACOUSTIC: REGAL ERA INSTRUMENTS

REGAL MODEL 27 – birch, mahogany, or maple body, round or square neck with 12 or 14 frets, holes at the end of the fingerboard, available in two-tone walnut finish, mfg. 1933-1942.

| | N/A | $1,700 - 2,000 | $1,100 - 1,300 | |

This model was produced in California. In 1939, three-segment f-holes were added to specifications of the Model 25.

REGAL MODEL 37 – mahogany body, round or square neck with 12 or 14 frets, bound body, available in Sunburst finish, mfg. 1933-1937.

| | N/A | $1,850 - 2,100 | $1,200 - 1,350 | |

Some models were produced with bound fingerboards, and this model was also available as a California.

REGAL MODEL 45 – spruce top, mahogany back and sides, four-ply top binding, single-ply back binding, ebony fingerboard, round or square neck, mfg. 1933-37.

| | N/A | $2,000 - 2,350 | $1,300 - 1,500 | |

REGAL MODEL 46/47 – aluminum body dobro lite or luma lite body, 14-fret round neck joint, slotted headstock, silver finish with gold highlights, mfg. 1935-1942.

| | N/A | $1,900 - 2,250 | $1,300 - 1,500 | |

In 1937, the finish was changed to a mahogany or maple grain paint. In 1939, the model was changed to the number 47.

REGAL MODEL 55 – spruce top, mahogany back and sides, arched back, bound body, round or square neck, chrome hardware with inlays, mfg. 1933-34.

| | N/A | $2,250 - 2,750 | $1,400 - 1,750 | |

REGAL MODEL 62/65 – brass body with nickel plating, Spanish dancer etching on the back, solid headstock, mfg. 1935-1942.

| | N/A | $2,100 - 2,500 | $1,350 - 1,600 | |

By 1937, the rosewood fingerboard was documented. In 1939, the Model 62 was changed to the 65.

ANGELUS – birch body, round or square neck, three-segment f-holes, 12 large round holes in the coverplate, simulated binding by paint, slotted peghead, Walnut, Natural, or Sunburst finish, mfg. 1933-36.

| | N/A | $1,700 - 2,000 | $1,100 - 1,300 | |

ACOUSTIC: GARDENA/MOSRITE PRODUCTION MODELS 1965-69

In 1965, standard production of Dobros was underway again in Gardena, CA. Ed Dopyera's son Emil Dopyera, along with a few partners, received a license to build instruments under the Dobro trademark. In 1966, Mosrite founder, Semie Moseley, purchased Dobro and continued producing the same models that were introduced a year earlier and eventually moving production to the Mosrite production facility in Bakersfield, CA. The Mosrite/Dobro era lasted until 1969 when Mosrite went bankrupt and production ceased. Instruments produced in Gardena, CA under the Dopyera-ownership have serial numbers stamped on the top of the headstock. Instruments produced in Bakersfield, CA under Mosrite ownership have serial numbers stamped in the fingerboard toward the body. No serial number lists exist for either era of manufacture.

C-3 "THE MONTEREY" – Spanish guitar configuration, compact body with mahogany back and sides and a maple top, top and back body binding with double top purfling, set slim adj. neck, 14/19-fret rosewood fingerboard with dot inlays, standard headstock, three-per-side tuners, C-style resonator with two diamond hole plate round soundholes, trapeze tailpiece, available in Natural finish, 23.25 in. scale, mfg. 1965-69.

| | N/A | $1,000 - 1,200 | $625 - 750 | |

* **C-3E "The Monterey Electric"** – similar to the C-3 "The Monterey," except has a single coil Dobro pickup two knobs (v, tone), and a jack on the face of the guitar, available in Natural finish, mfg. 1965-69.

| | N/A | $1,200 - 1,500 | $700 - 850 | |

C-60 "THE AVALON" – Spanish guitar configuration, standard body with unspecified wood construction, top and back body binding, set slim adj. neck, 14/20-fret rosewood fingerboard with dot inlays, standard headstock, three-per-side tuners, C-style resonator with two diamond hole plate round soundholes, trapeze tailpiece, available in Candy Apple Red or Dark Metallic Blue finish, 24.625 in. scale, mfg. 1965-67.

| | N/A | $1,000 - 1,200 | $625 - 750 | |

* **C-60E "The Avalon Electric"** – similar to the C-60 "The Avalon," except has a single coil Dobro pickup two knobs (v, tone), and a jack on the face of the guitar, available in Candy Apple Red or Metallic Blue finish, mfg. 1965-67.

| | N/A | $1,200 - 1,500 | $700 - 850 | |

C-65 "THE PLAINSMAN" – Spanish guitar configuration, standard body with rounded shoulders and Ribbon Grained African mahogany, select maple, or mahogany back and sides with a maple top construction, top and back body binding with double top purfling, set slim adj. neck, 14/20-fret rosewood fingerboard with dot inlays, standard headstock, three-per-side tuners, C-style resonator with two diamond hole plate round soundholes, trapeze tailpiece, available in Natural finish, 24.625 in. scale, mfg. 1966-67.

| | N/A | $1,000 - 1,200 | $625 - 750 | |

* **C-65E "The Plainsman Electric"** – similar to the C-65 "The Plainsman," except has a single coil Dobro pickup two knobs (v, tone), and a jack on the face of the guitar, available in Natural finish, mfg. 1966-67.

| | N/A | $1,200 - 1,500 | $700 - 850 | |

MSR/NOTES	100%	EXCELLENT	AVERAGE	LAST MSR

D-12 "THE COLUMBIA" – 12-string Spanish guitar configuration, standard body with ribbon grained African mahogany or figured curly maple, top and back body binding, set slim adj. neck, 14/20-fret rosewood fingerboard with dot inlays, bound slotted headstock, six-per-side open-style banjo tuners, D-style resonator with two diamond hole plate round soundholes, trapeze tailpiece, available in Natural finish, 24.625 in. scale, mfg. 1966-67.

| | N/A | $850 - 1,000 | $600 - 700 | |

* **D-12E "The Columbia Electric"** – similar to the D-12 "The Columbia," except has a single coil Dobro pickup two knobs (v, tone), and a jack on the face of the guitar, available in Natural finish, mfg. 1966-67.

| | N/A | $1,000 - 1,250 | $625 - 750 | |

D-12S "THE LEXINGTON" – 12-string Steel guitar configuration, standard body with ribbon grained African mahogany or figured curly maple, top and back body binding, set slim adj. square neck, 14/20-fret rosewood fingerboard with dot inlays, bound slotted headstock, six-per-side open-style forward-facing banjo tuners, D-style resonator with two diamond hole plate round soundholes, trapeze tailpiece, available in Natural finish, 24.625 in. scale, mfg. 1966-67.

| | N/A | $850 - 1,000 | $600 - 700 | |

* **D-12SE "The Lexington Electric"** – similar to the D-12S "The Lexington," except has a single coil Dobro pickup two knobs (v, tone), and a jack on the face of the guitar, available in Natural finish, mfg. 1966-67.

| | N/A | $1,000 - 1,250 | $625 - 750 | |

D-40 "THE TEXARKANA" – Spanish guitar configuration, standard body with unspecified wood construction, top and back body binding, set slim adj. neck, 14/20-fret rosewood fingerboard with dot inlays, standard headstock, three-per-side tuners, D-style resonator with two diamond hole plate round soundholes, trapeze tailpiece, available in Candy Apple Red, Dark Metallic Blue, or Mahogany Sunburst finish, 24.625 in. scale, mfg. 1965-67.

| | N/A | $1,000 - 1,200 | $625 - 750 | |

* **D-40E "The Texarkana Electric"** – similar to the D-40 "The Texarkana," except has a single coil Dobro pickup two knobs (v, tone), and a jack on the face of the guitar, available in Candy Apple Red, Dark Metallic Blue, or Mahogany Sunburst finish, mfg. 1965-67.

| | N/A | $1,200 - 1,500 | $700 - 850 | |

D-40S "THE BLUE GRASS" – Steel guitar configuration, standard body with unspecified wood construction, top and back body binding, set slim adj. square neck, 14/20-fret bound rosewood fingerboard with inlaid frets and dot inlays, slotted headstock, three-per-side open-style forward-facing banjo tuners, C-style resonator with two diamond hole plate round soundholes, trapeze tailpiece, available in Candy Apple Red, Dark Metallic Blue, or Mahogany Sunburst finish, 24.625 in. scale, mfg. 1965-67.

| | N/A | $1,000 - 1,200 | $625 - 750 | |

* **D-40SE "The Blue Grass Electric"** – similar to the D-40 "The Texarkana," except has a single coil Dobro pickup two knobs (v, tone), and a jack on the face of the guitar, available in Natural finish, mfg. 1965-67.

| | N/A | $1,200 - 1,500 | $700 - 850 | |

D-50 "THE RICHMOND" – Spanish guitar configuration, standard body with ribbon grained African mahogany or figured curly maple, top and back body binding with double top purfling, set slim adj. neck, 14/20-fret rosewood fingerboard with dot inlays, standard headstock, three-per-side tuners, D-style resonator with two diamond hole plate round soundholes, trapeze tailpiece, available in Natural finish, 24.625 in. scale, mfg. 1965-69.

| | N/A | $1,200 - 1,500 | $700 - 850 | |

* **D-50E "The Richmond Electric"** – similar to the D-50 "The Richmond," except has a single coil Dobro pickup two knobs (v, tone), and a jack on the face of the guitar, available in Natural finish, mfg. 1965-69.

| | N/A | $1,400 - 1,750 | $850 - 1,050 | |

D-50S "THE UNCLE JOSH" – Steel guitar configuration, standard body with ribbon grained African mahogany or figured curly maple, top and back body binding with double top purfling, set slim adj. square neck, 14/20-fret bound rosewood fingerboard with dot inlays, slotted headstock, three-per-side open-style forward facing banjo tuners, D-style resonator with two diamond hole plate round soundholes, trapeze tailpiece, available in Natural finish, 24.625 in. scale, mfg. 1965-69.

| | N/A | $1,200 - 1,500 | $700 - 850 | |

* **D-50SE "The Uncle Josh Electric"** – similar to the D-50S "The Uncle Josh," except has a single coil Dobro pickup two knobs (v, tone), and a jack on the face of the guitar, available in Natural finish, mfg. 1965-69.

| | N/A | $1,400 - 1,750 | $850 - 1,050 | |

D-100 "THE CALIFORNIAN" – Spanish guitar configuration, symmetrical double rounded cutaway body with unspecified wood construction, top and back double body binding, set slim adj. neck, 18/22-fret rosewood fingerboard with dot inlays, standard headstock, three-per-side tuners, D-style resonator with two diamond hole plate round soundholes, trapeze tailpiece, two single coil pickups, four knobs (v and tone for each pickup), three-way pickup switch, available in Black or Cherry finish, 24.625 in. scale, mfg. 1965-69.

| | N/A | $1,650 - 2,000 | $1,000 - 1,200 | |

* **D-100-12 "The Californian 12-String"** – similar to the D-100-12 "The Californian," except in 12-string configuration with a slotted headstock and six-per-side tuners, mfg. 1965-69.

| | N/A | $1,800 - 2,200 | $1,100 - 1,350 | |

MSR/NOTES	100%	EXCELLENT	AVERAGE	LAST MSR

ACOUSTIC: ACOUSTIC SERIES

MAHOGANY TROUBADOUR (DWTRUMH) – available in Natural finish, mfg. 1996-2000.

	N/A	$700 - 800	$450 - 525	$1,499

SPRUCE TOP TROUBADOUR (DWTRUSP) – similar to the Mahogany Troubadour, except has a spruce top, mfg. 1996-2000.

	N/A	$775 - 900	$525 - 600	$1,699

ACOUSTIC: ARTIST SIGNATURE SERIES

The Artist Signature models are limited edition models that are signed up on the headstock by the Artist involved with the specialty design (Dobro also offers the same design in an unsigned/un-numbered edition as well).

AL PERKINS LTD (DW PERKINS LTD) – hollow style, bound figured maple top/back/sides, two f-holes, single cone resonator with engraved pointsettia palmplate, 12/19-fret bound rosewood fingerboard with pearl dot inlay (dots begin at 5th fret), spider bridge/trapeze tailpiece, solid peghead with logo decal/signature, gold hardware, three-per-side tuners, available in Trans. Black finish, mfg. 1996-2003.

	N/A	$1,800 - 2,050	$1,100 - 1,250	$3,738

* *Al Perkins (DW Perkins)* – similar to the Al Perkins Ltd., except has no signature on peghead, mfg. 1996-2005.

	N/A	$1,900 - 2,200	$1,200 - 1,350	$3,500

JERRY DOUGLAS LTD (DWJDS LTD) – hollow style with internal soundposts and tone bars, bound mahogany top/back/sides, two screened/three smaller uncovered soundholes, single cone resonator with squared sound holes, mahogany neck, 12/19-fret bound rosewood fingerboard with pearl dot inlay (dots begin at 5th fret), spider bridge/trapeze tailpiece, solid peghead with logo decal/signature, chrome hardware, three-per-side tuners, available in Natural finish, 25 in. scale, mfg. 1996-2005.

	N/A	$2,600 - 3,100	$1,500 - 1,750	$4,799

* *Jerry Douglas (DWJDS)* – similar to the Jerry Douglas Ltd., except has no signature on peghead, mfg. 1996-2005.

	N/A	$1,900 - 2,200	$1,200 - 1,350	$3,500

JOSH GRAVES LTD (DWJOSH LTD) – hollow style, bound wood body, two screened soundholes, single cone resonator, 12/19-fret rosewood fingerboard with pearl dot inlay, spider bridge/trapeze tailpiece, solid peghead with logo decal/signature, chrome hardware, three-per-side tuners, available in Sunburst finish, 25 in. scale, mfg. 1996-2005.

	N/A	$2,600 - 3,100	$1,500 - 1,750	$4,799

This model is based on Graves' own 1928 Model 37.

* *Josh Graves (DWJOSH)* – similar to the Josh Graves Ltd., except has no signature on peghead, mfg. 1996-2005.

	N/A	$1,900 - 2,200	$1,200 - 1,350	$3,500

PETE BROTHER OSWALD KIRBY LTD (DWOS LTD) – hollow style, bound wood body, two screened soundholes, single cone resonator with parallelogram soundwell holes, 12/19-fret rosewood fingerboard with pearl dot inlay (position markers begin at 5th fret), 'V'-shaped roundneck, metal high-nut adaptor, spider bridge/trapeze tailpiece, slotted peghead with logo decal/signature, chrome hardware, three-per-side tuners, available in Sunburst finish, mfg. 1996-2003.

	N/A	$1,800 - 2,100	$1,100 - 1,250	$3,738

This model is based on Kirby's own 1928 Model 27.

* *Pete Brother Oswald Kirby (DWOS)* – similar to the Pete Brother Oswald Kirby Ltd., except has no signature on peghead, mfg. 1996-2003.

	N/A	$1,400 - 1,600	$875 - 1,000	$2,738

PHIL LEADBETTER (DWLEDBET) – hollow style, ivoroid bound flamed maple top/back/sides, two screened soundholes, single cone spider resonator with fanned sound holes, mahogany neck, 12/19-fret bound rosewood fingerboard with pearl dot inlay and 12th fret signature inlay, spider bridge/trapeze tailpiece, solid peghead with logo decal/signature, chrome hardware, three-per-side tuners, available in Sunburst finish, 25 in. scale, mfg. 2004-present.

MSR $2,779	$2,500	$1,350 - 1,675	$800 - 1,000	

PHIL LEADBETTER MAHOGANY "LIMITED EDITION" (DWLEDMAH) – solid mahogany top, back, and sides, two round soundholes, single cone spider resonator with fanned sound holes, mahogany neck, 12/19-fret bound rosewood fingerboard with pearl dot inlay and 12th fret signature inlay, bound mahogany headstock overlay with logo decal/signature, three-per-side Schaller tuners with ebony buttons, spider bridge/trapeze tailpiece, Fishman resonator pickup/electronics, chrome hardware, available in Trans. Cinnamon finish, 25 in. scale, limited edition run of 50 instruments, mfg. 2008-present.

MSR $3,887	$3,500	$1,700 - 2,100	$1,025 - 1,275	

TOM SWATZELL LTD (DWTS LTD) – hollow style, bound wood body, two screened/three smaller uncovered soundholes, single cone resonator with engraved diamond palmplate/coverplate, 12/19-fret bound ebony fingerboard with abalone diamond inlay (position markers begin at 5th fret), spider bridge/trapeze tailpiece, slotted peghead with logo decal/signature, chrome hardware, three-per-side tuners, available in Sunburst finish, mfg. 1996-2003.

	N/A	$1,800 - 2,100	$1,100 - 1,250	$3,738

* *Tom Swatzell (DWTS)* – Similar to the Tom Swatzell Ltd., except has no signature on peghead, mfg. 1996-2003.

	N/A	$1,400 - 1,600	$875 - 1,000	$2,738

MSR/NOTES	100%	EXCELLENT	AVERAGE	LAST MSR

ACOUSTIC: BOTTLENECK SERIES

Bottleneck Series instruments are specifically designed for bottleneck-style guitar playing, and feature a flat 14/19-fret fingerboard, biscuit bridge, and a single 9.5 in. resonator cone.

CHROME-PLATED 90 (DM90) – hollow style, chrome plated bell brass body, two f-holes, single cone resonator, maple neck, 14/19-fret rosewood fingerboard with white dot inlay, biscuit bridge/trapeze tailpiece, chrome hardware, solid peghead, three-per-side tuners, available in Chrome finish, disc. 2000.

	N/A	$1,000 - 1,150	$650 - 750	$1,799

90 DELUXE (DM90 DLX) – similar to the Chrome-Plated 90, except features a bound ebony fingerboard with pearl diamond inlays, sand-blasted Palm Tree scene on front and back, disc. 2000.

	N/A	$1,200 - 1,350	$750 - 875	$2,099

STEEL BODY 90 (DS90) – similar to the Chrome-Plated 90, except has a steel body, available in Amberburst or Darkburst finish, mfg. 1996-2000.

	N/A	$700 - 800	$450 - 525	$1,499

HULA BLUES (DWHB) – hollow style, maple top, two f-holes, single cone resonator, maple back/sides/neck, 12/19-fret rosewood fingerboard with pearl dot inlay, spider bridge/trapeze tailpiece, chrome hardware, slotted peghead, three-per-side tuners, available in Brown/Cream or Green/Cream screened Hawaiian scenes (front and back) finish, disc. 2000.

	N/A	$850 - 1,000	$600 - 700	$1,099

ACOUSTIC: DM33 (THE METAL BODY) SERIES

33 Series instruments have round necks, two f-holes (instead of mesh-covered soundholes) biscuit bridge, and a 10.5 in. inverted resonator cone.

DM33 – hollow style, chrome plated bell brass body, two f-holes, single cone resonator, maple neck, 14/19-fret rosewood fingerboard with white dot inlay, biscuit bridge/trapeze tailpiece, chrome hardware, three-per-side tuners, available in California Girl, Dobro D, Gator, Hawaiian (palm trees), Sand-blasted Flower, or Sailboat finish on back, disc. 2005.

	N/A	$1,600 - 1,850	$875 - 1,000	$2,945

In 1996 the Sand-blasted Flower finish was discontinued and all the other finishes were introduced.

DM33 POWDERCOAT (DS33) – similar to the DM33 except features a black, silver, bronze or gray powder coat (black and gray disc. 2002), disc. 2003.

	N/A	$1,150 - 1,300	$650 - 750	$2,142

DM20 (DECO) – similar to the DM33 except features the "Deco" engraving, disc. 2003.

	N/A	$1,600 - 1,850	$1,000 - 1,150	$3,165

DM36 (ROSE) – similar to the DM33 except features the "Rose" engraving, disc. 2005.

	N/A	$2,150 - 2,500	$1,300 - 1,500	$3,854

DM75 (LILY OF THE VALLEY) – similar to the DM33 except features the "Lily of the Valley" engraving, disc. 2005.

	N/A	$2,750 - 3,250	$1,750 - 2,000	$4,870

DM1000 (DOBRO SHIELD) – similar to the DM33 except features the "Dobro Shield" engraving, mfg. 1972-1997, 2002-05.

	N/A	$3,200 - 3,700	$2,000 - 2,300	$5,742

DM3000 (CHRYSANTHEMUM) – similar to the DM33 except features the "Chrysanthemum" engraving, disc. 2005.

	N/A	$3,700 - 4,200	$2,200 - 2,550	$6,577

33 DELUXE MESA (MODEL DM33 DLX M) – similar to the Chrome Plated 33, except has mesa style sand-blasted design on back, mfg. 1996-2000.

	N/A	$1,100 - 1,250	$650 - 750	$2,099

STEEL 33 (MODEL DS33) – similar to the Chrome Plated 33, except has steel body, available in Amberburst or Darkburst finish, mfg. 1996-2000.

	N/A	$700 - 800	$450 - 525	$1,499

WOOD 33 (MODEL DW33) – similar to the Chrome Plated 33, except has three-ply laminated maple body, available in Natural finish, mfg. 1996-2000.

	N/A	$650 - 750	$400 - 475	$1,299

ACOUSTIC: ROUNDNECK SERIES

The 60 Roundneck Series, like their Squareneck counterparts, have a 12/19 fingerboard, three-ply laminated wood bodies, 10.5 in. resonator, and a original-style spider bridge. The Roundneck series has a rounded (Spanish) neck.

CLASSIC 60 AMBER – similar to 60 Classic, except has bound body, available in Amber finish, disc. 1996.

	N/A	$1,050 - 1,250	$750 - 900	$1,149

This model was also available with a square neck (Model DW60 A S).

MSR/NOTES	100%	EXCELLENT	AVERAGE	LAST MSR

CLASSIC 60 MAHOGANY (MAHOGANY CLASSIC MODEL DW60 MN) – similar to 60 Classic, except has mahogany body, two screened/three clear soundholes, bound body/fingerboard/peghead, pearl diamond/dot fingerboard inlay, available in Natural finish, disc. 1996.

	N/A	$1,050 - 1,250	$750 - 900	$1,249

This model was also available with a square neck (Model DW60 MN S).

CLASSIC 60 NATURAL (NATURAL CLASSIC MODEL DW60 N) – similar to 60 Classic, except has bound body, available in Natural finish, disc. 1996.

	N/A	$1,050 - 1,250	$750 - 900	$1,149

This model was also available with a square neck (Model DW60 N S).

CLASSIC 60 SUNBURST (MODEL DW60 S) – similar to 60 Classic, except has bound body, available in Three-Tone Sunburst finish, disc. 1996.

	N/A	$1,050 - 1,250	$750 - 900	$1,199

This model was also available with a square neck (Model DW60 S S).

CLASSIC 60 WALNUT (WALNUT CLASSIC MODEL DW60 WN) – hollow style, walnut top, two screened/three clear soundholes, single cone resonator, walnut back/sides, maple neck, 14/19-fret bound ebony fingerboard with pearl vine inlay, spider bridge/trapeze tailpiece, chrome hardware, slotted peghead w/logo decal, three-per-side tuners w/plastic buttons, available in Natural finish, disc. 1996.

	N/A	$1,050 - 1,250	$750 - 900	$1,299

This model was also available with a square neck (Model DW60 WN S).

DW60 (F-60) – hollow style, three-ply laminated maple top/back/sides, two screened/three smaller uncovered soundholes, single cone resonator, maple neck, 12/19-fret rosewood fingerboard with white dot inlay, spider bridge/trapeze tailpiece, solid peghead with logo decal, chrome hardware, three-per-side tuners, available in Amber, Natural, or Sunburst finish, disc. 2000.

	N/A	$1,250 - 1,500	$900 - 1,050	$1,399

* **DWF60RDB** – similar to 60 Classic, available in Darkburst finish, disc. 2005.

	N/A	$1,100 - 1,250	$600 - 700	$1,988

DW90 – figured maple body, two f-Holes, spider-style resonator, poinsetta cover plate, single body binding, 14/19-fret flat fingerboard with dot inlay, three-per-side tuners, nickel plated hardware, available in Vintage Sunburst, Trans. Red, Trans. Blue, Tran. Green, Trans. Black, or Natural finish, deluxe hardshell case included, disc. 2005.

	N/A	$1,300 - 1,500	$775 - 900	$2,499

* **DW90C** – similar to the DW90 except has a single cutaway and only one f-hole, disc. 2005.

	N/A	$1,350 - 1,550	$800 - 925	$2,599

* **Wood Body 90 Deluxe (DW90 DLX)** – similar to the DW90, except features a bound peghead, bound ebony fingerboard with pearl diamond inlay, mfg. 1996-2000.

	N/A	$900 - 1,050	$550 - 650	$1,799

* **Wood Body 90 Soft Cutaway (DWSFT)** – similar to the DW90, except has single rounded cutaway, slotted headstock, multiple soundholes in two diamond-shaped groups, available in Natural or Darkburst finish, disc. 2000.

	N/A	$775 - 900	$475 - 550	$1,599

DOBROLEKTRIC (DELEK) – figured maple single cutaway body, single upper body f-hole, single body binding, biscuit style resonator, poinsettia cover plate, two pickups (nickel bridge transducer and black P-90 neck), three knobs, available in Vintage Sunburst finish, slimline deluxe hardshell case included, disc. 2005.

	N/A	$1,400 - 1,600	$850 - 975	$2,595

The Dobrolektric was also available in Blackburst and Wine Red finishes for a short time.

F60 CLASSIC (F-HOLE CLASSIC, DWF60) – hollow style, laminated maple top, two f-holes, single cone resonator, maple back/sides/neck, 12/19-fret rosewood fingerboard with pearl dot inlay, spider bridge/trapeze tailpiece, slotted peghead with logo decal, chrome hardware, three-per-side tuners with plastic buttons, available in Blackburst, Tobacco Burst, or Vintage Burst finish, disc. 2000.

	N/A	$525 - 600	$325 - 375	$1,099

HOUND DOG (U.S. MFG., DWHOUNDR) – laminated and figure maple body, open sound well construction, two f-holes, no body binding, round neck, spider style resonator, fan cover plate, Fishman resonator pickup, nickel plated hardware, available in hand-rubbed brown finish, gig-bag included, mfg. 2003-present.

MSR $1,599	$1,440	$750 - 950	$450 - 550	

* **Hound Dog 60 (U.S. Mfg., DWHOUND60R)** – similar to the Hound Dog, except has soundholes and body binding (classic 60 Dobro style appointments), mfg. 2004-05.

	N/A	$700 - 800	$400 - 475	$1,285

MSR/NOTES	100%	EXCELLENT	AVERAGE	LAST MSR

HOUND DOG ROUND NECK (DWHOUNDRN) – plain maple body, two f-holes, rounded mahogany neck, 12/19-fret rosewood fingerboard with pearl dot inlays, mahogany headstock overlay with Dobro logo, three-per-side Grover tuners, spider bridge with ebony capped maple base, Dobro Cone resonator, nickel-plated hardware, available in Vintage Brown finish, 25 in. scale, mfg. 2007-present.

| MSR $589 | $350 | $200 - 250 | $120 - 150 | |

* *Hound Dog Deluxe Roundneck (DWHOUNDLX)* – similar to the Hound Dog Roundneck, except has a figured maple body, two small round soundholes with screens, and a Fishman pickup, mfg. 2007-present.

| MSR $833 | $500 | $275 - 350 | $150 - 210 | |

MISSISSIPPI VOODOO – single cutaway mahogany body with figured maple top, "lizard" shaped f-hole, no resonator, poinsettia cover plate, gold plated hardware, VooDoo Magic Pickups, three knobs, available in Heritage Cherry Sunburst, Sunrise, or Vintage Brown finishes, disc. 2005.

| | N/A | $1,600 - 1,850 | $1,000 - 1,150 | $2,899 |

ZEPHYR SUNBURST (DW60 ZSC) – single sharp cutaway hollow style, maple top, multiple soundholes, single cone resonator, bound body, maple back/sides/neck, 19-fret ebony fingerboard with abalone seagull inlay, spider bridge/trapeze tailpiece, chrome hardware, slotted peghead, three-per-side tuners with plastic buttons, available in Sunburst finish, disc. 1995.

| | N/A | $700 - 800 | $400 - 475 | $1,399 |

ACOUSTIC: SPECIAL EDITION SERIES

Special Edition models were offered with round (Spanish) or square (Hawaiian) necks (square neck models were designated with an **S** after the model code).

CURLY MAPLE SPECIAL (DWS60 C) – hollow style, curly maple back/sides, single cone resonator, maple neck, 12/19-fret rosewood fingerboard with white dot inlay, spider bridge/trapeze tailpiece, solid peghead with logo decal, chrome hardware, three-per-side tuners, available in Natural, disc. 1995.

| | N/A | $925 - 1,075 | $550 - 650 | $1,799 |

* *Koa Special (DWS60 K)* – similar to the Curly Maple Special, except has koa back and sides, disc. 1995.

| | N/A | $1,400 - 1,600 | $725 - 850 | $2,799 |

* *Mahogany Special (DWS60 M)* – similar to the Curly Maple Special, except has mahogany back and sides, disc. 1995.

| | N/A | $775 - 900 | $450 - 525 | $1,599 |

* *Rosewood Special (DWS60 R)* – similar to the Curly Maple Special, except has rosewood back and sides, disc. 1995.

| | N/A | $1,150 - 1,300 | $700 - 800 | $1,999 |

ACOUSTIC: SQUARENECK SERIES

The 60 Squareneck Series is constructed similar to the Roundneck models, except have a squared (Hawaiian) neck for lap steel-style playing, high nut, and two mesh-covered soundholes.

27 DELUXE (DW27 DLX) – hollow style, laminated figured maple top/back/sides, two smaller screened soundholes, single cone resonator with parallelogram sound holes, maple neck, 12/19-fret rosewood fingerboard with elaborate pearl inlay, spider bridge/trapeze tailpiece, solid peghead with logo decal, chrome hardware, three-per-side tuners, available in Vintage Burst, mfg. 1996-2005.

| | N/A | $1,850 - 2,200 | $1,100 - 1,400 | $3,037 |

27 DELUXE BUBINGA DOBRO – solid bubinga top, back, and sides, ivoroid top and back binding, dual screened soundholes, solid mahogany square neck, 12/19-fret ivoroid-bound solid ebony fingerboard with MOP Lyre inlays, ivoroid-bound ebony headstock overlay with MOP Dobro logo, three-per-side nickel mini-Grover tuners, spun aluminum cone, spider bridge with ebony-capped maple saddles, nickel dobro tailpiece, nickel poinsettia cover plate, available in Antique Natural lacquer finish, 3.6 in. body depth, custom formfitting hardshell case and certificate of authenticity included, mfg. fall 2008-present.

| MSR $4,443 | $4,000 | $2,325 - 2,900 | $1,400 - 1,750 | |

F-60 SQUARENECK (DW60) – hollow style, laminated maple top/back/sides, two screened/three smaller uncovered soundholes, single cone resonator with squared sound holes, maple neck, 12/19-fret rosewood fingerboard with pearl dot inlay, spider bridge/trapeze tailpiece, solid peghead with logo decal, chrome hardware, three-per-side tuners, available in Amberburst, Natural, or Sunburst finish, disc. 2000.

| | N/A | $1,250 - 1,500 | $900 - 1,050 | $1,399 |

* *60 Squareneck Darkburst (DW60 SDB)* – similar to 60 Squareneck, available in Darkburst finish, mfg. 2000-05.

| | N/A | $1,100 - 1,250 | $600 - 700 | $1,983 |

60-D CLASSIC SQUARENECK (DW60SVSB) – hollow style, laminated maple top, two f-holes, single cone resonator, maple back/sides/neck, 12/19-fret rosewood fingerboard with pearl dot inlay, spider bridge/trapeze tailpiece, slotted peghead with logo decal, chrome hardware, three-per-side tuners with plastic buttons, available in Blackburst (disc.), Tobacco Burst (disc.), or Vintage Sunburst finish, disc. 2005.

| | N/A | $1,250 - 1,400 | $700 - 800 | $2,281 |

* *Model 63 (Dobro 8-String DW63)* – similar to the F60 Squareneck, except has eight-string configuration, two screened/three smaller uncovered soundholes, four-per-side slotted headstock, redesigned bridge, available in Natural or Sunburst finish, mfg. 1996-2000.

| | N/A | $650 - 750 | $400 - 475 | $1,399 |

MSR/NOTES	100%	EXCELLENT	AVERAGE	LAST MSR

HOUND DOG (U.S. MFG., DWHOUNDS) – laminated and figure maple body, open sound well construction, two f-holes, no body binding, square neck, spider style resonator, fan cover plate, Fishman resonator pickup, nickel plated hardware, available in hand-rubbed Brown finish, gig-bag included, mfg. 2003-05.

	N/A	$700 - 850	$425 - 500	$999

Hound Dog 60 (U.S. Mfg., DWHOUND60S) – similar to the Hound Dog, except has soundholes and body binding (classic 60 Dobro style appointments), mfg. 2004-05.

	N/A	$650 - 750	$400 - 475	$1,285

HOUND DOG SQUARE NECK (DWHOUNDSN) – plain maple body, two f-holes, square mahogany neck, 12/19-fret rosewood fingerboard with pearl dot inlays, mahogany headstock overlay with Dobro logo, three-per-side Grover tuners, spider bridge with ebony capped maple base, Dobro Cone resonator, nickel-plated hardware, available in Vintage Brown finish, 25 in. scale, mfg. 2007-present.

MSR $589	$350	$200 - 250	$120 - 150	

Hound Dog Deluxe Squareneck (DWHOUNDLXS) – similar to the Hound Dog Squareneck, except has a figured maple body, two small round soundholes with screens, and a Fishman pickup, mfg. 2007-present.

MSR $833	$500	$275 - 350	$160 - 210	

ACOUSTIC BASS

Resonator-equipped Acoustic bass models debuted in 1995. Some models listed were available with an optional fretless fingerboard.

MODEL D DELUXE (DBASS) – hollow style, bound laminated maple top/back/sides, two screened/three smaller uncovered soundholes, single cone resonator, maple neck, 18/24-fret rosewood fingerboard with white dot inlay, spider bridge/trapeze tailpiece, solid peghead with logo decal, chrome hardware, two-per-side tuners, available in Darkburst finish, mfg. 1995-2000.

	N/A	$1,000 - 1,150	$600 - 700	$1,899

Model D Deluxe Natural (DBASS N) – similar to the Model D Deluxe in construction, available in Natural finish, mfg. 1995-2000.

	N/A	$1,050 - 1,200	$600 - 700	$1,999

MODEL F (FBASS) – similar to the Model D, except has two f-holes, available in Black Burst, Tobacco Burst, or Vintage Burst finish, mfg. 1996-2000.

	N/A	$725 - 850	$425 - 500	$1,499

This model was not available in fretless configuration.

Model F Deluxe (FBASS DLX) – similar to the Model F in construction, available in Dark Burst finish, mfg. 1996-2000.

	N/A	$1,000 - 1,150	$600 - 700	$1,899

This model was not available in fretless configuration.

Model F Deluxe Natural (FBASS DLX N) – similar to the Model F in construction, available in Natural finish, mfg. 1996-2000.

	N/A	$1,050 - 1,200	$600 - 700	$1,999

This model was not available in fretless configuration.

MODEL F DELUXE 5 STRING (DBASS DLX 5) – similar to the Model F, except has a five-string configuration, available in Dark Burst finish, mfg. 1996-2000.

	N/A	$1,200 - 1,350	$700 - 800	$2,099

Model F Deluxe 5 String Natural (DBASS DLX N 5) – similar to the Model F Deluxe five-string in construction, available in Natural finish, mfg. 1996-2000.

	N/A	$1,250 - 1,400	$750 - 850	$2,199

D-100 CALIFORNIAN BASS (MARK X) – slim line semi-hollow dual cutaway bound body, maple neck, Type D resonator, 30.25 in. scale, 20-fret rosewood fingerboard with dot inlay, adjustable bridge/metal tailpiece, chrome hardware, two-per-side tuners, two exposed pole piece pickups, volume/tone controls, three-way selector toggle switch (controls plus a .25 in. jack mounted to celluloid controls plate), available in Cherry, Cherry Sunburst, or Natural finish, mfg. 1966-69.

	N/A	$750 - 900	$425 - 500	$349

DOITSCH

Guitars previously produced by Harmony in Chicago, IL during the late 1930s and early 1940s. See chapter on House Brands.

The Doitsch trademark was used on a line of acoustic guitars built by the Harmony company in Chicago, IL. Little else is known about who sold the guitars and how long they were produced. Any further information on Doitsch can be submitted directly to Blue Book Publications. Source: Michael Wright, *Vintage Guitar Magazine*.

MSR/NOTES	100%	EXCELLENT	AVERAGE	LAST MSR

DOLCE

Unknown manufacture date or location. See chapter on House Brands.

This trademark has been identified as the House Brand used by such stores as Marshall Fields, Macy's, and Gimbles. Source: Willie G. Moseley, *Stellas & Stratocasters*.

DOMINO

Instruments previously manufactured in Japan circa mid- to late 1960s. Distributed by Maurice Lipsky Music Company, Inc., in New York, NY.

These Japanese-produced guitars and basses were imported to the U.S. market by the Maurice Lipsky company in New York, NY (Domino was a division of The Orpheum Manufacturing Company). Domino offered a wide range of Vox- and Fender-derived solid body models, and Gibson-esque 335 models. In 1967, the Domino design focus spotlighted copies of Fender's Jazzmaster, Jaguar and Mustang models renamed the Spartan and the Olympic.

The entire Domino product line featured Japanese hardware and pickups. Domino's Thunder-Matic line of drums featured six-ply shells, and internal adjustable mufflers. Sources: Michael Wright, *Guitar Stories*, Volume One and Domino catalog courtesy John Kinnemeyer, JK Lutherie.

The **Mark V Nylon** model was a classical-style acoustic with laminated top/back/sides, round soundhole, a slotted headstock, tied bridge, and featured three-per-side tuners (retail list was $90). For further information regarding Domino electric guitars, please refer to the *Blue Book of Electric Guitars*.

DONNELL, KEN

Instruments previously built in Chico, CA during the late 1980s and early 1990s. Distributed by Donnell Enterprises of Chico, CA.

Luthier Ken Donnell offered an acoustic bass that was optionally augmented with a magnetic pickup in the soundhole or an internal Donnell Mini-Flex microphone system. Currently, Boom basses are not in production while Donnell focuses on the development and production of the Donnell Mini-Flex microphone system.

This internal mini-microphone installs inside the acoustic guitar with no modifications to the guitar itself. The mic and gooseneck clip to an interior brace near the soundhole, and the cable runs along the bass side of the fingerboard to the output jack. Other models are installed through the endblock of the guitar in place of the strap button. The Mini-Clip series is offered in a number of different models (featuring different low impedance microphones).

ACOUSTIC

Boom basses have a cedar soundboard, mahogany back, sides, and neck, and rosewood fingerboards and bridges. The tuning machines are chrome Schallers. The basses have a 32 in. scale (45.5 in. overall), and a six inch depth. The neck joined the non-cutaway body at the 14th fret, and had 19 frets overall. The original suggested list price (direct from the company) was $1,600.

DOOLIN GUITARS

Instruments previously produced in Portland, OR between 1997 and 2011.

CONTACT INFORMATION
DOOLIN GUITARS
Phone No.: 503-236-2424
doolinguitars.com

Luthier Mike Doolin handcrafted acoustic guitars in his Portland, OR shop between 1997 and 2011. Doolin utilized several modern designs including a double cutaway body style, adjustable neck angle, and a pinless bridge. Doolin offered four standard body styles including a jumbo, OM, dreadnought, and classical and all models started at $6,000. Doolin also built custom instruments, but they must be in double cutaway configuration with spiral soundhole rosette, headstock shape, and bridge shape. Doolin retired from professional lutherie in 2011 and is no longer taking orders for guitars.

DORADO

Instruments previously produced in Japan circa early 1970s. Distributed in the U.S. by the Baldwin Piano and Organ Company in Cincinnati, OH.

The Dorado trademark was briefly used by Baldwin (during its Gretsch ownership) on a product line of Japanese-built acoustics and electric guitars and basses. Dorado instruments are of decent quality, but are often found at slightly inflated asking prices due to the attachment of the Gretsch name. Remember, these are 1970s Japanese guitars imported in by Gretsch during their phase of Baldwin ownership! Source: Walter Murray, Frankenstein Fretworks; and Michael Wright, *Vintage Guitar Magazine*.

ACOUSTIC

MISC. ACOUSTIC MODELS – various configurations and styles including dreadnoughts, concerts, folks, jumbos, and classicals, mfg. early 1970s.

	N/A	$175 - 225	$110 - 140	

DREAM GUITARS

Instruments commissioned from premier luthiers from around the world and select preowned instruments. Located in Weaverville, Western North Carolina. Previously located in New Jersey.

Dream Guitars offers the finest hand crafted instruments by many of the top small-production builders. They also commission limited editions, known as Dream Series - high-end guitars featuring the finest tonewoods and unique appointments. The goal of these series' are to give the luthier an opportunity to build their finest instruments without limitations. Owner Paul Heumiller is a member of ASIA and GAL and an active player in his own right. Recording Artist Al Petteway is a consultant for Dream Guitars and records samples of all the instrument on the Dream Guitar's website. A premier shop run by players for players. For more information contact Dream Guitars directly.

CONTACT INFORMATION
DREAM GUITARS
59 Azalea Drive
Weaverville, NC 28787
Phone No.: 828-658-9795
Fax No.: 828-658-9190
www.dreamguitars.com
paul@dreamguitars.com

DRIVE

Acoustic guitars previously produced in China during the early 2000s. Distributed by Switchmusic.com, Inc. in Ontario, CA.

Drive is a trademark of the Switchmusic.com, Inc. company that produces entry level guitars at competitive prices. Their products include the Traditional Series of guitars that are similar to popular American models (Stratocaster, Les Paul, Jazz Bass), and they also have original designs such as the Wild Fire models. Drive also produced a few acoustic models.

DUNWELL GUITAR

Guitars currently produced in Nederland, CO since 1994.

Luthier Alan Dunwell produces hand-built custom flattop acoustic guitars in his shop outside of Nederland, CO. Dunwell runs a one-man shop and every guitar is constructed entirely one at a time by Alan. The base price for a guitar is $5,599 and several options and features are available. Typical construction time is between six and nine months. For more information, visit Dunwell's website or contact him directly.

CONTACT INFORMATION
DUNWELL GUITAR
1891 CR 68-J, MSR
Nederland, CO 80466
Phone No.: 303-939-8870
www.dunwellguitar.com
alan@dunwellguitar.com

DUPONT, GUITARES MAURICE

Please refer to the G section in this text.

DURANGO (PREVIOUS MFG.)

Instrument production and dates of production unknown. Distributed by Sayre Woods Music & Band Instrument Company of Madison Township, NJ.

Guitarist/Blue Book reader Kenneth Heller offers this as yet unspecified Durango trademark for your inspection. The inside label reads "Distributed by Sayre Woods Music & Band Instrument Company of Madison Township, New Jersey"; model "# SAY 622 in.; serial "#-283 in. (or perhaps G000315). Source: Kenneth Heller.

DURANGO (CURRENT MFG.)

Instruments currently produced in Asia. Distributed by Saga Musical Instruments of San Francisco, CA.

Durango guitars are budget student models offered by Saga music. These acoustics come in a small variety of styles (grand concert, dreadnought, and jumbo) as well as three different trim levels (Standard, Deluxe, and Professional). Guitars retail between $195 and $325. For more information visit Durango's website or contact Saga directly.

CONTACT INFORMATION
DURANGO (CURRENT MFG.)
Distributed by Saga Music
PO Box 2841
South San Francisco, CA 94080
Phone No.: 650-558-5558
Fax No.: 650-871-7590
www.sagamusic.com
info@sagamusic.com

DYER, W.J. & BRO.

Guitars previously produced during the 1900s and 1910s in Chicago, IL. Also see Maurer, Prairie State, Euphonon, Wm. C. Stahl, and Larson Brothers.

From the 1880s to the 1930s, the Dyer store in St. Paul, MN was *the* place for musical merchandise for the Midwest in the areas northwest of Chicago. They sold about anything music related on the market at that time. The Larson brothers of Maurer & Co., Chicago were commissioned to build a line of Symphony harp-guitars and Symphony harp-mandolin orchestra pieces along with the J.F. Stetson brand of guitars. They started building these great instruments circa 1905.

The original design of these harp-style instruments came from that of Chris Knutsen who had been building that style since 1898. The early Larsons showed a resemblance to the Knutsen ideas but evolved to a final design by 1912. The harp-guitars are labeled **Style #4** through **#8** where the higher the number, the better the grade of material and intricacy of the trim. The Style #4 is very plain with dot inlays in the fingerboard and no binding on the back. The Style #8 has a pearl trimmed top, fancy peghead inlay and the beautiful tree-of-life fingerboard. This tree-of-life pattern is also used on the fanciest Maurers and Prairie States having the twelve-fret-to-the-body necks.

The harp-mandolin series includes a harp-mandola and harp-mando-cello also in different degrees of ornamentation. Some of the Stetson guitars are Larson-made, but others were possibly made by Harmony, Lyon & Healy, or others. If the Stetson trademark is burned into the inside back strip, it is probably a Larson. Source: Hartman, Robert Carl, *The Larsons' Creations: Guitars and Mandolins*.

E SECTION
EASTMAN

Instruments currently produced in China. Distributed in the U.S. by Eastman Strings.

Eastman Strings was founded by Qian Ni in 1992. Qian came from China to the U.S. to study music, and, at first, started importing violins from his hometown in China. Shortly after this he founded a workshop with several master violinmakers, using old world techniques. Now they produce a wide variety of instruments including guitars, violins, cellos, basses, bows, and other accessories. For models with exposed pickups, refer to the *Blue Book of Electric Guitars*. For more information, visit Eastman's website or contact them directly.

CONTACT INFORMATION
EASTMAN
2138 Pomona Boulevard
Pomona, CA 91768
Phone No.: 800-624-0270
Fax No.: 800-390-7416
www.eastmanguitars.com
info@eastmanstrings.com

ACOUSTIC ARCHTOP

Eastman produces both flattops and archtops. Archtop models include the Uptown Professional series with models **AR800** (disc. 2006, last MSR was $1,895), **AR804** (disc. 2009, last MSR was $1,995), **AR804C** Cutaway (disc. 2009, last MSR was $2,195), **AR805** (MSR $1,995), **AR805C** Cutaway (disc. 2009, last MSR was $2,195), the **AR810** (disc. 2009, last MSR was $2,095), and the **AR810C** Cutaway (disc. 2009, last MSR was $2,295). The Uptown Luxury series include the **AR900** (disc. 2006, last MSR was $2,895), **AR904** (disc. 2009, last MSR was $2,895), the **AR904C** Cutaway (disc. 2009, last MSR was $3,095), **AR905** (disc. 2009, last MSR was $2,995), the **AR905C** Cutaway (disc. 2009, last MSR was $3,195), the **AR910** (disc. 2006, last MSR was $3,095), and the **AR910C** Cutaway (disc. 2009, last MSR was $3,295). The 800/900 series feature oval soundholes. The 804/904 series have a suspended neck over the body. The 805/905 series have f-holes. The 810/910 series have a 17 in. body with f-holes.

In 2004, Jim Fisch started working at Eastman Guitars and after his sudden death in 2006, Eastman introduced a line of guitars named after him in 2007. The Jim Fisch Mahogany Archtop Guitar comes in a variety of configurations. Models include the **AR604** (disc. 2009, last MSR was $1,695), the **AR604C** Cutaway (disc. 2009, last MSR was $1,795), the **AR605** (MSR $1,695), the **AR605C** Cutaway (disc. 2009, last MSR was $1,795), the **AR610** (MSR $1,795), and the **AR610C** Cutaway (disc. 2009, last MSR was $1,895).

ACOUSTIC FLATTOP

Flattop guitars include the Super Jumbo series with models **SJ400** (disc. 2004, last MSR $950), **SJ600** (disc. 2004, last MSR $1,250), and the **SJ800** (disc. 2004, last MSR $1,650). Standard flattop and flatback acoustic guitars come in a variety of configurations and all have spruce tops. Entry level models with Sitka spruce tops and mahogny backs include the **AC312** (2008-2010, last MSR was $695), **AC312CE** Cutaway Electric (2008-2010, last MSR was $995), **AC320** (2008-present, MSR $795), **AC320CE** Cutaway Electric (2008-present, MSR $945), and **AC330-12-String** (2008-2010, last MSR was $795). Entry level models with Sitka spruce tops and Indian rosewood backs include the **AC412** (2008-2010, last MSR was $995), **AC412CE** Cutaway Electric (2008-2010, last MSR was $1,295), **AC420** (2008-present, MSR $995), **AC420CE** Cutaway Electric (2008-present, MSR $1,145), and **AC430-12-String** (2008-2010, last MSR was $1,095). Mahogany-backed models include the **AC510** (disc. 2010, last MSR was $1,250), the **AC510C** Cutaway (disc. 2010, last MSR was $1,350), the **AC515** (disc. 2010, last MSR was $1,250), the **AC515C** Cutaway (MSR $1,350), the **AC515-12** (MSR $1,550), the **AC520** (MSR $1,250), and the **AC520C** Cutaway (MSR $1,350). Maple-backed models include the **AC610** (disc. 2010, last MSR was $1,350), the **AC610C** Cutaway (disc. 2010, last MSR was $1,450), the **AC615** (disc. 2010, last MSR was $1,350), the **AC615C** Cutaway (disc. 2010, last MSR was $1,450), the **AC615-12** (disc. 2010, last MSR was $1,650), the **AC620** (disc. 2010, last MSR was $1,350), and the **AC620C** Cutaway (disc. 2010, last MSR was $1,450). Rosewood-backed models include the **AC710** (disc. 2010, last MSR was $1,350), the **AC710C** Cutaway (disc. 2010, last MSR was $1,450), the **AC715** (disc. 2010, last MSR was $1,350), the **AC715C** Cutaway (disc. 2010, last MSR was $1,450), the **AC715-12** (disc. 2010, last MSR was $1,650), the **AC720** (MSR $1,395), and the **AC720C** Cutaway (disc. 2010, last MSR was $1,450).

Archback jumbo guitars were introduced in 2005. Mahogany backed models include the the **AJ615** (disc. 2010, last MSR was $1,450), the **AJ615C** Cutaway (disc. 2010, last MSR was $1,550), **AJ616** (disc. 2010, last MSR was $1,350), the **AJ616C** Cutaway (disc. 2010, last MSR was $1,650), the **AJ616CE** Cutaway Electric (MSR $1,695), the **AJ617** (disc. 2010, last MSR was $1,650), and the **AJ617C** Cutaway (disc. 2010, last MSR was $1,750). Maple-backed models include the **AJ815** (disc. 2007, last MSR was $1,450), the **AJ815C** Cutaway (disc. 2007, last MSR was $1,450), the **AJ816** (disc. 2010, last MSR was $1,650), the **AJ816C** Cutaway (disc. 2007, last MSR was $1,550), the **AJ816CE** Cutaway Electric (MSR $1,995), the **AJ817** (disc. 2007, last MSR was $1,650), and the **AJ817C** Cutaway (disc. 2007, last MSR was $1,650).

- **Add $200 for electronics.**

ECCLESHALL

Instruments currently built in England since the early 1970s.

Luthier Christopher J. Eccleshall is known for the high quality guitars that he produces. Eccleshall also builds violins, mandolins, and banjos. Some of his original designs carry such model designations like **Excalibur, EQ,** and **Craftsman**. Luthier Eccleshall was also the first UK maker to have Japanese-built solid body guitars. Eccleshall also is an authorized repairer of Gibson, Guild, and Martin. Source: Tony Bacon and Paul Day, *The Guru's Guitar Guide*.

CONTACT INFORMATION
ECCLESHALL
36 Clarendon Road
Ipplepen, Devon TQ12 5QS England
Phone No.: +44 (0)1803 812885
www.eccleshallguitars.co.uk
chris@eccleshallguitars.co.uk

EHLERS & BURNS

Instruments previously custom built in Portland, OR from 1974 to 1984.

The E & B (Ehlers & Burns) trademark was used by luthiers Rob Ehlers and Bruce Burns during a ten-year period. Most instruments produced then were custom ordered. After 1984, Bruce Burns was no longer involved in the construction of the instruments. For more information, refer to Ehlers Guitars.

EHLERS GUITARS

Instruments previously produced between 1968 and 2011 in Mexico, Portland, OR and Santa Monica, CA.

CONTACT INFORMATION
EHLERS GUITARS
www.ehlersguitars.com

Luthier Rob Ehlers first started building acoustic guitars in 1968. His first guitars were built in Santa Monica, CA with Ren Ferguson of Gibson fame. In 1971, he moved to Portland, OR and continued to produced various sized acoustic guitars. In 1973, Bruce Burns came to work with Rob and they later developed the 15 1/2 cutaway model, which was smaller than a dreadnought but bigger than a 000. Ehlers moved to Mexico circa 2000, where he continued to build guitars one at a time. In 2005, his brother began working with him and along with one other employee they built about 45-50 guitars per year with no CNC or mass-production equipment during construction. Models started at $4,000, and Ehlers had recently introduced a new line of guitars that started at $3,200. Ehlers passed away in November, 2011.

EICHELBAUM GUITARS

Instruments currently built in Ojai, CA. Previously built in Santa Barbara, CA.

CONTACT INFORMATION
EICHELBAUM GUITARS
304 South Blanche Street
Ojai, CA 93023
Phone No.: 800-451-9811
www.eichelbaumguitars.com
david@eichelbaumguitars.com

David Eichelbaum has been building and repairing guitars in his California workshop since 1990. Since 1994, he has focused full-time on his own line of acoustic flattop guitars and currently offers several contemporary "fingerstyle" models as well as vintage-styled models to suit a wide range of playing styles. All models are constructed from master grade woods and are presented in a Deluxe Carlton Case. Current base price for all models is $8,400. Eichelbaum continues to perform major restorations and repairs on vintage Fender and Gibson guitars and is also an authorized Martin warranty center. For more details and information visit Eichelbaum's website or contact them directly.

EISELE

Instruments currently built in Kailua, HI.

CONTACT INFORMATION
EISELE
53-524 Kamehameha Hwy A
Hauula, HI 96717
Phone No.: 808-254-5679

Donn H. Eisele began playing guitar about thirty years ago, and started collecting in the past ten years. In 1989, Eisele began building guitars as a hobby; he decided to pursue it full time in early 1995. To find the date of the guitar, get a mirror and look at the underside of the top of the guitar.

Eisele offers a range of both flattop and archtop acoustic guitars. All models have a wide range of custom features available, and both prices include a hardshell case.

Eisele's flattop guitars include such standard features as mahogany back and sides, one piece or laminated mahogany neck, Sitka spruce or Western red cedar top, ebony or rosewood fingerboard with dot inlays, ebony or rosewood bridge, single body binding (white, ivoroid, or tortoiseshell), chrome Schaller tuners, and a nitrocellulose lacquer finish. The Standard list price begins at $2,500. The **F-00** has a 15 in. body similar to a Gibson L-00, while the **F-OM's** 15 in. body resembles a Martin OM. The **F-100** is the 16 in. version of the F-00, and the **F-J** model is a 16 in. jumbo shaped like a Gibson J-185. The 17 in. **F - SJ** jumbo resembles a Gibson J-200.

Eisele's Archtop guitar is featured in a 16 in. or 17 in. body, and the Standard has a list price beginning at $4,750. The Archtop includes such standard features as hand carved back of big leaf maple with matching sides, one-piece or laminated figured maple neck, hand carved Englemann or Sitka spruce top, ebony fingerboard/finger rest/bridge/tailpiece, black/white/black body purfling, ivoroid fingerboard binding, gold Schaller tuners, and a nitrocellulose lacquer finish.

EKO

Trademark of instruments currently built in the Czech Republic, Asia, Spain (classical), and Italy. EKO is now part of the E Group, which is split into EKO (Italian distributor of musical instruments), Esound (Italian distributor of musical instruments), Etek (professional audio producer and world wide musical instruments distributor), and Res (service society). Instruments were formerly built in Italy from the early 1960s through 1987. Distribution in the U.S. market by the LoDuca Bros. of Milwaukee, WI.

The LoDuca Bros. musical distribution company was formed in 1941 by brothers Tom and Guy LoDuca. Capitalizing on money made through their accordion-based vaudevillian act, lessons, and accordion repair, the LoDucas began importing and selling Italian accordions. Throughout the 1940s and 1950s, the LoDucas built up a musical distributorship with accordions and sheet music. By the late 1950s, they were handling Magnatone amplifiers and guitars.

In 1961, the LoDucas teamed up with Italy-based Oliviero Pigini & Company to import guitars. Pigini, one of the LoDuca's accordion manufacturers, had formed the EKO company in anticipation of the boom in the guitar market. The LoDucas acted as technical designers and gave input on EKO designs (as well as being the exclusive U.S. dealers), and EKO built guitars for their dealers. Some of the sparkle finishes were no doubt inspired by the accordions produced in the past. In fact, the various on/off switches and tone settings are down right reminiscent of accordion voice settings! The plastic covered-guitars lasted through to the mid-1960s, when more conventional finishes were offered. EKO also built a number of guitars for Vox, Goya, and Thomas companies.

By 1967 EKO had established dealers in fifty-seven countries around the world. During the late 1960s and early 1970s the guitar market began to get soft, and many guitar builders began to go out of business. EKO continued on, but cut back the number of models offered. In the late 1970s, EKO introduced a custom shop branch that built neck-through designed guitars for other trademarks. Once such company was D'Agostino, and EKO produced the **Bench Mark** models from 1978 to 1982.

The EKO company kept producing models until 1985. By the mid-1980s, the LoDuca Bros. company had begun concentrating on guitar case production, and stopped importing the final Alembic-styled set-neck guitars that were being produced. The original EKO company's holdings were liquidated in 1987.

Currently, the EKO trademark has again been revived in Italy, and appears on entry level solid body guitars built in various countries. The revived company is offering a wide range of acoustic, classical, and solid body electric guitars and amplifiers - all with contemporary market designs. EKO history source: Michael Wright, *Guitar Stories*, Volume One.

ACOUSTIC

The current EKO product line has a wide range of classical (**Conservatorio** and **Studio** series), classical models with EQ and piezo bridges (**Classic EQ**), jumbo-style acoustic/electrics (**Electro-Acoustic** series), and Dreadnought models (**Acoustic** series). The current acoustic models all have different, re-styled headstocks from the earlier EKO Italian-production models. Most EKO models in average original condition are priced in the $150-$350 price range, depending on condition, originality, and overall appeal.

RANGER 6 – dreadnought style, Gibson Hummingbird/Dove style pickguard, dot inlay, natural finish, mfg. 1967-early 1980s.

	N/A	$300 - 350	$150 - 200

* *Ranger 6 Electra* – similar to the Ranger 6, except has electronics with two knobs on face of guitar, mfg. 1967-early 1980s.

	N/A	$325 - 400	$175 - 225

RANGER 12 – dreadnought style, 12-string configuration, Gibson Hummingbird/Dove style pickguard, block inlay, natural finish, mfg. 1967-early 1980s.

	N/A	$350 - 425	$200 - 250

* *Ranger 12 Electra* – similar to the Ranger 12, except has electronics with two knobs on face of guitar, mfg. 1967-early 1980s.

	N/A	$400 - 475	$225 - 275

EL CID

Instruments previously produced in Asia. Previously distributed by the L.A. Guitar Works of Reseda, CA.

El Cid classical guitars were offered in **King** and **Queen** designated models that have slotted headstocks, solid spruce or cedar tops, and rosewood or lacewood back/sides. List price for either model was $799 (with hardshell case).

ELECA

Instruments currently produced in China. Distributed by Eleca International Inc. in Chino, CA.

Eleca instruments are produced in China and distributed throughout the United States. They produce a variety of electric and acoustic guitars. Most acoustic guitars are based off of popular American designs, such as the dreadnoughts, classicals, folk guitars, and Ovation's bowlback design. Most of their products are offered at a competitive price. For more information please refer to the website.

ELGER

Instruments previously produced in Ardmore, PA between 1959 and 1965. Elger began importing instruments produced in Japan during the early 1960s.

Elger instruments were distributed in the U.S. by the Elger Company of Ardmore, PA. The roots of the Elger company were founded in 1954 by Harry Rosenbloom when he opened Medley Music in Bryn Mawr, PA. In 1959, Rosenbloom decided to produce his own acoustic guitars as the Elger Company (named after his children, Ellen and Gerson). Rosenbloom soon turned from U.S. production to Japanese when the Elger company became partners with Hoshino Gakki Gen, and introduced the Ibanez trademark to the U.S. market. Elger did maintain the Pennsylvania facilities to check incoming shipments and correct any flaws prior to shipping merchandise out to their dealers. For further company history, see Ibanez. Source: Michael Wright, *Guitar Stories, Volume One.*

Japanese-imported models included the **Avondale Classic** (Model 7280/7281), the **Philadelphian** (Model 7282), the **Newport** (Model 7283/7284), and the **Haverford** 12-String (Model 7285/7286). Used acoustic guitars are generally priced between $150 and $300 in excellent condition.

ELLIOTT, JEFFREY R.

Instruments currently built in Portland, OR since 1966.

Jeffrey R. Elliott has been building guitars since 1966, produces a limited number of instruments each year, and has a 12-year waiting list. He is currently not accepting new commissions until further notice; however, those interested can visit the Pre-Owned page on his website to learn of instruments currently available. His classical guitars are constructed

MSR/NOTES	100%	EXCELLENT	AVERAGE	LAST MSR

in the Torres/Hauser design tradition, while his steel string guitars are designed especially for fingerstyle playing utilizing his hybrid X-and-fan top bracing system and pinless bridge design. All instruments are tailored to the individual both acoustically and aesthetically. Clientele include Julian Bream, Leo Kottke, Ralph Towner, Earl Klugh, Burl Ives, Jonathan Leathwood, and Dick Weissman. The base price for 2013 is $18,000, with an additional charge for certain options: rare woods, cutaways, carved rosettes, additional strings, custom gears and cases, and electronics. All instruments are French polished, and Alessi tuners and a high quality hardshell case are standard. Visit Elliott's website for full details, to view the extensive photo gallery, and learn more.

EMERALD

Instruments previously built in Donegal, Ireland between 1999 and 2007.

Luthier Alistair Hay built carbon fiber guitars under the Emerald Guitar name between 1999 and 2007. Hay started working on a carbon fiber guitar in 1999 and the first models were launched at the 2003 NAMM show. The bodies and neck are constructed out of carbon fiber and have elaborate designs and colors. Hay ceased production of Emerald Guitars in 2007 to persue other interests, but he still may offer custom guitars in the future on a one-off basis.

Emerald offered three different series of guitars with the **Artisan, Fusion,** and the **Opus**. The Opus series features the carbon-fiber body, Graphtech nut, saddle, and bridge pins, and a Fishman Classic 4 or LR Boggs IRT electronic system. The **Opus X10** is a folk style, the **X20** is a dreadnought style, and the **X30** is a super jumbo. The Artisan series has everything the Opus does along with elaborate inlays and LR Boggs I-Beam, RT Blender, or Fishman Prefix Pro electronics system. The models are numbered just like the Opus. (**X10, X20,** and **X30**). The Fusion represents the middle ground between the Artisan and the Opus. This model is only available as the X10, (X20 and X30 configurations were available early on). All X10 and X30 models are available in a seven-string or 12-string configuration. All guitars are single cutaways and feature the cool emerald color, as well as other finishes. Emerald also produced the XB-Bass series in a four-string and five-string configurations.

EMPERADOR

Instruments previously built in Japan by the Kasuga company between circa 1966 and 1992. Distributed by Westheimer Musical Instruments of Chicago, IL.

The Emperador trademark was a brand name used in the U.S. market by the Westheimer Musical Instruments of Chicago, IL. The Emperador trademark was the Westheimer company's entry level line to their Cort products line through the years. Emperador models are usually shorter-scaled entry level instruments, and the trademark can be found on both jazz-style thinline acoustic/electric archtops and solid body electric guitars and basses. Acoustic flattop models can be found priced used between $150 and $250 in excellent condition.

ENCORE

Instruments currently produced in Asia. Distributed by John Hornby Skewes & Co., Ltd. of Garforth (Leeds), England and in North America by MIDC Ltd. in Markham, Ontario, Canada.

The Encore trademark is a brand name of UK importer John Hornby Skewes & Co., Ltd. The company was founded in 1965 by its namesake, Mr. John Hornby Skewes. The Encore line consists of solidly built guitars and basses that feature designs based on popular American favorites. Encore instruments are of medium to good quality, and their model E83 bass was named "Most Popular U.K. Bass Guitar" from 1992 to 1995. For more information, visit JHS's website or contact them directly.

CONTACT INFORMATION
ENCORE
Distributed by John Hornby Skewes &
Co. Ltd.
Leeds, United Kingdom
www.jhs.co.uk
info@jhs.co.uk

North American Distributor: MIDC Ltd.
860 Denison St. Unit 11
Markham, Ontario L3R 4HA Canada
Phone No.: 866-607-7030
Fax No.: 905-258-0140
sales@midc.ca

Encore's acoustic line includes the **W-255** dreadnought (MSR $275), the **EA255** acoustic/electric dreadnought (MSR $340), the **CEA-255** cutaway acoustic/electric, and three classical models.

ENSENADA

Instruments previously produced in Japan, during the late 1960s and 1970s. Distributed by Strum & Drum in Chicago, IL.

The Ensenada trademark was a brand name used by U.S. importers Strum & Drum of Chicago, IL. Strum and Drum were later owners of the National trademark, acquired when Valco's holdings were auctioned off. Ensenada instruments were distributed between the late 1960s and circa 1974. Source: Michael Wright, *Guitar Stories*, Volume One.

EPI

Trademark of instruments previously produced in China or Indonesia. Distributed by Epiphone (Gibson Musical Instruments) of Nashville, TN.

Epi stringed instruments were an entry level line to the Epiphone range of guitars and basses.

ACOUSTIC

EC-100 (MODEL EC10) – available in Natural Matte finish, disc.

	N/A	$65 - 95	$35 - 55	$189

ED-100 (MODEL ED10) – available in Natural Matte finish, disc.

	N/A	$70 - 100	$35 - 55	$209

EPIPHONE

Instruments currently produced in China and Indonesia since 1997. Previously produced in Korea between 1983 and 2004. Epiphone is a division of and distributed by Gibson Musical Instruments of Nashville, TN. The original Epiphone company was based in New York, NY from 1904 to 1953; and later in Philadelphia, PA from 1954 to 1957. When Epiphone was purchased by Gibson, production moved to Kalamazoo, MI from 1958 to 1969; then to Japan from 1970 to 1983. Some specialty models were built in Nashville, TN in 1982 to 1983, also from 1989 to 1994.

CONTACT INFORMATION
EPIPHONE
A division of Gibson
645 Massman Drive
Nashville, TN 37210
Phone No.: 800-444-2766
www.epiphone.com

HISTORY: 1863-1957

According to family history, Anastasios Stathopoulo (b. 1863) began constructing musical instruments in his home town of Sparta, Greece in 1873. He moved to the U.S. with his family is 1903, settling in New York City, where he produced a full range of stringed instruments bearing his own name up until the time of his death in 1915. The company, which soon became known as The House of Stathopoulo, continued under the direction and ownership of his wife, Marianthe (b. 1875) and eldest son, Epaminondas (Epi [b. 1893]).

Following Marianthe's death in 1923, The House of Stathopoulo was incorporated with Epi as president and majority shareholder, his sister Alkminie (Minnie [1897-1984]) as treasurer, and brother Orpheus (Orphie [1899-1973]) as secretary. They immediately announced that"[t]he new policy of business [would be] the production of banjos, tenor banjos, banjo mandolins, banjo guitars, and banjo ukuleles under the registered trademark of Epiphone." The name "Epiphone" was a combination of Epi's nickname with "phone," the Greek word for sound. Their elegant Recording line of tenor banjos was considered to be among the finest ever made. These were joined in the late 1920s by a full line of Recording model guitars. In 1928, the company's name was changed to The Epiphone Banjo Co.

The Masterbilt series of guitars was introduced in 1931 and marked Epiphone's entrance into the production of modern, carved, f-hole archtop guitars, based on violin construction principles. Indeed, at the time of their introduction, the Masterbilt guitar line was the most complete selection of "f"-hole guitars available from any instrument maker in the world. Complementary Spanish and Hawaiian flattop models and carved-top mandolins were likewise included under the Masterbilt Aegis. Soon, Epiphone advertisements would claim that it was "The World's Largest Producer of First Grade Fretted Instruments." Whether this was an accurate boast or not, it set the stage for a two-decade rivalry between Epiphone and its largest competitor, Gibson.

By 1935, the company was now known simply as Epiphone, Inc., and was producing its Electar brand of electric Hawaiian and Spanish guitars, as well as amplifiers which were designed by electronics pioneer and Danelectro founder, Nat Daniels (1912-1994). That same year marked the introduction of the flagship 18.375 in. Emperor model archtop guitar and signaled the redesign and enlargement of the company's entire Masterbilt archtop line.

Notable Epiphone innovations in this era included the first patented electronic pickup with individual pole pieces and the distinctive Frequensator tailpiece. Both were designed by salesman and acknowledged jack-of-all-trades, Herb Sunshine (1906-1988), and in production by 1937. In 1940, the company also introduced a full line of well respected bass violins produced under the watchful eye of the youngest of the Stathopoulo brothers, Frixo (1905-1957), who had joined the firm in the early 1930s.

During this period, Epiphone's growing product line was considered to be second to none, and could boast such endorsers as George Van Eps (with the Ray Noble Orchestra), Carmen Mastren (with Tommy Dorsey), Allan Reuss (with Benny Goodman's band), and many, many more.

Epi Stathopoulo died from leukemia in 1943 at the age of forty-nine, and this, combined with the many hardships incurred during World War II, set the company on a downward spiral. Orphie Stathopoulo, who took over as president, was unable to recapture the momentum of the prewar years, and constant friction between he and his brother Frixo (now vice-president) began to pull the company apart at the seams.

In 1951, simmering labor problems resulted in a strike which shut down the New York plant for several months. During this time, Orphie sold a stake in the business to the large distribution company, Continental Music. Continental moved production to Philadelphia, and most instruments manufactured from 1952 to 1957 were made there. It is doubtful, however, if much was produced in the final two years, as Epiphone was rapidly being overtaken by new entrants into the guitar market, notably Fender and Guild, the later of which had ironically been started by many former Epiphone employees under the leadership of Alfred Dronge and former Epiphone executive George Mann.

HISTORY: 1957-PRESENT (GIBSON ERA)

It had become increasingly apparent that Epiphone was no longer capable of developing the new products necessary to capture the imagination of the guitar-buying public and its financial viability had come to an end. Following Frixo's sudden death in 1957, Orphie, now the company's sole owner, approached Gibson president Ted McCarty, who had previously expressed interest in buying Epiphone's bass violin production. A deal was signed and trucks were dispatched from Kalamazoo to New York and Philadelphia to make the move. Records during this time period indicate that the out-of-work ex-Epiphone workers in New Berlin, New York "celebrated" by hosting a bonfire behind the plant with any available lumber (both finished and unfinished!). When the vans returned to the Gibson warehouse in Michigan, McCarty realized (much to his surprise) that not only had he received the bass-making operation, but all the jigs, fixtures, and machinery necessary for making guitars, plus much of the work in progress. For the sum of $20,000, Gibson had acquired its once mighty rival (including what would become the most profitable trademark) lock, stock, and barrel.

It was decided that Epiphone would be re-established as a first rate guitar manufacturer, so that Gibson's parent company CMI (Chicago Musical Instruments) could offer a product comparable in every way to Gibson. This was done primarily as a way of offering music stores which, due to existing contractual obligations in a particular sales area, were not allowed to carry the exclusive Gibson line. The Epiphone brand could now be offered to competing retailers who were also carrying many of the other

MSR/NOTES	100%	EXCELLENT	AVERAGE	LAST MSR

well-known brands which were distributed by the giant CMI. Though Epiphone was set up as an autonomous company, in a separate part of the Gibson complex, parallel product lines were soon established, and Gibson was (in effect) competing with itself.

After Epiphone moved to Kalamazoo, instruments were built in the U.S through 1969. Epiphone boomed along with Gibson during the mid-1960s, but by the late 1960s, the guitar boom had busted. In 1969, Gibson only shipped 2,526 Epiphone guitars, which was 86 percent drop from only four years ago. Gibson also found that Epiphone was actually competing with itself for sales. To make things worse, Gibson's parent company CMI, was hurting financially and in the last few days of 1969, ECL bought CMI. By this time, Gibson was already looking for a way to keep Epiphone afloat and importing guitars with Epiphone on the headstock seemed to be the only answer.

After about a year of researching imported guitars, Epiphone production was entirely moved overseas. Instruments were originally built by the Matsumoku factory (of Lyle fame) in Japan between 1970 and 1983. At the time, Matsumoku was considered the second best Japanese producer only behind Ibanez. In the fall of 1970, an entirely new line of Epiphone-branded guitars was introduced, but they did not resemble old Epiphones in the least bit. In fact, most of these guitars were already in production for other trademarks and Epiphone was simply applied to the headstock. Epiphone spent the first part of the 1970s without much identity, but throughout the 1970s, more individual models were introduced. The FT and PR series of acoustics sold relatively well, and Epiphone showed some creative prowess with the Scroll and Genesis Series electrics and the Nova acoustic series. Epiphone also introduced reissues of their popular electric archtop models (Casino, Emperor, Riviera, and Sheraton) in 1982.

By the early 1980s, it was evident that Japanese production was becoming too pricey due to the changing ratio of the dollar/yen. Norlin shopped production and by 1983 it had moved to the Samick factory in Korea. Production remained in Korea largely through 2004, although Epiphones have been produced in a variety of factories and countries over the years. The mid-1980s is a cloudy time for Epiphone, mainly because of the struggles Gibson was going through. When Gibson was sold to Henry Juszkiewicz, David Berryman, and Gary Zebrowski in 1986, not much was going on with Epiphone. With the boom of Asian-built guitars in the late 1980s, Gibson's new ownership group jumped on bandwagon and began rebuilding Epiphone. Instead of introducing a line of original or other manufacturers copied models, Gibson used Epiphone as sort of a budget brand. By the late 1980s, Les Pauls, Flying Vs, and SGs were being produced with an Epiphone logo! Epiphone has also returned to its roots by offering several reissues of their popular guitars of the 1950s and 1960s.

In 2003, Epiphone introduced the Elitist Series, which is designed to be a premium line of guitars based on popular Gibson and Epiphone models. In 2004, all production of Epiphone guitars moved to either China or Indonesia.

Source: N.Y. Epiphone information by L.B. Fred and Jim Fisch, *Epiphone: The House of Stathopoulo*, additional Epiphone history courtesy Walter Carter, *Epiphone: The Complete History*.

ACOUSTIC ARCHTOP: MFG. 1931-1970

BEVERLY – flat spruce top, two segmented f-holes, raised black pickguard, mahogany arched back, mahogany sides/neck, 14/20-fret rosewood fingerboard with pearl dot inlay, adjustable rosewood bridge/trapeze tailpiece, blackface peghead, three-per-side tuners, available in Brown finish, 13 in. body width, mfg. 1931-37.

	N/A	$750 - 950	$450 - 550	

For historical interest, this instrument originally sold for $35.

BLACKSTONE – carved spruce top, f-holes, raised black pickguard, bound body, maple back/sides, 14/20-fret bound rosewood fingerboard with pearl dot inlay, adjustable rosewood bridge/trapeze tailpiece, bound blackface peghead with pearl logo inlay, three-per-side plate mounted tuners, available in Ebony or Sunburst finish, 14.75 in. body width, mfg. 1931-1951.

1931-1932	N/A	$1,075 - 1,350	$650 - 800	
1933-1935	N/A	$950 - 1,200	$575 - 725	
1936-1939	N/A	$800 - 1,000	$475 - 600	
1940-1944	N/A	$675 - 850	$400 - 500	
1945-1951	N/A	$550 - 700	$350 - 425	

The Ebony finish was briefly available from 1931 to 1932. In 1933, engraved pearloid peghead overlay with pearl Masterbilt banner peghead inlay was added. In 1934, 15.5 in. body width, mahogany back/sides, redesigned unbound peghead with redesigned inlay replaced original part/designs. In 1936, 16.375 in. body, parallelogram fingerboard inlay replaced original part/design, auditorium style body, maple back/sides, diamond/script logo peghead inlay replaced original part/designs. In 1939, center dip style peghead replaced original part/design. In 1941, Blonde finish became an option. In 1945, abalone oval peghead inlay and logo were introduced. In 1946, diamond peghead inlay and plastic inlays were introduced.

* ***Blackstone Tenor*** – similar to the Blackstone, except in four-string tenor configuration, mfg. 1937-1949.

	N/A	$650 - 800	$400 - 500	

BROADWAY – carved spruce top, f-holes, raised black pickguard, multi-bound body, walnut back/sides, mahogany neck, 14/20-fret bound ebony fingerboard with pearl diamond inlay, adjustable ebony bridge/trapeze tailpiece, blackface peghead with pearl Masterbilt banner/logo inlay, three-per-side nickel tuners, available in Sunburst finish, 16.375 in. body width, mfg. 1931-1958.

1931-1938 Walnut Body	N/A	$2,000 - 2,500	$1,200 - 1,500	
1939-1942 Maple Body	N/A	$2,200 - 2,750	$1,325 - 1,650	
1943-1950	N/A	$1,800 - 2,250	$1,075 - 1,350	
1951-1958	N/A	$1,600 - 2,000	$950 - 1,200	

MSR/NOTES	100%	EXCELLENT	AVERAGE	LAST MSR

An example of a Broadway courtesy Cam Water

In 1934, walnut back, bound pickguard, block fingerboard inlay, vine/block logo peghead inlay, gold hardware replaced original part/designs; carved back added to design. In 1937, 17.375 in. body width, redesigned pickguard/tailpiece/logo replaced original part/designs, bound peghead replaced original part/design, and Frequensator tailpiece was introduced. In 1939, maple back/sides, center dip peghead replaced original part/designs.

In 1941, Blonde finish was an option. In 1945, pearl flower peghead inlay replaced original part/design. In 1951, f-holes with painted corners were introduced.

* ***Bretton Tenor*** – tenor version of the Broadway model, 15.5 in. body width, mfg. 1931-36.

	N/A	$950 - 1,200	$600 - 725	

This tenor model was originally called the Bretton from its introduction in 1931 to 1936. The name was changed to Broadway Tenor in 1937.

* ***Broadway Tenor*** – similar to the Broadway, except in four-string tenor configuration, mfg. 1937-1949.

1937-1942	N/A	$950 - 1,200	$575 - 725	
1943-1949	N/A	$850 - 1,050	$500 - 625	

* ***Broadway Regent*** – similar to the Broadway, except features a single rounded cutaway body, mfg. 1948-1958.

	N/A	$2,000 - 2,500	$1,200 - 1,500	

BYRON – carved spruce top, mahogany back/sides, single body binding, mahogany neck, 20-fret rosewood fingerboard with dot inlay, f-holes, three-per-side tuners with plastic buttons, nickel hardware, tortoiseshell pickguard, trapeze tailpiece, available in Sunburst Top finish, 15.375 in. body width, mfg. 1949-1955.

	N/A	$450 - 550	$275 - 325	

This model may have been available as early as 1939.

DE LUXE – carved spruce top, two f-holes, multi-bound body, black/white diagonal purfling on top, figured maple back/sides, five-piece carved figured maple neck, 14/20-fret bound rosewood fingerboard with pearl slotted diamond inlay, adjustable rosewood bridge/trapeze tailpiece, bound blackface peghead with pearl Masterbilt banner inlay, three-per-side gold die cast tuners, available in Natural or Sunburst finish, 16.375 in. body width, mfg. 1931-1957.

1931-1937 Trapeze Tailpiece	N/A	$3,200 - 4,000	$1,925 - 2,400	
1937-1944 Frequensator Tailpiece	N/A	$3,000 - 3,750	$1,800 - 2,250	
1945-1949	N/A	$2,800 - 3,500	$1,675 - 2,100	
1950-1957	N/A	$2,400 - 3,000	$1,450 - 1,800	

* **Add 10% for Natural finish.**

In 1934, floral fingerboard inlay, vine/logo peghead inlay replaced original part/designs, raised white pickguard was added. In late 1935 (grand auditorium style), a 17.375 in. body width, redesigned black pickguard, bound f-holes, resigned tailpiece replaced original part/designs, cloud fingerboard inlay, script peghead logo replaced the original parts and designs. In 1937, a Frequensator tailpiece replaced the original tailpiece. In 1939, Natural finish became an option, and a center dip headstock was introduced. In 1949, De Luxe Regent (cutaway body) was introduced.

* ***Empire (De Luxe Tenor)*** – tenor version of the De Luxe model, 15.5 in. body width, mfg. 1931-37.

	N/A	$2,000 - 2,500	$1,200 - 1,500	

* ***De Luxe Regent*** – similar to the De Luxe, except has a single round cutaway body, mfg. 1949-1953.

	N/A	$3,200 - 4,000	$1,925 - 2,400	

In 1950, some models were produced with unbound f-holes. In 1951, f-holes with pointed corners were introduced.

* ***De Luxe Cutaway*** – similar to the De Luxe Regent, just renamed in 1953, mfg. 1953-1970.

1953-1957 Epiphone Mfg.	N/A	$3,000 - 3,750	$1,800 - 2,250	
1958-1964 Gibson Mfg.	N/A	$4,400 - 5,500	$2,650 - 3,300	
1965-1970	N/A	$4,000 - 5,000	$2,400 - 3,000	

Under Gibson ownership, this model was reintroduced in 1958/1959. In 1959, 70 instruments were produced in Gibson's Kalamazoo plant. By 1965, the model was available by special order; and discontinued in 1970.

MSR/NOTES	100%	EXCELLENT	AVERAGE	LAST MSR

DEVON – carved spruce top, mahogany back/sides, single bound body, mahogany neck, 20-fret rosewood fingerboard with oval inlay, f-holes, three-per-side tuners, nickel hardware, bound tortoiseshell logo with 'E' logo, Frequensator tailpiece, available in Sunburst top or Natural finish, 17.375 in. body width, mfg. 1949-1957.

	N/A	$1,200 - 1,500	$725 - 900

* **Add 10% for Natural finish.**

In 1954, Natural finish was introduced. In 1955 a metal peghead plate was introduced.

EMPEROR – carved spruce top, multi-bound f-holes, raised bound tortoise pickguard, multi-bound body, maple back/sides/neck, carved back, 14/20-fret bound ebony fingerboard with pearl split block inlay, adjustable ebony bridge/logo engraved trapeze tailpiece, bound peghead with pearl vine/logo inlay, three-per-side gold tuners, available in Cremona Brown Sunburst finish, 18.5 in. body width, mfg. 1935-1957.

An example of a Emperor courtesy Blue Book Archive

1935-1938	N/A	$4,400 - 5,500	$2,650 - 3,300
1939-1949	N/A	$3,800 - 4,750	$2,275 - 2,850
1950-1957	N/A	$3,200 - 4,000	$1,925 - 2,400

* **Add 10% for Natural finish.**

In 1937, Frequensator tailpiece replaced original part/designs. In 1939, pearl block/abalone triangle fingerboard, center dip peghead replaced original part/designs; Natural finish was an option. By 1946, rosewood fingerboard replaced original part/design. By 1948, an abalone V inlay was introduced. In 1948, Emperor Regent (cutaway body) was introduced. In 1950, the E logo appeared on the pickguard. In 1951 f-holes with painted corners were introduced. In 1952 a truss-rod cover was introduced on the peghead. For historical interest, this instrument originally sold for $400. A limited number of cutaway Emperors bearing the label Soloist Emperor were produced between 1941-42.

* ***Emperor Regent (New York Mfg.)*** – similar to Emperor, except has single round cutaway, mfg. 1948-1953.

	N/A	$4,400 - 5,500	$2,650 - 3,300

* **Add 10% for Natural finish.**

* ***Emperor Cutaway*** – similar to Emperor Regent, just renamed in 1953, mfg. 1953-1970.

1953-1957 Epiphone Mfg.	N/A	$4,400 - 5,500	$2,650 - 3,300
1958-1964 Gibson Mfg.	N/A	$4,000 - 5,000	$2,400 - 3,000
1965-1970	N/A	$3,600 - 4,500	$2,150 - 2,700

* **Add 10% for Natural finish.**

HOWARD ROBERTS CUSTOM – single sharp cutaway ES-175-style body, arched spruce top, maple back and sides, seven-piece laminated neck, Tree-of-Life headstock inlay, single Johnny Smith pickup attached to the fingerboard, ebony bridge base, tune-o-matic bridge, ES-175 bail fern tailpiece, oval sound hole, nickel hardware, one tone and one volume control, available in Black, Sunburst, or Brown finish, 25.5 in. scale, 16.25 in. lower bout, 3.375 in. depth, mfg. 1965-68.

	N/A	$2,600 - 3,250	$1,550 - 1,950	$825

OLYMPIC – carved spruce or poplar top, mahogany back/sides, single body binding, mahogany neck, segmented f-holes, 20-fret rosewood fingerboard with dot inlay, small black pickguard, three-per-side tuners with plastic buttons, available in Golden Brown and Brown with Sunburst top, 13 in. body width, mfg. 1931-1949.

1931-1939	N/A	$675 - 850	$400 - 500
1940-1949	N/A	$650 - 800	$400 - 500

In 1933, the body was changed to 13.625 in. width, trapeze tailpiece, rounded end fingerboard with dot inlay, and a sunburst finish were introduced. In 1934 the Masterbilt and Epiphone in banner logos appeared on headstock. By 1936, the Masterbilt logo was removed, the body was changed to 15.25 in. wide, cello f-holes with squared edges, and a single bound top were introduced. In 1939, a center dip peghead and a script decal with tail logo was introduced. In 1943, the tail was removed from the logo, and some featured a pearl logo. Some models have appeared with no body binding.

* ***Olympic Tenor*** – tenor version of the Olympic model, mfg. 1937-1949.

	N/A	$600 - 750	$350 - 450

MSR/NOTES	100%	EXCELLENT	AVERAGE	LAST MSR

RITZ – carved spruce top, maple back/sides, tortoiseshell body binding, cello style f-holes, cherrywood neck, 20-fret rosewood fingerboard with dot inlay, trapeze tailpiece, available in Natural opaque finish only, 15.25 in. body width, mfg. 1940-49.

	N/A	$725 - 900	$450 - 550	

* **Ritz Tenor** – tenor version of the Ritz model, mfg. 1941-49.

	N/A	$650 - 800	$400 - 500	

ROYAL – carved spruce top, mahogany back and sides, single body binding, segmented f-holes, two-piece mahogany neck, 20-fret rosewood fingerboard with dot inlay, black pickguard, trapeze tailpiece, available in Brown with Sunburst top finish, 15.5 in. body width, mfg. 1931-35.

	N/A	$1,400 - 1,750	$850 - 1,050	

In 1933, American walnut back/sides replaced original part/design.

SPARTAN – carved spruce top, round soundhole, raised black pickguard, one stripe rosette, bound body, maple back/sides, mahogany neck, 14/20-fret bound rosewood fingerboard with pearl dot inlay, adjustable rosewood bridge/nickel trapeze tailpiece, bound peghead with pearl wedge/logo inlay, three-per-side nickel tuners, available in Sunburst finish, 16.375 in. body width, mfg. 1934-1949.

	100%	EXCELLENT	AVERAGE	
1934-1939	N/A	$800 - 1,000	$475 - 600	
1940-1949	N/A	$725 - 900	$425 - 550	

In 1936, carved back added to design; f-holes, walnut back/sides, block fingerboard inlay, Greek column/logo peghead inlay replaced original part/designs. In 1939, center dip peghead replaced original part/design. In 1941, white mahogany back/sides replaced original part/design, Blonde finish was an option. In 1947, plastic inlay material was used instead of pearl and a notched, diamond peghead inlay was introduced. For historical interest, this instrument originally sold for $100.

* **Regent Tenor** – similar to the Spartan, except has a bound body, mahogany back/sides, trapeze tailpiece, 15.5 in. body width, mfg. 1934-36.

	N/A	$650 - 800	$375 - 475	

This model originally was the companion tenor model to the Spartan guitar. Discontinued in favor of the Spartan Tenor, introduced in 1937.

* **Spartan Tenor** – similar to the Regent Tenor, 15.5 in. body width, mfg. 1937-1949.

	N/A	$525 - 650	$325 - 400	

TRIUMPH – 15.5 in. body width, carved spruce top, f-holes, raised black pickguard, bound body, walnut back/sides, mahogany neck, 14/20-fret bound rosewood fingerboard with pearl diamond inlay, adjustable rosewood bridge/trapeze tailpiece, bound peghead with pearl Masterbilt banner/logo inlay, three-per-side nickel tuners, available in Blonde or Sunburst finish, mfg. 1931-1958.

	100%	EXCELLENT	AVERAGE	
1931-1933 Laminated	N/A	$1,475 - 1,850	$900 - 1,100	
1934-1939 Solid	N/A	$1,600 - 2,000	$950 - 1,200	
1940-1949	N/A	$1,475 - 1,850	$900 - 1,100	
1950-1958	N/A	$1,400 - 1,750	$850 - 1,050	

• **Add 10% for Natural finish.**

In 1933, the body was changed to 16.375 in. width and laminated maple back and sides were introduced with a single bound top and back. In 1934, solid maple back/sides, unbound peghead with pearl fleur-de-lis/logo inlay replaced original part/designs; carved back added to design. In 1935, redesigned script peghead logo replaced original part/design. In 1936, the body was changed to 17.375 in. width, cello f-holes with squared edges, triple bound top, single bound back, bound peghead, bound pickguard, and flat tailpiece were introduced. In 1937, Frequensator tailpiece and center dip headstock were introduced. In 1941, Blonde finish was optional. In 1947, redesigned pickguard with stylized E, column peghead inlay replaced original part/designs. In 1950, f-holes with painted corners were introduced. For historical interest, this instrument originally sold for $125.

* **Triumph Regent** – similar to Triumph, except has single round cutaway, mfg. 1948-1953.

	N/A	$2,200 - 2,750	$1,325 - 1,650	

* **Triumph Cutaway** – similar to Triumph Regent, just renamed in 1953, reintroduced by Gibson in 1958, available by special order only in 1965, mfg. 1953-1970.

	100%	EXCELLENT	AVERAGE	
1953-1957 Epiphone Mfg.	N/A	$2,200 - 2,750	$1,325 - 1,650	
1958-1964 Gibson Mfg.	N/A	$2,000 - 2,500	$1,200 - 1,500	
1965-1970	N/A	$1,875 - 2,350	$1,125 - 1,400	

* **Hollywood Tenor** – tenor version of the Triumph, mfg. 1931-36.

	N/A	$1,600 - 2,000	$950 - 1,200	

This model was originally called the Hollywood from its introduction in 1934 to 1936. The name was changed to Triumph Tenor in 1937.

* **Triumph Tenor** – similar to the Hollywood Tenor, mfg. 1937-1957.

	N/A	$1,400 - 1,750	$850 - 1,050	

MSR/NOTES	100%	EXCELLENT	AVERAGE	LAST MSR

TUDOR – carved spruce top, curly maple back/sides, carved back, three-ply body binding, five-ply maple/mahogany neck, segmented f-holes, bound black pickguard, gold hardware, trapeze tailpiece, available in Brown with Sunburst top, 16.375 in. body width, mfg. 1933-37.

	N/A	$3,200 - 4,000	$1,925 - 2,400	

In 1934, a bound pickguard, and vine peghead inlay with block letter logo were introduced.

ZENITH – carved spruce top, f-holes, raised black pickguard, bound body, maple back/sides, mahogany neck, 14/20-fret rosewood fingerboard with pearl dot inlay, adjustable rosewood bridge/trapeze tailpiece, blackface peghead, three-per-side single unit nickel tuners with plastic buttons, available in Sunburst finish, 13.625 in. body width, mfg. 1931-1958.

1931-1933	N/A	$875 - 1,100	$525 - 650	
1934-1947	N/A	$950 - 1,200	$575 - 725	
1948-1958	N/A	$750 - 950	$450 - 575	

In 1933, single binding on the top and back, a black raised pickguard, square end fingerboard with dot inlay, a rounded top peghead with Zenith logo engraved diagonally were introduced. In 1934, 14.375 in. body width, walnut back/sides replaced original part/designs, pearl wedge/logo peghead inlay, three tuners on a strip, were introduced, and sunburst finish was an option. In 1936, 16.375 in. body width, cello f-holes with squared edges, diamond/script logo peghead inlay, and individual tuners were introduced. In 1939 a center dip peghead was introduced. By 1949, maple back and sides were introduced and Blond finish became available. In 1950, f-holes with painted corners were introduced. In 1951, a pearl oval peghead inlay was introduced. This instrument originally sold for $50.

* *Melody Tenor* – tenor version of the Zenith, walnut back/side, 13.25 in. body width, mfg. 1931-36.

	N/A	$1,075 - 1,350	$650 - 800	

In 1934, walnut back and sides were introduced. This model was originally called the Melody from its introduction in 1931-36. The name was changed to Zenith Tenor in 1937.

* *Zenith Tenor* – similar to the Melody tenor, 13.25 in. body width, mfg. 1937-1957.

	N/A	$950 - 1,200	$575 - 725	

ACOUSTIC ARCHTOP: RECORDING MODELS

Recording Model archtop guitars feature an asymmetrical body with angled cutaway on treble bout. Some models had flattops, others an arched top (see descriptions below). Recording Model guitars are relatively rare in the vintage guitar market. These models were introduced during the 1920s, and discontinued around 1931.

RECORDING MODEL A – graduated spruce top, maple or mahogany back/sides, single black body binding, 25 in. scale, rosewood fingerboard with dot inlay, three-per-side tuners, pin bridge or trapeze tailpiece, available in Natural or Natural with shaded top finish.

	N/A	$1,400 - 1,750	$900 - 1,125	

RECORDING MODEL B – similar to Recording Model A, except features bound rosewood fingerboard with paired diamond inlay.

	N/A	$1,800 - 2,250	$1,075 - 1,350	

RECORDING MODEL C – similar to Recording Model A, except features carved spruce top, bound ebony fingerboard with paired diamond inlay, single white body binding, available in Shaded Top finish.

	N/A	$2,200 - 2,750	$1,325 - 1,650	

Some models may have rosewood fingerboards with block inlay; some may have a black pickguard.

RECORDING MODEL D – similar to Recording Model A, except features carved spruce top, bound ebony fingerboard with pearloid block inlay, single white body binding, black pickguard, available in Shaded Top finish.

	N/A	$2,800 - 3,500	$1,675 - 2,100	

RECORDING MODEL E – similar to Recording Model A, except features carved spruce top, laminated curly maple body, three-ply white body binding, bound ebony fingerboard with celluloid blocks with floral engraving, black pickguard, gold plated tuners, available in Shaded top finish.

	N/A	$3,400 - 4,250	$2,050 - 2,550	

ACOUSTIC: AJ (ADVANCED JUMBO) SERIES

In 2004, Epiphone decided to rename all the current AJ series models. The AJ-10 became the AJ-100, the AJ-15 turned into the AJ-200, and the AJ-18S became the AJ-200S. However there were no changes to specs on these models.

AJ-28S (MODEL EAT1) – similar to AJ-15, except has a solid spruce top, bound body/fingerboard/headstock, diamond fingerboard inlay/block inlay at 12th fret, rosewood headstock veneer, available in Ebony, Natural, or Vintage Sunburst finish, mfg. 1998-2002.

	N/A	$235 - 285	$140 - 180	$569

* *AJ-2812S (Model EA28)* – similar to AJ-28S except in a twelve-string model, six-per-side tuners, chrome hardware, available in Natural Satin finish, disc. 2000.

	N/A	$275 - 325	$150 - 200	$679

* *AJ-2812SE (MODEL EE28)* – similar to the AJ2812S, except has piezo pickup with Epiphonic-Six preamp and EQ, disc. 2002.

	N/A	$325 - 375	$200 - 250	$749

MSR/NOTES	100%	EXCELLENT	AVERAGE	LAST MSR

AJ-30 CE (MODEL EEA3) – similar to AJ-15 E, except has single rounded cutaway body, dot fingerboard inlay/block inlay at 12th fret, piezo pickup, Electar Epiphone 6 preamp system, available in Ebony, Natural, or Vintage Sunburst finish, mfg. 1998-2000, reintroduced 2001-02.

	N/A	$300 - 350	$170 - 220	$729

When this model was reintroduced it featured Epiphonic-Six Chorus electronics and had a model designation of EE6C.

AJ-35S (MODEL EAT2) – similar to AJ-15, except has a solid spruce top, triple-ply body binding, abalone rosette, dot fingerboard inlay/block inlay at 12th fret, rosewood headstock veneer, gold hardware, available in Ebony, Natural, or Vintage Sunburst finish, mfg. 1998-2000.

	N/A	$275 - 325	$150 - 200	$679

AJ-40 TLC (MODEL EE4C) – similar to AJ-15 E, except has single rounded cutaway body, no pickguard, bound body, dot fingerboard inlay/block inlay at 12th fret, gold hardware, piezo pickup, Electar Epiphonic 2000 preamp system (equipped with Epiphonic-Six preamp/EQ as of 2001), available in Ebony, Natural, or Vintage Sunburst finish, mfg. 1998-2002.

	N/A	$300 - 350	$175 - 225	$699

AJ-45S (MODEL EAA8) – similar to AJ-15, except has a solid spruce top, 24.75 in. scale, bound body, blackface headstock with screened logo, tortoiseshell pickguard, three-per-side vintage-style tuners, available in Vintage Sunburst finish, mfg. 1998-2000, 2002.

	N/A	$250 - 300	$150 - 200	$649

The AJ-45S is based on Gibson's J-45 model.

* AJ-45SE (MODEL EEA8) – similar to the AJ-45S, except features a piezo pickup and either Electar Epiphone 6 or Epiphonic-Six electronics, available in Vintage Sunburst finish, mfg. 1998-99.

	N/A	$350 - 425	$225 - 275	

AJ-100 (AJ-10, MODEL EAJ1) – slope-shouldered Advanced Jumbo-style body, select spruce top, mahogany back and sides, black body binding, round soundhole with multi-ring rosette, set mahogany neck, 14/20-fret rosewood fingerboard with dot inlays, black headstock overlay with Epiphone logo, three-per-side chrome tuners, rosewood bridge, black pickguard, available in Ebony, Natural, or Vintage Sunburst finish, 25.5 in. scale, mfg. 1999-2011.

	$100	$60 - 80	$35 - 50	$182

* AJ-100CE (AJ-10CE, MODEL EE1C) – similar to the AJ-100CE, except has single cutaway and electronics, available in Natural or Vintage Sunburst (disc.) finish, mfg. 2002-present.

MSR $248	$150	$85 - 105	$50 - 65	

AJ-200 (AJ-15, MODEL EAA1) – sloped shoulder jumbo style, select spruce top, round soundhole, black pickguard, bound body, stripe rosette, mahogany back/sides/neck, 14/20-fret fingerboard with pearl dot inlay, rosewood bridge with black bridgepins, three-per-side chrome tuners, available in Ebony, Natural, or Vintage Sunburst finish, mfg. 1998-2005.

	N/A	$95 - 120	$50 - 70	$299

* AJ-200L Left-Handed (AJ-15L, Model EAA2) – similar to AJ-200 (AJ-15), except in left-handed configuration, available in Natural finish, mfg. 1998-2000, 2002-05.

	N/A	$100 - 135	$60 - 80	$332

* AJ-1512 (Model EAA3) – similar to AJ-15, except in a twelve-string configuration, six-per-side tuners, available in Natural finish, mfg. 1998-2000.

	N/A	$135 - 175	$85 - 115	$349

* AJ-200E (AJ-15E, Model EEA1) – similar to the AJ-15E, except has a piezo pickup and electronics, mfg. 1998-2004.

	N/A	$125 - 150	$85 - 115	$332

AJ-200S (AJ-18S, MODEL EAA4) – similar to AJ-15, except has a solid spruce top, single rounded cutaway body, no pickguard, diamond fingerboard inlay/block inlay at 12th fret, gold hardware, available in Ebony (disc.), Natural, or Vintage Sunburst (disc.) finish, mfg. 1998-2010.

	$200	$110 - 140	$70 - 90	$332

* AJ-18SL (Model EAA5) – similar to AJ-18S, except in a left-handed configuration, available in Natural finish, mfg. 1998-2001.

	N/A	$120 - 150	$75 - 100	$414

* AJ-200SCE (Model EEC2, AJ-18SCE, Model EEA2) – similar to AJ-15 E, except has single rounded cutaway body, no pickguard, diamond fingerboard inlay/block inlay at 12th fret, gold hardware, piezo pickup, Electar Epiphone 6 preamp system (equipped with Epiphonic-Six preamp/EQ as of 2001), available in Ebony (disc.), Natural, or Vintage Sunburst (disc.) finish, mfg. 1998-2010.

	$300	$160 - 210	$100 - 130	$499

* AJ-212S (Model EAT2, AJ-212S, Model EAA6) – similar to AJ-18S, except in a twelve-string configuration, six-per-side tuners, available in Natural finish, mfg. 1998-2000, 2002-04.

	N/A	$175 - 225	$110 - 140	$449

* AJ-1812SL (Model EAA7) – similar to AJ-18S, except in a left-handed twelve-string configuration, six-per-side tuners, available in Natural finish, mfg. 1998-2000.

	N/A	$175 - 225	$110 - 140	$454

MSR/NOTES	100%	EXCELLENT	AVERAGE	LAST MSR

AJ-220S (MODEL EA22) – slope-shouldered dreadnought body, solid Sitka spruce top, mahogany back and sides, round soundhole with multi-ring rosette, multi-ply binding, mahogany neck, 14/20-fret bound rosewood fingerboard with dot inlays, black headstock overlay, three-per-side nickel tuners, rosewood bridge, tortoise pickguard, available in Natural or Vintage Sunburst (2012-present) finish, 25.5 in. scale, 1 11/16 in. nut width, mfg. 2010-present.

MSR $261	$200	$95 - 120	$55 - 70	

* AJ-220SCE (Model EE2S) – similar to the AJ-220S, except has a single smooth cutaway and NanoFlex electronics, available in Ebony (2012-present), Natural, or Vintage Sunburst (2012-present) finish, mfg. 2010-present.

MSR $392	$300	$140 - 175	$85 - 105	

»AJ-220SCE Robot (Model EEAT) – similar to the AJ-220SCE, except has the robotic Tuning Lite system, available in Ebony, Natural, or Vintage Sunburst finish, mfg. 2012-present.

MSR $832	$500	$300 - 375	$175 - 225	

AJ-300S (MODEL EA3J) – slope shoulder jumbo style, solid spruce top, rosewood back/sides, mahogany neck, 14/20-fret rosewood fingerboard with diamond inlay and 12th fret block inlay, pickguard with stylized E, gold hardware, available in Natural or Vintage Sunburst finish, mfg. 2004-05.

	N/A	$200 - 250	$120 - 150	$499

AJ-500M MASTERBILT (MODEL EMJM) – jumbo style, premium solid Sitka spruce top, premium solid rosewood back/sides, body/neck binding, mahogany neck, 14/20-fret rosewood fingerboard with dot inlay, tortoiseshell pickguard, nickel hardware, available in Natural, Natural Satin (disc. 2011), or Vintage Sunburst (disc.) finish, mfg. 2004-present.

MSR $832	$500	$300 - 350	$175 - 225	

* AJ-500ME Masterbilt Electric (Model EMJME) – similar to the AJ-500M, except has Baggs electronics, available in Natural Satin or Vintage Sunburst finish, mfg. 2004-2011.

	$550	$325 - 400	$200 - 250	$915

* AJ-500R Masterbilt (Model EMJR) – similar to the AJ-500M, except has premium rosewood solid back and sides, mfg. 2004-2011.

	$600	$350 - 425	$225 - 275	$999

»AJ-500RE Masterbilt Electric (Model EMJRE) – similar to the AJ-500R, except has L.R. Baggs electronics, mfg. 2004-2011.

	$700	$425 - 500	$275 - 325	$1,165

AJ-500RC MASTERBILT (MODEL EMJCS) – southern jumbo style, premium solid cedar top, premium solid rosewood back/sides, body/neck binding, mahogany neck, 12/20-fret rosewood fingerboard with diamond inlay, open-style headstock with three-per-side gold tuners, tortoiseshell pickguard, nickel hardware, Natural Satin finish, 25.5 in. scale, mfg. 2006-08.

	N/A	$350 - 425	$225 - 275	$999

ACOUSTIC: BLUEGRASS SERIES

BISCUIT RESOPHONIC (MODEL EFB1) – resonator model with round neck, chrome hardware, two f-holes, available in Black, Brown, Heritage Cherry Sunburst, Red Brown Mahogany, or Translucent Blue finish, disc. 2008.

	N/A	$200 - 250	$120 - 150	$582

SPIDER RESOPHONIC (MODEL EFSP) – similar to Biscuit Resophonic, except has square neck, two mesh-covered soundholes, slotted headstock, disc.

	N/A	$225 - 275	$130 - 170	$569

MD-100 – metal resophonic guitar, chrome/brass body, round mahogany neck, rosewood fingerboard with dot inlay, three-per-side tuners, chrome finish, mfg. 2003-08.

	N/A	$325 - 400	$200 - 250	$915

ACOUSTIC: CLASSICAL SERIES (NEW YORK & GIBSON MFG.)

ALHAMBRA (NEW YORK) – spruce top, curly maple back/sides, round soundhole, single body binding, mahogany neck, 12/20-fret rosewood fingerboard, pickguard with treble side extension, rosewood bridge, slotted headstock with center dip, 14.375 in. body width, mfg. 1938-1941.

	N/A	$800 - 1,000	$525 - 600	

Also available with a 14-fret neck.

BARCELONE (EC300, GIBSON) – maple back/sides, 25.5 in. scale, black body binding, gold hardware, pearloid tuner buttons, 14.25 in. body width, sharp back edge, rosewood finish on back/sides, mfg. 1963-68.

	N/A	$750 - 900	$500 - 575	

CLASSIC (EC150, GIBSON) – spruce top, mahogany back/sides, tortoise body binding, sharp back edge, 14.25 in. wide, mfg. 1963-1970.

	N/A	$550 - 650	$325 - 400	

In 1965, a Standard Heel was introduced.

MSR/NOTES	100%	EXCELLENT	AVERAGE	LAST MSR

CONCERT (NEW YORK) – maple back/sides, multiple-body bindings, bound 12-fret clear of body rosewood fingerboard (extends over soundhole), rosewood bridge, slotted peghead with dip, gold hardware, available in Natural finish, 16.5 in. body width, mfg. 1938-1941.

| | N/A | $1,000 - 1,250 | $625 - 750 | |

A 14-fret fingerboard was also available.

ENTRADA (EC90, GIBSON) – petite-sized classical guitar, natural top, mahogany back and sides, standard rounded neck heel, pointed headstock corners, 13.25 in. width, 22.75 in. scale, mfg. 1963-69.

| | N/A | $550 - 650 | $325 - 400 | |

ESPANA (EC200, GIBSON) – maple back/sides, black bound body, sharp back edge, available in Walnut finish, mfg. 1962-68.

| | N/A | $600 - 700 | $375 - 450 | |

MADRID (EC30, GIBSON) – classical style, mahogany back/sides, tortoiseshell celluloid binding, rounded neck heel, pointed peghead corners, available in Natural finish, mfg. 1962-69.

| | N/A | $425 - 500 | $275 - 325 | |

SEVILLE (NEW YORK MFG. 1938-1941) – classical style, spruce top, round soundhole, mahogany back/sides, mahogany neck, 12/20-fret rosewood extended fingerboard, rosewood bridge, slotted headstock, available in Natural finish, 14.375 in. body width, mfg. 1938-1941.

| | N/A | $750 - 900 | $500 - 575 | |

* *Seville (EC100, Gibson Mfg. 1961-1970)* – classical style, mahogany back/sides, 25.5 in. scale, tortoise body binding, available in Natural finish, 14.25 in. body width, mfg. 1961-1970.

| | N/A | $525 - 600 | $325 - 400 | |

The Seville model was offered with a ceramic pickup between 1961 and 1963 as the Seville Electric.

ACOUSTIC: CLASSICAL SERIES (1970S MODELS)

MODEL 6512 – classical body style, spruce top, mahogany back and sides, round soundhole with wooden marquetry, brown celluloid binding, mahogany neck, 12/19-fret rosewood fingerboard, slotted headstock with rosewood overlay, three-per-side open-style nickel-plated tuners, rosewood tied bridge, Natural finish, 25.625 in. scale, mfg. 1970-71.

| | N/A | $100 - 150 | $50 - 75 | |

MODEL 6514 – classical body style, spruce top, rosewood back and sides, round soundhole with wooden marquetry, brown celluloid binding, mahogany neck, 12/19-fret rosewood fingerboard, slotted headstock with rosewood overlay, three-per-side open-style gold-plated tuners, rosewood tied bridge, Natural finish, 25.625 in. scale, mfg. 1970-71.

| | N/A | $150 - 200 | $95 - 120 | |

CO-60 (CONCERT 60) – classical body style, spruce top, rosewood back and sides, round soundhole with wooden marquetry, mahogany neck, 12/19-fret ebony fingerboard, slotted headstock with rosewood overlay, three-per-side open-style gold-plated tuners, rosewood tied bridge, Natural finish, 25.625 in. scale, mfg. 1976-79.

| | N/A | $200 - 250 | $120 - 150 | |

EC-15 – classical body style, spruce top, mahogany back and sides, round soundhole with wooden marquetry, mahogany neck, 12/19-fret rosewood fingerboard, slotted headstock with rosewood overlay, three-per-side open-style tuners, rosewood tied bridge, Natural finish, 25.625 in. scale, mfg. 1976-79.

| | N/A | $95 - 120 | $50 - 75 | |

EC-20 – classical body style, spruce top, mahogany back and sides, round soundhole with wooden marquetry, rosewood celluloid binding, mahogany neck, 12/19-fret rosewood fingerboard, slotted headstock with rosewood overlay, three-per-side open-style gold-plated tuners with ivoroid buttons, rosewood tied bridge, Natural finish, 25.625 in. scale, mfg. 1972-77.

| | N/A | $95 - 120 | $50 - 75 | |

EC-22 – classical body style, spruce top, rosewood back and sides, round soundhole with wooden marquetry, celluloid binding, center line back inlay, mahogany neck, 12/19-fret rosewood fingerboard, slotted headstock with rosewood overlay, three-per-side open-style gold-plated tuners, rosewood tied bridge, Natural finish, 25.625 in. scale, mfg. 1972-74.

| | N/A | $120 - 150 | $75 - 95 | |

EC-23 – classical student body style, spruce top, specially designed bracing to strengthen top, student-sized neck, mfg. 1973 only.

| | N/A | $120 - 150 | $75 - 95 | |

EC-24 – classical body style, cedar top, rosewood back and sides, round soundhole with wooden marquetry, celluloid binding, center line back inlay, mahogany neck, 12/19-fret rosewood fingerboard, slotted headstock with rosewood overlay, three-per-side open-style gold-plated tuners, rosewood tied bridge, Natural finish, 25.625 in. scale, mfg. 1972-74.

| | N/A | $135 - 175 | $85 - 110 | |

EC-25 – classical body style, cedar top, rosewood back and sides, round soundhole with wooden marquetry, rosewood celluloid binding, mahogany neck, 12/19-fret ebony fingerboard, slotted headstock with rosewood overlay, three-per-side open-style gold-plated tuners, rosewood tied bridge, Natural finish, 25.625 in. scale, mfg. 1970-77.

| | N/A | $175 - 225 | $100 - 135 | |

MSR/NOTES	100%	EXCELLENT	AVERAGE	LAST MSR

ACOUSTIC: CLASSICAL SERIES (RECENT & CURRENT MFG.)

BARCELONA CE (MODEL EC7C) – single soft cutaway body, solid spruce top, mahogany body and neck, rosewood fingerboard, 25.5 in. scale, gold hardware, Piezo/Epi-Six pickup and preamp/EQ, available in Antique Natural finish, mfg. 1999-2000.

	N/A	$375 - 450	$225 - 275	$899

C-25 (MODEL EC25) – classical style, available in Natural Satin finish, disc. 2000.

	N/A	$100 - 135	$50 - 75	$269

C-70 CE (MODEL EOC7) – classic style, single rounded cutaway body, spruce top, round soundhole, bound body, wooden inlay rosette, rosewood back/sides, mahogany neck, 19-fret rosewood fingerboard, rosewood tied bridge, rosewood peghead veneer with circles/star design, three-per-side chrome tuners with pearl buttons, piezo pickup, volume/three-band EQ, available in Natural finish, disc. 2000.

	N/A	$275 - 325	$150 - 200	$649

* *Selena C-70 CE (Model EESE)* – similar to the C-70 CE, except features Selena signature graphic on body, available in Black finish, mfg. 1997 only.

	N/A	$375 - 450	$225 - 275	$899

CLASSICA (MODEL EC70) – top of the line traditional classical model, solid spruce top, rosewood body and fingerboard, mahogany neck, 25.5 in. scale, gold hardware, available in Antique Natural finish, mfg. 1999-2000.

	N/A	$275 - 325	$150 - 200	$649

EN-5 (C-5, MODEL EC05) – 3/4 size classical size, similar to the EN-10 (C-10), available in Natural finish, mfg. 2003-04.

	N/A	$50 - 75	$25 - 40	$149

EN-10 (C-10, MODEL EC15) – classical style body, mahogany body and neck, spruce top, chrome hardware, available in Natural Satin finish, mfg. 1997-2006.

	N/A	$60 - 85	$30 - 45	$165

EN-40 (C-40, MODEL EC40) – classical style, available in Natural gloss finish, disc. 2005.

	N/A	$120 - 150	$60 - 80	$299

EN-546C MASTERBILT (MODEL EM46C) – classical style single cutaway, premium solid cedar top, premium solid rosewood back and sides, body binding, mahogany neck, 12/19 rosewood fingerboard, open-style headstock, natural finish, mfg. 2004-05.

	N/A	$425 - 500	$275 - 325	$1,099

* *EN-546CE Masterbilt (EM46CE)* – similar to the EN-546C, except has Baggs element electronics, mfg. 2004-08.

	N/A	$375 - 450	$250 - 300	$1,082

EN-552 MASTERBILT (MODEL EM52) – classical style, premium solid cedar top, premium solid rosewood back and sides, body binding, mahogany neck, 12/19 rosewood fingerboard, open-style headstock, natural finish, mfg. 2004-05.

	N/A	$375 - 450	$225 - 275	$982

GRANADA (MODEL EC60) – traditional classical body, Select Spruce top, mahogany back and sides, rosewood fingerboard, bound body, 25.5 in. scale, gold hardware, available in Antique Natural finish, mfg. 1999-2001.

	N/A	$150 - 200	$90 - 120	$419

SST CLASSIC (MODEL ECS1/ECS2) – nylon-string configuration, single smooth cutaway chambered mahogany body, select spruce top, round soundhole with rosette, top binding, mahogany neck, 12/19-fret rosewood fingerboard with no inlays, 1.75 in. (SST Classic 1.75) or 2 in. (SST Classic 2.0, 2007-2011) neck width, slotted headstock with three-per-side banjo open-style chrome tuners, rosewood bridge, Shadow Nanoflex pickup system, available in Natural finish, 25.5 in. scale, mfg. 2007-present.

MSR $582	$350	$200 - 250	$120 - 150	

VALENCIA CE (MODEL EC6C) – single smooth cutaway classical mahogany body, select spruce top, rosewood fretboard, nylon string, open style tuners, body binding, Epiphonic Six preamp, gold hardware, Antique Natural finish, mfg. 2002-03.

	N/A	$275 - 325	$150 - 200	$699

This model is the same as the Granada except features a cutaway and electronics.

* *Valencia CE Left-Handed (Model EC6CL)* – similar to the Valencia CE except in left-handed configuration, mfg. 2002-03.

	N/A	$275 - 325	$150 - 200	$724

ACOUSTIC: DOVE & HUMMINGBIRD SERIES

These models are based off of Gibson's Dove and Hummingbird, respectively.

DOVE (MODEL EADV) – double parallelogram fingerboard inlay, dove artwork on tortoiseshell pickguard, moustache-style bridge with wing inlay, bound fingerboard, available in Cherry (disc.) or Natural finish, mfg. 1998-2000, reintroduced 2003-present.

MSR $499	$300	$175 - 225	$110 - 140	

MSR/NOTES	100%	EXCELLENT	AVERAGE	LAST MSR

DOVE A/E (MODEL EEDV) – double parallelogram fingerboard inlay, dove artwork on tortoiseshell pickguard, moustache-style bridge with wing inlay, bound fingerboard, piezo pickup, Electar preamp system, available in Cherry and Natural finish, based on Gibson's Dove acoustic guitar, mfg. 1998-99.

	N/A	$275 - 325	$150 - 200	$679

HUMMINGBIRD (MODEL EAHB) – dreadnought style, bound body, double parallelogram block inlays, flowers/hummingbird artwork on tortoiseshell pickguard, three-per-side chrome vintage-style tuners, available in Heritage Cherry Sunburst finish, current mfg.

MSR $499	$300	$175 - 225	$110 - 140	

ACOUSTIC: EARLY 1970S JAPAN NUMBERED MODELS

In 1970, Epiphone moved all production overseas and the first models to be produced in Japan feature no model name but a four digit model number instead. This configuration only lasted for two years, and by 1972, the entire Epiphone line was renamed again.

MODEL 6730 – dreadnought body style, spruce top, mahogany back and sides, round soundhole with multi-ring rosette, multi-layer binding, three-piece bolt-on neck, 14/20-fret rosewood fingerboard with dot inlays, black headstock overlay with Epiphone logo, three-per-side chrome tuners, adj. rosewood bridge, black pickguard, Natural finish, 25.5 in. scale, mfg. 1970-71.

	N/A	$100 - 150	$50 - 75	

* *Model 6735 12-String* – similar to the Model 6730, except in 12-string configuration with six-per-side tuners, mfg. 1970-71.

	N/A	$125 - 175	$75 - 100	

MODEL 6732 – Grand Auditorium 000-style body, spruce top, mahogany back and sides, round soundhole with multi-ring rosette, multi-layer binding, three-piece bolt-on neck, 14/20-fret rosewood fingerboard with dot inlays, black headstock overlay with Epiphone logo, three-per-side chrome tuners, adj. rosewood bridge, black pickguard, Natural finish, 24.75 in. scale, mfg. 1970-71.

	N/A	$100 - 150	$50 - 75	

MODEL 6830 – dreadnought body style, spruce top, rosewood back and sides, round soundhole with decorative rosette, multi-layer binding, three-piece bolt-on neck, 14/20-fret bound rosewood fingerboard with large block inlays, bound black headstock overlay with Epiphone logo, three-per-side chrome tuners, adj. rosewood bridge, black pickguard, Natural finish, 25.5 in. scale, mfg. 1970-71.

	N/A	$150 - 200	$95 - 120	

* *Model 6834 12-String* – similar to the Model 6830, except in 12-string configuration with six-per-side tuners, mfg. 1970-71.

	N/A	$175 - 225	$110 - 140	

MODEL 6832 – Grand Auditorium 000-style body, spruce top, rosewood back and sides, round soundhole with decorative rosette, multi-layer binding, three-piece bolt-on neck, 14/20-fret bound rosewood fingerboard with large block inlays, bound black headstock overlay with Epiphone logo, three-per-side chrome tuners, adj. rosewood bridge, black pickguard, Natural finish, 24.75 in. scale, mfg. 1970-71.

	N/A	$150 - 200	$95 - 120	

ACOUSTIC: EJ, ELVIS PRESLEY EJ, & SJ SERIES

EJ-100 (MODEL EA1J, SJ-15, MODEL EAS1) – super jumbo acoustic, mahogany body with spruce top, mahogany neck, rosewood fingerboard with dot inlays, round soundhole, black pickguard, three-per-side tuners, chrome hardware, available in Natural Satin finish, disc. 2004.

	N/A	$140 - 180	$90 - 120	$365

EJ-200 (MODEL EAJ2) – jumbo J-200-style body, spruce top, maple back and sides, round soundhole with three-ring rosette, three-stripe body binding, maple neck, 14/20-fret bound pointed fingerboard with pearl crown inlay, bound headstock with black overlay and pearl crown/logo inlay, three-per-side gold tuners, rosewood mustache bridge with pearl block inlay, white black dot bridge pins, tortoise pickguard with engraved flowers/pearl dot inlay, available in Ebony, Natural, or Vintage Sunburst finish, disc. 2011.

	$400	$225 - 275	$130 - 170	$665

* *EJ-212* – similar to the EJ-200, except has 12-string configuration with six-per-side tuners, available in Black, Natural, or Vintage Sunburst finish, disc. 1999.

	N/A	$350 - 425	$225 - 275	$819

* *EJ-200 CE/EJ-200 SCE (MODEL EEJ2)* – similar to the EJ-200 (Model EAJ2), except has a piezo bridge pickup with volume/tone controls, available in Black, Natural, or Vintage Sunburst finish, current mfg.

MSR $665	$400	$250 - 300	$150 - 190	

EJ-200 ELVIS PRESLEY (MODEL EAEP) – similar to the EJ-200, except has special fingerboard inlay, yellow Elvis graphic on lower bout, special graphic pickguard, available in Black finish, disc. 1999.

	N/A	$325 - 375	$200 - 250	$799

* *EJ-200 CE Elvis Presley (Model EEEP)* – similar to the Elvis Presley EJ-200, except features single rounded cutaway, piezo bridge pickup, volume/tone controls, available in Black finish, disc. 1999.

	N/A	$425 - 500	$250 - 300	$999

MSR/NOTES	100%	EXCELLENT	AVERAGE	LAST MSR

EJ-200E ELVIS PRESLEY SIGNATURE SECOND VERSION (EAEP) – Super Jumbo-style body, spruce top, maple back and sides, round soundhole with multi-layer three-ring rosette, multi-layer binding, maple neck, 14/20-fret bound rosewood fingerboard with custom "Elvis Presley" with a star on each end inlays, black headstock overlay with pearl logo and crown inlay, three-per-side gold tuners, historic rosewood moustache bridge with four-piece pearl inlays, custom tortoise pickguard with special shape designs, Nanoflex pickup, eSonic preamp electronics, available in Antique Natural finish, 25.5 in. scale, mfg. 2008-2011.

	$500	$300 - 350	$175 - 225	$832

EJ-300S (MODEL EAJ3) – Super Jumbo body style, solid spruce top, rosewood back/sides, mahogany neck, full binding, 14/20-fret rosewood fingerboard with crown inlays, tortoiseshell pickguard with flower inlay, gold hardware, available in Natural or Vintage Sunburst finish, mfg. 2004-06.

	N/A	$250 - 300	$140 - 180	$665

* EJ-300SCE (Model EEJC) – similar to the EJ-300S, except has a single cutaway with electronics, mfg. 2004 only.

	N/A	$325 - 375	$175 - 225	$832

EL-00 – rounded cutaway mahogany body, solid spruce top, mahogany neck, 19-fret rosewood fingerboard with dot inlay, round soundhole, tortiseshell pickguard with E logo, three-per-side-tuners, E logo on truss rod cover, chrome hardware, available in Vintage Sunburst finish, based on Gibson's L-00, mfg. 2001-present.

MSR $499	$300	$175 - 225	$110 - 140	

EO-1 – rounded cutaway, spruce top, round soundhole, three-stripe bound body/rosette, mahogany back/sides/neck, 21-fret bound rosewood fingerboard with pearl dot inlay, rosewood bridge with white black dot pins, rosewood veneer on bound peghead with star/crescent inlay, three-per-side chrome tuners, available in Natural finish, mfg. 1992-2000.

	N/A	$275 - 325	$150 - 200	$630

EO-2 (MODEL EO2E) – rounded cutaway folk style, arched walnut top, oval soundhole, three-stripe bound body/rosette, walnut back/sides, mahogany neck, 21-fret bound rosewood fingerboard with pearl dot inlay, rosewood bridge with white black dot pins, rosewood veneer on bound peghead with star/crescent inlay, three-per-side chrome tuners, piezo pickup, volume/tone controls, available in Natural finish, mfg. 1992-97.

	N/A	$350 - 425	$175 - 225	$799

This model has a wooden butterfly inlay between the soundhole and bridge.

SJ-18S (MODEL EAS2) – super jumbo, mahogany body and neck, rosewood fingerboard with split diamond inlays, three-per-side tuners, solid spruce top, rosewood bridge, round soundhole, tortoise pickguard, gold hardware, available in Ebony, Natural Satin, or Vintage Sunburst finish, mfg. 2000-03.

	N/A	$175 - 225	$110 - 140	$449

SJ-18SCE – single rounded cutaway super jumbo mahogany body, solid spruce top, mahogany neck, rosewood fingerboard, split diamond inlays, Piezo pickup, Epiphonic Six preamp, body and neck binding, gold hardware, available in Natural or Vintage sunburst finish, mfg. 2000-03.

	N/A	$300 - 350	$150 - 200	$699

ACOUSTIC: ELITIST SERIES

ELITIST L-00 (MODEL ELOO JAPAN) – solid spruce top, solid mahogany back, mahogany sides, 1-piece mahogany set neck with rosewood fingerboard and 19 frets, bone nut, rosewood bridge, nickel hardware, Grover tuners, available in Vintage Sunburst finish, 25.5 in. scale, mfg. 2003-04.

	N/A	$800 - 1,000	$475 - 600	$1,537

* Elitist L-00 Jim Croce (Model ELCLO Japan) – similar to the Elitist L-00, except is a Jim Croce signature, mfg. 2004-05.

	N/A	$875 - 1,100	$525 - 650	$2,152

ELITIST J-45 (MODEL ELJ5 JAPAN) – jumbo body style, solid spruce top, solid mahogany back, mahogany sides, one-piece mahogany set neck with rosewood fingerboard, 20 frets, bone nut and saddle, rosewood bridge, nickel hardware, Grover tuners, available in Vintage Sunburst or Natural finish, 24.75 in. scale, mfg. 2003-04.

	N/A	$875 - 1,100	$525 - 650	$1,614

ELITIST '65 TEXAN (ELTX JAPAN) – solid spruce top, solid mahogany back, mahogany sides, one-piece mahogany set neck with rosewood fingerboard and 20 frets, bone nut, rosewood bridge, intonated, adjustable saddle, nickel hardware, Grover tuners, available in Natural or Vintage Sunburst finish, 25.5 in. scale, mfg. 2003-04.

	N/A	$875 - 1,100	$525 - 650	$1,614

ELITIST J-200 (MODEL ELJ2 JAPAN) – jumbo body style, solid spruce top, solid maple back and sides, five-piece maple and rosewood set neck with Ebonized rosewood fingerboard, bone nut and saddle, 24kt. gold plated hardware, Grover tuners with Imperial buttons, available in Vintage Sunburst or Natural finish, 25.5 in. scale, mfg. 2003-04.

	N/A	$1,000 - 1,250	$600 - 750	$2,152

MSR/NOTES	100%	EXCELLENT	AVERAGE	LAST MSR

ELITIST 1964 USA TEXAN PAUL MCCARTNEY SIGNATURE – slope shouldered dreadnought style, solid spruce top, solid mahogany back, mahogany sides, one-piece mahogany neck, 14/20-fret rosewood fingerboard with parallelogram inlays, three-per-side tuners, rosewood bridge, tortoise pickguard with E logo, nickel hardware, Natural finish, 25.5 in. scale, mfg. 2005 only.

	N/A	$3,200 - 4,000	$1,925 - 2,400	$7,998

This model is also available in left-handed configuration.

ACOUSTIC: FT SERIES (U.S. MFG.)

FT DE LUXE – spruce top, maple back/sides, round soundhole, multiple body binding, maple neck, bound rosewood fingerboard with cloud inlay, tortoiseshell pickguard, trapeze tailpiece, vine peghead inlay, gold hardware, available in Natural and Sunburst finishes, 16.5 in. body width, mfg. 1939-1942.

	N/A	$3,400 - 4,250	$2,050 - 2,550	

This model is similar to the De Luxe Archtop, except in a flattop configuration.

* *FT De Luxe Cutaway (Deluxe Regent, FT-210)* – similar to the FT De Luxe, except features a single rounded cutaway body, flower peghead inlay, 17.375 in. body width, mfg. 1954-57.

	N/A	$4,000 - 5,000	$2,400 - 3,000	

FT 27 – spruce top, mahogany back/sides, bound top, 14/20-fret rosewood fingerboard with dot inlay, Masterbilt peghead decal, rosewood bridge, available in Sunburst finish, 14.5 in. body width, mfg. 1935-1941.

	N/A	$825 - 1,000	$550 - 625	

FT 30 (CABALLERO) – 00-style, mahogany top, round soundhole, tortoiseshell pickguard, mahogany back/sides/neck, 14/20-fret rosewood fingerboard with pearl dot inlay, rosewood bridge with white pins, three-per-side tuners with plastic buttons, available in Natural finish, 14.5 in. body width, mfg. 1941-49, 1958-1970.

1941-1949	N/A	$1,000 - 1,250	$600 - 750	
1958-1961	N/A	$800 - 1,000	$475 - 600	
1962-1964	N/A	$650 - 800	$400 - 500	
1965-1970	N/A	$525 - 650	$325 - 400	

The FT 30 was renamed the Caballero by Gibson in 1958. In 1958, tortoise pickguard with logo was introduced. In 1961, non-logo pickguard replaced original part/design. In 1963, adjustable saddle replaced original part/design.

FT 37 – spruce top, quartered walnut back/sides, cherry neck, 20-fret rosewood fingerboard with dot inlay, tortoiseshell pickguard, rosewood bridge, three-per-side tuners with plastic buttons, available in Yellow Sunburst top and Natural finish, 15.5 in. body width, mfg. 1935-1941.

	N/A	$1,100 - 1,350	$700 - 825	

FT 45 (CORTEZ) – 00-style, spruce top, round soundhole, tortoise pickguard, white body binding, walnut back/sides, cherry neck, 20-fret rosewood fingerboard with pearl dot inlay, rosewood bridge with white pins, metal logo plate mounted on peghead, three-per-side tuners, available in Natural or Sunburst finish, 14.5 in. body width, mfg. 1941-49, 1958-1970.

1941-1949	N/A	$1,200 - 1,500	$725 - 900	
1958-1964	N/A	$1,400 - 1,750	$850 - 1,050	
1965-1970	N/A	$1,000 - 1,250	$600 - 750	

The FT 45 was renamed the Cortez by Gibson in 1958, mfg. 1958 to 1970. In 1962, Natural finish with adjustable bridge became an option.

FT 50 – 00-style, spruce top, round soundhole, mahogany back/sides, tortoiseshell body binding, cherry neck, tortoise pickguard, 14/20-fret bound rosewood fingerboard with dot inlay, rosewood bridge, three-per-side tuners with plastic buttons, available in Natural finish, 14.5 in. body width, mfg. 1941-49.

	N/A	$1,300 - 1,600	$825 - 975	

FT 75 – spruce top, curly maple back/sides, multiple body binding, mahogany neck, 20-fret bound rosewood fingerboard with parallelogram inlay, rosewood bridge, three-per-side open back tuners, available in Cherry Burst, Natural, or Sunburst finish, 16.5 in. body width, mfg. 1935-1942.

	N/A	$1,450 - 1,700	$900 - 1,100	

FT 79 (TEXAN) – dreadnought style, spruce top, walnut back/sides, cherry neck, 20-fret bound rosewood fingerboard with parallelogram inlay, rosewood bridge, three-per-side open back tuners, available in Natural and Sunburst finish, 16.5 in. body width, mfg. 1941-1970.

1941-1949 Old Body Style	N/A	$2,750 - 3,250	$1,750 - 2,100	
1949-1958 New Body Style	N/A	$2,250 - 2,750	$1,400 - 1,700	
1958-1964	N/A	$3,250 - 4,000	$2,050 - 2,450	
1965-1970	N/A	$2,750 - 3,250	$1,750 - 2,100	

In 1949, a new jumbo body style was introduced. In 1954, curly maple back/sides replaced original part/design. The FT 79 was renamed the Texan by Gibson in 1958, mfg. 1958-1970.

MSR/NOTES	100%	EXCELLENT	AVERAGE	LAST MSR

* *Texan Reissue (Model EATX)* – contemporary model, available in Natural or Vintage Sunburst finish, mfg. 1996-2002.

	N/A	$325 - 400	$200 - 250	$799

FT 85 (SERENADER) – 12-string configuration, 14.25 in. body width, mahogany back/sides, 25.5 in. scale, adjustable saddle, dot fingerboard inlay, available in Walnut finish, mfg. 1963-1970.

1963-1964	N/A	$1,000 - 1,250	$625 - 750	
1965-1970	N/A	$825 - 1,000	$550 - 625	

FT 90 (EL DORADO) – squared shoulder dreadnought, spruce top, mahogany back and sides, multiple body binding, bound fingerboard with single parallelogram inlay, oval headstock inlay, available in Natural finish, mfg. 1963-1970.

1963-1964	N/A	$2,200 - 2,750	$1,325 - 1,650	
1965-1970	N/A	$1,800 - 2,250	$1,075 - 1,350	

FT 95 (FOLKSTER) – 14.25 in. body width, spruce top, mahogany back/sides, rosewood fingerboard with dot inlay, two white pickguards, mfg. 1966-1970.

	N/A	$725 - 900	$425 - 550	

FT 98 (TROUBADOUR) – squared shoulder dreadnought style, spruce top, maple back/sides, multiple body binding, 12/19-fret rosewood fingerboard with slotted block inlay, two white pickguards, solid peghead, gold hardware, available in Walnut finish, mfg. 1963-1970.

1963-1964	N/A	$2,000 - 2,500	$1,200 - 1,500	
1965-1970	N/A	$1,800 - 2,250	$1,075 - 1,350	

FT 110 (FRONTIER) – dreadnought style, spruce top, curly maple back/sides, five-piece cherry neck, 20-fret bound rosewood fingerboard with slotted block inlay, rosewood bridge, three-per-side open back tuners, available in Natural and Sunburst finish, 16.5 in. body width, mfg. 1941-1970.

1941-1949 Old Body Style	N/A	$3,200 - 4,000	$1,925 - 2,400	
1949-1958 New Body Style	N/A	$3,000 - 3,750	$1,800 - 2,250	
1958-1964	N/A	$2,800 - 3,500	$1,675 - 2,100	
1965-1970	N/A	$2,400 - 3,000	$1,450 - 1,800	

In 1949, a new jumbo body style was introduced. The FT 110 was renamed the Frontier by Gibson in 1958, mfg. 1958-1970.

* *Frontier Reissue (Model EAFT)* – contemporary reissue, available in Natural and Vintage Sunburst finish, disc.

	N/A	$375 - 450	$225 - 275	$899

» *Frontier Reissue Left-Handed (Model EAFTL)* – similar to the Frontier Reissue, except in left-handed configuration, available in Natural or Vintage Sunburst finish, mfg. 1997-98.

	N/A	$550 - 650	$375 - 450	$1,269

FT 112 (BARD) – 12-string configuration, spruce top, mahogany back/sides, multiple-bound body, adj. saddle, stylized E logo, oval peghead inlay, Sunburst or Walnut finishes, 24.75 in. scale, 16.25 in. width, mfg. 1962-69.

An example of a FT 112 courtesy John Beeson, The Music Shoppe

1962-1964	N/A	$1,400 - 1,750	$850 - 1,050	
1965-1969	N/A	$1,200 - 1,500	$725 - 900	

This model was available with maple back and sides in walnut finish.

FT 120 (EXCELLENTE) – squared shoulder dreadnought style, spruce top, rosewood back/sides, multiple body binding, round soundhole, bound ebony fingerboard with cloud inlay, pearl and abalone peghead inlay, eagle inlay on pickguard, tune-o-matic bridge, gold hardware, available in Natural finish, mfg. 1963-1970.

1963-1965	N/A	$5,600 - 7,000	$3,500 - 4,200	
1966-1970	N/A	$4,800 - 6,000	$2,900 - 3,600	

MSR/NOTES	100%	EXCELLENT	AVERAGE	LAST MSR

* **Excellente Reissue (Model EAEX)** – contemporary reissue, available in Natural and Vintage Sunburst finish, disc. 2000.

	N/A	$525 - 600	$300 - 350	$1,249

ACOUSTIC: FT SERIES (1970S KOREA/JAPAN MFG.)

FT-120 – Grand Auditorium 000-style body, laminated spruce top, mahogany back and sides, multi-ply body binding, bolt-on neck, 14/20-fret rosewood fingerboard with dot inlay, three-per-side tuners, black pickguard, rosewood bridge, chrome hardware, Natural or Sunburst finish, mfg. 1976-1980.

	N/A	$75 - 100	$45 - 60	

FT-130 (CABALLERO) – Grand Auditorium 000-style body, laminated spruce top, mahogany back and sides, multi-ply body binding, three-piece bolt-on neck, 14/20-fret rosewood fingerboard with dot or block (later models) inlays, three-per-side tuners, black pickguard, rosewood bridge, chrome hardware, Natural, Maple, or Sunburst finish, mfg. 1972-1980.

	N/A	$100 - 135	$60 - 75	

FT-132 – Grand Auditorium 000-style body, spruce top, mahogany back/sides, laminated mahogany neck, rosewood fingerboard with dot inlay, multiple body binding, chrome hardware, Natural finish, mfg. 1972-73.

	N/A	$100 - 135	$60 - 75	

FT-133 (DE-LUXE) – Grand Auditorium 000-style body, laminated spruce top, mahogany back and sides, multi-ply body binding, bolt-on neck, 14/20-fret rosewood fingerboard with block inlays, three-per-side tuners, black pickguard, rosewood bridge, chrome hardware, Natural finish, mfg. 1976-77.

	N/A	$120 - 150	$70 - 90	

FT-134 – Grand Auditorium 000-style student model, spruce top, mahogany back and sides, special design bracing for more strength, pickguard, chrome hardware, Natural finish, mfg. 1973 only.

	N/A	$100 - 135	$60 - 75	

FT-135 (CORTEZ) – Grand Auditorium 000-style body, laminated spruce top, rosewood back and sides, multiple body binding, three-piece bolt-on neck, rosewood fingerboard with block inlays, three-per-side chrome tuners, black pickguard, rosewood adj. bridge, Natural finish, mfg. 1972-78.

	N/A	$175 - 225	$100 - 130	

FT-140 – dreadnought style body, laminated spruce top, nato back and sides, three-piece bolt-on neck, 14/20-fret rosewood fingerboard with pearl dot inlays and zero fret, three-per-side chrome tuners, black pickguard, rosewood bridge with black buttons, available in Natural finish, mfg. 1976-1980.

	N/A	$120 - 150	$70 - 90	$145

FT-145 (TEXAN) – dreadnought body style, laminated spruce top, mahogany back and sides, multi-ply body binding, three-piece bolt-on neck, 14/20-fret rosewood fingerboard with dot inlays, three-per-side chrome tuners, available in Maple, Natural, or Sunburst finish, mfg. 1972-1980.

	N/A	$175 - 225	$100 - 130	

This model was also available in left-hand configuration. Sunburst and Maple finishes were added in the late 1970s.

FT-146 (TEXAN DELUXE) – dreadnought body style, laminated spruce top, mahogany back and sides, multi-ring soundhole rosette, multi-ply body binding, three-piece bolt-on neck, 14/20-fret bound rosewood fingerboard with block inlays, bound headstock, three-per-side chrome tuners, available in Natural finish, mfg. 1976-77.

	N/A	$175 - 225	$100 - 130	

FT-147 – dreadnought body style, laminated spruce top, highly figured mahogany back and sides, multi-ring soundhole rosette, multi-ply body binding, three-piece bolt-on neck, 14/20-fret bound rosewood fingerboard with dot inlays, French Heel design, three-per-side chrome tuners, available in Natural finish, mfg. 1973 only.

	N/A	$200 - 250	$120 - 150	

FT-150/FT-150BL (BARD) – dreadnought body style, laminated spruce top, rosewood (FT-150) or maple (FT-150BL) back and sides, multi-ply body binding, herringbone-style purfling, three-piece bolt-on neck, 14/20-fret rosewood fingerboard with dot inlays, three-per-side chrome tuners, rosewood bridge, available in Natural finish, mfg. 1972-1980.

	N/A	$250 - 300	$145 - 190	

FT-155 – dreadnought-style body, spruce top, highly figured ash back and sides, soundhole purfling rings, multiple body binding, 14/20-fret rosewood fingerboard with dot inlays, three-per-side chrome tuners, Natural finish, mfg. 1972-73.

	N/A	$275 - 325	$150 - 200	

FT-160 (TEXAN 12-STRING) – 12-string configuration, dreadnought-style body, laminated spruce top, mahogany back and sides, multiple body binding, three-piece bolt-on neck, 14/20-fret rosewood fingerboard with dot inlays, six-per-side chrome tuners, rosewood bridge, black pickguard, available in Natural or Sunburst finish, mfg. 1972-1980.

	N/A	$175 - 225	$100 - 130	

MSR/NOTES	100%	EXCELLENT	AVERAGE	LAST MSR

FT-165 (DE-LUXE 12-STRING) – 12-string configuration, dreadnought-style body, laminated spruce top, rosewood back and sides, multiple body binding, three-piece bolt-on neck, 14/20-fret rosewood fingerboard with block inlays, six-per-side chrome tuners, rosewood bridge, black pickguard, available in Natural finish, mfg. 1972-1980.

	N/A	$250 - 300	$145 - 190	

FT-200 "THE MONTICELLO" – embossed eagle featured on peghead, star inlays on fingerboard, non-adj. bridge, mfg. circa mid-1970s.

	N/A	$200 - 250	$120 - 150	

FT-335 – Grand Auditorium 000-style body, spruce top, rosewood back and sides, round soundhole with decorative rosette, three-piece bolt-on neck, 14/20-fret rosewood fingerboard with block inlays, three-per-side tuners, fixed rosewood bridge, black pickguard, mfg. 1974 only.

	N/A	$275 - 325	$150 - 200	

FT-350/FT-350BL – dreadnought-style body, spruce top, maple (FT-350BL) or rosewood (FT-350) back and sides, multi-ply body binding, three-piece bolt-on neck, 14/20-fret rosewood fingerboard with block inlays, bound headstock, three-per-side chrome tuners, non-adj. rosewood bridge, available in Natural finish, mfg. 1974-78.

	N/A	$300 - 350	$175 - 225	

FT-365 – 12-string configuration, dreadnought-style body, spruce top, rosewood back and sides, round soundhole with decorative rosette, three-piece bolt-on neck, 14/20-fret rosewood fingerboard with block inlays, bound headstock, six-per-side tuners, fixed rosewood bridge, black pickguard, mfg. 1974 only.

	N/A	$300 - 350	$175 - 225	

FT-550 – dreadnought-style body, select spruce top, three-piece (jacaranda/natural curly maple/jacaranda) back (Martin D-35 style), fixed full heel neck, 14/20-fret bound rosewood fingerboard with block inlays, bound headstock, three-per-side tuners, non-adj. rosewood bridge, black pickguard, Natural finish, mfg. 1974-78.

	N/A	$300 - 375	$175 - 225	

FT-565 – 12-string configuration, dreadnought-style body, select spruce top, three-piece (jacaranda/natural curly maple/jacaranda) back (Martin D-35 style), fixed full heel neck, 14/20-fret bound rosewood fingerboard with block inlays, bound headstock, six-per-side tuners, non-adj. rosewood bridge, black pickguard, Natural finish, mfg. 1974-76.

	N/A	$300 - 375	$175 - 225	

FT-570BL/FT-570SB – Jumbo-style body (Gibson J-200-style), select spruce top, select mahogany (FT-570SB) or maple (FT-570BL) back and sides, three-piece birch neck, 14/20-fret bound rosewood fingerboard with block inlays, bound headstock, three-per-side tuners, rosewood bridge, large black pickguard, available in Natural (FT-570BL) or Sunburst (FT-570SB) finish, mfg. 1974-75.

	N/A	$325 - 400	$200 - 250	

ACOUSTIC: MADRID & NAVARRE SERIES

MADRID (MFG. 1931-1941) – spruce top, curly maple back/sides, tortoiseshell body binding, 12/19-fret fingerboard, available in Natural finish, 16.5 in. body width, mfg. 1931-1941.

1931-1935	N/A	$2,500 - 3,000	$1,500 - 1,875	
1936-1941	N/A	$2,000 - 2,500	$1,200 - 1,500	

This model was originally introduced as an f-hole guitar, Hawaiian (or Spanish) style. In 1936, the Madrid was re-designated as a jumbo size, round soundhole, Hawaiian style only.

NAVARRE – Hawaiian style, spruce top, mahogany back/sides/neck, round soundhole, 20-fret bound rosewood fingerboard with dot inlay, tortoiseshell pickguard, rosewood bridge, three-per-side tuners with plastic buttons, available in Brown finish, 16.5 in. body width, mfg. 1931-1941.

	N/A	$1,650 - 2,000	$1,100 - 1,350	

ACOUSTIC: NOVA SERIES

NOVA 180 – uniquely-shaped jumbo body style, laminated spruce top, laminated nato back and sides, oval soundhole with rosette, one-piece nato neck, 14/21-fret rosewood fingerboard with dot inlays, black headstock overlay, three-per-side chrome tuners, bowed rosewood bridge, triangular black pickguard, Natural finish, mfg. 1977-79.

	N/A	$200 - 250	$120 - 150	

NOVA 245 – 12-string configuration, uniquely-shaped jumbo body style, laminated spruce top, laminated nato back and sides, oval soundhole with rosette, one-piece nato neck, 14/21-fret rosewood fingerboard with block inlays, bound black headstock overlay with design, six-per-side chrome tuners, bowed rosewood bridge, triangular black pickguard, Natural finish, mfg. 1977-79.

	N/A	$250 - 300	$135 - 175	

NOVA 295 – uniquely-shaped jumbo body style, solid spruce top, laminated rosewood back and sides, oval soundhole with rosette, three-piece nato neck, 14/21-fret rosewood fingerboard with block inlays, black headstock overlay, three-per-side chrome tuners, bowed rosewood bridge, triangular black pickguard, Natural finish, mfg. 1977-79.

	N/A	$250 - 300	$135 - 175	

MSR/NOTES	100%	EXCELLENT	AVERAGE	LAST MSR

NOVA 390 – uniquely-shaped jumbo body style, solid spruce top, laminated rosewood back and sides, oval soundhole with rosette, multi-ply top and back binding, three-piece maple neck, 14/21-fret bound rosewood fingerboard with hump block inlays, bound black headstock overlay with design, three-per-side gold tuners, bowed rosewood bridge, triangular black pickguard, Natural finish, mfg. 1977-79.

	N/A	$300 - 350	$175 - 225	

Epiphone also produced the Nova 390J, but specifications are unknown.

ACOUSTIC: PLAYER PACKS

In 1998, Epiphone began offering guitar and accessory packages for "one-stop shopping" experience for mostly entry level and a few mid-grade guitars. Nearly all (if not all) Epiphone Player Packs contain a gigbag, tuner, strap, and picks, while a few have guitar amplifiers and an extra set of strings. The values shown here are based on the entire package - if you only have the guitar or various parts of the Player Pack, the value will be less. A few of these packages feature guitars that are sold separately in Epiphone's product line, and they can be valued individually in other categories of the Epiphone section.

AJ-10/AJ-100 PLAYER PACK (MODEL PPGR-EAJ1) – entry level acoustic guitar package that includes an Epiphone AJ-10/AJ-100 acoustic guitar with a select spruce top, mahogany back and sides, a rosewood fingerboard and bridge, and available in Ebony or Natural finish, gigbag, tuner, strap, picks, and instructional video or DVD, mfg. 1999-2004.

	N/A	$110 - 140	$65 - 85	$329

In 2004, this model was renamed from the AJ-10 to the AJ-100.

AJ-220ST PREMIUM PACK (MODEL PPGR-EA2T) – entry level acoustic guitar package that includes an Epiphone AJ-200 advanced jumbo acoustic guitar with a solid Sitka spruce top, mahogany back and sides, a rosewood fingerboard and bridge, Shadow Sonic Tuner (built-in), and available in Natural or Vintage Sunburst (2012-present) finish, strap, picks, metal wall hanger, and instructional DVD, mfg. 2010-present.

MSR $320	$200	$120 - 150	$70 - 90	

C-5/N-5/EN-5 CLASSICAL PLAYER PACK (MODEL PPCG-EC05) – entry-level 3/4-sized classical guitar package that includes an Epiphone EN5 3/4-sized classical guitar with a select spruce top, mahogany back and sides, a rosewood fingerboard and bridge, and available in Natural finish, gigbag, tuner, strap, picks, and instructional video or DVD, mfg. 1999-2000, 2003-04.

	N/A	$65 - 85	$35 - 50	$199

In 2004, this model changed from the C-5 to the N-5 or EN-5.

C-10/N-10/EN-10 CLASSICAL PLAYER PACK (MODEL PPCG-EC15) – entry-level classical guitar package that includes an Epiphone EN10 classical guitar with a select spruce top, mahogany back and sides, a rosewood fingerboard and bridge, and available in Natural finish, gigbag, tuner, strap, picks, and instructional video or DVD, mfg. 1998-2006.

	N/A	$100 - 125	$60 - 75	$249

In 2004, this model changed from the C-10 to the N-10 or EN-10.

DR-90 PLAYER PACK (MODEL PPGR-EA9D) – entry level acoustic guitar package that includes an Epiphone DR-90 dreadnought acoustic guitar (only available as part of the package) with a select spruce top, mahogany back and sides, a rosewood fingerboard and bridge, and available in Natural finish, gigbag, tuner, strap, picks, and instructional DVD, mfg. 2005-2010.

	$150	$95 - 120	$50 - 75	$229

* DR-90S Player Pack (Model PPGR-EA9DS) – similar to the DR-90 Player Pack, except has a DR-90S acoustic guitar (only available as part of the package) with a solid spruce top, mfg. 2005-2010.

	$200	$120 - 150	$70 - 95	$332

DR-90T PLAYER PACK (MODEL PPGR-EA9T) – entry level acoustic guitar package that includes an Epiphone DR-90 dreadnought acoustic guitar (only available as part of the package) with a select spruce top, mahogany back and sides, a rosewood fingerboard and bridge, Shadow Sonic Tuner (built-in), and available in Natural or Vintage Sunburst (2012-present) finish, strap, picks, metal wall hanger, and instructional DVD, mfg. 2010-present.

MSR $224	$150	$95 - 120	$55 - 70	

PR-4E PLAYER PACK (MODEL PPGR-EEP4) – mid-level acoustic/electric guitar package that includes an Epiphone PR-4E single cutaway folk acoustic/electric guitar (only available as part of the package) with a select spruce top, mahogany back and sides, a rosewood fingerboard and bridge, pickup/electronics, and available in Natural finish, Epiphone Studio 15C acoustic guitar amplifier with chorus (only available as part of the package), gigbag, tuner, strap, picks, an extra set of strings, and instructional DVD, mfg. 2006-present.

MSR $347	$200	$120 - 150	$70 - 90	

PR-100 PLAYER PACK (MODEL PPGR-EANT) – entry level acoustic guitar package that includes an Epiphone PR-100 dreadnought acoustic guitar with a select spruce top, mahogany back and sides, a rosewood fingerboard and bridge, and available in Ebony or Natural finish, gigbag, tuner, strap, picks, and instructional video or DVD, mfg. 1998-2002.

	N/A	$110 - 140	$65 - 85	$329

ACOUSTIC: PRESENTATION (PR/DR) SERIES

The Presentation Series was introduced in the mid-1970s and has been a cornerstone in Epiphone's acoustic line up ever since. In 2004, Epiphone changed the model prefixes from "PR" to "DR". While the prefix changed and in some cases a different number

MSR/NOTES	100%	EXCELLENT	AVERAGE	LAST MSR

was assigned, there was no change to the actual model. Since Korean production halted in 2004, Epiphone probably used the new model designations to distinguish origin of manufacture on the guitar.

An example of a PR-5 E courtesy Epiphone

PR-5 E (MODEL EEP5) – single sharp cutaway folk style, figured maple top, round soundhole, multi-bound body/rosette, mahogany back/sides/neck, 20-fret bound rosewood fingerboard with pearl diamond slot inlay, rosewood bridge with white black dot pins, blackface peghead with pearl crown/logo inlay, three-per-side gold tuners, piezo bridge pickup, four-band EQ, available in Ebony, Natural, or Vintage Sunburst finish, mfg. 1992-present.

MSR $499	$300	$175 - 225	$100 - 135	

* **PR-5 E Artist (Model EEA5)** – available in Heritage Cherry Sunburst, Vintage Sunburst, or White (disc. 1999) finish, disc.

	N/A	$325 - 400	$175 - 225	$799

* **PR-5 E Left-Handed (Model EEP5L)** – similar to the PR-5 E, except in a left-handed configuration, available in Natural finish, current mfg. - single rounded solid mahogany body, solid spruce top, mahogany neck, RW fingerboard with split diamond inlay, binding, Shadow Classic P-4 preamp (2003-05), available in Natural, Heritage Cherry Sunburst, Trans. Amber, Trans. Red, Trans. Blue, Trans. Black, or Tobacco Sunburst finish, disc. 1998, reintroduced 2003-05.

	N/A	$250 - 300	$150 - 200	$615

PR-6 E (MODEL EEP6) – single rounded solid mahogany body, solid spruce top, mahogany neck, RW fingerboard with split diamond inlay, binding, Shadow Classic P-4 preamp (2003-06), available in Natural, Heritage Cherry Sunburst, Trans. Amber, Trans. Red, Trans. Blue, Trans. Black, or Tobacco Sunburst finish, disc. 1998, reintroduced 2003-06.

	N/A	$300 - 350	$175 - 225	$749

This model was also available with rosewood back/sides (PR-6ER, Last MSR $749).

* **PR-6E Left-Handed (Model EEP6L)** – similar to the PR-6E except in left-handed configuration, available in Natural or Trans. Amber finish, mfg. 2003-05.

	N/A	$300 - 375	$175 - 225	$799

PR-7 E (MODEL EEP7) – similar to the PR-5E except has a bird's-eye maple top, slim taper neck, and Epiphonic 2000, available in Heritage Cherry Sunburst, Natural, Orange Sunburst, Trans. Black, or Vintage Cherry Sunburst, disc. 2002.

	N/A	$300 - 350	$175 - 225	$749

DR-100 (PR-100, MODEL EA10) – dreadnought style, spruce top, round soundhole, black pickguard, stripe rosette, mahogany back/sides/neck, 14/20-fret rosewood fingerboard with dot inlay, rosewood bridge with black pins, three-per-side chrome tuners, available in Ebony, Natural Gloss, Wine Red (disc.), or Vintage Sunburst finish, mfg. 1997-present.

MSR $182	$100	$60 - 80	$35 - 50	

Also available with an ash top at no additional charge (Model PR-100A). Also was available in a single cutaway design for an additional $50 (Model PR-100C). Wine Red added in 2002.

* **PR-100-12 (Model EA12)** – similar to the PR-100 except in 12-string configuration, available in Natural finish, disc. 2003.

	N/A	$95 - 120	$55 - 80	$332

PR-150 – dreadnought-style body, select spruce top, mahogany back and sides, black body binding, round soundhole with three-ring rosette (5/9/5 grouping), set mahogany neck, 14/20-fret rosewood fingerboard with dot inlays, black headstock overlay with Epiphone logo, rosewood bridge with black bridge pins, black pickguard with "E" logo, chrome hardware, available in Natural or Vintage Sunburst finish, current mfg.

MSR $199	$130	$75 - 100	$45 - 60	

This is part of Epiphone's Special Run Series and is only available through select retailers.

DR-200 (PR-200, MODEL EA20) – dreadnought style, spruce top, round soundhole, black pickguard, stripe rosette, bound body, mahogany back/sides/neck, 14/20-fret rosewood fingerboard with pearl dot inlay, rosewood bridge with white pins, three-per-side chrome tuners, available in Natural Satin finish, mfg. 1992-2005.

1992-1999	N/A	$150 - 200	$95 - 120	
2000-2005	N/A	$90 - 120	$50 - 70	$299

In 1998, Ebony, Natural Gloss, and Vintage Sunburst finishes were introduced (previously a $15 option).

MSR/NOTES	100%	EXCELLENT	AVERAGE	LAST MSR

* DR-212 12-String (Model EA2T) – similar to the DR-200, except in 12-string configuration and six-per-side tuners, available in Natural finish, mfg. 2005-present.

MSR $282	$170	$95 - 120	$55 - 70	

* PR-200 E (Model EE20) – similar to the DR-200 (PR-200), except has electronics, available in Natural finish, mfg. 1992-2001.

	N/A	$130 - 160	$80 - 110	$329

* DR-200S (Model EA2S) – similar to the DR-200, except has a solid spruce top, mfg. 2005-2010.

	$200	$110 - 140	$70 - 90	$332

»DR-200SLH (Model EA2SL) – similar to the DR-200S, except is in left-handed configuration, mfg. 2005 only.

	N/A	$130 - 160	$75 - 95	$445

DR-200CE (MODEL EE2C, PR-350 CE, MODEL EE3C) – single rounded cutaway dreadnought style body, select spruce top, mahogany back and sides, body binding, mahogany neck, 14/20-fret rosewood fingerboard with split diamond inlays, tortoise pickguard with E logo, piezo pickup, Epiphonic-Six preamp, chrome hardware, available in Ebony, Natural, or Vintage Sunburst finish, mfg. 1993-2010.

	$230	$130 - 160	$80 - 100	$332

In 1998, Ebony and Vintage Sunburst finishes were introduced (previously a $10 option).

DR-220S (MODEL EAS2) – square-shouldered dreadnought body, solid Sitka spruce top, mahogany back and sides, round soundhole with multi-ring rosette, multi-ply binding, mahogany neck, 14/20-fret bound rosewood fingerboard with dot inlays, black headstock overlay, three-per-side nickel tuners, rosewood bridge, tortoise pickguard, available in Natural finish, 25.5 in. scale, 1 11/16 in. nut width, mfg. 2010-2011.

	$200	$110 - 140	$70 - 90	$319

DR-300S (MODEL EA03) – dreadnought style, solid spruce top, rosewood back/sides, mahogany neck, 14/20-fret rosewood fingerboard with diamond inlays, body/neck binding, tortoise pickguard with stylized E, gold hardware, available in Natural or Vintage Sunburst finish, mfg. 2004-07.

	N/A	$175 - 225	$110 - 140	$499

PR-350 (MODEL EA35) – dreadnought style, spruce top, round soundhole, tortoise pickguard with stylized E, three-stripe bound body/rosette, mahogany back/sides/neck, 14/20-fret rosewood fingerboard with pearl snowflake inlay, pearl crown/logo inlay, three-per-side chrome tuners, available in Natural finish, mfg. 1992-2000.

	N/A	$200 - 250	$120 - 150	$369

In 1998, Ebony and Vintage Sunburst finishes were introduced (previously a $10 option).

* DR-350-12 (Model EA2T, PR-350-12, Model EA3T) – similar to the PR-350 S, except has 12-string configuration, available in Natural finish, disc. 2004.

	N/A	$225 - 275	$135 - 170	$331

»PR-350 12 E (Model EE3T) – similar to DR-350-12 (PR-350-12), except has electronics, available in Natural finish, mfg. early 1990s-1998.

	N/A	$250 - 300	$150 - 190	$529

* PR-350 C (Model EA3C) – similar to the PR-350, except has a single rounded cutaway, available in Ebony, Natural, or Vintage Sunburst finish, mfg. 1993-99.

	N/A	$225 - 275	$135 - 170	$409

* PR-350 E (Model EE35) – similar to the PR-350, except has electronics, available in Ebony, Natural, or Vintage Sunburst finish, mfg. early 1990s-1998.

	N/A	$225 - 275	$135 - 175	$459

* PR-350 M (Model EM35) – similar to the PR-350, except has a mahogany top, mfg. 1994-98.

	N/A	$150 - 200	$90 - 120	$379

»PR-350 ME (Model EME5) – similar to PR-350 M, except has a piezo bridge pickup and electronics, mfg. 1993-98.

	N/A	$200 - 250	$120 - 150	$499

* DR-350 S (PR-350 S, Model EAO5) – similar to the PR-350, except has a solid spruce top, available in Ebony, Natural, or Vintage Sunburst finish, mfg. 1992-2004.

	N/A	$225 - 275	$135 - 175	$382

»DR-350 S Left-Handed (Model EASL, PR-350 S, Model EA2T) – similar to the PR-350 S, except in left-handed configuration, available in Natural finish, mfg. early 1990s-2000, 2002-04.

	N/A	$225 - 275	$135 - 175	$415

* DR-350 SM (PR-350 SM, Model EO35) – similar to the PR-350, except has solid mahogany back and sides, available in Natural Satin finish, mfg. 2003-04.

	N/A	$325 - 375	$200 - 250	$832

MSR/NOTES	100%	EXCELLENT	AVERAGE	LAST MSR

* *PR-350 SO (Model EM35)* – similar to the PR-350, except has solid ovangkol back and sides, available in Natural Satin finish, mfg. 2003 only.

	N/A	$425 - 500	$250 - 300	$999

* *PR-350 SR (Model ER35)* – similar to the PR-350, except has solid rosewood back and sides, available in Natural Satin finish, mfg. 2003-04.

	N/A	$425 - 500	$250 - 300	$999

PR-400 (MODEL EA40) – available in Natural finish, mfg. 1997-99.

	N/A	$175 - 225	$110 - 140	$459

DR-500M MASTERBILT (MODEL EMM5) – dreadnought style, premium solid Sitka spruce top, premium solid mahogany back and sides, body/neck binding, mahogany neck, 14/20-fret rosewood fingerboard with diamond inlays, nickel hardware, available in Natural (2007-2011) or Natural Satin finish, mfg. 2004-2011.

	$500	$300 - 350	$175 - 225	$832

* *DR-500MCE Masterbilt (Model EMEC)* – similar to the DR-500M Masterbilt, except has a single smooth cutaway and Shadown NanoMag/NanoFlex pickups with eSonic-2 stereo electronics, available in Natural (2012-present) or Vintage Sunburst finish, mfg. 2010-present.

MSR $999	$600	$350 - 425	$225 - 275	

* *DR-500ME Masterbilt (Model EMM5E)* – similar to the DR-500M Masterbilt, except has L.R. Baggs electronics, available in Natural Satin finish, mfg. 2004-2011.

	$550	$325 - 400	$200 - 250	$915

* *DR-500P Masterbilt (Model EMP5)* – similar to the DR-500M, except has solid maple back and sides, gold hardware, and headstock binding, available in Natural Satin finish, mfg. 2004-2010.

	$550	$325 - 400	$200 - 250	$915

• **Add $100 for Baggs electronics (Model DR-500ME, EMP5E, disc. 2005).**

* *DR-500R Masterbilt (Model EMR5)* – similar to the DR-500P, except has solid rosewood back and sides, available in Natural Satin finish, mfg. 2004-2011.

	$600	$350 - 425	$225 - 275	$999

• **Add $100 for Baggs electronics (Model DR-500RE, EMR5E, disc. 2005).**

»*DR-500RA Masterbilt (Model EMRA5)* – similar to the DR-500R, except has abalone binding, and available in Natural Satin or Vintage Sunburst finish, mfg. 2004-05.

	N/A	$650 - 750	$400 - 475	$1,598

PR-500 – dreadnought-style body, spruce top, mahogany back and sides, round soundhole with multi-ring rosette, tortoiseshell with black and white multi-ply binding, mahogany neck, 14/20-fret rosewood fingerboard, three-per-side tuners, rosewood bridge, pickguard with "E" logo, available in Natural finish, 25.5 in. scale, mfg. early 1980s.

	N/A	$300 - 350	$175 - 225	

PR-550 – dreadnought-style body, spruce top, rosewood back and sides, round soundhole with multi-ring rosette, black and white multi-ply binding, mahogany neck, 14/20-fret rosewood fingerboard, three-per-side tuners, rosewood bridge, pickguard with "E" logo, available in Natural finish, 25.5 in. scale, mfg. early 1980s.

	N/A	$300 - 375	$175 - 225	

PR-600 – Grand Auditorium 000-style body, laminated spruce top, two-piece mahogany back, mahogany sides, round soundhole with herringbone design purfling ring, tortoise top and back body binding, one-piece mahogany neck, 14/20-fret rosewood fingerboard with dot inlays, scripted Epiphone logo on headstock, three-per-side chrome tuners, available in Antique Sunburst or Natural finish, 25.5 in. scale, mfg. 1980-mid-1980s.

	N/A	$325 - 400	$200 - 250	

PR-650 – slope-shouldered dreadnought, laminated spruce top, mahogany back and sides, round soundhole with concentric brown rings, tortoise top and back body binding, one-piece mahogany neck, 14/20-fret rosewood fingerboard with dot inlays, scripted Epiphone logo on headstock, three-per-side chrome tuners, rosewood bridge, teardrop-shaped pickguard, available in Antique Sunburst or Natural finish, 25.5 in. scale, mfg. 1980-mid-1980s.

	N/A	$250 - 300	$150 - 190	

* *PR-650-12* – similar to the PR-650 except in 12-string configuration with six-per-side tuners, mfg. 1980-mid-1980s.

	N/A	$250 - 300	$150 - 190	

PR-715 – dreadnought-style body, laminated spruce top, two-piece bookmatched rosewood back, rosewood sides, round soundhole with herringbone rosette, brown herringbone top binding/inlay, one-piece mahogany neck, 14/20-fret rosewood fingerboard with dot inlays, scripted Epiphone logo on headstock, three-per-side chrome tuners, rosewood bridge, available in Antique Cherry Sunburst, Antique Sunburst, or Natural finish, mfg. 1981-mid-1980s.

	N/A	$175 - 225	$110 - 140	

MSR/NOTES	100%	EXCELLENT	AVERAGE	LAST MSR

* *PR-715-12* – similar to the PR-715, except in 12-string configuration with six-per-side tuners, mfg. 1980-mid-1980s.

| | N/A | $200 - 250 | $120 - 150 | |

PR-720 S – dreadnought style, solid spruce top, round soundhole, no pickguard, three-stripe rosette, bound body, African ovangkol back/sides, mahogany neck, 14/20-fret rosewood fingerboard with pearl diamond inlay, rosewood bridge with white pins, three-per-side gold tuners, available in Natural finish, mfg. 1992 only.

| | N/A | $225 - 275 | $120 - 150 | |

PR-725 – dreadnought-style body, laminated spruce top, two-piece mahogany back, mahogany sides, round soundhole with concentric rings, laminated maple top and back binding, one-piece mahogany neck, 14/20-fret rosewood fingerboard with dot inlays, scripted Epiphone logo inlaid in MOP on headstock, three-per-side chrome tuners, rosewood bridge, available in Natural finish, 25.5 in. scale, mfg. circa 1975-mid-1980s.

| | N/A | $175 - 225 | $95 - 125 | |

* *PR-725S* – similar to the PR-725, except has a solid spruce top, mfg. 1979-mid-1980s.

| | N/A | $225 - 275 | $115 - 145 | |

PR-735 – dreadnought style body, laminated spruce top, rosewood back and sides, round soundhole with concentric brown rings, laminated maple top and back body binding, one-piece mahogany neck, 14/20-fret maple-bound rosewood fingerboard with dot inlays, maple-bound headstock with scripted logo inlaid in MOP, three-per-side tuners, rosewood bridge, teardrop-shaped black pickguard, available in Natural finish, 25.5 in. scale, mfg. 1979-mid-1980s.

| | N/A | $225 - 275 | $120 - 150 | |

* *PR-735S* – similar to the PR-735, except has a solid spruce top, mfg. 1979-mid-1980s.

| | N/A | $250 - 300 | $135 - 175 | |

PR-745 – dreadnought-style body, laminated spruce top, rosewood back and sides, round soundhole with concentric rings, laminated maple top and back binding, one-piece mahogany neck, 14/20-fret rosewood fingerboard with dot inlays, scripted Epiphone logo inlaid in MOP on headstock, three-per-side chrome tuners, rosewood bridge, available in Natural finish, 25.5 in. scale, mfg. circa 1975-79.

| | N/A | $250 - 300 | $135 - 175 | |

PR-755S – dreadnought-style body, solid spruce top, three-piece rosewood back, rosewood sides, round soundhole with concentric brown rings, laminated maple top and back body binding, one-piece mahogany neck, 14/20-fret maple-bound rosewood fingerboard with dot inlays, scripted Epiphone logo inlaid in MOP, three-per-side gold tuners, ebony bridge, available in Antique Cherry Sunburst, Antique Sunburst, or Natural finish, 25.5 in. scale, mfg. 1979-mid-1980s.

| | N/A | $300 - 350 | $175 - 225 | |

PR-765 – dreadnought-style body, solid spruce top, rosewood back and sides, round soundhole with concentric rings, multi-ply body binding, one-piece mahogany neck, 14/20-fret bound rosewood fingerboard with abalone/MOP block inlays, bound black headstock with scripted Epiphone logo and decorative floral design inlaid in MOP on headstock, three-per-side tuners, rosewood bridge, available in Natural finish, 25.5 in. scale, mfg. circa 1975-79.

| | N/A | $300 - 350 | $175 - 225 | |

PR-775 S – dreadnought style, solid spruce top, round soundhole, tortoiseshell pickguard, abalone bound body/rosette, rosewood back/sides, mahogany neck, 14/20-fret bound rosewood fingerboard with abalone pearl block/triangle inlay, rosewood bridge with white black dot pins, rosewood veneer on bound peghead with crescent/star/logo inlay, three-per-side chrome tuners, available in Natural finish, disc. 1996.

| | N/A | $200 - 250 | $135 - 175 | $500 |

* *PR-775-12* – similar to the PR-775 S, except in 12-string configuration, disc. 1996.

| | N/A | $200 - 250 | $135 - 175 | $500 |

PR-775 SCE (MODEL EO77) – single rounded cutaway body, gold hardware, Electar preamp system, available in Antique Natural finish, mfg. 1997-99.

| | N/A | $325 - 400 | $200 - 250 | $799 |

PR-795AE – acoustic electric Presentation guitar, available in Natural, Antique Sunburst, or Antique Cherry Sunburst finish, mfg. 1980-mid-1980s.

| | N/A | $250 - 300 | $120 - 150 | |

PR-800 S (MODEL EA80) – available in Natural finish, disc. 1998.

| | N/A | $275 - 325 | $150 - 200 | $619 |

* *PR-800 SE (Model EE80)* – similar to the PR-800 S, except has an Electar preamp system, available in Natural finish, disc. 1999.

| | N/A | $300 - 350 | $200 - 250 | $719 |

ACOUSTIC: SIGNATURE SERIES

CHET ATKINS SST STUDIO (MODEL ECSS) – semi-solid thinline acoustic, mahogany set neck, maple top, rosewood fingerboard with dot inlays, three-per-side tuners, Shadow piezo pickup, passive electronics, gold hardware, available in Ebony, Heritage Cherry Sunburst (disc. 2000), or Natural finish, disc. 2005.

| | N/A | $275 - 325 | $150 - 200 | $665 |

MSR/NOTES	100%	EXCELLENT	AVERAGE	LAST MSR

Chet Atkins CE (Model ECCE) – nylon string version of Chet Atkins SST, banjo style tuners, available in Ebony or Natural finish, mfg. 1995-2005.

	N/A	$275 - 325	$175 - 225	$665

Chet Atkins Custom (Model ECSF) – available in Heritage Cherry Sunburst or Natural finish, disc.

	N/A	$300 - 350	$175 - 225	$699

Chet Atkins Deluxe (Model ECBE) – available in Heritage Cherry Sunburst or Natural finish, disc.

	N/A	$325 - 375	$200 - 250	$749

DAVE NAVARRO "JANE" (MODEL EEDN) – single smooth cutaway dreadnought-style body, solid Sitka spruce top, solid mahogany back and sides, round soundhole with multi-ring abalone rosette, multi-ply body binding, mahogany neck, 14/20-fret bound ebony fingerboard with MOP Unicursal hexagram inlays, bound black headstock overlay, "Jane" on truss rod cover, three-per-side chrome tuners, ebony bridge, tree/bird pickguard, Shadow NanoFlex pickup, eSonic preamp, available in Ebony finish, 25.5 in. scale, 1.725 in. nut width, mfg. 2010-present.

MSR $999	$600	$350 - 425	$200 - 250	

JEFF "SKUNK" BAXTER (MODEL EAJB) – available in Ebony, Red Brown Mahogany, Natural, or Vintage Sunburst finish, disc. 2005.

	N/A	$350 - 425	$200 - 250	$832

JOAN SEBASTIAN "SONADOR" (MODEL EEJS) – single smooth cutaway jumbo-style body, solid Sitka spruce top, mahogany back and sides, round soundhole with multi-ring abalone rosette, multi-ply body binding, mahogany neck, 14/20-fret rosewood fingerboard with dot inlays, black headstock overlay with Epiphone logo, cross, heart, and horseshoe inlays, three-per-side chrome tuners, rosewood moustache bridge with horseshoe inlays, Piezo Element pickup, AT-3000 preamp, available in Antique Natural finish, 25.5 in. scale, 1.725 in. nut width, mfg. 2011-present.

MSR $499	$300	$175 - 225	$100 - 135	

JOAN SEBASTIAN "TRIUNFADORA" (MODEL EEJS) – single smooth cutaway jumbo-style body, solid Sitka spruce top, rosewood back and sides, round soundhole with custom hearts rosette, white body binding with abalone purfling, mahogany neck, 14/20-fret bound rosewood fingerboard with cross inlays, black headstock overlay with Epiphone logo, cross, heart, and horseshoe inlays, three-per-side gold Imperial tuners, rosewood moustache bridge with horseshoe inlays, Shadow NanoFlex pickup, eSonic preamp, available in Antique Natural finish, 25.5 in. scale, 1.725 in. nut width, mfg. 2011-present.

MSR $999	$600	$350 - 425	$200 - 250	

JOHN LENNON AJ/EJ-160 E (MODEL EEEJ) – dreadnought style, bound body/fingerboard, trapezoid fingerboard inlay, built-in pickup, volume/tone controls (on top), tortoiseshell pickguard, screened "John Lennon" signature on body, available in Natural (1997-98) or Vintage Cherry Sunburst finish, mfg. 1997-present.

MSR $832	$500	$300 - 375	$175 - 225	

PAUL MCCARTNEY 1964 TEXAN (JAPAN MFG., MODEL EEMT) – slope shouldered dreadnought style, solid spruce top, solid mahogany back, mahogany sides, one-piece mahogany neck, 14/20-fret rosewood fingerboard with parallelogram inlays, three-per-side tuners, rosewood bridge, tortoise pickguard with E logo, nickel hardware, Natural finish, 25.5 in. scale, mfg. 2006-2010.

	$2,850	$1,650 - 2,000	N/A	$4,700

This model is also available in left-handed configuration. This model is not to be confused with the McCartney model produced in the U.S. during 2005 (see Elitist Series).

ROY ORBISON SIGNATURE BARD LIMITED EDITION (EABR) – 12-string configuration, square-shouldered dreadnought-style based on the Epiphone Bard, solid spruce top, laminated mahogany back and sides, round soundhole with multi-ring rosette, cream body binding, set three-piece 1960s slim taper mahogany neck, 14/20-fret rosewood fingerboard with dot inlays, black headstock overlay with Epiphone logo and pearl design, back of headstock has Orbison's signature along with the notation of the first measure for "Oh Pretty Woman," six-per-side nickel tuners with cream buttons, rosewood bridge, tortoise pickguard with "E" foil logo, available in Antique Natural finish, custom hard shell case with Orbison's signature and sunglasses graphics, certificate of authenticity, and photo included, mfg. late 2009-2010.

	$800	$475 - 550	$300 - 350	$1,332

ACOUSTIC: SQ SERIES (DON EVERLY & NEIL DIAMOND)

DON EVERLY SQ-180 (MODEL EAQ1) – star fingerboard inlay, soundhole-surrounding pickguard, available in Ebony finish, disc. 2000, reintroduced 2002-04.

	NA	$475 - 550	$300 - 350	$519

NEIL DIAMOND SQ-180 (MODEL EAND) – maple body, select spruce top, mahogany neck, rosewood fingerboard with diamond-shaped inlays, 24.75 in. scale, facsimile signature on headstock, gold hardware, available in Black Metallic finish, mfg. 1999-2000, reintroduced 2002.

	N/A	$425 - 500	$250 - 300	$599

MSR/NOTES	100%	EXCELLENT	AVERAGE	LAST MSR

ACOUSTIC: MISC. & REISSUE SERIES

BLUESMASTER/THE SONGWRITER (MODEL EABM) – Grand Auditorium-sized Parlor-style body, solid spruce top, mahogany back and sides, round soundhole with three-ring rosette, multi-ply body binding, mahogany neck, 12/18-fret bound rosewood fingerboard with pearl dot inlays, bound headstock with black overlay and Epiphone logo, "Blues Master" on truss rod cover, three-per-side chrome tuners, rosewood bridge, available in Ebony, Natural, or Vintage Sunburst finish, 24.75 in. scale, mfg. 1994-98.

	N/A	$325 - 400	$175 - 225	$679

In 1997, the Bluesmaster was renamed The Songwriter and the name was changed on the truss rod cover.

CABALLERO/EL CABALLERO (MODEL EECB) – single rounded cutaway jumbo body, solid spruce top, mahogany back and sides, round soundhole with five-ring rosette, multi-ply body binding, mahogany neck, 14/20-fret rosewood fingerboard with Mesa-Moon Southwestern motif inlays, black headstock overlay with Epiphone logo and cactus Southwestern motif inlays, uniquely-shaped rosewood bridge with Southwestern motif inlays, piezo pickup with para EQ, available in Natural finish, 25.5 in. scale, mfg. 1997-99.

	N/A	$525 - 600	$375 - 425	$1,299

While Epiphone listed this model in their catalog and price list as the "Caballero," the label on the inside of the guitar and truss rod cover may have "El Caballero" listed.

EF-500M MASTERBILT (EMF1) – folk style, premium solid Sitka spruce top, premium solid mahogany back and sides, body/neck binding, mahogany "V" neck, 14/20-fret rosewood fingerboard with diamond inlays, nickel hardware, available in Natural Satin or Vintage Sunburst finish, mfg. 2004-2011.

	$550	$325 - 400	$200 - 250	$915

* ***EF-500R Masterbilt (EMF3)*** – similar to the EF-500M, except has solid rosewood back and sides, gold hardware, and headstock binding, mfg. 2004-2011.

	$600	$350 - 425	$225 - 275	$999

»***EF-500RCE Masterbilt (EM3C)*** – similar to the EF-500R, except has L.R. Baggs electronics, mfg. 2004-05.

	N/A	$425 - 500	$275 - 325	$1,216

»***EF-500RCCE Masterbilt (EM3CC)*** – similar to the EF-500R, except has a single cutaway, solid cedar top, and L.R. Baggs electronics, available in Natural Satin finish, mfg. 2006-present.

MSR $1,332	$800	$475 - 575	$300 - 350	

* ***EF-500RA Masterbilt (EMF3A)*** – similar to the EF-500R, except has abalone binding, and available in Natural Satin or Vintage Sunburst finish, mfg. 2004-2011.

	$900	$550 - 650	$375 - 450	$1,498

EXPEDITION TRAVEL GUITAR (MODEL EAEX) – travel-sized guitar, solid spruce top, mahogany back and sides, round soundhole with multi-ring rosette, mahogany neck, 14/20-fret rosewood fingerboard, black headstock overlay with Epiphone logo, three-per-side chrome tuners, rosewood bridge, available in Natural finish, 22 in. scale, 1.68 in. nut width, gig bag included, mfg. 2010-2011.

	$200	$130 - 160	$80 - 100	$365

INSPIRED BY 1964 TEXAN (EETX) – slope-shouldered dreadnought-style based on the Epiphone Texan (AJ), solid spruce top, solid mahogany back and sides, round soundhole with multi-ring rosette, five-ply top and back body binding, set 1960s slim taper mahogany neck, 14/20-fret rosewood fingerboard with MOP parallelogram inlays, black headstock overlay with Epiphone logo and pearl design, three-per-side nickel tuners with cream buttons, rosewood bridge, tortoise pickguard with "E" foil logo, Shadow NanoFlex low impedance pickup, Shadow Sonic soundhole mounted electronics, available in Antique Natural or Vintage Cherryburst finish, mfg. late 2009-present.

MSR $665	$400	$250 - 300	$150 - 190	

PERFORMER ME (MODEL EEP6) – single cutaway folk style body, flame maple top, back, and sides, round soundhole with abalone rosette, abalone binding, mahogany neck, 14/20-fret bound rosewood fingerboard with dot inlays, black headstock overlay, three-per-side chrome tuners, rosewood bridge, Epiphone eSonic2 stereo preamp system, available in Trans. Black finish, mfg. 2007-2011.

	$500	$300 - 350	$175 - 225	$832

* ***Performer SE (Model EEP6)*** – similar to the Performer ME, except has a solid Sitka spruce top, available in Natural finish, mfg. 2007-2010.

	$500	$300 - 350	$175 - 225	$832

SST STUDIO (MODEL EEST) – steel-string configuration, single smooth cutaway chambered mahgaony body, flame maple top, top binding, mahogany neck, 14/24-fret extended rosewood fingerboard with no inlays, black headstock overlay with three-per-side chrome tuners, rosewood bridge, Shadow Nanoflex pickup system, available in Ebony finish, 25.5 in. scale, mfg. 2007-2011.

	$350	$200 - 250	$120 - 150	$582

ACOUSTIC ELECTRIC BASS

EL CAPITAN (MODEL EBEC) – jumbo style, maple body, set-in maple neck, 34 in. scale, rosewood fingerboard with dot inlay, piezo bridge pickup, Para-EQ preamp system, available in Ebony, Natural, or Vintage Sunburst finishes, disc. 2000.

	N/A	$150 - 200	$120 - 150	$949

MSR/NOTES	100%	EXCELLENT	AVERAGE	LAST MSR

* **El Capitan Cutaway (Model EBC4)** – similar to El Capitan, except features a single rounded cutaway body, available in Ebony (disc.), Natural (disc.), or Vintage Sunburst finish, disc. 2011.

	$400	$225 - 275	$130 - 160	$665

» **El Capitan Cutaway Fretless (Model EBC4F)** – similar to El Capitan, except features a single rounded cutaway body, fretless fingerboard, available in Ebony, Natural, or Vintage Sunburst finish, disc. 1998.

	N/A	$275 - 325	$150 - 200	$1,099

* **El Capitan Cutaway Five-String (Model EBC5)** – similar to El Capitan, except features a single rounded cutaway body, five-string configuration, 3/2-per-side tuners, available in Ebony, Natural, or Vintage Sunburst finish, disc. 2000.

	N/A	$275 - 325	$150 - 200	$1,049

» **El Capitan Cutaway Fretless Five-String (Model EBC5F)** – similar to the El Capitan 5 String Cutaway, except features a fretless fingerboard, available in Ebony, Natural, or Vintage Sunburst finish, disc. 2000.

	N/A	$300 - 350	$175 - 225	$1,049

EL SEGUNDO (MODEL EBS3) – jumbo mahogany body, laminated maple top, maple set neck, rosewood fingerboard with dot inlays, two-per-side tuners, bound body, chrome hardware, Epiphonic-Six preamp with Shadow piezo pickup, available in Natural finish, mfg. 2007-08.

	N/A	$130 - 160	$80 - 100	$382

* **El Segundo Cutaway (Model EBS4)** – similar to the El Segundo, except has a single cutaway, available in Natural or Vintage Sunburst finish, disc. 2006.

	N/A	$225 - 275	$135 - 175	$582

ERNIE BALL'S EARTHWOOD

Instruments previously produced in San Luis Obispo, CA in the early to mid-1970s.

After finding great success with prepackaged string sets and custom gauges, Ernie Ball founded the Earthwood company to produce a four-string acoustic bass guitar. George Fullerton built the prototype, as well as helping with other work before moving to Leo Fender's CLF Research company in 1974. Earthwood offered both the acoustic bass guitar and a lacquer finished solid body guitar with large sound chambers in 1972, but production was short lived (through February 1973). In April of 1975, bass guitar operations resumed on a limited basis for a number of years.

EROS

Instruments previously produced in Japan between the early 1970s and the early 1980s.

The Eros trademark is the brand name of a UK importer. These guitars were generally entry level copies of American designs. Source: Tony Bacon and Paul Day, *The Guru's Guitar Guide*.

ESPAÑA

Instruments previously produced in Finland by Landola. Distributed in the U.S. by España Guitars (Buegeleisen & Jacobson) in New York, NY.

The España trademark was used and distributed by Buegeleisen & Jacobson (B&J) in New York, New York. In the early 1960s, B&J started importing acoustic guitars under the España trademark that were made by Landola in Finland. Unlike many distributors at the time, B&J did not own the España trademark - it was actually owned by Landola. To further confuse the matter, B&J marketed España guitars as being produced in Sweden instead of Finland! España acoustic instruments mainly consist of mid-level classical guitars, although they produced dreadnoughts as well. In circa 1963, Landola began building electric guitars and by the late 1960s/early 1970s, thin hollowbody and solidbody electric guitars began appearing with the España trademark. The España trademark eventually disappeared in the mid-1970s - a few years later than many other European factories ceased production. Landola, however, continues to produce guitars in Finland.

ACOUSTIC: CLASSICAL MODELS

2000 – nylon string configuration, 25 in. scale, spruce top, round soundhole, mahogany back/sides, 18-fret rosewood fingerboard, seven-piece mahogany neck, rosewood bridge, three-per-side tuners, available in Natural finish, mfg. circa early 1970s.

	N/A	$75 - 95	$45 - 60	$100

* **2001 (3/4 Size)** – similar to the 2000, except features a 22 in. scale, rosewood bridge with inlay, available in Natural finish, length 35 in., body width 16.25 in., body thickness 3.75 in., mfg. circa early 1970s.

	N/A	$75 - 95	$45 - 60	$110

2002 – nylon string configuration, spruce top, round soundhole, mahogany back/sides, marquetry on back, 18-fret rosewood fingerboard, seven-piece mahogany neck, rosewood bridge with inlay, three-per-side tuners, available in Natural finish, body width 18.25 in., body thickness 4.25 in., 25 in. scale, mfg. circa early 1970s.

	N/A	$95 - 120	$60 - 75	$125

MSR/NOTES	100%	EXCELLENT	AVERAGE	LAST MSR

2004 – nylon string configuration, 25.5 in. scale, spruce top, round soundhole, rosewood back/sides, 18-fret rosewood fingerboard, seven-piece mahogany neck, rosewood bridge, three-per-side tuners, available in Natural finish, body width 18.875 in., body thickness 4.375 in., mfg. circa early 1970s.

	N/A	$120 - 150	$75 - 95	$165

2006 – similar to the 2004, except has additional inlay, rosewood bridge with inlay, three-per-side gold-plated tuners, available in Natural hand-rubbed finish, mfg. circa early 1970s.

	N/A	$150 - 200	$95 - 120	$250

ACOUSTIC: DREADNOUGHT MODELS

2100 – dreadnought style, 25 in. scale, spruce top, round soundhole, mahogany back/sides, 21-fret rosewood fingerboard, seven-piece mahogany neck, rosewood bridge, three-per-side tuners, Natural finish, length 18 in., body thickness 3.875 in., mfg. circa early 1970s.

	N/A	$75 - 95	$45 - 60	$100

2102 – similar to the 2100, available in Natural finish, length 18.25 in., body thickness 4.25 in., mfg. circa early 1970s.

	N/A	$75 - 95	$45 - 60	$125

2104 – similar to the 2100, except features round soundhole with inlay, rosewood back/sides, adjustable bridge, Natural finish, length 18.875 in., body thickness 4.375 in., mfg. circa early 1970s.

	N/A	$95 - 120	$60 - 75	$165

2106 – dreadnought style, 25 in. scale, spruce top, round soundhole with inlay, rosewood back/sides, 21-fret rosewood fingerboard, seven-piece mahogany neck, rosewood bridge, three-per-side tuners, Natural finish, length 20 in., body thickness 4.375 in., mfg. circa early 1970s.

	N/A	$120 - 150	$75 - 95	$175

2108 12-STRING – similar to the 2106, except has 12-string configuration, six-per-side tuners, 18-fret rosewood fingerboard, additional inlay, available in Natural finish, length 20 in., body thickness 4.375 in., mfg. circa early 1970s.

	N/A	$135 - 175	$80 - 105	$195

2114 TENOR – dreadnought style, 23 in. scale, spruce top, round soundhole, mahogany back/sides, 20-fret rosewood fingerboard, seven-piece mahogany neck, adjustable rosewood bridge, three-per-side tuners, available in Natural finish, length 18.25 in., body thickness 4.25 in., mfg. circa early 1970s.

	N/A	$75 - 95	$45 - 60	$125

ESPANOLA

Instruments previously produced in Korea. Distributed by V.J. Rendano Music Company, Inc. of Youngstown, OH.

The wide range of Espanola acoustic guitars are designed and priced with the entry level or student guitarist in mind. Suggested new retail prices range from $200 up to $450 on the Korean-produced acoustic guitar models; $450 on the resonator-style models; $125 to $300 on four Paracho, Mexico classicals; and $350 to $550 on four-string acoustic bass guitars.

ESPANOLA, GUITARRAS

Please refer to the G section in this text.

ESTEBAN, ANTONIO

Instruments currently produced in Spain.

Antonio Esteban classical guitars are currently available in the European market. **Models 10** and **30** are constructed with mahogany (bubinga on **Model 20**) bodies, Canadian cedar tops, and palisander fingerboards and bridges. The top-of-the-line **Model 40** has a palisander body, and ebony fingerboard. Antonio Esteban also offers a Flamenco model (**Model 40 F**) with tap plates and a palisander fingerboard.

ESTESO

Guitars previously built in Spain.

The Esteso label indicated instruments built by Domingo Esteso (1882-1937). Originally trained at the Madrid workshop of Manuel Ramirez, Esteso later set up shop in the same town, and his instruments were widely praised. Source: Tony Bacon, *The Ultimate Guitar Book*.

ESTEVE

Instruments currently built in Alboraya (Valencia), Spain. Distributed by Fernandez Music in Irvine, CA.

Esteve was established by Francisco Esteve, Manuel Adalid Sr., and Antonio Monfort in 1957. Esteve guitars are built in an artisan workshop in Spain, and have solid tops as well as traditional Spanish integrated neck/body construction. There is a wide range of classical and flamenco guitars available, as well as requintos and special models (bass, contrabass, and an octave guitar).

CONTACT INFORMATION
ESTEVE
Distributed by Fernandez Music
Box 5153
Irvine, CA 92616
Phone No.: 949-856-1537
Fax No.: 949-856-1529
www.fernandezmusic.com
ron@fernandezmusic.com

ACOUSTIC NYLON/CLASSICAL

There are several models currently offered by Esteve. The classic models start at $525 and go up from there. The different variations range from different sizes to the different types of woods that are used. There are also **Deluxe Classical** models that retail upwards towards $7,500.

Flamenco models (with a clear tap plate) feature sycamore back and sides and double rosewood purfling (retail list $895). The **Deluxe Artisan Flamenco models** range from $1,495 (solid Mukali with ebony fingerboard) up to $3,000 (Indian rosewood body). Wooden tuning pegs (instead of metal) are an additional $100.

Esteve also offers some acoustic electric models as well as a variety of different sized guitars. For more information and to find that perfect model for you, refer to their website.

EUPHONON

Instruments previously produced by the Larson Brothers between circa 1934 and 1944.

The Euphonon brand of guitars and mandolins was made by the Larson brothers of Maurer & Co. in Chicago from circa 1934 till the demise of the company in 1944. In 1934, there were a number of Euphonon guitars in different combinations of the old style twelve-fret to the body necks, slotted pegheads, with elevated pickguards, or without pickguards. This was a transition year which probably saw the beginning of the fourteen-fret to the body sizes also. They all had the new purfling consisting of a series of black and white stripes side-by-side around the body edges, and soundhole that was to remain the style for the Euphonon brand except when the abalone trim was used on the top-of-the-line guitars. By 1935, the larger bodies with narrower necks were the norm.

The Larsons made Euphonon guitars in two main types: the traditional round-hole and the dreadnought. The round-hole guitar sizes range from 15 in. student grade to 16 in., 17 in., 19 in., and a very rare 21 in. in the better and best grades. Many of the better and all of the best grades have laminated top braces and laminated necks. Euphonons have backs and sides made of oak, maple, mahogany, or rosewood.

Some of the fret markers used on the Euphonons and the larger Prairie State guitars are the same as the ones used on the earlier Maurers and Prairie States of the smaller body sizes. The fancier trimmed instruments often have engraved pearl fret markers along with a similar inlay on each end of the bridge. The Euphonon guitars are quite rare, of very high quality, and are sought by players and collectors.

For more information regarding other Larson-made brands, see Maurer, Prairie State, Wm. C. Stahl, W.J. Dyer, and The Larson Brothers. Source: Hartman, Robert Carl, *The Larsons' Creations: Guitars and Mandolins*.

ACOUSTIC

Just like any other instrument associated with the Larson Brothers, Euphonon guitars are very valuable and each instrument should be examined and appraised seperately. Euphonon instruments are typically viewed as the entry-level model because of their lack of a truss rod in most cases. Regardless, guitars start around $15,000 with very plain appointments and can climb above $30,000 for a fancy model. Original condition also plays a major role in the overall value.

EUPHONON COMPANY

See Walter Lipton.

EVERETT GUITARS

Instruments currently built in Decatur, GA.

Luthier Kent Everett has been crafting guitars since 1977. Everett had eighteen years experience in performing guitar repairs during his early days working and later owning Atlanta Guitar Works. In 1990, he closed Atlanta Guitar Works and started Everett Guitars. During the peak of the mid-1990s, Everett was producing fifty-four guitars a year. Now, he produces six to eight instruments a year. Current order time is around three years if the guitar is ordered today. Refer to Everett's website for more information.

CHRONOLOGY

The following information is a chronological order of events/instruments by Kent Everett.

1977-1990: All of these guitar were built as "one off" instruments, and you will find a variety of: archtop guitars, archtop electric guitars, mandolins, a dobro or two, electric guitars (with the patented Everett body shape), and of course acoustic instruments. There are not many of these guitars out there. I was only building six to ten instruments a year and unless someone dies and you can pry the guitar from their cold clammy hands, you probably will not find one.

1991-1996: 30 - 50 guitars annually, Serial Number = guitar number/year. These are the beginning years of my guitar production full time. It grew from four guitars a month to five instruments per month and all were acoustic steel-string guitars. There are 30 guitars out there with walnut or rosewood back and sides, satin finish, and cedar or spruce tops that are called the "Artist" series. I used these guitars to develop my production and they sold for less than $1,000 each including case. After that I started using the rosewood and spruce combination primarily. All solid wood instruments featured abalone rosettes, ivoroid or tortous plastic bindings. The early guitars with rosewood fingerboard and later ones with ebony boards. The earlier ones listed new for $1,650 and the later ones went for a $1,860 list price. They were all sold through stores and discounted a bit.

MSR/NOTES	100%	EXCELLENT	AVERAGE	LAST MSR

1997-1999: 50 guitars annually, Serial Number = guitar number / year. These guitars were called the Emerald Series guitars. Most of them had a little emerald somewhere on the fingerboard (usually the 12th fret) and were constructed with Rosewood, spruce, and wood bindings predominately. Again, these were primarily sold through stores with the list price going form $1,860 to $2,100. Upgraded instruments included the Silver Series ($3,200), the Sierra Series ($3,400) and the Elite Series ($3,600).

1999 - 2001: 50 guitars annually, Serial Number = guitar number / year. The Milano Series replaced the Emerald Series with a base price of $2,885 and rose to $3,200. Instruments featured all wood bindings, exotic wood veneers, wood-bound sound hole, wood-bound headstock, use of color veneers, and Schaller tuners with ebony buttons. Upgraded guitars include the Sierra Series ($3,600) and the Elite Series ($3,900).

2001: 20 guitars, Serial Number = guitar number / year. This was a transitional year for Everett guitars. During 2001, the Everett Laurel Series started to grow to the point where the Everett Milano production backed down to two guitars per month, and the list price rose to $4,200. These were primarily custom orders.

The Laurel Series - 1st edition, (Numbers 1 - 29). The Laurel Series included 128 guitars that Everett built in conjunction with a high quality factory called Terada in Nagoya Japan. The Laurel First Edition featured a solid Sitka top with laminated rosewood back and sides, and all had highly flame maple bindings, maple rosette, and rosewood fingerboard and bridge. List price $1,375, (cutaway add $175)

2002: The Laurel Standard (Numbers 30 - 78). All instruments feature solid wood, rosewood fingerboards and bridges, and a maple line rosette. List price $1,875 (cutaway add $175).

Beginning in 2002, the Elan Everett was only available as a custom order. These guitars were built and sold only directly from the workshop of Everett guitars, only the finest materials are used, and they are built one at a time by Kent Everett. Prices ranged between $5,600 and $6,400. These instruments are signed and dated individual works of art.

2003: The Laurel Select (Numbers 79 - 128) is introduced upgrading the Laurel Series with ebony fingerboards, abalone rosettes, and custom tuners with ebony buttons. List prices started at $2,100 (cutaway add $175). Due to the problems associated with international business, 2003 was the last year of the Everett Laurel Series guitars.

2003-2004: The Everett Elan is offered at $6,200 and the Everett Concert Classical at $6,200. The Elan and Concert Classical are built entirely by Kent Everett in his shop in Atlanta and are only available by custom order. Orders at this point grew to a three-year back log.

2004-2005: The Everett Celona and Azalea are added. No more than three Celonas or three Azaleas are scheduled to be built each year. The Celona is not built to custom order, but is used to try new ideas, woods, etc, They are built in between the Elan orders and pricing starts at $5,200. The Azalea is built entirely by Everett and is used as the example guitar for the "Art of the Guitar" construction class held at the Everett workshop. 2004 Azalea prices start at $2,300. 2005 Azalea prices (material upgrade) started at $3,800.

2005-2008: The Everett Elan became the custom order Everett model. Prices ranged between $8,900 and $12,500. Series is scheduled to end in 2008. In 2006 Everett stopped taking Elan orders in order to get caught up.

2008: The Alienzo replaces the Elan as the custom order Everett (prices range between $10,400 and $14,000. The Metrocaster is introduced as a thin body handmade acoustic electric (prices start at $8,400). The Valentino is a new concept in building a guitar that combines fine art work and fine instrument craftsmanship (prices start at $23,000).

ACOUSTIC

Current models include the **Metrocaster** (prices start at $9,750) thin body acoustic instrument, the **Alienzo** (prices start at $10,500) replaces the Elan as the custom order Everett guitar, and the **Valentino** (prices start at $23,000) a mixture of high end acoustic guitar building and fine art. In 2009, the Catalina (prices start at $5,800) was introduced. The "average" Everett Guitar sells for $14,500. 2011 pricing ranges from $9,600 for a beautifully appointed custom guitar to $18,000 for a museum level guitar with exposition appointments. The Laurel guitar was built by the Terada factory in Japan. Each guitar was inspected in Atlanta before it was sold. There were 125 instruments produced over a three-year period.

LAUREL – Indian rosewood back and sides, solid Sitka top, ebony fingerboard, bridge, tuner buttons, and bridgepins, flamed maple binding, heart abalone inlays, three-per-side tuners, available as the O Model (Orchestra), A Model (Auditorium), or D Model (Dreadnought), mfg. 2000-03.

	N/A	$1,350 - 1,750	$950 - 1,100	$2,100

- **Add $50 for single cutaway.**
- **Add $100 for 12-string configuration.**

EVERGREEN MOUNTAIN INSTRUMENTS

Instruments currently built in Cove, OR.

Jerry Nolte has been producing handcrafted instruments since 1971. Nolte's guitars are available in six-string, twelve-string, tenor, and bass configurations. His acoustics feature cedar or spruce tops; three-piece mahogany necks; rosewood fingerboard and bridge; back and sides of American black walnut, maple, koa, and cherry; and hand-rubbed violin varnish. The order process includes a $350 down payment, which is non-refundable. Base prices vary from model to model, but are generally in the $2,000 range plus options. Nolte also produces a line of mandolins. For more information visit Evergreen Mountain Instruments' website or contact them directly.

CONTACT INFORMATION
EVERGREEN MOUNTAIN INSTRUMENTS
1608 Jasper
Cove, OR 97824
Phone No.: 541-568-4687
www.eoni.com/~emi/
emi@eoni.com

EVERLY GUITARS

Guitars previously produced in Portland, OR between 1982 and 2001. See Steinegger Guitars.

Luthier Robert Steinegger (Steinegger Guitars) built the Ike Everly Model under the company name Everly Guitars. For more information, refer to Steinegger Guitars.

NOTES

F SECTION

FAIR LADY

Instruments previously produced in China during the late 1990s and early 2000s. Distributed by Kwo Hsiao Company, Ltd., of Taipei, Taiwan.

The Kwo Hsiao Company, Ltd. offered a wide range of student level to intermediate grade acoustic guitar models. Models ranged from classical-style nylon strings to dreadnought and jumbo style models (some with single rounded cutaways), and include models with built-in piezo bridge pickups and preamp systems. Models featured a spruce top, nato wood back and sides, rosewood fingerboard and bridge, and a solid headstock with three-per-side chrome tuners. It is unknown if they were ever distributed into the U.S.

FASCINATOR

Guitars previously produced in Kalamazoo, MI during the 1930s and 1940s. See chapter on House Brands.

This Gibson-built budget line of guitars has been identified as a House Brand of the Tonk Bros. company of Chicago, IL. While built to the same standards as other Gibson guitars, these guitars lack the one true Gibson touch: an adjustable truss rod. House Brand Gibsons were available to musical instrument distributors in the late 1930s and early 1940s. Source: Walter Carter, *Gibson Guitars: 100 Years of an American Icon*.

FAUSTO CARRERA GUITARS

Instruments currently produced in Quito, Ecuador.

Luthier Fausto Moya Carrera builds hand-crafted guitars in his Ecuador workshop. After going to work with Senor Nunoz while in high school, he eventually purchased the shop along with his father and has been building guitars ever since. Carrera uses high-quality tonewoods and builds all guitars strictly by hand.

FAVILLA

Instruments previously built in New York City, NY between 1890 and 1973.

In 1888, brothers John and Joseph Favilla left their home country of Italy and moved to Manhattan in New York City. Two years later, they founded Favilla Brothers, which later became Favilla Guitars, Inc. The workshop moved to Brooklyn in 1929, and later back to Manhattan.

Frank Favilla (John's elder son) began running the facility in the late 1940s. The company moved to larger facilities in Brooklyn in 1959, and in 1965 moved to a 20,000-square-foot plant out in Long Island. The larger facilities employed between fifteen and twenty workers, and the staff produced about three thousand acoustic guitars a year. Higher production costs were one of the factors that led to the plant closing in 1973.

In 1970, Tom Favilla (third generation) began importing guitars from Japan. Japanese Favillas had the company name in script; American-built Favillas will have the family crest on the headstock. Source: Tom Wheeler, *American Guitars*.

Early models produced before WWII will command the most money in the vintage marketplace, but they are rarely encountered. Most models that show up in the used marketplace are from the 1960s and early 1970s when Favilla was at its height of production. Most American-made acoustics from this era are valued between $300 and $700 depending on condition and configuration. Imported Japanese models will command much less between $100 and $300.

FENDER

Instruments currently produced in Corona, CA (U.S.), Mexico, Japan, Tianjin (China), and Korea. Distributed by the Fender Musical Instruments Corporation of Scottsdale, AZ. The Fender trademark was established circa 1948 in Fullerton, CA.

CONTACT INFORMATION
FENDER
17600 North Perimeter Drive
Scottsdale, AZ 85255
Phone No.: 480-596-9690
Fax No.: 480-367-5262
www.fender.com
custserv@fenderusa.com

Clarence Leonidas Fender was born in 1909, and raised in Fullerton, California. As a teenager, he developed an interest in electronics, and soon was building and repairing radios for fellow classmates. After high school, Leo Fender held a bookkeeping position while he did radio repair at home. After holding a series of jobs, Fender opened up a full-scale radio repair shop in 1939. In addition to service work, the Fender Radio Service store soon became a general electronics retail outlet. However, the forerunner to the Fender Electric Instruments company was a smaller, two-man operation that was originally started as the K & F company in 1945. Leo Fender began modestly building small amplifiers and electric lap steels with his partner, Clayton Orr Doc Kaufman. After K & F dissolved, Fender then formed the Fender Electric Instrument company in 1946, located on South Pomona Avenue in Fullerton, California. The company sales, though slow at first, began to expand as his amplifiers and lap steels began meeting acceptance with West Coast musicians. In 1950, Fender successfully developed the first production solid body electric guitar. Originally the Broadcaster, the name was quickly changed to the Telecaster after the Gretsch company objected to the infringement of their Broadkaster drum sets.

Soon Fender's inventive genius began designing new models through the early 1950s and early 1960s. The Fender Precision Bass guitar was unveiled in 1951. While there is some kind of an existing background for the development of an electric solid body guitar, the notion of a 34 in. scale instrument with a fretted neck that could replace an upright acoustic doublebass was completely new to the music industry. The Precision bass (so named because players could fret the note precisely), coupled with a Fender Bassman amplifier, gave the bass player more sonic projection. Fender then followed with another design in 1954, named the Stratocaster. The simplicity in design, added to the popular sounds and playability, makes this design the most copied worldwide. Other popular models of guitars, basses, and amplifiers soon followed.

By 1964, Fender's line of products included electric guitars, basses, steel guitars, effects units, acoustic guitars, electric pianos, and a variety of accessories. Leo's faltering health was a factor in putting the company up for sale, and he first offered it to Don Randall (the head of Fender Sales) for a million and a half dollars. Randall opened negotiations with the Baldwin Piano & Organ company, but when those negotiations fell through, he offered it to the conglomerate CBS (who was looking to diversify the company holdings). Fender (FEIC) was purchased by CBS on January 5, 1965 (actually in December of 1964) for thirteen million dollars. Leo Fender was kept on as a special consultant for five years, and then left when then contract was up in 1970. Due to a ten-year no compete clause, the next Leo Fender-designed guitars did not show up in the music industry until 1976 (Music Man).

While Fender was just another division of CBS, a number of key figures left the company. Forrest White, the production manager, left in 1967 after a dispute in producing solid state amplifiers. Don Randall left in 1969, disenchanted with corporate life. George Fullerton, one of the people involved with the Stratocaster design, left in 1970. Obviously, the quality in Fender products did not drop the day Leo Fender sold the company. Dale Hyatt, another veteran of the early Fender days, figured that the quality on the products stayed relatively stable until around 1968 (Hyatt left in 1972). But a number of cost-cutting strategies, and attempts to produce more products had a deteriorating effect. This reputation leads right to the classic phrase heard at vintage guitar shows, "Pre-CBS?"

In the early 1980s, the Fender guitar empire began to crumble. Many cost-cutting factors and management problems forced CBS to try various last ditch efforts to salvage the instrument line. In March of 1982, Fender (with CBS' blessing) negotiated with Kanda Shokai and Yamano Music to establish Fender Japan. After discussions with Tokai (who built a great Fender Strat replica, among other nice guitars), Kawai, and others, Fender finally chose Fuji Gen Gakki (based in Matsumoto, about 130 miles northwest of Tokyo). In 1983, the Squier series was built in Japan, earmarked for European distribution. The Squier trademark came from a string-making company in Michigan (V.C. Squier) that CBS had acquired in 1965.

In 1984, CBS decided to sell Fender. Offers came in from IMC (Hondo, Charvel/Jackson), and the Kaman Music Corporation (Ovation). Finally, CBS sold Fender to an investment group led by William Schultz in March for twelve and a half million dollars. This investment group formally became the Fender Musical Instruments Corporation (FMIC). As the sale did not include production facilities, USA guitar production ceased for most of 1985. It has been estimated that 80% of the guitars sold between late 1984 and mid-1986 were made in Japan. Soon after, a new factory was built in Corona, California, and USA production was restored in 1986 and continues to this day. FMIC expanded their company by purchasing Sunn amplifiers in 1987.

In 1990, the Fender (FMIC) company built an assembly facility in Mexico to offset rising costs of Asian production due to the weakening of the American dollar in the international market. Fender also experimented with production based in India from 1989 to 1990. The Fender (FMIC) company currently manufactures instruments in China, Japan, Korea, Mexico, and the U.S. In 1991, Fender relocated its headquarters from Corona, California to Scottsdale, Arizona. This is where they are today. In 1992, the amplifier custom shop was opened.

As FMIC began to expand in the 1990s, they also started to buy into other interests. The Guild guitar company has been making high-quality instruments since 1952, but the company went up for the sale in the early '90s. Fender completed the sale in 1995 and began building instruments in the Custom Shop in Nashville, Tennessee in 1996. Fender also picked up Manuel Rodriguez guitars for classical guitars handcrafted in Spain.

As reported in the March 1998 edition of MMR, Fender CEO Schultz sent out a letter to Fender dealers (dated January 9, 1998) which discussed the company establishing a limited number of Fender mail-order catalog dealers. Fender has announced specific guidelines as to what is allowed in mail-order catalog sales. Most importantly, Fender "announced a minimum advertised price (MAP) policy applicable to mail-order catalogs only," stated Schultz, "The MAP for mail-order catalogs is set at a maximum 30 percent off the Fender suggested retail price, and will be enforced unilaterally by Fender." What this does to the Fender retail price overall is basically lower the bar - but the impact on regular guitar stores has not been fully realized. While it's one thing to buy because of a discounted price through a catalog, it's a different situation to walk into a dealer's shop and be able to "test drive" a guitar before it is purchased. Retail music stores have to be aware that there is now an outside source (not under their control) that dictates minimum sales prices -- the national catalogs. Of course, retail shops still control the maximum sale price applied to an instrument. Readers familiar with the *Blue Book of Electric Guitars* will note both the manufacturer's suggested retail price and the appropriate discounted price (100% listing) under currently produced models.

In 1998, Fender opened up a new 177,000-square-foot manufacturing facility in Corona, California. This is a state-of-the-art facility that can pump out 350 guitars a day and the factory discharges 95% clean air. In Summer 2002, Fender announced the purchase of the Gretsch guitar line. This buy-out went into effect January 1, 2003. In 2003, Fender also aquired the rights to SWR Amplifiers. In 2005, Fender expaned their vast line once again by aquiring Tacoma/Olympia/Orpheum. Fender's line now includes Fender, Squier, Gretsch, Guild, Benedetto, Jackson, Charvel, Tacoma, Olympia, Orpheum, Sunn, and SWR. In 2012, Fender moved its headquarters from Scottsdale to a larger space in North Scottsdale.

(Source for earlier Fender history: Richard R. Smith, *Fender: The Sound Heard 'Round the World*.)

PRODUCTION MODEL CODES

Current Fender instruments are identified by a part number that consists of a three-digit location/facility code and a four-digit model code (the two codes are separated by a hyphen). An example of this would be:

MSR/NOTES	100%	EXCELLENT	AVERAGE	LAST MSR

(The 096-9900 part number is the Chinese-built Tiki-Coustic Femme Fatale Limited Edition.)

As Fender guitars are built in a number of locations worldwide, the three-digit code will indicate where production took place (this does not indicate where the parts originated, however; just assembly of components). The first digit differentiates between Fender bridges and Floyd Rose tremolos, but since all Fender acoustics do not have Floyd Rose tremolos this number will always be 0.

The second/third digit combination designates the production location:

10 U.S. MFG. (Corona, CA)	19 U.S. MFG. (Corona, CA)	33 Korea MFG.
11 U.S. MFG. (Corona, CA)	25 Japan MFG.	96 China MFG.
13 Mexico	26 Korea MFG.	The four digits on the other side
15 U.S. MFG. Custom Shop	27 Japan MFG.	of the hyphen continue defining the

model. The fourth/fifth digit combination is the product designation. The sixth digit defines left-handedness, or key parts inherent to that product. The final seventh digit indicates which type of wood fingerboard. The eighth digit indicates what type of case the guitar comes with. An eighth digit of "3" indicates a gig-bag, a "5" means the guitar comes with no case, a "7" indicates that the guitar comes with a standard case, and an "8" means it comes with a deluxe case. The last numbers (ninth and tenth) indicate the finish/color.

06 Black	21 Natural	39 Trans. Grey
09 Candy Apple Red	27 Trans. Blue	48 Trans. Green
20 Trans. Amber	32 Sunburst	94 Trans. Violet

ACOUSTIC: 1963-1970 PRODUCTION MODELS

Before Fender introduced their full line of acoustic guitars designed by Roger Rossmeisl in 1963, they also sold a few Fender-branded guitars that were built by Harmony.

CONCERT – dreadnought style, spruce top, round soundhole, maple back/sides, bound top/back, bolt-on maple neck with neckplate, 20-fret rosewood fingerboard with pearl dot inlays, six-per-side chrome tuners, rosewood bridge with white bridgepins, single-ply pickguard, aluminum support rod (through body), available in Natural finish, 15.375 in. body width, 25.5 in. scale, mfg. 1963-1970.

1963-1965	N/A	$725 - 900	$425 - 550
1966-1970	N/A	$650 - 800	$375 - 475

In 1966, mahogany, rosewood, vermillion, or zebrawood back and sides were an option. In 1968, Sunburst finish was an option.

KING – dreadnought style, spruce top, round soundhole, mahogany back/sides, multiple bound top/back, bolt-on maple neck with neckplate, 21-fret bound rosewood fingerboard with pearl dot inlays, six-per-side chrome tuners, aluminum support rod (through body), available in Natural finish, 25.5 in. scale, 15.625 in. body width, mfg. 1963-66.

N/A	$875 - 1,100	$525 - 650

This model was optional with back and sides of Brazilian rosewood, Indian rosewood, vermillion, or zebrawood.

KINGMAN (FIRST VERSION) – similar to the King model, available in Natural or Sunburst finish, mfg. 1966-1971.

N/A	$800 - 1,000	$475 - 600

In 1968, maple, rosewood, or vermillion back and sides were optional in addition to Black, Custom Colors, and Antigua finishes.

MALIBU (FIRST VERSION) – dreadnought style, spruce top, round soundhole, mahogany back/sides, mahogany neck, one-ply bound top, 14/20-fret rosewood fingerboard with dot inlay, rosewood bridge, available in Black, Mahogany, or Sunburst finish, 25.5 in. scale, 14.875 in. body width, mfg. 1965-1971.

N/A	$525 - 650	$325 - 400

NEWPORTER – dreadnought style, spruce top, round soundhole, mahogany back/sides, mahogany neck, one-ply bound top, 14/20-fret rosewood fingerboard with dot inlay, rosewood bridge, available in Mahogany finish, 25.5 in. scale, 14.375 in. body width, mfg. 1965-1971.

1965-1968 Spruce Top	N/A	$375 - 450	$250 - 300
1968-1971 Mahogany Top	N/A	$325 - 400	$200 - 250

In 1968, a Mahogany top, three-ply pickguard, and Black finish were introduced.

PALOMINO – dreadnought style, spruce top, mahogany back and sides, round soundhole with two rope pattern and two black rings, top and back binding, maple neck, 14/20-fret rosewood fingerboard with dot inlays, Strat-style headstock with maple overlay, six-on-one-side tuners with plastic buttons, rosewood bridge, 15.375 in. body width, 25.5 in. scale, available in Black Vermillion, Natural, or Sunburst finish, mfg. 1968-1971.

N/A	$525 - 600	$325 - 400

REDONDO – similar to the Newporter, except features a spruce top, mfg. 1969-1971.

N/A	$400 - 500	$250 - 300

SHENANDOAH – similar to the Kingman, except features 12-string configuration, six-per-side tuners, available in Natural, Black, Sunburst, or Antigua finishes, mfg. 1965-1971.

Natural, Black, or Sunburst finishes	N/A	$625 - 750	$425 - 500
Antigua Finish	N/A	$850 - 1,000	$500 - 600

In 1967 Antiqua finish was introduced. In 1968, Black and Sunburst finishes were introduced.

MSR/NOTES	100%	EXCELLENT	AVERAGE	LAST MSR

VILLAGER – similar to the Malibu, except in 12-string configuration and six-per-side tuners, mfg. 1965-69.

	N/A	$525 - 650	$325 - 400	

In 1969, Sunburst finish was optional.

WILDWOOD ACOUSTIC – similar to the Kingman, except features beechwood back/sides, three-ply pickguard, block fingerboard inlay, available in injected-dye colors (primary colors of green, blue, and gold), mfg. 1966-1971.

	N/A	$1,200 - 1,500	$725 - 900	

The Wildwood finish was the result of a seven-year process in Germany where dye was injected into growing beech trees. Veneers for laminating were available after the beech trees were harvested. The value depends upon how much the guitar has faded. It will command a premium if it has little fading.

ACOUSTIC: CALIFORNIA SERIES

The California series was introduced circa 1982. Models were produced in Japan from 1982 to 1985 and then Korea from 1985 until 1994. The California Series was reintroduced in 2005, and instruments are produced in China. The first three models are the Kingman, Malibu, and Sonoran. For the first versions of the Kingman and Malibu models, refer to Acoustic: Dreadnought 1963-1970 Mfg. Many California Series models were updated in 2012 with three-ply pickguards, a bone nut and saddle, and a vintage-style Fender "Viking" bridge along with new production model codes.

AVALON (NO. 094-5801) – folk style, spruce top, round soundhole, black pickguard, three-stripe bound body/rosette, mahogany back/sides/neck, 14/20-fret bubinga fingerboard with pearl dot inlay, bubinga strings through bridge, six-per-side die-cast tuners, available in Natural or Wine Red finish, mfg. 1985-1994.

	N/A	$200 - 250	$120 - 150	$301

Later models have Nato back and sides.

BALBOA – single cutaway style, solid spruce top, mahogany back and sides, original Fender electronics, Natural finish, mfg. 1983-87.

	N/A	$300 - 375	$175 - 225	$650

CAPISTRANO – single cutaway style, solid spruce top, rosewood back and sides, original Fender electronics, Natural finish, mfg. 1983-87.

	N/A	$250 - 300	$150 - 200	$525

CATALINA (NO. 094-5201) – dreadnought style, spruce top, round soundhole, black pickguard, three-stripe bound body/rosette, mahogany back/sides/neck, 14/20-fret rosewood fingerboard with pearl dot inlay, rosewood bridge with white black dot pins, six-per-side die-cast tuners, available in Black finish, mfg. 1983-1994.

	N/A	$250 - 300	$140 - 175	$372

CONCORD (NO. 094-4600) – similar to Catalina, except has bubinga fingerboard/bridge, available in Natural finish, mfg. 1987-1994.

	N/A	$200 - 250	$120 - 150	$301

DEL MAR – dreadnought style, spruce top, rosewood back and sides, 14/20-fret rosewood fingerboard with dot inlay, Strat-style headstock with six-per-side tuners, rosewood bridge, tortoiseshell pickguard, Natural finish, mfg. 1983-89.

	N/A	$250 - 300	$140 - 175	$340

EL RIO – dreadnought style, spruce top, sycamore back and sides, 14/20-fret rosewood fingerboard with dot inlay, Strat-style headstock with six-on-one-side tuners, rosewood bridge, tortoiseshell pickguard, Natural finish, mfg. 1983-87.

	N/A	$250 - 300	$140 - 175	$520

KINGMAN "10" (NO. 096-8100) – single cutaway dreadnought style body, solid cedar top, laminated rosewood back and sides, scalloped bracing, round soundhole with Polynesian Surf Glyph rosette, multiple body binding, abalone purfling, maple soft C-shaped neck, 14/20-fret bound rosewood fingerboard with white Tropical Sunset inlays, Stratocaster-style headstock, six-on-one-side vintage Fender-style chrome tuners with white buttons, rosewood bridge with compensated saddle, Fishman Aero pickup and electronics with three-band EQ and electronic tuner, available in Natural finish, 25.3 in. scale, mfg. spring-winter 2009.

	N/A	$325 - 400	$175 - 225	$800

KINGMAN S SECOND VERSION (NO. 096-8010) – dreadnought style body, solid spruce top, solid mahogany back, laminated mahogany sides, top and back binding, round soundhole with checkered rosette, mahogany neck, 14/20-fret rosewood fingerboard with dot inlay, Stratocaster-style headstock with six-on-one-side chrome tuners, rosewood bridge, black pickguard, Natural finish, 25.3 in. scale, mfg. 2006-07.

	N/A	$300 - 375	$175 - 225	$714

* *Kingman SCE Cutaway Electric (No. 096-8015)* – similar to the Kingman, except has a single smooth cutaway and Fishman Classic IV pickups, electronics, and tuner, mfg. 2006-07.

	N/A	$325 - 400	$200 - 250	$786

KINGMAN SCE THIRD VERSION (NO. 096-8014/8601) – single cutaway dreadnought style body, solid spruce top, laminated mahogany back and sides, top and back binding, round soundhole with checkered rosette, maple vintage C-shaped neck, 14/20-fret bound rosewood fingerboard with white pearloid block inlays, Stratocaster-style headstock with six-on-one-side chrome tuners, rosewood bridge, available in 3-Color Sunburst with a black pickguard or Natural finish with a gold pickguard, 25.3 in. scale, mfg. 2008-present.

MSR $680	$480	$275 - 325	$160 - 200	

MSR/NOTES	100%	EXCELLENT	AVERAGE	LAST MSR

* *Kingman SCE Left-Handed (No. 096-8018)* – similar to the Kingman SCE Third Version, except in left-handed configuration, available in Natural finish with a gold pickguard, mfg. 2008-09.

	N/A	$300 - 350	$175 - 225	$700

LA BREA (NO. 094-4706/4721/4732/4742) – single round cutaway dreadnought style, spruce top, round soundhole, black pickguard, three-stripe bound body/rosette, mahogany back/sides/neck, 21-fret rosewood fingerboard with pearl dot inlay, rosewood bridge with white black dot pins, six-per-side chrome tuners, acoustic pickup, volume/tone control, available in Black, Maple, Natural, or Sunburst finish, mfg. 1987-1994.

	N/A	$250 - 300	$140 - 175	$480

* **Add 15% for figured maple top/back/sides.**

LAGUNA – spruce top, redwood back and sides, mfg. 1986-88.

	N/A	$250 - 300	$140 - 175	$475

MALIBU SECOND VERSION (NO. 094-5301) – dreadnought style, sycamore top, round soundhole, black pickguard, sycamore back/sides, mahogany neck, 14/20-fret rosewood fingerboard with pearl dot inlay, rosewood bridge with white black dot inlay, six-per-side die-cast tuners, available in Dark Violin Sunburst finish, mfg. 1983-1994.

	N/A	$225 - 275	$120 - 150	$385

MALIBU THIRD VERSION (NO. 096-8000) – folk-style body, solid spruce top, solid mahogany back, laminated mahogany sides, top and back binding, round soundhole with checkered rosette, mahogany neck, 14/20-fret rosewood fingerboard with dot inlay, Stratocaster-style headstock with six-on-one-side chrome tuners, rosewood bridge, Natural finish, 24.75 in. scale, mfg. 2006-07.

	N/A	$300 - 375	$175 - 225	$714

* *Malibu SCE Cutaway Electric (No. 096-8005)* – similar to the Malibu Second Version, except has a single smooth cutaway and Fishman Classic IV pickups, electronics, and tuner, mfg. 2006-07.

	N/A	$325 - 400	$200 - 250	$786

MAILBU CE FOURTH VERSION (NO. 096-8008/8608) – single cutaway folk-style body, spruce top, laminated mahogany back and sides, top and back binding, round soundhole with checkered rosette, maple vintage C-shaped neck, 14/20-fret bound rosewood fingerboard with pearl dot inlays, Stratocaster-style headstock with six-on-one-side chrome tuners with aged white plastic buttons, rosewood bridge, gold pickguard, Fender FTE3-TN electronics, available in Natural finish, 24.75 in. scale, mfg. 2009-present.

MSR $400	$280	$160 - 200	$95 - 120	

MALIBU SCE FOURTH VERSION (NO. 096-8004/8602) – single cutaway folk-style body, solid spruce top, laminated mahogany back and sides, top and back binding, round soundhole with checkered rosette, maple vintage C-shaped neck, 14/20-fret bound rosewood fingerboard with white pearloid block inlays, Stratocaster-style headstock, six-on-one-side chrome tuners with aged white plastic buttons, rosewood bridge, Fishman Aero electronics, available in 3-Color Sunburst with a black pickguard or Natural finish with a gold pickguard, 24.75 in. scale, mfg. 2008-2013.

	$480	$275 - 325	$140 - 175	$680

* *Malibu SCE Left-Handed (No. 096-8007)* – similar to the Malibu SCE Fourth Version, except in left-handed configuration, available in Natural finish with a gold pickguard, mfg. 2008 only.

	N/A	$275 - 325	$140 - 175	$650

MONTARA (NO. 094-5706/5721/5732/5742) – single round cutaway dreadnought style, spruce top, oval soundhole, bound body, multi-ring rosette, mahogany back/sides/neck, convex back, 21-fret rosewood fingerboard with pearl dot inlay, rosewood bridge with white pins, six-per-side die-cast tuners with pearl buttons, acoustic pickup, volume/treble/mid/bass controls, available in Black, Maple, Natural, or Sunburst finish, mfg. 1990-94.

	N/A	$325 - 400	$175 - 225	$650

* **Add 10% for flame maple top/back/sides/neck.**

MONTCLAIR – dreadnought style, solid spruce top, mahogany back and sides, 22-fret rosewood fingerboard with snowflake inlay, Strat-style headstock with six-per-side tuners, rosewood bridge, tortoiseshell pickguard, mfg. 1987-88.

	N/A	$275 - 325	$150 - 200	$435

NEWPORTER (NO. 094-5001) – dreadnought style, mahogany top, round soundhole, black pickguard, three-stripe bound body/rosette, mahogany back/sides/neck, 14/20-fret rosewood fingerboard with pearl dot inlay, rosewood bridge with white black dot pins, six-per-side die-cast tuners, Natural finish, mfg. 1983-1994.

	N/A	$175 - 225	$110 - 140	$326

NEWPORTER TRAVELER (NO. 096-8029) – mini-dreadnought style body, laminated spruce top, laminated mahogany back and sides, round soundhole with checkered rosette, mahogany neck, 14/20-fret rosewood fingerboard with white dot inlays, Stratocaster-style headstock with mahogany overlay, six-per-side chrome tuners with white plastic buttons, rosewood bridge, Natural finish, 22.6 in. scale, mfg. 2012-13.

	$280	$160 - 200	$95 - 120	$400

REDONDO (NO. 094-5101) – similar to the Newporter, except has spruce top, available in Natural finish, mfg. 1983-1994.

	N/A	$200 - 250	$120 - 150	$337

MSR/NOTES	100%	EXCELLENT	AVERAGE	LAST MSR

REDONDO CE (NO. 096-8610) – single cutaway dreadnought-style body, laminated spruce top, laminated mahogany back and sides, multiple body binding, round soundhole with checkered rosette, maple vintage C-shaped neck, 14/20-fret rosewood fingerboard with pearl dot inlays, Stratocaster-style headstock, six-on-one-side chrome tuners with aged white plastic buttons, rosewood bridge, three-ply gold pickguard, Fender Isys III electronics with tuner, available in Natural finish, 25.3 in. scale, mfg. 2012-present.

MSR $400	$280	$160 - 200	$95 - 120	

SAN LUIS REY (NO. 094-5410) – dreadnought style, solid spruce top, round soundhole, black pickguard, rosewood back/sides, mahogany neck, 14/20-fret rosewood fingerboard with pearl snowflake inlay, six-per-side chrome tuners, available in Natural finish, mfg. 1990-94.

	N/A	$250 - 300	$140 - 175	$444

SAN MARINO (NO. 094-5110) – similar to the San Luis Rey, except has three-stripe bound body/rosette, mahogany back/sides/neck, 14/20-fret rosewood fingerboard with pearl dot inlay, available in Natural finish, mfg. 1990-1994.

	N/A	$225 - 275	$120 - 150	$372

SAN MIGUEL (NO. 094-5105) – single round cutaway dreadnought style, spruce top, round soundhole, black pickguard, three-stripe bound body/rosette, mahogany back/sides/neck, 14/20-fret rosewood fingerboard with pearl dot inlay, rosewood bridge with white black dot pins, six-per-side tuners, Natural finish, mfg. 1990-94.

	N/A	$200 - 250	$120 - 150	$362

This model was also available in left-handed configuration (Model 094-5106).

SANTA MARIA (NO. 094-4400) – similar to the Newporter, except in 12-string configuration, has spruce top, tortoise pickguard, available in Natural finish, mfg. 1988-1994.

	N/A	$200 - 250	$120 - 150	$362

SANTA ROSA – double cutaway semi-acoustic body, similar to the Stratacoustic, unknown body wood, possibly basswood, matching Strat-style headstock with six-per-side tuners, 22-fret rosewood fingerboard, simple electronics, available in various finishes, mfg. 1989-90.

	N/A	$200 - 250	$110 - 140	$739

SONORAN (NO. 096-8020) – dreadnought style body, spruce top, mahogany back and sides, top and back binding, round soundhole with checkered rosette, mahogany neck, 14/20-fret rosewood fingerboard with dot inlay, Stratocaster-style headstock with six-per-side chrome tuners, rosewood bridge, black pickguard, Natural finish, 25.3 in. scale, mfg. 2006-07.

	N/A	$140 - 180	$85 - 105	$357

* *Sonoran CE Cutaway Electric (No. 096-8025)* – similar to the Sonoran, except has a single smooth cutaway and Fishman Classic IV pickups, electronics, and tuner, available in Natural finish, mfg. 2006-07.

	N/A	$175 - 225	$100 - 135	$429

SONORAN S SECOND VERSION (NO. 096-8022/8606) – dreadnought style body, solid spruce top, laminated mahogany back and sides, top and back binding, round soundhole with checkered rosette, vintage C-shaped maple neck, 14/20-fret rosewood fingerboard with white dot inlays, Stratocaster-style headstock with six-per-side chrome tuners, rosewood bridge, gold pickguard, Natural finish, 25.3 in. scale, mfg. 2008-present.

MSR $430	$300	$160 - 200	$95 - 120	

* *Sonoran SCE Cutaway Electric Second Version (No. 096-8024/8604)* – similar to the Sonoran S Second Version, except has a single smooth cutaway and Fender FTE-3 electronics, available in Natural finish, mfg. 2008-present.

MSR $500	$350	$175 - 225	$110 - 140	

» *Sonoran SCE Custom Color Second Version (No. 096-8026/8604)* – similar to the Sonoran SCE Cutaway Electric Second Version, except available in various custom color finishes including Black (2009-present), Candy Apple Red, Firemist Silver (2009-10), Lake Placid Blue, Olympic White (2013 only), Shell Pink (new 2014), Shoreline Gold (2007-09), or Surf Green (2007-09, reintroduced 2014) finish, mfg. summer 2007-present.

MSR $500	$350	$175 - 225	$110 - 140	

Early models may have Fishman Classic IV electronics.

» *Sonoran SCE Cutaway Electric Left-Handed (No. 096-8027/8605)* – similar to the Sonoran SCE Second Version, except in left-handed configuration, available in Natural finish with a gold pickguard, mfg. 2008-present.

MSR $600	$430	$200 - 250	$120 - 150	

» *Sonoran SCE Cutaway Electric Thinline (No. 096-8609)* – similar to the Sonoran SCE Second Version, except has a thin 3 in. body, available in Natural finish, mfg. 2012-present.

MSR $500	$350	$175 - 225	$110 - 140	

SONORAN SCE '67 LIMITED (NO. 096-8028) – single cutaway dreadnought-style body, solid spruce top, laminated Milkwood back and sides, round soundhole with checkerboard rosette, scalloped X bracing, mulit-ply body binding, vintage C-shaped maple neck, 14/20-fret rosewood fingerboard with white dot inlays, Strat-style headstock with matching Milkwood overlay, six-on-one-side vintage-style chrome tuners with white buttons, rosewood bridge, gold pickguard, Fender FTE-3TN electronics with built-in tuner, available in Natural finish, 25.3 in. scale, mfg. 2010 only.

	$400	$275 - 325	$150 - 200	$650

Milkwood, as used on the Sonoran SCE '67, appears similar to Fender's Wildwood guitars in the late 1960s.

MSR/NOTES	100%	EXCELLENT	AVERAGE	LAST MSR

SONORAN BUCKET (NO. 096-8616) – single cutaway dreadnought style body, flame maple top, laminated mahogany back and sides, round soundhole with T-Bucker pinstriped rosette, multi-ply body binding, maple neck, 14/20-fret rosewood fingerboard with white dot inlays and 12th fret "F" logo inlay, Stratocaster-style headstock, six-per-side chrome tuners, rosewood bridge, Fishman Isys III pickup/electronics, available in Flame Burst finish, 25.3 in. scale, mfg. 2013 only.

	$350	$175 - 225	$110 - 140	$500

VILLAGER 12-STRING (NO. 096-8060/8607) – 12-string configuration, dreadnought style body, solid spruce top, laminated mahogany back and sides, top and back binding, round soundhole with checkered rosette, soft C-shaped maple neck, 14/20-fret rosewood fingerboard with white dot inlays, Fender electric 12-string-style headstock with six-per-side chrome tuners, rosewood bridge, gold pickguard, Fishman Isys III electronics, Natural finish, 25.3 in. scale, mfg. 2011-present.

MSR $630	$430	$225 - 275	$135 - 170	

ACOUSTIC: CLASSICAL CG SERIES

CG stands for classical guitars (with nylon strings), and they are built in Asia.

CG-5 (NO. 094-0500) – classical style, nato top/back/sides, round soundhole, nato neck, 12/18-fret rosewood fingerboard, slotted headstock, three-per-side chrome tuners, available in Satin finish, mfg. 1995-98.

	N/A	$60 - 75	$35 - 45	$155

CG-7 (NO. 094-0700) – similar to the CG-5, except features spruce top, meranti back/sides, 12/19-fret fingerboard, available in Gloss finish, mfg. 1995-2005.

	N/A	$70 - 90	$40 - 55	$186

CG-11 (NO. 094-1100) – similar to CG-7, except has Nato back, sides, and neck, 20 frets, 25.3 in. scale, available in Natural finish, disc. 2001.

	N/A	$120 - 150	$70 - 95	$320

* CG-11 E Electric (No. 094-1101) – similar to the CG-11, except has Fender Passive Piezo electronics, mfg. summer 1998-2005.

	N/A	$135 - 175	$80 - 100	$343

CG-21 S (NO. 094-2100) – similar to CG-11, except has solid spruce top, rosewood back and sides, rosewood fingerboard, gold tuners, available in Natural finish, mfg. 1999-2005.

	N/A	$175 - 225	$95 - 120	$500

CG-24 SCE (NO. 094-2405) – classical body with cutaway, solid cedar top, ovangkol back and sides, Nato neck, rosewood fingerboard, wood mosaic rosette, multi-ABS body binding, brown neck binding, 18 frets, gold tuners, Fender Piezo Transducer pickup with Onboard Active Preamp, three-band EQ plus Mid Sweep, available in Natural finish, 25.3 in. scale, mfg. summer 1999-2005.

	N/A	$225 - 275	$120 - 150	$571

CG-25 SCE (NO. 094-2505) – classical style with cutaway design, solid cedar top, round soundhole, ovangkol back/sides, nato neck, 12/19-fret rosewood fingerboard, slotted headstock, three-per-side gold tuners, piezo transducer, active EQ, available in Gloss finish, mfg. 1995-99.

	N/A	$275 - 325	$150 - 200	$699

CG-35SCE (NO. 094-3505) – single cutaway design, solid cedar top, rosewood back and sides, mahogany neck, rosewood fingerboard with dot position markers, 25.6 in. scale, Piezo pickup with Fishman Classic 4 Preamp, available in Natural Gloss finish, mfg. 2000-01.

	N/A	$300 - 350	$175 - 225	$749

ACOUSTIC: CLASSIC DESIGN (CD) SERIES

The Classic Design series replaced the DG Series dreadnought models and many of the classical designs. Dreadnought models have a CD prefix and classical models have a CDN prefix. You may notice that many new CD models correspond to old CG and DG models (CG-21 is now the CDN-210, DG-22S is now the CD-220 S, etc.). In 2011, Fender updated a majority of their Classic Design models and changes included a MOP acrylic soundhole rosette, new pickguard, compensated bridge design, different bridge pins, and smaller 3mm dot fingerboard inlays. Fender's part number changed on these guitars as well to start at 096-15XX.

CD-60 (NO. 096-0600/1539) – dreadnought style, spruce top, mahogany back and sides, black body binding, round soundhole with multi-ring black (2006-2010) or MOP acrylic (2011-present) rosette, nato neck, 14/20-fret sonokeling fingerboard with regular sized dots (2006-2010) or small dots (2011-present) inlays, three-per-side chrome tuners, sonokeling bridge, black pickguard, available in Black, Natural, or Sunburst finish, 25.3 in. scale, mfg. 2006-present.

MSR $330	$230	$120 - 150	$70 - 90	

* CD-60 CE Cutaway Electric (No. 096-0605/0620/1536) – similar to the CD-60, except has a single smooth cutaway and Fishman Mini Q electronics (2006-08), Fender F3TN (2009-2010), or Fishman Isys III (2011-present) electronics, available in Black, Natural, or Sunburst finish, mfg. 2006-present.

MSR $430	$300	$160 - 200	$95 - 120	

»**CD-60CELH Cutaway Electric Left-Handed (No. 096-0625)** – similar to the CD-60CE Cutaway Electric, except in left-handed configuration, available in Natural finish, mfg. 2008 only.

	N/A	$160 - 200	$95 - 120	$450

MSR/NOTES	100%	EXCELLENT	AVERAGE	LAST MSR

* **CD-60 All Mahogany (No. 096-1596)** – similar to the CD-60, except has an all-mahogany laminated body, available in Natural finish, mfg. 2013-present.

| MSR $300 | $200 | $110 - 135 | $70 - 85 | |

»**CD-60CE All Mahogany (No. 096-1590)** – similar to the CD-60 All Mahogany, except has a single smooth cutaway and Fishman Isys III electronics, available in Natural finish, mfg. 2013-present.

| MSR $430 | $270 | $150 - 190 | $95 - 115 | |

CD-100 (NO. 096-1000/1535) – dreadnought style, spruce top, mahogany back and sides, black body binding, round soundhole with multi-ring black (2006-2010) or MOP acrylic (2011, 2013-present) rosette, nato neck, 14/20-fret rosewood fingerboard with regular sized dots (2006-2010) or small dots (2011, 2013-present) inlays, three-per-side chrome tuners, rosewood bridge, black pickguard, available in Natural finish, 25.3 in. scale, mfg. 2006-2011, 2013-present.

| MSR $280 | $200 | $120 - 150 | $70 - 95 | |

* **CD-100 LH Left-Handed (No. 096-1020/1534)** – similar to the CD-100, except in left-handed configuration, mfg. 2006-2011, 2013-present.

| MSR $330 | $230 | $135 - 175 | $85 - 110 | |

* **CD-100-12 12-String (No. 096-1012/1533)** – similar to the CD-100, except in 12-string configuration with six-per-side tuners, mfg. 2006-2011, 2013-present.

| MSR $330 | $250 | $135 - 175 | $80 - 100 | |

* **CD-100 CE Cutaway Electric (No. 096-1005/1006/1532)** – similar to the CD-100, except has a single smooth cutaway and Fender CE301 (2006-08), Fender FTE-3TN (2009-2010), or Fishman Isys III (2011, 2013-present) electronics, mfg. 2006-2011, 2013-present.

| MSR $380 | $250 | $140 - 180 | $85 - 105 | |

»**CD-100 CE LH Cutaway Electric Left-Handed (No. 096-1025/1026/1531)** – similar to the CD-100 CE Cutaway Electric, except in left-handed configuration, mfg. 2006-2011, 2013-present.

| MSR $500 | $350 | $175 - 225 | $105 - 130 | |

CD-110 E ELECTRIC (NO. 096-1101) – dreadnought style, spruce top, nato back and sides, body binding, nato neck, 14/20-fret rosewood fingerboard with dot inlay, matching headstock with three-per-side chrome tuners, rosewood bridge, black pickguard, Fishman Classic IV electronics, available in Black finish, 25.3 in. scale, mfg. 2006-08.

| | N/A | $140 - 180 | $80 - 100 | $360 |

* **CD-110CE Cutaway Electric (096-1101/1102/1530)** – similar to the CD-110E Electric, except has a single smooth cutaway with Fishman Classic IV (2009 only), Fender AGE-TN (2010 only), or Fishman Presys (2011-13) electronics, mfg. 2009-2013.

| | $270 | $140 - 175 | $85 - 105 | $380 |

CD-140 S (NO. 096-1400/1518) – dreadnought style, solid spruce top, mahogany back and sides, black body binding, nato neck, 14/20-fret rosewood fingerboard with dot inlay, three-per-side chrome tuners, rosewood bridge, tortoiseshell pickguard, available in Natural finish, 25.3 in. scale, mfg. 2006-present.

| MSR $300 | $200 | $110 - 135 | $70 - 85 | |

* **CD-140S LH Left-Handed (No. 096-1420)** – similar to the CD-140S, except in left-handed configuration, mfg. 2006-09.

| | N/A | $150 - 200 | $90 - 120 | $385 |

* **CD-140S-12 12-String (No. 096-1405)** – similar to the CD-140S, except in 12-string configuration with six-per-side tuners, mfg. 2006-09.

| | N/A | $160 - 210 | $95 - 125 | $400 |

* **CD-140S CE Cutaway Electric (No. 096-1412/1514)** – similar to the CD-140S, except has a single smooth cutaway and Fishman Classic IV with tuner (2006-2010) or Fishman Presys (2011-present) electronics, available in Black or Natural finish, mfg. 2006-present.

| MSR $430 | $300 | $160 - 195 | $95 - 120 | |

CD-160 E-12 ELECTRIC 12-STRING (NO. 096-1613) – 12-string configuration, dreadnought style, spruce top, nato back and sides, body binding, mahogany neck, 14/20-fret rosewood fingerboard with snowflake inlay, matching headstock with inlaid pearl logo and six-per-side chrome tuners, rosewood bridge, black pickguard, Fishman Classic IV electronics with tuner, available in Black or Natural (2008 only) finish, 25.3 in. scale, mfg. 2006-08.

| | N/A | $200 - 250 | $120 - 150 | $500 |

* **CD-160 SE-12 Electric 12-String (No. 096-1614/1522)** – similar to the CD-160 E-12 Electric 12-String except has a solid spruce top and Fishman Sonicore pickup and Fishman Aero active electronics with three-band EQ and electronic tuner (2009-2010) or Fishman Presys (2011-present), available in Black (2009-2012) or Natural finish, mfg. 2009-present.

| MSR $630 | $430 | $225 - 275 | $130 - 165 | |

MSR/NOTES	100%	EXCELLENT	AVERAGE	LAST MSR

CD-220 S (ASIAN STRIPED EBONY/BUBINGA/DAO, NO. 096-2201/02/03) – dreadnought style, solid spruce top, Asian Striped Ebony, Bubinga, or Dao back and sides, black body binding, nato neck, 14/20-fret rosewood fingerboard with dot inlay, three-per-side gold tuners, rosewood bridge, tortoise pickguard, available in Natural finish, 25.3 in. scale, mfg. 2006-08.

	N/A	$175 - 225	$110 - 140	$450

*** CD-220 SCE Cutaway Electric (Asian Striped Ebony/Bubinga/Dao, No. 096-2206/07/08)** – similar to the CD-200 S Asian Striped Ebony (2006-08), Bubinga, or Dao (2006-08), except has a single smooth cutaway and Fishman Classic 4 electronics with tuner, mfg. 2006-2010.

	$400	$250 - 300	$140 - 175	$600

CD-220 SCE (ASH BURL/OVANGKOL, NO. 096-1500/1501) – single cutaway dreadnought style body, solid spruce top, Ash Burl (1500) or Ovangkol (1501) back and sides, black body binding, round soundhole with abalone rosette, nato neck, 14/20-fret rosewood fingerboard with small dot inlays, MOP Fender headstock logo, three-per-side gold tuners, rosewood bridge, tortoise pickguard, Fishman Presys electronics, available in Natural finish, 25.3 in. scale, mfg. 2011-present.

MSR $700	$430	$250 - 300	$145 - 180	

*** CD-220CE All Zebrano (No. 096-1504)** – similar to the CD-200SCE, except has laminated Zebrano top, back, sides, and headstock overlay, available in Natural finish, mfg. 2013-present.

MSR $630	$400	$225 - 275	$135 - 170	

CD-230 SCE (NO. 096-1503) – single cutaway dreadnought style body, solid spruce top, Ash Burl (1500) or Ovangkol (1501) back and sides, black body binding, round soundhole with abalone rosette, nato neck, 14/20-fret rosewood fingerboard with small dot inlays, MOP Fender headstock logo, three-per-side gold tuners, rosewood bridge, tortoise pickguard, Fishman Presys electronics, available in Natural finish, 25.3 in. scale, mfg. 2011-13.

	$400	$225 - 275	$135 - 170	$630

CD-280S (NO. 096-0281/1512) – dreadnought-style body, solid spruce top, laminated rosewood back and sides, scalloped X bracing, round soundhole with three ring multi ABS (2009-2010) or MOP (2011-present) rosette, multi ABS body binding, mahogany neck, 14/20-fret rosewood fingerboard with white dot (2009-2010) or small dot (2011-present) inlays, rosewood headstock overlay with gold decal (2009-2010) or MOP (2011-present) logo, three-per-side chrome tuners, rosewood bridge, tortoise shell pickguard, available in Natural finish, 25.3 in. scale, mfg. spring 2009-present.

MSR $450	$330	$160 - 200	$95 - 120	

*** CD-280SCE Cutaway Electric (No. 096-0280/1510)** – similar to the CD-280S, except has a single smooth cutaway and Fender FTE3-TN preamp and active electronics with three-band EQ and chromatic tuner (2009-2010) or Fishman Isys III electronics (2011-present), available in Natural finish, mfg. spring 2009-present.

MSR $630	$430	$225 - 275	$130 - 165	

CD-290SCE/CJ-290SCE CUTAWAY ELECTRIC (NO. 096-0290/1565) – single cmooth cutaway jumbo-style body, solid spruce top, laminated flame maple back and sides, scalloped X bracing, round soundhole with three ring multi ABS (2009-2010) or abalone (2011-present) rosette, multi ABS body binding, maple neck, 14/20-fret rosewood fingerboard with regular sized white dot (2009-2010) or small dot (2011-present) inlays, rosewood headstock overlay with gold decal (2009-2010) or MOP (2011-present) logo, three-per-side chrome (2009-2010) or gold (2011-present) tuners, rosewood bridge, tortoise shell pickguard, Fishman Aero pickup and active electronics with three-band EQ and electric tuner (2009-2010) or Fishman Presys electronics (2011-present), available in Natural finish, 24.75 in. scale, mfg. spring 2009-present.

MSR $750	$500	$260 - 325	$160 - 195	

*** CJ290S (No. 096-1562)** – similar to the CJ290SCE, except has no cutaway and no electronics, available in Natural finish, mfg. 2013 only.

	$380	$200 - 250	$120 - 150	$600

*** CJ290SCE-12 12-String (No. 096-1561)** – similar to the CJ290SCE, except in 12-string configuration with six-per-side tuners, available in Natural finish, mfg. 2013-present.

MSR $850	$550	$300 - 375	$180 - 225	

CD-320AS (NO. 096-0321) – dreadnought-style body, solid spruce top, solid mahogany back and sides, scalloped X bracing, round soundhole with three ring MOP rosette, multi ABS body binding, mahogany neck, 14/20-fret rosewood fingerboard with MOP dot inlays, rosewood headstock overlay with MOP logo, three-per-side gold tuners, rosewood bridge, tortoise shell pickguard, available in Natural finish, 25.3 in. scale, mfg. 2012-present.

MSR $850	$600	$350 - 425	$200 - 250	

*** CD-320ASCE Cutaway Electric (No. 096-0320)** – similar to the CD-320ASCE, except has a single smooth cutaway and Fishman Presys pickup/electronics, available in Natural finish, mfg. 2012-present.

MSR $1,050	$750	$400 - 500	$250 - 300	

MSR/NOTES	100%	EXCELLENT	AVERAGE	LAST MSR

CD-360SCE/CA-360SCE CUTAWAY ELECTRIC (NO. 096-0360/1570) – single cmooth cutaway auditorium-style body, solid spruce top, laminated mahogany back and sides (2009-2010) or solid mahogany back with laminated mahogany sides (2011-present), scalloped X bracing, round soundhole with three ring multi ABS (2009-2010) or MOP (2011-13) rosette, multi ABS B/W body binding, mahogany neck, 14/20-fret rosewood fingerboard with white regular sized dot (2009-2010) or small dot (2011-13) inlays, rosewood headstock overlay with gold decal (2009-2010) or MOP (2011-13) logo, three-per-side chrome tuners, rosewood bridge, tortoise shell pickguard, Fishman Aero pickup and active electronics with three-band EQ and electric tuner (2009-2010) or Fishman Presys electronics (2011-13), available in Natural finish, 25.3 in. scale, mfg. spring 2009-2013.

	$430	$225 - 275	$135 - 170	$650

CDN-90/CN-90 (NO. 096-0900) – classical nylon-string style, spruce top, mahogany back and sides, multi-layer body binding, nato neck, 12/18-fret rosewood fingerboard, three-per-side open-style chrome tuners with white buttons, rosewood bridge, available in Natural finish, 25.3 in. scale, mfg. 2006-present.

MSR $300	$200	$100 - 130	$60 - 75	

CDN-110 E ELECTRIC (No. 097-1101) – classical nylon-string style, spruce top, nato back and sides, multi-layer body binding, nato neck, 12/18-fret rosewood fingerboard, three-per-side open-style chrome tuners with white buttons, rosewood bridge, passive piezo pickup, electronics, available in Natural finish, 25.5 in. scale, mfg. 2006-07.

	N/A	$140 - 180	$80 - 100	$357

CDN-210S (NO. 097-2100) – classical nylon-string style, solid spruce top, rosewood back and sides, multi-layer body binding, mahogany neck, 12/18-fret rosewood fingerboard, three-per-side open-style gold tuners with white buttons, rosewood bridge, available in Natural finish, 25.6 in. scale, mfg. 2006-07.

	N/A	$200 - 250	$120 - 150	$500

CDN-240 SCE/CN-240 SCE CUTAWAY ELECTRIC (NO. 097-2405) – classical nylon-string style, solid cedar top, wood mosaic rosette, rosewood back and sides, multi-layer body binding, mahogany neck, 12/18-fret rosewood fingerboard, three-per-side open-style gold tuners with pearl buttons, rosewood bridge, available in Natural finish, 25.3 in. scale, mfg. 2006-2012.

	$350	$175 - 225	$105 - 130	$500

* *CN-240SCE Cutaway Electric Thinline (No. 097-2406)* – similar to the CN-240SCE, except has a thin 3 in. body, available in Natural finish, mfg. 2012-present.

MSR $500	$350	$175 - 225	$105 - 130	

CF-100 FOLK (NO. 096-1462) – folk-style body, laminated spruce top, laminated mahogany back and sides, multi-ply body binding, round soundhole with MOP acrylic rosette, mahogany neck, 14/20-fret rosewood fingerboard with small dot inlays, three-per-side chrome tuners, rosewood bridge, available in Natural finish, 25.3 in. scale, mfg. 2013 only.

	$180	$105 - 130	$65 - 80	$280

* *CF-100CE Folk Cutaway Electric (No. 096-1463)* – similar to the CF-100, except has a single smooth cutaway and Fishman Isys III electronics, mfg. 2013 only.

	$230	$135 - 170	$80 - 100	$330

CF-140S (NO. 096-1460) – folk style, solid spruce top, mahogany back and sides, round soundhole with MOP rosette, black body binding, mahogany neck, 14/20-fret rosewood fingerboard with MOP dot inlays, rosewood headstock overlay with MOP logo, three-per-side chrome tuners, rosewood bridge, no pickguard, available in Natural finish, 25.3 in. scale, mfg. 2012-present.

MSR $300	$200	$110 - 135	$70 - 85	

* *CF-140SCE Cutaway Electric (No. 096-1461)* – similar to the CF-140S, except has a single smooth cutaway and Fishman Presys pickup/electronics, available in Natural finish, mfg. 2012-present.

MSR $430	$300	$160 - 195	$95 - 120	

CN-140S (NO. 096-1465) – classical style, solid cedar top, rosewood back and sides, traditional fan bracing, round soundhole with vintage Fender rosette, black body binding, mahogany neck, 12/19-fret rosewood fingerboard, slotted headstock with rosewood overlay, three-per-side open-style chrome tuners, rosewood tied bridge, no pickguard, available in Natural finish, 25.3 in. scale, mfg. 2012-present.

MSR $350	$250	$130 - 165	$80 - 100	

CN-320AS (NO. 096-0323) – classical-style body, solid cedar top, solid rosewood back and sides, traditional fan bracing, round soundhole with vintage Fender 70s rosette, ivoroid body binding, mahogany neck, 12/19-fret ebony fingerboard, slotted headstock with rosewood overlay with MOP logo, three-per-side open-style gold tuners, rosewood bridge, no pickguard, available in Natural finish, 25.3 in. scale, mfg. 2012-present.

MSR $1,000	$700	$350 - 450	$225 - 275	

CP-100 PARLOR (NO. 096-1571) – parlor-style body, laminated spruce top, laminated mahogany back and sides, multi-ply body binding, round soundhole with MOP acrylic rosette, mahogany neck, 14/20-fret rosewood fingerboard with small dot inlays, three-per-side chrome tuners, rosewood bridge, available in Sunburst finish, 24.875 in. scale, mfg. 2013-present.

MSR $280	$180	$105 - 130	$65 - 80	

MSR/NOTES	100%	EXCELLENT	AVERAGE	LAST MSR

ACOUSTIC: DREADNOUGHT AG SERIES

AG Series acoustics were discontinued in 1994, in favor of the DG Series. AG Series models were produced in Asia.

AG-10 – dreadnought style, spruce top, round soundhole, black pickguard, five-stripe bound body/rosette, mahogany back/sides/neck, 14/20-fret rosewood fingerboard with pearl dot inlay, rosewood bridge with black white dot pins, six-per-side chrome tuners, available in Natural finish, mfg. 1994 only.

	N/A	$100 - 130	$50 - 70	$230

AG-15 – similar to AG-10, except has a High Gloss finish, mfg. 1994 only.

	N/A	$125 - 150	$55 - 80	$250

AG-20 – similar to AG-10, except has rosewood back/sides, mfg. 1994 only.

	N/A	$130 - 170	$60 - 90	$281

AG-25 – single round cutaway dreadnought style, spruce top, round soundhole, black pickguard, mahogany back/sides/neck, 20-fret rosewood fingerboard with pearl dot inlay, rosewood bridge with black white dot pins, six-per-side chrome tuners, piezo bridge pickup, volume/tone slide control, available in Natural finish, mfg. 1994 only.

	N/A	$135 - 175	$70 - 95	$337

ACOUSTIC: DREADNOUGHT DG SERIES

The DG Series acoustics are steel-string dreadnought designs that were produced in Asia and introduced in 1995. They replaced the AG and Spring Hill series, and the entire DG series was discontinued in 2005 with the introduction of the Classical Design (CD) Series in 2006.

DG-3 VALUEPAK (NO. 095-0300) – dreadnought style, spruce top, round soundhole, black pickguard, nato back/sides, 14/20-fret rosewood fingerboard with white dot inlay, six-per-side die-cast tuners, available in Natural finish, mfg. 1995-99.

	N/A	$95 - 120	$60 - 75	$319

DG-5 (NO. 095-0500) – dreadnought style, nato top/back/sides, round soundhole, 14/20-fret rosewood fingerboard, rosewood bridge, black plastic pickguard, three-per-side chrome tuners, available in Black, Natural, or Sunburst finish, hard case included, mfg. 1995-98, 2004-05.

	N/A	$120 - 150	$70 - 95	$267

DG-6 (NO. 095-0600) – dreadnought style, Laminated Agathis top, back and sides, Nato neck with rosewood fingerboard, dot inlays, rosewood bridge, compensated Urea saddle, 25.3 in. scale, chrome tuners, black pickguard, available in Natural satin (-021) finish, mfg. 1999-2000.

	N/A	$95 - 120	$60 - 75	$190

In 2001, this guitar was introduced as a Squier model. Refer to Squier for current mfg.

DG-7 (NO. 095-0700) – dreadnought style, spruce top, round soundhole, meranti back/sides, 14/20-fret rosewood fingerboard, rosewood bridge, pickguard, three-per-side chrome tuners, available in High Gloss Natural finish, mfg. 1995-2000, 2003-05.

	N/A	$100 - 135	$65 - 85	$229

DG-8(S) VALUE PACK (NO. 095-0800/0801) – dreadnought style, Nato (early models) or solid spruce (later models) top, Nato back and sides, round soundhole, 14/20-fret rosewood fingerboard with white dot inlay, three-per-side chrome tuners, also included is a gig bag, tuner, polish cloth, picks, DVD, chord book, string winder and an extra set of strings, available in Black (2013-present) or Natural finish, mfg. 1995-present.

MSR $350	$200	$130 - 160	$80 - 100	

In 2013, this model was upgraded with a slightly reshaped pickguard, 1970s style rosewood bridge, different sized fingerboard dot inlays, and a MOP acrylic rosette.

DG-9 (NO. 095-0900) – dreadnought style, select spruce top, round soundhole, mahogany back/sides, 14/20-fret rosewood fingerboard, rosewood bridge, black pickguard, three-per-side chrome tuners, available in Satin finish, mfg. 1997-2002.

	N/A	$120 - 150	$70 - 95	$266

DG-10 (NO. 095-1000) – dreadnought style, select spruce top, round soundhole, mahogany back/sides, 14/20-fret rosewood fingerboard, rosewood bridge, black pickguard, three-per-side chrome tuners, available in Satin finish, mfg. 1995-96, reintroduced 2003-05.

	N/A	$95 - 120	$60 - 75	$257

DG-10 CE Cutaway Electric (No. 095-1005) – similar to the DG-10, except has a single cutaway and electronics, mfg. 1995-2005.

	N/A	$120 - 150	$70 - 95	$385

»***DG-10 CE LH Cutaway Electric Left Handed (No. 095-1025)*** – similar to the DG-10 CE Cutaway Electric, except in left-handed configuration, mfg. 1998-2005.

	N/A	$135 - 175	$75 - 100	$400

DG-10 LH Left Handed (No. 095-1020) – similar to the DG-10, except in a left-handed configuration, mfg. 1995-2005.

	N/A	$100 - 135	$65 - 85	$285

MSR/NOTES	100%	EXCELLENT	AVERAGE	LAST MSR

* **DG-10-12 12-String (No. 095-1012)** – similar to the DG-10, except in a 12-string configuration, mfg. 1995-2005.

| | N/A | $120 - 150 | $70 - 95 | $315 |

DG-11 (NO. 095-1100) – dreadnought style, spruce top, round soundhole, nato back/sides, 14/20-fret rosewood fingerboard with dot inlay, rosewood bridge, black pickguard, three-per-side chrome tuners, available in Black, Sunburst, or Natural Gloss finish, mfg. 1998-2005.

| | N/A | $120 - 150 | $70 - 95 | $286 |

* **DG-11 E Electric (No. 095-1101)** – similar to the DG-11, except has a pickup and electronics, mfg. summer 1998-2005.

| | N/A | $130 - 165 | $75 - 100 | $329 |

DG-14 S (NO. 095-1400) – dreadnought style, solid Spruce top, maple back and sides, nato neck, rosewood fingerboard, dot inlays, 20 frets, Natural Gloss Wood-Tone finish, 25.3 in. scale, disc. 2005.

| | N/A | $135 - 175 | $75 - 100 | $357 |

* **DG-14 SCE Cutaway Electric (No. 095-1405)** – similar to the DG-14 S, except has a single cutaway and electronics, mfg. 2003-2005.

| | N/A | $160 - 200 | $100 - 130 | $429 |

* **DG-14 LH Left Handed (No. 095-1420)** – similar to the DG-14, except in a left-handed configuration, mfg. 1999-2005.

| | N/A | $150 - 190 | $95 - 120 | $364 |

* **DG-14 S-12 12-String (No. 095-1412)** – similar to Model DG-14 S, only in 12-string configuration, available in Natural Wood-Tone finish, mfg. 1999-2005.

| | N/A | $160 - 200 | $100 - 130 | $386 |

DG-15 (NO. 095-1500) – similar to the DG-10 model, available in Jet Black, Gloss Sunburst, or Natural finishes, mfg. 1995-98.

| | N/A | $135 - 175 | $75 - 100 | $359 |

DG-16 (NO. 095-1600) – dreadnought style, spruce top, round soundhole, mahogany back/sides, 14/20-fret rosewood fingerboard with snowflake inlay, rosewood bridge, black pickguard, three-per-side die-cast tuners, available in Black, Sunburst, or Natural gloss finish, mfg. 1998-2005.

| | N/A | $135 - 175 | $75 - 100 | $371 |

* **DG-16 LH Left Handed (No. 095-1620)** – similar to the DG-10, except in a left-handed configuration, available in Natural or Black finish, mfg. 1999-2003.

| | N/A | $150 - 190 | $95 - 120 | $380 |

* **DG-16-12 12-String (No. 095-1612)** – similar to Model DG-16, except in 12-string configuration, available in Natural Gloss or Black finish, disc. 2005.

| | N/A | $160 - 200 | $100 - 130 | $400 |

»**DG-16E-12 12-String Electric (No. 095-1613)** – similar to the DG-16-12 12-String, except has a pickup and electronics, mfg. 1999-2005.

| | N/A | $175 - 225 | $110 - 140 | $471 |

DG-20 S (NO. 095-2000) – dreadnought style, solid spruce top, round soundhole, mahogany back/sides, 14/20-fret rosewood fingerboard, rosewood bridge, tortoiseshell pickguard, three-per-side chrome tuners, available in Natural Gloss finish, mfg. 1995-2004.

| | N/A | $175 - 225 | $110 - 140 | $400 |

* **DG-20 SCE Cutaway Electric (No. 095-2005)** – similar to the DG-20 S, except has a single cutaway, pickup, and electronics, mfg. 1995-2005.

| | N/A | $250 - 300 | $150 - 200 | $600 |

DG-21 S (NO. 095-2100) – dreadnought style, solid spruce top, round soundhole, rosewood back/sides, 14/20-fret rosewood fingerboard, rosewood bridge, tortoiseshell pickguard, three-per-side gold die-cast tuners, available in Natural Gloss finish, mfg. 1995-2005.

| | N/A | $175 - 225 | $110 - 140 | $450 |

DG-22 S (NO. 095-2200) – dreadnought style, solid spruce top, round soundhole, figured maple back/sides, 14/20-fret rosewood fingerboard, rosewood bridge, tortoiseshell pickguard, three-per-side gold die-cast tuners, available in Cherry, Natural, Crimson Red Burst (1999-2005), Blue Burst (1999-2005), or Sunburst Gloss finish, mfg. 1995-2005.

| | N/A | $200 - 250 | $120 - 150 | $543 |

In 2005, Dao, Asian Striped Ebony, and Bubinga replaced the original design.

* **DG-22 SCE Cutaway Electric (No. 095-2205)** – similar to the DG-22 S, except has a single cutaway, pickup, and electronics, available in Blue Burst (1999-2005), Cherry, Crimson Red Burst (1999-2005), Natural, or Sunburst finish, mfg. 1995-2005.

| | N/A | $275 - 325 | $150 - 200 | $714 |

In 2005, Dao, Asian Striped Ebony, or Bubinga replaced the back and sides, and a solid spruce was introduced for the top.

MSR/NOTES	100%	EXCELLENT	AVERAGE	LAST MSR

DG-24 (NO. 095-2400) – dreadnought style, wood bound mahogany top/back/sides, round soundhole, wood inlay rosette, 14/20-fret rosewood fingerboard, rosewood bridge, three-per-side chrome die-cast tuners with pearloid buttons, available in Satin finish, mfg. 1997-2003.

	N/A	$200 - 250	$120 - 150	$500

DG-25 S (NO. 095-2500) – dreadnought style, solid cedar top, mahogany back and sides, round soundhole, wood inlay rosette, 14/20-fret rosewood fingerboard, rosewood bridge, three-per-side chrome die-cast tuners with pearloid buttons, available in Satin finish, mfg. 1997-2005.

	N/A	$225 - 275	$135 - 175	$571

DG-27 SCE CUTAWAY ELECTRIC (NO. 095-2705) – dreadnought-style body with Florentine cutaway, solid spruce top, premium mahogany back and sides, mahogany neck, rosewood fingerboard with dot inlays, rosewood bridge, Compensated Urea saddle, chrome tuners, Piezo pickup, volume control and active three-band EQ, Mid Sweep, tortoiseshell pickguard, available in Natural or Black finish, 25.6 in. scale, disc. 2002.

	N/A	$250 - 300	$150 - 200	$650

DG-30 S/DG-31 S (NO. 095-3100) – dreadnought style, solid Englemann spruce top, round soundhole, mahogany back/sides, 14/20-fret rosewood fingerboard, rosewood bridge, three-per-side chrome die-cast tuners, available in Natural Gloss finish, mfg. 1995-99.

	N/A	$200 - 250	$120 - 150	$549

In 1996, all of the DG-30 S models were changed to DG-31S, and tops were specified as Englemann spruce.

* **DG-30 SCE/DG-31 SCE Cutaway Electric (No. 095-3005/3105)** – similar to the DG-30 S/DG-31 S, except has a single cutaway, Fishman Acoustic Matrix pickup, onboard preamp, and volume/3-band EQ/mid-sweep controls, available in Black, Cherry Sunburst, or Natural Gloss finish, mfg. 1995-99.

	N/A	$300 - 350	$175 - 225	$799

In 1996, the model changed to the DG-31 SCE and the top was specified as Englemann spruce. DG-30 SCE models feature Fender One Way Mono electronics.

* **DG-30 S/DG-31 S LH Left Handed (No. 095-3120)** – similar to the DG-31, except in a left-handed configuration, mfg. 1995-99.

	N/A	$200 - 250	$120 - 150	$559

* **DG-30-12/DG-31-12 12-String (No. 095-3112)** – similar to the DG-31, except in a 12-string configuration, spruce top, six-per-side tuners, available in Natural Gloss finish, mfg. 1995-99.

	N/A	$225 - 275	$135 - 175	$529

DG-40 S/DG-41 S (NO. 095-4000/4100) – dreadnought style, solid Englemann spruce top, round soundhole, rosewood back/sides, 14/20-fret rosewood fingerboard, rosewood bridge, tortoiseshell pickguard, three-per-side gold die-cast tuners, available in Gloss finish, mfg. 1995-2000.

	N/A	$225 - 275	$135 - 175	$599

In 1996, all model DG-40 S models were changed to the DG-41 S and the top was specified as Englemann spruce.

* **DG-40 SCE/DG-41 SCE Cutaway Electric (No. 095-4005/4105)** – similar to the DG-40 S/DG-41 S, except has a single cutaway, a Fishman Acoustic Matrix Professional pickup, onboard preamp, and electronics, mfg. 1995-2000.

	N/A	$325 - 400	$200 - 250	$999

In 1996, the model was changed to the DG-41 S, the top was specified as Englemann spruce. DG-40 S models will have Fender Mono Two-Way electronics.

* **DG-40 S-12/DG-41 S-12 12-String (No. 095-4012/4112)** – similar to the DG-41, except in 12-string configuration, available in Natural Gloss finish, mfg. 1995-2000.

	N/A	$250 - 300	$150 - 200	$689

DG-60 – dreadnought-style body, laminated spruce top, laminated mahogany back and sides, round soundhole with multi-ring rosette, scalloped X bracing, multi-ply body binding, nato neck, 14/20-fret sonokeling (Indian rosewood) fingerboard with white dot inlays, three-per-side chrome tuners, sonokeling bridge, black pickguard, available in Natural finish, 25.3 in. scale, current mfg.

MSR $225	$160	$95 - 120	$50 - 75	

This model is not part of Fender's standard catalog. It is produced for and sold by select retailers including Guitar Center and Musician's Friend.

DG-100 – dreadnought-style body, solid Englemann spruce top, laminated mahogany back and sides, round soundhole with multi-ring abalone rosette, scalloped X bracing, multi-ply body binding, nato neck, 14/20-fret bound rosewood fingerboard with white dot inlays, black headstock overlay, three-per-side gold tuners, rosewood bridge, tortoise pickguard, available in Natural finish, 25.3 in. scale, disc.

	$250	$135 - 175	$75 - 100	$324

This model was not part of Fender's standard catalog. It was produced for and sold by select retailers including Guitar Center and Musician's Friend.

DG-200SCE – single cutaway dreadnought-style body, solid spruce top, laminated rosewood back and sides, round soundhole with multi-ring abalone rosette, scalloped X bracing, multi-ply body binding, nato neck, 14/20-fret bound rosewood fingerboard with white dot inlays, black headstock overlay, three-per-side gold tuners, rosewood bridge, tortoise pickguard, Fishman Aero pickup and electronics with tuner, available in Natural finish, 25.3 in. scale, current mfg.

MSR $600	$400	$225 - 275	$120 - 150	

This model is not part of Fender's standard catalog. It is produced for and sold by select retailers including Guitar Center and Musician's Friend.

MSR/NOTES	100%	EXCELLENT	AVERAGE	LAST MSR

ACOUSTIC: ENSENADA SERIES

The Ensenada Series are named after the city that they are produced in, Ensenada, Mexico.

ENSENADA ESA-10/ESD-10/ESM-10/ESV-10 12 FRET (NO. 096-6300/6000/6100/6200) – grand auditorium, dreadnought, mini-jumbo, or orchestra 12-fret body style, solid spruce top, solid palo escrito back and sides, Vintage-style Grover tuners, Natural finish, mfg. 2005-07.

	N/A	$550 - 625	$325 - 400	$1,214

Each model has the same type of wood and construction; the only difference is the body style/size. The ESA-10 and ESV-10 12 Fret were introduced in 2006.

* ***Ensenada ESA-10E/ESD-10E/ESM-10E/ESV-10E 12-Fret (No. 096-6305/6005/6105/6205)*** – similar to the Ensenada acoustic models, except they have Fishman Ellipse VT Electronics with the controls mounted in the soundhole, mfg. summer 2005-07.

	N/A	$625 - 725	$400 - 475	$1,429

All Enesenada models feature the same wood and construction; the only difference is the body size. The ESA-10E and ESV-10E 12-Fret were introduced in 2006.

ACOUSTIC: F SERIES

The F-Series were introduced in 1969. The F-Series replaced the initial acoustic line and were discontinued sometime after 1980. The first initial models were the **F-1000**, **F-1010**, **F-1030**, **F-1040**, **F-1050**, **F-1060**, and **F-1070-12**. These models were priced between $33 and $197. Secondhand market prices on these guitars are around $50 - $100. The F-3 and F-5 models (1980-81 mfg.) are budget instruments that bring about $30 - $50 today. These era of guitars can be distinguished by their notched headstock. The FC-Series was introduced about the same time and included classical models.

Another F-Series was introduced in the early 1980s and are known as the Standard Series. See the Standard Series for more information.

F-15 – concert style, spruce top, Nato back and sides, mahogany neck, 14/20-fret rosewood fingerboard, adjustable rosewood bridge, black pickguard, Natural finish, 25.5 in. scale, mfg. 1972-1981.

	N/A	$50 - 70	$20 - 30	

F-25 – auditorium style, spruce top, Nato back and sides, mahogany neck, 14/20-fret rosewood fingerboard, adjustable rosewood bridge, black pickguard, Natural finish, 24.75 in. scale, mfg. 1972-1981.

	N/A	$50 - 70	$20 - 30	

F-35 – dreadnought style, spruce top, Ovangkol back and sides, mahogany neck, 14/20-fret rosewood fingerboard, adjustable rosewood bridge, black pickguard, Natural finish, 25.5 in. scale, mfg. 1972-1981.

	N/A	$55 - 75	$25 - 35	

F-45 – concert folk style, spruce top, two-piece mahogany back and sides, mahogany neck, 12/19-fret rosewood fingerboard, open style headstock, rosewood bridge, Natural finish, 24.75 in. scale, mfg. 1972-late 1970s.

	N/A	$90 - 120	$50 - 70	

This model is supposed to be strung with both nylon and steel strings.

F-50 – grand concert style, solid spruce top, rosewood back and sides, mahogany neck, rosewood fingerboard, rosewood bridge, Natural finish, mfg. 1980 only.

	N/A	$175 - 225	$100 - 130	

F-55-12 – 12-string configuration, dreadnought style, spruce top, Bubinga back and sides, mahogany neck, 14/20-fret rosewood fingerboard, adjustable rosewood bridge, black pickguard, Natural finish, 25.5 in. scale, mfg. 1972-1980.

	N/A	$150 - 200	$90 - 120	

F-65 – dreadnought style, spruce top, simulated abalone binding, rosewood back and sides, mahogany neck, 14/20-fret rosewood fingerboard with snowflake inlays, adjustable rosewood bridge, black pickguard, Natural finish, 25.5 in. scale, mfg. 1972-1981.

	N/A	$150 - 200	$90 - 120	

F-75 – dreadnought style, solid spruce top, rosewood back and sides, mahogany neck, 14/20-fret rosewood fingerboard, rosewood bridge, black pickguard, Natural finish, 25.5 in. scale, mfg. 1974-1980.

	N/A	$175 - 225	$100 - 130	

F-80-12 – 12-string configuration, dreadnought style, solid spruce top, rosewood back and sides, mahogany neck, 14/20-fret rosewood fingerboard, rosewood bridge, black pickguard, Natural finish, 25.5 in. scale, mfg. 1977-1981.

	N/A	$175 - 225	$100 - 130	

F-85 – dreadnought style, solid spruce top, three-piece rosewood back and sides, mahogany neck, 14/20-fret ebony fingerboard, ebony bridge, black pickguard, Natural finish, 25.5 in. scale, mfg. 1974-1980.

	N/A	$200 - 250	$120 - 150	

MSR/NOTES	100%	EXCELLENT	AVERAGE	LAST MSR

F-95 – dreadnought style, solid spruce top, full body binding, three-piece Jacaranda back and sides, mahogany neck, 14/20-fret ebony fingerboard, ebony bridge, black pickguard, Natural finish, 25.5 in. scale, mfg. 1974-1980.

	N/A	$225 - 275	$120 - 150	

F-115 – dreadnought style, solid spruce top, full body abalone binding, three-piece rosewood back and sides, mahogany neck, 14/20-fret ebony fingerboard with butterfly inlays, butterfly F logo on headstock, ebony bridge, black pickguard, Natural finish, 25.75 in. scale, mfg. 1977-1987.

	N/A	$300 - 375	$150 - 200	

FC-10/20/30/40 – classical style guitars, spruce or cedar top, various binding options, Chitora or rosewood back and sides, mahogany neck, 12/19-fret rosewood fingerboard, rosewood fingerboard, open style headstock, rosewood bridge, Natural finish, mfg. 1972-1981.

FC-10/20	N/A	$90 - 120	$50 - 70	
FC-30/40	N/A	$125 - 175	$70 - 90	

FJ-70 – jumbo style, solid spruce top, rosewood back and sides, mahogany neck, rosewood fingerboard, rosewood bridge, Natural finish, mfg. late 1980-81.

	N/A	$175 - 225	$100 - 130	

ACOUSTIC: GRAND SERIES (GA, GC, GD, & GN MODELS)

Fender recently introduced Grand series guitars, which includes the Auditorium and Concert models. These guitars offer more styles than just the dreadnought they have produced for several years.

GA-43S NATURAL (NO. 095-4300) – custom-designed body shape, solid AA Grade spruce top, solid mahogany back, rosewood fingerboard with dot position markers, three-per-side tuners, available in Natural (-021) finish, mfg. 2001-04.

	N/A	$250 - 300	$150 - 200	$665

* **GA-43 SCE Cutaway Electric (No. 095-4305)** – similar to the GA-43 S, except has a single cutaway, pickup, and electronics, mfg. 2000-09.

	N/A	$425 - 500	$275 - 325	$1,000

GA-45S NATURAL (NO. 095-4500) – similar to GA-43S, custom-designed body shape, solid AA Grade spruce top, solid mahogany back, rosewood fingerboard with dot position markers, three-per-side tuners, available in Natural (-021) finish, mfg. 2001-04.

	N/A	$300 - 350	$175 - 225	$765

* **GA-45 SCE Cutaway Electric (No. 095-4505)** – similar to the GA-45 S, except has a single cutaway, pickup, and electronics, mfg. 2001-09.

	N/A	$450 - 525	$300 - 350	$1,050

» **GA-45 SCE Cutaway Electric Left-Handed (No. 095-4525)** – similar to the GA-45 SCE except in left-handed configuration, available in Natural finish, mfg. 2002-04.

	N/A	$450 - 525	$300 - 350	$1,029

GC-12 (NO. 095-1200) – economy version of the GC-23S, spruce top, Nato back, sides and neck, rosewood fingerboard with dot position markers, chrome-plated covered tuners, three-per-side tuners, available in Natural Gloss finish, mfg. 2000-08.

	N/A	$110 - 140	$70 - 90	$280

GC-23 S (NO. 095-2300) – grand concert style, solid spruce top, round soundhole, mahogany back/sides, 14/20-fret rosewood fingerboard, rosewood bridge, three-per-side chrome die-cast tuners, available in Natural Gloss finish, mfg. 1997-2008.

	N/A	$140 - 180	$85 - 110	$350

GC-42S (NO. 094-4200) – non-cutaway design, solid AA grade spruce top, solid mahogany back, rosewood fingerboard, die-cast silver tuning machines, abalone fret markers, 20 frets, tortoiseshell-style binding, available in Natural finish, mfg. 2001-04.

	N/A	$275 - 325	$150 - 200	$665

GD-47 S (NO. 095-4700) – non-cutaway, solid AA grade spruce top, rosewood back and sides, three-per-side gold die-cast Grover tuning keys, rosewood fingerboard, Nato neck, 20 abalone rosette frets, tortoiseshell-style binding, available in Natural finish, mfg. 2002-04.

	N/A	$325 - 400	$200 - 250	$800

* **GD-47 SCE Cutaway Electric (No. 094-4705)** – similar to the GD-47 S, except has a single cutaway and Fender Fishman 4 ACLR Pickup System, available in Natural finish, mfg. 2002-07.

	N/A	$400 - 500	$250 - 300	$1,000

* **GD-47 S 12 12-String (No. 095-4712)** – similar to the GD-47 S except in 12-string configuration and six-per-side tuners, mfg. 2002-04.

	N/A	$350 - 425	$200 - 250	$857

» **GD-47 12 SCE 12-String Cutaway Electric (No. 095-4717)** – similar to the GD-47 12 12-String, except has a single cutaway and electronics, mfg. summer 2005-07.

	N/A	$425 - 525	$275 - 325	$1,071

MSR/NOTES	100%	EXCELLENT	AVERAGE	LAST MSR

GN-45SCE (NO. 094-4505) – single cutaway design, solid AA grade spruce top, solid rosewood back, rosewood fingerboard, die-cast gold tuning machines, abalone fret markers, 20 frets, tortoiseshell-style binding, Fender/Fishman exclusive ACLR preamp, Piezo pickup, available in Natural finish, mfg. 2001-07.

	N/A	$400 - 500	$250 - 300	$1,000

ACOUSTIC: GEMINI SERIES

The Gemini series were introduced subsequently or after the second F-Series in the mid-1980s. These guitars were built in Korea, distributed in the US by MIDCO, and produced until roughly 1990.

GEMINI I – classical style, spruce top, Nato back and sides, mfg. 1984-88.

	N/A	$135 - 175	$85 - 110	$165

GEMINI II – dreadnought style, spruce top, Nato back and sides, 14/20-fret rosewood fingerboard, rosewood bridge, black pickguard, Natural finish, mfg. 1984-87.

	N/A	$150 - 200	$95 - 120	$189

* *Gemini IIE* – similar to the Gemini II, except has electronics, mfg. 1987-1990.

	N/A	$175 - 225	$110 - 140	$260

GEMINI III – dreadnought style, spruce top, mahogany back and sides, 14/20-fret rosewood fingerboard, rosewood bridge, Black finish, mfg. 1987-88.

	N/A	$175 - 225	$110 - 140	$209

GEMINI IV – dreadnought style, spruce top, mahogany back and sides, 14/20-fret rosewood fingerboard, rosewood bridge, White finish, mfg. 1987-1990.

	N/A	$200 - 250	$120 - 150	$240

ACOUSTIC: GLOBAL DESIGN SERIES

GDC-100 SCE (NO. 095-8000) – single cutaway concert-style body, solid spruce top, laminated ash back/sides, nato neck, rosewood fingerboard with 12th fret Fender inlay, round soundhole with rosette, chrome hardware, Piezo pickup with active electronics, available in Natural finish, mfg. 2004-07.

	N/A	$250 - 300	$150 - 190	$571

GDC-200 SCE (NO. 095-8001) – single sharp cutaway concert-style body, solid spruce top, laminated ash back/sides, nato neck, rosewood fingerboard with 12th fret Fender inlay, round soundhole with rosette, chrome hardware, Piezo pickup with active electronics, available in Natural finish, mfg. 2004-07.

	N/A	$250 - 300	$150 - 190	$571

GDO-200 (NO. 095-8905) – orchestra style body, laminated quilt ash top, laminated ash back/sides, nato neck, rosewood fingerboard with 12th fret Fender inlay, round soundhole with rosette, chrome hardware, available in Trans. Green (2006-07), Trans. Gray (2006-07), or Trans. Violet finish, mfg. 2004-08.

	N/A	$140 - 180	$80 - 105	$350

GDO-300 (NO. 095-8906) – orchestra-style body, laminated quilt maple top, laminated mahogany back/sides, nato neck, rosewood fingerboard with 12th fret Fender inlay, round soundhole with rosette, chrome hardware, available in Trans. Amber, Trans. Blue (2006-07), or Trans. Green (2006-07) finish, mfg. 2004-08.

	N/A	$140 - 180	$80 - 105	$350

GDO-500S (NO. 095-8200) – orchestra style body, solid cedar top, solid ovangkol back/sides, round soundhole with rosette, mahogany neck, 14/20-fret rosewood fingerboard with dot and 12th fret "F" inlay, three-per-side chrome tuners, available in Natural or Sunburst finish, mfg. summer 2006-07.

	N/A	$350 - 425	$200 - 250	$857

* *GDO-500SE Electric (No. 095-8205)* – similar to the GDO-500S, except has Fishman Classic IV T electronics, mfg. summer 2006-07.

	N/A	$375 - 475	$225 - 275	$929

GDP-100 (NO. 095-8901) – parlor-style body, laminated spruce top, laminated mahogany back/sides, mahogany neck, rosewood fingerboard with 12th fret Fender inlay, round soundhole with rosette, chrome hardware, Natural finish, mfg. 2004-08.

	N/A	$120 - 150	$75 - 90	$300

GDS-500SE (NO. 095-8100) – slope-shouldered dreadnought style body, solid spruce top, solid mahogany back/sides, round soundhole with rosette, mahogany neck, 14/20-fret rosewood fingerboard with 12th fret "F" inlay, Fishman Classic IV T electronics, chrome hardware, available in Natural or Sunburst finish, mfg. 2006-07.

	N/A	$375 - 475	$225 - 275	$929

MSR/NOTES	100%	EXCELLENT	AVERAGE	LAST MSR

ACOUSTIC: JUMBO/MINI-JUMBO SERIES (SJ & JG MODELS)

SJ-64 S (NO. 095-6400) – super jumbo body, solid spruce top, rosewood back and sides, mahogany neck, bound neck and body, rosewood fingerboard with split block position markers, 20 frets, 25.6 in. scale, gold die-cast tuners, available in Natural Gloss finish, disc. 2002.

	N/A	$250 - 300	$135 - 175	$700

SJ-65 S (NO. 095-6500) – super jumbo body, similar to SJ-64 S, except has flamed maple back and sides, maple neck, available in Natural Gloss finish, disc. 2002.

	N/A	$275 - 325	$150 - 200	$720

JG-12 CE-12 12-STRING (NO. 095-1217) – mini-jumbo style with cutaway design, spruce top, round soundhole, mahogany back/sides, 14/20-fret rosewood fingerboard, rosewood bridge, six-per-side chrome die-cast tuners, Fender piezo pickup, onboard preamp, volume/three-band EQ/mid-sweep controls, available in Satin finish, mfg. 1998-2009.

	N/A	$200 - 250	$120 - 150	$480

JG-26 SCE (NO. 095-2605) – mini-jumbo style with cutaway design, solid cedar top, round soundhole, mahogany back/sides, 14/20-fret rosewood fingerboard, rosewood bridge, three-per-side gold die-cast tuners with pearloid buttons, Fishman Acoustic Matrix pickup, onboard preamp, volume/three-band EQ/mid-sweep controls, available in Satin finish, mfg. 1997-2009.

	N/A	$250 - 300	$150 - 200	$550

ACOUSTIC: RESONATOR SERIES

FR-48 RESONATOR (NO. 095-4800) – steel body resonator, custom Fender f-holes, mahogany neck, 19-fret rosewood fingerboard with dot inlay, Micarta saddle bridge, chrome die-cast three-per-side tuners, available in chrome finish, mfg. 2003-09.

	N/A	$400 - 475	$250 - 300	$950

FR-50 RESONATOR (NO. 095-5000/5002) – spruce top, mahogany back and sides, custom Fender f-holes, chrome finished resonator, round (Model 095-5000) or square (Model 095-5002, 2000-09) mahogany neck, 14/19-fret rosewood fingerboard with dot inlays, three-per-side chrome tuners, available in Sunburst or Black (Round Neck model only, 2000-09) finish, 25.3 in. scale, mfg. 2000-present.

MSR $600	$450	$225 - 275	$135 - 170	

* *FR-50 CE Cutaway Electric (No. 095-5005)* – similar to the FR-50 Resonator, except has a single cutaway, Fender Telecaster neck pickup, and a Fishman bridge pickup, with two knobs on body, Sunburst finish only, mfg. 2003-present.

MSR $1,100	$800	$375 - 475	$225 - 275	

FR-55 HAWAIIAN RESONATOR (NO. 095-5053) – nickel-plated metal body, Continental Eastern European hand spun cone, two Fender f-holes, square mahogany neck, 14/19-fret rosewood fingerboard with dot inlays, rosewood headstock overlay with gold Fender logo, three-per-side chrome tuners, ebony bridge with hard maple top, bell brass nickel-plated tailpiece, available in chrome Hawaiian finish, 24.875 in. scale, mfg. 2012-present.

MSR $1,000	$650	$375 - 450	$225 - 275	

RESO-TELE (NO. 095-5010) – single cutaway Tele-style maple body, F-shaped soundhole in upper bass bout, bolt-on maple neck, 21-fret maple fingerboard with black dot inlays, Tele-style headstock, six-on-one-side tuners, hand-spun resonator cone, maple biscuit bridge, single Tele-style single coil pickup, Fishman Powerchip under-saddle pickup, two knobs (MV, pickup blend), chrome hardware, available in 2-Color Sunburst finish, 25.5 in. scale, mfg. 2013-present.

MSR $1,100	$800	$500 - 600	$250 - 325	

ACOUSTIC: SIGNATURE MODELS

ALKALINE TRIO MALIBU (NO. 096-8325) – folk-style body, laminated mahogany top, laminated mahogany back and sides, scalloped X bracing, heart-shaped soundhole with decorative rosette, multiple body bindings, maple neck, 14/20-fret bound rosewood fingerboard with dot inlays, Strat-style headstock, six-on-one-side tuners with cream plastic buttons, rosewood bridge, white bridge pins with black dots, available in Natural finish, 25.5 in. scale, mfg. 2012-present.

MSR $350	$250	$135 - 170	$80 - 100	

BUDDY MILLER SIGNATURE (NO. 096-9700) – slope-shouldered dreadnought style, solid Sitka spruce top, solid mahogany back and sides, round soundhole with checkered rosette, checkered top binding, mahogany neck, 14/20-fret rosewood fingerboard with dot inlays, Strat-style headstock Buddy Miller's signature and six-on-one-side Vintage-style chrome tuners, slight moustache-style rosewood bridge, pickguard, Fishman Ellipse Aura electronics, available in Natural or Sunburst (2008-09) finish, 25.75 in. scale, made in Mexico, mfg. 2007-09.

	N/A	$750 - 900	$475 - 550	$1,800

DICK DALE LIMITED EDITION MALIBU CE (NO. 096-8401) – single cutaway folk Malibu-style body, laminated spruce top, laminated mahogany back and sides, round soundhole with checkerboard rosette, scalloped X bracing, multi-ply body binding, vintage C-shaped maple neck, 14/20-fret bound rosewood fingerboard with white dot inlays, reverse Strat-style headstock with Black finish overlay and Dick Dale signature, six-on-the-other-side vintage-style chrome tuners with aged white plastic buttons, rosewood bridge, Fender FTE3-TN electronics with chromatic tuner, available in Surfer's Choice Artwork finish, 24.75 in. scale, mfg. 2010 only.

	$350	$200 - 250	$120 - 150	$450

This model was produced in commemoration of the 45th Anniversary of Dick Dale's album "Surfer's Choice."

MSR/NOTES	100%	EXCELLENT	AVERAGE	LAST MSR

DICK DALE SIGNATURE MALIBU SCE (NO. 096-8400) – single cutaway folk Malibu-style body, solid spruce top, laminated mahogany back and sides, round soundhole with checkerboard rosette, scalloped X bracing, multi-ply body binding, vintage C-shaped maple neck, 14/20-fret bound rosewood fingerboard with pearloid block inlays, reverse Strat-style headstock with matching finish overlay and Dick Dale signature, six-on-the-other-side vintage-style chrome tuners with aged white plastic buttons, rosewood bridge, dual red pickguards, Fishman Presys pickup and electronics with tuner, available in Surfin' Red finish, 24.75 in. scale, deluxe hardshell case included, mfg. 2010-present.

| MSR $1,000 | $650 | $375 - 450 | $225 - 275 | |

* *Dick Dale Signature Malibu SCE Left-Handed (No. 096-8420)* – similar to the Dick Dale Signature Mailbu SCE, except in left-handed configuration, available in Surfin' Red finish, mfg. 2010-present.

| MSR $1,050 | $700 | $400 - 475 | $250 - 300 | |

DUANE PETERS SONORAN SCE '61 (NO. 096-8407) – single cutaway dreadnought-style body, solid spruce top, laminated mahogany back and sides, scalloped X bracing, round soundhole, ivoroid body binding, maple vintage C-shaped neck, 14/20-fret ivoroid-bound rosewood fingerboard with pearl dot inlays, Stratocaster-style headstock with black/white checkerboard overlay, six-on-one-side chrome tuners, rosewood bridge, Fishman Isys III pickup and electronics with tuner, available in custom diagonal orange/black finish with Duane Peters graphics on the top and back and Natural sides, 25.3 in. scale, mfg. 2012 only.

| | $400 | $250 - 300 | $150 - 190 | $550 |

ELVIS KINGMAN (NO. 096-8408) – dreadnought-style body, solid spruce top, laminated wildwood back and sides, scalloped X bracing, multiple body binding, round soundhole with dual checkered rosette, maple neck, 14/20-fret ivoroid-bound rosewood fingerboard with white pearloid block inlays, Stratocaster-style headstock with Elvis signature, six-on-one-side chrome tuners, rosewood bridge, three-ply gold pickguard, available in Natural finish, 25.3 in. scale, mfg. 2012-present.

| MSR $600 | $400 | $250 - 300 | $150 - 190 | |

J5 SIGNATURE (NO. 095-8801) – single sharp cutaway, solid spruce top, laminated premium mahogany back/sides, mahogany neck, rosewood fingerboard with "5" inlay at 5th fret, white pickguard, white body and neck binding, large headstock with three-per-side tuners very close together, Fishman Classic 4 preamp, black hardware, available in black finish only, mfg. 2004-2010.

| | $630 | $375 - 450 | $225 - 275 | $900 |

JIMMY DALE SIGNATURE KINGMAN SCE (NO. 096-8405) – single cutaway dreadnought Kingman-style body, solid mahogany top, back, and sides, round soundhole with checkerboard rosette, scalloped X bracing, multi-ply body binding, vintage C-shaped maple neck, 14/20-fret bound rosewood fingerboard with pearloid block inlays, Strat-style headstock with Natural overlay and Jimmy Dale signature, six-on-one-side vintage-style chrome tuners with aged white plastic buttons, rosewood bridge, dual tortoise pickguards, Fishman Presys pickup and electronics with tuner, available in Natural finish, 24.75 in. scale, deluxe hardshell case included, mfg. 2010-present.

| MSR $900 | $650 | $375 - 450 | $225 - 275 | |

JOHN SEVERSON SURF FEVER/WOODY SONORAN SCE (NO. 096-8040/8042) – single cutaway dreadnought-style body, solid spruce top, laminated mahogany back and sides, top and back binding, round soundhole, vintage C-shaped maple neck, 14/20-fret rosewood fingerboard with white dot inlays, Stratocaster-style headstock, six-per-side chrome tuners with white plastic buttons, rosewood bridge, available in Surf Fever (Black/Red/White graphics top with black back, sides, and headstock overlay) or Woody (Woody graphics on top with Natural back, sides, and headstock overlay) finish, 25.3 in. scale, mfg. late 2008-09.

| | N/A | $200 - 250 | $120 - 150 | $500 |

ROY EMORY "LOYALTY" PARLOR (NO. 096-8551) – parlor-style body, laminated spruce (Vintage Sunburst finish) or laminated ash (Ash Butterscotch) top, laminated mahogany back and sides (Vintage Sunburst finish) or laminated ash back and sides (Ash Butterscotch), round soundhole with herringbone rosette, herringbone body binding, set soft V-shaped mahogany (Vintage Sunburst finish) or maple (Ash Butterscotch) neck, bound 12/19-fret rosewood fingerboard with diamond inlays and 12th fret Loyalty inlay, 1970s-style bound Fender headstock with black overlay (Vintage Sunburst finish) or natural overlay (Ash Butterscotch finish), three-per-side chrome tuners, rosewood bridge, tortoise (Vintage Sunburst finish) or gold (Ash Butterscotch finish) pickguard, Fishman Isys III pickup/electronics, available in Ash Butterscotch or Vintage Sunburst finish, 25.3 in. scale, mfg. 2013-present.

| MSR $430 | $280 | $180 - 210 | $90 - 110 | |

ROY EMORY "LOYALTY" SLOPE SHOULDER DREADNOUGHT (NO. 096-8550) – slope-shoulder dreadnought body-style, laminated spruce (Vintage Sunburst finish) or laminated ash (Ash Butterscotch) top, laminated mahogany back and sides (Vintage Sunburst finish) or laminated ash back and sides (Ash Butterscotch), round soundhole with herringbone rosette, herringbone body binding, set soft V-shaped mahogany (Vintage Sunburst finish) or maple (Ash Butterscotch) neck, bound 14/20-fret rosewood fingerboard with diamond inlays and 12th fret Loyalty inlay, 1970s-style bound Fender headstock with black overlay (Vintage Sunburst finish) or natural overlay (Ash Butterscotch finish), three-per-side chrome tuners, rosewood bridge, tortoise (Vintage Sunburst finish) or gold (Ash Butterscotch finish) pickguard, Fishman Isys III pickup/electronics, available in Ash Butterscotch or Vintage Sunburst finish, 25.3 in. scale, mfg. 2013-present.

| MSR $500 | $350 | $230 - 265 | $115 - 140 | |

TERRI CLARK SIGNATURE (NO. 095-8105) – slope-shouldered dreadnought-style body, AA solid spruce top, solid rosewood back and sides, scalloped X bracing, round soundhole with abalone rosette, multi-layer binding, mahogany neck, 14/20-fret rosewood fingerboard with abalone dots and 12th fret "F" inlays, stylized abalone and pearl "TC" and Fender logo headstock inlay, three-per-side chrome tuners, rosewood bridge, black bridge pins with abalone dots, tortoise pickguard, Fishman Matrix Natural I electronics, available in Natural finish, 25.3 in. scale, case included, mfg. summer 2008 only.

| | N/A | $450 - 525 | $275 - 325 | $1,000 |

MSR/NOTES	100%	EXCELLENT	AVERAGE	LAST MSR

TIM ARMSTRONG HELLCAT ACOUSTIC (NO. 096-8300) – concert-style body, solid mahogany top, laminated mahogany back and sides, Fender advanced scalloped bracing, round soundhole with decorative rosette, cream body bindings, maple neck, 14/20-fret rosewood fingerboard with Hellcat and 12th fret Double Skull inlays, black headstock overlay with large Fender logo, Tim Armstrong Signature truss rod cover, three-per-side vintage Fender-style tuners with cream plastic buttons, rosewood vintage-style Fender Viking bridge with compensated saddle, black bridge pins with white dots, four-ply tortoise shell pickguard, Fender FTE3-TN pickup and active electronics with three-band EQ and chromatic tuner, availalbe in Natural Satin finish, 25.3 in. scale, Tim Armstrong "Let's Go" strap included, mfg. spring 2009-present.

MSR $450	$300	$175 - 225	$110 - 140

Tim Armstrong Hellcat Acoustic 12-String (No. 096-8312) – similar to the Tim Armstrong Hellcat Acoustic, except in 12-string configuration with six-per-side tuners, available in Natural Satin finish, mfg. 2013-present.

MSR $600	$400	$225 - 275	$135 - 170

»*Tim Armstrong Hellcat Acoustic 12-String Left-Handed (No. 096-8313)* – similar to the Tim Armstrong Hellcat Acoustic 12-String, except in left-handed configuration, available in Natural Satin finish, mfg. spring 2009-present.

MSR $650	$450	$250 - 300	$150 - 190

Tim Armstrong Hellcat Acoustic Left-Handed (No. 096-8320) – similar to the Tim Armstrong Hellcat Acoustic, except in left-handed configuration, availalbe in Natural Satin finish, mfg. spring 2009-present.

MSR $530	$380	$200 - 250	$120 - 150

TIM ARMSTRONG HELLCAT DELUXE (NO. 096-8314) – concert-style body, solid mahogany top, laminated mahogany back and sides, Fender advanced scalloped bracing, round soundhole with 70s F-style rosette, cream body bindings, maple neck, 14/20-fret rosewood fingerboard with pearl dot inlays, black headstock overlay with large Fender logo, Tim Armstrong Signature truss rod cover, three-per-side vintage Fender-style tuners with cream plastic buttons, rosewood vintage-style Fender Viking bridge with compensated saddle, black bridge pins with white dots, four-ply tortoise shell pickguard, Fishman Neo-D soundhole system electronics, availalbe in Natural Satin finish, 25.3 in. scale, Tim Armstrong "Let's Go" strap and tolex case with gold interior included, mfg. 2013-present.

MSR $700	$450	$250 - 300	$150 - 190

Tim Armstrong Hellcat Deluxe Left-Handed (No. 096-8315) – similar to the Tim Armstrong Hellcat Deluxe, except in left-handed configuration, availalbe in Natural Satin finish, mfg. 2013-present.

MSR $800	$550	$275 - 350	$150 - 200

VINCE RAY "UNLUCKY 13" (NO. 096-9910) – single cutaway dreadnought-style body, laminated spruce top, laminated mahogany back and sides, scalloped X bracing, round soundhole with pinstriping design rosette, multi-ply ivory color body binding, nato neck, 14/20-fret ivory-bound rosewood fingerboard with 12th fret "F" in a diamond pinstriping motif inlay by Vince Ray, black headstock overlay with Fender logo and pinstriping motif inlay, three-per-side chrome tuners, rosewood bridge, black bridge pins with white dots, white pickguard with Vince Ray graphics, Fender FTE-3TN electronics, available in Black finish with "Unlucky 13" Hot Rod graphics and pinstriping, 25.3 in. scale, mfg. summer 2008 only.

	N/A	$200 - 250	$120 - 150	$450

VINCE RAY VOODOO BUCKET 300CE (NO. 096-8078) – single cutaway dreadnought-style body, laminated spruce top, laminated mahogany back and sides, scalloped X bracing, round soundhole with Vince Ray design rosette, multi-ply ivory body binding, set C-shaped mahogany neck, 14/20-fret bound rosewood fingerboard with dot inlays and 12th fret "F" logo inlay, matching finish headstock overlay with Fender logo and Voodoo graphics, three-per-side chrome tuners, Viking-style rosewood bridge, white bridge pins with black dots, Fishman Isys III electronics, available in custom Vince Ray Voodoo graphics finish, 25.3 in. scale, mfg. 2013-present.

MSR $500	$350	$200 - 250	$120 - 150

ACOUSTIC: SPRINGHILL (LS/SB) SERIES

Springhill Series models were produced in Spring Hill, TN.

LS-10 – dreadnought style, solid spruce top, round soundhole, tortoiseshell pickguard, mahogany back/sides/neck, 14/20-fret bound rosewood fingerboard with pearl dot inlay, rosewood bridge with black pearl dot pins, ebony veneered peghead with pearl logo inlay, three-per-side chrome tuners, available in Natural finish, mfg. 1994-95.

	N/A	$875 - 1,000	$525 - 600	$1,700

LS-20 (NO. 095-4000) – similar to LS-10, except has rosewood back/sides, ebony fingerboard/bridge, gold tuners, mfg. 1994-95.

	N/A	$1,050 - 1,200	$650 - 750	$2,075

• **Add $200 for Fishman electronics and left-handed configuration LS-20LH (Model 095-4020-320)**

LS-30 – similar to LS-10, except has figured maple back/sides, ebony fingerboard/bridge, bound peghead, gold tuners, mfg. 1994-95.

	N/A	$950 - 1,100	$550 - 650	$2,000

LS-40C – single sharp cutaway dreadnought style, solid spruce top, round soundhole, tortoiseshell pickguard, mahogany back/sides/neck, 14/20-fret bound rosewood fingerboard with pearl dot inlay, rosewood bridge with black pearl dot pins, ebony veneered peghead with pearl logo inlay, three-per-side chrome tuners, available in Natural finish, disc. 1994.

	N/A	$950 - 1,100	$550 - 650	$1,900

MSR/NOTES	100%	EXCELLENT	AVERAGE	LAST MSR

LS-50C – similar to LS-40C, except has rosewood back/sides, ebony fingerboard/bridge, gold tuners, disc. 1994.

	N/A	$1,050 - 1,200	$650 - 750	$2,100

LS-60C – similar to LS-40C, except has figured maple back/sides, ebony fingerboard/bridge, bound peghead, gold tuners, disc. 1994.

	N/A	$1,100 - 1,250	$650 - 750	$2,200

SB-15 (NO. 095-4515) – jumbo style, solid spruce top, round soundhole, tortoise pickguard, mahogany back/sides/neck, 14/20-fret bound rosewood fingerboard with pearl dot inlay, rosewood bridge with black pearl dot pins, ebony veneered peghead with pearl logo inlay, three-per-side chrome tuners, available in Natural or Sunburst finish, mfg. 1994-96.

	N/A	$875 - 1,000	$525 - 600	$1,875

SB-25 (NO. 095-4525) – similar to SB-15, except has rosewood back/sides, ebony fingerboard/bridge, gold tuners, mfg. 1994-96.

	N/A	$950 - 1,100	$600 - 700	$2,075

SB-35 (NO. 095-4535) – similar to SB-15, except has figured maple back/sides, ebony fingerboard/bridge, bound peghead, gold tuners, mfg. 1994-96.

	N/A	$900 - 1,050	$550 - 650	$2,175

SB-45C (NO. 095-4545) – single sharp cutaway jumbo style, solid spruce top, round soundhole, tortoiseshell pickguard, mahogany back/sides/neck, 14/20-fret bound rosewood fingerboard with pearl dot inlay, rosewood bridge with black pearl dot pins, ebony veneered peghead with pearl logo inlay, three-per-side chrome tuners, available in Natural finish, mfg. 1994-96.

	N/A	$900 - 1,050	$550 - 650	$2,075

SB-55C (NO. 095-4555) – similar to SB-45C, except has rosewood back/sides, ebony fingerboard/bridge, gold tuners, mfg. 1994-96.

	N/A	$1,000 - 1,150	$600 - 700	$2,275

SB-65C (NO. 095-4565) – similar to SB-45C, except has figured maple back/sides, ebony fingerboard/bridge, bound peghead, gold tuners, mfg. 1994-96.

	N/A	$1,050 - 1,200	$600 - 700	$2,375

ACOUSTIC: STANDARD (F) SERIES

The Standard Series was introduced in 1982 after most of the F-Series models were disc. The Standard Series feature a swooping style headstock. There are several other Standard models including the F-240A, F-250, F-260S, F-265C, F-270SCE, F-310-12, F-330-12, F-360S-12, and classical models FC-100, FC-110, FC-120, and FC-130S.

F-200 – grand concert style, spruce top, mahogany back and sides, 14/20-fret rosewood with dot inlay, Natural finish, mfg. 1982-88.

	N/A	$120 - 150	$75 - 95	$245

F-210 – dreadnought style, spruce top, mahogany back and sides, 14/20-fret rosewood with dot inlay, Natural finish, mfg. 1982-88.

	N/A	$125 - 150	$75 - 95	$265

Also available in left-hand configuration.

* **F-210S** – similar to the F-210, except has a solid spruce top, mfg. 1988-1990.

	N/A	$140 - 180	$90 - 110	$325

F-220SB – dreadnought style, spruce top, mahogany back and sides, 14/20-fret rosewood with diamond inlay, tortoise pickguard, Sunburst finish, mfg. 1982-88.

	N/A	$120 - 150	$75 - 95	$275

F-230 – dreadnought style, spruce top, rosewood back and sides, 14/20-fret rosewood with dot inlay, Natural finish, mfg. 1982-88.

	N/A	$140 - 180	$90 - 110	$325

* **F-230CE** – similar to the F-230, except has a single cutaway and electronics, mfg. 1988-1990.

	N/A	$170 - 210	$100 - 130	$425

ACOUSTIC: SX SERIES

600 SX (NO. 095-0600) – dreadnought style, spruce top, round soundhole, tortoise pickguard, five-stripe bound body/rosette, nato back/sides/neck, 14/20-fret rosewood fingerboard with pearl dot inlay, rosewood bridge with white black dot pins, rosewood veneered peghead with pearl logo inlay, three-per-side chrome tuners, available in Natural finish, mfg. 1994-95.

	N/A	$150 - 200	$95 - 125	$449

800 SX (NO. 095-0800) – similar to 600 SX, except has rosewood back/sides, gold hardware, mfg. 1994-95.

	N/A	$175 - 225	$110 - 140	$519

1000 SX (NO. 095-1000) – dreadnought style, solid spruce top, round soundhole, three-stripe bound body/rosette, mahogany back/sides/neck, 14/20-fret rosewood fingerboard with pearl dot inlay, strings through rosewood bridge, bound rosewood veneered peghead with pearl logo inlay, three-per-side chrome tuners, available in Natural finish, mfg. 1992-95.

	N/A	$300 - 350	$150 - 200	$709

MSR/NOTES	100%	EXCELLENT	AVERAGE	LAST MSR

1100 SX (NO. 095-1100) – similar to 1000 SX, except has rosewood back/sides, ebony fingerboard/bridge, gold tuners, mfg. 1992-95.

| | N/A | $350 - 400 | $175 - 225 | $819 |

1105 SXE (NO. 095-1105) – dreadnought style, solid spruce top, round soundhole, three-stripe bound body/rosette, mahogany neck, rosewood back/sides, 14/20-fret ebony fingerboard with pearl dot inlay, strings through ebony bridge, bound rosewood veneered peghead with pearl logo inlay, three-per-side gold tuners, piezo pickup, volume/treble/bass/mix controls, available in Natural finish, mfg. 1992-95.

| | N/A | $400 - 475 | $200 - 250 | $882 |

1200 SX (NO. 095-1200) – dreadnought style, solid spruce top, round soundhole, three-stripe bound body/rosette, mahogany back/sides/neck, 14/20-fret rosewood fingerboard with pearl dot inlay, strings through rosewood bridge, bound rosewood veneered peghead with pearl logo inlay, three-per-side chrome tuners, available in Natural finish, mfg. 1992-95.

| | N/A | $425 - 500 | $225 - 275 | $964 |

1300 SX (NO. 095-1300) – similar to 1200 SX, except has rosewood back/sides, ebony fingerboard with pearl snowflake inlay, ebony bridge, gold tuners, mfg. 1992-95.

| | N/A | $550 - 650 | $275 - 325 | $1,173 |

1500 SX (NO. 095-1500) – jumbo style, solid spruce top, round soundhole, black pickguard, rosewood back/sides, mahogany neck, 14/20-fret rosewood fingerboard with pearl block inlay, strings through rosewood bridge, bound rosewood veneered peghead with pearl logo inlay, three-per-side gold tuners, available in Natural finish, mfg. 1992-95.

| | N/A | $475 - 550 | $225 - 275 | $964 |

1505 SX (NO. 095-1505) – similar to 1500 SX, except has sycamore back/sides, available in Sunburst Top finish, mfg. 1992-95.

| | N/A | $525 - 600 | $275 - 325 | $1,015 |

1600 SXE (NO. 095-1600) – jumbo style, solid spruce top, round soundhole, black pickguard, rosewood back/sides, mahogany neck, 14/20-fret rosewood fingerboard with pearl block inlay, strings through rosewood bridge, bound rosewood veneered peghead with pearl logo inlay, three-per-side gold tuners, piezo pickup, volume/treble/bass/mix controls, available in Natural finish, mfg. 1993-95.

| | N/A | $550 - 650 | $300 - 350 | $1,066 |

2100 SX (NO. 095-2100) – single round cutaway classic style, solid cedar top, round soundhole, five-stripe bound body, wood inlay rosette, ovangkol back/sides, nato neck, 19-fret rosewood fingerboard, rosewood bridge, rosewood veneered peghead, three-per-side gold tuners with pearloid buttons, available in Natural finish, mfg. 1994-95.

| | N/A | $375 - 450 | $225 - 275 | $679 |

ACOUSTIC: T-BUCKET SERIES

T-BUCKET 100CE (NO. 096-8075) – single cutaway dreadnought-style body, laminated spruce top, laminated mahogany back and sides, scalloped X bracing, round soundhole with pinstriping design rosette, multi-ply body binding, set C-shaped mahogany neck, 14/20-fret rosewood fingerboard with dot inlays and 12th fret "F" logo inlay, black headstock overlay with Fender logo and pinstriping motif inlay, three-per-side chrome tuners, rosewood bridge, white bridge pins with black dots, Fishman Isys III pickup/electronics, available in 3-Color Sunburst finish, 25.3 in. scale, mfg. 2013-present.

| MSR $400 | $250 | $165 - 190 | $80 - 100 | |

T-BUCKET 200 (NO. 096-8050) – orchestra-style body, laminated figured ash top, laminated ash back and sides, scalloped X bracing, round soundhole with pinstriping design rosette, multi-ply ivory body binding, nato neck, 14/20-fret ivory-bound rosewood fingerboard with 12th fret "F" in a diamond pinstriping motif inlay by Vince Ray, black headstock overlay with Fender logo and pinstriping motif inlay, three-per-side chrome tuners, rosewood bridge, white bridge pins with black dots, available in Trans. Violet finish, 25.2 in. scale, mfg. summer 2008-09.

| | N/A | $140 - 180 | $85 - 110 | $360 |

T-BUCKET 200CE (NO. 096-8052/8080) – single cutaway folk-style body, laminated flame maple top, laminated mahogany back and sides, scalloped X bracing, round soundhole with pinstriping design (2013 only) or holographic (2013-present) rosette, multi-ply ivory body binding, mahogany neck, 14/20-fret ivory-bound rosewood fingerboard with dot inlays and 12th fret "F" in a diamond pinstriping motif inlay by Vince Ray (2012 only) or regular "F" logo inlay (2013-present), black headstock overlay with Fender logo and pinstriping motif inlay, three-per-side chrome tuners, rosewood bridge, white bridge pins with black dots, available in Trans. Black finish, 25.3 in. scale, mfg. 2012-present.

| MSR $450 | $300 | $175 - 225 | $110 - 140 | |

T-BUCKET 300 (NO. 096-8051) – orchestra-style body, laminated quilted maple top, laminated mahogany back and sides, scalloped X bracing, round soundhole with pinstriping design rosette, multi-ply ivory body binding, nato neck, 14/20-fret ivory-bound rosewood fingerboard with 12th fret "F" in a diamond pinstriping motif inlay by Vince Ray, black headstock overlay with Fender logo and pinstriping motif inlay, three-per-side chrome tuners, rosewood bridge, white bridge pins with black dots, available in Amber finish, 25.2 in. scale, mfg. summer 2008-09.

| | N/A | $140 - 180 | $85 - 110 | $360 |

* *T-Bucket 300 CE Cutaway Electric (No. 096-8005/8079)* – similar to the T-Bucket 300, except has a single cutaway, laminated flame maple (Trans. Black and Trans. Blue finishes), laminated quilted maple (3-Color Sunburst and Amber finishes), or laminated quilt ash (new 2013, Trans. Dark Brown or Trans. Violet), and Fender FTE-3TN electronics, available in 3-Color Sunburst, Amber, Trans. Black, Trans. Blue, Trans. Dark Brown (2013-present), or Trans. Violet (2013-present) finish, mfg. summer 2008-present.

| MSR $450 | $300 | $175 - 225 | $110 - 140 | |

In 2013, this model was upgraded with a holographic rosette, regular 12th fret "F" logo inlay, and a Graphtech Nubone nut and compensated bridge saddle.

MSR/NOTES	100%	EXCELLENT	AVERAGE	LAST MSR

T-BUCKET 400 CE (NO. 096-8055/8076) – single cutaway dreadnought-style body, laminated flame maple top, back, and sides, scalloped X bracing, round soundhole with pinstriping design (2011-12) or holographic (2013-present) rosette, multi-ply ivory body binding, mahogany neck, 14/20-fret ivory-bound rosewood fingerboard with 12th fret "F" in a diamond pinstriping motif inlay by Vince Ray (2011-12) or regular "F" logo inlay (2013-present), flame maple matching finish headstock overlay with Fender logo and pinstriping motif inlay, three-per-side chrome tuners, rosewood bridge, white bridge pins with black dots, Fishman Isys III electronics, available in Natural finish, 25.2 in. scale, mfg. 2011-present.

| MSR $550 | $350 | $200 - 250 | $120 - 150 | |

ACOUSTIC: MISC. MODELS

D'AQUISTO MASTERBUILT ULTRA ACOUSTIC (U.S. MFG., NO. 010-2070) – Single round cutaway hollow figured maple body (17 in.width), arched bound spruce top, bound f-holes, set-in maple neck, raised bound ebony pickguard, 22-fret bound ebony fingerboard with pearl block inlay, adjustable ebony bridge/ebony trapeze tailpiece, bound peghead with pearl fan/logo inlay, three-per-side gold tuners with ebony buttons, available in Antique Burst and Natural finish, mfg. 1994-2001.

| | N/A | $7,000 - 8,500 | $4,000 - 5,000 | $15,030 |

* Add $250 for pickguard mounted custom Kent Armstrong floating pickup (with volume and tone controls) as Model 010-2080 (last MSR $15,530).

FA-100 (NO. 095-0816) – dreadnought-style body, laminated spruce top, laminated agathis back and sides, X bracing, round soundhole with multi-ring rosette, black/white body binding, laminated agathis neck, 14/20-fret rosewood fingerboard with white dot inlays, three-per-side chrome tuners, rosewood bridge, available in Natural finish, 25.3 in. scale, includes gig bag, mfg. 2012-present.

| MSR $170 | $100 | $50 - 75 | $30 - 40 | |

FA-100 Pack (No. 095-0815) – similar to the FA-100, except includes an electronic tuner and stap as part of a package, mfg. 2012-present.

| MSR $200 | $130 | $70 - 95 | $40 - 55 | |

FA-125S PACK (NO. 095-0870) – folk-style body, solid spruce top, laminated mahogany back and sides, scalloped X bracing, round soundhole with multi-ring rosette, black/white body binding, nato neck, 14/20-fret rosewood fingerboard with white dot inlays, three-per-side chrome tuners, rosewood bridge, available in Natural finish, 25.3 in. scale, includes gig bag, tuner, strings, string winder, picks, and instructional booklet, mfg. 2009-2012.

| | $200 | $120 - 150 | $75 - 95 | $350 |

FA-130 ACOUSTIC/ELECTRIC PACK (NO. 095-0810) – single cutaway concert-style body, laminated spruce top, laminated basswood back and sides, X bracing, round soundhole with multi-ring rosette, aged body binding, nato neck, 14/20-fret aged bound rosewood fingerboard with white dot inlays, matching finish headstock overlay with gold logo, three-per-side chrome tuners, rosewood bridge, black pickguard, Fishman Ion T pickup and electronics with chromatic tuner, available in Black finish, 25.3 in. scale, includes Fender SA-10 acoustic guitar amplifier, gig bag, cable, strap, strings, string winder, picks, and instructional DVD, mfg. summer 2009-present.

| MSR $400 | $250 | $140 - 180 | $85 - 110 | |

KINGMAN "C" USA (NO. 096-0213) – dreadnought-style body, solid Englemann spruce top, solid mahogany back and sides, forward-shifted scalloped X bracing, round soundhole with checkered rosette, aged white body binding, maple vintage C-shaped neck with rolled edges, 14/20-fret aged white-bound rosewood fingerboard with dot inlays, Stratocaster-style headstock, six-on-one-side nickel tuners, rosewood bridge, Fishman Matrix Infinity electronics with volume and tone controls, available in Fiesta Red finish, 25.625 in. scale, deluxe hardshell tolex case, leather strap, and certificate of authenticity included, mfg. 2012-present.

| MSR $2,660 | $1,900 | $1,150 - 1,425 | $700 - 875 | |

KINGMAN USA SELECT (NO. 096-0211) – dreadnought-style body, solid Englemann spruce top, solid mahogany back and sides, forward-shifted scalloped X bracing, round soundhole with checkered rosette, aged white body binding, maple vintage V-shaped neck, 14/20-fret aged white-bound rosewood fingerboard with dot inlays, Stratocaster-style headstock with maple overlay, six-on-one-side nickel tuners, rosewood bridge, three-ply gold pickguard, Fishman Sonitone electronics with volume and tone controls, available in 3-Color Sunburst finish, 25.625 in. scale, deluxe hardshell tolex case, leather strap, and certificate of authenticity included, mfg. 2012-present.

| MSR $2,450 | $1,800 | $1,100 - 1,350 | $650 - 825 | |

MA-1 (NO. 094-0100-021) – 3/4 scale mini-acoustic, Laminated Agathis top, back, and sides, Nato neck with rosewood fingerboard, chrome, open-gear tuners, 18 frets, 23.3 in. scale, available in Natural finish, disc. 2001.

| | N/A | $50 - 70 | $25 - 35 | $150 |

In 2001 this model became part of the Squier line. See Squier for current mfg.

MA-1 3/4 STEEL (NO. 096-3001) – 3/4-sized Grand Concert body, laminated agathis top, laminated sapele back and sides, round soundhole with multi-ring rosette, nato neck, 12/18-fret rosewood fingerboard with dot inlays, three-per-side chrome tuners, rosewood bridge, available in Natural finish, 23.3 in. scale, mfg. 2012-present.

| MSR $220 | $130 | $70 - 90 | $45 - 55 | |

Prior to 2012, this model was offered in the Squier line.

MA-2 (NO. 094-0200-021) – similar to MA-1, except has laminated spruce top, 20 frets, chrome, covered tuners, rosewood bridge, Compensated Urea saddle, multi-ABS inlays on soundhole and body edge, black neck binding, available in Natural finish, mfg. 1999-2000.

| | N/A | $60 - 85 | $40 - 60 | $189 |

MSR/NOTES	100%	EXCELLENT	AVERAGE	LAST MSR

MC-1 3/4 NYLON (NO. 096-3000) – 3/4-sized classical-style body, laminated agathis top, laminated sapele back and sides, round soundhole with multi-ring rosette, nato neck, 12/18-fret rosewood fingerboard with dot inlays, slotted headstock, three-per-side open-style chrome tuners with pearloid buttons, rosewood bridge, available in Natural finish, 23.3 in. scale, mfg. 2012-present.

MSR $220	$130	$70 - 90	$45 - 55	

Prior to 2012, this model was offered in the Squier line.

MOAI MADNESS TIKI (NO. 096-9903) – single cutaway dreadnought style, spruce top, mahogany back and sides, round soundhole with rings, nato neck, 14/20-fret rosewood fingerboard with dot and 12th fret Tiki mask inlay, three-per-side tuners, rosewood bridge, small black pickguard, Fishman Mini-Q electronics, chrome hardware, available in Tiki Blue finish with Moai Madness Tiki graphics, 25.5 in. scale, made in China, limited run of 600 guitars, mfg. fall 2007 only.

	N/A	$250 - 300	$135 - 175	$571

TIKI-COUSTIC FEMME FATALE LIMITED EDITION (NO. 096-9900) – single cutaway dreadnought style, spruce top, mahogany back and sides, round soundhole with rings, mahogany neck, 14/20-fret rosewood fingerboard with 12th fret Tiki inlay, three-per-side tuners, rosewood bridge, small black pickguard, Fishman Mini-Q electronics, chrome hardware, available in Natural finish, 25.5 in. scale, made in China, limited mfg. first quarter of 2007 only.

	N/A	$250 - 300	$135 - 175	$571

TIKI-COUSTIC MONKEY BUSINESS LIMITED EDITION (NO. 096-9901) – dreadnought style, spruce top, mahogany back and sides, round soundhole with rings, mahogany neck, 14/20-fret rosewood fingerboard with dot inlays, black headstock with three-per-side chrome tuners, rosewood bridge, Fishman Mini-Q electronics, available in Black finish, 25.5 in. scale, made in China, limited mfg. second quarter of 2007 only.

	N/A	$250 - 300	$135 - 175	$571

TIKI UNIQUIET VILLAGE (NO. 096-9902) – single cutaway dreadnought style, spruce top, mahogany back and sides, round soundhole with rings, nato neck, 14/20-fret rosewood fingerboard with dot and 12th fret Tiki mask inlay, three-per-side tuners, rosewood bridge, small black pickguard, Fishman Mini-Q electronics, chrome hardware, available in Tiki Green finish with Tiki graphics, 25.5 in. scale, made in China, limited run of 600 guitars, mfg. summer 2007 only.

	N/A	$250 - 300	$135 - 175	$571

TRAVEL GUITAR TG-4S (NO. 095-0040-321) – travel size acoustic model, solid spruce top, Nato back, sides and neck, rosewood fingerboard with dot position markers, three-per-side chrome covered tuners, comes with gig bag, available in Natural finish, mfg. 2000-08.

	N/A	$120 - 150	$70 - 95	$300

ACOUSTIC ELECTRIC: ELECTRACOUSTIC SERIES

ACOUSTASONIC STRATOCASTER (MEX. MFG. NO. 013-9700) – alder hollow body, oval oblong soundhole, maple M-Shaped neck, 22-fret rosewood fingerboard with dot inlay, six-on-one-side tuners, rosewood bridge, three in-bridge Piezo pickups, no pickguard, three knobs, chrome hardware, available in Crimson Red Trans., Ebony Trans., Pewter, or Sapphire Blue Trans., finish, mfg. 2004-09.

	N/A	$500 - 575	$325 - 375	$1,100

JZM DELUXE (NO. 096-7700) – acoustic Jazzmaster/Jaguar-style body, spruce top, solid mahogany back, laminated mahogany sides, oval soundhole, maple Jazzmaster/Jaguar neck, 21-fret rosewood fingerboard with dot inlays, Jazzmaster/Jaguar-style headstock with six-on-one side tuners, rosewood bridge, interchangeable black, white, and tortoiseshell pickguards, single exposed Telecaster pickup, Fishman Classic IV MB electronics, chrome hardware, available in Sunburst or Trans. Amber finish, 25.5 in. scale, made in South Korea, mfg. 2007-09.

	N/A	$375 - 450	$225 - 275	$900

STRATACOUSTIC (NO. 095-7400) – solid spruce top, double cutaway design, state-of-the-art one-piece fiberglass body, bolt-on neck with rosewood fingerboard, dot position markers, thinline body, trademark Stratocaster style headstock, Fender Fishman Classic 4 Preamp, die-cast tuners, available in Black or Olympic White finish, mfg. 2000-05.

	N/A	$150 - 200	$95 - 120	$429

This model was discontinued as a Fender brand and reintroduced as a Squier (see section).

STRATACOUSTIC DELUXE (NO. 096-7400) – acoustic Stratocaster-style body, spruce top, solid mahogany back, laminated mahogany sides, oval soundhole, maple Stratocaster neck, 21-fret rosewood fingerboard with dot inlays, Strat-style headstock with six-on-one side tuners, rosewood bridge, interchangeable black, white, and tortoiseshell pickguards, single exposed Telecaster pickup, Fishman Classic IV MB electronics, chrome hardware, available in Black or Sunburst finish, 25.5 in. scale, made in South Korea, mfg. 2007-09.

	N/A	$375 - 450	$225 - 275	$900

STANDARD STRATACOUSTIC (NO. 096-7300) – acoustic Stratocaster-style body, laminated spruce top, one-piece fiberglass back and sides, X bracing, oval soundhole, C-shaped maple neck, 21-fret rosewood fingerboard with dot inlays, Strat-style headstock with six-on-one side chrome tuners, rosewood bridge, BG3-TN electronics with volume, bass, mid, and treble controls and a built-in tuner, available in Black or Walnut Stain (2009 only) finish, 25.5 in. scale, made in South Korea, mfg. 2009-present.

MSR $400	$280	$150 - 190	$95 - 120	

MSR/NOTES	100%	EXCELLENT	AVERAGE	LAST MSR

TELECOUSTIC STANDARD – single round cutaway style, spruce top, oval soundhole, basswood back/sides, maple neck, 22-fret rosewood fingerboard, rosewood bridge with white pins, six-per-side chrome tuners with plastic buttons, piezo bridge pickup, volume/treble/bass slide controls, available in Antique Burst, Black, or Natural finish, mfg. 1993-95.

	N/A	$425 - 500	$300 - 350	$960

* *Telecoustic Custom* – similar to Telecoustic Standard, except has bound solid spruce top, mahogany back/sides/neck, pau ferro fingerboard, pau ferro/ebony laminate bridge, Schaller tuners with pearl buttons, active electronics, available in Antique Burst and Natural finish, mfg. 1993-95.

	N/A	$775 - 900	$475 - 550	$2,150

* *Telecoustic Deluxe* – similar to Telecoustic Standard, except has mahogany back/sides/neck, rosewood/ebony laminate bridge, pearl tuner buttons, mfg. 1993-95.

	N/A	$550 - 650	$350 - 400	$1,160

TELECOUSTIC (NO. 095-7500) – solid spruce top, single cutaway, state-of-the-art one-piece fiberglass body, bolt-on neck with rosewood fingerboard, dot position markers, thinline body, trademark Telecaster headstock design, die-cast tuners, Fender Fishman Classic 4 Preamp, available in Inca Silver, Sunburst (2002-05), Natural (2002-05), or Candy Apple Red finish, mfg. 2000-05.

	N/A	$150 - 200	$95 - 120	$429

This model was discontinued as a Fender brand and reintroduced as a Squier (see section).

TELECOUSTIC DELUXE (NO. 096-7500) – acoustic Telecaster-style body, spruce top, solid mahogany back, laminated mahogany sides, oval soundhole, maple Telecaster neck, 21-fret rosewood fingerboard with dot inlays, Telecaster-style headstock with six-on-one side tuners, rosewood bridge, interchangeable black, white, and tortoiseshell pickguards, single exposed Telecaster pickup, Fishman Classic IV MB electronics, chrome hardware, available in Candy Apple Red or Sunburst finish, 25.5 in. scale, made in South Korea, mfg. 2007-09.

	N/A	$375 - 450	$225 - 275	$900

STANDARD TELECOUSTIC (NO. 096-7310) – acoustic Telecaster-style body, laminated spruce top, one-piece fiberglass back and sides, X bracing, oval soundhole, C-shaped maple neck, 21-fret rosewood fingerboard with dot inlays, Tele-style headstock with six-on-one side chrome tuners, rosewood bridge, BG3-TN electronics with volume, bass, mid, and treble controls and a built-in tuner, available in Black or Walnut Stain (2009 only) finish, 25.5 in. scale, made in South Korea, mfg. 2009-present.

MSR $400	$280	$150 - 190	$95 - 120	

ACOUSTIC ELECTRIC BASS

BG-29 (NO. 095-2900-021) – slimline dreadnought style with cutaway design, maple top, round soundhole, maple back/sides, 14/20-fret rosewood fingerboard, rosewood bridge, two-per-side chrome die-cast tuners, Fishman Acoustic Matrix pickup, onboard preamp, volume/three-band EQ/mid-sweep controls, available in Gloss Black (1997-present) or Natural Satin (1995-2007) finish, gig bag included, mfg. 1995-2008.

	N/A	$350 - 425	$225 - 275	$800

BG-31 (NO. 095-3100) – non-cutaway design, laminated spruce top, laminated mahogany back/sides, rosewood fingerboard with dot inlays, chrome die-cast tuners, two-per-side tuners, Piezo with APC-Pro Pre-Amp, available in Candy Apple Red (2003-06) or Metallic Black finish, 32 in. scale, mfg. 2003-2011.

	$400	$225 - 275	$125 - 165	$550

BG-32 (NO. 095-3200) – non-cutaway design, spruce top, mahogany back and sides, rosewood fingerboard with dot position markers, chrome die-cast tuners, two-per-side tuners, Fishman Classic 4 Preamp and pickup, Natural Satin finish, mfg. 2000-08.

	N/A	$300 - 350	$175 - 225	$650

CB-100CE BASS (NO. 096-1560) – single cutaway dreadnought-style body, laminated spruce top, laminated mahogany back and sides, scalloped X bracing, round soundhole with MOP acrylic design rosette, mulit-ply body binding, set maple Jazz Bass profile neck, 17/22-fret rosewood fingerboard with pearl dot inlays, traditional headstock, two-per-side chrome tuners, rosewood bridge, black pickguard, Fishman Isys III pickup/electronics, available in Natural finish, 34 in. scale, mfg. 2013-present.

MSR $450	$300	$170 - 210	$100 - 120	

GB-41 SCE (NO. 095-4105) – single cutaway solid mahogany body, solid AA spruce top, mahogany neck, 24-fret rosewood fingerboard with dot inlays, two-per-side Hipshot chrome tuners, Fishman Classic 4 with ACLR pickup and electronics, available in Natural finish, mfg. 2003-09.

	N/A	$450 - 525	$300 - 350	$1,050

KINGMAN BASS SCE (NO. 096-8200/8603) – single cutaway Kingman-style bass dreadnought body, solid spruce top, laminated mahogany back and sides, special acoustic bass X bracing, round soundhole with checkerboard rosette, mulitple body binding, maple Jazz Bass C-shaped neck, 15/20-fret aged binding rosewood fingerboard with pearl block inlays, Jazz Bass headstock, four-on-one-side chrome tuners, rosewood bridge, vintage-inspired gold pickguard, Fishman Sonicore pickup, Fishman Aero electronics with three-band EQ and electronic tuner, available in Natural finish, 34 in. scale, mfg. summer 2009-present.

MSR $730	$530	$275 - 325	$160 - 200	

MSR/NOTES	100%	EXCELLENT	AVERAGE	LAST MSR

T-BUCKET BASS (NO. 096-8009) – grand concert-style bass body, laminated flame maple top, laminated mahogany back and sides, special acoustic bass X bracing, round soundhole with inlaid pinstriping rosette, ivory body binding, mahogany neck, 15/22-fret ivory-bound rosewood fingerboard with pearl dot inlays and 12th fret inlaid "F" and pinstriping motif inlays, black headstock overlay with Fender logo and pinstriping design inlay, two-per-side chrome tuners, rosewood bridge, Fishman Sonicore pickup, Fishman Isys III system electronics with electronic tuner, available in 3-Tone Sunburst finish, 32 in. scale, mfg. 2012-present.

MSR $550	$400	$225 - 275	$135 - 170	

VICTOR BAILEY SIGNATURE (NO. 095-3300) – single cutaway body, solid spruce top with Dao overlay, round soundhole, abalone rosette, solid dao back/sides/neck, rosewood fingerboard, two-per-side gold Hipshot tuners, Fishman Classic IV electronics, available in Natural finish, 34 in. scale, mfg. 2005-2010.

	$900	$575 - 675	$350 - 425	$1,300

* *Victor Bailey Signature Five-String (No. 095-3305)* – similar to the Victor Bailey Signature, except in five-string configuration with 3/2-per-side tuners, mfg. 2007-2010.

	$1,000	$625 - 725	$375 - 450	$1,400

FERNANDES

Instruments currently produced in Japan, China, Korea, and Taiwan. Distributed by Fernandes Guitars/Kaysound Imports Inc. in Champlain, NY. Fernandes has been producing guitars since 1969.

CONTACT INFORMATION
FERNANDES
5 Coton Lane
Champlain, NY 12919
Phone No.: 800-343-0353
www.fernandesguitars.com
fernandesguitars@kaysound.com

In 1969, Fernandes Company Ltd. (based in Tokyo, Japan) was established to produce quality classical guitars at an affordable price. Over the next twenty years, Fernandes expanded the line and became one of the largest selling guitar manufacturers in the world. Fernandes is the number one selling guitar in Japan, and at times has held as much as 40% of the Japanese market.

In late 1992, Fernandes Company Ltd. began distributing their entire line of guitars to the U.S. market as Fernandes Guitars U.S.A., Inc. Fernandes Company Ltd. uses only the top facilities located in Japan, Taiwan, China, and Korea to produce their guitars. Once the factory is done manufacturing the guitars, they are shipped to the United States where they are inspected and set up again.

Even though Fernandes started out building classical guitars, by the time they were available in the U.S. they had stopped producing them. The first acoustic guitar to show up for Fernandes wasn't until 1997 with the FAA-500. This model evolved into the Reyna, while the Palisade series was introduced in 1999. Fernandes discontinued all acoustic guitars in 2004. In 2006, they reintroduced a small line of Palisade guitars. Up until 2006, Fernandes was distributed by Fernandes Guitars International Inc., in Chatsworth, CA and in 2007, Fernandes Guitars/Kaysound Imports Inc. became the exclusive distributor. For more information, visit Fernandes' website, or contact them directly.

ACOUSTIC: PALISADE SERIES

The Palisade Series was disc. in 2004, but reintroduced in 2006 with three entirely new models.

PALISADE CC50 – classical-style body, rosewood sides/back, solid spruce top, nato neck, 20-fret rosewood fingerboard, rosewood bridge, three-per-side open tuners, under-the-bridge saddles, Piezo pickup, active preamp, four-band EQ, available in Natural finish, mfg. 2001-04.

	N/A	$250 - 300	$135 - 175	$500

PALISADE D30 – dreadnought body, spruce top with "X"-bracing, Sapele back and sides, nato set neck, rosewood fingerboard with dot position markers, 20 medium frets, chrome covered tuners, rosewood bridge, available in Black, Natural, or Dark Red finish, 25.25 in. scale, mfg. 1999-2004.

	N/A	$125 - 150	$60 - 90	$240

* *Palisade D30-12 12-String* – similar to Palisade D30, except in a 12-string configuration, available in Natural finish, mfg. 2000-04.

	N/A	$120 - 150	$65 - 90	$250

PALISADE DC34 – similar to Palisade D30, except has a single cutaway, available in Natural finish, mfg. 1999-2000.

	N/A	$135 - 175	$95 - 125	$339

PALISADE D36 – dreadnought body, solid spruce top, sapele back and sides, nato neck, 20-fret rosewood fingerboard with dot inlay, three-per-side chrome tuners, rosewood bridge, black pickguard, Natural finish, mfg. 2001 only.

	N/A	$130 - 170	$90 - 110	$300

PALISADE D38 – similar to Palisade D30, except has mahogany back and sides, bound body and neck, tortoise pickguard, available in Natural Gloss finish, mfg. 1999-2004.

	N/A	$150 - 200	$90 - 120	$330

PALISADE DC50 – dreadnought body with single cutaway, spruce top with "X"-bracing, mahogany back and sides, nato set neck, piezo pickup under the bridge saddle, volume, bass, middle, treble, chrome die cast tuners, rosewood bridge, available in Natural or Black finish, 25.25 in. scale, mfg. 1999-2004.

	N/A	$150 - 200	$90 - 120	$330

MSR/NOTES	100%	EXCELLENT	AVERAGE	LAST MSR

PALISADE PD16C – single cutaway folk-style body, solid spruce top, mahogany back and sides, black and white ring rosette, contour binding, mahogany neck, 22-fret fingerboard with triangle trapezoid inlays, three-per-side chrome tuners, rosewood bridge, available in Black, Blue Burst, or Natural finish, mfg. 2006-present.

MSR $399	$300	$150 - 200	$90 - 120	

* *Palisade PD16C EQ* – similar to the Palisade PD16C, except has Shadow LC-4 electronics and pickup, mfg. 2006-present.

MSR $449	$350	$175 - 225	$105 - 130	

PALISADE PD18C EQ – single cutaway dreadnought body, solid spruce top, mahogany back and sides, black and white ring rosette, contour binding, mahogany neck, 22-fret fingerboard with triangle trapezoid inlays, three-per-side chrome tuners, rosewood bridge, Shadow electronics and pickup, available in Black, Natural, or Dark Red finish, mfg. 2006-present.

MSR $449	$350	$175 - 225	$105 - 130	

ACOUSTIC: FAA & REYNA SERIES

FAA-400 ACOUSTIC/ELECTRIC – single rounded cutaway body, spruce top, molded back, set-in nato neck, multi-layer binding, 22-fret rosewood fingerboard, rosewood bridge, chrome hardware, three-per-side tuners, bridge mounted piezo pickup, active preamp/three-band EQ, available in Natural finish, 25.25 in. scale, disc. 1998.

	N/A	$250 - 300	$135 - 175	$519

REYNA STANDARD – single cutaway hollowbody, select spruce top, molded back and sides, nato set neck, rosewood fingerboard with dot position markers, 22 frets, three-per-side tuners, piezo pickup mounted under the bridge saddle, volume/tone controls, chrome tuners, rosewood bridge, bound body and neck, available in Black, White, or Vintage Natural finish, mfg. 2000, 2003-04.

	N/A	$90 - 120	$40 - 60	$200

* *Reyna (FAA-500)* – similar to the FAA-400, except features a bound flame maple top, bound neck, active preamp with volume/bass/mid/treble slider controls, available in Three-Tone Sunburst, Black Burst, Cherry Sunburst, or Natural finish, mfg. 1997-98.

	N/A	$200 - 250	$120 - 150	$549

Early versions of the FAA-500 were also available in Antique Sunburst and Greyburst finishes.

* *Reyna Custom* – similar to the Reyna Standard, except has a select spruce top, split trapezoid inlays, and gold hardware, available in See-Thru Black, White, or Cherry Sunburst finish, mfg. 2003-04.

	N/A	$130 - 170	$75 - 100	$300

FERRINGTON, DANNY

Instruments previously built in Santa Monica, CA between 1980 and the early 2000s.

Luthier Danny Ferrington was born and raised in Louisiana. Ferrington's father, Lloyd, was a cabinet maker who had previously played guitar and bass in a local country western combo. Ferrington's first experiences with woodworking were in his father's shop in Monroe, LA.

Ferrington accepted an apprenticeship in 1975 at the Old Time Pickin' Parlour in Nashville, TN. He spent the next five years working with noted acoustic guitar builder Randy Woods. Ferrington's first acoustic was built in 1977, and he continued to hone his craft after that.

In 1980, Ferrington moved to Los Angeles, CA. Ferrington spent a number of years experimenting with different designs, and tones from instruments, and continued building custom guitars. Many of the features on the custom guitars are developed through discussions with the musician commissioning the piece. It is estimated that by 1992, Ferrington had constructed over one hundred custom instruments.

In the late 1980s, the Kramer guitar company was offering several models designed by Ferrington. After Kramer went under, the Ferrington Guitar Company of Long Branch, NJ offered essentially the same models (KFS-1, KFT-1, and KFB-1) with Ferrington on the headstock. These models featured a maple neck, rosewood fingerboard, acoustic body, three-band EQ, and a thinline bridge transducer. Source: Kate Geil, et al, the *Ferrington Guitars Book*.

FINE RESOPHONIC

Instruments currently produced in Vitry Sur Seine, France since 1988.

Luthiers Mike Lewis and Pierre Avocat produce resonator guitars as well as resonator mandolins, ukuleles, and electric resonators. Resonators are available in various configurations including single, tri-cone, and spider bridge models and wood or metal bodies. Custom models are also available. Prices start at €3,500. For more information, visit their website or contact them directly.

CONTACT INFORMATION
FINE RESOPHONIC
3 Voie Coypel
Vitry Sur Seine, 94400 France
Phone No.: 33 (1) 46 77 86 17
Fax No.: 33 (1) 46 77 86 17
www.fineresophonic.com
fine-resophonic@wanadoo.fr

FINOCCHIO GUITARWORKS

Instruments currently produced in Easton, PA.

Luthier Frank Finocchio has been building guitars for over twenty-five years now. He specializes in acoustic, flattop, arch top, and classical instruments. Frank is also known as a teacher of restoring and building guitars. He teaches his workshop four times a year. Frank learned many of his traits from working at Martin Guitars and was a major developer for the DXM guitar. Finocchio is also an authorized Martin repair site. For more information on either Finocchio's workshops or custom built guitars refer to his website.

CONTACT INFORMATION
FINOCCHIO GUITARWORKS
20 South Maple Street
Easton, PA 18042
Phone No.: 610-258-5154
www.finocchioguitar.com
ffino@enter.net

FIRST ACT

Instruments currently produced in Boston, MA and China since 1995. Distributed by First Act of Boston, MA.

First Act Inc. produces a full line of musical instruments ranging from guitars to amplifiers. They produce a line of guitars built in the U.S., a custom shop in the U.S., and a line of guitars built in China. The company's custom products are matched by a commitment to make music more accessible for everyone - challenging the idea that quality instruments have to be expensive and sold in a handful of places. First Act makes it possible for people from all backgrounds to play music. You may also recognize many First Act guitars in 2006-07 model Volkswagons, as they teamed together to sell cars and guitars packaged together. Anybody who bought a Volkswagon model in the last quarter of 2006, got a First Act guitar (matching color) that could be plugged into the VW's aux. input on the radio. In 2007, First Act expanded and moved their custom shop within Boston to allow for more custom instrument production. For more information on First Act or their custom shop instruments, please contact the company directly.

CONTACT INFORMATION
FIRST ACT
745 Boylston Street
Boston, MA 02116
Phone No.: 617-226-7888
Phone No.: 888-551-1551
Fax No.: 617-226-7890
www.firstact.com

FISCHER, PAUL

Acoustic guitars currently produced in Oxfordshire, United Kingdom since 1956.

Luthier Paul Fischer builds fine classical guitars at his studio in the United Kingdom. Fischer started his career in 1956 when he studied under the renowned harpsichord builder Robert Goble. He later took his harpsichord making skills to the guitar and lute maker David Rubio, at the same time extending his making range to early fretted plucked instruments and the modern classical guitar. He remained as manager of the Rubio workshop for six years before establishing his own studio in 1975.

Since then he has become one of England's most prominent classical guitar builders and has built guitars for players including the Assad Brothers, Paulo Bellinati and Jason Vieaux. In 2006, Fischer celebrated his 50th anniversary as an instrument maker with a special classical guitar. For more information, visit Fischer's website.

CONTACT INFORMATION
FISCHER, PAUL
West End Studio, 19 West End
Chipping Norton, Oxfordshire OX7 5EY
United Kingdom
Phone No.: +44 (0)1608 642792
www.paulfischerguitars.com
paul@paulfischerguitars.com

FIVE STAR

Unknown production location and date. See chapter on House Brands.

While this trademark has been identified as a House Brand, the retailer or distributor has not yet been identified. These smaller-bodied acoustics have the logo and star position markers painted on, as opposed to the inlay work of a more expensive guitar. Source: Willie G. Moseley, *Stellas & Stratocasters*.

FLANDERS CUSTOM GUITARS

Instruments previously built in New England between 1979 and the early 2000s. Previously distributed by Fretboard Corner in Lake Ronkonkoma, NY.

Building his first guitar in 1979, Martin Flanders has managed to walk the fine line between old world craftsmanship and modern vision. Flanders gained experience and respect for quality by restoring antique furniture in his father's shop. Living in New England (where select tone woods exist) has afforded Flanders the thrill of harvesting his own stock. Luthier Flanders' business strategy consists of marketing his custom-built guitars at a price customers would expect to pay for a "production" instrument.

Flanders offered several acoustic models including the, **Model 300 Executive**, which is a single cutaway acoustic archtop, the **Soloist**, and the **Bostonian**.

FLEISHMAN INSTRUMENTS

Instruments currently built in Sebastopol, CA. Previously built in Boulder, CO. Fleishman has been building guitars since 1975.

Luthier Harry Fleishman has been designing and building high quality, innovative acoustic guitars and basses since 1975. He is well known for his multi-wood topped guitars, mixing tonewoods to increase the harmonic complexity of his guitars. Harry pioneered the use of multiple scale instruments to retain the sweetness of trebles while increasing the

CONTACT INFORMATION
FLEISHMAN INSTRUMENTS
1533 Welter Ct.
Sebastopol, CA 95472
Phone No.: 707-823-3537
www.fleishmaninstruments.com
hfguitars@gmail.com

clarity and depth of basses. His double soundhole guitars have great depth without boominess. The asymmetry of his designs offers both access to upper frets and increased depth and clarity. Tapered, contoured and scalloped bodies make his guitars comfortable and highly playable. While many luthiers use his ideas, Harry has made good use of the Wechter Access Panel, through which he voices his finished instruments. Harry's work is sought by performers and collectors around the world. He has worked as a consultant to several companies, and has made presentations at many *Guild of American Luthiers* conventions on topics ranging from guitar design to acoustic instrument amplification. He was formerly director of the American School of Lutherie, and is currently director of Luthiers School International. Harry also designs for Fender Musical Instruments Company, Boulder Basses, and Jackson Guitars.

Harry Fleishman builds innovative, unusual acoustic steel-string and nylon guitars. They are for the most part custom, one-of-a-kind instruments. For more information and to view a few of Harry's more than 350 instruments, visit Fleishman's website or contact him directly.

FLETA

Instruments previously built in Barcelona, Spain from 1927 to 1977.

Luthier Ignacio Fleta (1897-1977) built classical guitars in Spain that reflected the influence of Antonio de Torres, but featured some of Fleta's design ideas as well. Fleta would varnish the inside of the guitar as well, with the intent of brightening the sound. Fleta also added an extra strut under the treble side of the top as a means of increasing volume. Source: Tony Bacon, *The Ultimate Guitar Book*.

FLETCHER BROCK STRINGED INSTRUMENTS

Instruments currently produced in Seattle, WA since 1992. Previously produced in Ketchum, ID.

Luthier Fletcher Brock builds custom archtop acoustic instruments and specializes in the mandolin family and archtop guitars. Brock has produced mandolins, mandolas, octave mandolins, mandocellos, archtop guitars, flattop guitars, citterns, and bouzoukis. Almost all guitars are customly built to order and Fletcher produces around fifteen instruments a year. For more information and pricing inquiries, contact Fletcher directly.

CONTACT INFORMATION
FLETCHER BROCK STRINGED INSTRUMENTS
1417 NE Boat Street
Seattle, WA 98105
Phone No.: 206-547-2168
www.fletcherbrock.com
fletcher@fletcherbrock.com

FOGGY MOUNTAIN GUITARS

Acoustic guitars currently produced in China since 2005.

Foggy Mountain Guitars are budget to entry-level acoustic guitars imported from China. Unlike most Chinese manufacturers that are built by CNC machines, Foggy Mountain Guitars are actually built by Chinese luthiers. Models are available in several configurations including dreadnoughts, dreandought cutaways, folk cutaways, classicals, and acoustic basses. Prices typically range between $150 and $500. In 2006, Foggy Mountain introduce the Mason Williams Signature Line including the Mason Williams Commemorative model. For more information, visit Foggy Mountain's website or contact them directly.

CONTACT INFORMATION
FOGGY MOUNTAIN GUITARS
401 Loop 336W. Suite B
Conroe, TX 77301
Phone No.: 936-756-2400
Fax No.: 936-588-2445
www.foggymountainguitars.com
sales@foggymountainguitars.com

FOLEY GUITARS

Instruments currently built in Moravia, NY. Previously produced in Andover, NJ. Foley has been producing guitars since 1988. Distributed by Foley Guitars, Inc. in Moravia, NY.

Luthier Ed Foley has been hand crafting high quality acoustic guitars since the late 1980s. Many of his guitars can be found with a large number of Austin and Nashville artists, as well as other recording professionals. Foley headstocks are quite distinctive, for they have a recycled Ivory piano key cut into a steer scull! Foley also uses a MOP Foley logo if preferred. Foley builds less than ten guitars a year. In addition to his custom bracing, Foley also uses graphite along side of the truss rod to reinforse his necks and improve sustain. For more information, visit Foley's website or contact them directly.

CONTACT INFORMATION
FOLEY GUITARS
Moravia, NY 13118
Phone No.: 973-903-4884
www.foleyguitars.com
edfoley@foleyguitars.com

Ordering a Foley acoustic is exactly like ordering a custom built guitar. True to form, the price list runs three pages; the customer starts at the top of page one and makes the necessary choices as the list is run down. At the end of the choices for the model, the customer totals up all additional charges, and that is the retail price. All Foley guitars come with a hardshell case and John Pearse strings.

The base list price for a Foley acoustic is $5,850 (and that begins with any body size). A left-handed configuration is no extra charge; but a body cutaway adds $650 and the 12-string configuration is an additional $850. The basic model consists of a scalloped brace Sitka spruce top, mahogany sides, two-piece mahogany back, ivoroid or tortoiseshell body binding, black and white rings rosette, dot fingerboard inlay, 24.9 in. or 25.4 in. scale, rosewood fingerboard and bridge, three-per-side chrome Schaller tuners, and choice of black, tortoise, or no pickguard.

Any other custom choice carries an additional cost, such as a choice of Engelmann spruce (or flame koa or Alpine or German spruce) top for $400 (each), Brazilian rosewood back and sides ($6,500 for quarter sawn), flame koa for $1,150 or flame maple, birdseye maple, or quilted maple for $850 (each). The list of options is actually staggering, but the end result is a custom built guitar the way the customer wanted it.

FONTANILLA GUITARS

Classical guitars currently produced in San Francisco, CA since 1987.

Luthier Allan Fontanilla is a self-taught builder who focuses on acoustic classical guitars. Fontanilla's guitars range from traditional conservative methods to non-traditional modern designs. Every guitar is entirely custom built (standard specifications are available), and Fontanilla works alone in his shop. Fontanilla also offers repairs. For more information, visit Fontanilla's website or contact him directly.

CONTACT INFORMATION
FONTANILLA GUITARS
PO Box 31423
San Francisco, CA 94131
www.fontanilla.com
allan@fontanilla.com

FOSTER GUITARS

Instruments previously built in Covington, LA, between the late 1960s/early 1970s and 2011.

Luthier Jimmy Foster offered repair and restoration work in addition to his guitar designs, and had worked in the New Orleans area for over twenty five years. In addition to his standard models (listed below), Foster also offered custom orders available with choice of woods, inlays, and trim. Jimmy passed away on April 26, 2011. For the AT series refer to the Foster section in the *Blue Book of Electric Guitars*.

CONTACT INFORMATION
FOSTER GUITARS
76353 Eugene Wallace Rd.
Covington, LA 70435
Phone No.: 985-892-9822
Phone No.: 1-888-317-4146
Fax No.: 985-871-7833
www.fosterguitars.com
jimmy@fosterguitars.com

The **FT-1** (Last MSR was $2,450) featured a flat top, 17 in. body width, spruce top, body binding, mahogany back/sides/neck, 25.5 in. scale, ebony fingerboard, ebony bridge, and an ebony headstock overlay. A piezo bridge pickup was available for an additional $150.

The **Prodigy 1** (Last MSR was $2,450) featured a 17 in. cut-a-way body bound body, Sitka spruce top, mahogany back and sides, ebony fingerboard, bridge, and headstock, 25.5 in. scale, and 3.5 in. depth. The **Prodigy 2** (Last MSR was $3,250) is similar to the Prodigy 1, except has a carved mahogany back and an even 3 in. body. The standard **Prodigy** (Last MSR starts at $3,900) was available with a carved spruce or cedar top, and select mahogany back/sides. The **Prodigy Elite** (Last MSR starts at $9,500) is the top-of-the-line model with master grade spruce or cedar top and master grade quilted maple back/sides.

* **Add $450 for seven-string configuration (Prodigy models only).**

FRAMUS

Instruments currently produced in Markneukirchen, Germany. Distributed by Warwick GmbH & Co. Music Equipment Kg of Markneukirchen, Germany. Instruments were previously produced in Germany from the late 1940s through the mid-1970s. In 1996, the trademark was reintroduced in Europe. Distributed in the U.S. by Dana B. Goods of Ventura, CA.

When Frederick Wilfer returned to his home town of Walthersgrun at the end of World War II, he realized that the American-controlled Sudetenland area was soon to fall under control of the Russian forces. With the help of the Americans, Wilfer succeeded in resettling a number of violin makers from Schonbach to Franconia (later in the district of Erlangen). Between 1945 and 1947, Wilfer continued to find homes and employment for the Schonbach violin makers.

In 1946, Wilfer founded the Framus production company, the company name an acronym for Franconian Musical instruments. As the company established itself in 1946, Wilfer drew on the knowledge of his violin builder from Schonbach to produce a range of musical instruments including violins and cellos. The new Framus company expanded out of its first couple of production buildings, eventually building a new factory in Bubenreuth in 1955.

The first Framus electric guitars appeared in the 1950s. Due to the presence of American servicemen stationed there, the influence of rock-'n-roll surfaced earlier in Germany than other European countries. As a result, German guitar builders had a head start on answering the demand caused by the proliferation of pop groups during the 1960s. Furthermore, as the German production increased, they began exporting their guitars to other countries (including the U.S.). The Framus company stayed active in producing acoustic and electric guitars, and electric basses until the mid-1970s.

In the 1970s, increased competition and serious price undercutting from firms in the Asian market had a serious effect on established companies. Unfortunately, one aspect was to force a number of firms into bankruptcy - and Framus was one of those companies in 1975. However, Wilfer did have the opportunity to watch his son, Hans-Peter Wilfer, establish his own company in 1982 (see Warwick). Warwick's success allowed Hans-Peter to re-introduce the Framus trademark to the European musical market in 1996. In honor of his father Frederick, Hans-Peter chose to use the world-famous Framus trademark when he began offering guitar models in 1996 (source: Hans Peter Wilfer, Warwick GmbH & Co. Music Equipment Kg; and Tony Bacon and Paul Day, *The Guru's Guitar Guide*).

ACOUSTIC & SERIALIZATION

In order to properly date the year of issue, most Framus guitars had a separate pair of digits after the main serial number. If the separate pair is present, the two numbers will indicate the year. Current Framus instruments, including the electric guitars and handwired tube guitar amps, are produced at the Warwick facility. Acoustic instruments are no longer produced by Framus. Currently, Framus instruments are available in England, Germany, Sweden, and Switzerland; worldwide distribution is in the planning stages.

The majority of Framus acoustic guitars were produced in the 1960s. Some of the models that were produced inlcude the Texan, King, Blueridge, Tenor, Hootenany, and the Camping King. Used prices for these instruments range anywhere between $300 and $700, depending on the model.

MSR/NOTES	100%	EXCELLENT	AVERAGE	LAST MSR

GAUCHO – small acoustic body, spruce top, arched mahogany back, mahogany sides, round soundhole, bolt-on mahogany neck, 21-fret rosewood fingerboard, black headstock overlay with Framus logo and design, string guide, three-per-side tuners, bolt-on large adj. rosewood fingerboard, tortoise pickguard, nickel hardware, available in Natural or Sunburst finish, mfg. 1960s.

	N/A	$250 - 300	$125 - 175	

FRANCISCAN

Instruments previously produced in Indonesia. Previously distributed in the U.S. by Kaman Musical Instruments of Bloomfield, CT.

The Franciscan line offered a full line of beginner, student, and intermediate quality guitars, as well as mandolins. Most of the instruments in the line retailed between $75 and $175. The last Franciscan model was produced in 1998. These guitars then became Castillas and all of those have since become Montana guitars. Sources: Walter Murray, *Frankenstein Fretworks*, & Tim Campbell, Kaman Music.

Models included the **CS-3**, which has a 3/4 size acoustic with a classical-style slotted headstock, 12/18-fret fingerboard, black pickguard, trapeze-style tailpiece, pearloid tuner buttons, and a two-tone Sunburst finish (last MSR $75). The **CS-19** (last MSR $100) is a full sized acoustic folk guitar, with spruce top, round soundhole, black rosette, black body binding, nato back and sides, 14/20-fret laminated fretboard with pearl dot inlay, three-per-side chrome tuners, and hardwood bridge with black bridge pins. The **CS-20 E** is similar in construction to the **CS-19**, except also has a transducer pickup (last MSR $150).

FRANCONIA

Instruments previously built in Japan between 1980 and 1985.

The Franconia trademark was a brand name used by a UK importer. The guitars were generally entry level to mid quality copies of American designs. Source: Tony Bacon and Paul Day, *The Guru's Guitar Guide*.

FRANKLIN GUITAR COMPANY

Instruments previously built in Franklin, MI, Idaho, and Seattle, WA between 1976 and the mid-1990s.

Luthier Nick Kukich began the Franklin Guitar Company in Franklin, MI during 1975. Kukich moved the company to Idaho and ultimately to Seattle, WA. It is estimated that he built around thirty-six guitars a year, offered in OM and jumbo body styles. Kukich's acoustic guitars feature Engelmann spruce tops, Indian (or Brazilian) rosewood and koa back/sides, mahogany necks, ebony fingerboards and bridges, and herringbone purfling. Options such as a left-hand configuration, cutaway body design, or inlay/ornamentation was available by customer's specifications. Nick quit producing guitars for apparent health reasons and production of guitars stopped by the mid-1990s.

FREDDY'S FRETS

Instruments currently built in Welland (Ontario), Canada.

Luthier Freddy Gabrsek is currently offering a number of handcrafted acoustic and electric guitar models. Steel string acoustic guitars start at $3,500 with Sapele back and sides. Indian rosewood and curly white maple back and sides are optional. Electronics can be added as well. For further information regarding specifications and complete pricing, contact Freddy's Frets directly.

CONTACT INFORMATION
FREDDY'S FRETS
2520 Merritt Rd.
Welland, ON L3B 5N5 Canada
Phone No.: 905-384-0303
Phone No.: 866-204-4075
Fax No.: 905-384-0014
www.freddysfrets.com
freddy@freddysfrets.com

FRESHMAN

Instruments previously built in Japan during the mid-1960s.

As an inexpensive, entry level guitar, the Freshman trademark is quite apt: a senior, it isn't. In fact, it's not even close to a sophomore! Source: Tony Bacon and Paul Day, *The Guru's Guitar Guide*. The Freshman brand was reintroduced in the early 2000s as a guitar manufacturer based in England.

FRETLIGHT

Guitars currently produced overseas. Distributed by Optek Music Systems, Inc. in Reno, NV.

The Fretlight instructional guitar was developed by Optek Music Systems, Inc. (they also developed Smartlight several years ago). The fingerboard has built in LEDs, and when connected to a computer, the fingerboard will light up indicating where to place your fingers. Every guitar comes with a CD-ROM that has built in lessons, and more software packs can be purchased. For more information, visit Fretlight's website or contact them directly.

CONTACT INFORMATION
FRETLIGHT
4750 Longley Lane, Suite 201
Reno, NV 89502
Phone No.: 800-575-6511
Fax No.: 775-201-0007
www.fretlight.com
info@fretlight.com

The **FG-401** (MSR $400) features a thinline Tele-shaped body with a spruce top and mahogany back and sides. The **FG-405** (MSR $530) is similar to the FG-401, except it has a piezo pickup with three-band electronics on-board.

FRITZ BROTHERS

Instruments currently built in Albion, Mendocino County, CA. Previously built in Mobile, AL circa 1988.

CONTACT INFORMATION
FRITZ BROTHERS
31300 Middle Ridge Rd.
Albion, CA 95410
Phone No.: 707-937-6060
http://fritzbrothersguitars.com/
fritzbro@mcn.org

Luthier Roger Fritz met Marc Fisher in Nashville in 1987. Together with guitarist Roy Buchanan they formed Fritz Brothers guitars, which was relocated to Alabama a year later. During 1988, the Fritz Brothers began building the Roy Buchanan Bluesmaster model; Buchanan died later that year (a portion of the sales goes to Buchanan's estate).

Roger is now making guitars and other instruments out of his shop in Albion, California. He builds many different models that are partly inspired by classic designs with his own twist. For more information, visit Fritz Brothers' website or contact them directly. Source: Tom Wheeler, *American Guitars*.

FROGGY BOTTOM GUITARS

Instruments currently built in Newfane, VT since 1970. Distributed by Froggy Bottom Guitars.

CONTACT INFORMATION
FROGGY BOTTOM GUITARS
PO Box 246
Chelsea, VT 05038
Phone No.: 802-685-2205
www.froggybottomguitars.com
froggy@froggybottomguitars.com

Luthier Michael Millard visited Michael Gurian's workshop in 1970 and was offered a job after his college graduate program was eliminated. Millard built his first Froggy Bottom guitar (a modified Gurian JM) in his apartment's kitchen in late 1970. In 1973, Millard moved with Gurian to New Hampshire and continued to work for him until 1974 when he left to start building his own guitars exclusively. Millard continued building Froggy Bottom guitars one at a time through the rest of the 1970s and most of the 1980s. As his guitars became more popular and widespread, demand started to pour in from guitar stores and dealerships. By the mid-1980s, Millard started attending NAMM shows, began developing a dealer network, and started selling guitars wholesale for the first time. Froggy Bottom is now the trio of Andy Mueller, Eric Goodenough and Millard, enhanced by the unique engraving skills of long-time collaborator Petria Mitchell. In 2008, the company moved to a new, off-the-grid post and beam workshop in central Vermont and produces about one hundred high-end acoustic guitars annually.

These instruments have won an *Acoustic Guitar* Magazine "Players Choice Award" in each of the years that poll has been conducted. Froggy Bottom is somewhat unusual in that they refuse to use their high-profile clients in their advertising, instead they prefer to deal with the functional needs of players directly and personally.

For more information, visit Froggy Bottom's website or contact them directly.

Froggy Bottom Guitars are available in several different body shapes/styles as well as several trim levels and body wood configurations.

Body Shape/Style:

Small Body Guitars: Parlor Model L, Parlor 12-fret (P12), Parlor 14-fret (P14), Concert 12-fret (A12), Grand Concert Model M, Grand Concert 12-fret (H12), Grand Concert 14-fret (H14).

Full-Size Guitars: Dreadnought 12-fret (D12), Dreadnought 14-fret (D), Model F12, Model F14, Model K, Model SJ.

Jumbo Guitars: Model B-12, Model G, Model J.

Trim Levels:

Basic: The Basic style offers maple trim, a single herringbone rosette ring, eight-ply top purfling, mother-of-pearl peghead logo, a Brazilian rosewood bridge, and chrome Schaller tuners. This option is now discontinued.

Standard: The Standard options go one step up with an ebony bridge, abalone position markers, an abalone logo, two-ring rosette, maple end inlay and heel cap, and back and side purfling.

Deluxe: Further options in the Deluxe category include an abalone rosette, curly maple neck heel trim, Gold Schaller tuners, a bound headstock, and a distinctive fretboard inlay.

Limited: The Limited style option offers an abalone back seam inlay and abalone top trim inlay to the preceding steps.

Custom: The Custom style is entirely different as it is typically a player's own choices on the guitar. When there have been some serious alterations to the body and ornamentation, it is classified as Custom.

Body Wood: Standard woods include mahogany, East Indian rosewood, maple, walnut, and koa. Prices start at just over $6,000 and models with options range up to well over $10,000.

- Add $100 for Gold Schaller tuners.
- Add $150 for nickel finish Waverly G-98 tuners.
- Add $200 for Gold finish Waverly G-98 tuners.
- Add $150 for oversized soundhole.
- Add $160 for bound headstock (six-string models).
- Add $200 for left-handed configuration.
- Add $200 for curly maple heel grafts.
- Add $225 for engraved Mammoth Ivory heel cap.
- Add $295-$395 for various fingerboard inlays.
- Add $350 for a slotted headstock.
- Add $450 for 12-string configuration (full-sized and jumbo models only).
- Add $550 for a Sunburst finish top.
- Add $700 (and up) for Florentine or Venetian cutaway body.
- Add $2,500 and up for Madagascar rosewood.

FRONTIER

Instruments previously produced in Japan during the early 1980s.

Frontier guitars are decent to good quality original designs as well as copies of American designs. The puzzling model that there appears to be no information on is the signature model of Norris Fant. Guitar collectors. Source: Tony Bacon and Paul Day, *The Guru's Guitar Guide*.

FYLDE

Instruments currently built in Penrith (Cumbria), England since 1973.

CONTACT INFORMATION
FYLDE
www.fyldeguitars.com
rogerbucknall@fyldeguitars.com

Roger Bucknall began building guitars at age nine (back in the late 1950s), and continued occasionally building until he was twenty-one. While he was running a folk club, Bucknall soon had a large number of orders for his designs from artists such as Gordon Giltrap, Nic Jones, and John James. A friend offered to finance his new endeavor, and Roger moved to the Fylde coast of Lancashire in 1973 to begin producing guitars. He continued to expand the business through the 1970s, and by the end of the decade had a staff of around twelve people building twenty guitars a week. Roger estimates that half of the production was being sold to the U.S., the rest in Europe.

In the later half of 1979 to 1980, Roger suffered through personal family problems, coupled with a fading market and struggling finances. In 1980, Fylde Instruments Ltd. was closed down. He continued making about 100 guitars a year under the Fylde Guitars name. He also launched a business making snooker and pool cues. Bucknall sold the snooker business in 1992 and re-invested in guitar making.

With traditional wood supplies becoming scarce, Bucknall sought a source of renewable new materials for his guitars, and was committed to not purchasing any more rosewood or ebony unless the wood came from a substantial source.

In addition to the numerous guitar models, Fylde Guitars also offers a number of models from the Mandolin family, such as the Mandola, Cittern, Portuguese Mandola, Bouzouki, and Mandolin.

Since about 2008, most of Roger's instruments are supplied directly to the customer, and not through shops. His clientele includes Ritchie Blackmore, Pete Townshend, Eric Bibb, Lisa Hannigan, Gordon Giltrap, Ken Nicol, Duck Baker, Seth Lakeman, Tristan Sueme, John Smith, Martin Simpson, Dave Swarbrick, Martin Carthy, and hundreds of household names. Much of Rogers work is now commissions for individual customers. Roger also offers unique one off instruments made according to Roger's own preferences and sold exclusively as "Personal Selection". All prices are listed in pounds and a price list is available on their website where you can find detailed information about every Fylde instrument.

ACOUSTIC

The clever folks at Fylde named many of the current guitar models after characters in Shakespeare plays (which, in the long run, is more entertaining than a simple model number). The **Ariel** model has a slotted headstock, and a body design somewhere between a nylon and steel-string guitar design. The Ariel features a cedar top, mahogany back and sides, and a 12/19-fret ebony neck with a 629 mm scale length.

The **Goodfellow** is slightly larger than the Ariel, and has a 14/20-fret rosewood fingerboard.

If you combine a single cutaway with a Hot Club-era Selmer acoustic, the results may be a **Caliban**. The D-shaped soundhole and deep cutaway mark this model, constructed with a cedar top, Indian rosewood back and sides, and ebony fingerboard and bridge.

The **Egyptian** features a spruce top, an oval soundhole, and bridge/metal tailpiece with its deep cutaway and Indian rosewood back and sides. Both models feature a 24-fret fingerboard.

The **Falstaff** and **Oberon** models share similar construction such as spruce tops, Indian rosewood back and sides, and an ebony fingerboard and bridge. The Falstaff has a dreadnought body appearance and a 648 mm scale, while the Oberon leans toward a grand concert style and 629 mm scale.

Fylde's **Orsino** acoustic is a dreadnought-style guitar with a cedar top and mahogany back and sides.

The deep-bodied jumbo-style **Magician** features a cedar top, walnut back and sides, a five-piece laminated neck, and an ebony fingerboard and bridge. The **Alchemist** was developed from the Magician, being just 10% smaller, and the **Alexander** is a simplification of the Alchemist shape, made from Cedar and Sapele, but without a cutaway

The **Leonardo** is half way between the Magician and Alchemist, with a fairly shallow body for a little extra comfort in playing. It has Maple back and sides with a laminated maple neck with a broad heel to fit the cutaway and a Sitka Spruce soundboard. An Indian Rosewood model is also available.

All models can have pick-ups fitted.

Fylde also make three signature models based on long acquaintants with **Gordon Giltrap**, **Eric Bibb**, and **Ken Nicol**, and have recently added a **Tenor** guitar to the range.

ACOUSTIC BASS

Fylde has three models of acoustic bass, the **King John** (860 mm scale) and the **Sir Toby** (762 mm scale). Both basses feature mahogany back and sides, a voiced cedar top, and rosewood fingerboard and bridge but have now been discontinued. The **Magician** acoustic bass is still available.

G SECTION
GADOTTI GUITARS

Instruments currently produced in Sao Paolo, Brazil, Orlando, FL, and other U.S. locations since 1997.

CONTACT INFORMATION
GADOTTI GUITARS
Orlando, FL
Phone No.: 812-486-5836
www.gadotti-guitars.com/english/
jsmith@nascoinc.com

Luthier Jeanfranco Biava Gadotti is originally from Sao Paolo, Brazil and started building guitars under the direction of Brazilian luthier Marcio Benedetti in 1997. Gadotti moved to the U.S. in 1999 and continued to build under luthier Mark Eshenbaugh. In 2002, Gadotti settled in Orlando, FL where he currently builds guitars today. Gadotti currently offers a variety of custom acoustic and electric instruments that feature unique designs. His **Nylon String King** (MSR $3,699) features a chambered body with a soundhole that goes all the way through the body. For more information, visit Gadotti's website or contact him directly.

GAGLIANO

Instruments previously produced in Korea. Distributed by Avnet, Inc.

Gagliano acoustic guitars have the Gagliano trademark name in gold script on the headstock, while their internal label states "Meisel Music, a subsidiary of Avnet, Inc." One model observed, the Model 2060, may or may not be indicative of the entire product line: The different components are of various levels of quality and state of technology. For example, the neck is a decent quality nato, with an adjustable truss rod. This neck is about as good a quality as you could expect on this genre of instrument. On the other hand, the bridge is made of plastic and the soundboard is plywood, with a paper-like laminate to make it look like spruce. The internal bracing is also a mish-mash of technological styles. Source: Walter Murray, Frankenstein Fretworks.

GALIANO

Acoustic guitars previously produced in New York, NY during the early 1900s.

Luthiers Antonio Cerrito and Raphael Ciani built acoustic guitars, mandolins, and other instruments under the Galiano trademark. They also used the Galiano brand on instruments built by other companies, most notably the Oscar Schmidt Guitar Company. Known examples feature arch tops with mid-grade appointments. Any further information can be submitted directly to Blue Book Publications.

GALLAGHER GUITARS

Instruments currently built in Wartrace, TN since 1965. Distributed by J.W. Gallagher & Sons of Wartrace, TN.

CONTACT INFORMATION
GALLAGHER GUITARS
PO Box 128
Wartrace, TN 37183
Phone No.: 931-389-6455
Fax No.: 931-389-6455
www.gallagherguitar.com
don@gallagherguitar.com

The Gallagher family settled in Wartrace (about sixty miles southeast of Nashville) back in the late 1820s. John William Gallagher was born in 1915, and in 1939 he established a furniture making business. Don Gallagher was born in 1947, and grew up among the tools and wood in the family's woodworking shop. The furniture business converted to guitar production later in the 1960s. Gallagher and his son Don produced twenty-four guitars in their first year.

In 1976, Don Gallagher took over management of the business, three years before the luthier community lost J.W. Gallagher in 1979. Don Gallagher continues to build acoustic guitars in the family tradition. Source: Tom Wheeler, *American Guitars*.

Gallagher guitars have been built in very limited numbers. From the opening year of 1965 to 1990, only 2,064 guitars were made. According to the Gallagher catalog, early instruments had paper labels. The serial number on these labels indicate the year and month the guitar was made. Starting in 1970, the serialization began to reflect the number of guitars that had been built. This number, along with the model number, is stamped on the neck block inside every Gallagher guitar.

ACOUSTIC

All Gallagher guitars are meticulously handcrafted, using the finest woods available at the workshop. Hardshell cases are an extra charge, at $150 for a standard hardshell case or $575 for a Calton case, which is custom made for Gallagher instruments.

The first Gallagher guitar model was built back in 1965, and was designated the G-50 in honor of J.W. Gallagher's age at the time. In 1968, both Doc and Merle Watson began playing guitars crafted by J.W. and Don. In 1974, Doc Watson requested particular features in a guitar that was built for him, and it was the basis for the Doc Watson model. In 1975, Merle recieved the first cutaway version of this model. The first GC-70 was built in 1968, for country artist Grandpa Jones. The 71 Special was introduced in 1970. The 72 Special was introduced in late 1977.

Price options apply to guitars where the feature is not part of the standard package (i.e. the Steve Kaufman comes standard with Sunburst finish so you would not add $275).

- Add $250 for left-handed configuration.
- Add $300 for Fishman Acoustic Matrix system.
- Add $300 for maple binding.
- Add $400 for a modified body (12/20-fret fingerboard).
- Add $500 for Sunburst finish.
- Add $550 for single cutaway body design.
- Add $550 for a slotted headstock.
- Add $600 for 12-string configuration.

MSR/NOTES	100%	EXCELLENT	AVERAGE	LAST MSR

71 SPECIAL – dreadnought style, rosewood back/sides/neck, Sitka spruce top with voiced bracing, maple B/N/H binding, round soundhole with herringbone purfling and inlay, 14/20-fret ebony fingerboard with abalone snowflake inlays, MOP bell flower headstock inlay, three-per-side tuners, ebony bridge, chrome hardware, Natural finish, mfg. 1970-present.

MSR $4,299	$3,700	$2,150 - 2,600	$1,500 - 1,750	

72 SPECIAL – dreadnought style, rosewood back/sides/neck, Sitka spruce top with voiced bracing, maple B/N/H binding, round soundhole with abalone purfling and inlay, 14/20-fret ebony fingerboard with abalone snowflake inlays, MOP bell flower headstock inlay, three-per-side tuners, ebony bridge, chrome hardware, Natural finish, mfg. 1977-present.

MSR $5,199	$4,450	$2,600 - 3,150	$1,825 - 2,100	

75 SPECIAL – dreadnought style, rosewood back/sides/neck, Sitka spruce top with voiced bracing, abalone pearl trim top, sides and back, maple B/N/H binding, round soundhole with abalone purfling and inlay, 14/20-fret ebony fingerboard with special pattern and dot inlays, MOP bell flower headstock inlay, three-per-side tuners, ebony bridge, chrome hardware, Natural finish, current mfg.

MSR $7,999	$6,800	$4,000 - 4,800	N/A	

DOC WATSON – dreadnought style, African mahogany back/sides/neck, Sitka spruce top with voiced bracing, black body binding, round soundhole with herringbone purfling and inlay, 14/20-wide fret ebony fingerboard with MOP dot inlays, three-per-side tuners, ebony bridge, tortoise pickguard, chrome hardware, Natural finish with zig-zag back strip, current mfg.

MSR $3,599	$3,100	$1,800 - 2,200	$1,250 - 1,450	

DOC WATSON SIGNATURE – dreadnought style, African mahogany back/sides/neck, Sitka spruce top with voiced bracing, maple body binding, round soundhole with herringbone purfling and inlay, 14/20-wide fret ebony fingerboard with MOP diamond and square inlays with 14th fret Doc Watson singnature inlay, maple headstock binding, three-per-side tuners, ebony bridge, tortoiseshell pickguard, chrome hardware, Natural finish with zig-zag back strip, current mfg.

MSR $3,999	$3,400	$2,000 - 2,400	$1,400 - 1,600	

G-45 – dreadnought style, African mahogany back/sides/neck, Sitka spruce top, black body binding, round soundhole with W/B/W purfling and inlay, 14/20-fret ebony fingerboard with MOP dot inlays, three-per-side tuners, ebony bridge, tortoiseshell pickguard, chrome hardware, Natural finish, disc. 2008.

	N/A	$1,450 - 1,750	$1,025 - 1,175	$2,899

G-50 – dreadnought style, African mahogany back/sides/neck, Sitka spruce top, ivoroid body binding, round soundhole with W/B/W purfling and inlay, 14/20-fret ebony fingerboard with MOP dot inlays, ivoroid-bound headstock, three-per-side tuners, ebony bridge, tortoiseshell pickguard, chrome hardware, Natural finish, current mfg.

MSR $3,199	$2,725	$1,600 - 1,950	$1,125 - 1,300	

G-65 – dreadnought style, rosewood back/sides/neck, Sitka spruce top, ivoroid B/N/H binding, round soundhole with B/W/B purfling and inlay, 14/20-fret ebony fingerboard with MOP dot inlays, unbound headstock with MOP inlaid G, three-per-side tuners, ebony bridge, tortoiseshell pickguard, chrome hardware, Natural finish, current mfg.

MSR $3,399	$2,900	$1,700 - 2,050	$1,200 - 1,375	

G-70/A-70/GC-70/GA-70 – auditorium, dreadnought, grand auditorium, or grand concert style, rosewood back/sides/neck, Sitka spruce top, ivoroid body binding, round soundhole with herringbone purfling and inlay, 14/20-fret ebony fingerboard with MOP diamond and square inlays, ivoroid-bound headstock, three-per-side tuners, ebony bridge, tortoiseshell pickguard, chrome hardware, Natural finish, current mfg.

MSR $3,999	$3,400	$2,000 - 2,400	$1,400 - 1,600	

GC SHORT-SCALE – grand concert style, Sitka spruce top with voice bracing, rosewood back and sides, round soundhole with herringbone purfling and inlay, ebony fingerboard with abalone snowflake inlays, three-per-side tuners, ebony bridge, tortoiseshell pickguard, chrome hardware, Natural finish, 24.75 in. scale, disc. 2009.

	N/A	$2,000 - 2,400	$1,400 - 1,600	$3,999

RAGTIME SPECIAL – auditorium style, African mahogany back/sides/neck, Sitka spruce top with voice bracing, round soundhole with herringbone purfling and inlay, ebony fingerboard with abalone snowflake inlays, three-per-side tuners, ebony bridge, tortoiseshell pickguard, chrome hardware, Natural finish, current mfg.

MSR $3,750	$3,250	$1,900 - 2,300	$1,350 - 1,550	

STEVE KAUFMAN SIGNATURE – dreadnought single cutaway style, rosewood back/sides/neck, Engleman spruce top, voiced top and back bracing, ivoroid body binding, round soundhole with abalone purfling and inlay, 14/20-wide fret ebony fingerboard with dot and 14th fret Steve Kaufman signature inlays, ivoroid bound MOP bell flower headstock inlay, three-per-side tuners, ebony bridge, tortoiseshell pickguard, Fishman electronics, chrome hardware, Sunburst finish, current mfg.

MSR $5,499	$4,700	$2,750 - 3,300	$1,925 - 2,200	

GALLAGHER, KEVIN

See Omega Instruments in the O section.

MSR/NOTES	100%	EXCELLENT	AVERAGE	LAST MSR

GALLOUP GUITARS

Instruments currently built in Big Rapids, MI since 1992.

CONTACT INFORMATION
GALLOUP GUITARS
10840 Northland Drive
Big Rapids, MI 49307
Phone No.: 231-796-5611
Phone No.: 800-278-0089
www.galloupguitars.com
bryan@galloupguitars.com

Luthier Bryan Galloup has been a guitar repairman on vintage guitars for several years. Galloup began building his own guitars in 1992, and went full time in guitar building in 1995.

Galloup's techniques of neck resetting, fretting, and bridge and bridge plate replacing were featured in the Guild of American Luthier's *American Luthier* publication. Galloup is also the repair and modification columnist for The Association of Stringed Instrument Artisans' quarterly magazine.

In addition to his acoustic guitar models, Galloup also runs the Bryan Galloup's School of Guitar Building and Repair, which is a fully equipped wood working shop that is designed to handle the most advanced repairs, restorations, and custom ordered acoustic and electric guitars. Students during the eight-week class are outfitted with their own workbench, hand tools, and supplies and receive a hands-on education in the lutherie arts. There is also a twenty-four-week Masters course available. For more information, visit Galloup's website or contact them directly.

Galloup's acoustic guitar models include the **G-1 American Classic** (disc., last list was $2,650), the **GD-1 Classic Deluxe** (disc., last list was $3,800), **GS-2 Hutchinson** (disc., last list was $2,975), and the **GE-3 Hired Hand** (disc., last list was $2,495). Currently the models have different names: the **G-1 Big Mitten**, the **G-2 Northern Light**, and the **G-3 Solstice**. Other models include the **Eclipse**, **Florentine**, and **Baritone**.

GARRISON GUITARS

Instruments previously produced in St. John's, Newfoundland, Canada between 2000 and circa 2008.

Chris Griffiths started his first company in 1993 at the age of nineteen, which was called Griffiths Guitar Works. They sold high end instruments only and did repair work. Towards the end of the 1990s the idea of Garrison guitars was in full swing and the Garrison guitar was released at the 2000 NAMM show. What separates this guitar from others is the Griffiths Active Bracing System. This system intergrates the binding, bridge plate, neck and bracing all into one glass fiber component. Guitars can be produced at a rate of forty-five seconds each. In August, 2007, Gibson purchased Garrison Guitars, and after continued to produce Garrison-branded guitars for a short while, but quickly converted the factory to produce the Gibson-branded Songmaker Series that lasted about a year.

ACOUSTIC: AG SERIES

The AG series uses part of the Active Bracing System. The guitar's top bracing and bridge are composed of the Griffiths Active TopBrace and the rest of the guitar is built with wood components. In 2006, a grand concert and parlor body style were introduced. They are available in all series, except the parlor is not available as a 12-string. The Dreadnought has a prefix of AGD, Grand Concert of AGGC, and the Parlor has a prefix of AGP.

200 SERIES – dreadnought, grand concert, or parlor style, nato back and sides, spruce top, ivory colorbody binding, round soundhole with multi-ring rosette, nato neck, 14/20-fret rosewood fingerboard with dot inlay, three-per-side tuners, rosewood bridge, black pickguard, chrome hardware, available in Black, Blue, Green, Natural, or Red finish, 24.25 in. scale, mfg. 2003-08.

	N/A	$100 - 150	$60 - 80	$250

- Add 12.5% (Last MSR was $282) for colors besides Natural finish.
- Add 35% (Last MSR was $340) for 12-string configuration.
- Add 55% (Last MSR was $390) for single cutaway and electronics.
- Add 90% (Last MSR was $480) for 12-string configuration, a single cutaway, and electronics.

300 SERIES – dreadnought, grand concert, or parlor style, ash back and sides, ash top, ivory colorbody binding, round soundhole with multi-ring rosette, nato neck, 14/20-fret rosewood fingerboard with dot inlay, ash headstock with three-per-side tuners, rosewood bridge, black pickguard, chrome hardware, available in Black, Blue, Green, Natural, or Red finish, 24.25 in. scale, mfg. 2003-08.

	N/A	$150 - 200	$95 - 120	$340

- Add 10% (Last MSR was $372) for colors besides Natural finish.
- Add 25% (Last MSR was $430) for 12-string configuration.
- Add 40% (Last MSR was $480) for single cutaway and electronics.
- Add 70% (Last MSR was $570) for 12-string configuration, a single cutaway, and electronics.

400 SERIES – dreadnought, grand concert, or parlor style, mahogany back and sides, solid cedar top, ivory color body binding, round soundhole with multi-ring rosette, nato neck, 14/20-fret rosewood fingerboard with dot inlay, rosewood headstock with three-per-side tuners, rosewood bridge, black pickguard, chrome hardware, available in Black or Natural finish, 24.25 in. scale, mfg. 2003-08.

	N/A	$160 - 210	$95 - 120	$370

- Add 10% (Last MSR was $402) for Black finish.
- Add 25% (Last MSR was $460) for 12-string configuration.
- Add 40% (Last MSR was $525) for single cutaway and electronics.
- Add 65% (Las MSR was $615) for 12-string configuration, a single cutaway, and electronics.

MSR/NOTES	100%	EXCELLENT	AVERAGE	LAST MSR

500 SERIES – dreadnought, grand concert, or parlor style, sycamore back and sides, solid spruce top, ivory colorbody binding, round soundhole with multi-ring rosette, nato neck, 14/20-fret rosewood fingerboard with dot inlay, flamed sycamore headstock with three-per-side tuners and MOP logo, rosewood bridge, black pickguard, chrome hardware, available in Blue, Green, Natural, or Red finish, 24.25 in. scale, mfg. 2003-08.

	N/A	$190 - 240	$120 - 150	$430

- Add 7.5% for Blue, Green, or Red finishes.
- Add 20% (Last MSR was $520) for 12-string configuration.
- Add 35% (Last MSR was $585) for single cutaway and electronics.
- Add 55% (Last MSR was $675) for 12-string configuration, a single cutaway, and electronics.

600 SERIES – dreadnought, grand concert, or parlor style, mahogany back and sides, solid spruce top, ivory colorbody binding, round soundhole with abalone multi-ring rosette, nato neck, 14/20-fret rosewood fingerboard with dot inlay, rosewood headstock with three-per-side tuners and MOP logo, rosewood bridge, tortoiseshell pickguard, gold hardware, available in Natural finish, 24.25 in. scale, mfg. 2003-08.

	N/A	$225 - 275	$130 - 170	$480

- Add 22.5% (Last MSR was $590) for 12-string configuration.
- Add 35% (Last MSR was $650) for single cutaway and electronics.
- Add 57.5% (Last MSR was $760) for 12-string configuration, a single cutaway, and electronics.

700 SERIES – dreadnought, grand concert, or parlor style, rosewood back and sides, solid cedar top, ivory colorbody binding, round soundhole with abalone contemporary square rosettes, nato neck, 14/20-fret rosewood fingerboard with dot inlay, rosewood headstock with three-per-side tuners and MOP logo, rosewood bridge, tortoiseshell pickguard, gold hardware, available in Natural finish, 24.25 in. scale, mfg. 2003-08.

	N/A	$250 - 300	$150 - 190	$550

- Add 20% (Last MSR was $550) for 12-string configuration.
- Add 30% (Last MSR was $720) for single cutaway and electronics.
- Add 50% (Last MSR was $830) for 12-string configuration, a single cutaway, and electronics.

AGLE-1 LIMITED EDITION – grand concert body style, solid cedar top, solid ovankol back and sides, maple body binding, abalone purfling and rosette, mahogany neck, abalone vine fingerboard inlay, three-per-side gold Grover tuners, bone nut and saddle, Natural finish, 100 instruments scheduled to be produced, mfg. 2006-07.

	N/A	$400 - 475	$225 - 275	$850

- Add 37.5% (Last MSR was $1,170) for a single cutaway and Fishman Classic 4T electronics.

AGSP-1 LIMITED EDITION – super thin line grand concert body style, quilted ash top, ash back and sides, nato neck, three-per-side tuners, four-band EQ electronics, available in Black, Blue, Natural, or Red finish, shipped quarterly only, mfg. 2006-07.

	N/A	$220 - 270	$130 - 170	$460

- Add 7.5% (Last MSR was $482) for Black, Blue, or Red finish.

ACOUSTIC: G SERIES

The G-Series features the full Griffiths Active Bracing System. The glass-fibre composite is used in the bracing, bridge, binding, and the neck. The wood components are then attached to this frame. In 2006, a grand concert and parlor body style were introduced. They are available in all series, except the parlor is not available as a 12-string. The Dreadnought has a prefix of GD, Grand Concert of GGC, and the Parlor has a prefix of GP. In 2007, birch body, neck, and headstock binding became optional.

4 SERIES – dreadnought, grand concert, or parlor style, solid sapele back and sides, solid Sitka spruce top, black body binding, round soundhole with Herringbone wood pattern inlay, mahogany neck, 14/20-fret rosewood fingerboard with dot inlay, three-per-side tuners, rosewood bridge, tortoiseshell pickguard, chrome hardware, Buzz Feiten Tuning System, Natural finish, 25.4 in. scale, disc. 2008.

	N/A	$375 - 450	$200 - 250	$800

- Add 12.5% (Last MSR was $900) for high-gloss finish.
- Add 12.5% (Last MSR was $900) for birch body binding.
- Add 15% (Last MSR was $930) for 12-string configuration.
- Add 25% (Last MSR was $1,000) for birch body, neck, and headstock binding.
- Add 35% (Last MSR was $1,070) for Fishman Prefix Pro electronics.
- Add 50% (Last MSR was $1,200) for 12-string configuration and Fishman Prefix Pro electronics.
- Add 52.5% (Last MSR was $1,220) for a single cutaway and Fishman Prefix Pro electronics.
- Add 70% (Last MSR was $1,350) for 12-string configuration, a single cutaway, and Fishman Prefix Pro electronics.

20 SERIES – dreadnought, grand concert, or parlor style, solid birch back and sides, solid cedar top, black body binding, round soundhole with herringbone wood inlay, mahogany neck, 14/20-fret rosewood fingerboard with dot inlay, three-per-side tuners, rosewood bridge, black pickguard, chrome hardware, Buzz Feiten Tuning System, Natural finish, 25.4 in. scale, disc. 2008.

	N/A	$300 - 350	$175 - 225	$650

- Add 15% (Last MSR was $750) for high-gloss finish.
- Add 15% (Last MSR was $750) for birch body binding.
- Add 20% (Last MSR was $780) for 12-string configuration.
- Add 25% (Last MSR was $820) for Fishman Prefix Pro electronics.
- Add 30% (Last MSR was $850) for birch body, neck, and headstock binding.
- Add 45% (Last MSR was $950) for 12-string configuration and Fishman Prefix Pro electronics.
- Add 50% (Last MSR was $970) for a single cutaway and Fishman Prefix Pro electronics.
- Add 70% (Last MSR was $1,100) for 12-string configuration, a single cutaway, and Fishman Prefix Pro electronics.

MSR/NOTES	100%	EXCELLENT	AVERAGE	LAST MSR

25 SERIES – dreadnought, grand concert, or parlor style, solid birch back and sides, solid cedar top, black body binding, round soundhole with contemporary wood pattern inlay, mahogany neck, 14/20-fret ebony fingerboard with dot inlay, three-per-side tuners, ebony bridge, tortoiseshell pickguard, gold hardware, Buzz Feiten Tuning System, Natural hardware, 25.4 in. scale, mfg. 2002-08.

	N/A	$375 - 450	$200 - 250	$800

- Add 12.5% (Last MSR was $900) for high-gloss finish.
- Add 12.5% (Last MSR was $900) for birch body binding.
- Add 15% (Last MSR was $930) for 12-string configuration.
- Add 25% (Last MSR was $1,000) for birch body, neck, and headstock binding.
- Add 35% (Last MSR was $1,070) for Fishman Prefix Pro electronics.
- Add 50% (Last MSR was $1,200) for 12-string configuration and Fishman Prefix Pro electronics.
- Add 52.5% (Last MSR was $1,220) for a single cutaway and Fishman Prefix Pro electronics.
- Add 70% (Last MSR was $1,350) for 12-string configuration, a single cutaway, and Fishman Prefix Pro electronics.

30 SERIES – dreadnought, grand concert, or parlor style, solid birch back and sides, solid Sitka spruce top, black body binding, round soundhole with herringbone pattern wood inlay, mahogany neck, 14/20-fret rosewood fingerboard with dot inlay, three-per-side tuners, rosewood bridge, black pickguard, chrome hardware, Buzz Feiten Tuning System, Natural finish, 25.4 in. scale, disc. 2008.

	N/A	$325 - 400	$180 - 220	$700

- Add 15% (Last MSR was $800) for high-gloss finish.
- Add 15% (Last MSR was $800) for birch body binding.
- Add 17.5% (Last MSR was $830) for 12-string configuration.
- Add 25% (Last MSR was $870) for Fishman Prefix Pro electronics.
- Add 27.5% (Last MSR was $900) for birch body, neck, and headstock binding.
- Add 42.5% (Last MSR was $1,000) for 12-string configuration and Fishman Prefix Pro electronics.
- Add 45% (Last MSR was $1,020) for a single cutaway and Fishman Prefix Pro electronics.
- Add 65% (Last MSR was $1,150) for 12-string configuration, a single cutaway, and Fishman Prefix Pro electronics.

35 SERIES – dreadnought, grand concert, or parlor style, solid birch back and sides, solid Sitka spruce top, black body binding, round soundhole with contemporary wood pattern inlay, mahogany neck, 14/20-fret ebony fingerboard with dot inlay, three-per-side tuners, ebony bridge, tortoiseshell pickguard, gold hardware, Buzz Feiten Tuning System, Natural finish, 25.4 in. scale, mfg. 2003-08.

	N/A	$400 - 475	$225 - 275	$850

- Add 12.5% (Last MSR was $950) for high-gloss finish.
- Add 12.5% (Last MSR was $950) for birch body binding.
- Add 17.5% (Last MSR was $830) for 12-string configuration.
- Add 22.5% (Last MSR was $1,050) for birch body, neck, and headstock binding.
- Add 32.5% (Last MSR was $1,120) for Fishman Prefix Pro electronics.
- Add 50% (Last MSR was $1,270) for a single cutaway and Fishman Prefix Pro electronics.
- Add 60% (Last MSR was $1,370) for 12-string configuration and Fishman Prefix Pro electronics.
- Add 80% (Last MSR was $1,520) for 12-string configuration, a single cutaway, and Fishman Prefix Pro electronics.

40 SERIES – dreadnought, grand concert, or parlor style, solid sapele back and sides, solid Sitka spruce top, black body binding, round soundhole with contemporary wood pattern inlay, mahogany neck, 14/20-fret ebony fingerboard with dot inlay, three-per-side tuners, ebony bridge, tortoiseshell pickguard, gold hardware, Buzz Feiten Tuning System, Natural finish, 25.4 in. scale, disc. 2008.

	N/A	$450 - 525	$275 - 325	$1,000

- Add 10% (Last MSR was $1,100) for high-gloss finish.
- Add 10% (Last MSR was $1,100) for birch body binding.
- Add 25% (Last MSR was $1,250) for 12-string configuration.
- Add 20% (Last MSR was $1,200) for birch body, neck, and headstock binding.
- Add 27.5% (Last MSR was $1,270) for Fishman Prefix Pro electronics.
- Add 42.5% (Last MSR was $1,420) for a single cutaway and Fishman Prefix Pro electronics.
- Add 52.5% (Last MSR was $1,520) for 12-string configuration and Fishman Prefix Pro electronics.
- Add 67.5% (Last MSR was $1,670) for 12-string configuration, a single cutaway, and Fishman Prefix Pro electronics.

41 SERIES – dreadnought, grand concert, or parlor style, solid sapele back and sides, solid sapele top, black body binding, round soundhole with Herringbone wood pattern inlay, mahogany neck, 14/20-fret rosewood fingerboard with dot inlay, three-per-side tuners, rosewood bridge, black pickguard, chrome hardware, Buzz Feiten Tuning System, Natural finish, 25.4 in. scale, mfg. 2003-08.

	N/A	$425 - 500	$250 - 300	$900

- Add 10% (Last MSR was $1,000) for high-gloss finish.
- Add 10% (Last MSR was $1,000) for birch body binding.
- Add 15% (Last MSR was $1,030) for 12-string configuration.
- Add 22.5% (Last MSR was $1,100) for birch body, neck, and headstock binding.
- Add 30% (Last MSR was $1,170) for Fishman Prefix Pro electronics.
- Add 47.5% (Last MSR was $1,320) for a single cutaway and Fishman Prefix Pro electronics.
- Add 60% (Last MSR was $1,450) for 12-string configuration and Fishman Prefix Pro electronics.
- Add 80% (Last MSR was $1,520) for 12-string configuration, a single cutaway, and Fishman Prefix Pro electronics.

MSR/NOTES	100%	EXCELLENT	AVERAGE	LAST MSR

50 SERIES – dreadnought, grand concert, or parlor style, solid rosewood back and sides, solid Sitka spruce top, black body binding, round soundhole with contemporary wood pattern inlay, mahogany neck, 14/20-fret ebony fingerboard with dot inlay, three-per-side tuners, ebony bridge, tortoiseshell pickguard, gold hardware, Buzz Feiten Tuning System, Natural finish, 25.4 in. scale, disc. 2008.

	N/A	$575 - 700	$350 - 425	$1,300

- Add 7.5% (Last MSR was $1,40) for high-gloss finish.
- Add 7.5% (Last MSR was $1,400) for birch body binding.
- Add 20% (Last MSR was $1,550) for 12-string configuration.
- Add 15% (Last MSR was $1,200) for birch body, neck, and headstock binding.
- Add 20% (Last MSR was $1,570) for Fishman Prefix Pro electronics.
- Add 32.5% (Last MSR was $1,720) for a single cutaway and Fishman Prefix Pro electronics.
- Add 40% (Last MSR was $1,820) for 12-string configuration and Fishman Prefix Pro electronics.
- Add 52.5% (Last MSR was $1,970) for 12-string configuration, a single cutaway, and Fishman Prefix Pro electronics.

ACOUSTIC BASS

AGAB BASS – single cutaway bass configuration, select spruce top, maghogany back and sides, four-band active electronics, mfg. 2006-08.

	N/A	$240 - 290	$140 - 180	$500

GASSER, MARK

See Backwoods Guitars in the B section.

GAY

Instruments previously built in Edmonton (Alberta), Canada between circa early/mid-1950s and the mid-1970s.

Luthier Frank Gay maintained his guitar building and repair services for more than two decades in Edmonton. A formidable jazz and classical guitarist, his flattop acoustics were the most recognizable instrument. Oddly enough, his biggest endorsers were country western artists (one notable player was Webb Pierce). Gay guitars are recognized by the exaggerated checkerboard rosette inlays, six-on-a-side headstocks, and the occasional heart-shaped soundhole. Source: Teisco Del Rey, *Guitar Player Magazine*.

GENEVA

Instruments previously produced in the Czech Republic 1981-1999. Distributed by the Geneva International Corporation of Wheeling, IL.

Geneva acoustic guitars were produced in the Czech Republic from 1981 to 1999, and carry the same European traditions of quality workmanship. Geneva guitars feature a different bridge design that changes the pitch of the string crossing the bridge's saddle, adding to the transfer of vibrations from the strings to the top via the bridge.

ACOUSTIC: PRO DREADNOUGHT STYLE SERIES

D 1 P – dreadnought style, solid cedar top, round soundhole, laminated mahogany back/sides, mahogany neck, rosewood fingerboard with white dot inlay, rosewood bridge, three-per-side Schaller tuners, available in Natural matte finish, disc. 1999.

	N/A	$425 - 500	$250 - 300	$739

D 5 P – dreadnought style, solid spruce top, round soundhole, solid rosewood back/sides, mahogany neck, ebony fingerboard with abalone inlay, ebony bridge, three-per-side gold tuners, available in Natural High Gloss finish, disc. 1999.

	N/A	$850 - 950	$525 - 600	$1,439

D 61 – dreadnought style, solid cedar top, round soundhole, laminated mahogany back/sides, mahogany neck, rosewood fingerboard with white dot inlay, rosewood bridge, three-per-side Schaller tuners, available in Natural Matte finish, disc. 1999.

	N/A	$375 - 450	$200 - 250	$659

D 62 – dreadnought style, solid spruce top, round soundhole, solid rosewood back/sides, mahogany neck, rosewood fingerboard with white dot inlay, rosewood bridge, three-per-side Schaller tuners, available in Natural High Gloss finish, disc. 1999.

	N/A	$875 - 1,000	$525 - 600	

D 63 – dreadnought style, solid spruce top, round soundhole, solid rosewood back/sides, mahogany neck, ebony fingerboard with abalone inlay, ebony bridge, three-per-side gold tuners, available in Natural High Gloss finish, disc. 1999.

	N/A	$875 - 1,000	$525 - 600	$1,499

JV 61 – jumbo style, single rounded cutaway, solid cedar top, round soundhole, laminated mahogany back/sides, mahogany neck, rosewood fingerboard with white dot inlay, rosewood bridge, three-per-side Schaller tuners, available in Natural Matte finish, disc. 1999.

	N/A	$375 - 450	$200 - 250	$695

ACOUSTIC: PRO ROUNDBACK STYLE SERIES

Z 122 12-STRING – roundback body design, 12-string configuration, solid spruce top, round soundhole, ebony fingerboard with abalone inlay, ebony bridge, six-per-side tuners, available in Natural High Gloss finish, disc. 1999.

	N/A	$650 - 750	$375 - 450	$999

MSR/NOTES	100%	EXCELLENT	AVERAGE	LAST MSR

Z V 62 6-STRING – roundback body design, solid spruce top, round soundhole, ebony fingerboard with abalone inlay, ebony bridge, three-per-side tuners, available in Natural High Gloss finish, disc. 1999.

	N/A	$525 - 600	$300 - 350	$869

ACOUSTIC: SELECT SERIES

The **GS-10** features a spruce top, round soundhole, rosewood back/sides, bound body, rosewood fingerboard with white diamond-shaped inlays, rosewood bridge, black teardrop-shaped pickguard, three-per-side tuners, and is available in a high gloss finish. The **GS-20** is similar to the GS-10, except features a rounded cutaway body; the **GS-21** is similar to the GS-20 and has an on-board preamp (9-volt) with EQ controls. Series was discontinued in 1999.

GIANNINI

Instruments currently built in Brazil. Distributed by Etros Music, LLC in Sunrise, FL. Giannini has been producing guitars since 1900.

CONTACT INFORMATION
GIANNINI
U.S. Distribution: Etros Music, LLC
10362 NW 55th Street
Sunrise, FL 33351
Phone No.: 954-746-2777
Fax No.: 954-746-2777
www.gianniniguitars.com
info@etrosmusic.com

In 1890 Tranquillo Giannini left Italy and migrated to San Paulo, Brazil where he began manufacturing guitars. The company eventually became one of the largest manufacturers of guitars in Brazil. They also produced a line of mandolins, craviolas, cavaquinhos, and violas. In the early 1970s, Giannini was distributed in the U.S. by Giannini Guitars at 75 Frost Street, Westbury (New York 11590). If that address seems somewhat familiar, that may be because it was shared by Westbury Guitars, the Merson company, and later Korg USA. Giannini Guitars are still available and distributed by Etros Music, LLC. For more information, visit Giannini's website or contact them directly.

ACOUSTIC

Giannini currently produces a wide range of acoustic guitars including classicals and misc. acoustic/electrics. The **Study Series** (MSR $180-$380) represent beginner models and are available in a variety of configurations. The **Brazil & Performance Series** ($280-$950) are classicals and cutaways with and without electronics in several configurations. The **Classical Series** ($380-$580) are classical models. The **Handcrafted Series** ($900-$2,700) are the highest-end models Giannini produces, and they are constructed with all solid woods. Giannini also produces the unique Craviola in six models, seven-strings classicals in six models, Cavaquinhos, 10 Str Brazilian Violas, and Mandolins.

CRA-65 – dreadnought style, yellow spruce top, round soundhole, Brazilian rosewood back/sides, 19-fret rosewood fingerboard and bridge, three-per-side tuners, available in Natural finish, length 40 in., body width 15.25 in., body thickness 4 in., mfg. circa early 1970s.

	N/A	$275 - 325	$125 - 175	$160

CRA-125 – dreadnought style, spruce top, round soundhole, Brazilian rosewood back/sides, 20-fret rosewood fingerboard, rosewood bridge, three-per-side tuners, available in Natural finish, length 43 in., body width 15.25 in., body thickness 4 in., mfg. circa early 1970s.

	N/A	$350 - 425	$175 - 225	$175

CRA 6N CRAVIOLA – nylon strings, spruce top, round soundhole, Brazilian rosewood back/sides, 19-fret rosewood fingerboard and bridge, three-per-side tuners, available in Natural finish, length 40 in., body width 15.25 in., body thickness 4 in., mfg. circa early 1970s.

	N/A	$300 - 350	$150 - 200	$150

This model was also available in a 12-string configuration. The Craviola is the "kidney bean-shaped" body Giannini model that turns up occasionally in the secondary market. This model may also have a Merson company label.

GIBSON

Instruments currently produced in Bozeman, MT since 1989, intermittently in Nashville, TN since 1974, and St. John's, Newfoundland, Canada since 2007. Previously produced in Kalamazoo, MI between 1894 and 1984. Distributed by the Gibson Guitar Corporation in Nashville, TN.

CONTACT INFORMATION
GIBSON
Gibson Montana
1894 Orville Way
Bozeman, MT 57915 USA
Phone No.: 406-587-4117
Fax No.: 406-587-9109
www.gibson.com/acoustics

Gibson Headquarters/Corporate
309 Plus Park Blvd.
Nashville, TN 37217
Phone No.: 615-871-4500
Fax No.: 615-884-9411
www.gibson.com
service@gibson.com

Gibson acoustic instruments were previously produced in Kalamazoo, Michigan from 1896 to 1984. The Gibson Mandolin-Guitar Manufacturing Company, Limited (which evolved into the Gibson Guitar Corporation) produced acoustic instruments in Kalamazoo, Michigan from 1902 to 1984. Gibson banjos, mandolins, and Dobros are currently manufactured by Original Acoustic Instruments (OAI), located in the Opryland Mall, in Nashville, Tennessee.

Gibson solid body and semi-hollowbody electrics are currently produced in Nashville & Memphis, Tennessee -- please refer to the *Blue Book of Electric Guitars* for both up-to-date pricing and information.

Luthier Orville H. Gibson was born in Chateaugay, New York in 1856. He moved west to Kalamazoo, Michigan. City records from 1896-1897 indicate a business address of 114 South Burdick for O.H. Gibson, Manufacturer, Musical Instruments. By 1899-1902, the city directories indicate a change to the second floor of 104 East Main.

The Gibson Mandolin-Guitar Manufacturing Company, Limited, was established at 2:55 p.m. on October 11, 1902. The agreement was formed by John W. Adams (pres.), Samuel H. Van Horn (treasurer), Sylvo Reams (sec. and also production mgr.), Lewis Williams (later secretary and gen. mgr.), and Leroy Hornbeck. Orville Gibson was not one of the founding partners, but had a separate contract to be a consultant and trainer. Gibson was also the first to purchase 500 shares of the new company's stock. In 1915, Gibson and the company negotiated a new agreement in which Orville was to be paid a monthly salary for the rest of his life. Orville, who had some troubles with his health back in 1911, was treated in 1916 at the psychiatric center of St. Lawrence State hospital in Ogdensburg, New York. Orville Gibson died of endocarditis on August 21, 1918.

In 1906 the company moved to 116 East Exchange Place, and the name was changed to Gibson Mandolin Guitar Company. In 1917, production facilities were opened at Parsons Street (the first of a total of five buildings at that location). Chicago Musical Instruments (CMI) acquired controlling interest in Gibson, Inc. in 1944. Maurice H. Berlin (president of CMI) became general secretary and treasurer of Gibson. From this date, the Gibson Sales Department became located in Chicago while the Kalamazoo plant concentrated on production.

In 1935, Gibson began investigating a prototype electric pickup. Musician Alvino Rey started research with engineers at the Lyon & Healy company (See Washburn) in Chicago, and a year later the research was moved in-house to Kalamazoo. In late 1935, Gibson debuted the hexagonal pickup on a lap steel model; this same pickup was applied to an archtop guitar and offered as the ES (Electric Spanish) 150 in 1936. The ES-150 was used by jazz guitarist Charlie Christian, and this model is still known as the "Charlie Christian" model.

After the release of Leo Fender's Broadcaster (later Telecaster) model, Gibson and guitarist Les Paul collaborated in the release of the solid body Gibson Les Paul in 1952. This model was refined with the introduction of the tune-o-matic bridge/stop tailpiece combination, and P.A.F. humbuckers through the 1950s. Under the direction of then Gibson president Ted McCarty, the Gibson company attempted to throw off the tag of being "stodgy" and old fashioned when they introduced the Flying V and Explorer models in the late 1950s. In this case, they pre-judged the public's tastes by about ten years! As guitar players' tastes changed in the late 1950s, Gibson discontinued the single cutaway Les Paul model in favor of the double cutaway SG in 1960. As the popularity of the electric blues (as championed by Eric Clapton and Michael Bloomfield) grew during the 1960s, Gibson reissued the Les Paul in 1968.

Gibson acquired Epiphone in 1957, and production of Gibson-made Epiphones began in 1959, and lasted until 1969. In 1970, production moved to Japan (or, the Epiphone name was then applied to imported instruments).

In December of 1969, E.C.L. Industries, Inc. took control of CMI. Gibson, Inc. stayed under the control of CMI until 1974, when it became a subsidiary of Norlin Industries (Norlin is named after H. Norton Stevens, President of E.C.L. and Maurice H. Berlin, President of CMI). A new factory was opened in Nashville, Tennessee during 1969.

In 1980, Norlin decided to sell Gibson. Norlin also relocated some of the sales, marketing, administration, and finance personnel from Chicago to the Nashville plant. Most Gibson production took place in Nashville after 1980, and the Kalamazoo plant was used mostly for custom orders. In 1983, then-Gibson president Marty Locke informed plant manager Jim Deurloo that the Kalamazoo plant would close. Final production was in June of 1984, and the plant closed three months later. [On a side note: Rather than give up on the sixty-five-year-old facilities, Jim Deurloo, Marv Lamb, and J.P. Moats started the Heritage Guitar Company in April of 1985. The company is located in the original 1917 building.]

In January of 1986, Henry Juszkiewicz (current CEO), David Berryman (current president), and Gary Zebrowski bought Gibson for five million dollars. Since the sale in 1986, the revived Gibson USA company has been at work to return to the level of quality the company had reached earlier. Expansion of the acoustic guitar production began in Bozeman, Montana during 1989.

Gibson's Historic Collection models were introduced in 1991, and during 1993, the Custom Shop moved into a separate production facility on Massman Drive. Custom Shop instruments built at Gibson's Custom Shops (both Nashville, TN and Bozeman, MT plants) began using their own Gibson Custom Art Historic logo on the back of the headstock in 1996. The Gibson Custom, Art, and Historic division is responsible for producing Historic Collection models, commemorative guitars, custom-ordered and special edition guitars.

In the tail end of 1996, both the Dobro production facilities in California and the Montana mandolin facilities were closed down. Current Dobro production was resumed in Nashville at the OAI facility in the Opryland Mall beginning 1997, and banjo and mandolin manufacture followed shortly.

In 1998, Gibson opened up a new dealer level for specialty guitars, both acoustic and electric. The Gibson Historic Collection Award Dealer models are only available through approximately thirty-seven Award Level dealers, and feature specific year/model designated custom instruments at an upscale price.

Gibson started the new millennium in perhaps its best shape in a long time. With the Montana plant now producing consistently high quality acoustic instruments (perhaps their best ever), and the electric models being led by the extensive offerings from the Gibson Custom, Art, and Historic Division, this legendary American guitar company seems to be in great shape for the next century of guitar manufacturing.

During 2001, Gibson opened up a new production facility in Memphis, TN, primarily manufacturing ES-335 type electric instruments and variations. At the end of 2001, Gibson Guitar Corp. purchased Baldwin, longtime manufacturer of pianos and organs.

During 2002, Gibson purchased long time guitar retailer Valley Arts Guitars, and opened up a separate retail store in downtown Nashville.

During 2004, Gibson introduced their Americana Series of acoustic electric guitars, featuring two models, the Ranger and the Pioneer Cutaway. Both models are based on the Chet Atkins SST solid body acoustic concept, and are manufactured by Gibson USA, located in Nashville.

In 2005, the Custom Shop in Bozeman released Designer Customs, Historic Collection, Historic Signature, and Master Museum Collection instruments in limited quantities - many of them are limited to less than twenty-four per month.

Beginning 2006, all Montana Gibson acoustics are equipped with an active bridge pickup with the exception of the Advanced Jumbo, Robert Johnson L-1, and Arlo Guthrie LG-2.

In mid-2007, Gibson bought Garrison Guitars in St. John's, Newfoundland, Canada and began building a line of traditional-shaped acoustic guitars in their factory that are branded Gibson.

Sources include: Gibson.com, Walter Carter, *Gibson Guitars: 100 Years of an American Icon*; and Tom Wheeler, *American Guitars*.

GIBSON ACOUSTIC IDENTIFYING FEATURES: HEADSTOCK LOGO

The most consistent and easily found feature that goes across all models of Gibson production is the logo, or lack of one, found on the peghead. The very earliest instruments made are generally found with a star inside a crescent design, or a blank peghead, and labels inside the body. This lasted until approximately 1902.

From 1902 to the late 1920s, "The Gibson," inlaid in pearl and placed at a slant, is found on the peghead. In the late 1920s, this style of logo was changed to having "The Gibson" read straight across the peghead as opposed to being slanted. Peghead lettering was done in silver stencil from the mid-late 1920s, then were white silk screened until 1942, when it changed to gold. Pearl logos were also different.

Flattop acoustics production began during 1926, and these instruments generally do not have "The" on the inlay (they just have "Gibson" in script writing). By about 1931-32, this was the established peghead logo for Gibson. Just before WWII, Gibson began making the lettering on the logo thicker and this became standard on most pre-war instruments. Right after WWII, the styling of the logo remained but it became slanted once again.

In 1947, the logo that is still in use today made its debut. This logo has a block styling with the "G" having a tail, the "i" dot is touching the "G," the "b" and "o" are open and the "n" is connected at the bottom. The logo is still slanted. By 1951, the dot on the "i" was no longer connected to the "G." In 1967, the logo styling became even more squared (pentographed) with the "b" and "o" becoming closed and the "i" dot being removed.

In 1970, Gibson replaced the black tinted piece of wood that had been used on the peghead face with a black fiber that the logo and other peghead inlay were placed into. With the change in peghead facing came a slightly smaller logo lettering. In 1972, the "i" dot reappeared on the peghead logo. In 1981, the "n" is connected at the top of the "o." There are a few models through the years that do not follow this timeline (i.e.: reissues and limited editions), but most of the production instruments can be found with the above feature changes.

GIBSON ACOUSTIC IDENTIFYING FEATURES: TUNERS

The configuration of the Kluson tuners used on Gibson instruments can be used to date an instrument. Before 1959, all Kluson tuners with plastic buttons had a single ring around the stem end of the button. In 1960, this was changed to a double ring configuration. Early 1950s tuners have no writing in the center line. Mid-1950s to late 1950s production features Kluson deluxe tuners with single line marking. By the mid-1960s, a two-line marking states "Kluson Deluxe."

GIBSON ACOUSTIC IDENTIFYING FEATURES: PEGHEAD VOLUTE

"Made in USA" was stamped into the wood in back of the peghead beginning in 1969. Another dating feature of Gibsons is the use of a peghead volute found on instruments made between 1970 and 1973. Also, in 1965 Gibson switched from 17 degrees to 14 degrees on the tilt of the peghead. Before 1950, peghead thickness varied, getting narrower towards the top of the peghead. After 1950, pegheads all became one uniform thickness, from bottom to top.

GIBSON COMMON ABBREVIATIONS

- C - Cutaway
- D - Dreadnought or Double
- E - Electric
- ES - Electric (Electro) Spanish
- GS - Gut String

- J - Jumbo
- LE - Limited Edition
- MOP - Mother-of-Pearl
- S - Spanish, SolidBody, Special or Super
- SG - Solid Guitar

- SJ - Super Jumbo
- T - Tremolo or Thinline
- V - Venetian or Vibrato

GIBSON ACOUSTIC FINISH CODES

Current Gibson finish codes with abbreviations include the following:

- AC - Antique Cherry Back & Sides
- AN - Antique Natural
- AT - Antique Walnut Back & Sides

- EB - Ebony
- HC - Heritage Cherry Sunburst
- NAT - Natural

- VCS - Vintage Cherry Sunburst
- VS - Vintage Sunburst

GIBSON PRODUCTION MODELS CODES & SHIPMENT TOTALS

For ease in identifying current Gibson production guitar models in this section, the Gibson Family Code/SKU may follow the model's name in parentheses (in some cases, only the alphabetical prefix is listed, as the individual finishes and/or colors will result in the rest of the code). This also is true when brackets[] are encountered within a family code.

For anyone who is interested in individual Gibson model production totals from 1937 to 1979 (including guitars, basses, artist models, custom models, mandolins, banjos, ukuleles, steel guitars, effects, and amps), we recommend that you read *Gibson Shipment Totals 1937-1979* by Larry Meiners.

Gibson acoustic archtop models that include "floating" pickups or built-in acoustic/electric pickups are listed in the acoustic electric category at the end of the Gibson section.

ACOUSTIC: GENERAL INFORMATION

Lloyd Loar came to Gibson as an acoustic engineer in 1919. He is widely known for bringing many new innovations to Gibson guitars in the 1920s. Some of these innovations included elevated fingerboards, longer necks on mandolins, and the f-hole mandolins and guitars. These instruments were named **Style 5**, and designated the Master Model Series. Approximately 250 guitars and mandolins were personally inspected by Loar. Some guitars made since 1924 may have the virzi tone producer, which is an oval-shaped wood sounding board suspended from the top. Loar left Gibson in 1924, and the guitars he designed will command a premium in the secondary marketplace.

For organizational consideration, the category names and variations have been listed in alphabetical sequence. In the numbered series, models will start with the lowest number, and end with the highest. Named models will appear at the end of the categories

MSR/NOTES	100%	EXCELLENT	AVERAGE	LAST MSR

whenever possible. The following categories appear in this order: B Series, Blue Ridge/Blues King Series, C Models, Centennial Series, CL Series, Dove Series, Everly Brothers Series, Folksinger/Gospel Series, Hall of Fame Models, Hummingbird Series, Jumbo/J and SJ Models, L Series, LG Series, Mark Series, Misc., Model O & U Series, Songbird Series, Songwriter Series, Super 300/Super 400 Series, Working Man & Working Musician Series. The current and recent Gibson Historic Collection models can be found after these categories. Acoustic electric models can be found at the end of this section, under the Acoustic Electric category. In some cases, acoustic electric models/submodels may appear as a variation in the acoustic section.

While the thought of a Sunburst finished Les Paul brings many players (and collectors) a case of the warm fuzzies, Gibson acoustic guitar collectors are more partial to a Natural finish acoustic over a similar model finished in Sunburst. As a result, there is a premium for Natural finished Gibson acoustics.

ACOUSTIC: B SERIES

Several tops of the B Series guitars have cracked and been repaired. The values in this section reflect guitars in original uncracked condition. Values will be impacted negatively based on the amount of cracks and the condition and overall quality of the repairs.

B-15 – small body, spruce top, round soundhole, tortoiseshell pickguard, one-stripe rosette, bound top, mahogany back/sides/neck, 14/20-fret rosewood fingerboard with pearl dot inlay, rosewood bridge with white pins, three-per-side tuners with plastic buttons, available in Natural finish, 14.5 in. body width, over 12,000 mfg. 1967-1971.

1967-1969	N/A	$550 - 700	$350 - 425	
1970-1971	N/A	$475 - 600	$275 - 350	

B-20 – mahogany back/sides, black binding, standard peghead, 14.5 in. body width, approx. 500 mfg. 1971-72.

	N/A	$475 - 600	$275 - 350	

B-25/B-25N – small body, spruce top, mahogany back, laminated mahogany sides, round soundhole with single ring rosette, three-ply top body binding, single-ply back binding, mahogany neck, 14/20-fret rosewood fingerboard with pearl dot inlays, blackface headstock overlay (1962-69) or no overlay (1970-77) with decal logo, three-per-side nickel tuners with plastic buttons, rosewood bridge (1962-63, circa 1969-1977) or plastic bridge (1963-1968) with adjustable saddle (1962-69) and white pins, long tortoise pickguard, available in Cherry Sunburst (B-25) or Natural (B-25N) finish, 14.25 in. body width, 24.75 in. scale, mfg. 1962-1977.

1962-1963 Wood Bridge	N/A	$1,400 - 1,750	$850 - 1,050	
1963-1968 Plastic Bridge	N/A	$1,200 - 1,500	$775 - 950	
1969-1977	N/A	$1,000 - 1,250	$600 - 750	

From 1962 to 1968 the bridge featured an upper belly and in 1969 it was changed to a lower belly. In 1972, a black outer layer was added to the body binding.

* **B-25 3/4/B-25N 3/4** – similar to the B-25, except has a 3/4 sized body, 12.75 in. body width, available in Cherry Sunburst or Natural (1966-68) finish, mfg. 1962-68.

1961-1963 Wood Bridge	N/A	$1,000 - 1,250	$600 - 750	
1963-1968 Plastic Bridge	N/A	$800 - 1,000	$475 - 600	

* **B-25-12/B-25-12N** – spruce top, round soundhole, tortoiseshell pickguard, bound body/rosette, mahogany back/sides/neck, 14/20-fret rosewood fingerboard with pearl dot inlay, reverse belly rosewood bridge with white pins, blackface peghead with decal logo, six-per-side tuners with plastic buttons, available in Cherry Sunburst and Natural finishes, mfg. 1962-1977.

1962-1964	N/A	$1,300 - 1,600	$775 - 975	
1965-1969	N/A	$1,125 - 1,400	$675 - 850	
1970-1977	N/A	$950 - 1,200	$575 - 700	

In 1963, strings-through-bridge replaced the original design, with no bridge pins. In 1965, the redesigned reverse bridge replaced the previous design, and a trapeze tailpiece added. In 1970, a standard bridge with white pins replaced the previous design, there was no trapeze tailpiece, and the Cherry Sunburst finish was discontinued.

* **B-25 12 Historic Reissue** – similar to the B-25 12, available in Vintage Sunburst finish, limited mfg. 2005 only.

	N/A	$1,400 - 1,750	$850 - 1,050	$3,459

B-45-12/B-45-12N – slope shouldered large body, spruce top, round soundhole, tortoise pickguard, two-stripe bound body/rosette, mahogany back/sides/neck, 14/20-fret rosewood fingerboard with pearl dot inlay, rosewood bridge with adjustable saddle, trapeze tailpiece, blackface peghead with pearl split diamond inlay/logo decal, six-per-side nickel tuners with plastic buttons, available in Tobacco Sunburst, Natural and Cherry Sunburst finish, 16 in. wide body, mfg. 1961-1979.

1961-1962	N/A	$1,875 - 2,350	$1,125 - 1,400	
1962-1964	N/A	$1,600 - 2,000	$950 - 1,200	
1965-1969	N/A	$1,400 - 1,750	$850 - 1,050	
1970-1979	N/A	$1,125 - 1,400	$675 - 850	

In 1962, reverse belly bridge with pins, adjustable saddle replaced original part/design. In 1964, string through reverse belly bridge replaced previous part/design, Natural finish (Model B-45-12 N) became an option. In 1965, rectangular bridge/trapeze tailpiece replaced previous part/design. In 1970, redesigned pickguard, 12/20-fret fingerboard, standard bridge with pins, Tobacco Sunburst finish became an option.

MSR/NOTES	100%	EXCELLENT	AVERAGE	LAST MSR

ACOUSTIC: BLUE RIDGE SERIES

BLUE RIDGE – slope shouldered body style, solid spruce top, round soundhole, black pickguard, three-stripe bound body/rosette, laminated rosewood back/sides, mahogany neck, 14/20-fret rosewood fingerboard with pearl dot inlay, reverse belly rosewood bridge with black white dot pins, blackface peghead with screened logo, three-per-side chrome tuners, available in Natural finish, approx. 5,000 mfg. 1968-1975.

	100%	EXCELLENT	AVERAGE	
1968-1969	N/A	$950 - 1,200	$575 - 725	
1970-1975	N/A	$800 - 1,000	$475 - 600	

In 1969, a standard bridge replaced the original design. In 1973, a low impedance pickup became an option (however, only one was shipped). Less than 20 left-hand instruments were made from 1971 to 1975.

* **Blue Ridge 12** – similar to Blue Ridge, except in 12-string configuration with six-per-side tuners, approximately 370 mfg. 1970-78.

	N/A	$800 - 1,000	$475 - 600	

ACOUSTIC: C (CLASSICAL) SERIES

The following models represent classical instruments, and all models have a dual slotted headstock. 14.25 in. wide by 19 in. long, by 4.5 in. deep, 25.5 in. scale.

C-L – student model, thin shouldered dreadnought shape, transducer pickup, abalone rosette, two-point tortoiseshell celluloid pickguard, mahogany back, non-gloss finish, approx. 3,750 mfg. 1969-1971.

	N/A	$325 - 400	$200 - 250	

C-0 – classical style, spruce top, mahogany back and sides, round soundhole with decorative Spanish rosette, black body binding, mahogany neck, 12/19-fret rosewood fingerboard, slotted headstock with center stripe and Gibson decal logo, three-per-side open-style chrome tuners with plastic buttons, rosewood wraparound bridge, 14.25 in. body width, 19 in. body length, 4.5 in. body depth, 25.5 in. scale, over 15,000 produced, mfg. 1962-1971.

1962-1964	N/A	$525 - 650	$325 - 400	
1965-1971	N/A	$400 - 500	$250 - 300	

The C-0 and C-1 are very similar with the only differences listed in literature indicating the C-0 has a one-piece top and back while the C-1 has a two-piece top and back.

C-1 – spruce top, round soundhole, bound body, two-stripe rosette, mahogany back/sides/neck, 12/19-fret rosewood fingerboard, rosewood wraparound bridge, three-per-side nickel tuners with plastic buttons, available in Natural finish, over 14,000 mfg. 1957-1971.

1957-1964	N/A	$550 - 700	$325 - 400	
1965-1971	N/A	$475 - 600	$300 - 350	

In 1966, wooden inlay rosette, chrome tuners replaced original part/design.

* **C-1 D Laredo** – similar to C-1, except has rounded peghead, mfg. 1963-1970.

1963-1964	N/A	$600 - 750	$375 - 450	
1965-1970	N/A	$525 - 650	$325 - 400	

* **C-1 E** – similar to C-1, except has ceramic bridge pickup, approx. 675 mfg. 1960-68.

1960-1964	N/A	$650 - 800	$400 - 475	
1965-1971	N/A	$550 - 700	$325 - 400	

* **C-1 S** – similar to C-1, except has petite student size body, approx. 865 mfg. 1961-67.

1961-1964	N/A	$525 - 650	$325 - 400	
1965-1967	N/A	$450 - 550	$275 - 325	

C-2 – spruce top, round soundhole, bound body, two-stripe rosette, maple back/side, mahogany neck, 12/19-fret rosewood fingerboard, rosewood wraparound bridge with pearl block inlay, three-per-side nickel tuners with plastic buttons, available in Natural Top/Mahogany back/side finish, approx. 960 mfg. 1960-1970.

1960-1964	N/A	$675 - 850	$400 - 500	
1965-1970	N/A	$550 - 700	$325 - 400	

In 1966, a redesigned rosette and a peghead replaced the original design.

C-4 – similar to C-2, except has gold tuners, available in Natural top/rosewood back/sides finish, approx. 150 mfg. 1962-68.

1962-1964	N/A	$750 - 950	$450 - 575	
1965-1968	N/A	$675 - 850	$400 - 500	

C-6 RICHARD PICK CUSTOM – classic style, spruce top, round soundhole, tortoiseshell bound body, wooden inlay rosette, Brazilian rosewood back/sides, mahogany neck, 12/19-fret ebony fingerboard, wraparound rosewood bridge, rosewood veneered peghead, three-per-side gold tuners, available in Natural finish, approx. 450 mfg. 1958-1970.

1958-1964	N/A	$1,050 - 1,300	$650 - 800	
1965-1970	N/A	$950 - 1,200	$575 - 725	

In 1966, pearl block bridge inlay was added.

MSR/NOTES	100%	EXCELLENT	AVERAGE	LAST MSR

C-8 GRAND CLASSIC – similar to C-6, except has different rosette pattern, narrow peghead, approx. 110 mfg. 1962-69.

1962-1964	N/A	$1,400 - 1,750	$850 - 1,050	
1965-1969	N/A	$1,200 - 1,500	$725 - 900	

C-100 – mahogany back, ebony fingerboard, standard width slotted peghead, labeled "Master Style," satin non-gloss finish, approx. 430 mfg. 1970-71.

	N/A	$350 - 450	$225 - 275	

C-200 – mahogany back and sides, similar to C-100 model, except has gloss finish, approx. 200 mfg. 1971-72.

	N/A	$450 - 550	$275 - 325	

C-300 – mahogany back and sides, wood binding, wider rosette, rosewood fingerboard, narrow peghead with dip in center of top, approx. 65 mfg. 1971-72.

	N/A	$575 - 700	$350 - 425	

C-400 GRAND – similar to C-500, except has chrome plated hardware, approx. 30 mfg. 1971-72.

	N/A	$775 - 950	$475 - 575	

C-500 – rosewood back and sides, decorative Spanish purfling, abalone and ivory bridge inlays, laminated mahogany/ebony neck, ebony fingerboard, narrow peghead with dip in center of top, gold plated hardware, mfg. 1969-1970.

	N/A	$925 - 1,150	$575 - 700	

C-800 – rosewood back and sides, mfg. 1969-1970.

	N/A	$1,075 - 1,350	$650 - 800	

C-1000 – rosewood back and sides, mfg. 1969-1970.

	N/A	$1,200 - 1,500	$725 - 900	

FLAMENCO 2 – classical styling, spruce top, round soundhole, two white pickguards, tortoiseshell bound body, wooden inlay rosette, cypress back/side, mahogany neck, 12/19-fret rosewood fingerboard, rosewood wraparound bridge with pearl block inlay, rosewood veneered peghead with logo decal, three-per-side nickel tuners with plastic buttons, available in Natural Top/Mahogany back/side finish, approx. 300 mfg. 1963-68.

1963-1964	N/A	$1,400 - 1,750	$850 - 1,050	
1965-1967	N/A	$1,200 - 1,500	$725 - 900	

ACOUSTIC: CENTENNIAL SERIES

During 1994, Gibson began offering the acoustic Centennial series models to celebrate Gibson's 100-year anniversary (1894 to 1994). There were twelve models in the program, and they were released at the rate of one new model per month. No more than 101 instruments of each model were produced. Gibson's plan was to have 100 dealers that year, with each one committed to a package of 12 guitars. Those dealers received a custom-made oak and glass humidfied display cabinet at no charge to display each new model.

Models included the 1929 L-2 (Jan. 1994), 1933 Century (Feb. 1994), 1934 Gibson Jumbo (Mar. 1994), 1934 Roy Smeck Radio Grande (April 1994), 1938 Super Jumbo 200 (May 1994), 1939 Super Jumbo 100 (June 1994), 1940 Jumbo 55 (July 1994), 1948 SJ-200N Aug. 1994), 1950 CF-100E (Sept. 1994), 1951 J-185 (Oct. 1994), 1963 Hummingbird (Nov. 1994), and the J-200 Rose (Dec. 1994).

ACOUSTIC: CF SERIES

CF-100 – single sharp cutaway small body, spruce top, mahogany back and sides, round soundhole with single ring rosette, body binding, mahogany neck, 14/20-fret bound rosewood fingerboard with pearl trapezoid inlays, black headstock overlay with pearl Gibson logo and crown inlay, three-per-side nickel tuners, rosewood reverse bridge with two pearl dot inlays, white bridge pins, tortoise teardop pickguard (1950-mid-1950s) or larger J-35 pre-war-style pickguard (mid-1950s-1959), available in Sunburst finish, 14.125 in. body width, 19.5 in. body length, 4.5 in. deep, 24.75 in. scale, approx. 1,675 mfg. 1950-59.

1950-1955	N/A	$3,400 - 4,250	$2,050 - 2,550	
1956-1959	N/A	$3,000 - 3,750	$1,800 - 2,250	

Early models may have a gold logo or no logo at all.

* **CF-100 E** – similar to the CF-100, except has a single coil pickup mounted between the end of the fingerboard and soundhole and two knobs mounted on the lower treble bout (v, tone), approx. 1,250 mfg. 1951-59.

1951-1955	N/A	$3,800 - 4,750	$2,275 - 2,850	
1956-1959	N/A	$3,400 - 4,250	$2,050 - 2,550	

ACOUSTIC: CL SERIES

The Custom Acoustic Line Series was manufactured 1997-98. Most models featured the Gibson Advanced Bracing pattern and factory-installed transducer.

MSR/NOTES	100%	EXCELLENT	AVERAGE	LAST MSR

CL-20 STANDARD PLUS (CL20) – solid Sitka spruce top, round soundhole, black body binding, solid mahogany back/sides, 14/20-fret rosewood fingerboard with abalone snowflake inlay, moustache-style rosewood bridge with white bridge pins, three-per-side gold tuners, batwing-shaped tortoiseshell pickguard, available in Antique Natural finish, mfg. 1997-98.

	N/A	$875 - 1,100	$525 - 650	$1,499

This model did not feature the installed transducer. The regular CL-20 has a laminated arched back.

CL-30 DELUXE (CL30) – solid Sitka spruce top, round soundhole, multi-ply body binding, solid African bubinga back/sides, 14/20-fret rosewood fingerboard with abalone floret inlay, rosewood headstock veneer, mother-of-pearl headstock logo/abalone floret inlay, moustache-style rosewood bridge with white bridgepins, three-per-side gold tuners, batwing-shaped tortoise pickguard, available in Antique Natural gloss lacquer finish, mfg. 1997-98.

	N/A	$950 - 1,200	$575 - 725	$1,849

* *CL-35 Deluxe Cutaway (CL35)* – similar to the CL-30, except features a single Venetian cutaway body, available in Antique Natural gloss lacquer finish, mfg. 1997-98.

	N/A	$1,075 - 1,350	$650 - 800	$1,949

CL-40 ARTIST (CL40) – solid Sitka spruce top, round soundhole, abalone rosette, multi-ply body binding, solid rosewood back/sides, 14/20-fret ebony fingerboard with abalone angel wing inlay, mother-of-pearl headstock logo/abalone angel wing inlay, moustache-style ebony bridge with abalone dot bridgepins, three-per-side gold tuners, batwing-shaped tortoise pickguard, available in Antique Natural Gloss Lacquer finish, mfg. 1997-98.

	N/A	$1,200 - 1,500	$725 - 900	$2,649

* *CL-45 Artist Cutaway (CL45)* – similar to the CL-40, except features a single Venetian cutaway body, available in Antique Natural Gloss Lacquer finish, mfg. 1997-98.

	N/A	$1,400 - 1,750	$850 - 1,050	$2,749

CL-50 SUPREME (CL50) – solid Sitka spruce top, round soundhole, abalone rosette, abalone body binding, solid rosewood back/sides, 14/20-fret ebony fingerboard with abalone autumn leaf inlay, bound headstock, mother-of-pearl headstock logo/abalone autumn leaf inlay, moustache-style ebony bridge with abalone dot bridgepins, three-per-side gold tuners, batwing-shaped tortoiseshell pickguard, available in Antique Natural Gloss Lacquer finish, mfg. 1997-98.

	N/A	$3,000 - 3,750	$1,800 - 2,250	$4,999

This model was available with a tree-of-life fingerboard inlay (with cost upcharge).

ACOUSTIC: DOVE SERIES

DOVE – square-shouldered dreadnought-style body, spruce top, figured maple back and sides, round soundhole with three ring rosette, three-stripe bound body, 14/20-fret bound ebony fingerboard with pearl parallelogram inlay, black headstock overlay with pearl plant/logo inlay, three-per-side nickel tuners, tortoiseshell pickguard with dove inlay, enlarged rosewood bridge with black pearl dot pins, pearl dove inlay on bridge wings, available in Natural or Cherry Sunburst finish, mfg. 1962-1996.

1962-1964	N/A	$4,800 - 6,000	$2,875 - 3,600	
1965-1966	N/A	$3,400 - 4,250	$2,050 - 2,550	
1967-1968	N/A	$2,800 - 3,500	$1,675 - 2,100	
1969-1970	N/A	$2,400 - 3,000	$1,450 - 1,800	
1971-1984	N/A	$2,000 - 2,500	$1,200 - 1,500	
1985-1996	N/A	$1,800 - 2,250	$1,075 - 1,350	$2,450

• **Add 10-20% for Natural finish.**

In 1969, adjustable bridge replaced original part/design. In 1970, non-adjustable bridge replaced previous part/design. In 1975, ebony fingerboard replaced original part/design. In 1996, the '60s Dove model superseded the original Dove model (see listing below).

DOVE REISSUE HISTORIC – dreadnought body, solid Sitka spruce top, round soundhole, three-ply bound body/rosette, flamed maple back/sides, maple neck, 14/20-fret bound rosewood fingerboard with pearl parallelogram inlay, rosewood dove-wing bridge with mother-of-pearl inlay, black white dot bridgepins, bound blackface peghead with abalone crown/logo inlay, three-per-side gold tuners, tortoiseshell pickguard with engraved dove inlay, available in Antique Cherry (Natural top and Cherry finish back/sides) Lacquer finish, mfg. 2005-08.

	N/A	$1,800 - 2,250	$1,075 - 1,350	$4,108

• **Subtract 5% if w/o active pickup (became standard 2006).**

100 mfg. beginning 2005. This model's name was changed to Dove Reissue Historic during 2005.

Beginning 2006, this model included an active pickup.

DOVE ARTIST – solid Sitka spruce top, Indian rosewood back/sides, mahogany neck, ebony fingerboard/bridge, mother-of-pearl wing bridge and fretboard inlays, includes active tranducer pickup, available in Antique Natural finish, mfg. 1999-2005.

	N/A	$1,350 - 1,650	$825 - 1,000	$3,119

* *Dove Artist Cutaway EC* – similar to the Dove Artist, except has a single cutaway, mfg. 1999-2005.

	N/A	$1,400 - 1,750	$850 - 1,050	$3,227

MSR/NOTES	100%	EXCELLENT	AVERAGE	LAST MSR

ELVIS PRESLEY DOVE (ARTIST MODEL ACDO) – square shouldered dreadnought body, solid spruce top, maple back and sides, mahogany neck, rosewood fingerboard and bridge, Elvis Presley signature engraved on truss rod cover, distinctive black pickguard, available in Black Lacquer finish, mfg. 2001-2010.

	100%	EXCELLENT	AVERAGE	LAST MSR
	$3,650	$2,000 - 2,350	$1,400 - 1,650	$4,697

* **Subtract 5% if w/o active pickup (became standard 2006).**

This model was available in left-hand configuration at no extra charge. An active pickup became standard on this model during 2006.

DOVES IN FLIGHT (ACDFACGH1) – dove dreadnought style, hand select solid spruce top, round soundhole, bound body, flamed maple back/sides, three-piece maple neck, 14/20-fret bound ebony fingerboard with pearl parallelogram inlay, ebony dove-tail bridge with dove inlay, white bridgepins, blackface peghead with mother-of-pearl "3 Doves in Flight"/logo inlay, Custom Shop seal on back of headstock, three-per-side gold tuners, tortoise pickguard with engraved dove inlay, available in Antique Cherry (Natural top and Cherry back and sides) Lacquer finish, mfg. 1997-98.

	100%	EXCELLENT	AVERAGE	LAST MSR
	N/A	$3,600 - 4,500	$2,150 - 2,700	$5,499

NEW DOVES IN FLIGHT CUSTOM (MODEL SSDF) – customer selected back/side wood, features 28 mother-of-pearl doves inlaid in fingerboard, pickguard, and bridge, ebony neck and fingerboard, abalone top trim and rosette, available in Antique Cherry finish, mfg. by MT Custom Shop beginning 1999.

	100%	EXCELLENT	AVERAGE	LAST MSR
	$6,250	$3,050 - 3,800	$1,900 - 2,250	$8,077

Gibson's Doves In Flight model has a special serialization system of DF YNNNY, where the first and last digits indicate the last two digits of the year it was produced and the middle three are the production ranking for that year.

* *Doves in Flight Rosewood (Model SSDF)* – similar to the New Doves In Flight Custom, except has a rosewood fingerboard and rosewood bridge, available in Antique Cherry, limited availability 2012-2013.

	100%	EXCELLENT	AVERAGE	LAST MSR
	$5,000	$3,250 - 3,750	$1,625 - 2,000	$6,450

SUPER DOVE (MODEL SJSD) – single cutaway jumbo-style body, AAA Sitka spruce top, AAA eastern curly maple back and sides, round soundhole with abalone rosette, multi-ply body binding, mahogany neck, 14/20-fret bound ebony fingerboard with 12th fret MOP dove inlays, black bound headstock overlay with Gibson logo and crown inlays, three-per-side gold Grover Keystone tuners, ebony bridge with MOP dove inlays, custom dove pickguard, Fishman Aura Pro pickup, available in Antique Natural or Vintage Sunburst finish, 3 in. body depth, mfg. 2009-2012.

	100%	EXCELLENT	AVERAGE	LAST MSR
	$3,900	$2,050 - 2,550	$1,250 - 1,550	$5,024

ACOUSTIC: EVERLY BROTHERS SERIES

EVERLY BROTHERS – spruce top, round soundhole, two tortoiseshell pickguards, two-stripe bound body/rosette, maple back/sides, one-piece mahogany neck, 14/20-fret rosewood fingerboard with pearl star inlay, reverse belly adjustable bridge with pearl dot inlay, blackface peghead with pearl star/logo inlay, three-per-side gold tuners, available in Black, Cherry Sunburst, Natural top/Red back/sides, or Natural top/Walnut back/sides (rare, approx. 45 mfg. 1963 only) finishes, approx. 440 mfg. 1962-1971.

	100%	EXCELLENT	AVERAGE	LAST MSR
1962-1964	N/A	$9,500 - 12,000	$5,750 - 7,250	
1965-1967	N/A	$7,250 - 9,000	$4,500 - 5,500	
1968-1972	N/A	$4,800 - 6,000	$2,900 - 3,600	

This model also known as Model J-180. In 1968, black pickguards, Natural Top/Walnut Back/Sides finish replaced original part/design.

* *The Everly J-180 (AC18)* – jumbo style, spruce top, round soundhole, two black pickguards, multistripe bound body/rosette, figured maple back/sides/neck, 14/20-fret bound rosewood fingerboard with pearl star inlay, rosewood mustache bridge with pearl star inlay/white pins, multibound blackface peghead with pearl star/logo inlay, three-per-side nickel tuners, available in Antique Ebony or Heritage Cherry Sunburst finishes, mfg. 1994-97.

	100%	EXCELLENT	AVERAGE	LAST MSR
	N/A	$1,400 - 1,750	$850 - 1,050	$2,000

* *Everly Cutaway* – similar to The Everly, except has single sharp cutaway, tortoiseshell pickguards, gold tuners, transducer pickups/preamp system, available in Antique Ebony or Heritage Cherry Sunburst finishes, mfg. 1994-97.

	100%	EXCELLENT	AVERAGE	LAST MSR
	N/A	$1,400 - 1,750	$850 - 1,050	$2,300

ACOUSTIC: FOLKSINGER & GOSPEL SERIES

F-25 (FOLKSINGER) – small body, spruce top, round soundhole, two white pickguards, two-stripe bound body/rosette, mahogany back/sides/neck, 12/18-fret rosewood fingerboard with pearl dot inlay, rosewood reverse belly bridge with white pins/two pearl dot inlay, blackface peghead with screened logo, three-per-side nickel tuners with plastic buttons, available in Natural finish, approx. 3,350 mfg. 1963-1970.

	100%	EXCELLENT	AVERAGE	LAST MSR
1963-1964	N/A	$1,200 - 1,500	$725 - 900	
1965-1970	N/A	$950 - 1,200	$575 - 725	

In 1969, the body and peghead were redesigned, a standard bridge replaced the original design, and white pickguards were discontinued.

MSR/NOTES	100%	EXCELLENT	AVERAGE	LAST MSR

FJ-N (FOLKSINGER JUMBO) – jumbo body, spruce top, round soundhole, two white pickguards, three-stripe bound body/rosette, mahogany back/sides/neck, 12/18-fret bound rosewood fingerboard with pearl trapezoid inlay, rosewood reverse bridge with white pins/two pearl dot inlay, blackface peghead with pearl crown/logo inlay, three-per-side nickel tuners with plastic buttons, available in Natural finish, approx. 650 mfg. 1963-68.

1963-1964	N/A	$2,800 - 3,500	$1,675 - 2,100	
1965-1968	N/A	$2,000 - 2,500	$1,200 - 1,500	

GOSPEL (1973-1980 MFG.) – dreadnought body, spruce top, round soundhole, tortoiseshell pickguard, three-stripe bound body/rosette, laminated maple back/sides, maple neck, 14/20-fret ebony fingerboard with pearl dot inlay, ebony bridge with black pearl dot pins, blackface peghead with dove/logo decals, three-per-side chrome tuners, available in Walnut (approx. 270 mfg.) or Natural (most common) finish, mfg. 1973-1980.

	N/A	$750 - 950	$475 - 575	

GOSPEL (1993-1996 MFG.) – dreadnought style, spruce top, round soundhole, tortoiseshell pickguard, multistripe bound body/rosette, mahogany back/sides/neck, 14/20-fret rosewood fingerboard with pearl dot inlay, rosewood bridge with white pins, blackface peghead with screened vase/logo, three-per-side nickel tuners with pearloid buttons, available in Antique Natural or Natural top/Antique Walnut back/sides finishes, mfg. 1993-96.

	N/A	$950 - 1,200	$575 - 725	$1,050

* *Gospel AV (1993-1996 Mfg.)* – similar to Gospel, except has transducer pickup/preamp system, available in Antique Natural, Natural top/Antique Walnut back/sides or Vintage Sunburst finish, mfg. 1993-96.

	N/A	$1,075 - 1,350	$650 - 800	$1,350

ACOUSTIC: HALL OF FAME MODELS

Hall of Fame models celebrate a famous artist's association with a specific acoustic guitar. All Hall of Fame models are numbered, limited editions.

BUDDY HOLLY MODEL J-45 (ACBH) – J-45 style, solid Sitka spruce top, round soundhole, bound body, mahogany back/sides, 14/20-fret bound rosewood fingerboard with pearl dot inlay, rosewood bridge, black bridgepins, blackface peghead with abalone banner/logo inlay, three-per-side nickel tuners, teardrop-shaped black pickguard, available in Vintage Sunburst lacquer finish, total production of 750 instruments (250 instruments a year), mfg. 1995-97.

	N/A	$2,200 - 2,750	$1,325 - 1,650	$4,999

This model has a certificate of authenticity signed by Maria Elena Holly (Buddy Holly's widow).

ELVIS KING OF ROCK J-200 MODEL (ACEP) – J-200 style, solid Sitka spruce top, round soundhole, bound body, maple back/sides, 14/20-fret bound ebony fingerboard with ten mother-of-pearl crown inlays, custom ebony bridge, white bridgepins, bound blackface peghead with mother-of-pearl crown/logo inlay, three-per-side gold tuners, bound black pickguard with mother-of-pearl crown inlay, available in Ebony Lacquer finish, mfg. 1997-98, reintroduced 2002-04.

	N/A	$1,800 - 2,250	$1,075 - 1,350	$4,000

This limited edition model was scheduled for 250 instruments. All models certified and endorsed by Graceland.

* *Elvis Presley Signature Model (Mfg. 1997-98, ACEP)* – similar to the Elvis King of Rock model, except features a premium Sitka spruce top, flamed maple back/sides, Elvis Presley fingerboard inlay with two stars, custom engraved "Elvis" pickguard, bound blackface peghead with mother-of-pearl flowerpot/logo inlay, ebony moustache bridge with pearl inlay, available in Antique Natural Lacquer finish, mfg. 1997-98.

	N/A	$2,800 - 3,500	$1,675 - 2,100	$7,999

The Elvis Presley Signature model was based on the custom J-200 used by Elvis during his 1969 concert at the International Hotel in Las Vegas. Built in cooperation with Graceland, this limited edition model was scheduled for 250 instruments. Models have a signed certificate of authenticity.

* *Elvis Presley Signature J-200 Model (New 2002, ACEP)* – similar to earlier model, except has Elvis Presley name inlaid into truss rod cover, available in Antique Natural Lacquer finish, mfg. 2002 only.

	N/A	$1,600 - 2,000	$950 - 1,200	$5,000

SJ HANK WILLIAMS JR. MODEL (ACJS) – super Jumbo (SJ) style, solid Sitka spruce top, round soundhole, multi-ply bound body/rosette, mahogany back/sides, 14/20 bound rosewood fingerboard with pearl parallelogram inlay, rosewood bridge, black bridgepins, blackface peghead with pearl logo inlay, three-per-side nickel Kluson-style tuners, teardrop-shaped black pickguard, available in Vintage Sunburst Lacquer finish, mfg. 1997-98.

	N/A	$2,000 - 2,500	$1,200 - 1,500	$4,999

ACOUSTIC: HG (HAWAIIAN) SERIES

HG (HAWAIIAN) – approx. 15 mfg. 1953 only.

	N/A	$5,500 - 7,000	$3,500 - 4,250	

HG-0 (HAWAIIAN) – approx. 165 mfg. 1937-circa 1941.

	N/A	$3,600 - 4,500	$2,150 - 2,700	

MSR/NOTES	100%	EXCELLENT	AVERAGE	LAST MSR

HG-00 (HAWAIIAN) – L-00 style body, 14 3/4 in. wide by 19 1/4 in. long, mahogany back/sides, bound top, high bone nut, 12/19-fret fingerboard, Natural finish, approx. 625 mfg. 1932-circa 1946.

	N/A	$3,000 - 3,750	$1,800 - 2,250	

HG-20 (HAWAIIAN) – dreadnought style body with four f-holes plus round soundhole, maple back/sides, limited mfg. 1929-1933.

	N/A	$3,000 - 3,750	$1,800 - 2,250	

HG-22 (HAWAIIAN) – similar to HG-20, 14 in. wide body, very limited mfg. 1929-1932.

	N/A	$3,400 - 4,250	$2,050 - 2,550	

HG-24 (HAWAIIAN) – dreadnought style body, Brazilian rosewood back/sides, with four f-holes plus round soundhole, limited mfg. 1929-1932.

	N/A	$7,250 - 9,000	$4,250 - 5,500	

HG-CENTURY (HAWAIIAN, CENTURY OF PROGRESS) – 14 3/4 in. long, approx. 30 mfg. 1937-38.

	N/A	$3,200 - 4,000	$1,925 - 2,400	

ACOUSTIC: HUMMINGBIRD SERIES

HUMMINGBIRD/HUMMINGBIRD CUSTOM – dreadnought style, spruce top, round soundhole, tortoiseshell pickguard with engraved floral/hummingbird pattern, three-stripe bound body/rosette, mahogany back/sides/neck, 14/20-fret bound rosewood fingerboard with pearl parallelogram inlay, rosewood bridge with black pearl dot pins, blackface peghead with pearl plant/logo inlay, three-per-side gold tuners with pearl buttons, available in Vintage Cherry Sunburst (most common) or Natural finish, mfg. 1960-1996.

	100%	EXCELLENT	AVERAGE	LAST MSR
1960-1964	N/A	$3,800 - 4,750	$2,275 - 2,850	
1965-1966	N/A	$2,800 - 3,500	$1,675 - 2,100	
1967-1968	N/A	$2,400 - 3,000	$1,450 - 1,800	
1969-1970	N/A	$2,200 - 2,750	$1,325 - 1,650	
1971-1980	N/A	$1,875 - 2,350	$1,125 - 1,400	
1981-1984	N/A	$1,800 - 2,250	$1,075 - 1,350	
1985-1988	N/A	$1,325 - 1,650	$800 - 1,000	
1989-1996	N/A	$1,475 - 1,850	$900 - 1,100	$2,299

• **Add 10-20% for maple body (1962-63 only).**

In the early to mid-1970s, Gibson changed the name of the Hummingbird to the Hummingbird Custom; however, there was no change in the specifications. Between 1962 and 1963, some models were produced with maple back/sides. In 1966, adjustable saddle replaced original part/design. In 1970, non-adjustable saddle replaced previous part/design and chrome hardware replaced gold. In 1973, block fingerboard inlay replaced original part/design. In 1984, parallelogram fingerboard inlay replaced previous part/design. In 1996, the Early '60s Hummingbird model superseded the original Hummingbird model.

HUMMINGBIRD REISSUE – dreadnought style, solid Sitka spruce top, round soundhole, bound body, mahogany back/sides, 24.75 in. scale, 14/20-fret bound rosewood fingerboard with mother-of-pearl parallelogram inlay, rosewood bridge, black bridgepins, blackface peghead with abalone crown/logo inlay, three-per-side nickel tuners, tortoiseshell pickguard with floral/hummingbird design, available in Heritage Cherry Sunburst Lacquer finish, disc.

	N/A	$1,325 - 1,650	$800 - 1,000	$3,119

HUMMINGBIRD CUSTOM KOA (MODEL SSHC) – custom shop variation featuring hummingbird inlays on the headstock, pickguard, and bridge, beginning 2003, hummingbird inlays are also on ebony fingerboard, customer selected back/side wood, including koa (standard beginning 2003), mahogany neck, abalone top trim, engraved gold tuners, available in Antique Natural (2003-present), Heritage Cherry, or Sunburst finish, mfg. by the MT Custom Shop beginning 1999, 36 mfg. beginning 2005-2012.

	$6,000	$3,200 - 4,000	$1,925 - 2,400	$7,734

HUMMINGBIRD PRO – square-shouldered dreadnought body, solid Sitka spruce top, solid mahogany back and sides, round soundhole with traditional double ring rosette, multi-ply top binding, single-ply back binding, Marquetry back strip, mahogany neck with round neck 60s thin line profile and compound dovetail joint, 14/20-fret bound rosewood fingerboard with MOP parallelogram inlays, black headstock overlay with MOP Gibson logo and crown inlay, three-per-side nickel Grover Rotomatic tuners, traditional rosewood belly-up bridge, tortoise pickguard, L.R. Baggs Element electronics, available in Vintage Sunburst finish, Gibson custom hardshell case included, mfg. 2010-2011.

	$2,100	$1,200 - 1,500	$750 - 900	$2,953

* *Hummingbird Pro EC* – similar to the Hummingbird Pro, except has a single smooth cutaway and Fishman Prefix Plus electronics, available in Vintage Sunburst finish, Gibson custom hardshell case included, mfg. 2010-2011.

	$2,300	$1,300 - 1,650	$800 - 975	$3,235

HUMMINGBIRD SHERYL CROW ARTIST MODEL (MODEL ACSC) – solid Sitka spruce top, replica of a 1962 Country Western Model with antique lacquer finish and dark cherry stained sides, mahogany back/sides/neck, hummingbird pickguard without artwork, Sheryl Crow signed label, mfg. limited edition beginning 2000-2011.

	$2,800	$1,550 - 1,800	$950 - 1,100	$3,574

• **Subtract 5% if w/o active pickup.**

Beginning 2006, this model became standard with an active pickup.

MSR/NOTES	100%	EXCELLENT	AVERAGE	LAST MSR

HISTORIC HUMMINGBIRD (MODEL SSHB) – square shoulder dreadnought body, premium Sitka spruce, mahogany back and sides, mahogany neck, rosewood fingerboard with mother-of-pearl paralellogram inlays, mother-of-pearl crown in headstock, traditional Gibson rosewood bridge with mother-of-pearl inlays, nickel Grover kidney tuners, active preamp pickups, available in Heritage Cherry Sunburst or Wine Red (2013 limited availability) finish, 24.75 in. scale, mfg. 2005-present.

MSR $3,997	$3,300	$1,600 - 2,000	$950 - 1,200	

MAPLE HUMMINGBIRD (MODEL SSHM, LTD 2013) – square-shouldered dreadnought-style body, Sitka spruce top, maple back and sides, round shoundhole with double ring rosette, multi-ply top and back binding, set maple rounded profile neck, 14/20-fret bound rosewood fingerboard with MOP split parallelogram inlays, bound headstock with black overlay, MOP Gibson logo, and MOP torch inlays, three-per-side nickel Grover Rotomatic tuners, tortoise Hummingbird-style pickguard, rosewood bridge with MOP dot inlays, L.R. Baggs Element pickup and electronics, 24.75 in. scale, 1.725 in. nut width, available in Vintage Cherry (Sunburst) finish, hardshell case included, mfg. 2013-present.

MSR N/A	$3,300	$2,150 - 2,475	$1,075 - 1,325	

HUMMINGBIRD TRUE VINTAGE (MODEL SSHVP) – detailed edition of Gibson's original Hummingbird, square-shouldered dreadnought style, solid Sitka spruce top, solid mahogany back and sides, round soundhole with rosette, six-ply top binding, four-ply back binding, mahogany rounded neck, 14/20-fret Madagascar rosewood single-ply bound fingerboard with MOP split parallelogram inlays, black headstock with MOP crown and "Hummingbird" on truss rod cover, three-per-side gold keystone tuners, Madagascar rosewood bridge with MOP dots and white pins, tortoiseshell Hummingbird pickguard, available in Heritage Cherry Sunburst finish, 24.75 in. scale, mfg. 2007-present.

MSR $5,158	$4,000	$2,100 - 2,600	$1,350 - 1,600	

50th ANNIVERSARY 1960 HUMMINGBIRD – square-shouldered dreadnought body, Sitka spruce top, mahogany back and sides, round soundhole with traditional double ring rosette, multi-ply top and back binding, mahogany neck with compound dovetail joint, 14/20-fret bound rosewood fingerboard with MOP paralellogram inlays, black headstock overlay with Gibson logo and MOP "50" anniversary inlay, 50th Anniversary on truss rod cover, three-per-side gold Gotoh tuners with vintage-style tulip buttons, traditional rosewood belly-up bridge, 50th anniversary gold-painted hummingbird pickguard, available in Heritage Dark Cherry Sunburst finish, Gibson custom hardshell case and certificate of authenticity included, limited edition run of 200 instruments, mfg. 2010-2011.

	$4,700	$3,200 - 3,900	N/A	$6,018

* 50th Anniversary 1960 Hummingbird Koa – similar to the 50th Anniversary 1960 Hummingbird, except has Hawaiian koa back and sides with high glued top bracing, and an 18k gold "50" headstock inlay, available in Gold Honey Burst finish, Gibson custom hardshell case and certificate of authenticity signed by Ren Ferguson included, limited edition run of 50 instruments, mfg. 2010-2011.

	$7,500	$5,000 - 6,250	N/A	$10,748

* 50th Anniversary 1960 Hummingbird Rosewood – similar to the 50th Anniversary 1960 Hummingbird, except has exotic virgin rosewood back and sides hand selected by Ren Ferguson with high glued top bracing, and an 18k gold "50" headstock inlay, available in Heritage Dark Cherry Sunburst finish, Gibson custom hardshell case and certificate of authenticity signed by Ren Ferguson included, limited edition run of 50 instruments, mfg. 2010-2011.

	$7,500	$5,000 - 6,250	N/A	$10,748

HUMMINGBIRD QUILT (MODEL SSHBQ) – square-shouldered dreadnought-style body, Sitka spruce top, quilt maple back and sides, round soundhole with traditional double-ring rosette, multi-ply top and back binding, set mahogany rounded-profile neck, 14/20-fret bound rosewood fingerboard with MOP split parallelogram inlays, black headstock overlay with MOP Gibson logo and crown inlays, three-per-side Grover Rotomatic gold tuners, rosewood bridge, tortoise Hummingbird pickguard, L.R. Baggs Element pickup and electronics, 24.75 in. scale, 1.725 in. nut width, available in Cherry Sunburst finish, hardshell case included, new 2014.

MSR $4,771	$3,700	$2,400 - 2,800	$1,200 - 1,475	

ACOUSTIC: J-45/J-50 MODELS & VARIATIONS

J-45 – slope shouldered body, spruce top, round soundhole, tortoiseshell pickguard, three-stripe bound body/rosette, mahogany back/sides/neck, 14/19 (pre-war) or 14/20-fret rosewood fingerboard with pearl dot inlay, rosewood bridge with black pins, three-per-side nickel tuners

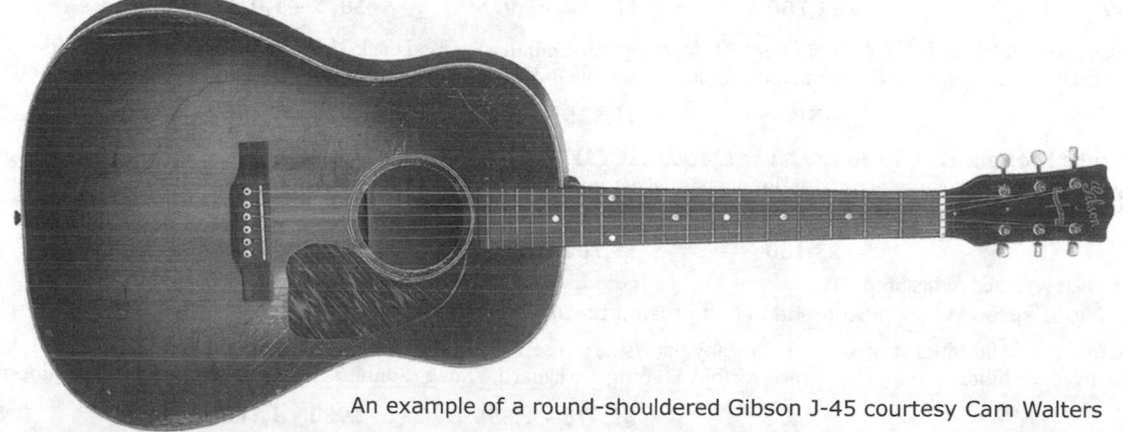

An example of a round-shouldered Gibson J-45 courtesy Cam Walters

MSR/NOTES	100%	EXCELLENT	AVERAGE	LAST MSR

with pearl buttons, available in Sunburst finish, mfg. 1942-1985.

1942	N/A	$8,800 - 11,000	$5,275 - 6,600	
1943-1946 Banner Logo	N/A	$8,000 - 10,000	$4,750 - 6,000	
1946-1949	N/A	$4,800 - 6,000	$2,900 - 3,600	
1950-1954	N/A	$4,500 - 5,500	$2,750 - 3,400	
1955-1957	N/A	$4,000 - 5,000	$2,400 - 3,000	
1958-1960	N/A	$3,600 - 4,500	$2,150 - 2,700	
1961-1962	N/A	$2,800 - 3,500	$1,675 - 2,100	
1963-1964	N/A	$2,400 - 3,000	$1,450 - 1,800	
1965-1966	N/A	$2,000 - 2,500	$1,200 - 1,500	
1967-1969 Round Shouldered	N/A	$1,725 - 2,150	$1,050 - 1,300	
1969-1972 Square Shouldered	N/A	$1,475 - 1,850	$875 - 1,100	
1973-1975	N/A	$1,400 - 1,750	$850 - 1,050	
1976-1985	N/A	$1,275 - 1,600	$750 - 950	

- **During WWII, Gibson used whatever materials were handy. A mahogany top J-45 will bring about 15% less than above values, but a mahogany back with rosewood or maple sides will bring 15% higher values. Add 25% for maple back/sides. Add a significant premium for rosewood back and sides (rare). Add 10-20% for Red or Black finish.**

This model was originally offered with a single stripe body binding. The banner peghead inlay was offered from 1942 to 1945. In 1942, multi-ply body binding was offered; In 1943, one stripe body binding replaced multi-ply body binding. In 1950, upper belly on bridge, three-stripe body binding replaced original part/design. In 1955, redesigned pickguard replaced original part/design. In 1956, adjustable bridge became an option. The fixed bridge was discontinued in late 1961. In 1962, Cherry Sunburst finish was offered. In 1968, belly under bridge replaced previous part/design. In 1969, redesigned body/pickguard replaced previous part/design. In 1971, non-adjustable saddle became standard. In 1975, redesigned pickguard, four-stripe top purfling, tortoise body binding replaced previous part/design. In 1981, three-stripe top purfling replaced previous part/design.

* ***J-45 Celebrity*** – similar to J-45, except has rosewood back/sides, abalone "The Gibson" and fern design peghead inlay, five-ply bound headstock, ebony fingerboard and bridge, seven-ply front and back binding, gold hardware, mfg. 1985 only.

	N/A	$1,725 - 2,150	$1,025 - 1,300	

Approximately 100 of these instruments were produced.

J-45 REISSUE/STANDARD (MODEL RS45/RS4S) – slope (round) shouldered dreadnought style, solid Sitka spruce top, round soundhole, white body binding, mahogany back/sides, 14/20-fret rosewood fingerboard with mother-of-pearl dot inlay, vintage-style rosewood reverse belly bridge, white bridgepins, blackface peghead with logo inlay, three-per-side vintage-style nickel tuners, teardrop-shaped black pickguard, available in Antique Natural, Vintage Cherry Sunburst (disc. 2003), or Vintage Sunburst, mfg. 1984-present.

MSR $3,072	$2,200	$1,300 - 1,600	$750 - 900	

- **Add $81 for Bubinga color in Antique Natural (disc. 2002, reintroduced 2004 by Custom Shop).**
- **Subtract 5% if w/o transducer pickup.**

Beginning in 1984, the J-45 Reissue was available in Ebony, Natural and Sunburst finishes. When the model was re-designated the Early J-45, the finish was changed to a Vintage Sunburst finish. Beginning 1999, model nomenclature was again changed back to the J-45, and a transducer pickup was added as standard equipment. Recent finishes include Antique Natural (Bubinga), Cherry, Ebony, Heritage Cherry Sunburst, Pre-War Vintage Sunburst, and Triburst. In 2009, this model was upgraded and improved.

* ***J-45 Cobraburst (Model RS45)*** – similar to the J-45 Reissue/Standard, except has a MOP Gibson headstock logo, black pickguard, available in Cobraburst finish, mfg. 2013-present.

MSR $3,029	$2,350	$1,525 - 1,750	$775 - 950	

* ***J-45 Standard Limited Edition Colors (Model RS45)*** – similar to the J-45 Reissue/Standard, except available in limited availability finishes including Gold Top, Pelham Blue, or Wine Red, mfg. 2013-present.

MSR $3,449	$2,700	$1,750 - 2,025	$875 - 1,075	

* ***J-45 Rosewood (Model RS4R)*** – similar to J-45, except has Indian rosewood back/sides, ebony fingerboard/bridge, gold hardware, and abalone fingerboard inlays, transducer pickup standard, available in Vintage Sunburst or Antique Natural finish, mfg. 1999-2008.

	N/A	$1,525 - 1,900	$925 - 1,150	$3,404

* ***J-45 Dwight Yoakam Honky Tonk Deuce (Model ACDYHT)*** – similar to J-45 reissue, except has solid Indian rosewood back/sides and bridge, V profile mahogany neck with double paralellogram inlays and dice at the 12th fret, tortoiseshell J-50 pickguard has mother-of-pearl dice inlays, available in Antique Natural or Vintage Sunburst finish, mfg. 2003-2012.

	$3,180	$1,700 - 2,100	$1,025 - 1,275	$4,099

- **Subtract 5% if w/o active preamp.**

Beginning 2006, a transducer pickup and active preamp became standard.

* ***J-45 Historic*** – solid Sitka spruce top, mahogany back/sides, rosewood bridge and fingerboard, mother-of-pearl dot inlays, scalloped and tuned bracing, body binding, nickel hardware, tortoise teardrop pickguard, Vintage Sunburst finish, Fishman active transducers, 670 mfg. 2005.

	N/A	$1,475 - 1,850	$900 - 1,100	$2,724

MSR/NOTES	100%	EXCELLENT	AVERAGE	LAST MSR

J-45 Rosewood Custom – similar to J-45 Rosewood, except has abalone top trim and no transducer, mfg. 1999-2005.

	N/A	$1,675 - 2,100	$1,000 - 1,250	$4,060

J-45 Custom Vine Rosewood (Model RS4V) – similar to J-45 Rosewood Custom, except has customer selected wood and elaborate custom vine fretboard inlays, available in Antique Natural or Vintage Sunburst finish, mfg. 1999-2012.

	$5,450	$2,900 - 3,600	$1,750 - 2,175	$7,047

J-45 Wartime Historic Signature – Vintage Sunburst, hand built by Ren Ferguson, limited mfg. beginning 2005.

	N/A	N/A	N/A	

This model was priced on request.

J-45 BRAD PAISLEY – Brad Paisley J-45 signature based on a 1942 Gibson J-45, rounded-shouldered dreadnought style, solid Adirondack red spruce top, solid mahogany back and sides, round soundhole with traditional double ring rosette, multi-ply top binding, single-ply back binding, one-piece mahogany modified "V" neck with a compound dovetail joint, 14/20-fret rosewood fingerboard with 1/4 inch MOP dot inlays and 12th fret MOP paisleys, AJ-style headstock with 17 degree angle, black overlay, pre-war Gibson logo, and banner emblem, Brad Paisley signature on truss rod cover, three-per-side vintage-style nickel tuners with white buttons, rosewood bridge with MOP dots and white pins, traditional tortoise pickguard with Brad Paisley engraved design, available in Cherry Sunburst finish, 24.75 in. scale, hardshell case included, mfg. 2010-12.

	$4,160	$2,650 - 3,300	$1,600 - 2,000	$5,364

J-45 CUSTOM (MODEL RS4C) – rounded shouldered dreadnought-style body, AA-grade Sitka spruce top, Indian rosewood back and sides, round soundhole with two ring abalone rosette, single-ply body binding, top herringbone purfling, dovetail neck joint, 14/20-fret rosewood fingerboard with pearl dot inlays, black headstock overlay with Gibson logo and MOP flower and vine inlay designed by Ren Ferguson, three-per-side gold Grover Rotomatic tuners, rosewood bridge with upper belly and two pearl dot inlays, cream bridge pins, tortoise pickguard, L.R. Baggs Element Active Acoustic Pickup System, available in Amberburst (2013 limited availability), Antique Natural, or Vintage Sunburst finish, mfg. 2009-present.

MSR $3,610	$2,800	$1,600 - 2,000	$975 - 1,200	

J-45 JOHN HIATT – John Hiatt J-45 signature based on his specifications, rounded-shouldered dreadnought style, solid Sitka spruce top, solid mahogany back and sides, round soundhole with traditional double ring rosette, multi-ply top binding, single-ply back binding, one-piece mahogany modified "V" neck with a compound dovetail joint, 14/20-fret rosewood fingerboard with 1/4 inch MOP dot inlays, CF-style headstock with 17 degree angle, black overlay, and gold block Gibson decal logo, John Hiatt signature on truss rod cover, three-per-side vintage-style nickel tuners with cream buttons, rosewood belly up bridge with MOP dots and white pins, teardrop firestripe pickguard, available in Tobacco Brown back and sides with a Tri-Burst top finish, 24.75 in. scale, hardshell case included, limited edition run of 100 instruments, mfg. 2010-12.

	$3,600	$2,000 - 2,500	$1,200 - 1,500	$4,696

J-45 RED SPRUCE (MODEL RS45, LTD 2013) – slope-shouldered dreadnought-style body, Red Adirondack spruce top, mahogany back and sides, round soundhole with single ring rosette, multi-ply top binding, single-ply back binding, set mahogany modified V profile neck, 14/20-fret rosewood fingerboard with MOP dot inlays, black headstock overlay with MOP Gibson logo, three-per-side open-style gold tuners, rosewood bridge with MOP dot inlays, tortoise pickguard, 24.75 in. scale, 1.725 in. nut width, available in Sunset Burst finish, hardshell case included, mfg. 2013-present.

MSR N/A	$5,000	$3,250 - 3,750	$1,625 - 2,000	

J-45 TRUE VINTAGE (MODEL RS4TP) – detailed edition of Gibson's original J-45, rounded-shouldered dreadnought style, solid Sitka spruce top, solid mahogany back and sides, round soundhole with rosette, four-ply top binding, single-ply back binding, mahogany V-shaped neck, 14/20-fret Madagascar rosewood fingerboard with MOP dot inlays, black headstock with Gibson logo, three-per-side nickel Gotoh tuners with white buttons, Madagascar rosewood bridge with MOP dots and white pins, tortoiseshell teardrop pickguard, available in Vintage Sunburst finish, 24.75 in. scale, mfg. 2007-present.

MSR $3,874	$3,000	$1,750 - 2,200	$1,050 - 1,325	

1942 J-45 LEGEND (MODEL H442) – detailed edition of a 1942 Gibson J-45, rounded-shouldered dreadnought style, solid Adirondack spruce top, solid mahogany back and sides, round soundhole with rosette, five-ply top binding, three-ply back binding, mahogany 1942 profile neck, 14/20-fret Madagascar rosewood fingerboard with MOP dot inlays, black headstock with script Gibson logo and banner, three-per-side reproduction nickel tuners with white buttons, Madagascar rosewood bridge with MOP dots and white pins, 1942 style celluloid teardrop pickguard, available in Vintage Sunburst finish, 24.75 in. scale, Red Line case included, limited production of 25 guitars per month, mfg. 2007-2012.

	$7,200	$4,000 - 4,750	$2,750 - 3,250	$9,301

MSR/NOTES	100%	EXCELLENT	AVERAGE	LAST MSR

J-50 – similar to J-45, except has Natural finish, mfg. 1945-1985.

	100%	EXCELLENT	AVERAGE
1945-1946 Banner Logo	N/A	$7,600 - 9,500	$4,550 - 5,700
1946-1949	N/A	$4,800 - 6,000	$2,900 - 3,600
1950-1954	N/A	$4,500 - 5,500	$2,750 - 3,400
1955-1957	N/A	$4,000 - 5,000	$2,400 - 3,000
1958-1960	N/A	$3,600 - 4,500	$2,150 - 2,700
1961-1962	N/A	$2,800 - 3,500	$1,675 - 2,100
1963-1964	N/A	$2,400 - 3,000	$1,450 - 1,800
1965-1966	N/A	$2,000 - 2,500	$1,200 - 1,500
1967-1969 Round Shouldered	N/A	$1,725 - 2,150	$1,050 - 1,300
1969-1972 Square Shouldered	N/A	$1,475 - 1,850	$875 - 1,100
1973-1975	N/A	$1,400 - 1,750	$850 - 1,050
1976-1985	N/A	$1,275 - 1,600	$750 - 950

During 1956, an adjustable bridge became an option, and in 1961, the fixed bridge was discontinued.

J-50 REISSUE HISTORIC (MODEL RS50) – spruce top, mahogany back/sides, traditional J-50 features, nickel hardware, available in Antique Natural finish, mfg. 1999-2008.

	100%	EXCELLENT	AVERAGE	LAST MSR
	N/A	$1,250 - 1,425	$775 - 900	$2,818

Also available in left-hand configuration beginning 2003, at no charge.

ACOUSTIC: J-160E MODELS & VARIATIONS

J-160 E – slope shouldered body, spruce top, round soundhole, tortoiseshell pickguard, two-stripe bound body/rosette, mahogany back/sides/neck, 15/19-fret bound rosewood fingerboard with pearl block/trapezoid inlay, rosewood bridge with white pins, adjustable saddle, blackface peghead with pearl crown/logo inlay, three-per-side nickel tuners, single coil pickup, volume/tone control, available in Sunburst finish, over 4,400 mfg. 1954-1979.

	100%	EXCELLENT	AVERAGE
1954-1959	N/A	$4,400 - 5,500	$2,650 - 3,300
1960-1964	N/A	$4,600 - 5,750	$2,750 - 3,450
1965-1969	N/A	$2,800 - 3,500	$1,675 - 2,100
1970-1979	N/A	$2,000 - 2,500	$1,200 - 1,500

This model was made popular because John Lennon played it. A model around the same time Lennon played it with the Beatles (approx. 1962-64) may add a premium to the price.

J-160 E (REISSUE) – similar to J-160 E, except has regular saddle, available in Vintage Sunburst finish, mfg. 1991-96.

	100%	EXCELLENT	AVERAGE	LAST MSR
	N/A	$1,550 - 1,950	$950 - 1,175	$1,900

J-160 E STANDARD (MODEL AS16) – patterned after the original J-160 E, Vintage Sunburst finish, J-45 body style, solid spruce top and mahogany back/sides, rosewood bridge and fretboard, P-100 pickup with nickel Gotch and Keystone buttons, limited mfg. 2003, reintroduced 2005-08.

	100%	EXCELLENT	AVERAGE	LAST MSR
	N/A	$1,550 - 1,950	$950 - 1,175	$3,171

J-160 E JOHN LENNON LIMITED EDITION – slope/round shoulder, laminated spruce top with ladder bracing, mahogany back/sides/neck, rosewood fingerboard and bridge, P-90 single coil pickup between fretboard/soundhole, Lennon signature truss rod cover, available in Vintage Sunburst finish, 24.75 in. scale, limited mfg. 2000 only.

	100%	EXCELLENT	AVERAGE	LAST MSR
	N/A	$1,500 - 1,750	$1,275 - 1,450	$3,500

J-160 E JOHN LENNON PEACE MODEL (MODEL RSJLP) – slope/round shoulder, solid Sitka spruce top, mahogany back/sides/neck, 15/20 rosewood fretboard with pearloid trapezoid inlays, P-100 stacked humbucker pickups, unsigned tortoise pickguard, Lennon signature truss rod cover, authentic replica strap, Antique Natural finish, limited edition with certificate of authenticity, mfg. 2003-present.

MSR $4,358	100%	EXCELLENT	AVERAGE
	$3,380	$1,800 - 2,250	$1,075 - 1,350

This model is patterned after John Lennon's original J-160 E guitar circa 1969, after he stripped away the psychedelic paint job he commissioned in 1967.

J-160 E JOHN LENNON COLLECTION SET – includes three separate J-160E variations - a Fab Four Model (Lennon Model 1), Magical Tour Model (Lennon Model 2), Bed-In Model (Lennon Model 3), only 47 sets were scheduled for production by the MT Custom Shop, limited mfg. 1999-2002.

	100%	EXCELLENT	AVERAGE	LAST MSR
	N/A	$24,750 - 28,500	$14,000 - 16,500	$50,000

    * *J-160 E John Lennon Bed-In* – mfg. 2001-02.

	100%	EXCELLENT	AVERAGE	LAST MSR
	N/A	$7,600 - 9,150	$4,650 - 5,250	$18,020

MSR/NOTES	100%	EXCELLENT	AVERAGE	LAST MSR

* J-160 E John Lennon Magical Tour – mfg. 2001-02.

	N/A	$7,600 - 9,150	$4,650 - 5,250	$18,020

* J-160 E John Lennon Fab Four – mfg. 2001-02.

	N/A	$7,600 - 9,150	$4,650 - 5,250	$18,020

70th ANNIVERSARY JOHN LENNON J-160E (RSJL) – slope-shouldered dreadnought-style body based on a 1950s/1960s J-160E, laminated Sitka spruce top, solid mahogany back and sides, traditional ladder bracing, round soundhole with traditional single ring rosette, multi-ply top binding, single-ply back binding, one-piece mahogany neck with round profile and compound dovetail joint, 15/20-fret bound rosewood fingerboard with MOP trapezoid inlays and John Lennon's birthdate (October 9, 1940) on the 12th fret, traditional J-160E headstock with black overlay, MOP Gibson logo, and John Lennon script signature, three-per-side vintage nickel Kluson-Gotoh tuners with tulip buttons, traditional belly up rosewood bridge with MOP dots and white pins, tortoise J-160E pickguard, single P-90 single coil pickup, two amber knobs (v, tone), available in Vintage Sunburst finish, 1.725 in. nut width, 24.75 in. scale, hardshell case and certificate of authenticity included, limited edition run of 500 instruments, mfg. 2010-11.

	$3,600	$2,100 - 2,600	$1,275 - 1,575	$4,728

* 70th Anniversary John Lennon J-160E "Imagine" – similar to the 70th Anniversary John Lennon J-160E, except has an all "Imagine" White finish including the headstock overlay, abalone John Lennon signature on headstock, hardshell case and certificate of authenticity included, limited edition run of 70 instruments, mfg. 2010-2011.

	$8,300	$4,750 - 6,000	N/A	$10,748

* 70th Anniversary John Lennon J-160E Museum – similar to the 70th Anniversary John Lennon J-160E, except has a thin Natural finish and John and Yoko caricature sketches on the lower treble bout, hardshell case and certificate of authenticity included, limited edition run of 70 instruments, mfg. 2010-2011.

	$11,000	N/A	N/A	$15,048

ACOUSTIC: J-180/J-185 MODELS & VARIATIONS

J-180 – spruce top, round soundhole, two tortoiseshell pickguards, three-stripe bound body/rosette, maple back/sides, one-piece mahogany neck, 14/20-fret rosewood fingerboard with pearl star inlay, reverse belly bridge with black white dot pins, blackface peghead with pearl star/logo inlay, three-per-side nickel tuners with pearloid buttons, available in Black finish, mfg. 1986-1991.

	N/A	$1,475 - 1,850	$900 - 1,100	

J-180 (RECENT MFG.) – solid Sitka spruce top, round soundhole, white body binding, maple back/sides, 14/20-fret bound rosewood fingerboard with mother-of-pearl star inlays, rosewood bridge, white bridgepins, blackface peghead with abalone star/logo inlay, three-per-side nickel tuners, "dual side" black pickguard, available in Ebony finish, disc. 2005.

	N/A	$1,200 - 1,500	$725 - 900	$2,571

* J-180 Dwight Yoakam Y2K Artist Model – solid Sitka spruce top, J-180 body with double pickguards and J-200 features including a mustache bridge, crown inlays, and figured maple back/sides/neck, rosewood fingerboard/bridge, Dwight Yoakam signed label, available in Antique Natural finish, 25.5 in. scale, limited edition mfg. 2000-2002, reintroduced 2005 only.

	N/A	$1,325 - 1,650	$800 - 1,000	$2,819

J-180 EC – solid spruce top, figured maple back/sides/neck, rosewood fingerboard and bridge, mother-of-pearl starburst or dot fingerboard inlays and abalone rosette, with onboard controls, available in Antique Walnut, Vintage Sunburst, or Ebony finish, mfg. 1999-2002.

	N/A	$1,075 - 1,350	$650 - 800	$2,571

• **Subtract $427 for dot inlays and Ebony finish.**

* Historic 1950s J-180 – similar to J-180 Reissue, Antique Ebony finish. Limited mfg. beginning 2005.

	N/A	N/A	N/A	

This model was priced on request.

J-180 BILLIE JOE ARMSTRONG (MODEL J8BJ) – jumbo J-180-style body, solid Sitka spruce top, solid maple back and sides, traditional J-180 X bracing, round soundhole with traditional double ring rosette, multi-ply top binding, single-ply back binding, one-piece mahogany neck with modified V profile and compound dovetail joint, 14/20-fret bound rosewood fingerboard with MOP graduated star inlays, AJ-style headstock with 17 degree angle tilt, black overlay, and MOP Gibson logo and star inlays, "Billie Joe" on truss rod cover, three-per-side Gotoh nickel tuners, traditional belly-up rosewood bridge with MOP dots and white pins, traditional double tortoise J-180-style transparent pickguards, Fishman VT pickup with soundhole mounted controls, available in Ebony finish, 16 in. body width, 1.725 in. nut width, 24.75 in. scale, hardshell case included, limited edition run of 100 instruments, mfg. 2011 only.

	$3,100	$1,750 - 2,150	$1,050 - 1,325	$4,023

J-185 – spruce top, round soundhole, tortoise pickguard, two-stripe bound body/rosette, figured maple back/sides, mahogany neck, 14/20-fret rosewood fingerboard with pearl parallelogram inlay, upper belly rosewood bridge with white pins, pearl cross bridge wings inlay, blackface peghead with pearl crown/logo inlay, three-per-side nickel tuners, available in Cremona Brown Burst (most common) or Natural finishes, mfg. 1951-59.

	N/A	$10,000 - 12,500	$6,000 - 7,500	

• **Add 30-40% for Natural finish.**

MSR/NOTES	100%	EXCELLENT	AVERAGE	LAST MSR

HISTORIC J-185 REISSUE (MODEL J885/J885A) – spruce top, maple back/sides, Maltese cross bridge wing inlays, pearl parallelogram fretboard inlays, available in Antique Natural or Vintage Sunburst finish, mfg. 1999-present.

| MSR $3,237 | $2,500 | $1,300 - 1,600 | $850 - 1,000 | |

J-185 12-String – similar to J-185 Reissue, except has 12 strings and flamed maple back/sides, available in Antique Natural finish, mfg. as a limited production 2000-2005.

| | N/A | $1,525 - 1,900 | $925 - 1,150 | $3,243 |

This model was available in left-hand configuration at no extra charge.

J-185 Custom Vine (Model J82K) – similar to J-185, except has custom vine fingerboard inlay, Antique Cherry or Antique Natural finish, mfg. 2005-08.

| | N/A | $2,600 - 3,250 | $1,550 - 1,950 | $6,366 |

J-185 TRUE VINTAGE (MODEL J88V) – detailed edition of Gibson's original J-185, jumbo style, solid Sitka spruce top, solid AAA flamed maple back and sides, round soundhole with rosette, four-ply top and back binding, mahogany V-shaped neck, 14/20-fret Madagascar rosewood single-ply bound fingerboard with MOP split parallelogram inlays, black headstock with MOP crown, three-per-side nickel Gotoh tuners, Madagascar rosewood bridge with two MOP Maltese crosses and white pins, tortoiseshell late 1950s J-185-style pickguard, available in Antique Natural or Vintage Sunburst finish, 24.75 in. scale, mfg. 2007-08.

| | N/A | $1,600 - 2,000 | $950 - 1,200 | $3,691 |

J-185 EC (BLUES KING ELECTRO, MODEL J8J5/J8J5A) – single cutaway Jumbo-style body, solid Sitka spruce top, flame maple back and sides, round shoundhole with double ring abalone rosette, multi-ply top binding, single-ply back binding, set flame maple comfort contour profile neck, 14/20-fret single-ply bound ebony fingerboard with MOP split block inlays, bound headstock with black overlay, MOP Gibson logo, and MOP torch inlays, three-per-side gold Grover Rotomatic tuners, tortoise pickguard, ebony bridge, Fishman Aura Pro electronics, 24.75 in. scale, available in Antique Sunburst or Vintage Sunburst finish, mfg. 1999-present.

| MSR $4,142 | $3,200 | $1,750 - 2,200 | $1,050 - 1,325 | |

J-185 EC MAHOGANY (MODEL J8JM) – single cutaway Jumbo-style body, solid Sitka spruce top, mahogany back and sides, round shoundhole with double ring abalone rosette, multi-ply top binding, single-ply back binding, set flame maple modified V-profile neck, 14/20-fret single-ply bound rosewood fingerboard with MOP split parallelogram inlays, bound headstock with black overlay, MOP Gibson logo, and MOP torch inlays, three-per-side nickel Grover Rotomatic tuners, tortoise pickguard, rosewood bridge with MOP dot inlays, Fishman Aura Pro electronics, 24.75 in. scale, 1.725 in. nut width, available in Antique Natural finish, hardshell case included, mfg. 2013-present.

| MSR N/A | $3,000 | $1,950 - 2,250 | $975 - 1,200 | |

J-185 EC ROSEWOOD (MODEL J88E/J88EA) – single cutaway Jumbo-style body, premium Sitka spruce top, Indian rosewood back and sides, round shoundhole with abalone rosette, four-ply top binding, single-ply back binding, set mahogany V profile neck, 14/20-fret single-ply birdsbeak bound ebony fingerboard with MOP split block inlays, bound headstock with black overlay, MOP Gibson logo, and MOP five-piece Les Paul Customs-style inlays, three-per-side gold Grover kidney tuners, tortoise pickguard, ebony bridge, Fishman Prefix Plus-T pickups, 24.75 in. scale, available in Antique Natural finish, mfg. 2006-present.

| MSR $4,398 | $3,400 | $1,800 - 2,250 | $1,075 - 1,350 | |

ACOUSTIC: J-200 MODELS & VARIATIONS

J-200/SJ-200 – spruce top, round soundhole, black pickguard with engraved floral pattern, figured maple back/sides/neck, 14/20-fret bound rosewood fingerboard with pearl crown inlay, rosewood mustache bridge with pearl block inlay, black pearl dot pins, bound peghead with pearl plant/logo inlay, three-per-side gold tuners with pearl buttons, available in Antique Walnut, Natural, or Vintage Sunburst finish, mfg. 1938-1942, and 1945-1996.

An example of a J-200 courtesy Dave Rogers, Dave's Guitar Shop

| 1938-1941 Stairstep Headstock | N/A | $120,000 - 150,000 | $72,500 - 90,000 | |
| 1941-1942 Standard Headstock | N/A | $90,000 - 120,000 | $55,000 - 67,500 | |

MSR/NOTES	100%	EXCELLENT	AVERAGE	LAST MSR
1945-1949	N/A	$12,000 - 15,000	$7,500 - 9,500	
1950-1954	N/A	$9,500 - 12,000	$5,800 - 7,250	
1955-1959	N/A	$8,800 - 11,000	$5,275 - 6,600	
1960-1964	N/A	$8,000 - 10,000	$4,800 - 6,000	
1965-1966	N/A	$5,600 - 7,000	$3,350 - 4,200	
1967-1969	N/A	$4,000 - 5,000	$2,400 - 3,000	
1970-1979	N/A	$2,500 - 3,000	$1,800 - 2,100	
1980-1989	N/A	$2,250 - 2,750	$1,500 - 1,800	
1990-1996	N/A	$2,000 - 2,500	$1,200 - 1,500	$2,700

- **Add 10-20% for Natural finish (1945-1964).**

When this model was introduced in 1938, it was known as the Super Jumbo (SJ-200) and it featured rosewood back and sides (only approx. 100 mfg.). Some prototypes made during late 1937 were labeled "Super Jumbo" and "L-5 Spec." In 1939, this model was renamed the Super Jumbo 200. In 1947, it was renamed in the company catalogs to the J-200. However, many instruments continued to be labeled SJ-200 well into the early 1950s. Pre-war instruments should be determined on a piece-by-piece basis as opposed to the usual market, as this model and many of Gibson's high end instruments were not manufactured during the war - thus, there simply aren't that many guitars available in the secondary marketplace.

When this model was originally released, it featured a single peghead binding. In 1948, Natural finish became an option. In 1960, adjustable saddle bridge became an option. In 1961, tune-o-matic bridge with pearl block inlay replaced original part/design. In 1969, adjustable saddle became standard. In 1971, ebony fingerboard replaced original part/design, non-adjustable bridge replaced previous part/design. In 1979, rosewood fingerboard replaced previous part/design. In 1994, Antique Ebony finish was introduced, pearl crown fingerboard inlay, gold hardware replaced previous part/design. In 1996, the '50s Super Jumbo 200 model superseded the J-200 model (see listing below.)

* **J-200 12-String** – similar to J-200, except has 12 strings, six-per-side tuners, disc. 1998.

	N/A	$2,000 - 2,500	$1,200 - 1,500	$3,200

* **J-200 Celebrity** – similar to J-200, except has ornate scroll type fingerboard inlay, fern peghead inlay, mfg. 1985 only.

	N/A	$2,600 - 3,250	$1,550 - 1,950	

* **J-200 Deluxe** – spruce top, round soundhole, black pickguard with engraved floral pattern/abalone dot inlay, abalone bound body/rosette, figured maple back/sides/neck, 14/20-fret bound ebony fingerboard with abalone crown inlay, ebony mustache bridge with abalone block inlay/white abalone dot pins, bound blackface peghead with abalone crown/logo inlay, three-per-side gold Grover Imperial tuners, available in Antique Natural or Vintage Sunburst finish, mfg. 1994-96.

	N/A	$2,200 - 2,750	$1,325 - 1,650	$5,200

- **Add 20% for rosewood back, sides, and neck.**

This model has a rosewood back/sides/neck as an option.

* **J-200 Jr.** – similar to J-200, except has smaller body, nickel tuners, disc. 1994.

	N/A	$1,400 - 1,750	$850 - 1,050	$1,800

This model was also offered in a 12-string configuration (Model J-200 Jr. 12-String).

HISTORIC SJ-200/J-200 STANDARD (J-200 REISSUE, MODEL SJ20/SJ22) – Sitka spruce top, round soundhole, abalone bound body/rosette, flame maple back/sides, maple neck, 14/20-fret bound Madagascar rosewood fingerboard with abalone crown inlays, Madagascar rosewood mustache bridge with abalone block inlay/white abalone dot pins, bound blackface peghead with abalone crown/logo inlay, three-per-side gold tuners, black pickguard with engraved floral pattern/abalone dot inlay, available in Antique Natural, Trans. Black (2013 limited availability), Vintage Sunburst, or Wine Red (2013 limited availability) finish, current mfg.

MSR $4,900	$3,800	$2,100 - 2,600	$1,275 - 1,575	

- **Subtract 5% if w/o active preamp.**

Beginning 2006, this model became standard with transducer pickup and active preamp.

* **J-200 Elite Custom** – similar to SJ-200 Reissue, except has ebony fingerboard and bridge, gold Imperial tuners, and abalone rosette, mfg. 1999-2004.

	N/A	$2,600 - 3,250	$1,550 - 1,950	$5,433

* **J-200 Pre-War Western Classic (Model SJ2C)** – Indian rosewood back/sides, maple neck with ebony bridge and fingerboard with mother-of-pearl block inlays, patterned after the 1937 Ray Whitley model, available in Vintage Sunburst finish, Custom Shop model, mfg. 1999-2012.

	$6,250	$3,050 - 3,800	$1,900 - 2,250	$8,077

* **J-200 Pre-War Western Classic Brazilian** – similar to SJ-200 Pre-War Western Classic, except back/sides are Brazilian rosewood, Custom Shop model, mfg. 2003 only.

	N/A	$4,800 - 6,000	$2,900 - 3,600	$9,038

* **J-200 Custom Brazilian** – similar to J-200 Reissue, except has Brazilian rosewood back/sides, mfg. by Custom Shop 2004.

	N/A	$4,000 - 5,000	$2,400 - 3,000	$9,038

MSR/NOTES	100%	EXCELLENT	AVERAGE	LAST MSR

* **SJ-200 Artist Supreme** – top-of-the-line Custom Shop model, Zircote back and sides, Sitka spruce top, multi-bound body with abalone at all joints, mother-of-pearl and abalone inlays on neck headstock and pickguard, ebony fretboard and bridge, A2 relief carved maple neck with contrasting color veneers, neck is sunbursted "V S," ebony multi-bound headstock overlayed with ebony, hand engraved tuners, designed by Ren Ferguson, mfg. 2003-2004.

N/A	$13,250 - 16,500	$8,000 - 10,000	$32,500

* **Prewar SJ-200 Historic Signature** – Vintage Sunburst finish, limited mfg. beginning 2005.

N/A	N/A	N/A

This model was priced on request.

J-200 CUSTOM (MODEL SJ2R) – Super Jumbo-style body, AAA-grade Sitka spruce top, AAA-grade curly maple back and sides, round soundhole with three-ring rosette (two five-ring groupings surrounding a large ring of abalone), multi-ply body binding, abalone purfling, tapered dovetail neck joint, 14/20-fret bound ebony fingerboard with MOP graduated crown inlays and rolled edges, multi-ply bound headstock with black overlay, script pearl logo, and MOP crown inlay, three-per-side gold Grover Imperial "stairstep" tuners, ebony mustache bridge with four block and two dot MOP inlays, white bridge pins with MOP dots, tortoise pickguard with floral/vine graphics, L.R. Baggs Element Active Acoustic Pickup System, available in Antique Natural or Vintage Sunburst finish, mfg. 2009-2012.

$4,750	$2,525 - 3,150	$1,525 - 1,900	$6,125

J-200 STUDIO (MODEL SJ5S) – Super Jumbo-style body, AA-grade Sitka spruce top, maple back and sides, round soundhole with single nine-ring rosette, multi-ply body binding, tapered dovetail neck joint, 14/20-fret rosewood fingerboard with pearl graduated crown inlays and rolled edges, black headstock overlay with pearl logo and pearl crown inlay, three-per-side nickel Grover Rotomatic tuners, rosewood mustache bridge, white bridge pins, tortoise pickguard, Fishman Aura Pro Acoustic Pickup System, available in Antique Natural finish, hardshell case included, mfg. 2009-2012.

$3,100	$1,650 - 2,100	$1,000 - 1,250	$3,978

SJ-200 TRUE VINTAGE (MODEL SJ2TP) – detailed edition of Gibson's 1950S SJ-200, jumbo style, solid Sitka spruce top, solid AAA flamed maple back and sides, round soundhole with rosette, six-ply top binding, four-ply back binding, mahogany rounded neck, 14/20-fret Madagascar rosewood single-ply bound fingerboard with MOP crown inlays, single-ply bound black headstock with MOP crown, three-per-side gold Gotoh tuners with white buttons, Madagascar rosewood moustache bridge with four MOP bar inlays and white pins, tortoiseshell 1950s J-200-style pickguard, available in Antique Natural or Vintage Sunburst finish, 24.75 in. scale, mfg. 2007-2012.

$5,050	$2,650 - 3,300	$1,575 - 1,975	$6,519

PETE TOWNSHEND J-200 SIGNATURE (MODEL SJPT) – Sitka spruce top, flame maple back and sides, flame maple neck, 20-fret Madagascar rosewood fingerboard with mother-of-pearl crown inlays and signature, 25 1/2 in. scale, slim profile selected by Pete Townshend, 1960s style Madagascar moustache bridge with mother-of-pearl inlays, gold kidney bean tuners, 60s style SJ-200 pickguard, multi-ply binding on top and back, Fishman System electronics, Antique Natural or Vintage Sunburst finish, mfg. 2005-2012.

$4,750	$2,525 - 3,150	$1,525 - 1,900	$6,152

RON WOOD SIGNATURE J-200 (MODEL ACRW) – J-200 style, hand select solid Sitka spruce top, round soundhole, bound body, flamed maple back/sides, flamed maple neck, 14/20-fret bound ebony fingerboard with abalone flame inlay, ebony moustache bridge with gold lip pearl inlay, white bridgepins, blackface peghead with mother-of-pearl "Ron Wood" signature/logo inlay, Custom Shop seal on back of headstock, three-per-side gold tuners, dual hand-engraved pickguards with a flame design, available in Antique Natural Lacquer finish, mfg. 1997-98.

N/A	$3,250 - 4,000	$2,100 - 2,500	$7,999

This model was designed in conjunction with guitarist Ron Wood (Rolling Stones). Wood personally signed the first 100 labels for this limited edition model. This Special Custom model was designed by Gibson Master Luthier Ren Ferguson, is specially numbered, and has a certificate of authenticity.

ELVIS PRESLEY KING OF ROCK J-200 (MODEL ACEP) – soliud Sitka spruce top, solid flame maple back and sides, maple neck, ebony fingerboard with mother-of-pearl crown inlays, multi-ply top and back binding, 25 1/2 in. scale, carved ebony bridge with mother-of-pearl inlays, gold tuners, Elvis signature truss rod cover, Elvis custom pickguard with mother-of-pearl crown, Ebony finish, mfg. 2005-2010.

$3,550	$1,900 - 2,300	$1,100 - 1,300	$4,562

Beginning 2006, this model became standard with transducer pickup and active preamp.

MONTANA GOLD J-200 (ACMGANGH1) – J-200 style, hand select solid spruce top, round soundhole, bound body, flamed maple back/sides, flamed maple neck, 14/20-fret bound ebony fingerboard with pearl block inlay, ebony moustache bridge with pearl inlay, white bridgepins, blackface peghead with mother-of-pearl "Harvested Wheat"/logo inlay, Custom Shop seal on back of headstock, three-per-side gold Imperial tuners, tortoise pickguard with engraved "Montana Gold"/Wheat inlay, available in Antique Natural Lacquer finish, mfg. 1997-98.

N/A	$2,200 - 2,750	$1,325 - 1,650	$4,399

This model's serial number is inside the guitar on the headblock. This Special Custom model was designed by Gibson Master Luthier Ren Ferguson, is specially numbered, and has a certificate of authenticity.

* **Montana Gold 200 Custom** – J-200 super jumbo size body, solid Sitka spruce top, highly flamed maple, koa (2005 only), or quilted maple (2005 only) back/sides/neck, ebony fingerboard, gold plated imperial tuners, special wheat inlays on pickguard and Montana Gold banner on both headstock and pickguard, available in Trans. Amber finish, Custom Shop model, mfg. 2001-2002, reintroduced 2004-2005.

N/A	$2,400 - 3,000	$1,450 - 1,800	$5,433

MSR/NOTES	100%	EXCELLENT	AVERAGE	LAST MSR

SUPER 200 CUSTOM – J-200 super jumbo size body with Super 400 appointments, solid Sitka spruce top, figured maple back and sides, ebony bridge and fingerboard, mother-of-pearl split block inlays, Venetian cutaway pickguard with headstock style inlay, available in Antique Natural or Vintage Sunburst finish, Custom Shop model, mfg. 2001-05.

	N/A	N/A	N/A	

This model was priced on request.

SOUTHERN JUMBO 200 HISTORIC – Antique Natural or Vintage Sunburst finish, 300 mfg. 2005.

	N/A	$1,950 - 2,400	$1,175 - 1,450	$4,238

J-200 CUSTOM VINE (SJ2V) – top-of-the-line custom SJ-200, featuring elaborate custom vine abalone fingerboard inlays, hand engraved pickguard, and abalone body trim, available in Antique Natural or Vintage Sunburst finish, custom shop model, mfg. 1999-2012.

	$9,700	$5,200 - 6,500	$3,100 - 3,900	$12,561

ACOUSTIC: JUMBO/ADVANCED JUMBO MODELS & VARIATIONS

JUMBO – round soundhole, stripe bound body/rosette, mahogany back/sides/neck, 14/19-fret rosewood fingerboard with pearl dot inlay, rectangular rosewood bridge with white pins, blackface peghead with pearl logo inlay, three-per-side nickel tuners, tortoise pickguard, available in Sunburst finish, mfg. 1934-36.

	N/A	$18,000 - 22,500	$10,750 - 13,500	

In 1935, fingerboard binding was added.

ADVANCED JUMBO (MFG. 1936-1940) – similar to jumbo, 16 in. wide, 20.25 in. long, and 4.5 in. deep, rosewood back/sides, pearl diamond/arrow fingerboard inlay, white black dot bridge pins, pearl diamond/arrow peghead inlay, available in Sunburst finish, approx. 300 mfg. 1936-1940.

	N/A	$48,000 - 60,000	$29,000 - 36,000	

JUMBO DELUXE – round shouldered dreadnought, 16 in. wide, mahogany back/sides, moustache shaped bridge with cutouts at bridge ends, height adj. saddle bearings, four semi-rectangular pearl inlays and two pearl dots on bridge, single bound top/back, unbound fingerboard, dot inlays, pearl logo, Sunburst finish, less than five made in 1938 only.

	N/A	N/A	N/A	

Extreme rarity factor precludes accurate pricing on this model.

ADVANCED JUMBO REISSUE (HLAJ - CURRENT, ACAJ-DISC.) – slope shouldered body, solid Sitka spruce top, round soundhole, bound body, Indian rosewood back/sides, 14/20-fret bound rosewood fingerboard with mother-of-pearl arrow inlay, rosewood bridge, white bridgepins, blackface peghead with abalone crown/logo inlay, three-per-side nickel tuners, "flame" colored pickguard, available in Vintage Sunburst, Antique Natural, or Antique Walnut (mfg. 2002-2003) Lacquer finish, disc. 1998, reintroduced 2002, 200 mfg. during 2005.

	N/A	$1,550 - 1,950	$950 - 1,175	$2,923

* Add $693 for Original 1930s Adirondack spruce top (2004-05).
* Subtract $172 for Original 1930s design with Sitka top (2004-05).

* *Advanced Jumbo Reissue Bird's-eye Maple* – similar to the Advanced Jumbo Reissue, except has bird's-eye maple back and sides, mfg. 1995-96.

	N/A	$2,500 - 3,000	$1,500 - 1,875	

ADVANCED JUMBO CUSTOM REISSUE (LUTHIER'S CHOICE HISTORIC SIGNATURE) – slope shouldered body, solid red spruce top, round soundhole, bound body, Brazilian rosewood back/sides, 14/20-fret bound rosewood fingerboard, three-per-side nickel Waverly tuners, available in Vintage Sunburst finish, mfg. 2001-05.

	N/A	$3,750 - 4,500	$2,500 - 3,000	

This model was priced on request.

ADVANCED JUMBO RED SPRUCE (MODEL HLAJRS, LTD 2013) – slope-shouldered dreadnought-style body, Red Adirondack spruce top, Bhilwara rosewood back and sides, round soundhole with double ring rosette, single-ply top and back binding, set mahogany modified V profile neck, 14/20-fret bound rosewood fingerboard with MOP diamond and arrows inlays, black headstock overlay with MOP script Gibson logo and diamond/arrows inlays, three-per-side open-style nickel tuners, rosewood bridge with MOP dot inlays, firestripe pickguard, 25.5 in. scale, 1.725 in. nut width, available in Vintage Sunburst finish, hardshell case included, mfg. 2013-present.

MSR N/A	$3,000	$1,950 - 2,250	$975 - 1,200	

RANDY SCRUGGS ADVANCED JUMBO – Randy Scruggs Advanced Jumbo signature based on a late 1930s Gibson AJ, rounded-shouldered dreadnought style, solid Sitka spruce top, solid east Indian rosewood back and sides, advanced X bracing, round soundhole with abalone rosette, multi-ply top binding with abalone trim, single-ply back binding, one-piece mahogany modified "V" neck with a compound dovetail joint, 14/20-fret rosewood fingerboard with MOP custom crown inlays, AJ-style headstock with 17 degree angle, black overlay, MOP script Gibson logo, and MOP custom crown inlay, Randy Scruggs signature on truss rod cover, three-per-side vintage-style open back nickel tuners, traditional rectangular rosewood bridge with MOP dots and white pins, traditional AJ firestripe pickguard, available in Vintage Sunburst finish, 25.5 in. scale, hardshell case included, limited edition run of 100 instruments, mfg. 2010-present.

MSR $4,696	$3,600	$1,925 - 2,400	$1,150 - 1,450	

MSR/NOTES	100%	EXCELLENT	AVERAGE	LAST MSR

ORIGINAL 1934 JUMBO – round shouldered body, solid Sitka (standard) or red (optional) spruce top, patterned after the original round shoulder model released in 1934, mahogany back/sides, Madagascar rosewood fingerboard, tapered headstock, 19 or 20 frets, 24.75 in. scale, 1930s Vintage Sunburst or Sunburst (mfg. 2003) finish, Custom Historic Collection, limited mfg. 2003, reintroduced 2005.

	N/A	$1,700 - 2,100	$1,025 - 1,275	$3,892

Gibson made 48 of these during 2005.

ORIGINAL 1934 JUMBO (MODEL RSOJ) – slope-shouldered dreadnought J-45-style body, Red Adirondack spruce top, mahogany back and sides, round soundhole with two-ring rosette, single-ply top and back binding, set mahogany period-correct V profile neck, 14/19-fret bound rosewood fingerboard with MOP dot inlays, black headstock overlay with MOP script Gibson logo, three-per-side vintage Waverly open-style gold tuners, rosewood bridge with MOP dot inlays, firestripe pickguard, 25 in. scale, 1.725 in. nut width, available in Vintage Sunburst finish, period correct hardshell case included, limited run of 100 instruments, mfg. 2013-present.

MSR $7,738	$6,000	$3,900 - 4,500	$1,950 - 2,400	

This model is replicated on collector Gary Burnett's 1934 Jumbo.

JACKSON BROWNE SIGNATURE MODEL 1 (MODEL RSJB1) – Jackson Brown Jumbo signature based on a 1930s Gibson Jumbo, rounded-shouldered dreadnought style, solid Adirondack red spruce top, solid farmed English Walnut back and sides, scalloped red spruce bracing, round soundhole with traditional three-ply rosette, multi-ply top binding, single-ply back binding, one-piece mahogany modified "V" neck with a compound dovetail joint, 12/19-fret bound rosewood fingerboard with abalone slotted diamond inlays, traditional tapered 1930s-style headstock with 17 degree angle, black overlay, and MOP Gibson logo, three-per-side gold Waverly tuners with ivoroid buttons, traditional rectangular rosewood bridge, firestripe pickguard, available in Vintage Sunburst finish, 4.55 in. body depth at neck block, 4.83 in. body depth at tail block, 1.805 in. nut width, 24.75 in. scale, hardshell case and certificate of authenticity included, mfg. 2011-12.

	$4,500	$2,600 - 3,250	$1,575 - 1,950	$5,803

* *Jackson Browne Signature Model A (Model RSJBA)* – similar to the Jackson Browne Signature Model 1, except has Trance Audio Amulet System with low impedance cable and outboard blue box, available in Vintage Sunburst finish, hardshell case and certificate of authenticity included, mfg. 2011-12.

	$6,000	$3,450 - 4,300	$2,100 - 2,600	$7,738

ACOUSTIC: JUMBO MISC. MODELS

J-10 – Gibson shipping records indicate approx. 30 mfg. 1971-73.

	N/A	N/A	N/A	

Extreme rarity factor precludes accurate pricing on this model.

J-15 (MODEL RS15) – slope-shouldered dreadnought J-45-style body, Sitka spruce top, walnut back and sides, round soundhole with multi-ring abalone rosette, multi-ply top binding, single-ply back binding, set maple neck, 14/20-fret walnut fingerboard with MOP dot inlays, black headstock overlay with natural Gibson logo, three-per-side mini Grover nickel tuners, walnut bridge, tortoise pickguard, L.R. Baggs Element pickup and electronics, 24.75 in. scale, 1.725 in. nut width, available in Antique Natural finish, hardshell case included, new 2014.

MSR $2,095	$1,500	$975 - 1,125	$500 - 600	

J-25 – slope shouldered body, laminated spruce top, round soundhole, tortoiseshell pickguard, bound body/rosette, synthetic back/sides bowl, mahogany neck, 14/20-fret rosewood fingerboard with pearl dot inlay, rosewood bridge with white pins, blackface peghead with screened logo, three-per-side nickel tuners with pearloid buttons, available in Natural finish, mfg. 1984-87.

	N/A	$475 - 600	$275 - 350	

J-29 ROSEWOOD (MODEL RS29) – slope-shouldered dreadnought J-45-style body, Sitka spruce top, rosewood back and sides, round soundhole with three-ply single ring rosette, multi-ply top binding, single-ply back binding, set mahogany neck, 14/20-fret rosewood fingerboard with MOP dot inlays, black headstock overlay with Gibson logo, three-per-side Grover nickel tuners, rosewood bridge, tortoise pickguard, L.R. Baggs Element pickup and electronics, 24.75 in. scale, 1.725 in. nut width, available in Antique Natural finish, hardshell case included, new 2014.

MSR $2,862	$2,250	$1,450 - 1,675	$725 - 900	

J-30 – dreadnought body, spruce top, round soundhole, tortoiseshell pickguard, three-stripe bound body/rosette, mahogany back/sides/neck, 14/20-fret rosewood fingerboard with pearl dot inlay, blackface peghead with pearl banner/logo inlay, rosewood bridge with black pins, three-per-side nickel tuners with pearloid buttons, available in Antique Walnut or Vintage Sunburst finish, mfg. 1985-1998.

	N/A	$800 - 1,000	$475 - 600	$1,400

In 1994, reverse bridge with rosewood pins replaced original part/design.

* *J-30 Cutaway* – similar to J-30, except has single round cutaway, reverse belly bridge with rosewood pins, transducer pickup/preamp system, available in Antique Walnut or Vintage Sunburst finish, mfg. 1994-98.

	N/A	$875 - 1,100	$525 - 650	$1,750

JUMBO 35 (J-35) – spruce top, round soundhole, bound body, one-ply stripe rosette, mahogany back/sides/neck, 14/19-fret rosewood fingerboard with pearl dot inlay, rosewood straight bridge with pearl dot inlay, white bridge pins, blackface peghead with screened logo, three-per-side tuners with plastic buttons, "tiger stripe" pickguard, available in Natural (approx. 25 mfg. 1941 only) or Sunburst finish, approx. 2,500 mfg. 1936-1942.

1936-1938	N/A	$12,000 - 15,000	$7,250 - 9,000	
1939-1942	N/A	$10,750 - 13,500	$6,500 - 8,000	

* **Add 10-20% for Natural finish.**

In 1939, Natural finish was also available. In 1941, both Natural and Sunburst finishes were available. 3-tone bar models bring slightly higher premium.

MSR/NOTES	100%	EXCELLENT	AVERAGE	LAST MSR

J-35 (1985-87 MFG.) – spruce top, round soundhole, tortoiseshell pickguard, three-stripe bound body/rosette, maple back/sides/neck, 14/20-fret rosewood fingerboard with pearl dot inlay, rosewood reverse bridge with white black dot pins, blackface peghead with screened logo, three-per-side tuners with plastic buttons, available in Cherry Sunburst finish, mfg. 1985-87.

	N/A	$800 - 1,000	$475 - 600	

J-35 1995 LIMITED EDITION – select solid Sitka spruce top, mahogany back/sides, ebony fingerboard and bridge, historic firestripe pickguard, advanced bracing pattern, vintage nickel tuners, 250 manufactured, mfg. 1995 only.

	N/A	$1,200 - 1,500	$725 - 900	

There is also a J-35 Fuller, which was made for Fuller's Vintage Guitar located in Houston, TX. 2002 MSR was $2,402.

J-35 (MODEL RS35, 2013 MFG.) – slope-shouldered dreadnought-style body, Sitka spruce top, mahogany back and sides, round soundhole with traditional ring rosette, multi-ply top binding, single-ply back binding, mahogany neck, 14/20-fret rosewood fingerboard with MOP dot inlays, black headstock overlay with gold script and banner Gibson decal, three-per-side nickel tuners with white buttons, rosewood bridge, 40s-style firestripe pickguard, L.R. Baggs Element pickup/electronics, available in Antique Natural finish, 24.75 in. scale, 1.725 in. nut width, black hardshell case included, mfg. 2013-present.

MSR $2,190	$1,700	$1,100 - 1,275	$550 - 675	

J-40 – square-shouldered dreadnought-style body, spruce top, mahogany back and sides, round soundhole with three-stripe rosette, double X-bracing, regular body binding (1971-1980) or tortoiseshell celluloid binding (1981-82), one-piece (1971-mid-1970s) or three-piece (mid-1970s-1982) mahogany neck, 14/20-fret rosewood fingerboard with pearl dot inlays, Natural finish (1971-77) or black (1977-1982) headstock overlay with decal logo, three-per-side Kluson Deluxe tuners with tulip buttons, rosewood bridge with bottom belly and no pins, black teardrop pickguard (1971-77) or large black pointed pickguard (1977-1982), available in Natural or Cherry Sunburst finish with Walnut back and sides, mfg. 1971-1982.

	N/A	$800 - 1,000	$475 - 600	

JUMBO 55 (J-55, 1939-1942 MFG.) – spruce top, round soundhole, tortoise pickguard, bound body, one-stripe rosette, mahogany back/sides/neck, 14/20-fret bound coffeewood fingerboard with pearl dot inlay, coffeewood mustache bridge with pearl dot inlay, white bridge pins, blackface stairstep peghead with pearl logo inlay, three-per-side tuners with amber buttons, available in Sunburst finish, approx. 325 mfg. 1939-1942.

1939-1940 Stairstep Headstock	N/A	$16,000 - 20,000	$9,500 - 12,000	
1940-1942 Regular Headstock	N/A	$14,500 - 18,000	$8,750 - 11,000	

In 1940, standard peghead replaced original design. In 1941, rosewood fingerboard, wings shaped rosewood bridge with pearl dot inlay replaced original part/design.

* J-55 (1972-1982 Mfg.) – slope shouldered body, spruce top, round soundhole, tortoise pickguard, bound body, three-stripe rosette, laminated mahogany back/sides, maple neck, 14/20-fret rosewood fingerboard with pearl dot inlay, rosewood bridge with black white dot pins, blackface peghead with pearl logo inlay, three-per-side chrome tuners, available in Natural finish, approx. 3,900 mfg. 1972-1982.

	N/A	$875 - 1,100	$525 - 650	

J-60 – dreadnought body, spruce top, round soundhole, tortoiseshell pickguard, three-stripe bound body/rosette, rosewood back/sides, mahogany neck, 14/20-fret rosewood fingerboard with pearl dot inlay, rosewood bridge with black pins, three-per-side nickel tuners with pearl buttons, available in Antique Natural or Vintage Sunburst finish, mfg. 1992-98.

	N/A	$1,200 - 1,500	$725 - 950	$1,999

J-60 TRADITIONAL (CL60) – square shoulder dreadnought, solid Sitka spruce top, round soundhole, abalone body binding, solid rosewood back/sides, 14/20-fret ebony fingerboard with pearl dot inlay, bound headstock with mother-of-pearl script logo, ebony belly bridge with white bridgepins, three-per-side gold tuners, teardrop-shaped tortoiseshell pickguard, available in Antique Natural Gloss Lacquer finish, mfg. 1997-98.

	N/A	$1,200 - 1,500	$725 - 950	$2,099

J-60 (MODEL SS60, 2013 MFG.) – square-shouldered dreadnought-style body, Sitka spruce top, Indian rosewood back and sides, round soundhole with double ring rosette, multi-ply top and back binding, set mahogany rounded profile neck, 14/20-fret rosewood fingerboard with MOP dot inlays, black headstock overlay with MOP script Gibson logo, three-per-side gold vintage open-style tuners, firestripe pickguard, rosewood bridge, L.R. Baggs Element pickup and electronics, 24.75 in. scale, 1.725 in. nut width, available in Antique Natural finish, hardshell case included, mfg. 2013-present.

MSR N/A	$3,000	$1,950 - 2,250	$975 - 1,200	

J-100/J-100 CUSTOM/SUPER JUMBO 100 (1939-1975 MFG.) – mahogany neck/back/sides, cedar top, 17 in. wide, black teardrop pickguard, rosewood belly bridge, four-ply top binding with black outer layer, black bound back, 25.5 in. scale, dot inlays, crown peghead inlay, pearl logo, approx. 140 mfg. 1939-1941, and approx. 290 mfg. 1972-1975.

1939-1941	N/A	$24,000 - 30,000	$14,500 - 18,000	
1972-1975	N/A	$1,400 - 1,750	$850 - 1,050	

• **Add 10%-15% for maple back/sides.**

This model was renamed the J-100 Custom in 1970. Moustache bridge and stairstep peghead became optional in 1972.

MSR/NOTES	100%	EXCELLENT	AVERAGE	LAST MSR

J-100 (1985-1991 MFG.) – spruce top, round soundhole, black pickguard, two-stripe bound body/rosette, maple back/sides/neck, 14/20-fret rosewood fingerboard with pearl dot inlay, rosewood bridge with black pins, three-per-side nickel tuners with pearl buttons, available in Natural finish, mfg. 1985-1991.

	N/A	$1,275 - 1,600	$750 - 950	

This model was available with a cedar top as an option.

J-100 (XTRA) – J-200 size super jumbo body, spruce top, round soundhole, black pickguard, two-stripe bound body/rosette, maple (mfg.1999-2005), Bubinga (2005 only), or mahogany (disc. 1998) back/sides/neck, 14/20-fret rosewood fingerboard with pearl dot inlay, rosewood bridge with black pins, blackface peghead with pearl crown logo inlay, three-per-side nickel (disc.) or gold tuners/hardware with pearloid buttons, available in Antique Natural (1999-2005), Black Cherry (mfg. 2003) Antique Walnut (disc. 2003), or Vintage Sunburst (disc. 1998) finish, mfg. 1991-97, 1999-2005.

	N/A	$1,200 - 1,500	$725 - 900	$2,703

* **Add approx. 5% for Black Cherry finish (mfg. 2003). Subtract approx. 5% if w/ maple back/sides.**
In 1994, tortoise pickguard, mustache bridge with rosewood (disc. 1998) or white (new 1999) pins replaced original part/design.

* ***J-100 Xtra Cutaway*** – similar to J-100 Xtra, except has single round cutaway, tortoiseshell pickguard, mustache bridge with rosewood pins, transducer pickup/preamp system, available in Antique Walnut and Vintage Sunburst finishes, mfg. 1994-98.

	N/A	$1,275 - 1,600	$775 - 950	$1,850

J-150 – J-200 size super jumbo body, spruce top, figured maple back/sides/neck (1999-2004) or rosewood back/sides (2005 only), rosewood fingerboard/bridge, engraved multi-color flower pattern pickguard, moustache bridge, with transducer, Antique Natural finish, mfg. 1999-2005.

	N/A	$1,450 - 1,800	$875 - 1,100	$3,379

J-190 EC SUPER FUSION – solid spruce top, flame maple back/sides/neck, gold hardware, features Gibson's dual pickup system (single coil pickup and acoustic transducer), available in Antique Natural and Vintage Sunburst (2001-04) finish, mfg. 1999-2004.

	N/A	$1,350 - 1,700	$825 - 1,025	$4,710

J-250 R – spruce top, round soundhole, black pickguard with engraved floral pattern, rosewood back/sides, mahogany neck, 14/20-fret bound rosewood fingerboard with pearl crown inlay, rosewood mustache bridge with pearl block inlay, black pearl dot pins, bound peghead with pearl crown/logo inlay, three-per-side gold tuners with pearl buttons, available in Natural finish, approx. 20 mfg. 1972-78.

	N/A	$2,400 - 3,000	$1,450 - 1,800	

J-250 MONARCH CUSTOM (MODEL AC2M) – J-200 Super Jumbo body, top-of-the-line model with solid spruce top, Brazilian rosewood back/sides, ebony bridge and fingerboard, Monarch crown fretboard inlays, extensive and elaborate mother-of-pearl and abalone bindings/inlays, available in Antique Natural or Vintage Sunburst (disc.) finish, Custom Shop model, 25.5 in. scale, limited mfg. beginning 2001-present.

MSR $27,704	$21,400	$11,500 - 14,000	N/A	

J-250 PRESENTATION – J-200 super jumbo body, top-of-the-line model with rare Schmetterling spruce top, select three-piece figured maple back, ebony fingerboard and SJ200 bridge, ancient Siberian mammoth bone saddle, bridge pins, and endpin, custom carved "volute" headstock with ebony overlays, hand carved solid mother-of-pearl nut, cloud mother-of-pearl fingerboard inlay, fleur-de-lis and scroll abalone and mother-of-pearl headstock inlays, multiple bound body, headstock, fingerboard, and rosette, handmade, bound caramel shell pickguard, MT Custom Shop Limited Edition, only 101 produced, mfg. 1995 only.

	N/A	$3,500 - 4,350	$2,150 - 2,650	

J-300 – similar to J-250 R, except has 12 strings, six-per-side tuners, only one mfg. 1973.

	N/A	N/A	N/A	

Extreme rarity precludes accurate pricing on this model.

J-1000 – rounded single cutaway body, spruce top, round soundhole, three-stripe bound body/rosette, rosewood back/sides, mahogany neck, 20 bound rosewood pointed fingerboard with pearl diamond inlay, rosewood mustache bridge with black pearl dot pins, bound blackface peghead with pearl diamond/logo inlay, three-per-side gold tuners, available in Natural finish, mfg. 1992 only.

	N/A	$1,600 - 2,000	$950 - 1,200	$1,999

J-1500 – rounded single cutaway body, spruce top, round soundhole, three-stripe bound body, abalone rosette, rosewood back/sides, mahogany neck, 20-fret bound ebony pointed fingerboard with abalone varied diamond inlay, ebony mustache bridge with white black dot pins, bound blackface peghead with abalone fleur-de-lis/logo inlay, three-per-side gold tuners, available in Natural finish, mfg. 1992 only.

	N/A	$1,800 - 2,250	$1,075 - 1,350	$2,750

J-2000/CUSTOM – single rounded cutaway body, spruce top, round soundhole, abalone bound body/rosette, rosewood back/sides, mahogany neck, 20-fret bound ebony point fingerboard with abalone leaf inlay, ebony bridge with white abalone dot pins, abalone leaf bridge wings inlay, bound peghead with leaf/logo inlay, three-per-side gold tuners with pearl buttons, piezo bridge pickup, endpin pickup jack, available in Antique Natural or Vintage Sunburst finish, disc. 1994.

	N/A	$2,600 - 3,250	$1,675 - 2,075	$4,010

MSR/NOTES	100%	EXCELLENT	AVERAGE	LAST MSR

J-2000 CUSTOM CUTAWAY – single rounded cutaway body, solid spruce top, customer selected back and side wood, mahogany neck, abalone top trim, "autumn leaf" fretboard, and headstock inlays, hand carved gold tuners, available in Antique Natural or Vintage Sunburst finish, limited mfg. beginning 1999 by MT Custom Shop.

	N/A	$2,800 - 3,500	$1,675 - 2,100	

This model was priced on request.

JG-0 – spruce top, round soundhole, bound body, one-stripe rosette, mahogany back/sides/neck, 14/20-fret rosewood fingerboard with pearl dot inlay, rosewood bridge with white pins, logo peghead decal, three-per-side tuners, available in Natural finish, approx. 550 mfg. 1970-75.

	N/A	$800 - 1,000	$475 - 600	

* *JG-12* – similar to the JG-0, except in 12-string configuration with six-per-side tuners, approx. 185 mfg. 1970 only.

	N/A	$850 - 1,050	$500 - 625	

CJ-165 MAPLE (MODEL LS65) – 15 in. SJ-200 body style, premium Sitka spruce top, premium AAA maple back and sides, 24 3/4 in. scale, four-ply top, single-ply back, V-shape profile, maple neck, Indian rosewood fingerboard with mother-of-pearl dot inlays, mini nickel Grover tuners, traditional Gibson rosewood bridge with mother-of-pearl dot inlays, abalone rosette, active preamp pickups, available in Vintage Sunburst or Antique Natural finish, mfg. 2006-08.

	N/A	$1,325 - 1,650	$800 - 1,000	$2,936

* *CJ-165EC Maple (Model LSSM)* – similar to the CJ-165 Maple, except has a single smooth cutaway and Fishman Ellipse Aura System electronics, available in Antique Natural or Vintage Sunburst finish, mfg. summer 2007-present.

MSR $3,762	$2,900	$1,600 - 1,900	$950 - 1,200	

CJ-165 ROSEWOOD (MODEL LS6R) – 15 in. SJ-200 body style, premium Sitka spruce top, premium Indian rosewood back and sides, mahogany neck, ebony fingerboard with mother-of-pearl paralellogram inlays, V-shape profile, four-ply top and single-ply back binding, 24 3/4 in. scale, traditional Gibson ebony bridge with mother-of-pearl dot inlays, abalone rosette, mini- Grover tuners, active preamp pickups, available in Vintage Sunburst or Antique Natural finish, mfg. 2006-08.

	N/A	$1,400 - 1,750	$850 - 1,050	$3,171

* *CJ-165EC Rosewood (Model LSSR)* – similar to the CJ-165 Rosewood, except has a single smooth cutaway and Fishman Ellipse Aura System electronics, available in Antique Natural or Vintage Sunburst finish, mfg. summer 2007-present.

MSR $3,762	$2,900	$1,600 - 1,900	$950 - 1,200	

SJ-100 (MODEL SJ1X) – premium Sitka spruce top, Bubinga back and sides, mahogany neck, Indian rosewood fingerboard with mother-of-pearl dot inlays, rosewood moustache bridge, single-ply top and back body binding, 25 1/2 in. scale, nickel hardware, tortoiseshell pickguard, active preamp electronics, Antique Natural finish, mfg. 2006-08.

	N/A	$1,250 - 1,550	$750 - 925	$2,936

1941 SJ-100 (MODEL SJ10) – Super Jumbo-style body, Sitka spruce top, mahogany back and sides, round soundhole with single ring rosette and bound soundhole edge, multi-ply top and back binding, mahogany rounded profile neck, 14/20-fret bound rosewood fingerboard with MOP dot inlays, J-200-style headstock with black overlay and MOP script Gibson logo, three-per-side nickel tuners with white buttons, 40s-style rosewood bridge with three MOP dots, AJ-style firestripe pickguard, L.R. Baggs Element pickup/electronics, available in Vintage Sunburst finish, 25.5 in. scale, 1.725 in. nut width, hardshell case included, mfg. 2013-present.

MSR $3,868	$3,000	$1,950 - 2,250	$975 - 1,200	

SJ-150 MAPLE (SJ15) – Super Jumbo body, premium Sitka Spruce top, maple back and sides, figured maple neck, 25 1/2 in. scale, round profile, Indian rosewood fingerboard with mother-of-pearl crown inlays, rosewood moustache bridge, six-ply top, four-ply back body binding, vintage style nickel Gotoh tuners, tortoise shell pickguard with engraved border, active preamp pickup, Antique Natural finish, mfg. 2006-08.

	N/A	$1,525 - 1,900	$925 - 1,150	$3,610

SJ-200 EC (MODEL SJS2) – Super Jumb body, premium Sitka spruice top, AAA flame maple back and sides, maple neck, 25 1/2 in. scale, round profile, Madagascar rosewood fingerboard with mother-of-pearl crown inlays, multi-ply binding with birdsbeak, rosewood moustache bridge with mother-of-pearl bar inlays, gold Gotoh tuners, tortoise shell J-200 pickup, six-ply top and four-ply back body binding, Fishman Prefix Premium Blend pickups, available in Antique Natural or Vintage Sunburst finish, mfg. 2006-08.

	N/A	$2,200 - 2,750	$1,325 - 1,650	$5,029

SJ-300 ROSEWOOD (MODEL SJ2E) – Super Jumbo body, AAA premium Sitka spruce top, premium Indian rosewood back and sides, mahogany neck, ebony fingerboard with abalone crown inlays, 25 1/2 in. scale, single-ply headstock, six-ply top, four-ply back binding, ebony moustache bridge with four abalone bar inlays, gold Grover Imperial tuners, tortoise sheel pickguard with abalone dots, active preamp pickup, available in Antique Natural or Vintage Sunburst finish, mfg. 2006-08.

	N/A	$2,600 - 3,250	$1,550 - 1,950	$5,901

ACOUSTIC: L SERIES

There is a great deal of confusion about the difference between the small bodied L-0 series and L-00 series guitars. The L-0 was introduced in 1926 in the "Robert Johnson" shape. By 1928, it was produced with a mahogany top, back and sides. The L-0 was redesigned circa 1930 as a Martin 00 shaped guitar. It had a spruce top, mahogany back and sides, and 12 frets were clear of the

MSR/NOTES	100%	EXCELLENT	AVERAGE	LAST MSR

body. By 1932 the L-0 had 14 frets to the body, and by 1933, it had been discontinued in favor of the more popular L-00. The L-0 was reintroduced in 1937 as a black guitar with a tortoiseshell celluloid pickguard and remained in the line until 1942.

The L-00 was introduced in 1932 with a spruce top, mahogany back and sides, Black finish and a white pickguard. By 1933, the L-00 was available in a Sunburst finish with a striped celluloid pickguard. The L-00 Series was discontinued in 1942.

In terms of L Series desirability, an early Robert Johnson style shaped instrument is less than the post-1930 design. A mahogany top is less valuable than spruce. Rosewood and maple sides with a mahogany back will add to the rarity and price, while a maple back and side will be even more desirabile. Brazilian rosewood back and sides are the most desirable in this series. 12 frets to the body will be less desirable than 14, while the infrequently encountered 13 fret Nick Lucas will be somewhere in between.

STYLE L – arched spruce top, round soundhole, bound body, wood inlay rosette, maple back/sides/neck, 13/19-fret ebony fingerboard with pearl dot inlay, ebony bridge/trapeze tailpiece, blackface peghead, three-per-side tuners, available in Orange Top finish, mfg. approx. 1902.

	N/A	$1,500 - 1,800	$1,000 - 1,200	

L-0 – spruce (1926-1928, 1937-1942) or mahogany (1928-1933) top, maple (1926-1928) or mahogany (1928-1933, 1937-1942) back and sides, round soundhole with two-stripe rosette, bound body, mahogany neck, 12/19-fret (1926-1932) or 14/19-fret (1932-1933, 1937-1942) ebonized fingerboard with pearl dot inlays, black headstock overlay with screened "The Gibson" (1926-1932) or "Gibson" (1932-1933, 1937-1942) logo, three-per-side tuners with plastic buttons, ebony pyramid (1926-1928), rosewood (1928-1933, 1937-1942) bridge, black bridge pins, extra white bridge pin below bridge pins (1928-1929), white (1931-1933, some 1937-1942) or celluloid (1937-1942) pickguard, available in Amber Brown (1926-1928), Amber (1928-1931), or Black (1931-1933, 1937-1942) finish, 13.5 in. (1926-1931) or 14.75 in. (1931-1933, 1937-1942) lower bout width, 25 in. (1926-1931) or 24.75 in. scale (1931-1933, 1937-1942) scale, mfg. 1926-1933, 1937-1942.

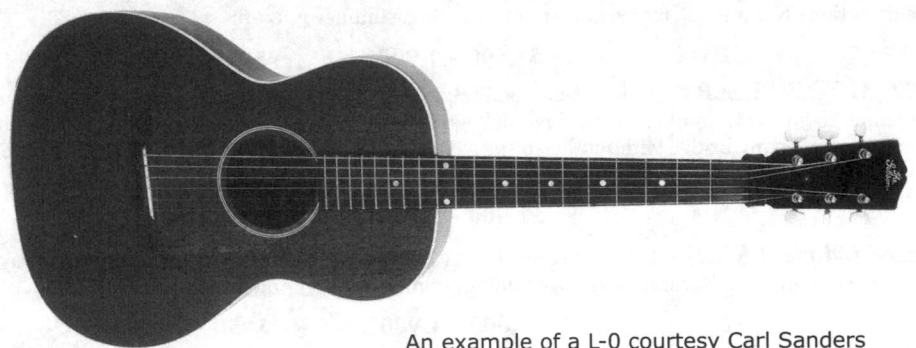

An example of a L-0 courtesy Carl Sanders

1926-1928 Maple	N/A	$3,200 - 4,000	$1,925 - 2,400	
1928-1931 Mahogany				
13.5 in. Body Width	N/A	$3,200 - 4,000	$1,925 - 2,400	
1931-1933 14.75 in. Body Width	N/A	$3,400 - 4,250	$2,050 - 2,550	
1937-1942	N/A	$3,400 - 4,250	$2,050 - 2,550	

L-00 – small body guitar, spruce top, mahogany back and sides, round soundhole with single multi ring rosette, top body binding, back body binding (1937-1946), mahogany neck, 14/19-fret rosewood fingerboard with pearl dot inlays, black headstock overlay with screened logo and "Only a Gibson is Good Enough" banner (1943-46), three-per-side tuners with plastic buttons, rosewood straight bridge, black bridge pins, tortoise or white pickguard, available in Ebony (1932-38), Natural (1941-46), or Sunburst top with mahogany red back and sides (1933-1946) finish, 14.75 in. body width, 19.25 in. body length, mfg. 1930-1946.

Ebony, 12-fret	N/A	$4,200 - 5,250	$2,525 - 3,150	
14-fret	N/A	$4,000 - 5,000	$2,400 - 3,000	

Models with maple back/sides command a premium (up to 50% for flamed maple). Early versions of this model have 12/19-fret fingerboards.

* **L-00 3/4** – similar to Model L-00, except has 3/4 size body, approx. 35 mfg. 1938-39 only.

	N/A	$4,250 - 5,250	$2,525 - 3,150	

L-00 (1936 REISSUE) – spruce top, round soundhole, two-stripe bound body/rosette, mahogany back/sides/neck, 14/19-fret bound rosewood fingerboard with pearl dot inlay, rosewood bridge with white pins, three-per-side nickel tuners with plastic buttons. Patterned after Gibson's older 00 size body, available in Antique Walnut, Vintage Sunburst, or Ebony (1999-2002) finish, mfg. 1992-96, reissued 1999-2002.

	N/A	$1,050 - 1,300	$650 - 800	$2,391

1937 L-00 (MODEL HL37) – detailed edition of a 1937 Gibson L-00, small body style, solid Adirondack spruce top, solid mahogany back and sides, round soundhole with rosette, single-ply top and back binding, mahogany 1937 profile V-shaped neck, 14/19-fret Madagascar rosewood fingerboard with MOP dot inlays, black headstock with script Gibson logo , three-per-side reproduction nickel tuners with white buttons, Madagascar rosewood bridge with MOP dots and white pins, 1937 style celluloid teardrop pickguard, available in Vintage Sunburst finish, 24.75 in. scale, Red Line case included, limited production of 25 guitars per month, mfg. 2007-present.

MSR $7,086	$5,500	$2,900 - 3,600	$1,750 - 2,175	

MSR/NOTES	100%	EXCELLENT	AVERAGE	LAST MSR

BLUES KING L-00 (MODEL LSBK) – parlor style, spruce top, round soundhole, tortoise pickguard, three-stripe bound body/rosette, mahogany back/sides/neck, 14/20-fret rosewood fingerboard with pearl dot inlay, straight rosewood bridge with white pins, blackface peghead with pearl logo inlay, three-per-side nickel tuners, available in Ebony (mfg. 2003) Antique Ebony (disc.), Natural top/Antique Walnut back/sides (disc.), Antique Natural (mfg. 2003), or Vintage Sunburst finish, mfg. 1994-96, reintroduced 2003-present.

1994-1996	N/A	$1,100 - 1,350	$675 - 825	
2003-Present MSR $3,098	$2,350	$1,250 - 1,550	$725 - 850	

* **Blues King Special** – similar to Blues King L-00, except has Indian rosewood back/sides, bound ebony fingerboard with pearl block inlay, ebony belly bridge with white pins, bound blackface peghead with pearl vase/logo inlay, transducer pickup/preamp system, available in Antique Natural or Vintage Sunburst finish, mfg. 1994-96.

	N/A	$1,200 - 1,500	$725 - 900	$2,500

NICK LUCAS (GIBSON SPECIAL) – slightly arched spruce top, mahogany back/sides/neck, bound body, bound rosewood fingerboard with dot inlay, rosewood bridge, "The Gibson" headstock logo, special round Nick Lucas label, this model underwent redesign several times in its short production span, originally introduced as a mahogany/spruce "Robert Johnson" shaped guitar with at least a 4.5 in. depth and 12 frets to the body, models can be found with 12, 13, and 14 fret-to-the-body fingerboards in mahogany, rosewood, and maple, available in Sunburst finish, original body width was 13.5 in., later mfg. was 14.75 in. wide, 19.25 in. long, 4.5 in. deep, mfg. circa 1928-1941, limited mfg. (probably less than 250 instruments).

1928-1930 Mahogany Body	N/A	$10,750 - 13,500	$6,500 - 8,000	
1929-1934 Rosewood Body	N/A	$20,000 - 25,000	$12,000 - 15,000	
1934-1941 Maple Body	N/A	$32,000 - 40,000	$19,250 - 24,000	
Four-String Tenor Configuration	N/A	$8,000 - 10,000	$4,750 - 6,000	

• **Subtract 20%-30% for tailpiece.**

In 1929, this model was redesigned in the L-00 body shape, retaining its deep body and 12-fret configuration. During 1930, most production featured rosewood back and sides, 13 frets to the body. During 1932, an adjustable bridge and tailpiece were listed as optional. In 1934, 14 frets to the body, mostly maple back and sides (mahogany on some), became standard. While this model was discontinued in 1938, the last production was shipped as late as 1941.

NICK LUCAS REISSUE CLASSIC (L-00 VARIANT) – solid spruce top, flame maple back/sides, rosewood fingerboard/bridge, patterned after the original Nick Lucas model, includes 1930s Nick Lucas label, available in Vintage Sunburst finish, mfg. 1999-2003.

	N/A	$2,000 - 2,500	$1,200 - 1,500	$2,989

* **Nick Lucas Elite (L-00 Variant)** – similar to Nick Lucas Reissue, except has Ebony fingerboard, maple neck, abalone Lucas style fretboard inlays, top trim, and rosette, vintage gold hardware, available in Antique Natural or Vintage Sunburst, mfg. 1999-2002.

	N/A	$2,800 - 3,500	$1,675 - 2,100	$4,040

* **Nick Lucas 1929 Reissue** – mahogany, maple, or rosewood, 12 or 14 frets, limited mfg. 2005.

	N/A	N/A	N/A	

This model was priced on request.

* **Nick Lucas 1929 Historic Signature** – Vintage Sunburst finish, mfg. by Custom Shop beginning 2005.

	N/A	N/A	N/A	

This model was priced on request.

* **Nick Lucas Historic Signature Koa Special** – similar to 1929 Historic Signature model, except has koa back/sides, mfg. by Custom Shop beginning 2005.

	N/A	N/A	N/A	

This model was priced on request.

L-1 ARCHTOP – carved spruce top, bound round soundhole, raised tortoiseshell pickguard, bound body, two-rope pattern rosette, birch back/sides, maple neck, 13/19-fret ebony fingerboard with pearl dot inlay, ebony bridge/trapeze tailpiece, slotted peghead, three-per-side tuners with plastic buttons, available in Orange Top/Mahogany finish, mfg. 1903-1925.

	N/A	$1,725 - 2,150	$1,025 - 1,300	

This model was also produced with maple back/sides. In 1918, Brown finish replaced original part/design. In 1920, a five-ring rosette replaced the original design.

L-1 FLATTOP – spruce top, round soundhole, bound body, three-ring rosette, mahogany back/sides, maple neck, 12/19-fret ebony fingerboard with pearl dot inlay, ebony pyramid bridge with black pins, painted peghead logo, three-per-side tuners with plastic buttons, mfg. 1926-1937.

1926-1931 12/13-Fret Body	N/A	$4,200 - 5,250	$2,525 - 3,150	
1932-1937 14-Fret Body	N/A	$4,000 - 5,000	$2,400 - 3,000	

This model was produced in the "Robert Johnson" body shape between 1926-28 - Sunburst finish became available in 1927. The body style changed to an L-0 shape circa 1929. By 1928, bound rosewood fingerboard, three-stripe bound body/rosette, rosewood belly bridge with white pins, Brown Sunburst finish replaced original part/design, extra bridge pin was added. In 1929, straight bridge replaced original design, extra bridge pin was discontinued. In 1931, the body and bridge were redesigned, unbound fingerboard replaced previous part/design. In 1932, single bound body, 14/19-fret fingerboard replaced previous part/design. From 1932-33, a tortoiseshell pickguard was added.

MSR/NOTES	100%	EXCELLENT	AVERAGE	LAST MSR

L-1 FLATTOP REISSUE – small body L-style guitar with a circular lower bout, spruce top, mahogany back and sides, round soundhole with two-stripe rosette, top and back binding, mahogany neck, 12/19-fret bound ebony fingerboard with pearl dot inlays, black headstock overlay with "The Gibson" logo, three-per-side nickel tuners with plastic buttons, rosewood bridge with pyramid ends, white bridge pins, available in Vintage Sunburst finish, 13.5 in. body width, 24.75 in. scale, mfg. 1991-95.

1991 1 of 100	N/A	$1,400 - 1,750	$850 - 1,050	
1992-1995	N/A	$1,200 - 1,500	$725 - 900	$1,400

This model was reintroduced in 1991 as a limited edition run of 100 instruments. In 1992, it was renamed the L-1 1992 Edition, and in 1993 it was discontinued as a standard production model. In 1994, it was reintroduced again simply as the L-1.

L-1 ROBERT JOHNSON (MODEL LSRL) – patterned after Robert Johnson's original L-1, shallow L-1 body, Sitka spruce top, mahogany back/sides/neck, ebony fingerboard, 12/19-fret, ebony bridge, period hardware, Robert Johnson signature at bottom of fingerboard, Vintage Sunburst only, 25 in. scale, mfg. summer 2003-present.

MSR $3,449	$2,700	$1,750 - 2,025	$875 - 1,075	

In 2009, this model was upgraded and improved.

L-2 ARCHTOP (1910-1923 MFG.) – carved spruce top, round soundhole, raised tortoise pickguard, bound body, three-rope pattern rosette, birch back/sides, maple neck, 13/19-fret ebony fingerboard with pearl dot inlay, adjustable ebony bridge/trapeze tailpiece, snakehead peghead with pearl logo inlay, three-per-side tuners with plastic buttons, available in Orange Top finish, mfg. 1910-1923.

	N/A	$1,800 - 2,250	$1,075 - 1,350	

* **L-2 Archtop (1924-26 Mfg.)** – carved spruce top, round soundhole, raised tortoiseshell pickguard, bound body, two-ring rosette, maple back/sides, mahogany neck, 13/19-fret bound ebony fingerboard with pearl dot inlay, adjustable ebony bridge/trapeze tailpiece, snakehead peghead with pearl logo inlay, three-per-side tuners with plastic buttons, available in Amber finish, mfg. 1924-26.

	N/A	$1,875 - 2,350	$1,125 - 1,400	

L-2 FLATTOP – spruce top, round soundhole, three-stripe body/rosette, bound body, rosewood back/sides, mahogany neck, 13/19-fret bound ebony fingerboard with pearl dot inlay, ebony pyramid bridge, blackface peghead with pearl logo inlay, three-per-side tuners with plastic buttons, available in Natural or Sunburst finish, mfg. 1929-1934.

Rosewood w/tailpiece	N/A	$8,000 - 10,000	$4,800 - 6,000	
Mahogany	N/A	$9,500 - 12,000	$5,750 - 7,250	

This model had a rosewood bridge 1929-1931. This model was also available with adjustable ebony bridge/trapeze tailpiece. In 1931, mahogany back/sides, 12/19-fret fingerboard replaced original part/design, gold sparkle inlay rosette/body, pearl flame peghead inlay were added. In 1932, rosewood back/sides, 13/19-fret fingerboard adjustable ebony bridge/trapeze tailpiece replaced previous part/design, raised pickguard was added, gold sparkle inlay no longer available. In 1933, top glued pickguard, ebony bridge with black pins replaced previous part/design. In 1934, 14/19-fret fingerboard replaced previous part/design.

L-3 – carved spruce top, bound round soundhole, raised tortoiseshell pickguard, bound body, three-ring wooden inlay rosette, birch back/sides, maple neck, 13/20-fret bound ebony fingerboard with pearl dot inlay, ebony bridge/trapeze tailpiece, blackface peghead with pearl logo inlay, three-per-side tuners with plastic buttons, available in Orange Top/Mahogany finish, mfg. 1902-1933.

1902-1928 Round Soundhole	N/A	$1,750 - 2,200	$1,075 - 1,325	
1928-1933 Oval Soundhole	N/A	$2,000 - 2,500	$1,200 - 1,500	

In 1928, an oval soundhole replaced original design.

L-4 – arched carved spruce top, oval soundhole, wooden inlay rosette, raised tortoiseshell pickguard, bound soundhole/body, maple back/sides, mahogany neck, 12/20-fret bound ebony pointed fingerboard with pearl dot inlay, ebony bridge/trapeze tailpiece with black pins, bound blackface peghead with pearl logo inlay, three-per-side tuners with buttons, available in Black finish, mfg. 1912-1956.

1912-1927 Oval Soundhole	N/A	$3,200 - 4,000	$1,925 - 2,400	
1928-1934 Round Soundhole	N/A	$3,400 - 4,250	$2,050 - 2,550	
1935-1939 F-Holes	N/A	$2,800 - 3,500	$1,675 - 2,100	
1940-1945	N/A	$2,800 - 3,500	$1,675 - 2,100	
1946-1956	N/A	$2,600 - 3,250	$1,550 - 1,950	

• **Add 20% for truss rod or snake head.**

16.25 in. by 20.25 in. body. In 1914, three-ring rosette, Mahogany finish replaced original part/design, Black and Orange finishes became an option. In 1918, Mahogany Sunburst finish replaced previous part/design. By 1920, rosette and peghead logo inlay were redesigned. In 1923, tailpiece pins were removed. In 1927, rosette was redesigned. In 1928, round soundhole 14/20-fret unbound fingerboard, unbound peghead replaced original part/design, two-ring rosette, redesigned peghead logo replaced previous part/design. By 1933, bound fingerboard replaced previous part/design, pearl diamond peghead inlay was added. In 1935, f-holes, bound pickguard, redesigned fingerboard inlay, redesigned trapeze tailpiece, bound peghead with lily inlay replaced previous part/design. In 1937, unbound pickguard replaced previous part/design, round soundhole was an option.

In 1940, Natural finish was an option. In 1941, unbound peghead replaced previous part/design. In 1946, bound pickguard, multi-bound body replaced previous part/design. In 1947, laminated pickguard, parallelogram fingerboard inlay replaced previous part/design.

* **L-4 C** – single pointed cutaway body, arched spruce top, f-holes, raised laminated pickguard, bound body, carved maple back/sides, mahogany neck, 19-fret bound rosewood fingerboard with pearl parallelogram inlay, adjustable rosewood bridge/trapeze tailpiece, blackface

MSR/NOTES	100%	EXCELLENT	AVERAGE	LAST MSR

peghead with pearl flowerpot/logo inlay, three-per-side tuners with plastic buttons, available in Natural or Sunburst finish, mfg. 1949-1970.

1949-1959	N/A	$2,800 - 3,500	$1,675 - 2,100	
1960-1964	N/A	$2,400 - 3,000	$1,450 - 1,800	
1965-1969	N/A	$1,800 - 2,250	$1,075 - 1,350	
1970-1971	N/A	$1,600 - 2,000	$950 - 1,200	

L-4 A CUTAWAY – jumbo cutaway body with solid Sitka spruce top, curly maple (disc. 2004) or rosewood back/sides/neck, 14/20 rosewood fingerboard with mother-of-pearl trapezoid inlays, rosewood bridge, gold Grover tuners, Fishman Prefix Plus pickup, available in Antique Natural, Vintage Sunburst, Blue Jean (2003), Chet Orange (2003), Emerald (2003), Antique Cherry (2003), Ice Blue (2003), Ebony (2003), Antique Walnut (2004), and Natural Gloss Top, mfg. 2003-05.

	N/A	$1,125 - 1,400	$675 - 850	$2,703

L-5 – carved spruce top, f-holes, raised multi-bound pickguard, multi-bound body, carved figured maple back/sides, figured maple/ebony neck, 14/20-fret bound ebony pointed fingerboard with pearl dot inlay, adjustable ebony bridge/trapeze tailpiece, multi-bound blackface snakehead peghead with pearl flowerpot/logo inlay, three-per-side silver plate tuners with pearl buttons, Master Model/Lloyd Loar signature labels, available in Natural or Cremona Brown Sunburst finish, limited in mfg. 1922-1958.

1922-1924 Lloyd Loar	N/A	$40,000 - 50,000	$24,000 - 30,000	
1925-1927 Master Model	N/A	$22,000 - 27,500	$13,250 - 16,500	
1928-1932	N/A	$10,000 - 12,500	$6,000 - 7,500	
1933-1934	N/A	$8,000 - 10,000	$4,800 - 6,000	
1935-1940	N/A	$6,000 - 7,500	$3,600 - 4,500	
1941-1949	N/A	$5,600 - 7,000	$3,350 - 4,200	
1950-1958	N/A	$5,200 - 6,500	$3,125 - 3,900	

- **Add 10-20% for Natural finish (1939-1958).**

Models signed by Lloyd Loar (1922 to 1924).

Some early versions of this instrument have birch back/sides. In 1925, gold tuners replaced original part/design. In 1927, Master Model label was discontinued. In 1929, flat fingerboard with block inlay replaced original part/design, individual tuners replaced previous part/design. In 1935, The Advanced L-5's larger body (17 inches across lower bout by 21 in. long), binding, tailpiece, peghead replaced original part/design, redesigned fingerboard replaced previous part/design. In 1936, bound f-holes replaced original part/design. In 1937, gold tailpiece with silver insert, Grover Imperial tuners replaced previous part/design. In 1939, redesigned tailpiece replaced previous part/design, pearloid pickguard, Natural finish became an option. In 1948, one or two pickguard mounted pickups became an option.

Current production instruments (1934 L-5) are part of the Historic Collection Series, found at the end of this section.

* L-5 P (Premiere)/L-5 C – single rounded cutaway body, arched spruce top, bound f-holes, raised multi-bound pearloid pickguard, multi-bound body, carved figured maple back/sides, figured maple neck, 14/20-fret multi-bound ebony pointed fingerboard with pearl block inlay, adjustable ebony bridge/gold trapeze tailpiece with silver insert, multi-bound blackface peghead with pearl flowerpot/logo inlay, three-per-side gold tuners, available in Natural or Sunburst finish, mfg. 1939-1989.

1939-1947 Premiere	N/A	$12,000 - 15,000	$7,250 - 9,000	
1948-1949	N/A	$10,750 - 13,500	$6,500 - 8,000	
1950-1959	N/A	$9,500 - 12,000	$5,750 - 7,250	
1960-1964	N/A	$7,600 - 9,500	$4,550 - 5,700	
1965-1969	N/A	$6,000 - 7,500	$3,600 - 4,500	
1970-1975	N/A	$5,200 - 6,500	$3,125 - 3,900	
1976-1989	N/A	$4,800 - 6,000	$2,900 - 3,600	

- **Add 10-20% for Natural finish.**

In 1948, renamed L-5 C, and 1 or 2 pickguard mounted pickups became an option.

* L-5 CT – similar to L-5 C, except has thin body, shorter scale length, available in Red finish, approx. 35 mfg. 1959-1961.

	N/A	$14,500 - 18,000	$8,750 - 11,000	

Also referred to as the George Gobel model with two humbucker pickups, two volume/tone controls, and a three-position switch became options. George Gobel's personal guitar was non-electric.

L-7 – arched spruce top, f-holes, raised bound black pickguard, bound body, carved maple back/sides, mahogany neck, 14/19-fret bound rosewood fingerboard with pearl multi-design inlay, adjustable rosewood bridge/trapeze tailpiece, bound blackface peghead with pearl fleur-de-lis/logo inlay, three-per-side tuners with plastic buttons, available in Natural or Sunburst (most common) finish, 16 or 17 in. body, approx. 1,200 mfg. 1932-1956.

1932-1934 16 in. Body	N/A	$4,000 - 5,000	$2,400 - 3,000	
1935-1942 17 in. Body	N/A	$4,000 - 5,000	$2,400 - 3,000	
1943-1949	N/A	$3,400 - 4,250	$2,050 - 2,550	
1950-1956	N/A	$2,400 - 3,000	$1,450 - 1,800	

- **Add 10-20% for Natural finish.**

Original body size was 16 in. In 1934, Advanced body (17 in. wide by 21 in. long) fingerboard/peghead inlay, trapeze tailpiece replaced original part/design. In 1937, redesigned trapeze tailpiece replaced previous part/design. In 1939, Natural finish became

MSR/NOTES	100%	EXCELLENT	AVERAGE	LAST MSR

available. In 1942, multi-bound body, parallelogram fingerboard inlay, crown peghead inlay replaced previous part/design. In 1944, redesigned trapeze tailpiece replaced previous part/design. In 1948, laminated pickguard replaced previous part/design, and one or two pickguard mounted pickups became options.

* **L-7 C** – single rounded cutaway body, arched spruce top, f-holes, raised black laminated pickguard, bound body, carved maple back/sides, mahogany neck, 14/19-fret bound rosewood fingerboard with pearl parallelogram inlay, adjustable rosewood bridge/trapeze tailpiece, bound blackface peghead with pearl crown/logo inlay, three-per-side tuners with plastic buttons, available in Natural or Sunburst (most common) finish, mfg. 1948-1972.

1948-1959	N/A	$4,400 - 5,500	$2,650 - 3,300	
1960-1964	N/A	$3,400 - 4,250	$2,050 - 2,550	
1965-1969	N/A	$3,200 - 4,000	$1,925 - 2,400	
1970-1972	N/A	$3,000 - 3,750	$1,800 - 2,250	

This model had one or two pickguard mounted pickups as an option. In 1957, redesigned trapeze tailpiece replaced original part/design.

* **L-7 E/ED/NED** – similar to the L-7, except has either one pickup (L-7 E) or two pickups (L-7 ED), available in Sunburst (most common) or Natural (L-7 CNED) finish, limited mfg. 1948-1954.

	N/A	$4,400 - 5,500	$2,650 - 3,300	

»**L-7 CE/CED/CEN** – similar to the L-7C, except has either one (L-7CE) or two pickups (L-7 CED), available in Sunburst (most common) or Natural (L-7 CEN) finish, mfg. 1948-1954.

	N/A	$4,800 - 6,000	$2,875 - 3,600	

L-7C REISSUE (MODEL SJL7) – classic L-7 archtop single cutaway body style, arched solid Sitka spruce top, solid maple arched back, maple sides, two f-holes, multi-ply top and back binding and marquetry, maple neck, 14/19-fret rosewood single-ply bound fingerboard with MOP split parallelogram inlays, bound black headstock with MOP Gibson logo and crown inlay, three-per-side nickel Gotoh tuners with pearloid Keystone buttons, adj. rosewood bridge, trapeze tailpiece, raised black pickguard, available in Vintage Sunburst finish, 25.5 in. scale, mfg. 2007-2012.

	$5,750	$3,000 - 3,750	$1,800 - 2,250	$7,421

L-10 (1931-39 MFG.) – 16 or 17 in. body, arched spruce top, f-holes, raised tortoiseshell pickguard, carved maple back/sides, mapleneck, 14/19-fret bound ebony fingerboard with pearl dot inlay, adjustable ebony bridge/wrapover trapeze tailpiece, blackface peghead with pearl logo inlay, three-per-side nickel tuners, available in Black finish, mfg. 1931-39.

1931-1934	N/A	$3,600 - 4,500	$2,150 - 2,700	
1935-1939	N/A	$3,600 - 4,500	$2,150 - 2,700	

Original body size was 16 in. In 1934, Advanced Body (17 in. wide by 21 in. long), bound pickguard, checkered top binding, double triangle fingerboard inlay, redesigned trapeze tailpiece, bound peghead with pearl vase inlay, Red Mahogany finish replaced original part/design. In 1935, redesigned tailpiece, redesigned peghead inlay replaced previous part/design.

L-10 (CS-CAL10VSNH) – reissue of original L-10 mfg. in 1929, carved spruce top, carved figured maple back and sides, muli-ply checkerboard binding on top, single ply white binding on back, one-piece mahogany neck, 19-fret ebony with 6 fret extension fingerboard, split L-10 inlays, Waverly button tuners, nickel hardware, rosewood bridge, bale tailpiece, ES rounded profile, includes Custom Shop case, certificate of authenticity and custom care kit, Vintage Sunburst finish only, built in Nashville, mfg. 2004-08.

	N/A	$2,800 - 3,500	$1,675 - 2,100	$6,821

L-12 – acoustic hollowbody, arched spruce top, carved maple back/sides, two f-holes, bound body, mahogany neck, 14/19-fret bound ebony fingerboard with elaborate hollow rectangle inlays that have a different design in each one, bound black headstock overlay with a pearl vase/design and logo inlays, three-per-side gold tuners, adjustable ebony bridge, trapeze tailpiece, raised bound black pickguard, available in Red Mahogany Sunburst finish, 16 in. body width (1930-34) or 17 in. body width (1934-1955), mfg. 1930-1955.

1930-1934 16 in. Body	N/A	$4,400 - 5,500	$2,650 - 3,300	
1935-1939 17 in. Body	N/A	$4,200 - 5,250	$2,525 - 3,150	
1940-1949	N/A	$3,400 - 4,250	$2,050 - 2,550	
1950-1955	N/A	$2,800 - 3,500	$1,675 - 2,100	

In 1934, multi-bound pickguard/top/peghead, parallelogram fingerboard inlay, diamond/star peghead inlay replaced original part/design. In 1937, redesigned tailpiece replaced original part/design. In 1941, bound pickguard/peghead, crown peghead inlay replaced previous part/design.

* **L-12 P (Premiere)** – similar to L-12, except has single round cutaway, approx. 90 mfg. 1947-1950.

	N/A	$4,800 - 6,000	$2,875 - 3,600	

L-20 SPECIAL (MODEL AC2L) – small body acoustic, solid Sitka spruce top, solid Indian rosewood back and sides, round soundhole with two-stripe multi ring rosette, multi-ply body binding, 12/17-fret bound ebony fingerboard with MOP block inlays, bound black headstock overlay with pearl logo and torch inlays, three-per-side gold tuners with plastic buttons, ebony bridge with white pins, piezo bridge pickup, endpin pickup jack, available in Antique Natural or Vintage Sunburst finish, 24.75 in. scale, 14.75 in. body width, special hardshell case included, mfg. 1993-94.

	N/A	$1,400 - 1,750	$850 - 1,050	$1,999

MSR/NOTES	100%	EXCELLENT	AVERAGE	LAST MSR

L-30 – arched spruce top, f-holes, raised black pickguard, bound body, maple back/sides, mahogany neck, 14/19-fret ebony fingerboard with pearl dot inlay, adjustable ebony bridge/trapeze tailpiece, blackface peghead with screened logo, three-per-side tuners with plastic buttons, available in Black finish, mfg. 1935-1943.

	N/A	$1,275 - 1,600	$775 - 950	

In 1936, Dark Mahogany Sunburst finish replaced original part/design. In 1938, rosewood bridge replaced original part/design. 14 3/4 in. wide, 19 1/4 in. long.

L-37 – similar to L-30, except has Red Mahogany Sunburst finish, mfg. 1935-1941.

	N/A	$1,400 - 1,750	$850 - 1,050	

In 1936, Brown Sunburst finish replaced original part/design.

L-47 – arched spruce top, f-holes, raised bound pickguard, tortoise bound body, maple back/sides, mahogany neck, 14/19-fret ebony fingerboard with pearl dot inlay, adjustable ebony bridge/trapeze tailpiece, blackface peghead with screened logo, three-per-side tuners with plastic buttons, available in Natural or Sunburst finish, mfg. 1940-43.

	N/A	$1,450 - 1,800	$875 - 1,100	

L-48 – arched mahogany top, f-holes, raised black pickguard, bound body, mahogany back/sides/neck, 14/19-fret rosewood fingerboard with pearl dot inlay, adjustable rosewood bridge/trapeze tailpiece, blackface peghead with screened logo, three-per-side tuners, available in Cremona Brown Sunburst finish, mfg. 1946-1970.

	100%	EXCELLENT	AVERAGE	LAST MSR
1946-1949	N/A	$1,400 - 1,750	$850 - 1,050	
1950-1959	N/A	$1,275 - 1,600	$750 - 950	
1960-1964	N/A	$1,075 - 1,350	$650 - 800	
1965-1970	N/A	$875 - 1,100	$525 - 650	

A few early instruments have spruce tops, trapezoid fingerboard inlay. In 1952, spruce top, maple back, mahogany sides replaced original part/design. In 1957, mahogany top replaced previous part/design, some instruments found with mahogany back also.

L-50 – arched spruce top, f-hole/round soundhole, black pickguard, bound body, maple back/sides, mahogany neck, 14/19-fret ebony fingerboard with trapezoid or pearl dot inlay, adjustable ebony bridge/trapeze tailpiece, blackface peghead with screened logo, three-per-side tuners with plastic buttons, available in Dark Mahogany Sunburst finish, mfg. 1932-1970.

	100%	EXCELLENT	AVERAGE	LAST MSR
1932-1934 14.75 in. Body	N/A	$1,600 - 2,000	$950 - 1,200	
1934-1942 16 in. Body	N/A	$1,800 - 2,250	$1,075 - 1,350	
1943-1949	N/A	$1,600 - 2,000	$950 - 1,200	
1950-1959	N/A	$1,325 - 1,650	$800 - 1,000	
1960-1964	N/A	$1,125 - 1,400	$675 - 850	
1965-1970	N/A	$950 - 1,200	$575 - 725	

In 1934, redesigned body (16.25 in. body width, 20.25 in. long, arched back), raised pickguard, redesigned tailpiece replaced original part/design. In 1935, orchestra style body replaced previous part/design, arched back replaced original part/design. In 1936, redesigned tailpiece replaced previous part/design. In 1943, redesigned tailpiece replaced original part/design, three-per-side plate mounted tuners replaced original part/design. In 1946, bound pickguard/fingerboard with pearl trapezoid inlay replaced original part/design, redesigned tailpiece, three-per-side tuners with plastic buttons replaced previous part/design. In 1949, laminated pickguard replaced previous part/design.

L-75 – arched spruce top, f-holes, bound body, mahogany back/sides, mahogany neck, 14/19-fret pearloid fingerboard with pearl multi-design inlay in blocks of rosewood, adjustable rosewood bridge/trapeze tailpiece, pearloid veneered peghead, rosewood diamond peghead inlay with pearl logo, three-per-side tuners with plastic buttons, available in Natural or Sunburst finish, mfg. 1932-39.

	100%	EXCELLENT	AVERAGE	LAST MSR
1932-1934 14.75 in. Body	N/A	$1,800 - 2,250	$1,075 - 1,350	
1934-1939 16 in. Body	N/A	$2,000 - 2,500	$1,200 - 1,500	

In 1934, redesigned body/tailpiece, bound rosewood fingerboard with pearl dot inlay, blackface peghead with pearl vase logo inlay replaced original part/design. In 1935, carved back replaced original part/design, orchestra style body, redesigned peghead inlay replaced previous part/design, raised pickguard added. 16.25 in. by 20.25 in. body.

L-130 – features Gibson's Advanced 00 body design, spruce top, bubinga back/sides, rosewood fingerboard/bridge, mahogany neck, abalone fingerboard inlays and rosette, active transducer, available in Antique Natural finish, mfg. 1999-2005.

	N/A	$1,000 - 1,250	$600 - 750	$2,391

L-140 – similar to L-130, except has Indian rosewood back/sides, and ebony fingerboard/bridge, mfg. 1999-2005.

	N/A	$1,200 - 1,500	$725 - 900	$3,109

L-150 CUSTOM – custom shop model with customer selected wood, without active transducer pickup, available in Antique Natural finish, mfg. 1999-2002, reintroduced 2004.

	N/A	$2,400 - 3,000	$1,450 - 1,800	$5,748

MSR/NOTES	100%	EXCELLENT	AVERAGE	LAST MSR

L-200 EMMYLOU HARRIS (MODEL LSL2) – custom shop model with newly designed body that's smaller and thinner than the SJ-200, new bracing, includes Schertler Bluestick transducer pickup system, SJ-200 features include flame maple back/sides, mother-of-pearl crest fingerboard inlays, moustache bridge, and engraved pickguard, available in Antique Natural or Vintage Sunburst finish, mfg. 2002-present.

MSR $3,913	$3,000	$1,600 - 2,000	$950 - 1,200	

L-C/CENTURY (CENTURY OF PROGRESS) – L-style small body, spruce top, curly maple back and sides, round soundhole with two ring rosette, three-ply (1933-38) or single-ply (1938-1941) body binding, mahogany neck, 14/19-fret three-ply bound pearloid fingerboard, notched pearl diamonds inlaid in rosewood block fingerboard inlays, black-bound headstock with pearloid veneer with rosewood wedge and pearl slotted diamond/Gibson logo inlay (1933-38), or unbound headstock with rosewood veneer and stickpin inlay (1938-1941), three-per-side tuners with plastic buttons, rosewood straight bridge with white pins, tortoise pickguard, 14 3/4 in. body width, 19 1/4 in. body length, available in Sunburst finish, mfg. 1933-1941.

1933-1938 Pearloid Headstock	N/A	$5,000 - 6,000	$3,000 - 3,750	
1938-1941 Rosewood Headstock	N/A	$4,000 - 5,000	$2,500 - 3,250	

In 1938, two types of rosewood headstock veneer replaced the pearloid veneer. One featured a pearl diamond inlay and the other was bound with pearl slotted diamond/logo inlays. Rare examples have a black truss rod cover. Several variations of the L-C/Century exist including multiple fingerboard and headstock designs and inlays.

ELVIS COSTELLO "CENTURY OF PROGRESS" (MODEL LSEC) – L-00-style body, Adirondack spruce top, Hard Rock Eastern maple back and sides, single-ply top and back binding, Honduras mahogany neck, 14/20-fret bound pearloid fingerboard with Madagascar rosewood/MOP diamond rectangular inlays, bound headstock with pearloid overlay and rosewood inlay, three-per-side nickel reproduction tuners with ivory buttons, Madagascar bridge, white bridge pins, 1936-style celluloid-striped pickguard, label signed by Elvis Costello, available in Vintage Sunburst finish, 24.75 in. scale, limited edition run of 300 instruments, black hardshell case included, mfg. 2008-present.

MSR $5,858	$4,500	$2,400 - 3,000	$1,450 - 1,800	

Each guitar is numbered in sequence from 1 to 300 and comes with a hardbound certificate of authenticity with Costello's signature imprinted in silver. The case features black hardware, black velvet lining, and a plaque adorning Costello and Gibson.

L-JR. – carved spruce top, round bound soundhole, birch back/sides, maple neck, 13/19-fret ebony fingerboard with pearl dot inlay, ebony bridge/trapeze tailpiece, tortoiseshell plate with black pins on trapeze tailpiece, slotted peghead, three-per-side tuners with plastic buttons, available in Brown finish, body width 13.5 in., mfg. 1919-1926.

	N/A	$1,075 - 1,350	$650 - 800	

* **L-Jr. models with truss rod or factory black finish command a higher premium.**

The L-Jr. model is a "budget" version of the L-1 archtop.

KEB' MO' BLUESMASTER (MODEL LSKM) – L-style body, Adirondack red spruce top, mahogany back and sides, traditional L-00 X-braced top, round soundhole with traditional double ring rosette, cream top and back binding, herringbone purfling, one-piece mahogany neck with custom Keb' Mo' profile, 12/19-fret bound East Indian rosewood fingerboard with MOP dot inlays, 17 degree angle Advanced Jumbo-style headstock with taper, cream binding, and black overlay, MOP Gibson logo and crown inlay, three-per-side vintage open back nickel tuners, "Keb' Mo'" on truss rod cover, traditional lower belly East Indian rosewood bridge, L.R. Baggs Element electronics with soundhole-mounted volume control, available in Antique Natural or Vintage Sunburst finish, 25 in. scale, hardshell case included, mfg. 2010-present.

MSR $3,223	$2,500	$1,625 - 1,875	$825 - 1,000	

ACOUSTIC: LG SERIES

LG-0 – mahogany top, round soundhole, black pickguard, bound body, one-stripe rosette, mahogany back/sides/neck, 14/20-fret rosewood fingerboard with pearl dot inlay, rosewood straight bridge with pearl dot inlay, white bridge pins, blackface peghead with screened logo, three-per-side nickel tuners with plastic buttons, available in Natural finish, mfg. 1958-1974.

An example of a LG-0 courtesy John Beeson, The Music Shoppe

1958-1961 Rosewood Bridge	N/A	$800 - 1,000	$475 - 600	
1962-1964 Plastic Bridge	N/A	$725 - 900	$450 - 550	
1965-1969	N/A	$600 - 750	$350 - 450	
1970-1974	N/A	$475 - 600	$275 - 350	

MSR/NOTES	100%	EXCELLENT	AVERAGE	LAST MSR

In 1962, plastic screw-on bridge replaced original part/design. In 1963, redesigned tortoise pickguard replaced original part/design. In 1966, rosewood reverse bridge replaced previous part/design. In 1969, spruce top, standard bridge replaced previous part/design. In 1970, veneerless peghead replaced original part/design, black pickguard replaced previous part/design.

LG-1 – spruce top, round soundhole, tortoiseshell pickguard, bound body, one-stripe rosette, mahogany back/sides/neck, 14/19-fret rosewood fingerboard with pearl dot inlay, rosewood straight bridge with pearl dot inlay, black bridge pins, blackface peghead with screened logo, three-per-side nickel tuners with plastic buttons, available in Sunburst finish, approx. 27,000 mfg. 1947-1968.

1947-1949	N/A	$1,525 - 1,900	$925 - 1,150
1950-1961 Rosewood Bridge	N/A	$1,400 - 1,750	$850 - 1,050
1962-1964 Plastic Bridge	N/A	$1,200 - 1,500	$725 - 900
1965-1968	N/A	$950 - 1,200	$550 - 700

In 1955, redesigned pickguard, 14/20-fret fingerboard replaced original part/design. In 1962, plastic screw-on bridge replaced original part/design.

LG-2 – red spruce top, round soundhole, tortoiseshell pickguard, bound body, one-stripe rosette, mahogany back/sides/neck, 14/19-fret rosewood fingerboard with pearl dot inlay, rosewood straight bridge with pearl dot inlay, black bridge pins, blackface peghead with screened logo, three-per-side nickel tuners with plastic buttons, available in Cherry Sunburst or Golden Sunburst finish, mfg. 1942-1962.

1942-1946	N/A	$3,000 - 3,750	$1,800 - 2,250
1947-1949	N/A	$2,400 - 3,000	$1,450 - 1,800
1950-1954	N/A	$2,200 - 2,750	$1,325 - 1,650
1955-1958	N/A	$2,000 - 2,500	$1,200 - 1,500
1959-1962	N/A	$1,800 - 2,250	$1,075 - 1,350

- **Add 20% for banner headstock and striped pickguard (produced 1942) variations.**
- **Add 15% for mahogany back with maple or rosewood sides.**
- **Add 25% for maple sides and back.**
- **Add 40%-60% for Brazilian rosewood back and sides.**
- **Subtract 15% for mahogany top.**

During WWII, Gibson used whatever materials were available to construct instruments. Consequently, there are LG-2's found with mahogany tops, maple back/sides/neck, no truss rods and other little differences from other production models found before and after the war. In 1955, redesigned pickguard, 14/20-fret fingerboard replaced original part/design. In 1961, Cherry Sunburst finish replaced original part/design.

* LG-2 3/4 – similar to LG-2, except has 3/4 size body, mfg. 1949-1968.

1949-1954	N/A	$1,800 - 2,250	$1,075 - 1,350
1955-1961	N/A	$1,600 - 2,000	$950 - 1,200
1962-1964	N/A	$1,400 - 1,750	$850 - 1,050
1965-1968	N/A	$1,200 - 1,500	$725 - 950

ARLO GUTHRIE LG-2 3/4 (MODEL LSAG) – patterned after the LG-2 that Woody Guthrie gave to Arlo Guthrie in 1953, similar to LG-2 3/4, except has Sitka spruce top, 14/20-fret, mahognay neck/back/sides, available in Vintage Sunburst, limited mfg. 2003, reintroduced 2005-present.

MSR $2,681	$2,080	$1,075 - 1,350	$650 - 800

LG-2 AMERICAN EAGLE (MODEL LSAE) – LG-style small body, Sitka spruce top, mahogany back and sides, round soundhole with single ring rosette, multi-ply top binding, single-ply back binding, mahogany V-profile neck, 14/19-fret rosewood fingerboard with MOP dot inlays, black headstock overlay with modern gold Gibson decal, three-per-side nickel tuners with white buttons, rosewood bridge, no pickguard, L.R. Baggs Element pickup/electronics, available in Antique Natural finish, 24.75 in. scale, 1.725 in. nut width, black hardshell case included, mfg. 2013-present.

MSR $2,449	$1,900	$1,225 - 1,425	$625 - 750

LG-3 – spruce top, round soundhole, tortoiseshell pickguard, three-stripe bound body/rosette, mahogany back/sides/neck, 14/19-fret rosewood fingerboard with pearl dot inlay, rosewood straight bridge with pearl dot inlay, white bridge pins, blackface peghead with banner/logo decal, three-per-side nickel tuners with plastic buttons, available in Natural finish, mfg. 1942-1963.

1942-1945	N/A	$3,200 - 4,000	$1,925 - 2,400
1946-1949	N/A	$2,800 - 3,500	$1,675 - 2,100
1950-1954	N/A	$2,400 - 3,000	$1,450 - 1,800
1955-1961 Rosewood Bridge	N/A	$2,200 - 2,750	$1,325 - 1,650
1962-1963 Plastic Bridge	N/A	$2,000 - 2,500	$1,200 - 1,500

In 1955, teardrop pickguard was replaced by the longer Gibson style pickguard with a single point, 14/20-fret fingerboard replaced original part/design. In 1961, adjustable bridge replaced original part/design. In early 1962, reverse rosewood bridge with adjustable saddle replaced previous part/design. In late 1962, plastic screw-on bridge replaced previous part/design. The LG-3 has a "X-braced" top. In 1963, the LG-3 was renamed the B-25N.

MSR/NOTES	100%	EXCELLENT	AVERAGE	LAST MSR

LG-12 – mahogany back/sides, 12-string, large belly bridge with bridge pins, adj. saddle, 14 .125 in. wide, long pickguard with point at upper bout (some models had teardrop pickguard), single black soundhole ring, single-bound top, unbound back, three-piece neck, 18-fret rosewood fingerboard, 24.75 in. scale, dot inlays, no peghead veneer, available in Natural top finish, light mahogany finish on back and sides, approx. 1,150 mfg. 1967-1973.

1967-1969	N/A	$950 - 1,200	$575 - 725	
1970-1973	N/A	$800 - 1,000	$475 - 600	

This model does not appear in the Gibson shipping total records until 1970. Non-adj. saddle and teardrop pickguard were introduced in 1970.

ACOUSTIC: MARK SERIES

All of the following instruments have these features: sloped shouldered body, spruce top, round soundhole, removable pickguard, bound body, mahogany neck, 14/20-fret fingerboard, fan bridge, three different replaceable saddles, blackface snakehead peghead, three-per-side tuners. Available in Natural and Sunburst finishes (unless otherwise noted).

MK-35 – spruce top, two-stripe rosewood soundhole cap, mahogany back/sides, rosewood fingerboard with pearl dot inlay, nickel tuners, Natural or Sunburst finish, approx. 5,225 mfg. 1975-78.

	N/A	$675 - 800	$425 - 500	

* **MK-35-12** – similar to MK-35, except has 12 strings, six-per-side tuners, mfg. 1977 only.

	N/A	$725 - 850	$450 - 525	

Only twelve of these instruments were produced.

MK-45-12 – spruce top, 12-string, very limited mfg. 1975-78.

	N/A	N/A	N/A	

Extreme rarity precludes accurate pricing on this model.

MK-53 – spruce top, multi-bound body, two-stripe rosewood soundhole cap, maple back/sides, rosewood fingerboard with pearl dot inlay, nickel tuners. Approx. 1,425 mfg. 1975-78.

	N/A	$750 - 900	$475 - 550	

MK-72 – spruce top, three-stripe rosette, rosewood back/sides, three-piece ebony/rosewood/ebony fingerboard with pearl dot inlay, nickel tuners. Approx. 1,225 mfg. 1975-78.

	N/A	$850 - 1,000	$600 - 700	

MK-81 – spruce top, three-stripe rosewood rosette cap, multi-bound body, rosewood back/sides, ebony fingerboard with block abalone inlays, gold tuners. Approx. 430 mfg. 1975-79.

	N/A	$950 - 1,100	$650 - 775	

MK-99 – spruce top, round soundhole with two-stripe rosewood soundhole cap, red stripe bound body, purple stained rosewood back/sides, purple stained maple neck, 14/20-fret red stripe bound ebony fingerboard with abalone bowtie inlay, ebony fan bridge with silver red dot pins, blackface red bound peghead, three-per-side gold tuners, available in Natural finish, mfg. 1977 only.

	N/A	N/A	N/A	

Extreme rarity precludes accurate pricing on this model. This model was handcrafted and signed by Richard Schneider while he was Gibson's Master Luthier. Less than twelve instruments are known to have been made.

ACOUSTIC: MODEL O & STYLE U HARP SERIES

MODEL O – arched spruce top, oval soundhole, bound body, wood inlay rosette, walnut back/sides, mahogany neck, 12/20-fret bound pointed rosewood fingerboard with pearl dot inlay, rosewood bridge/trapeze tailpiece with black pearl dot pins, bound blackface peghead with pearl logo inlay, friction tuners, available in Black Top finish, mfg. 1902-07.

	N/A	$6,000 - 7,500	$3,600 - 4,500	

The Model O had features from both archtop and flattop construction. Some models have an 18 in. body width. This model was also available in a Presentation version, which is extremely rare (the last recorded sale of a Presentation model was for $15,000). In 1906, a slotted peghead was introduced.

STYLE O ARTIST – single sharp cutaway body, carved spruce top, scrolled upper bass bout, oval soundhole, raised tortoiseshell pickguard, bound body, wood inlay rosette, maple back/sides, mahogany neck, 15/22-fret bound extended ebony fingerboard with pearl dot inlay, ebony bridge/trapeze tailpiece with black pearl dot pins, bound blackface peghead with pearl fleur-de-lis/logo inlay, three-per-side diecast tuners, available in Amber, Black, Mahogany Stain, or Mahogany Sunburst finish, mfg. 1908-1923.

	N/A	$8,000 - 10,000	$4,800 - 6,000	

In 1914, Amber and Mahogany finishes replaced original finishes. In 1918, redesigned pickguard/peghead inlay replaced original part/design. Mahogany Sunburst finish replaced previous finish.

STYLE U HARP GUITAR – six-string/9 or 10 bass string configuration, round soundhole, scroll on upper bass bout, maple back and sides, bound soundhole, mahogany bridge, ebony fingerboard with dot inlay, veneer peghead, available in Black Top/Dark Mahogany back/sides finish, body width 21 in., mfg. 1902-1939.

	N/A	$8,000 - 10,000	$4,800 - 6,000	

Although this model stayed listed in Gibson catalogs until 1939, it's unlikely that models were manufactured after 1924.

MSR/NOTES	100%	EXCELLENT	AVERAGE	LAST MSR

ACOUSTIC: NOUVEAU BY GIBSON SERIES

The Nouveau by Gibson Series feature bodies and necks that were produced in Japan and then shipped to the U.S. where they were assembled and completed. The Nouveau guitars were introduced into the Gibson line in 1986, but by late 1987, they were moved to the Epiphone line and changed to Nouveau by Epiphone. A line of electric guitars was offered as well.

NV 6 – dreadnought-style body, spruce top, mahogany back and sides, round soundhole with three-ring rosette, multi-ply body binding, mahogany neck, 14/20-fret ebony fingerboard with custom shape inlays, black headstock overlay with pearl "Nouveau" logo across the top and seven-stripe pearl diamond inlay with a vertical "Gibson" logos three-per-side chrome tuners, ebony bridge, tortoise pickguard, available in Natural finish, mfg. 1986-87.

	N/A	$425 - 500	$250 - 300	

* **NV 6R** – similar to the NV 6, except has rosewood back and sides, available in Natural finish, mfg. 1986-87.

	N/A	$475 - 550	$275 - 325	

»**NV 6R-S** – similar to the NV 6R, except has a solid spruce top, available in Natural finish, mfg. 1987 only.

	N/A	$525 - 600	$300 - 375	

* **NV 6T** – similar to the NV 6, except has tortoiseshell celluloid binding, available in Natural finish, mfg. 1987 only.

	N/A	$475 - 550	$275 - 325	

* **NV 12** – similar to the NV 6, except in 12-string configuration with six-per-side tuners, available in Natural finish, mfg. 1986-87.

	N/A	$525 - 600	$300 - 375	

ACOUSTIC: SONGBIRD SERIES

SONGBIRD – square shoulder body similar to the Hummingbird & Dove Series, solid spruce top, mahogany back/sides/neck, morado fingerboard/bridge, contoured two-point pickguard, gloss finished top with satin back, available in Antique Walnut finish, mfg. 1999-2002.

	N/A	$800 - 1,000	$475 - 600	$1,846

SONGBIRD DELUXE – similar to Songbird, except has Indian rosewood back/sides/fingerboard/bridge, abalone fingerboard inlays and rosette, includes active transducer pickup, available in Antique Natural finish, mfg. 1999-2002.

	N/A	$1,000 - 1,250	$600 - 750	$2,399

* **Songbird Deluxe Cutaway EC** – similar to the Songbird Deluxe, except has a single cutaway, mfg. 2001-02.

	N/A	$1,075 - 1,350	$650 - 800	$2,507

SONGBIRD DELUXE KOA – similar to Songbird, except has koa back/sides, limited mfg. 2003 only.

	N/A	$1,200 - 1,500	$725 - 900	$3,027

ACOUSTIC: SONGMAKER SERIES

Gibson's Songmaker Series are produced in St. John's, Newfoundland, Canada at the Garrison Guitar Factory. These guitars offer traditional shapes and styles with all solid woods and tasteful appointments. Gibson bought Garrison Guitars in mid-2007.

CQM – Grand Concert-style body, solid spruce top, solid quilted maple back and sides, round soundhole with three-ring rosette, tortoise body binding, mahogany neck, 14/20-fret rosewood-bound ebony fingerboard with abalone dot inlays, black headstock overlay, three-per-side chrome Gibson tuners, ebony belly bridge, white bridge pins, tortoiseshell pickguard, Natural finish with High Gloss overcoat, 25.5 in. scale, hardshell case included, mfg. 2008-09.

	N/A	$1,000 - 1,150	$600 - 700	$2,159

* **CQM-CE Cutaway Electric** – similar to the CQM, except has a single smooth cutaway and Fishman Prefix Pro Blend electronics, mfg. 2008-09.

	N/A	$1,250 - 1,550	$750 - 900	$2,839

CSM – Grand Concert-style body, solid spruce top, solid mahogany back and sides, round soundhole with three-ring rosette, white body binding, mahogany neck, 14/20-fret rosewood-bound ebony fingerboard with abalone dot inlays, black headstock overlay, three-per-side chrome Gibson tuners, ebony belly bridge, white bridge pins, tortoiseshell pickguard, Natural finish with High Gloss overcoat, 25.5 in. scale, hardshell case included, mfg. 2008-09.

	N/A	$500 - 575	$300 - 375	$1,119

* **CSM-CE Cutaway Electric** – similar to the CSM, except has a single smooth cutaway and Fishman Prefix Pro Blend electronics, mfg. 2008-09.

	N/A	$700 - 825	$450 - 525	$1,599

CSR – Grand Concert-style body, solid spruce top, solid rosewood back and sides, round soundhole with three-ring rosette, white body binding, mahogany neck, 14/20-fret rosewood-bound ebony fingerboard with abalone dot inlays, black headstock overlay, three-per-side chrome Gibson tuners, ebony belly bridge, white bridge pins, tortoiseshell pickguard, Natural finish with High Gloss overcoat, 25.5 in. scale, hardshell case included, mfg. 2008-09.

	N/A	$600 - 700	$375 - 450	$1,359

MSR/NOTES	100%	EXCELLENT	AVERAGE	LAST MSR

* CSR-CE Cutaway Electric – similar to the CSM, except has a single smooth cutaway and Fishman Prefix Pro Blend electronics, mfg. 2008-09.

	N/A	$850 - 1,000	$550 - 650	$1,839

DQM – Dreadnought-style body, solid spruce top, solid quilted maple back and sides, round soundhole with three-ring rosette, tortoise body binding, mahogany neck, 14/20-fret rosewood-bound ebony fingerboard with abalone dot inlays, black headstock overlay, three-per-side chrome Gibson tuners, ebony belly bridge, white bridge pins, tortoiseshell pickguard, Natural finish with High Gloss overcoat, 25.5 in. scale, hardshell case included, mfg. 2008-09.

	N/A	$1,000 - 1,150	$600 - 700	$2,159

* DQM-CE Cutaway Electric – similar to the DQM, except has a single smooth cutaway and Fishman Prefix Pro Blend electronics, mfg. 2008-09.

	N/A	$1,250 - 1,550	$750 - 900	$2,839

DSM – Dreadnought-style body, solid spruce top, solid mahogany back and sides, round soundhole with three-ring rosette, white body binding, mahogany neck, 14/20-fret rosewood-bound ebony fingerboard with abalone dot inlays, black headstock overlay, three-per-side chrome Gibson tuners, ebony belly bridge, white bridge pins, tortoiseshell pickguard, Natural finish with High Gloss overcoat, 25.5 in. scale, hardshell case included, mfg. 2008-09.

	N/A	$500 - 575	$300 - 375	$1,119

* DSM-CE Cutaway Electric – similar to the DSM, except has a single smooth cutaway and Fishman Prefix Pro Blend electronics, mfg. 2008-09.

	N/A	$700 - 825	$450 - 525	$1,599

DSR – Dreadnought-style body, solid spruce top, solid rosewood back and sides, round soundhole with three-ring rosette, white body binding, mahogany neck, 14/20-fret rosewood-bound ebony fingerboard with abalone dot inlays, black headstock overlay, three-per-side chrome Gibson tuners, ebony belly bridge, white bridge pins, tortoiseshell pickguard, Natural finish with High Gloss overcoat, 25.5 in. scale, hardshell case included, mfg. 2008-09.

	N/A	$600 - 700	$375 - 450	$1,359

* DSR-CE Cutaway Electric – similar to the DSM, except has a single smooth cutaway and Fishman Prefix Pro Blend electronics, mfg. 2008-09.

	N/A	$850 - 1,000	$550 - 650	$1,839

ACOUSTIC: SONGWRITER SERIES

SONGWRITER – square shoulder body similar to the Hummingbird & Dove Series, solid Sitka spruce top, solid mahogany back/sides/neck, morado fingerboard with pearloid trapezoid inlays, gold Grover Kidney tuners and tortoiseshell three-point mini-hummingbird shape pickguard, available in Natural Gloss Top/Satin Back finish, mfg. 2003-05.

	N/A	$800 - 1,000	$500 - 600	$1,846

SONGWRITER DELUXE CUSTOM (MODEL SSPD) – dreadnought-style body, AA-grade Sitka spruce, rosewood back and sides, hand-scalloped radiused top bracing, round soundhole with three-ring rosette (5/7/5 grouping with a large center ring of abalone), multi-ply wood binding, abalone purfling, 14/20-fret wood-bound ebony fingerboard with custom design MOP inlays and rolled edges, black headstock overlay with wood binding, 1920s-style pearl logo, and pearl design inlay, three-per-side gold Grover Rotomatic tuners, ebony bridge with lower belly, white bridge pins, tortoise pickguard, L.R. Baggs Element Active Acoustic Pickup System electronics, available in Antique Natural or Vintage Sunburst finish, mfg. 2009-2011.

$3,350	$1,850 - 2,200	$1,100 - 1,300		$4,298

* Songwriter Deluxe Custom EC Cutaway (Model SSPC) – similar to the Songwriter Deluxe Custom, except has a single smooth cutaway, available in Antique Natural or Vintage Sunburst finish, mfg. 2009-2011.

$3,350	$1,850 - 2,200	$1,100 - 1,300		$4,298

SONGWRITER DELUXE STANDARD (MODEL SSDD) – dreadnought-style body, AA-grade Sitka spruce, rosewood back and sides, hand-scalloped radiused top bracing, round soundhole with three-ring rosette (5/7/5 grouping with a large center ring of abalone), multi-ply wood binding, 14/20-fret ebony fingerboard with three-piece arrow/diamond MOP inlays and rolled edges, black headstock overlay with wood binding, pearl logo, and pearl crown inlay, three-per-side gold Grover Rotomatic tuners, ebony bridge with lower belly, ebony bridge pins with pearl dots, tortoise pickguard, Fishman Aura Pro Acoustic Pickup System electronics, available in Antique Natural or Vintage Sunburst finish, mfg. 2009-2012.

$3,250	$1,725 - 2,150	$1,050 - 1,300		$4,205

* Songwriter Deluxe Standard EC Cutaway (Model SSDC) – similar to the Songwriter Deluxe Standard, except has a single smooth cutaway, available in Antique Natural or Vintage Sunburst finish, mfg. 2009-2012.

$3,250	$1,725 - 2,150	$1,050 - 1,300		$4,205

MSR/NOTES	100%	EXCELLENT	AVERAGE	LAST MSR

SONGWRITER DELUXE "STUDIO" (MODEL SSSD) – similar to Songwriter, except has solid rosewood back/sides, abalone double paralellogram fingerboard inlays and rosette, ebony fingerboard and bridge, includes Fishman active transducer pickup, available in Antique Natural finish, mfg. 2003-present.

MSR $3,223	$2,500	$1,275 - 1,600	$750 - 950	

In 2009, this model became the Songwriter Deluxe Studio.

* *Songwriter Deluxe Cutaway "Studio" (Model SSCD)* – similar to the Songwriter Deluxe, except has a single cutaway, mfg. 2003-present.

MSR $3,352	$2,600	$1,350 - 1,700	$825 - 1,025	

In 2009, this model became the Songwriter Deluxe Studio.

* *Special Songwriter Deluxe Brazilian* – features Brazilian rosewood back/sides. Antique Natural finish only, mfg. by Custom Shop, limited mfg. 2003 only.

	N/A	$1,800 - 2,250	$1,075 - 1,350	$3,892

* *Custom Songwriter Deluxe 12-String Brazilian* – similar to Special Songwriter Deluxe Brazilian, except is 12-string, limited mfg. 2003 only.

	N/A	$2,000 - 2,500	$1,200 - 1,500	$4,324

SONGWRITER DELUXE 12-STRING (MODEL SD12) – square shoulder small dreadnought body, premium Sitka spruce top, Indian rosewood back and sides, 25 1/2 in. scale, six-ply top, single-ply back binding, mahogany neck, ebony fingerboard with mother-of-pearl paralellogram inlays, abalone rosette, tradtional Gibson ebony bridge, gold Grover kidney tuners, tortoise Custom Line pickguard, transducer pickup with active preamp, Antique Natural finish, mfg. 2006-08.

	N/A	$1,400 - 1,750	$850 - 1,050	$3,132

TRAVELING SONGWRITER (MODEL SSTS) – cutaway thin body design with rear soundhole, solid Sitka spruce top, solid mahogany back/sides and neck, Indian rosewood fingerboard with dot inlays, sculpted rosewood bridge, gold tuners, active transducer with onboard electronics, special design Gibson sculpted pickguard, scalloped 1930s style bracing, Antique Natural finish, includes special lightweight travel case, mfg. 2005-2011.

	$3,000	$1,750 - 2,000	$1,075 - 1,225	$3,893

ACOUSTIC: SOUTHERN JUMBO (SJ) MODELS & VARIATIONS

SJ (SOUTHERNER JUMBO/COUNTRY WESTERN) – spruce top, round soundhole, black pickguard, two-stripe bound body/rosette, mahogany back/sides/neck, 14/20-fret bound rosewood fingerboard with pearl parallelogram inlays, rosewood bridge with white pins, blackface peghead with pearl banner logo inlay, three-per-side nickel tuners, available in Sunburst finish, mfg. 1942-1978.

An example of a SJ courtesy Willie's American Guitars

1942-1945	N/A	$9,500 - 12,000	$5,800 - 7,250	
1946-1949	N/A	$6,000 - 7,500	$3,600 - 4,500	
1950-1954	N/A	$5,200 - 6,500	$3,150 - 3,900	
1955-1959	N/A	$4,800 - 6,000	$2,875 - 3,600	
1960-1962 Round Shoulder	N/A	$4,200 - 5,250	$2,525 - 3,150	
1962-1964 Square Shoulder	N/A	$3,600 - 4,500	$2,150 - 2,700	
1965-1966	N/A	$2,800 - 3,500	$1,675 - 2,100	
1967-1969	N/A	$2,400 - 3,000	$1,450 - 1,800	
1970-1972	N/A	$1,600 - 2,000	$950 - 1,200	
1973-1978	N/A	$1,475 - 1,850	$900 - 1,100	

• **Add 15% for mahogany back and rosewood or maple sides, and 25% for maple back/sides. Add a 15%-25% for early striped pickguard, depending on condition. Add a significant premium for rosewood back and sides (rare).**

During WWII, Gibson used whatever materials were handy. Banner peghead inlay mfg. 1942-45, disc. 1946. A few early models

MSR/NOTES	100%	EXCELLENT	AVERAGE	LAST MSR

are found with rosewood back/sides. In 1946, the banner inlay on the peghead was discontinued. In 1949, upper belly bridge replaced original part/design. In 1954, Natural finish became an option. In 1955, redesigned pickguard replaced original part/design. In 1956, the SJ in Natural finish was renamed the Country-Western Jumbo. In 1960, this new designation was again renamed the SJN (See SJN listing below). In mid to late 1962, adjustable saddle replaced original part/design; redesigned body/pickguard replaced previous part/design. In 1969, standard style bridge replaced previous part/design. In 1970, non-adjustable saddle replaced previous part/design. In 1974, four-stripe body/two-stripe neck binding replaced original part/design.

* **SJN (SJN Country Western, Country-Western Jumbo)** — similar to SJ (Southern Jumbo), except has tortoiseshell pickguard, available in Natural finish, mfg. 1954-1978.

1954-1959	N/A	$4,800 - 6,000	$2,875 - 3,600	
1960-1962 Round Shoulder	N/A	$4,200 - 5,250	$2,525 - 3,150	
1962-1964 Square Shoulder	N/A	$3,600 - 4,500	$2,150 - 2,700	
1965-1966	N/A	$2,800 - 3,500	$1,675 - 2,100	
1967-1969	N/A	$2,400 - 3,000	$1,450 - 1,800	
1970-1972	N/A	$1,600 - 2,000	$950 - 1,200	
1973-1978	N/A	$1,475 - 1,850	$900 - 1,100	

In 1956, the SJ in Natural finish was renamed the Country-Western Jumbo. In 1960, this new designation was again renamed the SJN. In 1962, the SJN was again called the Country-Western.

SJ-45 DELUXE — spruce top, round soundhole, tortoise pickguard, abalone bound body, three-stripe rosette, rosewood back/sides, mahogany neck, 14/20-fret bound rosewood fingerboard with pearl flower inlay, rosewood bridge with white pins, bound blackface peghead with pearl banner/logo inlay, three-per-side gold tuners, available in Antique Natural or Special Vintage Sunburst finishes, mfg. 1994-98.

	N/A	$1,725 - 2,150	$1,050 - 1,300	$4,010

SJ ROSEWOOD — rounded-shouldered dreadnought based on a circa 1942/1943 SJ, rosewood back and sides, unbound rosewood fingerboard with double parallelogram inlays, 1940s-style Gibson logo with "Only a Gibson is Good Enough" banner, rosewood bridge with pearl dots on either side, limited mfg. 1991-94.

	N/A	$1,600 - 2,000	$950 - 1,200	

According to reports, Gibson produced 15 of these guitars with Indian rosewood and 5 with Brazilian rosewood in 1991. 66 were produced in 1992 (all in Indian rosewood), none in 1993, and one Indian rosewood version in 1994.

SOUTHERN JUMBO (SJ, HISTORIC) — J-45 style body, solid spruce top, mahogany back/sides/neck, bound rosewood fingerboard and bridge, vintage styling, available in Vintage Sunburst (disc., reintroduced 2004) or Triburst '47 (mfg. 2002-03) finish, mfg. 1999-2008.

	N/A	$1,600 - 2,000	$950 - 1,200	$3,090

SOUTHERN JUMBO TRUE VINTAGE — detailed edition of Gibson's late 1940s SJ, rounded-shouldered style, solid Sitka spruce top, solid mahogany back and sides, round soundhole with rosette, six-ply top binding, four-ply back binding, mahogany V-shaped neck, 14/20-fret Madagascar rosewood single-ply bound fingerboard with MOP split parallelogram inlays, black headstock with MOP logo, three-per-side nickel Gotoh tuners with white buttons, Madagascar rosewood bridge with MOP dots and white pins, tortoiseshell SJ pickguard, available in Vintage Sunburst finish, 24.75 in. scale, mfg. 2007-08.

	N/A	$2,000 - 2,500	$1,200 - 1,500	$3,883

AARON LEWIS SOUTHERN JUMBO (MODEL RSAL) — Aaron Lewis SJ signature based on his 1951 SJ, rounded-shouldered dreadnought-style body, solid Sitka spruce top, solid mahogany back and sides, Gibson 1930s advanced X bracing, round soundhole with traditional double ring rosette, multi-ply top and back binding, one-piece mahogany modified "V" neck with a compound dovetail joint, 14/20-fret rosewood fingerboard with pearloid parallelogram inlays, AJ-style headstock with 17 degree angle, black overlay, and gold Gibson logo decal, Aaron Lewis silhouette on truss rod cover, three-per-side vintage-style Kluson nickel tuners with white buttons, traditional belly down rosewood bridge with MOP dots and white pins, teardrop tortoise pickguard, available in Vintage Sunburst finish, 1.725 in. nut width, 24.75 in. scale, hardshell case and certificate or authenticity included, limited edition run of 363 instruments, mfg. 2010-12.

	$2,950	$1,600 - 2,000	$950 - 1,200	$3,799

* **Aaron Lewis Southern Jumbo Aged (Model RSAL)** — similar to the Aaron Lewis Southern Jumbo, except are hand aged and distressed in the Gibson Montana Art Shop, available in Vintage Sunburst finish, hardshell case and certificate or authenticity included, limited edition run of 37 instruments, mfg. 2010-12.

	$6,600	$4,000 - 5,000	N/A	$8,598

Gibson also produced an additional 13 Aaron Lews Southern Jumbos that were aged and signed and personally played by Aaron Lewis. MSR on these are $17,198.

THE KRISTOFFERSON SJ (MODEL RSKK) — slope-shouldered dreadnought, AAA-grade Sitka spruce top, pattern-grade quarter-sawn mahogany, hand-scalloped radiused bracing, round soundhole with two-ring rosette (3/7 grouping), multi-ply body binding, 14/20-fret bound rosewood fingerboard with split parallelogram and 12th fret "UFW" logo MOP inlays, black headstock overlay with pearl logo and crown inlay, three-per-side chrome tuners, rosewood bridge with upper belly and two pearl dot inlays, white bridge pins, 50s-style tortoise pickguard, Fishman Matrix Natural 1 Pickup System, available in Vintage Sunburst finish, mfg. 2009-2012.

	$3,300	$1,750 - 2,200	$1,050 - 1,325	$4,246

MSR/NOTES	100%	EXCELLENT	AVERAGE	LAST MSR

TRADITIONAL SOUTHERN JUMBO (MODEL RSSJ) – slope-shouldered dreadnought-style body, solid Sitka spruce top, mahogany back and sides, round soundhole with double ring rosette, multi-ply top and back binding, set mahogany modified V profile neck, 14/20-fret bound rosewood fingerboard with MOP split parallelogram inlays, black headstock overlay with MOP Gibson logo and crown inlays, three-per-side nickel Grover Rotomatic tuners, rosewood bridge with MOP dot inlays, tortoise pickguard, L.R. Baggs Element pickup and electronics, 24.75 in. scale, 1.725 in. nut width, available in Vintage Sunburst finish, hardshell case included, mfg. 2013-present.

MSR N/A	$3,050	$1,975 - 2,275	$1,000 - 1,225	

WOODY GUTHRIE BANNER SOUTHERN JUMBO (MODEL RSWG) – similar body size as J-45, mahogany back/sides/ neck, Sitka spruce top, rosewood fingerboard with pearloid parallelogram inlays, rosewood bridge, Gotch tuners with Fishman matrix pickup, gold script, includes Woody's famous sign, "This Machine Kills Facists", Vintage Sunburst finish, mfg. 2004-2012.

	$2,430	$1,275 - 1,600	$750 - 950	$3,128

In 2009, this model was upgraded and improved.

SHERYL CROW SOUTHERN JUMBO SPECIAL EDITION (MODEL RSSC) – slope-shouldered dreadnought-style body, Adirondack red spruce top, mahogany back and sides, round soundhole with traditional double-ring rosette, multi-ply top and back binding, set mahogany modified "V"-profile neck, 14/20-fret bound rosewood fingerboard with MOP split parallelogram inlays, black headstock overlay with gold script Gibson logo "Only a Gibson is Good Enough" banner decal, three-per-side Waverly open-style nickel tuners with white buttons, rosewood bridge, tortoise pickguard, Trance Audio Amulet System electronics (Model A only), 24.75 in. scale, 1.725 in. nut width, available in Vintage Sunburst finish, hardshell case included, limited availability 2012/2013.

	$3,350	$2,175 - 2,500	$1,100 - 1,350	$4,300

ACOUSTIC: STAR, STARBURST, EAS, & EC SERIES

Models are listed in chronological order according to their release dates. The EC-20 and EC-30 models were incorporated into the Electric J Series in 1999.

THE STAR – single sharp cutaway jumbo body, rosewood fingerboard with dot inlays, star inlay on headstock, three-ply pickguard, available in Antique Ebony or Sunburst (1992 only) finish, 16 in. body width, mfg. 1991-94.

	N/A	$1,200 - 1,500	$725 - 900	

STARBURST/STARBURST STANDARD/SUNBURST FLAME (MODEL ASSF) – single pointed cutaway jumbo body, solid maple top, solid figured maple back and sides, multi-ply top and back body binding, round soundhole with multi-ring rosette, 14/20-fret rosewood fingerboard with multi star MOP inlays, pearl headstock logo and multiple star inlays, three-per-side gold tuners, bowed rosewood bridge with three star inlays on the bass side, no pickguard, piezo pickup and preamp, available in Antique Natural, Amber, Black Cherry, Blue, Cherry, Gray, Green, Peach, Purple, or Red finish, 24.75 in. scale, special hardshell case included, mfg. 1992-94.

	N/A	$1,200 - 1,500	$725 - 900	$1,899

This model was introduced as the Starburst and shortly changed to the Starburst Standard and Starburst Flame depending on the finish.

STARBURST ELITE (MODEL ASSE) – single pointed cutaway jumbo body, solid quilted maple top, solid figured maple back and sides, multi-ply top and back body binding, round soundhole with multi-ring rosette, 14/20-fret bound ebony fingerboard with multi star MOP inlays, bound headstock with pearl logo and multiple star inlays, three-per-side gold tuners, bowed ebony bridge with three star inlays on the bass side, tortoise pickguard, piezo pickup and preamp, available in Antique Natural, Amber, or Vintage Sunburst finish, 24.75 in. scale, ultra hardshell case included, mfg. 1992-94.

	N/A	$1,400 - 1,750	$850 - 1,050	$2,299

STARBURST STUDIO (MODEL ASSS) – single pointed cutaway jumbo body, solid Sitka spruce top, solid figured maple back and sides, multi-ply top and back body binding, round soundhole with multi-ring rosette, 14/20-fret rosewood fingerboard with single star inlays, pearl headstock logo and multiple star inlays, three-per-side nickel tuners, bowed rosewood bridge with three star inlays on the bass side, no pickguard, piezo pickup and preamp, available in Antique Natural, Cherry, Ebony, or Vintage Sunburst finish, 24.75 in. scale, standard hardshell case included, mfg. 1992-94.

	N/A	$950 - 1,200	$575 - 725	$1,599

EAS CLASSIC/STANDARD (MODEL ASES) – single rounded cutaway jumbo body, solid Sitka spruce top, arched laminated maple back, maple sides, round soundhole with two multi-stripe rings rosette, single-ply body binding, maple neck, 20-fret unbound rosewood fingerboard with pearl dot inlays, blackface headstock with screened logo, three-per-side nickel or gold tuners, rosewood bridge with upper belly and white pins, tortoise pickguard, piezo pickup with three-band EQ, available in Antique Ebony, Antique Natural, Cherry, Ivory, Vintage Cherry, or Vintage Sunburst finish, 24.75 in. scale, standard hardshell case included, mfg. 1992-95.

	N/A	$700 - 875	$425 - 525	$1,299

In 1993, a double cutaway model was offered and the guitar was renamed the EAS Standard.

EAS DELUXE (MODEL ASED) – single rounded cutaway jumbo body, solid flamed maple top, arched laminated maple back, maple sides, round soundhole with two multi-stripe rings rosette, single-ply body binding, maple neck, 14/20-fret bound rosewood fingerboard with pearl trapezoid inlays, blackface headstock with pearl logo and crown inlays and "Deluxe" engraved on the truss rod cover, three-per-side nickel tuners with plastic buttons, rosewood bridge with upper belly and white pins, ivory pickguard, piezo pickup with three-band EQ, available in Vintage Cherry Sunburst finish, 24.75 in. scale, standard hardshell case included, mfg. 1992-94.

	N/A	$800 - 1,000	$475 - 600	$1,499

MSR/NOTES	100%	EXCELLENT	AVERAGE	LAST MSR

EC-10 STANDARD (MODEL EC10) – single rounded cutaway jumbo body, solid Sitka spruce top, arched maple back, solid maple sides, round soundhole with abalone pearl rosette, black top binding with white line, 14/20-fret rosewood fingerboard with pearl dot inlays, black headstock overlay with screened logo, three-per-side nickel or gold (Emerald Forest Green finish only) tuners, moustache-style rosewood bridge with white bridgepins, batwing-shaped black pickguard, piezo pickup with volume/brilliance/three-band EQ controls, phase switch, available in Blue, Cherry, Ebony, or Emerald Forest Green (1998 only) finish, 24.75 in. scale, 15.875 in. body width, case included, mfg. 1997-98.

	N/A	$800 - 1,000	$475 - 600	$1,699

* **Add 10% (Last MSR was $1,799) for Emerald Forest finish with gold hardware.**

EC-20 STARBURST (MODEL EC20) – single rounded cutaway jumbo body, solid Sitka spruce top, arched maple back, solid maple sides, round soundhole with abalone pearl rosette, multi-ply top binding and single-ply back binding, 14/20-fret rosewood fingerboard with multi star MOP inlays, black headstock overlay with screened logo and multi star inlays, three-per-side gold tuners, moustache-style rosewood bridge with white bridgepins and three stars on the bass side, batwing-shaped tortoiseshell pickguard, piezo pickup with volume/brilliance/treble contour/bass frequency/notch controls, phase switch, available in Antique Natural, Blue, or Trans. Cherry finish, 24.75 in. scale, 15.875 in. body width, case included, mfg. 1997-98.

	N/A	$1,325 - 1,650	$800 - 1,000	$2,149

This model was also available with abalone floret fingerboard inlays, a floral headstock inlay, and no bridge inlays. This model was replaced by the J-180 EC Cutaway in 1999 and can be found in the J Series section.

EC-30 BLUES KING ELECTRO (MODEL EC30) – single rounded cutaway jumbo body, solid Sitka spruce top, arched maple back, solid maple sides, round soundhole with abalone pearl rosette, multi-ply top binding and single-ply back binding, 14/20-fret bound ebony fingerboard with split pearl MOP parallelogram inlays, bound black headstock overlay with pearl logo and double handled vase over dots inlays, three-per-side gold tuners, moustache-style ebony bridge with white bridgepins, batwing-shaped tortoiseshell pickguard, piezo pickup with vvolume/brilliance/treble contour/bass frequency/notch controls, phase switch, available in Antique Natural finish, 24.75 in. scale, 15.875 in. body width, case included, mfg. 1997-98.

	N/A	$1,400 - 1,750	$850 - 1,050	$2,999

This model was replaced by the J-185 EC Cutaway in 1999 and can be found in the J Series section.

ACOUSTIC: SUPER 300/SUPER 400 SERIES

For current Super 400 Series pricing, please refer to the individual listings under Gibson Historic Collection Acoustic Models section. Please refer to the *Blue Book of Electric Guitars* for CES Models.

SUPER 300 – same dimensions as the Super 400, arched spruce top, f-holes, raised multi-ply black pickguard, figured maple back/sides, multiple bound body, three-piece figured maple/mahogany neck, 14/20-fret bound Brazilian rosewood fingerboard with pearl parallelogram inlay, adjustable rosewood bridge/nickel trapeze tailpiece, multi-bound blackface peghead with pearl crown/logo inlay, three-per-side nickel tuners, available in Golden Sunburst finish, approx. 200 mfg. 1948-1955.

1948-1949	N/A	$4,000 - 5,000	$2,400 - 3,000	
1950-1955	N/A	$3,600 - 4,500	$2,150 - 2,700	

* *Super 300 C* – similar to Super 300, except has a single rounded cutaway, very limited mfg. 1957-58.

	N/A	$4,800 - 6,000	$2,900 - 3,600	

SUPER 400 – non-cutaway body, carved spruce top, carved maple back and sides, two bound f-holes, multiple bound body, three-piece figured maple neck, model name engraved into heel cap, 13/20-fret bound ebony fingerboard with point on bottom, pearl split block fingerboard inlays, multi-bound blackface headstock with pearl five-piece split diamond/logo inlay, pearl three-piece split diamond inlay on back of headstock, three-per-side engraved gold tuners, adj. rosewood bridge with pearl triangle inlays, gold trapeze tailpiece with engraved model name, raised multi-bound tortoiseshell pickguard, available in Brown Sunburst or Natural finish, 24.75 in. (1934-35) or 25.5 in. scale (1936-1955), 18 in. body width, 21.75 in. body width, 3.5 in. body depth, mfg. 1934-1955.

1934-1936	N/A	$12,000 - 15,000	$7,250 - 9,000	
1936-1941	N/A	$10,000 - 12,500	$6,000 - 7,500	
1945-1949	N/A	$8,000 - 10,000	$4,800 - 6,000	
1950-1955	N/A	$6,800 - 8,500	$4,100 - 5,100	

* **Add 10-25% for Natural finish.**
* **Add 10-25% for highly flamed maple.**

In 1936, the upper bout was widened to 13.625 in. In 1937, Grover Imperial tuners became an option. In 1938, Kluson Sealfast tuners replaced original part/design. In 1939, Natural finish became an option. In 1941, engraved heel cap and rosewood bridge with pearl inlay were discontinued. This model, like many of Gibson's high end instruments, was not manufactured during World War II.

* *Super 400 Premier (Super 400 C)* – similar to the Super 400, except has a single rounded cutaway, multi-bound pearloid pickguard, rigid Varitone tailpiece, available in Brown Sunburst (most common) or Natural finish, limited mfg. 1939-1983 (typically less than 25 were produced each year with that number shrinking throughout the years).

1939-1942	N/A	$18,000 - 22,500	$10,750 - 13,500	
1944-1949	N/A	$10,750 - 13,500	$6,500 - 8,000	
1950-1959	N/A	$9,500 - 12,000	$5,750 - 7,250	
1960-1964	N/A	$8,800 - 11,000	$5,300 - 6,600	
1965-1969	N/A	$6,000 - 7,500	$3,600 - 4,500	

MSR/NOTES	100%	EXCELLENT	AVERAGE	LAST MSR
1970-1974	N/A	$4,800 - 6,000	$2,900 - 3,600	
1975-1983	N/A	$4,400 - 5,500	$2,650 - 3,300	

* Add 50-100% for Natural finish on prewar models (1939-1942).
* Add 20-30% for Natural finish on postwar models (1944-1983).

Some early models were produced with solid metal tuners. In 1942, no model name was indicated on the heel cap. This model, like many of Gibson's high end instruments, was not manufactured during WWII. In 1948, this model was renamed the Super 400 C. In 1949, rosewood fingerboard replaced original part/design. In 1953, ebony fingerboard replaced previous part/design. By 1957, metal tuners replaced original part/design. Current production instruments (1939 Super 400 Premier in Natural or Cremona Brown) are part of the Historic Collection Series, and can be found at the end of this section.

ACOUSTIC: TG (TENOR) SERIES

TG-0 TENOR – four-string tenor configuration, all mahogany body, round soundhole, tortoiseshell body binding, mahogany neck, 14/19-fret rosewood fingerboard with dot inlays, black headstock overlay with Gibson logo, two-per-side tuners with pearl buttons, rosewood bridge with white pins, black pickguard, most common Gibson tenor guitar, L-0 body style 1927-1933, LG-0 body style 1960-1974, mahogany body, light amber finish during L-0 production, Natural Mahogany finish 1960-1974, early mfg. 1927-1933, and over 2,500 mfg. 1960-1974.

	100%	EXCELLENT	AVERAGE	
1927-1933	N/A	$2,000 - 2,500	$1,200 - 1,500	
1960-1964	N/A	$1,000 - 1,250	$600 - 750	
1965-1969	N/A	$650 - 800	$375 - 475	
1970-1974	N/A	$525 - 650	$325 - 340	

TG-00 TENOR – four string, based on L-00 body style, 23 in. scale, approx. 250 mfg. 1937-circa 1941.

	N/A	$1,600 - 2,000	$950 - 1,200	

TG-1 TENOR – four string, based on L-1 body style, mahogany back/sides, bound body, mfg. 1927-1937.

	N/A	$1,800 - 2,250	$1,075 - 1,350	

TG-2 TENOR – four string, only two made, mfg. 1939-1940.

	N/A	N/A	N/A	

Extreme rarity factor precludes accurate pricing on this model.

TG-25 TENOR – four string, B-25 body style, mahogany back/sides, Sunburst or Natural finish, approx. 890 mfg. 1962-1973.

	100%	EXCELLENT	AVERAGE	
1962-1964	N/A	$950 - 1,200	$575 - 725	
1965-1973	N/A	$750 - 950	$450 - 575	

TG-50 TENOR – four string, archtop tenor configuration based on the L-50, mahogany back/sides, available in Sunburst or Natural finish, mfg. 1934-1963.

	100%	EXCELLENT	AVERAGE	
1934-1939	N/A	$1,800 - 2,250	$1,075 - 1,350	
1940-1949	N/A	$1,600 - 2,000	$950 - 1,200	
1950-1963	N/A	$1,400 - 1,750	$850 - 1,050	

ACOUSTIC: WORKING MAN/WORKING MUSICIANS SERIES

Working Musician and Working Man models were available in limited quantities.

WORKING MUSICIAN 00 – features Gibson's new Advanced 00 body design, spruce top, mahogany back/sides/neck, morado fingerboard and bridge, gloss top with satin back and sides, available in Antique Walnut finish, mfg. 1999-2000.

	N/A	$600 - 700	$425 - 500	$1,439

BLUESBENDER (WM00) – small body, Sitka spruce top, round soundhole, mahogany back/sides, three-per-side nickel tuners, available in Antique Walnut satin finish, mfg. 1998 only.

	N/A	$600 - 700	$450 - 525	$1,099

SONGWRITER DREADNOUGHT (WM10) – dreadnought style, Sitka spruce top, round soundhole, mahogany back/sides, three-per-side nickel tuners, available in Antique Walnut satin finish, mfg. 1998 only.

	N/A	$600 - 700	$450 - 525	$1,099

WORKING MAN 45 (WM45) – soft round shouldered dreadnought style, Sitka spruce top, round soundhole, mahogany back/sides, three-per-side nickel tuners, available in Antique Walnut satin finish, mfg. 1988-2005.

	N/A	$875 - 1,100	$525 - 650	$2,160

WORKING MUSICIAN J-180 – Jumbo J-180-style body, solid spruce top, solid mahogany back and sides, round soundhole with multi-ring rosette, black body binding, mahogany neck, 14/20-fret morado fingerboard with MOP dot inlays, black headstock overlay, three-per-side gold kidney tuners, morado bridge, tortoise pickguard, available in Antique Walnut finish with gloss top and satin back and sides, 24.75 in. scale, mfg. 1999-2000.

	N/A	$775 - 900	$450 - 525	$1,639

MSR/NOTES	100%	EXCELLENT	AVERAGE	LAST MSR

ACOUSTIC: MISC. MODELS

CHICAGO 35 – slope shoulder dreadnought style, spruce top, round soundhole, tortoise pickguard, three-stripe bound body/rosette, mahogany back/sides/neck, 14/19-fret rosewood fingerboard with pearl cross inlay, rosewood straight bridge with white pins, blackface peghead with screened logo, three-per-side nickel tuners, transducer pickup/preamp system, available in Antique Natural or Special Vintage Sunburst finish, mfg. 1994-96.

	N/A	$875 - 1,100	$525 - 650	$2,000

GS-1 – classic style, round soundhole, bound body, three-stripe rosette, bound body, two-stripe rosette, mahogany back/sides/neck, 12/19-fret rosewood fingerboard, rosewood tied bridge with pearl cross inlay, blackface peghead with screened logo, three-per-side tuners with plastic buttons, available in Natural finish, approx. 140 mfg. 1950-56.

	N/A	$950 - 1,200	$575 - 725	

This series has gut strings.

* **GS-2** – similar to GS-1, except has maple back/sides, approx. 175 mfg. 1954-1959.

	N/A	$950 - 1,200	$575 - 725	

* **GS-5 (Custom Classic)** – similar to GS-1, except has rosewood back/sides, approx. 85 mfg. 1954-1959.

	N/A	$1,400 - 1,750	$850 - 1,050	

This model was originally designated the Custom Classic in 1954. In 1957, it was renamed the GS-5.

GS-35 – classical style, spruce top, round soundhole, bound body, two-stripe rosette, mahogany back/sides/neck, 12/19-fret ebony fingerboard, rosewood tied bridge, solid blackface peghead with screened logo, three-per-side tuners with plastic buttons, available in Natural finish, approx. 40 mfg. 1939-1941.

	N/A	$2,000 - 2,500	$1,200 - 1,500	

This series has gut strings.

GS-85 – similar to GS-35, except has rosewood back/sides, pearl bridge inlay, approx. 25 mfg. 1939-1941.

	N/A	$3,800 - 4,750	$2,275 - 2,850	

This series has gut strings.

HARLEY DAVIDSON LIMITED EDITION ACOUSTIC – smaller J-style body, solid Sitka spruce top, solid maple back and sides, round soundhole with two ring rosette, white ivoroid binding, maple neck, 14/20-fret bound ebony fingerboard with large diamond inlays, black headstock overlay with Gibson logo and Harley Davidson shield logo, three-per-side nickel Grover Rotomatic tuners, ebony bridge, double black Everly Brothers-style pickguards with script "Harley Davidson" on treble bout pickguard, 100th Anniversary label, available in Antique Ebony finish, 24.75 in. scale, black hardshell case with Harley Davidson orange lining and certificate of authenticity included, limited edition run of 1,500 instruments sold through Harley Davidson dealers, mfg. 1994-95.

	N/A	$1,600 - 2,000	$950 - 1,200	

A limited number of these guitars were produced in left-handed configuration.

HERITAGE – dreadnought body, round soundhole, tortoiseshell pickguard, two-stripe bound body/rosette, laminated rosewood back/sides, mahogany neck, 14/20-fret ebony fingerboard with pearl dot inlay, reverse ebony bridge with white pins, adjustable saddle, blackface peghead with logo decal, three-per-side nickel tuners, available in Natural finish, mfg. 1965-1982.

1965-1968	N/A	$1,400 - 1,750	$850 - 1,050	
1969-1982	N/A	$1,075 - 1,350	$650 - 800	

Several Heritage Deluxe models were mfg. in 1968 only. In 1968, standard bridge replaced original part/design. In 1969, black pickguard, pearl diamond/curlicue/logo peghead inlay replaced original part/design. In 1971, pearl block fingerboard inlay replaced original part/design, redesigned bridge with pearl curlicue inlay replaced previous part/design. In 1973, bound fingerboard replaced original part/design.

* **Heritage 12** – similar to Heritage, except has 12 strings, six-per-side tuners, approx. 140 mfg. 1968-1970.

	N/A	$1,200 - 1,500	$725 - 900	

JUBILEE – 3/4 size square shouldered body, spruce top, round soundhole, black pickguard, bound body/rosette, mahogany back/sides/neck, 14/20-fret rosewood fingerboard with pearl dot inlay, adjustable rosewood bridge, three-per-side tuners, available in Natural finish, approx. 255 mfg. 1970-71.

	N/A	$725 - 900	$450 - 550	

* **Jubilee 12-string** – similar to Jubilee, except in 12-string configuration with six-per-side tuners, approx. 75 mfg. 1970-71.

	N/A	$800 - 1,000	$475 - 600	

* **Jubilee Deluxe** – similar to Jubilee, except has rosewood back and sides, multi-wooden binding/purfling, approx. 165 mfg. 1970 only.

	N/A	$950 - 1,200	$575 - 725	

MSR/NOTES	100%	EXCELLENT	AVERAGE	LAST MSR

MONTANA GOLD CUSTOM (MODEL ACMG) – super jumbo style, solid Sitka spruce top, Eastern curly maple back and sides, round soundhole with rosette, six-ply top binding, four-ply back binding, black and white checker board marquetry, Eastern curly maple rounded neck, 14/20-fret ebony single-ply bound with birdsbeak fingerboard, MOP block inlays, single-ply bound black headstock with Gibson logo and special MOP wheat and banner inlays, three-per-side gold Imperial tuners, ebony moustache bridge with MOP bar inlays and white pins, tortoiseshell J-200 pickguard with Montana Gold logo and wheat, available in Antique Natural finish, 25.5 in. scale, mfg. 2007-2012.

	$5,150	$2,800 - 3,500	$1,675 - 2,100	$6,661

This model was designed by Ren Ferguson. 48 guitars were scheduled for production in 2007. Gibson's Montana Gold Custom model has a special serialization system of MG YNNNY, where the first and last digits indicate the last two digits of the year it was produced and the middle three are the production ranking for that year.

PIONEER CUTAWAY – round shouldered cutaway dreadnought (L-00 design), spruce top, mahogany back/neck, 25.5 in. scale, traditional Gibson script headstock logo, features Chet Atkins SST design with new body chambering process, Gibson Hex Piezo bridge transducer, 14/20-fret with pearloid dot inlays, lightweight, available in Antique Natural or Vintage Sunburst, mfg. 2004-06.

	N/A	$950 - 1,200	$575 - 725	$2,338

This model is part of the Americana Series, and was manufactured by Gibson USA in Nashville.

PLECTRUM MODELS – four-string, spruce top, mahogany back/sides/neck, 14 3/4 in. by 19 1/4 in., 27 in. scale, 22-fret fingerboard, Sunburst finish. Gibson made less than 10 of these instruments between 1937 and 1955. The two models were the PG-00 and the PG-1 (more common).

	N/A	N/A	N/A	

Extreme rarity factor precludes accurate pricing on this model.

RANGER – L-00 body design, patterned after Chet Atkins SST acoustic concept, spruce top with acoustically chambered mahogany back, mahogany neck with 14/20-fret rosewood fingerboard with pearloid dots, Gibson Hex Piezo bridge transducer, traditional script Gibson headstock logo, Saddle Brown or Natural Satin finish, mfg. 2004-06.

	N/A	$850 - 1,050	$525 - 625	$2,018

This model is part of the Americana Series and is manufactured by Gibson USA in Nashville.

ROY SMECK RADIO GRANDE – spruce top, 16 in. wide, 20.25 in. long, 4.5 in. deep, round soundhole, tortoiseshell pickguard, bound body, one-stripe rosette, rosewood back/sides, mahogany neck, 12/19-fret bound rosewood fingerboard with pearl varying diamond inlay, rosewood straight bridge with black pearl dot pins, blackface peghead with screened model name/logo, three-per-side tuners with plastic buttons, available in Natural finish, less than 100 mfg. 1934-39.

	N/A	$13,250 - 16,500	$8,000 - 10,000	

* *Roy Smeck Stage Deluxe* – similar to Radio Grande, except has mahogany back/sides, pearl dot fingerboard inlay, white pearl dot bridge pins, available in Sunburst finish, mfg. 1934-1942.

	N/A	$6,000 - 7,500	$3,600 - 4,500	

Two styles of this model were available; Standard and Hawaiian. The Standard model had the logo only screened on the peghead. The Hawaiian model featured inlaid ivoroid pieces instead of frets. The ivoroid pieces were usually replaced by frets, making the original ivoroid inlay configuration more desired by collectors. In 1935, bound fingerboard with varying pearl diamond inlay replaced original part/design.

* *Roy Smeck Radio Grande Reissue Historic Signature* – Vintage Sunburst finish, mfg. by Custom Shop beginning 2005.

	N/A	N/A	N/A	

This model was priced on request.

* *Roy Smeck Stage Deluxe Reissue* – Vintage Sunburst finish, mfg. by Custom Shop beginning 2005.

	N/A	N/A	N/A	

This model was priced on request.

GIBSON HISTORIC COLLECTION ACOUSTIC MODELS

The instruments in this series are reproductions of Gibson classics, mostly manufactured by the Custom Shop in Nashville, TN. These guitars are manufactured to the exact specifications of their original release and in several cases, use the same tooling when available. The Gibson Historic Collection first debuted in 1991, and is now formally part of the Gibson Custom, Art, Historic Division. Historic Collection instruments are produced in limited quantities. Historic Collection instruments may also be found under individual category or model names. The few guitars that do show up in the secondary marketplace are usually in Excellent+ (95% - 98% condition).

MASTER MUSEUM COLLECTION (MODEL ACMC) – built by Ren Ferguson at MT custom shop, and each instrument is a one-of-a-kind, only one available per month, mfg. 2005-present.

Current MSR is $46,223.

1934 L-5 NON-CUTAWAY (MODEL HSL5) – multi-bound body, carved spruce top, layered tortoiseshell pickguard, bound f-holes, maple back/sides/neck, 20-fret bound pointed ebony fingerboard with pearl block inlay, ebony bridge with pearl inlay on wings, model name engraved trapeze tailpiece with chrome insert, multi-bound blackface peghead with pearl flame/logo inlay, three-per-side gold tuners, available in Cremona Brown Sunburst finish, mfg. 1995-2008.

	N/A	$3,200 - 4,000	$1,925 - 2,400	$6,774

MSR/NOTES	100%	EXCELLENT	AVERAGE	LAST MSR

L-5 CT (MODEL HSLC) – single rounded cutaway bound hollow thinline body, carved spruce top, bound f-holes, solid maple back/sides, five-piece laminated maple neck, 20-fret bound pointed ebony fingerboard with pearl block inlay, ebony bridge/model name engraved trapeze tailpiece with chrome insert, multi-ply bound blackface peghead with pearl flowerpot/logo inlay, three-per-side Schaller M-6 tuners, gold hardware, layered tortoiseshell pickguard, available in Natural (NA, disc.), Vintage Sunburst (VS), or Faded Cherry (FC, disc.) finish, 17 in. body width, mfg. 1998-2010.

	$8,900	$5,000 - 6,000	N/A	$12,588

- Add 27.5-30% (Last MSR was $16,115) for Natural finish.
- Subtract 12.5% (Last MSR was $10,588) for Faded Cherry finish.

This model is also available with two '57 Classic Humbucker pickups (see *Blue Book of Electric Guitars*).

1939 SUPER 400 PREMIER (HS4PNAGH) – single round cutaway body, arched spruce top, bound f-holes, raised multi-bound pearloid pickguard, figured maple back/sides, multiple bound body, three-piece figured maple/mahogany neck, model name engraved into heel cap, 14/20-fret bound ebony fingerboard with point on bottom, pearl split block fingerboard inlay, adjustable rosewood bridge with pearl triangle wings inlay, gold unhinged PAF trapeze tailpiece with engraved model name, multi-bound blackface peghead with pearl five-piece split diamond/logo inlay, pearl three-piece split diamond inlay on back of peghead, three-per-side gold Grover Imperial tuners, available in Natural or Cremond Brown Burst finish, disc. 1998.

	N/A	$6,100 - 7,150	$3,200 - 3,700	$14,719

ACOUSTIC ELECTRIC: GENERAL INFORMATION

The following Acoustic Electric category names appear in this order: Chet Atkins Series, J Series (numbered), L Series, Les Paul Series, and Misc. Even though many of Gibson's current acoustic models now have either transducer or active transducer pickups, only those acoustic electric models with the traditional Gibson E suffix or visible pickup with controls will appear in this section.

- Add 15%-30% for Natural finish, depending on the model (including rarity factor), configuration, and original condition. Add approx. 10% for left-hand models on current/recent mfg.

ACOUSTIC ELECTRIC: CHET ATKINS SERIES

Gibson's Chet Atkins Series was produced in Nashville, TN and part of Gibson USA until 2002, and produced in Bozeman, MT as part of Gibson Acoustic until 2005.

CHET ATKINS CE (ARCE) – single rounded cutaway mahogany body with hollow sound chambers, solid spruce top, round soundhole with plastic bowl insert and wood inlay rosette, two-stripe body binding, mahogany neck, 12/19-fret rosewood (1981-1996) or ebony (1996-2005) fingerboard, slotted headstock with rosewood overlay, three-per-side gold tuners with pearl buttons, tied rosewood bridge, Gibson piezo bridge pickups, volume/tone control, active electronics, available in Alpine White (1981-1994), Antique Natural, Cedar (1994-95), Ebony (1990-94), or Wine Red (1990-2002) finish, 1.8 in. nut width, 25.5 in. scale, mfg. late 1981-2005.

1981-1995	N/A	$1,200 - 1,500	$725 - 900	
1996-2005	N/A	$1,075 - 1,350	$650 - 800	$1,898

- Add 10-20% (Last MSR was $3,248) for Antique Natural finish.

This model was produced in Nashville until 2002 when production moved to Montana through 2005. Approximately the first 1,000 instruments were stamped with a unique serial number consisting of a letter prefix followed by three digits. This series started with A 001, ran through A 100 then switched to B 001, ran through B 100 all the way up to K 100.

* ***Chet Atkins True Cedar CE (ARER)*** – similar to the Chet Atkins CE, except has a True Cedar top, available in Antique Natural finish, mfg. 1999-2002.

	N/A	$1,200 - 1,500	$725 - 900	$3,398

* ***Chet Atkins CEC (ARCC)*** – similar to the Chet Atkins CE, except has an ebony fingerboard and 2 in. nut width, available in Antique Natural, Cedar (1994-95), Ebony, or Wine Red (1990-2002) finish, mfg. late 1981-2005.

1981-1995	N/A	$1,200 - 1,500	$725 - 900	
1996-2005	N/A	$1,075 - 1,350	$650 - 800	$1,998

- Add 10-20% (Last MSR was $3,263) for Antique Natural finish

This model was produced in Nashville until 2002 when production moved to Montana through 2005. Approximately the first 1,000 instruments were stamped with a unique serial number consisting of a letter prefix followed by three digits. This series started with A 001, ran through A 100 then switched to B 001, ran through B 100 all the way up to K 100.

» ***Chet Atkins True Cedar CEC (ARCR)*** – similar to the Chet Atkins CEC, except has a True Cedar top, available in Antique Natural finish, mfg. 1999-2002.

	N/A	$1,200 - 1,500	$725 - 900	$3,548

CHET ATKINS STUDIO CE (ARSE) – single rounded cutaway hollow mahogany body with Chet Atkins signature on upper bass bout, solid spruce top, multi-ply body binding with black outer layer, no soundhole, three-piece mahogany neck, 24-fret extended ebony fingerboard with no inlays, slotted headstock with rosewood overlay and gold Gibson logo, three-per-side open-style gold tuners with plastic buttons, flared bridge ends (1993-2000) or "bird and beak" bridge (2004-05), bridge-mounted piezo pickup, individual string volume controls accessed internally, controls mounted on rim (1993-2000) or on upper bass bout (2004-05), available in Antique Natural finish, 1.8 in. nut width, 26 in. scale, mfg. 1993-99, 2004-05.

	N/A	$1,450 - 1,800	$875 - 1,100	$4,214

MSR/NOTES	100%	EXCELLENT	AVERAGE	LAST MSR

* ***Chet Atkins Studio CEC (ARST)*** – similar to the Chet Atkins Studio CE, except a 2 in. nut width, available in Antique Natural finish, mfg. 1993-2000, 2004-05.

	N/A	$1,450 - 1,800	$875 - 1,100	$4,322

CHET ATKINS SST (ARSS) – single round cutaway mahogany body with Chromyte (balsa) center, solid spruce top with Chet Atkins signature on upper bass bout, simulated round soundhole with soundhole insert, signature, and prewar script Gibson logo (1987-1993) or no soundhole (1993-2005), body binding, set mahogany neck, 14/21-fret extended ebony fingerboard with pearl dots (1987-1993) or stars (1993-2005) inlays, black headstock overlay with no logo (1987-1993) or pearl Gibson logo and star inlay (1993-2005), three-per-side gold tuners, standard ebony bridge (1987-1993) or ebony bridge with upper belly with pearl star inlays, black pearl dot pins, transducer bridge pickup, controls on top (1987-1993) or on rim (1993-2005), active electronics, available in Alpine White (1987-1993), Antique Natural, Ebony, Heritage Cherry Sunburst (1994-2005), or Wine Red finish, mfg. 1987-2005.

1987-1993	N/A	$1,200 - 1,500	$725 - 900	
1993-2005	N/A	$1,075 - 1,350	$650 - 800	$2,398

• **Add 10-20% (Last MSR was $2,498) for Antique Natural finish.**

* ***Chet Atkins SST 12*** – similar to the Chet Atkins SST, except in 12-string configuration with six-per-side tuners, available in Alpine White, Ebony, or Wine Red finish, mfg. 1989-1994.

	N/A	$1,275 - 1,600	$750 - 950	$1,250

» ***Chet Atkins SST 12 Flame Top*** – similar to Chet Atkins SST 12, except has a flame maple top, available in Antique Natural, Heritage Cherry Sunburst, Trans. Amber (1994 only), or Trans. Red finish, mfg. 1993-94.

	N/A	$1,350 - 1,750	$850 - 1,050	$2,179

* ***Chet Atkins SST Flame Top*** – similar to the Chet Atkins SST, except has a flamed maple top, available in Antique Natural, Heritage Cherry Sunburst, Trans. Amber (1994-95), or Trans. Red (1993-94) finish, mfg. 1993-95.

	N/A	$1,275 - 1,600	$750 - 950	$2,179

ACOUSTIC ELECTRIC: CITATION & KALAMAZOO SERIES

CITATION – single round cutaway multi-bound body, carved spruce top, bound f-holes, raised multi-bound flamed maple pickguard, figured maple back/sides/neck, 20-fret multi-bound pointed fingerboard with pearl cloud inlay, adjustable ebony bridge with pearl fleur-de-lis inlay on wings, gold trapeze tailpiece with engraved model name, multi-bound ebony veneered peghead with abalone fleur-de-lis/logo inlay, abalone fleur-de-lis inlay on back of peghead, floating pickup with volume control on pickguard, three-per-side gold engraved tuners, 17 in. wide, 20.5 in. long, 3 in. deep, available in Faded Cherry Sunburst, Honeyburst or Natural finish, only 14 mfg. 1969-1979.

	N/A	$16,000 - 20,000	$9,500 - 12,000	

Less than 14 Citations were made between 1969 and 1979. In 1982, Gibson produced three more (by customer request). Current production instruments are part of the Historic Collection Series (see Gibson Historic Collection Acoustic Models).

KALAMAZOO AWARD – top-of-the-line archtop mfg. in Kalamazoo, Michigan, circa 1978-1984, similar dimensions as the Citation, except is 4 inches deep, trapeze tailpiece has eagle inlay and pickguard has eagle landing in tree branch, floating pickup with volume control on pickguard, available in Natural or Sunburst finish, less than 30 mfg. 1978-1984.

	N/A	$9,500 - 12,000	$6,000 - 7,500	

• **Add 10-20% for Natural finish.**

The Kalamazoo Award model followed the Citation in production.

ACOUSTIC ELECTRIC: LC SERIES

LC-1 CASCADE CUTAWAY (LSC1) – single cutaway L-00-style body, solid cedar top, quilted maple (2003-04) or rosewood (2005-06) back and sides, multi-ply body binding, round soundhole with abalone rosette, set figured maple neck, 14/20-fret rosewood fingerboard with MOP dot inlays, black headstock overlay with pearl Gibson logo and crown inlay, three-per-side vintage gold tuners, sculpted Indian rosewood bridge, Schertler Bluestick transducer pickup with volume control, available in Antique Natural or Vintage Sunburst finish, 24.75 in. scale, hardshell case included, mfg. 2003-06.

	N/A	$1,200 - 1,500	$750 - 950	$2,818

LC-2 SONOMA CUTAWAY (LSC2) – single cutaway L-00-style body, solid cedar top, solid walnut (2003-04) or quilted maple (2005-06) back and sides, multi-ply body binding, round soundhole with abalone rosette, set mahogany neck, 14/20-fret ebony fingerboard with abalone floret inlays, bound headstock with black overlay, pearl Gibson logo, and MOP crown inlay, three-per-side vintage gold tuners, sculpted ebony bridge, Schertler Bluestick transducer pickup with volume control, available in Antique Natural or Vintage Sunburst finish, 24.75 in. scale, hardshell case included, mfg. 2003-06.

	N/A	$1,400 - 1,750	$850 - 1,050	$3,665

LC-3 CALDERA CUTAWAY (LSC3) – single cutaway L-00-style body, solid cedar top, solid flamed koa back and sides, multi-ply body binding, round soundhole with abalone rosette, set mahogany neck, 14/20-fret ebony fingerboard with abalone autumn leaf inlays, bound headstock with black overlay, pearl Gibson logo, and MOP crown inlay, three-per-side vintage gold tuners, sculpted ebony bridge, Schertler Bluestick transducer pickup with volume control, available in Antique Natural or Vintage Sunburst finish, 24.75 in. scale, hardshell case included, mfg. 2003-04.

	N/A	$1,600 - 2,000	$950 - 1,200	$4,194

MSR/NOTES	100%	EXCELLENT	AVERAGE	LAST MSR

ACOUSTIC ELECTRIC: LES PAUL SERIES

LES PAUL JUMBO – slope shouldered body, single rounded cutaway, spruce top, round soundhole, tortoiseshell pickguard, two-stripe bound body/rosette, bookmatched rosewood back/sides, mahogany neck, 19-fret rosewood fingerboard with pearl dot inlay, rosewood bridge with black and white dot pins, three-per-side chrome tuners, low impedance single coil pickup, volume/treble/mid/bass controls, two-position switch, available in Natural finish, approx. 140 mfg. 1969-1973.

	N/A	$2,800 - 3,500	$1,675 - 2,100	

LES PAUL ACOUSTIC (CSLPA) – features LP style hollow mahogany body with carved figured maple top, unique bridge is carved directly into top, button type tailpiece with dark bridgepins, L.R. Baggs piezo pickup, tone and volume controls, traditional LP unbound rosewood fingerboard with trapezoid inlays, available in Tangerine Burst (TBG) or Translucent Black (TBK), limited mfg. 2001-02.

	N/A	$2,400 - 3,000	$1,450 - 1,800	$5,680

This model was produced by the Nashville Gibson Custom Shop, and was part of the Custom Collection.

LES PAUL ACOUSTIC PLAIN TOP – features LP style solid mahogany body with plain maple top, relief carved Pro Shop bridge, L.R. Baggs piezo pickup, tone and volume controls, traditional LP unbound rosewood fingerboard with trapezoid inlays, nickel hardware, available in Tangerine Burst (TBG) Washed Cherry (WC) or Trans Black (TB), mfg. 2003-04.

	N/A	$1,600 - 2,000	$950 - 1,200	$3,856

This model was produced by the Nashville Gibson Custom Shop, and was part of the Custom Collection.

ACOUSTIC ELECTRIC: MISC.

The Custom Acoustic Line Series was manufactured 1994-98. Models featured the Gibson Advanced Bracing pattern and included a factory-installed transducer with onboard controls.

ACAPULCO GOLD KOA CUSTOM – advanced 00 body, solid koa top/back/sides, abalone rosette, mother-of-pearl floret fretboard inlays, equipped with Schertler Bluestick pickup system, supplied with certificate of authenticity, 24 mfg. July, 2003.

	N/A	$1,650 - 2,000	$1,100 - 1,350	$3,459

ACOUSTIC FIREBIRD CUSTOM (MODEL SSFB) – patterned after the J-30, square shoulder dreadnought, Sitka spruce top, quilted Western maple back/sides, curly maple neck with ebony fingerboard with mother-of-pearl/abalone flame inlays, pickguard has engraved flames, 24.75 in. scale, 14/20-fret, active Fishman pickup, gold Grover tuners, Antique Cherry finish, limited mfg. by Custom Shop beginning 2002-2012.

$4,460	$2,400 - 3,000	$1,450 - 1,800	$5,763

BOSSA NOVA – nylon string configuration, single round cutaway body, spruce top, round soundhole, two-stripe bound body/rosette, rosewood back/sides, mahogany neck, 20-fret rosewood fingerboard, rosewood tied bridge, classical style slotted peghead, three-per-side nickel tuners with plastic buttons, ceramic bridge pickup, available in Natural finish, seven mfg. 1971-73.

	N/A	N/A	N/A	

Extreme rarity factor precludes accurate pricing on this model.

MAUI WOWIE KOA CUSTOM – round shoulder J-45 style body, solid koa top/back/sides, abalone dot fretboard inlays, equipped with Schertler pickup system, includes custom shop label, decal insignia, and supplied with certificate of authenticity, 24 mfg. July, 2003.

	N/A	$1,750 - 2,100	$1,150 - 1,400	$3,892

GILBERT GUITARS, JOHN AND WILLIAM

Instruments currently built outside San Francisco, CA.

Luthier John Gilbert built his first classical guitar in 1965 as a hobby. By 1974, after performing repair work in addition to his guitar building, Gilbert was concentrating on building full time. In 1991, Gilbert was joined by his son Bill. Gilbert's classical guitars have been favored by a large number of professional players. The design features a responsive projection of volume and tone coloration that depends on the guitarist's playing. Between 1974 and 1991, John Gilbert built an estimated 120 guitars and Bill, who builds a limited number of guitars annually, has produced an estimated 130 guitars for a total of around 250. For more information on Gilbert Guitars refer to the website.

CONTACT INFORMATION
GILBERT GUITARS, JOHN AND WILLIAM
5760 Forked Horn Place
Paso Robles, CA 93446
Phone No.: 805-776-3738
http://wgilbertguitars.com
bill@wgilbertguitars.com

GILCHRIST

Instruments currently built in Australia.

CONTACT INFORMATION
GILCHRIST
www.gilchristmandolins.com
info@gilchristmandolins.com

Australian luthier Stephen Gilchrist is known for his high quality mandolins, mandolas, and mandocellos. Gilchrist began building instruments in 1976, and spent 1980 in the U.S. working in Nashville, TN at Gruhn Guitars. After 1980, Gilchrist returned to Australia where he continues to produce mandolins as well as a few guitars. Gilchrist has built a number of acoustic and electric guitars; most of the electric guitars were built between 1987 and 1988. Currently, Gilchrist focuses on the mandolin family. To make identification of these guitars a bit difficult, some models do not have the Gilchrist name anywhere on the instrument and none of them have a serial number. For further information regarding current model specifications and pricing, visit Gilchrist's website or contact them directly.

GIRDIS, ROBERT

Instruments previously produced in Seattle, WA between the early 1980s and 2009.

In 1978, luthier Robert Girdis began his studies in guitar construction at the Northwest School of Instrument Design in Seattle, WA. After his first year of intensive studies apprenticeship, Girdis stayed on for a second year as a teaching assistant. In 1981, Girdis established his own workshop of Guemes Island (Washington), sharing a large workshop with a boat builder.

After a short time at work in an Anacortes boat yard, Girdis formed a collaboration with a local wildlife artist to make fifty realistic carved cedar duck decoys. Girdis also served as assistant to Guemes Island's artist/sculptor Phillip McCracken, working on several sculptures in progress in wood, stone, and bronze. Returning to his own shop, Girdis began fashioning commissioned guitars and dulcimers as well as performing instrument repair work. Dulcimer construction offered Girdis the chance to experiment with several different designs, and different exotic woods. Girdis then began to focus on building acoustic guitars, and accepting more commissions for steel string models.

Girdis has been featured in *Frets* Magazine, focusing on the artistic side of the craft. Girdis' guitars are noted for their big acoustic sound and attention to detail in the construction. Models were available in dreadnought and parlor styles and a number of configurations were available. Girdis passed away in June, 2009.

GITANE

Instruments currently produced in China since the early 2000s. Distributed by Saga Music in San Francisco, CA.

Gitane is a trademark of Saga Music that offers Gypsy Jazz, Maccaferri-style acoustic guitars produced in Asia. Guitarist John Jorgensen popularized the Jazz-style guitar and also has a signature model through Gitane. For more information, visit Saga's website or contact them directly.

CONTACT INFORMATION
GITANE
PO Box 2841
South San Francisco, CA 94080
Phone No.: 650-558-5558
Fax No.: 650-871-7590
www.sagamusic.com
info@sagamusic.com

Gitane offers several models in a variety of configurations and styles. The **DG-255** (MSR $950) features a solid spruce top, premium rosewood back and sides, and an oval soundhole, the **DG-250** (MSR $995) features a solid spruce top, premium rosewood back and sides, and an oval soundhole, the **DG-250M** (MSR $1,050) features a solid spruce top, bird's-eye maple back and sides, and an oval soundhole, and the **D-500** (MSR $950) is a Maccaferri-style jazz guitar with a solid spruce top, premium rosewood back and sides, and a large D-shaped soundhole. The John Jorgensen Signature Series includes the **DG-300** (MSR $1,495) that features a solid spruce top, figured Santos rosewood back and sides, and an oval soundhole, the **DG-320** (MSR $1,495) that features a solid spruce top, figured Santos rosewood back and sides, and a large D-shaped soundhole, and the **DG-330 Tuxedo Modele** (MSR $1,495) that features a solid spruce top, mahogany back and sides, an oval soundhole and an all-black finish.

GIVENS, ROBERT L.

Instruments previously built between circa 1960 and 1992.

Luthier Robert L. Givens began building guitars, mandolins, and banjo necks in 1960. Shortly after high school, he moved to Nashville, TN where he partnered with dobro player Tut Taylor. The two of them bought the old Harmony guitar factory and began building instruments as a contractor for Baldwin. He built mandolins for Baldwin under the "Ode" trademark, but he also began building his own custom instruments at that time. This partnership didn't last very long, and soon, Givens had moved to Australia where he lived for several years and worked as a welder. After the Vietnam War, Givens moved back to the U.S. in the early 1970s. He eventually ended up in Northern Idaho, and in 1979 local luthier Steve Weill met Givens. Shortly thereafter, Weill started to work for Givens and became his only employee over all the years that he built instruments. Most Givens instruments were built during the 1980s and early 1990s, but Givens always remained an independent luthier. His mandolins became so popular that in order to continue working, he moved to a secret location, didn't list his telephone number, and only notified customers when their instruments were done. By the early 1990s, many people thought Givens was going to start mass producing his instruments. Unfortunately, Givens developed lymphatic cancer in the early 1990s and since he refused to see a doctor until it was too late, the cancer couldn't be treated. Givens became ill during late 1992, and in March 1993, he died at the age of 50.

Since Givens' death, his instruments have become very popular/collectible - especially his mandolins. Givens' mandolins are known for being very loud but they don't lose any tone the louder they get. His mandolins were also built very well. It is estimated that Givens built 700 mandolins, 200 guitars, and a few hundred banjo necks. Givens also built about 800 mandolins for Tut Taylor's GTR company early in his career.

GLEN BURTON GUITARS

Instruments previously produced in China during the 2000s. Distributed by United States Music in Franklin Square, NY.

Glen Burton offers a line of beginner/entry-level guitars that started as low as $25. Acoustic guitars were mainly limited to dreadnoughts, although several variations were available. These are strictly budget guitars with little value.

MSR/NOTES	100%	EXCELLENT	AVERAGE	LAST MSR

GLEN MORGAN GUITARS

Guitars currently produced in Skiatook, OK.

CONTACT INFORMATION
GLEN MORGAN GUITARS
Skiatook, OK
Phone No.: 866-660-7834
www.glenmorganguitars.com
glen@glenmorganguitars.com

Luthier Glen Morgan and his daughter, Alisa Everitt build acoustic and electric guitars in their shop in Oklahoma. Morgan guitars are built with high quality tonewoods and no laminate materials are used. In 2002, Morgan met Joesf Glaude and the two collaborated to created the Glen Morgan Harp Guitar. Morgan guitars are offered in several acoustic variations including the Type A Narrow Throat, Type B Wide Throat, Type C Cutaway, and Type D Harp Guitar. For more information, visit Mogan's website or contact them directly.

GLOBE

Guitars previously produced in the late 1950s and early 1960s. Also see Goodman and chapter on House Brands.

The Globe trademark has been identified as a House Brand of the Goodman Community Discount Center, circa 1958-1960. Source: Willie G. Moseley, *Stellas & Stratocasters*.

GODIN

Instruments currently produced in La Patrie, Quebec, Princeville, Quebec, and/or Berlin, NH since 1987. Distributed by Godin Guitars (previously La Si Do, Inc.) in Baie D'Urfe Quebec, Canada.

CONTACT INFORMATION
GODIN
19420 Avenue Clark-Graham
Baie D Urfe, Quebec H9X 3R8 Canada
Phone No.: 514-457-7977
Fax No.: 514-457-5774
www.godinguitars.com
info@godinguitars.com

Robert Godin has been a mainstay in the guitar building industry since 1972. At the age of seven, Godin got his first guitar and he has never looked back. By the time he was 15, he was working at La Tosca Musique in Montreal selling guitars and learning about minor repairs and set up work. Before long, Godin's passion for guitar playing was eclipsed by his fascination with the construction of the instruments themselves. In 1968, Godin set up a custom guitar shop in Montreal called Harmonilab, which quickly became known for its excellent work and musicians were coming from as far away as Quebec City to have their guitars adjusted. Harmonilab was the first guitar shop in Quebec to use professional strobe tuners for intonating guitars.

Although Harmonilab's business was flourishing, Godin was full of ideas for the design and construction of acoustic guitars. In 1972, the Norman Guitar Company was born. From the beginning the Norman guitars showed signs of the innovations that Godin would eventually bring to the guitar market. Perhaps the most significant item about the Norman history is that it represented the beginning of guitar building in the village of La Patrie, Quebec. La Patrie has since become an entire town of guitar builders.

By 1978, Norman guitars had become quite successful in Canada and France, while at the same time the people in La Patrie were crafting replacement necks and bodies for the electric guitar market. Before long, there was a lineup at the door of American guitar companies that wanted Godin's crew to supply all their necks and bodies.

Before the actual Godin tradmark appeared on a guitar, Godin introduced the Seagull acoustic line in 1980, the La Paterie line of classical guitars in 1982, and the Simon & Patrick line of acoustic guitars in 1985. Since Godin's factory had been producing necks and bodies for various American guitar companies since 1978, he combined that knowledge with his background in acoustic guitar design for an entirely new product. The Acousticaster debuted in 1987, and represented the first design under the Godin name. The Acousticaster was designed to produce an acoustic sound from an instrument that was as easy to play as the player's favorite electric guitar. This was achieved through the help of a patented mechanical harp system inside the guitar. Godin now presents a full line of Acousticaster-style instruments as well as full electric solidbody guitars. Today, Godin Guitars employs close to 500 people in four factories located in La Patrie and Princeville, Quebec (Canada), and Berlin, New Hampshire. Intial company history courtesy Robert Godin and Katherine Calder (Artist Relations), La Si Do, Inc. (Godin Guitars), June 5, 1996.

PRODUCTION MODEL CODES

Godin is currently using a system similar to the original Gretsch system, in that the company is assigning both a model name and a four, five, or six-digit number that indicates the color finish specific to that guitar model. Thus, the four, five, or six-digit code will indicate which model and color a guitar is from just one number. References in this text will list the four, five, or six-digit variances for color finish within the model designations.

ACOUSTIC ELECTRIC: A SERIES

A 6 SIX-STRING ACOUSTIC/ELECTRIC – single rounded cutaway semi-hollow chambered light maple body, solid cedar top, mahogany neck, 22-fret rosewood fingerboard with offset dot inlay, solid peghead with Godin logo, three-per-side black tuners, rosewood bridge with white bridgepins, L.R. Baggs ribbon transducer, volume/three-band EQ slider controls, on-board preamp, available in Blue (7486), CognacBurst (7479), or Natural (7523) Semi-gloss finish, 25.5 in. scale, disc.

	N/A	$350 - 425	$225 - 275	$795

• **Add 10% for Black High Gloss finish (9435).**

MSR/NOTES	100%	EXCELLENT	AVERAGE	LAST MSR

A 6 SECOND VERSION – single cutaway two chambered body, solid cedar top, silver leaf maple back and sides, no soundhole, mahogany neck, 22-fret rosewood fingerboard, three-per-side black tuners, rosewood bridge, Custom Godin under-saddle transducer, preamp controls mounted in the upper bass bout, available in Black high-gloss (25299), CognacBurst semi-gloss (25312), or Natural (25336) semi-gloss finish, 25.5 in. scale, disc. 2006.

	N/A	$300 - 350	$175 - 225	$652

* Add 15% (Last MSR $619) for Black high-gloss finish.

* *A 6 Ultra* – similar to the A 6 Second Version, except has a single exposed humbucker pickup in the neck position, available in Black high-gloss (30309), CognacBurst high-gloss (30286), Natural semi-gloss (30293), or Trans. Red (2012-present, 036196) finish, mfg. 2007-present.

MSR $839	$700	$400 - 475	$250 - 300	

* Add 12.5% (MSR $949) for Black, Cognac, or Trans. Red high-gloss finish.

A 11 GLISSENTAR – 11-string nylon-string configuration, single cutaway two chambered body, solid cedar bound top, silver leaf maple back and sides, no soundhole, mahogany neck, fretless ebony fingerboard, bound headstock with three-per-side chrome tuners, rosewood bridge, Custom Godin under-saddle transducer, preamp controls mounted in the upper bass bout, available in Natural semi-gloss finish (17706), 25.5 in. scale, current mfg.

MSR $1,195	$1,000	$575 - 650	$325 - 400	

A 12 12-STRING ACOUSTIC/ELECTRIC – similar to the A 6, except in 12-string configuration, has a maple neck, and six-per-side tuners, available in Black High Gloss finish (9619) or Blue (10653), CognacBurst (10646), or Natural (9602) Semi-gloss finish, mfg. 1997-disc.

	N/A	$500 - 550	$300 - 350	$845

* Add 10% for Black High Gloss finish (9619).

A 12 SECOND VERSION 12-STRING – similar to the A 6 Second Version, except in 12-string configuration and has a rock maple neck, available in Natural semi-gloss finish only (25343), current mfg.

MSR $895	$750	$425 - 525	$275 - 325	

ACS NYLON WITH SYNTH ACCESS "2-VOICE" – nylon string configuration single rounded cutaway semi-hollow chambered light maple body, cedar (2009-present) or maple (disc. 2008) top, mahogany neck, 22-fret ebony fingerboard with offset dot inlay, five small soundholes on upper bass bout, slotted peghead with "R. Godin" signature logo, three-per-side gold tuners with pearloid buttons, rosewood tied bridge, six individual micro transducer bridge saddles, RMC hexaphonic multi sensors, volume/three-band EQ/synth volume slider controls, two synth (program up/down) push buttons, on board preamp, 13-pin connector for Roland GR series guitar synths, available in CognacBurst (disc., 9381) and Natural (7745/32150) Semi-gloss finishes and Black Pearl (11872/32174) and Blue (disc. 2007, 9428) High Gloss finish, current mfg.

MSR $1,315	$1,050	$575 - 725	$325 - 400	

* Add 7.5% (MSR $1,395) for Trans. Blue High Gloss finish (Model 9428) or Black Pearl high gloss finish (Model 11872/32174).

* *ACS Slim Nylon With Synth Access* – similar to the ACS Nylon, except with a narrower neck, available in Natural (18864/32167) or Black Pearl (18871/32181) finish, current mfg.

MSR $1,315	$1,050	$575 - 725	$325 - 400	

* Add 7.5% (MSR $1,295) for Black Pearl high gloss finish.

* *ACS Lightburst Flame Nylon With Synth Access* – similar to the ACS Nylon, except has a flame maple top, available in Lightburst Flame high gloss finish (34017) finish, mfg. 2010-present.

MSR $1,495	$1,200	$650 - 800	$375 - 450	

ACOUSTIC ELECTRIC: ACOUSTICASTER SERIES

Early Acousticaster models have a black or creme colored controls plate in the bass horn bout.

ACOUSTICASTER 6 (MODEL 3518) – single cutaway semi-hollow maple body, solid spruce top, fan bracing with mechanical harp (18 tuned metal tines), rock maple neck, 25.5 in. scale, 22-fret maple or rosewood fingerboard with offset dot inlay, six-per-side gold tuners, rosewood bridge with white bridgepins, L.R. Baggs bridge transducer, volume/active three-band EQ, available in Black High Gloss finish (maple fingerboard: 3471; rosewood fingerboard: 3518), disc.

	N/A	$400 - 450	$250 - 300	$899

This model was initially available in Aqua and White finishes.

* *Acousticaster 6 Left (Model 3532)* – similar to the Acousticaster 6, except in left-handed configuration and is available only with a rosewood fingerboard, available in Black High Gloss finish, disc.

	N/A	$475 - 550	$300 - 350	$1,039

* *Acousticaster 6 Deluxe (Model 3594)* – similar to Acousticaster 6, except has semi-hollow mahogany body, available in Natural High Gloss finish (maple fingerboard: 3563; rosewood fingerboard: 3594), current mfg.

MSR $1,195	$1,000	$575 - 650	$325 - 400	

This model was initially available in Cherryburst, Cognacburst, or Natural finish.

ACOUSTICASTER 12 – similar to Acousticaster, except has 12 strings, six-per-side tuners, available Black or White finish, disc. 1996.

	N/A	$425 - 500	$225 - 275	$960

MSR/NOTES	100%	EXCELLENT	AVERAGE	LAST MSR

* **Acousticaster Deluxe 12** – Similar to Acousticaster, except in 12-string configuration, has semi-hollow mahogany body, and six-per-side tuners, available in Cognacburst or Natural finish, disc. 1996.

	N/A	$475 - 550	$300 - 350	$1,039

This model was initially available in Cherryburst, Cognacburst, or Natural finish.

ACOUSTIC ELECTRIC: MULTIAC SERIES

All MultiAc semi-acoustic models feature a dual-chambered mahogany body, solid spruce top, and mahogany neck. **Synth Access** models have an RMC hexaphonic multi-sensor, while the **Duet** models feature the L.R. Baggs Duet system.

MULTIAC NYLON STRING WITH SYNTH ACCESS (MODEL 4690/4713) – nylon string configuration single cutaway two-chambered mahogany body, bound spruce top, mahogany neck, 22-fret ebony fingerboard with offset dot inlay, five small soundholes on upper bass bout, slotted peghead with "R. Godin" signature logo, three-per-side gold tuners with pearloid buttons, rosewood tied bridge, six individual micro transducer bridge saddles, RMC hexaphonic multi-sensors, volume/three-band EQ/synth volume slider controls, two synth (program up/down) push buttons, on-board preamp, 13-pin connector for Roland GR series guitar synths, available in Natural Semi-gloss finish, 25.5 in. scale, current mfg.

MSR $1,895	$1,580	$850 - 1,050	$500 - 625	

* **Multiac Nylon String With Synth Access Fretless (12817/19717)** – similar to the Multiac Nylong String With Synth Access, except has a fretless fingerboard, available in Natural Semi-gloss finish, current mfg.

MSR $1,895	$1,580	$850 - 1,050	$500 - 625	

* **Multiac Nylon String With Synth Access Left-Handed (036073)** – similar to the Multiac Nylong String With Synth Access, except in left-handed configuration, available in Natural Semi-gloss finish, mfg. 2012-present.

MSR $1,995	$1,650	$875 - 1,100	$525 - 650	

MULTIAC GRAND CONCERT SA WITH SYNTH ACCESS (MODEL 12817) – nylon string configuration single cutaway Grand Concert style guitar, two-chambered mahogany body with solid cedar top, mahogany neck and ebony fingerboard, width at nut 2 in., Custom RMC Polydrive electronics with a 13-pin connector for direct access to Roland GR Series and Axon AX100 guitar synths, available in semi-gloss or High Gloss Natural finish, current mfg.

MSR $1,895	$1,580	$850 - 1,050	$500 - 625	

* **Multiac Grand Concert Duet (Model 16471)** – similar to Grand Concert With Synth Access except has rosewood fingerboard and a custom L.R. Baggs Duet System (Ribbon Transducer and Internal Microphone), available in Semi Gloss or High Gloss Natural finishes, mfg. 2000-08.

	N/A	$750 - 900	$475 - 550	$1,640

* **Multiac Grand Concert Duet Ambiance (Model 31498)** – similar to the Grand Concert SA With Synth Access except has custom Fishman Aura electronics, blendable sound imaging mic with 4 individual mic settings, and dual source pre-amp with feedback control, available in Lightburst (32495) or Natural (31498) high gloss finish, mfg. 2009-present.

MSR $1,895	$1,580	$850 - 1,050	$500 - 625	

MULTIAC NYLON DUET (MODEL 7615/7608) – similar to MultiAc Nylon String With Synth Access, except has rosewood fingerboard, L.R. Baggs Duet system (ribbon transducer and internal microphone), available in Natural semi-gloss finish, disc. 2008.

	N/A	$750 - 900	$475 - 550	$1,640

* **MultiAc Nylon Duet Custom Shop** – similar to MultiAc Nylon Duet, except has ebony fingerboard, abalone bound body/neck/headstock, abalone bridge inlay, available in Black (4836) and Natural (4843) High Gloss finish, mfg. 1998-99.

	N/A	$1,300 - 1,500	$775 - 900	$2,745

MULTIAC NYLON DUET AMBIANCE (MODEL 032266) – nylon string configuration, single cutaway chambered mahogany body, solid spruce top, mahogany neck, 22-fret ebony fingerboard with offset dot inlays, slotted headstock with "R. Godin" signature logo, three-per-side open-style gold tuners with pearloid buttons, rosewood tied bridge, Custom Fishman electronics, under-saddle transducer, blendable sound imaging mic with four individual mic settings, volume, treble, mid, bass, and blend control sliders, available in Natural Semi-gloss finish (032266), 1.9 in. nut width, 25.5 in. scale, gig bag included, mfg. mid-2011-present.

MSR $1,895	$1,580	$850 - 1,050	$500 - 625	

MULTIAC NYLON ENCORE (MODEL 035045) – nylon string configuration, single cutaway chambered silver leaf maple body, solid cedar top, mahogany neck, 22-fret rosewood fingerboard with offset dot inlays, slotted headstock with "R. Godin" signature logo, three-per-side open-style gold tuners with pearloid buttons, rosewood tied bridge, blendable custom dual source electronics with under-saddle transducer and acoustic soundboard transducer, volume, treble, mid, bass, and blend control sliders, available in Natural Semi-gloss finish (035045), 1.875 in. nut width, 25.5 in. scale, mfg. 2011-present.

MSR $1,045	$850	$475 - 575	$275 - 325	

* **Multiac Nylon Encore Left-Handed (035878)** – similar to the Multiac Nylong Encore, except in left-handed configuration, available in Natural Semi-gloss finish, mfg. 2012-present.

MSR $1,145	$950	$500 - 625	$300 - 375	

MSR/NOTES	100%	EXCELLENT	AVERAGE	LAST MSR

MULTIAC STEEL STRING WITH SYNTH ACCESS (MODEL 4812/4775) – steel string configuration single cutaway two-chambered mahogany body, bound spruce top, mahogany neck, 22-fret ebony fingerboard with offset dot inlay, five small soundholes on upper bass bout, slotted peghead with "R. Godin" signature logo, three-per-side gold tuners with pearloid buttons, rosewood tied bridge, six individual micro transducer bridge saddles, RMC hexaphonic multi-sensors, volume/three-band EQ/synth volume slider controls, two synth (program up/down) push buttons, on-board preamp, 13-pin connector for Roland GR series guitar synths, available in Natural semi-gloss finish, 25.5 in. scale, disc. 2010.

	$1,350	$775 - 925	$475 - 550	$1,640

- Add 10% for Blue (disc., Model 7905) or CognacBurst (disc., Model 7912) finish.

* *MultiAc Steel Duet (Model 7646/7639)* – similar to MultiAc Steel String With Synth Access, except has rosewood fingerboard, L.R. Baggs Duet system (ribbon transducer and internal microphone), available in Natural semi-gloss finish, disc. 2010.

	$1,350	$775 - 925	$475 - 550	$1,640

- Add 10% for Blue (disc., Model 7899) or CognacBurst (disc., Model 7622) finish.

* *MultiAc Steel Duet Custom Shop* – similar to MultiAc Steel Duet, except has ebony fingerboard, abalone bound body/neck/head stock, abalone bridge inlay, available in Black (4881) or Natural (4898) high-gloss finish, mfg. 1998-99.

	N/A	$1,300 - 1,500	$775 - 900	$2,845

MULTIAC STEEL DUET AMBIANCE – single cutaway chambered mahogany body, solid spruce top, mahogany neck, 22-fret ebony fingerboard with offset dot inlays, slotted headstock with "R. Godin" signature logo, three-per-side open-style gold tuners with pearloid buttons, rosewood tied bridge, Custom Fishman electronics, under-saddle transducer, blendable sound imaging mic with four individual mic settings, volume, treble, mid, bass, and blend control sliders, available in Sunburst (035953) or Trans. Red (035946) High-gloss finish, 1.715 in. nut width, 25.5 in. scale, gig bag included, mfg. 2012-present.

MSR $1,895	$1,580	$850 - 1,050	$500 - 625	

MULTIAC SPECTRUM STEEL STRING – single cutaway chambered mahogany body, solid spruce top, mahogany neck, 22-fret ebony fingerboard with small offset dot inlays, slotted headstock, three-per-side open-style tuners, ebony bridge, single Seymour Duncan lipstick pickup with separate volume and tone controls, custom RMC electronics with 13-pin output for computer access, chrome hardware, available in Black (31245), Cognac Burst/Lightburst (2008-2011, 31221), or Natural (31238) high-gloss finish, 25.5 in. scale, mfg. 2008-present.

MSR $1,995	$1,580	$850 - 1,050	$500 - 625	

ACOUSTIC: MISC. MODELS

5TH AVENUE ARCHTOP ACOUSTIC – non-cutaway body, Canadian wild cherry top, back, and sides, two f-holes, cream body binding, silver leaf maple neck, 14/21-fret rosewood fingerboard with dot inlays up to the 12th fret, contoured high-gloss headstock, three-per-side chrome tuners, adj. rosewood bridge, trapeze tailpiece, raised pickguard, available in Black (Model 31276), Cognac Burst (31252), or Natural (31269) finish, 16 in. body width, 24.84 in. scale, mfg. 2008-present.

MSR $655	$550	$300 - 375	$175 - 225	

- Add 27.5% (MSR $825) for a floating P-90 pickup with two knobs (v, tone).

MULTIOUD (MODEL 035014) – 11-string configuration, based on the Middle-Eastern Oud 11-string guitar, single cutaway two-chambered mahogany body, solid spruce top, 10 small round and 5 slotted soundholes, multi-ply body binding, mahogany neck, ebony fretless fingerboard, slotted headstock, 5/6-per-side open-style chrome tuners, rosewood tied bridge, custom voiced electronics with bridge and microphone options, Fishman Aura electronics with built-in chromatic tuner, available in Natural high-gloss (035014) finish, 1.6 in. nut width, 23.03 in. scale, mfg. 2011-present.

MSR $1,945	$1,600	$900 - 1,100	$525 - 625	

* *Multioud Fretted (Model 036493)* – similar to the Multioud, except has a fretted fingerboard, mfg. 2012-present.

MSR $1,945	$1,600	$900 - 1,100	$525 - 625	

* *Multioud Steel-String (Model 036509)* – similar to the Multioud, except in steel-string configuration, mfg. 2012-present.

MSR $1,945	$1,600	$900 - 1,100	$525 - 625	

ACOUSTIC ELECTRIC BASS

A 4 SEMI-ACOUSTIC BASS – single rounded cutaway semi-hollow chambered maple body, solid cedar top, maple neck, 22-fret rosewood fingerboard with offset dot inlay, blackface peghead with Godin logo, four-on-one-side gold tuners, strings-through rosewood bridge, L.R. Baggs ribbon transducer, volume/three-band EQ slider controls, onboard preamp, available in Black (10585), CognacBurst (10141), or Natural (10134) Semi Gloss finish, 34 in. scale, disc. 2004.

	N/A	$425 - 500	$250 - 300	$996

- Add 10% for Black High Gloss finish.

* *A 4 Semi-Acoustic Fretless Bass* – similar to the A 4 Semi-Acoustic Bass, except features a fretless ebony fingerboard, available in Black (10578), CognacBurst (10165), or Natural (10158) semi-gloss finish, disc. 2006.

	N/A	$550 - 650	$275 - 325	$1,142

- Add 10% for Black High Gloss finish.

MSR/NOTES	100%	EXCELLENT	AVERAGE	LAST MSR

* *A 4 Semi-Acoustic Bass With Synth Access* – similar to the A 4 Semi-Acoustic Bass, has custom RMC electronics with a 13-pin output for Roland and many other Synth devices, available in Natural finish (28627), mfg. 2006-2011.

	$1,000	$600 - 700	$325 - 375	$1,196

- **Add 10% (Last MSR was $1,296) for fretless configuration with an ebony fingerboard (Model 28627).**

»*A 4 Ultra Semi-Acoustic Bass With Synth Access* – similar to the A 4 Semi-Acoustic Bass with Synth Access, except has an additional Lace Sensor Low-Profile pickup with side-mounted volume and tone knobs, available in Natural finish (33652), mfg. 2010-present.

MSR $1,395	$1,150	$625 - 750	$350 - 425	

- **Add 10% (MSR $1,495) for fretless configuration with an ebony fingerboard (Model 33645).**

A 5 SEMI-ACOUSTIC BASS FIVE-STRING (MODEL 10585/16556) – similar to Model A 4, except in a five-string configuration, available in high-gloss Black, semi-gloss Natural or Cognac Burst finish, mfg. 2000-04.

	N/A	$500 - 600	$300 - 350	$1,146

* *A 5 Semi-Acoustic Fretless Bass Five-String (Model 16587)* – similar to the A-5, except in fretless configuration, mfg. 2003-06.

	N/A	$650 - 750	$375 - 450	$1,298

* *A 5 Semi-Acoustic Bass With Synth Access Five-String* – similar to the A 5 Semi-Acoustic Bass, has custom RMC electronics with a 13-pin output for Roland and many other Synth devices, available in Natural finish (28771), mfg. 2006-2011.

	$1,100	$650 - 750	$350 - 425	$1,346

- **Add 10% (Last MSR was $1,446) for fretless configuration with an ebony fingerboard (Model 28634).**

»*A 5 Ultra Semi-Acoustic Bass With Synth Access Five-String* – similar to the A 5 Semi-Acoustic Bass with Synth Access, except has an additional Lace Sensor Low-Profile pickup with side-mounted volume and tone knobs, available in Natural finish (33621), mfg. 2010-present.

MSR $1,545	$1,300	$700 - 850	$400 - 475	

- **Add 7.5% (MSR $1,645) for fretless configuration with an ebony fingerboard (Model 33638).**

ACOUSTIBASS – single cutaway routed out maple body, bound spruce top, thumb rest, bolt-on maple neck, fretless ebony fingerboard, strings-through ebony bridge, four-per-side gold tuners, piezo bridge pickup, four-band EQ, available in Aqua, Black or White finishes, disc. 1996.

	N/A	$450 - 525	$275 - 325	$1,060

* *AcoustiBass Deluxe (Model 3754)* – similar to AcoustiBass, except has routed out mahogany body, available in Cherryburst, Cognacburst and Natural finishes, disc. 1998.

	N/A	$525 - 625	$325 - 375	$1,159

GOLDENTONE

Instruments previously produced in Japan during the 1960s.

The Goldentone trademark was used by U.S. importer Elger and its partner Hoshino Gakki Ten as one of the brand names used in their joint guitar producing venture. Hoshino in Japan was shipping Fuji Gen Gakki-built guitars marketed in the U.S. as Goldentone, Elger, and eventually Ibanez. These guitars featured original body designs in the early to mid-1960s. Source: Michael Wright, *Guitar Stories*, Volume One.

GOODALL GUITARS

Instruments currently built in Fort Bragg, CA. Distributed by Goodall Guitars, Inc. in Fort Bragg, CA.

CONTACT INFORMATION
GOODALL GUITARS
541 South Franklin Street
Fort Bragg, CA 95437
Phone No.: 707-962-1620
www.goodallguitars.com
contact@goodallguitars.com

Luthier James Goodall grew up in Spring Valley, California. Apparently, there must be something in the water, for a number of high profile luthiers (such as Greg Deering, Geoff Stelling, and Larry and Kim Breedlove) have sprung from the same area. Prior to building his first acoustic guitar, Goodall's woodworking experience was limited to his surfboard building during high school (of course, having a father with wood carving knowledge certainly helps). After his initial success, Goodall began building guitars for friends, which lead to a backlog of orders by the mid-1970s. Goodall moved to full-time guitar building in 1972.

In 1984, Goodall relocated his shop to Mendocino, California. From 1984 to 1992, he produced an average of around forty guitars a year. From 1992 to 2008, Goodall moved off the continental U.S. to Kailua-Kona, Hawaii. His shop had nine employees, and shipped ten instruments a week. In 2009, Goodall moved back to the California from Hawaii and continues to build instruments in Fort Bragg, CA. For further information regarding pricing, specifications, and dealer listings please visit Goodall Guitars' website or contact them directly.

Goodall builds steel and nylon string guitars and offers a wide range of custom options, including wood choices, fingerboard inlay, and body binding. Fine woods of maple, myrtle, bubinga, palo escrito, Honduran rosewood, cocobolo, Macassar ebony, quilted mahogany, or Brazilian rosewood back and sides. Top woods include adirondack, Sitka, engelmann, Port Orford white cedar, redwood, cedar, koa, mahogany, German or Italian spruce.

The following prices and descriptions apply to the following models: **Parlor** (14 in. bout, 25 in. scale), **Grand Concert** (15 in. bout), **Concert Jumbo** (15.875 in. bout), **Standard** (16 in. bout), and **Jumbo** (17 in. bout) Series. These guitars feature: Alaskan Sitka spruce top, round soundhole, abalone rosette, ebony binding, 14/20-fret ebony fingerboard with abalone dot inlays, ebony bridge with black white dot pins, three-per-side chrome Gotoh tuners, available in natural finish (with satin finish neck), current mfg. Prices are $5,700 for mahogany back and sides with rosewood or maple binding, $5,700 for East Indian Rosewood back and sides, with curly koa binding, $6,700 for curly koa back/sides with rosewood or curly maple binding, $6,200 for curly maple back and sides with rosewood or curly koa binding, and $6,200 for curly walnut back and sides with curly maple binding. Add $400 for the Jumbo. Add $800 for the Jumbo Baritone.

The **Royal Hawaiian** has curly Koa top/back/sides, pearl rosette with island scene fretboard inlay, ebony fretboard and bridge, and peghead venner, gold Gotoh tuners with ebony buttons, purpleheard wood bindings, 1.75 in. satin finish neck, 25.5 in. scale, and comes in natural finish. The Royal Hawaiian is available in all box sizes for a retail price of $9,500.

The **Traditional OM** and **Dreadnought** models feature: mahogany or East Indian rosewood back and sides, herringbone rosette and top purfling, chevron marquetry backstrip, MOP notched square fretboard inlay, ebony peghead, tortise pickguard, nickel Waverly tuners with ivoroid or ebony knobs, 1.75 in. or 1.69 in. neck width, 25.5 in. scale, and maple binding. These guitars retail for $6,200 with a bear claw Sitka spruce top, and $7,000 for an Adirondack spruce top. Add $400 for 28 in. scale baritone configuration.

The **Aloha** model features a solid Sitka spruce top, koa or mahogany back & sides, rosewood fretboard & bridge, koa peghead veneer, pearl inlay with MOP dots, chrome Gotoh tuners, 25.5 in. scale, and ebony binding. This guitar is available in all box sizes, and retails for $5,200.

The **Pacific** model features a master red cedar top, AAA curly maple back and sides, dark curly koa B/N/H binding, fancy abalone rosette, MOP notched square fingerboard and bridge inlays, and a curly maple headstock veneer with gold tuners with ebony buttons. This guitar is available in Parlor (25 in. scale) or Grand Concert (25.5 in. scale) sizes and retails for $7,500.

The **Crossover Nylon String** model features a red cedar or Port Orford white cedar top, AAA East Indian rosewood or Palo Escrito back and sides, radial cut padauk wood rosette, no fingerboard inlays, an ebony slotted headstock with precision ebony tuners, and a clear pickguard. This guitar has a 14-fret neck, 25.5 in. scale, and retails for $8,000.

- Add $200 for left-handed configuration.
- Add $600 for 12-string configuration.
- Add $800 for a bent cutaway body configuration.
- Add $900 for a sharp cutaway body configuration.

GOODMAN

Instruments previously produced in the early 1960s. See chapter on House Brands.

The Goodman trademark has been identified as a House Brand of the Goodman Community Discount Center, between circa 1961 and 1964. Previously, the company used the trademark of Globe. Source: Willie G. Moseley, *Stellas & Stratocasters*.

GOODMAN GUITARS

Instruments currently built in Brewster, NY.

Luthier Brad Goodman took to woodworking in his early childhood, and by the end of high school had completed several guitars and mandolins. Over the past twenty years, Goodman has continued to refine his guitar building skills by building lutes, mandolins, and acoustic flattop and archtop guitars. Goodman is currently focusing on a series of archtop models.

Goodman archtops have similar construction features like AAA figured maple back and sides, Sitka spruce tops, three-piece curly maple necks, ebony fingerboard/tailpiece/bridge/pickguard/peghead veneers. Instruments also feature multiple-layer binding, abalone side dots, gold Schaller tuners, and clear lacquer finishes. Acoustic flattops started at $2,000 and acoustic archtops started at $2,800. Goodman also has a business that sells instrument wood. For more information visit Goodman's website or contact him directly.

GOWER

Instruments previously produced in Nashville, TN between 1955 and the 1960s.

Luthier J.W. Gower began building custom acoustic and electric guitars out of his garage in 1955. His son Randy would later come on to work with him as they began to mass-produce an acoustic line of guitars. In the mid-1960s, Gower, Billy Grammer, and Clyde Reid formed a partnership (RG&G) to build a good acoustic guitar at a fair price. Gower built the first prototype and many of this family members also worked at the Grammer factory. By 1967, Gower had left Grammer to work on his own guitars. It is unknown how long Gower produced guitars after he left Grammer.

Very little specific model information is known about Gower guitars. Most acoustics feature a square-shouldered dreadnought body shape and examples have varied with wood types and options. Used values on these guitars ranged between $1,000 and $1,500 in excellent condition.

MSR/NOTES	100%	EXCELLENT	AVERAGE	LAST MSR

GOYA

Guitars previously produced in Sweden between the late 1950s and the early-1970s, in Japan, Korea, and Taiwan between the early 1970s and 1996. Distributed by Hershman Musical Instrument Company in New York, NY between the late 1950s and 1970, by Kustom Electronics, Inc. between 1970 and 1972, by Dude Inc. between 1972 and 1976, and by The Martin Guitar Company in Nazareth, PA between 1976 and 1996.

The Goya trademark was originally used by the Hershman Musical Instrument Company in New York City, NY in the 1950s on models built by Sweden's Levin company (similar models were sold in Europe under the company's Levin trademark). Levin built high quality acoustic flattop, classical, and archtop guitars as well as mandolins. A large number of rebranded Goya instruments were imported to the U.S. market.

In the late 1950s, solid body electric guitars and basses built by Hagstrom (also a Swedish company) were rebranded Goya and distributed in the U.S. as well. In 1963 the company changed its name to the Goya Musical Instrument Corporation.

Goya was purchased by Avnet (see Guild) in 1966, and continued to import instruments such as the Rangemaster in 1967. By the late 1960s, electric solid body guitars and basses were then being built in Italy by the EKO company. Avnet then sold the Goya trademark to Kustom Electronics. It has been estimated that the later Goya instruments of the 1970s were built in Japan.

The C.F. Martin company later acquired the Levin company, and bought the rights to the Goya trademark from a company named Dude, Inc. in 1976. Martin imported a number of guitar, mandolin, and banjo string instruments from the 1970s through to 1996. While this trademark is currently discontinued, the rights to the name are still held by the Martin Guitar company.

The Goya company featured a number of innovations that most people are not aware of. Goya was the first classic guitar line to put the trademark name on the headstock, and also created the ball end classic guitar string. Levin-Era Goya models feature interior paper label with the Goya trademark in a cursive style, and designated "Made by A.B. Herman Carlson Levin - Gothenburg, Sweden." Model and serial number appear on the label, as well as on the neck block.

ACOUSTIC: 1960S-1970S MFG.

G-10 – classical style, figured birch back and sides, clear spruce top, plastic ebony top body binding, round soundhole with multi-colored inlay, slotted headstock, three-per-side tuners, brass hardware, Natural finish, mfg. 1960s.

	N/A	$200 - 250	$120 - 150	

This model was also available in a 3/4 size.

G-13 – classical style, mahogany back/sides/neck, Alp spruce top, black and white body binding, round soundhole with multi-colored inlay, rosewood fingerboard, slotted headstock, three-per-side tuners, nickel hardware, Natural finish, mfg. 1960s.

	N/A	$250 - 300	$150 - 190	

G-17 – classical grand concert size style, mahogany back/sides/neck, Alp spruce top, black and decorative body binding, round soundhole with multi-colored inlay, truss-rod in neck, rosewood fingerboard, slotted headstock, three-per-side tuners, rosewood bridge, nickel hardware, Natural finish, mfg. 1960s.

	N/A	$275 - 350	$160 - 210	

ACOUSTIC

G-1 – classic style, spruce ply top, round soundhole, bound body, rosette decal, mahogany stain ply back/sides, nato neck, 12/19-fret ebonized fingerboard, ebonized tied bridge, three-per-side chrome tuners with white buttons, available in Natural finish, disc. 1996.

	N/A	$60 - 80	$35 - 50	$115

G-2 – similar to the G-1, except has rosewood stain ply back/sides, three-per-side chrome tuners with pearloid buttons, available in Natural finish, disc. 1996.

	N/A	$75 - 100	$40 - 60	$155

G-3 – dreadnought style, spruce ply top, round soundhole, black pickguard, bound body, rosette decal, mahogany stain ply back/sides, nato neck, 14/20-fret ebonized fingerboard with pearl dot inlay, ebonized bridge with white pins, screened peghead logo, three-per-side chrome diecast tuners, available in Natural finish, disc. 1996.

	N/A	$65 - 85	$40 - 50	$135

G-4 – similar to the G-3, except has rosewood stain ply back/sides, rosewood bridge with white pins, available in Natural finish, disc. 1996.

	N/A	$80 - 110	$45 - 65	$170

G-120 – classic style, spruce top, round soundhole, bound body, wood inlay rosette, mahogany back/sides/neck, 12/18-fret rosewood fingerboard, rosewood tied bridge, three-per-side chrome tuners, available in Natural finish, disc. 1996.

	N/A	$120 - 150	$70 - 95	$260

G-125 – similar to the G-120, except has a 12/19-fret rosewood fingerboard, available in Natural finish, disc. 1996.

	N/A	$130 - 160	$70 - 95	$290

G-145 – classic style, cedar top, round soundhole, bound body, wood inlay rosette, rosewood back/sides, mahogany neck, 12/19-fret rosewood fingerboard, rosewood tied bridge, three-per-side gold tuners, available in Natural finish, disc. 1996.

	N/A	$175 - 225	$100 - 130	$350

MSR/NOTES	100%	EXCELLENT	AVERAGE	LAST MSR

* **G-145 S** – similar to G-145, except has solid cedar top, disc. 1996.

| | N/A | $200 - 250 | $120 - 150 | |

G-215 – grand concert style, spruce top, round soundhole, black pickguard, three-stripe bound body/rosette, mahogany back/sides/neck, 14/20-fret rosewood fingerboard with pearl dot inlay, rosewood bridge with white black dot pins, rosewood veneered peghead with screened logo, three-per-side chrome tuners, available in Natural finish, disc. 1996.

| | N/A | $160 - 210 | $90 - 120 | $330 |

* **G-215 L** – similar to the G-215, except in left-handed configuration, disc. 1996.

| | N/A | $160 - 210 | $90 - 120 | $350 |

G-230 S – similar to G-215, except has solid spruce top, tortoiseshell pickguard, gold tuners, disc. 1996.

| | N/A | $180 - 230 | $110 - 140 | $405 |

G-300 – dreadnought style, spruce top, round soundhole, black pickguard, bound body, three-stripe rosette, mahogany back/sides/neck, 14/20-fret rosewood fingerboard with pearl dot inlay, rosewood bridge with black white dot pins, screened peghead logo, three-per-side diecast tuners, available in Natural or Sunburst finish, disc. 1996.

| | N/A | $130 - 160 | $70 - 95 | $300 |

* **G-300 L** – similar to the G-300, except in left-handed configuration, disc. 1996.

| | N/A | $130 - 160 | $70 - 95 | $320 |

G-312 – similar to the G-300, except has three-stripe bound body/rosette, three-per-side chrome tuners, available in Natural or Sunburst finish, disc. 1996.

| | N/A | $175 - 225 | $100 - 130 | $360 |

G-316 H – dreadnought style, spruce top, round soundhole, tortoise pickguard, herringbone bound body/rosette, rosewood back/sides, mahogany neck, 14/20-fret rosewood fingerboard with pearl dot inlay, rosewood bridge with white black dot pins, screened peghead logo, three-per-side chrome tuners, available in Natural finish, disc. 1996.

| | N/A | $200 - 250 | $110 - 140 | $480 |

G-318 C – single round cutaway dreadnought style, spruce top, round soundhole, black pickguard, three-stripe bound body/rosette, mahogany back/sides/neck, 14/20-fret rosewood fingerboard with pearl dot inlay, rosewood bridge with black white dot pins, screened peghead logo, three-per-side chrome tuners, available in Natural finish, disc. 1996.

| | N/A | $175 - 225 | $100 - 130 | $375 |

G-330 S – dreadnought style, solid spruce top, round soundhole, tortoiseshell pickguard, multibound body/rosette, rosewood back/sides/neck, 14/20-fret bound ebonized rosewood fingerboard with pearl dot inlay, rosewood bridge with white black dot pins, bound peghead with pearl torch inlay, three-per-side gold tuners, available in Natural finish, disc. 1996.

| | N/A | $250 - 300 | $130 - 160 | $555 |

G-335 S – similar to the G-330 S, except has herringbone bound body/rosette, rosewood back/sides, mahogany neck, 14/20-fret bound rosewood fingerboard with pearl snowflake/tree of life inlay, available in Natural finish, disc. 1996.

| | N/A | $250 - 300 | $140 - 170 | $580 |

G-415 – dreadnought style, spruce top, round soundhole, black pickguard, multibound body/rosette, mahogany back/sides/neck, 14/20-fret rosewood fingerboard with pearl dot inlay, rosewood bridge with black white dot pins, screened peghead logo, six-per-side chrome tuners, available in Natural finish, disc. 1996.

| | N/A | $180 - 230 | $110 - 140 | $390 |

ACOUSTIC ELECTRIC

G-312 E – dreadnought style, spruce top, round soundhole, black pickguard, bound body, three-stripe rosette, mahogany back/sides/neck, 14/20-fret rosewood fingerboard with pearl dot inlay, rosewood bridge with black white dot pins, screened peghead logo, three-per-side diecast tuners, piezo bridge pickup, volume/tone controls, available in Natural finish, disc. 1996.

| | N/A | $200 - 250 | $110 - 140 | $475 |

G-318 CE – single round cutaway dreadnought style, spruce top, round soundhole, black pickguard, three-stripe bound body/rosette, mahogany back/sides/neck, 14/20-fret rosewood fingerboard with pearl dot inlay, rosewood bridge with black white dot pins, screened peghead logo, three-per-side chrome tuners, piezo bridge pickup, volume/tone control, available in Natural finish, disc. 1996.

| | N/A | $225 - 275 | $130 - 160 | $515 |

G-500 – single round cutaway hollow style, round soundhole, multibound body/rosette, mahogany back/sides/neck, 20-fret bound rosewood fingerboard with pearl dot inlay, rosewood bridge with white black dot pins, bound peghead with screened logo, three-per-side chrome tuners, piezo bridge pickup, three-band EQ, available in Black, Blueburst, or Natural finish, disc. 1996.

| | N/A | $275 - 325 | $150 - 200 | $600 |

MSR/NOTES	100%	EXCELLENT	AVERAGE	LAST MSR

G-600 – single sharp cutaway Dreadnought body, spruce top, round soundhole, black pickguard, multibound body/rosette, mahogany back/sides/neck, 14/20-fret rosewood fingerboard with pearl dot inlay, rosewood bridge with black white dot pins, bound peghead with screened logo, three-per-side chrome tuners, piezo bridge pickup, three-band EQ, available in Black or Natural finish, disc. 1996.

	N/A	$275 - 325	$150 - 200	$580

GRACIA GUITARS

Instruments currently produced in Buenos Aires, Argentina. Distributed in the U.S. by the Port Bourbon Trading Company in Carlisle, KY. Previously distributed by California Guitar Works in Huntington Beach, CA.

Gracia guitars was founded by Don Dionisio Garcia and they have been produced since the 1950s. Gracia produces a large quantity of nylon string classical guitars as well as a few select steel string models. Models range in prices from $280 to $1,300. For more information contact the distribution company via email.

CONTACT INFORMATION
GRACIA GUITARS
Distributor: Port Bourbon Trading Company
PO Box 329
Carlisle, KY 40311
Phone No.: 859-473-3100
portbourbontrading@gmail.com

GRAF, OSKAR

Instruments previously built in Clarendon, Ontario (Canada) between 1970 and 2013.

Luthier Oskar Graf has handcrafted classical and steel-string acoustic guitars since the late 1960s. In addition, Graf offered acoustic bass guitars, solid body upright string basses, eight- and ten-string classical guitars as well as custom designs and restorations. Graf has also built flamenco-style guitars and lutes through the years, and estimates that he has produced maybe 400 guitars (mostly as commissioned pieces). Instruments feature cedar and spruce tops, and rosewood and koa backs and sides. Graf is now officially retired, but may still build an occasional instrument from time to time (and possibly sell it!) For more information, visit Graf's website or contact him directly.

All Oskar Graf instruments need to be appraised and evaluated on a case-by-case basis. Most used instruments start at $10,000 and go up from there.

CONTACT INFORMATION
GRAF, OSKAR
PO Box 2502
Clarendon, Ontario K0H 1J0 Canada
Phone No.: 613-279-2610
www.grafguitars.com
oskar@grafguitars.com

GRAMMER

Instruments previously built in Nashville, TN circa early 1960s until 1971.

RG & G was founded in the Spring of 1965 in Nashville, Tennessee, by Grand Ole Opry performer Billy Grammer. The company was very active in the Nashville area, and many local performers used these acoustic guitars during the 1960s. The factory burned down in April, 1968 and was rebuilt in June, 1968. RG & G was reformed as Grammer Guitars in the fall of 1968.

The Grammer Guitar company was later sold to Ampeg (circa unknown, late 1960s), and the later models have an Ampeg "A" logo on the front of the headstock below the Grammer name. Grammer went out of business in 1971; the company's assets (but not the trademark name) were sold at a bankruptcy auction the same year. Billy Grammer died on August 10, 2011 after a long illness. Sources: George Gruhn, *Vintage Guitar Magazine*, Walter Murray of *Frankenstein Fretworks*, and Tom Wheeler, *American Guitars*.

ACOUSTIC

In general, Grammer guitars can be distinguished by their batwing-shaped headstock and typically feature a crown-shaped bridge, although some may have a moustache bridge. They feature solid spruce tops, and the fingerboard inlay has dot fretmarkers with double dots at frets 3, 7, and 17 and triple dots at 12 position. The pickguards and headstock overlays were layered black on white plastic. The pickguards were asymetrical and the headstock features the name "The Grammer Guitar." Most guitars were finished in Natural but there were some unusual colorations used such as a greenburst and a bright yellow clearcoat. Chrome Grover Roto-Matic tuners were standard on most models. Early models made under RG & G ownership have a paper label in the soundhole that reads RG & G on the label. Besides the G Series that is listed, Grammer also produced the slightly smaller S Series, the 12-String R Series, the tenor T Series, and the baby B Series.

G-10 – dreadnought style, Alpine spruce top, Brazilian rosewood back and sides, cherry neck, 20-fret ebony fingerboard with dot inlays, inlaid veneer headstock, three-per-side tuners, ebony bridge, large black pickguard, available in Natural finish, 15.5 in. lower body width, 24.625 in. scale, mfg. mid-1960s-early 1970s.

	N/A	$1,650 - 2,000	$1,000 - 1,200	

G-20 – dreadnought style, Alpine spruce top, maple back and sides, maple neck, 20-fret rosewood fingerboard with dot inlays, inlaid veneer headstock, three-per-side tuners, rosewood bridge, large black pickguard, available in Blue Sunburst, Green Sunburst, Natural, Sunburst, or Red Sunburst finish, 15.5 in. lower body width, 24.625 in. scale, mfg. mid-1960s-early 1970s.

	N/A	$1,550 - 1,800	$950 - 1,100	

G-30 – dreadnought style, Sitka spruce top, mahogany back and sides, mahogany neck, 20-fret rosewood fingerboard with dot inlays, inlaid veneer headstock, three-per-side tuners, rosewood bridge, large black pickguard, available in Natural or Sunburst finish, 15.5 in. lower body width, 24.625 in. scale, mfg. mid-1960s-early 1970s.

	N/A	$1,350 - 1,600	$900 - 1,050	

MSR/NOTES	100%	EXCELLENT	AVERAGE	LAST MSR

G-40 – dreadnought style, Alpine spruce top, exotic wood back and sides including Prima Vera, Satinwood, and Avodire, matching exotic wood neck, 20-fret ebony fingerboard with dot inlays, inlaid veneer headstock, three-per-side tuners, ebony bridge, large black pickguard, available in Natural finish, 15.5 in. lower body width, 24.625 in. scale, mfg. mid-1960s-early 1970s.

| | N/A | $1,650 - 2,000 | $1,000 - 1,200 | |

Grammer used this model as their custom model, and it is possible to find custom appointments not listed.

JOHNNY CASH MODEL – features a gray/black "Silverburst" finish, Brazilian rosewood back and sides.

| | N/A | $2,000 - 2,500 | $1,300 - 1,650 | |

Johnny Cash's Grammar Guitar sold at auction in 2004 for $131,000.

MERLE HAGGARD MODEL – features a slotted headstock with rear-facing tuners, Brazilian rosewood back and sides with a blonde center stripe on the back, spruce top, has Merle Haggard in white script writing on the headstock.

| | N/A | $1,250 - 1,500 | $800 - 900 | |

GRAND

Instruments currently produced in China. Distributed by Grand International in Hong Kong.

Grand produces entry level dreadnoughts, classicals, and acoustic basses. There are various models and options offered. For more information, visit Grand's website or contact them directly.

CONTACT INFORMATION
GRAND
www.grandintl.com
info@grandintl.com

GRANDE

Instruments previously built in Japan during the mid- to late 1970s. Imported by Jerry O'Hagan in St. Louis Park, MN.

Between 1975 and 1979, Jerry O'Hagan imported the Japanese-built Grande acoustic guitars to the U.S. market. O'Hagan later went on to produce the American-built solid body electric O'Hagan guitars between 1979 and 1983. Source: Michael Wright, *Guitar Stories*, Volume One.

GRANT

Instruments previously produced in Japan from the 1970s through the 1980s.

The Grant trademark was the brandname of a UK importer, and the guitars were medium quality copies of American designs. Source: Tony Bacon and Paul Day, *The Guru's Guitar Guide*.

GRANTSON

Instruments previously produced in Japan during the mid-1970s.

These entry level guitars featured designs based on popular American models. Source: Tony Bacon and Paul Day, *The Guru's Guitar Guide*.

GRD (GUITAR RESEARCH AND DESIGN)

Instruments previously built in South Strafford, VT between 1978 and 1982. Distributed initially by United Marketing International of Grapevine, TX; distribution was later retained by Guitar Research and Design.

For a full history on GRD, see the *Blue Book of Electric Guitars*. For more information on Charles Fox, see the Charles Fox section in the C section.

The 1978 GRD brochure featured six acoustic models, but also mentioned six- and ten-string classic guitars, baroque, flamenco, and smaller-sized steel stringed instruments, which were available on a custom basis. All braces are fully scalloped, tapered, and float free of the linings. The phenolic fretboard is relieved over the soundboard. Upper linings are individual tentalones, back linings are solid bent rosewood. The nut and saddle are solid brass (interchangeable saddles of bone, phenolic, and epoxy graphite were available in special order). The body/neck connection was a Spanish-style foot and shelf neck/body joint.

GRD acoustics feature a solid rosewood back and sides, peghead overlay, back linings, center web, bindings, and trim. The standard soundboard was spruce; cedar was optional. GRD necks are Honduran mahogany with the head and arm spliced instead of being band sawn from one piece. Headstocks featured three-per-side gold-plated Schaller tuners.

On-board electronics featured a transducer pickup and tone control system that required no preamp-- one pickup was mounted beneath the bridge, and the second was mounted beneath the fretboard. The on-board electronics featured volume, tone, and balance controls. The output jacks were flush mounted, and the guitars had Strap Lock fittings.

The model **F** and **F 1** were full-sized acoustics with a jumbo-esque (tight waist) body style, 660 mm scale, and 21-fret fingerboard. The F 1 model has a single Florentine-style cutaway. The **T** and **T 1** acoustics were full sized models with a dreadnought-style body, 630 mm scale, and 21-fret fingerboard. The T 1 model has a single Florentine-style cutaway. The shallow body **S 1** and **S 2** models have a 645 mm scale, and a 21-fret fingerboard. The S 1 has a single Florentine-style cutaway; the S 2 is a double (dual) cutaway body.

Prices are still relatively unknown for used GRD models because so few of them are circulating in the market.

GREAT DIVIDE GUITARS

Instruments currently produced in China since 2009. Distributed by Two Old Hippies, LLC in Spirit Lake, IA.

Tom Bedell began importing guitars from Japan in the mid-1960s under the Bedell name when he was just 14 years old. After leaving the music industry and working as a political consultant and for the Pure Fishing Company, Bedell and his wife bought The Great Divide guitar shop in Aspen, Colorado. They renamed it Two Old Hippies, and Bedell began importing guitars again under the Bedell and Great Divide Guitars names. Great Divide currently offers a full line of acoustic guitars For more information, visit Great Divide's website or contact Two Old Hippies directly.

CONTACT INFORMATION

GREAT DIVIDE GUITARS

Two Old Hippies Office
PO Box 557
Spirit Lake, IA 51360
Phone No.: 877-264-3356
www.greatdivideguitars.com
service@twooldhippies.com

Two Old Hippies Store
111 S. Monarch Street
Aspen, CO 81611
Phone No.: 970-925-7492
www.twooldhippies.com

GRECO

Instruments currently produced in Japan since the 1960s.

Greco instruments were imported to the U.S. through Goya Guitars/Avnet. Avnet was the same major company that also acquired Guild in 1966. Source: Michael Wright, *Guitar Stories*, Volume One.

GREENFIELD GUITARS

Guitars currently produced in Montreal, Quebec, Canada since 1997.

Luthier Michael Greenfield builds acoustic guitars out of his Montreal shop. Each guitar is individually is crafted and constructed by Greenfield, and he uses the finest materials in his guitars. Because of this care to detail, he only produces twelve guitars a year. Acoustic models include steel-strings and nylon-strings.

GREEN MOUNTAIN GUITARS

Instruments currently built in Bradford, VT.

Green Mountain Guitars was started by Glen DeRusha, and is currently run by him and his family. Glen grew up in Cloquet, MN and loved to play guitar and craft things out of wood. He worked for years building furniture and cabinets. Glen attended Roberto-Venn school of Luthiery in Phoneix, AZ where he learned the skills and techniques for building guitars. He then repaired and restored guitars for some time when he was able to start building his own guitars. Green Mountain Guitars currently produce dreadnoughts, jumbos, and orchestra models. Prices start around $1,500. For more information visit Green Mountain's website or contact them directly.

CONTACT INFORMATION

GREEN MOUNTAIN GUITARS

39 Saddleback Road
Bradford, VT 05033
Phone No.: 802-222-9012
www.greenmountainguitars.com
glen@greenmountainguitars.com

GREMLIN

Instruments previously built in Asia. Distributed in the U.S. market by Midco International of Effingham, IL.

Gremlin guitars are designed for the entry level or student guitarist.

GRETSCH

Instruments currently produced in Japan, Korea, Indonesia, and China since 1989. Distributed by Fender Musical Instruments Corporation (FMIC) in Scottsdale, AZ since 2003. Instruments were originally produced in New York City, NY from the early 1900s to 1970, in Booneville, AR from 1970 to 1979, and various other assembly locations between 1979 and 1981. Previously distributed by the Fred Gretsch Company of Savannah, GA from 1989 to 2002.

Friedrich Gretsch was born in 1856, and emigrated to America when he was 16. In 1883 he founded a musical instrument shop in Brooklyn which prospered. The Fred Gretsch Company began manufacturing instruments in 1883 (while Friedrich maintained his proper name, he "Americanized" it for the company). Gretsch passed away unexpectedly (at age 39) during a trip to Germany in April 1895, and his son Fred (often referred to as Fred Gretsch, Jr. in company histories) took over the family business (at 15!). Gretsch Sr. expanded the business considerably by 1916. Beginning with percussion, ukuleles, and banjos, Gretsch introduced guitars in the early 1930s, developing a well respected line of archtop orchestra models. In 1926 the company acquired the rights to K. Zildjian Cymbals, and debuted the Gretsch tenor guitar. During the Christmas season of 1929, the production capacity was reported to be 100,000 instruments (stringed instruments and drums); and a new midwestern branch was opened in Chicago, Illinois. In March of 1940 Gretsch acquired the B & D trademark from the Bacon Banjo Corporation. Fred Gretsch, Sr. retired in 1942.

William Walter Gretsch assumed the presidency of the company until 1948, and then Fred Gretsch, Jr. took over the position. Gretsch, Jr. was the primary president during the great Gretsch heyday, and was ably assisted by such notables as Jimmy Webster and Charles "Duke" Kramer (Kramer was involved with the Gretsch company from 1935 to his retirement in 1980, and was even involved after his retirement!). During the 1950s, the majority of Gretsch's guitar line was focused on electric six-

CONTACT INFORMATION

GRETSCH

A division of FMIC
8860 East Chaparral Road, Ste. 100
Scottsdale, AZ 85250-2610
Phone No.: 480-596-9690
Fax No.: 480-596-1384
www.gretschguitars.com
custserve@fenderusa.com

MSR/NOTES	100%	EXCELLENT	AVERAGE	LAST MSR

string Spanish instruments. With the endorsement of Chet Atkins and George Harrison, Gretsch electrics became very popular with both country and rock 'n roll musicians through the 1960s.

Outbid in their attempt to buy Fender in 1965, the D.H. Baldwin company bought Gretsch in 1967, and Gretsch, Jr. was made a director of Baldwin. Baldwin had previously acquired the manufacturing facilities of England's James Ormstron Burns (Burns Guitars) in September 1965, and Baldwin was assembling the imported Burns parts in Booneville, Arkansas. In a business consolidation, The New York Gretsch operation was moved down to the Arkansas facility in 1970. Production focused on Gretsch, and Burns guitars were basically discontinued.

In January of 1973, the Booneville plant suffered a serious fire. Baldwin made the decision to discontinue guitar building operations. Three months later, long-time manager Bill Hagner formed the Hagner Musical Instruments company and formed an agreement with Baldwin to build and sell Gretsch guitars to Baldwin from the Booneville facility. Baldwin would still retain the rights to the trademark. Another fire broke out in December of the same year, but the operation recovered. Baldwin stepped in and regained control of the operation in December of 1978, the same year that they bought the Kustom Amplifier company in Chanute, Kansas. Gretsch production was briefly moved to the Kansas facility, and by 1982 they moved again to Gallatin, Tennessee. 1981 was probably the last date of guitar production, but Gretsch drum products were continued at Tennessee. In 1983 the production had again returned to Arkansas.

Baldwin had experimented briefly with guitar production at their Mexican organ facilities, producing perhaps 100 Southern Belle guitars (basically renamed Country Gentlemans) between 1978 and 1979. When Gretsch production returned to Arkansas in 1983, the Baldwin company asked Charles Kramer to come out of retirement and help bring the business back (which he did). In 1984, Baldwin also sold off their rights to Kustom amps. In 1985 Kramer brokered a deal between Baldwin and Fred Gretsch, III that returned the trademark back to the family.

Kramer and Gretsch, III developed the specifications for the reissue models that are currently being built by the Terada company in Japan.

On January 1, 2003, Gretsch guitars was sold to Fender (FMIC) as the exclusive distributor, producer, developer, and marketer of Gretsch.

Gretsch guitars are in the Fender booth now at the NAMM shows, and Fred is still consulting for Gretsch guitars. In 2010, Gretsch discontinued production on most of their acoustic guitars including the entire Rancher Series.

Charles "Duke" Kramer first joined the Gretsch company at their Chicago office in 1935. When Kramer first retired in 1980, he formed D & F Products. In late 1981, when Baldwin lost a lease on one of their small production plants, Kramer went out and bought any existing guitar parts (about three 42-foot semi-trailers worth!). While some were sold back to the revitalized Gretsch company in 1985, Kramer still made the parts available through his D & F Products company. Duke passed away on July 28, 2005 at the age of 88.

PRODUCTION MODEL CODES

The Gretsch company assigned a name and a four-digit number to each guitar model. However, they also assigned a different, yet associated number to the same model in a different color or component assembly. This system helped expedite the ordering system, says Charles Duke Kramer. You could look at an invoice and know exactly which model and color the guitar was from one number. References in this text, while still incomplete, will list variances in the model designations.

Current Gretsch models may have a G preface to the four-digit code, and also letters at the end that designate different bridge configuration (like a Bigsby tremolo), or a cutaway body style. Many of the reissue models also have a hyphen and four digit year following the primary model number designation that indicate a certain vintage-style year.

For further information regarding Gretsch electric models, please refer to the *Blue Book of Electric Guitars*. Gretsch archtop models with built-in pickups can be found in the Gretsch Electric section of the Electric edition.

ACOUSTIC ARCHTOP: 1930S-1970S MFG.

Gretsch made at least two other models (an un-named archtop and a model called the Jet 21), and information is very scarce on them. Many Gretsch acoustic guitars could be special ordered in a tenor version. Synchromatic models are the most popular/collectible Gretsch acoustic archtops - especially models with the "cat's-eye" soundholes. Crumbling and breaking binding is a very common problem with many Gretsch guitars and to find all original models with binding intact is nearly impossible.

CORSAIR (MODEL 6014/6015/6016) — carved spruce top, arched maple back, maple sides, two f-holes, single binding on top and back, three-piece maple neck, 14/20-fret rosewood fingerboard with large block, hump, or thumbnail inlays, bound headstock with three-per-side tuners, adj. rosewood bridge, "G" tailpiece, tan pickguard with no logo, available in Bordeaux Burgundy (6016), Natural (6015), or Sunburst (6014) finish, 16 in. body width, 24.5 in. scale, mfg. 1955-1960.

	100%	EXCELLENT	AVERAGE
1955-1959	N/A	$850 - 1,000	$600 - 700
1959-1960	N/A	$750 - 900	$550 - 650

• **Add 10-20% for Natural finish.**

In 1957, hump block fingerboard inlays replaced the large block inlays. In 1959, a single cutaway body design, ebony bridge, and thumbprint fingerboard inlays were introduced.

MSR/NOTES	100%	EXCELLENT	AVERAGE	LAST MSR

ELDORADO (MODEL 6040/6041) – single round cutaway body, arched spruce top, maple back/sides, two f-holes, triple-bound top and back, maple neck, 21-fret bound ebony fingerboard with pearloid hump top and black/white/black slash block inlay, triple-bound black face headstock with slanted logo inlay and "Synchromatic"/tusk decoration, three-per-side gold tuners, adj. ebony stairstep bridge, "G" logo trapeze tailpiece, triple-bound raised pickguard, gold hardware, available in Natural (6041) or Sunburst (6040) finish, 18 in. body width, mfg. 1955-1970.

1955-1959	N/A	$2,250 - 2,750	$1,500 - 1,800	
1960-1964	N/A	$1,800 - 2,250	$1,250 - 1,500	
1965-1970	N/A	$1,650 - 2,000	$1,100 - 1,350	

* **Add 10-20% for Natural finish.**

This model was introduced in 1955 as a custom order only. In 1959 or 1960, thumbprint fingerboard inlays replaced humptop inlays and the "Gretsch" logo replaced the "Synchromatic" logo. By 1968, Natural finish was disc.

FLEETWOOD/ELDORADO (MODEL 6038/6039) – single round cutaway body, arched spruce top, maple back/sides, two f-holes, triple-bound top and back, maple neck, 21-fret bound ebony fingerboard with pearloid hump top and black/white/black slash block inlay, triple-bound black face headstock with "Synchromatic" logo, three-per-side gold tuners, adj. ebony stairstep bridge, "G" logo trapeze tailpiece, triple-bound raised pickguard, gold hardware, available in Natural (6039) or Sunburst (6038) finish, 17 in. body width, mfg. 1955-1969.

1955-1958 Fleetwood	N/A	$2,100 - 2,500	$1,400 - 1,700	
1959-1964 Eldorado	N/A	$1,650 - 2,000	$1,150 - 1,400	
1965-1969 Eldorado	N/A	$1,200 - 1,500	$850 - 1,050	

This model is similar to the Eldorado, except has a smaller body and "Synchromatic " logo on the headstock. In 1959 or 1960, thumbprint fingerboard inlays replaced humptop inlays. By 1968, Natural finish was disc.

MODEL 25 – carved spruce top, arched maple back, maple sides, two f-holes, no body binding, three-piece maple neck, 14/20-fret ebony fingerboard with dot inlays, rosewood covered headstock with a pearl scroll logo placed diagonally and three-per-side tuners, non adj. ebony bridge, trapeze tailpiece, dark red/brown Sunburst finish 16 in. body width, 24.5 in. scale, mfg. 1933-39.

	N/A	$600 - 700	$425 - 500	

MODEL 30 – carved spruce top, arched maple back, maple sides, two unbound f-holes, single bound top, three-piece maple neck, 14/20-fret bound rosewood fingerboard with pearl dot inlays, rosewood rounded top headstock with a pearl scroll logo inlaid diagonally and three-per-side tuners, adj. maple bridge, trapeze tailpiece, black Bakelite pickguard, nickel-plated hardware, dark red/brown Sunburst finish, 16 in. body width, 24.5 in. scale, mfg. 1939-1949.

	N/A	$675 - 800	$500 - 575	

MODEL 35 – carved spruce top, arched maple back, maple sides, two f-holes, single bound top and back, three-piece maple/rosewood neck, 14/20-fret ebony fingerboard with pearloid dot inlay, rosewood peghead veneer with pearl logo inlay, three-per-side diecast tuners, ebony bridge, trapeze tailpiece, raised bound black pickguard, available in Dark Red Sunburst finish, 16 in. body width, 24.5 in. scale, mfg. 1933-1949.

	N/A	$750 - 900	$500 - 600	

In 1936, an adjustable maple bridge and black plastic peghead veneer replaced the original design. By 1939, a three-stripe body binding, rosewood fingerboard, tortoiseshell tuner buttons, nickel-plated hardware, and Brown Sunburst finish became standard.

MODEL 50 – carved spruce top, arched maple or avoidire back, figured maple sides, two f-holes, triple-bound top and single boudn back, three-piece maple neck, 14/20-fret bound ebony or rosewood pointed end fingerboard with pearloid diamond inlays, black plastic veneer peghead with pearl scroll inlay and vertical lines, three-per-side nickel tuners with tortoiseshell or white buttons, adj. maple bridge, trapeze tailpiece, raised triple-bound bakelite black pickguard, available in Brown Sunburst finish, 16 in. body width, 24.5 in. scale, mfg. 1936-1949.

	N/A	$850 - 1,000	$600 - 700	

This model also available with a round soundhole (Model 50R), which was produced between 1936 and 1939. In the late 1930s, avoidire replaced maple in the back, a rosewood fingerboard replaced the ebony, white tuner buttons replaced the tortoiseshell, and a crosspiece was placed in the middle of the tailpiece. By 1940, dot fingerboard inlays were replaced by diamonds.

MODEL 65 – carved spruce top, arched maple back, maple sides, two f-holes, four-ply top and back body binding, three-piece maple neck, 14/20-fret bound ebony fingerboard with notched diamond inlays, rosewood covered headstock with a vertical floral inlay, pearl scroll logo placed diagonally, and three-per-side tuners, non adj. ebony bridge, trapeze tailpiece, dark red/golden amber Sunburst finish 16 in. body width, 24.5 in. scale, mfg. 1933-39.

	N/A	$900 - 1,100	$625 - 750	

In 1936, an adj. maple bridge and a black plastic veneer headstock with a center dip style was introduced.

MODEL 75 – arched spruce top, raised bound tortoise pickguard, f-holes, bound body, figured maple back/sides, three-piece maple neck, 14/20-fret bound rosewood pointed end fingerboard with pearloid block inlay, adjustable rosewood stairstep bridge/nickel trapeze tailpiece, black face peghead with large floral/logo inlay, three-per-side nickel tuners, available in Brown Sunburst finish, body width 16 in., mfg. 1939-1949.

	N/A	$1,050 - 1,250	$750 - 900	

Early models had bound pegheads. By 1940, a three-stripe bound pickguard/body replaced the original design, and the pickguard was also enlarged.

MODEL 100F – arched spruce top, arched maple back, maple sides, two f-holes, two-stripe bound body, three-piece maple/rosewood neck, 14/20-fret bound rosewood fingerboard with small diamond inlays, rosewood veneer headstock with fern inlay and pearl scroll logo, three-per-side gold

MSR/NOTES	100%	EXCELLENT	AVERAGE	LAST MSR

tuners, adj. ebony bridge, trapeze tailpiece, raised single-bound tortoiseshell pickguard, available in dark red/golden amber Sunburst finish, 16 in. body width, 24.5 in. scale, mfg. 1933-39.

| | N/A | $1,050 - 1,250 | $750 - 900 | |

This model was also produced with a round soundhole (Model 100R) between 1933 and 1938. In 1936, a tortoiseshell pickguard replaced the black and the headstock was changed from a rosewood veneer to a black plastic veneer with a center dip design. This model was renamed the Synchromatic 100 in 1939 (see listing).

MODEL 150 (ARTIST) – carved spruce top, arched maple back, maple sides, two f-holes, multiple bound top and back, three-piece maple neck, 14/20-fret bound ebony fingerboard with pearl block inlays, bound blackface headstock with large pearl design that covers most of the headstock and "Artist" logo inlay, three-per-side gold tuners with engraved buttons, adj. ebony bridge, trapeze tailpiece, raised bound tortoiseshell pickguard with floral engraving around edges, gold hardware, available in Sunburst finish, 16 in. body width, 24.5 in. scale, mfg. 1935-38.

| | N/A | $1,400 - 1,750 | $950 - 1,100 | |

MODEL 250 – arched spruce top, arched maple back, maple sides, bound cat's-eye soundholes, five-ply bound top and back and pearl top border, three-piece maple neck, 14/20-fret bound ebony fingerboard with trapezoid or misc. inlays, bound blackface headstock with a pointed top and two pearl quarter notes/logo inlay, three-per-side gold tuners with pearloid buttons, adj. stylized ebony bridge, trapeze tailpiece, raised bound tortoise pickguard with two musical note inlays, available in Sunburst finish, 16 in. body width, 24.5 in. scale, mfg. 1936-38.

| | N/A | $1,600 - 2,000 | $1,000 - 1,250 | |

A tenor version of the Model 250 was also available (Model 240).

NEW YORKER (MODEL 6050) – non-cutaway archtop body, spruce top, rock maple back and sides, two f-holes, single (1949-1970) or triple (mid-1940s-1949) bound top, single bound back, bound (mid-1940s-1949) or unbound (1949-1970) 14/20-fret rosewood fingerboard with blcck (mid-1940s-1970) or dot (1949-1970) inlay, three-per-side tuners, adj. rosewood bridge, trapeze tailpiece, tortoiseshell celluloid pickguard, 16 in. body width, available in Sunburst finish, mfg. 1949-1970.

	100%	EXCELLENT	AVERAGE	
1940s	N/A	$800 - 1,000	$475 - 600	
1949-1954	N/A	$650 - 800	$375 - 475	
1955-1970	N/A	$525 - 650	$325 - 400	

The original New Yorker featured a round headstock with a stenciled logo of the T-roof Gretsch through circle and New Yorker vertically. In 1949, a lightning bolt was added to the logo. In 1955, a headstock with a rounded top and sharper corners was introduced. Some models produced in the late 1960s feature a rectangle-shaped headstock that is similar to flattop guitars with a Gretsch plaque.

SYNCHROMATIC (MODEL 6038/6039) – single cutaway, carved spruce top, arched laminated maple back, laminated maple sides, two double-bound f-holes, multiple-bound top and back, maple neck, bound rosewood fingerboard with slashed hump block inlays, bound headstock with a rounded top and "Synchromatic" logo, three-per-side stairstep tuners, stairstep rosewood bridge, "G" tailpiece, bound pickguard, gold-plated hardware, available in Natural (Model 6039) or Sunburst (Model 6038) finish, mfg. 1951-55.

| | N/A | $1,800 - 2,250 | $1,250 - 1,500 | |

In 1955, this model became the Fleetwood (see listing).

SYNCHROMATIC 75 – arched spruce top, carved maple back, maple sides, two unbound f-holes, four-ply bound top and back, three-piece maple/rosewood neck, bound ebony fingerboard with pointed end and large block inlays, black plastic headstock veneer with scroll "Gretsch" logo across the top and large floral design, three-per-side tuners with metal buttons, stylized stairstep rosewood bridge, harp tailpiece, raised triple-bound pickguard, nickel hardware, available in Sunburst finish, 16 in. body width, 24.5 in. scale, mfg. 1939-1949.

| | N/A | $950 - 1,200 | $575 - 725 | |

The earliest models may have a trapeze tailpiece, only single-ply binding on the top and back, an unbound headstock, and a single-bound smaller pickguard.

SYNCHROMATIC 100 (MODEL 6014/6015) – carved spruce top, arched maple back, maple sides, two f-holes, tortoiseshell celluloid binding, three-piece maple neck, 14/20-fret rosewood fingerboard with various symmetrical inlays, rounded top headstock with clipped edges, large fern pattern inlay, three-per-side tuners, stairstep bridge, harp tailpiece, raised pickguard that extends below the bridge, available in Natural or Sunburst finish, 16 in. body width, 24.5 in. scale, mfg. 1939-1955.

	100%	EXCELLENT	AVERAGE	
1939-1949	N/A	$875 - 1,100	$525 - 650	
1949-1955	N/A	$800 - 1,000	$475 - 600	

• **Add 15-20% for Natural finish.**

In 1946, a double bound top and back, bound pickguard, and bound f-holes were introduced, the fingerboard inlays were changed to large blocks, and the headstock changed to an unbound rounder design with the "Synchromatic" logo. In 1947, the headstock became bound with a rounded top design. In 1949, the Synchromatic was assigned the Model 6014 number and Sunburst finish became standard. In 1951, Natural finish became avaialble again and was assigned the Model 6015 number. In 1952, binding was removed from the f-holes, headstock, and pickguard. In 1955, the Synchromatic 100 was renamed the Corsair (see listing).

SYNCHROMATIC 115 – carved spruce top, arched maple back, maple sides, two unbound f-holes, tortoiseshell binding on top and back, three-piece maple/rosewood neck, bound ebony fingerboard with pointed end and large block inlays, black plastic headstock veneer with scroll "Synchromatic" logo above (1946-1947) or below (1947-1949) the A- and B-string tuners, three-per-side tuners with metal buttons, stylized stairstep rosewood bridge, harp tailpiece, raised triple-bound pickguard, nickel hardware, available in Trans. Blonde finish, 16 in. body width, 24.5 in. scale, mfg. 1946-49.

| | N/A | $1,100 - 1,350 | $750 - 900 | |

The earliest models may have a trapeze tailpiece, only single-ply binding on the top and back, an unbound headstock, and a single-bound smaller pickguard.

MSR/NOTES	100%	EXCELLENT	AVERAGE	LAST MSR

SYNCHROMATIC 160 (MODEL 6028) – carved spruce top, carved curly maple back, curly maple sides, two double-bound cat's-eye soundholes, tortoiseshell bound body, five-piece maple/rosewood neck, 14/20-fret four-ply bound rosewood fingerboard with large pearl block inlay, bound blackface headstock with pearl "Gretsch" logo on top and "Synchromatic" logo above the E-string tuners inlays, three-per-side chrome Grover tuners, adj. stylized rosewood bridge, harp tailpiece, raised bound tortoiseshell pickguard, chrome-plated hardware, available in Natural (6029) or Sunburst (6028) finish, 17 in. body width, 26 in. scale, mfg. 1939-1951.

1939-1943	N/A	$1,325 - 1,650	$800 - 1,000	
1947-1951	N/A	$1,200 - 1,500	$725 - 900	

In 1942, Natural finish with tortoiseshell binding became available. This model was disc. in 1943 but reintroduced in 1947 with some models having slight changes: an ebony fingerboard, no headstock indents above the E string tuners, and gold-plated hardware. In 1948, the Synchromatic 160 was assigned Model 6029 for Natural finish and Model 6028 for Sunburst finish.

SYNCHROMATIC 200 – carved spruce top, carved flame maple back, flame maple sides, two double-bound cat's-eye soundholes, wide multiple-binding on top and back, five-piece maple/rosewood neck, 14/20-fret bound rosewood fingerboard with hump block inlays, bound blackface headstock with indents above the E string tuners, pearl "Gretsch" logo on top and "Synchromatic" logo above the A and B-string tuners inlays, three-per-side chrome Grover tuners with engraved buttons, adj. stylized rosewood bridge, harp tailpiece, raised bound tortoiseshell pickguard, gold-plated hardware, available in Natural or Sunburst finish, 17 in. body width, 26 in. scale, mfg. 1939-1949.

	N/A	$1,700 - 2,100	$1,150 - 1,400	

SYNCHROMATIC 300 (MODEL 6036/6037) – carved spruce top, carved flame maple back, curly maple sides, two double-bound cat's-eye soundholes, wide multiple-binding on top and back, five-piece maple/rosewood neck, 14/20-fret five-ply bound rosewood fingerboard with gold sparkle hump block inlays, bound blackface headstock with indents above the E string tuners, pearl "Gretsch" logo on top and "Synchromatic" logo above the A and B-string tuners inlays, three-per-side chrome Grover tuners with engraved buttons, adj. stylized rosewood bridge, harp tailpiece, raised bound tortoiseshell pickguard, gold-plated hardware, available in Natural (6037) or Sunburst (6036) finish, 17 in. body width, 26 in. scale, mfg. 1939-1955.

1939-1950	N/A	$2,500 - 3,000	$1,750 - 2,100	
1951-1955	N/A	$2,100 - 2,500	$1,400 - 1,700	

* **Add 10-20% for Natural finish.**

In 1941, Natural finish was introduced. In 1948, the Synchromatic 300 was assigned Model 6036 for Sunburst finish and Model 6037 for Natural finish. In 1951, f-holes, a stairstep bridge, "G" tailpiece, triple bound top and back, single bound pickguard and fingerboard, slashed hump block fingerboard inlays, and a rounded top headstock were introduced.

SYNCHROMATIC 400 (MODEL 6040/6041) – carved spruce top, carved flame maple back, curly maple sides, two double-bound cat's-eye soundholes, wide multiple-binding with gold sparkle on top and back, five-piece maple/rosewood neck, 14/20-fret five-ply white/gold bound rosewood fingerboard with slashed hump block inlays, bound blackface headstock with indents above the E string tuners, pearl angled "Gretsch" logo on top and crossed "Synchromatic" logo slanted between the tuners, three-per-side chrome Grover tuners with engraved buttons, adj. stylized rosewood bridge, harp tailpiece with gold and chrome plating, raised white/gold sparkle bound tortoiseshell pickguard, gold-plated hardware, available in Natural (6041) or Sunburst (6040) finish, 18 in. body width, 26 in. scale, mfg. 1940-1955.

1939-1950	N/A	$5,000 - 6,000	$3,250 - 4,000	
1951-1955	N/A	$4,500 - 5,500	$2,750 - 3,500	

* **Add 10-20% for Natural finish.**

In 1948, the Synchromatic 400 was assigned Model 6040 for Sunburst finish and Model 6041 for Natural finish. In 1951, f-holes, a stairstep bridge, "G" tailpiece, triple bound top and back, single bound pickguard and fingerboard, slashed hump block fingerboard inlays, and a rounded top headstock with no indents were introduced. In 1952, a rounded-top headstock was introduced. In 1955, this model was replaced by the Eldorado (see listing).

SYNCHROMATIC/CONSTELLATION 6030/6031 – single round cutaway body, arched spruce top, laminated maple back and sides, two double bound f-holes, triple bound top and back, three-piece maple/rosewood neck, 19-fret bound rosewood fingerboard with pearloid block inlay, bound black face rounded headstock with pearl logo "Synchromatic" inlay, three-per-side gold tuners, raised bound tortoise pickguard, adj. rosewood stairstep bridge, harp tailpiece, gold hardware, available in Natural (6031) or Sunburst (6030) finish, 17 in. body width, mfg. 1951-1960.

1951-1955	N/A	$1,475 - 1,850	$900 - 1,100	
1955-1960	N/A	$1,350 - 1,700	$825 - 1,025	

This model was originally released as the Synchromatic, and in 1955 it was changed to the Constellation. In 1955, hump top block fingerboard inlays, an ebony bridge, and a "G" logo trapeze tailpiece were introduced.

ACOUSTIC ARCHTOP: RECENT MFG.

Early Synchromatic models have bulb-shaped pegheads. Fingerboard inlay listed as the standard, though models are also found with split block, thumb print and other inlay styles.

SYNCHROMATIC G400 (NO. 260-0100) – arched spruce top, raised bound tortoiseshell pickguard, bound cat's-eye soundholes, three-stripe bound body, arched maple back, maple sides/neck, 14/20-fret bound rosewood fingerboard with pearl split hump block inlay, adjustable stylized ebony bridge/step trapeze tailpiece, bound blackface peghead with pearl model name/logo inlay, three-per-side gold tuners, available in Black (disc. 2009) or Sunburst finish, mfg. 1991-2012.

	$1,500	$950 - 1,100	$550 - 700	$2,125

MSR/NOTES	100%	EXCELLENT	AVERAGE	LAST MSR

Synchromatic G400 C (No. 260-0101) – similar to Synchromatic except has single round cutaway, available in Sunburst finish, mfg. 1991-2009.

| | N/A | $950 - 1,200 | $575 - 725 | $2,950 |

Blonde Maple Synchromatic G400 MC – similar to Synchromatic C, except has Blonde Maple finish, available in Natural finish, mfg. 1991-96.

| | N/A | $1,000 - 1,150 | $625 - 775 | $1,850 |

Synchromatic G400 CV (G6040MCSS, No. 260-0107) – similar to Synchromatic C, except has a Filtertron pickup and a Bigsby tremolo bridge, available in Blonde or Sunburst finish, mfg. 1994-2009.

| | N/A | $1,075 - 1,350 | $650 - 800 | $2,950 |

• **Add 5% for Blonde finish.**

Synchromatic G400JV Jimmie Vaughan (No. 260-0110) – similar to the Synchromatic G400, except is the Jimmie Vaughan signature version, arched solid spruce top, solid maple back and sides, two cat's-eye soundholes, mulitple top and back binding, three-piece maple neck, 14/20-fret bound ebony fingerboard with slashed hump block inlays, multiple-bound headstock with slanted "Gretsch" and "Synchromatic" logos, three-per-side Grover Imperial tuners, compensated rosewood synchronized bridge, harp tailpiece, tortoiseshell pickguard that covers most of the treble soundhole, Fishman Archtop pickup system, two knobs under the pickguard (v, tone), available in Natural finish, 17 in. body width, 3.5 in. body depth, 25.5 in. scale, mfg. summer 2006-2011.

| $2,350 | $1,450 - 1,700 | $950 - 1,100 | $3,325 |

SYNCHROMATIC 17 IN. LIMITED EDITION (MODEL G450) – similar to the Synchromatic, except features handcarved spruce top, floating Jazz pickup, available in Walnut Stain finish, body width 17 in., mfg. 1997-2002.

| | N/A | $1,250 - 1,500 | $950 - 1,100 | $4,000 |

This Limited Edition model comes with a Certificate of Authenticity signed by Fred Gretsch.

Synchromatic 17 In. Maple Limited Edition (Model G450 M) – similar to the 17 in. Synchromatic Limited Edition, except features a carved maple top, mfg. 1997-2002.

| | N/A | $1,400 - 1,700 | $1,050 - 1,200 | $4,300 |

SYNCHROMATIC THINLINE G460 – similar to the Synchromatic, except features a laminated spruce top, available in Orange finish, mfg. 1997-2003.

| | N/A | $750 - 875 | $550 - 650 | $1,525 |

Maple Synchromatic G460 M – similar to the Orange Synchromatic, except features a laminated maple top, mfg. 1997-2002.

| | N/A | $650 - 775 | $500 - 575 | $1,295 |

SYNCHROMATIC G100 (NO. 251-5830) – non-cutaway Synchromatic-style archtop body, spruce top, laminated maple back and sides, two f-holes, vintage white body binding, maple neck, 20-fret bound rosewood fingerboard with pearl block inlays, black headstock with Gretsch Synchromatic logo and three-per-side tuners, Gretsch rosewood adj. stairstep bridge, trapeze tailpiece, raised tortoise pickguard, chrome hardware, available in Black (2009 only), Natural, or Sunburst finish, 25.5 in. scale, mfg. summer 2006-09.

| | N/A | $425 - 500 | $225 - 275 | $1,000 |

ELDORADO 18 IN. CARVED TOP (MODEL G410) – similar to the Eldorado (Model 6040). Synchromatic Jazz Model, available in Sunburst (G410) or Natural (G410 M) finishes, body width 18 in., mfg. 1991-2001.

| | N/A | $1,800 - 2,100 | $1,300 - 1,500 | $5,700 |

• **Add $300 for model in Natural finish (Model G410 M). Shaded finish added and Sunburst finish discontinued in 1999.**

ACOUSTIC FLATTOPS: 1930S-1970S MFG.

Gretsch first produced flattop acoustics around the same time they introduced archtop acoustics in 1933. However, the flattops weren't nearly as popular and very little is known about the earliest models. These models include the **Broadkaster**, **Castillian**, **Rhumba**, and the **Number 40 Hawaiian** model. Gretsch (and part of Baldwin) also produced some little-known models during the late 1960s and 1970s. Some of these models include the **Deluxe** and the **Supreme** as well as two unnamed models: a 12-string and a jumbo. Gretsch flattop guitars were built very poorly and cheaply and they didn't sound very good - a stark contrast to their electric counterparts. Therefore, they aren't very collectible in the used marketplace.

BURL IVES (MODEL 6004) – spruce top, mahogany back and sides, round soundhole with nine-ply ring, double bound top, mahogany neck, 14/19-fret rosewood fingerboard with pearloid dot inlay, black peghead face with Gretsch and Burl Ives logos, three-per-side tuners with plastic buttons, rosewood bridge with black pins, tortoiseshell teardrop-shaped pickguard, available in Natural finish, 14.25 in. body width, mfg. 1952-54.

| | N/A | $525 - 650 | $325 - 400 | |

ELECTRO CLASSIC (MODEL 6006/7495) – classical style, specifications unknown, on-board piezo under bridge pickup and electronics (by Baldwin), mfg. 1969-1973.

| | N/A | $550 - 700 | $350 - 425 | |

This model was originally numbered 6006 but it was changed to 7495 in 1971.

MSR/NOTES	100%	EXCELLENT	AVERAGE	LAST MSR

MODEL 6003/GRAND CONCERT/JIMMIE RODGERS/FOLK – spruce top, mahogany back and sides, round soundhole, four-ply bound top, mahogany neck, 14/19-fret rosewood fingerboard with pearloid dot inlay, black peghead face with Gretsch logo with a circle and parallelogram inlay, three-per-side tuners with plastic buttons, rosewood bridge with black pins, tortoiseshell teardrop-shaped pickguard, available in Natural finish, 14.25 in. body width, mfg. 1951-1975.

1951-1959

Model 6003/Grand Concert	N/A	$625 - 750	$450 - 525	
1959-1963 Jimmie Rodgers	N/A	$600 - 700	$425 - 500	
1963-1965 Folk Singing	N/A	$550 - 650	$400 - 475	
1965-1969 Folk	N/A	$500 - 575	$325 - 400	
1969-1975 Folk	N/A	$425 - 500	$275 - 325	

This model was originally introduced as the Model 6003. In 1955, this model was named the Grand Concert (Model 6003) and a slanted peghead logo was introduced. In 1959, this model was renamed the Jimmy Rogers Model (endorsed by 1950s/1960s pop star Jimmie Rogers). In 1963, it was renamed the Folk Singing Model and a 14.5 in. body width and 24.5 in. scale were introduced. In 1965, it was renamed Folk Model. In 1967, a zero fret was introduced and the logo was placed straight across the headstock. In 1969, a mahogany top (Model 6004) and Sunburst finish (Model 6002) became optional.

OZARK SOFT STRING (MODEL 6005) – classical style, spruce top, rosewood back and sides, round soundhole, double-bound top and back, rosewood fingerboard with no inlays, slotted headstock with three-per-side open-style tuners, rosewood bridge, available in Natural finish, 16 in. body width, mfg. 1965-68.

	N/A	$525 - 650	$325 - 400	

RANCHER (MODEL 6022/7525) – laminated spruce top with stylized "G" brand on the bass bout, maple arched back, maple sides, triangle soundhole with rosette, four-ply bound top, double bound back, maple neck, 14/21-fret bound rosewood fingerboard with pearloid block inlays engraved with cows and cactus, black face bound peghead with pearl steer head/logo inlay, three-per-side gold tuners, adj. rosewood bridge mounted on triangular rosewood base, tortoiseshell, gold, or tan pickguard with engraved longhorn steer head, available in Golden Red finish, 17 in. body width, 25.5 in. scale, mfg. 1954-1973.

1954-1959	N/A	$3,500 - 4,250	$2,500 - 3,000	
1960-1964	N/A	$3,000 - 3,500	$2,000 - 2,500	
1965-1969	N/A	$2,250 - 2,750	$1,500 - 1,800	
1970-1973	N/A	$1,800 - 2,250	$1,200 - 1,500	

By 1957, a gold pickguard replaced the tortoiseshell, and hump block fingerboard inlay with no engraving replaced the original design. In 1959, a tan pickguard replaced the gold pickguard and thumbnail fingerboard inlays replaced hump block inlays. In 1961, the G brand on the bass bout was removed, and a horseshoe peghead inlay was introduced. In 1969, a zero fret was introduced. In 1971, the Rancher's model number was changed to 7525.

RANCHER FIRST REISSUE (1975-1980 MFG.) – similar to the Rancher (Model 7525), except has a "G" brand logo on the treble bout, block fingerboard inlays with engraved cows and cacti, a rosewood bridge with white pins, and a horseshoe peghead inlay, mfg. 1975-1980.

	N/A	$1,700 - 2,100	$1,150 - 1,400	

In 1978, tri-saddle bridge with white pins replaced original parts/design.

SHO-BRO HAWAIIAN RESONATOR (MODEL 6031/7705) – non-cutaway body, select spruce top, maple back and sides, large resonator with two small screened soundholes, multiple-bound top and back, laminated maple neck, 12/24-fret bound white celluloid fingerboard with playing card symbol inlays (hearts, clubs, etc.), bound headstock with "Sho Bro" logo (no Gretsch logo) and three-per-side tuners, combination metal bridge/trapeze tailpiece, chrome hardware, available in Natural finish, 16.5 in. body width, 4.5 in. body depth, 25.25 in. scale, mfg. 1969-1978.

	N/A	$650 - 800	$375 - 475	

This model was originally numbered 6031, but in 1971, it was renumbered 7705. A seven-string version was also available between 1972 and 1978 with 4/3-per-side tuners (Model 7710).

SHO-BRO SPANISH RESONATOR (MODEL 6030/7715) – non- or sharp single-cutaway body, select spruce top, mahogany back and sides, large resonator with two small screened soundholes, multiple-bound top and back, laminated mahogany neck, 14/21-fret bound rosewood fingerboard with dot inlays, bound headstock with "Sho Bro" logo (no Gretsch logo) and three-per-side tuners, combination metal bridge/trapeze tailpiece, chrome hardware, available in Natural finish, 16.5 in. body width, mfg. 1969-1978.

	N/A	$600 - 750	$350 - 450	

This model was offered with two distinct variations: cutaway and non-cutaway. The cutaway model had a thinner body than the non-cutaway style. In 1971, this model was renumbered 7715 from 6030.

SILVER CLASSIC/CLASSIC HAUSER (MODEL 6000/6001) – classical style, grand concert-sized body, spruce top, mahogany back and sides, round soundhole with decorative inlaid purfling, black top and back binding, mahogany neck, rosewood fingerboard with no inlays, slotted headstock with three-per-side open-style tuners, rosewood bridge, available in Natural finish, 14.25 in. body width, 3.75 in. body depth, mfg. 1961-1972.

	N/A	$350 - 450	$225 - 275	

* **Add 25% for Model 6000 appointments (decorative back and headstock).**

The Model 6000 Hauser (sometimes called the Golden Classic) featured a decorated back and inlaid headstock.

MSR/NOTES	100%	EXCELLENT	AVERAGE	LAST MSR

SUN VALLEY (MODEL 6010/7514/7515) – spruce top, laminated Brazilian rosewood back with stripe and sides, round soundhole with rosette, four-ply bound top, single-bound back, 14/20-fret bound ebony fingerboard with dot inlay, rosewood bridge with black pins, bound headstock with pearl logo and three-per-side chrome tuners, tortoiseshell pickguard, available in Natural (6010, 7515) or Sunburst (7514) finish, 15.5 in. body width, 24.5 in. scale, mfg. 1959-1977.

1959-1964	N/A	$800 - 1,000	$475 - 600	
1965-1969	N/A	$650 - 800	$375 - 475	
1970-1977	N/A	$525 - 650	$325 - 400	

In 1971, this model was renumbered 7515. By 1973, Sunburst finish became optional (Model 7514).

SUN VALLEY REISSUE MODEL G6010 – dreadnought style, solid spruce top, triangle soundhole, three-stripe bound body, floral pattern rosette, rosewood back/sides, mahogany neck, 14/20-fret bound rosewood fingerboard with pearl diamond inlay, pearl scroll inlay at 12th fret, rosewood bridge with black pearl dot pins, pearl floral bridge wing inlay, bound blackface peghead with pearl floral/logo inlay, three-per-side gold tuners, available in Natural finish, mfg. 1991-disc.

	N/A	$525 - 600	$375 - 450	$1,250

SYNCHROMATIC 300F FLATTOP – spruce top, maple arched back and sides, triangle soundhole, mulit-bound top and back, maple neck, 14/21-fret bound rosewood fingerboard with pearloid slashed hump top block inlay, bound cloud headstock with indents below the E strings, a straight "Gretsch" logo at the top, and "Synchromatic" logo above the A and B string tuner posts, three-per-side gold tuners, adj. rosewood stairstep bridge, harp tailpiece, raised pickguard, available in Natural top, dark back/side finish, mfg. 1947-1955.

	N/A	$1,800 - 2,250	$1,200 - 1,500	

This model was originally custom built for Buddy Starcher.

SYNCHROMATIC 400F FLATTOP (MODEL 6042) – spruce top, maple arched back and sides, triangle soundhole, mulit-bound top and back with tortoiseshell layer, maple neck, 14/21-fret bound rosewood fingerboard with pearloid slashed hump top block inlay, bound cloud headstock with indents below the E strings and a pointed top, a slanted "Gretsch" logo at the top, and a Synchromatic/tusk ornamental logo, three-per-side enclosed Grover gold tuners, adj. rosewood stairstep bridge, harp tailpiece, raised pickguard, available in Natural top, Sunburst back/side finish, 18 in. body width, mfg. 1947-1955.

	N/A	$3,750 - 4,500	$2,500 - 3,000	

By 1949, an adj. bridge with a large triangular base, metal string anchor plate, and a non-raised pickguard were all introduced. In 1949, this model was numbered 6042.

SYNCHROMATIC JUMBO 125F (MODEL 6021) – spruce top, figured maple arched back and sides, triangle soundhole with rosette, mulitple bound top and back, maple neck, 14/21-fret bound rosewood fingerboard with pearloid block inlay, adj. rosewood bridge with triangular base, slanted metal string anchor plate, black face headstock with "Synchromatic" inlay above the A and B string tuner posts, three-per-side diecast tuners, tortoiseshell pickguard, available in Natural top, Sunburst back and side finish, 17 in. body width, 26 in. scale, mfg. 1947-1954.

	N/A	$2,250 - 2,750	$1,500 - 1,850	

Some models were finished in White with tortoiseshell binding all around, other models came with single body binding. This model was renamed into two different models in 1955: The Rancher and the Town and Country (see listings).

SYNCHROMATIC X75F/SYNCHROMATIC SIERRA (MODEL 6007) – spruce top, arched maple back, maple sides, triangular soundhole, maple neck, rosewood fingerboard with block inlays, black headstock with "Gretsch" and "75" logos, three-per-side tuners, trapezoid-shaped bridge, straight-mounted metal string-anchor plate, available in Sunburst finish, 16 in. body width, mfg. 1947-1955.

	N/A	$1,200 - 1,500	$725 - 900	

In 1949, this model was renamed the Synchromatic Sierra and numbered 6007.

TOWN AND COUNTRY – spruce top, maple arched back and sides, triangle soundhole with rosette, mulitple bound top and back, maple neck, 14/21-fret bound rosewood fingerboard with pearloid block inlay, black face headstock with three-per-side diecast tuners, adj. rosewood bridge with triangular base, slanted metal string anchor plate, tortoiseshell pickguard, available in Natural finish, 17 in. body width, 25.5 in. scale, mfg. 1954-59.

	N/A	$1,650 - 2,000	$1,100 - 1,350	

WAYFARER JUMBO (MODEL 6008) – dreadnought style, spruce top, red maple back and sides, round soundhole with rosette, mulitple bound top and back, red maple neck, 14/21-fret ebonized rosewood triple-bound rosewood fingerboard with pearl split block inlay, rosewood bridge with white pins, black face headstock with logo inlay, three-per-side Grover chrome tuners, lucite pickguard with engraved sailboat/logos, available in Natural finish with Cherry back and sides, 16 in. body width, mfg. 1969-1971.

	N/A	$850 - 1,000	$600 - 700	

ACOUSTIC FLATTOPS: RECENT MFG.

CRIMSON FLYER G6020 – single round cutaway body, solid spruce top, triangle soundhole, multi-bound body, floral pattern rosette, chestnut back/sides, two-piece mahogany neck, 22-fret rosewood fingerboard with pearl dot inlay, pearl scroll inlay at 12th fret, pearl floral bridge wing inlay, bound body matching headstock with pearl logo inlay, three-per-side gold tuners, rosewood bridge with black pearl pins, active ceramic pickup, volume/tone control, available in Cherry Sunburst finish, mfg. 1991-96.

	N/A	$625 - 750	$400 - 475	$1,350

* *Crimson Flyer V G6020 V* – similar to Crimson Flyer, except has rosewood/metal tune-o-matic bridge/Bigsby vibrato, disc.

	N/A	$800 - 950	$525 - 600	$1,650

MSR/NOTES	100%	EXCELLENT	AVERAGE	LAST MSR

NIGHTBIRD G6030 – single round cutaway body, solid spruce top, maple back/sides, triangle soundhole, three-stripe bound body, floral pattern rosette, twp-piece mahogany neck, 21-fret bound rosewood fingerboard with pearl dot inlay, pearl scroll inlay at 12th fret, bound blackface peghead with pearl logo inlay, three-per-side gold tuners, rosewood bridge with black pearl dot pins, pearl floral pattern bridge wing inlay, active ceramic pickup, volume/tone control, available in Ebony finish, disc.

	N/A	$550 - 650	$375 - 450	$1,200

* *Nightbird V (Model 6030 V)* – similar to Nightbird, except has rosewood/metal tune-o-matic bridge/Bigsby vibrato tailpiece, disc.

	N/A	$675 - 800	$450 - 525	$1,500

RANCHER SECOND REISSUE MODEL G6022 (NO. 260-0202) – spruce top with G brand, bound triangle soundhole, tortoise pickguard with engraved steerhead, three-stripe bound body, maple back/sides/neck, 14/21-fret bound rosewood fingerboard with western motif engraved pearl block inlays, rosewood bridge with black white dot pins, bound peghead with pearl steerhead/logo inlay, three-per-side gold tuners, available in Orange Satin finish, mfg. 1991-2009.

	N/A	$900 - 1,050	$550 - 650	$1,950

* *Rancher 1954 Reissue Model G6022-1954* – similar to Rancher Second Reissue Model G6022, except is based on the 1954 Rancher model specifications, mfg. 1997-2002.

	N/A	$950 - 1,100	$600 - 700	$1,650

* *Rancher 12-String Model G6022-12 (No. 260-0204)* – similar to Rancher Second Reissue Model G6022, except in 12-string configuration and six-per-side tuners, disc. 2003.

	N/A	$950 - 1,100	$600 - 700	$1,775

»*Rancher 12-String Cutaway Model G6022-C/12* – similar to Rancher 12-String Model G6022-12, except has a single round cutaway, a single coil pickup, and volume/tone controls, disc.

	N/A	$1,000 - 1,150	$625 - 750	$1,600

* *Rancher Acoustic/Electric Model G6022E (No. 260-0206)* – similar to Rancher Second Reissue Model G6022, except has a Fishman Acoustic Matrix pickup and electronics, mfg. 2007-09.

	N/A	$1,050 - 1,250	$625 - 775	$2,450

* *Rancher C Cutaway Model G6022C (No. 260-0203)* – similar to Rancher Second Reissue Model G6022, except has a single round cutaway and pickup/electronics, disc. 2009.

	N/A	$1,075 - 1,300	$650 - 800	$2,500

* *Rancher CV Model G6022CV* – similar to Rancher Second Reissue Model G6022, except has single round cutaway, no pickguard, adjust-a-matic metal bridge with rosewood base/Bigsby vibrato, single coil pickup, volume/tone control, disc. 1999.

	N/A	$1,050 - 1,250	$700 - 800	$1,750

* *Rancher Double Neck Model G6022-6/12* – similar to the Rancher Second Reissue Model G6022, except has two necks in six-string and 12-string configurations, mfg. 1997-2002.

	N/A	$1,650 - 2,000	$1,100 - 1,350	$3,200

* *Rancher Sweet 16 Model G6012 (No. 260-0200)* – similar to the Rancher Second Reissue, except is available in Natural, Purple, Candy Apple Red, Regal Blue, Tangerine, Black, Tobacco Burst, or Anniversary Green finish, disc. 2003.

	N/A	$1,000 - 1,150	$625 - 750	$1,875

WHITE FALCON RANCHER MODEL G6022 CWFF (NO. 260-0101) – single round cutaway jumbo style, solid spruce top with "G" brand, tortoiseshell pickguard, bound triangle soundhole, gold sparkle bound body, maple back/sides/neck, 21-fret gold sparkle bound rosewood fingerboard with western motif engraved pearl block inlays, rosewood bridge with black white dot pins, gold sparkle bound peghead with gold sparkle inlay, three-per-side gold tuners, internal acoustic pickup, volume/3-band EQ controls, available in White finish, mfg. 1994-2009.

	N/A	$1,250 - 1,500	$825 - 975	$2,950

* *White Falcon Rancher with Fishman Pickup (Model G6022 CWFF)* – similar to the White Falcon Rancher, except features a Fishman transducer pickup, mfg. 1997-2002.

	N/A	$1,350 - 1,650	$900 - 1,050	$2,800

ACOUSTIC: HISTORIC/FLATTOP SERIES

In 2000, Gretsch launched its first budget series called the Historic Series, which were basically all models based on popular vintage Gretsch models produced overseas. Most price points were between $600 and $1,000 - a price that Gretsch guitars hadn't offered since the 1950s and 1960s. These new guitars received a lukewarm response and the entire Historic Series was discontinued in 2003. However, some of the popular models went on to other series. For acoustic guitars, only the Rancher and dreadnought-style guitars survived and they are currently the only two budget models Gretsch produces today. Every model that is not part of Gretsch's big-name line is included here with the exception of the Rancher models that can be found in the Rancher section.

AMERICANA COLLECTION G45X0 (No. 270-300X) – 3/4-sized small-bodied acoustic, unspecified wood construction, round soundhole, 18-fret fingerboard, three-per-side tuners, available in four western-themed finishes/graphics with one released quarterly: The Wild West Sweethearts (Q1 2007, Red finish G4530 No. 270-3003), The Showdown (Q2 2007, Gray/Black Sunburst, G4510, No. 270-3001),

MSR/NOTES	100%	EXCELLENT	AVERAGE	LAST MSR

Sundown Serenade (Q3 2007, Brown Sunburst, G4500, No. 270-3000), and Way Out West (Q4 2007, Green, G4520, No. 270-3002), 13 in. body width, 3.75 in. body depth, 24 in. scale, made in Indonesia, mfg. 2007 only.

	N/A	$65 - 80	$40 - 50	$150

DREADNOUGHT G3503/3520/3523 (NO. 270-130X) – 16 in. dreadnought acoustic six-string, solid Sitka spruce top, rosewood back and sides, 25.5 in. scale, maple neck with rosewood fingerboard, neoclassical position markers, three-per-side tuners, available in Aged Natural (Model G3503), Satin Natural (G3523, 2001-03), or Satin Tobacco Sunburst (G3520, 2001-03) finish, mfg. 2000-03.

	N/A	$175 - 225	$110 - 140	$400

* **Add 60% (Last MSR $640) for Aged Natural (non-Satin) finish.**

Gretsch also produced versions of this model with Quilted Maple and Tiger Maple (specifications unknown).

* *Dreadnought Acoustic/Electric G360X (No. 270-130X)* – similar to Historic Series Dreadnought acoustic model except, has a Fishman Frefix pickup system with built-in preamp and tone circuit, available in Aged Natural (Model G3603) or Black (Model G3601) finish, mfg. 2000-03.

	N/A	$375 - 450	$225 - 275	$880

* *Dreadnought 12-String G3523-12 (No. 270-1307)* – similar to the Dreadnought except in 12-string configuration, and six-per-side tuners, available in Natural Satin finish, mfg. 2000-03.

	N/A	$250 - 300	$150 - 200	$460

DREADNOUGHT G503X (NO. 270-2110) – dreadnought style, solid spruce top, laminated maple backand sides, maple neck, rosewood fingerboard, triangle soundhole, tortoise pickguard, rosewood bridge, gold hardware, available in Tobacco Sunburst, Orange Stain, Black, or Natural finish, mfg. 2003-08.

	N/A	$275 - 325	$175 - 225	$600

* *Dreadnought Cutaway Electric G503XC (No. 270-2001)* – similar to the Dreadnought, except has a single cutaway with Fishman Prefix electronics, mfg. 2003-08.

	N/A	$375 - 450	$225 - 275	$860

DREADNOUGHT G3553 (NO. 270-1802) – dreadnought style body, available in Natural, Black (G3551), Blue (G3557), or Red (G3559) finishes, mfg. 2000-03.

	N/A	$200 - 230	$130 - 150	$320

This model was part of the Synchromatic Series.

GRAND CONCERT G3303/3366/3373 (NO. 270-1201/3) – 15 in. grand concert acoustic six-string, cutaway or non-cutaway design, solid Sitka spruce and hardwood top, rosewood/hardwood sides and back, 25.5 in. scale, maple neck with rosewood fingerboard, neoclassical inlays, gold hardware, three-per-side tuners, available in Aged Natural (Model G3303), Deep Red Stain (Model G3366), or Natural Maple (Model G3373) finish, mfg. 2000-03.

	N/A	$225 - 275	$140 - 175	$520

* **Add 20% (Last MSR $620) for non-cutaway version (Model G3303).**

* *Grand Concert Acoustic/Electric G3400 (No. 270-1202)* – similar to Historic Series Grand Concert acoustic model except, has a Fishman Prefix pickup system with built-in preamp and tone circuit, available in Aged Natural finish, disc. 2003.

	N/A	$375 - 450	$225 - 275	$860

HAWAIIAN G3100/3101/3105 (NO. 270-1101) – 16 in. auditorium acoustic six-string, solid Sitka spruce top, mahogany back and sides, maple neck with rosewood fingerboard, neoclassical position markers, three-per-side tuners, available in Black (Model G3101), Tobacco Sunburst (Model G3100), or Vintage Sunburst (Deluxe version, Model G3105) finish, 24.75 in. scale, mfg. 2000-03.

	N/A	$250 - 300	$150 - 200	$620

* **Add 35% for Deluxe Model with celluloid fingerboard and headstock and Vintage Sunburst finish (Model G3105).**

* *Hawaiian Acoustic/Electric G3201/3203/3205 (No. 270-1102)* – similar to the Historic Series Hawaiian acoustic model except, has a Fishman Prefix pickup with built-in preamp and tone circuit, gold hardware, faux tortoiseshell pickguard, available in Aged Natural (Model G3203), Black (Model G3201), or Vintage Sunburst (Deluxe Version only, Model G3205) finish, mfg. 2000-03.

	N/A	$375 - 450	$225 - 275	$880

* **Add 25% (Last MSR $1,100) for Deluxe model with Vintage Sunburst finish (Model G3205).**

RANCHER JUMBO CUTAWAY ACOUSTIC/ELECTRIC MODEL G502XC (NO. 270-2001) – jumbo style single cutaway body, solid spruce top, laminated maple backand sides, mahogany neck, rosewood fingerboard, triangle soundhole, tortoiseshell pickguard, rosewood bridge, Fishman Prefix electronics, gold hardware, available in Black, Natural, Orange Stain, or Tobacco Sunburst finish, mfg. 2003-08.

	N/A	$375 - 450	$225 - 275	$860

RANCHER JUNIOR CUTAWAY ACOUSTIC/ELECTRIC MODEL G501X (NO. 270-1202/2020) – similar to the Rancher design except has a smaller 15 in. wide body, has a Fishman Prefix pickup and preamp system, available in Black, Blue (2002-03), Natural (2004-08), Orange Stain, Purple (2002-03), Red (2002-03), or Tobacco Sunburst finish, mfg. 2000-08.

	N/A	$375 - 450	$225 - 275	$860

In 2004, this model was moved from the Historic Collection (Model G341X, No. 270-1202) and placed in the Flattop Series (Model G501X, No. 270-2020).

MSR/NOTES	100%	EXCELLENT	AVERAGE	LAST MSR

RESONATOR G3170 (NO. 270-1601) – 14 in. body, 25.3 in. scale, laminated maple top, back and sides, maple neck with rosewood fingerboard, neoclassical position markers, chrome plated resonator, three-per-side tuners, available in Tobacco Sunburst finish, mfg. 2000-03.

	N/A	$475 - 550	$325 - 375	$800

SIERRA JUMBO G3738 (NO. 270-1502) – 17 in. Jumbo acoustic six-string, maple top, back and sides, maple neck, 25.5 in.scale, three-per-side tuners, mfg. 2001-03.

	N/A	$300 - 350	$175 - 225	$700

* *Sierra Jumbo G3713 (No. 270-1900)* – similar to the Sierra Jumbo except has a solid Sitka spruce top, 16 in. wide bout, and mahogany neck, disc. 2003.

	N/A	$375 - 450	$225 - 275	$900

* *Sierra Jumbo 12-String G3700-12 (No. 270-1504)* – similar to the Sierra Jumbo except in 12-string configuration, six-per-side tuners, mfg. 2000-03.

	N/A	$400 - 475	$250 - 300	$960

* *Sierra Jumbo Acoustic/Electric G370X (No. 270-1502)* – 17 in. jumbo body, 25.5 in. scale, solid Sitka spruce top, mahogany back and sides, maple neck with rosewood fingerboard, neoclassical position markers, three-per-side tuners, French soundhole, Fishman Prefix pickup with built-in preamp and tone circuit, available in Tobacco Sunburst, Black (G3701), or Natural (G3703) finish, mfg. 2000-03.

	N/A	$400 - 475	$250 - 300	$920

SYNCHROMATIC JR. G3900 (NO. 251-0107) – 15 in. body, single cutaway archtop design, laminated maple top, back and sides, maple neck with rosewood fingerboard, three-per-side tuners, neoclassical position markers, single neck-mounted jazz style pickup, available in Tobacco Sunburst (G3900), Metallic Gold (G3967), or Vintage Sunburst (G3905) finish, 24.75 in. scale, mfg. 2000-03.

	N/A	$500 - 600	$300 - 350	$1,100

- Add 10% (Last MSR $1,200) for left-handed configuration (Model G3900LH).
- Add 15% (Last MSR $1,280) for Metallic Gold finish (Model G3967).
- Add 17.5% (Last MSR $1,300) for Vintage Sunburst finish (Model G3905).

STANDARD FOLK G1653 (NO. 270-1800) – folk style body, Neo-Classical "Thumbnail" Inlay position markers, bound fingerboard, triple bound body, aged B/W/B rosette, adjustable truss rod, available in Natural or Red (G1659) finish, mfg. 2000-03.

	N/A	$120 - 150	$75 - 95	$280

This model was part of the Synchromatic Series.

ACOUSTIC ELECTRIC BASS

ACOUSTIC FRETTED BASS G6175 (NO. 260-0900) – single round cutaway body, spruce top, triangle soundhole, three-stripe bound body, floral pattern rosette, maple back/sides/neck, 23-fret bound rosewood fingerboard with pearl dot inlay, pearl scroll inlay at 12th fret, rosewood strings through bridge, bound blackface peghead with pearl logo inlay, two-per-side gold tuners, active ceramic pickup, volume/tone control, available in Orange Stain finish, mfg. 2000-03.

	N/A	$775 - 900	$500 - 600	$1,725

* *Acoustic Fretless Bass G6176* – similar to the Acoustic Fretted Bass, except has fretless fingerboard, disc. 2003.

	N/A	$775 - 900	$500 - 600	$1,725

ACOUSTIC FRETTED BASS WESTERN G6175W (NO. 260-0903) – similar to the G6175 except in Western style, available in Orange Stain finish, disc. 2003.

	N/A	$850 - 1,000	$550 - 650	$1,975

GREVEN GUITARS

Instruments currently built in Portland, OR since 1971. Previously built in Bloomington, IN.

CONTACT INFORMATION
GREVEN GUITARS
1415 SE Taylor
Portland, OR 97214
Phone No.: 503-233-8525
Fax No.: 503-233-8525
www.grevenguitars.com
grevenguitars@msn.com

Luthier John Greven has been building guitars since 1971, and he worked at Gruhn Guitars repairing and restoring instruments before he started building his own. While Greven has always been building good sounding acoustics, he is perhaps better known for the outstanding quality of his inlay work. In the mid-1990s, Greven devised a faux tortoiseshell material that can be used as pickguards or body binding without the problems encountered by the real material. This faux shell is called "Tor-tis." The base price for a mahogany guitar is $3,500 and a rosewood or other special material guitar starts at $5,200. For more information on his instruments or inlay work visit Greven's website or contact him directly.

GRIFFIN STRING INSTRUMENTS

Acoustic instruments currently produced in Greenwich, NY since 1976.

Luthier Kim Griffin was born in 1952 and began repairing string instruments of all types in 1975. He then attended the School of Guitar Research and Design in 1977 learning steel string and classical guitar building methods from George Morris and Charles Fox. Since then, he has built steel string acoustic and electric guitars, mandolins, banjos, and hammered dulcimers in Greenwich, New York. Griffin builds custom one of a kind, hand built instruments and offers five different guitar shapes: A (parlor), B (00 size), C (classical), GC (grand concert), and D (rounded dreadnought). Prices start at $2,900 and a minimum deposit of $1,250 secures a place on the waiting list (currently 12- 18 months). For more information contact Griffin directly.

CONTACT INFORMATION
GRIFFIN STRING INSTRUMENTS
5264 Rt. 113
Greenwich, NY 12834
Phone No.: 518-695-5382
www.kimgriffinguitars.com
griffin.guitars@juno.com

GRIMES GUITARS

Instruments currently built in Kula, HI since 1972.

Luthier Stephen Grimes originally apprenticed with a violin maker and set up his own mandolin shop in Port Townsend, WA in 1972, assembling archtop mandolins. In 1974, Grimes began handcrafting archtop guitars, as well as a few steel string flattop models. In 1982, Grimes introduced a semi-hollow archtop, two steel string flattops, and a half-sized flattop. Grimes also moved to Hawaii in 1982, and continues to produce guitars on a custom basis. Grimes estimates that he produces about twenty guitars a year (half of them are archtops, and half of them are double soundhole flattops in steel or nylon configurations). Customers have choices on size, woods used, color of finish, inlay work, electronic packages, and the neck profile. For more information, contact Grimes directly.

CONTACT INFORMATION
GRIMES GUITARS
1520 Kamehameiki Road
Kula, HI 96790
Phone No.: 808-878-2076
Fax No.: 808-878-2076
www.grimesguitars.com
grimesguitars@gmail.com

Grimes' models include several models. The **Beamer**, a double soundhole flattop acoustic that is constructed with highly figured wood (list $6,500, Nylon-string version is $6,900). The **Hapa** model is similar to the Beamer with two soundholes, but it features a cutaway body (list $6,600, nylon-string version is $7,000). The **LC Model** is an oval center hole flattop guitar designed for Larry Coryell introduced in 2003 (list $6,900, nylon-string version is $7,400). The **Kula Rose** is an archtop guitar with a single cutaway (list $10,500). The **Jazz Nouveau** is an archtop model with a flat back in curly maple or curly koa (list $9,000). The **Montreux** is an archtop model with arched and arched top and back, European spruce top, and figured German maple back and sides (list $12,800). The **Jazz Laureate** is a full body arch top with select aged German and Austrian tone woods (list $16,000). A nylon-string archtop lists for $10,500, and the "Tiny Grimes" mini parlor lists for $5,500.

Grimes has also produced anniversary models. The 25th Anniversary model was released in 1999 and is still available for $22,000. The 30th Anniversary model lists for $26,000, and Stephen is currently taking orders for the 35th Anniversary, which was released in 2008. All guitars are custom and have many possible options. Contact Grimes directly for more information.

GRIMSHAW

Instruments previously produced in England between the 1950s and the late 1970s.

While this company is best known for its high quality archtop guitars, they also produced a notable semi-hollowbody design in the mid-1950s called the Short-Scale. In the early 1960s, Emile Grimshaw introduced the Meteor solid body guitar. The company then focused on both original and copies of American designs from the late 1960s on. Source: Tony Bacon and Paul Day, *The Guru's Guitar Guide*.

GROSSMAN BROTHERS

Also Grossman Music Company and Grossman Music Corp. See chapter on House Brands.

Grossman Brothers (also Grossman Music Company and Grossman Music Corp) was a large mail order distribution company that sold several brands of guitars mainly during the 1930s and 1940s. Before World War II, the majority of guitars were sold through mail-order distributors. Brands and trademark dates of Grossman are Capitol (1933), Champion (1932), Crestline (1957), Dixie (1948), Duplex (1937), KlearTone (1923), Masterfonic (1937), and Trophy (1945). The trademark date is the earliest date most of these guitars were probably produced. KlearTone is probably the most well-known brand out of all the names Grossman distributed, and these guitars were probably produced by various manufacturers including Harmony, Kay, Regal, and Gibson. It's also possible that Grossman affixed their name to some guitars. Source: Tom Wheeler, *American Guitars* and Walter Murray, Frankenstein Fretworks.

GROVES CUSTOM GUITARS

Instruments currently built in Tucson, AZ.

Luthier Gordon S. Groves is currently offering handcrafted guitar models built to customers' specifications. Groves also operates a guitar repair shop. For more information contact luthier Groves directly.

CONTACT INFORMATION
GROVES CUSTOM GUITARS
1130 South Highland Ave.
Tucson, AZ 85719
Phone No.: 520-628-3390

GRUEN ACOUSTIC GUITARS

Instruments currently produced in Sonoma County, CA and previously produced in Chapel Hill, NC since 1999.

Luthier Paul Gruen has been playing guitar since the 1960s, and since 1998 has been building a hybrid form of acoustic guitar incorporating elements of flattop, archtop, and Selmer/Mac construction. These guitars have five soundholes, and any combination of one or two of the oval soundholes can be plugged to change the tone. Guitars are available in 16 in., 17 in., and 18 in. variations. Prices start at $2,385. For more information visit Gruen's website or contact him directly.

GUDELSKY MUSICAL INSTRUMENTS

Instruments previously built in Vista, CA between 1985 and 1996.

Luthier Harris Paul Gudelsky (1964-1996) had apprenticed to James D'Aquisto before starting Gudelsky Musical Instruments. Gudelsky's personal goal was to try to build a more modern version of the archtop guitar. Gudelsky offered a small line of instruments exclusively on a customer order basis that included hollowbody archtops (acoustic and electric/acoustic) ranged from $4,290 to $5,500, semi-hollowbodies ranged from $4,235 to $4,400, and set-neck solid bodies ranged from $2,450 to $3,500. Paul Gudelsky was found fatally shot at his Vista, California home in May, 1996.

GUGINO

Instruments previously built in Buffalo, NY between the 1930s and 1940s.

Luthier Carmino Gugino built instruments that featured high quality conventional building (frets, finish, carving, etc.) combined with very unconventional design ideas. As detailed by Jay Scott, certain models feature necks that screw on to the body, or have asymmetrical bodies, or an archtop that has a detachable neck/body joint/bridge piece that is removable from the body. Source: Teisco Del Rey, *Guitar Player* magazine.

GUILD

Instruments currently produced in New Hartford, CT since 2008 and China since the mid-2000s. Previously produced in New York City, NY between 1952 and 1956, Hoboken, NH between late 1956 and 1968, Westerly, RI between 1969 and the early 2000s, Nashville, TN between 1997 and the early 2000s, Corona, CA between 1999 and 2006, and Tacoma, WA between 2006 and 2008. Distributed by Cordoba Music Group in Santa Monica, CA since 2014.

Contrary to the stories about a "guild of old world-style craftsmen" gathering to build these exceptional guitars, Guild was founded in 1952 by Alfred Dronge (who did hire great guitar builders). Dronge, a Jewish emigrant from Europe, grew up in New York City and took jobs working for various music stores on Park Row. Dronge became an accomplished musician who played both banjo and guitar, and loved jazz music. His experience in teaching music and performing in small orchestras led to the formation of the Sagman and Dronge music store.

After World War II, Dronge gave up the music store in favor of importing and distributing Italian accordions. The Sonola Accordion Company was successful enough to make Dronge a small fortune. It is with this reputation and finances that Dronge formed Guild Guitars, Inc. with ex-Ephiphone sales manager George Mann. Incidentally, the Guild name came from a third party who was involved with a guitar amplifier company that was going out of business. As the plant was closing down Dronge and Gene Detgen decided to keep the name. The Guild company was registered in 1952.

As the original New York-based Epiphone company was having problems with the local unions, they decided to move production down to Philadelphia. Dronge took advantage of this decision and attracted several of their ex-luthiers to his company. Some of the workers were of Italian ancestry, and felt more comfortable remaining in the Little Italy neighborhood rather than moving to Pennsylvania.

The company was originally located in a New York loft from 1952 through 1956. They expanded into a larger workshop in Hoboken, New Jersey, in late 1956. Finally, upon completion of new facilities, Guild moved to its current home in Westerly, Rhode Island, in 1969.

As pop music in the 1960s spurred on a demand for guitars, musical instrument companies expanded to meet the business growth. At the same time, large corporations began to diversify their holdings. Most people are aware of the CBS decision to buy Fender in 1965, or Baldwin Piano's purchase of the Burns trademark and manufacturing equipment in 1967. In 1966, electronic parts producer Avnet Inc. bought Guild Musical Instruments, and Alfred Dronge stayed on as president. Dronge also hired Jim Deurloo (of Gibson and later Heritage fame) as plant manager in December 1969. Deurloo's commitment to quality control resulted in better consistency of Guild products.

Tragedy occurred in 1972 as Alfred Dronge was killed in an aircraft crash. The relationships he built with the members of the company dissipated, and the driving force of twenty years since the inception was gone. However, Leon Tell (Guild's vice president from 1963 to 1973) became the company president in 1973 and maintained that position until 1983.

In mid-August of 1986, Avnet sold Guild to a management/investment group from New England and Tennessee. Officers of the newly formed Guild Music Corporation included company President Jerre R. Haskew (previously Chief Executive Officer

MSR/NOTES	100%	EXCELLENT	AVERAGE	LAST MSR

and President of the Commerce Union Bank of Chattanooga, TN), Executive Vice President of Plant and Operations George A. Hammerstrom, and Executive Vice President of Product Development and Artist Relations George Gruhn (Gruhn later left the company in early 1988).

Unfortunately, the remaining members of the investment group defaulted on bank obligations in November of 1988, leading to a court supervised financial restructuring. The Faas Corporation of New Berlin, WI (now U.S. Musical Corporation) bought Guild in January, 1989. Solid body guitar production was discontinued in favor of acoustic and acoustic-electric production (a company strength) although some electric models were reissued in the mid-1990s.

In 1995, Fender Musical Instruments Corporation (FMIC) of Scottsdale, AZ bought Guild, which was the financial assistance they needed to continue producing guitars. Gradually throughout the late 1990s, Guild grew back into a commercial and financial success with the introduction of more acoustic guitars as well as the resurgence of electric guitars. In 1997, Guild opened a new Custom Shop in Nashville, TN. In 1999, Robert Benedetto signed a formal agreement with FMIC to redesign both the Artist Award and X700 Stuart Models, which were produced in Westerly, RI. While the trademark Guild harp-style tailpiece remains, a MOP "Benedetto" logo was inlaid in the 19th fret on both models. In 2001, all Guild guitar production was moved to Corona, CA because the Westerly location needed a complete overhaul of its facility. In 2004, FMIC bought the Tacoma guitar company in Tacoma, WA mainly for a location to build acoustic guitars. By 2006, all electric Guild production was disc. (excluding the Johnny Smith Award) and FMIC decided to use the Guild trademark strictly on acoustic guitars, where production was merged with the newly acquired Tacoma plant. Also in 2006, after seven years of a partnership, FMIC and Benedetto amicably split ways. In late 2007, FMIC purchased Kaman Music Corporation and in early 2008, they moved production of Guild acoustic guitars from the Tacoma, WA factory to Kaman's manufacturing facility in New Hartford, CT. In 2014, (FMIC) sold Guild to the Cordoba Music Group in Santa Monica, CA.

Reference source for early Guild history: Hans Moust, *The Guild Guitar Book*; contemporary history courtesy Jay Pilzer; Bendetto model information courtesy of Cindy Benedetto.

IDENTIFYING FEATURES/GENERAL INFORMATION

According to noted authority and Guild enthusiast Jay Pilzer, there are identifying features on Guild instruments that can assist in determining their year of production. For information regarding archtop models with floating or built-in pickups, please refer to the *Blue Book of Electric Guitars*.

Knobs on Electrics: 1953-58 transparent barrel knobs; 1959-63 transparent yellowish top hat knobs with Guild logo in either chrome or gold; 1964-72 black top hat knobs, Guild logo, tone or vol; circa 1990-present black top hat with Guild logo, no numbers or tone/vol.

Electric Pickguards: Except for the Johnny Smith/Artist Award (which used the stairstep pickguard), Guild pickguards were rounded, following the shape of the guitar until 1963 when the stairstep became standard on archtop electrics.

Acoustic Pickguards: Most models have a distinct Guild shape in either tortoiseshell or black with rounded edges that follow the line of guitar, except the F-20, M-20, and new **A** series which have teardrop pickguards.

Headstock Inlays: The earliest were simple Guild inverted **V** with triangular insert, with **G** logo below, later the triangular insert disappears, Chesterfield introduced on some models by 1957. In general the more elaborate the headstock, the higher price the instrument.

Several acoustic Guild guitars were available with a pickup and/or electronics as well as left-handed configurations. For the most part, electronics were a $200 option on top of retail, and left-handed version retailed for the same amount.

- **Add $150 for electronics on guitars where they are not a standard feature.**

ACOUSTIC ARCHTOP

All Guild hollow body acoustic archtop guitars were available with optional pickups. Guild also produced another model called the A-600B. They only built one for display at the 1968 NAMM show although it was listed in Guild price lists until 1973. This guitar features unusual specs such as an oval soundhole and checkered binding.

A-50 GRANADA/CORDOBA – non-cutaway bound hollow body, laminated arched spruce top, two f-holes, laminated maple back and sides, three-piece mahogany/maple neck, 14/20-fret rosewood fingerboard with pearl dot inlays, blackface peghead with screened logo, three-per-side nickel tuners, raised black pickguard, adjustable rosewood bridge/trapeze tailpiece, available in Sunburst finish, 16.25 in. body width, 24.75 in. scale, mfg. 1956-1972.

	N/A	$950 - 1,200	$575 - 725	

In 1959, a one-piece mahogany neck was introduced and Blonde finish became available (Model A-50B). In 1961 the A-50 Granada was renamed the A-50 Cordoba.

A-150 SAVOY – single round cutaway bound hollow body, solid spruce top, two f-holes, laminated maple back and sides, three-piece mahogany/maple neck, 20-fret rosewood fingerboard with block inlays, blackface headstock with Chesterfield crown and column logo/inlay, three-per-side nickel tuners, adj. rosewood bridge, trapeze tailpiece, raised black pickguard, nickel-plated hardware, available in Blonde or Sunburst finish, 17 in. body width, 24.75 in. scale, mfg. 1958-1973.

	N/A	$1,800 - 2,250	$1,075 - 1,350	

MSR/NOTES	100%	EXCELLENT	AVERAGE	LAST MSR

A-350/A-350B/A-375 STRATFORD – single round cutaway hollow body, arched spruce top, two bound f-holes, multi-ply binding, solid curly maple back and sides, three-piece maple/walnut neck, 20-fret bound rosewood fingerboard with pearl block inlays, multibound blackface headstock with "G" logo inlay, three-per-side tuners, adj. rosewood bridge, harp tailpiece, raised black laminated pickguard, gold-plated hardware, available in Blonde (A-375 or A-350B) or Sunburst (A-350) finish, 24.75 in. scale, mfg. circa 1956-1973.

1956-1959	N/A	$2,200 - 2,750	$1,325 - 1,650	
1960-1972	N/A	$1,800 - 2,250	$1,075 - 1,350	

• **Add 10% for Natural finish (Model A-375 or A-350B).**

In 1959, a G shield headsock logo/inlay was introduced. In 1960, an ebony fingerboard and bridge was introduced. The Blonde version of this guitar was called the A-375 Stratford until 1960 and A-350B after 1960.

A-500/A-500B/A-550 STUART – single round cutaway hollow body, bound arched solid spruce top, two bound f-holes, solid curly maple back and sides, three-piece walnut/maple neck, 20-fret bound rosewood fingerboard with pearl block inlays with abalone V wedges, bound headstock with pearl G shield logo/inlay, three-per-side Imperial tuners, adj. rosewood bridge, stylized trapeze tailpiece, bound tortoise pickguard, gold-plated hardware, available in Natural or Sunburst finish, 24.75 in. scale, mfg. circa 1956-1969.

	N/A	$2,400 - 3,000	$1,450 - 1,800	

• **Add 10% for Natural finish (Model A-550 Stuart or A-500B).**

In 1959, a five-piece maple/walnut neck and an ebony fingerboard and bridge were introduced. The Blonde version of this guitar was called the A-550 Stuart until 1960 and A-500B after 1960.

CA-100/CA-100B CAPRI – single sharp cutaway hollow body, arched bound solid spruce top, two f-holes, laminated maple back and sides, three-piece mahogany/maple neck, 20-fret bound rosewood fingerboard with pearl block inlays, blackface headstock with G logo/inlay, three-per-side tuners, adj. rosewood bridge, trapeze tailpiece, raised bound black pickguard, nickel-plated hardware, available in Blonde (CA-100B) or Sunburst (CA-100) finish, 16.375 in. body width, 24.75 in. scale, mfg. 1956-1973.

	N/A	$1,400 - 1,750	$850 - 1,050	

In 1957, a Chesterfield crown and column headstock logo/inlay was introduced. In 1960, a harp tailpiece was introduced. Blonde finish was available between 1961 and 1972.

ACOUSTIC: CLASSICAL MODELS (MARK, CCE, ETC. PREFIX)

Guild also offered a Jose Feliciano model called the Mark 50. It was available with maple or rosewood back and sides, a slotted headstock, and Natural or Sunburst finish.

CCE-100 – classical nylon string configuration, single round cutaway solidbody, spruce top, mahogany back and sides, oval soundhole routing, bound body, wood inlay rosette, mahogany neck, 24-fret rosewood fingerboard, three-per-side chrome tuners, rosewood bridge, transducer pickup, four-band EQ with preamp, available in Natural satin finish, mfg. 1993-94.

	N/A	$775 - 900	$475 - 550	$1,199

* **CCE-100 HG** – similar to CCE-100, except has gold hardware and a Natural high gloss finish, mfg. 1994 only.

	N/A	$875 - 1,000	$550 - 625	$1,399

MARK I – nylon string classical configuration, mahogany top, mahogany back and sides, round soundhole with simple marquetry rosette, three-piece mahogany neck, 12/19-fret rosewood fingerboard, three-per-side nickel tuners, tied rosewood bridge, available in Natural satin finish, 14.5 in. body width, 25.5 in. scale, mfg. 1961-1972.

1961-1969	N/A	$450 - 550	$275 - 325	
1970-1972	N/A	$325 - 400	$190 - 240	

MARK II – nylon string classical configuration, spruce top, mahogany back and sides, round soundhole with red/black/white ring, tortoiseshell celluloid top and back binding, three-piece mahogany neck, 12/19-fret rosewood fingerboard, three-per-side nickel tuners, tied rosewood bridge, available in Natural satin finish, 14.5 in. body width, 25.5 in. scale, mfg. 1961-1986.

1961-1969	N/A	$475 - 600	$275 - 350	
1970-1979	N/A	$450 - 550	$275 - 325	
1980-1986	N/A	$400 - 500	$250 - 300	

MARK III – nylon string classical configuration, spruce top, mahogany back and sides, round soundhole with floral pattern ring, three-ply tortoiseshell celluloid top and back binding, three-piece mahogany neck, 12/19-fret rosewood fingerboard, rosewood headstock overlay, three-per-side nickel tuners, tied rosewood bridge, available in Natural satin finish, 14.5 in. body width, 25.5 in. scale, mfg. 1961-1986.

1961-1969	N/A	$550 - 700	$350 - 425	
1970-1979	N/A	$525 - 650	$325 - 400	
1980-1986	N/A	$475 - 600	$275 - 350	

MARK IV – nylon string classical configuration, spruce top, figured pearwood, flamed maple (1962-63), or rosewood (1961, 1978-1986) back and sides, round soundhole with floral pattern ring, four-ply tortoiseshell celluloid top and back binding, three-piece mahogany neck, 12/19-fret rosewood fingerboard, rosewood headstock overlay, three-per-side gold tuners, tied ebony bridge, available in Natural satin finish, 14.5 in. body width, 25.5 in. scale, mfg. 1961-1986.

1961-1969	N/A	$750 - 950	$450 - 575	
1970-1979	N/A	$675 - 850	$400 - 500	
1980-1986	N/A	$550 - 700	$350 - 425	

In 1966, a rosewood bridge was introduced.

MSR/NOTES	100%	EXCELLENT	AVERAGE	LAST MSR

MARK V – nylon string classical configuration, spruce top, flamed maple (1961-63) or rosewood back and sides, round soundhole with floral pattern ring, ebony top and back binding, three-piece mahogany neck, 12/19-fret rosewood fingerboard, ebony headstock overlay, three-per-side gold engraved tuners, ebony bridge, available in Natural satin finish, 14.5 in. body width, 25.5 in. scale, mfg. 1961-1987.

1961-1963 Maple	N/A	$1,200 - 1,500	$850 - 1,000	
1961-1969 Rosewood	N/A	$2,000 - 2,500	$1,200 - 1,500	
1970-1979	N/A	$800 - 1,000	$475 - 600	
1980-1987	N/A	$600 - 750	$350 - 450	

In 1966, a rosewood bridge was introduced.

MARK VI – nylon string classical configuration, spruce top, rosewood back and sides, round soundhole with floral pattern ring, natural wood top and back binding, three-piece mahogany neck, 12/19-fret rosewood fingerboard, ebony headstock overlay, three-per-side gold engraved tuners, ebony bridge, available in Natural satin finish, 14.5 in. body width, 25.5 in. scale, mfg. 1962-1987.

1962-1969	N/A	$1,800 - 2,250	$1,075 - 1,350	
1970-1979	N/A	$1,000 - 1,250	$600 - 750	
1980-1987	N/A	$800 - 1,000	$475 - 600	

In 1966, a rosewood bridge with pearl inlays was introduced.

MARK VII CUSTOM – nylon string classical configuration, spruce top, rosewood back and sides, round soundhole with floral pattern ring, natural wood top and back binding, three-piece mahogany neck, 12/19-fret ebony fingerboard, ebony headstock overlay, three-per-side gold engraved tuners, ebony bridge, available in Natural satin finish, 14.5 in. body width, 26.25 in. scale, mfg. 1962-1987.

1962-1969	N/A	$2,000 - 2,500	$1,200 - 1,500	
1970-1979	N/A	$1,125 - 1,400	$675 - 850	
1980-1987	N/A	$950 - 1,200	$575 - 725	

In 1966, a rosewood bridge with pearl inlays was introduced.

MKS-10 – nylon string configuration, single rounded cutaway solidbody, spruce top, routed mahogany back, round sounhole with decorative rosette, mahogany neck, 12/19-fret rosewood fingerboard with no inlays, slotted headstock with three-per-side open tuners, rosewood bridge, Fishmann TASS pickup, available in Black, Natural, or Sunburst finish, 14.75 in. body width, 24.75 in. scale, mfg. 1984-86.

	N/A	$600 - 700	$375 - 450	

MKS-11 – nylon string configuration, single sharp cutaway body with an acoustic sound chamber, spruce top, routed mahogany back, oval soundhole, mahogany neck, 12/19-fret rosewood fingerboard with no inlays, slotted headstock with three-per-side open tuners, rosewood bridge, Fishmann TASS pickup, available in Black, Natural, or Sunburst finish, 14.75 in. body width, 2.75 in. body depth, 24.75 in. scale, mfg. 1984 only.

	N/A	$600 - 700	$375 - 450	

MKS-44 – nylon string configuration, single rounded cutaway solidbody, spruce top, routed mahogany back, oval sounhole, mahogany neck, 14/24-fret bound rosewood fingerboard with no inlays, solid headstock with Chesterfield inlay and three-per-side tuners, rosewood bridge, Fishmann TASS pickup, available in Black, Natural, or Sunburst finish, 14.75 in. body width, 24.75 in. scale, mfg. 1984 only.

	N/A	$600 - 700	$375 - 450	

ACOUSTIC: CONTEMPORARY SERIES

CD-1 (NO. 380-9990) – dreadnought-style body, solid Sitka spruce top, solid rosewood back and sides, round soundhole with Madagascar rosewood and ivoroid, red, and black accent lines rosette, mutli-layer ivoroid binding, Guild neck block system, one-piece mahogany neck, 14/21-fret Madagascar rosewood fingerboard with abalone dot inlays, rosewood headstock overlay with MOP logo and shield inlay, three-per-side chrome Gotoh tuners, Madagascar rosewood bridge, tortoise shell pickguard, available in Antique Burst, Ice Tea Burst, or Natural finish, 25.5 in. scale, deluxe hardshell case included, mfg. summer 2008 only.

	N/A	$1,050 - 1,300	$650 - 800	$2,600

CO-1 (NO. 380-6000) – F-30 Orchestra-style body, solid western red cedar top, solid mahogany back and sides, round soundhole with Madagascar rosewood and ivoroid, red, and black accent lines rosette, mutli-layer ivoroid binding, Guild neck block system, one-piece mahogany neck, 14/21-fret Madagascar rosewood fingerboard with dot inlay, three-per-side Gotoh tuners, Madagascar rosewood bridge and end pins, tortoiseshell pickguard, available in Natural finish, mfg. summer 2006-08.

	N/A	$925 - 1,150	$550 - 700	$2,300

* CO-1C Cutaway (No. 380-6100) – similar to the CO-1C, except has a single Schoenberg-style cutaway and D-TAR Wavelength Load and Lock pickup and electronics, available in Natural finish, mfg. summer 2006-08.

	N/A	$1,000 - 1,250	$600 - 750	$2,500

CO-2 (NO. 380-8000) – F-30 Orchestra-style body, solid red spruce top, solid mahogany back and sides, round soundhole with Madagascar rosewood and ivoroid, red, and black accent lines rosette, mutli-layer ivoroid binding, Guild neck block system, one-piece mahogany neck, 14/21-fret ebony fingerboard with dot inlay, three-per-side Gotoh chrome tuners, ebony bridge, available in Antique Burst, Ice Tea Burst, or Natural finish, mfg. summer 2007-08.

	N/A	$1,000 - 1,250	$600 - 750	$2,500

MSR/NOTES	100%	EXCELLENT	AVERAGE	LAST MSR

* *CO-2C Cutaway (No. 380-8100)* – similar to the CO-2, except has a single Venetian-style cutaway and D-TAR Wavelength Load and Lock pickup and electronics, available in Antique Burst, Ice Tea Burst, or Natural finish, mfg. summer 2007-08.

	N/A	$1,075 - 1,350	$650 - 800	$2,700

CV-1 (NO. 380-5000) – F-40 Orchestra-style body, solid spruce top, Indian rosewood back and sides, round soundhole with Madagascar rosewood and ivoroid, red, and black accent lines rosette, mutli-layer ivoroid binding, Guild neck block system, one-piece mahogany neck, 14/21-fret Madagascar rosewood fingerboard with dot inlay, MOP headstock logo and inlay with three-per-side Gotoh tuners, Madagascar rosewood bridge and end pins, tortoiseshell pickguard, available in Antique Burst, Ice Tea Burst, or Natural finish, mfg. summer 2006-08.

	N/A	$1,000 - 1,250	$600 - 750	$2,500

* *CV-1C Cutaway (No. 380-5100)* – similar to the CV-1C, except has a single sharp cutaway and D-TAR Wavelength Load and Lock pickup and electronics, available in Antique Burst, Ice Tea Burst, or Natural finish, mfg. summer 2006-08.

	N/A	$1,075 - 1,350	$650 - 800	$2,700

CV-2 (NO. 380-7000) – F-40 Orchestra-style body, solid red spruce top, solid flame maple back and sides, round soundhole with Madagascar rosewood and ivoroid, red, and black accent lines rosette, mutli-layer ivoroid binding, Guild neck block system, one-piece mahogany neck, 14/21-fret ebony fingerboard with dot inlay, MOP headstock logo and inlay with three-per-side chrome Gotoh tuners, ebony bridge, available in Antique Burst, Ice Tea Burst, or Natural finish, mfg. summer 2007-08.

	N/A	$1,125 - 1,400	$675 - 850	$2,800

* *CV-2C Cutaway (No. 380-7100)* – similar to the CV-2, except has a single Florentine-style cutaway and D-TAR Wavelength Load and Lock pickup and electronics, available in Antique Burst, Ice Tea Burst, or Natural finish, mfg. summer 2007-08.

	N/A	$1,200 - 1,500	$725 - 900	$3,000

ACOUSTIC: CUSTOM SHOP

In 1997, Guild opened a Custom Shop in Nashville, Tennessee. Guild Custom Shop models are built in limited quantities.

45TH ANNIVERSARY – F-style body based on the original F-44, solid Sitka spruce top, solid flame maple back and sides, round soundhole, mutli-ply body binding, abalone purfling/rosette, 14/20-fret bound ebony fingerboard with pearl blocks/abalone V insert inlays, bound headstock with abalone G shield/logo inlay, engraved flame maple truss rod cover, three-per-side gold tuners, ebony bridge, available in Natural finish, limited run of 45, mfg. 1997 only.

	N/A	$3,200 - 3,700	$2,200 - 2,600	$4,500

This 45th Anniversary model commemorates Guild's beginning in 1952.

DECO DREADNOUGHT (NO. 395-0850) – dreadnought style, solid AAA spruce top, bookmatched rosewood back, solid rosewood sides, scalloped bracings, round soundhole, abalone rosette, abalone top binding, three-piece mahogany neck, 14/20-fret bound ebony fingerboard with abalone Deco inlays, bound headstock with abalone shield/logo inlay, ebony bridge, three-per-side gold tuners, abalone-bound black pickguard, available in Natural high gloss lacquer finish, case included, mfg. 1997-2000.

	N/A	$2,700 - 3,200	$1,500 - 1,800	$3,799

FINESSE DREADNOUGHT (NO. 395-0805) – dreadnought style, solid AAA spruce top, scalloped bracings, round soundhole, herringbone rosette, bookmatched rosewood back, solid rosewood sides, tortoiseshell bound top, three-piece mahogany neck, 14/20-fret ebony fingerboard with abalone dot inlays, abalone shield and logo headstock inlays, three-per-side gold tuners, ebony bridge, tortoiseshell pickguard, Fishman Matrix Natural II pickup, available in Natural high gloss lacquer finish, case included, mfg. 1997-98.

	N/A	$2,500 - 3,000	$1,500 - 1,800	$2,699

VALENCIA CONCERT (NO. 395-3550) – small body narrow waist concert body style based on the F-40 Valencia, solid AAA spruce top, solid highly figured maple back and sides, shaved bracings, round soundhole, abalone rosette, abalone top binding, solid figured maple neck, 14/20-fret bound ebony fingerboard with abalone Deco inlays, bound peghead with abalone shield/logo inlay, three-per-side gold tuners, ebony bridge, black pickguard, available in Black, Blonde, Antique Burst, or Torino Red high gloss lacquer finish, case included, mfg. 1998-2003.

	N/A	$3,000 - 3,500	$2,100 - 2,500	$4,300

* *Valencia Cutaway (No. 395-3560)* – similar to the Valencia Concert except has a custom Florentine Cutaway and Fishman Matrix pickup, mfg. 2001-03.

	N/A	$2,700 - 3,200	$1,900 - 2,300	$4,800

ACOUSTIC: DREADNOUGHT MODELS (D, DV, G PREFIX)

All models in this series have dreadnought style bodies. DV models feature shaved or hand scalloped top bracing and are designed to sound like a vintage guitar that is already broken in.

D-4 (NO. 350-0100) – dreadnought style, solid spruce top, arched mahogany back, solid mahogany sides, round soundhole, three-stripe bound body/rosette, mahogany neck, 14/20-fret rosewood fingerboard with pearl dot inlays, snakehead-shaped headstock with three-per-side chrome tuners, rosewood bridge with white black dot pins, tortoiseshell pickguard, available in Natural hand rubbed satin finish, 15.75 in. body width, 25.625 in. scale, mfg. 1992-2002.

	N/A	$550 - 650	$375 - 450	$850

MSR/NOTES	100%	EXCELLENT	AVERAGE	LAST MSR

* D-4 12 12-String (Model 350-0900) – similar to the D-4, except in 12-string configuration and six-per-side tuners, available in Natural hand rubbed satin finish, mfg. 1992-99.

	N/A	$650 - 750	$475 - 550	$1,049

* D-4G (Model 350-0140) – similar to the D-4, except has a high gloss finish, mfg. 1998-2002.

	N/A	$600 - 700	$425 - 500	$950

* D-4HG – similar to the D-4, except has a high gloss finish available in Natural or Sunburst finish, mfg. 1992 only.

	N/A	$600 - 700	$425 - 500	$999

* D-4M (No. 350-0100) – similar to the D-4, except has a solid mahogany top, mfg. 1999-2002.

	N/A	$550 - 650	$375 - 450	$799

D-6(S) – dreadnought style, solid spruce top, bookmatched mahogany back, mahogany sides, round soundhole, three-stripe bound body/rosette, mahogany neck, 14/20-fret rosewood fingerboard with pearl dot inlays, snakehead-shaped headstock with three-per-side gold tuners, rosewood bridge with white black dot pins, tortoiseshell pickguard, available in Natural hand rubbed satin finish, 15.75 in. body width, 25.625 in. scale, mfg. 1992-95.

	N/A	$650 - 800	$475 - 550	$950

* D-6HG – similar to the D-6 except has a Natural or Sunburst high gloss finish, mfg. 1992-95.

	N/A	$700 - 850	$525 - 600	$1,100

D-15 MAHOGANY RUSH – dreadnought style, mahogany top/back/sides, round soundhole, three-stripe rosette, mahogany neck, 14/20-fret rosewood fingerboard with pearl dot inlays, three-per-side chrome tuners, rosewood bridge with white black dot pins, tortoiseshell pickguard, available in Black, Natural, or Wood Grain Red finish, 15.75 in. body width, 25.625 in. scale, mfg. 1983-88.

	N/A	$650 - 750	$525 - 600	$850

* D-15 12 Mahogany Rush 12-String – similar to the D-15, except in 12-string configuration and six-per-side tuners, available in Natural Mahogany or Woodgrain Red finish, mfg. 1983-85.

	N/A	$675 - 800	$525 - 600	$850

* D-15HG/D-16 Mahogany Rush – similar to the D-15 Mahogany Rush, except has a Natural gloss finish, mfg. 1983-88.

	N/A	$675 - 800	$525 - 600	

In 1987, this model was renamed the D-15 with a high gloss finish.

* D-17 Mahogany Rush – similar to the D-15 Mahogany Rush, except has a bound top and back and a Natural gloss finish, mfg. 1983-86.

	N/A	$700 - 850	$550 - 650	

»D-17 12 Mahogany Rush 12-String – similar to the D-17 Mahogany Rush, except in 12-string configuration and six-per-side tuners, mfg. 1984 only.

	N/A	$750 - 900	$575 - 675	

D-25 BLUEGRASS (NO. 350-0200) – dreadnought style, solid spruce or mahogany top, arched laminated mahogany or flat solid mahogany back, solid mahogany sides, round soundhole, black bound body, three-stripe rosette, mahogany neck, 14/20-fret rosewood fingerboard with pearl dot inlay, three-per-side chrome tuners, rosewood bridge with white black dot pins, tortoiseshell pickguard, available in Antique Burst, Black (1980-1999), Cherry Red (1968-1986), Mahogany, Natural or Woodgrain Red high gloss finish, 15.75 in. body width, 25.5 in. scale, mfg. 1968-2000.

1968-1978	N/A	$875 - 1,100	$525 - 650	
1979-1989	N/A	$750 - 900	$500 - 600	
1990-1999	N/A	$700 - 825	$425 - 500	$1,249

In 1969, a larger pickguard and a headstock with no veneer and a silkscreen logo were introduced. In 1976, a spruce top with either an arched laminated or solid flat mahogany back became optional, black top and back binding was introduced, and Shaded Mahogany and Cherry finishes were standard. In 1980, Black or Sunburst finish became optional. In 1987, listed colors were Black, Mahogany, Natural, Sunburst, and Woodgrain Red.

* D-212/D-25-12/D-225 12-String (Model 350-1000) – similar to the D-25 Bluegrass except in 12-string configuration and six-per-side tuners, available in Antique Burst, Black, Cherry, Mahogany, Natural, or Sunburst high gloss finish, mfg. 1981-1992, 1996-99.

1981-1992	N/A	$800 - 950	$625 - 750	
1996-1999	N/A	$750 - 875	$525 - 625	$1,249

This model was called the D-212 between 1981 and 1987 when it was renamed the D-25-12. In 1998, it was renamed the D-225.

* D-25C Cutaway – similar to the D-25 Bluegrass, except has a single smooth cutaway, mfg. 1983-85.

	N/A	$800 - 950	$625 - 750	

D-25 SECOND VERSION (NO. 380-0000) – dreadnought style, solid mahogany top/back/sides, round soundhole with rosette, single-ply white top and back binding, mahogany neck, 14/20-fret rosewood fingerboard with pearl dot inlays, three-per-side chrome tuners, rosewood bridge, black pickguard, available in Amber, Brown Sunburst, Honey Blonde Red Trans., Sapphire Blue Trans., or Seafoam Green finish, mfg. 1999-2003.

	N/A	$750 - 875	$475 - 550	$1,200

MSR/NOTES	100%	EXCELLENT	AVERAGE	LAST MSR

D-30 (NO. 350-1200) – dreadnought style, solid spruce top, arched maple back, solid maple sides, round soundhole, multi-ply top and back binding, mahogany neck, 14/20 rosewood fingerboard with pearl dot inlays, Chesterfield headstock inlay, three-per-side chrome tuners, tortoiseshell pickguard, available in Antique Burst (1997-99), Black, Blonde, Sunburst, or Woodgrain high gloss finish, 15.75 in. body width, 25.625 in. scale, mfg. 1987-1999.

	N/A	$950 - 1,100	$700 - 850	$1,400

D-35 BLUEGRASS – dreadnought style, solid spruce top, mahogany back/sides, round soundhole, bound body, one-stripe rosette, mahogany neck, 14/20-fret rosewood fingerboard with pearl dot inlays, black headstock overlay with screened logo, three-per-side chrome tuners, rosewood bridge with white black dot pins, tortoiseshell pickguard, available in Natural finish, 15.75 in. body width, 25.5 in. scale, mfg. 1968-1987.

	N/A	$1,050 - 1,250	$750 - 900	

In 1969, a larger pickguard was introduced, and the veneer from the headstock was removed and a silkscreen logo was added.

D-40 BLUEGRASS JUBILEE – dreadnought style, solid spruce top, mahogany back and sides, round soundhole, bound body, three-stripe rosette, three-piece mahogany neck, 14/20-fret rosewood fingerboard with pearl dot inlays, pearl Chesterfield/logo peghead inlay, three-per-side chrome tuners, rosewood bridge with white black dot pins, tortoiseshell pickguard, available in Natural finish, mfg. 1963-1992.

1963-1969	N/A	$1,650 - 2,000	$1,100 - 1,300	
1970-1979	N/A	$1,400 - 1,750	$950 - 1,150	
1980-1992	N/A	$1,250 - 1,500	$800 - 1,000	

* **D-40C Bluegrass Jubilee Cutaway** – similar to the D-40 Bluegrass Jubilee, except has a single sharp cutaway, mfg. 1975-1991.

1975-1979	N/A	$1,400 - 1,750	$950 - 1,150	
1980-1991	N/A	$1,250 - 1,500	$800 - 1,000	

D-40 SECOND VERSION (NO. 380-0100) – dreadnought style, solid spruce top, solid mahogany back and sides, round soundhole with rosette, multi-ply top and back binding, mahogany neck, 14/20-fret rosewood fingerboard with pearl dot inlays, black headstock overlay with pearl Chesterfield and logo inlays, three-per-side chrome tuners, rosewood bridge, tortoise pickguard, available in Antique Burst, Black, Natural, or Trans. Red lacquer finish, 25.625 in. scale, mfg. 1999-2003.

	N/A	$900 - 1,050	$675 - 800	$1,700

* **D40CE Cutaway Electric (No. 380-3106)** – similar to the D40 Second Version, except has a single cutaway and Fishman Prefix Pro Blend pickup/electronics, available in Antique Burst, Black, Natural, or Red Trans. finish, mfg. 2003 only.

	N/A	$1,300 - 1,450	$1,000 - 1,125	$2,000

* **D-40 Richie Havens Signature (No. 380-0110)** – similar to the D-40 except has a double pickguard setup and signature on truss rod cover, available in Black or Natural finish, mfg. 2003-09.

	N/A	$1,200 - 1,400	$700 - 850	$2,800

»**D-40 Richie Havens Signature Electric (No. 380/385-0115)** – similar to the D-40 Richie Havens Signature, except has Fishman electronics, available in Black or Natural finish, mfg. 2003-2013.

	$2,700	$1,400 - 1,750	$850 - 1,050	$3,400

D-40 BLUEGRASS JUBILEE THIRD VERSION (NO. 380/385-6300) – dreadnought style based on the 1963 model, solid red spruce top, solid mahogany back and sides, round soundhole, classic Guild rosette, tortoiseshell binding, one-piece mahogany neck, 14/20-fret Indian rosewood fingerboard with dot inlays, three-per-side Grover Rotomatic chrome tuners, Indian rosewood bridge with bone pins, tortoiseshell pickguard, available in Antique Burst or Natural finish, 25.5 in. scale, mfg. summer 2006-2013.

	$2,600	$1,350 - 1,675	$800 - 1,000	$3,300

* Add 2.5% (MSR $3,350) for Antique Burst finish.

This model was also available in left-handed configuration (No. 385-6320).

* **D-40 Bluegrass Jubilee Third Version Electric (No. 380/385-6305/3607)** – similar to the D-40 Bluegrass Jubilee Third Version, except has D-TAR Wavelength electronics, available in Antique Burst or Natural finish, mfg. summer 2006-2013.

	$2,890	$1,450 - 1,800	$875 - 1,100	$3,650

* Add 2.5% (MSR $3,750) for Antique Burst finish.

This model is also available in left-handed configuration (No. 385-6327).

D-40 STANDARD (NO. 385-5300) – dreadnought body style, solid Sitka spruce top, solid mahogany back and sides, red spruce bracing, round soundhole with multi-ring rosette, ivoroid body binding, slim profile mahogany neck, 14/20-fret rosewood fingerboard with pearl dot inlays, mahogany headstock overlay with pearl Guild logo, three-per-side chrome Gotoh tuners, rosewood bridge with bone pins, tortoise pickguard, available in Natural high gloss finish, 25.625 in. scale, hardshell case included, mfg. summer 2010-12.

	$1,800	$1,050 - 1,300	$650 - 800	$2,500

This model is also available in left-handed configuration (No. 385-5320).

MSR/NOTES	100%	EXCELLENT	AVERAGE	LAST MSR

* ***D-40CE Standard Cutaway Electric (No. 385-5306)*** – similar to the D-40 Standard, except has a single smooth cutaway and a D-TAR Wave-Length end pin mounted preamp with volume and tone controls, available in Natural high gloss finish, hardshell case included, mfg. 2011-present.

| MSR $3,200 | $2,550 | $1,325 - 1,650 | $800 - 1,000 | |

This model is also available in left-handed configuration (No. 385-5326).

D-44 BLUEGRASS JUBILEE – dreadnought style, solid spruce top, pearwood back and sides, round soundhole, five-stripe bound body/ rosette, mahogany neck, 14/20-fret ebony fingerboard with pearl dot inlays, pearl Chesterfield/logo peghead inlay, three-per-side chrome tuners, ebony bridge with white black dot pins, tortoiseshell pickguard, available in Natural or Sunburst finish, 15.75 in. body width, 25.5 in. scale, mfg. 1965-1972.

| | N/A | $1,325 - 1,650 | $800 - 1,000 | |

* ***D-44M Bluegrass Jubilee*** – similar to the D-44 Bluegrass Jubilee, except has maple back and sides, mfg. circa 1971-79.

| | N/A | $1,325 - 1,650 | $800 - 1,000 | |

D-46 – dreadnought body, solid spruce top, ash back and sides, round soundhole, multi-ply top binding, ash neck, 14/20-fret ebony fingerboard with dot inlays, Chesterfield headstock inlay, three-per-side chrome tuners, ebony bridge, black pickguard, available in Natural or Sunburst finish, mfg. 1980-85.

| | N/A | $1,150 - 1,350 | $850 - 1,000 | |

D-47CE – single sharp cutaway dreadnought style, spruce top, mahogany back and sides, oval soundhole, mahogany neck, 14/20-fret rosewood fingerboard with dot inlays, Chesterfield headstock inlay, three-per-side tuners, rosewood bridge, Fishman TASS pickup, available in Black, Natural, or Sunburst finish, 15.75 in. body width, 24.75 in. scale, mfg. 1983-85.

| | N/A | $1,100 - 1,300 | $800 - 950 | |

D-48 – dreadnought style, spruce top, laminated arched mahogany back, solid mahogany sides, scalloped bracing, round soundhole, multi-ply binding, mahogany neck, 14/20-fret rosewood fingerboard with dot inlays, three-per-side tuners, rosewood bridge, available in Natural or Sunburst finish, mfg. 1992 only.

| | N/A | $1,000 - 1,150 | $750 - 900 | $1,495 |

D-50 BLUEGRASS SPECIAL – dreadnought style, solid spruce top, rosewood back and sides, round soundhole, five-stripe bound body/ rosette, three-piece mahogany neck, 14/20-fret ebony fingerboard with pearl dot inlays, pearl Chesterfield/logo peghead inlay, three-per-side chrome tuners, ebony bridge with white black dot pins, tortoiseshell pickguard, available in Natural or Antique Burst finish, mfg. 1963-1993.

1963-1969 (Brazilian)	N/A	$2,400 - 3,000	$1,450 - 1,800	
1970-1979 (Indian)	N/A	$1,400 - 1,750	$850 - 1,050	
1980-1993	N/A	$1,200 - 1,500	$725 - 900	$1,395

In 1968, the Chesterfield headstock inlay was introduced. In 1974, a one-piece mahogany neck was introduced. In 1975, an ebony bridge was introduced. In 1987, scalloped bracing and a snakehead headstock was introduced.

* ***D-50-12/D-312 12-String*** – similar to the D-50 Bluegrass Special, except in 12-string configuration and six-per-side tuners, mfg. 1986-87.

| | N/A | $1,300 - 1,600 | $800 - 1,000 | |

D-50 SECOND VERSION (NO. 380-0300) – dreadnought style, spruce top, rosewood back and sides, round soundhole with rosette, multi-ply black and white top and back binding, mahogany neck, 14/20-fret ebony fingerboard with MOP dot inlays, black headstock overlay with Chesterfield/logo pearl inlays, three-per-side chrome tuners, rosewood bridge, tortoiseshell pickguard, available in Antique Burst or Natural finish, 25.625 in. scale, disc. 2003.

| | N/A | $1,100 - 1,300 | $750 - 900 | $1,900 |

* ***D50CE Cutaway Electric (No. 380-3306)*** – similar to the D50 Second Version, except has a single cutaway and Fishman Prefix Pro Blend pickup/electronics, available in Natural or Antique Burst finish, disc. 2003.

| | N/A | $1,300 - 1,450 | $1,000 - 1,150 | $2,200 |

D-50 BLUEGRASS SPECIAL THIRD VERSION (NO. 380/385-6400) – dreadnought style based on the 1963 model, solid red spruce top, solid rosewood back and sides, round soundhole, classic Guild rosette, tortoiseshell binding, one-piece mahogany neck, 14/20-fret ebony fingerboard with dot inlays, three-per-side Grover Rotomatic chrome tuners, rosewood bridge with bone pins, tortoiseshell pickguard, available in Antique Burst or Natural finish, 25.5 in. scale, mfg. summer 2006-present.

| MSR $3,400 | $2,700 | $1,350 - 1,700 | $825 - 1,025 | |

• **Add 2.5% (MSR $3,450) for Antique Burst finish.**

This model is also available in left-handed configuration (No. 385-6420).

* ***D-50 Bluegrass Special Third Version Electric (No. 380/385-6405/6407)*** – similar to the D-50 Bluegrass Special Third Version, except has D-TAR Wavelength electronics, available in Antique Burst or Natural finish, mfg. summer 2006-present.

| MSR $3,750 | $3,000 | $1,475 - 1,850 | $875 - 1,100 | |

• **Add 2.5% (MSR $3,800) for Antique Burst finish.**

This model is also available in left-handed configuration (No. 385-6427).

MSR/NOTES	100%	EXCELLENT	AVERAGE	LAST MSR

D-50 STANDARD (NO. 385-5400) – dreadnought body style, solid Sitka spruce top, solid Indian rosewood back and sides, red spruce bracing, round soundhole with multi-ring rosette, ivoroid body binding, slim profile mahogany neck, 14/20-fret rosewood fingerboard with pearl dot inlays, mahogany headstock overlay with pearl Guild logo, three-per-side chrome Gotoh tuners, rosewood bridge with bone pins, tortoise pickguard, available in Antique Burst (2012 only) or Natural high gloss finish, 25.625 in. scale, hardshell case included, mfg. summer 2010-2012.

	$2,000	$1,125 - 1,400	$675 - 850	$2,700

• Add 2.5% (Last MSR was 2,750) for Antique Burst finish.

This model is also available in left-handed configuration (No. 385-5420).

* D-50CE Standard Cutaway Electric (No. 385-5406) – similar to the D-50 Standard, except has a single smooth cutaway and a D-TAR Wave-Length end pin mounted preamp with volume and tone controls, available in Antique Burst (2012-present) or Natural high gloss finish, hardshell case included, mfg. 2011-present.

MSR $3,300	$2,650	$1,350 - 1,700	$825 - 1,025

• Add 2.5% (MSR $3,350) for Antique Burst finish.

This model is also available in left-handed configuration (No. 385-5426).

D-52 – dreadnought body, solid spruce top, rosewood back and sides, round soundhole with herringbone soundhole ring, scalloped bracing, mahogany neck, 14/20-fret ebony fingerboard with dot inlays, Chesterfield headstock inlay, three-per-side chrome tuners, ebony bridge, available in Natural or Sunburst finish, 15.75 in. body width, 25.625 in. scale, mfg. 1983-84.

	N/A	$1,300 - 1,550	$1,000 - 1,150

D-55 (TV MODEL)/D-65 (NO. 350-0300/380-0500) – dreadnought style, solid spruce top, bookmatched rosewood back, solid rosewood sides, round soundhole, three-stripe body binding, abalone rosette, three-piece mahogany neck, 14/20-fret bound ebony fingerboard with pearl block/abalone wedge inlays, bound headstock with pearl shield/logo inlay, three-per-side gold tuners, ebony bridge with white abalone dot pins, maple endpin wedge, tortoiseshell pickguard, available in Antique Burst, Ice Tea Burst, or Natural lacquer finish, case included, 15.75 in. body width, 25.5 in. scale, mfg. 1968-1987, 1990-present.

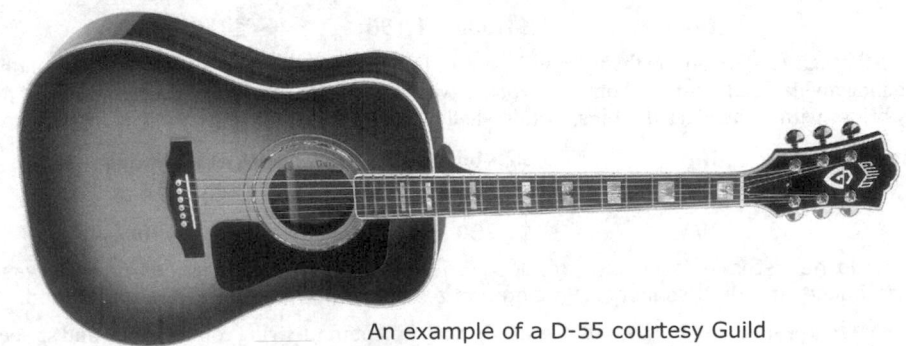

An example of a D-55 courtesy Guild

1968-1969	N/A	$2,400 - 2,850	$1,500 - 1,800
1970-1979	N/A	$2,000 - 2,300	$1,200 - 1,500
1980-1987	N/A	$1,650 - 1,950	$1,050 - 1,250
1990-1998	N/A	$1,500 - 1,900	$1,000 - 1,200
1999-Present MSR $3,900	$2,950	$1,450 - 1,875	$900 - 1,125

• Add 2.5% (MSR $3,950) for Antique Burst finish.

This model was a special order only between 1968 and 1973 and was originally called the TV Model D-55. In 1972, an ebony bridge was introduced. In 1973, a three-piece padouk/maple neck was introduced. In 1987, this model was renamed the D-65, but it was disc. later that year. In 1990, this model was reintroduced as the D-55, with a few minor changes: a larger headstock and 25.625 in. scale. This model is also available in left-handed configuration (No. 385-0520).

* D-55 Electric (No. 380-0505/0507) – similar to the D-55 (TV Model)/D-65, except has Fishman (disc. 2006) or D-TAR Wavelength electronics (summer 2006-present), available in Antique Burst or Natural finish, mfg. summer 2006-present.

MSR $4,200	$3,200	$1,650 - 2,050	$1,000 - 1,250

• Add 2.5% (MSR $4,250) for Antique Burst finish.

This model is also available in left-handed configuration (No. 385-0527).

D-60/D-66 – dreadnought style, spruce top, rosewood back and sides, round soundhole, scalloped bracing, multi-ply top and back binding, mahogany neck, 14/20-fret bound ebony fingerboard with slotted diamond inlays, bound snakehead-shaped headstock with G shield logo inlay, three-per-side tuners, available in Natural finish, 15.75 in. body width, 25.625 in. scale, designed by George Gruhn, mfg. 1984-1990.

	N/A	$1,650 - 2,000	$1,100 - 1,300

In 1987, this model was renamed the D-60.

MSR/NOTES	100%	EXCELLENT	AVERAGE	LAST MSR

D-60 SECOND VERSION (NO. 350-1600) – dreadnought style, solid spruce top, flame maple back and sides, round soundhole with abalone ring, multi-ply top and back binding, maple neck, 14/20-fret bound ebony fingerboard with pearl/abalone block/V insert inlays, bound large black headstock overlay with G shield logo/inlay, three-per-side gold tuners, ebony bridge, black pickguard, available in Antique Burst or Natural finish, 15.75 in. body width, 25.625 in. scale, mfg. 1998-2000.

| | N/A | $1,400 - 1,750 | $1,000 - 1,200 | $2,200 |

D-62 – dreadnought style, spruce top, mahogany back and sides, round soundhole, 14/20-fret rosewood fingerboard with small slotted squares and diamonds inlay, snakehead-shaped headstock with three-per-side tuners, designed by George Gruhn, mfg. 1984-85.

| | N/A | $1,500 - 1,800 | $1,000 - 1,200 | |

Early versions of this model may only have fingerboard inlays at the 5th, 7th, and 9th frets.

D-64 – dreadnought style, spruce top, maple back and sides, round soundhole, multi-ply top and back binding, 14/20-fret bound ebony fingerboard with notched diamonds inlay, bound snakehead-shaped headstock with G shield logo/inlay, three-per-side chrome tuners, designed by George Gruhn, mfg. 1984-86.

| | N/A | $1,500 - 1,900 | $1,000 - 1,200 | |

D-70 LIMITED EDITION – dreadnought style, spruce top, rosewood back and sides, round soundhole with pearl ring, multi-ply top and back binding with maple outer layer, scalloped bracing, mahogany neck, 14/20-fret ebony fingerboard with humptop trapezoid inlay, ivory nut, bound headstock with G shield logo inlay, ebony truss rod cover, three-per-side gold tuners, ebony bridge with an ivory saddle, available in Natural finish, 15.75 in. body width, 25.625 in. scale, mfg. 1981-85.

| | N/A | $2,200 - 2,700 | $1,600 - 1,900 | |

* *D-70C Carved Limited Edition* – similar to the D-70 Limited Edition, except has a carved neck, mfg. 1983-85.

| | N/A | $2,300 - 2,800 | $1,650 - 1,950 | |

DK-70 PEACOCK LIMITED EDITION – dreadnought style, koa body, ebony fingerboard with abalone cloud inlays, abalone Guild logo inlay on headstock, abalone peacock inlay on pickguard, available in Natural finish, mfg. 1995-96.

| | N/A | $2,300 - 2,850 | $1,650 - 2,000 | $4,999 |

The projected production run of this model was 50 pieces. It is estimated that only half were actually completed.

D-80/D-100 – dreadnought style, solid spruce top, solid rosewood back/sides, scalloped bracing, round soundhole, maple bound body, abalone purfling/rosette, three-piece mahogany/maple neck, 14/20-fret maple bound ebony fingerboard with abalone crown inlay, maple bound peghead with abalone shield/logo inlay, three-per-side gold tuners, ebony bridge with white abalone dot pins, maple endpin wedge, black pickguard, available in Natural or Sunburst finish, mfg. 1983-87, 1990-98.

| | N/A | $3,000 - 3,500 | $1,950 - 2,300 | $3,600 |

* *D-80C/D-100C (No. 350-0400)* – similar to the D-80/D-100, except has a handcarved neck heel, available in Antique Burst or Natural high gloss lacquer finish, case included, mfg. 1983-87, 1990-2000.

| | N/A | $3,100 - 3,600 | $2,000 - 2,400 | $4,000 |

DV-4 (NO. 350-0150/380-0040/383-0040) – dreadnought style, solid spruce top, solid mahogany back and sides, round soundhole with rings, body binding, one-piece mahogany neck, 14/20-fret rosewood fingerboard with pearl dot inlays, natural headstock with Guild logo, three-per-side chrome tuners, rosewood bridge, tortoiseshell pickguard, available in Natural Satin finish, 25.625 in. scale, mfg. 1999-2000, reintroduced summer 2007-2011.

| 1999-2000 | N/A | $600 - 700 | $375 - 450 | |
| 2007-2011 | $800 | $500 - 600 | $325 - 400 | $1,100 |

DV-6 (NO. 350-0500) – dreadnought style, solid spruce top, solid Indian rosewood back and sides, shaved bracing, round soundhole, vintage herringbone rosette, mahogany neck, 14/20-fret rosewood fingerboard with dot inlay, three-per-side gold tuners, tortoiseshell pickguard, available in Natural hand rubbed satin finish, case included, mfg. 1995-98, reintroduced summer 2007-2011.

| 1995-1998 | N/A | $675 - 800 | $425 - 500 | |
| 2007-2011 | $840 | $550 - 650 | $350 - 425 | $1,200 |

* *DV-6 HG (No. 350-0600)* – similar to the DV-6, except available in Antique Burst or Natural high gloss lacquer finish, case included, mfg. 1995-98.

| | N/A | $850 - 1,000 | $600 - 700 | $1,300 |

DV-25 (NO. 350-0250) – dreadnought style, solid spruce top, solid mahogany back and sides, round soundhole with rings, body binding, one-piece mahogany neck, 14/20-fret rosewood fingerboard with pearl dot inlays, black headstock with Guild logo, three-per-side chrome tuners, rosewood bridge, tortoiseshell pickguard, available in Antique Sunburst, Black, or Natural finish, 25.625 in. scale, mfg. 1999-2000.

| | N/A | $650 - 750 | $425 - 500 | $1,185 |

DV-52 (NO. 350-0700) – dreadnought style, solid spruce top, solid rosewood back and sides, round soundhole, hand-scalloped bracing, multi-ply body binding with cream outer layer, abalone rosette, mahogany neck, 14/20-fret ebony fingerboard with pearl dot inlay, black headstock overlay with pearl Chesterfield and logo inlay, three-per-side gold tuners, ebony bridge with white black dot pins, black pickguard, available in Natural satin lacquer finish, case included, mfg. 1992-2000.

| | N/A | $1,000 - 1,200 | $750 - 900 | $1,550 |

MSR/NOTES	100%	EXCELLENT	AVERAGE	LAST MSR

* **DV-52 HG (No. 350-0800)** – similar to the DV-52, except available in Antique Burst or Natural high gloss lacquer finish, case included, mfg. 1992-2000.

	N/A	$1,100 - 1,300	$800 - 950	$1,700

DV-62 – dreadnought style, solid spruce top, rosewood back and sides, round soundhole, herringbone bound body/rosette, mahogany neck, 14/20-fret ebony fingerboard with pearl dot inlay, pearl Chesterfield/logo headstock inlay, three-per-side gold tuners, ebony bridge with white black dot pins, tortoiseshell pickguard, available in Natural or Sunburst finish, mfg. 1993-95.

	N/A	$1,250 - 1,450	$850 - 1,000	$1,500

DV-72 – dreadnought style, solid AAAA feathered spruce top, solid rosewood back and sides, round soundhole with turquoise rosette, cream body binding, herringbone top purfling, herringbone backstripe, multi-ply B/W back purfling, mahogany neck, 14/20-fret ebony fingerboard with turquoise triangles in pearl block inlays, black headstock overlay with pearl Guild logo and turquoise sheild inlays, three-per-side Grover Super Rotomatic chrome tuners, ebony bridge with inlaid turquoise triangles, available in Natural or Sunburst finish, limted edition run of 200 instruments, serial number starts with LK, mfg. 1993 only.

	N/A	$1,400 - 1,750	$1,000 - 1,200	

DV-74 PUEBLO (LIMITED EDITION) – dreadnought style, solid spruce top, herringbone top binding, rosewood back and sides, ebony fingerboard with South Sea coral/onyx/turquoise/nickel silver Southwestern motif, South Sea coral/onyx/turquoise/nickel silver design on rosette, chrome silver hardware, Grover Imperial tuners, mfg. 1996 only.

	N/A	$2,100 - 2,500	$1,400 - 1,700	$2,499

In 1996, Guild announced that only 50 of these guitars would be constructed, but it is not known if the full production run was completed.

G-37 – square shouldered dreadnought style, solid spruce top, laminated arched maple back, maple sides, round soundhole, bound body, three-stripe rosette, mahogany neck, 14/20-fret rosewood fingerboard with pearl dot inlays, pearl logo headstock inlay, three-per-side chrome tuners, rosewood bridge with white black dot pins, tortoise pickguard, available in Black, Natural, or Sunburst finish, 15.75 in. body width, 5 in. body depth, 25.5 in. scale, mfg. 1972-1987.

1972-1979	N/A	$1,000 - 1,200	$725 - 850	
1980-1987	N/A	$900 - 1,050	$650 - 750	

In 1976, a laminated maple neck and a Chesterfield headstock logo were introduced. In 1987, this model was renamed the D-30.

G-41 – rounded shouldered dreadnought style, solid spruce top, mahogany back and sides, round soundhole, bound body, three-stripe rosette, mahogany neck, 14/20-fret rosewood fingerboard with pearl dot inlays, pearl Chesterfield and logo headstock inlays, three-per-side chrome tuners, rosewood bridge with white black dot pins, tortoise pickguard, available in Black, Natural, or Sunburst finish, 17 in. body width, 5 in. body depth, 26.25 in. scale, mfg. 1974-77.

	N/A	$1,300 - 1,550	$850 - 1,000	

G-75 – 3/4-sized square shouldered dreadnought style, solid spruce top, rosewood back and sides, round soundhole, bound body, three-stripe rosette, mahogany neck, 14/20-fret ebony fingerboard with pearl dot inlays, pearl Chesterfield and logo headstock inlays, three-per-side chrome tuners, ebony bridge with white black dot pins, black pickguard, available in Natural finish, 15 in. body width, 5 in. body depth, 25.5 in. scale, mfg. 1975-77.

	N/A	$1,250 - 1,450	$850 - 1,000	

This model is basically a D-50 with a 3/4-sized body.

G-212 12-STRING – 12-string configuration, dreadnought style, solid spruce top, mahogany back and sides, round soundhole, tortoiseshell celluloid body binding, three-stripe rosette, mahogany neck, double truss rods, 14/20-fret rosewood fingerboard with no inlays, pearl Chesterfield/logo peghead inlay, six-per-side chrome Guild tuners, rosewood bridge with white black dot pins, tortoise pickguard, available in Natural or Sunburst finish, 15.75 in. body width, 25.5 in. scale, mfg. 1974-1983.

	N/A	$1,150 - 1,350	$800 - 950	$895

This model is a 12-string version of the D-40.

G-312 12-STRING – 12-string configuration, dreadnought style, solid spruce top, rosewood back and sides, round soundhole, seven-ply white ivoroid body binding, three-stripe rosette, three-piece mahogany neck, double truss rods, 14/20-fret ebony fingerboard with no inlays, pearl Chesterfield/logo peghead inlay, six-per-side chrome Schaller tuners, rosewood bridge with white black dot pins, black pickguard, available in Natural or Sunburst finish, 15.75 in. body width, 25.5 in. scale, mfg. 1974-1985.

1974-1979	N/A	$1,350 - 1,750	$900 - 1,100	
1980-1985	N/A	$1,100 - 1,400	$750 - 900	$1,130

This model is a 12-string version of the D-50.

ACOUSTIC: F-STYLE MODELS (F, GF, GV PREFIX)

Models in this series are based on Guild's F orchestra style guitars, however not every model follows this design - especially in the 12-string versions. By the late 1980s, Guild abandoned use of the F Series with these type of guitars and reassigned them to the new Traditional Acoustic Series that are all cutaway electrics. After the late 1980s, guitars were split up into JF models for jumbos or GF for orchestra models.

MSR/NOTES	100%	EXCELLENT	AVERAGE	LAST MSR

F-20 TROUBADOR – small body narrow waist body style, solid spruce top, maple (1956-1958) or mahogany (1959-1987) back and sides, round soundhole, single rosette, body binding, mahogany neck, 14/20-fret rosewood fingerboard with pearl dot inlays, blackface headstock with screened logo, three-per-side chrome tuners, rosewood bridge with white pins, tortoiseshell pickguard, available in Natural or Sunburst top with Mahogany Stain back and sides finish, 13.75 in. body width, 4.125 in. body depth, 24.75 in. scale, mfg. 1956-1987.

1956-1958	N/A	$1,400 - 1,700	$900 - 1,100	
1959-1969	N/A	$1,200 - 1,450	$850 - 1,000	
1970-1979	N/A	$1,000 - 1,200	$675 - 800	
1980-1987	N/A	$800 - 950	$550 - 650	

In 1976, a few dimensions were changed with a deeper 4.25 in. body depth and a longer 25.5 in. scale.

* **F-20 3/4** – similar to the F-20 Troubador, except has a 3/4-sized body, 13.125 in. body width, 3.75 in. body depth, 22.5 in. scale, mfg. 1969-1977.

	N/A	$900 - 1,050	$650 - 750	

* **M-20(S) Economy** – similar to F-20 Troubador, except has an all mahogany body and a satin finish, mfg. 1958-1972, 1977-78.

1958-1969	N/A	$1,150 - 1,400	$800 - 950	
1970-1978	N/A	$1,000 - 1,150	$600 - 750	

F-20 STANDARD (NO. 385-1200) – concert body style, solid Sitka spruce top, solid mahogany back and sides, red spruce bracing, round soundhole with ivoroid multi-ring rosette, ivoroid body binding, black/ivoroid/black purfling, slim profile mahogany neck, 14/20-fret rosewood fingerboard with pearl dot inlays, mahogany headstock overlay with pearl Guild logo, three-per-side chrome Gotoh tuners, rosewood bridge with bone pins, tortoise pickguard, available in Natural high gloss finish, 25.5 in. scale, hardshell case included, mfg. 2013-present.

MSR $2,800	$2,100	$1,200 - 1,500	$725 - 900	

This model is also available in left-handed configuration (No. 385-1220).

* **F-20E Standard Electric (No. 385-1206)** – similar to the F-20 Standard, except has D-TAR Wave-Length end pin mounted preamp with volume and tone controls, available in Natural high gloss finish, hardshell case included, mfg. 2013-present.

MSR $3,100	$2,450	$1,250 - 1,575	$750 - 950	

This model is also available in left-handed configuration (No. 385-1226).

F-30 ARAGON – small body narrow waist body style, solid spruce top, maple (1954-1958) or mahogany (1959-1986) back and sides, round soundhole, single rosette, bound body, mahogany neck, 14/20-fret rosewood fingerboard with pearl dot inlays, blackface headstock with screened logo, three-per-side chrome tuners, rosewood bridge with white pins, black pickguard, available in Natural top/Mahogany Stain back/sides finish, 15 in. body width, 4 in. body depth, 25.5 in. scale, mfg. 1954-1986.

1954-1958	N/A	$1,750 - 2,200	$1,150 - 1,400	
1959-1969	N/A	$1,400 - 1,750	$1,000 - 1,150	
1970-1979	N/A	$1,200 - 1,450	$850 - 1,000	
1980-1986	N/A	$1,000 - 1,200	$700 - 800	

In 1957, a larger pickguard and a G shield logo headstock inlay were introduced. In 1959, a 24.75 in. scale neck was introduced. In the early 1960s, a Chesterfield headstock inlay was introduced. In 1969, a silkscreen headstock logo was introduced. In 1970, a wider 15.5 in. body and a longer 25.5 in. scale neck was introduced.

* **F-30R Aragon** – similar to the F-30 Aragon, except has rosewood back and sides, mfg. 1973-75, 1976-78.

1973-1975	N/A	$1,450 - 1,850	$1,100 - 1,200	
1976-1978	N/A	$1,300 - 1,650	$900 - 1,050	

This model was disc. in late 1975 and reintroduced in 1976 with slightly different specs including an F-50 style neck and deluxe trimmings.

* **M-30 Del Rio** – similar to the F-30 Aragon, except has an all mahogany body and a black pickguard, mfg. 1959-1964.

	N/A	$1,200 - 1,450	$850 - 1,000	

F-30 HR/M-20 SECOND VERSION (NO. 350-5300) – small body narrow waist body style, solid mahogany top, solid mahogany back/sides, round soundhole, 14/20-fret rosewood fingerboard with dot inlays, blackface headstock with Chesterfield and logo inlays, three-per-side chrome tuners, tortoise pickguard, available in Natural hand rubbed satin finish, case included, 13.75 in. body width, 24.75 in. scale, mfg. 1998-2000.

	N/A	$725 - 850	$525 - 600	$1,000

This model was first introduced as the F-30HR (a satin hand-rubbed finish version of the F-30), but it was renamed the M-20 to coincide with the relationship of the vintage F-30 and the M-20 guitars.

F-30 HG SECOND VERSION (NO. 350-5400) – small body narrow waist body style, solid spruce top, solid mahogany back and sides, round soundhole, 14/20-fret rosewood fingerboard with dot inlays, blackface headstock with Chesterfield and logo inlays, three-per-side chrome tuners, tortoise pickguard, available in Antique Burst, Black, or Natural high gloss finish, case included, 15 in. body width, 24.75 in. scale, mfg. 1998-2000.

	N/A	$850 - 1,000	$600 - 700	$1,400

* **F-30 R Second Version (No. 350-5500)** – similar to the F-30 HG, except has rosewood back and sides, an ebony fingerboard, and gold tuners, available in Antique Burst or Natural high gloss finish, case included, mfg. 1998-2000.

	N/A	$1,000 - 1,150	$700 - 850	$1,600

MSR/NOTES	100%	EXCELLENT	AVERAGE	LAST MSR

F-30 ARAGON THIRD VERSION (NO. 380/385-6500) – orchestra-style body, solid red spruce top, solid mahogany back and sides, round soundhole with rings, tortoise body binding, three-piece mahogany neck, 14/20-fret rosewood fingerboard with pearl dot inlays, rosewood headstock overlay with G and Guild logo inlays, three-per-side chrome Gotoh tuners, rosewood bridge, available in Antique Burst, Ice Tea Burst (2007-08), or Natural finish, 25.5 in. scale, mfg. 2007-present.

MSR $3,300	$2,500	$1,275 - 1,600	$750 - 950	

• **Add 2.5% (MSR $3,350) for Antique Burst finish.**

This model is also available in left-handed configuration (No. 385-6520).

* F-30 Aragon Third Version Electric (No. 380/385-6506/6507) – similar to the F-30 Aragon Third Version, except has D-TAR Wavelength electronics, available in Antique Burst, Ice Tea Burst (2007-08), or Natural finish, mfg. 2007-present.

MSR $3,650	$2,800	$1,400 - 1,750	$850 - 1,050	

• **Add 2.5% (MSR $3,700) for Antique Burst finish.**

This model is also available in left-handed configuration (No. 385-6527).

F-30 STANDARD (NO. 385-5500) – orchestra body style, solid Sitka spruce top, solid mahogany back and sides, red spruce bracing, round soundhole with multi-ring rosette, ivoroid body binding, slim profile mahogany neck, 14/20-fret rosewood fingerboard with pearl dot inlays, mahogany headstock overlay with pearl Guild logo, three-per-side chrome Gotoh tuners, rosewood bridge with bone pins, tortoise pickguard, available in Natural high gloss finish, 25.5 in. scale, hardshell case included, mfg. summer 2010-2012.

	$1,800	$1,050 - 1,300	$625 - 775	$2,500

This model is also available in left-handed configuration (No. 385-5520).

* F-30CE Standard Cutaway Electric (No. 385-5506) – similar to the F-30 Standard, except has a single smooth cutaway and a D-TAR Wave-Length end pin mounted preamp with volume and tone controls, available in Natural high gloss finish, hardshell case included, mfg. 2011-present.

MSR $3,100	$2,450	$1,250 - 1,575	$750 - 950	

This model is also available in left-handed configuration (No. 385-5526).

* F-30R Standard Rosewood (No. 385-5700) – similar to the F-30 Standard, except has solid Indian rosewood back and sides, available in Antique Burst (2012 only) or Natural high gloss finish, hardshell case included, mfg. summer 2010-2012.

	$2,000	$1,125 - 1,400	$675 - 850	$2,700

• **Add 2.5% (Last MSR was $2,750) for Antique Burst finish.**

This model is also available in left-handed configuration (No. 385-5720).

»F-30RCE Standard Rosewood Cutaway Electric (No. 385-5706) – similar to the F-30R Standard Rosewood, except has a single smooth cutaway and a D-TAR Wave-Length end pin mounted preamp with volume and tone controls, available in Antique Burst (2012-present) or Natural high gloss finish, hardshell case included, mfg. 2011-present.

MSR $3,300	$2,650	$1,350 - 1,700	$825 - 1,025	

• **Add 2.5% (MSR $3,350) for Antique Burst finish.**

This model is also available in left-handed configuration (No. 385-5726).

F-40 BLUEGRASS/VALENCIA – small body narrow waist concert body style, solid spruce top, maple back and sides, round soundhole, two-stripe rosette, multi-ply body binding, three-piece mahogany/maple neck, 14/20-fret bound rosewood fingerboard with six or seven pearloid block inlays, blackface headstock with pearl G shield and logo inlay, three-per-side chrome tuners, rosewood bridge with white pins, tortoiseshell celluloid pickguard, available in Natural or Sunburst finish, 16 in. body width, 4.25 in. body depth, 25.5 in. scale, mfg. 1954-1963, 1973-1983.

1954-1956	N/A	$2,600 - 3,100	$1,750 - 2,100	
1957-1963	N/A	$2,300 - 2,800	$1,600 - 1,950	
1973-1983	N/A	$1,400 - 1,700	$1,000 - 1,150	

Models produced between 1954 and 1957 do not have an inlay in the first fret. In 1957, a larger pickguard and Chesterfield headstock logo were introduced. When this model was reintroduced in 1973, it was called the Bluegrass F-40. Later models may have a maple neck.

F-40 VALENCIA SECOND VERSION (NO. 380/385-6600) – grand orchestra-style body, solid red spruce top, solid mahogany back and sides, round soundhole with rings, tortoise body binding, three-piece mahogany neck, 14/20-fret rosewood fingerboard with pearl dot

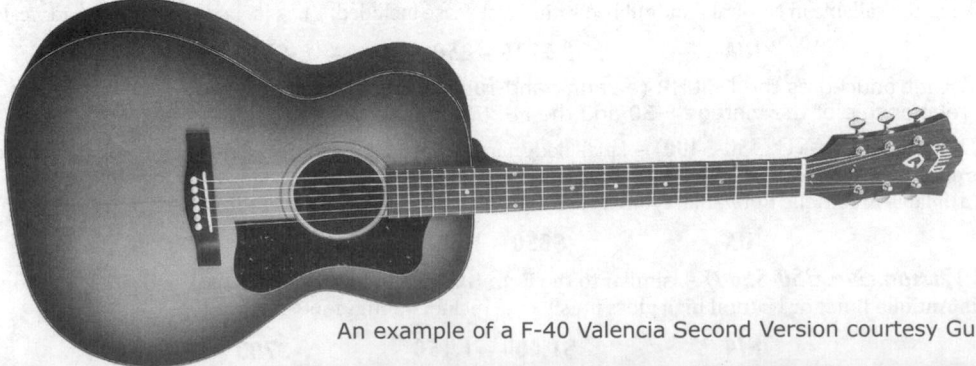

An example of a F-40 Valencia Second Version courtesy Guild

MSR/NOTES	100%	EXCELLENT	AVERAGE	LAST MSR

inlays, rosewood headstock overlay with G and Guild logo inlays, three-per-side chrome Gotoh tuners, rosewood bridge, available in Antique Burst, Ice Tea Burst (2007-09), or Natural finish, 25.5 in. scale, mfg. 2007-present.

MSR $3,300	$2,650	$1,350 - 1,700	$825 - 1,025	

* Add 2.5% (MSR $3,350) for Antique Burst finish.

This model is also available in left-handed configuration (No. 385-6630).

* **F-40 Valencia Second Version Electric (No. 380/385-6606/6607)** – similar to the F-40 Valencia Second Version, except has D-TAR Wavelength electronics, available in Antique Burst, Ice Tea Burst (2007-08), or Natural finish, mfg. 2007-present.

MSR $3,650	$2,800	$1,400 - 1,750	$850 - 1,050	

* Add 2.5% (MSR $3,700) for Antique Burst finish.

This model is also available in left-handed configuration (No. 385-6637).

F-42 – folk body style, spruce top, mahogany back and sides, round soundhole, plain ivoroid body binding, 14/20-fret rosewood fingerboard with small slotted diamond and square inlays, snakehead-shaped headstock with a raised pearloid logo, three-per-side tuners, rosewood bridge, 16 in. body width, designed by George Gruhn, mfg. 1984-85.

	N/A	$1,400 - 1,750	$1,000 - 1,150	

F-44/GF-60M – folk body style, spruce top, maple back and sides, round soundhole, multi-ply body binding, 14/20-fret bound ebony fingerboard with notched diamond inlays, snakehead-shaped headstock with G shield pearloid logo, three-per-side chrome tuners, rosewood bridge, 16 in. body width, designed by George Gruhn, mfg. 1984-89.

	N/A	$1,800 - 2,250	$1,150 - 1,350	

In 1987, this model was renamed the GF-60M and gold hardware was introduced.

F-46/GF-60R/GF-55 – folk body style, spruce top, rosewood back and sides, round soundhole, multi-ply body binding, 14/20-fret bound ebony fingerboard with notched diamond inlays, snakehead-shaped headstock with G shield pearloid logo, three-per-side chrome tuners, rosewood bridge, 16 in. body width, designed by George Gruhn, mfg. 1984-1991.

	N/A	$1,650 - 2,050	$1,050 - 1,250	

In 1987, this model was renamed the GF-60R and gold hardware was introduced. In 1990, this model was renamed the GF-55.

* **GF-60C Cutaway** – similar to the F-46/GF-60R/GF-55, except has a single sharp cutaway, designed by George Gruhn, mfg. 1989 only.

	N/A	$1,700 - 2,100	$1,100 - 1,300	

F-47 BLUEGRASS – folk body style, spruce top, mahogany back and sides, round soundhole with four rings, multi-ply body binding, three-piece mahogany neck, 14/20-fret bound rosewood fingerboard with eight pearloid block inlays, black headstock with Chesterfield and logo inlay, three-per-side chrome tuners, rosewood bridge, Bluegrass (horses and horseshoe design) or regular tortoiseshell pickguard, available in Natural finish, 16 in. body width, 25.5 in. scale, mfg. 1963-1976.

1963-1969	N/A	$2,000 - 2,400	$1,200 - 1,500	
1970-1976	N/A	$1,600 - 2,000	$1,100 - 1,300	

This guitar is very similar to the F-40 that was discontinued in the same year, with the exception of mahogany back and sides.

F-47M (NO. 380/385-4000) – grand orchestra-sized body, solid red spruce, solid flame maple back and sides, round soundhole with rings rosette, white body bindings with multi-laminate purfling, three-piece mahogany neck, dovetail neck joint, 20-fret rosewood fingerboard with MOP block inlays, MOP crest headstock inlay, three-per-side nickel Gotoh tuners, rosewood bridge, tortoiseshell pickguard, chrome hardware, available in Antique Burst, Blonde, or Ice Tea Burst (2007-09) finish, 25.625 in. scale, deluxe hardshell case included, mfg. summer 2007-present.

MSR $3,600	$2,800	$1,400 - 1,750	$850 - 1,050	

* Add 2.5% (MSR $3,650) for Antique Burst finish.

This model is also available in left-handed configuration (No. 385-4020).

* **F-47MC (No. 380/385-4106/4107)** – similar to the F-47M, except has a single Florentine cutaway and D-TAR Wavelength electronics, available in Antique Burst, Blonde/Natural, or Ice Tea Burst (2007-08) finish, mfg. summer 2007-present.

MSR $3,900	$3,000	$1,525 - 1,900	$925 - 1,125	

* Add 2.5% (MSR $3,950) for Antique Burst finish.

This model is also available in left-handed configuration (No. 385-4127).

* **F-47M Electric (No. 380/385-4006/4007)** – similar to the F-47M, except has D-TAR Wavelength electronics, available in Antique Burst or Natural finish, mfg. 2009-present.

MSR $3,950	$3,000	$1,525 - 1,900	$925 - 1,125	

* Add 2.5% (MSR $4,000) for Antique Burst finish.

This model is also available in left-handed configuration (No. 385-4027).

* **F-47R (No. 380/385-3000)** – similar to the F-47M, except has solid rosewood back and sides, available in Antique Burst, Ice Tea Burst (2007-08), or Natural finish, mfg. summer 2007-present.

MSR $3,600	$2,800	$1,400 - 1,750	$850 - 1,050	

* Add 2.5% (MSR $3,650) for Antique Burst finish.

This model is also available in left-handed configuration (No. 385-3020).

MSR/NOTES	100%	EXCELLENT	AVERAGE	LAST MSR

»F-47RC (No. 380/385-3106/3107) – similar to the F-47R, except has a single Florentine cutaway, available in Antique Burst, Ice Tea Burst (2007-08), or Natural finish, mfg. summer 2007-present.

MSR $3,900	$3,000	$1,525 - 1,900	$925 - 1,125	

- **Add 2.5% (MSR $3,950) for Antique Burst finish.**

This model is also available in left-handed configuration (No. 385-3127).

»F-47R Electric (No. 380/385-3006/3007) – similar to the F-47R, except has D-TAR Wavelength electronics, available in Antique Burst or Natural finish, mfg. 2009-present.

MSR $3,950	$3,000	$1,525 - 1,900	$925 - 1,125	

- **Add 2.5% (MSR $4,000) for Antique Burst finish.**

This model is also available in left-handed configuration (No. 385-3027).

GF-25 – folk style with a rounded bass bout, spruce top, arched mahogany back and sides, dark top and back binding, mahogany neck, rosewood fingerboard with dot inlays, snakehead-style headstock with Guild logo, three-per-side tuners, available in Black (1987-88), Mahogany (1987-88), Natural, Sunburst, or Woodgrain Red (1987-88) finish, 16 in. body width, 25.625 in. scale, designed by George Gruhn, mfg. 1987-1992.

	N/A	$850 - 1,000	$675 - 825	

* **GF-25 C Cutaway** – similar to the GF-25, except has a single sharp cutaway and a Chesterfield headstock inlay, designed by George Gruhn, mfg. 1988-1991.

	N/A	$1,000 - 1,150	$800 - 950	

GF-30 – folk style with a rounded bass bout, spruce top, flat maple back, maple sides, multi-ply top and back binding, maple neck, rosewood fingerboard with dot inlays, snakehead-style headstock with Chesterfield and Guild logo inlays, three-per-side chrome tuners, available in various finishes, 16 in. body width, 25.625 in. scale, designed by George Gruhn, mfg. 1987-1991.

	N/A	$1,050 - 1,250	$750 - 900	

* **GF-30C Cutaway** – similar to the GF-30, except has a single sharp cutaway, designed by George Gruhn, mfg. 1987-89.

	N/A	$1,100 - 1,300	$800 - 950	

GF-40 – folk style with a rounded bass bout, spruce top, flat mahogany back, mahogany sides, multi-ply top and back binding, mahogany neck, rosewood fingerboard with dot inlays, snakehead-style headstock with Chesterfield and Guild logo inlays, three-per-side chrome tuners, available in various finishes, 16 in. body width, 25.625 in. scale, designed by George Gruhn, mfg. 1987-88.

	N/A	$1,050 - 1,250	$750 - 900	

GF-50 – folk style with a rounded bass bout, spruce top, flat rosewood back, rosewood sides, multi-ply top and back binding, mahogany neck, rosewood fingerboard with dot inlays, snakehead-style headstock with Chesterfield and Guild logo inlays, three-per-side chrome tuners, available in various finishes, 16 in. body width, 25.625 in. scale, designed by George Gruhn, mfg. 1987-1991.

	N/A	$1,200 - 1,450	$850 - 1,000	

GV-52 – F-style body, solid spruce top, rosewood back and sides, round soundhole, bound body, herringbone rosette, mahogany neck, 14/20-fret ebony fingerboard with pearl dot inlays, blackface headstock with pearl Chesterfield/logo inlay, three-per-side gold tuners, ebony bridge with white black dot pins, tortoise pickguard, available in Natural finish, 16 in. body width, mfg. 1994-95.

	N/A	$1,050 - 1,250	$750 - 900	$1,199

GV-70 – F-style body, solid spruce top, rosewood back and sides, round soundhole with abalone rosette, bound body, mahogany neck, 14/20-fret ebony fingerboard with abalone dot inlays, blackface headstock with abalone Chesterfield/logo inlay, three-per-side gold tuners, ebony bridge with white black dot pins, tortoise pickguard, available in Natural gloss finish, 16 in. body width, mfg. 1994-95.

	N/A	$1,350 - 1,700	$1,000 - 1,200	$1,799

GV-72 – F-style body, solid spruce top, rosewood back and sides, round soundhole with exotic stone rosette, bound body, herringbone purfling, mahogany neck, 14/20-fret ebony fingerboard with exotic stone dot inlays, blackface headstock with exotic stone G shield and logo inlay, three-per-side gold tuners, ebony bridge with white black dot pins, tortoise pickguard, available in Natural gloss finish, 16 in. body width, mfg. 1993 only.

	N/A	$1,400 - 1,750	$1,050 - 1,250	

ACOUSTIC: GAD SERIES

GAD stands for the Guild Acoustic Design series. Most guitars in this series are based on traditional designs including many Guild originals, and they are all built in China. In mid-2011, an all-new GAD line of acoustics was introduced replacing the "GAD" models with "D-, F-, and M-" models.

GAD-4N (NO. 381-0904) – single cutaway Hauser nylon string classical body, solid spruce top, solid mahogany back and sides, special spruce bracing, round soundhole with wood rosette, wood body binding, one-piece mahogany neck with rosewood insert, 12/18-fret ebony fingerboard with no inlays, rosewood overlay slotted headstock with three-per-side open-style chrome tuners, rosewood bridge, Seymour Duncan Timberline electronics, available in Natural finish, 25.59 in. scale, mfg. 2007-2011.

$900	$625 - 725	$325 - 400		$1,400

MSR/NOTES	100%	EXCELLENT	AVERAGE	LAST MSR

GAD-5N (NO. 381-0905) – single cutaway Hauser nylon string classical body, solid western red cedar top, solid African padauk back and sides, special spruce bracing, round soundhole with wood rosette, wood body binding, one-piece mahogany neck with rosewood insert, 12/18-fret ebony fingerboard with no inlays, rosewood overlay slotted headstock with three-per-side open-style chrome tuners, rosewood bridge, Seymour Duncan Timber-line electronics, available in Natural finish, 25.59 in. scale, mfg. 2007-2011.

	$900	$625 - 725	$325 - 400	$1,400

GAD-25 (NO. 381-0100) – dreadnought body, solid mahogany top, solid mahogany back and sides, wood binding, three-piece mahogany neck, 20-fret Indian rosewood fingerboard with dot inlay, three-per-side tuners, Indian rosewood bridge, tortoise pickguard, chrome hardware, available in Natural finish, mfg. summer 2005-2011.

	$600	$375 - 450	$200 - 250	$900

GAD-30 (NO. 381-0200) – orchestra body, solid spruce top, solid mahogany back and sides, wood binding, one-piece mahogany neck, 20-fret Indian rosewood fingerboard with dot inlay, three-per-side tuners, Indian rosewood bridge, tortoise pickguard, chrome hardware, available in Amber Sunburst (2007-09), Antique Sunburst, Ice Tea Burst (2005-08), or Natural finish, mfg. summer 2005-2011.

	$730	$475 - 550	$250 - 300	$1,100

* Add 5% (Last MSR was $1,150) for Antique Burst finish.

* *GAD-30E (No. 381-0205)* – similar to the GAD-30, except has Fishman Matrix 1 electronics, mfg. summer 2005-2011.

	$900	$575 - 675	$300 - 375	$1,350

* Add 5% (Last MSR was $1,400) for Antique Burst finish.

* *GAD-30R (No. 381-0300)* – similar to the GAD-30, except has solid Indian rosewood back and sides, mfg. summer 2005-2011.

	$760	$500 - 600	$275 - 325	$1,200

* Add 5% (Last MSR was $1,250) for Antique Burst finish.

» *GAD-30RE (No. 381-0305)* – similar to the GAD-30R, except has Fishman Matrix 1 electronics, mfg. summer 2005-2011.

	$930	$625 - 725	$325 - 400	$1,450

* Add 2.5% (Last MSR was $1,500) for Antique Burst finish.

GAD-30PCE (NO. 381-0356) – single cutaway orchestra style body, solid Sitka spruce top, solid African padauk back and sides, round soundhole with rings, wood body binding, one-piece mahogany neck, dovetail neck joint, 14/20-fret rosewood fingerboard with diamond and snowflake inlays, Chesterfield and logo headstock inlays, three-per-side Grover chrome tuners, rosewood bridge with ebony pins, black pickguard, available in Antique Burst, Ice Tea Burst (2007-08), or Natural finish, 25.5 in. scale, mfg. 2007-2011.

	$1,030	$650 - 775	$350 - 425	$1,530

* Add 2.5% (Last MSR was $1,580) for Antique Burst finish.

GAD-40 (NO. 381-1400) – dreadnought body, solid Sitka spruce top, solid mahogany back and sides, wood binding, mahogany neck, 14/20-fret rosewood fingerboard with diamond inlays, rosewood bridge, clear pickguard, rosewood headstock overlay, three-per-side chrome tuners, available in Antique Burst or Natural finish, mfg. 2010-2011.

	$650	$425 - 500	$225 - 275	$1,000

* Add 5% (Last MSR was $1,050) for Antique Sunburst finish.

* *GAD-40C (NO. 381-0400)* – similar to the GAD-40, except has a single smooth cutaway, available in Ice Tea Burst or Natural finish, mfg. 2004-07.

	N/A	$450 - 550	$275 - 325	$1,008

» *GAD-40CE (No. 381-0405)* – similar to the GAD-40C, except has a single Venetian cutaway and Fishman Acoustic Matrix electronics, available in Antique Burst (2010-2011), Ice Tea Burst, (2005-08) or Natural finish, mfg. 2005-2011.

	$900	$625 - 725	$325 - 400	$1,400

* Add 2.5% (Last MSR was $1,450) for Antique Burst finish.

GAD-50 (NO. 381-0500) – dreadnought body, solid spruce top, solid Indian rosewood back and sides, mahogany neck, 20-fret rosewood fingerboard with diamond inlays, rosewood bridge, wood binding, clear pickguard, rosewood peghead cap, nickel hardware, available in Amber Sunburst (2004-08), Antique Sunburst, Ice Tea Burst (2004-08), or Natural finish, mfg. 2004-2011.

	$750	$500 - 575	$250 - 300	$1,150

* Add 5% (Last MSR was $1,200) for Antique Burst finish.

* *GAD-50E (No. 381-0500)* – similar to the GAD-40C, except has Fishman Acoustic Matrix electronics, available in Amber Sunburst (2005-08), Antique Sunburst, Ice Tea Burst (2005-08), or Natural finish, mfg. 2005-2011.

	$900	$625 - 725	$325 - 400	$1,400

* Add 2.5% (Last MSR was $1,450) for Antique Burst finish.

* *GAD-50L (No. 381-0520)* – similar to the GAD-50, except in left-handed configuration, available in Amber Sunburst (2005-08), Ice Tea Burst (2005-08), or Natural finish, mfg. summer 2005-2011.

	$830	$550 - 650	$275 - 325	$1,280

MSR/NOTES	100%	EXCELLENT	AVERAGE	LAST MSR

GAD-50PCE (NO. 381-2506) – single cutaway dreadnought style body, solid Sitka spruce top, solid African padauk back and sides, round soundhole with rings, wood body binding, one-piece mahogany neck, dovetail neck joint, 14/20-fret rosewood fingerboard with diamond and snowflake inlays, Chesterfield and logo headstock inlays, three-per-side Grover chrome tuners, rosewood bridge with ebony pins, black pickguard, Fishman Matrix 1 electronics, available in Antique Burst, Ice Tea Burst (2007-08), or Natural finish, 25.5 in. scale, mfg. 2007-2011.

	$1,000	$675 - 800	$375 - 450	$1,580

• Add 2.5% (Last MSR was $1,630) for Antique Burst finish.

GAD-C1 (NO. 381-0901) – Hauser nylon string classical style, solid western red cedar top, solid mahogany back and sides, special spruce bracing, round soundhole with wood rosette, wood body binding, one-piece mahogany neck with rosewood insert, 12/18-fret ebony fingerboard with no inlays, rosewood overlay slotted headstock with three-per-side open-style chrome tuners, rosewood bridge, available in Natural finish, 25.59 in. scale, mfg. 2007-2011.

	$700	$450 - 525	$225 - 275	$1,050

GAD-C2 (NO. 381-0902) – Spanish nylon string classical style, solid western red cedar top, solid Indian rosewood back and sides, special spruce bracing, round soundhole with wood rosette, wood body binding, one-piece mahogany neck with rosewood insert, 12/18-fret ebony fingerboard with no inlays, rosewood overlay slotted headstock with three-per-side open-style chrome tuners, rosewood bridge, available in Natural finish, 25.59 in. scale, mfg. 2007-2011.

	$800	$500 - 600	$275 - 325	$1,200

GAD-C3 (NO. 381-0903) – German nylon string classical style, solid AAA Sitka spruce top, solid AAA Indian rosewood back and sides, special spruce bracing, round soundhole with wood rosette, wood body binding, multi-color purfling, one-piece mahogany neck with rosewood insert, 12/18-fret ebony fingerboard with no inlays, rosewood overlay slotted headstock with three-per-side open-style chrome tuners, rosewood bridge, available in Natural finish, 25.59 in. scale, mfg. 2007-2011.

	$850	$550 - 650	$300 - 350	$1,300

GAD-F20 (NO. 381-9000) – concert-style body, solid Sitka spruce top, solid mahogany back and sides, round soundhole with rings, flame maple body binding, one-piece mahogany neck, dovetail neck joint, 14/20-fret rosewood fingerboard with MOP dot inlays, MOP headstock logo, three-per-side vintage chrome tuners, rosewood bridge with cream pins, tortoiseshell pickguard, available in Ice Tea Burst (2007-08) or Natural finish, 13.75 in. lower body width, 24.75 in. scale, deluxe hardshell case included, mfg. late 2007-2011.

	$730	$475 - 550	$250 - 300	$1,100

* *GAD-F20E Electric (No. 381-9006)* – similar to the GAD-F20, except has Fishman Matrix 1 electronics, mfg. late 2007-2011.

	$900	$575 - 675	$300 - 375	$1,350

GAD-F40 (NO. 381-0600) – grand orchestra style body based on the 1955 F-40 Valencia model, solid spruce top, solid flame maple back and sides, round soundhole with rings, wood body binding, one-piece mahogany neck, dovetail neck joint, 14/20-fret ebony fingerboard with diamond and snowflake inlays, Chesterfield and logo headstock inlays, three-per-side Grover chrome tuners, ebony bridge with ebony pins, black pickguard, available in Antique Burst (2010-2011), Black, Blonde, or Ice Tea Burst (2007-08) finish, 25.5 in. scale, mfg. 2007-2011.

	$1,000	$675 - 775	$350 - 425	$1,550

• Add 2.5% (Last MSR was $1,600) for Antique Burst finish.

* *GAD-F40E Electric (No. 381-0605)* – similar to the GAD-F40, except has Fishman Matrix 1 electronics, mfg. 2007-2011.

	$1,150	$750 - 900	$425 - 500	$1,800

• Add 2.5% (Last MSR was $1,850) for Antique Burst finish.

GAD-F40P (NO. 381-0800) – grand orchestra style body based on the 1955 F-40 Valencia model, solid spruce top, solid African Padauk back and sides, round soundhole with rings, wood body binding, one-piece mahogany neck, dovetail neck joint, 12/20-fret rosewood fingerboard with diamond and snowflake inlays, Chesterfield and logo headstock inlays, three-per-side Grover chrome tuners, rosewood bridge with ebony pins, black pickguard, available in Amber Sunburst (2007-08), Ice Tea Burst (2007-08), or Natural finish, 25.5 in. scale, mfg. 2007-2011.

	$800	$500 - 600	$275 - 325	$1,200

* *GAD-F40PE Electric (No. 381-0805)* – similar to the GAD-F40P, except has Fishman Matrix 1 electronics, mfg. 2007-2011.

	$950	$625 - 725	$325 - 400	$1,450

GAD-F212 12-STRING (NO. 381-3400) – 12-string configuration, grand orchestra style body based on the 1955 F-40 Valencia model, solid spruce top, solid mahogany back and sides, round soundhole with rings, wood body binding, three-piece mahogany/maple neck, dovetail neck joint, 14/20-fret rosewood fingerboard with dot inlays, Chesterfield and logo headstock inlays, six-per-side Grover mini-chrome tuners, rosewood bridge with ebony pins, black pickguard, available in Ice Tea Burst (2007-08) or Natural finish, 25.5 in. scale, mfg. 2007-2011.

	$800	$500 - 600	$275 - 325	$1,200

* *GAD-F212E 12-String Electric (No. 381-3405)* – similar to the GAD-F212, except has Fishman Matrix 1 electronics, mfg. 2007-2011.

	$950	$625 - 725	$325 - 400	$1,450

MSR/NOTES	100%	EXCELLENT	AVERAGE	LAST MSR

GAD-G212 (NO. 381-3200) – 12-string configuration, dreadnought body, solid Sitka spruce top, solid mahogany back and sides, wood binding, one-piece mahogany neck, 20-fret Indian rosewood fingerboard with diamond inlay, six-per-side tuners, Indian rosewood bridge, tortoise pickguard, chrome hardware, available in Amber Burst (2005-08), Antique Burst, Ice Tea Burst (2005-08), or Natural finish, mfg. summer 2005-2011.

	$800	$500 - 600	$275 - 325	$1,200

* Add 5% (Last MSR was $1,250) for Antique Burst finish.

* *GAD-G212E (No. 381-3205)* – similar to the GAD-G212, except has Fishman Matrix 1 electronics, mfg. summer 2005-2011.

	$950	$625 - 725	$325 - 400	$1,450

* Add 2.5% (Last MSR was $1,500) for Antique Burst finish.

GAD-JF30 (NO. 381-3000) – jumbo body, solid spruce top, solid AAA flamed maple back and sides, mahogany neck, 20-fret ebony fingerboard with diamond inlays, rosewood bridge, wood binding, clear pickguard, rosewood peghead cap, nickel hardware, available in Antique Sunburst, Blonde, or Ice Tea Burst (2004-08) finish, mfg. 2004-2011.

	$1,000	$675 - 775	$350 - 425	$1,550

* Add 2.5% (Last MSR was $1,600) for Antique Burst finish.

* *GAD-JF30E (No. 381-3005)* – similar to the GAD-JF30, except has Fishman Matrix 1 electronics, available in Amber Sunburst (2007 only), Antique Burst, Blonde, or Ice Tea Burst (2007 only), mfg. 2007-2011.

	$1,150	$750 - 900	$425 - 500	$1,800

* Add 2.5% (Last MSR was $1,850) for Antique Burst finish.

* *GAD-JF30-12 12-String (No. 381-3500)* – similar to the GAD-JF30, except in 12-string configuration and six-per-side tuners, available in Antique Burst, Blonde, or Ice Tea Burst (2007-08) finish, mfg. 2007-2011.

	$1,150	$750 - 900	$425 - 500	$1,800

* Add 2.5% (Last MSR was $1,850) for Antique Burst finish.

»*GAD-JF30-12E 12-String Electric (No. 381-3505)* – similar to the GAD-JF30-12, except has Fishman Matrix 1 electronics, available in Antique Burst, Blonde, or Ice Tea Burst (2007-08) finish, mfg. 2007-2011.

	$1,350	$900 - 1,050	$475 - 550	$2,050

* Add 2.5% (Last MSR was $2,100) for Antique Burst finish.

GAD-JF48 (NO. 381-3100) – jumbo body, solid spruce top, solid mahogany back and sides, wood binding, one-piece mahogany neck, 20-fret Indian rosewood fingerboard with diamond inlays, Indian rosewood bridge, tortoise pickguard, rosewood peghead cap, chrome hardware, available in Amber Burst, Antique Sunburst, Black, Ice Tea Burst (2005-06), or Natural finish, mfg. summer 2005-08.

	N/A	$475 - 600	$275 - 350	$1,120

* *GAD-JF48E (No. 381-3105)* – similar to the GAD-JF48, except has Fishman Matrix 1 electronics, available in Amber Burst, Antique Burst, or Natural finish, mfg. 2007-08.

	N/A	$550 - 700	$350 - 425	$1,344

GAD-M20 (NO. 381-8000) – concert-style body, solid mahogany top, solid mahogany back and sides, round soundhole with rings, one-piece mahogany neck, dovetail neck joint, 14/20-fret rosewood fingerboard with MOP dot inlays, MOP headstock logo, three-per-side vintage chrome tuners, rosewood bridge with cream pins, tortoiseshell pickguard, available in Natural finish, 13.75 in. lower body width, 24.75 in. scale, deluxe hardshell case included, mfg. 2008-2012.

	$600	$375 - 450	$200 - 250	$900

* *GAD-M20E Electric (No. 381-8006)* – similar to the GAD-M20, except has Fishman Matrix 1 electronics, mfg. 2008-2012.

	$750	$500 - 575	$250 - 300	$1,150

D-125 (NO. 381-0110) – dreadnought body, solid mahogany top, solid mahogany back and sides, round soundhole with MOP rosette, black ABS binding, mahogany neck, 14/20-fret rosewood fingerboard with pearl dot inlays, rosewood headstock overlay with Guild logo, three-per-side tuners, rosewood bridge, tortoise pickguard, chrome hardware, available in Cherry Red (2013-present) or Natural finish, 25.5 in. scale, 1.6875 in. nut width, mfg. late 2011-present.

MSR $740	$530	$300 - 375	$175 - 225	

* *D-125-12 12-String (No. 381-0120)* – similar to the D-125, except in 12-string configuration with six-per-side tuners, available in Natural finish, 25.5 in. scale, 1.875 in. nut width, mfg. late 2011-present.

MSR $840	$630	$350 - 425	$200 - 250	

* *D-125-CE Cutaway Electric (No. 381-0115)* – similar to the D-125, except has a single cutaway and Fishman Sonicore soundhole pickup and electronics, available in Cherry Red or Natural finish, mfg. 2013-present.

MSR $1,000	$750	$425 - 525	$250 - 325	

MSR/NOTES	100%	EXCELLENT	AVERAGE	LAST MSR

D-140 (NO. 381-1410) – dreadnought body, solid spruce top, solid mahogany back and sides, round soundhole with MOP rosette, multi-ply B/W binding, mahogany neck, 14/20-fret rosewood fingerboard with pearl dot inlays, rosewood headstock overlay with Guild logo, three-per-side chrome tuners, rosewood bridge, black pickguard, available in Natural finish, 25.5 in. scale, 1.6875 in. nut width, mfg. late 2011-present.

MSR $900	$650	$350 - 450	$200 - 250	

* D-140CE Cutaway Electric (No. 381-0415) – similar to the D-140, except has a single smooth cutaway and Fishman Sonicore electronics, available in Natural finish, mfg. late 2011-present.

MSR $1,150	$850	$450 - 575	$250 - 325	

D-150 (NO. 381-0510) – dreadnought body, solid spruce top, solid rosewood back and sides, round soundhole with MOP rosette, ivoroid body binding, mahogany neck, 20-fret rosewood fingerboard with pearl dot inlays, rosewood headstock overlay with Guild logo, three-per-side tuners, rosewood bridge, black pickguard, chrome hardware, available in Natural finish, 25.5 in. scale, 1.6875 in. nut width, mfg. late 2011-present.

MSR $1,040	$750	$425 - 525	$250 - 325	

* D-150CE Cutaway Electric (No. 381-0515) – similar to the D-150, except has a single smooth cutaway and Fishman Sonicore electronics, available in Natural finish, mfg. late 2011-present.

MSR $1,270	$950	$525 - 650	$325 - 400	

* D-150L Left-Handed (No. 381-0530) – similar to the D-150, except in left-handed configuration, available in Natural finish, mfg. late 2011-present.

MSR $1,150	$830	$450 - 575	$250 - 325	

F-130 (NO. 381-0210) – orchestra body, solid spruce top, solid mahogany back and sides, round soundhole with MOP rosette, multi-ply B/W binding, mahogany neck, 14/20-fret rosewood fingerboard with pearl dot inlays, rosewood headstock overlay with Guild logo, three-per-side tuners, rosewood bridge, black pickguard, chrome hardware, available in Natural finish, 25.5 in. scale, 1.75 in. nut width, mfg. late 2011-present.

MSR $900	$650	$350 - 450	$200 - 250	

* F-130CE Cutaway Electric (No. 381-0215) – similar to the F-130, except has a single smooth cutaway and Fishman Sonitone electronics, available in Natural finish, mfg. late 2011-present.

MSR $1,150	$850	$450 - 575	$250 - 325	

* F-130R Rosewood (No. 381-0310) – similar to the F-130, except has solid rosewood back and sides, available in Natural finish, mfg. late 2011-present.

MSR $1,000	$750	$425 - 525	$250 - 325	

»F-130RCE Rosewood Cutaway Electric (No. 381-0315) – similar to the F-130R Rosewood, except has solid rosewood back and sides, available in Natural finish, mfg. late 2011-present.

MSR $1,270	$950	$525 - 650	$325 - 400	

F-150R (NO. 381-4010) – jumbo body, solid spruce top, solid rosewood back and sides, round soundhole with MOP rosette, ivoroid body binding, black/cream/black purfling, mahogany neck, 14/20-fret rosewood fingerboard with pearl block inlays, rosewood headstock overlay with Guild logo, three-per-side tuners, rosewood bridge, black pickguard, gold hardware, available in Natural finish, 25.5 in. scale, 1.6875 in. nut width, mfg. late 2011-present.

MSR $1,420	$1,050	$575 - 725	$350 - 425	

* F-150RCE Cutaway Electric (No. 381-4016) – similar to the F-150R, except has a single smooth cutaway and Fishman Sonitone electronics, available in Natural finish, mfg. late 2011-present.

MSR $1,680	$1,250	$675 - 850	$400 - 500	

* F-1512 12-String (No. 381-4510) – similar to the F-150R, except in 12-string configuration with six-per-side tuners, available in Natural finish, 1.875 in. nut width, mfg. late 2011-present.

MSR $1,620	$1,200	$650 - 825	$400 - 475	

»F-1512E 12-String Electric (No. 381-4516) – similar to the F-1512, except has Fishman Sonitone electronics, available in Natural finish, mfg. late 2011-present.

MSR $1,830	$1,350	$750 - 925	$450 - 550	

M-120 (NO. 381-8100) – concert-style body, solid mahogany top, solid mahogany back and sides, round soundhole with MOP rosette, mahogany neck, 14/20-fret rosewood fingerboard with pearl dot inlays, rosewood headstock overlay with Guild logo, three-per-side tuners, rosewood bridge with cream pins, black pickguard, nickel hardware, available in Cherry Red (2013-present) or Natural finish, 24.75 in. scale, 1.6875 in. nut width, mfg. late 2011-present.

MSR $740	$530	$300 - 375	$175 - 225	

* M-120E Electric (No. 381-8106) – similar to the M-120, except has Fishman Sonitone electronics, available in Cherry Red (2013-present) or Natural finish, mfg. late 2011-present.

MSR $915	$680	$375 - 475	$225 - 275	

MSR/NOTES	100%	EXCELLENT	AVERAGE	LAST MSR

GC-2 (NO. 381-0912) – nylon string classical-style, solid cedar top, solid rosewood back and sides, special spruce bracing, round soundhole with wood mosaic rosette, rosewood body binding, multi-ply maple/rosewood purfling, mahogany neck with rosewood insert, 12/18-fret ebony fingerboard with no inlays, rosewood overlay slotted headstock, three-per-side open-style chrome tuners with black buttons, rosewood bridge, available in Natural finish, 25.5 in. scale, 2 in. nut width, mfg. late 2011-present.

MSR $1,200	$900	$500 - 625	$300 - 375	

GN-5 (NO. 381-0915) – single cutaway nylon string classical body, solid cedar top, solid rosewood back and sides, special spruce bracing, round soundhole with wood mosaic rosette, rosewood body binding, multi-ply maple/rosewood purfling, mahogany neck, 12/18-fret ebony fingerboard with no inlays, rosewood overlay slotted headstock, three-per-side open-style nickel tuners with black buttons, rosewood bridge, Fishman Sonitone electronics, available in Natural finish, 25.5 in. scale, 1.75 in. nut width, mfg. late 2011-present.

MSR $1,330	$1,000	$550 - 700	$325 - 400	

ACOUSTIC: JUMBO MODELS (F, JF, JV PREFIX)

All models in this series have jumbo style bodies, round soundholes, and tortoiseshell pickguards.

F-48 NAVARRE – jumbo body style, spruce top, mahogany back and sides, round soundhole with four rings, multi-ply body binding, three-piece mahogany/maple neck, 14/20-fret bound rosewood fingerboard with eight pearloid block inlays, black headstock with Chesterfield and logo inlay, three-per-side chrome tuners, rosewood bridge, tortoiseshell pickguard, available in Natural or Sunburst finish, 17 in. body width, 4.625 in. body depth, 25.5 in. scale, mfg. 1972-75.

	N/A	$1,500 - 1,850	$1,000 - 1,200	

F-50 NAVARRE/JF-65M – jumbo body style, spruce top, curly maple back and sides, round soundhole with four rings, multi-ply body binding, three-piece mahogany/maple neck, 14/20-fret bound rosewood fingerboard with eight pearloid block inlays, black bound headstock overlay with G logo inlay, three-per-side gold-plated Kluson Deluxe tuners, rosewood bridge, tortoiseshell pickguard, available in Natural or Sunburst finish, 17 in. body width, 4.5 in. body depth, 25.5 in. scale, mfg. 1954-1987.

1954-1956	N/A	$3,200 - 3,800	$2,200 - 2,700	
1957-1962	N/A	$2,800 - 3,300	$1,950 - 2,300	
1963-1969	N/A	$2,300 - 2,800	$1,400 - 1,750	
1970-1979	N/A	$2,100 - 2,500	$1,250 - 1,500	
1980-1987	N/A	$1,750 - 2,250	$1,100 - 1,400	

In 1956, a maple neck with a walnut strip, pearl block fingerboard inlays, and the G shield headstock inlay were introduced. In 1957, pearl block fingerboar inlays with V inserts were introduced. In 1962, an ebony fingerboard was introduced. In 1966 a "cloud" bridge with two points was introduced. In 1967 the body was deepend to 5 in. Around 1972, some guitars were constructed with ebony bridges and black pickguards were introduced. In 1987, this model was renamed the JF-65M.

* F-50 R Navarre/JF-65R – similar to the F-50 Navarre, except has rosewood back and sides, mfg. 1965-1987.

1965-1969	N/A	$4,250 - 5,250	$2,750 - 3,250	
1970-1974	N/A	$2,250 - 2,750	$1,400 - 1,750	
1975-1979	N/A	$2,100 - 2,500	$1,250 - 1,500	
1980-1987	N/A	$1,750 - 2,200	$1,100 - 1,400	

Brazilian rosewood was used on the back and sides until circa 1969. In 1966 a "cloud" bridge with two points was introduced. In 1967 the body was deepend to 5 in. In 1969, a rosewood bridge was introduced. Around 1970, some guitars had a flat laminated back with one-piece mahogany necks. Around 1972, some guitars were constructed with ebony bridges and three-piece padouk/maple necks and black pickguards were introduced. Around 1977, some guitars had three-piece mahogany/maple necks. In 1987, this model was renamed the JF-65R.

F-50 SECOND VERSION (NO. 380/385-2400) – jumbo body style, AAA spruce top, arched curly maple back, curly maple sides, round soundhole with four rings, multi-ply body binding, three-piece mahogany/maple neck, 14/20-fret bound ebony fingerboard with eight MOP block inlays with abalone V inserts, black bound headstock overlay with G shield and logo inlay, three-per-side gold-plated Grover Rotomatic tuners, rosewood bridge, tortoiseshell pickguard, available in Antique Burst, Black (disc. 2008), Blonde, Ice Tea Burst (disc. 2008), Natural (disc.), or Red Trans. (disc.) finish, 17 in. body width, 4.8 in. body depth, 25.625 in. scale, mfg. 2002-present.

MSR $3,900	$3,000	$1,550 - 1,950	$950 - 1,175	

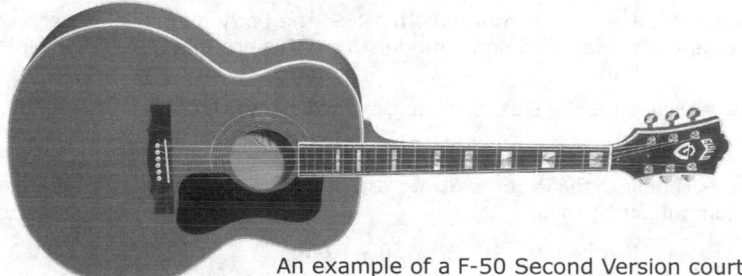

An example of a F-50 Second Version courtesy Guild

• **Add 2.5% (MSR $3,950) for Antique Burst finish.**
This model is also available in left-handed configuration (No. 385-2420).

MSR/NOTES	100%	EXCELLENT	AVERAGE	LAST MSR

* **F-50 Second Version Electric (No. 380/385-2406/2407)** – similar to the F-50 Second Version, except has Fishman (disc. 2006), or D-TAR Wavelength (summer 2006-present) electronics, mfg. 2002-present.

MSR $4,250	$3,200	$1,650 - 2,050	$1,000 - 1,250	

  • Add 2.5% (MSR $4,300) for Antique Burst finish.
  This model is also available in left-handed configuration (No. 385-2427).

* **F-50R Second Version (No. 380/385-2800)** – similar to the F-50 Second Version, except has rosewood back and sides, available in Antique Burst, Ice Tea Burst (disc. 2009), or Natural finish, mfg. 2002-present.

MSR $4,000	$3,000	$1,550 - 1,950	$950 - 1,175	

  • Add 2.5% (MSR $4,050) for Antique Burst finish.
  This model is also available in left-handed configuration (No. 385-2820).

» **F-50R Second Version Electric (No. 380/385-2806/2807)** – similar to the F-50R Second Version, except has Fishman (disc. 2006), or D-TAR Wavelength (summer 2006-present) electronics, mfg. 2002-present.

MSR $4,350	$3,300	$1,675 - 2,100	$1,000 - 1,250	

  • Add 2.5% (MSR $4,400) for Antique Burst finish.
  This model is also available in left-handed configuration (No. 385-2827).

F-50 STANDARD (NO. 385-1400) – jumbo body style, solid Sitka spruce top, arched laminated maple back, solid maple sides, red spruce bracing, round soundhole with multi-ring rosette, ivoroid body binding, slim profile mahogany neck, 14/20-fret rosewood fingerboard with pearl dot inlays, mahogany headstock overlay with pearl Guild logo, three-per-side chrome Gotoh tuners, rosewood bridge with bone pins, tortoise pickguard, available in Antique Burst (2012 only) or Natural high gloss finish, 25.625 in. scale, hardshell case included, mfg. summer 2010-12.

	$2,100	$1,150 - 1,450	$700 - 875	$2,800

  • Add 2.5% (Last MSR was $2,850) for Antique Burst finish.
  This model is also available in left-handed configuration (No. 385-1420).

* **F-50CE Standard Cutaway Electric (No. 385-1406)** – similar to the F-50 Standard, except has a single smooth cutaway and a D-TAR Wave-Length end pin mounted preamp with volume and tone controls, available in Natural high gloss finish, hardshell case included, mfg. 2011-present.

MSR $3,400	$2,750	$1,400 - 1,750	$850 - 1,050	

  • Add 2.5% (MSR $3,150) for Antique Burst finish.
  This model is also available in left-handed configuration (No. 385-1426).

F-112 STANDARD 12-STRING – jumbo body based on the F-30 specs, solid spruce top, mahogany back and sides, round soundhole, single rosette, tortoiseshell body binding, mahogany neck, 14/20-fret rosewood fingerboard with pearl dot inlays, blackface headstock with Chesterfield and logo inlays, six-per-side chrome tuners, rosewood bridge with white pins, tortoise pickguard, available in Natural finish, 15.25 in. body width, 4.5 in. body depth, 25.5 in. scale, mfg. 1968-1982.

1968-1969	N/A	$1,100 - 1,400	$750 - 850	
1970-1982	N/A	$900 - 1,100	$600 - 700	

The earliest models may not have the Chesterfield headstock inlay. In 1976, the body size changed to 15.375 in. body width and 4.875 in. body depth.

F-212 12-STRING – 12-string configuration, jumbo body based on the F-47 specs, solid spruce top, mahogany back and sides, round soundhole, single rosette, tortoiseshell body binding, three-piece mahogany/maple neck, 14/20-fret rosewood fingerboard with no inlays, blackface headstock with Guild logo inlay, six-per-side chrome tuners, rosewood bridge with white pins, tortoise pickguard, available in Natural finish, 16 in. body width, 4.875 in. body depth, 25.5 in. scale, mfg. 1964-1985.

1964-1969	N/A	$1,400 - 1,750	$1,050 - 1,250	
1970-1979	N/A	$1,000 - 1,250	$750 - 900	
1980-1985	N/A	$900 - 1,100	$675 - 800	

In 1968, a Chesterfield headstock inlay was introduced. In 1969, the body dimensions were changed as the body was slightly narrower at 15.875 in. and deeper at 5 in., and some models from this era may have a one-piece neck. In 1976, the body was widened back to the orignal size of 16 in.

* **F-212C 12-String Cutaway** – similar to the F-212 12-String, except has a single sharp cutaway, mfg. 1976-1981.

	N/A	$1,250 - 1,550	$950 - 1,100	

* **F-212E 12-String Electric** – similar to the F-212 12-String, except has an exposed pickup above the soundhole and two knobs (v, tone) mounted on the face of the guitar, mfg. 1965-1974.

1965-1969	N/A	$1,450 - 1,850	$1,000 - 1,200	
1970-1974	N/A	$1,100 - 1,350	$750 - 900	

MSR/NOTES	100%	EXCELLENT	AVERAGE	LAST MSR

* **F-212 XL 12-String Standard** – similar to F-212, except has larger body and an ebony fingerboard, 21 in. body length, 17 in. body width, 5 in. body depth, mfg. 1966-1986.

	N/A	$1,200 - 1,450	$900 - 1,050	

In 1977, an ebony bridge was introduced.

F-212XL 12-STRING SECOND VERSION (NO. 350-2400) – 12-string configuration, jumbo body style, based on the original F-212XL Standard 12-String, solid spruce top, solid mahogany back and sides, round soundhole with rings, top and back body binding, mahogany neck, 14/20-fret ebony fingerboard with no inlays, black headstock overlay with Chesterfield and logo inlays, six-per-side chrome tuners, ebony bridge, available in Antique Burst, Black, or Natural finish, 25.625 in. scale, mfg. 1998-2000.

	N/A	$1,100 - 1,350	$800 - 950	$1,800

F-212XL STANDARD (NO. 385-1700) – 12-string configuration, jumbo body style, solid Sitka spruce top, solid mahogany back and sides, red spruce bracing, round soundhole with multi-ring rosette, ivoroid body binding, slim profile mahogany neck, 14/20-fret rosewood fingerboard with pearl dot inlays, mahogany headstock overlay with pearl Guild logo, six-per-side chrome Gotoh tuners, rosewood bridge with bone pins, tortoise pickguard, available in Natural high gloss finish, 25.625 in. scale, hardshell case included, mfg. summer 2010-present.

MSR $3,200	$2,000	$1,125 - 1,400	$675 - 850	

This model is also available in left-handed configuration (No. 385-1720).

* **F-212XLCE Standard Cutaway Electric (No. 385-1706)** – similar to the F-212XL Standard, except has a single smooth cutaway and a D-TAR Wave-Length end pin mounted preamp with volume and tone controls, available in Natural high gloss finish, hardshell case included, mfg. 2011-present.

MSR $3,500	$2,300	$1,275 - 1,600	$825 - 1,025	

This model is also available in left-handed configuration (No. 385-1726).

F-312 ARTIST 12-STRING – 12-string configuration, jumbo body based on the F-47 specs, solid spruce top, rosewood back and sides, round soundhole, single rosette, tortoiseshell body binding, three-piece mahogany/maple neck, 14/20-fret ebony fingerboard with no inlays, blackface headstock with Guild logo inlay, six-per-side chrome tuners, ebony bridge with white pins, tortoise pickguard, available in Natural finish, 15.875 in. body width, 5 in. body depth, 25.5 in. scale, mfg. 1964-1974.

1964-1969 Brazilian Rosewood	N/A	$2,200 - 2,750	$1,400 - 1,750	
1970-1974 Indian Rosewood	N/A	$1,300 - 1,600	$950 - 1,100	

F-412 CUSTOM 12-STRING – 12-string configuration, jumbo body based on the F-50 specs, solid spruce top, maple arched back, maple sides, round soundhole, single rosette, tortoiseshell body binding, three-piece maple/walnut neck, 14/20-fret ebony fingerboard with abalone block inlays with MOP V inserts, blackface headstock with G Shield and Guild logo inlays, six-per-side chrome tuners, rosewood bridge with white pins, tortoise pickguard, available in Natural or Sunburst finish, 17 in. body width, 5 in. body depth, 25.5 in. scale, mfg. 1968-1987.

1968-1974	N/A	$2,200 - 2,750	$1,400 - 1,750	
1975-1979	N/A	$2,100 - 2,500	$1,300 - 1,600	
1980-1987	N/A	$1,750 - 2,150	$1,100 - 1,350	

This model was available by special order only between 1968 and 1974. In 1976, an ebony bridge was introduced. In 1987, this model was renamed the JF-65M-12.

F-412 12-STRING SECOND VERSION (NO. 380/385-2500) – 12-string configuration, jumbo body, solid spruce top, figured maple back and sides, round soundhole, multibound body, three-stripe rosette, mahogany neck, 14/20-fret bound ebony fingerboard with abalone block inlay and MOP V inserts, bound blackface headstock with pearl G shield and Gretsch logo inlays, six-per-side gold tuners, ebony bridge with white pins, black pickguard, available in Antique Burst, Blonde, Natural (disc.), Ice Tea Burst (disc. 2008), or Red Trans. (disc.) finish, 21 in. body length, 17 in. body width, 5 in. body depth, 25.625 in. scale, mfg. 2002-present.

MSR $4,000	$3,000	$1,600 - 2,000	$950 - 1,200	

• **Add 2.5% (MSR $4,050) for Antique Burst finish.**

This model is also available in left-handed configuration (No. 385-2520).

* **F-412 12-String Second Version Electric (No. 380/385-2505/2506/2507)** – similar to the F-412 12-String Second Version, except has Fishman (disc. 2006), or D-TAR Wavelength (summer 2006-present) electronics, mfg. 2002-present.

MSR $4,300	$3,400	$1,750 - 2,150	$1,025 - 1,275	

• **Add 2.5% (MSR $4,350) for Antique Burst finish.**

This model is also available in left-handed configuration (No. 385-2527).

F-512 CUSTOM/JF-65R-12 12-STRING – 12-string configuration, jumbo body based on the F-50R specs, solid spruce top, maple arched back, maple sides, round soundhole, single rosette, tortoiseshell body binding, three-piece mahogany/maple neck, 14/20-fret ebony fingerboard with abalone block inlays with MOP V inserts, blackface headstock with G Shield and Guild logo inlays, six-per-side chrome tuners, rosewood bridge with white pins, tortoise pickguard, available in Natural finish, 17 in. body width, 5 in. body depth, 25.5 in. scale, mfg. 1968-1987.

1968-1974	N/A	$2,150 - 2,650	$1,300 - 1,600	
1975-1979	N/A	$1,950 - 2,400	$1,200 - 1,500	
1980-1987	N/A	$1,650 - 2,100	$1,000 - 1,200	

This model was available by special order only between 1968 and 1974. In 1976, an ebony bridge was introduced. In 1987, this model was renamed the JF-65R-12.

MSR/NOTES	100%	EXCELLENT	AVERAGE	LAST MSR

F-512 12-STRING SECOND VERSION (NO. 380/385-2900) – 12-string configuration, jumbo body, solid spruce top, rosewood back and sides, round soundhole, multibound body, three-stripe rosette, mahogany neck, 14/20-fret bound ebony fingerboard with abalone block inlay and MOP V inserts, bound blackface headstock with pearl G shield and Gretsch logo inlays, six-per-side gold tuners, ebony bridge with white pins, black pickguard, available in Antique Burst, Ice Tea Burst (disc. 2008), or Natural finish, 21 in. body length, 17 in. body width, 5 in. body depth, 25.625 in. scale, mfg. 2002-present.

| MSR $4,400 | $3,500 | $1,800 - 2,250 | $1,075 - 1,350 | |

• Add 2.5% (MSR $4,450) for Antique Burst finish.

This model is also available in left-handed configuration (No. 385-2920).

* *F-512 12-String Second Version Electric (No. 380/385-2905/2906/2907)* – similar to the F-512 12-String Second Version, except has Fishman (disc. 2006), or D-TAR Wavelength (summer 2006-present) electronics, mfg. 2002-present.

| MSR $4,700 | $3,800 | $1,925 - 2,400 | $1,150 - 1,450 | |

• Add 2.5% (MSR $4,750) for Antique Burst finish.

This model is also available in left-handed configuration (No. 385-2927).

F-612 CUSTOM 12-STRING – 12-string configuration, jumbo body based on the F-50 specs, solid spruce top, rosewood back and sides, round soundhole with checker inlay ring, white body binding and checkered purfling, three-piece mahogany/maple neck, 14/20-fret ebony fingerboard with fancy MOP inlays, checkered-bound blackface headstock with G Shield and Guild logo inlays, six-per-side gold Grover tuners, rosewood bridge with fancy MOP inlays, tortoise pickguard, available in Natural or Sunburst finish, 18 in. body width, 5 in. body depth, 25.5 in. scale, mfg. 1970-73.

| | N/A | $3,200 - 4,000 | $2,500 - 3,000 | |

• Add 25-50% for Brazilian rosewood back and sides.

This model was never listed in a catalog and was only available by special order. Early models may have Brazilian rosewood back and sides.

JF-4 – jumbo style body, solid spruce top, mahogany back and sides, bound body, three-stripe rosette, mahogany neck, 14/20-fret rosewood fingerboard with pearl dot inlays, wood headstock overlay with Guild logo, three-per-side chrome tuners, rosewood bridge with white black dot pins, tortoiseshell pickguard, available in Natural satin finish, mfg. 1992-95.

| | N/A | $650 - 750 | $350 - 425 | $880 |

* *JF-4-HG* – similar to the JF-4, except available in Natural or Sunburst high gloss finish, mfg. 1992-93.

| | N/A | $700 - 800 | $400 - 475 | $995 |

* *JF-4 12 S 12-String* – similar to the JF-4, except in 12-string configuration and six-per-side tuners, mfg. 1993-94.

| | N/A | $700 - 800 | $400 - 475 | $995 |

» *JF-4-12-HG 12-String* – similar to the JF-4-12 12-String, except available in Natural or Sunburst high gloss finish, mfg. 1993 only.

| | N/A | $725 - 850 | $425 - 500 | $1,195 |

JF-30 (NO. 350-2000/380-2000) – jumbo body style, solid spruce top, arched maple back, solid curly maple sides, bound body, three-stripe rosette, maple neck, 14/20-fret rosewood fingerboard with pearl dot inlay, rosewood bridge with white black dot pins, pearl Chesterfield/logo headstock inlays, three-per-side gold tuners, available in Blonde, Black, or Antique Burst, Red Trans., high gloss finish, case included, mfg. 1987-2003.

| | N/A | $1,050 - 1,250 | $750 - 900 | $1,800 |

* *JF-30C Cutaway* – similar to the JF-30, except has a single cutaway, mfg. 1988 only.

| | N/A | $1,150 - 1,350 | $850 - 1,000 | |

* *JF-30-12 12-String (No. 350-2500/380-2100)* – similar to JF-30, except in 12-string configuration and six-per-side tuners, available in Blonde, Black, Red Trans., and Antique Burst, high gloss finish, case included, mfg. 1987-2003.

| | N/A | $1,100 - 1,300 | $750 - 900 | $1,900 |

JF-50R – jumbo body style, spruce top, rosewood back and sides, multi-ply top and back binding, mahogany neck, ebony fingerboard with dot inlays, snakehead-shape headstock with Chesterfield and Guild logo inlays, three-per-side tuners, ebony bridge, available in various finishes, 17 in. body width, 25.625 in. scale, mfg. 1987-88.

| | N/A | $1,400 - 1,700 | $950 - 1,100 | |

JF-55 (NO. 350-2100) – jumbo body style, solid spruce top, solid rosewood back and sides, scalloped bracing, three-stripe bound body, abalone rosette, mahogany neck, 14/20-fret bound ebony fingerboard with pearl block/abalone wedge inlays, bound peghead with pearl shield/logo inlay, three-per-side gold tuners, ebony bridge with white abalone dot pins, maple endpin wedge, available in Antique Burst (837) or Natural (821) high gloss finish, case included, mfg. 1989-2000.

| | N/A | $1,400 - 1,750 | $950 - 1,150 | $2,400 |

* *JF-55-12 12-String (Model 350-2600)* – similar to the JF-55, except in 12-string configuration and six-per-side tuners, available in Natural or Antique Burst high gloss finish, case included, mfg. 1991-2000.

| | N/A | $1,450 - 1,800 | $1,000 - 1,200 | $2,500 |

MSR/NOTES	100%	EXCELLENT	AVERAGE	LAST MSR

JF-65 SECOND VERSION (NO. 350-2900) – jumbo style body, solid spruce top, arched maple back, solid curly maple sides, three-stripe bound body, abalone rosette, maple neck, 14/20-fret bound ebony fingerboard with pearl block/abalone wedge inlays, bound headstock with pearl shield/logo inlays, three-per-side gold tuners, ebony bridge with white abalone dot pins, maple endpin wedge, available in Blonde or Antique Burst finish, case included, mfg. summer 1997-2001.

	N/A	$1,450 - 1,800	$950 - 1,100	$2,300

* *JF-65 12 Second Version 12-String (Model 350-2700)* – similar to the JF-65 Second Version, except in 12-string configuration and six-per-side tuners, available in Blonde or Antique Burst high gloss finish, case included, mfg. 1987-2001.

	N/A	$1,450 - 1,800	$950 - 1,100	$2,400

JF-100 JUMBO – jumbo body style, solid spruce top, scalloped bracing, maple bound body, abalone purfling, abalone rosette, solid rosewood back and sides, three-piece mahogany neck with maple center strip, 14/20-fret maple bound ebony fingerboard with abalone crown inlay, maple bound headstock with abalone shield/logo inlay, three-per-side tuners, ebony bridge with white abalone pins, maple endpin wedge, ebony endpin, available in Natural finish, mfg. 1992-95.

	N/A	$3,200 - 3,700	$2,000 - 2,500	$3,700

* *JF-100 C Cutaway (No. 350-2200)* – similar to the JF-100, except has hand carved heel, available in Antique Burst or Natural high gloss lacquer finish, case included, mfg. 1994-2000.

	N/A	$3,300 - 4,000	$2,100 - 2,600	$4,300

* *JF-100 12 12-String* – similar to the JF-100, except in 12 string configuration and six-per-side tuners, mfg. 1992-95.

	N/A	$3,000 - 3,500	$1,900 - 2,300	$4,000

» *JF-100 C 12 12-String Cutaway (No. 350-2800)* – similar to JF-100 12-String, except has a hand carved heel, available in Antique Burst or Natural high gloss lacquer finish, case included, mfg. 1994-2000.

	N/A	$3,300 - 4,000	$2,100 - 2,600	$4,500

JV-52 – jumbo style, solid spruce top, rosewood back and sides, round soundhole, bound body, herringbone rosette, mahogany neck, 14/20-fret ebony fingerboard with pearl dot inlays, blackface headstock with pearl Chesterfield and logo inlay, three-per-side gold tuners, ebony bridge with white black dot pins, tortoiseshell pickguard, available in Natural finish, 17 in. body width, mfg. 1994-95.

	N/A	$1,150 - 1,400	$750 - 900	$1,250

ACOUSTIC: MISC./SOLIDBODY MODELS

The S-4 CE Specialist models were previously called the Songbird models. The S-4 CE has a body the size of a Bluesbird, and has a routed-out acoustic chamber in the mahogany body that is capped with an X-braced solid spruce top.

A-25HR – concert size body, spruce top, mahogany back and sides, black binding, rosewood fingerboard with dot inlays, three-per-side tuners, rosewood bridge, tortoiseshell pickguard, available in Antique Burst or Natural hand-rubbed satin finish, 15 in. body width, mfg. 1995-97.

	N/A	$525 - 600	$400 - 450	$999

* *A-25HG* – similar to the A-25HR, except has a high gloss lacquer finish, mfg. 1995-97.

	N/A	$700 - 800	$450 - 525	$1,099

A-50 – concert size body, spruce top, rosewood back and sides, black binding, abalone rosette, ebony fingerboard with dot inlays, three-per-side tuners, ebony bridge, tortoiseshell pickguard, available in Antique Burst or Natural hand-rubbed satin finish, 15 in. body width, mfg. 1996-97.

	N/A	$750 - 875	$475 - 550	$1,499

AD-3 ARCOS (NO. 383-0080) – dreadnought-style body, solid Sitka spruce top, arched laminated mahogany back, laminated mahogany sides, round soundhole with koa rosette, black ABS body binding with white/black purfling, mahogany neck, 14/20-fret rosewood fingerboard with pearl dot inlays, rosewood headstock overlay with Guild logo, three-per-side chrome tuners, rosewood bridge, ivory colored plastic bridge pins with abalone dots, black pickguard, available in Natural finish, 25.625 in. scale, 1.6875 in. nut width, deluxe polyfoam case included, mfg. 2012-present.

MSR $760	$550	$300 - 375	$175 - 225	

* *AD-3CE Arcos Cutaway Electric (No. 383-0106)* – similar to the AD-3 Arcos, except has a single smooth cutaway and Fishman Presys Plus electronics, available in Natural finish, mfg. 2012-present.

MSR $1,000	$750	$400 - 500	$250 - 300	

AD-5CE ARCOS (NO. 383-0506) – single cutaway dreadnought-style body, solid Sitka spruce top, arched laminated rosewood back, laminated rosewood sides, round soundhole with koa rosette, white ABS body binding with black/white/black purfling, mahogany neck, 14/20-fret rosewood fingerboard with pearl dot inlays, rosewood headstock overlay with Guild logo, three-per-side chrome tuners, rosewood bridge, ivory colored plastic bridge pins with abalone dots, black pickguard, Fishman Presys Plus electronics, available in Natural finish, 25.625 in. scale, 1.6875 in. nut width, deluxe polyfoam case included, mfg. 2013-present.

MSR $1,100	$800	$450 - 575	$250 - 325	

AO-3 ARCOS CUTAWAY ELECTRIC (NO. 383-0306) – single cutaway Orchestra-style body, solid Sitka spruce top, arched laminated mahogany back, laminated mahogany sides, round soundhole with koa rosette, black ABS body binding with white/black purfling, mahogany neck, 14/20-fret rosewood fingerboard with pearl dot inlays, rosewood headstock overlay with Guild logo, three-per-side chrome tuners, rosewood bridge, ivory colored plastic bridge pins with abalone dots, black pickguard, Fishman Presys Plus electronics, available in Natural finish, 25.5 in. scale, 1.75 in. nut width, deluxe polyfoam case included, mfg. 2012-present.

MSR $1,000	$750	$400 - 500	$250 - 300	

MSR/NOTES	100%	EXCELLENT	AVERAGE	LAST MSR

AO-5CE ARCOS (NO. 383-0706) – single cutaway orchestra-style body, solid Sitka spruce top, arched laminated rosewood back, laminated rosewood sides, round soundhole with koa rosette, white ABS body binding with black/white/black purfling, mahogany neck, 14/20-fret rosewood fingerboard with pearl dot inlays, rosewood headstock overlay with Guild logo, three-per-side chrome tuners, rosewood bridge, ivory colored plastic bridge pins with abalone dots, black pickguard, Fishman Presys Plus electronics, available in Natural finish, 25.625 in. scale, 1.6875 in. nut width, deluxe polyfoam case included, mfg. 2013-present.

MSR $1,100	$800	$450 - 575	$250 - 325	

CLASSIC (PRESTIGE SERIES) – single cutaway slimline hollow body, spruce top, curly maple back and sides, round soundhole with rings, multi-ply body binding, mahogany neck, 14/20-fret rosewood fingerboard with pearl dot inlays, black headstock overlay with pearl Chesterfield and Guild headstock logo, three-per-side chrome tuners, rosewood bridge, tortoiseshell pickguard, Guild transducer pickup with two knobs for electronics, available in Blonde finish, mfg. 1990-91.

	N/A	$950 - 1,100	$675 - 800	

CR-1 CROSSROADS DOUBLE E (NO. 395-6120) – doubleneck configuration with one six- and one 12-string neck, chambered all mahogany body that is hollow under the 12-string and solid under the six-string, two mahogany necks, 12-string neck specs: oval soundhole, 22-fret rosewood fingerboard with pearl dot inlays, bound headstock with pearl G shield and logo inlays, six-per-side chrome tuners, rosewood bridge with white pins, Fishman Acoustic Matrix electronics, six-string neck specs: 20-fret bound rosewood fingerboard with abalone and pearl block inlays, bound headstock with pearl G shield and logo inlays, Tune-O-Matic bridge, stop tailpiece, two exposed Slash Seymour Duncan humbucker pickups, four knobs (two v, two tone), three-way pickup switch, chrome hardware, available in Black, Crimson Trans., or White finish, mfg. 1993, 1998-2000.

	N/A	$2,600 - 3,250	$1,575 - 1,950	$4,900

A AAA maple top finished in custom colors was also available. This model was designed in conjunction with Slash (Guns 'N Roses, Velvet Revolver).

CR-1 CROSSROADS SINGLE E – single cutaway, spruce top, routed mahogany back and sides, cream top binding, rosewood fingerboard with dot inlays, three-per-side gold tuners, EMG S2 pickup and transducer pickup, available in Amber, Black, or Woodgrain finish, mfg. 1993-94.

	N/A	$1,200 - 1,500	$725 - 900	$1,299

DS-48 CE – single sharp cutaway solidbody, routed mahogany back, oval soundhole, Fishman TASS pickup, available in Black, Natural, or Sunburst finish, mfg. 1983-84.

	N/A	$900 - 1,100	$650 - 800	

EXCELLENCE (PRESTIGE SERIES) – single cutaway slimline hollow body, spruce top, curly maple back and sides, round soundhole with rings, multi-ply body binding, mahogany neck, 14/20-fret rosewood fingerboard with pearl block with abalone V insert inlays, bound black headstock overlay with pearl G shield and Guild headstock logo, three-per-side gold tuners, rosewood bridge, tortoiseshell pickguard, Guild transducer pickup with two knobs for electronics, available in Blonde or Sunburst finish, mfg. 1990-91.

	N/A	$1,050 - 1,250	$750 - 900	

FS-20 CE – single sharp cutaway solidbody, spruce top, routed mahogany back, oval soundhole, Fishman TASS pickup and electronics, other specs unknown, mfg. 1986-87.

	N/A	$850 - 1,000	$625 - 750	

FS-46 (CE) – single sharp cutaway solid body, spruce top, mahogany back, routed oval soundhole, mahogany neck, 14/24-fret bound rosewood fingerboard with dot inlays, Chesterfield and Guild logo inlays, three-per-side tuners, rosewood bridge, Fishman TASS electronics, available in Black, Natural, or Sunburst finish, 16 in. body width, 24.75 in. scale, mfg. 1983-86.

	N/A	$700 - 825	$525 - 625	

* **FS-46-6 (CE)** – similar to the FS-46 (CE), except has a maple fingerboard with black dot inlays and a Strat-style headstock with six-on-one-side tuners, mfg. 1983-85.

	N/A	$775 - 925	$525 - 625	

* **FS-46-12 (CE) 12-String** – similar to the FS-46 (CE), except in 12-string configuration and six-per-side tuners, mfg. 1983-85.

	N/A	$900 - 1,050	$650 - 750	

FS-48 DECEIVER – single sharp cutaway solidbody, oval soundhole, maple fingerboard with black dot inlays, pointed headstock with six-on-one-side tuners, one piezo pickup and one EMG humbucker hidden between the soundhole and bridge, mfg. 1985 only.

	N/A	$800 - 950	$650 - 750	

S-4 CE HR (NO. 350-6000) – Bluesbird-style solid mahogany body with (routed out) acoustic chamber, solid spruce top, round soundhole, three-stripe bound body/rosette, mahogany neck, 22-fret rosewood fingerboard with pearl dot inlay, three-per-side chrome tuners, rosewood bridge with white black dot pins, tortoise pickguard, transducer bridge pickup, volume/concentric treble/bass control, (Fishman Acoustic Matrix preamp on later models), available in Natural hand rubbed satin finish, case included, mfg. 1992-2000.

	N/A	$1,000 - 1,200	$650 - 800	$1,300

* **S-4 CE HG/Songbird (No. 350-6100)** – similar to the S-4 CE HR, except has a pearl Chesterfield/logo peghead inlay, gold tuners, and available in a Black, Natural, or White high gloss finish, case included, mfg. 1987-2000.

	N/A	$1,200 - 1,450	$850 - 1,000	$1,500

This model was called the Songbird until 1998 when it was changed to the high gloss version of the S-4 CE HR. A Songbird Custom model was available in 1989 with gold tuners and a black, red, or white top finish with black back and sides.

MSR/NOTES	100%	EXCELLENT	AVERAGE	LAST MSR

* *S-4 CE BG Barry Gibb Signature (No. 350-6100)* – similar to the S-4 CE HG, except is available in Crimson Red Trans. or Sapphire Blue Trans. custom high gloss finish, mfg. 1998-2002.

	N/A	$1,250 - 1,550	$900 - 1,050	$1,550

This model was designed in conjunction with Barry Gibb (BeeGees). List price includes deluxe hardshell case. In 2000, Sapphire Blue Trans. finish was discontinued. In 2001, Metallic Blue finish was introduced.

STANDARD (PRESTIGE SERIES) – single cutaway slimline hollow body, spruce top, curly maple back and sides, round soundhole with rings, body binding, mahogany neck, 14/20-fret rosewood fingerboard with pearl dot inlays, Guild headstock logo, three-per-side chrome tuners, rosewood bridge, Guild transducer pickup with two knobs for electronics, available in Black finish, mfg. 1990-91.

	N/A	$750 - 900	$525 - 600	

STUDIO 24/S-60 STUDIO – double cutaway body, spruce top, maple back and sides, redesigned neck joint that allows access to upper frets, notched diamond inlays, snakehead-shape headstock, mfg. 1986-89.

	N/A	$2,300 - 2,700	$1,650 - 1,900	

This model was designed in conjunction with George Gruhn.

WILLY PORTER SIGNATURE (NO. 380-9006) – single cutaway F-40-style body, solid AAA Sitka spruce top, solid flame maple back and sides, round soundhole with Madagascar rosewood and ivoroid, red, and black accent lines rosette, special binding package, Guild neck block system, one-piece mahogany neck, 21-fret Madagascar rosewood fingerboard with small abalone dot inlays, three-per-side nickel Gotoh tuners, Madagascar rosewood bridge with bone pins for the bass strings and ebony pins for the treble strings, Fishman Elipse Matrix Blend electronics, available in Antique Burst, Blonde, or Ice Tea Burst, 25.5 in. scale, mfg. summer 2007-2010.

$2,500	$1,500 - 1,750	$950 - 1,100	$3,300

ACOUSTIC: TRUE AMERICAN SERIES (DCE PREFIX)

DCE-1 TRUE AMERICAN (NO. 350-1306) – single cutaway dreadnought style, solid spruce top, mahogany back/sides/neck, round soundhole, bound body, three-stripe rosette, 20-fret rosewood fingerboard with dot inlay, three-per-side gold tuners, rosewood bridge with white black dot pins, black pickguard, transducer pickup, Fishman Acoustic Matrix system, available in Natural (021) hand rubbed satin finish, mfg. 1993-2000.

	N/A	$675 - 800	$475 - 550	$1,200

* *DCE-1 HG (No. 350-1406)* – similar to the DCE-1, except it features a high gloss finish available in Antique Burst, Black, Cherry (1998 only), Natural (1999-2000), or Trans. Red (1999-2000), mfg. 1997-2000.

	N/A	$800 - 950	$550 - 650	$1,400

DCE-3 (NO. 350-1456) – single cutaway dreadnought style, solid spruce top, flame maple back and sides, round soundhole with three-stripe rosette, multi-ply body binding, mahogany neck, 14/20-fret ebony fingerboard with dot inlays, black headstock overlay with Chesterfield and Guild inlays, three-per-side gold tuners, ebony bridge with white black dot pins, tortoiseshell pickguard, transducer pickup, Fishman Prefix Pro electronics, available in Antique Burst, Black, Blonde, or Tennessee Orange finish, mfg. 1998-2000.

	N/A	$900 - 1,075	$625 - 725	$1,450

DCE-5 TRUE AMERICAN (NO. 350-1506) – single cutaway dreadnought style, solid spruce top, rosewood back and sides, round soundhole with three-stripe rosette, multi-ply body binding, mahogany neck, 14/20-fret ebony fingerboard with dot inlays, black headstock overlay with Chesterfield and Guild inlays, three-per-side gold tuners, ebony bridge with white black dot pins, black pickguard, transducer pickup, Fishman Blender electronics, available in Antique Burst or Natural nitrocellulose finish, mfg. 1994-2000.

	N/A	$925 - 1,050	$575 - 650	$1,750

ACOUSTIC ELECTRIC: TRADITIONAL SERIES (F PREFIX)

All models in this series have single rounded cutaway folk style body, oval soundhole, tortoiseshell pickguard, three-stripe bound body/rosette, transducer pickup, volume/four-band EQ preamp system with built in phase reversal, unless otherwise listed.

F-4 CE (NO. 350-3006) – single smooth cutaway body, solid spruce top, mahogany back and sides, oval soundhole, bound body, mahogany neck, 14/20-fret rosewood fingerboard with pearl dot inlays, three-per-side chrome tuners, rosewood bridge with white black dot pins, Fishman Acoustic Matrix system, available in Natural Hand Rubbed satin finish, case included, mfg. 1992-99.

	N/A	$700 - 800	$400 - 475	$1,285

* *F-4 CE HG (No. 350-3106)* – similar to the F-4 CE, except available in Antique Burst, Black, Crimson Red Transparent, or Teal Green Trans. high gloss finish, case included, mfg. 1998-99.

	N/A	$750 - 850	$450 - 525	$1,470

* *F-4 CE MH* – similar to the F-4 CE, except has an all mahogany body, available in Amber finish, mfg. 1992-95.

	N/A	$700 - 800	$400 - 475	$1,050

F-5 CE (NO. 350-3206) – single cutaway body, solid spruce top, rosewood back and sides, oval soundhole, mahogany neck, 14/20-fret rosewood fingerboard with pearl dot inlay, three-per-side chrome Grover tuners, rosewood bridge with white black dot pins, Fishman Acoustic Matrix system, available in Black, Natural, or Antique Burst high gloss lacquer finish, case included, mfg. 1992-99.

	N/A	$850 - 1,000	$550 - 650	$1,570

MSR/NOTES	100%	EXCELLENT	AVERAGE	LAST MSR

* FF-5 CE – similar to the F-5 CE, except has a deep body, mfg. 1992-95.

	N/A	$1,000 - 1,150	$625 - 750	$1,299

F-25 CE – solid spruce top, mahogany back/sides/neck, 24-fret rosewood fingerboard with pearl dot inlay, rosewood bridge with white black dot pins, three-per-side chrome Grover tuners, volume control, concentric treble/bass control, active preamp, available in Black, Natural or Sunburst finish, mfg. 1991-92.

	N/A	$850 - 1,000	$550 - 650	$1,195

F-30 CE – solid spruce top, flame maple back/sides, mahogany neck, 24-fret rosewood fingerboard with pearl dot inlay, rosewood bridge with white black dot pins, pearl Chesterfield/logo peghead inlay, three-per-side gold Grover tuners, available in Black, Blonde, Natural, or Sunburst finish, mfg. 1992-95.

	N/A	$1,000 - 1,150	$625 - 750	$1,495

F-45 CE – solid spruce top, mahogany back/sides/neck, rosewood fingerboard with pearl dot inlay, rosewood bridge with white black dot pins, pearl Chesterfield/logo peghead inlay, three-per-side gold Grover tuners, available in Black, Blonde, Natural, or Sunburst finish, mfg. 1983-1992.

	N/A	$1,050 - 1,200	$700 - 800	

In 1985, curly maple back and sides, an oval soundhole, a bound rosewood fingerboard, and a Chesterfield headstock logo were introduced. This model was renamed the GF-45CE for a brief period in 1987, and a snakehead-style headstock was introduced.

* F-45C-12 12-String – similar to the F-45 CE, except in 12-string configuration, available in Black, Natural, or Sunburst finish, mfg. 1984 only.

	N/A	$1,100 - 1,300	$750 - 900	

F-47 CE HR (NO. 350-3606) – single smooth cutaway grand concert-style body, solid spruce top, solid mahogany back, laminated mahogany sides, scalloped bracing, round soundhole with rings, multi-ply binding, mahogany neck, 14/20-fret bound rosewood fingerboard with pearloid block inlays, black headstock overlay with logo and Chesterfield pearl inlays, three-per-side chrome tuners, rosewood bridge, tortoise pickguard, available in Natural satin finish, 25.625 in. scale, mfg. 2000-01.

	N/A	$850 - 1,000	$550 - 650	$1,500

* F-47CE HG (No. 350-3406) – similar to the F-47CE HR, except available in an Antique Burst, Black, or Natural high gloss finish, mfg. 1999-2001.

	N/A	$1,000 - 1,200	$625 - 750	$1,800

»F-47 MCE (No. 350-3706/380-3606) – similar to the F-47 CE HG except has a solid flame maple back and laminated flame maple sides, available in Blonde, Black, Antique Burst, or Red Trans. finish, mfg. 2000-03.

	N/A	$1,250 - 1,400	$775 - 900	$2,400

»F-47 RCE (No. 350-3506/380-3506) – similar to the F-47CE HG, except has rosewood back and sides, available in Natural or Antique Burst high gloss finish, mfg. 1999-2003.

	N/A	$1,300 - 1,450	$825 - 950	$2,400

F-65 CE (NO. 350-3306) – single cutaway body, solid spruce top, curly maple back and sides, oval soundhole with abalone rosette, multi-ply body binding, mahogany neck, 14/20-fret bound ebony fingerboard with pearl block/abalone wedge inlays, bound headstock with pearl shield/logo inlay, three-per-side gold Grover tuners, ebony bridge with white abalone dot pins, Fishman Prefix On-Board Blender system, available in Antique Burst, Black, Blonde, Crimson Red Trans., Sapphire Blue Trans., or Teal Green Trans. high gloss finish, case included, mfg. 1992-2001.

	N/A	$1,350 - 1,650	$950 - 1,100	$2,299

Early versions of this model had optional figured maple top with Amber and Sunburst finishes. In 1994, transducer pickup, and preamp were introduced.

ACOUSTIC/ACOUSTIC ELECTRIC BASS

B-4 E (NO. 350-4006) – single rounded cutaway folk style body, solid spruce top, arched mahogany back, mahogany sides, oval soundhole, three-stripe bound body/rosette, mahogany neck, 14/20-fret rosewood fingerboard with pearl dot inlays, two-per-side chrome tuners, rosewood bridge with white black dot pins, tortoiseshell pickguard, transducer pickup, volume/four-band EQ control, Fishman Acoustic Matrix preamp, available in Natural hand rubbed satin finish, case included, mfg. 1993-99.

	N/A	$1,000 - 1,200	$750 - 900	$1,356

Early models were available with gold hardware and later models were available with fretless fingerboards.

* B-4 E HG (No. 350-4206) – similar to the B-4 E, except has multiple-ply body binding and available in an Antique Burst, Black, Crimson Red Trans., or Teal Green Trans. high gloss finish, case included, mfg. 1994-95, 1998-99.

	N/A	$1,000 - 1,200	$750 - 900	$1,500

Later models were available with fretless fingerboards.

* B-4 E MH – similar to the B-4E, except has a mahogany top, mfg. 1995-96.

	N/A	$900 - 1,050	$650 - 750	$1,150

MSR/NOTES	100%	EXCELLENT	AVERAGE	LAST MSR

B-50/B-30 – grand concert style body, spruce top, arched mahogany back, mahogany sides, round soundhole, three-stripe bound body/rosette, mahogany neck, 14/20-fret rosewood fingerboard with pearl dot inlay, black pointed headstock with pearl Chesterfield and Guild logo inlays, two-per-side chrome tuners, rosewood bridge with split saddle and white pins, tortoiseshell pickguard, available in Natural or Sunburst finish, 30.75 in. scale, mfg. 1975-1997.

	100%	EXCELLENT	AVERAGE	LAST MSR
1975-1987 B-50	N/A	$1,400 - 1,700	$950 - 1,100	
1987-1997 B-30	N/A	$1,200 - 1,450	$850 - 1,000	$1,400

In 1987, this model was renamed the B-30.

* **B-50E/B-30 E Electric (No. 350-4406)** – similar to the B-50/B-30, except has a transducer pickup and electronics (Fishman Acoustic Matrix system on later models), available in Natural or Antique Burst high gloss lacquer finish, case included, mfg. 1983-1999.

	100%	EXCELLENT	AVERAGE	LAST MSR
1983-1987 B-50E	N/A	$1,500 - 1,850	$1,050 - 1,250	
1987-1999 B-30E	N/A	$1,300 - 1,600	$900 - 1,050	$2,000

In 1987, this model was renamed the B-30E and an arched laminated mahogany back and solid mahogany sides were listed. Later models were available with fretless fingerboards.

* **B-30 ET Thinline** – similar to the B-30E, except has thinline body style, disc. 1992.

	100%	EXCELLENT	AVERAGE	LAST MSR
	N/A	$1,350 - 1,700	$950 - 1,100	$1,595

B-54CE STANDARD BASS (NO. 385-1806) – single cutaway Jumbo body, solid Sikta spruce top, arched maple back, solid maple sides, round soundhole with multi-ring ivoroid rosette, ivoroid binding, black/ivoroid/black purfling, set mahogany neck, 17/22-fret rosewood fingerboard with pearl dot inlays, mahogany headstock overlay with pearl Guild logo, two-per-side chrome Gotoh tuners, rosewood bridge, Fishman Matrix Infinity pickup with end-pin mounted preamp, available in Blonde finish, 34 in. scale, deluxe hardshell case included, mfg. 2012-present.

MSR $3,500	$2,600	$1,400 - 1,750	$850 - 1,050	

B-500 C – single cutaway body, spruce top, maple back and sides, round soundhole, inlaid logo, two-per-side tuners, special design Guild transducer and pre amp with volume/concentric treble/bass controls, available in Natural or Sunburst finish, mfg. 1992-93.

	N/A	$1,400 - 1,700	$1,000 - 1,200	$1,695

FB-46CE – single cutaway thinbody based on the FS-46CE guitar, spruce top, mahogany back and sides, round soundhole, maple or mahogany neck, maple or rosewood fingerboard with dot inlays, Fishman TASS pickup, available in Black, Natural, or Sunburst finish, mfg. 1983 only.

	N/A	$950 - 1,100	$675 - 800	

GUITARES MAURICE DUPONT

Instruments currently built in France. Previously distributed by Paul Hostetter of Santa Cruz, CA.

After spending a number of years repairing and restoring Selmer/Maccaferri guitars, luthier Maurice Dupont began building Selmer replicas that differ in the fact the Dupont features a one-piece neck with adjustable trussrod inside (Selmers had a three-piece neck), and better construction materials. Dupont also hand builds his own classical, flamenco, steel-string, and archtop guitars. Both the **Excellence** and **Privilege** archtops are offered in 16 in. or 17 in. bodies, and with a Florentine or Venetian cutaway. For further information you can try contacting Dupont directly but it is unknown if he is still producing guitars.

GUITAR FACTORY

Instruments currently built in Orlando, FL.

The Guitar Factory has been building and repairing guitars since 1972. They offer an Electric/Acoustic E/A 6 or 12 model with mono or dual output. A wide variety of exotic wood's, a hollow-neck-through-body two-octave instrument. Prices start at $3,600. Various options include pickup configuration, choice of different woods, and hardware. They also build neck-thru basses and a line of 000 acoustics called Orange Blossom. For further information regarding specifications, other models and pricing, visit Guitar Factory's website or contact them directly.

GUITAR FARM

Instruments previously built in Sperryville, VA.

The Guitar Farm offered hand crafted guitar models.

GUITARRAS ALMANSA S.A.

Instruments currently produced in Almansa, (Albacete) Spain. Distributed in the USA by Ruben Flores, located in Seal Beach, CA.

Guitarras Almansa guitars are handcrafted in Almansa, Spain under directorship of Pedro-Angel Lopez.
Almansa Classical guitars are constructed to 650 (25.6 in.), 636, 580, and 544 mm scales and in various models for children,

students, and professional guitarists. Classical Models 401 through 436 are Studio models with solid cedar tops and laminated mahogany, bubinga, and rosewood back and sides. Conservatory models 457 through 461 are of solid cedar or spruce tops with solid Indian Rosewood back and sides. The Concert guitars are fully handcrafted with solid cedar or German Spruce tops, back, and sides of Indian Rosewood or brazilian Rosewood of the finest quality. Many models of classical guitar are built in regular and thin body cutaways with pickups for students and professionals. Almansa also buids Flamenco guitars; models 447 and 449 as well as the Professional model. These have German Spruce tops and solid cypress back and sides. Studio Flamenco models 413 and 415 have solid spruce tops and sycamore back and sides. Also available are regular and thin body Flamenco Cutaway models with pickups. All feature clear pickguards.

MSR: Classical Models 401 ($490), 402 ($560), 403 ($630), 424 ($720), 434 ($790), 435 ($990), 436 ($1,290), 457 ($1,630), 459 ($2,140), 461 ($2890). Flamenco Models 413 ($690), 415 ($1,040), 447 ($1,420), 449 ($2,240), Professional ($4,200). Cadete Models are special order. Senorita Models are special order. Bandurrias: 403 ($630), 434 ($790), and 435 ($990). Lauds: 403 ($630), and 434 ($790). Professional Rosewood ($4,300), Professional Jacaranda ($5,400), Grand Professional Jacaranda (inquire).

GUITARRAS LA ESPAÑOLA

Instruments previously built in Paracho (Michoacan), Mexico.

Guitarras Española handcrafted classical guitars through three generations. The guitars were built of exotic Mexican woods in the artisan tradition workshop, and feature cedar tops, mahogany or walnut sides, as well as Siricote or Palo Escrito woods.

GUITARS FROM SPAIN

Distributor located in Boca Raton, FL.

EMAC Music imports and distributes classical, flamenco, and acoustic/electric guitars from Spain. Currently, they distribute Amalio Burguet, Antonio Sanchez, Antonio Picado, and Prudencio Saez. For more information, visit EMAC's website or contact them directly.

CONTACT INFORMATION
GUITARS FROM SPAIN
1498 SW 1st Street
Boca Raton, FL 33486
Phone No.: 561-393-1933
Phone No.: 866-396-1933
Fax No.: 561-347-0291
www.guitarsfromspain.com
info@guitarsfromspain.com

GURIAN, MICHAEL

Instruments previously built in New York City, NY, Hinsdale, NH, and West Swanzey, NJ between 1965 and 1981/82.

Luthier Michael Gurian built quality classical and steel string acoustic guitars, as well as being a major American wood supplier. He debuted his classical designs in 1965 and offered steel string designs four years later. In 1971, at the encouragement of vintage retailer Matt Umanov, Gurian designed a cutaway model that later became a regular part of the product line.

In the early 1970s, Gurian moved his production facilities from New York City, NY to Hinsdale, NH. Gurian's four story mill building housed a large band saw (for slabbing logs), two resaws (cutting slabs to dimension), and various planers. During this time period, Gurian imported ebony, rosewood, mansonia, and spruce; his U.S. sources supplied walnut, maple, and other woods. Disaster struck in 1979, as a fire consumed their current stock of guitars as well as tooling and machinery. Gurian rebuilt by later that year in West Swanzey, NJ and continued producing guitars until 1982.

Michael Gurian may have stopped offering guitars in 1982, but he still continues to be a major presence in the guitar building industry. Gurian serves as a consultant in guitar design, and his company offers guitar fittings (such as bridge pins) and supplies, custom built marquetry, and guitar-building tools based on his designs. Gurian was perhaps one of the first smaller guitar producers to combine production techniques with hand crafted sensibilities. Guitars produced at the New Hampshire site were built in three distinct phases. In Phase One, the basic guitar parts (tops, backs, necks, fingerboards, etc.) were produced in large lots and inventoried. Gurian's factory did use carving lathes to "rough out" the neck blanks, and heated hydraulic presses to bend the guitar sides. During Phase Two, the company's luthiers would choose "kits" from the part supplies and construct the guitar individually. This allowed the luthiers control over individual guitar's construction and tuning. Finally, in Phase Three, the finished guitars were sent to the finishing technicians to spray the finish. This method would guarantee a similarity in the finishes from one guitar to the next. It is estimated that around 5,000 Gurian guitars were built. Sources: The Alembic Report *Guitar Player* magazine, and Tom Wheeler, *American Guitars*, and David Johnson.

MODEL OVERVIEW/GENERAL INFORMATION

The models listed in the following categories are the most common Gurian guitars encountered in the used market; however, other variations do exist and because of the obscurity of these guitars, they need to be evaluated on a case-by-case basis. Size 2, Size 3, and Jumbo models were all available in left-handed configuration, with a wide neck, and with electronics. The standard Gurian neck was narrow in comparison to other acoustic necks with a 1.625 in. wide nut. Brazilian rosewood and koa back and sides were also offered although not on a standard production basis. Brazilian models are indicated by a B in the model name and koa models are indicated by a K in the model name. It appears that Gurian stopped using Brazilian rosewood in the mid-1970s. Gurian also built a handful of Size 1 (parlor sized) guitars that are extremely rare. These guitars feature Brazilian rosewood back and sides and they do not have labels or serial numbers.

Almost all Gurian guitars feature a Brazilian rosewood bridge and bridgeplate and an ivory saddle and nut. Guitars that were equipped with pickguards featured a thin black teardrop-style guard. Tuners were chrome Schallers on standard models and gold Schallers or Grovers on custom and fancier models.

• **Add 30% for custom wide neck.**

MSR/NOTES	100%	EXCELLENT	AVERAGE	LAST MSR

ACOUSTIC: CLASSICAL/FLAMENCO MODELS

Early classical models were simply called the CL without any designation in the model name indicating what type of back and side woods were used. Gurian also offered Flamenco guitars called the FLC, but too few of these guitars exist to establish a used market value.

CLM – classical body style, cedar top, mahogany back and sides, wood bindings, round soundhole with rosette, mahogany neck, ebony fingerboard, ivory nut, slotted headstock with three-per-side open-style tuners, Brazilian rosewood bridge with an ivory saddle, Natural finish, mfg. mid 1960s-early 1980s.

	N/A	$1,000 - 1,500	$700 - 1,000	

CLR – classical body style, cedar top, Indian rosewood back and sides, decorative wood bindings, round soundhole with rosette, mahogany neck, ebony fingerboard, ivory nut, slotted headstock with three-per-side open-style gold-plated tuners, Brazilian rosewood bridge with an ivory saddle, Natural finish, mfg. mid 1960s-early 1980s.

	N/A	$1,100 - 1,700	$900 - 1,200	

ACOUSTIC: CUTAWAY MODELS

CMPH – single sharp cutaway mid-sized body, spruce top, curly maple back and sides, wood body binding, herringbone purfling, round soundhole with herringbone rosette, ebony fingerboard, ivory nut, three-per-side tuners, Brazilian rosewood bridge with an ivory saddle, available in Natural finish, mfg. late 1970s-early 1980s.

	N/A	$3,000 - 4,000	$1,800 - 2,500	

* **CMPH Electric** – similar to the CMPH, except has Frap GF100 electronics, mfg. late 1970s-early 1980s.

	N/A	$3,000 - 4,000	$1,800 - 2,500	

CRH – single sharp cutaway mid-sized body, spruce top, Indian rosewood back and sides, wood body binding, herringbone purfling, round soundhole with herringbone rosette, ebony fingerboard, ivory nut, three-per-side tuners, Brazilian rosewood bridge with an ivory saddle, available in Natural finish, mfg. late 1970s-early 1980s.

	N/A	$2,300 - 3,100	$1,400 - 2,000	

* **CRH Electric** – similar to the CRH, except has Frap GF100 electronics, mfg. late 1970s-early 1980s.

	N/A	$2,300 - 3,100	$1,400 - 2,000	

ACOUSTIC: SIZE 2/SIZE 3/JUMBO MODELS

S2M – small-sized body, spruce top, mahogany back and sides, wood body binding, round soundhole with wooden rosette, mahogany neck, ebony fingerboard, ivory nut, three-per-side tuners, Brazilian rosewood bridge with an ivory saddle, pickguard, available in Natural finish, mfg. 1970s-early 1980s.

	N/A	$1,800 - 2,300	$1,300 - 1,600	

S2R – small-sized body, spruce top, East Indian rosewood back and sides, wood body binding, round soundhole with wooden rosette, mahogany neck, ebony fingerboard, ivory nut, three-per-side tuners, Brazilian rosewood bridge with an ivory saddle, pickguard, available in Natural finish, mfg. 1970s-early 1980s.

	N/A	$2,000 - 2,500	$1,400 - 1,800	

* **S2R3H** – similar to the S2R, except has a three-piece back, herringbone purflings, and upgraded gold tuners, mfg. 1970s-early 1980s.

	N/A	$1,800 - 2,250	$1,150 - 1,400	

S3M – mid-sized body, spruce top, mahogany back and sides, wood body binding, round soundhole with wooden rosette, mahogany neck, ebony fingerboard, ivory nut, three-per-side tuners, Brazilian rosewood bridge with an ivory saddle, pickguard, available in Natural finish, mfg. 1970s-early 1980s.

	N/A	$2,000 - 2,500	$1,400 - 1,800	

S3R – mid-sized body, spruce top, East Indian rosewood back and sides, wood body binding, round soundhole with wooden rosette, mahogany neck, ebony fingerboard, ivory nut, three-per-side tuners, Brazilian rosewood bridge with an ivory saddle, pickguard, available in Natural finish, mfg. 1970s-early 1980s.

	N/A	$2,500 - 3,200	$1,500 - 2,000	

* **S3R3H** – similar to the S3R, except has a three-piece back, herringbone purflings, and upgraded gold tuners, mfg. 1970s-early 1980s.

	N/A	$2,000 - 2,500	$1,350 - 1,700	

JM – jumbo-sized body, spruce top, mahogany back and sides, wood body binding, round soundhole with wooden rosette, mahogany neck, ebony fingerboard, ivory nut, three-per-side tuners, Brazilian rosewood bridge with an ivory saddle, pickguard, available in Natural finish, mfg. 1970s-early 1980s.

	N/A	$1,700 - 2,100	$1,250 - 1,500	

JR – jumbo-sized body, spruce top, East Indian rosewood back and sides, wood body binding, round soundhole with wooden rosette, mahogany neck, ebony fingerboard, ivory nut, three-per-side tuners, Brazilian rosewood bridge with an ivory saddle, pickguard, available in Natural finish, mfg. 1970s-early 1980s.

	N/A	$2,500 - 3,200	$1,500 - 2,000	

* **JR3H** – similar to the JR, except has a three-piece back, herringbone purflings, and upgraded gold tuners, mfg. 1970s-early 1980s.

	N/A	$2,000 - 2,500	$1,350 - 1,700	

NOTES

H SECTION
HAGSTROM

Instruments currently produced overseas since 2004. Instruments previously produced in Sweden between 1957 and 1983. Distributed by U.S. Music Corp. in Buffalo Grove, IL. Previously distributed by American Music & Sound (AM&S) in Agoura Hills, CA between 2004 and 2009. Early distributors included the Hershman Musical Instrument Company of New York (under Goya logo) and Selmer, U.K. (under Futurama logo). In the mid-1970s, Ampeg became the U.S. distributor.

CONTACT INFORMATION
HAGSTROM
Distributed by U.S. Music Corp.
1000 Corporate Grove Drive
Buffalo Grove, IL 60089
Phone No.: 847-949-0444
Phone No.: 800-877-6863
Fax No.: 847-949-8444
www.hagstromguitars.com
guitar.support@usmusiccorp.com

Hagstrom first began building guitars and basses in 1957, although many models appeared under the Futurama trademark in England (distributed by Selmer, U.K.) and either Hagstrom or Goya (distributed by Hershman Musical Instrument Company).

Hagstrom produced roughly 130,000 electric guitars and basses from 1958 to 1981 in Alvdalen, Sweden. During the early '80s until 1983, a few instruments were manufactured under the Hagstrom name in Japan. Due to quality concerns and ever increasing competition, the doors were eventually closed in 1983.

Distributors included the Hershman Musical Instrument Company of New York, the Merson Musical Supply Company of Westbury, New York, Selmer, U.K. and eventually Ampeg. The evolution of the Hagstrom line was rapid, and approximately sixty-five different models of guitars and basses were produced. (Featured here are the more popular and well-known models.) Early in its history, guitars were marketed in the U.K. as Futurama and in the US as Goya, Kent (a name that rarely appeared on the guitar and should not be confused with Kent trademark guitars) or Hagstrom. By 1965, all guitars were identified as Hagstrom.

Hagstrom produced both solid body and semi-hollowbody electrics, as well as an archtop model designed by luthier James L. D'Aquisto. Also introduced was the first eight-string bass (four pairs of strings) and the "fastest neck in the world" which was accomplished by using an H shape "expander stretcher" truss, a design that has allowed the necks to remain true even to this day.

In 2004, Hagstrom announced that they were building guitars again. This line was officially introduced at the 2005 NAMM show. Hagstrom has always been known for their electric designs, but this new line of guitars featured standard acoustic models that lasted one year. For more information contact Hagstrom directly.

The **O78S** (disc. last MSR was $325) is an Orchestra 7/8 sized body with a solid spruce top, and mahogany back/sides/neck. The **O78SC** (disc. last MSR was $395) is the same as the O78S, except it has a single cutaway. The **O100S** (disc. last MSR was $395) is the same as the O78S, except it is a full-sized body. The **O102S** (disc. last MSR was $395) is the same as the O100S, except has a solid cedar top. The **D100** (disc. last MSR was $275) is a dreadnought body with a spruce top, and basswood sides/back. The **D100S** (disc. last MSR was $395) is similar to the D100, except has a solid spruce top, and mahogany back/sides/neck. The **C102** (disc. last MSR was $395) is a classical style with a solid cedar top, and mahogany back/sides/neck. The **O103S** (disc. last MSR was $395) is a grand auditorium style with a solid mahogany top, and mahogany back/sides/neck.

Currently, Hagstrom offers a line of acoustic guitars that retails between $425 and $995 and these instruments are available in dreadnought and NG body styles.

HALFLING BY RIBBECKE

Instruments currently produced in the USA since 2005. Distributed by the Ribbecke Guitar Company in Healdsburg, CA.

CONTACT INFORMATION
HALFLING BY RIBBECKE
PO Box 697
Healdsburg, CA 95448
Phone No.: 707-431-0125
www.ribbeckehalfling.com
info@rgcguitars.com

Luthier Tom Ribbecke has been hand crafting guitars since the early 1970s, and in 2004, he formed the Ribbecke Guitar Corporation to produce more guitars while being able to focus more time on his independent lutherie. The first brand under the Ribbecke Guitar Corporation is Halfling, and the first guitar to be built is the Bobby Vega Halfling Acoustic Bass. All Halfling guitars are built in the USA by accomplished luthiers and the entire operation is overseen by Ribbecke himself. With the Ribbecke Guitar Corporation, they are able to produce more guitars while using CNC technology. For more information, visit Halfling's website or contact them directly.

ACOUSTIC

The **Pin Bridge Halfling Guitar** (MSR $6,500) is a fully acoustic guitar with an internal B-Band pickup and electronics.

ACOUSTIC BASS

The **PB-1 Arch Back Pin Bridge Bass** (MSR $6,500) features a solid western red cedar top that is flatter on the base side and arched on the treble side, an arched back, a B-Band pickup, and the soundhole is located in the upper bass bout. The **FB-1 Flat Back Pin Bridge Bass** (disc. 2008, last MSR was $4,750) is the same as the PB-1 Arch Back Bass, except has a flat back. The **BV-1 Bobby Vega Bass** (MSR $7,500) is similar to the PB-1 Arch Back Bass, except is is slightly heavier and has a built-in bridge pickup by Rick Turner. The Bobby Vega Bass was also available with a neck pickup (**BV-N1**, Last MSR was $5,000), and an Artist Series version with custom choices is available through the custom shop (MSR starts at $7,500). The **Five-String Vega Halfling Bass** (MSR $8,500) has a floating custom Kent Armstrong pickup.

HALL, WILLIAM & SON

Instruments previously built in New York City, NY, during the 1800s.

William Hall was a guitar dealer in New York City between circa 1820 and 1874. Hall did business at several addresses in New York - most of which were on Broadway. He conducted business on and off with two partners, John Firth and Sylvanus Pond, and they did business under many names including Firth, Hall, and Pond, Firth & Hall, and Firth, Pond, and Company. Hall also did business with his son James, and the business was called Hall & Son or W.M. Hall & Son. Hall's principle business was a dealership, but he did have a manufacturing facility with thirty employees where they built pianos. It is unlikely that his shop produced many (if any) guitars. The guitars sold under Hall's name (Firth & Pond as well) were made predominantly (almost exclusively) by James Ashborn of Torrington, CT. Ashborn produced two main styles of guitars were identified as Model 1 and Model 2. This designation of models is also used on the guitars made for Hall and others.

Limited number of these guitars are still in existence. Most models that appear are the parlor style. Original instruments in excellent condition could bring more than $1,000 in the marketplace. Source: Walter Murray, Frankenstein Fretworks.

HANNAH

Instruments previously built in Vancouver, B.C., Canada between 1995 and 2006.

Luthier Rod Hannah hand built both dreadnought and 000-sized 12-fret acoustic guitars in "short lot" sizes (approximately four instruments at a time). Hannah guitars were built with recording and performing musicians in mind. Prices started around $4,500 U.S.D.

HARMONY

Instruments currently produced in China and Korea since 2007. Previously produced in the Chicago, IL area between the 1890s and 1975, and in various Asian countries including Korea from the mid-1970s through the early 2000s. Distributed by The Original Harmony Guitar Company, Inc. in Palatine, IL. See Chapter on House Brands.

The Harmony Company of Chicago, IL was one of the largest American musical instrument manufacturers. Harmony has the historical distinction of being the largest "jobber" house in the nation, producing stringed instruments for a number of different wholesalers. Individual dealers or distributors could get stringed instruments with their own brand name on it (as long as they ordered a minimum of 100 pieces). At one time the amount of instruments being produced by Harmony made up the largest percentage of stringed instruments being manufactured in the U.S. market (archtops, flattops, electric Spanish, Hawaiian bodies, ukuleles, banjos, mandolins, violins, and more).

Harmony was founded by Wilhelm J.F. Schultz in 1892. Schultz, a German immigrant and former foreman of Lyon & Healy's drum division, started his new company with four employees. By 1884, the number of employees had grown to forty, and Shultz continued to expand into larger and larger factories through 1904. Shultz built Harmony up to a 125 employee workforce (and a quarter of a million dollars in annual sales) by 1915.

In 1916, the Sears, Roebuck Company purchased Harmony, and seven years later the company had annual sales of 250,000 units. Max Adler, a Sears executive, appointed Jay Kraus as vice-president of Harmony in 1925. The following year Kraus succeeded founder Wilhelm Schultz as president, and continued expanding production. In 1930, annual sales were reported to be 500,000 units, with 35 to 40 percent being sold to Sears (catalog sales). Harmony had no branch offices, territorial restrictions, or dealer reps - wholesalers purchased the musical instruments and aggressively sold to music stores.

Harmony bought several trademarks from the bankrupt Oscar Schmidt Company in 1939, and their Sovereign and Stella lines were Harmony's more popular guitars. In 1940, Krause bought Harmony by acquiring the controlling stock, and continued to expand the company's production to meet the market boom during the 1950s and 1960s. Mr. Kraus remained president until 1968, when he died of a heart attack. Charles Rubovits (who had been with Harmony since 1935) took over as president, and remained in that position for two years. Kraus' trust still maintained control over Harmony, and trust members attempted to form a conglomerate by purchasing Chicago-based distributor Targ & Dinner and a few other companies. Company (or more properly the conglomerate's) indebtedness and the cheap mid-grade guitars that were being imported from Asia, led to a liquidation auction to satisfy creditors - although Harmony continued to turn in impressive annual sales figures right up until the company was dissolved in 1975.

In the late 1970s, the Harmony trademark was sold and licensed for use on a line of Asian-built guitars. From the late 1970s through the 1990s, Harmony was mainly used on cheap entry-level guitars that were often sold through mass merchandisers. The trademark and licensing agreements were also bought and sold several times throughout this period. In 2000, MBT International began to distribute Harmony guitars with a line of acoustic and electric instruments mainly based on popular American designs; however, by 2001, this licensing agreement was dissolved.

Current Harmony president Charlie Subecz bought the Harmony trademark in the mid-1990s, and by the mid-2000s, he decided to reintroduce the Harmony guitar line. Instead of using Harmony as simply a budget brand of copied models, Subecz went to work on offering vintage Harmony guitars that were reminiscent of the 1950s and 1960s. Unfortunately, no blueprints or records existed on Harmony's vintage guitars, so Subecz and his crew had to obtain physical examples of these guitars. Examples were then sent to Korea where they were precisely duplicated and readied for production.

MSR/NOTES	100%	EXCELLENT	AVERAGE	LAST MSR

Harmony currently offers a line of vintage reproduction guitars as well as a custom line of guitars that feature newer designs and technology. For more information, visit Harmony's website or contact them directly.

Harmony company history courtesy Tom Wheeler, *American Guitars*, Harmony model information courtesy John Kinnemeyer of JK Lutherie, Ryland Fitchett of Rockohaulix, Ronald Rothman of *Rothman's Guitars*.

IDENTIFYING RE-BRANDED HARMONY TRADEMARKS

Harmony reportedly made fifty-seven "different" brands throughout their productive years. Early models featured the Harmony trademark, or remained unlabeled for the numerous wholesalers. In 1928 Harmony introduced the **Roy Smeck Vita** series, and two years later the **Grand Concert** and **Hawaiian** models debuted. The **Vagabond** line was introduced in 1931, the **Cremona** series in 1934, and **Patrician** guitars later in 1938.

As Harmony was purchased by Sears, Roebuck in 1916, Harmony built a number of **Silvertone** models. Harmony continued to sell to Sears even after Kraus bought the company. Harmony bought a number of trademarks from the bankrupt Oscar Schmidt Company in 1939 (such as **La Scala, Stella, Sovereign**), as well as expanding their own brand names with **Valencia, Monterey, Harmony Deluxe, Johnny Marvin, Vogue**, and many (like Carelli from the mid-1930s) that are being researched today. Although the Kay company built most of the **Airline** guitars for the Montgomery Ward stores, Harmony was subcontracted to build Airlines to meet the seasonal shopping rush. National (Valco) supplied resonator cones for some Harmony resonator models, and probably bought guitar parts from Harmony in return. Harmony also built guitars under the **Barclay** trademark, and these guitars were basically copies of the Harmony line from that era.

HARMONY PRODUCTION & PRICING

The Harmony company of 4600 South Kolin Avenue in Chicago, Illinois built a great number of guitars. Harmony catalogs in the early 1960s proudly proclaimed "we've produced millions of instruments but we make them one at a time." Harmony guitars can be found practically anywhere: the guitar shop, the antique shop, the flea market, the Saturday garage sale right around the corner. Due to the vast numbers of Harmony guitars and because the majority of them were entry level models, the vintage guitar market's response is a collective shrug of the shoulders as it moves on to the higher dollar American-built Fenders and Gibsons, etc.

As a result, the secondary Harmony guitar market is rather hard to pin down. Outside of a few hardy souls like Willie Moseley, Ronald Rothman, Paul Day, and Tony Bacon, very little has been written about Harmony guitar models as a means to identify them. As a result, rather than use the exact model designations, most dealers tend to offer a "Harmony Acoustic," or a "'60s Harmony Archtop" through their ads or at guitar shows. It becomes difficult to track the asking prices of various models if the information regarding that model is not available.

The majority of Harmony guitars encountered today are generally part of the millions produced during the 1960s through the company's closing in 1975. As most of them were entry level models, condition (especially physical condition) becomes a bit more critical in pricing. A dead mint Harmony Rocket is worth the money because it's clean - a beat up, player's grade Rocket might not be worth a second look to the interested party. However, the market interest is the deciding factor in pricing- the intrinsic value of (for example) a laminated body Harmony archtop will be the deciding factor in the asking price to the public.

The *Blue Book of Acoustic Guitars* continues to seek out additional input on Harmony models, specifications, dates of production, and any serialization information. Any information on Harmony guitars can be submitted directly to the *Blue Book of Acoustic Guitars*.

Most Harmony guitars have been played and are in the average condition range. Most of these guitars are valued under $300. However, there are some models that may bring more money, especially if they are in excellent condition. We have listed some of the most popular models from the 1960s and 1970s. Keep in mind that Harmony produced hundreds of different models over the years. It is unrealistic to provide every single model ever produced because we simply do not have adequate information to make model descriptions. The information listed is from catalogs. Nine out of ten Harmony guitars are going to be in average condition and valued under $300.

Harmony models also carried the series designation on the headstock (i.e. Broadway, Monterey, Patrician, Sovergin, etc.) in addition to the Harmony trademark.

For further information on solid body electric and archtop electric guitars refer to the *Blue Book of Electric Guitars*.

ACOUSTIC: ARCHED TOP SERIES

The 1200 Series Arched Guitars were originally designated the Auditorium models; in 1969, they were renamed to Archtone models.

H 945 MASTER (AUDITORIUM SIZE) – celluloid bound hollow body, arched hardwood top/back, two f-holes, 20-fret ebonized maple fingerboard with white block inlay, three-per-side tuners, chrome hardware, adjustable ebonized bridge/raised tailpiece, raised shell pickguard with stenciled Master logo, available in Sunburst lacquer finish, length 40 in., body width 15.75 in., disc. circa 1972.

	N/A	$250 - 300	$150 - 200	$59.95

H 950 MONTEREY LEADER – celluloid bound hollow body, arched hardwood top/back, two f-holes, 20-fret ebonized maple fingerboard with white dot inlay, three-per-side tuners, chrome hardware, adjustable ebonized bridge/raised tailpiece, raised black pickguard with stenciled M logo, available in Figured Red Sunburst finish, length 40 in., body width 15.75 in., disc. circa 1972.

	N/A	$300 - 375	$200 - 250	$69.95

* *HTG 950 Monterey Tenor (TG 950)* – similar to the H 950, except in Tenor (four-string) configuration, available in Figured Red Sunburst finish, disc. circa 1972.

	N/A	$400 - 475	$225 - 275	$69.50

MSR/NOTES	100%	EXCELLENT	AVERAGE	LAST MSR

H 954 BROADWAY (AUDITORIUM SIZE) – bound hollowbody, arched select hardwood top/hardwood back/sides, two f-holes, 20-fret ebonized maple fingerboard with white dot inlay, three-per-side tuners, chrome hardware, adjustable bridge/raised tailpiece, raised celluloid pickguard with stenciled design, available in Mahogany Sunburst finish, length 40.75 in., body width 15.75 in., disc. circa 1972.

	N/A	$300 - 350	$175 - 225	$74.50

* *H954 Broadway Tenor* – similar to the H954 Broadway, except in tenor configuration with four-strings, mfg. 1960s-early 1970s.

	N/A	$375 - 450	$250 - 300	

H 956 W MONTCLAIR (GRAND AUDITORIUM PROFESSIONAL) – bound hollowbody, arched hardwood top/hardwood back/sides, two f-holes, 20-fret bound fingerboard with white dot inlay, three-per-side tuners, chrome hardware, adjustable bridge/raised tailpiece, raised white pickguard, available in Black finish, length 40.5 in., body width 16.5 in., disc. circa 1965.

	N/A	$275 - 325	$150 - 200	$65

* *H 956 Montclair* – similar to the H 956 W, except features white block fingerboard inlay, available in Black finish, length 40.5 in., body width 16.5 in., mfg. 1966-67.

	N/A	$275 - 325	$150 - 200	$75

H 1213 ARCHTONE (H 1214 BLONDE, H 1215 BROWN MAHOGANY) – hollowbody with white striped edges, arched birch top/birch back/sides, 16 in. body width, two f-holes, 14/19-fret hard maple fingerboard with white dot inlay, three-per-side tuners, chrome hardware, adjustable bridge/raised tailpiece, raised celluloid pickguard with stenciled Harmony logo, serial numbers inside body, available in Shaded Brown Sunburst (Model H 1213), Blonde Ivory Enamel with Grained effect (Model H 1214), Gloss Brown Mahogany with Grained effect (Model H 1215), or Two-Tone Blue finish, disc. circa 1972.

	N/A	$200 - 250	$100 - 150	$49.95

The hard maple fingerboard was "grained to resemble rosewood," according to the 1961 Harmony catalog. The Two-Tone paint finish was known as the Catalina model.

* *HTG 1215 Archtone Tenor* – similar to the H 1215 Archtone, except in Tenor (four-string) configuration, available in Gloss Brown Mahogany finish with Grained effect, disc. circa 1972.

	N/A	$425 - 500	$250 - 300	$49.95

H 1300 CREMONA – bound body, arched spruce top/maple back, two segmented f-holes, 20-fret rosewood fingerboard with pearlette block inlay, pearlette inlaid logo on rosewood peghead veneer, three-per-side tuners, chrome hardware, adjustable bridge/raised tailpiece, raised black pickguard, available in Shaded Brown finish, length 41 in., body width 16.5 in., disc. circa 1972.

	N/A	$425 - 500	$250 - 300	

* *H 1310 Cutaway* – similar to the H 1300 Cremona, except has a single cutaway, disc. circa 1972.

	N/A	$475 - 550	$275 - 325	$149.50

* *H 1311 Cutaway Blonde* – similar to the H 1310, available in Blonde finish, disc. circa 1965.

	N/A	$525 - 600	$300 - 350	$105

H 1325 MONTEREY (GRAND AUDITORIUM) – celluloid bound hollowbody, arched spruce top/hardwood back/sides, two f-holes, 20-fret bound fingerboard with white dot inlay, three-per-side tuners, chrome hardware, adjustable bridge/raised tailpiece, raised shell pickguard with stenciled M logo, available in Shaded Brown finish, length 41 in., body width 16.25 in., disc. circa 1972.

	N/A	$375 - 450	$225 - 275	$79.50

H 1407 PATRICIAN (AUDITORIUM SIZE) – shell celluloid bound hollowbody, arched spruce top/mahogany back/sides, mahogany neck, two f-holes, 20-fret rosewood fingerboard with white dot inlay, three-per-side tuners, chrome hardware, adjustable bridge/raised tailpiece, raised shell celluloid pickguard with stencilled P logo, available in Natural finish, length 40.75 in., body width 15.75 in., disc. circa 1972.

	N/A	$325 - 400	$175 - 225	$79.50

H 1456 MONTEREY (GRAND AUDITORIUM PROFESSIONAL) – celluloid bound hollowbody, arched select spruce top/ maple back, two segmented f-holes, 20-fret celluloid bound rosewood fingerboard with pearlette block inlay, three-per-side tuners, chrome hardware, adjustable bridge/raised tailpiece, raised brown pickguard with stenciled M logo, available in Sunburst finish, length 40.5 in., body width 16.5 in., disc. circa 1968.

	N/A	$400 - 475	$250 - 300	$85

* *H 1457 Monterey Blonde* – similar to the H 1456, except features raised white pickguard with stenciled M logo, available in Blonde finish, disc. circa 1965.

	N/A	$475 - 550	$275 - 325	$78

ACOUSTIC: CLASSICAL SERIES

Classic Series models are classical guitars with Harmony's "Fan-Rib" construction (a Spanish-style fan-braced top).

H 171 CLASSIC/FOLK – nylon string, 25.25 in. scale, spruce top, round soundhole, hardwood back/sides/neck, 12/19-fret ebonized maple fingerboard, slotted headstock, pinless bridge, three-per-side Waverly tuners, available in Pumpkin finish, length 36 in., body width 13.125 in., mfg. 1969-circa 1971.

	N/A	$150 - 200	$95 - 120	$49.95

The H 171 does not have the fan-rib bracing.

MSR/NOTES	100%	EXCELLENT	AVERAGE	LAST MSR

H 172 – nylon string, 25.25 in.scale, bound spruce top, fan ribbed, round soundhole with marquetry inlay, hardwood back/sides/neck, 12/19-fret ebonized maple fingerboard, rosewood pinless bridge, three-per-side Waverly tuners, available in Pumpkin finish, length 38.5 in., body width 14.625 in., mfg. 1971-circa 1973.

	N/A	$225 - 275	$100 - 150	$79.95

H 173 – nylon string, bound select spruce top, bound round soundhole, hardwood back/sides/neck, 12/19-fret ebonized maple fingerboard, ebonized maple tie bridge, three-per-side tuners, squared slotted headstock, available in Natural finish, Length 38.5 in., Body Width 14.625 in., disc. 1971.

	N/A	$225 - 275	$100 - 150	$79.50

H 174 – nylon string, bound seasoned spruce top, round soundhole with inlay, mahogany back/sides/neck, 12/19-fret fingerboard, rosewood tie bridge, three-per-side tuners, rounded slotted headstock, available in Natural finish, length 38.5 in., body width 14.625 in., disc. circa 1968.

	N/A	$250 - 300	$125 - 175	$95

H 175 – nylon string, 25.25 in.scale, black bound select spruce top, fan ribbed, round soundhole with wood marquetry inlay, mahogany neck, hard maple back/sides, 12/19-fret ebonized maple fingerboard, slotted headstock with wood marquetry inlay, pinless bridge with wood marquetry inlay, three-per-side Waverly tuners, available in Natural finish, length 38.5 in., body width 14.625 in., mfg. 1967-circa 1973.

	N/A	$275 - 325	$150 - 200	$135

H 177 – nylon string, 25.25 in.scale, bound seasoned spruce top, bound back, fan ribbed, round soundhole with marquetry inlay, mahogany back/sides/neck, 12/19-fret ebonized hard maple fingerboard, pinless rosewood bridge, slotted headstock, three-per-side Waverly tuners, available in Pumpkin finish, length 38.5 in., body width 14.625 in., mfg. 1969-circa 1973.

	N/A	$250 - 300	$125 - 175	$99.50

H 937 STUDENT GUITAR – nylon string, 24.25 in.scale, hardwood top, round soundhole, hardwood back/sides, 18-fret ebonized maple fingerboard, slotted headstock, pinless bridge, three-per-side Waverly tuners, available in Natural finish, length 36 in., body width 13.125 in., mfg. 1969-circa 1971.

	N/A	$125 - 175	$75 - 100	$41.50

ACOUSTIC: FLATTOP SERIES

H 150 STUDIO SPECIAL (3/4 SIZE) – dreadnought style, celluloid bound hardwood top, round soundhole, hardwood back/sides, 12/18-fret ebonized maple fingerboard, pinless bridge, white celluloid pickguard, three-per-side tuners, available in Natural finish, length 34.25 in., body width 13.125 in., disc. 1971.

	N/A	$125 - 175	$75 - 100	$41.50

H 151 BEST BEGINNERS (3/4 SIZE) – dreadnought style, bound hardwood top, celluloid edge binding, round soundhole, hardwood back/sides, 12/18-fret maple fingerboard, bolted-on pinless bridge, black celluloid batwing pickguard with vine design, solid blackface headstock, three-per-side Waverly tuners, available in Shaded Brown finish, length 34.25 in., body width 13.125 in., body thickness 3.25 in., disc. 1971.

	N/A	$125 - 175	$75 - 100	$41.50

Harmony designated the H 151 the "Best Beginners or 'Loaner' Guitar."

H 159 JUMBO – dreadnought style, 25.25 in.scale, hardwood top, white striped edge/black pin line, white celluloid bindings, round soundhole with simulated marquetry inlay, hardwood back/sides, 20-fret ebonized maple fingerboard with white dot inlay, ebonized maple pin bridge with white bridgepins, black pickguard with small logo design, three-per-side Waverly tuners, available in Natural Top/Dark Brown Rosewood body stain finish, length 40.75 in., body width 16 in., body thickness 4.25 in., mfg. circa 1969-1970.

	N/A	$150 - 200	$100 - 125	$59.95

H 162 GRAND CONCERT – dreadnought style, 24.25 in.scale, spruce top, round soundhole, mahogany back/sides, hardwood neck, 14/19-fret rosewood fingerboard with white dot inlay, adjustable truss rod, rosewood pin bridge, shell celluloid pickguard, three-per-side tuners, available in Natural lacquer finish, length 39 in., body width 15.125 in., disc. 1970.

	N/A	$300 - 350	$175 - 225	$64.50

* *H 162 3/4* – similar to the H 162, except in smaller (3/4) size configuration, Length 32 in., body width 11.25 in., disc. 1970.

	N/A	$250 - 300	$125 - 175	$64.50

* *H 165 Grand Concert Mahogany* – similar to the H 162, except features a mahogany top, Brazilian rosewood fingerboard, pinless bridge, disc. 1970.

	N/A	$250 - 300	$125 - 175	$64.50

It is unknown if Brazilian rosewood was actually used.

H 162/1 FOLK (GRAND CONCERT SIZE) – dreadnought style, 24.25 in.scale, spruce top, round soundhole, mahogany back/sides, 19-fret rosewood fingerboard, adjustable truss rod, pinned bridge, black pickguard, three-per-side Waverly tuners, available in Natural finish, length 39 in., body width 15.125 in., mfg. 1971-72.

	N/A	$300 - 350	$175 - 225	$64.50

* *H 162 3/4* – similar to the H 162/1, available in Natural finish, length 39 in., body width 15.125 in., mfg. 1971-72.

	N/A	$250 - 300	$125 - 175	$64.50

MSR/NOTES	100%	EXCELLENT	AVERAGE	LAST MSR

* *H 165/1 Folk Mahogany (Grand Concert Size)* – similar to the H 162/1, except features a mahogany top and pinless bridge, length 39 in., body width 15.125 in., mfg. 1971-72.

	N/A	$250 - 300	$125 - 175	$64.50

H 166 FOLK – dreadnought style, 24.25 in.scale, spruce top, white body binding, round soundhole, hardwood back/sides/neck, 19-fret bound rosewood fingerboard with white dot inlay, pin bridge, three-per-side Waverly tuners, black batwing-pickguard with small "H" logo, white truss rod cover, available in Pumpkin Top/Dark Rosewood stain gloss finish, length 40 in., body width 15.125 in., disc. 1971.

	N/A	$325 - 375	$200 - 250	$74.50

H 167 FOLK – dreadnought style, spruce top, round soundhole, hardwood back/sides, 19-fret bound rosewood fingerboard with white dot inlay, rosewood pin bridge with white bridgepins, six-on-a-side tuners, white truss rod cover, black "batwing" pickguard with small "H" logo, available in Natural finish, length 39 in., body width 15.125 in., mfg. circa 1969-1970.

	N/A	$325 - 375	$200 - 250	$74.50

* *H 168 Folk* – similar to the H 167 Folk, available in Pumpkin Top/Dark Rosewood Body Color finish, length 39 in., body width 15.125 in., mfg. circa 1969-1970.

	N/A	$325 - 375	$200 - 250	$74.50

H 180 GRAND CONCERT – dreadnought style, bound selected spruce top, round soundhole, mahogany back/sides, 19-fret bound rosewood fingerboard with white dot inlay, adjustable saddle rosewood pin bridge with white bridgepins, black pickguard with design pattern, sic-per-side Waverly tuners, available in Antique Mahogany (Antique limed grain over Dark Rosewood stain) finish, length 39 in., body width 15.125 in., mfg. circa 1969-1970.

	N/A	$350 - 425	$225 - 275	$104.50

H 181 GRAND CONCERT – similar to the H 180, except features inlaid rings rosette, available in Pumpkin Top/Dark Rosewood stain finish, Length 39 in., Body Width 15.125 in., mfg. circa 1969-1970.

	N/A	$350 - 425	$225 - 275	$104.50

H 182 GRAND CONCERT – dreadnought style, 24.25 in. scale, bound selected spruce top, round soundhole, mahogany back/sides/neck, 19-fret bound rosewood fingerboard with white dot inlay, bound blackface headstock with decorative design, adjustable pin bridge, teardrop-shaped black pickguard, three-per-side Waverly tuners with white buttons, white truss rod cover, available in Pumpkin Top/Dark Rosewood body finish, length 40 in., body width 15.125 in., disc. 1971.

	N/A	$350 - 425	$225 - 275	$104.50

ACOUSTIC: SOVEREIGN FLATTOP SERIES

H 164 "JET SET" SOVEREIGN FOLK GUITAR – dreadnought style, 24.25 in. scale, select spruce top, bound body, round soundhole with inlaid rings, hardwood back/sides/neck, 14/19-fret rosewood fingerboard with white dot inlay, rosewood pin bridge, white edged tear-drop shaped black pickguard with small "H" design, three-per-side Waverly tuners, available in Jet Black gloss finish, length 39 in., body width 15.125 in., mfg. circa 1971.

	N/A	$275 - 325	$150 - 200	$74.50

HTG 1201 TENOR GUITAR – tenor (four-string) configuration, spruce top/mahogany back/sides, round soundhole, mahogany neck, celluloid edge binding, 14/20-fret fingerboard with white dot inlay, ebonized pin bridge, shell celluloid pickguard, two-per-side tuners, available in Natural finish, length 34 in., body width 13.125 in., disc. circa 1972.

	N/A	$325 - 400	$200 - 250	$82.50

H 1203 GRAND CONCERT SPECIAL (WESTERN SPECIAL) – dreadnought style, 24.25 in.scale, select spruce top/mahogany back/sides, round soundhole, mahogany neck, 19-fret rosewood fingerboard with white dot inlay, adjustable truss rod, pinless rosewood bridge, three-per-side Waverly tuners, available in Natural finish, length 40 in., body width 15.125 in., disc. circa 1972.

	N/A	$550 - 650	$350 - 425	$98.50

The H 1203 model was originally designated the Western Special. In 1966, it was re-designated the Grand Concert Special.

H 1204 "JET SET" SOVEREIGN GRAND CONCERT – dreadnought style, 24.25 in.scale, rosewood top, round soundhole, hardwood back/sides, 19-fret rosewood fingerboard, adjustable truss rod, adjustable pin bridge, three-per-side Waverly tuners, available in Natural finish, length 40 in., body width 15.125 in., mfg. circa 1971.

	N/A	$350 - 425	$250 - 300	$99.50

H 1260 JUMBO – jumbo style, 25.25 in.scale, spruce top/mahogany back/sides, round soundhole, mahogany neck, shell edge binding, 19-fret rosewood fingerboard with white dot inlay, pinless bridge, teardrop-shaped pickguard, three-per-side Waverly tuners, available in Natural finish, length 40.25 in., body width 16 in., body thickness 4 5/16 in., disc. circa 1972.

	N/A	$525 - 600	$300 - 350	$119.50

H 1264 "JET SET" SOVEREIGN JUMBO – dreadnought style, 25.25 in.scale, bound spruce top, round soundhole with wood marquetry inlay, hardwood back/sides, 14/19-fret rosewood fingerboard with white block inlays, adjustable mustache-style bridge with white pins, two black batwing pickguards (one on each side of the soundhole), three-per-side Waverly tuners, available in Jet Black gloss finish, length 41.5 in., body width 16 in., body thickness 4 5/64 in., mfg. 1971-circa 1972.

	N/A	$600 - 700	$350 - 425	$159.50

MSR/NOTES	100%	EXCELLENT	AVERAGE	LAST MSR

H 1266 SOVEREIGN DELUXE JUMBO – dreadnought style, 25.25 in. scale, bound spruce top, round soundhole, mahogany back/sides, 14/19-fret rosewood fingerboard with white block inlays, adjustable mustache-style bridge with white pins, two black batwing pickguards (one on each side of the soundhole), three-per-side Waverly tuners, available in Sunburst finish, length 41.5 in., body width 16 in., body thickness 4 5/64 in., mfg. 1969-circa 1972.

	N/A	$550 - 650	$350 - 425	$169.50

* *H 1265 Sovereign Deluxe Jumbo* – similar to the H 1266, except features two-piece black "State of Alaska"-shaped pickguard, available in Sunburst finish, length 41.5 in., body width 16 in., body thickness 4.08 in., mfg. 1967-68.

	N/A	$600 - 700	$350 - 425	$159.50

The H 1265 was the forerunner to the H 1266 model (the H 1266 has a "more sensible" pickguard scheme).

ACOUSTIC: 12-STRING SERIES

Many of Harmony's catalogs make the following statement: "You do not tune a 12-string guitar as high as regular 6-string guitar pitch." As a result, the *Blue Book of Acoustic Guitars* offers a caution that current owners of these same models may want to tune down to avoid any structural problems (bridges separating or pulling off, top warpage, etc.).

H 1230 GRAND CONCERT 12-STRING – select spruce top, round soundhole, mahogany back/sides, bound body, mahogany neck, 12/18-fret tapered rosewood fingerboard with white dot position markers, solid headstock, dual-saddle rosewood bridge/chrome metal tailpiece, six-per-side Waverly tuners, black batwing pickguard with silk-screened design, available in Pumpkin Top/Dark stain body finish, length 40.75 in., body width 15.125 in., 25.25 in. scale, mfg. circa 1969-circa 1971.

	N/A	$225 - 275	$125 - 175	$129.50

H 1270 JUMBO 12-STRING – select spruce top, round soundhole, mahogany back/sides, bound body, 12/18-fret rosewood fingerboard with white dot position markers, slotted headstock, dual-saddle rosewood bridge/chrome metal tailpiece, six-per-side Waverly tuners, teardrop-shaped black pickguard, available in Natural finish, length 40.5 in., body width 16 in., body thickness 4.31 in., 25.25 in. scale, mfg. 1963-circa 1972.

	N/A	$475 - 550	$325 - 375	$164.50

ACOUSTIC ELECTRIC

H 55 SOVEREIGN DUAL PURPOSE – dreadnought style, spruce top, round soundhole, mahogany back/sides, 20-fret rosewood fingerboard with white dot inlay, pinless bridge, black teardrop-shaped pickguard, three-per-side Waverly tuners, pickup (concealed under fingerboard), volume/tone controls, available in Natural finish, length 40 in., body width 15.125 in., body thickness 3.75 in., 24.25 in. scale, disc. 1971 (as H 55), 1972-75 (as H 655).

	N/A	$325 - 375	$200 - 250	$137.50

This model is designated Harmony and Sovereign on the black peghead. In circa 1973, the H 55 model was redesignated the H 655.

HARPTONE

Guitars previously built in Newark, NJ between 1966 and the mid-1970s.

The Harptone company was a commercial successor to the Felsberg Company (circa 1893). During the 1930s, Harptone was more known for musical instrument accessories, although a few guitars were built between 1924 and 1942.

In the 1960s, The Harptone Manufacturing Corporation was located at 127 South 15th Street in Newark, NJ (07107) and Harptone's main guitar designer at the time was Stan Koontz (who also designed Standel and his own signature guitars). Harptone's guitar product line consisted of mainly flattop acoustics, electric archtops, and electric basses. Harptone instruments were built between 1966 and the mid-1970s when the company went out of business.

When Micro-Frets closed operations in Maryland in either 1974 or 1975, the company assets were purchased by David Sturgill. Sturgill, who served as the company president of Grammer Guitars for three years, let his sons John and Danny gain access to leftover Micro-Frets parts. In addition to those parts, they had also purchased the remains of the Harptone guitar company. The two assembled a number of solid body guitars which were then sold under the Diamond-S trademark. Unfortunately, that business venture did not catch on, and dissolved sometime in 1976. For further information regarding Harptone electric models, please refer to the *Blue Book of Electric Guitars*. Company history courtesy Tom Wheeler, *American Guitars*.

ACOUSTIC

Harptone also offered most of their guitars in a Deluxe version that featured rosewood back and sides, elaborate inlays, and other high-end appointments. Retail prices on these guitars were typically about twice a standard version and while these guitars may command a premium over the standard guitars today, don't expect them to draw twice the values listed.

EAGLE (E-6) – dreadnought body style, Sitka spruce top, arched mahogany back, mahogany sides (curly maple back and sides were optional), round soundhole, ivoroid top and back body binding, 20-fret rosewood fingerboard, double truss rod, three-per-side Grover tuners, black pickguard, rosewood pin bridge, available in Natural or Sunburst finish, 15.625 in. body width, 4.875 in. body depth, 24.625 in. scale, mfg. 1966-mid-1970s.

	N/A	$850 - 1,000	$500 - 600	$225

MSR/NOTES	100%	EXCELLENT	AVERAGE	LAST MSR

* *Eagle 12-String (E-12)* – similar to the Eagle (E-6), except in 12-string configuration and six-per-side tuners, mfg. 1966-mid-1970s.

	N/A	$900 - 1,100	$550 - 650	$250

FOLK MASTER (F-6NC) – similar to the Sultan (S-6NC), except has a 17 in. body width, mfg. 1966-mid-1970s.

	N/A	$900 - 1,100	$550 - 650	$330

* *Folk Master 12-String (F-12NC)* – similar to the Folkmaster (F-6NC), except in 12-string configuration and six-per-side tuners, mfg. 1966-mid-1970s.

	N/A	$1,000 - 1,200	$600 - 700	

LARK (L-6) – jumbo body style, Sitka spruce top, mahogany back and sides, round soundhole, ivoroid top and back body binding, 20-fret rosewood fingerboard, double truss rod, three-per-side Grover tuners, black pickguard, rosewood pin bridge, available in Natural or Sunburst finish, 17 in. body width, 4.875 in. body depth, 24.625 in. scale, mfg. 1966-mid-1970s.

	N/A	$900 - 1,100	$550 - 650	$270

* *Lark 12-String (L-12)* – similar to the Lark (L-6), except in 12-string configuration and six-per-side tuners, mfg. 1966-mid-1970s.

	N/A	$1,000 - 1,200	$600 - 700	

PIONEER (P-6) – jumbo body style, Sitka spruce top, arched mahogany back, mahogany sides, round soundhole, ivoroid top and back body binding, 20-fret rosewood fingerboard, double truss rod, three-per-side Grover tuners, black pickguard, adj. rosewood bridge, available in Natural or Sunburst finish, 16 in. body width, 4.875 in. body depth, 24.625 in. scale, mfg. 1966-mid-1970s.

	N/A	$850 - 1,000	$500 - 600	$225

* *Pioneer 12-String (P-12)* – similar to the Pioneer (P-6), except in 12-string configuration and six-per-side tuners, mfg. 1966-mid-1970s.

	N/A	$900 - 1,100	$550 - 650	

RENZI 100 – nylon string, Alpine spruce top, round soundhole, mahogany back/sides, 19-fret rosewood fingerboard, hand-engraved headstock, rosewood bridge, three-per-side German tuners, available in Natural finish, 25.625 in. scale, mfg. 1966-mid-1970s.

	N/A	$750 - 900	$425 - 500	$250

* *Renzi 200* – similar to the Renzi 100, except features maple back/sides, available in Natural finish, mfg. 1966-mid-1970s.

	N/A	$850 - 1,000	$500 - 600	$350

SULTAN (S-6NC) – single cutaway jumbo body style, Sitka spruce top, curly maple back and sides, round soundhole, dark top and back body binding, curly maple neck, 20-fret rosewood fingerboard, double truss rod, three-per-side Grover tuners, black pickguard, adj. rosewood bridge, available in Natural finish, 16 in. body width, 4.875 in. body depth, 24.625 in. scale, mfg. 1966-mid-1970s.

	N/A	$1,000 - 1,200	$600 - 700	$269

* *Sultan 12-String (S-12NC)* – similar to the Sultan (S-6NC), except in 12-string configuration and six-per-side tuners, mfg. 1966-mid-1970s.

	N/A	$1,100 - 1,300	$625 - 750	$295

ZODIAC (Z-6) – dreadnought body style, Sitka spruce top, rosewood back and sides, round soundhole, ivoroid top and back body binding, 20-fret bound rosewood fingerboard with pearl block inlays, double truss rod, MOP headstock inlays, three-per-side Grover tuners, black pickguard, rosewood pin bridge, available in Natural finish, 15.625 in. body width, 4.875 in. body depth, 24.625 in. scale, mfg. 1966-mid-1970s.

	N/A	$1,150 - 1,400	$650 - 800	$350

* *Zodiac 12-String (Z-12)* – similar to the Zodiac (Z-6), except in 12-string configuration and six-per-side tuners, mfg. 1966-mid-1970s.

	N/A	$1,250 - 1,500	$700 - 850	$375

HARRIS, RICHARD

Instruments previously built in Indianapolis, IN.

Luthier Richard Harris built custom acoustic Tele-style guitars. The models are all acoustic, but are shaped with the single cutaway body like a Tele. Information is unknown about pricing on these guitars and how many were built.

HASCAL HAILE

Instruments previously produced in Tompkinsville, KY between the late 1960s and 1986.

Luthier Hascal Haile built mostly classical guitars in his Kentucky home basement shop between the late 1960s and the time of his death in 1986. Haile was a furniture maker for much of his life, but he had always been a musician and decided to build instruments full-time beginning in the late 1960s. Haile built guitars for many artists including Waylon Jennings, Roy Clark, and Bobby Goldsboro, but his most famous customer was Chet Atkins. Haile actually built Atkins' prototype for the now-famous Gibson solidbody classical guitar. Haile was still building instruments when he passed away in 1986. Haile's classicals are quite valuable today often bringing over $5,000.

HAUSER GUITARS

Instruments currently built in Reisbach, Germany. Instruments built in Munich, Germany since the early 1900s.

CONTACT INFORMATION
HAUSER GUITARS
Clemens-Seidl-Str. 5-7
Reisbach, D-94419 Germany
Phone No.: ++49-8734-932506
Fax No.: ++49-8734-7665
www.hauserguitars.com
hauser.hermann@t-online.de

Hauser Guitars was founded by Josef Hauser (1854-1939) in the early 1900s when he rented a barn close to Munich and built his first zithers, guitars, lutes, mandolins, and violins. Hauser received a letter of recommendation from Duke Maximilian that stated "Königlicher Bayerischer Hoflieferant." Hauser's son Hermann Hauser I (1882-1952), learned the art of lutherie from his father and eventually took over the workshop. Hauser I began to focus more on guitars and Andres Segovia took notice of Hauser's instruments. Segovia started playing Hauser guitars in 1924 and continued playing them through 1979. Hermann Hauser II built several guitars for Segovia and Hermann Hauser III built one for him in 1979. Hauser I also used the Torres guitar as a prototype and was a further development for the modern classical guitar. Hauser I's son Hermann Hauser II (1911-1988) started working at the Hauser guitar shop in 1926, and all instruments from 1953 through 1983 were signed by him.

Hermann Hauser III (1958-) began building instruments in August, 1974 in the same shop as his father, Hauser II, although they built instruments separately. Hauser III's daughter Kathrin Hauser (1982-, born 100 years after Hermann Hauser I) passed her examination as an instrument builder in 2007 and they currently build Hauser guitars together in their Reisbach workshop. Hauser estimates that they produce about seventeen guitars per year.

Hauser instruments are known for being well-built with high quality woods, but more importantly the sound of the guitars is unbelievable. All used guitars should be evaluated on a case-by-case basis. For more information and a full history of Hauser Guitars, visit Hauser's website or contact them directly.

HAUVER GUITARS

Acoustic guitars currently produced in Sharpsburg, MD.

CONTACT INFORMATION
HAUVER GUITARS
3663 Harpers Ferry Road
Sharpsburg, MD 21782
Phone No.: 304-876-8181
www.hauverguitars.com
michael@hauverguitars.com

Luthier Michael Hauver builds acoustic guitars with the famous ladder bracing of the 1920s and 1930s. Hauver started repairing and restoring guitars several years ago and after attending Charles Fox's American School of Lutherie in 1999, he decided to start building his own guitars. He was inspired by the Stella guitars of the 1920s that feature ladder or lateral bracing on the top so his guitars feature this type of construction. Several models are available including the Jumbo and Barbeque Bob, and prices start at $2,400. For more information, visit Hauver's website or contact him directly.

HAWK

Instruments previously built in West Germany during the early 1960s. Also see Framus and Klira.

The Hawk trademark was a brand name used by a UK importer. Instruments imported into England were built by either Framus or Klira in Germany, and are identical to their respective builder's models. Source: Tony Bacon and Paul Day, *The Guru's Guitar Guide*.

HAYNES

Instruments previously manufactured in Boston, MA from 1865 to the early 1900s.

The Oliver Ditson Company, Inc. was formed in 1835 by music publisher Oliver Ditson (1811-1888). Ditson was a primary force in music merchandising, distribution, and retail sales on the East Coast. He also helped establish two musical instrument manufacturers: The John Church Company of Cincinnati, OH and Lyon & Healy (Washburn) in Chicago, IL.

In 1865, Ditson established a manufacturing branch of his company under the supervision of John Haynes, called the John C. Haynes Company. This branch built guitars for a number of trademarks, such as Bay State, Tilton, and Haynes Excelsior. Source: Tom Wheeler, *American Guitars*.

HAYNIE, LES

Instruments previously built in Eureka Springs, AR during the 1990s.

Les Haynie built custom guitars in his shop in Eureka Springs in the 1990s, and he is currently part-owner of Blue Moon Music in Fayetteville, AR.

HEIDEN STRINGED INSTRUMENTS

Instruments currently built in Creston, British Columbia, Canada since circa 2010. Previously produced in Chilliwac, British Columbia, Canada between 1974 and circa 2010. Distributed by Heiden Stringed Instruments of Creston, British Columbia, Canada.

CONTACT INFORMATION
HEIDEN STRINGED INSTRUMENTS
1155 Simmons Rd.
Creston, British Columbia V0B 1G7
Canada
Phone No.: 250-428-7450
www.heideninstruments.ca
info@heideninstruments.ca

Luthier Michael Heiden is currently handcrafting some very high quality acoustic guitar models and mandolins. Current guitar models include the **Jumbo**, **Junior**, **OM**, and **Dreadnought**. Heiden has produced other style models in the past and several types of woods are available for construction. For further information regarding model specifications, custom orders, and pricing, visit Heiden's website or contact him directly.

MSR/NOTES	100%	EXCELLENT	AVERAGE	LAST MSR

HENDERSON, WAYNE

Instruments currently built in Mouth of Wilson, VA.

Guitars currently built in Virgina. Wayne is also the host of the Wayne C. Henderson Music Festival and Guitar Competition that is held every third week in June. For more information contact Henderson directly.

CONTACT INFORMATION
HENDERSON, WAYNE
388 Tucker Road
Mouth of Wilson, VA 24363
www.waynehenderson.org
gerald@waynehenderson.org

HENDERSON, WILLIAM

Instruments previously built in the U.S. Distributed by Kirkpatrick Guitar Studios of Baltimore, MD.

Luthier William Henderson built high quality classical guitars for a short while in the 1990s and possibly into the 2000s.

HENRY GUITAR COMPANY

Instruments previously built in Atlanta, GA, 1997-2000, and in Asheville, NC 1994-97.

Luthier Jeff Henry studied under Nick Apollonio of Rockport, Maine before forming his own company. Henry offered five different handcrafted acoustic guitar models, as well as custom options. Henry guitars carry a stylized H on the headstock, as well as a full label inside the soundhole.

Jeff Henry offered five different acoustic guitar models: the **ML**, his smallest instrument with lively response, **LJ**, a Little Jumbo that combines the balance of a ML with the power of a full body, the **Jumbo**, a full sized acoustic, the **D**, a dreadnought sized acoustic; and the **SD**, which is similar to the **D** except had sloped shoulders.

Henry guitars were offered with other custom options such as installed pickups, and additional wood choices on the soundboard, or back and sides. These are some of the option prices for the guitars:

All five models were available in either the Standard or Deluxe package, and the prices included a hardshell case. The **Standard** package (last retail was $1,500) had a Sitka spruce or western red cedar soundboard, mahogany back and sides, a rosewood fingerboard and bridge, pearl dots inlay, ivoroid or tortoiseshell body binding, a herringbone rosette, a tortoiseshell pickguard, and Grover tuners. More upscale was the Deluxe package (last retail was $2,100). The **Deluxe** offers the same Sitka spruce or western red cedar soundboard, a mahogany back with a hardwood backstrip, mahogany sides, a bound ebony fingerboard, ebony bridge, abalone diamond inlays, abalone bridge inlay, rosewood or maple mitered body binding, an abalone rosette, a tortoiseshell pickguard, and Schaller tuners.

- Add $25 for an exotic wood pickguard. Add $75 for an exotic wood rosette. Add $200 for a cutaway body configuration. Add $200 for a 12-string configuration.

HERITAGE

Instruments currently built in Kalamazoo, MI since 1984. The company was incorporated on April 1, 1985. The Lasar Music Corporation, located in Brentwood, TN is the exclusive sales and marketing company for Heritage Guitars, Inc. Heritage stopped producing acoustic guitars in 2000.

CONTACT INFORMATION
HERITAGE
Manufacturing
225 Parsons Street
Kalamazoo, MI 49007
Phone No.: 269-385-5721
Fax No.: 269-385-3519
www.heritageguitar.com

Sales/Marketing: Lasar Music Corporation
500 Wilson Pike Circle Suite 204
Brentwood, TN 37027
Phone No.: 615-377-4913
Fax No.: 615-377-4986

The Heritage Guitar Company opened in 1985 setting up shop in the original Gibson factory that had moved from Kalamazoo, MI to Nashville, TN a year earlier. While Heritage currently focuses on hollowbody, semi-hollowbody, and solidbody electric guitars, they have also experminented with acoustic instruments. Most Heritage acoustic instruments were produced during the 1990s. Heritage also built mandolins and a banjo model on a "Limited Availability" basis.

The Kalamazoo Standard Banjo (retail list $2,700) has a bound curly maple resonator/neck, maple rim, bound ebony fingerboard with mother-of-pearl inlays, and chrome hardware, available in Honey Stain finish. For more company history refer to the *Blue Book of Electric Guitars*. For more information, visit Heritage's website or contact them directly.

ACOUSTIC

Heritage's acoustic instruments are available on a limited basis.

H-450 – dreadnought style, solid spruce top, round soundhole, white bound body, wooden inlay rosette, black pickguard, mahogany back/sides, maple neck, 14/20-fret rosewood fingerboard with mother-of-pearl dot inlay, rosewood bridge with white pins, three-per-side chrome tuners, available in Antique Sunburst or Natural finish on top; Walnut finish on back/sides/neck, 25.5 in. scale, disc. 1990.

	N/A	$450 - 525	$250 - 300	$850

H-480 – narrow waist rounded single cutaway style, solid spruce top, oval soundhole, white bound body/rosette, carved mahogany back, solid mahogany sides, mahogany neck, 14/21-fret rosewood fingerboard with mother-of-pearl dot inlay, rosewood bridge with white pins, three-per-side chrome tuners, available in Antique Sunburst or Natural finish on top, Walnut finish on back/sides/neck, 25.5 in. scale, disc. 1990.

	N/A	$450 - 525	$250 - 300	$850

HFT-445 (H-445) – dreadnought style, solid spruce top, round soundhole, white bound body and wooden inlay rosette, black pickguard, mahogany back/sides, maple neck, 14/20-fret rosewood fingerboard with pearl dot inlay, rosewood bridge with white pins, three-per-side chrome tuners, available in Antique Sunburst or Natural finish, mfg. 1987-2000.

	N/A	$675 - 800	$425 - 500	$1,400

- Add 10% for Natural finish.

MSR/NOTES	100%	EXCELLENT	AVERAGE	LAST MSR

HFT-475 – single sharp cutaway jumbo style, solid spruce top, round soundhole, five-stripe bound body and rosette, black pickguard, mahogany back/sides/neck, 20-fret bound rosewood fingerboard with pearl block inlay, rosewood bridge with white pins, bound peghead, three-per-side chrome tuners, available in Antique Sunburst or Natural finish, disc. 1999.

	N/A	$1,050 - 1,200	$650 - 750	$2,050

- **Add 10% for Natural finish.**
- **Add 25% for a DeArmond pickup.**

HFT-485 – jumbo style, solid spruce top, round soundhole, three-stripe bound body/rosette, rosewood pickguard, rosewood back/sides, mahogany neck, 14/21-fret bound rosewood fingerboard with pearl block inlay, rosewood bridge with white pins, bound peghead, three-per-side chrome tuners, available in Antique Sunburst or Natural finish, disc. 1999.

	N/A	$1,100 - 1,250	$725 - 850	$2,300

- **Add 10% for Natural finish.**

HERMANOS, CONDE

See Conde Hermanos in the C Section.

HERNANDEZ Y AGUADO

Instruments previously built in Madrid, Spain between the 1940s and the 1970s.

Luthiers Manuel Hernandez and Victoriano Aguado combined guitar making skills to build world class classical guitars. According to a newspaper article in the late 1960s or early 1970s, Hernandez had built almost 400 guitars. All guitars were built by hand in his small Madrid shop. Source: Tony Bacon, *The Ultimate Guitar Book*.

HIGHLAND GUITAR COMPANY

Instruments currently produced overseas. Distributed by AudioOne Corporation in Bolton, Ontario, Canada.

The Highland Guitar Company offers a variety of acoustic, acoustic-electric, electric, and bass guitars. These guitars were designed in North America and they are produced overseas. More than 30 different models are currently available and prices range from the mid-$200s up to the mid-$800s. For more information, visit Highland's website or contact their distributor directly.

> **CONTACT INFORMATION**
> **HIGHLAND GUITAR COMPANY**
> *Headquarters*
> www.highlandguitarcompany.com
> sales@highlandguitarcompany.com

> **CONTACT INFORMATION**
> **HIGHLAND GUITAR COMPANY**
> *North American Distributor: AudioOne Corporation*
> 60 Healey Rd. Unit #11
> Bolton, Ontario L7E 5A6 Canada
> Phone No.: 888-276-9372
> www.AudioOne.ca

HILL, DENNIS

Instruments currently built in Panama City, Florida. Distributed by Dennis Hill and Leitz Music, Inc. of Panama City, Florida.

> **CONTACT INFORMATION**
> **HILL, DENNIS**
> *Distributed by Leitz Music, Inc.*
> 508 Harrison Avenue
> Panama City, FL 32401
> Phone No.: 850-769-0111
> Phone No.: Studio: 850-784-1527
> Fax No.: 850-785-1779

Dennis Hill has a tradition of music in his life that reaches back to his father, who was a dance band musician. After a five-year career in the U.S. Navy (Hill received his Honorable Discharge in 1969), Hill became the student to classical guitar teacher Ernesto Dijk. As Hill's interest in guitars grew, he met Augustino LoPrinzi in 1987. Hill finally became a sales representative for LoPrinzi's guitars, and studied guitarmaking at LoPrinzi's shop. Hill spent days in the shop as LoPrinzi's shadow observing construction techniques and finishing methods. For the sake of efficiency, Hill and LoPrinzi agreed to reserve in depth question and answer sessions for breakfast/lunch meetings (Those encounters now highly regarded and much appreciated by Hill). All building was done after hours in Hill's art studio (Hill lived as a portrait artist and art teacher at that time). In 1992, Hill moved to Panama City and established his own shop. For further information contact Leitz Music, Inc. directly (early source: Hal Hammer).

Hill currently builds classical, flamenco, and archtop guitars as well as violins employing traditional Spanish and Italian construction styles. Woods include European or Englemann spruce or cedar tops, cedar, mahogany or maple necks, cypress, maple, mahogany or rosewood back and sides, ebony fingerboards, and rosewood or maple binding and trim. Classical models start at $8,000, flamenco models start at $6,000, and the archtop guitar starts at $9,500. The Vioin starts at $7,500.

HILL GUITAR COMPANY

Instruments currently built in Ben Lomond, CA since 2007. New World Guitars are imported from China. Previously produced in Felton, CA where Master Series and signature guitars were built between 2001 and 2007. Distributed by the Hill Guitar Company of Ben Lomond, CA. See Also New World Guitar Company.

> **CONTACT INFORMATION**
> **HILL GUITAR COMPANY**
> 8011 Highway 9
> Ben Lomond, CA 95005
> Phone No.: 831-336-9317
> Phone No.: 800-262-8858
> Fax No.: 831-336-9428
> www.hillguitar.com
> khill@hillguitar.com

Kenny Hill has been a professional classical guitarist for twenty-five years, and has performed extensively throughout the United States and Mexico. His ability and experience as a performer result in a special gift for making an instrument that is very playable and appealing to the player, as well as the audience.

He has been awarded two major grants from the California Arts Council. One of those grants was to establish a guitar building program inside Soledad State Prison. He continues to act as a guitar building consultant, there and in other prisons. He is also the founder and director of the New World Guitar Co., listed elsewhere in this directory. Mr. Hill is a regular contributor to several national magazines, including *Guitar, Soundboard,* and *American Lutherie,* (Biography courtesy Kenny Hill, September 1997).

Kenny Hill has built quality concert classical and flamenco guitars since 1975. He builds about 25 guitars per year in his shop in the mountains outside of Santa Cruz, California. The Performance and Signature Series guitars are built in Hill's shop located in Felton, CA.

ACOUSTIC: MASTER SERIES (US)

All Master Series guitars are produced in the U.S. Hill guitars are characterized as having a clear and warm sound, with excellent balance and separation. The neck and action are among the most playable available anywhere.

The **Signature Series** are Hill's finest models and can be entirely customized. The base price for the Signature is $6,500 and every guitar is individually hand-built.

The **11-String** (disc., last MSR was $9,995) is an 11-string classical-style guitar, that was introduced in 2006 and features an offset neck with seven strings over the fingerboard and four harp-style strings, Englemann spruce top, Indian rosewood back and sides, Spanish cedar neck, ebony fingerboard, open-style headstock, and Natural finish.

The **Barcelona Model** (disc., last MSR was $2,995) was produced through 2002 and was built in the style of Ignacio Fleta guitars, with a western red cedar top, Indian rosewood back/sides, 650 mm scale, ebony fingerboard, and a slotted headstock with three-per-side Fustero tuners. In 2003, this model was renamed the Fleta.

The **Classic Crossover** (last MSR was $4,495) was introduced in 2003 and features Indian rosewood back and sides, an Englemann spruce top, mahogany neck, Sloane machines, 1.875 in. neck, radiused fingerboard, and French polish finish. Variations include Brazilian rosewood, Qulited and flamed maple, lacquer finish, and Schatten pickups.

The **Fleta** (disc., last MSR was $4,195) was introduced in 2004 and is based from an Ignacio Fleta design, with Indian rosewood back and sides, a Western red cedar top, Spanish cedar neck, Gotoh machines, French polish finish, dove tail neck joint construction, and the interior is finished. Variations include a spruce top and Brazilian rosewood.

The **Hauser '37** (MSR $5,495) was introduced in 2004 and is a replica of the Metropolitan Museum's Segovia Hauser as documented by Richard Brune. Specs, materials and building processes are consistent with the original and features include Indian rosewood back and sides, a European spruce top, mahogany neck, Schaller, Ruber machines, and French polish finish.

The **La Triana Flamenco** (disc., last MSR was $1,750) was disc. in 2003 and it was built in the style of Santos Hernandez guitars with a Canadian spruce top, cypress back/sides, 650 mm scale, ebony fingerboard, and a slotted headstock with three-per-side Schaller (or peg) tuners.

The **London Model** (19th Century, last MSR $1,995) was produced through 2002 and it was built in the style of Louis Panormo guitars. It featured a Canadian spruce top, rosewood back/sides, 635 mm scale, ebony fingerboard, and slotted headstock with three-per-side Sloane tuners. This style of guitar is nicknamed "Cacahaute" (Peanut) because of its size and distinctive shape. In 2003, this model was renamed the Panormo.

The **Madrid Model** (disc., last MSR was $1,995) was disc. in 2003 and was built in the style of Jose Ramirez guitars, with a western red cedar top, Indian rosewood back/sides, 650 mm scale, ebony fingerboard, and a slotted headstock with three-per-side Gotoh tuners.

The **Palo Escrito** was a student model disc. in 2003 that featured a cedar top, palo escrito back and sides, ebony or granadillo fingerboard, Spanish cedar neck, classical style headstock, and Natural finish.

The **Panormo** (MSR $7,495) comes from a Luis Panormo design with Indian rosewood back and sides, an Englemann spruce top, Spanish cedar neck, Rubner machines, and French polish finish. Variations include maple, Brazilian rosewood, and seven- and eight-string configurations.

The **Prodigy** (disc., last MSR was $1,295) was a smaller parlor-sized student guitar that featured an Englemann spruce top, palo escrito back/sides, 650 mm scale, granadillo fingerboard, and a slotted headstock with three-per-side Gotoh tuners. Variations included Indian rosewood back and sides and a French polish finish.

The **Rodriguez** (disc., last MSR was $3,995) comes from a Miguel Rodriguez design with Indian or Brazilian rosewood back and sides, a Western red cedar top, Spanish cedar neck, Gotoh machines, and French polish finish. Variations include a spruce top.

The **Ruck** (disc., last MSR was $3,995) was designed and licensed by Robert Ruck. This guitar features the prominent Ruck sound ports, Indian or Brazilian rosewood back and sides, a Western red cedar top, Spanish cedar neck, Gotoh machines, and French polish finish. Variations include Qulited maple and Koa.

The **Torres 1856** (MSR $5,495) is a replica of Antonio de Torres' 1856 guitar. It features Indian rosewood back and sides, an Englemann spruce top, Spanish cedar neck, Rubner machines, and French polish finish. Variations include quilted and flamed maple, 650mm, 640mm, 630mm scale lengths, a 1.875 in. neck, and a single cutaway.

The **Torres FE 18** (MSR $5,495) is a replica of Antonio de Torres' FE 18 guitar. It features Indian rosewood, maple, or cypress back and sides, an Englemann spruce top, Spanish cedar neck, Gotoh machines, and French polish finish. Scale lengths are available in 640mm or 630mm scale lengths.

- Add $165 for a Schatten pickup.
- Add $450 for a single cutaway.
- Add $400 for a Spanish cedar top.
- Add $350 for maple back and sides.
- Add $2,000 (minimum charge) for Brazilian rosewood back and sides.

ACOUSTIC: PERFORMANCE SERIES

The Performance Series was introduced in 2010, and is a modern classical guitar for active musicians with models available in Stage, Parlor, and Crossover variations. Standard features of the Performance Series feature a solid or double top, lattice or fan bracing, sound ports, all French polish finish, and truss rod. Variations include cutaway, stage, optional string lengths and body sizes, tonewoods. Base price for the Performance Series is $5,500.

ACOUSTIC: SIGNATURE SERIES

The Signature Series is Hill's top-of-the-line guitar with models available in classical, flamenco, and parlor variations. Standard features of the Signature Series feature a double top, lattice or fan bracing, elevated fingerboard, sound ports, all French polish finish, and truss rod. Variations include Stand up model with wedge shaped body and strap buttons, arm rest, optional string lengths, cutaway, parlor size body, tonewoods. Base price for the Signature Series is $7,500.

CUSTOM & NEW WORLD SERIES

The New World Guitars are imported from China. Kenny goes to the different sites where these guitars are built and oversees the design, technique, and quality control. All guitars have a final setup in California at the Hill Guitar Company. A few of the models in the New World Guitar line were previously produced in the U.S., but all production shifted to China in 2003.

HIRADE

See Takamine (Hirade Series) in the T section.

HOFFMAN GUITARS

Instruments currently built in Minneapolis, MN since 1971.

Luthier Charlie Hoffman and Hoffman Guitars offers both high quality handcrafted guitars and high quality instrument repair services. Hoffman Guitars is the factory authorized warranty service for Martin, Gibson, Guild, Fender, Taylor, and other manufacturers.

To date, Charlie Hoffman has built over 610 handcrafted guitars, which are played by such guitarists as Tim Sparks, Dakota Dave Hull, Ann Reed, and many others. For more information, visit Hoffman's website or contact him directly.

Given the nature of hand building custom guitars, the following information is more of a guide than an exact specification for the commissioned guitar.

The **Concert Model** was designed with a fingerpicking player in mind, and also works well with vocal accompaniment. This Concert Model is available with a cutaway body, or a 12-fret (body joins the neck at the 12th fret) configuration: body length 18.75 in., depth 4.5 in., lower bout 15.25 in.

Hoffman's **Dreadnought** model is built along the lines of the classic Martin Dreadnought shape, with a somewhat "stiff" top (to accentuate the treble) and a slightly deeper body. This model is also available with a cutaway body, or a 12-fret (body joins the neck at the 12th fret) configuration: body length 20 in., depth 5 in., lower bout 15.6 in.

The **0** guitar is patterned after the numerous parlor guitars of the 1900s to the 1930s, particularly the C.F. Martin 0 size guitar and is standard with a 12-fret neck. It is optional in a slotted or solid headstock: body length 19 in., depth 4.125 in., lower bout 13.75 in.

The **Jumbo** is a 16 in. body (similar to the Gibson J-185), which has a thinner 4 in. body for a more balanced tone and 24.75 scale.

The **00** is based on the Martin 00 style and is available in 12- or 14-fret configurations.

Hoffman's primary body shapes are all priced the same by the nature of the body woods that determine the construction. African mahogany and East Indian body woods retail at $4,600, highly flamed maple starts at $4,800, koa starts at $5,000+, and cocobolo start at $5,000. Brazilian rosewood and other body woods are also available - please inquire for more information. A harp guitar with a mahogany body starts at $9,500.

- **Wood binding and cases are now standard items as of 2004. Carved heels, electronics, and inlays can all be added (call for estimate).**
- Add $150 for a pyramid bridge.
- Add $150 for an abalone soundhole rosette.
- Add $150 for an abalone back center strip.
- Add $150 for a wedge body.
- Add $200 for a soundport.
- Add $250 for contrasting wood/abalone soundhole rosette.

- Add $300-500 for an Adirondack spruce top.
- Add $450 for a slotted headstock with Waverly gears.
- Add $350 for 12-string configuration.
- Add $400 for German (or Italian) spruce top.
- Add $450 for abalone top edging.
- Add $450 for a cutaway body.
- Add $700 for arm bevel.

CONTACT INFORMATION
HOFFMAN GUITARS
2219 East Franklin Ave.
Minneapolis, MN 55404
Phone No.: 612-338-1079
www.hoffmanguitars.com
hoffmanguitars@qwestoffice.net

HÖFNER

Instruments currently produced from 1887-1949 in Schonbach, and 1950-present in Bubenreuth, and Hagenau, Germany. Acoustic instruments are currently produced overseas. Distributed in the U.S. by CMI (Classic Musical Instruments) of Pleasant Prairie, WI.

The Höfner instrument making company was originally founded by Karl Höfner in 1887. Originally located in Schonbach (in the area now called Czech Republic), Höfner produced fine stringed instruments such as violins, cellos, and double basses. Karl's two sons, Josef and Walter, joined the company in 1919 and 1921 (respectively), and expanded Höfner's market to North American and the Far East. Production of guitars began in 1925, in the area that was to become East Germany during the "Cold War" era. Following World War II, the Höfner family moved to West Germany and established a new factory in Bubenreuth in 1948. By 1950, new production facilities in Bubenreuth and

CONTACT INFORMATION
HÖFNER
Distributed by CMI (Classic Musical Instruments)
PO Box 580713
Pleasant Prairie, WI 58158
Phone No.: 262-942-4811
Phone No.: 888-942-2642
Fax No.: 262-671-4280
www.hofner.com
rob.olsen@hofner.com

Hanenau were staffed by over 300 Hofner employees.

The first Höfner electric archtop debuted in the 1950s. While various guitar models were available in Germany since 1949 (and earlier, if you take in the over 100 years of company history), Höfners were not officially exported to England until Selmer of London took over distributorship in 1958. Furthermore, Selmer's British models were specified for the U.K. only - and differ from those available in the German market.

The concept of a violin-shaped bass was developed by Walter Höfner (Karl's son) in 1956. Walter's idea to electrically amplify a bass was new for the company, but the hollow body model itself was based on family design traditions. The 500/1 model made its debut at the Frankfurt Music Fair the same year. While most people may recognize that model as the Beatle Bass popularized by Paul McCartney, the Höfner company also produced a wide range of solid, semi-hollow, and archtop designs that were good quality instruments.

Until 1997, Höfner products were distributed by EMMC (Entertainment Music Marketing Corporation, which focused on distributing the 500/1 Reissue violin electric bass. In 1998, distribution for Höfner products in the U.S. market was changed to Boosey & Hawkes Musical Instruments, Inc. of Libertyville, Illinois. Boosey & Hawkes wasted no time in introducing three jazz-style semi-hollow guitar models, which includes a New President (Model HP-55) model guitar. Distribution was handled by the Music Group until 2005. In 2006, CMI (Classic Musical Instruments) took over distribution, (Höfner history source: Gordon Giltrap and Neville Marten, *The Höfner Guitar - A History*; and Tony Bacon, *The Ultimate Guitar Book*, Current Höfner product information courtesy Rob Olsen, Höfner).

MODEL DATING INFORMATION

Höfner began installing adjustable truss-rods in their guitar necks beginning in 1960. Any model prior to that year will not have a truss-rod cover.

Between the late 1950s and early 1970s, Höfner produced a number of semi-hollow or hollowbody electric guitars and basses that were in demand in England. English distribution was handled by **Selmer** of London, and specified models that were imported. In some cases, English models are certainly different from the domestic models offered in Germany.

ACOUSTIC ARCHTOP MODELS

The models listed below have not been priced individually. In general, Höfner prices range as follows. Guitars produced between 1951 and 1964 (pre-Beatles era) are generally priced between $250 and $450. Instruments produced from the mid-'60s through the mid-'80s will command slightly more, usually in the $650-$850 range. As with any maker, prices are based on configuration, originality factor and condition. Used clean big-body hollowbody guitars had been advertised nationally for $750 to $950, with the more ornate models carrying an asking price of $1,500 to $2,200.

MODEL 455 – archtop hollowbody, laminated maple top, back and sides, rosewood fingerboard with white celluloid inlays, three-per-side tuners, black and white celluloid binding on top, back, and f-holes, red-white celluloid inlays on headstock, white pickguard, lyre tailpiece, available in Cherry Red shaded finish, mfg. 1951-1968.

MODEL 455/S – similar to Model 455 except in a single cutaway design, mfg. 1961-1970.

* *Model 455/S/B* – similar to 455/S except in Blonde finish, mfg. 1963-67.

MODEL 4550 – similar to the Model 455 except features a larger archtop body, laminated maple top, back and sides, bound top, back, fingerboard, and f-holes, rosewood fingerboard, celluloid band position markers, white pickguard, three-per-side tuners, lyre tailpiece, Shaded Brown finish, also available in a single cutaway model (Model 4550/S), mfg. 1955-1966.

MODEL 456 – archtop hollowbody, flame maple back and sides, rosewood fingerboard, celluloid band position markers, bound top, back, fingerboard and f-holes, red, black, or white headstock, white pickguard, lyre tailpiece, three-per-side tuners, available in Dark Brown Sunburst finish or Blonde (Model 456/b), mfg. 1951-1961.

Subvariations include Model 456/S with single cutaway and 456/S/b, single cutaway with blonde finish, mfg. 1961-62

MODEL 457 – archtop hollowbody, nicely flamed maple back and sides, spruce top, bound top, back, fingerboard and f-holes, headstock decorated with gold-plated clef and staff, three-per-side tuners, celluloid band position markers, available in Brown Sunburst or Blonde finish, Model 457/b, mfg. 1954-1994.

Subvariations include Model 457/S, single cutaway version and Model 457/S/b, single cutaway design with Blonde finish, mfg. 1961-1970.

MODEL 458 – archtop hollowbody, laminated maple top and back, bound top, back, fingerboard and f-holes, celluloid band position markers, decorated headstock, three-per-side tuners, white pickguard, lyre tailpiece, available in highly polished Black finish, mfg. 1954-1966.

Also available in single cutaway design, Model 458/S, mfg. 1961-66.

MODEL 461/S – archtop hollowbody, single cutaway design, bound top, backand f-holes, additional small oval soundhole in the traditional location, harp tailpiece, three-per-side tuners, black and white celluloid decoration on the headstock with stylized arrow, split trapezoid position markers, unusually shaped f-holes, available in highly polished Black finish only, mfg. 1954-1964.

MODEL 462 – archtop hollowbody, flamed maple back and sides, selected spruce top, elliptical sound holes, two-piece tailpiece, bound top, back, fingerboard and f-holes, headstock has gold plated clef and staff, celluloid band position markers (one wideand two narrow), three-per-side tuners, white pickguard, available in Light Brown Varnish finish, mfg. 1951 only.

* *Model 462/S* – similar to Model 462 except in a single cutaway design, available in Light Brown Varnish finish, mfg. 1954-1970.

MODEL 463 – archtop hollowbody, sapeli mahogany backand sides, selected spruce top, bound mahogany fingerboard, split trapezoid position markers, wooden inlaysand celluloid bindings on top and back, wooden inlays around f-holes, harp tailpiece, three-per-side tuners,

MSR/NOTES	100%	EXCELLENT	AVERAGE	LAST MSR

white pickguard, available in Shaded Brown finish, mfg. 1952-1994.

Also available in single cutaway design, Model 463/S, mfg. 1961-1970.

MODEL 464/S – archtop hollowbody, single cutaway design, spruce top, flame maple back and sides, bound top, back, fingerboard and f-holes, eliptical sound holes, one additional rhombic soundhole located in the traditional position, celluloid band position markers (two wide and two narrow), lyre tailpiece, three-per-side tuners, white pickguard, available in Dark Wine Red finish, mfg. 1954-1968.

MODEL 465 – archtop hollowbody, well selected fine spruce top, rosewood back and sides, ebony fingerboard, woodand celluloid bindings on top, back, fingerboard and f-holes, MOP headstock inlays (bell-flowers) and position markers (one narrow rectangle flanked by two pentagons that resemble arrowheads), lucite pickguard, three-per-side tuners, lyre tailpiece, Shaded Brown finish, mfg. 1951-1962.

Also available in a single cutaway design, Model 465/S, mfg. 1961-1970.

MODEL 470/S – archtop hollowbody, single cutaway design, selected spruce top, best quality flame maple back and sides, wooden flower inlays on back, ebony fingerboard and headstock, bound top, back, fingerboard and f-holes, three-per-side tuners, MOP headstock inlays (lillies) and position markers (one narrow rectangle flanked by two pentagons that resemble arrowheads), rosewood pickguard, available in high polish Blonde finish, mfg. 1961-1994.

MODEL 471 – archtop hollowbody, enlarged body, selected spruce top, flame maple back and sides, florentine cutaway, celluloid bound top and back, ebony fingerboard with split trapezoid MOP inlays, elaborate headstock inlays, three-per-side tuners, harp tailpiece, Blonde finish, mfg. 1969-1977.

MODEL 477 – archtop hollowbody, spruce top, flame maple back and sides, florentine cutaway, three-dot position markers, three-per-side tuners, harp tailpiece, bound top, back, fingerboard and f-holes, black pickguard, available in high polish Yellow-red Shaded finish, mfg. 1969-1994.

ACOUSTIC: CURRENT FLATTOP MODELS

Höfner also offers a line of entry-level acoustic guitars. The Classic series feature laminated woods and standard appointments. Retail prices start at $459. The Master Luthier series feature all solid woods and they are built in Germany. Prices start at $2,399.

HAS01 – dreadnought style, spruce top, catalpa back and sides, rosewood fingerboard and bridge, black pickguard, chrome hardware, Natural finish, disc. 2005.

	N/A	$70 - 90	$40 - 60	$200

*** HAS01CE** – similar to the HAS01, except has a single cutaway and active electronics, disc. 2005.

	N/A	$100 - 150	$50 - 75	$300

HAS05 – dreadnought or grand concert style, solid spruce top, mahogany back and sides, full binding, rosewood fingerboard and bridge, shell pickguard, gold-plated hardware, Natural finish, disc. 2005.

	N/A	$95 - 125	$50 - 75	$270

HAS07 – dreadnought style, solid spruce top, rosewood back and sides, full binding, rosewood fingerboard and bridge, shell pickguard, gold-plated hardware, Natural finish, disc. 2005.

	N/A	$110 - 160	$70 - 90	$320

*** HAS07-12ET 12-String** – similar to the HAS07, except in 12-string configuration, six-per-side tuners, and electronics, disc. 2005.

	N/A	$140 - 190	$95 - 120	$400

HA-GC/HA-GA/HA-JC-03 – grand concert (GC), grand auditorium (GA), or Jumbo cutaway (JC) body style, solid spruce top, exotic lacewood back and sides, rosewood fingerboard, three-per-side Grover tuners, rosewood bridge, B-Band A3.2 pickup and electronics, Natural finish, mfg. 2006-present.

MSR $679	$475	$250 - 300	$120 - 150	

HA-GA/HA-JC-05 – grand auditorium (GA), or jumbo cutaway (JC) body style, solid spruce top, flame maple back and sides, mahogany wood binding, rosewood fingerboard, three-per-side Grover tuners, rosewood bridge, B-Band A3.2 pickup and electronics, Natural finish, mfg. 2006-present.

MSR $799	$560	$300 - 375	$175 - 225	

HA-GC/HA-GA/HA-JC-07 – grand concert (GC), grand auditorium (GA), or jumbo cutaway (JC) body style, solid spruce top, rosewood back and sides, mahogany wood binding, rosewood fingerboard, three-per-side Grover tuners, rosewood bridge, B-Band A3.2 pickup and electronics, Natural finish, mfg. 2006-present.

MSR $849	$600	$325 - 400	$200 - 250	

HOHNER

Instruments currently produced in Korea, although earlier models from the 1970s were built in Japan. Currently distributed in the U.S. by Hohner, Inc. in Glen Allen, VA.

The Hohner company was founded in 1857, and is currently the world's largest manufacturer and distributor of harmonicas. Hohner offers a wide range of solidly constructed musical instruments. The company has stayed contemporary with the current market by licensing designs and parts from Ned Steinberger, Claim Guitars (Germany), and Wilkinson hardware. Hohner started producing guitars in the 1970s. In 1986, HSS was established by Hohner to become a distributor to all of Hohner's products (guitars, drums,

CONTACT INFORMATION

HOHNER

Distributed by Hohner, Inc.
1000 Technology Park Drive
Glen Allen, VA 23059
Phone No.: 804-515-1900
Phone No.: 800-446-6010
Fax No.: 804-515-0347
www.hohnerusa.com
info@hohnerusa.com

MSR/NOTES	100%	EXCELLENT	AVERAGE	LAST MSR

accessories, etc.). HSS was also the distributor for Crafter Guitars in the late 1990s and early 2000s. For more information, visit Hohner's website, or contact them directly.

ACOUSTIC: CLASSICAL (HC) MODELS

All models in this series have a round soundhole, bound body, wooden inlay rosette, 14/19-fret ebonized fingerboard, nylon strings, tied bridge, three-per-side diecast tuners (unless otherwise noted).

HC02P – student model, solid spruce top, mahogany back and sides, classical style tuners, available in Natural finish, gig bag included, mfg. 2004-present.

| MSR $130 | $99 | $50 - 65 | $30 - 40 | |

HC03 STUDENT MODEL – 3/4 size body, available in Natural finish, current mfg.

| MSR $100 | $75 | $40 - 60 | $25 - 35 | |

HC06 – spruce top, mahogany back/sides, available in Natural finish, current mfg.

| MSR $140 | $90 | $45 - 60 | $25 - 35 | |

* *HC06E* – similar to the HC06 except has Shadow electronics, current mfg.

| MSR $170 | $125 | $80 - 100 | $50 - 65 | |

HC09 – full-size body, mahogany neck, back and sides, spruce top, rosewood fingerboard, 18 frets, multi-ply binding, classical gold tuners, available in Natural finish, current mfg.

| MSR $200 | $150 | $90 - 115 | $55 - 75 | |

* *HC09E* – similar to the HC09 except has Shadow electronics, current mfg.

| MSR $250 | $190 | $100 - 130 | $70 - 90 | |

* *HC09TE Thinline Electric* – similar to the HC09 except has a thinline-style single cutaway body and Shadow electronics, available in Black or Natural finish, mfg. 2007-present.

| MSR $270 | $200 | $110 - 140 | $75 - 95 | |

HC15 – mahogany back/sides/top/neck, available in Natural Mahogany finish, disc. 1999.

| | N/A | $90 - 115 | $55 - 75 | $189 |

HC20 – spruce top, Philippine mahogany back/sides, available in Natural finish, disc. 1999.

| | N/A | $130 - 160 | $90 - 110 | $269 |

HC30 – classical style, solid Sitka spruce top, ovangkol back and sides, gold tuners, available in Natural finish, current mfg.

| MSR $330 | $250 | $125 - 175 | $80 - 110 | |

HC35S – solid spruce top, rosewood back/sides, available in Natural finish, disc. 1999.

| | N/A | $175 - 225 | $120 - 140 | $399 |

HC620 – classical style, solid Sitka spruce top, mahogany back and sides, chrome hardware, available in Natural finish, mfg. 2004-06.

| | N/A | $100 - 130 | $60 - 80 | $229 |

HMC10 – spruce top, mahogany back/sides/neck, available in Natural finish, mfg. 1991-96.

| | N/A | $125 - 150 | $75 - 100 | $220 |

HMC30 – similar to HMC10, except has rosewood back/sides, mfg. 1991-96.

| | N/A | $150 - 200 | $100 - 125 | $300 |

ACOUSTIC: DESIGNER SERIES

DM-700S – dreadnought body, solid spruce top, curly maple back and sides, multi-ring rosette, body binding, 14/20-fret rosewood fingerboard with three point inlays, matching headstock with three-per-side Grover tuners, rosewood bridge, chrome hardware, Natural finish, mfg. 2005-present.

| MSR $750 | $525 | $325 - 400 | $175 - 225 | |

DMC-725S – single cutaway dreadnought body, solid Sitka spruce top, curly maple back and sides, multi-ring rosette, body binding, 14/20-fret rosewood fingerboard with three point inlays, matching headstock with three-per-side Grover tuners, rosewood bridge, Shadow P7 electronics, chrome hardware, Natural finish, mfg. 2005-present.

| MSR $800 | $575 | $350 - 425 | $200 - 250 | |

GM-750M – single cutaway grand auditorium body, figured maple top/back/sides, multi-ring rosette, body binding, 14/20-fret rosewood fingerboard with three point inlays, matching headstock with three-per-side Grover tuners, rosewood bridge, Shadow P7 electronics, chrome hardware, Natural finish, mfg. 2005-present.

| MSR $850 | $600 | $375 - 450 | $225 - 275 | |

MSR/NOTES	100%	EXCELLENT	AVERAGE	LAST MSR

GM-750S – single cutaway grand auditorium body, solid spruce top, figured maple back and sides, multi-ring rosette, body binding, 14/20-fret rosewood fingerboard with three point inlays, matching headstock with three-per-side Grover tuners, rosewood bridge, Shadow P7 electronics, chrome hardware, Natural finish, mfg. 2005-present.

MSR $900	$650	$400 - 475	$250 - 300	

JM-775 – single cutaway jumbo body, figured maple top/back/sides, multi-ring rosette, body binding, 14/20-fret rosewood fingerboard with cloud inlays, matching headstock with three-per-side Grover tuners, rosewood bridge, Shadow P7 electronics, chrome hardware, Natural finish, mfg. 2005-present.

MSR $900	$650	$400 - 475	$250 - 300	

ACOUSTIC: DREADNOUGHT 500 SERIES

DK500 – dreandought-style body, Java koa top, back, and sides, round soundhole with multi-ring abalone rosette, multi-ply top and back body binding, one-piece mahogany neck, 14/20-fret bound rosewood fingerboard with oval abalone pearl inlays, bound koa headstock overlay, three-per-side chrome Grover tuners, rosewood bridge, tortoise pickguard, available in Natural High Gloss finish, mfg. 2008-present.

MSR $330	$220	$140 - 170	$85 - 110	

* **DK500CE Cutaway Electric** – similar to the DK500, except has a single rounded cutaway and Fishman Classic 4T Blend electronics with a Sonocore pickups, available in Natural High Gloss finish, mfg. 2008-present.

MSR $530	$350	$200 - 250	$120 - 150	

DL500 – dreandought-style body, Lacewood top, back, and sides, round soundhole with multi-ring abalone rosette, multi-ply top and back body binding, one-piece mahogany neck, 14/20-fret bound rosewood fingerboard with oval abalone pearl inlays, bound Lacewood headstock overlay, three-per-side chrome Grover tuners, rosewood bridge, tortoise pickguard, available in Natural High Gloss finish, mfg. summer 2008-09.

	N/A	$140 - 170	$85 - 110	$330

* **DL500CE Cutaway Electric** – similar to the DL500, except has a single rounded cutaway and Fishman Classic 4T Blend electronics with a Sonocore pickups, available in Natural High Gloss finish, mfg. summer 2008-09.

	N/A	$200 - 250	$120 - 150	$530

DR500 – dreandought-style body, solid spruce top, rosewood back and sides, round soundhole with multi-ring abalone rosette, multi-ply top and back body binding, one-piece mahogany neck, 14/20-fret bound rosewood fingerboard with oval abalone pearl inlays, black bound headstock overlay, three-per-side chrome Grover tuners, rosewood bridge, tortoise pickguard, available in Natural High Gloss finish, mfg. 2008-09.

	N/A	$140 - 170	$85 - 110	$330

* **DR500CE Cutaway Electric** – similar to the DR500, except has a single rounded cutaway and Fishman Classic 4T Blend electronics with a Sonocore pickups, available in Natural High Gloss finish, mfg. 2008-present.

MSR $530	$350	$200 - 250	$120 - 150	

DR550 – dreandought-style body, solid cedar top, solid rosewood back and sides, round soundhole with multi-ring abalone rosette, maple top and back body binding, one-piece mahogany neck, 14/20-fret maple-bound rosewood fingerboard with custom inlays, black headstock overlay with pearl logo, three-per-side gold Grover tuners with ebony buttons, ebony bridge, tortoise pickguard, available in Matte Natural finish, mfg. 2008-present.

MSR $750	$500	$300 - 375	$175 - 225	

* **DR550CE Cutaway Electric** – similar to the DR550, except has a single rounded cutaway and Fishman Classic 4T Blend electronics with a Sonocore pickups, available in Natural finish, mfg. 2008-present.

MSR $900	$600	$375 - 450	$225 - 275	

ACOUSTIC: EA & EC MODELS

EA55CEQ – single cutaway body, spruce top, oval soundhole, bound body, striped rosette, ashwood back/sides, mahogany neck, 22-fret rosewood fingerboard with white dot inlay, rosewood bridge, two-per-side chrome tuners, piezo bridge pickup, volume/four-band EQ controls, available in Natural or Trans. Red finish, disc. 2001.

	N/A	$225 - 275	$125 - 175	$499

* **EA12 12-String** – similar to EA55CEQ, except features a 12-string configuration, and six-per-side tuners, available in Trans. Black finish, disc. 1999.

	N/A	$250 - 300	$150 - 200	$569

EA60CEQ – similar to EA55CEQ, except features maple top, available in Trans. Blue or Trans. Black finish, disc. 2001.

	N/A	$225 - 275	$125 - 175	$525

EA65CEQ – medium body size, single cutaway, solid Sitka spruce top, ovangkol back and sides, gold die cast tuners, Shadow electronics, available in Natural finish, current mfg.

MSR $550	$390	$225 - 275	$140 - 175	

MSR/NOTES	100%	EXCELLENT	AVERAGE	LAST MSR

EA95CEQ "EL BACHATERO" – medium-size body with cutaway, mahogany neck and sides, arched mahogany back, spruce top, rosewood fingerboard with mother-of-pearl diamond position markers, 24 frets, Shadow four-band EQ with anti-feedback switch, Shadow pickup, die-cast tuners, three-per-side tuners, available in Black, Natural, Trans. Red, or Trans. Blue finish, disc. 2003.

	N/A	$225 - 275	$125 - 175	$525

EA100CEQ – similar to EA55CEQ, except features a flamed maple top, available in Natural finish, disc. 1999.

	N/A	$275 - 325	$175 - 225	$599

EA120CEQ – similar to EA55CEQ, except features a solid cedar top, available in Natural finish, disc. 2001.

	N/A	$275 - 325	$175 - 225	$629

EA140CEQ – jumbo size body with cutaway, rosewood back and sides, solid cedar top, mahogany neck, rosewood fingerboard, 20 frets, Shadow four-band EQ with anti-feedback switch, Shadow pickup, die-cast tuners, three-per-side tuners, available in Natural finish, disc. 2001.

	N/A	$300 - 350	$200 - 250	$649

EC280CEQ (EC280EQ) – single cutaway classical style, spruce top, round soundhole, bound body, striped rosette, mahogany back/sides/neck, 19-fret rosewood fingerboard, rosewood bridge, slotted headstock, three-per-side gold tuners, piezo bridge pickup, volume/four-band EQ controls, available in Natural finish, disc. 2003.

	N/A	$225 - 275	$125 - 175	$499

ACOUSTIC: EBONY/800 SERIES

EBCG CLASSICAL EBONY – classical style, solid spruce top, striped ebony backand sides, 19-fret solid ebony fingerboard with dot inlay, Circle of Sound rosette soundhole, ebony bridge, gold hardware with ebonite keys, Natural finish, mfg. 2004-06.

	N/A	$225 - 275	$125 - 175	$549

* *EBCE Classical Ebony Cutaway Electric* – similar to the EBCG Classical Ebony, except has a single cutaway and Shadow P7 electronics, mfg. 2004-06.

	N/A	$275 - 325	$150 - 200	$649

EBDG DREADNOUGHT EBONY – dreadnought style, solid spruce top, striped ebony backand sides, solid ebony fingerboard with dot inlay, Circle of Sound rosette soundhole, ebony bridge, gold hardware, Natural finish, mfg. 2004-06.

	N/A	$275 - 325	$150 - 200	$649

* *EBDE Dreadnought Ebony Cutaway Electric* – similar to the EBDG Dreadnought Ebony, except has a single cutaway and Shadow P7 electronics, mfg. 2004-06.

	N/A	$325 - 375	$175 - 225	$749

CE800S – classical style, solid spruce top, striped ebony back and sides, maple body binding with abalone purfling, round soundhole with ring rosette, mahogany neck, 12/19-fret solid ebony fingerboard, slotted headstock, three-per-side open-style gold tuners with ebony buttons, ebony bridge, available in Natural finish, mfg. 2007-09.

	N/A	$275 - 325	$175 - 225	$650

* *CE800E* – similar to the CE800S, except has a single smooth cutaway and Shadow preamp/electronics, available in Natural finish, mfg. 2007-09.

	N/A	$325 - 375	$200 - 250	$750

DE800S – dreadnought style, solid spruce top, striped ebony back and sides, maple body binding with abalone purfling, round soundhole with ring rosette, mahogany neck, 14/20-fret solid ebony fingerboard with oval pearl inlays, vertical Hohner headstock inlay, three-per-side open-style gold Grover tuners, ebony bridge, available in Natural finish, mfg. 2007-09.

	N/A	$350 - 425	$200 - 250	$800

GE800E – single cutaway grand auditorium style, solid spruce top, striped ebony back and sides, maple body binding with abalone purfling, round soundhole with ring rosette, mahogany neck, 14/20-fret solid ebony fingerboard with oval pearl inlays, vertical Hohner headstock inlay, three-per-side open-style gold Grover tuners, ebony bridge, Shadow P7 electronics, available in Natural finish, mfg. 2007-09.

	N/A	$375 - 450	$225 - 275	$850

ACOUSTIC: ECLIPSE SERIES

ECA600 – single cutaway bowlback-style body, solid spruce top, cross-woven spherical alder bowl back, small oval soundhole with four oval soundholes in the upper bass bout, maple body binding with herringbone purfling, two-piece mahogany neck, 22-fret extended rosewood fingerboard with oval pearl inlays, moon headstock inlay, three-per-side gold Grover tuners, rosewood bridge with two moon inlays, ANP41 preamp/electronics, available in Aged Natural, Amber, Deep Purple Burst, or Tobacco Sunburst finish, mfg. 2007-09.

	N/A	$400 - 475	$250 - 300	$900

* *ECA612 12-String* – similar to the ECA600, except in 12-string configuration and six-per-side tuners, available in Aged Natural, Amber, Deep Purple Burst, or Tobacco Sunburst finish, mfg. 2007-09.

	N/A	$450 - 525	$275 - 325	$1,000

MSR/NOTES	100%	EXCELLENT	AVERAGE	LAST MSR

ECA800 – single cutaway bowlback-style body, solid spruce top, cross-woven spherical alder bowl back, small oval soundhole with four oval soundholes in the upper bass bout, maple body binding with abalone purfling, five-piece mahogany/maple neck, 22-fret extended ebony fingerboard with oval pearl inlays, moon headstock inlay, three-per-side gold Grover tuners with ebony buttons, ebony bridge with two moon inlays, ANP41 preamp/electronics, available in Amber, Deep Purple Burst, Emerald Burst, or Grey Ghost finish, mfg. 2007-09.

	N/A	$575 - 675	$350 - 425	$1,300

* ***ECA800EX*** – similar to the ECA800, except has a bubinga, flame maple, or quilted maple top, available in Deep Purple Burst (quilted maple), Honey Burst (quilted maple), Tiger Flame (flame maple), or Waterfall Bubinga (bubinga) finish, mfg. 2007-09.

	N/A	$625 - 725	$400 - 475	$1,400

ECT60 – travel-sized single cutaway bowlback-style body, spruce top, cross-woven spherical alder bowl back, small oval soundhole with four oval soundholes in the upper bass bout, ivoroid body binding, three-piece mahogany neck, 20-fret Sonokelin fingerboard with oval pearl inlays, three-per-side chrome tuners, Sonokelin bridge, available in Natural finish, mfg. 2007-09.

	N/A	$200 - 250	$120 - 150	$500

ACOUSTIC: MISC. MODELS

AMERICANA SERIES – dreadnought style, solid spruce top, walnut back and sides, mahogany neck, 20-fret rosewood fingerbaord with dot inlay, rosewood bridge, Natural finish with either American Eagle, Golden Gate Bridge, Statue of Liberty, or Mount Rushmore graphics, mfg. 2004 only.

	N/A	$275 - 325	$175 - 225	$589

HAG21 – single round cutaway classic style, solid maple body, spruce top, round soundhole, bound body, wooden inlay rosette, mahogany neck, 20-fret rosewood fingerboard with white dot inlay, rosewood bridge with white pins, three-per-side chrome tuners, piezo bridge pickup, volume/tone control, available in Natural finish, mfg. 1990-92.

	N/A	$250 - 300	$150 - 200	$500

* ***HAG22*** – similar to HAG21, except has dreadnought style body, available in Sunburst finish, disc. 1992.

	N/A	$250 - 300	$150 - 200	$500

HAG250P – half-size body, nylon strings, available in Natural finish, current mfg.

MSR $60	$45	$20 - 30	$10 - 15	

HAG294 – small body, spruce top, round soundhole, bound body, five-stripe rosette, black pickguard, mahogany back/sides/neck, 12/18-fret ebonized fingerboard with white dot inlay, ebonized bridge, three-per-side diecast tuners, available in Natural finish, mfg. 1991-96.

	N/A	$50 - 75	$35 - 45	$110

* ***HAG294C*** – similar to HAG294, except has classical body styling, disc. 1996.

	N/A	$50 - 75	$35 - 45	$110

HF70 – 3/4 size, spruce top, round soundhole, bound body, black pickguard, mahogany back/sides/neck, 14/20-fret rosewood fingerboard with white dot inlay, rosewood bridge with white pins, three-per-side covered tuners, available in Natural finish, disc. 2001.

	N/A	$110 - 140	$60 - 90	$269

HF75 – concert size steel string body, solid Sitka spruce top, ovangkol back and sides, pearloid position markers and bridge inlays, 18 frets, gold open style tuners, available in Natural finish, current mfg.

MSR $380	$270	$150 - 200	$95 - 120	

HFX – cutaway body, Engleman solid spruce top, mahogany back and sides, 20-fret rosewood fingerboard, abalone position markers and soundhole inlay, Shadow Megatech 8 digital preamp with 20 factory presets and 20 user presets, onboard effects include reverb, Delay, tremolo, Chorus, Flanger, Compressor, Noise gate, and Phase reverb switch, available in Natural finish, disc. 2001.

	N/A	$400 - 475	$250 - 300	$849

TWP600 – single cutaway dreadnought style, spruce top, triangular soundhole, bound body, three-stripe rosette, mahogany back/sides/neck, 20-fret rosewood fingerboard with white dot inlay, rosewood bridge with white pins, three-per-side chrome tuners, piezo bridge pickup, three-band EQ system, available in Black, Blue Sunburst, Natural, or Pumpkin Burst finish, mfg. 1992-96.

	N/A	$250 - 300	$150 - 200	$550

ACOUSTIC: TRADITIONAL (HW) MODELS

HW03 STUDENT MODEL – 3/4 size, spruce top, round soundhole, bound body, black pickguard, mahogany back/sides/neck, 14/20-fret fingerboard, nylon string tied bridge, three-per-side open tuners, available in Natural finish, current mfg.

MSR $150	$100	$60 - 75	$30 - 45	

HW90 – dreadnought style, solid Sitka spruce top, ovangkol back and sides, gold die-cast tuners, tortise shell pickguard, O series dot inlays, available in Natural finish, current mfg.

MSR $400	$280	$150 - 200	$95 - 120	

* ***HW90-12 12-String*** – similar to the HW90, except in 12-string configuration and six-per-side tuners, current mfg.

MSR $450	$320	$175 - 225	$110 - 140	

MSR/NOTES	100%	EXCELLENT	AVERAGE	LAST MSR

* ***HW90LH Left-Handed*** – similar to the HW90, except in left-handed configuration, current mfg.

MSR $420	$295	$160 - 210	$100 - 130	

HW200 – auditorium-size body, mahogany back, sides and neck, spruce top, hardwood fingerboard, 18 frets, open tuners, adjustable tension rod, available in Natural finish, current mfg.

MSR $120	$90	$45 - 60	$25 - 35	

HW220 – dreadnought-size body, mahogany back, sides and neck, spruce top, hardwood fingerboard, 20 frets, open tuners, adjustable tension rod, available in Natural finish, current mfg.

MSR $150	$105	$60 - 80	$35 - 45	

HW300 COUNTRYMAN (HW-300CM) – dreadnought style, mahogany top, round soundhole, single body binding, five-stripe rosette, black pickguard, mahogany back/sides/neck, 14/20-fret rosewood fingerboard with white dot inlay, rosewood bridge with white pins, three-per-side open tuners, available in Gloss Natural, Natural Satin, Sunburst, Trans. Black, Trans. Blue, Trans. Red, or Trans. Wine Red finish, mfg. 1994-present.

MSR $200	$140	$85 - 100	$50 - 70	

In 2005, the HW300 was new and improved with changes including Countryman - a new model name!

* ***HW312 12-String*** – similar to the HW300 Countryman, except in 12-string configuration and six-per-side tuners, available in Gloss Natural finish, mfg. 2007-present.

MSR $270	$190	$120 - 150	$80 - 100	

* ***HW300CE Cutaway Electric*** – similar to the HW300 Countryman, except has a single cutaway and Fishman Ion+ electronics, available in Sunburst, Trans. Black, or Trans. Wine Red finish, mfg. summer 2008-present.

MSR $340	$240	$140 - 175	$90 - 110	

* ***HW300E*** – similar to the HW300 except has Shadow electronic, available in Amber, Gloss, or Sunburst finish, disc. 2003.

	N/A	$110 - 140	$70 - 90	$249

HW350 JOURNEYMAN – dreadnought style, select spruce top, round soundhole, single body binding, five-stripe rosette, tortoise pickguard, mahogany back/sides/neck, 14/20-fret rosewood fingerboard with white dot inlay, rosewood bridge, three-per-side tuners, chrome hardware, available in Natural Satin finish, hardshell case included, mfg. 2005-present.

MSR $250	$175	$110 - 140	$60 - 80	

* ***HW350CE Cutaway Electric*** – similar to the HW350 Journeyman, except has a single cutaway and Fishman Ion+ electronics, available in Sunburst, Trans. Black, or Trans. Wine Red finish, mfg. summer 2008-present.

MSR $400	$280	$170 - 210	$110 - 140	

HW400 (HMW400) – dreadnought body, spruce top, round soundhole, bound body, five-stripe rosette, black pickguard, mahogany back/sides/neck, 14/20-fret rosewood fingerboard with white dot inlay, rosewood bridge with white pins, three-per-side covered tuners, available in Natural or Sunburst finish, mfg. 1990-99.

	N/A	$115 - 150	$70 - 90	$269

* Add $20 for left-handed configuration (Model HW400 LH).
* Add $50 for Black finish.

* ***HW12 12-String*** – similar to the HW400, except features ashwood back/sides, multiple body binding, bound neck/headstock, 12-string configuration, and six-per-side covered tuners, available in Natural finish, disc. 1999.

	N/A	$150 - 200	$110 - 130	$339

HW420 – dreadnought-size body, Siberian willow top, back and sides, mahogany neck, rosewood fibgerboard, 20 frets, die-cast tuners, multi-ply binding, available in Natural, Trans. Black, Cherry Sunburst, Tobacco, Emerald Green, or Amber finishes, disc. 2004.

	N/A	$120 - 150	$70 - 95	$269

HW440 – dreadnought-size body with cutaway, mahogany back, side, top and neck, rosewood fingerboard, 20 frets, passive pickup with volume and tone control, die-cast tuners, available in Natural, Tobacco, Trans. Black, or Trans. Wine Red finish, current mfg.

MSR $330	$250	$125 - 175	$80 - 110	

* Add 5% (MSR $350) for left-handed configuration (Model HW440LH).
* Add 25% for White finish (Model HW440G WT).

HW600 – dreadnought body, solid Sitka spruce top, mahogany back and sides, chrome hardware, available in Natural finish, mfg. 2004-present.

MSR $250	$175	$110 - 140	$60 - 80	

HW605 – jumbo body, solid Sitka spruce top, mahogany backand sides, chrome hardware, available in Natural finish, mfg. 2004-06.

	N/A	$100 - 130	$60 - 80	$239

HW640 – dreadnought-size body, maple back, sides and neck, solid Sitka spruce top, rosewood fingerboard, 20 frets, tortoiseshell-style binding, satin finish, die-cast tuners, available in Natural or Sunburst (2006-present) finish, current mfg.

MSR $350	$250	$135 - 175	$80 - 110	

* Add 5% (MSR $370) for left-handed configuration (Model HW640LH).

MSR/NOTES	100%	EXCELLENT	AVERAGE	LAST MSR

HW645 – concert body, solid Sitka spruce top, maple backand sides, chrome hardware, available in Natural finish, mfg. 2004-06.

	N/A	$125 - 175	$75 - 100	$299

HW655 – dreadnought-size body, rosewood back and sides, solid Sitka spruce top, maple neck, rosewood fingerboard, 20 frets, tortoiseshell-style binding, die-cast tuners, available in Natural Gloss finish, disc. 2003.

	N/A	$175 - 225	$100 - 130	$399

HW660CEQ – dreadnought-size body with cutaway, maple back, sides and neck, solid Sitka spruce top, rosewood fingerboard, 20 frets, Shadow four-band EQ with anti-feedback switch, Shadow pickup, die-cast tuners, available in Natural finish, disc. 2003.

	N/A	$275 - 325	$150 - 200	$599

HW700S – dreadnought body, solid spruce top, round soundhole, bound body, black pickguard, mahogany back/sides/neck, 14/20-fret rosewood fingerboard with white dot inlay, rosewood bridge with white pins, three-per-side deluxe tuners, available in Natural finish, disc. 1999.

	N/A	$175 - 225	$100 - 125	$389

HW720S – similar to HW700S, except features rosewood back and sides, available in Natural finish, disc. 1999.

	N/A	$200 - 250	$125 - 150	$469

HW750S – similar to HW700S, except features solid cedar top, ashwood back and sides, available in Natural finish, disc. 1999.

	N/A	$225 - 275	$125 - 150	$499

HMW600 – similar to HMW400, except has herringbone binding and rosette, enclosed chrome tuners, available in Black and Natural finishes, disc. 1996.

	N/A	$100 - 150	$70 - 95	$290

HMW1200 – similar to HMW400, except has 12-string configuration, six-per-side tuners, disc. 1996.

	N/A	$150 - 200	$100 - 125	$325

ACOUSTIC ELECTRIC BASS

EAB40 – single cutaway body, spruce top, oval soundhole, bound body, striped rosette, ashwood back/sides, mahogany neck, 22-fret rosewood fingerboard with white dot inlay, rosewood bridge, two-per-side chrome tuners, piezo bridge pickup, volume/four-band EQ controls, available in Natural finish, disc. 2001.

	N/A	$300 - 350	$200 - 250	$625

* **Add $70 for maple top with Sunburst finish (Model EAB50).**

EAB65 – medium sized body with single cutaway, solid Sitka spruce top, ovangkol back and sides, pearloid O series dot markers and bridge inlays, 20-fret fingerboard, Shadow electronics, gold die-cast tuners, available in Natural finish, mfg. 2002-present.

MSR $650	$450	$275 - 325	$175 - 225	

* **Add 2.5% (MSR $670) for left-handed configuration.**

TWP600B – single cutaway dreadnought style, spruce top, triangle soundhole, bound body, three-stripe rosette, mahogany back/sides/neck, 20-fret rosewood fingerboard with white dot inlay, strings through rosewood bridge, two-per-side chrome tuners, piezo electric bridge pickup, three-band EQ system, available in Black, Blue Sunburst, Natural, Pumpkin Burst, or Trans. Red finish, mfg. 1992-96.

	N/A	$325 - 375	$225 - 275	$650

HOLIDAY

Guitars previously produced by various manufacturers during the 1960s. See chapter on House Brands.

The Holiday trademark has been identified as a House Brand distributed by Montgomery Wards and Alden's department stores. Author/researcher Willie G. Moseley also reports seeing a catalog reprint showing Holiday instruments made by Harmony, Kay, and Danelectro. Acoustic instruments include flattops, archtops, and mandolins. Source: Willie G. Moseley, *Stellas & Stratocasters*.

HOLLENBECK GUITARS

Instruments previously built in Lincoln, IL between 1970 and 2008.

Luthier Bill Hollenbeck took a serious interest in guitars as a youth, and used to modify his own instruments in his attempt to improve them. Hollenbeck has a Master's Degree in Industrial and Technology and taught electronics to high school students for twenty-five years. During his teaching years, Hollenbeck met well-known midwestern luthier Bill Barker in 1970. Hollenbeck served as Barker's apprentice for twenty years as he learned the art of guitar construction. In 1990, Hollenbeck left his career in education to devote himself full-time to guitar building, restoration, and repair. Hollenbeck was featured at the Smithsonian Institute in 1996 during a week-long celebration of electric guitars. Then in 1998, he built one of the 18 in. Ebony-n-Blue guitars for the Scott Chinery collection, which was on display at the Smithsonian. Hollenbeck built mainly Jazz guitars and most of them feature a floating humbucker pickup. Refer to the *Blue Book of Electric Guitars* for complete model listings. Hollenbeck passed away on April 4, 2008.

HOLLISTER GUITARS

Instruments previously built in Dedham, MA during the 1990s and possibly into the 2000s.

Luthier Kent Hollister offered high quality, custom built guitars. The **Archtop** (last MSR $3,000) was available without a pickup (making it structurally acoustic), but most guitars were installed with pickups. Refer to the *Blue Book of Electric Guitars* for more electric guitar information.

HOLST, STEPHEN

Instruments currently built in Eugene, OR since 1984.

CONTACT INFORMATION
HOLST, STEPHEN
82722 Bear Creek Road
Creswell, OR 97426
Phone No.: 541-895-2362
www.pacinfo.com/~sholst/
sholst@pacinfo.com

Luthier Stephen Holst began building guitars in 1984, and through inspiration and refinement developed the models currently offered. Holst draws on his familiarity of Pacific Northwest tonewoods in developing tonal qualities in his handcrafted instruments. Holst specifically works with the customer commissioning the instrument, tailoring the requests to the specific guitar. Current models include archtop guitars, semi-hollow archtops, flat top guitars, and mandolin family instruments. For more information, visit Holst's website or contact him directly.

Holst's acoustic line includes a nylon string guitar available that starts at $4,000, a line of flattop acoustic guitars that start at $4,000, and archtops that start at $3,300.

HOMENICK

Guitars previously produced in the New York City area during the 1930s and 1940s.

The late Jim Fisch had a Homenick Style B guitar in his collection, but not much more is known about this guitar. The guitar is built in the style of D'Angelico and appears to be of high quality. Any further information on Homenick can be submitted directly to Blue Book Publications. Source: Scott Freilich, *20th Century Guitar*.

HONDO

Instruments previously produced in China and Taiwan between 1993 and 2005, in Korea between 1984 and 1987, and in Japan between 1974 and 1983. Distributed by Musicorp, Inc. in North Charleston, SC. The Hondo company was founded in 1969.

The Hondo guitar company was originally formed in 1969 when Jerry Freed and Tommy Moore of the International Music Corporation (IMC) of Fort Worth, TX, combined with the recently formed Samick company. IMC's intent was to introduce modern manufacturing techniques and American quality standards to the Korean guitar manufacturing industry.

The Hondo concept was to offer an organized product line and solid entry level market instruments at a fair market price. The original Korean products were classical and steel-string acoustic guitars, and in 1972, the first crudely-built Hondo electrics were introduced. However, two years later the product line took a big leap forward in quality under the new Hondo II logo. Hondo also began offering limited production guitars in Japan in 1974.

By 1975, Hondo had distributors in seventy countries worldwide, and they began producing other stringed instruments such as banjos and mandolins. In 1976, over 22,000 of the Bi-Centennial banjos were sold. The company also made improvements to the finish quality on their products, introduced scalloped bracing on acoustics, and began using a higher quality brand of tuning machines.

Hondo was one of the first overseas guitar builders to feature American-built DiMarzio pickups on the import instruments beginning in 1978. By this year, a number of Hondo II models featured designs based on classic American favorites. In 1979, over 790,000 Hondo instruments were sold worldwide. All guitar production returned to Korea in 1983, and at that point, the product line consisted of 485 different models!

In 1985, IMC acquired the major interest in the Charvel/Jackson company, and began dedicating more time and interest in the higher end guitar market. By 1987, Hondo had ceased operations and the trademark was put into hiatus. In 1989, Jerry Freed started the Jerry Freed International company, and acquired the rights to the Hondo trademark in 1991 (the "Est. 1969" tag line was added to the Hondo logo at this time). Freed began distribution of a new line of Hondo guitars. In 1993, the revamped company was relocated to Stuart, FL, and models were produced in China and Taiwan.

The Hondo Guitar Company was purchased by MBT International in 1995 and began offering Hondo guitars through their large Musicorp distribution catalog. MBT continued to offer a full line of entry-level acoustic guitars, electric guitars, and guitar amplifiers through the late 1990s and early 2000s. In 2005, MBT International/Musicorp was acquired by Kaman Music. The distribution side of the company is now solely referred to as Musicorp leaving the MBT trademark for their lighting and sound division. Shortly thereafter, Kaman/Musicorp phased out the Hondo brand in favor of their other trademarks including Arbor and J.B. Player. Currently, there are no Hondo-branded instruments available in the U.S. Sources: Tom Malm, MBT International, and Michael Wright, *Guitar Stories*, Volume One.

Hondo offered a wide range of dreadnought and classical style guitars. The models most recently produced included the **H18** (last MSR was $289), the **H18-B** (last MSR was $309), the **H18L** (last MSR was $299), the **H18-E** (last MSR was $349), the **H18-12** (last MSR was $309), the **H28** (last MSR was $329), the **H50** (last MSR was $219), the **H50P** (last MSR was $199), the **H60** (last MSR was $249), the **H60S** (last MSR was $239), the **H115** (last MSR was $169), the **H124AM** (last MSR was $299), the **H125** (last MSR was $285), the 12-string **H-180**, the **H305** Classical (last MSR was $139), the **H320** Classical (last MSR was $189), the

H330 Classical (last MSR was $299), the **H012N** Nylon, the **H012S** Steel, the **H015N** Nylon, and the **H015S** Steel, and the **H1000** acoustic/electric bass.

The Deluxe Series was first offered in 1982, and featured 11 classical and 22 steel string acoustic models.

The Professional Series was introduced in 1982, and had a number of classical and steel string models.

Standard Series guitars were also introduced in the early 1980s, was a beginner's line of acoustic guitars.

HOOTENANNY

Unknown location and date of manufacturer. See chapter on House Brands.

The Hootenanny trademark has been identified as a "sub-brand" from the budget line of Chris guitars by the Jackson-Guldan company. However, another source suggests that the trademark was marketed by the Monroe Catalog House. Source: Willie G. Moseley, *Stellas & Stratocasters*.

HOPF

Instruments previously built in Germany from the late 1950s through the mid-1980s.

The Hopf name was established back in 1669, and lasted through the mid-1980s. The company produced a wide range of good quality solid body, semi-hollow, and archtop guitars from the late 1950s on. While some of the designs do bear an American design influence, the liberal use of local woods (such as beech, sycamore, or European pine) and certain departures from conventional styling give them an individual identity. Hopf produced electric guitars through the 1970s, and has focused on classical guitars since. In 2006, Eastwood Guitars reissued the Hopf Saturn 63 with a few minor improvements. Source: Tony Bacon, *The Ultimate Guitar Book*.

HOPF, DIETER

Instruments currently built in Germany. Distributed by Luthier Music Corporation, of New York City, NY.

Dieter Hopf is concentrating on building classical instruments only. Hopf has roots in the music business all the way back to the early 1900s (see Hopf). Luthier Music Corporation distributes his instruments in the US and prices start at $1,600 and go over $6,000. For more information visit Hopf's website or contact Luthier Music Corporation directly.

CONTACT INFORMATION	CONTACT INFORMATION
HOPF, DIETER	**HOPF, DIETER**
Distribution: Luthier Music Corporation	*Factory*
341 West 44th Street	www.hopfguitars.com
New York, NY 10036	gitarren-hopf@t-online.de
Phone No.: 212-397-6038	
Fax No.: 212-397-6048	
www.luthiermusic.com	
guitar@luthiermusic.com	

HOUND DOG

Instruments previously produced in Gardena, CA during the late 1960s and in Japan during the mid-1970s.

The Dopyeras introduced the Hound Dog trademark under OMI (Original Musical Instruments) as a line of resonator guitars. In the mid-1970s, the Hound Dog trademark was used on a line of Japanese flattop acoustic guitars. Most guitars can be identified by the Hound Dog logo on the headstock. Source: Walter Carter and George Gruhn, *Gruhn's Guide to Vintage Guitars*.

HOWARD (U.S. MFG.)

Instruments previously built in New York, NY circa 1930s.

The construction technique and overall appearance indicate the possibility that Epaminondas "Epi" Stathopoulos' Epiphone company built instruments under the Howard trademark for a dealer or distributor. Models that have appeared in the vintage guitar market have the Howard brand name and fleur-de-lis inlaid on the headstock. The dealer or distributor involved in the Howard trademark has yet to be identified. Source: Paul Bechtoldt, *Vintage Guitar Magazine*, February 1996.

HOWELL & FORSYTH

Guitars currently produced in Campbell, CA.

Luthiers Joshua Howell and David Forsyth Schooler build high-quality acoustic guitars in their Campbell, CA shop. Guitars are inspired by Spanish design and they are available in steel and nylon string configurations. Guitar series include the H&F Studio Series and the J. Howell Signature Series. For more information, visit Howell & Forsyth's website or contact them directly.

CONTACT INFORMATION
HOWELL & FORSYTH
1091 Florence Way
Campbell, CA 95008
Phone No.: 408-379-5000
Fax No.: 408-378-6819
www.howellandforsyth.com
info@howellandforsyth.com

HOWE-ORME

Instruments previously built in the late 1800s and early 1900s. Distributed by the Elias Howe Company in Boston, MA.

Elias Howe, Jr. founded the Elias Howe Company in Boston, MA and after his death in 1895, his sons William H. Howe and Edward F. Howe produced Howe-Orme branded instruments during the late 1890s and early 1900s. George L. Orme was from Ottawa, Ontario, Canada and was a partner in the J.L. Orme & Son company that he also became involved in after his father's death. J.L. Orme & Son retailed musical instruments and also published sheet music in Canada. It is unknown how Howe and Orme became associated with one another, although Orme shared a patent with James S. Back for a "raised longitudinal belly ridge" for use on guitars and mandolins. This patent was later refined and a new one was issued to Edward Howe in 1897.

Howe-Orme offered a variety of acoustic guitars as well as other instruments, but they were most successful with mandolins. Their guitars also featured several innovative designs including the longitudinal belly ridge, an adjustable/detachable neck, and a zero fret. Several patents were awarded to Howe-Orme and guitars often feature many of these numbers on them. It is unknown how many guitars were actually produced, but it appears that most designs are similar to Martin's of the same era. Any further information on Howe-Orme can be submitted directly to Blue Book Publications.

HOYER

Instruments currently produced. Previously produced in West Germany from the late 1950s through the late 1980s. Distributed by Ritter USA LLC in New York, NY.

The Hoyer company was founded in 1874 and produced a wide range of good to high quality solid body, semi-hollow body, and archtop guitars, with some emphasis on the latter during the 1960s. During the early 1970s, there was some production of solidbodied guitars with an emphasis on classic American designs.

The Hoyer trademark was re-introduced in the 1990s with the cheerful "A Legend is Back!" motto. Martin Ritter's firm Ritter Brands Ltd. purchased the Hoyer guitar brand name and trademarks in 2009. At the 2010 Summer NAMM Show, Hoyer launched the new USA Hoyer Electric Guitar collection, but they are currently not offering any acoustic guitars. For more information, visit Hoyer's website or contact them directly.

Hoyer does not currently offer any acoustic guitars, but in the 1990s they offered several acoustic models (primarily dreadnought designs) and two resonator guitar models. Models fall under the **Select Top Series** (laminated bodies), **Solid Top Series** (solid wood top and laminated back and sides), and the **Electric Acoustic Series** (which has Fishman Matrix and Prefix systems).

The five Hoyer classical and flamenco acoustic models were built in Spain, and were offered in the **Solid Top Series** (laminated wood back and sides) or the **Solid Body Series** (Solid Body Series models still have a solid wood top).

Both the classical style **HC-150E** and **HC-200E** models have an L.R. Baggs RT preamp and ribbon pickup. Both have a solid cedar top, rosewood back and sides, and ebony fingerboards.

CONTACT INFORMATION
HOYER
U.S. Distributor: Ritter USA LLC
PO Box 4668 #14030
New York, NY 10163-4668
Phone No.: 347-404-5088
Fax No.: 347-710-8819
www.ritterusa.com
cbac@mac.com

Headquarters/Factory
www.hoyerguitars.com

HUIPE, BENITO

Instruments currently built in Paracho, Mexico.

Benito Huipe started making guitars in his hometown of Paracho (Michoacan) Mexico, but in his youth, he moved to Los Angeles, California, where he perfected his craft during his twenty-two years there. While he makes all types of guitars, he is particularly known for the high quality of his flamenco guitars. In 1994, he returned to live permanently in Paracho, and continues to produce guitars.

Huipe's basic flamenco guitar of cypress and either spruce or cedar sells from $2,500 to $3,500. Huipe's guitars were previously distributed by Casa Talamantes of Albuquerque, NM. It is unknown who is distributing Benito's guitars today.

HUMPHREY, THOMAS

See Thomas Humperey Guitars in the T section.

HUTTL

Instruments previously built in Germany between the 1950s and the 1970s.

The Huttl trademark may not be as well-known as other German guitar builders such as Framus, Hopf, or Klira. While their designs may be as original as the others, the quality of workmanship is still fairly rough in comparison. Research continues into the Huttl trademark.

HUVARD, ANTHONY J.

Instruments currently built in Sandston, VA, since 1964.

Luthier Anthony J. Huvard builds a limited number of high quality guitars. Huvard also offers a very comprehensive website called Luthiers Around The World, which offers information regarding independent luthiers and lutherie products. For more information, visit Huvards' website or contact him directly.

CONTACT INFORMATION
HUVARD, ANTHONY J.
PO Box 130
Sandston, VA 23150
www.cybozone.com/luthier/

HYUNDAI

Instruments previously built in Korea. Distributed in the U.S. through Hyundai Guitars of West Nyack, NY.

Hyndai offered a range of entry-level to medium quality guitars designed for beginning students that have designs based on popular American classics.

I SECTION
IBANEZ

Instruments currently produced in Japan since the early 1960s, Korea since the 1980s, and China since the early 2000s. Ibanez guitars are distributed in the U.S. by Ibanez USA (Hoshino) in Bensalem, PA. Other distribution offices include Quebec (for Canada), Sydney (for Australia), and Auckland (for New Zealand).

CONTACT INFORMATION
IBANEZ
Distributed by Hoshino, Inc.
1726 Winchester Road
Bensalem, PA 19020
Phone No.: 215-638-8670
Phone No.: 800-669-4226
Fax No.: 215-245-8583
www.ibanez.com

The Ibanez trademark originated from the Fuji plant in Matsumoto, Japan. In 1932, the Hoshino Gakki Ten, Inc. factory began producing instruments under the Ibanez trademark. The factory and offices were burned down during World War II, and were revived in 1950. By the mid-1960s, Hoshino was producing instruments under various trademarks such as Ibanez, Star, King's Stone, Jamboree, and Goldentone.

In the mid-1950s, Harry Rosenbloom opened the Medley Music store outside Philadelphia. As the Folk Music boom began in 1959, Rosenbloom decided to begin producing acoustic guitars and formed the Elger company (named after Rosenbloom's children, Ellen and Gerson). Elger acoustics were produced in Ardmore, Pennsylvania between 1959 and 1965.

In the 1960s, Rosenbloom traveled to Japan and found a number of companies that he contracted to produce the Elger acoustics. Later, he was contacted by Hoshino to form a closer business relationship. The first entry level solid body guitars featuring original designs first surfaced in the mid-1960s, some bearing the Elger trademark, and some bearing the Ibanez logo. One of the major keys to the perceived early Ibanez quality is due to Hoshino shipping the guitars to the Elger factory in Ardmore. The arriving guitars would be re-checked, and set up prior to shipping to the retailer. Many distributors at the time would just simply ship product to the retailer, and let surprises occur at the unboxing. By reviewing the guitars in a separate facility, Hoshino/Ibanez could catch any problems before the retailer - so the number of perceived flawed guitars was reduced at the retail/sales end. In England, Ibanez was imported by the Summerfield Brothers, and sometimes had either the CSL trademark or no trademark at all on the headstock. Other U.K. distributors used the Antoria brand name, and in Australia they were rebranded with a Jason logo.

In the early 1970s, the level of quality rose as well as the level of indebtedness to classic American designs. It has been argued that Ibanez' reproductions of Stratocasters and Les Pauls may be equal to or better than the quality of Norlin era Gibsons or CBS era Fenders. In any event, the unauthorized reproductions eventually led to Fender's objections to Tokai's imports (the infamous headstock sawing rumour), and Norlin/Gibson taking Hoshino/Ibanez/Elger into court for patent infringement.

When Ibanez began having success basically reproducing Gibson guitars and selling them at a lower price on the market, Norlin (Gibson's owner at the time) sent off a cease-and-desist warning. Norlin's lawyers decided that the best way to proceed was to defend the decorative (the headstock) versus the functional (body design), and on June 28th, 1977 the case of Gibson vs. Elger Co. opened in Philadelphia Federal District Court. In early 1978, a resolution was agreed upon: Ibanez would stop reproducing Gibsons if Norlin would stop suing Ibanez. The case was officially closed on February 2, 1978.

The infringement lawsuit ironically might have been the kick in the pants that propelled Ibanez and other Japanese builders to get back into original designs. Ibanez stopped building Gibson exact reproductions, and moved on to other designs. By the early 1980s, certain guitar styles began appealing to other areas of the guitar market (notably the Hard Rock/Heavy Metal genre), and Ibanez's use of famous endorsers probably fueled the appeal. Ibanez's continuing program of original designs and artist involvement continued to work in the mid- to late 1980s, and continues to support their position in the market today (source: Michael Wright, *Guitar Stories*, Volume One).

In 2011, Ibanez announced that they were bringing all U.S. distribution to the Hoshino Bensalem, PA location.

MODEL DATING IDENTIFICATION

In addition to the Ibanez company's model history, a serialization chart is provided in the back of the *Blue Book of Acoustic Guitars* to further aid the dating of older Ibanez guitars (not all potentiometer builders use the EIA source code, so overseas-built potentiometer codes on Japanese guitars may not help in the way of clues).

1959-1967: Elger Acoustics are built in Ardmore, Pennsylvania; and are distributed by Medley Music, Grossman Music (Cleveland), Targ and Dinner (Chicago), and the Roger Balmer Company on the west coast. Elger imported from Japan the Tama acoustics, Ibanez acoustics, and some Elger electrics.

1971-1977: The copy era begins for Ibanez (Faithful Reproductions) as solid body electrics based on Gibson, Fender, and Rickenbacker models (both bolt-ons and set-necks) arrive. These are followed by copies of Martin, Guild, Gibson, and Fender acoustics. Ibanez opens an office and warehouse outside of Philadelphia, Pennsylvania to maintain quality control on imported guitars in 1972.

1973: Ibanez's Artist series acoustics and electrics are debuted. In 1974, the Artist-style neck joint; later in 1976 an Artist Les Paul arrives. This sets the stage for the LP variant double cutaway Artist model in 1978.

1975: Ibanez began to use a meaningful numbering system as part of their warranty program. In general, the letter stands for the month (January = A, February = B, etc.) and the following two digits are the year.

1981-1987: In 1984, the Lonestar acoustics are introduced, and Ibanez responds to the MIDI challenge of Roland by unveiling the IMG-2010 MIDI guitar system.

1992-1993: The ATL acoustic/electric design is unveiled, and RT Series guitars debut in 1993. This overview, while brief, will hopefully identify years, trends, and series. For further information and deeper clarification, please refer to Michael Wright's *Guitar Stories*, Volume One.

MSR/NOTES	100%	EXCELLENT	AVERAGE	LAST MSR

ACOUSTIC: AMBIANCE SERIES

The Ambiance Series features large, resonant bodies with arched backs and Fishman Aero preamps.

AMBIANCE A100E – single smooth cutaway Ambiance-style body, spruce top, arched mahogany back, mahogany sides, round soundhole with laser-engraved wood rosette, single-ply body binding, mahogany neck, 14/21-fret rosewood fingerboard with small dot inlays, bound matching finish headstock overlay with logo, three-per-side chrome tuners, rosewood bridge, Fishman Sonicore pickup and Aero preamp with onboard tuner, available in Black or Natural finish, 25.2 in. scale, mfg. 2009-2010.

	$350	$225 - 275	$120 - 150	$500

* *Ambiance A100LE Left-Handed* – similar to the the Ambiance A100E, except in left-handed configuration, available in Natural finish, mfg. 2010 only.

	$380	$225 - 275	$120 - 150	$543

* *Ambiance A1012E 12-String* – similar to the the Ambiance A100E, except in 12-string configuration with six-per-side tuners, available in Black finish, mfg. 2010 only.

	$400	$250 - 300	$135 - 175	$571

AMBIANCE A200E – single smooth cutaway Ambiance-style body, flame maple top, arched flame maple back, flame maple sides, round soundhole with abalone rosette, multi-ply body binding, mahogany neck, 14/21-fret bound rosewood fingerboard with no inlays, bound matching finish headstock overlay with logo, three-per-side gold tuners, rosewood bridge, Fishman Sonicore pickup and Aero+ preamp with onboard tuner, available in Trans. Blue Sunburst (2010 only), Trans. Brown, Trans. Gray, Trans. Red, or Trans. Violet Sunburst (2010 only) finish, 25.2 in. scale, mfg. 2009-2010.

	$450	$275 - 325	$150 - 200	$643

AMBIANCE A300E – single smooth cutaway Ambiance-style body, quilted maple top, arched quilted maple back, quilted maple sides, round soundhole with abalone rosette, multi-ply body binding, mahogany neck, 14/21-fret bound rosewood fingerboard with no inlays, bound matching finish headstock overlay with logo, three-per-side gold tuners, rosewood bridge, Fishman Sonicore pickup and Aero Blend preamp with onboard tuner, available in Trans. Black Cherry Sunburst, Trans. Emerald Burst (2010 only), or Vintage Violin finish, 25.2 in. scale, mfg. 2009-2010.

	$500	$300 - 375	$175 - 225	$714

ACOUSTIC: ARTWOOD (AC, AG, AJ, & AW) SERIES

AC10 – grand concert body, solid Sitka spruce top, mahogany back/sides/neck, rosewood fingerboard with dot inlay, tortoise pickguard, Natural finish, mfg. 2000-04.

	N/A	$150 - 200	$95 - 120	$343

AC12 – grand concert body, solid Sitka spruce top, mahogany backand sides, three-ring rosette, body binding, maple neck, 14/20-fret rosewood fingerboard with dot inlay, three-per-side tuners, rosewood bridge, tortoise pickguard, chrome hardware, Natural High Gloss finish, mfg. 2005-06.

	N/A	$140 - 180	$80 - 110	$343

AC30 – grand concert style body, solid Englemann spruce top, mahogany back and sides, round soundhole with abalone rosette, maple body binding, mahogany neck, 14/20-fret maple bound rosewood fingerboard with brown dot inlays, three-per-side gold tuners with brown pearloid buttons, rosewood bridge, tortoise pickguard, available in Natural High Gloss finish, mfg. 2007-2010.

	$250	$140 - 180	$80 - 110	$357

AC35ECE – single smooth cutaway grand concert style body, solid cedar top, rosewood back and sides, round soundhole with abalone rosette, maple body binding, mahogany neck, 14/20-fret maple bound rosewood fingerboard with brown dot inlays, three-per-side gold tuners with brown pearloid buttons, rosewood bridge, tortoise pickguard, B-Band UST pickup, Ibanez SRTn preamp, available in Natural High Gloss finish, mfg. 2007-2010.

	$350	$225 - 275	$125 - 175	$500

AC50 LG – OM-style body, solid Sitka spruce top, round soundhole, tortoiseshell pickguard, maple back/sides/neck, 14/20-fret rosewood fingerboard with pearl dot inlay, rosewood bridge with white black dot pins, Ibanez/'AW' logo on peghead, chrome hardware, three-per-side die-cast tuners available in Natural Low Gloss finish, mfg. 1998-2002.

	N/A	$140 - 180	$90 - 115	$340

AC70 LG – similar to the AC50 LG, except features mahogany back/sides, available in Natural Low Gloss finish, mfg. 1997-99.

	N/A	$175 - 225	$100 - 125	$399

AC100 – OM-style body, solid Sitka spruce top, round soundhole, tortoiseshell pickguard, bound body, mahogany back/sides/neck, 14/20-fret rosewood fingerboard with pearl dot inlay, rosewood bridge with white black dot pins, Ibanez/'AW' logo on peghead, chrome hardware, three-per-side die-cast tuners, available in Natural Low Gloss finish, mfg. 1997 only.

	N/A	$225 - 275	$125 - 175	$449

AC110 – grand concert body, solid Sitka spruce top, walnut backand sides, abalone rosette, maple body binding, 14/20-fret rosewood fingerboard with abalone diamond inlay, three-per-side tuners, rosewood bridge, tortoiseshell pickguard, gold hardware, Natural High Gloss finish, mfg. 2005-06.

	N/A	$200 - 250	$120 - 150	$500

MSR/NOTES	100%	EXCELLENT	AVERAGE	LAST MSR

AC240 – grand concert style body, solid mahogany top, mahogany back and sides, round soundhole with abalone rosette, cream body binding, mahogany neck, 14/20-fret rosewood fingerboard with pearl dot inlays, black headstock overlay with Ibanez and "AW" inlays, three-per-side chrome tuners, rosewood bridge, tortoise pickguard, available in Natural Open Pore finish, 25 in. scale, mfg. 2011-present.

MSR $450	$300	$175 - 225	$105 - 130	

* *AC240E Electric* – similar to the AC240, except has a Fishman Sonicore pickup, and Ibanez SST Shape Shifter preamp with tuner, available in Open Pore Natural finish, mfg. 2012-present.

MSR $600	$400	$250 - 300	$135 - 175	

AC300 FIRST VERSION – similar to the AC100, except features rosewood back/sides, bound fingerboard/peghead, abalone dot fingerboard inlay, Grover tuners, available in Natural Gloss finish, mfg. 1996-98.

	N/A	$275 - 325	$175 - 225	$599

AC300 SECOND VERSION – grand concert style body, solid Englemann spruce top, mahogany back and sides, round soundhole with abalone rosette, multi-ply body binding, mahogany neck, 14/20-fret bound rosewood fingerboard with pearl dot inlays, bound black headstock overlay with Ibanez and "AW" inlays, three-per-side chrome tuners, rosewood bridge, black pickguard, available in Cherry Sunburst (2012-present), Light Violin Sunburst (2012-present), or Natural High Gloss finish, 25 in. scale, mfg. 2011-present.

MSR $450	$300	$175 - 225	$105 - 130	

* *AC300ECE Cutaway Electric* – similar to the AC300 Second Version, except has a single smooth cutaway, Fishman Sonicore pickup, and Ibanez SST Shape Shifter preamp with tuner, available in Natural High Gloss finish, mfg. 2011-present.

MSR $600	$400	$250 - 300	$135 - 175	

AC350ECE CUTAWAY ELECTRIC – single smooth cutaway grand concert style body, solid cedar top, mahogany back and sides, round soundhole with abalone rosette, multi-ply body binding, mahogany neck, 14/20-fret bound rosewood fingerboard with pearl dot inlays, bound rosewood headstock overlay with Ibanez and "AW" inlays, three-per-side chrome tuners, rosewood bridge, black pickguard, available in Natural High Gloss finish, 25 in. scale, mfg. 2011-present.

MSR $600	$400	$250 - 300	$135 - 175	

AC900 – similar to the AC100, except features solid Engelmann spruce top, rosewood back/sides, bound fingerboard/peghead, abalone snowflake fingerboard inlay, gold hardware, Grover tuners, available in Antique Stained Gloss finish, mfg. 1996-98.

	N/A	$500 - 575	$350 - 425	$1,099

AC3000 – Grand Concert-style body, solid Englemann spruce top, solid mahogany back and sides, round soundhole with abalone rosette, multi-ply rosewood body binding, mahogany neck, 14/20-fret rosewood-bound rosewood fingerboard with abalone dot inlays, bound headstock with rosewood overlay and Ibanez/"AW" logos, three-per-side gold Grover tuners with brown pearloid knobs, rosewood bridge, Advantage bridge pins, black pickguard, available in Natural gloss finish, gig bag included, mfg. summer 2010-2012.

	$600	$350 - 450	$200 - 250	$900

AG200 – tight waist/rounded lower bout body with single rounded cutaway, solid Engelmann spruce top, round soundhole, tortoiseshell pickguard, bound body, mahogany back/sides/neck, 14/20-fret rosewood fingerboard with pearl diamond inlay, rosewood bridge with snowflake inlay, white black dot pins, Ibanez/'AW' logo on peghead, chrome hardware, three-per-side Grover tuners, available in Natural Low Gloss finish, mfg. 1996-97.

	N/A	$300 - 350	$175 - 225	$669

* *AG200E Electric* – similar to the AG200 execpt has a Slim Jim pickup, volume/three-band EQ controls, available in Natural Gloss finish, mfg. 1997-98.

	N/A	$350 - 425	$225 - 275	$829

AG600E – similar to the AG200 E, except features Mexican abalone rosette/binding, bound fingerboard/peghead, snowflake inlay on bridge, Fishman pickup, volume/three-band EQ controls, available in Natural Gloss finish, mfg. 1996-98.

	N/A	$475 - 550	$300 - 350	$999

AJ30ECE – single smooth cutaway jumbo style body, solid Englemann spruce top, maple back and sides, round soundhole with abalone rosette, maple body binding, maple neck, 14/20-fret maple bound rosewood fingerboard with brown dot inlays, matching headstock, three-per-side gold tuners with brown pearloid buttons, rosewood bridge, tortoise pickguard, Fishman Sonicore pickup, Ibanez AEQ-SST shape shifter preamp, available in Honey Sunburst High Gloss finish, mfg. 2007-08.

	N/A	$230 - 285	$135 - 170	$529

AJ200 CE CUTAWAY ELECTRIC – single cutaway jumbo body, solid Englemann Spruce top, flamed maple back & sides, tortoiseshell pickguard, Fishman Acoustic Matrix pickup and Prefix Plus EQ, three-per-side tuners, gold hardware, available in Antique Violin High Gloss finish, mfg. 2004-06.

	N/A	$375 - 450	$225 - 275	$857

AJ307 CE SEVEN-STRING – seven-string configuration, tight waist/rounded lower bout body with single rounded cutaway, solid Sitka spruce top, round soundhole, tortoiseshell pickguard, bound body, rosewood back/sides/neck, 14/20-fret rosewood fingerboard with abalone dot inlay, rosewood bridge with white bridgepins, Ibanez/AW logo on peghead, gold hardware, 4/3-per-side Grover tuners, Fishman transducer, volume/three-band EQ controls, available in Natural Gloss finish, mfg. 1997-2006.

	N/A	$475 - 550	$300 - 350	$1,129

MSR/NOTES	100%	EXCELLENT	AVERAGE	LAST MSR

AW10 – dreadnought body, solid Sitka spruce top, mahogany back and sides, tortiseshell pickguard, chrome hardware, Natural finish, mfg. 2000-03.

	N/A	$140 - 170	$100 - 120	$320

* *AW10CE Cutaway Electric* – similar to the AW10 except has a single cutaway, Fishman Sonicore pickup and Ibanez AEQ-SS EQ, Natural finish, mfg. 2000-03.

	N/A	$230 - 270	$130 - 160	$480

AW12 – dreadnought body, solid Sitka spruce top, mahogany back and sides, tortoiseshell pickguard, chrome hardware, available in Black or Natural finish, mfg. 2004-06.

	N/A	$140 - 180	$80 - 110	$343

* *AW12CE Cutaway Electric* – similar to the AW12, except has a single cutaway body with a Fishman Sonicore pickup and AEQ-SS EQ, available in Natural finish, mfg. 2004-06.

	N/A	$225 - 275	$130 - 170	$529

AW20 – dreadnought body, solid Sitka spruce top, maple back and sides, tortiseshell pickguard, chrome hardware, available in Honey Gloss Sunburst or Gloss Burgundy Sunburst (2003-04) finish, mfg. 2003-06.

	N/A	$145 - 185	$80 - 110	$371

* *AW20CE Cutaway Electric* – Similar to the AW20 except has a single cutaway, Fishman Sonicore pickup and Ibanez AEQ-SS EQ, mfg. 2003-06.

	N/A	$225 - 275	$130 - 170	$529

AW30 – dreadnought style body, solid Englemann spruce top, mahogany back and sides, round soundhole with abalone rosette, maple body binding, mahogany neck, 14/20-fret maple bound rosewood fingerboard with brown dot inlays, three-per-side gold tuners with brown pearloid buttons, rosewood bridge, tortoise pickguard, available in Dark Violin Sunburst (2009-2010) or Natural High Gloss finish, mfg. 2007-2010.

	$250	$140 - 180	$80 - 110	$357

* *AW30ECE Cutaway Electric* – similar to the AW30, except has a single smooth cutaway, a Fishman Sonicore pickup, and an Ibanez AEQ-SST shape shifter preamp, available in Dark Violin Sunburst (2009-2010) or Natural High Gloss finish, mfg. 2007-2010.

	$350	$225 - 175	$120 - 150	$500

»*AW30LECE Cutaway Electric Left-Handed* – similar to the AW30ECE Cutaway Electric, except in left-handed configuration, available in Natural High Gloss finish, mfg. 2007-2010.

	$370	$240 - 290	$135 - 185	$529

AW35RECE – single smooth cutaway dreadnought style body, solid cedar top, rosewood back and sides, round soundhole with abalone rosette, maple body binding, mahogany neck, 14/20-fret maple bound rosewood fingerboard with brown dot inlays, three-per-side gold tuners with brown pearloid buttons, rosewood bridge, tortoise pickguard, B-Band UST pickup, Ibanez SRTn preamp, available in Natural High Gloss finish, mfg. 2007-2010.

	$400	$250 - 300	$125 - 175	$571

AW40 – dreadnought body, solid Sitka spruce top, mahogany backand sides, abalone rosette, body binding, maple neck, 20-fret rosewood fingerboard with abalone tree-of-life inlay, three-per-side tuners, rosewood bridge, tortoise pickguard, gold hardware, Natural High Gloss finish, mfg. 2005-07.

	N/A	$175 - 225	$105 - 130	$429

AW50 – dreadnought style body, solid Sitka spruce top, sapele back and sides, round soundhole with multi ring rosette, single-ply black body binding, mahogany neck, 14/20-fret rosewood fingerboard with pearl dot inlays, rosewood headstock overlay with Ibanez and "AW" inlays, three-per-side chrome tuners, rosewood bridge, available in Natural High Gloss finish, 25.5 in. scale, mfg. 2012-present.

MSR $300	$200	$120 - 150	$70 - 90	

* *AW50ECE Cutaway Electric* – similar to the AW50, except has a single smooth cutaway, Ibanez under saddle pickup, and Ibanez SPT Shape Shifter preamp with tuner, available in Natural High Gloss finish, mfg. 2012-present.

MSR $450	$300	$175 - 225	$105 - 130	

AW70 (FIRST VERSION) – dreadnought style body, solid Sitka spruce top, round soundhole, tortoiseshell pickguard, bound body, mahogany back/sides/neck, 14/20-fret rosewood fingerboard with pearl dot inlay, rosewood bridge with white black dot pins, Ibanez/'AW' logo on peghead, chrome hardware, three-per-side die-cast tuners, available in Natural Low Gloss finish, mfg. 1997-99.

	N/A	$175 - 225	$100 - 125	$399

AW70 LG – dreadnought style, solid Sitka spruce top, round soundhole, tortoiseshell pickguard, bound body, mahogany back/sides/neck, 14/20-fret rosewood fingerboard with pearl dot inlay, rosewood bridge with white black dot pins, Ibanez/'AW' logo on peghead, chrome hardware, three-per-side die-cast tuners, Slim Jim pickup, volume/three-band EQ controls, available in Natural Low Gloss finish, mfg. 1998-99.

	N/A	$175 - 225	$100 - 125	$399

MSR/NOTES	100%	EXCELLENT	AVERAGE	LAST MSR

* AW70 CE LG Limited Edition – similar to the AW70 LG, except features a single rounded cutaway body, available in Natural Low Gloss finish, mfg. 1998-99.

	N/A	$275 - 325	$175 - 225	$599

AW70 (SECOND VERSION) – dreadnought style body, solid Sitka spruce top, sapele back and sides, round soundhole with multi ring rosette, multi-ply black/white body binding, mahogany neck, 14/20-fret bound rosewood fingerboard with pearl dot inlays, bound rosewood headstock overlay with Ibanez and "AW" inlays, three-per-side chrome tuners, rosewood bridge, available in Black or Natural High Gloss finish, 25.5 in. scale, mfg. 2012-present.

MSR $375	$250	$150 - 190	$90 - 115	

* AW70ECE Cutaway Electric (Second Version) – similar to the AW70 (Second Version), except has a single smooth cutaway, Ibanez under saddle pickup, and Ibanez SPT Shape Shifter preamp with tuner, available in Black, Natural, or Trans. Blue Sunburst High Gloss finish, mfg. 2012-present.

MSR $525	$350	$225 - 275	$135 - 170	

AW100 – dreadnought style body, solid Sitka spruce top, round soundhole, tortoiseshell pickguard, bound body, mahogany back/sides/neck, 14/20-fret rosewood fingerboard with pearl dot inlay, rosewood bridge with white black dot pins, Ibanez/'AW' logo on peghead, chrome hardware, three-per-side die-cast tuners, available in Natural gloss finish, mfg. 1996-98, 2000-06.

	N/A	$200 - 250	$120 - 150	$500

When this model was reintroduced in 2000, Englemann spruce was used.

* AW100 CE Cutaway Electric – dreadnought style body with single rounded cutaway, solid Sitka spruce top, round soundhole, tortoiseshell pickguard, bound body, mahogany back/sides/neck, 14/20-fret rosewood fingerboard with pearl dot inlay, rosewood bridge with white black dot pins, Ibanez/'AW' logo on peghead, chrome hardware, three-per-side die-cast tuners, Slim Jim pickup, volume/three-band EQ controls, available in Natural gloss finish, mfg. 1996-98, 2000-06.

	N/A	$300 - 350	$175 - 225	$714

* **Add 5% for Black gloss finish (Model AW100 CE BK).**

When this model was reintroduced in 2000, Englemann spruce was used.

»AW100LCE Cutaway Electric Left-Handed – similar to the AW100CE Cutaway Electric except in left-handed configuration, disc. 2006.

	N/A	$300 - 375	$175 - 225	$757

AW112 NT – similar to AW100, except in 12-string configuration, six-per-side tuners, available in Natural gloss finish, mfg. 1997-2000.

	N/A	$275 - 325	$175 - 225	$600

AW120 – dreadnought body, solid Englemann spruce top, mahogany back and sides, no pickguard, gold hardware, available in Resonant Dark Violin finish, mfg. 2004-07.

	N/A	$200 - 250	$120 - 150	$500

* AW120CE Cutaway Electric – similar to the AW120, except has a single cutaway body with a Fishman Sonicore pickup and AEQ-SSR EQ, mfg. 2004-07.

	N/A	$300 - 375	$175 - 225	$714

AW130BG/FM/RGECE CUTAWAY ELECTRIC – single smooth cutaway dreadnought style body, solid Englemann spruce top, bubinga (BG), flamed maple (FM), or Ranggu (RG) back and sides, round soundhole with abalone rosette, maple body binding, mahogany neck, 14/20-fret maple bound rosewood fingerboard with brown dot inlays, three-per-side gold tuners with brown pearloid buttons, rosewood bridge, tortoise pickguard, Fishman Sonicore pickup, Fishman Classic 4T Blend preamp, available in Natural (BG, RG), or Vintage Violin (FM) High Gloss finish, mfg. 2007 only.

	N/A	$350 - 450	$225 - 275	$857

AW200 – dreadnought body, solid Englemann spruce top, flamed maple back and sides, mahogany neck, rosewood fingerboard and bridge, dot inlay, three-per-side tuners, matching headstock, available in Natural (disc.) or Vintage Violin finishes, mfg. 1996, 2000-06.

	N/A	$250 - 300	$125 - 175	$571

* AW200CE Cutaway Electric – similar to the AW200 except has a Fishman Acoustic Matrix and Fishman prefix EQ, mfg. 2000-06.

	N/A	$350 - 425	$200 - 250	$857

AW250 – dreadnought style body, solid cedar top, mahogany back and sides, round soundhole with wooden rosette, multi-ply body binding, mahogany neck, 14/20-fret rosewood fingerboard with pearl dot inlays, rosewood headstock overlay with Ibanez and "AW" inlays, three-per-side chrome tuners, rosewood bridge, available in Rustic Brown Low Gloss finish, 25 in. scale, mfg. 2011-present.

MSR $450	$300	$175 - 225	$105 - 130	

* AW250ECE Cutaway Electric – similar to the AW250, except has a single smooth cutaway, Fishman Sonicore pickup, and Ibanez SST Shape Shifter preamp with tuner, available in Rustic Brown Low Gloss finish, mfg. 2011-present.

MSR $600	$400	$250 - 300	$135 - 175	

MSR/NOTES	100%	EXCELLENT	AVERAGE	LAST MSR

AW300 FIRST VERSION – similar to the AW100, except features rosewood back/sides, abalone dot inlay, gold Grover tuners, available in Natural gloss finish, mfg. 1996-2000, reintroduced 2003-06.

	N/A	$250 - 300	$150 - 200	$600

* *AW300CE Cutaway Electric First Version* – similar to the AW300, except features rosewood back/sides, abalone dot inlay, gold Grover tuners, Fishman pickup, volume/three-band EQ controls, mfg. 2002-06.

	N/A	$400 - 475	$250 - 300	$929

AW300 SECOND VERSION – dreadnought style body, solid Englemann spruce top, mahogany back and sides, round soundhole with abalone rosette, multi-ply body binding, mahogany neck, 14/20-fret bound rosewood fingerboard with pearl dot inlays, bound rosewood headstock overlay with Ibanez and "AW" inlays, three-per-side chrome tuners, rosewood bridge, black or tortoise pickguard, available in Dark Violin Sunburst, Natural (2011 only), or Vintage Sunburst High Gloss finish, 25 in. scale, mfg. 2011-present.

MSR $450	$300	$175 - 225	$105 - 130	

* *AW300ECE Cutaway Electric Second Version* – similar to the AW300, except has a single smooth cutaway, Fishman Sonicore pickup, and Ibanez SST Shape Shifter preamp with tuner, available in Cherry Sunburst (2012-present), Dark Violin Sunburst, Natural (2011, 2013-present), or Vintage Sunburst high gloss finish, mfg. 2011-present.

MSR $600	$400	$250 - 300	$135 - 175	

»*AW300LECE Cutaway Electric Left-Handed* – similar to the AW300ECE Cutaway Electric Second Version, except in left-handed configuration, available in Natural finish, mfg. 2011-present.

MSR $645	$430	$260 - 325	$160 - 200	

* *AW300L Left-Handed* – similar to the AW300 Second Version, except in left-handed configuration, available in Natural finish, mfg. 2011-present.

MSR $495	$330	$200 - 250	$120 - 150	

AW380ECE CUTAWAY ELECTRIC – single smooth cutaway dreadnought style body, solid Englemann spruce top, rosewood back and sides, round soundhole with abalone rosette, multi-ply body binding, mahogany neck, 14/20-fret bound rosewood fingerboard with pearl dot inlays, bound rosewood headstock overlay with Ibanez and "AW" inlays, three-per-side chrome tuners, rosewood bridge, black pickguard, Fishman Sonicore pickup, Ibanez SST Shape Shifter preamp with tuner, available in Natural High Gloss finish, 25 in. scale, mfg. 2011-12.

	$450	$300 - 350	$175 - 225	$675

AW400 – dreadnought body, solid Englemann spruce top, mahogany sides and solid mahogany back, mahogany neck, rosewood fingerboard, tortoiseshell pickguard, Natural finish, gold hardware, mfg. 2001 only.

	N/A	$275 - 325	$125 - 175	$600

* *AW400CE Cutaway Electric* – similar to the AW400 except has a Fishman Acoustic Matrix and Fishman prefix EQ, Natural finish, mfg. 2001 only.

	N/A	$425 - 500	$300 - 350	$900

AW500 – similar to the AW100, except features solid Engelmann spruce top, rosewood back/sides, herringbone rosette/body binding, abalone snowflake inlay, gold Grover tuners, available in Natural Gloss finish, mfg. 1996-98, 2002-06.

	N/A	$275 - 325	$150 - 200	$643

* *AW500CE Cutaway Electric* – similar to the AW500, except features rosewood back/sides, abalone dot inlay, gold Grover tuners, Fishman pickup, volume/three-band EQ controls, mfg. 2002-06.

	N/A	$425 - 500	$275 - 325	$971

AW600 – similar to the AW100, except features solid Engelmann spruce top, rosewood back/sides, Mexican abalone rosette/body binding, abalone snowflake inlay, gold Grover tuners, available in Natural gloss finish, mfg. 1996-97.

	N/A	$325 - 400	$175 - 225	$749

AW700 – dreadnought body, solid Englemann spruce top, quilted maple back and sides, abalone and wood vine rosette, maple body and neck binding, maple neck, 22-fret rosewood fingerboard with diamond inlays, abalone inlaid matching headstock with three-per-side tuners, rosewood bridge with abalone inlays, gold hardware, Natural High Gloss finish, mfg. 2005-06.

	N/A	$350 - 425	$200 - 250	$857

AW800 – dreadnought style body, solid Englemann spruce top, solid mahogany back and sides, round soundhole with abalone rosette, white/black body binding, mahogany neck, 14/20-fret bound rosewood fingerboard with pearl dot inlays, three-per-side gold tuners with brown pearloid buttons, rosewood bridge, tortoise pickguard, available in Natural High Gloss finish, mfg. 2007-08.

	N/A	$300 - 375	$175 - 225	$714

* *AW800ECE Cutaway Electric* – similar to the AW800, except has a single smooth cutaway, a B-Band UST pickup, and a B-Band A-5 preamp, available in Natural High Gloss finish, mfg. 2007 only.

	N/A	$350 - 450	$225 - 275	$900

MSR/NOTES	100%	EXCELLENT	AVERAGE	LAST MSR

* *AW800R* – similar to the AW800, except has solid rosewood back and sides, available in Natural High Gloss finish, mfg. 2007-08.

	N/A	$350 - 425	$225 - 275	$857

»*AW800RECE Cutaway Electric* – similar to the AW800R, except has a single smooth cutaway, a B-Band UST pickup, and a B-Band A-5 preamp, available in Natural High Gloss finish, mfg. 2007 only.

	N/A	$425 - 525	$260 - 325	$1,043

AW900 AN – similar to the AW100, except features solid Engelmann spruce top, rosewood back/sides, Mexican abalone rosette/body binding, abalone snowflake inlay, gold Grover tuners, available in Antique Stained gloss finish, mfg. 1996-98.

	N/A	$500 - 575	$325 - 375	$1,099

AW1050CE CUTAWAY ELECTRIC – single cutaway dreadnought body, solid Western Canadian Red Cedar top, solid mahogany back and sides, maple body and neck binding, Fishman Acoustic Matrix pickup and Prefix Plus EQ, abalone headstock, fingerboard and bridge inlays, available in Resonant Low Gloss finish, mfg. 2004-06.

	N/A	$600 - 725	$375 - 450	$1,429

AW1400 – dreadnought body, solid Englemann spruce top, solid rosewood back and sides, abalone rosette, maple body binding, maple neck, 22-fret rosewood fingerboard with abalone diamond inlays, abalone inlaid headstock with three-per-side tuners, rosewood bridge with abalone inlays, gold hardware, Natural High Gloss finish, mfg. 2005-06.

	N/A	$500 - 575	$300 - 350	$1,143

AW3000 – dreadnought body, solid Englemann spruce top, solid mahogany back and sides, round soundhole with abalone rosette, multi-ply rosewood body binding, mahogany neck, 14/20-fret rosewood-bound rosewood fingerboard with abalone dot inlays, bound headstock with rosewood overlay and Ibanez/"AW" logos, three-per-side gold Grover tuners with brown pearloid knobs, rosewood bridge, Advantage bridge pins, black pickguard, available in Natural gloss finish, gig bag included, mfg. 2010-present.

MSR $900	$600	$350 - 450	$200 - 250	

* *AW3000CE Cutaway Electric* – similar to the AW3000, except has a single smooth cutaway, L.R. Baggs Element pickup, and L.R. Baggs EAS-VTC endpin preamp with soundhole mounted controls, available in Natural High Gloss finish, gig bag included, mfg. summer 2010-present.

MSR $1,200	$800	$475 - 600	$275 - 350	

AW3080 – dreadnought body, solid Englemann spruce top, solid rosewood back and sides, round soundhole with abalone rosette, mahogany rosewood body binding, mahogany neck, 14/20-fret mahogany-bound rosewood fingerboard with abalone dot inlays, bound headstock with rosewood overlay and Ibanez/"AW" logos, three-per-side gold Grover tuners with brown pearloid knobs, rosewood bridge, Advantage bridge pins, black pickguard, available in Natural high gloss finish, gig bag included, mfg. 2011-12.

	$700	$425 - 525	$260 - 325	$1,050

ACOUSTIC: ARTWOOD STUDIO SERIES

The Artwood Studio Series of guitars represent Ibanez's highest-quality Artwood-style guitars. All models feature solid wood for the top, back, and sides, decorative appointments, Ibanez Exclusive Fast Action Set-up Technology (F.A.S.T.) adjustable neck, and flying top construction that was developed by Swiss luthier Lukas Brunner that allows the guitar to vibrate evenly for better resonance and projection.

ACS1150ECE – single sloped cutaway Grand Concert body, solid cedar top, solid rosewood back and sides, round soundhole with abalone rosette, maple binding, mahogany F.A.S.T. adjustable neck, 14/20-fret ebony fingerboard, black headstock overlay with Ibanez and AW inlays, three-per-side gold Grover tuners with brown pearloid knobs, ebony bridge, clear pickguard, B-Band UST pickup and A5T preamp, available in Natural High Gloss finish, mfg. 2008-09.

	N/A	$550 - 650	$350 - 425	$1,286

AJS1180ECE – single sloped cutaway semi-jumbo body, solid Englemann spruce top, solid flamed maple back and sides, round soundhole with abalone rosette, maple binding, mahogany F.A.S.T. adjustable neck, 14/20-fret ebony fingerboard, flamed maple headstock overlay with abalone Ibanez and AW inlays, three-per-side gold Grover tuners with brown pearloid knobs, ebony bridge, clear pickguard, B-Band UST pickup and A5T preamp, available in Natural High Gloss finish, mfg. 2008-09.

	N/A	$625 - 725	$400 - 475	$1,429

AWS1000ECE – single sloped cutaway dreadnought body, solid Sitka spruce top, solid mahogany back and sides, round soundhole with abalone rosette, maple binding, mahogany F.A.S.T. adjustable neck, 14/20-fret ebony fingerboard, black headstock overlay with Ibanez and AW inlays, three-per-side gold Grover tuners with brown pearloid knobs, ebony bridge, clear pickguard, B-Band UST pickup and A5T preamp, available in Natural High Gloss finish, mfg. 2008-09.

	N/A	$500 - 575	$300 - 375	$1,143

ACOUSTIC: CHARLESTON SERIES

CR80 – auditorium style, spruce top, bound f-holes, three-layer black pickguard, nato back/sides, mahogany neck, 14/22-fret bound rosewood fingerboard with pearl dot inlay, rosewood bridge with white black dot pins, blackface peghead with screened logo, three-per-side chrome tuners, available in Brown Sunburst or Cherry Sunburst finish, mfg. 1994-96.

	N/A	$200 - 250	$125 - 175	$500

MSR/NOTES	100%	EXCELLENT	AVERAGE	LAST MSR

* **CR100E** – similar to CR80, except has thinner body, piezo bridge pickup, four-band EQ, disc. 1996.

	N/A	$300 - 350	$175 - 225	$700

ACOUSTIC: CLASSIC/G ELITE (GA/G) SERIES

GA1 – 1/2-sized classical style, spruce top, agathis back and sides, round soundhole, wood inlay rosette, mahogany neck, 12/18-fret rosewood fingerboard, slotted headstock, three-per-side open-style chrome tuners, rosewood tied bridge, available in Natural Gloss finish, 20.9 in. scale, mfg. 2013-present.

MSR $165	$110	$70 - 85	$45 - 55	

GA2 – 3/4-sized classical style, spruce top, agathis back and sides, round soundhole, wood inlay rosette, mahogany neck, 12/19-fret rosewood fingerboard, slotted headstock, three-per-side open-style chrome tuners, rosewood tied bridge, available in Natural Gloss finish, 22.8 in. scale, mfg. 2013-present.

MSR $180	$120	$75 - 90	$45 - 60	

GA3 – classical style, spruce top, agathis or catalpa back and sides, round soundhole, wood inlay rosette, mahogany neck, 12/19-fret rosewood fingerboard, slotted headstock, three-per-side open-style chrome tuners, rosewood tied bridge, available in Natural Gloss finish, current mfg.

MSR $195	$130	$80 - 100	$45 - 60	

GA5 – classical style, spruce top, round soundhole, wood inlay rosette, mahogany back/sides, mahogany neck, 12/19-fret rosewood fingerboard, rosewood tied bridge, three-per-side chrome tuners, available in Natural Gloss finish, mfg. 1998-present.

MSR $270	$180	$110 - 140	$70 - 85	

* **GA5TCE Cutaway Electric** – similar to the GA5 except has a single cutaway and a Piezo Transducer with a three-band EQ, current mfg.

MSR $375	$250	$150 - 190	$95 - 120	

GA6 CE CUTAWAY ELECTRIC – classical style body with single rounded cutaway, spruce top, round soundhole, wood inlay rosette, mahogany back and sides, mahogany neck, 12/19-fret rosewood fingerboard, rosewood tied bridge, three-per-side gold tuners, piezo pickup, volume/4-band EQ, available in Natural gloss finish, mfg. 1998-present.

MSR $375	$250	$150 - 190	$95 - 120	

GA7 – similar to the GA5, except features rosewood back/sides, gold tuners, available in Natural Gloss finish, mfg. 1998-2000.

	N/A	$100 - 130	$70 - 90	$229

GA10 – classical style, spruce top, round soundhole, bound body, wood inlay rosette, nato back/sides, mahogany neck, 12/19-fret rosewood fingerboard, rosewood tied bridge, rosewood peghead veneer, three-per-side chrome tuners with pearloid buttons, available in Natural Gloss finish, mfg. 1994-96, 1998-99.

	N/A	$110 - 140	$80 - 100	$259

GA30 – similar to the GA10, except features mahogany back/sides, gold tuners, available in Natural gloss finish, mfg. 1998-99.

	N/A	$130 - 160	$90 - 110	$299

GA35TCE CUTAWAY ELECTRIC – single cutaway thinline classical style, spruce top, mahogany back and sides, round soundhole, wood inlay rosette, mahogany neck, 14/21-fret rosewood fingerboard, slotted headstock with black overlay and gold Ibanez logo, three-per-side open-style gold tuners, rosewood tied bridge, Fishman Sonicore pickup, Ibanez AEQ210T electronics with onboard tuner, available in Dark Violin Sunburst finish, 25.6 in. scale, mfg. 2013-present.

MSR $450	$300	$175 - 225	$105 - 130	

GA60S CE CUTAWAY ELECTRIC – single cutaway classical style, solid spruce top, round soundhole, wood inlay rosette, mahogany back/sides, mahogany neck, 12/19-fret rosewood fingerboard, rosewood tied bridge, Fishman Acoustic Matrix pickup and AEQ-SS EQ, three-per-side classical tuners, available in Natural Gloss finish, mfg. 2004-07.

	N/A	$175 - 225	$105 - 130	$429

G100 – classical nylon-string body, solid spruce top, mahogany back and sides, round soundhole with classical Mosaic design rosette, mahogany neck, 12/19-fret rosewood fingerboard, slotted headstock, three-per-side open-style chrome tuners, rosewood tied bridge, available in Natural High Gloss finish, mfg. 2008-2010.

	$200	$120 - 150	$75 - 95	$286

G200ECE – single smooth cutaway classical nylon-string body, solid spruce top, mahogany back and sides, round soundhole with classical Mosaic design rosette, mahogany body binding, mahogany neck, 12/19-fret rosewood fingerboard, slotted headstock, three-per-side open-style gold tuners, rosewood tied bridge, B-Band UST pickup and Ibanez SRTn preamp, available in Natural High Gloss finish, mfg. 2008-2010.

	$300	$175 - 225	$110 - 140	$429

G480 – classical nylon-string body, solid cedar top, rosewood back and sides, round soundhole with classical Mosaic design rosette, rosewood body binding, mahogany neck with Spanish joint construction, 12/19-fret rosewood fingerboard, slotted headstock, three-per-side open-style gold tuners, rosewood tied bridge, available in Natural High Gloss finish, mfg. 2008-2010.

	$300	$175 - 225	$110 - 140	$429

MSR/NOTES	100%	EXCELLENT	AVERAGE	LAST MSR

* **G480ECE Cutaway Electric** – similar to the G480, except has a single smooth cutaway, a B-Band UST pickup, and B-Band A3T preamp, mfg. 2008-2010.

	$400	$250 - 300	$135 - 175	$571

G850 – classical nylon-string body, solid cedar top, solid mahogany back and sides, round soundhole with classical Mosaic design rosette, mahogany body binding, mahogany neck with Spanish joint construction, 12/19-fret ebony fingerboard, slotted headstock, three-per-side open-style gold tuners with black knobs, ebony tied bridge, available in Natural High Gloss finish, mfg. 2008-2010.

	$400	$250 - 300	$135 - 175	$571

* **G850ECE Cutaway Electric** – similar to the G850, except has a single smooth cutaway, a B-Band UST pickup, and B-Band A5T preamp, mfg. 2008-2010.

	$500	$300 - 375	$175 - 225	$714

GM500CE CUTAWAY ELECTRIC – single cutaway classical Grand Concert-style body, solid cedar top, rosewood back and sides, round soundhole with abalone and wood inlay rosette, multi-ply body binding, mahogany neck, 12/19-fret rosewood fingerboard, slotted headstock with rosewood overlay and gold Ibanez logo, three-per-side open-style gold tuners, rosewood tied bridge, Fishman Sonicore pickup, Ibanez AEQ210T electronics with onboard tuner, available in Natural finish, 25.6 in. scale, mfg. 2013-present.

MSR $675	$450	$300 - 250	$175 - 225	

ACOUSTIC: CONCORD SERIES

Ibanez produced several acoustic guitars during the 1970s and the 1980s. The Concord series was probably the most popular and included several copies of American designs. Most of the popular designs (Gibson, Martin, etc.) can be found priced between $500 and $700. Less popular designs are somewhere between $300 and $450.

ACOUSTIC: DAYTRIPPER SERIES

DT5 – similar to the DT10 except has covered tuners, disc. 2000.

	N/A	$100 - 130	$70 - 90	$230

DTMA (10) ACOUSTIC – spruce top, mahogany back/sides, rosewood fingerboard with pearl dot inlay, rosewood bridge, chrome die-cast tuners, available in Natural Gloss finish, mfg. 1998-2008.

	N/A	$110 - 140	$70 - 90	$271

* **DT 10 CA Cutaway Acoustic** – similar to the DT 10 except has a single cutaway, available in Natural Gloss finish, mfg. 1998-99.

	N/A	$140 - 170	$100 - 120	$329

DTME CUTAWAY ELECTRIC – similar to the DTMA except has a single cutaway and Piezo transducer with two-band EQ, available in Gloss Trans. Blue, mfg. 2000-08.

	N/A	$150 - 190	$90 - 120	$386

DT100E – mini-dreadnought-style body, spruce top, mahogany back and sides, round soundhole with three groups of rings rosette, multi-ply body binding, mahogany neck, 14/20-fret bound rosewood fingerboard with white dot inlays, mahogany headstock overlay with logo, three-per-side chrome tuners, rosewood bridge, tortoise pickguard, onboard tuner (no pickup/electronics), available in Natural finish, mfg. 2009-2011.

	$200	$120 - 150	$75 - 95	$300

* **DT100ECE Cutaway Electric** – similar to the DT100E, except has a single cutaway, piezo pickup, and AEQ200T electronics with two-band EQ, available in Natural finish, mfg. 2009-2011.

	$250	$135 - 175	$85 - 105	$375

ACOUSTIC: EXOTIC WOOD (EW) SERIES

In 2010, Ibanez introduced new preamp electronics in all of their Exotic Wood (EW) guitars. The SRTc preamp features chorus, phase reverse with anti-feedback frequency, and an onboard tuner.

An example of a 2008 Ibanez EW20AS Quilted Ash Courtesy Chad Speck, Encore Music

MSR/NOTES	100%	EXCELLENT	AVERAGE	LAST MSR

EW20BG BUBINGA – AEL style body, figured bubinga top/back/sides, abalone rosette, 14/20-fret rosewood fingerboard with 12th fret inlay, matching headstock, rosewood bridge, chrome hardware, Natural High Gloss finish, mfg. 2006 only.

	N/A	$175 - 225	$105 - 135	$429

EW20KOE KOA CUTAWAY ELECTRIC – AEL style single cutaway body, figured koa top/back/sides, abalone rosette, 14/20-fret rosewood fingerboard with 12th fret inlay, matching headstock, rosewood bridge, B-Band pickup and Ibanez electronics, chrome hardware, Natural High Gloss finish, mfg. summer 2006-07.

	N/A	$325 - 400	$200 - 250	$786

EW20AS QUILTED ASH – AEL style body, quilted ash top/back/sides, abalone rosette, 14/20-fret rosewood fingerboard with 12th fret inlay, matching headstock, rosewood bridge, chrome hardware, Natural High Gloss finish, mfg. 2005-2010.

	$270	$150 - 200	$95 - 120	$386

* *EW20ASE Quilted Ash Cutaway Electric* – similar to the EW20AS Ash, except has a single sharp cutaway and a B-Band UST pickup with Ibanez SRTn (2005-09) or SRTc (2010-present) electronics, mfg. summer 2005-present.

MSR $600	$400	$250 - 300	$135 - 175	

»*EW20LASE Quilted Ash Cutaway Electric Left-Handed* – similar to the EW20ASE Quilted Ash Cutaway Electric, except in left-handed configuration, mfg. summer 2008-2011.

	$430	$275 - 325	$150 - 200	$645

»*EW2012ASE Quilted Ash Cutaway Electric 12-String* – similar to the EW20ASE Quilted Ash Cutaway Electric, except in 12-string configuration with six-per-side tuners, mfg. summer 2008-present.

MSR $720	$480	$300 - 375	$175 - 225	

EW20 MBE BURL MAPLE CUTAWAY ELECTRIC – AEL style single cutaway body, burled maple top/back/sides, abalone rosette, 14/20-fret rosewood fingerboard with 12th fret inlay, matching headstock, rosewood bridge, B-Band pickup, Ibanez SRTn (2007 only) or SRTc (2010-2011) electronics, chrome hardware, Natural High Gloss finish, mfg. second half 2007, reintroduced 2010-2011.

	$430	$275 - 325	$150 - 200	$645

EW20QM QUILTED MAPLE – AEL style body, quilted maple top/back/sides, abalone rosette, 14/20-fret rosewood fingerboard with 12th fret inlay, matching headstock, rosewood bridge, chrome hardware, Natural High Gloss finish, mfg. 2005-06.

	N/A	$200 - 250	$120 - 150	$471

* *EW20QME Quilted Maple Cutaway Electric* – similar to the EW20QM Quilted Maple, except has a single sharp cutaway and a B-Band UST pickup with Ibanez SRTn (2006-09) or SRTc (2010-12) electronics, mfg. 2006-2012.

	$450	$275 - 325	$150 - 200	$675

EW20SG MANGO-WOOD – single cutaway thinline EW body, spalted Mango-Wood top, back, and sides, round soundhole with abalone rosette, multi-ply cream binding, mahogany neck, 14/20-fret bound rosewood fingerboard with 11-13th fret design inlays, Mango-Wood headstock overlay with logo, three-per-side chrome tuners, rosewood bridge, B-Band UST pickup, Ibanez SRTn (2009 only) or SRTc (2010-2011) electronics, available in Natural High Gloss finish, mfg. 2009-2011.

	$500	$300 - 375	$175 - 225	$750

EW20SME SPALTED MAPLE CUTAWAY ELECTRIC – AEL style single cutaway body, spalted maple top/back/sides, abalone rosette, 14/20-fret rosewood fingerboard with 12th fret inlay, matching headstock, rosewood bridge, B-Band pickup, Ibanez SRTn preamp, chrome hardware, Natural High Gloss finish, mfg. 2007-mid-2008.

	N/A	$300 - 350	$175 - 225	$714

EW20ZW ZEBRA WOOD – AEL style body, zebra wood top/back/sides, abalone rosette, 14/20-fret rosewood fingerboard with 12th fret inlay, matching headstock, rosewood bridge, chrome hardware, Natural High Gloss finish, mfg. 2005-06.

	N/A	$150 - 200	$90 - 120	$400

* *EW20ZWE Zebra Wood Cutaway Electric* – similar to the EW20ZW Zebra Wood, except has a single sharp cutaway and a B-Band UST pickup with Ibanez SRTn (2007-09) or SRTc (2010-present) electronics, mfg. 2007-present.

MSR $600	$400	$250 - 300	$135 - 175	

EWC30ASE FIGURED ASH CUTAWAY ELECTRIC – mini AEL-style single cutaway body, figured ash top/back/sides, abalone rosette, 14/20-fret rosewood fingerboard with 12th fret inlay, matching headstock, rosewood bridge, B-Band UST pickup with Ibanez SRTn (2007-09) or SRTc (2010-2011) electronics, chrome hardware, Natural Resonant Low Gloss finish, mfg. 2007-2011.

	$400	$250 - 300	$135 - 175	$600

EWC30EBE EBONY CUTAWAY ELECTRIC – mini AEL-style single cutaway body, ebony top/back/sides, mahogany body binding, abalone rosette, 14/20-fret mahogany-bound rosewood fingerboard with 12th fret inlay, matching headstock, three-per-side chrome tuners, rosewood bridge, B-Band UST pickup, Ibanez SRTc preamp, available in Natural Resonant Low Gloss finish, mfg. 2010-2011.

	$450	$275 - 325	$150 - 200	$675

MSR/NOTES	100%	EXCELLENT	AVERAGE	LAST MSR

EWC30PDE PADAUK CUTAWAY ELECTRIC – mini AEL-style single cutaway body, padauk top/back/sides, abalone rosette, 14/20-fret rosewood fingerboard with 12th fret inlay, matching headstock, rosewood bridge, B-Band UST pickup with Ibanez SRTn (2007-09) or SRTc (2010 only) electronics, chrome hardware, Natural Resonant Low Gloss finish, mfg. summer 2007-2010.

	$400	$250 - 300	$135 - 175	$571

EW35ABE OLIVE ASH BURL CUTAWAY ELECTRIC LIMITED EDITION – single cutaway EW-style body, olive ash burl top, back, and sides, mahogany body binding, round soundhole with abalone rosette, mahogany neck, 14/20-fret mahogany-bound rosewood fingerboard with 11th-13th fret design inlay, matching finish olive ash burl headstock overlay with pearl Ibanez logo, three-per-side gold tuners, rosewood bridge, B-Band UST pickup, Ibanez SRTc preamp with chorus, phase reverse, and anti-feedback, available in Natural high gloss finish, 25.25 in. scale, mfg. 2011 only.

	$500	$300 - 375	$175 - 225	$750

EW35SPE SAPELE POMMELE – single cutaway EW-style body, sapele pommele top, back, and sides, mahogany body binding, round soundhole with abalone rosette, mahogany neck, 14/20-fret mahogany-bound rosewood fingerboard with 11th-13th fret design inlay, matching finish sapele pommele headstock overlay with pearl Ibanez logo, three-per-side gold tuners, rosewood bridge, B-Band UST pickup, Ibanez SRTc preamp with chorus, phase reverse, and anti-feedback, available in Natural high gloss finish, 25.25 in. scale, mfg. 2012-present.

MSR $750	$500	$300 - 375	$175 - 225	

EWN28BGE BUBINGA NYLON – single cutaway thinline mini EW body, bubinga top, back, and sides, round soundhole with laser-engraved wood rosette, mahogany binding, mahogany neck, 14/20-fret mahogany-bound rosewood fingerboard, slotted headstock with matching finish bubinga overlay, three-per-side gold classical tuners with white buttons, rosewood tied bridge, B-Band UST pickup with Ibanez SRTn (2008-09) or SRTc (2010-2011) electronics, available in Natural High Gloss finish, mfg. 2008-2011.

	$450	$275 - 325	$150 - 200	$675

EWN28KOE KOA NYLON – single cutaway thinline mini EW body, koa top, back, and sides, round soundhole with laser-engraved wood rosette, mahogany binding, mahogany neck, 14/20-fret mahogany-bound rosewood fingerboard, slotted headstock with matching finish koa overlay and abalone logo inlay, three-per-side gold classical tuners with white buttons, rosewood tied bridge, B-Band UST pickup with Ibanez SRTn (2008-09) or SRTc (2010-2011) electronics, available in Natural High Gloss finish, mfg. 2008-2011.

	$550	$325 - 400	$175 - 225	$825

EWN28SYE FLAMED SYCAMORE NYLON – single cutaway thinline mini EW body, flamed sycamore top, back, and sides, round soundhole with laser-engraved wood rosette, mahogany binding, mahogany neck, 14/20-fret mahogany-bound rosewood fingerboard, slotted headstock with matching finish flamed sycamore overlay and abalone logo inlay, three-per-side gold classical tuners with white buttons, rosewood tied bridge, B-Band UST pickup with Ibanez SRTn (2008-09) or SRTc (2010-2011) electronics, available in Natural High Gloss finish, mfg. 2008-2011.

	$400	$250 - 300	$135 - 175	$600

EW40CB COCOBOLO – single cutaway thinline EW body, Cocobolo top, back, and sides, round soundhole with abalone rosette, rosewood binding, mahogany neck, 14/20-fret rosewood-bound rosewood fingerboard with 11-13th fret design inlays, Cocobolo headstock overlay with logo, three-per-side gold tuners with brown pearloid knobs, rosewood bridge, B-Band UST pickup with Ibanez SRTn (2009 only) or SRTc (2010 only) electronics, available in Natural High Gloss finish, mfg. 2009-2010.

	$550	$325 - 400	$200 - 250	$786

EW50MPS MONKEY-POD – single cutaway thinline EW body, solid Monkey-Pod top, Monkey-Pod back and sides, round soundhole with abalone rosette, rosewood binding, mahogany neck, 14/20-fret rosewood-bound rosewood fingerboard with 11-13th fret design inlays, Monkey-Pod headstock overlay with logo, three-per-side gold tuners with brown pearloid knobs, rosewood bridge, B-Band UST pickup with Ibanez SRTn (2009 only) or SRTc (2010-2011) electronics, available in Natural High Gloss finish, mfg. 2009-2011.

	$500	$300 - 375	$175 - 225	$750

ACOUSTIC: LONESTAR SERIES

LS 370 – dreadnought-style body, spruce top, flame maple back and sides, round soundhole with three-ring rosette, multi-ply body binding, maple neck, 14/20-fret bound maple fingerboard with pearl dot inlays, bound pointed maple headstock, six-on-side chrome tuners, rosewood bridge, available in Natural finish, mfg. 1984 only.

	N/A	$250 - 300	$150 - 190	

ACOUSTIC: MASA SERIES

FX72 – single cutaway MASA style body, spruce top, mahogany back and sides, oval soundhole, mahogany neck, 14/20-fret rosewood fingerboard with dot inlay, rosewood bridge, three-per-side tuners, AP2 Magnetic pickup and Fishman Sonicore pickup, 3MX EQ, chrome hardware, Natural finish, mfg. 2004-06.

	N/A	$250 - 300	$125 - 175	$600

GX90 BK – dreadnought size body with MASA 90 System (Magnetic Acoustic Solid-top Acoustic). Ibanez AP1 magnetic pickup located at neck/body joint, AEQ3M equalizer and EQ phase switch, solid Sitka Spruce top, mahogany neck, back, and sides, die-cast tuners, rosewood bridge and fretboard, available in Black High Gloss finish, mfg. 1999-2000.

	N/A	$325 - 375	$200 - 250	$699

MSR/NOTES	100%	EXCELLENT	AVERAGE	LAST MSR

SX90 BK – similar to GX90 BK, except has single cutaway design and smaller body, 24.75 in. neck, modified triangle soundhole, available in Black High Gloss finish, mfg. 1999-2000.

	N/A	$375 - 450	$225 - 275	$799

JX70 – similar to GX90 BK, except has sharp single cutaway original design and smaller body, available in Trans. Deep Blue or Trans. Blue Sunburst finish, mfg. 2001-02.

	N/A	$225 - 275	$125 - 175	$500

SX72 – single cutaway MASA style body, figured ash top/back/sides, oval soundhole, mahogany neck, 14/20 fret rosewood fingerboard with dot inlay, rosewood bridge, three-per-side tuners, AP2 Magnetic pickup & Fishman Sonicore pickup, 3MX EQ, chrome hardware, available in Trans. Black Cherry or Trans. Blue Sunburst finish, mfg. 2004-06.

	N/A	$250 - 300	$125 - 175	$600

ACOUSTIC: MONTAGE SERIES

The Montage Series of guitars offer the guitarist the best of both worlds with a true acoustic and electric in the same instrument. Features include: five different sound choices from full acoustic to straight electric, individual electronics for acoustic and electric (acoustic electronics are mounted on the side of the guitar, electric controls are mounted on the face of the guitar on the upper bass bout), and Ibanez's exclusive Fast Action Set-Up Technology (F.A.S.T.) adj. neck.

MONTAGE MSC350 – single cutaway Ibanez original MSC-style body, spruce top, mahogany back and sides, two oval soundholes both on the bass bout, white (Black finish) or black (Pearl White finish) body binding, mahogany neck 14/20-fret rosewood fingerboard with double dot inlays at the 12th fret, matching finish headstock, three-per-side chrome tuners, rosewood bridge, single Ibanez AP10 magnetic exposed pickup and an Ibanez piezo acoustic pickup, Ibanez M300 preamp, four knobs on face of guitar (g, v, tone, anti-feedback), three-way acoustic/electric pickup switch, traditional acoustic electronics on rim, available in Black or Pearl White (summer 2010-2011) High Gloss finish, mfg. 2010-2011.

	$500	$300 - 375	$175 - 225	$714

MONTAGE MSC380FM – single cutaway Ibanez original MSC-style body, flamed maple top, back, and sides, two oval soundholes both on the bass bout, multi-ply body binding, mahogany neck, 14/20-fret bound rosewood fingerboard with double dot inlays at the 12th fret, matching finish flamed maple headstock overlay, three-per-side chrome tuners, rosewood bridge, single Ibanez AP10 magnetic exposed pickup and an Ibanez piezo acoustic pickup, Ibanez M300 preamp, four knobs on face of guitar (g, v, tone, anti-feedback), three-way acoustic/electric pickup switch, traditional acoustic electronics on rim, available in Trans. Red High Gloss finish, mfg. 2011 only.

	$550	$325 - 400	$200 - 250	$825

MONTAGE MSC380QM – single cutaway Ibanez original MSC-style body, quilted maple top, back, and sides, two oval soundholes both on the bass bout, multi-ply body binding, mahogany neck, 14/20-fret bound rosewood fingerboard with double dot inlays at the 12th fret, matching finish flamed maple headstock overlay, three-per-side chrome tuners, rosewood bridge, single Ibanez AP10 magnetic exposed pickup and an Ibanez piezo acoustic pickup, Ibanez M300 preamp, four knobs on face of guitar (g, v, tone, anti-feedback), three-way acoustic/electric pickup switch, traditional acoustic electronics on rim, available in Vintage Violin High Gloss finish, mfg. 2011 only.

	$600	$375 - 450	$225 - 275	$900

MONTAGE MSC500 – single cutaway AEL-style body, solid spruce top, mahogany back and sides, two oval soundholes both on the bass bout, mahogany neck with F.A.S.T. adj. neck, 24-fret extended rosewood fingerboard with double dot inlays at the 12th fret, matching finish headstock, three-per-side chrome tuners, rosewood bridge, single Ibanez AP9 magnetic exposed chrome pickup and a B-Band UST acoustic pickup, Ibanez HBP multi-function preamp, available in Metallic Black High Gloss finish, mfg. 2008-09.

	N/A	$375 - 450	$225 - 275	$857

MONTAGE MSC550 – single cutaway AEL-style body, flamed maple top, back, and sides, two oval soundholes both on the bass bout, B/W multi-layer binding, mahogany neck with F.A.S.T. adj. neck, 24-fret extended bound rosewood fingerboard with double dot inlays at the 12th fret, flamed maple matching finish headstock, three-per-side gold tuners, rosewood bridge, single Ibanez AP9 magnetic exposed gold pickup and a B-Band UST acoustic pickup, Ibanez HBP multi-function preamp, available in Trans. Red High Gloss finish, mfg. 2008-2010.

	$650	$400 - 475	$250 - 300	$929

MONTAGE MSC650 – single cutaway AEL-style body, quilted maple top, back, and sides, two oval soundholes both on the bass bout, B/W multi-layer binding, mahogany neck with F.A.S.T. adj. neck, 24-fret extended bound rosewood fingerboard with double dot inlays at the 12th fret, flamed maple matching finish headstock, three-per-side gold tuners, rosewood bridge, single Ibanez AP9 magnetic exposed gold pickup and a B-Band UST acoustic pickup, Ibanez HBP multi-function preamp, available in Vintage Violin High Gloss finish, mfg. 2008-2010.

	$700	$425 - 500	$275 - 325	$1,000

MONTAGE MSC700 – single cutaway AEL-style body, solid cedar top, rosewood back and sides, two oval soundholes both on the bass bout, maple binding, mahogany neck with F.A.S.T. adj. neck, 24-fret extended maple-bound ebony fingerboard with double dot inlays at the 12th fret, rosewood headstock overlay, three-per-side gold tuners with brown pearloid knobs, ebony bridge, single Ibanez AP9 magnetic exposed gold pickup and a B-Band UST acoustic pickup, Ibanez HBP multi-function preamp, available in Natural High Gloss finish, mfg. 2008-2010.

	$750	$475 - 550	$300 - 350	$1,071

MONTAGE MSC750 – single cutaway AEL-style body, koa top, back, and sides, two oval soundholes both on the bass bout, B/W multi-layer binding, mahogany neck with F.A.S.T. adj. neck, 24-fret extended maple-bound ebony fingerboard with double dot inlays at the 12th fret, koa headstock overlay, three-per-side gold tuners with brown pearloid knobs, ebony bridge, single Ibanez AP9 magnetic exposed gold pickup and a B-Band UST acoustic pickup, Ibanez HBP multi-function preamp, available in Natural High Gloss finish, mfg. 2008 only.

	N/A	$450 - 575	$275 - 350	$1,143

MSR/NOTES	100%	EXCELLENT	AVERAGE	LAST MSR

ACOUSTIC: N SERIES

N600 – single cutaway classical style, cedar top, round soundhole, five-stripe bound body, wooden inlay rosette, mahogany back/sides/neck, 21-fret rosewood fingerboard with pearl dot inlays, rosewood bridge with white black dot pins, three-per-side chrome die-cast tuners, piezo pickup, volume/three-band EQ controls, available in Natural finish, mfg. 1992-94.

	N/A	$275 - 325	$175 - 225	$600

N601 N – similar to the N600, except features slotted peghead, gold hardware, three-per-side open classic tuners, available in Natural finish, mfg. 1992-94.

	N/A	$300 - 350	$200 - 250	$680

N700 D – single rounded cutaway dreadnought style, spruce top, round soundhole, five-stripe bound body, wooden inlay rosette, ovankol back/sides, mahogany neck, 21-fret rosewood fingerboard with snowflake inlays, rosewood bridge with white black dot pins, three-per-side gold die-cast tuners, piezo pickup, volume/three-band EQ controls, available in Natural finish, mfg. 1992-94.

	N/A	$325 - 375	$200 - 250	$700

N800 – single cutaway jumbo style, flame maple top, round soundhole, abalone bound body and rosette, flame maple back/sides, mahogany neck, 21-fret bound rosewood fingerboard with abalone block inlays, rosewood bridge with black white dot pins, bound peghead, three-per-side chrome die-cast tuners, piezo pickup, Matrix four-band EQ, available in Trans. Blue or Trans. Violin finish, mfg. 1992-94.

	N/A	$375 - 450	$250 - 300	$850

N900 S – similar to N800, except has solid spruce top, gold die-cast tuners, disc. 1994.

	N/A	$500 - 575	$325 - 375	$1,100

ACOUSTIC: PERFORMANCE SERIES

PC5 – miniature jumbo style, spruce top, round soundhole, black body binding, five-stripe rosette, nato back/sides/neck, 14/20-fret rosewood fingerboard with pearl dot inlay, rosewood bridge with white black dot pins, three-per-side chrome covered tuners, Mini Jumbo models specifications: body length 19 in., body width 14.5 in., body depth 3.75 in., available in Natural low gloss finish, mfg. 1998-2006.

	N/A	$100 - 130	$60 - 80	$257

PC15 – Grand Concert body, spruce top, mahogany back and sides, round soundhole with a three-ring rosette, multi-ply body binding, mahogany neck, 14/20-fret bound rosewood fingerboard with pearl dot inlays, standard headstock with gold Ibanez and "PF" logo decals, three-per-side chrome tuners, black pickguard, rosewood bridge, available in Open Pore Vintage Sunburst or Vintage Sunburst high gloss finish, 25.5 in. scale, mfg. 2013-present.

MSR $270	$180	$110 - 140	$70 - 85	

* *PC15WC* – similar to the PC15, except available in Natural finish and hardshell case included, mfg. 2013-present.

MSR $300	$200	$120 - 150	$75 - 90	

»*PC15ECEWC Cutaway Electric* – similar to the PC15WC, except has a single smooth cutaway, Ibanez piezo pickup, and Ibanez AEQ200T preamp, available in Natural high gloss finish, hardshell case included, mfg. 2013-present.

MSR $405	$270	$150 - 200	$95 - 120	

PC25 – Grand Concert body, spruce top, mahogany back and sides, round soundhole with a three-ring rosette (5/9/5 grouping with a large pearl center ring), multi-ply body binding, mahogany neck, 14/21-fret bound rosewood fingerboard with pearl dot inlays, standard headstock with gold Ibanez and "PF" logo decals, three-per-side chrome tuners, tortoise pickguard, available in Natural high gloss finish, 25.5 in. scale, hardshell case included, mfg. summer 2009-2012.

	$230	$140 - 175	$85 - 105	$345

* *PC25ECE Cutaway Electric* – similar to the PC25, except has a single smooth cutaway, Ibanez piezo pickup, and Ibanez AEQ200T preamp, available in Natural high gloss finish, hardshell case included, mfg. summer 2010-12.

	$280	$150 - 200	$95 - 120	$420

PC300CE CUTAWAY ELECTRIC – similar to the PC-5, except has a sharp cutaway original design body and a piezo transducer with three-band EQ, disc. 2004.

	N/A	$175 - 225	$100 - 130	$429

PF GUITAR JAM PACK (IJP1) PACKAGE – dreadnought style, spruce top, round soundhole, black pickguard, three-stripe rosette, nato back/sides, mahogany neck, 14/20-fret rosewood fingerboard with pearl dot inlay, rosewood bridge with black pins, three-per-side covered tuners, available in Natural low gloss finish, disc. 2003.

	N/A	$150 - 180	$110 - 130	$320

The different Ibanez Jam Pack combinations included a PF guitar, gig bag, instructional video, electronic tuner, extra strings, strap, chord chart, picks, and a free subscription to *Plugged In* (the official Ibanez newsletter).

* *PF Guitar Jam Pack (IJP1 BK) Package* – similar to the IJP1 Jam Pack, available in Black finish, mfg. 1997-2003.

	N/A	$160 - 190	$115 - 135	$340

MSR/NOTES	100%	EXCELLENT	AVERAGE	LAST MSR

* PF Guitar Jam Pack (IJP1 SM) Package – similar to the IJP1 Jam Pack, except features Grand Concert size acoustic, available in Natural finish, mfg. 1998-99.

	N/A	$150 - 180	$115 - 135	$330

* PF Guitar Jam Pack (IJP1 CL) Package – similar to the IJP1 Jam Pack, except features Classical acoustic, available in Natural finish, mfg. 1998-99.

	N/A	$140 - 170	$105 - 125	$319

PF GUITAR JAM PACK (IJP1 DE AMP) PACKAGE – dreadnought style, spruce top, round soundhole, black pickguard, three-stripe rosette, nato back/sides, mahogany neck, 14/20-fret rosewood fingerboard with pearl dot inlay, rosewood bridge with black pins, three-per-side covered tuners, available in Natural low gloss finish, disc. 1999.

	N/A	$250 - 300	$160 - 190	$549

The Jam Pack included an acoustic/electric model PF guitar, 10 watt acoustic amp, gig bag, instructional video, electronic tuner, extra strings, strap, chord chart, picks, and a free subscription to *Plugged In* (the official Ibanez newsletter). Everything must be included to bring the full value.

PF3 – dreadnought style, spruce top, round soundhole, black pickguard, bound body, three-stripe rosette, nato back/sides, mahogany neck, 14/20-fret rosewood fingerboard with pearl dot inlay, rosewood bridge with black white dot pins, three-per-side chrome tuners, available in Natural finish, mfg. 1994-97, reintroduced 2003-04.

	N/A	$120 - 150	$75 - 100	$280

Models produced between 2003 and 2004 came with a case.

PF5 – dreadnought style, spruce top, round soundhole, bound body, five-stripe rosette, mahogany back/sides/neck, 14/20-fret rosewood fingerboard with pearl dot inlay, rosewood bridge with white black dot pins, three-per-side chrome covered tuners, available in Black or Natural gloss finish, mfg. 1992-2006.

	N/A	$100 - 130	$60 - 80	$257

In 1994, a black pickguard was introduced.

* PF5L Left-Handed – similar to the PF5 except in left-handed configuration, available in Natural Gloss finish, disc. 2006.

	N/A	$120 - 150	$70 - 90	$286

* PF5S Solid Top – similar to PF5, except features solid spruce top, pearl snowflake fingerboard inlay, mfg. 1994-96.

	N/A	$175 - 225	$100 - 130	$390

* PF512 12-String – similar to PF5, except in 12-string configuration and six-per-side tuners, available in Natural low gloss finish, mfg. 1994-2006.

	N/A	$130 - 170	$90 - 110	$329

* PF5CE Cutaway Electric – similar to the PF5 except has a single smooth cutaway and electronics, available in Natural gloss finish, mfg. 1994-2010.

$300	$175 - 225	$100 - 130	$429

»PF5LCE Cutaway Electric Left-Handed – similar to the PF5CE Cutaway Electric except in left-handed configuration, mfg. 2006-2010.

$300	$175 - 225	$100 - 130	$429

* PF5 DE Electric – similar to the PF5, except has electronics, available in Natural gloss finish, mfg. 1998-2000.

	N/A	$150 - 180	$90 - 120	$340

PF10 – dreadnought style, spruce top, round soundhole, bound body, five-stripe rosette, mahogany back/sides/neck, 14/20-fret rosewood fingerboard with pearl dot inlay, rosewood bridge with black white dot pins, three-per-side chrome die-cast tuners, available in Natural Gloss finish, mfg. 1991-99.

	N/A	$140 - 170	$90 - 110	$319

• Add $20 for left-handed configuration (Model PF10 L). Add $60 for Black gloss finish (Model PF10 BK). When this option was discontinued in 1998, the list price for a PF10 BK was $399.

In 1994, black pickguard was introduced.

* PF1012 12-String – similar to PF10, except in 12-string configuration and six-per-side tuners, available in Natural Gloss finish, disc.

	N/A	$160 - 190	$110 - 130	$369

* PF10CE Cutaway Electric – similar to the PF5 CE, except features three-per-side chrome die-cast tuners, available in Natural Gloss finish, mfg. 1992-98.

	N/A	$250 - 300	$160 - 190	$549

PF15 FIRST VERSION – dreadnought body style, spruce top, mahogany back/sides/neck, 14/20-fret rosewood fingerboard with dot inlay, black pickguard, PF logo on headstock, three-per-side tuners, chrome hardware, available in Marine Sunburst or Trans. Red Sunburst finish, mfg. 2004-06.

	N/A	$120 - 150	$70 - 90	$286

MSR/NOTES	100%	EXCELLENT	AVERAGE	LAST MSR

* *PF15CE Cutaway Electric First Version* – similar to the PF15, except has a single cutaway and a Fishman Sonicore pickup and EQ, available in Black finish, mfg. 2004-09.

	N/A	$200 - 250	$120 - 150	$500

PF15 SECOND VERSION – dreadnought body, spruce top, mahogany back and sides, round soundhole with three-ring rosette, multi-ply body binding, mahogany neck, 14/20-fret bound rosewood fingerboard with pearl dot inlays, standard headstock with gold Ibanez and "PF" logo decals, three-per-side chrome tuners, black pickguard, available in Light Violin Sunburst or Trans. Red Sunburst high gloss finish, 25.5 in. scale, mfg. 2013-present.

MSR $270	$180	$110 - 140	$70 - 85	

* *PF1512 12-String* – similar to the PF15, except in 12-string configuration with six-per-side tuners, available in Natural finish, mfg. 2013-present.

MSR $300	$200	$120 - 150	$75 - 90	

* *PF15ECE Cutaway Electric* – similar to the PF15, except has a single smooth cutaway, Ibanez piezo pickup, and Ibanez AEQ200T preamp, available in Black or Trans. Blue high gloss finish, mfg. 2013-present.

MSR $330	$220	$135 - 170	$80 - 100	

»*PF15ECEWC Cutaway Electric* – similar to the PF15ECE Cutaway Electric, except has available in Natural high gloss finish, hardshell case included, mfg. 2013-present.

MSR $405	$270	$150 - 200	$95 - 120	

* *PF15L Left-Handed* – similar to the PF15, except in left-handed configuration, available in Natural finish, mfg. 2013-present.

MSR $300	$200	$120 - 150	$75 - 90	

* *PF15WC* – similar to the PF15, except available in Natural finish and hardshell case included, mfg. 2013-present.

MSR $300	$200	$120 - 150	$75 - 90	

PF18 S – similar to the PF10, except features solid spruce top, available in Natural Gloss finish, mfg. 1992-98.

	N/A	$190 - 230	$120 - 140	$440

* *PF18 S CE Cutaway Electric* – similar to the PF18S except has a single cutaway and electronics available in Natural gloss finish, mfg. 1994-96.

	N/A	$275 - 325	$150 - 200	$600

PF20 – similar to PF10, except features flame maple top, three-per-side chrome enclosed tuners, available in Traditional Violin finish, mfg. 1991-96.

	N/A	$170 - 210	$95 - 125	$370

In 1994, a black pickguard was introduced.

PF25 FIRST VERSION – similar to PF10, except features herringbone body binding, oak back/sides, 14/20-fret rosewood fingerboard with pearl snowflake inlay, available in Natural finish, mfg. 1994-96.

	N/A	$170 - 210	$95 - 125	$360

PF25 SECOND VERSION – dreadnought body, spruce top, mahogany back and sides, round soundhole with a three-ring rosette (5/9/5 grouping with a large pearl center ring), multi-ply body binding, mahogany neck, 14/20-fret bound rosewood fingerboard with pearl dot inlays, standard headstock with gold Ibanez and "PF" logo decals, three-per-side chrome tuners, tortoise pickguard, available in Natural high gloss finish, 25.5 in. scale, hardshell case included, mfg. summer 2009-2012.

	$230	$140 - 175	$85 - 105	$345

* *PF25ECE Cutaway Electric* – similar to the PF25 Second Version, except has a single smooth cutaway, Ibanez piezo pickup, and Ibanez AEQ200T preamp, available in Light Violin Sunburst (2010-2011) or Natural (2012 only) high gloss finish, hardshell case included, mfg. summer 2010-12.

	$280	$150 - 200	$95 - 120	$420

PF28ECE CUTAWAY ELECTRIC – single cutaway dreadnought body, flamed maple top, mahogany back and sides, round soundhole with decorative rosette, multi-ply body binding, mahogany neck, 14/20-fret bound rosewood fingerboard with pearl dot inlays, matching finish flame maple headstock with gold Ibanez and "PF" logo decals, three-per-side chrome tuners, available in Dark Violin Sunburst, Trans. Red Sunburst, or Vintage Violin high gloss finish, 25.5 in. scale, mfg. 2012-present.

MSR $450	$300	$175 - 225	$105 - 130	

PF30 – similar to PF10, except features cedar top, three-per-side chrome enclosed tuners, available in Natural finish, mfg. 1991-92.

	N/A	$135 - 165	$80 - 100	$290

PF30S – dreadnought body, solid Englemann spruce top, mahogany back and sides, round soundhole with a three-ring rosette (5/9/5 grouping with a large pearl center ring), black body binding, mahogany neck, 14/20-fret bound rosewood fingerboard with pearl dot inlays, standard headstock with rosewood overlay, gold Ibanez and "PF" logo decals, three-per-side chrome tuners, tortoise pickguard, available in Natural high gloss finish, 25.5 in. scale, mfg. summer 2010-2011.

	$200	$120 - 150	$70 - 90	$300

MSR/NOTES	100%	EXCELLENT	AVERAGE	LAST MSR

* **PF30SECE Cutaway Electric** – similar to the PF30S, except has a single smooth cutaway, Fishman Sonicore pickup, and Ibanez AEQ-SST Shape Shifter preamp, available in Natural high gloss finish, mfg. summer 2010-2011.

	$300	$175 - 225	$100 - 135	$450

PF40 – similar to PF10, except features flame maple top, three-per-side chrome diecast tuners. Available in Natural finish, mfg. 1991-96.

	N/A	$175 - 225	$100 - 130	$430

In 1994, black pickguard was introduced, spruce top, flame maple back/sides replaced original parts.

* **PF40 FM** – similar to PF40, except has flame maple top, available in Natural or Trans. Blue finish, mfg. 1994-96.

	N/A	$225 - 275	$125 - 175	$500

PF50 – dreadnought style, spruce top, round soundhole, herringbone bound body and rosette, rosewood back/sides, mahogany neck, 14/20-fret bound rosewood fingerboard with abalone dot inlay, rosewood bridge with black abalone dot pins, bound peghead, three-per-side chrome diecast tuner, available in Natural finish, mfg. 1991-94.

	N/A	$190 - 230	$120 - 140	$430

* **PF50 S** – similar to PF50, except has solid spruce top, disc. 1994.

	N/A	$250 - 300	$125 - 175	$550

* **PF50 12** – similar to PF50, except has 12-string configuration, six-per-side tuners, disc. 1994.

	N/A	$200 - 240	$130 - 150	$480

PF75 M – similar to PF50, except features flame maple back/sides, maple neck, 14/20-fret bound maple fingerboard with black dot inlays, rosewood bridge with white abalone dot pins, bound peghead with abalone Ibanez logo inlay, available in Natural finish, mfg. 1992-96.

	N/A	$250 - 300	$125 - 175	$550

PF80 V – similar to the PF50, except has an ovangkol top, back, and sides, available in Natural finish, mfg. 1994-98.

	N/A	$140 - 170	$90 - 110	$320

PF105S – dreadnought body style, solid spruce top, mahogany back and sides, mahogany neck, 14/20-fret rosewood fingerboard with dot inlay, tortoise pickguard, PF logo on headstock, three-per-side tuners, chrome hardware, available in Natural finish, mfg. 2004 only.

	N/A	$120 - 150	$75 - 100	$290

PF300NT – similar to the PF50, disc. 2000.

	N/A	$145 - 175	$90 - 110	$330

* **PF300CE-NT** – similar to the PF300NT, except has a Piezo transducer with a three-band EQ, disc. 2000.

	N/A	$200 - 250	$100 - 150	$450

PN15 – parlor body, spruce top, mahogany back and sides, round soundhole with a two-ring rosette, multi-ply body binding, mahogany neck, 12/18-fret bound rosewood fingerboard with pearl dot inlays, standard headstock with gold Ibanez and "PF" logo decals, three-per-side chrome tuners, black pickguard, rosewood bridge, available in Brown Sunburst high gloss finish, 24.4 in. scale, mfg. summer 2012-present.

MSR $270	$180	$110 - 140	$70 - 85	

ACOUSTIC: RAGTIME SERIES

R001 – parlor style, solid spruce top, round soundhole, wooden inlay binding and rosette, rosewood back/sides/neck, 14/20-fret rosewood fingerboard, rosewood bridge with white black dot pins, gold hardware, three-per-side die-cast tuners, available in Natural finish, mfg. 1992-94.

	N/A	$275 - 325	$150 - 200	$600

R300 – similar to the R001, except features cedar top, mahogany back/sides/neck, chrome hardware, available in Natural finish, mfg. 1992-94.

	N/A	$175 - 225	$100 - 130	$400

R302 – similar to R001, except features 12-string configuration, six-per-side tuners, cedar top, mahogany back/sides/neck, chrome hardware, available in Natural finish, disc. 1994.

	N/A	$200 - 250	$120 - 150	$450

R350 – similar to R001, except features cedar top, ovankol back/sides, mahogany neck, chrome hardware, available in Natural finish, disc. 1994.

	N/A	$200 - 250	$120 - 150	$450

ACOUSTIC: SAGE SERIES

The Sage Series of guitars were inspired by the "1st Golden Age of Ibanez Acoustics" that have a retro/vintage look and feel.

SGT110 – grand concert style body, spruce top, mahogany back and sides, round soundhole with pearloid rosette, black/white binding, mahogany neck, 14/20-fret rosewood fingerboard with pearl dot inlays, three-per-side chrome tuners, rosewood bridge, available in Natural (tortoise pickguard) or Vintage Sunburst (black pickguard) high gloss finish, mfg. 2007-2012.

	$180	$100 - 130	$60 - 80	$270

MSR/NOTES	100%	EXCELLENT	AVERAGE	LAST MSR

SGT120 – dreadnought style body, spruce top, mahogany back and sides, round soundhole with pearloid rosette, black/white binding, mahogany neck, 14/20-fret rosewood fingerboard with pearl dot inlays, three-per-side chrome tuners, rosewood bridge, black or tortoise (Natural finish only) pickguard, available in Black (2007-2011), Natural, Trans. Blue Sunburst, Trans. Red Sunburst, or Vintage Sunburst high gloss finish, mfg. 2007-2012.

	$180	$100 - 130	$60 - 80	$270

* *SGT120L Left-Handed* – similar to the SGT120, except in left-handed configuration, available in Natural high gloss finish, mfg. 2007-2012.

MSR $300	$200	$110 - 140	$70 - 90	

* *SGT122 12-String* – similar to the SGT120, except in 12-string configuration and six-per-side tuners, available in Natural high gloss finish, mfg. 2007-2012.

	$230	$140 - 175	$85 - 105	$345

SGT130 – jumbo style body, spruce top, mahogany back and sides, round soundhole with pearloid rosette, black/white binding, mahogany neck, 14/20-fret rosewood fingerboard with pearl dot inlays, three-per-side chrome tuners, rosewood bridge, black pickguard, available in Black high gloss finish, mfg. 2007-2011.

	$200	$110 - 140	$70 - 90	$300

* *SGE130 Electric* – similar to the SGT130, except has a tortoise pickguard and Ibanez AP3 pickup with AEQ200MT electronics, available in Dark Violin Sunburst, Honey Sunburst, or Vintage Sunburst high gloss finish, mfg. summer 2009-2011.

	$250	$150 - 190	$95 - 120	$375

SGT220E – dreadnought style body, spruce top, mahogany back and sides, round soundhole with pearloid rosette, multi-ply black/white binding, mahogany neck, 14/20-fret rosewood fingerboard with pearl block inlays, black headstock overlay with gold Ibanez logo, three-per-side chrome tuners, rosewood bridge, black pickguard, onboard tuner, available in Black high gloss finish, mfg. 2012 only.

	$200	$110 - 140	$70 - 90	$300

* *SGE220 Electric* – similar to the SGT220E, except has an Ibanez AP3 mangnetic pickup mounted over the soundhole and Ibanez AEQ200MT preamp with 2-band EQ and onboard tuner, available in Cherry Sunburst or Vintage Sunburst high gloss finish, mfg. 2012-present.

MSR $375	$250	$150 - 190	$90 - 110	

SGT520 – dreadnought style body, solid spruce top, mahogany back and sides, round soundhole with pearloid rosette, black/white binding, mahogany neck, 14/20-fret rosewood fingerboard with pearl dot inlays, three-per-side chrome tuners, rosewood bridge, tortoiseshell pickguard, available in Vintage Sunburst high gloss finish, mfg. 2007-2011.

	$220	$130 - 160	$75 - 100	$330

ACOUSTIC: TALMAN SERIES

An example of a Talman TCY20E Second Version Courtesy Ibanez

TALMAN TCY10 – double cutaway unique body style, spruce top, mahogany back/sides/neck, 20-fret rosewood fingerboard with dot inlay, Ibanez Piezo pickup and two-band EQ, three-per-side tuners, chrome hardware, available in Black, Metallic Silver Sunburst (2013-present), or Trans. Blue Sunburst finish, mfg. 2000-present.

MSR $375	$250	$145 - 190	$90 - 115	

TALMAN TCY15 FIRST VERSION – similar to the TCY10 except has black hardware and triangle inlays, available in Galaxy Violet or Galaxy Magenta, mfg. 2000-03.

	N/A	$170 - 220	$110 - 130	$380

TALMAN TCY15E SECOND VERSION – offset double cutaway unique-style Talman body, spruce top, mahogany back and sides, oval soundhole with single ring rosette, black body binding, mahogany neck, 16/20-fret rosewood fingerboard with pearl dot inlays, matching finish headstock overlay with "Talman" logo, three-per-side black tuners, rosewood bridge, Ibanez piezo pickup, Ibanez AEQ200T preamp, available in Red or Yellow (2011-12) finish, 25.5 in. scale, mfg. summer 2010-12.

	$230	$140 - 175	$85 - 105	$345

MSR/NOTES	100%	EXCELLENT	AVERAGE	LAST MSR

TALMAN TCY20 FIRST VERSION – double cutaway unique body style, figured ash top/back/sides mahogany neck, 20-fret rosewood fingerboard with dot inlay, Ibanez piezo pickup and two-band EQ, three-per-side tuners, chrome hardware, available in Trans. Red or Vintage Violin finish, mfg. 2004-2010.

	$300	$175 - 225	$100 - 130	$429

TALMAN TCY20E SECOND VERSION – offset double cutaway unique-style Talman body, figured ash top, back, and sides, oval soundhole with abalone rosette, multi-ply body binding, mahogany neck, 16/20-fret bound rosewood fingerboard with pearl dot inlays, matching finish figured ash headstock overlay with "Talman" logo, three-per-side black tuners, rosewood bridge, Ibanez piezo pickup, Ibanez AEQ200T preamp, available in Trans. Red Sunburst or Vintage Violin finish, 25.5 in. scale, mfg. 2011-12.

	$300	$175 - 225	$100 - 135	$450

TALMAN TCM50 – double cutaway unique body style, figured ash top, mahogany back/sides/neck, 20-fret rosewood fingerboard with dot inlay, pickguard, AP2 Magnetic soundhole pickup, AEQ200M EQ, three-per-side tuners, chrome hardware, available in Natural (2012-present) or Vintage Brown Sunburst finish, mfg. 2004-present.

MSR $450	$300	$175 - 225	$105 - 130	

TALMAN TCM60 – double cutaway unique body style, spruce top, mahogany back/sides/neck, 20-fret rosewood fingerboard with dot inlay, three-per-side tuners, white pickguard with heart graphic, AP2 Magnetic soundhole pickup, AEQ200M EQ, chrome hardware, available in Baby Blue, Lilac, Orange (2006-08), or Pink (2007-09) finish, mfg. summer 2006-09.

	N/A	$150 - 200	$95 - 120	$400

TALMAN TCY74 – offset double cutaway unique-style Talman body, mahogany top, back, and sides, oval soundhole with wooden rosette, multi-ply body binding, mahogany neck, 16/20-fret bound rosewood fingerboard with pearl dot inlays, matching finish mahogany headstock overlay with "Talman" logo, three-per-side chrome tuners, rosewood bridge, Fishman Sonicore pickup, Fishman Sonitone preamp, available in Open Pore Natural finish, 25.5 in. scale, mfg. 2013-present.

MSR $450	$300	$175 - 225	$100 - 135	

ACOUSTIC: MISC. MODELS

Ibanez's Vintage models feature tempered mahogany necks (thinner and flatter profile) and synthetic Ivorex nuts and saddles.

EP5 EUPHORIA STEVIE VAI – single sharp cutaway body thin body, solid Englemann spruce top, mahogany back and sides, mulit-bound body, oval soundhole with Stevie Vai logo wood rosette, mahogany neck, 14/24-fret extended rosewood fingerboard with 12th fret Steve Vai inlay, black headstock overlay with pearl Ibanez logo, three-per-side gold Grover tuners with brown pearloid buttons, rosewood bridge, Fishman Sonicore pickup, Ibanez AEQ210TF preamp with tuner, available in Black Pearl High Gloss finish, 25.3 in. scale, mfg. 2011-present.

MSR $900	$600	$350 - 450	$200 - 250	

EP7 EUPHORIA STEVIE VAI – single sharp cutaway body, quilted maple top/back/sides, mahogany neck, rosewood fingerboard with tree-of-life green pearl inlay, body binding, rosewood bridge, oval soundhole with Stevie Vai signature, B-Band UST pickup and A5 EQ, gold hardware, available in Resonant Forest Green finish, mfg. 2004-05.

	N/A	$625 - 750	$425 - 500	$1,429

EP9 EUPHORIA STEVIE VAI – single sharp cutaway body, solid Englemann spruce top, solid mahogany back and sides, multi-bound body, oval soundhole with Stevie Vai logo wood rosette, mahogany neck, 14/24-fret extended bound rosewood fingerboard with tree-of-life green pearl inlay, abalone headstock inlay with three-per-side gold Grover tuners with buttons, rosewood bridge, Fishman AURA electronics, available in Resonant Root Beer Low Gloss finish, mfg. 2006-2010.

	$1,200	$750 - 950	$475 - 550	$1,714

EP10 EUPHORIA STEVIE VAI – single sharp cutaway body thin body, solid Englemann spruce top, solid mahogany back and sides, brown/black swirl body binding, abalone top inlay, oval soundhole with Stevie Vai logo metal plate rosette, mahogany neck, 14/24-fret brown/black-bound extended rosewood fingerboard with tree-of-life inlay, black headstock overlay with pearl Ibanez logo, three-per-side gold Grover tuners with brown pearloid buttons, rosewood bridge, Fishman Acoustic Matrix pickup, Fishman Aura IC preamp with Steve Vai original sound preset, available in Black Pearl High Gloss finish, 25.3 in. scale, mfg. 2011-present.

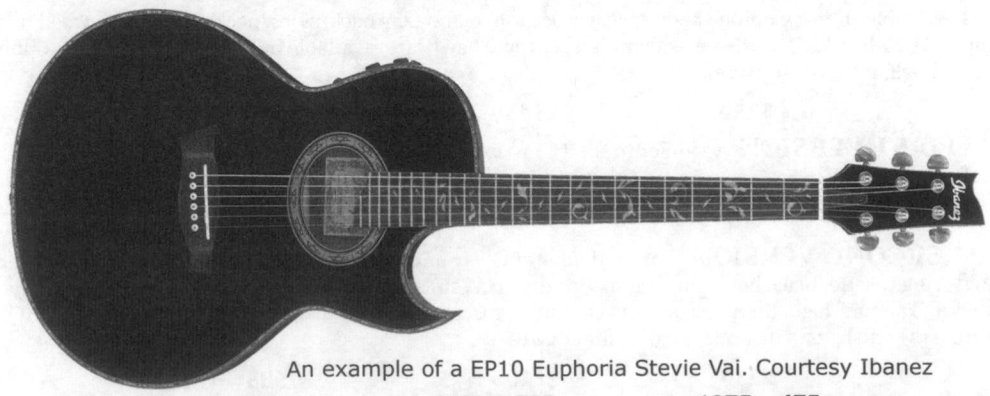

An example of a EP10 Euphoria Stevie Vai. Courtesy Ibanez

MSR $1,650	$1,100	$625 - 775	$375 - 475	

MSR/NOTES	100%	EXCELLENT	AVERAGE	LAST MSR

JSA5 JOE SATRIANI – single sharp cutaway Joe Satriani original body style, solid Englemann spruce top, mahogany back and sides, round soundhole with abalone rosette, multi-ply body binding, mahogany neck, 14/20-fret bound rosewood fingerboard with pearl dot inlays, black headstock overlay with Ibanez logo and Joe Satriani signature, three-per-side chrome Grover tuners, rosewood bridge, Fishman Sonicore pickup, Fishman Presys preamp with onboard tuner, available in Black (2010-12) or Vintage Burst (2013-present) high gloss finish, mfg. 2010-present.

MSR $900	$600	$350 - 450	$200 - 250	

JSA10 JOE SATRIANI – single sharp cutaway Joe Satriani original body style, solid Englemann spruce top, solid rosewood back and sides, round soundhole with abalone rosette, abalone body binding, mahogany neck, 14/20-fret bound ebony fingerboard with pearl dot inlays, black headstock overlay with Ibanez logo and Joe Satriani signature, three-per-side chrome Grover tuners, ebony bridge, Fishman Acoustic Matrix pickup, Fishman Ellipse VT preamp, available in Black high gloss finish, mfg. 2010-12.

	$1,000	$625 - 750	$375 - 450	$1,500

JSA20 JOE SATRIANI – single sharp cutaway Joe Satriani original body style, solid Englemann spruce top, solid rosewood back and sides, round soundhole with abalone rosette, abalone body binding, mahogany neck, 14/20-fret bound ebony fingerboard with pearl dot inlays, black headstock overlay with Ibanez logo and Joe Satriani signature, three-per-side chrome Grover tuners, ebony bridge, Fishman Acoustic Matrix pickup, Fishman Aura Pro preamp with Joe Satriani preset sound, available in Vintage Burst high gloss finish, mfg. 2013-present.

MSR $1,950	$1,300	$800 - 1,000	$475 - 600	

PGA1000 PAUL GILBERT – single cutaway AEF-style body, flame maple top, back, and sides, round soundhole with abalone rosette, multi-ply body binding, one-piece maple neck, 22-fret bound rosewood fingerboard with trapezoid inside of pearl block inlays, matching finish flame maple bound headstock overlay with Ibanez logo and Paul Gilbert inlay, three-per-side chrome tuners with pearl buttons, rosewood bridge with pearl f-holes, white pickguard with Paul Gilbert signature, Fishman Matrix electronics, available in Marine Blue or Trans. Red finish, mfg. 1998-2000.

	N/A	$475 - 600	$275 - 350	$1,000

This model was not factory cataloged.

TULSA TU5 – grand concert style, round soundhole, bound body, three-stripe rosette, nato back/sides, mahogany neck, 14/20-fret rosewood fingerboard with pearl dot inlay, rosewood bridge with black white dot pins, black pickguard, three-per-side chrome tuners, available in Natural finish, mfg. 1994-96.

	N/A	$110 - 140	$70 - 90	$250

V70 – dreadnought body, spruce top, mahogany back/sides/neck, 14/20-fret rosewood fingerboard, black pickguard, chrome hardware, available in Black, Natural, or Vintage Sunburst (2005-06) finish, mfg. 2004-06.

	N/A	$75 - 100	$40 - 60	$200

* **V70L Left-Handed** – similar to the V70 except in left-handed configuration, available in Natural finish, mfg. 2004-06.

	N/A	$80 - 110	$50 - 70	$229

* **V7012 12-String** – similar to the V70, except in 12-string configuration and six-per-side tuners, available in Natural finish, mfg. summer 2005-06.

	N/A	$100 - 130	$60 - 80	$257

* **V70 CE Cutaway Electric** – similar to the V70, except has a single cutaway with a piezo transducer and two-band EQ, available in Black, Natural, or Trans. Blue Sunburst (2006-2012) finish, mfg. 2004-2012.

	$200	$120 - 150	$70 - 90	$300

V100 CE NT – dreadnought style body with single rounded cutaway, spruce top, round soundhole, body binding, mahogany back/sides, tempered mahogany neck, 14/20-fret rosewood fingerboard with pearl dot inlay, rosewood bridge with white bridgepins, three-per-side chrome die-cast tuners, tortoiseshell pickguard, available in Natural gloss finish, piezo bridge pickup, EQ30 volume/three-band EQ, mfg. 1998-99.

	N/A	$225 - 275	$140 - 170	$550

VC70 – grand concert body, spruce top, mahogany back/sides/neck, 14/20-fret rosewood fingerboard, black pickguard, chrome hardware, available in Natural finish, mfg. 2004-06.

	N/A	$75 - 100	$40 - 60	$200

VS100 NT – dreadnought style, spruce top, round soundhole, body binding, mahogany back/sides, tempered mahogany neck, 14/20-fret rosewood fingerboard with pearl dot inlay, rosewood bridge with white bridgepins, three-per-side chrome die-cast tuners, tortoise pickguard, available in Black or Natural gloss finish, mfg. 1998-2000.

	N/A	$170 - 210	$95 - 125	$370

ACOUSTIC ELECTRIC: AE, AEG, AES, & ATL SERIES

AE10 – single rounded cutaway dreadnought style, spruce top, bound body, three-stripe rosette, mahogany back/sides, mahogany neck, 14/21-fret rosewood fingerboard with pearl dot inlay, rosewood bridge with white black dot pins, wood peghead with screened plant/logo, three-per-side chrome die-cast tuners, piezo bridge pickup, AEQ-20 volume/tone/four-band EQ slider controls, available in Natural low gloss finish, mfg. 1996-98.

	N/A	$200 - 250	$120 - 150	$449

MSR/NOTES	100%	EXCELLENT	AVERAGE	LAST MSR

* AEG10 – similar to the AE10 except has a Fishman Sonicore pickup and Ibanez AEZ-SS electronics, available in Gloss Black, Metallic Red (2007-08), Trans. Blue Sunburst (2009-2012), Trans. Red Sunburst (disc.), Trans. Purple (disc.), or Vintage Sunburst finish, mfg. 2001-2012.

	$300	$175 - 225	$105 - 130	$450

»AEG10 II – similar to the AEG10 except has Ibanez AEQ-SP1 electronics, available in Blue Sunburst, Gloss Black, or Vintage Sunburst finish, mfg. 2013-present.

MSR $450	$300	$175 - 225	$105 - 130	

»AEG10NE Nylon-String – similar to the AE10G except in nylon classical-string configuration with a slotted headstock and tied bridge, available in Flat Black (2006-2012), Gloss Tangerine, Trans. Red Sunburst (disc.), or Trans. Purple (disc.) finish, mfg. 2001-2012.

	$300	$175 - 225	$100 - 130	$450

»AEG10N II Nylon-String – similar to the AEG10N Nylon String except has Ibanez AEQ-SP1 electronics, available in Black Flat or Gloss Tangerine finish, mfg. 2013-present.

MSR $450	$300	$175 - 225	$105 - 130	

AE18 – similar to the AE10 (with the Ibanez AEQ system), available in Natural Gloss finish, mfg. 1997-98.

	N/A	$275 - 325	$150 - 200	$599

* AE18 BK/TRS – similar to the AE18, available in Black Gloss or Trans. Red Sunburst finishes, mfg. 1998-2003.

	N/A	$275 - 325	$175 - 225	$600

* AE18 NT – similar to AE18, except has Fishman Sonicore electronics with four-band EQ, available in Natural gloss finish, disc. 2003.

	N/A	$250 - 300	$150 - 200	$549

* AE18 TBU – similar to the AE18, available in Trans. Blue Gloss finish, mfg. 1998-2000.

	N/A	$275 - 325	$150 - 200	$599

* AEF18 – similar to the AE18, available in Black, Natural, Trans. Brown Sunburst, or Trans. Violet Sunburst finish, mfg. 2000-08.

	N/A	$200 - 250	$120 - 150	$500

* AEF1812 12-String – similar to the AE18, except in 12-string configuration with six-per-side tuners, available in Natural finish, mfg. 2000-08.

	N/A	$300 - 375	$175 - 225	$714

AE20 – similar to the AE10, except featured nato back/sides, 22-fret rosewood fingerboard with pearl dot inlay, available in Natural gloss finish, mfg. 1994-96.

	N/A	$325 - 375	$200 - 250	$700

* AE20 N – similar to AE20, except has classic style body/peghead, no fingerboard inlay, rosewood tied bridge, three-per-side tuners with pearloid buttons, disc. 1996.

	N/A	$325 - 375	$200 - 250	$700

AE25 (TB, TS) – single rounded cutaway dreadnought style, flame maple top, bound body, three-stripe rosette, bound body, maple back/sides, mahogany neck, 21-fret bound rosewood fingerboard with abalone dot inlay, rosewood bridge with white black dot pins, black peghead with screened plant/logo, three-per-side gold die-cast tuners, piezo bridge pickup, volume/tone/three-band EQ slider controls, available in Trans. Blue (TB) and Tobacco Sunburst (TS) finishes, disc. 1999.

	N/A	$325 - 375	$200 - 250	$699

In 1998, Transparent Blue finish was discontinued.

AE30 TP – similar to AE18, except has flame maple top, maple back and sides, abalone/pearl block fingerboard inlays, gold hardware, Fishman Sonicore pickup and Ibanez AEQ40 four-band EQ, available in Trans. Purple finish, mfg. 1999-2001.

	N/A	$325 - 375	$200 - 250	$699

* AE30MS/TVS – similar to the AE30 except is in Gloss Marine Sunburst, Gloss Trans. Cherry Sunburst, or Trans. Violet Sunburst finish, mfg. 2000-03.

	N/A	$325 - 375	$200 - 250	$640

AE40 – single rounded cutaway dreadnought style, figured maple top, bound body, three-stripe rosette, nato back/sides, mahogany neck, 22-fret bound rosewood fingerboard with abalone/pearl block inlay, rosewood bridge with white black dot pins, bound peghead with screened plant/logo, three-per-side gold die-cast tuners with pearloid buttons, piezo bridge pickup, volume/tone/four-band EQ controls, available in Honey Sunburst, Red Sunburst, or Trans. Blue finish, mfg. 1994-96.

	N/A	$425 - 500	$250 - 300	$900

* AE60S – similar to the AE40, except features solid spruce top, ovangkol back/sides, bound blackface peghead with screened plant/logo, available in Natural finish, mfg. 1994-96.

	N/A	$475 - 550	$275 - 325	$1,000

MSR/NOTES	100%	EXCELLENT	AVERAGE	LAST MSR

AEG25 – single cutaway mid-depth AEG body, quilted maple top, mahogany back and sides, round soundhole with abalone rosette, multi-ply binding, mahogany neck, 14/20-fret bound rosewood fingerboard with pearl dot inlays, matching finish quilted maple headstock overlay with Ibanez logo and floral design inlays, three-per-side chrome tuners, rosewood bridge, Fishman Sonicore pickup, Ibanez AEQ-SST Shape Shifter electronics with onboard tuner, available in Brown Sunburst, Trans. Black, or Trans. Red finish, 25.5 in. scale, mfg. summer 2009-2012.

	$350	$200 - 250	$120 - 150	$525

AES10E – single sharp cutaway mini-jumbo body, quilted ash top/back/sides, body binding, 14/21-fret rosewood fingerboard with dot inlay, matching headstock with three-per-side tuners, rosewood bridge, Fishman Sonicore pickup, Ibanez AEQ-SST electronics, chrome hardware, available in Amber or Trans. Blue Sunburst High Gloss finish, mfg. 2005-2010.

	$400	$250 - 300	$135 - 175	$571

AES20E CUTAWAY ELECTRIC – single sharp cutaway mini-jumbo body, spruce top mahogany back and sides, body binding, diamond shaped soundhole with abalone rosette, 14/21-fret rosewood fingerboard with diamond inlay, matching headstock with three-per-side tuners, rosewood bridge, Fishman Sonicore pickup, Ibanez AEQ-SST electronics, chrome hardware, Black High Gloss finish, mfg. 2005-2010.

	$400	$250 - 300	$135 - 175	$571

ATL10 – single cutaway hollow style, spruce top, oval soundhole, bound body, three-stripe rosette, maple back/sides/neck, 22-fret rosewood fingerboard with pearl dot inlays, rosewood bridge with white pearl dot pins, 6-per-side black diecast tuners, piezo pickup, volume/three-band EQ controls, available in Black or Blue Night finish, mfg. 1992-96.

	N/A	$250 - 300	$125 - 175	$550

ACOUSTIC ELECTRIC: AEF SERIES

AEF18E – single smooth cutaway AEF-style body, spruce top, mahogany back and sides, round soundhole with fire rosette, multi-ply body binding, mahogany neck, 14/20-fret bound rosewood fingerboard with pearl dot inlays, matching finish headstock overlay with Ibanez and "AE" decals, three-per-side chrome tuners, rosewood bridge, Ibanez piezo pickup, Ibanez SPT Shape Shifter preamp with tuner, available in Black or Dark Violin high gloss finish, 25.25 in. scale, mfg. 2011-present.

MSR $450	$300	$175 - 225	$100 - 130	

* *AEF1812E 12-String* – similar to the AEF18E, except in 12-string configuration with six-per-side tuners, available in Black high gloss finish, mfg. 2011-present.

MSR $570	$380	$230 - 285	$140 - 175	

* *AEF18LE Left-Handed* – similar to the AEF18E, except in left-handed configuration, available in Black (new 2013) or Natural high gloss finish, mfg. 2011-present.

MSR $495	$330	$190 - 240	$115 - 145	

AEF20CSNE – nylon string configuration, single cutaway body, solid cedar top, arched mahogany back, mahogany sides, mahogany rosette, mahogany neck, 14/21-fret rosewood fingerboard, rosewood bridge, Ibanez B-Band pickup & AEQ-SRT electronics, gold hardware, Resonant Low Gloss finish, mfg. 2005-08.

	N/A	$250 - 300	$135 - 175	$571

AEF30 – single cutaway body, flamed maple top, arched maple back, mahogany neck, 14/21-fret rosewood fingerboard with block abalone inlay, rosewood bridge, Ibanez B-Band pickup and AEQ-SSR EQ, gold hardware, available in Cherry Violin (2006-08), Marine Sunburst, Orange Sunburst (disc.), Trans. Violet Sunburst, Trans. Black, or Vintage Violin (2006-08) finish, mfg. 2004-08.

	N/A	$275 - 325	$150 - 200	$643

AEF30E – single smooth cutaway AEF-style body, flamed maple top, back, and sides, round soundhole with pearloid rosette, multi-ply body binding, mahogany neck, 14/20-fret bound rosewood fingerboard with pearl and abalone black inlays, matching finish flamed maple headstock ovleray with Ibanez and "AE" design pearl inlays, three-per-side gold tuners, rosewood bridge, Fishman Sonicore pickup, Ibanez SST Shape Shifter preamp with tuner, available in Trans. Blue Sunburst, Trans. Hibiscus Sunburst (2011-12), Trans. Violet Sunburst, or Vintage Violin high gloss finish, 25.25 in. scale, mfg. 2011-present.

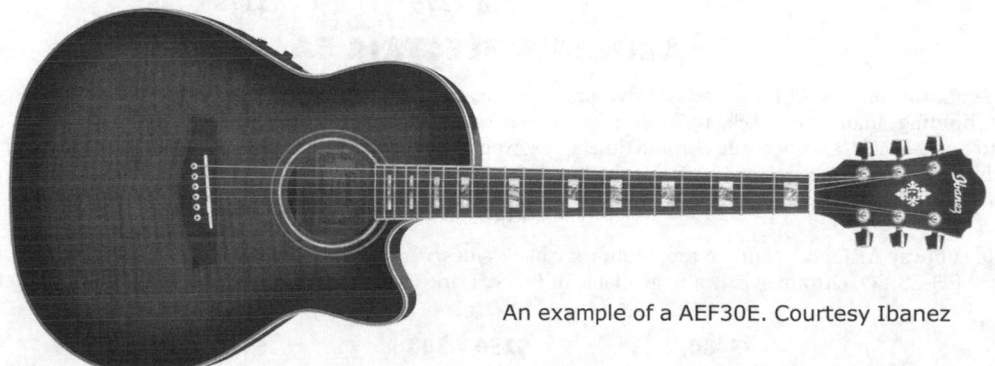

An example of a AEF30E. Courtesy Ibanez

MSR $600	$400	$250 - 300	$135 - 175	

MSR/NOTES	100%	EXCELLENT	AVERAGE	LAST MSR

AEF37 – single cutaway body, quilted maple top/back/sides, mahogany neck, 14/21-fret rosewood fingerboard with block abalone inlay, rosewood bridge, Ibanez B-Band pickupand AEQ-SSR EQ, gold hardware, available in Sunset Gold or Trans. Cherry Sunburst finish, mfg. 2004-08.

	N/A	$325 - 400	$200 - 250	$786

AEF37E – single smooth cutaway AEF-style body, quilted maple top, back, and sides, round soundhole with abalone rosette, multi-ply body binding, mahogany neck, 14/20-fret bound rosewood fingerboard with pearl and abalone black inlays, matching finish quilted maple headstock ovleray with Ibanez and "AE" design pearl inlays, three-per-side gold tuners, rosewood bridge, Fishman Sonicore pickup, Ibanez SST Shape Shifter preamp with tuner, available in Trans. Black Cherry Sunburst or Trans. Emerald Sunburst high gloss finish, 25.25 in. scale, mfg. 2011-present.

MSR $675	$450	$275 - 325	$150 - 200	

AEF100E ELECTRIC – single cutaway body, quilted maple top/back/sides, abalone body binding, abalone rosette, mahogany neck, 14/21-fret rosewood fingerboard with three breeze inlays, rosewood bridge, Fishman Aura Blender electronics, gold hardware, Antique Cherry Violin Gloss finish, mfg. 2005-07.

	N/A	$650 - 750	$400 - 475	$1,429

ACOUSTIC ELECTRIC: AEL SERIES

AEL10 – single cutaway AEL body, spruce top, mahogany back/sides/neck, 14/20-fret rosewood fingerboard with dot inlay, Fishman Sonicore pickup, Ibanez AEQ-SS EQ, chrome hardware, available in Black finish, mfg. 2004-2011.

	$330	$190 - 240	$115 - 145	$495

* *AEL10L Left-Handed* – similar to the AEL10 except in left-handed configuration, mfg. 2004-2010.

	$330	$190 - 240	$115 - 145	$471

AEL20 – single cutaway AEL body, flamed maple top, maple back/sides maple neck, 14/20-fret rosewood fingerboard with dot inlay, Fishman Sonicore pickup, Ibanez AEQ-SS EQ, gold hardware, available in Deep Purple Sunburst (2007-08), Trans. Black (2008-present), Trans. Blue Sunburst, Trans. Red Sunburst, or Vintage Violin (2008 -present) finish, mfg. 2004-present.

MSR $600	$400	$250 - 300	$150 - 185	

* *AEL2012 12-String* – similar to the AEL20, except in 12-string configuration with six-per-side tuners, available in Trans. Black finish, mfg. 2008-present.

MSR $675	$450	$275 - 350	$160 - 200	

AEL30SE – single cutaway AEL body, solid Englemann spruce top, mahogany back and sides, round soundhole with abalone rosette, multi-ply body binding, mahogany neck, 14/20-fret rosewood fingerboard with pearl and abalone block inlays, black or matching finish headstock overlay with pearl Ibanez and fluer-de-lis inlays, three-per-side gold tuners, rosewood bridge, Fishman Sonicore pickup, Ibanez AEQ-SST Shape Shifter preamp with tuner, available in Black (2011-12), Dark Violin Sunburst, or Vintage Violin (2011-12) finish, 25.6 in. scale, mfg. 2011-present.

MSR $675	$450	$275 - 350	$160 - 200	

AEL50CS – single cutaway AEL body, solid cedar top, rosewood back/sides, mahogany neck, 14/20 fret rosewood fingerboard with dot inlay, maple body and neck binding, Fishman Sonicore pickup, Ibanez AEQ-SS EQ, gold hardware, available in Natural finish, mfg. 2004 only.

	N/A	$300 - 350	$175 - 225	$650

AEL50SE CUTAWAY ELECTRIC – single cutaway AEL body, solid spruce top, flamed sycamore back and sides, maple body and neck binding, round soundhole with abalone rosette, mahogany neck, 14/20-fret rosewood fingerboard with wood vine inlay, three-per-side tuners, rosewood bridge with inlay, Ibanez B-Band SQR pickup, Ibanez AEQ-SRT electronics, gold hardware, available in Natural Resonant Low Gloss finish, mfg. 2005-2010.

	$500	$300 - 375	$175 - 225	$714

ACOUSTIC ELECTRIC BASS

AEB5E – single cutaway full-size AEB-style bass body, spruce top, agathis back and sides, round soundhole with two-ring rosette (5/9 grouping), multi-ply body binding, mahogany neck, 15/22-fret bound rosewood fingerboard with pearl dot inlays, black headstock overlay with gold Ibanez logo and floral decals, two-per-side chrome tuners, rosewood bridge, Ibanez piezo pickup and AEQ-202T electronics with two-band EQ and onboard tuner, available in Black or Natural high gloss finish, mfg. summer 2009-present.

MSR $300	$200	$120 - 150	$70 - 90	

AEB10 – single cutaway AEL body, spruce top, mahogany back/sides/neck, 22-fret rosewood fingerboard with dot inlay, Fishman Sonicore pickup, Ibanez AEQ-SS EQ, chrome hardware, available in Black, Dark Violin Sunburst (2009-present), or Natural (2004-2012) finish, mfg. 2004-present.

MSR $600	$400	$250 - 300	$150 - 185	

MSR/NOTES	100%	EXCELLENT	AVERAGE	LAST MSR

AEB30 – four-string bass single cutaway AEF body, spruce top, mahogany back/sides/neck, rosewood fingerboard with dot inlay, Ivorex saddle, Fishman Sonicore pickup and AEQ-SS electronics, Natural finish, disc. 2003.

	N/A	$325 - 375	$200 - 250	$700

AEB305 FIVE-STRING – similar to the AEB30 except in five-string configuration and 3/2-per-side tuners, available in Natural finish, disc. 2006.

	N/A	$350 - 425	$225 - 275	$814

AEB45 – four-string bass single cutaway AEF body, spruce top, ovangkol back/sides mahogany neck, rosewood fingerboard with dot inlay, Shadow pickup and four-band EQ, Natural finish, disc. 2000.

	N/A	$325 - 375	$200 - 250	$700

EWB10ASE FIGURED ASH – single sharp cutaway AEL-style body, figured ash top, back, and sides, round soundhole with white ring rosette, mahogany neck, 22-fret rosewood fingerboard with 10-14-fret hurricane inlay, two-per-side chrome tuners, rosewood bridge, Fishman Sonicore pickup, Ibanez AEQ-SST Shape Shifter preamp, available in Black Open Pore Low Gloss finish, 34 in. scale, mfg. 2007-2010.

	$450	$275 - 325	$150 - 200	$643

EWB20QHFE QUILTED MAHOGANY – single sharp cutaway AEL-style body, quilted mahogany top, back, and sides, round soundhole with abalone rosette, mahogany neck, 22-fret rosewood fingerboard with no inlays, quilted mahogany matching finish headstock overlay, two-per-side chrome tuners, rosewood bridge, Fishman Sonicore pickup, Ibanez AEQ-SST Shape Shifter preamp, available in Natural High Gloss finish, 34 in. scale, mfg. 2008-09.

	N/A	$375 - 450	$225 - 275	$857

EWB20SME SPALTED MAPLE – single sharp cutaway AEL-style body, spalted maple top, back, and sides, round soundhole with abalone rosette, mahogany neck, 22-fret rosewood fingerboard with 10-14-fret hurricane inlay, matching headstock with two-per-side chrome tuners, rosewood bridge, Fishman Sonicore pickup, Ibanez AEQ-SST Shape Shifter preamp, available in Natural Gloss finish, 34 in. scale, mfg. summer 2007-2010.

	$650	$400 - 475	$250 - 300	$929

EWB20WNE CORDIA – single sharp cutaway AEL-style body, Cordia top, back, and sides, round soundhole with abalone rosette, mahogany neck, 22-fret rosewood fingerboard with 10-14-fret hurricane inlay, matching headstock with two-per-side chrome tuners, rosewood bridge, Fishman Sonicore pickup, Ibanez AEQ-SST Shape Shifter preamp, available in Natural gloss finish, 34 in. scale, mfg. 2007-2011.

	$500	$300 - 375	$175 - 225	$750

* EWB205WNE Cordia Five-String – similar to the EWB20WNE Cordia, except in five-string configuration and 3/2-per-side tuners, mfg. 2007-2011.

	$550	$325 - 400	$200 - 250	$825

SGBE110 SAGE BASS – grand concert body, spruce top, mahogany back and sides, round soundhole with multi-ring pearloid rosette, multi-ply body binding, mahogany neck, 15/20-fret bound rosewood fingerboard with pearl dot inlays, black headstock overlay with gold Ibanez logo, two-per-side chrome tuners, rosewood bridge, black (Vintage Sunburst finish) or tortoise (Antique Natural finish) pickguard, Ibanez under saddle pickup, Ibanez AEQ202T preamp with 2-band EQ and onboard tuner, available in Antique Natural or Vintage Sunburst high gloss finish, 32 in. scale, mfg. 2012-present.

MSR $450	$300	$175 - 225	$105 - 130	

INDIANA

Guitars currently produced in China. Distributed by SHS International in Indianapolis, IN.

SHS International offers the Indiana line of acoustic guitars that are available in a variety of series. Guitars are mainly aimed at entry-level students, but they do offer some mid-grade models. For more information, visit Indiana's website or contact them directly.

CONTACT INFORMATION
INDIANA
1922 W. Banta Rd
Indianapolis, IN 46217
www.shsint.net
sales@shsaudio.com

INTERDONATI, PHILIP

Guitars previously produced in Staten Island, NY during the 1920s and 1930s.

Luthier Philip Interdonati built mainly flattop acoustic guitars, but he also produced acoustic archtops as well. The best-known Interdonati model is a 000-sized guitar that was very decorated and features one of the first scalloped fingerboards. Interdonati guitars were also very well built and they have become very collectible today. Each Interdonati guitar needs to be evaluated individually, but models have sold for over $5,000 with high decorations. Source: Tony Marcus, *Acoustic Guitar*.

ITHACA STRINGED INSTRUMENTS

Instruments currently built in Trumansburg, NY.

After a long association with Ithaca Guitar Works, luthiers Eric Aceto and Dan Hoffman established their own company in 1997. The company offers the **Oneida** acoustic/electric guitar (MSR $4,800), the Oneida Jazz guitar (MSR $9,000), parlor acoustic guitars, and a variety of other scrolled acoustic instruments, including electric mandolins and violins. For further information, visit Ithaca Stringed Instruments' website or contact them directly.

CONTACT INFORMATION

ITHACA STRINGED INSTRUMENTS
6115 Mount Road
Trumansburg, NY 14886
Phone No.: 607-387-3544
Fax No.: 607-387-3544
www.ithacastring.com
eric@ithacastring.com

NOTES

J SECTION

JACKSON, DOUGLAS R.

Instruments currently built and distributed by Douglas R. Jackson Guitar Shop in Destin, FL.

CONTACT INFORMATION
JACKSON, DOUGLAS R.
175 Stahlman Ave.
Destin, FL 32541
Phone No.: 850-654-1048
Fax No.: 850-654-1048
drjguitars@juno.com

Luthier Douglas R. Jackson handcrafts his own acoustic and electric guitars, which are built on commission. On occasion, Jackson may build a model on speculation, but that is not the norm. All models are marketed through his guitar shop.

Jackson attended a guitar building school in the Spring of 1977. While enrolled, he was hired by the school to teach and perform repairs. Jackson taught two classes in the 1977 school year, and helped build over 150 instruments (plus his own personal guitars and repairs). Jackson then went to work for a vintage guitar dealer on and off for three years, while he studied just about anything he could get his hands on. During this research phase, Jackson continued to build three or four guitars a year (in addition to his shop repairs).

In 1986, Jackson moved from Arizona to his present location in Destin, FL (the Pensacola/Fort Walton Beach area). Jackson currently owns and operates a 1,500-square-foot building that houses his guitar shop and manufacturing equipment (biography courtesy Douglas R. Jackson).

Jackson estimates that he has built close to 150 instruments consisting of acoustic and electric six-string and twelve-string guitars, electric basses and mandolins, resonator guitars, ukuleles, and dulcimers.

The majority of Jackson's acoustic guitars have been the dreadnought style, with his own scalloped bracing pattern. These dreadnought models feature herringbone trim on the front, back, back center strip, and soundhole; ebony fingerboards, bridges, and peghead laminates; curly maple binding, mother-of-pearl inlay; and spruce tops. The backs and sides are constructed out of either mahogany, Indian rosewood, curly koa, curly claro walnut, or curly maple (although other woods have been used through the years). Jackson now regularly makes a body size the same as a resonator or "classical in a steel-string."

Acoustic prices start at $3,000 for a plain mahogany body and go up according to the woods and appointments used. A used one in good condition may sell for $1,000 to $2,000, depending on how fancy a model it is.

JACOBACCI

Guitars previously produced in France between the 1930s and the 1990s.

JACOBSON, PAUL H.

Classical guitars currently produced in Cleveland, MO (a suburb of Kansas City) since 1974.

CONTACT INFORMATION
JACOBSON, PAUL H.
21116 SE Clover Hills Rd.
Cleveland, MO 64734
Phone No.: 816-658-3701
Fax No.: 816-658-3500
www.pjguitar.com
paulj_website@pjguitar.com

Luthier Paul H. Jacobson, along with help from his wife Carol, build classical acoustic guitars at their shop called The Guitar Workshop, Inc. Jacobson built his first classical guitar in 1974 while working as an apprentice with Macario Briseño. During his early years as a luthier, Jacobson built a number of acoustic and twelve-string guitars in addition to classicals. Since 1980, Jacobson has been focusing solely on classical guitars and in 1984, he began building guitars full time. Jacobson's classical guitars are well-known throughout the world and he has gained a reputation for his experience with intonation. He has also repaired and customized several classical guitars. Guitars start at $6,900. Visit Jacobson's website to contact him directly regarding further information, prices, and options. Early history courtesy Hal Hammer, Jr.

JAIME JULIA

Previously distributed by Manufacturas Alhambra S.L. of Muro del Alcoy, Spain.

Jaime Julia brand nylon string classical guitars were distributed by Manufacturas Alhambra S.L. of Muro del Alcoy, Spain. Suggested retail in the U.S. was $4,261.

JAMBOREE

Instruments previously produced in Japan.

The Jamboree trademark was a brand name used by U.S. importers Elger/Hoshino of Ardmore, PA. Jamboree, along with others like Goldentone, King's Stone, and Elger were all used on Japanese guitars imported to the U.S. Elger/Hoshino evolved into Hoshino USA, the distributor of Ibanez guitars. Source: Michael Wright, *Guitar Stories, Volume One*.

JAMMER

Instruments previously produced in Asia. Previously distributed by VMI Industries (Vega Musical Instruments) of Brea, CA.

Jammer instruments were designed with the entry level and student guitarist in mind.

MSR/NOTES	100%	EXCELLENT	AVERAGE	LAST MSR

JASMINE

Instruments currently produced in Asia since 1994. Distributed by KMC Music in Bloomfield, CT.

The Jasmine trademark is a division of KMC Music (previously Kaman Music), who also represents Ovation, Takamine, Adamas, and Applause. Jasmine guitars are viewed as an entry level step into the Takamine product line. Jasmine guitars may not be as ornate, and may feature different construction methods than Takamine models. For more information, visit Jasmine's website or contact KMC Music directly.

CONTACT INFORMATION
JASMINE
Distributed by KMC Music
55 Griffin Road South
Bloomfield, CT 06002-0507
Phone No.: 860-243-7105
Phone No.: 800-647-2244
Fax No.: 860-243-7287
www.jasmineguitars.com
askus@takamine.com

ACOUSTIC: C CLASSICAL SERIES

C-20 – classical body style, spruce top, nato back and sides, round soundhole, rosewood fingerboard, three-per-side open-style chrome tuners, rosewood bridge, Natural finish, current mfg.

MSR $259	$150	$95 - 120	$55 - 75	

C-22 – classical style, agathis top, round soundhole, hardwood back/sides, nato neck, 12/19-fret rosewood fingerboard, rosewood tied bridge, three-per-side chrome tuners with pearloid buttons, available in Natural finish, disc. 2003.

	N/A	$90 - 125	$60 - 80	$249

C-23 – classic style, spruce top, round soundhole, bound body, wood inlay rosette, mahogany back/sides, nato neck, 12/19-fret rosewood fingerboard, rosewood tied bridge, three-per-side chrome tuners with pearloid buttons, available in Natural finish, mfg. 1994-2003.

	N/A	$105 - 140	$70 - 90	$289

C-26 – classic style, spruce top, round soundhole, three-stripe bound body, wood inlay rosette, mahogany back/sides, nato neck, 12/19-fret rosewood fingerboard/bridge, three-per-side gold tuners with pearloid buttons, available in Natural finish, disc. 1994.

	N/A	$125 - 175	$75 - 100	$280

C-27 – classic style, cedar top, round soundhole, bound body, wood inlay rosette, mahogany back/sides, nato neck, 12/19-fret rosewood fingerboard, rosewood tied bridge, three-per-side chrome tuners with pearloid buttons, available in Natural finish, mfg. 1994-98.

	N/A	$80 - 120	$50 - 70	$200

C-28 – classic style, spruce top, round soundhole, three-stripe bound body, wood inlay rosette, rosewood back/sides, nato neck, 12/19-fret rosewood fingerboard, tied rosewood bridge, three-per-side gold tuners with pearloid buttons, available in Natural finish, disc. 1992.

	N/A	$150 - 200	$90 - 120	$350

C-36 S – classic style, solid spruce top, round soundhole, three-stripe bound body, wood inlay rosette, rosewood back/sides, nato neck, 12/19-fret rosewood fingerboard, tied rosewood bridge with marquetry inlay, three-per-side gold tuners with pearloid buttons, available in Natural finish, mfg. 1994-98.

	N/A	$225 - 275	$125 - 175	$520

C-48 M – single round cutaway classic style, figured maple top, round soundhole, three-stripe bound body, wood inlay rosette, figured maple back/sides, nato neck, 12/19-fret rosewood fingerboard, tied rosewood bridge, figured maple veneered peghead, three-per-side gold tuners with pearloid buttons, available in Natural finish, mfg. 1994-98.

	N/A	$225 - 275	$125 - 175	$500

RQ-28 – requinto style, spruce top, round soundhole, bound body, wood inlay rosette, rosewood back/sides, nato neck, 12/19-fret extended rosewood fingerboard, tied rosewood bridge with marquetry inlay, three-per-side gold tuners with pearloid buttons, available in Natural finish, mfg. 1994-98.

	N/A	$175 - 225	$100 - 135	$420

ACOUSTIC: S DREADNOUGHT SERIES

S-31 – dreadnought style, spruce top, round soundhole, black pickguard, three-stripe bound body/rosette, nato back/sides/neck, 14/20-fret rosewood fingerboard with pearl dot inlay, rosewood bridge with white pins, three-per-side chrome tuners, available in Black finish, mfg. 1994-2003.

	N/A	$170 - 220	$90 - 120	$389

S-32 – dreadnought style, spruce top, round soundhole, black pickguard, three-stripe bound body/rosette, nato back/sides/neck, 14/20-fret rosewood fingerboard with pearl dot inlay, rosewood bridge with white pins, three-per-side chrome diecast tuners, available in Natural gloss finish, disc. 2003.

	N/A	$110 - 150	$70 - 90	$269

* **S-312 12-String** – similar to the S-32, except in 12-string configuration, six-per-side tuners, five-stripe bound body/rosette, available in Natural gloss finish, disc. 2004.

	N/A	$130 - 170	$80 - 100	$319

S-33 – dreadnought style, spruce top, round soundhole, black pickguard, stripe bound body/rosette, mahogany back/sides, nato neck, 14/20-fret rosewood fingerboard with pearl dot inlay, rosewood bridge with white black dot pins, three-per-side chrome diecast tuners, available in Natural or Vintage Sunburst finish, current mfg.

MSR $369	$180	$110 - 140	$60 - 85	

Also available in left-handed configuration.

MSR/NOTES	100%	EXCELLENT	AVERAGE	LAST MSR

S-34C – dreadnought style single cutaway mahogany body, laminated spruce top, mahogany neck, 14/21-fret rosewood fingerboard with dot inlay, three-per-side-tuners, rosewood bridge, chrome hardware, available in Natural finish, mfg. 2001-present.

| MSR $249 | $130 | $75 - 100 | $50 - 65 | |

* *S-34CFM* – similar to the S-34C, except has flame maple back and sides, available in Natural finish, mfg. 2011-present.

| MSR $299 | $200 | $120 - 150 | $70 - 95 | |

»*ES-34CFM* – similar to the S-34CFM, except has a pickup with Jasmine preamp, available in Natural finish, mfg. 2011-present.

| MSR $409 | $300 | $150 - 200 | $90 - 120 | |

S-35 – dreadnought style nato bound body, spruce top, mahogany neck, 14/20-fret rosewood fingerboard with dot inlay, three-per-side-tuners, rosewood bridge, black pickguard, chrome hardware, available in Natural finish, mfg. 2001-present.

| MSR $179 | $100 | $60 - 80 | $35 - 50 | |

* *S-35QA* – similar to the S-35, except has quilted ash back and sides, available in Natural finish, mfg. 2010-present.

| MSR $269 | $180 | $110 - 140 | $65 - 85 | |

S-36 (FIRST VERSION) – dreadnought style, agathis top, walnut back and sides, round soundhole, nato neck, three-per-side chrome tuners, mfg. 1990s.

| | N/A | $100 - 150 | $60 - 80 | |

S-36 (SECOND VERSION) – dreadnought body, spruce top, figured nato back and sides, rosewood fingerboard, three-per-side chrome tuners, rosewood bridge, available in Natural gloss finish, gig bag included, mfg. 2011-present.

| MSR $349 | $175 | $110 - 140 | $60 - 80 | |

S-37 – dreadnought style, agathis top, round soundhole, black pickguard, bound body, three-stripe rosette, ovangkol back and sides, nato neck, 14/20-fret rosewood fingerboard with pearl dot inlay, rosewood bridge with white pins, three-per-side die-cast tuners, available in Natural finish, mfg. 1994-98.

| | N/A | $100 - 150 | $60 - 80 | $250 |

S-38 – dreadnought style, solid spruce top, round soundhole, black pickguard, three-stripe bound body/rosette, mahogany back/sides, nato neck, 14/20-fret bound rosewood fingerboard with pearl dot inlay, rosewood bridge with white pins, three-per-side chrome die-cast tuners, available in Natural finish, disc. 2003.

| | N/A | $140 - 170 | $80 - 100 | $319 |

* *S-38 S* – similar to the S-38, except features solid spruce top, available in Natural finish, disc. 2003.

| | N/A | $160 - 190 | $100 - 120 | $389 |

S-40 – dreadnought style, round soundhole, black pickguard, three-stripe bound body/rosette, nato neck, 14/20-fret bound rosewood fingerboard with pearl dot inlay, rosewood bridge with white black dot pins, bound peghead, three-per-side chrome diecast tuners, available in Natural finish, disc. 1992.

| | N/A | $150 - 200 | $90 - 120 | $350 |

S-41 – dreadnought style, spruce top, round soundhole, black pickguard with white outline, three-stripe bound body/rosette, daowood back/sides, nato neck, 14/20-fret bound rosewood fingerboard with pearl dot inlay, rosewood bridge with white black dot pins, three-per-side chrome die-cast tuners, available in Black finish, disc. 1994.

| | N/A | $150 - 200 | $90 - 120 | $360 |

S-46 – dreadnought style, spruce top, round soundhole, black pickguard with white outline, three-stripe bound body/rosette, daowood back/sides, nato neck, 14/20-fret bound rosewood fingerboard with pearl dot inlay, rosewood bridge with white black dot pins, three-per-side chrome die-cast tuners, available in White finish, disc. 1992.

| | N/A | $150 - 200 | $90 - 120 | $360 |

S-49 – dreadnought style, mahogany top, round soundhole, black pickguard, three-stripe bound body/rosette, mahogany back/sides, nato neck, 14/20-fret bound rosewood fingerboard with pearl dot inlay, rosewood bridge with white black dot pins, bound peghead, three-per-side chrome diecast tuners, available in Natural finish, disc. 1992.

| | N/A | $150 - 200 | $90 - 120 | $360 |

S-60 – dreadnought style, spruce top, round soundhole, black pickguard, three-stripe bound body/rosette, rosewood back/sides, nato neck, 14/20-fret fingerboard with pearl dot inlay, rosewood bridge with white black dot pins, three-per-side chrome diecast tuners, available in Natural finish, disc. 1992.

| | N/A | $160 - 210 | $95 - 125 | $390 |

S-70 – dreadnought style, spruce top, round soundhole, black pickguard, three-stripe bound body/rosette, Hawaiian koa back/sides, nato neck, 14/20-fret rosewood fingerboard with pearl dot inlay, rosewood bridge with white black dot pins, three-per-side chrome diecast tuners, available in Natural finish, disc. 1994.

| | N/A | $175 - 225 | $110 - 140 | $400 |

MSR/NOTES	100%	EXCELLENT	AVERAGE	LAST MSR

S-80 S – dreadnought style, solid spruce top, round soundhole, black pickguard, three-stripe bound body/rosette, jacaranda back/sides, nato neck, 14/20-fret bound rosewood fingerboard with pearl dot inlay, rosewood bridge with white black dot pins, bound peghead, three-per-side gold diecast tuners, available in Natural finish, disc. 1998.

	N/A	$300 - 350	$150 - 200	$630

S-341 – dreadnought body, spruce top, lacewood back and sides, rosewood fingerboard, three-per-side chrome tuners, rosewood bridge, available in Black gloss finish, hardshell case included, mfg. 2011-present.

MSR $369	$200	$120 - 150	$70 - 90	

ACOUSTIC: STUDIO SERIES

Studio models are correctly proportioned sized classical models, and are available in 1/4 size, 1/2 size, 3/4 size, and full sized scale lengths. Studio Series models come equipped with a quality gig bag and shoulder strap.

STUDIO – classical style, spruce top, round soundhole, mahogany back/sides, nato neck, 12/19-fret rosewood fingerboard, rosewood tied bridge, slotted peghead, three-per-side chrome tuners, available in Natural finish, current mfg.

MSR $239 - 269	$130 - 160	$80 - 120	$40 - 60	

Retail prices were the following: JS141 1/4 size, 22.5 in. scale, $239; JS241 1/2 size, 23 5/16 in. scale, $249; JS341 3/4 size, 24.75 in. scale, $259; JS441 full size, 25.687 in. scale, $269.

ACOUSTIC ELECTRIC: ES SERIES

All models in this series have the following features: single round cutaway folk-style, round soundhole, three-stripe bound body/rosette, 21-fret bound rosewood fingerboard with pearl dot inlay, rosewood bridge with white black dot pins, body matching bound peghead, three-per-side chrome die cast tuners, crystal bridge pickups, three-band EQ, unless otherwise listed.

ES-31 C – single rounded cutaway dreadnought style body, spruce top, round soundhole, black pickguard, three-stripe bound body/rosette, nato back/sides/neck, 14/20-fret rosewood fingerboard with pearl dot inlay, rosewood bridge with white pins, three-per-side chrome tuners, piezo bridge pickup, DJ-2 two-band EQ, available in Black finish, mfg. 1994-2004, 2010-present.

MSR $389	$250	$150 - 190	$90 - 120	

ES-32 C – single rounded cutaway dreadnought style, spruce top, round soundhole, black pickguard, five-stripe bound body/rosette, mahogany back/sides, nato neck, 14/20-fret rosewood fingerboard with pearl dot inlay, rosewood bridge with white black dot pins, three-per-side chrome tuners, piezo bridge pickup, DJ-2 two-band EQ, available in Natural finish, mfg. 1994-2004.

	N/A	$150 - 190	$100 - 120	$369

* **ES-312 12-String** – similar to the ES-32 C, except features non-cutaway body, nato back and sides, 12-string dreadnought style, six-per-side tuners, available in Natural finish, mfg. 1994-2003.

	N/A	$150 - 180	$100 - 120	$369

ES-33 C – single round cutaway dreadnought style, spruce top, round soundhole, black pickguard, stripe bound body/rosette, mahogany back/sides, nato neck, 14/20-fret rosewood fingerboard with pearl dot inlay, rosewood bridge with white black dot pins, three-per-side chrome diecast tuners, piezo bridge pickup, three-band EQ control, available in Natural finish, current mfg.

MSR $469	$250	$135 - 175	$85 - 110	

* **ES-33 C-TOB** – similar to ES-33 C, except has single round cutaway, six crystal bridge pickups, two-band EQ control, available in Trans. Orangeburst finish, disc. 1998.

	N/A	$220 - 270	$130 - 160	$490

ES-34 C – single cutaway NEX body style, spruce top, nato back and sides, round soundhole, rosewood fingerboard with dot inlay, three-per-side chrome tuners, rosewood bridge, black pickguard, passive electronics, Natural finish, disc. 2007.

	N/A	$110 - 140	$70 - 90	$349

ES-35C – single cutaway dreadnought-style body, spruce top, nato back and sides, rosewood fingerboard, three-per-side tuners, rosewood bridge, pickup and Jasmine preamp, available in Natural or Wine Red gloss finish, mfg. 2011-present.

MSR $399	$250	$135 - 175	$80 - 100	

ES-40 C – single round cutaway dreadnought style, round soundhole, black pickguard, three-stripe bound body/rosette, nato neck, 14/20-fret bound rosewood fingerboard with pearl dot inlay, rosewood bridge with white black dot pins, bound peghead, three-per-side chrome diecast tuners, piezo bridge pickup, two-band EQ control, available in Natural finish, disc. 1994.

	N/A	$160 - 210	$95 - 125	$390

ES-41 C – dreadnought single cutaway, spruce top, nato back/sides/neck, three-per-side chrome tuners, Black finish, mfg. 1990s.

	N/A	$140 - 180	$90 - 120	

ES-45 C – dreadnought style single cutaway nato body, spruce top, mahogany neck, 14/21-fret rosewood fingerboard with dot inlay, two-band EQ electronics, three-per-side-tuners, rosewood bridge, chrome hardware, available in Natural finish, mfg. 2001-present.

MSR $399	$170	$120 - 160	$80 - 100	

MSR/NOTES	100%	EXCELLENT	AVERAGE	LAST MSR

ES-49 C – dreadnought single cutaway, mahogany top, mahogany back and sides, nato neck, three-per-side chrome tuners, Mahogany finish, mfg. 1990s.

	N/A	$200 - 250	$120 - 150	

ES-341C – single cutaway dreadnought-style body, spruce top, lacewood back and sides, rosewood fingerboard, three-per-side tuners, rosewood bridge, pickup and Jasmine preamp, available in Black gloss finish, hardshell case included, mfg. 2011-present.

MSR $469	$250	$135 - 175	$80 - 100	

ACOUSTIC ELECTRIC: TC SERIES

TC-28 C – single round cutaway classic style, spruce top, round soundhole, three-stripe bound body, wood inlay rosette, rosewood back/sides, nato neck, 12/19-fret rosewood fingerboard, tied rosewood bridge, three-per-side gold tuners with pearloid buttons, piezo bridge pickup, four-band EQ, available in Natural finish, disc. 2003.

	N/A	$280 - 330	$150 - 180	$629

TC-29 C – single round cutaway classic style, cedar top, round soundhole, three-stripe bound body, wood inlay rosette, rosewood back/sides, nato neck, 19-fret rosewood fingerboard, tied rosewood bridge with wood marquetry inlay, three-per-side gold tuners with pearloid tuners, piezo bridge pickup, three-band EQ, available in Natural finish, mfg. 1994-98.

	N/A	$300 - 350	$150 - 200	$650

TC-30 C – similar to the TC-28 C, except has walnut back/sides, available in Amber finish, disc. 2003.

	N/A	$280 - 330	$150 - 180	$629

TC-38 C – classic style single cutaway body, spruce top, rosewood back and sides, nato neck, three-per-side gold plated tuners, available in Pumpkin finish, mfg. 1990s.

	N/A	$275 - 325	$150 - 180	

TC-48 MC – single round cutaway classic style, figured maple top, round soundhole, three-stripe bound body, wood inlay rosette, figured maple back/sides, nato neck, 12/19-fret rosewood fingerboard, tied rosewood bridge, figured maple veneered peghead, three-per-side gold tuners with pearloid buttons, piezo bridge pickup, four-band EQ, available in Natural finish, mfg. 1994-98.

	N/A	$300 - 350	$150 - 200	$650

ACOUSTIC ELECTRIC: TS SERIES

TS-26 C – mahogany top/back/sides, abalone body purfling, nato neck, pearl diamond fingerboard inlay, black white dot bridge pins, gold diecast tuners, available in White/Black finish, mfg. 1994-98.

	N/A	$300 - 350	$150 - 200	$650

TS-33 C – single rounded cutaway body, spruce top, mahogany back/sides, nato neck, rosewood fingerboard, rosewood bridge with black pins, gold diecast tuners, available in Natural finish, disc. 2003.

	N/A	$250 - 300	$150 - 200	$569

TS-38 C – single rounded cutaway dreadnought body, spruce top, round soundhole, rosewood back/sides, nato neck, 14/20-fret rosewood fingerboard with pearl dot inlay, rosewood bridge with white bridgepins, chrome diecast tuners, available in Natural finish, disc. 2003.

	N/A	$250 - 300	$150 - 200	$559

TS-41 C – single round cutaway dreadnought style, spruce top, round soundhole, black pickguard with white outline, three-stripe bound body/rosette, daowood back/sides, nato neck, 14/20-fret bound rosewood fingerboard with pearl dot inlay, rosewood bridge with white black dot pins, three-per-side chrome diecast tuners, bridge pickup, four-band EQ control, available in Black finish, disc. 1994.

	N/A	$200 - 250	$100 - 130	$450

TS-46 C – single round cutaway dreadnought style, spruce top, round soundhole, black pickguard with white outline, three-stripe bound body/rosette, daowood back/sides, nato neck, 14/20-fret bound rosewood fingerboard with pearl dot inlay, rosewood bridge with white black dot pins, three-per-side chrome die-cast tuners, bridge pickup, four-band EQ control, available in White finish, disc. 1992.

	N/A	$200 - 250	$100 - 130	$450

TS-49 C – single round cutaway dreadnought style, mahogany top, round soundhole, black pickguard, three-stripe bound body/rosette, mahogany back/sides, nato neck, 14/20-fret bound rosewood fingerboard with pearl dot inlay, rosewood bridge with white black dot pins, bound peghead, three-per-side chrome diecast tuners, bridge pickup, four-band EQ control, available in Natural finish, disc. 1992.

	N/A	$200 - 250	$100 - 130	$450

TS-50 C – rounded cutaway dreadnought style, spruce top, round soundhole, black pickguard, three-stripe bound body/rosette, flame maple back/sides, maple neck, 20-fret bound rosewood fingerboard with pearl dot inlay, rosewood bridge with white black dot pins, body matching peghead, three-per-side chrome die-cast tuners, bridge pickup, four-band volume/EQ control, available in Blue Stain, Ebony Stain, or Red Stain finishes, disc. 1994.

	N/A	$275 - 325	$150 - 200	$600

TS-52 C MR – single round cutaway dreadnought style, ash top, round soundhole, black trilamated pickguard, ash back/sides, nato neck, 20-fret bound rosewood fingerboard with pearl dot inlay, rosewood bridge with white black dot pins, body matching bound peghead with screened logo, three-per-side chrome die cast tuners, piezo bridge pickup, four-band EQ, available in a Red Stain finish, mfg. 1994-98.

	N/A	$325 - 375	$200 - 250	$700

MSR/NOTES	100%	EXCELLENT	AVERAGE	LAST MSR

* **TS-52 C ME** – similar to the TS-52 CMR, except in an Ebony Stain finish, mfg. 1994-98.

	N/A	$325 - 375	$200 - 250	$700

TS-58 – jumbo style, cedar top, round soundhole, tortoise pickguard, three-stripe bound body, wood inlay rosette, daowood back/sides, nato neck, 14/20-fret bound rosewood fingerboard with pearl diamond dot inlay, rosewood bridge with white black dot pins, bound peghead, three-per-side gold diecast tuners, piezo bridge pickup, four-band EQ control, available in Natural finish, disc. 1998.

	N/A	$300 - 350	$150 - 200	$650

TS-60 – dreadnought style, spruce top, round soundhole, black pickguard, three-stripe bound body/rosette, rosewood back/sides, nato neck, 14/20-fret fingerboard with pearl dot inlay, rosewood bridge with white black dot pins, three-per-side chrome diecast tuners, piezo bridge pickup, four-band EQ, available in Natural finish, disc. 1994.

	N/A	$225 - 275	$125 - 175	$500

* **TS-60 C** – similar to TS-60, except has single round cutaway, disc. 1994.

	N/A	$250 - 300	$140 - 180	$550

TS-74 C – single round cutaway dreadnought style, cedar top, round soundhole, tortoise pickguard, five-stripe bound body, wood inlay rosette, daowood back/sides, nato neck, 20-fret bound rosewood fingerboard with pearl diamond inlay, rosewood bridge with white black dot pins, bound blackface peghead with screened logo, three-per-side gold diecast tuners, piezo bridge pickup, four-band EQ, available in Natural finish, mfg. 1994-98.

	N/A	$325 - 375	$175 - 225	$700

TS-90 C-DW (DARK WALNUT) – burled mahogany top/back/sides, nato neck, available in a Dark Walnut Stain finish, mfg. 1994-2003.

	N/A	$325 - 375	$175 - 225	$699

* **TS-90 C-LW** – similar to the TS-90 C-DW (Dark Walnut), except finished in a Light Walnut Stain, mfg. 1994-98.

	N/A	$325 - 375	$175 - 225	$740

TS-91 C – similar to TS-74 C, except features daowood top/back/sides, nato neck, available in Black finish, disc. 2003.

	N/A	$275 - 325	$150 - 200	$629

TS-92 C – similar to the TS-91 C, except features flame maple top/back/sides, maple neck, available in Red Stain finish, disc. 1994.

	N/A	$225 - 275	$125 - 175	$520

TS-93 C-A – similar to TS-90 C-DW, except features silky oak top/back/sides, maple neck, available in Amber finish, mfg. 1994-98.

	N/A	$325 - 375	$150 - 200	$680

TS-95 C – similar to the TS-91 C, except features flame maple top/back/sides, maple neck, available in Ebony Stain finish, disc. 1994.

	N/A	$225 - 275	$125 - 175	$520

TS-96 C – similar to the TS-91 C, except features daowood top/back/sides, nato neck, black white dot bridge pins, available in White finish, disc. 1994.

	N/A	$200 - 250	$100 - 150	$480

TS-97 C – similar to the TS-91 C, except features cedar top, daowood back/sides, nato neck, pearl diamond fingerboard inlay, gold die-cast tuners, available in Natural finish, disc. 1998.

	N/A	$275 - 325	$150 - 200	$600

TS-98 C-FM – similar to TS-93 C-A, except features flame maple top/back/sides, maple neck, available in Cherry Sunburst or Blue Stain finish, mfg. 1994-98.

	N/A	$300 - 350	$150 - 200	$680

TS-99 C – similar to the TS-91 C, except features daowood top/back/sides, nato neck, available in Walnut Sunburst finish, disc. 1994.

	N/A	$200 - 250	$125 - 150	$480

TS-612 – dreadnought style, spruce top, round soundhole, black pickguard, three-stripe bound body/rosette, rosewood back/sides, nato neck, 14/20-fret bound rosewood fingerboard with pearl dot inlay, rosewood bridge with white black dot pins, six-per-side chrome diecast tuners, piezo bridge pickup, four-band EQ, available in Natural finish, disc. 1994.

	N/A	$250 - 300	$140 - 180	$560

* **TS-612 C** – similar to 612-TS, except has single round cutaway, mfg. 1994-98.

	N/A	$325 - 375	$175 - 225	$720

ACOUSTIC ELECTRIC BASS

ES-50 C – single rounded cutaway body, spruce top, nato back and sides, round soundhole, nato neck, 14/20-fret bound rosewood fingerboard with dot inlay, two-per-side chrome diecast tuners, rosewood bridge with white black dot pins, piezo bridge pickup, two-band EQ control, available in Natural gloss finish, mfg. 2011-present.

MSR $469	$250	$135 - 175	$80 - 100	

MSR/NOTES	100%	EXCELLENT	AVERAGE	LAST MSR

ES-100 C – single rounded cutaway body, round soundhole, black pickguard, nato neck, 14/20-fret bound rosewood fingerboard with dot inlay, rosewood bridge with white black dot pins, bound peghead, two-per-side chrome diecast tuners, piezo bridge pickup, two-band EQ control, available in Maple (ES-100 C-M), Natural (ES-100 C-4), or Sunburst (ES-100 C-1) finishes, mfg. 1994-2003.

	N/A	$325 - 375	$175 - 225	$739

JAY G

Guitars previously built in Columbus, OH during the 1950s and the 1960s. See chapter on House Brands.

This trademark has been identified as a sub-brand from the budget line of Chris guitars by the Jackson-Guldan company of Columbus, OH. Source: Willie G. Moseley, *Stellas & Stratocasters*.

JAY TURSER

Instruments currently produced in Asia since 1997. Distributed by U.S. Music Corp. in Buffalo Grove, IL. Previously distributed by American Music & Sound (AM&S) in Agoura Hills, CA.

The Jay Turser brand of guitars was created by Tommy Rizzi at Music Industries Corp. in the late 1990s. Initially, Jay Turser instruments consisted of student and entry-level guitars that were based on popular American designs. As the line expanded through the 2000s, mid-level guitars and original designs have been introduced and Jay Turser currently offers a wide variety of guitars, basses, and guitar amplifiers. For more information visit their website or contact them directly.

CONTACT INFORMATION
JAY TURSER
Distributed by U.S. Music Corp.
1000 Corporate Grove Drive
Buffalo Grove, IL 60089
Phone No.: 847-949-0444
Phone No.: 800-877-6863
Fax No.: 847-949-8444
www.jayturser.com
guitar.support@usmusiccorp.com

ACOUSTIC

JTA-15S – parlor style, solid spruce top, rosewood back and sides, rosewood fingerboard, chrome tuners, available in Natural finish, mfg. 2004-06.

	N/A	$120 - 150	$70 - 90	$300

JTA-30S – dreadnought style, solid spruce top, rosewood back and sides, B/N/H binding, rosewood fingerboard, gold tuners, available in Natural Gloss or Natural Matte finish, mfg. 2004-06.

	N/A	$95 - 120	$55 - 75	$240

* **Add 5% for left-handed configuration (Model JTA-30S-LH).**
* **Add 10% for 12-string configuration (Model JTA-30S-12).**
* **Add 20% for a single cutaway and electronics (Model JTA-30SC).**

JTA-40CEQ – single cutaway thinline acoustic, select spruce top, mahogany back and sides, rosewood fingerboard with dot position markers, three-per-side tuners, rosewood bridge, four-band EQ, volume control, available in Natural, Trans. Blue, Trans. Red, or Black finish, mfg. 2001-06.

	N/A	$120 - 150	$70 - 90	$300

* **JTA-40-12CEQ** – single cutaway thinline acoustic, 12-string, select spruce top, mahogany back and sides, four-band EQ, available in Black finish, mfg. 2001-06.

	N/A	$130 - 170	$80 - 100	$330

JTAC-43 – single cutaway western-style body, mahogany top, back, and sides, B/N/H binding, rosewood fingerboard, rosewood bridge, gold tuners, available in Black, Natural Mahogany, Trans. Blue, or Trans. Red finish, mfg. 2004-06.

	N/A	$50 - 75	$30 - 40	$150

* **Add 35% for electronics.**

JTAC-45CEQ – single cutaway western-style body, spruce top, mahogany back, and sides, brown marble pearl body and headstock binding, rosewood fingerboard, rosewood bridge, gold tuners, available in Natural Gloss finish, mfg. 2004-06.

	N/A	$65 - 90	$40 - 50	$180

* **Add 35% for electronics.**

JTA-49 – slope-shouldered dreadnought body, select spruce top, mahogany back and sides, body and neck binding, rosewood fingerboard, rosewood bridge, chrome tuners, tortoiseshell pickguard, available in Vintage Sunburst finish, mfg. 2004-08.

	N/A	$60 - 80	$40 - 50	$175

* **Add 15% (Last MSR was $200) for electronics.**

JTAC-66T – thinline cutaway acoustic, spruce top, nato neck, nato back and sides, rosewood fingerboard with dot position markers, three-per-side tuners, one volume and one tone control, available in Trans. Black, Trans. Blue, or Trans. Red finish, mfg. 2001-06.

	N/A	$80 - 110	$50 - 65	$200

* **Add 15% for left-handed configuration.**

JTA-67/NG – dreadnought size acoustic, Canadian spruce top, Honduras mahogany neck, Honduras mahogany back and sides, rosewood bridge, black pickguard, dot position markers, available in Natural finish, mfg. 2001-06.

	N/A	$80 - 110	$50 - 65	$200

* **Add $20 for left-handed configuration. Add $40 for solid spruce top (JTA-67S).**

MSR/NOTES	100%	EXCELLENT	AVERAGE	LAST MSR

JTA-68NM – dreadnought size acoustic, Canadian Spruce top, mahogany back and sides, herringbone binding, Honduras Mahogany neck, bound neck and headstock, three-per-side die-cast tuners, rosewood bridge, available in Natural Matte finish, mfg. 2001-06.

	N/A	$90 - 120	$60 - 75	$230

JTA-69EQ/NM – dreadnought size cutaway acoustic, Canadian spruce top, Honduras mahogany back and sides, rosewood fingerboard with dot position markers, herringbone binding, rosewood bridge, three-per-side die-cast tuners, bound neck and headstock, four-band EQ, available in Natural Matte finish, mfg. 2001-06.

	N/A	$125 - 170	$80 - 100	$320

JTA-100 – dreadnought style, spruce top, mahogany back and sides, laser-cut Lady Liberty soundhole, rosewood fingerboard, molded back with cream binding, four-band EQ, Natural Gloss finish, mfg. 2004-06.

	N/A	$150 - 190	$95 - 120	$380

JTA-600CE – single cutaway full body acoustic, flame maple top, die-cast tuners, three-band EQ, available in Tobacco Sunburst finish, mfg. 2001-02.

	N/A	$160 - 190	$100 - 130	$349

JTNC-EQ – cutaway classical acoustic electric, spruce top, mahogany back and sides, four-band EQ, rosewood fingerboard, rosewood bridge, inlaid wood rosette, available in Natural finish, mfg. 2001-02.

	N/A	$120 - 160	$70 - 90	$299

ACOUSTIC: PREMIER SERIES

JTA-D – dreadnought, laminated spruce top, mahogany back and sides, body binding, round soundhole, 14/20-fret rosewood fingerboard with dot inlay, three-per-side white pearl die-cast tuners, rosewood bridge, available in Black, Trans. Blue, or Trans. Red finish, mfg. 2003-06.

	N/A	$90 - 130	$50 - 70	$250

JTA-DQ – dreadnought, quilted maple top, mahogany back and sides, white/black body binding, round soundhole with abalone rosette, mahogany neck, 14/20-fret rosewood fingerboard with dot and 12th fret block inlay, three-per-side white pearl die cast tuners, rosewood bridge, available in Trans. Black, Trans. Blue, Trans. Red, Purple Sunburst, or Natural Gloss finish, mfg. 2003-06.

	N/A	$120 - 170	$70 - 90	$315

* *JTA-DQ-12* – similar to the JTA-DQ, except in 12-string configuration, available in Natural Gloss finish, mfg. 2003-08.

	N/A	$125 - 175	$75 - 95	$350

JTA-DS – dreadnought, solid spruce top, flame maple back and sides, white/black body binding, round soundhole with abalone rosette, mahogany neck, 14/20-fret rosewood fingerboard with vine inlay, three-per-side gold die-cast tuners, rosewood bridge, available in Natural finish, mfg. 2003-06.

	N/A	$150 - 200	$90 - 120	$390

JTA-EGL – single cutaway, spruce top, mahogany back and sides, white/black body binding, abalone eagle soundhole, mahogany neck, 14/20-fret rosewood fingerboard with block inlay, three-per-side gold die cast tuners, rosewood bridge, active four-band EQ, available in Black, Purple Sunburst, Trans. Blue, or Trans. Red finish, mfg. 2003-06.

	N/A	$175 - 225	$110 - 140	$450

JTA-HEART – single cutaway, spruce top, mahogany back and sides, white/black body binding, abalone heart soundhole inlay, mahogany neck, 14/20-fret rosewood fingerboard with heart inlay, three-per-side chrome die-cast tuners, rosewood bridge, active four-band EQ, available in Black, Purple Sunburst, Trans. Blue, or Trans. Red finish, mfg. 2004-06.

	N/A	$200 - 250	$120 - 150	$500

JTA-SQCE – single cutaway, solid spruce top, quilt maple back and sides, abalone body binding, round soundhole with white pearl rosette, mahogany neck, 14/20-fret rosewood fingerboard with dot inlay, three-per-side gold die cast tuners, rosewood bridge, active four-band EQ, available in Trans. Black, Purple Sunburst, Trans. Blue, Trans. Red or Natural Gloss finish, mfg. 2003-06.

	N/A	$200 - 250	$120 - 150	$500

JTA-VC20 – classical style, select spruce top, mahogany back and sides, round soundhole with wood rosette, black and cream binding, mahogany neck, rosewood fingerboard, open style headstock, three-per-side white tuners, rosewood bridge, electronics, four-band EQ, Natural finish, mfg. 2003-06.

	N/A	$120 - 160	$70 - 90	$330

J.B. PLAYER

Instruments currently produced in Asia and the Artista Classical Series is produced in Spain since the 1980s. Distributed by Musicorp, Inc. in North Charleston, SC.

The J.B. Player trademark was founded in the 1980s where production was briefly based in the U.S. In 1989, MBT International bought the trademark and have continued to build and distribute the J.B Player name (MBT International later became Musicorp). J.B. Player offered a wide range of entry to beginner level acoustic guitars, electric solid body guitars, and basses. Currently J.B. Player only offers acoustic guitars and basses. For more information, visit Musicorp's website or contact them directly.

CONTACT INFORMATION
J.B. PLAYER
Distributed by Musicorp, Inc.
PO Box 63366
N. Charleston, SC 29419
Phone No.: 843-745-8501
Phone No.: 800-641-6931
Fax No.: 843-745-8502
www.musicorp.com
kmcmcpsales@kmcmusic.com

MSR/NOTES	100%	EXCELLENT	AVERAGE	LAST MSR

ACOUSTIC: ARTISTA CLASSICAL SERIES

J.B. Player's Artista Series guitars are all made in Spain.

FLAMENCO – classical-style body, Oregon pine top, sycamore back and sides, round soundhole with decorative rosette, mahogany neck, 12/19-fret rosewood fingerboard, slotted headstock with three-per-side open-style gold tuners, tied rosewood bridge, Natural finish, current mfg.

MSR $499	$375	$200 - 250	$120 - 150	

GRANADA – classical-style body, Oregon pine top, mahogany back and sides, round soundhole with decorative rosette, mahogany neck, 12/19-fret rosewood fingerboard, slotted headstock with three-per-side open-style tuners, tied rosewood bridge, Natural finish, current mfg.

MSR $359	$270	$140 - 180	$90 - 110	

MORENA – classical-style body, Oregon pine top, rosewood back and sides, round soundhole with decorative rosette, mahogany neck, 12/19-fret rosewood fingerboard, slotted headstock with three-per-side open-style tuners, tied rosewood bridge, Natural finish, current mfg.

MSR $449	$340	$175 - 225	$110 - 140	

SEGOVIA – classical-style body, solid cedar top, rosewood back and sides, round soundhole with decorative rosette, mahogany neck, 12/19-fret rosewood fingerboard, slotted headstock with three-per-side open-style gold tuners, tied rosewood bridge, Natural finish, current mfg.

MSR $675	$500	$300 - 350	$175 - 225	

ACOUSTIC: ARTIST SERIES

JBA-1010 – grand auditorium style, flame maple top, round soundhole, multiple-ply body binding, mahogany back/sides, nato neck, 14/20-fret rosewood fingerboard with dot inlay, rosewood bridge with white dot pins, three-per-side diecast tuners, available in Sunburst finish, mfg. 1998-2003.

	N/A	$150 - 200	$100 - 125	$399

JBA-1150 – auditorium style, solid cedar top, round soundhole, multiple-ply body binding, rosewood back/sides, mahogany neck, 14/20-fret rosewood fingerboard with dot inlay, rosewood bridge with white dot pins, blackface peghead, three-per-side tuners, available in Natural finish, mfg. 1998-2003.

	N/A	$225 - 275	$150 - 200	$525

JBA-1200 – dreadnought style, solid cedar top, black pickguard, round soundhole, mahogany back/sides/neck, 14/20-fret rosewood fingerboard with dot inlay, rosewood bridge with white dot pins, three-per-side diecast tuners, available in Natural finish, disc. 2003.

	N/A	$175 - 225	$100 - 150	$430

* **Add $110 for two-piece mahogany back and sides (Model JBA-1250).**
* **Add $290 for two-piece ovangkol back and sides (Model JBA-1275).**

* *JBA-1200-12* – similar to the JBA-1200, except features a 12-string configuration, six-per-side tuners, available in Natural finish, disc. 1998.

	N/A	$200 - 250	$95 - 125	$475

JBA-1500 – similar to the JBA-2000, except features mahogany back and sides, no abalone rosette, black pickguard, disc. 1998.

	N/A	$175 - 225	$90 - 120	$395

JBA-1520 – similar to the JBA-2000, except features mahogany back and sides, abalone-style rosette, black pickguard, mfg. 1998-2003.

	N/A	$130 - 170	$80 - 110	$299

JBA-2000 – dreadnought style, solid spruce top, tortoiseshell pickguard, round soundhole, four-stripe bound body, abalone rosette, rosewood back/sides, mahogany neck, 14/20-fret bound rosewood fingerboard with abalone block inlay, rosewood bridge with white black dot pins, three-per-side gold tuners, available in Natural finish, mfg. 1994-96.

	N/A	$225 - 275	$125 - 175	$540

JBA-2200 – similar to the JBA-2000, except features back and sides, herringbone rosette/body binding, bound fingerboard with pearl palm tree inlay, disc. 2003.

	N/A	$275 - 325	$175 - 225	$620

ACOUSTIC: JB SERIES (CURRENT MFG.)

JB10C – classical style, agathis top, nato back/sides/neck, body binding, open style headstock, gold tuners, natural finish, current mfg.

MSR $179	$100	$60 - 80	$35 - 45	

JB18 – auditorium style, spruce top, mahogany back/sides, multi-layer body binding, rosewood fingerboard and bridge, chrome tuners, natural finish, current mfg.

MSR $199	$110	$65 - 85	$40 - 50	

JB20 – auditorium style, spruce top, nato back/sides/neck, body binding, chrome tuners, natural finish, current mfg.

MSR $215	$120	$70 - 90	$45 - 55	

Also available in left-handed configuration (MSR $219).

MSR/NOTES	100%	EXCELLENT	AVERAGE	LAST MSR

* *JB20 12-String* – similar to the JB20, except in 12-string configuration and six-per-side tuners, current mfg.

MSR $265	$150	$85 - 115	$50 - 65	

JB36 – auditorium style, spruce (Natural finish) or nato (Black finish) top, nato back and sides, round soundhole with decorative rosette, single-ply binding, rosewood fingerboard with pearl-type inlays, three-per-side chrome tuners, rosewood bridge, available in Black or Natural finish, 36 in. overall length, current mfg.

MSR $159	$90	$50 - 65	$30 - 40	

JB85S – dreadnought style, solid spruce top, mahogany back and sides, round soundhole with diamond rosette, maple body binding, mahogany neck, 14/20-fret maple-bound rosewood fingerboard with brown dot inlays, maple-bound headstock overlay, three-per-side gold tuners, rosewood bridge, tortoise pickguard, Natural gloss finish, 25.5 in. scale, mfg. 2008-present.

MSR $259	$145	$80 - 110	$50 - 65	

JB90S – dreadnought style, solid spruce top, mahogany back/sides/neck, multi-layer body binding, rosewood fingerboard and bridge, gold tuners, Natural finish, disc. 2007.

	N/A	$110 - 140	$70 - 90	$235

ACOUSTIC: RIDGEVILLE SERIES

J.B. Player's **Ridgeville** series offered three different model acoustic guitars. The **JBR-20** Dreadnought (last MSR $229) has a spruce top, mahogany back and sides, and die-cast tuners. The **JBR-30** Dreadnought (last MSR $259) has a spruce top and ovangkol back and sides. The **JBR-10 C** classical (last MSR $199) has an agathis top, mahogany back and sides, and plank-style tuners. All models were available in a Natural finish.

ACOUSTIC: STANDARD SERIES

JB-95 COUNTRY JUMBO – jumbo style, maple top, round soundhole, three-stripe bound body/rosette, mahogany back/sides, mahogany neck, 14/20-fret rosewood fingerboard with pearl dot inlay, rosewood bridge with black bridgepins, three-per-side chrome tuners, available in Natural satin finish, mfg. 1998-2003.

	N/A	$120 - 150	$70 - 90	$290

JB-402 – dreadnought style, spruce top, round soundhole, black pickguard, bound body, five-stripe rosette, nato back/sides/neck, 14/20-fret bound rosewood fingerboard with pearl dot inlay, rosewood bridge with white black dot pins, three-per-side chrome diecast tuners, available in Natural finish, disc. 2003.

	N/A	$115 - 145	$65 - 85	$275

JB-403 – similar to JB-402, except has multiple-ply body binding, available in Natural finish, mfg. 1991-94, 1998-2003.

	N/A	$130 - 170	$80 - 110	$299

JB-405-12 – dreadnought style, 12-string configuration, spruce top, round soundhole, black pickguard, stripe bound body/rosette, ash back/sides, bound mahogany neck, 14/20-fret bound rosewood fingerboard with pearl dot inlay, rosewood bridge with white black dot pins, six-per-side chrome diecast tuners, available in Natural finish, disc. 2003.

	N/A	$140 - 180	$90 - 110	$335

JB-407 – dreadnought style, ash top, round soundhole, black pickguard, bound body, five-stripe rosette, ash back/sides, nato mahogany neck, 14/20-fret bound fingerboard with pearl dot inlay, rosewood bridge with white black dot pins, three-per-side chrome diecast tuners, available in Tobacco Sunburst finish, disc. 2003.

	N/A	$110 - 140	$60 - 80	$280

This model had an optional acoustic pickup, active volume/three-band EQ (JB-407 E). This option discontinued in 1998.

JB-408 – similar to the JB-407, except features mahogany neck, available in Trans. Blonde finish, mfg. 1998-2003.

	N/A	$135 - 175	$80 - 110	$325

JB-409 – dreadnought style, spruce top, round soundhole, black pickguard, bound body, five-stripe rosette, mahogany back/sides/neck, 14/20-fret bound fingerboard with pearl dot inlay, rosewood bridge with white black dot pins, three-per-side chrome diecast tuners, available in Black, Natural, or Tobacco Sunburst finish, mfg. 1998-2003.

	N/A	$130 - 170	$80 - 100	$315

* *JBL-409* – similar to the JB-409, except features a left-handed configuration, available in Black, Natural, or Tobacco Sunburst finish, mfg. 1998-2003.

	N/A	$140 - 180	$90 - 110	$330

JB-450 – dreadnought style, spruce top, round soundhole, black pickguard, imitation abalone bound body/rosette, ash back/sides, mahogany neck, 14/20-fret bound rosewood fingerboard with hexagon imitation abalone inlay, rosewood bridge with white black dot pins, three-per-side chrome diecast tuners, available in Natural finish, disc. 2003.

	N/A	$130 - 160	$80 - 100	$315

JB-502 – dreadnought style, spruce top, round soundhole, black pickguard, bound body, five-ring rosette, mahogany finishes nato back/sides, nato neck, 14/20-fret rosewood fingerboard with pearl dot inlay, rosewood bridge with black bridgepins, three-per-side chrome diecast tuners, available in Natural finish, mfg. 1998-2003.

	N/A	$150 - 190	$90 - 110	$360

MSR/NOTES	100%	EXCELLENT	AVERAGE	LAST MSR

* *JB-502-12* – similar to JB-502 except features a 12-string configuration, six-per-side tuners, available in Natural finish, mfg. 1998-2003.

	N/A	$160 - 210	$120 - 140	$395

JB-505 – classical style, spruce top, round soundhole, herringbone bound body, wooden inlay rosette, ash back/sides, mahogany neck, 12/18-fret rosewood fingerboard, rosewood bridge, three-per-side chrome tuners with nylon buttons, available in Natural finish, disc. 1994.

	N/A	$100 - 135	$60 - 80	$260

JB-506 – similar to JB-502 except features a blackface peghead, available in Violin (shaded Brown Sunburst) finish, mfg. 1998-2003.

	N/A	$150 - 200	$110 - 130	$375

JB-1000 – dreadnought style, spruce top, oval soundhole, black pickguard, three-stripe bound body/rosette, mahogany back/sides/neck, 14/20-fret bound rosewood fingerboard with pearl dot inlay, rosewood bridge with white black dot pins, three-per-side chrome tuners, available in Black or White (White finish model has black chrome tuners) finishes, disc. 1996.

	N/A	$140 - 170	$100 - 120	$325

• **Add $70 for flame maple top and jacaranda back/sides (available in Natural finish).**

JB-5000 – classical style, spruce top, round soundhole, bound body, wooden inlay rosette, mahogany back/sides/neck, 12/18-fret rosewood fingerboard, rosewood bridge, three-per-side gold tuners with pearloid buttons, available in Natural finish, disc. 1994.

	N/A	$150 - 180	$110 - 130	$350

JB-8000 – similar to the JB-1000, except features round soundhole, bound body, five-stripe rosette, rosewood back/sides, available in Natural finish, disc. 1994.

	N/A	$170 - 220	$120 - 150	$425

JB-9000 – similar to the JB-1000, except features round soundhole, bound body, five-stripe rosette, available in Tobacco Sunburst finish, disc. 1996.

	N/A	$160 - 210	$120 - 140	$395

* *JB-9000-12* – similar to JB-9000, except has 12 strings, black white dot pins, six-per-side tuners, available in Natural finish.

	N/A	$170 - 220	$120 - 145	$410

ACOUSTIC ELECTRIC: ARTIST SERIES

JB-300 E – single round cutaway dreadnought style, maple top, black pickguard, round soundhole, three-stripe bound body/rosette, ash back/sides, mahogany neck, 20-fret bound rosewood fingerboard with pearl dot inlay, rosewood bridge with white black dot pins, bound blackface peghead with screened logo, three-per-side chrome tuners, acoustic pickup, volume/presence/three-band EQ control, available in Brownburst, Cherryburst, Natural, or White finishes, mfg. 1994-2003.

	N/A	$175 - 225	$110 - 140	$440

JBA-50 CEQ NYLON STRING – single rounded cutaway body, flame maple top, round soundhole, maple back/sides, mahogany neck, 12/19-fret rosewood fingerboard, rosewood tied bridge, slotted headstock, three-per-side gold tuners with white buttons, piezo pickup, active electronics, available in Sunburst finish, mfg. 1998-2003.

	N/A	$225 - 275	$125 - 175	$525

JBA-65 CEQ – single rounded cutaway folk-style body, flame maple top, round soundhole, ash back/sides, mahogany neck, 14/20-fret rosewood fingerboard with white diamond inlay, rosewood bridge with white bridgepins, three-per-side gold tuners, piezo pickup, three-band EQ, presence control, active electronics, pop-out battery compartment, available in Natural (JBA-65 NCEQ) or Tobacco Sunburst (JBA-65 CEQ) finishes, mfg. 1998-2003.

	N/A	$250 - 300	$150 - 200	$599

JBA-97 CEQ – single rounded cutaway jumbo-style body, spruce top, round soundhole, mahogany back/sides/neck, 14/20-fret rosewood fingerboard with white dot inlay, rosewood bridge with white bridgepins, three-per-side gold tuners, piezo pickup, three-band EQ, presence control, active electronics, pop-out battery compartment, available in Natural satin finishes, mfg. 1998-2003.

	N/A	$215 - 265	$120 - 160	$495

JBA-260 – single cutaway alder body with carved tone chambers, spruce top, f-hole, mahogany neck, 21-fret rosewood fingerboard with dot inlay, rosewood bridge with black pins, six-per-side diecast tuners, piezo pickup, volume/tone controls, available in Natural finish, disc. 1998.

	N/A	$350 - 425	$200 - 250	$740

JBA-910 – single round cutaway body, solid cedar top, round soundhole, body binding, three-ring rosette, mahogany back/sides/neck, 14/20-fret bound rosewood fingerboard with pearl dot inlay, rosewood bridge with black bridgepins, three-per-side gold Schaller tuners with white pearloid buttons, piezo pickup, three-band EQ, active electronics, 1/4 in. and XLR outputs, available in Natural finishes, disc. 2003.

	N/A	$350 - 425	$200 - 250	$775

KJ-330-PU – single rounded cutaway body, tiger maple top, oval soundhole, abalone bound body/rosette, tiger maple back/sides, mahogany neck, 20-fret bound rosewood fingerboard with pearl split block inlay, rosewood bridge with white black dot pins, three-per-side gold tuners with amber buttons, acoustic pickup, four-band EQ, active electronics, available in Brownburst or Natural finishes, mfg. 1994-2003.

	N/A	$300 - 350	$175 - 225	$675

MSR/NOTES	100%	EXCELLENT	AVERAGE	LAST MSR

KJ-609-WPU – single round cutaway body, spruce top, round soundhole, three-stripe bound body, abalone rosette, maple back/sides, mahogany neck, 14/20-fret rosewood fingerboard with pearl dot inlay, 12th fret pearl horns inlay, rosewood bridge with white black dot pins, three-per-side chrome tuners, acoustic pickup, active four-band EQ, active electronics, available in Natural finish, mfg. 1994-2003.

	N/A	$300 - 350	$175 - 225	$660

KJ-705-WPU – similar to the KJ-609-WPU, except features mahogany back/sides/neck, available in Tobacco Sunburst finish, disc. 1998.

	N/A	$350 - 425	$200 - 250	$720

ACOUSTIC ELECTRIC: JBEA SERIES (CURRENT MFG.)

JBEA15 "BLOOM" – single rounded cutaway thin body, spruce top, basswood back and sides, round soundhole with three ring rosette, multi-ply top binding, single-ply back binding, Catalpa neck, 14/22-fret bound rosewood fingerboard with dot inlays, matching finish headstock, three-per-side chrome tuners, rosewood bridge, four-band electronics, available in Aqua Green, Black, Pink, or Powder Blue finish, mfg. 2007-present.

MSR $199	$110	$65 - 85	$40 - 50	

JBEA20 – single cutaway dreadnought, spruce top, nato back/sides/neck, single ply b/n binding, tortoiseshell pickguard, electronics, chrome tuners, natural finish, current mfg.

MSR $219	$120	$70 - 95	$45 - 55	

JBEA25 – single rounded cutaway dreadnought style body, spruce top, mahogany back and sides, round soundhole with decorative rosette, mahogany neck, 14/20-fret rosewood fingerboard with brown dot inlays, matching finish headstock overlay, three-per-side chrome tuners, rosewood bridge, pickguard, Barcus-Berry Realm I pickup and electronics, available in Black, Natural, Trans. Blue, or Walnut finish, 25.5 in. scale, current mfg.

MSR $219	$120	$70 - 95	$45 - 55	

JBEA35 – offset double cutaway uniquely-shaped body, spruce top, mahogany back and sides, round soundhole with large ring rosette, mahogany neck, 14/19-fret bound rosewood fingerboard with offset dot inlays, matching finish headstock overlay, three-per-side chrome tuners, rosewood bridge, one single coil pickup mounted in soundhole and one saddle pickup, Barcus-Berry Realm II electronics, available in Black, Natural, Sunburst, or Trans. Blue finish, current mfg.

MSR $249	$140	$80 - 105	$50 - 65	

JBEA60 – single cutaway grand concert, spruce top, agathis back/sides nato neck, single ply b/n binding, redwood fingerboard and bridge, four-band EQ, chrome tuners, Natural, Red Sunburst, or Trans. Black finish, disc. 2007.

	N/A	$120 - 150	$75 - 95	$280

JBEA80 – single rounded cutaway dreadnought style body, solid spruce top, mahogany back and sides, round soundhole with three-ring decorative rosette, multi-ply body binding, mahogany neck, 14/20-fret bound rosewood fingerboard with pearl dot inlays, three-per-side chrome tuners, rosewood bridge, tortoise pickguard, four-band electronics, Natural gloss finish, 25.5 in. scale, disc. 2007.

	N/A	$130 - 160	$75 - 100	$299

JBEA85 – single rounded cutaway dreadnought style body, solid spruce top, mahogany back and sides, round soundhole with diamond rosette, maple body binding, mahogany neck, 14/20-fret maple-bound rosewood fingerboard with brown dot inlays, maple-bound headstock overlay, three-per-side gold tuners, rosewood bridge, tortoise pickguard, Barcus-Berry Realm III pickup and electronics, Natural gloss finish, 25.5 in. scale, current mfg.

MSR $369	$200	$120 - 160	$75 - 95	

ACOUSTIC ELECTRIC BASS

JBA-3000 EAB – single round cutaway folk-style, select spruce top, round soundhole, three-stripe bound body/rosette, mahogany back/sides/neck, 22-fret bound rosewood fingerboard with pearl dot inlay, rosewood strings thru bridge, two-per-side chrome tuners, acoustic pickup, active three-band EQ, available in Natural finish, mfg. 1994-2003.

	N/A	$300 - 350	$175 - 225	$720

JBEAB 3500/3600/3700 – single cutaway body, spruce or ash top, mahogany back and sides, abalone body binding, abalone rosette, rosewood fingerboard and bridge, four-band EQ, two-per-side gold tuners, Natural, Trans. Black, or Trans. Red finish, disc. 2010.

	$330	$175 - 225	$110 - 140	$440

JBEAB 4000 – five-string configuration, single cutaway body, flame maple top, mahogany back/sides/neck, abalone body binding, abalone rosette, rosewood fingerboard and bridge, four-band EQ, 3/2-per-side gold tuners, Natural finish, disc. 2010.

	$350	$190 - 240	$120 - 150	$465

JDS

Instruments previously built in Asia. Distributed by Wolf Imports of St. Louis, MO.

JDS Limited Edition instruments were medium quality acoustic and solid body electric guitars that feature designs based on popular American classics.

JEDSON

Instruments previously produced in Japan from the late 1960s through the late 1970s.

The Jedson trademark appears on entry to student level acoustic guitars; some models with original design and some models based on classic American designs. source: Tony Bacon and Paul Day, *The Guru's Guitar Guide*.

JHS

Instruments previously built in Japan during the late 1970s.

The initials in the JHS trademark were the initials of the UK importer John Hornby Skewes, who founded his import company in 1965 (See Encore). The instruments featured both original designs as well as those based on classic American designs. The line focused primarily on solid body guitars, much like the Encore line today Source: Tony Bacon and Paul Day, *The Guru's Guitar Guide*.

JISHENG

Instruments currently produced in China. Currently there is no U.S. distributor.

Jisheng Musical Instruments Manufacturing Ltd. is currently offering a wide range of classical and dreadnought acoustic guitar models, as well as some acoustic/electric dreadnought models (some with single cutaway bodies). The company also produces violin models, and numerous gig bag/carrying bags for guitars, drums, and other musical instruments.

JOHN HOW GUITARS

Instruments currently produced in Cool, CA since the 1990s.

Luthier John How builds guitars at his shop in the Sierra Foothills in Northern California. How has played guitars since the 1970s and played in several bands during the 1980s, but he did not get involved into building until he met violin maker John Harrison who helped him build a violin. After his violin, he decided to build a guitar and his first piece was a dreadnought-shaped guitar. How has since focused on smaller body sizes, specifically inspired by Gibson's L Series. How has also gained a reputation for his ladder bracing that he employs on select guitars. How offers guitars in parlor, concert, and grand concert-sized bodies and are available with ladder bracing or traditional X bracing. He also offers an "FP" model that stands for fingerpicker. Prices start at $3,295 for ladder braced parlor and concert guitars and at $3,695 for ladder braced grand concert and all other X-braced guitars. Several options are available as well. For more information, visit John How's website or contact him directly.

CONTACT INFORMATION
JOHN HOW GUITARS
2395 Indian Rock Rd.
Cool, CA 95614
Phone No.: 530-863-6137
www.johnhowguitars.com
johow@johnhowguitars.com

JOHN PEARSE

Instruments previously built in Center Valley, PA between 1996 and 1998. Distributed by Breezy Ridge Instruments, Inc. in Center Valley, PA.

Starting with Herman Weissenborn's unusual styling, Breezy Ridge Instruments modified the design specifications and created a unique new generation of slide guitars. The John Pearse Vintage Acoustic Steel Guitars were available in four different models for the time span of about two years. If the company name seems familiar, it's because Breezy Ridge is connected with John Pearse Strings - and John Pearse Strings has been producing guitar strings for quite some time.

All models feature 37.875 in. overall body length, 2.875 in. body depth, 10.25 in. treble bout width, and 15.375 in. bass bout width. The **#100 ACJ** (last MSR $1,695) has a solid acajoux top/back/sides/fingerboard, rosewood bridge, orange wood binding, and a vintage satin finish. The **#200 APM** (last MSR $1,795) has an Engelmann spruce top, maple back and sides, rosewood fingerboard/bridge/binding, and vintage satinized Gold varnish; while the **#300 BW** has figured manzoniza walnut back/sides/fingerboard, rosewood and orange wood rope binding (last MSR $1,995). Pearse's **#400 BAF** (last MSR $1,995) has highly figured afromosia top/back/sides/fingerboard, rosewood bridge, rosewood and orange wood rope binding, and a vintage satin finish.

JOHNSON

Instruments currently produced in Asia since the mid-1990s. Distributed by the Music Link in Brisbane, CA.

Johnson is a trademark of The Music Link in Brisbane, CA and they offer a wide range of acoustic guitars and resonators, as well as electric guitars, guitar amplifiers, and other music related accessories. Prices are mainly aimed at the entry level and student guitarists, however they have recently introduced some higher end models. For more information, visit Johnson's website or contact The Music Link directly.

CONTACT INFORMATION
JOHNSON
Distributed by The Music Link
31067 San Clemente Street
Hayward, CA 94544
Phone No.: 415-570-0970
Fax No.: 415-570-0651
www.johnsongtr.com
info@johnsongtr.com

ACOUSTIC: DREADNOUGHTS & JUMBOS

The **Carolina Series** were designed by Greg Rich, produced between 2006 and 2008, and they represent Johnson's higher end acoustic guitars. Models in the Carolina Series I include the **JD-16** (disc. last MSR was $400), **JD-17** (disc. last MSR was $450), **JO-16** (disc. last MSR was $400), and the **JO-17** (disc. last MSR was $450). The Carolina Series II feature solid back and sides and models include the **JD-26** (disc. last MSR was $600), **JD-27** (disc. last MSR was $800), **JO-26** (disc. last MSR was $600), and the **JO-27** (disc. last MSR was $800).

MSR/NOTES	100%	EXCELLENT	AVERAGE	LAST MSR

The **Herringbone Series** feature herringbone purfling and rosette. Models include the **Herringbone Dreadnought JD-D30** (MSR $195), the **JG-D35** with a solid spruce top (MSR $237), **Herringbone 000** (MSR $184), **Herringbone 000 Electric** (MSR $299), **Herringbone 000 Solid Top** (MSR $232), and the **Herringbone 000 Electric Solid Top** (MSR $339).

The **Songwriter Series I** feature a Canadian Sitka spruce top and they are available as a six-string dreadnought **JG-670** (MSR $185), twelve-string dreadnought **JG-670-12** (MSR $250), and a twelve-string dreadnought left-handed **JG-674-12** (MSR $290).

The **Songwriter Series II** feature solid tops and are available as a JD-06 dreadnought with mahogany back and sides (MSR $210), **JD-06-12** dreadnought 12-string (MSR $270), **JD-06-CFE** dreadnought cutaway with mahogany back and sides and electronics, **JD-07** dreadnought with rosewood back and sides ($240), **JO-06** 000-style with mahogany back and sides (MSR $210), **JO-07** 000-style with rosewood back and sides (MSR $240), **JJ-06** jumbo with mahogany back and sides (MSR $250), and the **JJ-06-CFE** jumbo cutaway with mahogany back and sides and electronics (MSR $380).

The **Player Series** are Johnson's entry-level series and models include the **JG-608**, **JG-610** dreadnought (MSR $110), **JG-610 3/4** (MSR $90), **JG-610 1/2** (MSR $90), **618** (MSR $130), **JG-620** (MSR $150), **JG-620-C Cutaway** (MSR $180), **JG-620-CE** cutaway electric (MSR $227), **JG-624-C** left-handed model (MSR $200), and the **JG-624CE** left handed electric cutaway (MSR $247). The **JG-650-T** (MSR $179) is a single cutaway dreadnought with electronics. The **JG-420** (MSR $160) is a 000-sized guitar.

The **Red Cliff Mahogany Dreadnought** features an all-mahogany body and is available as a regular dreadnought (MSR $185), cutaway dreadnought (MSR $195), cutaway dreadnought with electronics (MSR $299).

Other models include The Jumbo Cutaway **JG-740** (disc. last MSR was $199), **Player Deluxe Dreadnought** (disc. last MSR was $172), and the **JG-TR1 Trailblazer** (MSR $140) is a small bodied travel-size guitar.

Acoustic basses include the **JG-622-E** Deep Body Jumbo (MSR $330), **JG-672-E** Songwriter Series Bass (MSR $360), and the **JG-702-CE** cutaway acoustic/electric bass (MSR $309).

ACOUSTIC MODELS – various designs, spruce tops, various back and sides, various appointments, various finishes, current mfg.

Low End	$80 - 120	$50 - 60	$30 - 40
Middle	$100 - 140	$60 - 80	$40 - 50
High End	$150 - 250	$90 - 120	$50 - 70

ACOUSTIC: METAL BODY & RESONATORS

Resonator models feature chrome-plated bell brass bodies, mahogany necks, 14/19-fret rosewood fingerboards, and three-per-side Gotoh tuners. The **JM-998 Style O** is modeled after the pre-WWII guitars and retails for $678. The **JM-998-C Style 0-Cutaway** has a single rounded cutaway body (disc. Last MSR $1,650). It was also available with a biscuit pickup as the **JM-998-CE** (disc. Last MSR $1,850). Other Sterling Style O models include the full body **JM-998-D Style 0** is the same as the cutaway model (disc., Last MSR $895); the **JM-998-R Style 0** full body model has a different pattern on the resonator plate (disc., Last MSR $895).

Johnson Tricone resonator guitars are modeled after the original, pre-World War II guitars. Models included chrome-plated bell brass bodies, mahogany necks, 12/19-fret rosewood fingerboards, and three-per-side Gotoh tuners. The **JM-991 Style I** plain body (no design) model lists at $824. The JM-991 Style I Squareneck is also available (MSR $854). The **JM-992 Style II** (disc., Last MSR $2,295) has the Wild Rose engraved design; the **JM-993 Style III** (disc., Last MSR $2,995) has the engraved Lily of the Valley design; and the **JM-993 Style IV** (disc. Last MSR $3,595) has the engraved Chrysanthemum design. There are also painted resonators available, model **JM-996**.

Johnson wood body resonators typically have spruce or mahogany bodies with different types of resonators. The **JR-200 Chicago Blues** (disc., last MSR was $328) has a die-cast Spider Bridge, is available with a roundneck or squareneck, and comes in Blueburst or Sunburst finish. The **JR-400 Nashville Slide Model** (disc., last MSR was $499) has a Sandcast Spider Bridge, is meant for slide guitar, and was available in Natural, Mahogany, Sunburst, or Cherryburst finish. The **JR-410 Delta Blues** (MSR $430) is available in roundneck or squareneck configurations. The **JR-440 Bass** (disc., last MSR was $595, $675 with a pickup) is the bass equivilent to the JR-400. The **JR-500 Classic Trolian** (disc., last MSR was $495) has MOP position markers and a hard maple biscuit bridge. The **JR-520-EM Electric Swamp Stomper** (MSR $440) is like the JR-500 except has a single cutaway and a built in humbucking pickup with a spun aluminum resonator. The **JR-550 Bottle Slide Triolian** (MSR $370) is a wood body resonator with a slotted headstock. This model is also available as the **JR-550-FEN** (MSR $450).

JOHNSON GUITARS

Instruments previously built in Talkkeetna, AK during the 1980s and 1990s.

Luthier Johnson started building guitars in 1981. Originally working out of a gutted R.V. trailer, Johnson operated a one-man shop located in his home in rural Alaska, located at the base of Mt. McKinley (North America's tallest mountain). Johnson narrowed down his line of guitar models to a few select models; and as the single builder gave close attention to each commissioned guitar during construction. Johnson offered such custom options as a custom size or design, Englemann spruce or cedar tops, flame walnut back and sides, and onboard electronics. A standard hard shell case was included in the retail prices.

Johnson offered five acoustic models and one archtop model. All models featured a Sitka spruce top, East Indian rosewood back and sides, 25.5 in.scale ebony fingerboard. The **Size A** Concert listed at $2,000, and was also available in a Classical version at $2,500. The **Size C** Grand Auditorium listed at $2,000, as well as the **Size D** Dreadnought and the **Size E** Jumbo.

The single cutaway **American Archtop** model had a hand carved Sitka or Engelmann spruce top, flame maple back, sides, and neck, two f-holes, and an ebony fingerboard, tailpiece, and bridge (last list price was $4,000).

MSR/NOTES	100%	EXCELLENT	AVERAGE	LAST MSR

JON KAMMERER GUITARS

Instruments currently manufactured by Jon Kammerer Guitars located in Keokuk, IA, since 2000.

CONTACT INFORMATION
JON KAMMERER GUITARS
222 Timea Street
Keokuk, IA 52632
Phone No.: 319-526-7651
Fax No.: 319-526-7649
www.jonkammererguitars.com
jonkammerer@earthlink.net

Luthier Jon Kammerer originally started manufacturing his unique acoustic instruments because of a 1995 thesis project for industrial design school. After much research, it was determined that up to two-thirds of the sound waves in an acoustic guitar bounce into a corner and directly back onto themselves, canceling each other. Also, the standard boxy appearance of an acoustic guitar had not been changed for a long time. This led to his experimentation with both ceramic and fiberglass guitar bodies. Utilizing state-of-the-art CAD/CAM software and computer controlled milling machines, every wood part in a Kammerer guitar is machine made to high tolerances. The unique contoured body is cut out of two blanks, then precisely glued at the center. All Kammerer instruments include a dual action truss rod, four-screw neck, Gotoh tuning machines, cast acrylic saddle and nut, strap mounting buttons, and a hard shell case. In 2002, Jon started producing electric guitars as well. For more information or custom ordering, contact Kammerer directly or visit his website.

Jon Kammerer makes both acoustics and acoustic electrics, with or without cutaway, and in various colors/finishes. A standard satin acoustic guitar is (MSR $995), gloss acoustic guitar (MSR $1,250), single cutaway satin (MSR $1,085), and a single cutaway gloss (MSR $1,430). Options include one flame color inlay (MSR $200), multi color flame inlay ($300), etched flame inlay ($50), L.R. Baggs pickup with preamp ($200+), single cutaway body ($180), deep body ($100), translucent color finish ($200), or solid primary color ($200).

JOSHUA GUITARS

Instruments previously manufactured in Northridge, CA during the 1990s.

Joshua guitars feature quality woods with sound ports on the side of the body. Joshua guitars were produced in the 1990s and possibly into the early 2000s. These guitars were built in California and offered at a competitive price point.

ACOUSTIC ELECTRIC

Joshua Guitars utilize maple tops (available in four different Sunburst colors), and a glass fiber deep back body with onboard four-band EQ peizo pickup system. Models included the **JAE-750F** ($375 last MSR), the **JAE-850F** ($389 last MSR), and the **JAE-900** ($399 last MSR). Newer models released included the **JSP-1000** and the **JSP-2000 AE**.

JAE MODELS – glass fiber deep back body, maple top, various appointments, four-band electronics, various finishes, mfg. 1990s.

Low End	N/A	$125 - 175	$75 - 95	
High End	N/A	$175 - 250	$95 - 125	$375-400

JSP MODELS – higher end models than the JAE series, flamed maple tops, various other features, mfg. late 1990s-early 2000s.

	N/A	$200 - 300	$100 - 150

J. REYNOLDS

Instruments currently produced in Asia. Distributed by Musicorp, Inc. in North Charleston, SC.

CONTACT INFORMATION
J. REYNOLDS
Distributed by Musicorp, Inc.
PO Box 63366
N. Charleston, SC 29419
Phone No.: 843-745-8501
Phone No.: 800-641-6931
Fax No.: 843-745-8502
www.musicorp.com
sales.kmcmcp@kmcmusic.com

J. Reynolds offers entry level guitars based on popular American designs at a competitive price. For more information visit their website.

Student-sized acoustic models include the **JR12S** (MSR $120), **JR14** (MSR $95), **JR15S** (MSR $125), **JR45** (MSR $130), **JR60** (disc. 2010, last MSR was $125), and the **JR68S** (disc. 2010, last MSR was $180). Nylon classical acoustic models include the **JRC10** (MSR $125), **JRC10E** (2008-present, MSR $185), **JR12N** (MSR $120), and the **JR15N** (MSR $125). Dreadnought acoustic models include the **JR65** (MSR $140), **JR70** (MSR $165), **JR70AE** (MSR $205), and the **JR78S** (MSR $210). Other models include the **JRC18S** (disc., last MSR was $170) and the **JR1000** acoustic/electric bass (MSR $250).

JTG OF NASHVILLE

Instruments previously built in Japan and Mexico. Distributed by JTG of Nashville in Nashville, TN.

The JTG of Nashville company imported Japanese and Mexican acoustic guitars. JTG is no longer importing guitars and they focus mainly on children's toys and books.

J3

Guitars previously produced overseas. Distributed by Codel Enterprises in Bethel, CT.

Codel Enterprises imported the J3 guitar line that included acoustic guitars as well as electric guitars and basses. These guitars are mainly entry level to the intermediate guitar player.

JUDD GUITARS

Instruments previously built in Cranbrook (British Columbia), Canada.

Judd custom instruments were produced in Cranbrook, British Columbia. Very little information is known about the company and what kind of guitars they produced.

JUNIOR

Instruments previously produced by Gibson between 1919 and 1926. See chapter on House Brands.

This trademark has been identified as a Gibson built budget line available from 1919 through 1926. The pegheads carry no logo, and essentially are no-frills versions of low-end Gibsons. They will have a label different from the standard Gibson label of the time, but still credit Gibson as the manufacturer. As a Gibson-built budget line instrument these guitars do not have an adjustable truss rod in the neck. Source: Walter Carter, *Gibson Guitars: 100 Years of an American Icon*.

NOTES

K SECTION
KAKOS, STEPHEN

Instruments currently built in Mound, MN since 1984.

CONTACT INFORMATION
KAKOS, STEPHEN
1720 Finch Lane
Mound, MN 55364
Phone No.: 952-472-4732
kakosg@aol.com

Luthier Stephen Kakos began building classical guitars in 1972, and turned to full time building in 1975. Kakos concentrates specifically on classical acoustics, although he has built a few flamenco guitars on request. His Standard Model has Indian rosewood back and sides, Engelmann spruce or cedar top, mahogany or Spanish cedar neck, Sloan cast bronze tuners, and a French Polish finish (Retail $6,000 & up). In addition to guitar building, Kakos also performs some repairs and restorations. For further information on models and pricing, please contact luthier Kakos directly.

KALAMAZOO

Acoustic guitars built by Gibson between the late 1930s and early 1940s. See chapter on House Brands.

In the late 1930s, the Gibson guitar company decided to offer their own entry level guitars. While similar to models built for other distributors (Cromwell, Fascinator, or Capital) in construction, the Kalamazoo line was originally only offered for about five years. Models included flattop and archtop acoustics, lap steels (and amps), and mandolins.

Pre-war Kalamazoo instruments, like other Gibson budget instruments, do not have an adjustable truss rod (a key difference), have different construction techniques, and have no identifying Gibson logo.

In the mid-1960s, Gibson again released an entry level series of guitars under the Kalamazoo trademark, except all models were electric solid body guitars (except a flattop acoustic). The body profile of late 1960s models then switched to even dual cutaways. The second run of Kalamazoo models came to an end in the early 1970s. These post-war models do feature an adjustable truss rod.

Kalamazoo serial numbers are impressed into the back of the headstock, and feature six digits like the regular Gibson line. However, the Kalamazoo numbers do not match or correspond with the Gibson serialization. Sources: Walter Carter, *Gibson Guitars: 100 Years of an American Icon* and George Gruhn and Walter Carter: *Gruhn's Guide to Vintage Guitars*.

MSR/NOTES	100%	EXCELLENT	AVERAGE	LAST MSR

ACOUSTIC

KG-11 – flattop acoustic, mahogany back and sides, binding on top, squared peghead, no pickguard, 14.75 in. width, 17.5 in. long, Sunburst top with Mahogany back and sides finish, mfg. 1933-1941.

	N/A	$875 - 1,100	$525 - 650	

In 1936, a pickguard was introduced and followed the contour of the body. This model was also available as the Senior, which featured a firestripe pickguard and Senior on the peghead. A tenor version of this model was also produced.

KG-14 – flattop acoustic, mahogany back and sides, rosewood fingerboard, binding on top, pickguard that follows contour of body, Gibson L-0 size, Sunburst finish, mfg. 1936-1940.

	N/A	$1,200 - 1,500	$750 - 950	

* **KHG-14 Hawaiian** – similar to the KG-14, except in Hawaiian configuration with a 12-fret neck, high nut, and straight saddle, available in Sunburst finish, mfg. 1936-1941.

	N/A	$1,200 - 1,500	$750 - 950	

* **KTG-14 Tenor** – similar to the KG-14, except in four-string tenor configuration with two-per-side tuners, available in Sunburst finish, mfg. 1936-1940.

	N/A	$800 - 1,000	$475 - 600	

KG-16 – acoustic archtop, spruce top, mahogany back and sides, f-holes, black pickguard, binding on top, rosewood fingerboard with dot inlay, adjustable bridge with trapeze tailpiece, Gibson L-30 size, Sunburst finish, mfg. 1939-1941.

	N/A	$1,050 - 1,300	$625 - 750	

In late 1936, the back recieved binding, and Sunburst finish was on the entire guitar. A tenor and Hawaiian version of this guitar were both produced.

KG-21 – acoustic archtop, spruce top, mahogany back and sides, f-holes, black pickguard, binding on top, rosewood fingerboard with dot inlay, adjustable bridge with trapeze tailpiece, Gibson L-50 size, 14.75 in. wide, Sunburst finish, mfg. 1936-1941.

	N/A	$1,000 - 1,250	$600 - 750	

In late 1936, the back recieved binding, and Sunburst finish was on the entire guitar. A tenor and Hawaiian version of this guitar were both produced.

KG-22 – acoustic archtop, carved spruce top, carved maple back and sides, pickguard, binding on body, rosewood fingerboard with dot inlay, adjustable bridge with trapeze tailpiece, Gibson L-50 size, 16 in. wide, Sunburst finish, mfg. 1940-1942.

	N/A	$1,000 - 1,250	$600 - 750	

A tenor and Hawaiian model were available.

MSR/NOTES	100%	EXCELLENT	AVERAGE	LAST MSR

KG-31 – acoustic archtop, spruce top, mahogany back and sides, f-holes, single-bound pickguard, binding on body, rosewood fingerboard with dot inlay, adjustable bridge with trapeze tailpiece, Gibson L-50 size, 16 in. wide, Sunburst finish, mfg. 1935-1940.

	N/A	$875 - 1,100	$525 - 650	

In 1936, binding was introduced on the entire body, pickguard, and fingerboard. A tenor and plectrum model were both available.

KG-32 – acoustic archtop, spruce top, maple back and sides, f-holes, single-bound pickguard, binding on body, rosewood fingerboard with dot inlay, adjustable bridge with trapeze tailpiece, Gibson L-50 size, 14.75 in. wide, Sunburst finish, mfg. 1939-1942.

	N/A	$1,000 - 1,250	$600 - 750	

An oriole model with a bird on the headstock was produced in Natural finish between 1940 and 1942. 1 Hawaiian model was produced.

KALIL

Instruments currently built in McComb, MS.

Luthier Edward E. Kalil builds instruments to custom order. Kalil currently offers acoustic steel and nylon models, as well as solid body electrics. Costs will vary due to complexity of the design and appointments.

Kalil began building guitars after attending a class at Guitar Research and Design (GRD) run by Charles Fox in South Strafford, VT. Kalil's class instructor was George Morris. Kalil has been a member of the Guild of American Luthiers (G.A.L.) since 1981, and a member of A.S.I.A. (Association of Stringed Instrument Artisans) since 1988.

Kalil instruments can be easily identified by the "Kalil" headstock logo. Kalil also offers the Lick En Stik travel guitar, a full-scale instrument with a compact body and built-in amp (with variable distortion). For further information, visit Kalil's website or contact him directly.

CONTACT INFORMATION
KALIL
132 S. Front Street
McComb, MS 39648
Phone No.: 504-450-5468
members.aol.com/edekalil/eddie.html
edekalil@aol.com

KAMICO

Acoustic guitars previously produced by Kay in Chicago, IL during the late 1940s and early 1950s. See chapter on House Brands.

Kamico was a House Brand of the Kay Guitar company that was started in the late 1940s. As one of the leading suppliers of House Brand guitars, Kay also supplied the Kamico entry level budget line of guitars to various musical instrument distributors. Source: Willie G. Moseley, *Stellas & Stratocasters*.

KANSAS

Instruments previously built near Lawrence, KS between circa 1910 and the early 1940s.

The Kansas guitar company, located outside of Lawrence, KS built acoustic guitars from circa 1910 to World War II. During the war, the company switched over to producing gun stocks. After the war (circa 1946 to 1948) the company was sold to the employees, then went out of business.

A Kansas trademark later showed up on guitars featured by the Sears, Roebuck catalog until the catalog folded in 1991. It is unknown whether or not the two Kansas trademarks were related.

KATHY WINGERT GUITARS

Instruments currently produced in Rancho Palos Verdes, CA since 1996.

Luthier Kathy Wingert builds custom-made handcrafted acoustic guitars. For more information visit Wingert's website or contact her directly.

Guitars start at $12,500 with several options are available. Body styles include the Model CM Concert Muse, Model E Grand Concert, Model F Baritone, Model F Grand Auditorium, Model D Grand Festival, Parlor Guitar, Vintage Style 12-Fret Model D, and a Harp Guitar. Standard woods include a Sitka or German spruce or cedar top, Indian rosewood or mahogany back and sides, wood binding, mahogany neck, ebony fingerboard and ebony bridge. Wingert also produces the Elite series, which are available as a limited edition only. All orders require a 20% down payment.

CONTACT INFORMATION
KATHY WINGERT GUITARS
28364 South Western Avenue #451
Rancho Palos Verdes, CA 90275
Phone No.: 310-522-9596
www.wingertguitars.com
kathy@wingertguitars.com

KAUFFMAN LUTHERIE

Instruments currently produced in San Francisco, CA.

Luthier Steve Kauffman builds high quality acoustic guitars in California. Kauffman began guitar building by looking at different variations of tonal qualities, especially in bracing systems and wood combinations. He built his first guitar in the early 1970s when he was a teenager. He also apprenticed with Steve Klein many years ago. They developed several projects together with Klein the designer and Kauffman the builder. Kauffman still builds Klein guitars, but he also builds his own line of guitars. All instruments are hand built by Kauffman in his San Francisco shop. The base price for his guitars is $9,500 for the New Parlor and the Small Kauffman, and $10,000 for the Large Kauffman. For more information contact luthier Kauffman directly.

CONTACT INFORMATION
KAUFFMAN LUTHERIE
San Francisco, CA
Phone No.: 925-283-6520
www.kauffmanguitars.com
steven@kauffmanguitars.com

KAWAKAMI GUITARS

Instruments currently produced in Japan and Canada.

Luthier Yusuke Kawakami builds uniquely shaped acoustic guitars in his Japanese and Canadian shops. Kawakami uses Sitka spruce and Canadian flamed maple for his bodies and they are all inlaid with ornate abalone pearl. Ritchie Blackmore is also an endorser for Kawakami. For more information, visit Kawakami's website or contact him directly.

CONTACT INFORMATION
KAWAKAMI GUITARS
Japan Shop
1811-5 Nakaedo
Kani-City, Gifu 509-0202 Japan
Phone No.: 0574-62-1744
www.kawakamiguitars.com
yusukekawakami@gmail.com

CONTACT INFORMATION
KAWAKAMI GUITARS
Canada Shop
#106-60 Orwell St.
North Vancouver, British Columbia V7J
1A5 Canada
Phone No.: 604-240-6861

KAY

Instruments currently produced in Asia. Previously built in Chicago, IL between the 1930s and the late 1960s and in Japan during 1970s. Distributed by the Kay Guitar Company in Newport Beach, CA. See chapter on House Brands.

CONTACT INFORMATION
KAY
PO Box 8798
Newport Beach, CA 92658
www.kayguitar.com

The roots of the Kay Musical Instruments company began back in 1890, when the Groeschel Company of Chicago, Illinois first began building bowl-back (or potato bug) mandolins. In 1918 Groeschel was changed to the Stromberg-Voisenet Company, and incorporated in 1921. Vice-president C.G. Stromberg directed production of guitars and banjos under the Mayflower trademark (See Mayflower). This Stromberg is not to be confused with luthier Charles Stromberg (and son Elmer) of Boston, Massachusetts. Stromberg-Voisenet introduced the process of laminating wood tops and backs in 1924, and also began arching instruments' tops and backs. Henry Kay Kuhrmeyer, who later became company president, offered use of his middle name on the more popular Kay-Kraft series of Stromberg-Voisenet's guitars, mandolins and banjos.

The Kay era began when Henry Kay Kuhrmeyer bought the Stromberg-Voisenet company in 1928. Kuhrmeyer renamed the company Kay Musical Instruments in 1931, and began mass-producing stringed instruments in large volume. Kay, like Washburn at the turn of the century, claimed production of almost 100,000 instruments a year by the mid-1930s. Kay instruments were both marketed by the company themselves and produced for jobbers (distributors) and retail houses under various names. Rather than produce a list here, the *Blue Book of Acoustic Guitars* has attempted to identify Kay-produced House Brands throughout the alphabetical listing in this text. Many of these instruments were entry level or student instruments then, and should be considered entry level even now. But as Jay Scott (author of *50's Cool: Kay Guitars*) points out, "True, the vast majority of Kay's student-grade and intermediate guitars were awful. But the top of each line - banjo, guitar and mandolin (especially the acoustic and electric jazz guitars and flattop acoustics) - were meritorious pieces of postwar musical art."

Kay introduced upright basses in 1937, and marketed them under both the Kay trademark and under K. Meyer (a clever abbreviation of Kuhrmeyer?). After Leo Fender debuted his Precision electric bass at the 1951 NAMM trade show, Kay was the first company to join Fender in the electric bass market as they introduced their K-162 model in 1952. Kay also went on to produce some of the coolest mixtures of classic archtop design and '50s modern acrylic headstocks on the "Gold K" line that debuted in 1957.

The Kay Musical Instrument company was sold to an investment group headed by Sydney Katz in 1955. Katz, a former manager of Harmony's service department, was more aggressive and competitive in the guitar market. Kay's production facilities expanded to try to meet the demand of the guitar market in the late 1950s and early 1960s. A large number of guitars were produced for Sears under their Silvertone trademark. At the peak of the guitar boom in 1964, Kay moved into a new million dollar facility located near Chicago's O'Hare Airport.

Unfortunately, by 1965 the guitar market was oversaturated as retail demand fell off. While Kay was still financially sound, Katz sold the company to Seeburg. Seeburg, a large jukebox manufacturer based in Chicago, owned Kay for a period of two years. At this time, the whole guitar industry was feeling the pinch of the economy. Seeburg wanted to maintain their niche in the industry by acquiring Valco Guitars, Inc. (See National or Dobro) and producing their own amplifiers to go with the electric Kay guitars. Bob Keyworth, the executive vice-president in charge of Kay, suggested the opposite: Seeburg should sell Kay to Valco.

Robert Engelhardt, who succeeded Louis Dopyera in Valco's ownership in 1962, bought Kay from Seeburg in June 1967. Valco moved into the Kay facilities, but Engelhardt's company was under financed from the beginning. Engelhardt did make some deal with an investment group or financial company, but after two years the bills couldn't be paid. The investment group just showed up one day, and changed the plant locks. By 1969 or 1970, both Valco Guitars Inc., and the Kay trademark were out of business.

The rights to the Kay name were acquired by Sol Weindling and Barry Hornstein, who were importing Teisco Del Rey (Kawai) guitars to the U.S. market with their W.M.I. importing company. W.M.I. begins putting the Kay name on the Teisco products beginning in 1973, and continued on through the 1970s. In 1980, Tony Blair of A.R. Enterprises purchased the Kay trademark. The Kay trademark is now on entry level/beginner guitars built in Asia. Source: 1950s/1960s company history courtesy Jay Scott, *50's Cool: Kay Guitars*, contemporary history courtesy Michael Wright, *Vintage Guitar Magazine*, individual model listings: Michael Wright, *Guitar Stories*, Volume Two.

MSR/NOTES	100%	EXCELLENT	AVERAGE	LAST MSR

ACOUSTIC ARCHTOP

K-11/K-8911/RHYTHM SPECIAL – single cutaway archtop style, solid spruce top, curly maple back and sides, two bound f-holes, B/N/H W/B/W binding, 14/19-fret rosewood fingerboard withshark fin inlays, inlaid pearl rosewood headstock logo with three-per-side chrome plated Kluson tuners, white pickguard, rosewood bridge, trapeze tailpiece, Sunburst or Blonde finish, mfg. 1952-1960.

	N/A	$1,000 - 1,250	$600 - 750	

In 1957, this model was renumbered the K8911. In 1958, a Kelvinator headstock replaced the old style.

K-21/K-8921/MASTERPIECE – single cutaway archtop style, solid spruce top, curly maple back and sides, two bound f-holes, B/N/H W/B/W binding, 14/19-fret ebony rosewood fingerboard with split block and oval inlays, inlaid MOP ebony headstock logo with three-per-side chrome plated Kluson tuners, white pickguard with logo, ebony bridge, trapeze tailpiece with detail, Sunburst or Blonde finish, 17 in. body, mfg. 1952-59.

	N/A	$1,125 - 1,400	$675 - 850	

In 1957, this model was renumbered the K8921. In 1958, a Kelvinator headstock replaced the old style.

K-44/ARTIST – archtop style, solid spruce top, curly maple back and sides, two f-holes, front and back body binding, 14/19-fret Brazillian rosewood fingerboard with block inlays, painted celluloid headstock with three-per-side tuners, white pickguard, rosewood bridge, trapeze tailpiece, Honey Sunburst finish, 17 in. body, mfg. 1947-1951.

	N/A	$475 - 600	$275 - 325	

K-45/PROFESSIONAL – archtop style, solid spruce top, curly maple back and sides, two f-holes, front and back body binding, 14/19-fret Brazillian rosewood fingerboard with block inlays, engraved celluloid headstock with three-per-side tuners, white pickguard, rosewood bridge, trapeze tailpiece, Natural finish, 17 in. body, mfg. 1952-54.

	N/A	$550 - 700	$350 - 425	

K-46/ARTIST – archtop style, solid spruce top, curly maple back and sides, two f-holes, front and back body W/B/W binding, 14/19-fret Brazillian rosewood fingerboard with pearl shark fin inlays, inlaid pearl headstock logo with three-per-side tuners, white pickguard, rosewood bridge, trapeze tailpiece, Sunburst finish, 17 in. body, mfg. 1947-1951.

	N/A	$475 - 600	$275 - 325	

K-48 ARTIST – archtop style, solid spruce top, highly flamed maple back and sides, two bound f-holes, B/N/H W/B/W binding, 14/19-fret ebony rosewood fingerboard with split block and oval inlays, inlaid pearl ebony headstock logo with three-per-side chrome plated Kluson tuners, white pickguard, rosewood bridge, trapeze tailpiece with detail, Sunburst or Blonde finish, 17 in. body, mfg. 1947-1951.

	N/A	$950 - 1,200	$575 - 725	

ACOUSTIC FLATTOP

K-24 – solid spruce top, curly maple back and sides, one round soundhole, body binding, 4/19-fret ebony fingerboard with block inlay, ebony headstock with inlaid MOP logo, ebony bridge, white pickguard, Sunburst finish, mfg. 1947-1951.

	N/A	$600 - 750	$350 - 450	

K-26 – J-200 style, spruce top, mahogany back and sides, round soundhole, body binding, 14/19-fret rosewood fingerboard with block inlay, rosewood headstock, rosewood bridge, white pickguard, Sunburst finish, mfg. 1947-1951.

	N/A	$725 - 900	$425 - 550	

K-27 – J-200 style, solid spruce top, curly maple back and sides, round soundhole, body binding, 14/19-fret ebony fingerboard with block inlay, ebony headstock with inlaid MOP logo, ebony bridge, pickguard, Sunburst finish, mfg. 1952-1956.

	N/A	$1,200 - 1,500	$725 - 900	

KAY KRAFT

Instruments produced in Chicago, IL during the 1930s. Also see Kay.

Henry Kay Kuhrmeyer, who worked his way up from company secretary, treasurer, and later president of Stromberg-Voisenet, lent his middle name to a popular selling line of guitars, mandolins, and banjos. When Kuhrmeyer gained control of Stromberg-Voisenet and changed the name to Kay Musical Instruments, he continued to use the Kay Kraft trademark (sometimes hyphenated as Kay-Kraft). Instruments using this trademark could thus be either Stromberg-Voisenet or Kay (depending on the label) but was still produced by the same company in the same facilities.

K.D. DAVIS GUITARS

Instruments previously built in Sonoma, CA during the 1990s.

Luthier Kevin D. Davis built handcrafted custom guitars during the 1990s and possibly into the early 2000s.

KEL KROYDON

Guitars previously produced in Kalamazoo, MI by Gibson during the early 1930s. See chapter on House Brands.

Faced with the severe American Depression of the 1930s, Gibson general manager Guy Hart converted most of company production to toy manufacturing as a means to keep his workforce employed. Kalamazoo Playthings produced wood blocks

| MSR/NOTES | 100% | EXCELLENT | AVERAGE | LAST MSR |

and wooden pull-toys from 1931 to 1933, while the Kel Kroyden offshoot built toy sailboats. Wood bodies, strings, and masts!

Kel Kroydon brand guitars seem to appear at the same time period that Kel Kroyden Toys were introduced. The "Kel" lettering is horizontal on the headstock, while "Kroydon" is lettered vertically. Source: Walter Carter, *Gibson Guitars: 100 Years of an American Icon*.

ACOUSTIC

KK-1 – small L-0-sized body, round soundhole, body binding, swooping pointed headstock, available in Natural finish with floral pattern on the top, mfg. early 1930s.

N/A	$2,600 - 3,250	$1,550 - 1,950

KELLER, MICHAEL L.

Instruments currently built in Rochester, MN since 1975.

CONTACT INFORMATION
KELLER, MICHAEL L.
2207 30th Avenue S.E.
Rochester, MN 55904
Phone No.: 507-288-9226
www.kellerguitar.com
michael@kellerguitars.com

Michael Keller currently builds world class instruments using the finest tonewoods in the heart of Southern Minnesota. He uses extreme precision when building guitars, and no shortcuts are used. Michael's guitars have even impressed the likes of the famous guitar builder James Olsen, who is also from Minnesota. Contact Keller for any information and any custom work you may be interested in.

Models start at $5,200 and include the **KLM Rose**, **OO-K Parlor**, **Jumbo**, and **Baritione**. A **Baby** half size starts at $4,800 and the **12-String** model starts at $5,400. The **Bauhaus** features a jumbo-style body with an offset soundhole, side port, and a dropped shoulder and it starts at $6,450. Standard features include East Indian rosewood back and sides, Sitka spruce or red cedar top, ebony fingerboard with MOP dot inlays, bridge, and peghead veneer, adjustable truss rod, chrome Schaller tuners, tortoiseshell body binding, and a fully compensated bone nut and saddle.

There are several options available including the body wood, inlays, body options, and neck options. A custom built instrument is also a possiblity - contact Keller directly to discuss a guitar.

- **Add $300 for flamed maple.**
- **Add $200 for a red wood or Adirondack spruce top.**
- **Add $350 for a single cutaway.**
- **Add $400 for zirocote.**
- **Add $600 for flamed koa.**

KELLISON, T. R.

Instruments previously built in Billings, MT from 1978 to the 1990s.

Luthier T.R. Kellison handcrafted custom instruments from 1978 to the 1990s.

KEMPF, DAVID GUITARS

Instruments currently produced in Bivins, TX.

CONTACT INFORMATION
KEMPF, DAVID GUITARS
Rt. 1 Box 87
Bivins, TX 75555
Phone No.: 903-796-9639
dkguitars@aol.com

David Kempf guitars feature solid wood construction, wood bindings and bound fretboards, and every model is a concert sized (000) fingerstyle guitar. For more information including pricing, contact Kempf directly.

KEN BEBENSEE GUITARS AND BASSES

Instruments currently built in North San Juan, CA. Previously built in Nevada City and San Luis Obispo, CA.

CONTACT INFORMATION
KEN BEBENSEE GUITARS AND BASSES
29085A Highway 49
North San Juan, CA 95960
Phone No.: 530-292-0156
www.kbguitars.com
ken@kbguitars.com

Luthier Ken Bebensee began building basses and guitars in high school as a musician trying to develop his own style. While studying engineering and industrial technology at Cal Poly State University (San Luis Obispo), Bebensee continued to refine and improve on his designs. In 1983, Bebensee began offering custom built instruments. Bebensee works out of an old wooden shop in San Luis Obispo, and custom creates a handful of instruments per year. Bebensee's instruments are custom built from the highest grade of sustained yield, exotic woods. Bebensee estimates that he has created over eighty instruments since 1983. In 2001/02, KB Guitars and Basses relocated to Nevada City, CA. In 2004, they relocated again to North San Juan, CA. For more information visit Bebensee's website or contact him directly.

ACOUSTIC/ACOUSTIC BASS

Models include a flattop acoustic/electric (MSR starts at $3,220), an archtop acoustic (MSR starts at $5,220), an acoustic/electric bass (MSR starts at $3,450 for four-string configuration, and $3,590 for five-string configuration), and an archtop acoustic bass (MSR starts at $5,480).

MSR/NOTES	100%	EXCELLENT	AVERAGE	LAST MSR

KEN FRANKLIN GUITARS

Acoustic guitars currently produced in Ukiah, CA since 2003.

Luthier Ken Franklin builds custom acoustic guitars in his California workshop. He built his first guitar in the 1970s, but has been in business as Ken Franklin Guitars since 2003. Guitars are constructed with sculpted braces, graduated top thickness, and personally selected tone woods. Ken Franklin works with each customer individually and guitars typically price between $3,600 and $5,000. For more information, visit Ken Franklin's website or contact him directly.

CONTACT INFORMATION
KEN FRANKLIN GUITARS
2790 Oak Court Road
Ukiah, CA 95482
Phone No.: 707-468-9609
www.franklinguitars.com
franklinsk@att.net

KEN PARKER ARCHTOPS

Instruments currently produced in Gloucester, MA.

Ken Parker is best-known for co-designing the Parker Fly guitar with Larry Fishman in the early 1990s, but he has been involved in building guitars, most notably archtops since the mid-1970s. Parker took a job with the now defunct Stuyvesant Music in New York City, working both in the repair shop as well as building Guitar Man instruments. Parker's background in repairing and customizing guitars became the groundwork for the innovative design of the Fly guitar. Parker introduced the Fly guitar in 1992 and continued on with Parker until 2003 when his company was purchased by U.S. Music Corp. Parker has been building a variety of archtop guitars since under Ken Parker Archtops. For more information, visit Parker's website or contact him directly.

CONTACT INFORMATION
KEN PARKER ARCHTOPS
17 Kondelin Road #5
Gloucester, MA 01930
kenparkerarchtops.com
kensarchtopguitars@gmail.com

KENT

Instruments previously produced in Korea and Japan circa 1960s. Distributed in the U.S. by Buegeleisen & Jacobson of New York, NY; Maxwell Meyers in TX; Southland Musical Merchandise Corporation in NC; and Harris Fandel Corporation in MA.

The Kent trademark was used on a full line of acoustic and solid body electric guitars, banjos, and mandolins imported into the U.S. market during the 1960s. Some of the earlier Kent guitars were built in Japan by either the Teisco company or Guyatone, but the quality level at this time is down at the entry or student level. The majority of the models were built in Korea. The address for Kent Guitars (as distributed by Buegeleisen & Jacobson) during the 1960s was 5 Union Square, New York, New York 10003, (Source: Walter Murray, Frankenstein Fretworks; and Michael Wright, *Guitar Stories, Volume One*).

ACOUSTIC

Many of the Kent models were patterned after Gibson models. For example, the Kent **KF-340** is roughly a Gibson Dove knock-off, as it includes the dove motif pickguard, double parallelogram pearl fingerboard inlay, and moustache bridge assembly with pearl dove inlay. Notable design differences include the **KF-340**'s zero fret (which the Dove does not), chrome tuners instead of gold, and an obvious quality level. The **KF-340** was available in Natural and Black finishes. A Kent KF-340 in average condition brings around $100 in value.

MISC. FLATTOP MODELS – various configurations and appointments, mfg. 1960s.

	N/A	$100 - 150	$50 - 75	

KENTARE GUITARS

Instruments currently produced in Vietnam and Romania since 2003. Distributed by Liikanen Guitars in Helsinki, Finland.

Liikanen Guitars introduced the Kantare trademark in 2003 as a more affordable option to their Liikanen Guitars equipped with Lens Resonance System tops (LRS). Kantare Guitars are high quality guitars manufactured with the "LRS" system top and are exclusively manufactured for Liikanen guitars in two factories in Vietnam and Romania. Models cover sizes from three-quarter to full-size. For further information regarding specifications and pricing, contact Kentare Guitars directly.

CONTACT INFORMATION
KENTARE GUITARS
Helsinki, Finland
www.kantareguitars.com
info@kantareguitars.com

KEVIN RYAN GUITARS

Instruments currently produced in Westminster, CA since 1989.

Luthier Kevin Ryan builds high quality instruments in California. Ryan's models use newer technology to accommodate today's demands such as scale length to complement alternate tunings and light bracing. Many woods and options are available. For more information and to order a guitar contact Ryan directly.

CONTACT INFORMATION
KEVIN RYAN GUITARS
14082 Willow Lane
Westminster, CA 92683
Phone No.: 714-379-0944
Phone No.: 800-311-1527
Fax No.: 714-379-0975
www.ryanguitars.com
kevin@ryanguitars.com

KEYSTONE STATE

See Weymann & Son in the W section.

MSR/NOTES	100%	EXCELLENT	AVERAGE	LAST MSR

KIMAXE

Instruments previously produced in Korea and China. Distributed by Kenny & Michael's Co., Inc. of Los Angeles, CA.

Kimaxe guitars were manufactured by Sang Jin Industrial Company, Ltd., which has a head office in Seoul, Korea and manufacturing facilities in four different places (Inchon, Bupyong, and Kongju, Korea; Tien Jin, China). Sang Jin Industrial Company, Ltd. is better known as a main supplier of guitars to world famous companies such as Fender, Hohner, and other buyers' own brand names for the past ten years. Sang Jin built almost 10,000 guitars for these accounts each month. In 1994, Sang Jin established its own subsidiary (Kenny and Michael's Company) in Los Angeles in order to distribute their own lines of Kimaxe electric guitars and Corina acoustic guitars. It is unknown if Sang Jin still builds guitars under the Kimaxe trademark.

KIMBARA

Instruments previously produced in Japan from the late 1960s to 1990 and in China from 1995 to the late 1990s. Previously distributed in the U.K. by FCN Music.

The Kimbara trademark was a brand name used by a UK importer on these Japanese-produced budget level instruments. Kimbara acoustics were first introduced in England in the late 1960s. During the 1970s, the Kimbara trademark was also applied to a number of solid body guitars based on classic American designs as well. Kimbara instruments are generally mid to good quality budget models, and a mainstay in the British market through 1990.

In 1995, FCN Music began importing Chinese-built classical and dreadnought acoustic guitars into England. Retail price-wise, the reborn line is back in its traditional niche. Source: Jerry Uwins, *Guitar Magazine* (UK).

KIMBERLY

Instruments previously produced in Seoul, Korea and China during the 1990s and 2000s, and in Japan between circa 1960s to early 1970s. Distributed by the Kimex Trading Co., Ltd. in Seoul, Korea. Previously distributed by Lafayette Company catalog sales.

Kimberly guitars were originally manufactured by Kawai Guitars (and pianos), located in Hamamatsu, Japan, and imported by Limmco, Inc., owned by Bob Seidman. The company tried to fill the void left by the discontinuance of the Kay & Harmony trademarks. Recent production of guitars under the Kimberly trademark was the Kimex Trading Co., Ltd. of Seoul, Korea. Kimex produced a number of guitar and bass models that favor classic American designs, and are designed with the entry level guitarist and student in mind. Source: Mr. Bob Seidman, Seidman Sales, Ft. Lauderdale, FL.

KINGSLIGHT GUITARS

Guitars currently produced in Bremerton, WA since 2010. Previously produced in Taos, NM between 1979 and 1983 and Portage, MI between 1983 and 2010.

CONTACT INFORMATION
KINGSLIGHT GUITARS
3709 NE Liverpool Drive
Bremerton, WA 98311
Phone No.: 360-633-7026
www.kingslightguitars.com
john@kingslightguitars.com

Luthier John Kingslight builds custom acoustic guitars in his Michigan shop. In 1979, after Kingslight had apprenticed with John Dillon, he built his first acoustic guitar. He built four more guitars before he started working as a carpenter and woodworker. In the early 2000s, he returned to guitar making, which he currently does today. Models are designed on traditional acoustic shapes, but Kingslight offers several options. Prices start around $3,000. For more information, visit Kingslight's website or contact him directly.

KINGSTON

Instruments previously produced in Japan between 1958 and 1967. Distributed in the U.S. by Westheimer Importing Corporation in Chicago, IL.

The Kingston brand name was used by U.S. importer Westheimer Importing Corporation in Chicago, IL. Jack Westheimer, who was one of the original guitar importers and distributors, later went on to become president of Cort Musical Instruments in Northbrook, IL. The Kingston trademark was used on a product line of acoustic and solid body electric guitars, electric bass guitars, banjos, and mandolins imported into the U.S. market during the 1960s. It has been estimated that 150,000 guitars were sold in the U.S. during the 1960s. Some of the earlier Kingston guitars were built in Japan by either the Teisco company or Guyatone. Source: Michael Wright, *Guitar Stories*, Volume One.

ACOUSTIC

MISC. ACOUSTIC FLATTOPS – various configurations and appointments, mfg. late 1950s-1960s.

	N/A	$125 - 175	$70 - 95	

KING'S STONE

Instruments previously produced in Japan.

The King's Stone trademark was a brand name used by U.S. importers Elger/Hoshino of Ardmore, PA. King's Stone, along with others like Goldentone, Jamboree, and Elger were all used on Japanese guitars imported to the U.S. Elger/Hoshino evolved into Hoshino USA, distributor of Ibanez guitars. Source: Michael Wright, *Guitar Stories, Volume One*.

KINSCHERFF GUITARS

Instruments currently built in Canyon Lake, TX.

Luthier James Kinscherff has been hand crafting fine acoustic guitars for many years. Kinscherff built his first guitar in 1978 and the first guitar to bear the Kinscherff name on it was built in 1990. While Kinscherff has performed some repair work in the past (and accepts some currently), his main focus has been on building guitars. Until 2003, Kinscherff built guitars in Austin, TX when he relocated to the Briarwood Ranch, which is east of Wimberly in the Texas Hill Country. In November, 2006 Kinscherff moved again to Canyon Lake, TX. James estimates that he builds eighteen to twenty guitars a year. The base price for guitars, including the hardshell case, is $5,500. For further information regarding his acoustic guitars, please contact luthier Kinscherff directly.

CONTACT INFORMATION
KINSCHERFF GUITARS
1191 Dawnridge Dr.
Canyon Lake, TX 78133
Phone No.: 830-899-6699
www.kinscherff.com
jaime@kinscherff.com

KISO GUITARS

Instruments previously produced in Japan during the late 1990s and early 2000s. Previously distributed by Go-En International in Glen Ellen, CA.

Kiso Guitars was a collaboration between luthiers of the Kiso Valley in Japan and Steve Klein in California. They teamed up to produce the KisoKlein guitar, which had several unique features including a neck joint that bolts on with no heel and an Impedance matching bridge. The Kiso name came from the Kiso Valley of Japan where many fine examples of woodworking came from. Kiso sold guitars at a "Players's price," which means if the guitar was purchased at a dealer or through Kiso, the buyer paid the same price.

The KisoKlein Orchestra Model **OMK-1** (last MSR was $3,300) was available with a spruce or cedar top. The **OMK-2** (last MSR was $3,500) featured koa back and sides. A Dreadnought **DK-1** (last MSR was $3,300) model was also available. Kiso also teamed up with Ribbecke to produce an archtop jazz guitar.

KLEARTONE

Instruments previously produced in the 1920s and 1930s. See Chapter on House Brands.

KlearTone (notice the capital T) was a house brand build by various manufacturers including Harmony, Kay, Regal, and Gibson. These guitars include acoustic archtops but may include other variations as well. These guitars were distributed by Grossman Brothers of Cleveland, OH. The headstock may read "As Good as it Sounds." Information courtesy: Walter Murray, Frankenstein Fretworks.

KLEIN, STEVE

Instruments currently produced in Sonoma, CA since 1976.

Steve Klein first began building electric guitars in Berkeley, CA in 1967. A year later, Klein's grandfather introduced him to Dr. Michael Kasha at the University of California in Berkeley. Klein built his first acoustic after that meeting. He briefly attended the California College of Arts and Crafts in 1969, but left to continue building guitars. In 1970, Klein built his second acoustic guitar. He moved to Colorado in the winter of 1970-1971; later that summer he was offered, but did not accept, a job at The American Dream guitar shop back in San Diego (this shop was later bought by Bob Taylor and Kurt Listug, and grew into Taylor Guitars).

CONTACT INFORMATION
KLEIN, STEVE
521 Broadway
Sonoma, CA 95476
Phone No.: 707-996-2196
www.kleinguitars.com
info@kleinguitars.com

The third guitar Steve Klein built also had Kasha-inspired designs. Klein travelled to Detroit via Colorado, and met Richard Schneider. Schneider was building Kasha-style classical guitars at the time, and Klein thought that he was going to stay and apprentice with Schneider. Schneider looked at Klein's current guitar and said "Congratulations, you're a guitar builder," and sent Klein back home.

In the fall of 1972 Klein received his business license. He designed the current acoustic body shape and flying brace, and started work on the Electric Bird guitar. Later the next summer, Klein had finished the first L-457 acoustic; and by 1974 had finished three more acoustics, his first twelve-string guitar, and the first small (39.6) body. Klein made a deal with Clayton Johnson (staff member of "Bill Gramm Presents") to be able to get into concerts to show guitars to professional musicians. Klein got to meet such notables as Stills, Crosby, Young, David Lindly, Doc Watson, Roy Buchanan, John Sebastion (Loving Spoonful), and others. In the summer of 1975, Klein went to Los Angeles with guitars and met J.D. Souther; he also received a commission from Joni Mitchell, and set up shop in Oakland.

In 1976, Klein finally settled into his current shop space in Sonoma. He continued building and designing guitars while doing some repair work. Two years later he finished Joni Mitchell's guitar, and the Electric Bird as well. In 1979, Klein met Steve Kauffman at a G.A.L. convention in Boston. That same year, Klein and Carl Margolis began developing a small electric model that was nicknamed Lumpy by David Lindly. Klein also did a side project of antique repair, furniture, and chairs for George Lucas at the Skywalker Ranch. On a more personal note, Klein married Lin Marie DeVincent in the spring of 1985, and Michael Hedges played at their wedding.

The MK Electric model was designed in conjunction with Ronnie Montrose in 1986. By 1988 the small Klein electric design was finished, and was debuted at a trade show in 1989. Klein Electric Division was later started that same year, and Steve Klein began designing an acoustic Harp guitar for Michael Hedges. A year later the acoustic Harp project was dropped in favor of an electrical Harp design instead (Hedges and guitar appeared on the cover of the October 1990 issue of *Guitar Player* magazine).

In the early 1990s, Klein began designing an acoustic bass guitar for and with Bob Taylor of Taylor Guitars. The first prototypes were assembled by Steve Kauffman in 1993. A large acoustic guitar order came in from Japan a year later, and the shipment was sent in 1995. In order to concentrate on the acoustic guitar production, Klein sold his Electric Division to Lorenzo German that same year, and the Electric Division still operates out of the original Klein Sonoma facilities. The Taylor/Klein acoustic bass went into production in 1995, and currently there is a waiting period on acoustic models.

In 1997, Klein went into business with Ed Dufault and opened Klein's Sonoma Music. Located on Broadway in Sonoma, CA, the music shop services the local community as well as offering acoustic guitars built by Klein and other high grade builders like Michael Lewis. For more information, visit Klein's website or contact him directly.

Klein currently focuses his attention on acoustic guitar building. His **Basic Klein Acoustic Guitar** features Indian Rosewood or walnut back and sides, a spruce top, rosewood neck, ebony bridge and fretboard, and gold plated tuners with Ebony buttons. The **M-43** starts at $7,500 and $7,500 with an oval hole in the upper bout. The model **S-39.6** carries a list price of $11,500; and the **L-45.7** is $12,000. The N-36.5 is also available. Klein offers a fairly fancy ornamentation package including mother-of-pearl snowflake inlays on the guitars. Optional custom features included a 12-string configuration, Florentine cutaway with hidden heel, and use of Brazilian rosewood.

KLEPPER, HOWARD

Guitars currently produced in Berkeley, CA since 2001.

Luthier Howard Klepper builds custom acoustic instruments in his Berkeley, CA shop. Klepper began working on guitars in 1968 and built his first guitar in 1977. Over the years, Klepper has met several important figures in the guitar industry, and much of this has to do with his location in California. However, the guitar market became saturated in the late 1970s, and Klepper went back to school. Klepper taught law and philosophy for almost twenty years when he retured to Berkeley in 1997. He leased a warehouse and started doing woodturning, but he eventually came back to guitar building in 2001.

CONTACT INFORMATION
KLEPPER, HOWARD
Berkeley, CA
Phone No.: 510-684-5187
www.klepperguitars.com
howard@klepperguitars.com

Klepper builds all kind of instruments including classicals, carved archtops, and even solidbody electrics. Every guitar is custom built and therefore is a one-of-a-kind model and Klepper only builds about ten guitars a year. Prices on flattop acoustic guitars start at $5,750 and several options are available. For more information, visit Klepper's website or contact him directly.

KNAGGS GUITARS

Instruments currently produced in Greensboro, MD since 2009.

Knaggs Guitars was founded by former PRS employees Joe Knaggs and Peter Wolf in 2009. Luthier Knaggs and a small team of craftsmen make all of their guitars in their Greensboro, MD workshop while marketing guru Wolf handles the promotion and marketing side of the business. All guitars are named after American Indian river names and special attention is paid to the woods used in their instruments. Knaggs offers acoustic guitars, electric guitars, and electric basses and their instruments typically have a street price between $3,500 and $4,500. For more information, visit Knagg's website or contact them directly.

CONTACT INFORMATION
KNAGGS GUITARS
Design Studio
205 Dutcher Road
Queenstown, MD 21658
www.knaggsguitars.com

KNIGHT GUITARS

Instruments currently built in Surrey, England since the 1970s.

Luthier Dick Knight (1907-1996) was a well respected British guitar maker, and examples of his work were collected worldwide. Knight (born Stanley Charles Knight) specialized in archtop guitar construction, notably the Imperial model. While Knight began building his first guitars in the 1930s, he became more prominent in the 1970s (and 1980s), and featured such clients as Dave Gilmour, Paul McCartney, Pete Townshend, and Mike Rutherford (among others).

CONTACT INFORMATION
KNIGHT GUITARS
England
Phone No.: +44 (0) 1932 353 131
www.knight-guitars.com
info@knight-guitars.com

During Knight's formative years in the 1930s he worked for Lagonda, the motor vehicle manufacturer. After work, Knight would construct wood items at home, and lost the tips of his fingers in an accident. As this accident prevented him from playing guitar, he turned to making instruments as a hobby.

At the outbreak of World War II Knight met Ben and Lew Davis (the owners of Selmers music shop in London), as well as Joe Van Straten (Selmers' shop manager). In addition to instrument repair, Van Straten suggested the two work on producing a quality English archtop. When finances would not permit the business to carry on, Selmers asked Knight to produce some guitars.

Later, when Knight's wife became ill, he left his work at Selmers and professional guitar making for seventeen years. During this time period, he did produce a number of instruments under the "Knight" logo. Some of his earliest models do not have a name on the headstock. In addition to his archtop models, Knight produced flattop acoustic, solid body and **335**-style guitars. All Knight's instruments were produced with the same high degree of quality.

Recently, Knight's son-in-law Gordon Wells has been continuing to produce guitars and keep the Knight name alive in the guitar-building world. For more information, visit Knight's website. Source: Keith Smart, *The Zemaitis Guitar Owners Club.*

MSR/NOTES	100%	EXCELLENT	AVERAGE	LAST MSR

KNUTSEN

Instruments previously built by Christopher J. Knutsen in Los Angeles, CA circa WWI-1930.

While Weissenborn has become the prestige, and at the same time generic, name for wooden hollow-neck Hawaiian guitars, nevertheless the innovator of this design may well have been Christopher J. Knutsen (1856-1930), also a pioneer of harp-guitar designs (which were later licensed by the estimable Larson Brothers). And Knutsen often combined these two seemingly disparate concepts.

He also made harp-ukuleles, harp mandolins and even the occasional standard instrument, but even a plain roundneck guitar might bear some charming feature testifying to his eccentricity - like an angled metal bracket fixed to neck and body with wing nuts which took the place of the neck's heel. Knutsen was granted a U.S. design patent on the harp guitar in 1898 (he also had Canadian patents in which he attempted to sell a percentage).

He spent most of his life in Seattle and environs, moving to Los Angeles around 1916, interestingly close to the beginnings of the Hawaiian music phenomenon which swept through the mainland after the Panama Pacific Exposition held in San Francisco in 1915. Knutsen aficionados have been trying to determine whether he might have made any Hawaiian guitars during his residency in Washington. If so, such a hypothetical guitar could be a historical Holy Grail, especially if it pre-dated the Exposition.

While some instruments from Washington bear the paper label reading "Harp Guitar Factory," there's little to suggest that his Los Angeles operation was any more than a one-man shop. And while there is an unmistakable exchange of design ideas going back and forth between Weissenborn and Knutsen, there is no concrete evidence that the two ever worked together or one for the other.

Early Hawaiian guitar designs showed a variety of neck joints - from slight extensions of the body up to true hollow necks. While Weissenborn also made some square, solid-neck Hawaiians, Knutsen made several instruments with partial hollow necks; in other words, the headstock joints might be somewhere between the third and twelfth frets. One headstock sports original six-per-side tuners, perhaps thirty years before Merle Travis's Bigsby or the Fender Broadcaster.

The closest semblance to sales literature for Knutsen's offerings are the picture labels showing examples of his work found in some instruments.

(Many labels have name, business and address information only.) Unlike Weissenborn styles 1 through 4, Knutsen's instruments are not so conveniently identified and have to be considered individually. Some are very plain, while others are extraordinarily elaborate.

Koa and mahogany bodies (sometimes with spruce tops) are the most common woods for body construction. Familiar Knutsen design touches include rope binding (usually larger than Weissenborn's), harp sub-bass and treble strings, a fretboard inlays often mixing shapes, angled back braces and minimal top bracing. Some instruments feature dramatically figured one-piece backs with the grain pattern running at an angle somewhere between crossways or lengthwise. Seeing the variety and ambition of Knutsen's optimistic designs can't help but make the observer think this builder was a colorful benign eccentric.

Knutsen has been disparaged widely in vintage-instrument circles (his instruments are for the most part, woefully under built), but when they hold - or have been patched back together, they usually sound great. Builder and author Rick Turner said it best when he proclaimed Knutsen "a brilliant hack." His Hawaiian harp guitars are warm, resonant and responsive, but not as haunting and bright as most Weissenborns.

Perhaps the only way to identify an unlabeled Knutsen is to compare other Knutsen instruments. While codifying his designs flies in the face of organization and logic, seeing a few of his creations conveys the notion that Knutsen is better understood by feel and experience than by facts and statistics.

Because there are no standard models of Knutsen instruments, establishing prices becomes largely a matter of finding common ground between selling and buying parties. Weissenborn and other similar instruments can be a guide, with the most important factors being sound, condition and playability. The latter two can be a sticking point for Knutsen instruments, because they are so fragile. Some types of Knutsen instruments lend themselves to functional restoration better than others-e.g., Hawaiian guitars better than harp-guitars with many sub-bass and treble strings. Some guitars that began as Spanish guitars might better be considered as Hawaiians after three generations of cracking and warping.

ACOUSTIC

For Knutsen & Hawaiian guitars, prices can run from $700-$1,000 for a plain, much-repaired example, to the $3,000+ range for a pristine specimen (it does happen). Harp instruments tend to fetch similar prices, with the more elaborate harp guitars running to $5,000 and beyond (the publisher wishes to express his thanks to Mr. Ben Elder for making this information available).

LOW END HAWAIIAN – Hawaiian style similar to Weissenborn, many examples may have been repaired or are in extremely poor condition, mfg. 1910s-1930s.

	N/A	$1,500 - 2,000	$1,000 - 1,200	

HIGH END HAWAIIAN – Hawaiian style similar to Weissenborn, very rare instruments, if any exist at all, in original condition, mfg. 1910s-1930s.

	N/A	$2,500 - 3,000	$1,650 - 2,000	

KNUTSON LUTHIERY

Instruments currently built in Forestville, CA, since 1978.

Luthier John Knutson has been building and repairing stringed instruments in and around the San Francisco Bay area since 1978. As a custom builder of acoustic, archtop, and electric instruments, Knutson has produced hundreds of guitars, mandolins, dulcimers, and basses (including custom double- and triple-neck combinations). For further information contact luthier John Knutson directly.

CONTACT INFORMATION
KNUTSON LUTHIERY
PO Box 945
Forestville, CA 95436
Phone No.: 707-887-2709
www.knutsonluthiery.com
john@knutsonluthiery.com

Knutson is currently producing the **Songbird** Archtop guitar (list $7,500), the **Songbird** Archtop mandolin (list $3,750), the **Flattop** acoustic (list $3,250), and the **Nightlife** Archtop Guitar (list $7,500). General archtop guitars start at $6,500. Flattop Steelstring guitars start at $3,250. Songbird steelstring guitars start at $3,500. Nylon string guitars start at $3,250. Also in current production is the new **Messenger** hybrid archtop guitar (list $3,500). All instruments are limited edition, numbered, signed, and handcrafted by the luthier. John Knutson holds the exclusive rights to the Songbird, Messenger, and Ecotone trademarks.

KOHNO

Instruments currently built in Japan since the mid-1960s. Distributed by Cordoba Music Group previously (Tornavoz Music) in Santa Monica, CA.

Luthier Masaru Kohno was noted as being the leading Japanese classical-style guitar maker in author Tony Bacon's *Ultimate Guitar Book* (1991). Kohno studied under luthier Arcangel Fernandez in his Madrid workshop, and later opened his own operation in Tokyo during the late 1960s. Masaru Kohno died of cancer in 1998. Kohno's nephew Masaki-Sakurai began working for Kohno in 1978, and continued the guitar operation after he died. Masaki-Sakurai currently produces guitars under the trademark Sakura-Kohno. For more information contact Cordoba Music Group or visit their website.

CONTACT INFORMATION
KOHNO
Factory
Tokyo, Japan
www.kohno-guitar.org
msakurai@kohno-guitar.org

U.S. Distributor: Cordoba Music Group
1455 19th Street
Santa Monica, CA 90404
Phone No.: 310-586-1180
Fax No.: 310-586-1181
www.cordobaguitars.com

KONA (CURRENT MFG.)

Instruments currently produced in Asia, since 2001. Distributed by M&M Merchandisers of Ft. Worth, TX.

Since 1976, M&M Merchandisers has been a national wholesaler of musical instruments and consumer electronics. Tiring of quality issues usually associated with the entry level guitars offered to them at the time, M&M decided to make a change to better serve their dealer base. In July of 2001 M&M introduced their Kona brand of import electric guitars, acoustic guitars, and guitar amplifiers (as well as Z.Z. Ryder and Trinity River acoustic guitars) to have better control over the quality and features offered. The K1 is the entry-level acoustic guitar that retails for $250. The K1E has electronics and retails for $280. A signature series is also available with more options. For more information contact M&M Merchandisers.

CONTACT INFORMATION
KONA (CURRENT MFG.)
Distributed by M&M Merchandisers
1923 Bomar Ave.
Fort Worth, TX 76103
Phone No.: 800-299-9035
www.konaguitars.com
chuck@mmwholesale.com

KOONTZ

Instruments previously built in Linden, NJ, during the 1970s and 1980s. Also see Standel and Harptone.

Luthier Stan Koontz designed several different models of acoustic and electric guitars and basses for Bob Crooks' Standel company. The instruments were built in Harptone's New Jersey facilities, and have the Standel logo on the peghead. Koontz also built his own custom guitars that featured such striking innovations as side-mounted electronics and a hinged internal f-hole cover. Stan passed away in the late 1980s. Source: Tom Wheeler, *American Guitars*.

KRAMER

Acoustic instruments currently produced overseas. Instruments previously produced in Neptune, NJ. Kramer Guitars is currently a division of Gibson Musical Instruments, located in Nashville, TN.

CONTACT INFORMATION
KRAMER
A Division of Gibson
645 Massman Drive
Nashville, TN 37210
Phone No.: 800-444-2766
www.kramerguitars.com

For a full history on Kramer, please refer to the *Blue Book of Electric Guitars*. In the late 1980s, Kramer introduced acoustic models that were designed by Danny Ferrington. These were produced until about 1991. In 1995, Kramer introduced a new line of guitars, but they did not last very long. In 1997, the Gibson corporation acquired the Kramer trademark. By 1998, Gibson was displaying Kramer trademarked models at the Summer NAMM industry show, and ads in the print media followed a month later. Gibson did not pay much attention to Kramer for the rest of the 1990s and early 2000s. In 2006, at Winter NAMM, Kramer displayed a full line of guitars in their own booth - located not even close to Gibson! Kramer produces several replicas of their old guitars overseas, as well as a few reissue models in the U.S. For more information, contact Kramer directly or visit their website.

ACOUSTIC

The Kramer Ferringtons were thinline, hollowbody acoustics with bridge mounted piezo pickup systems, volume and tone controls. The six-tuners-per-side headstocks and slimmer profile necks felt more like an electric guitar, and the instruments could be used in performances with minimal feedback problems.

MSR/NOTES	100%	EXCELLENT	AVERAGE	LAST MSR

Current Kramer acoustic models include the **D-100** (MSR $149), **D-200S** (MSR $215), and **D-200SCE** (MSR $283). Value packs of these guitars were also available.

FERRINGTON II KFS2 – offset double cutaway acoustic body, round soundhole, six-per-side tuners on a pointy headstock, chrome tuners, rosewood bridge, one volume and two tone knobs, available in Black, Red, or White finish, mfg. 1986-1991.

	N/A	$450 - 550	$250 - 325	$550

FERRINGTON II KFT2 – single cutaway acoustic body, round soundhole, six-per-side tuners on a pointy headstock, chrome tuners, rosewood bridge, one volume and two tone knobs, available in Black, Red, or White finish, mfg. 1986-1991.

	N/A	$450 - 550	$250 - 325	$550

ACOUSTIC/ELECTRIC BASS

KFB-1 FERRINGTON BASS – offset double cutaway hollow maple body, rounded triangular soundhole with five-ring rosette, three-ply body binding, bolt-on maple Kramer electric neck, 21-fret bound rosewood fingerboard with custom Kramer inlays or fretless fingerboard, hockey stick-style headstock with black overlay and four-on-one-side chrome tuners, rosewood bridge, Thinline transducer pickup with volume and three-band EQ, available in Black, Natural, Red, or White finish, 34 in. scale, mfg. 1987-1990.

	N/A	$400 - 500	$250 - 300	

KFB-2 FERRINGTON BASS – offset double cutaway hollow maple body, rounded triangular soundhole with five-ring rosette, single-ply body binding, bolt-on maple Kramer electric neck, 21-fret rosewood fingerboard with dot inlays, hockey stick-style headstock with black overlay and four-on-one-side chrome tuners, rosewood bridge, Thinline transducer pickup with volume and three-band EQ, available in Black, Natural, Red, or White finish, 34 in. scale, mfg. 1987-1990.

	N/A	$375 - 450	$225 - 275	

KREMONA

Instruments currently produced in Kazanlak, Bulgaria. Distributed by Kremona USA Inc. in Folsom, CA.

Kremona was established in 1924 and produces and distributes stringed musical instruments. Instruments are distributed in the U.S., Russia, and Germany. They produce acoustic guitars along with violins, violas, cellos, and other stringed instruments. All acoustic guitars are classical nylon stringed models and retail prices are typically between $300 and $500. Contact Kremona for more information.

CONTACT INFORMATION
KREMONA
Factory
Kazanlak, Bulgaria
Phone No.: +359 431 635 63
Fax No.: +359 431 632 77
www.kremona.com
info@kremona.com

CONTACT INFORMATION
KREMONA
U.S. Distribution: Kremona USA, Inc.
Distributed by Kremona, Inc.
2202 Ferry Circle
Folsom, CA 95630
Phone No.: 916-355-8585
Fax No.: 240-465-4796
www.kremona.com
nick@kremona.com

KRUSA GUITARS

Instruments currently produced outside of Nashville, TN since the late 1990s.

Luthier Kipp Krusa builds custom acoustic guitars in his shop outside of Nashville, TN. In 1993, Krusa went to school at The Northwest School of Wooden Boatbuilding in Port Townshend, WA where he began to learn the art of woodworking. In 1994, he began experimenting with guitar building and attended the Timeless Instruments School of Lutherie. During the mid-1990s, be continued to build commercial fishing boats while he assembled a shop to construct guitars. Several luthiers lended their advice to Krusa along the way, and he was an apprentice at Froggy Bottom Guitars for three years. Krusa offers five base models with the **Monarch** (prices start at $3,800), **Kyoto** (prices start at $3,800), **Mesa** (prices start at $3,800), **Fat Cat** (prices start at $4,200), and the **Mojito** (prices start at $4,200), and several options are available. For more information, visit Krusa's website, or contact him directly.

CONTACT INFORMATION
KRUSA GUITARS
566 Doug Hill Rd
Bon Aqua, TN 37025
Phone No.: 615-412-5650
Phone No.: 931-623-0730
www.krusaguitars.com
kkrusa@bellsouth.net

K & S

Instruments previously built in Mexico in the 1990s. Previously distributed by K & S Guitars of Berkeley, CA.

George Katechis and Marc Silber (K & S), two noted guitar experts, reintroduced the Acoustic Hawaiian Slide Guitar in the 1990s. This type of guitar was developed in the 1920s and enjoyed moderate success before being overtaken by the louder, resonator-driven National-style guitars of the early 1930s. The recent instruments are modeled after designs by Weissenborn, Hilo, and Knutsen.

Prices started at $700 for these solid wood acoustic Hawaiian Slide Guitars. Wood options include Canadian cedar top and Spanish Cedar body; Sitka Spruce top and Spanish cedar, Honduras mahogany, maple, or California koa (acacia) body, or all California koa. Instruments are bound and feature Van Gent tuners.

KYLE, DOUG

Instruments currently built in Hampstead (Devon), England.

Doug Kyle is currently offering handcrafted guitars, and Kyle is known for his Selmer-style instruments.

L SECTION
LA CADIE

Instruments previously built in Vancouver, B.C., Canada between 1995 and 2006.

Luthier Rod Hannah hand built both dreadnought and 000 12-Fret acoustic guitars in "short lot" sizes (approximately four instruments at a time). Retail list prices started at $3,000.

LACE MUSIC PRODUCTS

Also Lace Helix. Instruments currently built in China. Instruments previously built in Huntington Beach, CA. Distributed by AGI (Actodyne General Inc.) of Huntington Beach, CA. Lace has been building guitars since 1999.

CONTACT INFORMATION
LACE MUSIC PRODUCTS
5596 Corporate Drive
Cypress, CA 90630
Phone No.: 714-898-2776
Fax No.: 714-893-1045
www.lacemusic.com
info@lacemusic.com

Lace Music Products was started in the family garage by Don Lace, Sr. in 1979. They first produced pickups and other electronics. Fender really put them on the map when many of their guitars featured Lace pickups. Lace ventured down the instrument building path with the ergonomically correct Lace Helix Twisted Neck. The Twisted Neck has a twenty-degree twist that follows the natural twist of the player's hand as it travels up and down the fingerboard. While the prototypes were introduced during 1997, production finally began in late 1999. Lace discontinued producing the Twisted Neck circa 2005. They currently focus on an imported line of acoustic and electric guitars that feature Lace pickups. For more information visit Lace's website, or contact the company directly.

MSR/NOTES	100%	EXCELLENT	AVERAGE	LAST MSR

ACOUSTIC

* **Add 10% (Last MSR was $100) for a Lace California Acoustic Male pickup.**
* **Add 15% (Last MSR was $150) for a Lace Acoustic Blade pickup.**

LD-310 – dreadnought style, laminated spruce top, laminated mahogany back and sides, multi-layer soundhole rings, mahogany neck, 14/20-fret rosewood fingerboard with dot inlay, three-per-side chrome tuners, rosewood bridge, black pickguard, Natural finish, disc.

	N/A	$120 - 150	$70 - 90	$300

LD-350SE – dreadnought style, solid spruce top, solid rosewood back and sides, maple/abalone rosette and body binding, mahogany neck, maple/abalone bound 14/20-fret rosewood fingerboard with abalone cucumber seed inlay, three-per-side gold tuners, rosewood bridge, Lace Hybrid Technology electronics with a piezo and Lace Blade sensor and HT preamp, Natural finish, disc.

	N/A	$450 - 525	$225 - 275	$1,000

LF-130CE – single cutaway folk style, laminated ash top, laminated ash back and sides, imitation abalone rosette and body binding, mahogany neck, 14/20-fret rosewood fingerboard with offset dot inlay, three-per-side chrome tuners with pearl buttons, rosewood bridge, Lace Hybrid Technology electronics with a piezo and Lace Blade sensor and HT preamp, Black finish, disc.

	N/A	$200 - 250	$120 - 150	$500

LF-150SCE – single cutaway folk style, solid spruce top, laminated rosewood back and sides, abalone/maple rosette, maple body binding, mahogany neck, 14/20-fret rosewood fingerboard with Acryl vine inlay, three-per-side gold tuners with pearl buttons, rosewood bridge, Lace Hybrid Technology electronics with a piezo and Lace Blade sensor and HT preamp, Natural finish, disc.

	N/A	$300 - 375	$150 - 200	$700

LACEY GUITARS

Instruments currently built in Kingston Springs, TN.

CONTACT INFORMATION
LACEY GUITARS
PO Box 634
Kingston Springs, TN 37082
Phone No.: 615-504-3005
www.laceyguitars.com
mark@laceyguitars

Luthier Mark Lacey studied formal training in musical instrument technology at the London School of Design, and Lacey has been repairing and building fine instruments since 1974. During that time, he spent two years at Gruhn Guitars in Nashville, TN, where he gained insight from noted vintage guitar expert George Gruhn. Lacey's flattop guitars start at $8,000 and archtops start at $10,000. The top-of-the-line archtop starts at $25,000 and several options are available. For more information or to order visit Lacey's website or contact him directly.

LACOTE

Instruments previously built in Paris, France during the early to mid-1800s.

Luthier Rene Lacote was hand building acoustic guitars during the first half of the nineteenth century. According to author Tony Bacon, Lacote is sometimes credited with the invention of the scalloped fingerboard. Many of Lacote's guitars featured relatively small bodies braced with "transverse" strutting inside the top.

During the late 18th century, the European guitar was moving away from earlier designs containing five or six "courses" (a "course" was a pair of strings) to the simple six single string design. This design is closer to what the modern "classical" guitar looks like today. Lacote's designs in the 1830s followed the six-string models. Source: Tony Bacon, *The Ultimate Guitar Book*.

LADY LUCK

Instruments previously produced in Korea between 1986 and the late 1990s. Distributed in the U.S., Europe, and South America by Lady Luck Industries, Inc. in Cary, IL.

President Terresa Miller offered a wide range of imported, affordable guitars that were designed for beginning students up to working professionals. Lady Luck guitar models were designed in the U.S. (specifications and colors). Lady Luck also offered several models of electric bass guitars along with a line of acoustic and electric guitars. In addition to the Lady Luck and Nouveau brands, Lady Luck Industries also distributed Adder Plus pickups and EV Star Cables. Most acoustic guitars retailed between $100 and $400.

LAFAYETTE (KOREA MFG.)

Instruments previously built in Korea during the 1990s. Distributed by the More Company in Pooler, GA.

The More Company, distributors of Synsonic instruments, also offered a wide range of acoustic and acoustic/electric guitars as well as solid body electric guitars and basses.

LÂG

Instruments currently produced. Distributed in the U.S. by Korg USA in Melville, NY.

Lâg guitars became available in the U.S. through Korg USA in 2010. Retail prices range between $280 and $975. For more information, visit their website or contact them directly.

CONTACT INFORMATION
LÂG
U.S. Distributor: Korg USA
316 South Service Road
Melville, NY 11747-3201
Phone No.: 631-390-6800
www.korg.com
support@korgusa.com

CONTACT INFORMATION
LÂG
Headquarters
www.lagguitars.co.uk

LA GUITAR FACTORY

Instruments currently produced in Charlotte, NC since 1997.

The LA Guitar Factory consists of luthiers Ari Lehtela and Luke Luther. They use a wide variety of materials to produce acoustic and electric guitars, primarily hollow body archtop jazz electrics. They also produce bass guitars along with a variety of other products. Several options available on each guitar. For more information, visit LA Guitar Factory's website.

CONTACT INFORMATION
LA GUITAR FACTORY
8125-B Old Concord Road
Charlotte, NC 28213
Phone No.: 704-599-4410
www.laguitarfactory.com

LAGUNA

Instruments currently produced in Indonesia since 2008. Distributed by Laguna (Guitar Center) in Laguna Beach, CA.

Guitar Center introduced the Laguna line of guitars in 2008 as a private label for all of GC's selling outlets including Musician's Friend. The line of acoustic and electric guitars retail between $300 and $1,400, and were designed by guitarists for guitarists. For more information, visit Laguna's website.

CONTACT INFORMATION
LAGUNA
668 North Coast Highway, #101
Laguna Beach, CA 92651
playlaguna.com
info@playlaguna.com

Acoustic models include the **LD1 Little Brat** (MSR $300), **LD2 Little Brat** (MSR $500), **LG4CETR** (disc., last MSR was $800), **LG4CEBUB** (disc., last MSR was $800), **LG6CEOVK** (disc., last MSR was $1,000), **LG6CERW** (disc., last MSR was $1,000), and the **LG300CE** (MSR $800). Acoustic/electric bass models include the **LAB5CE** (disc., last MSR was $700) and the **LAB7CE** (disc., last MSR was $1,000).

LA JOLLA LUTHIERS

Instruments previously built in San Diego, CA.

Luthier Wayne Harris and his shop produced both steel-string and classical guitar models. Both models feature the unusual "Bi-Level" design (developed by Roger Pytlewski), in which the guitar's top is bent into two levels; the levels connect in a ten-degree "ramp" where the bridge is located. The purpose of this design (as addressed in their advertising) was "to increase the instrument's high overtones and overall perceived brilliancy and volume."

It is estimated that Harris built about one hundred instruments a year. **The Collector's Series Bi Level** steel string model is a dreadnought-sized guitar with a Sitka spruce top, Brazilian rosewood body, fan bracing, adjustable truss rod, and mahogany neck (last MSR was $2,167).

LAKEWOOD

Instruments currently built in Giessen, Germany. Represented in North America by Bill Dixon in Boothbay Harbor, ME.

Luthier Martin Seeliger founded Lakewood Guitars in 1985. Seeliger apprenticed for three years with luthier Manfred Pletz, and then worked as a repairman for local music shops. His experience restoring and repairing different types and brands of acoustic guitars was utilized when he began designing his own style of acoustic steel string instruments. Lakewood guitars have a distinct wedge-shaped side profile, and both the top and back are slightly arched for strength and volume. These guitars are essentially custom shop models with dozens of options available. They build about 2,000 instruments a year. For more information contact Lakewood directly.

CONTACT INFORMATION

LAKEWOOD
Factory
Zum Bahnhof 6a
Giessen, D - 35394 Germany
Phone No.: +49 - (0)641 - 43038
Fax No.: +49 - (0)641 - 491398
www.lakewood.de
info@lakewood.de

Bill Dixon, North American Rep
PO Box 552
Boothbay Harbor, ME 04358
www.lakewood.de
bigartdog@aol.com

Lakewood is like a custom shop where the customer starts with a basic models and adds options accordingly. The main option is the back and sides of the guitar that determines the number of the guitars. For instance, a model D-14 is a dreadnought body with solid mahogany back and sides. Use the following chart to add or subtract to the standard value. There are also several other options such as the top, neck, headstock, tuners, fingerboard, binding, inlays, finishes, etc. Just about every option has a price adjustment with it. Contact Lakewood for a quote. When evaluating used Lakewood guitars, every option must be considered. Used prices start around $1,000 - 1,500 for guitars in excellent condition plus options.

Lakewood now uses Shadow pickups. Previous models feature B-Band electronics.

The **Auditorium Model A** (MSR $2,595) standard features include an Engleman spruce top, East Indian rosewood back and sides, round soundhole, rosewood binding, mahogany neck, ebony fingerboard, rosewood slotted peghead, three-per-side tuners, gold hardware, and Natural finish.

The **Classic Cutaway Model M CCP** (MSR $2,995) standard features include an Engleman spruce top, East Indian rosewood back and sides, round soundhole, rosewood binding, mahogany neck, ebony fingerboard, rosewood slotted peghead, three-per-side tuners, gold hardware, and Natural finish.

The **Dreadnought Model D** (MSR $2,495) standard features include an Engleman spruce top, East Indian rosewood back and sides, round soundhole, rosewood binding, mahogany neck, ebony fingerboard, rosewood flat peghead, three-per-side tuners, gold hardware, and Natural finish.

The **Grand Concert Model M** (MSR $2,495) standard features include an Engleman spruce top, East Indian rosewood back and sides, round soundhole, rosewood binding, mahogany neck, ebony fingerboard, rosewood flat peghead, three-per-side tuners, gold hardware, and Natural finish.

The **Jumbo Model J** (MSR $2,695) standard features include an Engleman spruce top, East Indian rosewood back and sides, round soundhole, rosewood binding, mahogany neck, ebony fingerboard, rosewood flat peghead, three-per-side tuners, gold hardware, and Natural finish.

- Style 14: Solid mahogany back and sides, subtract $242.
- Style 18: Solid ovangkol back and sides, subtract $181.
- Style 20: Solid maple back and sides, subtract $121.
- Style 22: Solid walnut back and sides, subtract $97.
- Style 24: Solid figured claro walnut back and sides, add $726.
- Style 32: Solid East Indian Rosewood back and sides, standard equipment, included in Standard price.
- Style 34: Solid padauk back and sides, add $91.
- Style 36: Solid cypress back and sides, add $169.
- Style 38: Solid cherry back and sides, no upcharge.
- Style 40: Solid pear back and sides, no upcharge.
- Style 42: Solid yew back and sides, add $605.
- Style 48: Solid macassar ebony back and sides, add $1,210.
- Style 50: Solid flamed maple back and sides, add $423.
- Style 52: Solid flamed myrtle back and sides, add $726.
- Style 54: Solid Brazillian rosewood back and sides, add $2,177.
- Style 55: Solid Brazillian rosewood, selected vertical grain back and sides, add $3,145.
- Style 56: Solid flamed koa back and sides, add $1,210.

LA MANCHA

Instruments currently built in Paracho (Michoacan) Mexico. Distributed by La Mancha Guitars of Nashville, TN.

Jerry Roberts has been providing fine classical guitars for over a quarter century. In 1996, Roberts debuted the La Mancha line, which offers handcrafted guitars inspired by Fleta, Friederick, Gilbert, Hauser, Ramierez, Romanillos, Ruck, and other legendary makers. La Mancha guitars are handmade by a team of highly skilled Mexican luthiers who are supervised by California luthiers Kenny Hill and Gil Carnal. Guitars start at $1,995. For more information, visit La Mancha's website or contact Jerry Roberts directly.

CONTACT INFORMATION

LA MANCHA
Distributed by La Mancha Guitars
PO Box 41023
Nashville, TN 37204
Phone No.: 615-269-3929
www.lamancha.com
jerryrobertsguitars@gmail.com

LANDOLA

Instruments currently built in Pietarsaari, Finland.

Landola has a tradition of guitar building that stretches back to 1942. In the late 1980s, Landola entered into a contract with Peavey to produce acoustic guitars for the U.S. company. Unfortunately, the company was not geared up for the production numbers that Peavey had projected, and this particular agreement had near disastrous results for the company.

CONTACT INFORMATION

LANDOLA
Pietarsaari, Finland
www.landola.fi
landola@landola.fi

MSR/NOTES	100%	EXCELLENT	AVERAGE	LAST MSR

However, Landola bounced back, and is currently offering a number of good quality acoustic guitar models. For further information regarding specific models and pricing, contact Landola Guitars directly or visit their website.

Landola offers several models of quality acoustic guitars. Models are constructed with spruce or cedar tops, mahogany or rosewood back/sides, arctic birch or mahogany necks. Models are classified into their respective series. The Artist A Series has a large jumbo sized body. The Artist AC Cutaway Series is the Artist with a cutaway. The Classical Series are classical style guitars. The D Series are Dreadnought style guitars. The J Series are jumbo style guitars. The LR (Landola Ragtime) Series are small bodied almost like parlor guitars. Models are also available in 12-string configurations, electronics, and almost all models are available with curly birch.

LANGE

See Paramount & Orpheum.

In the late 1890s, William L. Lange was a partner in Rettberg & Lange, a major East coast banjo producer and distributor. Lange expanded the company into the William L. Lange Company in the early 1920s, and supplied the C. Bruno & Son distributor with both **Paramount** and **Orpheum** banjo lines. In 1934, Lange debuted the Paramount guitar series - and some of the models were built by the C.F. Martin guitar company. Lange was quick to add Orpheum-branded guitars, and some of those models were built by Chicago's Kay company.

Lange's company went out of business in the early 1940s, but New York distributor Maurice Lipsky resumed distribution of Orpheum guitars in 1944. By the late 1940s, the Paramount guitar line was distributed by Gretsch & Brenner. Source: Tom Wheeler, *American Guitars.*

LANGEJANS GUITARS

Instruments currently built in Holland, MI, since 1971.

Delwyn (Del) Langejans started Del's Guitar Gallery in 1970 and a year later was building his own guitar with the name "Langejans" on the headstock. Del is past serial number 1,268 and is dedicated full time to building and reparing guitars. He is a warranty service for several brands and he also warranties any Langejans guitar for two years to the original owner. Del makes nylon and steel guitars in a variety of configurations and prices start at $3,495 for most models. For information refer to Del's website.

LA PATRIE

Instruments currently built in La Patrie, Quebec, Canada since 1982. Distributed by Godin Guitars (previously La Si Do, Inc.) in Baie D'Urfe Quebec, Canada.

The village of La Patrie, Quebec has long been associated with Robert Godin as far back as the introduction of the Norman Guitar Company in 1972. Other Godin trademark instruments have been built there for years, so it was fitting that the line of classical guitars introduced in 1982 should bear the name of the La Patrie village. For full overall company history, see Godin. For more information, visit La Patrie's website or contact Godin Guitars directly.

ACOUSTIC

All instruments in this series have the following features, unless otherwise listed: classic style, round soundhole, bound body, wood marquetry rosette, Honduras mahogany neck, 12/19-fret rosewood fingerboard, slotted peghead, three-per-side gold tuners with pearloid buttons. Available in a Natural finish of special alcohol lacquer (mfg. 1982-present). Models may be optionally equipped in a hardshell case.

COLLECTION (MODEL 0463) – solid spruce top, solid rosewood back/sides, ebony tied bridge, high gloss lacquer finish, current mfg.

MSR $825	$700	$350 - 450	$200 - 250	

- **Add 20% (MSR $975) for EPM/Quantum electronics (Model 0470).**

CONCERT (MODEL 0425) – solid cedar top, mahogany back/sides, rosewood tied bridge, high gloss lacquer finish, current mfg.

MSR $585	$480	$240 - 290	$135 - 170	

- **Add 10% (MSR $640) for left-handed configuration (Model 0449).**
- **Add 22.5% (MSR $715) for EPM/Quantum electronics (Model 0432).**
- **Add 32.5% (MSR $769) for left-handed configuration with EPM/Quantum electronics (Model 0456).**

* *Concert Cutaway (Model 25084)* – similar to the Concert, except has a single cutaway, mfg. 2004-2011.

	$550	$275 - 325	$150 - 200	$675

»*Concert Cutaway Electric (Model 25091)* – similar to the Concert Cutaway, except has EPM/Quantum electronics, mfg. 2004-present.

MSR $850	$700	$350 - 425	$200 - 250	

MSR/NOTES	100%	EXCELLENT	AVERAGE	LAST MSR

ETUDE (MODEL 0340) – solid cedar top, mahogany back/sides, rosewood tied bridge, lacquer satin finish, current mfg.

| MSR $495 | $400 | $200 - 250 | $120 - 150 | |

- Add 10% (MSR $545) for left-handed configuration (Model 0364).
- Add 25% (MSR $620) for EPM/Quantum electronics (Model 0357).
- Add 35% (MSR $669) for left-handed configuration with EPM/Quantum electronics (Model 0371).

HYBRID CUTAWAY (MODEL 28740/28757) – single cutaway classical body, solid cedar top, mahogany back and sides, mahogany neck, rosewood fingerboard, rosewood bridge, Quantum Burst II electronics, available in Black (28740) or Light Burst (28757) finish, mfg. 2006-present.

| MSR $1,095 | $900 | $450 - 550 | $275 - 325 | |

MOTIF (MODEL 8841) – similar to the Etude, except features a more compact body, available in semi-gloss lacquer finish, mfg. 1998-present.

| MSR $495 | $400 | $200 - 250 | $120 - 150 | |

- Add 25% (MSR $620) for EPM/Quantum electronics (Model 8858).

PRESENTATION (MODEL 0388) – solid spruce top, rosewood back/sides, rosewood tied bridge, semi-gloss lacquer finish, current mfg.

| MSR $725 | $600 | $300 - 375 | $175 - 225 | |

- Add 17.5% (MSR $850) for EPM/Quantum electronics (Model 0395).

LARK IN THE MORNING

Instruments currently produced overseas. Distributed by Lark In The Morning in Fort Bragg, CA.

Lark In The Morning distributes several thousand different types of music products. Lark's catalog includes guitars, harp guitars, Cuban tres, Puerto Rican quatro, travel guitars, citterns, bajo sexto, vihuela, guitarrone, octave mandolins, steel guitars, and many other instruments. Even though they represent several trademarks, they also offer their own line of guitars (and other instruments) that display the name "Lark In The Morning." For more information on their numerous stringed instruments and pricing, please contact the Lark In The Morning directly.

CONTACT INFORMATION
LARK IN THE MORNING
PO Box 799
Fort Bragg, CA 95437
Phone No.: 877-964-5569
Fax No.: 707-964-1979
www.larkinthemorning.com
info@larkinam.com

LARRIVÉE

Instruments currently produced in Vancouver, British Columbia (Canada), since 1982 and Oxnard, CA since 2001. Previously produced in Toronto, Ontario between 1968 and 1977 and in Victoria, British Columbia between 1977 and 1982. Distributed by Larrivée Guitars, Ltd. in Vancouver, British Columbia, Canada, and in the U.S. by Jean Larrivée Guitars USA Inc. in Oxnard, CA.

CONTACT INFORMATION
LARRIVÉE
U.S. Factory/Distribution
1070 Yarnell Place
Oxnard, CA 93033
Phone No.: 805-487-9980
www.larrivee.com
info@larrivee.com

Canada Factory/Distribution
780 E. Cordova Street
Vacouver, British Columbia V6A 1M3
Canada
Phone No.: 604-253-7111
Fax No.: 604-253-5447
www.larrivee.com
info@larrivee.com

Luthier Jean Larrivée met German classical guitar luthier Edgar Mönch and began studying classical guitar at the age of 20. Larrivée moved to Toronto and apprenticed with Mönch and learned to build classical guitars. Larrivée built two guitars under Mönch's leadership and then he began to build guitars by himself at his home workshop. Larrivée guitars was officially started in 1968, and he moved into his first true workshop in 1970, which was above a theater. After exclusively building classical guitars, Larrivée built his first steel string guitar in 1971. Larrivée continued to experiment with guitar building by introducing his own body styles/shapes, different bracings, and other technologies not previously used. In 1972, Jean Larrivée married his wife Wendy, who designs and engraves inlays on many of Larrivée's guitars.

Larrivée grew throughout the 1970s, and by 1976, Larrivée had eight employees and they were building between twenty-five and thirty guitars a month. In 1977, Larrivée moved operations to the island city of Victoria, British Columbia, which provided access to the wet coastal forests on the west coast of North America. In 1982, Larrivée decided to move to the mainland of British Columbia just as most acoustic guitar manufacturers were going through their toughest times. Instead of consolidating operations, Larrivée began building solidbody electric guitars in 1983. Larrivée's first electric line lasted through 1989 when the acoustic guitar market improved to the point where he solely focus on acoustics again.

The 1990s marked a resurgence in guitar building as they moved to an 11,000 square foot factory in 1991 where they employed thirty-five people and built twenty-five guitars a day. In 1997, Larrivée introduced their lowest priced model in their lineup with the D-03, which would firmly establish Larrivée in the acoustic guitar world. In 1998, they moved into another new factory with 33,000 square foot and by now they had 100 employees and they were producing sixty to seventy-two guitars per day. In 2001, Larrivée opened a new factory in southern California ten days before 9/11. Although production slowed for the next two years, Larrivée overhauled some of their production and streamlined production where only the 3 Series of guitars are produced in Canada, and all remaining models are built in the U.S. In 2005, Larrivée introduced their Traditional Series of guitars that are based on traditional designs of the "golden era" of guitar manufacturing. In 2008, Larrivée

MSR/NOTES	100%	EXCELLENT	AVERAGE	LAST MSR

ventured into the solidbody electric realm with their RS-4 model.

Larrivée continues to offer several body shapes, including a few of Larrivée's own designs, and several decoration levels ranging from plain satin-finished models to highly ornate decorative models. For more information, visit Larrivée's website or contact them directly.

NUMERICAL SUFFIXES & MODEL OPTIONS

Numerical suffixes listed below indicate individualized features per model suffix.

05 Mahogany Standard (mahogany back/sides). 09 Standard (pearl logo peghead inlay). 10 Deluxe (abalone purfling on top, abalone/pearl fingerboard inlay, peghead bordered by inlaid silver, hand-engraved Eagle, Gryphon, Pelican or Seahorse on headstock). 19 Special (abalone/pearl fingerboard inlay, hand-engraved Eagle, Gryphon, Pelican or Seahorse on headstock). 50 Standard (ebony fingerboard [pearl dot inlay available on request], pearl logo peghead inlay).

60 Special (Eagle [with feather fingerboard inlay], Stallion and Tiger peghead inlay). 70 DeLuxe (abalone purfled body/rosette, Eagle [with feather fingerboard inlay], Stallion and Tiger peghead inlay). 72 Presentation (abalone purfling on all bound edges, abalone rosette, abalone/pearl fingerboard inlay, peghead bordered by inlaid silver, hand-engraved Dancing Ladies, Genies, Jester, Mermaid on Seahorse or Tamborine Lady inlay on headstock, bridge wing inlays). All instruments are available in left-handed versions at no additional charge. All instruments are also available with following options:

Unless otherwise noted, all Larrivée models are constructed with the same standard materials: spruce top, round soundhole, wood body binding, wooden inlay rosette, transparent pickguard, rosewood or figured maple back/sides, mahogany neck, bound ebony fingerboard, ebony bridge with black pearl dot pins, and three-per-side chrome tuners.

- **A 12-string variation is available in the following models for an additional $190: Cutaway, Cutaway Jumbo, Dreadnought, Jumbo, Larrivee and Larrivée Jumbo Series. Add $140 for Fishman Matrix pickup.**
- **Add $280 for Fishman pickup with preamp.**
- **Add $375 for 2005 inlay designs including Flying Eagle, Seahorse, and Dragon.**
- **Add $1,000 for Brazilian rosewood (when available).**

ACOUSTIC: ANNIVERSARY & LIMITED EDITION SERIES

L-19 CALIFORNIA ANNIVERSARY – Larrivee body style, Indian rosewood back and sides, solid Sitka spruce top, mahogany neck, African ebony fingerboard and bridge, multi-layer rosewood body binding, soundhole with abalone rosette, headstock volute, palm tree with logo headstock and 12th fret California inlays, transparent pickguard, gloss finish, mfg. 2003 only.

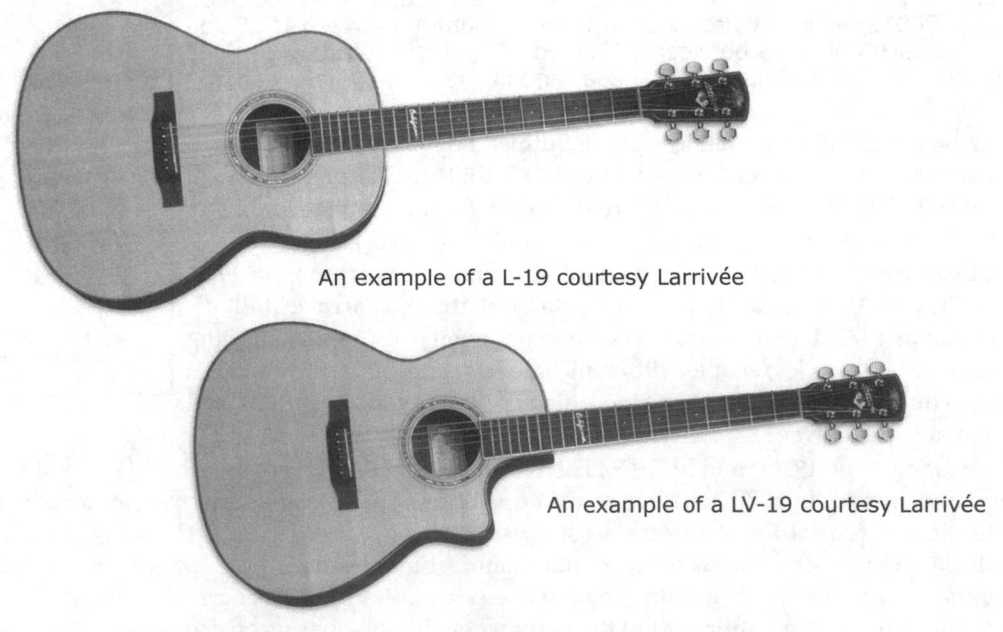

An example of a L-19 courtesy Larrivée

An example of a LV-19 courtesy Larrivée

	N/A	$1,250 - 1,400	$800 - 925	$2,598

- **Add $225 for a Venetian cutaway (Model LV-19 CA).**

This model was also available as an Orchestra body shape (Model OM-19 CA).

L-19 LVE – 16 in. body, solid Sitka spruce top, solid rosewood back and sides, mahogany neck, ebony fingerboard with vine inlays, ebony bridge with wing inlays, abalone rosette, tortoiseshell pickguard, headstock with vine inlay, natural finish, mfg. 2004-05.

	N/A	$1,700 - 1,950	$975 - 1,125	$3,699

- **Add $225 for single Venetian cutaway (Model LV-19 LVE).**

MSR/NOTES	100%	EXCELLENT	AVERAGE	LAST MSR

OM-19 LVE – similar to the L-19 LVE, except in OM body style, mfg. 2004-06.

	N/A	$1,700 - 1,950	$975 - 1,125	$3,699

ACOUSTIC: CLASSIC/FINGERSTYLE SERIES

Classical specifications: 66 mm scale, 15 in. lower bout.

LSV-11 FINGERSTYLE – single Venetian cutaway body, solid Canadian Sitka spruce top, solid Indian rosewood back and sides, enlarged round soundhole with abalone rosette, one-piece South American mahogany neck, 14/19-fret ebony fingerboard with deluxe abalone fingerboard inlays, bound headstock with MOP logo and three-per-side chrome Ping tuners and black buttons, ebony pyramid bridge with ebony/ablone pins, optional electronics, Natural finish, 15.125 in. body width, 4.125 in. depth, 24.75 in. scale, mfg. summer 2006-present.

MSR $4,023	$3,050	$1,650 - 2,000	$1,100 - 1,300	

- Add 7.5% (MSR $4,343) for L.R. Baggs pickup and electronics No-Cut iMix.
- Add 7.5% (MSR $4,323) for L.R. Baggs pickup and electronics with iMix Notch system.

L-30 STANDARD – classic style, unbound fingerboard, tied bridge, three-per-side gold tuners with pearl buttons, disc.

	N/A	$1,050 - 1,200	$675 - 800	$2,395

* *C-30 Cutaway* – similar to the L-30, except features single Florentine cutaway body, disc.

	N/A	$1,300 - 1,500	$785 - 1,000	$2,695

LS-30 – solid Sitka spruce top, rosewood back and sides, ebony fingerboard, rosewood bridge, open-style headstock, mfg. 2004-06.

	N/A	$1,300 - 1,500	$800 - 925	$2,799

* *LSV-30 Cutaway* – similar to the LS-30, except has a single cutaway, mfg. 2004-06.

	N/A	$1,400 - 1,600	$850 - 1,000	$3,099

ACOUSTIC: CUTAWAY SERIES

The instruments in this series have the Larrivee body style with a single sharp cutaway, specifications: 25.5 in. scale, 20.25 in. length, 16 in. lower bout, 4 in. max depth.

C-03 RE ROSEWOOD STANDARD – features a Fishman Prefix+ pickup, disc.

	N/A	$700 - 850	$475 - 550	$1,495

C-05 MAHOGANY STANDARD – disc.

	N/A	$1,000 - 1,200	$725 - 850	$1,895

C-09 ROSEWOOD STANDARD FIRST VERSION – disc.

	N/A	$1,250 - 1,500	$900 - 1,050	$2,295

C-09 ROSEWOOD SELECT SECOND VERSION – single sharp cutaway Larrivée body, solid Canadian Sitka spruce top, solid Indian rosewood back and sides, round soundhole with marquetry rosette, symmetrical parabolic Canadian Sitka spruce X-bracing, Canadian maple body binding, one-piece mahogany neck, 14/20-fret ivoroid-bound ebony fingerboard with microdot inlays, rosewood headstock overlay with Sterling silver bordering and MOP logo, three-per-side chrome Schaller tuners, ebony bridge, clear pickguard, available in Natural gloss finish, archtop hardshell case included, mfg. summer 2008-present.

MSR $3,793	$2,850	$1,600 - 1,950	$1,050 - 1,250	

C-10 ROSEWOOD DELUXE FIRST VERSION – disc.

	N/A	$1,650 - 2,000	$1,100 - 1,300	$2,795

C-10 ROSEWOOD DELUXE SECOND VERSION – single sharp cutaway Larrivée body, solid Canadian Sitka spruce top, solid Indian rosewood back and sides, round soundhole with marquetry rosette, symmetrical parabolic Canadian Sitka spruce X-bracing, abalone pearl purfling, one-piece mahogany neck, 14/20-fret ivoroid-bound ebony fingerboard with deluxe pearl custom inlays, rosewood headstock overlay with Sterling silver bordering and MOP logo, three-per-side chrome Schaller tuners, ebony bridge with deluxe pearl wing inlays, clear pickguard, available in Natural gloss finish, archtop hardshell case included, mfg. summer 2008-present.

MSR $4,598	$3,450	$2,000 - 2,350	$1,250 - 1,500	

ACOUSTIC: CUTAWAY JUMBO SERIES

All the instruments in this series have jumbo Larrivée body styles with a single sharp cutaway.

LCJ-05 MAHOGANY STANDARD – disc.

	N/A	$1,050 - 1,250	$750 - 875	$1,995

LCJ-09 ROSEWOOD STANDARD – disc.

	N/A	$1,300 - 1,550	$925 - 1,075	$2,495

LCJ-10 ROSEWOOD DELUXE – disc.

	N/A	$1,700 - 2,050	$1,125 - 1,325	$2,995

LCJ-72 PRESENTATION – disc.

	N/A	$2,750 - 3,250	$1,800 - 2,100	$5,995

MSR/NOTES	100%	EXCELLENT	AVERAGE	LAST MSR

ACOUSTIC: CUTAWAY SMALL BODY SERIES

Fashioned after the Larrivee small body style, these instruments have a single sharp cutaway.

CS-05 MAHOGANY STANDARD – disc.

	N/A	$1,000 - 1,200	$725 - 850	$1,895

CS-09 ROSEWOOD STANDARD – disc.

	N/A	$1,200 - 1,500	$850 - 1,000	$2,295

CS-10 ROSEWOOD DELUXE – disc.

	N/A	$1,650 - 2,000	$1,100 - 1,300	$2,795

CS-72 PRESENTATION – disc.

	N/A	$2,750 - 3,250	$1,800 - 2,100	$5,995

ACOUSTIC: D-LITE SERIES

All instruments in this series have slightly smaller dreadnought-style bodies, and have an optional gig bag. Specifications: 24.5 in. scale, 19 in. length, 15 in. lower bout, 4.5 in. max depth.

D-LITE – dreadnought style, solid spruce top, wood fiber body binding, round soundhole, mahogany back/sides, mahogany neck, 14/20-fret ebony fingerboard, three-per-side chrome tuners, ebony bridge with white bridgepins (satin) pickguard, available in Natural satin finish, mfg. 1997-99.

	N/A	$350 - 425	$225 - 275	$749

L-LITE – similar to the D-Lite, except features Larrivée body (Larrivée Series) design, available in Natural satin finish, mfg. 1997-99.

	N/A	$350 - 425	$225 - 275	$749

ACOUSTIC: DREADNOUGHT SERIES

All instruments in this series have dreadnought-style bodies. Specifications: 25.5 in. scale, 19 .75 in. length, 16 in. lower bout, 4.5 in. max depth.

D-02 MAHOGANY STANDARD – disc. 2001.

	N/A	$325 - 400	$200 - 250	$699

* Add $100 for Fishman Deluxe SC pickup (Model D02E).

D-03 MAHOGANY STANDARD – Canadian Sitka spruce top, mahogany back and sides, multi-strip rosette, Canadian maple body binding, mahogany neck, ivoroid bound ebony fingerboard, three-per-side tuners, ebony bridge, tortoiseshell pickguard, current mfg.

MSR $1,516	$1,150	$625 - 775	$400 - 475	

* Add 10% (disc. 2010, last MSR was $1,666) for L.R. Baggs electronics.
* Add 17.5% (2010-present, MSR $1,796) for L.R. Baggs Element Notch electronics.

* **D-03R Rosewood Standard** – similar to the D-03, except has rosewood back/sides, current mfg.

MSR $1,707	$1,300	$725 - 875	$475 - 550	

* Add 10% (disc. 2010, last MSR was $1,857) for L.R. Baggs electronics.
* Add 17.5% (2010-present, MSR $1,987) for L.R. Baggs Element Notch electronics.

* **D-03W Walnut Standard** – similar to the D-03, except has walnut back/sides, disc. 1999.

	N/A	$450 - 525	$275 - 325	$899

* **DV-03 Mahogany Standard Cutaway** – similar to D-03, except has a single Venetian cutaway, disc.

	N/A	$675 - 825	$425 - 500	$1,199

* Add 15% for Fishman Prefix Plus electronics (Model DV-03E).

D-04 MAHOGANY STANDARD – disc.

	N/A	$725 - 850	$425 - 500	$1,599

* Add $100 for Fishman Deluxe SC pickup (Model D-04E), disc. 2000.
* Add $200 for Fishman Prefix Plus pickup (Model D-04E).
* Add $300 for Venetian cutaway (Model DV-04).

D-05 MAHOGANY SELECT – Canadian Sitka spruce top, mahogany back and sides, abalone rosette, Canadian multi-layer maple body binding, mahogany neck, 14/20-fret ivoroid bound ebony fingerboard with micro dot inlays, MOP headstock inlay, three-per-side tuners, ebony bridge, beveled tortoiseshell pickguard, current mfg.

MSR $2,528	$1,900	$1,100 - 1,300	$675 - 825	

* Add 12.5% (MSR $2,848) for electronics (Model D-05E).

This model was also available with a mahogany top (Model D-05MT).

* **DV-05 Mahogany Select Cutaway** – similar to the D-05 Select Mahogany, except has a single cutaway, disc.

	N/A	$1,150 - 1,350	$725 - 875	$1,949

* Add 15% for electronics (Model DV-05E).

MSR/NOTES	100%	EXCELLENT	AVERAGE	LAST MSR

D-09 ROSEWOOD ARTIST – Canadian Sitka spruce top, rosewood back and sides, abalone rosette, Canadian multi-layer maple body binding, mahogany neck, 14/20-fret ivoroid bound ebony fingerboard with micro dot inlays, sterling silver headstock border with MOP inlay, three-per-side tuners, ebony bridge, beveled tortoiseshell pickguard, current mfg.

MSR $2,988	$2,250	$1,250 - 1,550	$850 - 1,000	

* Add 10% (MSR $3,308) for electronics (Model D-09E).

* *DV-09 Rosewood Artist Cutaway* – similar to the D-09 Rosewood Artist, except has a single cutaway, disc.

	N/A	$1,300 - 1,600	$900 - 1,050	$2,398

* Add 12.5% for electronics (Model DV-09E).

D-10 ROSEWOOD DELUXE – Canadian Sitka spruce top, rosewood back and sides, abalone rosette, abalone purfling, mahogany neck, 14/20-fret ivoroid bound ebony fingerboard with deluxe abalone inlays, sterling silver headstock border with MOP inlay, three-per-side tuners, ebony bridge with abalone wing inlays, beveled tortoiseshell pickguard, current mfg.

MSR $3,793	$2,850	$1,600 - 1,950	$1,050 - 1,250	

* Add 5% (MSR $4,093) for electronics (Model D-10E).

* *DV-10 Rosewood Deluxe* – similar to the D-10 Rosewood Deluxe, except has a single cutaway, disc.

	N/A	$1,650 - 2,000	$1,100 - 1,300	$2,998

* Add 7.5% for electronics (Model DV-10E).

D-72 PRESENTATION – disc.

	N/A	$2,500 - 3,000	$1,700 - 1,950	$5,495

* Add $225 for Fishman Prefix Pro Blender pickup (Model D-72E).

ACOUSTIC: KOA SERIES

All instruments in this series have single sharp cutaway style bodies, koa top/back/sides, seashell fingerboard/bridge wing inlay, dolphin peghead inlay, disc. 1994.

C-20 – Larrivée style body, disc. 1994.

	N/A	$1,050 - 1,200	$675 - 800	$2,110

CJ-20 – Larrivée jumbo style body, disc. 1994.

	N/A	$1,100 - 1,250	$700 - 825	$2,210

CS-20 – Larrivée small style body, disc. 1994.

	N/A	$1,050 - 1,200	$675 - 800	$2,110

ACOUSTIC: LARRIVÉE SERIES

All instruments in this series have Larrivée-style bodies. Specifications: 25.5 in. scale, 20.25 in. length, 16 in. lower bout, 4 in. max depth.

L-02 MAHOGANY STANDARD – disc.

	N/A	$325 - 400	$200 - 250	$699

* Add $100 for Fishman Deluxe SC pickup (L-02E).

L-03 MAHOGANY STANDARD – Canadian Sitka spruce top, mahogany back and sides, multi-strip rosette, Canadian maple body binding, mahogany neck, ivoroid bound ebony fingerboard, three-per-side tuners, ebony bridge, tortoiseshell pickguard, current mfg.

MSR $1,516	$1,150	$625 - 775	$400 - 475	

* Add 10% (disc. 2010, last MSR was $1,666) for L.R. Baggs electronics (Model L-03E).
* Add 17.5% (2010-present, MSR $1,796) for L.R. Baggs Element Notch electronics (Model L-03E).

* *L-03R Rosewood Standard* – similar to the L-03, except has rosewood back and sides, current mfg.

MSR $1,707	$1,300	$725 - 875	$475 - 550	

* Add 10% (disc. 2010, last MSR was $1,857) for L.R. Baggs electronics.
* Add 17.5% (2010-present, MSR $1,987) for L.R. Baggs Element Notch electronics.

»*LV-03RE Rosewood Standard Cutaway* – similar to the L-03R Rosewood Standard, except has a single cutaway and L.R. Baggs (disc. 2010) or L.R. Baggs Element Notch (2010-present) electronics, current mfg.

MSR $2,382	$1,800	$1,000 - 1,250	$625 - 750	

* *L-03W Walnut Standard* – similar to the L-03, except has walnut back and sides, disc. 1999.

	N/A	$450 - 525	$275 - 325	$899

* *L-03-12E 12-String* – similar to the L-03 Mahogany Standard, except in 12-string configuration, six-per-side tuners, and L.R. Baggs (disc. 2010) or L.R. Baggs Element Notch (2010-present) electronics, current mfg.

MSR $2,090	$1,575	$875 - 1,100	$550 - 650	

MSR/NOTES	100%	EXCELLENT	AVERAGE	LAST MSR

* *LV-03E Mahogany Standard Cutaway* – similar to L-03E Mahogany Standard, except has a single Venetian cutaway body and L.R. Baggs (disc. 2010) or L.R. Baggs Element Notch (2010-present) electronics, current mfg.

MSR $2,193	$1,650	$925 - 1,150	$575 - 675	

L-04 MAHOGANY STANDARD – disc. 2001.

	N/A	$650 - 800	$375 - 450	$1,299

- Add $100 for Fishman Deluxe SC pickup (Model L-04E, disc. 2000.).
- Add $200 for Fishman Prefix Pro pickup (Model L-04E, mfg. 2001 only).
- Add $300 for Venetian cutaway (Model LV-04).
- Add $400 for Venetian cutaway and Fishman Deluxe SC pickup (Model LV-04E).

L-05 MAHOGANY SELECT – Canadian Sitka spruce top, mahogany back and sides, abalone rosette, Canadian multi-layer maple body binding, mahogany neck, 14/20-fret ivoroid bound ebony fingerboard with micro dot inlays, MOP headstock inlay, three-per-side tuners, ebony bridge, beveled tortoiseshell pickguard, current mfg.

MSR $2,528	$1,900	$1,100 - 1,300	$675 - 825	

- Add 12.5% (MSR $2,848) for L.R. Baggs iMix Notch electronics (Model L-05E).

Also available with a mahogany top (Model L-05-MT).

* *L-05-12 Mahogany Select 12-String* – similar to the L-05 Mahogany Select, except in 12-string configuration and six-per-side tuners, current mfg.

MSR $2,758	$2,075	$1,200 - 1,400	$750 - 900	

* *LV-05 Mahogany Select Cutaway* – similar to the L-05 Mahogany Select, except has a single cutaway, current mfg.

MSR $2,873	$2,150	$1,250 - 1,450	$775 - 925	

- Add 10% (MSR $3,193) for L.R. Baggs iMix Notch electronics (Model LV-05E).

L-09 ROSEWOOD ARTIST – Canadian Sitka spruce top, rosewood back and sides, abalone rosette, Canadian multi-layer maple body binding, mahogany neck, 14/20-fret ivoroid bound ebony fingerboard with micro dot inlays, sterling silver headstock border with MOP inlay, three-per-side tuners, ebony bridge, beveled tortoiseshell pickguard, current mfg.

MSR $2,988	$2,250	$1,250 - 1,550	$850 - 1,000	

- Add 10% (MSR $3,308) for L.R. Baggs iMix Notch electronics (Model L-09E).
- Add 20% (disc., Last MSR was $3,598) for AURA Electronics (Model L-09 AURA).

* *L-09-12 Rosewood Artist 12-String* – similar to the L-09 Rosewood Artist, except in 12-string configuration and six-per-side tuners, current mfg.

MSR $3,218	$2,425	$1,350 - 1,650	$900 - 1,050	

* *LV-09 Rosewood Artist Cutaway* – similar to the L-09 Rosewood Artist, except has a single cutaway, current mfg.

MSR $3,333	$2,500	$1,400 - 1,700	$950 - 1,100	

- Add 10% (MSR $3,633) for electronics (Model LV-09E).
- Add 17.5% (MSR $3,933) for AURA Electronics (Model LV-09 AURA).

L-10 ROSEWOOD DELUXE – Canadian Sitka spruce top, rosewood back and sides, abalone rosette, abalone purfling, mahogany neck, 14/20-fret ivoroid bound ebony fingerboard with deluxe abalone inlays, sterling silver headstock border with MOP inlay, three-per-side tuners, ebony bridge with abalone wing inlays, beveled tortoiseshell pickguard, current mfg.

MSR $3,793	$2,850	$1,600 - 1,950	$1,050 - 1,250	

- Add 5% (MSR $4,093) for L.R. Baggs iMix Notch electronics (Model L-10E).
- Add 15% (disc., last MSR was $4,393) for AURA Electronics (Model L-10 AURA).

* *L-10-12 Rosewood Deluxe 12-String* – similar to the L-10 Rosewood Artist, except in 12-string configuration and six-per-side tuners, current mfg.

MSR $4,023	$3,050	$1,700 - 2,050	$1,150 - 1,350	

* *LV-10 Rosewood Deluxe Cutaway* – similar to the L-10 Rosewood Artist, except has a single cutaway, current mfg.

MSR $4,138	$3,125	$1,750 - 2,100	$1,200 - 1,400	

- Add 5% (MSR $4,438) for L.R. Baggs iMix Notch electronics (Model LV-10E).
- Add 15% (disc., last MSR was $4,738) for AURA Electronics (Model LV-10 AURA).

L-72 PRESENTATION – disc.

	N/A	$2,500 - 3,000	$1,700 - 1,950	$5,495

- Add $225 for Fishman Prefix Pro Blender pickup (Model L-72E).

ACOUSTIC: LARRIVÉE JUMBO SERIES

All instruments in this series have Larrivée Jumbo-style bodies.

LJ-05 MAHOGANY STANDARD – disc.

	N/A	$850 - 1,000	$550 - 650	$1,599

LJ-09 ROSEWOOD STANDARD – disc.

	N/A	$1,100 - 1,350	$750 - 900	$2,099

MSR/NOTES	100%	EXCELLENT	AVERAGE	LAST MSR
LJ-10 ROSEWOOD DELUXE – disc.				
	N/A	$1,400 - 1,750	$1,000 - 1,150	$2,749
LJ-72 PRESENTATION – disc.				
	N/A	$2,600 - 3,050	$1,750 - 2,000	$5,695

ACOUSTIC: LARRIVÉE OM SERIES

All instruments in this series have Larrivée OM-style bodies. Specifications: 25.5 in. scale, 20.25 in. length, 16 in. lower bout, 4 in. max depth.

OM-02 MAHOGANY STANDARD – disc.

	N/A	$325 - 400	$200 - 250	$699

* *OM-2E* – similar to OM-02, except has Fishman Deluxe SC pickup, disc.

	N/A	$375 - 450	$225 - 275	$799

OM-03 MAHOGANY STANDARD – Canadian Sitka spruce top, mahogany back and sides, multi-strip rosette, Canadian maple body binding, mahogany neck, ivoroid bound ebony fingerboard, three-per-side tuners, ebony bridge, tortoiseshell pickguard, current mfg.

MSR $1,516	$1,150	$625 - 775	$400 - 475	

* Add 10% (disc. 2010, last MSR was $1,666) for L.R. Baggs electronics.
* Add 17.5% (2010-present, MSR $1,796) for L.R. Baggs Element Notch electronics.

* *OM-03R Rosewood Standard* – similar to the OM-03, except has rosewood back and sides, current mfg.

MSR $1,707	$1,300	$725 - 875	$475 - 550	

* Add 10% (disc. 2010, last MSR was $1,857) for L.R. Baggs electronics.
* Add 17.5% (2010-present, MSR $1,987) for L.R. Baggs Element Notch electronics.

* *OM-03W Walnut Standard* – similar to the OM-03, except features walnut back and sides, disc. 1999.

	N/A	$450 - 525	$275 - 325	$899

OM-04 STANDARD MAHOGANY – disc.

	N/A	$600 - 700	$350 - 425	$1,299

* *OM-04E* – similar to OM-04, except has Fishman Deluxe SC pickup, current mfg.

	N/A	$675 - 800	$450 - 525	$1,499

OM-05 MAHOGANY SELECT – Canadian Sitka spruce top, mahogany back and sides, abalone rosette, Canadian multi-layer maple body binding, mahogany neck, 14/20-fret ivoroid bound ebony fingerboard with micro dot inlays, MOP headstock inlay, three-per-side tuners, ebony bridge, beveled tortoiseshell pickguard, current mfg.

MSR $2,528	$1,900	$1,100 - 1,300	$675 - 825	

* Add 12.5% (MSR $2,848) for L.R. Baggs iMix Notch (disc. 2010) or L.R. Baggs Element Notch (2010-present) electronics (Model OM-05E). This model was also available with a mahogany top (Models OM-05MT).

* *OMV-05 Mahogany Select Cutaway* – similar to the OM-05 Mahogany Select, except has a single cutaway, disc. 2006.

	N/A	$1,150 - 1,350	$700 - 850	$2,249

* Add 15% for electronics (Model OM-05E, Last MSR $2,549).

OM-09 ROSEWOOD ARTIST – Canadian Sitka spruce top, rosewood back and sides, abalone rosette, Canadian multi-layer maple body binding, mahogany neck, 14/20-fret ivoroid bound ebony fingerboard with micro dot inlays, sterling silver headstock border with MOP inlay, three-per-side tuners, ebony bridge, beveled tortoiseshell pickguard, current mfg.

MSR $2,988	$2,250	$1,250 - 1,550	$850 - 1,000	

* Add 10% (MSR $3,308) for L.R. Baggs iMix Notch electronics (Model OM-09E).

* *OMV-09 Rosewood Artist Cutaway* – similar to the OM-09 Rosewood Artist, except has a single cutaway, disc. 2006.

	N/A	$1,300 - 1,600	$875 - 1,025	$2,698

* Add 10% for electronics (Model OMV-09E, Last MSR $2,998).

OM-10 ROSEWOOD DELUXE – Canadian Sitka spruce top, rosewood back and sides, abalone rosette, abalone purfling, mahogany neck, 14/20-fret ivoroid bound ebony fingerboard with deluxe abalone inlays, sterling silver headstock border with MOP inlay, three-per-side tuners, ebony bridge with abalone wing inlays, beveled tortoiseshell pickguard, current mfg.

MSR $3,793	$2,850	$1,600 - 1,950	$1,050 - 1,250	

* Add 5% (MSR $4,093) for L.R. Baggs iMix Notch electronics (Model OM-10E).

* *OMV-10 Rosewood Deluxe Cutaway* – similar to the OM-10 Rosewood Artist, except has a single cutaway, disc. 2006.

	N/A	$1,650 - 2,000	$1,075 - 1,275	$3,298

* Add 5% (Last MSR $3,498) for electronics (Model OMV-10E).

MSR/NOTES	100%	EXCELLENT	AVERAGE	LAST MSR
OM-72 PRESENTATION – disc.				
	N/A	$2,500 - 3,000	$1,700 - 1,950	$5,495

* Add $225 for Fishman Prefix Pro Blender pickup (Model OM-72E).

ACOUSTIC: LARRIVÉE SMALL SERIES

All instruments in this series have Larrivée Small-style bodies.

MSR/NOTES	100%	EXCELLENT	AVERAGE	LAST MSR
LS-05 MAHOGANY STANDARD – disc.				
	N/A	$750 - 900	$500 - 600	$1,595
LS-09 ROSEWOOD STANDARD – disc.				
	N/A	$1,000 - 1,200	$725 - 850	$1,995
LS-10 ROSEWOOD DELUXE – disc.				
	N/A	$1,200 - 1,500	$850 - 1,000	$2,495
LS-72 PRESENTATION – disc.				
	N/A	$2,500 - 3,000	$1,700 - 1,950	$5,495

ACOUSTIC: LARRIVÉE OO SERIES

All instruments in this series have Larrivée 00-style bodies.

MSR/NOTES	100%	EXCELLENT	AVERAGE	LAST MSR
00-05 MAHOGANY STANDARD – disc.				
	N/A	$750 - 900	$500 - 600	$1,595
00-09 ROSEWOOD STANDARD – disc.				
	N/A	$1,000 - 1,200	$725 - 850	$1,995
00-10 ROSEWOOD DELUXE – disc.				
	N/A	$1,200 - 1,500	$850 - 1,000	$2,495
00-72 PRESENTATION – disc.				
	N/A	$2,500 - 3,000	$1,700 - 1,950	$5,495

ACOUSTIC: JUMBO SERIES

All instruments in this series have Jumbo-style bodies. Specifications: 25.5 in. scale, 20.625 in. length, 17 in. lower bout, 4.75 in. max depth.

MSR/NOTES	100%	EXCELLENT	AVERAGE	LAST MSR
J-05 MAHOGANY STANDARD – disc. 2003.				
	N/A	$1,000 - 1,200	$725 - 850	$1,899

* Add $225 for electronics and a pickup (Model J-05E).
* Add $225 for a Venetian cutaway (Model JV-05).

MSR/NOTES	100%	EXCELLENT	AVERAGE	LAST MSR
J-09 ROSEWOOD STANDARD – disc. 2003.				
	N/A	$1,200 - 1,500	$850 - 1,000	$2,448

* Add $225 for electronics and a pickup (Model J-09E).
* Add $225 for a Venetian cutaway (Model JV-09).

MSR/NOTES	100%	EXCELLENT	AVERAGE	LAST MSR
J-10 ROSEWOOD DELUXE – disc. 2003				
	N/A	$1,650 - 2,000	$1,100 - 1,300	$3,048

* Add $225 for electronics and a pickup (Model J-10E).
* Add $225 for a Venetian cutaway (Model JV-10).

MSR/NOTES	100%	EXCELLENT	AVERAGE	LAST MSR
J-72 PRESENTATION – disc.				
	N/A	$2,500 - 3,000	$1,700 - 1,950	$5,695

ACOUSTIC: PARLOR SERIES

0-01 MH PARLOR GUITAR – parlor sized body 13.25 in. width, South American mahogany back/sides, solid Sitka spruce top, mahogany neck, ebony fingerboard and bridge, transparent pickguard, satin finish, mfg. 2002-03.

MSR/NOTES	100%	EXCELLENT	AVERAGE	LAST MSR
	N/A	$325 - 400	$200 - 250	$729

* Add $95 for Indian rosewood back and sides (Model O-01 RW).
* Add $75 for Canadian flamed maple back and side (Model O-01 FM).
* Add $115 for Hawaiian koa back and sides (Model O-01 KA).

P-05 – 13.25 in. body, solid Sitka spruce top, solid mahogany back and sides, multi-strip maple body binding, mahogany neck, 12/19-fret ebony fingerboard, ebony bridge, tortoiseshell pickguard, three-per-side tuners, available in Natural finish, mfg. 2004-present.

MSR/NOTES	100%	EXCELLENT	AVERAGE	LAST MSR
MSR $1,895	$1,425	$800 - 950	$550 - 625	

MSR/NOTES	100%	EXCELLENT	AVERAGE	LAST MSR

P-09 – similar to the P-05, except has rosewood back and sides, mfg. 2004-present.

MSR $2,010	$1,525	$875 - 1,025	$575 - 675	

* *P-09 TSB* – similar to the P-09, except has a flamed maple back and sides with a Sunburst top finish, mfg. 2004-06.

	N/A	$1,050 - 1,250	$700 - 800	$2,429

* *PV-09 Cutaway* – similar to the P-09, except has a single Venetian cutaway, mfg. 2007-present.

MSR $2,355	$1,775	$1,050 - 1,200	$675 - 775	

ACOUSTIC: TRADITIONAL SERIES

0-50 – 0-sized body, Sitka Spruce top, solid mahogany back and sides, maple body binding with herringbone, tortoiseshell pickguard, mahogany neck, 12/19-fret ebony fingerboard with dot inlay, ebony bridge, three-per-side tuners, Natural finish, mfg. 2005 only.

	N/A	$1,200 - 1,500	$750 - 950	$2,849

* Add 35% for full sunburst finish (Model 0-50 FSB).

0-60 – similar to the 0-50, except has rosewood back and sides, mfg. 2005 only.

	N/A	$1,400 - 1,750	$850 - 1,050	$3,398

00-50 – 00-sized body, Sitka Spruce top, solid mahogany backand sides, maple body binding with herringbone, tortoiseshell pickguard, mahogany neck, 12/19-fret ebony fingerboard with dot inlay, ebony bridge, three-per-side tuners, Natural finish, mfg. 2005-06.

	N/A	$1,200 - 1,500	$750 - 950	$2,849

* Add 35% for full sunburst finish (Model 00-50 FSB).

00-60 – similar to the 00-50, except has rosewood back and sides, mfg. 2005-06.

	N/A	$1,400 - 1,750	$850 - 1,050	$3,398

* Add 10% for partial sunburst finish (Model 00-60 FSB).

000-50 TRADITIONAL – 15 in. body, Sitka Spruce top, solid mahogany back and sides, maple body binding with herringbone, tortoisesell pickguard, mahogany neck, 12/19-fret ebony fingerboard with dot inlay, ebony bridge, three-per-side tuners, Natural finish, mfg. 2004-present.

MSR $3,563	$2,675	$1,500 - 1,800	$1,050 - 1,250	

* Add 27.5% (MSR $4,563) for complete Tobacco Sunburst finish (Model 000-50 TSB).

000-60 TRADITIONAL – similar to the 000-50, except has rosewood back and sides, mfg. 2004-present.

MSR $4,138	$3,100	$1,750 - 2,150	$1,150 - 1,350	

* Add 30% for full sunburst finish (Model 000-60 FSB, disc.).

D-50 TRADITIONAL – dreadnought body style, South American mahogany back and sides, solid Sitka spruce top, mahogany neck, African ebony fingerboard and bridge, Canadian flamed maple body binding, enlarged soundhole with abalone rosette, headstock volute, MOP headstock and fingerboard inlays, tortoiseshell pickguard, gloss finish, mfg. 2003-present.

MSR $2,988	$2,250	$1,200 - 1,500	$850 - 1,000	

* Add 10% (MSR $3,288) for L.R. Baggs No-Cut iMix System electronics (Model D-50E).

* *DV-50 Traditional Cutaway* – similar to the D-50 Traditional, except has a single cutaway, mfg. 2003-05.

	N/A	$1,250 - 1,550	$900 - 1,050	

* Add 10% for electronics (Model DV-50E).

D-60 TRADITIONAL – similar to the D-50, except has Indian rosewood back and sides, mfg. 2003-present.

MSR $3,563	$2,675	$1,500 - 1,800	$1,050 - 1,250	

* Add 7.5% (MSR $3,863) for L.R. Baggs No-Cut iMix System electronics (Model D-60E).
* Add 10% for slotted headstock (Model D-60H, disc.).

* *DV-60 Traditional Cutaway* – similar to the D-60, except has a single cutaway, mfg. 2003-05.

	N/A	$1,550 - 1,850	$1,100 - 1,300	

* Add 7.5% for electronics (Model D-60).

OM-50 TRADITIONAL – similar to the D-50, except in an Orchestra Model body, mfg. 2004-present.

MSR $2,988	$2,250	$1,200 - 1,500	$850 - 1,000	

* Add 10% (MSR $3,288) for L.R. Baggs No-Cut iMix System electronics (Model OM-50E).
* Add 35% (MSR $3,988) for Total Sunburst (Model OM-50 TSB).

* *OMV-50 Traditional Cutaway* – similar to the OM-50, except has a single cutaway, mfg. 2004-06.

	N/A	$1,250 - 1,550	$900 - 1,050	$2,649

* Add 7.5% (Last MSR $2,849) for electronics (Model OMV-50E).

OM-60 TRADITIONAL – similar to the D-60 Traditional, except in OM body style, mfg. 2004-present.

MSR $3,563	$2,675	$1,500 - 1,800	$1,050 - 1,250	

* Add 7.5% (MSR $3,863) for L.R. Baggs No-Cut iMix System electronics (Model OM-60E).
* Add 12.5% (MSR $3,963) for Total Sunburst (Model OM-60 TSB).

MSR/NOTES	100%	EXCELLENT	AVERAGE	LAST MSR

OMV-60 Traditional Cutaway – similar to the OM-60 Traditional, except has a single cutaway, mfg. 2004-06.

	N/A	$1,550 - 1,850	$1,100 - 1,300	$3,099

- Add 7.5% (Last MSR $3,299) for electronics (Model OMV-60E).

SD-50 TRADITIONAL – 15 in. body, Sitka Spruce top, sold Honduran mahogany back and sides, maple body binding with herringbone, tortoiseshell pickguard, mahogany neck, 12/19-fret ebony fingerboard with diamond inlay, ebony bridge, rosewood headstock overlay, three-per-side tuners, Natural finish, mfg. 2004-present.

MSR $3,563	$2,675	$1,500 - 1,800	$1,050 - 1,250	

- Add 10% (MSR $3,863) for L.R. Baggs No-Cut iMix System electronics (Model SD-50E).
- Add 27.5% (MSR $4,563) for a Total Tobacco Sunburst finish (Model SD-50 TSB).

SD-60 TRADITIONAL – similar to the SD-50, except has rosewood back and sides, mfg. 2004-present.

MSR $4,138	$3,100	$1,750 - 2,150	$1,150 - 1,350	

- Add 7.5% (MSR $4,438) for L.R. Baggs No-Cut iMix System electronics (Model SD-60E).
- Add 10% (MSR $4,538) for a Sunburst top (Model SD-60 SBT).

BT-60 Baritone – similar to the SD-60, except in baritone configuration and 27 in. scale, mfg. 2005-06.

	N/A	$1,800 - 2,250	$1,150 - 1,400	$3,749

ACOUSTIC/ELECTRIC BASS

B-03RE BASS – rounded body, solid Canadian Sitka spruce top, solid Indian rosewood back and sides, round soundhole with three-ring rosette, symmetrical parabolic Canadian Sitka spruce X-bracing, Canadian maple body binding, one-piece mahogany neck, handfit dovetail neck joint, 14/19-fret ivoroid-bound ebony fingerboard with microdot inlays, black headstock overlay with pearl logo, two-per-side chrome tuners, ebony bridge, L.R. Baggs Element Notch system electronics, available in Natural Satin finish, mfg. summer 2008-present.

MSR $2,428	$1,825	$1,000 - 1,250	$625 - 750	

LARSON BROTHERS

Instruments previously manufactured by Larson Brothers of Maurer & Co. 1900-1944. Also see Maurer and Prairie State.

Carl Larson immigrated from Sweden during the 1880s and began working in the musical instrument trade in the Chicago area. He soon sent for younger brother August who also had a great aptitude for woodworking. In 1900, August and other investors bought out Robert Maurer's Chicago-based business of manufacturing guitars and mandolins. August and Carl ran the business and maintained the Maurer & Co. name throughout their careers which ended with the death of August in 1944. During that period they produced a vast array of stringed instruments including guitars, harp guitars, mandolin orchestra pieces and harp mandolin orchestra pieces, and a few ukes, taro-patches, tiples, and mandolinettos. Through the years the styles changed and so did the basic sizes of guitars and mandolins. They were built larger starting in the mid-1930s to accommodate the demand from players for more volume.

The Larson brothers house brand was "Maurer" up to the transition period of the larger body instruments when the Euphonon brand was initiated for guitars and mandolins. The Maurer brand was used on guitars and mandolin orchestra pieces of many designs during that approximate thirty-five-year period. The guitars ranged from oak body small guitars to pearl and abalone trimmed guitars and mandolins having tree-of-life inlays on the fingerboards. These are beautifully made instruments of the highest quality, but even the less fancy models are well made in the tradition of the Larson brothers' craftsmanship. The guitars with the 12-frets-to-the-body neck sizes came in widths of 12.75 in., 13.5 in., 14 in. and 15 in.

The Larson brothers also built guitars, harp guitars, and mandolin orchestra pieces for Wm. C. Stahl of Milwaukee and W.J. Dyer of St. Paul, as well as other assorted suppliers who put their own name on the Larsons' products. Stahl and Dyer claimed to be the makers - a common practice during those "progressive years."

The Prairie State brand was added in the mid-1920s for guitars only. These followed the styles of the better and best grade Maurer models but incorporated one of three main systems of steel rods running the length of the guitar body. August was awarded three patents for these ideas which included side items such as adjustable bridges, fingerboards, and necks.

The Prairie State guitars and the better and best grade Maurers and Stahls had a system of laminated top braces. August patented this idea in 1904 making the Larsons pioneers in designing the first guitars made for steel strings which are the only kind they ever made. The laminated braces were continued in the larger Prairie States and the better and best grade models of the Euphonon brand. An occasional Maurer brand instrument may be found in the larger size bodies which I attribute to those sold by Wack Sales Co. of Milwaukee during this later period. This outlet was not offered the Euphonon brand, so they sold them under the Maurer name.

The Larson brothers sold their wares to many prominent players from the radio stations in Chicago, mainly WLS and WJJD. These stations put on country music shows with live performances and became very popular. The Larsons also built three guitars for Les Paul, one of which was a step in developing the solid body guitar. A Larson fingerboard can be seen on what Les called "The Log" which he submitted to Gibson to sell his solid body idea. Gene Autry and Patsy Montana bought Euphonon guitars from the Larsons' shop in 1937.

The main brands produced by the Larsons were Maurer, Prairie State, Euphonon, W.J. Dyer, and Wm. C. Stahl. J.F. Stetson was Dyer's brand for their regular flattop guitar, while the Dyer label was used for the "Symphony" series of harp-guitars and harp-mandolin family instruments.

The Larson brands were burned into the center inside back strip below the soundhole. Typically, if an instrument was altered from standard, it was not branded. This led to many not having any markings. All of the instruments built by the Larsons were handmade. Their degree of craftsmanship made them wonderful instruments to play and ensured that they would become highly collectible. Many people believe that the Larsons' products are as good as Martins and Gibsons, and some believe that they are better. The Larson-built Dyer brand harp guitars are considered the best harp guitars ever made.

More information regarding the individual brands can be found under their brand names: Maurer, Prairie State, Euphonon, Wm. C. Stahl and W.J. Dyer.

Information courtesey: Robert Carl, *The Larsons' Creations, Guitars and Mandolins.*

LASKIN, WILLIAM (GRIT)

Instruments currently built in Toronto, Canada.

William "Grit" Laskin has been building concert-level guitars for more than 43 years. His steel-string, classical and flamenco guitars are known and coveted around the world. Players of his instruments include: K.D. Lang, Ben Mink, Rik Emmett, Tom Cochrane, Jesse Cook, Wayne Johnson, Tom Chapin, Garnet Rogers, Stan Rogers, Ottmar Liebert, Ken Whiteley, James Keelaghan, Cathy Fink, Lillebjorn Nilsen. Commissions from guitarmaker colleagues and others within the trade include Bill Collings (Collings Guitars, Texas), Roger Sadowsky (Sadowsky Guitars, New York), Dick Boak (director, Martin Guitars, PA), Larry Sifel (pres., Pearlworks, MD). His current waiting list of commissions is 25 months long.

In 1997, he received Canada's prestigious Saidye Bronfman Award For Excellence, the first and only instrument maker to be so honored. He is also an elected fellow of the Royal Canadian Academy of the Arts, and included both in the University Of Toronto's "Who's Who In Canada" as well as the Encyclopedia of Music In Canada. In 2010, he received the Estelle Klein Lifetime Achievement Award and most recently, on June 30, 2012 he was awarded the Order Of Canada, which is Canada's highest civilian honor for those who enhance the national fabric.

In addition to building the instruments, Laskin uses them as "canvases" for his engraved inlay art. He is now internationally acknowledged as having single-handedly taken the tradition of musical instrument decoration beyond the purely decorative. For Laskin, the inlay medium has become a tool for communication, not merely embellishment. For more information, visit Laskin's website or contact him directly.

Laskin's steel string guitars start at $15,900, Flamenco guitars start at $16,500, and classical guitars start at $16,900. Inlay art is $95 per hour. As of June, 2014, the earliest delivery of a guitar is September, 2016 and to secure a spot on the waiting list requires a deposit of 20% of the base price.

LAUNHARDT

Previously Launhardt & Kobs. Instruments currently produced in Wetslar, Germany since the 1980s.

German luthier Thomas Launhardt builds high quality acoustic guitar as well as archtop jazz guitars and solidbody guitars. Most Launhardt instruments have "LUK" on the headstock. In 1999, Launhardt changed the name of the company from Launhardt & Kobs to Launhardt.

Classical models include the **Prelude, Sarabande, Bourree,** and **Romantika** with slotted headstocks and traditional Spanish-style bodies. Jumbo-style models include the six-string **Jack D**. and the twelve-string **William D**. The **Averell D**. akustik (acoustic bass) model has a single rounded cutaway body, and a 865 mm scale length.

L BENITO GUITARS

Acoustic guitars currently produced in Chile since 2001. Distributed in the U.S. by L&B Marketing Inc. in Stone Mountain, GA.

Luthier Lito Benito builds a wide range of quality acoustic guitars in his Chile factory. Benito worked at Taylor Guitars where he eventually became the head of final assembly. In 1997, he moved to Mexico, and Taylor set him up to build guitars. In 2001, he moved to Chile and worked on building the infrastructure to make guitars in such an undeveloped nation. Benito uses a unique wood in his guitars call Alerce - a 3,000 year old tonewood. For more information, contact Benito directly.

LEACH, H.G.

Instruments currently built in Cedar Ridge, CA.

CONTACT INFORMATION
LEACH, H.G.
PO Box 1315
Cedar Ridge, CA 95924
Phone No.: 530-477-2938
www.leachguitars.com
harv@leachguitars.com

Harvey G. Leach has been building musical instruments for over forty years. Leach, a former furniture maker from Vermont, began building banjos and mandolins early on in his musical instrument career. In 1979, he built his first guitar, and then gave it to his wife as a wedding present. All H.G. Leach guitars are individually handcrafted, and built to the owner's specifications. He estimates that twenty to twenty-five guitars are built each year; a basic model may take a week's worth of work (spread out over a three-week time period), and a fancier model with mother-of-pearl inlays may take five times as long.

Leach decided that he wanted to focus more time on his inlay work and started the company Cutting Edge Inlays. This reduced his building to only about twelve guitars instead of thirty a year.

Leach is also committed to environmental concerns, and produces his guitars with domestic or foreign sustainable yield mahogany and Brazilian (or Bolivian) rosewood. Leach also uses a UV cured lacquer finish (a nitrocellulose finish is available on request).

Luthier Leach offers a wide range of inlay, abalone trim, wood appointments, and other options to all of his creations (the list is two columns long!). As a result, the custom-ordered guitar is a custom-built guitar, right to the customer's specifications. All list prices include a hardshell case. For more information, visit Leach's website or contact him directly.

Leach builds all of his guitars as a custom shop where each guitar starts with a base model and options are priced accordingly. Naked Canvas guitars start at $8,000, Limited Edition themes can be added starting at $2,800, and archtop guitars start at $8,500.

LEBEDA, JIRI

Instruments currently produced in the Czech Republic since 1978.

Luthier Jiri Lebeda has been offering a wide range of lutherie services in the Czech Republic since the late 1970s. Lebeda offers regular lutherie services like set-ups and repair, as well as handcrafting mandolins, custom instruments, and special custom inlay work. Lebeda also offers design and technology research of fretted instruments, building prototypes and special series instruments, and building special tools. Lebeda currently focuses primarily on building mandolins and resonator guitars. It is rumoured that Lebeda has gone on hiatus from instrument building, and it is unknown if or when he will resume production.

LEHMANN STRINGED INSTRUMENTS

Guitars currently produced in Rochester, NY since 1971.

CONTACT INFORMATION
LEHMANN STRINGED INSTRUMENTS
34 Elton St.
Rochester, NY 14607
Phone No.: 585-902-8663
www.lehmannstrings.com
bernie@lehmannstrings.com

Luthier Bernie Lehmann builds custom acoustic and archtop guitars in his Rochester, NY shop. He also serves as a full stringed instrument service shop. Lehmann builds all kinds of instruments including classical guitars, lutes, mandolins, and several other one-off pieces. His main production instruments consist of classical guitars, flattop guitars, gypsy-style guitars, and archtop guitars. Prices start at $3,350 for flattops and $3,500 for classicals. For more information, visit Lehmann's website or contact him directly.

LEIF HANSSON

Guitars previously produced in Olso, Norway.

Leif Hansson guitars were produced in Norway and at least two examples have been seen in the U.S. Source: Walter Murray, Frankenstein Fretworks.

LEVIN

Instruments currently built in Sweden. Instruments were previously built in Sweden from 1900 to 1977. In the early 1970s, Levin was purchased by the Martin Guitar Company of Nazareth, Pennsylvania.

The Levin company of Sweden was founded by luthier Herman Carlson Levin in 1900, and the first guitar and mandolin factory was set up in Goteburg, Sweden. Prior to establishing his factory, luthier Levin had a shop in Manhattan.

Levin was purchased in the early 1970s by the Martin Guitar company. While early Levin models had some "Martin-esque" qualities prior to the sale, they definitely showed Martin influence afterwards. Production focused on flat-tops after the company changed hands. The last Levin guitars were built in 1977 (source: Aad Overseem, The Netherlands).

Levin guitars was purchased by Bertil Josefson and they are now producing guitars again. They make small wood classic guitars, but no longer make dreadnoughts.

Levin built very good quality single cutaway, one (or two) pickup archtops between the 1930s and the 1960s, as well as flattop guitars, banjos, mandolins, lutes, and other stringed instruments. It is estimated that the company built more than 560,000 instruments while in business. The Model 119 was one guitar to be made by Levin and it featured a small, narrow-waisted, folk six-string, solid spruce top, 12/18 neck with dot position markers, three-per-side tuners, no pickguard, red and green rosette. Values are still unknown on used Levin instruments.

LEVITCH

Levitch Guitar Works. Instruments previously built in Scotch Plains, NJ, from the late 1980s until the 1990s.

Luthier Richard Levitch offered custom handmade acoustic and electric guitars from the late 1980s through the 1990s. Levitch apprenticed to luthier Sam Koontz in Linden, New Jersey, for five years before building on his own. Levitch guitars may have also been produced in Prescott, Arizona. In addition to his acoustic guitar models, Levitch offered electric guitars with a retail price starting at $950 plus options.

The Basic **Artisan** model (last list $950) featured a dreadnought or 15.5 in. round body, Sitka spruce top, mahogany (or maple or Indian rosewood) back and sides, maple or mahogany neck, ebony or rosewood fingerboard and bridge, black headpiece with mother-of-pearl or abalone inlay, gold-plated or nickel-plated tuners, plastic or wood binding, and an oval or round soundhole. The Artisan was finished with gloss or satin lacquer, and the price included a hardshell case.

Options included an Engelmann spruce top (add $125), rounded or sharp cutaway (add $150), Fishman bridge pickup (add $200), and others. Levitch offered the following optional tonewoods for the back and sides of his Artisan model: figured bubinga, quilted and flame maple, Eucalyptus, Australian figured lacewood, figured paduak, figured walnut, and figured myrtle (add $150), flamed koa (add $200), Brazilian rosewood and quilted mahogany.

LEWIS, MICHAEL A.

Instruments currently built in Grass Valley, CA, since 1993.

CONTACT INFORMATION
LEWIS, MICHAEL A.
20807 E. Spring Ranches Rd.
Grass Valley, CA 95949
Phone No.: 530-272-4124
www.michaellewisinstruments.com
michaellewisinstruments@wildblue.net

Luthier Michael A. Lewis began offering handcrafted banjos and mandolins in 1981. Lewis, a stringed instrument repairman since 1981, began making both flattop and archtop guitars in 1993. In 1999, Lewis chose to focus exclusively on the carved plate instruments. Until 2011, Lewis made authorized replicas of John D'Angelico's Excel and New Yorker models (prices started at $18,000). Lewis is a repair and restoration shop for original D'Angelico guitars and an authorized service center for Martin. For more information visit Lewis' website or contact him directly.

Archtop models include the **Studio**, **Standard**, **Deluxe**, and **Supreme**. These are states of trim and material selection, and may be applied to 16 in., 17 in., 17.5 in., or 18 in. body sizes. Most Lewis instruments are custom ordered and therefore unique, leaving the model designation somewhat vague. Regular archtop prices start at $7,200 and climb to over $20,000, and are determined by selection of materials, design, and other appointments. The overall design and structure is strongly influenced by D'Aquisto's and D'Angelico's work, but has some other concepts and considerations factored in. Built as acoustic instruments, they are also available with the option of Bartolini hum canceling jazz pickups and controls mounted on the pickguard.

LIIKANEN GUITARS

Instruments currently built in Helsinki, Finland, since 1986.

CONTACT INFORMATION
LIIKANEN GUITARS
Helsinki, Finland
www.liikanenguitars.com
keijo.liikanen@kolumbus.fi

Liikanen Musical Instruments is a company formed by three experienced luthiers to construct high class concert acoustic guitars. The company was founded by Kauko Liikanen in 1986, who has been building guitars for more than twenty years. Kauko's brother, Keijo Liikanen, joined the company in 1990. A German guitar teacher Uwe Florath joined the team in 1999. In 2000, the company invented and patented new construction for an acoustic guitar top. Since then every Liikanen guitar is build with the "Lens Resonance System top." Models include six-string, seven-string and ten-string classical guitars as well as an eleven-string alto guitar. For further information regarding specifications and pricing, contact Liikanen Musical Instruments directly.

LINCOLN

Instruments previously produced in Japan between the late 1970s and the early 1980s.

Lincoln instruments featured both original designs and designs based on classic American favorites; most guitars are considered to be of good quality. Source: Tony Bacon and Paul Day, *The Guru's Guitar Guide*.

LINDELL

Instruments previously produced in Japan during the mid-1960s.

Research continues into the Lindell trademark, as the producing company in Japan and the American distributor has yet to be identified.

LINE 6

Acoustic instruments currently produced since 2005. Electric instruments currently produced since 2002. Amplifiers and other modeling devices currently produced in Agoura Hills, CA since 1996. Distributed by Line 6 in Agoura Hills, CA.

CONTACT INFORMATION
LINE 6
29901 Agoura Rd.
Agoura Hills, CA 91301-2513
Phone No.: 818-575-3600
Fax No.: 818-575-3601
www.line6.com

Line 6 was established in 1996. Even though they are a relatively new company, they have been very successful. Line 6 products can be described as taking musical products, such as amplifiers, and combining with up-to-date technology. Line 6's first patent was a

MSR/NOTES	100%	EXCELLENT	AVERAGE	LAST MSR

digital modeling amp, which almost all amplifier companies have given a try at now. This was a result of realizing the need to get a number of amplifier tones out of one amplifier. Not only was this Line 6's idea, but this is the theory behind all modeling amps. The AxSys 212 was the first product to hit the shelves in 1996, and many amplifiers followed. Shortly thereafter, another idea was tackled by the staff at Line 6; to make an amplifier that would sound great in the recording studio. The POD was the answer to this, as it could plug into a tape recorder, or even a computer. This is a kidney shaped device that has all the effects with a line out jack for recording purposes. Line 6 is currently still producing state-of-the-art amps and leading the industry as far as technology. They have also released the Variax guitar, which is a modeling type of guitar. In 2005, an acoustic Variax model was introduced. For more information refer to their website.

ACOUSTIC

VARIAX ACOUSTIC 300 – nylon or steel string configuration, single cutaway body, spruce top, mahogany back and sides, round soundhole, mahogany neck, 19-fret rosewood fingerboard (nylon) or 21-fret rosewood fingerboard with dot inlays (steel), slotted headstock (nylon) three-per-side tuners, rosewood bridge, volume controls, digital display with ten presets, available in Natural finish, 25.5 in. scale (steel) or 25.9 in. scale (nylon), mfg. 2005-2012.

	$600	$350 - 425	$200 - 250	$840

VARIAX ACOUSTIC 700 – single cutaway body, cedar top, mahogany back and sides, mahogany neck, 24-fret extended rosewood fingerboard with snowflake inlays, three-per-side tuners, rosewood bridge, 16 guitar models, electronics, available in Black, Natural, or Sunburst finish, 25.5 in. scale, mfg. 2005-2010.

	$1,200	$750 - 900	$475 - 550	$1,680

LIPTON, WALTER

Instruments currently built in Orford, NH.

CONTACT INFORMATION
LIPTON, WALTER
PO Box 100-J
Orford, NH 03777
Phone No.: 603-353-4882

Luthier Walter Lipton builds an estimated ten handcrafted acoustic guitars each year. Lipton's retail list prices start around $3,000, and he offers both steel-string and classical-style guitars. Lipton specializes in aged woods (10 to 20 years) and engraved mother-of-pearl inlays. Lipton also operates the Euphonon Co., a parts supply house that offers woods, luthier tools, strings, and fretted instrument parts. Lipton is currently building guitars with luthier Bill Tippin.

LOAR, THE

Instruments currently produced overseas since 2005. Distributed by The Music Link in Hayward, CA.

CONTACT INFORMATION
LOAR, THE
Distributed by The Music Link
31067 San Clemente Street
Hayward, CA 94544
Phone No.: 415-570-0970
Fax No.: 415-570-0651
www.theloar.com
info@themusiclink.net

The Loar brand is a division of The Music Link. These acoustic instruments were designed by famous engraver Greg Rich and were inspired by Lloyd Loar, who designed many famous instruments for Gibson in the 1920s. The Loar brand has a series of archtop models with many traditional appointments that Loar used when he designed guitars. For more information, contact The Music Link, or visit their website.

ACOUSTIC

LH-200 – small 1930s-style body, solid spruce top, mahogany back and sides, round soundhole with single ring rosette, ivoroid binding, 14/19-fret rosewood fingerboard with dot inlays, bound black headstock overlay with flower pot or fern abalone inlays, three-per-side chrome Butterbean tuners, rosewood bridge, black pickguard, available in Natural or Sunburst finish, 25.5 in. scale, mfg. 2008-present.

MSR $668	$500	$275 - 325	$150 - 200	

LH-250 – small 1930s-style body, solid spruce top, solid mahogany back and sides, round soundhole with single ring rosette, ivoroid binding, 14/19-fret rosewood fingerboard with dot inlays, bound black headstock overlay with abalone/MOP logo, three-per-side chrome Butterbean tuners, rosewood bridge, black pickguard, available in Natural or Sunburst finish, 25.5 in. scale, mfg. 2010-present.

MSR $734	$550	$300 - 375	$180 - 225	

LH-300 – L-style body, solid hand-carved spruce top, maple back and sides, two f-holes, ivoroid binding, mahogany neck with vintage "V" profile, 14/19-fret bound rosewood fingerboard with dot inlays, black headstock overlay with abalone/MOP fleur-de-lis inlay and logo, three-per-side chrome Butterbean tuners, adj. ebony bridge, nickel-plated trapeze tailpiece, available in Tobacco Sunburst finish, 24.75 in. scale, mfg. 2010-present.

MSR $800	$600	$350 - 425	$200 - 250	

* *LH-350* – similar to the LH-350, except has a single sharp cutaway, Kent Armstrong humbucker pickup, and a raised tortoise pickguard with a single volume knob mounted on it, available in Tobacco Sunburst finish, 24.75 in. scale, mfg. 2010-present.

MSR $1,000	$750	$425 - 525	$250 - 300	

MSR/NOTES	100%	EXCELLENT	AVERAGE	LAST MSR

LH-400/LH-500 – L-style body, solid arched select spruce top, solid flamed maple arched back and sides, round soundhole with rosette (LH-400) or two f-holes (LH-500), multi-ply binding, 14/19-fret rosewood fingerboard with dot inlays, flower pot or fern abalone/MOP headstock inlays, three-per-side chrome Butterbean tuners, adj. ebony bridge, trapeze tailpiece, raised tortoiseshell pickguard, available in Natural or Sunburst finish, mfg. 2005-08.

	N/A	$600 - 750	$350 - 450	$1,400

* **Add 7.5% (Last MSR was $1,500) for a floating pickup (LH-500 only).**

LH-600 – L-style body, hand-carved hand-graduated spruce top, hand-carved flamed maple back, flamed maple sides, two f-holes, ivory binding, 14/19-fret bound rosewood fingerboard with dot inlays, flower pot or fern abalone/MOP headstock inlays, three-per-side chrome Butterbean tuners, adj. ebony bridge, trapeze tailpiece, available in Natural or Sunburst finish, 24.75 in. scale, mfg. 2008-present.

MSR $1,334	$1,000	$575 - 700	$325 - 400	

LH-700 – L-style body, solid hand-carved AAA spruce top, solid hand-carved AAA flamed maple arched back and sides, two f-holes, ivoroid binding, flame maple neck, 14/19-fret bound ebony fingerboard with dot inlays, bound black headstock overlay with flower pot abalone/MOP inlays, three-per-side chrome Gotoh tuners, adj. ebony bridge, trapeze tailpiece, available in Sunburst finish, 24.75 in. scale, hardshell case included, mfg. 2010-present.

MSR $2,000	$1,500	$850 - 1,050	$500 - 625	

LO-16 – L-00-style body, solid spruce top, mahogany back and sides, round soundhole with single ring rosette, ivoroid binding, mahogany neck, 14/19-fret rosewood fingerboard with dot inlays, black headstock overlay with MOP fleur-de-lis and logo inlays, three-per-side nickel Grover tuners, rosewood bridge, black or white pickguard, available in Black or Natural finish, 24.75 in. scale, mfg. 2010-present.

MSR $534	$400	$255 - 275	$130 - 165	

LONE STAR

Instruments previously made in Paracho, Mexico. Distributed by LPD Music International in Madison Heights, MI.

Lone Star guitars were produced in the mountain village of Paracho, Mexico, which has a two-hundred-year heritage of guitar building. Lone Star guitars are available with laminate, solid cedar, or solid spruce tops and are designed for the beginning to intermediate student. Besides guitars, they also produce a variety of other instruments including requintos, mandolins, and bajo sextos. The Dallas dreadnought model retailed for $475. The San Marcos Classical retailed for $199 and the El Paso classical retailed for $475. Prices on the other models ran from $150 to $500. In the late 2000s, LPD Music decided to change the name of their guitars from Lone Star to Paracho Elite Guitars.

LOPRINZI

Instruments previously built in Rosemont, Hopeville, and Plainsboro, NJ from 1972 to 1980.

Thomas R. LoPrinzi, along with his brother Augustino, originally founded LoPrinzi guitars in New Jersey in early 1972. The business grew from a two- and three-man operation into a staff of eighteen employees. Modern production techniques enabled the LoPrinzi brothers to pare the number of employees back to seven while still producing sixty to eighty guitars a month in the late 1970s. Augustino LoPrinzi, tired of overseeing production, sold the business to Maark Corporation (a subsidiary of AMF). His brother Thomas was then named president of LoPrinzi Guitars. The AMF-owned company continued producing guitars for a number of years, and finally closed the doors in 1980. Years later, Augustino called AMF to request his old trademark back. Working with vice president Dick Hargraves, Augustino officially had the trademark transferred back, and has combined it to form the current "Augustino LoPrinzi" line of classical guitars (source: Hal Hammer).

LoPrinzi guitars were available in three styles: Standard, Folk, and Twelve-String. Early designs featured German silver Spruce tops and Brazilian rosewood; later models had tops built out of Canadian and Alaskan spruce, and bodies constructed with Indian rosewood, flamed maple, and Honduran mahogany. All models have an adjustable truss rod, ebony fingerboard, pearl or abalone inlays, and a rosewood bridge.

ACOUSTIC

LR-15 – dreadnought-style body, spruce top, rosewood back and sides, round soundhole with multi-ring rosette, multi-ply body binding, mahogany neck, 14/20-fret ebony fingerboard with dot inlays, three-per-side gold tuners, rosewood bridge, available in Natural finish, mfg. 1970s.

	N/A	$1,200 - 1,500	$750 - 950	

LR-20 – classical style, spruce top, rosewood back and sides, round soundhole, mahogany neck, ebony fingerboard with dot inlays, gold hardware, available in Natural finish, mfg. 1970s.

	N/A	$1,200 - 1,500	$750 - 950	

LOPRINZI, AUGUSTINO

Instruments currently built in Florida.

CONTACT INFORMATION
LOPRINZI, AUGUSTINO
1929 Drew Street
Clearwater, FL 33765
Phone No.: 727-447-2276
Fax No.: 727-446-7704
www.augustinoloprinzi.com
loprinzi@gate.net

A self-taught guitar builder, LoPrinzi's original Flemmington, NJ barber shop also had a guitar workshop in the back. After ten years dividing his interests, LoPrinzi (and his brother Thomas) founded LoPrinzi guitars in New Jersey in 1972. The business grew from a two- and three-man operation into a staff of eighteen employees. Modern production techniques enabled the LoPrinzi brothers to pare the number of employees back to seven while still producing sixty to eighty guitars a month in 1975. LoPrinzi, tired of overseeing production, sold the business to Maark Corporation (a subsidiary of AMF). Refusing to sign a "Non-compete" clause, LoPrinzi opened "Augustino Guitars" two weeks later - and literally right next door to his original plant! He continued to produce guitars there until 1978, and then moved to Florida. The AMF-owned LoPrinzi company continued producing guitars for a number of years, and finally closed the doors in 1980. Years later, Augustino called AMF to request his old trademark back. Working with vice president Dick Hargraves, Augustino officially had the trademark transferred back, and has combined it to form the current "Augustino LoPrinzi" line of guitars.

In 1994, Augustino was joined by his daughter Donna LoPrinzi Chavis and together they began producing over 200 instruments per year. While the actual business was turned over to Donna in 2003, Augustino has stayed on and continues building guitars. The LoPrinzi's current production is nearly 25 instruments per month.

Through the years, Augustino LoPrinzi has consulted or designed instruments for many companies including Guild, Martin, Kramer, Fender, and others. His high quality limited production classical guitars feature quality tonewoods, and range in price from $3,000 to $10,000. LoPrinzi also builds several flamenco models, steel string acoustics and ukuleles. For further information regarding models, availability, and pricing, visit LoPrinzi's website or contact him directly.

LORD

Instruments previously built in Japan during the 1960s.

Guitars with the Lord trademark originated in Japan, and were distributed in the U.S. by the Halifax company. Used Lord acoustic guitars can generally be found priced between $75 and $150 depending upon condition. Source: Michael Wright, *Guitar Stories*, Volume One.

LOTUS

Acoustic guitars previously produced in Korea, China, and/or India during the 1990s. Distributed by Midco International in Effingham, IL.

Lotus is a trademark of Musicorp (previously Midco International). In the 1990s, they offered a wide range of acoustic and electric guitars that were designed for the student and/or entry level player. In the 2000s, Musicorp stopped offering guitars under the Lotus trademark to focus on bluegrass instruments, specifically banjos and mandolins.

LOWDEN

Instruments currently produced in Northern Ireland. Instruments previously produced in Japan from 1981 to 1985. Lowden has been producing guitars since 1973.

CONTACT INFORMATION
LOWDEN
34 Down Business Park, Belfast Road
Downpatrick, County Down BT30 9UP
Northern Ireland
Phone No.: +44 (0)284 461 9161
Fax No.: +44 (0)284 461 7043
www.georgelowden.com
sumitra@georgelowden.com

In 1973, luthier George Lowden began designing and manufacturing hand-built guitars in Ireland. Demand outgrew the one-person effort and the production of some models were farmed out to luthiers in Japan in 1981. However, full production was returned to Ireland in 1985. In 1988, the flat acoustic market took its toll on the small company and Lowden was forced to close its doors. The company was placed in receivership, similar to Chapter 11 bankruptcy, and Lowden was bought out by a group. George signed licensing papers so he could still oversee guitar production and they could use his designs. In 1989, George moved to France, where he started building guitars as an independent luthier. George moved back to Ireland in 1990. From 1990 to 1998, Lowden released many new models, and became an established guitar company. In 1998, George put together a new holding company that bought a controlling interest in Lowden. George has since built a new factory and Lowden continues to introduce new models. For more information, refer to Lowden's website or contact them directly.

ACOUSTIC: ORIGINAL SERIES

Lowden offers four main body styles, and they are each available in various configurations. All models with the same configurations are priced the same (for example, a Model 10 Folk is the same price as a Model 10 Jumbo). The four body styles are dreadnought (D), jumbo (O), mini-folk (F), and small-body (S). The dreadnought body style was discontinued in 2003.

- Add $100 (MSR $115) for a low profile neck.
- Add $265 (MSR $310) for a narrower neck (43.5 mm/56 mm).
- Add $290 (disc., last MSR was $385) for Baggs Ribbon system electronics.
- Add $290 (disc., last MSR was $385) for Fishman Matrix electronics.
- Add $480 (MSR $565) for Fishman Elipse blend electronics.

MSR/NOTES	100%	EXCELLENT	AVERAGE	LAST MSR

MODEL 10 – dreadnought, jumbo, mini-folk, or small-body style, cedar top, round soundhole, wood bound body, wood inlay rosette, mahogany back/sides, five-piece mahogany/rosewood neck, 14/20-fret ebony fingerboard, rosewood veneered peghead with pearl logo inlay, three-per-side custom gold tuners with amber buttons, rosewood bridge, available in Natural finish, disc. 2007.

	N/A	$1,850 - 2,150	$1,100 - 1,300	$3,995

* *Model 10 12 String* – similar to Model 10, except in 12-string configuration and six-per-side tuners, disc. 2007.

	N/A	$2,050 - 2,450	$1,250 - 1,450	$4,520

* *Model 10 Cutaway* – similar to the Model 10, except has a single cutaway, disc. 2007.

	N/A	$2,050 - 2,450	$1,250 - 1,450	$4,540

MODEL 12 – similar to Model 10, except has a spruce top, disc. 2007.

	N/A	$1,850 - 2,150	$1,100 - 1,300	$3,995

* *Model 12 12 String* – similar to Model 12, except in 12-string configuration and six-per-side tuners, disc. 2007.

	N/A	$2,050 - 2,450	$1,250 - 1,450	$4,520

* *Model 12 Cutaway* – similar to the Model 12, except has a single cutaway, disc. 2007.

	N/A	$2,050 - 2,450	$1,250 - 1,450	$4,540

MODEL 22 – dreadnought, jumbo, or mini-folk, body style, cedar top, round soundhole, wood bound body, wood inlay rosette, mahogany back/sides, mahogany/sycamore five-piece neck, 14/20-fret ebony fingerboard, rosewood bridge, rosewood veneered peghead with pearl logo inlay, three-per-side gold tuners with amber buttons, available in Natural finish, disc. 1994, reintroduced 2008-present.

MSR $4,575	$3,900	$2,175 - 2,625	$1,275 - 1,600	

* *Model 22 12-String* – similar to O-22, except in 12-string configuration and six-per-side tuners, disc. 1994, reintroduced 2008-present.

MSR $5,210	$4,450	$2,475 - 3,000	$1,425 - 1,825	

* *Model 22 Cutaway* – similar to the Model-22, except in has a single cutaway, mfg. 2008-present.

MSR $5,170	$4,400	$2,450 - 2,975	$1,400 - 1,800	

MODEL 23 – dreadnought, jumbo, mini-folk, or small-body style, cedar top, round soundhole, wood bound body, abalone/wood inlay rosette, walnut back/sides, mahogany/sycamore five-piece neck, 14/20-fret ebony fingerboard, rosewood bridge, rosewood veneered peghead with pearl logo inlay, three-per-side gold tuners with amber buttons, available in Natural finish, current mfg.

MSR $4,670	$4,000	$2,200 - 2,700	$1,275 - 1,600	

* *Model 23 12-String* – similar to the Model 23, except in 12-string configuration and six-per-side tuners, current mfg.

MSR $5,305	$4,500	$2,500 - 3,050	$1,450 - 1,850	

* *Model 23 Cutaway* – similar to the Model 23, except has a single cutaway, current mfg.

MSR $5,265	$4,475	$2,475 - 3,025	$1,425 - 1,825	

* *Model 23S* – folk style, German spruce top, round soundhole, wood bound body, abalone/wood inlay rosette, walnut back/sides, mahogany/sycamore five-piece neck, 14/20-fret ebony fingerboard, rosewood bridge, rosewood veneered peghead with pearl logo inlay, three-per-side gold tuners with ebony buttons, available in Natural finish, mfg. 1994-95.

	N/A	$2,100 - 2,500	$1,200 - 1,500	$2,390

MODEL 25 – dreadnought, jumbo, mini-folk, or small-body style, cedar top, round soundhole, wood bound body, wood inlay rosette, Indian rosewood back/sides, mahogany/rosewood five-piece neck, 14/20-fret ebony fingerboard, rosewood bridge, pearl logo inlay and rosewood veneer on peghead, three-per-side gold tuners with amber buttons, available in Natural finish, current mfg.

MSR $4,670	$4,000	$2,200 - 2,700	$1,275 - 1,600	

* *Model 25 12-String* – similar to the Model 25, except in 12-string configuration and six-per-side tuners, current mfg.

MSR $5,305	$4,500	$2,500 - 3,050	$1,450 - 1,850	

* *Model 25 Cutaway* – similar to the Model 25, except has a single cutaway, current mfg.

MSR $5,265	$4,475	$2,475 - 3,025	$1,425 - 1,825	

MODEL 32 – similar to the Model-25, except has a spruce top and pearl tuner buttons, current mfg.

MSR $4,775	$4,050	$2,275 - 2,750	$1,325 - 1,675	

* *Model 32 12-String* – similar to Model 32, except in 12-string configuration and six-per-side tuners with pearl buttons, mfg. 1993-present.

MSR $5,410	$4,600	$2,575 - 3,100	$1,500 - 1,900	

* *Model 32 Cutaway* – similar to the Model 32, except has a single cutaway, current mfg.

MSR $5,370	$4,575	$2,550 - 3,075	$1,475 - 1,875	

MODEL 34 – similar to Model 22, except is only available in Folk-style, has a spruce top, and koa back and sides, mfg. 1994-95.

	N/A	$1,400 - 1,600	$875 - 1,000	$3,190

MSR/NOTES	100%	EXCELLENT	AVERAGE	LAST MSR

ACOUSTIC: PREMIER SERIES

All Premier Guitars are available in the four distinctive Lowden body configurations (O, F, D, S). Dreadnought models were discontinued in 2003. These Premier guitars are Lowden's top-of-the-line models with premium woods and features. In mid-2006, the Lowden 50 Series was released, which is the new top-of-the-line model in the Original Series. These guitars are built on a very limited production and prices start at $8,075. Each guitar should be individually appraised.

PREMIER 35 – dreadnought, jumbo, mini-folk, or small body style, cedar or Sitka spruce top, figured blackwood, Brazilian rosewood, cocobolo, figured koa, figured myrtle, quilted maple, East Indian rosewood, figured Walnut, or Ziricote back and sides, abalone, rosewood, sycamore, mahogany, walnut rosette, blackwood or rosewood binding, sycamore/rosewood/mahogany purfling, five-piece maple/walnut/rosewood neck, 14/20-fret rosewood/sycamore bound ebony fingerboard, East Indian rosewood headstock overlay with three-per-side gold Gotoh 510 tuners with ebony buttons, Brazilian rosewood bridge, Tusq/bone nut/saddle, clear pickguard, Natural finish, mfg. 1996-present.

MSR $5,835	$5,000	$2,750 - 3,350	N/A	

- Add 5% for figured walnut back and sides (MSR $6,165).
- Add 5% for quilted maple, figured myrtle, or figured blackwood back and sides (disc., last MSR was $5,860).
- Add 10% for Alpine Spruce or Redwood top (MSR $6,185).
- Add 20% for figured koa, cocobolo, or Ziricote back and sides (MSR $6,975).
- Add 15% for an Adirondack spruce top (MSR $6,695).
- Add 80% for Brazilian rosewood back and sides (Rio model, MSR $10,125).

* *Premier 35 12-String* – similar to the Premier 35, except in 12-string configuration and six-per-side tuners, mfg. 1996-2007.

	N/A	$2,800 - 3,300	N/A	$5,770

- Add 2.5% for figured walnut back and sides (MSR $5,950).
- Add 5% for quilted maple, figured myrtle, or figured blackwood back and sides (MSR $6,070).
- Add 10% for figured koa, cocobolo, or Ziricote back and sides (MSR $6,465)
- Add 85% for Brazilian rosewood back and sides (Rio model, MSR $10,465).

* *Premier 35 Cutaway* – similar to the Premier 35, except has a single cutaway, mfg. 1996-present.

MSR $6,715	$5,700	$3,200 - 3,850	N/A	

- Add 5% for figured walnut back and sides (MSR $7,045).
- Add 5% for quilted maple, figured myrtle, or figured blackwood back and sides (MSR $6,660).
- Add 10% for Alpine Spruce or Redwood top (MSR $6,985).
- Add 17.5% for figured koa, cocobolo, or Ziricote back and sides (MSR $7,855).
- Add 12.5% for an Adirondack spruce top (MSR $7,575).
- Add 80% for Brazilian rosewood back and sides (Rio model, MSR $10,925).

PREMIER 38 – dreadnought, jumbo, mini-folk, or small body style, dark cedar top, Brazilian rosewood back and sides, abalone, rosewood, sycamore, mahogany, walnut rosette, sycamore binding, rosewood/abalone purfling, five-piece mahogany/rosewood neck, 14/20-fret rosewood/pear bound ebony fingerboard with abalone leaf inlays, East Indian rosewood headstock overlay with three-per-side gold Gotoh 510 tuners with ebony buttons, Brazilian rosewood bridge, Tusq/bone nut/saddle, clear pickguard, Natural finish, mfg. 1996-present.

MSR $11,750	$10,000	$5,600 - 6,750	N/A	

* *Premier 38 Cutaway* – similar to the Premier 38, except has a single cutaway, mfg. 1996-2007.

	N/A	$5,200 - 6,200	N/A	$11,200

ACOUSTIC ELECTRIC: STAGE & JAZZ SERIES

LS - 1 (LSE-I) – Venetian cutaway folk style, spruce top, round soundhole, wood bound body, wood inlay rosette, mahogany two-piece neck, 20-fret ebony fingerboard, rosewood bridge, pearl logo inlay and rosewood veneer on peghead, three-per-side gold tuners with pearl buttons, transducer bridge pickup, available in Natural finish, disc. 2004.

	N/A	$1,550 - 1,800	$950 - 1,100	$3,550

* *LS - 11 (LSE-II)* – similar to LSE-I, except has Indian rosewood back/sides, disc. 2004.

	N/A	$1,550 - 1,800	$950 - 1,100	$3,550

S25 JAZZ – nylon string configuration, small body with cutaway, same specifications as the Model 25, except features slotted peghead, three-per-side tuners with pearloid buttons, transducer bridge pickup, preamp, mfg. 1993-present.

MSR $5,795	$4,950	$2,750 - 3,350	$1,600 - 2,000	

S32 JAZZ – nylon string configuration, small body with cutaway, Western Red cedar top, East Indian rosewood back and sides, slotted peghead, three-per-side tuners with pearloid buttons, Headway pickup system, preamp, mfg. 2004-07.

	N/A	$2,400 - 2,800	$1,450 - 1,650	$5,175

LUCENA

Instruments previously distributed by Music Imports of San Diego, CA.

Music Imports offered a number of quality Lucena guitar models.

LUCIDA GUITARS

Instruments currently produced in Asia and Spain. Distributed by The Music Link of Hayward, CA.

Lucidea is a trademark of the The Music Link and they produce classical acoustic guitars as well as other Spanish-style instruments. Prices are aimed at students, but they also offer mid-level guitars as well. Prices range from $150 to $1,000. For more information, visit Lucida's website or contact The Music Link directly.

CONTACT INFORMATION
LUCIDA GUITARS
Distributed by The Music Link
31067 San Clemente Street
Hayward, CA 94544
Phone No.: 415-570-0970
Fax No.: 415-570-0651
www.lucidaguitars.com
info@themusiclink.net

LUNA GUITARS

Instruments currently produced overseas since 2005. Distributed by Luna Guitars in Tampa, FL.

Yvonne de Villers started Luna Guitars in 2005. Yvonne watched her mother, Hilda, play bass for forty years, and she also saw the toll a heavy bass was taking on her mother's body. Yvonne envisoned a guitar fit for the female body, but that would also engage the mind and spirit. Luna guitars are built for the female body and feature artwork by Yvonne. Guitars are also priced reasonably with models starting under $100. Most acoustic models range from $100 to around $750. For more information contact Luna directly.

CONTACT INFORMATION
LUNA GUITARS
4924 West Waters Ave.
Tampa, FL 33634
Phone No.: 800-793-5273
www.lunaguitars.com
lunaquestions@lunaguitars.com

LUTHIER

Instruments currently built in Spain. Distributed by Luthier Music Corporation of New York, NY.

The Luthier Music Corporation imports classical and flamenco guitars from Spain to the U.S. market. Models range from Student and Advanced Student up to Concert level acoustics. Luthier Music Corporation also distributes the Luthier brand nylon strings. Prices range from $525 to $4,995. For further information regarding models and pricing, contact the Luthier Music Corporation directly.

CONTACT INFORMATION
LUTHIER
Distributed by Luthier Music Corporation
341 West 44th Street
New York, NY 10036
Phone No.: 212-397-6038
Fax No.: 212-693-6048
www.luthiermusic.com
guitar@luthiermusic.com

LYLE

Instruments previously built in Japan between 1969 and 1980. Distributed by the L.D. Heater company in Portland, OR.

The Lyle product line consisted of acoustic and acoustic/electric archtop guitars, as well as solid body electric guitars and basses. These entry level to intermediate quality guitars featured designs based on popular American models. These instruments were manufactured by the Matsumoku company, which supplied models for both the Arai (Aria, Aria Pro II) company and the early 1970s Epiphone models. Used prices on Lyle guitars are typically between $100 and $150 depending on condition. Source: Michael Wright, *Vintage Guitar Magazine*.

ACOUSTIC

MISC. ACOUSTIC MODELS – various configuration, mfg. 1969-1980.

Low End	N/A	$150 - 200	$95 - 120
Middle Grade	N/A	$250 - 300	$135 - 175
High End	N/A	$325 - 400	$175 - 225

LYS

Acoustic guitars previously built in Canada between 1980 and 1983.

Lys guitars were produced by Unisonic who was founded by Robert Godin (Godin Guitars) and Claude Boucher (Boucher is the son of Normand Boucher who founded Norman Guitars). The guitars were designed by Claude Boucher and the team at Unisonic. In 1982, the Unisonic facilities closed and LaSiDo, Inc. bought the trademark. Guitars were produced into 1983 when the design was modified to become Seagull guitars. The first generation of Lys guitars have a dovetail neck joint and the second generation have a bolt-on neck. Most acoustic guitars are dreadnought in design. Information courtesy: Daniel Laroche.

NOTES

M SECTION
MACCAFERRI

Instruments previously produced in Italy circa 1923. Instruments designed for the Selmer company in France date between 1931 and 1932. Maccaferri instruments were produced in America circa the early 1950s to the early 1990s.

Italian-born luthier Mario Maccaferri (1900-1993) was a former classical guitarist turned guitar designer and builder. Born in Bologna, Italy in 1900, Maccaferri began his apprenticeship to luthier/guitarist Luigi Mozzani in 1911. At age sixteen, Maccaferri began classical guitar studies at the Academy in Siena, and graduated with highest possible honors in 1926.

Between 1931 and 1932, Maccaferri designed and built a series of instruments for the French Selmer company. Although they were used by such notables as Django Reinhardt, a dispute between the company and Maccaferri led to a short production run. In the two years (1931-1932) that Maccaferri was with Selmer, he estimated that perhaps two hundred guitars were built.

In 1936 Maccaferri moved to New York. He founded Mastro Industries, which became a leading producer of plastic products such as clothespins (which he invented during World War II), acoustical tiles, and eventually Arthur Godfrey ukuleles.

In 1953, Maccaferri introduced another innovative guitar made out of plastic. This archtop guitar featured a through-neck design, three-tuners-per-side headstock, and two f-holes. Despite the material involved, Maccaferri did not consider them to be a toy. Along with the archtop model Maccaferri produced a flattop version. But the 1953 market was not quite prepared for this new design, and Maccaferri took the product off the market and stored them until around 1980 (then released them again).

In the mid-1950s, Maccaferri was on friendly terms with Nat Daniels of Danelectro fame. As contemporaries, they would gather to discuss amplification in regards to guitar design, but nothing came of their talks. Maccaferri stayed busy with his plastics company and was approached by Ibanez in the early 1980s to endorse a guitar model. As part of the endorsement, Maccaferri was personally signing all the labels for the production run.

The Maccaferri-designed instruments were produced by the atelier of Henri Selmer and Co. of Paris, France between 1931 and 1932 as the Selmer model Concert. However, due to the dispute between the company and Maccaferri, experts estimate that less than three hundred were made (note Maccaferri's estimate, above). Source: George Gruhn and Dan Forte, *Guitar Player* magazine, February 1986; and Paul Hostetter, Guitares Maurice Dupont.

MSR/NOTES	100%	EXCELLENT	AVERAGE	LAST MSR

ACOUSTIC

G-30 FLATTOP – single cutaway hollow plastic body, f-holes, neck-thru body, 20-fret fingerboard with large white dot inlays, elaborate tailpiece, bridged molded in the top, three-per-side banjo-style tuners, available in White finish, mfg. 1953-mid 1950s.

	N/A	$325 - 400	$200 - 250	

G-40 ARCHTOP – single cutaway hollow archtop plastic body, f-holes, neck-thru body, 20-fret fingerboard with large white dot inlays, elaborate tailpiece, three-per-side banjo-style tuners, available in White finish, mfg. 1953-mid 1950s.

	N/A	$375 - 450	$225 - 275	

MACDONALD, S.B. CUSTOM INSTRUMENTS

Instruments currently built in Huntington (Long Island), NY, since 1991.

Luthier Scott B. MacDonald has been building and restoring stringed instruments since 1991. His instruments are built by special order and designed around the artist. MacDonald offers acoustic, electric, and resophonic instruments. MacDonald is also a warranty/authorized repair center for Gibson, Martin, and Taylor.

MacDonald produces a range of electric instruments as well. Refer to the *Blue Book of Electric Guitars* for more information. For more information, a gallery, and sounds on MacDonald guitars, visit his website or contact him directly.

CONTACT INFORMATION
MACDONALD, S.B. CUSTOM INSTRUMENTS
22 Fairmont Street
Huntington, NY 11743
Phone No.: 631-421-9056
customguitars.com
scott@customguitars.com

MAC YASUDA GUITARS

Instruments previously built in Old Hickory, TN with final production (inlays) in California. Distributed by Mac Yasuda Enterprises of Irvine, CA. Also Masterbilt Guitars.

Mac Yasuda is internationally recognized as a vintage guitar authority and collector, and has been writing on the topic of vintage instruments for well over two decades. Many may not realize that Yasuda is also a first-rate musician who has appeared on stage at the WSM Grand Ole Opry. Yasuda began performing country music on a local radio show in Kobe, Japan at the age of seventeen, and joined the "Rodeo Rangers" as a singer a year later. This group gained popularity on radio and in nightclubs in western Japan.

In 1970, Yasuda arrived in the U.S. to study at Michigan Technological University. He traveled to Nashville, and later purchased his first vintage guitar from a Denver pawnshop. Since then, virtually thousands of vintage instruments have passed through his hands.

MSR/NOTES	100%	EXCELLENT	AVERAGE	LAST MSR

In the late 1980s, Yasuda met Greg Rich. Rich was then acquiring a reputation for his custom musical instruments created for a major guitar producer (located in Nashville). These specialized custom instruments had immediate appeal in the collectibles market. In 1992, Rich collaborated with Mark Taylor (see Tut Taylor, Crafters Of Tennessee) to create a company to produce his latest custom designs. Mac Yasuda contracted Rich and Taylor to produce his namesake high quality, custom guitars. Mac Yasuda guitars debuted at the 1997 NAMM show, but Rich left the Masterbilt company shortly thereafter. It is unknown how many guitars were actually produced.

MADEIRA

Instruments previously built in Japan between the early 1970s and late 1980s. Distributed by Guild.

The Madeira line was first imported in to augment Guild sales in the U.S. between 1973 and 1974. Between the early 1970s and late 1980s, Guild consistently imported acoustic guitars to serve as a budget line for Guild. When Guild was sold to the Faas Corporation in 1988, they discontinued the Madeira line to focus on Guild production. A few electric guitar lines were offered under the Madira line as well. Source: Michael Wright, *Vintage Guitar Magazine*.

ACOUSTIC

MISC. ACOUSTIC MODELS – various configurations and appointments, models numbers include A-4, A-5, A-7, A-9, A-10, A-12A, A-14, A-14-12, A-15B, A-16, A-17M, A-18, A-25M, A-25R, A-25CE, A-30M, A-35, A-70, and AM-12, mfg. early 1970s-late 1980s.

	100%	EXCELLENT	AVERAGE
Low End Models	N/A	$175 - 250	$100 - 150
High End Models	N/A	$400 - 500	$250 - 300

Generally, the higher the number of the guitar is, the higher quality it is.

MAESTRO BY GIBSON

Instruments currently produced overseas. Distributed by the Gibson Guitar Corporation in Nashville, TN.

The Maestro by Gibson brand was developed by Gibson to sell entry level guitars and accessories for the beginner guitarist. The Maestro trademark has previously been used on a line of accordion amplifiers in the 1960s and they have retained it throughout the years. Maestro produces two acoustic dreadnought guitars in 38 in. and 41 in. body lengths. Maestro also offers two full size electric guitars with a Les Paul Junior style and SG style as well as a mini Flying V model and numerous accessories. For more information, visit Gibson's website or contact them directly.

CONTACT INFORMATION
MAESTRO BY GIBSON
309 Plus Park Blvd.
Nashville, TN 37217
Phone No.: 615-871-4500
Fax No.: 615-884-9411
www.gibson.com

MAGNUM OPUS GUITARS

Guitars currently produced in Marina Del Ray, CA since 2006.

Magnum Opus Guitars offers custom-built acoustic guitars that are entirely built by hand. In fact, Magnum doesn't use any CNC in their construction. Only fine tonewoods and great detail are used for these guitars. Several different variations are available and prices on most guitars are generally around $5,000. For more information, visit Magnum Opus' website or contact them directly.

CONTACT INFORMATION
MAGNUM OPUS GUITARS
578 Washington Blvd, Suite 149
Marina Del Ray, CA 90292
Phone No.: 310-902-9960
www.magnumopusguitars.com

MAINGARD GUITARS

Instruments currently produced in Cape Town, South Africa.

Master craftsman Marc Maingard, an accomplished composer, musician, and performer, began repairing his own guitars in the early 1970s, and because of the lack of luthiers in South Africa, he created a steady job repairing guitars in the area. Maingard became an apprentice under an English cabinetmaker and at the same time started building violins and cellos under the direction of Brian Lisus. Maingard also worked and studied with Santa Cruz guitars in California during the early 1980s as well as with James D'Aquisto, and spending many hours with Hose Oirbe in San Diego perfecting his classical guitar sound. Currently, Maingard builds a variety of acoustic and classical guitars in his South African shop and is the only authorized repairman for Gibson, Martin, and Ovation guitars in the area. Maingard offers a variety of guitars ranging from classicals to dreadnoughts to archtops. Marc is also a recognized inlay artist offering an exciting selection of custom trim details and inlays using the world's finest pearl, abalone, gold, silver, and rare gems. Maingard Guitars are all made in a humidity controlled environment with precious and rare woods quartersawed and well-seasoned. All guitars carry CITES certification, are in Lacey Act Compliance, and Maingard is a Brazilian rosewood (old growth) specialist. For more information, visit Maingard's website or contact him directly.

CONTACT INFORMATION
MAINGARD GUITARS
PO Box 22711
Scarborough
Cape Town, 7975 South Africa
Phone No.: +27217801236
www.maingardguitars.com
marc@maingardguitars.com

MAIZE, DAVE

Instruments currently built in Cave Junction, OR.

Luthier Dave Maize handbuilds acoustic and acoustic bass guitars with wood he has milled from prized trees or from growth of old timbers. His guitars are known for their tone and state-of-the-art design. Maize builds a select number of guitars each year so it allows him to spend more time on each model. Players currently using Maize instruments include, Jack Casady, Phil Lesh, Adam Clayton, and Jeff Ament. Maize was previously located in Talent, Oregon. For more information visit Maize's website or contact him directly.

CONTACT INFORMATION
MAIZE, DAVE
PO Box 2129
Cave Junction, OR 97523
Phone No.: 541-592-4535
www.maizeguitars.com
dave@maizeguitars.com

ACOUSTIC & ACOUSTIC BASS

Dave Maize instruments typically have spruce, redwood or cedar tops and bodies of figured claro walnut, bigleaf maple, myrtlewood, or other select woods. Standard features include solid wood construction (including binding), Sperzel locking tuners, double action truss rod, bolt-on walnut neck, and a beautiful peghead inlay. Maize offers several custom options (cutaway body, electronics, etc.). Acoustic models include the Auditorium Model (MSR starts at $4,150), Dread Model (MSR starts at $4,250), and the Baritone (MSR $4,00). Acoustic bass guitars include a four-string (MSR starts at $4,500) and five-string with a high C string (MSR starts at $4,800).

MANEA GUITARS

Previously Manea Custom Guitars. Instruments currently built in Nashville, TN.

Luthier Dumitru Manea has always been interested in woodworking, and the Romanian boy emegrated to the United States at the age of twenty-one. He continued to work in America as a woodworker until he eventually started building guitars. Manea produced guitars under Manea Custom Guitars for several years until circa 2006 when he started a new company simply called Manea Guitars. Manea currently builds custom acoustic guitars including a variety of violin family acoustical instruments, as well as electric guitars. For more information and a complete listing of the instruments Manea builds, visit his website or contact him directly.

CONTACT INFORMATION
MANEA GUITARS
2817 West End Ave. #126-276
Nashville, TN 37203-1453
Phone No.: 615-627-7081
www.maneaguitars.com
manea1310@yahoo.com

Both the steel string model **M-2000** and classical model **AV-1** feature hand-carved spruce or cedar tops, mahogany or cedar necks and Indian rosewood back and sides. Both models feature ebony fingerboards and bridges, and a number of additionally priced design options. In addition to the AV-1, Manea also offers two student models (**MP-14** Steel String and **ME-14** Classical). Prices start at $2,500 for student models and at $3,500 for standard models. Manea has also produced the **Tribute Guitar** that is dedicated to the U.S. service men and women who have died fighting in the Middle East.

MANSON

A.B. Manson & Company. Instruments currently built in Devon, England since the late 1970s.

Stringed instruments bearing the Manson name come from two separate operations. Acoustic guitars, mandolins, bouzoukis (and even triplenecks!) are built by Andrew Manson at A.B. Manson & Company. Electric guitars and electric basses are built by Hugh Manson at Manson Handmade Instruments. Andrew and Hugh Manson have been applying their luthier skills for over thirty years. Both Mansons draw on a wealth of luthier knowledge as they tailor the instrument directly to the player commissioning the work.

CONTACT INFORMATION
MANSON
Crediton, Devon England
www.andymanson.co.uk/
andy@andymanson.co.uk

Hand sizing (for neck dimensions), custom wiring, or custom choice of wood - it's all done in-house. Both facilities are located in Devon, and both Mansons build high quality instruments respective of their particular genre. Models include the **Dove, Heron**, and **Sandpiper**. Manson instruments can be dated by the first two digits of the respective instrument's serial number. For further information regarding model specifications, pricing, and availability, please contact either Andrew or Hugh Manson directly. Source: Tony Bacon and Paul Day: *The Guru's Guitar Guide.*

MANUEL & PATTERSON

Instruments currently produced in Abita Sprins, LA since 1990. Distributed by the Abita Springs Guitar Company.

Luthiers Joe Manuel and Phil Patterson have been building guitars since 1990 and acoustic guitars since 1993. The two came to work together at a music store in Covington, LA in the mid-1980s. They successfully ran the guitar shop through the 1980s and in 1990 they set out to build a guitar. They built two electric guitars before building their first acoustic guitar in 1993. They continued to work at the music store while building guitars on the side until 2004, when the owner of the store decided to get out of the business. Manuel and Patterson decided to start the Abita Springs Guitar Company to build and fix guitars and abandoned the retail business for good.

CONTACT INFORMATION
MANUEL & PATTERSON
Abita Springs Guitar Company LLC
PO Box 1869
Abita Springs, LA 70420
Phone No.: 985-892-4403
www.mpguitar.com
info@mpguitar.com

Manuel and Patterson build a variety of custom acoustic guitars. While they offer a several standard body shapes/styles, just about anything can be customized to the customer's liking. Guitars start at $4,500. For more information, visit their website or contact them directly.

MANZANITA GUITARS

Instruments currently built in Rosdorf, Germany, since 1993.

CONTACT INFORMATION
MANZANITA GUITARS
Rosdorf, Germany
www.manzanita.de
info@manzanita.de

Manzanita Guitars was founded in 1993 by Moritz Sattler and Manfred Pietrzok. However, Manfred put the first label for a Manzanita in a guitar in 1985. During their first year of cooperation, they concentrated on building acoustic steel string guitars, blending traditional shapes with design and construction ideas that soon became accepted as typical for Manzanita Guitars.

Today they offer a wide variety of custom-made flattop, hollow neck and resophonic guitars. Musicians using Manzanita Guitars include David Lindley, Ron Wood and Gero Drnek (Fury in the Slaughterhouse). Prices vary since each instrument is "one of a kind" in every way. For more information refer to their website.

MANZER GUITARS

Instruments currently built in Toronto, Canada since 1974.

CONTACT INFORMATION
MANZER GUITARS
65 Metcalfe Street
Toronto, Ontario M4X 1R9 Canada
Phone No.: 416-927-1539
www.manzer.com
linda@manzer.com

Luthier Linda Manzer was first inspired to build stringed instruments after seeing Joni Mitchell perform on a dulcimer in 1969. Manzer began building full time in 1974, and apprenticed under Jean Claude Larrivée until 1978. In 1983, Manzer spent several months with James D'Aquisto while learning the art of archtop guitar building. Manzer gained some industry attention after she completed Pat Metheny's "Pikasso" multi-necked guitar (the model has four necks sharing one common body and 42 strings). In 1990, Manzer was commissioned by the Canadian Museum of Civilization to create a guitar for one of their displays. In addition to building the high quality guitar that she is known for, Manzer included inlay designs in the shape of one of Canada's endangered species on the neck. The extra ornamentation served as a reminder for environmental concerns. Noted players using Manzer guitars include Pat Metheny, Bruce Cockburn, and Carlos Santana. For more information visit Manzer's website or contact her directly.

ACOUSTIC: ARCHTOP SERIES

All Manzer archtops use only highest grade aged spruce tops and curly maple back, sides, and neck. Other features include an ebony fingerboard, bridge, and floating pickguard, as well as a gold plated height adjustment for the ebony tailpiece, and Schaller machine heads. Body depth is 3 in. at the side and 5 in. at the middle, a scale length of 25.25 in. (64 cm), and an overall length of 41 in. (104.5 cm) - except the Absynthe, which is 43 in. long (109 cm). Prices typically start over $20,000.

The **Au Naturel** is 17 in. wide across the lower bout, and features all wood binding, highest grade woods, Orchid inlay and signature on the peghead, plain fingerboard, and art deco f-holes. This model is available in a Blonde finish.

The **Blue Note** model has a five-ply maple/mahogany top and back, with curly maple sides and a body width of 16 in. Other features include an "In body" custom made PAF pickup that delivers rich warm tone with on-board volume and tone controls. Finished in a Light Tangerine Honey Burst, with all ebony appointments. The **JazzCAT** is a 17 in. all wood model with contemporary **A** soundholes, bevelled veneered peghead, and Manzer signature inlay. This model is equipped with a Manzer JazzCAT pickup with adjustable pole pieces, and is finished in Honey Tangerine. The 18 in. **Absynthe** has deluxe binding, highest grade woods, ebony bound fingerboard with split block inlay, and Orchid with engraved mother-of-pearl scroll inlay of peghead. This model is available in Blonde or custom colors.

Models introduced in 2004 include "The Trio." These three guitars include the **Wildwood**, **Classic Archtop**, and the **Paradiso**.

ACOUSTIC: FLATTOP SERIES

There are several Manzer flattop models, each with their own "personality." Prices start over $18,000. Again, construction features aged spruce or Western cedar, Indian rosewood, and ebony. Manzer's most popular model, the **Manzer Steel String** has a 25.5 in. scale, rosewood back and sides, and an ebony fingerboard. The **Baritone** features a longer 29 in. scale. The longer scale supports the lower tuning (either low B to B, or low A to A) thus giving guitars access to a fuller voice. Back and sides are constructed of curly koa, and the fingerboard and bridge are ebony. The **Cowpoke** shares construction similarities with the standard Manzer, but features a larger and deeper body. Original inspiration was derived from a tall guy who wanted a Manzer, only bigger! The **Classical** offers a design that accommodates both traditional classical playing and modern jazz styles. A **12-string** configuration flattop is also offered. The **Little Manzer Steel** and the **Little Manzer Classical** are also available.

MAPSON, JAMES L.

Instruments currently built in Santa Ana, CA, since 1995.

CONTACT INFORMATION
MAPSON, JAMES L.
3230 South Susan Street
Santa Ana, CA 92704
Phone No.: 714-754-6566
www.mapsonguitars.com
guitar_info@mapsoneng.com

Luthier James L. Mapson individually tailors both acoustic and electro-coustic archtop guitars by commission, balancing both design and construction to achieve performance goals for the professional musician. Beginning his career in 1995, James is largely self-taught. After considerable study of construction theory, he settled upon pursuing the D'Angelico approach, passed down and further developed by James L. D'Aquisto and subsequently by John Monteleone. Today Jim continues this approach to acoustic design, as well as his own designs to improve the electric archtop for performance and recording-minded clientele. Noted players using Mapson's instruments include Mundell Lowe, Ron Eschete, Frank Potenza and John Abercrombie. For more information contact Mapson directly.

Acoustic models do not have exposed pickups. The **Solo** is a 16 or 17 in. body Neo-classic acoustic archtop and lists for $7,500. The **Lusso** is a 16 or 17 in. body traditional acoustic archtop and lists for $12,500. The **Avante** is a 17 or 18 in. body advanced acoustic archtop and lists for $7,500. There is only one of these built per year and in the past two were built per year.

Electric models have exposed pickups. The **Bopcity** is a 16 in. electric archtop and lists for $5,550. The **Jazz Standard** is a 15 in. tinline body available in a flat back with arch top for $4,500 or arched back and top for $5,500. The **Jazz Bandit** is a 13.5 in. thinline body available in a flat back with arch top for $4,500 or arched back and top for $5,500.

MAPLE LAKE

See Wechter in the W section.

MARATHON

Unknown production location and date. See chapter on House Brands.

This trademark had been identified as a House Brand previously used by Abercrombie & Fitch during the 1960s. However, a number of newer guitars sporting the same trademark have been recently spotted. These guitars were built in Korea by the Samick company, and serve as an entry level instrument for the novice guitarist. Source: Willie G. Moseley.

MARCHIONE GUITARS

Instruments currently handcrafted in Houston, TX. Previously produced in New York (Manhattan), NY, since 1993.

CONTACT INFORMATION
MARCHIONE GUITARS
1312 Willard Street
Houston, TX 77006
Phone No.: 713-522-7221
www.marchione.com
marchioneguitars@yahoo.com

Stephen Marchione builds recording quality archtop and special commission guitars. Marchione's clientele primarily consists of New York's top studio and stage players, and he has received commissions from the likes of Mark Whitfield, Mike Moreno, John Abercrombie, Vernon Reed, and Mark Knopfler. Other notables playing Marchione's guitars are George Wadenius (Steely Dan's *Alive in America* CD), Mark Stewart (Bang on a Can's *Music for Airports* CD), and Kenny Brescia and Ira Seigel (soundtrack for the Broadway smash *Rent*).

Marchione approaches his craft from many different angles. He understands players' sound and comfort needs as a guitar player himself. Marchione also seriously studies the great guitar and violin instruments in order to build archtop guitars that function as pinnacle pieces. When a player brings in a D'Aquisto or D'Angelico to Marchione's studio, Marchione scrutinizes the instrument's construction, draws blueprints, and then quizzes the player about the instrument's best qualities. These important elements are then incorporated into his own designs.

The violin tradition has also figured prominently in Marchione's building. A hands-on understanding of cello arching is crucial to Marchione's ability to recreate the arching subtleties that imbue his archtop guitars with full acoustic volume and tambour. Marchione's friendship with violin maker Guy Rabut has impressed upon Marchione the importance of incorporating centuries of stringed instrument knowledge.

Personal musicianship, an exacting approach to guitar making, and the experience of hand building over four hundred acoustic archtops, neck-throughs, and electric guitars are the groundwork for each and every Marchione guitar.

The **Marchione Archtop** is available in 16 in. with prices beginning at the following marks depending on choice of materials and design theme (MSR $16,500-$22,000), 17 in. (MSR $22,000-$25,000), or 18 in. (MSR $26,000-$35,000) body widths, and features a hollow body archtop, AAAAA Englemann Spruce top, highly figured maple back and sides, two f-holes, all wood binding, African ebony fingerboard, MOP headstock inlay, three-per-side tuners, narrow pickguard, fancy tailpiece, hand wound floating pickup, and is available in various finishes.

The **Whitfield Archtop** (MSR $19,500) features a hollow body archtop, AAAAA Englemann Spruce top, highly figured maple back and sides, two f-holes, single ply all wood binding, sugar maple neck, African ebony fingerboard, African ebony MOP and zulu headstock inlay, three-per-side tuners, narrow African ebony pickguard, fancy tailpiece with zulu wood, hand wound floating pickup, and available in Red finish.

Marchione has a new **15 in. Whitfield Archtop** (MSR $16,500) available that features a European Alpine spruce top, European flamed maple back and sides, an American sugar maple neck, African ebony fittings, binding, and fingerboard, hand-wound, very warm, full out-put humbucker pickup, stainless steel fretwire, locking Sperzel tuners, and Schaller Strap Locks, and the finish is nitrocellulose lacquer.

MARCO POLO

Instruments previously built in Japan circa early 1960s. Distributed by the Marco Polo Company of Santa Ana, CA.

The Marco Polo product line offered acoustic flattops, thinline hollowbody acoustic/electric guitars, and solid body electric guitars and basses. These inexpensive Japanese-built instruments were the first to be advertised by its U.S. distributors, Harry Stewart and the Marco Polo company. While the manufacturers are currently unknown, it is estimated that some of the acoustics were built by Suzuki, and some electric models were produced by Guyatone. Source: Michael Wright, *Vintage Guitar Magazine.*

ACOUSTIC

MISC. ACOUSTIC MODELS – various configurations and appointments, mfg. 1960s.

	N/A	$150 - 200	$95 - 120	

MSR/NOTES	100%	EXCELLENT	AVERAGE	LAST MSR

MARK WESCOTT GUITARS

Instruments currently built in Somers Point, NJ, since 1980.

Mark Wescott's approach to guitar building is one of innovative design that is based on the importance of sound and the interaction between the guitar and the player. Wescott is one of the growing number of modern builders who are systematically re-examining the mechanics of how a guitar produces sound.

Wescott's background in music began early as he grew up in a musical family where violins, violas, and cellos were always present. While Wescott first trained as an apprentice in cabinet making and furniture restoration, his musical background led him back to creating high quality acoustic guitars.

In 1980, Wescott built his first guitar under the guidance of George Morris, while attending the Charles Fox Guitar Research and Design School (GRD). Several years later, Wescott attended Richard Schneider's Kasha Design Seminar. Wescott continued on as resident luthier for three years at Schneider's Lost Mountain Center for the Guitar; it was there that he acquired a solid background in the Kasha method of radial soundboard bracing. This method was first invented by Dr. Michael Kasha, and pioneered by Master Luthier Richard Schneider.

Wescott designs his guitars (including the most recent **Intrepid** model) using the Kasha system of soundboard design. Asymmetrical radial soundboard bracing in conjunction with the impedance matching bridge enables Wescott to tailor the tonal response of the instrument. The **Intrepid** model is available in six-string and seven-string configurations, and features a Sitka spruce top, East Indian rosewood back and sides, Honduran mahogany neck, 24-fret ebony fingerboard, Kasha-type bridge, three-per-side Schaller mini tuners, graphite soundboard braces, Wechter-style access panel (trap door) tail block. Commissioned retail price is $8,000, and comes complete with deluxe hardshell case.

MARLING

Instruments previously produced in Japan during the mid-1970s.

As the Italian-based EKO guitar company was winding down, they were marketing EKO guitar copies built in Japan (although they may have been built by EKO). EKO offered a number of Marling acoustic models, as well as electric guitars. These guitar models were poor quality compared to the 1960s Italian EKOs. Source: Michael Wright, *Guitar Stories, Volume One*.

ACOUSTIC

MISC. ACOUSTIC MODELS – various configurations including classical and dreadnought designs, Natural finish, mfg. 1960s.

N/A	$75 - 125	$30 - 50

MARONI

Instruments previously produced in Italy in the mid-1960s.

Reader Gene Van Alstyne of Cushing, OK called in this classical-styled guitar, built by luthier Farfisa. The guitar has a zero fret, a split saddle, 38 mm tuning pegs, and a "Made in Italy" label in the soundhole. When the Farfisa name was uttered, the immediate talk turned to those 1960s organs. A connection, perhaps? Any further information would be appreciated and can be submitted directly to the *Blue Book of Acoustic Guitars*.

MARTELLE

Instruments previously built in Kalamazoo, MI by Gibson during the late 1930s and early 1940s. See chapter on House Brands.

The distributor of this Gibson-built budget line of guitars has not yet been identified. Built to the same standards as other Gibson guitars, they lack the one true Gibson touch: an adjustable truss rod. House Brand Gibsons were available to musical instrument distributors in the late 1930s and early 1940s. These guitars may be worth some heavy money if they are authentic. More research is underway to accurately price them. However, when currently pricing them we recommend getting a few opinions. Source: Walter Carter, *Gibson Guitars: 100 Years of an American Icon*.

MARTIN

Instruments currently manufactured in Nazareth, PA since 1839 and in Mexico (Backpacker Series) since the mid-1990s. Previously produced in New York, NY between 1833 and 1839. Distributed by Martin in Nazareth, PA.

CONTACT INFORMATION
MARTIN
510 Sycamore Street
Nazareth, PA 18064-9233
Phone No.: 610-759-2837
Fax No.: 610-759-5757
www.martinguitar.com
info@martinguitar.com

Christian Frederick Martin, Sr. (1796-1873) came from a woodworking (cabinet making) family background. He learned guitar building as an employee of Johann Stauffer, and worked his way up to becoming Stauffer's foreman in Vienna, Austria. Martin left Stauffer in 1825, and returned to his birthplace in Markneukirchen, Germany. Martin got caught up in an ongoing dispute between the violin makers' guild and the cabinet makers' guild. Martin and his family emigrated to America in the fall of 1833, and by the end of the year set up a full-line music store. The Martin store dealt in all types of musical instruments, sheet music, and repairs, as well as Martin's Stauffer-style guitars.

After six years, the Martin family moved to Nazareth, Pennsylvania. C.A. Zoebich & Sons, their New York sales agency, continued to hold "exclusive" rights to sell Martin guitars, so the Martin guitars retained their New York labels until a business falling-out occurred in 1898. The Martin family settled outside of town, and continued producing guitars that began to reflect less of a European design in favor of a more straightforward design. Christian Martin favored a deeper, lower bout, Brazilian rosewood for the back and sides, cedar for necks, and a squared-off slotted peghead (with three tuners per side). Martin's scalloped X-bracing was developed and used beginning in 1850 instead of the traditional "fan" bracing favored by Spanish luthiers (fan bracing is favored on classical guitars today).

In 1852, Martin standardized his body sizes, with Size 1 being the largest and Size 3 being the smallest (size 2 and 2 1/2 were also included). Two years later, a larger Size 0 and a smaller Size 5 "Terz" were added to the line. Martin also standardized his style (or design) distinctions in the mid-1850s, with the introduction of Style 17 in 1856 and Styles 18 and 27 a year later. Thus, every Martin guitar has a two-part name: size number and style number. Martin moved into town in 1857 (a few blocks north of town square), and built his guitar building factory right next door within two years.

The C.F. Martin & Company was announced in 1867, and in three years a wide range of styles was available. A larger body size, the Size 00, or Grand Concert, debuted in 1877. Under the direction of C.F. Martin, Jr. (1825-1888), the company decided to begin producing mandolins, which caused the business split with their New York sales agency. Martin bowl-back mandolins were first offered in 1895 - three years before the snowflake inlay Style 42 became available. In 1898, Martin began serializing their guitars. Martin estimated that 8,000 guitars had been built between 1833 and 1898, so started the serialization with number 8,000. Ever since 1898, Martin has serial numbered their guitars (excluding the Backpacker and Little Martin guitars) using a straightforward numerical sequence. At the end of each year, the last serial number is recorded and this provides a very accurate way to date Martin guitars back to 1898. In 1902, the 15 in. wide Size 000 "Grand Auditorium" was introduced, and more pearl inlay on Martin guitars was introduced in 1902, which led to the fancier Style 45 two years later.

A major materials change occurred in 1916, as mahogany replaced cedar as the chosen wood for neck building, and white celluloid (ivoroid) became the new binding material in 1918. The Martin company also took a big technological leap in 1922, as they adapted the Model 2-17 for steel strings instead of gut strings (all models would switch to steel string configuration by 1929). To help stabilize the new amount of stress in the necks, an ebony bar was embedded in the neck (the ebony bar was replaced by a steel T-Bar in 1934). Martin briefly built banjos in the early to mid-1920s, and also built a fair share of good quality ukuleles and tiples.

In 1929, Martin was contacted by Perry Bechtel who was looking for a flattop guitar with fourteen frets clear of the body (Martin's models all joined at the twelfth fret). The company responded by building a 000 Grand Auditorium model with a square-shouldered body and slimmed down 14/20-fret neck. This new model was announced in the 1930 catalog as the OM (Orchestra Model), and the 14/20-fret neck was adopted by almost all models in the production line by 1934. Martin also began stamping the model name into the neck block of every guitar in 1931.

Martin responded to the up-and-coming popularity of jazz guitars and began offering archtop models in the early 1930s. The three C models were introduced in 1931, the R-18 two years later, and the F-7 (the shape that eventually became the profile of the M, 0000, and J models) in 1935. Martin archtop production lasted until 1942. The archtops of 1931 have since been overshadowed by another model that debuted that year - Martin's 16 in. wide dreadnought size. Guitar players were asking for more volume, but instead of making a bigger "0000" body, Martin chose to design a new type of acoustic guitar. Martin was already building a similar type of guitar originally as a model for the Oliver Ditson company in 1916; they just waited for the market to catch up to them!

The Dreadnought acoustic (so named after large World War I battleships) with X-bracing is probably the most widely copied acoustic guitar design in the world today. A look at today's music market could confirm a large number of companies building a similar design, and the name "Dreadnought" has become an industry standard.

In 1938, the X-bracing (on Dreadnought models only) was shifted back to approximately two inches from soundhole, presumably to strengthen the top. In 1939, the neck was narrowed slightly. In mid-1944, the Martin company stopped the practice of "scalloping" (shaving a concave surface) the braces on their guitar tops. 1947 saw the end of herringbone trim on the guitar tops, due to a lack of consistent sources (either German or American). The first two dozen (or so) 1947 D-28 models did have herringbone trim. Some thirty years later, Martin's HD-28 model debuted with the "restored" scalloped bracing and herringbone trim (this model is still in production today).

The folk boom of the late 1950s increased the demand for Martin guitars. The original factory produced around 6,000 guitars a year, which wasn't enough to keep up with demand. Martin began construction on a new facility in 1964, and when the new plant opened a year later, production began to exceed 10,000 guitars a year. While expansion of the market is generally a good thing, the limited supply of raw materials was detrimental. In 1969, Brazil put an embargo on rosewood logs exported from their country. To solve this problem, Martin switched over to Indian rosewood in 1969, and Brazilian rosewood from legal sources does show up on certain limited edition models from time to time.

The 1970s was a period of fluctuation for the Martin company. Many aggressive foreign companies began importing products to the U.S., and were rarely challenged by complacent U.S. manufacturers. To combat the loss of sales in the entry-level market, Martin started the Sigma line of overseas-produced guitars for dealers. Martin also bought Levin, the Swedish guitar company, in 1973. The Size M, developed in part by Mark Silber, Matt Umanov, and Dave Bromberg, debuted in 1977. Martin's second try at electric guitars with the E Series were introduced in 1979 and produced through 1983. A failed attempt at union organization at the Martin plant also occurred in the late 1970s. Martin's Custom Shop was formally opened in 1979, and set the tone for other manufacturers' custom shop concepts.

The late C.F. Martin III, who had steered the company through the Great Depression, said that 1982 was the most devastating year in the company's history. The balance of the 1980s produced some innovations and radical changes at the Martin company. It was 1985 when current CEO and Chairman of the Board Chris F. Martin IV assumed his duties at the youthful age of 28. The Martin Guitar of the Month program, a limited production/custom guitar offering, was introduced in 1984 (and continued through 1994, prior to the adoption of the Limited Edition series) as well as the new Jumbo J Series. Martin introduced two radical changes in the mid-1980s with the adjustable truss rod and a thinner neck profile. Martin had always maintained the theory that a properly built guitar wouldn't need a truss rod, but they finally began using Gibson's patented system in 1985. The thinner neck or "low-profile neck" as it was often referred to as was inspired by Taylor Guitars. By the end of the 1980s, both of these features were standard equipment across the board for Martin. In 1986, Martin introduced the Style 16, which was intended to be a special run of affordable guitars that were offered at the annual NAMM show, and these guitars have evolved into standard production models, which continue to be Martin's most affordable all solid wood guitars. The Korean-built Stinger line of solid body electrics was offered the same year as the Shenandoah line of Japanese-produced parts/U.S. assembly.

In 1988, Martin discontinued the Style 18 1/9/1 grouping soundhole rosette configuration and replaced it with the 5/9/5 grouping used on Style 28 and other models. In 1992, Martin introduced the Backpacker travel guitar that is built in their Mexican manufacturing facility. In 1993, Martin introduced the 1 Series of guitars that featured a combination of solid and laminated woods. Martin continued to expand and experiment with other wood styles with the introduction of the all-laminated Road Series in 1996, and the new high-pressure laminate X Series in 1998. Guitars with Smartwood and aluminum tops solidify Martin's commitment to exploring other options for building guitars as wood supplies get tighter. Martin also adheres to the guidelines and conservation efforts set by such organizations as the Forest Stewardship Council (FSC), Rainforest Foundation International, and SmartWood Certified Forestry (Certified Wood products).

In 1996, Martin introduced the first version of their semi-annual Sounding Board magazine that highlights new Martin models and a news briefing about what is going on with Martin. During 1999, Martin proudly opened up its new 85,000-square-foot addition where production rose to 225 guitars per day. This new efficient technology also has enabled Martin to keep consistent high quality production within the U.S., while actually lowering consumer costs.

At the 2001 summer NAMM Show in Nashville, TN, Martin showcased yet another milestone in its company's history with instrument number 750,000. This Peacock Deluxe flattop was the most elaborate and ornate Martin guitar manufactured at the time, with over 2,000 handcut pieces of shell inlayed on the back, sides, pickguard, and neck.

During 2002, Martin continued to expand its line of regular models, with prices ranging from $619 to $25,000! Additionally, Martin released eighteen new special and limited editions at the winter NAMM Show, and eleven new special/limited editions at the Nashville Summer NAMM Show. With this new lineup, Martin continues to be the leader in acoustic instruments, covering a wide variety of price points, building materials, and both vintage and high-tech guitar construction techniques.

In 2003, Martin introduced the Little Martin (LX) Series of guitars that are constructed out of HPL and built in Martin's Mexican manufacturing facility. Serial number 800,000 (a CFM3 Commemorative) was announced at the Anaheim winter NAMM show in January of 2003. During mid-2003, the first Martin resonator guitar was introduced (Alternative II resonator). Longtime Martin employee Mike Longworth also passed away in 2003.

In 2004, Martin unveiled a company milestone at the Anaheim NAMM Show with the Millionth Martin Guitar, serial numbered 1,000,000. This is the most elaborate guitar the company has ever manufactured, and to help commemorate this historic event, Martin announced that it would be producing a D-100 Deluxe limited edition, priced at $100,000, with only fifty scheduled to be manufactured. Martin also announced the collaboration with archtop builder Dale Unger to produce a limited amount of Martin f-hole archtops (two models, the CF-1, and CF-2) with a choice of either a Seymour Duncan or Kent Armstrong pickup.

In late 2004, Martin began construction of a new Visitor's Center and Museum on the site of the old factory. The Martin Visitor's Center and Museum was completed during late 2005, and over 130 instruments are featured in the museum. Also in 2004, Chris Martin and his wife gave birth to a daughter named Claire Frances Martin and in 2005 she already had her own signature model with the Baby Claire!

In 2006, Martin introduced the Custom Artist Series that feature guitars designed by selected artists, but they are not built to any limited quantities or set orders.

In 2008, Martin celebrated the 175th Anniversary of their company (1833-2008) with three 175th Anniversary models: the DX 175th Anniversary Limited Edition, 00 Stauffer 175th Anniversary Limited Edition, and America's Guitar 175th Anniversary Limited Edtition.

In 2009, Martin celebrated the 75th Anniversary of the "modern" dreadnought body shape (1934-2009) with two anniversary models: The D-18 and D-28 75th Anniversary editions.

In 2010, Chris Martin IV, celebrated his 55th birthday and Martin released a lmited edition CFM IV 55th Anniversary D-28 based on a 1955 D-28.

In 2011, Martin produced their 1.5 millionth guitar called DaVinci Unplugged. Inlaid by Harvey Leach and engraved by Bob Hergert, this guitar features Mona Lisa on the headstock, the Last Supper on the pickguard, and the Vitruvian Man on the back.

Sources: Mike Longworth, *Martin Guitars: A History*; Walter Carter, *The Martin Book: A Complete History of Martin Guitars*; and Tom Wheeler, *American Guitars*.

VISUAL IDENTIFICATION FEATURES

Martin has been in the same small town for 160 years and serialization has remained intact and consistent since its first instrument. When trying to determine the year of an instrument's construction, some quick notes about features can be helpful. The few notes contained herein are for readily identifying the instrument upon sight and are by no means meant to be used for truly accurate dating of an instrument. All items discussed are for flattop steel string guitars and involve instruments that are standard production models.

The earliest dreadnoughts, and indeed just about all instruments produced with a neck that joins the body at the twelfth fret, have bodies that are bell-shaped on the top, as opposed to the more square-shouldered styles of most dreadnoughts. Between 1929 and 1934, Martin began placing fourteen-fret necks on most of their instruments and this brought about the square-shouldered body style. A few models maintained twelve-fret necks into the late 1940s and several had a twelve-fret neck until the late 1980s.

Turn-of-the-century instruments have square-slotted pegheads with the higher end models (models 42 and 45) displaying an intricate pearl fern inlay that runs vertically up the peghead. This was replaced by a vertical inlay known as the flowerpot or the torch inlay, in approximately 1905. In 1932, the "C.F. Martin & Co. Est. 1833" scroll logo began appearing on certain models' pegheads. By approximately 1934, a solid peghead with a vertical pearl "C.F. Martin" inlay had replaced the former peghead design.

Bridges from the 1900s are rectangular with pyramid wings. In approximately 1929, the belly bridge replaced the rectangle bridge. This bridge has a straight slot cut across the entire length of the center section of the bridge. In 1965, the straight cut saddle slot was changed to a routed slot. It was in approximately 1936, that Martin began using the tied bridge on their classical instruments.

Pickguards were not standard features on instruments until 1931 (1930 on some OM models) when tortoiseshell pickguards were introduced. In 1967, black pickguards became standard. In 1969, Martin stopped using Brazilian rosewood for its regular production instruments, ending with serial number 254498. As a result, premiums are being asked for instruments manufactured from this exotic wood. After 1969, Martin began to use East Indian rosewood backs and sides on standard production instruments in Style 21 or higher (D-21, D-28, etc.); and mahogany backs and sides on Style 20 or lower (D-18, D-1220, etc.) production models.

INSTRUMENTS BUILT FOR OTHER TRADEMARKS (BRAND NAMES)

Martin did build guitars for other retailers, teachers, and musical instrument distributors; unlike Harmony's or Kay's house brands, though, "retitled" Martins were the exception and not the rule. If any of these trademarks are spotted, here's a partial hint to origin:

Bacon Banjo Company: Around 1924, Martin supplied a number of guitars without Martin stamps or labels. However, most of the Bacon-trademarked guitars were built by Regal (Chicago, Illinois).

Belltone: Only a few Style 3K guitars, mandolins, and ukuleles were built for the Perlburg and Halpin company of New York City, New York.

Bitting Special: Both guitars and mandolins were built for this well-known music teacher in Bethlehem, Pennsylvania between 1916 and 1919.

Briggs Special: Sixty-five specially trimmed mandolin models were built for the Briggs Music shop in Utica, New York circa 1914 to 1919.

C. Bruno: Long before they were acquired by Kaman Music, C. Bruno was associated with C.F. Martin in 1838. Guitars carry a paper label that says "C.F. Martin & Bruno." Later C. Bruno & Sons guitars were not built by Martin.

William Foden: Concert guitarist and teacher William Foden had his own series of Foden Specials built by Martin. These models were primarily sold to his students between 1900 and 1920. Foden's insistence on a twenty-fret fingerboard is now a standard feature on Martin guitars.

J.A. Handley: J.A. Handley was an instructor in Lowell, Massachusetts. He is credited with the development of the Style 6A mandolin.

Jenkins: This dealer in Kansas City, Missouri sold Martin ukuleles, renumbered #35 (Style 1) and #40 (Style 2).

Montgomery Ward: Martin had a short term deal with the Montgomery Ward company circa 1932. Martin supplied mahogany guitars, flat mandolins, and ukuleles.

Vahdah Olcott-Bickford: Vahdah Olcott-Bickford was a well-known concert artist and teacher. Guitars built to her specifications were called a Style 44, or Soloist.

Paramount: Paramount ordered about thirty special resonator models under the Paramount logo. Paramount was well known for their banjo models, which were not Martin instruments.

Rolando: The Rolando trademark shows up on a series of Martin-built koa Hawaiian-style guitars ordered by the Southern California Music Company (circa 1917-1920). Records also show a direct sale to J.J. Milligan Music.

Rudick's: The Rudick's firm of Akron, Ohio ordered a number of OO-17 guitars with the number O-55 stamped inside (circa 1935).

William J. Smith: The William J. Smith firm of New York City, New York had Martin-built ukuleles, taro patches and tiples in stock circa 1917.

Stetson: W.J. Dyer & Bro., known for their association with Larson Brothers acoustics, also specified three guitars for their Stetson trademark circa 1922.

S.S. Stewart: Distributors Buegeleisen and Jacobson of New York City, New York ordered ukuleles and other stringed instruments with their S.S. Stewart label circa 1923 to 1925.

John Wanamaker: The Wanamaker department store in Philadelphia, Pennsylvania ordered special models circa 1909.

H.A. Weymann & Son: The Weymann firm of Philadelphia, Pennsylvania was known for their banjos; Martin built a number of ukuleles and taro patches models around 1925.

Wolverine: The Wolverine trademark was applied to Martin-built guitars and mandolins for the Grinnell Brothers of Detroit, Michigan. Wolverine instruments carry the regular Martin serial numbers.

Rudolph Wurlitzer: The Wurlitzer music store chain ordered special model guitars between 1922 and 1924.

Information on "Retitled" Martin instruments courtesy: Mike Longworth, *Martin Guitars: A History*; Walter Carter, *The Martin Book: A Complete History of Martin Guitars*, and Tom Wheeler, *American Guitars*.

COMMON MARTIN ABBREVIATIONS

0 - Concert
00 - Grand Concert
000 - Grand Auditorium
0000 - Grand Auditorium
A - Ash
AE - Acoustic/Electric
B - Acoustic Bass or Brazilian
BK - Black
BR - Brazilian Rosewood
B/W/B - Black/White/Black binding or rosette

C - Cutaway, Classic, or Classical
CEO - Chief Executive Officer
C.I.T.E.S. - Convention for International Trade of Endangered Species (July 1, 1975)
D - Dreadnought
DB - Deep Body
E - Electronics
EMP - Employee
FMG - Figured Mahogany
G - Gut (later nylon) String

GE - Golden Era
GM - Grand Marquis
GOM - Guitar of the Month
GT - Gloss Top
H - Herringbone or Hawaiian
HP - Herringbone Pearl
HPL - High Pressure Laminate
J - Jumbo
K - Koa (back and sides)
K2 - Koa (top, back, and sides)
L - Left-Hand

LE - Limited Edition
LS (LSH) - Large Soundhole
M - Mahogany
MB - Maple binding
MP - Morado Rosewood
N - Martin Classical Shape (non-low-profile neck)
OM - Orchestra Model
P - Plectrum or Low Profile

Q - Old Style non adj. neck (1985-current)
R - Rosewood
S - Special or Special Order (pre-1995)
S - 12-Fret Slotted Neck
SE - Signature Edition
SP - Special (post-1995) or Special Appointments

SW - Smart Wood Certified
T - Tenor
V - Vintage (suffix for models after 1983)
VS - Vintage Sunburst
W - Walnut
W/B/W - White/Black/White binding or rosette
X - X Series

ACOUSTIC GUITARS: GENERAL INFORMATION & PRICING OPTIONS

Because of the large amount of guitar series and the sheer volume of guitars that Martin has produced over the years, this section has been split up into several categories designed to make location and accessibility easier. Martin first broke their guitar line into separate "Series" in 1996. All regular production models were transferred into the newly designated "Standard" Series. No specifications or features were changed, so all standard production models built before 1996 are included in the Standard Series as well. The Standard Series is then broken down into several sub-categories that divides these guitars into their various sizes such as the Dreadnought, 0 Concert, 00 Grand Concert, 000 Grand Auditorium, 0000/M Grand Auditorium, Jumbo, and OM Orchestra Model Series. All other guitars are divided into their respective series, which Martin has made very clear and precise since 1996.

Martin offers several guitars with electronics as standard equipment (models are designated with E); however, electronics can be added to just about any model that Martin produces. Several electronic/pickup combinations are available as factory equipment and the following add-ons only apply to guitars without standard factory electronics. For example, you would not add any additional value to the Model DC-15E since the pickup is already included in the price.

- **Add 50% for original Sunburst finish on pre-WWII instruments.**
- **Add $125 (Last MSR was $159) for Thinline 332 Passive Piezo Pickup (disc. mid-2009).**
- **Add $150 (Last MSR was $199) for Martin Thinline 332 Plus (disc. mid-2009).**
- **Add $195 (MSR $259) for Martin Thinline Gold Plus Natural 1 electronics.**
- **Add $195 (Last MSR was $259) for Martin Thinline Gold Plus Maximum electronics (disc. mid-2009).**
- **Add $175 (Last MSR was $229) for Fishman Aero + electronics (offered second half of 2009 only).**
- **Add $225 (Last MSR was $299) for Fishman Ellipse Blend electronics (2005-06).**
- **Add $250 (MSR $329) for Fishman Ellipse Matrix Blend (2007-present).**
- **Add $160 (Last MSR was $209) for Fishman Classic 4 Sonicore (disc. mid-2009).**
- **Add $175 (Last MSR was $239) for Fishman Prefix electronics (mid-2001-06).**
- **Add $210 (Last MSR was $279) for Fishman Prefix Plus electronics (disc. 2007).**
- **Add $225 (Last MSR was $299) for Fishman Prefix Pro electronics (disc. mid-2009).**
- **Add $230 (Last MSR was $309) for Fishman Prefix Pro Blend electronics (disc. 2006).**
- **Add $350 (Last MSR was $459) for Fishman Prefix Premium Blend electronics (disc. 2009).**
- **Add $250 (Last MSR was $339) for Fishman Prefix Stereo Onboard Blender electronics (disc. 2003).**
- **Add $150 (MSR $229) for Fishman Presys + electronics (new 2010).**
- **Add $150 (Last MSR was $200) for Rare Earth single coil soundhole pickup (disc. 2000).**
- **Add $175 (Last MSR was $250) for Rare Earth humbucker soundhole pickup (disc. 2000).**
- **Add $325 (Last MSR was $450) for Rare Earth blender soundhole pickup (disc. 2000).**
- **Add $225 (Last MSR was $299) for Sli Matrix EQ electronics (disc. 2002).**
- **Add $100 (Last MSR was $150) for System 1 electronics (disc. 2000).**
- **Add $210 (MSR $279) for Matrix Infinity electronics (summer 2009-present).**

MARTIN GUITARS MADE BEFORE 1898

Any Martin guitar built before 1898 usually needs to be identified and evaluated on an individual basis. Although Martin introduced standard body sizes and styles by the mid-1800s, they are not as streamlined as they became in 1898. Martin also offered variations on their popular style numbers and it is unknown how many of each model were produced making evaluation extremely difficult. Most Martin guitars built before 1898 are considered antiques as they were produced decades before the "Golden Age" of guitars came around. Approximately 8,000 guitars were built between 1833 and 1898. Contact Blue Book Publications directly for more information regarding Martin guitars built before 1898.

ACOUSTIC: SMALL BODIED GUITARS (SIZES 1/4, 1/2, 3/4, 1, 2, 2 1/2, & 3)

In 1898, when Martin standardized their configurations, several small bodied models were carried over. Certain models were extremely popular and were produced for several years (such as Size 1 and Size 2) while others were only produced in very limited quantities (such as Size 1/4, Size 1/2, Size 3/4, and Size 3). By 1938, all of these models had been discontinued as larger jumbo and dreadnought guitars were quickly becoming the popular acoustic instrument. Most models that were produced in large quantities are individually listed and valued in this section because they are traded quite often in the used marketplace. Other limited quantity models (typically less than 5 produced) are not individually listed because of their lack of market activity. However, we have mentioned all of these guitars including how many and what years they were produced.

Early **Size 1/4** instruments have dimensions of a 6 3/16 in. lower bout width, 2.875 in. body depth, 12 in. body length, and 17 in. scale.

Late **Size 1/4** instruments have dimensions of a 8 5/16 in. lower bout width, 3 9/16 in. body depth, 12 1/16 in. body length, and a 17 in. scale.

Size 1/2 instruments have dimensions of a 10.125 in. lower bout width, 3.375 in. body depth, 15 1/16 in. body length, and 20.875 in. scale.

MSR/NOTES	100%	EXCELLENT	AVERAGE	LAST MSR

Size 1 instruments have dimensions of a 12 3/4 in. lower bout width, 4 3/16 in. body depth, 18.875 in. body length, and 24.9 in. scale.

Size 2 instruments have dimensions of a 12 in. lower bout width, 4 in. body depth, 18 1/4 in. body length, and 24.5 in. scale.

Size 2 1/2 instruments have dimensions of a 11 5/8 in. lower bout width, 3.875 in. body depth, 17.875 in. body length, and 24.5 in. scale.

Size 3 instruments have dimensions of a 11.25 in. lower bout width, 3 3/16 in. body depth, 17.375 in. body length, and 23.875 in. scale.

Martin produced a variety of different small bodied-sized guitars that were built in very limited quantities. Size 1/4 limited quantity Martin's include 22 **Model 1/4-18** guitars (1918-1931), 14 **Model 1/4-28** guitars (1972, 1981), and six **1/4-12-String** guitars (1918). Size 1/2 limited quantity Martin's include 18 **Model 1/2-18** guitars (1918-19), and one **Model 1/2-21** guitar (1919 only). Size 3/4 limited quantity Martin's include four **Model 3/4-18** guitars (1921) and one **Model 3/4-21** (1921). Size 2 limited quantity Martin's include two **Model 2-34**s (1898, although this was a popular configuration before 1898 as well), one **Model 2-40** (1909 only), two **Model 2-42**s (1900 only), four **Model 2-45**s (1925-27), and two **Model 2-45T** tenors (1927-28). Size 2 1/2 limited quantity Martin's include five **Model 2 1/2-30** guitars (1901-1914) and one **Model 2 1/2-42** guitar (1911 only). Size 3 limited quanity Martin's include only one **Model 3-17** that was produced in 1908; however, the Model 3-17 was a popular configuration prior to 1898.

MODEL 1-17 (FIRST VERSION) – Size 1 body, spruce top, mahogany back and sides, round soundhole with three black rings rosette, three-ply top binding with rosewood outer layer, rosewood back binding, ebony fingerboard with two dot inlays at the 7th fret, rectangular bridge, total production of 145 instruments, mfg. 1906-1917.

	N/A	$1,800 - 2,250	$1,075 - 1,350	

MODEL 1-17 (SECOND VERSION) – Size 1 body, mahogany top, back, and sides, round soundhole with three B/W/B rings rosette, no body binding, rosewood fingerboard with two dot inlays at the 7th fret, rectangular bridge, optional pickguard (1932-34), available in Natural flat finish, total production of 1,130 instruments, mfg. 1931-34.

	N/A	$2,200 - 2,750	$1,325 - 1,650	

* ***Model 1-17P Plectrum*** – similar to the Model 1-17 (Second Version), except in four-string plectrum configuration with two-per-side tuners and a 27 in. scale, total production of 272 instruments, mfg. 1928-1931.

	N/A	$1,800 - 2,250	$1,075 - 1,350	

Martin also produced one Model 1-17P Plectrum in five-string configuration (1939).

MODEL 1-18 – Size 1 body, spruce top, rosewood (1899-1917) or mahogany (1917-1927) back and sides, round soundhole with wood colored rope pattern (1899-1902) or three-stripe rosette (1/9/1 grouping between 1902 and 1927), five-ply top binding, single-ply back binding with outer rosewood layer, black backstripe, ebony fingerboard with no inlays (1899-1902) or dot inlays (1902-1927), total production of 964 instruments, mfg. 1899-1927.

1899-1917 Rosewood	N/A	$2,400 - 3,000	$1,450 - 1,800	
1917-1927 Mahogany	N/A	$2,200 - 2,750	$1,325 - 1,650	

Martin also produced three Model 1-18H Hawaiian guitars (1918), one Model 1-18P Plectrum five-string guitar (1930), and three Model 1-18T Tenor guitars (1927).

* ***Model 1-18K Koa*** – similar to the Model 1-18, except has koa back and sides, total production of 46 instruments, mfg. 1917-19.

	N/A	N/A	N/A	

Extreme rarity precludes accurate pricing.

MODEL 1-21 – Size 1 body, spruce top, rosewood back and sides, round soundhole with three-stripe rosette (herringbone ring between two groups of five rings), five-ply top binding with outer rosewood layer, two-ply back binding with outer rosewood layer, herringbone backstripe, ebony fingerboard with slotted diamond inlays, total production of 575 instruments, mfg. 1898-1926.

	N/A	$3,200 - 4,000	$1,925 - 2,400	

The Model 1-21 was also a popular configuration prior to Martin's standardization of configurations in 1898 - every guitar built before 1898 in this configuration should be evaluated and appraised on a case-by-case basis. Martin also produced one Model 1-21P Plectrum guitar (1931).

MODEL 1-27 – Size 1 body, spruce top, Brazilian rosewood back and sides, round soundhole with five-stripe rosette (pearl center ring in four groups of five rings), ivory top binding, green/brown wood diagonal pattern top purfling, three-ply back binding with outer ivory layer, zig-zag backstripe, ebony ivory-bound fingerboard, ivory headstock binding, total production of 13 instruments, mfg. 1898-1907.

	N/A	$5,600 - 7,000	$3,350 - 4,200	

The Model 1-27 was also a popular configuration prior to Martin's standardization of configurations in 1898 - every guitar built before 1898 in this configuration should be evaluated and appraised on a case-by-case basis.

MODEL 1-28 – Size 1 body, spruce top, Brazilian rosewood back and sides, round soundhole with three-stripe rosette (5/9/5 grouping), ivory top binding (1898-1918) or ivoroid top binding (1918-1923), herringbone top purfling, three-ply back binding with outer ivory layer (1898-1918) or ivoroid layer (1918-1923), zig-zag backstripe, ebony fingerboard with no inlays (1898-1901) or slotted diamond inlays (1901-1923), total production of 238 instruments, mfg. 1898-1923.

	N/A	$5,600 - 7,000	$3,350 - 4,200	

The Model 1-28 was also a popular configuration prior to Martin's standardization of configurations in 1898 - every guitar built before 1898 in this configuration should be evaluated and appraised on a case-by-case basis.

* ***Model 1-28P Plectrum*** – similar to the Model 1-28, except in four-string plectrum configuration with two-per-side tuners and a 27 in. scale, total production of 19 instruments, mfg. 1928-1930.

	N/A	$3,200 - 4,000	$1,925 - 2,400	

MSR/NOTES	100%	EXCELLENT	AVERAGE	LAST MSR

MODEL 1-30 – Size 1 body, spruce top, Brazilian rosewood back and sides, round soundhole with pearl ring rosette, herringbone top purfling, ebony ivory-bound (1898-1918) or ivoroid-bound (1918-1919) fingerboard, ivory-bound (1898-1918) or ivoroid-bound (1918-1919) headstock, total production of 78 instruments, mfg. 1898-1919.

	N/A	$6,400 - 8,000	$3,850 - 4,800	

The Model 1-30 was also a popular configuration prior to Martin's standardization of configurations in 1898 - every guitar built before 1898 in this configuration should be evaluated and appraised on a case-by-case basis.

MODEL 1-34 – Size 1 body, spruce top, Brazilian rosewood back and sides, round soundhole with pearl ring rosette, ivory top binding, herringbone top purfling, ivory back binding, ebony ivory-bound fingerboard, ivory-bound headstock, ivory bridge, total production of 11 instruments, mfg. 1898-1904.

	N/A	N/A	N/A	

Extreme rarity precludes accurate pricing.

MODEL 1-42 – Size 1 body, spruce top, Brazilian rosewood back and sides, round soundhole with pearl ring rosette, pearl top bordering that also goes around the fingerboard, ebony ivory-bound (1898-1918) or ivoroid-bound (1918-1919) fingerboard with snowflake inlays (snowflakes on three frets between 1898 and 1901 and on five frets between 1901 and 1919), ivory-bound (1898-1918) or ivoroid-bound (1918-1919) headstock, ivory (1898-1918) or ebony (1918-19) bridge, total production of 44 instruments, mfg. 1898-1919.

	N/A	$10,000 - 12,500	$6,000 - 7,500	

The Model 1-42 was also a popular configuration prior to Martin's standardization of configurations in 1898 - every guitar built before 1898 in this configuration should be evaluated and appraised on a case-by-case basis.

MODEL 1-45 – Size 1 body, spruce top, Brazilian rosewood back and sides, round soundhole with pearl ring rosette, pearl top bordering that also goes around the fingerboard, pearl side bordering, zipper-pattern backstripe, ebony ivory-bound (1904-1918) or ivoroid-bound (1918-1919) fingerboard with snowflake inlays (snowflakes on five frets between 1904 and 1914 and on eight frets between 1914 and 1919), ivory-bound (1904-1918) or ivoroid-bound (1918-1919) headstock, ivory (1904-1918) or ebony (1918-19) bridge, total production of 6 instruments, mfg. 1904-1919.

	N/A	$22,000 - 27,500	$13,250 - 16,500	

MODEL 2-17 (FIRST VERSION) – Size 2 body, spruce top, mahogany back and sides, round soundhole with three black rings, three-ply top binding with rosewood outer layer, rosewood back binding, ebony fingerboard with two dot inlays at the 7th fret, rectangular bridge, total production of 6 instruments, mfg. 1910 only.

	N/A	$1,800 - 2,250	$1,075 - 1,350	

MODEL 2-17 (SECOND VERSION) – Size 2 body, mahogany top, back, and sides, round soundhole with three thin B/W/B rings rosette, three-ply top binding with outer rosewood layer, rosewood back binding (no back binding in 1930), thin black backstripe, rosewood fingerboard with two dot inlays at the 7th fret, rectangular bridge, available in Natural finish, total production of 6,044 instruments, mfg. 1922-1930.

	N/A	$2,200 - 2,750	$1,325 - 1,650	

* **Model 2-17H Hawaiian** – similar to the Model 2-17 Second Version, except in Hawaiian configuration with a flat fingerboard with flush frets, a high nut, and a non-slanted saddle, total production of 551 instruments, mfg. 1927-1931.

	N/A	$2,200 - 2,750	$1,325 - 1,650	

* **Model 2-17T Tenor** – similar to the Model 2-17 Second Version, except in four-string tenor configuration and two-per-side tuners, total production of 45 instruments, mfg. 1927-28.

	N/A	$1,600 - 2,000	$950 - 1,200	

#25 (MODEL 2-17 THIRD VERSION) – Size 2 body, mahogany top, back, and sides, round soundhole with three thin B/W/B rings rosette, no body binding, rosewood fingerboard with two dot inlays at the 7th fret, rectangular bridge, available in Natural finish, total production of 775 instruments, mfg. 1929-1930.

	N/A	$2,400 - 3,000	$1,450 - 1,800	

This is actually the third version of the Model 2-17 although it was referred to as the #25. This designation comes from Martin dropping the price $25 from the previous Model 2-17 by eliminating the body bindings. In 1930, this model was reinstated as the Model 2-17.

MODEL 2-17 FOURTH VERSION – Size 2 body, mahogany top, back, and sides, round soundhole with three thin B/W/B rings rosette, no body binding, rosewood fingerboard with two dot inlays at the 7th fret, rectangular bridge, no pickguard (1930-32) or tortoise pickguard (optional between 1932 and 1934 and standard from 1934), available in Natural finish, total production of 612 instruments, mfg. 1930-38.

	N/A	$2,600 - 3,250	$1,550 - 1,950	

MODEL 2-18 – Size 2 body, spruce top, rosewood (1898-1917) or mahogany (1917-1938) back and sides, round soundhole with wood colored rope pattern (1898-1902) or three-stripe rosette (1/9/1 grouping between 1902 and 1938), five-ply top binding, single-ply back binding with outer rosewood (1898-1932), black (1932-36), or tortoise (1936-38) layer, black backstripe, ebony fingerboard with no inlays (1898-1902) or dot inlays (1902-1938), total production of 100 instruments, mfg. 1898-1938.

1898-1917 Rosewood	N/A	$2,750 - 3,250	$1,800 - 2,250	
1917-1938 Mahogany	N/A	$2,200 - 2,750	$1,450 - 1,800	

Martin also produced one Model 2-18G with gut-string configuration (1954).

MSR/NOTES	100%	EXCELLENT	AVERAGE	LAST MSR

🎸 * **Model 2-18T Tenor** – similar to the Model 2-18, except in four-string tenor configuration and two-per-side tuners, total production of 345 instruments, mfg. 1928-1930.

| | N/A | $1,800 - 2,250 | $1,075 - 1,350 | |

MODEL 2-21 – Size 2 body, spruce top, rosewood back and sides, round soundhole with three-stripe rosette (single herringbone ring between two groups of five rings), five-ply top binding with outer rosewood layer, two-ply back binding with outer rosewood layer, herringbone backstripe, ebony fingerboard with slotted diamond inlays, total production of 12 instruments, mfg. 1898-1929.

| | N/A | $3,200 - 4,000 | $1,925 - 2,400 | |

The Model 2-21 was also a popular configuration prior to Martin's standardization of configurations in 1898 - every guitar built before 1898 in this configuration should be evaluated and appraised on a case-by-case basis. Martin also produced one Model 2-21T Tenor guitar (1928).

MODEL 2-27 – Size 2 body, spruce top, Brazilian rosewood back and sides, round soundhole with five-stripe rosette (pearl center ring in four groups of five rings), ivory top binding, green/brown wood diagonal pattern top purfling, three-ply back binding with outer ivory layer, zig-zag backstripe, ebony ivory-bound fingerboard, ivory headstock binding, total production of 8 instruments, mfg. 1898-1907.

| | N/A | $4,800 - 6,000 | $2,875 - 3,600 | |

The Model 2-27 was also a popular configuration prior to Martin's standardization of configurations in 1898 - every guitar built before 1898 in this configuration should be evaluated and appraised on a case-by-case basis.

MODEL 2-28T TENOR – tenor configuration, Size 2 body, spruce top, Brazilian rosewood back and sides, round soundhole with three-stripe rosette (5/9/5 grouping), ivoroid top binding, herringbone top purfling, three-ply back binding with outer ivoroid layer, zig-zag backstripe, ebony fingerboard with slotted diamond inlays, two-per-side tuners, total production of 35 instruments, mfg. 1929-1930.

| | N/A | $3,400 - 4,250 | $2,050 - 2,550 | |

MODEL 2-30 – Size 2 body, spruce top, Brazilian rosewood back and sides, round soundhole with pearl ring rosette, herringbone top purfling, ebony ivory-bound (1902-1918) or ivoroid-bound (1918-1921) fingerboard, ivory-bound (1902-1918) or ivoroid-bound (1918-1921) headstock, wood bridge, total production of 7 instruments, mfg. 1902-1921.

| | N/A | $5,600 - 7,000 | $3,350 - 4,200 | |

MODEL 2-44 – Size 2 body, spruce top, Brazilian rosewood back and sides, round soundhole with three ring rosette (5/9/5 grouping), six-ply top binding with outer ivoroid layer, three-ply back binding with outer ivoroid layer, wide white backstripe surrounded by smaller black and white lines, ebony ivoroid-bound fingerboard with no inlays, ivoroid-bound headstock with "Soloist" or "Olcott-Bickford Artist Model" inlaid, total production of 4 instruments, mfg. 1930 only.

| | N/A | $20,000 - 25,000 | $12,500 - 15,000 | |

These guitars were specially built for performer Vahdah Olcott-Bickford.

MODEL 2 1/2-17 – Size 2 1/2 body, spruce top, mahogany back and sides, round soundhole with three black rings, three-ply top binding with rosewood outer layer, rosewood back binding, ebony fingerboard, total production of 38 instruments, mfg. 1909-1914.

| | N/A | $1,750 - 2,200 | $1,050 - 1,325 | |

MODEL 2 1/2-18 – Size 2 1/2 body, spruce top, rosewood (1898-1917) or mahogany (1917-1923) back and sides, round soundhole with wood colored rope pattern (1898-1902) or three-stripe rosette (1/9/1 grouping between 1902 and 1923), five-ply top binding with outer rosewood layer, rosewood back binding, black backstripe, ebony fingerboard with no inlays (1898-1902) or dot inlays (1902-1923), total production of 58 instruments, mfg. 1898-1923.

| 1898-1917 Rosewood | N/A | $2,600 - 3,250 | $1,550 - 1,950 | |
| 1917-1923 Mahogany | N/A | $2,000 - 2,500 | $1,200 - 1,500 | |

The Model 2 1/2-18 was also a popular configuration prior to Martin's standardization of configurations in 1898 - every guitar built before 1898 in this configuration should be evaluated and appraised on a case-by-case basis.

MODEL 2 1/2-21 – Size 2 1/2 body, spruce top, rosewood back and sides, round soundhole with three-stripe rosette (single herringbone ring between two groups of five rings), five-ply top binding with outer rosewood layer, two-ply back binding with outer rosewood layer, herringbone backstripe, ebony fingerboard with slotted diamond inlays, total production of 29 instruments, mfg. 1910-1921.

| | N/A | $3,600 - 4,500 | $2,150 - 2,700 | |

MODEL 2 1/2-28 – Size 2 1/2 body, spruce top, Brazilian rosewood back and sides, round soundhole with three-stripe rosette (5/9/5 grouping), ivory (1909-1918) or ivoroid (1918-1923) top binding, herringbone top purfling, three-ply back binding with outer ivory (1909-1918) or ivoroid (1918-1923) layer, zig-zag backstripe, ebony fingerboard with slotted diamond inlays, two-per-side tuners, total production of 18 instruments, mfg. 1909-1923.

| | N/A | $3,600 - 4,500 | $2,150 - 2,700 | |

ACOUSTIC: SIZE 5 MODELS

Martin's Size 5 guitar body is the only Model number guitar to be produced after the 1930s. The Model 5-18 was produced through 1989 and various other models have been produced as one-offs during the 20th century. The Size 5 is also often referred to as a "Terz" guitar because they are often tuned one-third higher than standard guitars. In the late 1990s, the Size 5 guitar was introduced with the Size 5 Mini Martin and the reintroduction of the 5-15 in Martin's mahogany 15 Series. The small body size has also been utilized on Claire's Guitar - a limited edition model built for Chris Martin's daughter, Claire.

MSR/NOTES	100%	EXCELLENT	AVERAGE	LAST MSR

Size 5 dimensions: 11.25 in. lower bout width, 3.875 in. body depth, 16 in. body length, and 21.4 in. scale (1898-1924) or 22 in. scale (1924-present).

Martin produced five other Size 5 guitars in limited quantities including three **Model 5-30s** (1900-02), one **Model 5-34** (1899), one **Model 5-35** (1971), two **Model 5-42s** (1921-22), and one **Model 5-45** (1922). For the recent production of the Model 5-15, refer to the 15 Series.

MODEL 5-15T – tenor configuration, Size 5 body, mahogany top, back, and sides, round soundhole with three thin W/B/W rings, no binding, mahogany neck, rosewood fingerboard with single dot inlays, two-per-side tuners, rectangular bridge, available in Natural non-gloss finish, 22 in. scale, total production of 1,325 instruments, mfg. 1949-1963.

	N/A	$1,075 - 1,350	$650 - 800	

The Model 5-15T and the Model 5-17T are very similar with the only difference being non-gloss finish versus gloss finish. However, there was no overlap in production so dating by serial number will provide an accurate year and model of guitar.

MODEL 5-16 – Size 5 body, spruce top, mahogany back and sides, round soundhole with three-stripe rosette (1/9/1 grouping), black outer body binding, mahogany neck, 12/19-fret rosewood fingerboard, three-per-side chrome tuners, rosewood bridge with black white dot pins, available in Natural finish, total production of 127 instruments, mfg. 1962-63.

	N/A	$1,600 - 2,000	$950 - 1,200	

MODEL 5-17 (FIRST VERSION) – Size 5 body, spruce top, mahogany back and sides, round soundhole with three black soundhole rings, three-ply top binding with outer rosewood layer, rosewood back binding, mahogany neck, 12/19-fret unbound ebony fingerboard, three-per-side die-cast tuners with nickel buttons, rosewood bridge with black pins, available in Dark finish, total production of 14 instruments, mfg. 1912-16.

	N/A	$1,475 - 1,850	$950 - 1,175	

MODEL 5-17 (SECOND VERSION) – Size 5 body, mahogany top, back, and sides, round soundhole with three thin W/B/W soundhole rings, three-ply top binding with outer rosewood layer (1927-1930) or no top binding (1930-1943), rosewood back binding (1927-1930) or no back binding (1930-1943), thin black back stripe, mahogany neck, 12/19-fret unbound rosewood fingerboard with double dot inlays at the 7th fret, three-per-side die-cast tuners with nickel buttons, rectangular rosewood bridge with black pins, available in Natural finish, total production of 218 instruments, mfg. 1927-1943.

	N/A	$1,600 - 2,000	$950 - 1,200	

* *Model 5-17T Tenor* – similar to the Model 5-17 (Second Version), except in four-string tenor configuration with two-per-side tuners and 22 in. scale, total production of 3,666 instruments, mfg. 1927-1949.

	N/A	$1,125 - 1,400	$675 - 850	

MODEL 5-18 – Size 5 body, spruce top, rosewood (1898-1917) or mahogany (1917-1989) back and sides, round soundhole with colored rope pattern rosette (1898-1902) or three-stripe rosette (1/9/1 grouping between 1902 and 1988 and 5/9/5 grouping between 1988 and 1989, rings weren't actually inlaid until the mid 1930s), five-ply top binding and single-ply back binding with rosewood (1898-1932), black (1932-36, 1966-1989), or tortoise (1936-1966) outer layer, black back stripe, unbound ebony fingerboard with no inlays (1898-1902) or dot inlays (1902-1989), three-per-side tuners, rectangular bridge, total production of 2,774 instruments, mfg. 1898-1989.

1898-1917 Rosewood Back & Sides	N/A	$2,600 - 3,250	$1,550 - 1,950	
1917-1932 Mahogany Back & Sides	N/A	$3,000 - 3,750	$1,800 - 2,250	
1933-1944	N/A	$2,800 - 3,500	$1,675 - 2,100	
1945-1949	N/A	$2,200 - 2,750	$1,325 - 1,650	
1950-1959	N/A	$1,800 - 2,250	$1,075 - 1,350	
1960-1969	N/A	$1,400 - 1,750	$850 - 1,050	
1970-1989	N/A	$1,200 - 1,500	$725 - 900	

Martin also produced two Model 5-18G guitars with gut-string configuration (1954 and 1956), three Model 5-18K guitars with koa top, back, and sides (1921, 1937), and four Model 5-18T tenor guitars (1940, 1954, 1961, 1962). This model was available as a special order toward the end of the production run.

MODEL 5-21 – Size 5 body, spruce top, rosewood back and sides, round soundhole with three-stripe rosette (single herringbone ring between two groups of five rings), five-ply top binding with outer rosewood layer, two-ply back binding with outer rosewood layer, herringbone backstripe, ebony fingerboard with slotted diamond inlays, total production of 118 instruments, mfg. 1902-1927, and one produced in 1977.

	N/A	$2,600 - 3,250	$1,550 - 1,950	

* *Model 5-21T Tenor* – similar to the Model 5-21, except in four-string tenor configuration with two-per-side tuners, total production of 312 instruments, mfg. 1927-1928.

	N/A	$2,000 - 2,500	$1,200 - 1,500	

MODEL 5-28 – Size 5 body, spruce top, Brazilian rosewood (1901-1939, 1968-69) or Indian rosewood (1969-1981, 1988) back and sides, round soundhole with three-stripe rosette (5/9/5 grouping), ivory (1901-1918), ivoroid (1918-1939), or white (1968-1981, 1988) top binding, herringbone top purfling (1901-1939) or six-ply top purfling with outer white layer (1968-1981, 1988), three-ply back binding with outer ivory (1901-1918), ivoroid (1918-1939), or white (1968-1981, 1988) layer, zig-zag backstripe (1901-1939) or chainlink back stripe (1968-1981, 1988), unbound ebony fingerboard with slotted diamond inlays (1901-1939) or dot inlays (1968-1981, 1988), total production of 26 instruments, mfg. 1901-1939 (15 produced), 1968-1981 (10 produced), and 1988 (one produced).

1901-1923 Gut Bracing	N/A	$2,800 - 3,500	$1,675 - 2,100	
1935-1939 Steel Bracing	N/A	$4,400 - 5,500	$2,825 - 3,525	
1968-1969 Brazilian Rosewood	N/A	$4,000 - 5,000	$2,400 - 3,000	
1969-1981, 1988 Indian Rosewood	N/A	$2,000 - 2,500	$1,200 - 1,500	

Martin also produced one Model 5-28G guitar with gut strings (1939) and one Model 5-28T tenor guitar (1939).

MSR/NOTES	100%	EXCELLENT	AVERAGE	LAST MSR

ACOUSTIC: SIZE 7 MODELS

The 7/8-sized (Size 7) dreadnought was one of Chris Martin's first ideas in the early 1980s. After a trip in Japan, he noticed how large standard dreadnought guitars looked on the small frame of a Japanese guitar player. He came back to the factory and started to build the 7-28 - a 7/8-sized dreadnought with standard 28 style appointments. Unfortunately, the Size 7 body style never took off and only a couple hundred were ever produced. Size 7 dimensions: 13 11/16 in. lower bout width, 14.375 in. body depth, 17.5 in. body length, and 23 in. scale.

MODEL 7-28 – 7/8-sized Dreadnought-style body, spruce top, Indian rosewood back and sides, round soundhole with three ring rosette (5/9/5 grouping), six-ply top body binding with outer white layer, three-ply back binding with outer white layer, unbound ebony fingerboard, three-per-side tuners, black pickguard, available as a special order item, mfg. 1980-1993.

	N/A	$1,800 - 2,250	$1,075 - 1,350	$2,380

MODEL 7-37K – 7/8-sized Dreadnought-style body, spruce top, koa back and sides, round soundhole with pearl ring rosette, white outer top body binding, unbound ebony fingerboard with slotted diamond inlays at the fifth and ninth frets, three-per-side tuners, tortoise pickguard, limited edition run of 95 instruments, mfg. 1980-87.

	N/A	$2,000 - 2,500	$1,200 - 1,500	

ACOUSTIC: STANDARD SERIES

Martin's Standard Series was formally introduced in 1996, but the majority of standard Martin guitars built before the mid-1980s appear in this series. As Martin began expanding into limited editions, special editions, vintage reissues, and other "non-standard" guitars, they realized that they needed a series for their regular guitars to appear in. The Standard Series continues traditional building methods with various modern technologies mixed in. There really was no change in specifications or construction when the Standard Series was introduced, aside from the designation of the Standard Series.

The Standard Series encompasses several models and body styles, so they are broken out into each body style numerically/alphabetically and then listed numerically within each sub-category.

ACOUSTIC: STANDARD CONCERT (0) SERIES

Size 0 (Concert) guitars feature a lower bout width of 13.5 inches, 4.25 (14-fret) or 4 3/16 (12-fret) in. depth, 18.375 (14-fret) or 19.125 (12-fret) in. length, and 24.9 in. scale.

For the Model 0-55, refer to the 00-17 listed in the Grand Concert Series.

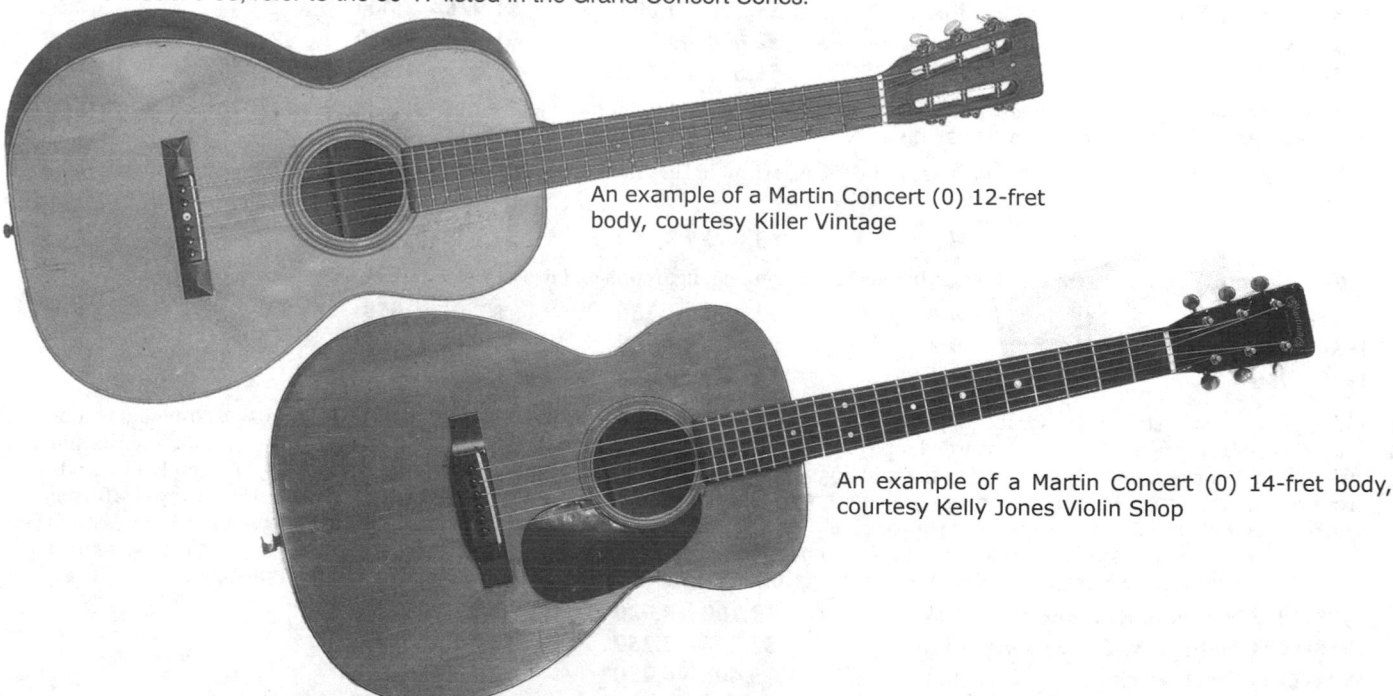

An example of a Martin Concert (0) 12-fret body, courtesy Killer Vintage

An example of a Martin Concert (0) 14-fret body, courtesy Kelly Jones Violin Shop

0-15 – concert body style, mahogany top, back, and sides, round soundhole with thin three-stripe (W/B/W) rosette, no binding, mahogany neck, 14/20-fret rosewood fingerboard with single white dot inlays, rosewood headstock overlay with logo decal, three-per-side nickel tuners with plastic buttons, rectangular rosewood bridge, white bridge pins, tortoiseshell pickguard, available in Natural Satin finish, mfg. 1935, 1940-1961.

1935	N/A	$2,600 - 3,250	$1,550 - 1,950
1940-1945	N/A	$2,400 - 3,000	$1,450 - 1,800
1946-1949	N/A	$2,200 - 2,750	$1,325 - 1,650
1950-1955	N/A	$2,000 - 2,500	$1,200 - 1,500
1956-1961	N/A	$1,800 - 2,250	$1,075 - 1,350

The 0-15 and 0-17 models are nearly identical with the only differences being the 0-17 has body binding and a gloss finish.

MSR/NOTES	100%	EXCELLENT	AVERAGE	LAST MSR

* **0-15H Hawaiian** – similar to the 0-15, except in Hawaiian configuration with a flat fingerboard with flush frets, a high nut, and a non-slanted saddle, mfg. 1939 only.

| | N/A | $2,400 - 3,000 | $1,450 - 1,800 | |

* **0-15T Tenor** – similar to the 0-15, except in four-string tenor configuration and two-per-side tuners, mfg. 1960-63.

| | N/A | $1,075 - 1,350 | $650 - 800 | |

0-16 – concert body style, spruce top, mahogany back and sides, round soundhole with three-stripe rosette (1/9/1 grouping), three-ply top binding with black outer layer, mahogany neck, 14/20-fret rosewood fingerboard, three-per-side tuners, rectangular rosewood bridge, black bridge pins, tortoise pickguard, Natural finish, six total guitars produced, mfg. 1961 only.

| | N/A | $1,875 - 2,350 | $1,125 - 1,400 | |

0-16NY – concert body style, spruce top, mahogany back and sides, round soundhole with three-stripe rosette, black binding, mahogany neck, 12/19-fret extra-wide rosewood fingerboard with no inlays, slotted headstock with gold foil logo, three-per-side open-style tuners with plastic buttons, rosewood bridge with black bridge pins, available in Natural Satin finish, available as a Special Order, mfg. 1961-1995.

1961-1969	N/A	$2,000 - 2,500	$1,200 - 1,500	
1970-1979	N/A	$1,800 - 2,250	$1,075 - 1,350	
1980-1989	N/A	$1,600 - 2,000	$950 - 1,200	
1990-1995	N/A	$1,400 - 1,750	$850 - 1,050	

0-17 FIRST VERSION – concert body style, spruce top, mahogany back and sides, round soundhole with three black rings, three-ply top binding with rosewood outer layer, rosewood back binding, cedar (1906-1916) or mahogany (1916-17) neck, 12/20-fret ebony fingerboard with pearl dot inlay, slotted headstock, three-per-side nickel tuners with plastic buttons, ebony bridge, black bridge pins, available in Natural finish, mfg. 1906-1917.

| | N/A | $1,875 - 2,350 | $1,125 - 1,400 | |

0-17 SECOND VERSION – concert body style, mahogany top, back, and sides, round soundhole with three thin W/B/W rings, three-ply top binding with rosewood outer layer (1929-1930, no binding after 1930), mahogany neck, 12/20-fret (1929-1931) or 14/20-fret (1932-1948, 1966-68) rosewood fingerboard with double pearl dot inlays, slotted (1929-1934) or solid (1929-1934) headstock, three-per-side open-style nickel tuners with plastic buttons (1929-1934) or regular tuners (1934-1948, 1966-68), rectangular rosewood bridge, black bridge pins, no pickguard (1929-1934) tortoise pickguard (1932-1948), or black pickguard (1966-68), available in Natural gloss finish, mfg. 1929-1948, 1966-68.

1929-1931 12-Fret	N/A	$2,200 - 2,750	$1,325 - 1,650	
1932-1939 14-Fret	N/A	$3,200 - 4,000	$1,925 - 2,400	
1940-1948	N/A	$2,600 - 3,250	$1,550 - 1,950	
1966-1968	N/A	$1,800 - 2,250	$1,075 - 1,350	

A pickguard was optional between 1932 and 1934. The 0-17 and 0-15 models are nearly identical with the only differences being the 0-17 has body binding and a gloss finish.

* **0-17H Hawaiian** – similar to the 0-17 Second Version, except in Hawaiian configuration with a flat fingerboard with flush frets, a high nut, and a non-slanted saddle, mfg. 1930-39.

| | N/A | $3,000 - 3,750 | $1,800 - 2,250 | |

* **0-17T Tenor** – similar to the 0-17, except in four-string tenor configuration and two-per-side tuners, mfg. 1932-1960.

1932-1933	N/A	$1,400 - 1,750	$850 - 1,050	
1934-1939	N/A	$2,000 - 2,500	$1,200 - 1,500	
1940-1960	N/A	$1,200 - 1,500	$800 - 950	

0-18 – concert body style, solid spruce top, Brazilian rosewood (1898-1917) or mahogany (1918-1993) back and sides, round soundhole with various rosette configurations (colored-wood rope pattern between 1898 and 1902, white lines grouped 1/9/1 between 1902 and the mid-1930s, white inlaid lines grouped 1/9/1 between the mid-1930s and 1988, and 5/9/5 grouping between 1988 and 1993), five-ply top binding with rosewood (1898-1932), black (1932-1936, 1966-1993) or tortoise (1936-1966) outer layer, cedar (1898-1916) or mahogany (1916-1993) neck, 12/19-fret (1898-1934) or 14/20-fret (1934-1993) ebony fingerboard with no inlays (1898-1902) or pearl dot inlays (1902-1993), slotted (1898-1934) or solid (1934-1993) headstock, three-per-side open-style brass tuners with ivory buttons (1898-1934) or regular tuners (1934-1993), pyramid ebony bridge with black pearl dot pins, available in Natural finish, available as a Special Order, mfg. 1898-1993.

1898-1917 Brazilian Rosewood	N/A	$3,200 - 4,000	$1,925 - 2,400	
1918-1924 Mahogany, Gut Bracing	N/A	$2,600 - 3,250	$1,550 - 1,950	
1924-1933 Steel Bracing	N/A	$3,400 - 4,250	$2,050 - 2,550	
1934-1939	N/A	$4,800 - 6,000	$2,875 - 3,600	
1940-1945 Scalloped Bracing	N/A	$3,600 - 4,500	$2,150 - 2,700	
1946-1949	N/A	$3,200 - 4,000	$1,925 - 2,400	
1950-1954	N/A	$2,800 - 3,500	$1,675 - 2,100	
1955-1959	N/A	$2,400 - 3,000	$1,450 - 1,800	
1960-1964	N/A	$2,200 - 2,750	$1,325 - 1,650	
1965-1969	N/A	$1,800 - 2,250	$1,075 - 1,350	
1970-1979	N/A	$1,475 - 1,850	$900 - 1,100	
1980-1995	N/A	$1,200 - 1,500	$725 - 900	$2,330

• **Add 25-50% for Sunburst finish during the 1930s.**

MSR/NOTES	100%	EXCELLENT	AVERAGE	LAST MSR

Martin also produced one 0-18 in Hawaiian configuration (Model 0-18H, 1920 only) and three 0-18s in the new 14-fret style (Model 0-18S, 1932 only).

* **0-18K Koa** – similar to the 0-18, except has koa top, back, and sides, mfg. 1918-1935.

	N/A	$3,400 - 4,250	$2,050 - 2,450	

* **0-18T Tenor** – similar to the 0-18, except in four-string tenor configuration and two-per-side tuners, available as a Special Order, mfg. 1929-1993.

	100%	EXCELLENT	AVERAGE	LAST MSR
1929-1932	N/A	$2,200 - 2,750	$1,325 - 1,650	
1936-1939	N/A	$4,000 - 5,000	$2,400 - 3,000	
1940-1944	N/A	$2,600 - 3,250	$1,550 - 1,950	
1945-1946	N/A	$2,200 - 2,750	$1,325 - 1,650	
1947-1959	N/A	$1,600 - 2,000	$950 - 1,200	
1960-1969	N/A	$1,400 - 1,750	$850 - 1,050	
1970-1979	N/A	$1,075 - 1,350	$650 - 800	
1980-1993	N/A	$925 - 1,150	$550 - 700	$2,330

Martin also produced 31 0-18Ts that were specially built for Carl Fisher in New York City (Model 0-18T Carl Fisher, 1930 only), two 0-18T electric tenor instruments (Model 0-18TE, 1959, 1962), five 0-18T eight-string tenor instruments (Model 0-18T8, 1969-1970), and one unspecified 0-18T (Model 0-18TD, 1977 only).

0-21 – concert body style, solid spruce top, rosewood back and sides, round soundhole with three ring rosette (5/herringbone/5 grouping between 1898 and 1947, 1/9/1 grouping between 1947 and 1948), five-ply top binding, two-ply back binding with rosewood (1898-1932), black (1932-1936), or tortoise (1936-1948) outer layer, herringbone backstripe, cedar (1898-1916) or mahogany (1916-1948) neck, 12/19-fret ebony (1898-1941) or rosewood (1941-48) fingerboard with slotted diamond inlays (1898-1944) or pearl dot inlays (1944-48), slotted headstock, three-per-side open-style brass tuners with ivory buttons, pyramid ebony bridge, ebony bridge pins with pearl dots, available in Natural finish, mfg. 1898-1948.

	100%	EXCELLENT	AVERAGE	
1898-1929	N/A	$4,800 - 6,000	$2,875 - 3,600	
1930-1939	N/A	$7,600 - 9,500	$4,550 - 5,700	
1940-1944	N/A	$4,800 - 6,000	$2,875 - 3,600	
1945-1948 (Non-scalloped bracing)	N/A	$4,000 - 5,000	$2,400 - 3,000	

Three 0-21s were produced with 14-fret body styles and fingerboards and a solid headstock in 1930. Martin also produced one 0-21 in Hawaiian configuration (Model 0-21H, 1918 only) and one 0-21 in plectrum configuration (Model 0-21P, 1929 only).

* **0-21K Koa** – similar to the 0-21, except has koa top, back, and sides, mfg. 1919-1929.

	N/A	$4,800 - 6,000	$2,875 - 3,600	

* **0-21T Tenor** – similar to the 0-21, except in four-string tenor configuration and two-per-side tuners, mfg. 1929-1935.

	N/A	$4,800 - 6,000	$2,875 - 3,600	

0-28 – concert body style, solid spruce top, Brazilian rosewood back and sides, round soundhole with three-ring rosette (5/9/5 grouping), ivory (1898-1918), ivoroid (1918-1931, 1937), or non-grained white (1969 only) binding, herringbone (1898-1931, 1937) or six-ply with white outer layer (1969) purfling, cedar (1898-1916) or mahogany (1916-1931, 1937, 1969) neck, 12/19-fret ebony fingerboard with no inlays (1898-1901), slotted diamond inlays (1901-1931, 1937) or pearl dot inlays (1969), slotted headstock, three-per-side brass tuners with ivory buttons, pyramid ebony bridge, ebony bridge pins with pearl dots, available in Natural finish, mfg. 1898-1931, 1937, 1969.

	100%	EXCELLENT	AVERAGE	
1898-1927 Gut Bracing	N/A	$6,400 - 8,000	$3,850 - 4,800	
1925-1929 Steel Bracing	N/A	$7,600 - 9,500	$4,550 - 5,700	
1930-1931, 1937	N/A	$8,800 - 11,000	$5,275 - 6,600	

Martin also produced one 0-28 with electronics (Model 0-28E, 1963 only), two 0-28s in Hawaiian configuration (Model 0-28H, 1928 only), two 0-28s with wide necks (Model 0-28NY, 1968-69), and one 0-28 in plectrum configuration (Model 0-28P, 1930 only).

* **0-28K Koa** – similar to the 0-28, except has koa top, back, and sides, mfg. 1917-1935.

	N/A	$6,400 - 8,000	$3,850 - 4,800	

* **0-28T Tenor** – similar to the 0-28, except in four-string tenor configuration and two-per-side tuners, mfg. 1930-31, 1941, 1961, 1964.

	100%	EXCELLENT	AVERAGE	
1930-1931	N/A	$6,000 - 7,500	$3,600 - 4,500	
1941	N/A	$4,800 - 6,000	$2,875 - 3,600	

0-30 – concert body style, solid spruce top, Brazilian rosewood back and sides, round soundhole with pearl rosette, ivory (1899-1918) or ivoroid (1918-1921) top and back binding, cedar (1899-1916) or mahogany (1916-1921) neck, 12/19-fret ivory (1899-1918) or ivoroid (1918-1921) bound ebony fingerboard with pearl dot inlays, ivory (1899-1918) or ivoroid (1918-1921) slotted headstock, three-per-side open-style silver brass tuners, pyramid ebony bridge, ebony bridge, ebony bridge pins with pearl dots, available in Natural finish, mfg. 1899-1921.

	N/A	$6,800 - 8,500	$4,100 - 5,100	

MSR/NOTES	100%	EXCELLENT	AVERAGE	LAST MSR

0-34 – concert body style, solid spruce top, Brazilian rosewood back and sides, round soundhole with pearl rosette, ivory top and back binding, herringbone top purfling, cedar neck, 12/19-fret ivory-bound ebony fingerboard with pearl slotted diamond inlays at the 5th and 9th frets and a Maltese cross at the 7th fret, ivory-bound slotted headstock, three-per-side open-style silver brass tuners, pyramid ivory bridge, ebony bridge pins with pearl dots, available in Natural finish, mfg. 1898-99, 1907.

	N/A	$7,200 - 9,000	$4,300 - 5,400	

0-40 – concert body style, solid spruce top, Brazilian rosewood back and sides, round soundhole with pearl rosette, pearl top ivoroid top and back binding, pearl top borders and no pearl around the fingerboard on the top of the guitar, cedar neck, 12/19-fret unbound ebony fingerboard with pearl snowflake inlays, slotted headstock with three-per-side open-style silver brass tuners, pyramid ivory bridge, ebony bridge pins with pearl dots, available in Natural finish, total production of six instruments, mfg. 1912-13.

	N/A	N/A	N/A	

Extreme rarity precludes accurate pricing.

0-42 – concert body style, solid spruce top, Brazilian rosewood back and sides, round soundhole with pearl rosette, ivory (1898-1918) ivoroid (1918-1942) top and back binding, pearl top borders that go around the fingerboard on the top of the guitar, zipper-pattern backstripe, cedar (1898-1916) or mahogany (1916-1942) neck, 12/19-fret ivory (1898-1918) or ivoroid (1918-1942) bound ebony fingerboard with pearl snowflake inlays that started at the 3rd fret (1898-1901) or the 5th fret (1901-1942), ivory (1898-1918) or ivoroid (1918-1942) bound slotted headstock, three-per-side open-style silver tuners with pearl buttons, pyramid ivory bridge (1898-1918) or ebony bridge (1918-1942), ebony bridge pins with pearl dots, available in Natural finish, mfg. 1898-1942.

1898-1927 Gut Bracing	N/A	$10,000 - 12,500	$6,000 - 7,500	
1927-1942 Steel Bracing	N/A	$14,000 - 17,500	$8,500 - 10,500	

0-44 – concert body style, solid spruce top, Brazilian rosewood back and sides, round soundhole with three-stripe rosette (5/9/5 grouping), six-ply top binding with ivory (1913-1918) or ivoroid (1918-1931) outer layer, three-ply back binding with ivory (1913-1918) or ivoroid (1918-1931) outer layer, wide white backstripe surrounded by smaller black and white lines, cedar (1913-16) or mahogany (1916-1931) 12/19-fret ivory (1913-1918) or ivoroid (1918-1931) bound ebony fingerboard, ivory (1913-1918) or ivoroid (1918-1931) bound slotted headstock, three-per-side open-style tuners, available in Natural finish, total production of 17 guitars, mfg. 1913-1931.

	N/A	$18,000 - 22,500	$10,750 - 13,500	

Some 0-44s may have "Soloist" inlaid on the headstock. There were also a few 0-44s specially made for Vahdah Olcott-Bickford that have non-herringbone-style top and back binding and have "Olcott-Bickford Artist Model" inlaid on the headstock.

0-45 – concert body style, solid spruce top, Brazilian rosewood back and sides, round soundhole with pearl rosette, ivory (1904-1918) or ivoroid (1918-1939) top and back binding, pearl top borders that go around the fingerboard on the top of the guitar, pearl around sides, zipper-pattern backstripe, cedar (1904-1916) or mahogany (1916-1939) neck, 12/19-fret ivory (1904-1918) or ivoroid (1918-1939) bound ebony fingerboard with pearl snowflake/diamond inlays that start at the 5th fret (1904-1914) or the 1st fret (1914-1939), ivory (1904-1918) or ivoroid (1918-1939) bound headstock with pearl torch inlay (1904-1934) or vertical block CF Martin logo inlay (1934-39), three-per-side open-style brass tuners with ivory buttons, pyramid ivory bridge (1904-1918) or ebony bridge (1918-1939), ebony bridge pins, no pickguard (1904-1932) or tortoise pickguard (1932-1939), available in Natural finish, mfg. 1904-1939.

1904-1927 Gut Bracing	N/A	$28,000 - 35,000	$16,750 - 21,000	
1927-1930 Steel Bracing	N/A	$40,000 - 50,000	$24,000 - 30,000	

ACOUSTIC: STANDARD GRAND CONCERT (00) SERIES

Size 00 (Grand Concert) guitars feature a lower bout width of 14 5/16 (14-fret) or 14.125 (12-fret) in., 4.125 (14-fret) or 4 1/16 (12-fret) in. depth, 18.875 (14-fret) or 19.625 (12-fret) in. length, and 24.9 in. scale.

Martin produced one 0012-35 in 1973 that featured 12-string configuration and a three-piece Indian rosewood back.

00-16C CLASSICAL – classical Grand Concert body style, solid spruce top, mahogany back and sides, round soundhole with three-stripe rosette (1/9/1 grouping), dark outer top binding, black back stripe, mahogany neck, 12/19-fret rosewood fingerboard with no inlays, slotted headstock, three-per-side open-style tuners with pearl buttons, tied rosewood bridge, available in Natural finish, available as a Special Order, mfg. 1962-1982, 1988.

1962-1964	N/A	$1,350 - 1,700	$825 - 1,025	
1965-1969	N/A	$1,200 - 1,500	$725 - 900	
1970-1979	N/A	$850 - 1,125	$525 - 650	
1980-1982, 1988	N/A	$800 - 1,000	$475 - 600	$2,330

Martin also offered a 00-16C with ash back and sides (00-16CA, 1988 only), a 00-16C with maple back and sides (00-16CM, 1988 only), and a 00-16 C that is a regular non-classical maple version (00-16M, 1988 only).

00-17 FIRST VERSION – Grand Concert body style, spruce top, mahogany back and sides, round soundhole with three black rings, three-ply top binding with rosewood outer layer, rosewood back binding, cedar (1908-1916) or mahogany (1916-17) neck, unbound ebony fingerboard, rectangular ebony bridge, available in Natural finish, mfg. 1908-1917.

	N/A	$2,400 - 3,000	$1,450 - 1,800	

MSR/NOTES	100%	EXCELLENT	AVERAGE	LAST MSR

An example of a Martin Grand Concert (00) 12-fret body, courtesy Bilton Beeslyn

An example of a Martin Grand Concert (00) 14-fret body, courtesy Willie Del Mar

00-17 SECOND VERSION – Grand Concert body style, mahogany top, back, and sides, round soundhole with three thin W/B/W rings, no binding, thin black back stripe, mahogany neck, 12/19-fret (1930-34) or 14/20-fret (1934-1960, 1982-88) rosewood fingerboard with pearl dot inlays, slotted headstock (1930-34) or solid headstock (1934-1960, 1982-88), three-per-side open-style tuners (1930-34) or regular tuners (1934-1960, 1982-88), rectangular rosewood bridge, no pickguard (1930-34), tortoise pickguard (1932-1960), or black pickguard (1982-88), available in Natural finish, total production of 13,407 instruments, mfg. 1930-1960, 1982-88.

1930-1933	N/A	$2,800 - 3,500	$1,675 - 2,100
1934-1939	N/A	$3,600 - 4,500	$2,150 - 2,700
1940-1945	N/A	$3,200 - 4,000	$1,925 - 2,400
1946-1949	N/A	$2,800 - 3,500	$1,675 - 2,100
1950-1960	N/A	$2,400 - 3,000	$1,450 - 1,800
1982-1988	N/A	$1,400 - 1,750	$850 - 1,050

Rudick's of Akron, OH ordered 12 00-17s in 1935, but they are stamped 0-55 at the request of Rudick's. Martin also produced one 00-17 as a plectrum model (Model 00-17P, 1941).

* *00-17 Hawaiian* – similar to the 00-17 Second Version, except in Hawaiian configuration with a flat fingerboard with flush frets, a high nut, and a non-slanted saddle, total production of 20 instruments, mfg. 1934-35.

	N/A	$3,200 - 4,000	$1,925 - 2,400

00-18 – Grand Concert body style, spruce top, Brazilian rosewood (1898-1917) or mahogany (1917-1993) back and sides, round soundhole with various rosettes (colored wood rope rosette between 1898 and 1902, white line rosette grouped 1/9/1 between 1902 and the mid-1930s, inlaid white lines grouped 1/9/1 between the mid-1930s and 1988, and inlaid 5/9/5 grouping between 1988 and 1993), five-ply top binding, single-ply back binding with rosewood (1898-1932), black (1932-36, 1966-1993), or tortoise (1936-1966) outer layer, black backstripe, cedar (1898-1916) or mahogany (1916-1993) neck, 12/19-fret (1898-1934) or 14/20-fret (1934-1993) unbound ebony (1898-1939) or rosewood (1935-1993) fingerboard with no inlays (1898-1902) or pearl dot inlays (1902-1993), slotted (1898-1934) or solid (1934-1993) headstock, three-per-side open-style tuners (1898-1934) or regular tuners (1934-1993), rectangular (1898-1929) or belly (1929-1993) ebony bridge, no pickguard (1898-1932) tortoise pickguard (1932-1966), or black pickguard (1966-1993), Natural finish, 24.9 in. scale, available as a Special Order, mfg. 1898-1993.

1898-1917 Brazilian Rosewood	N/A	$4,500 - 5,500	$2,400 - 3,000
1917-1924 Mahogany Gut Bracing	N/A	$4,000 - 5,000	$2,400 - 3,000
1924-1934 Steel Bracing 12-Fret	N/A	$4,800 - 6,000	$2,875 - 3,600
1934-1939 14-Fret	N/A	$8,000 - 10,000	$4,800 - 6,000
1940-1945 Scalloped Bracing	N/A	$6,400 - 8,000	$3,850 - 4,800
1945-1946 Unscalloped Bracing	N/A	$4,800 - 6,000	$2,875 - 3,600
1947-1949	N/A	$4,000 - 5,000	$2,400 - 3,000

Continues on next page.

MSR/NOTES	100%	EXCELLENT	AVERAGE	LAST MSR
1950-1954	N/A	$3,200 - 4,000	$1,925 - 2,400	
1955-1959	N/A	$2,800 - 3,500	$1,675 - 2,100	
1960-1969	N/A	$2,400 - 3,000	$1,450 - 1,800	
1970-1979	N/A	$1,800 - 2,250	$1,075 - 1,350	
1980-1993	N/A	$1,400 - 1,750	$850 - 1,050	$2,480

- **Add 20-30% for Sunburst finish on 1930s models.**

The rosewood fingerboard was formally introduced in 1940, but examples have been found with rosewood as early as 1935.

* **00-18C Classical** – similar to the 00-18, except in classical nylon string configuration with a 12-fret body, 12/19-fret fingerboard, slotted headstock, fan bracing, and a tied bridge, 26.44 in. scale, total production of 4,351 instruments, available as a Special Order, mfg. 1962-1992.

	100%	EXCELLENT	AVERAGE	LAST MSR
1962-1964	N/A	$1,400 - 1,750	$850 - 1,050	
1965-1969	N/A	$1,200 - 1,500	$725 - 900	
1970-1979	N/A	$1,075 - 1,350	$650 - 800	
1980-1992	N/A	$950 - 1,200	$575 - 725	$2,480

* **00-18E Electric** – similar to the 00-18, except has a single exposed pickup in the upper part of the soundhole and two knobs on the lower treble bout (v, tone), total production of 593 instruments, mfg. 1959-1964.

	100%	EXCELLENT	AVERAGE
	N/A	$3,200 - 4,000	$1,925 - 2,400

* **00-18G Gut String** – similar to the 00-18, except in classical nylon string configuration with X-bracing, fan patterned, and a pin tied bridge, total production of 5,140 instruments, mfg. 1936-1962.

	100%	EXCELLENT	AVERAGE
1936-1939	N/A	$1,850 - 2,250	$1,200 - 1,500
1940-1949	N/A	$1,650 - 2,000	$1,100 - 1,350
1950-1962	N/A	$1,400 - 1,750	$1,000 - 1,200

This model was replaced by the 00-18C Classical in 1962.

* **00-18H Hawaiian** – similar to the 00-18, except in Hawaiian configuration with a flat fingerboard with flush frets, a high nut, and a non-slanted saddle, total production of 255 instruments, mfg. 1935-1941.

	100%	EXCELLENT	AVERAGE
	N/A	$6,400 - 8,000	$3,850 - 4,800

Most of the 00-18H Hawaiian models were in finished in Sunburst.

* **00-18K Koa** – similar to the 00-18, except has koa top, back, and sides, total production of 61 instruments, mfg. 1918-1934.

	100%	EXCELLENT	AVERAGE
	N/A	$5,600 - 7,000	$3,350 - 4,200

* **00-18T Tenor** – similar to the 00-18, except in four-string tenor configuration and two-per-side tuners, total production of six instruments, mfg. 1931, 1936, 1938-1940.

	100%	EXCELLENT	AVERAGE
	N/A	$3,750 - 4,500	$2,500 - 3,000

00-21 – Grand Concert body style, spruce top, Brazilian rosewood (1898-1969) or Indian rosewood (1969-1995) back/sides, round soundhole with herringbone rosette (1898-1947, three stripes with 5/herringbone/5 grouping) or regular rosette (1/9/1 grouping), five-ply top binding, two-ply back binding with rosewood (1898-1932), black (1932-36, 1966-1995), or tortoise (1936-1966) outer layer, herrinbgone backstripe (1898-1947), cedar (1898-1916) or mahogany (1898-1916) neck, 12/19-fret unbound ebony (1898-1947) or rosewood (1947-1995) fingerboard with slotted diamond (1898-1944) or pearl dot (1944-1995) inlays, slotted headstock (1898-1990) or solid headstock (1990-95) with rosewood overlay and screened logo, three-per-side open-style chrome tuners with pearl knobs (1898-1990) or regular tuners (1990-95), rectangular (1898-1929) or belly (1929-1995) ebony (1898-1947) or rosewood (1947-1995) bridge, black bridge pins with white dots, no pickguard (1898-1932), tortoise pickguard (1932-1966), or black pickguard (1966-1995), available in Natural finish, 24.9 in. scale, available as a Special Order, mfg. 1898-1995.

	100%	EXCELLENT	AVERAGE	LAST MSR
1898-1925 Gut Bracing	N/A	$6,400 - 8,000	$3,850 - 4,800	
1926-1930 Steel Bracing	N/A	$7,200 - 9,000	$4,300 - 5,400	
1931-1939	N/A	$8,000 - 10,000	$4,800 - 6,000	
1940-1944 Scalloped Bracing	N/A	$7,200 - 9,000	$4,300 - 5,400	
1945-1946 Unscalloped Bracing	N/A	$6,400 - 8,000	$3,850 - 4,800	
1947-1949	N/A	$6,000 - 7,500	$3,600 - 4,500	
1950-1959	N/A	$5,600 - 7,000	$3,350 - 4,200	
1960-1969 Brazilian Rosewood	N/A	$5,200 - 6,500	$3,125 - 3,900	
1969-1979 Indian rosewood	N/A	$2,600 - 3,250	$1,550 - 1,950	
1980-1990 Slotted Headstock	N/A	$2,400 - 3,000	$1,450 - 1,800	
1990-1995 Solid Headstock	N/A	$2,200 - 2,750	$1,325 - 1,650	$2,730

Martin also produced one reissue model with Brazilian rosewood back and sides (Model 00-21B, 1985 only), three models strung for nylon strings (Model 00-21G, 1937-38), three Hawaiian models (Model 00-21H, 1914, 1952, and 1955), and two tenor models (Model 00-21T, 1934 only).

MSR/NOTES	100%	EXCELLENT	AVERAGE	LAST MSR

* **00-21NY** – similar to the 00-21, except has no pickguard, no fingerboard inlays, and a wide fingerboard, total production of 906 instruments, mfg. 1961-65.

	N/A	$4,000 - 5,000	$2,400 - 3,000	

00-25K KOA – Grand Concert body style, solid spruce top, koa back and sides, round soundhole with three-stripe rosette (5/9/5 grouping), five-ply top binding with black outer layer, black back binding, chainlink back stripe, mahogany neck, 14/20-fret unbound rosewood fingerboard with pearl dot inlays, three-per-side chrome tuners, rosewood bridge, black bridge pins with white dots, tortoise pickguard, Natural finish, 24.9 in. scale, total production of 128 instruments, mfg. 1980, 1985, and 1988.

	N/A	$1,600 - 2,000	$950 - 1,200	

* **00-25K2 Koa** – similar to the 00-25K Koa, except has a koa top, total production of 54 instruments, mfg. 1980-89.

	N/A	$1,800 - 2,250	$1,075 - 1,350	

00-28 – Grand Concert body style, solid spruce top, Brazilian rosewood (1898-1941, 1958) or Indian rosewood (1977, 1984) back and sides, round soundhole with three-stripe rosette (5/9/5 grouping), ivory (1898-1918), ivoroid (1918-1941, 1958), or non-grained white (1977, 1984) top binding, herringbone top purfling (1898-1941) or six-ply top inlay with white outer layer (1958, 1977, 1984), three-ply back binding with ivory (1898-1918), ivoroid (1918-1941, 1958), or non-grained white (1977, 1984) outer layer, zigzag (1898-1941) or chainlink (1958, 1977, 1984) back stripe, cedar (1898-1916) or mahogany (1916-1941, 1958, 1977, 1984) neck, 12/19-fret unbound ebony fingerboard with no inlays (1898-1901), slotted diamond inlays (1901-1941), or pearl dot inlays (1958, 1977, 1984), slotted headstock with rosewood overlay, three-per-side open-style tuners, rectangular (1898-1929) or belly (1929-1941, 1958, 1977, 1984) ebony bridge, no pickguard (1898-1932), tortoise pickguard (1932-1941, 1958), or black pickguard (1977, 1984), available in Natural finish, 24.9 in. scale, total production of 758 instruments, mfg. 1898-1941, 1958, 1977, and 1984.

1898-1924	N/A	$8,000 - 10,000	$4,800 - 6,000	
1925-1941	N/A	$16,000 - 20,000	$9,500 - 12,000	
1958, 1977, 1984	N/A	$5,600 - 7,000	$3,350 - 4,200	

Martin also produced two tenor 00-28 instruments (Model 00-28T, 1931, 1940).

* **00-28C Classical** – similar to the 00-28, except in classical nylon string configuration with fan bracing and a tied bridge, 26.44 in. scale, total production of 1,411 instruments, available as a Special Order, mfg. 1962-1992.

1966-1969 Brazilian rosewood	N/A	$2,600 - 3,250	$1,500 - 1,950	
1969-1992 Indian rosewood	N/A	$1,400 - 1,750	$850 - 1,050	$2,760

* **00-28G Gut String** – similar to the 00-28, except in classical nylon string configuration with X-bracing, fan patterned, and a pin tied bridge, total production of 1,531 instruments, mfg. 1936-1962.

1936-1939	N/A	$4,000 - 5,000	$2,600 - 3,200	
1940-1949	N/A	$3,200 - 4,000	$1,925 - 2,400	
1950-1952	N/A	$2,800 - 3,500	$1,675 - 2,100	

This model was replaced by the 00-28C Classical in 1962.

* **00-28K Hawaiian Koa** – similar to the 00-28, except in Hawaiian configuration with koa back and sides, a flat fingerboard with flush frets, a high nut, and a non-slanted saddle, total production of 40 instruments, mfg. 1919-1921, 1926-1933.

1919-1921	N/A	$8,000 - 10,000	$4,800 - 6,000	
1926-1933	N/A	$9,500 - 12,000	$5,750 - 7,250	

00-30 – Grand Concert body style, spruce top, Brazilian rosewood back and sides, round soundhole with pearl rosette, ivory (1899-1918) or ivoroid (1918-1921) top and back binding, herringbone top purfling, cedar (1899-1916) or mahogany (1916-1921) neck, 12/19-fret ivory (1899-1918) or ivoroid (1918-1921) bound ebony fingerboard, slotted headstock, three-per-side open-style tuners, rectangular ebony bridge, Natural finish, 24.9 in. scale, total production of 101 instruments, mfg. 1899-1921.

	N/A	$10,000 - 12,500	$6,000 - 7,500	

00-34 – Grand Concert body style, spruce top, Brazilian rosewood back and sides, round soundhole with pearl rosette, ivory top and back binding, herringbone top purfling, cedar neck, 12/19-fret ivory-bound ebony fingerboard with slotted diamond inlays at the 5th and 9th frets and a Maltese cross inlay at the 7th fret, slotted headstock, three-per-side open-style tuners, rectangular ebony bridge, Natural finish, 24.9 in. scale, total production of six instruments, mfg. 1898-99.

	N/A	$10,000 - 12,500	$6,000 - 7,500	

00-40 – Grand Concert body style, spruce top, Brazilian rosewood back and sides, round soundhole with pearl rosette, ivory top and back binding, pearl top border, cedar neck, 12/19-fret ivory-bound ebony fingerboard with snowflake inlays starting at the fifth fret, slotted headstock, three-per-side open-style tuners, rectangular ivory bridge, Natural finish, 24.9 in. scale, total production of one instrument, mfg. 1913 only.

	N/A	N/A	N/A	

Extreme rarity precludes accurate pricing.

* **00-40H Hawaiian** – similar to the 00-40, except in Hawaiian configuration with a flat fingerboard with flush frets, a high nut, and a non-slanted saddle, total production of 244 instruments, mfg. 1928-1939.

	N/A	$18,500 - 22,500	$12,000 - 15,000	

MSR/NOTES	100%	EXCELLENT	AVERAGE	LAST MSR

* ***00-40K Koa*** – similar to the 00-40, except has koa top, back, and sides, total production of nine instruments, mfg. 1917-18, 1930.

| | N/A | $22,500 - 27,500 | $15,000 - 18,500 | |

The first three guitars produced with koa were actually stamped as regular 00-40s.

00-41 – Grand Concert body style, solid spruce top, Indian rosewood back and sides, round soundhole with pearl rosette, white top and back binding, pearl top borders, zipper-pattern back stripe, mahogany neck, bound ebony fingerboard with hexagonal pearl inlays, bound headstock with vertical block Martin logo, ebony belly bridge, black pickguard, Natural finish, 24.9 in. scale, total production of five instruments, mfg. 1972-75.

| | N/A | N/A | N/A | |

Extreme rarity precludes accurate pricing.

00-42 – Grand Concert body style, spruce top, Brazilian rosewood back and sides, round soundhole with pearl rosette, ivory (1898-1918) or ivoroid (1918-1942) top and back binding, pearl border around top and where the fingerboard meets the body, zipper-pattern back stripe, cedar (1898-1916) or mahogany (1916-1942) neck, 12/19-fret ivory (1898-1918) or ivoroid (1918-1942)-bound ebony fingerboard with snowflake inlays that start at the fifth fret, ivory (1898-1918) or ivoroid (1918-1942)-bound slotted headstock, three-per-side open-style tuners, rectangular (1898-1929) or belly (1929-1942, 1973) ivory (1898-1918) or ebony (1918-1942) bridge, no pickguard (1898-1932) or tortoise pickguard (1932-1942), Natural finish, 24.9 in. scale, total production of 503 instruments, mfg. 1898-1942, 1973.

| 1898-1927 Gut Bracing | N/A | $20,000 - 25,000 | $13,000 - 16,500 | |
| 1927-1942 Steel Bracing | N/A | $25,000 - 30,000 | $16,500 - 20,000 | |

Martin produced one 00-42 in 1973 that featured Indian rosewood back and sides and a black pickguard. Martin also produced three 00-42s with classical nylon-string configuration (Model 00-42G, 1936-39), and one 00-42 with a koa top, back, and sides (Model 00-42K, 1919 only).

00-44 – Grand Concert body style, spruce top, Brazilian rosewood back and sides, round soundhole with three-stripe rosette (5/9/5 grouping), six-ply top binding with ivory (1913-18) or ivoroid (1918-1922) outer layer, three-ply back binding with ivory (1913-18) or ivoroid (1918-1922) outer layer, wide white backstripe surrounded by smaller black and white lines, cedar (1913-16) or mahogany (1916-1922) neck, 12/19-fret ivory (1913-18) or ivoroid (1918-1922)-bound ebony fingerboard, ivory (1913-18) or ivoroid (1918-1922)-bound slotted headstock, rectangular ebony bridge, Natural finish, 24.9 in. scale, total production of six instruments, mfg. 1913-1922.

| | N/A | $36,000 - 45,000 | $21,500 - 27,000 | |

This model was specially built for performer Vahdah Olcott-Bickford. Some models may have "Soloist" or "Olcott-Bickford Artist Model" inlaid on the headstock. Martin also produced two 00-44 classical nylon-string guitars (Model 00-44G, 1938).

00-45 – Grand Concert body style, spruce top, Brazilian rosewood (1904-1938) or Indian rosewood (1970-1993) back and sides, round soundhole with pearl rosette, ivory (1904-1918) or ivoroid (1918-1938, 1970-1993) top binding, pearl inlay border around top and fingerboard where it meets the top, pearl inlays around sides, zipper-pattern back stripe, cedar (1904-1916) or mahogany (1916-1938, 1970-1993) neck, 12/19-fret (1904-1934, 1970-1993) or 14/20-fret (1934-38) ivory (1904-1918), ivoroid (1918-1938), or white (1970-1993)-bound ebony fingerboard with snowflake inlays (1904-1938) or hexagonal inlays (1970-1993), ivory (1904-1918), ivoroid (1918-1938), or white (1970-1993)-bound slotted (1904-1934, 1970-1993) or solid (1934-38) headstock with torch inlay (1904-1934) or vertical block Martin logo inlay (1934-38, 1970-1993), three-per-side open-style tuners (1904-1934, 1970-1993) or regular tuners (1934-38), rectangular (1904-1929) or belly (1929-1938, 1970-1993) ivory (1904-1918) or ebony (1918-1938, 1970-1993) bridge, Natural finish, 24.9 in. (1904-1938) or 25.4 in. (1970-1993) scale, available as a Special Order, mfg. 1904-1938, 1970-1993.

1904-1927 Gut Bracing	N/A	$40,000 - 50,000	$24,000 - 30,000	
1927-1938 Steel Bracing	N/A	$60,000 - 75,000	$36,000 - 45,000	
1970-1979	N/A	$3,600 - 4,500	$2,150 - 2,700	
1980-1993	N/A	$3,200 - 4,000	$1,925 - 2,400	$6,860

Martin also produced two reissue 00-45s with Brazilian rosewood back and sides (Model 00-45B, 1985 only), one 00-45 with a koa top, back, and sides (Model 00-45K, 1919 only), and an undisclosed amount of 00-45s with non-scalloped braces (Model 00-45N, 1989-1993).

ACOUSTIC: STANDARD GRAND AUDITORIUM (000) SERIES

Size 000 (Auditorium) guitars feature a lower bout width of 15 in., 4.125 (14-fret) or 4 1/16 (12-fret) in. depth, 19.375 (14-fret) or 20 7/16 in. length, and 24.9 (most common) or 25.4 (1924-1934 mfg., 12-fret only) in. scale.

Martin produced a variety of different 000-style guitars that were built in very limited quantities. These models include one **000-17** (1911 only), one **000-30** (1919 only), one **000-40** (1909 only), one **000-40 Hawaiian** (Model 000-40H, 1933 only), one **000-41** (1975 only), and three **000-44**s that were specially built for performer Vahdah Olcott-Bickford (1917-19).

000-16(M) – Grand Auditorium body style, solid spruce top, solid mahogany back and sides, round soundhole with three-stripe rosette (5/9/5 grouping), tortoise top and back binding, mahogany neck, 14/20-fret rosewood fingerboard with slotted diamond inlays, rosewood headstock overlay with raised gold foil logo, three-per-side chrome tuners, rosewood bridge, black bridge pins with pearl dots, tortoise pickguard, Natural satin finish, 24.9 in. scale, mfg. 1989-1995.

| | N/A | $1,050 - 1,300 | $625 - 775 | $1,680 |

Refer to the 16 Series for the 000-16(T). The 000-16M designation only lasted for 1989 and in 1990 it was changed to the 000-16.

MSR/NOTES	100%	EXCELLENT	AVERAGE	LAST MSR

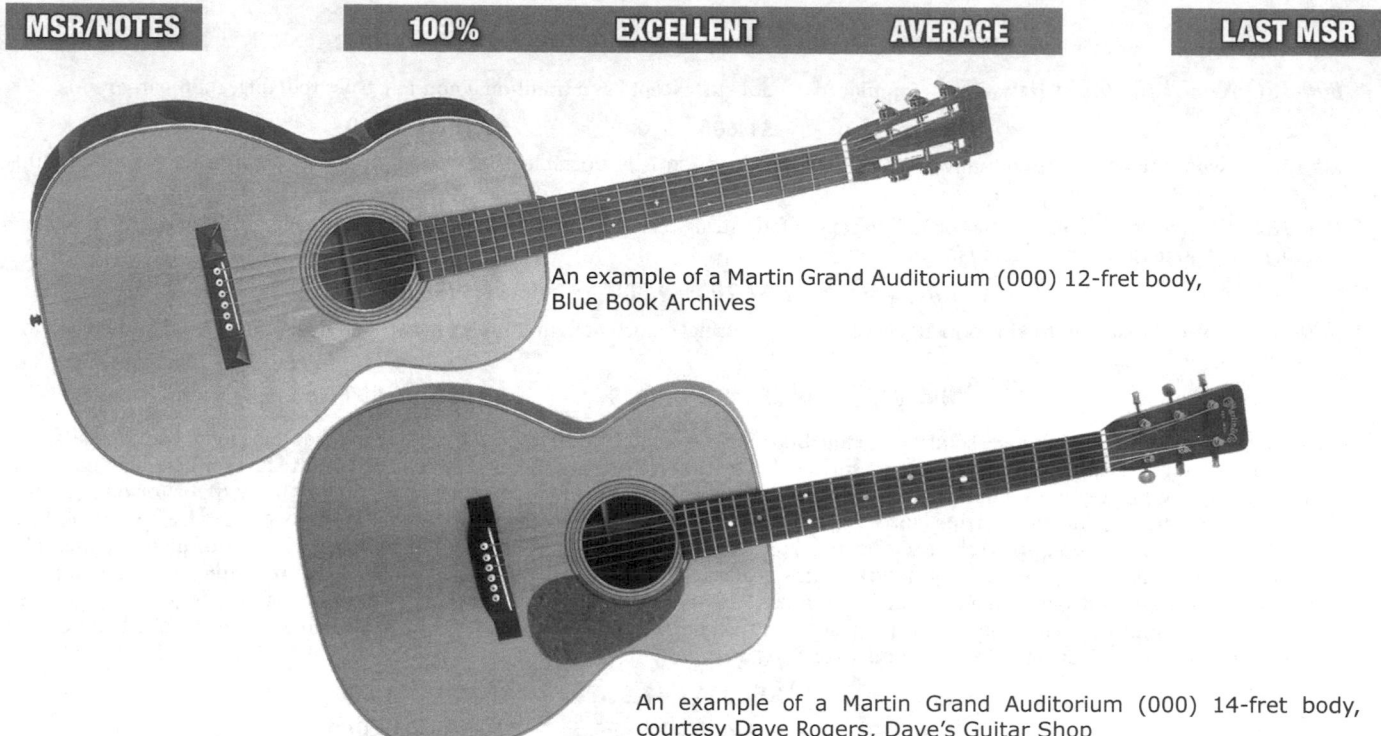

An example of a Martin Grand Auditorium (000) 12-fret body, Blue Book Archives

An example of a Martin Grand Auditorium (000) 14-fret body, courtesy Dave Rogers, Dave's Guitar Shop

* **000-C16/000C-16 Cutaway** – similar to the 000-16(M), except has a single rounded cutaway, oval soundhole with single nine-ring rosette, pearl dot fingerboard inlays, all black bridge pins, and Natural high-gloss finish, mfg. 1990-95.

	N/A	$1,125 - 1,400	$675 - 850	$1,860

Refer to the 16 Series for the 000C-16(T) model.

000-17 – Grand Auditorium body style, mahogany top, back, and sides, round soundhole with three thin W/B/W line rosette, no body binding, thin black back stripe, mahogany neck, rosewood fingerboard with pearl dot inlay, mahogany headstock overlay with three-per-side tuners, tortoise pickguard, available in Natural finish, total production of 25 instruments, 24.9 in. scale, mfg. 1952 only.

	N/A	$4,000 - 5,000	$2,400 - 3,000	

000-18 – Grand Auditorium body style, solid spruce top, Brazilian rosewood (1911-17) or mahogany (1918-present) back and sides, round soundhole with three-stripe rosette (1/9/1 grouping between 1911 and the mid-1930s, inlaid 1/9/1 grouping between the mid-1930s and 1988, and 5/9/5 grouping since 1988), five-ply top binding, single ply back binding with rosewood (1911-1932), black (1932-26, 1966-present), or tortoise (1936-1966) outer layer, black back stripe, cedar (1911-16) or mahogany (1916-present) neck, 12/19-fret (1911-1934) or 14/20-fret (1934-present) ebony fingerboard with Style 28 pearl dot inlays, slotted (1911-1934) or solid (1934-present) headstock with rosewood overlay and raised gold foil logo, three-per-side brass tuners with ivory buttons (1911-1934) or regular tuners (1934-present), ebony rectangular (1911-1929) or belly (1929-present) bridge, black bridge pins with pearl dots, no pickguard (1911-1932), tortoise pickguard (1932-1966), or black pickguard (1966-present), available in Natural finish, 24.9 in. scale, mfg. 1911-present.

1911-1926	N/A	$10,000 - 12,000	$7,000 - 8,500
1927-1934 12-Fret Body	N/A	$14,000 - 17,500	$8,500 - 10,500
1934-1939 14-Fret Body	N/A	$12,000 - 15,000	$7,250 - 9,000
1940-1944 Scalloped Bracing	N/A	$9,500 - 12,000	$5,750 - 7,250
1945-1949 Unscalloped Bracing	N/A	$5,750 - 7,000	$4,000 - 5,000
1950-1954	N/A	$4,000 - 5,000	$2,500 - 3,000
1955-1959	N/A	$3,200 - 4,000	$1,925 - 2,400
1960-1964	N/A	$2,750 - 3,500	$1,800 - 2,200
1965-1969	N/A	$2,400 - 3,000	$1,450 - 1,800
1970-1974	N/A	$2,000 - 2,500	$1,350 - 1,600
1975-1979	N/A	$1,800 - 2,250	$1,075 - 1,350
1980-1989	N/A	$1,600 - 2,000	$1,100 - 1,300
1990-1999	N/A	$1,450 - 1,800	$850 - 1,075
2000-Present MSR $2,999	$2,300	$1,275 - 1,600	$850 - 1,000

• **Add 25-50% for Sunburst finish on 1930s models.**

Martin also produced one 000-18 in 12-string configuration (Model 000-18 12-String, 1913 only), one 000-18 in classical nylon-string configuration (Model 000-18G, 1955 only), one 000-18 in Hawaiian configuration (Model 000-18H, 1938 only), and three 000-18s with 12-fret necks in the 1970s (Model 000-18S, 1976-77).

MSR/NOTES	100%	EXCELLENT	AVERAGE	LAST MSR

* ***000-18Q Non-Adjustable Truss Rod*** – similar to the 000-18, except has a traditional non-adj. truss rod, mfg. 1986-early 1990s.

	N/A	$1,600 - 2,000	$1,100 - 1,300	

This model was not listed individually in Martin's price lists, so it is possible that it was priced the same as a regular 000-18. Production was very limited.

* ***000-18P Plectrum*** – similar to the 000-18, except in four-string plectrum configuration with two-per-side tuners and a 27 in. scale, total production of 46 instruments, mfg. 1930 only.

	N/A	$7,200 - 9,000	$4,325 - 5,400	

* ***000-18T Tenor*** – similar to the 000-18, except in four-string tenor configuration with two-per-side tuners, total production of five instruments, mfg. 1930-1941.

	N/A	$6,400 - 8,000	$3,850 - 4,800	

000-21 – Grand Auditorium body style, solid spruce top, Brazilian rosewood (1902-1954, 1965) or Indian rosewood (1979) back and sides, round soundhole with three-stripe rosette (herringbone surrounded by two five ring groupings between 1902 and 1947, non-herringbone with 1/9/1 grouping after 1947), five-ply top binding, two-ply back binding with rosewood (1902-1932), black (1932-36, 1979), or tortoise (1936-1954, 1965) outer layer, herringbone back stripe (1902-1948), cedar (1902-1916) or mahogany (1916-1954, 1965, 1979) neck, 12/19-fret (1902-1934) or 14/20-fret (1934-1954, 1965, 1979) ebony (1902-1947) or rosewood (1947-1954, 1965, 1979) fingerboard with slotted diamond inlays (1902-1944) or pearl dot inlays (1944-1954, 1965, 1979), slotted headstock (1902-1934) or solid headstock (1934-1954, 1965, 1979), with rosewood overlay and raised gold foil logo, three-per-side brass tuners with ivory buttons (1902-1934) or regular tuners (1934-1954, 1965, 1979), ebony rectangular (1902-1929) or belly (1929-1954, 1965, 1979) bridge, black bridge pins with pearl dots, available in Natural finish, 24.9 in. scale, total production of 9,005 instruments, mfg. 1902-1954, 1965, 1979.

1902-1931	N/A	$14,000 - 17,500	$9,500 - 11,500	
1934-1939	N/A	$16,000 - 20,000	$10,500 - 13,000	
1940-1944	N/A	$9,500 - 12,000	$5,700 - 7,125	
1945-1947 Non Scalloped Bracing	N/A	$7,600 - 9,500	$4,550 - 5,700	
1948-1959, 1965	N/A	$5,600 - 7,000	$3,350 - 4,200	
1979	N/A	$2,500 - 3,000	$1,650 - 2,000	

Martin also produced two 000-21s in 10-string configuration (1902 only), one 000-21 in 12-string configuration (1921 only), four 000-21s in harp configuration with extra sub-bass strings (mfg. 1902-09), and one 000-21 in the 1970s with a 12-fret neck (Model 000-21S, 1977 only).

000-28 – Grand Auditorium body style, solid spruce top, Brazilian rosewood (1902-1969) or Indian rosewood (1969-present) back and sides, round soundhole with three-ring rosette (5/9/5 grouping), ivory (1902-1918), ivoroid (1918-1966), or non-grained white (1966-present) top binding, herringbone top purfling (1902-1947) or six-ply top inlay with white outer layer (1947-present), three-ply back binding with ivory (1902-1918), ivoroid (1918-1966), or non-grained white (1966-present) back binding, zigzag (1902-1947) or chainlink (1947-present) back stripe, cedar (1902-1916) or mahogany (1916-present) neck, 12/19-fret (1902-1934) or 14/20-fret (1934-present) ebony fingerboard with slotted diamond inlays (1902-1944) or pearl dot inlays (1944-present), slotted (1902-1934) or solid (1934-present) headstock with rosewood overlay and raised gold foil logo, three-per-side open-style brass tuners with ivory buttons (1902-1934) or regular tuners (1934-present), ebony rectangular (1902-1929) or belly (1929-present) bridge, black bridge pins with pearl dots, available in Natural finish, 24.9 in. scale, mfg. 1902-present.

1902-1924	N/A	$18,000 - 22,500	$10,800 - 13,500	
1925-1934 12-Fret Body	N/A	$26,000 - 32,500	$15,500 - 19,500	
1934-1938 14-Fret Body	N/A	$32,000 - 40,000	$19,250 - 24,000	
1939-1944	N/A	$22,000 - 27,500	$13,250 - 16,500	
1945-1947 Herringbone	N/A	$18,000 - 22,500	$10,750 - 13,500	
1947-1949 Non-Herringbone	N/A	$9,500 - 12,000	$5,700 - 7,125	
1950-1954	N/A	$8,000 - 10,000	$5,500 - 6,500	
1955-1959	N/A	$7,200 - 9,000	$4,325 - 5,400	
1960-1964	N/A	$6,000 - 7,500	$4,000 - 5,000	
1965-1969 Brazilian Rosewood	N/A	$5,200 - 6,500	$3,125 - 3,900	
1969-1979 Indian rosewood	N/A	$1,850 - 2,250	$1,250 - 1,500	
1980-1989	N/A	$1,650 - 2,000	$1,100 - 1,300	
1990-1999	N/A	$1,500 - 1,850	$1,050 - 1,250	
2000-Present MSR $3,349	$2,500	$1,350 - 1,700	$950 - 1,100	

* **Add 25-50% for Sunburst finish on 1930s models.**
* **Add 7.5% (MSR $3,599) for Sunburst or Ambertone finish on 2014 and later models.**

Martin also produced one 000-28 in 10-string configuration (1902 only), one 000-28 in 12-string configuration (1936 only), two 000-28s with Style 45 necks (Model 000-28-45, 1938-39), one 000-28 with electronics (Model 000-28E, 1970 only), one 000-28 in Hawaiian configuration (Model 000-28H, 1949 only), one 000-28 in harp configuration with extra sub-bass strings (1906 only), two 000-28 models with the suffix HX (specifications unknown, 1965 only), one 000-28 with a koa top, back, and sides (Model 000-28K, 1921 only), two 000-28s with 12-fret bodies/necks and wide fingerboards (Model 000-28NY, 1962 only), three 000-28s in plectrum configuration (Model 000-28P, 1930 only), and one 000-28 in tenor configuration (Model 000-28T, 1929 only).

MSR/NOTES	100%	EXCELLENT	AVERAGE	LAST MSR

* ***000-28B Brazilian*** – similar to the 000-28, except has Brazilian rosewood back and sides, total production of six instruments, mfg. 1985 only.

| | N/A | $5,000 - 6,000 | $3,500 - 4,200 | |

* ***000-28C Classical*** – similar to the 000-28, except in classical nylon string configuration with fan bracing and a tied bridge, total production of 560 instruments, mfg. 1962-69.

| | N/A | $3,400 - 4,250 | $2,050 - 2,550 | |

* ***000-28F 12-Fret*** – similar to the 000-28, except has a 12-fret neck, total production of 10 instruments, mfg. 1964-67.

| | N/A | $5,800 - 7,000 | $4,000 - 4,800 | |

* ***000-28G Gut String*** – similar to the 000-28, except in classical nylon string configuration with X-bracing, fan patterned, and a pin tied bridge, total production of 17 instruments, mfg. 1937-1955.

| | N/A | $6,000 - 7,500 | $3,600 - 4,500 | |

* ***000-28H Herringbone*** – similar to 000-28, except has herringbone top purfling, a herringbone back inlay strip, and a tortoise pickguard, mfg. 2000-mid-01.

| | N/A | $1,500 - 1,800 | $1,050 - 1,250 | $2,850 |

* ***000-28Q Non-Adjustable Truss Rod*** – similar to the 000-28, except has a traditional non-adj. truss rod, mfg. 1986-early 1990s.

| | N/A | $1,650 - 2,000 | $1,150 - 1,350 | |

This model was not listed individually in Martin's price lists, so it is possible that it was priced the same as a regular 000-28.

* ***000-28S 12-Fret*** – similar to the 000-28, except has a 12-fret neck, total production of 31 instruments, mfg. 1974-77.

| | N/A | $1,650 - 2,000 | $1,150 - 1,350 | |

* ***000-28V*** – similar to the 000-28, except has Brazilian rosewood back and sides, scalloped bracing, ivoroid binding, herringbone top purfling, zigzag back stripe, V-shaped neck, chrome tuners, white bridge pins with tortoise dots, and a tortoise pickguard, Natural finish with Aging Toner top, total production of 17 instruments, mfg. 1983-84.

| | N/A | $5,000 - 6,000 | $3,500 - 4,200 | |

The 000-28V was one of the first guitars Martin produced based on "Vintage specifications," and was one of the forerunners to the Vintage Series Martin would release several years later.

000-42 – Grand Auditorium body style, solid spruce top, Brazilian rosewood (1918-1948) or East Indian rosewood (2004-present) back and sides, round soundhole with three-stripe rosette (abalone pearl ring between two groups of five rings), ivoroid (1918-1948) or grained ivoroid (2004-present) top and back binding, abalone pearl top inlay that goes around the fingerboard, zipper pattern back stripe, mahogany (1918-1948) or select hardwood (2004-present) neck, 12/19-fret (1918-1934) or 14/20-fret (1934, 2004-present) ivory (1918-1948) or grained ivoroid (2004-present)-bound ebony fingerboard with abalone pearl diamond/snowflake inlays, ivory (1918-1948) or grained ivoroid (2004-present) slotted (1918-1934) or solid (1934-1948, 2004-present) headstock with rosewood overlay and abalone pearl vertical block Martin inlay, three-per-side open-style silver tuners with pearl buttons (1918-1934) or regular tuners (1934-1948, 2004-present), ebony bridge, black bridge pins with pearl dots, available in Natural finish, 24.9 in. scale, mfg. 1918-1948, summer 2004-present.

1918-1925	N/A	$40,000 - 50,000	$24,000 - 30,000	
1930-1939	N/A	$60,000 - 75,000	$37,500 - 45,000	
1940-1948	N/A	$48,000 - 60,000	$28,800 - 36,000	
2004-Present MSR $6,799	$5,100	$2,800 - 3,500	$1,675 - 2,100	

000-45 – Grand Auditorium body style, solid spruce top, Brazilian rosewood (1907-1942) or Indian rosewood (1970-1985) back and sides, round soundhole with pearl rosette, ivory (1907-1918) or ivoroid (1918-1942, 1970-1985) top and back binding, pearl top borders that go around the fingerboard, zipper-pattern back stripe, cedar (1907-1916) or mahogany (1916-1942, 1970-1985) neck, 12/19-fret (1907-1934) or 14/20-fret (1934-1942, 1970-1985) ivory (1907-1918), ivoroid (1918-1942), or white (1970-1985)-bound ebony fingerboard with pearl diamond/snowflake inlays (1907-1942) or hexagaonal inlays (1970-1985), ivory (1907-1918), ivoroid (1918-1942), or white (1970-1985)-bound slotted (1907-1934) or solid (1934-1942, 1970-1985) headstock with rosewood overlay and torch inlay (1907-1934) or vertical block Martin logo (1934-1942, 1970-1985), three-per-side silver tuners with pearl buttons (1907-1934) or regular tuners (1934-1942, 1970-1985), ivory (1907-1918) or ebony (1918-1942, 1970-1985) bridge, black bridge pins with pearl dots, no pickguard (1907-1932), tortoise pickguard (1932-1942), or black pickguard (1970-1985), available in Natural finish, 24.9 in. scale, total production of 327 instruments, mfg. 1907-1942, 1970-1985.

1907-1919	N/A	$40,000 - 50,000	$24,000 - 30,000	
1920-1927 Gut Bracing	N/A	$56,000 - 70,000	$33,500 - 42,000	
1927-1929 Steel Bracing	N/A	$80,000 - 100,000	$55,000 - 65,000	
1934-1939	N/A	$120,000 - 150,000	$75,000 - 95,000	
1940-1942	N/A	$95,000 - 120,000	$60,000 - 75,000	
1970-1985	N/A	$5,500 - 6,500	$3,750 - 4,500	$6,530

Martin also produced three 000-45s in seven-string configuration (1911-31), two 000-45s in the 1980s with Brazilian rosewood back and sides (Model 000-45B, 1985 only), two 000-45s in Hawaiian configuration (Model 000-45H, 1937), one 000-45 with a lyre head (1914 only), and one 000-45 with a vine fingerboard inlay (1912 only).

MSR/NOTES	100%	EXCELLENT	AVERAGE	LAST MSR

* ***000-45N*** – similar to the 000-45, except has a non-scalloped bracing and a standard profile neck, mfg. 1989-early 1990s.

	N/A	$5,000 - 6,000	$3,500 - 4,250	

This model was not listed individually in Martin's price lists, so it is possible that it was strictly a custom order instrument.

* ***000-45S/S-00045 12-Fret*** – similar to the 000-45, except has a 12-fret neck, total production of 19 instruments, mfg. 1974-76.

	N/A	$5,000 - 6,000	$3,500 - 4,250	

ACOUSTIC: STANDARD GRAND AUDITORIUM (0000/M) SERIES

Size M guitars feature a lower bout width of 16 in., a body depth of 4.125 in., 20.125 in. length, and 25.4 in. scale.

An example of a Martin Grand Auditorium (0000/M) 14-fret body, courtesy Martin

0000-28H – Grand Auditorium 0000 body style, solid spruce top, solid rosewood back and sides, round soundhole with three-stripe Style 28 rosette (5/9/5 grouping), white body binding, herringbone purfling, zig-zag back inlay, mahogany neck, 14/20-fret ebony fingerboard with pearl dot inlays, rosewood headstock overlay with gold foil logo, three-per-side chrome tuners, ebony bridge, white bridge pins with black dots, tortoise pickguard, available in Natural finish, 25.4 in. scale, mfg. 1997-2000.

	N/A	$1,675 - 2,100	$1,000 - 1,250	$2,770

CM-0089 – Grand Auditorium 0000 body style, solid spruce top, three-piece rosewood back, rosewood sides, round soundhole with three-stripe rosette (5/9/5 grouping), six-ply top binding, three-ply back binding with white outer layer, W/B/W back stripes, mahogany neck, 14/20-fret ebony fingerboard with pearl dot inlays, three-per-side chrome tuners, rosewood bridge, white bridge pins with black dots, tortoiseshell pickguard, available in Natural finish, total production of 25 guitars, mfg. 1979 only.

	N/A	N/A	N/A	

This guitar was built as a promotion by Fantasy Records for a David Bromberg album.

M-18 – Grand Auditorium 0000 body style, solid spruce top, solid mahogany back and sides, round soundhole with three-stripe rosette (1/9/1 grouping between 1984 and 1987, 5/9/5 grouping in 1988), five-ply top binding, single-ply back binding with black outer layer, mahogany neck, 14/20-fret rosewood fingerboard with pearl dot inlay, three-per-side chrome tuners, rosewood bridge, black bridge pins with white dots, black pickguard, available in Natural finish, total production of 106 instruments, mfg. 1984-88.

	N/A	$1,200 - 1,500	$850 - 1,000	$1,550

The earliest M-18s were produced with ebony fingerboards and bridges and three models have a Blue/Red/White finish.

MC-28 CUTAWAY – single rounded cutaway Grand Auditorium 0000 body style, solid spruce top, rosewood back and sides, oval soundhole with nine ring rosette, six-ply top binding, three-ply back binding with white outer layer, chainlink back stripe, mahogany neck, 14/22-fret ebony fingerboard with pearl dot inlays, rosewood headstock overlay with gold logo, three-per-side chrome tuners, ebony bridge, white bridge pins with black dots, black pickguard, available in Natural finish, mfg. 1981-1996.

	N/A	$1,700 - 2,100	$1,150 - 1,350	$2,810

M-35/M-36 – Grand Auditorium 0000 body style, solid Sitka spruce top, solid three-piece rosewood back, solid rosewood sides, round soundhole with three-stripe rosette (5/9/5 grouping), six-ply top binding, three-ply back binding with white outer layer, mahogany neck, 14/20-fret bound ebony fingerboard with pearl dot inlays, rosewood headstock overlay with gold foil logo, three-per-side chrome tuners, rosewood bridge, white bridge pins with black dots, tortoise pickguard, available in Natural finish, 25.4 in. scale, mfg. 1978-1996, reintroduced summer 2007-present.

1978-1989	N/A	$1,725 - 2,150	$1,025 - 1,300	
1990-1996	N/A	$1,475 - 1,850	$900 - 1,100	
2007-Present MSR $3,349	$2,500	$1,350 - 1,700	$850 - 1,075	

This guitar was originally called the M-35, but after 26 guitars were produced, it was renamed the M-36.

MC-37K KOA CUTAWAY – single rounded cutaway Grand Auditorium 0000 body style, solid spruce top, figured koa back and sides, oval soundhole with abalone pearl rosette, multi-ply top binding, back binding, mahogany neck, 14/22-fret ebony fingerboard with abalone flake inlays at the 5th, 7th, and 9th frets, rosewood headstock overlay with gold foil logo, three-per-side chrome tuners, ebony bridge, white bridge pins with black dots, tortoiseshell pickguard, available in Amber Stain finish, available as a Special Order, total production of 53 instruments (18 produced between 1981 and 1982, 35 produced between 1988 and 1933), mfg. 1981-82, 1988-1993.

	N/A	$2,250 - 2,650	$1,600 - 1,850	$2,000

MSR/NOTES	100%	EXCELLENT	AVERAGE	LAST MSR

M-38/0000-38 – Grand Auditorium 0000 body style, solid Sitka spruce top, solid rosewood back and sides, round soundhole with three-stripe Style 45 abalone pearl rosette (5/9/5 grouping), seven-ply top binding, three-ply back binding with white outer layer, zipper pattern back strip, mahogany neck, 14/20-fret bound ebony fingerboard with pearl dot inlays, bound headstock with rosewood overlay and gold foil logo, three-per-side chrome tuners, rosewood bridge, white bridge pins with black dots, tortoise pickguard, available in Natural finish, 25.4 in. scale, mfg. 1978-1997, reintroduced 2007-2011.

1977-1989	N/A	$2,200 - 2,750	$1,325 - 1,650	
1990-1997	N/A	$2,000 - 2,500	$1,200 - 1,500	
2007-2011	$3,300	$1,850 - 2,300	$1,100 - 1,375	$4,399

For 1997 and 1997 only, the M-38 model was redesignated the 0000-38. When this guitar was reintroduced in 2007, it was called the M-38. Martin also offered the **M-38N** with a standard neck (early 1990s).

* *M-38 Koa Special* – similar to the M-38, except has solid highly flamed koa back, sides, and headstock overlay, Style 45 snowflake fingerboard inlays, and gold hardware, available in Natural finish, Geib-style case included, mfg. 2009-2010.

	$4,700	$2,850 - 3,300	$1,900 - 2,200	$6,299

M-64 – Grand Auditorium 0000 body style, solid Sitka spruce top, solid flamed maple back and sides, round soundhole with three-stripe rosette (5/9/5 grouping), six-ply top binding, three-ply back binding with tortoise outer layer, mahogany neck, 14/20-fret ebony fingerboard with pearl dot inlays, ebony headstock overlay with gold foil logo, three-per-side chrome tuners, ebony bridge, white bridge pins with tortoise dots, tortoise pickguard, available in Natural finish, 25.4 in. scale, available as a Special Order, mfg. 1985-1995.

	N/A	$1,400 - 1,750	$1,000 - 1,150	$2,520

MC-68 CUTAWAY – single rounded cutaway Grand Auditorium 0000 body style, solid spruce top, figured maple back and sides, oval soundhole with nine-stripe rosette, six-ply top binding, three-ply back binding with white outer layer, chainlink back strip, mahogany neck, 14/22-fret bound ebony fingerboard with pearl dot inlays, bound headstock with rosewood overlay and abalone pearl vertical Martin logo, three-per-side gold tuners, ebony bridge, white bridge pins with black dots, tortoise pickguard, available in Natural or Sunburst finish, 25.4 in. scale, available as a Special Order, mfg. 1985-1995.

	N/A	$2,400 - 3,000	$1,450 - 1,800	$2,930

ACOUSTIC: STANDARD DREADNOUGHT (D) SERIES

Martin also produced 75 **D-21 Special Edition** guitars with Indian rosewood back and sides (1985).

Size D (dreadnought) guitars feature a lower bout width of 15.625 in., 4.875 in. (14-fret) or 4.75 in. (12-fret) in. depth, 20 (14-fret) or 20 15/16 (12-fret) in. length, and 25.4 in. scale.

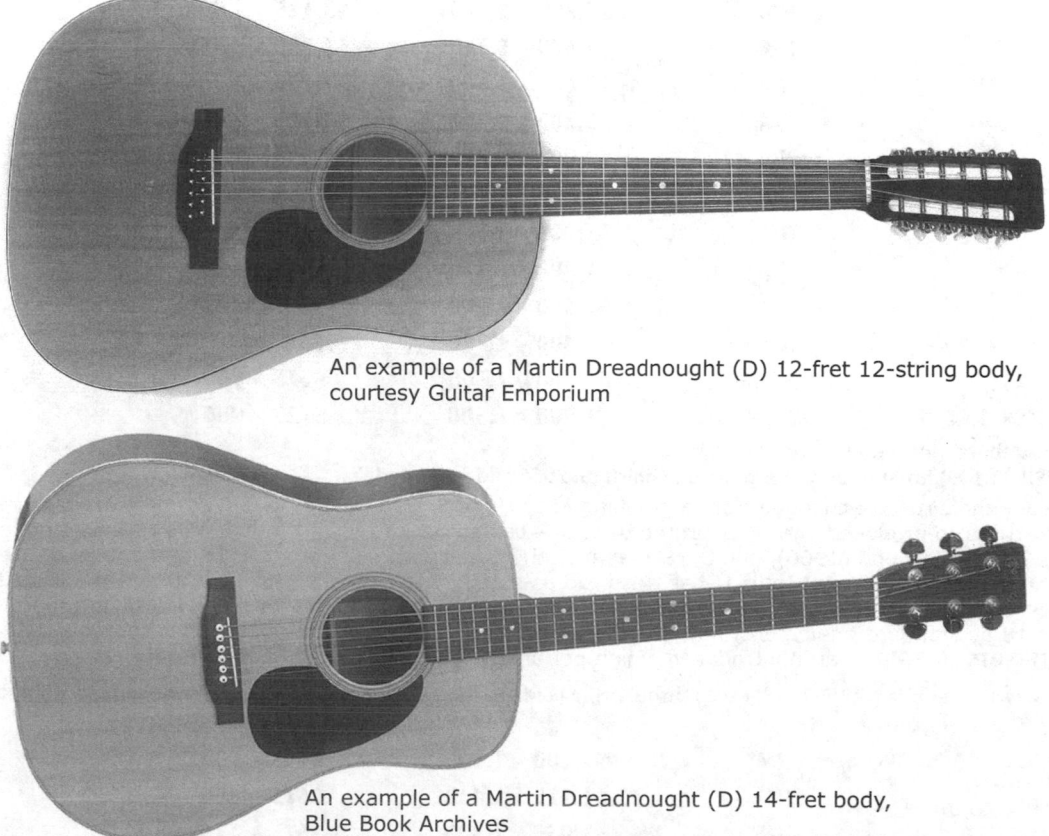

An example of a Martin Dreadnought (D) 12-fret 12-string body, courtesy Guitar Emporium

An example of a Martin Dreadnought (D) 14-fret body, Blue Book Archives

MSR/NOTES	100%	EXCELLENT	AVERAGE	LAST MSR

D-16H – dreadnought body style, solid spruce top, solid mahogany back and sides, round soundhole with herringbone rosette, zigzag back stripe, mahogany neck, 14/20-fret rosewood fingerboard with dot inlays, three-per-side chrome Grover tuners (1991-92) or Gotoh tuners (1993-95), rosewood bridge, Natural satin finish, offered in limited quantities, mfg. 1991-95.

	N/A	$950 - 1,200	$575 - 725	$1,640

* **D-16A Ash** – similar to the D-16H, except has ash back and sides, limited availability, a total of 818 guitars were produced, mfg. 1987-88, 1990.

	N/A	$1,100 - 1,350	$800 - 950	

* **D-16K Koa** – similar to the D-16, except has koa back and sides, black binding, and Natural gloss finish, limited availability, total production of 390 guitars, mfg. 1986 only.

	N/A	$1,200 - 1,500	$850 - 1,000	

* **D-16W Walnut** – similar to the D-16H, except has walnut back and sides and black body binding, limited availability, total production of 138 guitars, mfg. 1987, 1990.

	N/A	$1,100 - 1,350	$800 - 950	

D-16M/D-16 – dreadnought-style body, spruce top, mahogany back and sides, round soundhole with three-ring rosette (5/9/5 grouping), tortoise body binding, mahogany neck, rosewood headstock overlay with gold decal logo, three-per-side chrome Grover tuners, rosewood bridge, tortoise pickguard, Natural satin finish, 25.4 in. scale, total production of 2,120 instruments, mfg. 1986-1990.

	N/A	$850 - 1,050	$500 - 625	

D-18 – dreadnought body style, solid spruce top, mahogany back and sides, round soundhole with three-stripe purfling/rosette, five-ply top binding, one-ply back binding with rosewood (1932-36), tortoise (1936-1966), or black (1966-present) outer layer, 12/19-fret (1932-34) or 14/20-fret (1934-present), ebony fingerboard (1932-1947) or rosewood fingerboard (1947-present) with pearl dot inlays, three-per-side chrome tuners, ebony bridge (1932-1947) or rosewood bridge (1947-present) with black white dot pins, tortoise (1936-1966) or black (1966-present) pickguard, available in Natural or Sunburst (optional) finish, 25.4 in. scale, mfg. 1932-present.

	100%	EXCELLENT	AVERAGE	LAST MSR
1932-1934 12-Fret Body	N/A	$48,000 - 60,000	$28,800 - 36,000	
1934-1938 14-Fret Body	N/A	$36,000 - 45,000	$21,500 - 27,000	
1939-1941	N/A	$18,000 - 22,500	$10,750 - 13,500	
1942-1944 Scalloped	N/A	$14,000 - 17,500	$8,500 - 10,500	
1944-1946 Unscalloped	N/A	$11,000 - 13,500	$7,500 - 9,000	
1947-1949	N/A	$8,000 - 10,000	$5,500 - 6,500	
1950-1952	N/A	$5,200 - 6,500	$3,125 - 3,900	
1953-1959	N/A	$4,600 - 5,750	$2,750 - 3,450	
1960-1962	N/A	$3,600 - 4,500	$2,150 - 2,700	
1963-1965	N/A	$3,200 - 4,000	$1,925 - 2,400	
1966-1967	N/A	$3,000 - 3,500	$1,850 - 2,250	
1968-1969	N/A	$2,500 - 3,000	$1,650 - 2,000	
1970-1974	N/A	$2,000 - 2,500	$1,200 - 1,500	
1975-1979	N/A	$1,800 - 2,250	$1,075 - 1,350	
1980-1989	N/A	$1,600 - 2,000	$950 - 1,200	
1990-1999	N/A	$1,400 - 1,750	$850 - 1,050	
2000-2011	$2,000	$1,200 - 1,500	$725 - 900	
2012-Present MSR $2,899	$2,200	$1,200 - 1,500	$725 - 900	

- Add 50% for Sunburst finish mfg. during the 1930s.
- Add 10% (MSR $3,149) for Sunburst or Ambertone finish on 2014 and later models.

In 1988, the soundhole rosette changed from a grouping of 1/9/1 to 5/9/5. The first two D-18 prototypes were actually stamped D-1 (1931). Martin also produced one DC-1 prototype with a carved back (1934), three D-18H Hawaiian guitars (1934-36), two D-18H models with Huda wood (1966), one D-18M (specifications/features unknown, 1961), and one D-18T Tenor guitar (1962). In 1985, Martin introduced an adjustable U-bar truss rod as standard equipment; however, they also offered a non-adjustable square bar truss rod through the early 1990s and these guitars are stamped **D-18Q**. In 1987, Martin introduced a new low-profile neck on the D-18 as standard equipment; however, they continued to offer their old neck style through 1989 and these guitars are stamped **D-18P**. In 2012, Martin introduced a high performance neck standard on the D-18.

* **D12-18 12-String** – similar to the D-18, except in 12-string configuration and six-per-side tuners, available as a Special Order, mfg. 1973-1995.

	100%	EXCELLENT	AVERAGE	LAST MSR
1973-1979	N/A	$1,200 - 1,500	$725 - 900	
1980-1989	N/A	$1,125 - 1,400	$675 - 850	
1990-1995	N/A	$1,050 - 1,300	$625 - 775	$2,350

MSR/NOTES	100%	EXCELLENT	AVERAGE	LAST MSR

* D-18E Electric – similar to the D-18, except has two single coil exposed DeArmond pickups, a mixing switch, one volume control, and two tone controls, mfg. 1958-59.

	N/A	$3,600 - 4,500	$2,150 - 2,700	

* D-18P – similar to the D-18, except has a slimmer, faster profile high performance neck with a nut width of 1.75 in., mfg. 2011 only.

	$2,000	$1,175 - 1,375	$775 - 900	$2,599

This model is different than the earlier D-18P that was produced in the late 1980s and early 1990s.

D-18S – slope-shouldered dreadnought 12-fret body style, solid spruce top, mahogany back and sides, round soundhole with three-stripe purfling/rosette, five-ply top binding, one-ply back binding with black outer layer, 12/20-fret rosewood fingerboard with pearl dot inlays, slotted headstock with raised gold foil logo, three-per-side open-style chrome tuners, rosewood bridge, black pickguard, available in Natural finish, 25.4 in. scale, available as a Special Order, total production of 1,637 instruments, mfg. 1967-1993.

1967-1969	N/A	$2,800 - 3,500	$1,675 - 2,100	
1970-1974	N/A	$2,400 - 3,000	$1,450 - 1,800	
1975-1979	N/A	$2,200 - 2,750	$1,325 - 1,650	
1980-1993	N/A	$1,725 - 2,150	$1,025 - 1,300	$2,330

D-19 – dreadnought body style, solid spruce top, mahogany back and sides, round soundhole with three-stripe (5/9/5 grouping) rosette, five-ply top binding with black outer ring, three-ply back binding, mahogany neck, 14/20-fret rosewood fingerboard with pearl dot inlays, rosewood headstock overlay with logo decal, three-per-side chrome tuners, rosewood bridge, black pickguard, available in Dark Brown finish, 25.4 in. scale, mfg. 1976-1988.

	N/A	$1,675 - 2,100	$1,000 - 1,250	

* D-19M Mahogany – similar to the D-19, except has a mahogany top, mfg. 1980-88.

	N/A	$1,475 - 1,850	$900 - 1,100	

D12-20 12-STRING – 12-string configuration, dreadnought body style, solid spruce top, mahogany back and sides, round soundhole with three-stripe rosette (1/9/1 grouping between 1964 and 1988 and 5/9/5 grouping between 1988 and 1991), five-ply top binding, one-ply back binding with tortoise (1964-66) or black (1966-1991) outer layer, chainlink back stripe, mahogany neck, 12/20-fret rosewood fingerboard with pearl dot inlays, slotted headstock, six-per-side open-style chrome tuners with white plastic buttons, rosewood bridge, tortoise (1964-66) or black (1966-1991) pickguard, available in Natural finish, total production of 10,350 instruments, available as a Special Order, mfg. 1964-1991.

1964-1969	N/A	$1,475 - 1,850	$875 - 1,100	
1970-1979	N/A	$1,325 - 1,650	$800 - 1,000	
1980-1991	N/A	$1,200 - 1,500	$725 - 900	$2,480

One six-stringed version of the D-12-20 was produced in 1969 called the SD6-20.

D-21 – dreadnought body style, solid spruce top, Brazilian rosewood back and sides, round soundhole with herringbone rosette (1/9/1 grouping), five-ply top binding, one-ply back binding with tortoise (1955-1966) or black (1966-69) outer layer, mahogany neck, 14/20-fret Brazilian rosewood fingerboard with pearl dot inlays, three-per-side chrome tuners, Brazilian rosewood bridge, tortoise (1955-1966) or black (1966-69) pickguard, Natural finish, total production of 2,933 instruments, mfg. 1955-1969.

1956-1959	N/A	$6,000 - 7,500	$3,600 - 4,500	
1960-1962	N/A	$5,600 - 7,000	$3,350 - 4,200	
1963-1964	N/A	$5,200 - 6,500	$3,125 - 3,900	
1966-1969	N/A	$4,800 - 6,000	$2,875 - 3,600	

Martin also produced one D-21V guitar with Brazilian rosewood back and sides (1984).

D-21 SPECIAL – dreadnought body style, solid Sitka spruce top, solid East Indian rosewood back and sides, three ring herringbone rosette, rosewood top binding, herringbone back purfling, select hardwood neck, 14/20-fret, ebony fingerboard with diamond abalone inlays, three-per-side nickel Gotoh tuners, ebony bridge, tortoiseshell pickguard, available in Natural or Sunburst gloss finish, 25.4 in. scale, mfg. 2008-2011.

	$2,900	$1,725 - 2,025	$1,150 - 1,350	$3,849

D-25K – dreadnought body style, solid spruce top, koa back and sides, round soundhole with three stripe rosette (5/9/5 grouping), bound body, five-ply top binding with black outer layer, mahogany neck, 14/20-fret rosewood fingerboard with pearl dot inlays, rosewood headstock overlay with screened logo, three-per-side chrome tuners, rosewood bridge, tortoise pickguard, available in Natural finish, total production of 925 instruments, mfg. 1980-89.

	N/A	$1,800 - 2,250	$1,075 - 1,350	$1,610

* D-25K2 – similar to the D-25K, except has a koa top and black pickguard, total production of 512 instruments, mfg. 1980-89.

	N/A	$1,925 - 2,400	$1,150 - 1,450	$1,735

MSR/NOTES	100%	EXCELLENT	AVERAGE	LAST MSR

D-28 – dreadnought body style, solid spruce top, Brazilian rosewood (1931-1969) or Indian rosewood (1969-present) back and sides, round soundhole with three stripe rosette (5/9/5 grouping), ivoroid (1931-1966) or non-grained white (1966-present) body binding, herringbone top purfling (1931-1947) or six-ply top inlay with white outer layer (1947-present), three-ply back binding with ivoroid (1931-1966) or non-grained white (1966-present) outer layer, zigzag (1931-1946), narrow chainlink (1947), or wide chainlink (1948-present) back stripe, 12/20-fret (earliest models only) or 14/20-fret ebony fingerboard with pearl slotted diamond inlays (1931-1946) or pearl dot inlays (1946-present), three-per-side chrome tuners, ebony bridge with white bridge pins and black dots, tortoise (1934-1966) or black (1966-present) pickguard, available in Natural finish, 25.4 in. scale, mfg. 1931-present.

1931-1934 12-Fret Body	N/A	$140,000 - 175,000	$75,000 - 100,000	
1934-1938 14-Fret Body	N/A	$100,000 - 125,000	$60,000 - 75,000	
1939-1941	N/A	$60,000 - 75,000	$32,000 - 40,000	
1942-1944 Scalloped	N/A	$48,000 - 60,000	$28,800 - 36,000	
1944-1946 Herringbone	N/A	$24,000 - 30,000	$14,500 - 18,000	
1947-1949 Non-Herringbone	N/A	$12,000 - 15,000	$7,250 - 9,000	
1950-1952	N/A	$10,000 - 12,500	$6,000 - 7,500	
1953-1959	N/A	$8,800 - 11,000	$5,275 - 6,600	
1960-1962	N/A	$6,400 - 8,000	$3,850 - 4,800	
1963-1965	N/A	$5,600 - 7,000	$3,350 - 4,400	
1966-1969 Brazilian Rosewood	N/A	$4,800 - 6,000	$2,875 - 3,600	
1969-1979 Indian Rosewood	N/A	$2,000 - 2,500	$1,200 - 1,500	
1980-1989	N/A	$1,800 - 2,250	$1,075 - 1,350	
1990-1999	N/A	$1,600 - 2,000	$950 - 1,200	
2000-Present MSR $3,149	$2,400	$1,400 - 1,750	$850 - 1,050	

• **Add 7.5% (MSR $3,399) for Sunburst or Ambertone finish on 2014 and later models.**

In 1944, scalloped bracing was disc. Martin produced seven D-2 models that were prototypes for the D-28 (1931-34). Martin also produced two D-28 models with cocobolo wood (1987), two **D-28G** models with gut strings (1937, 1961), two **D-28H** Hawaiian models (1934, 1936), and one **D-28T** tenor model (1964). Martin also produced 30 **D-28SW** guitars with 12-fret neck bodies and slotted headstocks for the Wurlitzer music store (1962-68). In 1985, Martin introduced an adjustable U-bar truss rod as standard equipment; however, they also offered a non-adjustable square bar truss rod through the early 1990s and these guitars are stamped **D-28Q** (total production of 417 instruments). In 1987, Martin introduced a new low-profile neck on the D-28 and stamped these guitars **D-28P**; however, they continued to offer their old neck style through 1989 and these guitars are stamped D-28 (total production of 1,322 instruments).

* ***D12-28 12-String*** – similar to the D-28, except in 12-string configuration and six-per-side tuners, mfg. 1970-present.

1970-1979	N/A	$1,600 - 2,000	$1,100 - 1,350	
1980-1989	N/A	$1,500 - 1,850	$1,000 - 1,200	
1990-1999	N/A	$1,450 - 1,750	$1,000 - 1,150	
2000-Present MSR $3,299	$2,500	$1,350 - 1,700	$950 - 1,100	

* ***D-28E Electric*** – similar to the D-28, except has two single coil exposed gold DeArmond pickups, four knobs (two v, two tone), a three-way pickup switch, and gold hardware, total production of 238 instruments, mfg. 1959-1964.

	N/A	$4,400 - 5,500	$2,650 - 3,300	

* ***D-28P*** – similar to the D-28, except has a slimmer, faster profile high performance neck with a nut width of 1.75 in., mfg. 2011-13.

	$2,400	$1,400 - 1,750	$850 - 1,050	$3,149

This model is different than the earlier D-28P that was produced in the late 1980s and early 1990s.

* ***D-28V*** – contemporary reissue of the vintage D-28 with Brazilian rosewood back and sides, scalloped bracing, ivoroid binding, herringbone top purfling, W/B/W back stripe, a V-shaped neck, slotted diamond fingerboard inlays, and a tortoise pickguard, total production of 268 instruments, mfg. 1983-85.

	N/A	$4,800 - 6,000	$2,875 - 3,600	

* ***DC-28 Cutaway*** – similar to the D-28, except has single rounded cutaway, oval soundhole, and 14/22-fret fingerboard, available as a Special Order, mfg. 1981-1996.

1981-1989	N/A	$1,875 - 2,350	$1,125 - 1,400	
1990-1996	N/A	$1,750 - 2,200	$1,050 - 1,325	$2,810

Martin also produced one DC-28P with a low-profile neck before the P suffix was dropped from the name (1988).

* ***DC-28E Cutaway Electric*** – similar to the D-28, except has a single cutaway and Fishman Ellipse Aura electronics, mfg. summer 2006-2010.

	$2,900	$1,725 - 2,025	$1,150 - 1,350	$3,849

MSR/NOTES	100%	EXCELLENT	AVERAGE	LAST MSR

* HD-28 Herringbone – similar to the D-28, except has scalloped bracing, bold herringbone purfling/top inlay, zigzag back purfling, and a tortoise color pickguard, mfg. 1976-present.

	100%	EXCELLENT	AVERAGE	LAST MSR
1976-1979	N/A	$2,125 - 2,650	$1,275 - 1,600	
1980-1989	N/A	$1,925 - 2,400	$1,150 - 1,450	
1990-1999	N/A	$1,800 - 2,250	$1,075 - 1,350	
2000-Present MSR $3,649	$2,700	$1,475 - 1,850	$1,025 - 1,200	

The HD-28 is really an updated version of a late 1930s/1940s D-28 that featured herringbone purfling. Martin also produced two HD-28 models with cocobolo wood (1987), and unknown number of **HD-28MP** models with Bolivian rosewood back and sides (1990), an unknown number of **HD-28N** models with scalloped bracing (1989), and one **HD-28V** contemporary reissue model with Brazilian rosewood back and sides (1984). In 1987, Martin introduced a new low-profile neck on the HD-28 as a standard feature; however, they continued to offer their old neck style through 1989 and these guitars are stamped **HD-28P** (total production of 1,959 instruments).

»HD-28MP – similar to the HD-28, except has solid Madagascar rosewood back and sides, grained ivoroid binding, and a slimmer, faster profile high performance neck with a nut width of 1.75 in., mfg. summer 2011-2012.

	100%	EXCELLENT	AVERAGE	LAST MSR
	$3,500	$2,050 - 2,400	$1,375 - 1,600	$4,599

»HD-282R Herringbone – similar to the HD-28, except has a larger soundhole with two rows of herringbone rosette, mfg. 1992-95.

	100%	EXCELLENT	AVERAGE	LAST MSR
	N/A	$1,650 - 2,000	$1,150 - 1,350	$2,730

»CHD-28 Herringbone Cedar – similar to the HD-28, except has a cedar top, mfg. 1991-95.

	100%	EXCELLENT	AVERAGE	LAST MSR
	N/A	$1,650 - 2,000	$1,150 - 1,350	$2,610

»LHD-28 Herringbone Larch – similar to the HD-28, except has a larch top, mfg. 1991-93.

	100%	EXCELLENT	AVERAGE	LAST MSR
	N/A	$1,650 - 2,000	$1,150 - 1,350	$2,340

»Custom 15/Custom HD-28 Rosewood – similar to the HD-28, except has a V-shaped neck, unbound ebony fingerboard with slotted-diamond inlays, chrome tuners, and a tortoiseshell pickguard, mfg. 1980-1995.

	100%	EXCELLENT	AVERAGE	LAST MSR
	N/A	$2,000 - 2,500	$1,200 - 1,500	$3,260

The Custom 15 was named after the 15th custom-ordered guitar of 1980.

D-28S – slope-shouldered dreadnought 12-fret body style, solid spruce top, Brazilian rosewood (1954-1969) or Indian rosewood (1969-1993) back and sides, round soundhole with three-stripe rosette (5/9/5 grouping), five-ply top ivoroid (1954-1966) or non-grained white (1966-1993) binding, three-ply back binding with ivoroid (1954-1966) or non-grained white (1966-1993) outer layer, wide chainlink backstrip, 12/20-fret ebony fingerboard with pearl dot inlays, slotted headstock with raised gold foil logo, three-per-side open-style chrome tuners, ebony bridge, tortoise (1954-1966) or black (1966-1993) pickguard, available in Natural finish, 25.4 in. scale, available as a Special Order, total production of 1,789 instruments, mfg. 1967-1993.

	100%	EXCELLENT	AVERAGE	LAST MSR
1954-1959	N/A	$10,000 - 12,500	$6,000 - 7,500	
1960-1962	N/A	$8,000 - 10,000	$4,750 - 6,000	
1963-1965	N/A	$6,800 - 8,500	$4,100 - 5,100	
1966-1969 Brazilian Rosewood	N/A	$6,400 - 8,000	$3,850 - 4,800	
1969-1979 Indian Rosewood	N/A	$2,400 - 3,000	$1,450 - 1,800	
1980-1993	N/A	$2,200 - 2,750	$1,325 - 1,650	$2,620

* Custom 15S/Custom HD-28S Rosewood – similar to the D-28S, except has a V-shaped neck, herringbone purfling, unbound ebony fingerboard with slotted-diamond inlays, chrome tuners, and a tortoiseshell pickguard, mfg. 1995 only.

	100%	EXCELLENT	AVERAGE	LAST MSR
	N/A	$2,200 - 2,750	$1,325 - 1,650	$3,670

The Custom 15 was named after the 15th custom-ordered guitar of 1980.

D-35 – dreadnought body style, solid spruce top, three-piece Brazilian rosewood (1965-69) or Indian rosewood (1969-present) back, Brazilian rosewood (1965-69) or Indian rosewood (1969-present) sides, round soundhole with 5/9/5 grouping ring rosette, six-ply top body binding, three-ply back binding with white outer layer, side binding with two black lines, mahogany neck, 14/20-fret bound ebony fingerboard with pearl dot inlays, rosewood headstock overlay with logo and three-per-side chrome tuners, ebony bridge with white bridge pins and black dots, tortoise (1965-69) or black (1969-present) pickguard, available in Natural or Sunburst (optional) finish, 25.4 in. scale, mfg. 1965-present.

	100%	EXCELLENT	AVERAGE	LAST MSR
1965-1969 Brazilian Rosewood	N/A	$4,400 - 5,500	$2,650 - 3,300	
1969-1979 Indian Rosewood	N/A	$1,850 - 2,250	$1,200 - 1,500	
1980-1989	N/A	$1,650 - 2,000	$1,150 - 1,350	
1990-1999	N/A	$1,500 - 1,850	$1,050 - 1,250	
2000-Present MSR $3,249	$2,500	$1,325 - 1,650	$925 - 1,075	

• **Add 7.5% (MSR $3,499) for Sunburst or Ambertone finish on 2014 and later models.**

In 1967, black pickguard replaced tortoisehell pickguard. In 1969, Martin transitioned from Brazilian rosewood to Indian rosewood back and sides, but a few guitars from 1969 have been encountered with a combination of Brazilian and Indian rosewood because of the three-piece back (Brazilian rosewood wings with an Indian rosewood center). Martin also produced one SD8-35 eight-string guitar (1969). In 1985, Martin introduced an adjustable U-bar truss rod as standard equipment; however, they also offered a non-adjustable square bar truss rod through the early 1990s and these guitars are stamped **D-35Q** (total production of 289 instruments). In 1987, Martin introduced a new low-profile neck on the D-35 and stamped these guitars **D-35P**; however, they continued to offer their old neck style through 1990 and these guitars are stamped **D-35** (total production of 1,485 instruments).

MSR/NOTES	100%	EXCELLENT	AVERAGE	LAST MSR

* **D-35MP** – similar to the D-35, except has solid Madagascar rosewood back and sides, grained ivoroid binding, and a slimmer, faster profile high performance neck with a nut width of 1.75 in., mfg. summer 2011-2012.

	$3,200	$1,900 - 2,200	$1,300 - 1,550	$4,199

* **D-35V** – contemporary reissue of the vintage D-35 with Brazilian rosewood back and sides, a V-shaped neck, mitered binding on the fingerboard, a tortoise pickguard, and an Aging Toner top finish, total production of 50 instruments, mfg. 1984 only.

	N/A	$4,000 - 5,000	$2,400 - 3,000	

* **HD-35 Herringbone** – similar to the D-35, except has scalloped bracing, bold herringbone purfling/top inlay, zigzag back purfling, and a tortoise color pickguard, mfg. 1978-present.

	100%	EXCELLENT	AVERAGE	LAST MSR
1978-1989	N/A	$1,875 - 2,350	$1,125 - 1,400	
1990-1999	N/A	$1,675 - 2,100	$1,000 - 1,250	
2000-Present MSR $3,849	$2,900	$1,550 - 1,950	$1,150 - 1,350	

In 1987, Martin introduced a new low-profile neck on the HD-35 and stamped these guitars **HD-35P**; however, they continued to offer their old neck style through 1989 and these guitars are stamped D-35 (total production of 166 instruments).

»**CHD-35 Herringbone Cedar** – similar to the HD-35, except has a cedar top, mfg. 1992-95.

	N/A	$1,900 - 2,300	$1,250 - 1,500	$2,960

»**LHD-35 Herringbone Larch** – similar to the HD-35, except has a larch top, mfg. 1992 only.

	N/A	$1,900 - 2,300	$1,250 - 1,500	$2,660

D-35S – slope-shouldered dreadnought 12-fret body style, solid spruce top, three-piece Brazilian rosewood (1966-69) or Indian rosewood (1969-present) back, Brazilian rosewood (1966-69) or Indian rosewood (1969-present) sides, round soundhole with 5/9/5 grouping ring rosette, six-ply top body binding, three-ply back binding with white outer layer, side binding with two black lines, mahogany neck, 14/20-fret bound ebony fingerboard with pearl dot inlays, slotted headstock with rosewood overlay and logo, three-per-side open-style chrome tuners, ebony bridge with white bridge pins and black dots, tortoise (1966-69) or black (1969-present) pickguard, available in Natural finish, 25.4 in. scale, available as a Special Order, total production of 1,831 instruments, mfg. 1966-1993.

	100%	EXCELLENT	AVERAGE	LAST MSR
1966-1969 Brazilian Rosewood	N/A	$5,750 - 7,000	$3,750 - 4,500	
1969-1979 Indian Rosewood	N/A	$2,000 - 2,500	$1,300 - 1,600	
1980-1993	N/A	$1,800 - 2,250	$1,250 - 1,450	$2,760

Martin also produced three **D-35SW** models that were built for the Wurlitzer music store (1966-68) and one **SD-35S9** nine-string guitar for Fat Johnson (New Christy Minstrels, 1968).

* **D12-35 12-String** – similar to the D-35S, except in 12-string configuration and six-per-side tuners, available as a Special Order, total production of 6,480 instruments, mfg. 1965-1992.

	100%	EXCELLENT	AVERAGE	LAST MSR
1965-1969 Brazilian Rosewood	N/A	$3,800 - 4,750	$2,275 - 2,850	
1969-1979 Indian Rosewood	N/A	$1,600 - 2,000	$950 - 1,200	
1980-1993	N/A	$1,475 - 1,850	$875 - 1,100	$2,760

D-37K – dreadnought body style, solid spruce top, figured koa back and sides, round soundhole with pearl ring rosette, six-ply top binding, three-ply back binding with white outer layer, mahogany neck, 14/20-fret ebony fingerboard with diamond and triangle inlays at the 5th and 9th frets and a Maltese cross at the 7th fret, koa headstock overlay with logo decal, three-per-side chrome tuners, ebony bridge with white bridge pins with black dots, tortoiseshell pickguard, available in Amber Stain finish, mfg. 1980-1995.

	N/A	$2,200 - 2,750	$1,325 - 1,650	$2,740

* **D-37K2** – similar to the D-37K, except has a figured koa top and black pickguard, mfg. 1980-1995.

	N/A	$2,400 - 3,000	$1,450 - 1,800	$2,920

In 1982, one D-37K2 with herringbone purfling was produced (Model HD-37K2).

D-40 – dreadnought body style, solid spruce top, solid East Indian rosewood back and sides, round soundhole with Style 45 abalone pearl rosette, white body binding, Style 45 mosaic back purfling, mahogany neck, 14/20-fret bound ebony fingerboard with abalone hexagon inlays, bound headstock with East Indian rosewood overlay and Style 45 abalone pearl logo, three-per-side gold tuners, ebony bridge, tortoise color pickguard, available in Natural Gloss finish, 25.4 in. scale, mfg. 1997-mid-2005.

	N/A	$1,800 - 2,250	$1,075 - 1,350	$3,799

D-41 – dreadnought body style, solid spruce top, solid Brazilian rosewood (1969 only) or East Indian rosewood back and sides, round soundhole with Style 45 abalone pearl rosette, white body binding, abalone pearl top inlays, Style 45 mosaic back purfling, mahogany neck, 14/20-fret bound ebony fingerboard with abalone hexagon inlays, bound headstock with East Indian rosewood overlay and Style 45 abalone pearl logo, three-per-side gold tuners, ebony bridge, tortoise color pickguard, available in Natural Gloss finish, 25.4 in. scale, mfg. 1969-present.

	100%	EXCELLENT	AVERAGE	LAST MSR
1969 Brazilian Rosewood	N/A	$17,000 - 21,000	$11,500 - 14,000	
1969-1979 Indian Rosewood	N/A	$3,200 - 4,000	$1,925 - 2,400	
1980-1989	N/A	$2,600 - 3,250	$1,550 - 1,950	
1990-1999	N/A	$2,400 - 3,000	$1,450 - 1,800	
2000-Present MSR $5,299	$4,000	$2,150 - 2,700	$1,300 - 1,625	

Continues on next page.

MSR/NOTES	100%	EXCELLENT	AVERAGE	LAST MSR

- **Add 5% (MSR $5,549) for Sunburst or Ambertone finish on 2014 and later models.**

In 1986, Martin introduced an adjustable U-bar truss rod as standard equipment on the D-41; however, they also offered a non-adjustable square bar truss rod through the early 1990s and these guitars are stamped **D-41Q** (total production of seven instruments). Martin also offered the **D-41N** with a standard neck.

* *D-41 Special* – similar to D-41, except has grained ivoroid bindings and heelcap, abalone snowflake fingerboard inlays, and an Aging Toner top finish, mfg. 2004-2011.

	100%	EXCELLENT	AVERAGE	LAST MSR
	$3,900	$2,350 - 2,750	$1,550 - 1,825	$5,199

* *HPD-41 Herringbone* – similar to the D-41, except has a forward shifting bracing, herringbone pearl rosette, top binding, and back strip, mfg. 1999-mid-2001.

	100%	EXCELLENT	AVERAGE	LAST MSR
	N/A	$2,500 - 3,000	$1,650 - 2,000	$5,399

D-41S – slope-shouldered dreadnought 12-fret body style, solid spruce top, solid East Indian rosewood back and sides, round soundhole with Style 45 abalone pearl rosette, white body binding, abalone pearl top inlays, Style 45 mosaic back purfling, mahogany neck, 12/20-fret bound ebony fingerboard with abalone hexagon inlays, slotted bound headstock with East Indian rosewood overlay and Style 45 abalone pearl logo, three-per-side gold tuners, ebony bridge, tortoise color pickguard, available in Natural Gloss finish, 25.4 in. scale, available as a Special Order, total production of 17 instruments, mfg. 1970-1993.

	100%	EXCELLENT	AVERAGE	LAST MSR
1970-1979	N/A	$3,750 - 4,500	$2,500 - 3,000	
1980-1993	N/A	$2,800 - 3,500	$1,675 - 2,100	$3,720

* *D12-41 12-String* – similar to the D-41S, except in 12-string configuration and six-per-side tuners, total production of 8 instruments, mfg. 1988-1992.

	100%	EXCELLENT	AVERAGE	LAST MSR
	N/A	$2,500 - 3,000	$1,650 - 2,000	$3,860

D-42 – dreadnought body style, solid spruce top, solid East Indian rosewood back and sides, round soundhole with Style 45 abalone pearl rosette, grained ivoroid body binding, abalone pearl with B/WB boltaron top inlays, B/W boltaron back and side inlays, mahogany neck, 14/20-fret bound ebony fingerboard with Style 45 pearl snowflake inlays, bound headstock with rosewood overlay and select abalone pearl block logo inlay, three-per-side gold tuners with butterbean knobs, ebony bridge with white bridge pins and abalone pearl dots, tortoiseshell pickguard, available in Natural Gloss finish with Aging Toner, 25.4 in. scale, mfg. 1996-present.

	100%	EXCELLENT	AVERAGE	LAST MSR
MSR $6,799	$5,100	$2,800 - 3,500	$1,675 - 2,100	

In 1934, one D-42 was produced with special features (Model D-42S).

* *D-42K Koa* – similar to the D-42, except has highly flamed Hawaiian koa back and sides, mfg. 2000-mid-2008.

	100%	EXCELLENT	AVERAGE	LAST MSR
	N/A	$3,400 - 4,250	$2,050 - 2,550	$6,049

»*D-42K2 Koa* – similar to the D-42K Koa, except also has a solid highly flamed Hawaiian koa top, mfg. 2000-mid-05.

	100%	EXCELLENT	AVERAGE	LAST MSR
	N/A	$3,600 - 4,500	$2,150 - 2,700	$6,449

* *D-42V* – contemporary reissue of the vintage D-42 with Brazilian rosewood back and sides, scalloped bracing, ivoroid binding, a V-shaped neck, and hexagon fingerboard inlays, total production of 12 instruments, mfg. 1985 only.

	100%	EXCELLENT	AVERAGE	LAST MSR
	N/A	$7,200 - 9,000	$4,325 - 5,400	

D-45 – dreadnought body style, solid spruce top, solid Brazilian rosewood (1933-1942, 1968-69) or Indian rosewood (1969-present) back and sides, round soundhole with abalone pearl rosette, ivoroid (1933-1942) or white (1968-present) body binding, abalone pearl top, back, and side inlays, Style 45 zigzag back strip, mahogany neck, 14/20-fret ivoroid (1933-1942) or white (1968-present) bound ebony fingerboard with snowflake (1933-39) or hexagonal (1940-42, 1968-present) inlay, bound headstock with rosewood overlay and abalone block logo inlay, three-per-side gold tuners, ebony bridge with white bridge pins and abalone dots, tortoise (1933-1942) or black (1968-present) pickguard, available in Natural finish, 25.4 in. scale, mfg. 1933-1942, 1968-present.

	100%	EXCELLENT	AVERAGE	LAST MSR
1933-1942 See Notes	N/A	N/A	N/A	
1968-1969 Brazilian Rosewood	N/A	$32,000 - 40,000	$19,250 - 24,000	
1969-1979 Indian Rosewood	N/A	$5,800 - 7,250	$3,475 - 4,350	
1980-1989	N/A	$4,800 - 6,000	$2,875 - 3,600	
1990-1999	N/A	$4,600 - 5,750	$2,750 - 3,450	
2000-Present MSR $10,599	$8,000	$4,400 - 5,500	$2,650 - 3,300	

The prices of Prewar D-45s are constantly increasing. According to Martin production records, only 91 instruments were produced between 1933 and 1942. Currently, the market has only accounted for 72 of the 91. Furthermore, 25 of the 72 have been refinished or oversprayed. Depending on the original condition, prewar D-45s are currently priced in the $350,000 - $500,000 range, and refinished or oversprayed instruments will sell for considerably less (approx. $150,000 - $200,000). As values on this model continue to rise, especially for pre-WWII mfg., originality has become increasingly important, affecting values up to 25% or more in today's original condition dominated marketplace. Original frets, tuners, bridges, bridge pins, bridge plates, and especially finish have become more critical to determining the final value. The *Blue Book of Acoustic Guitars* highly recommends that several professional appraisals be secured before buying/selling/trading any pre-war Martin D-45.

Martin also produced two **SD12-45** 12-string guitars with standard 14-fret neck bodies (1971, 1973), one **D-45P** guitar with a low profile neck (1987), and an unknown number of **D-45N** guitars with standard necks (1989-early 1990s). In 1986, Martin introduced an adjustable U-bar truss rod as standard equipment; however, they also offered a non-adjustable square bar truss rod through the early 1990s and these guitars are stamped **D-45Q** (total production of 32 instruments).

MSR/NOTES	100%	EXCELLENT	AVERAGE	LAST MSR

* **D-45 Koa** – similar to the D-45, except has solid highly flamed Hawaiian koa back and sides and grained ivoroid bindings, mfg. 2006-mid-2008.

	N/A	$4,800 - 6,000	$2,875 - 3,600	$9,599

* **D-45V** – contemporary reissue of the vintage D-45 with Brazilian rosewood back and sides, scalloped bracing, ivoroid binding, a V-shaped neck, and snowflake fingerboard inlays, a tortoise pickguard, and an Aging Toner top finish, total production of 62 instruments, mfg. 1983-85.

	N/A	$12,000 - 15,000	$7,250 - 9,000	

D-45S – slope-shouldered dreadnought body style, solid spruce top, solid Brazilian rosewood (1969 only) or Indian rosewood back and sides, round soundhole with abalone pearl rosette, white body binding, abalone pearl top, back, and side inlays, Style 45 zigzag back strip, mahogany neck, 12/20-fret white bound ebony fingerboard with hexagonal inlays, slotted bound headstock with rosewood overlay and abalone block logo inlay, three-per-side open-style gold tuners, ebony bridge with white bridge pins and abalone dots, black pickguard, available in Natural finish, 25.4 in. scale, available as a Special Order, mfg. 1969-1993.

1969 Brazilian Rosewood	N/A	$34,000 - 42,500	$20,500 - 25,500	
1969-1979 Indian Rosewood	N/A	$6,000 - 7,500	$3,600 - 4,500	
1980-1993	N/A	$5,200 - 6,500	$3,125 - 3,900	$6,860

* **D12-45 12-String** – similar to the D-45S, except in 12-string configuration and six-per-side tuners with pearl buttons, available as a Special Order, total production of 87 instruments, mfg. 1969-1992.

1969-1979	N/A	$5,500 - 6,500	$3,750 - 4,500	
1980-1992	N/A	$5,000 - 6,000	$3,500 - 4,250	$7,020

Although this guitar was first produced during the era of Brazilian rosewood, it is unknown if one has been encountered.

D-60 – dreadnought body style, solid spruce top, bird's-eye maple back and sides, round soundhole with three ring rosette, three-stripe bound body/rosette, tortoise body binding, maple neck, 14/20-fret ebony fingerboard with pearl dot inlays, ebony-bound headstock with bird's-eye maple overlay, three-per-side gold tuners with ebony buttons, ebony bridge with white bridge pins and red dots, tortoise pickguard, available in Natural finish, 25.4 in. scale, mfg. 1989-1995.

	N/A	$1,475 - 1,850	$875 - 1,100	$3,060

D-62 – dreadnought body style, solid spruce top, flame maple back and sides, round soundhole with three ring rosette, three-stripe bound body/rosette, tortoise body binding, maple neck, 14/20-fret ebony fingerboard with pearl dot inlays, three-per-side chrome tuners with pearl buttons, ebony bridge with white bridge pins and red dots, tortoise pickguard, available in Natural finish, 25.4 in. scale, total production of 142 instruments, mfg. 1987-1995.

	N/A	$1,475 - 1,850	$875 - 1,100	$2,420

D-76 (BICENTENNIAL LIMITED EDITION) – dreadnought body style, solid spruce top, Indian rosewood three-piece back, Indian rosewood sides, round soundhole with herringbone rosette, six-ply top binding, three-ply black binding with white outer layer, herringbone back stripes, mahogany neck with brass plate on neck block, 14/20-fret ebony fingerboard with pearl star inlays, rosewood headstock overlay with pearl eagle/logo inlays, three-per-side gold tuners, ebony bridge, white bridge pins with black dots, black pickguard, available in Natural finish, mfg. 1975-76.

	N/A	$3,000 - 3,750	$1,800 - 2,250	

A total of 2,274 models were built, (200 in 1975, 1,976 in 1976, and 98 built exclusively for employees [Model D-76 E]).

ACOUSTIC: STANDARD JUMBO (J) SERIES

Size J (Jumbo) guitars feature a lower bout width of 16 in., a body depth of 4.875 in., 20.125 in. length, and 25.4 in. scale. J Series models had the "M" suffix as part of the model designation until 1990. All J Series models have scalloped braces.

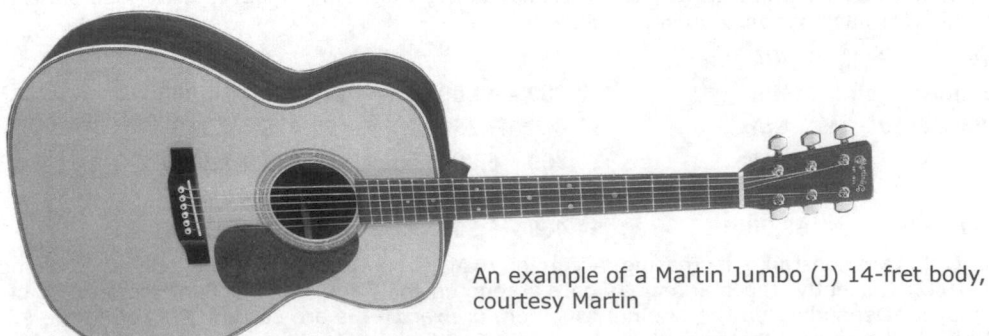

An example of a Martin Jumbo (J) 14-fret body, courtesy Martin

J-18(M) – jumbo body style, solid spruce top, mahogany back and sides, round soundhole with three-stripe rosette (1/9/1 grouping between 1985 and 1988 and 5/9/5 grouping between 1988 and 1996), five-ply top binding, single-ply back binding with tortoise outer layer, mahogany neck, 14/20-fret rosewood fingerboard with pearl diamond and square inlays, rosewood headstock overlay with gold logo, three-per-side Schaller chrome tuners with ebony buttons, rosewood bridge, black bridge pins with white dots, tortoiseshell pickguard, available in Natural finish, mfg. 1987-1996.

	N/A	$1,200 - 1,500	$725 - 900	$2,300

MSR/NOTES	100%	EXCELLENT	AVERAGE	LAST MSR

J-21(M) – jumbo body style, solid spruce top, rosewood back and sides, round soundhole with three-stripe rosette, five-ply top black binding, single-ply back binding with black outer layer, chainlink backstripe, mahogany neck, 14/20-fret rosewood fingerboard, rosewood headstock overlay with gold logo, three-per-side chrome tuners, rosewood bridge, black bridge pins with white dots, tortoiseshell pickguard, available in Natural finish, available as a Special Order, mfg. 1985-1996.

	N/A	$1,725 - 2,150	$1,025 - 1,300	$2,520

GRAND J-28LSE BARITONE – baritone configuration, Grand Jumbo-style body, solid Sitka spruce top, solid East Indian rosewood back and sides, standard X progressively scalloped tone bars bracing, round soundhole with Style 28 three ring rosette (5/9/5 grouping), white boltaron binding, multiple B/W boltaron top and back inlay, select hardwood neck, 14/20-fret white Boltaron-bound ebony fingerboard with Style 28 pearl dot inlays, solid East Indian rosewood headstock overlay with gold C.F. Martin & Co. logo, three-per-side chrome Grover tuners with large buttons, ebony belly bridge, white bridge pins with black dots, black pickguard, D-TAR Wave-Length Multi-Source electronics, available in Natural polished gloss or optional Sunburst gloss finish, Geib-style case included, 27.5 in. scale, mfg. 2011-present.

MSR $3,999	$3,000	$1,675 - 2,100	$1,000 - 1,250	

HJ-28 – jumbo body style, solid spruce top, solid rosewood back and sides, round soundhole with black and white Style 28 rosette, white body binding, mahogany neck, 14/20-fret ebony fingerboard with pearl dot inlays, rosewood headstock overlay with gold foil logo, three-per-side chrome tuners, ebony bridge, white bridge pins with black dots, tortoise pickguard, Natural polished gloss finish, 25.4 in. scale, mfg. 1996-2000.

	N/A	$1,850 - 2,250	$1,200 - 1,500	$2,850

GRAND J-35E – Grand Jumbo-style body, solid Sitka spruce top, solid three-piece East Indian rosewood back, solid East Indian rosewood sides, standard X progressively scalloped tone bars bracing, round soundhole with Style 28 three ring rosette (5/9/5 grouping), white boltaron binding, multiple B/W boltaron top and side inlay, B/W boltaron back inlay, select hardwood neck, 14/20-fret white Boltaron bound ebony fingerboard with pearl dot inlays, solid East Indian rosewood headstock overlay with gold C.F. Martin & Co. logo, three-per-side chrome Grover tuners with large buttons, ebony belly bridge, white bridge pins with black dots, black pickguard, D-TAR Wave-Length Multi-Source electronics, available in Natural polished gloss or optional Sunburst gloss finish, Geib-style case included, 25.4 in. scale, mfg. summer 2009-2011.

	$3,000	$1,800 - 2,100	$1,200 - 1,400	$3,999

J-40(M) – jumbo body style, solid spruce top, solid East Indian rosewood back and sides, round soundhole with three-ring (5/9/5 grouping, 1985-1995) or Style 45 abalone pearl rosette (1996-present), eight-ply top binding, four-ply back binding with white outer layer, mahogany neck, 14/20-fret bound ebony fingerboard with reduced abalone pearl hexagon inlays, unbound headstock with rosewood overlay and regular logo (1985-1995) or bound headstock with rosewood overlay and select abalone pearl Martin block logo, three-per-side gold tuners, ebony bridge, white bridge pins with abalone pearl dots, black pickguard (1985-1995) or tortoise pickguard (1996-present), available in Natural or Sunburst (optional) polished gloss finish, 25.4 in. scale, mfg. 1985-present.

1985-1995	N/A	$2,050 - 2,450	$1,400 - 1,700	
1996-Present MSR $4,649	$3,500	$1,875 - 2,350	$1,125 - 1,400	

* **J12-40(M) 12-String** – similar to the J-40(M), except in 12-string configuration and six-per-side gold tuners with ebony buttons, mfg. 1985-1996.

	N/A	$1,875 - 2,350	$1,125 - 1,400	$3,350

* **J-40(M)BK Black** – similar to the J-40(M), except has a gloss Black finish with matching Black finish headstock, mfg. 1988-1996.

	N/A	$2,050 - 2,450	$1,400 - 1,700	$3,470

* **J-40MC/JC-40 Cutaway** – similar to the J-40(M), except has single rounded cutaway, an oval soundhole, and a low-profile adj. neck, mfg. 1987-1996.

	N/A	$2,100 - 2,500	$1,400 - 1,700	$3,390

GRAND J-12-40E SPECIAL – 12-string configuration, Grand Jumbo-style body, solid Sitka spruce top, solid East Indian rosewood back and sides, standard X progessively scalloped tone bars bracing, round soundhole with Style 45 three ring rosette (5/9/5 grouping with a large center ring of abalone), grained ivoroid binding, multiple B/W boltaron top and back inlay, B/W boltaron side inlay, select hardwood neck, 14/20-fret grained ivoroid bound ebony fingerboard with long pattern diamond and squares inlays, grained ivoroid-bound headstock with solid East Indian rosewood overlay and CMF Martin abalone pearl logo, six-per-side gold tuners with small buttons, ebony belly bridge, white bridge pins with abalone pearl dots, Delmar tortoise pickguard, D-TAR Wave-Length Multi-Source electronics, available in Natural gloss finish with an Aging toner top, Geib-style case included, 17 in. lower bout, 25.4 in. scale, mfg. 2009-2011.

	$3,900	$2,350 - 2,750	$1,550 - 1,825	$5,199

J-41 SPECIAL – jumbo body style, solid Sitka spruce top, East Indian rosewood back and sides, round soundhole with Style 45 abalone pearl rosette, grained ivoroid binding, abalone pearl with B/W/B top inlays, B/W back inlays, mahogany neck, 14/20-fret bound ebony fingerboard Style 45 select pearl snowflake inlays, bound headstock with Indian rosewood overlay and abalone block Martin logo, three-per-side gold tuners, ebony vintage belly drop in long saddle bridge, Natural polished gloss finish with Aging Toner top, 25.4 in. scale, mfg. summer 2004-06.

	N/A	$2,100 - 2,500	$1,400 - 1,700	$4,849

J-65(M) – jumbo body style, solid spruce top, flamed maple back and sides, round soundhole with three-stripe rosette (5/9/5 grouping), six-ply top binding, three-ply back binding with tortoise outer layer, zipper pattern backstripe, mahogany neck, 14/20-fret tortoise-bound ebony fingerboard with pearl dot inlays, rosewood headstock overlay with gold logo, three-per-side gold tuners with pearl buttons, ebony bridge, white bridge pins with tortoise dots, tortoiseshell pickguard, available in Natural finish, mfg. 1985-1995.

	N/A	$1,725 - 2,150	$1,025 - 1,300	$2,520

MSR/NOTES	100%	EXCELLENT	AVERAGE	LAST MSR

* *J12-65(M) 12-String* – similar to the J-65(M), except in 12-string configuration and six-per-side tuners, available as a Special Order, mfg. 1985-1995.

| | N/A | $2,000 - 2,500 | $1,200 - 1,500 | $2,610 |

* *CMJ-65/Custom J-65* – similar to the J-65(M), except has white binding, hexagonal fingerboard inlays, white bridge pins with pearl dots, a black pickguard, and available in Cherry Sunburst finish, designed around the special guitar that C.F. Martin IV used at clinics/demonstrations, mfg. 1993-94.

| | N/A | $2,000 - 2,500 | $1,350 - 1,650 | $2,900 |

» *Custom J-65E Electric* – similar to the CMJ-65/Custom J-65, except has MEQ-932 acoustic amplification system, mfg. 1993-94.

| | N/A | $2,150 - 2,650 | $1,400 - 1,750 | $3,070 |

ACOUSTIC: STANDARD ORCHESTRA (OM) SERIES

Size OM (Orchestra Model) guitars feature a lower bout width of 15 inches, 4.125 in. depth, 19.375 in. length, and 25.4 in. scale.

An example of a Martin Orchestra (OM) 14-fret body, courtesy Martin

OM-18 – orchestra body style, solid spruce top, mahogany back and sides, round soundhole with rope pattern rosette (1/9/1 grouping), five-ply top binding, single-ply back binding with rosewood outer layer (1930-31) or black outer layer (1932-33), black backstripe, mahogany neck, 14/20-fret ebony fingerboard with pearl dot inlays, solid headstock with three-per-side banjo-style tuners with ivoroid buttons (1930-31) or regular right angle tuners (1931-33), ebony belly bridge, black bridge pins, small tortoiseshell pickguard (1930-31) or larger tortoiseshell pickguard (1932-33), available in Natural or Sunburst finish, 25.4 in. scale, total production of 765 instruments, mfg. 1930-33.

| 1930-1931 | N/A | $22,000 - 27,500 | $13,250 - 16,500 | |
| 1932-1933 | N/A | $20,000 - 25,000 | $12,000 - 15,000 | |

* **Add 25-50% for Sunburst finish.**

Martin also produced one **OM-18T** in tenor configuration (1931).

* *OM-18P Plectrum* – similar to the OM-18, except in four-string plectrum configuration with two-per-side tuners and a 27 in. scale, total production of 95 instruments, mfg. 1930-31.

| | N/A | N/A | N/A | |

Extreme rarity precludes accurate pricing.

OM-21 – orchestra body style, solid Sitka spruce top, solid East Indian rosewood back and sides, round soundhole with Style 28 rosette, tortoise color binding, select hardwood neck, 14/20-fret rosewood fingerboard with Style 28 dot inlays, rosewood headstock overlay with raised gold foil logo, three-per-side chrome tuners, rosewood bridge, black bridge pins with white dots, available in Natural or Sunburst (optional) finish, 25.4 in. scale, mfg. 1993-present.

1993-1999	N/A	$1,275 - 1,600	$750 - 950	
2000-2011	$2,000	$1,225 - 1,425	$800 - 950	
2012-Present MSR $3,099	$2,400	$1,325 - 1,650	$800 - 1,000	

* **Add 7.5% (MSR $3,349) for Sunburst or Ambertone finish on 2014 and later models.**

In 2012, Martin introduced a high-performance neck standard on the OM-21.

* *OM-21 Special* – similar to the OM-21, except has a three-stripe patterned herringbone rosette, fine herringbone backstripe, multiple black/maple top inlay, maple back binding, solid black ebony endpiece with maple fiber inlay, an ebony fingerboard with Style 21 select abalone square inlays, a large old-style Martin logo, three-per-side Gotoh nickel open-geared tuners, ebony bridge, ebony bridge pins with ivoroid dots, and a Delmar tortoise color beveled pickguard, mfg. 2007-2011.

| | $2,900 | $1,700 - 2,000 | $1,150 - 1,325 | $3,799 |

OM-28 – orchestra body style, solid spruce top, Brazilian rosewood (1929-1933) or Indian rosewood (1990-96) back and sides, round soundhole with three-ring rosette (5/9/5 grouping), ivoroid (1929-1933) or white (1990-96) top and back binding, zig-zag backstripe, mahogany neck, 14/20-fret ebony fingerboard with slotted diamond inlays, rosewood headstock overlay, three-per-side chrome banjo tuners (1929-1931) or regular right angle tuners (1932-33, 1990-96), ebony pyramid bridge (1929-1930) or belly bridge (1931-33, 1990-96), white bridge pins with black dots, small tortoise (1929-1931), large tortoise (1932-33) or black (1990-96) pickguard, available in Natural finish, 25.4 in. scale, mfg.

MSR/NOTES	100%	EXCELLENT	AVERAGE	LAST MSR

1929-1933 (total production of 487 instruments) and 1990-96.

1929-1931 Banjo tuners	N/A	$72,000 - 90,000	$43,000 - 54,000	
1932-1933 Regular tuners	N/A	$52,000 - 65,000	$31,000 - 39,000	
1990-1996	N/A	$1,600 - 2,000	$950 - 1,200	

Martin also produced five **OM-28P** in plectrum neck configuration (1931-32), one **OM-28T** in tenor neck configuration (1930), six **SOM-28** reissues of the OM-28 (1969), and one **OM-28V** contemporary reissue with Brazilian rosewood back and sides (1984).

* ***OMC-28E Cutaway Electric*** – similar to the OM-28, except has a single cutaway and Fishman Ellipse Aura System electronics, mfg. summer 2006-09.

	N/A	$1,800 - 2,250	$1,075 - 1,350	$3,849

OM-35 – orchestra body style, solid Sitka spruce top, solid three-piece Indian rosewood back, solid Indian rosewood sides, round soundhole with Style 28 rosette, white boltaron binding, B/W/B top inlay, B/W back inlay, mulitple B/W side inlay, Style 35 back purfling, mahogany neck, 14/20-fret ebony fingerboard with Style 28 pearl dot inlays, rosewood headstock overlay with raised gold foil logo, three-per-side Gotoh tuners with large buttons, ebony belly bridge, white bridge pins with black dots, black pickguard, Natural polished gloss finish, 25.4 in. scale, mfg. 2003-mid-2007.

	N/A	$1,600 - 2,000	$950 - 1,200	$3,349

OM-41 SPECIAL – orchestra body style, solid Sitka spruce top, solid East Indian rosewood back and sides, round soundhole with Style 45 three ring abalone pearl rosette, grained ivoroid binding, Style 41 abalone top inlay, B/W boltaron back inlay, select hardwood neck, 14/20-fret bound ebony fingerboard with Style 45 abalone pearl snowflake inlays, bound headstock with rosewood headstock overlay and abalone pearl vertical block Martin logo, three-per-side gold tuners with butterbean knobs, ebony bridge, white bridge pins with abalone pearl dots, tortoise pickguard, Natural polished gloss finish with Aging Toner, 25.4 in. scale, mfg. 2005-06.

	N/A	$2,400 - 3,000	$1,450 - 1,800	$4,849

OM-42 – orchestra body style, solid Sitka spruce top, solid East Indian rosewood back and sides, round soundhole with Style 45 three-ring abalone pearl rosette, grained ivoroid binding, abalone pearl with B/W/B boltaron top inlay, B/W boltaron back inlay, Style 45 back purfling, select hardwood neck, 14/20-fret ebony fingerboard with Style 45 select abalone pearl snowflake inlays, bound headstock with rosewood overlay and select abalone pearl vertical Martin block inlay, three-per-side gold Gotoh open-geared tuners with butterbean knobs, ebony bridge with two abalone pearl snowflake inlays, white bridge pins with abalone pearl dots, tortoise color beveled pickguard, available in Natural or Sunburst (optional) polished gloss with Aging Toner finish, 25.4 in. scale, mfg. 1999-present.

MSR $6,799	$5,100	$2,800 - 3,500	$1,675 - 2,100	

In 1930, Martin built two OM-42 models with roughly the same specifications of the modern OM-42.

* ***OM-42 Koa*** – similar to the OM-42 Koa, except has solid highly flamed Hawaiian koa back and sides, mfg. 2005-mid-2008.

	N/A	$3,400 - 4,250	$2,050 - 2,550	$6,049

OM-45/SOM-45 – orchestra body style, solid spruce top, Brazilian rosewood (1930-32) or Indian rosewood (1977-1993) back and sides, round soundhole with abalone pearl rosette, ivoroid (1930-32) or white (1977-1993) top and back binding, abalone pearl top and side inlays, zipper pattern backstripe, mahogany neck, 14/20-fret ivoroid (1930-32) or white (1977-1993) bound ebony fingerboard with abalone snowflake (1930-32) or hexagonal (1977-1993) inlays, ivoroid (1930-32) or W/B/W (1977-1993) bound rosewood headstock overlay with abalone pearl toch (1930-32) or vertical block Martin logo (1977-1993) inlay, three-per-side gold banjo-style tuners with ivoroid buttons (1930-31) or regular tuners (1931-32, 1977-1993), ebony bridge, white bridge pins with abalone dots, small tortoise (1930-31) or large tortoise (1931-32, 1977-1994) pickguard, Natural finish, available as a Special Order, mfg. 1930-32 (total production of 40 instruments) and 1977-1993 (total production of 184 instruments).

1930-1932	N/A	$220,000 - 275,000	$135,000 - 165,000	
1977-1993	N/A	$5,200 - 6,500	$3,125 - 3,900	$6,530

The first OM-45 "reissue" models were stamped SOM-45 and there were 56 of these produced. The OM-45 is a very rare instrument, and original finish and parts make a huge difference in value. The *Blue Book of Acoustic Guitars* highly recommends obtaining several appraisals before buying, selling, or trading this model.

* ***OM-45 Deluxe*** – similar to the OM-45, except has abalone pearl pickguard inlay and abalone snowflake bridge wing inlays, total production of 14 instruments, mfg. 1930 only.

	N/A	$300,000 - 375,000	$180,000 - 225,000	

Only 14 instruments were built, which makes the OM-45 Deluxe a very rare instrument, and original finish and parts make a huge difference in value. The *Blue Book of Acoustic Guitars* highly recommends obtaining several appraisals before buying, selling, or trading this model.

ACOUSTIC: 1 SERIES

The 1 Series is one of Martin's middle-level line of guitars. For the 1 Series, Martin retained the size and appointments of their traditional models, but they redesigned all the structural components of the guitar. The most notable change was the cantilevered A-frame bracing pattern but other new designs included a neck-to-body joint, a stress-free neck, beveled front and rear blocks, and an angled bridge hole pattern. All tops featured solid spruce (except the C-1R has cedar), backs were constructed of either solid mahogany or laminated East Indian rosewood, and sides were made of three-ply laminated mahogany or East Indian Rosewood. The first 1 Series guitar (D-1) was introduced in 1993 and by the time Martin split their guitars into series in 1996, the line had

MSR/NOTES	100%	EXCELLENT	AVERAGE	LAST MSR

rapidly expanded to include several dreadnoughts, jumbos, orchestras, 00s, and 000s. By the early 2000s, many models were discontinued and the series became grouped with the Road Series. By 2005 the entire line of guitars had been discontinued and the basses held on through 2006. Amid the economic recession of 2009, Martin reintroduced the 1 Series in attempts to keep their production line busy and to offer the customer a solid-wood Martin at an affordable price. The new 1 Series are very similar to the original 1 Series, except the guitars are constructed with all solid woods. By 2011, Martin was only produced two 1 Series models. 1 Series models that were produced originally are referred to as the "First Version" and the new 1 Series are referred to as the "Second Version."

00-1 – 00-style body, solid Sitka spruce top, solid two-piece mahogany back with Style 18 plain black fiber purfling, laminated mahogany sides, round soundhole with Style 28 black and white rosette, tortoise color body binding, mahogany neck, 14/20-fret rosewood fingerboard with Style 28 dot inlays, solid rosewood headstock overlay with three-per-side chrome tuners, rosewood bridge, tortoiseshell pickguard, available in Natural Satin finish, 25.4 in. scale, mfg. 1996-2000.

	N/A	$600 - 700	$375 - 450	$1,250

* *00-1R Rosewood* – similar to the 00-1, except features laminated East Indian rosewood back and sides, mfg. 1996-97.

	N/A	$625 - 750	$400 - 475	$1,450

000-1 – 000-style body, solid Sitka spruce top, solid two-piece mahogany back with Style 18 plain black fiber purfling, laminated mahogany sides, round soundhole with Style 28 black and white rosette, tortoise color body binding, mahogany neck, 14/20-fret rosewood fingerboard with Style 28 dot inlays, solid rosewood headstock overlay with three-per-side chrome tuners, rosewood bridge, tortoiseshell pickguard, available in Natural Satin finish, 25.4 in. scale, mfg. summer 1995-mid 2005.

	N/A	$625 - 650	$400 - 475	$1,299

* *000C-1 Cutaway* – similar to the 000-1, except has a single cutaway, mfg. 1997 only.

	N/A	$650 - 775	$425 - 500	$1,300

»*000C-1E Cutaway Electric* – similar to the 000C-1, except has Fishman Prefix electronics, mfg. 1997-2000.

	N/A	$675 - 825	$450 - 525	$1,499

* *000-1R Rosewood* – similar to the 000-1, except has laminated East Indian rosewood back and sides, mfg. summer 1995-2002.

	N/A	$650 - 775	$425 - 500	$1,329

0000-1 – orchestra-style body, solid Sitka spruce top, solid two-piece mahogany back with Style 18 plain black fiber purfling, laminated mahogany sides, round soundhole with Style 28 black and white rosette, tortoise color body binding, mahogany neck, 14/20-fret rosewood fingerboard with Style 28 dot inlays, solid rosewood headstock overlay with three-per-side chrome tuners, rosewood bridge, tortoiseshell pickguard, available in Natural Satin finish, 25.4 in. scale, mfg. 1997-2000.

	N/A	$625 - 750	$400 - 475	$1,099

C-1R – classical-style body, solid cedar top, Humphrey-style lattice bracing, laminated two-piece rosewood back, laminated rosewood sides, round soundhole with wooden classical Mosaic rosette, black body binding, Humphrey Classical-style spanish cedar neck, 12/19-fret rosewood fingerboard with no inlays, slotted headstock with rosewood overlay, three-per-side open-style brass sidemount tuners with pearloid buttons, rosewood bridge, no pickguard, available in Natural Satin finish, 25.5 in. scale, mfg. 1997-mid-2002.

	N/A	$800 - 950	$550 - 650	$1,575

D-1 FIRST VERSION – dreadnought style body, solid Sitka spruce top, solid two-piece mahogany back with Style 18 plain black fiber purfling, laminated mahogany sides, round soundhole with Style 28 black and white rosette, tortoise color body binding, mahogany neck, 14/20-fret rosewood fingerboard with Style 28 dot inlays, solid rosewood headstock overlay with three-per-side chrome tuners, rosewood bridge, tortoiseshell pickguard, available in Natural Satin finish, mfg. 1993-mid-2005.

	N/A	$625 - 750	$400 - 475	$1,299

* *D12-1 12-String* – similar to the D-1, except in 12-string configuration and six-per-side tuners, mfg. 1996-mid-2001.

	N/A	$650 - 800	$425 - 500	$1,300

* *DC-1 Cutaway* – similar to the D-1, except has a single cutaway, mfg. 1996-99.

	N/A	$650 - 775	$425 - 500	$1,300

»*DC-1E Cutaway Electric* – similar to the DC-1, except has Fishman Prefix electronics, mfg. 1997-mid-2005.

	N/A	$675 - 825	$450 - 525	$1,749

* *D-1R Rosewood* – similar to the D-1, except has laminated East Indian rosewood back and sides, mfg. 1995-2002.

	N/A	$650 - 775	$425 - 500	$1,329

»*DC-1R Rosewood Cutaway* – similar to the D-1R, except has a single cutaway, mfg. summer 1998-99.

	N/A	$650 - 800	$425 - 500	$1,499

MSR/NOTES	100%	EXCELLENT	AVERAGE	LAST MSR

D-1 SECOND VERSION – dreadnought-style body, solid Sitka spruce top, solid sapele back and sides, modified hybrid "X" scalloped bracing, round soundhole with three ring Style 28 rosette (5/9/5 grouping), black boltaron binding, rust Stratabond neck, 14/20-fret rosewood fingerboard with Style 28 dot inlays, rosewood pattern HPL headstock overlay, three-per-side chrome tuners with small buttons, rosewood bridge, white bridge pins with black dots, black pickguard, available in Natural Satin finish, 25.4 in. scale, case included, mfg. 2009-2010.

	$900	$500 - 600	$300 - 350	$1,199

* **D-1E Electric Second Version** – similar to the D-1 Second Version, except has Fishman Presys+ pickup/electronics, available in Natural Satin finish, mfg. 2010 only.

	$1,000	$600 - 700	$325 - 400	$1,349

* **D-1GT Second Version** – similar to the D-1 Second Version, except has a polished gloss top, mfg. 2011-present.

MSR $1,349	$1,050	$525 - 675	$300 - 375	

* **DC-1E Cutaway Electric Second Version** – similar to the D-1 Second Version, except has a single smooth cutaway and Fishman pickup/electronics, available in Natural Satin finish, mfg. 2009-2010.

	$1,100	$625 - 775	$325 - 400	$1,499

D-2R – dreadnought style body, solid Sitka spruce top, laminated two-piece East Indian rosewood back with Style 28 checkered purfling, laminated East Indian rosewood sides, round soundhole with Style 28 black and white rosette, white body binding, mahogany neck, 14/20-fret black micarta fingerboard with Style 28 dot inlays, solid rosewood headstock overlay with three-per-side chrome tuners, rosewood bridge, black pickguard, available in Natural Satin finish, mfg. 1996-2002.

	N/A	$650 - 775	$425 - 500	$1,399

D-3R – dreadnought style body, solid Sitka spruce top, laminated three-piece East Indian rosewood back with Style 35 W/B/W purfling, laminated East Indian rosewood sides, round soundhole with Style 28 black and white rosette, white body binding, mahogany neck, 14/20-fret bound black micarta fingerboard with Style 28 dot inlays, solid rosewood headstock overlay with three-per-side chrome tuners, rosewood bridge, black pickguard, available in Natural Satin finish, mfg. 1996-2002.

	N/A	$650 - 800	$425 - 500	$1,479

J-1 – jumbo style body, solid Sitka spruce top, solid two-piece mahogany back with Style 18 plain black fiber purfling, laminated mahogany sides, round soundhole with Style 28 black and white rosette, tortoise color body binding, mahogany neck, 14/20-fret rosewood fingerboard with Style 28 dot inlays, solid rosewood headstock overlay with three-per-side chrome tuners, rosewood bridge, tortoiseshell pickguard, available in Natural Satin finish, 25.4 in. scale, mfg. 1997-2000.

	N/A	$600 - 700	$375 - 450	$1,099

* **JC-1E Cutaway Electric** – similar to the J-1, except has a single cutaway and Fishman Prefix electronics, mfg. summer 1998-2000.

	N/A	$625 - 750	$400 - 475	$1,499

OM-1 FIRST VERSION – orchestra-style body, solid Sitka spruce top, solid two-piece mahogany back with Style 18 plain black fiber purfling, laminated mahogany sides, round soundhole with Style 28 black and white rosette, tortoise color body binding, mahogany neck, 14/20-fret rosewood fingerboard with Style 28 dot inlays, solid rosewood headstock overlay with three-per-side chrome tuners, rosewood bridge, tortoiseshell pickguard, available in Natural Satin finish, 25.4 in. scale, mfg. 1999-2001.

	N/A	$625 - 750	$400 - 475	$1,099

OM-1 SECOND VERSION – orchestra-style body, solid Sitka spruce top, solid sapele back and sides, modified hybrid "X" scalloped bracing, round soundhole with three ring Style 28 rosette (5/9/5 grouping), black boltaron binding, rust Stratabond neck, 14/20-fret rosewood fingerboard with Style 28 dot inlays, rosewood pattern HPL headstock overlay, three-per-side chrome tuners with small buttons, rosewood bridge, white bridge pins with black dots, black pickguard, available in Natural Satin finish, 25.4 in. scale, case included, mfg. 2009-2010.

	$900	$500 - 600	$300 - 350	$1,199

* **OM-1E Electric Second Version** – similar to the OM-1 Second Version, except has Fishman Presys+ pickup/electronics, available in Natural Satin finish, mfg. 2010 only.

	$1,000	$600 - 700	$325 - 400	$1,349

* **OM-1GT Second Version** – similar to the OM-1 Second Version, except has a polished gloss top, mfg. 2011-present.

MSR $1,349	$1,050	$525 - 675	$300 - 375	

* **OMC-1E Cutaway Electric Second Version** – similar to the OM-1 Second Version, except has a single smooth cutaway and Fishman pickup/electronics, available in Natural Satin finish, mfg. 2009-2010.

	$1,100	$625 - 775	$325 - 400	$1,499

ACOUSTIC: 15 SERIES

Martin's 15 Series feature all solid mahogany or solid sapele top, back, and sides. Because of the lower price of mahogany wood, Martin offers these guitars as a middle-level option. Other features of the 15 Series include no body, fingerboard, or headstock bindings and A-frame bracing. The first 15 Series guitar was the D-15 and it was introduced in 1997. Several other models popped up during the late 1990s and early 2000s including jumbos, orchestras, 00s, and 000s, and the 15 Series continued to be a strong line in Martin's catalog throughout the 2000s.

MSR/NOTES	100%	EXCELLENT	AVERAGE	LAST MSR

00-15 – 00 body style, solid mahogany or solid sapele (2003-present) top, back, and sides, round soundhole with gold and black Herringbone rosette, select hardwood neck, 14/20-fret rosewood fingerboard with Style 28 dot inlays, solid rosewood headstock overlay with raised gold foil logo, three-per-side chrome tuners with small buttons, rosewood bridge, tortoise color pickguard, available in Natural Satin finish, 25.4 in. scale, mfg. summer 1998-2010.

	$950	$550 - 650	$350 - 425	$1,249

00-15M – 00-style Grand Concert body, solid mahogany top, back, and sides, round soundhole with single ring rosette, A-Frame X solid Sitka spruce bracing, mahogany neck, 14/20-fret rosewood fingerboard with short pattern diamond and square inlays, solid rosewood headstock overlay with raised gold foil logo, three-per-side open-geared chrome tuners with butterbean knobs, rosewood bridge with lower belly, Delmar tortoise color pickguard, available in Natural Satin finish, 25.4 in. scale, 300 Series case included, mfg. summer 2010-present.

MSR $1,549	$1,200	$625 - 775	$400 - 475	

00C-15AE CUTAWAY ELECTRIC – 00 thin body style, solid mahogany, back, and sides, round soundhole with gold and black Herringbone rosette, select hardwood neck, 14/20-fret rosewood fingerboard with Style 28 dot inlays, solid rosewood headstock overlay with raised gold foil logo, three-per-side chrome tuners with small buttons, rosewood bridge, tortoise color pickguard, Fishman Sonicore Classic 4 electronics, available in Natural Satin finish, 25.4 in. scale, mfg. 2000-01.

	N/A	$575 - 675	$400 - 475	$1,349

000-15 – 000 body style, solid mahogany or solid sapele (2003-present) top, back, and sides, round soundhole with gold and black Herringbone rosette, select hardwood neck, 14/20-fret rosewood fingerboard with Style 28 dot inlays, solid rosewood headstock overlay with raised gold foil logo, three-per-side chrome tuners with small buttons, rosewood bridge, tortoise color pickguard, available in Natural Satin finish, 25.4 in. scale, mfg. summer 1998-2010.

	$950	$550 - 650	$350 - 425	$1,249

* ***000C-15E Cutaway Electric*** – similar to the 000-15, except has a single cutaway and Fishman System 1 electronics, mfg. 1999-2002.

	N/A	$650 - 800	$475 - 550	$1,499

000-15M – 000-style Grand Auditorium body, solid mahogany top, back, and sides, round soundhole with single ring rosette, A-Frame X solid Sitka spruce bracing, mahogany neck, 14/20-fret rosewood fingerboard with long pattern diamond and square inlays, solid rosewood headstock overlay with raised gold foil logo, three-per-side open-geared chrome tuners with butterbean knobs, rosewood bridge with lower belly, Delmar tortoise color pickguard, available in Natural Satin finish, 25.4 in. scale, 300 Series case included, mfg. 2010-present.

MSR $1,549	$1,200	$625 - 775	$400 - 475	

* ***000-15SM*** – similar to the 000-15M, except has a 000 12-fret body style with a 12/20-fret fingerboard and slotted headstock, available in Natural Satin finish, 300 Series case included, mfg. summer 2011-present.

MSR $1,849	$1,400	$750 - 950	$450 - 575	

000-15S – 000 12-fret body style, solid mahogany or solid sapele (2003-09) top, back, and sides, round soundhole with gold and black Herringbone rosette, select hardwood neck, 12/20-fret rosewood fingerboard with Style 28 dot inlays, slotted headstock with solid rosewood overlay and raised gold foil logo, three-per-side open-style Schaller chrome tuners with acrylic buttons, rosewood bridge, tortoise color pickguard, available in Natural Satin finish, 25.4 in. scale, mfg. 2000-09.

	N/A	$725 - 900	$425 - 550	$1,629

5-15 – small Size 5 body style, solid mahogany or solid sapele (2003-present) top, back, and sides, round soundhole with gold and black Herringbone rosette, select hardwood neck, 12/18-fret rosewood fingerboard with Style 28 dot inlays, solid rosewood headstock overlay with raised gold foil logo, three-per-side chrome tuners with small buttons, rosewood bridge, available in Natural Satin finish, 21.5 in. scale, mfg. summer 2002-06.

	N/A	$625 - 750	$400 - 475	$1,199

D-15 – dreadnought body style, solid mahogany or solid sapele (2003-present) top, back, and sides, round soundhole with gold and black Herringbone rosette, select hardwood neck, 14/20-fret rosewood fingerboard with Style 28 dot inlays, solid rosewood headstock overlay with raised gold foil logo, three-per-side chrome tuners with small buttons, rosewood bridge, tortoise color pickguard, available in Natural Satin finish, 25.4 in. scale, mfg. 1997-2010.

	$950	$550 - 650	$350 - 425	$1,249

* ***DC-15E Cutaway Electric*** – similar to the D-15, except has a single cutaway and Fishman System 1 electronics (early models) or Fishman Prefix Pro electronics (later models), mfg. summer 1998-2010.

	$1,350	$825 - 975	$525 - 625	$1,899

D-15M – dreadnought body style, solid mahogany top, back, and sides, round soundhole with single ring rosette, A-Frame X solid Sitka spruce bracing, mahogany neck, 14/20-fret rosewood fingerboard with long pattern diamond and square inlays, solid rosewood headstock overlay with raised gold foil logo, three-per-side open-geared chrome tuners with butterbean knobs, rosewood bridge with lower belly, Delmar tortoise color pickguard, available in Natural Satin finish, 25.4 in. scale, 300 Series case included, mfg. 2010-present.

MSR $1,549	$1,200	$625 - 775	$400 - 475	

* ***DC-15ME*** – similar to the D-15M, except has a single smooth cutaway and Shadow NanoMag electronics, available in Natural Satin finish, 300 Series case included, mfg. summer 2011-present.

MSR $1,899	$1,450	$850 - 1,000	$500 - 600	

MSR/NOTES	100%	EXCELLENT	AVERAGE	LAST MSR

D-15S – slope shouldered 12-fret body style, solid mahogany (2003-present) or solid sapele top, back, and sides, round soundhole with gold and black Herringbone rosette, select hardwood neck, 12/20-fret rosewood fingerboard with Style 28 dot inlays, slotted headstock with solid rosewood overlay and raised gold foil logo, three-per-side open-style Schaller chrome tuners with acrylic buttons, rosewood bridge, tortoise color pickguard, available in Natural Satin finish, 25.4 in. scale, mfg. summer 2001-09.

	N/A	$675 - 850	$400 - 500	$1,629

J-15 – jumbo body style, solid mahogany or solid sapele (2003-2010) top, back, and sides, round soundhole with gold and black Herringbone rosette, select hardwood neck, 14/20-fret rosewood fingerboard with Style 28 dot inlays, solid rosewood headstock overlay with raised gold foil logo, three-per-side chrome tuners with small buttons, rosewood bridge, tortoise color pickguard, available in Natural Satin finish, 25.4 in. scale, mfg. summer 1999-2010.

	$950	$550 - 650	$350 - 425	$1,249

* *J12-15 12-String* – similar to the J-15, except in 12-string configuration and six-per-side tuners, mfg. 2000-07.

	N/A	$575 - 725	$350 - 425	$1,399

* *JC-15E Cutaway Electric* – similar to the J-15, except has a single cutaway and Fishman Sonicore Classic 4 electronics, mfg. summer 2000-mid-2001.

	N/A	$650 - 800	$425 - 500	$1,349

OM-15 – orchestra body style, solid mahogany top, back, and sides, round soundhole with gold and black herringbone rosette, select hardwood neck, 14/20-fret rosewood fingerboard with Style 28 dot inlays, solid rosewood headstock overlay with raised gold foil logo, three-per-side chrome tuners with small buttons, rosewood bridge, tortoise color pickguard, available in Natural Satin finish, 25.4 in. scale, mfg. summer 2000-02.

	N/A	$450 - 525	$325 - 375	$979

* *OMC-15E Cutaway Electric* – similar to the OM-15, except has a single cutaway body, either a solid mahogany (2003-present) or solid sapele top, back, and sides, and Fishman Prefix Plus electronics, mfg. summer 2001-07.

	N/A	$775 - 975	$450 - 575	$1,899

ACOUSTIC: 16 SERIES

The 16 Series represents Martin's top-end modern series of guitars (the Standard and Vintage Series both cost more and have higher appointments, but they are based on Martin's traditional and vintage designs). Guitars in the 16 Series are constructed out of all solid woods and use Martin's Hybrid X bracing system. Several models have been produced under the 16 Series and they continue to be very popular.

There are some models that have 16 in their name that won't appear in the 16 Series. When Martin split their entire line into specific series in 1996, the 16 Series took on a new role. Previously, a few 16 models were offered, but their specifications varied between model and the Style 16 never really represented a full line like the Style 18 or Style 28, for instance. For models produced before 1996 that are of the 16 nature, refer to their respective section in the Standard categories. In mid-2009, Martin began using black Richlite for many of their bridges and fingerboards in the 16 Series that replaced black Micarta versions.

00-16DBM – 00-style deep body, solid mahogany top, solid mahogany back and sides, round soundhole with mosaic wood rosette, mahogany neck, 14/20-fret rosewood fingerboard with pearl dot inlays, slotted headstock with mahogany overlay, three-per-side chrome open-style tuners, rosewood bridge, black pickguard, Natural clear top and polished Gloss back and sides finish, 25.4 in. scale, mfg. summer 1999-2004.

	N/A	$800 - 950	$550 - 625	$1,729

00C-16DB – single cutaway deep 00-style body, solid spruce top, solid mahogany back and sides, round soundhole with mosaic wood rosette, mosaic back inlays, tortoise color body binding, mahogany neck, 14/20-fret ebony fingerboard with diamond and square abalone inlays, slotted headstock with rosewood overlay, three-per-side chrome sidemount tuners, ebony bridge, black pickguard, Natural polished Gloss finish, 25.4 in. scale, mfg. summer 1998-2000.

	N/A	$650 - 775	$475 - 550	$1,450

00C-16DBGTE – single smooth cutaway Grand Concert 00 14-fret-style deep body, solid Sitka spruce top, solid mahogany sides, hybrid X scalloped bracing, round soundhole with bold herringbone rosette, black boltaron binding, select hardwood modified low oval neck, 14/20-fret black micarta (first half of 2009 only) or black Richlite (mid-2009-2010) fingerboard with Style 28 pearl dot inlays, solid East Indian rosewood headstock overlay with gold foil logo, three-per-side chrome tuners with small buttons, black micarta (first half of 2009 only) or black Richlite (mid-2009-2010) belly bridge, white bridge pins with black dots, tortoise pickguard, Roland AP-1 electronics, available in Natural satin finish with a polished gloss top, 25.4 in. scale, hardshell case included, mfg. 2009-2010.

	$1,650	$1,000 - 1,150	$675 - 800	$2,199

00C-16DBRE – single cutaway grand concert 00-style body, solid Sitka spruce top, East Indian rosewood back and sides, round soundhole with single ring rosette, white boltaron body binding, mulitple B/W boltaron top inlays, B/W boltaron back inlays, Style 45 back purfling, select hardwood neck, 14/20-fret striped ebony fingerboard with Style 28 abalone dot inlays, East Indian rosewood headstock overlay with raised gold foil logo, three-per-side chrome tuners with small buttons, ebony belly bridge, Fishman Ellipse Matrix Blend electronics, Natural polished gloss finish, 25.4 in. scale, mfg. summer 2005-summer 2009.

	N/A	$1,400 - 1,700	$925 - 1,075	$3,099

MSR/NOTES	100%	EXCELLENT	AVERAGE	LAST MSR

00C-16FMBUAE – single cutaway thin grand concert 00-style body, solid Pacific Big Leaf flame maple top, back, and sides, round soundhole with single ring of Blue Paua pearl rosette, two-piece maple neck, 14/20-fret black Micarta fingerboard with Style 18 old style abalone dot inlays, Trans. Blue flame maple headstock with three-per-side gold Gotoh tuners, black Micarta bridge, no pickguard, Fishman Prefix Pro Blender electronics, available in Trans. Blue polished gloss finish, 25.4 in. scale, mfg. 2003-04.

	N/A	$1,450 - 1,700	$1,100 - 1,275	$3,299

00C-16GTAE – single cutaway thin grand concert 00-style body, solid Sitka spruce top, solid mahogany back and sides, round soundhole with triple ring rosette, black body binding, mahogany neck, 14/20-fret black Micarta fingerboard with single dot inlays, three-per-side chrome tuners, black Micarta bridge, tortoise color pickguard, Fishman Prefix Pro electronics, Natural polished gloss top and satin back and sides finish, 25.4 in. scale, mfg. 2002 only.

	N/A	$750 - 875	$525 - 625	$1,649

000-16T – auditorium 000-style body, solid spruce top, solid mahogany back and sides, round soundhole with herringbone rosette, tortoise color body bindings, mahogany neck, 14/20-fret rosewood fingerboard with diamond and square abalone inlays, rosewood headstock overlay with raised gold foil logo, three-per-side chrome tuners, rosewood bridge with diamond abalone inlays, tortoise color pickguard, Natural Satin finish with an Aging Toner top, mfg. 1996-97.

	N/A	$725 - 850	$525 - 625	$1,650

* *000-16TR Rosewood* – similar to the 000-16(T), except has solid rosewood back and sides, mfg. 1996-97.

	N/A	$800 - 925	$575 - 675	$1,850

* *000C-16T Cutaway* – similar to the 000-16T, except has a single cutaway, mfg. 1996-97.

	N/A	$800 - 925	$575 - 675	$1,850

000-16GT – auditorium 000-style body, solid Sitka spruce top, solid mahogany back and sides, round soundhole with bold herringbone rosette, black boltaron body binding, select hardwood neck, 14/20-fret black Micarta (2000-mid-2009) or black Richlite (mid-2009-present) fingerboard with Style 28 pearl dot inlays, East Indian rosewood headstock overlay with raised gold foil logo, three-per-side chrome tuners with small buttons, black Micarta (2000-mid-2009) or black Richlite (mid-2009-present) bridge, tortoise color pickguard, Natural polished gloss top and satin back and sides finish, mfg. 2000-present.

MSR $1,499	$1,150	$625 - 775	$425 - 500	

* *000-16RGT Rosewood* – similar to the 000-16GT, except has solid Indian rosewood back and sides and a bound fingerboard, mfg. 2001-05.

	N/A	$725 - 875	$525 - 650	$1,649

»*000C-16RGTE Rosewood Cutaway Electric* – similar to the 000-16RGT, except has a single cutaway and Fishman Prefix Pro electronics, mfg. 2000-03.

	N/A	$850 - 975	$575 - 675	$1,939

»*000C-16RGTE Premium Rosewood Cutaway Electric* – similar to the 000-16RGT, except has a single cutaway and Fishman Prefix Premium Onboard Blender electronics, mfg. summer 2003-mid-2005.

	N/A	$900 - 1,025	$625 - 725	$2,099

»*000C-16RGTE Aura Rosewood Cutaway Electric* – similar to the 000-16RGT, except has a single cutaway and Aura Sound Reinforcement System electronics, mfg. 2005-2010.

	$1,750	$1,050 - 1,250	$725 - 850	$2,349

* *000C-16GTE Cutaway Electric* – similar to the 000-16GT, except has Fishman Prefix Pro electronics, mfg. summer 1999-2003.

	N/A	$775 - 900	$550 - 650	$1,699

* *000C-16GTE Premium Cutaway Electric* – similar to the 000-16GT, except has a single cutaway and Fishman Prefix Premium Onboard Blender electronics, mfg. summer 2003-09.

	N/A	$900 - 1,050	$600 - 675	$1,999

000-16SGT – auditorium 000 12-fret-style body, solid spruce top, solid mahogany back and sides, round soundhole with wood herringbone rosette, black body binding, mahogany neck, 12/20-fret black Micarta fingerboard with Style 28 pearl dot inlays, slotted headstock with solid rosewood overlay, three-per-side open-style chrome tuners, black Micarta bridge, tortoise color pickguard, Natural polished gloss top and satin back and sides, 25.4 in. scale, mfg. summer 2000-05.

	N/A	$725 - 850	$500 - 600	$1,699

* *000-16SRGT Rosewood* – similar to the 000-16SGT, except has solid rosewood back and sides, mfg. 2002 only.

	N/A	$750 - 900	$525 - 625	$1,669

000C-16SGTNE NYLON STRING CUTAWAY ELECTRIC – nylon string configuration, single cutaway auditorium 000 12-fret-style body, Western red cedar top, solid mahogany back and sides, single ring blue Paua pearl rosette, black body binding, Style 45 mosaic back purfling, mahogany neck, 12/20-fret rosewood fingerboard with no inlays, slotted headstock with three-per-side open-style gold tuners, rosewood bridge, no pickguard, Fishman Prefix Pro Blend electronics with a Sound Board Transducer, Natural polished gloss top and satin back and sides finish, 26.44 in. scale, mfg. summer 2002-06.

	N/A	$1,050 - 1,250	$725 - 850	$2,299

MSR/NOTES	100%	EXCELLENT	AVERAGE	LAST MSR

* *000C-16SRNE Nylon String Rosewood Cutaway Electric* – similar to 000C-16SGTNE Nylon String Cutaway Electric, except has solid East Indian rosewood back and sides, white body binding, and polished gloss back and sides finish, mfg. 2003-05.

	N/A	$1,225 - 1,400	$775 - 925	$2,699

5-16GT – size 5 small body style, solid spruce top, solid mahogany back and sides, round soundhole with Style 17 rosette, black boltaron body binding, select hardwood neck, 12/18-fret black Micarta fingerboard with Style 28 pearl dot inlays, solid rosewood headstock overlay with raised gold foil logo, three-per-side chrome tuners, black Micarta bridge, no pickguard, Natural polished gloss top and satin back and sides finish, 21.38 in. scale, mfg. 2003-04.

	N/A	$625 - 725	$450 - 525	$1,329

D-16(T) FIRST VERSION – dreadnought style, solid spruce top, solid mahogany back and sides, multi-ring herringbone rosette, tortoise color binding, herringbone back strip, mahogany neck, 14/20-fret rosewood fingerboard with abalone diamond and square inlays, solid rosewood headstock overlay with raised gold foil logo, three-per-side chrome tuners with small buttons, rosewood bridge with abalone diamond inlays, tortoise color pickguard, available in Natural Satin finish, 25.4 in. scale, mfg. 1995-98.

	N/A	$750 - 875	$550 - 625	$1,650

In 1998, the "T" was dropped from the model name and it was called the D-16 from here on out.

* *D-16(T)R Rosewood First Version* – similar to the D-16(T) First Version, except has solid East Indian rosewood back and sides, mfg. 1996-98.

	N/A	$1,150 - 1,300	$775 - 900	$1,850

In 1998, the "T" was dropped from the model name and it was called the D-16 from here on out.

D-16 SECOND VERSION – dreadnought style, solid Sitka spruce top, solid sapele back and sides, single pearl rosette, tortoise color binding, multiple layer black/white top inlay, Style 45 back purfling, select hardwood neck, 14/20-fret striped ebony fingerboard with Style 28 dot inlays, solid rosewood headstock overlay with raised gold foil logo, three-per-side chrome tuners with small buttons, striped ebony bridge, tortoise color pickguard, available in Natural polished gloss finish, 25.4 in. scale, mfg. 2004-summer 2009.

	N/A	$925 - 1,150	$550 - 700	$2,199

* *D-16R Rosewood Second Version* – similar to the D-16 Second Version, except has solid East Indian rosewood back and sides, mfg. 2004-summer 2009.

	N/A	$1,000 - 1,250	$600 - 750	$2,399

»*DC-16RE Rosewood Cutaway Electric* – similar to the D-16R Second Version, except has a single cutaway, single ring of blue Paua pearl rosette with B/W/B fiber on both sides, black Micarta fingerboard and bridge, and Bluestick from Schertler electronics, mfg. summer 2002-03.

	N/A	$1,075 - 1,225	$750 - 875	$2,399

»*DC-16RE Premium Rosewood Cutaway Electric* – similar to D-16R Rosewood Second Version, except has a single cutaway and Fishman Premium electronics, mfg. 2004-mid-2005.

	N/A	$1,250 - 1,400	$875 - 1,000	$2,679

»*DC-16RE Aura Rosewood Cutaway Electric* – similar to D-16R Second Version, except has a single cutaway and Fishman Aura sound reinforcement system electronics, mfg. 2005-summer 2009.

	N/A	$1,350 - 1,700	$825 - 1,025	$3,099

* *DC-16E Cutaway Electric* – similar to the D-16 Second Version, except has a single cutaway, single ring of blue Paua pearl rosette with B/W/B fiber on both sides, black Micarta fingerboard and bridge, and Bluestick from Schertler electronics, mfg. 2003 only.

	N/A	$1,025 - 1,175	$750 - 875	$2,199

* *DC-16E Premium Cutaway Electric* – similar to the D-16 Second Version, except has a single cutaway and Fishman Premium electronics, mfg. 2004-mid-07.

	N/A	$1,050 - 1,300	$650 - 800	$2,649

* *DC-16E Koa Cutaway Electric* – similar to the D-16 Second Version, except has a single cutaway, solid figured koa back and sides, and Fishman Ellipse System electronics, mfg. summer 2005-07.

	N/A	$1,200 - 1,500	$750 - 950	$2,999

D-16GT – dreadnought style, solid Sitka spruce top, solid mahogany back and sides, bold herringbone rosette, black boltaron binding, select hardwood neck, 14/20-fret black Micarta (1999-mid-2009) or black Richlite (mid-2009-present) fingerboard with Style 28 dot inlays, solid rosewood headstock overlay with raised gold foil logo, three-per-side chrome tuners with small buttons, black Micarta (1999-mid-2009) or black Richlite (mid-2009-present) bridge, tortoise color pickguard, Natural gloss top and satin back and sides finish, 25.4 in. scale, mfg. 1999-present.

MSR $1,499	$1,150	$625 - 775	$425 - 500	

* *D-16RGT Rosewood* – similar to the D-16GT, except has solid East Indian rosewood back and sides, mfg. summer 2000-present.

MSR $1,799	$1,350	$750 - 925	$525 - 600	

MSR/NOTES	100%	EXCELLENT	AVERAGE	LAST MSR

»*DC-16RGTE Rosewood Cutaway Electric* – similar to the D-16RGT Rosewood, except has a single cutaway and Fishman Prefix Pro electronics, mfg. 2000-03.

	N/A	$850 - 975	$625 - 725	$1,939

»*DC-16RGTE Premium Rosewood Cutaway Electric* – similar to the D-16RGT, except has a single cutaway and Fishman Prefix Premium Blend electronics, mfg. summer 2003-mid-2005.

	N/A	$900 - 1,050	$675 - 800	$2,099

»*DC-16RGTE Aura Rosewood Cutaway Electric* – similar to the D-16RGT, except has a single cutaway and Fishman Aura sound reinforcement system electronics, mfg. 2005-2010.

	$1,750	$1,050 - 1,250	$725 - 850	$2,349

* *DC-16GTE Cutaway Electric* – similar to the D-16GT, except has a single cutaway body Fishman Prefix Pro electronics mfg. summer 1999-2003.

	N/A	$750 - 875	$550 - 650	$1,699

* *DC-16GTE Premium Cutaway Electric* – similar to the D-16GT, except has a single cutaway and Fishman Prefix Premium Blend electronics, mfg. summer 2003-09.

	N/A	$900 - 1,050	$600 - 675	$1,999

* *DC-16GTE Sapele Cutaway Electric* – similar to the D-16GT, except has a single smooth cutaway, solid sapele back and sides, multiple B/W boltaron top inlay, and Roland AP-1 electronics, mfg. 2010-present.

MSR $2,299	$1,750	$950 - 1,200	$575 - 725	

* *DC-16OGTE Ovangkol Cutaway Electric* – similar to the D-16GT, except has a single smooth cutaway, solid ovangkol back wings with a solid East Indian rosewood wedge, solid ovangkol sides, white boltaron binding, multiple B/W boltaron top inlay, fingerboard binding, and Roland AP-1 electronics, mfg. 2009-present.

MSR $2,299	$1,750	$950 - 1,200	$575 - 725	

D-16 ADIRONDACK – dreadnought-style body, solid Adirondack spruce top, solid mahogany back and sides, Hybrid X scalloped bracing, round soundhole with three-ring Old Style 18 rosette (1/9/1 grouping), tortoise color body binding, multiple B/W boltaron top inlay, Style 18 back purfling, select hardwood modified V-shaped neck, 14/20-fret striped ebony fingerboard with Old Style 18 pearl dot inlays, solid East Indian rosewood headstock overlay with raised gold foil logo, three-per-side chrome tuners with large buttons, striped ebony belly bridge, tortoise color beveled pickguard, Natural polished gloss finish with Vintage Toner top, 25.4 in. scale, case included, mfg. summer 2009-present.

MSR $2,799	$2,100	$1,200 - 1,500	$725 - 900	

D-16 LYPTUS – dreadnought body style, solid Sitka spruce top, solid Lyptus back and sides, round soundhole with single ring rosette, black boltaron binding, Style 18 top inlay, Style 28 back inlay, Spanish cedar neck, 14/20-fret black Micarta rosewood fingerboard with Style 28 abalone dot inlays, solid rosewood headstock overlay, three-per-side gold Gotoh tuners with large knobs, black Micarta bridge, tortoiseshell pickguard, Natural polished gloss top and polished gloss with maple stain back and sides, 25.4 in. scale, mfg. summer 2003-mid-05.

	N/A	$875 - $1,025	$625 - 775	$2,049

HD-16R ADIRONDACK – dreadnought style-body, solid Adirondack spruce top, solid East Indian rosewood back and sides, Hybrid X scalloped bracing, round soundhole with three-ring Style 28 rosette (5/9/5 grouping), grained ivoroid body binding, fine herringbone top inlay, B/W boltaron back inlays, HD zigzag back purfling, select hardwood neck, 14/20-fret striped ebony fingerboard with long pattern diamonds and squares inlays, solid East Indian rosewood headstock overlay with raised gold foil logo, three-per-side chrome tuners with large buttons, striped ebony bridge, Natural polished gloss finish with Vintage Toner top, 25.4 in. scale, case included, mfg. summer 2008-present.

MSR $3,099	$2,300	$1,325 - 1,650	$800 - 1,000	

HD-16RLSH – dreadnought body style, solid Sitka spruce top, solid East Indian rosewood back and sides, oversized soundhole with herringbone rosette, white boltaron body binding, fine herringbone top inlays, black/white boltaron back inlays, select hardwood neck, 14/20-fret striped ebony fingerboard with Style 28 dot inlays, solid rosewood headstock overlay with raised gold foil logo, three-per-side chrome tuners with small buttons, striped ebony bridge, Natural polished gloss with aging toner top and satin back and sides finish, 25.4 in. scale, mfg. 2007-present.

MSR $2,799	$2,100	$1,200 - 1,500	$725 - 900	

HDC-16RE – single smooth cutaway dreadnought-style body, solid Sitka spruce top, solid East Indian rosewood back and sides, hybrid X scalloped bracing, round soundhole with three-ring Style 28 rosette (5/9/5 grouping), grained ivoroid binding, fine herringbone top inlay, B/W boltaron back inlay, HD zig-zag back purfling, select hardwood modified V-shape neck, 14/20-fret solid striped ebony fingerboard with long pattern diamonds and squares inlays, solid East Indian rosewood headstock overlay with C.F. Martin & Co. gold foil logo, three-per-side chrome tuners with small buttons, solid striped ebony belly bridge, white bridge pins with tortoise color dots, Delmar tortoise color pickguard, Fishman Aura Pro electronics, available in Natural polished gloss finish with a Vintage Toner top or optional Sunburst top, 25.4 in. scale, hardshell case include, mfg. summer 2009-2010.

	$2,400	$1,500 - 1,800	$950 - 1,150	$3,299

HOMC-16RE – single smooth cutaway 000-14 Orchestra-style body, solid Sitka spruce top, solid East Indian rosewood back and sides, hybrid X scalloped bracing, round soundhole with three ring Style 28 rosette (5/9/5 grouping), grained ivoroid binding, fine herringbone top inlay, B/W boltaron back inlay, HD zig-zag back purfling, select hardwood modified V-shaped neck, 14/20-fret solid stiped ebony fingerboard with long pattern diamonds and squares inlays, solid East Indian rosewood headstock overlay with C.F. Martin & Co. gold foil logo, three-per-side chrome tuners with small buttons, solid stiped ebony belly bridge, white bridge pins with tortoise color dots, Delmar tortoise color pickguard,

MSR/NOTES	100%	EXCELLENT	AVERAGE	LAST MSR

Fishman Aura Pro electronics, available in Natural polished gloss finish with a Vintage Toner or optional Sunburst top, hardshell case included, 25.4 in. scale, mfg. summer 2009-2010.

	$2,400	$1,500 - 1,800	$950 - 1,150	$3,299

J12-16GT 12-STRING – 12-string configuration, jumbo body style, solid Sitka spruce top, solid mahogany back and sides, round soundhole with bold herringbone rosette, black boltaron binding, select hardwood neck, 14/20-fret black Micarta (2000-mid-2009) or black Richlite (mid-2009-2013) fingerboard with Style 28 dot inlays, solid rosewood headstock overlay with raised gold foil logo, six-per-side chrome tuners with small buttons, black Micarta (2000-mid-2009) or black Richlite (mid-2009-2013) bridge, tortoise color pickguard, Natural polished gloss top and satin back and sides finish, 25.4 in. scale, mfg. 2000-mid-2013.

	$1,350	$750 - 950	$450 - 575	$1,799

JC-16GTE CUTAWAY ELECTRIC – jumbo body style, solid spruce top, solid mahogany back and sides, round soundhole with multi-colored wooden mosaic rosette, black body binding, herringbone multi color back purfling, select hardwood neck, 14/20-fret Macassar ebony fingerboard with Style 28 dot inlays, three-per-side chrome tuners, Macassar ebony bridge, black pickguard, Fishman Prefix Pro electronics with a Co-polymer pickup, Natural polished gloss top and satin back and sides finish, 25.4 in. scale, mfg. 2000-03.

	N/A	$750 - 900	$500 - 600	$1,739

* *JC-16GTE Premium Cutaway Electric* – similar to the JC-16GTE, except has a black Micarta fingerboard and bridge and Fishman Prefix Premium Blend electronics, mfg. 2004-05.

	N/A	$850 - 1,000	$650 - 800	$1,999

* *JC-16RGTE Rosewood Cutaway Electric* – similar to the JC-16GTE, except has solid East Indian rosewood back and sides, mfg. 2000-03.

	N/A	$850 - 1,000	$600 - 700	$1,939

»*JC-16RGTE Premium Rosewood Cutaway Electric* – similar to the JC-16GTE, except has a black Micarta fingerboard and bridge and Fishman Prefix Premium Blend electronics, mfg. 2004-mid-2008.

	N/A	$925 - 1,150	$550 - 700	$2,199

»*JC-16RGTE Aura Rosewood Cutaway Electric* – similar to the JC-16RGTE, except has a black Micarta fingerboard and Fishman Aura sound reinforcement system electronics, mfg. summer 2008-2010.

	$1,850	$1,150 - 1,350	$725 - 875	$2,499

* *JC-16WE Walnut Cutaway Electric* – similar to JC-16GTE, except has a solid Sitka spruce top, solid walnut sides, solid walnut two-piece back, single ring rosette with blue Paua pearl and B/W inlay, a black Micarta fingerboard and bridge, gold tuners, Bluestick from Schertler electronics, and an all polished gloss body, mfg. summer 2002-03.

	N/A	$1,000 - 1,200	$725 - 850	$2,249

»*JC-16WE Premium Walnut Cutaway Electric* – similar to JC-16WE, except Fishman Premium Blend electronics, mfg. 2004-05.

	N/A	$1,100 - 1,350	$800 - 950	$2,649

JC-16ME AURA – single cutaway jumbo body style, solid Sitka spruce top, solid European flame maple back and sides, round soundhole with single ring rosette, white boltaron binding, multiple B/W boltaron top inlays, B/W/B back and side boltaron inlays, Style 45 back purfling, select hardwood neck, 14/20-fret bound striped ebony fingerboard with Style 28 dot inlays, solid rosewood headstock overlay with raised gold foil logo, three-per-side chrome tuners with small buttons, striped ebony bridge, tortoise color pickguard, Fishman Aura electronics, 25.4 in. scale, mfg. 2006-09.

	N/A	$1,400 - 1,700	$925 - 1,075	$3,099

* *JC-16RE Aura* – similar to the JC-16ME Aura, except has solid East Indian rosewood back and sides, mfg. 2006-mid-2011.

	$2,300	$1,400 - 1,700	$925 - 1,075	$3,099

M-16GT – 0000 body style, solid Sitka spruce top, solid mahogany back and sides, round soundhole with bold herringbone rosette and single Style 18 rings on either side, black boltaron binding, select hardwood neck, 14/20-fret black Micarta fingerboard with Style 28 dot inlays, solid rosewood headstock overlay with raised gold foil logo, three-per-side chrome tuners with small buttons, black Micarta bridge, tortoise color pickguard, Natural polished gloss top and satin back and sides finish, 25.4 in. scale, mfg. summer 2001-02.

	N/A	$625 - 725	$425 - 500	$1,279

* *MC-16GTE Cutaway Electric* – similar to the M-16GT Cutaway, except has a single cutaway and Fishman Prefix Stereo onboard blender electronics, mfg. 2002-03.

	N/A	$825 - 950	$575 - 675	$1,699

* *MC-16GTE Premium Cutaway Electric* – similar to the M-16GT, except has a single cutaway and Fishman Prefix Premium Blend electronics, mfg. 2004 only.

	N/A	$850 - 1,000	$575 - 675	$1,849

OM-16GT – orchestra body style, solid Sitka spruce top, solid mahogany back and sides, bold herringbone rosette, black boltaron binding, select hardwood neck, 14/20-fret black Micarta fingerboard with Style 28 dot inlays, solid rosewood headstock overlay with raised gold foil logo, three-per-side chrome tuners with small buttons, black Micarta bridge, tortoise color pickguard, Natural gloss top and satin back and sides finish, 25.4 in. scale, mfg. summer 2000-mid-2005.

	N/A	$625 - 750	$425 - 500	$1,399

MSR/NOTES	100%	EXCELLENT	AVERAGE	LAST MSR

OMC-16E CUTAWAY ELECTRIC – single cutaway orchestra body style, solid Sitka spruce top, solid sapele back and sides, round soundhole with single ring of blue Paua pearl and B/W/B fiber on both sides rosette, tortoise color body binding, Style 18 top inlays, Style 28 back inlays, Style 45 back purfling, solid Spanish cedar neck, 14/20-fret black Micarta fingerboard with Style 28 abalone dot inlays, three-per-side gold Gotoh tuners, black Micarta bridge, tortoise color pickguard, Bluestick from Schertler electronics, Natural polished gloss finish, 25.4 in. scale, mfg. 2003 only.

| | N/A | $950 - 1,100 | $675 - 800 | $2,199 |

* **OMC-16E Premium Cutaway Electric** – similar to OMC-16E Cutaway Electric, except has Fishman Prefix Premium Blend electronics, mfg. 2004-mid-2007.

| | N/A | $1,075 - 1,350 | $650 - 800 | $2,649 |

* **OMC-16RE Rosewood Cutaway Electric** – similar to the OMC-16E, except has solid East Indian rosewood back and sides, mfg. 2003 only.

| | N/A | $1,000 - 1,200 | $700 - 850 | $2,399 |

» **OMC-16RE Premium Rosewood Cutaway Electric** – similar to the OMC-16RE Rosewood Cutaway Electric, except has Fishman Prefix Premium Blend electronics, mfg. 2004-mid-2005.

| | N/A | $1,250 - 1,500 | $775 - 925 | $2,799 |

* **OMC-16WE Walnut Cutaway Electric** – similar to the OMC-16E, except has solid Walnut back and sides and Fishman Gold Plus Natural I electronics, mfg. 2002-03.

| | N/A | $975 - 1,125 | $675 - 800 | $2,199 |

OMC-16E MAPLE CUTAWAY ELECTRIC – single cutaway orchestra body style, solid Sitka spruce top, solid European flame maple back and sides, round soundhole with single ring rosette, white boltaron binding, multiple B/W boltaron top inlays, B/W/B back and side boltaron inlays, Style 45 back purfling, select hardwood neck, 14/20-fret bound striped ebony fingerboard with Style 28 dot inlays, solid rosewood headstock overlay with raised gold foil logo, three-per-side chrome tuners with small buttons, striped ebony bridge, tortoise color pickguard, Fishman Ellipse Matrix Blend electronics, 25.4 in. scale, mfg. 2005-09.

| | N/A | $1,300 - 1,550 | $850 - 1,000 | $2,899 |

* **OMC-16E Koa Cutaway Electric** – similar to the OMC-16E Maple Cutaway Electric, except has solid koa back and sides, mfg. 2005-09.

| | N/A | $1,400 - 1,700 | $925 - 1,075 | $3,099 |

* **OMC-16RE Aura Rosewood Cutaway Electric** – similar to the Model OMC-16E Maple Cutaway Electric, except has solid East Indian rosewood back and sides and Fishman Onboard Aura sound reinforcement system electronics, mfg. 2005-summer 2009.

| | N/A | $1,400 - 1,700 | $925 - 1,075 | $3,099 |

OMC-16OGTE OVANGKOL CUTAWAY ELECTRIC – single smooth cutaway Grand Auditorium 000 14-fret-style body, solid Sitka spruce top, solid ovangkol back wings with a solid East Indian rosewood wedge, solid ovangkol sides, hybrid X scalloped bracing, round soundhole with bold herringbone rosette, white boltaron binding, multiple B/W boltaron top inlay, select hardwood modified low oval neck, 14/20-fret bound black micarta (first half of 2009 only) or black Richlite (mid-2009-present) fingerboard with Style 28 pearl dot inlays, solid East Indian rosewood headstock overlay with gold foil logo, three-per-side chrome tuners with large buttons, black micarta (first half of 2009 only) or black Richlite (mid-2009-present) belly bridge, white bridge pins with black dots, tortoise pickguard, Roland AP-1 electronics, available in Natural satin finish with a polished gloss top, 25.4 in. scale, hardshell case included, mfg. 2009-present.

| MSR $2,299 | $1,750 | $950 - 1,200 | $575 - 725 | |

OMC-16GTE SAPELE CUTAWAY ELECTRIC – single smooth cutaway Grand Auditorium 000 14-fret-style body, solid Sitka spruce top, solid sapele back and sides, hybrid X scalloped bracing, round soundhole with bold herringbone rosette, black boltaron binding, multiple B/W boltaron top inlay, select hardwood modified low oval neck, 14/20-fret black Richlite fingerboard with Style 28 pearl dot inlays, solid East Indian rosewood headstock overlay with gold foil logo, three-per-side chrome tuners with large buttons, black Richlite belly bridge, black bridge pins with white dots, Delmar tortoise pickguard, Roland AP-1 electronics, available in Natural satin finish with a polished gloss top, 25.4 in. scale, hardshell case included, mfg. 2010-present.

| MSR $2,299 | $1,750 | $950 - 1,200 | $575 - 725 | |

ACOUSTIC: SPECIAL 16 SERIES

In addition to the 16 Series, Martin also offered a Special Edition line of 16 Series guitars. This series was introduced in late 1996 with most production starting in 1997. The Special 16 Series featured the same woods and bracing that the regular 16 Series has, but added features including an abalone pearl rosette, a Style 45 multi-colored back inlay strip, and gold hardware. The Special 16 Series was initially offered as a limited edition and in 1997 only 2,500 guitars in the entire line were going to be produced, but production became more standard in the late 1990s and early 2000s. Most models were discontinued by the early 2000s, but the SPD-K Koa models were produced until 2005.

SP00-16RST – grand concert 00 12-fret body style, solid spruce top, solid rosewood back and sides, round soundhole with abalone pearl rosette, tortoise color body binding, Style 45 mosaic back inlay strip, mahogany neck, 12/20-fret striped ebony fingerboard with abalone square and diamond inlays, Stauffer-style headstock with raised gold foil logo, six-on-one-side gold tuners, striped ebony bridge, no pickguard, Natural polished gloss finish, mfg. summer 1999-mid-2001.

| | N/A | $1,200 - 1,450 | $800 - 950 | $2,550 |

MSR/NOTES	100%	EXCELLENT	AVERAGE	LAST MSR

SP00C-16AE – single cutaway grand concert 00 body style, solid spruce top, solid mahogany back and sides, round soundhole with abalone pearl rosette, tortoise color body binding, Style 45 mosaic back inlay strip, mahogany neck, 14/20-fret rosewood fingerboard with abalone square and diamond inlays, three-per-side gold tuners, rosewood bridge, onboard electronics, Natural polished gloss finish, mfg. 2000 only.

	N/A	$1,000 - 1,200	$725 - 850	$2,250

SP000-16(T) – auditorium 000 body style, solid spruce top, solid mahogany back and sides, round soundhole with abalone pearl rosette, tortoise color body binding, Style 45 mosaic back inlay strip, mahogany neck, 14/20-fret rosewood fingerboard with abalone square and diamond inlays, three-per-side gold tuners, rosewood bridge with two abalone diamond inlays, tortoise pickguard, Natural gloss with Aging Toner top finish, mfg. 1997-2000.

	N/A	$850 - 1,000	$600 - 700	$1,800

In 1998, the "T" was dropped from the model name and it was called the 000-16 from 1998 on.

* SP000-16(T)R Rosewood – similar to SP000-16(T), except has solid East Indian rosewood back and sides, mfg. 1997-2000.

	N/A	$950 - 1,100	$675 - 800	$2,000

In 1998, the "T" was dropped from the model name and it was called the 000-16R Rosewood from 1998 on.

»SP000C-16(T)R Rosewood Cutaway – similar to the SP 000-16(T)R Rosewood, except has a single cutaway, mfg. 1997-2000.

	N/A	$1,000 - 1,150	$700 - 850	$2,300

In 1998, the "T" was dropped from the model name and it was called the 000C-16R Rosewood Cutaway from 1998 on.

* SP000C-16 Cutaway – similar to SP000-16(T), except has a single cutaway, mfg. 1999 only.

	N/A	$900 - 1,050	$625 - 750	$2,100

»SP000C-16E Cutaway Electric – similar to SP000C-16 Cutaway, except has Fishman Prefix Pro electronics, mfg. 1999-2000.

	N/A	$950 - 1,100	$675 - 800	$2,250

SPD-16(T) SPECIAL – dreadnought body style, solid spruce top, solid mahogany back and sides, round soundhole with abalone pearl rosette, tortoise color body binding, Style 45 mosaic back inlay strip, mahogany neck, 14/20-fret rosewood fingerboard with abalone square and diamond inlays, three-per-side gold tuners, rosewood bridge with two abalone diamond inlays, tortoise pickguard, Natural gloss with Aging Toner top finish, mfg. 1997-2000.

	N/A	$750 - 900	$525 - 625	$1,800

In 1998, the "T" was dropped from the model name and it was called the SPD-16 from 1998 on.

* SPD-16B Black – similar to the SPD-16(T), except has an all Black Gloss finish with a white rosette and matching finish headstock, mfg. summer 1998-mid-2001.

	N/A	$950 - 1,100	$675 - 800	$2,250

* SPD-16E Electric – similar to the SPD-16(T), except has Fishman Prefix electronics, mfg. summer 1999 only.

	N/A	$850 - 1,000	$600 - 700	$1,950

* SPD-16K Koa – similar to the SPD-16(T), except has solid flamed koa back and sides, mfg. 2000-05.

	N/A	$1,150 - 1,400	$800 - 950	$2,599

»SPD-16K2 Koa – similar to the SPD-16K, except has a solid flamed koa top, mfg. 2000-mid-05.

	N/A	$1,200 - 1,500	$850 - 1,000	$3,099

* SPD-16M Maple – similar to the SPD-16(T), except has solid flamed maple back and sides, mfg. summer 1998-mid-2001.

	N/A	$850 - 1,000	$600 - 700	$1,950

* SPD-16(T)R Rosewood – similar to the SPD-16 (T), except has solid East Indian rosewood back and sides, mfg. 1997-2001.

	N/A	$950 - 1,100	$675 - 800	$2,050

In 1998, the "T" was dropped from the model name and it was called the SPD-16R from 1998 on.

»SPD12-16R Rosewood 12-String – similar to the SPD-16(T)R, except in 12-string configuration and six-per-side tuners, mfg. summer 1999-2002.

	N/A	$1,000 - 1,150	$700 - 850	$2,319

»SPDC-16(T)R Rosewood Cutaway – similar to the SPD-16(T)R, except has a single cutaway, mfg. 1997-2000.

	N/A	$1,000 - 1,200	$700 - 850	$2,100

* SPD-16W Walnut – similar to the SPD-16(T), except has solid walnut back and sides, mfg. summer 1998-mid-2001.

	N/A	$850 - 1,000	$600 - 700	$1,950

SPJC-16E – single cutaway jumbo body style, solid spruce top, solid mahogany back and sides, round soundhole with abalone pearl rosette, tortoise color body binding, Style 45 mosaic back inlay strip, mahogany neck, 14/20-fret Macassar ebony fingerboard with abalone square and diamond inlays, three-per-side gold tuners, Macassar bridge, tortoise pickguard, Natural gloss with Aging Toner top finish, 25.4 in. scale, mfg. 2000-02.

	N/A	$950 - 1,100	$675 - 800	$2,459

MSR/NOTES	100%	EXCELLENT	AVERAGE	LAST MSR

* *SPJC-16RE* – similar to SPJC-16E, except has solid rosewood back and sides, mfg. 2000-03.

	N/A	$1,050 - 1,250	$750 - 875	$2,659

SPOM-16 – orchestra body style, solid spruce top, solid mahogany back and sides, round soundhole with abalone pearl rosette, tortoise color body binding, Style 45 mosaic back inlay strip, mahogany neck, 14/20-fret rosewood fingerboard with abalone square and diamond inlays, three-per-side gold tuners, rosewood bridge with two abalone diamond inlays, tortoise pickguard, Natural gloss with Aging Toner top finish, mfg. summer 1999-mid-2001.

	N/A	$850 - 1,000	$600 - 700	$1,950

ACOUSTIC: 17 SERIES

The 17 Series is very similar to the all mahogany or sapele 15 Series, except for all gloss finish bodies, hybrid scalloped bracing, body bindings, and gold hardware. The 17 Series was introduced in 2000 - three years after the introduction of the 15 Series - and was produced until 2004. Fewer models were offered in the 17 Series and with the high price points of these guitars, Martin realized that customers would rather buy a traditional 16 Series guitar rather than a fancy all mahogany 17 Series.

D-17 – dreadnought body style, solid mahogany or solid sapele (2003-present) top, back, and sides, tortoiseshell binding with Style 18 inlays, Style 18 black fiber back purfling, round soundhole with Style 17 rosette, mahogany neck, 14/20-fret black Micarta fingerboard with Style 28 dot inlays, black Micarta headstock overlay with raised gold foil logo, three-per-side gold tuners with small buttons, black Micarta bridge, tortoise color pickguard, available in Natural Gloss finish, 25.4 in. scale, mfg. summer 2000-04.

	N/A	$800 - 950	$550 - 650	$1,729

* *DC-17E Cutaway Electric* – similar to the D-17, except has a single cutaway and Fishman Prefix Stereo blender electronics, mfg. 2002 only.

	N/A	$950 - 1,100	$625 - 750	$2,199

* *D-17GT* – similar to the D-17, except has only has a gloss top and satin back and sides, mfg. 2002 only.

	N/A	$675 - 800	$450 - 525	$1,499

D-17M – dreadnought 14-fret body style, solid Sitka spruce top, solid mahogany back and sides, tortoise color binding, round soundhole with single ring rosette, select hardwood modified low oval neck, 14/20-fret Morado fingerboard with short pattern diamond and squares inlays, solid headstock with East Indian rosewood overlay and raised gold foil logo, three-per-side nickel tuners with butterbean buttons, Morado belly bridge, tortoise color pickguard, available in Natural Satin with shaded top finish, 25.4 in. scale, 1.6875 in. nut width, hardshell case included, mfg. 2013-present.

MSR $1,999	$1,500	$850 - 1,050	$525 - 650	

00-17 – dreadnought body style, solid mahogany or solid sapele (2003-present) top, back, and sides, tortoiseshell binding with Style 18 inlays, Style 18 black fiber back purfling, round soundhole with Style 17 rosette, mahogany neck, 14/20-fret black Micarta fingerboard with Style 28 dot inlays, black Micarta headstock overlay with raised gold foil logo, three-per-side gold tuners with small buttons, black Micarta bridge, tortoise color pickguard, available in Natural Gloss finish, 25.4 in. scale, mfg. summer 2000-03.

	N/A	$800 - 1,000	$550 - 650	$1,650

000-17S – 000 12-fret body style, solid mahogany or solid sapele (2003-present) top, back, and sides, tortoiseshell binding with Style 18 inlays, Style 18 black fiber back purfling, round soundhole with Style 17 rosette, mahogany neck, 14/20-fret black Micarta fingerboard with Style 28 dot inlays, slotted headstock with black Micarta overlay and raised gold foil logo, three-per-side open-style gold tuners with small buttons, black Micarta bridge, tortoise color pickguard, available in Natural Gloss finish, 25.4 in. scale, mfg. summer 2002-03.

	N/A	$850 - 1,000	$600 - 700	$1,899

000-17SM – 000 12-fret body style, solid Sitka spruce top, solid mahogany back and sides, tortoise color binding, round soundhole with single ring rosette, select hardwood modified low oval neck, 12/20-fret Morado fingerboard with short pattern diamond and squares inlays, slotted headstock with East Indian rosewood overlay and gold foil logo, three-per-side open-style nickel tuners with ivory buttons, Morado belly bridge, tortoise color pickguard, available in Natural Satin with shaded top finish, 25.4 in. scale, 1.75 in. nut width, hardshell case included, mfg. 2013-present.

MSR $2,149	$1,600	$900 - 1,125	$550 - 675	

ACOUSTIC: BACKPACKER SERIES

The Backpacker Travel Guitar was developed by luthier/designer Bob McNally in 1994. Backpackers have shown up in the most unusual of places, from the Space Shuttle to the Himalayas! Models are currently produced in Martin's Mexican facility located in Navojoa, Sonora, Mexico.

* **Add 50% (MSR $469) for factory installed Martin 332 Thinline bridge pickup.**
* **Add 50% for factory installed System 1 pickup (Classical Backpacker only, disc. 2004).**

BACKPACKER – thin travel-style "paddle-shaped" body, solid spruce top, solid wood back and sides, round soundhole, one-piece mahogany neck, 15-fret hardwood fingerboard with white dot inlays, three-per-side chrome mini tuners, hardwood bridge, white bridge pins with black dots, available in Natural finish, 24 in. scale, mfg. 1992-present.

MSR $329	$200	$120 - 150	$75 - 95	

In the early 2000s, the Backpacker was upgraded with a slightly reshaped body, wider headstock, and the Martin logo was moved from beneath the fingerboard to the traditional place on the headstock.

MSR/NOTES	100%	EXCELLENT	AVERAGE	LAST MSR

BACKPACKER CLASSICAL – thin classical nylon-string travel-style "paddle-shaped" body, solid spruce top, solid wood back and sides, round soundhole, one-piece mahogany neck, 15-fret hardwood fingerboard with white dot inlays, three-per-side chrome mini tuners, hardwood bridge, available in Natural finish, 24 in. scale, padded combo bag included, mfg. 1995-present.

MSR $329	$200	$120 - 150	$75 - 95	

In the mid-2000s, the Backpacker Classical was upgraded with a slightly reshaped body, wider headstock, and the Martin logo was moved from beneath the fingerboard to the traditional place on the headstock.

ACOUSTIC: CLASSICAL (N/C) SERIES

Size N (Classical) guitars feature a lower bout width of 14 7/16 in., 4.125 in. depth, 19.125 in. length, and 26.375 or 25.4 (early Mfg.) in. scale.

N-10 – classical-style body, spruce top, mahogany back and sides, fan bracing, round soundhole with decorative wooden rosette, five-ply wood top binding with outer black layer, three-ply wood back binding with outer black layer, 12/18-fret unbound rosewood fingerboard with no inlays, slotted headstock with decal logo, three-per-side open-style tuners with pearloid buttons (1970-1993), rosewood tied bridge, Natural finish, 25.4 in. scale (1968-1970) or 26.44 in. scale (1970-1993), total production of 835 instruments (280 in 25.4 in. scale and 555 in 26.44 in. scale), available as a special order, mfg. 1968-1993.

1968-1969 25.4 in. scale	N/A	$1,400 - 1,750	$1,000 - 1,150	
1970-1979 26.44 in. scale	N/A	$1,300 - 1,600	$950 - 1,100	
1980-1993	N/A	$1,200 - 1,450	$850 - 1,000	$2,620

In 1970, a pointed headstock was introduced.

N-20 – classical-style body, spruce top, Brazilian rosewood (1968-69) or Indian rosewood (1969-1995) back and sides, fan bracing, round soundhole with decorative wooden rosette, five-ply wood top binding with outer black layer, three-ply wood back binding with outer black layer, W/B/W back stripe, 12/18-fret unbound ebony fingerboard with no inlays, slotted headstock with decal logo, three-per-side open-style tuners with pearloid buttons, rosewood tied bridge, Natural finish, 25.4 in. scale (1968-1970) or 26.44 in. scale (1970-1995), total production of 1,101 instruments (277 in 25.4 in. scale and 824 in 26.44 in. scale), available as a special order, mfg. 1968-1995.

1968-1969 Brazilian Rosewood	N/A	$4,800 - 6,000	$2,875 - 3,600	
1969-1979 Indian Rosewood	N/A	$2,000 - 2,500	$1,200 - 1,500	
1980-1995	N/A	$1,800 - 2,250	$1,100 - 1,350	$3,190

In 1970, a pointed headstock was introduced. Martin also produced two **N-20B** models with Brazilian rosewood back and sides (1985-86).

MARTIN/HUMPHREY C-TSH CLASSICAL (STANDARD SERIES) – solid Englemann spruce top, round soundhole, rose-patterned mosaic rosette, solid East Indian two-piece back with (style 45) mosaic inlay strip, solid East Indian rosewood sides, rosewood/black/white body binding, classic neck shape incorporates neck to body shape and sound board arching, mahogany neck, 12/19 "elevated" ebony fingerboard, slotted headstock, three-per-side gold tuners with white buttons, available in Natural Gloss finish, mfg. 1996-mid 2002.

	N/A	$2,000 - 2,500	$1,200 - 1,500	$3,850

In 1996, luthier Thomas Humphrey contracted a standardized design of his Millennium design to the C.F. Martin Guitar company (see Thomas Humphrey).

ACOUSTIC: LITTLE MARTIN (LX) SERIES

The Little Martin Series are constructed out of the same High Pressure Laminate (HPL) that is used on Martin's X Series. The Little Martin (LX) Series are much smaller than regular Martin's and are targeted for travel, recreation, student use, or beginners. The overall length of the LX is 34 in. compared to 40.5 in. for a regular Martin dreadnought and scale size is 23 in. compared to 25.4 in. Every LX guitar has the same small body shape, but Martin has made several colors and features available. The first LX model was introduced in summer 2003, and they continue to produce all models that have been introduced.

LXM LITTLE MARTIN – downsized 0 body style, HPL textured spruce patterned top, HPL textured mahogany pattern back and sides, gold and black herringbone-style rosette, rust Stratabond neck, 14/20-fret East Indian rosewood fingerboard, HPL mahogany pattern headstock overlay, three-per-side chrome tuners with small buttons, East Indian rosewood bridge, no pickguard, available in Natural semi-gloss finish, 23 in. scale, padded gig bag included, mfg. summer 2003-present.

MSR $409	$290	$175 - 225	$105 - 130	

* *LX Little Martin Black* – similar to the LXM, except has HPL Jett Black top, back and sides, black Micarta fingerboard, a HPL Jett Black headstock overlay, and black Micarta bridge, mfg. 2004-present.

MSR $409	$290	$175 - 225	$105 - 130	

* *LX Little Martin Color* – similar to the LXM, except comes in four different color patterns (Blue, Pink, Purple, or Red) for the top, back, sides, and headstock overlay, black Micarta fingerboard, and a black Micarta bridge, mfg. 2007-summer 2009.

	N/A	$175 - 225	$110 - 140	$419

* *LXME Little Martin Electric* – similar to the LXM, except has Fishman Mini Q electronics, mfg. summer 2003-present.

MSR $489	$370	$225 - 275	$135 - 170	

MSR/NOTES	100%	EXCELLENT	AVERAGE	LAST MSR

* **LXM Little Martin Java Mahogany** – similar to the LXM, except has HPL Java Mahogany top, back, sides, and headstock overlay, mfg. summer 2006-2010.

	$280	$165 - 215	$100 - 130	$399

* **LXM Tenor** – similar to the LXM Little Martin, except in four-string tenor configuration and two-per-side tuners, mfg. 2008-mid-2011.

	$450	$250 - 300	$135 - 175	$599

* **LXM Tres** – similar to the LXM Little Martin, except the strings are arranged and tuned in three pairs to produce open chords, padded gigbag included, mfg. 2009-mid-2011.

	$350	$220 - 270	$130 - 160	$499

LX1 LITTLE MARTIN – downsized 0 body style, solid Sitka spruce top, HPL textured mahogany pattern back and sides, mulitple B/W Boltaron with red fiber rosette, rust Stratabond neck, 14/20-fret East Indian rosewood fingerboard, HPL mahogany pattern headstock overlay, three-per-side chrome tuners with small buttons, East Indian rosewood fingerboard, no pickguard, available in Natural semi-gloss finish, 23 in. scale, padded gig bag included, mfg. summer 2004-present.

MSR $429	$300	$175 - 225	$110 - 140	

* **LX1E Little Martin Electric** – similar to the LX1, except has Fishman Mini Q electronics, mfg. summer 2004-present.

MSR $519	$400	$235 - 285	$140 - 175	

LXK2 LITTLE MARTIN – downsized 0 body style, HPL Hawaiian koa patterned top, HPL Hawaiian koa patterned back and sides, gold and black herringbone-style rosette, natural Stratabond neck, 14/20-fret East Indian rosewood fingerboard, HPL koa pattern headstock overlay, three-per-side chrome tuners with small buttons, East Indian rosewood bridge, no pickguard, available in Natural semi-gloss finish, 23 in. scale, padded gig bag included, mfg. 2004-present.

MSR $409	$290	$175 - 225	$105 - 130	

LX ELVIS PRESLEY LITTLE MARTIN – downsized Concert 0-style body, HPL textured spruce patterned top, HPL textured black back and sides, gold and black three-ring rosette, natural Stratabond modified low oval neck, 14/20-fret black micarta fingerboard with no inlays, HPL jett black headstock overlay with silver logo, Elvis silhouette, and Elvis signature, three-per-side chrome tuners with small buttons, black micarta belly bridge with drop-in saddle, white bridge pins with black dots, no pickguard, available in Natural semi-gloss finish with a custom leather cover graphic top, 23 in. scale, padded gig bag included, mfg. 2009-2011.

	$530	$300 - 375	$175 - 225	$699

LX JIMMY BUFFET LITTLE MARTIN – downsized Concert 0-style body, HPL top, HPL koa wood pattern back and sides, modified X Series solid Sitka spruce bracing, round soundhole, natural Stratabond modified low oval neck, 14/20-fret black Richlite fingerboard with no inlays, HPL jett black headstock overlay with silver logo, palm tree logo, and Jimmy Buffet signature, three-per-side chrome tuners with small buttons, black Richlite belly bridge with compensated white tusq saddle, white bridge pins with black dots, no pickguard, available in Natural semi-gloss finish with a custom design top by Dan Rizzie, 23 in. scale, padded gig bag included, limited edition run of 300 instruments, mfg. 2010 only.

	$500	$300 - 350	$175 - 225	$649

LX REALTREE HD LITTLE MARTIN – downsized 0 body style, HPL textured custom Realtree hardwoods camo patterned top, HPL textured custom Realtree hardwoods camo patterned back and sides, natural Stratabond neck, 14/20-fret black Micarta fingerboard, HPL custom Realtree hardwoods pattern headstock overlay, three-per-side Gotoh Cosmo black tuners, black Micarta (summer 2005-summer 2009) or black Richlite (summer 2009-2010) bridge, no pickguard, 23 in. scale, padded gig bag with Realtree pattern included, mfg. summer 2005-2010.

	$480	$300 - 350	$175 - 225	$649

ACOUSTIC: PERFORMING ARTIST SERIES

DCPA1 PERFORMING ARTIST/PLUS – single cutaway dreadnought 14-fret-style body, solid Sitka spruce top, solid East Indian rosewood back and sides, hybrid X scalloped solid Sitka spruce bracing, round soundhole with two-ring abalone rosette, solid ovangkol binding, multiple B/W fiber top inlay, solid ovangkol back purfling, select hardwood Performing Artist profile neck, 14/20-fret ovangkol-bound ebony fingerboard with arrows and squares inlays, solid ovangkol-bound square headstock with ebony overlay and abalone CMF Martin vertical block logo, three-per-side gold tuners with large buttons, ebony Performing Artist belly bridge, Delmar tortoise pickguard, bone bridge pins with pearl dots, Fishman F1 Aura (2010-mid-2012) or Fishman F1 Aura+ (mid-2012-present) electronics with two low-profile knobs and LED display, available in Natural polished gloss finish (Sunburst optional), 25.4 in. scale, brown hardshell case included, mfg. 2010-present.

MSR $3,999	$3,000	$1,900 - 2,250	$1,200 - 1,500	

DCPA1 MADAGASCAR ROSEWOOD PERFORMING ARTIST – single cutaway dreadnought 14-fret-style body, solid Adirondack Sitka spruce top, solid Madagascar rosewood back and sides, standard X scalloped forward shifted solid Sitka spruce bracing, round soundhole with Style 45 two-ring abalone rosette, grained ivoroid binding, Style 41 abalone top inlay, black/maple fiber inlay, Style 45 Golden era back purfling, select hardwood Performing Artist profile neck, 14/20-fret grained ivoroid-bound ebony fingerboard with alternative torch inspired inlays, grained ivoroid-bound square headstock with Madagascar rosewood overlay and abalone CMF Martin vertical block logo, three-per-side gold tuners with large buttons, ebony Performing Artist belly bridge, Delmar tortoise pickguard, bone bridge pins with pearl dots, Fishman F1 Aura electronics with two low-profile knobs and LED display, available in Natural polished gloss finish (Sunburst optional), 25.4 in. scale, brown hardshell case included, mfg. 2012 only.

	$4,900	$2,900 - 3,600	$1,750 - 2,175	$6,499

MSR/NOTES	100%	EXCELLENT	AVERAGE	LAST MSR

DCPA3 PERFORMING ARTIST – single cutaway dreadnought 14-fret-style body, solid Sitka spruce top, solid East Indian rosewood back and sides, hybrid X scalloped solid Sitka spruce bracing, round soundhole with two-ring rosette, white boltaron binding, multiple B/W boltaron top inlay, select hardwood Performing Artist profile neck, 14/20-fret white boltaron-bound black Richlite fingerboard with MOP offset dot inlays, square headstock with ebony overlay and gold foil CMF Martin horizontal script logo, three-per-side chrome tuners with large buttons, black Richlite Performing Artist belly bridge, Delmar tortoise pickguard, white bridge pins with black dots, Fishman F1 Aura electronics with two low-profile knobs and LED display, available in Natural polished gloss finish, 25.4 in. scale, hardshell case included, mfg. 2011-mid-2012.

	$2,000	$1,175 - 1,375	$775 - 900	$2,599

DCPA4 PERFORMING ARTIST – single cutaway dreadnought 14-fret-style body, solid Sitka spruce top, solid sapele back and sides, hybrid X scalloped solid Sitka spruce bracing, round soundhole with two-ring rosette, black boltaron binding, select hardwood Performing Artist profile neck, 14/20-fret black Richlite fingerboard with offset dot inlays, square headstock with East Indian rosewood overlay and gold foil CMF Martin horizontal script logo, three-per-side chrome tuners with large buttons, black Richlite Performing Artist belly bridge, Delmar tortoise pickguard, white bridge pins with black dots, Fishman F1 Analog electronics with two low-profile knobs and LED display, available in Natural polished gloss finish, 25.4 in. scale, hardshell case included, mfg. 2011-present.

MSR $1,649	$1,250	$700 - 875	$425 - 525	

* *DCPA4 Rosewood Performing Artist* – similar to the DCPA4 Performing Artist, except has solid East Indian rosewood back and sides, available in Natural polished gloss finish, mfg. summer 2012-present.

MSR $1,849	$1,400	$775 - 975	$450 - 575	

DCPA4 SIRIS PERFORMING ARTIST – single cutaway dreadnought 14-fret-style body, solid Sitka spruce top, solid East Indian rosewood back and sides, hybrid X scalloped solid Sitka spruce bracing, round soundhole with two-ring rosette, white boltaron binding, B/W/B boltaron top inlay, select hardwood Performing Artist profile neck, 14/20-fret black Richlite fingerboard with Style 28 dot inlays, square headstock with East Indian rosewood overlay and gold foil CMF Martin horizontal script logo, three-per-side chrome tuners with large buttons, black Richlite Performing Artist belly bridge, Delmar tortoise pickguard, white bridge pins with black dots, Fishman F1 Analog electronics with two low-profile knobs and LED display, available in Natural polished gloss finish, 25.4 in. scale, hardshell case included, mfg. 2012-present.

MSR $1,849	$1,400	$775 - 975	$450 - 575	

DCPA5 PERFORMING ARTIST – single cutaway dreadnought 14-fret-style body, solid Sitka spruce top, mahogany pattern HPL (high pressure laminate) back and sides, hybrid X scalloped solid Sitka spruce bracing, round soundhole with two-ring rosette, Brown Stratabond Performing Artist profile neck, 14/20-fret black Richlite fingerboard with offset dot inlays, square headstock with mahogany pattern HPL overlay and gold foil CMF Martin horizontal script logo, three-per-side chrome tuners with large buttons, black Richlite Performing Artist belly bridge, Delmar tortoise pickguard, white bridge pins with black dots, Fishman F1 Analog electronics with two low-profile knobs and LED display, available in Natural polished gloss finish, 25.4 in. scale, mfg. 2013-present.

MSR $1,099	$800	$450 - 575	$275 - 350	

DCPA5K PERFORMING ARTIST – single cutaway dreadnought 14-fret-style body, solid Sitka spruce top, koa HPL (high pressure laminate) back and sides, hybrid X scalloped solid Sitka spruce bracing, round soundhole with two-ring rosette, Brown Stratabond Performing Artist profile neck, 14/20-fret black Richlite fingerboard with offset dot inlays, square headstock with koa HPL overlay and gold foil CMF Martin horizontal script logo, three-per-side chrome tuners with large buttons, black Richlite Performing Artist belly bridge, Delmar tortoise pickguard, white bridge pins with black dots, Fishman F1 Analog electronics with two low-profile knobs and LED display, available in Natural polished gloss finish, 25.4 in. scale, mfg. 2012-present.

MSR $1,099	$800	$450 - 575	$275 - 350	

GPCPA1 PERFORMING ARTIST/PLUS – single cutaway Grand Performance 14-fret-style body, solid Sitka spruce top, solid East Indian rosewood back and sides, hybrid X scalloped solid Sitka spruce bracing, round soundhole with two-ring abalone rosette, solid ovangkol binding, multiple B/W fiber top inlay, solid ovangkol back purfling, select hardwood Performing Artist profile neck, 14/20-fret ovangkol-bound ebony fingerboard with arrows and squares inlays, solid ovangkol-bound square headstock with ebony overlay and abalone CMF Martin vertical block logo, three-per-side gold tuners with large buttons, ebony Performing Artist belly bridge, Delmar tortoise pickguard, bone bridge pins with pearl dots, Fishman F1 Aura (2010-mid-2012) or Fishman F1 Aura+ (mid-2012-present) electronics with two low-profile knobs and LED display, available in Natural polished gloss finish (Sunburst optional), 25.4 in. scale, brown hardshell case included, mfg. 2010-present.

MSR $3,999	$3,000	$1,900 - 2,250	$1,200 - 1,500	

GPCPA1 MADAGASCAR ROSEWOOD PERFORMING ARTIST – single cutaway Grand Performance 14-fret-style body, solid Adirondack Sitka spruce top, solid Madagascar rosewood back and sides, standard X scalloped forward shifted solid Sitka spruce bracing, round soundhole with Style 45 two-ring abalone rosette, grained ivoroid binding, Style 41 abalone top inlay, black/maple fiber inlay, Style 45 Golden era back purfling, select hardwood Performing Artist profile neck, 14/20-fret grained ivoroid-bound ebony fingerboard with alternative torch inspired inlays, grained ivoroid-bound square headstock with Madagascar rosewood overlay and abalone CMF Martin vertical block logo, three-per-side gold tuners with large buttons, ebony Performing Artist belly bridge, Delmar tortoise pickguard, bone bridge pins with pearl dots, Fishman F1 Aura electronics with two low-profile knobs and LED display, available in Natural polished gloss finish (Sunburst optional), 25.4 in. scale, brown hardshell case included, mfg. 2012 only.

	$4,900	$2,900 - 3,600	$1,750 - 2,175	$6,499

GPCPA2 PERFORMING ARTIST – single cutaway Grand Performance 14-fret-style body, solid Sitka spruce top, solid three-piece East Indian rosewood back, solid East Indian rosewood sides, hybrid X scalloped solid Sitka spruce bracing, round soundhole with two-ring abalone rosette, grained ivoroid binding, multiple B/W fiber top inlay, select hardwood Performing Artist profile neck, 14/20-fret grained ivoroid-bound black Richlite fingerboard with scalloped diamond inlays, square headstock with ebony overlay and gold foil CMF Martin horizontal script logo, three-per-side gold tuners with large buttons, black Richlite Performing Artist belly bridge, Delmar tortoise pickguard, white bridge pins with pearl dots, Fishman F1 Aura electronics with two low-profile knobs and LED display, available in Natural polished gloss finish, 25.4 in. scale, hardshell case included, mfg. 2011-mid-2012.

	$2,600	$1,575 - 1,850	$1,050 - 1,225	$3,499

MSR/NOTES	100%	EXCELLENT	AVERAGE	LAST MSR

GPCPA2 MAHOGANY PERFORMING ARTIST – single cutaway Grand Performance 14-fret-style body, solid certified European spruce top, solid certified mahogany back and sides, hybrid X scalloped solid Sitka spruce bracing, round soundhole with two-ring pearl rosette, white binding, multiple B/W fiber top inlay, select hardwood Performing Artist profile neck, 14/20-fret bound black Richlite fingerboard with dot inlays, square headstock with mahogany overlay and gold foil CMF Martin horizontal script logo, three-per-side gold tuners with large buttons, black Richlite Performing Artist belly bridge, Delmar tortoise pickguard, white bridge pins with pearl dots, Fishman F1 Aura+ electronics with two low-profile knobs and LED display, available in Natural polished gloss finish, 25.4 in. scale, hardshell case included, mfg. summer 2012-present.

| MSR $3,399 | $2,500 | $1,450 - 1,800 | $850 - 1,075 | |

GPCPA3 PERFORMING ARTIST – single cutaway Grand Performance 14-fret-style body, solid Sitka spruce top, solid East Indian rosewood back and sides, hybrid X scalloped solid Sitka spruce bracing, round soundhole with two-ring rosette, white boltaron binding, multiple B/W boltaron top inlay, select hardwood Performing Artist profile neck, 14/20-fret white boltaron-bound black Richlite fingerboard with MOP offset dot inlays, square headstock with ebony overlay and gold foil CMF Martin horizontal script logo, three-per-side chrome tuners with large buttons, black Richlite Performing Artist belly bridge, Delmar tortoise pickguard, white bridge pins with black dots, Fishman F1 Aura electronics with two low-profile knobs and LED display, available in Natural polished gloss finish, 25.4 in. scale, hardshell case included, mfg. 2011-mid-2012.

| | $2,000 | $1,175 - 1,375 | $775 - 900 | $2,599 |

GPCPA3 SAPELE PERFORMING ARTIST – single cutaway Grand Performance 14-fret-style body, solid Sitka spruce top, solid Sapele back and sides, hybrid X scalloped solid Sitka spruce bracing, round soundhole with two-ring rosette, black boltaron binding, select hardwood Performing Artist profile neck, 14/20-fret black Richlite fingerboard with Style 28 Ecru Corian dot inlays, square headstock with rosewood overlay and gold foil CMF Martin horizontal srcipt logo, three-per-side chrome tuners with large buttons, black Richlite Performing Artist belly bridge, Delmar tortoise pickguard, white bridge pins with black dots, Fishman F1 Aura+ electronics with two low-profile knobs and LED display, available in Natural polished gloss finish, 25.4 in. scale, hardshell case included, mfg. summer 2012-present.

| MSR $2,199 | $1,700 | $950 - 1,175 | $575 - 725 | |

GPCPA4 PERFORMING ARTIST – single cutaway Grand Performance 14-fret-style body, solid Sitka spruce top, solid sapele back and sides, hybrid X scalloped solid Sitka spruce bracing, round soundhole with two-ring rosette, black boltaron binding, select hardwood Performing Artist profile neck, 14/20-fret black Richlite fingerboard with offset dot inlays, square headstock with East Indian rosewood overlay and gold foil CMF Martin horizontal script logo, three-per-side chrome tuners with large buttons, black Richlite Performing Artist belly bridge, Delmar tortoise pickguard, white bridge pins with black dots, Fishman F1 Analog electronics with two low-profile knobs and LED display, available in Natural polished gloss finish, 25.4 in. scale, hardshell case included, mfg. 2011-present.

| MSR $1,649 | $1,250 | $700 - 875 | $425 - 525 | |

* **GPC12PA4 12-String Performing Artist** – similar to the GPCPA4 Performing Artist, except in 12-string configuration with six-per-side tuners, available in Natural polished gloss finish, mfg. summer 2012-present.

| MSR $1,849 | $1,400 | $775 - 975 | $450 - 575 | |

* **GPCPA4 Rosewood Performing Artist** – similar to the GPCPA4 Performing Artist, except has solid East Indian rosewood back and sides, available in Natural polished gloss finish, mfg. summer 2012-present.

| MSR $1,849 | $1,400 | $775 - 975 | $450 - 575 | |

GPCPA4 SAPELE PERFORMING ARTIST FSC – single cutaway Grand Performance 14-fret-style body, solid FSC certified Sitka spruce top, solid FSC certified sapele back and sides, hybrid X scalloped solid FSC certified Sitka spruce bracing, round soundhole with two-ring rosette, black boltaron binding, solid FSC certified mahogany Performing Artist profile neck, 14/20-fret FSC certified black Richlite fingerboard with offset dot inlays, square headstock with FSC certified mahogany overlay and gold foil CMF Martin horizontal script logo, three-per-side chrome tuners with large buttons, black FSC certified Richlite Performing Artist belly bridge, Delmar tortoise pickguard, white bridge pins with black dots, Fishman F1 Analog electronics with two low-profile knobs and LED display, available in Natural polished gloss finish, 25.4 in. scale, hardshell case included, mfg. 2012-present.

| MSR $1,799 | $1,400 | $775 - 950 | $450 - 575 | |

GPCPA4 SIRIS PERFORMING ARTIST – single cutaway Grand Performance 14-fret-style body, solid Sitka spruce top, solid East Indian rosewood back and sides, hybrid X scalloped solid Sitka spruce bracing, round soundhole with two-ring rosette, white boltaron binding, B/W/B boltaron top inlay, select hardwood Performing Artist profile neck, 14/20-fret black Richlite fingerboard with Style 28 dot inlays, square headstock with East Indian rosewood overlay and gold foil CMF Martin horizontal script logo, three-per-side chrome tuners with large buttons, black Richlite Performing Artist belly bridge, Delmar tortoise pickguard, white bridge pins with black dots, Fishman F1 Analog electronics with two low-profile knobs and LED display, available in Natural polished gloss finish, 25.4 in. scale, hardshell case included, mfg. 2012-present.

| MSR $1,849 | $1,400 | $775 - 975 | $450 - 575 | |

GPCPA5 PERFORMING ARTIST – single cutaway Grand Performance 14-fret-style body, solid Sitka spruce top, mahogany pattern (high pressure laminate) back and sides, hybrid X scalloped solid Sitka spruce bracing, round soundhole with two-ring rosette, Brown Stratabond Performing Artist profile neck, 14/20-fret black Richlite fingerboard with offset dot inlays, square headstock with mahogany pattern HPL overlay and gold foil CMF Martin horizontal script logo, three-per-side chrome tuners with large buttons, black Richlite Performing Artist belly bridge, Delmar tortoise pickguard, white bridge pins with black dots, Fishman F1 Analog electronics with two low-profile knobs and LED display, available in Natural polished gloss finish, 25.4 in. scale, 1.75 in. nut width, mfg. 2013-present.

| MSR $1,099 | $800 | $450 - 575 | $275 - 350 | |

MSR/NOTES	100%	EXCELLENT	AVERAGE	LAST MSR

GPCPA5K PERFORMING ARTIST – single cutaway Grand Performance 14-fret-style body, solid Sitka spruce top, koa HPL (high pressure laminate) back and sides, hybrid X scalloped solid Sitka spruce bracing, round soundhole with two-ring rosette, Brown Stratabond Performing Artist profile neck, 14/20-fret black Richlite fingerboard with offset dot inlays, square headstock with koa HPL overlay and gold foil CMF Martin horizontal script logo, three-per-side chrome tuners with large buttons, black Richlite Performing Artist belly bridge, Delmar tortoise pickguard, white bridge pins with black dots, Fishman F1 Analog electronics with two low-profile knobs and LED display, available in Natural polished gloss finish, 25.4 in. scale, mfg. 2012-present.

| MSR $1,099 | $800 | $450 - 575 | $275 - 350 | |

GPCPA MAHOGANY PERFORMING ARTIST – single cutaway Grand Performance 14-fret-style body, solid certified European spruce top, solid certified mahogany back and sides, hybrid X scalloped solid certified European spruce bracing, round soundhole with two-ring rosette, grained ivoroid binding, multiple B/W boltaron top inlay, solid certified mahogany Performing Artist profile neck, 14/20-fret grained ivoroid-bound black Richlite fingerboard with offset dot inlays, square headstock with solid certified mahogany overlay and gold foil CMF Martin horizontal srcipt logo, three-per-side gold tuners with large buttons, black Richlite Performing Artist belly bridge, Delmar tortoise pickguard, white bridge pins with pearl dots, Fishman F1 Aura electronics with two low-profile knobs and LED display, available in Natural polished gloss finish, 25.4 in. scale, slate gray hardshell case included, mfg. 2011-mid-2012.

| | $2,500 | $1,525 - 1,775 | $1,025 - 1,200 | $3,399 |

OMCPA1 PERFORMING ARTIST/PLUS – single cutaway Grand Auditorium/000 14-fret-style body, solid Sitka spruce top, solid East Indian rosewood back and sides, hybrid X scalloped solid Sitka spruce bracing, round soundhole with two-ring abalone rosette, solid ovangkol binding, multiple B/W fiber top inlay, solid ovangkol back purfling, select hardwood Performing Artist profile neck, 14/20-fret ovangkol-bound ebony fingerboard with arrows and squares inlays, solid ovangkol-bound square headstock with ebony overlay and abalone CMF Martin vertical block logo, three-per-side gold tuners with large buttons, ebony Performing Artist belly bridge, Delmar tortoise pickguard, bone bridge pins with pearl dots, Fishman F1 Aura (2010-mid-2012) or Fishman F1 Aura+ (mid-2012-present) electronics with two low-profile knobs and LED display, available in Natural polished gloss finish (Sunburst optional), 25.4 in. scale, brown hardshell case included, mfg. 2010-present.

| MSR $3,999 | $3,000 | $1,900 - 2,250 | $1,200 - 1,500 | |

OMCPA3 PERFORMING ARTIST – single cutaway Grand Auditorium/000 14-fret-style body, solid Sitka spruce top, solid East Indian rosewood back and sides, hybrid X scalloped solid Sitka spruce bracing, round soundhole with two-ring rosette, white boltaron binding, multiple B/W boltaron top inlay, select hardwood Performing Artist profile neck, 14/20-fret white boltaron-bound black Richlite fingerboard with MOP offset dot inlays, square headstock with ebony overlay and gold foil CMF Martin horizontal script logo, three-per-side chrome tuners with large buttons, black Richlite Performing Artist belly bridge, Delmar tortoise pickguard, white bridge pins with black dots, Fishman F1 Aura electronics with two low-profile knobs and LED display, available in Natural polished gloss finish, 25.4 in. scale, hardshell case included, mfg. 2011-12.

| | $2,000 | $1,175 - 1,375 | $775 - 900 | $2,599 |

OMCPA4 PERFORMING ARTIST – single cutaway Grand Auditorium/000 14-fret-style body, solid Sitka spruce top, solid sapele back and sides, hybrid X scalloped solid Sitka spruce bracing, round soundhole with two-ring rosette, black boltaron binding, select hardwood Performing Artist profile neck, 14/20-fret black Richlite fingerboard with offset dot inlays, square headstock with East Indian rosewood overlay and gold foil CMF Martin horizontal script logo, three-per-side chrome tuners with large buttons, black Richlite Performing Artist belly bridge, Delmar tortoise pickguard, white bridge pins with black dots, Fishman F1 Analog electronics with two low-profile knobs and LED display, available in Natural polished gloss finish, 25.4 in. scale, hardshell case included, mfg. 2011-present.

| MSR $1,649 | $1,250 | $700 - 875 | $425 - 525 | |

* *OMCPA4 Rosewood Performing Artist* – similar to the OMCPA4 Performing Artist, except has solid East Indian rosewood back and sides, available in Natural polished gloss finish, mfg. summer 2012-present.

| MSR $1,849 | $1,400 | $775 - 975 | $450 - 575 | |

ACOUSTIC: RETRO SERIES

D-18E RETRO – dreadnought-style body, solid Sitka spruce top, solid mahogany back and sides, standard X scalloped forward shifted bracing, round soundhole with Style 18 three-stripe rosette (1/9/1 grouping), tortoise color binding, multiple-ply B/W boltaron top inlay, old Style 18 back purfling, select hardwood neck with modified low oval profile with Performing Artist taper, 14/20-fret ebony fingerboard with old Style 18 green abalone dot inlays, East Indian rosewood headstock overlay with raised gold foil logo, three-per-side nickel open-geared tuners with butterbean knobs, vintage ebony belly bridge with drop-in long saddle, black bridge pins with white dots, beveled tortoise pickguard, Fishman F1 Aura Plus electronics, Natural polished gloss finish with Aging Toner top, 1.75 in. nut width, 25.4 in. scale, case included, mfg. summer 2012-present.

| MSR $3,399 | $2,600 | $1,450 - 1,825 | $875 - 1,100 | |

D-45E RETRO – dreadnought-style body, solid Sitka spruce top, solid East Indian rosewood back and sides, standard "X" scalloped forward shifted bracing, round soundhole with Style 45 three-stripe abalone pearl rosette (5/9/5 grouping), grained ivoroid binding, Style 45 abalone pearl with B/W/B boltaron top and side inlay, Style 45 abalone pearl with B/W boltaron back inlay, Style 45 back purfling, select hardwood neck with modified low profile and Peforming Artist taper, 14/20-fret grained ivoroid-bound ebony fingerboard with Style 45 select abalone pearl snowflake inlays, grained ivoroid-bound rosewood headstock overlay with abalone pearl vertical block Martin logo, three-per-side gold open-geared tuners with butterbean knobs, 1930s-style ebony belly bridge with drop-in long saddle, white bridge pins with ablone pearl dots, beveled tortoise pickguard, Fishman F1 Aura Plus electronics, available in Natural or Sunburst polished gloss finish with Aging Toner top, 1.75 in. nut width, 25.4 in. scale, case included, mfg. summer 2012-present.

| MSR $11,999 | $9,000 | $5,200 - 6,500 | N/A | |

MSR/NOTES	100%	EXCELLENT	AVERAGE	LAST MSR

HD-28E RETRO – dreadnought-style body, solid Sitka spruce top, solid East Indian rosewood back and sides, standard "X" scalloped forward shifted bracing, round soundhole with Style 28 three-stripe rosette (5/9/5 grouping), grained ivoroid binding, bold herringbone top inlay, zigzag HD pattern back purfling, select hardwood neck with modified low oval profile with Performing Artist taper, 14/20-fret ebony fingerboard with pearl diamond and square inlays, rosewood headstock overlay with raised gold foil logo, three-per-side nickel open-geared tuners with butterbean knobs, 1930s-style ebony belly bridge with drop-in long saddle, white bridge pins with tortoise dots, beveled tortoise pickguard, Fishman F1 Aura Plus electronics, Natural polished gloss finish with Aging Toner top, 1.75 in. nut width, 25.4 in. scale, case included, mfg. summer 2012-present.

| MSR $4,499 | $3,400 | $1,950 - 2,425 | $1,175 - 1,475 | |

OM-28E RETRO – orchestra-style body, solid Sitka spruce top, solid East Indian rosewood back and sides, standard "X" scalloped bracing, round soundhole with Style 28 three-stripe rosette (5/9/5 grouping), grained ivoroid binding, bold herringbone top inlay, HD zigzag pattern back purfling, select hardwood neck with modified low oval profile and Performing Artist taper, 14/20-fret ebony fingerboard with pearl diamond and square inlays, rosewood headstock overlay with raised gold foil logo, three-per-side nickel open-geared tuners with butterbean knobs, 1930s-style ebony belly bridge with drop-in long saddle, white bridge pins with tortoise dots, beveled tortoise pickguard, Fishman F1 Aura Plus electronics, Natural polished gloss finish with Aging Toner top, 1.75 in. nut width, 25.4 in. scale, case included, mfg. summer 2012-present.

| MSR $4,499 | $3,400 | $1,950 - 2,425 | $1,175 - 1,475 | |

ACOUSTIC: ROAD SERIES

The Road Series represented Martin's most affordable all-wood guitars for many years. Guitars feature solid spruce tops, three-ply laminated mahogany or rosewood back and sides, and are available in a variety of configurations. The DM was the first Road Series guitar to debut in 1996 and several other models were introduced during the late 1990s and early 2000s. By the mid-2000s, Martin had thinned out their entry-level guitars and merged the diminishing 1 Series with the Road Series. Since these two series were so similar, they discontinued the entire 1 Series by 2006 and continued on with the Road Series through mid-2009. In mid-2009, Martin reintroduced the 1 Series and discontinued the Road Series, but the Road Series was reintroduced in 2011 with the DRS1.

00C-ME/00C-MAE THIN BODY – 00-style single cutaway thin body, solid spruce top, laminated back and sides, bold herringbone rosette, black boltaron binding, select hardwood neck with Mortise/Tenon neck joint, 14/20-fret East Indian rosewood fingerboard with Style 28 dot inlays, East Indian rosewood headstock overlay with raised gold foil logo, three-per-side chrome tuners with small buttons, East Indian rosewood bridge, black pickguard, Fishman Classic 4 Sonicore electronics, available in Natural Satin finish, 25.4 in. scale, mfg. summer 1998-2000.

| | N/A | $650 - 775 | $475 - 575 | $1,450 |

In 1999, this model was renamed the 00C-MAE.

00M – 00-style body, solid spruce top, laminated back and sides, bold herringbone rosette, black boltaron binding, select hardwood neck with Mortise/Tenon neck joint, 14/20-fret East Indian rosewood fingerboard with Style 28 dot inlays, East Indian rosewood headstock overlay with raised gold foil logo, three-per-side chrome tuners with small buttons, East Indian rosewood bridge, tortoiseshell pickguard, available in Natural Satin finish, 25.4 in. scale, mfg. winter 2001 only.

| | N/A | $425 - 500 | $275 - 325 | $925 |

000M – 000-style body, solid spruce top, laminated back and sides, bold herringbone rosette, black boltaron binding, select hardwood neck with Mortise/Tenon neck joint, 14/20-fret East Indian rosewood fingerboard with Style 28 dot inlays, East Indian rosewood headstock overlay with raised gold foil logo, three-per-side chrome tuners with small buttons, East Indian rosewood bridge, tortoiseshell pickguard, available in Natural Satin finish, 25.4 in. scale, mfg. 1997-mid 2009.

| | N/A | $525 - 625 | $325 - 400 | $1,199 |

* **000CME Cutaway Electric** – similar to the 000M, except has a single cutaway body and Fishman Classic 4 electronics, mfg. summer 1999-2000.

| | N/A | $600 - 700 | $375 - 450 | $1,300 |

* **000R Rosewood** – similar to the 000M, except has laminated rosewood back and sides, mfg. summer 1998-2000.

| | N/A | $550 - 650 | $350 - 425 | $1,099 |

DM – dreadnought style, solid spruce top, laminated back and sides, bold herringbone rosette, black boltaron binding, select hardwood neck with Mortise/Tenon neck joint, 14/20-fret East Indian rosewood fingerboard with Style 28 dot inlays, East Indian rosewood headstock overlay with raised gold foil logo, three-per-side chrome tuners with small buttons, East Indian rosewood bridge, tortoiseshell pickguard, available in Natural Satin finish, 25.4 in. scale, mfg. 1996-mid 2009.

| | N/A | $525 - 625 | $325 - 400 | $1,199 |

* **DM-12 12-String** – similar to the DM, except in 12-string configuration and six-per-side tuners, mfg. 1997-mid 2009.

| | N/A | $650 - 750 | $400 - 475 | $1,449 |

* **DCM Cutaway** – similar to the DM, except has a single cutaway, mfg. 1997-98.

| | N/A | $550 - 650 | $350 - 425 | $1,150 |

» **DCME Cutaway Electric** – similar to DCM Cutaway, except has Fishman Classic 4 Sonicore electronics, mfg. summer 1998-mid 2009.

| | N/A | $775 - 925 | $475 - 575 | $1,799 |

MSR/NOTES	100%	EXCELLENT	AVERAGE	LAST MSR

* DR Rosewood – similar to the DM, except has laminated rosewood back and sides, mfg. 1997-mid 2009.

	N/A	$625 - 725	$375 - 450	$1,399

»DCRE Rosewood Cutaway Electric – similar to the DR, except has a single cutaway and Fishman System One electronics, mfg. summer 1999 only.

	N/A	$800 - 950	$500 - 600	$1,500

DRS1 – dreadnought style, solid sapele top, back, and sides, round soundhole with single ring rosette, Rust Stratabond neck, 14/20-fret black Richlite fingerboard with white ABS dot inlays, Indian rosewood pattern HPL headstock overlay with raised gold foil logo, three-per-side chrome tuners with small buttons, black Richlite bridge, white bridge pins with black dots, black pickguard, Fishman Sonitone electronics, available in Natural Satin finish, 25.4 in. scale, mfg. 2011-present.

MSR $999	$750	$425 - 525	$275 - 325	

DRS2 – dreadnought style, solid Sitka spruce top, solid sapele top, back, and sides, round soundhole with single ring rosette, Rust Stratabond neck, 14/20-fret black Richlite fingerboard with white ABS dot inlays, Indian rosewood pattern HPL headstock overlay with raised gold foil logo, three-per-side chrome tuners with small buttons, black Richlite bridge, white bridge pins with black dots, black pickguard, Fishman Sonitone electronics, available in Natural Satin finish, 25.4 in. scale, mfg. 2012-present.

MSR $1,099	$800	$450 - 575	$275 - 350	

JM – jumbo style, solid spruce top, laminated back and sides, bold herringbone rosette, black boltaron binding, select hardwood neck with Mortise/Tenon neck joint, 14/20-fret East Indian rosewood fingerboard with Style 28 dot inlays, East Indian rosewood headstock overlay with raised gold foil logo, three-per-side chrome tuners with small buttons, East Indian rosewood bridge, tortoiseshell pickguard, available in Natural Satin finish, 25.4 in. scale, mfg. summer 1998-2002.

	N/A	$425 - 500	$300 - 350	$949

OMM – Orchestra-style (OM) body, solid spruce top, laminated back and sides, bold herringbone rosette, black boltaron binding, select hardwood neck with Mortise/Tenon neck joint, 14/20-fret East Indian rosewood fingerboard with Style 28 dot inlays, East Indian rosewood headstock overlay with raised gold foil logo, three-per-side chrome tuners with small buttons, East Indian rosewood bridge, tortoiseshell pickguard, available in Natural Satin finish, 25.4 in. scale, mfg. 2000-02.

	N/A	$400 - 475	$300 - 350	$949

ACOUSTIC: VINTAGE SERIES

0-28VS – Concert 12-fret body style, solid Sitka spruce top, solid East Indian rosewood back and sides, standard "X" scalloped bracing, round soundhole with Style 28 three-stripe rosette (5/9/5 grouping), grained ivoroid binding, fine herringbone top inlay, B/W boltaron back inlay, HD zig-zag back stripe, modified V-shaped select hardwood neck, 12/20-fret ebony fingerboard with short pattern diamond and squares inlays, slotted headstock with rosewood headstock overlay and raised gold foil logo, three-per-side Waverly nickel open-style tuners with butterbean knobs, ebony pyramid bridge with long saddle, white bridge pins with black dots, Natural polished gloss finish with Aging Toner top, 24.9 in. scale, Geib-style case included, mfg. 2009-present.

MSR $4,599	$3,500	$2,000 - 2,500	$1,200 - 1,500	

00-18V – Grand Concert body style, solid Sitka spruce top, solid mahogany back and sides, standard "X" scalloped bracing, round soundhole with old Style 18 three-stripe rosette (1/9/1 grouping), tortoise color binding, multiple-ply B/W boltaron top inlay, Style 18 back purfling, select hardwood neck, 14/20-fret ebony fingerboard with old Style 18 pearl dot inlays, rosewood headstock overlay with raised gold foil logo, three-per-side Gotoh nickel open-geared tuners with butterbean knobs, vintage ebony belly bridge with drop-in long saddle, black bridge pins with white dots, beveled tortoise pickguard, Natural polished gloss finish with Aging Toner top, 24.9 in. scale, mfg. 2003-present.

MSR $3,599	$2,700	$1,525 - 1,900	$925 - 1,150	

00-28VS – Grand Concert 12-fret body style, solid Sitka spruce top, solid East Indian rosewood back and sides, standard "X" scalloped bracing, round soundhole with Style 28 three-stripe rosette (5/9/5 grouping), grained ivoroid binding, fine herringbone top inlay, B/W boltaron back inlay, HD zig-zag back stripe, Modified V-shaped select hardwood neck, 12/20-fret ebony fingerboard with short pattern diamond and squares inlays, slotted headstock with rosewood headstock overlay and raised gold foil logo, three-per-side Waverly nickel open-style tuners with butterbean knobs, ebony pyramid bridge with long saddle, white bridge pins with black dots, Natural polished gloss finish with Aging Toner top, 24.9 in. scale, Geib-style case included, mfg. 2009-present.

MSR $4,599	$3,500	$2,000 - 2,500	$1,200 - 1,500	

000-28EC ERIC CLAPTON – Grand Auditorium body style, solid Sitka spruce top, solid East Indian rosewood back and sides, standard "X" scalloped bracing, round soundhole with bold herringbone three-stripe rosette (5/9/5 grouping), grained ivoroid binding, fine herringbone top inlay, B/W boltaron back inlay, zigzag pattern back purfling, select hardwood neck, 14/20-fret ebony fingerboard with long pattern pearl diamond and square inlays and Eric Clapton's signature in the 20th fret, rosewood headstock overlay with raised gold foil logo, three-per-side Gotoh nickel open-geared tuners with butterbean knobs, vintage ebony belly bridge with drop-in long saddle, white bridge pins with black dots, beveled tortoise pickguard, available in Natural or Sunburst polished gloss finish with Aging Toner top, 24.9 in. scale, mfg. 1997-present.

MSR $4,599	$3,500	$1,875 - 2,350	$1,125 - 1,400	

• Add 5% (MSR $4,849) for Sunburst finish.

MSR/NOTES	100%	EXCELLENT	AVERAGE	LAST MSR

000-28VS – Grand Auditorium body style, solid Sitka spruce top, solid East Indian rosewood back and sides, standard "X" scalloped bracing, round soundhole with Style 28 three-stripe rosette (5/9/5 grouping), grained ivoroid binding, bold herringbone top inlay, B/W boltaron back inlay, zigzag pattern back purfling, select hardwood neck, 12/19-fret ebony fingerboard with short pattern square and diamond pearl inlays, slotted headstock with rosewood overlay and raised gold foil logo, three-per-side Waverly nickel side-mount tuners with butterbean knobs, vintage ebony belly bridge with drop-in long saddle, white bridge pins with black dots, no pickguard, available in Natural or Sunburst polished gloss finish with Aging Toner top, 25.4 in. scale, mfg. 1999-present.

| MSR $4,499 | $3,400 | $1,850 - 2,300 | $1,150 - 1,450 | |

D-18V(M) – dreadnought body style, solid Sitka spruce top, solid mahogany back and sides, round soundhole with old Style 18 three-stripe rosette (1/9/1 grouping), tortoise color binding, multiple-ply B/W boltaron top inlay, Style 18 back purfling, select hardwood neck, 14/20-fret ebony fingerboard with old Style 18 pearl dot inlays, rosewood headstock overlay with raised gold foil logo, three-per-side Gotoh nickel open-geared tuners with butterbean knobs, vintage ebony belly bridge with drop-in long saddle, black bridge pins with white dots, beveled tortoise pickguard, Natural polished gloss finish with Aging Toner top, 25.4 in. scale, mfg. 1996-2011.

| | $2,500 | $1,500 - 1,750 | $1,050 - 1,200 | $3,349 |

The M was dropped from the D-18VM designation after 1998 and called the D-18V from 1999 through 2011.

* D-18VE Electric – similar to the D-18V(M), except has Fishman Ellipse Blend System electronics, mfg. summer 2004-06.

| | N/A | $1,550 - 1,800 | $1,050 - 1,200 | $3,499 |

D-18V(M)S – 12-fret dreadnought body style, solid Sitka spruce top, solid mahogany back and sides, round soundhole with old Style 18 three-stripe rosette (1/9/1 grouping), tortoise color binding, multiple-ply B/W boltaron top inlay, Style 18 back purfling, select hardwood neck, 12/19-fret ebony fingerboard with old Style 18 pearl dot inlays, slotted headstock with rosewood overlay and raised gold foil logo, three-per-side Waverly nickle side-mount tuners with butterbean knobs, vintage ebony belly bridge with drop-in long saddle, black bridge pins with white dots, beveled tortoise pickguard, available in Natural or Sunburst polished gloss finish with Aging Toner top, 25.4 in. scale, mfg. 1996-2011.

| | $2,900 | $1,700 - 2,000 | $1,150 - 1,325 | $3,799 |

The M was dropped from the D-18VMS designation after 1998 and called the D-18VS from 1999 through 2011.

D-28V – dreadnought body style, solid spruce top, Brazilian rosewood back and sides, scalloped X bracing, ivoroid binding, herringbone top purfling, W/B/W back stripe, slotted diamond fingerboard inlays, tortoise pickguard, Natural finish, total production of 268 instruments, mfg. 1983-85.

| | N/A | $4,750 - 5,500 | $3,250 - 3,750 | $2,600 |

HD-28V(R) – dreadnought body style, solid Sitka spruce top, solid East Indian rosewood back and sides, standard "X" scalloped forward shifted bracing, round soundhole with Style 28 three-stripe rosette (5/9/5 grouping), grained ivoroid binding, bold herringbone top inlay, B/W boltaron back inlay, zigzag pattern back purfling, select hardwood neck, 14/20-fret ebony fingerboard with pearl diamond and square inlays, rosewood headstock overlay with raised gold foil logo, three-per-side Gotoh nickel open-geared tuners with butterbean knobs, vintage ebony belly bridge with drop-in long saddle, white bridge pins with tortoise dots, beveled tortoise pickguard, Natural polished gloss finish with Aging Toner top, 25.4 in. scale, mfg. 1996-present.

| MSR $4,399 | $3,300 | $1,800 - 2,250 | $1,075 - 1,350 | |

Before 1996 and before the Vintage Series was created, this model existed as the Custom HD-28 (See Standard Dreadnought Series). The R was dropped from the HD-28VR designation after 1998 and called the HD-28V from 1999 to the present.

* HD-28VE Electric – similar to the HD-28V(R), except has Fishman Ellipse Blend System electronics, mfg. summer 2004-06.

| | N/A | $1,875 - 2,350 | $1,125 - 1,400 | $4,199 |

* HD-28LSV Large Soundhole – similar to the HD-28V(R), except has a large soundhole, no fingerboard inlays, nickel enclosed tuners with large buttons, and black bridge pins with abalone dots, mfg. 1998-mid-2005.

| | N/A | $2,100 - 2,500 | $1,400 - 1,700 | $4,149 |

This model is based on a 1934 D-28 once owned by Clarence White (Kentucky Colonels).

HD-28VS – 12-fret dreadnought body style, solid Sitka spruce top, solid East Indian rosewood back and sides, standard "X" scalloped bracing, round soundhole with Style 28 three-stripe rosette (5/9/5 grouping), grained ivoroid binding, bold herringbone top inlay, B/W boltaron back inlay, zigzag pattern back purfling, select hardwood neck, 12/19-fret ebony fingerboard with long pattern square and diamond pearl inlays, slotted headstock with rosewood overlay and raised gold foil logo, three-per-side Waverly nickel side-mount tuners with butterbean knobs, vintage ebony belly bridge with drop-in long saddle, white bridge pins with tortoise dots, beveled tortoise pickguard, available in Natural or Sunburst polished gloss finish with Aging Toner top, 25.4 in. scale, mfg. 1996-present.

| MSR $4,449 | $3,300 | $1,850 - 2,300 | $1,100 - 1,375 | |

Before 1996 and before the Vintage Series was created, this model existed as the Custom HD-28S (See Standard Dreadnought Series).

D-45V(R) – dreadnought body style, solid Sitka spruce top, solid East Indian rosewood back and sides, round soundhole with Style 45 three-stripe abalone pearl rosette (5/9/5 grouping), grained ivoroid binding, abalone pearl with B/W/B boltaron top and side inlay, abalone pearl with B/W boltaron back inlay, Style 45 back purfling, select hardwood neck, 14/20-fret grained ivoroid-bound ebony fingerboard with Style 45 select abalone pearl snowflake inlays, grained ivoroid-bound rosewood headstock overlay with abalone pearl vertical block Martin logo, three-per-side Gotoh gold open-geared tuners with butterbean knobs, vintage ebony belly bridge with drop-in long saddle, white bridge pins with ablone pearl dots, beveled tortoise pickguard, available in Natural or Sunburst polished gloss finish with Aging Toner top, 25.4 in. scale, mfg. 1997-present.

| MSR $11,599 | $8,700 | $5,000 - 6,250 | N/A | |

The R was dropped from the D-45VR designation after 1998 and called the D-45V from 1999 to the present.

MSR/NOTES	100%	EXCELLENT	AVERAGE	LAST MSR

* **D-45V Brazilian** – similar to D-45V(R), except has Brazilian rosewood back and sides, mfg. 1983-85.

	N/A	$11,000 - 13,500	$7,000 - 8,500	

OM-18V – orchestra body style, solid Sitka spruce top, solid mahogany back and sides, round soundhole with old Style 18 three-stripe rosette (1/9/1 grouping), tortoise color binding, multiple-ply B/W boltaron top inlay, Style 18 back purfling, select hardwood neck, 14/20-fret ebony fingerboard with old Style 18 pearl dot inlays, rosewood headstock overlay with raised gold foil logo, three-per-side Gotoh nickel open-geared tuners with butterbean knobs, vintage ebony belly bridge with drop-in long saddle, black bridge pins with white dots, beveled tortoise pickguard, Natural polished gloss finish with Aging Toner top, 25.4 in. scale, mfg. 1999-mid-2008.

	N/A	$1,525 - 1,900	$925 - 1,150	$3,199

OM-28V(R) – orchestra body style, solid Sitka spruce top, solid East Indian rosewood back and sides, standard "X" scalloped bracing, round soundhole with Style 28 three-stripe rosette (5/9/5 grouping), grained ivoroid binding, bold herringbone top inlay, B/W boltaron back inlay, zigzag pattern back purfling, select hardwood neck, 14/20-fret ebony fingerboard with pearl diamond and square inlays, rosewood headstock overlay with raised gold foil logo, three-per-side Gotoh nickel open-geared tuners with butterbean knobs, vintage ebony belly bridge with drop-in long saddle, white bridge pins with tortoise dots, beveled tortoise pickguard, Natural polished gloss finish with Aging Toner top, 25.4 in. scale, mfg. 1996-present.

MSR $4,399	$3,300	$1,800 - 2,250	$1,075 - 1,350	

The R was dropped from the OM-28VR designation after 1998 and called the OM-28V from 1999 to the present.

ACOUSTIC: X SERIES

Martin's X Series guitars were introduced in summer 1998 and they feature a High Pressure Laminate (HPL) for several parts of the guitar. This series was created because Martin wanted to start using alternative materials in their guitar building process and they also wanted to offer a guitar that even the beginner could afford. All X Series guitars feature traditional Martin designs using the HPL technology. HPL is composed of highly compressed wood fibers that are pre-finished and textured once they are constructed. This provides the guitars with an authentic looking wood finish and texture that guitar players come to expect. The material is also very durable. In mid-2009, Martin began using black Richlite for all bridges and fingerboards in the X Series that replaced earlier Indian rosewood and black micarta versions. In mid-2010, Martin introduced Fisman Sonitone electronics on all previous acoustic instruments meaning every guitar in the X Series is now an acoustic/electric. Models that were previously acoustic now have an "AE" suffix, and they also added these electronics without raising the price

00CXMAE CUTAWAY ELECTRIC – 00-style single cutaway body, HPL spruce patterned top, HPL mahogany patterned textured back and sides, herringbone decal rosette, natural Stratabond neck, 14/20-fret black Micarta fingerboard with no inlays, HPL mahogany patterned headstock overlay, three-per-side chrome tuners, black Micarta bridge, no pickguard, Fishman Classic 4 Sonicore electronics, available in Natural semi-gloss finish, 25.4 in. scale, mfg. 2000-summer 2001.

	N/A	$400 - 475	$275 - 325	$799

* **00CXAE Color (Red/Navy/Black) Cutaway Electric** – similar to the 00CXMAE Cutaway Electric, except has Black, Navy (mfg. 2000-summer 2001), or Red (mfg. 2000-summer 2001) HPL top, back, sides, and headstock overlay, mfg. 2000-mid-2013.

	$700	$400 - 500	$275 - 325	$949

* **00CXRAE Cutaway Electric** – similar to the 00CXMAE Cutaway Electric, except has HPL rosewood patterned textured back and sides and a HPL rosewood patterned headstock overlay, mfg. 2000-summer 2001.

	N/A	$400 - 475	$275 - 325	$799

00CX1AE BLACK CUTAWAY ELECTRIC – 00-style single cutaway body, solid spruce top, HPL black satin back and sides, herringbone decal rosette, natural Stratabond neck, 14/20-fret black Micarta fingerboard with no inlays, HPL black headstock overlay, three-per-side chrome tuners, black Micarta bridge, no pickguard, Fishman Prefix Pro electronics, available in Natural semi-gloss finish, 25.4 in. scale, mfg. 2003-05.

	N/A	$425 - 500	$275 - 325	$999

00X1/00X1AE JAVA MAHOGANY – 00-sized grand concert body, solid Sitka spruce top, "Java Mahogany" HPL figured wood grain laminate back and sides, round soundhole with grained ivoroid multi-ply rosette, natural Stratabond neck, 14/20-fret rosewood (2007-mid-2009) or black Richlite (mid-2009-present) fingerboard, "Java Mahogany" headstock overlay, three-per-side chrome tuners, rosewood (2007-mid-2009) or black Richlite (mid-2009-2011) bridge, tortoise pickguard, Fishman Sonitone electronics (Model 00X1AE, summer 2010-2011), available in Natural finish, 25.4 in. scale, mfg. 2007-2011.

	$500	$300 - 350	$175 - 225	$719

000XM – 000-style body, HPL spruce patterned top, HPL mahogany patterned textured back and sides, black and gold herringbone-style rosette, select hardwood neck, 14/20-fret East Indian rosewood fingerboard with no inlays, HPL mahogany patterned headstock overlay, three-per-side chrome tuners, East Indian rosewood bridge, tortoiseshell pickguard, available in Natural semi-gloss finish, 25.4 in. scale, mfg. 1999-2000.

	N/A	$275 - 325	$150 - 200	$599

* **000XE Black Electric** – similar to the 000XM, except has a HPL Jett Black top, back, and sides, a HPL Jett Black headstock overlay, no pickguard, and Fishman Prefix Pro electronics, mfg. summer 2001-summer-2005.

	N/A	$425 - 500	$325 - 375	$929

» **000CXE Black Cutaway Electric** – similar to the 000XE, except has a single cutaway, mfg. 2002-mid-2013.

	$800	$450 - 550	$275 - 325	$1,049

MSR/NOTES	100%	EXCELLENT	AVERAGE	LAST MSR

000X1/000X1AE – 000-style body, solid Sitka spruce top, HPL mahogany patterned textured back and sides, multiple B/W boltaron rosette with red fiber, rust Stratabond neck, 14/20-fret East Indian rosewood (2000-mid-2009) or black Richlite (mid-2009-present) fingerboard with no inlays, HPL mahogany patterned headstock overlay, three-per-side chrome tuners with small buttons, belly-style East Indian rosewood (2000-mid-2009) or black Richlite (mid-2009-present) bridge, tortoiseshell pickguard, Fishman Sonitone electronics (Model 00X1AE, summer 2010-present), available in Natural semi-gloss finish, 25.4 in. scale, mfg. summer 2000-present.

MSR $749	$550	$300 - 375	$175 - 225	

* **000CX1E Cutaway Electric** – similar to the 000X1, except has a single cutaway body and Fishman Pro Prefix electronics, mfg. 2002 only.

	N/A	$475 - 550	$350 - 400	$1,049

000X1RGT – Grand Auditorium 000 14-fret-style body, solid Sitka spruce top, HPL Indian rosewood patterned textured back and sides, A-Frame X-1 bracing, round soundhole with Style 28 three-ring rosette overlay (5/9/5 grouping), natural Stratabond modified low oval neck, 14/20-fret black micarta (first half of 2009 only) or black Richlite (mid-2009-summer-2010) fingerboard with no inlays, HPL Indian rosewood patterned headstock overlay, three-per-side chrome tuners with small buttons, black micarta (first half of 2009 only) or black Richlite (mid-2009-summer 2010) belly bridge with drop-in saddle, white bridge pins with black dots, tortoise pickguard, available in Natural polished gloss finish, 25.4 in. scale, mfg. 2009-summer 2010.

	$700	$450 - 525	$325 - 375	$999

* **000CX1RGTE Cutaway Electric** – similar to the 000X1RGT, except has a single smooth cutaway and Fishman Aero electronics, available in Natural polished gloss finish, mfg. summer 2009-summer 2010.

	$900	$575 - 675	$375 - 450	$1,299

DXM/DXMAE – dreadnought body style, HPL spruce pattern top, HPL textured mahogany pattern back and sides, gold and black herringbone-style rosette, rust Stratabond neck, 14/20-fret Morado (early models), East Indian rosewood (disc. mid-2009), or black Richlite (mid-2009-present) fingerboard, HPL mahogany pattern headstock overlay, three-per-side chrome tuners with small buttons, Morado (early models) East Indian rosewood (disc. mid-2009), or black Richlite (mid-2009-present) bridge, tortoiseshell pickguard, Fishman Sonitone electronics (Model DXMAE, summer 2010-present), available in Natural semi-gloss finish, 25.4 in. scale, mfg. summer 1998-present.

MSR $699	$500	$275 - 350	$150 - 200	

* **D12XM 12-String** – similar to the DXM, except in 12-string configuration and six-per-side tuners, mfg. 1999-summer 2000.

	N/A	$325 - 400	$200 - 250	$699

* **DCXE Black Cutaway Electric** – similar to the DXM, except has a single cutaway, Jett Black top, back, and sides, a Jett Black headstock overlay, and Fishman Prefix Pro electronics, mfg. summer 2001-mid-2013.

	$800	$450 - 550	$275 - 325	$1,049

* **DCXM Cutaway** – similar to the DXM, except has a single cutaway body, mfg. first half of 1999 only.

	N/A	$300 - 375	$200 - 250	$699

»**DCXME Cutaway Electric** – similar to the DCXM, except has Fishman Classic 4 Sonicore electronics, mfg. summer 1999-2001.

	N/A	$350 - 425	$250 - 300	$769

* **DXB Black** – similar to the DXM, except has a black top, back, and sides, Macassar ebony fingerboard, black headstock overlay, and Macassar bridge, available in Gloss Black finish, mfg. 1999 only.

	N/A	$350 - 400	$225 - 275	$649

* **DXBR Brazilian Rosewood** – similar to the DXM, except has HPL Brazilian rosewood grained back and sides, available in Natural gloss finish, mfg. 1999 only.

	N/A	$350 - 425	$225 - 275	$749

* **DXME Electric** – similar to the DXM, except has Fishman Classic 4 Sonicore electronics, available in Natural semi-gloss finish, mfg. summer 1998-2012.

	$650	$350 - 450	$200 - 250	$869

* **DXR Rosewood** – similar to the DXM, except has laminated rosewood back and sides, mfg. 1999 only.

	N/A	$275 - 325	$150 - 200	$649

DX1/DX1AE – dreadnought body style, solid Sitka spruce top, HPL textured mahogany pattern back and sides, multiple B/W boltaron rosette with red fiber, rust Stratabond neck, 14/20-fret East Indian rosewood (2000-mid-2009) or black Richlite (mid-2009-present) fingerboard, HPL mahogany pattern headstock overlay, three-per-side chrome tuners with small buttons, East Indian rosewood (2000-mid-2009) or black Richlite (mid-2009-present) bridge, tortoiseshell pickguard, Fisman Sonitone electronics (Model DX1AE, summer 2010-present), available in Natural semi-gloss finish, 25.4 in. scale, mfg. 2000-present.

MSR $749	$550	$300 - 375	$175 - 225	

* **D12X1/D12X1AE 12-String** – similar to the DX1, except in 12-string configuration and six-per-side tuners, mfg. summer 2000-present.

MSR $849	$650	$350 - 450	$200 - 250	

* **DX1E Electric** – similar to DX1, except has Fishman Classic 4 Sonicore electronics, mfg. 2006-2012.

	$700	$375 - 475	$225 - 275	$929

MSR/NOTES	100%	EXCELLENT	AVERAGE	LAST MSR

»DCX1E Cutaway Electric – similar to the DX1E Electric, except has a single cutaway, mfg. summer 2000-mid-2012.

	$700	$450 - 525	$300 - 350	$999

***DX1K/DX1KAE Koa** – similar to the DX1, except has HPL koa back and sides, and a HPL koa headstock overlay, mfg. 2004-present.

MSR $749	$550	$300 - 375	$175 - 225	

»DCX1KE Koa Cutaway Electric – similar to the DX1K Koa, except has a single cutaway and Classic 4 Sonicore electronics, mfg. 2004-mid-2012.

	$700	$450 - 525	$300 - 350	$999

***DX1R/DX1RAE Rosewood** – similar to the DX1, except has HPL Indian rosewood back and sides, and a HPL Indian rosewood headstock overlay, mfg. 2001-present.

MSR $749	$550	$300 - 375	$175 - 225	

»DCX1RE Rosewood Cutaway Electric – similar to the DX1R Rosewood, except has a single cutaway and Fishman Classic 4 Sonicore electronics, mfg. 2004-mid-2012.

	$700	$450 - 525	$300 - 350	$999

»DCX1RGTE Rosewood Gloss Top Cutaway Electric – similar to the DX1RGT Rosewood Gloss Top, except has a single smooth cutaway and Fishman Aero electronics, available in Natural polished gloss finish, mfg. summer 2009-summer 2010.

	$900	$575 - 675	$375 - 450	$1,299

»DX1RGT Rosewood Gloss Top – similar to the DX1R, except has a Style 28 rosette, black micarta fingerboard with Style 28 mini inlays, and a Natural gloss finish, mfg. 2008-summer 2010.

	$700	$450 - 525	$300 - 350	$999

DX1 TAWNY SATINWOOD – dreadnought style, solid Sitka spruce top, "Tawny Satinwood" HPL figured wood grain laminate back and sides, round soundhole with rosewood, maple and koa Art Deco rosette, natural Stratabond neck, 14/20-fret rosewood fingerboard with Style 45 maple hexagon inlays, "Tawny Satinwood" headstock overlay, three-per-side chrome tuners, rosewood bridge, available in Natural finish, 25.4 in. scale, mfg. 2007-mid-2009.

	N/A	$450 - 525	$300 - 350	$999

***DXC1E Tawny Satinwood** – similar to the DX1 Satin Tawnywood, except has a single cutaway Fishman Classic 4T electronics, mfg. summer 2007-mid-2009.

	N/A	$600 - 700	$350 - 425	$1,349

DXK2/DXK2AE – dreadnought body style, HPL Hawaiian koa patterned top, HPL Hawaiian koa patterned back and sides, gold and black herringbone-style rosette, natural Stratabond neck, 14/20-fret East Indian rosewood (mid-2002-mid-2009) or black Richlite (mid-2009-present) fingerboard, HPL koa pattern headstock overlay, three-per-side chrome tuners with small buttons, East Indian rosewood (mid-2002-mid-2009) or black Richlite (mid-2009-present) bridge, no pickguard, Fisman Sonitone electronics (Model DXK2AE, summer 2010-present), available in Natural semi-gloss finish, 25.4 in. scale, mfg. summer 2002-present.

MSR $699	$500	$275 - 350	$150 - 200	

OMCX1KE – 000-style single cutaway body, solid Sitka spruce top, textured HPL koa patterned back and sides, multiple B/W boltaron rosette with red fiber, natural Stratabond neck, 14/20-fret East Indian rosewood (2008-mid-2009) or black Richlite (mid-2009-present) fingerboard with no inlays, HPL koa patterned headstock overlay with standard logo, three-per-side chrome tuners with small buttons, belly East Indian rosewood (2008-mid-2009) or black Richlite (mid-2009-2012) bridge, no pickguard, Fishman Classic 4T electronics, available in Natural finish, 25.4 in. scale, mfg. 2008-2012.

	$800	$450 - 550	$275 - 325	$1,099

OMCXK2E – 000-style single cutaway body, HPL koa patterned top, HPL textured koa patterned back and sides, gold and black herringbone decal rosette, natural Stratabond neck, 14/20-fret East Indian rosewood fingerboard, HPL koa wood pattern headstock overlay and printed logo, three-per-side chrome tuners with small knobs, belly-style East Indian rosewood bridge, Fishman Classic 4T electronics, 25.4 in. scale, mfg. summer 2006-mid-2009.

	N/A	$475 - 550	$275 - 325	$1,049

ORIGINS – dreadnought body style, HPL top, HPL textured Indian rosewood pattern back and sides, X-Series solid Sitka spruce bracing, round soundhole, rust Stratabond modified low profile neck, 14/20-fret black Richlite fingerboard, HPL Indian rosewood pattern headstock overlay, three-per-side chrome tuners with small buttons, black Richlite belly bridge, white bridge pins with black dots, available in Natural Satin finish with a custom graphic top designed by Robert F. Goetzl, 25.4 in. scale, 300 Series case included, mfg. first half of 2010 only.

	$700	$450 - 525	$300 - 350	$999

ACOUSTIC: ARCHTOP C, F, & R SERIES

Martin was one of the first guitar companies to start producing acoustic archtop guitars in the early 1930s. Other large manufacturers including Gibson and Epiphone were also experimenting with these violin-inspired designs and Martin saw archtops as an opportunity. Instead of developing an entirely new line of guitars, they simply modified their existing models with arched tops and backs. The first archtops were based on Martin's new OM-style body and were labeled "C" models. The entry level "R" Series of archtops was introduced

MSR/NOTES	100%	EXCELLENT	AVERAGE	LAST MSR

in 1932 and were based on Martin's Grand Concert 00-style body. In 1935, Martin introduced a third variation with their top-of-the-line F Series that were based on an enlarged Grand Auditorium 000-style body (the F model was actually closer in size to Martin's 0000-size body; however, that variation wasn't introduced until several years later). Unfortunately, Martin's archtops encountered several problems that doomed their success. The guitars were too small in comparison to other archtops and they did not produced enough sound. The sound of Martin's archtops is also very unique as they used predominately rosewood and mahogany back and sides as opposed to the more popular maple. The guitars themselves were actually hard to play - instead of designing a new guitar for archtops, Martin simply added an arched top. The problem was that the neck was tilted back at an extreme angle to clear to the higher top and that made the guitar difficult to play.

Tailpiece variations were common on all of Martin's archtop guitars.

Size C dimensions: 15 in. lower bout width, 4 3/16 in. body depth, 19.375 in. body length, and 24.9 in. scale.

Size F dimensions: 16 in. lower bout width, 4.125 in. body depth, 20.125 in. body length, and 24.9 in. scale.

Size R dimensions: 14.625 in. lower bout width, 4.25 in. body depth, 18.875 in. body length, and 24.9 in. scale.

Martin also produced two **F-5** guitars that featured a maple body (1940 only), two **R-15** prototypes that featured maple or birch back and sides (1934), and one **R-21** with rosewood back and sides (1938).

C-1 – Grand Auditorium 000-style body, carved spruce top, arched mahogany back, mahogany sides, round soundhole (1931-34) or two f-holes (1932-1942), black outer layer body binding (1931-35) or three-ply binding with outer ivoroid layer (1935-1942), mahogany neck, 14/20-fret unbound rosewood (1931-34) or ebony (1934-1942) fingerboard with white dot inlays, vertical pearl Martin (1931-32) or CF Martin (1932-34) logo inlay or decal (1934-1942) on headstock, three-per-side nickel tuners, rosewood bridge, trapeze tailpiece, raised black pickguard, available in Sunburst finish, total production of 1,235 instruments (449 with round soundhole, 786 with f-holes), mfg. 1931-1942.

1931-1934 Round Soundhole	N/A	$2,400 - 3,000	$1,450 - 1,800	
1932-1942 F-Holes	N/A	$2,200 - 2,750	$1,325 - 1,650	

Martin also produced one C-1 12-string with a round soundhole (1932). The C-1 has features that are similar to Martin's Style 18 appointments.

* **C-1P Plectrum** – similar to the C-1, except in four-string plectrum configuration with two-per-side tuners and a 27 in. scale, total production of 10 instruments (nine with a round soundhole and one with f-holes), mfg. 1931-33, 1939.

	N/A	N/A	N/A	

Extreme rarity precludes accurate pricing.

* **C-1T Tenor** – similar to the C-1, except in four-string tenor configuration with two-per-side tuners, total production of 154 instruments (71 with a round soundhole and 83 with f-holes), mfg. 1931-38.

1931-1933 Round Soundhole	N/A	$2,200 - 2,750	$1,325 - 1,650	
1933-1938 F-Holes	N/A	$2,000 - 2,500	$1,200 - 1,500	

C-2 – Grand Auditorium 000-style body, carved spruce top, arched Brazilian rosewood back, Brazilian rosewood sides, round soundhole (1931-33) or two f-holes (1932-1942), three-ply body binding with outer ivoroid layer, 14/20-fret unbound (1931-35) or ivoroid-bound (1935-1942) ebony fingerboard with slotted diamond inlays (1931-35) or hexagaonal inlays starting at the third fret (1939-1942), unbound headstock overlay with vertical CF Martin logo, three-per-side nickel tuners, rosewood bridge, trapeze tailpiece, raised unbound (1931-35) or ivoroid-bound (1935-1942) plastic black pickguard, available in Darkened top (1931-34) or shaded (1934-1942) finish, total production of 709 instruments (269 with round soundhole, 440 with f-holes), mfg. 1931-1942.

1931-1933 Round Soundhole	N/A	$3,600 - 4,500	$2,150 - 2,700	
1932-1942 F-Holes	N/A	$3,400 - 4,250	$2,050 - 2,550	

Martin also produced one C-2 12-String (1932, f-hole configuration), and two C-2P plectrum models (1931). The C-2 has features that are similar to Martin's Style 28 appointments.

* **C-2T Tenor** – similar to the C-2, except in four-string tenor configuration with two-per-side tuners, total production of 17 instruments (15 with a round soundhole and 2 with f-holes), mfg. 1931-34, 1936.

	N/A	N/A	N/A	

Extreme rarity precludes accurate pricing.

C-3 – Grand Auditorium 000-style body, carved spruce top, arched Brazilian rosewood back, Brazilian rosewood sides, round soundhole (1931-33) or two f-holes (1933-34), five-ply top body binding with outer ivoroid layer, zipper pattern back stripe, 14/20-fret ivoroid-bound ebony fingerboard with snowflake inlays starting at the first fret, ivoroid-bound headstock overlay with vertical CF Martin logo, three-per-side gold tuners, rosewood bridge, gold trapeze tailpiece, raised unbound (1931-33) plastic pickguard with pearl inlays and B/W plastic bordering (1933-34), available in Darkened top finish, total production of 111 instruments (53 with round soundhole, 58 with f-holes), mfg. 1931-34.

1931-1933 Round Soundhole	N/A	$6,000 - 7,000	$4,000 - 5,000	
1933-1934 F-Holes	N/A	$5,500 - 6,500	$3,700 - 4,500	

Martin also produced one C-3T with a tenor neck (1934). The C-3 has features that are similar to Martin's Style 45 appointments.

F-1 – Grand Auditorium-style body, carved spruce top, arched mahogany back, mahogany sides, two f-holes, three-ply top and back body binding with outer ivoroid layer, mahogany neck, 14/20-fret unbound ebony fingerboard with white dot inlays, unbound headstock overlay with standard decal logo, three-per-side nickel tuners, adj. ebony bridge, nickel-plated trapeze tailpiece, raised black pickguard, available in dark back and sides with a Shaded top finish, total production of 91 instruments, mfg. 1940-42.

	N/A	$1,800 - 2,250	$1,200 - 1,500	

Martin also produced one F-1S 12-string (1941). The F-1 has features that are similar to Martin's Style 18 appointments.

MSR/NOTES	100%	EXCELLENT	AVERAGE	LAST MSR

F-2 – Grand Auditorium-style body, carved spruce top, arched Brazilian rosewood back, Brazilian rosewood sides, two f-holes, three-ply top and back body binding with outer ivoroid layer, zigzag back stripe, mahogany neck, 14/20-fret ivoroid-bound ebony fingerboard with pearl hexagonal inlays starting at the third fret, unbound headstock overlay with vertical CF Martin logo, three-per-side nickel tuners, adj. ebony bridge, nickel-plated trapeze tailpiece, raised ivoroid-bound black pickguard, available in dark back and sides with a Shaded top finish, total production of 47 instruments, mfg. 1940-42.

| | N/A | $2,200 - 2,750 | $1,325 - 1,650 | |

One F-2 was produced with maple back and sides (1941). The F-2 has features that are similar to Martin's Style 28 appointments.

F-7 – Grand Auditorium-style body, carved spruce top, arched Brazilian rosewood back, Brazilian rosewood sides, two f-holes, seven-ply top body binding with outer ivoroid layer, multi-ply back binding, zipper back stripe, mahogany neck, 14/20-fret ivoroid-bound ebony fingerboard with pearl (1935-37) or pearloid (1937-1942) hexagonal inlays starting at the third fret, three-ply headstock binding with outer ivoroid layer, vertical CF Martin logo, three-per-side nickel tuners, adj. ebony bridge, nickel-plated trapeze tailpiece, raised ivoroid-bound black pickguard, available in dark back and sides with a Shaded top finish, total production of 187 instruments, mfg. 1935-1942.

| | N/A | $6,000 - 7,500 | $3,600 - 4,500 | |

One F-7S guitar was produced with a round soundhole (1936).

F-9 – Grand Auditorium-style body, carved spruce top, arched Brazilian rosewood back, Brazilian rosewood sides, two f-holes, seven-ply top body binding with outer ivoroid layer, multi-ply back binding, zipper back stripe, mahogany neck, 14/20-fret ivoroid-bound ebony fingerboard with W/BW inlays near the edge and pearl or pearloid hexagonal inlays starting at the first fret, three-ply headstock binding with outer ivoroid layer, vertical CF Martin logo, three-per-side gold tuners, adj. ebony bridge, gold-plated trapeze tailpiece, raised black pickguard with three-ply binding and outer ivoroid layer, available in dark back and sides with a Shaded Golden Brown top finish, total production of 72 instruments, mfg. 1935-1942.

| | N/A | $12,000 - 15,000 | $7,200 - 9,000 | |

R-17 – Grand Concert-style body, arched mahogany top and back, mahogany sides, two three-piece (1934-37) or one-piece (1937-1942) f-holes, 14/20-fret rosewood fingerboard with white dot inlays, unbound headstock with decal logo, three-per-side nickel single unit tuners, rosewood bridge, nickel-plated trapeze tailpiece, raised black pickguard, available in dark back and sides with a Golden Brown Sunburst top finish, total production of 940 instruments, mfg. 1934-1942.

| | N/A | $1,400 - 1,750 | $1,000 - 1,150 | |

R-18 – Grand Concert-style body, arched (1933-37) or carved (1937-1942) spruce top, arched mahogany back, mahogany sides, round soundhole (1933 only) or two three-piece (1933-37) or one-piece (1937-1942) f-holes, four-ply body binding with outer black layer, 14/20-fret rosewood fingerboard with white dot inlays, unbound headstock with decal logo, three-per-side nickel single unit tuners, rosewood bridge, nickel-plated trapeze tailpiece, raised tortoiseshell or black pickguard, available in dark back and sides with a Golden Brown Sunburst top finish, total production of 1,927 instruments (approx. 400 produced with round soundhole), mfg. 1933-1942.

| 1933 Round Soundhole | N/A | $2,000 - 2,500 | $1,300 - 1,600 | |
| 1933-1942 F-Holes | N/A | $1,800 - 2,250 | $1,200 - 1,500 | |

Martin also produced four R-18P guitars in plectrum configuration (1934-36). The first few R-18 archtop guitars were actually stamped 00-18S. In 1933, the R-18 retailed for $55 plus $8 for a hardshell case.

* **R-18T Tenor** – similar to the R-18, except in four-string tenor configuration with two-per-side tuners, total production of 133 instruments, mfg. 1934-1941.

| | N/A | $1,400 - 1,750 | $850 - 1,050 | |

ACOUSTIC: GUITAR OF THE MONTH/YEAR

Wherever possible, both pricing and the number of instruments made are provided in the individual listings. Where N/As appear, accurate secondary marketplace pricing cannot be provided, since these instruments do not trade sufficiently enough to list pricing.

The models listed below are in chronological sequence (the original year of manufacture appears after the model name).

As customer demand opened up for specified, limited edition models, Martin announced the Guitar of the Month program in October, 1984. This ambitious plan to offer an announced custom-built limited edition model every month was scaled back to four or five models per year. This program continued through 1994, when Martin switched to annual offerings of limited/special editions. Between 1984 and 1985, Guitar of the Month models had special paper labels signed by C.F. Martin III and C.F. Martin IV. Special/limited editions after 1986 are signed by C.F. Martin IV (unless otherwise listed below).

Some Guitar of the Month models are built in a "fixed," predetermined production amount, while others may be "open-ended" and are limited to the number sold (or ordered) through the calender year.

Prior to 1995, these Limited Edition models were labeled separately for domestic (U.S.) and foreign markets: a model may be #1 of 100 in the U.S., while the next model may be numbered #1 of 12 (overseas). Thus, the total production may be 112 for this model (and not the number given on the U.S. label). Separate foreign label editions are marked with a (*). In 1995, Martin began to issue one label worldwide.

Martin special editions are typically commemorative models which pay tribute to those Martin models which have been historically significant - these include the Golden Era Series, certified wood models, and other special editions. Special editions do not have a total quantity assigned to each variation, and are made as demand dictates. Limited editions are usually associated with a particular artist or event, and the quantity of each variation is usually determined at the time of release. In many cases, a portion of the sales go to charities of the artist's choice. Limited editions are usually made for a limited time and are available until the variation

MSR/NOTES	100%	EXCELLENT	AVERAGE	LAST MSR

sells out. Sometimes, a sellout can occur in a few weeks (i.e., Jimmy Buffet Signature HD-18JB 1998), while other guitars may not sell out for years.

Whenever possible, the year a special/limited edition was introduced is listed after the model name in parentheses. In many cases, these instruments will continue to be listed on Martin's price sheets until they are sold out. On recently manufactured special and limited editions, unless the model is marked special edition in parentheses after the model name, you can assume that the model is a limited edition.

Guitar of the Month models are usually identified with a suffix. For example, a HD-28BLE (1990) is an HD-28 with Brazilian rosewood back and sides. Due to the limited production numbers (and fierce loyalty of Martin guitar owners), these specialty guitars trade only infrequently in the acoustic vintage market. Most models encountered are in Excellent to Mint condition (i.e. well cared for).

For readers new to Martin products, please note: Aging Toner finish, or a " Toned Top" model refers to the golden-toned lacquer that is shot on the top (soundboard) of the guitar. The following models are listed as to the features that differ from similarly designated stock models (for that year).

A special note from Martin: "As a general rule, Martin has produced two prototypes of each limited edition in order to develop model specifications and help determine production costs. Generally these prototypes are not for sale. However, due to factory space constrictions, many prototypes have already or eventually may be sold." When buying/selling/trading these rare Martin factory prototypes, it is recommended that you get as much original paperwork as possible to establish provenance, as well as documenting legal ownership.

The source material for Martin's Guitar of the Month series is courtesy of Dick Boak, Martin Guitar Company. Additional detailed information can be found in Jim Washburn and Richard Johnson's *Martin Guitars: An Illustrated Celebration of America's Premier Guitarmaker*, Rodale Books, 1997; or Walter Carter's *The Martin Book: A Complete History of Martin Guitars*, GPI Books, 1995).

Whenever possible, pricing (including original MSRs) and the number of instruments are listed for the following models, whether they are guitars of the month, special editions, or limited editions. N/As indicate that the rarity factor and lack of activity in the secondary marketplace (especially those older models with high demand) preclude accurate pricing.

As a rule of thumb, many instruments listed in this section that are five years or older are typically worth at least 65%-75% value at the time of production, but there are exceptions (i.e. Eric Clapton, etc.). It is recommended that you follow this niche marketplace by studying dealer listings and the Internet and eBay for possible listings and current prices. Remember, even though some of these special models are relatively rare and now almost twenty years old, it doesn't necessarily mean that they are valued higher than a similar current production model with the same appointments and features. One exception is any model made with Brazilian rosewood, as values for this South American tone wood have skyrocketed in recent years.

00-18V (GOM, OCTOBER, 1984) – Grand Concert 00-style body, tortoise binding, ebony fingerboard, gold tuners, tortoise pickguard, ebony bridge, Natural finish with Aging Toner top, 25.4 in. scale, limited edition run of nine instruments, mfg. 1984 only.

N/A	$1,675 - 2,100	$1,000 - 1,250	$1,520

00-21LE (GOM, SEPTEMBER, 1987) – Grand Concert 14-fret 00-style body, scalloped bracing, herringbone rosette, tortoise binding, 14-fret ebony fingerboard, slotted headstock, three-per-side tuners with pearloid buttons, rectangular ebony bridge, black bridgepins with white dots, optional tortoise pickguard, Natural finish with Aging Toner top, 24.9 in.scale, limited edition run of 19 instruments (18 domestic, 1 foreign), mfg. 1987 only.

N/A	$2,200 - 2,750	$1,325 - 1,650	$2,350

D3-18 (GOM, 1991) – dreadnought 14-fret-style body, three-piece back, white purfling, tortoise-bound ebony fingerboard with MOP diamonds and squares inlay, three-per-side chrome tuners with embossed "M" on buttons, diamond inlays on bridge ends, black bridgepins with white dots, tortoise pickguard, Natural finish with Aging Toner top, limited edition run of 80 instruments (72 domestic, 8 foreign), mfg. 1991 only.

N/A	$1,600 - 2,000	$950 - 1,200	$2,398

D-18LE (1986-1987, LIMITED EDITION) – dreadnought-style body, quilted or flamed mahogany back and sides, scalloped bracing, tortoise binding, herringbone backstrip, V-shaped neck, ebony fingerboard, three-per-side gold tuners with ebony buttons, ebony bridge, black bridge pins with white dots, tortoiseshell pickguard, available in Natural finish, limited edition run of 30 instruments, 1986-87.

N/A	$1,800 - 2,250	$1,075 - 1,350	

D-18MB (GOM, 1990) – dreadnought-style body, Engelmann spruce top (the underside of the top is signed by the foreman at the Martin factory), X-bracing, flamed maple binding/backstrip/peghead veneer, ebony tuner buttons, white bridgepins with red dots, Natural finish with Aging Toner top, limited edition run of 99 instruments (96 domestic, 3 foreign), mfg. 1990 only.

N/A	$2,000 - 2,500	$1,200 - 1,500	$2,300

D-18 SPECIAL (D-18 GOM, 1989) – dreadnought-style body, scalloped braces, rosewood binding, low profile neck, diamonds and squares fingerboard inlay, three-per-side Grover tuners, tortoiseshell pickguard, black bridge pins with pearl dots, limited edition run of 28 instruments (15 domestic, 13 foreign), mfg. 1989 only.

N/A	$2,000 - 2,500	$1,200 - 1,500	$1,950

D-18V (GOM, SEPTEMBER 1985) – dreadnought-style, tortoise binding, V-shaped neck, ebony fingerboard, ebony bridge, tortoiseshell pickguard, limited edition run of 56 instruments, mfg. 1985 only.

N/A	$1,800 - 2,250	$1,075 - 1,350	$1,640

MSR/NOTES	100%	EXCELLENT	AVERAGE	LAST MSR

D-18 VINTAGE (1992) – dreadnought-style, scalloped braces, three-ring rosette (1/9/1 grouping), tortoise binding, V-shaped low profile neck, ebony fingerboard, logo stamped on back of headstock, three-per-side Grover tuners, ebony bridge with saddle slot, tortoiseshell pickguard, black bridge pins with white dots, available in Natural finish with Aging Toner top, limited edition run of 218 instruments (215 domestic, 2 foreign), mfg. 1992 only.

	N/A	$1,800 - 2,250	$1,075 - 1,350	$1,998

D-21LE (GOM, NOVEMBER 1985) – dreadnought-style, Indian rosewood back and sides, herringbone rosette, tortoise binding, V-shaped neck, rosewood fingerboard, rosewood bridge, tortoiseshell pickguard under finish, limited edition run of 75 instruments, mfg. 1985 only.

	N/A	$1,675 - 2,100	$1,000 - 1,250	$1,550

D-28 1935 SPECIAL (GOM, 1993) – dreadnought-style based on 1935 specifications, Indian rosewood back and sides, scalloped bracing, ivoroid binding, zigzag back stripe, V-shaped neck, square tapered peghead with Brazilian rosewood veneer, bridge with a saddle slot through the middle, tortoise pickguard, available in Natural or Dark Sunburst finish, limited edition run of 237 instruments (217 domestic, 20 foreign), mfg. 1993 only.

	N/A	$2,400 - 3,000	$1,450 - 1,800	$3,800

D-28 CUSTOM (GOM, NOVEMBER, 1984) – dreadnought-style, Indian rosewood back and sides, scalloped braces, ebony fingerboard with snowflake inlays, unbound headstock with torch inlay and stamped logo on back, limited edition run of 43 instruments, mfg. 1984 only.

	N/A	$2,400 - 3,000	$1,450 - 1,800	$2,000

D-28LSH (GOM, 1991) – dreadnought style, Indian rosewood back and sides, large soundhole with two pearl soundhole rings, ivoroid binding, herringbone top inlay, 22-fret fingerboard with snowflake inlay, three-per-side gold tuners with ebony tuner buttons inlaid with snowflakes, snowflake inlay on bridge ends, tortoise pickguard, available in Natural finish with Aging Toner top, limited edition run of 211 instruments (200 domestic, 11 foreign), mfg. 1991 only.

	N/A	$2,200 - 2,750	$1,325 - 1,650	$4,398

The underside of the top is signed by C.F. Martin IV and company employees. The label is signed by Les Wagner, who retired in 1991 after 47 years service with Martin guitar company.

D-40BLE (GOM, 1990) – dreadnought-style body, Engelmann spruce top, Brazilian rosewood back and sides, X bracing, pearl rosette, white top binding, three-ply back binding, single black line side binding, pearl top inlay that does not go around the fingerboard, bound ebony fingerboard with snowflake inlay, two six-point snowflake inlay on bridge, bound headstock, three-per-side engraved gold tuners with "M" buttons, white bridge pins with pearl dots, tortoise pickguard, label signed by CFM IV and Mike Longworth, limited edition run of 58 instruments (50 domestic, 8 foreign), Mark Leaf hardshell case included, mfg. 1990 only.

	N/A	$6,400 - 8,000	$3,850 - 4,800	$5,598

D-41BLE (GOM, 1989) – dreadnought-style body, Engelmann spruce top, Brazilian rosewood back and sides, scalloped braces, low profile neck, pearl bound fingerboard with hexagon inlays, pearl bound headstock, three-per-side gold tuners with large ebony buttons, tortoise pickguard, available in Natural finish with Aging Toner top, limited edition run of 39 instruments (31 domestic, 8 foreign), mfg. 1989 only.

	N/A	$5,600 - 7,000	$3,350 - 4,200	$4,800

D-42LE (GOM, 1988) – dreadnought-style body, scalloped bracing, white binding, low profile neck, small hexagonal fingerboard inlays, three-per-side gold tuners with large ebony buttons, tortoiseshell pickguard, limited edition run of 75 instruments (69 domestic, 6 foreign), mfg. 1988 only.

	N/A	$3,200 - 4,000	$1,925 - 2,400	$3,300

The underside of the top is signed by CF Martin IV and the company foremen.

D-45 GENE AUTRY (GOM, 1994) – dreadnought-style body designed after Autry's 1933 D-45, scalloped bracing, neck joins at 12th fret, "Gene Autry" pearl script fingerboard inlay or snowflake inlays with 15th fret "Gene Autry" inlay, torch inlay on headstock, decal logo on back of headstock, three-per-side Waverly tuners, label signed by Gene Autry, limited edition run of 66 instruments (50 domestic, 16 foreign), mfg. 1994 only.

	N/A	$17,000 - 21,500	$10,000 - 13,000	$22,000

D-45KLE (GOM, 1991) – dreadnought-style body, Engelmann spruce top, flamed koa back and sides, ivoroid binding, snowflake fingerboard inlay, pearl bound Brazilian rosewood headstock overlay, tortoise pickguard, three-per-side gold tuners with embossed "M" on buttons, snowflake bridge inlays, available in Natural finish with Aging Toner top, Mark Leaf case included, limited edition run of 54 instruments (50 domestic, 4 foreign), mfg. 1991 only.

	N/A	$6,400 - 8,000	$3,850 - 4,800	$7,800

The underside of the top was signed by company employees.

D-45LE (GOM, SEPTEMBER, 1987) – dreadnough-style body, Brazilian rosewood back and sides, pearl bound fingerboard with hexagon outline inlays, pearl bound headstock, hexagon outline at bridge ends, three-per-side gold tuners with ebony buttons, tortoiseshell pickguard, limited edition run of 50 instruments (44 domestic, 6 foreign), mfg. 1987 only.

	N/A	$16,000 - 20,000	$9,500 - 12,000	$7,500

D-45S DELUXE (GOM, 1992) – dreadnought-style body based on a 1937 D-45S (12-fret-style with a solid headstock), Brazilian rosewood back and sides, scalloped braces, ivoroid binding, neck joins body at 12th fret, pearl border on fingerboard, snowflake fingerboard inlay, solid headstock with pearl borders, three-per-side gold tuners with ebony buttons and pearl "M" inlay, snowflake inlay at bridge ends, tortoiseshell pickguard, available in Natural finish with Aging Toner top, limited edition run of 60 instruments (50 domestic, 10 foreign), mfg. 1992 only.

	N/A	$7,200 - 9,000	$4,325 - 5,400	$9,760

MSR/NOTES	100%	EXCELLENT	AVERAGE	LAST MSR

D-45 DELUXE (GOM, 1993) – dreadnought-style body, bear claw figured spruce top, Brazilian rosewood back and sides, ivoroid binding, pearl-bordered fingerboard with highly figured pearl tree-of-life inlays, headstock pearl borders, three-per-side gold tuners with large gold buttons embossed with "M," bridge inlay, pickguard inlay, fossilized ivory bridge pins with pearl dots, black pickguard, available in Natural finish with Aging Toner top, limited edition run of 60 instruments (50 domestic, 10 foreign), mfg. 1993 only.

	N/A	$17,000 - 21,500	$10,000 - 13,000	$18,200

D-62LE (GOM, OCTOBER, 1986) – dreadnought-style, flamed maple back and sides, tortoiseshell binding, snowflake fingerboard inlay, tortoiseshell pickguard, white bridge pins with tortoiseshell dots, label signed by CFM IV, limited edition run of 48 instruments (46 domestic, 2 foreign), mfg. 1986 only.

	N/A	$1,800 - 2,250	$1,075 - 1,350	$2,100

D-93 (GOM, 1993) – dreadnought-style body, mahogany back and sides, white binding, herringbone rosette, herringbone back stripe, bound ebony fingerboard with diamonds and squares inlay/"CFM" script inlay at third fret, bound Brazilian rosewood headstock overlay, three-per-side gold tuners with ebony buttons, diamond inlay at bridge ends, tortoiseshell pickguard, white bridge pins with red dots, available in Natural finish with Aging Toner top, limited edition run of 165 instruments (148 domestic, 17 foreign), mfg. 1993 only.

	N/A	$2,600 - 3,250	$1,550 - 1,950	$3,000

This model commemorated 160 years of guitar building for Martin's 160th anniversary (1833-1993).

HD-18LE (GOM, OCTOBER, 1987) – dreadnought-style body, scalloped bracing, tortoiseshell binding, herringbone top inlay, diamonds and squares fingerboard inlay, three-per-side tuners, with ebony tuner buttons, black bridge pins with white dots, tortoise pickguard, available in Natural finish with Aging Toner top, limited edition run of 51 instruments (50 domestic, 1 foreign), mfg. 1987 only.

	N/A	$2,000 - 2,500	$1,200 - 1,500	$2,250

Only 51 instruments were sold (50 domestic, 1 foreign).

HD-28BLE (GOM, 1990) – dreadnought-style body, Brazilian rosewood back and sides, low profile neck, ivoroid binding, herringbone top inlay, herringbone rosette, diamonds and squares fingerboard inlay, ivoroid bound headstock, three-per-side chrome tuners, tortoiseshell pickguard, white bridge pins with red dots, available in Natural finish with Aging Toner top, limited edition run of 108 instruments (100 domestic, 8 foreign), mfg. 1990 only.

	N/A	$5,600 - 7,000	$3,350 - 4,200	$3,900

HD-28BSE (1987) – dreadnought-style body, Brazilian rosewood back and sides, ivoroid binding, V-shaped neck, slotted diamond fingerboard inlays, three-per-side gold tuners with ebony buttons, tortoiseshell pickguard available in Natural finish with Aging Toner top, limited edition run of 93 instruments (88 domestic, 5 foreign), mfg. 1987 only.

	N/A	$5,200 - 6,500	$3,125 - 3,900	$3,300

The underside of these tops were signed by CFM IV and company supervisors.

HD-28 C.T.B. (GOM, 1992, CUSTOM TORTOISE BOUND) – dreadnought-style body, tortoise binding, herringbone back stripe, MOP diamonds and squares fingerboard inlay and 12th fret CFM script inlay, slotted headstock with torch pattern inlay, brand stamp on back of headstock, three-per-side gold tuners with embossed "M" on buttons, tortoiseshell pickguard, white bridge pins with red dots, available in Natural finish with Aging Toner top, limited edition run of 97 instruments (89 domestic, 8 foreign), mfg. 1992 only.

	N/A	$2,600 - 3,250	$1,550 - 1,950	$3,800

Only 97 instruments were sold (89 domestic, 8 foreign).

HD-28C LSH (GOM, 1993) – single cutaway dreadnought-style body, scalloped bracing, large round soundhole, herringbone top inlay, rosewood headstock overlay, white bridgepins with red dots, tortoise pickguard, built-in pickup, available in Sunburst finish, limited edition, mfg. 1993 only.

	N/A	$1,800 - 2,250	$1,075 - 1,350	

HD-28GM GRAND MARQUIS (GOM, 1989) – dreadnought-style body, Indian rosewood back and sides, scalloped bracing, herringbone rosette, tortoiseshell binding, herringbone top inlay and backstripe, snowflake fingerboard inlays, vertical CF Martin logo on headstock and "Grand Marquis" decal on back of headstock, three-per-side gold tuners with embossed "M" on buttons, snowflake inlay on bridge ends, tortoise pickguard, black bridge pins with abalone dots, limited edition run of 120 instruments (112 domestic, 8 foreign), mfg. 1989 only.

	N/A	$3,000 - 3,500	$2,100 - 2,500	$3,198

HD-28GM LSH GRAND MARQUIS (GOM, 1994) – dreadnought-style body, large soundhole with two herringbone soundhole rings, tortoiseshell binding, herringbone top inlay, unbound ebony fingerboard with snowflake and 12th fret pearl "Grand Marquis" inlays, "CF Martin" pearl logo inlay on headstock, three-per-side gold tuners with embossed "M" on buttons, snowflake inlay on bridge, tortoise pickguard, available in Gloss Natural finish with Aging Toner or Shaded top (Sunburst), limited edition run of 151 instruments (106 domestic in Natural finish, 9 foreign in Natural finish, 36 domestic in Sunburst, and 6 foreign in Sunburst), mfg. 1994 only.

	N/A	$2,400 - 3,000	$1,450 - 1,800	

* Add 10% for Sunburst finish (Last MSR $4,830).

HD-28LE (GOM, DECEMBER, 1985) – dreadnought-style body, scalloped bracing, ivoroid binding, herringbone top purfling, V-shaped neck, diamonds and squares fingerboard inlay, square headstock, tortoise pickguard under finish, white bridgepins with red dots, available in Natural finish with Aging Toner top, limited edition run of 87 instruments, mfg. 1985 only.

	N/A	$2,600 - 3,250	$1,550 - 1,950	$2,100

MSR/NOTES	100%	EXCELLENT	AVERAGE	LAST MSR

HD-28M (GOM, 1988) – dreadnought-style body, mahogany back and sides, scalloped bracing, herringbone top inlay, diamonds and squares inlay, gold tuners with large pearloid buttons, tortoise pickguard, white bridge pins with tortoiseshell dots, available in Natural finish with Aging Toner top, limited edition run of 81 instruments (77 domestic, 4 foreign), mfg. 1988 only.

	N/A	$1,800 - 2,250	$1,075 - 1,350	$2,170

HD-28PSE (GOM, 1988) – dreadnought-style body, scalloped bracing, low-profile neck, squared off headstock, ivoroid binding, herringbone top purfling, snowflake fingerboard inlays, three-per-side chrome tuners with ebony tuner buttons, white bridge pins with tortoiseshell dots, tortoiseshell pickguard, available in Natural finish with Aging Toner top, limited edition run of 96 instruments (93 domestic, 3 foreign), mfg. 1988 only.

	N/A	$2,400 - 3,000	$1,450 - 1,800	$2,750

The underside of the top was signed by CFM IV and company supervisors.

HD-28SE (GOM, SEPTEMBER, 1986) – dreadnought-style body, ivoroid binding, herringbone top inlay, V-shaped neck, diamonds and squares fingerboard inlay, ebony tuner buttons, tortoiseshell pickguard under finish, available in Natural finish, limited edition run of 138 instruments (130 domestic, 8 foreign), mfg. 1986 only.

	N/A	$2,100 - 2,500	$1,400 - 1,750	$2,300

The underside of these tops were signed by CFM III, CFM IV, and company foremen.

HJ-28 (GOM, 1992) – Jumbo-style, Indian rosewood back and sides, round soundhole with three ring rosette (5/9/5 grouping), ivoroid binding, herringbone top inlay, unbound ebony fingerboard with diamonds and squares inlay, three-per-side chrome tuners with embossed "M" on buttons, tortoiseshell pickguard, white bridge pins with red dots, available in Natural finish with Aging Toner top, limited edition run of 69 instruments (56 domestic, 13 foreign), mfg. 1992 only.

	N/A	$2,600 - 3,250	$1,550 - 1,950	$3,050

Only 69 instruments were sold (56 domestic, 13 foreign).

HJ-28M (GOM, 1994) – jumbo-style body based on the specs of an HD-28, mahogany back and sides, ivoroid binding, herringbone top inlay, herringbone back stripe, striped Madagascar ebony fingerboard, three-per-side chrome tuners with large ebony buttons and pearl "M" inlay, striped Madagascar ebony bridge, tortoiseshell pickguard, white bridge pins with tortoise dots, available in Natural finish with Aging Toner top, limited edition run of 72 instruments (60 domestic, 12 foreign), mfg. 1994 only.

	N/A	$3,200 - 4,000	$1,925 - 2,400	$3,900

HOM-35 (GOM, 1989) – Orchestra-style body, Brazilian rosewood sides, three-piece back, ivoroid binding top and back binding, herringbone top inlay, low-profile neck, 14/20-fret ivoroid-bound ebony fingerboard with diamonds and squares inlays, Martin stamp on back of headstock, three-per-side gold tuners, tortoiseshell OM-style pickguard, white bridge pins with red dots, available in Natural finish with Aging Toner top, 25.4 in. scale, limited edition run of 60 instruments (96 domestic, 3 foreign), mfg. 1989 only.

	N/A	$4,400 - 5,500	$2,650 - 3,300	$4,000

J-21MC (GOM, 1986) – single cutaway jumbo body style, round soundhole with nine ring rosette, black binding, tortoiseshell pickguard, chrome tuners with ebony buttons, limited edition run of 56 instruments (55 domestic, 1 foreign), mfg. 1986 only.

	N/A	$1,800 - 2,250	$1,075 - 1,350	$1,750

J-40MBLE (GOM, NOVEMBER, 1987) – jumbo-style body, Brazilian rosewood back and sides, snowflake fingerboard inlay, gold tuners with large pearloid buttons, tortoise pickguard, available in Natural finish with Aging Toner top, limited edition run of 17 instruments (16 domestic, 1 foreign), mfg. 1987 only.

	N/A	$4,400 - 5,500	$2,650 - 3,300	$3,000

J-45M CUSTOM DELUXE (GOM, DECEMBER, 1986) – jumbo-style body, Englemann or European spruce top, Indian rosewood back and sides, pearl rosette, tortoise binding, pearl bordering, zipper pattern back stripe, pearl bound ebony fingerboard with hexagonal inlays, three-per-side gold tuners with small ebony buttons, black bridge pins with pearl dots, pearl hexagon outline inlay on bridge tips, pearl-bound tortoise pickguard, limited edition run of 17 instruments (16 domestic, 1 foreign), mfg. 1986 only.

	N/A	$4,400 - 5,500	$2,650 - 3,300	$6,900

M-21 CUSTOM (GOM, DECEMBER, 1984) – Grand Auditorium 0000/M-style body, Indian rosewood back and sides, round soundhole with three-ring rosette (5/9/5 grouping), five-ply top binding with tortoise outer layer, single-ply back binding with tortoise outer layer, unbound rosewood fingerboard with slotted diamond inlays, tortoiseshell pickguard, black bridge pins with white dots, available in Natural finish with Aging Toner top, limited edition run of 16 instruments, mfg. 1984 only.

	N/A	$1,800 - 2,250	$1,075 - 1,350	$1,600

M2C-28 (GOM, 1988) – double cutaway Grand Auditorium 0000/M-style body, single pearl ring rosette, zipper-pattern backstripe, three-per-side gold self-locking tuners with small ebony buttons, white bridge pins with pearl dots, optional pickguard, optional thinline pickup, limited edition run of 22 instruments (20 domestic, 2 foreign), mfg. 1988 only.

	N/A	$2,400 - 3,000	$1,450 - 1,800	$2,700

OM-28LE (GOM, OCTOBER, 1985) – Orchestra-style body, ivoroid binding, V-shaped neck, diamonds and squares fingerboard inlays, tortoiseshell pickguard under finish, available in Natural finish with Aging Toner top, limited edition run of 41 instruments (39 domestic, 2 foreign), mfg. 1985 only.

	N/A	$2,400 - 3,000	$1,450 - 1,800	$2,180

MSR/NOTES	100%	EXCELLENT	AVERAGE	LAST MSR

OMC-28 (GOM, 1990) – single cutaway Orchestra-style body, scalloped bracing, oval soundhole, low profile neck, MOP "C.F. Martin" headstock inlay, three-per-side gold tuners with small pearloid buttons, white bridgepins with red dots, tortoiseshell pickguard, limited edition run of 76 instruments (74 domestic, 2 foreign), mfg. 1990 only.

	N/A	$1,800 - 2,250	$1,075 - 1,350	$3,148

OM-21 SPECIAL (GOM, 1991) – Orchestra-style body, herringbone rosette, tortoise binding, herringbone back stripe, striped Macassar ebony fingerboard with MOP diamonds and squares inlay, striped ebony bridge, tortoiseshell-bound headstock with MOP Martin logo inlay, three-per-side gold tuners with pearloid buttons, white bridgepins with red dots, OM-style tortoiseshell pickguard, available in Natural finish with Aging Toner top, limited edition run of 36 instruments (32 domestic, 4 foreign), mfg. 1991 only.

	N/A	$2,000 - 2,500	$1,200 - 1,500	$3,998

OM-28 PERRY BECHTEL (GOM, 1993) – Orchestra-style body, wood purfling rosette, ivoroid binding, herringbone top inlay, diamonds and squares fingerboard inlay, Brazilian rosewood headstock overlay, three-per-side chrome tuners with embossed "M" on buttons, pyramid bridge, tortoise pickguard, label signed by Mrs. Ina Bechtel, available in Natural finish with Aging Toner finish, limited edition run of 94 instruments (50 domestic, 16 foreign), mfg. 1993 only.

	N/A	$3,800 - 4,750	$2,275 - 2,850	$4,000

OM-40LE (GOM, 1994) – Orchestra-style body, Indian rosewood back and sides, double narrow pearl rosette, double pearl border on top, unbound ebony fingerboard with snowflake inlays, "CF Martin" pearl logo on headstock, three-per-side gold tuners with large ebony buttons and pearl four-point snowflake inlays, white bridge pins with pearl dots, available in Natural and Sunburst finish, limited edition run of 86 instruments (45 domestic and 12 foreign in Natural finish, and 20 domestic and 9 foreign in Sunburst finish), mfg. 1994 only.

	N/A	$3,600 - 4,500	$2,150 - 2,750	

* **Add 10% (Last MSR was $7,430) for Sunburst finish.**

ACOUSTIC: LIMITED EDITION SERIES

Martin's Guitar of the Month/Year program was popular, but by the mid-1990s, they realized that it wasn't enough (or at times it wasn't often enough) to release custom guitars each month. Martin decided to introduce a new line called the Limited Edition Series that included guitars that were built specifically for someone, a special event, or a significant era and have a set number of instruments produced or a limited ordering period where the quantity is set afterwards. Eric Clapton pioneered the Limited Edition Series with his signature 000-42EC in 1995. Martin now introduces their Limited Edition Series guitars typically twice a year at each NAMM show (Winter and Summer) and they highlight them in their semi-annual publication called *The Sounding Board*.

Currently, over 150 guitars have been released in Martin's Limited Edition Series and the list is very extensive. Rather than list every model in one giant category, we have broken them out into separate sub-categories for ease of searching. Models are alphabetized by their model number rather than the person, event, or era the guitar was built for. For instance, the D-42 Peter Frampton is listed under "D" instead of "P" or "F." Numbered models are also featured first followed by all letter prefix models. In most model descriptions, the production total is listed as well as the year of manufacture. Keep in mind that the production totals are taken from Martin's records and actual production totals may be different from what is listed. The year of manufacture is also taken from Martin's price list and the years when the respective guitar was offered. Many times, Martin has introduced a Limited Edition guitar at a NAMM show, they sell out of the run during the show, and production of these guitars do not start until several weeks if not months after the show. It is entirely possible to find a Limited Edition Martin that was produced after the years listed in the model descriptions.

ACOUSTIC: LIMITED EDITION MODELS NUMBERED (0, 00, 000, 0000)

0-28 IAN ANDERSON (2004) – Concert 12-fret 0-style body, solid Adirondack spruce top, solid East Indian rosewood back and sides, round soundhole with custom rosette, grained ivoroid binding, fine herringbone top inlay, B/W fiber back and side inlay, select hardwood neck, 12/20-fret ebony fingerboard with long pattern diamond and square inlays and 20th fret Ian Anderson signature inlay, slotted headstock solid East Indian rosewood overlay and small old style logo, three-per-side Waverly/Sloane tuners with small ivoroid knobs, ebony pyramid-style long saddle bridge, white bridge pins with black dots, no pickguard, label signed by CFM IV and Ian Anderson and numbered in sequence, Fishman Gold Plus Natural I electronics, Natural polished gloss with Vintage Toner top finish, 24.9 in. scale, case included, limited edition run of 87 instruments, mfg. 2004 only.

	N/A	$3,000 - 3,750	$1,800 - 2,250	$5,499

0-45JB JOAN BAEZ (1998) – Concert 12-fret 0-style body, solid Sitka spruce top, solid East Indian rosewood back and sides, standard X scalloped bracing, round soundhole with three-ring Style 45 rosette (5/9/5 grouping with a large center ring of abalone pearl), grained ivoroid binding, Style 45 abalone pearl top, back, and side inlays, Style 45 back purfling, mahogany neck, 12/19-fret ebony grained ivoroid-bound fingerboard with Style 45 snowflake and 19th fret Joan Baez signature inlays, grained ivoroid-bound slotted headstock with solid Indian rosewood overlay and torch inlay, logo stamp on back of headstock, three-per-side gold side-mount Irving Sloane tuners with grained ivoroid buttons, ebony bridge with long saddle, fossilized ivory bridge pins with pearl dots, tortoise color pickguard, two labels with one signed by Joan Baez and one under the top, Natural polished gloss finish with Aging Toner top, 24.9 in. scale, case included, limited edition run of 59 instruments, mfg. 1998 only.

	N/A	$4,400 - 5,500	$2,650 - 3,300	$9,850

This model was the first artist signature model in Martin's "Woman & Music" program.

0-45S STEPHEN STILLS (2007) – Concert 0-style body based on Stills' original 0-45 built between 1904 and 1939, solid Adirondack spruce top, solid Madagascar rosewood back and sides, Style 45 rosette, grained ivoroid body binding, abalone with B/W/B top and back inlays, mahogany neck, 12/19-fret grained ivoroid bound ebony fingerboard with MOP Golden Era Style 45 snowflake inlays, bound slotted headstock with rosewood overlay and vertical block "CMF Martin" inlaid logo, three-per-side open-style Waverly brass tuners with small ivoroid knobs, pyramid ebony bridge, available in Natural Gloss finish, 24.9 in. scale, label signed by Chris Martin IV and Stephen Stills, limited edition run of 91 instruments, mfg. summer 2007-09.

	N/A	$7,200 - 9,000	$4,325 - 5,400	$15,999

MSR/NOTES	100%	EXCELLENT	AVERAGE	LAST MSR

00 STAUFFER 175TH (2008) – Grand Concert 12-fret 00-style body, solid Englemann spruce top, solid Madagascar rosewood back and sides, Style 45 rosette, grained ivoroid binding, fine herringbone top inlay, black/white boltaron back/side inlays, fine pattern herringbone back purfling, select hardwood neck, grained ivoroid heelcap, 12/20-fret grained ivoroid-bound ebony fingerboard with 12th fret 175th Anniversary banner inlay, hook-shaped original Martin/Stauffer-style headstock, six-on-one-side Gotoh nickel engraved Stauffer-style tuners with coin-shaped buttons, pyramid ebony bridge with drop-in long saddle, no pickguard, signed by CFM IV and individually numbered, available in Natural Gloss finish, 24.9 in. scale, limited edition run of 50 instruments, mfg. 2008 only.

	N/A	$4,000 - 5,000	$2,400 - 3,000	$8,999

00-16DB WOMEN AND MUSIC (1997) – Grand Concert 14-fret 00-style body with extra deep sides, solid spruce top, solid mahogany back and sides, round soundhole with classical-style wood mosaic rosette, black binding, mahogany neck, 14/19-fret ebony fretboard with diamonds and squares inlay, slotted headstock with rosewood overlay and gold logo, three-per-side Waverly open-style tuners, ebony belly bridge, black bridge pins with white dots, available in Natural finish, limited edition run of 97 instruments, mfg. summer 1997 only.

	N/A	$1,000 - 1,250	$600 - 750	$2,100

This model was the first guitar in Martin's Women and Music Program that feature guitars specifically built for women.

* **00-16DBR Women and Music Rosewood (1998)** – similar to the 00-16DB Women and Music, except has solid Indian rosewood back and sides, mfg. 1998 only.

	N/A	$1,075 - 1,350	$650 - 800	$2,400

00-17SO SINGOUT (2000) – Grand Concert 14-fret 00-style body, solid mahogany top, back, and sides, Hybrid scalloped bracing, round soundhole with single ring rosette, tortoise color binding, 14/20-fret ebony fingerboard with custom inlays, solid mahogany headstock overlay with logo, three-per-side tuners, ebony belly bridge, white bridge pins, tortoise color pickguard, Natural gloss finish, 25.4 in. scale, case included, limited edition run of 50 instruments, mfg. 2000 only.

	N/A	$1,400 - 1,750	$850 - 1,050	$2,399

00-18CTN ELIZABETH COTTEN (2001) – Grand Concert 14-fret 00-style body, solid Sitka spruce top, solid mahogany back and sides, standard X scalloped bracing, round soundhole with three-ring Style 18 rosette (1/9/1 grouping), tortoise color binding, multiple B/W top inlay, mahogany neck, 14/20-fret ebony fingerboard with single abalone pearl dots, 12th fret freight train, and 20th fret Elizabeth Cotten signature inlays, ebony headstock overlay with large old style logo, three-per-side nickel Gotoh tuners with oval buttons, ebony belly bridge, black bridge pins with white dots, tortoise color pickguard, label signed by CFM IV and Mr. Larry H. Ellis Sr. (Cotten's grandson), Natural polished gloss finish with Vintage Toner top, 24.9 in. scale, case included, limited edition run of 76 instruments, mfg. early 2001 only.

	N/A	$2,000 - 2,500	$1,200 - 1,500	$3,299

00-18SH STEVE HOWE (1999) – Grand Concert 14-fret 00-style body, solid Englemann spruce top, solid mahogany back and sides, standard X scalloped bracing, old Style 18 three-ring rosette (1/9/1 grouping), tortoise colored binding, Style 18 top inlay and back purfling, mahogany neck, 14/20-fret ebony fingerboard with abalone dots and 19-20th fret Steve Howe signature inlays, solid East Indian rosewood headstock overlay with old style logo, three-per-side nickel Gotoh tuners with oval buttons, ebony belly bridge, black bridge pins with white dots, tortoise color pickguard, label signed by CFM IV and Steve Howe, Natural polished gloss finish with Vintage Toner top, 24.9 in. scale, case included, limited edition run of 250 instruments, mfg. 1999-2000.

	N/A	$1,800 - 2,250	$1,075 - 1,350	$2,950

00-18 TIM O'BRIEN (2008) – Grand Concert 14-fret 00-style body, solid Adirondack spruce top, solid mahogany back and sides, standard X scalloped bracing, round soundhole with three ring rosette (1/7/1 grouping with a large middle ring of abalone pearl), black Boltaron binding, multiple B/W Boltaron top inlay, solid Madagascar rosewood strip back purfling, select hardwood full thickness V profile neck with 30s style ebony heel, 14/20-fret ebony fingerboard with long pattern Golden Era diamonds and squares inlays, solid Madagascar rosewood headstock overlay with large Golden Era-style logo, three-per-side nickel Waverly tuners with oval buttons, ebony belly bridge, ebony bridge pins with abalone pearl dots, tortoise color pickguard, label signed by Tim O'Brien and numbered in sequence, Natural polished gloss finish with Aging Toner top, 25.4 in. scale, case included, limited edition run of 100 instruments, mfg. summer 2008-2011.

	$4,400	$2,500 - 3,000	$1,600 - 1,900	$5,499

00-21 KINGSTON TRIO (2007) – Grand Auditorium 14-fret 00-style body built in tribute to the 50th Anniversary of the Kingston Trio, solid Italian Alpine spruce top, solid East Indian rosewood back and sides, Style 28 rosette, tortoise color binding, Style 21 top inlay, mahogany neck, 12/20-fret unbound ebony fingerboard with abalone square inlays, open-style headstock with rosewood overlay, three-per-side Waverly brass tuners with small ivoroid buttons, ebony bridge with drop-in long saddle, tortoise pickguard, label signed by Chris Martin IV and Bob Shane, available in Natural Gloss finish, 24.9 in. scale, limited edition run of 100 instruments, mfg. summer 2007-mid-2009.

	N/A	$2,600 - 3,250	$1,550 - 1,950	$6,299

00-37K STEVE MILLER (2000) – Grand Concert 12-fret 00-style body, solid Englemann spruce top, solid flamed Hawaiian koa back and sides, standard X scalloped bracing, round soundhole with three-ring Style 45 rosette (5/9/5 grouping with large center ring of abalone pearl), grained ivoroid binding, fine herringbone top inlay, B/W/B back and side inlays, Style 45 back purfling, mahogany neck, 12/20-fret grained ivoroid-bound bony fingerboard with no inlays, bound slotted headstock with ebony overlay and alternate pattern abalone pearl torch inlay, logo stamp on back of headstock, three-per-side side-mount gold Waverly/Sloane tuners with grained ivoroid buttons, ebony belly bridge, ebony bridge pins with pearl dots, no pickguard, label signed by CFM IV and Steve Miller, Natural polished gloss finish with Vintage Toner top, 24.9 in. scale, case included, limited edition run of 68 instruments, mfg. summer 2000 only.

	N/A	$3,600 - 4,500	$2,150 - 2,750	

* **00-37K2 Steve Miller (2000)** – similar to the 00-37K Steve Miller, except has a solid flamed Hawaiian koa top, limited edition run of 68 instruments, mfg. summer 2000 only.

	N/A	$4,000 - 5,000	$2,400 - 3,000	

MSR/NOTES	100%	EXCELLENT	AVERAGE	LAST MSR

00-40 STAUFFER (1997) – Grand Concert 12-fret 00-style body, bookmatched solid Sitka spruce top, solid East Indian rosewood back and sides, scalloped bracing, round soundhole with three-ring Style 45 rosette (5/9/5 grouping with a large center ring of abalone pearl), grained ivoroid binding, multiple B/W top inlays, mahogany neck, 12/20-fret ebony fingerboard with Style 45 snowflake pattern inlays, Stauffer-style headstock with black Boltaron overlay and gold foil logo, six-on-one-side gold custom tuners with elongated variable length knobs, ebony pointed belly bridge with pyramid wings, fossilized ivory bridge pins with abalone pearl dots, no pickguard, Natural polished gloss finish with Vintage Toner top and Black ebonized finish on the back of the neck, 24.9 in. scale, case included, limited edition run of 75 instruments, mfg. 1997 only.

	N/A	$4,800 - 6,000	$2,850 - 3,600	$7,900

00-42 LINDA RONSTADT (2009) – Grand Concert 12-fret 00-style body based on an early 1900s 00-42, solid Adirondack spruce top, solid Madagascar rosewood back and sides, Style 45 rosette (5/9/5 grouping with a large center ring of abalone), grained ivoroid binding, Style 42 abalone top inlay that goes around the fingerboard, B/W back and side inlay, Style 45 back purfling, modified V select hardwood neck, 12/19-fret grained ivoroid-bound ebony fingerboard with Style 45 select abalone snowflake and 19th fret Linda Ronstadt signature inlays, open-style headstock with solid Madagascar rosewood overlay and golden era CF Martin block abalone pearl logo, three-per-side Waverly brass tuners with small ivoroid buttons, ebony pyramid bridge with drop-in saddle, label signed by Linda Ronstadt and numbered in sequence, available in Natural Gloss finish, 24.9 in. scale, limited edition run of 150 instruments, Geib-style case included, mfg. 2009-2011.

	$8,000	$4,700 - 5,400	N/A	$9,999

00-42K ROBBIE ROBERTSON (2007) – Grand Concert 12-fret 00-style body based on Robertson's 1919 00-45K Koa, solid Italian spruce top, solid highly flamed maple koa back and sides, Style 45 rosette, grained ivoroid binding, abalone with B/W/B Boltaron top inlay, B/W/B back inlay, mahogany neck, 12/19-fret grained ivoroid with B/W/B inlay bound ebony fingerboard with Style 45 snowflake inlays, open-style headstock with rosewood overlay and pearl torch inlays, three-per-side Waverly brass tuners with small ivoroid buttons, ebony pyramid bridge with drop-in saddle, label signed by Robbie Robertson, available in Natural Gloss finish, 24.9 in. scale, limited edition run of 100 instruments, mfg. summer 2007-09.

	N/A	$3,600 - 4,500	$2,150 - 2,750	$8,799

* **00-42K2 Robbie Robertson (2007)** – similar to the 00-42K Robbie Robertson, except has a solid highly flamed koa top, limited edition run of 100 instruments, mfg. summer 2007-09.

	N/A	$3,800 - 4,750	$2,275 - 2,850	$8,999

00-45S 1902 (2002) – Grand Concert 12-fret 00-style body based on four prototype 1902 Martins that eventually became the Style 45 Martins in 1904, solid Adirondack spruce top, solid Brazilian rosewood back and sides, standard bracing, three-ring Style 45 rosette (5/9/5 grouping with a large middle ring of abalone pearl), grained ivoroid binding, Style 42 abalone pearl with black/maple/black fiber top, back, and side inlays, Style 45 Golden Era back purfling, select hardwood neck, 12/19-fret grained ivoroid-bound ebony fingerboard with elaborate abalone and MOP Tree Of Life inlays, slotted headstock with with solid Brazilian rosewood overlay and abalone pearl flower pot inlays, three-per-side open-style Waverly/Sloane tuners with small iovorid knobs, white Micarta pyramid bridge with drop-in saddle, fossilized ivory bridge pins with black pearl dots, tortoise color pickguard with ablone pearl inlays that is positioned directly below the soundhole, label signed by CFM IV and numbered in sequence, Natural polished gloss with Vintage Toner top finish, 24.9 in. scale, hardshell vintage-style coffin case included, limited edition run of 60 instruments, mfg. 2002-04.

	N/A	$10,500 - 12,500	$7,500 - 9,000	$25,000

00-45 STAUFFER (1997) – Grand Concert 12-fret 00-style body, bookmatched solid Sitka spruce top, solid Brazilian rosewood back and sides, scalloped bracing, round soundhole with three-ring Style 45 rosette (5/9/5 grouping with a large center ring of abalone pearl), grained ivoroid binding, Style 45 abalone pearl top inlay that goes around the fingerboard, mahogany neck, 12/20-fret grained ivoroid-bound ebony fingerboard with Style 45 snowflake pattern inlays, Stauffer-style headstock with black Boltaron overlay and gold foil logo, six-on-one-side gold custom tuners with elongated variable length knobs, ebony pointed belly bridge with pyramid wings, fossilized ivory bridge pins with abalone pearl dots, no pickguard, Natural polished gloss finish with Vintage Toner top and Black ebonized finish on the back of the neck, 24.9 in. scale, case included, limited edition run of 25 instruments, mfg. 1997 only.

	N/A	$10,000 - 12,500	$6,000 - 7,500	$20,000

000-16RGD GODFREY DANIELS (2002) – Grand Auditorium 14-fret 000-style body, solid Sitka spruce top, solid East Indian rosewood back and sides, 0001 hybrid scalloped bracing, round soundhole with three ring Style 45 rosette (5/9/5 grouping with a large middle ring of abalone pearl), tortoise color binding, multiple B/W top inlay, solid Spanish cedar neck, 14/20-fret black Micarta fingerboard with custom inlays including abalone pearl modified snowflakes at the 1st, 3rd, 7th, 9th, and 16th frets, music note at the 5th fret, 12th-13th fret "Godfrey Daniels" signature, and 20th fret "Est. 1976" inlays, solid East Indian rosewood headstock overlay with raised gold foil logo, three-per-side gold Gotoh tuners with large knobs, black Micarta belly bridge with two abalone pearl snowflake inlays, black bridge pins with white dots, tortoise color beveled pickguard, two labels with one signed by CFM IV and Dave Fry and numbered in sequence and the other bearing signatures from several folk musicians, Natural polished gloss finish with Aging Toner top and Dark Filler back and sides, 25.4 in. scale, case included, limited edition run of 100 instruments, mfg. 2002-mid 2003.

	N/A	$1,400 - 1,750	$1,000 - 1,150	$2,849

000-18 MC MARTIN CARTHY (2003) – Grand Auditorium 14-fret 000-style body, solid Sitka spruce top, solid mahogany back and sides, 000 non-scalloped bracing, three-ring old Style 18 rosette (15/1 grouping), tortoise color binding, multiple B/W Boltaron top inlay, B/W Boltaron back and side inlay, mahogany neck, 14/20-fret ebony fingerboard with old Style 18 abalone pearl dot inlays, solid Indian rosewood headstock overlay with gold foil logo, three-per-side nickel Waverly tuners with Butterbean knobs, ebony belly bridge, brass bridge pins for treble strings and black bridge pins with abalone dots for bass strings, tortoise color pickguard, label signed by CFM IV and Martin Carthy and numbered in sequence, Natural polished gloss finish with Aging Toner top and Dark Mahogany back and sides, 24.9 in. scale, case included, limited edition of 88 instruments, mfg. 2003 only.

	N/A	$1,650 - 2,000	$1,100 - 1,350	$3,199

MSR/NOTES	100%	EXCELLENT	AVERAGE	LAST MSR

000-28B NORMAN BLAKE (2004) – Grand Auditorium 12-fret 000-style body, solid Adirondack spruce top, solid Brazilian rosewood back and sides, unique top bracing pattern/scalloped bracing, round soundhole with three-ring Style 28 black/white fiber rosette (5/9/5 grouping), grained ivoroid binding, fine herringbone top inlay, B/W fiber back inlay, select hardwood neck, 12/19-fret ebony fingerboard with unique pattern diamond and square inlays, slotted headstock with solid Brazilian rosewood overlay and Golden Era-style logo, three-per-side open-style Waverly/Sloane tuners with small ivoroid knobs, ebony vintage belly drop-in long saddle bridge, fossil ivory bridge pins with black pearl dots, tortoise color pickguard, label signed by CFM IV and Norman Blake and numbered in sequence, Natural polished gloss with Aging Toner top finish, 24.9 in. scale, case included, limited edition run of 52 instruments, mfg. 2004 only.

	N/A	$6,000 - 7,000	$4,250 - 5,000	$9,999

000-28ECB ERIC CLAPTON (2002) – Grand Auditorium 14-fret 000-style body, solid Sitka spruce top, solid Brazilian rosewood back and sides, round soundhole with Style 45 rosette (5/9/5 grouping with a large center ring of fine herringbone), grained ivoroid binding, fine herringbone top inlay, B/W/B boltaron back inlay, multiple B/W side inlay, select hardwood neck, 14/20-fret ebony fingerboard with long pattern diamond and square inlays bordered in MOP and 20th fret Eric Clapton signature inlay, solid Brazilian rosewood headstock overlay with large old style logo, three-per-side nickel Waverly tuners with butterbean knobs, ebony belly bridge, fossil ivory bridge pins with black dots, tortoise color pickguard, label signed by CFM IV and Eric Clapton and numbered in sequence, Natural polished gloss with Vintage Toner top finish, 24.9 in. scale, case included, limited edition run of 500 instruments, mfg. 2002-04.

	N/A	$6,250 - 7,500	$4,500 - 5,250	$9,999

000-28LD LONNIE DONEGAN (2002) – Grand Auditorium 14-fret 000-style body, solid Sitka spruce top, solid East Indian rosewood back and sides, round soundhole with three ring Style 45 rosette (5/9/5 grouping with a large middle ring of blue paua pearl, grained ivoroid binding, B/W/B top inlay, B/W back inlay, mahogany neck, 14/20-fret ebony fingerboard with custom inlays consisting of a crown at the 3rd fret, "SKIFFLE" spelled out between the 5th and 17th frets, and "LONNIE DONEGAN" between the 19th and 20th frets, solid Indian rosewood headstock overlay with old style logo and abalone pearl rat and "G.O.W.R." inlays, ebony belly bridge, white bridge pins with tortoise dots, black beveled pickguard, Fishman Gold Plus Natural II electronics, label signed by CFM IV and Lonnie Donegan and numbered in sequence, 1935-style Sunburst polished gloss finish top with Dark Filler back and sides, 24.9 in. scale, case included, limited edition run of 72 instruments, mfg. 2002 only.

	N/A	$2,250 - 2,750	$1,500 - 1,850	$4,099

   * *000-28LDB Lonnie Donegan Brazilian (2002)* – similar to the 000-28LD Lonnie Donegan, except has solid Brazilian rosewood back, sides, and headstock overlay, limited edition run of 75 instruments, mfg. 2002-mid-2003.

	N/A	$5,500 - 6,500	$3,750 - 4,500	$8,219

000-28M ERIC CLAPTON (2009) – Grand Auditorium 14-fret 000-style body, solid Carpathian spruce top, solid Madagascar rosewood back and sides, round soundhole with Style 45 rosette (5/9/5 grouping with a large center ring of fine herringbone), grained ivoroid binding, fine herringbone top inlay, B/W/B boltaron back and side inlay, modified V-shaped select hardwood neck, 14/20-fret ebony fingerboard with long pattern diamond and square inlays bordered in MOP and 20th fret Eric Clapton signature inlay, solid Madagascar rosewood headstock overlay with gold foil logo, three-per-side nickel Waverly tuners with butterbean knobs, ebony belly bridge with drop-in saddle, bone bridge pins with black dots, tortoise color pickguard, label signed by Eric Clapton and numbered in sequence, Natural polished gloss with a Natural or Sunburst Vintage Toner top finish, 24.9 in. scale, case included, limited edition run of 461 instruments, mfg. 2009 only.

	N/A	$3,400 - 4,250	$2,050 - 2,550	$6,749

   • **Add 5% (Last MSR was $6,999) for Sunburst finish.**

000-40Q2GN GRAHAM NASH (2003) – Grand Auditorium 14-fret 000 style body, solid quilted mahogany top, back, and sides, 000/scalloped bracing, round soundhole with three-ring Style 45 rosette (5/9/5 grouping with a large middle ring of abalone pearl), tortoise color binding, bold herringbone top inlay, B/W Boltaron back and side inlays, mahogany neck, 14/20-fret ebony fingerboard with Style 42 abalone pearl Snowflakes and 18th-20th fret Graham Nash signature inlays, ebony headstock overlay with white outline, red heart with MOP wings, and logo, three-per-side gold Waverly tuners with butterbean knobs, ebony belly bridge, black bridge pins with pearl dots, tortoise pickguard, label signed by CFM IV and Graham Nash and numbered in sequence, Natural polished gloss finish with Dark Stain top and Dark Mahogany Stain back and sides, 24.9 in. scale, case included, limited edition run of 147 instruments, mfg. 2003 only.

	N/A	$2,750 - 3,250	$1,800 - 2,250	$4,699

000-40S MARK KNOPFLER (2006) – Grand Concert 12-fret 000-style body, Italian Alpine spruce top, Indian rosewood back and sides, round soundhole with special historical rosette, grained ivoroid binding, bold herringbone top inlay, black/white Boltaron back inlay, fine pattern herringbone back purfling, select hardwood neck, 12/20-fret grained ivoroid-bound ebony fingerboard with Style 42 select abalone snowflake inlays, bound slotted headstock with East Indian rosewood overlay and MOP logo, three-per-side Waverly/Sloane tuners with small ivroid knobs, ebony pyramid style bridge with drop-in saddle, fossilized ivory bridge pins with black dots, no pickguard, Natural polished gloss with Aging Toner top finish, label signed by C.F. Martin IV and Mark Knopfler and numbered in sequence, 25.4 in. scale, case included, limited edition run of 155 instruments, mfg. summer 2006 only.

	N/A	$3,250 - 3,750	$2,250 - 2,750	$6,999

000-40SPR PETER ROWAN (2001) – Grand Auditorium 12-fret 000-style body, solid Sitka spruce top, solid mahogany back and sides, 000-12 scalloped bracing, round soundhole with three-ring Style 45 rosette (5/9/5 grouping with a large center ring of blue paua shell), tortoise color binding, multiple B/W top, back, and side inlays, mahogany neck, 12/20-fret ebony fingerboard with phases of the moon inlays and 20th fret Peter Rowan signature inlay, slotted headstock with ebony overlay, B/W border, and abalone pearl clouds and moon inlay (no logo), ebony pyramid bridge, black bridge pins with abalone dots, tortoise color beveled pickguard, label signed by CFM IV and Peter Rowan and numbered in sequence, Natural polished gloss finish with Aging Toner top and Dark Mahogany Stain back and sides, 25.4 in. scale, case included, limited edition run of 87 instruments, mfg. summer 2001 only.

	N/A	$2,400 - 2,800	$1,600 - 1,950	$4,999

MSR/NOTES	100%	EXCELLENT	AVERAGE	LAST MSR

000-42EC ERIC CLAPTON (1995) – Grand Concert 14-fret 000-style body, solid Sitka spruce top, solid East Indian rosewood back and sides, herringbone rosette, ivoroid body binding, herringbone top inlay, mahogany neck, 14/20-fret grained ivoroid-bound ebony fingerboard with abalone pearl custom inlays and 20th fret MOP Eric Clapton signature inlay, bound headstock with East Indian rosewood overlay and large abalone pearl vertical block logo, three-per-side gold tuners with butterbean knobs, ebony belly bridge with snowflake inlays, tortoise color pickguard, available in Natural or Sunburst polished gloss top finish and Natural back and sides, 24.9 in. scale, case included, limited edition run of 461 instruments (433 finished in Natural, 28 finished in Sunburst), mfg. 1995 only.

	N/A	$6,250 - 7,500	$4,500 - 5,250	$8,100

- **Add 10-15% (Last MSR was $8,320) for Sunburst finish.**

000-42ECB ERIC CLAPTON (2000) – Grand Auditorium 14-fret 000-style body, solid Engelmann spruce top, solid Brazilian rosewood back and sides, standard X scalloped bracing, round soundhole with three-ring Style 45 rosette (5/9/5 grouping with a large center ring of abalone pearl), grained ivoroid binding, Style 42 with B/W wood fiber top inlay, B/W back and side inlays, mahogany V-shaped neck, 14/20-fret grained ivoroid-bound fingerboard with Style 45 heart pearl snowflake inlays and bordered in MOP and 20th fret Eric Clapton signature inlay, bound headstock with solid Brazilian rosewood overlay and alternate torch abalone pearl inlay, logo stamp on back of headstock, three-per-side gold Waverly tuners with butterbean knobs, ebony belly bridge with six point heart pearl snowflake inlays bordered in MOP, fossilized ivory bridge pins with black pearl dots, labeld signed by CFM IV and Eric Clapton, Natural polished gloss finish with Vintage Toner top, 24.9 in. scale, case with combination lock included, limited edition run of 200 instruments, mfg. 2000 only.

	N/A	$10,750 - 13,500	$6,500 - 8,000	$15,000

000-42M ERIC CLAPTON (2008) – Grand Auditorium 14-fret 000-style body based on the 000-42ECB Eric Clapton Signature produced in 2000, solid Carpathian spruce top, solid Madagascar rosewood back and sides, Style 45 rosette, grained ivoroid binding, Style 42 black/maple/black fiber top inlay, black/maple fiber back and side inlays, select hardwood neck, grained ivoroid with black/maple fiber inlay heelcap, 14/20-fret grained ivoroid-bound ebony fingerboard with select abalone Style 45 snowflake inlays and Eric Clapton's signature in Agoya between the 19th and 20th frets, bound headstock with solid Madagascar rosewood overlay and select abalone alternate torch inlays, three-per-side Waverly nickel tuners with ivoroid butterbean knobs, belly-style ebony bridge with bone saddle, tortoiseshell pickguard, signed by Eric Clapton and individually numbered, available in Natural Gloss or Sunburst finish, 24.9 in. scale, limited edition run of 250 instruments, mfg. 2008 only.

	N/A	$4,800 - 6,000	$2,900 - 3,600	$9,749

- **Add 2.5% (Last MSR was $9,999) for Sunburst finish.**

000-45JR JIMMIE RODGERS (1997) – Grand Auditorium 12-fret 000-style body, solid bookmatched Adirondack spruce top, solid Brazilian rosewood back and sides, scalloped forward-shifted bracing, round soundhole with three-ring Style 45 rosette (5/9/5 grouping with a large center ring of pearl), grained ivoroid binding, Style 45 abalone pearl with B/W/B top inlay, mahogany neck, 12/19-fret grained ivoroid-bound ebony fingerboard with pearl MOP "JIMMIE RODGERS" and diamond/square/snowflake inlays, bound slotted headstock with solid Brazilian rosewood overlay and MOP "BLUE YODEL" inlay (no logo), three-per-side gold Waverly open-geared side-mount tuners with ivoroid buttons, ebony pyramid bridge with MOP snowflake inlays, fossilized ivory bridge pins with abalone pearl dots, label signed by CFM IV, Natural polished gloss finish with Vintage Toner top, 25.4 in. scale, case included, limited edition run of 100 instruments, mfg. 1997 only.

	N/A	$10,750 - 13,500	$6,500 - 8,100	$25,000

This model is the replica of Jimmie Rodgers' 1928 000-45 and these guitars were offered with an optional "THANKS" printing on the back.

000-45S STEPHEN STILLS (2005) – Grand Auditorium 12-fret 000-style body, solid Adirondack spruce top, solid East Indian rosewood back and sides, round soundhole with three-ring Style 45 rosette (5/9/5 grouping with large middle ring of abalone pearl), grained ivoroid binding, Style 42 abalone pearl with multiple black/white top inlay, abalone pearl with B/W/B back and side inlays, Style 45 Golden Era back purfling, solid mahogany neck, 12/20-fret grained ivoroid-bound ebony fingerboard with Golden Era Style 45 snowflake and 18th-20th fret MOP Stephen Stills signature inlays, bound slotted headstock with East Indian rosewood overlay and large abalone vertical block logo, three-per-side open-style gold Waverly/Sloane tuners with small ivoroid knobs, pyramid ebony bridge with drop-in saddle, fossil ivory bridge pins with black pearl dots, no pickguard, label signed by Stephen Stills and CFM IV, numbered in sequence, and includes a photo of the album cover, Natural polished gloss finish with Vintage Toner top and dark filler back and sides, 25.4 in. scale, case included, limited edition run of 91 instruments, mfg. 2005 only.

	N/A	$6,000 - 7,500	$3,600 - 4,500	$12,999

000C STEVE MILLER (2005) – single cutaway Grand Auditorium 14-fret 000-style body, solid Engelmann spruce top, solid quilted mahogany back and sides, hybrid scalloped bracing, round soundhole with three-ring Style 45 rosette (5/9/5 grouping with large middle ring of abalone pearl), grained ivoroid binding, fine herringbone top inlay, B/W/B Boltaron back and side inlay, Style 45 back purfling, select hardwood neck, 14/20-fret grained ivoroid-bound ebony fingerboard with no inlays, bound headstock with ebony overlay and special select pearl 1902-style inlay, three-per-side nickel open-geared Gotoh tuners with Butterbean knobs, ebony vintage belly bridge with drop-in long saddle, ebony bridge pins with abalone pearl dots, black beveled pickguard, Fishman Ellipse System electrincs, two labels with one signed by CFM IV, Steve Miller, and Dick Boak, and numbered in sequence, and the other with Steve Miller Pegasus logo, Natural polished gloss finish with Vintage Toner top and Dark Mahogany back, sides, and neck, 24.9 in. scale, case included, limited edition run of 383 instruments, mfg. 2005 only.

	N/A	$2,100 - 2,500	$1,500 - 1,800	$4,499

A portion of the proceeds from this guitar supported The Snake River Alliance, an Idaho-based community organization working through research, education, and community advocacy for peace and justice, the end of nuclear weapons production facilties, and responsible solutions to nuclear waste and contamination.

000C-16RB BABYFACE (2000) – single cutaway 14-fret 000-style body, solid Italian Alpine spruce top, solid East Indian rosewood back and sides, Hybrid X scalloped bracing, round soundhole with three-ring Style 45 rosette (5/9/5 grouping with a large center ring of abalone pearl), grained ivoroid binding, fine herringbone top inlay, B/W back inlay, HD-28-style zig-zag back purfling, mahogany neck, 14/20-fret long pattern abalone pearl diamond and squares and 20th fret Babyface signature inlay, solid Indian rosewood headstock overlay with logo, three-per-side chorme Gotoh tuners

MSR/NOTES	100%	EXCELLENT	AVERAGE	LAST MSR

with butterbean knobs, ebony belly bridge, black bridge pins with white dots, no pickguard, label signed by CFM IV and Kenny Edmonds (Babyface), Natural polished gloss finish with Vintage Toner top, 24.9 in. scale, case included, limited edition run of 100 instruments, mfg. 2000-mid 2001.

	N/A	$1,350 - 1,650	$950 - 1,100	$2,850

000C-28 ANDY SUMMERS (2006) – single cutaway Grand Auditorium 14-fret 000-style body, solid Italian Alpine spruce top, solid East Indian rosewood back and sides, three-ring fine herringbone rosette (5/9/5 grouping), black and white check binding, B/W Boltaron back and side inlays, Style 45 back purfling, select hardwood neck, 14/20-fret grained ivoroid-bound ebony fingerboard with MOP Buddhist Mudhra, Yin/Yang, and 20th fret Andy Summers' signature inlays, bound headstock with ebony overlay and MOP Lotus flower inlay (no logo), three-per-side nickel Waverly tuners with butterbean knobs, pyramid Stauffer-style ebony bridge, ebony bridge pins with abalone pearl dots, Fishman Ellipse Matrix Blend electronics, label signed by CFM IV and Andy Summers and numbered in sequence, Natural polished gloss with Aging toner top finish, 24.9 in. scale, case included, limited edition run of 87 instruments, mfg. 2006 only.

	N/A	$2,750 - 3,250	$1,850 - 2,250	$5,999

000C-28SMH MERLE HAGGARD (2001) – single cutaway Grand Auditorium 12-fret 000-style body, solid Sitka spruce top, solid East Indian rosewood back and sides, three-ring Style 45 rosette (5/9/5 grouping with a large center ring of abalone pearl), grained ivoroid binding, fine herringbone top inlay, mahogany neck, 12/20-fret ebony fingerboard with long pattern abalone pearl diamonds and square inlays and 20th fret Merle Haggard signature inlay, slotted headstock with solid East Indian rosewood headstock overlay with MOP "Blue Yodel #13" inlay and CFM stamp on back of headstock, three-per-side open-style nickel Waverly tuners with butterbean knobs, ebony belly bridge, ebony bridge pins with abalone pearl dots, no pickguard, label signed by CFM IV and Merle Haggard, Natural polished gloss finish with Aging Toner top, 25.4 in. scale, case included, limited edition run of 122 instruments, mfg. early 2001 only.

	N/A	$2,500 - 3,000	$1,750 - 2,100	$4,799

000CBD DION (2002) – single cutaway Grand Auditorium 14-fret 000-style body, solid Sitka spruce top, solid mahogany back and sides, 0001 Hybrid, 1 Style/scalloped bracing, round soundhole with a single ring rosette (large middle ring of blue paua pearl with B/W/B fiber on both sides), black Boltaron binding, B/W top inlay, multiple B/W back and side inlays, mahogany neck, 14/20-fret ebony fingerboard with long pattern diamond and squares inlays and 19th-20th fret "The Wanderer" inlay, ebony headstock overlay with abalone pearl New York City skyline and Dion signature inlays and a raised silver foil logo, three-per-side chrome Schaller tuners with large ebony knobs, ebony belly bridge with two abalone pearl bird inlays, black beveled pickguard, Fishman Gold Plus Natural II electronics, label signed by CFM IV and Dion and numbered in sequence, Black polished gloss finish, 25.4 in. scale, case included, limited edition run of 57 instruments, mfg. 2002 only.

	N/A	$2,800 - 3,500	$1,675 - 2,100	$3,299

000CDG DOUG GRETH (2011) – single cutaway Grand Auditorium 12-fret 000-style body, solid certified European spruce top, solid certified mahogany back and sides, unique A-frame X bracing, round soundhole with Celtic Knot design rosette, grained ivoroid binding, multi-ply B/W top inlay, B/W/B Boltaron back inlay, Style 45 back purfling, solid certified mahogany neck, 12/20-fret grained black Richlite fingerboard with no inlays, slotted headstock with black Corian overlay and gold script logo, three-per-side brass open-geared Gotoh tuners with pearl buttons, black Richlite classic bridge with drop-in saddle, no pickguard, Fishman F1 analog electrincs, two labels with one signed by CFM IV and numbered in sequence, and the other with FSC mixed sources, Natural polished gloss finish with Mellow Yellow toner top, 26.44 in. scale, case included, limited edition run of 48 instruments, mfg. summer 2011 only.

	$2,400	$1,400 - 1,650	$950 - 1,100	$2,999

000-ECHF BELLEZZA BIANCA (2006) – Grand Auditorium 14-fret 000-style body, solid Engelmann Spruce top, solid Pacific Big Leaf flame maple back and sides, round soundhole with custom design rosette (black and silver diamond pattern with white fiber inlay borders), grained ivoroid binding, fine herringbone top inlay, multiple B/W Boltaron back and side inlay, select hardwood neck, 14/20-fret grained ivoroid-bound ebony fingerboard with Style 45 select abalone pearl snowflakes and abalone/MOP "Bellezza Bianaca" 20th fret inlays, bound headstock with ebony overlay and select pearl alternate torch pattern inlay (no logo), three-per-side silver-plated Gotoh tuners, ebony belly bridge, ebony bridge pins with abalone pearl dots, black pickguard, label signed by CFM IV, Eric Clapton, Hiroshi Fujiwara, and Dick Boak, White polished gloss finish (the entire body, neck, and back of the headstock are all White), 24.9 in. scale, case included, limited edition run of 410 instruments, mfg. 2006 only.

	N/A	$3,600 - 4,500	$2,150 - 2,750	$5,999

000-ECHF BELLEZZA NERA (2004) – Grand Auditorium 14-fret 000-style body, solid Engelmann Spruce top, solid East Indian rosewood back and sides, round soundhole with custom design rosette (black and silver diamond pattern with white fiber inlay borders), grained ivoroid binding, fine herringbone top inlay, multiple B/W Boltaron back and side inlay, mahogany neck, 14/20-fret grained ivoroid/mitered-bound ebony fingerboard with Style 45 select abalone pearl snowflakes and abalone/MOP "Bellezza Nera" 20th fret inlays, bound headstock with ebony overlay and select pearl alternate torch pattern inlay (no logo), three-per-side silver-plated Schaller tuners with large knobs, ebony belly bridge, ebony bridge pins with abalone pearl dots, no pickguard, label signed by CFM IV, Eric Clapton, Hiroshi Fujiwara, and Dick Boak, Black polished gloss finish (the entire body, neck, and back of the headstock are all Black), 24.9 in. scale, case included, limited edition run of 476 instruments, mfg. summer 2004 only.

	N/A	$3,600 - 4,500	$2,150 - 2,750	$5,999

000-JBP JIMMY BUFFETT POLLYWOG (2003) – Grand Auditorium 12-fret 000-style body, solid Sitka spruce top, solid mahogany back and sides, hybrid scalloped bracing, round soundhole with single ring rosette (large ring of blue Paua pearl surrounded by B/W/B fiber), tortoise color binding, rope wood with B/W/B top inlay, B/W Boltaron back and side inlay, select hardwoods neck, 12/20-fret ebony fingerboard abalone pearl dots, 5th fret MOP ship wheel, and 20th fret Jimmy Buffet signature inlays, ebony headstock overlay with ship porthole/palm tree inlay (no logo), three-per-side gold Gotoh tuners with butterbean knobs, ebony straight-line bridge with drop-in saddle, black bridge pins with pearl dots, tortoise color pickguard, label signed by CFM IV and Jimmy Buffett and numbered in sequence, Natural polished gloss finish with Vintage Toner top and Dark Mahogany Stain back and sides, 25.4 in. scale, Honey Winn Skai Oxen leatherette covering case included, limited edition run of 305 instruments, mfg. 2003 only.

	N/A	$2,600 - 3,250	$1,550 - 1,950	$3,699

MSR/NOTES	100%	EXCELLENT	AVERAGE	LAST MSR

000-JBS JIMMY BUFFETT SHELLBACK (2003) – Grand Auditorium 12-fret 000-style body, solid mahogany top, solid mahogany back and sides, hybrid scalloped bracing, round soundhole with single ring rosette (large ring of blue Paua pearl surrounded by B/W/B fiber), tortoise color binding, rope wood with B/W/B top inlay, B/W Boltaron back and side inlay, select hardwoods neck, 12/20-fret ebony fingerboard abalone pearl dots, 5th fret MOP ship wheel, and 20th fret Jimmy Buffet signature inlays, ebony headstock overlay with ship porthole/palm tree inlay (no logo), three-per-side gold Gotoh tuners with butterbean knobs, ebony straight-line bridge with drop-in saddle, black bridge pins with pearl dots, tortoise color pickguard, label signed by CFM IV and Jimmy Buffett and numbered in sequence, Natural polished gloss finish with Dark Stain top and Dark Mahogany Stain back and sides, 25.4 in. scale, Honey Winn Skai Oxen leatherette covering case included, limited edition run of 168 instruments, mfg. 2003 only.

	N/A	$1,850 - 2,250	$1,200 - 1,500	$3,699

000X HIPPIE (2007) – Grand Auditorium 14-fret 000-style body, HPL top, back, and sides, round soundhole, mortise neck, 14/20-fret black Micarta fingerboard with no inlays, matching finish headstock with graphics, three-per-side black Gotoh tuners, black Micarta bridge, available in custom Hippie multi-color finish with Peace and Love graphics, orange back, yellow sides, 25.4 in. scale, limited edition run of 200 instruments, mfg. summer 2007 only.

	N/A	$1,000 - 1,250	$600 - 750	$1,249

0000-28H AG ARLO GUTHRIE (1997) – Grand Auditorium 14-fret 0000/M-38-style body, solid Sitka spruce top, solid East Indian rosewood back and sides, round soundhole with three-ring Style 45 rosette (5/9/5 grouping with a large center ring of abalone pearl), grained ivoroid binding, bold herringbone top inlay, B/W back inlay, Style 45 back purfling, mahogany neck, 14/20-fret ebony fingerboard with circles and arrows, 12-13th and 16th fret "Alice"s Restaurant 30th," and 20th fret Arlo Guthrie signature inlays, solid East Indian rosewood headstock overlay with raised gold logo and engraved pearl representation of Alice's restaurant peghead inlay, three-per-side chrome Schaller tuners with large ebony buttons, solid Brazilian rosewood belly bridge, white bridge pins with pearl dots, tortoise color pickguard, label signed by CFM IV and Arlo Gutherie, Natural polished gloss finish with Vintage Toner top, 25.4 in. scale, denim-covered case included, limited edition run of 30 instruments, mfg. summer 1997 only.

	N/A	$2,600 - 3,250	$1,550 - 1,950	$4,750

* *0000-1228H AG Arlo Guthrie 12-String (1997)* – similar to the 0000-28H AG Arlo Guthrie, except in 12-string configuration and six-per-side tuners, limited edition run of 30 instruments, mfg. summer 1997 only.

	N/A	$2,800 - 3,500	$1,675 - 2,100	$4,950

ACOUSTIC: LIMITED EDITION MODELS STARTING WITH A-D

In 2011, Martin produced the **CS-21-11** (MSR $6,499) and the **CS-35-11** (MSR $6,999) with Madagascar rosewood back and sides. In 2012, Martin produced the **CS-D18-12** (MSR $6,499) with Sinker mahogany and a 12-fret body, the **CS-D28-12** (MSR $6,999) with Cocobolo, and the **CS-D28-12 Sunburst** (MSR $7,249).

AMERICA'S GUITAR (2008) – dreadnought 14-fret-style body, solid Adirondack spruce top, solid Madagascar rosewood back and sides, Style 28 black/maple fiber rosette, solid Hawaiian koa binding, fine herringbone top inlay, select hardwood neck, 14/20-fret ebony fingerboard with select abalone diamonds and squares inlays bordered in MOP and a 12th fret 175th Anniversary logo inlay, regular headstock with solid ebony overlay and MOP "Martin 1833-2008 America's Guitar" logo inlay, three-per-side Waverly nickel tuners with butterbean knobs, 1930s-style belly ebony bridge with drop-in long saddle, tortoiseshell pickguard, two labels (one signed by CFM IV number in sequence and one with photo of CFM IV and family), available in Natural Gloss finish, 25.4 in. scale, limited edition run of 175 instruments, mfg. 2008 only.

	N/A	$3,600 - 4,500	$2,150 - 2,750	$7,499

ARTS AND CRAFTS (2006) – dreadnought 14-fret-style body, bearclaw solid Sitka spruce top, solid flame mahogany back and sides, D-OM scalloped bracing, round soundhole with bold herringbone rosette (5/9/5 grouping), solid East Indian rosewood binding, bold herringbone top inlay, maple and black fiber back inlay, select hardwood neck, 14/20-fret ebony fingerboard with gingko leaf inlays, East Indian rosewood headstock overlay with large vertical block logo, three-per-side Antique Gold tuners with large knobs, pyramid Stauffer-style ebony bridge, ebony bridge pins, leather pickguard, label signed by CFM IV, Natural polished gloss with Aging toner top finish, 25.4 in. scale, brown leather case included, limited edition run of 100 instruments, mfg. 2006 only.

	N/A	$2,750 - 3,250	$1,850 - 2,250	$5,799

ARTS & CRAFTS 2 (2008) – Grand Auditorium 14-fret 000-style body, solid Englemann spruce top, solid German White oak back and sides, bold herringbone with black/maple fiber rosette, solid East Indian rosewood binding, bold Herringbone top inlay, black/maple fiber back inlay, select hardwood neck, 12/20-fret ebony fingerboard with gold MOP Ginkgo leaf inlays, regular headstock with solid East Indian rosewood overlay and gold MOP block-style Martin logo, three-per-side Gotoh antique gold tuners with large buttons, pyramid Stauffer-style ebony bridge with bone saddle, no pickguard, signed by CFM IV and individually numbered, available in Natural Gloss finish, 25.4 in. scale, limited edition run of 100 instruments, mfg. 2008-09.

	N/A	$2,900 - 3,500	$1,900 - 2,200	$6,499

CLAIRE'S GUITAR (2005) – size 5/Terz 12-fret-style body, solid Sitka spruce top, solid Brazilian rosewood back and sides, round soundhole with three-ring Style 45 rosette (5/9/5 grouping with a large middle ring of abalone pearl), grained ivoroid binding, Style 41 abalone pearl top inlay, B/W Boltaron back inlay, select hardwood neck, 12/18-fret ebony fingerboard with custom pearl "CFM" building blocks, square and diamonds, and an 18th-fret footprint inlays, solid Brazilian rosewood headstock overlay with gold logo, three-per-side gold Waverly tuners with butterbean knobs, ebony square long saddle bridge, bone bridge pins with Awabi ribbon pearl dots, Natural polished gloss with Aging Toner top finish, 21.4 in. scale, label signed by CFM IV and Diane S. Repyneck, case included, limited edition run of 100 instruments, mfg. 2005-mid-06.

	N/A	$2,600 - 3,250	$1,575 - 1,950	$6,999

MSR/NOTES	100%	EXCELLENT	AVERAGE	LAST MSR

CLAIRE 2 (2007) – Size 5/Terz 12-fret-style body, solid Adirondack spruce top, solid European flamed maple back and sides, Style 45 rosette, grained ivoroid binding, Style 41 top inlay, mahogany neck, 12/18-fret ebony fingerboard with Style 45 pearl snowflake inlays, black ebony headstock overlay with alternative torch pattern pearl inlay, three-per-side gold Waverly tuners with ivoroid butterbean buttons, ebony bridge, available in Natural finish with Trans. Pink back and sides, 21.38 in. scale, limited edition run of 100 instruments, mfg. 2007-mid-2010.

	$5,500	$3,200 - 3,700	$1,950 - 2,300	$6,799

CMSH STING CLASSICAL (1998) – classical nylon-string configuration, Martin/Humphrey-style body, solid western red cedar top, solid quilted mahogany back and sides, round soundhole with wooden rosette (light and dark brown lines of natural wood with thin stripes of black and white), tortoise color body binding, B/W top, back, and side inlays, mahogany neck, 12/19-fret ebony fingerboard with inset abalone pearl bordering, abalone pearl dots with 19th fret Sting signature inlay, slotted headstock with ebony overlay and raised gold foil logo, three-per-side open-style gold tuners with pearl buttons, ebony tied bridge, Martin/Fishman Thinline Gold Plus system, Natural finish with Aging Toner top, limited edition run of 250 instruments, mfg. 1998 only.

	N/A	$2,400 - 3,000	$1,450 - 1,800	$4,450

CONCEPT IV (2004) – single cutaway Jumbo 14-fret-style body, solid Sitka spruce top, solid soft red curly maple back and sides, round soundhole with single ring rosette (large pearl ring surrounded by B/W/B fiber), two-piece maple neck, 14/20-fret black Boltaron-bound black Micarta fingerboard with hollow pearl hexagon inlays, solid maple headstock overlay with matching finish and gold foil logo, three-per-side gold Gotoh tuners, black Micarta belly bridge with hollow pearl hexagon inlays, black bridge pins with pearl dots, no pickguard, Fishman Prefix Premium Stereo Onboard Blender electronics, available in Englehart Firemist Blue Pigment polished gloss finish, 25.4 in. scale, case included, limited edition run of 15 instruments, mfg. 2004 only.

	N/A	$1,850 - 2,150	$1,200 - 1,500	$3,999

COWBOY II (2001) – Grand Auditorium 14-fret 000-style body, High Pressure Laminate (HPL) top with custom Cowboy Breakfast Scene graphic designed by Robert Armstrong, Sol Durango HPL back and sides with textured finish, 000-1 A-frame bracing, round soundhole, Brown Stratabond neck, 14/20-fret black Micarta fingerboard with old Style 18 abalone pearl dot inlays, Jett Black HPL headstock overlay with raised old style raised gold foil logo, three-per-side black Gotoh tuners, black Micarta belly bridge, no pickguard, label numbered in sequence with total, case included, 25.4 in. scale, hard shell case included, limited edition run of 500 instruments, mfg. early 2001 only.

	N/A	$475 - 550	$325 - 400	$999

COWBOY III (2001) – Grand Auditorium 14-fret 000-style body, High Pressure Laminate (HPL) top with custom Cowboy Bucking Bronco Scene graphic designed by Robert Armstrong, Arroyo Durango HPL back and sides with textured finish, 000-1 A-frame bracing, round soundhole, Olive Stratabond neck, 14/20-fret black Micarta fingerboard with old Style 18 abalone pearl dot inlays, Jett Black HPL headstock overlay with raised old style raised gold foil logo, three-per-side black Gotoh tuners, black Micarta belly bridge, no pickguard, label numbered in sequence with total, case included, 25.4 in. scale, hard shell case included, limited edition run of 750 instruments, mfg. summer 2001 only.

	N/A	$475 - 550	$325 - 400	$1,099

COWBOY IV (2003) – Grand Auditorium 14-fret 000-style body, High Pressure Laminate (HPL) top with custom Cowboy Branding Guitar Scene graphic designed by Robert Armstrong, Red Rock Durango HPL back and sides with textured finish, 000-1 A-frame bracing, round soundhole, Rust Stratabond neck, 14/20-fret black Micarta fingerboard with old Style 18 abalone pearl dot inlays, Jett Black HPL headstock overlay with raised old style raised gold foil logo, three-per-side black Gotoh tuners, black Micarta belly bridge, no pickguard, label numbered in sequence with total, case included, 25.4 in. scale, includes padded gig bag, limited edition run of 250 instruments, mfg. 2003-mid-05.

	N/A	$475 - 550	$325 - 400	$1,199

COWBOY V (2006) – Little Martin-style body, High Pressure Laminate (HPL) top with custom Cowboy graphic designed by Robert Armstrong, HPL back with crosswalk pattern, HPL sides, modified X bracing, round soundhole, natural Stratabond neck, 14/20-fret black Micarta fingerboard, Jett Black HPL headstock overlay with logo, three-per-side Cosmo black Gotoh tuners, black Micarta belly bridge, numbered in sequence with total, 23 in. scale, includes padded gig bag, limited edition run of 500 instruments, mfg. summer 2006-09.

	N/A	$300 - 350	$175 - 225	$599

CS-OM-13 (2013) – Orchestra 14-fret 000-style body, solid high altitude Swiss spruce top, solid Madagascar rosewood back and sides, round soundhole with three-ring Style 28 rosette (5/9/5 grouping), quilted bubinga binding, bold herringbone, multi-ply black/maple fiber top inlay, black/maple/black back binding, select hardwood Custom Shop #1 profile neck, 14/20-fret quilted bubinga-bound ebony fingerboard with pearl scalloped diamond and red spiny Recon stone with MOP border inlays, solid Madagascar rosewood headstock overlay with script logo, three-per-side Waverly nickel tuners with snakewood knobs, ebony belly bridge, black bridge pins with white dots, tortoise color pickguard, Natural polished gloss finish, 25.4 in. scale, case included, limited edition run of 80 instruments, mfg. 2013-present.

MSR $6,899	$5,500	$2,950 - 3,700	N/A	

D12-42RM ROGER MCGUINN (1999) – 12-string configuration, dreadnought 14-fret-style body, solid Sitka spruce top, solid East Indian rosewood back and sides, standard X bracing, round soundhole with three-ring Style 45 rosette (5/9/5 grouping with a large center ring of abalone pearl), grained ivoroid binding, abalone pearl with W/B top inlays, B/W Boltaron back and side inlays, abalone pearl back purfling, mahogany neck, 14/20-fret grained ivoroid-bound ebony fingerboard with Style 45 abalone pearl hexagon inlays and 20th fret Roger McGuinn signature inlay, bound headstock with solid Indian rosewood overlay and large abalone pearl vertical block logo, six-per-side gold Schaller M6 tuners with small pearl buttons, ebony belly bridge, white bridge pins with pearl dots, tortoise color pickguard, Gold Plus Natural II electronics, label signed by CFM IV and Roger McGuinn, Natural polished gloss finish with Vintage Toner top, 24.9 in. scale, denim case included, limited edition run, mfg. 1999 only.

	N/A	$3,000 - 3,500	$2,100 - 2,500	$6,900

MSR/NOTES	100%	EXCELLENT	AVERAGE	LAST MSR

D-16BH BECK (2001) – dreadnought 14-fret-style body with shallow 000-style body depth, solid Sitka spruce top, solid East Indian rosewood back and sides, D1 Hybrid scalloped bracing, round soundhole with three-ring Style 45 rosette (5/9/5 grouping with large center ring of abalone pearl), tortoise color binding, B/W/B top, back, and side inlays, solid Spanish cedar neck, 14/20 ebony fingerboard with abalone dot inlays and 20th fret Beck signature inlay, solid East Indian rosewood headstock overlay with raised gold foil logo, three-per-side chrome Gotoh tuners with small ebony knobs, ebony belly bridge, tortoise color beveled pickguard, Fishman Gold Plus Natural II electronics, label signed by CFM IV and Beck and numbered in sequence, Natural polished gloss finish with Vintage Toner top and Dark Filler back and sides, 25.4 in. scale, case included, limited edition run of 99 instruments, mfg. summer 2001 only.

	N/A	$1,100 - 1,350	$750 - 900	$2,950

D-18 75TH ANNIVERSARY EDITION (2009) – dreadnought 14-fret-style body, solid Adirondack spruce top, solid mahogany back and sides, standard X scalloped forward-shifted bracing, round soundhole with three-ring old Style 18 rosette (1/9/1 grouping), black boltaron binding, multiple B/W boltaron top inlay, Style 18 back purfling, modified V select hardwood neck, 14/20-fret ebony fingerboard with old Style 18 dot inlays, solid Madagascar rosewood headstock overlay with gold foil logo and "75th Anniversary Edition 1934-2009" inscription, three-per-side chrome Waverly tuners with butterbean buttons, 1930s-style ebony belly bridge with long saddle, solid black ebony bridge pins, tortoise color pickguard, label signed by CFM IV and numbered in sequence, Natural polished gloss finish with Aging Toner top, 25.4 in. scale, 545V75 Harptone case with 75th Anniversary Edition embroidery included, mfg. 2009 only.

	N/A	$2,400 - 3,000	$1,450 - 1,800	$5,199

D-18 1955 CFM IV (2010) – dreadnought-style body based on a 1955 D-18, solid Sitka spruce top, solid quilted mahogany back and sides, standard X rear-shifted solid Sitka spruce bracing, round soundhole with three-ring old Style 18 rosette (1/9/1 grouping), tortoise color binding, multiple B/W boltaron top inlay, old Style 18 back purfling, mahogany modified V-shaped neck, 14/20-fret ebony fingerboard with 1955 era Style 18 dot inlays, rounded headstock corners with solid Madagascar rosewood overlay and gold foil C.F. Martin & Co. logo, three-per-side Grover Deluxe nickel tuners with oval buttons, 1930s-style belly ebony bridge with drop-in long saddle, Delmar tortoise color pickguard, label signed by CFM IV and numbered in sequence, available in Natural Gloss finish with Aging Toner top, 25.4 in. scale, limited edition run of 55 instruments, 545E Geib-style case included, mfg. summer 2010-2011.

	$3,800	$2,125 - 2,475	$1,400 - 1,650	$4,699

D18 ANDY GRIFFITH (2003) – dreadnought 14-fret-style body, bearclaw Sitka spruce top, solid quilted mahogany back and sides, D-OMLE/forward shifted bracing, round soundhole with three-ring Style 18 rosette (1/5/1 grouping of black/white fiber), tortoise color binding, multiple layer B/W top inlay, single tortoise color back stripe, select hardwood neck, 14/20-fret solid Brazilian rosewood fingerboard with old Style 18 MOP dot inlays and 20th fret Andy Griffith signature inlay, solid Brazilian rosewood headstock overlay with large old style logo, three-per-side nickel Grover Deluxe tuners (Kluson style), solid Brazilian rosewood vintage belly-style bridge with drop in long saddle, black bridge pins, clear pickguard, label signed by CFM IV and Andy Griffith and numbered in sequence, Natural polished gloss finish with Aging Toner top and Dark Mahogany back and sides, limited edition run of 311 instruments, mfg. summer 2003 only.

	N/A	$2,000 - 2,500	$1,200 - 1,500	$3,699

D-18CW CLARENCE WHITE (2001) – dreadnought 14-fret-style body, solid Adirondack spruce top, solid quilted mahogany back and sides, standard X scalloped forward-shifted bracing, round soundhole with a single ring rosette (large ring of abalone pearl surrounded by B/W/B wood fiber), tortoise color binding, multiple B/W top, back, and side inlays, fine herringbone back purfling, mahogany neck, 14/20-fret ebony fingerboard with 20th fret Clarence White signature, solid Indian rosewood headstock overlay with old Style logo, three-per-side nickel Waverly tuners with Butterbean knobs, ebony belly bridge with a long saddle, ebony bridge pins with abalone pearl dots, tortoise color pickguard, label signed by CFM IV and Michelle White Bledsoe, Natural polished gloss finish with Aging Toner top, 25.4 in. scale, case included, limited edition run of 292 instruments, mfg. early 2001 only.

	N/A	$1,650 - 2,000	$1,100 - 1,350	$3,999

D-18DC DAVID CROSBY (2002) – dreadnought 14-fret body-style, solid Engelmann spruce top, solid quilted mahogany back and sides, DOM forward shifted/scalloped bracing, round soundhole with three-ring Style 45 rosette (5/9/5 grouping with a large center ring of blue paua pearl), tortoise color binding, B/W top, back, and side inlays, Style 45 back purfling, solid mahogany neck, 14/20-fret ebony fingerboard with abalone dot inlays and 20th fret "David Crosby" signature inlay, solid ebony headstock overlay with raised gold foil logo and abalone pearl Schooner ship inlay, three-per-side nickel Waverly tuners with butterbean knobs, ebony belly bridge, black bridge pins with abalone dots, tortoise color beveled pickguard, label signed by CFM IV and David Crosby and numbered in sequence, Natural polished gloss finish with Vintage Toner top and Maple Stain/Dark Filler back and sides, 25.4 in. scale, case included, limited edition run of 250 instruments, mfg. 2002 only.

	N/A	$2,000 - 2,500	$1,200 - 1,500	$3,799

D-18GL GORDON LIGHTFOOT (2000) – dreadnought 14-fret-style body, solid Englemann spruce top, solid quilted mahogany back and sides, standard X scalloped forward-shifted bracing, round soundhole with three-ring Style 45 rosette (5/9/5 grouping with large center ring of abalone pearl), tortoise color binding, B/W Style 18 top inlay, Style 18 back purfling, mahogany neck, 14/20-fret ebony fingerboard with abalone dots, 12th fret silhouette of the Edmund Fitzgerald, and 19-20th fret Gordon Lightfoot signature inlays, solid Indian rosewood headstock overlay with old Style logo, three-per-side chrome Gotoh tuners with oval buttons, ebony belly bridge, tortoise color pickguard, label signed by CFM IV and Gordon Lightfoot, Natural polished gloss finish with Vintage Toner top, 25.4 in. scale, case included, limited edition run of 61 instruments, mfg. summer 2000 only.

	N/A	$1,850 - 2,250	$1,200 - 1,500	$3,499

D-21JC JIM CROCE (2000) – dreadnought 14-fret-style body, solid Sitka spruce top, solid East Indian rosewood back and sides, standard X scalloped forward-shifted bracing, round soundhole with old Style 18 rosette, black Boltaron binding, multiple B/W top and side inlays, mahogany neck, 14/20-fret ebony fingerboard with Style 28 abalone dots, 3rd fret dime, and 19-20th fret Jim Croce signature inlays, solid Indian rosewood headstock overlay with old Style logo, three-per-side chrome Grover 102C tuners, ebony belly bridge, black bridge pins with white dots, black pickguard, two labels with one signed by CFM IV and Ingrid Croce and one with a photo of Jim Croce and an imprint of his signature, Natural polished gloss finish with Vintage Toner top, 25.4 in. excale, case included, limited edition run of 73 instruments, mfg. 2000 only.

	N/A	$3,200 - 4,000	$1,925 - 2,400	$3,450

MSR/NOTES	100%	EXCELLENT	AVERAGE	LAST MSR

* **D-21JCB Jim Croce Brazilian (2000)** – similar to the D-21JC Jim Croce, except has solid Brazilian rosewood back, sides, and headstock overlay, limited edition run of 73 instruments, mfg. 2000-mid 2001.

	N/A	$6,000 - 7,500	$3,600 - 4,500	$8,745

D-28 75TH ANNIVERSARY EDITION (2009) – dreadnought 14-fret-style body, solid Adirondack spruce top, solid Madagascar rosewood back and sides, standard X scalloped forward-shifted bracing, round soundhole with three-ring Style 28 rosette (5/9/5 grouping), grained ivoroid binding, multiple fine herringbone top inlay, B/W fiber back inlay, HD zig-zag back purfling, modified V select hardwood neck, 14/20-fret ebony fingerboard with golden era long pattern diamond and squares inlays, solid Madagascar rosewood headstock overlay with gold foil logo and "75th Anniversary Edition 1934-2009" inscription, three-per-side chrome Waverly tuners with butterbean buttons, 1930s-style ebony belly bridge with long saddle, fossilized ivory bridge pins with black dots, tortoise color pickguard, label signed by CFM IV and numbered in sequence, Natural polished gloss finish with Aging Toner top, 25.4 in. scale, 545V75 Harptone case with 75th Anniversary Edition embroidery included, mfg. 2009 only.

	N/A	$3,600 - 4,500	$2,150 - 2,900	$7,599

D-28 1955 CFM IV (2010) – dreadnought-style body based on a 1955 D-28, solid Sitka spruce top, solid Madagascar rosewood back and sides, standard X rear-shifted solid Sitka spruce bracing, round soundhole with three-ring Style 28 rosette (5/9/5 grouping), grained ivoroid binding, multiple B/W boltaron top inlay, B/W boltaron back inlay, Style 28 back purfling, select hardwood modified V-shaped neck, 14/20-fret ebony fingerboard with Style 28 dot inlays, rounded headstock corners with solid Madagascar rosewood overlay and gold foil C.F. Martin & Co. logo, three-per-side Kluson Waffleback nickel tuners with oval buttons, 1930s-style belly ebony bridge with drop-in long saddle, Delmar tortoise color pickguard, label signed by CFM IV and numbered in sequence, available in Natural Gloss finish with Aging Toner top, 25.4 in. scale, limited edition run of 55 instruments, 545E Geib-style case included, mfg. 2010 only.

	$5,200	$3,250 - 3,900	N/A	$6,499

D-28CWB CLARENCE WHITE (2002) – dreadnought 14-fret body style designed after Clarence White's 1935 D-28, solid Adirondak spruce top, solid Brazilian rosewood back and sides, standard X scalloped forwarded shifted bracing, large round soundhole with two-ring Style 28 black/white fiber rosette (9/5 grouping), grained ivoroid binding, fine herringbone top inlay, black/maple fiber back inlay, select hardwood neck, 14/21-fret ebony bound fingerboard that extends over the soundhole, solid Brazilian rosewood headstock overlay with a Golden Era logo, three-per-side Waverly nickel tuners with Butterbean knobs, ebony belly bridge with long saddle, white bridge pins with black dots, authentic tortoiseshell patterned pickguard, label signed by CFM IV and Michelle White Bledsoe and numbered in sequence, Natural polished gloss finish with Aging Toner top, 25.4 in. scale, case included, limited edition run of 150 instruments, mfg. summer 2002-04.

	N/A	$5,500 - 6,500	$3,500 - 4,250	$9,999

For the D-28CW Clarence White standard production model without Brazilian rosewood, refer to the Special Edition Series.

D-28DM DEL McCOURY (2002) – dreadnought 14-fret-style body, solid Adirondack spruce top, solid East Indian rosewood back and sides, DOM forward-shifted/scalloped bracing, three-ring rosette (1/5/1 grouping with a large center ring of blue paua pearl), grained ivoroid binding, B/W/B top inlay, B/W back inlay, HD zigzag back purfling, solid mahogany neck, 14/20-fret ebony fingerboard with lapis dot inlays outlined in MOP and optional 20th fret "Del McCoury" signature inlay, solid Brazilian rosewood headstock overlay with old style logo, three-per-side nickel Waverly W-16 tuners, ebony belly bridge, ebony bridge pins with lapis dots outlined by aluminum rings, tortoise color beveled pickguard, label signed by CFM IV and Del McCoury and numbered in sequence, Natural polished gloss finish with Aging Toner top and Dark Filler back and sides, 25.4 in. scale, case included, limited edition run of 115 instruments, mfg. summer 2002-mid 2003.

	N/A	$2,600 - 3,250	$1,575 - 1,950	$4,899

D-28HW HANK WILLIAMS SR. (1998) – dreadnought 14-fret-style body, solid Sitka spruce top, solid Brazilian rosewood back and sides, DOM forward-shifted scalloped bracing, round soundhole with Style 28 wood fiber rosette, grained ivoroid binding, fine herringbone with wood fiber top and back inlays, HD zig-zag back purfling, mahogany neck, 14/20-fret ebony fingerboard with diamond and square inlays and 20th fret Hank Williams signature inlay, solid Brazilian rosewood headstock overlay with large old Style logo, three-per-side chrome Waverly tuners, ebony belly bridge with long saddle, fossil ivory bridge pins with tortoise color dots, tortoise color beveled pickguard, label signed by CFM IV, Natural polished gloss finish with Aging Toner top and Dark Filler back and sides, 25.4 in. scale, case included, limited edition run of 150 instruments, mfg. 1998 only.

	N/A	$7,000 - 9,500	$4,550 - 5,700	$9,000

This guitar commemorates the 75th birthday anniversary of Hank Williams, Sr. and is modeled closely after his original 1944 D-28.

D-28KTBS BOB SHANE (2003) – dreadnought 14-fret-style body, solid Sitka spruce top, solid East Indian rosewood back and sides, D-OMLE scalloped bracing, round soundhole with three-ring Style 28 rosette (5/9/5 grouping of black/white fiber), grained ivoroid binding, B/W/B top inlay, B/W back inlay, mahogany neck, 14/20-fret ebony fingerboard with MOP Style 28 dots, 11th-13th fret "The Kingston Trio," and 20th fret Bob Shane inlays, solid Indian rosewood headstock with large old style logo, three-per-side chrome Grover tuners, ebony belly bridge with drop-in saddle, white bridge pins with tortoise dots, tortoise color pickguard, label signed by CFM IV and Bob Shane and numbered in sequence, Natural polished gloss with Aging Toner top finish, 25.4 in. scale, case included, limited edition run of 19 instruments, mfg. 2003 only.

	N/A	$1,850 - 2,250	$1,200 - 1,500	$3,799

* **D-28KTBSDG Bob Shane Double Guard (2003)** – similar to the D-28KTBS Bob Shane, except has a large Josh White-style double black pickguard that covers most of the upper body, limited edition run of 32 instruments, mfg. 2003 only.

	N/A	$2,000 - 2,400	$1,350 - 1,650	$3,999

MSR/NOTES	100%	EXCELLENT	AVERAGE	LAST MSR

D-28LF LESTER FLATT (1998) – dreadnought 14-fret-style body, solid Sitka spruce top, solid Brazilian rosewood back and sides, standard X bracing, round soundhole with Style 28 rosette, grained ivoroid binding, Style 28 top inlay and back purfling, mahogany neck, 14/20-fret ebony fingerboard with specially designed custom Mike Longworth inlays, solid Brazilian rosewood headstock overlay with old Style logo, three-per-side nickel Gotoh tuners with oval buttons, ebony belly bridge with long saddle, white bridge pins with tortoise dots, tortoise color pickguard available in standard size or special Flatt oversize, label signed by CFM IV and pre-printed Lester Flatt, Natural polished gloss finish with Aging Toner, 25.4 in. scale, case included, limited edition run of 50 instruments, mfg. summer 1998 only.

	N/A	$6,000 - 7,000	$4,250 - 5,000	$8,500

D-28M ELVIS PRESLEY (2008) – dreadnought-style body based on Presley's 1955 D-28 with a custom-tooled leather cover with his name across the lower bout, solid Adirondack spruce top, solid Madagascar rosewood back and sides, Style 28 rosette, grained ivoroid multiple black/white boltaron binding, select hardwood neck, MOP TCB lightning bolt graphic in black micarta neck heel, 14/20-fret ebony fingerboard with select abalone star inlays bordered in MOP, regular headstock with solid ebony overlay and black/white abalone Elvis Presley graphic silhouette, three-per-side Grover Deluxe nickel tuners (Kluson-style), vintage belly ebony bridge with drop-in long saddle, black pickguard, two labels (Elvis label with holographic sticker numbered in sequence, an album cover label), available in Natural Gloss finish, 25.4 in. scale, limited edition run of 175 instruments, mfg. 2008-mid-2010.

	$9,200	$5,500 - 6,250	N/A	$11,499

D-28M MERLE TRAVIS (2008) – dreadnought 14-fret-style body, solid Adirondack spruce top, solid Madagascar rosewood back and sides, standard X scalloped forward-shifted bracing, round soundhole with three-ring Style 28 rosette (5/9/5 grouping), grained ivoroid binding, fine herringbone top inlay, black/maple fiber back inlay, HD zig-zag back purfling, curly maple low-profile neck, 14/20-fret ebony fingerboard with custom heart/club/diamond/square inlays, Bigsby-style headstock with figured walnut overlay and Bigsby logo inlay, small old style Martin logo on back of headstock, six-on-one-side nickel Grover Vintage Deluxe tuners, solid Brazilian rosewood bridge, bone bridge pins with tortoise dots, black unique Travis-shaped pickguard, label signed by CFM IV, Thom Bresh, and Fred Gretsch and numbered in sequence, Natural polished gloss finish with Aging Toner top, 25.4 in. scale, case included, mfg. summer 2008-2010.

	$6,400	$3,700 - 4,400	$2,500 - 2,900	$7,999

D-28 SPECIAL "WALK THE LINE" (2005) – special black D-28 made exclusively for the movie "Walk The Line", labled inside "To commemorate the release of 'Walk the Line' - Original Motion Picture Soundtrack" In memory of Johnny Cash 1932-2003. Limited production of 12 instruments, no. 1 given to Joaquin Phoenix, remaining 11 were given away through various contests, mfg. 2005 only.

	N/A	N/A	N/A	

Extreme rarity precludes accurate pricing on this model.

D-35 30TH ANNIVERSARY (1995) – dreadnought 14-fret-style body, solid spruce top, three-piece back with solid East Indian rosewood wings and a solid Brazilian rosewood center wedge, solid East Indian rosewood sides, ivoroid binding, mitered fingerboard binding, "1965-1995" logo inlaid at 20th fret, tortoiseshell pickguard, three-per-side gold tuners with "M" buttons, available in Natural finish, limited edition run of 207 instruments, mfg. 1995 only.

	N/A	$2,400 - 3,000	$1,450 - 1,800	$4,000

D-35 ERNEST TUBB (2003) – dreadnought 14-fret-style body, solid Italian Alpine spruce, three-piece back with solid East Indian rosewood wings and a solid Brazilian rosewood center wedge, solid East Indian rosewood sides, round soundhole with three-ring Style 45 rosette (5/9/5 grouping with a large middle ring of abalone pearl), tortoise color binding, rope wood with B/W/B top inlay, B/W Boltaron back inlay, multiple B/W side inlay, Women and Music mosaic back purfling, mahogany neck, 14/20-fret ebony fingerboard with custom inlays including 5th fret State of Texas silhouette, 7th fret pearl diamond, 9th fret pearl Lone Star, and 12th and 15th fret Style 42 inlays, tortoise-bound solid Brazilian rosewood headstock overlay with longhorn cattle skull and gold logo, ebony belly bridge, white bridge pins with tortoise color dots, Fishman Gold Plus Natural II electronics, label signed by CFM IV and Talmadge Tubb and numbered in sequence, available in Natural or Sunburst (optional) polished gloss finish with Vintage Toner top and Dark Filler back and sides, 25.4 in. scale, leatherette covering case included, limited edition run of 90 instruments, mfg. summer 2003 only.

	N/A	$3,000 - 3,500	$2,100 - 2,500	$4,499

D-37W LUCINDA WILLIAMS (2003) – dreadnought 14-fret-style body, solid Engelmann spruce top, solid flamed claro walnut back and sides, D-OMLE scalloped bracing, rround soundhole with three-ring Style 45 rosette (5/9/5 grouping with a large middle ring of abalone pearl), grained ivoroid binding, bold herringbone top inlay, B/W/B back inlay, mahogany neck, 14/20-fret ebony fingerboard with Foden-style inlays on the 5th, 7th, and 9th frets, solid flamed claro walnut headstock overlay with Aztec two-headed multi-color serpent inlay and gold foil logo, three-per-side nickel Waverly W-16 tuners, ebony belly bridge, white bridge pins with tortoise dots, tortoise pickguard, label signed by CFM IV and Lucinda Williams and numbered in sequence, Natural polished gloss with Vintage Sunburst top and Dark Filler back and sides finish, 25.4 in. scale, case included, limited edition run, mfg. summer 2003 only.

	N/A	$3,400 - 4,250	$2,050 - 2,550	$4,999

D-40DM DON MCLEAN (1998) – dreadnought 14-fret-style body, solid Englemann spruce, solid East Indian rosewood back and sides, standard X scalloped forward-shifted bracing, round soundhole with three-ring Style 45 rosette (5/9/5 grouping with a large center ring of abalone pearl), white Boltaron binding, multiple B/W Boltaron top and side inlays, B/W Boltaron back inlay, Style 45 back purfling, mahogany neck, 14/20-fret white Boltaron-bound ebony fingerboard with American Pie hexagon themed inlays and 20th fret Don McLean signature inlay, White Boltaron-bound headstock with ebony overlay, MOP modified torch inlay and logo, three-per-side gold Schaller M6 tuners with large pearl buttons, ebony belly bridge, white bridge pins with pearl dots, tortoise color pickguard, label signed by CFM IV and Don McLean and has McLean's hand-colored thumbs up logo, Natural polished gloss finish with Aging Toner top, 25.4 in. scale, tweed case included, limited edition run of 71 instruments, mfg. summer 1998-2000.

	N/A	$4,000 - 5,000	$2,400 - 3,000	$5,750

MSR/NOTES	100%	EXCELLENT	AVERAGE	LAST MSR

D-40FMG (1995) – dreadnought 14-fret-style body, solid Sitka spruce, solid quilted mahogany back and sides, standard X scalloped bracing, round soundhole with three-ring Style 45 rosette (5/9/5 grouping with a large center ring of abalone pearl), tortoise top and back binding, multiple B/W top, back, and side inlays, Style 45 back purfling, mahogany neck, 14/20-fret tortoise-bound ebony fingerboard with hexagon pearl inlays, tortoise-bound headstock with rosewood overlay, MOP vertical block logo, three-per-side gold Gotoh tuners, ebony belly bridge, white bridge pins with pearl dots, tortoise color pickguard, label signed by CFM IV, Natural polished gloss finish , 25.4 in. scale, case included, limited edition run of 150 instruments, mfg. 1995 only.

| | N/A | $4,800 - 6,000 | $2,850 - 3,600 | |

D-40QM (1996) – dreadnought 14-fret-style body, solid Sitka spruce, solid quilted maple back and sides, standard X scalloped forward-shifted bracing, round soundhole with three-ring Style 45 rosette (5/9/5 grouping with a large center ring of abalone pearl), tortoise top and back binding, multiple B/W top, back, and side inlays, Style 45 back purfling, mahogany neck, 14/20-fret tortoise-bound ebony fingerboard with hexagon pearl inlays, tortoise-bound headstock with rosewood overlay, MOP vertical block logo, three-per-side gold tuners, ebony belly bridge, white bridge pins with pearl dots, tortoise color pickguard, label signed by CFM IV, Natural polished gloss finish , 25.4 in. scale, case included, limited edition run of 200 instruments, mfg. 1996 only.

| | N/A | $2,250 - 2,750 | $1,500 - 1,850 | |

D-41DF DAN FOGELBERG (2001) – dreadnought 14-fret-style body, solid Sitka spruce top, solid East Indian rosewood back and sides, D OM non-scalloped bracing, round soundhole with three-ring Style 45 rosette (5/9/5 grouping with a large center ring of abalone pearl), grained ivoroid binding, abalone pearl with B/W/B top inlays, B/W back inlays, mahogany neck, 14/20-fret ebony fingerboard with original Style 41 hexagon block inlays and 20th fret Dan Fogelberg inlay, bound headstock with solid East Indian rosewood overlay and large vertical abalone pearl block-style logo, three-per-side gold Grover tuners with large knobs, ebony belly bridge, black pickguard, label signed by CFM IV and Dan Fogelberg and numbered in sequence, Natural polished gloss finish with Aging Toner top and Dark Filler back and sides, 25.4 in. scale, case included, limited edition run of 141 instruments, mfg. summer 2001 only.

| | N/A | $3,600 - 4,500 | $2,150 - 2,750 | $4,750 |

D-41GJ GEORGE JONES (2000) – dreadnought 14-fret-style body, solid Englemann spruce top, solid East Indian rosewood back and sides, DOM forward-shifted scalloped bracing, round soundhole with three-ring Style 45 rosette (5/9/5 grouping with a large center ring of abalone pearl), grained ivoroid binding, Style 41 abalone pearl top and back inlays, Style 45 back purfling, mahogany neck, 14/20-fret grained ivoroid-bound ebony fingerboard with abalone pearl scalloped hexagon inlays and 19th-20th fret George Jones signature inlay, bound headstock with solid East Indian rosewood overlay and large abalone pearl vertical block inlay, three-per-side gold Waverly tuners with butterbean knobs, ebony belly bridge, white bridge pins with abalone dots, tortoise color pickguard, label signed by CFM IV and George Jones and numbered in sequence, Natural polished gloss finish with Aging Toner top and Dark Filler back and sides, 25.4 in. scale, case included, limited edition run of 100 instruments, mfg. summer 2000 only.

| | N/A | $3,200 - 4,000 | $1,925 - 2,400 | |

D-41K PURPLE MARTIN (2013) – dreadnought 14-fret-style body, solid Adirondack spruce top, solid highly flamed koa back and sides, three-ring Style 45 rosette (5/9/5 grouping with a large middle ring of abalone pearl), grained ivoroid binding, Style 41 abalone pearl with multiple B/W fiber top inlays, B/W Boltaron back inlay, select hardwood modified low profile neck, 14/20-fret grained ivoroid-bound ebony fingerboard with bird theme inlays, bound headstock with rosewood overlay and old style abalone inlay, three-per-side gold tuners with engraved C.F. Martin knobs, ebony belly bridge with bird inlays, bone bridge pins with select pearl dots, black pickguard with purple martin inlay, label signed by CFM IV and numbered in sequence, Natural polished gloss with againe Toner top finish, 25.4 in. scale, 1.75 in. nut width, case included, limited edition run of 50 instruments, mfg. 2013-present.

| MSR $9,999 | $8,000 | $4,200 - 5,250 | N/A | |

D-42 FLAMED MAHOGANY (2006) – dreadnought 14-fret-style body, solid Adirondack spruce top, solid flame mahogany back and sides, round soundhole with three-ring Style 45 rosette (5/9/5 grouping with a large middle abalone pearl ring), grained ivoroid binding, abalone pearl with B/W/B fiber top inlays, B/W Boltaron back and side inlays, select hardwood neck, 14/20-fret grained ivoroid-bound ebony fingerboard with abalone pearl decorative inlays, bound headstock with ebony overlay and logo, three-per-side gold Gotoh tuners with ebony buttons, ebony belly bridge, tortoise shell pickguard, label signed by CFM IV and numbered in sequence, Natural polished gloss finish with mahogany stain, case included, limited edition run of 30 instruments, mfg. summer 2006 only.

| | N/A | $6,000 - 7,000 | $4,250 - 5,000 | $9,999 |

D-42JC JOHNNY CASH (1997) – dreadnought 14-fret-style body, solid Sitka spruce top, solid East Indian rosewood back and sides, round soundhole with three-ring Style 45 rosette (5/9/5 grouping with a large center ring of abalone pearl), grained ivoroid binding, Style 42 abalone pearl top inlay, multiple B/W back and side inlays, Style 45 back purfling, mahogany neck, 14/20-fret grained ivoroid-bound ebony fingerboard with abalone stars and 20th fret Johnny Cash signature inlays, bound headstock with ebony overlay and large vertical block logo inlay, three-per-side gold Gotoh tuners with butterbean knobs, ebony belly bridge, white bridge pins with pearl dots, black pickguard, label signed by CFM IV and Johnny Cash, Black polished gloss finish, 25.4 in. scale, case included, limited edition run of 200 instruments but only 80 were produced and sold, mfg. summer 1997-98.

| | N/A | $4,750 - 5,500 | $3,000 - 3,750 | $8,200 |

D-42 PETER FRAMPTON (2006) – dreadnought 14-fret-style body, solid Adirondack spruce top, solid East Indian rosewood back and sides, three-ring Style 45 rosette (5/9/5 grouping with a large middle ring of abalone pearl), grained ivoroid binding, abalone pearl with multiple B/W fiber top inlays, B/W Boltaron back inlay, select hardwood neck, 14/20-fret grained ivoroid-bound ebony fingerboard with abalone pearl Style 42 snowflakes and 20th Peter Frampton signature inlays, bound headstock with ebony overlay and old style abalone camel inlay, three-per-side gold Waverly tuners with ivroid butterbean knobs, ebony belly bridge, camel bone bridge pins with select pearl dots, tortoise color pickguard, label signed by CFM IV and Peter Frampton, Natural polished gloss with Vintage Toner top finish, 25.4 in. scale, case included, mfg. summer 2006 only.

| | N/A | $4,250 - 5,000 | $3,000 - 3,500 | $7,799 |

MSR/NOTES	100%	EXCELLENT	AVERAGE	LAST MSR

D-45 CELTIC KNOT (2004) – dreadnought 14-fret-style body, solid Adirondack spruce top, solid Brazilian rosewood back and sides, D-OMLE forward shifted bracing, round soundhole with three-ring Style 45 rosette (5/9/5 grouping with a large middle ring of abalone pearl), grained ivoroid binding, abalone pearl with black/maple/black fiber top, back, and side inlays, select hardwood neck, 14/20-fret grained ivoroid/ mitered-bound ebony fingerboard with Awabi and Paua Celtic knot design inlays, bound headstock with solid Brazilian rosewood overlay and Awabi large vertical block inlay, three-per-side gold Gotoh tuners with celtic buttons, ebony 1930s-style belly bridge with long saddle, fossil ivory bridge pins with black pearl dots, tortoise color beveled pickguard, label signed by C.F. Martin IV and numbered in sequence, Natural polished gloss finish with Vintage Toner top and Dark Filler back and sides, case included, limited edition run of 30 instruments, mfg. 2004-06.

	N/A	$16,500 - 20,000	$11,000 - 13,500	$35,000

D-45 C.F. MARTIN SR. SIGNATURE (1996) – dreadnought 14-fret-style body, solid Sitka spruce top, solid East Indian rosewood back and sides, scalloped forward-shifted bracing, round soundhole with three-ring Style 45 rosette (5/9/5 grouping with a large center ring of abalone pearl), grained ivoroid binding, Style 45 abalone pearl top inlay that goes around the fingerboard, Style 45 abalone pearl back purfling, mahogany neck, 14/20-fret grained ivoroid-bound ebony fingerboard with abalone pearl bordering and abalone Style 45 snowflake inlays, ivoroid-bound headstock with abalone pearl bordering, large abalone pearl vertical block logo, three-per-side gold open geared tuners with Butterbean knobs, ebony belly bridge with abalone pearl snowflake inlays, tortoise color pickguard, Natural polished gloss finish, 25.4 in. scale, case included, limited edition run of 114 instruments, mfg. 1996 only.

	N/A	$6,250 - 7,500	$4,500 - 5,250	$11,000

This model commemorates the 200 year anniversary of Martin founder C.F. Martin, Sr.'s birthday (1796).

* **_D-45 C.F. Martin Sr. Deluxe Commemorative (1996)_** – similar to the D-45 C.F. Martin Sr. Signature, except has solid Brazilian rosewood back, sides, and headstock overlay and more ornate inlays, limited edition run of 91 instruments, mfg. 1996 only.

	N/A	$12,500 - 15,000	$9,000 - 10,500	$19,500

D-45 MIKE LONGWORTH (2005) – dreadnought 14-fret-style body, solid Adirondack spruce top, solid East Indian rosewood back and sides, forward shifted/scalloped bracing, round soundhole with three-ring Style 45 rosette (5/9/5 grouping with large middle ring of abalone pearl), grained ivoroid binding, abalone pearl with black/maple/black fiber top, back, and side inlays, Golden Era Style 45 back purfling, select hardwood neck, 14/20-fret grained ivoroid-bound ebony fingerboard with Golden Era D-45 snowflake inlays, bound headstock with solid East Indian rosewood overlay and abalone pearl torch and logo inlays, three-per-side gold Waverly tuners with butterbean knobs, ebony 1930s-style belly bridge, fossil ivory bridge pins with black pearl dots, tortoise color pickguard, two labels with one signed by CFM IV and Sue Longworth and the other with total production, Natural polished gloss finish with Vintage Toner top and Dark Filler back and sides, 25.4 in. scale, case included, limited edition run of 91 instruments, mfg. 2005-mid-06.

	N/A	$6,000 - 7,000	$4,250 - 5,000	$13,999

D-45SS STEPHEN STILLS (1998) – dreadnought 14-fret-style body, solid Italian Alpine spruce, solid Brazilian rosewood back and sides, standard X scalloped forward-shifted bracing, round soundhole with three-ring Style 45 rosette (5/9/5 grouping with a large center ring of abalone pearl), grained ivoroid binding, abalone pearl with B/W/B top inlay, abalone pearl with B/W back and side inlays, Style 45 back purfling, mahogany neck, 14/20-fret grained ivoroid-bound ebony fingerboard with snowflakes or optional hexagon pearl inlays and 17-20th fret Stephen Stills signature inlay, bound headstock with solid Brazilian rosewood overlay and large abalone pearl vertical block logo, three-per-side gold Waverly W-16 tuners, ebony belly bridge with a long saddle, fossilized ivory bridge pins with pearl dots, tortoise color pickguard with southern cross inlay, label signed by CFM IV and Stephen Stills, Natural polished gloss finish with Vintage Toner top, 25.4 in. scale, case included, limited edition run of 91 instruments, mfg. summer 1998-mid-1999.

	N/A	$16,000 - 20,000	$9,500 - 12,000	$19,000

D-50 DELUXE (2001) – dreadnought 14-fret-style body, solid Sitka spruce with heavy bearclaw, CITES certified select Brazilian rosewood back and sides, D-OMLE forward-shifted bracing, round soundhole with three-ring rosette (5/9/5 grouping with a large middle ring of herringbone pearl), grained ivoroid binding, herringbone pearl with B/W/B fiber top inlays, abalone pearl with B/W/B fiber back and sides inlays, multi-layer fiber/heart pearl/BWB fiber back purfling, floral pattern abalone inlays on the bottom and top sides as well as around the neck joint, mahogany neck, 14/19-fret grained ivoroid-bound ebony fingerboard with custom abalone Tree of Life inlay bordered in MOP, solid Brazilian rosewood headstock overlay with abalone pearl bordering and Tree of Life/MOP inlays, three-per-side gold Waverly hand engraved tuners with butterbean knobs, ebony belly bridge with abalone pearl Tree of Life/MOP inlays, black beveled pickguard with abalone pearl/MOP Tree of Life inlay, fossil ivory bridge pins with star sapphire dots bordered in 14 karat gold, label signed by CFM IV and numbered in sequence, Natural polished gloss finish, 25.4 in. scale, special leather hardshell case with onboard humidity/temparture gauge included, limited edition run of 50 instruments, mfg. early 2001 only.

	N/A	$20,000 - 25,000	$12,000 - 15,000	$50,000

D-50 KOA DELUXE (2003) – dreadnought 14-fret-style body, solid Adirondack spruce top, solid highly flamed Hawaiian koa back and sides, standard X scalloped forward-shifted bracing, custom three-ring abalone pearl/herringbone rosette, grained ivoroid binding, Style 50 abalone pearl/herringbone with B/W/B fiber top inlay, abalone pearl with B/W/B fiber back and side inlays, custom fiber, paua pearl, herringbone pearl, and B/W/B back purfling mahogany neck, 14/20-fret grained ivoroid-bound ebony fingerboard with elaborate abalone pearl inlays, bound headstock with solid highly flamed Hawaiian koa overlay and elaborate abalone pearl inlays and logo, three-per-side hand-engraved gold Waverly tuners with Butterbean knobs, ebony belly bridge with elaborate inlays, fossilized ivory bridge pins with star sapphire dots bordered in 14 kt gold settings, black Micarta pickguard with MOP Tree of Life inlay, label signed by C.F. Martin IV and numbered in sequence, Natural polished gloss with Aging Toner top finish, case included, limited edition run of 50 instruments, mfg. 2003-2011.

	$40,000	$23,000 - 26,500	$15,000 - 17,500	$50,000

D-100 DELUXE (2004) – dreadnought 14-fret-style body, solid Adirondack spruce top, solid Brazilian back and sides, standard X scalloped forward shifted bracing, custom three-ring abalone pearl/herringbone rosette, grained ivoroid binding, Style 50 abalone pearl/herringbone with B/W/B fiber top inlay, abalone pearl with B/W/B fiber back and side inlays, custom pearl back inlay with logo and model name, mahogany neck, 14/20-fret grained ivoroid-bound ebony fingerboard with elaborate abalone pearl inlays, bound headstock with solid Brazilian rosewood

MSR/NOTES	100%	EXCELLENT	AVERAGE	LAST MSR

overlay and elaborate abalone pearl inlays and logo, three-per-side hand-engraved gold Waverly tuners with butterbean knobs, ebony belly bridge with elaborate inlays, fossilized ivory bridge pins with green tourmaline dots bordered in 14 kt gold settings, black Micarta pickguard with MOP Tree of Life inlay, label signed by C.F. Martin IV and numbered in sequence, Natural polished gloss with Aging Toner top finish, black leather case with black velvet interior included, limited edition run of 50 instruments, mfg. 2004-present.

MSR $114,999	$92,000	$50,000 - 60,000	N/A	

The D-100 Deluxe was designed to commemorate Martin's one millionth guitar and all the fancy inlay work was inspired by the special one millionth guitar that Larry Robinson built. The serial number range for these guitars run between 10000001 and 1000050.

D-180 (2013) – dreadnought 14-fret-style body, solid Adirondack spruce top, solid Madagascar rosewood back and sides, three-ring D-180 rosette (5/9/5 grouping with a large middle ring of abalone pearl), grained ivoroid binding, Style 42 abalone pearl with multiple B/W fiber top inlays, black/maple/black back inlay, abalone pearl with black/maple/black side inlay, select hardwood modified V profile neck, 14/20-fret grained ivoroid-bound ebony fingerboard with 180th anniversary design inlays, grained ivoroid bound headstock with solid Madagascar rosewood overlay and 180th anniversary abalone inlay, three-per-side Waverly gold tuners with butterbean knobs, ebony 1930s-style belly bridge with 180th anniversary inlays, fossilized ivory bridge pins with black pearl dots, tortoise color pickguard, label signed by CFM IV and numbered in sequence, Natural polished gloss with Vintage Toner top finish, 25.4 in. scale, 1.75 in. nut width, case with 180th anniversary design included, mfg. 2013-present.

MSR $18,000	$14,000	$7,600 - 9,500	N/A	

DCRNS NED STEINBERGER (TRANSACTION, 2002) – single cutaway dreadnought 14-fret-style body, solid Sitka spruce top, solid East Indian rosewood back and sides, modified hybrid/solid 1 Style scalloped bracing, round soundhole with three ring Style 45 rosette, black Boltaron binding, multiple B/W top inlay, B/W back inlay, Style 35 back purfling, mahogany neck with patented Transaction System that allows the player to adjust the neck angle without loosening the strings, 14/20-fret black Micarta fingerboard with no inlays, solid ebony headstock overlay with raised gold foil logo, three-per-side black anodized Steinberger "Auto Trim" tuners with C.F. Martin logo, black Micarta bridge, black pickguard, Fishman Prefix Stereo Onboard Blender electronics, label signed by CFM IV and Ned Steinberger, Natural polished gloss finish with Dark Filler back and sides, 25.4 in. scale, case included, limited edition run of 100 instruments, mfg. 2002-03.

	N/A	$1,850 - 2,250	$1,200 - 1,500	$3,649

DC TREY ANASTASIO (2005) – single cutaway dreadnought 14-fret-style body, solid Italian Alpine spruce top, three-piece back with solid East Indian rosewood wings and a solid flamed koa wedge, solid East Indian rosewood sides, D1 Hybrid scalloped bracing, round soundhole with three-ring Style 45 rosette (5/9/5 grouping with a large middle ring of abalone pearl), grained ivoroid binding, fine herringbone top inlay, black/white side inlay, select hardwood neck, 14/20-fret grained ivoroid-bound ebony fingerboard with unique diamonds and square pattern and 19th-20th fret Trey Anastasio signature inlays, bound headstock with solid flamed koa overlay and large vertical block logo, three-per-side gold Gotoh tuners with ebony knobs, ebony belly bridge, label signed by CFM IV and Trey Anastasio and numbered in sequence, Natural polished gloss finish with Vintage Toner top and Dark Filler back and sides, 25.4 in. scale, case included, limited edition run of 141 instruments, mfg. summer 2005-mid-06.

	N/A	$2,500 - 3,000	$1,750 - 2,100	$5,199

The entire production run of 141 instruments includes both the regular DC Trey Anastasio and the electric version.

* DCE Trey Anastasio Electric (2005) – similar to the DC Trey Anastasio, except has Fishman Ellipse System electronics, mfg. summer 2005-mid-06.

	N/A	$2,700 - 3,200	$1,850 - 2,250	$5,499

DM3MD DAVE MATTHEWS (1999) – dreadnought 14-fret-style body, solid Engelmann spruce top, three-piece back with solid East Indian rosewood wings and a solid African Padauk center wedge, solid East Indian rosewood sides, three-ring Style 45 rosette (5/9/5 grouping with a large center ring of abalone pearl), grained ivoroid binding, rope pattern top inlay, multiple red/white/black back inlay, mahogany neck, 14/20-fret ebony fingerboard with long pattern diamond and squares and 20th fret Dave Matthews signature inlays, three-piece headstock with solid East Indian rosewood wings and a solid African Padauk center wedge, gold foil logo, three-per-side chrome Gotoh tuners with Butterbean knobs, ebony belly bridge, white bridge pins with tortoise dots, tortoise color pickguard, label signed by CFM IV and Dave Matthews, Natural polished gloss finish with Vintage Toner top, 25.4 in. scale, hardshell case included, limited edition run of 234 instruments, mfg. 1999 only.

	N/A	$2,800 - 3,500	$1,675 - 2,100	$3,250

D-NIGHT DIVE (2004) – dreadnought 14-fret-style body, bearclaw Sitka spruce top, solid Brazilian rosewood back and sides, round soundhole with three-ring Style 45 rosette (5/9/5 grouping with a large middle ring of abalone pearl), black Boltaron binding, abalone pearl with B/W/B top inlay, B/W back and side inlays, select hardwoods neck, 14/20-fret ebony fingerboard with special "Night Dive" custom inlays designed by William "Grit" Laskin of Pearl Works that continue up through the headstock, ebony headstock overlay, three-per-side chrome Schaller tuners with large ebony knobs, ebony belly bridge, black bridge pins with pearl dots, no pickguard, label signed by CFM IV amd Grit Laskin and Larry Sifel of Pearl Works and numbered in sequence, Natural polished gloss finish with Aging Toner top and Dark Filler back and sides, 25.4 in. scale, Calton hardshell case included, limited edition run of 15 instruments, mfg. 2004-05.

	N/A	$9,500 - 11,000	$6,500 - 7,500	$19,999

A total of 15 combined instruments between the D-Night Dive and the OM-Night Dive were produced.

DOOBIE-42 TOM JOHNSTON (2007) – dreadnought 14-fret-style body based on a D-42, solid Englemann spruce top, solid East Indian rosewood back and sides, three-ring rosette (5/9/5 grouping with a large middle ring of bold herringbone), grained ivory top binding, Style 42 top inlay, black/white Boltaron back inlay, mahogany neck, 14/19-fret bound ebony fingerboard with Style 45 snowflake and 12th fret quarter note inlays, bound rosewood headstock overlay with special logo, three-per-side gold Waverly tuners, ebony bridge with inlaid hands giving the "OK" symbol, tortoise pickguard, label signed by Tom Johnston, available in Natural finish, 25.4 in. scale, 545E Geib style case with hemp exterior included, limited edition run of 35 instruments, mfg. early 2007 only.

	N/A	$3,400 - 4,250	$2,050 - 2,550	$8,499

MSR/NOTES	100%	EXCELLENT	AVERAGE	LAST MSR

DSR SUGAR RAY (2002) – dreadnought 14-fret-style body with contiguous rounded edges, solid mahogany top, back, and sides, round soundhole with triple ring rosette with a center ring of black bordered rippled pearl, mahgoany neck, 14/20-fret ebony fingerboard with green abalone ripple dog paws and dog bone inlays and 20th fret "Sugar Ray" signature inlay, ebony headstock overlay with raised gold foil logo and MOP bulldog head inlay, three-per-side chrome Schaller tuners with large ebony knobs, ebony belly bridge, black bridge pins with abalone dots, black beveled pickguard, two labels with one signed by CFM IV and individually numbered and one signed by the members of Sugar Ray, polished gloss finish with Red Toner top and Red Stain back and sides, hardshell case included, 25.4 in. scale, mfg. summer 2002-mid-2003.

	N/A	$1,400 - 1,750	$950 - 1,150	$2,499

DX 175TH (2008) – dreadnought-style body, HPL top, HPL rosewood-grained back and sides, round soundhole, natural Stratabond neck, 14/20-fret Indian rosewood fingerboard with no inlays, regular headstock with HPL Indian rosewood pattern overlay, three-per-side Gotoh Cosmo black tuners, solid East Indian rosewood bridge, no pickguard, available in Natural Gloss finish with custom design 175th Anniversary graphic by Robert F. Goetzl, 25.4 in. scale, mfg. 2008-mid-2010.

	$750	$450 - 525	$275 - 325	$999

ACOUSTIC: LIMITED EDITION MODELS STARTING WITH E-L

EMP-NS EMPLOYEE MODEL (2000) – dreadnought 14-fret-style body, solid spruce top, solid flamed maple back and sides, A-frame Hybrid scalloped X bracing, round soundhole with abalone pearl rosette, black binding, mahogany neck, 14/20-fret ebony fingerboard, three-per-side tuners, ebony belly bridge, black pickguard, Natural polished gloss top and Black gloss Trans. back and sides finish, 25.4 in. scale, case included, limited edition run of 199 instruments, mfg. 2000 only.

	N/A	$1,400 - 1,750	$950 - 1,100	$2,299

FELIX (2004) – Little Martin-style body, High Pressure Laminate (HPL) top, Jett Black HPL back and sides, round soundhole, natural Stratabond neck, 14/20-fret black Micarta fingerboard with no inlays, HPL black headstock overlay with Felix The Cat graphic and printed logo, three-per-side chrome tuners with small knobs, black Micarta bridge, available in Red Felix The Cat graphics, 23 in. scale, Felix The Cat gig-bag included, limited edition run of 756 instruments, mfg. 2004 only.

	N/A	$425 - 500	$275 - 325	$549

FELIX II (2006) – Little Martin-style body, High Pressure Laminate (HPL) top, back, and sides, round soundhole, natural Stratabond neck, 14/20-fret black Micarta fingerboard with no inlays, HPL black headstock overlay with Felix The Cat graphic and printed logo, three-per-side Black Cosmo Gotoh tuners, black Micarta bridge, available in custom black and white Felix The Cat graphics, 23 in. scale, limited edition run of 625 instruments, mfg. 2006 only.

	N/A	$425 - 500	$275 - 325	$599

FELIX III (2007) – Little Martin-style body, high pressure laminate (HPL) top, back, and sides, round soundhole, mortise neck, 14/20-fret black Micarta fingerboard with no inlays, HPL headstock overlay with matching finish and Felix The Cat graphic, three-per-side black Gotoh tuners, black Micarta bridge, available in custom rainbow finish with Felix The Cat graphics, 23 in. scale, limited edition run of 1,000 instruments, mfg. 2007-mid-2010.

	$500	$300 - 350	$175 - 225	$649

GPC-42E AMAZON ROSEWOOD (2011) – single cutaway Grand Performer 14-fret-style body, solid Adirondack spruce top, solid Amazon rosewood back and sides, standard X scalloped forward shifted bracing, three-ring rosette Style 45 rosette (5/9/5 grouping with a large middle abalone pearl ring), grained ivoroid binding, Style 42 abalone pearl top inlay, maple/black back inlay, Style 45 back purfling, mahogany Performing Artist profile neck, 14/20-fret grained ivoroid-bound ebony fingerboard with alternative torch-inspired inlays, grained ivoroid-bound square taper headstock with ebony overlay and custom abalone design inlay and logo, three-per-side gold Waverly tuners with butterbean knobs, ebony belly Performing Artist bridge, tortoise color pickguard, label signed C.F. Martin IV and numbered in sequence, polished gloss finish with aging toner top, 25.4 in. scale, limited edition run of 25 instruments, mfg. 2011 only.

	$8,000	N/A	N/A	$9,999

HAWAIIAN X (2002) – Grand Auditorium 14-fret 000-style body, Hawaiian Luau Custom High Pressure Laminate (HPL) top, koa wood pattern HPL textured back and sides, 000-1 A-frame bracing, round soundhole, brown Stratabond neck, 14/20-fret black Micarta fingerboard with Style 18 abalone pearl dot inlays, koa wood pattern HPL textured headstock overlay with raised gold foil logo, three-per-side black Gotoh tuners with CFM logo, black Micarta belly bridge, label numbered in sequence, custom Hawaiian Luau graphic finish by R. Armstrong, 25.4 in. scale, hardshell case included, limited edition run of 500 instruments, mfg. 2002-05.

	N/A	$600 - 750	$350 - 450	$1,099

HD-18JB JIMMY BUFFET (1998) – dreadnought 14-fret-style body, solid Sitka spruce top, solid mahogany back and sides, standard X scalloped forward-shifted bracing, round soundhole with three-ring Style 45 rosette (5/9/5 grouping with a large center ring of abalone pearl), grained ivoroid binding, fine herringbone top inlay, B/W Boltaron back and side inlays, fine herringbone back purfling, mahogany neck, 14/20-fret ebony fingerboard with Style 42 snowflakes and 20th fret Jimmy Buffet signature inlays, ebony headstock overlay with windswept palm tree inlay and gold foil logo, three-per-side chrome Gotoh tuners with butterbean knobs, ebony belly bridge, black bridge pins with pearl dots, tortoise color pickguard, label signed by CFM IV and Jimmy Buffet, Natural polished gloss finish with Vintage Toner top, 25.4 in. scale, tweed case included, limited edition run of 424 instruments, mfg. 1998 only.

	N/A	$3,600 - 4,500	$2,150 - 2,750	$3,650

MSR/NOTES	100%	EXCELLENT	AVERAGE	LAST MSR

HD-28KM KEVIN MOORE "KEB' MO'" (2001) – dreadnought 14-fret-style body, solid Englemann spruce top, solid flamed Hawaiian koa back and sides, standard X scalloped forward-shifted bracing, round soundhole with three-ring Style 45 rosette (5/9/5 grouping with large center ring of abalone pearl), grained ivoroid binding, fine herringbone top inlay, B/W/B back and side inlays, HD zig-zag back purfling, mahogany neck, 14/20-fret ebony fingerboard with long pattern abalone pearl diamond and squares inlays and 20th fret Keb' Mo' signature inlay, ebony headstock with old Style logo, three-per-side gold Schaller M6 tuners with large ebony buttons, ebony belly bridge, white bridge pins with tortoise dots, tortoise color pickguard, label signed by CFM IV and Kevin Moore, Natural polished gloss finish with Vintage Toner top, 25.4 in. scale, case included, limited edition run of 250 instruments, mfg. early 2001 only.

	N/A	$2,000 - 2,500	$1,200 - 1,500	$3,999

HD-28 SO (1995) – dreadnought body style, solid Sitka spruce top, solid East Indian rosewood back and sides, standard "X" scalloped forward shifted bracing, round soundhole with Style 28 three-stripe rosette (5/9/5 grouping), grained ivoroid binding, bold herringbone top inlay, B/W boltaron back inlay, zigzag pattern back purfling, select hardwood neck, 14/20-fret ebony fingerboard with pearl diamond and square inlays and MOP "Sing Out!" inlay, slotted headstock with rosewood overlay and raised gold foil logo, three-per-side Gotoh nickel open-geared tuners with Butterbean knobs, vintage ebony belly bridge with drop-in long saddle, white bridge pins with tortoise dots, beveled tortoise pickguard, label signed by CFM IV and Pete Seeger, Natural polished gloss finish with Aging Toner top, 25.4 in. scale, limited edition run of 45 instruments, mfg. 1995 only.

	N/A	$2,400 - 3,000	$1,450 - 1,800	$4,500

This model commemorates the 45th Anniversary of *Sing Out!* magazine.

HD-35 NANCY WILSON (2006) – dreadnought 14-fret-style body, solid Englemann spruce top, solid East Indian rosewood back wings with a Bubinga wedge, solid East Indian rosewood sides, three-ring Style 45 rosette (5/9/5 grouping with a large middle ring of abalone pearl), grained ivoroid binding, bold herringbone top inlay, B/W Boltaron back inlay, multiple B/W Boltaron side inlay, HD zig-zag back purfling, select hardwood neck, 14/20-fret grained ivoroid-bound ebony fingerboard with abalone dots on 5th, 7th, 9th, and 15th frets and a Heart Insignia on the 12th fret inlays, ebony headstock overlay with large old style logo and special Nancy Wilson inlay, three-per-side gold Gotoh tuners with large ebony knobs, ebony belly bridge, tortoise color pickguard, label signed by signed by CFM IV and Nancy Wilson and numbered in sequence, Natural polished gloss finish, 25.4 in. scale, case included, limited edition run of 101 instruments, mfg. summer 2006 only.

	N/A	$2,400 - 3,000	$1,450 - 1,800	$4,399

HD-35SJC JUDY COLLINS (2002) – dreadnought 12-fret body-style, solid Sitka spruce top, three-piece back with solid East Indian rosewood wings and a solid Pacific Big Leaf maple center wedge, solid East Indian rosewood sides, round soundhole with three-ring Style 45 rosette (5/9/5 grouping with a large center ring of abalone pearl), grained ivoroid binding, fine herringbone top inlay, multiple B/W back and side inlay, 00-21 Golden Era back purfling, solid mahogany neck, 12/19-fret grained ivoroid/mitered-bound ebony fingerboard with abalone pearl Style 45 snowflake inlays, bound headstock with solid ebony overlay, raised silver foil logo, and abalone pearl Wildflower inlays, ebony belly bridge, white bridge pins with abalone pearl dots, black pickguard, label signed by CFM Iv and Judy Collins and numbered in sequence, Natural polished gloss with Vintage Toner top and Dark Filler back/sides, 25.4 in. scale, case included, limited edition run of 50 instruments, mfg. 2002 only.

	N/A	$2,400 - 3,000	$1,450 - 1,800	$5,149

* *HD12-35SJC Judy Collins 12-String (2002)* – similar to the HD-35SJC Judy Collins, except in 12 string-configuration and six-per-side tuners, limited edition run of 33 instruments, mfg. 2002 only.

	N/A	$2,600 - 3,250	$1,550 - 1,950	$5,349

HD-40LSH TOM PAXTON (2004) – dreadnought 14-fret-style body, bearclaw Sitka spruce top, solid East Indian rosewood back and sides, forward shifted/scalloped bracing, large round soundhole with three-ring Style 45 rosette (5/9/5 grouping with large middle ring of abalone pearl), grained ivoroid binding, fine herringbone top inlay, black/white back inlay, HD zig-zag back purfling, mahogany neck, 14/20-fret grained ivoroid/mitered-bound ebony fingerboard with diamond and square long pattern and 20th fret MOP Tom Paxton signature inlays, bound headstock with ebony overlay, Tom Paxton face with hat inlay, and pearl logo logo, three-per-side nickel Waverly tuners with Butterbean knobs, ebony vintage belly bridge, ebony bridge pins with abalone dots, tortoise color beveled pickguard, label signed by CFM IV and Tom Paxton and numbered in sequence, Natural polished gloss finish with Vintage Toner top and Dark Filler back and sides, 25.4 in. scale, case included, limited edition run of 30 instruments, mfg. summer 2004 only.

	N/A	$2,250 - 2,750	$1,500 - 1,850	$4,899

HD-40MK MARK KNOPFLER (2001) – dreadnought 14-fret-style body, solid Italian Alpine spruce top, solid East Indian rosewood back and sides, DOM forward shifted scalloped bracing, round soundhole with three-ring rosette (5/9/5 grouping with large center ring of bold herringbone), grained ivoroid binding, bold herringbone top inlay, B/W back inlay, mahogany neck, 14/20-fret grained ivoroid/mitered-bound ebony fingerboard with Style 42 snowflake inlays and 18-20th fret Mark Knopfler signature inlay, bound headstock with solid East Indian rosewood overlay and MOP logo, three-per-side nickel Waverly tuners with butterbean knobs, ebony belly bridge, black bridge pins with white dots, tortoise color beveled pickguard, label signed by CFM IV and Mark Knopfler and numbered in sequence, Natural polished gloss finish with Vintage Toner top and Dark Filler back and sides, 25.4 in. scale, case included, limited edition run of 251 instruments, mfg. summer 2001 only.

	N/A	$2,800 - 3,500	$1,675 - 2,100	$4,999

HD-40MS MARTY STUART (1996) – dreadnought 14-fret-style body, solid Sitka spruce top, solid East Indian rosewood back and sides, standard X scalloped forward-shifted bracing, round soundhole with herringbone pearl rosette, grained ivoroid binding, fine herringbone top inlay, B/W back inlay, fine herringbone back purfling, mahogany neck, 14/20-fret ebony fingerboard with 103-piece Marty Stuart designed pearl/abalone/recomposite stone fingerboard inlay (steer horns, horseshoes, dice, hearts, and flowers) and 20th fret Marty Stuart signature inlay, grained ivoroid-bound headstock with solid Indian rosewood overlay and gold foil logo, three-per-side gold Gotoh tuners with Butterbean knobs, ebony belly bridge, white bridge pins with pearl dots, tortoise color pickguard, label signed by CFM IV and Marty Stuart, Natural polished gloss finish, 25.4 in. scale, case included, limited edition run of 250 instruments, mfg. 1996 only.

	N/A	$2,800 - 3,500	$1,675 - 2,100	$5,400

MSR/NOTES	100%	EXCELLENT	AVERAGE	LAST MSR

HD-40 TOM PETTY (2004) – dreadnought 14-fret-style body, solid Italian Alpine spruce top, solid East Indian rosewood back and sides, round soundhole with three-ring Style 45 rosette (5/9/5 grouping with a large middle ring of abalone pearl), grained ivoroid binding, bold herringbone top inlay, multiple B/W back inlay, select hardwood neck, 14/20-fret grained ivoroid/mitered-bound ebony fingerboard with "Phases Of The Moon" motif inlays (new moon at first fret in brown lip pearl, rest in awabi, stars in paua) and 20th fret Tom Petty signature, bound headstock with ebony overlay abalone pearl torch inlays (no logo), three-per-side gold Schaller tuners with large ebony knobs, ebony belly bridge, ebony bridge pins with abalone pearl dots, tortoise pickguard, Fishman Gold Plus Natural II electronics, label signed by CFM IV and Tom Petty and numbered in sequence, Natural polished gloss finish with Vintage Toner top and Dark Filler back and sides, 25.4 in. scale, case included, limited edition run of 274 instruments, mfg. 2004 only.

	N/A	$3,600 - 4,500	$2,150 - 2,750	$4,999

* *HD12-40 Tom Petty 12-String (2004)* – similar to the HD-40 Tom Petty, except in 12-string configuration and six-per-side tuners with small ebony knobs, limited edition run of 90 instruments, mfg. 2004 only.

	N/A	$3,800 - 4,750	$2,275 - 2,850	$5,199

HDC-40 TRAVIS TRITT (2007) – single cutaway dreadnought 14-fret thin 000-depth-style body, solid Adirondack spruce top, solid East Indian rosewood back and sides, Style 45 herringbone pearl rosette, grained ivoroid binding, bold herringbone top inlay, black/white Boltaron back inlay, mahogany neck, 14/20-fret grained ivoroid bound ebony fingerboard with MOP Vine of Harmonics and Travis Tritt's signature between the 18th and 19th frets inlays, rosewood headstock overlay with "CMF Martin" logo, three-per-side gold tuners with large buttons, ebony bridge with island scroll inlays, black pickguard with vine inlays, label signed by Travis Tritt, available in Natural finish, 25.4 in. scale, limited edition run of 40 instruments, mfg. summer 2007 only.

	N/A	$3,200 - 4,000	$1,925 - 2,400	$8,999

HDN NEGATIVE (2002) – dreadnought 14-fret-style body, solid Englemann spruce top, solid East Indian rosewood back and sides, three-ring Style 45 rosette (5/9/5 grouping with a large center ring of abalone pearl), black Boltaron binding, bold herringbone top inlay, B/W Boltaron back inlay, B/W side inlay, HD zig-zag back purfling, solid mahogany neck, 14/20-fret black Boltaron-bound white Micarta fingerboard with abalone pearl Style 45 snowflake inlays, black-bound headstock with white Micarta overlay and abalone pearl torch inlays, three-per-side chrome tuners with large ebony buttons, white Micarta belly bridge, white Micarta beveled pickguard, black label signed by CFM IV and Dick Boak and numbered in sequence, available in Black polished gloss finish, 25.4 in. scale, case included, mfg. summer 2002-mid-2003.

	N/A	$2,200 - 2,750	$1,325 - 1,650	$3,699

HDO GRAND OLE OPRY (2000) – dreadnought 14-fret-style body, solid Sitka spruce top, solid East Indian rosewood back and sides, D1 hybrid/scalloped bracing, round soundhole with three-ring Style 45 rosette (5/9/5 grouping with a large middle ring of abalone pearl), grained ivoroid binding, fine herringbone top inlay, B/W Boltaron back inlay, HD zig-zag back purfling, select hardwood neck, 14/20-fret white Micarta fingerboard with red "WSM Grand Ole Opry" and 19th-20th fret "1925-2000" inlays, ebony headstock overlay with abalone pearl WSM microphone inlay and gold foil logo, three-per-side nickel open-geared Gotoh tuners with Butterbean knobs, ebony belly bridge, white bridge pins with tortoise color dots, tortoise beveled pickguard, two labels with one signed by CFM IV and numbered in sequence and one with the Ryman Auditorium, Natural polished gloss finish with Vintage Toner top and Dark Filler back and sides, 25.4 in. scale, case included, limited edition run of 650 instruments, mfg. 2000-04.

	N/A	$1,800 - 2,250	$1,075 - 1,350	$3,350

HTA KITTY WELLS (2002) – dreadnought 14-fret-style body with 000-style body depth, solid Englemann spruce top, solid East Indian rosewood back and sides, D1 hybrid/scalloped bracing, round soundhole with three-ring Style 45 rosette (5/9/5 grouping with large center ring of abalone pearl), grained ivoroid binding, fine herringbone top inlay, B/W back inlay, HD zigzag back purfling, solid mahogany neck, 14/20-fret ebony fingerboard with long pattern diamond and squares inlays and 5th fret abalone crown inlay outlined in MOP, ebony headstock overlay with abalone pearl Honky Tonk Angel inlay (no logo), three-per-side chrome Schaller tuners with large pearloid knobs, ebony belly bridge, tortoise color beveled pickguard, label signed by CFM IV, Kitty Wells, and Johnny Wright and numbered in sequence, Natural polished gloss finish with Vintage Toner top and Dark Filler back and sides, 25.4 in. scale, case included, limited edition run of 70 instruments, mfg. summer 2002-mid-2003.

	N/A	$1,900 - 2,350	$1,250 - 1,550	$3,299

JC-16KWS KENNY WAYNE SHEPERD (2001) – single cutaway jumbo-style body, solid Sitka spruce top, solid Sapele back and sides, J1 Hybrid scalloped bracing, round soundhole with three-ring Style 45 rosette (5/9/5 grouping with a large center ring of blue Paua shell), black Boltaron binding, multiple black/white/blue top, back, and side inlays, mahogany neck, 14/20-fret ebony fingerboard with blue Azurite teardrops bordered in pearl and 19-20th fret Kenny Wayne Sheperd signature inlays, ebony headstock overlay with raised silver foil logo, three-per-side chrome Schaller tuners with large ebony knobs, ebony belly bridge, black bridge pins with abalone dots, black pickguard, Fishman Gold Plus Natural II electronics, label signed by CFM IV and Kenny Wayne Sheperd and numbered in sequence, Blue polished gloss top with Black polished gloss back and sides finish, 25.4 in. scale, case included, limited edition run of 198 instruments, mfg. early 2001 only.

	N/A	$1,400 - 1,750	$850 - 1,050	$3,179

JC BUDDY GUY (2006) – single cutaway Jumbo-style body, solid Adirondack spruce top, solid East Indian rosewood back and sides, round soundhole with black Micarta rosette with turquoise dots, grained ivoroid binding, B/W/B Boltaron top inlay, multiple B/W Boltaron back inlay, B/W Boltaron side inlay, select hardwood neck, 14/20-fret grained ivoroid-boudn ebony fingerboard with turquoise polka dot pattern and a 12th fret "BG" inlays, bound headstock with ebony overlay and turquoise large vertical block logo, three-per-side chrome Gotoh tuners with large ebony knobs, ebony belly bridge with turquoise dot inlays, ebony bridge pins with turquoise dots, black pickguard, Fishman Gold Plus VT electronics with two knobs (v, tone) mounted on the face of the guitar, label signed by C.F. Martin IV and Buddy Guy and numbered in sequence, Natural polished gloss finish, 25.4 in. scale, case included, limited edition run of 36 instruments, mfg. summer 2006 only.

	N/A	$2,500 - 3,000	$1,750 - 2,100	$6,399

MSR/NOTES	100%	EXCELLENT	AVERAGE	LAST MSR

JDP DIANE PONZIO (2003) – jumbo 14-fret-style body, solid Sitka spruce top, solid three-piece back with East Indian rosewood wings and an Indian rosewood wedge, special forward-shifted pattern/scalloped bracing, round soundhole with three-ring Style 45 rosette (5/9/5 grouping with a large middle ring of abalone pearl), white Boltaron binding, B/W/B top inlay, multiple B/W Boltaron back inlay, B/W side inlay, mahogany neck, 14/20-fret bound ebony fingerboard with pearl reduced-size hexagon inlays, bound headstock with solid Indian rosewood overlay and select pearl vertical block logo inlay, three-per-side gold Gotoh tuners with large knobs, ebony belly bridge, black bridge pins with pearl dots, black pickguard, label signed by CFM IV and Diane Ponzio, available in Sunburst polished gloss finish on the top and Natural polished gloss finish with Dark Filler on the back and sides, 25.4 in. scale, hardshell case included, limited edition run of 101 instruments, mfg. 2003 only.

	N/A	$2,100 - 2,500	$1,400 - 1,750	$3,999

JLJCR JONNY LANG (2000) – single cutaway jumbo-style body, solid Sitka spruce top, laminated Indian rosewood back and sides, Hybrid X scalloped bracing, round soundhole with double B/W/B rosette, black Boltaron binding, W/B Boltaron top inlay, mahogany neck, 14/20-fret ebony fingerboard with hexagon outline and 19-20th fret Jonny Lang signature inlays, solid rosewood headstock overlay with silver foil logo, three-per-side chrome tuners with large ebony buttons, ebony belly bridge, black bridge pins, no pickguard, Fishman Prefix Onboard Blender electronics, label signed by CFM IV and Jonny Lang, Natural polished gloss top finish and Natural satin back and sides finish, 25.4 in. scale, case included, limited edition run of 111 instruments, mfg. 2000-mid 2001.

	N/A	$1,150 - 1,400	$850 - 1,000	$2,750

KINGSTON TRIO SET (1997) – Martin introduced a three-piece set including a guitar, tenor guitar, and banjo to commemorate the 40 Year Anniversary of the Kingston Trio. The three-piece set includes a custom D-28 guitar, an 0-18T tenor guitar, and a Vega Long-Neck Folk Model banjo. These instruments are a limited edition of 40 sets and each instrument contains a label signed by CFM IV, Bob Shane, Nick Reynolds, George Grove, and John Stewart. Martin also announced that an unspecified number of the D-28 guitars (named the D-28KT) would be released in addition to the 40 initial sets although none were ever constructed or prototyped. Specifications:

D-28: dreadnought 14-fret-style body, solid spruce top, solid East Indian rosewood back and sides, scalloped forward-shifted bracing, round soundhole with rosette, grained ivoroid binding, mahogany neck, 14/20-fret ebony fingerboard with 1950s-era MOP Style 28 dot inlays, solid Brazilian rosewood headstock overlay with old Style logo, three-per-side gold Vintage-style open-geared tuners with Butterbean knobs, ebony belly bridge, ebony belly bridge with long saddle, white bridge pins with tortoise color dots, tortoise color beveled pickguard, Natural polished gloss finish, 25.4 in. scale.

0-18T Tenor: four-string tenor configuration, Concert 0-style body, select Sitka spruce top, mahogany back and sides, round soundhole with Style 18 rosette, tortoise color binding, ebony fingerboard, two-per-side gold Vintage tuners with butterbean knobs, ebony bridge, Natural finish.

Vega Banjo: constructed by the Deering Banjo Company, ebony fingerboard with MOP dot inlays and fifth fret "The Kingston Trio, 1957-1997" inlays, nickel-plated hardware.

Set of all three	N/A	$6,100 - 7,000	$4,450 - 5,000	
D-28 only	N/A	$2,500 - 3,000	$1,750 - 2,100	
0-18T only	N/A	$1,400 - 1,750	$950 - 1,100	$12,500

ACOUSTIC: LIMITED EDITION MODELS STARTING WITH M-Z

M3M GEORGE MARTIN (2005) – Grand Auditorium 14-fret M/0000-style body, solid Italian Alpine spruce top, solid mahogany back wings with a solid quilted mahogany wedge, solid mahogany sides, three-ring Style 45 rosette (5/9/5 grouping with a large middle ring of abalone pearl), grained ivoroid binding, fine herringbone top inlay, B/W/B Boltaron back and side inlays, select hardwood neck, 14/20-fret grained ivoroid-bound ebony fingerboard with Style 42 snowflake pattern, 5th fret "5," and 20th fret George Martin signature inlays, bound headstock with solid mahogany wings and solid mahogany quilted wedge overlay and long "M" inlay, three-per-side gold Waverly tuners with Butterbean knobs, belly ebony bridge, tortoise color J-40 pickguard, label signed by C.F. Martin IV and Sir George Martin and numbered in sequence, Natural polished gloss with Aging Toner top finish, 25.4 in. scale, case included, limited edition run of 127 instruments, mfg. summer 2005-mid-06.

	N/A	$3,000 - 3,750	$1,800 - 2,250	$5,699

M3SC SHAWN COLVIN (2002) – Grand Auditorium 14-fret 0000/M-style body, solid Engelmann spruce top, three-piece back with solid mahogany wings and a solid East Indian rosewood center wedge, solid mahogany sides, J1 hybrid scalloped bracing, round soundhole with s single ring rosette (abalone pearl with wood fiber inlays), tortoise color binding, multiple B/W top inlay, B/W back and side inlays, Style 35 back purfling with black fiber strip on each side, solid mahogany neck, 14/20-fret ebony fingerboard with no inlays, three-piece headstock with mahogany wings and an Indian rosewood wedge separated by B/W inlays, raised gold foil logo, three-per-side chrome Schaller tuners with large ebony knobs, ebony belly bridge, tortoise color beveled pickguard, Fishman Gold Plus Natural I electronics, label signed by CFM IV and Shawn Colvin and numbered in sequence, Natural polished gloss finish with Vintage Toner top and Maple Stain/Dark Filler back and sides, 25.4 in. scale, case included, limited edition run of 120 instruments, mfg. 2002 only.

	N/A	$1,600 - 2,000	$950 - 1,200	$3,199

M-42 DAVID BROMBERG (2006) – Grand Auditorium 14-fret M/0000-style body, solid Italian Alpine spruce top, solid East Indian rosewood back and sides, round soundhole with three-ring Style 45 rosette (5/9/5 grouping with a large middle ring of abalone pearl), grained ivoroid binding, Style 42 with B/W/B Boltaron top inlay, black/white Boltaron back and side inlays, select hardwood neck, 14/20-fret grained ivoroid-bound ebony fingerboard with narrow Style 45 select abalone snowflakes and MOP Bromberg signature between the 18th and 20th frets inlays, bound headstock with solid East Indian rosewood overlay and large vertical block logo inlay, three-per-side gold Gotoh tuners with large knobs, ebony belly bridge, white bridge pins with abalone pearl dots, tortoise color pickguard, label signed by CFM IV and David Bromberg and numbered in sequence, Natural polished gloss with Aging Toner top finish, 25.4 in. scale, case included, limited edition run of 83 instruments, mfg. summer 2006 only.

	N/A	$3,600 - 4,500	$2,150 - 2,750	$6,999

MSR/NOTES	100%	EXCELLENT	AVERAGE	LAST MSR

MC-12-41 RICHIE SAMBORA (2006) – 12-string configuration, single cutaway Grand Auditorium 14-fret M/0000-style body, solid Italian Alpine spruce top, solid Madagascar rosewood back and sides, round soundhole with three-ring Style 45 rosette (5/9/5 grouping with a large middle ring of abalone pearl), grained ivoroid binding, Style 41 abalone pearl with B/W/B Boltaron top inlay, B/W Boltaron back and side inlays, select hardwood neck, 14/20-fret ebony fingerboard with abalone pearl hexagons bordered in MOP and Richie Sambora's signature between the 19th and 20th fret inlays, ebony headstock overlay with abalone pearl/MOP modified torch inlay (no logo), three-per-side gold Gotoh tuners with small buttons, pyramid Stauffer-style ebony bridge, fossilized ivory bridge pins with pearl dots, black beveled pickguard, Martin Gold Plus Natural 1 electronics, label signed by CFM IV and Richie Sambora and numbered in sequence, Amber Sunburst polished gloss top and Natural polished gloss back and sides finish, 25.4 in. scale, case included, limited edition run of 200 instruments, mfg. 2006-mid-2009.

	N/A	$3,200 - 4,000	$1,925 - 2,400	$7,199

MC-40 ERIC JOHNSON (2003) – single cutaway Grand Auditorium 14-fret M/0000-style body, solid Engelmann spruce, solid East Indian rosewood back and sides, round soundhole with a single ring of abalone pearl surrounded by B/W fibers, grained ivoroid binding, blue fiber with B/W/B Boltaron top and back inlays, B/W/B Boltaron side inlay, Southwestern marquetry (brown and blue arrows) back purfling, mahogany neck, 14/20-fret grained ivoroid/mitered-bound ebony fingerboard with planetary inlays, bound headstock with ebony overlay and engraved MOP angel and logo inlays, three-per-side nickel Waverly tuners with Butterbean knobs, ebony belly bridge, ebony bridge pins with abalone pearl dots, label signed by CFM IV and Eric Johnson and numbered in sequence, Natural polished gloss finish with Adobe toner top and Dark Filler back and sides, 25.4 in. scale, hardshell case with burgundy interior included, limited edition run of 90 instruments, mfg. summer 2003 only.

	N/A	$2,400 - 3,000	$1,450 - 1,800	$4,999

MC-DSM (2008) – single cutaway Grand Auditorium M/0000-style body, solid Italian Alpine spruce top, solid highly flamed Hawaiian koa back and sides, single ring fine herringbone rosette, ebony binding, black/white boltaron top/back/side inlays, select hardwood neck, black ebony heelcap with black/white boltaron inlay, 14/20-fret ebony-bound ebony fingerboard with select abalone foden inlays, regular headstock with solid ebony overlay and select abalone pearl logo inlay, three-per-side Waverly nickel tuners with oval buttons, straightline ebony bridge with drop-in saddle, no pickguard, individually numbered, available in Natural Gloss finish, 25.4 in. scale, limited edition run of 100 instruments, mfg. 2008-mid-2010.

	$6,400	$3,700 - 4,400	$2,500 - 2,900	$7,999

MPFF PHILLY FOLK FESTIVAL (2002) – Grand Auditorium 14-fret 0000/M-style body, solid Engelmann spruce top, solid East Indian rosewood back and sides, J1 hybrid scalloped bracing, round soundhole with three-ring Style 45 rosette (5/9/5 grouping with a large center ring of abalone pearl), grained ivoroid binding, bold herringbone top inlay, B/W back and side inlays, solid mahogany neck, 14/20-fret grained ivoroid/mitered-bound ebony fingerboard with Style 42 snowflake, 4th-5th fret MOP smiling banjo, and 19th-20th fret "Philadelphia Folk Festival" inlays, bound ebony headstock with alternate torch pearl inlay and C.F. Martin stamp on the back of the headstock, solid Brazilian rosewood belly bridge, white bridge pins with abalone dots, tortoise color beveled pickguard, two labels with one signed by CFM IV and David Baskin and the other signed by the Philly Folk Festival even participants and numbered in sequence, Natural polished gloss finish with Vintage Toner top and Dark Filler back and sides, 25.4 in. scale, case included, limited edition run of 85 instruments, mfg. 2002 only.

	N/A	$1,500 - 1,850	$1,000 - 1,250	$3,449

MTV 1 UNPLUGGED (1996) – dreadnought 14-fret-style body, solid Sitka spruce top, split-back and sides with solid mahogany on the treble side and solid East Indian rosewood on the bass side, scalloped X bracing, round soundhole with three-ring Style 45 rosette (5/9/5 grouping with a large center ring of abalone pearl), tortoise color binding, B/W top inlay, mahogany neck, 14/20-fret ebony fingerboard with paua shell wide block letter "UNPLUGGED" inlays, rosewood headstock overlay with MOP "MTV" inlay and gold foil logo, three-per-side chrome tuners with ebony buttons, ebony belly bridge, Natural satin finish (gloss finish optional), 25.4 in. scale, limited edition run of 697 instruments, mfg. 1996 only.

	N/A	$1,100 - 1,350	$800 - 950	$2,450

MTV 2/MTV 2G "MTV UNPLUGGED" (2003) – Grand Auditorium 14-fret 000-style body, solid Sitka spruce top, split-back with solid Pacific Big Leaf Flame maple on the treble side and solid Indian rosewood on the bass side, hybrid Style 1 scalloped bracing, round soundhole with three-ring Style 45 rosette (5/9/5 grouping with a large middle ring of abalone pearl), tortoise color binding, multiple B/W top inlay, B/W Boltaron back inlay, fine pattern herringbone back purfling, select hardwoods neck, 14/20-fret ebony fingerboard with wide Blue Paua letters spelling "UNPLUGGED" from top to bottom of the fingerboard, solid East Indian rosewood headstock overlay with MOP "MTV" logo and gold foil logo, three-per-side chrome Gotoh tuners with large ebony knobs, ebony belly bridge, black bridge pins with pearl dots, clear pickguard, label signed by CFM IV and numbered in sequence, available in Natural semi-gloss top with satin back and sides (MTV 2) or Natural polished gloss with Dark Filler back and sides (MTV 2G) finish, 25.4 in. scale, hardshell case included, limited edition run of 200 instruments, mfg. 2003-04.

	N/A	$1,000 - 1,200	$725 - 850	$2,749

* **Add 10% (Last MSR was $2,999) for polished gloss top, back, and sides finish (MTV 2G).**

N-20WN WILLIE NELSON (1998) – classical nylon-string configuration, N-style body, solid Sitka spruce top, solid East Indian rosewood back and sides, non-scalloped bracing, round soundhole with wood mosaic binding, black Boltaron binding, multiple B/W top inlay, Style 35 back purfling, mahogany neck, 12/19-fret ebony fingerboard with 5th fret MOP state of Texas with star in the middle inlay, 12th fret wester letter style "TRIGGER" inlay, and 19th fret Willie Nelson signature inlay, slotted headstock with solid East Indian rosewood overlay and small old style logo, three-per-side side-mount Irving Sloane tuners, solid East Indian rosewood tied bridge with square ends, Fishman pickup that is a replica of the original Baldwin pickup, label signed by CFM IV and Willie Nelson, Natural polished gloss finish with Yellow Stain top and Dark Filler back and sides, 25.4 in. scale, case included, limited edition run of 70 instruments, mfg. summer 1998-99.

	N/A	$3,200 - 4,000	$1,925 - 2,400	$5,500

MSR/NOTES	100%	EXCELLENT	AVERAGE	LAST MSR

* **N-20WNB Willie Nelson Brazilian (1998)** – similar to the N-20WN Willie Nelson, except has solid Brazilian rosewood back, sides, and headstock overlay, limited edition run of 30 instruments, mfg. summer 1998-99.

	N/A	$8,000 - 9,500	$5,500 - 6,500	$9,800

NUB X (2008) – single cutaway Grand Auditorium 14-fret 000-style body, HPL top, HPL Jett Black textured back and sides, round soundhole, natural Stratabond neck, 14/20-fret black Micarta fingerboard with no inlays, regular headstock with HPL Jett Black overlay, three-per-side Gotoh Cosmo black tuners, belly-style black Micarta bridge, no pickguard, Fishman Classic 4T electronics, available in a light blue finish with custom "Nub" graphics by Nub Graphix, 25.4 in. scale, limited run of 200 instruments, mfg. 2008-mid 2009.

	N/A	$600 - 750	$350 - 450	$1,299

NWD GEORGE NAKASHIMA (2000) – dreadnought 14-fret-style body, solid Italian Alpine spruce top, solid high figured Claro Walnut back and sides, DOM forward-shifted scalloped bracing, round soundhole with single ring rosette (large ring of blue paua pearl surrounded by B/W/B fiber on each side), solid East Indian rosewood binding, multiple B/W wood fiber top and back inlays, two Indian rosewood bowtie inlays on the back, maple neck with a walnut center stripe, 14/20-fret ebony fingerboard with flower petals and 20th fret George Nakashima signature inlays, solid figured Claro walnut headstock overlay with logo and Nakashima Crest abalone pearl inlay, three-per-side nickel Waverly tuners with Butterbean knobs, ebony belly bridge, fossil ivory bridge pins with black pearl dots, tortoise color beveled pickguard, two labels with one signed by CFM IV and Mira Nakashima and the other with a picture of George Nakashima, Natural polished gloss top with Aging Toner and satin back and sides finish, 25.4 in. scale, case included, limited edition run of 100 instruments, mfg. 2000-mid 2001.

	N/A	$2,250 - 2,750	$1,500 - 1,850	$4,750

OM-28 JOHN MAYER (2003) – Orchestra 14-fret 000-style body, solid Engelmann spruce top, solid East Indian rosewood back and sides, round soundhole with three-ring Style 45 rosette (5/9/5 grouping with a large middle ring of abalone pearl), grained ivoroid binding, bold herringbone top inlay, B/W Boltaron back and side binding, mahogany neck, 14/20-fret ebony fingerboard with small pearl dots inlays, 12th-13th fret MOP triangle with dots inlays, and 20th fret John Mayer signature inlay, solid Indian rosewood headstock overlay with silver outline and logo, ebony belly bridge, white bridge pins with abalone dots, tortoise color beveled pickguard, signed by CFM IV and John Mayer and numbered in sequence, Fishman Gold Plus Natural I electronics, Natural polished gloss finish with Vintage Toner top and Dark Filler back and sides, 25.4 in. scale, case included, limited edition run of 404 instruments, mfg. summer 2003-mid-05.

	N/A	$4,400 - 5,500	$2,650 - 3,300	$4,499

OM-28M ROSEANNE CASH (2008) – Grand Auditorium 14-fret 000-style body, solid Adirondack spruce top, solid Madagascar rosewood back and sides, Style 45 rosette, grained ivoroid binding, bold herringbone top inlay, black/white boltaron back inlays, select hardwood neck, grained ivoroid heelcap, 14/20-fret ebony fingerboard with MOP diamond and sqaure inlays and "CASH" inlaid between the 19th and 20th fret, regular headstock with solid ebony overlay and special colored MOP rose inlays, three-per-side Gotoh open-geared nickel tuners with butterbean knobs, vintage belly-style ebony bridge with drop-in long saddle, tortoiseshell pickguard, signed by Roseanne Cash and individually numbered, available in Natural Gloss, 25.4 in. scale, limited edition run of 100 instruments, mfg. 2008-09.

	N/A	$3,400 - 4,250	$2,050 - 2,750	$6,999

OM-40 RORY BLOCK (2004) – Orchestra 14-fret 000-style body, solid Englemann spruce top, solid East Indian rosewood back and sides, scalloped bracing, round soundhole with three-ring Style 45 rosette (5/9/5 grouping with a large middle ring of abalone pearl), grained ivoroid binding, bold herringbone top inlay, B/W Boltaron back inlay, select hardwood neck, 14/20-fret grained ivoroid-bound ebony fingerboard with MOP highway signs designs and 20th fret Rory Block signature inlays, bound headstock with ebony overlay and MOP antique car and logo inlays, three-per-side nickel Waverly tuners with butterbean knobs, ebony belly bridge, ebony bridge pins with abalone pearl dots, tortoise color beveled pickguard, label signed by C.F. Martin IV and Rory Block and numbered in sequence, Natural polished gloss finish with Vintage Toner top, 25.4 in. scale, case included, limited edition run of 38 instruments, mfg. summer 2004 only.

	N/A	$2,500 - 3,000	$1,750 - 2,100	$5,199

OM-42 FLAMED MAHOGANY (2006) – Orchestra 14-fret 000-style body, solid Adirondack spruce top, solid flamed mahogany back and sides, OM scalloped bracing, three-ring rosette Style 45 rosette (5/9/5 grouping with a large middle abalone pearl ring), grained ivoroid binding, abalone pearl with multiple black/white fiber top inlay, black/white Boltaron back and side inlays, Style 45 back purfling, select hardwood neck, 14/20-fret grained ivoroid-bound ebony fingerboard with "Vine of Harmonics" abalone inlay designed by Dick Boak, square taper headstock with ebony overlay and C.F. Martin in abalone script, three-per-side gold Gotoh tuners with ebony buttons, ebony belly bridge, tortoise color pickguard, label signed C.F. Martin IV and numbered in sequence, polished gloss top with aging toner, 25.4 in. scale, limited edition run of 30 instruments, mfg. summer 2006 only.

	N/A	$5,500 - 6,500	$3,750 - 4,500	$9,999

OM-42PS PAUL SIMON (1997) – Grand Concert 14-fret OM-style body, solid Sitka spruce top, solid East Indian rosewood back and sides, round soundhole with three-ring Style 45 rosette (5/9/5 grouping with a large center ring of abalone pearl), tortoise color binding, Style 42 abalone pearl top inlay, Style 45 multi-colored mosaic back inlay, mahogany neck, 14/20-fret tortoise color-bound ebony fingerboard with Style 42 abalone pearl snowflake inlays and 20th fret MOP Paul Simon signature inlay, tortoise color-bound with reverse B/W inlay headstock with rosewood overlay and large vertical block logo, three-per-side nickel Waverly tuners with ivoroid buttons, ebony belly bridge with Style 42 abalone pearl snowflake inlays, teardrop-shaped tortoise color pickguard, label signed by CFM IV and Paul Simon, Natural polished gloss finish with Vintage Toner top, 25.4 in. scale, case included, limited edition run of 500 instruments but only 223 were produced and sold, mfg. 1997 only.

	N/A	$4,000 - 4,750	$3,000 - 3,500	$8,000

MSR/NOTES	100%	EXCELLENT	AVERAGE	LAST MSR

OM-42 TASMANIAN BLACKWOOD (2011) – Orchestra 14-fret 000-style body, solid Adirondack spruce top, solid flamed Tasmanian blackwood back and sides, standard X scalloped bracing, three-ring rosette Style 45 rosette (5/9/5 grouping with a large middle abalone pearl ring), solid European flamed maple binding, Style 42 abalone pearl top inlay, black/maple/black back inlay, Style 45 back purfling, select hardwood modified V neck, 14/20-fret solid European flamed maple-bound ebony fingerboard with Style 42 golden era snowflake inlays, square taper headstock with ebony overlay and custom abalone design inlay, three-per-side gold tuners with engraved butterbean knobs, ebony belly bridge with drop-in long saddle, tortoise color pickguard, label signed C.F. Martin IV and numbered in sequence, polished gloss top with aging toner, 25.4 in. scale, limited edition run of 8 instruments, mfg. summer 2011 only.

	$8,000	N/A	N/A	$9,999

OM-45 ROY ROGERS (2006) – Grand Auditorium 14-fret 000-style body, solid Adirondack spruce top, solid East Indian rosewood back and sides, three-ring Style 45 rosette (5/9/5 grouping with a large middle ring of abalone pearl), grained ivoroid binding, abalone pearl with black/maple/black fiber top, back, and side inlays, Style 45 back purfling, select hardwood neck, 14/20-fret grained ivoroid/mitered-bound ebony fingerboard with D-45 snowflake inlays, bound headstock with solid East Indian rosewood overlay and abalone pearl torch inlay (no logo), three-per-side gold tuners with butterbean knobs, 1930s-style ebony belly long saddle bridge with abalone pearl snowflake inlays, fossil ivory bridge pins with black pearl dots, Greven tortoise pickguard with pearl floral pattern, label signed by CFM IV and Roy Rogers, Jr. and numbered in sequence, Natural polished gloss finish with Vintage Toner top and Dark Filler back and sides, 25.4 in. scale, case included, limited edition run of 84 instruments, mfg. 2006 only.

	N/A	$6,500 - 8,000	$4,500 - 5,500	$14,999

* OM-45B Roy Rogers (2006) – similar to the OM-45 Roy Rogers, except has solid Brazilian rosewood back and sides, limited edition run of 14 instruments, mfg. 2006 only.

	N/A	$16,000 - 20,000	$9,500 - 12,000	$29,999

OMC-18VLJ LAURENCE JUBER (2002) – single cutaway Orchestra 14-fret 000-style body, solid Adirondack spruce top, solid mahogany back and sides, round soundhole with old Style 18 rosette, tortoise color binding, multiple B/W top inlay, mahogany neck, 14/20-fret ebony fingerboard with abalone pearl dot inlays at the 5th, 7th, and 9th frets, solid Brazilian rosewood headstock overlay with large old style logo, three-per-side nickel Waverly tuners with butterbean knobs, ebony belly bridge, black bridge pins with abalone dots, no pickguard, label signed by CFM IV and Laurence Juber and numbered in sequence, polished gloss finish with Aging Toner top and Dark Mahogany Stain back and sides, 25.4 in. scale, case included, limited edition run of 133 instruments, mfg. 2002 only.

	N/A	$2,000 - 2,500	$1,200 - 1,500	$4,449

OMC-28 LAURENCE JUBER (2004) – single cutaway Orchestra 14-fret 000-style body, solid Adirondack spruce top, solid East Indian rosewood back and sides, OM scalloped bracing, round soundhole with three-ring Style 28 B/W fiber rosette (5/9/5 grouping), grained ivoroid binding, fine herringbone top inlay, B/W fiber back inlay, select hardwood neck, 14/20-fret ebony fingerboard with no inlays, solid East Indian rosewood headstock overlay with large old style logo, three-per-side nickel Waverly tuners with Butterbean knobs, ebony belly bridge, fossil ivory bridge pins with black dots, label signed by C.F. Martin IV and Laurence Juber and numbered in sequence, Natural polished gloss finish with Aging Toner top and Dark Filler back and sides, 25.4 in. scale, case included, limited edition run of 133 instruments, mfg. 2004 only.

	N/A	$2,600 - 3,250	$1,550 - 1,950	$4,999

* OMC-28B Laurence Juber (2004) – similar to the OMC-28 Laurence Juber, except has solid Brazilian rosewood back, sides, and headstock overlay, limited edition run of 50 instruments, mfg. 2004 only.

	N/A	$6,000 - 7,500	$3,600 - 4,500	$9,999

OMC-41 RICHIE SAMBORA (2006) – single cutaway Orchestra 14-fret 000-style body, solid Italian Alpine spruce top, solid Madagascar rosewood back and sides, round soundhole with three-ring Style 45 rosette (5/9/5 grouping with a large middle ring of abalone pearl), grained ivoroid binding, Style 41 abalone pearl with B/W/B Boltaron top inlay, B/W Boltaron back and side inlays, select hardwood neck, 14/20-fret ebony fingerboard with abalone pearl hexagons bordered in MOP and Richie Sambora's signature between the 19th and 20th fret inlays, ebony headstock overlay with abalone pearl/MOP modified torch inlay (no logo), three-per-side gold Gotoh tuners with small buttons, pyramid Stauffer-style ebony bridge, fossilized ivory bridge pins with pearl dots, black beveled pickguard, Martin Gold Plus Natural 1 electronics, label signed by CFM IV and Richie Sambora and numbered in sequence, Amber Sunburst polished gloss top and Natural polished gloss back and sides finish, 25.4 in. scale, case included, limited edition run of 200 instruments, mfg. 2006-mid-2009.

	N/A	$3,600 - 4,500	$2,150 - 2,750	$6,999

OMC ARTINGER CUSTOM (2005) – unique one-of-a-kind custom OM model mfg. in collaboration with PA luthier Matt Artinger, bear claw Adirondack spruce top, Indian rosewood sides and back, bordered with abalone pearl, elliptical soundhole, assymetrical bridge, hollow hexagon fingerboard inlays, contoured armrest on lower bass side bout, side port, scalloped nut, flamed koa trim, gloss top. One-of-a-kind model mfg. 2005 only.

	N/A	N/A	N/A	

Extreme rarity precludes accurate pricing on this model.

OMCE CLARO (2008) – Grand Auditorium 14-fret 000-style body, solid Sitka spruce top, solid highly figured claro walnut back and sides, hybrid X scalloped bracing, round soundhole with a multi-ply abalone pearl ring rosette, grained ivoroid binding, multiple B/W Boltaron top inlay, B/W Boltaron back inlay, Style 45 back purfling, select hardwood modified low oval neck, 14/20-fret striped ebony fingerboard with small pearl dot inlays, solid highly figured claro walnut headstock overlay with raised gold foil logo, three-per-side gold tuners with small buttons, striped ebony belly bridge, white bridge pins with abalone pearl dots, tortoise color pickguard, Fishman Matrix Infinity, label numbered in sequence, Natural polished gloss finish, 25.4 in. scale, case included, limited edition run of 150 instruments, mfg. summer 2008-2010.

	$2,200	$1,400 - 1,600	$875 - 1,025	$2,999

MSR/NOTES	100%	EXCELLENT	AVERAGE	LAST MSR

OM FIGURED KOA (2010) – Grand Auditorium/000 14-fret-style body, solid Adirondack spruce top, solid highly flamed koa back and sides, standard X scalloped Golden Era-style solid Adirondack spruce bracing, round soundhole with three-ring Style 45 rosette (5/9/5 grouping with a large center ring of abalone), grained ivoroid binding, Style 42 abalone top inlay, B/W/B boltaron back and side inlays, Style 45 Golden Era back purfling, select hardwood low profile neck, 14/20-fret grained ivoroid-bound ebony fingerboard with Style 45 MOP hexagon inlays bordered in blue paua and blue paua diamonds inlaid within the hexagons, grained ivoroid-bound square tapered headstock with ebony overlay and blue Paua Flower pot design inlay, three-per-side gold open-geared tuners with engraved buttons, 1930s-style ebony belly bridge with drop in saddle, bone bridge pins with pearl dots, Delmar tortoise pickguard, label signed by CFM IV and numbered in sequence with total, available in Natural polished gloss finish with Aging Toner top, 25.4 in. scale, Geib-style case included, limited edition run of 20 instruments, mfg. 2010 only.

	$8,000	**N/A**	**N/A**	**$9,999**

The OM Figured Koa was Martin's 2010 NAMM Show guitar and could only be ordered in person at the Anaheim Winter NAMM Show 2010.

OM NEGATIVE (2007) – Orchestra 14-fret 000-style body, solid Englemann spruce top, solid East Indian rosewood back and sides, Style 45 rosette, black Boltaron binding, bold herringbone top inlay, black/white Boltaron back inlay, mortise neck, 14/20-fret black Boltaron bound white Micarta fingerboard with Style 45 snowflake inlays, white Micarta headstock overlay with abalone torch inlays, three-per-side chrome tuners with large ebony buttons, white Micarta bridge, white pickguard, available in Black finish, 25.4 in. scale, label signed by Dick Boak, limited edition run of 60 instruments, mfg. summer 2007 only.

	N/A	**$3,200 - 4,000**	**$1,925 - 2,400**	**$5,599**

This guitar featured reverse appointments where everything that is supposed to be light (top, back, sides, etc.) is dark and everything that is supposed to be dark (finerboard, pickguard, bridge, etc.) is light.

PS2 PAUL SIMON (2002) – Grand Auditorium 14-fret 000-style body, solid Sitka spruce top, solid East Indian rosewood back and sides, round soundhole with three ring Style 45 rosette (5/9/5 grouping with a center ring of blue paua pearl), tortoise color binding, multiple B/W top inlay, B/W back and side inlays, mahogany neck, 14/20-fret ebony fingerboard with long pattern paua diamond and square inlays and 18th-20th-fret MOP Paul Simon signature inlay, ebony headstock overlay with raised gold foil logo and green malachite/blue lapis reconstituted stone world inlay, three-per-side nickel-plated tuners with butterbean knobs, ebony belly bridge, tortoise color beveled pickguard, label signed by CFM IV and Paul Simon and numbered in sequence, Natural polished gloss finish with Aging Toner top and Dark Filler back and sides, 24.9 in. scale, mfg. summer 2002-mid-2003.

	N/A	**$2,200 - 2,750**	**$1,325 - 1,650**	**$3,499**

SPNAMM NAMM 100TH ANNIVERSARY (2001) – single cutaway Grand Auditorium 14-fret 000-style body, solid Sitka spruce top, solid mahogany back and sides, 0001 Hybrid scalloped bracing, round soundhole with three-ring Style 45 rosette (5/9/5 grouping with large middle ring of abalone pearl), tortoise color binding, mahogany neck, 14/20-fret striped ebony fingerboard with modified snowflake inlays, solid East Indian rosewood headstock overlay with raised gold foil logo, three-per-side gold Gotoh tuners with large knobs, ebony belly bridge with two abalone pearl snowflake inlays, black beveled pickguard, Fishman Prefix Onboard Blender electronics, label with 100th NAMM Anniversary, Sunburst polished gloss top and Natural polished gloss back and sides with Maple Stain/Dark Filler, 25.4 in. scale, hardshell case included, limited edition run of 100 instruments, mfg. early 2001 only.

	N/A	**$1,400 - 1,750**	**$950 - 1,150**	**$2,499**

SS-D35-13 (2013) – dreadnought 14-fret-style body, solid Englemann spruce top, three-piece back with solid Madagascar rosewood wings and a cocobolo wavey center wedge, solid Madagascar rosewood sides, round soundhole with three-ring Style 45 rosette (5/9/5 grouping with a large middle abalone ring), grained ivoroid binding, Style 42 abalone top inlay that goes around the fingerboard, B/W Boltaron back inlay, multiple B/W boltaron side inlay, Style 35 back purfling, select hardwood mod low oval profile neck, 14/20-fret grained ivoroid-bound ebony fingerboard with Style 42 snowflake inlays with MOP borders, solid Madagascar rosewood with cocobolo wedge headstock overlay with script MOP logo, three-per-side Waverly gold tuners with butterbean knobs, 1930-style ebony belly bridge, bone bridge pins with select pearl dots, tortoise pickguard, lable signed by Chris Martin IV and numbered in sequence, optional electronics, available in Natural polished gloss finish with aging toner top, 25.4 in. scale, custom case included, limited edition run of 30 instruments, mfg. 2013-present.

MSR $9,999	**$8,000**	**$4,200 - 5,250**	**N/A**	

STING MINI (2005) – Size 5/Terz 12-fret-style body, Western red cedar top, Sustainable Solomon Padauk back and sides, three-ring Style 45 rosette (5/9/5 grouping with large middle ring of abalone pearl), tortoise color binding, fine herringbone top inlay, B/W back inlay, mahogany neck, 12/18-fret Sustainable Katalox fingerboard with abalone pearl diamond and square and 18th-fret Sting signature inlays, Sustainable Soloman Padauk headstock overlay with gold logo, three-per-side nickel Gotoh open-geared tuners with butterbean knobs, Sustainable square Katalox bridge, white bridge pins with tortoise dots, label signed by C.F. Martin IV and Sting, Natural polished gloss finish, case included, limited edition run of 100 instruments, mfg. summer 2005-mid-06.

	N/A	**$1,950 - 2,350**	**$1,250 - 1,550**	**$3,999**

SW00-DB MACHICHE (2006) – Grand Concert 14-fret deep-style body designed by the Women and Music Task Team, solid rescued Sitka spruce, sustainable Machiche back and sides, round soundhole with cherry, machiche and maple pattern rosette, grained ivoroid binding, rope design with black/maple/black fiber top inlay, black/maple/black back inlay, solid Sustainable cherry neck, 14/20-fret Katalox fingerboard with Style 28 cherry and maple position dots, solid Sustainable Machiche headstock overlay with vertical block CMF Martin logo, three-per-side Gotoh antique bright copper tuners, solid Sustainable Katalox belly bridge, two labels and numbered in sequence with total, Natural polished gloss finish, 25.4 in. scale, limited edition run of 125 instruments, mfg. summer 2006-summer 2007.

	N/A	**$1,275 - 1,600**	**$750 - 950**	**$2,999**

MSR/NOTES	100%	EXCELLENT	AVERAGE	LAST MSR

TATTOO (2004) – Grand Auditorium 14-fret 000-style body, High Pressure Laminate (HPL) top with traditional tattoo custom art, Tawny Satinwood HPL textured back and sides, round soundhole, Stratabond neck, 14/20-fret Morado fingerboard with old Style 18 abalone pearl dot inlays, HPL headstock overlay with matching finish and traditional tattoo custom art, Morado belly bridge, black bridge pins with abalone dots, no pickguard, tattoo paper label and numbered in sequnce, White finish, 25.4 in. scale, dark brown western motif case with mauve plush interior and custom Jodi Head tattoo themed strap, limited edition run of 100 instruments, mfg. summer 2004 only.

| | N/A | $625 - 750 | $425 - 500 | $1,299 |

ACOUSTIC: SPECIAL EDITION MODELS NUMBERED MODELS, A-D

00-16DBFM WOMEN & MUSIC – Grand Concert 14-fret deep 000-style body, solid Sitka spruce top, Pacific Big Leaf flamed maple back and sides, round soundhole with Women & Music mosaic rosette, solid mahogany binding, black/white/black/rope wood top inlay, B/W/B back inlay, Women & Music back purfling, maple neck with mahogany stripe, 14/20-fret ebony fingerboard with MOP diamond and pearl short pattern inlays, slotted headstock with solid Pacific Big Leaf flamed maple overlay and small raised foil logo, three-per-side open-style gold Waverly tuners with Butterbean knobs, ebony belly bridge, black bridge pins with MOP dots, black teardrop pickguard, two labels with one signed by CFM IV and one with the Women & Music mission statement, Natural polished gloss finish with Autumn Maple toner, 25.4 in. scale, case included, mfg. summer 2000-03.

| | N/A | $1,100 - 1,450 | $800 - 950 | $2,839 |

000-18 NORMAN BLAKE – Grand Auditorium-style body that has a 14-fret style body with a 12-fret style neck, differet bracing, and a smaller 00-sized soundhole, solid Italian Alpine spruce top, solid mahogany back and sides, Style 28 rosette, tortoise color body binding, mahogany neck, 12/19-fret ebony fingerboard with unique diamond and square inlays, rosewood headstock overlay, three-per-side Waverly nickel tuners with ivoroid butterbean knobs, ebony bridge, tortise pickguard, label signed by Norman Blake, available in Natural Gloss finish, 24.9 in. scale, mfg. summer 2007-mid-2011.

| | $3,800 | $2,150 - 2,600 | $1,300 - 1,550 | $4,699 |

000-18 WG WOODY GUTHRIE – Grand Auditorium 14-fret 000-style body, solid spruce top, solid bookmatched mahogany back and sides, round soundhole with three-ring rosette (1/5/1 grouping), tortoise binding, V-shaped mahogany neck, 14/20-fret ebony with abalone dot inlays and "Woody Gutherie" signature on the 20th fret, tapered headstock with old style Martin decal logo, three-per-side nickel tuners with Butterbean knobs, ebony belly bridge, tortoise pickguard, label signed by Arlo Gutherie, Nora Gutherie, Harold Levinthal, and CFM IV, Natural finish, mfg. summer 1999-mid-2001.

| | N/A | $2,000 - 2,500 | $1,200 - 1,500 | $3,150 |

000-28 NORMAN BLAKE – Grand Auditorium 12-fret 000-style body, solid Adirondack spruce top, solid East Indian rosewood back and sides, round soundhole with three-ring Style 28 black/white fiber rosette (5/9/5 grouping), grained ivoroid binding, fine herringbone top inlay, black/maple fiber back inlay, HD zig-zag back purfling, select hardwood neck, 12/19-fret ebony fingerboard with Maltese diamond and square long pattern inlays, slotted headstock with solid East Indian rosewood overlay and Golden Era logo, three-per-side open-style Waverly tuners with small ivoroid buttons, ebony vintage belly drop-in long saddle bridge, fossilized ivory bridge pins with black pearl dots, tortoise color beveled pickguard, Natural polished gloss finish with Aging toner top, label signed and numbered by C.F. Martin IV and Norman Blake, case included, 24.9 in. scale, mfg. 2004-mid-2008.

| | N/A | $2,400 - 3,000 | $1,450 - 1,800 | $5,299 |

000CE AL CHERRY (FSC CERTIFIED WOOD) – single cutaway Grand Auditorium 14-fret 000-style body, Graffiti pattern aluminum top, solid certified cherry back and sides, A-Frame X bracing, round soundhole with no rosette, black Boltaron binding, certified Cherry modified low oval neck, 14/20-fret certified Katalox fingerboard with small dot inlays, solid certified cherry headstock overlay with raised silver foil logo, three-per-side chrome tuners with small buttons, certified Katalox belly bridge, aluminum bridge pins with black dot inalys, Fishman Aero Blend electronics, two lables with one for the model name and the other for the FSC certification, aluminum polished gloss top and satin Classic Cherry Stain back and sides finish, 25.4 in. scale, case included, mfg. summer 2008-2010.

| | $1,850 | $1,100 - 1,300 | $750 - 900 | $2,499 |

000C NYLON – single cutaway Grand Auditorium 12-fret 000-style body, solid Sitka spruce top, solid sapele back and sides, unique A-frame X bracing, round soundhole with single ring bold herringbone rosette, tortoise color binding, multi-ply B/W boltaron top inlay, B/W Boltaron back inlay, solid select hardwood neck, 12/20-fret black Richlite fingerboard with no inlays, slotted headstock with East Indian rosewood overlay and gold script logo, three-per-side brass open-geared Gotoh tuners with pearloid buttons, black Richlite classic bridge with drop-in saddle, no pickguard, Fishman F1 analog electrincs, Natural polished gloss finish, 26.44 in. scale, 1.875 in. nut width, case included, mfg. 2012-present.

| MSR $1,949 | $1,500 | $875 - 1,100 | $525 - 650 | |

ALTERNATIVE II – single cutaway Grand Auditorium 14-fret 000-style body, solid graffiti pattern aluminum top, Jett Black High Pressue Laminate (HPL) back and sides, alternative pattern bracing, round soundhole, black Stratabond neck, 14/20-fret black Micarta fingerboard with small dot inlays, solid graffiti pattern aluminum headstock overlay with metallic black foil logo, three-per-side Cosmo black Gotoh tuners, black Micarta belly bridge, black bridge pins with white dots, Fishman Prefix Pro electronics, 25.4 in. scale, case included, mfg. 2002-03.

| | N/A | $550 - 650 | $375 - 450 | $1,199 |

* *Alternative II Resonator* – similar to the Alternative II, except has a hand-spun aluminum resonator cone, spider bridge, and Fishman Prefix Pro Resonator system electronics, mfg. summer 2003-07.

| | N/A | $650 - 800 | $400 - 500 | $1,499 |

MSR/NOTES	100%	EXCELLENT	AVERAGE	LAST MSR

ALTERNATIVE III – single cutaway dreadnought 14-fret-style body, solid graffiti pattern aluminum top, Jett Black High Pressue Laminate (HPL) back and sides, alternative pattern bracing, round soundhole, black Stratabond neck, 14/20-fret black Micarta fingerboard with small dot inlays, solid graffiti pattern aluminum headstock overlay with metallic black foil logo, three-per-side Cosmo black Gotoh tuners, black Micarta belly bridge, black bridge pins with white dots, Fishman Prefix Pro electronics, 25.4 in. scale, case included, mfg. 2002-03.

	N/A	$550 - 650	$375 - 450	$1,199

ALTERNATIVE X – single cutaway Grand Concert 14-fret 00 thin-style body, solid graffiti pattern aluminum top, Jett Black High Pressue Laminate (HPL) back and sides, alternative pattern bracing, round soundhole, black Stratabond neck, 14/20-fret black Micarta fingerboard with small dot inlays, solid graffiti pattern aluminum headstock overlay with metallic black foil logo, three-per-side Cosmo black Gotoh tuners, black Micarta belly bridge, black bridge pins with white dots, Fishman Prefix Pro electronics, 25.4 in. scale, case included, mfg. 2001-mid-2013.

	$1,000	$550 - 700	$350 - 425	$1,299

* *Alternative XMIDI* – similar to the Alternative X, except has Roland MIDI GK-KIT-G electronics with three knobs and a switch on the face of the guitar, mfg. 2003-mid-2005.

	N/A	$675 - 800	$475 - 550	$1,599

* *Alternative XT* – similar to the Alternative X, except has a "CFM" Martin logo grille soundhole cover, a tune-o-matic bridge, Bigsby vibrato tailpiece, a DiMarzio Fast Track 2 humbucker pickup, and two knobs and a coil tap switch on the face of the guitar, mfg. summer 2002-mid-2005.

	N/A	$700 - 850	$500 - 600	$1,469

CAR TALK – dreadnought 14-fret-style body, solid Englemann spruce top, solid East Indian rosewood back and sides, standard X scalloped forward-shifted bracing, round soundhole with a Style 45 three-ring rosette (5/9/5 grouping with a large middle ring of abalone pearl), grained ivoroid binding, bold herringbone top inlay, B/W Boltaron back and side inlays, select hardwood neck, 14/20-fret ebony fingerboard with custom assorted car-related pearl inlays and 20th-fret Tom and Ray signatures inlay, ebony headstock overlay with Click and Clack cartoon inlay and large old style logo, three-per-side chrome Gotoh tuners with car themed engraved knobs, ebony belly bridge, ebony bridge pins with abalone dots, black pickguard with Car Talk credits artwork, two labels with one signed by Tom and Ray Magliozzi and numbered in sequence (no total) and the other with a photo of the Magliozzis, special case with nickel hardware and Car Talk license plate included, 25.4 in. scale, mfg. summer 2008-mid-2010.

	$5,200	$2,600 - 3,250	$1,550 - 1,950	$6,499

This model honors Tom and Ray Magliozzi who perform a show on National Public Radio and are known as Click and Clack, the Tappett Brothers.

CEO'S CHOICE CEO-1 – dreadnought 14-fret-style body, solid Sitka spruce top, solid mahogany back and sides, round soundhole with three-ring Style 45 rosette (5/9/5 grouping with a large middle ring of abalone pearl), black binding, fine herringbone top inlay, mahogany neck, 14/20-fret ebony fingerboard with hollow pearl hexagon inlays and CF Martin IV's signature on the 20th fret, East Indian rosewood headstock overlay with raised gold foil logo, three-per-side gold tuners with ebony button, ebony belly bridge with hollow pearl hexagon inlays, tortoiseshell pickguard, label signed by CF Martin IV, Natural finish, 25.4 in. scale, case included, total production of 128 instruments, mfg. 1997 only.

	N/A	$1,525 - 1,900	$925 - 1,150	$2,600

* *CEO's Choice CEO-1R* – similar to the CEO's Choice CEO-1, except has solid East Indian rosewood back and sides, total production of 191 instruments, mfg. 1997 only.

	N/A	$1,675 - 2,100	$1,000 - 1,250	$2,800

CEO'S CHOICE CEO-2 – dreadnought 14-fret-style body, solid spruce top, laminated Macassar striped ebony back and sides, three-ring Style 45 rosette (5/9/5 grouping with a large middle abalone pearl ring), black binding, fine herringbone top inlay, 14/20-fret ebony fingerboard with hollow hexagon inlay and C.F. Martin IV's signature on the 20th fret, three-per-side gold enclosed tuners with ebony buttons, ebony bridge with hollow hexagon inlays, tortoise pickguard, label signed by C.F. Martin IV, Natural finish, 25.4 in. scale, mfg. 1998 only.

	N/A	$1,600 - 2,000	$950 - 1,200	$2,900

CEO'S CHOICE CEO-3 – dreadnought 14-fret-style body, solid spruce top, veneered Brazilian rosewood back and sides, round soundhole with three-ring Style 45 rosette (5/9/5 grouping with a large middle abalone pearl ring), multiple body binding, mahogany neck, 14/20-fret ebony fingerboard with hollow pearl hexagon inlays, tortoise headstock overlay, three-per-side gold tuners with tortoise buttons, ebony belly bridge with two hollow pearl hexagon inlays, black pickguard, label signed by CFM IV, Unique gold top finish, 25.4 in. scale, limited production of 150 instruments, mfg. 1999 only.

	N/A	$1,675 - 2,100	$1,000 - 1,250	$3,500

CEO'S CHOICE CEO-4 – slope-shouldered dreadnought 14-fret-style body, solid Adirondack spruce top, solid mahogany back and sides, modified hybrid bracing, round soundhole with thin two-ring black/white rosette, white Boltaron binding, black top inlay, black Boltaron back and side inlays, mahogany neck, 14/20-fret black Micarta fingerboard with Style 28 pearl dot inlays, solid Indian rosewood headstock overlay with raised gold foil logo, three-per-side gold Gotoh tuners with large knobs, black Micarta belly bridge, white bridge pins with tortoise color dots, black beveled pickguard, Sunburst polished gloss finish, label signed by CFM IV, 25.4 in. scale, case included, mfg. 2001-03.

	N/A	$1,325 - 1,650	$800 - 1,000	$2,500

* *CEO's Choice CEO-4R* – similar to the CEO-4, except has solid East Indian rosewood back and sides, mfg. 2002-mid-2010.

	$2,400	$1,450 - 1,750	$950 - 1,100	$3,249

MSR/NOTES	100%	EXCELLENT	AVERAGE	LAST MSR

CEO'S CHOICE CEO-5 – dreadnought 12-fret-style body, solid Sitka spruce top, solid sapele back and sides, hybrid scalloped bracing, round soundhole with a three-ring herringbone pearl rosette (5/9/5 grouping), grained ivoroid binding, herringbone with black/white fiber top inlay, B/W/B back inlay, Style 18 back purfling, mahogany neck, 12/20-fret ebony fingerboard with gold color frets and old Style 18 abalone pearl dot inlays, slotted headstock with solid Indian rosewood overlay and gold logo, three-per-side gold side-mount Schaller tuners with acrylic knobs, ebony belly bridge, white bridge pins with abalone dots, tortoise color beveled pickguard, label signed by CFM IV, Natural polished gloss finish with Aging Toner top, 25.4 in. scale, case included, mfg. 2001-04.

	N/A	$1,500 - 1,850	$1,000 - 1,200	$2,799

CEO'S CHOICE CEO-6 – dreadnought 14-fret slope shouldered-style body, solid Adirondack spruce (Natural or Sunburst finish) or solid Sitka spruce (Black finish) top, solid East Indian rosewood back and sides, modified hybrid X scalloped solid Sitka spruce bracing, round soundhole with a singe-ring rosette (5 grouping), grained ivoroid binding, multiple B/W fiber top inlay, B/W fiber back inlay, Style 45 Golden Era back purfling, select hardwood Performing Artist profile neck, 14/20-fret ebony fingerboard with Style 28 pearl dot inlays, solid headstock with solid ebony overlay and pearl Martin logo, three-per-side gold Grover tuners with large buttons, 1930s-style ebony belly bridge, bone bridge pins with black dots, tortoise color (Natural or Sunburst) or black (Black finish) beveled pickguard, Fishman F1 Aura electronics, label signed by CFM IV, available in Black (2013-present) ,Natural, or Sunburst polished gloss finish, 25.4 in. scale, Geib-style case included, mfg. 2011-present.

MSR $4,499	$3,300	$1,900 - 2,250	$1,250 - 1,475	

  • **Subtract 10% (MSR $3,999) for Black finish.**

CF-1 – single cutaway archtop body, laminated Alpine spruce top, laminated European flamed maple back and sides, two f-holes, archtop crossbrace bracing, U-shaped flamed maple neck, 14/21-fret ebony fingerboard with no inlays, black micarta headstock overlay with raised gold foil "American Archtop" and "Martin" logos, three-per-side gold Gotoh tuners with ebony buttons, floating ebony bridge, ebony trapeze tailpiece, ebony finger rest pickguard, single Kent Armstrong floating pickup, single black volume knob mounted on the pickguard, available in Black (summer 2005-present), Natural, or Sunburst polished gloss finish, 17 in. body width, 3 in. body depth, 25 in. scale, mfg. 2004-mid-2009.

	N/A	$2,000 - 2,500	$1,200 - 1,500	$4,649

  • **Add 10% (Last MSR was $5,149) for Sunburst finish.**
  • **Add 15% (Last MSR was $5,399) for Black finish.**

* *CF-2* – similar to the CF-2, except has a thinner 2.5 in. body, two Seymour Duncan humbucker pickups, four knobs (two v, two tone), and a three-way pickup switch, mfg. 2004-mid-2009.

	N/A	$2,200 - 2,750	$1,325 - 1,650	$5,149

  • **Add 10% (Last MSR was $5,649) for Sunburst finish.**
  • **Add 15% (Last MSR was $5,899) for Black finish.**

CONCEPT J – single cutaway Jumbo-style body with rounded edges, solid spruce top, solid maple back and sides, round soundhole with abalone rosette, 14/20-fret ebony fingerboard with hollow hexagon inlay and C.F. Martin IV's signature on the 20th fret, three-per-side tuners, ebony bridge with hollow hexagon inlays, active electronics, available in "Holographic" finish (made with suspended metallic particles), mfg. 1998-99.

	N/A	$2,100 - 2,500	$1,400 - 1,750	$4,100

CONCEPT II – single cutaway Grand Auditorium 14-fret 000-style body, spruce top, curly maple back and sides, three-per-side gold tuners, on-board EQ or Gold+Plus electronics, available in contiguous holographic opalescent gloss lacquer finish, mfg. summer 1999-2001.

	N/A	$1,850 - 2,250	$1,200 - 1,500	$4,199

CONCEPT III – single cutaway Grand Auditorium 14-fret 000-style body, solid Sitka spruce top, solid soft red curly maple back and sides, round soundhole with single ring blue paua/pearl rosette, two-piece maple neck, 14/20-fret black Micarta fingerboard, solid maple headstock overlay with black foil logo, three-per-side black Gotoh tuners with L-5 buttons, black Micarta belly bridge, black bridge pins with pearl dots, no pickguard, label signed by CFM IV, available in polished gloss finish with firemist gold pigment, 25.4 in. scale, case included, mfg. 2003 only.

	N/A	$1,400 - 1,750	$1,000 - 1,150	$3,299

COWBOY X – Grand Auditorium 14-fret 000-style body, high pressure laminate (HPL) top with Robert Armstrong's cowboy campfire scene, HPL back and sides with "Dreamy Illusion" color, round soundhole, black Stratabond neck, 14/20-fret black Micarta fingerboard with pearl dot inlays, HPL headstock overlay with gold foil logo, three-per-side black tuners, black Micarta belly bridge, limited production of no more than 250 instruments, mfg. summer 2000 only.

	N/A	$675 - 800	$475 - 550	$999

CSN GERRY TOLMAN – dreadnought style, solid Englemann spruce, solid East Indian rosewood back and sides, Style 45 rosette, grained ivoroid bold herringbone body binding, mahogany neck, 14/20-fret bound ebony fingerboard with special Crosby, Stills, Nash, and Young design inlays, bound ebony headstock overlay with "Martin" and "CSN" inlays, three-per-side nickel open geared tuners with butterbean knobs, ebony pyramid Stauffer-style bridge, tortoise pickguard, label signed by Crosby, Stills, and Nash, available in Natural Gloss finish, 25.4 in. scale, mfg. 2007-09.

	N/A	$2,400 - 3,000	$1,450 - 1,800	$5,199

Gerry Tolman was the manager for Crosby, Stills, & Nash. A portion of the proceeds from this guitar go to the Tolman estate to fund college for his two children.

D-7 ROGER MCGUINN – seven-string configuration with a double G string based on the HD-7 Roger McGuinn model, solid Sitka spruce top, solid East Indian rosewood back and sides, bold Herringbone rosette, grained ivoroid body binding, mortise neck, 14/20-fret ebony fingerboard with diamond and squares inlaid in hard rock maple inlays, ebony headstock overlay, three-per-side chrome tuners, ebony bridge, tortoise pickguard, label signed by Roger McGuinn, available in Natural Gloss finish, 25.4 in. scale, mfg. 2007-mid-2011.

	$2,500	$1,450 - 1,700	$950 - 1,100	$3,099

MSR/NOTES	100%	EXCELLENT	AVERAGE	LAST MSR

D-12 DAVID CROSBY – dreadnought-style 14-fret body, solid Carpathian spruce top, solid quilted mahogany back and sides, standard X bracing, round soundhole with three ring Style 45 rosette (5/9/5 grouping with a large center ring of abalone), tortoise color binding, multiple B/W boltaron top, back, and sides inlays, Style 45 back purfling, solid hard maple low profile neck, 12/18-fret ebony fingerboard with abalone dot inlays and MOP David Crosby signature inlay in the 17th fret, ebony headstock overlay with gold foil logo and sailboat inlay, six-per-side chrome Grover tuners with small buttons, ebony belly bridge, ebony bridge pins with abalone pearl dots, tortoise pickguard, label signed by David Crosby and numbered in sequence, available in Natural polished gloss finish with Vintage Toner top, 25.4 in. scale, Geib-style case included, mfg. summer 2009-2011.

	$4,900	$3,000 - 3,750	$2,000 - 2,500	$6,099

This model has a 14-fret-style dreadnought body, but the neck meets it at the 12th fret and the long scale pushes the bridge to the middle of the top.

D-18 SS (SHORT SCALE) – dreadnought 14-fret-style body, solid Sitka spruce top, solid mahogany back and sides, standard X scalloped forward shifted bracing, three-ring Style 18 rosette (1/9/1 grouping), tortoise color binding, multiple B/W boltaron top inlay, Style 18 back purfling, select hardwood modified V-shaped neck, 14/20-fret ebony fingerboard with old Style 18 dot inlays, solid East Indian rosewood headstock overlay with gold foil logo, three-per-side nickel open-geared with butterbean knobs, vintage belly ebony bridge with drop-in saddle, black bridge pins with white dots, Delmar tortoise color pickguard, available in Natural polished gloss finish, 24.9 in. scale, mfg. summer 2009-2012.

	$2,500	$1,600 - 1,950	$1,100 - 1,300	$3,299

D-28CW CLARENCE WHITE – dreadnought 14-fret body style designed after Clarence White's 1935 D-28, solid Adirondak spruce top, solid East Indian rosewood back and sides, standard X scalloped forwarded shifted bracing, large round soundhole with two-ring Style 28 black/white fiber rosette (9/5 grouping), grained ivoroid binding, fine herringbone top inlay, black/maple fiber back inlay, select hardwood neck, 14/21-fret ebony bound fingerboard that extends over the soundhole, solid East Indian rosewood headstock overlay with a Golden Era logo, three-per-side Waverly nickel tuners with butterbean knobs, ebony belly bridge with long saddle, white bridge pins with black dots, authentic tortoiseshell patterned pickguard, label signed by CFM IV and Michelle White Bledsoe and numbered in sequence, Natural polished gloss finish with Aging Toner top, 25.4 in. scale, mfg. summer 2002-present.

MSR $5,599	$4,400	$2,400 - 3,000	$1,450 - 1,800	

For the D-28CWB Clarence White model with Brazilian rosewood, refer to the Limited Edition Series.

D-28 ELVIS PRESLEY – dreadnought-style body based on Presley's 1955 D-28, solid Carpathian spruce top, solid East Indian rosewood back and sides, Style 28 rosette, grained ivoroid multiple black/white boltaron binding, select hardwood neck, MOP TCB lightning bolt graphic in black micarta neck heel, 14/20-fret ebony fingerboard with select abalone star inlays bordered in MOP, regular headstock with solid ebony overlay and black/white abalone Elvis Presley graphic silhouette, three-per-side Grover Deluxe nickel tuners (Kluson-style), vintage belly ebony bridge with drop-in long saddle, black pickguard, two labels (Elvis label with holographic sticker numbered in sequence, an album cover label), available in Natural Gloss finish, 25.4 in. scale, mfg. 2008-mid-2010.

	$5,600	$3,300 - 3,800	$2,200 - 2,500	$6,999

* D-28 Elvis Presley CVR – similar to the D-28 Elvis Presley, except has a custom-tooled leather cover with Presley's name inscribed across the lower bout, mfg. 2008-mid-2010.

	$6,800	$4,100 - 4,600	$2,500 - 2,800	$8,499

D-35 JOHNNY CASH – dreadnought-style body, solid Engelmann spruce top, solid East Indian rosewood back and sides, round soundhole with Style 45 three-stripe rosette (5/9/5 grouping with a large center ring of abalone pearl), grained ivoroid binding, multiple B/W Boltaron top and side inlay, B/W/B Boltaron back inlay, HD zig-zag back purfling, 14/20-fret grained ivoroid-bound ebony fingerboard with select abalone stars bordered in MOP and 20th fret Johnny Cash signature inlays, grained ivroid-bound solid East Indian rosewood headstock overlay with large old style logo, three-per-side chrome Grover 102C tuners, ebony belly bridge, black bridge pins with abalone pearl dots, black beveled pickguard, label signed by C.F. Martin IV and John Carter Cash, Black polished gloss finish, 25.4 in. scale, black case with black interior and hardware included, mfg. summer 2006-present.

MSR $5,799	$4,600	$2,500 - 3,100	$1,500 - 1,875	

DC AURA – single cutaway dreadnought 14-fret-style body, solid Sitka spruce top, solid East Indianrosewood back and sides, hybrid X scalloped bracing, round soundhole with three-ring Style 45 rosette (5/9/5 grouping with a large middle ring of abalone pearl), white Boltaron binding, abalone pearl with B/W/B Boltaron top inlay, B/W Boltaron back inlay, B/W Boltaron side inlay, Style 45 back purfling, select hardwood neck, 14/20-fret bound ebony fingerboard with pearl hexagon outline inlays, bound headstock with pearl overlay and MOP logo, three-per-side gold Gotoh tuners with large ebony buttons, ebony belly bridge with pearl hexagon outlines, ebony bridge pins with abalone pearl dots, black beveled pickguard, Fishman Prefix Aura system electronics, Natural polished gloss finish, 25.4 in. scale, mfg. 2004-mid-2011.

	$2,900	$1,750 - 2,050	$1,150 - 1,350	$3,849

DCE BLACK (SUSTAINABLE WOOD) – single cutaway dreadnought style, solid Sitka spruce top, solid poplar back and sides, Style 28 overlay rosette, White Boltaron body binding, cherry/Mortise neck, 14/20-fret black Micarta fingerboard with Style 28 simulated pearl dot inlays, poplar headstock overlay, three-per-side chrome tuners, black Micarta bridge, black pickguard, Fishman Aura Pro Electronics, available in Black Gloss finish, 25.4 in. scale, mfg. summer 2007-mid-2009.

	N/A	$1,600 - 2,000	$950 - 1,200	$3,499

This guitar is part of the Sustainable Wood Series that feature woods that have been harvested from forests managed in an ecologically responsible manner.

MSR/NOTES	100%	EXCELLENT	AVERAGE	LAST MSR

D CHERRY (FSC CERTIFIED WOOD) – dreadnought 14-fret-style body, solid certified European spruce top, solid certified cherry back and sides, standard X bracing, Style 28 three-ring rosette (5/9/5 grouping), white boltaron binding, multiple B/W Boltaron top inlay, B/W Boltaron back inlay, black Boltaron side inlay, certified mahogany low profile neck, 14/20-fret certified black Richlite fingerboard with Style 28 bone dot inlays, certified cherry headstock overlay with gold foil logo, three-per-side chrome Grover tuners with large knobs, black Richlite belly bridge, white bridge pins with black dots, black pickguard, MiSi simple jack electronics, two labels with one with FSC certification and one with model name, Natural polished gloss finish, 25.4 in. scale, case included, mfg. summer 2009-mid-2013.

	$2,200	$1,400 - 1,700	$1,000 - 1,150	$2,899

DITSON DREADNAUGHT 111 – body designed after the original 1916-1930 Dreadnaught (notice spelling), solid Adirondack spruce, solid mahogany back and sides, single ring rosette, Brazilian rosewood body binding, mahogany neck, 12/19-fret ebony fingerboard with dot inlays at the 5th, 7th, and 9th frets, open-style headstock with Brazilian rosewood overlay, three-per-side Waverly brass open geared tuners with small ivoroid knobs, ebony bridge, small tortoise pickguard, reissue paper label signed by Chris Martin IV, available in Natural Gloss finish, 25.4 in. scale, mfg. 2007-09.

	N/A	$2,800 - 3,500	$1,675 - 2,100	$6,599

DITSON DREADNAUGHT 333 – dreadnought 12-fret-style body, solid Adirondack spruce top, solid Mahogany back and sides, standard X scalloped bracing, round soundhole with Ditson-style multi-ring rosette, grained ivoroid binding, multiple B/W Boltaron top inlay, B/W Boltaron back inlay, select hardwood Modified V-shaped neck, 12/19-fret bound ebony fingerboard with Style 333 snowflake, diamond, and oval inlays, slotted headstock with solid Brazilian rosewood overlay, three-per-side open-style Waverly tuners with small ivoroid buttons, pyramid ebony bridge with drop-in long saddle, bone bridge pins with tortoise dots, label signed by CFM IV, Natural polished gloss finish with Ditson 333 Toner top, 25.4 in. scale, case included, mfg. summer 2008-2010.

	$5,600	$3,300 - 3,800	$2,200 - 2,500	$6,999

D MAHOGANY (FSC CERTIFIED WOOD) – dreadnought 14-fret-style body, solid certified European spruce top, solid certified mahogany back and sides, standard X scalloped forward-shifted bracing, Style 18 three-ring rosette (1/9/1 grouping), tortoise color binding, multiple B/W Boltaron top inlay, B/W Boltaron back inlay, certified mahogany modified V neck, 14/20-fret certified Katalox fingerboard with old Style 18 bone dot inlays, certified mahogany headstock overlay with gold foil logo, three-per-side nickel open-geared tuners with butterbean knobs, certified Katalox 1930s-style belly bridge with drop-in long saddle, bone bridge pins with black dots, tortoise color pickguard, two labels with one with FSC certification and one with model name, Natural polished gloss finish with Aging Toner top, 25.4 in. scale, case included, mfg. 2009-mid-2013.

	$2,700	$1,500 - 1,800	$1,050 - 1,200	$3,599

D MUNINGA 08 (FSC CERTIFIED WOOD) – dreadnought 14-fret-style body, solid certified four-piece Adirondack spruce top, solid certified Muninga back and sides, standard X scalloped forward-shifted bracing, Style 28 three-ring rosette (5/9/5 grouping), grained ivoroid binding, multiple B/W Boltaron top inlay, B/W Boltaron back inlay, grained ivoroid back purfling, certified mahogany modified V neck, 14/20-fret certified Katalox fingerboard with long pattern Golden Era diamonds and squares inlays, certified Muninga headstock overlay with Golden Era-style logo, three-per-side nickel Gotoh open-geared tuners with butterbean knobs, certified Katalox 1930s-style belly bridge with drop-in saddle, bone bridge pins with black dots, Delmar tortoise color pickguard, two labels with one with FSC certification and one with model name and numbered in sequence, 1935 Sunburst polished gloss top and Natural polished gloss back and sides finish, 25.4 in. scale, case included, limited edition run of 17 instruments, mfg. summer 2008 only.

	N/A	$1,600 - 2,000	$950 - 1,200	$3,399

DVM VETERAN'S MODEL – dreadnought 14-fret-style body, solid Sitka spruce top, East Indian rosewood back and sides, hybrid X scalloped bracing, round soundhole with three-ring Style 45 rosette (5/9/5 grouping with a large middle abalone pearl ring), black Boltaron binding, bold herringbone inlay, black/white Boltaron back and side inlay, select hardwood neck, 14/20-fret ebony fingerboard with MOP 3rd fret eagle, "VETERANS" spelled across frets 5 through 12, small stars at the 15th and 17th fret, and 20th fret red/yellow logo inlays, ebony headstock overlay with raised gold foil logo and the five Armed Forces applied insignia pins (Army, Marines, Navy, Air Force, and Coast Guard), three-per-side gold Gotoh tuners with Butterbean knobs, ebony belly bridge, black bridge pins with abalone pearl dots, black beveled pickguard, Natural polished gloss finish with Aging Toner top, label signed by CFM IV and numbered in sequence, 25.4 in. scale, case included, supplied with two genuine steel dog tags with serial number, mfg. 2002-mid-2008.

	N/A	$1,800 - 2,250	$1,075 - 1,350	$3,449

ACOUSTIC: SPECIAL EDITION MODELS E-Z

EMP-1 EMPLOYEE MODEL – single cutaway Grand Auditorium 14-fret 000-style body, solid spruce top, solid three-piece ovangkol back with rosewood center wedge, solid ovangkol sides, round soundhole with wooden rosette, 14/20-fret fingerboard with offset dot inlays, abalone pearl peghead logo, three-per-side gold tuners with ebony buttons, ebony belly bridge, black bridge pins with abalone pearl dots, no pickguard, available in Natural finish, total production of 262 instruments, mfg. 1998 only.

	N/A	$1,650 - 2,000	$1,100 - 1,300	$2,450

EMP-2 EMPLOYEE MODEL – single cutaway dreadnought 14-fret thin-style body, solid spruce top, Tzalam SmartWood back and sides, round soundhole with arrow pattern rosette (turquoise, brown, beige, and black colors), 14/20-fret fingerboard with New Zealand Paua shell flying saucer inlays, abalone pearl ukulele headstock inlay with no logo, three-per-side chrome tuners, black pickguard, available in Natural finish, mfg. 1999 only.

	N/A	$1,400 - 1,750	$950 - 1,150	$2,700

GRAPHITE II – single cutaway Grand Concert 14-fret 00 thin-style body, graphite top, Jett Black High Pressure Laminate (HPL) back and sides, 00X A-frame bracing, round soundhole, black Stratabond neck, 14/20-fret black Micarta fingerboard with small dot inlays, Jett Black HPL headstock overlay with silver logo, three-per-side black Gotoh tuners, black Micarta belly bridge, black bridge pins with white dots, no pickguard, Fishman Prefix Pro electronics, hand-rubbed top finish, 25.4 in. scale, case included, mfg. 2003-04.

	N/A	$625 - 750	$425 - 500	$1,349

MSR/NOTES	100%	EXCELLENT	AVERAGE	LAST MSR

GRAPHITE X – single cutaway dreadnought 14-fret-style body, graphite top, Jett Black High Pressure Laminate (HPL) back and sides, 00X A-frame bracing, round soundhole, black Stratabond neck, 14/20-fret black Micarta fingerboard with small dot inlays, Jett Black HPL headstock overlay with silver logo, three-per-side black Gotoh tuners, black Micarta belly bridge, black bridge pins with white dots, no pickguard, Fishman Prefix Pro electronics, hand-rubbed top finish, 25.4 in. scale, case included, mfg. summer 2002-03.

	N/A	$625 - 750	$425 - 500	$1,349

HD-7 ROGER MCGUINN – seven-string configuration, dreadnought-style body, solid Sitka spruce top, solid East Indian rosewood back and sides, round soundhole with Style 45 three-ring rosette (5/9/5 grouping with a large middle ring of abalone pearl), grained ivoroid binding, bold herringbone top inlay, B/W Boltaron back and side inlay, select hardwood neck, 14/20-fret grained ivoroid-bound ebony fingerboard with Style 45 hexagonal position markers and 20th fret Roger McGuinn signature, grained ivoroid-bound headstock with solid East Indian rosewood overlay and abalone pearl vertical block CMF Martin logo, 3/4-per-side Schaller gold tuners with small ebony buttons, ebony belly bridge with 7th string point, white bridge pins with abalone pearl dots, tortoise color beveled pickguard, label signed by C.F. Martin IV and Roger McGuinn, Natural polished gloss finish with Vintage Toner top, 25.4 in. scale, hardshell case included, mfg. 2005-08.

	N/A	$2,350 - 2,950	$1,400 - 1,750	$5,599

McGuinn's unique seven-string dreadnought Martin features a double G string instead of the typical added top or bottom string on traditional seven-string guitars. The extra G string is tuned an octave higher than the regular G string.

HM BEN HARPER – Grand Auditorium 0000-style body based on Harper's personal M-38, solid Adirondack spruce top, solid East Indian rosewood back and sides, three-ring bold herringbone rosette, grained ivoroid binding, bold herringbone top inlay, black/maple fiber back and side inlays, select hardwood neck, grained ivoroid with black/maple fiber inlay heelplate, 14/20-fret ebony fingerboard with Style 28 Blue Paua and ebony target inlays, regular headstock with solid ebony overlay and mandarin orange/kiwi target composite stone inlay, three-per-side Gotoh chrome tuners with large buttons, belly ebony bridge with white tusq saddle, tortoiseshell pickguard, Fishman Ellipse Matrix Blend electronics, signed by Harper and individually numbered, available in Natural Gloss finish, 25.4 in. scale, mfg. 2008-09.

	N/A	$2,800 - 3,500	$1,675 - 2,100	$6,499

JDP II (DIANE PONZIO) – jumbo-style body, solid Italian Alpine spruce top, solid mahogany back and sides, hybrid X scalloped forward-shifted bracing, large round soundhole with custom Madagascar rosewood/mahogany triangle design rosette, tortoise color binding, black/maple/black fiber top inlay, black/maple back inlay, fine herringbone back purfling, select hardwood low profile neck, 14/20-fret ebony fingerboard with pearl dot inlays, slotted headstock with ebony overlay and gold logo, three-per-side nickel Waverly tuners with ivoroid Butterbean knobs, solid East Indian rosewood belly bridge, white bridge pins with black dots, Delmar tortoise color pickguard, label signed by Diane Ponzio and numbered in sequence, Natural polished gloss finish, 25.4 in. scale, case included, mfg. summer 2008-mid-2011.

	$2,700	$1,625 - 1,875	$1,000 - 1,225	$3,599

MC-38 STEVE HOWE – single cutaway M/0000 14-fret-style body, solid Carpathian spruce top, solid East Indian rosewood back and sides, standard bracing, elliptical soundhole with a single ring of abalone pearl, grained ivoroid binding, multiple B/W Boltaron top inlay, B/W Boltaron back and side inlay, select hardwood low profile neck, 14/22-fret ebony fingerboard with Style 42 snowflake inlays and 20th-21st fret Steve Howe signature inlay, slotted headstock with ebony overlay, gold foil logo, and yin/yang inlay, three-per-side brass Waverly open-geared tuners with small ivoroid buttons, ebony belly bridge with snowflake inlays, white bridge pins with black dots, black pickguard, label signed by Steve Howe and numbered in sequence, available in Natural polished gloss finish with Vintage Toner top, 25.4 in. scale, case included, mfg. summer 2009-mid-2011.

	$5,300	$3,300 - 4,000	$2,200 - 2,700	$6,599

MC ADIRONDACK 1 – single cutaway Grand Auditorium 0000-style body, solid Adirondack red spruce top, solid Spanish cedar back and sides, single ring abalone rosette, grained ivoroid herringbone body binding, mortise neck, 14/20-fret ebony fingerboard, ebony headstock overlay, three-per-side gold tuners, ebony bridge, Fishman Ellipse Matrix Blend electronics, available in Natural Gloss finish, 25.4 in. scale, mfg. summer 2007-09.

	N/A	$1,800 - 2,250	$1,075 - 1,350	$3,999

MINI-MARTIN – Size 5/Terz 12-fret-style body, solid Sitka spruce top, solid East Indian rosewood back and sides, round soundhole with three-ring Style 45 abalone pearl rosette (5/9/5 grouping), grained ivoroid binding, fine herringbone top inlay, black/white Boltaron back inlay, HD zig-zag back purfling, select hardwood neck, 12/18-fret ebony fingerboard with long pattern diamonds and squares inlays, solid East Indian rosewood headstock overlay with large old style logo, three-per-side nickel Waverly tuners with butterbean knobs, ebony bridge, white bridge pins with tortoise colored dots, no pickguard, label signed by CFM IV and Dick Boak, Natural polished gloss finish with Vintage Toner top, 21.4 in. scale, case included, mfg. 1999-mid-2009.

	N/A	$1,800 - 2,250	$1,075 - 1,350	$4,099

OMC ARTINGER 1 – single smooth cutaway Orchestra-style body solid Sitka spruce top, solid East Indian rosewood back and sides, elliptical soundhole with laser-cut koa binding that is at an oblique angle, special oval sound port on the lower bass side, figured Hawaiian koa binding, mortise neck, 14/22-fret striped ebony fingerboard with aluminum jogged dot inlays, ebony headstock overlay, three-per-side chrome tuners with ebony buttons, striped ebony bridge, Martin Gold Plus Natural 1 pickup, label signed by Matt Artiger, available in Natural Gloss finish with a triangle beneath the soundhole and black arm bevel on the lower bass bout, 25.4 in. scale, mfg. 2007-mid-2009.

	N/A	$2,000 - 2,500	$1,200 - 1,500	$4,599

OMC AURA – single cutaway Grand Auditorium 14-fret 000-style body, solid Sitka spruce top, solid East Indianrosewood back and sides, hybrid X scalloped bracing, round soundhole with three-ring Style 45 rosette (5/9/5 grouping with a large middle ring of abalone pearl, white Boltaron binding, abalone pearl with B/W/B Boltaron top inlay, Style 28 back inlay, B/W Boltaron side inlay, Style 45 back purfling, select hardwood neck, 14/20-fret bound ebony fingerboard with pearl hexagon outline inlays, bound headstock with ebony overlay and MOP logo, three-per-side gold Gotoh tuners with large ebony buttons, ebony belly bridge with pearl hexagon outlines, ebony bridge pins with abalone pearl dots, black beveled pickguard, Fishman Prefix Aura system electronics, Natural polished gloss finish, 25.4 in. scale, mfg. 2004-mid-2011.

	$2,900	$1,750 - 2,050	$1,150 - 1,350	$3,849

MSR/NOTES	100%	EXCELLENT	AVERAGE	LAST MSR

OMC CHERRY (SUSTAINABLE WOOD) – single cutaway Grand Auditorium-style body, solid Sitka spruce top, solid sustainable cherry wings with solid sustainable maple wedge back, solid sustainable cherry sides, single ring rosette with leaf pattern, grained ivoroid binding, bold herringbone/sustainable cherry top inlay, B/W/B boltaron back and side inlays, bold herringbone/sustainable cherry back purfling, sustainable cherry neck, grained ivoroid heelplate, 14/20-fret sustainable Katalox fingerboard with Style 28 sustainable cherry dot inlays, regular headstock with solid sustainable maple overlay and regular logo, three-per-side Gotoh nickel open-geared tuners with oval buttons, belly sustainable Katalox bridge with white tusq saddle, no pickguard, Fishman Ellipse Aura electronics, available in Natural Gloss finish, 25.4 in. scale, mfg. 2008-mid-2013.

	$2,700	$1,550 - 1,800	$1,000 - 1,150	$3,599

This guitar is part of the Sustainable Wood Series that feature woods that have been harvested from forests managed in an ecologically responsible manner.

OMCE MAHOGANY (FSC CERTIFIED WOOD) – single cutaway Grand Auditorium 000-style body, solid certified European spruce top, solid certified mahogany back and sides, hybrid X scalloped solid certified European spruce top, round soundhole with three-ring Style 28 rosette (5/9/5 grouping), grained ivoroid binding, multiple B/W boltaron top inlay, B/W/B boltaron back and side inlays, solid certified mahogany modified low oval-shaped neck, grained ivoroid heelplate, 14/20-fret black Richlite fingerboard with old Style 18 bone dot inlays, square taper headstock with solid certified mahogany overlay and gold foil logo, three-per-side chrome tuners with large buttons, belly black Richlite bridge with white tusq saddle, Delmar tortoise color pickguard, MiSi simple jack electronics, two labels (one with FSC mixed source and one with model name), available in Natural Gloss finish with Aging Toner top, 25.4 in. scale, molded hardshell case included, mfg. 2010-mid-2012.

	$2,400	$1,350 - 1,675	$825 - 1,025	$3,099

This guitar is part of the Sustainable Wood Series that feature woods that have been harvested from forests managed in an ecologically responsible manner.

OMCE SEAFOAM GREEN – single cutaway Grand Auditorium-style body, solid Englemann spruce top, solid Pacific Big Leaf flame maple back and sides, hybrid X scalloped bracing, round soundhole with three-ring rosette (5/9/5 grouping), grained ivoroid binding, fine herringbone with B/W Boltaron top inlay, B/W Boltaron back and side inlays, fine herringbone back purfling, solid hard maple modified low oval profile neck, grained ivoroid heelplate, 14/20-fret rosewood fingerboard with long pattern diamonds and squares inlays, Pacific Big Leaf flame maple Seafoam Green finish headstock overlay with large old style logo, three-per-side Gotoh nickel open-geared tuners with oval buttons, rosewood belly bridge, aluminum bridge pins, ivoroid pickguard, Fishman Matrix Infinity electronics, Seafoam Green polished gloss finish, 25.4 in. scale, vintage tweed case included, mfg. summer 2008-09.

	N/A	$1,800 - 2,250	$1,075 - 1,350	$4,199

OMCE WALNUT – single cutaway Grand Auditorium-style body, solid Englemann spruce top, solid black walnut back and sides, standard X scalloped bracing, round soundhole with single ring laser cut walnut rosette with WAM Southwest design, tortoise color binding, blue/maple/black fiber top inlay, maple/blue/black fiber back inlays, Southwestern marquetry back purfling, select hardwood modified low profile neck, solid black walnut heelplate, 14/20-fret ebony fingerboard with red, white, and blue Southwestern inlays, black walnut headstock overlay with red/blue arrowhead inlay and raised silver foil logo, three-per-side chrome tuners with large buttons, ebony belly bridge, ebony bridge pins with aluminum dots, Fishman Matrix Infinity electronics, Natural polished gloss finish, 25.4 in. scale, case included, mfg. summer 2008-2010.

	$2,200	$1,250 - 1,500	$850 - 1,000	$2,899

OMC FINGERSTYLE 1 – single cutaway Grand Auditorium 14-fret 000-style body, solid Sitka spruce top, solid Spanish cedar back and sides, hybrid X scalloped bracing, round soundhole with single ring rosette (grouping of nine rings with a large ring of colored material), grained ivoroid binding, fine herringbone top inlay, B/W back Boltaron inlay, B/W/B side Boltaron inlay, select hardwood neck, 14/20-fret ebony fingerboard with no inlays, solid ebony headstock overlay with raised gold foil logo, three-per-side gold Gotoh tuners with L5 buttons, ebony belly bridge, black bridge pins with abalone pearl dots, no pickguard, Fishman Ellipse Matrix Blend electronics, Natural polished gloss finish, 25.4 in. scale, Slate Gray case included, mfg. 2005-09.

	N/A	$1,600 - 2,000	$950 - 1,200	$3,899

OMCGTE CHERRY (SUSTAINABLE WOOD) – single cutaway Grand Auditorium 14-fret 000-style body, solid rescued Sitka spruce top, solid sustainable cherry back and sides, A-Frame X bracing, Style 28 three-ring rosette (5/9/5 grouping), grained ivoroid binding, multiple B/W top inlay, B/W/B Boltaron back and side inlays, bold herringbone/sustainable cherry back purfling, sustainable cherry neck, grained ivoroid heelplate, 14/20-fret sustainable Katalox fingerboard with Style 28 sustainable cherry dot inlays, regular headstock with solid sustainable cherry overlay and raised gold foil logo, three-per-side chrome tuners with small buttons, sustainable Katalox belly bridge with white tusq saddle, white bridge pins with black dots, tortoise color pickguard, Fishman Aero Blend electronics, Natural polished gloss top with satin Classic Cherry Stain back and sides finish, 25.4 in. scale, Slate Gray case included, mfg. summer 2008-mid-2013.

	$2,100	$1,200 - 1,500	$725 - 900	$2,799

This guitar is part of the Sustainable Wood Series that feature woods that have been harvested from forests managed in an ecologically responsible manner.

OMCRE – single cutaway Orchestra-style body, solid Carpathian spruce top, solid East Indian rosewood back and sides, Style 28 overlay rosette, grained ivoroid fine herringbone body binding, features Babicz's Continually Adjustable Neck that allows for string height adj. without detuning or changing the saddle, 14/20-fret ebony fingerboard with small abalone diamond inlays, ebony headstock overlay, three-per-side nickel open geared tuners with butterbean knobs, ebony pyramid Stauffer-style bridge, tortoise pickguard, Fishman Aura Pro electronics, available in Natural Gloss finish, 25.4 in. scale, mfg. summer 2007-mid-2009.

	N/A	$1,600 - 2,000	$950 - 1,200	$3,499

MSR/NOTES	100%	EXCELLENT	AVERAGE	LAST MSR

OMC RED BIRCH (SUSTAINABLE WOOD) – single cutaway Orchestra-style body, solid Sitka spruce top, solid sustainable red birch back and sides, cherry back center wedge, cherry with red birch leaf pattern rosette, grained ivoroid binding, mortise neck, 14/20-fret Katalox fingerboard with Style 28 cherry dot inlays, red birch headstock overlay, three-per-side chrome tuners, Katalox bridge, Fishman Ellipse Aura electronics, available in Natural Gloss finish, 25.4 in. scale, mfg. 2007 only.

	N/A	$1,400 - 1,750	$850 - 1,050	$2,999

This guitar is part of the Sustainable Wood Series that feature woods that have been harvested from forests managed in an ecologically responsible manner.

OMJM JOHN MAYER – Grand Auditorium 14-fret 000-style body, solid Engelmann spruce top, solid East Indian rosewood back and sides, hybrid X scalloped bracing, round soundhole with Style 45 three-ring rosette (5/9/5 grouping with a large middle ring of abalone pearl), bold herringbone top inlay, B/W Boltaron back inlay, select hardwood neck, 14/20-fret ebony fingerboard with MOP dot and 12th fret double dot with square inlays, solid East Indian rosewood headstock overlay with large old style silver logo, three-per-side nickel Gotoh open-geared tuners with butterbean knobs, ebony belly bridge, white bridge pins with abalone pearl dots, tortoise color beveled pickguard, Martin Gold Plus Natural 1 electronics, label signed by C.F. Martin IV and John Mayer, Natural polished gloss finish with Vintage Toner top, 25.4 in. scale, case included, mfg. 2006-present.

MSR $4,349	$3,400	$1,875 - 2,350	$1,125 - 1,400	

POW MIA – dreadnought-style body, solid Sitka spruce top, solid mahogany back and sides, round soundhole with single ring of paua with B/W/B inlay rosette, white Boltaron binding, multiple B/W Boltaron top inlay, B/W/B back and side binding, Style 45 back purfling, select hardwood neck, 14/20-fret ebony fingerboard with Eagle, POW, Five-Point Star, MIA, Double Tear Drop, and Single Tear Drop custom inlays, black ebony headstock overlay with POW/MIA pin inlay and raised silver foil logo, three-per-side chrome Gotoh tuners with large knobs, ebony belly bridge, label signed and numbered by C.F. Martin IV, Black polished gloss finish, 25.4 in. scale, case with American flag lining included, mfg. 2006-mid-2010.

	$4,600	$2,700 - 3,200	$1,700 - 2,000	$5,799

STING SWC – classical-style body, solid Sitka spruce top, solid certified Machiche back and sides, round soundhole with a wide-banded tortoise color rosette, tortoise color binding, solid certified cherry neck, 12/19-fret Katalox patented Humphrey elevated fingerboard with Sting's signature on the 19th fret, slotted headstock with three-per-side open-style tuners, Katalox tied bridge, no pickguard, Martin/Fishman Gold+Plus electronics, label signed by Sting and CFM IV, Natural finish, mfg. 1999-2000.

	N/A	$1,400 - 1,750	$850 - 1,050	$3,500

SWD CERTIFIED WOOD – dreadnought 14-fret-style body, solid rescued Sitka spruce top, solid Sustainable cherry back and sides, A-frame X-bracing, round soundhole with five-ring rosette (large tortoise color ring with ivoroid surrounded by blue and white inlays), red tortoise color binding, black/grained ivoroid top inlay, Sustainable cherry neck, 14/20-fret solid Sustainable Katalox fingerboard with Style 28 imitation pearl dots, tortoise color headstock with raised gold foil logo, three-per-side gold Gotoh tuners with large buttons, solid Sustainable Katalox belly bridge, white bridge pins with tortoise color dots, tortoise color pickguard, Natural polished gloss finish, 25.4 in. scale, case included, mfg. 1998-2000.

	N/A	$750 - 900	$500 - 600	$1,399

* SWDGT (Certified Wood) – similar to the SWD Certified Wood, except has a polished gloss top with satin back and sides, mfg. summer 2000-present.

MSR $1,849	$1,400	$800 - 1,000	$475 - 600	

SWD RED BIRCH CERTIFIED WOOD – dreadnought 14-fret-style body, solid rescued Sitka spruce top, Sustainable solid red birch back and sides, D1 A-frame non-scalloped bracing, round soundhole with single ring rosette (five-ring grouping), tortoise color binding, thin black Style 18 top inlay style, multiple layer black/white Boltaron back inlay, Sustainable cherry neck, 14/20-fret Sustainable Katalox fingerboard with Style 28 pearl dot inlays, Sustainable red birch headstock overlay with gold foil logo, three-per-side gold Gotoh tuners with large knobs, Katalox belly bridge, white bridge pins with black dots, tortoise color pickguard, Natural polished gloss finish with Autumn Maple toner, 25.4 in. scale, case included, mfg. summer 2003-04.

	N/A	$750 - 900	$500 - 600	$1,849

SWJGT CERTIFIED WOOD – jumbo-style body, solid rescued Sitka spruce top, solid Sustainable cherry back and sides, A-frame non-scalloped bracing, round soundhole with five-ring rosette (large tortoise color ring surrounded by small black rings), tortoise color binding, black/ivoroid top inlay, Sustainable cherry neck, 14/20-fret solid Sustainable Katalox fingerboard with Style 28 dot inlays, tortoise color headstock with raised gold foil logo, three-per-side gold Gotoh tuners with large buttons, solid Sustainable Katalox belly bridge, white bridge pins with tortoise color dots, tortoise color pickguard, Natural polished gloss top with Aging Toner and Satin back and sides finish, 25.4 in. scale, case included, mfg. summer 2002-04.

	N/A	$725 - 850	$500 - 575	$1,649

SWMGT CERTIFIED WOOD – Grand Auditorium 14-fret 0000-style body, solid rescued Sitka spruce top, solid Sustainable cherry back and sides, A-frame non-scalloped bracing, round soundhole with five-ring rosette (large tortoise color ring surrounded by small black rings), tortoise color binding, black/ivoroid top inlay, Sustainable cherry neck, 14/20-fret solid Sustainable Katalox fingerboard with Style 28 dot inlays, tortoise color headstock with raised gold foil logo, three-per-side gold Gotoh tuners with large buttons, solid Sustainable Katalox belly bridge, white bridge pins with tortoise color dots, tortoise color pickguard, Natural polished gloss top with Aging Toner and Satin back and sides finish, 25.4 in. scale, case included, mfg. summer 2002-03.

	N/A	$675 - 800	$475 - 550	$1,550

MSR/NOTES	100%	EXCELLENT	AVERAGE	LAST MSR

SWOM CERTIFIED WOOD – Grand Auditorium 14-fret 000-style body, solid rescued Sitka spruce top, solid Sustainable cherry back and sides, A-frame X-bracing, round soundhole with five-ring rosette (large tortoise color ring with ivoroid surrounded by blue and white inlays), red tortoise color binding, black/grained ivoroid top inlay, Sustainable cherry neck, 14/20-fret solid Sustainable Katalox fingerboard with Style 28 imitation pearl dots, tortoise color headstock with raised gold foil logo, three-per-side gold Gotoh tuners with large buttons, solid Sustainable Katalox belly bridge, white bridge pins with tortoise color dots, tortoise color pickguard, Natural polished gloss finish, 25.4 in. scale, case included, mfg. 2000 only.

	N/A	$675 - 800	$475 - 550	$1,450

* *SWOMGT Certified Wood* – similar to the SWOM Certified Wood, except has a polished gloss top with satin back and sides, mfg. summer 2000-present.

MSR $1,849	$1,400	$800 - 1,000	$475 - 600	

XC1T ELLIPSE – single cutaway Grand Auditorium 14-fret 000-style body, soliud Sitka spruce top, Tawny Satinwood HPL textured back and sides, A-Frame X bracing, round soundhole with custom East Indian rosewood, maple, and koa rosette, Natural Stratabond neck, 14/20-fret striped ebony fingerboard with no inlays, Tawny Satinwood HPL textured headstock overlay with black logo, three-per-side Gotoh Cosmo black tuners, striped ebony belly bridge, black bridge pins with abalone pearl dots, no pickguard, Fishman Ellipse Matrix Blend electronics, label designed by Cyndi Fritz with WAM group aproval, 25.4 in. scale, case included, mfg. 2006-2012.

	$950	$550 - 675	$350 - 425	$1,249

ACOUSTIC: AUTHENTIC GOLDEN ERA/MARQUIS SERIES

Martin's Authentic, Golden Era, and Marquis Series of guitars are all reissues from Martin's "Golden Era" of production in the 1930s. Since most Martin guitars produced between the early 1930s and WWII are very valuable today, they decided to offer a line of guitars that would faithfully reproduce those specifications. Golden Era guitars feature all Golden Era appointments including Brazilian rosewood tonewoods when applicable. The first Golden Era instrument was the D-18 and it appeared in 1995. Marquis models appeared in the mid-2000s and they are very similar to the Golden Era models, except they use East Indian rosewood instead of the pricy Brazilian rosewood. Since Brazilian rosewood is hard to find, they discontinued many of the Golden Era models that used Brazilian and replaced them with Marquis models in the mid-2000s. Martin's Authentic Series of guitars are as close as you can get to the real thing. Each Authentic model is designed on a specific model and year and is recreated to the original specifications.

00-21GE GOLDEN ERA – Grand Concert body style based on a 1920s 12-fret 00-21, solid spruce top, rosewood back and sides, 12/20-fret ebony fingerboard with inlays at the 5th, 7th, and 9th frets, slotted headstock, three-per-side open-style tuners, ebony belly bridge, tortoise pickguard, Natural finish, mfg. 1998-99.

	N/A	$2,200 - 2,750	$1,325 - 1,650	$3,950

000-18 AUTHENTIC 1937 – Grand Auditorium body style based on a 1937 14-fret 000-18, solid Adirondack spruce top, solid mahogany back and sides, standard X scalloped forward shifted bracing, round soundhole with old Style 18 three-stripe rosette (1/9/1 grouping), tortoise color binding, multiple B/W Boltaron top inlay, solid Brazilian rosewood back stripe, authentic 1937 Barrel & Heel mahogany neck, 14/20-fret ebony fingerboard with old Style 18 dot inlays, solid Brazilian rosewood headstock overlay with Golden Era-style logo, three-per-side Waverly nickel tuners with oval buttons, ebony 1930s-style belly bridge with long saddle, ebony bridge pins, Delmar tortoise beveled pickguard, available in Natural or Sunburst polished gloss finish with Aging Toner top, 24.9 in. scale, authentic-style case included, mfg. 2008-mid-2011.

	$6,900	$3,850 - 4,500	N/A	$8,599

• **Add 2.5% (Last MSR was $8,849) for Sunburst finish.**

000-18GE GOLDEN ERA – Grand Auditorium body style based on a 1937 14-fret 000-18, solid Adirondack spruce top, solid mahogany back and sides, standard X scalloped forward shifted bracing, round soundhole with old Style 18 three-stripe rosette (1/9/1 grouping), tortoise color binding, multiple B/W Boltaron top inlay, solid Brazilian rosewood back stripe, modified V with 30s-style heel select hardwood neck, 14/20-fret ebony fingerboard with old Style 18 dot inlays, solid Brazilian rosewood headstock overlay with Golden Era-style logo, three-per-side Gotoh open-geared nickel tuners with butterbean buttons, ebony 1930s-style belly bridge with long saddle, ebony bridge pins, tortoise beveled pickguard, labeled signed by CFM IV, available in Natural or Sunburst polished gloss finish with Aging Toner top, 24.9 in. scale, case included, mfg. 2006-present.

MSR $4,499	$3,400	$1,925 - 2,400	$1,150 - 1,450	

• **Add 5% (MSR $4,749) for Sunburst finish.**

000-18 MARQUIS – Grand Auditorium body style inspired by Martin's 1930s vintage models, solid Adirondack spruce top, solid mahogany back and sides, standard X scalloped bracing, round soundhole with old Style 18 three-stripe rosette (1/9/1 grouping), tortoise color binding, multiple B/W Boltaron top inlay, solid Madagascar rosewood back stripe, modified V with 30s-style heel select hardwood neck, 14/20-fret ebony fingerboard with old Style 18 dot inlays, solid Madagascar rosewood headstock overlay with Golden Era-style logo, three-per-side Gotoh open-geared nickel tuners with oval buttons, ebony 1930s-style belly bridge with long saddle, ebony bridge pins, tortoise beveled pickguard, available in Natural polished gloss finish with a Natural Aging Toner or 1935 Sunburst polished gloss top, 24.9 in. scale, case included, mfg. summer 2009-2010.

	$3,400	$2,025 - 2,400	$1,350 - 1,575	$4,499

• **Add 5% (Last MSR was $4,749) for Sunburst finish.**

000-28 12-FRET GOLDEN ERA – Grand Auditorium 12-fret 000-style body, bookmatched solid Sitka spruce top, solid East Indian rosewood back and sides, scalloped X bracing, round soundhole with three-ring Style 28 rosette (5/9/5 grouping), ivoroid binding, fine herringbone top inlay, mahogany neck, 12/20-fret ebony fingerboard with abalone diamonds and squares inlay, slotted headstock with solid Indian rosewood overlay and gold foil logo, three-per-side chrome open-style Waverly-Sloane tuners, ebony pyramid bridge, optional pickguard, Natural polished gloss finish with Aging Toner top, case included, limited edition run of 367 instruments, mfg. 1996 only.

	N/A	$2,750 - 3,250	$1,850 - 2,250	$4,000

MSR/NOTES	100%	EXCELLENT	AVERAGE	LAST MSR

000-42 MARQUIS – Grand Auditorium body style based on a 1930s 14-fret 000-42, solid Adirondack spruce top, solid East Indian rosewood back and sides, standard X scalloped bracing, round soundhole with Style 45 three-stripe rosette (5/9/5 grouping with a large middle ring of abalone pearl), grained ivoroid binding, abalone pearl with black/maple/black top inlay, black/maple fiber back inlay, Style 45 Golden Era back stripe, modified V with 30s-style heel select hardwood neck, 14/20-fret ebony fingerboard with Style 42 snowflake inlays, solid East Indian rosewood headstock overlay with Golden Era-style logo, three-per-side Gotoh open-geared nickel tuners with oval buttons, ebony 1930s-style belly bridge with long saddle, white bridge pins with black dots, Delmar tortoise beveled pickguard, Natural polished gloss finish with Aging Toner top, 24.9 in. scale, case included, mfg. 2007-09.

	N/A	$3,600 - 4,500	$2,150 - 2,750	$7,499

D-18 AUTHENTIC 1937 – dreadnought body style based on a 1937 14-fret D-18, solid Adirondack spruce top, solid mahogany back and sides, standard X scalloped forward shifted bracing, round soundhole with old Style 18 three-stripe rosette (1/9/1 grouping), Delmar tortoise color endpiece, black boltaron binding, multiple B/W boltaron top inlay, solid Brazilian rosewood back stripe, select hardwood neck, 14/20-fret ebony fingerboard with old Style 18 dot inlays, solid Brazilian rosewood headstock overlay with large Golden Era-style logo, three-per-side Waverly nickel tuners with butterbean knobs, ebony 1930s-style belly bridge with long saddle, ebony bridge pins, Delmar tortoise color beveled pickguard, available in Natural or Sunburst (2008-2012) polished gloss finish with Aging Toner top, 25.4 in. scale, authentic-style case included, mfg. summer 2005-2012.

	$7,000	$3,800 - 4,750	N/A	$8,899

- Add 2.5% (Last MSR $9,149) for Sunburst finish.

D-18 AUTHENTIC 1939 – dreadnought body style based on a 1939 14-fret D-18, solid Adirondack spruce top, solid mahogany back and sides, standard X scalloped forward shifted bracing, round soundhole with old Style 18 three-stripe rosette (1/9/1 grouping), Delmar tortoise color endpiece, tortoise color binding, multiple B/W boltaron top inlay, solid Madagascar rosewood back stripe, mahogany authentic 1939 barrel & heel neck, 14/20-fret ebony fingerboard with old Style 18 abalone dot inlays, solid Madagascar rosewood headstock overlay with large Golden Era-style logo, three-per-side Waverly nickel tuners with butterbean knobs, ebony 1930s-style belly bridge with long saddle, ebony bridge pins, Delmar tortoise color beveled pickguard, available in Natural Aging Toner polished gloss finish, 25.4 in. scale, 1.6875 in. nut width, authentic-style case included, mfg. 2013-present.

MSR $6,749	$5,300	$2,875 - 3,600	N/A	

D-18 GOLDEN ERA (FIRST VERSION) – dreadought 14-fret body style based on a 1937 D-18 abalone dot pattern on fingerboard, Brazilian rosewood headstock overlay, old style logo, available in Natural or Sunburst finishes, mfg. 1995 only.

	N/A	$2,200 - 2,750	$1,325 - 1,650	$3,100

- Add 10% (Last MSR was $3,320) for Sunburst finish.

Only 320 instruments were sold (272 in Natural finish and 48 in Sunburst finish). This model was based on a 1937 D-18 with similar features that are found on the current D-18VM (Vintage Series) models. The Second Version D-18 Golden Era is based on a 1934 D-18.

D-18GE GOLDEN ERA (SECOND VERSION) – dreadnought body style based on a 1934 14-fret D-18, solid Adirondack spruce top, solid mahogany back and sides, standard X scalloped forward shifted bracing, round soundhole with old Style 18 three-stripe rosette (1/9/1 grouping), black boltaron binding, multiple B/W boltaron top inlay, select hardwood neck, 14/20-fret ebony fingerboard with old Style 18 dot inlays, solid Brazilian rosewood headstock overlay with Golden Era-style logo, three-per-side Waverly nickel tuners with butterbean buttons, ebony 1930s-style belly bridge with long saddle, black bridge pins, tortoise beveled pickguard, Natural or Sunburst (summer 2005-present) polished gloss finish with Aging Toner top, 25.4 in. scale, case included, mfg. summer 1999-present.

MSR $4,499	$3,400	$1,925 - 2,400	$1,150 - 1,450	

- Add 5% (MSR $4,749) for Sunburst finish.

D-18 MARQUIS – dreadnought 14-fret body style inspired by Martin's 1930s vintage models, solid Adirondack spruce top, solid mahogany back and sides, standard X scalloped forward shifted bracing, round soundhole with old Style 18 three-stripe rosette (1/9/1 grouping), black Boltaron binding, multiple B/W Boltaron top inlay, solid Madagascar rosewood back stripe, modified V select hardwood neck, 14/20-fret ebony fingerboard with old Style 18 dot inlays, solid Madagascar rosewood headstock overlay with Golden Era-style logo, three-per-side Waverly open-geared nickel tuners with oval buttons, ebony 1930s-style belly bridge with long saddle, ebony bridge pins, tortoise beveled pickguard, available in Natural polished gloss finish with a Natural Aging Toner or 1935 Sunburst polished gloss top, 25.4 in. scale, case included, mfg. summer 2009-2010.

	$3,400	$2,025 - 2,400	$1,350 - 1,575	$4,499

- Add 5% (Last MSR was $4,749) for Sunburst finish.

D-28 AUTHENTIC 1931 – dreadnought body style based on a 1931 12-fret D-28, solid Adirondack spruce top, solid Madagascar rosewood back and sides, standard X scalloped bracing, round soundhole with Authentic 1931 Style 28 three-stripe rosette (5/9/5 grouping), grained ivoroid binding, fine herringbone top inlay, B/W boltaron back inlay, HD zig-zag back stripe, mahogany Authentic 1931 barrel & heel neck, 12/19-fret ebony fingerboard with short pattern diamond and square inlays, slotted solid Madagascar rosewood headstock overlay, three-per-side Waverly nickel open-style tuners with butterbean buttons, ebony 1930s-style belly bridge with long saddle, ivory bridge pins with black dots, Delmar tortoise color beveled pickguard, available in Natural polished gloss finish with Aging Toner top, 25.4 in. scale, authentic-style case included, mfg. 2013-present.

MSR $8,499	$6,700	$3,600 - 4,500	N/A	

D-28 AUTHENTIC 1937 – dreadnought body style based on a 1937 14-fret D-28, solid Adirondack spruce top, solid Brazilian rosewood back and sides, standard X scalloped forward shifted bracing, round soundhole with Style 28 three-stripe rosette (5/9/5 grouping), grained ivoroid binding, fine herringbone top inlay, B/W boltaron back inlay, HD zig-zag back stripe, mahogany neck, 14/20-fret ebony fingerboard with long pattern diamond and square inlays, solid Brazilian rosewood headstock overlay with Golden Era-style logo, three-per-side Gotoh nickel open-geared tuners with butterbean buttons, ebony 1930s-style belly bridge with long saddle, antique white bridge pins with black dots, Delmar tortoise color beveled pickguard, available in Natural polished gloss finish with Aging Toner top, 25.4 in. scale, authentic-style case included, mfg. 2007-mid-2009.

	N/A	$16,000 - 20,000	$9,500 - 12,000	$39,999

MSR/NOTES	100%	EXCELLENT	AVERAGE	LAST MSR

D-28 AUTHENTIC 1941 – dreadnought body style based on a 1941 14-fret D-28, solid Adirondack spruce top, solid Madagascar rosewood back and sides, standard X scalloped circa 1941 rear-shifted bracing, round soundhole with Style 28 three-stripe rosette (5/9/5 grouping), grained ivoroid binding, bold herringbone top inlay, B/W boltaron back inlay, HD zig-zag back stripe, mahogany authentic 1941 barrel & heel profile neck, 14/20-fret ebony fingerboard with long pattern diamond and square inlays, solid Madagascar rosewood headstock overlay with Golden Era-style logo, three-per-side Waverly nickel open-geared tuners with oval buttons, ebony belly bridge with long saddle, alternative ivory bridge pins with black dots, Delmar tortoise color beveled pickguard, available in Natural polished gloss finish with Aging Toner top, 25.4 in. scale, authentic-style case included, mfg. 2013-present.

| MSR $7,999 | $6,300 | $3,350 - 4,200 | N/A | |

D-28GE GOLDEN ERA – dreadnought body style based on a 1930s 14-fret D-28, solid Adirondack spruce top, solid Brazilian rosewood back and sides, standard X scalloped forward shifted bracing, round soundhole with old Style 28 three-stripe rosette (5/9/5 grouping), grained ivoroid binding, fine herringbone top inlay, select hardwood neck, 14/20-fret ebony fingerboard with diamond and square inlays, solid Brazilian rosewood headstock overlay with Golden Era-style logo, three-per-side Waverly nickel tuners with butterbean buttons, ebony 1930s-style belly bridge with long saddle, white bridge pins with black dots, tortoise beveled pickguard, Natural polished gloss finish with Aging Toner top, 25.4 in. scale, case included, mfg. 1999-2004, reintroduced summer 2005-mid-06.

| | N/A | $7,000 - 8,500 | $5,000 - 6,000 | $14,999 |

D-28 MARQUIS – dreadnought body style based on a 1930s 14-fret D-28, solid Adirondack spruce top, solid East Indian rosewood back and sides, standard X scalloped forward shifted bracing, round soundhole with Style 28 three-stripe rosette (5/9/5 grouping), grained ivoroid binding, fine herringbone top inlay, black/maple fiber back inlay, HD zig-zag back stripe, select hardwood neck, 14/20-fret ebony fingerboard with long pattern diamond and square inlays, solid East Indian rosewood headstock overlay with Golden Era-style logo, three-per-side Gotoh nickel open-geared tuners with butterbean buttons, ebony 1930s-style belly bridge with long saddle, fossilized ivory bridge pins with black dots, tortoise beveled pickguard, available in Natural or Sunburst polished gloss finish with Aging Toner top, 25.4 in. scale, case included, mfg. summer 2004-present.

| MSR $5,499 | $4,300 | $2,350 - 2,950 | $1,425 - 1,775 | |

• **Add 5% (MSR $5,749) for Sunburst finish.**

* *D-28 Marquis Madagascar* – similar to the D-28 Marquis, except has Madagascar rosewood back, sides, and headstock overlay, available in Natural polished gloss finish with Aging Toner top, mfg. summer 2007-mid-2009.

| | N/A | $3,200 - 4,000 | $1,925 - 2,400 | $7,599 |

D-28 MUSEUM EDITION 1941 – dreadnought body style based on the 1941 14-fret D-28 (serial number 79103) that is on display in the Martin Museum, solid Adirondack spruce top, solid Madagascar rosewood back and sides, standard X scalloped authentic-style bracing, round soundhole with Style 28 three-stripe rosette (5/9/5 grouping), grained ivoroid binding, bold herringbone top inlay, B/W boltaron back inlay, HD zig-zag back stripe, authentic 1941 barrel and heel mahogany neck, 14/20-fret ebony fingerboard with long pattern diamond and square inlays, solid Madagascar rosewood headstock overlay with Golden Era-style logo, three-per-side Waverly nickel tuners with oval buttons, ebony 1930s-style belly bridge with long saddle, antique white bridge pins with black dots, Delmar tortoise color beveled pickguard, available in Natural polished gloss finish with Aging Toner top, 25.4 in. scale, Harptone case included, mfg. 2009-2012.

| | $12,000 | $6,750 - 8,250 | N/A | $15,499 |

D-45 AUTHENTIC 1942 – dreadnought body style based on a 1942 14-fret D-45, solid Adirondack spruce top, solid Brazilian rosewood back and sides, standard X scalloped rear shifted Golden Era solid Aidrondack spruce bracing, round soundhole with Style 45 three-stripe rosette (5/9/5 grouping with a large middle ring of abalone pearl), grained ivoroid binding, Style 42 abalone pearl top inlay that goes around the fingerboard, Style 45 abalone pearl back inlay, Style 45 Golden Era back stripe, mahogany neck with an authentic 1942 barrel and heel, 14/20-fret grained ivoroid-bound ebony fingerboard with abalone pearl hexagon inlays, grained ivoroid-bound solid Brazilian rosewood headstock overlay with Golden Era-style verical block Martin logo, three-per-side Waverly gold tuners with butterbean buttons, ebony 1930s-style belly bridge with long saddle, alternative ivory bridge pins with pearl dots, tortoise beveled pickguard, Natural polished gloss finish, 25.4 in. scale, Harptone case included, mfg. 2011-present.

| MSR $59,999 | $48,000 | N/A | N/A | |

D-45GE GOLDEN ERA – dreadnought body style based on a 1930s 14-fret D-45, solid Adirondack spruce top, solid Brazilian rosewood back and sides, standard X scalloped forward shifted bracing, round soundhole with Style 45 three-stripe rosette (5/9/5 grouping with a large middle ring of abalone pearl), grained ivoroid binding, abalone pearl top inlay that goes around the fingerboard, abalone pearl back and side inlays, Style 45 Golden Era back stripe, mahogany neck, 14/20-fret grained ivoroid-bound ebony fingerboard with abalone pearl snowflake inlays, grained ivoroid-bound solid Brazilian rosewood headstock overlay with Golden Era-style verical block Martin logo, three-per-side Waverly gold tuners with butterbean buttons, ebony 1930s-style belly bridge with long saddle, white bridge pins with abalone pearl dots, tortoise beveled pickguard, Natural polished gloss finish with Aging Toner top, 25.4 in. scale, special leather case included, mfg. summer 2000-04.

| | N/A | $12,000 - 15,000 | $7,200 - 9,000 | $20,500 |

D-45 MARQUIS – dreadnought body style based on a 1930s 14-fret D-45, solid Adirondack spruce top, solid East Indian rosewood back and sides, standard X scalloped forward shifted bracing, round soundhole with Style 45 three-stripe rosette (5/9/5 grouping with a large middle ring of abalone pearl), grained ivoroid binding, abalone pearl top inlay that goes around the fingerboard, abalone pearl back inlay, Style 45 Golden Era back stripe, mahogany neck, 14/20-fret grained ivoroid-bound ebony fingerboard with abalone pearl snowflake inlays, grained ivoroid-bound solid East Indian rosewood headstock overlay with Golden Era-style verical block Martin logo, three-per-side Waverly gold tuners with butterbean buttons, ebony 1930s-style belly bridge with long saddle, fossilized ivory bridge pins with black pearl dots, tortoise beveled pickguard, Natural polished gloss finish with Aging Toner top, 25.4 in. scale, case included, mfg. summer 2006-mid-2008.

| | N/A | $7,200 - 9,000 | $4,325 - 5,400 | $12,999 |

MSR/NOTES	100%	EXCELLENT	AVERAGE	LAST MSR

D-45S AUTHENTIC 1936 – dreadnought body style based on a 1936 14-fret D-45, solid Adirondack spruce top, solid Brazilian rosewood back and sides, standard X scalloped bracing, round soundhole with Style 45 three-stripe rosette (5/9/5 grouping with a large middle ring of abalone pearl), grained ivoroid binding, Style 42 abalone pearl top inlay that goes around the fingerboard, Style 45 abalone pearl back and side inlay, Style 45 Golden Era back stripe, mahogany neck with an authentic 1936 barrel and heel, 14/20-fret grained ivoroid-bound ebony fingerboard with abalone snowflake inlays, grained ivoroid-bound solid Brazilian rosewood headstock overlay with Golden Era-style verical block Martin logo, three-per-side Waverly gold tuners with butterbean buttons, ebony 1930s-style belly bridge with long saddle, ivory colored bridge pins with pearl dots, tortoise beveled pickguard, Natural polished gloss finish, 25.4 in. scale, Harptone case included, mfg. 2013-present.

| MSR $59,999 | $48,000 | N/A | N/A | |

OM-18 AUTHENTIC 1933 – orchestra body style based on a 1933 14-fret OM-18, solid Adirondack spruce top, solid mahogany back and sides, standard X scalloped bracing, round soundhole with old Style 18 three-stripe black/white fiber rosette (1/5/1 grouping), black boltaron binding, multiple black/white boltaron top inlay, mahogany authentic 1933 barrel & heel profile neck, 14/20-fret ebony fingerboard with old style 18 dot inlays, solid Madagascar rosewood headstock overlay with gold logo, three-per-side Waverly nickel tuners with butterbean buttons, ebony belly bridge with long saddle, black bridge pins, tortoise beveled pickguard, Aging Toner polished gloss finish with 1933 Chris Hillman top, 25.4 in. scale, case included, mfg. 2013-present.

| MSR $6,499 | $5,000 | $2,725 - 3,400 | $1,650 - 2,050 | |

OM-18GE GOLDEN ERA – orchestra body style based on a 1930 14-fret OM-18, solid Adirondack spruce top, solid mahogany back and sides, standard X scalloped bracing, round soundhole with old Style 18 three-stripe black/white fiber rosette (1/5/1 grouping), Brazilian rosewood binding, multiple black/maple/black fiber top inlay, 30s-style V select hardwood neck, 14/20-fret ebony fingerboard with abalone dot inlays at the 5th, 7th, and 9th frets, solid Brazilian rosewood headstock overlay with no logo, three-per-side Waverly nickel banjo-style tuners with ivoroid buttons, ebony 1930s-style belly bridge with long saddle, ebony bridge pins, tortoise beveled pickguard, Natural polished gloss finish with Aging Toner top, 25.4 in. scale, case included, mfg. 2003-09.

| | N/A | $2,400 - 3,000 | $1,450 - 1,800 | $4,899 |

OM-28GE GOLDEN ERA – orchestra body style based on a 1930s 14-fret OM-28, solid Adirondack spruce top, solid Brazilian rosewood back and sides, scalloped bracing, round soundhole with old Style 28 black/maple three-stripe rosette (5/9/5 grouping), grained ivoroid binding, fine herringbone top inlay, 30s-style modified V select hardwood neck, 14/20-fret ebony fingerboard with short pattern diamond and square inlays, solid Brazilian rosewood headstock overlay with Golden Era-style logo, three-per-side Gotoh nickel open-geared tuners with butterbean buttons, ebony 1930s-style belly bridge with long saddle, fossilized ivory bridge pins with black dots, tortoise pickguard, Natural polished gloss finish with Aging Toner top, 25.4 in. scale, case included, mfg. summer 2003-mid-2006.

| | N/A | $7,000 - 8,500 | $5,000 - 6,000 | $14,999 |

OM-28 MARQUIS – orchestra body style based on a 1930s 14-fret OM-28, solid Adirondack spruce top, solid East Indian rosewood back and sides, standard X scalloped bracing, round soundhole with Style 28 three-stripe rosette (5/9/5 grouping), grained ivoroid binding, fine herringbone top inlay, black/maple fiber back inlay, HD zig-zag back stripe, select hardwood neck, 14/20-fret ebony fingerboard with short pattern diamond and square inlays, solid East Indian rosewood headstock overlay with Golden Era-style logo, three-per-side Gotoh nickel open-geared tuners with butterbean buttons, ebony 1930s-style belly bridge with long saddle, fossilized ivory bridge pins with black dots, tortoise beveled pickguard, available in Natural polished gloss finish with Aging Toner top, 25.4 in. scale, case included, mfg. 2005-present.

| MSR $5,499 | $4,300 | $2,350 - 2,950 | $1,425 - 1,775 | |

* *OM-28 Marquis Madagascar* – similar to the OM-28 Marquis, except has solid Madagascar rosewood back, sides, and headstock overlay, mfg. summer 2007-mid-2009.

| | N/A | $3,200 - 4,000 | $1,925 - 2,400 | $7,599 |

OM-45GE GOLDEN ERA – orchestra body style based on a 1933 14-fret OM-45, solid Adirondack spruce top, solid Brazilian rosewood back and sides, scalloped bracing, round soundhole with Style 45 three-stripe rosette (5/9/5 grouping with a large middle ring of abalone pearl), grained ivoroid binding, abalone pearl and B/M/B fiber top inlays that goes around the fingerboard, abalone pearl with B/M/B fiber back and side inlays, Style 45 Golden Era back stripe, mahogany neck, 14/20-fret grained ivoroid-bound ebony fingerboard with abalone pearl snowflake inlays, grained ivoroid-bound solid Brazilian rosewood headstock overlay with Golden Era-style verical block Martin logo, three-per-side Waverly gold tuners with butterbean buttons, ebony 1930s-style belly bridge with long saddle, fossilized ivory bridge pins with black pearl dots, tortoise beveled pickguard, Natural polished gloss finish with Vintage Toner top, 25.4 in. scale, case included, mfg. summer 1998, summer 2000-04.

| | N/A | $12,000 - 15,000 | $7,200 - 9,000 | $20,500 |

For the first run of this guitar, 14 instruments were produced in 1998. This number was chosen because 14 guitars were originally made in 1930.

OM-45 MARQUIS – orchestra body style based on a 1930s 14-fret OM-45, solid Adirondack spruce top, solid East Indian rosewood back and sides, standard X scalloped bracing, round soundhole with Style 45 three-stripe rosette (5/9/5 grouping with a large middle ring of abalone pearl), grained ivoroid binding, abalone pearl top inlay that goes around the fingerboard, abalone pearl back inlay, Style 45 Golden Era back stripe, mahogany neck, 14/20-fret grained ivoroid-bound ebony fingerboard with abalone pearl snowflake inlays, grained ivoroid-bound solid East Indian rosewood headstock overlay with Golden Era-style verical block Martin logo, three-per-side Waverly gold tuners with butterbean buttons, ebony 1930s-style belly bridge with long saddle, fossilized ivory bridge pins with black pearl dots, tortoise beveled pickguard, Natural polished gloss finish with Aging Toner top, 25.4 in. scale, case included, mfg. 2005-mid-2008.

| | N/A | $6,000 - 7,500 | $3,600 - 4,500 | $12,999 |

MSR/NOTES	100%	EXCELLENT	AVERAGE	LAST MSR

ACOUSTIC: CUSTOM ARTIST SERIES

Custom Artist Series guitars bear an interior label signed by the artist and C.F. Martin IV, and are numbered in sequence.

- **These models are available in left hand at no additional charge.**

0-18T NICK REYNOLDS – tenor configuration, Concert 0 14-fret-style body, solid Sitka spruce top, solid mahogany back and sides, standard X solid Sitka spruce bracing, round soundhole with old Style 18 rosette (1/9/1 grouping), select hardwood top inlay, B/W boltaron back inlays, Style 18 back purfling, select hardwood tenor neck, 14/20-fret ebony fingerboard with abalone dots and 20th fret Nick Reynolds signature inlays, solid headstock with solid Madagascar rosewood overlay and C.F. Martin & Co. gold foil logo, two-per-side chrome Grover tuners with large buttons, ebony tenor bridge with drop-in long saddle, black bridge pins with white dots, tortoise color pickguard, two labels, one signed by Nick Reynolds and numbered in sequence, one photographic label, Natural polished gloss finish with Aging Toner top, 23 in. scale, Geib style case included, mfg. summer 2010-2011.

	$3,150	$1,750 - 2,050	$1,175 - 1,375	$3,899

00-18H GEOFF MULDAUR – Grand Concert 00 12-fret-style body, solid Adirondack spruce top, solid mahogany back and sides, round soundhole with old Style 18 rosette, tortoise color binding, multiple B/W top inlays, B/W boltaron inlays, Style 18 back stripe, select hardwood neck, 12/20-fret ebony fingerboard with abalone dot inlays, slotted headstock with ebony overlay, three-per-side open-style Waverly tuners with ivoroid knobs, ebony belly bridge, black pickguard, label signed by Geoff Muldaur and C.F. Martin IV, Sunburst polished gloss finish with aging toner top, 24.9 in. scale, mfg. summer 2006-mid-2011.

	$4,200	$2,350 - 2,750	$1,550 - 1,825	$5,199

00-18S JOHN MELLENCAMP – Grand Concert 00 12-fret-style body, solid Carpathian spruce top, solid quilted mahogany back and sides, standard X scalloped bracing, round soundhole with old Style 18 rosette (1/9/1 grouping), tortoise color binding, multiple B/W boltaron top inlays, B/W boltaron back inlays, Style 18 back purfling, select hardwood low profile neck, 12/20-fret ebony fingerboard with abalone dots and 20th fret John Mellencamp signature inlays, slotted headstock with solid Madagascar rosewood overlay, three-per-side open-style gold Waverly tuners with ivoroid knobs, ebony pyramid bridge with drop-in saddle, solid black ebony bridge pins, no pickguard, label signed by John Mellencamp and numbered in sequence, Natural satin finish with Aging Toner top, 24.9 in. scale, mfg. 2009-mid-2010.

	$4,500	$2,500 - 2,950	$1,675 - 1,950	$5,599

* 00-18S *John Mellencamp Gloss* – similar to the 00-18S John Mellencamp, except has a polished gloss finish with an Aging Toner top, mfg. 2009-mid-2010.

	$4,800	$2,700 - 3,150	$1,800 - 2,100	$5,999

00-42SC JOHN MAYER – Grand Concert 12-fret 00-style body based on John Mayer's 00-42, solid Sitka spruce top, solid cocobolo back and sides, custom Style 45 rosette (5/9/5 grouping with a large center ring of abalone), grained ivoroid binding, Style 42 abalone top inlay that goes around the fingerboard, black/maple/black back and side inlay, Style 45 black mosaic back purfling, modified V select hardwood neck, 12/19-fret grained ivoroid-bound ebony fingerboard with Style 42 paua pearl snowflake inlays, open-style grained ivoroid-bound headstock with solid cocobolo overlay and golden era CF Martin block abalone pearl logo, three-per-side Waverly brass tuners with small ivoroid buttons, ebony pyramid bridge with drop-in saddle, label signed by John Mayer, available in Natural Gloss finish, 24.9 in. scale, custom case included, mfg. 2013-present.

MSR $9,999	$8,000	$4,700 - 5,400	N/A	

00-DB JEFF TWEEDY – Grand Concert 14-fret 00-style body, solid FSC certified mahogany top, solid FSC certified mahogany back and sides, hybrid X scalloped FSC certified European spruce bracing, round soundhole with three-ring rosette, tortoise binding, B/W top inlay, black back purfling, FSC certified mahogany modified V-shaped neck, tortoise heelcap, 14/20-fret black Richlite fingerboard with Foden-style inlays, solid-square tapered headstock with FSC certified mahogany headstock overlay and regular logo, three-per-side nickel tuners with butterbean knobs, black Richlite bridge, black bridge pins, tortoise pickguard, Natural polished gloss finish with Sunburst top, 1.75 in. nut width, 25.4 in. scale, molded case included, mfg. summer 2012-present.

MSR $2,999	$2,400	$1,325 - 1,650	$800 - 1,000	

000-18 KENNY SULTAN – 000-sized body, solid Adirondack spruce top, solid flamed mahogany back and sides, single ring herringbone pearl rosette, tortoise color biding, mahogany neck, 14/20-fret ebony fingerboard with diamond and square pattern inlays, ebony headstock overlay, three-per-side Waverly nickel tuners with butterbean knobs, ebony bridge, tortoise pickguard, label signed by Kenny Sultan, available in Sunburst Gloss finish, 24.9 in. scale, mfg. 2007-mid-2010.

	$4,100	$2,300 - 2,700	$1,525 - 1,800	$5,099

000C DAVID GRAY – single cutaway Grand Auditorium 14-fret 000-style body, solid Italian Alpine spruce top, mahogany back and sides, select hardwood neck, 14/20-fret ebony fingerboard with old style 18 abalone pearl inlays, ebony headstock with herringbone inlay and silver foil logo, Gotoh nickel open geared tuners with butterbean knobs, ebony belly bridge, Martin Gold Plus Natural 1 electronics, label signed by C.F. Martin IV and David Gray, Natural polished gloss finish with vintage toner top, case included, 24.9 in. scale, mfg. summer 2006-07.

	N/A	$2,000 - 2,500	$1,200 - 1,500	$3,799

000C-MR STEVE MILLER – single cutaway Grand Auditorium 14-fret 000-style body, solid Adirondack spruce top, solid Pacific Big Leaf maple back and sides, standard X scalloped solid Sitka spruce bracing, round soundhole with three-ring Style 45 rosette (5/9/5 grouping with a large ring of abalone), grained ivoroid binding, multiple B/W boltaron top inlay, B/W/B Boltaron back and side inlay, Style 45 back purfling, hard maple modified low oval neck, 14/20-fret grained ivoroid-bound ebony fingerboard with no inlays, grained ivoroid-bound square tapered headstock with ebony overlay and 1902 alternative torch inlay, three-per-side nickel open-geared tuners with butterbean knobs, ebony belly bridge with bone saddle, black ebony bridge pins with pearl dots, black pickguard, Fishman Matrix Infinity electronics, label signed by Steve Miller and numbered in sequence, available in Red polished gloss finish, 24.9 in. scale, Geib-style case included, mfg. 2010-mid-2013.

	$5,400	$2,925 - 3,400	$1,950 - 2,275	$6,499

MSR/NOTES	100%	EXCELLENT	AVERAGE	LAST MSR

5-18 MARTY ROBBINS – Size 5/Terz 12-fret-style body, solid Adirondack spruce top, solid mahogany back and sides, standard X bracing, round soundhole with three-ring old Style 18 rosette (1/9/1 grouping), tortoise color binding, multiple B/W Boltaron binding, Style 18 back purfling, select hardwood modified low oval neck, 12/18-fret ebony fingerboard with old Style 18 dots, 5th fret Texas, and 7th fret star inlays, solid Madagascar rosewood headstock overlay with standard CF Martin & Co. logo, three-per-side open-geared nickel tuners with butterbean knobs, Size 5 ebony bridge with long saddle, black bridge pins with white dots, Delmar tortoise color pickguard, label signed by Ronnie Robbins and numbered in sequence, available in Natural polished gloss finish with Aging Toner top, case included, mfg. summer 2009-mid-2011.

	$3,100	$1,700 - 2,000	$1,150 - 1,350	$3,799

D-18 DEL McCOURY 50TH ANNIVERSARY – dreadnought 14-fret-style body, solid Adirondack spruce top, solid mahogany back and sides, standard X scalloped, rear shifted solid Adirondack spruce bracing, round soundhole with three-ring old Style 18 rosette (1/9/1 grouping), tortoise color binding, multiple B/W boltaron top inlay, Style 18 back purfling, mahogany rounded full thickness V-shaped neck with a 30s-style heel, 14/20-fret ebony fingerboard with old Style 18 dot inlays, square tapered headstock with solid Madagascar rosewood overlay and gold foil standard logo, three-per-side Waverly nickel open-geared tuners with oval buttons, ebony belly bridge with compensated bone saddle, black ebony bridge pins with abalone pearl dots, Delmar tortoise pickguard, two labels (one signed by Del McCoury and numbered in sequence with total production, one for 50th Anniversary), available in Natural polished gloss finish with aging toner top, 25.4 in. scale, Geib-style case included, limited edition run of 50 instruments, mfg. first half of 2010 only.

	$3,750	$2,025 - 2,375	$1,350 - 1,575	$4,499

D-28 DAN TYMINSKI – dreadnought 14-fret-style body, solid Adirondack spruce top, solid East Indian rosewood back and sides, standard X scalloped rear shifted bracing (Golden Era-style), round soundhole with three-ring Style 28 rosette (5/9/5 grouping), grained ivoroid binding, bold herringbone top inlay, B/W fiber back inlay, HD zig-zag back purfling, select hardwood modified V neck, 14/20-fret ebony fingerboard with diamond & squares long pattern Golden Era inlays, solid East Indian rosewood headstock overlay with CF Martin & Co. logo, three-per-side Waverly open-geared nickel tuners with oval buttons, ebony belly bridge, ebony bridge pins, Delmar tortoise color pickguard, label signed by Dan Tyminski and numbered in sequence, available in Natural polished gloss finish with Aging Toner top, 25.4 in. scale, case included, mfg. summer 2009-mid-2013.

	$4,150	$2,325 - 2,700	$1,550 - 1,800	$5,149

D-28M THE MAMAS AND THE PAPAS – dreadnought 14-fret-style body, solid Carpathian spruce top, solid Madagascar rosewood back and sides, standard X scalloped rear shifted bracing, round soundhole with three-ring Style 28 rosette (5/9/5 grouping), grained ivoroid binding, multi-ply B/W boltaron top inlay, multi-ply B/W boltaron back inlay, HD zig-zag back purfling, solid mahogany low profile neck, 14/20-fret ebony fingerboard with Style 28 MOP dot inlays, ebony headstock overlay with CF Martin & Co. logo and pearl silhouette of the band, three-per-side Grover chrome tuners with large buttons, ebony belly bridge, bone bridge pins with select pearl dots, Delmar tortoise color pickguard, two labels: one signed by C.F. Martin IV and Michelle Phillips and numbered in sequence and one photographic label, available in Natural polished gloss finish with Aging Toner top, 25.4 in. scale, case included, limited run of 100 instruments, mfg. 2012-present.

MSR $4,999	$4,000	$2,400 - 3,000	$1,450 - 1,800	

D-35 SETH AVETT – dreadnought 14-fret-style body, solid high altitude spruce top, three-piece back with solid East Indian rosewood wings and a flamed koa center wedge, solid East Indian rosewood sides, round soundhole with three-ring Style 28 rosette (5/9/5 grouping with a large middle herringbone ring), grained ivoroid binding, fine herringbone top inlay, B/W Boltaron back inlay, multiple B/W boltaron side inlay, Style 35 back purfling, select hardwood Performing Artist profile neck, 14/20-fret grained ivoroid-bound ebony fingerboard with custom Avett copper snowflake inlays, solid East Indian rosewood headstock overlay with large golden era style gold logo, ebony belly bridge, white bridge pins with tortoise color dots, black pickguard, Martin Gold Plus Natural 1 electronics, available in Natural polished gloss finish 25.4 in. scale, custom case included, mfg. 2013-present.

MSR $3,999	$3,200	$1,675 - 2,100	$1,000 - 1,250	

D-41 PORTER WAGONER – dreadnought-style body, solid Englemann spruce top, solid East Indian rosewood back and sides, Style 45 rosette, grained ivoroid binding, abalone pearl with B/W/B boltaron top inlay, B/W boltaron back inlay, select hardwood neck, 14/20-fret ebony fingerboard with scalloped hexagon inlays, solid East Indian rosewood headstock overlay with select abalone pearl Martin block logo inlay, three-per-side Gotoh gold open-geared tuners with butterbean knobs, belly ebony bridge, special Porter Wagoner pickguard, two labels (one signed by Wagoner and Marty Stuart and one with Wagoner photo "Wagonmaster" numbered in sequence), available in Natural Gloss finish, 25.4 in. scale, mfg. 2008-09.

	N/A	$2,800 - 3,500	$1,675 - 2,150	$5,999

D JOHN SEBASTIAN – slope-shouldered dreadnought 14-fret-style body, solid Adirondack spruce top, solid highly figured koa back and sides, standard X scalloped bracing, round soundhole with three-ring Style 45 rosette (5/9/5 grouping with a large ring of abalone), solid East Indian rosewood binding, fine herringbone top inlay, multi-ply B/W boltaron back inlay, fine herringbone back purfling, select hardwood Performing Artist profile neck, 14/20-fret ebony fingerboard with John Sebastian design MOP inlays, East Indian rosewood headstock overlay with abalone Martin logo, three-per-side Waverly nickel tuners with snakewood knobs, 1930-style ebony belly bridge, bone bridge pins with pearl dots, no pickguard, two labels: one signed by John Sebastian and numbered in sequence and one photographic label, available in Natural polished gloss finish with Amber Burst top, 25.4 in. scale, case included, limited run of 44 instruments, mfg. 2013-present.

MSR $7,999	$6,400	$3,350 - 4,200	N/A	

HD DIERKS BENTLEY – dreadnought-style body, solid Adirondack spruce top, solid East Indian rosewood back and sides, standard X scalloped forward shifted bracing, round soundhole with red, white, and blue herringbone rosette, grained ivoroid binding, red, white, and blue herringbone top inlay, red, white, and blue back purfling, select hardwood modified V-shaped neck, grained ivoroid heelcap, 14/20-fret ebony fingerboard with Style 28 MOP dot inlays and 12th fret Phoenix inlay, Madagascar rosewood headstock overlay with gold foil logo, three-per-side Waverly nickel tuners with butterbean knobs, ebony belly bridge, bone (white) bridge pins with tortoise dots, tortoise pickguard, Natural polished gloss finish, 1.6875 in. nut width, 25.4 in. scale, Geib hardshell case included, mfg. summer 2012-present.

MSR $4,999	$4,000	$2,150 - 2,700	$1,300 - 1,625	

MSR/NOTES	100%	EXCELLENT	AVERAGE	LAST MSR

HD ELLIOT EASTON – dreadnought-style body, solid Adirondack spruce top, quilted mahogany back and sides, standard X scalloped forward shifted bracing, round soundhole with fine herringbone rosette, grained ivoroid binding, fine herringbone top inlay, B/W boltaron back inlay, HD zig-zag back stripe, select hardwood neck, grained ivoroid heelcap, 14/20-fret ebony fingerboard with diamond and square inlays, Indian rosewood headstock overlay with large old style logo, three-per-side Waverly gold tuners with butterbean knobs, ebony belly bridge, white bridge pins with tortoise dots, tortoise pickguard, Natural polished gloss finish with with aging toner top, label signed by C.F. Martin IV and Elliot Easton, 25.4 in. scale, mfg. summer 2006-mid-2008.

	N/A	$2,200 - 2,750	$1,325 - 1,650	$4,899

* *HDE Elliot Easton Electric* – similar to the HD Elliot Easton, except has Fishman Ellipse Aura electronics, mfg. summer 2006-mid-2008.

	N/A	$2,325 - 2,900	$1,400 - 1,750	$5,399

HJ-38 STEFAN GROSSMAN – jumbo-style body, solid Sitka spruce top, solid Madagascar rosewood back and sides, Style 45 rosette, grained ivoroid binding, fine herringbone top inlay, B/W/B boltaron back inlay, select hardwood neck, grained ivoroid with B/W/B boltaron inlay heelcap, 14/20-fret ebony fingerboard with Maltese diamond and square inlays, solid Madagascar rosewood headstock overlay with select abalone pearl Golden Era Martin block logo inlay, three-per-side Waverly gold tuners with butterbean knobs, belly ebony bridge, tortoiseshell pickguard, label signed by Stefan Grossman and numbered in sequence, available in Natural Gloss finish, 25.4 in. scale, mfg. 2008-mid-2011.

	$4,200	$2,350 - 2,750	$1,550 - 1,825	$5,199

JSO SING OUT! PETE SEEGER 60TH ANNIVERSARY – jumbo 14-fret-style body, solid Sitka spruce top, solid East Indian rosewood back and sides, standard X progressively scalloped tone bars, triangular soundhole with single ring rosette (5 grouping), grained ivoroid binding, bold herringbone top inlay, B/W boltaron back inlay, HD zig-zag back purfling, mahogany low oval neck, 15/21-fret ebony fingerboard, solid ebony headstock overlay with CF Martin & Co. logo and abalone Pete Seeger signature and banjo inlay, three-per-side chrome Grover tuners with large buttons, ebony Stauffer-style pyramid bridge, ebony bridge pins with paua pearl dots, two black pickguards, label signed by Pete Seeger and CFM IV, available in Natural polished gloss finish with Aging Toner top, 27.5 in. scale, Geib-style case included, mfg. 2011-mid-2013.

	$4,000	$2,250 - 2,650	$1,500 - 1,750	$4,999

* *J12SO Sing Out! Pete Seeger 60th Anniversary 12-String* – similar to the JSO Sing Out! Pete Seeger 60th Anniversary, except in 12-string configuration with six-per-side tuners, available in Natural polished gloss finish with Aging Toner top, mfg. 2011-mid-2013.

	$4,200	$2,375 - 2,750	$1,575 - 1,850	$5,249

M-21 STEVE EARLE – Grand Auditorium 14-fret 0000/M-style body, solid Italian Alpine spruce top, solid East Indian rosewood back and sides, standard X scalloped forward-shifted bracing, round soundhole with three-ring old Style 18 rosette (1/9/1 grouping), tortoise color binding, multiple B/W Boltaron top inlay, B/W Boltaron back inlay, Style 28 back purfling, select hardwood low profile neck, 14/20-fret rosewood fingerboard with pearl dot inlays, solid Indian rosewood headstock overlay with large old style logo, three-per-side nickel Waverly tuners with Butterbean knobs, rosewood belly bridge, black bridge pins with white dots, tortoise color pickguard, label signed by Steve Earle and Matt Umanov and numbered in sequence, Natural polished gloss finish with Aging Toner top, 25.4 in. scale, Slate Gray case included, mfg. summer 2008-2011.

	$3,400	$1,925 - 2,250	$1,300 - 1,500	$4,299

M-30 JORMA KAUKONEN – 0000/M-style body, solid Italian Alpine spruce top, solid East Indian rosewood back and sides, standard X scalloped forward shifted solid Sitka spruce bracing, large round soundhole with two-ring Style 45 rosette (5/9 grouping with a large ring of abalone - inner ring is not present), grained ivoroid binding, Style 30 multi-colored parallelogram top inlay, B/W boltaron back and side inlay, Style 30 multi-colored parallelogram back purfling, mahogany modified V-shaped neck, 14/20-fret grained ivoroid-bound ebony fingerboard with select pearl long pattern Maltese diamond and square inlays and "Jorma" signature across the 19th and 20th frets, grained ivoroid-bound square tapered headstock with solid East Indian rosewood overlay, abalone logo, and modified abalone torch inlay, three-per-side Waverly nickel open-geared tuners with ivoroid oval buttons, ebony belly bridge with compensated bone saddle, bone bridge pins with pearl dots, Delmar tortoise pickguard, two labels (one signed by Jorma Kaukonen and numbered in sequence and one Fur Peace Ranch), available in Natural polished gloss with Aging Toner top finish, 25.4 in. scale, Geib-style case included, mfg. 2010-mid-2013.

	$5,150	$2,800 - 3,250	$1,875 - 2,175	$6,199

M3H CATHY FINK – Grand Auditorium 14-fret 0000-style body, solid Adirondack spruce top, solid East Indian rosewood back with solid flamed Hawaiian koa wedge, solid East Indian rosewood sides, round soundhole with three ring Style 45 rosette (5/9/5 grouping with an abalone pearl center), grained ivoroid binding, fine herringbone top inlay, B/W boltaron back and side inlays, Style 45 back stripe, select hardwood neck, grained ivoroid heelcap 14/20-fret grained ivoroid-bound ebony fingerboard with Style 42 MOP snowflake and 12th fret "two hands" inlays, grained ivoroid-bound ebony headstock overlay with abalone torch pattern inlay, three-per-side Gotoh gold tuners with large ebony knobs, ebony belly bridge, white bridge pins with abalone pearl dots, Natural polished gloss finish with Vintage Toner top, label signed by C.F. Martin IV and Cathy Fink, 25.4 in. scale, black denim case included, mfg. summer 2006-07.

	N/A	$2,000 - 2,500	$1,200 - 1,500	$4,399

MC-18 WOODY MANN – single smooth cutaway M/0000 14-fret-style body, solid Adirondack spruce top, solid mahogany back and sides, standard X scalloped forward shifted bracing, large round soundhole with three ring old Style 18 rosette, solid East Indian rosewood binding, multiple B/W fiber top inlay, B/W fiber back inlay, Style 18 back purfling, select hardwood low profile neck, 14/20-fret ebony fingerboard with no inlays, solid Madagascar rosewood headstock overlay with CF Martin & Co. logo, three-per-side Waverly nickel open-geared tuners with ebony buttons, straight ebony bridge with drop-in saddle, label signed by Woody Mann and numbered in sequence, available in Natural polished gloss finish with Aging Top toner, 25.4 in. scale, case included, mfg. summer 2009-2011.

	$4,400	$2,400 - 2,800	$1,600 - 1,850	$5,299

MSR/NOTES	100%	EXCELLENT	AVERAGE	LAST MSR

MC3H MARCY MARXER – single cutaway Grand Auditorium 14-fret 0000-style body, solid Adirondack spruce top, solid East Indian rosewood back with solid flamed Hawaiian koa wedge, solid East Indian rosewood sides, round soundhole with three ring Style 45 rosette (5/9/5 grouping with an abalone pearl center), grained ivoroid binding, fine herringbone top inlay, B/W boltaron back and side inlays, Style 45 back stripe, select hardwood neck, grained ivoroid heelcap14/20-fret grained ivoroid-bound ebony fingerboard with Style 42 MOP snowflake and 12th fret "two hands" inlays, grained ivoroid-bound ebony headstock overlay with abalone torch pattern inlay, three-per-side Gotoh gold tuners with large ebony knobs, ebony belly bridge, white bridge pins with abalone pearl dots, Natural polished gloss finish with Vintage Toner top, label signed by C.F. Martin IV and Marcy Marxer, 25.4 in. scale, black denim case included, mfg. summer 2006-07.

	N/A	$2,200 - 2,750	$1,325 - 1,650	$4,799

OM-30DB PAT DONOHUE – Grand Auditorium 14-fret 000 deep-style body, solid Adirondack spruce top, solid East Indian rosewood back and sides, standard X scalloped bracing, round soundhole with three-ring Style 45 rosette (5/9/5 grouping with a large middle ring of abalone pearl), grained ivoroid binding, Style 30 multi-colored top inlay, B/W Boltaron back inlay, Style 30 multi-colored back purfling, mahogany modified V neck, 14/20-fret grained ivoroid-bound ebony fingerboard with Style 30 abalone pearl snowflake inlays and 12th fret "PD" inlays, grained ivoroid-bound slotted headstock with solid East Indian rosewood overlay and select abalone pearl torch pattern inlays, three-per-side gold Waverly tuners with small ivoroid buttons, ebony pyramid bridge with drop-in saddle, camel bone bridge pins with select pearl dots, Delmar tortoise color pickguard, label signed by Pat Donohue and numbered in sequence, Natural polished gloss finish with Aging Toner top, 25.4 in. scale, Geib-style case included, mfg. summer 2008-mid-2010.

	$5,100	$3,050 - 3,550	$2,050 - 2,400	$6,799

OM CHRIS HILLMAN – Grand Auditorium 14-fret 000-style body, solid Adirondack spruce top, solid East Indian rosewood back and sides, standard X scalloped bracing, round soundhole with three-ring herringbone rosette (two five grouping rings with a large center ring of herringbone), tortoise binding, fine herringbone top inlay, B/W Boltaron back and side inlay, HD zig-zag back purfling, mahogany low profile neck, 14/20-fret grained tortoise color-bound ebony fingerboard with Style 45 select abalone snowflake inlays and 20th fret Chris Hillman signature inlay, ebony headstock overlay with select abalone pearl logo and roping cowboy inlays, three-per-side nickel Waverly tuners with ebony buttons, ebony belly bridge with drop-in saddle, white bridge pins with tortoise color dots, Delmar tortoise color pickguard, label signed by Chris Hillman and numbered in sequence, Natural polished gloss finish with a 1932 Sunburst top, 25.4 in. scale, Geib-style case included, mfg. 2009-mid-2010.

	$5,600	$3,150 - 3,700	$2,100 - 2,450	$6,999

OM JEFF DANIELS – Grand Auditorium 14-fret 000-style body, solid Adirondack spruce top, solid Madagascar rosewood back and sides, standard X scalloped bracing, round soundhole with three-ring Style 42 wood fiber rosette, grained ivoroid binding, bold herringbone top inlay, B/W wood fiber back inlay, HD-28-style zig-zag strip back purfling, mahogany modified V-shaped neck with 1930s-style heel, grained ivoroid heelcap, 14/20-fret ebony fingerboard with special select abalone diamond and square long pattern inlays and 12th fret MOP happy/ sad theatrical masks inlays, Madagascar rosewood headstock overlay with Golden Era Style 45 block letter abalone pearl logo, three-per-side Waverly nickel tuners with butterbean knobs, ebony belly bridge, bone (white) bridge pins with black dots, tortoise pickguard, Natural polished gloss finish with 1932 shaded top, label personally signed by Jeff Daniels and numbered in sequence, 1.75 in. nut width, 25.4 in. scale, Geib hardshell case included, mfg. summer 2012-mid-2013.

	$4,000	$2,150 - 2,700	$1,300 - 1,625	$4,999

OMC-18 LAURENCE JUBER – 000-style body, solid Adirondack spruce top, solid Mahogany back and sides, Style 28 old Style Wood fiber inlays rosette, tortoise color binding, mulitple B/W boltaron top inlay, select hardwood neck, ebony heelcap, 14/20-fret ebony fingerboard with abalone pearl dot inlays, solid Madagascar rosewood headstock overlay with large old style logo, three-per-side Gotoh nickel open-geared tuners with Butterbean knobs, belly ebony bridge, no pickguard, label signed by Laurence Juber and numbered in sequence, available in Natural Gloss finish, 25.4 in. scale, mfg. 2008-mid-2010.

	$3,800	$2,150 - 2,525	$1,450 - 1,700	$4,799

OMC-28M LAURENCE JUBER – single cutaway Grand Auditorium 14-fret 000-style body, solid Adirondack spruce top, solid Madagascar rosewood back and sides, round soundhole with Style 28 rosette, grained ivoroid binding, fine herringbone top inlay, black/maple fiber back inlay, HD zig-zag back inlay, select hardwood neck, grained ivoroid heelcap, 14/20-fret ebony fingerboard, solid Madagascar rosewood headstock overlay with large old style logo, three-per-side Waverly nickel tuners with butterbean knobs, ebony belly bridge, fossilized ivory bridge pins with black dots, Natural polished gloss finish with Aging Toner top, label signed by Laurence Juber, 25.4 in. scale, case included, mfg. summer 2006-mid-2011.

	$4,500	$2,600 - 3,050	$1,750 - 2,050	$5,799

OMC JACQUES STOTZEM – single cutaway 000-style body, solid Sitka spruce top, solid East Indian rosewood back and sides, old Style 18 rosette, tortoise color binding, multiple B/W boltaron top inlay, B/W boltaron back and side inlays, Style 35 back stripe, mahogany neck, 14/20-fret ebony fingerboard with no inlays, rosewood headstock overlay, three-per-side Gotoh nickel open geared tuners with butterbean knobs, ebony bridge, tortoise pickguard, Fishman Ellipse Matrix Blend electronics, label signed by Chris Martin IV and Jacques Stotzem and numbered in sequence, available in Natural Gloss finish, 25.4 in. scale, mfg. 2007-mid 2009.

	N/A	$1,600 - 2,000	$950 - 1,200	$3,499

OMC-LJ PRO LAURENCE JUBER – single cutaway Grand Auditorium 000 14-fret-style body, solid Adirondack spruce top, solid Pacific big leaf flamed maple back and sides, standard X scalloped forward shifted solid Adriondack spruce bracing, round soundhole with three-ring Style 28 rosette (5/9/5 grouping), grained ivoroid binding, fine herringbone top inlay, B/W fiber back inlay, HD zig-zag back purfling, Eastern hard maple modified V-shaped neck, 14/20-fret ebony fingerboard with no inlays, square tapered headstock with ebony overlay and standard gold foil logo, three-per-side Waverly nickel open-geared tuners with butterbean knobs, ebony belly bridge with compensated bone saddle, ebony bridge pins, no pickguard, D-TAR Wave-Length electronics, label signed by Laurence Juber and numbered in sequence, available in Natural polished gloss with Aging Toner top finish, 25.4 in. scale, Geib-style case included, mfg. 2010-mid-2013.

	$4,400	$2,475 - 2,900	$1,650 - 1,925	$5,499

MSR/NOTES	100%	EXCELLENT	AVERAGE	LAST MSR

OMM JOHN RENBOURN – Grand Auditorium 14-fret 000-style body, solid Italian Alpine spruce top, solid Madagascar rosewood back and sides, standard X scalloped bracing, round soundhole with three-ring Style 28 rosette (5/9/5 grouping), grained ivoroid binding, fine herringbone top inlay, B/W Boltaron back inlay, fine herringbone back purfling, mahogany low profile neck, 14/20-fret ebony fingerboard with Pentangle MOP inlays, slotted headstock with ebony overlay with abalone unicorn inlays, three-per-side nickel tuners with ivoroid buttons, ebony pyramid bridge, solid black ebony bridge pins, no pickguard, label signed by John Renbourn and numbered in sequence, Natural polished gloss finish with aging toner top, 25.4 in. scale, Geib-style case included, mfg. summer 2011-mid-2013.

	$4,400	$2,500 - 3,000	$1,600 - 1,900	$5,499

ACOUSTIC BASS/ACOUSTIC ELECTRIC BASS

00C-16GTAE BASS (16 SERIES) – single cutaway grand concert 00-style body, solid Sitka spruce top, solid mahogany back and sides, round soundhole with bold herringbone rosette, black boltaron body binding, select hardwood neck, 17/23-fret East Indian rosewood fingerboard with no inlays, East Indian rosewood headstock overlay with raised gold foil logo, two-per-side Gotoh Cosmo black bass tuners, East Indian rosewood bridge, tortoise color pickguard, Fishman Prefix Pro Bass System electronics, Natural polished gloss top and satin back and sides, 34.15 in. scale, mfg. 2006-mid-2011.

	$1,600	$1,000 - 1,150	$650 - 775	$2,199

ALTERNATIVE X BASS (SPECIAL EDITION SERIES) – single cutaway Grand Concert 14-fret 00 thin-style body, solid graffiti pattern aluminum top, Jett Black High Pressue Laminate (HPL) back and sides, X-bass bracing, round soundhole, black Stratabond neck, 17/23-fret ebony fingerboard with no inlays, solid graffiti pattern aluminum headstock overlay with metallic black foil logo, two-per-side black Gotoh tuners with large knobs, ebony belly bridge, black bridge pins with white dots, Fishman Prefix Pro Bass electronics, 34.15 in. scale, case included, mfg. 2004-05.

	N/A	$750 - 900	$525 - 600	$1,549

BM (ROAD SERIES) – solid spruce top, round soundhole, black body binding, laminated mahogany back/sides, mahogany neck, 14/20 rosewood fingerboard with white dot inlay, single band herringbone rosette, tortoiseshell pickguard, two-per-side chrome tuners, available in Natural Satin finish, mfg. 1998-2001.

	N/A	$600 - 700	$400 - 475	$1,299

B-1 (1 SERIES) – solid spruce top, solid two-piece mahogany back with Style 18 plain black fiber purfling, laminated mahogany sides, round soundhole with Style 28 black and white rosette, tortoise color body binding, mahogany neck, 17/23-fret rosewood fingerboard with no inlays, solid rosewood headstock overlay with two-per-side chrome tuners, rosewood bridge, tortoiseshell pickguard, available in Natural Satin finish, 34 in. scale, mfg. 1997-2006.

	N/A	$850 - 1,000	$600 - 700	$1,749

* **B-1E Electric (1 Series)** – similar to the B-1 (1 Series), except has Fishman Prefix Plus Bass System electronics, mfg. summer 2002-06.

	N/A	$950 - 1,100	$625 - 750	$2,049

BC-15E CUTAWAY ELECTRIC BASS (15 SERIES) – single cutaway bass body style, solid mahogany or solid sapele (2003-present) top, back, and sides, round soundhole with gold and black Herringbone rosette, select hardwood neck, 17/23-fret rosewood fingerboard with no inlays, solid rosewood headstock overlay with raised gold foil logo, two-per-side Gotoh chrome tuners, rosewood bridge, tortoise color pickguard, Fishman Gold Plus electronics (early models) or Fishman Prefix Pro electronics (later models) available in Natural Satin finish, 34.15 in. scale, mfg. summer 1999-2009.

	N/A	$950 - 1,200	$575 - 725	$2,099

BC-16GTE CUTAWAY ELECTRIC BASS (16 SERIES) – single cutaway bass body style, solid Sitka top, solid mahogany back and sides, bass A-frame X bracing, round soundhole with bold Herringbone rosette, black Boltaron binding, select hardwood neck, 17/23-fret rosewood fingerboard with no inlays, solid East Indian rosewood headstock overlay with raised gold foil logo, two-per-side Gotoh Cosmo black chrome tuners, rosewood bridge, white bridge pins with black dots, tortoise color pickguard, Fishman Prefix Plus T Bass system electronics, Natural polished gloss top with Natural Satin back and sides finish, 34.15 in. scale, case included, mfg. summer 2008-2012.

	$1,950	$1,125 - 1,400	$675 - 850	$2,599

BCPA4 PERFORMING ARTIST BASS – single cutaway jumbo bass-style body, solid Sitka spruce top, solid sapele back and sides, bass A-frame X solid Sitka spruce bracing, round soundhole with two-ring rosette, black boltaron binding, select hardwood special bass profile neck, 17/23-fret ebony fingerboard with no inlays, square headstock with East Indian rosewood overlay and gold foil CMF Martin horizontal script logo, two-per-side Gotoh bass chrome tuners, ebony Performing Artist belly bridge, Delmar tortoise pickguard, white bridge pins with black dots, Fishman F1 Analog electronics with two low-profile knobs and LED display, available in Natural polished gloss finish, 34 in. scale, hardshell case included, mfg. 2013-present.

MSR $1,999	$1,500	$850 - 1,050	$525 - 650	

B-40 – jumbo style, solid spruce top, round soundhole, black pickguard, five-stripe bound body/rosette, rosewood back/sides, mahogany neck, 17/23-fret ebony fingerboard, ebony bridge with white black dot pins, rosewood peghead veneer, two-per-side chrome tuners, available in Natural finish, mfg. 1988-1996.

	N/A	$1,200 - 1,500	$850 - 1,000	$2,900

* **BC-40** – similar to B-40, except has single round cutaway, oval soundhole, mfg. 1990-96.

	N/A	$1,300 - 1,650	$950 - 1,100	$3,120

MSR/NOTES	100%	EXCELLENT	AVERAGE	LAST MSR

* **B-540** – similar to B-40, except has five strings, striped ebony fingerboard/bridge, 5/2-per-side tuners, mfg. 1992-95.

	N/A	$1,300 - 1,650	$950 - 1,100	$2,790

B-65 – similar to B-40, except has tortoiseshell pickguard, figured maple back/sides, mfg. 1987-1995.

	N/A	$1,300 - 1,650	$950 - 1,100	$2,610

STING SWB BASS (SPECIAL EDITION SERIES) – Grand Concert-style bass body, solid Sitka spruce top, certified cherry back and sides, round soundhole with single ring black and white rosette, certified cherry neck, 17/23-fret Katalox fingerboard with Sting's signature on the 20th fret, certified cherry headstock overlay with two-per-side gold tuners, Katalox bridge, tortoiseshell pickguard, Martin/Fishman Gold+Plus electronics, Natural polished gloss finish with Vintage Toner top, 34 in. scale, mfg. 1999-2000.

	N/A	$1,400 - 1,750	$1,000 - 1,150	$2,950

MARVEL

Instruments previously built in Japan circa 1950s to mid-1960s. Also see Premier.

The Peter Sorkin Music Company of New York, NY was an importer/distributor of Premier guitars and amplifiers. Many Premier guitars were built in New York using Italian or other foreign parts, and sometimes the instruments would be rebranded, including Marvel, Royce, Bell-Tone, or Strad-O-Lin. Marvel guitars have been identified as the budget line distributed by Sorkin. Marvel guitars may be completely imported or have parts that are imported, which would make the guitar partially U.S. built. Source: Michael Wright, *Guitar Stories*, Volume One.

ACOUSTIC

MISC. ACOUSTIC ARCHTOPS – various configurations, trapeze tailpieces, raised pickguards, mfg. late 1950s-early 1960s.

	N/A	$275 - 350	$150 - 200	

MARWIN

Unknown production location and date. See Chapter on House Brands.

Marwin was a House Brand, but who they represented has yet to be identified. Most examples seem to be built by Harmony during the late 1930s and early 1940s, and some were built by Kay possibly in the early 1950s. Any further information on Marwin can be submitted directly to Blue Book Publications. Source: Walter Murray, Frankenstein Fretworks.

MASTER

Instruments currently built in Los Angeles, CA.

Luthier George Gorodnitski has been building fine handcrafted acoustic and semi-hollowbody electric guitars for over thirty years. Acoustic guitars start at $4,000 and archtops start at $5,000. For further information, please contact luthier Gorodnitski directly.

CONTACT INFORMATION
MASTER
7336 Santa Monica Blvd.
W. Hollywood, CA 90046
www.master-guitars.com
info@master-guitars.com

MASTERBILT

See Epiphone or Mac Yasuda Guitars.

The Masterbilt trademark has been used by Mac Yasuda Guitars, and most recently by Epiphone on high-end acoustic line.

MASTERTONE

Instruments previously produced in Kalamazoo, MI by Gibson between the 1920s and 1940s. See chapter on House Brands.

While the Mastertone designation was applied to high end Gibson banjos in the 1920s, the Mastertone trademark was used on a Gibson-produced budget line of electric guitars beginning in 1941. Some acoustic "Hawaiian" guitars from the 1930s by Gibson also carried the Mastertone label. While built to the same standards as other Gibson guitars, they lack the one "true" Gibson touch: an adjustable truss rod. House Brand Gibsons were available to musical instrument distributors in the late 1930s and early 1940s. Source: Walter Carter, *Gibson Guitars: 100 Years of an American Icon*.

MATES, TOM

Instruments currently built in England.

Luthier Tom Mates produces handcrafted acoustic guitars. One notable player using a rather ornately inlaid version is Dave Pegg of Jethro Tull. Source: Tony Bacon, *The Ultimate Guitar Book*.

MATON

Instruments currently produced in Australia since 1946.

CONTACT INFORMATION
MATON
6 Clarice Road Box Hill
Victoria, 3128 Australia
Phone No.: 61 3 9896 9500
Fax No.: 61 3 9896 9501
www.maton.com.au
sales@maton.com.au

Maton is Australia's longest established guitar manufacturer, and the Maton trademark was established in 1946 by British emigre Bill May, a former woodworking teacher. His trademark name was a combination of his last name and tone, which is what every luthier seeks.

In the 1940s, it was a commonly held belief among Australian guitarists and musical instrument retailers that American guitars were the best in the world. But that didn't stop Bill May from questioning why Australians shouldn't build their own guitars. As May related in a 1985 interview, "I wanted to make better guitars, beyond what people thought you had the ability to do. People asked 'How do you think you can do it, you've never been to see how it's done and what do you know about it? And it's Australia. You don't know anything here. If you want good instruments, you have to wait and get them from America.' But I didn't believe that."

May was raised with craftsman skills and a positive attitude, both for his own self esteem and for his country. Bill May originally completed his apprenticeship in cabinet making, and later an honors course in art and graphic design before he spent ten years as a woodwork teacher. When May couldn't find a decent sounding guitar in a reasonable price range, he began building guitars in the garage of his Thornbury home. While there was no wealth of guitar building information back in the 1940s, May learned from the various guitars that passed through his hands. Production tools for the time period were the same sort used by furniture craftsmen, like chisels, planes, or the occasional belt-sander or bench saw. Rather than knock out copies of American models, May produced designs that were distinctive in appearance and sound and featured Australian woods and distinctly Australian names. After the humble beginnings in his garage, a factory was established outside of Melbourne in 1951. Maton guitars began to be offered through local stores; by the mid-1960s Maton instruments had established a solid reputation throughout Australia.

May passed away on his 75th birthday in 1993, but the company continues to produce quality guitars. In 2003, Maton moved to their current premises in Clarice Road in Box Hill. The company currently builds over 8000 instruments a year and includes acoustics and electric guitars, basses and ukuleles. For more information, visit Maton's website. Sources: Company history courtesy John Stephenson, *The Maton Book* (1997) and Mark Mansour (2012). Additional model descriptions courtesy Linda Kitchen (Bill May's daughter) and Haidin Demaj, Maton Guitars.

Maton has been focused on producing quality acoustic guitars for the past several years. Current models feature Canadian Sitka spruce tops, Queensland maple and walnut as well as Tasmanian and Victorian blackwood on the back and sides. Other timbers include Brazilian and Indian rosewood, and rock maple. Most models feature solid wood back and sides. The acoustic/electric models feature an installed AP5 pickup and on-board preamp built by Australian piezo manufacturer GEC-Marconi. Maton's guitars retail starting at $799 and climb up to $4,200.

MATSUOKA, RYOJI

Instruments currently produced in Japan since the mid- to late 1970s. Previously distributed by Tornavoz Music in Santa Monica, CA and Unicord in Westbury, NY.

Japanese luthier Ryoji Matsuoka offered good quality classical guitars during the 1970s. Guitars were offered as part of the M Series with models starting at M-20 and ranging by ten digit increments up to the M-100. The higher the number of the guitar, the higher quality materials were used. In 1976, prices ranged between $270 and $1,050. In the late 2000s, Tornavoz Music began importing another line of Matsuoka guitars including the 706 (MSR $1,399) and the 710 (MSR $2,199).

MATTHEW MUSTAPICK GUITARS

Instruments currently produced in Soquel, CA since 2003.

CONTACT INFORMATION
MATTHEW MUSTAPICK GUITARS
2714 Lafayette Street
Soquel, CA 95073
Phone No.: 831-465-6803
mustapickguitars.com
matt@mustapickguitars.com

Luthier Matthew Mustapick began building guitars in 2003 after leaving his job at an Internet company in the heart of Silicone Valley. Mustapick learned the art of building guitars through talking with other builders, reading books and literature, researching the Internet, and playing guitars to find out as much about them as he could. He offers five main models with the **Aurora**, **Arena OM**, **Classical**, **Concert Nylon Crossover**, and the **Deep Baritone**. Mustapick also offers several options and because each guitar is hand built, each model can be custom ordered. Mustapick uses several features that have become more popular in 21st century playing such as the Kevin Ryan-style body bevel, the Linda Manzer-style wedge body, and multi-scale designs. Prices start at $5,100 for the Aurora and Arena OM, $5,200 for the Deep Baritone, and $5,300 for the Classical and Concert Nylon Crossover. For more information, visit Mustapick's website or contact him directly.

MAUEL GUITARS

Instruments previously produced in Auburn, CA between 1995 and 2011.

Luthier Hank Mauel built high-quality acoustic guitars out of the highest quality traditional tonewoods in a variety of styles. Model styles included the OM, Deep Bodied OM, 0, 00, 000, 12-fret, 12-fret dreadnought, dreadnought, grand auditorium, grand concert, parlor, and small jumbo. Mauel temporarily cut back his production in 2006 and 2007, but returned to full-time building in April 2007 until he ceased instrument production altogether in 2011.

MAURER & CO.

Instruments previously produced by the Larson Brothers between 1900 and the mid-1940s. Also see Larson Brothers.

The Maurer brand was used by Robert Maurer prior to 1900 and by the Larson brothers, Carl and August, starting in 1900. The Larsons produced guitars, ukes, and mandolin family instruments under this brand until the mid-1930s when they, and the rest of the industry, changed designs from the small body guitars with slot pegheads and twelve-frets-to-the-body necks to larger bodies with necks becoming narrower but extending the fingerboard to now have fourteen frets to the body.

The most commonly found Maurer instrument is the flattop guitar having either X-bracing or straight, ladder-type bracing. Some of the X-braced instruments have the laminated X-braces which were patented by August in 1904. The Maurers were offered in student grade, intermediate grade and best grade. The Maurer brand was also used on the harp guitar, uke, taro-patch, mandolinetto, mandola, octave mandolin, mando-cello, and mando-bass.

The style of the Maurers was carried through in the instruments sold to Wm. C. Stahl and the Prairie State brand. They ranged from the very plain to the pearl and abalone trimmed with the fanciest having a beautiful tree-of-life fingerboard. The Maurers are high quality instruments and are more commonly found than the other Larson brands. Information courtesey: Robert Carl, *The Larsons' Creations, Guitars and Mandolins*.

MAXINE

Instruments currently produced in China. Distributed by Bejing Eternal Musical Instrument Corp. Ltd.

Maxine is a company that makes an endless number of guitars. Pretty much any color, design, and configuration is available. They are mainly entry level guitars and don't sell for much. It is unknown whether a U.S. distributor has been established yet. For more information visit their website.

CONTACT INFORMATION
MAXINE
Distributed by the Eternal Musical Instrument Corp. Ltd.
www.embmusic.com
xsma@embmusic.com

MAXTONE

Instruments currently produced in Taiwan. Distributed by the Ta Feng Long Enterprises Company, Ltd. in Tai Chung, Taiwan and in Singapore by the Renner Piano Company.

Maxtone instruments are designed with the entry level to student quality guitars. They produce a whole range of guitars and prices are mainly between $100 and $200. For further information, visit Renner Piano Company's website.

CONTACT INFORMATION
MAXTONE
Distributed by the Renner Piano Company
Peace Centre, Singapore
www.renner.com.sg
support@renner.com.sg

MAYA

Instruments previously produced in Japan from the mid-1970s through the mid-1980s.

Maya guitars span the range of entry level to medium quality acoustic, solidbody, semi-hollowbody, and archtops that feature both original designs and other designs based on classic American favorites. The Maya company also produced a secondary trademark called "El Maya" that featured good quality Fender-based designs as well as some originals. Source: Tony Bacon and Paul Day, *The Guru's Guitar Guide*.

MAYFLOWER

Instruments previously built in Chicago, IL between 1918 and 1928.

The Groeschel Company of Chicago, IL first began building bowl-back (or "potato bug") mandolins in 1890. Guitars were also manufactured under the Flower & Grochsl trademark. In 1918 Groeschel was changed to the Stromberg-Voisenet Company, who produced guitars and banjos under the Mayflower trademark. This Stromberg company is not to be confused with luthier Charles Stromberg (and son Elmer) of Boston, MA. Henry Kay Kuhrmeyer bought the Stromberg-Voisenet company in 1928, and renamed it Kay Musical Instruments in 1931 (See Kay).

McALISTER GUITARS

Instruments currently produced in Gig Harbor, WA since 2005. Previously produced in Watsonville, CA between 1997 and 2005.

Luthier Roy McAlister produces high quality instruments on a custom-order basis. His guitars start out at a base price of $6,200 and options are added on after that. Models come in a Dreadnought-style, Jumbo, Concert, and Lucas, which is designed to have the presence of a large guitar with the playability of a small one. McAlister also builds a contemporary line of guitars based on his own design and a Vintage Series of pre-war replicas. In 2005, McAlister moved from Watsonville, CA to Gig Harbor, WA. For more information visit McAlister's website or contact him directly.

CONTACT INFORMATION
McALISTER GUITARS
Gig Harbor, WA 98332
Phone No.: 206-322-1601
www.mcalisterguitars.com
info@mcalisterguitars.com

McCOLLUM GUITARS

Instruments previously produced in Colfax, CA between 1994 and early 2009.

Luthier Lance McCollum began building guitars in the 1980s, and started building McCollum guitars full-time in 1994. McCollum was a die-hard fan of the dovetail neck joint and he built guitars with the tonal complexity of a grand piano as each note sounded independently but at the same time, they blended all the way up the fingerboard. McCollum was also known for his selection of beautiful tonewoods and elaborate rosettes. McCollum's clients included Alex de Grassi, Todd Hallawell, Roger Hodgson, Dougie MacLean, and Doug Smith, and it is estimated that McCollum built between 250 and 300 guitars. McCollum passed away on February 1, 2009 of an abdominal aortic aneurysm.

In McCollumn's last price list (2008), all basic guitar styles started at $6,500 with additional options. Models included a baritone, bass, classical, dreadnought, grand-auditorium, Kayleigh Jumbo, Madrone 00, Meghann 000, and Skyforest Parlor. The Kevin Doubleneck started at $9,000, Classical models started at $9,000, and a harp guitar started at $6,500. Options include different woods, headstocks, fingerboards, bridges, inlays, etc.

McCURDY GUITARS

Instruments currently built in New York City, NY.

Luthier Ric McCurdy has been producing custom guitars since 1983. Originally based in Santa Barbara, CA, he moved to New York City in 1991 where he studied archtop guitar building with Bob Benedetto. Since then, he has been concentrating on fine archtop and electric guitars for musicians. McCurdy has built and repaired guitars for several artists including John Abercrombie, Sheryl Bailey, Joe Beck, Paul Bollenbeck, Joe Cocker, Kenny Loggins, Jimmy Vivano, Jack Wilkins, and Jimmy Wyble. For model listings on electric archtops, refer to the *Blue Book of Electric Guitars*. For further information visit McCurdy's website or contact McCurdy directly.

CONTACT INFORMATION
McCURDY GUITARS
19 Hudson Street
New York, NY 10013
Phone No.: 212-274-8352
Fax No.: 212-274-8352
www.mccurdyguitars.com
mccurdygtr@aol.com

McELROY GUITARS

Instruments currently built in Seattle, WA, since 1995.

Brent McElroy has been building guitars since circa 1995. McElroy's guitars are hand built. Guitars are based on traditional designs with McElroy's own twist on things. For more information contact McElroy directly.

CONTACT INFORMATION
McELROY GUITARS
6750 Murray Ave. SW
Seattle, WA 98136
Phone No.: 206-728-9055
www.mcelroyguitars.com
brent@mcelroyguitars.com

Base price for guitars is $6,500. Standard features include a Sitka or Englemann spruce or cedar top, Indian rosewood or Honduras mahogany back/sides/neck, wood binding, hand crafted wood rosette, ebony fingerboard with MOP dot inlays, ebony or Brazilian rosewood headstock overlay with wood binding and Gotoh 510 tuning machines. The **Standard** Model has fourteen frets to the body: 12 in. upper bout, 16 in. lower bout, 20 in. body length, 41 in. overall length, and a 25.4 in. scale length. The **000/OM** Model has fourteen frets to the body: 11.5 in. upper bout, 15.25 in. lower bout, 19 in. body length, 40 in. overall length, and a 24.9 in. (000) or 25.4 in. (OM) scale length. The **00** Model has twelve frets to the body: 9.75 in. upper bout, 14.125 in. lower bout, 19.625 in. body length, 38 in. overall length, and a 24.9 in. scale length. The **Classical** Model has a body design and dimensions that are based on the 1937 Hauser that belonged to Segovia, and the top bracing is based on the de Jonge lattice style. Everything else is based on McElory's intuition. The Mac 1 and the Mac 5, which is based on Martin's smallest guitar -- the Style 5 -- were both discontinued in 2005.

McGILL GUITARS

Instruments currently built in Nashville, TN, since 1976.

CONTACT INFORMATION
McGILL GUITARS
808 Kendall Drive
Nashville, TN 37209
Phone No.: 615-354-0070
www.mcgillguitars.com
conecaster@aol.com

Paul McGill is an American guitar maker and has been making guitars for 36 years dating back to 1976. His early career was mentored by makers such as Charles Fox where he studied for a few months at the Earthworks. After returning to Georgia for a few years, he relocated to Madison, WI where he was influenced by Robert Ruck. McGill spent his years in Wisc. refining his craft and building many types of guitars, Classical, Steel String and a few carved top instruments. In 1982, he made the guitar that was eventually used by Muriel Anderson to win the Winfield competition. He also made guitars for many local artists including Barbara Koimman of Timbuk 3. In 1985, McGill took a position on the staff at Gruhn Guitars in Nashville, TN.

After moving to Nashville, he made guitars and worked for Gruhn as a restorationist and repairman. In 1986, he made a guitar that would be used by Earl Klugh to record his *Solo Guitar* album. McGill left Gruhn's in 1988 and setup shop in the Berry Hill section of Nashville in 1989. By this point Paul was focused on classical guitar making. In 1992, he made a Delvecchio-style guitar at Earl Klugh's request. The next four years were focused on perfecting the Brazilian resonator guitars. This type of guitar was used extensively by Chet Atkins, who was exposed by the Brazilian Legend Nato Lima of Los Indios Tabajaras. Paul made three resonator guitars for Chet - one was a gift from Earl Klugh. The last of these is featured in Chet's final publication *Me and my guitars*. Paul Also made resonators for Nato, Jim Stafford, Don Potter, John Standerfer, and Steve Earl.

In 1996, McGill moved to his current location in West Nashville. He also envisioned his Nylon String electric model the Super Acoustic Classical Electric, or Super ACE. The first of these models were made in June, 1998. Peter White acquired one of these guitars in 1999 and it has been his main instrument on stage since, Marc Antoine also acquired one that year.

In 2007, Paul was commisioned by the legendary Jimmy Wyble to make a Super ACE for him. After a long absence, Jimmy returned to the Musician's Institute where he was a founding instructor and became exposed to the Super Ace through instructor David Oakes. Jimmy bought a Super Ace with the intention of leaving it with Larry Koonse and Jimmy passed in 2010. Paul delivered the guitar in 2008 and since 2009, Larry Koonse has worked with the instrument, including The Autumn recording with Billy Childs. Paul is known for classical, nylon string electric, and resophonic guitars. His latest model is a Steel string model in the style of the ACE the Super Steel. For more information and a custom quotation, please contact McGill directly.

McKNIGHT GUITARS

Instruments currently produced in Morral, OH since 1992.

CONTACT INFORMATION
McKNIGHT GUITARS
PO Box 6
Morral, OH 43337
Phone No.: 740-465-2371
mcknightguitars.com
tim@mcknightguitars.com

Luthier Tim McKnight and his wife Mary, build acoustic guitars in their Morral, OH shop. McKnight was originally a mechanical engineer and he would repair guitars at night. In the mid-1980s, Mary bought him a guitar kit so he could assemble his own instrument. Although it took around eight years to complete the guitar, it inspired McKnight to begin building guitars full-time in 1992. Guitars are constructed by Tim, and Mary handles the binding, rosettes, inlays, and other exterior aspects. McKnight offers seven body styles including the Jumbo Mac, MacNaught, Highlander OM-D, Skeeter, Mini Mac, Slope MacNaught, and the Deacon. Several woods come standard, but there is a full list of options available. Guitars start at $5,500. For more information, visit McKnight's website or contact them directly.

McPHERSON GUITARS

Instruments currently built in Sparta, WI since 2001.

CONTACT INFORMATION
McPHERSON GUITARS
1204 Roberts Road, PO Box 260
Sparta, WI 54656
Phone No.: 608-366-1407
www.mcphersonguitars.com
info@mcphersonguitars.com

The original three soundhole McPherson guitar was initially designed and developed in the early 1980s. After years of exhaustive testing and R&D McPherson Guitars (luthier Matt McPherson) was incorporated in December, 2001 and released their perfected hand-built design. The McPherson guitar combines exquisite master craftsmanship with cutting edge guitar design which features their Offset Soundhole Technology, state-of-the art bracing, and their unique "no touch" Cantilevered Neck Design. Collectively, these technologies allow the top of the instrument to vibrate and resound to its fullest potential. For more information on McPherson Guitars or to hear the sound of their guitars go to McPherson's website and download a free copy of Sunset Drive or contact McPherson Guitars directly.

Standard models start at $6,400, and include redwood, cedar, or spruce tops and options for East Indian rosewood, Granadillo or African mahogany back and sides. But with stunning top upgrades such as Port Orford cedar, Adirondack red spruce and flamed redwood - or custom back and sides options including flamed walnut, quilted maple, wavy mahogany, striped Macassar ebony, koa, Madagascar rosewood and more. The luthiers at McPherson stand ready to create the custom guitar of your dreams. All guitars come complete with three custom bone saddles, Buzz Feiten Tuning System, a factory installed L.R. Baggs pickup system as well as a custom hard shell case which includes built-in humidity control. For more information or to hear the stunning sound of McPherson Guitars visit their website and download a copy of their free sampler "Sunset Drive," or contact McPherson Guitars directly.

MEGAS GUITARS

Instruments currently built in San Francisco, CA since 1989.

CONTACT INFORMATION
MEGAS GUITARS
Phone No.: 503-289-8788
Fax No.: 503-289-8789
www.megasguitars.com
ted@megasguitars.com

Luthier Ted Megas has been building guitars since 1975, and in 1989 began building archtop guitars, which represented the best combination of his musical interests and his knowledge and skills as a woodworker. Megas builds about seven of his quality instruments each year. For more information, please contact luthier Megas directly.

Megas currently builds three archtop models. All his guitars have hand carved Spruce tops, hand carved, highly figured maple backs with matching sides, solid ebony fingerboard, bridge, pickguard, and peg overlay, figured hard maple neck and adjustable truss rod, high gloss Nitro-cellulose lacquer finish, and come with a five-ply hardshell case. All models are made in 16 in., 17 in., and 18 in. bodies.

The **Athena** is classically styled with multi-lined plastic bindings throughout; split block MOP inlays on fingerboard; abalone dot side position markers; X-bracing; MOP nut; precision machined brass tailpiece construction with ebony overlay; and Schaller tuning machines with ebony buttons. List prices range from the 16 in. body width ($8,200), 17 in. width ($8,600), and the 18 in. width ($9,300).

The **Apollo** features wood bindings, abalone, dot side position makers, X-bracing; cello style f-holes, MOP nut, precision machined brass tailpiece construction with ebony overlay, and Schaller tuning machines with ebony buttons. List prices range from the 16 in. body width ($7,200), 17 in. width ($7,575), and the 18 in. width ($8,200).

The **Spartan** has a single bound body, neck, and peg head, parallel bracing, bone nut, ebony tailpiece with brass anchor, and gold Gotoh tuning machines. List prices range from the 16 in. body width ($6,075), 17 in. width ($6,425), and the 18 in. width ($6,900).

* **Add $300 for built-in or floating Kent Armstrong pickup.**

MELLO, JOHN F.

Instruments currently built in Kensington, CA, since 1973.

Since 1973, John Mello has been building classical and small-bodied steel-string guitars, with an emphasis on clarity, projection, and providing the player with a wide dynamic range and broad palette of colors to interpret his/her music. His building is informed by extensive experience in restoring master instruments by both historic and contemporary makers, and his guitars have been exhibited at the Renwick Gallery of the Smithsonian Institution, played on recordings by Douglas Woodful Harris and Alex de Grassi, and gained him mention as one of America's seventeen best classical guitar makers by *Musician Magazine*. Handmade Mello guitars retail between $8,500 and $10,000. For more information, contact John directly or visit his website.

CONTACT INFORMATION
MELLO, JOHN F.
437 Colusa Ave.
Kensington, CA 94707
Phone No.: 510-528-1080
Fax No.: 510-528-1080
www.johnfmello.com
jfm@lmi.net

MELO GUITARS

Instruments currently built in Sabadell, Catalonia, Spain.

Josep Melo has a family backround that allows him to combine intellectual work with craftsmanship. He has studied with James L. D'Aquisto, José L. Romanillos and Steve Klein, as well as a number of other luthiers from around the world. Melo produces acoustic, classical, acoustic archtops, and electric archtops with all different types of designs and patterns. Retail prices start around 2,000 euros. For more information contact Melo Guitars directly.

CONTACT INFORMATION
MELO GUITARS
Sabadell, Spain
www.meloguitars.com
josepmelo@meloguitars.com

MELOPHONIC

Instruments previously built by Valco in Chicago, IL, circa mid-1960s.

Melphonic resonator guitars were built by Valco (see Valco or Dobro). Source: Michael Wright, *Vintage Guitar Magazine*.

MENKEVICH GUITARS

Instruments currently built in Philadelphia, PA, since 1970.

Luthier Michael Menkevich has been handcrafting quality guitars for a number of years. He builds classical guitars from original designs to reproductions of popular models. For more information concerning model specifications and pricing, please contact luthier Menkevich directly.

CONTACT INFORMATION
MENKEVICH GUITARS
624 Stetson Road
Elkins Park, PA 19027
Phone No.: 215-635-0694
Fax No.: 215-635-0694
menkguitar@yahoo.com

MERRILL

Instruments previously produced in New York, NY circa late 1880s.

Company president Neil Merrill began experimenting with aluminum in the mid-1880s. He debuted his aluminum-bodied guitars in 1894 and offered a wide range of stringed instruments based on this design. Source: Tom Wheeler, *American Guitars*.

MERMER GUITARS

Instruments currently built in Sebastian, FL, since 1983.

Luthier Richard Mermer, Jr. is producing concert quality, handcrafted instruments designed and built for the individual. Steel string, nylon string, electric-acoustic instruments, and acoustic Hawaiian steel guitars are offered. All Mermer guitars feature solid wood construction, choice of select tone woods, decorative wood binding, custom wood and stone inlay, custom scale lengths, fully compensated saddles and precision intonation, adjustable truss rod, choice of hardware and accessories, and optional pickup and microphone installation. Mermer produces about twelve instruments a year. For a list of options and additional information refer to their website.

CONTACT INFORMATION
MERMER GUITARS
PO Box 782132
Sebastian, FL 32978
Phone No.: 772-388-0317
www.mermerguitars.com
rmermer@mermerguitars.com

MESROBIAN

Instruments currently built in Salem, MA, since 1995.

Luthier Carl Mesrobian began woodworking at the age of seven, and received his first guitar at the age of fourteen. Like many luthiers, Carl worked on making furniture cabinets after completing a program in this industry in Boston. After this he began repairing guitars, and eventually made two of his own. Carl then attended Dick Boak's guitar making class in New Jersey, and has been producing guitars ever since. All standard production models come equipped with pickup and hardshell case - refer to the *Blue Book of Electric Guitars* for model listings. For further information visit Mesrobian's website or contact him directly.

CONTACT INFORMATION
MESROBIAN
23 Woodside Street
Salem, MA 01970
Phone No.: 978-740-6986
www.cmesrobian.com
cmesrobian@verizon.net

MICHAEL DOLAN CUSTOM GUITARS

Instruments currently built in Upper Lake, Lake County, CA. Dolan has been in business since 1977.

Luthier Michael Dolan has been handcrafting quality guitars for over thirty-five years. After Dolan graduated from Sonoma State University with a Bachelor of Arts degree in Fine Arts, he went to work for a prestigious bass and guitar manufacturer.

Dolan's full service shop offers custom built guitars and basses (solid body, arch-top, acoustic, neck-through, bolt-on, set-neck, and headless), custom ukuleles, as well as repairs. He works in domestic and exotic woods, and uses hardware and electronics from all well-known manufacturers. Finishes include a standard acrylic top coat/polyester base, nitrocellulose, and hand rubbed oil.

As luthier Dolan likes to point out, a "Custom Guitar is a unique expression of the vision of a particular individual. Because there are so many options and variables, offering a price list has proven to be impractical." However, Dolan's prices generally run between $2,000 and $4,000. Prices are determined by the nature of the project, and the costs of components and building materials.

Working with their custom guitar order form, Michael Dolan can provide a firm up-front price quote. All custom guitars are guaranteed for tone, playability, and overall quality. For more information contact Michael Dolan directly.

CONTACT INFORMATION
MICHAEL DOLAN CUSTOM GUITARS
9820 Middle Creek Rd.
Upper Lake, CA 95485
Phone No.: 707-275-8821
www.dolanguitars.com
mndolan@sbcglobal.net

MICHAEL DUNN CUSTOM GUITARS

Instruments currently built in Vancouver (British Columbia), Canada.

Michael Dunn apprenticed for three years under maestros Jose Orti and Jose Ferrer at George Bowden's workshop in Palma De Mallorca, Spain during the mid-1960s. As a guitarist, Dunn was fascinated by Django Reinhardt's acoustic style of jazz. Dunn's interest in the Maccaferri guitar design, along with his background of the Spanish guitar-building tradition, is the basis for his modern interpretation of Maccaferri-styled models. Dunn also offers two classical style models, a flamenco style acoustic, and a Weissenborn-style acoustic Hawaiian guitar. Dunn builds about twenty guitars a year. For more information, visit Dunn's directly or contact him directly.

CONTACT INFORMATION
MICHAEL DUNN CUSTOM GUITARS
2457 Dundas St.
Vancouver, BC V5K 1P5 Canada
Phone No.: 604-524-1943
www.michaeldunnguitars.com
guitarbuilder@shaw.ca

Dunn uses spruce or cedar for the tuned soundboard, and an ebony fingerboard on top of a Honduran mahogany neck. Models have a brass tailpiece, and are finished with a French polish process. A slotted peghead is optional. The **Mystery Pacific** model was developed from the original design patented by Mario Maccaferri in 1930. The Mystery Pacific is fitted with an internal soundbox and reflector, and possesses the D-shaped soundhole, cedar soundboard, and rosewood back and sides. The **Stardust** has an oval soundhole, and features paduak or a similar medium density tropical hardwood for the back and sides. The scale length of the **Belleville** is 670 mm, as compared to the Stardust's 640 mm scale. Construction of the longer-scaled Belleville is similar to the Stardust model. The **Daphne** has no internal soundbox or reflector. The **Patenotte** is a gypsy guitar based on the Patenotte guitar from France.

In addition to the Maccaferri-derived models, Dunn also builds a 660 mm scale Classical guitar, a 1939 Hauser-type Classical (650 mm scale length) guitar, a Flamenco model, and a Weissenborn-style acoustic Hawaiian guitar model. Guitars start at $3,800 and guitars with an internal sound box start at $4,500.

MICHAEL KELLY

Instruments currently produced overseas. Distributed by Hanser Music Group (previously HHI) in Hebron, KY. Michael Kelly has been producing guitars since 1999.

Michael Kelly produces a variety of guitars that have unique characteristics but are affordable. They became bored with the same-old designs that were on the market and decided to produce guitars with a little flare. They started by producing acoustic guitars, acoustic basses, mandolins, and archtops. The guitars feature nice woods and ornate inlays. In the 2000s, they introduced electric archtop jazz guitars and solidbody electric models. For more information contact Michael Kelly directly.

CONTACT INFORMATION
MICHAEL KELLY
www.michaelkellyguitars.com
info@michaelkellyguitars.com

U.S. Distributor: Hanser Music Group
3015 Kustom Drive
Hebron, KY 41048
Phone No.: 859-817-7100
Phone No.: 877-363-6444
Fax No.: 859-817-7150
www.hansermusicgroup.com
info@hansermusicgroup.com

MICHELETTI GUITARS

Instruments currently produced in Willits, CA since 1980.

Luthier Rick Micheletti has been producing acoustic guitars in Northern California since 1980. He taught himself how to build first, but was dissatisfied with the results. He attended the Vermont Intrument Workshop under the instructor, George Morris. He has been building guitars ever since. Rick's goal is to make guitars that inspire musicians. He also encourages customers to be involved in the design of the guitar. He builds some general models and offers options. The base price for guitars is $3,900. For further information, visit Micheletti's website or contact him directly.

CONTACT INFORMATION
MICHELETTI GUITARS
19590 Shafer Ranch Road
Willits, CA 95490
Phone No.: 707-459-0820
www.michelettiguitars.com
rick@michelettiguitars.com

MIRABELLA GUITARS

Guitars currently produced in Babylon, NY since 1997.

Considered one of the premier builders of today's archtop guitar, luthier Cristian Mirabella has incorporated the skills learned and refined over the past thirty-three years into the construction and development of his work today. True to the fundamentals of tradition, but pushing the possibilities of innovative design, Mirabella's instruments offer a blend of visual art and acoustic science. This has set Mirabella apart, drawing great acknowledgment for his elegant designs, refined harmonics, balanced and full tone, as well as the flawless playability of his instruments. For more information, visit Mirabella's website or contact him directly.

CONTACT INFORMATION
MIRABELLA GUITARS
PO Box 482
Babylon, NY 11702
Phone No.: 631-842-3819
www.mirabellaguitars.com
mirguitars@aol.com

MIRAGE

Instruments previously produced in Taiwan during the late 1980s.

Entry level to intermediate quality guitars based on classic American designs. Source: Tony Bacon and Paul Day, *The Guru's Guitar Guide*.

MIRAGE GUITAR WORKS, LLC

Instruments previously produced in Manchester, MD and Korea between the 1980s and 2007. Previously built in Etters, PA from 1978-early 1980s.

Luthier Paul Gobat is the founder of Mirage Guitar Works (MGW). MGW opened in 1978, and the first guitars were primarily built from acrylic sheet or cast polyester. In 1985, Gobat started building guitars out of wood but continues to produce guitars mainly out of alternative materials. Guitars are built in very limited productions and many are built as full custom instruments. In 1998, MGW started an import series from Korea. These guitars are solidbodies with high-quality appointments. Only 50 guitars were built at a time, and a total of 500 built in a series. Gobat worked to introduce one new model a year and discontinue one after five hundred are built. In 2004, a series of acoustic guitars was introduced as a limited production of around fifty guitars a year. By 2006, acoustic instruments were standard production. In February 2007, a catastrophic fire destroyed Mirage's production facilities including the tooling, templates, drawings, and special tools.

The **B Series** consists of dreadnought guitars that feature a AAAA Himalayan spruce top and figured solid mahogany back and sides. It was available as a six-string (last MSR was $1,511) and a twelve-string (last MSR was $1,547). A cutaway is available for an additional $89 and electronics for $100.

The **C Series** are folk-style guitars that have a AAA Himalayan spruce top, laminated curly maple back and sides, and abalone and ABS binding and rosette. These guitars were available as a six-string (last MSR was $954) or a twelve-string (last MSR was $1,102). A cutaway is available for an additional $100 and electronics for $100.

The **F Series** are also folk-style guitars with a AAA Himalayan spruce top, laminated Indian rosewood back and sides, and wood binding and rosette. These guitars were available as a cutaway six-string (last MSR was $955) or a cutaway twelve-string (last MSR was $1,006). Add electronics for $100.

The **E and G Series** feature more common woods in place of the more expensive/rare woods. Gobat calls them his "Save the Trees" guitars. The E6 (last MSR was $569) features a solid sycamore top with laminated sapele back and sides. The G6 (last MSR was $589) features a solid cedar top with laminated sycamore back and sides and Sonokeling fingerboard and bridge.

MIRANDA GUITARS

Guitars currently produced in the San Francisco Bay Area, CA.

Miranda Guitars was founded by Phil Green with the vision of developing a full-sized guitar that had the portability of a violin, but still had the full-bodied sound of an acoustic. Miranda's travel guitars feature a center mahogany body/neck with detachable acrylic sides, an aluminum side support arm, and a piezo pickup. Models are available as a nylon-string CFX-200 and steel-string S-250. Both guitars sell for $1,395 and Miranda only sells factory direct. For more information, visit Miranda's website or contact them directly.

CONTACT INFORMATION
MIRANDA GUITARS
PO Box 175
Los Altos, CA 94023-0175
Phone No.: 650-948-9454
Fax No.: 650-917-1176
www.mirandaguitars.com
sales@miranda-tech.com

MITCHELL, BIL GUITARS

Instruments currently built in Bucks County, PA, since 1979. Previously located in Wall, NJ, Mitchell relocated and expanded his shop to Riegelsville, PA in 2003.

Bil Mitchell has been designing and crafting high-end acoustic and electric guitars since 1979. Bil's longevity as a full-time luthier has firmly established him as a consummate craftsman focusing primarily on flat top acoustic guitars. He and his partner Sarah Dieterichs operate the Guitar Parlor, offering custom guitars, extensive repairs, and a retail showroom.

Bil Mitchell has no affiliation with the import line of "Mitchell" guitars. His early logo is displayed as Mitchell on the headstock, but every acoustic guitar built since 1995 displays an "M" logo and sound hole label marked "Bil Mitchell". A

CONTACT INFORMATION
MITCHELL, BIL GUITARS
705 Durham Road, PO Box 284
Riegelsville, PA 18077
Phone No.: 610-749-2520
www.guitarparlor.net

number of acoustic basses, archtop, solid bodies, and hybrid guitars were also manufactured. Call Bil Mitchell directly to identify. For more information, contact Bil Mitchell directly.

Bil Mitchell currently crafts two lines of acoustic guitars. The Homegrown line is a 100% handmade solid wood guitar, made without the use of any prefabricated or outsourced parts. A limited number of options keep the Homegrown an affordable, custom quality guitar. Currently available on the OM and 00-concert body style, appointments include: cherry, mahogany or black walnut tonewoods, sitka or engleman soundboard, 14-fret, 25.5 in. scale on OM and 12-fret, 24.5 in. scale on 00-concert, cherry neck, rosewood fingerboard with Persian eye position markers, rosewood bridge, 1.75 in. nut width, maple binding, three ring rosette, high gloss nitro lacquer and three-per side Grover mini tuners. List price of $2,100 for cherry and $2,500 for walnut and mahogany. Add $300 for a cutaway. Hard shell case included.

The Bil Mitchell line is Bil's truly custom heirloom line of guitars. Available in Parlor, 00-concert, 00 De Luxe, OM, Dreadnought and Jumbo body styles. Base model standard appointments include: choice of black walnut or mahogany tone wood with sitka or engleman soundboard, ebony head stock overlay, fingerboard and bridge, mahogany soft V hand profiled neck, diamond inlay pattern, profusely flamed maple head stock, fingerboard, body, and bridge binding, head stock underlay and heel capping, carbon fiber and spruce laminated X brace, high gloss nitro lacquer finish and Waverly or Schaller tuners. Three ply archtop hard shell case included. Base price for above appointments is $4,500 for 00 Deluxe, OM, Jumbo and Dread models and $5,000 for the Parlor and 00-concert because of slotted headstock.

Being truly custom models, a wide range of woods, custom neck widths, and appointments are available. Mitchell specializes in custom inlay design and extensive hand cut inlay patterns on his Bil Mitchell guitars.

M&M MERCHANDISERS, INC.

Instruments currently distributed in Fort Worth, TX. M&M Merchandisers have been distributing instruments since 1976.

Since 1976 M&M Merchandisers has been a national wholesaler of musical instruments and consumer electronics. Tiring of quality issues usually associated with the entry level guitars offered to them at the time, M&M decided to make a change to better serve their dealer base. In July of 2001 M&M introduced their Kona, Trinity River & Z.Z. Ryder brands of import acoustic and electric guitars to have better control over the quality and features offered. These guitars are aimed at the entry market with retails ranging from $179 to $399 with one goal in mind reflecting the company's mantra "Exceeding Your Expectations." They are also distributors for many guitar, amplifier, mandolin, ukulele, drum, and accessory trademarks. Non-guitar-related products include DJ products, sheet music, cables, home speakers, etc. For more information, visit M&M's website, or contact them directly.

CONTACT INFORMATION
M&M MERCHANDISERS, INC.
1923 Bomar Ave.
Fort Worth, TX 76103-2102
Phone No.: 817-339-1400
Fax No.: 800-299-9035
www.mmwholesale.com
sales@mmwholesale.com

MOLL CUSTOM INSTRUMENTS

Instruments currently built in Springfield, MO, since 1996.

Luthier Bill Moll builds premium custom crafted acoustic flattops and and acoustic and electric archtop guitars. Moll instruments are designed and built to perform acoustically before any electronics are considered. Much of Moll's training comes from his years in the violin business, and several construction aspects of his guitars reflect this. Moll's wife Denise has been studying lutherie since 1997 and continues to help in the shop. For more information, visit Moll's website or contact him directly.

CONTACT INFORMATION
MOLL CUSTOM INSTRUMENTS
2304 E. Cardinal
Springfield, MO 65804
Phone No.: 877-838-7348
www.mollinst.com
billmoll@sbcglobal.net

Moll offers three body styles in the SJ, OM, and 000 and in two trim levels. The LI trim level starts at $4,000 and the LX trim level starts at $6,000.

MONTALVO

See Casa Montalvo.

MONTANA

Instruments previously produced in Korea during the early 1990s. Distributed by the Kaman Music Corporation in Bloomfield, CT.

Kaman Music imported the Montana line of acoustic and acoustic/electric guitars priced for novice and intermediate players.

MONTCLAIR

Unknown production location and date. See chapter on House brands.

This trademark has been identified as a House Brand of Montgomery Wards. Source: Willie G. Moseley, *Stellas & Stratocasters*.

MONTELEONE, JOHN

Instruments currently built in Islip, NY, since 1976.

CONTACT INFORMATION
MONTELEONE, JOHN
PO Box 52
Islip, NY 11751
Phone No.: 631-277-3620
www.monteleone.net
john@monteleone.net

Luthier John Monteleone has been building guitars and mandolins since the mid-1970s. A contemporary of James D'Aquisto, Monteleone performed repair and restoration work for a number of years while formulating his own archtop designs. Monteleone's archtop guitars feature such unique ideas as a flush-set truss rod cover, recessed tuning machine retainers, and a convex radius headstock. For further information, please contact luthier John Monteleone directly.

The following numbers are Monteleone base prices bearing in mind that virtually every guitar is customized to a large degree and Monteleone makes only ten or twelve guitars per year. These are pre-Met show prices, and given the response to the show, prices are expected to go up five to ten percent.

The **Grand Artist Scroll** is around $85,000

The **Eclipse** is around $39,000

The **Radio Flyer** is around $59,000

The **Radio City** is around $59,000

The **Quattroport** is around $35,000

The **Tri-Port** in various versions is around $39,000

The **Grand Artist Mandolin** is between $24,000 to $29,000

These are all average prices including a base price and some customer customization. All guitars at this time are built specifically for customers, which Monteleone builds one at a time by himself.

Custom Guitars also include a **Seven String Radio Flyer**, a **Gotham City** and a **Hexaphone**, all in the $35,000 to $40,000 range.

Some unique qualities of Monteleone Guitars is that their tuner buttons are specially made to be the letter M, cast in metal. Unlike other builders, Monteleone headstocks vary by the model, though the cast brass M's do not. The stylized "Monteleone" is trademarked and the numbers of guitars are small enough that authenticity of guitars can be verified by a call to the artist.

MOON GUITARS LTD. (SCOTLAND)

Instruments currently built in Glasgow, Scotland, since 1979.

CONTACT INFORMATION
MOON GUITARS LTD. (SCOTLAND)
974 Pollokshaws Road
Glasgow, G41 2HA Scotland
Phone No.: 0044(0)141 632 9526
Fax No.: 0044(0)141 632 4928
www.moonguitars.co.uk
moon@moonguitars.co.uk

Moon Guitars was established by Jimmy Moon in 1979, and the Moon Guitars name has become synonymous with custom built instruments of very high quality as they are producing modern instruments with strong traditional roots. Originally, Moon Guitars produced acoustic guitars, mandolins, mandolas, and dulcimers. Moon moved into the electric market during the eighties, producing for an impressive client list of famous names. A shift in the market caused them to return to building acoustics and mandolins - including the Model T mandolin used by Steve Earle.

They now produce high quality affordable acoustic guitars from the Standard Series through to the Master Series - built with exotic timbers such as African Rosewood, Black Acacia and Koa. Moon also manufacture signature models for Bryan Adams and Dougie MacLean and continue to produce the entire mandolin family range of instruments. For further information, visit Moon Guitars' website or contact them directly.

MOONSTONE

Instruments currently built in Eureka, CA (guitar production has been in different locations in California since 1972). Distributed directly by Moonstone Guitars of Eureka, CA.

CONTACT INFORMATION
MOONSTONE
PO Box 757
Eureka, CA 95502
Phone No.: 707-445-9045
www.moonstoneguitars.com
steve@moonstoneguitars.com

In 1972, self-taught luthier Steve Helgeson began building acoustic instruments in an old shingle mill located in Moonstone Heights, California. By 1974, Helgeson moved to Arcata, California, and began producing electric Earth Axe guitars. By 1976, Helgeson had moved to a larger shop and increased his model line and production. Helgeson hit boom sales in the early 1980s, but tapered off production after the market shifted in 1985. Rather than shift with the trends, Helgeson preferred to maintain his own designs. In 1988, a major disaster in the form of a deliberately set fire damaged some of his machinery. Steve's highly figured wood supply survived only a minor scorching. Helgeson moved and reopened his workshop in 1990 at the current location in Eureka, California, where he now offers a wide range of acoustic and electric guitars and basses. In addition to the standard models, Moonstone also offers custom guitars designed in accordance with the customer's request. All current prices include a hardshell case.

All Moonstone instruments are constructed from highly figured woods. Where burl wood was not used in the construction, the wood used is highly figured. Almost all necks are reinforced with veneers or stringers. Bass necks are reinforced with through body graphite stringers. Moonstone has always utilized exotic woods such as African purpleheart, paduak, wenge, koa, mahogany, Sitka and Engelmann spruce, Myrtlewood, and black burl walnut.

Some older models can also be found with necks entirely made of graphite composite with phenolic fingerboards. Helgeson

MSR/NOTES	100%	EXCELLENT	AVERAGE	LAST MSR

commissioned Modulus Graphite to produce these necks, and used them on models like the Eclipse Standard, Deluxe Basses, Vulcan Standard and Deluxe guitars, the M-80, D-81 Eagle 6- and 12-string models, as well as the D-81 Standard and the Moondolin (mandolin). In 1981, most wood necks were reinforced with a Graphite Aluminum Honeycomb Composite (G.A.H.C.) beam with stainless steel adjustment rod. For more information contact Moonstone directly.

ACOUSTIC

All necks currently are reinforced with .375 in. by .5 in. U channel graphite beam with a .1875 in. adjustment rod.

Moonstone has guitars that are based off of traditional popular designs. The 000-42 features Brazillian rosewood and retails for $8,180. The 000-45 has fifty-year old Brazillian rosewood and retails for $10,180. The OM-45 has koa wood and lists for $7,830. Model styles 00, 000, and OM all retail for $4,400. Moonstone also offers an SJ-19, B-95 Baritone, and J-99 Baritone model. Retail on all of these is $4,900.

D-81 EAGLE 6 – spruce top, round soundhole, black pickguard, bound body, wood inlay rosette, quilted maple back/sides, graphite neck, 14/20-fret bound phenolic fingerboard with abalone vine inlay, eagle shape ebony bridge with black pins, walnut burl peghead veneer with abalone halfmoon/logo inlay, three-per-side gold tuners, available in Natural finish, mfg. 1981-84.

	N/A	$1,100 - 1,250	$650 - 750	$2,075

* **D-81 Eagle 12** – similar to D-81 Eagle 6, except has 12 strings, six-per-side tuners.

	N/A	$1,200 - 1,350	$675 - 800	$2,255

J-90 – Sitka spruce top, round soundhole, bound body, rifling twist rosette, wenge back/sides/neck, 14/20-fret bound ebony fingerboard with abalone/pearl flower/vine inlay, ebony bridge with pearl flower wing inlay, black pearl dot bridge pins, ebony peghead veneer with abalone halfmoon/logo inlay, three-per-side gold tuners, available in Natural finish, mfg. 1992-present.

MSR $4,400	N/A	N/A	N/A	

* Add $650 for J-90 Eagle Makassar ebony with top rim inlay and full vine inlay.

J-90 EAGLE – similar to the J-90, except features carved eagle bridge, bird fingerboard inlays, disc. 2005.

	N/A	N/A	N/A	$3,600

This model was an option with quilted Pacific or Canadian flame maple, rosewood, curly koa, or paduak back and sides, cutaway body design, abalone top purfling, and an Engelmann spruce top.

* **J-90 Eagle Macassar Ebony** – similar to the J-90 Eagle, except has Makassar ebony back and sides, disc. 2005.

	N/A	N/A	N/A	$5,050

* **J-90 Eagle Koa** – similar to the J-90 Eagle, except has koa back and sides, disc. 2005.

	N/A	N/A	N/A	$7,295

* **J-90 Eagle Brazilian Rosewood** – similar to the J-90 Eagle, except has Brazilian rosewood back and sides, disc. 2005.

	N/A	N/A	N/A	$12,620

J-99 – slope shouldered jumbo body, 17 in. width, Asian rosewood back and sides, 12/19-fret fingerboard with bird inlay, three-per-side gold tuners, available in Natural finish, current mfg.

MSR $4,400	N/A	N/A	N/A	

ACOUSTIC BASS

B-95 – Englemann spruce top, round soundhole, 35 in. scale, wenge (or rosewood or curly koa or paduak or burl maple) back/sides/neck, ebony fingerboard with abalone filled mother-of-pearl inlays, two-per-side tuners, available in Natural finish, current mfg.

MSR $4,900	N/A	N/A	N/A	

* **B-95 Five-String** – similar to the B-95, except in five-string configuration, 3/2-per-side tuners, current mfg.

MSR $5,200	N/A	N/A	N/A	

MORGAN GUITARS

Instruments currently built in North Vancouver (British Columbia), Canada, since 1981.

Morgan acoustic guitars are hand crafted by luthier David Iannone, and feature premier woods and construction techniques. Iannone began building guitars in 1981. His apprenticeship carried on a guitar lineage that dates back to the very birth of the modern classic guitar. Morgan Guitars, named after his first son, is Welsh for "working by the sea" (which he does).

CONTACT INFORMATION
MORGAN GUITARS
3007 Plymouth Drive
Vancouver, BC V7H 1C6 Canada
Phone No.: 604-929-0292
Fax No.: 604-929-5517
www.morganguitars.com
inquiry@morganguitars.com

Morgan guitars all share the following features: high grade spruce or cedar top, rosewood (or mahogany or maple) back and sides, one-piece mahogany neck, bound ebony fingerboard, wood binding and purfling, wood marquetry or abalone rosette, transparent or tortoiseshell pickguard, and Morgan engraved machine heads.

Morgan Rosewood model guitars are offered in configurations like the **Concert, OM, Dreadnought**, and **OO** models (list $2,850 each); **Florentine Cutaway** ($3,350); **Venetian Cutaway** ($3,200). **Classic** (disc., last MSR was $2,510); **Traditional Jumbo**

($3,000), **Jumbo 12 String** ($3,250), and the **Concert 12 String** ($3,080).

Morgan Mahogany model guitars are offered in configurations like the **Concert, OM, Dreadnought**, and **OO** models (list $2,600 each); **Venetian Cutaway** ($2,925), **Traditional Jumbo** ($2,700), **Jumbo 12-String** ($2,925), and the **Concert 12-String** ($2,815).

Options include a figured maple back and sides, koa back and sides, Brazilian rosewood back and sides (call for quote), and other custom options.

MORGAN MONROE

Instruments currently produced in China. Distributed by SHS International in Indianapolis, IN. Previously produced in Korea.

Morgan Monroe is a line of traditional acoustic guitars, as well as resonators, mandolins, and banjos. Most of these instruments are middle grade with prices retailing under $1,000. For more information, refer to their website.

CONTACT INFORMATION
MORGAN MONROE
1922 W. Banta Rd
Indianapolis, IN 46217
www.morganmonroe.com
sales@shsaudio.com

MORIDAIRA

Instruments previously produced in Japan. Also see Morris.

The Moridaira company is an OEM manufacturer of guitars for other companies, under different trademark names. The company has produced a wide range of entry level to very good quality guitars through the years, depending on the outside company's specifications. Circa 2003, they were no longer an OEM manufacturer.

MORRELL

Instruments previously built in TN. Distributed by the Joe Morrell Music Distributing Company of Bristol, TN.

The Joe Morrell Music Distributing company sells products wholesale to music dealers, instrument repair personnel, and instrument builders. Their current catalog offers a wide range of Morrell stringed instruments all built in the U.S., such as resonator guitars, lap steel guitars, dulcimers, and flaptop mandolins. In addition, the Morrell company also lists music songbooks, instructional videos, guitar cases, name brand guitar strings and accessories, guitar/banjo/violin parts, drum heads and drum parts, and other music store accessories. Besides their own U.S.-built Morrell instruments, the Morrell company offers low cost, quality acoustic and electric instruments from overseas manufacturers.

Additional Morrell stringed instruments include their Tennessee Mountain dulcimer (last MSR was $120), Tennessee Flattop Mandolin (last MSR was $300), and Lap Steel guitars. A two-octave student model in natural finish has a retail price of $219.95 (black or red sparkle finish is $50 extra), and the three-octave Professional model Joe Morrell Pro 6 or Little Roy Wiggins eight-string had a last MSR of $400 each.

Morrell is currently offering the **FlintHill** series of resonator guitars, available in roundneck and square neck models. These resonator models feature a maple top, walnut back and sides, walnut neck, ebony fingerboard, and three-per-side closed tuners. Models are available in Natural (**Model MDR-1/MDS-1**) and Tobacco Sunburst (**Model MDR-2/MDS-2**) finishes. All resonator models had a retail list price of $799. Morrell also stocks replacement parts for performing repairs on other resonator models.

MORRIS

Instruments currently produced in Japan. Distributed in the USA by Moridaria USA Inc, in Fairfield, CA. Guitars were produced 1967-1980s, and 2001-present.

Toshio Moridaira founded Morris guitars in 1967. Moridaira got the name Morris when an employee at the Gibson factory nicknamed him that during a visit in 1964. In 1974, Morris displayed guitars at the NAMM show for the first time. They produced acoustic guitars and a thinline Ovation-style Tornado series until the 1980s. Morris guitars were re-introduced in 2001 with the S Series and are distributed in the U.S. by Moridaira, USA Inc. Morris guitars are advertised as "Made for Fingerpickers," for the high end hand crafted acoustic guitar. For more information contact Morris directly.

CONTACT INFORMATION
MORRIS
Distributed by Moridaira USA, Inc.
4476 Green Valley Road
Fairfield, CA 94585
Phone No.: 707-864-1442
Fax No.: 707-864-1209
moridairausa@att.net

The Morris S Series represent the current line of acoustic guitars. Retail prices start at $900 with the Mini Western and climb to $5,000 for the Grand Auditorium. Some of the higher end models are handcrafted and the other models are built by machine. Fine woods are used and optional on most models.

MORSE, JOHN DAVID

Instruments currently built in Santa Cruz, CA since 1978. Luthier Morse is currently concentrating on violin making.

Luthier John David Morse combined his artistic backgrounds in music, sculpture, and woodcarving with the practical scientific knowledge of stress points and construction techniques to produce a superior modern archtop guitar. Morse, a descendant of Samuel Morse (the telegraph and Morse code), studied under fine violin makers Henry Lannini and Arthur Conner to learn the wood carving craft. Morse still combines scientific processes in his building, and has identified means to recreate his hand graduated tops.

Morse is currently making high quality violins. A number of his violins are currently in use with the San Francisco Symphony, and he is building models for concertmaster Ramond Kobler and conductor Herbert Blomstedt. Any potential commissions for archtop guitar models should be discussed directly with luthier Morse.

MORTORO GUITARS

Instruments currently built in Miami, FL, since 1991.

CONTACT INFORMATION
MORTORO GUITARS
PO Box 161225
Miami, FL 33116-1225
Phone No.: 305-238-7947
www.motoroguitars.com
info@mortoroguitars.com

Luthier Gary Mortoro has been building handcrafted instruments since 1991, under the guidance and direction of Master Luthier and Archtop Builder Robert Benedetto. Gary's dedication to the crafting of his guitars combined with his playing ability has resulted in an instrument not only of fine detail and craftsmanship, but of exquisite sound and beauty. Some of the players who own a Mortoro guitar are George Benson, Tony Mottola, Jimmy Vivino, Rodney Jones, Gene Bertoncini, Joe Cinderella, and Jimmy Buffet.

Mortoro currently offers six different models that are available in carved or laminate versions. For further information, please contact Gary Mortoro directly.

Carved models have select tops and backs with matching sides and neck. **Laminate** models feature laminated tops and backs, with necks and sides of flamed maple. All models feature a single cutaway and come in 14 in., 16 in., or 17 in. bodies. Body thickness is up to the player's choice. Motoro guitars feature ebony for the fingerboard, pickguard, bridge, and tailpiece, Pearl inlay, Schaller tuners, and a floating Mortoro pickup by Kent Armstrong. Models come with a hard shell case and warranty. A number of options; custom colors, custom inlays, seven-string models, etc. are also available.

For complete model listings please refer to the *Blue Book of Electric Guitars*.

MOSRITE

Instruments previously produced in Bakersfield, CA during the 1960s. Earlier models built in Los Angeles, CA during the mid- to late 1950s. Distribution in the 1990s was handled by Unified Sound Association, Inc. Production of Mosrite guitars ceased in 1994. There were other factory sites around the U.S. during the 1970s and 1980s. Other notable locations include Carson City, NV, Jonas Ridge, NC, and Booneville, AR (previous home of Baldwin-operated Gretsch production during the 1970s).

Luthier/designer Semie Moseley (1935-1992) was born in Durant, Oklahoma. The family moved to Bakersfield, California when Moseley was nine years old, and Semie left school in the seventh grade to travel with an evangelistic group playing guitar.

Moseley, eighteen, was hired by Paul Barth to work at Rickenbacker in 1953. While at Rickenbacker, Moseley worked with Roger Rossmeisl. Rossmeisel's "German carve" technique was later featured on Moseley's guitar models as well. Moseley was later fired from Rickenbacker in 1955 for building his own guitar at their facilities. In the later years, Moseley always credited Barth and Rossmeisl (and the Rickenbacker company) for his beginning knowledge in guitar building.

With the help of Reverend Ray Boatright, who co-signed for guitar building tools at Sears, Moseley began building his original designs. The Mosrite trademark is named after **Mos**eley and Boat**right** ("-rite"). After leaving Rickenbacker, Moseley built custom instruments for various people around southern California, most notably Joe Maphis (of "Town Hall Party" fame). Moseley freelanced some work with Paul Barth's "Barth" guitars, as well as some neck work for Paul Bigsby.

After traveling for several months with another gospel group, Moseley returned to Bakersfield and again set up shop. Moseley built around twenty guitars for Bob Crooks (Standel). When Crooks asked for a Fender-styled guitar model, Moseley flipped a Stratocaster over, traced the rough outline, and built the forerunner to the "Ventures" model!

After Nokie Edwards (Ventures) borrowed a guitar for a recording session, Stan Wagner (Ventures Manager) called Moseley to propose a business collaboration. Mosrite would produce the instruments, and use the Venture's organization as the main distributor. The heyday of the Mosrite company was the years between 1963 and 1969. When the demand set in, the company went from producing thirty-five guitars a month to fifty and later three hundred. The Mosrite facility had 105 employees at one point, and offered several different models in addition to the Ventures model (such as the semi-hollowbody Celebrity series, the Combo, and the Joe Maphis series).

In 1963, investors sold the Dobro trademark to Moseley, who built the first 100 or 150 out of parts left over from the Dobro plant in Gardenia. Later Bakersfield Dobros can be identified by the serial number imprinted on the end of the fingerboard. The Mosrite company did not build the amplifiers which bear the Mosrite trademark; another facility built the Mosrite amplifiers and fuzz pedals, and paid for the rights to use the Mosrite name.

The amplifier line proved to be the undoing of Mosrite. While some of the larger amplifiers are fine, one entry level model featured a poor design and a high failure rate. While covering for returns, the Ventures organization used up their line of credit at their bank, and the bank shut down the organization. In doing so, the Mosrite distribution was shut down as well. Moseley tried a deal with Vox (Thomas Organ) but the company was shut down in 1969. Moseley returned to the Gospel music circuit, and transferred the Dobro name to OMI in a series of negotiations.

Between the mid-1970s and the late 1980s, Moseley continued to find backers and sporadically build guitars. In 1972, *Guitar Player* magazine reported, "Semie Moseley is now working with Reinhold Plastics, Inc. to produce Mosrite of California guitars." Later that year, Moseley set up a tentative deal with Bud Ross at Kustom (Kustom Amplifiers) in Chanute, Kansas. Moseley was going to build a projected 200 guitars a month at his 1424 P Street location, and Ross' Kustom Electronics was going to be the distributor. This deal fell through, leaving Moseley free to strike up another deal in April of 1974 with Pacific Music Supply Company of Los Angeles, California. Pacific Music Supply Company had recently lost their Guild account, and was looking for another guitar line to distribute. One primary model in 1974 was the solid body Model 350 Stereo. The Brass Rail model was developed around 1976/1977. While shopping around his new model with "massive sustain," Moseley met a dealer in Hollywood Music in Los Angeles. This dealer had connections in Japan, and requested that Moseley begin recreating the original-style Ventures models. Moseley set out to build thirty-five to fifty of these reproductions per month for a number of months. Several years after Moseley recovered from an illness in 1983, he began rebuilding his dealer network with a number of models like the V-88, M-88, and Ventures 1960's Reissues. These models were built at his Jonas Ridge location.

Moseley's final guitar production was located in Booneville, Arkansas. The Unified Sound Association was located in a converted Walmart building, and an estimated 90% to 95% of production was earmarked for the Japanese market.

Moseley passed away in 1992. His two biggest loves were gospel music, and building quality guitars. Throughout his nearly forty year career, he continued to persevere in his guitar building. Unified Sound Association stayed open through 1994 under the direction of Loretta Moseley, and then later closed its doors as well, (Information courtesy of Andy Moseley and Hal Hammer [1996]; additional information courtesy Willie G. Moseley, *Stellas and Stratocasters*, and Tom Wheeler, *American Guitars*, Mosrite catalogs and file information courtesy John Kinnemeyer, JK Lutherie, model dating estimations courtesy Carlos Juan, Collectables & Vintage '95, Stuttgart, Germany).

MODEL IDENTIFICATION

Mosrite guitars are easily identifiable by the "M" notch in the top of the headstock. Mosrite models produced in the 1960s have a "M" initial in a edged circle, and "Mosrite" (in block letters) "of California" (in smaller script) logo.

Contrary to vintage guitar show information in the current "Age of Fender mania," Mosrite instruments were not available in those (rare) Fender finishes like "Candy Apple Red" and "Lake Placid Blue." Catalog colors were identified as Blue or Red. Mosrite did offer option colored finishes like Metallic Blue and Metallic Red.

Semie's designs offered numerous innovations, most notable being the Vibra-Mute vibrato. This item was designed for the Ventures models and can be used to help identify early Mosrite instruments. The early vibratos (pre-1977) have Vibra-Mute and Mosrite on them, while later vibratos have Mosrite alone on them. More distinction can be made among the earliest instruments with Vibra-Mutes by observing the casting technique used. While the early vibratos were sandcast, later units were diecast (once funding was available).

During the heyday of Mosrite production in Bakersfield, model designations in the catalog would list a **Mark I** to designate a 6-string model, **Mark XII** to indicate the 12-string version, and **Mark X** to designate the bass model within a series. These Mark designations are a forerunner to - but not the same usage as - the later **1967-1969 Mark** "No Logo" series.

PRODUCTION DATES

Mosrite models in this edition of the *Blue Book of Acoustic Guitars* feature estimated dates of production for each model. Just as it is easy to take for granted a sunny day in the summer until it rains, most dealers and collectors take a Mosrite model as "just a Mosrite" without really double checking the true nature of **which** model it really is. Of course, the corollary of this way of thinking is to assume that the Mosrite in question is going to end up in the Far East with the rest of them! Was Johnny Ramone the only American guitar player to use these guitars? Are there no mega-Mosrite collectors? Ventures fans unite!

The *Blue Book of Acoustic Guitars* is actively seeking additional input on Mosrite models, specifications, date of production, and any serialization information. This section is the official "Line Drawn in the Sand" for Mosrite fans -- assume that this is the drawing board, or the foundation to build upon. Any extra information gathered on Mosrite will be updated in future editions of the *Blue Book of Acoustic Guitars*. For the time being, assume that all production dates are either CIRCA and/or ESTIMATED.

For further information regarding Mosrite electric models, please refer to the *Blue Book of Electric Guitars*.

ACOUSTIC: BALLADERE & SERENADE MODELS

· The D-8 Memphis five-string banjo was built between 1966 and 1969, and featured a maple top/back/sides, single body binding, 26 in.scale, East Indian rosewood fingerboard, Type C resonator and cover plate, 12 round mini-soundholes arranged around the resonator, bridge/metal tailpiece. The D-8 Memphis was available in a Blonde finish, and had a new retail list price of $229.00 (in 1966).

BALLADERE I (MODEL 401) – dreadnought style, 3.25 in. body depth, bound spruce top, round soundhole, mahogany back/sides, 24.5 in. scale, 14/20-fret Indian rosewood fingerboard, rosewood bridge with white bridgepins, three-per-side chrome enclosed tuners, available Natural or Transparent Sunburst finish, mfg. 1966-69.

| | N/A | $1,000 - 1,250 | $600 - 750 | $198 |

* *Balladere II (Model 402)* – similar to the Balladere I, except features rosewood back/sides, two-color laminated line purfling (top and back), bound fingerboard, available Natural or Transparent Sunburst finish, body thickness 5 in., mfg. 1968-69.

| | N/A | $1,200 - 1,500 | $725 - 900 | $398 |

SERENADE – dreadnought style, spruce top, round soundhole, mahogany back/sides, mahogany neck, celluloid double binding on body, 14/20-fret rosewood fingerboard with dot inlay, rosewood bridge with white bridgepins, black celluloid batwing pickguard, three-per-side Kluson tuners, available in Natural Spruce Top/Shaded Burgundy high gloss finish, mfg. 1965-69.

| | N/A | $800 - 1,000 | $475 - 600 | $198 |

A similar model, the Seranade I (Model 401) featured maple back and sides, and was available in Natural Spruce Top, Transparent Cherry Red and Transparent Sunburst finishes.

MSR/NOTES	100%	EXCELLENT	AVERAGE	LAST MSR

ACOUSTIC: MOBRO MODELS

The "Mobro" name is derived from "Mosrite Dobro"; in other words, Dobro models built by the Mosrite company.

MOBRO STANDARD – resonator style, hollow wood body, two mesh-covered mini-soundholes in upper bouts, 14/20-fret fingerboard, chrome resonator, bridge/metal tailpiece, Mosrite-style headstock, "Mosrite/Mobro" headstock logos, three-per-side chrome tuners, available in Natural finish, mfg. 1972-73.

	N/A	$500 - 575	$275 - 325	$349

* *Mobro Standard E* – similar to the Mobro Standard, except features one single coil pickup, available in Natural finish, mfg. 1972-73.

	N/A	$500 - 575	$275 - 325	$429

MOBRO STEEL – similar to Mobro Standard, except features a metal body, available in chrome finish, mfg. 1972-73.

	N/A	$500 - 575	$275 - 325	$349

* *Mobro Steel E* – similar to the Mobro Steel, except features one single coil pickup, available in chrome finish, mfg. 1972-73.

	N/A	$600 - 700	$350 - 425	$429

MOSSMAN

Instruments currently produced in Sulphur Springs, TX since 1989. Instruments previously built in Winfield, KS from 1969 to 1977. Some models were available from Mossman's private shop after 1977.

CONTACT INFORMATION
MOSSMAN
1813 Main Street
Sulphur Springs, TX 75482
Phone No.: 903-885-4992
tony@mossman-guitars.com

Luthier Stuart Mossman originally built acoustic guitars in his garage in 1969. Mossman then founded the S. L. Mossman Company, and set up a factory to produce guitars. Mossman inspected each finished guitar before shipping; the scale of the Mossman factory was to build eight to ten guitars a day (at the most). Actually, when discussing acoustic guitars, it is probably proper to say complete eight to ten guitars a day, as the actual construction would take longer to complete (gluing the bodies, neck/body joint assembly and set up, etc.). It is estimated that around 1,400 guitars had been built between 1970 and 1975, when a fire struck the factory in February. With the support of local businessmen, Mossman returned to production. However, due to a disagreement with his distributors, the Mossman company closed shop in August of 1977. Stuart Mossman then opened a private shop, and offered a number of instruments privately.

In 1989, John Kinsey of Dallas, Texas resurrected the Mossman trademark. In mid-1990, Bob Casey joined the company as a part owner. The company operated in a suburb of Dallas until August of 1991 when it was moved to an old dairy barn in Sulpher Springs, Texas. The company has operated in Sulphur Springs since then. The Mossman line of acoustic guitars is still regarded as one of the finest handmade instruments in the country, (Company history courtesy John Kinsey, Mossman Guitars).

Mossman Guitars manufactures basically the same models as Stuart Mossman manufactured in Winfield, Kansas. Some of the lower line models have been discontinued, but the mainstream line (Texas Plains, Winter Wheat, South Wind, and Golden Era) continue to be produced. Several improvements have been made to the standard models, such as scalloped bracing being made a standard feature. Mossman Guitars, Inc. has also developed the "next step in the evolution of X-bracing," they refer to it as Suspension Bracing. This modification helps projection as well as producing a clear, clean punch on the lower end. For further information on Texas-made or Kansas-made Mossman instruments, please contact Mossman Guitars, Inc. directly.

ACOUSTIC

In 1975, a fire started in the finishing area at Mossman Guitars. While no employees were hurt and the machinery suffered minor losses, the company's supply of Brazilian rosewood was depleted. Models that featured Brazilian rosewood before the fire were converted to Indian rosewood after the fire (a minor instrument dating tip).

FLINT HILLS – dreadnought style, 25 .75 in. scale, sitka spruce top, round soundhole, East Indian rosewood back/sides, 20-fret ebony fingerboard, ebony pin bridge, three-per-side Grover (or Schaller) tuners, available in Natural finish, mfg. 1969-1977.

	N/A	$1,600 - 2,000	$950 - 1,200	$350

This model was an option with abalone top and soundhole inlay as the Flint Hills Custom (retail list $525).

GOLDEN ERA – dreadnought style, 25 .75 in. scale, German spruce top with abalone inlay, round soundhole, abalone trim, Brazilian rosewood back/sides, 20-fret ebony fingerboard, black pickguard, adjustable ebony bridge with white pins, three-per-side gold Grover (or Schaller) tuners, available in Natural finish, mfg. 1969-1977.

	N/A	$2,600 - 3,250	$1,550 - 1,950	$750

This model was an option with abalone tree-of-life floral inlay as the Golden Era Custom (retail list price $900).

GREAT PLAINS – dreadnought style, 25 .75 in. scale, German spruce top, round soundhole, herringbone inlay, Brazilian rosewood back/sides, 20-fret ebony fingerboard, ebony pin bridge, three-per-side Grover (or Schaller) tuners, available in Natural finish, mfg. 1969-1977.

	N/A	$1,400 - 1,750	$850 - 1,050	$425

TENNESSEE FLATTOP – dreadnought style, 25.75 in. scale, sitka spruce top, round soundhole, black plastic body binding, Honduran mahogany back/sides, 20-fret rosewood fingerboard, adjustable bridge, three-per-side Grover (or Schaller) tuners, available in Natural finish, mfg. 1969-1977.

	N/A	$1,200 - 1,500	$725 - 900	$350

MTD

Instruments currently built in Kingston, NY since 1994.

CONTACT INFORMATION
MTD
3 Lauren Court
Kingston, NY 12401
Phone No.: 845-246-0670
Fax No.: 845-246-1670
www.mtdbass.com
mike@mtdbass.com

Kingston Series Distributor: Dana B. Goods
4054 Transport Street, Unit A,
Ventura, CA 93003
Phone No.: 800-741-0109
www.danabgoods.com

Luthier Michael Tobias has been handcrafting guitars and basses since 1977. The forerunner of MTD, Tobias Guitars was started in Orlando, Florida in April 1977. Tobias' first shop name was the Guitar Shop, and he sold that business in 1980 and moved to San Francisco to be partners in a short-lived manufacturing business called Sierra Guitars. The business made about fifty instruments and then Tobias left San Francisco in May of 1981 to start a repair shop in Costa Mesa, California.

Several months later, Tobias left Costa Mesa and moved to Hollywood. Tobias Guitars continued to repair instruments and build custom basses for the next several years with the help of Bob Lee and Kevin Almieda (Kevin went on to work for Music Man). The company moved into 1623 Cahuenga Boulevard in Hollywood and after a year quit the repair business. Tobias Guitars added Bob McDonald, lost Kevin to Music Man, and then got Makoto Onishi. The business grew in leaps and bounds. In June of 1988 the company had so many back orders that it did not accept any new orders until the January NAMM show in 1990.

After several attempts to move the business to larger, better-equipped facilities, Michael Tobias sold Tobias Guitars to Gibson on January 1, 1990. Late in 1992, it was decided that in the best corporate interests, Tobias Guitars would move to Nashville. Michael Tobias left the company in December 1992, and was a consultant for Gibson as they set up operations in Nashville.

By contractual agreement, after Tobias' consulting agreement with Gibson was up, he had a one-year non-competition term. That ended in December 1993. During that time, Tobias moved to The Catskills in upstate New York and set up a small custom shop. Tobias started designing new instruments and building prototypes in preparation for his new venture. The first instruments were named Eclipse. There are fifty of these instruments and most of them are 35 in. bolt-ons. There are three neck-throughs. Tobias finally settled on MTD as the company name and trademark. As of 1997 he had delivered 250 MTD instruments, including bolt-on basses, guitars, neck-through basses, and acoustic bass guitars.

Michael Tobias is currently building nearly one hundred instruments per year, with the help of Chris Hofschneider (who works two days per week). Chris has at least fifteen years experience, having worked for Sam Koontz, Spector Guitars, Kramer, and being on the road with bands like Bon Jovi and other New Jersey-based bands. Michael Tobias is also doing design and development work for other companies, such as Alvarez, Brian Moore Guitars, Modulus Guitars, Lakland, American Showster (with Chris Hofschneider) and the new Czech-built Grendel basses (source: Michael Tobias, MTD fine handmade guitars and basses).

ACOUSTIC BASS

All MTD instruments are delivered with a wenge neck/wenge fingerboard, or maple neck/rosewood fingerboard; 21 frets plus a "Zero" fret, 35 in. scale length. Prices include plush hard shell cases. The standard finish for body and neck is a satin catalyzed urethene. Wood choices for bodies: swamp ash, poplar, and alder. Other woods, upon request, may require up charges. Exotic tops are subject to availability. Beginning 2000, all MTD Basses come equipped with the Buzz Feiten Tuning System. Models can be ordered in 34 in. or 35 in. scale. MTD basses are all electric as of 2002.

* Add $100 for a lined fretless neck.
* Add $150 for a hand rubbed oil stain.
* Add $300 for wenge.
* Add $200 for satin epoxy coating on lined or unlined fretless fingerboard.
* Add $200 for epoxy/oil urethane finished maple fingerboard.
* Add $200 for a 24-fret fingerboard.

* Add $400 for Lacquer finish: Sunburst (Amber or Brown), See-Throughs (Transparency) of Red, Coral Blue, or Honey Gold. Add $300 for a korina, African satinwood (Avadore), or lacewood body.
* Add $500 for a 10 Top of burl, flamed, or quilted maple, myrtle, or mahogany.
* Add $150 for Highlander system.
* Add $175 for Fishman Transducer.

ABG 4 – four-string acoustic bass, flamed myrtle back and sides, spruce top, mfg. 1994-2001.

	100%	EXCELLENT	AVERAGE	LAST MSR
	N/A	$1,550 - 1,800	$1,150 - 1,300	$2,750

ABG 5 – five-string acoustic bass, flamed myrtle back and sides, spruce top, mfg. 1994-2001.

	100%	EXCELLENT	AVERAGE	LAST MSR
	N/A	$1,650 - 1,900	$1,150 - 1,300	$2,900

MITCHELL

Instruments currently produced in China.

CONTACT INFORMATION
MITCHELL
www.musiciansfriend.com/mitchell

Mitchell is a trademark used by Musician's Friend and Guitar Center as a brand of imported acoustic guitars. Mitchell guitars are offered in a variety of traditional shapes with optional solid spruce tops and electronics. Guitars retail between $250 and $900 and generally sell new for half the retail price.

N SECTION
NAGOYA

Guitars previously produced in Japan during the 1970s.

Nagoya guitars were produced by the Suzuki Violin Company in Nagoya Japan. These acoustic guitars have a striking resemblance to Martin guitars of the same era. Many players report that these guitars play very well and have a nice sound. Any further information on Nagoya can be submitted directly to Blue Book Publications.

NASH

Instruments previously built in Markneukirchen, Germany 1996-2000. Previously distributed in the U.S. by Musima North America of Tampa, FL.

Nash acoustic guitars debuted in the United States, Canadian, and South American markets in 1996. The guitars were built by Musima, Germany's largest acoustic guitar manufacturer (the company headquarters in Markneukirchen, Germany are near the Czech border). In 1991, Musima was purchased by industry veteran Helmet Stumpf. Nash guitars were offered through 2000 and models included the MW600, MW700, and MW800.

NASHVILLE GUITAR COMPANY

Instruments currently built in Nashville, TN since 1985.

Luthier/musician Marty Lanham began working on stringed instruments in San Francisco during the late 1960s, and moved to Nashville in 1972. He accepted a job at Gruhn Guitar's repair shop, and spent eight years gaining knowledge and lutherie insight. In 1985, Lanham went into business custom building his own acoustic guitars. Nashville Guitar's custom steel string acoustic models feature German or sitka spruce tops; mahogany, koa, Indian or Brazilian rosewood, Tasmanian blackwood, and Malagasy kingwood back

and sides, mahogany neck, and an ebony or rosewood fingerboard. They also offer museum-quality restorations. For more information, visit Nashville's website or contact them directly.

NATIONAL

Instruments previously produced in Los Angeles, CA during the mid-1920s to the mid-1930s. Instruments produced in Chicago, IL from mid-1930s to 1969. After National moved production to Chicago in the mid-1930s, they formally changed the company name to Valco (but still produced National brand guitars). Instruments produced in Japan circa 1970s. Distributed by Strum'N Drum of Chicago, IL. When Valco went out of business in 1969, the National trademark was acquired by Strum'N Drum, who then used the trademark on a series of Japanese built guitars.

The Dopyera family emigrated from the Austro-Hungary area to Southern California in 1908. In the early 1920s, John and Rudy Dopyera began producing banjos in Southern California. They were approached by guitarist George Beauchamp to help solve his "volume" (or lack thereof) problem with other instruments in the vaudeville orchestra. In the course of their conversation, the idea of placing aluminum resonators in a guitar body for amplification purposes was developed. John Dopyera and his four brothers (plus some associates like George Beauchamp) formed National in 1925.

The initial partnership between Dopyera and Beauchamp lasted for about two years, and then John Dopyera left National to form the Dobro company. National's corporate officers in 1929 consisted of Ted E. Kleinmeyer (pres.), George Beauchamp (sec./gen. mgr.), Adolph Rickenbacker (engineer), and Paul Barth (vice pres.). In late 1929, Beauchamp left National, and joined up with Adolph Rickenbacker to form Ro-Pat-In (later Electro String/Rickenbacker).

At the onset of the American Depression, National was having financial difficulties. Louis Dopyera bought out the National company; and as he owned more than 50% of the stock in Dobro, "merged" the two companies back together (as National Dobro). In 1936, the decision was made to move the company to Chicago, Illinois. Chicago was a veritable hotbed of mass produced musical instruments during the early to pre-World War II 1900s. Manufacturers like Washburn and Regal had facilities, and major wholesalers and retailers like the Tonk Bros. and Lyon & Healy were based there. Victor Smith, Al Frost, and Louis Dopyera moved their operation to Chicago, and in 1943 formally announced the change to Valco (The initials of their three first names: Victor-Al-Louis Company). Valco worked on war materials during World War II, and returned to instrument production afterwards. Valco produced the National/Supro/Airline fiberglass body guitars in the 1950s and 1960s, as well as wood-bodied models.

In 1969 or 1970, Valco Guitars, Inc. went out of business. The assets of Valco/Kay were auctioned off, and the rights to the National trademark were bought by the Chicago, Illinois-based importers Strum'N Drum. Strum'N Drum, which had been importing Japanese guitars under the Norma trademark, were quick to introduce National on a line of Japanese produced guitars that were distributed in the U.S. market. Author/researcher Michael Wright points out that the National "Big Daddy170 bolt-neck black LP copy was one of the first models that launched the Japanese "Copy Era" of the 1970s.

Early company history courtesy Bob Brozman, *The History and Artistry of National Resonator Instruments*; model descriptions compiled by Dave Hull, "Copy Era" National information courtesy Michael Wright.

MSR/NOTES	100%	EXCELLENT	AVERAGE	LAST MSR

ACOUSTIC: SINGLE CONE MODELS

STYLE O – nickel plated bell brass body, 2 f-holes, maple neck, 12/19-fret ebonized maple fingerboard with pearl dot inlay, 3-per-side tuners, available with Sandblasted Hawaiian Scene on body, mfg. 1930-1941.

	100%	EXCELLENT	AVERAGE	
Spanish 12-Fret	N/A	$3,200 - 4,000	$1,900 - 2,400	
Spanish 14-Fret	N/A	$2,800 - 3,500	$1,675 - 2,100	
Hawaiian	N/A	$2,200 - 2,750	$1,325 - 1,650	

* **The 12-fret guitars with rolled in f-holes command a premium (produced for about one year).**

The first few hundred Style O models featured steel bodies. The Hawaiian Style O has a wooden neck. Some 14-fret models may have parallelogram fingerboard inlays. Until 1933, the f-holes were flat cut. After 1933, the f-holes were rolled in (these are the rarest and most expensive Style O models). In late 1934, 14-fret fingerboard replaced 12-fret fingerboard.

STYLE N – German silver body, 12/19-fret fingerboard, square headstock with pearloid overlay (no sandblasting or etching design), mfg. 1930-34.

	100%	EXCELLENT	AVERAGE	
Spanish 12-Fret	N/A	$5,600 - 7,000	$3,500 - 4,200	

THE DON #1 – German silver body, 14/20-fret fingerboard with dot inlay, available with plain body with engraved edged borders.

	100%	EXCELLENT	AVERAGE	
Spanish 14-Fret	N/A	$8,000 - 10,000	$4,800 - 6,000	

The Don guitar models are fairly rare and are rarely traded in the vintage market.

* **The Don #2** – similar to The Don #1, except features pearloid headstock overlay, pearl square fingerboard inlay, available with geometric engraving.

	100%	EXCELLENT	AVERAGE	
Spanish 14-Fret	N/A	$12,000 - 15,000	$7,500 - 9,500	

* **The Don #3** – similar to The Don #1, except features pearloid headstock overlay, pearl square fingerboard inlay, available with Floral Pattern engraving.

	100%	EXCELLENT	AVERAGE	
Spanish 14-Fret	N/A	16,000 - 20,000	$9,500 - 12,000	

DUOLIAN – thinner gauge steel body, 2 flat cut f-holes, mahogany or maple neck, 12/19-fret dyed maple fingerboard with pearl or ivoroid dot inlay, mfg. 1931-1940.

	100%	EXCELLENT	AVERAGE	
Spanish 12-Fret	N/A	$2,800 - 3,500	$1,675 - 2,100	
	N/A	$2,600 - 3,250	$1,550 - 1,950	

After 1933, rolled in f-holes replaced flat cut f-holes. In 1935 a 14/20-fret fingerboard was introduced with a basswood neck. Before 1938, Duolian models featured a crystalline paint finish.

TRIOLIAN – wooden body, 2 flat cut f-holes, 12/19-fret fingerboard, available in Light Green finish with a light overspray of several colors; neck, fingerboard, and peghead featured matching finish, decals were then placed on the body; early models feature a bouquet design, later models feature a hula girl design, mfg. 1928-1941.

	100%	EXCELLENT	AVERAGE	
1928 (Tricone)	N/A	$2,800 - 3,500	$1,675 - 2,100	
1928-1929 Wood Body	N/A	$2,600 - 3,250	$1,550 - 1,950	
1929-1934	N/A	$2,800 - 3,500	$1,675 - 2,100	
1935-1941	N/A	$2,200 - 2,750	$1,325 - 1,650	

Only 12 of the 1928 Tricone Triolian models exist, making this an extremely rare model. In 1929, steel body replaced wooden bodies. In 1933, rolled in f-holes replaced flat cut f-holes. In 1935, 14/20-fret fingerboard replaced 12/19-fret fingerboards. The first Triolians were an attempt to make a budget tricone. National then almost immediately switched to a single resonator cone on the wooden body; a steel body was later adopted.

ACOUSTIC: TRICONE MODELS

The Tricone Nationals came in two configurations: round neck (**Spanish**) and square neck (**Hawaiian**). The round neck was basically a "German Silver" body with an attached wooden neck, while the square neck was a hollow extension of the body (all the way up to the attached wooden headstock). The tenor and plectrum instruments were built on a smaller triangular shaped body and only came in the Spanish style.

Generally speaking, the plectrum instruments will command a premium over the tenors. All of these instruments feature minor (and sometimes not so minor) changes through the years; a good place to research those would be Bob Brozman's fine work: *National Resonator Instruments* (published by Center Stream Publications).

STYLE 1 – German silver body, mahogany neck, ebony fingerboard with pearl dot inlay, National logo decal on headstock, available in Plain (no engraving) body, mfg. 1928-1941.

	100%	EXCELLENT	AVERAGE	
Spanish	N/A	$4,800 - 6,000	$2,900 - 3,600	
Hawaiian	N/A	$2,800 - 3,500	$1,675 - 2,100	
Plectrum	N/A	$2,000 - 2,500	$1,200 - 1,500	
Tenor	N/A	$1,800 - 2,250	$1,075 - 1,350	

Style 1 models below serial number 380 have a rosewood fingerboard instead of ebony. Tenor and plectrum models feature maple necks.

MSR/NOTES	100%	EXCELLENT	AVERAGE	LAST MSR

STYLE 2 – German silver body, mahogany neck, ebony fingerboard with pearl dot inlay, National logo decal on headstock, available in a Wild Rose engraving pattern, mfg. 1927-1939.

Spanish	N/A	$8,000 - 10,000	$4,800 - 6,000	
Hawaiian	N/A	$4,000 - 5,000	$2,400 - 3,000	
Plectrum	N/A	$2,200 - 2,750	$1,325 - 1,650	
Tenor	N/A	$2,000 - 2,500	$1,200 - 1,500	

Style 2 models below serial number 400 have a rosewood fingerboard instead of ebony. Tenor and plectrum models feature maple necks.

STYLE 3 – German silver body, mahogany neck, ebony fingerboard with pearl square inlay, engraved National logo inlay on ebony peghead overlay (some models feature a pearloid engraved overlay), available in a Lily of the Valley engraving pattern, mfg. 1928-1941.

Spanish	N/A	$14,000 - 17,500	$8,500 - 10,500	
Hawaiian	N/A	$6,500 - 8,000	$3,900 - 4,850	
Plectrum	N/A	$4,000 - 5,000	$2,400 - 3,000	
Tenor	N/A	$3,800 - 4,750	$2,300 - 2,850	

Tenor and plectrum models feature maple necks.

STYLE 4 – German silver body, mahogany neck, ebony fingerboard with pearl square inlay, engraved National logo inlay on pearloid peghead overlay, available in a Chrysanthemum engraving pattern, mfg. 1928-1941.

Spanish	N/A	$18,000 - 22,500	$10,500 - 13,500	
Hawiian	N/A	$6,800 - 8,500	$4,100 - 5,100	

STYLE 35 – nickel plated brass body, mahogany neck (Spanish) or integral neck (Hawaiian), ebony fingerboard with pearl dot inlay, black and white celluloid peghead overlay, available in a Sandblasted Scene of a minstrel, colored with airbrushed enamel, mfg. 1936-1940.

Spanish	N/A	$22,000 - 27,500	$13,250 - 16,500	
Hawaiian	N/A	$8,800 - 11,000	$5,275 - 6,600	

The Style 35 is extremely rare. The Hawaiian featured an ebonoid fingerboard.

STYLE 97 – nickel plated brass body, mahogany neck (maple neck on Hawaiian), ebony fingerboard with pearl dot inlay, black and white celluloid peghead overlay, available in a Sandblasted Scene of a female surfer, colored with airbrushed enamel, mfg. 1936-1940.

Spanish	N/A	$10,000 - 12,500	$6,000 - 7,500	
Hawaiian	N/A	$6,800 - 8,500	$4,100 - 5,100	
Plectrum	N/A	$4,200 - 5,250	$2,500 - 3,150	
Tenor	N/A	$4,000 - 5,000	$2,400 - 3,000	

Tenor and plectrum models feature maple necks, single resonator cone. The Style 97 is extremely rare. The Hawaiian featured an ebonoid fingerboard. The Hawaiian models tend to price closer to their Spanish sisters, because they are convertible.

ACOUSTIC: WOODEN BODY MODELS

Wooden body Nationals have a single resonator cone.

ARAGON – 18 in. body width, spruce top, maple back and sides, 14-fret fingerboard with parallelogram inlays, mfg. circa 1938-1941.

	N/A	$7,200 - 9,000	$4,325 - 5,400	

Bodies for the Aragon model were produced by Harmony or Kay.

EL TROVADOR – laminated mahogany body, mahogany neck, 12-fret fingerboard with pearl dot inlay, slotted peghead, mfg. 1932-33.

	N/A	$2,400 - 3,000	$1,450 - 1,800	

The El Trovador model featured a Kay-built body.

ESTRALIA, ROSITA, TROJAN – wooden body, mfg. circa 1930s to 1940s.

	N/A	$950 - 1,200	$575 - 725	

Most of the wooden body Nationals (Estralia, Rosita, and Trojan) seen today are one of these models. These guitars feature Harmony bodies, usually of birch or basswood. In the words of National expert Bob Brozman, they produce a "mushy sound."

HAVANA – spruce top, 14-fret fingerboard, mfg. circa 1938-1941.

	N/A	$1,000 - 1,250	$600 - 750	

Not much is known about this guitar. The Havana was apparently introduced around the same time as the Aragon, and featured a Kay-built body.

ACOUSTIC: NON-RESONATOR MODELS

MODEL 1150 CONCERT – Martin 000-style concert body, spruce top, mahogany back and sides, round soundhole with ring rosette, ivoroid body binding, mahogany neck, 14/19-fret rosewood fingerboard with dot inlays, three-per-side tuners, rosewood bridge, pickguard, available in Natural finish, mfg. 1948-late 1950s.

	N/A	$950 - 1,200	$575 - 725	

MSR/NOTES	100%	EXCELLENT	AVERAGE	LAST MSR

MODEL 1155 JUMBO – SJ-style jumbo body, spruce top, mahogany back and sides, round soundhole with ring rosette, ivoroid body binding, mahogany neck, 14/20-fret rosewood fingerboard with dot inlays, three-per-side tuners, rosewood bridge, pickguard, available in Golden Shaded Sunburst finish, mfg. 1948-1961.

	N/A	$1,800 - 2,250	$1,075 - 1,350	

The 1155 appeared in several variations according to National's catalog. Later models may feature Natural finish and an electric model was offered in the late 1950s as well.

NATIONAL RESO-PHONIC GUITARS

Instruments currently built in San Luis Obispo, CA since 1988.

Founders Don Young and McGregor Gaines met in 1981. Both worked off-and-on at OMI (the former Dobro Co.) but left due to disagreements with management over production and quality. They established the National Reso-Phonic Guitar Co. in 1988 producing wood body single resonator guitars. In 1992, they made their first metal body reproduction of the Style "O" single cone that was soon followed by the Style "1" Tricone. They continue to make reproductions of older Nationals as well as innovations. For additional information concerning specifications and availability contact National Reso-Phonic Guitars directly.

CONTACT INFORMATION
NATIONAL RESO-PHONIC GUITARS
871 Via Esteban #C
San Luis Obispo, CA 93401
Phone No.: 805-546-8442
Fax No.: 805-546-8430
www.nationalguitars.com
natres@nationalguitars.com

SINGLE CONE RESONATORS

National Reso-Phonic Guitars offers additional resonator instruments including ukuleles, basses, baritone guitars and mandolins.

BENDAWAY RADIO TONE – single rounded cutaway body, maple top/back/sides, slotted upper bout sound ports, maple neck, single resonator, 15/19-fret rosewood fingerboard with ivoroid dot inlay, biscuit bridge, nickel hardware, blackface peghead with logo/art deco design, three-per-side tuners, available in light or dark amber finish, disc. 2005.

	N/A	$850 - 1,000	$500 - 600	$1,760

DELPHI – hollow steel body, two f-holes, maple or mahogany round or square neck, 12/19-fret ivoroid bound rosewood fingerboard with ivoroid dots, single resonator, biscuit bridge, nickel hardware, slotted headstock with logo, three-plate nickel tuners, baked wrinkle finish in a variety of colors, disc. 2010.

	$1,950	$1,275 - 1,500	$750 - 925	$2,300

In 2006, a maple neck replaced the mahogany neck.

* ***Delphi Deluxe*** – similar to the Delphi, except has MOP fingerboard diamond inlays and an ivoroid headstock with an engraved logo, disc. 2010.

	$2,200	$1,425 - 1,700	$850 - 1,050	$2,600

* ***Delphi Vintage Steel*** – similar to the Delphi, except has a steel finish, disc. 2010.

	$2,200	$1,425 - 1,700	$850 - 1,050	$2,600

»***Delphi Vintage Steel Deluxe*** – similar to the Delphi Vintage Steel, except has MOP fingerboard diamond inlays and an ivoroid headstock with an engraved logo, disc. 2010.

	$2,475	$1,600 - 1,875	$950 - 1,150	$2,900

EL TROVADOR – hollow mahogany body, two f-holes, multi-laminate top binding, three-ply ivoroid/black/ivoroid back binding, mahogany neck, 12/19-fret ivoroid-bound ebony fingerboard with MOP dot inlays, rosewood slotted headstock overlay with decal logo, ivoroid truss rod cover, three-per-side open-style tuners, biscuit bridge, 9.5 in. single cone resonator, satin nickel hardware, available in Natural finish, 14.5 in. lower bout width, 4 in. body depth, 25 21/32 in. scale, mfg. summer 2006-present.

MSR $3,400	$2,875	$1,800 - 2,150	$1,075 - 1,325	

This model is styled on a Kay resonator body shape.

ESTRALITA DELUXE – hollow bound wood body, lam. anagre top, lam. walnut back, walnut sides, two f-holes, walnut neck, 12/19-fret bound rosewood fretboard, slotted headstock with pearloid overlay, MOP diamond fretboard inlay, single resonator, biscuit bridge, nickel hardware, three-per-side plate tuners, available in Amber Burst finish, mfg. 2001-present.

MSR $2,900	$2,450	$1,550 - 1,825	$900 - 1,125	

This model replaces the plainer Estralita, made 1997-2001.

M-2 – hollow bound mahogany laminated body, mahogany sides and neck, two f-holes, 12/19-fret bound rosewood fretboard, solid headstock with pearloid overlay, MOP diamond fretboard inlay, single resonator, biscuit bridge, satin nickel hardware, three-per-side plate tuners, 25 in. scale, current mfg.

MSR $2,700	$2,275	$1,425 - 1,700	$850 - 1,050	

The M-2 replaced the M-1, produced 1991-94 (with non-adjustable truss rod) and a last MSR of $1,800.

MODEL D – hollow body, bound laminated spruce top, laminated walnut back, walnut sides, round screened sound ports, walnut round or square neck, 12/19-fret bound ebony fingerboard with ivoroid dots, slotted headstock with silkscreen logo, spider resonator and spider bridge, nickel-plated hardware, three-per-side plate tuners, 25. in scale, disc. 2010.

	$2,300	$1,475 - 1,750	$875 - 1,075	$2,700

Also available as a Deluxe with engraved coverplate, MOP diamond inlay, pearloid headstock overlay, quarter match walnut lam. back for $3,100.

MSR/NOTES	100%	EXCELLENT	AVERAGE	LAST MSR

* **Model D Western** – similar to the Model D, except has a quarter matched laminated walnut burl back, two f-holes (no small soundholes), rope binding, MOP arrowhead fingerboard inlays, and a ivoroid headstock overlay, available in Sunburst finish, disc. 2009.

| | N/A | $2,025 - 2,350 | $1,150 - 1,350 | $3,914 |

REPLICON – brass Style O body that has been aged, maple neck, ebony fingerboard, antiqued decal logo, biscuit bridge, 9.5 in. resonator, all parts of the guitar have been aged to look like it is a relic, current mfg.

| MSR $3,800 | $3,200 | $1,925 - 2,400 | $1,175 - 1,450 | |

RESO ROCKET – hollow steel body, single rounded cutaway to 17th fret, grillwork upper bout sound port, bound ebony fingerboard with MOP diamond inlays, maple neck, solid peghead, pearloid headstock overlay, three-per-side plate nickel tuners, baked wrinkle finish in a variety of colors, current mfg.

| MSR $3,100 | $2,700 | $1,750 - 2,075 | $1,050 - 1,275 | |

* Add 7.5% (MSR $3,300) for Vintage Steel.
* Add 15% (MSR $3,700) for Brass with nickel finish.

RESOLECTRIC – solid mahogany single rounded cutaway with flame maple laminated top, single resonator 14/21-fret rosewood fingerboard with ivoroid inlay, biscuit bridge, solid peghead with logo, three-per-side tuners, ivoroid pickguard, P-90 single coil pickup, Highlander pickup, magnetic volume/Highlander volume/tone chickenhead knob controls, three-way toggle switch, nickel hardware, available in Light or Dark Amber finish, current mfg.

| MSR $2,700 | $2,200 | $1,375 - 1,625 | $850 - 1,000 | |

Earlier models may have a lipstick tube single coil pickup instead of the creme colored P-90 single coil pickup. Similar model, ResoLectric Jr., available with painted maple body, P-90 only, satin nickel hardware for $1,300 in black or red, $1,400 in ivory.

STYLE "O" AND STYLE "N" – hollow nickel-plated brass body, two f-holes, maple neck, 12/19-fret bound ebony fingerboard with ivoroid dot, single resonator, biscuit bridge, slotted peghead with metal logo shield, three-per-side plate nickel tuners, nickel hardware, available in etched Hawaiian design front and back (Style "O") or bright nickel mirror finish (Style "N," disc. 2005), current mfg.

| MSR $3,300 | $2,800 | $1,700 - 2,025 | $1,000 - 1,250 | |

* Add 5% for Style N finish.

Previously available with a fully etched body (Style EN) for $2,750.

* **Style "O" Deluxe** – similar to the Style "O", except has a slightly figured maple neck, MOP fingerboard diamond inlays, an ivoroid headstock with an engraved logo, and a hand-engraved border, current mfg.

| MSR $3,800 | $3,200 | $1,925 - 2,400 | $1,175 - 1,450 | |

* **Style "O" 14-Fret** – similar to the Style "O", except has a folk-style body, 14/19-fret ebony fingerboard, solid headstock with engraved MOP inlay, and a chicken-foot coverplate for the resonator, mfg. 2006-present.

| MSR $3,300 | $2,800 | $1,750 - 2,075 | $1,050 - 1,275 | |

STYLE 3 – similar to the Style 3 Tricone, except has a single cone resonator, two f-holes, disc. 2010.

| | $5,275 | $3,400 - 4,050 | N/A | $6,200 |

TRICONE RESONATORS

POLYCHROME TRICONE – hollow steel body, grillwork upper bout sound ports, maple neck, 12/19-fret bound rosewood fingerboard with ivoroid dots, three resonators, T-bridge, nickel hardware, blackface headstock with logo/art deco design, E-plate tuners, available in baked wrinkle finish in a variety of colors, current mfg.

| MSR $2,700 | $2,300 | $1,475 - 1,750 | $875 - 1,075 | |

* **Polychrome Tricone Baritone** – similar to the Polychrome Tricone, except in baritone configuration, 27 in. scale, current mfg.

| MSR $3,200 | $2,725 | $1,750 - 2,075 | $1,050 - 1,275 | |

* **Polychrome Tricone Cutaway** – similar to the Polychrome Tricone, except has a single cutaway, mfg. 2006-present.

| MSR $3,200 | $2,725 | $1,750 - 2,075 | $1,050 - 1,275 | |

STYLE 1 TRICONE – hollow nickel-plated brass body, grillwork upper bout sound ports, mahogany neck, 12/19-fret bound ebony fingerboard with ivoroid dot inlay, three 6 in. resonators, T-bridge, nickel hardware, slotted peghead with metal logo shield, three-per-side plate tuners, current mfg.

| MSR $3,700 | $3,150 | $1,925 - 2,400 | $1,175 - 1,450 | |

Also available with an etched body (Style 1-E) for $3,360.

* **Style 1.5 Tricone** – similar to the Style 1 Tricone, except has engraved border front, back and sides, current mfg.

| MSR $4,400 | $3,700 | $2,350 - 2,800 | $1,400 - 1,725 | |

* **Style 1 Tricone Baritone** – similar to the Style 1 Tricone, except in baritone configuration, 27 in. scale, current mfg.

| MSR $3,900 | $3,325 | $2,150 - 2,525 | $1,275 - 1,550 | |

* **Style 1 Tricone Cutaway** – similar to the Style 1 Tricone, except has a single cutaway, mfg. 2006-present.

| MSR $4,200 | $3,550 | $2,250 - 2,700 | $1,325 - 1,650 | |

MSR/NOTES	100%	EXCELLENT	AVERAGE	LAST MSR

STYLE 2 TRICONE – similar to the Style 1 except has Rose engraving on front, back, sides; MOP diamond inlay on fingerboard, ivoroid heelcap and headstock overlay with engraved logo; Waverly three-plate tuners, current mfg.

| MSR $4,700 | $4,000 | $2,525 - 3,000 | $1,500 - 1,850 | |

STYLE 3 TRICONE – hollow nickel-plated brass body, "louver" upper bout soundports, mahogany neck, 12/19-fret bound ebony fingerboard with mother-of-pearl dot inlay, tri-cone resonator, bridge/chrome trapeze tailpiece, slotted peghead, ivoroid headstock overlay with logo, three-per-side chrome tuners, available in hand-engraved Lily of the Valley finish, current mfg.

| MSR $6,900 | $5,850 | $3,750 - 4,450 | N/A | |

STYLE 4 TRICONE – similar to the Style 3, except has Chrysanthemum engraving on body, current mfg.

| MSR $7,700 | $6,500 | $4,200 - 4,950 | N/A | |

STYLE 5 TRICONE – similar to the Style 3, except has Acanthus engraving on body, disc. 2005.

| | N/A | $4,000 - 5,000 | N/A | $6,850 |

VINTAGE STEEL TRICONE – hollow steel body, grillwork upper bout sound ports, maple neck, 12/19-fret bound ebony fingerboard with ivoroid dots, three 6 in. resonators, T-bridge, blackface headstock with logo/art deco design, three-per-side plate tuners, nickel hardware, available in Satin Nickel finish, disc. 2010.

| | $2,550 | $1,650 - 1,950 | $975 - 1,200 | $3,000 |

* *Vintage Steel Tricone Cutaway* – similar to the Vintage Steel Tricone, except has a single cutaway, mfg. 2006-2010.

| | $2,975 | $1,925 - 2,275 | $1,150 - 1,400 | $3,500 |

BASS RESONATORS

RTB BASS – single cutaway maple body, lined soundholes by neck, hard rock maple neck, 24-fret ebony fretted or fretless fingerboard with dot inlay, ivoroid binding, two-per-side tuners, chrome hardware, Sunburst finish, disc. 2005.

| | N/A | $1,250 - 1,450 | $725 - 850 | $2,350 |

STYLE N BASS – brass body plated with nickel, two f-soundholes by neck, hard rock maple neck, 24-fret ebony fretted or fretless fingerboard with dot inlay, ivoroid binding, two-per-side tuners, chrome hardware, chrome finish, disc. 2005.

| | N/A | $1,400 - 1,600 | $750 - 900 | $2,650 |

WB BASS – maple body, two f-holes by neck, 24-fret ebony fretted or fretless fingerboard with dot inlay, ivoroid binding, two-per-side tuners, chrome hardware, Sunburst finish, disc. 2005.

| | N/A | $1,150 - 1,350 | $650 - 750 | $2,250 |

NAVARRO, FRANCISCO

Acoustic guitars currently produced in Mexico. Distributed in the U.S. by Memorial Music Imports in Houston, TX (Ron Hudson, president).

Luthier Francisco Navarro builds classical, flamenco, and grand concert style nylon-stringed guitars. Navarro is a famous luthier in Mexico, and he won a national competition in 1989 for his guitar designs. Navarro's guitars are now available in the U.S. through Memorial Music Imports. For more information, visit Navarro's website or contact them directly.

CONTACT INFORMATION
NAVARRO, FRANCISCO
U.S. Distributor: Memorial Music Imports
12649 Memorial Dr.
Houston, TX 77024
Phone No.: 713-461-1060
Fax No.: 713-461-1060
www.francisconavarro.com
francisconavarro_2001@yahoo.com

NEW WORLD GUITAR COMPANY

Instruments currently designed, supervised, and distributed by Hill Guitar Company in Felton, CA and built in China. Previously produced in Ben Lomond, CA.

New World Guitar Company was established in 1995 by American luthier Kenny Hill, in association with Swiss luthier Gil Carnal and guitar dealer Jerry Roberts. These guitars are made exclusively by world class craftsmen in China. Kenny has traveled to each manufacturing site, trained the staff, and oversaw the design, technique and quality control of each model. New World craftsmen have also been trained in the Hill shop in California, and Kenny visits production sites periodically to review guitar production. There are two lines of guitars currently in production: Player and Estudio. For more information contact New World directly.

CONTACT INFORMATION
NEW WORLD GUITAR COMPANY
Distributed by the Hill Guitar Company
8011 Highway 9
Ben Lomond, CA 95005
Phone No.: 831-336-9317
Phone No.: 800-262-8858
Fax No.: 831-336-9428
www.hillguitar.com
khill@hilguitar.com

ACOUSTIC: ARTISAN SERIES

The Artisan line was transferred from the Hill Master Series and features handmade traditional Spanish style construction and French polish finishes. Most Artisan Series models have been discontinued, but 1-2 a month are still produced.

MSR/NOTES	100%	EXCELLENT	AVERAGE	LAST MSR

ALMERIA MODEL – built in the style of Antonio de Torres guitars, Englemann spruce top, Indian rosewood back/sides, Spanish cedar neck, ebony fingerboard, slotted headstock with three-per-side Schaller tuners, 650 mm scale, disc.

	$1,425	$900 - 1,100	$500 - 600	$1,995

FINGERSTYLE – single cutaway body, Englemann spruce top, Indian rosewood back/sides, Spanish cedar neck, ebony fingerboard, slotted headstock with three-per-side Schaller tuners, optional electronics, 650 mm scale, disc. 2006.

	N/A	$900 - 1,100	$500 - 600	$1,995

LA CURVA – cutaway classical model, spruce or cedar top, rosewood or cypress back and sides, ebony fingerboard, Schaller tuners, available in Natural finish, disc.

	$1,550	$1,050 - 1,250	$675 - 800	$2,195

LA TRIANA – traditional flamenco-style guitar, Englemann spruce top, cypress back/sides, Spanish cedar neck, ebony fingerboard, slotted headstock with three-per-side Gotoh tuners, 650 mm scale, disc.

	$1,425	$900 - 1,100	$500 - 600	$1,995

MADRID – built in the style of Jose Ramirez guitars, western red cedar top, Indian rosewood back/sides, Spanish cedar neck, ebony fingerboard, slotted headstock with three-per-side Schaller tuners, 650 mm scale, disc.

	$1,425	$900 - 1,100	$500 - 600	$1,995

MUNICH MODEL – built in the style of Herman Hauser I guitars, Canadian spruce top, Indian rosewood back/sides, 640 or 650 mm scale, ebony fingerboard, slotted headstock with three-per-side Schaller tuners, disc.

	$1,425	$900 - 1,100	$500 - 600	$1,995

ACOUSTIC: ESTUDIO SERIES

The Estudio Series represents New World Guitar's entry-level guitar line. These instruments feature solid tops and laminated back and sides.

ESTUDIO CLASSICAL (90S/90C) – classical style, solid spruce or solid cedar top, Indian rosewood back and sides, round soundhole with rosette, rosewood fingerboard, bone nut, slotted headstock with three-per-side open-style tuners, tied bridge, bone saddle, lacquer Natural finish, 650 mm (25.6 in.) scale, current mfg.

MSR $895	$895	$525 - 650	$325 - 400	

The Estudio Classical is also available in 480mm (18.9 in.), 520mm (20.5 in.), 580mm (22.8 in.), and 615mm (24.2 in.) scale lengths.

* *Estudio Fingerstyle Cutaway (90S/90C Cutaway)* – similar to the Estudio Classical (90S/90C), except has a single cutaway, current mfg.

MSR $995	$995	$575 - 725	$350 - 425	

ESTUDIO CLASSICAL (628S/628C) – classical style, solid spruce or solid cedar top, Indian rosewood back and sides, round soundhole with rosette, rosewood fingerboard, bone nut, slotted headstock with three-per-side open-style tuners, tied bridge, bone saddle, lacquer Natural finish, 628mm (24.75 in.) scale, current mfg.

MSR $895	$895	$525 - 650	$325 - 400	

ACOUSTIC: PLAYER SERIES

The Player Series is New World Guitar's mid-grade line. These guitars feature solid tops, back, and sides.

PLAYER CLASSICAL (130S/130C) – classical style, solid spruce or solid cedar top, solid Indian rosewood back and sides, round soundhole with rosette, ebony fingerboard, bone nut, slotted headstock with three-per-side open-style tuners, tied bridge, bone saddle, lacquer Natural finish, 650mm (25.6 in.) scale, current mfg.

MSR $1,695	$1,695	$1,000 - 1,250	$600 - 750	

The Player Classical is also available in 615mm Parlor (24.2 in.) and 640mm (25.2 in.) scale lengths.

* *Player Classical Cutaway (130S/130C Cutaway)* – similar to the Model 130S/130C, except has a single cutaway, current mfg.

MSR $1,795	$1,795	$1,050 - 1,300	$625 - 775	

PLAYER CLASSICAL (628S/628C) – classical style, solid spruce or solid cedar top, solid Indian rosewood back and sides, round soundhole with rosette, ebony fingerboard, bone nut, slotted headstock with three-per-side open-style tuners, tied bridge, bone saddle, lacquer Natural finish, 24.75 in. scale, current mfg.

MSR $1,695	$1,695	$1,000 - 1,250	$600 - 750	

PLAYER FINGERSTYLE (FS S/C FINGERSTYLE) – single cutaway classical fingerstyle, solid spruce or solid cedar top, solid Indian rosewood back and sides, round soundhole with rosette, narrow neck, ebony fingerboard, bone nut, slotted headstock with three-per-side open-style tuners, tied bridge, bone saddle, lacquer Natural finish, 650mm (25.6 in.) scale, current mfg.

MSR $1,795	$1,795	$1,050 - 1,300	$625 - 775	

PLAYER FLAMENCO – classical Flamenco design, solid spruce or solid cedar top, solid Indian rosewood back and sides, round soundhole with rosette, narrow neck, ebony fingerboard, bone nut, slotted headstock with three-per-side open-style tuners, tied bridge, bone saddle, lacquer Natural finish, 650mm (25.6 in.) scale, current mfg.

MSR $1,695	$1,695	$1,000 - 1,250	$600 - 750	

NICKERSON

Instruments currently built in Ashville, NC since 2006. Previously built in Northampton, MA between the early 1980s and 2005.

CONTACT INFORMATION
NICKERSON
Phone No.: 828-252-4093
www.nickersonguitars.com
nickersonguitars@hotmail.com

Luthier Brad Nickerson, born and raised on Cape Cod, Massachusetts, has been building archtop guitars since 1982. Nickerson attended the Berklee College of Music, and worked in the graphic arts field for a number of years. While continuing his interest in music, Nickerson received valuable advice from New York luthier Carlo Greco, as well as Cape Cod violin builder Donald MacKenzie. Nickerson also gained experience doing repair work for Bay State Vintage Guitars (Boston), and The Fretted Instrument Workshop (Amherst, Massachusetts). With his partner Lyn Hardy, Nickerson builds archtop, flattop, and electric guitars on a custom order basis. Nickerson is also available for restorations and repair work. In 2006, Nickerson moved to Ashville, NC where he currently teaches classes on building guitars. For more information, visit Nickerson's website or contact him directly.

Nickerson's instruments are constructed out of Sitka or European spruce tops, European cello or figured maple back and sides, and ebony tailpiece, bridge, and compound radius fingerboard.

The **Corona** (MSR starts at $6,500) features Sitka or European spruce top, figured maple back/sides, multiple-ply body binding, bound fingerboard/peghead/finger rest, macassar ebony tailpiece/finger rest/peghead, gold Schaller M6 tuners with ebony buttons, available in Blonde, Cherry Sunburst, Brown Sunburst, or custom color nitrocellulose finishes, body width 17 in., body depth 3 in. (or 3.125 in.).

The **Equinox** (MSR starts at $8,000) features European spruce top, European cello maple back/sides, all wood binding, macassar ebony tailpiece/finger rest/peghead veneer, gold Schaller M6 tuners with ebony buttons or Waverly gold tuners, available in Blonde finish, body width 18 in.

The **FC3** (MSR starts at $2,800) is a flattop model, single rounded cutaway, Sitka or European spruce top, wood purfling, cherry binding, Indian rosewood back/sides, laminated walnut neck, 25.25 in. scale, 20-fret fingerboard with pearl diamond inlays, macassar ebony peghead veneer, Schaller M6 mini tuners, available in Natural finish, body width 16 in., body depth 3.375 in. (or 4.375 in.). The **FC3S** (MSR starts at $2,800) is similar to the FC3, except has a narrower body width of 15 in. Both models are also offered in a non-cutaway body version as the Model F3 and F3S.

The **Solstice** (L'Anima MSR starts at $3,800) features a Sitka spruce top, maple back/sides, rock maple neck, body binding, macassar ebony tailpiece/finger rest, macassar ebony or figured maple or burl peghead veneer, Schaller M tuners, available in Shaded Brown, Reddish Brown, and Burnt Tangerine nitrocellulose finishes, body width 15.5 in., body depth 3 in. (or 2.875 in.).

The **Skylark** (MSR starts at $2,700) features a semi-hollow mahogany body, carved spruce top, ivoroid body binding, macassar ebony tailpiece/finger rest/peghead veneer, Schaller M6 mini tuners, available in custom color nitrocellulose finish, body width 14.375 in., body depth 1.75 in.

The **Virtuoso** (MSR starts at $5,700) features a European spruce top, European maple back/sides, all wood binding, macassar ebony tailpiece/finger rest, macassar ebony or figured maple or burl peghead veneer, gold Schaller M6 tuners with ebony buttons, available in Shaded Brown, Reddish Brown, and Burnt Tangerine nitrocellulose finishes, body width 17 in., body depth 3 in. (or 3.125 in.).

- **Add $200 for pickup with endpin jack.**
- **Add $400 for left-handed configuration.**
- **Add $500 for 7-string configuration.**

NOBLE

Instruments previously produced in Italy circa 1950s to 1964. Production models were then built in Japan circa 1965 to 1969. Distributed by Don Noble and Company of Chicago, IL.

Don E. Noble, accordionist and owner of Don Noble and Company (importers), began business importing Italian accordions. By 1950, Noble was also importing and distributing guitars (manufacturer unknown). In 1962 the company began distributing EKO and Oliviero Pigini guitars, and added Wandre instruments the following year.

In the mid-1960s, the Noble trademark was owned by importer/distributor Strum 'N Drum of Chicago. The Noble brand was then used on Japanese-built solid body electrics (made by Tombo) through the late 1960s.

When the Valco/Kay holdings were auctioned off in 1969, Strum 'N Drum bought the rights to the National trademark. Strum 'N Drum began importing Japanese-built versions of popular American designs under the National logo, and discontinued the Noble trademark during the same time period. Source: Michael Wright, *Vintage Guitar Magazine*.

NOBLE, ROY

Instruments currently built in Little Rock, CA since the late 1950s. Distributed by the Stringed Instument Division of Missoula, MT.

CONTACT INFORMATION
NOBLE, ROY
8140 East Avenue U
Little Rock, CA 93543
Phone No.: 661-944-5548
www.roynoble.net
roynoble@adelphia.net

Luthier Roy Noble has been handcrafting acoustic guitars for several years. Noble has been plying his guitar building skills since the 1950s, when he first began building classical instruments after studying the construction of Jose Ramirez's Concert models. Noble later moved to a dreadnought steel string acoustic design in the late 1950s and early 1960s as he practiced his craft repairing vintage instruments, and has produced anywhere from two to twenty guitars a year since then. Noble constantly experimented with the traditional uses of tonewoods, and his designs reflect the innovative use of coco bolo in bridges, and western red cedar for tops.

MSR/NOTES	100%	EXCELLENT	AVERAGE	LAST MSR

In 1964/1965, Noble replaced the top and neck on Clarence White's pre-war Martin D-28 when it came in for repairs (this instrument is currently owned by Tony Rice). White so enjoyed the sound that he later recorded with two Noble acoustics in many of his studio recordings.

Noble currently offers two models, a concert size acoustic or a dreadnought-sized six or twelve-string acoustic. Models are built in one of three configurations. The Standard features mahogany and Indian rosewood construction, while the Deluxe features mahogany, Indian rosewood, koa, pau ferro, or coco bolo. The Custom offers construction with koa, pau ferro, coco bolo or CITES certified Brazilian rosewood. For further information regarding models, specifications, and pricing please visit Noble's website or contact him directly. Source: Michael R. Stanger and Greg Boyd, Stringed Instrument Division.

Standard dreadnought and concert models start at $2,800, semi-custom dreadnought and concert models start at $3,000, and custom dreadnought and concert models start at $3,600. Several options are available for each level as well.

NOBLES, TONY

Instruments currently built in Waverly, TX. Distributed exclusively by Hill Country Guitars in Wimberly, TX.

Luthier Tony Noble builds high quality acoustic guitars and resonators in his Texas shop. Nobles also writes a column for *Vintage Guitar Magazine*. For more information, visit Hill Country's website or contact them directly.

CONTACT INFORMATION
NOBLES, TONY
11 Old Kyle Road, Suite 200
Wimberly, TX 78676
Phone No.: 512-847-8677
www.hillcountryguitars.com
info@hillcountryguitars.com

NORMA

Instruments previously built in Japan between 1965 and 1970 by the Tombo company. Distributed by Strum 'N Drum, Inc., in Chicago, IL.

These Japanese built guitars were distributed in the U.S. market by Strum 'N Drum, Inc. of Chicago, IL. Strum 'N Drum also distributed the Japanese-built Noble guitars of the mid to late 1960s, and National solidbody guitars in the early 1970s. Source: Michael Wright, *Guitar Stories*, Volume One.

NORMAN

Instruments currently built in La Patrie, Quebec, Canada since 1972. Distributed by Godin Guitars (previously La Si Do, Inc.) in Baie D'Urfe Quebec, Canada.

CONTACT INFORMATION
NORMAN
Distributed by Godin Guitars
19420 Ave. Clark Graham
Baie d' Urfe, PQ H9X 3R8
Phone No.: 514-457-7977
Fax No.: 514-457-5774
www.normanguitars.com
info@normanguitars.com

Cabinet maker Normand Boucher from La Patrie, Quebec, built his first guitar in 1967 and in 1968, he set up shop and began producing guitars under the Norman trademark. In 1972, Boucher left the cabinet industry to start building guitars full-time and it is around this same year he met Robert Godin on a hunting trip in La Patrie. Godin founded Sibécor that same year and became the exclusive distributor of the trademark. The company grew in the 1970s and became quite successful. Meanwhile, Godin started Unisonic in 1975 with Norman's son Claude to build classical guitars. By 1979, Normand Boucher and Robert Godin had different views and the contract with Sibécor was cancelled, Boucher started his own distribution. However, Godin owned the entire contact network that made it tough for Boucher to do business. In 1980, the Norman factory burned to the ground and everything was lost forcing Boucher to start over. He continued to produce guitars until the mid '80s when he sold Norman Guitars. It went through two different ownerships before Godin bought the trademark circa 1989. Today, Godin electric guitars are built "down the hill" in the old Norman shop while acoustic guitars are produced in the old Unisonic shop "up the hill." Normand Boucher died in 1997, Claude Boucher went on to build guitars under the Boucher trademark, and Robert Godin is currently president of Godin Guitars and the network of trademarks under Godin Guitars. For more information, visit Norman's website or contact Godin Guitars directly. Source: Daniel Laroche.

ACOUSTIC: PROTÉGÉ (B15/B18) SERIES

B-15 – dreadnought style, wild cherry top, round soundhole, black pickguard, bound body, black ring rosette, wild cherry back/sides, mahogany neck, 14/21-fret rosewood fingerboard with pearl dot inlay, rosewood bridge with white black dot pins, three-per-side chrome tuners, available in Almond Brown (summer 2011-present, 035571), Brown (disc. 2011, 0593), Burgundy (disc. 2004), Natural (disc. 2004), or TobbacoBurst (disc. 2004) finish, current mfg.

MSR $465	$380	$200 - 250	$120 - 150	

- Add 10% for left-handed configuration (disc.).
- Add 42.5% (Last MSR was $535) for Fishman Classic 4T electronics (disc. 2009, 027293).
- Add 25% (MSR $585) for Fishman Presys electronics (2010-present, 027293/035564).

* **B-15 12-String** – similar to the B-15, except in 12-string configuration and six-per-side tuners, disc. 2003.

	N/A	$175 - 225	$110 - 140	$436

- Add 10% for a left-handed configuration.
- Add 30% for Fishman Basic EQ electronics.
- Add 40% for a left-handed configuration and Fishman Basic EQ electronics.

MSR/NOTES	100%	EXCELLENT	AVERAGE	LAST MSR

B-18 – similar to the B-15, except has a solid cedar top, available in Black (021017), Burgundy (021024), or Tobacco Burst (021048) finish, current mfg.

MSR $475	$390	$200 - 250	$120 - 150	

- Add 37.5% (Last MSR was $575) for Fishman Classic 4T electronics (disc. 2009, 027323/027316/027309).
- Add 27.5% (MSR $600) for Fishman Presys electronics (2010-present, 027323/027316/027309).

* B-18 12-String – similar to the B-18, except in 12-string configuration with six-per-side tuners, available in Natural finish (021109), current mfg.

MSR $615	$500	$275 - 325	$150 - 200	

- Add 10% (disc. 2007, last MSR was $585) for left-handed configuration.
- Add 25% (Last MSR was $735) for Fishman Classic 4 electronics (disc. 2009, 027354).
- Add 25% (MSR $757) for Fishman Presys electronics (2010-present, 027354).

* B-18 Cedar – similar to the B-18, except has a solid cedar top, available in Natural finish (021000), current mfg.

MSR $488	$400	$200 - 250	$120 - 150	

- Add 10% (MSR $539) for left-handed configuration (021123).
- Add 32.5% (Last MSR was $595) for Fishman Classic 4 electronics (disc. 2009, 027330).
- Add 25% (MSR $619) for Fishman Presys electronics (2010-present, 027330).
- Add 40% (Last MSR was $635) for left-handed configuration with Fishman Classic 4 electronics (disc. 2009, 027347).
- Add 37.5% (MSR $669) for left-handed configuration with Fishman Presys electronics (2010-present, 027347).

»B-18 Cutaway Cedar – similar to the B-18 Cedar, except has a single cutaway, available in Black (028108), Natural (2011 only, 028092), or Tobacco Burst (028115) finish, mfg. 2008-2011.

	$480	$250 - 300	$150 - 190	$585

- Add 15% (disc. 2009, Last MSR was $669) for Fishman Classic 4T electronics.

»B-18 Cutaway Cedar Electric – similar to the B-18 Cedar Cutaway, except has Fishman Presys electronics, available in Black (028054), Natural (2011-present, 028047), or Tobacco Burst (028061) finish, mfg. 2010-present.

MSR $715	$580	$300 - 375	$175 - 225	

* B-18 Folk Cedar – similar to the B-18, except in folk body configuration and has a solid cedar top, available in Burgundy (034888) or Tobacco Burst (034857) finish, mfg. 2011-present.

MSR $475	$390	$200 - 250	$120 - 150	

- Add 27.5% (MSR $600) for Fishman Presys electronics (034864/034871).

ACOUSTIC: ENCORE (B20) SERIES

B-20 – dreadnought style, solid spruce top, round soundhole, black pickguard, bound body, one ring rosette, cherry back/sides, mahogany neck, 14/21-fret rosewood fingerboard with pearl dot inlay, rosewood bridge with white black dot pins, three-per-side chrome tuners, available in Natural semi-gloss finish (000890), current mfg.

MSR $569	$470	$250 - 300	$150 - 190	

- Add 7.5% (MSR $609) for left-handed configuration (000951).
- Add 32.5% (Last MSR was $649) for Fishman Basic EQ/Classic 4 electronics (disc. 2009, 027378).
- Add 22.5% (MSR $700) for Fishman Basic Presys electronics (2010-present, 027378).
- Add 42.5% (Last MSR was $689) for left-handed configuration with Fishman Basic EQ/Classic 4 electronics (disc. 2009, 027385).
- Add 27.5% (MSR $749) for left-handed configuration with Fishman Presys electronics (2010-present, 027385).
- Add 50% for Fishman Prefix EQ electronics (disc.).

* B-20 HG High Gloss – similar to B-20, available in Black (027477) or Natural (001019) high gloss lacquer finish, current mfg.

MSR $656	$550	$285 - 335	$160 - 200	

- Add 10% (disc. 2007, last MSR was $607) for left-handed configuration.
- Add 7.5% (MSR $729) for Black finish.
- Add 27.5% (Last MSR was $725) for Fishman Classic 4 Electronics (disc. 2009, 027415/027484).
- Add 17.5% (MSR $795) for Fishman Presys Electronics (2010-present, 027415).
- Add 27.5% (MSR $879) for Fishman Presys Electronics in Black finish (2010-present, 027484).
- Add 60% for Fishman Prefix EQ electronics (disc.).
- Add 75% for Fishman Blender EQ electronics (disc.).

* B-20 12-String – similar to the B-20, except in 12-string configuration with six-per-side tuners, available in Natural semi-gloss finish (000920), current mfg.

MSR $699	$570	$300 - 350	$175 - 225	

- Add 5% for left-handed configuration (disc.).
- Add 22.5% (Last MSR was $769) for Fishman Classic 4 electronics (disc. 2009, 027439).
- Add 20% (MSR $829) for Fishman Presys electronics (2010-presenet, 027439).
- Add 50% for Fishman Prefix EQ electronics (disc.).
- Add 70% for Fishman Blender EQ electronics (disc.).

MSR/NOTES	100%	EXCELLENT	AVERAGE	LAST MSR

* **B-20 Cutaway** – similar to the B-20, except has single rounded cutaway, available in Natural semi-gloss finish (000517), disc. 2011.

	$530	$275 - 325	$150 - 200	$649

* Add 25% (Last MSR was $785) for Fishman Classic 4 electronics (disc. 2009, 027453).
* Add 50% for Fishman Prefix EQ electronics (disc.).
* Add 70% for Fishman Blender EQ electronics (disc.).

»**B-20 Cutaway Electric** – similar to the B-20 Cutaway, except has Fishman Presys electronics, available in Natural semi-gloss finish (027453), mfg. 2010-present.

MSR $785	$650	$325 - 425	$175 - 225	

»**B-20 Cutaway HG** – similar to B-20 Cutaway, except has a Natural high gloss finish, disc. 2007.

	N/A	$300 - 350	$175 - 225	$684

* Add 42.5% (Last MSR was $963) for Fishman Prefix EQ electronics.
* Add 60% for Fishman Blender EQ electronics (disc.).

B-20 FOLK – similar to B-20, except has folk-style body, available in Natural semi-gloss finish (033157), current mfg.

MSR $569	$470	$250 - 300	$150 - 190	

* Add 10% (disc. 2007, last MSR was $515) for left-handed configuration.
* Add 32.5% (Last MSR was $649) for Fishman Basic EQ/Classic 4 electronics (disc. 2009, 033140).
* Add 22.5% (MSR $700) for Fishman Presys electronics (2010-present, 033140).
* Add 65% for Fishman Prefix EQ electronics (disc.).

* **B-20 Cutaway Folk** – similar to the B20 Folk, except in a single cutaway body, available in Natural finish (033133), disc. 2011.

	$530	$275 - 325	$150 - 200	$649

* Add 25% (Last MSR was $785) for Fishman Classic 4 Electronics (disc. 2009, 033126).

»**B-20 Cutaway Folk Electric** – similar to the B20 Folk Cutaway, except has Fishman Presys Electronics, available in Natural finish (033126), mfg. 2010-present.

MSR $797	$650	$325 - 425	$175 - 225	

B-20 MINI-JUMBO – similar to the B-20, except in mini-jumbo configuration, available in Natural finish (033171), mfg. 2005-present.

MSR $569	$470	$250 - 300	$150 - 190	

* Add 52.5% (Last MSR was $785) for Fishman Classic 4T electronics (disc. 2009, 033164).
* Add 22.5% (MSR $700) for Fishman Presys electronics (2010-present, 033164).

ACOUSTIC: STUDIO SERIES

ST-30 – dreadnought style, solid spruce top, mahogany back and sides, mahogany neck, rosewood fingerboard, rosewood bridge, mfg. 1980s-1990s.

	N/A	$300 - 350	$175 - 225	

ST-40 – dreadnought style, solid cedar top, round soundhole, black pickguard, bound body, three-stripe rosette, mahogany back/sides/neck, 14/21-fret rosewood fingerboard with pearl dot inlay, rosewood bridge with white black dot pins, three-per-side chrome tuners, available in Natural semi-gloss finish (001071), current mfg.

MSR $769	$630	$325 - 425	$200 - 250	

* Add 27.5% (Last MSR was $695) for Fishman Classic 4 electronics (disc. 2009, 027514).
* Add 17.5% (MSR $899) for Fishman Presys electronics (2010-present, 027514).
* Add 50% for Fishman Prefix EQ electronics (disc.).
* Add 80% for Fishman Blender EQ electronics (disc.).

* **ST-40 Cutaway Electric** – similar to the ST-40, except has a single cutaway and Fishman Prefix (2004-09) or Presys (2010-present) electronics, available in Natural finish (031351), mfg. 2004-present.

MSR $977	$800	$400 - 500	$250 - 300	

* **ST-40 Folk** – similar to the ST-40, except in folk body configuration, available in Natural finish (034031), mfg. 2010-present.

MSR $769	$630	$325 - 425	$200 - 250	

* Add 17.5% (MSR $899) for Fishman Presys electronics (034239).

ST-68 – dreadnought style, solid spruce top, round soundhole, black pickguard, bound body, three-ring wooden inlay rosette, solid rosewood back, rosewood sides, mahogany neck, 14/21-fret ebony fingerboard with pearl dot inlay, ebony bridge with white black dot pins, three-per-side chrome tuners, available in Natural high gloss finish (001255), current mfg.

MSR $1,281	$1,000	$525 - 600	$350 - 425	

* Add 10% for left-handed configuration (disc.).
* Add 25% (Last MSR was $1,379) for Fishman Prefix EQ electronics (disc. 2009, 031665).
* Add 25% (MSR $1,429) for Fishman Presys electronics (2010-present, 031665).
* Add 30% for Fishman Blender EQ electronics (disc).

MSR/NOTES	100%	EXCELLENT	AVERAGE	LAST MSR

* **ST-68 Cutaway** – similar to ST-68, except has a single rounded cutaway body, available in Natural high gloss finish (008346), mfg. 1998-2011.

	$1,200	$625 - 750	$425 - 500	$1,449

- Add 20% (Last MSR was $1,549) for Fishman Prefix EQ electronics (disc. 2009, 031672).
- Add 7.5% (Last MSR was $1,595) for Fishman Presys electronics (2010-2011, 031672).
- Add 30% for Fishman Blender EQ electronics (disc.).

»**ST-68 Cutaway Electric** – similar to ST-68 Cutaway, except has A6T electronics, available in Natural high gloss finish (035885), mfg. 2012-present.

MSR $1,639	$1,350	$675 - 850	$400 - 500	

STUDIO B-50 – dreadnought style, solid spruce top, round soundhole, black pickguard, bound body, three-ring wooden inlay rosette, maple back/sides, mahogany neck, 14/21-fret rosewood fingerboard with pearl dot inlay, rosewood bridge with white black dot pins, three-per-side chrome tuners, available in Natural high gloss finish (021390), current mfg.

MSR $830	$680	$350 - 425	$215 - 265	

- Add 40% (Last MSR was $989) for Fishman Prefix EQ electronics (disc. 2009, 031344).
- Add 17.5% (MSR $989) for Fishman Presys electronics (2010-present, 031344).
- Add 60% for Fishman Blender EQ electronics (disc.).

* **Studio B-50 12-String** – similar to B-50, except has 12-string configuration and six-per-side tuners, available in Natural high gloss finish, disc. 2007.

	N/A	$325 - 400	$200 - 250	$757

- Add 37.5% (Last MSR was $1,036) for Fishman Prefix EQ electronics.
- Add 50% for Fishman Blender EQ electronics (disc.).

NORTHWOOD GUITARS

Instruments currently built in the Shuswap region of British Columbia, Canada since 2007. Previously built in Langley, British Columbia, Canada between 1994 and 2006.

Northwood Guitars started in 1994 in the Fraser valley of British Columbia. Currently located in the Shuswap region of B.C., John McQuarrie builds flat-top solid wood steel string guitars using locally grown Engelmann spruce. For more information, please refer to their website or contact them directly.

CONTACT INFORMATION
NORTHWOOD GUITARS
650 Caouette Rd.
Sorrento, BC V0E 2W1 Canada
Phone No.: 250-803-8118
www.northwoodguitars.com
northwoodguitars@telus.net

Guitar models are available in most styles including; Dreadnought, OM, MJ, 000, 00 as well as both Venetian and Florentine cutaways. Suggested retail prices start at $3,595.00 including case.

NORTHWORTHY

Instruments currently built in England since 1987.

Northworthy currently offers hand crafted acoustic guitars, as well as custom and left-handed models. Previous original design solid body guitars are generally of very good quality, and feature such model designations as the **Dovedale**, **Edale**, and **Milldale**. Models include classical and dreadnought styles (also a few others), as well as a range of

CONTACT INFORMATION
NORTHWORTHY
Derbyshire, England
Phone No.: +44 1335 370806
www.northworthy.com
info@northworthy.com

mandolins, mandolas, octave mandolins, bozoukis, and electric instruments. All instruments are built individually by hand and take into account the customers' preferences regarding neck dimensions, materials and finishes. Prices start at £1,500. For more information, visit Northworthy's website or contact them directly.

NORWOOD

Guitars previously produced in the U.S. during the 1950s.

The Norwood tradmark has shown up on an acoustic guitar that features the "Adjustomatic" neck that can raise or lower the neck to adjust string action. This is similar to the Jeff Babicz patent on his adjustable neck. Very little else is known about this guitar and any information can be submitted directly to Blue Book Publications.

O SECTION
OAHU

Instruments previously built by Kay from the 1930s-1960s, however the Oahu trademark has been used all the way into the 1980s. Previously distributed by the Oahu Publishing Company of Cleveland, OH.

The Oahu Publishing Company offered Hawaiian and Spanish-style acoustic guitars, lap steels, sheet music, and a wide range of accessories during the Hawaiian music craze of pre-war America. Catalogs stress the fact that the company is a major music distributor, but the instruments were really built by the Kay Musical Company. They produced a number of Hawaiian style guitars in the 1930s and 1940s, primarily. In the late 1930s, Oahu developed a line of lap steel guitars and amplifiers. Information courtesy: Michael Wright, *Guitar Stories*, Volume Two.

MSR/NOTES	100%	EXCELLENT	AVERAGE	LAST MSR

ACOUSTIC

MODEL 50K/53K/55K – parlor student size guitars in various configurations, all mahogany body, round or square neck, open or regular style headstock, Natural or Sunburst finish, mfg. 1930s.

	N/A	$250 - 300	$150 - 200	

MODEL 64K/65K – full size Hawaiian guitar, all mahogany body, round soundhole, white binding, square neck (65K) or round neck (64K), available in Natural or Sunburst finish, mfg. 1930s.

	N/A	$350 - 425	$200 - 250	

MODEL 65M – full size Hawaiian guitar, all mahogany body, round soundhole, checkered binding, available in Natural or Sunburst finish, mfg. 1930s.

	N/A	$475 - 600	$275 - 350	

MODEL 66K/67K – concert size Hawaiian guitar, all mahogany body, round soundhole, white binding, square neck (66K) or round neck (67K), available in Natural or Sunburst finish, mfg. 1930s.

	N/A	$475 - 550	$275 - 325	

MODEL 68K/69K DELUXE JUMBO – full size Hawaiian body, spruce top, Brazilian rosewood back and sides, round soundhole with abalone rosette, abalone body binding, square neck (68K) or round neck (69K), rosewood fingerboard with vine inlay, rosewood bridge, standard headstock with inlays and three-per-side tuners, available in Natural finish, mfg. 1930s

	N/A	$3,200 - 4,000	$1,950 - 2,400	

MODEL 71K/72K JUMBO – full size Hawaiian body, spruce top, rosewood back and sides, round soundhole, white body binding, square neck (71K) or round neck (72K), rosewood fingerboard with dot inlay, rosewood bridge, 3-per-side tuners, available in Sunburst finish with floral design, mfg. 1930s

	N/A	$1,600 - 2,000	$950 - 1,200	

The earlier version of this guitar is the Model 68B, which has a black pickguard.

OAKLAND

Instruments previously produced in Japan from the late 1970s through the early 1980s.

These good quality solid body guitars featured both original designs and designs based on classic American favorites. Source: Tony Bacon and Paul Day, *The Guru's Guitar Guide*.

ODC

Instruments previously produced circa 2000. Previously distributed by L.A. Guitar Works in Reseda, CA.

The ODC Odyssey guitar uses the Sound Port Technology system. This patented system has three dobro-style ports on the sides of the guitar that project sound to the player. This way, the sound has more than one place to exit rather than a single round soundhole. The result gives many different options for tonal qualities and a surround sound effect.

ACOUSTIC

ODYSSEY 2000 – single smooth cutaway dreadnought style, solid spruce top, mahogany back/sides/neck, vertical sound channels and three dobro-style sound ports on the side, 14/22-fret rosewood fingerboard with pearl block inlay, three-per-side tuners, rosewood bridge, Piezo pickup with 4-band EQ, gold tuners, available in Black or Natural finish, mfg. circa 2000.

	N/A	$350 - 425	$200 - 250	$699

ODELL

Instruments previously produced by the Vega Guitar Company of Boston, MA, and distributed through the Vega Guitar catalog circa early 1930s to the early 1950s.

Odell acoustic guitars with slotted headstocks were offered through early Vega Guitar catalogs in the early 1930s. In the 1932 catalog, the four Odell models were priced above Harmony guitars, but were not as pricey as the Vega models.

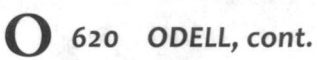

MSR/NOTES	100%	EXCELLENT	AVERAGE	LAST MSR

The four Odell acoustic models featured in the 1932 catalog have a round soundhole, three-per-side brass or nickel-plated tuners, slotted headstock, pearl position dots, and are described as full standard size or concert size. The **Model A** had a white spruce top, mahogany body/neck, black and white purfling, blackwood fingerboard/bridge, and a 1930s list price of $15! The **Model B** featured a mahogany top/body/neck, and rosewood fingerboard/bridge (new list $20). The professional **Model C** had a black and white pyralin bound white spruce top, mahogany body, and a new price of $25. The quartet was rounded out by a four-string **Tenor Guitar** ($15) with mahogany top/body/neck, with the neck joining the body at the 15th fret. Models in excellent condition are found used typically between $400 and $800 depending upon the style.

OLD KRAFTSMAN

Instruments previously produced by Gibson and Kay circa 1930s-1960s. See chapter on House Brands.

This trademark has been identified as a House Brand of Speigel, and was sold through the Speigel catalogs. The Old Kraftsman brand was used on a full line of acoustic, thinline acoustic/electric, and solid body guitars from circa 1930s to the 1960s. Old Kraftsman instruments were probably built by various companies in Chicago, including Kay and some models by Gibson. Source: Michael Wright, *Vintage Guitar Magazine*.

ACOUSTIC

MISC. ACOUSTIC MODELS – various configurations including archtops, various appointments, various finishes, mfg. 1930s-1960s.

	100%	EXCELLENT	AVERAGE	
1930s	N/A	$425 - 500	$250 - 300	
1950s-1960s	N/A	$300 - 350	$175 - 225	

OLSEN AUDIO

Instruments previously built in Saskatoon, Saskatchewan, Canada.

Luthier Bryan Olsen built guitars and performed repairs for a number of years. One project featured a metal bodied tricone-style resonator guitar with a single cutaway. The body shape has been designed from the ground up, and has an innovative stacked cone tray assembly.

OLSON, JAMES A.

Instruments currently built in Circle Pines, MN, since 1977.

CONTACT INFORMATION
OLSON, JAMES A.
11840 Sunset Ave.
Circle Pines, MN 55014
Phone No.: 763-780-5301
Fax No.: 763-780-8513
www.olsonguitars.com
jolson@olsonguitars.com

Luthier James A. Olson began building acoustic guitars full time in 1977. Olson had previous backgrounds in woodworking and guitar playing, and combined his past favorites into his current occupation. Olson's creations have been used by James Taylor (since 1989), Phil Keaggy, Sting, Leo Kottke, Justin Hayward (Moody Blues), and Kathy Mattea.

Olson handcrafts sixty guitars a year, and currently has a waiting list. All models are custom made with a wide variety of options to choose from. Olson builds in either the **SJ** (Small Jumbo) or **Dreadnought** configuration, and features East Indian rosewood back and sides, a Sitka spruce or western red cedar top, and a five-piece laminated neck (rosewood center, maple, and mahogany outer sections). Either configuration also offers an ebony fingerboard, bridge, and peghead overlay, tortoiseshell bound body, bound headstock and side purfling, herringbone top purfling, mother-of-pearl fingerboard position dots, a carved volute on back of the headstock, chrome Schaller tuners, and gloss nitro-cellulose lacquer finish. Olson will accomodate most requests for $12,500. For a complete listing of available options, or for further information visit Olson's website or contact him directly.

OLYMPIA

Instruments previously produced in Korea until 2006. Distributed by Fender Musical Instrument Corporation in Scottsdale, AZ. Previously distributed by Tacoma Guitars USA of Tacoma, WA.

Olympia instruments are engineered and set up in the U.S., and feature a number of dreadnought and jumbo body style models with designs based on the U.S.-produced Tacoma acoustic guitars. Guitars are priced affordable. Tacoma's distribution was switched to Fender in 2005, and along with that came the Olympia line of guitars. By 2006, Olympia guitars had disappeared from Fender's website and the status of the brand is unknown.

ACOUSTIC: CLASSICAL AND DREADNOUGHT SERIES

OC2/OD2/OP2 (NO. 039-5100/5110/5120) – 3/4 sized models, classical, dreadnought, or parlor design, spruce top, catalpa back and sides, Natural finish, disc. 2006.

	100%	EXCELLENT	AVERAGE	LAST MSR
	N/A	$70 - 90	$30 - 50	$200

OC5 (NO. 039-0200) – classical nylon string configuration, spruce top, mahogany back and sides, rosewood fingerboard and bridge, Amber Gloss finish, disc. 2006.

	100%	EXCELLENT	AVERAGE	LAST MSR
	N/A	$150 - 180	$95 - 120	$367

MSR/NOTES	100%	EXCELLENT	AVERAGE	LAST MSR

* *OC5CE (No. 039-0210)* – similar to the OC5, except is in single cutaway configuration with active 4-band electronics, disc. 2006.

	N/A	$180 - 230	$120 - 150	$467

OC10S (NO. 039-0100) – classical nylon string configuration, solid spruce top, mahogany back and sides, rosewood fingerboard and bridge, Natural Gloss finish, disc. 2006.

	N/A	$170 - 210	$105 - 135	$433

* *OC10SCE (No. 039-0110)* – similar to the OC10S, except is in single cutaway configuration with active 4-band electronics, disc. 2006.

	N/A	$210 - 260	$130 - 160	$533

OD3 (NO. 039-5130) – dreadnought style, spruce top, mahogany back and sides, rosewood fingerboard and bridge, Natural finish, disc. 2006.

	N/A	$105 - 130	$60 - 80	$283

OD4SB (NO. 039-5400) – dreadnought style, spruce top, mahogany back and sides, rosewood fingerboard and bridge, gold hardware, Sunburst finish, disc. 2006.

	N/A	$115 - 145	$65 - 85	$317

OD5 (NO. 039-5500) – dreadnought style, spruce top, mahogany back and sides, white binding, rosewood fingerboard and bridge, Natural finish, disc. 2006.

	N/A	$110 - 140	$65 - 85	$300

OD10S (NO. 039-5200) – dreadnought style, solid spruce top, mahogany back and sides, mulit-bound B/H, abalone rosette, rosewood fingerboard and bridge, Natural finish, disc. 2006.

	N/A	$180 - 230	$120 - 150	$467

* *OD10SCE (No. 039-5220)* – similar to the OD10S, except has a single cutaway, active 4-band EQ, and a digital tuner, disc. 2006.

	N/A	$225 - 275	$130 - 170	$550

ACOUSTIC: WING SOUNDHOLE SERIES

OMC1CE (NO. 039-1600) – orchestra model style, single cutaway, solid cedar top, MisChief wing soundhole, solid mahogany back and sides, Fishman Classic 4 electronics, Natural Satin finish, disc. 2006.

	N/A	$225 - 275	$130 - 160	$583

OMC11CE6 (NO. 039-1300) – orchestra model style, single cutaway, ash top/back/sides, MisChief wing soundhole, solid mahogany back and sides,Tacoma E6 Miratone electronics and LR Baggs pickup, electronics, available in Natural, Trans. Black, or Trans. Blue Gloss finish, disc. 2006.

	N/A	$275 - 325	$150 - 200	$667

ACOUSTIC BASS

OB3CE (NO. 039-1000) – single cutaway bass style, spruce top, mahogany back and sides, wing soundhole, set neck, Fishman Classic 4 electronics, Natural finish, 34 in. scale, disc. 2006.

	N/A	$220 - 270	$140 - 180	$563

OMEGA INSTRUMENTS

Instruments currently built in Saylorsburg, PA, since 1996. Distributed by Kevin Gallagher Guitars, Inc. in Saylorsburg, PA.

Luthier Kevin Gallagher is currently offering a range of quality, handcrafted acoustic guitars from his shop in Saylorsburg. Gallagher's Omega Instruments are offered in dreadnought, jumbo (and mini-jumbo), grand concert, and "000" style guitar models. In addition to a well-built, good sounding instrument, Gallagher also offers high quality inlay work that ranges from simple dots to a full fingerboard vine inlay.

OPTEK

See Fretlight.

OPUS

Instruments previously produced in Japan during the mid-1970s

The Opus trademark is a brand name of U.S. importers Ampeg/Selmer. Source: Michael Wright, *Guitar Stories,* Volume One.

ORBIT

Instruments previously built in Japan during the mid- to late 1960s. See Teisco Del Rey.

The Orbit trademark is the brand name of a UK importer. Orbit guitars were produced by the same folks who built Teisco guitars in Japan, so while there is the relative coolness of the original Teisco design, the entry level quality is the drawback. Source: Tony Bacon and Paul Day, *The Guru's Guitar Guide.*

ORIGINAL HOUND DOG

Instruments previously produced in Japan during the mid-1990s.

The Original Hound Dog trademark has appeared on many different resonator guitars, but according to sources, it has only appeared on a line of acoustic flattops that were produced in Japan during the mid-1970s. These acoustics are similar to many popular Martin acoustics from the 1970s including a D-35-style guitar with a three-piece back. Serial numbers are six digits inked on the back of the headstock similar to Gibson's serial numbers from the 1960s and 1970s. Any further information on the Original Hound Dog trademark can be submitted directly to Blue Book Publications.

ORIGINAL MUSIC INSTRUMENT COMPANY, INC (OMI)

Instruments currently produced in Nashville, TN (previous production was located in Long Beach, CA through December, 1996). Distributed by Gibson Guitar Corporation of Nashville, TN.

CONTACT INFORMATION
ORIGINAL MUSIC INSTRUMENT COMPANY, INC (OMI)
641 Massman Drive
Nashville, TN 37210
Phone No.: 615-871-9585
www.gibson.com
service@gibson.com

In 1960, Emil Dopyera and brothers Rudy and John founded the Original Music Instrument company to build resonator guitars. They soon resumed production on models based on their wood-body Dobros. In the late 1960s, OMI also began production of metal-bodied resonators roughly similar to their old National designs. Ron Lazar, a Dopyera nephew, took over the business in the early 1970s. In 1993, OMI was sold to the Gibson Guitar Corporation, and in 1997/1998 production moved to Nashville, TN. For further information on OMI/Dobro, see current model listings under Dobro. Early company history courtesy Bob Brozman, *The History and Artistry of National Resonator Instruments*.

ORIOLO GUITARS

Instruments currently produced in Korea and China since 2010. Distributed by Oriolo Guitars in Hamburg, NJ.

CONTACT INFORMATION
ORIOLO GUITARS
123 Route 23 S.
Hamburg, NJ 07419
Phone No.: 866-973-8880
Fax No.: 973-209-8899
www.oriologuitars.com
don@oriologuitars.com

Don Oriolo founded Oriolo Guitars in 2010 and officially launched the brand at the 2010 Summer NAMM show. Oriolo owns the Felix the Cat trademark and has developed his own line of guitars with unique designs featuring Felix the Cat. Oriolo worked with luthier Tony DiDomencio to make his designs reality and guitars are all produced overseas. Guitars are targeted for the entry-level to mid-range market. For more information, visit Oriolo's website or contact them directly.

ORISKANY STRINGED INSTRUMENTS

Instruments currently produced in Huntingdon, PA since 2002.

CONTACT INFORMATION
ORISKANY STRINGED INSTRUMENTS
7951 Oriskany Lane
Huntingdon, PA 16652
Phone No.: 814-643-3588
www.oriskanyguitars.com
luthiers@oriskanyguitars.com

Luthiers Curtis Rockwell and Johanna Mutti build custom acoustic guitars in the rolling hills of central Pennsylvania. Oriskany offers three basic body styles (A, B, and C) and base prices start at $4,000 with several options available. They build about twelve guitars a year and they also do instrument repair. For more information, visit Oriskany's website or contact them directly.

ORLANDO

Instruments previously produced in Japan during the mid-1970s.

Orlando guitars produced a line of acoustic guitars in the Japanese craze of guitars during the 1970s. Classical and other models were available with basic features. One classical model featured a very blonde body with a regular style headstock. Most guitars can be found for under $100 used. Information courtesy: Steve Cherne.

ORPHEUM

Instruments previously manufactured in Chicago, IL during the 1930s and 1940s, in Japan during the 1960s, and in Asia, between 2001 and 2006. Instruments Distributed by William L. Lange Company of New York, NY, and by C. Bruno & Son until 1942. Distributed by Maurice Lipsky Music Company, Inc., of New York, NY between 1944 and the early 1970s, by Tacoma Guitars between 2001 and 2004 and by Fender Musical Instruments Corporation between 2005 and 2006. Also see Lange.

The Orpheum trademark goes back to 1901. Orpheum guitars were first introduced by distributor William L. Lange Company of New York in the mid-1930s. The Orpheum brand instruments were also distributed by C. Bruno & Son during this early period. It is estimated that some of the Orpheum models were built in Chicago, IL by the Kay company.

Lange's company went out of business in the early 1940s, but New York distributor Maurice Lipsky resumed distribution of Orpheum guitars circa 1944. The Maurice Lipsky Music Company continued distributing Orpheum guitars, through to the 1960s (see also Domino).

Until more research is done in the Orpheum area, prices will continue to fluctuate. Be very cautious in the distinction between the American models and the later overseas models produced in Japan. "What the market will bear" remains the watchword for Orpheums.

MSR/NOTES	100%	EXCELLENT	AVERAGE	LAST MSR

In 2001, Tacoma reintroduced the Orpheum brand name on a line of acoustic instruments. In 2005, when Fender bought Tacoma and related trademarks, Orpheum became only a bluegrass trademark as mandolins, resonators, and banjos were offered. By 2006, Orpheum no longer appeared with Fender, and the status of the trademark is unknown. Sources: Tom Wheeler, *American Guitars*, Orpheum Manufacturing Company catalog courtesy John Kinnemeyer, JK Lutherie.

ORVILLE/ORVILLE BY GIBSON

Guitars previously produced in Japan between the mid-1980s and early 1990s. Distributed in the Japanese market only.

Orville and Orville by Gibson guitars are actually Japanese-built guitars that Gibson licensed. Gibson signed a deal with Fuji Gen Gakki to build Gibson-approved copies in their Japanese factory and distribute them in the Japanese market. All guitars are exact copies of authentic Gibson instruments including J-45s, J-160Es, J-200s, Doves, Hummingbirds, Chet Atkins thinbodies, L-00s, L-1s, as well as a line of electric guitars and basses. Since these guitars were designed for Japanese distribution only, very few were imported into the U.S. market although more examples are showing up. Prices generally run between $800 and $1,200 on used instruments in excellent condition. Look for more information in further editions of the *Blue Book of Acoustic Guitars*.

OSCAR SCHMIDT

Instruments currently built in China. Previously produced in Korea between the 1970s and early 2000s. Distributed by U.S. Music Corp. in Buffalo Grove, IL. Oscar Schmidt originally produced guitars in the U.S. between the late 1800s to circa 1939.

CONTACT INFORMATION
OSCAR SCHMIDT
Distributed by U.S. Music Corp.
1000 Corporate Grove Drive
Buffalo Grove, IL 60089
Phone No.: 847-949-0444
Phone No.: 800-877-6863
Fax No.: 847-949-8444
www.oscarschmidt.com
guitar.support@usmusiccorp.com

The original Oscar Schmidt company was based in Jersey City, New Jersey, and was established in the late 1800s by Oscar Schmidt and his son, Walter. The Oscar Schmidt company produced a wide range of stringed instruments and some of the trade names utilized were Stella, Sovereign, and LaScala among others. The company later changed its name to Oscar Schmidt International, and in 1935 or 1936 followed with the Fretted Instrument Manufacturers. After the company went bankrupt, the Harmony Company of Chicago, Illinois purchased rights to use Oscar Schmidt's trademarks in 1939.

In the late 1970s, the Oscar Schmidt trademark was revived by the Washburn International Company of Illinois. Oscar Schmidt currently offers acoustic, electric, and bass guitars as well as other instruments such as ukuleles and banjos for the beginning student up to the intermediate player. Source: Tom Wheeler, *American Guitars*.

ACOUSTIC: CLASSICAL

OC1 – classical body, agathis top, mahogany back and sides, nylon strings, available in Natural Satin finish, current mfg.

MSR $130	$80	$40 - 60	$20 - 30	

OC9 – classical body, mahogany top, back and sides, nylon strings, available in Natural finish, current mfg.

MSR $160	$95	$60 - 80	$30 - 40	

OC11 – classical body, select spruce top, mahogany back and sides, available in Natural finish, current mfg.

MSR $210	$125	$80 - 100	$50 - 65	

* OC11 CE – similar to the OC11, except has a single cutaway with electronics, current mfg.

MSR $320	$190	$100 - 130	$60 - 80	

OCHS – 1/2-sized classical body, select spruce top, Catalpa sides and back, round soundhole with classical-style rosette, mahogany neck, 12/19-fret rosewood fingerboard, slotted headstock, three-per-side open-style tuners, rosewood tied bridge, high-gloss Natural finish, mfg. 2008-present.

MSR $116	$70	$40 - 50	$20 - 30	

ACOUSTIC: DREADNOUGHT/FOLK MODELS

OF2 – folk style, spruce top, mahogany back and sides, mahogany neck, rosewood fingerboard, black pickguard, matching headstock, adjustable truss rod, chrome hardware, available in Cherry Sunburst, Natural, Pink, Trans. Blue, or Trans. Green finish, current mfg.

MSR $200	$120	$70 - 95	$35 - 50	

OG1 – dreadnought style, spruce top, catalpa back and sides, mahogany neck, rosewood fingerboard, black pickguard, chrome hardware, available in Black, Flame Yellow Sunburst, Natural, Trans. Blue, or Trans. Red finish, current mfg.

MSR $170	$100	$50 - 75	$30 - 40	

OG2 – dreadnought style, spruce top, mahogany back and sides, mahogany neck, rosewood fingerboard, black pickguard, matching headstock, adjustable truss rod, chrome hardware, available in Black, Natural, Trans. Blue, Trans. Red, or White finish, current mfg.

MSR $200	$120	$70 - 95	$35 - 50	

* Add 5% (MSR $210) for left-handed configuration.
* Add 10% (MSR $220) for flame top (Model OG2F, mfg. 2005-present, Yellow Sunburst or Black Cherry).

MSR/NOTES	100%	EXCELLENT	AVERAGE	LAST MSR

* OG2 CE Cutaway Electric – similar to the OG2, except has a single cutaway with electronics, available in Blue, Natural, Trans. Red, White (disc.), or Yellow Sunburst finish, current mfg.

MSR $300	$180	$100 - 130	$60 - 80	

• **Add 10% (MSR $330) for flame top (Model OG2 CEF, 2006-present).**

OG2M – dreadnought body, mahogany top, back and sides, available in Natural finish, disc. 2003.

	N/A	$100 - 130	$60 - 80	$269

• **Add $10 for Transparent Red and Transparent finishes.**

OG2N – dreadnought body, select spruce top, mahogany back and sides, available in Natural finish, disc. 2003.

	N/A	$105 - 135	$65 - 85	$279

• **Add $30 for left-hand model (OG2NLH).**

OG3 – dreadnought style, select spruce top, mahogany back and sides, decorative rosette, mahogany neck, rosewood fingerboard, black pickguard, adjustable truss rod, chrome hardware, available in Natural finish, current mfg.

MSR $310	$190	$110 - 140	$70 - 90	

* OG312 12-String – similar to the OG3, except in 12-string configuration and six-per-side tuners, current mfg.

MSR $320	$195	$110 - 140	$70 - 90	

» OG312 CE 12-String Cutaway Electric – similar to the OG312, except has a single cutaway and electronics, current mfg.

MSR $420	$250	$150 - 190	$95 - 120	

OG3S – dreadnought body, solid spruce top, mahogany back and sides, Schaller tuners, available in High Gloss Natural finish, mfg. 2001-03.

	N/A	$125 - 175	$75 - 100	$369

OG5SW – dreadnought style, solid mahogany top, solid mahogany back and sides, decorative rosette, mahogany neck, rosewood fingerboard, matching headstock, black pickguard, adjustable truss rod, chrome hardware, available in Natural finish, mfg. 2004-06.

	N/A	$125 - 165	$80 - 100	$390

OG6S – dreadnought style, solid spruce top, rosewood back and sides, herringbone top binding, bound neck and headstock, mahogany neck, rosewood fingerboard, matching headstock, tortoise pickguard, adjustable truss rod, gold hardware, available in Natural finish, current mfg.

MSR $390	$240	$135 - 175	$90 - 110	

OG8 CE CUTAWAY ELECTRIC – single cutaway folk-style, spruce top, catalpa back and sides, decorative rosette, mahogany neck, rosewood fingerboard, three-per-side chrome tuners, rosewood bridge, pickup and active electronics, available in Black or Natural finish, mfg. 2006-present.

MSR $300	$180	$100 - 130	$60 - 80	

OG10 CE CUTAWAY ELECTRIC – jumbo single cutaway style, hardwood flame top/back/sides, herringbone top binding, bound neck, mahogany neck, rosewood fingerboard, matching headstock, tortoise pickguard, adjustable truss rod, electronics and pickup, chrome hardware, available in Natural, Trans. Blue, Trans. Red, or White finish, current mfg.

MSR $320	$195	$110 - 140	$70 - 90	

OG11 CE CUTAWAY ELECTRIC – dreadnought body with single cutaway, select spruce top, rosewood fingerboard, dot position markers, 3-per-side tuners, passive pickups, available in Natural finish, disc. 2003.

	N/A	$150 - 200	$100 - 125	$399

• **Add $70 for Ash top. Available in Antique Natural and Transparent Red finishes.**

OG20 CE CUTAWAY ELECTRIC – dreadnought body, ash top, active pickups, rosewood fingerboard with dot position markers, available in Trans Red, Trans Blue, Black Pearl, or Metallic Apple finishes, disc. 2003.

	N/A	$175 - 225	$110 - 140	$449

OG240 – dreadnought body, select spruce top, mahogany back and sides, 3-per-side tuners, black pickguard, available in Natural finish, disc. 2003.

	N/A	$90 - 110	$50 - 65	$199

OG260 – similar to Model OG240, except has basswood top, back and sides, available in Semi-Satin finish, disc. 2003.

	N/A	$100 - 130	$60 - 90	$249

OGHS – 1/2-size dreadnought body, select spruce top, Catalpa back and sides, round soundhole with three-ring rosette, white binding with tortoise top border inlay, mahogany neck, 14/20-fret bound rosewood fingerboard with pearl dot inlays, three-per-side chrome tuners, rosewood moustache bridge, no pickguard, available in high-gloss Black or Natural finish, mfg. 2008-present.

MSR $146	$90	$50 - 70	$30 - 40	

ACOUSTIC ELECTRIC BASS

OB100 – single cutaway body, spruce top, mahogany back and sides, mahogany neck, body and neck binding, 22-fret rosewood fingerboard, matching headstock, rosewood bridge, electronics, chrome hardware, available in Black or Natural finish, current mfg.

MSR $480	$295	$150 - 200	$100 - 125	

OSTHOFF, JOHN GUITARS

Guitars currently produced in Becket, MA.

Luthier John Osthoff builds guitars in his one-man shop in Becket, MA. All guitars are individually built from start to finish by Osthoff and guitars start at $3,850. Models are available in four main sizes including auditorium, dreadnought, jumbo, and the O Series. A Custom Series is also available and several options are available on all guitars. For more information visit Osthoff's website or contact him directly.

CONTACT INFORMATION
OSTHOFF, JOHN GUITARS
52 Pill Drive
Becket, MA 01223
Phone No.: 413-623-6106
www.osthoffguitars.com
luthier@osthoffguitars.com

OUTBOUND

Instruments previously built in Boulder, CO between 1990 and 2002.

Outbound produced a scaled down travel guitar that maintains the look of a regular acoustic.

OVATION

Instruments currently produced in China, Korea, and Indonesia. Previously built in New Hartford, CT between 1967 and 2014. Distributed by KMC Music in Bloomfield, CT.

The Ovation guitar company, and the nature of the Ovation guitar's synthetic back are directly attributed to founder Charles H. Kaman's experiments in helicopter aviation. Kaman, who began playing guitar back in high school, trained in the field of aeronautics and graduated from the Catholic University in Washington, D.C. His first job in 1940 was with a division of United Aircraft, home of aircraft inventor Igor Sikorsky. In 1945, Kaman formed the Kaman Aircraft Corporation to pursue his helicopter-related inventions.

CONTACT INFORMATION
OVATION
Distributed by KMC Music
55 Griffin Road South
Bloomfield, CT 06002-0507
Phone No.: 860-379-7575
Phone No.: 800-813-1634
Fax No.: 860-243-7287
www.ovationguitars.com
askus@ovationguitars.com

As the company began to grow, the decision was made around 1957 to diversify into manufacturing products in different fields. Kaman initially made overtures to the Martin company, as well as exploring both Harmony and Ludwig drums. Finally, the decision was made to start fresh. Due to research in vibrations and resonances in the materials used to build helicopter blades, guitar development began in 1964 with employees John Ringso and Jim Rickard. In fact, it was Rickard's pre-war Martin D-45 that was used as the "test standard." In 1967, the Ovation company name was chosen, incorporated, and settled into its "new facilities" in New Hartford, Connecticut. The first model named that year was the Balladeer.

Ovation guitars were debuted at the 1967 NAMM show. Early players and endorsers included Josh White, Charlie Byrd, and Glen Campbell. Piezo pickup equipped models were introduced in 1972, as well as other models. During the early 1970s, Kaman Music (Ovation's parent company) acquired the well-known music distributors Coast, and also part of the Takamine guitar company. By 1975, Ovation decided to release an entry level instrument, and the original Applause/Medallion/Matrix designs were first built in the U.S. before production moved into Korea.

In 1986, Kaman's oldest son became president of Kaman Music. Charles William Bill Kaman II had begun working in the Ovation factory at age 14. After graduating college in 1974, Bill was made Director of Development at the Moosup, Connecticut plant. A noted Travis Bean guitar collector (see Kaman's Travis Bean history later in this book), Bill Kaman remained active in the research and development aspect of model design. Kaman helped design the Viper III, and the UK II solid bodies.

Bill Kaman gathered all branches of the company under one roof as the Kaman Music Corporation (KMC) in 1986. As the Ovation branch was now concentrating on acoustic and acoustic/electric models, the corporation bought the independent Hamer company in 1988 as the means to re-enter the solid body guitar market. In 2007, Ovation returned from nearly twenty years in electric hiatus with the VXT Hybrid model. This guitar has both acoustic and electric capabilities with two exposed humbucker pickups and a Fishman bridge pickup. In late 2007, the Fender Musical Instrument Corporation (FMIC) acquired Kaman Music, which included Ovation. In 2008, Kaman Music changed the name of their company to KMC Music. On January 31, 2011 Charles Kaman passed away at the age of 91. In June 2014, Fender closed the Ovation factory in Connecticut leaving only overseas production of Ovation guitars. Source: Walter Carter, *The History of the Ovation Guitar*.

FOUR DIGIT MODEL CODES

Ovation instruments are identified by a four digit model code. The individual numbers within the code will indicate production information about that model.

The first digit is (generally) 1.

The second digit describes the type of guitar:

1 Acoustic roundbacks or semi-hollow electric

2 Solidbody or semi-hollow electric

3 Ultra acoustics

4 Solidbody

5 Acoustic/Electric cutaway Adamas and II/Elite/Ultra electric

6 Acoustic//Electric roundback

7 Deep

8 Shallow

The third digit indicates the depth of the guitar's bowl:

1 Standard

2 Artist

3 Elite/Matrix electric deep bowl

4 Matrix shallow bowl

5 Custom Balladeer/Legend/Legend 12/Custom Legend 12/Anniversary

6 Cutaway electric, deep bowl

7 Cutaway electric, shallow bowl

8 Adamas

MSR/NOTES	100%	EXCELLENT	AVERAGE	LAST MSR

The fourth digit indicates the model (for the first 8 acoustics):

1 Balladeer	4 Josh White	7 Glen Campbell Artist Balladeer
2 Deluxe Balladeer	5 12-String	8 Glen Campbell 12-String
3 Classic	6 Contemporary Folk Classic	

The color code follows the hyphen after the four digit model number. Colors available on Ovation guitars:

1 Sunburst	6 White	9 Brown
2 Red	7 LTD Nutmeg/Anniversary Brown/ Beige/Tan	B Barnwood (a grey to black sunburst)
4 Natural		
5 Black	8 Blue	H Honeyburst

ACOUSTIC: GENERAL INFORMATION

Ovation is currently offering a 8-string Mandolin (**Model MM68**) and 8-string Mandocello (**Model MC868**). Both models feature a solid Sitka spruce top, 21-fret ebony fingerboard, gold hardware, and onboard preamp. The Mandolin has a list price of $1,499, and the Mandocello is $2,199.

Select Ovation acoustic/electric models can be ordered with a factory installed **Roland GK-2** synthesizer interface as an option. This option includes a magnetic hex pickup, synth/guitar mix controls, and a controller output jack.

All Ovation acoustic and acoustic/electric instruments have a synthetic rounded back/sides construction. The model number in parenthesis following the name is the current assigned **Model Number**.

In 1976/1977, Ovation debuted the Medallion series guitars -- which was later renamed the Matrix series. These models were produced in the U.S., and featured a wood top, synthetic bowl back, and plastic headstock overlay. The original list price was $249.

Ovation has released several Anniversary models over the years as many guitar companies do, to commemorate how many years they have been in business. Several of these models haven't been circulated in the secondary market and little is known about them.

ACOUSTIC: ADAMAS SERIES

All Adamas models have a composite top consisting of 2 carbon-graphite layers around a birch core, and carved fiberglass body binding. There are also 11 various sized soundholes with leaf pattern maple veneer around them, situated around the upper bouts on both sides of the fingerboard. The Adamas model was introduced in 1976, and discontinued in 1999. This model was discontinued under the Ovation label, and Adamas became its own name. See Adamas in the A section for models produced since 1999.

ADAMAS 6 ACOUSTIC (MODEL 1187) – carbon graphite composite top, mahogany neck, 14/24-fret walnut extended fingerboard with maple/ebony inlay, 11 various sized soundholes with leaf pattern maple veneer around them, walnut bridge with carved flower designs, carved flower design on peghead, 3-per-side gold tuners, available in Blue finish, mfg.1977-1990.

1977-1979	N/A	$1,600 - 2,000	$950 - 1,200
1980-1990	N/A	$1,275 - 1,600	$750 - 950

* *Adamas 6 Acoustic Wide Neck (Model 1189)* – similar to the Adamas 6 Acoustic, except has a wide neck, mfg. 1979-1990.

N/A	$1,275 - 1,600	$750 - 950

ADAMAS 6 ELECTRIC (MODEL 1687) – carbon graphite composite top, mahogany neck, 14/24-fret walnut extended fingerboard with maple/ebony inlay, 11 various sized soundholes with leaf pattern maple veneer around them, walnut bridge with carved flower designs, carved flower design on peghead, 3-per-side gold tuners, 6 piezo bridge pickups, volume/3-band EQ controls, active OP-24 preamp, available in Blue finish, mfg.1977-1998.

N/A	$1,275 - 1,600	$750 - 950	$3,099

Earlier models may have Beige, Black, Brown, or Red finishes.

* *Adamas 6 Electric Wide Neck (Model 1689)* – similar to the Adamas 6 Electric, except has a wide neck, mfg. 1979-1993.

N/A	$1,275 - 1,600	$750 - 950	$2,799

ADAMAS 6 CUTAWAY ACOUSTIC (MODEL 1587) – carbon graphite composite top, single Venetian cutaway body, mahogany neck, 14/24-fret walnut extended fingerboard with maple/ebony inlay, 11 various sized soundholes with leaf pattern maple veneer around them, no soundholes on cutaway side, walnut bridge with carved flower designs, carved flower design on peghead, 3-per-side gold tuners, available in red, blue, or black finish, mfg.1979-1998.

N/A	$1,275 - 1,600	$750 - 950	$3,199

ADAMAS CUTAWAY ELECTRIC (MODEL 6581) – deep lyrachord bowl, carbon graphite/birch composite top, mahogany neck, 14/24-fret ebony extended fingerboard, ebony bridge, natural peghead with Adamas logo, 3-per-side gold tuners, Optima pickup system, available in High Gloss Black or Opaque Burgundy finish, mfg. 1998 only.

N/A	$1,050 - 1,300	$625 - 775	$2,499

ADAMAS 12 ACOUSTIC (MODEL 1188) – carbon graphite composite top, 12-string configuration, mahogany neck, 14/24-fret walnut extended fingerboard with maple/ebony inlay, 11 various sized soundholes with leaf pattern maple veneer around them, walnut bridge with carved flower designs, carved flower design on peghead, 3-per-side gold tuners, available in Blue finish, mfg.1978-1990.

N/A	$1,400 - 1,750	$850 - 1,050

MSR/NOTES	100%	EXCELLENT	AVERAGE	LAST MSR

ADAMAS 12 ELECTRIC (MODEL 1688) – carbon graphite composite top, 12-string configuration, mahogany neck, 14/24-fret walnut extended fingerboard with maple/ebony inlay, 11 various sized soundholes with leaf pattern maple veneer around them, walnut bridge with carved flower designs, carved flower design on peghead, 3-per-side gold tuners, 6 piezo bridge pickups, volume/3-band EQ controls, active OP-24 preamp, available in black or blue finish, mfg.1978-1998.

	N/A	$1,350 - 1,700	$825 - 1,025	$3,299

ADAMAS SMT (MODEL 1597) – mid-depth Lyrachord bowl, carbon graphite/birch composite top, mahogany neck, 14/24-fret ebony extended fingerboard, ebony bridge, blackface peghead with Adamas logo, 3-per-side gold tuners, CP-100 pickup, Optima pickup system, available in Natural Graphite finish, mfg. 1998-99.

	N/A	$750 - 950	$450 - 575	$1,899

* *Adamas SMT 12-String (Model 1598)* – similar to Adamas Model 1597, except in a 12-string configuration, available in Natural Graphite and Red Graphite finish, mfg. 1999 only.

	N/A	$800 - 1,000	$475 - 600	$1,999

* *Adamas SMT Round Soundhole (Model 6591)* – similar to the Adamas SMT, except has a round soundhole, available in Natural Graphite or Ruby Graphite finish, mfg. 1999 only.

	N/A	$675 - 850	$400 - 500	$1,749

ADAMAS Q (MODEL Q181) – deep carbon graphite bowl, carbon graphite top, through body graphite neck, 14/24-fret ebony extended fingerboard, ebony bridge, blackface peghead with Adamas logo, 3-per-side gold tuners, available in Natural Graphite finish, mfg. 1998 only.

	N/A	$2,600 - 3,250	$1,550 - 1,950	$5,999

ACOUSTIC: ADAMAS II SERIES

Similar to the original Adamas series, the Adamas II featured the standard Ovation headstock and bridge instead of the carved walnut, and a five piece mahogany and maple laminate neck instead of the solid walnut neck. The Adamas II model was introduced in early 1982; the series was discontinued in 1998. In 1994, soundholes were added to the treble bout.

ADAMAS II (MODEL 1681) – composite top, mahogany/maple 5-piece neck, 14/24-fret walnut extended fingerboard with maple/ebony triangle inlay, walnut bridge, walnut veneer on peghead, 3-per-side gold tuners, available in Black, Blue, or Blue Green finish, mfg. 1981-1997.

	N/A	$1,150 - 1,450	$700 - 875	$2,399

ADAMAS II CUTAWAY (MODEL 1581) – similar to Adamas II, except has venetian cutaway, no soundholes on cutaway side, available in Blue finish, mfg. 1982-1998.

	N/A	$1,200 - 1,500	$725 - 900	$2,499

In 1994, soundholes on cutaway side were introduced.

ADAMAS II CUTAWAY SHALLOW (MODEL 1881) – similar to Adamas II, except has shallow bowl body, venetian cutaway, available in Black or Blue Green finish, mfg. 1993-98.

	N/A	$1,200 - 1,500	$725 - 900	$2,499

ADAMAS II 12 (MODEL 1685) – similar to Adamas II, except has 12 strings, 6-per-side tuners, available in Black finish, mfg. 1981-1998.

	N/A	$1,275 - 1,600	$750 - 950	$2,599

ADAMAS II 12 SHALLOW (MODEL 1885) – similar to Adamas II, except has shallow bowl body, 12 strings, 6-per-side tuners, available in Black finish, mfg. 1993-98.

	N/A	$1,275 - 1,600	$750 - 950	$2,699

ACOUSTIC: BALLADEER SERIES

The Balladeer was the first model introduced by the Ovation company in 1967. For the Classic Balladeer refer to the Classic series.

An example of a Cutsom Balladeer Electric courtesy Dave Rogers, Dave's Guitar Shop

CUSTOM BALLADEER ACOUSTIC (MODEL 1112) – spruce top, round soundhole, five-stripe bound body, leaf pattern rosette, five-piece mahogany/maple neck, 14/20-fret ebony fingerboard, 12th fret pearl diamond/dot inlay, three-per-side nickel tuners, walnut strings through bridge with pearl dot inlay, available in Black, Natural, Sunburst, or White finish, mfg. 1976-1990.

	N/A	$350 - 450	$225 - 275	

MSR/NOTES	100%	EXCELLENT	AVERAGE	LAST MSR
* *Custom Balladeer 12 Acoustic (Model 1155)* – similar to the Custom Balladeer Acoustic, except in 12-string configuration, mfg. 1982-1990.				
	N/A	$400 - 500	$250 - 300	

CUSTOM BALLADEER ELECTRIC (MODEL 1612/1712) – spruce top, round soundhole, 5-stripe bound body, leaf pattern rosette, 5-piece mahogany/maple neck, 14/20-fret ebony fingerboard, 12th fret pearl diamond/dot inlay, walnut strings through bridge with pearl dot inlay, 3-per-side nickel tuners, 6 piezo bridge pickups, volume control, 3-band EQ, FET preamp, available in Black, Natural, Sunburst, or White finish, mfg. 1976-1996.

MSR/NOTES	100%	EXCELLENT	AVERAGE	LAST MSR
	N/A	$400 - 500	$250 - 300	$995

This model has cedar top as an option. In 1994, the pearl dot bridge inlay was discontinued.

MSR/NOTES	100%	EXCELLENT	AVERAGE	LAST MSR
* *Custom Balladeer Cutaway Electric (Model 1860/1862)* – similar to Custom Balladeer, except has single round cutaway, shallow bowl body, mfg. 1989-1996.				
	N/A	$450 - 550	$275 - 325	$1,095
* *Custom Balladeer 12 Electric (Model 1655/1755)* – similar to Custom Balladeer Electric, except in 12-string configuration, mfg. 1982-1993.				
	N/A	$475 - 600	$275 - 350	$1,250

STANDARD BALLADEER (MODEL 1111) – folk-style, solid Sitka spruce top, round soundhole, 5-stripe bound body, leaf pattern rosette, cedro neck, 14/20-fret rosewood fingerboard with pearl dot inlay, rosewood strings through bridge with pearl dot inlay, 3-per-side chrome tuners, available in Natural finish, mfg. 1966-1983, 1993-2001.

MSR/NOTES	100%	EXCELLENT	AVERAGE	LAST MSR
1966-1979	N/A	$325 - 400	$190 - 240	
1980-1983	N/A	$275 - 350	$170 - 210	
1993-2001	N/A	$240 - 300	$145 - 180	$849
* *Standard Balladeer 12-String (Model 1151)* – similar to the Balladeer, except in 12-string configuration, mfg. 1996-99.				
	N/A	$275 - 350	$170 - 210	$899
* *Artist Balladeer (Model 1121)* – similar to the Standard Balladeer, except in shallow bowl configuration, mfg. 1968-1990.				
1966-1979	N/A	$350 - 450	$225 - 275	
1980-1990	N/A	$325 - 400	$190 - 240	

STANDARD BALLADEER ELECTRIC (MODEL 1611/1711) – similar to Standard Balladeer, except has piezo bridge pickups, 4-band EQ, available in Natural, Cadillac Green (disc.), Cherry Cherryburst (disc.), or Sunburst finish, mfg. 1983-85, 1993-2000, 2005-07.

MSR/NOTES	100%	EXCELLENT	AVERAGE	LAST MSR
1983-1985	N/A	$450 - 550	$275 - 325	
1993-2000	N/A	$400 - 500	$250 - 300	
2005-2007	N/A	$350 - 450	$225 - 275	$1,299
* *Artist Balladeer Electric (Model 1621)* – similar to the Standard Balladeer Electric, except in shallow bowl configuration, mfg. 1971-1990.				
1971-1979	N/A	$525 - 650	$325 - 400	
1980-1990	N/A	$450 - 550	$275 - 325	
* *Standard Balladeer Electric 12-String (Model 1751)* – similar to the Balladeer, except in 12-string configuration, mfg. 1996-98.				
	N/A	$600 - 700	$350 - 425	$1,149
* *Standard Balladeer LX (Model 1771LX)* – similar to the Standard Balladeer, except has LX upgrades including enhanced scalloped LX bracing, advanced neck system, Ovation Original Patented Pickup, and Op-Pro preamp, available in Natural, Cherry Cherry Burst, or Black finish, mfg. 2004-08.				
	N/A	$700 - 850	$450 - 525	$1,649

STANDARD BALLADEER CUTAWAY ELECTRIC (MODEL 1661/1761) – similar to Standard Balladeer, except has single round cutaway, deep bowl, piezo bridge pickups, 4-band EQ, available in Black, Natural, Cadillac Green, or Cherry Cherryburst finish, mfg. 1982-2000.

MSR/NOTES	100%	EXCELLENT	AVERAGE	LAST MSR
	N/A	$450 - 550	$275 - 325	$1,049
* *Standard Balladeer Cutaway Electric Mid-Depth (Model 1771)* – similar to Standard Balladeer except has a mid-depth bowl body, available in Natural, Black, or Cherry Cherryburst finish, mfg. 1998-2007.				
	N/A	$525 - 650	$325 - 400	$1,299

STANDARD BALLADEER SUPER SHALLOW CUTAWAY ELECTRIC (MODEL 1561/1861) – similar to Standard Balladeer, except has single round cutaway, super shallow bowl, piezo bridge pickups, 4-band EQ, available in Black, Natural, Cadillac Green (disc.), or Cherry Cherry Burst finish, mfg. 1984-2007.

MSR/NOTES	100%	EXCELLENT	AVERAGE	LAST MSR
	N/A	$525 - 650	$325 - 400	$1,299

MSR/NOTES	100%	EXCELLENT	AVERAGE	LAST MSR

* Standard Balladeer Super Shallow Cutaway 12 Electric (Model 6751) – similar to the Standard Balladeer, except in 12-string configuration and six-per-side tuners, available in Black, Natural, or Cherry Cherry Burst finish, mfg. 1998-2007.

	N/A	$600 - 750	$375 - 450	$1,499

»Standard Balladeer Super Shallow Cutaway Electric 12-String LX (Model 6751LX) – similar to the Standard Balladeer Super Shallow Cutaway 12 Electric, except has LX upgrades including enhanced scalloped LX bracing, advanced neck system, Ovation Original Patented Pickup, and Op-Pro preamp, available in Natural finish, mfg. 2007-08.

	N/A	$800 - 950	$525 - 600	$1,849

* Standard Balladeer Super Shallow Cutaway Electric LX (Model 1861LX) – similar to the Standard Balladeer Super Shallow Cutaway, except has LX upgrades including enhanced scalloped LX bracing, advanced neck system, Ovation Original Patented Pickup, and Op-Pro preamp, available in Black or Cherry Cherry Burst finish, mfg. summer 2005-08.

	N/A	$700 - 850	$450 - 525	$1,649

STANDARD BALLADEER CONTOUR CUTAWAY LX (MODEL 2771LX) – single cutaway deep body with a contoured back, solid Sitka spruce top, Scalloped LX bracing, round soundhole with oakleaf rosette, bound rosewood fingerboard with dot/diamond inlays, standard Ovation headstock, three-per-side chrome tuners, rosewood bridge, original patented pickup, available in Black, Cherry Cherry Burst, or Natural finish, 25.25 in. scale, mfg. 2008-09.

	N/A	$700 - 850	$450 - 525	$1,649

* Standard Balladeer Contour Cutaway 12-String LX (Model 2751LX) – similar to the Standard Balladeer Contour Cutaway, except in 12-string configuration with six-per-side tuners, available in Natural finish, mfg. 2008-09.

	N/A	$800 - 950	$525 - 600	$1,849

STANDARD BALLADEER (MODEL 1771AX) – single cutaway mid-depth body, AA solid spruce top, scalloped X bracing, round soundhole with hand-inlaid rosette, multi-ply body binding, five-piece satin finish mahogany/maple neck, 14/20-fret bound rosewood fingerboard with pearl dot and diamond inlays, black headstock overlay with Ovation logo, three-per-side chrome tuners, rosewood bridge, OCP-1 pickup, OP-Pro electronics, available in Black or Cherry Cherry Burst finish, 25.25 in. scale, mfg. summer 2008-2013.

	$700	$475 - 550	$300 - 350	$999

* Standard Balladeer Deep Contour Body (Model 2771AX) – similar to the Standard Balladeer, except has a deep contour body, available in Black or Cherry Cherry Burst finish, mfg. summer 2008-present.

MSR $999	$700	$475 - 550	$300 - 350	

»Standard Balladeer Deep Contour Body 12-String (Model 2751AX) – similar to the Standard Balladeer Deep Contour Body, except in 12-string configuration with six-per-side tuners, available in Black finish, mfg. summer 2008-present.

MSR $1,149	$800	$525 - 600	$325 - 375	

* Standard Balladeer Super Shallow Body (Model 1861AX) – similar to the Standard Balladeer, except has a super shallow body, available in Black or Cherry Cherry Burst finish, mfg. summer 2008-2011, reintroduced 2013 only.

	$700	$475 - 550	$300 - 350	$999

BALLADEER (MODEL 4861) – solid spruce top, super shallow cutaway body, satin finish mahogany neck with 20 frets, rosewood fingerboards-100 Thinline pickup, OP24 Plus Preamp and electronics, available in Sunburst, Natural, or Black finishes, mfg. 1999-2000.

	N/A	$350 - 425	$225 - 275	$799

BALLADEER SPECIAL (MODEL S771) – similar to Standard Balladeer except has Mid-Depth bowl body, available in Amberburst, Natural, Sundance (disc.), or Teardrop Burst (disc.) finish, mfg. 1999-2007.

	N/A	$475 - 600	$300 - 350	$1,299

* Balladeer Special Super Shallow (Model S861) – similar to Balladeer Special except has a Super Shallow bowl body, available in Natural, Sundance, or Teardrop Burst finish, mfg. 1999-2004.

	N/A	$550 - 650	$325 - 400	$929

BALLADEER 40TH ANNIVERSARY (MODEL K1111) – non-cutaway deep body, AA solid Sitka spruce top, round soundhole with original ribbon-style rosette, black/white multi-layer binding, 14/21-fret ebony fingerboard with dot inlay, three-per-side chrome tuners, Brazilian rosewood bridge, Natural finish, 25.25 in. scale, mfg. 2006 only.

	N/A	$1,150 - 1,350	$700 - 850	$2,499

VINTAGE BALLADEER (MODEL 1771VL) – single cutaway mid-depth body, solid spruce top, scalloped X bracing, round soundhole, five-piece mahogany/maple neck, 20-fret rosewood fingerboard with pearl dot and diamonds inlays, three-per-side chrome tuners, walnut bridge, OCP-1K pickup, Vintage Ovation FET pre-amp, available in Sunburst finish, mfg. 2013 only.

	$850	$550 - 650	$300 - 350	$1,199

* Vintage Balladeer Shallow Body (Model 1627VL) – similar to the Vintage Balladeer, except has no cutaway and a shallow body, available in Natural finish, mfg. 2013 only.

	$850	$550 - 650	$300 - 350	$1,199

MSR/NOTES	100%	EXCELLENT	AVERAGE	LAST MSR

ACOUSTIC: CELEBRITY SERIES

The Celebrity series represents Ovation's entry level guitars in their product line.

An example of a Celebruty Cutaway
courtesy Dave Rogers, Dave's Guitar Shop

CELEBRITY ACOUSTIC (MODEL CC-11) – spruce top, round soundhole, 5-stripe bound body, leaf pattern rosette, mahogany neck, 14/20-fret bound rosewood fingerboard with pearl dot inlay, walnut bridge with pearloid dot inlays, rosewood veneer on peghead, 3-per-side chrome tuners, available in Barn board, Brownburst, Natural, or Sunburst finish, mfg. 1984-1996.

	N/A	$175 - 225	$100 - 130	$400

- **Add $100 for 12-string configuration (Model CC-15, Disc.). Add $200 for 12-string configuration, piezo bridge pickups, 4-band EQ (Model CC-65, Disc.). Available in Natural finish.**
- * *Celebrity Electric (Model CC-67)* – similar to Celebrity, except has piezo bridge pickups, 4-band EQ, available in Barn board, Brownburst, or Natural finish, mfg. 1984-1996.

	N/A	$225 - 275	$135 - 175	$500

CELEBRITY ACOUSTIC (MODEL CC-01) – deep bowl, spruce top, round soundhole, bound body, leaf pattern rosette, two-piece mahogany neck, 14/20-fret bound rosewood fingerboard with dot inlay, three-per-side chrome tuners, walnut bridge with pearloid dot inlays, rosewood veneer on peghead, available in Natural or Mahogany finish, mfg. 1997-2005.

	N/A	$175 - 225	$100 - 135	$430

- * *Celebrity Shallow Electric (Model CC-57/CC-057)* – similar to Celebrity Electric, except features a super shallow cutaway bowl, available in Black, Honey Burst, Mahogany, Natural, or Ruby Red finish, mfg. 1990-93, 1996-2006.

	N/A	$275 - 325	$140 - 190	$600

- * *Celebrity Mid-Depth Electric (Model CC-047)* – similar to the Celebrity except has a mid-depth cutaway bowl, available in Natural finish, mfg. 1997-98.

	N/A	$325 - 375	$175 - 225	$700

CELEBRITY BALLADEER (MODEL CA24) – single cutaway, mid-depth body, spruce top, round soundhole, nato neck, 14/20-fret rosewood fingerboard with acrylic dot inlays, three-per-side chrome tuners, walnut bridge, Ovation Slimline pickup, OP4B electronics, available in Sunburst finish, 25.25 in. scale, mfg. 2013 only.

	$250	$160 - 195	$90 - 105	$359

CELEBRITY CUTAWAY (MODEL CC026) – similar to the Celebrity, except has a mid-depth body, available in Natural finish, mfg. 2000-05.

	N/A	$200 - 250	$130 - 160	$440

- * *Celebrity Cutaway (Model CK047)* – similar to the Model CC026, except has a spruce top, dot and diamond fingerboard inlays, modified A bracing, and an Ovation Slimline pickup, available in Black Cherry Burst Quilt, Black Flake, or Figured Koa finish, mfg. 2005-06.

	N/A	$300 - 375	$175 - 225	$714

- **Add 5% for Figured Koa finish.**
- » *Celebrity Cutaway Left-Handed (Model LCC047)* – similar to the Celebrity Cutaway (Model CK047), except in left-handed configuration, available in Honey Burst finish, mfg. 2005-present.

MSR $830	$580	$350 - 425	$200 - 250	

- * *Celebrity Cutaway Color (Model CK057)* – similar to the Celebrity Cutaway except is available in Dark Blue Pearl, Silver Satin Pearl, or Deep Purple Quilted finish, mfg. 2002-05.

	N/A	$275 - 325	$150 - 200	$640

- **Add $50 for Deep Purple Quilted finish.**

CELEBRITY NYLON STRING (MODEL CC059) – similar to the Celebrity, except in nylon string configuration with open tuners, available in Natural Cedar finish, mfg. 2002-2013.

	$450	$300 - 350	$175 - 225	$650

CELEBRITY TREKKER (MODEL CC-012/TC-012) – compact mini body, spruce top, round soundhole, bound body, leaf pattern rosette, two-piece mahogany neck, short scale 14/20-fret bound rosewood fingerboard with dot inlay, walnut bridge with pearloid dot inlays, rosewood veneer on peghead, three-per-side chrome tuners, piezo bridge pickup, available in Black (disc.) or Natural finish, mfg. 2000-08.

	N/A	$100 - 130	$50 - 75	$270

MSR/NOTES	100%	EXCELLENT	AVERAGE	LAST MSR

* *Celebrity Trekker (Model TS-212)* – similar to Trekker Model CC-012 except has mutli-soundholes, available in Natural finish, mfg. 2000-05.

	N/A	$200 - 250	$120 - 150	$486

CELEBRITY CLASSIC (MODEL CC-13/1113) – classical style, spruce top, round soundhole, 5-stripe bound body, leaf pattern rosette, mahogany neck, 12/19-fret bound rosewood fingerboard, walnut bridge, 3-per-side gold tuners with pearloid buttons, available in Natural finish, mfg. 1984-1996.

	N/A	$175 - 225	$100 - 130	$400

* Add $100 for piezo bridge pickups, 4-band EQ (Model 1613). Available in Natural finish (mfg. 1994 to 1996). Add $200 for venetian cutaway, piezo bridge pickups, volume/tone control (Model 1663).

* *Celebrity Classic Electric (Model CC-63/CC-163/1613)* – similar to the Celebrity Classic, except has electronics with piezo bridge pickups and 4-band EQ, mfg. 1984-1996.

	N/A	$300 - 350	$150 - 200	$670

* *Celebrity Classic Super Shallow Electric (Model CC-53/CC-153)* – similar to the Celebrity Classic, except has a single cutaway super shallow body and electronics with piezo bridge pickups and preamp, mfg. 1992-96.

	N/A	$300 - 350	$150 - 200	

CELEBRITY CUTAWAY ELECTRIC (MODEL CC-68/CC-147) – single round cutaway, spruce top, round soundhole, 5-stripe bound body, leaf pattern rosette, mahogany neck, 20-fret bound rosewood fingerboard with pearloid diamond/dot inlay, walnut bridge with pearloid dot inlay, walnut veneer on peghead, 3-per-side chrome tuners, 6 piezo bridge pickups, volume/tone control, available in Barn Board, Brownburst, Natural, or Sunburst finish, mfg. 1991-96.

	N/A	$325 - 375	$175 - 225	$750

CELEBRITY 12 (MODEL CC-15) – similar to the Celebrity Acoustic, except in 12-string configuration and six-per-side tuners, available in Sunburst of Natural finish, mfg. 1990-96.

	N/A	$250 - 300	$125 - 175	$570

* *Celebrity 12 Electric (Model CC-65/CC-165)* – similar to the Celebrity 12 Acoustic, except has electronics with piezo bridge pickups and 4-band EQ, available in Natural or Sunburst finish, mfg. 1990-96.

	N/A	$300 - 350	$150 - 200	$670

CELEBRITY/CELEBRITY STANDARD CUTAWAY MID-DEPTH (MODEL CC24/CS24) – single cutaway mid-depth body, laminated spruce or quilted maple (Natural finish only) top, round soundhole, nato neck, 14/22-fret rosewood fingerboard, three-per-side tuners, walnut bridge, Slimline Under Saddle Pickup, OP4BT electronics, gold hardware, available in Black, Figured Koa (new 2014), Flamed Koa (2013 only), Honey Burst (2013 only), Honey Burst Flamed Maple (2013 only), Natural, Natural Quilt Maple (2007-present), Nutmeg Burled Maple (2012-present), Ruby Red, Sunburst (2013-present), Trans Black Flamed Maple (2013-present), or White Pearl (2013 only) finish, 25.25 in. scale, mfg. summer 2005-present.

MSR $530	$370	$225 - 275	$135 - 170	

* Add 22.5% (MSR $650) for Figured Koa, Flamed Koa, Honey Burst Flamed Maple, Natural Quilt Maple, Nutmeg Burled Maple, or Trans Black Flamed Maple finish.

In 2014, the model name changed to Celebrity Standard (Model CS24).

* *Celebrity Cutaway Mid-Depth Solid Spruce (Model CC24S)* – similar to the Celebrity Cutaway Mid-Depth (Model CC24), except has a solid spruce top and abalone dot fingerboard inlays, available in Natural or Tuscan Tan Burst finish, mfg. 2008-2011.

	$400	$225 - 275	$135 - 175	$549

CELEBRITY CUTAWAY SUPER SHALLOW (MODEL CC28) – single cutaway super-shallow body, laminated spruce or quilted maple (Natural finish only) top, round soundhole, nato neck, 14/22-fret rosewood fingerboard, three-per-side tuners, walnut bridge, Slimline Under Saddle Pickup, OP4BT electronics, gold hardware, available in Amber Waterfall Bubinga (2009-2013), Black, Flamed Koa (2013 only), Honey Burst (2013 only), Honey Burst Flamed Maple (2013 only), Honey Burst Quilt (2008-2013), Natural (2007-08, reintroduced 2013 only), Natural Quilt (2007 only), Nutmeg Burled Maple (2013 only), Ruby Red, Sunburst (2013 only), or Trans. Black Burst Flame (2009-2013) finish, 25.25 in. scale, mfg. 2006-2013.

	$370	$225 - 275	$135 - 170	$530

* Add 22.5% (MSR $650) for Amber Waterfall Bubinga, Flamed Koa, Honey Burst Flamed Maple, Honey Burst Quilt, Natural Quilt, Nutmeg Burled Maple, or Trans. Black Burst finish.

CELEBRITY CUTAWAY DEEP BODY (MODEL CC29S) – single cutaway deep body, solid cedar top, modified quintad bracing, round soundhole with abalone rosette, nato neck, 14/20-fret rosewood fingerboard with abalone micro dot inlays, three-per-side chrome tuners with PVC coating, rosewood bridge, Slimline Under Saddle Pickup, OP4BT electronics, available in Natural Cedar or New England Burst finish, 25.25 in. scale, gig bag included, mfg. 2012-13.

	$420	$275 - 325	$150 - 200	$599

CELEBRITY CUTAWAY MID-DEPTH 12-STRING (MODEL CC045/CC245) – 12-string configuration, single cutaway mid-depth body, laminated spruce top, round soundhole, nato neck, 14/22-fret rosewood fingerboard, six-per-side tuners, walnut bridge, Slimline Under Saddle Pickup, OP4BT electronics, chrome hardware, available in Honey Burst finish, 25.25 in. scale, mfg. 2006-2013.

	$480	$300 - 350	$175 - 225	$680

MSR/NOTES	100%	EXCELLENT	AVERAGE	LAST MSR

CELEBRITY DX (MODEL CDX24) – single cutaway mid-depth body, AA solid Sitka spruce top, round soundhole, abalone purfling rosette, black/white body binding, two-piece mahogany neck, 14/23-fret extended bound rosewood fingerboard with pearl diamond inlays, three-per-side gold tuners with pearl buttons, rosewood bridge, OCP-1K pickup and OP-Pro electronics, available in Black, Deep Red Trans. (2008 only), or Sunburst (2006-07) finish, mfg. 2006-08.

	N/A	$400 - 475	$250 - 300	$950

CELEBRITY SE (MODEL CSE24) – single cutaway mid-depth body, solid Sitka spruce top, round soundhole, abalone rosette, black/white body binding, two-piece nato neck, 14/23-fret extended bound rosewood fingerboard with pearl triangle inlays, three-per-side gold tuners, rosewood bridge, OCP-1K pickup and OP-30 electronics, available in Black or Cherry Cherry Burst finish, mfg. 2006-08.

	N/A	$325 - 400	$200 - 250	$790

ACOUSTIC: CELEBRITY DELUXE/CELEBRITY ELITE SERIES

The Celebrity Deluxe/Celebrity Elite series features the same multiple soundholes of the Adamas and Elite designs on a laminated spruce or cedar top.

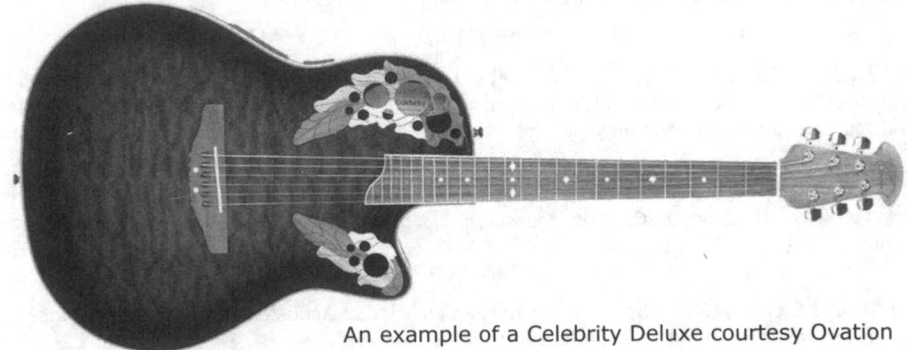

An example of a Celebrity Deluxe courtesy Ovation

CELEBRITY DELUXE (MODEL CC-267) – cedar top, multi-sized soundholes with leaf pattern maple veneer, 5-stripe bound body, mahogany neck, 14/23-fret bound rosewood extended fingerboard with pearl diamond/dot inlay, rosewood strings through bridge, rosewood veneered peghead with logo decal, 3-per-side gold tuners, piezo bridge pickups, 4-band EQ, available in Antique Sunburst or Natural finishes, mfg. 1992-95.

	N/A	$300 - 350	$150 - 200	$710

This model has spruce and sycamore tops as an option.

* *Celebrity Deluxe Cutaway (Model CC-268)* – similar to Celebrity Deluxe, except has single round cutaway, available in Black, Natural, or Wineburst finish, mfg. 1992-95.

	N/A	$325 - 375	$175 - 225	$740

• **Add $20 for Wineburst finish.**

* *Celebrity Deluxe Mid-Depth Cutaway (Model CC-247)* – similar to the Celebrity Deluxe, except has a single cutaway and mid-depth body, mfg. 1995-96.

	N/A	$350 - 425	$175 - 225	$830

CELEBRITY DELUXE (MODEL CS-247) – mid-depth Lyrachord bowl, solid spruce top, multi-sized soundholes with leaf pattern maple veneer, five-stripe bound body, two-piece nato neck, 14/23-fret bound rosewood extended fingerboard with pearl diamond/dot inlay, rosewood strings through bridge, rosewood veneered peghead with logo decal, three-per-side gold tuners, piezo bridge pickups, OP-24+ system, available in Natural finish, mfg. 1998-2005.

	N/A	$375 - 450	$200 - 250	$860

* *Celebrity Deluxe Left-Hand (Model LCS-247)* – similar to the Celebrity Deluxe, except in left-handed configuration, available in Black finish, mfg. 2002-08.

	N/A	$400 - 475	$225 - 275	$900

* *Celebrity Deluxe 12-String (Model CS-245)* – similar to the Celebrity Deluxe, except in 12-string configuration and six-per-side tuners, mfg. 1998-2005.

	N/A	$400 - 475	$225 - 275	$930

* *Celebrity Deluxe (Model CS-347)* – similar to the CS-247, except has a quilted maple or figured koa top, gold hardware, available in Black Cherry Burst Quilt or Figured Koa finish, mfg. 2005-06.

	N/A	$375 - 450	$200 - 250	$860

• **Add 5% (Last MSR $900) for flamed Koa wood.**

* *Celebrity Deluxe Arch Top (Model CSAT-47)* – similar to the CS-247, except has an arched top, available in Vintage Sunburst finish, mfg. 2005 only.

	N/A	$375 - 450	$200 - 250	$860

MSR/NOTES	100%	EXCELLENT	AVERAGE	LAST MSR

CELEBRITY DELUXE CUTAWAY SHALLOW (MODEL CC-257/CS-257) – similar to Celebrity Deluxe, except has spruce top, single round cutaway, shallow bowl body, OP-24 Plus preamp, available in Autumn Burst, Black, Blue Trans., Cherry Cherry Burst, Natural, Plum Burst, Ruby Red Burst, or Vintage Flame finish, mfg. 1992-2006.

	N/A	$350 - 425	$200 - 250	$790

- **Add 10% for Cherry Cherryburst Quilted Maple or Vintage Flame finishes.**

Autumn Burst finish added in 1999. In 1997, the model was renamed the CS-257.

* *Celebrity Deluxe Cutaway Shallow 12-String (Model CC-255/CS-255)* – similar to the Celebrity Deluxe Cutaway Shallow, except in 12-string configuration, available in Honey Burst finish, mfg. 1996-2006.

	N/A	$400 - 475	$225 - 275	$930

In 1997, this model was renamed the CS-257.

* *Celebrity Deluxe Cutaway Shallow Doubleneck (Model CSD255/CSE255)* – similar to the Celebrity Deluxe Cutaway Shallow, except has two necks with six- and 12-string configurations, available in Black Cherryburst (Model CSD255, disc.) or Blue Flame Maple (Model CSE255) finish, mfg. 2001-2012.

	$1,000	$675 - 775	$400 - 475	$1,429

CELEBRITY DELUXE/CELEBRITY ELITE CUTAWAY MID-DEPTH (MODEL CC-44/CE-44) – single cutaway mid-depth bowl, laminated spruce, quilted maple (Blue Burst finish only), or spalted maple top, multiple soundholes in exotic wood epaulets, nato neck, 14/23-fret extended rosewood fingerboard with small dot inlays, three-per-side tuners, walnut bridge, Slimline under saddle pickup, OP4BT electronics, chrome or gold hardware, available in Black, Blue Trans. (disc. 2013), Blue Burst Quilt (2007-present), Cherry Figured Ash (2013 only), Figured Koa (2011-present), Honey Burst (2013 only), Natural (2006-07, reintroduced 2013-present), Padauk (2013-present), Red Burst Burled Walnut (2011 only), Ruby Red Burst (2013-present), Spalted Maple (2009-present), Sunburst (new 2014), or White Pearl (2013 only) finish, 25.25 in. scale, mfg. 2006-present.

MSR $650	$450	$275 - 325	$150 - 200	

- **Add 17.5% (MSR $750) for Blue Burst Quilt, Cherry Figured Ash, Figured Koa, Padauk, Red Burst Burled Walnut, or Spalted Maple finish.**

In 2014, the model name changed to Celebrite Elite CE-44.

* *Celebrity Deluxe Cutaway Mid-Depth Solid Spruce (Model CC44S)* – similar to the Celebrity Deluxe Cutaway Mid-Depth (Model CC44), except has a solid spruce top and abalone dot fingerboard inlays, available in Amber Burst or Vintage Amber finish, mfg. 2008 only.

	N/A	$275 - 325	$160 - 200	$640

CELEBRITY DELUXE CUTAWAY SUPER SHALLOW (MODEL CC-48) – single cutaway super shallow bowl, laminated spruce, flame maple (Ruby Red Burst finish only), or Padauk (Figured Koa, Padauk, or Trans. Blue Quilt finish only) top, multiple soundholes in exotic wood epaulets, nato neck, 14/23-fret extended rosewood fingerboard with small dot inlays, three-per-side tuners, walnut bridge, Slimline under saddle pickup, OP4BT electronics, chrome or gold hardware, available in Black, Blue Trans./Trans. Blue Quilt, Flame Ruby Red Burst (2007-2013), Flamed Koa (2013 only), Honey Burst (2013 only), Natural (2006-07), Paduak (2010-13), or Ruby Red Burst (2013 only) finish, 25.25 in. scale, mfg. 2006-2013.

	$450	$275 - 325	$150 - 200	$650

- **Add 17.5% (MSR $750) for Flame Ruby Red Burst, Flamed Koa, Paduak, or Trans. Blue Quilt finish.**

CELEBRITY DELUXE CUTAWAY DEEP BODY (MODEL CC49S) – single cutaway deep body, solid spruce top, modified quintad bracing, multiple soundholes in exotic wood epaulets, nato neck, 14/23-fret extended rosewood fingerboard with abalone micro dot inlays, three-per-side chrome tuners with PVC coating, rosewood bridge, Slimline Under Saddle Pickup, OP4BT electronics, available in Vintage Amber finish, 25.25 in. scale, mfg. 2012-13.

	$500	$300 - 375	$175 - 225	$699

CELEBRITY DELUXE DX (MODEL CDX44) – single cutaway mid-depth body, AA solid Sitka spruce top, multi soundholes, oakleaf-style rosette, abalone body binding, two-piece mahogany neck, 14/23-fret extended bound rosewood fingerboard with pearl diamond inlays, three-per-side gold tuners with pearl buttons, rosewood bridge, OCP-1K pickup and OP-Pro electronics, available in Blue Trans. or Ruby Red Burst finish, mfg. 2006-08.

	N/A	$450 - 525	$275 - 325	$1,000

CELEBRITY DELUXE SE (MODEL CSE44) – single cutaway mid-depth body, solid Sitka spruce top, multi soundholes, oakleaf-style rosette, black/white body binding, two-piece nato neck, 14/23-fret extended bound rosewood fingerboard with pearl triangle inlays, three-per-side gold tuners, rosewood bridge, OCP-1K pickup and OP-30 electronics, available in Autumn Burst Birdseye (2008 only), Honey Burst, or Natural (2006-07) finish, mfg. 2006-09.

	N/A	$400 - 475	$250 - 300	$930

- **Add 5% (Last MSR was $960) for Autumn Burst Birdseye finish.**

ACOUSTIC: CLASSIC SERIES

CLASSIC ACOUSTIC (MODEL 1113) – classical style, cedar top, round soundhole, 5-stripe bound body, leaf pattern rosette, 5-piece mahogany/maple neck, 12/19-fret extended ebony fingerboard, walnut bridge, walnut veneer on peghead, 3-per-side gold tuners, available in Natural finish, mfg. 1967-1990.

1967-1973	N/A	$550 - 700	$350 - 425	
1974-1990	N/A	$475 - 600	$275 - 350	

MSR/NOTES	100%	EXCELLENT	AVERAGE	LAST MSR

CLASSIC ELECTRIC (MODEL 1613/1713) – classical style, cedar top, round soundhole, 5-stripe bound body, leaf pattern rosette, 5-piece mahogany/maple neck, 12/19-fret extended ebony fingerboard, walnut bridge, walnut veneer on peghead, 3-per-side gold tuners, piezo bridge pickup, volume/3-band EQ control, active preamp, available in Natural finish, mfg. 1982-1993.

	N/A	$400 - 500	$250 - 300	$1,420

* *Classic Cutaway Electric (Model 1663/1773)* – similar to Classic, except has venetian cutaway, available in Natural and White finish, mfg. 1982-1999.

	N/A	$450 - 550	$275 - 325	$1,520

This model had shallow bowl as an option.

CLASSIC CUTAWAY MID-DEPTH LX (MODEL 1773LX) – classical nylon configuration, single cutaway mid-depth Lyrachord GS body, solid Sitka cedar top, scalloped bracing, ANS, 12/19-fret ebony fingerboard, three-per-side open-style gold tuners with black buttons, ebony bridge, original patented pickup, OP-Pro electronics, available in Natural finish, 25.25 in. scale, mfg. 2006-2010.

	$1,900	$1,150 - 1,400	$700 - 850	$2,749

CLASSIC CUTAWAY DEEP CONTOUR LX (MODEL 2073LX) – classical nylon configuration, single cutaway deep contoured body, AAA solid cedar top, scalloped LX bracing, round soundhole with oak leaf pattern rosette, 12/19-fret ebony fingerboard, slotted headstock, three-per-side open-style gold tuners with black buttons, ebony bridge, original patented pickup, OP-Pro electronics, available in Natural finish, 25.25 in. scale, mfg. 2008-2010.

	$1,900	$1,150 - 1,400	$700 - 850	$2,749

CLASSIC ARTIST (MODEL 1123) – classical style, shallow bowl, cedar top, round soundhole, mfg. 1968-1975.

	N/A	$750 - 900	$425 - 500	

CLASSIC BALLADEER (MODEL 1122) – classical style, balladeer body, shallow bowl, flat ebony fingerboard with no inlays, 3-per-side tuners in a slotted headstock, mfg. 1972-78.

	N/A	$425 - 500	$275 - 325	

CLASSIC LEGEND ELECTRIC (MODEL 1763) – single round cutaway, AAA cedar top, round soundhole, 5-stripe bound body, leaf pattern rosette, 5-piece mahogany/maple neck, 19-fret ebony fingerboard, rosewood bridge, 3-per-side gold tuners with pearloid buttons, piezo bridge pickup, volume/3-band EQ control, OP-X preamp, available in Natural finish, mfg. 1982-1999.

	N/A	$750 - 875	$500 - 575	$1,649

• **Add $100 for Recording Model with OptiMax preamp (Model 1763-4RM).**

* *Classic Legend Electric Mid-Depth (Model 1773)* – similar to the Classic Legend Electric, except has a mid-depth body, mfg. 2000-03.

	N/A	$750 - 875	$500 - 575	$1,649

* *Classic Legend Electric Shallow (Model 1863)* – similar to the Nylon String Legend, except has a super shallow bowl, Natural finish, mfg. 1989-2005.

	N/A	$750 - 875	$500 - 575	$1,649

CONCERT CLASSIC (MODEL 1116) – classic style, spruce top, mahogany neck, 12/19-fret fingerboard with no inlay, 3-per-side chrome plated tuners in a slotted headstock, available in Natural or Sunburst finish, mfg. 1974-1990.

	N/A	$425 - 500	$275 - 325	

There was a prototype built with the same model in 1967 and called the Contemporary Folk Classic. It originally had a red, green, or blue bowl as an option.

CONCERT CLASSIC ELECTRIC (MODEL 1616) – classic style, spruce top, mahogany neck, 12/19-fret fingerboard with no inlay, 3-per-side chrome plated tuners in a slotted headstock, electronics with a pickup and single volume knob, available in Natural or Sunburst finish, mfg. 1974-1990.

	N/A	$475 - 550	$300 - 350	

ACOUSTIC: COLLECTOR'S SERIES

The Collector's Series offers limited edition guitars. Beginning in 1982, a different model is featured each year, and production of that model is limited to that year only. The following descriptions list the number of instruments built per model, and also the listed retail price. Information compiled by Paul Bechtoldt, and featured in Walter Carter's *The History of the Ovation Guitar* book. For whatever reason, a 2004 Collector's Edition never appeared in an Ovation catalog, price list, or on their website - it is unknown if one was ever produced.

1982 COLLECTOR'S (MODEL 1982-8) – bowl back acoustic guitar, round soundhole, mfg. 1982 only.

	N/A	$750 - 850	$475 - 550	$995

A total of 1,908 guitars were produced.

1983 COLLECTOR'S (MODEL 1983-B) – super shallow bowl, single cutaway, round soundhole, available in Barn board (exaggerated grain) finish, mfg. 1983 only.

	N/A	$750 - 850	$475 - 550	$995

A total of 2,754 guitars were produced.

MSR/NOTES	100%	EXCELLENT	AVERAGE	LAST MSR

1984 COLLECTOR'S (MODEL 1984-5) – Elite model design, Super shallow bowl, single cutaway, available in Ebony stain finish, mfg. 1984 only.

	N/A	$750 - 850	$475 - 550	$995

A total of 2,637 guitars were produced.

1985 COLLECTOR'S (MODEL 1985-1) – Elite model design, Super shallow bowl, single cutaway, available in Autumnburst finish, mfg. 1985 only.

	N/A	$725 - 850	$425 - 500	$1,095

A total of 2,198 guitars were produced.

* *1985 Collector's (Model 2985-1)* – similar to the 1985 Collector's model, except offered in limited quantities as a 12-string model, available in Autumnburst finish, mfg. 1985 only.

	N/A	$775 - 900	$450 - 525	$1,195

A total of 715 guitars were produced.

1986 COLLECTOR'S (MODEL 1986-6) – super shallow bowl, single cutaway, round soundhole, available in Pearl White finish, mfg. 1986 only.

	N/A	$725 - 850	$450 - 525	$1,095

A total of 1,858 guitars were produced.

* *1986 Collector's (Model 2986-6)* – similar to the 1986 Collector's model, except offered in limited quantities as a 12-string model, available in Pearl White finish, mfg. 1986 only.

	N/A	$775 - 900	$450 - 525	$1,195

A total of 392 guitars were produced.

1987 COLLECTOR'S (MODEL 1987-7) – Elite model design, deep bowl, single cutaway, available in Nutmeg stain finish, mfg. 1987 only.

	N/A	$1,100 - 1,250	$650 - 750	$1,800

A total of 820 guitars were produced.

* *1987 Collector's (Model 1987-5)* – similar to the 1987 Collector's model, except offered in limited quantities in a Black finish, mfg. 1987 only.

	N/A	$1,300 - 1,500	$750 - 875	$1,800

A total of 108 guitars were produced.

1988 COLLECTOR'S (MODEL 1988-P) – Elite model design, Super shallow bowl, single cutaway, available in a Pewter finish, mfg. 1988 only.

	N/A	$825 - 950	$500 - 575	$1,195

A total of 1,177 guitars were produced.

1989 COLLECTOR'S (MODEL 1989-8) – super shallow bowl, single cutaway, round soundhole, available in Blue Pearl finish, mfg. 1989 only.

	N/A	$850 - 975	$525 - 600	$1,299

A total of 981 guitars were produced.

1990 COLLECTOR'S (MODEL 1990-7) – Elite model design, bird's-eye maple top, deep bowl, single cutaway, available in Nutmeg finish, mfg. 1990 only.

	N/A	$900 - 1,050	$550 - 650	$1,599

A total of 500 guitars were produced.

* *1990 Collector's (Model 1990-1)* – similar to the 1990 Collector's model (1990-7), except offered in extremely limited quantities in a Sunburst finish, mfg. 1990 only.

	N/A	$950 - 1,100	$600 - 700	$1,599

A total of 50 guitars were produced.

* *1990 Collector's (Model 199S-7)* – similar to the 1990 Collector's model (1990-7), except offered in limited quantities with a Super shallow bowl and Nutmeg finish, mfg. 1990 only.

	N/A	$900 - 1,050	$550 - 650	$1,599

A total of 750 guitars were produced.

* *1990 Collector's (Model 199S-1)* – similar to the 1990 Collector's model (1990-7), except offered in limited quantities with a Super shallow bowl and a Sunburst finish, mfg. 1990 only.

	N/A	$950 - 1,050	$600 - 700	$1,599

A total of 100 guitars were produced.

1991 COLLECTOR'S (MODEL 1991-4) – single cutaway Balladeer deep bowl-style body, solid spruce top, round soundhole with elaborate rosette, multiple body bindings, 14/20-fret ebony fingerboard with single/double diamond and 12th fret "1991" inlay, natural headstock with "Ovation" and "25 years" decal, three-per-side chrome tuners, rosewood bridge, OP24 3-band electronics, available in Natural finish, mfg. 1991 only.

	N/A	$775 - 900	$475 - 550	$1,159

A total of 1,464 guitars were produced.

MSR/NOTES	100%	EXCELLENT	AVERAGE	LAST MSR

* 1991 Collector's (Model 1991-5) – similar to the 1991 Collector's, except available in Black Metallic finish, mfg. 1991 only.

	N/A	$825 - 950	$500 - 575	$1,159

A total of 292 guitars were produced.

1992 COLLECTOR'S (MODEL 1992-H) – Elite model design, quilted ash top, super shallow bowl, single cutaway, available in Honeyburst finish, mfg. 1992 only.

	N/A	$1,000 - 1,150	$625 - 675	$1,699

A total of 1,995 guitars were produced.

1993 COLLECTOR'S (MODEL 1993-4) – single round cutaway folk-style, solid spruce top, multi upper bout soundholes, 5-stripe bound body, multiple woods veneer around soundholes, medium bowl body, mahogany/padauk/ebony 5-piece neck, 22-fret ebony fingerboard with 12th fret banner inlay, strings through walnut bridge, maple logo inlay on peghead, 3-per-side gold Schaller tuners with ebony buttons, piezo bridge pickup, volume/3-band EQ control, active preamp, available in Natural finish, mfg. 1993 only.

	N/A	$850 - 975	$500 - 575	$1,499

A total of 1,537 guitars were produced.

1994 COLLECTOR'S (MODEL 1994-7) – single round cutaway folk style, solid spruce top, round soundhole, bound body, multi wood purfling, ash/ebony/pearl rosette, medium bowl body, mahogany/ebony/purpleheart 5-piece neck, 21-fret ebony extended fingerboard with 12th fret banner inlay, strings through ebony bridge, ebony veneered peghead with screened logo, 3-per-side gold tuners with ebony buttons, piezo bridge pickup, Optima EQ system, available in Nutmeg finish, mfg. 1994 only.

	N/A	$1,000 - 1,150	$600 - 700	$1,695

A total of 1,763 guitars were produced.

1995 COLLECTOR'S (MODEL 1995-7) – mid-depth bowl, single cutaway, round soundhole, available in Nutmeg finish, mfg. 1995 only.

	N/A	$1,100 - 1,250	$675 - 800	$1,899

A total of 1,502 guitars were produced.

1996 COLLECTOR'S (MODEL 1996-TPB) – solid Sitka spruce top, mid-depth bowl, single cutaway, five piece mahogany/maple/ebony neck, bound ebony fingerboard with mother-of-pearl inlay, Stereo HexFX piezo pickup system, 3+3 headstock, round soundhole, available in a Trans. Burgundy finish, mfg. 1996 only.

	N/A	$1,100 - 1,250	$675 - 800	$2,199

A total of 1,280 guitars were produced.

1997 COLLECTOR'S (MODEL 1997-7N) – narrow waist ("salon style") walnut-bound body, solid Sitka spruce top, round soundhole, maple leaf rosette, unbound 14/20-fret fingerboard, CP 100 piezo pickup system, 3-per-side slotted headstock with walnut veneer, onboard Stealth TS preamp, available in Nutmeg Stain finish, mfg. 1997 only.

	N/A	$1,000 - 1,150	$600 - 700	$1,799

This model is also available with a wider neck as Model 1997-7W. Every 1997 Collector's Series instrument is accompanied by a copy of Walter Carter's *The History of the Ovation Guitar* book.

1998 COLLECTOR'S (MODEL 1998) – single round cutaway style, figured maple top, laser cut leaf epaulets shaped with a cluster of 15 smaller soundholes, bound body, mid depth bowl body, 5-piece maple/mahogany neck, 22-fret rosewood fingerboard with 12th fret inlay, strings through rosewood bridge, 3-per-side tuners, piezo bridge pickup, OP-24E system, available in New England Burst finish, mfg. 1998 only.

	N/A	$900 - 1,050	$550 - 650	$1,649

1999 COLLECTOR'S (MODEL 1999) – single cutaway style, laser cut leaf epaulets with a cluster of 15 soundholes, red waterfall bubinga top, Optima preamp with tuner, 5-piece maple/mahogany neck, 22-fret ebony fingerboard, mid depth bowl body with light bracing, 3-per-side tuners, mfg. 1999 only.

	N/A	$950 - 1,100	$575 - 675	$1,749

2000 COLLECTOR'S (MODEL 2000-THA) – single cutaway style, laser cut leaf epaulets with a cluster of 15 soundholes, figured lacewood top, 5-piece mahogany/maple neck, "V" shaped neck, Optima preamp, Tru-Balance pickup, built in chromatic tuner, mid-depth body, 3-per-side tuners, gold Ovation tuners, available in Transparent Honey finish, mfg. 2000 only.

	N/A	$775 - 900	$475 - 550	$1,599

2001 COLLECTOR'S (MODEL 2001-FRA) – single cutaway style, laser cut leaf epaulets with a cluster of 15 soundholes, figured solid Redwood top, 5-piece mahogany/maple neck, Ovation Tru-Balance pickup, OP-24+C preamp, 3-band EQ, 2 mid frequencies, built in chromatic tuner, gold Ovation tuners, 3-per-side tuners, available in Figured Redwood Natural Gloss finish, mfg. 2001 only.

	N/A	$1,100 - 1,250	$650 - 750	$1,899

2002 COLLECTOR'S (MODEL 2002-AC) – mid depth single cutaway style, multi soundhole 5-piece epaulet, figured figured African Cherry top, ebony fingerboard and bridge, 12th fret MOP inlay, Ovation Tru-Balance pickup, OP-40 preamp, 3-band EQ, volume, built in chromatic tuner, gold Ovation tuners, 3-per-side tuners, available in African Cherry finish, mfg. 2002 only.

	N/A	$1,150 - 1,300	$700 - 825	$1,999

MSR/NOTES	100%	EXCELLENT	AVERAGE	LAST MSR

2003 COLLECTOR'S (MODEL 2003-VN) – mid depth single cutaway style, multi soundhole 5-piece epaulet, solid Sitka spruce top, ebony fingerboard and bridge, 12th fret LE inlay, Ovation Hi-Output pickup, OP-40 preamp, 3-band EQ, volume, built in chromatic tuner, gold Ovation tuners, 3-per-side tuners, available in Vintage Natural finish, mfg. 2003 only.

	N/A	$1,050 - 1,200	$675 - 775	$2,159

2005 COLLECTOR'S (MODEL 2005-ES) – single cutaway deep contour bowl, Englemann spruce top, LX bracing, round soundhole, abalone and trimmed ivory rosette, deluxe ebony fingerboard with 12th fret inlay, three-per-side tuners, original patented pickup, gold hardware, available in Natural finish, mfg. 2005 only.

	N/A	$950 - 1,100	$600 - 700	$1,999

2006 COLLECTOR'S (MODEL 2006-FKOA) – single cutaway deep contoured body, solid figured koa top, LX scalloped bracing, multiple soundholes inlaid in flame maple epaulet on the bass bout only, one-piece cedro neck, 14/23-fret ebony fingerboard with 12th fret Collector's inlay, three-per-side gold tuners with black buttons, ebony bridge, original patented pickup, VIP-5 electronics, 25.25 in. scale, available in Figured Koa finish, mfg. 2006 only.

	N/A	$1,250 - 1,450	$750 - 900	$2,829

2007 COLLECTOR'S (MODEL 2007-BCS) – single cutaway deep contoured body, solid bear claw spruce top, LX scalloped bracing, multiple soundholes inlaid in spalted maple epaulet on the bass bout only, one-piece cedro neck, 14/23-fret ebony fingerboard with flamed maple and 12th fret Collector's inlay, three-per-side black tuners with black buttons, ebony bridge, Ovation high-output pickup, VIP-5 electronics, 25.25 in. scale, available in Vintage Natural finish, mfg. 2007 only.

	N/A	$1,050 - 1,200	$650 - 800	$2,279

2008 COLLECTOR'S (MODEL 2008-5) – Adamas branded, single cutaway deep contoured body, graphite top, LX scalloped bracing, multiple soundholes inlaid in exotic woods epaulet on the bass bout only, brown patterned top inlay, 14/23-fret walnut fingerboard with gold leaf and 12th fret Collector's inlays, slotted headstock, three-per-side gold Schaller tuners, carved Walnut bridge, Ovation high-output pickup, VIP-5 electronics, 25.25 in. scale, available in Black finish, molded case included, mfg. 2008 only.

	N/A	$2,800 - 3,300	$1,800 - 2,100	$5,000

2009 COLLECTOR'S (MODEL 2009-FKOA) – deep contour body, solid figured koa top, scalloped bracing, round soundhole with abalone celtic knot rosette, abalone purfling, 14/20-fret ebony fingerboard with abalone celtic knot inlays, koa headstock overlay with Ovation logo, three-per-side gold tuners with pearl buttons, ebony bridge, OP Pro Studio with XLR electronics, available in Figured Koa (Natural) finish, 25.25 in. scale, limited edition run of 150 instruments, mfg. 2009 only.

	N/A	$1,600 - 1,900	$1,000 - 1,200	$3,599

2010 COLLECTOR'S LIMITED EDITION ELITE CUSTOM (MODEL 2078LE) – single cutaway deep contour body, solid Adirondack spruce top, scalloped X bracing, 11 multi-sized soundholes in the upper bass bout and four multi-sized soundholes in the treble bout both inlaid with walnut, oak, cherry, and hickory, cherry colored binding, 14/22-fret extended walnut fingerboard with cherry Elite-style tirangle inlays, three-per-side gold tuners, walnut bridge, Ovation High Output pickup, OP Pro Studio electronics, available in Natural Adirondack Spruce finish, 25.25 in. scale, mfg. 2010 only.

$2,000	$1,200 - 1,500	$750 - 950	$2,849

ACOUSTIC: COUNTRY ARTIST/FOLKLORE/JOSH WHITE SERIES

This series was introduced in 1967 as the Josh White Model (1114). Josh White was a blues and folk singer. He would actually visit the factory in the early days and they decided to make a guitar for him. Josh liked the wider neck Ovation offered that his current Guild did not. The Josh White model would become the fourth model in Ovation's product line. After he died in 1970, Ovation discontinued the model. In 1972, they reintroduced the same guitar (Model 1114), but as a different name, the Folklore. A new electric Folklore was introduced at the same time as the Model 1614. These models were produced until 1983, when they were discontinued again. In 1994, they reintroduced the Folklore once again, this time as the Model 6774.

The Country Artist was introduced to replace the Josh White model. The Josh Model was reintroduced in 1972, but it did not disc. the Country Artist model. The Country Artist model was produced into circa 1990, but was reintroduced in 1994 as a new model.

ARTIST CUTAWAY CONTOUR LX (MODEL 2773LX) – nylon-string configuration, single cutaway deep contoured body, solid-spruce top, scalloped LX bracing, round soundhole with inlaid tortoise rosette, 14/20-fret ebony fingerboard, slotted headstock, three-per-side open-style gold tuners with black buttons, ebony bridge, original patented pickup, OP-PRO electronics, available in Natural finish, 25.25 in. scale, mfg. 2008-2010.

$1,900	$1,150 - 1,400	$700 - 850	$2,749

ARTIST CUTAWAY MID-DEPTH LX (MODEL 6773LX) – nylon-string configuration, single cutaway mid-depth body, solid-spruce top, LX scalloped bracing, round soundhole with inlaid tortoise rosette, ANS, 14/20-fret ebony fingerboard, three-per-side open-style gold tuners with black buttons, ebony bridge, original patented pickup, OP-PRO electronics, available in Natural finish, 25.25 in. scale, mfg. 2006-2010.

$1,900	$1,150 - 1,400	$700 - 850	$2,749

MSR/NOTES	100%	EXCELLENT	AVERAGE	LAST MSR

COUNTRY ARTIST ACOUSTIC (MODEL 1124) – nylon string, classical style, shallow bowl, 14 frets clear of body, flat fingerboard, slotted 3-per-side tuners, mfg. 1971-1990.

| | N/A | $475 - 550 | $275 - 325 | |

COUNTRY ARTIST ELECTRIC (MODEL 1624) – nylon string, classical style, shallow bowl, 14 frets clear of body, flat fingerboard, slotted 3-per-side tuners, electronics and preamp, mfg. 1971-1990.

| | N/A | $525 - 600 | $300 - 375 | |

COUNTRY ARTIST CUTAWAY ELECTRIC (MODEL 1674) – nylon string, classical single cutaway body, shallow bowl, 14 frets clear of body, flat fingerboard, slotted 3-per-side tuners, electronics and preamp, mfg. 1982-1990.

| | N/A | $550 - 650 | $325 - 400 | |

COUNTRY ARTIST CUTAWAY ELECTRIC (MODEL 6773) – classical single cutaway body, mid-depth bowl, solid Sitka spruce top, round soundhole, inlaid rosette, five-piece maple and mahogany neck, 14/21-fret ebony fingerboard with 12th fret inlay, OP-X electronics, three-per-side slotted headstock, available in Natural finish, mfg. 1994-2005.

| | N/A | $825 - 950 | $550 - 650 | $1,849 |

COUNTRY ARTIST SPECIAL CUTAWAY ELECTRIC (MODEL S773) – similar to the Country Artist Model, mfg. 2001-04.

| | N/A | $525 - 600 | $350 - 425 | $1,149 |

FOLKLORE (MODEL 1114) – spruce top, round soundhole, mid-depth bowl back, inlaid rosette, 12/18-fret ebony fingerboard with dot inlays and 12th fret diamonds, walnut bridge, 3-per-side slotted headstock, available in Natural finish, mfg. 1972-1983.

| | N/A | $575 - 675 | $275 - 325 | |

* *Folklore Electric (Model 1614)* – similar to the Folklore, except has electronics, mfg. 1972-1983.

| | N/A | $625 - 725 | $300 - 375 | |

FOLKLORE (MODEL 6774) – single cutaway solid Sitka spruce top, round soundhole, mid-depth bowl back, inlaid rosette, five-piece mahogany/maple neck, 21-fret ebony fingerboard, walnut bridge, three-per-side slotted headstock, OP-X preamp, available in a Natural finish, mfg. 1994-2005.

| | N/A | $825 - 950 | $550 - 650 | $1,849 |

FOLKLORE CUTAWAY CONTOUR LX (MODEL 2774LX) – single cutaway deep contoured body, solid-spruce top, LX scalloped bracing, round soundhole with inlaid tortoise rosette, 14/20-fret ebony fingerboard, slotted headstock, three-per-side open-style gold tuners, ebony bridge, original patented pickup, OP-PRO electronics, available in Natural finish, 25.25 in. scale, mfg. 2008-2010.

| | $1,900 | $1,150 - 1,400 | $700 - 850 | $2,749 |

FOLKLORE CUTAWAY MID-DEPTH LX (MODEL 6774LX) – single cutaway mid-depth body, solid-spruce top, LX scalloped bracing, round soundhole with inlaid tortoise rosette, ANS, 14/20-fret ebony fingerboard, three-per-side open-style gold tuners with black buttons, ebony bridge, original patented pickup, OP-PRO electronics, available in Natural finish, 25.25 in. scale, mfg. 2006-2010.

| | $1,900 | $1,150 - 1,400 | $700 - 850 | $2,749 |

JOSH WHITE (MODEL 1114) – spruce top, round soundhole, mid-depth bowl back, inlaid rosette, 12/18-fret ebony fingerboard with dot inlays and 12th fret diamonds, walnut bridge, 3-per-side slotted headstock, available in Natural finish, mfg. 1967-1970.

| | N/A | $650 - 800 | $400 - 475 | |

JOSH WHITE 40TH ANNIVERSARY (K1114) – classical-style non-cutaway deep body, AA solid Sitka spruce top, round soundhole with oakleaf rosette, black/white multi-layer binding, 12/18-fret ebony fingerboard with dot and diamond inlays, open-style headstock with three-per-side chrome tuners and pearl buttons, Brazilian rosewood bridge, Natural finish, 25.25 in. scale, mfg. 2006 only.

| | N/A | $1,150 - 1,350 | $700 - 850 | $2,499 |

ACOUSTIC: CUSTOM LEGEND SERIES

Custom Legend models have an AAA grade solid Sitka spruce top, spruce struts, custom bracing, and the active OP-24 piezo electronics package.

An example of a Legend 12 Electric courtesy Dave Rogers, Dave's Guitar Shop

MSR/NOTES	100%	EXCELLENT	AVERAGE	LAST MSR

CUSTOM LEGEND (MODEL 1119) – spruce top, round soundhole, abalone bound body, abalone leaf pattern rosette, 14/20-fret bound ebony fingerboard with abalone diamond/dot inlay, strings through walnut bridge with carved flower design/pearl dot inlay, walnut veneered peghead with abalone logo inlay, 3-per-side gold tuners with pearloid buttons, available in Black, Natural, Sunburst, or White finish, mfg. 1974-1990.

	N/A	$700 - 825	$450 - 525	

CUSTOM LEGEND 12 (MODEL 1159) – similar to the Custom Legend, except in 12-string configuration, mfg. 1980-1990.

	N/A	$750 - 875	$475 - 550	

CUSTOM LEGEND ELECTRIC (MODEL 1619/1719) – spruce top, round soundhole, abalone bound body, abalone leaf pattern rosette, five-piece mahogany/maple neck, 14/20-fret bound ebony fingerboard with abalone diamond/dot inlay, strings through walnut bridge with carved flower design/pearl dot inlay, walnut veneered peghead with abalone logo inlay, three-per-side gold tuners with pearloid buttons, piezo bridge pickups, volume control, 3-band EQ, active preamp, available in Black, Natural, Sunburst, or White finish, mfg. 1974-1996, reintroduced 2005-07.

1974-1979	N/A	$800 - 950	$500 - 575	
1980-1996	N/A	$700 - 825	$450 - 525	
2005-2007	N/A	$850 - 1,050	$525 - 625	$2,149

This model was reintroduced in 2005 as part of the Traditional Series, with OP-50 electronics and available in Black finish.

* *Custom Legend 12 (Model 1759)* – similar to Custom Legend Electric, except in 12-string configuration, 6-per-side tuners, available in Black or Natural finish, mfg. 1980-1999.

	N/A	$950 - 1,100	$650 - 750	$2,099

* *Custom Legend Cutaway Electric (Model 1779)* – similar to Custom Legend except has a single cutaway and a mid-depth bowl body, available in Sunburst or Cherry Cherryburst finish, disc. 2007.

	N/A	$900 - 1,050	$525 - 600	$2,149

* *Custom Legend Special Order USA (Model 1779-USA)* – similar to the Custom Legend special order, except has custom American Flag graphics, mfg. 2002-03.

	N/A	$1,650 - 1,900	$1,050 - 1,200	$3,299

* *Custom Legend Special Order 12 String (Model 6759)* – similar to Custom Legend Special Order except in a 12-string configuration, available in Black or Natural finish, disc. 2004.

	N/A	$950 - 1,100	$650 - 750	$2,099

CUSTOM LEGEND CUTAWAY ELECTRIC (MODEL 1669/1769) – similar to Custom Legend, except has single rounded cutaway, available in Cherry Cherryburst, Cadillac Greenburst, and Sunburst finish, mfg. 1982-1993, 1996-99.

	N/A	$950 - 1,100	$600 - 700	$1,999

* *Custom Legend Cutaway Shallow Electric (Model 1569/1759)* – similar to Custom Legend, except has single round cutaway body, super shallow bowl, available in Black, Cherry Cherryburst, Natural, or Sunburst finish, mfg. 1984-2004.

	N/A	$950 - 1,100	$600 - 700	$1,999

CUSTOM LEGEND LX (MODEL C779LX) – single cutaway mid-depth bowl, AAA solid Sitka spruce top, round soundhole with hand-laid abalone rosette, deluxe ebony fingerboard with abalone dot and diamond inlays, three-per-side tuners, ebony bridge, Original Patented Pickups, gold hardware, available in Black or Cherry Cherry Burst finish, mfg. 2005-2010.

	$2,000	$1,200 - 1,500	$800 - 950	$2,899

* *Custom Legend LX Contour (Model C2079LX)* – similar to the Custom Legend LX, except has a deep contour body and oakleaf pattern rosette, mfg. summer 2005-2010.

	$2,000	$1,200 - 1,500	$800 - 950	$2,899

CUSTOM LEGEND AX (MODEL C2079AX) – single cutaway deep-depth bowl, AAA solid Sitka spruce top, scalloped X bracing, round soundhole with hand-laid abalone oak leaf rosette, white binding with abalone purfling, five-piece mahogany/maple neck, 14/20-fret bound ebony fingerboard with abalone dot and diamond inlays, black headstock overlay, three-per-side gold tuners with pearl buttons, ebony bridge, Ovation OCP-1K pickup, OP Pro Studio electronics, available in Black or Cherry Cherry Burst finish, 25.25 in. scale, case included, mfg. 2011-present.

MSR $1,569	$1,100	$650 - 800	$400 - 475	

CUSTOM LEGEND WITH ROLAND GR SYNTH (MODEL R 869) – similar to the Custom Legend, except has a factory installed Roland GR Series synthesizer interface, available in Natural finish, mfg. 1998 only.

	N/A	$1,150 - 1,300	$725 - 850	$2,499

CUSTOM LEGEND AL DI MEOLA SIGNATURE (MODEL 1769) – Custom Legend style body, deep cutaway, AAA Sitka spruce top, hand inlaid abalone purfling, ebony fingerboard and bridge, three-per-side 24kt. gold Ovation die cast tuners, abalone inlays, Ovation High Output or Ovation piezo electric pickup, OP-50 or OP-Pro preamp, available in Black or Natural finish, mfg. 1999-present.

MSR $4,299	$3,000	$1,675 - 2,100	$1,000 - 1,250	

MSR/NOTES	100%	EXCELLENT	AVERAGE	LAST MSR

CUSTOM LEGEND 30TH COMMEMORATIVE (MODEL 1719-30CM) – similar to the Custom Legend, top grade Bearclaw spruce top, custom inlays, available in Vintage Natural finish, mfg. 2004 only.

	N/A	$1,200 - 1,500	$750 - 900	$2,499

ACOUSTIC: ELITE SERIES

The Elite Series design is similar to the Adamas models, but substitutes a solid Spruce or solid cedar top in place of the composite materials. Standard models feature 22 soundholes of varying sizes, while the cutaway models only have 15 soundholes. Ovation also produced a small quantity of non-cutaway Elite LX Models that were numbered Model 1868LX.

ELITE (MODEL 1718) – spruce top, five-stripe bound body, five-piece mahogany/maple neck, 14/22-fret extended rosewood fingerboard with maple triangle inlay, walnut bridge, three-per-side gold tuners, six piezo bridge pickups, volume control, 3-band EQ, active OP-24 preamp, available in Black, Natural, Natural Cedar, Sunburst, or White finish, mfg. 1982-1997, 2005-07.

	N/A	$700 - 850	$450 - 525	$1,699

This model was reintroduced in 2005 as part of the Traditional Series, with OP-40 electronics and available in Sunburst or Black finishes.

* *Elite Cutaway (Model 1768)* – similar to Elite, except has single cutaway body, available in Sunburst, Black, White, or Natural finish, mfg. 1990-98.

	N/A	$775 - 900	$500 - 575	$1,699

A cedar top was optional from 1993-98.

* *Elite Cutaway 1996 Limited Edition (Model 1768-7 LTD)* – similar to the Elite Cutaway, except features an ebony fingerboard with 12th fret inlay, walnut bridge, fancy body binding, and gold hardware, available in Nutmeg finish, mfg. 1996 only.

	N/A	$1,000 - 1,200	$600 - 700	

* *Elite Deep Contour LX (Model 2078LX)* – similar to the Elite, except has a deep-contour bowl, and LX upgrades including enhanced scalloped LX bracing, advanced neck system, Ovation Original Patented Pickup, and Op-Pro preamp, available in Black, Black Cherry Burst, or Natural finish, mfg. 2006-2010.

	$1,750	$1,050 - 1,300	$625 - 750	$2,499

* *Elite Mid-Depth Model (Model 1778)* – similar to Elite Model 1768 except has a mid-depth bowl body, available in Natural, Black, or Black Cherryburst, mfg. 1998-2004.

	N/A	$650 - 750	$400 - 475	$1,360

* *Elite LX (Model 1778LX)* – similar to the Elite, except has LX upgrades including enhanced scalloped LX bracing, advanced neck system, Ovation Original Patented Pickup, and Op-Pro preamp, available in Black, Black Cherry Burst, Cherry Cherry Burst (disc.), Honey Burst (2008 only), or Natural finish, mfg. 2004-2010.

	$1,750	$1,050 - 1,300	$625 - 750	$2,499

* *Elite Left-Handed Mid-Depth Model (Model L778)* – similar to the Elite mid-depth, except in left-handed configuration, available in Natural or Black Cherryburst finishes, disc. 2003.

	N/A	$825 - 950	$525 - 600	$1,799

* *Elite Super Shallow Cutaway (Model 1868)* – similar to Elite, except has super shallow bowl body, single rounded cutaway, available in Black, Black Cherryburst, Natural, or Sunburst finishes, mfg. 1983-2004.

	N/A	$650 - 750	$400 - 475	$1,360

* Add $100 for Angel Step Walnut finish (Model 5868, mfg. 1993 only).

A cedar top was optional since 1993.

* *Elite 12 (Model 1758)* – similar to the Elite, except in 12-string configuration, available in Sunburst, Black, White, or Natural finish, mfg. 1989-1993.

	N/A	$775 - 900	$450 - 525	$1,575

* Add $100 for Angel Step Walnut finish (Model 5858, mfg. 1993 only).

* *Elite Shallow 12 (Model 1858)* – similar to Elite Shallow, except in 12-string configuration, available in Black Cherryburst or Sunburst finish, mfg. 1993-2004.

	N/A	$775 - 900	$450 - 525	$1,589

ELITE AX (MODEL 2078AX) – single cutaway deep-depth bowl, AA solid Sitka spruce top, scalloped X bracing, 11 multi-sized soundholes in the upper bass bout and four multi-sized soundholes in the treble bout both inlaid with exotic hardwoods, multi-ply binding, five-piece mahogany/maple neck, 14/22-fret extended bound ebony fingerboard with abalone triangle inlays, black headstock overlay, three-per-side gold tuners with pearl buttons, ebony bridge, Ovation OCP-1K pickup, OP Pro Studio electronics, available in Black or Black Cherry Burst finish, 25.25 in. scale, case included, mfg. 2011-present.

MSR $1,429	$1,000	$600 - 725	$375 - 450	

CUSTOM ELITE (MODEL CE-768) – spruce top, single cutaway body, deep bowl, 5-piece mahogany/maple neck, 22-fret extended rosewood fingerboard with maple triangle inlay, walnut bridge, 3-per-side gold tuners, piezo bridge pickup, volume control, 3-band EQ, active OP-X preamp, available in Black Cherryburst finish, mfg. 1996-99.

	N/A	$900 - 1,050	$600 - 700	$1,999

MSR/NOTES	100%	EXCELLENT	AVERAGE	LAST MSR

* **Custom Elite Deep Contour LX (Model C2078LX)** – similar to the Custom Elite, except has a deep-contour bowl, and LX upgrades including enhanced scalloped LX bracing, advanced neck system, Ovation Original Patented Pickup, and Op-Pro preamp, available in Black or Red Tear Drop finish, mfg. 2006-2010.

	$2,000	$1,200 - 1,500	$750 - 900	$2,899

* **Custom Elite Mid-Depth (Model CE-778)** – similar to Elite, except has Mid-Depth bowl body, available in Black Cherryburst finish, mfg. 1998-2007.

	N/A	$950 - 1,100	$575 - 650	$2,149

* **Custom Elite Shallow (Model CE-868)** – similar to Elite, except has super shallow bowl body, available in Black Cherryburst finish, mfg. 1996-2004.

	N/A	$900 - 1,050	$600 - 700	$1,999

* **Custom Elite LX (Model C778LX)** – similar to the Custom Elite, except has a AAA solid Sitka spruce top, custom laid epaulets, five-piece mahogany/maple neck, 14/22-fret ebony fingerboard with triangle inlays, three-per-side tuners, ebony bridge, OP-Pro preamp, OPP pickup, gold hardware, available in Black Cherry Burst or Red Tear Drop Burst finish, mfg. 2005-2010.

	$2,000	$1,200 - 1,500	$750 - 900	$2,899

CUSTOM ELITE AX (MODEL C2078X) – single cutaway deep-depth bowl, AAA solid Sitka spruce top, scalloped X bracing, 11 multi-sized soundholes in the upper bass bout and four multi-sized soundholes in the treble bout both inlaid with exotic hardwoods, white binding with abalone purfling, five-piece mahogany/maple neck, 14/22-fret extended bound ebony fingerboard with abalone triangle inlays, black headstock overlay, three-per-side gold tuners with pearl buttons, ebony bridge, Ovation OCP-1K pickup, OP Pro Studio electronics, available in Black or Red Teardrop Burst finish, 25.25 in. scale, case included, mfg. 2011-present.

MSR $1,569	$1,100	$650 - 800	$400 - 475	

ELITE SPECIAL (MODEL S778) – single cutaway mid-depth bowl, A Grade spruce top, rosewood slanted end fingerboard, walnut bridge, multi-soundhole five-piece epaulet, Thinline under-saddle pickup, OP30 preamp, three-per-side Ovation chrome tuners, available in Natural or Autumn Burst finish, mfg. 2000-07.

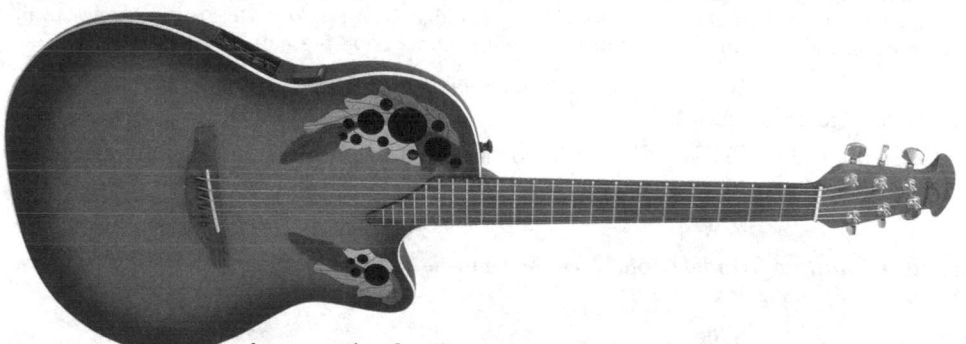

An example of a Elite Special courtesy John Beeson, The Music Shoppe

	N/A	$600 - 700	$375 - 450	$1,399

* **Elite Special (Model S868)** – similar to the Elite Special, except has a shallow body, available in Natural finish, mfg. 2000-04.

	N/A	$600 - 700	$375 - 450	$1,099

ELITE STANDARD (MODEL 6718) – spruce top, 5-stripe bound body, mahogany neck, 14/22-fret extended rosewood fingerboard, strings through rosewood bridge with pearl dot inlay, rosewood veneered peghead with ebony/maple logo inlay, 3-per-side chrome tuners, piezo bridge pickups, volume control, 3-band EQ, active preamp, available in Cherry Sunburst, Root Beer, or Vintage finish, mfg. 1993-96.

	N/A	$525 - 600	$325 - 375	$1,095

* **Elite Standard Cutaway (Model 6778)** – similar to Elite Standard, except has single round cutaway, available in Black, Black Cherryburst, Cadillac Greenburst (1998-99), Natural, or New England Burst (2005-06) finish, mfg. 1998-99, reintroduced 2005-07.

	N/A	$650 - 750	$400 - 475	$1,449

This model was reintroduced in 2005 as part of the Traditional Series, with OP-30 electronics and available in Black, New England Burst, or Sunburst finishes.

* **Elite Standard Deep Cutaway (Model 6768)** – similar to the Elite Standard, except has a deep body and single cutaway, available in Cherry Sunburst, Vintage, or Root Beer finishes, mfg. 1994-95.

	N/A	$550 - 650	$300 - 375	

* **Elite Standard LX (Model 6778LX)** – similar to the Standard Elite, except has LX upgrades including enhanced scalloped LX bracing, advanced neck system, Ovation Original Patented Pickup, and Op-Pro preamp, available in Black, Cherry Cherry Burst (2004-06), Natural, or New England Burst finish, mfg. 2004-08.

	N/A	$750 - 900	$475 - 550	$1,749

MSR/NOTES	100%	EXCELLENT	AVERAGE	LAST MSR

* **Elite Standard Cutaway Contour LX (Model 2778LX)** – similar to the Standard Elite, except has a deep contour body and LX upgrades including enhanced scalloped LX bracing, advanced neck system, Ovation Original Patented Pickup, and Op-Pro preamp, available in Black, Natural, or New England Burst finish, mfg. summer 2007-08.

	N/A	$750 - 900	$475 - 550	$1,749

» **Elite Standard Cutaway Contour 12-String LX (Model 2758LX)** – similar to the Elite Standard Cutaway Contour LX, except in 12-string configuration with six-per-side tuners, available in New England Burst, mfg. summer 2007-08.

	N/A	$850 - 1,000	$525 - 600	$1,949

* **Elite Standard LX (Model 6868LX)** – similar to the Elite Standard LX, except has a super shallow bowl, available in Black or New England Burst finish, mfg. summer 2005-08.

	N/A	$750 - 900	$475 - 550	$1,749

* **Elite Standard 12-String LX (Model 6758LX)** – similar to the Standard Elite LX, except in 12-string configuration with six-per-side tuners, available in New England Burst, mfg. 2005-08.

	N/A	$850 - 1,000	$525 - 600	$1,949

* **Elite Standard 12-String (Model 6758)** – similar to Elite Standard Cutaway, except in a 12-string variation, available in Natural and Black Cherryburst finish, mfg. 1998-99.

	N/A	$700 - 825	$425 - 500	$1,449

* **Elite Standard Cutaway Shallow (Model 6868)** – similar to Elite Standard Cutaway, except has a super shallow bowl body, available in Black, Black Cherry, or Natural finish, mfg. 1994-99.

	N/A	$650 - 750	$400 - 475	$1,349

In 1998, Aspen Blue finish was introduced.

ELITE STANDARD (MODEL 2778AX) – single cutaway deep contour body, AA solid spruce top, scalloped bracing, 11 multi-sized soundholes in the upper bass bout and 4 multi-sized soundholes in the upper treble bout both inlaid with exotic hardwoods, multi-ply binding, five-piece satin-finished mahogany/maple neck, 14/23-fret bound rosewood fingerboard with pearl dots and diamond inlays, black headstock overlay with Ovation logo, three-per-side chrome tuners, rosewood bridge, OCP-1 pickup, OP-Pro electronics, available in Black, Figured Koa (mfg. 2012 only), or New England Burst finish, 25.25 in. scale, mfg. summer 2008-present.

MSR $1,149	$800	$525 - 600	$300 - 350	

* Add 5% (MSR $1,199) for Figured Koa (disc.).

* **Elite Standard 12-String (Model 2758AX)** – similar to the Elite Standard, except in 12-string configuration with six-per-side tuners, available in New England Burst finish, mfg. summer 2008-present.

MSR $1,299	$900	$575 - 675	$325 - 400	

* **Elite Standard Super Shallow (Model 6868AX)** – similar to the Elite Standard, except has a super shallow body, available in Black or New England Burst finish, mfg. summer 2008-2011.

	$800	$525 - 600	$300 - 350	$1,149

ELITE T (MODEL 1778T) – single cutaway mid-depth body, solid spruce top, ebony fingerboard and bridge, multi 11-hole soundhole on bass side only, Ovation thinline pickup, OP-30 preamp, 3-per-side black tuners, available in Black, Lusty Red, or Pewter (disc.) finish, mfg. 2002-08.

	N/A	$625 - 750	$375 - 450	$1,429

* **Elite T Contour (Model 2078T)** – similar to the Elite T, except has a deep contoured body, available in Black finish, mfg. summer 2007-08.

	N/A	$625 - 750	$375 - 450	$1,429

» **Elite T Contour 12-String (Model 2058T)** – similar to the Elite T Contour, except in 12-string configuration and six-per-side tuners, available in Black finish, mfg. summer 2007-08.

	N/A	$700 - 850	$450 - 525	$1,629

* **Elite T Shallow (Model 1868T)** – similar to the Elite T, except has a super shallow body, mfg. 2002-08.

	N/A	$625 - 750	$375 - 450	$1,429

* **Elite T Shallow Blue/Purple Flame (Model 1778T-BTF/PTF)** – similar to the Elite T, except has a Blue Flame or Purple Flame (2006-08) top and headstock, mfg. 2005-08.

	N/A	$900 - 1,050	$550 - 650	$1,999

* **Elite T Shallow Red Flame (Model 1778T-RF)** – similar to the Elite T, except has a full body Red Flame finish, mfg. 2005 only.

	N/A	$950 - 1,100	$600 - 700	$1,999

* **Elite T Shallow 12-String (Model 6758T)** – similar to the Elite T mid-depth, except in 12-string configuration, six-per-side tuners, available in Black finish, mfg. 2005-08.

	N/A	$700 - 850	$450 - 525	$1,629

MSR/NOTES	100%	EXCELLENT	AVERAGE	LAST MSR

ELITE T (MODEL 1778TX/MODEL 1778TX-5) – single cutaway mid-depth body, AA solid spruce top, scalloped X bracing, 11 hole multi-sized soundholes on the upper bass bout, three-piece maple neck, 14/23-fret extended rosewood fingerboard, black headstock overlay with Ovation logo, three-per-side black tuners, black-finished rosewood bridge, OCP-1 pickup, OP-PRO electronics, available in Black, Black Gloss Spalted Maple (2010-2011), or Pewter (2009-2011) finish, 25.25 in. scale, mfg. summer 2008-present.

MSR $859	$600	$375 - 450	$225 - 275	

- **Add 7.5% (Last MSR was $929) for Black Gloss Spalted Maple finish.**
- **Add 10% (MSR $949) for Pewter finish.**

* *Elite T Deep Contour Body (Model 2078TX)* – similar to the Elite T, except has a deep contour body, available in Black or Pewter (2009-2011) finish, mfg. summer 2008-2013.

	$600	$375 - 450	$225 - 275	$859

- **Add 10% (MSR $949) for Pewter finish.**

»*Elite T Deep Contour Body 12-String (Model 2058TX/Model 2058TX-5)* – similar to the Elite T Deep Contour Body, except in 12-string configuration with six-per-side tuners, available in Black finish, mfg. summer 2008-present.

MSR $949	$660	$425 - 500	$250 - 300	

* *Elite T Super Shallow Body (Model 1868TX/Model 1868TX-5)* – similar to the Elite T, except has a super shallow body, available in Black finish, mfg. summer 2008-2013.

	$600	$375 - 450	$225 - 275	$859

ELITE TX D-SCALE (MODEL DS778TX/MODEL DS778TX-5) – single cutaway mid-depth body tuned a full step lower (D-G-C-F-A-D), solid A grade spruce top, scalloped X bracing, 11 soundholes in the upper bass bout, maple neck, 14/22-fret extended rosewood fingerboard with no inlays, satin black headstock overlay, three-per-side black tuners, rosewood bridge, Ovation OCP-1K pickup, OP Pro electronics, available in Black finish, 28.33 in. scale, mfg. 2011-present.

MSR $979	$680	$425 - 500	$275 - 325	

ELITE TX PREMIER (MODEL 1778TX) – single cutaway, mid-depth bowl, solid cedar top, 11 multi-sized soundholes on the upper bass bout, 14/23-fret fingerboard, black headstock overlay with Ovation logo, three-per-side black tuners, black-finished rosewood bridge, OCP-1 pickup, OP-PRO electronics, available in Black with Maple Epaulet (2013-present) or Natural Cedar Stain (disc. 2013) finish, mfg. 2012-present.

MSR $949	$650	$425 - 525	$235 - 285	

LEGEND ELITE (MODEL 1735) – deep bowl, cross between the Legend and the Elite, Sitka spruce top, 5-piece maple/mahogany neck, rosewood fingerboard, electronics, mfg. 1985-1990.

	N/A	$500 - 600	$250 - 300	

* *Legend Elite 12 (Model 1736)* – similar to the Legend Elite, except in 12-string configuration, mfg. 1985-1990.

	N/A	$550 - 650	$275 - 325	

ACOUSTIC: GLEN CAMPBELL SERIES

GLEN CAMPBELL BALLADEER ACOUSTIC (MODEL 1127) – Legend style, shallow bowl, inlaid rosette, 12/18-fret bound ebony fingerboard, diamond inlays and 12th fret "GC" inlay, gold tuners, mfg. 1968-1990.

	N/A	$525 - 600	$325 - 400	

GLEN CAMPBELL BALLADEER ELECTRIC (MODEL 1627) – Balladeer style, shallow bowl, inlaid rosette, 12/18-fret bound ebony fingerboard, diamond inlays and 12th fret "GC" inlay, gold tuners, electronics and pickup, mfg. 1971-1990.

	N/A	$600 - 700	$375 - 450	

GLEN CAMPBELL 12 ACOUSTIC (MODEL 1118) – Balladeer style, 12-string configuration, shallow bowl, inlaid rosette, 12/18-fret bound ebony fingerboard, diamond inlays and 12th fret "GC" inlay, gold tuners, mfg. 1968-1990.

	N/A	$650 - 750	$400 - 475	

GLEN CAMPBELL 12 ELECTRIC (MODEL 1618) – Balladeer style, 12-string configuration, shallow bowl, inlaid rosette, 12/18-fret bound ebony fingerboard, diamond inlays and 12th fret "GC" inlay, gold tuners, electronics and pickup, mfg. 1971-1982.

	N/A	$700 - 800	$450 - 525	

GLEN CAMPBELL 40TH ANNIVERSARY (MODEL 1627) – non-cutaway hand-made fiberglass cloth roundback body, solid Sitka spruce top, Ovation A bracing, round soundhole with oak leaf rosette, 14/20-fret ebony fingerboard with diamond and dot inlays, three-per-side Schaller gold tuners, truss rod cover with Glen Campbell signature, walnut bridge, original patented pickup, FET electronics, available in Natural finish, 25.25 in. scale, mfg. 2006 only.

	N/A	$1,150 - 1,350	$775 - 875	$2,599

GLEN CAMPBELL 12-STRING 40TH ANNIVERSARY (MODEL 1618) – 12-string configuration, Balladeer style, non-cutaway hand-made fiberglass cloth roundback body, solid Sitka spruce top, Ovation VT-12 bracing, round soundhole with oak leaf rosette, 12/18-fret ebony fingerboard with diamond and dot inlays, six-per-side Schaller open-style gold tuners with pearl buttons, truss rod cover with Glen Campbell signature, walnut bridge, original patented pickup, FET electronics, available in Sunburst finish, 25.25 in. scale, mfg. 2006 only.

	N/A	$1,200 - 1,400	$800 - 925	$2,699

MSR/NOTES	100%	EXCELLENT	AVERAGE	LAST MSR

ACOUSTIC: LEGEND SERIES

The Legend series was renamed from the Deluxe Balladeer series. The Legend series shares similar design patterns with the Custom Legend models, except a less ornate rosette and a standard Ovation bridge instead of the custom carved walnut version. Outside of the all acoustic Model 1117, Legend series models feature the active OP-24 preamp electronics. For the Legend Elite model refer to the Elite series.

LEGEND (MODEL 1117) – spruce top, round soundhole, 5-stripe bound body, leaf pattern rosette, 5-piece mahogany/maple neck, 14/20-fret bound rosewood fingerboard with pearl diamond/dot inlay, walnut bridge, walnut veneer on peghead, 3-per-side gold tuners, available in Black, Natural, Sunburst, or White finish, mfg. 1972-1999.

1972-1979	N/A	$650 - 750	$400 - 475	
1980-1989	N/A	$550 - 650	$350 - 425	
1990-1999	N/A	$475 - 550	$325 - 375	$999

In 1994, Cherry Cherryburst and Tobacco Sunburst finishes were introduced, bound ebony fingerboard replaced original parts/design, Sunburst and White finishes were discontinued.

LEGEND 12 (MODEL 1156) – similar to the Legend, except in 12-string configuration, mfg. 1982-late 1980s.

N/A	$600 - 700	$350 - 425	

LEGEND ELECTRIC (MODEL 1617/1717) – similar to Legend, except has piezo bridge pickup, volume control, 3-band EQ, OP-X active preamp on later models, available in Black, Cherry Cherryburst, or Natural finish, mfg. 1972-1998, reintroduced 2005-07.

N/A	$700 - 825	$450 - 525	$1,599

This model was reintroduced in 2005 as part of the Traditional Series, with OP-40 electronics and available in Natural or Black finish.

LEGEND 12 ELECTRIC (MODEL 1656/1756) – similar to Legend Electric, except in 12-string configuration, available in Cherry Cherryburst or Natural finish, mfg. 1982-1993.

N/A	$675 - 800	$425 - 500	$1,399

LEGEND CUTAWAY ELECTRIC (MODEL 1777) – similar to Legend, except has single round cutaway, mid-depth bowl, volume control, 3-band EQ, OP-X active preamp, available in Black, Cherry Cherryburst, Natural, or Red Stain finish, mfg. 1997-2007.

N/A	$700 - 825	$450 - 525	$1,599

* **Add $100 for Recording Model Telex mic/OptiMax preamp system (Model 1777-4RM).**

* *Legend LX (Model 1777LX)* – similar to the Legend, except has LX upgrades including enhanced scalloped LX bracing, advanced neck system, Ovation Original Patented Pickup, and Op-Pro preamp, available in Black, Cherry Cherry Burst (disc.), Natural, Red Tear Drop, or Trans. Burgundy (2008 only) finish, mfg. 2004-2010.

$1,700	$1,050 - 1,250	$600 - 700	$2,399

* *Legend LX 12-String (Model 6756LX)* – similar to the Legend, except in 12-string configuration, available in Amber Burst (2007 only), Black, or Natural finish, mfg. 2005-2010.

$1,750	$1,100 - 1,300	$625 - 750	$2,499

* *Legend LX Deep Contour (Model 2077LX)* – similar to the Legend, except has a deep contour body and LX upgrades including enhanced scalloped LX bracing, advanced neck system, Ovation Original Patented Pickup, and Op-Pro preamp, available in Black, Natural, or Trans. Burgundy finish, mfg. 2006-2010.

$1,700	$1,050 - 1,250	$600 - 700	$2,399

» *Legend LX Deep Contour 12-String (Model 2056LX)* – similar to the Legend LX Deep Contour (Model 2077LX), except in 12-string configuration, available in Black or Natural finish, mfg. summer 2007-2010.

$1,750	$1,100 - 1,300	$625 - 750	$2,499

* *Legend Cutaway Electric Deep (Model 1667/1767)* – similar to the Legend Cutaway Electric, except has a deep bowl, available in Cherry Cherryburst, Tobacco Burst, Black, or Natural finish, mfg. 1982-1995.

N/A	$600 - 700	$350 - 425	$1,299

* *Legend Cutaway Electric Super Shallow (Model 1567/1867)* – similar to Legend Cutaway Electric, except has a super shallow bowl body, available in Black, Cherry Cherryburst, Natural, or Red Stain finish, mfg. 1984-2004.

N/A	$600 - 700	$350 - 425	$1,289

HexFX electronics were available at no additional cost (Model 1867-HexFX).

* *Legend Cutaway Left Hand Model (Model L777)* – similar to Legend except in a left-handed configuration, mid-depth bowl body, available in Natural, Black, or Cherry Cherryburst finish, disc. 2004.

N/A	$775 - 900	$475 - 550	$1,699

* *Legend Cutaway Electric Shallow (Model 1677)* – similar to the Legend Cutaway Electric, except has a shallow bowl, mfg. 1982-1990.

N/A	$600 - 700	$350 - 425	

MSR/NOTES	100%	EXCELLENT	AVERAGE	LAST MSR

LEGEND AX (MODEL 2077AX) – single cutaway deep-depth bowl, AA solid Sitka spruce top, scalloped X bracing, round soundhole with pearl oak leaf rosette, multi-ply binding, five-piece mahogany/maple neck, 14/20-fret bound ebony fingerboard with abalone dot and diamond inlays, black headstock overlay, three-per-side gold tuners, ebony bridge, Ovation OCP-1K pickup, OP Pro Studio electronics, available in Black or Cherry Cherry Burst finish, 25.25 in. scale, case included, mfg. 2011-present.

MSR $1,429	$1,000	$600 - 725	$375 - 450	

* *Legend AX 12-String (Model 2056AX)* – similar to the Legend AX, except in 12-string configuration with six-per-side gold tuners, available in Black finish, 25.25 in. scale, mfg. 2013-present.

MSR $1,569	$1,100	$700 - 850	$400 - 475	

LEGEND 12 CUTAWAY ELECTRIC (MODEL 1866) – similar to Legend Cutaway electric, except has 12-string configuration, available in Black, Cherry Cherryburst, or Natural finish, mfg. 1989-2004, 2006-07.

	N/A	$750 - 900	$475 - 550	$1,799

HexFX electronics were available at no additional cost (Model 1866-HexFX).

LEGEND LIMITED (MODEL 1651) – similar to the Legend Electric, except has stereo electronics, available in Nutmeg finish, mfg. 1979-1988.

	N/A	$500 - 600	$325 - 375	

ACOUSTIC: LONGNECK SERIES

LONGNECK (MODEL DS 768) – similar to the Elite model six string, except has a scale length of 28 1/3 in. and is tuned one full step lower than a standard guitar, five-piece maple and mahogany neck, gold-plated hardware, and OP-X preamp, available in Natural or Cherry Cherryburst finish, mfg. 1994-99.

	N/A	$900 - 1,050	$575 - 675	$1,899

LONGNECK (MODEL DS 778) – similar to Model 768, mid-depth acoustic electric, available in Natural finish, disc. 2010.

	$1,950	$1,100 - 1,450	$700 - 850	$2,799

LONGNECK (MODEL DCS-247S) – similar to the longneck style, except has a solid spruce top, rosewood fingerboard, MOP inlays, Thinline pickup, OP-24+ preamp, gold hardware, available in Natural or Black finish, mfg. 2000-02.

	N/A	$375 - 450	$200 - 250	$800

ACOUSTIC: PINNACLE SERIES

The Pinnacle Series are made in Japan. They were first introduced internationally in 1987 and were introduced to the U.S. in 1990. They were discontinued in 1994, but reintroduced in 2002.

PINNACLE (MODEL 3712) – folk-style, spruce top, five-stripe bound body, leaf pattern rosette, mahogany neck, 14/20-fret rosewood fingerboard with white dot inlay, rosewood bridge with white dot inlay, rosewood veneer on peghead, three-per-side chrome tuners, six piezo bridge pickups, volume control, 3-band EQ, FET preamp, available in Barn Board, Black, Ebony Stain, Natural, Opaque Blue, Sunburst, Trans. Blue Stain, or White finish, mfg. 1991-93.

	N/A	$450 - 525	$250 - 300	$900

A Pinnacle Torch Top was also available in 1993 (Model 371T).

* *Pinnacle Shallow Cutaway (Model 3862)* – similar to Pinnacle, except has single round cutaway, shallow bowl body, mfg. 1991-94.

	N/A	$500 - 575	$300 - 350	$1,000

A Pinnacle Torch Top was also available in 1993 (Model 386T).

* *Pinnacle 12 Torch Top (Model 385T)* – similar to Pinnacle, except in 12-string configuration and has a torch top, available in Blue Stain, Cherry Sunburst, Natural Honey, Ebony Stain, or Sunburst finish, mfg. 1993 only.

	N/A	$550 - 650	$325 - 375	$1,250

PINNACLE (MODEL CU147) – single cutaway mid-depth body, AA grade solid Sitka spruce top, round soundhole with abalone rosette, two piece mahogany neck, rosewood fingerboard with abalone dot inlays, walnut bridge, three-per-side gold tuners, Ovation Thinline pickup, OP-30 preamp, available in Honey Burst finish, mfg. 2002-05.

	N/A	$350 - 425	$200 - 250	$790

PINNACLE DELUXE (MODEL CU247) – similar to the Pinnacle, except has quintad bracing, and mulit-soundholes with five-piece epaulet, available in Ruby Redburst finish, mfg. 2002-05.

	N/A	$400 - 475	$250 - 300	$930

ACOUSTIC: TANGENT SERIES

TANGENT (MODEL T257) – single cutaway super shallow body, spruce top, multi soundhole black epaulet, nato neck, dark rosewood fingerboard with abalone diamond inlay, Thin-line pickup, 2/4-per-side gunmetal gray tuners, available in Black finish, mfg. 2002-06.

	N/A	$350 - 425	$200 - 250	$814

MSR/NOTES	100%	EXCELLENT	AVERAGE	LAST MSR

TANGENT (MODEL 357) – similar to the Tangent, except has no epaulet soundhole inlays, available in Black Pearl or White Pearl finish, mfg. 2002-06.

	N/A	$350 - 425	$200 - 250	$814

TANGENT (MOB47) – similar to the Tangent design, except has a "surf" inspired design and surf board shaped soundholes, mid-depth body, nick-named "My Other Board," available in Blue Surf Burst, mfg. 2003-06.

	N/A	$375 - 450	$225 - 275	$860

TANGENT (MOB57) – similar to the Tangent MOB47, except has a shallow body, mfg. 2003-06.

	N/A	$375 - 450	$225 - 275	$860

ACOUSTIC: ULTRA/ULTRA DELUXE SERIES

The Ultra Deluxe models feature a solid spruce top, two piece mahogany neck, on-board OP-24Plus electronics, and a 20-fret bound rosewood fingerboard.

ULTRA ACOUSTIC (MODEL 1311/1312) – laminated spruce top, deep bowl, urelite (urethane) neck, 14/20-fret rosewood fingerboard with dot inlays, mfg. 1983-1991.

	N/A	$175 - 225	$100 - 135	$400

In 1985, a wood neck replaced the urethane neck.

ULTRA ELECTRIC (MODEL 1511/1512/1517) – laminated spruce top, deep bowl, urelite (urethane) neck, 14/20-fret rosewood fingerboard with dot inlays, electronics, mfg. 1983-1991.

	N/A	$275 - 325	$150 - 200	$600

In 1985, a wood neck replaced the urethane neck.

ULTRA DELUXE (MODEL 1317/1312-D) – spruce top, round soundhole, five-stripe bound body, leaf pattern rosette, 14/20-fret bound rosewood fingerboard with abalone diamond/dot inlay, walnut bridge with white dot inlay, rosewood veneer on peghead, three-per-side gold tuners, available in Barn Board, Black, Brownburst, Natural, or Sunburst finish, mfg. 1984-1996.

	N/A	$225 - 275	$125 - 175	$500

This model had a flame maple top with Brownburst finish as an option.

* *Ultra Deluxe Electric (Model 1517-D)* – similar to Ultra Deluxe, except has piezo bridge pickup, 4-band EQ, FET preamp, available in Black or Natural finish, mfg. 1985-1996.

	N/A	$275 - 325	$175 - 225	$600

Flame Maple top was optional with Brownburst finish.

ULTRA DELUXE 12 (MODEL 1315-D) – similar to the Ultra Deluxe, except in 12-string configuration with six-per-side tuners, mfg. 1990-93.

	N/A	$250 - 300	$150 - 200	$530

* *Ultra Deluxe 12 Electric (Model 1515-D)* – similar to the Ultra Deluxe, except in 12-string configuration with six-per-side tuners, piezo bridge pickups, 4-band EQ, preamp, available in Black or Natural finish, mfg. 1989-1995.

	N/A	$325 - 375	$175 - 225	$700

ULTRA DELUXE CUTAWAY (MODEL 1527-D) – similar to Ultra Deluxe, except has single round cutaway, piezo bridge pickup, volume/tone control, FET preamp, available in Barn Board, Brownburst, or Sunburst finish, mfg. 1984-1993.

	N/A	$350 - 400	$200 - 250	$730

* *Ultra Deluxe Shallow Cutaway (1528-D)* – similar to Ultra Deluxe, except has a single round cutaway, shallow bowl body, piezo bridge pickups, volume/tone control, FET preamp, available in Barn Board, Black, Brownburst, Natural, Redburst, Sunburst, or White finish, mfg. 1989-1995.

	N/A	$325 - 375	$175 - 225	$700

This model had a flame maple top with Brownburst finish as an option.

ULTRA (MODEL 2071) – single cutaway deep contour GS body, AA grade solid Sitka spruce top, scalloped LX bracing, round soundholes with classic Ovation abalone rosette, five-piece mahogany/maple neck, 14/20-fret rosewood fingerboard with pearl dot and diamond inlays, black headstock overlay, three-per-side chrome tuners, rosewood bridge, Ovation High-Output pickup, OP Pro preamp, available in Black (2008 only), Natural, or Sunburst (2008 only) finish, 25.25 in. scale, mfg. 2007-08.

	N/A	$550 - 650	$350 - 425	$1,279

This guitar was partially assembled overseas, shipped to the U.S. midway through production, and completed in Ovation's plant.

ULTRA (MODEL 2178) – single cutaway deep contour GS body, AA grade solid Sitka spruce top, scalloped LX bracing, multiple soundholes on either side of the fingerboard inlaid in five-piece extoic hardwood layering, five-piece mahogany/maple neck, 14/20-fret rosewood fingerboard with pearl dot and diamond inlays, black headstock overlay, three-per-side chrome tuners, walnut bridge, Ovation High-Output pickup, OP Pro preamp, available in Black, Black Cherry Burst, or Vintage Amber finish, 25.25 in. scale, mfg. 2008 only.

	N/A	$625 - 725	$375 - 450	$1,399

This guitar was partially assembled overseas, shipped to the U.S. midway through production, and completed in Ovation's plant.

MSR/NOTES	100%	EXCELLENT	AVERAGE	LAST MSR

ACOUSTIC: VIPER SERIES

The Viper was originally a solid body guitar from the mid-1970s to the early 1980s. The Viper name was then affixed to a 1990s acoustic/electric slim body design. The Viper model has a solid Spruce top and a mahogany body with acoustic chambers. An onboard active electronics package (volume and three band EQ) allows control over feedback.

VIPER (MODEL EA68) – single cutaway mahogany body with routed sound chamber, bound spruce top, 14 multi-size soundholes with various leaf wood overlay, five-piece mahogany/maple neck, 24-fret bound ebony fingerboard, strings through rosewood bridge, rosewood veneered peghead with screened logo, three-per-side gold tuners, six piezo bridge pickups, volume/3-band EQ controls, available in Black or Natural finish, mfg. 1994-2008.

	N/A	$1,100 - 1,300	$725 - 850	$2,499

VIPER 12-STRING (MODEL EA 58) – similar to the Viper, except in 12-string configuration, available in Black or Natural finish, mfg. 1996-98.

	N/A	$1,100 - 1,300	$725 - 825	$2,099

VIPER (MODEL CV68) – similar to the Viper, except has a rosewood fingerboard, walnut bridge, and has a Viper Thinline Graphic preamp, available in Black or Honey Burst finish, mfg. 2000-06.

	N/A	$400 - 475	$225 - 275	$860

VIPER NYLON (MODEL EA63) – similar to the Viper, except in six-string nylon variation, available in Black (1995-99) or Natural finish, mfg. 1995-2008.

	N/A	$1,100 - 1,300	$725 - 850	$2,499

VIPER YNGWIE MALMSTEEN NYLON SIGNATURE (MODEL YM63) – nylon-string configuration, single cutaway Viper-style chambered mahogany body, solid cedar top, two f-holes, multi-ply binding, set five-piece mahogany/maple neck, 14/20-fret ebony fingerboard, slotted headstock with ebony overlay, three-per-side open-style gold tuners with ebony buttons, walnut bridge, Ovation OCP-1K pickup, Viper 3-band electronics, available in Rossa Corsa Red or White finish, 25.25 in. scale, hardshell case included, mfg. 2012-present.

MSR $4,479	$3,200	$2,025- 2,475	$1,125 - 1,350	

VIPER YNGWIE MALMSTEEN STEEL SIGNATURE (MODEL YM68) – single cutaway Viper-style chambered mahogany body, solid cedar top, two f-holes, multi-ply binding, set five-piece mahogany/maple neck, 14/20-fret ebony fingerboard with diamond inlays, ebony headstock overlay, three-per-side gold tuners with ebony buttons, walnut bridge, Ovation OCP-1K pickup, Viper 3-band electronics, available in Rossa Corsa Red or White finish, 25.25 in. scale, hardshell case included, mfg. 2012-present.

MSR $4,479	$3,200	$2,025- 2,475	$1,125 - 1,350	

ACOUSTIC: MISC. MODELS

Although the New Hartford Artist Model RT521 (MSR $4,299) was listed in the 2014 Ovation price list, it appears it was never actually produced.

CLASSIC NYLON (MODEL 1773AX) – nylon-string configuration, single cutaway mid-depth body body, solid AA cedar top, inlaid pearl oak leaf rosette, five-piece mahogany/maple neck, 12/18-fret ebony fingerboard, slotted headstock, three-per-side gold tuners, walnut with black stain bridge, Ovation OCP-1K pickup, OP-Pro preamp with built-in tuner and 3-band EQ electronics, available in Natural finish, 26.2 in. scale, new 2014.

MSR $1,199	$850	$550 - 650	$300 - 350	

DJ ASHBA "DEMENTED SERIES" (MODEL DJA34) – single cutaway mid-depth body, spruce top, scalloped X bracing, 11 multi-sized soundholes in the upper bass bout, 14/22-fret extended rosewood fingerboard with 12th fret Custom Ashba inlays, black headstock overlay with Ashba inlays, three-per-side black tuners, rosewood bridge, Ovation Slimline pickup, OP-4BT electronics, available in four unique graphics designed by Ashba including Ashbaland (Model DJA34-AL), Bone Daddy (Model DJA34-BDY), Bone Yard (Model DJA34-BY), or Chrome Bone (Model DJA34-CHB), 25.25 in. scale, DJ Ashba gig bag included, mfg. 2010-13.

	$490	$300 - 375	$175 - 225	$700

iDea (MODEL CC24Si) – single cutaway mid-depth body, spruce top, modified X bracing, round soundhole with abalone rosette, white binding, mahogany neck, 14/20-fret bound rosewood fingerboard with abalone dot inlays, black headstock overlay with Ovation logo, three-per-side gold tuners, walnut bridge, Ovation Slimline pickup, iDea preamp/electronics with recording/playback capabilities and a USB connection, available in Black finish, 25.25 in. scale, mfg. 2010-12.

	$580	$350 - 425	$200 - 250	$829

iDea (MODEL CC44Si) – single cutaway mid-depth body, spruce top, matched lightweight bracing, 11 multi-sized soundholes in the upper bass bout and four multi-sized soundholes in the treble bout both inlaid with exotic hardwoods, white binding with abalone purfling, mahogany neck, 14/23-fret extended bound rosewood fingerboard with abalone dot inlays, black headstock overlay with Ovation logo, three-per-side gold tuners, walnut bridge, Ovation Slimline pickup, iDea preamp/electronics with recording/playback capabilities and a USB connection, available in Cherry Cherry Burst finish, 25.25 in. scale, mfg. 2010-12.

	$650	$400 - 475	$225 - 275	$929

MSR/NOTES	100%	EXCELLENT	AVERAGE	LAST MSR

iDea (MODEL CC54i) – single cutaway mid-depth body, spruce top, modified X bracing, three iDea elliptical soundholes, mahogany neck, 14/23-fret extended rosewood fingerboard with 12th fret "i" inlay, black headstock overlay with Ovation logo, three-per-side black tuners, rosewood bridge, Ovation original pickup, iDea preamp/electronics with recording/playback capabilities and a USB connection, available in Platinum finish, 25.25 in. scale, mfg. 2009-2010.

	$650	$400 - 475	$225 - 275	$929

The iDea preamp retrofit kit can be fitted for many Ovation guitars and it retails for $429.

MICK THOMPSON LIMITED EDITION (MODEL MT37) – single cutaway deep contour body, solid spruce top, scalloped X bracing, 11 multi-sized soundholes in the upper bass bout, white body binding, three-piece maple neck, 14/23-fret bound ebony fingerboard with "seven" inlaid between the 1st and 5th frets (2008-circa 2010) or no fingerboard inlays (circa 2010-present), black headstock overlay with Ovation logo, "seven" on truss rod cover (circa 2010-present), three-per-side tuners, black-stained walnut bridge, high output pickup, OP-Pro electronics, available in Black finish, 25.25 in. scale, mfg. summer 2008-2013.

	$670	$425 - 500	$250 - 300	$950

PACEMAKER/12-STRING (MODEL 1115) – 12-string configuration, unbound ebony fingerboard with dot/diamond inlays, three-per-side nickel tuners, mfg. 1968-1982.

1968-1972	N/A	$700 - 850	$425 - 500	
1973-1982	N/A	$525 - 625	$325 - 375	

In 1972, this model was renamed the Pacemaker.

PACEMAKER ELECTRIC (MODEL 1615) – similar to the Pacemaker 12-string, except has electronics, mfg. 1972-1982.

	N/A	$650 - 750	$375 - 450	

PARLOR (MODEL 5741) – narrow waist ("salon style") body, mid-depth bowl back, solid Sitka spruce top, round soundhole, inlaid rosette, five-piece mahogany/maple neck, unbound 14/21-fret ebony fingerboard, three-per-side headstock with walnut veneer, walnut bridge, CP 100 piezo pickup system, OP-X preamp, available in Brown Sunburst finish, mfg. 1998 only.

	N/A	$700 - 825	$400 - 475	$1,499

PATRIOT BICENTENNIAL – Custom Legend style, limited run of 1,776 guitars, features drum and flag with 1776/1976 graphics, mfg. 1976 only.

	N/A	$800 - 950	$500 - 600	

THUNDERBOLT – Legend style body, top has two lightning bolt soundholes instead of traditional soundholes, bound ebony fingerboard with no inlays, six-on-one side tuners, headstock with untraditional Ovation logo, available in White finish, mfg. 1988-1990.

	N/A	$450 - 525	$250 - 300	

VINTAGE LYRACHORD (MODEL 1627VL) – non-cutaway shallow Vintage Lyrachord body, solid spruce top, round soundhole with decorative rosette, multi-ply body binding, set five-piece mahogany/maple neck, 14/20-fret rosewood fingerboard with pearl dot/diamond inlays, walnut headstock overlay, three-per-side chrome tuners, walnut bridge, Ovation OCP-1K pickup, vintage Ovation FET electronics, available in Natural finish, 25.25 in. scale, mfg. 2012 only.

	$850	$500 - 625	$300 - 375	$1,199

VINTAGE LYRACHORD BALLADEER (MODEL 1771VL) – single cutaway mid-depth Vintage Lyrachord body, solid spruce top, scalloped X bracing, round soundhole with decorative rosette, multi-ply body binding, set five-piece mahogany/maple neck, 14/20-fret rosewood fingerboard with pearl dot/diamond inlays, walnut headstock overlay, three-per-side chrome tuners, walnut bridge, Ovation OCP-1K pickup, vintage Ovation FET electronics, available in Sunburst finish, 25.25 in. scale, mfg. 2012 only.

	$850	$500 - 625	$300 - 375	$1,199

VXT – single cutaway hybrid acoustic/electric design, one-piece chambered Honduras mahogany body, solid spruce top, one-piece Hounduras mahogany neck, 22-fret rosewood fingerboard with pearl dot inlays, standard Ovation headstock with three-per-side tuners, Fishman Power Bridge, two Seymour Duncan '59 humbucker pickups, three knobs (pickup v, tone, pickup blend), three-way pickup switch, active electronics, chrome hardware, available in Black, Caramel Burst, Cherry Trans., or Sunburst finish, 25.25 in. scale, mfg. 2007-09.

	N/A	$1,150 - 1,400	$725 - 875	$2,799

* **VXTD Deluxe** – similar to the VXT, except has a flame maple top, available in 59 Burst Flame or Brown Sugar Flame finish, mfg. 2008-09.

	N/A	$1,200 - 1,500	$750 - 900	$2,999

* **VXTS Standard** – similar to the VXT, except has a poplar body and two Seymour Duncan P-90 pickups available in Black or Titanium Silver finish, mfg. 2008-09.

	N/A	$1,100 - 1,350	$700 - 850	$2,699

ACOUSTIC ELECTRIC BASS

B778 BASS – single cutaway mid-depth cutaway body, solid spruce top, ebony fingerboard with MOP inlay, walnut bridge, multi soundhole five-piece epaulet, tru-balance pickup, OP-40 preamp, gold hardware, available in Black or Natural finish, mfg. 2000-2010.

	$2,275	$1,300 - 1,650	$850 - 1,050	$3,239

MSR/NOTES	100%	EXCELLENT	AVERAGE	LAST MSR

* NSB778 (Nikki Sixx Signature) Bass – similar to the B778 Bass, except has custom iron cross fingerboard inlays, matching headstock, and black hardware, available in Gray Flame Top or Red Flame top finish, 34 in. scale, mfg. 2006-2013.

	$2,650	$1,550 - 1,950	$1,000 - 1,200	$3,799

CELEBRITY (MODEL CC-074) – single round cutaway, spruce top, round soundhole, five-stripe bound body, leaf pattern rosette, mahogany neck, 20-fret bound rosewood fingerboard with pearloid diamond/dot inlay, walnut bridge with pearloid dot inlay, walnut veneer on peghead, two-per-side chrome tuners, piezo bridge pickups, volume/tone control, FET preamp, available in Ebony Stain, Natural, or Sunburst finish, mfg. 1993-96, 1998-2006.

	N/A	$400 - 475	$225 - 275	$860

CELEBRITY BASS (MODEL CC2474) – single cutaway mid-depth body, spruce top, modified quintad bracing, round soundhole with pearl ring rosette, three-piece nato neck, bound rosewood fingerboard with micro dot inlays, black headstock overlay with gold foil logo, two-per-side gold tuners, walnut bridge, Ovation Slimline pickup, OP4BT electronics, available in Black finish, 34 in. scale, disc. 2013.

	$460	$300 - 350	$175 - 225	$670

CELEBRITY DELUXE (MODEL CS-274/CC-274) – similar to the Celebrity, except features cedar top, multi-sized soundholes with leaf pattern maple veneers, 22-fret rosewood extended fingerboard with pearl dot inlay, rosewood strings through bridge, rosewood veneered peghead with logo decal, 2-per-side gold tuner, piezo bridge pickup, 4-band EQ, available in Antique Sunburst, Black, Natural, or Sunburst finishes, mfg. 1993-96.

	N/A	$350 - 425	$225 - 275	$800

This model has spruce and sycamore tops as an option.

* Celebrity Deluxe 5 (Model CS-275/CC-275) – similar to Celebrity Deluxe, except in five-string configuration, 19-fret fingerboard, 3/2-per-side chrome tuners, available in Black finish, mfg. 1994-98.

	N/A	$375 - 450	$225 - 275	$850

ELITE (MODEL D-868/B-768) – single round cutaway, spruce top, five-stripe bound body, multiple soundholes around the top bouts with leaf pattern veneer, five-piece mahogany/maple neck, 22-fret extended rosewood fingerboard with maple triangle inlay, walnut bridge, two-per-side gold tuners, piezo bridge pickup, volume/3-band EQ control, active preamp, available in Black, White, Natural, or Sunburst finish, mfg. 1990-99.

	N/A	$1,000 - 1,150	$650 - 750	$2,199

In 1994, bound fingerboard was introduced and Sunburst finish was disc.

* Elite 5 (Model B-5768) – similar to the Elite bass, except in five-string configuration and a 2/3 headstock design, available in Black, Sunburst, or Natural finish, mfg. 1995-98.

	N/A	$1,100 - 1,250	$700 - 825	$2,399

ELITE BASS (MODEL B778TX) – single cutaway mid-depth body, solid spruce top, scalloped X bracing, 11 soundholes in the upper bass bout, maple neck, 16/24-fret extended rosewood fingerboard with no inlays, satin black headstock overlay, two-per-side black tuners, walnut bridge, Ovation High-Output pickup, OP Pro electronics, available in Black finish, 34 in. scale, mfg. 2010-present.

MSR $979	$680	$425 - 500	$275 - 325	

VIPER BASS (MODEL EAB68) – single cutaway mahogany body with routed sound chamber, bound spruce top, 14 multi-size soundholes with various leaf wood overlay, five-piece mahogany/maple neck, 24-fret bound ebony fingerboard, strings through rosewood bridge, rosewood veneered peghead with screened logo, two-per-side gold tuners, four piezo bridge pickups, volume/3-band EQ controls, available in Black, Cherry Cherryburst, or Natural finish, mfg. 1994-98.

	N/A	$1,100 - 1,250	$700 - 825	$2,399

OZARK

Instruments currently produced in Korea, since the early 1980s. Distributed in the United Kingdom by Stentor Music Co. LTD.

Ozark guitars have been produced since the early 1980s. These guitars represent "excellent value at a modest price." They offer several different acoustic models as well as resonators, banjos, mandolins, and basses. For more information visit Ozark's website or contact Stentor Music directly.

CONTACT INFORMATION
OZARK
Distributed by Stentor Music Co. Ltd.
Albert Road North
Reigate, Surrey RH2 9EZ England
www.ozark-acoustic.com
ozark@stentor-music.com

NOTES

P SECTION
PACE

Instruments previously produced in Korea, circa early 1970s.

Pace brand guitars were moderate quality acoustics imported to the U.S. market. Source: Walter Murray, Frankenstein Fretworks.

MSR/NOTES	100%	EXCELLENT	AVERAGE	LAST MSR

ACOUSTIC

F-200 – spruce top, round soundhole, mahogany back and sides, black pickguard, 14/20-fret rosewood fingerboard, rosewood bridge with black bridge pins, three-per-side closed chrome tuners, Natural finish, mfg. 1970s.

	N/A	$125 - 175	$70 - 95	

PACK LEADER

Guitars previously produced during the early 2000s. Distributed by Pack Leader in Blackpool, England.

Although Roger Bucknall is most closely associated with the Pack Leader trademark, it appeared on a line of acoustic guitars in the early 2000s. Terry Pack distributed a wide line of acoustic guitars in various sizes and configurations.

PALMER

Instruments currently produced in Asia since the late 1980s. Distributed by Palmer Guitars USA in Miami, FL. Previously distributed by Chesbro Music Company in Idaho Falls, ID, and Tropical Music Corporation in Miami, FL.

The Palmer trademark was first introduced in the 1980s, initially distributed by the Chesbro Music Company, and later distributed by the Tropical Music Corporation. Palmer instruments are geared toward the entry level or student guitarist with a wide variety of instruments including solidbody electric and bass guitars, nylon-string acoustic guitars, and classical guitars, many of which are based on traditional American designs. Solidbody models were marketed under the trademark (or model designation) of Biscayne, Growler, Baby, and Six. The **Biscayne** trademark is still distributed by Tropical Music Corporation. Palmer guitars generally have a MAP or "street" price of between $100 and $500. For more information, visit Palmer's website or contact them directly.

PANORMO

Instruments previously built in London, England during the early nineteenth century.

During the early 1800s, luthier Louis Panormo ran a productive workshop in London. Panormo, the son of an Italian violin-maker, was one of the few outside of Spain that braced the tops of his acoustics with "fan-strutting," and advertised himself as the "only maker of guitars in the Spanish style." Source: Tony Bacon, *The Ultimate Guitar Book*.

PANTHEON GUITARS

Guitars currently produced in Lewiston, ME since 2000.

Pantheon Guitars was created by Patrick Theimer to allow several luthiers to use the same facilities to produce acoustic guitars. Dana Bourgeois along with six other luthiers build guitars in an old textile mill in Lewiston, ME. Although no guitars are actually branded Pantheon, they build all guitars for Bourgeois. For more information, refer to Bourgeois.

PAO CHIA

Instruments currently produced in China, since 1988. Distributed by the Guangzhou Bourgade Musical Instruments Factory Co. Ltd.

Pao Chia instruments have been produced since 1988. They produce an entire line of acoustic guitars, as well as classical guitars, and electric guitars and basses. These instruments are mainly entry level models at entry level prices. For more information in Chinese, refer to their website.

PARACHO ELITE GUITARS

Instruments currently made in Paracho, Mexico. Distributed by LPD Music International in Madison Heights, MI.

Paracho Elite guitars (previously Lone Star guitars) are produced in the mountain village of Paracho, Mexico, which has a two-hundred-year heritage of guitar building. Paracho Elite guitars are available with laminate, solid cedar, or solid spruce tops and are designed for the beginning to intermediate student. Besides guitars, they also produce a variety of other instruments including requintos, mandolins, and bajo sextos. The Dallas dreadnought model retails for $475. The San Marcos Classical retails for $199 and the El Paso classical retails for $475. Prices on the other models run from $150 to $500. For further information contact LPD Music International directly, or visit Paracho Elite's website.

MSR/NOTES	100%	EXCELLENT	AVERAGE	LAST MSR

PARAMOUNT

Instruments previously produced in America during the 1930s and 1940s. Also see Lange.

In 1934, the William L. Lange Company (New York) debuted the Paramount guitar series - and some of the models were built by the C.F. Martin guitar company. However, Lange's company went out of business in the early 1940s. In the late 1940s, the Paramount guitar line was reintroduced and distributed by Gretsch & Brenner. Source: Tom Wheeler, *American Guitars*.

ACOUSTIC

STYLE L – Resonator style guitar, only 36 produced, mfg. 1930s.

	N/A	$2,400 - 3,000	$1,450 - 1,800	

MISC. ARCHTOPS – various configurations, models start with a B prefix followed by 3 digits, mfg. 1930s-early 1940s.

	N/A	$1,100 - 1,400	$675 - 850	

PARKER

Acoustic instruments previously produced in China between 2006 and 2010. Distributed by U.S. Music Corp. in Buffalo Grove, IL. Parker has been producing electric guitars in Wilmington, MA and Mundelin, IL since 1992.

CONTACT INFORMATION
PARKER
Distributed by U.S. Music Corp.
1000 Corporate Grove Drive
Buffalo Grove, IL 60089
Phone No.: 847-949-0444
Phone No.: 800-877-6863
Fax No.: 847-949-8444
www.parkerguitars.com
guitar.support@usmusiccorp.com

Designer Ken Parker began building unconventional archtop guitars in the 1970s. He then took a job with (now defunct) Stuyvesant Music in New York City, working both in the repair shop as well as building Guitar Man instruments. Parker's background in repairing and customizing guitars became the groundwork for the innovative design of the Fly guitar.

In 1982, Parker met Larry Fishman (Fishman Transducers) while reviewing a prototype bass. Parker and Fishman joined forces, and attended the 1985 NAMM music industry show to gain financial backing for the new Fly model. The new guitar design attracted some interest in the market, but Parker and Fishman were interested in protecting the design, rather than let unauthorized versions show up in the marketplace. Around 1990, Korg USA (distributor of Marshall amplifiers and Korg keyboards in the U.S. market) took interest in the design and production applications. The Fly guitar debuted at the 1992 NAMM show. In 2003, they became a part of U.S. Music Corp., which also owns Washburn, Randall Amplifiers, and Oscar Schmidt. In 2006, Parker released their first full-acoustic models: the P6E and the P8E. In 2007, they expanded their acoustic line to two series, eight guitars, and one bass, but by 2010, Parker announced that they were discontinuing production of all their acoustic instruments.

ACOUSTIC: EVENT SERIES

P6E – single cutaway uniquely-shaped body, solid Sitka spruce top, mahogany back and sides, oval soundhole with pearl ring rosette, black or white body binding, set mahogany neck, 14/19-fret ebony fingerboard with offset microdot inlays, three-per-side gold tuners, ebony bridge with "P" inlay, Fishman hum-cancelling exposed pickup and Fishman Acoustic Matrix undersaddle pickup, four knobs (top-mounted v, side-mounted blend, b, t), available in Black, Pearl White, or Trans. Red finish, 25.5 in. scale, mfg. 2006-07.

	N/A	$675 - 800	$425 - 500	$1,500

P7E – single cutaway uniquely-shaped body, solid quilted sapele top, mahogany back and sides, oval soundhole with ring rosette, white body binding, set mahogany neck, 14/19-fret ebony fingerboard with large decorative inlays, three-per-side gold tuners, ebony bridge with "P" inlay, Fishman hum-cancelling exposed pickup and Fishman Acoustic Matrix undersaddle pickup, four knobs (top-mounted v, side-mounted blend, b, t), available in Natural finish, 25.5 in. scale, mfg. 2007-2010.

	$1,250	$775 - 925	$475 - 550	$1,800

P8E – single cutaway uniquely-shaped body, solid cedar top, solid flame maple back and sides, oval soundhole with pearl ring rosette, full rosewood body binding, set mahogany neck, 14/19-fret ebony fingerboard with offset microdot inlays, three-per-side gold tuners, ebony bridge with "P" inlay, Fishman hum-cancelling exposed pickup and Fishman Acoustic Matrix undersaddle pickup, four knobs (top-mounted v, side-mounted blend, b, t), available in Natural or Trans. Black (2006 only) finish, 25.5 in. scale, mfg. 2006-2010.

	$1,625	$1,000 - 1,200	$625 - 750	$2,300

P9E – single cutaway uniquely-shaped body, solid cedar top, solid Indian rosewood back, Indian rosewood sides, oval soundhole with ring rosette, rosewood body binding, set mahogany neck, 14/19-fret ebony fingerboard with offset microdot inlays, three-per-side gold tuners, ebony bridge with "P" inlay, Fishman hum-cancelling exposed pickup and Fishman Acoustic Matrix undersaddle pickup, four knobs (top-mounted v, side-mounted blend, b, t), available in Natural finish, 25.5 in. scale, mfg. 2007-2010.

	$1,650	$1,025 - 1,225	$650 - 775	$2,350

P10E – single cutaway uniquely-shaped body, solid Sitka spruce top top, bird's-eye maple back and sides, oval soundhole with ring rosette, red tortoiseshell body binding, set mahogany neck, 14/19-fret ivoroid fingerboard with large offset microdot inlays, flame maple headstock overlay with three-per-side gold tuners, ivoroid bridge with "P" inlay, Fishman hum-cancelling exposed pickup and Fishman Acoustic Matrix undersaddle pickup, four knobs (top-mounted v, side-mounted blend, b, t), available in Natural finish, 25.5 in. scale, mfg. 2007-2010.

	$1,700	$1,050 - 1,250	$650 - 800	$2,400

MSR/NOTES	100%	EXCELLENT	AVERAGE	LAST MSR

ACOUSTIC: INTRIGUE SERIES

PA22 – symmetrical body with two upper bout points, solid cedar top, solid sapele back, sapele sides, oval soundhole with checkered rosette, standard white/black body binding, five-piece mahogany neck, 14/20-fret rosewood fingerboard with offset dot inlays and "P" logo on bass end of board, rosewood headstock overlay with three-per-side gold tuners, rosewood bridge, black pickguard, available in Natural finish, 25.5 in. scale, mfg. 2007-2010.

	$1,090	$650 - 800	$400 - 475	$1,550

PA24 – symmetrical body with two upper bout points, solid Sitka spruce top, solid bird's-eye maple back, bird's-eye maple sides, oval soundhole with pearl rosette, red tortoiseshell body binding, five-piece mahogany neck, 14/20-fret ivoroid fingerboard with offset pearl dot inlays and "P" logo on bass end of board, bird's-eye maple headstock overlay with three-per-side gold tuners, ivoroid bridge, white pickguard, available in Natural finish, 25.5 in. scale, mfg. 2007-2010.

	$1,330	$850 - 1,000	$500 - 575	$1,900

PA28 – symmetrical body with two upper bout points, solid cedar top, solid Indian rosewood maple back, Indian rosewood bird's-eye maple sides, oval soundhole with pearl rosette, standard white/black body binding, five-piece mahogany neck, 14/20-fret ebony fingerboard with offset pearl dot inlays and "P" logo on bass end of board, rosewood headstock overlay with three-per-side gold tuners, ebony bridge, black pickguard, available in Natural finish, 25.5 in. scale, mfg. 2007-2010.

	$1,450	$900 - 1,050	$575 - 675	$2,050

ACOUSTIC ELECTRIC BASS

PAB40N – single cutaway uniquely-shaped American black walnut top/back/sides, sound slots in the upper bass bout, bass side thumb rest, white body binding, five-piece mahogany/maple neck, 24-fret extended ebony fingerboard with 12th fret offset pearl dot inlays, black walnut headstock overlay, two-per-side gold tuners, ebony bridge with "P" logo, Fishman piezo pickup, 4 Element Prefix Fishman preamp/electronics, available in Natural finish, 34 in. scale, mfg. 2007-mid-2009.

	$1,400	$900 - 1,050	$550 - 650	$2,000

PARKSONS

Instruments currently produced in Korea. Distributed by Paxphil in Korea.

Parksons produces an entire line of acoustic guitars as well as electrics, basses, banjos, mandolins, and resonators. These guitars are mainly entry level instruments that retail for under $200. Refer to their website for more information and a full listing of every guitar that they produce.

PARKWOOD

Guitars currently produced in Korea. Distributed by Praxis Musical Instruments in Orange, CA.

Parkwood Guitars feature all solid wood construction in their guitars, but they have kept the cost down unlike other solid wood guitars. Their Korea factory is very well documented and maintained. Guitars range in price from around $700 to $1,250. For more information, visit Parkwood's website or contact them directly.

PASAYE

Instruments currently produced in San Diego, CA. Distributed by Golden Hill Music.

Pasaye guitars are produced by Guitarras De Las Americas guitars, and their company name comes from the Central and South America theme of the guitars. These guitars are entirely hand built and they are although they look like normal 12-string guitars they actually Mexican folk guitars that are used in playing Norteno, Cajunto, Tejano, and Tex-Mex styles of music. They also have a full custom shop that can build just about anything. For more information, visit their website or contact them directly.

PATRICK JAMES EGGLE GUITARS

Instruments currently built in Oswestry, United Kingdom. Previously built in Hendersonville, NC.

Patrick James Eggle produces bespoke acoustic and electric instruments. Eggle started building guitars in the late 1970s. He spent much of the 1980s building and repairing guitars. In the early 1990s, he started building solidbody guitars under the name Patrick Eggle Guitars. In 1995, he left the company in pursuit to work alone. He spent the next few years doing repairs and building various instruments. In 2001, he started to build guitars again, but this time they were acoustic configurations. He worked in Bedforshire, England

MSR/NOTES	100%	EXCELLENT	AVERAGE	LAST MSR

for a while until he moved to the U.S. Flattop, archtop and solidbody guitars are currently produced in Oswestry, Shropshire. For more information, contact Eggle directly.

The **Skyland** is a Dreadnought style guitar and starts at £2,500. The **Etowah** is a 12-fret 000 style guitar and starts at £2,650 and $5,000 for the **Style 42** (disc.). The **Saluda** is a small body jumbo that starts at £2,850 and is available with a cutaway (£2,850), in 12-string configuration (£3,000), and in baritone configuration (£2,850). The **Linville** is an Orchestra model that starts at £2,300 and is also available as the **Gareth Pearson** model (£2,200) and a cutaway (£2,850). The **Kanuga** (MSR starts at £2,400) was introduced in 2007 and is also available in a 12-fret model (£3,200). A **Parlor** model is also available (£2,500). There are many options available as well.

PAUL REED SMITH GUITARS (PRS)

CONTACT INFORMATION
PAUL REED SMITH GUITARS (PRS)
380 Log Canoe Circle
Stevensville, MD 21666
Phone No.: 410-643-9970
Fax No.: 410-643-9980
www.prsguitars.com
custserv@prsguitars.com

Acoustic instruments currently produced in Stevensville, MD since 2009 and in Korea since 2012. Prototypes were previously produced in Annapolis, MD in 1992. Electric instruments currently produced in Stevensville, MD since 1996 and previously produced in Annapolis, MD from 1985 to 1996.

Paul Reed Smith started designing and building guitars in the 1970. By 1985, Paul Reed Smith Guitars was started as a company. Paul is known primarily for his highly figured tops on his electric guitars. In 1992, PRS Guitars first ventured down the acoustic route. Dana Bourgeois was brought on to design these guitars and with Paul's help they came up with three acoustic models. However, eleven instruments were built (all prototypes) and they never reached the production phase. No full-acoustic models have been produced and it is unknown what happened to the prototype instruments. In 2008, PRS began experimenting with acoustic models again in their Private Stock line, and in 2009, two production acoustic models, the Angelus Cutaway and Tonare Grand were introduced with several available options. In 2012, Korean-built SE models of the Angelus Cutaway were introduced. For a full history and electric guitar information, refer to the *Blue Book of Electric Guitars*.

ACOUSTIC: 1992

Since only eleven acoustics were manufactured, it is tough to put a value on these guitars. It is also unknown where the guitars ended up after the prototype run. Keep in mind that these specs were based on the models having a long production run. Since they never went into production, it is possible that many of the features listed never appeared on the guitar and the MSR is an arbitrary value. Three different acoustic models were produced.

The **Custom Cutaway** featured a single flat cutaway dreadnought style, spruce top, round soundhole, abalone bound body and rosette, figured maple back/sides, mahogany neck, 20-fret Brazilian rosewood fingerboard with abalone bird inlay, Brazilian rosewood bridge with ebony pearl dot pins, 3-per-side chrome locking PRS tuners, volume/tone control, preamp system, and was available in Amber Sunburst, Antique Natural, Black Cherry, Gray black, or Walnut Sunburst finish. Last MSR on this model was $2,590.

The **Mahogany Cutaway** featured a single flat cutaway dreadnought style, spruce top, round soundhole, wood bound body and rosette, mahogany back/sides/neck, 20-fret rosewood fingerboard, rosewood bridge with ebony pearl dot pins, rosewood veneer on peghead, 3-per-side chrome locking PRS tuners, volume/tone control, preamp system, and was available in Antique Natural, Black, or Natural finish. Last MSR on this model was $1,970.

The **Rosewood Signature** featured a dreadnought style, spruce top, round soundhole, abalone bound body and rosette, rosewood back/sides, mahogany neck, 20-fret Brazilian rosewood fingerboard with abalone bird inlay, Brazilian rosewood bridge with ebony pearl dot pins, 3-per-side gold locking PRS tuners, gold endpin, volume/tone control, preamp system, and was available in Antique Natural or Rosewood Sunburst finish. Last MSR on this model was $3,190.

ACOUSTIC: CURRENT MODELS

When Paul Reed Smith reintroduced their acoustic models in 2009, they produced two main body styles: the Angelus Cutaway and the Tonare Grande. In 2009, there was a base price of $5,330 for each model with a variety of options available that are listed below. In 2010, they introduced a standard and a custom version of each model and eliminated a number of the options. The additional prices below only apply to standard models produced in 2009, while all current options are listed within their respective models.

- Add $300 for a European/German AAAA spruce top.
- Add $450 for an Adirondack red spruce top.
- Add $1,050 for an Adirondack AAAA red spruce top.
- Add $1,500 for figured rosewood back and sides.
- Add $150 for any ebony fingerboard.
- Add $1,800 for Celtic cross inlays with a Celtic cross rosette/abalone ring.
- Add $750 for abalone top purfling.
- Add $525 for a PRS pickup system

ANGELUS CUTAWAY CUSTOM MODEL – single cutaway body, Adirondack spruce top, cocobolo back and sides, round soundhole with standard rosette, maple top purfling, Peruvian mahogany wide neck, 14/21-fret cocobolo fingerboard with bird inlays, bound headstock with PRS signature logo, three-per-side gold Robson hand-machined tuners, cocobolo bridge, optional electronics, Ameritage hardshell case included, 15.5 in. wide, mfg. 2010-13.

	$5,200	$3,350 - 4,100	$1,850 - 2,225	$5,780

- Add 10% (MSR $6,305) for PRS pickup system.
- Add $150 for an ebony fingerboard.
- Add $460 for Vintage Burst finish.
- Add $750 for abalone top purfling.

MSR/NOTES	100%	EXCELLENT	AVERAGE	LAST MSR

ANGELUS CUTAWAY STANDARD MODEL – single cutaway body, European/German (2009 only) spruce top, figured mahogany or rosewood (2009 only) back and sides, round soundhole with standard rosette, maple top purfling, Peruvian mahogany wide neck, 14/21-fret rosewood (2009 only) or cocobolo (2010-13) fingerboard with bird inlays, bound headstock with PRS signature logo, three-per-side gold Robson hand-machined tuners, rosewood (2009 only) or cocobolo (2010-13) bridge, optional electronics, Ameritage hardshell case included, 15.5 in. wide, mfg. 2009-13.

	$4,800	$3,100 - 3,750	$1,725 - 2,050	$5,330

- Add 10% (MSR $5,855) for PRS pickup system.
- Add $460 for Vintage Burst finish.

TONARE GRAND CUSTOM MODEL – non-cutaway body, Adirondack spruce top, cocobolo back and sides, round soundhole with standard rosette, maple top purfling, Peruvian mahogany wide neck, 14/21-fret cocobolo fingerboard with bird inlays, bound headstock with PRS signature logo, three-per-side gold Robson hand-machined tuners, cocobolo bridge, optional electronics, Ameritage hardshell case included, 16 in. wide, mfg. 2010-13.

	$5,200	$3,350 - 4,100	$1,850 - 2,225	$5,780

- Add 10% (MSR $6,305) for PRS pickup system.
- Add $150 for an ebony fingerboard.
- Add $460 for Vintage Burst finish.
- Add $750 for abalone top purfling.

TONARE GRAND STANDARD MODEL – non-cutaway body, European/German (2009 only) spruce top, figured mahogany or rosewood (2009 only) back and sides, round soundhole with standard rosette, maple top purfling, Peruvian mahogany wide neck, 14/21-fret rosewood (2009 only) or cocobolo (2010-13) fingerboard with bird inlays, bound headstock with PRS signature logo, three-per-side gold Robson hand-machined tuners, rosewood (2009 only) or cocobolo (2010-13) bridge, optional electronics, Ameritage hardshell case included, 16 in. wide, mfg. 2009-2013.

	$4,800	$3,100 - 3,750	$1,725 - 2,050	$5,330

- Add 10% (MSR $5,855) for PRS pickup system.
- Add $460 for Vintage Burst finish.

25th ANNIVERSARY "EMMA" ACOUSTIC – single cutaway body, AAAA Adirondack spruce top, Madagascar rosewood back and sides, round soundhole with standard rosette, snakewood binding, koa top purfling, curly mahogany wide neck, 14/21-fret Brazilian rosewood fingerboard with mammoth ivory 11th-13th fret 25th Anniversary Eagle inlay, bound headstock with Brazilian rosewood overlay and PRS mammoth ivory signature logo, three-per-side gold Robson hand-machined tuners, Brazilian rosewood bridge, PRS proprietary pickup system, Ameritage hardshell case included, 15.5 in. wide, limited mfg. 2010.

	$16,000	N/A	N/A	$20,000

- Add 10% (Last MSR was $5,855) for PRS pickup system.

PRS also produced a 25th Anniversary Tonare Grand in limited quantities for overseas distribution. The 25th Anniversary "Emma" Acoustic is only available in the U.S.

ACOUSTIC: SE SERIES

SE ANGELUS CUSTOM – single cutaway Angelus-style body, solid Sitka spruce top, solid rosewood back and sides, hybrid X bracing, round soundhole with large single ring rosette, multi-ply body binding, set mahogany standard-shape neck, 14/20-fret bound ebony fingerboard with bird inlays, bound headstock with black overlay and "SE Angelus" logo, three-per-side PRS-designed nickel tuners, ebony bridge, available in Natural finish, 15.5 in. body width, mfg. 2012-13.

	$800	$500 - 625	$300 - 375	$1,229

* **SE Angelus Custom Electric** – similar to the SE Angelus Custom, except has PRS electronics, available in Natural finish, mfg. 2012-present.

MSR N/A	$875	$525 - 650	$325 - 400	

SE ANGELUS STANDARD – single cutaway Angelus-style body, solid Sitka spruce top, solid mahogany back and sides, hybrid X bracing, round soundhole with large single ring rosette, multi-ply body binding, set mahogany standard-shape neck, 14/20-fret bound rosewood fingerboard with bird inlays, bound headstock with black overlay and "SE Angelus" logo, three-per-side PRS-designed nickel tuners, rosewood bridge, available in Natural finish, 15.5 in. body width, mfg. 2012-13.

	$700	$450 - 550	$275 - 350	$1,069

* **SE Angelus Standard Electric** – similar to the SE Angelus Standard, except has PRS electronics, available in Natural finish, mfg. 2012-present.

MSR N/A	$700	$450 - 550	$275 - 350	

PEAL

Instruments currently produced in Korea. Distributed by the Ye-Il International Company.

Peal produces a line of acoustic, electric, bass, and round back guitars that are mainly entry level instruments. For more information refer to their website.

CONTACT INFORMATION
PEAL
Distributed by Ye-Il International Company
www.guitar-peal.com
yeilint@netsgo.com

PEARL RIVER

Instruments currently produced in China.

Pearl River produces an entire line of acoustic guitars, as well as electric guitars. Pearl River guitars is a derivative of the Pearl River Guitar Company. They are mainly entry level instruments at entry level prices. For more information refer to their website.

CONTACT INFORMATION
PEARL RIVER
2260 S. Haven Avenue, Suite F
Ontario, CA 91761-0739
Phone No.: 909-673-9155
Fax No.: 909-673-9165
www.pearlriverpiano.com
wmk@pearlriverpiano.com

PEAVEY

Instruments currently built in Asia, Meridian, MS and Leaksville, MS. Distributed by Peavey Electronics Corporation of Meridian, MS since 1965. Peavey also has a factory and distribution center in Corby, England to help serve and service the overseas market.

CONTACT INFORMATION
PEAVEY
5022 Hartley Peavey Drive
Meridian, MS 39305
Phone No.: 601-483-5365
Fax No.: 601-486-1278
www.peavey.com
customerservice@peavey.com

Peavey Electronics is one of the very few major American musical instrument manufacturers still run by the original founding member and owner. Hartley Peavey grew up in Meridian, Mississippi and spent some time working in his father's music store repairing record players. He gained some recognition locally for the guitar amplifiers he built by hand while he was still in school, and decided months prior to college graduation to go into business for himself. In 1965, Peavey Electronics was started out of the basement of Peavey's parents home. Due to the saturated guitar amp market of the late 1960s, Peavey switched to building P.A. systems and components. By 1968, the product demand was great enough to warrant building a small cement block factory on rented land and hire another staff member.

The demand for Peavey products continued to grow, and by the early 1970s the company's roster had expanded to 150 employees. Emphasis was still placed on P.A. construction, although both guitar and bass amps were doing well. The Peavey company continued to diversify and produce all the components needed to build the finished product. After twelve years of manufacturing, the first series of Peavey guitars was begun in 1977, and introduced at the 1978 NAMM show. An advertising circular used by Peavey in the late '70s compared the price of an American built T-60 (plus case) for $350 versus the Fender Stratocaster's list price of $790 or a Gibson Les Paul for $998.50 (list). In light of those list prices, it's also easy to see where the Japanese guitar makers had plenty of maneuvering room during their "copy" era.

The "T-Series" guitars were introduced in 1978, and the line expanded from three models up to a total of seven in five years. In 1983, the product line changed, and introduced both the mildly wacky Mystic and Razer original designs (the Mantis was added in 1984) and the more conservative Patriot, Horizon, and Milestone guitars. The Fury and Foundation basses were also added at this time. After five years of stop tailpieces, the first Peavey "Octave Plus" vibratos were offered (later superseded by the Power bend model). Pickup designs also shifted from the humbuckers to single or double "blade" pickups.

Models that debuted in 1985 included the vaguely stratish Predator, and the first doubleneck (!), the Hydra. In response to the guitar industry shifting to "superstrat" models, the Impact was introduced in 1986. Guitars also had the option of a Kahler locking tremolo, and two offsprings of the '84 Mantis were released: The Vortex I or Vortex II. The Nitro series of guitars were available in 1987, as well as the Falcon, Unity, and Dyna-Bass. Finally, to answer companies like Kramer or Charvel, the Tracer series and the Vandenberg model(s) debuted in 1988.

As the U.S. guitar market grew more conservative, models like the Generation S-1 and Destiny guitars showed up in guitar shops. Peavey basses continued to evolve into sleeker and more solid instruments like the Palaedium, TL series or B Ninety. 1994 saw the release of the Midibase (later the Cyberbass) that combined magnetic pickups with a MIDI-controller section.

One of Peavey's biggest breakthroughs in recent years was the development of the Peavey EVH amplifier, developed in conjunction with Edward Van Halen. Due to the success and acceptance of the EVH 5150 amplifier, Van Halen withdrew his connection with his signature Ernie Ball model (which is still in production as the Axis model), and designed a "new" **Wolfgang** model with Peavey. This new model had a one year "waiting period" from when it was announced at the NAMM industry trade show to actual production. Many Peavey dealers who did receive early models generally sold them at new retail (no discount) for a number of months due to slow supply and re-supply.

Rather than stay stuck in a design "holding pattern," Peavey continues to change and revise guitar and bass designs, and they continue the almost twenty year tradition of American built electric guitars and basses, (Model History, nomenclature, and description courtesy Grant Brown, Peavey Repair section).

Information on virtually any Peavey product, or a product's schematic is available through Peavey Repair. Grant Brown, the head of the Repair section, has been with Peavey Electronics for over eighteen years.

In 1994, a series of Peavey acoustic guitars was announced. Although some models were shipped in quantity, the acoustic line was not as wide spread as other guitar models that were introduced. Another acoustic series was introduced circa 1999 and were produced until 2002. In 2003, a new line of acoustic guitars was introduced called the Briarwood Series. In 2005, Jack Daniel's acoustic guitars were introduced.

ACOUSTIC: BRIARWOOD SERIES

In 2007, the **Briarwood Stage Pack** (Last MSR was $200) was introduced and it features a Briarwood SP6 acoustic guitar, tuner, gig bag, picks, strap, an extra set of strings and a Learn to Play DVD.

MSR/NOTES	100%	EXCELLENT	AVERAGE	LAST MSR

BRIARWOOD CL-1 – classic style, spruce top, body binding, mahogany back/sides/neck, 14/20-fret rosewood fingerboard with dot inlay, open-style headstock and tuners, Natural finish, 25.5 in. scale, mfg. 2003-07.

	N/A	$100 - 125	$60 - 75	$250

BRIARWOOD DR-1 – dreadnought style, spruce top, body binding, mahogany back/sides/neck, 14/20-fret rosewood fingerboard with dot inlay, black pickguard, Natural finish, 25.5 in. scale, mfg. 2003-07.

	N/A	$80 - 100	$45 - 60	$200

* *Briarwood DR-112 12-String* – similar to the DR-1, except in 12-string configuration and six-per-side tuners, mfg. 2004-07.

	N/A	$95 - 120	$55 - 70	$230

BRIARWOOD DR-2ER – dreadnought style, spruce top, body binding, mahogany back/sides/neck, 14/20-fret rosewood fingerboard with dot inlay, tortoise pickguard, piezo pickup under bridge, available in Black or Natural finish, 25.5 in. scale, mfg. 2003-07.

	N/A	$120 - 150	$70 - 90	$290

- **Add 30% (Last MSR was $380) for Black finish with abalone binding and no pickguard.**

BRIARWOOD DR-3ERS/CDS – dreadnought style, solid spruce (ERS) or solid Cedar Top (CDS) top, body binding, mahogany back/sides/neck, 14/20-fret rosewood fingerboard with dot inlay, tortoise pickguard, piezo pickup under bridge, available in Natural finish, 25.5 in. scale, mfg. 2003-07.

	N/A	$140 - 175	$85 - 105	$340

BRIARWOOD DR-4CA EQ – dreadnought style, solid spruce top, abalone body binding, mahogany back/sides/neck, 14/20-fret rosewood fingerboard with dot inlay, tortoise pickguard, piezo pickup under bridge, 3-band EQ, available in Black, Natural, or Wine Red finish, 25.5 in. scale, mfg. 2003-07.

	N/A	$175 - 225	$105 - 130	$450

- **Add 10% (Last MSR was $500) for Black finish.**

BRIARWOOD DR-5CA EQ QT – dreadnought style, 25.5 in. scale, solid spruce with quilted maple top, abalone body binding, mahogany back/sides/neck, 14/20-fret rosewood fingerboard with dot inlay, piezo pickup under bridge, 3-band EQ, available in Purple finish, mfg. 2003-07.

	N/A	$225 - 275	$135 - 170	$550

BRIARWOOD FL-1 – jumbo (full) style, spruce top, body binding, mahogany back/sides/neck, 14/20-fret rosewood fingerboard with dot inlay, black pickguard, Natural finish, 25.5 in. scale, mfg. 2003-07.

	N/A	$100 - 125	$60 - 75	$250

ACOUSTIC: COMPACT CUTAWAY, DREADNOUGHT & JUMBO SERIES

Compact Cutaway Series: Two models comprise the Compact body design that featured a single cutaway: the **CC-37PE** ($1,099) had a five-piece mahogany/rosewood neck, piezo pickup system, and Schaller hardware; the **CC-3712PE** ($1,149) was the accompanying 12-string model.

Dreadnought Series: The **SD-9P** ($499) was the only model to feature a solid cedar top in the Dreadnought design. The **SD-11P** ($599) featured the same body design with a Spruce top and laminated mahogany sides and back, and the **DD-21P** ($699) substitutes laminated rosewood in place of the mahogany. The **SD-11PCE** ($759) featured a single cutaway and piezo under-the-bridge pickup system with 3-band EQ and volume control.

Jumbo Series: The **CJ-33PE** ($1,049) featured the Jumbo body design and a piezo system; the **CJ-3312PE** ($1,099) was the accompanying 12-string model.

ACOUSTIC: DELTA SERIES

BRIARWOOD – dreadnought style body, spruce top, mahogany back and sides, 20-fret rosewood fingerboard, compensated bridge saddles, 3-per-side tuners, chrome hardware, pickguard, Natural finish, disc. 2002.

	N/A	$95 - 130	$60 - 80	$230

CLARKSDALE – dreadnought body style, 25.5 in. scale, traditional X-bracing, spruce top, nato back, neck, and sides, bound body, rosewood fingerboard, 20-fret, sealed die-cast tuners, compensated bridge saddle, Satin finish on neck, gloss finish on body, chrome hardware, Natural finish, mfg. 1999-2000.

	N/A	$85 - 115	$50 - 70	$209

GLENDORA – western body style, solid spruce top, mahogany back and sides, traditional X-bracing, cream bound rosewood fingerboard, 20 frets, sealed die-cast tuners, chrome hardware, compensated bridge saddles, Satin finish on neck and headstock, Gloss finish on body, mfg. 2001-02.

	N/A	$225 - 275	$125 - 175	$500

* *Glendora 12* – similar to Glendora, except in a 12-string configuration, mfg. 2001 only.

	N/A	$325 - 375	$200 - 250	$675

MSR/NOTES	100%	EXCELLENT	AVERAGE	LAST MSR

INDIANOLA ER – western body style, 25.5 in. scale, traditional X-bracing, spruce top, mahogany back, sides, and neck, bound body, rosewood fretboard, 20 frets, sealed die-cast tuners, chrome hardware, compensated bridge saddle, Satin finish on neck, Gloss finish on body, available in Natural finish, mfg. 1999-2002.

	N/A	$125 - 175	$80 - 100	$310

McCOMB – 25.5 in. scale, solid cedar top, mahogany back and sides, cream bound rosewood fingerboard, sealed die-cast tuners, compensated bridge saddles, inlaid rosette, available in Satin finish, mfg. 2001-02.

	N/A	$225 - 275	$125 - 175	$500

TUPELO ER – western body style, 25.5 in. scale, traditional X-bracing, spruce top, mahogany back, neck, and sides, bound body, rosewood fingerboard, 20 frets, sealed die-cast tuners, chrome hardware, compensated bridge saddle, Satin finish, available in Natural finish, mfg. 1999-2002.

	N/A	$115 - 150	$75 - 95	$260

ACOUSTIC: MISC. MODELS

JACK DANIEL'S JDAG1 – dreadnought style, spruce top, rosewood back and sides, round soundhole with white filigree rosette, 14/20-fret rosewood fingerboard with pearl block inlay, Jack Daniel's on headstock with three-per-side tuners, Piezo pickup under bridge, chrome hardware, available in Black finish, mfg. 2005-present.

MSR $500	$380	$225 - 275	$125 - 175	

JACK DANIEL'S JDAG2 – dreadnought style, solid cedar top, mahogany back and sides, round soundhole with Jack Daniels inscribed filigree rosette, 14/20-fret rosewood fingerboard with 12th fret Old No. 7 inlay, Jack Daniel's on headstock with three-per-side tuners, Piezo pickup under bridge, chrome hardware, available in Natural finish, mfg. summer 2005-present.

MSR $800	$600	$350 - 425	$200 - 250	

JACK DANIEL'S JDAG3 – similar to the Jack Daniel's JDAG2, except has an Aged Barrel finish, mfg. 2006-present.

MSR $800	$600	$350 - 425	$200 - 250	

ACOUSTIC ELECTRIC

ABERDEEN – 25 in. scale, single cutaway body, ash top, mahogany back and sides, cream bound rosewood fingerboard, sealed die-cast tuners, compensated bridge saddles, piezo pickup with 4-band preamp. Satin finished neck and headstock, high gloss body, mfg. 2001-02.

	N/A	$275 - 325	$175 - 225	$600

ECOUSTIC – single rounded cutaway dreadnought style, cedar top, oval soundhole, bound body, 5-stripe rosette, mahogany back/sides, maple neck, 22-fret rosewood fingerboard with white dot inlay, rosewood bridge with white pins, 3-per-side gold tuners, piezo bridge pickup, 3-band EQ, available in Black, Natural, or Trans. Red finish, disc. 1999.

	N/A	$425 - 500	$250 - 300	$959

ECOUSTICATS – single rounded cutaway dreadnought style, maple top, oval soundhole, bound body, 5-stripe rosette, poplar back/sides, rock maple neck, 22-fret rosewood fingerboard with white dot inlay, rosewood ATS Tremolo bridge with white pins, 3-per-side chrome tuners, piezo bridge pickup, 3-band EQ, available in Black, Natural, or Trans. Red finish, mfg. 1995-99.

	N/A	$450 - 525	$275 - 325	$999

INDIANOLA AE – Western body style, 25.5 in. scale, traditional X-bracing, spruce top, mahogany back, neck, and sides, bound body, rosewood fingerboard, 20 frets, sealed die-cast tuners, compensated bridge saddle, chrome hardware, gloss finish on body, satin finish on neck, piezo under saddle bridge, preamp with 3-band EQ, rotary volume control, battery check LED and test button, switching jack, available in Natural finish, mfg. 1999-2002.

	N/A	$160 - 200	$100 - 130	$360

ROUTE 61 – 25" scale, solid spruce top, rosewood sides and back, single cutaway body, cream bound rosewood fingerboard, sealed die-cast tuners, piezo pickup with preamp, compensated bridge saddles, Satin finished neck and headstock, Gloss finished body, mfg. 2001-02.

	N/A	$325 - 375	$200 - 250	$700

TUPELO AE – western body style, 25.5 in. scale, spruce top, mahogany back, neck, and sides, bound body, rosewood fretboard, 20 frets, sealed die-cast tuners, chrome hardware, compensated bridge saddle, piezo under saddle bridge, 3-band EQ, rotary volume control, battery check LED and test button, switching jack, available in Natural Satin finish, mfg. 1999-2001.

	N/A	$190 - 240	$110 - 140	$440

PEDERSON, CRAIG

Instruments currently built in Brooklyn, NY. Distributed by Rudy's Music Shop of New York City, NY.

Luthier Craig Pederson has been building guitars for the past thirty-plus years. While currently based in New York (on the fourth floor of the Gretsch building!), Pederson has had workshops in Minneapolis, Minnesota as well as Albuquerque, New Mexico. Throughout his luthier career, Pederson has produced various acoustic guitar models, semi-hollowbody guitars, and archtop guitars.

In addition to his various guitar models, Pederson also produces mandolins, mandolas, and mandocellos. Flattop models start at $1,300 (add $200 for wood binding), and carved top models start at $3,200 (add $300 for wood binding).

MSR/NOTES	100%	EXCELLENT	AVERAGE	LAST MSR

All prices include a Harptone hardshell case. Pederson's **Archtop** guitars have a list price beginning at $4,000. Add $500 for wood binding on all guitar models (the following model prices quoted are for plastic body binding).

The **Pederson Nylon String** has a rounded body with venetian cutaway, round soundhole, set-in neck, rosette, 20-fret fingerboard, 3-per-side tuners. Retail pricing is $2,370 for both the cypress flamenco and rosewood classic versions.

The **Pederson Resonator** has a rounded body with florentine cutaway, set-in neck, 20-fret fingerboard, 3-per-side tuners, resonator, round covered soundhole on bass bout. Retail prices are $2,670 for either rosewood or curly maple, and $2,470 for mahogany.

The **Pederson Steel String** has a rounded body with florentine cutaway, round soundhole, set-in neck, rosette, 20-fret fingerboard, 3-per-side tuners. Retail pricing is $2,170 for the mahogany and $2,370 for rosewood or curly maple.

PEDERSON CUSTOM GUITARS

Formerly the Abyss Guitar Company. Instruments currently produced in Forest City, IA since 1997.

Luthier Kevin L. Pederson builds custom acoustic, electric solidbody, electric hollowbody, and bass guitars. Pederson founded Abyss guitars in 1997 and built under that trademark through early 2008 when he changed the name of his company to Pederson Custom Guitars. While all of Pederson's guitars are custom orders, they do offer a few standard models. Features of Pederson's guitars that make them unique include the highly figured tops and the ornate fingerboard inlays. For more information, including pricing, visit Pederson's website or contact him directly.

CONTACT INFORMATION
PEDERSON CUSTOM GUITARS
535 North 13 Street
Forest City, IA 50436
Phone No.: 641-590-2593
www.abyssguitars.com
kevin@abyssguitars.com

PEERLESS

Instruments currently produced in South Korea and Japan since 1970. Distributed in the U.S. by Guitars 'n Jazz in Summit, NJ.

Peerless began producing acoustic and arcthop guitars in Japan in 1970. Since then, Peerless has built guitars for Gretsch, Epiphone, and Alvarez. In the early years, Peerless was building nearly 30,000 instruments a month, but they currently produce less than 1,000 guitars a month to focus on quality instead of quantity. In late 2007, they moved to a new factory in Gimhae, Korea. Guitars currently range in price from $500 to $2,800. Martin Taylor is an endorser and has designed a signature model that is produced by Peerless Guitars. For more information, visit Peerless' website or contact them directly or their U.S. distributor.

CONTACT INFORMATION
PEERLESS

Factory/Headquarters
www.peerlessguitars.com
peerless@peerlessguitars.com

U.S. Distribution: Guitars 'n Jazz
407 Springfield Ave.
Summit, NJ 07901
Phone No.: 908-598-8010
www.guitarsnjazz.com
guitarsnjazz@comcast.net

PENCO

Instruments previously produced in Japan circa 1970s. Distributed by the Philadelphia Music Company of Philadelphia, PA.

This trademark has been identified as a House Brand of the Philadelphia Music Company of Philadelphia, Pennsylvania, the U.S. distributor of these Japanese-built instruments. The Penco (sometimes misspelled Pennco) brand name was applied to a full range of acoustic and solid body electric guitars, many entry level to intermediate quality versions of popular American designs. Source: Michael Wright, *Vintage Guitar Magazine*.

ACOUSTIC

MISC. ACOUSTIC MODELS – models include: A-6, A-13, A-14, A-15, A-16, A-17, A-18, A-22, A-170, and A-230, several variations and configurations, mfg. 1970s.

	100%	EXCELLENT	AVERAGE
Low End Models	N/A	$120 - 150	$70 - 90
High End Models	N/A	$150 - 200	$95 - 120

PENNCREST

Unknown production location and date. See chapter on House Brands.

This trademark has been identified as a House Brand of J.C. Penneys. Source: Willie G. Moseley, *Stellas & Stratocasters*.

PETE BACK CUSTOM GUITARS

Instruments previously built in Richmond (North Yorkshire), England between 1975 and 2006.

Luthier Pete Back is noted for his custom handcrafted guitars of the highest quality. His electric, folk, and classical guitar construction used the finest woods available. Pete had his own original designs, but would make whatever the guitarist required. He also offered repairs (refretting, set-ups, and resprays).

PETILLO GUITARS

Instruments currently manufactured in Ocean, NJ, since 1968.

Luthier Phillip J. Petillo began creating custom handcrafted instruments, repairing, and restoring guitars and other instruments in the 1960s. Petillo was one of the original co-designers of the Kramer aluminum neck guitar in 1976, and built the four prototypes for Kramer (BKL). Later, he severed his connections with the company.

Petillo made acoustic carved top and back guitars, flattop acoustics, semi-hollowbody guitars, and solid body guitars and basses. Petillo also made and repaired the bowed instruments. Petillo, a holder of a BS, MS, and PhD in Engineering, also offered his talents in Engineering for product development, research and development, engineering, and prototype building for the musical instruments industry.

Phillip and Lucille Petillo were the founders and officers of a research corporation that develops devices and technology for the medical industry. While seeming unrelated to the music industry, the Phil-Lu Incorporated company illustrated Petillo's problem-solving skills applied in different fields of study.

Petillo estimated that he hand built between eight and twenty guitars a year. Prices began at $1,200 and were priced by nature of design and materials utilized. Custom Marquetry Inlay and other ornamental work was priced by the square inch. Petillo offered 170 different choices of lumbers, veneers, and mother-of-pearl.

Restoration, alteration, and repair work were price quoted upon inspection of the instrument. In addition, he marketed his patented products such as Petillo Frets, the Acoustic Tonal Sensor, Petillo Strings and Polish, and a fret micro-polishing system. Petillo passed away due to a heart attack in 2010 at the age of 64, but his wife and five sons continue to build guitars.

Some of his clients included: Tal Farlow, Chuck Wayne, Jim Croce, Elvis Presley, James Taylor, Tom Petty, Howie Epstein, Dave Mason, The Blues Brothers, Bruce Springsteen, Gary Talent, Steve Van Zant, Southside Johnny, and many others. For more information, visit Petillo's website or contact them directly.

CONTACT INFORMATION
PETILLO GUITARS
1206 Herbert Ave.
Ocean, NJ 07712-4035
Phone No.: 732-531-6808
Fax No.: 732-531-3045
www.petilloguitars.com
Philluinc@aol.com

PETROS GUITARS

Instruments currently built in Kaukauna, WI since 1972.

Father and son luthiers Bruce and Matt Petros create about thirty hand-built guitars a year. They offer five body styles: the Parlor, the FS (Finger Style), the GC (Grand Concert) the D (Dreadnought), and the Jumbo. The Jumbo body is used for their largest guitar as well as their baritone. They also build a 12-fret slot-head FS, and a 12-fret 12-string GC. The Parlor is also a 12 fret. All body styles are available with an optional cutaway except the Parlor. Petros Guitars is also the inventor of Purflex®, a patented, flexible, designer purfling and a whole family of matching instrument appointments. For more information please refer to their website or contact them directly.

CONTACT INFORMATION
PETROS GUITARS
345 County Road CE
Kaukauna, WI 54130
Phone No.: 920-766-1295
www.petrosguitars.com
petros@petrosguitars.com

All Petros guitars feature a pre-stressed arched and graduated top with a proprietary bridge plate and back tilted, fully compensated saddle. There is also a unique neck profile that makes playing easier and less stressful. Wood bindings, hand made wooden tuner buttons and many other features are standard on all Petros guitars. All body styles are available as the base **Applecreek** model (the Studio Edition) starting at $18,000. Other models consisting of thematic add-ons are available in any body style as well and are named **The Celt**, **The African Rose**, **The Tunnel 13**, **The Yellow Rose**, **The Crown of Thorns**, **The Harvest**, and **The Baroque Parlor**. The limited edition, "Signature" instruments sell for $22,000. The African Rose features 100-year-old curly Redwood salvaged from Big River in Mendocino and the most unique African Rosewood they have ever seen. The Tunnel 13 model is using beautiful, virgin Redwood salvaged from a train tunnel built in the 1880s that was the location of the "Last Great American Train Robbery." Discontinued models include the **Jordan**, **High Cliff**, **The Rite of Spring**, **The Rose of Sharon**, **The Prairie**, and **The Crossover**.

PHIL

Instruments previously produced in South Korea by the Myung Sung Music Ind. Co during the 1990s and early 2000s.

The Myung Sung Music Ind. Co., Ltd. offered a wide range of well constructed acoustic and acoustic electric guitar models. There is a large variety of styles, configurations, colors, and affordable price points. Construction utilized top quality laminates, rosewood, spruce, mahogany, and build quality was top shelf. Acoustic electric models had onboard equalization. Although Phil tried to find a distributor in the U.S. for many years, it is likely these guitars were never officially distributed in America.

PHOENIX GUITAR COMPANY

Instruments currently produced in Phoenix, AZ. Phoenix has been producing guitars since 1994.

George Leach built his first guitar in 1989, and began building instruments under the name of GSL Guitars. In 1994, he formed the Phoenix Guitar Company, and hired several luthiers to build custom instruments and do repairs. After a couple of years, he closed the shop, because he wanted to build guitars rather than manage a store. During the next several years, he further developed his nylon string OM, and attended two archtop classes to expand his repertoire as a luthier. In addition, he started teaching a guitar making class, mainly to friends.

CONTACT INFORMATION
PHOENIX GUITAR COMPANY
7302 E. Helm #2005
Scottsdale, AZ 85260
Phone No.: 480-664-6315
www.phoenixguitarco.com
phoenixguitarco@gmail.com

In early 2006, George moved his shop into a larger building, and began focusing on his guitar making full time. He has partnered with Diana Huber, a former student from his guitar making class, and an excellent luthier in her own right. They will be expanding their guitar making class (a weekend only class), and expect to build 30 or so guitars per year, along with doing repairs. George and Diana currently build two models of steel string guitars, along with the nylon string OM, and a 17 inch archtop. For more information, visit Phoenix's website or contact them directly.

Serial numbers were attached to guitars and the following scheme can be used. Seven numbers were utilized MMYYXXX with MM being the month, YY being the year, and XXX being the production number starting with 001.

The **Nylon OM** was shaped on the Martin Orchestra Model and featured a western red cedar top with mahogany back and sides, and a bird decal on the headstock. The price was $1,600. A Deluxe model was available with rosewood back and sides, ebony fingerboard, bridge, and headstock overlay, and MOP bird decal on headstock. The price was $2,200. Other Martin copies were produced priced from $1,400 to $2,200. About 8 were built.

PIGNOSE

Instruments currently produced overseas. Distributed by Pignose in Las Vegas, NV.

CONTACT INFORMATION
PIGNOSE
570 W. Cheyenne Ave., Suite 80
North Las Vegas, NV 89030
Phone No.: 702-648-2444
Fax No.: 702-648-2440
www.pignoseamps.com

Pignose amplifiers have been around since 1972. A kid went to a distributor in Oakland with this prototype amp that was built in a wooden box. The idea of a portable, battery operated amp wasn't taken by storm from the distributor in Oakland. He later gave a prototype to Terry Kath of Chicago who took interest in the idea. The volume knob kept coming loose and he brought it his tech. The rubber knob was melted and when it was fixed, Terry said that it looked like a pig's nose. Some of the first models were produced with these "pignose" knobs, and there only two of them known in existence. It's funny how names sometimes come about.

This amp was one of the first that was completely portable amplifier. Now Pignose offers amps that are run strictly on DC battery power along with a rechargeable model. Not only are these amps novel ideas, they are also fairly cheap. They currently offer a wide range of products, including some tube models. They have also introduced an acoustic Dreadnought model, which retails for under $100. For more information visit Pignose's website or contact them directly.

PIMENTEL & SONS

Instruments currently built in Albuquerque, NM since 1951.

CONTACT INFORMATION
PIMENTEL & SONS
3316 Lafayette Dr NE
Albuquerque, NM 87107
Phone No.: 505-884-1669
www.pimentelguitars.com
info@pimentelguitars.com

Master Luthiers Rick Pimentel (born in El Paso, Texas), Robert Pimentel (born in Carlsbad New Mexico), and Victor Pimentel (also born in Carlsbad, New Mexico) learned the craft from their father, New Mexico Master Luthier Lorenzo Pimentel, originally born in Durango, Mexico who learned guitar making from his older brothers. Though trained as a baker, Pimentel moved to El Paso, Texas in 1948 to work for master violin maker Nagoles. In 1951, Pimentel started his own company building classical guitars, moved to Carlsbad, New Mexico, and then in 1963 moved to a permanent home in Albuquerque New Mexico where the late Lorenzo (and still surviving wife Josefina Founders) still reside. The company Pimentel & Sons consists of all family members including Rick Pimentel, Robert Pimentel, Victor Pimentel, who are all Master Luthiers, and Hector Pimentel and Gustavo Pimentel who are the musicians of the family. In the early 1970s, the company started building acoustic steel string guitars and to date there is a waiting period to get the best of their acoustics. In 2003, they designed a Variation of a guitar called the Acoustic and classical Electric Jazz Fussion guitars. Recently they designed a new model: the Dream Catcher series.

New Mexico governor Bill Richardson signed a bill to make an acoustic steel string Pimentel guitar called The New Mexico Sunrise the State guitar of New Mexico. Lorenzo Pimentel passed away in 2010 at the age of 82. For more information visit Pimentel's website or contact them directly.

Models include the **M-1 Custom** ($2,500), **W-1 Special** concert ($2,700), **Concert Classical** ($3,500), the **Grand Concert** ($5,000), **Dobre** ($8,000), **Pequeña Torres** Style Classical ($2,500). Flamenco Guitars include the **Studio Concert** ($3,000), **Concert Flamenco** ($5,000), and **Grand Concert** ($8,000).

Acoustic guitars include the **6 -M** Auditorium or Dreadnought ($3,000), **6 -R** Auditorium or Dreadnought ($4,500), 6-K Auditorium or Dreadnought ($5,000).

Small bodied acoustic guitars, Concert and mini Jumbos start at $3,000.

All Acoustics and Classical guitars can be built as a cutaway. All Acoustic models can be built as a 12 strings, please ask for pricing .

Acoustic bass guitars start at $3,500.

Specialty guitars, Requintos, Chile Pepper Fusion Jazz classical and Jazz Acoustics - The Dream Catcher Fusion Classical and Acoustics.The Southwestern Series Classical and Acoustics, The New Mexico series Classical and Acoustics. 7 & 10 string guitars Classical and Acoustics, please ask for pricing.

PINKHAM, RONALD

Instruments currently built in Glen Cove, ME. Distributed by Woodsound Studio of Glen Cove, ME.

CONTACT INFORMATION
PINKHAM, RONALD
Distributed by Woodsound Studio
PO Box 245
Glen Cove, ME 04846
Phone No.: 207-596-7407
www.woodsoundstudio.com
wdsound@midcoast.com

Luthier Ronald Pinkham currently offers high quality concert-grade classic and steel-string acoustic guitars, as well as cellos. Pinkham also has one of the largest orchestral and fretted instrument repair facilities in New England. For further information, visit Pinkham's website or contact him directly.

PLAYTIME

Guitars previously produced in Chicago, IL by either Kay or Harmony during the early 1940s.

The Playtime trademark has been identified as a House Brand for Sears. Playtime guitars mainly appeared in 1943 and 1944 catalogs and was sold as a budget brand to Sears popular Silvertone line. These guitars were probably made by Harmony, but a few examples look like they were built by Kay. Most guitars have arched plywood tops, but spruce was used as well. Source: Walter Murray, Frankenstein Fretworks.

PMC GUITARS

Instruments previously built in Asia. Previously distributed by Sound Trek Distributors of Tampa, FL.

PMC guitars were good quality acoustics designed for the entry or student level up to the medium grade player.

PRAIRIE STATE

Instruments previously produced between the mid-1920s and the early 1940s. Also see Larson Brothers.

The Larson brothers added the Prairie State brand to Maurer & Co. in the mid-1920s. This brand was used exclusively for guitars. The main difference between the Maurer and the Prairie State was the use of a support rod and an adjustable rod running the length of the guitar body from end block to neck block. These 12-fret-to-the-body guitars have the double rod system, which may vary according to the period it was made because August Larson was awarded three patents for these ideas. The rod closest to the soundhole is larger than the lower one, and, in some cases, is capable of making adjustments to the fingerboard height. The function of the lower rod is to change the angle of the neck. Most all Prairie States have laminated top braces and laminated necks. They were built in the lower bout widths of 13.5 in., 14 in., and 15 in. for the standard models, but special order guitars were built up to 21 in. wide. In the mid -1930s, the Prairie State guitars were built in the larger 14-fret-to-the-body sizes, all now sporting the large rod only. The common body widths of these are 15 in., 16 in., 17 in., 19 in., and a rare 21 in. The single cutaway style was used on one known 19 in. f-hole and one 21 in. guitar. The Prairie State guitar is rarer than the other Larson brands. They are of very high quality and are sought by players and collectors. The rigid body produces great sustain and a somewhat different sound from the Maurers and Euphonon guitars. Almost all the Prairie State guitars were made with beautiful rosewood back and sides except the f-hole models which were commonly made with maple bodies, all having select spruce tops. For more information regarding other Larson-made brands, see Maurer, Euphonon, Wm. C. Stahl, W.j. Dyer, and The Larson Brothers.

PRAIRIE VOICE

Unknown production location and date. See chapter on House Brands.

This trademark has been identified as a Harmony-built "Roy Rodgers" style guitar built specifically for the yearly Canadian "Calgary Stampede." Source: Willie G. Moseley, *Stellas & Stratocasters*.

PREMIER

Instruments currently produced in Korea, since the early 1990s. Instruments previously produced in New York from the 1930s-mid-1970s. Later models were manufactured in Japan. Previously distributed in the U.S. market during the 1990s by Entertainment Music Marketing Corporation (EMMC) in Deer Park, NY.

Premier was the brand name of the Peter Sorkin Music Company. Premier-branded solid body guitars were built at the Multivox company of New York, and distribution of those and the later Japanese built Premiers was handled by the Sorkin company of New York City, New York. Other guitars built and distributed (possibly as rebrands) were Royce, Strad-o-lin, Belltone, and Marvel.

Premier solid body guitars featured a double offset cutaway body, and the upper bout had a "carved scroll" design, bolt-on necks, a bound rosewood fingerboard, three-per-side headstocks (initially; later models featured six-on-a-side), and single coil pickups. Later models of the mid- to late 1960s featured wood bodies covered in sparkly plastic.

Towards the end of the U.S. production in the mid-1960s, the **Custom** line of guitars featured numerous body/neck/electronics/hardware parts from overseas manufacturers like Italy and Japan. The guitars were then assembled in the U.S. and available through the early 1970s.

Some models, like the acoustic line, were completely made in Japan during the early 1970s. Some Japanese-built versions of popular American designs were introduced in 1974, but were discontinued two years later. By the mid-1970s, both the Sorkin company and Premier guitars had ceased. Multivox continued importing and distributing Hofner instruments as well as Multivox amplifiers through the early 1980s. Entertainment Music Marketing Corporation began importing the Premier line again during the 1990s, but it is unknown who the distributor is today. Current Premier models are built in Korea, but they are mainly focused on solidbody guitars and basses. Source: Michael Wright, *Guitar Stories*, Volume One.

PRENKERT, RICHARD

Instruments currently built in near Sebastopol, CA since 1979.

Luthier Richard Prenkert builds high quality classical guitars in his shop near Sebastopol, CA. Prenkert graduated with a Bachelor of Arts degree in music from Sonoma State University in California, and has studied with George Sakellarion, Philip Rosheger, and Richard Stover. Prenkert began building guitars in 1979 when he co-owned a music shop in Santa Rosa, CA. Prekert classical guitars start at $6,000 and are available in a variety of high-quality tonewoods. Waiting time for delivery on a guitar is currently about five months, and Prenkert builds between fifteen and twenty guitars a year. For more information visit Prenkert's website or contact him directly.

CONTACT INFORMATION
PRENKERT, RICHARD
10992 Peaks Pike
Sebastopol, CA 95472
Phone No.: 707-829-6719
Fax No.: 707-829-6719
www.prenkertguitars.com
richard@prenkertguitars.com

PRUDENCIO SAEZ

Instruments currently produced in Spain. Distributed by Prudencio Seaz USA, Inc. in Boca Raton, FL.

Prudencio Saez classical acoustics are designed for the beginning to advancing player and are handmade in Spain. For more information visit Prudencio Vaez's website or contact the distributor directly.

Prudencio Saez guitars come in a variety of configurations and price ranges. Regular classical models range in price between $678 and $1,102, solid wood classical models range in price between $948 and $1,592, Flamenco models range in price between $1,382 and $1,592, and cutaway models range in price between $1,170 and $2,311.

CONTACT INFORMATION
PRUDENCIO SAEZ
1498 SW 1st Street
Boca Raton, FL 33486
Phone No.: 866-396-1933
Fax No.: 561-370-6999
www.prudenciosaezusa.com
info@prudenciosaezusa.com

PURE-TONE

Unknown production location and date. See chapter on House Brands.

This trademark has been identified as a House Brand of Selmer (UK). Source: Willie G. Moseley, *Stellas & Stratocasters*.

NOTES

_____

_____

_____

_____

_____

_____

_____

_____

_____

_____

_____

_____

_____

_____

_____

_____

_____

_____

_____

_____

_____

R SECTION
RAIMUNDO

Instruments currently built in Spain since 1968. Distributed by Rockbox Electronics in Campbell, CA.

CONTACT INFORMATION
RAIMUNDO
Factory
Pol. Fuente del Jarro-Paterna, Spain
www.guitarrasraimundo.com

U.S. Distributor: Rockbox Electronics
900 E. Hamilton Ave, Suite 100
Campbell, CA 95008
Phone No.: 408-287-4020
www.rockbox.com
info@rockbox.com

Manuel Raimundo first built guitars in 1968 with two partners: Jesús Grau and Antonio Aparicio. In 1974, they ventured out to some of the world's largest music fair. By 1980, Raimundo had twenty-five employees and they were building 12,000 guitars a year. In 1984, they exhibited in the U.S. for the first time. Guitars became available in the U.S. shortly thereafter. Production has steadily increased since then, and they have expanded into larger facilities several times. Raimundo offers a wide range of classical and flamenco-style acoustic guitars. Several models and variations are available. Prices range between $480 and $1,300. Instruments are currently distributed by Rockbox Electronics in Campbell, CA and previously distributed by Sam Ash Music, Luthier Music Corporation of New York, NY, and Music Imports of San Diego, CA. For more information, visit Raimundo's or Rockbox Electronics' website or contact them directly.

RAINSONG

All-Graphite acoustic guitars currently produced in Woodinville, WA since 2001. Projection Series and Parlor Series instruments previously produced until 2005 in Korea with soundboards built in Woodinville, WA. Distributed by RainSong Graphite Guitars. All-graphite instruments were previously produced in Maui, HI from 1994-2001.

CONTACT INFORMATION
RAINSONG
12604 NE 178th Street
Woodinville, WA 98072
Phone No.: 425-485-7551
Fax No.: 425-485-7274
www.rainsong.com
webinquiry@rainsong.com

RainSong Graphite Guitars was founded by Dr. John A Decker Jr. in Maui, Hawaii. Decker, a physicist with degrees in engineering, began researching and developing composite acoustic guitars in 1985. The goal was to produce a fine-sounding, high-quality composite acoustic guitar that would be impervious to changes in humidity and temperature. Members of the design team included Dr. Decker, noted luthier Lorenzo Pimentel and composites expert George Clayton. In December, 1994, after a prolonged R&D period, full production facilities were opened in Maui, Hawaii.

The first generation of RainSongs were built using traditional bracing patterns. By 1997, the company offered a complete range of acoustic guitars, acoustic basses and jazz archtops.

In 1998, Ashvin Coomar took over as the President/CEO of the company. With an engineering and business background, Coomar hit the road running. With the help of Dr. Decker, Coomar developed a new soundboard technology, Projection Tuned Layering™, that dramatically improved the volume and bass response of the instruments. In 1999, RainSong decided to narrow its line to one offering, the WS1000, that used the new Projection Tuned Layering™ technology. By late 2000, the company began leveraging the success of the WS1000 by introducing other models that used the same technology.

In 2001, RainSong relocated its entire operations to Woodinville, Washington. This move was based on economics - better access to materials and skilled craftsmen and lower shipping costs. The company currently employs seven people. Decker is now the Chairman and continues to reside in Maui, Hawaii.

RainSong introduced a revolutionary set of products in 2002 - the Projection Series and the Parlor guitars. These instruments are designed to provide the unique characteristics of graphite construction - unique sound, look and stability - in a more economical package. The soundboards are constructed using Projection Tuned Layering™ in Woodinville, Washington and shipped to Korea, where the instrument is completed using wood back/sides and neck. The instruments are then shipped to Woodinville for their final setup and inspections. For more information, contact Rainsong directly or visit their website.

MSR/NOTES	100%	EXCELLENT	AVERAGE	LAST MSR

ACOUSTIC

The Rainsong **Limited Edition** model features a Fishman Prefix Pro pickup system, and an abalone inlay on the 12th fret. They are available in Burgundy, Platinum, and Sapphire finishes. Only 300 models were scheduled in the Edition (last MSR was $1,995).

The **Russ Freeman Signature Jazz** model was available in six-string (last MSR was $2,995) and 12-string (last MSR was $3,295) configurations. RainSong guitars are optional with peghead inlay like the **Maui Girl**, **Modest Maui Girl**, and a **Whale** design. Prices range from $100 to $150 for peghead inlay.

6-STRING DREADNOUGHT – dreadnought size body, choice of 14/20- or 12/20-fret fingerboard, solid peghead, Schaller black tuning pegs, shark inlay design on the twelfth fret, side dot markers, Fishman Prefix transducer, volume/tone controls, disc. 2003.

	N/A	$1,300 - 1,500	$700 - 825	$2,195

* *12-String Dreadnought* – similar to the 6-string dreadnought, except features 12-string configuration, 6-per-side tuners, mfg. 1997-2003.

	N/A	$1,300 - 1,500	$700 - 825	$2,195

12-FRET WINDSONG – jumbo size single cutaway body, 12/20-fret fingerboard, solid peghead, Fishman Prefix transducer, Schaller black tuning pegs, shark inlay design on the twelfth fret, and side dot markers, disc.

	N/A	$1,300 - 1,500	$700 - 825	$2,195

MSR/NOTES	100%	EXCELLENT	AVERAGE	LAST MSR

* **14-Fret WindSong** – similar to the 12-Fret WindSong, except the neck joins the body at the 14th fret, 14/20 fingerboard, disc.

| | N/A | $1,300 - 1,500 | $700 - 825 | $2,195 |

* **12-String WindSong** – similar to the 14-Fret WindSong, except has 12-string configuration, 6-per-side tuners, mfg. 1997-2003.

| | N/A | $1,300 - 1,500 | $700 - 825 | $2,195 |

CLASSICAL – black unidirectional-graphite soundboard, 650 mm scale, 2 in. width at nut, slotted (open) peghead with 3-per-side tuners, gold Schaller tuners with ebony buttons, and abalone rosette, disc.

| | N/A | $1,300 - 1,500 | $700 - 825 | $2,195 |

The Classical model is patterned after Pimentel & Sons Grand Concert model.

DR1100 – dreadnought style, all-graphite top/back/sides/neck, 14/21-fret fingerboard with shark inlays, abalone rosette, mfg. 2000-06.

| | N/A | $1,200 - 1,500 | $750 - 950 | $2,795 |

Also available in left-handed configuration at no additional cost.

* **P-DR1100** – Projection series, similar to the DR-1100, except has a mahogany back/sides/neck, and graphite top, assembled in Korea, disc. 2005.

| | N/A | $450 - 525 | $300 - 350 | $999 |

FLAMENCO – similar to the Classical, except has solid headstock, disc. 2003.

| | N/A | $1,300 - 1,500 | $700 - 825 | $2,195 |

P-GA1100 – Projection series, deep body single cutaway style, graphite top, mahogany back/sides/neck, assembled in Korea, disc. 2005.

| | N/A | $550 - 650 | $350 - 400 | $1,182 |

P-MJ1100 – Projection series, slim body single cutaway style, graphite top, mahogany back/sides/neck, assembled in Korea, disc. 2005.

| | N/A | $550 - 650 | $350 - 400 | $1,182 |

WS1100 – deep body single cutaway style, all-graphite top/back/sides/neck, 14/21-fret fingerboard with shark inlays, abalone rosette, mfg. 2000-06.

| | N/A | $1,200 - 1,500 | $750 - 950 | $2,795 |

Also available in left-handed configuration at no additional cost.

* **A-WS1100** – similar to the WS-1100, except is part of the All-Graphite Advanced Series with all-graphite construction, dual action trussrod, pinless bridge, and other features, available in Black, Blue, Natural (2006 only), or Red finish, mfg. 2005-06.

| | N/A | $550 - 650 | $350 - 425 | $1,249 |

* Add 40% (Last MSR was $1,749) for Natural finish.

ACOUSTIC: HYBRID SERIES

Rainsong's Hybird Series that are composite guitars combining carbon fiber and glass fiber for the body.

H-DR1100N2 – dreadnought-style body, carbon/glass hybrid top, back and sides, no bracing, round soundhole with white ring rosette, graphite N2 neck, 14/21-fret composite fingerboard with white dot inlays, carbon headstock overlay, three-per-side chrome tuners, Natural Carbon fiber finish, 25.4 in. scale, hardshell case included, mfg. 2010-present.

| MSR $1,999 | $1,500 | $900 - 1,100 | $600 - 700 | |

H-OM1000N2 – single cutaway slim-body orchestra model-style body, carbon/glass hybrid top, back and sides, no bracing, round soundhole with white ring rosette, graphite N2 neck, 14/21-fret composite fingerboard with white dot inlays, carbon headstock overlay, three-per-side chrome tuners, Fishman Prefix Plus-T electronics, Natural Carbon fiber finish, 25.4 in. scale, hardshell included, mfg. 2010-present.

| MSR $2,399 | $1,800 | $1,075 - 1,325 | $725 - 850 | |

H-WS1000N2 – single cutaway full body orchestra model-style body, carbon/glass hybrid top, back and sides, no bracing, round soundhole with white ring rosette, graphite N2 neck, 14/21-fret composite fingerboard with white dot inlays, carbon headstock overlay, three-per-side chrome tuners, Fishman Prefix Plus-T electronics, Natural Carbon fiber finish, 25.4 in. scale, hardshell included, mfg. 2010-present.

| MSR $2,399 | $1,800 | $1,075 - 1,325 | $725 - 850 | |

ACOUSTIC: STUDIO SERIES

Rainsong's Studio Series feature the same hybrid construction of carbon and glass fiber with a tough, non-glossy Fine Texture finish.

S-DR1000N2 – dreadnought-style body, carbon/glass hybrid top, back and sides, no bracing, round soundhole with double white ring rosette, graphite N2 neck, 14/21-fret composite fingerboard with white dot inlays, carbon headstock overlay, three-per-side chrome tuners, Fishman Prefix+T electronics, non-glossy Fine Texture finish, 25.4 in. scale, deluxe gig bag included, mfg. 2011-present.

| MSR $1,868 | $1,400 | $850 - 1,025 | $550 - 650 | |

MSR/NOTES	100%	EXCELLENT	AVERAGE	LAST MSR

S-OM1000N2 – single cutaway slim-line orchestra model-style body, carbon/glass hybrid top, back and sides, no bracing, round soundhole with double white ring rosette, graphite N2 neck, 14/21-fret composite fingerboard with white dot inlays, carbon headstock overlay, three-per-side chrome tuners, Fishman Prefix+T electronics, non-glossy Fine Texture finish, 25.4 in. scale, deluxe gig bag included, mfg. 2011-present.

MSR $2,000	$1,500	$900 - 1,100	$600 - 700	

S-WS1000N2 – single cutaway full-body orchestra model-style body, carbon/glass hybrid top, back and sides, no bracing, round soundhole with double white ring rosette, graphite N2 neck, 14/21-fret composite fingerboard with white dot inlays, carbon headstock overlay, three-per-side chrome tuners, Fishman Prefix+T electronics, non-glossy Fine Texture finish, 25.4 in. scale, deluxe gig bag included, mfg. 2011-present.

MSR $2,000	$1,500	$900 - 1,100	$600 - 700	

ACOUSTIC ELECTRIC

6-STRING JAZZ GUITAR – single cutaway body, f-holes, 648 mm scale, 3+3 headstock, black Schaller tuning machines, graphite tailpiece, EMG 91 Custom pickup, Mike Christian tune-o-matic acoustic piezo bridge, volume/tone controls, 3-way pickup selector, disc.

	N/A	$1,450 - 1,650	$775 - 900	$2,495

* *12-String Jazz Guitar (StormSong)* – similar to the 6-String Jazz Guitar, except features a 12-string configuration, 6-per-side tuners, EMG 89R humbucker pickups, 5-way pickup selector, mfg. 1997-disc.

	N/A	$1,450 - 1,650	$775 - 900	$2,495

BI-JM1000N2 "BLACK ICE" – jumbo full-size body, all-graphite body with an all-graphite "Black Ice" top that features Rainsong's Projection Tuned Layering technique, round soundhole with abalone rosette, all-graphite N2 neck, 14/21 composite fingerboard with custom MOP shark inlays, graphite headstock overlay with logo, three-per-side chrome tuners, Fishman Prefix Plus T electronics, available in UV protective, high gloss, clear urethane finish, 25.4 in. scale, customized hardshell case included, mfg. 2011-present.

MSR $3,295	$2,475	$1,500 - 1,800	$1,000 - 1,200	

BI-OM1000N2 "BLACK ICE" – orchestra model body, all-graphite body with an all-graphite "Black Ice" top that features Rainsong's Projection Tuned Layering technique, round soundhole with abalone rosette, all-graphite N2 neck, 14/21 composite fingerboard with custom MOP shark inlays, graphite headstock overlay with logo, three-per-side chrome tuners, Fishman Prefix Plus T electronics, available in UV protective, high gloss, clear urethane finish, 25.4 in. scale, customized hardshell case included, mfg. 2012-present.

MSR $3,295	$2,475	$1,500 - 1,800	$1,000 - 1,200	

BI-WS1000N2 "BLACK ICE" – single cutaway full-size body, all-graphite body with an all-graphite "Black Ice" top that features Rainsong's Projection Tuned Layering technique, round soundhole with abalone rosette, all-graphite N2 neck, 14/21 composite fingerboard with custom MOP shark inlays, graphite headstock overlay with logo, three-per-side chrome tuners, Fishman Prefix Plus T electronics, available in UV protective, high gloss, clear urethane finish, 25.4 in. scale, customized hardshell case included, mfg. 2009-present.

MSR $3,295	$2,475	$1,500 - 1,800	$1,000 - 1,200	

CO-DR1000N2 "CONCERT" – dreadnought body, all-graphite body with an all-graphite unidirectional carbon top that features Rainsong's Projection Tuned Layering technique, round soundhole with abalone rosette, all-graphite N2 neck, 14/21 composite fingerboard with custom MOP shark inlays, graphite headstock overlay with logo, three-per-side chrome tuners, Fishman Prefix Plus T electronics, available in UV protective, high gloss, clear urethane finish, 25.4 in. scale, customized hardshell case included, mfg. 2012-present.

MSR $2,995	$2,250	$1,400 - 1,600	$875 - 1,000	

CO-JM1000N2 "CONCERT" – jumbo body, all-graphite body with an all-graphite unidirectional carbon top that features Rainsong's Projection Tuned Layering technique, round soundhole with abalone rosette, all-graphite N2 neck, 14/21 composite fingerboard with custom MOP shark inlays, graphite headstock overlay with logo, three-per-side chrome tuners, Fishman Prefix Plus T electronics, available in UV protective, high gloss, clear urethane finish, 25.4 in. scale, customized hardshell case included, mfg. 2012-present.

MSR $3,195	$2,400	$1,500 - 1,750	$925 - 1,075	

CO-OM1000N2 "CONCERT" – single cutaway orchestra body, all-graphite body with an all-graphite unidirectional carbon top that features Rainsong's Projection Tuned Layering technique, round soundhole with abalone rosette, all-graphite N2 neck, 14/21 composite fingerboard with custom MOP shark inlays, graphite headstock overlay with logo, three-per-side chrome tuners, Fishman Prefix Plus T electronics, available in UV protective, high gloss, clear urethane finish, 25.4 in. scale, customized hardshell case included, mfg. 2012-present.

MSR $3,195	$2,400	$1,500 - 1,750	$925 - 1,075	

CO-WS1000N2 "CONCERT" – single cutaway full-size body, all-graphite body with an all-graphite unidirectional carbon top that features Rainsong's Projection Tuned Layering technique, round soundhole with abalone rosette, all-graphite N2 neck, 14/21 composite fingerboard with custom MOP shark inlays, graphite headstock overlay with logo, three-per-side chrome tuners, Fishman Prefix Plus T electronics, available in UV protective, high gloss, clear urethane finish, 25.4 in. scale, customized hardshell case included, mfg. 2009-present.

MSR $3,195	$2,400	$1,500 - 1,750	$925 - 1,075	

DR1000 – dreadnought style, all-graphite top/back/sides/neck, 14/21-fret fingerboard with shark inlays, abalone rosette, Element electronics, mfg. 2000-present.

MSR $2,795	$2,100	$1,250 - 1,500	$875 - 1,000	

Also available in left-handed configuration at no additional cost.

MSR/NOTES	100%	EXCELLENT	AVERAGE	LAST MSR
* **P-DR1000** – Projection series, similar to the DR-1000, except has a mahogany back/sides/neck, and graphite top, Fishman Prefix Plus electronics, assembled in Korea, disc. 2005.				
	N/A	$525 - 625	$325 - 375	$1,149
JM1000 – jumbo style, all-graphite top/back/sides/neck, 14/21-fret fingerboard with shark inlays, abalone rosette, Element electronics, mfg. 2000-present.				
MSR $2,995	$2,250	$1,400 - 1,600	$875 - 1,000	
JM3000 – jumbo style, 12-string configuration, all-graphite top/back/sides/neck, 14/21-fret fingerboard with shark inlays, abalone rosette, Element electronics, mfg. 2000-present.				
MSR $3,195	$2,400	$1,500 - 1,750	$925 - 1,075	
OM1000 – orchestra single cutaway style, all-graphite top/back/sides/neck, 14/21-fret fingerboard with shark inlays, abalone rosette, Element electronics, mfg. 2000-present.				
MSR $2,995	$2,250	$1,400 - 1,600	$875 - 1,000	
P-GA1000 – Projection series, deep body single cutaway style, graphite top, mahogany back/sides/neck, Fishman Prefix Plus electronics, assembled in Korea, disc. 2005.				
	N/A	$625 - 675	$375 - 450	$1,332
P-MJ1000 – Projection series, slim body single cutaway style, graphite top, mahogany back/sides/neck, Fishman Prefix Plus electronics, assembled in Korea, disc. 2005.				
	N/A	$625 - 675	$375 - 450	$1,332
PARLOR W-PA1000 – parlor style body, graphite top, mahogany (MH), maple (MA), or rosewood (RW) backand sides, mahogany or maple neck, 12/19-fret rosewood fingerboard, rosewood bridge, Fishman Classic IV electronics, disc. 2005.				
	N/A	$400 - 475	$275 - 325	$899

* Add 5% for maple back and sides.
* Add 10% for rosewood back and sides.

MSR/NOTES	100%	EXCELLENT	AVERAGE	LAST MSR
SHORTY SFT – single cutaway orchestra body, all-graphite body with an all-graphite unidirectional carbon top that features Rainsong's Projection Tuned Layering technique, round soundhole with abalone rosette, all-graphite N neck, 12/18 composite fingerboard with no inlays, graphite headstock overlay with logo, three-per-side chrome tuners, Fishman Prefix Plus T electronics, available in UV protective, fine texture polyurethane finish, 24.875 in. scale, customized hardshell case included, mfg. 2012-present.				
MSR $2,265	$1,700	$1,000 - 1,250	$600 - 750	
* **Shorty SG** – similar to the Shorty SFT, except has a UV protective, high gloss urethane finish, customized hardshell case included, mfg. 2012-present.				
MSR $2,532	$1,900	$1,125 - 1,400	$675 - 850	
STAGESONG – similar to the Windsong Acoustic/Electric model, except has no soundhole in the top soundboard, disc.				
	N/A	$1,300 - 1,500	$700 - 825	$2,195
* **12-String StageSong** – similar to the StageSong, except in 12-string configuration and six-per-side tuners, mfg. 1997-disc.				
	N/A	$1,300 - 1,500	$700 - 825	$2,195
* **Stagesong Classical** – similar to the StageSong, except has classical stylings, disc.				
	N/A	$1,300 - 1,500	$700 - 825	$2,195
WS1000 – deep body single cutaway style, all-graphite top/back/sides/neck, 14/21-fret fingerboard with shark inlays, abalone rosette, Element electronics, mfg. 2000-present.				
MSR $2,995	$2,250	$1,400 - 1,600	$875 - 1,000	
* **A-WS1000** – similar to the WS-1000, except is part of the All-Graphite Advanced Series with all-graphite construction, dual action trussrod, pinless bridge, and other features, available in Black, Blue, Natural (2006-08), or Red finish, mfg. 2005-08.				
	N/A	$850 - 975	$525 - 600	$1,875

* Add 7.5% (Last MSR was $1,999) for Natural finish.

MSR/NOTES	100%	EXCELLENT	AVERAGE	LAST MSR
WS3000 – deep body single cutaway style, 12-string configuration, all-graphite top/back/sides/neck, 14/21-fret fingerboard with shark inlays, abalone rosette, Element electronics, mfg. 2000-present.				
MSR $3,195	$2,400	$1,500 - 1,750	$925 - 1,075	
WS9000 – deep body single cutaway nylon-string style, all-graphite top/back/sides/neck, 14/21-fret fingerboard with shark inlays, abalone rosette, Element electronics, mfg. 2000-06.				
	N/A	$1,400 - 1,600	$875 - 1,000	$2,995
WINDSONG ACOUSTIC/ELECTRIC – similar to the Windsong acoustic model, except has thinner body, oval soundhole, Fishman Axis-M transducer/preamp, and oval abalone rosette, disc.				
	N/A	$2,750 - 3,250	$1,400 - 1,600	$4,000

MSR/NOTES	100%	EXCELLENT	AVERAGE	LAST MSR

ACOUSTIC BASS

ACOUSTIC BASS – body patterned similar to the Windsong guitar, 844 mm scale, two-per-side tuners, solid headstock, abalone rosette, side dot fret markers, Fishman Prefix transducer/preamp, volume/tone controls, disc.

	N/A	$1,300 - 1,500	$700 - 825	$2,195

• **Add 20% for fretless fingerboard (Model Fretless Bass).**

STAGESONG BASS – similar to the Acoustic Bass, except has no soundhole in the top soundboard, disc.

	N/A	$1,300 - 1,500	$700 - 825	$2,195

RALEIGH

Instruments previously built in Chicago, IL. Distributed by the Aloha Publishing and Musical Instrument Company in Chicago, IL.

The Aloha company was founded in 1935 by J.M. Raleigh. True to the nature of a House Brand distributor, Raleigh's company distributed both Aloha instruments and amplifiers and Raleigh brand instruments through his Chicago office. Acoustic guitars were supplied by Harmony, and initial amplifiers and guitars for the Aloha trademark were supplied by the Alamo company of San Antonio, TX. By the mid-1950s, Aloha was producing their own amps, but continued using Alamo products. Source: Michael Wright, *Vintage Guitar Magazine.*

RAMIREZ, JOSÉ

Instruments currently built in Madrid, Spain. Distributed by Cordoba Music Group (previously Tornavoz Music) in Santa Monica, CA.

CONTACT INFORMATION
RAMIREZ, JOSÉ

U.S. Distributor: Cordoba Music Group
1455 19th Street
Santa Monica, CA 90404
Phone No.: 310-586-1180
Fax No.: 310-586-1181
www.cordobamusicgroup.com

José Ramirez (1858-1923), originally apprenticed with luthier Francisco Gonzalez, began the family business in 1882. Many well known players, such as Segovia, Tarrega, Sabicas, Llobet, Yepes, and others had used Ramirez guitars during the course of their careers. The Madrid-based family business then passed to José II (1885-1957), and then to José III (born 1922-1994).

The acoustic guitars today are built in the workshop that is supervised by José Ramirez IV. Ramirez IV, born in 1953, apprenticed in the family workshop when he was eighteen years old. By 1976, he had approached journeyman status, and within three years was working in maestro status. His sister, Amalia Ramirez (1955-), oversaw the business side of the company for a few years.

In the early 1980s, the family workshop employed seventeen workers and was producing 1,000 guitars a year. In the mid-1990s, the Ramirez workshop cut back production numbers to the amount the workshop could build without sub-contracting to outside builders. This level of supervision aids in maintaining the high quality of the guitars that carry the Ramirez name. José IV, passed away in 2000, and his sister Amalia took over the workshop after a short time away from the company. For more information contact the Cordoba Music Group directly.

The Concert Line represents Ramirez's top-end guitars. Prices range from $9,500 to $25,000 in this series. The R Series features guitars ranging in price from $1,799 to $3,759. The E Series is discontinued and featured guitars ranging from $2,469 to $4,899. The NE Series features guitars ranging in price from $2,110 to $4,250. A George Harrison model is available for $4,049.

RAMIERZ, MANUEL

Guitars previously produced in Madrid, Spain during the early 1900s.

Luthier Manuel Ramirez is the brother of noted Spanish classical builder José Ramirez. Several noted luthiers trained with Ramirez including Santos Hernandez, Enrique Garcia, Modesto Borreguero, and Domingo Esteso. Manuel worked with José for a few years, but after a fight between the two about moving shops, they never spoke again. Manuel built guitars until approximately the 1920s.

RANGE RIDER

Unknown production location and date. See chapter on House Brands.

This trademark has been identified as a House Brand of the Monroe Catalog House. Source: Willie G. Moseley, *Stellas & Stratocasters.*

RAREBIRD

Instruments currently built in Northern Georgia since 2007. Previously produced in Denver, CO between 1978 and 2006.

CONTACT INFORMATION
RAREBIRD

Phone No.: 720-364-6894
www.rarebirdguitars.com
mukster42@broomfield-designers.com

Luthier Philip Bruce Clay apprenticed in a small Denver repair shop from 1974 to 1976, where he learned the basics of guitar repair. Later, he attended the Guitar Research and Design Center in Vermont (under the direction of Charles Fox), and graduated in February of 1978.

The **Rarebird** concept has been to build a durable, high quality instrument ever since opening his shop. Custom options are

MSR/NOTES	100%	EXCELLENT	AVERAGE	LAST MSR

virtually limitless with over fifty species of hardwood on hand, and Clay's twenty-plus years of experience can help guide the customer to the tones so desired. Clay's approach is to simply talk the customer through the different options, systematically explaining the combinations. Having built over 1,200 instruments since 1978, Clay celebrated his 20th Anniversary in 1998.

Noted **Rarebird** features are multi-laminate necks and graphite reinforcements for stability, heelless bodies - either neck-through or set-in (glued in) for sustain and complete access, and semi-hollow guitar designs to achieve a rich and full balanced tone. For more information refer to Rarebird's website.

Rarebird produces the Aguila acoustic flattop. Prices start at $1,900 for standard production models, $2,300 for the deluxe model, and $2,700 for the artist model. Electric guitars and basses are available as well starting at $1,200 and $2,250 for custom made instruments.

RAYCO RESOPHONICS

Instruments currently produced in Smithers, British Columbia, Canada since 2002.

Luthiers Mark Thibeault and Jason Friesen build resophonic and Hawaiian-style guitars in their British Columbia shop. They use all solid woods with soundpost construction, dovetailed neck joints, ebony fingerboards, and all instruments feature a limited lifetime warranty. Thibeault and Friesen worked with Jean Larriveé and their resonator designs are inspired by Tim Scheerhorn. In November 2008, Rayco began to offer Scheerhorn cones and coverplates as an option on all models. Resophonic and Hawaiian instruments start at $3,200 with many options available. For more information, visit Rayco's website or contact them directly.

CONTACT INFORMATION
RAYCO RESOPHONICS
PO Box 3063, 3465 Poplar Road
Smithers, British Columbia V0J 2N0
Canada
Phone No.: 250-847-5001
rayco.ca
raycores@telus.net

RECORDING KING

Instruments previously produced in Kalamazoo, MI by Gibson, and in Chicago, IL by Kay, and New York, NY by Gretsch between the mid-1930s and the early 1940s. See chapter on House Brands.

The Recording King trademark was the House Brand of Montgomery Wards, and was used on a full range of acoustic flattops, electric lap steels, acoustic and electric archtop guitars, mandolins, and banjos. Instruments were built by a number of American manufacturers such as Gibson, Gretsch, and Kay between the 1930s through the early 1940s.

The high end models of the Recording King line were built by Gibson, but the low end models were built by other Chicago-based manufacturers. Recording King models built by Gibson will not have an adjustable truss rod (like other budget brands Gibson produced). Chances are that the low end, Chicago-built models do not either. Recording King had a number of endorsers, such as singing cowboy movie star Ray Whitley, country singer/songwriter Carson Robison, and multi-instrumental virtuoso Roy Smeck. Source: Walter Carter, *Gibson Guitars: 100 Years of an American Icon.*

ACOUSTIC ARCHTOP

M Series guitars were built by Gibson.

M-2 (1136/1254) – 16 in. wide body, carved top, maple back and sides, bound top, f-holes, rosewood fingerboard with dot inlay, pickguard, available in Sunburst finish, mfg. 1937-1941.

	N/A	$675 - 850	$400 - 500	

In 1938, this guitar was renamed the Model 1136 and featured changes such as full body binding, pickguard binding, peghead changed to a point with a crown graphic.

M-3/TONE CREST (1103/1137/1228/1282/1283) – 16 in. wide body, carved top, maple back and sides, tortoiseshell body binding, f-holes, bound rosewood fingerboard with dot inlay, cream pickguard, available in Natural (1283) or Sunburst (1282) finish, mfg. 1936-1941.

	N/A	$800 - 1,000	$475 - 600	

This model was originally a Tone Crest. In 1937, this guitar was renamed the Model 1228. In 1938, the model was change to the M-3 (1137) and featured changes such as a five-piece maple neck, full cream body binding, pickguard binding, peghead changed to a point with a crown graphic. In 1940, Natural finish became an option again (1103).

M-4 (1123) – 16 in. wide body, carved top, maple back and sides, mahogany neck, body binding, f-holes, bound rosewood fingerboard with dot inlay, bound peghead with 3-per-side tuners, bound pickguard, available in Natural or Sunburst finish, mfg. 1937-1940.

	N/A	$1,075 - 1,350	$650 - 800	

In 1938, this model was formally introduced as the M-4 and a five-ply neck was introduced.

M-5 (1285) – 16 in. wide body, carved top, maple back and sides, checkered top binding, single bound back, f-holes, bound rosewood fingerboard with diamond inlay, pickguard, checkered bound peghead with diamond and block inlays, chrome plated hardware, available in Natural or Sunburst finish, 4 in. body depth, mfg. 1936 only.

	N/A	$1,400 - 1,750	$850 - 1,050	

M-5 (1124) – 16 in. wide body, carved top, maple back and sides, checkered top binding, single bound back, f-holes, five-piece maple neck, bound rosewood fingerboard with three-piece inlay of rectangles and dots, pickguard, bound peghead with pearl inlays and graphic, chrome plated hardware, available in Natural or Sunburst finish, 4 in. body depth, mfg. 1937-38.

	N/A	$1,600 - 2,000	$950 - 1,200	

MSR/NOTES	100%	EXCELLENT	AVERAGE	LAST MSR

M-5 (1121) – 17 in. wide body, carved top, maple back and sides, five-ply top binding, three-ply back binding, f-holes, five-piece maple neck, bound rosewood fingerboard with large diamond inlays, pickguard, unbound peghead with reversed crown cutout and diamond inlays, trapeze tailpiece chrome plated hardware, available in Natural or Sunburst finish, 4 in. body depth, mfg. 1939-1941.

| | N/A | $1,800 - 2,250 | $1,075 - 1,350 | |

This model is also available with gold hardware (Model M-6).

RECORDING KING (CURRENT MFG.)

Instruments currently produced overseas since 2005. Distributed by The Music Link in Hayward, CA.

The Music Link distribution company reintroduced the Recording King trademark in 2005. Greg Rich of Gibson fame designed these mid-grade acoustic instruments and their product line consists of the Classic acoustic guitar series, the Western Collectible art guitar series, and banjos. Prices start at $340 and range up to $1,450 on Classic acoustic guitars. For more information, visit Recording King's website or contact The Music Link directly.

CONTACT INFORMATION
RECORDING KING (CURRENT MFG.)
Distributed by The Music Link
31067 San Clemente Street
Hayward, CA 94544
Phone No.: 415-570-0970
Fax No.: 415-570-0651
www.recordingking.com
info@themusiclink.net

REDGATE, JIM GUITARS

Instruments currently built in Adelaide, Australia. Distributed exclusively world-wide by Classic Guitars International in Santa Barbara, CA.

Luthier Jim Redgate was born in London, England in 1963 and his family emigrated to Australia in 1966. Redgate left school at the age of fifteen to begin a trade in the building industry. Much to the dismay of his employer, and after a four year award-winning apprenticeship, he changed direction to pursue a career in music.

Redgate has been building guitars since 1984. An accomplished player himself, he holds a Bachelor of Music Performance in Classical Guitar from the Elder Conservatorium. The relative isolation of Adelaide from the mainstream classical world resulted in Redgate developing his own unique building style and approach and his background in guitar playing is obvious in the design, playability, sound, and balance of his instruments. The popularity of his guitars spread and by the mid 1990's he was marketing worldwide.

CONTACT INFORMATION
REDGATE, JIM GUITARS
Factory/Headquarters
Port Noarlunga, Adelaide South
Australia
www.redgateguitars.com
jim@redgateguitars.com

*World-Wide Distributor: Classic Guitars
International*
3463 State St., #200
Santa Barbara, CA 93105
Phone No.: 805-390-1571
www.classicguitar.com
guitars@classicguitar.com

Always developing new ideas, Redgate is well-known for his arched back classical concert guitars with carbon fiber reinforced lattice bracing and two well received double top models, the "traditional" double top, with nomex core and flat back, and the ergonomic and immensely playable "WAVE" double top with its arched top and back and well elevated fingerboard. His high grade construction materials include rosewood, W.R. cedar, German spruce, ebony, and mahogany. To enhance the response and augment the rich classical tone he uses carbon fiber and Kevlar/Nomex to reinforce essential components in his instruments. Concert and recording artists including Ana Vidovic, Odair Assad, Slava Gregorian, Leonard Gregorian, Ralph Towner, and others play and record with Redgate guitars.

Redgate builds about fifteen guitars a year, with minimal use of power tools. Instruments are ordered through his agent, though custom requests can still be catered for. Guitars start at $12,950 and for further information, please contact Classic Guitars International directly.

REDONDO

Unknown production location and date. See chapter on House Brands.

This trademark has been identified as a House Brand of the Tosca Company. Source: Willie G. Moseley, *Stellas & Stratocasters*.

REEDMAN

Instruments previously built in Korea. Distributed by Reedman America in Whittier, CA.

The Reedman Musical Instrument company offered a wide range of good quality acoustic, acoustic/electric, and solid body electric guitars.

REGAL

Instruments currently produced in Korea. Distributed by Saga Musical Instruments of San Francisco, CA. Original Regal instruments produced beginning 1896 in Indianapolis, Indiana. Regal reappeared in Chicago, IL in 1908, possibly tied to Lyon and Healy (Washburn). U.S. production was centered in Chicago from 1908 through the late 1960s. Models from the mid-1950s to the late 1960s produced in Chicago, IL by the Harmony company. Some Regal models licensed to Fender, and some appear with Fender logo during the late 1950s to mid-1960s (prior to Fender's own flattop and Coronado series).

CONTACT INFORMATION
REGAL
Distributed by Saga Musical Instruments
PO Box 2841
South San Francisco, CA 94080
Phone No.: 650-558-5558
Fax No.: 650-871-7590
www.sagamusic.com
info@sagamusic.com

Emil Wulschner was a retailer and wholesaler in Indianapolis, Indiana during the 1880s. In the early 1890s he added his stepson to the company, and changed the name to "Wulschner and Son." They opened a factory around 1896 to build guitars and mandolins under three different trademarks: Regal, University, and 20th Century. Though Wulschner passed away in 1900, the factory continued on through 1902 or 1903 under control of a larger corporation. The business end of the company let it go when the economy faltered during those final years. This is the end of the original Regal trademarked instruments.

In 1904, Lyon & Healy (Washburn) purchased the rights to the Regal trademark, thousands of completed and works in progress instruments, and the company stockpile of raw materials. A new Regal company debuted in Chicago, Illinois in 1908 (it is not certain what happened during those four years) and it is supposed that they were tied to Lyon & Healy. The new company marketed ukuleles and tenor guitars, but not 6-string guitars.

However, experts have agreed that Regal built guitar models for other labels (Bruno, Weyman, Stahl, and Lyon & Healy) during the 1910-1920 era. Regal eventually announced that their six string models would be distributed through a number of wholesalers.

In 1930, the Tonk Bros. Company acquired the rights to the Washburn trademark when the then-current holder (J.R. Stewart Co.) went bankrupt. Regal bought the rights to the **Stewart** and **LeDomino** names from Tonk Bros., and was making fretted instruments for all three trademarks. Also in the early 1930s, Regal had licensed the use of Dobro resonators in a series of guitars. In 1934, they acquired the rights to manufacture Dobro brand instruments when National-Dobro moved to Chicago from California. Regal then announced that they would be joining the name brand guitar producers that sold direct to dealers in 1938. Regal was, in effect, another producer of House Brand guitars prior to World War II.

It has been estimated by one source that Regal-built Dobros stopped in 1940, and were not built from then on. During World War II, guitar production lines were converted to the war effort. After the war, the Regal Musical Instrument company's production was not as great as the pre-war production amounts. In 1954 the trademark and company fixtures were sold to Harmony. Harmony and Kay, were the other major producers of House Brand instruments. Regal guitars were licensed to Fender in the late 1950s, and some of the Harmony built "Regals" were rebranded with the Fender logo. This agreement continued up until the mid-1960s, when Fender introduced their own flattop guitars.

In 1987, Saga Musical Instruments reintroduced the Regal trademark to the U.S. market. Regal now offers a traditional resonator guitar in both a roundneck and squareneck versions. Saga, located in San Francisco, also offers the **Blueridge** line of acoustic instruments, as well as mandolins, and stringed instrument parts and replacement pieces.

Early Regal history courtesy John Teagle, *Washburn: Over One Hundred Years of Fine Stringed Instruments.*

ACOUSTIC

The **RD-30** (MSR $395) features the Power Reflex Tone Chamber and is available in roundneck or sqaureneck configurations. The **RD-38** (MSR $475) has more elaborate appointments including gold hardware. The **RD-40** (MSR $495) is Regal's most traditional resonator. The **RD-45** (disc.) roundneck resonator has a spruce top, solid 3+3 peghead, a 21-fret neck that joins at the 14th fret, and an adjustable truss rod. Available in Black, Cherryburst, Natural, and Sunburst. The all-mahogany version (**RD-45 M**, disc.) has a Gloss finish.

The **RD-45S** (disc.) squareneck resonator model also has a spruce top, and a more traditional slotted 3+3 peghead, as well as the 14/21-fret neck. The RD-45 S models are also available in Black, Cherryburst, Natural, and Sunburst. The all-mahogany version (**RD-45S M**, disc.) has a Gloss finish.

Regal briefly offered the **RD-65** resonator guitar. This roundneck model features all maple body construction, a mahogany neck, bound 14/21-fret rosewood fingerboard with mother-of-pearl position dots, solid three-per-side tuners, and a seven-ply white/black/white body binding. The **RD-65S** (disc.) squareneck model is similar in construction, except has a slotted 3+3 headstock, 12th fret neck joint, and all white body binding. Both models have a Sunburst finish. Regal's **RD-65M** (disc.) has a body constructed out of mahogany with the same specifications as the RD-65. The RD-65M has a dark-stained high gloss finish.

ACOUSTIC BASS

Regal also offered the **RD-05** resonator bass guitar. Similar to the RD-45 resonator guitar models, the RD-05 has 23-fret neck that joins the body at the 17th fret, a 2+2 solid headstock, a spruce top, and Sunburst finish.

REGENT

Instruments previously produced in Ottawa, Canada.

Regent produced guitars circa 1940s-1960s. The headstock features the name Regent in distinctive block lettering with one leg of the R extended to underline the rest of the word. They made both archtop and flattop models. Source: Walter Murray, Frankenstein Fretworks.

Two models have been encountered with the Regent brand. An archtop acoustic model P-13 features segmented f-holes, floating adjustable wood bridge, chome trapeze tailpiece, white plastic floating pickguard, single bound body, 14/20-fret fingerboard with dot markers, three-per-side tuners, and the label identifies S. Nathanson as the distributor.

A flattop acoustic (no model number) features a small parlor size body, spruce top, single bound body, cream teardrop pickguard, floating non-adjustable wood bridge, chrome tailpiece, 12/18-fret fingerboard with dot inlays, three-per-side tuners. This was labeled as a beginner guitar and was probably built in the late 1950s or early 1960s.

MSR/NOTES	100%	EXCELLENT	AVERAGE	LAST MSR

RENAISSANCE GUITAR COMPANY

Instruments currently manufactured in Santa Cruz, CA.

Renaissance Guitars are built by luthier Rick Turner, one of the original three partners that formed Alembic in 1970. In 1978, he left Alembic to form Turner Guitars, and opened a workshop in 1979 in Novato, California. Although artists such as Lindsey Buckingham favored Turner's guitars, the company was closed in 1981. Turner's records show that approximately 130 instruments were built during that time period (1979-1981).

CONTACT INFORMATION
RENAISSANCE GUITAR COMPANY
815 Almar Ave.
Santa Cruz, CA 95060-7440
Phone No.: 831-460-9144
Fax No.: 831-460-9146
www.renaissanceguitars.com
rick@renaissanceguitars.com

Rick Turner is well-known and respected for his innovative designs that oftentimes utilize a retro style with state-of-the-art construction, materials, and most importantly, his proprietary electronics, which give amazing results. As well as building instruments, Rick Turner has written countless columns on guitar building, repairs, and products profiles in guitar magazines. Turner reopened his guitar shop in 1989, and now offers a range of instruments under both the Renaissance and Rick Turner trademarks. For more information, visit Renaissance's website or contact them directly.

ACOUSTIC: COMPASS ROSE SERIES

Rick Turner and Renaissance Guitars also offered a line of traditional acoustic guitars. Guitars featured a AAA cedar or AAA spruce top, Indian rosewood back and sides, bound bodies, and othe features. Models are available as the **Deluxe Small Jumbo Guitar** (Last MSR was $5,450, $5,850 with a cutaway), **Deluxe Large Jumbo Guitar** (Last MSR was $5,950, $6,350 with a cutaway), and **Deluxe Baritone Jumbo Guitar** (Last MSR was $6,200, $6,600 with a cutaway). D-TAR 18 volt electronics can be added for $250. The Compass Rose Series was discontinued for guitars in 2008, but ukuleles are still available.

ACOUSTIC ELECTRIC: RENAISSANCE SERIES

RENAISSANCE STUDIO SPECIAL (RS6-SP) – uniquely-shaped single cutaway semi-acoustic body, walnut top, back and sides, no binding, Turner piezo bridge, 18 volt preamp, available in Satin Natural finish, current mfg.

| MSR $1,975 | $1,600 | $950 - 1,100 | $600 - 700 | |

- Add 2.5% (MSR $2,025) for classical nylon string configuration (RN6-STD).
- Add 5% (MSR $2,075) for hybrid nylon string configuration (RN6H-STD).

RENAISSANCE STAGE STANDARD (RS6-STD) – uniquely-shaped single cutaway semi-acoustic body, AAA cedar top, walnut back and sides, bound top, Turner piezo bridge, 18 volt preamp, available in Satin Natural finish, current mfg.

| MSR $2,385 | $1,900 | $1,100 - 1,300 | $675 - 800 | |

- Add 2.5% (MSR $2,450) for classical nylon string configuration (RN6-STD).
- Add 2.5% (MSR $2,435) for baritone configuration (RS6B-STD).
- Add 5% (MSR $2,510) for hybrid nylon string configuration (RN6H-STD).
- Add 10% (MSR $2,660) for 12-string configuration (RS12-STD).
- Add 15% (MSR $2,710) for 12-string baritone configuration (RS12B-STD).

RENAISSANCE HIGH (RS6-HI) – uniquely-shaped single cutaway semi-acoustic body, highly figured walnut top (optional AAA cedar or spruce top), walnut back and sides, hemp pattern rope purfling, matching headstock overlay, Turner piezo bridge, 18 volt preamp, available in Gloss Natural finish, disc. 2008.

| | N/A | $1,200 - 1,400 | $725 - 825 | $2,585 |

- Add 2.5% (Last MSR was $2,665) for baritone configuration (RS6B-HI).
- Add 5% (Last MSR was $2,700) for classical nylon string configuration (RN6-HI).
- Add 7.5% (Last MSR was $2,750) for hybrid nylon string configuration (RN6H-HI).
- Add 10% (Last MSR was $2,835) for 12-string configuration (RS12-HI).
- Add 12.5% (Last MSR was $2,915) for 12-string baritone configuration (RS12B-HI).

RENAISSANCE STEEL STRING (RSS-1) – cedar top, mahogany laminate back and sides, bound in black, mahogany neck with adjustable truss rod, 24-fret rosewood fingerboard (joins body at 14th fret), 25 21/32 in. scale, paua shell dot inlays and side dots, Turner "Reference Piezo" system, 18-volt Highlander Audio buffer electronics, one volume knob, Natural finish, disc. 1998.

| | N/A | $1,250 - 1,500 | $900 - 1,050 | $1,675 |

* **Renaissance Steel String (RSS-2)** – similar to the Renaissance Steel String (RSS-1), except features a Rosewood laminate back and sides, ebony fingerboard, tortoise celluloid binding with half-herringbone purfling around top, multiple veneer overlays on peghead, disc. 1998.

| | N/A | $1,450 - 1,750 | $950 - 1,100 | $2,050 |

* **Renaissance Nylon String (RNS-1)** – similar to the Renaissance Steel Strring (RSS-1), except in nylon string configuration, rosewood neck width at nut is 2 in. or 1.875 in., and paua shell side dots only, disc. 1998.

| | N/A | $1,250 - 1,500 | $900 - 1,050 | $1,650 |

»**Renaissance Nylon String (RNS-2)** – similar to the Renaissance Nylon String RNS-1, except features a rosewood laminate back and sides, ebony fingerboard, tortoise celluloid binding with half-herringbone purfling around top, multiple veneer overlays on peghead, disc. 1998.

| | N/A | $1,450 - 1,750 | $950 - 1,100 | $2,100 |

MSR/NOTES	100%	EXCELLENT	AVERAGE	LAST MSR

ACOUSTIC ELECTRIC BASS: RENAISSANCE SERIES

RENAISSANCE STUDIO SPECIAL BASS (RB4-SP) – uniquely-shaped single cutaway semi-acoustic body, walnut top, back and sides, no binding, fretted or fretless fingerboard, Turner piezo bridge, 18 volt preamp, available in Satin Natural finish, current mfg.

MSR $2,090	$1,675	$1,000 - 1,150	$625 - 725	

- **Add 10% (MSR $2,285) for five-string configuration (Model RB4-SP).**

RENAISSANCE STAGE STANDARD BASS (RB4-STD) – uniquely-shaped single cutaway semi-acoustic body, AAA cedar top, walnut back and sides, bound top, fretted or fretless fingerboard, Turner piezo bridge, 18 volt preamp, available in Satin Natural finish, current mfg.

MSR $2,540	$2,050	$1,200 - 1,450	$750 - 900	

- **Add 7.5% (MSR $2,750) for five-string configuration (Model RB5-STD).**

RENAISSANCE HIGH BASS (RB4-HI) – uniquely-shaped single cutaway semi-acoustic body, highly figured walnut top (optional AAA cedar or spruce top), walnut back and sides, hemp pattern rope purfling, fretted or fretless fingerboard, matching headstock overlay, Turner piezo bridge, 18 volt preamp, available in Gloss Natural finish, disc. 2008.

	N/A	$1,250 - 1,450	$750 - 850	$2,670

- **Add 10% (Last MSR was $2,915) for five-string configuration (Model RB5-HI).**

REX

See chapter on House Brands.

In the early 1900s, the Rex models were Kay-built student quality guitars distributed by the Fred Gretsch Manufacturing Company. By 1920 the Fred Gretsch Mfg. Co. had settled into its new ten story building in Brooklyn, New York, and was offering music dealers a very large line of instruments that included banjos, mandolins, guitars, violins, drums, and other band instruments. Gretsch distributed both the 20th Century and Rex trademarks prior to introduction of the Gretsch trademark in 1933.

Another Rex trademark has also been identified as a House Brand of the Great West Music Wholesalers of Canada by author/researcher Willie G. Moseley.

REX ARAGON

Instruments previously produced by Harmony circa 1940s. See chapter on House Brands.

Rex Aragon appears to be a House Brand of Harmony. Models include acoustic archtops but could include others as well. The headstock has Rex Aragon stenciled in white. Information courtesy: Walter Murray, Frankenstein Fretworks.

RIBBECKE GUITARS

Instruments currently built in Windsor, CA. Previously built in Healdsburg, Santa Rosa, and the San Francisco bay area in California.

Luthier Tom Ribbecke has been building and repairing guitars and basses in the San Francisco bay area since the early 1970s. Ribbecke's first lutherie business opened in 1975 in San Francisco's Mission District, and remained open and busy for ten years. In 1985, Ribbecke closed down the storefront in order to focus directly on client commissions.

Ribbecke guitars are entirely hand built by Ribbecke and his small staff of workers and they work directly with the customer when building a guitar. Beyond his signature and serial number of the piece, Ribbecke also offers a history of the origin of all materials involved in construction. In 2004, Ribbecke formed the Ribbecke Guitar Corporation that was created to put more guitars into players hands. American luthiers build the guitar with the aid of a CNC machine, and final set-up and inspection occurs at the Ribbecke shop. Under the new Ribbecke Guitar Corporation, they have introduced the Halfling by Ribbecke (see Halfling by Ribbecke) and Kiso (see Kiso) trademarks. Although Ribbecke does have standard production models, custom-built models can be created and several options are available on all models. In 2008, Ribbecke announced that he was going to stop taking orders for custom built guitars. For more information, visit Ribbecke's website or contact him directly. For more information on Ribbecke electric guitars, refer to the *Blue Book of Electric Guitars*.

The **Archtop Standard** is available in 16 in., 17 in., or 18 in. body widths and standard features include a Sitka spruce top, quality domestic figured maple back and sides, an ebony fingerboard, tailpiece, and pickguard, and gold hardware. Base price is $17,500 and several options are available. Earlier models were designated either a Monterey or Homage model. The Monterey features a cascade type peghead design and the Homage features a peghead design reminiscent of a D'Angelico.

The **Acoustic Steel String** features a spruce top, Indian rosewood back and sides, an ebony fingerboard with dot inlays, and an ebony bridge. Base price is $4,500 and several options are available.

The **Sound Bubble Steel String** features a solid carved top, Indian rosewood back and sides, an ebony fingerboard with dot inlays, and an ebony bridge. Base price is $6,000 and several options are available. The Sound Bubble, a slightly domed area on the bass side of the lower bout, increases the guitar's ability to translate the energy of the strings into sound. This design was patented in 1981 by artisan Charles Kelly and Tom Ribbecke.

The **Carved Top Acoustic Bass** features a solid carved spruce top with elliptical soundhole, maple back and sides, an ebony fingerboard with dot inlays, and chrome hardware. This model was discontinued when the Bobby Vega Halfling Bass was introduced and the last base price was $6,000.

RICHTER

Acoustic guitars previously produced in Chicago, IL during the 1930s. See chapter on House Brands.

The Richter trademark has been identified as a House Brand of Montgomery Wards. These guitars were built by the Richter Manufacturing Company in Chicago, IL during the 1930s. Most Richters are small bodied acoustics with relatively simple appointments. One example was found by Earl Oliver, and he claims that the guitar was built out of lesser materials, but the craftsmanship is excellent throughout the instrument. Dating is very precise as there is a physical date stamped in the guitar but no evidence of a serial number. Source: Bob Smith and Earl Oliver.

RICKENBACKER

Acoustic guitars previously produced in Santa Ana, CA between 1994 and 2006 and between 1958 and 1972. Distributed by Rickenbacker International Corporation of Santa Ana, CA. Rickenbacker electric instruments have been produced in CA since 1931.

> **CONTACT INFORMATION**
> **RICKENBACKER**
> 3895 S. Main Street
> Santa Ana, CA 92707
> Phone No.: 714-545-5574
> Fax No.: 714-754-0135
> www.rickenbacker.com
> sales@rickenbacker.com

In 1925, John Dopyera (and brothers) joined up with George Beauchamp and Adolph Rickenbacker and formed National to build resonator guitars. Beauchamp's attitudes over spending money caused John Dopyera to leave National and start the Dobro company. While at National, Beauchamp, Rickenbacker and Dopyera's nephew, Paul Barth, designed the **Frying Pan** electric lap steel. In 1929 or 1930, Beauchamp was either forced out or fired from National - and so allied himself with Adolph Rickenbacker (National's tool and die man) and Barth to form Ro-Pat-In.

In the summer of 1931, Ro-Pat-In started building aluminum versions of the Frying Pan prototype. Early models have "Electro" on the headstock. Two years later, Rickenbacker (or sometimes Rickenbacher) was added to the headstock, and Ro-Pat-In was formally changed to the Electro String Instrument Corporation. Beauchamp left Electro sometime in 1940, and Barth left in 1956 to form his own company.

In December of 1953, F.C. Hall bought out the interests of Rickenbacker and his two partners. The agreement stated that the purchase was complete, and Electro could "continue indefinitely to use the trade name Rickenbacker." Hall, founder of Radio-Tel and the exclusive Fender distributor, had his Fender distributorship bought out by Leo Fender and Don Randall. The Rickenbacker company was formed in 1965 as an organizational change (Electro is still the manufacturer, and Rickenbacker is the sales company). Rickenbacker instruments gained popularity as the Beatles relied on a number of their guitars in the 1960s. One slight area of confusion: the model names and numbers differ from the U.S. market to models imported in to the U.K. market during the short period in the 1960s when Rose Morris represented Rickenbacker in the U.K (at all other times, the model numbers worldwide have been identical to the U.S. market).

In 1984, John Hall (F.C. Hall's son) officially took control by purchasing his father's interests in both the Rickenbacker, Inc. and Electro String companies. Hall formed the Rickenbacker International Corporation (RIC) to combine both interests. In 1994, Rickenbacker introduced a line of acoustic guitars that was produced through 2006. However, luthier Paul Wilczynski aquired the license through Rickenbacker and John Hall to build Rickenbacker acoustics. Rickenbacker currently does not offer an acoustic line through their catalog; Rickenbacker acoustics are ordered directly from Wilczynski. Source: John C. Hall, Chief Executive Officer, Rickenbacker International Corporation; and Tom Wheeler, *American Guitars*). For further information regarding Rickenbacker electric models, please refer to the *Blue Book of Electric Guitars*.

ACOUSTIC

Rickenbacker currently offers the 5002V58 Mandolin, a vintage-style solid body electric mandolin based on a similar model issued in 1958. The current reproduction has a maple and walnut laminated body, eight-string configuration, and single coil pickups. Available in Fireglo or Mapleglo finishes (retail list is $1,619). All production acoustic models came with a standard case.

- **Add $250 for E3 electronics (Last MSR was $299).**

385 – dreadnought style, maple top, round soundhole, pickguard, checkered body/rosette, maple back/sides/neck, 21-fret rosewood fingerboard with pearl triangle inlay, rosewood bridge with white pins, available in Burst finishes, mfg. 1958-1972.

	100%	EXCELLENT	AVERAGE	
1958-1965	N/A	$2,000 - 2,500	$1,250 - 1,500	
1966-1972	N/A	$1,350 - 1,600	$850 - 1,000	

This model was also available in a classic style body (Model 385-S).

* *385-J* – similar to 385, except has jumbo style body, disc.

	100%	EXCELLENT	AVERAGE	
	N/A	$2,250 - 2,750	$1,450 - 1,750	

390 – a few prototypes were made (circa 1957), but this model was never put into production.

	100%	EXCELLENT	AVERAGE	
	N/A	N/A	N/A	

700 COMSTOCK (MODEL 700C) – jumbo style, bound spruce top, round soundhole, solid maple back/sides, 14/21-fret rosewood fingerboard with pearl triangle inlay, rosewood bridge, three-per-side tuners, chrome hardware, available in Natural finish, mfg. 1994-2006.

	100%	EXCELLENT	AVERAGE	LAST MSR
	N/A	$1,350 - 1,600	$825 - 1,000	$2,679

MSR/NOTES	100%	EXCELLENT	AVERAGE	LAST MSR

* *700 Comstock 12-String (Model 700C/12)* – similar to the 700 Comstock, except in 12-string configuration and six-per-side tuners, mfg. 1994-2006.

| | N/A | $1,400 - 1,675 | $850 - 1,025 | $2,789 |

700 SHASTA (MODEL 700S) – similar to the 700 Comstock, except has solid rosewood back and sides, mfg. 1994-2006.

| | N/A | $1,400 - 1,675 | $850 - 1,025 | $2,789 |

* *700 Shasta 12-String (Model 700S/12)* – similar to the 700 Shasta, except in 12-string configuration and six-per-side tuners, mfg. 1994-2006.

| | N/A | $1,450 - 1,750 | $875 - 1,100 | $2,899 |

730 LARAMIE (MODEL 730L) – dreadnought style, bound spruce top, round soundhole, solid maple back/sides, 14/21-fret rosewood fingerboard with pearl triangle inlay, rosewood bridge, three-per-side tuners, chrome hardware, available in Natural finish, mfg. 1994-2006.

| | N/A | $1,200 - 1,450 | $725 - 900 | $2,419 |

* *730 Laramie 12-String (Model 730L/12)* – similar to the 730 Laramie, except in 12-string configuration and six-per-side tuners, mfg. 1994-2006.

| | N/A | $1,275 - 1,525 | $750 - 950 | $2,529 |

730 SHILOH (MODEL 730S) – similar to the 730 Laramie, except has solid rosewood back and sides, mfg. 1994-2006.

| | N/A | $1,275 - 1,525 | $750 - 950 | $2,529 |

* *730 Shiloh 12-String (Model 730S/12)* – similar to the 730 Shiloh, except in 12-string configuration and six-per-side tuners, mfg. 1994-2006.

| | N/A | $1,325 - 1,600 | $800 - 1,000 | $2,639 |

760J JAZZ-BO – single rounded cutaway hollowbody, bound carved spruce top, set-in neck, solid maple sides, carved maple back, two bound cat's-eye f-holes, 14/21-fret rosewood fingerboard with pearl triangle inlay, adjustable rosewood bridge/metal trapeze tailpiece, three-per-side tuners, gold hardware, available in Natural or Sunburst finish, mfg. 1994-2006.

| | N/A | $2,700 - 3,250 | $1,625 - 2,025 | $5,389 |

RICKMANN

Instruments previously built in Japan during the late 1970s.

The Rickmann trademark was a brand name used by a UK importer. Instruments are generally intermediate quality copies of classic American designs. Source: Tony Bacon and Paul Day, *The Guru's Guitar Guide*.

RICO

See B.C. Rich in the B section.

RIEGER-KLOSS

See BD Dey in the B section.

RJP TECHNOLOGIES

Instruments previously produced overseas during the early 2000s. Distributed by Access Platform Inc. in Ontario, CA.

Luthier/designer Ronnie Parker was the CEO of RJP Technologies. Prior to his venture into musical instruments, Parker was a musician and audio engineer. His father John W. Parker is known for inventing the first self-propelled scissor lift. RJP Technologies has designed instruments for several large manufacturers including Washburn and Daisy Rock. During the early 2000s, RJP had its own line of guitars and basses, and according to most reviews they play very well and most reviewers give them a high rating. It is unknown if RJP Technologies is either designing or producing instruments any more.

RJP Technologies produced several acoustic models including dreadnoughts, 12-strings, small jumbos, and super jumbos. Retail prices generally ranged between $300 and $600 depending on the configuration and style.

RJS GUITARS

Instruments currently built in Fort Worth, TX since 1994.

Luthier R. Jeffrey Smith has been building guitars since 1994 and established the company with Steve Carson. He began building solidbody guitars and progressed to stunning archtop acoustics. RJS offers solidbody electrics, acoustic and electric archtops, and acoustic and electric flats. Archtop guitars are available in 16, 17, and 18 in. configurations with optional bindings and inlays. For more information, visit RJS' website or contact him directly.

MSR/NOTES	100%	EXCELLENT	AVERAGE	LAST MSR

ROB ALLEN GUITARS

Instruments currently built in Santa Monica, CA since 1996. Distributed by Rob Allen Guitars (Santa Monica), LA Bass Exchange (San Fernando Valley), and Rudy's Music (New York).

Luthier Rob Allen has a background as both a musical artist and a fine craftsman. It is a culmination of his experiences that make his instruments distinctly musical, organic in concept, and naturally appealing to the player. As a musician, Allen has played guitar with Melissa Etheridge (World Tour '92-'93), Ceremony (Geffen Records), and Kindred Spirit (I.R.S.). Allen has taught guitar at UCLA, and has recorded his own solo album (*Mysterious Measures*, released on the Suppletone label). Allen built his first electric guitar from raw materials at the age of seventeen, and shortly thereafter served as an apprentice to Seymour Duncan (Seymour Duncan Pickups) for three years. Allen has also had an apprenticeship with luthier Rick Turner, the co-founder of Alembic and now Rick Turner/Renaissance Guitars. In addition to working on his own designs, Allen has drawn from both of these modern pioneers. Since 1996, Allen has been handcrafting four- and five-string basses that feature internal hollow tone chambers, and Fishman piezo electronics (no magnetic pickups). Allen also built a line of RA series guitars and BB series Baritone guitars (for these instruments see the *Blue Book of Electric Guitars*). For more information, visit Allen's website or contact him directly.

CONTACT INFORMATION
ROB ALLEN GUITARS
1910 W. Rosecrans Ave.
Gardena, CA 90249
Phone No.: 310-324-4269
www.roballenguitars.com
info@roballenguitars.com

ACOUSTIC/ELECTRIC BASS

The **MB-2** features a sleek offset double cutaway swamp ash body with internal tone chambers, quilted maple top, bolt-on bird's-eye maple neck, fretless cocobola fingerboard, through-body stringing, carved cocobola bridge, two-per-side Hipshot Ultralite tuners, Fishman Acoustic Matrix Natural transducer, volume control (mounted on bridge), trim pot (in controls area in back), Fishman electronics, and is available in Tung Oil/Carnuba Wax finish. The four-string version starts at $2,300 and the five-string at $2,750. The **Mouse 30** is a shorter scale bass and starts at $2,000. The **Deep 4** and **Deep 5** are semi-hollow basses. They start at $3,800 for the four-string version and $4,100 for the five-string. There are several options available on every model and contact Allen for more information and pricing options.

* **Add 20% for left-hand configuration.**

MB-1 (SERIES 1) – similar to the MB-2, except features ultra premium wood selection, bound headstock, available in Natural, Plum, Red, Sunburst, or Vintage Amber gloss finish, disc.

	N/A	$1,200 - 1,500	$850 - 1,000	$2,000

* *MB-1 (SERIES 1) Five-String* – similar to the MB-1, except in five-string configuration, disc.

	N/A	$1,400 - 1,750	$900 - 1,100	$2,200

ROBERT GUITARS

Instruments currently built in British Columbia, Canada since the early 1980s.

Luthier Mikhail Robert was born in Moldavia, USSR in 1960 and he has been studying classical guitar and the violin since he was eight. Robert moved to Canada and studied math, physics, and guitars. In 1981, he built his first guitar, and by 1987, he had received international recognition for his guitar building. Robert builds a Concert Grand classical and a Short Scale classical, and prices on guitars start at $10,400 CAD. For more information, visit Robert Guitars's website or contact them directly.

CONTACT INFORMATION
ROBERT GUITARS
506 William St.
Victoria, BC V9A 3Y9 Canada
www.robertguitars.com
guitars@robertguitars.com

ROBERT TICE, LUTHIER

Instruments currently produced in Sciota, PA since 1979.

Bob Tice started producing guitars in 1979 and it is still a family owned business today, run by Bob, his wife, children, and friends. Tice offers all kinds of services related to stringed instruments (fretted and bowed) including repair, rentals, sales and building. For more information, visit Tice's website or contact him directly.

CONTACT INFORMATION
ROBERT TICE, LUTHIER
2503 Route 209
Sciota, PA 18354
Phone No.: 570-992-5695
Fax No.: 570-992-5695
www.roberttice.com
luthier@epix.net

RODRIGUEZ, MANUEL AND SONS

Instruments currently built in Madrid, Spain. Distributed in the U.S. by Musician's Friend in Medford, OR. Previously distributed in the U.S. market by Fender Musical Instruments Corporation of Scottsdale, AZ between the mid-1990s and 2005.

Luthier Manuel Rodriguez, grandson of noted flamenco guitarist Manuel Rodriguez Marequi, has been building classical style guitars for a number of years. He began learning guitar construction at the age of thirteen in Madrid and apprenticed in several shops before opening his own. Rodriguez

CONTACT INFORMATION
RODRIGUEZ, MANUEL AND SONS
www.guitars-m-r-sons.com

MSR/NOTES	100%	EXCELLENT	AVERAGE	LAST MSR

emigrated to Los Angeles in 1959 and professionally built guitars for nearly fifteen years. In 1973, Rodriguez returned to Spain and currently builds high quality instruments. U.S. distribution was handled by Fender between the mid-1990s and 2005.

ACOUSTIC

A (MODEL 094-9100) – classical style, solid Canadian red cedar top, round soundhole, Indian rosewood back and sides, sapele neck, rosewood fingerboard, three-per-side gold-plated standard tuners, available in Natural Gloss finish, current mfg.

| MSR $720 | $540 | $350 - 400 | $200 - 250 | |

B (MODEL 094-9140) – classical style, solid Canadian red cedar top, round soundhole, Indian rosewood back and sides, sapele neck, ebony fingerboard, three-per-side gold-plated standard tuners, available in Natural Gloss finish, current mfg.

| MSR $1,043 | $600 | $400 - 475 | $225 - 275 | |

C (MODEL 094-9180) – classical style, solid Canadian red cedar top, round soundhole, Indian rosewood back and sides, cedar neck with ebony reinforcement, ebony fingerboard, three-per-side goldplated standard tuners, available in Natural Gloss finish, current mfg.

| MSR $1,170 | $750 | $400 - 475 | $225 - 275 | |

C-1 (MODEL 094-9030) – classical style, solid Canadian red cedar top, round soundhole, Indian rosewood back and sides, sapele neck, rosewood fingerboard, three-per-side nickel-plated tuners, available in Natural Gloss finish, current mfg.

| MSR $580 | $400 | $200 - 250 | $120 - 150 | |

* **C-1 M (Model 094-9015)** – similar to the C-1, except features Natural Satin finish, current mfg.

| MSR $500 | $375 | $225 - 275 | $125 - 175 | |

C-3 (MODEL 094-9080) – classical style, solid Canadian red cedar top, round soundhole, Indian rosewood back and sides, sapele neck, rosewood fingerboard, three-per-side nickel-plated tuners, available in Natural Gloss finish, current mfg.

| MSR $830 | $500 | $300 - 375 | $200 - 250 | |

* **C-3 F (Model 094-9082)** – flamenco style, solid German spruce top, round soundhole, sycamore back and sides, sapele neck, rosewood fingerboard, three-per-side nickelplated tuners, available in Natural Gloss finish, current mfg.

| MSR $630 | $475 | $300 - 350 | $200 - 250 | |

CABALLERO 11 (MODEL 094-9110) – classical style, solid cedar top, round soundhole, Bubinga back and sides, saple neck, rosewood fingerboard, rosewood bridge, nickel hardware, available in Natural Gloss finish, mfg. 2004-present.

| MSR $415 | $250 | $150 - 200 | $95 - 120 | |

D (MODEL 094-9240) – classical style, solid Canadian red cedar top, round soundhole, Indian rosewood back and sides, Honduran cedar neck with ebony reinforcement, ebony fingerboard, three-per-side gold-plated standard tuners, available in Natural Gloss finish, current mfg.

| MSR $1,250 | $1,000 | $575 - 675 | $375 - 450 | |

* **D Rio (Model 094-9260)** – similar to the D, except has Brazilian rosewood back and sides, current mfg.

| MSR $1,660 | $1,500 | $750 - 875 | $475 - 550 | |

E (MODEL 094-9300) – classical style, solid Canadian red cedar top, round soundhole, solid Indian rosewood back and sides, Honduran cedar neck with ebony reinforcement, ebony fingerboard, three-per-side gold-plated standard tuners, available in Natural Gloss finish, current mfg.

| MSR $2,000 | $1,200 | $675 - 800 | $425 - 500 | |

FC (MODEL 094-9360) – classical style, solid Canadian red cedar top, round soundhole, solid Indian rosewood back/sides, Honduran cedar neck with ebony reinforcement, ebony fingerboard, 3-per-side gold-plated standard tuners, available in Natural Gloss finish, current mfg.

| MSR $3,500 | $1,750 | $1,100 - 1,350 | $700 - 850 | |

* **FCS (Model 094-9382)** – similar to the Model FC, except has a solid German Spruce top, mfg. 2004-present.

| MSR $2,280 | $1,750 | $1,100 - 1,250 | $700 - 825 | |

FF (MODEL 094-9280) – flamenco style, solid German cedar top, round soundhole, solid cypress back and sides, Honduran cedar neck with ebony reinforcement, ebony fingerboard, three-per-side gold-plated standard tuners, available in Natural Gloss finish, current mfg.

| MSR $2,256 | $1,200 | $650 - 750 | $400 - 475 | |

FG (MODEL 094-9400) – classical style, solid Canadian red cedar top, round soundhole, solid Indian rosewood back and sides, Honduran cedar neck with ebony reinforcement, ebony fingerboard, three-per-side gold-plated deluxe tuners, available in Natural Gloss finish, disc. 2003.

| N/A | $1,300 - 1,500 | $825 - 950 | $2,800 |

ACOUSTIC: HANDMADE CLASSICAL GUITARS

The following five models are completely handmade. The Brazilian rosewood used in Rodriguez guitars has been aged for over twenty-five years. CITES Treaty documentation is available upon request. List prices include a hardshell case. These guitars are special order instruments only.

MSR/NOTES	100%	EXCELLENT	AVERAGE	LAST MSR

NORMAN RODRIGUEZ (MODEL 094-9420) – classical style, solid Canadian red cedar top, round soundhole, solid Brazilian rosewood back and sides, Honduran cedar neck with ebony reinforcement, ebony fingerboard, three-per-side goldplated deluxe tuners, available in Natural Gloss finish, current mfg.

MSR $4,600	$3,700	$2,200 - 2,550	$1,450 - 1,650	

MANUEL RODRIGUEZ JR. (MODEL 094-9440) – classical style, solid Canadian red cedar top, round soundhole, solid Indian rosewood back and sides, Honduran cedar neck with ebony reinforcement, ebony fingerboard, three-per-side goldplated deluxe tuners, available in Natural Gloss finish, current mfg.

MSR $10,000	$4,000	$2,600 - 3,000	$1,750 - 2,000	

MANUEL RODRIGUEZ JR. (MODEL 094-9480) – classical style, solid Canadian red cedar top, round soundhole, solid Brazilian rosewood back and sides, Honduran cedar neck with ebony reinforcement, ebony fingerboard, three-per-side goldplated deluxe tuners, available in Natural Gloss finish, current mfg.

MSR $7,600	$6,100	$3,600 - 4,100	$2,400 - 2,800	

MANUEL RODRIGUEZ SR. (MODEL 094-9451) – classical style, solid Canadian red cedar top, round soundhole, solid Brazilian rosewood back and sides, Honduran cedar neck with ebony reinforcement, ebony fingerboard, three-per-side goldplated deluxe tuners, available in Natural Gloss finish, current mfg.

MSR $19,000	$15,500	$9,000 - 12,000	N/A	

100th ANNIVERSARY MODEL (MODEL 094-2005) – German spruce top, solid Madagascar Rosewood back and sides, signed by Manuel Sr., Manuel Jr., and Norman Rodriguez, limited to 100 pieces worldwide, mfg. 2005 only.

	$4,000	N/A	N/A	$5,000

ACOUSTIC ELECTRIC

Rodriguez Nylon String Acoustic Electrics feature a cutaway design and built-in electronics.

B CUTAWAY (MODEL 094-9150) – classical style with cutaway design, solid Canadian red cedar top, round soundhole, Indian rosewood back and sides, sapele neck, ebony fingerboard, three-per-side goldplated standard tuners, L.R. Baggs pickup, onboard preamp, volume/3-band EQ/mid-sweep controls, available in Natural Gloss finish, current mfg.

MSR $1,480	$1,125	$675 - 775	$450 - 525	

C CUTAWAY (MODEL 094-9190) – classical style with cutaway design, solid Canadian red cedar top, round soundhole, Indian rosewood back and sides, cedar neck with ebony reinforcement, ebony fingerboard, three-per-side goldplated standard tuners, L.R. Baggs pickup, onboard preamp, volume/3-band EQ/mid-sweep controls, available in Natural Gloss finish, current mfg.

MSR $2,043	$1,200	$775 - 900	$525 - 625	

FF CUTAWAY (MODEL 094-9290) – classical style with single cutaway, solid German Spruce top, solid cypress back and sides, Honduran Cedar neck with ebony reinforcement, ebony fingerboard, goldplated three-per-side tuners, Fishman Pro Blend Pickup system, gloss Natural finish, mfg. 2002-present.

MSR $2,256	$1,800	$1,200 - 1,350	$750 - 875	

ROGER

Instruments previously built in West Germany between the late 1950s and the mid-1960s.

Luthier Wenzel Rossmeisl built very good to high quality archtop guitars as well as a semi-solid body guitar called "Model 54." Rossmeisl derived the trademark name in honor of his son, Roger Rossmeisl.

Roger Rossmeisl (1927-1979) was raised in Germany and learned luthier skills from his father, Wenzel. One particular feature was the "German Carve," a feature used by Wenzel to carve an indented plane around the body outline on the guitar's top. Roger Rossmeisl then travelled to America, where he briefly worked for Gibson in Kalamazoo, MI (in a climate not unlike his native Germany). Shortly thereafter he moved to California, and was employed at the Rickenbacker company. During his tenure at Rickenbacker, Rossmeisl was responsible for the design of the Capri and Combo guitars, and custom designs. His apprentice was a young Semie Moseley, who later introduced the "German Carve" on his own Mosrite brand guitars. Rossmeisl left Rickenbacker in 1962 to help Fender develop their own line of acoustic guitars (Fender had been licensing Harmony-made Regals up till then), and later introduced the Montego and LTD archtop electrics.

ROGERS

Instruments previously produced by Selmer. See chapter on House Brands.

The Rogers trademark has been identified as a House Brand of Selmer in the United Kingdom. Source: Willie G. Moseley, *Stellas & Stratocasters*.

ROGUE

Instruments currently produced in China and/or Korea since the mid-1990s. Distributed by Musician's Friend in Medford, OR.

Musician's Friend distributes a full line of guitars, amplifiers, and other music related products through their mail order catalog. Musician's Friend introduced Rogue as their imported trademark on a line of guitars and amplifiers. For further information, visit Musician's Friend's website or contact them directly.

CONTACT INFORMATION
ROGUE
PO Box 4370
Medford, OR 97501
Phone No.: 800-449-9128
www.musiciansfriend.com

ROK AXE

Instruments previously produced in Korea during the 1990s and 2000s. Distributed by Muse in Inchon, Korea.

Rok Axe produced a wide range of entry level guitars and basses that are generally all copies of popular American models. Acoustic models included mostly dreadnought designs.

ROLF SPULER

Instruments currently produced in Switzerland. Distributed in the U.S. by Fine Guitar Consultants in San Diego, CA.

Swiss luthier Rolf Spuler builds a variety of guitars and basses in his shop. He is probably best known in the U.S. for designing the Ibanez Affirma Bass series that was produced in the early 1990s. As far as acoustic instruments, Spuler offers the Paradis model. In the mid-2000s, Spuler along with BridgeCo developed the first guitar to utilize firewire. This allowed the user to connect the guitar directly to a computer and track each string individually. For more information, visit Rolf Spuler's website or contact him directly.

CONTACT INFORMATION
ROLF SPULER
Headquarters
Gebenstorf, Switzerland
www.rolfspuler.com
welcome@rolfspuler.com

U.S. Distributor:
Fine Guitar Consultants
PO Box 15524
San Diego, CA 92175
Phone No.: 619-265-5900
www.fineguitarconsultants.com
rglick@fineguitarconsultants.com

ROYAL

Instruments previously built in England between 1981 and 1989.

Luthier Kevin Chilcott produced over 125 custom guitars in his English shop between 1981 and 1989. Chilcott apprenticed to English luthier Chris Eccleshall and became a self-employed luthier by the early 1980s. Chilcott built a wide range of instruments including acoustics, semi-hollowbodies, solidbody electrics, and a few NTB electric basses. Production increased every year with the most guitars produced between 1987 and 1989. Unfortunately, Chilcott was forced to retire from the guitar building business in 1989 due to a progressive disability. However, Chilcott has remained in the guitar industry performing some repairs, restorations, and other limited guitar production.

ROYALIST

Unknown place and date of manufacturer. See chapter on House Brands.

The Royalist trademark has been identified as a House Brand of the RCA Victor Records Store. Source: Willie G. Moseley, *Stellas & Stratocasters*.

ROY CUSTOM GUITARS

Instruments previously built in Sudbury, Ontario, Chelmsford, Ontario, and Ottawa, Quebec, Canada between the early 1980s and mid-2000s.

Luthier Rene Roy built hand-crafted acoustic and electric guitars in his Canadian shop. Customers could work directly with Roy to create and design a guitar. Acoustic models included the J-16 and J-17, as well as other custom orders. Roy retired from the guitar business in the mid-2000s.

R. TAYLOR GUITARS

Guitars currently produced in El Cajon, CA since 2006. Distributed by R. Taylor Guitars.

Luthier Robert Taylor, who founded and continues to run Taylor Guitars, custom builds acoustic guitars in his California shop. Taylor started out individually hand-building guitars, but the company has grown every year and they are currently producing thousands of guitars a year. However, Taylor wanted to get back to what he did best - individual custom-built guitars. R. Taylor Guitars is a stand-alone company from Taylor and they custom build a small number of guitars. The base price for R. Taylor guitars is $4,480 and there are several options available. For more information, visit R. Taylor's website or contact them directly.

CONTACT INFORMATION
R. TAYLOR GUITARS
1980 Gillespie Way
El Cajon, CA 92020-1096
Phone No.: 619-258-4032
Phone No.: 800-943-6782
www.rtaylorguitars.com

RUBEN FLORES GUITARS

Instruments currently built in Spain. Distributed in the U.S. by Ruben Flores in Seal Beach, CA.

Ruben Flores Classical and Flamenco guitars are handcrafted in Spain's foremost lutherie workshops employing the finest materials and workmanship. The Flores Classical guitars are constructed in scales of 48, 49, 54.4, 58, 63.6, and 65 centimeters. These guitars are designed to be played by children, young adults, and professionals. Many of the models are available with cutaways, regular or thin bodies, with onboard pickups. As with the classical guitars, Ruben Flores Flamenco Guitars come in a various models, some with cutaways, suitable for entry level, intermediate, and professional guitarists. Some Flamenco models are available with rosewood back and sides. For further information regarding pricing and model specifications, visit Flores' website or contact them directly.

CONTACT INFORMATION
RUBEN FLORES GUITARS
U.S. Distributor: Ruben Flores
PO Box 2746
Seal Beach, CA 90740-1746
Phone No.: 562-598-9800
Fax No.: 562-598-2459
www.rubenflores.com
rubenflores@verizon.net

ACOUSTIC

Classical models include the **100** (MSR $470) with a solid cedar top, mahogany back and sides, and a rosewood fingerboard, the **300** (MSR $580) with a solid cedar top, mahogany back and sides, and a rosewood fingerboard, the **400** (MSR $730) with a solid cedar top, rosewood back and sides, and an ebony fingerboard, the **500** (MSR $910) with a solid cedar top, rosewood back and sides, and an ebony fingerboard, the **600** (MSR $1,190) with rosewood back and sides and solid spruce top, the **700** (MSR $1,500) with solid rosewood back and sides and solid spruce top, the **900** (MSR $2,070) with solid rosewood back and sides and solid spruce top, the **910** (MSR $2,770) with solid rosewood back and sides and solid spruce top, and the **Professional** (MSR $3,990) with a solid cedar top, solid rosewood back and sides, and an ebony fingerboard.

Flamenco models include the **300** (MSR $640) with sycamore back and sides and a rosewood fingerboard, the **600** (MSR $950) with sycamore back and sides and an ebony fingerboard, the **700** (MSR $1,300) with solid cypress or rosewood back and sides, solid spruce top and ebony fingerboard, the **900** (MSR $2,160) with solid cypress or rosewood back and sides, solid spruce top and ebony fingerboard, and the **Professional** (MSR $3,900) with a solid spruce top, solid cypress or rosewood back and sides.

RUBIO, DAVID

Instruments previously built in New York City, NY, Spain, and England between the early 1960s and 2000.

English master luthier David Rubio apprenticed in Madrid, Spain at the workshop of Domingo Esteso, which was maintained by Esteso's nephews. In 1961, Rubio built guitars in New York City, NY. Returning to England in 1967, he set up a workshop and built guitars as well as violins, cellos, lutes, and other instruments. One of Rubio's apprentices was Paul Fischer, who has gone on to gain respect for his own creations. David died of cancer on October 21, 2000. Information courtesy Paul Fischer.

RUBIO, GERMAN VASQUEZ

Instruments currently produced in Los Angeles, CA.

Luthier German Vasquez Rubio builds classical and flamenco acoustic guitars in his Los Angeles shop. Rubio, originally from Mexico, built his first guitar at the age of sixteen in 1968 and has continued to build guitars ever since. Rubio offers several different models with prices ranging from approximately $2,000 to $7,500 and he will work closely with the customer to get them the right sounding instrument. For more information, visit Rubio's website or contact him directly.

CONTACT INFORMATION
RUBIO, GERMAN VASQUEZ
5117 W. Adams Blvd.
Los Angeles, CA 90016
Phone No.: 310-347-6207
www.guitarsbyGVR.com
arnazzi@guitarsbyGVR.com

RUCK, ROBERT

Instruments currently built in Eugene, OR. Previously built in Kauai, HI, Florida, Georgia, Washington, and Wisconsin.

Luthier Robert Ruck has been building high-quality classical and flamenco guitars since 1966. Ruck has a very lengthy order list therefore he is currently not taking new orders but he does have a cancellation list. Prices for classical guitars start at $7,750 and flamenco guitars start at $7,750. His guitars are available in several different sizes and configurations. For more information, contact Ruck directly.

CONTACT INFORMATION
RUCK, ROBERT
2507 Hawkins Lane
Eugene, OR 97405
http://www.maui.net/~rtadaki/ruck.html

RYAN, KEVIN

See Kevin Ryan Guitars in the K section.

NOTES

S SECTION
S-101

Instruments currently produced in China. Distributed by American Sejung Corporation in Ontario, CA.

The Sejung Musical Instrument Corporation produces the S-101 line of guitars and was introduced in 2002. They have a 600,000 square foot manufacturing facility and produce a wide variety of fretted instruments, guitar amplifiers, and pianos. Currently they produce a vast range of dreadnoughts, classicals, jumbos, 12-strings, and acoustic electrics. Most guitars are priced for the beginner player. For more information, visit their website.

CONTACT INFORMATION
S-101
Distributed by America Sejung Corporation
5300 East Ontario Mills Parkway, Suite 100
Ontario, CA 91764
Phone No.: 909-484-7498
Fax No.: 909-484-7890
www.sejungusa.com
sales@ascguitars.com

SAEHAN

Instruments currently built in Korea. Distributed by the Saehan International Co., Ltd. of Seoul, Korea.

The Saehan International company offers a wide range of acoustic guitars from standard to cutaway model dreadnoughts, jumbo style body designs, and acoustic/electric models. For further information, please contact the Saehan International company directly.

SAGA

Instruments currently imported and distributed in San Francisco, CA. Saga has been importing and distributing guitars since the late 1970s.

Saga imports and distributes a wide range of acoustic and electric guitars as well as resonators, banjos, mandolins, ukuleles, violins, violas, cellos, and accessories. For acoustic guitars and resonators, some of the brands that they currently represent include Blueridge, Durango, Regal, Gitane, Valencia, P. Saez, and A. Burguet. Guitars and mandolin kits are also available that bear the Saga name on the headstock. In the late 1980s and 1990s, Saga offered the Saga line of electric guitars. Saga also offers a wide range of parts. For more information or for a catalog, contact Saga directly or visit their website.

CONTACT INFORMATION
SAGA
PO Box 2841
South San Francisco, CA 94080
Phone No.: 650-558-5558
Fax No.: 650-871-7590
www.sagamusic.com
info@sagamusic.com

SAKASHTA GUITARS

See Taku Sakashta Guitars in the T section.

SAMICK

Instruments currently produced in Indonesia and Korea. Distributed by Samick Music Corporation in Gallatin, TN (previously located in Southern California). Samick has been producing guitars since 1965 and has been importing guitars into the U.S. since 1981.

For a number of years, the Samick corporation was the "phantom builder" of instruments for a number of other trademarks. In fact, when the Samick trademark was finally introduced to the U.S. guitar market, a number of consumers thought that the company was brand new! However, Samick has been producing both upright and grand pianos, as well as stringed instruments for more than forty years.

CONTACT INFORMATION
SAMICK
1329 Gateway Drive
Gallatin, TN 37066
Phone No.: 615-206-0077
Fax No.: 615-452-0451
www.gregbennettguitars.com
info@samickguitar.com

The Samick Piano Co. was established in Korea in 1958 by Hyo Ick Lee. By January of 1960 they had started to produce upright pianos, and within four years became the first Korean piano exporter. One year later in 1965, the company began manufacturing guitars, and by the early 1970s expanded to produce grand pianos and harmonicas as well. In 1973 the company incorporated as the Samick Musical Instruments Mfg. Co., Ltd. to reflect the diversity it encompassed. Samick continued to expand into guitar production. They opened a branch office in Los Angeles in 1978, a brand new guitar factory in 1979, and a branch office in West Germany one month before 1981.

Throughout the 1980s, Samick continued to grow, prosper, and win awards for quality products and company productivity. The Samick Products Co. was established in 1986 as an affiliate producer of other products, and the company was listed on the Korean Stock Exchange in September of 1988. With their size of production facilities (the company claims to be cranking out over a million guitars a year, according to a recent brochure), Samick could be referred to as modern day producer of House Brand guitars as well as their own brand. In the past couple of years Samick acquired Valley Arts, a guitar company known for its one-of-a-kind instruments and custom guitars. This merger stabilized Valley Arts as the custom shop wing of Samick, as well as supplying Samick with quality American designed guitars.

Samick continues to expand their line of guitar models through the use of innovative designs, partnerships with high exposure endorsees (like Blues Saraceno and Ray Benson), and new projects such as the Robert Johnson Commemorative and the D'Leco Charlie Christian Commemorative guitars. Currently, it is guesstimated that Samick produces fifty percent of the world's guitars (samick Company History courtesy Rick Clapper; Model Specifications courtesy Dee Hoyt).

MSR/NOTES	100%	EXCELLENT	AVERAGE	LAST MSR

In 1998, Samick decided to overhaul their entire line. They brought in Greg Bennett, who has been in the guitar industry for over twenty years, to create a sense of continuity throughout the entire line of guitars. In 2001, they stopped their previous line of guitars. In 2002, the Samick company was purchased by Jong-Sup Kim, and they introduced an entirely new line of guitars with Greg Bennett on every headstock, which is smaller as well. By combining Samick and Bennett, there is over seventy years of experience in guitars. The new line of guitars are called "Greg Bennett Design by Samick." In 2006, the Samick headquarters in the U.S. moved from City of Industry, CA to Gallatin, TN.

In addition to their acoustic and electric guitars and basses, Samick offers a wide range of other stringed instruments such as autoharps, banjos, mandolins, and violins. For more information, contact Samick directly or visit their website.

ACOUSTIC: AMERICAN CLASSIC SERIES

SC-330 S – classical style, solid spruce top, rosewood back and sides, gloss finish, mahogany set neck, rosewood fingerboard and bridge, 19 frets, gold standard tuners, disc. 2001.

	N/A	$250 - 300	$150 - 200	$600

SC-430 S N (LE GRANDE) – classical style, solid spruce top, round soundhole, bound body, wooden inlay rosette, rosewood back/sides, nato neck, 12/19-fret rosewood fingerboard, rosewood bridge, 3-per-side gold tuners, available in Natural finish, disc. 1999.

	N/A	$175 - 225	$100 - 150	$450

SC-433 – similar to the SC-430 S N, except features solid cedar top, laser-cut soundhole mosaic, mfg. 1997-2000.

	N/A	$175 - 225	$100 - 150	$450

SC-438 ES FS – classical style, solid cedar top, round soundhole, bound body, laser-cut sunflower mosaic, rosewood back/sides, nato neck, 12/19-fret rosewood fingerboard, rosewood bridge, 3-per-side gold tuners, piezo pickup, volume/3-band EQ slider controls, available in Natural finish, disc. 1999.

	N/A	$275 - 325	$160 - 210	$650

SR-100 – folk (wide shoulder/narrow waist) style, solid spruce top, round soundhole, bound body, multi stripe purfling/rosette, sapele back/sides, 14/20-fret rosewood fingerboard with dot inlay, rosewood bridge with black white dot pins, slotted headstock, 3-per-side chrome die-cast tuners, available in Natural finish, disc. 2000.

	N/A	$185 - 235	$120 - 160	$470

SR-200 – similar to the SR-100, except features jacaranda back/sides, snowflake fingerboard inlay, available in Natural finish, disc. 2000.

	N/A	$300 - 350	$175 - 225	$690

SW-790 S – dreadnought style, handmade, solid spruce top, round soundhole, bound body, multi stripe purfling/rosette, solid jacaranda back/sides, 14/20-fret ebony fingerboard with ornate abalone inlay, rosewood bridge with black white dot pins, tortoiseshell pickguard, 3-per-side chrome tuners, available in Natural finish, disc. 2001.

	N/A	$375 - 425	$200 - 250	$850

SJ-210 (MAGNOLIA) – jumbo style, sycamore top, round soundhole, black pickguard, 5-stripe bound body/rosette, nato back/sides/neck, 14/20-fret bound rosewood fingerboard with pearl dot inlay, rosewood bridge with white black dot pins, 3-per-side black chrome tuners, available in Black or White finish, disc. 1994.

	N/A	$120 - 160	$80 - 100	$330

SJD-210 – jumbo style body, spruce top, metal resonator/two screened soundholes, bound body, mahogany back/sides/neck, 14/20-fret bound rosewood fingerboard with pearl dot inlay, covered bridge/metal trapeze tailpiece, three-per-side chrome die-cast tuners, available in Natural finish, disc.

	N/A	$325 - 375	$175 - 225	$750

SJ-218 CE – jumbo style body with single rounded cutaway, spruce top, round soundhole, black pickguard, bound body, abalone rosette, nato back/sides/neck, 14/20-fret rosewood fingerboard with abalone dot inlay, rosewood bridge with white black dot pins, 3-per-side Gotoh tuners, piezo pickup, volume/3-band EQ slider controls, available in Natural finish, disc. 2000.

	N/A	$250 - 300	$150 - 200	$600

AMCT-CE – thin line depth dreadnought body with single florentine cutaway, solid spruce top, bound body, rosewood back/sides, mahogany neck, 14/20-fret bound extended rosewood fingerboard with abalone diamond inlay, ebony bridge and pins, 6-on-a-side chrome die-cast tuners, piezo bridge pickup, volume/3-band EQ slider controls, available in Natural (N), Trans. Purple (TP), or Vintage Sunburst (VSB), disc. 2001.

	N/A	$350 - 425	$200 - 250	$855

* **AMCT-CE/PBE** – similar to AMCT-CE, except has pink bird's-eye top, back, and sides, disc. 2001.

	N/A	$350 - 425	$200 - 250	$855

SW-218 CE TT – dreadnought style with single rounded cutaway, spruce top, laser cut round soundhole design, bound body, mahogany back/sides/neck, 14/20-fret rosewood fingerboard with white dot inlay, rosewood bridge with black white dot pins, 3-per-side die-cast tuners, piezo bridge pickup, volume/3-band EQ slider controls, XLR jack, available in Natural finish, disc. 2000.

	N/A	$230 - 280	$150 - 190	$570

MSR/NOTES	100%	EXCELLENT	AVERAGE	LAST MSR

EAG-88 (BLUE RIDGE) – single round cutaway flat-top body, spruce top, oval soundhole, bound body, wood purfling, abalone rosette, maple back/sides, mahogany neck, 24-fret bound extended rosewood fingerboard with pearl dot inlay, rosewood bridge, bound peghead with screened logo, 6-on-a-side black chrome tuners, piezo bridge pickup, volume/tone controls, available in Natural finish, disc. 1995.

	N/A	$200 - 250	$100 - 150	$500

Earlier models had a figured maple top, 22-fret bound rosewood fingerboard, and were available in Blue Burst, Natural, and Tobacco Sunburst finishes.

EAG-89 – similar to the EAG-88, except features a figured maple top, rosewood back/sides, gold tuners, available in Natural, Red Stain, or Sunburst finish, disc. 1995.

	N/A	$250 - 300	$150 - 200	$600

EAG-93 – thin line depth dreadnought body with single rounded cutaway, solid spruce top, oval soundhole, bound body, abalone purfling/rosette, rosewood back/sides, mahogany neck, 24-fret bound extended ebony fingerboard with pearl eagle inlay, rosewood bridge, abalone bound peghead with screened logo, 6-on-side tuners, black hardware, piezo bridge pickup, volume/3-band EQ slider controls, available in Natural finish, mfg. 1994-2001.

	N/A	$600 - 700	$350 - 400	$1,400

EAG-98 BLS – single cutaway design with flamed maple top, maple back and sides with sandstone finish, oval raised wood bound soundhole, rosewood fingerboard with dot inlays, 23 frets, rosewood bridge, black diecast tuners, EQ-700 System electronics, available in high gloss Trans. Blue finish, disc. 2001.

	N/A	$450 - 525	$250 - 300	$1,035

ACOUSTIC: ARTIST SERIES

EJ-1 – dreadnought style, spruce top, round soundhole, mahogany back/sides, 9-string configuration, rosewood bridge with black pins, chrome tuners, built-in guitar slide holder, available in Natural finish, mfg. 1997-2001.

	N/A	$250 - 300	$150 - 200	$597

ACOUSTIC: ARTIST CLASSICAL SERIES

Instruments in this series have a classical style body, round soundhole, bound body, wooden inlay rosette, 12/19-fret fingerboard, slotted peghead, tied bridge, 3-per-side chrome tuners as following features (unless otherwise listed).

SC-310 (SEVILLE) – select spruce top, mahogany back/sides/neck, rosewood fingerboard/bridge, available in Pumpkin finish, disc. 2001

	N/A	$145 - 185	$90 - 110	$375

SC-330 (DEL REY) – select spruce top, rosewood back/sides, mahogany neck, rosewood fingerboard/bridge, available in Pumpkin finish, disc. 2001.

	N/A	$225 - 275	$120 - 160	$555

SC-410 S – solid cedar top, sapele back/sides, mahogany neck, rosewood fingerboard/bridge, available in Pumpkin finish, mfg. 1997-2001.

	N/A	$195 - 235	$100 - 140	$525

SC-450 (LA TOUR) – select spruce top, sapele back/sides, nato neck, rosewood fingerboard/bridge, available in Pumpkin finish, disc. 2001.

	N/A	$170 - 210	$90 - 120	$420

* **SC-450 S (SC-430)** – similar to the SC-450, except features solid spruce top, available in Pumpkin finish, disc.

	N/A	$125 - 175	$70 - 90	$350

SCT-450 CE (GRANADA) – single round cutaway classical style, select spruce top, round soundhole, bound body, wooden inlay rosette, rosewood back/sides, nato neck, 12/19-fret rosewood fingerboard, rosewood bridge, rosewood peghead veneer, 3-per-side chrome tuners, active piezo pickup, volume/tone slider controls, available in Natural finish, disc.

	N/A	$280 - 330	$150 - 200	$660

ACOUSTIC: ARTIST CONCERT FOLK SERIES

Instruments in this series have a wide shoulder/narrow waist **folk**-style body, round soundhole, bound body, multi stripe purfling/rosette, 14/20-fret rosewood fingerboard with dot inlay, rosewood bridge with black white dot pins, 3-per-side chrome tuners as following features (unless otherwise listed).

SF-115 – select natural spruce top, mahogany back/sides/neck, chrome tuners, available in Natural finish, disc.

	N/A	$145 - 185	$90 - 110	$375

SF-210 (SF-210 M SWEETWATER) – select natural spruce top, mahogany back/sides/neck, die-cast chrome tuners, available in Natural finish, disc.

	N/A	$100 - 140	$60 - 80	$280

SF-291 (CHEYENNE) – solid spruce top, solid rosewood back/sides, nato neck, rosewood veneer on peghead, gold plated die-cast tuners, available in Natural finish, disc.

	N/A	$180 - 220	$100 - 135	$440

MSR/NOTES	100%	EXCELLENT	AVERAGE	LAST MSR

ACOUSTIC: ARTIST DREADNOUGHT SERIES

SW-21 NM – dreadnought style, select natural spruce top, round soundhole, black pickguard, ivory body binding, multi-stripe rosette, nato back/sides/neck, 14/20-fret rosewood fingerboard with white dot inlay, rosewood bridge with black pins, 3-per-side die-cast tuners, available in Natural finish, mfg. 1997-2000.

	N/A	$90 - 120	$50 - 70	$238

SW-015 D (SANTA FE) – dreadnought style, mahogany top, round soundhole, black pickguard, bound body, multi-stripe rosette, mahogany back/sides/neck, 14/20-fret rosewood fingerboard with white dot inlay, rosewood bridge with white black dot pins, 3-per-side die-cast tuners, available in Black, Natural, or White gloss finish, mfg. 1994-2001.

	N/A	$150 - 200	$90 - 120	$390

- **Add $15 for Black (BK) and White (WH) finishes.**

SW-115-12 – dreadnought style, 12-string configuration, select natural spruce top, round soundhole, black pickguard, bound body, multi-stripe rosette, mahogany back/sides/neck, 14/20-fret rosewood fingerboard with white dot inlay, rosewood bridge with white black dot pins, 6-per-side standard tuners, available in Natural finish, disc. 2001.

	N/A	$150 - 200	$90 - 120	$405

SW-115 DE – dreadnought style, select natural spruce top, round soundhole, black pickguard, bound body, multi-stripe rosette, mahogany back/sides/neck, 14/20-fret rosewood fingerboard with white dot inlay, rosewood bridge with white black dot pins, 3-per-side die-cast tuners, neck pickup, volume/tone controls, available in Black, Natural, or White gloss finish, mfg. 1994-2001.

	N/A	$180 - 220	$100 - 135	$435

- **Add $15 for Black (BK) and White (WH) finishes.**

SW-210 (GREENBRIAR) – dreadnought style, select natural spruce top, round soundhole, black pickguard, bound body, multi-stripe rosette, mahogany back/sides/neck, 14/20-fret rosewood fingerboard with white dot inlay, rosewood bridge black pins, 3-per-side die-cast tuners, available in Natural finish, disc. 2001.

	N/A	$175 - 225	$100 - 135	$450

* *SW-210 LH (Beaumont)* – similar to the SW-210, except in a left-handed configuration, disc. 2001.

	N/A	$175 - 225	$100 - 135	$465

* *SW-210 BB 1* – similar to the SW-210, except features select natural bamboo top/back/sides, available in Natural finish, mfg. 1997-99.

	N/A	$200 - 250	$120 - 150	$470

* *SW-210 S (Bluebird)* – similar to the SW-210, except features a solid spruce top, disc. 2001.

	N/A	$275 - 325	$125 - 175	$600

* *SW-210-12 (Savannah)* – similar to the SW-210, except in a 12-string configuration, 6-per-side tuners, disc. 2001.

	N/A	$225 - 275	$130 - 160	$525

SW-210 CE (LAREDO) – dreadnought style with single rounded cutaway, select natural spruce top, round soundhole, black pickguard, bound body, multi-stripe rosette, mahogany back/sides/neck, 14/20-fret rosewood fingerboard with white dot inlay, rosewood bridge with white black dot pins, 3-per-side die-cast tuners. piezo bridge pickup, volume/3-band EQ slider controls, available in Natural finish, disc. 2001.

	N/A	$300 - 350	$150 - 200	$645

SW-220 HS CE (AUSTIN) – dreadnought style with single rounded cutaway, solid cedar top, oval soundhole, 5-stripe bound body/rosette, cedar back/sides, maple neck, 14/20-fret bound rosewood fingerboard with pearl dot inlay, stylized pearl inlay at 12th fret, rosewood bridge with white black dot pins, cedar veneer on bound peghead, 3-per-side gold tuners, piezo pickup, volume/tone slider control, available in Natural finish, disc. 1994.

	N/A	$175 - 225	$100 - 135	$450

SW-230-12 HS (VICKSBURG) – dreadnought style, 12-string configuration, solid spruce top, round soundhole, black pickguard, bound body, herringbone purfling/rosette, rosewood back/sides, mahogany neck, 14/20-fret rosewood fingerboard with pearl dot inlay, rosewood bridge with black white dot pins, 6-per-side tuners gold die cast tuners, available in Natural finish, disc. 2001.

	N/A	$350 - 400	$200 - 250	$780

SW-250 (ASPEN) – dreadnought style, spruce top, round soundhole, black pickguard, 3-stripe bound body/rosette, sapele back/sides, nato neck, 14/20-fret rosewood fingerboard, rosewood bridge with white black dot pins, rosewood veneer on peghead, 3-per-side chrome tuners, available in Natural finish, disc. 1994.

	N/A	$90 - 125	$50 - 70	$250

SW-260-12 B (NIGHTINGALE 12) – dreadnought style, 12-string configuration, maple top, round soundhole, black pickguard, bound body, multi stripe purfling/rosette, mahogany back/sides/neck, 14/20-fret rosewood fingerboard with pearl dot inlay, rosewood bridge with black pins, 6-per-side chrome die-cast tuners, available in Black gloss finish, disc. 2001.

	N/A	$225 - 275	$120 - 160	$570

SW-260 CE N (GALLOWAY) – single rounded cutaway dreadnought style, maple top, round soundhole, tortoise pickguard, bound body, multi-stripe purfling/rosette, maple back/sides/neck, 14/20-fret bound rosewood fingerboard with pearl diamond/dot inlay, rosewood bridge with white black dot pins, bound peghead with pearl logo inlay, 3-per-side die-cast chrome tuners, piezo bridge pickup, volume/3-band EQ slider controls, available in Natural finish, disc. 2001.

	N/A	$300 - 350	$150 - 200	$720

- **Black finish added in 1999 at no additional charge.**

MSR/NOTES	100%	EXCELLENT	AVERAGE	LAST MSR

SW-270 HS NM (JASMINE) – dreadnought style, cedar top, round soundhole, black pickguard, bound body, herringbone purfling/rosette, walnut back/sides, mahogany neck, 14/20-fret bound rosewood fingerboard with pearl block inlay, bound peghead with pearl logo inlay, rosewood bridge with white black dot pins, 3-per-side chrome die-cast tuners, available in Natural finish, disc. 2001.

	N/A	$250 - 300	$125 - 175	$615

SW-292 S (NIGHTINGALE) – dreadnought style, solid spruce top, round soundhole, black pickguard, 3-stripe bound body/rosette, mock bird's-eye maple back/sides, nato neck, 14/20-fret bound rosewood fingerboard with pearl dot inlay, rosewood bridge with white black dot pins, bound headstock, 3-per-side chrome tuners, available in Trans. Black finish, disc. 1994.

	N/A	$125 - 175	$80 - 100	$350

SW-630 HS (LAUREL) – dreadnought style, solid spruce top, round soundhole, black pickguard, bound body, herringbone purfling/rosette, rosewood back/sides, mahogany neck, 14/20-fret bound rosewood fingerboard with pearl tree of life inlay, rosewood bridge with white black dot pins, bound peghead with pearl logo inlay, 3-per-side gold die-cast tuners, available in Natural finish, disc. 2001.

	N/A	$325 - 375	$175 - 225	$750

SW-730 SP – dreadnought style, solid spruce top, round soundhole, black pickguard, bound body, multi-stripe purfling/rosette, rosewood back/sides, mahogany neck, 14/20-fret ebony fingerboard with abalone dot inlay, ebony bridge with black white dot pins, bound peghead with abalone logo inlay, 3-per-side chrome tuners, available in Natural finish, mfg. 1994-96.

	N/A	$350 - 425	$200 - 250	$840

SW-790 SP – similar to the SW-730 SP, except features jacaranda back/sides, bound fingerboard, available in Natural finish, mfg. 1994-96.

	N/A	$300 - 350	$150 - 200	$720

SWT-210 CE – thin line depth dreadnought style with single rounded cutaway, spruce top, round soundhole, mahogany back/sides/neck, 14/20-fret rosewood fingerboard, rosewood bridge with white black dot pins, 3-per-side chrome tuners, piezo bridge pickup, volume/tone controls, available in Natural finish, disc. 2001.

	N/A	$300 - 350	$150 - 200	$705

SWT-217 CE ASHTR – thin line depth dreadnought style with single rounded cutaway, ash top, round soundhole, mahogany back/sides/neck, 14/20-fret bound rosewood fingerboard with pearl diamond inlay, rosewood bridge with white black dot pins, 3-per-side die-cast chrome tuners, piezo bridge pickup, volume/3-band EQ slider controls, available in Trans. Red finish, disc. 2001.

	N/A	$350 - 425	$200 - 250	$825

SDT-110 CE OSM – thin line depth dreadnought style with single rounded cutaway, kusu top/back/sides/headstock, round soundhole, tortoise pickguard, bound body, multi-stripe purfling/rosette, 14/20-fret bound rosewood fingerboard with pearl diamond/dot inlay, rosewood bridge with white black dot pins, bound peghead with pearl logo inlay, 3-per-side die-cast chrome tuners, piezo bridge pickup, volume/3-band EQ slider controls, available in Cherry Sunburst finish, disc. 2000.

	N/A	$225 - 275	$120 - 160	$570

ACOUSTIC: BARCELONA CLASSIC SERIES

C 1 – classical body style, nato top/back/sides, open style headstock, available in Black or Natural finish, mfg. 2005-present.

MSR $199	$130	$85 - 105	$40 - 60	

* C 1 CE – similar to the C 1, except has a single cutaway and passive electronics, Black finish, mfg. 2005-present.

MSR $309	$200	$120 - 160	$70 - 90	

* CT 1 CE – similar to the C 1, except has a thin body with a single cutaway and passive electronics, available in Black or Natural finish, mfg. 2005-present.

MSR $319	$210	$135 - 175	$80 - 100	

C 2 – classical body style, solid spruce top nato back and sides, single-ply cream binding, open style headstock, Natural finish, mfg. 2005-present.

MSR $249	$160	$110 - 140	$65 - 85	

* C 2 CE – similar to the C 2, except has a single cutaway and passive electronics, Natural finish, mfg. 2005-present.

MSR $369	$240	$135 - 175	$80 - 100	

C 3 – classical body style, solid spruce top, ovangkol back and sides, four-ply cream binding, open style headstock, Natural finish, mfg. 2005-present.

MSR $399	$260	$150 - 200	$90 - 120	

C 4 – classical body style, solid cedar top, sapele back and sides, six-ply white binding, open style headstock, Natural finish, mfg. 2005-present.

MSR $449	$290	$175 - 225	$110 - 140	

C 5 – classical body style, solid cedar top, rosewood back and sides, six-ply maple binding, open style headstock, Natural finish, mfg. 2005-present.

MSR $499	$325	$225 - 275	$120 - 150	

* CT 5 CE – similar to the C 5, except has a thinline single cutaway body and Fishman 4-Band electronics, mfg. 2005-present.

MSR $619	$400	$275 - 325	$150 - 200	

MSR/NOTES	100%	EXCELLENT	AVERAGE	LAST MSR

ACOUSTIC: BEAUMONT SERIES

D 7 – dreadnought style body, solid cedar top, rosewood sides and back, eight-ply white binding, tortise pickguard, three-per-side Grover tuners, chrome hardware, available in Natural finish, mfg. 2001-present.

| MSR $449 | $290 | $190 - 240 | $100 - 130 | |

* **D 7 12-String** – similar to the D 7, except in 12-string configuration, mfg. 2001-present.

| MSR $499 | $330 | $220 - 270 | $115 - 150 | |

»**D 7 12 CE** – similar to the D 7 12, except has a single cutaway with an active EQ and built-in tuner, mfg. 2011-present.

| MSR $569 | $370 | $260 - 310 | $125 - 175 | |

* **D 7 CE** – similar to the D 7, except has a single cutaway with an active EQ and built-in tuner, mfg. 2001-present.

| MSR $549 | $360 | $250 - 300 | $125 - 175 | |

OM 7 – orchestra model style body, solid cedar top, rosewood sides and back, eight-ply white binding, tortise pickguard, three-per-side Grover tuners, chrome hardware, available in Natural finish, mfg. 2001-present.

| MSR $419 | $280 | $190 - 240 | $100 - 130 | |

ACOUSTIC: BLACKBIRD SERIES

SMJ 17 CE – single sharp thin medium jumbo solid body, solid spruce top, maple sides and back, rosewood fingerboard with block inlays, abalone and black binding, three-per-side black Grover tuners, Fishman Classic 4-Band EQ, available in Black or Natural (2010-present) finish, mfg. 2006-present.

| MSR $919 | $600 | $400 - 475 | $250 - 300 | |

TMJ 17 CE – single sharp thin medium jumbo body, solid spruce top, maple sides and back, rosewood fingerboard with block inlays, abalone and black binding, three-per-side black Grover tuners, Fishman Classic 4-Band EQ, available in Black finish, mfg. 2000-present.

| MSR $719 | $470 | $300 - 375 | $175 - 225 | |

ACOUSTIC: CAROLINA SERIES

D 14 CE – dreadnought single cutaway body, solid cedar top, rosewood back and sides, herringbone trim, tortoise pickguard, electronics, three-per-side chrome Grover tuners, available in Natural finish, mfg. 2000-2011.

| | $550 | $325 - 375 | $175 - 225 | $879 |

SSJ 14/SJ14 – southern jumbo body, solid cedar top, rosewood back and sides, herringbone trim, tortoise pickguard, three-per-side chrome Grover tuners, available in Natural finish, mfg. 2000-09.

| | N/A | $225 - 275 | $115 - 150 | $639 |

* **SSJ 14 E/SJ 14 E** – similar to the SJ 14, except has Fishman Classic 4-Band EQ electronics, mfg. 2000-2010.

| | $525 | $325 - 375 | $175 - 225 | $839 |

ACOUSTIC: CHEYENNE SERIES

D 10 CE – dreadnought single cutaway style body, solid spruce top, mahogany sides and back, 8-ply white binding, tortoise pickguard, 3-per-side Grover tuners, chrome hardware, Fishman Classic 4-Band EQ, available in Natural, Wine Red, or Black finish, mfg. 2000-03.

| | N/A | $200 - 250 | $110 - 140 | $455 |

MJ 10 CE – medium jumbo single cutaway style body, solid spruce top, mahogany sides and back, 8-ply white binding, tortoise pickguard, 3-per-side Grover tuners, chrome hardware, Fishman Classic 4-Band EQ, available in Wine Red or Black finish, mfg. 2000-03.

| | N/A | $200 - 250 | $110 - 140 | $455 |

SMJ 10 CE – similar to the MJ 10 CE, except has a small body cutaway and a L.R. Baggs EQ, available in Black or Natural finish, mfg. 2000-present.

| MSR $749 | $500 | $325 - 400 | $200 - 250 | |

ACOUSTIC: CONTINENTAL SERIES

D 8 – dreadnought style body, solid cedar top, rosewood sides and back, abalone trim, tortoise pickguard, three-per-side Grover tuners, gold hardware, available in Natural finish, mfg. 2001-present.

| MSR $549 | $360 | $225 - 275 | $115 - 150 | |

* **D 8 CE** – similar to the D 8, except has a single cutaway with a Fishman classic 4-band EQ, mfg. 2001-present.

| MSR $699 | $460 | $325 - 400 | $175 - 225 | |

J 8 CE – jumbo style body, solid cedar top, rosewood sides and back, abalone trim, tortoise pickguard, 3-per-side Grover tuners, Fishman classic 4-band EQ, gold hardware, available in Natural finish, mfg. 2003 only.

| | N/A | $200 - 250 | $110 - 140 | $480 |

MSR/NOTES	100%	EXCELLENT	AVERAGE	LAST MSR

OM 8 CE – orchestra model style body, solid cedar top, rosewood sides and back, abalone trim, tortoise pickguard, three-per-side Grover tuners, Fishman classic 4-band EQ, gold hardware, available in Natural finish, mfg. 2003-present.

MSR $689	$450	$325 - 400	$175 - 225	

ACOUSTIC: EDEN PLAINS SERIES

D 4 – dreadnought style body, solid spruce top, ash sides and back, six-ply reverse binding, black pickguard, three-per-side Grover tuners, chrome hardware, available in Antique Natural, Trans. Red, Trans. Blue, Amber, or Trans. Black finish, mfg. 2001-09.

	N/A	$135 - 175	$80 - 100	$419

* D 4 CE – similar to the D 4, except has an Active EQ with built in tuner, mfg. 2001-present.

MSR $479	$320	$210 - 260	$110 - 140	

OM 4 CE – single cutaway orchestra body, solid spruce top, ash sides and back, six-ply reverse binding, black pickguard, three-per-side Grover tuners, electronics, chrome hardware, available in Antique Natural, Trans. Red, Trans. Blue, or Trans. Black finish, mfg. 2003-2010.

	$375	$210 - 260	$110 - 140	$599

ACOUSTIC: ELAN SERIES

D 11 CE – single cutaway dreadnought body, quilted maple top, sides, and back, rosewood fingerboard with offset inlays, three-per-side Grover tuners, Fishman Classic 4-band EQ, chrome hardware, available in Antique Natural finish, mfg. 2006-2010.

	$750	$500 - 575	$300 - 350	$1,199

TMJ 11 CE – single cutaway thin medium jumbo body, quilted maple top, sides, and back, rosewood fingerboard with offset inlays, 3-per-side Grover tuners, Fishman Classic 4-band EQ, chrome hardware, available in Trans. Red, Trans. Blue, Trans. Violet, or Trans. Black, mfg. 2000-04.

	N/A	$350 - 425	$200 - 250	$880

ACOUSTIC: EXOTIC WOOD SERIES

SD-50 – dreadnought style, spruce top, round soundhole, black pickguard, bound body, multi-stripe purfling/rosette, maple back/sides, mahogany neck, 14/20-fret rosewood fingerboard with pearl diamond/dot inlay, maple veneered peghead with pearl split diamond/logo inlay, rosewood bridge with white black dot pins, 3-per-side chrome tuners, available in Natural finish, mfg. 1994-95.

	N/A	$100 - 150	$60 - 80	$300

SD-60 S – dreadnought style, solid spruce top, round soundhole, black pickguard, bound body, multi-stripe purfling/rosette, bubinga back/sides, mahogany neck, 14/20-fret rosewood fingerboard with abalone diamond/dot inlay, rosewood bridge with white black dot pins, bubinga veneered peghead with abalone split diamond/logo inlay, 3-per-side chrome tuners, available in Natural finish, mfg. 1994-95.

	N/A	$175 - 225	$100 - 130	$450

SD-80 CS – dreadnought style, figured maple top, round soundhole, black pickguard, bound body, multi-stripe purfling/rosette, maple back/sides, mahogany neck, 14/20-fret bound rosewood fingerboard with abalone pearl diamond/dot inlay, bound peghead with abalone split diamond/logo inlay, rosewood bridge with white black dot pins, 3-per-side chrome tuners, available in Sunburst finish, mfg. 1994-95.

	N/A	$125 - 175	$80 - 100	$350

ACOUSTIC: GOLD RUSH SERIES

D1 – dreadnought body style, nato top, back, and sides, black binding, nato neck, 14/20-fret rosewood fingerboard with pearl dot inlays, rosewood bridge, abalone type rosette, three-per-side tuners, black pickguard, available in Black, Brown Sunburst, Cobalt Blue, Gloss Natural, Pearl White, Satin Natural, or Wine Red finish, mfg. 2001-present.

MSR $219	$140	$90 - 120	$50 - 70	

- Add 5% (MSR $229) for Gloss Natural, White, Black, Brown Sunburst, or Wine Red finish.
- Add 17.5% (MSR $259) for left-handed configuration.

* D1E – similar to the D1, except has PS-2000 passive electronics, Natural finish, mfg. 2001-03.

	N/A	$75 - 100	$40 - 60	$185

* D1CE – similar to the D1, except has a single cutaway and PS-2000 passive electronics, available in Black, Brown Sunburst, Cobalt Blue, or Natural finish, mfg. 2001-present.

MSR $319	$210	$135 - 175	$80 - 100	

- Add 10% (MSR $349) for left-handed configuration (2007-present).

OM1 – orchestra body style, nato top, back, and sides, black binding, nato neck, 14/20-fret rosewood fingerboard with pearl dot inlays, rosewood bridge, abalone type rosette, three-per-side tuners, black pickguard, available in Brown Sunburst finish, mfg. 2010-present.

MSR $225	$145	$100 - 130	$55 - 75	

ST6 1 – 36 in. student folk style body, nato top, back, and sides, nato neck, rosewood fingerboard, three-per-side tuners, available in Black, Brown Sunburst, Cobalt Blue, Gloss Natural, Red, or Satin Natural finish, mfg. 2001-present.

MSR $199	$130	$85 - 105	$40 - 60	

- Add 5% (MSR $209) for Black, Brown Sunburst, Cobalt Blue, Gloss Natural, or Red finish.

MSR/NOTES	100%	EXCELLENT	AVERAGE	LAST MSR

ST9 1 – 39 in. student folk style body, nato top, back, and sides, nato neck, rosewood fingerboard, three-per-side tuners, available in Black, Brown Sunburst, Cobalt Blue, Gloss Natural, or Satin Natural finish, mfg. 2001-present.

MSR $219	$140	$85 - 105	$40 - 60	

  • Add 2.5% (MSR $225) for Black, Brown Sunburst, Cobalt Blue, or Gloss Natural finish.

ACOUSTIC: IMPERIAL SERIES

D 9 – dreadnought style body, solid spruce top, maple sides and back, abalone trim, black reverse binding, pickguard, 3-per-side Grover tuners, chrome hardware, available in Natural finish, mfg. 2001-03.

	N/A	$140 - 190	$85 - 105	$360

* **D 9 CE** – similar to the D 9, except has a single cutaway with a Fishman classic 4-band EQ, available in Natural or Black finishes, mfg. 2001-03.

	N/A	$200 - 250	$110 - 140	$480

* **D 9 12 CE** – similar to the D 9 CE, except in 12-string configuration, available in Black finish, mfg. 2001-03.

	N/A	$225 - 275	$140 - 180	$525

J 9 CE – jumbo style sharp cutaway body, solid spruce top, maple sides and back, abalone trim, black reverse binding, pickguard, 3-per-side Grover tuners, chrome hardware, available in Natural or Black finish, mfg. 2001-03.

	N/A	$200 - 250	$110 - 140	$480

ACOUSTIC: KENSINGTON SERIES

D 3 – dreadnought style body, striped mahogany back, top, and sides, six-ply reverse binding, 14/20-fret rosewood fingerboard with dot inlays, pickguard, three-per-side tuners, available in Natural or Wine Red finish, mfg. 2001-present.

MSR $269	$180	$120 - 160	$70 - 90	

* **D 3 CE** – similar to the D 3, except has an AS-3000 active 2-band EQ, Natural finish, mfg. 2001-2011.

	$400	$225 - 275	$125 - 175	$639

OM 3 – dreadnought style body, striped mahogany back, top, and sides, six-ply reverse binding, 14/20-fret rosewood fingerboard with dot inlays, pickguard, three-per-side tuners, Natural finish, mfg. 2001-present.

MSR $299	$195	$120 - 160	$70 - 90	

ACOUSTIC: LAREDO SERIES

D 16 CE – dreadnought single cutaway body, solid cedar top, ovangkol sides and back, six-ply maple binding, three-per-side gold Grover tuners, Fishman Classic 4-Band EQ, available in Natural finish, mfg. 2000-03, 2006-2011.

	$675	$400 - 475	$200 - 250	$1,079

SSJ 16 E/SJ 16 E – southern jumbo body, solid cedar top, ovangkol sides and back, six-ply maple binding, three-per-side gold Grover tuners, Fishman Classic 4-Band EQ, available in Natural finish, mfg. 2000-03, 2006-09.

	N/A	$400 - 475	$200 - 250	$1,079

ACOUSTIC: PRO SERIES

All instruments in this series were handmade. This series was also known as the **Handcrafted Series**.

S-7 – concert style, spruce top, round soundhole, rosewood pickguard, bound body, multi stripe wood purfling/rosette, rosewood back/sides, mahogany neck, 14/20-fret bound ebony fingerboard with pearl dot inlay, ebony bridge with black white dot pins, pearl peghead logo inlay, 3-per-side chrome tuners, available in Natural finish, mfg. 1994-95.

	N/A	$300 - 350	$150 - 200	$700

SK-5 (MARSEILLES) – folk style, solid spruce top, round soundhole, tortoiseshell pickguard, wooden bound body, wooden inlay rosette, ovankol back/sides, nato neck, 14/20-fret bound rosewood fingerboard with pearl dot inlay, ebony bridge with white black dot pins, ovankol veneer on peghead with pearl logo inlay, 3-per-side chrome tuners, available in Natural finish, disc. 1994.

	N/A	$180 - 230	$100 - 130	$460

SK-7 (VERSAILLES) – similar to Marseilles, except has solid cedar top, rosewood back/sides, brown white dot bridge pins, disc. 1994.

	N/A	$300 - 350	$150 - 200	$700

S-7 EC (CHAMBRAY) – single round cutaway folk style, solid cedar top, round soundhole, rosewood pickguard, wooden bound body, wooden inlay rosette, rosewood back/sides, nato neck, 14/20-fret ebony fingerboard with pearl dot inlay, ebony bridge with black white dot pins, rosewood veneer on peghead with pearl logo inlay, 3-per-side Schaller gold tuners with pearl buttons, acoustic pickup, volume/tone control, preamp, available in Natural finish, disc. 1995.

	N/A	$475 - 550	$300 - 350	$1,100

SDT-10 CE – single round cutaway dreadnought style, ash top, round soundhole, tortoise pickguard, bound body, multi-stripe purfling/rosette, ash back/sides, maple neck, 14/20-fret bound rosewood fingerboard with pearl diamond/dot inlay, rosewood bridge with white black dot pins, bound peghead with pearl logo inlay, 3-per-side chrome tuners, piezo bridge pickup, 4-band EQ, available in Natural finish, mfg. 1994-95.

	N/A	$175 - 225	$100 - 130	$450

MSR/NOTES	100%	EXCELLENT	AVERAGE	LAST MSR

ACOUSTIC: REGENCY SERIES

ST6 2 – 36 in. student folk style guitar, nato sides and back, select spruce top, rosewood fingerboard, Natural finish, mfg. 2001-present.

MSR $229	$150	$90 - 110	$45 - 65	

ST9 2 – similar to the ST6 2, except is 39 in. body, available in Natural finish, mfg. 2001-present.

MSR $239	$155	$100 - 130	$50 - 70	

D2 – dreadnought style, nato sides and back, select spruce top, rosewood fingerboard with dot inlay, three-per-side tuners, single-ply cream binding, Natural finish, mfg. 2001-2011.

	$200	$110 - 140	$60 - 80	$319

* D2-12 12-String – similar to the D2, except is in 12-string configuration with six-per-side tuners, available in Natural finish, mfg. 2001-present.

MSR $329	$220	$140 - 190	$90 - 110	

* D2CE – similar to the D2, except has a single cutaway and PS-2000 passive electronics, available in Black or Natural finish, mfg. 2001-present.

MSR $419	$280	$200 - 250	$120 - 150	

J2 – jumbo style, nato sides and back, select spruce top, rosewood fingerboard with dot inlay, three-per-side tuners, single-ply cream binding, Natural finish, mfg. 2001-present.

MSR $289	$190	$120 - 160	$70 - 90	

OM2 – orchestra body style, nato sides and back, select spruce top, rosewood fingerboard with dot inlay, 3-per-side tuners, single-ply cream binding, Natural finish, mfg. 2001-present.

MSR $279	$180	$110 - 140	$65 - 85	

ACOUSTIC: REMINGTON SERIES

MJ 13 CE – single cutaway medium jumbo body, solid cedar top, striped mahogany back and sides, 6-ply reverse black binding, 3-per-side Grover chrome tuners, Fishman Classic 4-band EQ, available in Natural finish, mfg. 2000-03.

	N/A	$300 - 350	$150 - 200	$768

OM 13 CE – single cutaway orchestra model body, solid cedar top, striped mahogany back and sides, six-ply reverse black binding, three-per-side Grover chrome tuners, Fishman Classic 4-band EQ, available in Natural finish, mfg. 2000-03, 2006-09.

	N/A	$375 - 450	$200 - 250	$999

SMJ 13 CE – similar to the MJ13 CE, except has a solid body with a L.R. Baggs EQ, mfg. 2000-05.

	N/A	$400 - 475	$225 - 275	$996

* C SMJ 13 CE – similar to the SMJ 13 CE, except is a Classic, mfg. 2000-05.

	N/A	$450 - 525	$250 - 300	$1,156

ACOUSTIC: RIO GRANDE SERIES

D 15 E – dreadnought body, solid cedar top, ovangkol sides and back, turquoise dyed maple trim, maple binding, three-per-side gold Grover tuners, Fishman Classic 4-Band EQ, available in Natural finish, mfg. 2000-03, 2006-09.

	N/A	$325 - 400	$175 - 225	$919

OM 15 CE – Orchestra Model single cutaway body, solid cedar top, ovangkol sides and back, turquoise dyed maple trim, maple binding, three-per-side gold Grover tuners, Fishman Classic 4-Band EQ, available in Natural finish, mfg. 2000-03, 2006-present.

MSR $689	$450	$300 - 350	$175 - 225	

ACOUSTIC: SOLID WOOD SERIES

ASDML1 – dreadnought body, solid Sitka spruce top, solid mahogany back and sides, seven-ply binding, rosewood fingerboard with slotted square inlays, three-per-side Grover tuners, rosewood bridge, Natural finish, limited production, mfg. 2006-present.

MSR $669	$435	$300 - 350	$175 - 225	

* ASDML1 CE – similiar to the ASDML1, except has a single cutaway and Clearwave 50 Fishman 4-Band electronics, limited production, mfg. 2006-present.

MSR $849	$550	$350 - 425	$225 - 275	

ASDRL1 – dreadnought body, solid Sitka spruce top, solid rosewood back and sides, abalone trimmed maple binding, rosewood fingerboard with slotted square inlays, three-per-side Grover tuners, rosewood bridge, Natural finish, limited production, mfg. 2006-present.

MSR $949	$620	$400 - 500	$250 - 300	

MSR/NOTES	100%	EXCELLENT	AVERAGE	LAST MSR

* **ASDRL1 CE** – similiar to the ASDRL1, except has a single cutaway and Clearwave 50 Fishman 4-Band electronics, limited production, mfg. 2006-present.

| MSR $1,119 | $730 | $475 - 575 | $300 - 350 | |

ASMJR CE – single cutaway medium jumbo-sized body, solid Sitka spruce top, solid rosewood back and sides, abalone trimmed maple binding, rosewood fingerboard with slotted square inlays, three-per-side Grover tuners, rosewood bridge, Clearwave 50 Fishman 4-Band electronics, Natural finish, limited production, mfg. 2007-present.

| MSR $1,069 | $700 | $450 - 550 | $275 - 325 | |

ACOUSTIC: STANDARD CLASSICAL SERIES

Instruments in this series have a classical style body, round soundhole, bound body, marquetry rosette, 12/19-fret fingerboard, slotted peghead, tied bridge, 3-per-side tuners as following features (unless otherwise listed).

LC-006 – smaller scale (36 in. length) classical style, nato top/back/sides/neck, rosewood fingerboard/bridge, chrome tuners, available in Natural satin finish, mfg. 1997-2001.

| | N/A | $70 - 90 | $40 - 60 | $180 |

LC-009 – smaller scale (39 in. length) classical style, nato top/back/sides/neck, rosewood fingerboard/bridge, chrome tuners, available in Natural satin finish, mfg. 1997-2001.

| | N/A | $75 - 95 | $45 - 65 | $186 |

LC-015 G – nato mahogany top/back/sides/neck, rosewood fingerboard/bridge, chrome tuners, available in Natural gloss finish, mfg. 1994-2001.

| | N/A | $80 - 110 | $50 - 70 | $225 |

* **Available in Black finish for an additional $10 (LC-015 G BK).**

LC-025 G – natural spruce top, mahogany back/sides/neck, rosewood fingerboard/bridge, chrome tuners, available in Natural finish, mfg. 1994-2001.

| | N/A | $110 - 140 | $60 - 80 | $276 |

LC-034 G (NEW) – solid spruce top, ovankol back/sides, mahogany neck, rosewood fingerboard/bridge, gold plated tuners, available in Natural finish, mfg. 1997-2001.

| | N/A | $125 - 175 | $70 - 90 | $315 |

ACOUSTIC: STANDARD DREADNOUGHT SERIES

C-41 – dreadnought style, mahogany top, round soundhole, black pickguard, bound body, multi-stripe rosette, mahogany back/sides/neck, 14/20-fret rosewood fingerboard with dot inlay, rosewood bridge with black pins, 3-per-side chrome tuners, available in Black satin, Natural, or White satin finish, disc. 1995.

| | N/A | $70 - 90 | $40 - 60 | $160 |

LF-006 – smaller scale (36 in. length) folk style, nato top/back/sides/neck, bound body, round soundhole, rosewood fingerboard with dot inlay, rosewood bridge with black pins, 3-per-side chrome tuners, available in Natural satin finish, disc. 2001.

| | N/A | $70 - 90 | $40 - 60 | $186 |

* **Tobacco Sunburst finish added in 1999 for an additional $20 (LF-006G TS).**
* **Jewel Mist and Mint Julep added in 2000 for an additional $30 (LF-006G).**

LF-009 – smaller scale (39 in. length) folk style, nato top/back/sides/neck, bound body, round soundhole, rosewood fingerboard with dot inlay, rosewood bridge with black pins, 3-per-side chrome tuners, available in Natural satin finish, disc. 2001.

| | N/A | $80 - 100 | $50 - 70 | $192 |

* **Tobacco Sunburst finish added in 1999 for an additional $20 (LF-009G TS).**
* **Arizona Blue and Grape Mist finishes added in 2000 for an additional $20 (LF-009G).**

LF-015 – (full scale) folk style, nato top/back/sides/neck, bound body, round soundhole, rosewood fingerboard with dot inlay, rosewood bridge with black pins, 3-per-side chrome tuners, available in Natural satin finish, disc. 2001.

| | N/A | $85 - 115 | $50 - 70 | $234 |

LW-005 – dreadnought style, spruce top, nato back and sides, nato bolt-on neck, rosewood fingerboard and bridge, 20 frets, chrome enclosed gears, available in Natural Satin finish, mfg. 1999-2001.

| | N/A | $80 - 110 | $50 - 70 | $222 |

* **Add $18 for gloss finish (LW-005G).**
* **Add $48 for Black, Original Sunburst, Trans. Vintage, Trans. Blue and Vintage Sunburst finishes (LW-005G).**
* **LW-005G VS** – similar to LW-005, except has Vintage Sunburst gloss finish, mfg. 1999-2000.

| | N/A | $50 - 70 | $30 - 40 | $148 |

LW-015 – dreadnought style, nato top, round soundhole, black pickguard, bound body, multi-stripe rosette, nato back/sides/neck, 14/20-fret rosewood fingerboard with dot inlay, rosewood bridge with black pins, 3-per-side chrome tuners, available in Natural satin finish, mfg. 1994-2001.

| | N/A | $80 - 110 | $50 - 70 | $223 |

MSR/NOTES	100%	EXCELLENT	AVERAGE	LAST MSR

LW-015 LH – similar to the LW-015, except in a left-handed configuration, available in Natural satin finish, disc. 2001.

	N/A	$90 - 120	$60 - 80	$255

LW-015 G – similar to the LW-015, available in Black, Sunburst, or White gloss finish, disc. 2001.

	N/A	$90 - 120	$60 - 80	$252

LW-015 E – dreadnought style, nato top, round soundhole, black pickguard, bound body, multi-stripe rosette, nato back/sides/neck, 14/20-fret rosewood fingerboard with dot inlay, rosewood bridge with black pins, 3-per-side chrome tuners, piezo bridge pickup, volume/tone controls, available in Natural Satin finish, disc. 2001.

	N/A	$120 - 160	$70 - 90	$300

LWO-15 E LH – similar to the LW-015, except in a left-handed configuration, available in Natural Satin finish, disc. 2001.

	N/A	$120 - 160	$70 - 90	$315

LW-020 G – similar to the LW-015, except features solid natural Agathis top, 3-per-side enclosed tuners, available in Blonde (top only) finish, disc 2001.

	N/A	$110 - 150	$60 - 80	$270

LW-025 G – dreadnought style, spruce top, round soundhole, black pickguard, bound body, multi-stripe rosette, nato back/sides, mahogany neck, 14/20-fret rosewood fingerboard with dot inlay, rosewood bridge with white black dot pins, 3-per-side chrome die-cast tuners, available in Natural gloss finish, mfg. 1994-2001.

	N/A	$125 - 175	$70 - 90	$315

LW-025 G CEQ – dreadnought style with single rounded cutaway, spruce top, round soundhole, black pickguard, bound body, multi-stripe rosette, nato back/sides, mahogany neck, 14/20-fret rosewood fingerboard with dot inlay, rosewood bridge with white black dot pins, 3-per-side chrome die-cast tuners, piezo pickup, volume/EQ slider controls, available in Natural Gloss finish, mfg. 1997-2001.

	N/A	$170 - 215	$100 - 130	$435

• Add $25 for Trans. Green, Trans. Blue, and Trans. Red finishes.

LW-027 G – similar to the LW-025 G, except features ovankol back/sides, available in Natural gloss finish, disc. 2001.

	N/A	$140 - 190	$90 - 110	$375

LW-028 A NEW – similar to the LW-025 G, except features ivory body binding, 3-per-side Grover tuners, available in Natural satin finish, mfg. 1997-2001.

	N/A	$125 - 175	$70 - 90	$300

LW-028 SA – similar to LW-028, except has solid spruce top, Natural satin finish, disc. 2001.

	N/A	$135 - 185	$80 - 100	$324

Gloss finish available at no additional charge (LW-028 GSA).

LW-044 G CEQ NEW – similar to the LW-025 G CEQ, except features ovankol back/sides, ABS body binding, available in Natural Gloss finish, mfg. 1997-2001.

	N/A	$180 - 230	$90 - 120	$465

LW-060 GA – full size dreadnought, spruce top, rosewood back and sides, abalone inlay, mahogany set neck, rosewood fingerboard and bridge, 20 frets, gold Grover tuners, gloss Natural finish, mfg. 1999-2001.

	N/A	$200 - 250	$100 - 150	$493

Vintage Sunburst finish available at no extra charge (LW-060 GA VS).

ACOUSTIC: WINDSOR SERIES

D 6 – dreadnought style, solid spruce top, ovangkol back and sides, rosewood fingerboard, three-per-side Grover tuners, pickguard, chrome hardware, available in Natural finish, mfg. 2001-present.

MSR $419	$280	$190 - 240	$100 - 130	

D 6 CE – similar to the D 6, except has a single cutaway and an active EQ with built-in tuner, available in Natural finish, mfg. 2001-present.

MSR $569	$370	$250 - 300	$125 - 175	

OM 6 CE – single cutaway orchestra model style body, solid spruce top, ovangkol back and sides, rosewood fingerboard, three-per-side Grover tuners, pickguard, electronics, chrome hardware, available in Natural finish, mfg. 2005-present.

MSR $569	$370	$250 - 300	$125 - 175	

ACOUSTIC: WORTHINGTON SERIES

D 5 – dreadnought style, solid spruce top, striped mahogany back and sides, rosewood fingerboard, three-per-side Grover tuners, pickguard, chrome hardware, available in Natural finish, mfg. 2001-present.

MSR $349	$230	$140 - 190	$85 - 105	

MSR/NOTES	100%	EXCELLENT	AVERAGE	LAST MSR

* D 5 12 12-String – similar to the D 5, except in 12-string configuration, mfg. 2001-present.

| MSR $399 | $260 | $175 - 225 | $95 - 125 | |

* D 5 CE/D 5 B CE Cutaway Electric – similar to the D 5, except has a single cutaway and an active EQ with built in tuner, available in Natural or Wine Red finish, mfg. 2001-present.

| MSR $499 | $330 | $210 - 260 | $110 - 140 | |

In 2007, brown back and sides became optional (Model D 5 B CE).

»D 5 CE LH Cutaway Electric Left-Handed – similar to the D 5 CE, except in left-handed configuration, available in Natural finish, mfg. 2001-present.

| MSR $529 | $340 | $210 - 260 | $110 - 140 | |

* D 5 LH Left-Handed – similar to the D5, except in left-handed configuration, mfg. 2001-present.

| MSR $379 | $250 | $150 - 200 | $90 - 110 | |

* TD 5 CE – similar to the D 5, except has a thin body, available in Natural finish, mfg. 2001-2011.

| | $390 | $210 - 260 | $110 - 140 | $619 |

J 5 CE – jumbo style, solid spruce top, mahogany back and sides, rosewood fingerboard, three-per-side Grover tuners, pickguard, electronics, chrome hardware, available in Natural finish, mfg. 2005-present.

| MSR $469 | $310 | $210 - 260 | $110 - 140 | |

SSJ 5/SJ 5 – Southern Jumbo style, solid spruce top, striped mahogany back and sides, rosewood fingerboard, three-per-side Grover tuners, pickguard, chrome hardware, available in Natural finish, mfg. 2001-09.

| | N/A | $140 - 190 | $85 - 110 | $439 |

* TMJ 5 CE – similar to the SJ 5, except has a thin medium body with a single cutaway and an active EQ with built in tuner, available in Natural, Black, or Wine Red finish, mfg. 2001-present.

| MSR $459 | $300 | $210 - 260 | $110 - 140 | |

OM 5 – orchestra model style, solid spruce top, striped mahogany back and sides, rosewood fingerboard, three-per-side Grover tuners, pickguard, chrome hardware, available in Natural finish, mfg. 2001-present.

| MSR $349 | $230 | $140 - 190 | $85 - 110 | |

* OM 5 CE/OM 5 B CE – similar to the OM 5, except has a single cutaway and an active EQ with built in tuner, available in Natural finish, mfg. 2001-present.

| MSR $459 | $300 | $210 - 260 | $110 - 140 | |

In 2007, brown back and sides became optional (Model OM 5 B CE).

TT 65 TENNESSEE TRAVEL PACKAGE – travel pack that includes a Worthington Series 36 in. guitar with a solid spruce top and wine red striped mahogany back and sides, a padded gigbag, and a color merchandising box, available in Natural finish, current mfg.

| MSR $379 | $250 | $160 - 210 | $85 - 110 | |

ACOUSTIC ELECTRIC BASS: AMERICAN CLASSIC SERIES

HFB-590 N (KINGSTON) – single round cutaway flattop body, maple top, bound body, bound f-holes, maple back/sides/neck, 21-fret bound rosewood fingerboard with pearl dot inlay, strings through rosewood bridge, blackface peghead with pearl logo inlay, 2-per-side black chrome tuners, piezo bridge pickup, 4-band EQ, available in Natural finish, disc. 2000.

| | N/A | $350 - 425 | $200 - 250 | $850 |

Earlier models were also available in Black, Pearl White, and Tobacco Sunburst finishes.

HFB-690 RB TBK – similar to HF590, except has 5 strings, arched quilted maple top, 3/2-per-side tuners, available in Trans. Black finish, mfg. 1994-95 and 1999-2000.

| | N/A | $525 - 600 | $375 - 450 | $1,200 |

This model is also available with a bird's-eye maple top, maple satin neck, fretless fingerboard and Natural finish at no additional cost. (Model HFB5-690 RB FL N).

ACOUSTIC ELECTRIC BASS: CURRENT MFG. SERIES

ELAN AB 11 CE – single sharp cutaway thin medium jumbo body, quilted maple top, back, and sides, eight-ply binding, rosewood fingerboard, two-per-side chrome tuners, Fishman Classic 4-Band EQ, available in Amber finish, disc. 2010.

| | $750 | $525 - 625 | $300 - 375 | $1,199 |

REGENCY AB 2 – single cutaway medium jumbo body, select spruce top, nato sides and back, two-per-side chrome tuners, available in Natural finish, current mfg.

| MSR $499 | $330 | $225 - 275 | $130 - 175 | |

MSR/NOTES	100%	EXCELLENT	AVERAGE	LAST MSR

REMINGTON SOLID BODY SAB 13 – single cutaway body, cedar top, mahogany back, ablone dot inlays and rosette, rosewood fingerboard, two-per-side tuners, L.R. Baggs EQ system, available in Black (2010-disc.) or Natural (disc. 2009) finish, disc.

| | $875 | $550 - 650 | $325 - 400 | $1,399 |

SAND GUITARS

Instruments currently built in Laguna Beach, CA, since 1979.

CONTACT INFORMATION
SAND GUITARS
1027 N. Pacific Coast Hwy, Suite F
Laguna Beach, CA 92651
Phone No.: 949-497-5570
Fax No.: 949-497-0457
www.sandguitars.com
ksandca@aol.com

Luthier Kirk Sand began playing guitar at six years old and played professionally and taught until the age of nineteen when he moved from his hometown of Springfield, Illinois to Southern California to study classical guitar.

His love of the instrument led him to co-establish the Guitar Shoppe in 1972 with Jim Matthews in Laguna Beach, California, which produces some of the finest custom instruments built today as well as being one of the premier repair facilities on the West Coast. The head of the repair section is Mark Angus (see Angus Guitars) who works full-time as well as building his custom acoustics throughout the year.

By 1979, Kirk's twenty years of dedicated experience with guitars, guitar repair and restoration inspired him to begin building guitars of his own design. Sand guitars feature Sitka or Englemann spruce tops, Brazilian or Indian rosewood backs and sides, ebony fingerboards, and custom designed active electronics. Classical guitars start at $6,000 and steel string guitars start at $5,900. For further information, contact Sand Guitars directly.

SANDNER

Guitars previously produced between 1947 and 1958 in Germany.

The Sandner trademark was used on a series of acoustic archtops. These models may have "Alosa" or "Standard" on the headstock or tailpiece. The company was founded by Alois Sandner in Egerland, Germany and initially operated as a cottage industry. In 1953, the factory moved to Bubenreuth, Germany, and it had three employees until 1958. They offered approximately twenty models with a total production of less than 500 pieces. The company stopped producing guitars in 1957, but continued to offer stringed instruments.

SANOX

Instruments previously produced in Japan from the late 1970s through the mid-1980s.

Intermediate to good quality guitars featuring some original designs and some designs based on American classics (source: Tony Bacon and Paul Day, *The Guru's Guitar Guide*).

SANTA CRUZ

Instruments currently built in Santa Cruz, CA since 1976. Distributed by the Santa Cruz Guitar Company (SCGC) located in Santa Cruz, CA.

CONTACT INFORMATION
SANTA CRUZ
151 Harvey West Boulevard, Suite C
Santa Cruz, CA 95060
Phone No.: 831-425-0999
Fax No.: 831-425-3604
www.santacruzguitar.com
scgc@santacruzguitar.com

The Santa Cruz Guitar company has been creating high quality acoustic guitars since 1976. Founded by Richard Hoover, who first became interested in guitar building around 1969, and moved to Santa Cruz in 1972 where he studied once a week under a classical guitar builder. Hoover continued honing his skills through daily on-the-job training and talking with other builders. While he was learning the guitar building trade, Hoover was still playing guitar professionally. Hoover ran his own shop for a number of years, producing guitars under the "Rodeo" trademark.

The Santa Cruz Guitar Company was formed by Richard Hoover and two partners in 1976. Their objective was to build acoustic guitars with consistent quality. By drawing on building traditions of the classical guitar and violin builders, Hoover based the new company's building concept on wood choice, voicing the tops, and tuning the guitar bodies. The company's production of individually-built guitars has expanded by working with a group of established luthiers. Santa Cruz now offers several different guitar models with a wide variety of custom options. It is estimated that over half of the guitars are made to order to customer's specifications. For more information, contact Santa Cruz directly or visit their website.

ACOUSTIC ARCHTOP

ARCHTOP 16 INCH – single rounded 16 in. cutaway, bound carved Engelmann or Sitka spruce top, raised bound ebony pickguard, bound f-holes, multi-wood purfling, German maple back/sides/neck, 21-fret bound ebony fingerboard with abalone fan inlay, adjustable ebony bridge/fingers tailpiece, ebony veneered bound peghead with abalone logo inlay, 3-per-side tuners, gold hardware, pickups are an option, available in Natural finish, disc.

| | $8,500 | $5,200 - 5,850 | $3,300 - 3,800 | $10,500 |

* *Archtop 17 Inch* – similar to the Archtop, except has a 17 in. bout, disc.

| | $8,800 | $5,400 - 6,050 | $3,400 - 3,900 | $10,950 |

MSR/NOTES	100%	EXCELLENT	AVERAGE	LAST MSR

* ***Archtop 18 Inch*** – similar to the Archtop, except has a 18 in. bout, disc.

	$11,200	$6,500 - 7,500	$4,600 - 5,200	$14,000

ACOUSTIC

Santa Cruz offers a wide range of custom options on their guitar models. These options include different wood for tops, back/sides, tinted and Sunburst finishes, abalone, wood, or herringbone binding, and 12-string configurations. For current option pricing, availability, or further information, please contact the Santa Cruz Guitar Company directly.

All models have round soundholes with wood inlay rosettes, ivoroid body binding with wood purfling, and Natural finish (unless otherwise listed). The options are literally endless.

- Add $250 for cedar top.
- Add $250 for a mahogany top.
- Add $335 for German Spruce top (disc. 2008).
- Add $600 for a Carpathian spruce top.
- Add $600 for European spruce top.
- Add $550 for Hawaiian koa top.
- Add $900 for Adirondack spruce top.
- Add $400 for Sunburst finish top.
- Add $750 for German maple back and sides.
- Add $750 for Cocobolo rosewood back and sides.
- Add $2,000 for Hawaiian koa back and sides.
- Add $280 for Tinted top.
- Add $275 for abalone rosette.
- Add $650 for cutaway.
- Add $650 for 12-string configuration.
- Add $750 for figured mahogany back and sides.
- Add $900 for ziricote back and sides.
- Add $350 for short scale.

00 SKYE ERIC SKYE SIGNATURE – concert "00"-style body, Adirondack spruce top, cocobolo back and sides, scalloped bracing, round soundhole with multi-ring ivoroid rosette, ivoroid body binding, herringbone purfling, mahogany neck, 12/20-fret ivoroid-bound ebony fingerboard with 14th fret SCGC inlay, slotted headstock with cocobolo overlay, three-per-side open-style nickel Waverly tuners with ivoroid buttons, ebony bridge, available in Natural finish, 1 13/16 in. nut width, 24.9 in. scale, mfg. 2011-present.

MSR $6,950	$6,250	$3,500 - 4,200	N/A	

1929 0 MODEL – concert "0"-style body, mahogany top, back, and sides, scalloped bracing, round soundhole with single ring ivoroid/tortoise rosette, mahogany body binding with black purfling, mahogany neck, 12/19-fret ebony fingerboard, ebony headstock overlay with vintage-style period correct ivory grained celluloid script logo, three-per-side vintage nickel tuners with ebony buttons, ebony bridge, tortoise pickguard, available in Natural or Sunburst (2011-present) nitro cellulose finish, mfg. 2010-present.

MSR $3,800	$3,425	$1,875 - 2,300	$1,125 - 1,400	

- Add 10% (MSR $4,150) for Sunburst finish.

1929 00 MODEL – concert "00"-style body, mahogany top, back, and sides, scalloped bracing, round soundhole with single ring ivoroid/tortoise rosette, mahogany body binding with black purfling, mahogany neck, 12/19-fret ebony fingerboard, ebony headstock overlay with vintage-style period correct ivory grained celluloid script logo, three-per-side vintage nickel tuners with ebony buttons, ebony bridge, tortoise pickguard, available in Natural or Sunburst (2011-present) nitro cellulose finish, mfg. 2010-present.

MSR $3,800	$3,425	$1,875 - 2,300	$1,125 - 1,400	

- Add 10% (MSR $4,150) for Sunburst finish.

1929 000 MODEL – grand concert "000"-style body, mahogany top, back, and sides, scalloped bracing, round soundhole with single ring ivoroid/tortoise rosette, mahogany body binding with black purfling, mahogany neck, 12/19-fret ebony fingerboard, ebony headstock overlay with vintage-style period correct ivory grained celluloid script logo, three-per-side vintage nickel tuners with ebony buttons, ebony bridge, tortoise pickguard, available in Natural or Sunburst (2011-present) nitro cellulose finish, mfg. 2010-present.

MSR $3,900	$3,525	$1,925 - 2,350	$1,150 - 1,450	

- Add 7.5% (MSR $4,250) for Sunburst finish.

1934 D – dreadnought-style body, solid Adirondack spruce top, solid Brazilian rosewood back and sides, scalloped advanced X bracing, round soundhole with vintage-style ivoroid rosette, ivoroid body binding, herringbone purfling, 14/21-fret bound ebony fingerboard with 16th fret "SCGC" logo inlay, bound headstock with Brazilian rosewood overlay, three-per-side vintage nickel tuners, ebony bridge, dalmation pickguard, available in Natural finish, mfg. 2009-present.

MSR $18,550	$16,700	N/A	N/A	

This model is designed around the original dreadnought body style that debuted in 1934.

* ***1934 D Mahogany*** – similar to the 1934 D, except has mahogany back and sides, available in Natural finish, mfg. 2011-present.

MSR $8,950	$8,050	$4,500 - $5,350	N/A	

ARLEN ROTH SIGNATURE MODEL – F-style body, solid Sitka spruce top, solid Indian rosewood back and sides, round soundhole with violin purfle combo rosette, tortoise with ivoroid binding, ivoroid purfling, V neck shape with volute, 14/20-fret tortoise with ivoroid bound ebony fingerboard with Style 42 and 17th fret Arlen Roth signature block inlays, square bound headstock with solid Brazilian rosewood overlay and "SCGC" inlay, three-per-side nickel tuners, ebony pyramid bridge, tortoise pickguard, available in Arlen Sunburst top with clear back and sides finish, 25.375 in. scale, mfg. 2008-present.

MSR $4,950	$4,450	$2,500 - 3,000	$1,500 - 1,850	

BOB BROZMAN BARITONE – German spruce top, mahogany back and sides, three-per-side Waverly tuners, 12 frets to the body, no pickguard, available in Natural finish, 27 in. scale, mfg. 1997-present.

MSR $5,450	$4,900	$2,750 - 3,300	$1,625 - 2,050	

MSR/NOTES	100%	EXCELLENT	AVERAGE	LAST MSR

Bob Brozman Baritone Professional – similar to the Bob Brozman, except has koa back and sides and gold hardware, mfg. 1997-present.

MSR $7,250	$6,525	$3,650 - 4,350	N/A	

COWBOY SINGER 00 DON EDWARDS SIGNATURE – concert "00"-style body, mahogany top, back, and sides, scalloped bracing, round soundhole with three ring ivoroid/tortoise/ivoroid rosette, mahogany body binding, mahogany neck, 12/20-fret ebony fingerboard with 5th fret lone star inlay and 19th fret Don Edwards signature inlay, slotted headstock with ebony overlay and vintage-style period correct ivory grained celluloid script logo, three-per-side open-style gold Waverly tuners with snakewood buttons, ebony bridge, tortoise pickguard, available in Sunburst finish, 1 13/16 in. nut width, 24.75 in. scale, mfg. 2011-present.

MSR $4,850	$4,375	$2,425 - 2,900	$1,450 - 1,825	

FIREFLY – small concert F-style body designed for travel, cedar top, Indian rosewood back and sides, scalloped bracing, round soundhole with ivoroid rosette, ivoroid binding, FF combo purfling, S29 back stripe, 14/21-fret bound ebony fingerboard with small dot inlays, bound headstock with ebony overlay, three-per-side Gotoh mini chrome tuners, ebony bridge, available in Natural finish, 24 in. scale, mfg. 2007-present.

MSR $4,350	$3,425	$2,175 - 2,600	$1,300 - 1,625	

JANIS IAN MODEL (BLACK FINISH) – parlour-size with single rounded cutaway, Sitka spruce top, abalone rosette, Indian rosewood back/sides, mahogany neck, 14/20-fret bound ebony fingerboard with gold ring inlay/rude girl logo, ebony bridge with pearl dot bridgepins, three-per-side black Schaller tuners, L.R. Baggs pickup system, available in all Black finish, disc. 2005.

	N/A	$2,100 - 2,400	$1,200 - 1,350	$4,220

JANIS IAN MODEL (NATURAL FINISH) – single rounded cutaway parlour-size body, solid Sitka spruce top, solid mahogany back and sides, round soundhole with firefly rosette, ivoroid binding, firefly purfling, mahogany neck, 14/20-fret bound ebony fingerboard with "rude girl" inlays, bound headstock with ebony overlay, Janis Ian signature, and "SCGC" logo, three-per-side mini Gotoh chrome tuners, ebony bridge with pearl dot bridgepins, L.R. Baggs pickup system, available in Natural finish, 24.75 in. scale, mfg. 2009-present.

MSR $5,950	$5,350	$2,975 - 3,575	$1,800 - 2,250	

MODEL D – dreadnought style, Sitka spruce top, mahogany (disc. 2008) or Indian rosewood back and sides, mahogany neck, 14/20-fret bound ebony fingerboard, ebony bridge with black pearl dot pins, ebony veneer on bound peghead with pearl logo inlay, three-per-side chrome Scaller tuners, current mfg.

MSR $4,750	$4,275	$2,375 - 2,850	$1,425 - 1,775	

• Subtract 10% (Last MSR was $3,600) for mahogany back and sides.

Model D-Herringbone – similar to the Model D, except has herringbone purfling/appointments and only Indian rosewood back and sides, available in Natural finish, mfg. 2007-08.

	N/A	$1,900 - 2,300	$1,150 - 1,425	$3,800

Model D Pre-War – similar to Model D, except has advanced pre-war style X-bracing, enhanced bass response, available in Natural finish, current mfg.

MSR $3,950	$3,550	$1,975 - 2,375	$1,175 - 1,475	

• Subtract 12.5% (Last MSR was $3,150) for mahogany back and sides.

12-Fret D Model – Sitka spruce top, herringbone purfling/rosette, tortoise pickguard, mahogany back/sides, 12/20-fret ebony fingerboard with pearl diamond inlay, ebony bridge with pearl dot pins, ebony veneer on slotted peghead with pearl logo inlay, three-per-side Waverly tuners, current mfg.

MSR $4,750	$4,275	$2,375 - 2,850	$1,425 - 1,775	

• Add 5% for Indian rosewood back and sides.

Model DA1 – similar to the Model D, except features upgraded custom abalone top inlays, an ebony bridge and end pins, and Indian Rosewood back and sides, mfg. 2005-08.

	N/A	$2,350 - 2,800	$1,400 - 1,700	$4,700

MODEL F – Sitka spruce top, Indian rosewood back/sides, mahogany neck, 14/21-fret bound ebony fingerboard with abalone fan inlay, ebony bridge with black pearl dot pins, ebony veneer on bound peghead with pearl logo inlay, three-per-side chrome Schaller tuners, current mfg.

MSR $4,550	$4,100	$2,275 - 2,725	$1,375 - 1,700	

Model F Cutaway – similar to the Model F, except has a single cutaway, mfg. 2006 only.

	N/A	$2,100 - 2,500	$1,250 - 1,600	$3,995

MODEL FS – single rounded cutaway, red cedar top, Indian rosewood back/sides, mahogany neck, 21-fret ebony fingerboard, Brazilian rosewood binding, ebony bridge with black pearl dot pins, three-per-side gold Schaller tuners with ebony buttons, current mfg.

MSR $5,500	$4,950	$2,750 - 3,300	$1,650 - 2,050	

MODEL H – Sitka spruce top, mahogany (disc.) or Indian rosewood back and sides, mahogany neck, 14/20-fret bound ebony fingerboard, ebony bridge with black pearl pins, ebony veneer on bound peghead, three-per-side chrome Schaller tuners with ebony buttons, current mfg.

MSR $4,250	$3,825	$2,100 - 2,550	$1,250 - 1,550	

• Subtract 10% (Last MSR was $3,400) for mahogany back and sides.

MSR/NOTES	100%	EXCELLENT	AVERAGE	LAST MSR

* *Model H A/E* – spruce top, mahogany back/sides/neck, abalone top border and rosette, 21-fret ebony fingerboard with pearl/gold ring inlay, ebony bridge with black pearl dot pins, three-per-side gold Schaller tuners with ebony buttons, bridge pickup with micro drive preamp, disc. 2004.

	N/A	$2,500 - 3,000	$1,500 - 1,800	$5,000

* *Model H Studio* – similar to the Model H, except has Indian Rosewood back and sides, a single cutaway, and electronics with a Schertler Bluestick pickup, mfg. 2005-07.

	N/A	$2,000 - 2,400	$1,200 - 1,400	$3,950

* *Model H 13* – similar to the Model H, except has mahogany back and sides, a 13-fret neck clear of the body, mfg. 2005-present.

MSR $4,950	$4,450	$2,500 - 3,000	$1,500 - 1,850	

MODEL PJ – parlour-size, Sitka spruce top, mahogany back and sides, mahogany neck, herringbone border, 14/20-fret bound ebony fingerboard with diamond and squares inlay, ebony bridge with pearl dot bridgepins, three-per-side chrome Waverly tuners with ebony buttons, current mfg.

MSR $4,550	$4,100	$2,275 - 2,725	$1,375 - 1,700	

MODEL 00 – 00 14.5 in.body, solid sitka spruce top, mahogany (disc. 2007) or Indian rosewood back and sides, mahogany neck, herringbone border, 12/21-fret ebony fingerboard, slotted headstock, three-per-side tuners, Natural finish, current mfg.

MSR $4,650	$4,200	$2,325 - 2,800	$1,400 - 1,750	

  • Subtract 10% (Last MSR was $3,800) for mahogany back and sides.

MODEL 000-12 – Sitka spruce top, tortoise pickguard, mahogany (disc. 2007) or Indian rosewood back and sides, mahogany neck, 12/19-fret bound ebony fingerboard with pearl diamond and squares inlay, slotted headstock, ebony bridge with ebony mother-of-pearl dot pins, ebony peghead veneer, three-per-side Waverly W-16 tuners, 25.375 in. scale, mfg. 1995-present.

MSR $4,750	$4,275	$2,375 - 2,850	$1,425 - 1,775	

  • Subtract 15% (Last MSR was $3,800) for mahogany back and sides.

MODEL OM – Sitka spruce top, tortoise pickguard, mahogany (disc. 2008) or Indian rosewood back and sides, mahogany neck, 14/20-fret bound ebony fingerboard with pearl dot inlay, ebony bridge with black pearl dot pins, ebony peghead veneer, three-per-side chrome Waverly tuners, current mfg.

MSR $4,650	$4,200	$2,325 - 2,800	$1,400 - 1,750	

  • Subtract 10% (Last MSR was $3,850) for mahogany back and sides.

This model was also available in a short scale version.

* *Model OM-Prewar* – similar to Model OM, except has advanced X-bracing, enhanced bass response, available in Natural finish, current mfg.

MSR $3,950	$3,550	$1,975 - 2,375	$1,175 - 1,475	

  • Subtract 12.5% (Last MSR was $3,150) for mahogany back and sides.

OTIS TAYLOR SIGNATURE MODEL – F-style body, solid Italian spruce top, solid Madagascar rosewood back and sides, round soundhole with ivoroid/B/ivoroid rosette, ivoroid binding, FF combo purfling, S29 sideways back purfling, mahogany neck with rounded profile, ivoroid-bound ebony fingerboard that is fretted up to the 14th fret and fretless the rest of the way, small dot inlays and "OT" initial inlay on the fretless part, square bound headstock with ebony overlay and "SCGC" inlay, three-per-side nickel tuners with ivoroid buttons, ebony pyramid bridge, tortoise pickguard, available in Custom Tint top with clear back and sides finish, 25.375 in. scale, mfg. 2009-present.

MSR $5,225	$4,700	$2,600 - 3,150	N/A	

RS – Advanced Jumbo-style body, solid Sitka spruce top, solid mahogany back and sides, double tapered bracing, round 3.75 in. wide soundhole with ivoroid/B/maple/B combination rosette, tortoise binding, single B/W/B purfling, mahogany neck, 12/19-fret black bound ebony fingerboard with doppler-style inlays, ebony headstock overlay with "SCGC" logo inlay, three-per-side nickel open-back tuners with ivoroid buttons, ebony bridge, available in Tobacco Brown Sunburst finish, mfg. 2007-present.

MSR $4,950	$4,450	$2,500 - 3,000	$1,500 - 1,850	

SONIA – Model H-style body, Sitka spruce top, Indian rosewood back and sides, double tapered with bass scalloped bracing, round soundhole with multi-ring ivoroid rosette, ivoroid body binding, violin combo purfling, mahogany neck, 14/22-fret ivoroid-bound ebony fingerboard with custom SONiA inlays, bound ebony headstock overlay with SCGC inlay, three-per-side nickel tuners, ebony bridge, tortoise pickguard, available in Natural finish, 1 13/16 in. nut width, 25.375 in. scale, mfg. 2010-present.

MSR $4,500	$4,050	$2,250 - 2,700	$1,350 - 1,700	

  • Subtract 10% (Last MSR was $3,400) for mahogany back and sides.

STYLE 1 PARLOR – Parlor-style body based on Martin's Size 1, solid Sitka spruce top, solid Indian rosewood back and sides, scalloped bracing, round soundhole with ivoroid rosette, ivoroid binding, herringbone purfling, zipper back stripe, one-piece mahogany neck with a V-shape profile and volute, slotted bound headstock with ebony overlay and "SCGC" logo, three-per-side open-style nickel tuners with ivoroid buttons, ebony pyramid bridge, available in Clear finish, 24.75 in. scale, mfg. 2008-present.

MSR $4,750	$4,275	$2,375 - 2,850	$1,425 - 1,775	

TONY RICE MODEL – dreadnought style, Sitka spruce top, tortoise pickguard, herringbone bound body/rosette, Indian rosewood back/sides, mahogany neck, 14/20-fret bound ebony fingerboard with pearl logo inlay at 12th fret, Tony Rice signature on label, ebony bridge with black pearl dot pins, ebony peghead veneer, three-per-side chrome Waverly tuners, mfg. 1990-present.

MSR $5,350	$4,825	$2,675 - 3,225	$1,600 - 2,000	

This model was designed in conjunction with guitarist Tony Rice.

MSR/NOTES	100%	EXCELLENT	AVERAGE	LAST MSR

* **Tony Rice Professional** – similar to Tony Rice Model, except has German spruce top, Brazilian rosewood back and sides, 25.25 in. scale, enlarged soundhole, ivoroid/black/ivoroid binding on the fingerboard and peghead, gold Waverly tuners, available in Natural finish, mfg. 1990-present.

| MSR $13,900 | $12,500 | $7,000 - 8,350 | N/A | |

VINTAGE ARTIST – dreadnought style, Sitka spruce top, tortoise pickguard, herringbone body trim, mahogany back/sides/neck, 14/21-fret bound ebony fingerboard with pearl dot inlay, ebony bridge with black pearl dot pins, Brazilian rosewood veneer on bound peghead with pearl logo inlay, three-per-side Waverly tuners, disc. 2004, reintroduced 2007-present.

| MSR $5,350 | $4,825 | $2,675 - 3,225 | $1,600 - 2,000 | |

VINTAGE JUMBO – jumbo style, inspired by round-shouldered dreadnoughts of the 1940s, Sitka spruce top, mahogany back and sides, 14 frets to the body, round soundhole, three-per-side Waverly tuners, available in Sunburst finish, current mfg.

| MSR $4,950 | $4,450 | $2,500 - 3,000 | $1,500 - 1,850 | |

VINTAGE SOUTHERNER – similar to the Vintage Jumbo except in 24.75 in. scale and smaller rectangular shaped bridge, mfg. 2005-present.

| MSR $4,950 | $4,450 | $2,500 - 3,000 | $1,500 - 1,850 | |

* **Vintage Southerner Deluxe** – similar to the Vintage Southerner, except has highly flamed German maple back and sides, a maple neck, an ivoroid and black bound fingerboard and headstock, deeper cut and more purfling, and Tobacco Sunburst finish, mfg. 2005-09.

| | N/A | $2,825 - 3,400 | $1,700 - 2,100 | $5,650 |

ACOUSTIC BASS

TRUE ACOUSTIC BASS – D-style bass body, Sitka spruce top, mahogany back and sides, scalloped bracing, round soundhole with multi-ring herringbone rosette, ivoroid binding, zipper backstripe, mahogany neck, 15/21-fret black-bound ebony fingerboard, two-per-side tuners, belly bridge, available in Natural buffed/matte finish, 32 in. scale, mfg. 2010-present.

| MSR $5,250 | $4,725 | $2,600 - 3,150 | N/A | |

SANTA ROSA

Instruments currently built in Asia. Distributed by AR Musical Enterprises of Fishers, IN. Santa Rosa acoustic guitars are geared more towards the entry level or student guitarist.

SCHAEFER GUITARS

Instruments currently built in Austin, TX since 2009. Previously built in Hillsboro, TX and Fort Worth, TX until 2003, in Duluth, MN between 2003 and 2006, and in Bastrop, TX between 2007 and 2008.

Luthier Ed Schaefer studied classical guitar in college while working as a guitar tech at R.B.I. in the early 1970s. The Rhythm Band Instrument Company was a sister company of I.M.C. (International Music Corporation - See Hondo or Charvel/Jackson). Schaefer started producing his own guitars shortly thereafter and has been producing guitars ever since. Schaefer has produced in Texas for many years, except for a brief stint in Duluth, MN between 2003 and 2006.

In April 2008, Schaefer stopped taking commissions for new guitars except for building a few high-end models per year. Due to customer's requests and popular demand, Schaefer began taking limited commissions again in March 2009 and in June 2009, he opened a new shop in Austin, TX. Along with building guitars, Schaefer also offers guitar repairs and a luthier school. Schaefer reminds the customer that each model is only the starting point and several custom options are available. For more information or specific options, visit Schaefer's website or contact him directly.

SCHARPACH GUITARS

Instruments currently built in the Netherlands since 1979.

Guitarmaker Theo Scharpach was born near Vienna, Austria. He has been working in Bergeijk, the Netherlands for more than 30 years. Since more than 25 years he has been working together with Menno Bos who is now leading the workshop. Only ten to twelve exclusive handmade guitars are produced each year. Guitars are built only on commission. For more information contact Scharpach directly.

The **Classical Concert Model** has a two soundhole design with raised fingerboard, using only 1st quality, 100-year-old Brazilian rosewood with either spruce or cedar top. Standard is a unique semi-cutaway which, in combination with the raised fingerboard,

MSR/NOTES	100%	EXCELLENT	AVERAGE	LAST MSR

allows you to play in the highest registers, up to the 24th fret very easily. Construction techniques result in extremely long sustain with a well balanced mellow sound.

The **Blue Vienna Jazz Acoustic Archtop** is built using only the finest European cello-woods, and is available in Blue, Honey, and other finishes available (disc.).

The **Dolphin Classical Concert** is a jazz archtop model with nylon strings.

The **Original Selmer Design** is built in the style of Marrio Maccaferry, "Gypsy" style. Used by Tolga Emilio and Raphael Fays.

The **Steel String Jumbo** is available with or without cutaway, and is also available are 8-string, 12-string, and baritone models. The Model SKD was custom built for Steve Howe.

The **Arch** is a small, semi-acoustic model, nylon strings, used by Al di Meola.

The **Teardrop** is a jazz oriented style instrument.

In 2008, the **Vienna Apex** was developed as an exclusive and pure acoustic version created with our new bracing system called H.I.T. (Harmonic Integrated Topdesign). The top bracing no longer uses traditional cross bar or parallel bracing.

In 2012 the **Vienna Suprema** was introduced as the ultimate version of the Vienna Apex with no restrictions and limitation. The varnish and colouring is done by using old traditional techniques as used producing high quality bowed instruments like the Cello. The varnish is a dark shellac. The appearance is very traditional and elegant with no fancy inlays.

SCHECTER GUITAR RESEARCH

Instruments currently produced in Los Angeles, CA and in Korea (Diamond Series). Production of high quality replacement parts and guitars began in Van Nuys, CA in 1976.

CONTACT INFORMATION
SCHECTER GUITAR RESEARCH
10953 Pendleton St.
Sun Valley, CA 91352
Phone No.: 800-660-6621
Fax No.: 818-846-2727
www.schecterguitars.com
info@schecterguitars.com

The Schecter company, named after David Schecter, began as a repair/modification shop that also did some customizing. Schecter began making high quality replacement parts (such as Solid Brass Hardware, Bridges, Tuners, and the MonsterTone and SuperRock II pickups) and build-your-own instrument kits. This led to the company offering of quality replacement necks and bodies, and eventually to their own line of finished instruments. Schecter is recognized as one of the first companies to market tapped pickup assemblies (coil tapping can offer a wider range of sound from an existing pickup configuration). Other designers associated with Schecter were Dan Armstrong and Tom Anderson.

In 1994, Michael Ciravolo took over as the new director for Schecter Guitar Research. Ciravolo introduced new guitar designs the same year, and continues to expand the Schecter line with new innovations and designs.

In 1998, Schecter and Maestro Alex Gregory teamed up to offer the 7-String Limited Edition Signature model based on the patented specifications and neck profile of Gregory's original 1989 model. This signature model will be individually numbered, and comes with a signed Certificate of Authenticity (list $2,595) (source: Tom Wheeler, *American Guitars*).

By the mid-1980s, Schecter was offering designs based on early Fender-style guitars in models such as the Mercury, Saturn, Hendrix, and Dream Machine. In the late 1980s Schecter also had the U.S. built Californian series as well as the Japan-made Schecter East models. Recently they introduced an Acoustic line as well. For more information, visit Schecter's website or contact them directly.

ACOUSTIC

DIAMOND ACOUSTIC – single cutaway body, figured maple top over composite oval back (like Ovation), mahogany set-neck, 20-fret rosewood fingerboard with diamond inlays, body and neck binding, three-per-side Grover tuners, Diamond Piezo pickup, active 4-band EQ, chrome or gold hardware, available in Red Sunburst, Trans. Amber, Trans. Black, or Trans. Green Burst finish, disc. 2007.

	N/A	$175 - 225	$110 - 140	$399

* Add 12.5% (Last MSR was $449) for left-handed configuration, available in Trans. Amber finish.

* *Diamond Acoustic Elite* – similar to the Diamond Acoustic, except has a quilted maple top and abalone binding, available in Antique Brown Sunburst or Trans. Blue finish, disc. 2007.

	N/A	$225 - 275	$125 - 175	$499

* Add 10% (Last MSR was $549) for left-handed configuration, available in Trans. Blue finish.

* *Diamond Elite 12-String* – similar to the Diamond Elite, except in 12-string configuration, available in Antique Brown Sunburst finish, mfg. 2004-07.

	N/A	$250 - 300	$140 - 180	$549

* Add 10% (Last MSR was $599) for left-handed configuration.

GLP 1 GRANT LEE PHILLIPS – concert body style, solid mahogany top, back, and sides, ivory with vintage checkerboard binding, mahogany dove tail set-neck, 20-fret rosewood fingerboard with abalone and pearl stars inlays, three-per-side Grover tuners, Fishman Matrix Infinity pickup, rosewood bridge with bone compensated saddle, nickel hardware, available in Natural Gloss finish, 25.4 in. scale, case included, mfg. 2010-present.

MSR $1,219	$850	$550 - 675	$300 - 375	

MSR/NOTES	100%	EXCELLENT	AVERAGE	LAST MSR

HELLRAISER STAGE ACOUSTIC – single pointed cutaway body, quilted maple top, back, and sides, abalone (Black Cherry finish) or grey pearloid (See Thru Black finish) multi-ply body binding, mahogany dove tail set neck, 20-fret rosewood fingerboard with abalone or grey pearloid gothic crosses inlays, bound matching finish headstock, three-per-side Grover tuners, Custom Schecter Diamond Composite bridge with Graph Tech Black Tusq saddle and pins, rosewood rosette with gothic cross inlays, black chrome hardware, available in Black Cherry or See Thru Black finish, 25.5 in. scale, mfg. 2012-13.

	$400	$260 - 325	$145 - 175	$579

* *Hellraiser Studio Acoustic* – similar to the Hellraiser Stage Acoustic, except with a rounded single cutaway, available in Black Cherry or See Thru Black finish, 25.5 in. scale, mfg. 2012-13.

	$400	$260 - 325	$145 - 175	$579

OMEN EXTREME ACOUSTIC – single cutaway body, quilted maple top, sides, and back (Antique Amber or Black Cherry finish) or spruce top with rosewood sides and back (Vintage Sunburst finish), pearloid multi-ply body binding, mahogany dove tail set neck, 20-fret rosewood fingerboard with pearloid and abalone vector inlays, matching finish bound headstock, three-per-side Grover tuners, Custom Schecter Diamond composite bridge with Graph Tech Ivory Tusq saddle and pins, Fishman ISYS electronics, sonicore piezo, pearloid multi-ply rosette, chrome (Black Cherry or Vintage Sunburst finish) or gold (Antique Amber finish) hardware, available in Antique Amber, Black Cherry, or Vintage Sunburst finish, 25.5 in. scale, mfg. 2012-13.

	$350	$225 - 275	$125 - 150	$499

ORLEANS ACOUSTIC – single smooth cutaway dreadnought-style body, solid spruce top, solid mahogany back and sides, round soundhole with multi-ring rosette, body binding with abalone purfling, mahogany neck, 14/20-fret bound rosewood fingerboard with abalone dot inlays, bound headstock with logo and fleur-de-lis inlay, three-per-side Grover gold tuners, rosewood bridge with Graph Tech bridge pins, Fishman Prefix Plus T electronics, available in Natural finish, 25.5 in. scale, case included, mfg. 2009-2011.

	$850	$550 - 650	$300 - 350	$1,199

ROYAL ACOUSTIC – single smooth cutaway dreadnought-style body, solid spruce top, solid Indian rosewood back and sides, round soundhole with multi-ring rosette, creme body binding, mahogany neck, 14/20-fret bound rosewood fingerboard with creme dot inlays, bound headstock with logo and fleur-de-lis inlay, three-per-side Grover gold tuners, rosewood bridge with Graph Tech bridge pins, Fishman Prefix Plus T electronics, available in Vintage Sunburst finish, 25.5 in. scale, case included, mfg. 2009-2011.

	$850	$550 - 650	$300 - 350	$1,199

RS 1000 ROBERT SMITH – dreadnought body, spruce top, mahogany back and sides, B/N/H binding, white moon rosette, maple set-neck, 21-fret rosewood fingerboard with white pearl stars and moons inlays, three-per-side Grover tuners, rosewood bridge with bone saddle, chrome hardware, available in Gloss Black (disc. 2008) or Goth Black (2009-present) finish, 25.5 in. scale, mfg. 2006-present.

MSR $819	$580	$325 - 400	$175 - 225	

SW 3500 ACOUSTIC – single cutaway body, quilted maple top, South American Rosewood sides and back, mahogany set-neck, 22-fret rosewood fingerboard with dot inlays, body and neck binding, three-per-side Grover tuners, Fishman Piezo pickup and active 4-band EQ, chrome hardware, available in Black, Trans. Amber, or Vintage Natural Gloss finish, disc. 2006.

	N/A	$275 - 325	$150 - 200	$599

* Add 10% for left-handed configuration, available in Vintage Natural Gloss finish.

SCHEERHORN CUSTOM RESONATOR GUITARS

Instruments currently built in Kentwood, MI since 1989. Instruments are available through Scheerhorn or Elderly Instruments of Lansing, MI.

Luthier Tim Scheerhorn has background training as a tool and die maker, a tool engineer, and is a specialist in process automation for manufacturing. In the past, his hobbies generally involved rebuilding something - either boats or classic cars. But in 1986, Scheerhorn picked up a resonator guitar and later found himself immersed in the world of custom guitar building.

Although Scheerhorn did have prior experience setting up banjos and resonator guitars for other players, he had never built a musical instrument from scratch. He did possess a new OMI Dobro, and a Regal from the 1930s. In February of 1989, Scheerhorn began building guitars based on the Regal model and his own innovations. In the summer of 1989 the guitar was tested by Mike Auldridge (Seldom Scene) at the Winterhawk festival in New York. Encouraged by Auldridge's enthusiasm, Scheerhorn returned to his workshop and continued building.

Scheerhorn limits production to three or four instruments a month. All guitars are hand built by Scheerhorn.

Both Scheerhorn models share the same revised resonator design. The resonators are built of bright chrome plated brass, Spun Quarterman cone, and a spider bridge of aluminum. The bridge insert is made of hard maple with ebony tops. Both models also feature chrome Schaller M-6 tuning machines.

The **Curly Maple Regal Body** model has a bookmatched solid curly maple top, with matching sides and back. The three piece neck consists of curly maple and walnut, and has a 19-fret ebony fingerboard. The body and neck are bound in either an ivoroid or dark tortoise (Natural Blond finish), and finished in hand-rubbed lacquer. The **Curly Maple Large Body** model has similar specifications, but with a larger body size (longer, deeper, wider) for additional volume and projection.

The **Mahogany/Spruce Regal Body** model has a book-matched quartersawn Sitka spruce top, solid mahogany back and sides, and a two piece mahogany neck. The **Mahogany/Spruce Large Body** model has similar specifications, but with a larger body size for additional volume and projection.

Scheerhorn also builds a Weissenborn Style Reissue dubbed the "**Scheerhorn Hawaiian**." The body is constructed out of solid Figured Koa (top, back, and sides), and the peghead has a Curly Maple overlay. The bridge is cocobolo with a bone saddle, and the cocobolo fingerboard has Curly Maple binding and abalone inlays. This model also features Kluson style tuners, a built in McIntyre pickup, and a hand-rubbed lacquer finish.

Scheerhorn's newest model in the **Acoustic/Electric**, which features solid curly maple top/back/sides and neck, ebony fingerboard with flush frets, a 9" Quarterman cone and National-style coverplate, a Seymour Duncan mini-humbucker/McIntyre transducer pickups (with volume and tone for each system) and a 3-way selector switch. This model is wired for stereo.

SCHNEIDER, RICHARD

Instruments previously built in WA, and other locations. Distributed by the Lost Mountain Center for the Guitar of Carlsborg, WA.

In 1996, when luthier/designer Richard Schneider was asked what he considered his occupation, he simply replied, "I don't make guitars, I make guitar makers." While known for his Kasha-inspired acoustic guitar designs, Schneider also trained and encouraged younger builders to continue crafting guitars. At last count, some 21 full term apprentices had been taught in the craft of classical guitar design. Schneider is best known for his over 25 year collaboration with Dr. Michael Kasha, in their advanced design for the classical guitar. Kasha, the Director of Institute of Molecular Biophysics at Florida State University, worked with Schneider to pioneer an entirely new and scientific way of designing and constructing classical guitars. This advanced design has been the topic of controversy for a number of years in the classical guitar community.

Schneider first apprenticed with Juan Pimentel in Mexico City, Mexico from 1963 to 1965. Schneider served as proprietor of **Estudio be las Guitarra** from 1965 to 1972, which housed a guitar making workshop, retail store and music instruction studio. It was during this time period that Schneider began his collaboration with Dr. Kasha. In 1973, Schnieder became the director and owner of the Studio of Richard Schneider in Kalamazoo, Michigan. This studio was devoted solely to classical guitar design and fine construction using the Kasha/Schneider design. Schneider was a consultant to the Gibson Guitar company between 1973 and 1978. His duties included design, engineering, and production procedures for the **Mark** series guitars, which was based on the Kasha/Schneider design. He also designed the **The Les Paul** electric guitar model. In 1983, Schneider also engineered and built five **Taxi** prototypes for Silver Street, Inc. of Elkhart, Indiana.

In 1984, Schneider moved his family and workshop to Sequim, Washington. The Lost Mountain Center for the Guitar was founded in 1986 as a non-profit organization whose purposes include research, development, and information disseminating about improvements in guitar design. Schneider continued to make improvements to his Kasha/Schneider design, which made significant improvements to the tonal functions and playability. Luthier Richard Schneider passed away on January 31, 1997, (Biography courtesy Bob Fischer, Lost Mountain Center).

Schneider estimated that he constructed over two hundred guitars by 1996. Approximately sixty were handcrafted traditional concert guitars, while fifty models were the advanced Schneider/Kasha design. Rather than assign a serial number to his guitars, Schneider used to name them instead.

In addition to his own guitar designs, Schneider estimated that he had built over one hundred prototypes for the Gibson Guitar company, and Baldwin-era Gretsches.

Schneider met with Maestro Andres Segovia on eighteen separate occasions, and auditioned new instruments with Segovia on six of these visits for purposes of critique and analysis. After Segovia passed away, Schneider then consulted with guitarist Kurt Rodarmer, whose CD *The Goldberg Variations* features two of Schneider's guitars.

SCHOENBERG, ERIC

Instruments currently built in Tiburon, CA. Previous production was in MA. Nazareth, PA from 1985 to 1996. Schoenberg Guitars set up a new, separate production facility in MA in 1997.

CONTACT INFORMATION
SCHOENBERG, ERIC
106 Main Street
Tiburon, CA 94920
Phone No.: 415-789-0846
Fax No.: 415-789-0116
www.om28.com
eric@om28.com

Eric Schoenberg is regarded as one of the finest ragtime and finger style guitarists of the last twenty years. While operating out of the Music Emporium in Massachusetts, Schoenberg released a number of high quality acoustic guitars that were built in conjunction with the C.F. Martin company of Nazareth, Pennsylvania, and individually finished by either Schoenberg or luthier Dana Bourgeois. The Martin facilities assembled the bodies, then final touches were controlled by Schoenberg and Bourgeois. Luthier Bourgeois was involved in the project from 1986 to mid-1990. Luthier T.J. Thompson worked with Schoenberg from the mid-1990s until 1995. Beginning 1997, Schoenberg Guitars are individually handmade by several independent luthiers, including Bruce Sexauer of Petaluna, CA, and Robert Anderson of Victoria, British Columbia. For more information refer to their website.

Schoenberg debuted the **Soloist** model in the late 1980s. The Soloist was a modern version of a Martin OM-style acoustic, and featured top grade woods originally overseen by Bourgeois. The Soloist model featured a European spruce top, Brazilian back and sides, a one piece mahogany neck, 20-fret ebony fingerboard with diamond shaped pearl inlays, and Kluson-styled Grover tuning machines. Retail list price back in the late 1980s was $2,850 (which seems more than reasonable now!). Contact Schoenberg for a quote on a guitar.

MSR/NOTES	100%	EXCELLENT	AVERAGE	LAST MSR

SCHWARTZ, SHELDON

Instruments currently built in Toronto (Ontario), Canada.

Luthier Sheldon Schwartz currently offers high quality handcrafted acoustic guitars that are immaculately constructed. Schwartz began working on guitars at fifteen, and has had lutherie associations with such builders as Grit Laskin and Linda Manzer. In 1992, Schwartz began building full time, and attended vintage guitar shows to display his work. For more information, visit Schwartz's website or contact him directly.

CONTACT INFORMATION
SCHWARTZ, SHELDON
2717 Concession Road #5 RR1
Loretto, Ontario L0G 1L0 Canada
Phone No.: 905-729-0024
www.schwartzguitars.com
sheldon@schwartzguitars.com

Schwartz prefers working with the top quality, master grade woods for both appearance and tonal qualities. Depending on the commission, Schwartz also works in other woods such as Engelmann spruce, Bear claw Sitka spruce, and Brazilian rosewood and will negotiate rates on custom inlay work.

The **Advanced Auditorium Custom** (MSR $6,500) features a dreadnought-style body, Sitka spruce top, dovetail mahogany neck, bound ebony fingerboard with two abalone dots at 12th fret, East Indian back and sides, abalone rosette, rosewood binding/heelcap/headstock veneer, mitered top/back purfling, ebony bridge, solid Spanish cedar lining, bone nut and saddle, brass dot side position markers, three-per-side Schaller M6 tuning machines, 25.5 in. scale, 16.125 in. lower bout, and is available in Natural high gloss nitrocellulose finish.

The **Advanced Auditorium Elite** (disc. 2003, Last MSR was $3,900) is similar to the Advanced Auditorium Custom, except used all master-grade materials and features handpicked, color matched abalone top purfling.

The **Limited Edition Model** (disc. 2003, Last MSR was $4,900) is also similar to the Advanced Auditorium Custom, except has 130-year-old bird's-eye maple back and sides, reclaimed salmon trap soundboard, Brazilian rosewood fingerboard, bridge, binding, and front and back headstock veneers, gold tuners, and gold MOP 12-fret position marker.

The **Oracle Fingerstyle** (MSR $9,500) comes standard with a cutaway, bent wood-style arm rest, and three elliptical soundholes.

The **Pinnacle Fingerstyle** (MSR $7,500) features master grade Sitka spruce top, East Indian rosewood or mahogany back and sides, mahogany neck, and ebony fingerboard and bridge. This model is also available in seven-string configuration (MSR $7,800).

The **Schwartz Maple Series** (disc. 2003, Last MSR was $3,400-3,700) and features a single cutaway, curly or bird's-eye maple body, Brazillian rosewood fingerboard, bridges, and bindings.

* Add $550 for curly maple back and sides.
* Add $550 for Venetian (rounded) cutaway.
* Add $950 for curly koa back and sides.

SEAGULL

Instruments currently built in La Patrie, Quebec, Canada since 1980. Distributed by Godin Guitars (previously La Si Do, Inc.) in Baie D'Urfe Quebec, Canada.

CONTACT INFORMATION
SEAGULL
Distributed by Godin Guitars
19420 Ave. Clark Graham
Baie d Urfe, PQ H9X 3R8 Canada
Phone No.: 514-457-7977
Fax No.: 514-457-5774
www.seagullguitars.com
info@seagullguitars.com

In 1968, Robert Godin set up a custom guitar shop in Montreal called Harmonilab. Harmonilab quickly became known for its excellent work and musicians were coming from as far away as Quebec City to have their guitars adjusted.

Although Harmonilab's business was flourishing, Robert was full of ideas for the design and construction of acoustic guitars. So in 1972 the Norman Guitar Company was born. From the beginning the Norman guitars showed signs of the innovations that Godin would eventually bring to the guitar market. By 1978, Norman guitars had become quite successful in Canada and France.

In 1980, Godin introduced the Seagull guitar. With many innovations like a bolt-on neck (for consistent neck pitch), pointed headstock (straight string pull) and a handmade solid top, the Seagull was designed for an ease of play for the entry level to intermediate guitar player. Most striking was the satin lacquer finish. Godin borrowed the finishing idea that was used on fine violins, and applied it to the acoustic guitar. When the final version of the Seagull guitar went into production, Godin went about the business of finding a sales force to help introduce the Seagull into the U.S. market. Several independent U.S. sales agents jumped at the chance to get involved with this new guitar, and armed with samples, off they went into the market. A couple of months passed, and not one guitar was sold. Rather than retreat back to Harmonilab, Godin decided that he would have to get out there himself and explain the Seagull guitar concept. So he bought himself an old Ford Econoline van and stuffed it full of about 85 guitars, and started driving through New England visiting guitar shops and introducing the Seagull guitar. Acceptance of this new guitar spread, and by 1985 La Si Do was incorporated and the factory in La Patrie expanded to meet the growing demand. For full company history, see Godin.

ACOUSTIC: ARTIST SERIES

CAMEO CUTAWAY – full sized single cutaway body, solid spruce top, solid flame maple back and sides, mahogany neck, 14/21-fret rosewood fingerboard with dove inlay, rosewood bridge, optional Element (22632), I-Beam Duet (21895, disc. 2008), or Quantum II (2009 only, 22649) electronics, standard Quantum II (2010-present, 033461) electronics, high gloss natural lacquer, case included, mfg. 2003-present.

MSR $1,650	$1,350	$700 - 850	$450 - 525

* Subtract 20% (Last MSR was $1,290) for no electronics (21758).

MSR/NOTES	100%	EXCELLENT	AVERAGE	LAST MSR

GRAND ARTIST – solid spruce top, black pickguard, round soundhole, multi-stripe rosette, solid rosewood back, laminated rosewood sides, Honduran mahogany neck, 14/21-fret rosewood fingerboard with pearl dot inlay, bound headstock, rosewood bridge with white bridgepins, three-per-side chrome tuners, available in Natural high gloss finish (10561), 25 11/32 in. scale, mfg. 1993-99.

	N/A	$475 - 550	$325 - 375	$995

This model is designed to be a modern version of a "turn of the century" parlor guitar.

MOSAIC – full sized body, solid cedar top, solid mahogany back and sides, mahogany neck, 14/21-fret rosewood fingerboard with dove inlay, rosewood bridge, hand polished natural lacquer (21802/033515), case included, mfg. 2003-present.

MSR $1,050	$950	$475 - 550	$275 - 325	

- Add 25% for Element electronics (Model 22571, disc.).
- Add 20% (MSR $1,410) for Quantum II EQ electronics (2010-present, Model 22588/033508).
- Add 45% (Last MSR was $1,429) for I-Beam Duet electronics (Model 21949, disc. 2008).

* *Mosaic Cutaway* – similar to the Mosaic, except has a single cutaway (21765), mfg. 2003-09.

	N/A	$475 - 550	$300 - 350	$1,129

- Add 20% for Element electronics (Model 22670, disc.).
- Add 25% (Last MSR was $1,398) for Quantum II EQ electronics (Model 22656, 2009 only).
- Add 40% (Last MSR was $1,549) for I-Beam Duet electronics (Model 21901, disc. 2008).

* *Mosaic Folk* – similar to the Mosaic, except has a folk sized body (19885), mfg. 2004-09.

	N/A	$425 - 500	$275 - 325	$1,007

- Add 27.5% (Last MSR was $1,269) for Quantum II EQ electronics (Model 25107, 2009 only).
- Add 45% (Last MSR was $1,429) for I-Beam Duet electronics (Model 19908, disc. 2008).

»*Mosaic Cutaway Folk* – similar to the Mosaic Folk, except has a single cutaway and Quantum II electronics (033492), mfg. 2010-present.

MSR $1,450	$1,200	$675 - 825	$375 - 450	

PEPPINO SIGNATURE MODEL CUTAWAY – full sized single cutaway body, solid spruce top, solid rosewood back and sides, mahogany neck, 14/21-fret rosewood fingerboard with dove inlay, rosewood bridge, signature on headstock, optional I-Beam Duet (22663, disc. 2008) or Quantum II (26593, 2009 only) electronics, standard Quantum II (033485, 2010-present) electronics, high gloss Natural lacquer finish, mfg. 2003-present.

MSR $1,799	$1,500	$800 - 950	$500 - 600	

- Subtract 20% (Last MSR was $1,462) for no electronics (24995).

PORTRAIT CUTAWAY – full sized single cutaway body, solid spruce top, solid mahogany back and sides, mahogany neck, 14/21-fret rosewood fingerboard with dove inlay, rosewood bridge, high gloss Natural lacquer (21772), case included, mfg. 2003-09.

	N/A	$525 - 625	$300 - 375	$1,290

- Add 15% for Element electronics (Model 22618, disc.).
- Add 22.5% (Last MSR was $1,556) for Quantum II EQ electronics (Model 22625, 2009 only).
- Add 35% (Last MSR was $1,709) for I-Beam Duet electronics (Model 21918, disc. 2008).

STUDIO – full sized body, solid spruce top, solid rosewood back and sides, mahogany neck, 14/21-fret rosewood fingerboard with dove inlay, rosewood bridge, hand polished natural lacquer (21819), case included, mfg. 2003-09.

	N/A	$550 - 650	$325 - 400	$1,345

- Add 15% for Element electronics (Model 22557, disc.).
- Add 20% (Last MSR was $1,609) for Quantum II EQ electronics (Model 22564, 2009 only).
- Add 32.5% (Last MSR was $1,765) for I-Beam Duet electronics (Model 21956, disc. 2008).

* *Studio Burst* – similar to the Studio, except has a Sunburst finish (30255), mfg. 2007-09.

	N/A	$575 - 675	$350 - 425	$1,412

- Add 17.5% (Last MSR was $1,677) for Quantum II EQ electronics (Model 30262, 2009 only).
- Add 30% (Last MSR was $1,849) for I-Beam Duet electronics (Model 30279, 2007-08).

* *Studio Cutaway* – similar to the Studio, except has a single cutaway with optional Element (22595), I-Beam Duet (21932, disc. 2008), or Quantum II (22601, 2009 only) electronics, standard Quantum II (033478, 2010-present) electronics, mfg. 2003-present.

MSR $1,799	$1,450	$800 - 950	$500 - 600	

- Subtract 17.5% (Last MSR was $1,469) for no electronics (21796).

»*Studio 12 Burst 12-String* – similar to the Studio Burst, except in 12-string configuration and six-per-side tuners (30224), mfg. 2007-09.

	N/A	$600 - 700	$375 - 450	$1,469

- Add 17.5% (Last MSR was $1,729) for Quantum II EQ electronics (Model 30231, 2009 only).
- Add 30% (Last MSR was $1,899) for I-Beam Duet electronics (Model 30248, 2007-08).

ACOUSTIC: COASTLINE (S) SERIES

In 2006, the Coastline Series replaced the S Series. There were not a lot of physical changes except for a new polished lacquer finish and new model number designations.

MSR/NOTES	100%	EXCELLENT	AVERAGE	LAST MSR

S 6 ORIGINAL – dreadnought style bound body, solid cedar top, black pickguard, round soundhole, multi stripe rosette, wild cherry back/sides, mahogany neck, 14/21-fret rosewood fingerboard with pearl dot inlay, rosewood bridge with white black dot pins, blackface peghead with screened logo, three-per-side chrome tuners, available in Natural finish (10257/22229/29396), mfg. 1993-present.

MSR $507	$420	$210 - 260	$120 - 150	

- Add 25% (MSR $649) for Quantum EQ electronics (Model 22236/29426).
- Add 35% for Element electronics (disc.).

* **S 6 Original Left-Handed** – similar to the S 6, except in left-handed configuration (22250/29402), current mfg.

MSR $555	$450	$235 - 285	$135 - 170	

- Add 27.5% (MSR $695) for Quantum EQ electronics (Model 22267/29419).
- Add 30% for Element electronics (disc.).

* **S 6 Slim** – similar to the S 6 Original, except has a slim neck with a 1.72 in. nut width, available in Natural finish (28726), mfg. 2006-present.

MSR $507	$420	$210 - 260	$120 - 150	

- Add 25% (MSR $649) for Quantum EQ electronics (Model 28733).

S6+ CEDAR – similar to S6, except has a solid Cedar top, "+ version" uses a special staining process that results in a rich Violin Brown finish (10318), disc. 2002.

	N/A	$170 - 220	$100 - 130	$417

* **S6+ Spruce** – similar to S6, except has solid spruce top (10370), disc. 2002.

	N/A	$180 - 230	$105 - 135	$435

* **S6+ Burst** – similar to S6, except has Sunburst finish (1323), disc. 2002.

	N/A	$200 - 250	$120 - 160	$485

»**S6 + Cutaway Burst** – similar to S6 + Burst, except has a single cutaway, available in Sunburst finish (2160), disc. 2002.

	N/A	$275 - 325	$150 - 200	$580

* **S12 12-String** – similar to S6, except in 12-string configuration with six-per-side tuners, disc. 1998.

	N/A	$190 - 240	$100 - 130	$450

COASTLINE CEDAR GT (S6+ CEDAR GT) – similar to the S6+, except has a laquer finish with a gloss top (22281/29457), mfg. 2003-2011.

	$500	$265 - 315	$160 - 210	$609

- Add 25% (Last MSR was $759) for Quantum EQ electronics (Model 22298/29464).
- Add 30% for Element electronics (disc.).

* **S6+ Cedar GT Left** – similar to the Coastline Cedar GT (S6+ Cedar GT), except in left-handed configuration (22311), mfg. 2003-05.

	N/A	$275 - 325	$150 - 200	$539

- Add 30% for Quantum EQ electronics (Model 22328).
- Add 30% for Element electronics.

COASTLINE CEDAR BURST GT (S6+ BURST GT) – similar to the S6+, except has a Sunburst finish (22168/29433), mfg. 2003-2011.

	$520	$275 - 325	$165 - 210	$640

- Add 25% (Last MSR was $799) for Quantum EQ electronics (Model 22175/29440).
- Add 30% for Element electronics (disc.).

S6+ CUTAWAY CEDAR – similar to S6, except has a single cutaway (2214/22465), disc. 2006.

	N/A	$250 - 300	$140 - 180	$549

- Add 25% for Quantum EQ electronics (Model 22472).
- Add 25% for Element electronics.
- Add 30% for Quantum II electronics.

* **S6+ Cutaway Cedar Left** – similar to the S6+ Cutaway Cedar, except in left-handed configuration (22502), disc. 2006.

	N/A	$275 - 325	$150 - 200	$609

- Add 25% for Quantum EQ electronics (Model 22519).
- Add 25% for Element electronics.
- Add 30% for Quantum II electronics.

S 6 DELUXE – dreadnought style bound body, solid spruce top, black pickguard, round soundhole, multi stripe rosette, wild cherry back/sides, mahogany neck, 14/21-fret rosewood fingerboard with pearl dot inlay, rosewood bridge with white black dot pins, blackface peghead with screened logo, three-per-side chrome tuners, available in Honeyburst or Natural finish, disc. 1998.

	N/A	$180 - 230	$105 - 135	$435

This model has single round cutaway or left-hand version as an option.

MSR/NOTES	100%	EXCELLENT	AVERAGE	LAST MSR

* **S 12 Deluxe** – similar to S 6 Deluxe, except in 12-string configuration with six-per-side tuners, disc. 1998.

	N/A	$200 - 250	$125 - 160	$495

COASTLINE CEDAR 12 (S 12+) – similar to the S6+, except in 12-string configuration with six-per-side tuners (22106/29358), current mfg.

MSR $620	$500	$265 - 315	$160 - 200	

- Add 25% (MSR $769) for Quantum EQ electronics (Model 22113).
- Add 30% for Element electronics (disc.).

* **Coastline Cedar 12 Left (S12+ Left)** – similar to the Coastline Cedar 12 (S12+), except in left-handed configuration (22137/29365), mfg. 1999-present.

MSR $719	$550	$300 - 375	$175 - 225	

- Add 27.5% (MSR $869) for Quantum EQ electronics (Model 22144/29372).
- Add 30% for Element electronics (disc.).

COASTLINE CEDAR FOLK (S6+ FOLK) – Folk style body, solid cedar top, three-layer wild cherry back, wild cherry sides, silver leaf maple neck, 14/21-fret fingerboard with dot inlay, three-per-side chrome tuners, available in Natural semi-gloss lacquer finish (2474/29518/32549), mfg. 1999-present.

MSR $507	$400	$200 - 250	$110 - 140	

- Add 32.5% (MSR $649) for Quantum EQ electronics (Model 22700/32525/29525).
- Add 30% for Element electronics (disc.).

* **S6+ Folk Left** – similar to the Coastline Cedar Folk (S6+ Folk), except in left-handed configuration (2511), mfg. 1999-2006.

	N/A	$225 - 275	$120 - 150	$489

- Add 30% for Quantum EQ electronics (Model 22519).
- Add 30% for Element electronics.

* **S6+ Folk Cutaway** – similar to the S6+ Folk, except has a single cutaway (25022), mfg. 2004-06.

	N/A	$250 - 300	$140 - 180	$549

- Add 25% for Quantum Electronics (Model 25039).

COASTLINE CEDAR GRAND (S GRAND) – grand sized body, solid cedar top, three-layer wild cherry back, wild cherry sides, silver leaf maple neck, 14/21-fret fingerboard with dot inlay, three-per-side chrome tuners, available in Natural semi-gloss lacquer finish (8728/29242), mfg. 2002-present.

MSR $507	$400	$200 - 250	$110 - 140	

- Add 32.5% (MSR $649) for Quantum EQ electronics (Model 22687/29259).
- Add 35% for Element electronics (disc.).

S 6 MAHOGANY – dreadnought style bound body, solid cedar top, black pickguard, round soundhole, multi stripe rosette, mahogany back/sides/neck, 14/21-fret rosewood fingerboard with pearl dot inlay, rosewood bridge with white black dot pins, blackface peghead with screened logo, three-per-side chrome tuners, available in Natural finish (1767), disc.

	N/A	$200 - 250	$105 - 135	$450

This model has left-handed version as an option (Model 1804).

COASTLINE SPRUCE (S6+ SPRUCE) – similar to the S6+, except has a solid spruce top (22199/29532), current mfg.

MSR $570	$470	$250 - 300	$150 - 190	

- Add 25% (MSR $719) for Quantum EQ electronics (Model 22205/29549).
- Add 30% for Element electronics (disc.).

* **Coastline Spruce Cutaway Slim** – similar to the Coastline Spruce (S6+ Spruce), except has a single cutaway, thinner 1.72 in. width neck, and standard Quantum II electronics (30910), mfg. 2008-present.

MSR $799	$650	$325 - 400	$200 - 250	

COASTLINE S6 CRÉME BRULEE SEMI-GLOSS – dreadnought-style body, select pressure tested solid spruce top, Canadian wild cherry back and sides, round soundhole with rosette, cream body binding, integrated set silver maple neck, 14/21-fret rosewood fingerboard with dot inlays, Seagull-style headstock, three-per-side tuners, rosewood bridge, tortoise pickguard, available in Créme Brulee semi-gloss finish (036271), mfg. 2012-present.

MSR $609	$500	$265 - 315	$160 - 210	

- Add 25% (Last MSR was $759) for Quantum EQ electronics (Model 036288).

S 6 FLAME MAPLE CUTAWAY – round cutaway dreadnought style bound body, solid spruce top, round soundhole, herringbone rosette, maple back/sides, mahogany neck, 21-fret ebony fingerboard with offset dot inlay, ebony bridge with white black dot pins, bound flame maple veneered peghead with screened logo, three-per-side gold tuners, available in Blackburst or Natural finish (2375), disc.

	N/A	$400 - 475	$250 - 300	$895

* **S 6 Flame Maple Micro EQ** – similar to S 6 Flame Maple, except features piezo bridge pickup and onboard EQ (2399), disc.

	N/A	$500 - 575	$300 - 350	$1,084

MSR/NOTES	100%	EXCELLENT	AVERAGE	LAST MSR

SM6 (M6 GLOSS) – round cutaway dreadnought style bound body, solid spruce top, black pickguard, round soundhole, multi stripe rosette, mahogany back/sides/neck, 14/21-fret rosewood fingerboard with pearl dot inlay, rosewood bridge with white black dot pins, blackface peghead with screened logo, three-per-side chrome tuners, available in Natural finish (1927), disc.

| | N/A | $230 - 280 | $130 - 170 | $537 |

* **SM 12 (M12 Spruce)** – similar to SM 6 (M6 Gloss), except in 12-string configuration with six-per-side tuners (1972), disc.

| | N/A | $275 - 325 | $150 - 200 | $620 |

ACOUSTIC: MARITIME (M) SERIES

In 2006, the Maritime Series replaced the M Series. There were not a lot of physical changes except for a new polished lacquer finish and new model number designations.

MARITIME CEDAR GLOSS (M6) – full sized body, solid cedar top, mahogany back and sides, 14/21-fret fingerboard with dot inlay, tortoise pickguard, three-per-side chrome tuners, laquer finished Natural gloss top (29297/22342), mfg. 2003-08.

| | N/A | $225 - 275 | $130 - 170 | $581 |

* Add 30% for Quantum EQ electronics (Model 22359, disc.).
* Add 35% (Last MSR was $789) for Element electronics (Model 22366/29280).

MARITIME SPRUCE GLOSS (M6) – full sized body, solid spruce top, mahogany back and sides, 14/21-fret fingerboard with dot inlay, tortoise pickguard, three-per-side chrome tuners, high gloss lacquer Natural finish (22373/29303), disc. 2008.

| | N/A | $275 - 325 | $150 - 200 | $649 |

* Add 30% for Quantum EQ electronics (Model 22380, disc.).
* Add 32.5% (Last MSR was $859) for Element electronics (Model 22397/29310).

* **M6 Gloss Left-Handed** – similar to the Maritime Spruce Gloss (M6), except in left-handed configuration (22434), disc. 2006.

| | N/A | $300 - 350 | $175 - 225 | $639 |

* Add 30% for Quantum EQ electronics (Model 22441).
* Add 30% for Element electronics (Model 22458).

* **Maritime Cutaway Spruce Gloss** – similar to the Maritime Spruce Gloss (M6), except has a single cutaway and Quantum II electronics, gig bag included (31108), mfg. 2008 only.

| | N/A | $375 - 450 | $225 - 275 | $919 |

* **Maritime Spruce Gloss 12-String (M12)** – similar to the M6 Gloss, except in 12-string configuration with six-per-side tuners (22403/29266), disc. 2008.

| | N/A | $325 - 400 | $175 - 225 | $739 |

* Add 30% for Quantum EQ electronics (Model 22410, disc.).
* Add 30% (Last MSR was $949) for Element electronics (Model 22427/29273).

MARITIME MINI JUMBO (M J M 6) – mini jumbo body, solid spruce top, mahogany back and sides, 14/21-fret fingerboard with dot inlay, tortoise pickguard, three-per-side chrome tuners, High Gloss lacquer Natural finish (26562/29341), mfg. 2005-08.

| | N/A | $275 - 325 | $135 - 175 | $649 |

* Add 27.5% (Last MSR was $822) for Element electronics (Model 26579/29327).

* **Performer Mini Jumbo Cutaway (M J M 6)** – similar to the Maritime Mini Jumbo (M J M 6), except has a single cutaway, Quantum II electronics, and a lacquer finish gloss top and semi-gloss back and sides, Natural finish (26586/29334), mfg. 2005-08.

| | N/A | $425 - 500 | $225 - 275 | $972 |

MARITIME SWS SEMI-GLOSS – dreadnought-style body, select pressure tested solid spruce top, solid mahogany back and sides, round soundhole with rosette, multi-ply body binding, Honduras mahogany neck, 14/20-fret rosewood fingerboard with dot inlays up to the 12th fret, narrow headstock with mahogany overlay and Seagull logos, three-per-side tuners, rosewood bridge, tortoise pickguard, optional Godin Quantum I with tuner electronics, available in Natural Semi-Gloss finish (032686), mfg. 2009-present.

| MSR $769 | $630 | $325 - 400 | $200 - 250 | |

* Add 25% (MSR $925) for Godin Quantum I with tuner electronics (Model 32679).

* **Maritime SWS High-Gloss** – similar to the Maritime SWS, except is available in Natural High-Gloss finish (032419), mfg. 2009-present.

| MSR $869 | $700 | $375 - 450 | $225 - 275 | |

* Add 17.5% (MSR $1,019) for Godin Quantum I with tuner electronics (Model 32426).

MARITIME SWS CUTAWAY CRÉME BRULEE SEMI-GLOSS – single cutaway dreadnought-style body, select pressure tested solid spruce top, solid mahogany back and sides, round soundhole with rosette, multi-ply body binding, integrated set mahogany neck, 14/21-fret rosewood fingerboard with dot inlays, narrow Seagull-style headstock with mahogany overlay and Seagull logos, three-per-side tuners, rosewood bridge, no pickguard, Godin Quantum I with tuner electronics, available in Créme Brulee Semi-Gloss finish (036264), mfg. 2012-present.

| MSR $995 | $800 | $425 - 500 | $250 - 300 | |

MSR/NOTES	100%	EXCELLENT	AVERAGE	LAST MSR

MARITIME SWS FOLK HIGH-GLOSS – folk-style body, select pressure tested solid spruce top, solid mahogany back and sides, round soundhole with rosette, multi-ply body binding, Honduras mahogany neck, 14/20-fret rosewood fingerboard with dot inlays up to the 12th fret, narrow headstock with mahogany overlay and Seagull logos, three-per-side tuners, rosewood bridge, optional Godin Quantum I with tuner electronics, available in Natural High-Gloss finish (032396), mfg. 2009-present.

MSR $869	$700	$375 - 450	$225 - 275	

* Add 17.5% (MSR $1,019) for Godin Quantum I with tuner electronics (Model 32402).

MARITIME SWS MINI JUMBO HIGH-GLOSS – mini jumbo-style body, select pressure tested solid spruce top, solid mahogany back and sides, round soundhole with rosette, multi-ply body binding, Honduras mahogany neck, 14/20-fret rosewood fingerboard with dot inlays up to the 12th fret, narrow headstock with mahogany overlay and Seagull logos, three-per-side tuners, rosewood bridge, tortoise pickguard, optional Godin Quantum I with tuner electronics, available in Natural High-Gloss finish (032433), mfg. 2009-present.

MSR $869	$700	$375 - 450	$225 - 275	

* Add 17.5% (MSR $1,019) for Godin Quantum I with tuner electronics (Model 32440).

MARITIME SWS ROSEWOOD – dreadnought-style body, select pressure tested solid spruce top, solid rosewood back and sides, round soundhole with rosette, multi-ply body binding, Honduras mahogany neck with slim 1.72 in. nut width, 14/20-fret rosewood fingerboard with dot inlays up to the 12th fret, narrow headstock with mahogany overlay and Seagull logos, three-per-side tuners, rosewood bridge, tortoise pickguard, optional Godin Quantum I with tuner electronics, available in Natural Semi-Gloss finish (033607), mfg. 2010-present.

MSR $995	$800	$425 - 500	$250 - 300	

* Add 12.5% (MSR $1,145) for Godin Quantum I with tuner electronics (Model 033614).

ACOUSTIC: PERFORMER SERIES

PERFORMER CUTAWAY CEDAR (S6+ CUTAWAY CEDAR, MODEL 28535) – single cutaway dreadnought-style body, select solid cedar top, mahogany back and sides, round soundhole with rosette, silver leaf maple neck, three-per-side tuners, Quantum I or Quantum II electronics, case included, mfg. 2003-08.

	N/A	$325 - 400	$200 - 250	$815

* Add 7.5% (disc. 2007, Last MSR was $873) for Quantum II electronics (Model 29488/22540).
* Add 10% (Last MSR was $889) for left-handed configuration (Model 28788)

PERFORMER CUTAWAY FLAME MAPLE (MODEL 032464) – single cutaway dreadnought-style body, select pressure treated solid spruce top, flame maple back and sides, round soundhole with rosette, multi-ply body binding, silver leaf maple neck, 14/21-fret rosewood fingerboard with dot inlays up to the 12th fret, narrow headstock with flame maple overlay and Seagull logos, three-per-side chrome tuners, rosewood bridge, tortoise pickguard, Godin Quantum I electronics with tuner, available in Natural High Gloss finish, gig bag included, mfg. 2009-present.

MSR $925	$750	$375 - 475	$225 - 275	

PERFORMER CUTAWAY FOLK FLAME MAPLE (MODEL 032457) – single cutaway folk-style body, select pressure treated solid spruce top, flame maple back and sides, round soundhole with rosette, multi-ply body binding, silver leaf maple neck, 14/21-fret rosewood fingerboard with dot inlays up to the 12th fret, narrow headstock with flame maple overlay and Seagull logos, three-per-side chrome tuners, rosewood bridge, Godin Quantum I electronics with tuner, available in Natural High Gloss finish, gig bag included, mfg. 2009-present.

MSR $925	$750	$375 - 475	$225 - 275	

PERFORMER CUTAWAY MINI-JUMBO FLAME MAPLE (MODEL 032471) – single cutaway mini jumbo-style body, select pressure treated solid spruce top, flame maple back and sides, round soundhole with rosette, multi-ply body binding, silver leaf maple neck, 14/21-fret rosewood fingerboard with dot inlays up to the 12th fret, narrow headstock with flame maple overlay and Seagull logos, three-per-side chrome tuners, rosewood bridge, tortoise pickguard, Godin Quantum I electronics with tuner, available in Natural High Gloss finish, gig bag included, mfg. 2009-present.

MSR $925	$750	$375 - 475	$225 - 275	

PERFORMER FOLK CUTAWAY GT (S6+ FOLK CUTAWAY GT, MODEL 29471/28382) – single cutaway folk-style body, select solid cedar top, mahogany back and sides, round soundhole with rosette, silver leaf maple neck, Quantum I electronics, available in Natural finish with a Gloss top, case included, mfg. 2005-08.

	N/A	$325 - 400	$200 - 250	$815

ACOUSTIC: MISC. MODELS

25TH ANNIVERSARY MAHOGANY SPRUCE HG (MODEL 31313) – dreadnought-style body, solid spruce top, solid mahogany back and sides, round soundhole, mahogany neck, Indian rosewood fingerboard, rosewood headstock overlay, three-per-side deluxe gold tuners with cream buttons, Indian rosewood bridge, commemorative certificate, 25th Anniversary headstock logo, available in High Gloss natural finish, mfg. 2008 only.

	N/A	$325 - 400	$175 - 225	$869

25TH ANNIVERSARY CUTAWAY FLAME MAPLE (MODEL 31320) – single cutaway, solid spruce top, flame maple back and sides, round soundhole, silver leaf maple neck, Indian rosewood fingerboard, flame maple headstock overlay, three-per-side chrome tuners, Indian rosewood bridge, built-in electronics, commemorative certificate, 25th Anniversary headstock logo, mfg. 2008 only.

	N/A	$325 - 400	$175 - 225	$869

MSR/NOTES	100%	EXCELLENT	AVERAGE	LAST MSR

ENTOURAGE – dreadnought body style, select pressure tested solid cedar top, wild cherry back and sides, round soundhole with rings, cream body binding, Silver Leaf maple neck, 14/20-fret rosewood fingerboard with dot inlays, three-per-side chrome tuners, rosewood bridge, available in Rustic Burst semi-gloss varnish finish (Model 29822), 1.72 in. nut width, mfg. 2007-present.

MSR $477	$360	$200 - 250	$120 - 150	

  • Add 25% (MSR $605) for Quantum I electronics (Model 29839).

* *Entourage Cutaway* – similar to the Entourage, except has a single cutaway and standard Quantum I electronics (Model 033430), mfg. 2010-present.

MSR $659	$500	$300 - 350	$175 - 225	

»*Entourage Cutaway GT* – similar to the Entourage Cutaway, except has a gloss top, available in Burgundy (035199) or Rustic (035205) finish, mfg. 2011-present.

MSR $719	$550	$325 - 400	$200 - 250	

* *Entourage Grand* – similar to the Entourage, except has a grand concert body style (Model 035618), mfg. summer 2011-present.

MSR $477	$360	$200 - 250	$120 - 150	

  • Add 25% (MSR $605) for Quantum I electronics (Model 035625).

* *Entourage Mini-Jumbo* – similar to the Entourage, except has a mini-jumbo body style (Model 29846/032914), mfg. 2007-present.

MSR $499	$380	$210 - 260	$125 - 160	

  • Add 30% (MSR $649) for Quantum I electronics (Model 29853/032907).

SEAGULL NATURAL ELEMENTS DREADNOUGHT – dreadnought-style body, solid pressure-tested solid cedar with Natural Cherry back and sides, (036417), solid spruce top with Heart of Wild back and sides (036431), or solid spruce top with figured Amber Trail maple back and sides (036455), round soundhole with rosette, maple body binding, integrated set silver leaf maple neck, 14/21-fret rosewood fingerboard with dot inlays, Seagull-style headstock with flame maple overlay, three-per-side chrome tuners, rosewood bridge, B-band ACI.5T electronics with built-in tuner, available in Natural semi-gloss custom polished finish, mfg. 2012-present.

MSR $750	$550	$325 - 400	$200 - 250	

SEAGULL NATURAL ELEMENTS FOLK CUTAWAY – single cutaway folk-style body, solid pressure-tested solid cedar with Natural Cherry back and sides, (036394), solid spruce top with Heart of Wild back and sides (036424), or solid spruce top with figured Amber Trail maple back and sides (036479), round soundhole with rosette, maple body binding, integrated set silver leaf maple neck, 14/21-fret rosewood fingerboard with dot inlays, Seagull-style headstock with flame maple overlay, three-per-side chrome tuners, rosewood bridge, B-band ACI.5T electronics with built-in tuner, available in Natural semi-gloss custom polished finish, mfg. 2012-present.

MSR $800	$600	$350 - 425	$225 - 275	

SEAGULL NATURAL ELEMENTS MINI-JUMBO CUTAWAY – single cutaway mini jumbo-style body, solid pressure-tested solid cedar with Natural Cherry back and sides, (036400), solid spruce top with Heart of Wild back and sides (036448), or solid spruce top with figured Amber Trail maple back and sides (036462), round soundhole with rosette, maple body binding, integrated set silver leaf maple neck, 14/21-fret rosewood fingerboard with dot inlays, Seagull-style headstock with flame maple overlay, three-per-side chrome tuners, rosewood bridge, B-band ACI.5T electronics with built-in tuner, available in Natural semi-gloss custom polished finish, mfg. 2012-present.

MSR $800	$600	$350 - 425	$225 - 275	

SEBRING

Instruments previously built in Korea. Distributed by V.M.I. Industries of Brea, CA.

Sebring instruments are designed towards the intermediate level guitar student.

SEDONA

Instruments previously built in Asia. Distributed by V.M.I. Industries of Brea, CA.

Sedona offers a range of instruments that appeal to the beginning guitarist and entry level player.

SEGOVIA

Instruments previously produced in Korea and China. Previously distributed by the L.A. Guitar Works of Reseda, CA.

Segovia produces several acoustic models. These may include dreadnoughts, cutaways, folk styles, double arched, classical styles, and acoustic basses. A variety of woods and other features are used in construction. For more information contact their website.

SEKOVA

Instruments previously produced in Japan.

Sekova brand instruments were distributed in the U.S. market by the U.S. Musical Merchandise Corporation of New York, New York. Source: Michael Wright, *Guitar Stories*, Volume One.

MSR/NOTES	100%	EXCELLENT	AVERAGE	LAST MSR

HENRI SELMER & CO.

Instruments previously built in Paris, France between 1931 and 1952.

Between 1931 and 1932, Mario Maccaferri designed and built a series of instruments for the French Selmer company. They were originally referred to as the "modele Concert," and featured a "D" shaped soundhole. Although they were used by such notables as Django Reinhardt, a dispute between the company and Maccaferri led to a short production run. In the two years (1931-1932) that Maccaferri was with Selmer, he estimated that perhaps 200 guitars were built. After Macaferri left the business arrangement, the Selmer company continued to produce acoustic guitar models that featured an oval soundhole and a longer scale. All in all, an estimated 950 guitars were built (source: Paul Hostetter, Guitares Maurice Dupont).

SEXAUER

Instruments currently hand built in Petaluma, CA. Previously built in Sausalito, CA 1979-1999, and in Vancouver (British Columbia), Canada from 1967 through 1977.

CONTACT INFORMATION
SEXAUER
724 H Street
Petaluma, CA 94952
Phone No.: 707-782-1044
www.sexauerluthier.com
bruce@mojoluthier.com

Luthier Bruce Sexauer has been handcrafting contemporary flattop acoustic guitars since 1967. For the last several years, Sexauer has become increasingly interested in Archtop guitars, and in addition to his quality carved tops has become well-known for his highly innovative **Coo'stik Dominator** (a successful interpretation of the Selmer/Macaferri concept). For more information and options contact Sexauer directly.

While Sexauer continues to build true custom guitars, he also offers several standard models. The noted prices represent the simplest trim level, and most customers choose to indulge themselves somewhat more. The Parlor model starts at $6,000. The FT-15 ($7,50) is a concert sized flattop model, while the FT-16 ($7,500) is full sized. Sexauer offers a jazz-style hand carved archtop model in both a 16 in. body width, and 17 in. body width (JZ-17), and the prices range from $6,000-$10,000 for most models. For $12,500 it will build an instrument that "would intimidate almost anybody. His Coo'stik Dominator and the Blu'stik Harmonizer are also available.

SHANTI

Instruments currently built in Avery, CA, since 1985.

CONTACT INFORMATION
SHANTI
PO Box 310
Avery, CA 95224
Phone No.: 209-795-5299

Luthier Michael Hornick has been handcrafting acoustic guitars under the Shanti trademark for the past several years. All guitars are designed with input from the commissioning player, so specifications on woods and inlay work will vary. Contact Michael Hornick for further details.

Hornick produces about nine or ten guitars a year. In addition, Hornick hosts a mandolin-building course each year at the RockyGrass Festival in Lyons, Colorado; and has been affiliated with the Troubadour singer/songwriter competition in Telluride, Colorado for a good number of years.

SHENANDOAH

Instruments previously assembled from imported Japanese components in Nazareth, PA between 1983 and 1996. Distributed by the C.F. Martin Guitar Company of Nazarath, PA.

Shenandoah production began in 1983. Initially viewed as a way to offer entry level models for Martin dealers, Shenandoah models featured Japanese-built unfinished body and neck kits imported to the Martin plant for final assembly and finishing. However, Shenandoah guitars are not as ornate, and may feature different construction methods than the Martin models.

While this may have been cost effective to some degree, the labor intensive work of assembly and finishing at the Martin plant led Martin to considering producing the whole guitar in Nazareth - which led to the introduction of Martin's U.S.-built **Road** and **1** Series.

Instruments were produced in Japan and assembled in the U.S. between 1983 to 1993; full Japanese production was featured between 1994 and 1996. Shenandoah model codes add a -32 suffix after a Martin-style model designation. Thus, a D-1832 is Shenandoah's version of a D-18. Models carrying a CS prefix designation indicate a custom model, usually fancier than the standard version (custom models were built in limited runs of twenty-five instruments).

ACOUSTIC

Some models have a factory installed thinline bridge pickup. Most models feature a tortoiseshell pickguard, and laminated back/sides.

C-20 – classic style, solid spruce top, round soundhole, wooden bound body, wooden inlay rosette, rosewood back/sides, nato neck, 12/19-fret ebonized rosewood fingerboard, ebonized rosewood tied bridge, rosewood peghead veneer, 3-per-side gold tuners with pearl buttons, available in Natural or Yellow Stained Top finish.

	N/A	$600 - 700	$300 - 375	$1,280

This model had no factory installed pickup.

MSR/NOTES	100%	EXCELLENT	AVERAGE	LAST MSR

D-1832 – dreadnought style, solid spruce top, round soundhole, tortoise pickguard, 3-stripe bound body/rosette, mahogany back/sides, nato neck, 14/20-fret rosewood fingerboard with pearl dot inlay, rosewood bridge with black pins, rosewood peghead veneer, 3-per-side chrome tuners, available in Natural finish.

	N/A	$500 - 600	$250 - 300	$1,075

D-1932 – similar to D-1832, except has quilted mahogany veneer back/sides.

	N/A	$600 - 700	$300 - 375	$1,320

• Add $20 for 12-string version (D12-1932).

D-2832 – dreadnought style, solid spruce top, round soundhole, tortoise pickguard, three-stripe bound body/rosette, rosewood back/sides, nato neck, 14/20-fret ebonized rosewood fingerboard with pearl dot inlay, ebonized rosewood bridge with white black dot pins, rosewood peghead veneer, three-per-side chrome tuners, available in Natural finish, mfg. 1984-1992.

	N/A	$625 - 750	$325 - 400	$1,125

• Add $75 for 12-string version of this model (D12-2832).

* *HD-2832* – similar to D-2832, except has herringbone purfling.

	N/A	$650 - 800	$350 - 425	

D-3532 – similar to D-2832, except has bound fingerboard.

	N/A	$625 - 750	$325 - 400	$1,175

D-4132 – similar to D-2832, except has abalone bound body/rosette, bound fingerboard with abalone hexagon inlay, white abalone dot bridge pins, bound peghead, gold tuners.

	N/A	$850 - 1,000	$550 - 650	$1,750

D-6032 – similar to D-2832, tortoise binding, except has bird's-eye maple back/sides.

	N/A	$650 - 800	$350 - 425	$1,320

D-6732 – dreadnought style body, solid spruce top, round soundhole, tortoise pickguard, tortoise binding, 3-stripe rosette, quilted ash back/sides, nato neck, 14/20-fret bound ebonized rosewood neck with pearl dot inlay, pearl vine/diamond inlay at 12th fret, ebonized rosewood bridge with white black dot pins, bound peghead with quilted ash veneer, 3-per-side gold tuners with ebony buttons, available in Natural finish.

	N/A	$700 - 850	$400 - 475	$1,490

SE-2832 – single round cutaway folk style, solid spruce top, round soundhole, 3-stripe bound body/rosette, rosewood back/sides, nato neck, 14/21-fret bound ebonized rosewood fingerboard with pearl diamond inlay, ebonized rosewood bridge with white black dot pins, rosewood veneer peghead, 3-per-side chrome tuners, active EQ with volume/treble/mid/bass slider control, available in Natural or Sunburst Top finish.

	N/A	$650 - 800	$350 - 425	$1,470

SE-6032 – similar to SE-2832, except has tortoise binding, bird's-eye maple back/sides/peghead veneer, pearl tuner buttons, available in Burgundy Burst, Dark Sunburst, or Natural finish.

	N/A	$700 - 850	$400 - 475	$1,540

000-2832 – folk style, solid spruce top, round soundhole, tortoiseshell pickguard, 3-stripe bound body/rosette, rosewood back/sides, nato neck, 14/20-fret ebonized rosewood fingerboard with pearl dot inlay, ebonized rosewood bridge with white black dot pins, rosewood peghead veneer with abalone torch inlay, 3-per-side chrome tuners, available in Natural finish.

	N/A	$625 - 750	$325 - 400	$1,210

SHERWOOD

See chapter on House Brands.

This trademark has been identified as a House Brand of Montgomery Wards (source: Willie G. Moseley, *Stellas & Stratocasters*).

SHINANO

Instruments previously produced in Japan during the 1960s and 1970s.

Shinano was a trademark and possibly the name of a luthier who built classical guitars in Japan during the 1960s and 1970s. It is reported that Shinano guitars were distributed by Daion, but it is unknown if Shinano guitars were distributed in the U.S. by Daion's distributor MCI, Inc. in Waco, TX. Shinano guitars appear to built of mid- to high quality, but it is unknown if they were factory or hand-built. Any further information on Shinano can be submitted directly to Blue Book Publications.

SHO-BUD

Also Sho-Bro. Instruments previously built in the U.S. during circa early 1970s. Distributed through the Gretsch Guitar company catalog between 1972 and 1975; possibly as late as 1979.

While this company is best known for their pedal steel guitars, the company did produce a number of acoustic guitars. Sho-Bud and Sho-Bro guitars were designed by Shot Jackson (known for his Sho-Bud pedal steel guitars). Two models appear in the Gretsch catalogs of the early 1970s: The **Sho Bro**, a resonator with a single cutaway body and dot fingerboard inlays; and

MSR/NOTES	100%	EXCELLENT	AVERAGE	LAST MSR

the **Sho Bud**, a non-cutaway model with inlays similar to the Sho-Bud lap steels (the four suits of the card deck, information courtesy John Brinkmann, Waco Vintage Instruments; and John Sheridan).

Sho-Bro resonator guitars in the early 1970s featured a 17 in. body (4 5/8 in. body depth) with maple back and sides, bound rosewood fingerboard, 3-per-side polished plated geared tuners, metal resonator, 2 grill covered soundholes. The **Model 6031 Hawaiian** model has a squared neck, and playing card suites fingerboard inlays; the **Model 6030 Spanish** model has a rounded neck and "thumbprint" fingerboard inlays.

Later Sho-Bud acoustics have spruce tops and mahogany necks. The **Club (Model 7720)** features mahogany sides, and a 2-piece back; the **Diamond (Model 7722)** features rosewood sides and the 2-piece back. The **Heart (Model 7724)** has rosewood back and sides, mother-of-pearl inlays, and abalone purfling; the **Spade (Model 7726)** features a rosewood fingerboard, ebony bridge, and abalone bridge pins. The aptly named **Grand Slam (Model 7728)** has jacaranda back and sides, and an inlaid heel plate.

Sho-Bud and Sho-Bro acoustic guitars turn up infrequently at guitar shows. Average prices run from $600 to $1,000; buyers in the market have more control in the buy/sell arena by choking up on their wallets similar to big league baseball players choking up on their bats during a big ball game!

SHUTT

Instruments previously built in Topeka, Kansas circa 1900s.

Not much information is known about the Shutt instruments. Any further information on Shutt can be submitted directly to Blue Book Publications.

SIGMA

Instruments currently produced in Asia. Distributed by St. Louis Music, Inc. in St. Louis, MO. Previously produced in Japan between 1970 and 1983, Korea between 1983 and 1993, and Taiwan between 1994 and 2007. Final finishing/inspection occured in Nazareth, PA at the Martin factory.

In 1970, the Martin Guitar Company expanded its product line by introducing the Sigma line. The instruments begin their assembly in Japan, and then were shipped to Martin's factory in Nazareth, PA where they performed final finishing and setup. While Sigma was generally recognized and advertised as being around consistently since 1970, it has not appeared on a consistent basis from Martin. The last line of Martin guitars was produced until circa 1996, and a new line was introduced in 2006 that was distributed by Musicorp. In 2013, St. Louis Music, Inc. announced that they were managing and distributing the Sigma Line.

ACOUSTIC: CLASSICAL MODELS

CS-1 – classic style, spruce top, round soundhole, bound body, wooden inlay rosette, mahogany back/sides/neck, 20/19-fret ebonized fingerboard/tied bridge, 3-per-side chrome tuners, available in Antique Stain finish, disc. 1996.

	N/A	$70 - 100	$40 - 60	$210

CS-1 ST – classic style, solid spruce top, round soundhole, bound body, wood inlay rosette, mahogany back/sides/neck, 14/19-fret ebonized fingerboard, ebonized tied bridge, 3-per-side chrome tuners with nylon buttons, available in Natural finish, mfg. 1994-96.

	N/A	$130 - 160	$80 - 100	$335

CS-2 – classic style, spruce top, round soundhole, bound body, wooden inlay rosette, mahogany back/sides/neck, 20/19-fret ebonized fingerboard/tied bridge, 3-per-side chrome tuners, available in Natural finish, disc. 1994.

	N/A	$120 - 150	$70 - 90	$295

CS-4 – classic style, spruce top, round soundhole, bound body, wooden inlay rosette, mahogany back/sides/neck, 12/19-fret rosewood fingerboard, rosewood tied bridge, rosewood peghead veneer, 3-per-side chrome tuners with pearl buttons, available in Antique finish, disc. 1996.

	N/A	$135 - 165	$85 - 105	$340

CR-8 – classic style, solid spruce top, round soundhole, bound body, wooden inlay rosette, rosewood back/sides, mahogany neck, 12/19-fret ebonized fingerboard/tied bridge, 3-per-side gold tuners with pearl buttons, available in Natural finish, disc. 1996.

	N/A	$200 - 250	$100 - 150	$570

ACOUSTIC: DREADNOUGHT (DM) MODELS

DM-1 – dreadnought style, laminated spruce top, round soundhole, bound body, three-stripe rosette, laminated mahogany back and sides, mahogany neck, 14/20-fret rosewood fingerboard with pearl dot inlay, three-per-side chrome tuners, rosewood bridge with black pins, black pickguard, available in Natural or Black finish, disc. 2007.

	N/A	$135 - 175	$80 - 105	$335

* Add $25 for 12-string version (DM12-1).

* *DM-1 ST* – similar to the DM-1, except has a solid spruce top, available in Natural finish, mfg. 1994-2007.

	N/A	$160 - 210	$95 - 120	$415

MSR/NOTES	100%	EXCELLENT	AVERAGE	LAST MSR

»*DM-1ST CE Cutaway Electric* – similar to the DM-1ST, except has a single cutaway and electronics, disc. 2007.

	N/A	$225 - 275	$120 - 150	$530

»*DR-1 ST* – similar to DM-1 ST, except has rosewood back/sides, mfg. 1994-96.

	N/A	$140 - 170	$90 - 110	$375

»*DM12-1 ST 12-String* – similar to DM-1 ST, except in 12-string configuration and six-per-side tuners, mfg. 1994-96.

	N/A	$150 - 200	$100 - 120	$410

DM-2 – dreadnought style, spruce top, round soundhole, tortoiseshell pickguard, 3-stripe bound body/rosette, mahogany back/sides/neck, 14/20-fret rosewood fingerboard with pearl dot inlay, rosewood bridge with black white dot pins, 3-per-side chrome tuners, available in Natural finish, disc. 1994.

	N/A	$200 - 250	$110 - 140	$375

* **Add $45 for 12-string version (DM12-2).**

DM-2E/WH – similar to DM-2, except has ebonized fingerboard/bridge, acoustic pickup, 3-band EQ with volume control, available in White finish, disc. 1994.

	N/A	$225 - 275	$125 - 175	$630

* **Add $25 for single round cutaway, white black dot bridge pins. Available in Black finish (DM-2CE/B).**

DM-4 – dreadnought style, spruce top, round soundhole, black pickguard, 3-stripe bound body/rosette, mahogany back/sides/neck, 14/20-fret ebonized fingerboard with pearl dot inlay, pearl horizontal teardrop inlay at 12th fret, ebonized bridge with black white dot pins, rosewood peghead veneer, 3-per-side chrome tuners, available in Black or Natural finish, disc. 1996.

	N/A	$175 - 225	$105 - 130	$430

* **Add $30 for Black finish.**
* **Add $40 for 12-string version (DM12-4).**
* **Add $40 for left handed version (DM-4L).**
* **Subtract $20 for stained mahogany top (DM-4M).**

* **Add $45 for herringbone bound body/rosette (DM-4H).**
* **Add $45 for Antique and Tobacco Sunburst finishes (DM-4Y and DM-4S).**

In 1994, Antique finish (DM-4Y) was discontinued.

* *DM-4C* – similar to DM-4, except has single round cutaway, mfg. 1994-96.

	N/A	$200 - 250	$120 - 150	$505

* **Add $45 for Black finish.**

* *DM-4CV* – similar to DM-4, except has venetian cutaway, available in Violin finish, disc.

	N/A	$225 - 275	$135 - 170	$560

* *DM-4C/3B* – similar to DM-4, except has single round cutaway, acoustic pickup, 3-band EQ with volume control, available in Natural finish, disc. 1994.

	N/A	$300 - 350	$175 - 225	$715

* *DM12-4* – similar to DM-4, except has 12 strings, 6-per-side tuners, mfg. 1994-96.

	N/A	$200 - 250	$120 - 150	$470

DM-18 – dreadnought style, solid spruce top, round soundhole, tortoise pickguard, 3-stripe bound body/rosette, mahogany back/sides/neck, 14/20-fret ebonized fingerboard with pearl dot inlay, ebonized bridge with black white dot pins, abalone logo peghead inlay, 3-per-side chrome tuners, available in Natural finish, disc. 1996.

	N/A	$275 - 325	$150 - 200	$525

ACOUSTIC: DREADNOUGHT (DR, DT, & DV) MODELS

DR-2 – similar to DM-2, except has rosewood back/sides, ebonized fingerboard/bridge, disc. 1994.

	N/A	$225 - 275	$120 - 150	$510

DR-4H – similar to DM-4, except has tortoise pickguard, herringbone bound body/rosette, rosewood back/sides, available in Natural finish, disc.

	N/A	$275 - 325	$150 - 200	$510

DR-28 – dreadnought style, solid spruce top, round soundhole, tortoiseshell pickguard, 3-stripe bound body/rosette, rosewood back/sides, mahogany neck, 14/20-fret ebonized fingerboard with pearl dot inlay, ebonized bridge with white abalone dot pins, rosewood veneered peghead with abalone logo inlay, 3-per-side chrome tuners, available in Natural finish, disc. 1996.

	N/A	$300 - 350	$175 - 225	$620

* *DR-28H* – similar to DR-28, except has herringbone bound body, pearl diamond fingerboard inlay, disc. 1996.

	N/A	$325 - 400	$200 - 250	$670

* **Add $35 for 12-string version (DR12-28H), mfg. 1993-96.**

MSR/NOTES	100%	EXCELLENT	AVERAGE	LAST MSR

DR-35 – dreadnought style, solid spruce top, round soundhole, tortoiseshell pickguard, 5-stripe bound body/rosette, rosewood back/sides, mahogany neck, 14/20-fret bound ebonized fingerboard with pearl dot inlay, ebonized bridge with white abalone dot pins, bound rosewood veneered peghead with abalone logo inlay, 3-per-side chrome tuners, available in Natural finish, disc. 1996.

	N/A	$325 - 400	$200 - 250	$655

DR-41 – dreadnought style, solid spruce top, round soundhole, pearloid bound body/rosette, rosewood back/sides, mahogany neck, 14/20-fret bound rosewood fingerboard with abalone hexagon inlay, bound rosewood veneered peghead with abalone logo inlay, three-per-side chrome tuners, rosewood bridge with white abalone dot pins, tortoiseshell pickguard, available in Natural finish, disc. 2007.

	N/A	$300 - 350	$150 - 200	$675

DR-45 – dreadnought style, solid spruce top, round soundhole, tortoiseshell pickguard, abalone bound body/rosette, rosewood back/sides, mahogany neck, 14/20-fret abalone bound rosewood fingerboard with abalone hexagon inlay, rosewood bridge with white abalone dot pins, abalone bound rosewood veneered peghead with abalone logo inlay, 3-per-side gold tuners, available in Natural finish, mfg. 1994-96.

	N/A	$825 - 950	$525 - 600	$1,745

DT-4N – similar to DM-4, except has chestnut back/sides/peghead veneer, available in Violin finish, disc.

	N/A	$175 - 225	$100 - 130	$495

* Add $35 for Violin finish (DT-4).
* Add $75 for 12-string version (DT12-4).

DV-4 – similar to DM-4, except has ovangkol back/sides, available in Antique finish, disc. 1994.

	N/A	$250 - 300	$100 - 130	$595

ACOUSTIC: MISC. MODELS

FD-16M – folk style, spruce top, round soundhole, black pickguard, bound body, 3-stripe rosette, mahogany back/sides/neck, 14/20-fret ebonized fingerboard with pearl dot inlay, ebonized bridge with black pins, 3-per-side chrome tuners, available in Natural finish, mfg. 1994-96.

	N/A	$175 - 225	$100 - 130	$460

FDM-1 – similar to DM-1, except has folk style body, mfg. 1994-96.

	N/A	$90 - 120	$60 - 80	$255

GCS-1 – similar to DM-1, except has grand concert style body, disc. 1996.

	N/A	$120 - 150	$70 - 95	$260

GCS-2 – similar to DM-2, except has grand concert style body, disc. 1994.

	N/A	$150 - 200	$95 - 120	$420

GCS-4 – grand concert style, spruce top, round soundhole, black pickguard, 5-stripe bound body/rosette, mahogany back/sides/neck, 14/20-fret ebonized fingerboard with pearl dot inlay, horizontal teardrop inlay at 12th fret, ebonized bridge with black white dot pins, rosewood peghead veneer, 3-per-side chrome tuners, available in Natural finish, disc. 1996.

	N/A	$200 - 250	$120 - 150	$395

* **GCS-4C** – similar to GCS-4, except has single round cutaway, disc. 1994.

	N/A	$250 - 300	$135 - 175	$550

* **GCS-4C/3B** – similar to GCS-4, except has single round cutaway, acoustic pickup, 3-band EQ with volume control, disc. 1994.

	N/A	$300 - 350	$150 - 200	$715

000-18M – auditorium style, solid spruce top, round soundhole, tortoise pickguard, 3-stripe bound body, 5-stripe rosette, mahogany back/sides/neck, 14/20-fret ebonized fingerboard with pearl dot inlay, ebonized bridge with black white dot pins, rosewood peghead veneer with abalone logo inlay, 3-per-side chrome tuners, available in Antique finish, mfg. 1993-96.

	N/A	$190 - 240	$110 - 140	$525

* **000-18MC/3B** – similar to 000-18M, except has venetian cutaway, acoustic pickup, 3-band EQ with volume control, disc. 1994.

	N/A	$425 - 500	$225 - 275	$940

SE-1 – single round cutaway folk style, spruce top, round soundhole, 3-stripe bound body/rosette, mahogany back/sides/neck, 22-fret bound ebonized fingerboard with pearl dot inlay, ebonized bridge with white black dot pins, rosewood peghead veneer with abalone logo inlay, 3-per-side chrome tuners, acoustic pickup, volume/2-band EQ control, available in Black or Natural finish, mfg. 1994-96.

	N/A	$250 - 300	$120 - 150	$565

SE-18/2BC – single round cutaway folk style, spruce top, round soundhole, 3-stripe bound body/rosette, mahogany back/sides/neck, 22-fret bound ebonized fingerboard with pearl dot inlay, ebonized bridge with white black dot pins, rosewood peghead veneer with abalone logo inlay, 3-per-side chrome tuners, acoustic pickup, 2-band EQ with chorus effect, volume control, available in Black, Natural, Red, or Tobacco Sunburst finish, mfg. 1993-94.

	N/A	$400 - 475	$200 - 250	$905

* **SE-18/3B** – similar to SE-18/2BC, except has 3-band EQ with volume control, available in Natural or Tobacco Sunburst finish, mfg. 1993-94.

	N/A	$375 - 450	$200 - 250	$860

MSR/NOTES	100%	EXCELLENT	AVERAGE	LAST MSR

TB-1 – single cutaway 000-sized auditorium body, laminated spruce top, laminated mahogany back and sides, body binding, three-ring rosette, mahogany neck, 18/20-fret rosewood fingerboard with dot inlay, three-per-side chrome tuners, rosewood bridge, electronics, available in Black, Blue, or Natural finish, disc. 2007.

	N/A	$190 - 240	$130 - 160	$480

• **Add 7.5% for Black or Blue finish with gold tuners and neck binding.**

ACOUSTIC BASS

STB-M/E – jumbo style, spruce top, round soundhole, tortoise pickguard, 5-stripe bound body/rosette, maple back/sides/neck, 15/21-fret ebonized fingerboard with pearl dot inlay, ebonized strings through bridge with pearl dot inlay, maple peghead veneer, 2-per-side chrome tuners, acoustic pickup, 3-band EQ with volume control, available in Natural finish, mfg. 1993-96.

	N/A	$500 - 575	$325 - 375	$1,145

* *STB-R/E* – similar to STB-M, except has black pickguard, rosewood back/sides.

	N/A	$500 - 575	$325 - 375	$1,160

* *STB-M* – similar to STB-M/E, except has no acoustic pickup, 3-band EQ with volume control, mfg. 1994-96.

	N/A	$350 - 400	$200 - 250	$785

• **Add $15 for black pickguard, rosewood back/sides.**

SIGNET

Instruments previously produced in Japan circa early 1970s.

The Signet trademark was a brand name used by U.S. importers Ampeg/Selmer. Source: Michael Wright, *Guitar Stories*, Volume One.

SILVERTONE

Instruments currently produced in Asia and distributed by Samick. Instruments previously produced in the U.S. from circa 1940s-1970s. See chapter on House Brands.

CONTACT INFORMATION
SILVERTONE
Distributed by Samick Music Corporation
575 Airport Road
Gallatin, TN 37066
Phone No.: 615-206-0077
Fax No.: 615-452-0451
www.silvertoneguitar.com
info@smcmusic.com

This trademark has been identified as a House Brand owned and used by Sears and Roebuck between 1941 and 1970. There was no company or factory; Sears owned the name and applied it to various products from such manufacturers as Harmony, Valco, Danelectro, and Kay. Sears and Roebuck acquired Harmony in 1916 to control its respectable ukulele production. Harmony generally sold around forty percent of its guitar production to Sears. The following is a word of caution: Just because it says Silvertone, do not automatically assume it is a Danelectro! In fact, study the guitar to determine possible origin (Harmony, Valco and Kay were originally built in Illinois, Danelectro in New Jersey; so all were U.S. However, mid-1960s models were built in Japan by Teisco, as well!). Best of all, play it! If it looks good, and sounds okay - it was meant to be played. As most Silvertones were sold either through the catalog or in a store, they will generally be entry level quality instruments.

Certain Silvertone models have garnered some notoriety, such as the Danelectro-produced combination of guitar and amp-in-case. Sears also marketed the Teisco company's TRG-1 (or TRE-100) electric guitar with amp built in! This guitar has a six-on-a-side "Silvertone" headstock, and a single cutaway pregnant Telecaster body design (the small built-in speaker is in the tummy). Harmony produced a number of electric hollowbody guitars (like the Sovereign) for the Silvertone label; Kay also offered a version of their Thin Twin model as well as arch top models.

Today, Silvertone guitars are being produced by Samick. They have a wide variety of acoustic models from dreadnoughts to classicals. Prices are targeted to those who are entry to mid level guitar players. Paul Stanley of Kiss is an endorser of Silvertone now (c. 2002), and has an entire line of guitars including an acoustic model. For more information, contact Silvertone/Samick directly or visit their website.

ACOUSTIC: CURRENT MFG.

SD10 – dreadnought body style, nato mahogany top, back, and sides, pearloid rosette, 14/20-fret rosewood bridge with dot inlay, three-per-side chrome tuners, rosewood bridge, pickguard, High Gloss Black finish, current mfg.

MSR $182	$160	$100 - 130	$50 - 70	

SD20 – dreadnought body style, select spruce top, nato mahogany back, and sides, pearloid rosette, 14/20-fret rosewood bridge with dot inlay, three-per-side chrome tuners, rosewood bridge, pickguard, available in Natural, Trans. Black, Trans. Blue, or Trans. Red finish, current mfg.

MSR $229	$170	$110 - 140	$60 - 80	

* *SD20CE Cutaway Electric* – similar to the SD20, except has a single cutaway and electronics, available in Natural or Trans. Black finish, disc.

	$270	$140 - 180	$90 - 110	$360

MSR/NOTES	100%	EXCELLENT	AVERAGE	LAST MSR

SD50 – dreadnought body style, solid Sitka spruce top, striped mahogany back, and sides, abalone-style rosette, 14/20-fret rosewood bridge with dot inlay, three-per-side gold tuners, rosewood bridge, pickguard, available in Natural finish, disc.

	$270	$140 - 180	$90 - 110	$360

SF26 – folk body style, select spruce top, figured nato mahogany back and sides, pearloid rosette, 12/18-fret rosewood bridge with dot inlay, three-per-side chrome tuners, rosewood bridge, available in Natural finish, disc.

	$170	$90 - 120	$50 - 70	$228

SIMON & PATRICK

Instruments currently built in La Patrie, Quebec, Canada since 1985. Distributed by Godin Guitars (previously La Si Do, Inc.) in Baie D'Urfe Quebec, Canada.

CONTACT INFORMATION
SIMON & PATRICK
Distributed by Godin Guitars
19420 Clark Graham Ave.
Baie d'Urfe, QC H9X 3R8
Phone No.: 514-457-7977
Fax No.: 514-457-5774
www.simonandpatrick.com

Robert Godin set up a custom guitar shop in Montreal called Harmonilab in 1968. Harmonilab quickly became known for its excellent work and musicians were coming from as far away as Quebec City to have their guitars adjusted.

Although Harmonilab's business was flourishing, Robert was full of ideas for the design and construction of acoustic guitars. So in 1972 the Norman Guitar Company was born. From the beginning the Norman guitars showed signs of the innovations that Godin would eventually bring to the guitar market.

By 1978 Norman guitars had become quite successful in Canada and France. In 1980 Godin introduced the Seagull guitar. With many innovations like a bolt-on neck, pointed headstock and a handmade solid top, the Seagull was designed for an ease of play for the entry level to intermediate guitar player. Godin borrowed the finishing idea that was used on fine violins (a satin-finish lacquer), and applied it to the acoustic guitar.

Acceptance of this new guitar spread, and by 1985 La Si Do was incorporated and the factory in La Patrie expanded to meet the growing demand. In 1985 Godin introduced the Simon & Patrick line (named after his two sons) for people interested in a more traditional instrument. Simon & Patrick guitars still maintained a number of Seagull innovations. For full company history, see Godin.

ACOUSTIC: WOODLAND (S&P) SERIES

In 2006, the Woodland Series replaced the regular S&P models and the Vintage Burst Series replaced the Sunburst models. Most models are exactly the same with new number designations.

WOODLAND 6 CEDAR (S&P 6 CEDAR) – solid cedar top, wild cherry back and sides, rosewood fingerboard and bridge, three-per-side headstock, lacquer finish (Model 2719/28955), current mfg.

MSR $530	$440	$230 - 280	$135 - 170	

- Add 22.5% (MSR $665) for B-Band A3.2 Electronics (Model 20041/28962).
- Add 50% for B-Band NF-1 EQ electronics (Model 15276, disc.).
- Add 75% for B-Band NF-2 EQ electronics (Model 15283, disc.).

* *Woodland 6 Cedar Left (S&P 6 Cedar Left)* – similar to the Woodland 6 Cedar (S&P 6 Cedar), except in left-handed configuration (Model 2757/28979), current mfg.

MSR $570	$470	$250 - 300	$150 - 185	

- Add 25% (MSR $689) for B-Band A3.2 Electronics (Model 20065/28986).
- Add 50% for B-Band NF-1 EQ electronics (Model 15375, disc.).
- Add 75% for B-Band NF-2 EQ electronics (Model 15382, disc.).

* *S&P 6 Cedar Tobaccoburst* – similar to the Woodland 6 Cedar (S&P 6 Cedar), except has a Tobaccoburst finish (Model 13616), disc.

	N/A	$225 - 275	$125 - 175	$485

- Add $150 for B-Band NF-1 EQ electronics (Model 15290).
- Add $250 for B-Band NF-2 EQ electronics (Model 15306).

* *S&P 6 Cedar Cutaway* – similar to Woodland 6 Cedar (S&P 6 Cedar), except has a single cutaway (Model 2559), disc. 2003.

	N/A	$235 - 285	$135 - 185	$520

- Add $150 for B-Band NF-1 EQ electronics (Model 15177).
- Add $250 for B-Band NF-2 EQ electronics (Model 15283).

* *Woodland 6 Cutaway Cedar GT (S&P 6 Cedar Cutaway GT)* – similar to the Woodland 6 Cedar (S&P 6 Cedar), except has a single cutaway, B-Band A3.2 electronics, and a lacquer finish gloss top and semi-gloss back and sides (Model 25015/29013), disc. 2009.

	N/A	$375 - 450	$225 - 275	$909

* *Vintage Burst 6 Cedar (S&P 6 Cedar Sunburst)* – similar to the Woodland 6 Cedar (S&P 6 Cedar), except has a high-gloss Sunburst finish (Model 19915/28993), disc. 2009.

	N/A	$275 - 325	$150 - 200	$675

- Add 20% (Last MSR was $810) for B-Band A3.2 electronics (Model 19922/29006).

MSR/NOTES	100%	EXCELLENT	AVERAGE	LAST MSR

* *Vintage Burst 6 Cedar Cutaway (S&P 6 Cedar Cutaway Sunburst)* – similar to the Woodland 6 Cedar (S&P 6 Cedar), except has a single cutaway, B-Band A3.2 electronics, and a high-gloss Sunburst finish (Model 21666/29020), disc. 2009.

	N/A	$400 - 475	$250 - 300	$979

WOODLAND 12 CEDAR (S&P 12 CEDAR) – similar to Woodland 6 Cedar (S&P 6 Cedar), except in 12-string configuration with six-per-side tuners (2733/28870), disc. 2007.

	N/A	$250 - 300	$150 - 185	$536

- Add 25% (Last MSR was $672) for B-Band A3.2 Electronics (Model 20263/28887).
- Add 40% for B-Band NF-1 EQ electronics (Model 15351, disc.).
- Add 70% for B-Band NF-2 EQ electronics (Model 15368, disc.).

* *Woodland 12 Cedar Left (S&P 12 Cedar Left)* – similar to Woodland 12 Cedar (S&P 12 Cedar), except in left-handed configuration (Model 2771/28894), disc. 2007.

	N/A	$275 - 325	$165 - 205	$599

- Add 22.5% (Last MSR was $735) for B-Band A3.2 Electronics (Model 20287/28900).

* *Vintage Burst 12 Cedar (S&P 12 Cedar Sunburst)* – similar to the Woodland 12 Cedar (S&P 12 Cedar), except has a high-gloss Sunburst finish (Model 21628/28917), disc. 2009.

	N/A	$300 - 350	$175 - 225	$739

- Add 20% (Last MSR was $879) for A3.2 electronics (Model 28924).

S&P 6 CEDAR MAHOGANY – similar to the S&P 6, only has mahogany back and sides instead of wild-cherry, and has a satin lacquer finish (Model 2870), disc. 2003.

	N/A	$200 - 250	$120 - 160	$450

- Add $150 for B-Band NF-1 EQ electronics (Model 15450).
- Add $250 for B-Band NF-2 EQ electronics (Model 15467).
- Add $40 for left-handed configuration (Model 2894).

WOODLAND 6 SPRUCE (S&P 6 SPRUCE) – similar to the Woodland 6 Cedar (S&P 6 Cedar), except has a solid spruce top (Model 2795/29099), current mfg.

MSR $569	$470	$250 - 300	$150 - 190	

- Add 22.5% (MSR $705) for B-Band A3.2 Electronics (Model 20089/29105).
- Add 50% for B-Band NF-1 EQ electronics (Model 15375, disc.).
- Add 75% for B-Band NF-2 EQ electronics (Model 15184, disc.).

* *Woodland 6 Spruce Cutaway (S&P 6 Spruce Cutaway)* – similar to Woodland 6 Spruce (S&P 6 Spruce), except has a single cutaway and optional B-Band NF-1 EQ (Model 15191, disc.), B-Band NF-2 EQ (Model 15207, disc.), or B-Band A3.2 Electronics (Model 20249/29044), current mfg.

MSR $799	$650	$350 - 425	$200 - 250	

- Subtract 20% (Last MSR was $520) for no electronics (Model 2580/29037).
- Add 40% for B-Band NF-2 EQ electronics.

WOODLAND 12 SPRUCE (S&P 12 SPRUCE) – similar to Woodland 6 Spruce (S&P 6 Spruce), except in 12-string configuration with six-per-side tuners (Model 2818/28931), current mfg.

MSR $699	$570	$300 - 350	$175 - 225	

- Add 20% (MSR $829) for B-Band A3.2 Electronics (Model 20300/28948).
- Add 45% for B-Band NF-1 EQ electronics (Model 15436, disc.).
- Add 70% for B-Band NF-2 EQ electronics (Model 15443, disc.).

WOODLAND 6 SPRUCE MAHOGANY (S&P 6 SPRUCE MAHOGANY) – similar to the Woodland 6 Spruce (S&P 6 Spruce), except has mahogany back and sides instead of wild-cherry, and a satin lacquer finish (Model 2917/29051), disc. 2009.

	N/A	$250 - 300	$135 - 175	$599

- Add 22.5% (Last MSR was $735) for B-Band A3.2 electronics (Model 20188/29068).
- Add 40% for B-Band NF-1 EQ electronics (Model 15498, disc.).
- Add 70% for B-Band NF-2 EQ electronics (Model 15504, disc.).

* *Woodland Spruce Mahogany Left (S&P Spruce Mahogany Left)* – similar to the Woodland 6 Spruce Mahogany (S&P 6 Spruce Mahogany), except in left-handed configuration (Model 2931/29075), disc. 2007.

	N/A	$250 - 300	$130 - 180	$595

- Add 22.5% (Last MSR was $735) for B-Band A3.2 electronics (Model 20201/29082).

WOODLAND 6 FOLK (S&P 6 FOLK) – folk body, solid cedar top, red wild cherry back and sides, rosewood fingerboard and bridge, three-per-side tuners, lacquer finish (Model 17539/29112/32648), mfg. 2004-09.

	N/A	$200 - 250	$110 - 140	$487

- Add 30% (Last MSR was $627) for B-Band A3.2 Electronics (Model 20164/29129/32655).

MSR/NOTES	100%	EXCELLENT	AVERAGE	LAST MSR

* *Woodland 6 Folk Cutaway (S&P 6 Folk Cutaway)* – similar to the Woodland 6 Folk (S&P 6 Folk), except has a single cutaway (Model 25046/29150/32594), mfg. 2004-09.

	N/A	$260 - 310	$140 - 180	$607

- Add 22.5% (Last MSR was $749) for B-Band A3.2 Electronics (Model 25053/29167/32600).

* *Vintage Burst 6 Folk (S&P 6 Folk Sunburst)* – similar to the Woodland 6 Folk (S&P 6 Folk), except has a high-gloss Sunburst finish (Model 21598/29136/32617), disc. 2009.

	N/A	$275 - 325	$150 - 200	$675

- Add 20% (Last MSR was $810) for B-Band A3.2 Electronics (Model 21604/29143/32624).

WOODLAND MINI JUMBO (S&P MINI JUMBO) – mini-jumbo body, solid cedar top, red wild cherry back and sides, rosewood fingerboard and bridge, three-per-side headstock, lacquer finish (Model 26609/29211/32563), mfg. 2005-09.

	N/A	$210 - 260	$120 - 150	$525

- Add 27.5% (Last MSR was $659) for B-Band A3.2 Electronics (Model 26616/29228/32570).

* *Woodland Mini Jumbo Cutaway (S&P Mini Jumbo Cutaway)* – similar to the Woodland Mini Jumbo (S&P Mini-Jumbo), except has a single cutaway, B-Band A3.2 electronics, and a lacquer finish with a gloss top and semi-gloss back and sides (Model 26623/29235/32587), mfg. 2005-09.

	N/A	$375 - 450	$200 - 250	$929

WOODLAND 6 SPRUCE PARLOR (S&P 6 SPRUCE MAHOGANY PARLOR) – similar to the Woodland 6 Spruce Mahogany (S&P Spruce Mahogany), except in parlor body style (Model 14040/29174), disc. 2009.

	N/A	$220 - 270	$130 - 160	$549

- Add 25% (Last MSR was $685) for B-Band A3.2 Electronics (Model 20027/29181).

* *Vintage Burst 6 Parlor (S&P Parlor Sunburst)* – similar to the S&P Spruce Mahogany Parlor, except has a solid cedar top, red wild cherry back and sides, and a high-gloss Sunburst finish (Model 21567/29198), disc. 2009.

	N/A	$275 - 325	$150 - 200	$675

- Add 20% (Last MSR was $810) for B-Band A3.2 electronics (Model 21574/29204).

WOODLAND PRO FOLK SPRUCE – folk-style body, select pressure tested solid spruce top, solid mahogany back and sides, round soundhole with rosette, set mahogany neck, 14/20-fret rosewood fingerboard with dot inlays, three-per-side chrome tuners, rosewood bridge, optional electronics, available in Natural semi-gloss custom polished finish (Model 033713), mfg. 2010-present.

MSR $869	$700	$375 - 450	$200 - 250	

- Add 15% (MSR $999) for B-Band A3T electronics (Model 033706).

WOODLAND PRO FOLK SUNBURST – folk-style body, select pressure tested solid spruce top, solid mahogany back and sides, round soundhole with rosette, set mahogany neck, 14/20-fret rosewood fingerboard with dot inlays, slotted headstock with three-per-side open-style chrome tuners, rosewood bridge, optional electronics, available in Sunburst high-gloss custom polished finish (Model 034598), mfg. summer 2010-present.

MSR $899	$750	$400 - 475	$225 - 275	

- Add 12.5% (MSR $1,029) for B-Band A3T electronics (Model 034581).

WOODLAND PRO MINI-JUMBO SPRUCE – mini-jumbo-style body, select pressure tested solid spruce top, solid mahogany back and sides, round soundhole with rosette, set mahogany neck, 14/20-fret rosewood fingerboard with dot inlays, three-per-side chrome tuners, rosewood bridge, black pickguard, optional electronics, available in Natural semi-gloss custom polished finish (Model 033737), mfg. 2010-present.

MSR $849	$700	$375 - 450	$200 - 250	

- Add 15% (MSR $985) for B-Band A3T electronics (Model 033720).

WOODLAND PRO PARLOR SPRUCE – parlor-style body, select pressure tested solid spruce top, solid mahogany back and sides, round soundhole with rosette, set mahogany neck, 12/19-fret rosewood fingerboard with dot inlays, three-per-side chrome tuners, rosewood bridge, optional electronics, available in Natural (Model 033690) or Sunburst (2011-present, Model 035151) semi-gloss custom polished finish, mfg. 2010-present.

MSR $849	$700	$375 - 450	$225 - 275	

- Add 7.5% (MSR $899) for Sunburst finish (Model 035151).
- Add 15% (MSR $985) for B-Band A3T electronics (Model 033683).
- Add 22.5% (MSR $1,029) for Sunburst finish with B-Band A3T electronics (Model 035144).

WOODLAND PRO SPRUCE – dreadnought-style body, select pressure tested solid spruce top, solid mahogany back and sides, round soundhole with rosette, set mahogany neck, 14/20-fret rosewood fingerboard with dot inlays, three-per-side chrome tuners, rosewood bridge, black pickguard, optional electronics, available in Natural semi-gloss custom polished finish (Model 033676), mfg. 2010-present.

MSR $779	$630	$325 - 425	$175 - 225	

- Add 20% (MSR $912) for B-Band A3T electronics (Model 033669).

MSR/NOTES	100%	EXCELLENT	AVERAGE	LAST MSR

ACOUSTIC: PRO SERIES

S&P 6 PRO MAHOGANY (MODEL 2955) – similar to the S&P 6, except has a solid spruce top, mahogany back and sides, mahogany neck, and high gloss lacquer finish, disc. 2003.

	N/A	$325 - 375	$200 - 250	$685

- Add $125 for B-Band NF-1 EQ electronics (Model 15535).
- Add $200 for B-Band NF-2 EQ electronics (Model 15542).
- Add $40 for left-handed configuration (Model 3006).

S&P 6 PRO FLAME MAPLE (MODEL 3051) – similar to the S&P Pro Mahogany, except has flame maple sides and solid back, disc. 2003.

	N/A	$350 - 425	$225 - 275	$765

- Add $125 for B-Band NF-1 EQ electronics (Model 15573).
- Add $200 for B-Band NF-2 EQ electronics (Model 15580).
- Add $40 for left-handed configuration (Model 3105).

* *S&P 6 Pro Flame Maple Cutaway (Model 2665)* – similar to S&P 6 Pro Flame Maple, but body is in the cutaway configuration, disc. 2003.

	N/A	$400 - 475	$275 - 325	$895

- Add $125 for B-Band NF-1 EQ electronics (Model 15238).
- Add $200 for B-Band NF-2 EQ electronics (Model 15245).

S&P 6 PRO ROSEWOOD (MODEL 3150) – similar to the S&P Pro Mahogany, except has Indian rosewood back and sides, disc. 2003.

	N/A	$400 - 475	$275 - 325	$895

- Add $125 for B-Band NF-1 EQ electronics (Model 15610).
- Add $200 for B-Band NF-2 EQ electronics (Model 15627).
- Add $40 for left-handed configuration (Model 3204).

* *S&P 6 Pro Rosewood Cutaway (Model 2603)* – similar to S&P 6 Pro Rosewood, except features cutaway configuration, disc. 2003.

	N/A	$500 - 575	$300 - 350	$1,055

- Add $125 for B-Band NF-1 EQ electronics (Model 15214).
- Add $200 for B-Band NF-2 EQ electronics (Model 15221).

S&P 6 PRO QUILTED MAPLE (MODEL 3259) – similar to the S&P Pro Mahogany, except the back and sides are solid quilted maple, disc. 2003.

	N/A	$550 - 650	$350 - 425	$1,165

- Add $125 for B-Band NF-1 EQ electronics (Model 15658).
- Add $200 for B-Band NF-2 EQ electronics (Model 15665).
- Add $40 for left-handed configuration (Model 3303).

ACOUSTIC: SHOWCASE SERIES

In 2006, AER electronics were introduced.

S&P 6 SHOWCASE FLAME MAPLE – dreadnought body style, solid spruce top, flame maple mahogany back and sides, rosewood fingerboard, three-per-side tuners, available in Natural finish (Model 25152), mfg. 2004-present.

MSR $1,215	$1,000	$525 - 625	$300 - 375	

- Add 10% for B-Band A4.2 Electronics (disc., Model 25169).
- Add 10% for left-handed configuration (Model 25176, disc.).
- Add 15% (MSR $1,415) for A6T electronics (Model 033553, 2010-present).
- Add 20% (Last MSR was $1,419) for AER electronics (Model 28566, disc. 2009).
- Add 30% for left-handed configuration with B-Band A4.2 Electronics (Model 25183, disc.).

* *S&P Showcase Flame Maple Cutaway* – similar to the S&P 6 Showcase Flame Maple, except has a single cutaway and B-Band A4.2 (2004-05, Model 25268), AER electronics (2006-09, Model 028597) or A6T electronics (2010-present, Model 033270), mfg. 2004-present.

MSR $1,629	$1,330	$675 - 850	$400 - 500	

- Subtract 15% (Last MSR was $1,429) for no electronics (Model 025251).

S&P 6 SHOWCASE FOLK – folk body style, solid spruce top, rosewood back and sides, rosewood fingerboard, three-per-side tuners, B-Band A4.2 (2004-05, Model 25206), AER electronics (2006-09, Model 028580) or A6T electronics (2010-present, Model 033294), available in Natural finish (Model 25190), mfg. 2004-present.

MSR $1,529	$1,250	$650 - 800	$375 - 475	

- Subtract 15% (last MSR was $1,329) for no electronics (disc. 2011, Model 025190).

S&P 6 SHOWCASE MAHOGANY – dreadnought body style, solid spruce top, solid mahogany back and sides, rosewood fingerboard, three-per-side tuners, available in Natural finish (Model 25114), mfg. 2004-present.

MSR $1,095	$900	$500 - 575	$300 - 375	

- Add 10% for left-handed configuration (Model 25138, disc.).
- Add 20% for B-Band A4.2 Electronics (Model 25121, disc.).
- Add 17.5% (MSR $1,295) for A6T electronics (Model 033263, 2010-present).
- Add 25% (Last MSR was $1,265) for AER electronics (Model 28559, disc. 2009).
- Add 30% for left-handed configuration with B-Band A4.2 Electronics (Model 25145).

MSR/NOTES	100%	EXCELLENT	AVERAGE	LAST MSR

S&P 6 SHOWCASE ROSEWOOD – dreadnought body style, solid spruce top, rosewood back and sides, rosewood fingerboard, three-per-side tuners, available in Natural finish (Model 25213), mfg. 2004-present.

MSR $1,329	$1,080	$575 - 675	$350 - 425	

- Add 10% for left-handed configuration (Model 25237, disc.).
- Add 15% for B-Band A4.2 Electronics (Model 25220, disc.).
- Add 15% (MSR $1,529) for A6T electronics (Model 033294, 2010-present).
- Add 20% (Last MSR was $1,530) for AER electronics (Model 28573, disc. 2009).
- Add 25% for left-handed configuration with B-Band A4.2 Electronics (Model 25244, disc.).

* *S&P Showcase Rosewood Cutaway* – similar to the S&P 6 Showcase Rosewood, except has a single cutaway and B-Band A4.2 (2004-05, Model 25282), AER electronics (2006-09, Model 028603) or A6T electronics (2010-present, Model 033300), mfg. 2004-present.

MSR $1,749	$1,430	$725 - 900	$450 - 550	

- Subtract 15% for no electronics (Model 25275, disc. 2011).

ACOUSTIC: SONGSMITH SERIES

SONGSMITH – dreadnought body style, select pressure tested solid cedar top, wild cherry back and sides, round soundhole with rings, cream body binding, Silver Leaf maple neck, 14/20-fret rosewood fingerboard with dot inlays, three-per-side chrome tuners, rosewood bridge, available in Varnish Burst semi-gloss finish (Model 30088), mfg. 2007-present.

MSR $475	$360	$200 - 250	$120 - 150	

- Add 25% (MSR $605) for B-Band A3.2 electronics (Model 30095).

* *Songsmith Cutaway* – similar to the Songsmith, except has a single cutaway and B-BAND A3T electronics with built-in tuner, mfg. 2012-present.

MSR $675	$500	$300 - 350	$175 - 225	

* *Songsmith Folk* – similar to the Songsmith, except has a folk body style (Model 30101/33195), mfg. 2007-present.

MSR $475	$360	$200 - 250	$120 - 150	

- Add 25% (MSR $605) for B-Band A3.2 electronics (Model 30118/33188).

ACOUSTIC: CUTAWAY GT SERIES

CUTAWAY GT CEDAR – single cutaway dreadnought-style body, select pressure tested solid cedar top, red wild cherry back and sides, round soundhole with rosette, multi-ply body binding, set silver leaf maple neck, 14/20-fret rosewood fingerboard with dot inlays, three-per-side chrome tuners, rosewood bridge, black pickguard, standard B-Band A3T electronics, available in Natural semi-gloss custom polished finish with a gloss top (Model 033768), gig bag included, mfg. 2010-present.

MSR $929	$760	$400 - 475	$225 - 275	

* *Cutaway GT Vintage Burst Cedar* – similar to the Cutaway GT Cedar, except has a Vintage Burst semi-gloss custom polished finish with a gloss top (Model 033775), gig bag included, mfg. 2010-present.

MSR $979	$800	$425 - 500	$250 - 300	

CUTAWAY GT FOLK CEDAR – single cutaway folk-style body, select pressure tested solid cedar top, red wild cherry back and sides, round soundhole with rosette, multi-ply body binding, set silver leaf maple neck, 14/20-fret rosewood fingerboard with dot inlays, three-per-side chrome tuners, rosewood bridge, standard B-Band A3T electronics, available in Natural semi-gloss custom polished finish with a gloss top (Model 033744), gig bag included, mfg. 2010-present.

MSR $929	$760	$400 - 475	$225 - 275	

CUTAWAY GT MINI-JUMBO CEDAR – single cutaway Mini-Jumbo-style body, select pressure tested solid cedar top, red wild cherry back and sides, round soundhole with rosette, multi-ply body binding, set silver leaf maple neck, 14/20-fret rosewood fingerboard with dot inlays, three-per-side chrome tuners, rosewood bridge, standard B-Band A3T electronics, available in Natural semi-gloss custom polished finish with a gloss top (Model 033751), gig bag included, mfg. 2010-present.

MSR $929	$760	$400 - 475	$225 - 275	

ACOUSTIC: NATURAL ELEMENTS SERIES

S&P NATURAL ELEMENTS DREADNOUGHT – dreadnought-style body, solid pressure-tested solid cedar with Natural Cherry back and sides, (036325), solid spruce top with Heart of Wild back and sides (036356), or solid spruce top with figured Amber Trail maple back and sides (036387), round soundhole with rosette, maple body binding, integrated set silver leaf maple neck, 14/21-fret rosewood fingerboard with dot inlays, Seagull-style headstock with flame maple overlay, three-per-side chrome tuners, rosewood bridge, B-band ACI.5T electronics with built-in tuner, available in Natural semi-gloss custom polished finish, mfg. 2012-present.

MSR $750	$550	$325 - 400	$200 - 250	

S&P NATURAL ELEMENTS FOLK CUTAWAY – single cutaway folk-style body, solid pressure-tested solid cedar with Natural Cherry back and sides, (036318), solid spruce top with Heart of Wild back and sides (036332), or solid spruce top with figured Amber Trail maple back and sides (036370), round soundhole with rosette, maple body binding, integrated set silver leaf maple neck, 14/21-fret rosewood fingerboard with dot inlays, Seagull-style headstock with flame maple overlay, three-per-side chrome tuners, rosewood bridge, B-band ACI.5T electronics with built-in tuner, available in Natural semi-gloss custom polished finish, mfg. 2012-present.

MSR $800	$600	$350 - 425	$225 - 275	

MSR/NOTES	100%	EXCELLENT	AVERAGE	LAST MSR

S&P NATURAL ELEMENTS MINI-JUMBO CUTAWAY – single cutaway mini jumbo-style body, solid pressure-tested solid cedar with Natural Cherry back and sides, (036301), solid spruce top with Heart of Wild back and sides (036349), or solid spruce top with figured Amber Trail maple back and sides (036363), round soundhole with rosette, maple body binding, integrated set silver leaf maple neck, 14/21-fret rosewood fingerboard with dot inlays, Seagull-style headstock with flame maple overlay, three-per-side chrome tuners, rosewood bridge, B-band ACI.5T electronics with built-in tuner, available in Natural semi-gloss custom polished finish, mfg. 2012-present.

MSR $800	$600	$350 - 425	$225 - 275

SINGER

Instruments currently produced in China.

Singer produes a large amount of acoustic, electric, and bass guitars that are mainly based on popular American designs. They have some original designs as well. Currently, there is no American distributor. For more information contact their website.

CONTACT INFORMATION
SINGER
www.singercn.com
sggs@163.net

SLAMAN GUITARS

Instruments currently built in Den Haag, Netherlands since 1978. Distributed through Luthier Slaman's workshop, Casa Benelly in Den Haag, and La Guitarra Buena in Amsterdam.

CONTACT INFORMATION
SLAMAN GUITARS
Westeinde 58 2512 HE
Den Haag, The Netherlands
Phone No.: 31 (0)70 389 42 32
www.slamanguitars.com
slaman@ziggo.nl

Luthier Daniel Slaman began building classical guitars in 1978. Slaman participated in a guitar making Masterclass hosted by Jose L. Romanillos in 1988, and professes a strong design influence by Romanillos. In 1997, Slaman and Robert Benedetto presented guitar making workshops at the Instrument Museum in Berlin during the **History of the Guitar in Rock and Jazz** exhibition.

Slaman introduced a number of new acoustic models in 1996 as well. By slightly offsetting the body contour, Slaman produced a cutaway on his classical model (which allows access to all 20 frets); this model has been named the **Classic Access**. A variation named the **Flamenco Access** is in the works. Another model is a European jazz guitar inspired by the Selmer models built in France from 1932 to 1952. Slaman's **Modele Jazz** is offered as brand new, or with antique parts and distressing as the **Modele Jazz Patina**. List prices include a Hiscox case.

The majority of Slaman's instruments were built after 1992. Slaman currently produces between ten and fifteen handcrafted instruments a year, although archtop building is more time consuming and thus tends to slow down the building schedule.

Luthier Slaman uses European spruce for his classical guitar tops, and either Brazilian or Indian rosewood, cocobolo or maple for the back and sides. When building **flamenco instruments**, Slaman offers soundboards of either European spruce or Western red cedar, and bodies of Spanish cypress or rosewood.

The **North Sea Standard** 17 in. has a carved Sitka spruce top, two piece flamed maple back with matching sides/neck, ebony fingerboard with mother-of-pearl/Mexican green abalone inlays, ebony tailpiece/pickguard, Brazilian rosewood bridge/headplate, 3-per-side Schaller gold tuning machines. Available in hand-applied nitrocellulose finish, and an 18 in. or 18.5 in. wide body. List price includes a Calton DeLuxe fiberglass case. This model is available with an optional Benedetto S-6 suspended pickup. This model is available with select aged European Cello grade flamed maple back and sides as the North Sea Cello 17 in.

This model is available with special Thuya wood headplate/pickguard/bridge wings/tailpiece as the North Sea Special 17 in. The **North Sea Natural 17 in.** is similar to the North Sea Standard, except features all wood binding (no plastic) and no pearl inlay.

The **North Sea 7-String Swing** is similar to the North Sea, except in a 7-string configuration and 4/3-per-side headstock.

The **North Sea Orchestra** is similar to the North Sea, except has non-cutaway body style, 18 in. width (across lower bout), European spruce top, and European flamed maple back/sides/neck. Guitars are all priced in Euros.

SLINGERLAND

Instruments previously built in Chicago, IL from the mid-1930s to circa mid-1940s.

Slingerland is perhaps better known for the drums the company produced. The Slingerland Banjo and Drum Company was established in 1916 in Chicago. In terms of construction, a banjo and drum do have several similarities (the soundhead stretched over a circular frame and held by a retaining ring). The company introduced the Marvel line of carved top guitars in 1936. A catalog of the time shows that Slingerland guitars were also sold under various brand names such as Songster, College Pal, and May-Bell, as well as the Slingerland trademark (source: Tom Wheeler, *American Guitars*).

SMALLMAN GUITARS

Instruments currently built in Melbourne Victoria, Australia since the early 1980s.

Luthier Greg Smallman continues to push the mechanical limits on the classical guitar form. Though the instruments look conventional, Smallman utilizes a flexible criss-cross lattice-like internal strutting composed of balsawood reinforced by carbon fiber under a thin top to increase the volume of the guitar. Backs and sides are constructed from laminated rosewood, which reduces the amount of energy that they might absorb from the top, which also enhances the guitar's projection. Smallman favors cedar for his guitar tops (source: Tony Bacon, *The Ultimate Guitar Book*).

MSR/NOTES	100%	EXCELLENT	AVERAGE	LAST MSR

Luthier Smallman makes a small number of guitars each year, has a moderately high asking price, and has a long waiting list. 'Used' Smallman guitars rarely turn up on the secondary market.

SOBELL, STEFAN

Instruments currently built in England. Represented in the U.S. by Acoustic Music in Guilford, CT.

CONTACT INFORMATION
SOBELL, STEFAN
www.sobellinstruments.com, www.
sobellguitars.com
stefan@sobellguitars.com

Luthier Stefan Sobell was a pioneer in the development of the "cittern" (similar to a long necked mandolin) in the early 1970s (the cittern proved popular in the British Celtic music revival). Sobell then changed to building acoustic guitars in the early 1980s. Currently he produces about twelve guitars a year, mostly flattops with slightly curved backs and soundboards (the top and back feature a cylindrical arch). Sobell also builds citterns, mandolins, and Irish bouzoukis. For more information, visit Sobell's website or contact him directly.

SONNET

Instruments previously produced in Japan.

Sonnet guitars were distributed in the U.S. by the Daimaru New York Corporation of New York, New York (source: Michael Wright, *Guitar Stories, Volume One*).

SORRENTINO

Instruments previously built by Epiphone in New York, NY circa mid-1930s. Distributed by C.M.I. (Chicago Musical Instruments).

In the book, *Epiphone: The House of Stathopoulo*, authors Jim Fisch and L.B. Fred indicate that Sorrentino instruments were built by Epaminondas Stathopoulos' Epiphone company during the mid-1930s. Unlike other 1930s budget lines, the Sorrentinos are similar in quality and prices to Epiphones during this time period. Of the six models (Luxor, Premier, Artist, Avon, Lido, and Arcadia), two models were even higher priced than their Epiphone counterpart!

Sorrentinos share construction designs and serialization similar to same-period Epiphones, and headstock designs similar to the Epiphone-built Howard brand models. Sorrentinos, like budget line Gibsons, do not have a truss rod in the neck. Labels inside the body read: *Sorrentino Mfg. Co., USA* (source: Jim Fisch and L.B. Fred, *Epiphone: The House of Stathopoulo*).

SQUIER

Instruments currently produced in Mexico, Korea, and China. Distributed by the Fender Musical Instrument Corporation in Scottsdale, AZ. Previously produced in Japan.

CONTACT INFORMATION
SQUIER
A Division of FMIC
8860 Chapparral Road, Ste. 100
Scottsdale, AZ 85250-2618
Phone No.: 480-596-9690
Fax No.: 480-367-5262
www.squierguitars.com
custserv@fenderusa.com

In 1982, the Fender division of CBS established Fender Japan in conjunction with Kanda Shokai and Yamano music. Production of the Squier instruments began in 1983 at the Fugi Gen Gakki facilities in Matsumoto, Japan. The Squier trademark was based on the V.C. Squier string making company that produced strings for Fender in the 1950s, and was later aquired by Fender in 1965. Originally, the Squier trademark was intended for European distribution, but soon became a way for Fender to provide entry level instruments to its customers. Squier instruments are typically based off of the popular Fender designs. The Squier II series was introduced in 1986. In 1996 Fender greatly expanded its line with several models available at competitive prices. In 2012, Fender discontinued all production of Squier acoustic guitars and moved the MA-1 and MC-1 to the Fender line.

ACOUSTIC

MA-1 (NO. 093-0100-021) – 3/4 scale mini-acoustic, laminated agathis top, back, and sides, nato neck, 18-fret rosewood fingerboard, chrome, open-gear tuners, available in Natural finish, 23.3 in. scale, disc. 2011.

	100%	EXCELLENT	AVERAGE	LAST MSR
	$110	$60 - 80	$30 - 45	$200

This model is now branded as a Fender and can be found in the Fender section.

MC-1 (NO. 092-0100-021) – 3/4 scale nylon-string configuration, mini-classical body, laminated agathis top, back, and sides, nato neck, 18-fret rosewood fingerboard, open-gear tuners, available in Natural finish, 23.3 in. scale, disc. 2011.

	100%	EXCELLENT	AVERAGE	LAST MSR
	$100	$55 - 75	$30 - 40	$170

This model is now branded as a Fender and can be found in the Fender section.

HELLO KITTY ACOUSTIC (CHINA MFG. NO. 093-9000) – dreadnought style, basswood top/back/sides, round soundhole with rings, binding, nato neck, 14/20-fret rosewood fingerboard with dot inlays, black headstock with three-per-side chrome tuners, rosewood bridge, pickguard, available in Black or Pink finish with Hello Kitty graphics, 25.25 in. scale, mfg. 2007-08.

	100%	EXCELLENT	AVERAGE	LAST MSR
	N/A	$135 - 170	$80 - 100	$340

MSR/NOTES	100%	EXCELLENT	AVERAGE	LAST MSR

SA-100 ACOUSTIC PACK (NO. 093-0300/0315-021) – guitar value pack that includes a Squier SA-100 dreadnought guitar, a gig bag, pitch pipe, instruction book, picks, and a strap, available in Natural finish, disc. 2011.

	100%	EXCELLENT	AVERAGE	LAST MSR
	$100	$55 - 75	$30 - 40	$170

In 2010, this model was upgraded with a laminated spruce top, die-cast tuners, a real rosewood fingerboard and bridge, and nickel plated frets. The pack also now includes an electronic tuner.

SD-6 (DG-6, NO. 093-0600-021) – dreadnought style, laminated agathis top, back and sides, nato neck with rosewood fingerboard, dot inlays, rosewood bridge, compensated Urea saddle, chrome tuners, black pickguard, available in Candy Apple Red, Metallic Blue, Natural, or White (2001-05) satin finish, 25.3 in. scale, mfg. 2001-09.

	100%	EXCELLENT	AVERAGE	LAST MSR
	N/A	$85 - 110	$40 - 60	$230

* Add 15% (Last MSR was $250) for Candy Apple Red, Metallic Blue, or White finish.

STRATACOUSTIC (NO. 093-7400) – hollow Stratocaster shaped body, spruce top, round soundhole, one-piece fiberglass back and sides, bolt-on neck, 21-fret rosewood fingerboard with dot inlay, Stratocaster-style headstock with six-on-one-side chrome tuners, rosewood bridge, Fishman Classic 4 electronics with tuner, available in Black (2008 only) or Walnut Stain finish, mfg. 2006-08.

	100%	EXCELLENT	AVERAGE	LAST MSR
	N/A	$135 - 170	$80 - 100	$350

TELECOUSTIC (NO. 093-7500) – hollow Telecaster shaped body, spruce top, round soundhole, one-piece fiberglass back and sides, bolt-on neck, 21-fret rosewood fingerboard with dot inlay, Telecaster-style headstock with six-on-one-side chrome tuners, rosewood bridge, Fishman Classic 4 electronics with tuner, available in Black (2008 only) or Walnut Stain finish, mfg. 2006-08.

	100%	EXCELLENT	AVERAGE	LAST MSR
	N/A	$135 - 170	$80 - 100	$350

S.S. STEWART

Instruments also produced as Stewart & Bauer. Instruments previously produced in Philadelphia, PA, between circa 1878 and 1904, in Nazareth, PA by Martin guitars between circa 1923 and 1925, in Kalamazoo, MI by Gibson guitars between circa 1931 and 1932, and in Chicago, IL by Harmony during the 1950s and 1960s.

S.S. Stewart was established in the 1870s by Samuel Swain Stewart in Philadelphia, PA. Stewart initially sold banjos and was one of the first to apply mass production techniques to instrument building with good consequences. Stewart banjos were sold directly to the public while Acme-branded banjos also built by Stewart were sold by Sears, Roebuck, & Co. Stewart became partners with well-known guitar builder George Bauer and issued guitars under the Stewart & Bauer trademark from Philadelphia. Stewart passed away in 1898.

In 1915, distributor Buegeleisen & Jacobson purchased the S.S. Stewart trademark and used it intermittently. Between circa 1923 and 1925, Buegeleisen & Jacobson ordered ukuleles and other stringed instruments from Martin guitars in Nazareth, PA. In circa 1931, Buegeleisen & Jacobson contracted Gibson to build a guitar and banjo under the S.S. Stewart brand. The guitar was built in the style of a Gibson L-2 while the banjo was built in the style of a Gibson TB-11. The Stewart name also appears on a series of entry level to medium grade guitars built by Harmony in the 1950s and 1960s and others for Weymann. S.S. Stewart-branded guitars from this era are very similar in design to Harmony guitars from the same era. Source: Tom Wheeler, *American Guitars*, Mike Longworth, *Martin Guitars: A History,* and Paul Fox, *The Other Brands of Gibson.*

STAGG (CURRENT MFG.)

Instruments currently produced.

Stagg produces a wide variety of acoustic, electric, and bass guitars. They also produce guitar amplifiers, drums, keyboards, cables, and accessories. Currently, there is no U.S. distributor. Refer to their website for more information.

CONTACT INFORMATION
STAGG (CURRENT MFG.)
www.staggmusic.com

STAHL, WILLIAM C.

See Larson Brothers (1900-1944) in the L section.

William C. Stahl was a prominent music publisher and teacher of guitar, mandolin, and banjo in Milwaukee from the turn of the century to the early 1940s. He sold instruments to his students but also advertised heavily in the trade papers. The Larson brothers of Maurer & Co. in Chicago supplied most of his guitar and mandolin family instruments, and the remainder were made by Washburn, Regal, and others.

The Larson-made Stahl guitars followed the designs of the Maurer and Prairie State brands also built by the Larsons. The difference in the Stahl labeled guitars is that maple is used for bracing rather than spruce. Some of the top-of-the-line Stahl guitars have the Prairie State system of steel rods which strengthen the body and add sustain as well as help to produce a somewhat different sound from other Larson brands. The Larson-made Stahl instruments have a Stahl logo burned or stamped on the inside center strip. Author Robert Hartman believes that Stahl's paper label was also used on some Larsons, as well as the ones made by other builders. Stahl offered guitars and mandolins ranging in quality from student grade to the highest degree of presentation grade instruments.

STANSELL, LES GUITARS

Instruments currently produced in Pistol River, OR since 1979.

CONTACT INFORMATION
STANSELL, LES GUITARS
PO Box 6056
Pistol River, OR 97444
Phone No.: 541-698-7571
stansellguitars.com
les@stansellguitars.com

Luthier Les Stansell has been building classical and flamenco guitars in his Pistol River shop since the late 1970s. After completing a year-long course on instrument building, studying under the direction of luthier Anthony Huvard, Stansell began building guitars in 1979. In 1982, Stansell and his wife Mary, established the Pistol River Concert Association where he met many famous artists and formed friendships. For most of the 1980s and 1990s, Stansell worked as a carpenter and built custom furniture while he built guitars on the side. By the late 1990s, Stansell became very interested in flamenco design and began building guitars full-time. Stansell builds approximately five flamenco and classical guitars per year and they start at $5,400. For more information, visit Stansell's website.

STAUFFER

Instruments previously produced in Vienna, Italy in the early to mid-1800s.

Luthier George Stauffer (1778-1853) produced fine guitars in Vienna. He is also noted for training other guitar makers including C.F. Martin. He is also known for his inovations to instruments. Stauffer guitars can be worth quite a bit if they are original and the label indicates the guitar was built by him.

STEINEGGER GUITARS

Instruments currently produced in Portland, OR, since 1976.

CONTACT INFORMATION
STEINEGGER GUITARS
PO Box 25304
Portland, OR 97298
Phone No.: 503 644-1809
www.steinyguitars.com
steiny@aracnet.com

Robert Steinegger developed an interest in guitars while in high school. In 1969, Arthur Overholtzer coached him on classical guitar construction, and while attending school in Utah in 1973, he met Phil Everly of the Everly Brothers. In 1981, he was commissioned by Phil Everly to build an updated, improved version of the now highly collectible Gibson Everly Brothers Model. The "Ike Everly Model" was the result, and was built until 2002, when production was suspended (last retail price was $4,500). Only 57 were built. Robert Steinegger now builds other acoustic configurations, built per individual customer order. For more information contact Steinegger directly.

The **Oregon Grande** model retails for $5,900, and the **Oregon Grande Deluxe** model retails for $6,900. The **New Rosedale** model retails for $3,900, and the **New Rosedale Deluxe** model retails for $4,900. All models are round-bodied Jumbo style; also available on special order are the following body styles: Dreadnought, 12-fret Dreadnought "S", round-shouldered "J", and 12-fret "00". Steel strings only on all models.

- Add $350 for pointed cutaway.
- Add $500 for baritone (27 in. scale) configuration.
- Add $1,200 for Brazilian Rosewood, African Blackwood, or Camotillo Rosewood (D. Congestiflora).
- Add $195 for K&K pickup, installed.
- Hard-shell case is included; Shipping is extra.

STELLA

See Harmony. See Oscar Schmidt. Instruments previously produced by Oscar Schmidt in the early 1900s, produced by Harmony from the 1940s to the 1970s, and recently produced and distributed by MBT International from the late 1990s-early 2000s.

Stella was a name used on guitars by Oscar Schmidt in the late 1800s and early 1900s. Harmony purchased the trademark circa 1940 and produced instruments until circa 1970s. MBT International reintroduced the name in the late 1990s with a line of acoustic guitars and accessories priced competitively.

STEVENS CUSTOM GUITARS

Instruments currently built in Munchen (Munich), Germany.

CONTACT INFORMATION
STEVENS CUSTOM GUITARS
www.guitars.de/frameSCG.html

Werner Kozlik, Stefan Zirnbauer, and the other guitar builders at Stevens Custom Guitars are crafting high quality acoustic models. For additional information regarding models and specifications, please contact Stevens Custom Guitars directly.

STILES, GILBERT L.

Instruments previously built in Independence, WV and Hialeah, FL between 1960 and 1994.

Luthier/designer Gilbert L. Stiles (1914-1994) had a background of working with wood, be it millwork, logging or house building. In 1960, he set his mind to building a solid body guitar, and continued building instruments for over the next thirty years. In 1963, Stiles moved to Hialeah, FL. Later on in his career, Stiles also taught for the Augusta Heritage Program at the Davis and Elkins College in Elkins, WV.

Stiles built acoustic flattops, archtops, solid body electrics, mandolins, and other stringed instruments. It has been estimated that Stiles had produced over 1,000 solid body electric guitars and 500 acoustics during his career. His archtop and mandolins are still held in high esteem, as well as his banjos.

Stiles guitars generally have Stiles or G.L Stiles on the headstock, or Lee Stiles engraved on a plate at the neck/body joint of a bolt-on designed solid body. Dating a Stiles instrument is difficult, given that only the electric solids were given serial numbers consecutively, and would only indicate which number guitar it was, not when built. Source: Michael Wright, *Guitar Stories*, Volume One.

STOLL

Instruments currently built in Taunusstein Waldems, Germany since 1983. Previously distributed in the U.S. by Salwender International in Trabuco Canyon, CA.

CONTACT INFORMATION
STOLL
Schwalbacher Str. 18
Waldems, D-65529 Germany
Phone No.: +49 6126 589888
Fax No.: +49 6126 589889
www.stollguitars.de
post@Stollguitars.de

Christian Stoll began his lutherie career in the mid-1970s as an apprentice at Hopf guitars, then left to study under Dragan Musulin. Stoll finished his period of apprenticeship with Andreas Wahl, and founded the Stoll Guitar Company in 1983.

Between 1983 and 1985, Stoll produced custom orders for classical and steel string models (and some electric guitars and basses), and began to work on developing an acoustic bass guitar. In 1988, Stoll began adding other luthiers to his workshop, and currently has four on staff.

Stoll also offers the McLoud acoustic pickup system on a number of his acoustic models. This internal system features a piezo pickup, endpin jack, and a battery clip for 9-volt batteries. For more information, contact Stoll directly.

Stoll offers handcrafted steel string acoustic guitar and acoustic bass models. The models are built from quality wood, and inlays and trim are used sparingly as the emphasis is on tone and craftsmanship. Guitars are then finished in nitrocellulose lacquer or Shellac (French polish method).

Classical models feature solid cedar or spruce tops, rosewood or other exotic hardwood sides and backs, 20-fret ebony fingerboards, and Schaller tuners. The Steel String acoustics have solid spruce tops, maple or rosewood backs and sides, cedro necks, 21-fret rosewood or ebony fingerboards and chrome or gold Schaller tuners. All models are available with options like cutaways, left-handed configurations, and more. For both, classical and steel string models, they offer a wide range of tonewoods as for example Mango, Indian Silver Oak, Mahogany, Walnut, Violet Wood, Koa, Cypress. Prices start at 1,090€ for steel strings and 790€ for classical models. High class steel string and classical guitars feature Klaus Scheller tuners.

SPEXX acoustic basses feature a wider cutaway body design, solid spruce top, maple back and sides, a 21-fret ebony fingerboard, and gold Schaller tuners. Basses are available in fretless, left-handed, five- and six-string configurations. The basses also feature walnut backs and sides.

All guitars and basses are available with fanned frets.

STONEBRIDGE

Instruments currently produced in Velke Nemcice, Czech Republic since the mid-2000s.

CONTACT INFORMATION
STONEBRIDGE
Factory & Headquarters
Mestecko 27, 691 63
Velke Nemcice, Czech Republic
Phone No.: +420 519 417 062
www.furch.cz
info@furch.cz

CONTACT INFORMATION
STONEBRIDGE
U.S Distributor: Stonebridge Guitars
605 Lancaster St. West
Kitchener, Ontario N2K 1M5 Canada
Phone No.: 226-600-7853
www.stonebridgeguitars.com
todd@stonebridgeguitars.com

Luthier Frantisek Furch has been building acoustic guitars since 1981, and he and his staff have produced more than 60,000 guitars. In the mid-2000s, Furch introduced the Stonebridge trademark on his guitars to be sold through their North American distributor. Furch offers Stonebridge guitars in a variety of configurations including acoustic dreadnoughts, jumbos, and folk guitars. He also produces a line of traditional mandolins. For more information, visit Stonebridge's website or contact them directly.

STRADIVARI

Instruments previously built in Italy during the late 1600s.

While this renowned builder is revered for his violins, luthier Antonio Stradivari (1644-1737) did build a few guitars; a handful survive today. The overall design and appearance is reminiscent of the elegant yet simple violins that command such interest today (source: Tony Bacon, *The Ultimate Guitar Book*).

STRAD-O-LIN

Instruments previously produced in NY during the 1950s and 1960s. Later models manufactured in Japan.

Strad-O-Lin was a brand name of the Peter Sorkin Music Company. A number of solid body guitars were built at the Multivox company of New York, and distribution of those and the later Japanese built models were handled by the Sorkin company of New York City, New York. Other guitars built and distributed (possibly as rebrands) were Royce, Premier, Belltone, and Marvel.

STROMBERG

Instruments previously built in Boston, MA between 1906 and the mid-1950s.

The Stromberg business was started in Boston, Massachusetts in 1906 by Charles Stromberg (born in Sweden 1866) who immigrated to Boston in April 1886. Charles Stromberg was a master luthier. He specialized in banjo, drum, mandolin, and guitars after working for several years at Thompson and Odell (est. 1874), a Boston based firm that manufactured brass instruments, percussion instruments, fretted instruments, music publications, stringed instruments, and accessories. Thompson & Odell sold the manufacturing of the fretted instrument business to the Vega Company in Boston in 1905. Stromberg was one of the country's leading repairers of harps with his masterful ability in carving headstocks, replacing sound boards, and making new machine mechanisms. His reputation among Boston's early engravers, violin, drum, banjo, and piano makers was very high. Charles, in addition, repaired violins, cellos, and basses. Repairs were a steady source of income for the Stromberg business. His oldest son, Harry (born in Chelsea, Massachusetts 1890), worked with Charles from 1907 on and his youngest son, Elmer (born in Chelsea in 1895), apprenticed at the shop with older brother Harry from July 1910 until March 1917, when Elmer left the business to serve in World War I. He returned to the business in March 1919 after serving his country for two years in France.

At that time, the shop was located at 40 Sudbury Street and later moved to 19 Washington Street in early 1920s. Shop locations were in an area based in the heart of Boston's famous Scollay Square with burlesque and theater establishments. The Strombergs produced drums, mandolins, guitars, and banjos during the early 1920s from the 19 Washington Street location.

Throughout the 1920s (the Jazz Age of banjo music), the Strombergs produced custom tenor banjos. They competed with other banjo manufacturers, and were part of the eastern corridor in banjo manufacturing. The Stromberg reputation was very strong in Boston and the New England area. Banjoists who often desired a custom-made instrument chose the Stromberg banjo as it was highly decorative and the sound would carry for the player in large dance halls. In October of 1926, Elmer Stromberg applied for a patent for a series of tubes around the tone chamber of the banjo just under the head. This created a new sustaining sound and more volume and was called the "Cupperphone." The Stromberg Cupperphone banjo consisted of forty-one hollow, perforated metal tubes 13/16 in. high and 13/16 in. in diameter fitted to the wooden rim to produce a louder and clearer tone. This was an option for the banjos, and this Cupperphone feature made the Stromberg banjo one of the loudest and heaviest built in the country. The two models offered at this time were the Deluxe, and Marimba models. The patent was granted in June of 1928.

Harry Stromberg left the business in 1927. By the late 1920s, banjo players were beginning to switch from banjo to guitar to create deeper sounding rhythm sections in orchestras. As the style of music changed, the guitar needed to be heard better. While musicians' needs focused towards the guitar, the banjo's popularity declined and Elmer began producing archtop guitars for Boston musicians.

In June of 1927, the shop relocated to 40 Hanover Street where they began producing archtop guitars. By the early 1930s, banjo players began ordering guitars. As early as 1927, Elmer began taking guitar orders, and offered several types based on a 16 inch body, called the G series. The models G1, G2, and Deluxe models were offered featuring a small headstock, with laminated body and segmented f-holes.

HISTORY: 1930-PRESENT

During the American Depression of the 1930s, Elmer wanted as many musicians as possible to enjoy his instruments and kept the cost of the instrument affordable. After the Depression, the guitars began to change in looks and construction. By the mid-1930s (1935-37), musicians requested fancier models with larger bodies that could produce more volume. The Stromberg guitar went through at least two major headstock dimension sizes and designs and body specifications between 1936 and 1940. Elmer's response to players' needs (and the competition) was to widen the body on the G series guitars to 17.375 in., and add two more models: the 19 in. Master 400 model was introduced around 1937/38, and the Master 300 was introduced in the same time period. The larger body dimensions of the Master 300 and 400 made them the largest guitars offered from any maker.

Elmer's top-of-the-line model was the Master 400. This guitar would set the Stromberg guitar apart from other rhythm acoustic archtop guitars, especially during the swing era: Elmer added decorative pearl inlay to the headstock, additional binding, and a fine graduated top carving that would carry its sound volume across the brass sections of a large orchestra. By 1940, a new, longer headstock style and the single diagonal brace was added to Master series guitars, switching from a traditional parallel bracing to a single brace for yet more carrying power. The graduation of the tops also changed during this period. By 1940 to 1941, a single tension rod adjustment was added to the Master series (and was later added to the Deluxe and G series). By 1941, the G1 and G3 series body dimensions increased to 17.375 in., and featured a new tailpiece design that was "Y" shaped in design. The f-holes became non-segmented and followed the graceful design of the Deluxe model.

Elmer Stromberg built all of the guitars and the majority of banjos. His name never appeared on an instrument, with the exception of a Deluxe Cutaway (serial number 634, a short scale made for guitarist Hank Garland). Every label read Charles A. Stromberg and Son with a lifetime guarantee to the original purchaser. Elmer is described by many players who knew him as a gentle man with a heart of gold. He wanted to please his family of guitarists with the best instrument he could make.

Stromberg history and model specifications courtesy Jim Speros. Speros is currently compiling a Stromberg text, portions of which were supplied to this edition of the Blue Book of Acoustic Guitars. Interested parties can contact Speros through Stromberg Research, P.O. Box 51, Lincoln, Massachusetts 01773.

The apparent rarity of the individual guitars (it is estimated that only 640 guitars were produced), like D'Angelicos, combined with condition and demand, makes it difficult to set a selling price in the vintage market. The Blue Book of Acoustic Guitars recommends at least two or three professional appraisals or estimates before buying/selling/trading any Stromberg guitar (or any other Stromberg instrument, especially the banjos).

STROMBERG GUITAR IDENTIFICATION

Early G series (G1, G2, G3, Deluxe) from 1927-1930 has a 16 inch body and a label reading "40 Hanover Street, Tel Bowdoin 1228R-1728-M" (Stromberg's current business card). Narrow banjo-style headstock, Stromberg logo, Victorian-style, hand-painted with floral accents. Fingerboard (G1, G2, G3) mother-of-pearl inlays, diamond shape, oval at 14th fret. The Deluxe model featured solid pearl blocks position markers on an ebony fingerboard. The headstock was Victorian-style, engraved, hand-painted. Pressed back Indian rosewood or maple, carved spruce top, segmented f-holes. Trapeze-style tailpiece brass with chrome plating on models G1, G2, and G3 (gold plated on the Deluxe model). All shared rosewood bridge with adjustments for bridge height, top

MSR/NOTES	100%	EXCELLENT	AVERAGE	LAST MSR

location thumb adjustments. Bracing: two parallel braces, 3 ladder type braces.

Mid- to late 1930s (1935-37), the **G-100, G1, G3, Deluxe, Ultra Deluxe**, 17-3/8 inch body. Blonde finish guitars began appearing during the late 1930s. Construction featured a pressed back, carved spruce top, Grover tailpiece (chrome plated). Blue shipping labels inside guitar body read "Charles A. Stromberg & Son" in the late 1930s was typewritten or handwritten. The headstock shape changed to a larger bout and from the early 1930s had a laminated, embossed, plastic engraved Stromberg logo characterizing the new style. Bracing: dual parallel bracing top. The Master 400 had a "stubby" style headstock, parallel braced top, inlaid mother-of-pearl or Victorian laminated style.

1940S STYLE GUITARS

DELUXE – body size 17.375 in. wide x 20.75 in. length. Top: graduated and carved spruce .875 in. thickness. F-holes Ivoroid bound (white/black). Bridge: adjustable compensating rosewood. The pickguard was imitation tortoiseshell inlaid with white and black Ivoroid borders. Available in Natural or Sunburst finish. The ebony fingerboard had position markers solid pearl blocks. Bracing: single diagonal brace from upper bout to lower bout (1940-41). Tailpiece: 5 Cutout "Y" shaped (gold plated).

| | N/A | $7,600 - 9,500 | $4,500 - 5,700 | |

G-1 – body size 17.375 in. wide 20.75 in. length. Top: graduated and carved spruce .875 in. thickness. F-hole not bound. Bridge: adjustable compensating rosewood. The pickguard was imitation tortoiseshell inlaid with white and black Ivoroid borders. Available in Natural or Sunburst finish. The rosewood fingerboard had position markers of diamond shaped pearl with four indented circle cutouts in inner corners. Bracing: single diagonal brace from upper bout to lower bout (mid to late '40s). Tailpiece: 3 Cutout "Y" shaped (chrome plated).

| | N/A | $6,800 - 8,500 | $4,100 - 5,100 | |

G-3 – body size 17.375 in. wide x 20.75 in. length. Top: graduated and carved spruce .875 in. thickness. F-holes not bound. Bridge: adjustable compensating rosewood. The pickguard was imitation tortoiseshell inlaid with white and black Ivoroid borders. Available in Natural or Sunburst finish. The rosewood fingerboard had position markers of two segmented pearl blocks. Bracing: single diagonal brace from upper bout to lower bout (mid to late 1940s). Tailpiece: 3 Cutout "Y" shaped (gold plated).

| | N/A | $8,000 - 10,000 | $4,800 - 6,000 | |

MASTER 300 – body size 19 in. wide x 21.75 in. length. Top: carved and graduated spruce .875 in. thickness. F-holes bound white. Neck: rock maple with ebony fingerboard, position markers solid pearl block. Ivoroid binding on fingerboard (black and white). Bridge: adjustable compensating rosewood. The pickguard was imitation tortoiseshell inlaid with white and black Ivoroid borders. Available in Natural or Sunburst finish. Bracing: single diagonal brace from upper bout to lower bout (began about 1940). Tailpiece: 5 Cutout "Y" shaped with Stromberg engraving (gold plated).

| | N/A | $24,000 - 30,000 | $14,500 - 18,000 | |

MASTER 400 – body size 19 in. wide x 21.75 in. length. Top: carved and graduated spruce .875 in. thickness. F-holes bound white/black, neck was a 5 piece rock maple with Ivoroid binding (black and white) on fingerboard. The bridge was adjustable compensating rosewood and pickguard was imitation tortoiseshell that was inlaid with white and black Ivoroid borders. Available in Natural or Sunburst finish. Ebony fingerboard, position markers were three segmented pearl blocks. Bracing: single diagonal brace from upper bout to lower bout (began about 1940). Tailpiece: 5 Cutout "Y" shaped with Stromberg engraving (gold plated).

| | N/A | $36,000 - 45,000 | $21,500 - 27,000 | |

MODELS PRODUCED AFTER 1949

DELUXE – body size 17.375 in. wide x 20.75 in. length. Top: graduated and carved spruce .875 in. thickness. F-holes Ivoroid bound white/black. Bridge: adjustable compensating rosewood. The pickguard was imitation tortoiseshell inlaid with white and black Ivoroid borders. Available in Natural or Sunburst finish. Position markers were solid pearl blocks. Bracing: single diagonal brace from upper bout to lower bout. Tailpiece: 5 Cutout "Y" shaped with Stromberg engraving (gold plated).

| | N/A | $7,200 - 9,000 | $4,300 - 5,400 | |

G-3 CUTAWAY – body size 17.375 in. wide x 20.75 in. length. Top: graduated and carved spruce .875 in. thickness. F-hole unbound. Bridge: adjustable compensating rosewood. The pickguard was imitation tortoiseshell inlaid with white and black Ivoroid borders. Available in Natural or Sunburst finish. Rosewood fingerboard had position markers of split pearl blocks. Bracing: single diagonal brace from upper bout to lower bout. Tailpiece: 3 Cutout "Y" shaped (gold plated).

| | N/A | $9,500 - 12,000 | $5,700 - 7,125 | |

G-5 CUTAWAY – (introduced 1950): body size 17.375 in. wide x 20.75 in. length. Top: graduated and carved spruce 7/8 thickness. F-holes Ivoroid bound white. Bridge: adjustable compensating rosewood. Pickguard was imitation tortoiseshell inlaid with white and black Ivoroid borders. Available in Natural or Sunburst finish. Ebony fingerboard had position markers of solid pearl blocks. Bracing: single diagonal brace from upper bout to lower bout. Tailpiece: 3 Cutout "Y" shaped with Stromberg engraving (gold plated).

| | N/A | $16,000 - 20,000 | $9,500 - 12,000 | |

MASTER 400 – body size 18.375 in. wide x 21.75 in. length. Top: carved and graduated spruce .875 in. thickness. F-holes bound white/black. Neck: 5-piece rock maple. Ivoroid binding on fingerboard (black and white). Bridge: adjustable compensating rosewood. The pickguard was imitation tortoiseshell inlaid with white and black Ivoroid borders. Available in Natural or Sunburst finish. Ebony fingerboard had position markers of three segmented pearl blocks or solid pearl blocks. Bracing: single diagonal brace from upper bout to lower bout. Tailpiece: 5 Cutout "Y" shaped with the new Stromberg Logo engraved and gold plated.

| | N/A | $36,000 - 45,000 | $21,500 - 27,000 | |

STRUMSTICK

McNally Instruments. Instruments currently produced. Distributed by McNally Instruments in Rockaway, NJ.

Bob McNally designed the Strumstick, as well as the Backpacker model by Martin. The Strumstick is a guitar with three strings on it and no matter where you place your fingers, it creates a chord. This is achieved by making the entire fret-board a major scale, so there are no flats or sharps. It is intended for someone who does not know much about instruments, but is versatile enough for professionals to get a lot of use out of it. McNally has also introduced the model with different scales (Grand, Alto), different wood types (padouk, rosewood, koa), and more advanced models (four-string chromatic). The Standard Strumstick retails for $140. In 2006, McNally moved from Hibernia, NJ to Rockaway, NJ. For more information, contact the company directly.

CONTACT INFORMATION
STRUMSTICK
11 Longview Road
Rockaway, NJ 07866
Phone No.: 800-397-6563
Fax No.: 973-625-7794
www.strumstick.com
info@strumstick.com

STUDIO KING

See chapter on House Brands.

While this trademark has been identified as a House Brand, the distributor is currently unknown at this time. As information is uncovered, future listings in the *Blue Book of Acoustic Guitars* will be updated (source: Willie G. Moseley, *Stellas & Stratocasters*).

SUNGEUM

Instruments currently produced in Korea.

Sungeum is a guitar brand that was associated with Crafter guitars.

SUNLITE

Instruments currently produced overseas since 1984. Distributed in the U.S. by Sunlite Industrial Corp. in El Mote, CA.

Sunlite produces a wide variety of acoustic guitars that are priced affordable. Sunlite wants to help dealers help musicians find quality instruments that are affordable. They are also well-known in the drum world for their drum sets. Prices for acoustic guitars range from $80 to $400. For more information contact Sunlite directly.

CONTACT INFORMATION
SUNLITE
2436 Merced Ave.
El Monte, CA 91733
Phone No.: 626-448-8018
Fax No.: 626-448-9078
www.sunlitedrum.com
info@sunlitedrum.com

SUPERIOR

See chapter on House Brands.

While this trademark has been identified as a House Brand, the distributor is currently unknown. As information is uncovered, future editions of the *Blue Book of Acoustic Guitars* will be updated (source: Willie G. Moseley, *Stellas & Stratocasters*).

SUPERIOR (CURRENT MFG.)

Instruments currently produced in Mexico. Distributed by the Berkeley Musical Instrument Exchange in Berkeley, CA.

Superior is half of what used to be the K&S Guitar Company, which is no longer in business. Hawaiian style guitars are now built under the Superior name. For more information and pricing contact Berkeley Music.

CONTACT INFORMATION
SUPERIOR (CURRENT MFG.)
2923 Adeline Street
Berkeley, CA 94703
Phone No.: 510-548-7538
www.berkeleymusic.com
bmie@berkeleymusic.com

SUPERTONE

See chapter on House Brands.

This trademark has been identified as a House Brand of Sears, Roebuck and Company between 1914 to 1941. Instruments produced by various (probably) Chicago-based manufacturers, especially Harmony (then a Sears subsidiary). Sears used the Supertone trademark on a full range of guitars, lap steels, banjos, mandolins, ukuleles, and amplifiers.

In 1940, then-company president Jay Krause bought Harmony from Sears by acquiring the controlling stock, and continued to expand the company's production. By 1941, Sears had retired the Supertone trademark in favor of the new Silvertone name. Harmony, though a separate business entity, still sold guitars to Sears for sale under this new brand name (source: Michael Wright, *Vintage Guitar Magazine*).

SUPRO

See chapter on House Brands.

The Supro trademark was the budget brand of the National Dobro company (See National or Valco), who also supplied Montgomery Wards with Supro models under the Airline trademark. National offered budget versions of their designs under the Supro brand name beginning in 1935.

When National moved to Chicago in 1936, the Supro name was on wood-bodied lap steels, amplifiers, and electric Spanish arch top guitars. The first solid body Supro electrics were introduced in 1952, and the fiberglass models began in 1962 (there's almost thirty years of conventionally built guitars in the Supro history).

In 1962, Valco Manufacturing Company name was changed to Valco Guitars, Inc. (the same year that fiberglass models debuted). Kay purchased Valco in 1967, so there are some Kay-built guitars under the Supro brand name. Kay went bankrupt in 1968, and both the Supro and National trademarks were acquired by Chicago's own Strum 'N Drum company. The National name was used on a number of Japanese-built imports, but not the Supro name.

Archer's Music of Fresno, California bought the rights to the Supro name in the early 1980s. They marketed a number of Supro guitars constructed from new old stock (N.O.S.) parts for a limited period of time (source: Michael Wright, *Vintage Guitar Magazine*).

SUZUKI

Instruments currently built in Korea. Currently distributed in the U.S. market by Suzuki Guitars of San Diego, CA.

Suzuki, noted for their quality pianos, offered a range of acoustic and electric guitars designed for the beginning student to intermediate player. In 1996, the company discontinued the guitar line completely. Suzuki guitars are similar to other trademarked models from Korea at comparable prices. There are now guitars and amplifiers again available by Suzuki.

CONTACT INFORMATION
SUZUKI
PO Box 261030
San Diego, CA 92196
Phone No.: 858-566-9710
www.suzukimusic.com

SWARTELE GUITARS

Instruments currently manufactured in Rushville, NY.

Mr. Swartele worked for twenty-one years as a pattern maker before he began building guitars. He builds Model "D" guitars in small production lots of forty instruments and finalizes production in groups of five to six pieces. He uses Honduras mahogany for the back, sides and necks and European and Engelmann spruce for the tops as well as Northwestern red cedar. He has also used Sitka spruce. Necks are graphite reinforced and graphite is also used for the nut and saddle. Swartele guitars are known for their sustain and tonal balance. Instruments are finished in a Natural oil finish. Distributed by Sphere Sound in Rochester, New York.

CONTACT INFORMATION
SWARTELE GUITARS
Rushville, NY 14544
Phone No.: 585-554-3573
www.swartele.com

SWITCH

Instruments currently produced. Distributed by Switchmusic.com, Inc. in La Mirada, CA.

Switch produces a wide variety of acoustic guitars, electric guitars, electric basses, and guitar amplifiers. Most guitars are based on original designs and have unique features. All Switch guitars are built with Vibracell, which is a material different from wood but has the same type of response/tonal frequencies. In 2006, Switch introduced the Cedar Ridge trademark of acoustic guitars. MSR prices are between $400 and $700. Switch also produces custom and signature guitars. For more information contact Switch directly.

CONTACT INFORMATION
SWITCH
Distributed by Switchmusic.com, Inc.
15320 Valley View, Suite #9
La Mirada, CA 90638
Phone No.: 562-404-9777
www.switchmusic.com
info@switchmusic.com

NOTES

T SECTION
20TH CENTURY

Instruments previously produced by Regal (original company of Wulschner & Son) in the late 1890s through the mid-1900s.

Indianapolis retailer/wholesaler Emil Wulschner introduced the Regal line in the 1880s, and in 1896 opened a factory to build guitars and mandolins under the following three trademarks: Regal, 20th Century, and University. In the early 1900s, the 20th Century trademark was a sub-brand distributed by the Fred Gretsch Manufacturing Company. By 1920, the Fred Gretsch Mfg. Co. had settled into its new ten story building in Brooklyn, New York, and was offering music dealers a very large line of instruments that included banjos, mandolins, guitars, violins, drums, and other band instruments. Gretsch used both the 20th Century and Rex trademarks prior to introduction of the Gretsch trademark in 1933.

TACOMA

Instruments previously produced in Tacoma, WA between 1995 and early 2008. Distributed by Fender Musical Instrument Corporation (FMIC) in Scottsdale, AZ. Previously distributed by Tacoma Guitars direct sales force.

> **CONTACT INFORMATION**
> **TACOMA**
> *A Division of FMIC*
> www.tacomaguitars.com
> info@tacomaguitars.com

Tacoma was originally part of Young Chang Akki when the Korean piano company invested over $20 million in a 50 acre Tacoma sawmill plant. Young Chang was also producing cheap acoustic guitars at the same time when they decided they should start a private-label brand with the quality woods from the Tacoma plant. This project never got anywhere and in 1997, Young Chang introduced the Tacoma line of guitars. George Gruhn was a design consultant and developed the off center soundhole. By the late 1990s, Young Chang was facing financial trouble (later they filed for bankruptcy in 2004) and they sold the Tacoma line and saw-mill in 2000 to J.C. Kim. Tacoma Guitars never grew as much as many people thought they could under Kim. In late 2004, Fender Musical Instrument Corporation (FMIC) bought Tacoma from Kim. Fender's main reason to buy Tacoma was to provide more manufacturing space for their acoustic line (Guild). In late 2007, FMIC purchased Kaman Music Corporation and in early 2008, they announced that they were moving production of Tacoma acoustic guitars from the Tacoma, WA factory to Kaman's manufacturing facility in New Hartford, CT. Apparently, that never happened, and in April 2009, Fender told their Tacoma dealers that they were dropping the entire Tacoma product line. It is unknown if any Tacoma guitars were built in Connecticut or what Fender plans to do with the Tacoma brand/trademark.

GENERAL INFORMATION

The Tacoma guitar featured a unique bracing pattern called the Voice Support Bracing and have a unique soundhole shaped like a teardrop positioned on the bass bout for a different sound. All guitars came standard without electronics (with the exception of a few acoustic/electric models, the Papoose, and the Chief). If you wanted them, they were an option, which adds to the price shown. Finish was also an option. All guitars came standard in Natual but Black, Cherry Burst, Sunburst, Trans. Amber, Trans. Blueburst, and Trans. Cherry were all available for an upcharge. All models except for the Wing Series (Chief, Roadking, Thunderchief, and Thunderhawk) were available in left-handed configuration. There are also other options available such as inlay patterns, binding options, purfling, top options, tuner upgrades, and back and side options.

When Fender purchased Tacoma in 2004/05 they implemented their famous numbering scheme, which is XXX-XXXX-XXX. Guitars all start with 038 or 389. 038 indicates a guitar that was produced at the time of switchover. 389 indicates a guitar built under Fender's jurisdiction. Then four middle numbers indicate the production model and the last three are the finish color.

- **Add $125 for B-Band active electronics.**
- **Add $160 for L.R. Baggs Miratone electronics.**
- **Add $200 for Fishman Prefix Plus electronics.**
- **Add $150 - $200 for a color option.**

MSR/NOTES	100%	EXCELLENT	AVERAGE	LAST MSR

ACOUSTIC: CHIEF SERIES

C1C (NO. 038-1100) – similar to the Papoose, except has full sized body/neck, single rounded cutaway, cedar top, mahogany back and sides, 22-fret rosewood fingerboard and bridge, unbound body, 25.5 in. scale, mfg. 1997-2008.

	100%	EXCELLENT	AVERAGE	LAST MSR
	N/A	$475 - 550	$300 - 350	$1,039

- **Add 25% (Last MSR was $1,289) for Fishman Prefix Plus electronics (Model Chief C1CE4, No. 038-1104).**

CKK9C – similar to the C1C, except has a figured Koa body and tortise bound top, satin finish, disc. 2003.

	N/A	$600 - 700	$350 - 425	$1,279

CF26C – similar to the C1C, except has a sitka spruce top, figured maple back and sides, and tortoise bound top, Satin finish, disc. 2003.

	N/A	$675 - 800	$400 - 475	$1,499

CM28C – similar to the C1C, except has mahogany back and sides, and an ebony fingerboard and bridge, Gloss finish, disc. 2003.

	N/A	$650 - 775	$375 - 450	$1,449

MSR/NOTES	100%	EXCELLENT	AVERAGE	LAST MSR

ACOUSTIC: DREADNOUGHT SERIES

DM9 (NO. 038-2100) – dreadnought style, solid mahogany back and sides, solid Sitka spruce top, rosewood fingerboard with abalone dot position markers, three-per-side tuners, tortoise bound top, clear pickguard, herringbone rosette, branded logo on headstock, mfg. 2000-06.

An example of a DM9 courtesy Tacoma

	N/A	$450 - 525	$275 - 325	$999

* DM9-C Cutaway (No. 038-2110) – similar to DM9, except has a single cutaway, mfg. 2000-06.

	N/A	$525 - 600	$350 - 400	$1,172

* DM912 12-String (No. 038-9270) – similar to DM9, except in 12-string configuration and six-per-side tuners, mfg. 2000-03, 2005-06.

	N/A	$525 - 600	$325 - 400	$1,172

DM10 – dreadnought style, solid Sitka spruce top, round soundhole with abalone trim, mahogany back/sides, tortoise body binding, mahogany neck, 14/20-fret rosewood fingerboard with white dot inlay, rosewood bridge, 3-per-side headstock, chrome hardware, available in Natural satin finish, mfg. 1997-2003.

	N/A	$475 - 550	$300 - 350	$1,049

• **Add $250 for Fishman piezo pickup and active EQ (Model DM10E).**

DR12 – dreadnought style body, solid Sitka spruce top, solid rosewood back and sides, one-piece mahogany neck, rosewood fingerboard with abalone dot position markers, abalone rosette, rosewood bridge, chrome hardware, clear pickguard, ivoroid bound body and neck, Ivoroid logo inlaid on headstock, available in Natural Gloss top with Satin back and sides, mfg. 2000-02.

	N/A	$525 - 600	$325 - 375	$1,149

DM14 (NO. 038-3100) – dreadnought style, solid spruce top, round soundhole with abalone trim, mahogany back/sides, tortoise body binding, mahogany neck, 14/20-fret ebony fingerboard with white dot inlay, three-per-side tuners, ebony bridge, chrome hardware, mfg. 2004-06.

	N/A	$650 - 750	$375 - 450	$1,399

* DM14C Cutaway (No. 038-3120) – similar to the DM14, except has a single cutaway, mfg. 2003-06.

	N/A	$725 - 850	$400 - 475	$1,599

* DM1412 12-String – similar to the DM14, except in 12-string configuration, mfg. 2004 only.

	N/A	$700 - 825	$400 - 475	$1,540

DR14 (NO. 038-3200) – similar to the DM14, except has solid rosewood back and sides, mfg. 2002-06.

	N/A	$650 - 750	$375 - 450	$1,465

* DR14C Cutaway (No. 038-3210) – similar to the DR14, except has a single cutaway, mfg. 2004-06.

	N/A	$725 - 850	$425 - 500	$1,665

DK14 – similar to the DR14, except has figured koa back and sides, mfg. 2002-03.

	N/A	$675 - 800	$425 - 500	$1,299

DM16-C – dreadnought style with single cutaway, solid Sitka spruce top, solid mahogany back, solid sides, rosewood fingerboard with abalone dot position markers, abalone rosette, torrtoise bound body, inlaid ivoroid logo on headstock, rosewood bridge, available in Gloss Natural finish, disc. 2003.

	N/A	$700 - 825	$450 - 525	$1,349

DR16-R – similar to DM16-C, except has solid rosewood back. Natural Gloss finish, disc. 2003.

	N/A	$725 - 875	$475 - 550	$1,449

DM18 – dreadnought style body, solid Sitka spruce top, solid mahogany back and sides, rosewood fingerboard with abalone "Gingko" position markers, rosewood bridge, abalone rosette, tortoise bound body, 4-color top purfle, clear pickguard, inlaid ivoroid logo on headstock, available in Natural Gloss finish, disc. 2003.

	N/A	$650 - 750	$400 - 475	$1,239

* DM1812 12-String – similar to DM18, except in a 12-string configuration, Natural Gloss finish, mfg 2000-03.

	N/A	$675 - 800	$425 - 500	$1,389

MSR/NOTES	100%	EXCELLENT	AVERAGE	LAST MSR

DR20 – similar to the DM10, except features rosewood back/sides, herringbone pufling/ivoroid body binding, available in Natural gloss finish, mfg. 1997-2003.

	N/A	$675 - 800	$425 - 500	$1,299

• **Add $150 for Fishman Basic piezo pickup and active EQ (Model DR20E).**

DF21 – dreadnought style Sitka spruce top, figured maple back and sides, rosewood fingerboard and bridge, tortoise binding, pearl inlays, herringbone purfling, available in Gloss finish, mfg. 2001-03.

	N/A	$650 - 800	$400 - 500	$1,599

DM28 (NO. 038-4300) – dreadnought style, solid Sitka spruce top, round soundhole with abalone trim, mahogany back/sides/neck, tortoise body binding, mahogany neck, 14/20-fret ebony fingerboard with abalone inlay, ebony bridge, three-per-side headstock, gold hardware, mfg. 2004-06.

	N/A	$750 - 900	$450 - 525	$1,705

* *DM28C Cutaway (No. 389-4150)* – similar to the DM28, except has a single cutaway, mfg. 2005-06.

	N/A	$825 - 975	$500 - 600	$1,905

* *DM2812 12-String (No. 389-4160)* – similar to the DM28, except in 12-string configuration and six-per-side tuners, mfg. 2005-06.

	N/A	$800 - 950	$500 - 575	$1,865

DR28 (NO. 038-4400) – dreadnought style, solid Sitka spruce top, round soundhole with abalone trim, rosewood back/sides mahogany neck, tortoise body binding, mahogany neck, 14/20-fret ebony fingerboard with abalone inlay, ebony bridge, three-per-side headstock, gold hardware, mfg. 2004-06.

	N/A	$825 - 950	$475 - 550	$1,772

DR38 – dreadnought style body, solid Sitka spruce top, solid Rosewood back and sides, ebony fingerboard with abalone "Gingko" position markers, abalone top purfling, abalone rosette, ebony bridge, ivoroid bound body and neck, inlaid ivoroid logo on headstock, chrome hardware, clear pickguard, available in Natural Gloss finish, disc. 2003.

	N/A	$950 - 1,100	$600 - 700	$1,899

DK40 – dreadnought style Sitka spruce top, figured koa back and sides, ebony fingerboard and bridge, tortise binding, rosette and neck inlays, abalone purfle, available in Gloss finish, mfg. 2002-03.

	N/A	$1,000 - 1,200	$650 - 750	$1,999

DR55 – dreadnought style, red spruce body, Brazillian ebony fingerboard, ebony bridge, maple binding, abalone purfling and neck inlay, available in Gloss finish, mfg. 2002-03.

	N/A	$1,100 - 1,300	$675 - 800	$2,349

DR55 (NO. 389-4190) – dreadnought style, sitka spruce top, three-piece rosewood back and sides, ebony fingerboard and bridge, herringbone purfling and rosette, available in Gloss finish, mfg. 2002-06.

	N/A	$1,000 - 1,200	$650 - 750	$2,199

ACOUSTIC: JUMBO SERIES

JM9 (NO. 038-2300) – jumbo body, Sitka spruce top mahogany back and sides, rosewood fingerboard and bridge, tortoise top binding, herringbone rosette, disc. 2006.

An example of a JM9 courtesy Tacoma

	N/A	$525 - 600	$325 - 375	$1,172

JM16 – jumbo body, 25.5 in. scale, solid Sitka spruce top, solid mahogany back and sides, rosewood fingerboard with abalone dot position markers, rosewood bridge, ivoroid bound body, neck and headstock, ivoroid logo inlaid in the headstock, abalone rosette, chrome hardware, available in Gloss Natural finish, disc. 2001.

	N/A	$650 - 750	$375 - 450	$1,429

* *JM16C Cutaway* – similar to JM16, except has a single cutaway, available in Gloss Sunburst finish, disc. 2002.

	N/A	$675 - 800	$400 - 475	$1,499

MSR/NOTES	100%	EXCELLENT	AVERAGE	LAST MSR

* *JM1612C 12-String Cutaway* – similar to JM16C, except in a 12-string configuration, available in Natural Gloss finish, mfg. 2000-02.

| | N/A | $800 - 1,000 | $475 - 600 | $1,649 |

JF1912 – jumbo body, Sitka spruce top, figured maple back and sides, tortoise binding, 12-string configuration, Gloss finish, mfg. 2002-03

| | N/A | $900 - 1,050 | $600 - 700 | $1,749 |

JF21 – jumbo body, Sitka spruce top, figured maple back and sides, tortoise binding, herringbone purfling, Pearl Wave inlays, Gloss finish, disc. 2003.

| | N/A | $850 - 1,000 | $575 - 650 | $1,699 |

JF2812 12-STRING (NO. 389-6000) – 12-string configuration, jumbo style, solid Sitka spruce top, round soundhole with abalone trim, solid flamed maple back/sides mahogany neck, tortoise body binding, mahogany neck, 14/20-fret ebony fingerboard with abalone inlay, six-per-side tuners, ebony bridge, gold hardware, mfg. 2005-06.

| | N/A | $1,050 - 1,250 | $700 - 850 | $2,399 |

JK28C CUTAWAY (NO. 038-4600) – jumbo single cutaway style, solid Sitka spruce top, round soundhole with abalone trim, koa back/sides mahogany neck, tortoise body binding, mahogany neck, 14/20-fret ebony fingerboard with abalone inlay, three-per-side tuners, ebony bridge, gold hardware, mfg. 2004-06.

| | N/A | $950 - 1,100 | $625 - 725 | $2,132 |

JK50C CUTAWAY – rounded lower bout/slim waist style with single rounded cutaway, solid Sitka spruce top, round soundhole with abalone trim, koa back/sides, herringbone purfling/ivoroid body binding, mahogany neck, 14/20-fret bound rosewood fingerboard with abalone inlay, bound flamed koa peghead with maple logo inlay, rosewood bridge, 3-per-side headstock, chrome hardware, available in Natural satin finish, mfg. 1997-2003.

| | N/A | $1,000 - 1,150 | $675 - 800 | $1,899 |

JK50CE CUTAWAY ELECTRIC – rounded lower bout/slim waist style with single rounded cutaway, solid Sitka spruce top, round soundhole with abalone trim, koa back/sides, herringbone purfling/ivoroid body binding, mahogany neck, 14/20-fret bound rosewood fingerboard with abalone inlay, bound flamed koa peghead with maple logo inlay, rosewood bridge, three-per-side tuners, chrome hardware, Fishman Prefix system, available in Natural satin finish, mfg. 1997-2000.

| | N/A | $800 - 1,000 | $475 - 600 | $1,449 |

JR55 (NO. 389-6300) – jumbo body, Sitka spruce top, rosewood three-piece back and sides, maple binding, abalone purfling, rosette and neck inlays, Gloss finish, disc. 2006.

| | N/A | $1,050 - 1,250 | $675 - 800 | $2,399 |

ACOUSTIC: LITTLE JUMBO (E) SERIES

Lawrence Juber (LJ) Little Jumbo Series designed in conjunction with guitarist Lawrence Juber.

EM9 – small body jumbo, solid Sitka spruce top, solid mahogany back and sides, rosewood fingerboard with abalone dot position markers, rosewood bridge, tortoise bound top, clear pickguard, herringbone rosette, logo branded on headstock, available in Light Satin Natural finish, disc. 2003.

| | N/A | $450 - 525 | $275 - 325 | $999 |

* *EM9C Cutaway (No. 038-2200)* – similar to EM9, except has a single cutaway, mfg. 2000-07.

| | N/A | $500 - 625 | $300 - 375 | $1,239 |

EM10CE2 CUTAWAY ELECTRIC – single Florentine cutaway hollowbody, 3.25 in. deep, solid Sitka spruce top, solid mahogany back and sides, rosewood fingerboard with abalone dot position markers, rosewood bridge, tortoise bound neck and body, inlaid ivoroid logo on headstock, abalone rosette, Tacoma E2 Preamp system, available in Satin Natural finish, disc.

| | N/A | $550 - 650 | $350 - 425 | $1,189 |

EM14C CUTAWAY (NO. 038-3300) – little jumbo single cutaway style, solid spruce top, round soundhole with abalone trim, mahogany back/sides, tortoise body binding, mahogany neck, 14/20-fret ebony fingerboard with white dot inlay, ebony bridge, three-per-side headstock, chrome hardware, mfg. 2004-07.

| | N/A | $650 - 825 | $375 - 475 | $1,639 |

EM16CE4 CUTAWAY ELECTRIC – similar to EM10CE2, except has abalone "wave" position markers, available in Gloss Sunburst finish, disc.

| | N/A | $675 - 800 | $400 - 475 | $1,489 |

EM19 – similar to EM9, except has black hardware, inlaid ivoroid logo on headstock, ebony fingerboard, ebony bridge, ivoroid bound body, available in Gloss finish, disc. 2001.

| | N/A | $525 - 600 | $325 - 375 | $1,149 |

* *EM19C Cutaway* – similar to EM19, except has a single cutaway, available in Gloss finish, disc. 2002.

| | N/A | $600 - 750 | $375 - 450 | $1,499 |

MSR/NOTES	100%	EXCELLENT	AVERAGE	LAST MSR

EKK19C CUTAWAY – similar to EM19, except has a cutaway figured koa body, ebony fingerboard and bridge, and herringbone rosette, available in Gloss finish, mfg. 2003 only.

	N/A	$850 - 1,000	$575 - 650	$1,599

ER19C CUTAWAY – similar to EM19, except has rosewood back and sides, mfg. 2003 only.

	N/A	$800 - 950	$525 - 600	$1,599

ER22C CUTAWAY – similar to EM19C, except has solid cedar top, solid rosewood back and sides, available in Gloss Natural finish, disc. 2003.

	N/A	$850 - 1,000	$575 - 650	$1,599

ER28C CUTAWAY (NO. 038-4500) – little jumbo single cutaway style, solid Sitka spruce top, round soundhole with abalone trim, rosewood back/sides mahogany neck, tortoise body binding, mahogany neck, 14/20-fret ebony fingerboard with abalone inlay, ebony bridge, three-per-side headstock, gold hardware, mfg. 2004-07.

	N/A	$800 - 1,000	$475 - 600	$1,932

ECR38C CUTAWAY – single cutaway body, cedar top, rosewood back and sides, ebony fingerboard and bridge, abalone purfling and neck inlay, gloss finish, mfg. 2002-03.

	N/A	$1,100 - 1,300	$675 - 800	$2,199

ECR52C CUTAWAY – single cutaway body, Englemann spruce top, rosewood back and sides, koa binding, ebony fingerboard and bridge, abalone purfling and neck inlay, gloss finish, mfg. 2003 only.

	N/A	$1,200 - 1,400	$700 - 850	$2,399

EBZ24 CUTAWAY – single cutaway body, sitka spruce top, Brazilian rosewood back and sides, ivoroid binding, ebony fingerboard and bridge, abalone purfling and neck inlay, gloss finish, mfg. 2003 only.

	N/A	$1,250 - 1,500	$800 - 950	$2,649

ECR15NC CUTAWAY – nylon single cutaway body, cedar top, rosewood back and sides, ivoroid binding, rosewood fingerboard and bridge, inlaid rosewood rosette, gloss finish, mfg. 2002-03.

	N/A	$600 - 700	$375 - 450	$1,199

ER64NC CUTAWAY – similar to the ECR15NC, except has an Englemann spruce top, ebony fingerboard and bridge, and abalone purfling inlaid rosewood rosette, mfg. 2002-03.

	N/A	$950 - 1,100	$650 - 750	$1,899

ACOUSTIC: PAPOOSE SERIES

All Papoose guitars feature a small off-center teardrop-shaped pickguard and they are tuned a fifth above a regular guitar (ADGBEA - playing the Papoose is like playing a regular guitar capoed at the fifth fret).

P1 PAPOOSE (NO. 038-1400) – travel sized solid mahogany body and sides, cedar top, mahogany neck, 15/21-fret rosewood fingerboard with white dot inlay, quotation mark soundhole in bass bout, pinless bridge, three-per-side headstock, chrome hardware, 19.1 in. scale, mfg. 1997-2008.

	N/A	$375 - 450	$225 - 275	$799

* **P1E Papoose Electric (No. 389-1410)** – similar to the P1, except has a piezo pickup and an endpin jack (no electronics/controls), disc. 2008.

	N/A	$425 - 500	$250 - 300	$899

* **P112 Papoose 12-String (No. 038-1410)** – similar to the P1, except in 12-string configuration and six-per-side tuners, mfg. summer 2003-07.

	N/A	$375 - 475	$225 - 275	$932

»**P112E Papoose 12-String Electric (No. 038-1411)** – similar to the P112E Papoose except has a piezo pickup and an endpin jack (no electronics/controls), mfg. summer 2003-07.

	N/A	$425 - 525	$250 - 325	$1,032

P2 PAPOOSE – similar to the P1, except has rosewood back, sides, and fingerboard, and a bound body, mfg. 1997-2002.

	N/A	$400 - 475	$250 - 300	$779

P4KN PAPOOSE NYLON – Papoose sized figured koa body, nylon string configuration, ivoroid bound top, disc. 2003.

	N/A	$425 - 500	$250 - 300	$949

P6K PAPOOSE KOA – Papoose sized figured koa body, ebony fingerboard and bridge, gold hardware, ivoroid bound top, available in Gloss Natural finish, disc. 2003.

	N/A	$650 - 750	$400 - 475	$1,399

ACOUSTIC: PARLOR SERIES

PM9 – parlor style body, Sitka spruce top, mahogany back and sides, rosewood fingerboard and bridge, tortoise bound top, herringbone purfling, light satin finish, disc. 2003.

	N/A	$450 - 525	$275 - 325	$999

MSR/NOTES	100%	EXCELLENT	AVERAGE	LAST MSR

PR12 – parlor style body, Sitka spruce top, rosewood back and sides, rosewood fingerboard and bridge, ivoroid binding, gloss top and satin back and sides finish, mfg. 2002-03

	N/A	$550 - 650	$350 - 425	$1,149

PM20 – rounded lower bout/slim waist style, solid Sitka spruce top, round soundhole with abalone trim, mahogany back/sides, herringbone purfling/ivoroid body binding, 25.5 in. scale, mahogany neck, 14/20-fret bound rosewood fingerboard with white dot inlay, rosewood bridge, 3-per-side headstock, chrome hardware, available in Natural gloss finish, mfg. 1997-2003.

	N/A	$650 - 750	$425 - 500	$1,249

* **Add $250 for Fishman Prefix piezo pickup and active EQ (Model PM20E).**

PK30 – similar to the PM20, except features koa back/sides, bound flamed koa peghead with maple logo inlay, abalone position markers, available in Natural gloss finish, mfg. 1997-2003.

	N/A	$950 - 1,100	$650 - 750	$1,999

* **Add $250 for Fishman Prefix piezo pickup and active EQ (Model PK30E).**

PKK40 – parlor style body, figured koa body, ebony fingerboard and bridge, abalone purfling and floral neck inlay, gloss finish, disc. 2003.

	N/A	$1,650 - 2,000	$1,100 - 1,350	$3,399

PM28 (NO. 038-4700) – parlor style, spruce top, mahogany back and sides, abalone binding, round soundhole with rosette, three-per-side tuners, gold hardware, Natural finish, mfg. 2004-06.

	N/A	$750 - 875	$500 - 575	$1,732

ACOUSTIC: ROADKING DREADNOUGHT SERIES

The Roadking Series feature the off center teardrop soundhole in a dreadnought body style.

RM6 – dreadnought style body, same design as the Chief, Sitka spruce top, mahogany back and sides, sound hole on bass bout, rosewood fingerboard and bridge, unbound body, available in light satin finish, mfg. 2002-03.

	N/A	$350 - 425	$200 - 250	$799

* ***RM6C Cutaway (No. 038-1500)*** – similar to the RM6, except has a single cutaway, mfg. 2002-08.

	N/A	$475 - 550	$275 - 325	$1,065

* **Add 25% (Last MSR was $1,315) for Fishman Prefix Plus electronics (Model RM6CE4, No. 038-1504).**

RR8 – dreadnought style body, same design as the Chief, Sitka spruce top, rosewood back and sides, sound hole on bass bout, rosewood fingerboard and bridge, tortoise bound top, inlaid logo, available in satin finish, mfg. 2002-03.

	N/A	$450 - 525	$275 - 325	$999

* ***RR8C Cutaway*** – similar to the RR8, except has a single cutaway, mfg. 2002-03.

	N/A	$500 - 600	$300 - 375	$1,129

RMM9C CUTAWAY – dreadnought style single cutaway body, same design as the Chief, mahogany body, sound hole on bass bout, rosewood fingerboard and bridge, tortoise bound top, available in light satin finish, mfg. 2002-03.

	N/A	$450 - 525	$275 - 325	$999

RM26C CUTAWAY – dreadnought style single cutaway body, same design as the Chief, Sitka spruce top, mahogany back and sides, sound hole on bass bout, rosewood fingerboard and bridge, tortoise bound top, available in gloss finish, mfg. 2002-03.

	N/A	$600 - 700	$375 - 450	$1,279

ACOUSTIC BARITONE: THUNDERHAWK SERIES

The Thunderhawk Barione Series feature the off center tear drop soundhole, are tuned to baritone BEADGB, and have a 29 in. scale.

BM6C THUNDERHAWK CUTAWAY (NO. 038-1000) – baritone configuration, single smooth cutaway body, spruce top, mahogany back and sides, teardrop soundhole on bass bout, three-per-side tuners, mfg. 2004-08.

	N/A	$550 - 650	$350 - 425	$1,265

* **Add 20% (Last MSR was $1,515) for Fishman Prefix Plus electronics (Model BM6CE4, No. 038-1004).**

BM28C THUNDERHAWK CUTAWAY (NO. 389-2600) – baritone configuration, single smooth cutaway body, Sitka spruce top, figured mapleback and sides, teardrop soundhole on bass bout, ebony fingerboard and bridge, three-per-side tuners, mfg. 2005-07.

	N/A	$850 - 1,050	$500 - 625	$2,065

ACOUSTIC BASS: THUNDERCHIEF SERIES

The Thunderchief Bass series is just what it sounds. It is a bass version of the Chief series. All of these models have the soundhole in the upper bass bout. All models are available in fretless configuration for no additional cost (suffix F).

CB10C THUNDERCHIEF CUTAWAY BASS (NO. 038-1200) – single cutaway chief style body, Sitka spruce top, mahogany back and sides, rosewood fingerboard, unbound body, two-per-side tuners, mfg. 1999-2008.

	N/A	$525 - 625	$325 - 375	$1,239

* **Add 20% (Last MSR was $1,489) for Fishman Prefix Plus electronics (Model CB10CE4, No. 038-1204).**

MSR/NOTES	100%	EXCELLENT	AVERAGE	LAST MSR

* **CB105C Thunderchief Cutaway Bass Five-String (No. 389-1250)** – similar to the CB10C, except in five-string configuration and 3/2-per-side tuners, mfg. 1999-2008.

	N/A	$650 - 750	$375 - 450	$1,372

• Add 20% (Last MSR was $1,622) for Fishman Prefix Plus electronics (Model CB105CE4, No. 038-1254).

CB28C THUNDERCHIEF CUTAWAY BASS (NO. 389-3201) – single cutaway chief style body, Sitka spruce top, figured maple back and sides, ebony fingerboard, tortoise binding, pearl inlay, two-per-side tuners, gloss finish, mfg. 1999-2007.

	N/A	$925 - 1,150	$550 - 700	$2,265

* **CB285C Thunderchief Cutaway Bass Five-String (No. 389-3190)** – similar to the CB28C, except in five-string configuration and 3/2-per-side tuners, mfg. 1999-2007.

	N/A	$1,000 - 1,250	$600 - 750	$2,465

TAKAMINE

Instruments currently manufactured in Japan, China, and Korea since the early 1960s. Distributed by the KMC Music in Bloomfield, CT.

CONTACT INFORMATION
TAKAMINE
Distributed by KMC Music
55 Griffin Road South
Bloomfield, CT 06002-0507
www.takamine.com
info@takamine.com

Takamine was originally founded in Japan during the early 1960s and is named from the mountain near their factory in Sakashita, Japan. Mass Hirade, who has a line of classical guitars named after him in Takamine's line, came to work for Takamine in the late 1960s, and it was at this time when Takamine began to take off. Originally, Takamine built guitars for Martin's Sigma series through the Coast distributors. Kaman Music Corporation bought Coast in the mid-1970s, which forced Martin to contract their Sigma guitars to another company. At the same time Kaman/Ovation encouraged Takamine to start building guitars under their own trademark. Soon thereafter, Kaman started importing Takamine-branded guitars into the U.S. (Takamine was also distributed in many other countries). Most early models were copies of popular American designs - especially several Martin models. Not only are many of these guitars similar in design, but the logo was a near match other than the name. In the late 1970s, Takamine, along with many other Japanese manufacturers, were sued by a few American guitar builders, including Martin, for trademark infringement. Takamine agreed to stop using Martin's logo on their guitars and came up with their own. Guitars from this era are known to most guitar collectors as the pre-lawsuit era, and many of these instruments have become extremely collectible today.

Takamine continues to produce a wide variety of acoustic instruments ranging from entry-level guitars to highly ornate and limited edition models. While most guitars were produced in Japan, Takamine has shifted some production to Korea and China in the 2000s. Also, Takamine briefly entered the electric market with a few models in the 1980s. Takamine is still part of Kaman Music and is viewed as a traditional alternative to Ovation's bowl-back guitars. In late 2007, the Fender Musical Instrument Corporation (FMIC) bought Kaman Music, which included the Takamine brand. For more information, visit Takamine's website or contact them directly.

ACOUSTIC: G SERIES G10/G20/G30/G50/G70/G90 SERIES

This series was introduced in summer 2013.

GD-10 – dreadnought-style body, spruce top, mahogany back and sides, round soundhole, mahogany neck, 14/20-fret rosewood fingerboard with pearloid dot inlays, three-per-side chrome tuners, rosewood bridge, black pickguard, available in Satin Natural finish, mfg. summer 2013-present.

MSR $260	$180	$115 - 145	$65 - 80	

* **GD-10CE** – similar to the GD-10, except has a single cutaway and TP-E electronics, available in Satin Natural finish, mfg. summer 2013-present.

MSR $390	$270	$175 - 215	$100 - 115	

GD-20 – dreadnought-style body, solid cedar top, mahogany back and sides, round soundhole, mahogany neck, 14/20-fret rosewood fingerboard with pearloid dot inlays, three-per-side chrome tuners, rosewood bridge, no pickguard, available in Satin Natural finish, mfg. summer 2013-present.

MSR $360	$250	$160 - 200	$90 - 110	

GN-20 – NEX-style body, solid cedar top, mahogany back and sides, round soundhole, mahogany neck, 14/20-fret rosewood fingerboard with pearloid dot inlays, three-per-side chrome tuners, rosewood bridge, no pickguard, available in Satin Natural finish, mfg. summer 2013-present.

MSR $360	$250	$160 - 200	$90 - 110	

GD-30 – dreadnought-style body, solid spruce top, mahogany back and sides, round soundhole with pearloid rosette, mahogany neck, 14/20-fret rosewood fingerboard with pearloid dot inlays, three-per-side chrome tuners, rosewood bridge, black pickguard, available in Gloss Black or Gloss Natural finish, mfg. summer 2013-present.

MSR $410	$280	$185 - 225	$105 - 125	

* **GD-30-12 12-String** – similar to the GD-30, except in 12-string configuration with six-per-side tuners, available in Gloss Natural finish, mfg. summer 2013-present.

MSR $465	$320	$210 - 255	$115 - 140	

MSR/NOTES	100%	EXCELLENT	AVERAGE	LAST MSR

* GD-30CE – similar to the GD-30, except has a single cutaway and TP-4TD electronics, available in Gloss Black or Gloss Natural finish, mfg. summer 2013-present.

| MSR $540 | $370 | $245 - 295 | $135 - 160 | |

»GD-30CE-12 12-String – similar to the GD-30CE, except in 12-string configuration with six-per-side tuners, available in Gloss Natural finish, mfg. summer 2013-present.

| MSR $585 | $400 | $265 - 325 | $145 - 175 | |

GF-30CE – FXC-style body with single cutaway, solid spruce top, mahogany back and sides, round soundhole with pearloid rosette, mahogany neck, 14/20-fret rosewood fingerboard with pearloid dot inlays, three-per-side chrome tuners, rosewood bridge, black pickguard, TP-4TD electronics, available in Gloss Black, Gloss Brown Sunburst, or Gloss Natural finish, mfg. summer 2013-present.

| MSR $540 | $370 | $245 - 295 | $135 - 160 | |

GN-30 – NEX-style body, solid spruce top, mahogany back and sides, round soundhole with pearloid rosette, mahogany neck, 14/20-fret rosewood fingerboard with pearloid dot inlays, three-per-side chrome tuners, rosewood bridge, black pickguard, available in Gloss Black or Gloss Natural finish, mfg. summer 2013-present.

| MSR $410 | $280 | $185 - 225 | $105 - 125 | |

* GN-30CE – similar to the GN-30, except with a single cutaway, available in Gloss Black or Gloss Natural finish, mfg. summer 2013-present.

| MSR $540 | $370 | $245 - 295 | $135 - 160 | |

GD-51 – dreadnought-style body, solid spruce top, rosewood back and sides, round soundhole with abalone rosette, mahogany neck, 14/20-fret rosewood fingerboard with MOP dot inlays, three-per-side gold tuners, rosewood bridge, black pickguard, available in Gloss Brown Sunburst or Gloss Natural finish, mfg. summer 2013-present.

| MSR $505 | $350 | $225 - 280 | $125 - 150 | |

* GD-51CE – similar to the GD-51, except with a single cutaway and TP-4TD electronics, available in Gloss Brown Sunburst or Gloss Natural finish, mfg. summer 2013-present.

| MSR $610 | $420 | $275 - 325 | $155 - 185 | |

GN-51 – NEX-style body, solid spruce top, rosewood back and sides, round soundhole, mahogany neck, 14/20-fret bound rosewood fingerboard with MOP dot inlays, three-per-side gold tuners, rosewood bridge, black pickguard, available in Gloss Brown Sunburst or Gloss Natural finish, mfg. summer 2013-present.

| MSR $505 | $350 | $225 - 280 | $125 - 150 | |

* GN-51CE – similar to the GN-51, except with a single cutaway and TP-4TD electronics, available in Gloss Brown Sunburst or Gloss Natural finish, mfg. summer 2013-present.

| MSR $610 | $420 | $275 - 325 | $155 - 185 | |

GD-71CE – dreadnought-style body with single cutaway, solid spruce top, rosewood back and sides, round soundhole with abalone rosette, mahogany neck, 14/20-fret bound rosewood fingerboard with maple dots inlays, three-per-side gold tuners, rosewood bridge, tortoiseshell pickguard, TK40D electronics, available in Gloss Brown Sunburst or Gloss Natural finish, mfg. summer 2013-present.

| MSR $730 | $500 | $325 - 400 | $185 - 220 | |

GN-71CE – NEX-style body with single cutaway, solid spruce top, rosewood back and sides, round soundhole with abalone rosette, mahogany neck, 14/20-fret rosewood fingerboard with maple dots inlays, three-per-side gold tuners with amber buttons, rosewood bridge, tortoiseshell pickguard, TK40D electronics, available in Gloss Brown Sunburst or Gloss Natural finish, mfg. summer 2013-present.

| MSR $730 | $500 | $325 - 400 | $185 - 220 | |

GJ-72CE – jumbo-style body with single cutaway, solid spruce top, flame maple back and sides, round soundhole with abalone rosette, mahogany neck, 14/20-fret rosewood fingerboard with 12th fret abalone reversed mountain inlay, three-per-side gold tuners with pearl buttons, rosewood bridge, tortoiseshell pickguard, TK40D electronics, available in Gloss Brown Sunburst or Gloss Natural finish, mfg. summer 2013-present.

| MSR $800 | $550 | $350 - 450 | $200 - 240 | |

* GJ-72CE-12 12-String – similar to the GJ-72CE, except in 12-string configuration with six-per-side tuners, available in Gloss Brown Sunburst or Gloss Natural finish, mfg. summer 2013-present.

| MSR $860 | $600 | $375 - 475 | $215 - 260 | |

GD-93 – dreadnought-style body, solid spruce top, three-piece rosewood with quilt maple center back, rosewood sides, round soundhole with dark wood rosette, maple body binding, dark wood body purfling, mahogany neck, 14/20-fret bound rosewood fingerboard with abalone dot inlays, bound headstock, three-per-side gold tuners with black buttons, rosewood bridge, tortoiseshell pickguard, available in Gloss Natural finish, mfg. summer 2013-present.

| MSR $650 | $450 | $295 - 350 | $165 - 195 | |

* GD-93CE – similar to the GD-93, except with a single cutaway and TK40D electronics, available in Gloss Natural finish, mfg. summer 2013-present.

| MSR $800 | $550 | $350 - 450 | $200 - 240 | |

MSR/NOTES	100%	EXCELLENT	AVERAGE	LAST MSR

GN-93 – NEXT-style body, solid spruce top, three-piece rosewood back with quilt maple center, rosewood sides, round soundhole with dark wood rosette, maple body binding, dark wood body purfling, mahogany neck, 14/20-fret bound rosewood fingerboard with abalone dot inlays, bound headstock, three-per-side gold tuners with black buttons, rosewood bridge, tortoiseshell pickguard, available in Gloss Natural finish, mfg. summer 2013-present.

MSR $650	$450	$295 - 350	$165 - 195	

* **GN-93CE** – similar to the GN-93, except with a single cutaway and TK40D electronics, available in Gloss Natural finish, mfg. summer 2013-present.

MSR $800	$550	$350 - 450	$200 - 240	

GY-93 – New Yorker-style body, solid spruce top, three-piece rosewood back with quilt maple center, rosewood sides, round soundhole with dark wood rosette, maple body binding, dark wood body purfling, mahogany neck, 14/20-bound rosewood fingerboard with abalone dot inlays, bound headstock, three-per-side gold tuners with black buttons, rosewood bridge, no pickguard, available in Gloss Natural finish, mfg. summer 2013-present.

MSR $650	$450	$295 - 350	$165 - 195	

* **GY-93E** – similar to the GY-93, except has TK40D electronics, available in Gloss Natural finish, mfg. summer 2013-present.

MSR $800	$550	$350 - 450	$200 - 240	

ACOUSTIC: G SERIES MODELS STARTING WITH 1, 2, & MISC.

G-10 – dreadnought style, cedar top, round soundhole, bound body, multi-stripe purfling/rosette, mahogany back/sides/neck, 14/20-fret rosewood fingerboard, rosewood bridge with white black dot pins, 3-per-side gold tuners, available in Natural finish, mfg. 1994-99.

	N/A	$200 - 250	$100 - 150	$499

* **EG-10C** – similar to G-10, except has single round cutaway, crystal bridge pickups, 4-band EQ, available in Natural finish, mfg. 1994-2003.

	N/A	$400 - 475	$200 - 250	$860

EG-15C – similar to G-10, except has a gloss finish, disc. 2003.

	N/A	$450 - 525	$250 - 300	$1,000

EG-40C – NEX single cutaway body, solid cedar top, Sepele mahogany with solid back, rosewood fingerboard, N4B electronics, available in Gloss Natural finish, disc. 2003.

	N/A	$400 - 475	$200 - 250	$900

EG-45SC – small body acoustic electric with cutaway, solid spruce top, rosewood back and sides, N4B pre-amp system, gold tuners, Sante Fe position marker at the 12th fret, available in Natural finish, disc. 2003.

	N/A	$450 - 525	$250 - 300	$1,000

G-116 – classical body style, spruce top, nato back and sides, rosewood fingerboard, available in Gloss Natural finish, disc. 2005.

	N/A	$115 - 150	$70 - 90	$289

* **EG-116** – similar to the G-116, except has DJ2 electronics, disc. 2005.

	N/A	$170 - 210	$110 - 140	$399

G-124 – classical style, spruce top, round soundhole, bound body, wood marquetry rosette, nato or mahogany (2006-present) back/sides, mahogany neck, 12/19-fret rosewood fingerboard, tied rosewood bridge, three-per-side chrome tuners with plastic buttons, available in Natural finish, mfg. 1994-2001, 2006-2013.

	$200	$120 - 150	$70 - 90	$300

* **EG-124C** – similar to the G-124, except has a single cutaway and TP4T electronics, available in Natural finish, mfg. 2006-2013.

	$350	$200 - 250	$120 - 150	$500

* **G-124S** – similar to the G-124, except has a solid spruce top, mfg. 1994-2005.

	N/A	$200 - 250	$120 - 150	$499

* **EG-124SC** – similar to G-124, except has single round cutaway, solid spruce top, crystal bridge pickups, and 4-band EQ, available in Natural finish, mfg. 1994-2005.

	N/A	$325 - 375	$175 - 225	$759

G-128S – classical style, solid spruce top, rosewood back and sides, round soundhole, 12/19-fret rosewood fingerboard, open-style headstock with three-per-side gold tuners with pearl buttons, rosewood bridge, available in Natural finish, mfg. 2006-2013.

	$300	$175 - 225	$110 - 140	$450

EG-128SC – similar to the G-128S, except has a single cutaway and TP4T electonics, mfg. 2006-2013.

	$450	$275 - 325	$150 - 200	$650

EG-140SRC – small body acoustic electric with cutaway, solid spruce top, rosewood back and sides, gold tuners, N4B preamp system, available in Red Stain finish, disc.

	N/A	$400 - 475	$225 - 275	$949

MSR/NOTES	100%	EXCELLENT	AVERAGE	LAST MSR
EG-141SC – similar to EG-140SRC, except has spruce top, nato back and sides, available in Black Gloss finish, disc. 2003.				
	N/A	$350 - 425	$200 - 250	$850
G-220 – NEX style, spruce top, mahogany back and sides, rosewood fingerboard with dot inlays, three-per-side tuners, rosewood bridge, black pickguard, chrome hardware, Natural finish, mfg. 2005 only.				
	N/A	$120 - 150	$70 - 90	$289
* *EG-220C* – similar to the G-220, except has a single cutaway with TP-4 electronics, mfg. 2005 only.				
	N/A	$175 - 225	$110 - 140	$429
G-240/G-241 – dreadnought body style, spruce top, nato back and sides, rosewood fingerboard, available in Black (G-241), Natural (G-240), or Red Stain (G-240RS) finish, mfg. 1999-2005.				
	N/A	$120 - 160	$70 - 90	$299
EG-240/EG-241 – dreadnought body style, spruce top, nato back and sides, rosewood fingerboard, DJ2 electronics, available in Black (EG-241), Natural (EG-240), or Red Stain (EG-240RS) finishes, mfg. 1999-2005.				
	N/A	$150 - 200	$90 - 120	$369
• **Add 10% for Red Stain finish (Model G240 RS).**				
G260C – single cutaway FXC-style body, spruce top, nato back and sides, round soundhole with abalone ring rosette, top and back body binding, 14/20-fret rosewood fingerboard with dot inlays, three-per-side chrome tuners, available in Brown Sunburst, Gloss Black, Natural (mfg. 2009, reintroduced 2011), or Wine Red finish, mfg. 2007-mid-2013.				
	$250	$150 - 190	$85 - 110	$360
* *EG260C* – similar to the G260C, except has TP4T electronics, available in Brown Sunburst, Gloss Black, Natural (mfg. 2009, reintroduced 2011), or Wine Red finish, mfg. 2007-mid-2013.				
	$350	$200 - 250	$120 - 150	$500
EG630S – New Yorker-style body, solid cedar top, flame mahogany back and sides, round soundhole with abalone rosette, multi-ply body binding, mahogany neck, 14/20-fret rosewood fingerboard with dot inlays, slotted headstock with rosewood overlay and horizontal logo, three-per-side open-style gold tuners with white buttons, rosewood bridge, no pickguard, TP4T electronics, available in gloss Vintage Violin finish, mfg. 2011-12.				
	$550	$325 - 400	$200 - 250	$800

ACOUSTIC: G SERIES MODELS STARTING WITH 3

MSR/NOTES	100%	EXCELLENT	AVERAGE	LAST MSR
G-320 – dreadnought style, spruce top, mahogany back and sides, rosewood fingerboard, chrome hardware, available in Natural finish, mfg. 2005 only.				
	N/A	$120 - 150	$70 - 90	$289
* *EG-320C* – similar to the G-320, except has a single cutaway and TP-4 electronics, mfg. 2005 only.				
	N/A	$175 - 225	$110 - 140	$429
G-330 – dreadnought style, spruce top, mahogany back and sides, round soundhole, three-stripe bound body and rosette, mahogany neck, 14/20-fret rosewood fingerboard with white dot inlays, three-per-side chrome tuners, rosewood bridge with white pins, black pickguard, available in Black, Natural, or Red Stain finish, mfg. 1991-99.				
	N/A	$200 - 250	$100 - 125	$399
In 1993, Red Stain finish was introduced (discontinued 1994).				
* *G-330S* – similar to the G-330, except has a solid spruce top, available in Black or Natural finish, mfg. 1997-2005.				
	N/A	$175 - 225	$120 - 150	$439
• **Add 10% for Gloss Black finish (Model G-330SB).**				
* *GS-330S* – similar to the G-330, except has a solid cedar top, mfg. 2001-2012.				
	$300	$175 - 225	$120 - 150	$460
EGS-330SC – similar to G-330S, except has single round cutaway, crystal bridge pickups, 4-band EQ, available in Satin Natural finish, mfg. 1994-mid-2013.				
	$500	$325 - 375	$175 - 225	$740
• **Add 20% for left-hand model (disc., Model EG-330SLH).**				
• **Add 10% for Red Stain finish (disc., Model EG-330RC).**				
• **Add 10% for Ocean Blue Burst finish (disc., Model EG330OBB).**				
• **Subtract 10% for a spruce top and a satin finish (disc., Model EG330SC).**				
G-332 S – dreadnought style, solid spruce top, round soundhole, black pickguard, 3-stripe bound body and rosette, mahogany back/sides/neck, 14/20-fret rosewood fingerboard with white dot inlay, rosewood bridge with white pins, 3-per-side chrome tuners, available in Natural finish, disc. 2003.				
	N/A	$250 - 300	$150 - 200	$580

MSR/NOTES	100%	EXCELLENT	AVERAGE	LAST MSR

* **EG-332C** – similar to G-332, except has single round cutaway, crystal bridge pickups, 4-band EQ, available in Natural finish, mfg. 1994-2003.

	N/A	$350 - 400	$190 - 240	$800

G-334 – dreadnought style, spruce top, rosewood back/sides, round soundhole, wood bound body and rosette, mahogany neck, 14/20-fret bound rosewood fingerboard with pearl dot inlays, three-per-side gold tuners, rosewood bridge with white black dot pins, black pickguard, available in Natural or Black finish, disc. 1994.

	N/A	$200 - 250	$100 - 150	$500

* **EG-334SC** – similar to G-334, except has single rounded cutaway, ovangkol back and sides, crystal bridge pickups, 4-band EQ, available in Natural finish, mfg. 1994-2008.

	N/A	$375 - 450	$225 - 275	$899

* **EG-334SBC (EG-334RC)** – similar to G-334, except has single rounded cutaway, crystal bridge pickups, four-band EQ, available in Black Stain or Red Stain finish, mfg. 1994-2008.

	N/A	$375 - 450	$225 - 275	$899

G-335 12-STRING – dreadnought style, spruce top, round soundhole, black pickguard, three-stripe bound body and rosette, mahogany back/sides/neck, 14/20-fret rosewood fingerboard with white dot inlay, rosewood bridge with white pins, six-per-side chrome tuners, available in Natural finish, disc. 1999.

	N/A	$300 - 350	$150 - 200	$599

* **EG-335SC-12** – similar to the G-335, except has a single cutaway, solid spruce top and nato back and sides, mfg. 2000-06.

	N/A	$325 - 400	$200 - 250	$789

G-340 – dreadnought style, spruce top, mahogany back and sides, rosewood fingerboard, gold hardware, available in Natural finish, mfg. 2006-mid-2013.

	$250	$145 - 180	$90 - 110	$360

* **G-340LH Left-Handed** – similar to the G-340, except in left-handed configuration, mfg. 2011-mid-2013.

	$250	$145-180	$90-110	$360

* **G-340SC** – similar to the G-340, except has a solid spruce top and single cutaway, mfg. 2006-mid-2013.

	$300	$175 - 225	$110 - 140	$460

* **EG-340C/EG341C** – similar to the G-340, except has a single cutaway and TP4T electronics, available in Black (341, 2006-2011, reintroduced 2013) or Natural (340) finish, mfg. 2006-mid-2013.

	$350	$210 - 260	$125 - 160	$520

• **Add 2.5% for Black finish (Last MSR was $529).**

»**EG-340SC/EG-341SC** – similar to the EG-340C, except has a solid spruce top, available in Black (341) or Natural (340) finish, mfg. 2006-mid-2013.

	$500	$300 - 350	$175 - 225	$700

»**EG-340CLH Left-Handed** – similar to the EG-340C, except in left-handed configuration, available in Natural finish, mfg. 2008-mid-2013.

	$350	$210 - 260	$125 - 160	$520

EG-340DLX – single cutaway dreadnought-style body, solid Bearclaw spruce top, flame mahogany back and sides, round soundhole with abalone rosette, maple binding, abalone top purfling, mahogany neck, 14/20-fret maple-bound rosewood fingerboard with abalone snowflake inlays, bound headstock with rosewood overlay and vertical logo, three-per-side gold tuners with pearl buttons, rosewood bridge, tortoise pickguard, TP4T electronics, available in gloss Natural finish, mfg. 2012-mid-2013.

	$700	$425 - 525	$250 - 300	$1,000

EG-345C 12-STRING – 12-string configuration, dreadnought single cutaway style, spruce top, rosewood back and sides, rosewood fingerboard, TP4T electronics, available in Natural finish, mfg. 2006-mid-2013.

	$500	$300 - 350	$175 - 225	$700

G-360S – dreadnought style, solid spruce top, rosewood back and sides, abalone binding and rosette, rosewood fingerboard with snowflake inlays, gold hardware, available in Natural finish, mfg. 2006-2011.

	$500	$300 - 370	$180 - 220	$739

* **EG-360SC/EG-361SC** – similar to the G-360S, except has a single cutaway and TP4T electronics, available in Black (361, 2006-2010) or Natural (360) finish, mfg. 2006-2011, reintroduced 2013-mid 2013.

	$600	$350 - 425	$200 - 250	$859

EG-363SC – single smooth cutaway dreadnought-style body, solid spruce top, three-piece rosewood/quilted maple back, rosewood sides, round soundhole with abalone ring rosette, cream binding, mahogany neck, 14/20-fret rosewood fingerboard with small dots and 12th fret decorative inlays, black headstock overlay with vertical gold logo, three-per-side gold tuners with black buttons, ebony bridge, TP4T pickup/electronics, available in Natural finish, mfg. 2009-2012.

	$550	$325 - 400	$200 - 250	$800

MSR/NOTES	100%	EXCELLENT	AVERAGE	LAST MSR

* **EG-363SCLH Left-Handed** – similar to the EG-363SC, except in left-handed configuration, available in Natural finish, mfg. 2010-12.

	$550	$325 - 400	$200 - 250	$800

ACOUSTIC: G SERIES MODELS STARTING WITH 4

G-406S – New Yorker-style body, solid spruce top, three-piece rosewood/quilted maple back, rosewood sides, round soundhole with abalone ring rosette, cream binding, abalone purfling, mahogany neck, 14/20-fret rosewood fingerboard with pearl diamond inlays, black headstock overlay with vertical gold logo, three-per-side gold tuners with black buttons, ebony bridge, available in Natural finish, mfg. 2009-2012.

	$500	$300 - 350	$175 - 225	$700

EG416S – New Yorker-style body, solid spruce top, three-piece rosewood/quilted maple back and sides, round soundhole with abalone rosette, multi-ply body binding, mahogany neck, 14/20-fret rosewood fingerboard with dot inlays, rosewood headstock overlay with vertical logo, three-per-side gold tuners with black buttons, rosewood bridge, no pickguard, TP4T electronics, available in gloss Natural finish, mfg. 2010-12.

	$600	$350 - 450	$200 - 250	$860

GS-430S – grand auditorium NEX-style body, solid cedar top, mahogany back and sides, round soundhole with concentric rings, rosewood fingerboard with no inlays, three-per-side chrome tuners, available in Satin Natural finish, mfg. 2008-2012.

	$300	$175 - 225	$110 - 140	$460

EGS430SC – NEX single cutaway body, solid cedar top, nato back and sides, rosewood fingerboard, N4B electronics, available in Satin Natural finish, disc. 2005.

	N/A	$300 - 350	$150 - 200	$659

EG430SC – NEX-style body, single cutaway, solid cedar top, flame mahogany back and sides, round soundhole with abalone rosette, white body binding, mahogany neck, 14/20-fret rosewood fingerboard with dot inlays, black headstock overlay with vertical logo, three-per-side gold tuners, rosewood bridge, tortoise pickguard, TP4T electronics, available in gloss Vintage Violin (disc. 2013) or Wine Red (mfg. 2012-mid-2013) finish, mfg. 2011-mid-2013.

	$550	$350 - 425	$200 - 250	$800

G-440C – grand auditorium NEX single cutaway style, spruce top, mahogany back and sides, rosewood fingerboard, gold hardware, available in Natural finish, mfg. 2006-mid-2013.

	$250	$140 - 180	$90 - 110	$360

* **EG-440C** – similar to the G-440C, except has TP4T electronics, mfg. 2006-mid-2013.

	$400	$225 - 275	$135 - 175	$570

»**EG-440CST Flame Maple** – similar to the EG-440C, except has flame maple top, back, and sides, available in Trans. Black, Trans. Blue, or Trans. Red finish, mfg. 2009-mid-2013.

	$450	$275 - 325	$150 - 200	$650

»**EG-440CST Quilted Maple** – similar to the EG-440C, except has quilted maple top, back, and sides, available in Trans. Black, Trans. Blue, or Trans. Red finish, mfg. 2008 only.

	N/A	$250 - 300	$140 - 175	$589

»**EG-440SC** – similar to the EG-440C, except has a solid spruce top, mfg. 2006-mid-2013.

	$450	$275 - 325	$150 - 200	$650

EG444C – single cutaway NEX-style body, flame mahogany top, back, and sides, round soundhole with abalone rosette, white body binding, mahogany neck, 14/20-fret rosewood fingerboard with dot inlays, rosewood headstock overlay with vertical logo, three-per-side gold tuners, rosewood bridge, no pickguard, TP4T electronics, available in gloss Vintage Violin finish, mfg. 2011-mid-2013.

	$550	$350 - 425	$200 - 250	$800

EG450DLX-TBS – NEX-style body, solid spruce top, flame maple back and sides, round soundhole with abalone rosette, white body binding, mahogany neck, 14/20-fret rosewood fingerboard with oval MOP and abalone inlays, rosewood headstock overlay with vertical logo, three-per-side gold tuners, rosewood bridge, black pickguard with floral pattern, TP4T electronics, available in gloss Vintage Burst finish, mfg. 2011-12.

	$600	$350 - 450	$200 - 250	$870

EG450SMCSB – single cutaway NEX-style body, solid spruce top, flame maple back and sides, round soundhole with abalone rosette, white body binding, mahogany neck, 14/20-fret rosewood fingerboard with dot inlays, rosewood headstock overlay with vertical logo, three-per-side gold tuners, rosewood bridge, black pickguard, TP4T electronics, available in gloss Sunburst finish, mfg. 2010-12.

	$600	$350 - 450	$200 - 250	$870

EG451DLX – NEX-style body, solid spruce top, flame maple back and sides, round soundhole with abalone rosette, white body binding, mahogany neck, 14/20-fret rosewood fingerboard with oval MOP and abalone inlays, rosewood headstock overlay with vertical logo, three-per-side gold tuners, rosewood bridge, TP4T electronics, available in gloss Black finish, mfg. 2011-12.

	$600	$350 - 450	$200 - 250	$870

MSR/NOTES	100%	EXCELLENT	AVERAGE	LAST MSR

EG-460SC/EG-461SC – single cutaway NEX-style body, solid spruce top, rosewood back and sides, abalone binding and rosette, rosewood fingerboard with snowflake inlays, TP4T electronics, gold hardware, available in Black (EG-461SC, 2006-08) or Natural (EG-460SC) finish, mfg. 2006-2010.

	$600	$350 - 425	$200 - 250	$869

EG463SC – single cutaway NEX-style body, solid spruce top, three-piece rosewood/quilted maple back and sides, round soundhole with abalone rosette, white body binding, mahogany neck, 14/20-fret rosewood fingerboard with dots and 11-13th fret design inlays, rosewood headstock overlay with vertical logo, three-per-side gold tuners with black buttons, rosewood bridge, no pickguard, TP4T electronics, available in gloss Natural finish, mfg. 2010-12.

	$550	$350 - 425	$200 - 250	$800

EG481SCX – single cutaway NEX-style body, solid spruce top, mahogany back and sides, round soundhole with motorcycle chain rosette, white body binding, mahogany neck, 14/20-fret rosewood fingerboard with 12th fret cross inlays, black headstock overlay with vertical logo, three-per-side chrome tuners, rosewood bridge, no pickguard, TP4T electronics, available in gloss Black finish, mfg. 2009-mid-2013.

	$500	$300 - 375	$175 - 225	$740

ACOUSTIC: G SERIES MODELS STARTING WITH 5

G-501S – OM style body, solid spruce top, Bolivian rosewood back and sides, rosewood fingerboard, available in Gloss Natural finish, disc. 2009.

	N/A	$250 - 300	$140 - 180	$599

* **G501BF Butterfly** – similar to the G501S, except has a laminated spruce top, mahogany back and sides and a butterfly motif design along the lower treble bout, mfg. 2007-08.

	N/A	$240 - 290	$130 - 165	$589

»**EG501BF Butterfly Electric** – similar to the G501BF Butterfly, except has a solid spruce top and TK40 electronics, mfg. 2008 only.

	N/A	$375 - 450	$200 - 250	$849

* **EG-501S** – similar to the EG-501S, except has TK4NT electronics, disc. 2007.

	N/A	$350 - 425	$200 - 250	$789

G511SS – dreadnought-style body, solid cedar top, solid Sapele back and sides, round soundhole with herringbone rosette, cream body binding, herringbone purfling, mahogany neck, 14/20-fret rosewood fingerboard with dot inlays, rosewood headstock overlay with vertical logo, three-per-side chrome tuners, rosewood bridge, no pickguard, available in Satin Natural finish, mfg. 2010-11.

	$500	$300 - 375	$175 - 225	$739

* **EG511SSC** – similar to the G511SS, except has a single cutaway and TK40 electronics, available in Satin Natural finish, mfg. 2010-11.

	$600	$350 - 450	$200 - 250	$859

EG-522C – classical style single cutaway body, spruce top, nato back and sides, rosewood fingerboard, TK4NT electronics, available in Gloss Natural finish, disc. 2011.

	$600	$350 - 425	$200 - 250	$849

EG-523SC – jumbo style single cutaway body, solid spruce top, flamed maple back and sides, rosewood fingerboard, TK4NT electronics, available in Black, Blue (2005-06), Red (2005-06), or Natural Gloss finish, disc. mid-2013.

	$700	$425 - 525	$250 - 300	$1,000

* **EG-523CDX-HB** – similar to the EG-523SC, except has a three-piece quilt and flame maple back, available in Honey Burst finish, mfg. 2010-mid-2013.

	$850	$475 - 600	$275 - 350	$1,200

* **EG-523SC-12 12-String** – similar to the EG-523SC, except in 12-string configuration, available in Gloss Black or Gloss Natural finish, disc. mid-2013.

	$750	$450 - 550	$275 - 325	$1,090

»**EG-523CDX-HB-12 12-String** – similar to the EG-523SC-12 12-String, except has a three-piece quilt and flame maple back, available in Honey Burst finish, mfg. 2010-disc. mid-2013.

	$900	$525 - 650	$325 - 400	$1,290

G-530S(S) – dreadnought style body, spruce top, nato back and sides, rosewood fingerboard, Natural finish, disc. 2008, reintroduced 2010 only.

	$400	$240 - 290	$130 - 165	$589

* **G530SBF Butterfly** – similar to the G-530S, except has an inlaid abalone butterfly motif on the lower treble bout, available in Gloss Natural finish, mfg. 2007-08.

	N/A	$240 - 290	$130 - 165	$589

MSR/NOTES	100%	EXCELLENT	AVERAGE	LAST MSR

»*EG530SCBF Butterfly Electric Cutaway* – similar to the G-530SBF, except has a single cutaway and TK40 preamp/electronics, avaiable in Gloss Natural finish, mfg. 2007-08.

	N/A	$350 - 425	$200 - 250	$810

* *EG-530SC/SSC/EG-531SC/SSC* – dreadnought body with cutaway, spruce top, sapele back and sides, TK-4N preamp system, available in Black (531) or Natural Gloss (530) finish, disc. 2011.

	$600	$375 - 450	$200 - 250	$859

Also available in Red Stain finish (Model EG-530C-RS, disc.).

»*EG530SC-LH Left-Handed* – similar to the EG530SC, except in left-handed configuration and has nato back and sides, available in Gloss Natural finish, mfg. 2007-2011.

	$600	$375 - 450	$200 - 250	$859

»*EG531SCDR Dragon* – similar to the EG531SC, except available in Gloss Black finish with a dragon motif along the lower treble bout, mfg. 2008 only.

	N/A	$375 - 450	$200 - 250	$869

EG530DLX/EG531DLX – single smooth cutaway dreadnought-style body, solid spruce top, solid sapele back, sapele sides, round soundhole with abalone ring rosette, white body binding, abalone purfling, mahogany neck, 14/20-fret bound rosewood fingerboard with pearl diamond inlays, rosewood headstock overlay (Model EG530DLX) or black headstock overlay (Model EG531DLX) with vertical gold logo, three-per-side gold tuners with pearl buttons, rosewood bridge, TK40 pickup/electronics, available in Black (Model EG531DLX) or Natural (Model EG530DLX) gloss finish, mfg. 2009-2010.

	$700	$450 - 525	$275 - 325	$999

EG-535SC-12 12-STRING – similar to the EG-530SC, except in 12-string configuration, disc. 2008.

	N/A	$375 - 450	$200 - 250	$859

G536SHB – dreadnought-style body, solid spruce top, rosewood back and sides, round soundhole with herringbone rosette, ivory cab binding, herringbone top purfling, mahogany neck, 14/20-fret bound rosewood fingerboard with dot inlays, rosewood headstock overlay with vertical logo, three-per-side gold tuners with pearl buttons, rosewood bridge, no pickguard, available in gloss Natural finish, mfg. 2012-mid-2013.

	$630	$375 - 475	$225 - 275	$900

* *EG536SHB* – similar to the G536SHB, except has TK40 electronics, available in gloss Natural finish, mfg. 2012-mid-2013.

	$700	$425 - 525	$250 - 300	$1,000

EG-540SBF BUTTERFLY – Grand Auditorium NEX-style body, solid spruce top, mahogany back and sides, 14/21-fret rosewood fingerboard with small dot inlays, three-per-side chrome tuners, rosewood bridge, available in Gloss Natural finish with a butterfly motif along the lower treble bout, mfg. 2007-08.

	N/A	$240 - 290	$130 - 165	$589

* *EG-540SCBF Cutaway Butterfly* – similar to the EG-540BF, except has a single cutaway and TK40 electronics, mfg. 2007-08.

	N/A	$375 - 450	$200 - 250	$849

EG-540SC/SSC/EG-541SC/SSC – mini jumbo body with cutaway, solid spruce top, nato back and sides, TK-4N preamp system, chrome hardware, available in Black (EG-541), Natural, Red Stain, or Cherry Burst finish, disc. 2008, reintroduced 2010 only.

	$600	$375 - 450	$200 - 250	$869

* *EG-540C Flame Maple* – similar to the EG540SC/SSC, except has a flame maple body, available in Trans. Black, Trans. Blue, or Trans. Red finish, mfg. 2004-07.

	N/A	$325 - 400	$175 - 225	$785

EG540DLX/EG541DLX – single smooth cutaway NEX-style body, solid spruce top, solid sapele back, sapele sides, round soundhole with abalone ring rosette, white body binding, abalone purfling, mahogany neck, 14/20-fret bound rosewood fingerboard with pearl diamond inlays, rosewood headstock overlay (Model EG540DLX) or black headstock overlay (Model EG541DLX) with vertical gold logo, three-per-side gold tuners with pearl buttons, rosewood bridge, black pickguard, TK40 pickup/electronics, available in Black (Model EG541DLX) or Natural (Model EG540DLX) gloss finish, mfg. 2009-2010.

	$700	$450 - 525	$275 - 325	$999

EG543SC – single cutaway NEX-style body, flamed maple top/back/sides, round soundhole with concentric rings rosette, 14/20-fret rosewood fingerboard with pearl block inlays (abalone V inserts), three-per-side chrome tuners, rosewood bridge, tortoiseshell pickguard, TK40 preamp/electronics, available in Natural finish, mfg. 2007-08.

	N/A	$400 - 475	$225 - 275	$900

EG-544CK – single cutaway NEX-style body, figured koa top, koa back and sides, round soundhole with abalone rosette, white body binding, 14/20-fret bound rosewood fingerboard with abalone dot inlays, three-per-side gold tuners, rosewood bridge, TP4T pickup/electronics, available in Gloss Natural finish, mfg. early 2013 only.

	$650	$425 - 500	$235 - 280	$930

MSR/NOTES	100%	EXCELLENT	AVERAGE	LAST MSR

EG-560C – similar to EG-540C model, except is available in Blue Sunburst or Red Sunburst finish, disc. 2007.

	N/A	$300 - 375	$175 - 225	$749

EG-561C – similar to the EG-560CBS, except has Gloss Black finish, disc. 2010.

	$500	$300 - 375	$150 - 200	$735

EG-562C – nylon string configuration, single cutaway FXC classical-style body, spruce top, nato/ovangkol back and sides, rosewood fingerboard, slotted headstock, three-per-side open-style gold tuners, TV3/TV3N electronics, available in Gloss Natural finish, disc. 2005, reintroduced 2012 only.

	$600	$350 - 450	$200 - 250	$880

EG-568C – single cutaway Thinline FXC-style body, spruce top, nato/ovangkol back and sides, rosewood fingerboard, TV3 electronics, available in Gloss Natural, Gloss Black (disc. 2005), or Cherry Burst (disc. 2005) finish, disc. 2005, reintroduced 2012 only.

	$600	$350 - 450	$200 - 250	$880

The Cherry Burst finish has a flamed maple top.

EG-569C – single cutaway Thinline FXC-style body, ovangkol top, back, and sides, round soundhole with abalone rosette, white body binding, mahogany neck, 14/21-fret rosewood fingerboard with no inlays, matching finish headstock overlay, three-per-side chrome tuners, rosewood bridge, TV3N electronics, available in Burgundy finish, padded gig bag included, mfg. 2012 only.

	$600	$350 - 450	$200 - 250	$880

EGSF15 SC – single cutaway dreadnought body, solid spruce top, solid sapele back, sapele sides, round soundhole, southwest turquoise and wood rosette, rosewood fingerboard, three-per-side tuners, rosewood bridge, chrome hardware, Natural finish, mfg. 2004-08.

	N/A	$450 - 525	$275 - 325	$999

G5013SVFT – Orchestra Model-style body, solid spruce top, "fiddle-back" flamed maple back and sides, round soundhole with concentric rings rosette, top and back body binding, 14/20-fret rosewood fingerboard with dot inlays, three-per-side nickel tuners with ivory buttons, rosewood bridge, available in Antique Natural Violin finish, mfg. 2007-08.

	N/A	$240 - 290	$130 - 165	$589

EG5013SVFT – similar to the G5013SVFT, except has TK40 preamp/electronics, available in Antique Natural Violin finish, mfg. 2007-08.

	N/A	$375 - 450	$200 - 250	$849

G5403SVFT – NEX-style body, solid spruce top, "fiddle-back" flamed maple back and sides, round soundhole with concentric rings rosette, top and back body binding, 14/20-fret rosewood fingerboard with dot inlays, three-per-side nickel tuners with ivory buttons, rosewood bridge, available in Antique Natural finish, mfg. 2007-08.

	N/A	$240 - 290	$130 - 165	$589

EG5403SVFT – similar to the G5403S, except has TK40 preamp/electronics, available in Antique Natural finish, mfg. 2007-2008.

	N/A	$375 - 450	$200 - 250	$869

»*EG5403SCVFT Cutaway* – similar to the G5403S, except has a single cutaway, available in Antique Natural finish, mfg. 2008 only.

	N/A	$400 - 475	$225 - 275	$929

EG50TH – single cutaway dreadnought-style body, solid spruce top, mahogany back and sides, round soundhole with two ring gold rosette, ivory cab body binding, multi-ply top purfling, mahogany neck, 14/20-fret bound rosewood fingerboard with growing vine inlays, rosewood headstock overlay with vertical logo, three-per-side gold tuners, rosewood bridge, black inlayed pickguard with growing vine, TP4T pickup/electronics, available in gloss Natural finish, mfg. 2012 only.

	$700	$425 - 525	$275 - 325	$1,000

ACOUSTIC: TRADITIONAL/KEYSTONE (F) SERIES

In 2004, this line of guitars was renamed the Keystone Series.

EF-325SRC – dreadnought style, single rounded cutaway, solid spruce top, round soundhole, black pickguard, 5-stripe bound body/rosette, bubinga back/sides, mahogany neck, 14/20-fret bound rosewood fingerboard with pearl dot inlay, rosewood bridge with white black dot pins, 3-per-side chrome tuners, crystal bridge pickups, 3-band EQ, available in Clear Red finish, disc. 2003.

	N/A	$650 - 775	$375 - 450	$1,400

F-340 – dreadnought style, spruce top, round soundhole, black pickguard, 3-stripe bound body and rosette, mahogany back/sides/neck, 14/20-fret rosewood fingerboard with pearl dot inlay, rosewood bridge with black white dot pins, 3-per-side chrome tuners, available in Natural finish, disc. 1999.

	N/A	$350 - 425	$200 - 250	$769

EF-340SC – dreadnought body with cutaway, spruce top, mahogany back and sides, rosewood fingerboard, three-per-side tuners, piezo pickups, Graph EX preamp, 3-band EQ, Exciter control, volume, battery check, available in Natural or Sunburst (mfg. 2008-2010) finish, disc. 2003, reintroduced 2005-2010.

	$1,200	$750 - 900	$475 - 550	$1,719

• Add 10% for left-handed configuration (disc., Model EF-340C-LH).

MSR/NOTES	100%	EXCELLENT	AVERAGE	LAST MSR

* F-340S – similar to F-340, except has solid spruce top, disc. 1999.

	N/A	$375 - 450	$200 - 250	$899

* FD-340SC – similar to EF340C model except, has solid spruce top, DSP preamp, chromatic tuner, 10 factory presets, 10 write-your-own settings, dual digital reverb, bass, treble and parametric EQ, feedback absorber, available in Natural finish, disc.

	N/A	$700 - 850	$375 - 450	$1,369

F-341 – dreadnought style, spruce top, round soundhole, black pickguard, 5-stripe bound body and rosette, campnosparma back/sides, mahogany neck, 14/20-fret bound rosewood fingerboard with pearl dot inlay, rosewood bridge with white black dot pins, bound peghead, 3-per-side chrome tuners, available in Black finish, disc. 1996.

	N/A	$350 - 400	$200 - 250	$780

* EF-341 – similar to F-341, except has crystal bridge pickups, 3-band EQ, disc. 1999.

	N/A	$500 - 575	$275 - 325	$1,129

* EF-341SC – similar to F-341, except has single rounded cutaway, solid cedar top, crystal bridge pickups, 3-band EQ, current mfg.

MSR $1,800	$1,250	$725 - 900	$450 - 550	

Add 8% for left-handed configuration (Model EF-341SCLF).

* EF-341 Deluxe – similar to the EF-341SC, except has a solid spruce top, disc. 2004.

	N/A	$750 - 900	$475 - 550	$1,571

* TF-341 Deluxe – similar to the EF-341 Deluxe, except has Cool Tube electronics, mfg. 2004-05.

	N/A	$775 - 925	$475 - 550	$1,759

F-349 – dreadnought style, mahogany top, back, and sides, top body binding, round soundhole with rosette, mahogany neck, 14/20-fret rosewood fingerboard with dot inlays, black headstock with pre-lawsuit Takamine logo (early models) or regular Takamine logo (later models), three-per-side chrome tuners, rosewood bridge, black teardrop pickguard, available in Natural finish, mfg. late 1970s-1980s.

	N/A	$375 - 450	$225 - 275	

EF-350MHC – dreadnought body with cutaway, spruce top, maple back and sides, rosewood fingerboard, 3-per-side tuners, Graph EX preamp, 3-band EQ, volume, exciter control, available in Vintage Satin finish, disc.

	N/A	$600 - 700	$350 - 400	$1,299

EF-350SMC-SB – similar to EF-350MHC except, has solid spruce top, flamed maple back and sides, dot position markers, DSP preamp system, available in Sunburst finish, disc. 2010.

	$1,400	$850 - 1,000	$500 - 600	$1,929

F-360S – dreadnought style, solid spruce top, round soundhole, black pickguard, 5-stripe bound body/rosette, rosewood back/sides, 14/20-fret bound rosewood fingerboard with pearl dot inlay, rosewood bridge with white black dot pins, 3-per-side chrome tuners, available in Natural finish, disc. 1999.

	N/A	$475 - 550	$250 - 300	$1,089

* EF-360S – similar to the F-360S, except has electronics, disc.

	N/A	$550 - 650	$300 - 350	

• Add 10% for left-handed configuration (Model F-360SLH).

EF-360SC – dreadnought body with cutaway, solid spruce top, rosewood back and sides, rosewood fingerboard, CT4B preamp system, available in Natural finish, disc. 2010.

	$1,400	$850 - 1,000	$500 - 600	$1,929

FD-360SC – dreadnought body with cutaway, solid spruce top, rosewood back and sides, rosewood fingerboard, DSP preamp system, available in Natural finish, disc.

	N/A	$725 - 850	$450 - 525	$1,579

EF-381C 12-STRING – 12-string configuration, dreadnought style, single rounded cutaway, solid cedar or spruce top, round soundhole, black pickguard, five-stripe bound body/rosette, campnosperma or maple back/sides, mahogany neck, 14/20-fret rosewood fingerboard with pearl diamond/dot inlay, six-per-side chrome tuners, rosewood bridge w/white black dot pins, crystal bridge pickup, 3-band EQ, available in Black finish, current mfg.

MSR $1,900	$1,300	$775 - 950	$450 - 575	

EF-375 SW – dreadnought body style, solid Sitka spruce top, three-piece laminated rosewood/jacaranda back, laminated jacaranda sides, round soundhole with multi-ring rosette, wood body binding, 14/20-fret bound rosewood fingerboard with wood dot inlays, bound rosewood headstock overlay, three-per-side tuners, rosewood bridge, electronics with three slider knobs, available in Natural finish, mfg. late 1970s-early 1980s.

	N/A	$850 - 1,000	$600 - 700	

MSR/NOTES	100%	EXCELLENT	AVERAGE	LAST MSR

F-385 – dreadnought style, spruce top, round soundhole, black pickguard, 5-stripe bound body/rosette, mahogany back/sides/neck, 14/20-fret rosewood fingerboard with pearl dot inlay, rosewood bridge with black white dot pins, 6-per-side chrome tuners, available in Natural finish, disc. 1999.

	N/A	$375 - 450	$200 - 250	$859

* *EF-385* – similar to F-385, except has crystal bridge pickup, 3-band EQ, disc. 2003.

	N/A	$500 - 575	$275 - 325	$1,100

F-390S – jumbo-style body, solid spruce top, laminated rosewood back and sides, round soundhole with three ring rosette, multi-ply body binding, mahogany neck, 14/20-fret bound rosewood fingerboard with pearl block inlays, bound headstock with black overlay and Guild-style logo and inlays, three-per-side chrome tuners, rosewood bridge, black pickguard, available in Natural finish, mfg. 1970s-1980s.

	N/A	$400 - 500	$250 - 300	

F-400S 12-STRING – 12-string configuration, dreadnought-style body, solid spruce top, laminated rosewood back and sides, round soundhole with three ring rosette, multi-ply body binding, mahogany neck, 14/20-fret bound rosewood fingerboard with pearl dot inlays, bound headstock with black overlay and Guild-style logo and inlays, six-per-side gold tuners, rosewood bridge, black pickguard, available in Natural finish, mfg. 1970s-1980s.

	N/A	$475 - 600	$275 - 350	

EF-400SC 12-STRING – dreadnought body with cutaway, 12-string, solid spruce top, rosewood back and sides, rosewood fingerboard, DSP preamp system, available in Natural finish, disc. 2008.

	N/A	$850 - 1,000	$525 - 600	$1,959

ACOUSTIC: CLASSICAL SERIES

E-30 – single cutaway classical-style body, spruce top, rosewood back and sides, front and back body binding, oval soundhole with decorative rosette, mahogany neck, 12/20-fret (extends into soundhole) rosewood fingerboard with no inlays, slotted headstock with rosewood overlay, three-per-side open-style gold tuners with pearl buttons, rosewood tied bridge, 3-Band Palathetic electronics, available in Natural finish, 25 19/32 in. scale, mfg. late 1980s-1991.

	N/A	$325 - 400	$200 - 250	$750

C-128 – classical style, spruce top, round soundhole, 5-stripe bound body, wooden rosette, rosewood back/sides, mahogany neck, 12/19-fret rosewood fingerboard, rosewood bridge, 3-per-side gold tuners with nylon buttons, available in Natural finish, mfg. 1980s-2003.

	N/A	$325 - 375	$175 - 225	$700

* *EC-128* – similar to C-128, except has mahogany back/sides, crystal bridge pickups, 3-band EQ, mfg. 1980s-1999.

	N/A	$375 - 450	$200 - 250	$869

C-132S – classical style, solid cedar top, round soundhole, five-stripe bound body, wooden rosette, rosewood back/sides, mahogany neck, 12/19-fret rosewood fingerboard, three-per-side gold tuners with nylon buttons, rosewood bridge, available in Natural finish, mfg. 1980s-present.

MSR $1,400	$1,000	$550 - 700	$350 - 425	

* *EC-132C* – similar to C-132S, except has single rounded cutaway, spruce top, crystal bridge pickups, 3-band EQ, mfg. 1980s-2012.

	$1,100	$650 - 800	$375 - 475	$1,600

»*EC-132CLH Left-Handed* – similar to the EC-132C, except in left-handed configuration, disc. 2012.

	$1,200	$675 - 850	$400 - 500	$1,700

EC-132SC – similar to EC-132C, except has solid cedar top, DSP preamp system, available in Black (1995-2004) or Natural finish, mfg. 1995-2004, 2006-2012.

	$1,300	$750 - 925	$450 - 550	$1,850

* *CP-132SC* – similar to C-132S, except single rounded cutaway, crystal bridge pickup, parametric EQ, mfg. 1980s-1999.

	N/A	$550 - 650	$350 - 425	$1,249

TC-132SC – single cutaway classical body, solid cedar top, solid rosewood back, rosewood sides, round soundhole with marquettery rosette, rosewood fingerboard, three-per-side open-style tuners, rosewood bridge, CTP-1 Cool Tube electronics, gold hardware, available in Black (2004-05) or Natural finish, mfg. 2004-present.

MSR $2,000	$1,400	$800 - 1,000	$475 - 600	

TC-135 SC – similar to the TC-132 SC, except has a solid spruce top and 24-fret rosewood fingerboard, Natural finish only, mfg. 2005-present.

MSR $2,800	$1,900	$1,125 - 1,400	$675 - 850	

ACOUSTIC: HIRADE CLASSICAL SERIES

This series was designed by Mass Hirade, Takamine founder.

H-5 – classical style, solid cedar top, round soundhole, five-stripe wood bound body, wooden rosette, rosewood back/sides, mahogany neck, 12/19-fret ebony fingerboard, 3-per-side gold tuners with pearl buttons, ebony bridge, available in Natural finish, current mfg.

MSR $2,000	$1,400	$900 - 1,050	$525 - 625	

MSR/NOTES	100%	EXCELLENT	AVERAGE	LAST MSR

* **HE-5C** – similar to H-5 model, except has classical body with cutaway and electronics, available in Natural finish, mfg. 2000-04.

| | N/A | $1,000 - 1,150 | $600 - 700 | $2,149 |

* **TH-5** – similar to H-5 model, except has CTP-1 Cool Tube electronics, available in Natural finish, mfg. 2004-2012.

| | $1,600 | $1,050 - 1,200 | $650 - 750 | $2,300 |

» **TH-5C** – similar to TH-5 model, except has a single cutaway, available in Natural finish, mfg. 2004-present.

| MSR $2,400 | $1,750 | $1,000 - 1,250 | $600 - 750 | |

H-8 – similar to H-5, except features a solid spruce top, mfg. 1993-99.

| | N/A | $1,000 - 1,200 | $550 - 650 | $2,199 |

* **H-8SS** – similar to H-8, except has solid spruce top, solid rosewood back and sides, no electronics, available in Natural finish, mfg. 2000-present.

| MSR $2,800 | $1,900 | $1,200 - 1,450 | $725 - 875 | |

» **HE-8SS** – similar to H-8SS, except CT4B electronics, mfg. 2001-04.

| | N/A | $1,250 - 1,500 | $750 - 900 | $2,715 |

» **TH-8SS** – similar to H-8SS, except features CTP-1 Cool Tube electronics, mfg. 2004-2012.

| | $2,200 | $1,400 - 1,650 | $900 - 1,050 | $3,200 |

H-15 – classical style, solid spruce top, round soundhole, wood bound body, wooden rosette, rosewood back/sides, mahogany neck, 12/19-fret ebony fingerboard, ebony bridge with rosette matching inlay, 3-per-side gold tuners with pearl buttons, available in Natural finish, mfg. 1993-99.

| | N/A | $1,800 - 2,200 | $1,100 - 1,250 | $3,899 |

HP-7 – classical style, solid cedar top, round soundhole, 5-stripe wood bound body, wooden rosette, rosewood back/sides, mahogany neck, 12/19-fret ebony fingerboard, ebony bridge, 3-per-side gold tuners with pearl buttons, crystal bridge pickups, parametric EQ, available in Natural finish, mfg. 1980s-1999.

| | N/A | $1,100 - 1,250 | $725 - 850 | $2,349 |

HD-90/HE-90/HP-90 – classical body with cutaway, solid spruce top, rosewood back and sides, DSP preamp system, available in Natural finish, mfg. 1980s-2004.

| | N/A | $1,150 - 1,300 | $675 - 800 | $2,429 |

* **TH-90** – similar to the HE-90, except has CTP-1 Cool Tube electronics, mfg. 2004-present.

| MSR $2,900 | $2,000 | $1,300 - 1,500 | $750 - 900 | |

ACOUSTIC: LIMITED EDITION SERIES

1996 LIMITED EDITION – single cutaway NEX body, solid spruce top, rosewood back and sides, round soundhole with abalone/paduk/maple rosette, rosewood fingerboard with deco design inlays, three-per-side tuners, rosewood bridge, Accuracoustic electronics, chrome hardware, Black finish, mfg. 1996 only.

| | N/A | $1,050 - 1,200 | $550 - 650 | $2,000 |

1997 LIMITED EDITION – single cutaway NEX body, solid spruce top, koa back and sides, round soundhole with gecko rosette, rosewood fingerboard with gecko inlays, three-per-side tuners, rosewood bridge, Accuracoustic electronics, chrome hardware, Natural finish, mfg. 1997 only.

| | N/A | $900 - 1,100 | $500 - 600 | $1,800 |

1998 LIMITED EDITION – single cutaway NEX body, solid spruce top, Rio Grande Palisando back and sides, round soundhole with sun and moon abalone/pearl/rare woods rosette, rosewood fingerboard with abalone inlays, three-per-side tuners, rosewood bridge, Accuracoustic electronics, chrome hardware, Natural finish, mfg. 1998 only.

| | N/A | $950 - 1,150 | $550 - 650 | $1,900 |

1999 LIMITED EDITION – single cutaway NEX body, solid spruce top, rosewood back and sides, round soundhole with mountain rosette, rosewood fingerboard with 12th fret mountain inlay, three-per-side tuners, rosewood bridge, DSP electronics, chrome hardware, Natural finish, mfg. 1999 only.

| | N/A | $950 - 1,150 | $550 - 650 | $1,900 |

2000 LIMITED EDITION – single cutaway NEX body, solid Sitka spruce top, rosewood back and sides, round soundhole with olive branch rosette, rosewood fingerboard with dot and olive branch inlay, three-per-side tuners, rosewood bridge, Graph-EX electronics, gold hardware, Natural finish, mfg. 2000 only.

| | N/A | $1,000 - 1,200 | $550 - 650 | $1,950 |

This model is also available in left-handed configuration.

2001 LIMITED EDITION – single cutaway NEX body, solid spruce top, solid rosewood back, rosewood sides, round soundhole with dolphin rosette, rosewood fingerboard with 12th fret dolphin inlay, three-per-side tuners, rosewood bridge, electronics, gold hardware, Natural finish, mfg. 2001 only.

| | N/A | $1,000 - 1,200 | $550 - 650 | |

MSR/NOTES	100%	EXCELLENT	AVERAGE	LAST MSR

2002 LIMITED EDITION – single cutaway dreadnought body, solid Sitka spruce top, solid Indian rosewood back, Indian rosewood sides, round soundhole with whale rosette, ebony fingerboard with 12th fret whale inlay, three-per-side tuners, ebony bridge, CT-4B electronics, chrome hardware, Natural finish, mfg. 2002 only.

| | N/A | $1,000 - 1,200 | $550 - 650 | |

2003 LIMITED EDITION – single cutaway dreadnought body, solid spruce top, solid rosewood back, rosewood sides, round soundhole with eagle rosette, ebony fingerboard with 12th fret eagle eye and dot inlay, three-per-side tuners, ebony bridge, CT-4B electronics, gold hardware, Natural finish, mfg. 2003 only.

| | N/A | $1,100 - 1,300 | $600 - 700 | $2,400 |

2004 LIMITED EDITION – single cutaway dreadnought body, solid Sitka spruce top, solid Indian rosewood back and sides, round soundhole with Celestial Constellations rosette, ebony fingerboard with acrylic mirror inlays, three-per-side tuners, ebony bridge, CT-4B electronics, chrome hardware, Natural finish, mfg. 2004 only.

| | N/A | $1,100 - 1,300 | $600 - 700 | $2,400 |

2005 LIMITED EDITION – OM style body, solid spruce top, solid mahogany back and sides, round soundhole, cattail rosette below the soundhole made of wenge, silverheart, rosewood, and ovangkol, striped ebony fingerboard with wetland inlays, three-per-side tuners, ebony bridge, CT-4B electronics, chrome hardware, Natural finish, mfg. 2005 only.

| | N/A | $900 - 1,050 | $500 - 600 | $2,000 |

2006 LIMITED EDITION – OM-style single cutaway body, solid spruce top, solid Indian rosewood back, Indian rosewood sides, round soundhole with Tibetan Tantric rosette inlaid with koa, cocobolo, abalone, and lapis, 14/20-fret rosewood fingerboard with dot and Tibetan Tantric 12th fret inlays, three-per-side gold tuners, rosewood bridge, CT4B electronics, available in Natural finish, mfg. 2006 only.

| | N/A | $1,050 - 1,200 | $600 - 700 | $2,299 |

2007 LIMITED EDITION – dreadnought style, solid spruce top, solid mahogany back, mahogany sides, round soundhole with thunderclouds and lightning rosette, 14/20-fret ebony fingerboard with abalone lightning and raindrops inlays, matching finish headstock with three-per-side black chrome tuners, ebony bridge, CT4B electronics, available in Black finish, mfg. 2007 only.

| | N/A | $1,000 - 1,250 | $600 - 750 | $2,429 |

2008 LIMITED EDITION – NEX-style body, solid cedar top, solid mahogany back, mahogany sides, round soundhole with crescent view of earth as seen from the moon rosette, 14/20-fret ebony fingerboard with rising sun inlays, matching finish headstock with three-per-side black chrome tuners, ebony bridge, CT4B electronics, available in Black finish, mfg. 2008 only.

| | N/A | $1,050 - 1,250 | $600 - 700 | $2,429 |

2009 LIMITED EDITION – NEX-style grand auditorium body, solid spruce top, solid mahogany back, laminated mahogany sides, round soundhole with abalone rosette, cream body binding, mahogany neck, 14/20-fret bound ebony fingerboard with deluxe shell inlays, bound headstock with vertical logo, three-per-side gold tuners with pearl buttons, ebony bridge, large black pickguard with decorative vine/floral inlays, CTP-2 Cool Tube pickup/electronics, available in Vintage Sunburst finish with two floral inlay graphics at the bottom of the body, mfg. 2009 only.

| | N/A | $1,100 - 1,350 | $650 - 750 | $2,579 |

2010 LIMITED EDITION – single cutaway dreadnought-style body, solid spruce top, solid rosewood back, laminated rosewood sides, round soundhole with abalone rosette, cream body binding, Kimono cloth purfling, mahogany neck, 14/20-fret bound Kimono cloth fingerboard with deluxe inlays, bound headstock with Kimono cloth overlay and vertical logo, three-per-side gold tuners, Kimono cloth bridge, Kimono cloth pickguard, CTP-2 Cool Tube pickup/electronics, available in Natural finish, limited edition run of 280 instruments, mfg. 2010 only.

| | $2,380 | $1,550 - 1,900 | $950 - 1,200 | $3,399 |

2011 LIMITED EDITION – single cutaway NEX-style grand auditorium body, solid spruce top, solid mahogany back and sides, round soundhole with two ring gold braided string rosette, cream body binding, mahogany neck, 14/20-fret bound ebony fingerboard with goldfish inlays, bound headstock with vertical logo, three-per-side gold tuners with pearl buttons, rosewood bridge, CTP-2 Cool Tube pickup/electronics, available in Indigo Burst finish with two goldfish inlay graphics at the waists of the body, mfg. 2011 only.

| | $2,380 | $1,550 - 1,900 | $950 - 1,200 | $3,399 |

2012 LIMITED EDITION – single cutaway dreadnought-style body, white cap spruce top, rosewood back and sides, round soundhole with two ring gold rosette, white cab body binding, gold purfling, mahogany neck, 14/20-fret bound ebony fingerboard with growing vine inlays, bound headstock with vertical logo, three-per-side gold tuners, rosewood bridge, inlayed pickguard with growing vine, CTP-2 Cool Tube pickup/electronics, available in gloss Black finish, mfg. 2012 only.

| | $2,500 | $1,550 - 1,900 | $950 - 1,200 | $3,600 |

2012 LIMITED EDITION C – single cutaway classical-style body, solid spruce top, rosewood back and sides, oval soundhole with gold rosette, brown cab body binding, rope pattern purfling, mahogany neck, 12/20-fret ebony-bound ebony fingerboard with growing vine inlays, slotted headstock with "T" logo, three-per-side open-style gold tuners, rosewood tied bridge, CTP-2 Cool Tube pickup/electronics, available in gloss Black finish, mfg. 2012 only.

| | $2,500 | $1,550 - 1,900 | $950 - 1,200 | $3,600 |

MSR/NOTES	100%	EXCELLENT	AVERAGE	LAST MSR

2013 LIMITED EDITION – New Yorker-style body, solid spruce top, solid sapele back and sides, abalone rosette, ivory body binding, mahogany neck, 12/20-fret rosewood fingerboard with climber motif inlay, three-per-side chrome tuners with pearl buttons, rosewood bridge with split bone saddle, CT-4BII pre-amp system, available in gloss Natural finish, mfg. 2013 only.

	100%	EXCELLENT	AVERAGE	LAST MSR
	$1,900	$1,100 - 1,350	$600 - 725	$2,450

2013 LIMITED EDITION SE – New Yorker-style body, solid bearclaw spruce top, solid koa back and sides, round soundhole with spalted maple/cocobolo rosette, mahogany neck, 12/20-fret ebony fingerboard with climber motif inlay, three-per-side chrome tuners, rosewood bridge with split bone saddle, TLD pre-amp, available in gloss Natural finish, mfg. 2013 only.

	100%	EXCELLENT	AVERAGE	LAST MSR
	$3,900	$2,300 - 2,800	$1,275 - 1,525	$5,100

2014 LIMITED EDITION – single cutaway slope shoulder dreadnought-style body, solid spruce top, flame maple sides, solid flame maple back, abalone rosette, ivoroid body binding, b/h abalone purfling, mahogany neck, 12/20-fret ebony fingerboard with snow grouse "raicho" inlays, three-per-side cosmo black tuners, rosewood bridge with split bone saddle, CT4-DX preamp with 4-band EQ, volume control, onboard tuner and Palathetic under-saddle pickup, black pickguard with snow grouse design, black hardware, available in Transparent Black Burst, case included, 24.75 in. scale, new 2014.

MSR/NOTES	100%	EXCELLENT	AVERAGE	
MSR $5,100	$3,900	$2,300 - 2,800	$1,275 - 1,525	

Production was limited to 52 guitars worldwide. Each instrument was numbered and included a certificate of authenticity signed by the President of Takamine.

ACOUSTIC: NASHVILLE SERIES

EF-36 – dreadnought body style with single cutaway, solid spruce top, solid rosewood back and sides, round soundhole with snowflake rosette, 14/20-fret ebony fingerboard with dot inlays, three-per-side open gear gold tuners, ebony bridge, tortoiseshell pickguard, TLD Line Driver preamp/electronics, available in Gloss Natural finish, mfg. 2010-2011.

	100%	EXCELLENT	AVERAGE	LAST MSR
	$3,100	$2,000 - 2,450	$1,100 - 1,325	$4,449

EF-37 – dreadnought body style with single cutaway, solid spruce top, solid figured koa back and sides, round soundhole with snowflake rosette, 14/20-fret ebony fingerboard with dot inlays, three-per-side open gear gold tuners, ebony bridge, tortoiseshell pickguard, TLD Line Driver preamp/electronics, available in Gloss Natural finish, mfg. 2010-2011.

	100%	EXCELLENT	AVERAGE	LAST MSR
	$3,450	$2,225 - 2,700	$1,225 - 1,475	$4,949

EF340SBG – dreadnought style, solid spruce top, solid mahogany back and sides, round soundhole with concentric rings rosette, 14/20-fret ebony fingerboard with pearl dot inlays, three-per-side open gear antique nickel tuners, rosewood bridge, tortoiseshell pickguard, TLD Line Driver preamp/electronics, available in Gloss Natural finish, mfg. 2007-2012.

	100%	EXCELLENT	AVERAGE	LAST MSR
	$1,750	$1,000 - 1,250	$600 - 750	$2,499

* **TF340SBG** – similar to the EF340SBG, except has CTP-1 Cool Tube preamp/electronics, available in Gloss Natural finish, mfg. 2007-2012.

	100%	EXCELLENT	AVERAGE	LAST MSR
	$1,830	$1,050 - 1,300	$625 - 775	$2,599

NV-340S – dreadnought style, solid bear claw spruce top, solid mahogany back and sides, abalone rosette, abalone binding, ebony fingerboard with snowflake inlay, three-per-side tuners, ebony bridge, tortoise pickguard, gold hardware, Natural finish, mfg. 2003-04.

	100%	EXCELLENT	AVERAGE	LAST MSR
	N/A	$850 - 1,000	$500 - 600	$1,999

* **ENV-340S** – similar to the NV-340S, except has CTB-4 electronics, mfg. 2003-04.

	100%	EXCELLENT	AVERAGE	LAST MSR
	N/A	$1,000 - 1,150	$600 - 700	$2,286

* **ENV-340SC** – similar to the NV-340S, except has a single cutaway and CTB-4 electronics, mfg. 2003-04.

	100%	EXCELLENT	AVERAGE	LAST MSR
	N/A	$1,050 - 1,250	$650 - 750	$2,429

* **TNV-340S** – similar to the NV-340S, except has CTP-1 Cool Tube electronics, mfg. 2004-05.

	100%	EXCELLENT	AVERAGE	LAST MSR
	N/A	$1,100 - 1,300	$650 - 750	$2,439

* **TNV-340SC** – similar to the NV-340S, except has a single cutaway and CTP-1 Cool Tube electronics, mfg. 2004-08.

	100%	EXCELLENT	AVERAGE	LAST MSR
	N/A	$1,200 - 1,400	$700 - 800	$2,769

EF360SBG – dreadnought style, solid spruce top, solid rosewood back and sides, round soundhole with concentric rings rosette, 14/20-fret ebony fingerboard with pearl dot inlays, three-per-side open gear antique nickel tuners, rosewood bridge, tortoiseshell pickguard, TLD Line Driver preamp/electronics, available in Gloss Natural finish, mfg. 2007-2012.

	100%	EXCELLENT	AVERAGE	LAST MSR
	$2,000	$1,150 - 1,450	$700 - 875	$2,899

* **TF360SBG** – similar to the EF360SBG, except has CTP-1 Cool Tube preamp/electronics, available in Gloss Natural finish, mfg. 2007-2012.

	100%	EXCELLENT	AVERAGE	LAST MSR
	$2,100	$1,200 - 1,500	$725 - 900	$2,999

» **TF360SBG-MAG** – similar to the TF360SBG, except has a solid Adirondack spruce top and solid Madagascar rosewood back and sides, available in Gloss Natural finish, mfg. 2011 only.

	100%	EXCELLENT	AVERAGE	LAST MSR
	$3,800	$2,200 - 2,750	$1,325 - 1,650	$5,459

MSR/NOTES	100%	EXCELLENT	AVERAGE	LAST MSR

NV-360S – dreadnought style, solid bear claw spruce top, solid Indian rosewood back and sides, abalone rosette, abalone binding, ebony fingerboard with snowflake inlay, three-per-side tuners, ebony bridge, tortoise pickguard, gold hardware, Natural finish, mfg. 2001-04.

	N/A	$1,050 - 1,250	$700 - 800	$2,499

* **ENV-360S** – similar to the NV-360, except has CTB-4 electronics, mfg. 2001-04.

	N/A	$1,200 - 1,400	$750 - 900	$2,787

* **ENV-360SC** – similar to the NV-360, except has a single cutaway and CTB-4 electronics, mfg. 2001-04.

	N/A	$1,250 - 1,450	$750 - 900	$2,858

* **TNV-360S** – similar to the NV-360S, except has CTP-1 Cool Tube electronics, mfg. 2004-2011.

	$2,350	$1,400 - 1,700	$900 - 1,050	$3,359

* **TNV-360SC** – similar to the NV-360S, except has a single cutaway and CTP-1 Cool Tube electronics, mfg. 2004-2012.

	$2,550	$1,450 - 1,825	$875 - 1,100	$3,650

TF430SS – Grand Auditorium NEX-style body, solid cedar top, solid ovangkol back and sides, round soundhole with concentric rings rosette, body binding, 14/20-fret bound ebony fingerboard with small MOP dot inlays, bound headstock with "T" logo, three-per-side gold tuners with amber buttons, ebony bridge, CTP-1 electronics, available in Satin Sunburst finish, mfg. 2008-2010.

	$1,600	$1,000 - 1,150	$600 - 700	$2,299

NV-460S – NEX style, solid bear claw spruce top, solid Indian rosewood back and sides, abalone rosette, abalone binding, ebony fingerboard with snowflake inlay, three-per-side tuners, ebony bridge, tortoise pickguard, gold hardware, Natural finish, mfg. 2003-04.

	N/A	$1,050 - 1,250	$700 - 800	$2,499

* **ENV-460S** – similar to the NV-460S, except has a single cutaway and CTB-4 electronics, mfg. 2001-04.

	N/A	$1,250 - 1,450	$750 - 900	$2,858

* **TNV-460SC** – similar to the NV-460S, except has a single cutaway and CTP-1 Cool Tube electronics, mfg. 2004-2012.

	$2,550	$1,450 - 1,825	$875 - 1,100	$3,650

ENV-740S – OM style, solid bear claw spruce top, solid mahogany back and sides, abalone rosette, abalone binding, ebony fingerboard with snowflake inlay, three-per-side tuners, ebony bridge, tortoise pickguard, CTB-4 electronics, gold hardware, Natural finish, mfg. 2003-04.

	N/A	$1,000 - 1,150	$600 - 700	$2,286

* **TNV-740S** – similar to the ENV-470S, except has CTP-1 Cool Tube electronics, mfg. 2004-05.

	N/A	$1,050 - 1,250	$650 - 750	$2,439

TF740FS – single cutaway OM-style body, solid cedar top, solid mahogany back and sides, round soundhole with abalnoe rosette, 14/20-fret ebony fingerboard with pearl dot inlays, slotted headstock, three-per-side open-style gold tuners, ebony bridge, no pickguard, Cool Tube preamp/electronics, available in Gloss Natural finish, mfg. 2010-present.

MSR $2,900	$2,000	$1,150 - 1,450	$700 - 875	

ENV-760S – OM style, solid bear claw spruce top, solid Indian rosewood back and sides, abalone rosette, abalone binding, ebony fingerboard with snowflake inlay, three-per-side tuners, ebony bridge, tortoise pickguard, CTB-4 electronics, gold hardware, Natural finish, mfg. 2003-04.

	N/A	$1,200 - 1,400	$750 - 900	$2,787

* **TNV-760S** – similar to the ENV-760S, except has CTP-1 Cool Tube electronics, mfg. 2004-08, reintroduced 2011 only.

	$2,550	$1,450 - 1,825	$875 - 1,100	$3,649

* **TNV-760SC** – similar to the ENV-760S, except has a single cutaway and CTP-1 Cool Tube electronics, mfg. 2006-08.

	N/A	$1,500 - 1,750	$950 - 1,100	$3,429

EF-450/451DLX – NEX Grand Auditorium body style, solid spruce top, solid flamed maple back and sides, round soundhole with abalone ring rosette, 14/20-fret ebony fingerboard with creeping vine inlays, three-per-side gold deluxe tuners, ebony bridge, black pickguard with creeping vine design, TLD Line Driver preamp/electronics, available in Gloss Black (451) or Gloss Natural (450) finish, mfg. 2010-2011.

	$3,100	$2,000 - 2,450	$1,100 - 1,325	$4,449

ACOUSTIC: NATURAL/SUPER NATURAL SERIES

AN10S – dreadnought body style, solid cedar top, solid mahogany back and sides, rosewood fingerboard, available in Satin Natural, disc. 2005.

	N/A	$450 - 525	$250 - 300	$999

Also available in left-handed configuration (Model AN10-LH).

N-10 – dreadnought style, solid cedar top, round soundhole, 3-stripe bound body, 5-stripe rosette, mahogany back/sides/neck, 14/20-fret rosewood fingerboard, rosewood strings through bridge, 3-per-side gold tuners w/ amber buttons, available in Natural finish, disc. 1999.

	N/A	$400 - 475	$225 - 275	$949

MSR/NOTES	100%	EXCELLENT	AVERAGE	LAST MSR
* **EN-10** – similar to N-10, except has crystal bridge pickup, 3-band EQ, disc. 1999.				
	N/A	$525 - 600	$275 - 325	$1,239
* **EAN-10C** – similar to N-10, except has single rounded cutaway, crystal bridge pickup, 3-band EQ, available in Natural or Sunburst finish, disc. 2010.				
	$1,150	$700 - 850	$425 - 500	$1,649
This model was also available in left-handed configuration (Model EAN10C-LH).				
ETN-10C – dreadnought style body with single cutaway, solid cedar top, round soundhole, three-stripe bound body, multi-wood rosette, solid mahogany back/sides/neck, 14/20-fret rosewood fingerboard, rosewood strings through bridge, CT4B preamp, three-per-side chrome tuners, available in Satin Natural or Satin Tobacco Sunburst finish, mfg. 2010-12.				
	$1,250	$725 - 900	$450 - 550	$1,800
* **ETN-10C-LH Left-Handed** – similar to the ETN-10C, except in left-handed configuration, available in Satin Natural finish, mfg. 2010-12.				
	$1,400	$800 - 1,000	$475 - 600	$2,000
EN-12C-12 – dreadnought body with cutaway, 12-string, solid cedar top, Silky Oak back and sides, rosewood fingerboard, Graph EX pre-amp system, available in Natural finish, disc.				
	N/A	$675 - 800	$400 - 475	$1,579
N-15 – dreadnought style, solid cedar top, round soundhole, 3-stripe bound body, 5-stripe rosette, rosewood back/sides, mahogany neck, 14/20-fret rosewood fingerboard, rosewood strings through bridge, 3-per-side gold tuners with amber buttons, available in Natural finish, disc. 1999.				
	N/A	$500 - 575	$250 - 300	$1,139
* **NP-15C** – similar to N-15, except has single round cutaway, crystal bridge pickups, parametric EQ, disc. 1999.				
	N/A	$675 - 800	$400 - 475	$1,579
* **EAN-15C** – similar to N-15 model except, has single cutaway dreadnought body, DSP preamp system, padauk, ebony and maple rosette, available in Natural finish, mfg. 2001-04.				
	N/A	$750 - 900	$475 - 550	$1,786
* **TAN-15C** – similar to the EAN-15C, except has CTP-1/Cool Tube electronics, mfg. 2004-2012.				
	$1,650	$950 - 1,200	$550 - 700	$2,400
AN16S – dreadnought body style, solid spruce top, solid Indian rosewood back and sides, rosewood fingerboard, available in Gloss Natural, mfg. 2001-04.				
	N/A	$675 - 800	$425 - 500	$1,569
Also available in for left-handed configuration.				
* **EAN-16S** – similar to the AN16S, except has CT4B electronics, mfg. 2001-04.				
	N/A	$800 - 950	$525 - 600	$1,857
• **Add $15 for left-handed configuration (Model EAN-16S-LH).**				
* **EAN-16C** – similar to the EAN-16S, except has a single cutaway, mfg. 2001-04.				
	N/A	$800 - 950	$525 - 600	$1,857
This model was also available in left-handed configuration (Model EAN-16C-LH).				
* **EAN-16 KOA** – similar to the EAN-16S, except has a solid top with solid koa back and sides, mfg. 2003-04.				
	N/A	$900 - 1,050	$550 - 650	$2,072
* **TAN-16C** – similar to the EAN-16C, except has CTP-1 Cool Tube electronics, mfg. 2004-2012.				
	$1,650	$950 - 1,200	$550 - 700	$2,400
» **TAN-16C-12 12-String** – similar to the TAN-16C, except in 12-string configuration, mfg. 2007-08.				
	N/A	$1,050 - 1,250	$650 - 750	$2,399
» **TAN-16C-LH Left-Handed** – similar to the TAN-16C, except in left-handed configuration, available in Gloss Natural finish, mfg. 2004-2012.				
	$1,750	$1,050 - 1,300	$625 - 775	$2,550
* **TAN-16 KOA** – similar to the EAN-16S, except hasa solid top with solid koa back and sides and CTP-1 Cool Tube electronics, mfg. 2004-08.				
	N/A	$1,150 - 1,350	$700 - 825	$2,599
EN18C/NP-18C – dreadnought style, single rounded cutaway, solid spruce top, round soundhole, abalone bound body/rosette, rosewood back/sides, mahogany neck, 14/20-fret ebony fingerboard, ebony strings through bridge, abalone logo peghead inlay, three-per-side gold tuners with amber buttons, crystal bridge pickup, parametric EQ, available in Natural finish, disc. 1999.				
	N/A	$950 - 1,100	$600 - 700	$2,199
This model was distributed in the U.S. as the NP-18C, but the same guitar has been stamped the EN18C.				
N-20 – jumbo style, solid cedar top, round soundhole, 3-stripe bound body, 5-stripe rosette, mahogany back/sides/neck, 14/20-fret rosewood fingerboard, rosewood strings through bridge, 3-per-side gold tuners with amber buttons, available in Natural finish, disc. 1996.				
	N/A	$400 - 475	$225 - 275	$940

MSR/NOTES	100%	EXCELLENT	AVERAGE	LAST MSR

* **EN-20** – similar to N-20, except has crystal bridge pickup, 3-band EQ, disc. 1999.

| | N/A | $650 - 750 | $350 - 425 | $1,389 |

* **EAN-20C** – similar to N-20, except has CT4B electronics, disc. 2008.

| | N/A | $650 - 750 | $375 - 450 | $1,499 |

ETN-20C – jumbo body style, solid cedar top, round soundhole, three-stripe bound body, multi-wood rosette, solid mahogany back, mahogany sides and neck, 14/20-fret rosewood fingerboard, rosewood strings through bridge, CT4B preamp, three-per-side chrome tuners, available in Satin Natural finish, mfg. 2010-2011.

| | $1,200 | $700 - 875 | $425 - 500 | $1,719 |

NP-25C – jumbo style, single rounded cutaway, solid cedar top, round soundhole, 3-stripe bound body, 5-stripe rosette, mahogany back/sides/neck, 14/20-fret rosewood fingerboard, rosewood strings through bridge, 3-per-side gold tuners, crystal bridge pickups, parametric EQ, available in Natural finish, mfg. 1994-99.

| | N/A | $775 - 900 | $550 - 625 | $1,679 |

ND-25C – similar to NP-25C model, except has rosewood back sides and fingerboard, DSP preamp system, available in Natural finish, disc.

| | N/A | $800 - 925 | $550 - 625 | $1,729 |

EAN-30C – FXC/Aritist single cutaway body, solid cedar top, mahogany with solid back, rosewood fingerboard, CT4B electronics, Satin Natural finish, disc. 2008.

| | N/A | $650 - 750 | $375 - 450 | $1,499 |

* **ETN-30C** – similar to the EAN-30C, except has a multi-wood rosette and chrome tuners, available in Satin Natural finish, mfg. 2010-2011.

| | $1,200 | $700 - 875 | $425 - 500 | $1,719 |

N-40 – dreadnought style, solid red cedar top, round soundhole, 3-stripe bound body, 5-stripe rosette, mahogany back/sides/neck, 14/20-fret rosewood fingerboard, rosewood strings through bridge, 3-per-side gold tuners, available in Natural finish, mfg. 1994-99.

| | N/A | $400 - 475 | $325 - 375 | $949 |

* **EAN-40C** – similar to N-40, except has single round cutaway, crystal bridge pickups, 3-band EQ, mfg. 1994-2010.

| | $1,150 | $700 - 850 | $425 - 500 | $1,649 |

»**EAN-40C 12-String** – similar to the EAN-40C, except in 12-string configuration, six-per-side tuners, disc. 2008.

| | N/A | $700 - 825 | $425 - 500 | $1,639 |

»**EAN-40C-12LH Left-Handed 12-String** – similar to the EAN-40C, except in left-handed 12-string configuration with six-per-side tuners, disc. 2008.

| | N/A | $700 - 825 | $425 - 500 | $1,639 |

ETN-40C – NEX/Grand Auditorium body style with single cutaway, solid cedar top, round soundhole, three-stripe bound body, multi-wood rosette, solid mahogany back with mahogany sides and neck, 14/20-fret rosewood fingerboard, rosewood strings through bridge, CT4B preamp, three-per-side chrome tuners, available in Satin Natural finish, mfg. 2010-12.

| | $1,250 | $725 - 900 | $450 - 550 | $1,800 |

NP-45C – single cutaway NEX-style body, red cedar top, rosewood back and sides, round soundhole with five-stripe rosette, three-stripe bound body, mahogany neck, 14/20-fret rosewood fingerboard, three-per-side gold tuners, rosewood strings through bridge, crystal bridge pickups, parametric EQ, available in Natural finish, mfg. 1993-99.

| | N/A | $675 - 800 | $375 - 450 | $1,489 |

* **EAN-45C** – similar to the NP-45C, except has CT4B electronics, mfg. 2001-04.

| | N/A | $750 - 900 | $475 - 550 | $1,786 |

* **TAN-45C** – similar to the EAN-45C, except has CTP-1 Cool Tube electronics, mfg. 2004-2012.

| | $1,650 | $950 - 1,200 | $550 - 700 | $2,400 |

EAN-46C – similar to the EAN-45C, except has a solid spruce top, disc. 2003.

| | N/A | $800 - 925 | $475 - 550 | $1,700 |

TAN-55C – AXC body shape, solid cedar top, rosewood back and sides, round soundhole, concentric ring rosette, body binding, rosewood fingerboard, three-per-side tuners with amber buttons, CTP-1 Cool Tube electronics, gold hardware, available in Natural finish, mfg. 2005-08.

| | N/A | $950 - 1,100 | $550 - 650 | $2,199 |

EAN-60C – FXC nylon string single cutaway body, solid cedar top, mahogany back and sides, rosewood fingerboard, CT4B electronics, Satin Natural finish, disc. 2008.

| | N/A | $650 - 750 | $375 - 450 | $1,499 |

* **ETN-60C** – similar to the EAN-60C, except with multi-wood rosette and chrome tuners, available in Satin Natural finish, mfg. 2010-2011.

| | $1,200 | $700 - 875 | $425 - 500 | $1,719 |

MSR/NOTES	100%	EXCELLENT	AVERAGE	LAST MSR

NP-65C – "country classic" body style, single rounded cutaway, solid cedar top, round soundhole, 3-stripe bound body, wooden rosette, rosewood back/sides, mahogany neck, 20-fret ebony fingerboard, classic style ebony bridge, classic style peghead, 3-per-side gold tuners with amber buttons, crystal bridge pickups, parametric EQ, available in Natural finish, disc. 1999.

	N/A	$675 - 800	$375 - 450	$1,499

ND-65C – similar to NP-65C except, has rosewood fingerboard, DSP preamp system, available in Natural finish, disc.

	N/A	$750 - 875	$500 - 575	$1,629

EAN-70 – OM style body, solid cedar top, solid mahogany back, mahogany sides, round soundhole with tinted wood ring rosette, rosewood fingerboard, three-per-side tuners with amber buttons, CT4B electronics, gold hardware, Satin Natural finish, mfg. 2005-08.

	N/A	$650 - 750	$375 - 450	$1,499

* *EAN-70C* – similar to the EAN-70, except has a single cutaway, mfg. 2006-2010.

	$1,200	$750 - 900	$450 - 525	$1,719

ETN-70 – OM style body, solid cedar top, solid mahogany back, mahogany sides, round soundhole, multi-wood ring rosette, rosewood fingerboard, three-per-side chrome tuners, CT4B electronics, available in Satin Natural finish, mfg. 2010-2011.

	$1,200	$700 - 875	$425 - 500	$1,719

* *ETN-70C* – similar to the ETN-70, except with single cutaway, available in Satin Natural finish, mfg. 2010-2011.

	$1,200	$700 - 875	$425 - 500	$1,719

EAN-76 – OM style body, solid spruce top, solid rosewood back, rosewood sides, round soundhole with abalone rosette, rosewood fingerboard, 3-per-side tuners with amber buttons, CT4B electronics, gold hardware, Satin Natural finish, mfg. 2004 only.

	N/A	$850 - 1,000	$525 - 625	$1,857

* *TAN-76* – similar to the EAN-76, except has CTP-1 Cool Tube electronics, mfg. 2004-2011.

	$1,650	$950 - 1,175	$575 - 700	$2,349

» *TAN-76C* – similar to the TAN-76, except has a single cutaway, mfg. 2006-2010.

	$1,750	$1,050 - 1,250	$675 - 800	$2,499

EAN-77 – OM style body, solid cedar top, solid koa back and sides, round soundhole with abalone rosette, rosewood fingerboard, 3-per-side tuners with amber buttons, CT4B electronics, gold hardware, Satin Natural finish, mfg. 2004 only.

	N/A	$950 - 1,100	$600 - 700	$2,072

* *TAN-77* – similar to the EAN-77, except has CTP-1 Cool Tube electronics, mfg. 2004-2011.

	$1,900	$1,100 - 1,350	$650 - 800	$2,715

ACOUSTIC: PRO SERIES 1/2/3/4/5/6/7 SERIES

The Pro Series was introduced in 2013, and all models come with a hardshell case.

P1D – dreadnought-style body, solid cedar top, sapele back and sides, round soundhole with concentric rings rosette, mahogany neck, 14/20-fret rosewood fingerboard with pearl dot inlays, three-per-side chrome tuners, rosewood bridge with split bone saddle and pin-less base, black pickguard, CT4B2 pickup/electronics, available in Gloss Natural finish, mfg. 2013-present.

MSR $1,375	$950	$625 - 750	$350 - 400	

* *P1DC* – similar to the P1D, except has a single cutaway, available in Gloss Natural finish, mfg. 2013-present.

MSR $1,425	$1,000	$650 - 775	$350 - 425	

P1JC – jumbo single cutaway body, solid cedar top, sapele back and sides, round soundhole with concentric rings rosette, mahogany neck, 14/20-fret rosewood fingerboard with pearl dot inlays, three-per-side chrome tuners, rosewood bridge with split bone saddle and pin-less base, black pickguard, CT4B2 pickup/electronics, available in Gloss Natural finish, mfg. 2013-present.

MSR $1,500	$1,050	$675 - 825	$375 - 450	

* *P1JC12 12-String* – similar to the P1JC, except in 12-string configuration with six-per-side chrome tuners, available in Gloss Natural finish, mfg. 2013-present.

MSR $1,575	$1,100	$700 - 875	$400 - 475	

P1M – OM-style body, solid cedar top, sapele back and sides, round soundhole with concentric rings rosette, mahogany neck, 14/20-fret rosewood fingerboard with pearl dot inlays, three-per-side chrome tuners, rosewood bridge with split bone saddle and pin-less base, black pickguard, CT4B2 pickup/electronics, available in Gloss Natural finish, mfg. 2013-present.

MSR $1,375	$950	$625 - 750	$350 - 400	

P1NC – NEX-style body with single cutaway, solid cedar top, sapele back and sides, round soundhole with concentric rings rosette, mahogany neck, 14/20-fret rosewood fingerboard with pearl dot inlays, three-per-side chrome tuners, rosewood bridge with split bone saddle and pin-less base, black pickguard, CT4B2 pickup/electronics, available in Gloss Natural finish, mfg. 2013-present.

MSR $1,425	$1,000	$650 - 775	$350 - 425	

MSR/NOTES	100%	EXCELLENT	AVERAGE	LAST MSR

P2DC – dreadnought-style body with single cutaway, solid spruce top, sapele back and sides, round soundhole with concentric rings rosette, mahogany neck, 14/20-fret rosewood fingerboard with pearl dot inlays, three-per-side chrome tuners, rosewood bridge with split bone saddle and pin-less base, black pickguard, CT4B2 pickup/electronics, available in Gloss Natural finish, mfg. 2013-present.

MSR $1,500	$1,050	$675 - 825	$375 - 450	

P3D – dreadnought-style body, solid cedar top, solid saple back, sapele sides, round soundhole with concentric rings rosette, ivory body binding, mahogany neck, 14/20-fret rosewood fingerboard with wood dot-in-dot inlays, three-per-side gold tuners, rosewood bridge with split bone saddle and pin-less base, no pickguard, CT4B2 pickup/electronics, available in Satin Natural finish, mfg. 2013-present.

MSR $1,550	$1,100	$700 - 850	$375 - 475	

* **P3DC** – similar to the P3D, except has a single cutaway, available in Satin Natural finish, mfg. 2013-present.

MSR $1,595	$1,150	$725 - 875	$400 - 475	

»**P3DC12 12-String** – similar to the P3DC, except in 12-string configuration with six-per-side tuners, available in Satin Natural finish, mfg. 2013-present.

MSR $1,725	$1,250	$775 - 950	$425 - 525	

P3FCN – FXC-style body with single cutaway and nylon strings, solid cedar top, solid sapele back, sapele sides, round soundhole with concentric rings rosette, ivory body binding, mahogany neck, 14/20-fret rosewood fingerboard with wood dot-in-dot inlays, slotted headstock, three-per-side gold tuners with amber buttons, rosewood bridge with split bone saddle and pin-less base, no pickguard, CT4B2 pickup/electronics, available in Satin Natural finish, mfg. 2013-present.

MSR $1,595	$1,150	$725 - 875	$400 - 475	

P3MC – OM-style body with single cutaway, solid cedar top, solid sapele body, sapele sides, round soundhole with concentric rings rosette, ivory body binding, mahogany neck, 14/20-fret rosewood fingerboard with wood dot-in-dot inlays, three-per-side gold tuners, rosewood bridge with split bone saddle and pin-less base, no pickguard, CT4B2 pickup/electronics, available in Satin Natural finish, mfg. 2013-present.

MSR $1,595	$1,150	$725 - 875	$400 - 475	

P3NC – NEX-style body with single cutaway, solid cedar top, solid sapele back, sapele sides, round soundhole with concentric rings rosette, ivory body binding, mahogany neck, 14/20-fret rosewood fingerboard with wood dot-in-dot inlays, three-per-side gold tuners with amber buttons, rosewood bridge with split bone saddle and pin-less base, no pickguard, CT4B2 pickup/electronics, available in Satin Natural finish, mfg. 2013-present.

MSR $1,595	$1,150	$725 - 875	$400 - 475	

P3NY – New Yorker-style body, solid cedar top, solid sapele back, sapele sides, round soundhole with concentric rings rosette, ivory body binding, mahogany neck, 14/21-fret rosewood fingerboard with wood dot-in-dot inlays, slotted headstock, three-per-side gold tuners with amber buttons, rosewood with split bone saddle and pin-less base, no pickguard, CT4B2 pickup/electronics, available in Satin Natural finish, mfg. 2013-present.

MSR $1,595	$1,150	$725 - 875	$400 - 475	

P4DC – dreadnought-style body with single cutaway, solid spruce top, solid sapele back, sapele sides, round soundhole with concentric rings rosette, ivory body binding, mahogany neck, 14/20-fret rosewood fingerboard with wood dot-in-dot inlays, three-per-side gold tuners with amber buttons, rosewood bridge with split bone saddle and pin-less base, no pickguard, CT4B2 pickup/electronics, available in Gloss Natural finish, mfg. 2013-present.

MSR $1,860	$1,350	$825 - 1,025	$475 - 550	

P5DC – dreadnought-style body with single cutaway, solid spruce top, solid rosewood back, rosewood sides, round soundhole with abalone rosette, ivory body binding, mahogany neck, 14/20-fret rosewood fingerboard with abalone dot-in-dot inlays, three-per-side gold tuners, rosewood bridge with split bone saddle, tortoiseshell pickguard, CT4DX pickup/electronics, available in Gloss Natural finish, mfg. 2013-present.

MSR $2,350	$1,700	$1,050 - 1,300	$575 - 700	

P5J – jumbo-style body, solid spruce top, solid rosewood back, rosewood sides, round soundhole with abalone rosette, ivory body binding, mahogany neck, 14/20-fret rosewood fingerboard with abalone dot-in-dot inlays, three-per-side gold tuners, rosewood bridge with split bone saddle, tortoiseshell pickguard, CT4DX pickup/electronics, available in Gloss Natural finish, mfg. 2013-present.

MSR $2,400	$1,750	$1,075 - 1,325	$600 - 725	

* **P5JC** – similar to the P5J, except has a single cutaway, available in Gloss Natural finish, mfg. 2013-present.

MSR $2,450	$1,800	$1,100 - 1,350	$600 - 725	

P5NC – NEX-style body with single cutaway, solid spruce top, solid rosewood back, rosewood sides, round soundhole with abalone rosette, mahogany neck, 14/20-fret rosewood fingerboard with abalone dot-in-dot inlays, three-per-side gold tuners, rosewood bridge with split bone saddle, tortoiseshell pickguard, CT4DX pickup/electronics, available in Gloss Natural finish, mfg. 2013-present.

MSR $2,350	$1,700	$1,050 - 1,300	$575 - 700	

P6JC – jumbo-style body with single cutaway, solid spruce top, solid flame maple back, flame maple sides, round soundhole with MOP rosette, black/white body purfling, maple neck, 14/20-fret ivory-bound ebony fingerboard with MOP snowflake inlays, three-per-side gold tuners with pearl buttons, rosewood bridge, black pickguard, Palathetic pickup, CT4DX electronics, available in Gloss Brown Sunburst finish, mfg. 2013-present.

MSR $3,270	$2,400	$1,475 - 1,800	$825 - 975	

MSR/NOTES	100%	EXCELLENT	AVERAGE	LAST MSR

* *P6JC12 12-String* – similar to the P6JC, except in 12-string configuration with six-per-side tuners, available in Gloss Brown Sunburst finish, mfg. 2013-present.

| MSR $3,330 | $2,450 | $1,500 - 1,825 | $825 - 1,000 | |

P6N – NEX-style body, solid spruce top, solid flame maple back, flame maple sides, round soundhole with MOP rosette, ivory body binding, black/white purfling, maple neck, 14/20-fret ivory-bound ebony fingerboard with MOP snowflake inlays, three-per-side gold tuners with pearl buttons, rosewood bridge with bone saddle, black pickguard, Palathetic pickup, CT4DX electronics, available in Gloss Brown Sunburst finish, mfg. 2013-present.

| MSR $3,130 | $2,300 | $1,400 - 1,725 | $775 - 950 | |

* *P6NC* – similar to the P6N, except with a single cutaway, available in Gloss Brown Sunburst finish, mfg. 2013-present.

| MSR $3,200 | $2,350 | $1,450 - 1,750 | $800 - 950 | |

P7D – dreadnought-style body, solid spruce top, solid rosewood back and sides, round soundhole with abalone rosette, maple body binding, wood purfling, mahogany neck, 14/20-fret ebony fingerboard with abalone snowflake inlays, rosewood headstock overlay, three-per-side gold tuners, rosewood bridge with split bone saddle, tortoiseshell pickguard, CTP2 Cool Tube pickup/electronics, available in Gloss Natural finish, mfg. 2013-present.

| MSR $3,900 | $2,850 | $1,750 - 2,150 | $975 - 1,175 | |

* *P7DC* – similar to the P7D, except has a single cutaway, available in Gloss Natural finish, mfg. 2013-present.

| MSR $3,950 | $2,900 | $1,775 - 2,175 | $975 - 1,175 | |

P7JC – jumbo-style body with single cutaway, solid spruce top, solid rosewood back and sides, round soundhole with abalone rosette, maple body binding, wood purfling, mahogany neck, 14/20-fret ebony fingerboard, rosewood headstock overlay, three-per-side gold tuners, rosewood bridge with split bone saddle, tortoiseshell pickguard, CTP2 Cool Tube pickup/electronics, available in Gloss Natural finish, mfg. 2013-present.

| MSR $4,040 | $2,950 | $1,825 - 2,225 | $1,000 - 1,200 | |

P7NC – NEX-style body with single cutaway, solid spruce top, solid rosewood back and sides, round soundhole with abalone rosette, maple body binding, mahogany neck, 14/20-fret ebony fingerboard with abalone snowflake inlays, rosewood headstock overlay, three-per-side gold tuners, rosewood bridge with split bone saddle, tortoiseshell pickguard, CTP2 Cool Tube pickup/electronics, available in Gloss Natural finish, mfg. 2013-present.

| MSR $3,950 | $2,900 | $1,775 - 2,175 | $975 - 1,175 | |

ACOUSTIC: SANTA FE & NOVEAU SERIES

Santa Fe series instruments feature turquoise or abalone inlays and rosette designs with a Southwestern flavor.

PSF-15C – dreadnought style, single rounded cutaway, solid cedar top, round soundhole, 3-stripe bound body/black crow rosette, rosewood sides, bookmatched rosewood back, mahogany neck, 21-fret rosewood fingerboard with turquoise dot inlay, turquoise eagle inlay at 12th fret, black headstock, rosewood bridge, 3-per-side gold tuners, bridge pickup, preamp and parametric EQ, available in Natural finish, mfg. 1993-99.

| | N/A | $700 - 825 | $425 - 500 | $1,699 |

DSF-15C – similar to PSF-15C model except, has DSP preamp system, available in Natural Gloss finish, disc. 2003.

| | N/A | $800 - 925 | $475 - 550 | $1,749 |

PSF-35C – folk style, single rounded cutaway, solid cedar top, round soundhole, 3-stripe bound body/black crow rosette, rosewood back/sides, mahogany neck, 21-fret rosewood fingerboard with turquoise dot inlay, turquoise eagle inlay at 12th fret, open classical-style headstock, rosewood bridge, 3-per-side gold tuners with amber buttons, bridge pickup, preamp and parametric EQ, available in Natural finish, mfg. 1993-95.

| | N/A | $700 - 825 | $425 - 500 | $1,700 |

PSF-48C/DSF-48C – single cutaway NEX-style body, solid spruce top, rosewood back and sides, round soundhole, wood inlay rosette, multi-bound body, mahogany neck, 21-fret ebony fingerboard with green abalone eagle inlay, rosewood headstock overlay with abalone dot/logo inlay, three-per-side gold tuners with amber buttons, ebony bridge, piezo bridge pickup, parametric EQ, active electronics, available in Natural finish, mfg. 1993-2002.

| | N/A | $900 - 1,050 | $525 - 600 | $1,999 |

In 2000, the PSF-48C was updated with new electronics and renamed the DSF-48C.

EAC-48C – NEX style body, solid spruce top, solid rosewood back, rosewood sides, semi-precious stone rosette, rosewood fingerboard with semi-precious inlays, three-per-side tuners, rosewood bridge, CT4B electronics, chrome hardware, Natural finish, mfg. 2003-05.

| | N/A | $975 - 1,125 | $550 - 650 | $2,149 |

ESF-48C – similar to PSF-48C, except has electronics, available in Natural Gloss finish, disc. 2005.

| | N/A | $950 - 1,100 | $550 - 650 | $2,149 |

TSF-48C – similar to PSF-48C, except has Cool Tube electronics, available in Natural Gloss finish, mfg. 2006-present.

| MSR $2,800 | $2,000 | $1,125 - 1,400 | $675 - 850 | |

MSR/NOTES	100%	EXCELLENT	AVERAGE	LAST MSR

PSF-65C – folk style, single rounded cutaway, solid cedar top, round soundhole, 3-stripe bound body/black crow rosette, rosewood back/ sides, mahogany neck, 21-fret rosewood fingerboard with turquoise dot inlay, turquoise eagle inlay at 12th fret, open classical-style headstock, rosewood bridge, 3-per-side gold tuners, bridge pickup, preamp and parametric EQ, available in Natural finish, mfg. 1993-99.

	N/A	$700 - 825	$425 - 500	$1,699

The PSF-65C was designed for nylon string use.

EF-75S – OM body style, solid spruce top, solid Brazilian rosewood back and sides, ebony fingerboard, ebony bridge, TLD electronics, available in Natural finish, mfg. summer 2005-06.

	N/A	$2,000 - 2,300	$1,200 - 1,400	$4,149

TF77-PT – OM-style body, solid cedar top, solid koa back and sides, round soundhole with abalone rosette, multi-ply body binding, mahogany neck, 14/20-fret rosewood fingerboard with 11-12th fret Palm Tree inlays, black headstock overlay with vertical gold logo, three-per-side gold tuners with amber buttons, rosewood bridge, white bridge pins with black dots, no pickguard, Cool Tube pickup/electronics, available in Gloss Natural finish, mfg. 2011-present.

MSR $2,600	$1,800	$1,050 - 1,300	$625 - 775	

TF87-PT – New Yorker-style body, solid cedar top, solid koa back and sides, round soundhole with abalone rosette, multi-ply body binding, mahogany neck, 14/20-fret rosewood fingerboard with 11-12th fret Palm Tree inlays, slotted headstock with black overlay and horizontal gold logo, three-per-side open-style gold tuners with amber buttons, rosewood bridge, white bridge pins with black dots, no pickguard, Cool Tube pickup/electronics, available in Gloss Natural finish, mfg. 2011-12.

	$1,800	$1,050 - 1,300	$625 - 775	$2,600

ESF-93 – folk style, single rounded cutaway, solid cedar top, round soundhole, multi-bound, wood inlay rosette, silky oak back/sides, mahogany neck, 21-fret ebony fingerboard with turquoise eagle inlay, ebony bridge with white black dot pins, silky oak peghead veneer with turquoise dot/ abalone logo inlay, 3-per-side gold tuners with amber buttons, piezo bridge pickups, parametric EQ, active electronics. Available in Natural finish, mfg. 1993 only.

	N/A	$675 - 800	$400 - 475	$1,500

PSF-94 – folk style, single rounded cutaway, solid cedar top, round soundhole, multi-layer binding, wood inlay rosette, koa back/sides, mahogany neck, 20-fret rosewood fingerboard with abalone eagle inlay, rosewood strings through bridge, koa peghead veneer with abalone logo inlay, 3-per-side gold tuners with brown pearl buttons, piezo bridge pickups, parametric EQ, available in Natural finish, mfg. 1994 only.

	N/A	$825 - 975	$500 - 575	$1,850

EF-241S – jumbo body style, solid spruce top, mahogany back and sides, round sounhole with ring rosette, top and back body binding, 14/20- fret rosewood fingerboard with dot inlay, three-per-side chrome tuners, rosewood bridge, tortoise pickguard, CT4B electronics, available in Black finish, mfg. 2006-08.

	N/A	$725 - 875	$450 - 525	$1,715

* **TF-241DLX** – similar to the EF-241S, except has a single cutaway, solid mahogany back, abalone rosette, and CTP Cool Tube electronics, available in Black finish, mfg. 2006-08.

	N/A	$1,000 - 1,200	$600 - 700	$2,299

EF-250 SMC – jumbo single cutaway body, solid spruce top, solid flame maple back, flame maple sides, round soundhole with concentric ring rosette, body binding, ebony fingerboard with trapezoid abalone and wood inlays, flame maple headstock with three-per-side tuners, ebony bridge, CT4B electronics, gold hardware, available in Natural or Sunburst finishes, mfg. 2004 only.

	N/A	$1,100 - 1,300	$700 - 800	$2,572

* **TF-250 SMC** – similar to the EF-250 SMC, except has CTP-1 Cool Tube electronics, available in Gloss Natural (disc.) or Gloss Sunburst finish, mfg. 2004-2012.

	$2,400	$1,400 - 1,750	$850 - 1,050	$3,500

» **TF-250 SMC 12-String** – similar to the TF-250 SMC, except in 12-string configuration and six-per-side tuners, available in Natural or Sunburst finish, mfg. summer 2005-2010.

	$2,300	$1,400 - 1,650	$900 - 1,050	$3,299

EF-261SAN/SBL – Artist/FXC cutaway body, solid cedar top, mahogany back and sides, dot position inlays, Graph EX preamp system, available in Antique Stain Gloss or Gloss Black finishes, disc. 2011.

	$1,100	$675 - 800	$400 - 475	$1,579

EF-281S 12-STRING – similar to the EF-241S, except in 12-string configuration with six-per-side tuners, available in Black finish, mfg. 2006-08.

	N/A	$800 - 950	$500 - 575	$1,869

* **TF-281DLX 12-String** – similar to the EF-281S 12-String, except has a single cutaway, solid mahogany back, abalone rosette, and CTP Cool Tube electronics, available in Black finish, mfg. 2006-08.

	N/A	$1,050 - 1,250	$625 - 725	$2,449

MSR/NOTES	100%	EXCELLENT	AVERAGE	LAST MSR

EF-340SCGN – single cutaway dreadnought-style body, solid cedar top, mahogany back and sides, round soundhole with concentric ring rosette, black/white body binding, mahogany neck, 14/20-fret rosewood fingerboard with pearl dot inlays, mahogany headstock overlay with vertical silver logo, three-per-side nickel tuners, rosewood bridge, black bridge pins with white dots, black pickguard, CT4B pickup/electronics, available in Satin Antique finish, mfg. 2011-12.

	$1,000	$550 - 700	$350 - 425	$1,400

EF-440SCGN – single cutaway NEX-style body, solid cedar top, mahogany back and sides, round soundhole with concentric ring rosette, black/white body binding, mahogany neck, 14/20-fret rosewood fingerboard with pearl dot inlays, mahogany headstock overlay with vertical silver logo, three-per-side nickel tuners, rosewood bridge, black bridge pins with white dots, black pickguard, CT4B pickup/electronics, available in Satin Antique finish, mfg. 2011-12.

	$1,000	$550 - 700	$350 - 425	$1,400

EF444TBS – NEX-style body, solid spruce top, mahogany back and sides, round soundhole with concentric ring rosette, top and back body binding, 14/20-fret rosewood fingerboard with dot inlay, three-per-side chrome tuners, rosewood bridge, CT4B electronics, available in Gloss Tobacco Sunburst finish, mfg. 2008 only.

	N/A	$725 - 850	$450 - 525	$1,649

EF-450 SM – NEX body, solid spruce top, solid flame maple back, flame maple sides, round soundhole with concentric ring rosette, body binding, ebony fingerboard with dot abalone and pearl inlays, matching headstock with three-per-side tuners, ebony bridge, CT4B electronics, gold hardware, available in Sunburst finish, mfg. 2004 only.

	N/A	$1,100 - 1,300	$700 - 800	$2,572

*** TF-450 SM** – similar to the EF-450 SM, except has CTP-1 Cool Tube electronics, available in Natural or Sunburst finishes, mfg. 2004-2012.

	$2,400	$1,400 - 1,750	$850 - 1,050	$3,500

»**TF-450SMC** – similar to the TF-450 SM, except has a single cutaway, available in Sunburst finish, mfg. 2006-08, reintroduced 2010 only.

	$2,100	$1,350 - 1,550	$850 - 1,000	$3,005

EF-508KC – single cutaway NEX-style figured koa body, round soundhole with abalone rosette, bound body, bound rosewood fingerboard with abalone snowflake inlays, black headstock overlay with three-per-side gold tuners, rosewood bridge, Takamine Palethetic pickup, CT4B2 preamp/electronics, available in Natural finish, mfg. 2007-present.

MSR $2,000	$1,400	$800 - 1,000	$475 - 600	

EF-740SGN – OM-style body, solid cedar top, sapele back and sides, round soundhole with concentric ring rosette, black/white body binding, mahogany neck, 14/20-fret rosewood fingerboard with pearl dot inlays, sapele headstock overlay with vertical silver logo, three-per-side nickel tuners, rosewood bridge, black bridge pins with white dots, black pickguard, CT4B pickup/electronics, available in Satin Antique finish, mfg. 2009-2012.

	$1,000	$550 - 700	$350 - 425	$1,400

ACOUSTIC: SIGNATURE SERIES

GARTH BROOKS GB-7C – single cutaway dreadnought body, solid cedar top, rosewood back and sides, guitar-shaped soundhole that extends to fingerboard, concentric rings rosette, rosewood fingerboard, three-per-side tuners, rosewood bridge, CT-4B electronics, gold hardware, available in Natural finish, mfg. 1996-present.

MSR $2,200	$1,530	$875 - 1,100	$525 - 650	

Early models have Accuraacoustic electronics.

GLENN FREY EF360GF – dreadnought-style body, solid spruce top, solid rosewood back, rosewood sides, round soundhole with multi-ring rosette, white body binding with multi-ply top inlay, mahogany neck, 14/20-fret bound rosewood fingerboard with MOP dot inlays, rosewood headstock overlay with vertical silver logo, three-per-side chrome tuners, rosewood bridge, black pickguard, CT4B pickup/electronics, label individually signed by Glenn Frey, available in Natural gloss finish, hardshell case included, mfg. 2009-present.

MSR $2,480	$1,700	$1,000 - 1,250	$600 - 750	

JOHN JORGENSON JJ-325SRC – dreadnought body with cutaway, solid spruce top, abalone rosette, bubinga back and sides, rosewood fingerboard with abalone inlays, three-per-side tuners, rosewood bridge, white pickguard, DSP preamp system or CT4B preamp, gold hardware, available in Red Stain finish, mfg. 1999-present.

MSR $2,400	$1,650	$950 - 1,200	$575 - 725	

*** John Jorgenson 12-String JJ-325SRC12** – similar to the JJ-325, except in 12-string configuration, six-per-side tuners, available in Red Stain finish, mfg. 1999-present.

MSR $2,550	$1,750	$1,050 - 1,300	$625 - 775	

KENNY CHESNEY KC70 – Orchestra Model-style body, solid cedar top, solid mahogany back, mahogany sides, round soundhole with custom Kenny Chesney graphic rosette, 14/20-fret rosewood fingerboard with 12th fret custom inlays and 16-19th fret Kenny Chesney signature inlay, three-per-side gold tuners with amber buttons, rosewood bridge, CT4B electronics, available in Satin Natural finish, mfg. 2008-present.

MSR $2,800	$1,930	$1,125 - 1,400	$675 - 850	

MSR/NOTES	100%	EXCELLENT	AVERAGE	LAST MSR

STEVE WARINER SW-341SC – single cutaway dreadnought body, solid cedar top, solid mahogany back, mahogany sides, round soundhole, abalone rosette, abalone binding, rosewood fingerboard with snowflake and 12th fret SW inlays, three-per-side tuners with pearl buttons, rosewood bridge, CT-4B electronics, chrome hardware, available in Black finish, mfg. 1996-97, 2001-present.

| MSR $2,600 | $1,800 | $1,050 - 1,300 | $625 - 775 | |

The SW-341SC was produced for a short while in 1996 and 1997 before it officially became the Steve Wariner Signature model. These early models do not have 12th fret SW inlays.

TOBY KEITH EF250TK – single cutaway jumpo-style body, solid spruce top, flame maple back and sides, round soundhole with concentric rings, white body binding, mahogany neck, 14/20-fret bound ebony fingerboard with MOP/abalone block inlays, Toby Keith silhouette image on headstock medallion, three-per-side gold tuners, rosewood bridge with split bone saddle and pin-less base, tortoiseshell pickguard, Palathetic pickup, CT-4B2 preamp/electronics, available in gloss Sunburst finish, hardshell case included, mfg. 2013-present.

| MSR $3,600 | $2,500 | $1,625 - 1,975 | $900 - 1,075 | |

ACOUSTIC: MISC. MODELS

FLYING V ACOUSTIC/FLYING A – Flying V-style acoustic body, spruce top, rosewood back and sides, non-circular soundhole, body binding, mahogany neck, 14/20-fret rosewood fingerboard with dot inlays, three-per-side chrome tuners, rosewood bridge, on-board electronics, available in Natural, Metallic Blue, or Metallic Red finish, mfg. mid-1980s.

| | N/A | $1,000 - 1,200 | $650 - 800 | |

GRAND OLE OPRY 80TH ANNIVERSARY – single cutaway dreadnought-style body, Master Grade solid Sitka spruce top, Finest Grade Indian rosewood back and sides, round soundhole with an abalone ring rosette, top and back binding, abalone top inlay, 14/20-fret bound ebony fingerboard with Grand Ole Opry star inlays, bound headstock with abalone border and Grand Ole Opry logo, three-per-side gold tuners, ebony bridge, pickguard with dotted border, CTP-1 Cool Tube electronics, available in Gloss Natural finish, mfg. 2005 only.

| | N/A | $2,500 - 3,000 | $1,800 - 2,100 | $5,000 |

The guitar commemorates the 80th Anniversary of the Grand Ole Opry (1925-2005). 80 guitars were built - 40 were given to various Opry performers and the additional 40 were sold to the public.

G MINI – mini-style body, solid cedar top, mahogany back and sides, round soundhole with single ring rosette, single-ply binding, mahogany neck, 14/19-fret rosewood fingerboard with dot inlays, rosewood headstock overlay, three-per-side chrome tuners, rosewood bridge, no pickguard, available in Satin Natural finish, gig bag included, mfg. 2011-12.

| | $350 | $200 - 250 | $120 - 150 | $500 |

»**EG Mini** – similar to the GS Mini, except has V+T pickup/electronics, available in Gloss Black or Satin Natural finish, gig bag included, mfg. 2011-12.

| | $450 | $275 - 325 | $150 - 200 | $650 |

ACOUSTIC ELECTRIC BASS

(T)B-10 – 34 in. scale, single cutaway all maple body, spruce top, f-holes, striped ebony fretless fingerboard, DSP preamp system, 2 per side tuners, available in Red Stain finish, current mfg.

| MSR $4,300 | $2,950 | $1,700 - 2,125 | $1,025 - 1,275 | |

In 2004, the Cool Tube technology was introduced on this model changing the model to the TB-10.

EG512C – jumbo style single cutaway body, spruce top, rosewood/mahogany/maple/flamed maple back and sides, rosewood fingerboard, TK4NT electronics, available in Black or Natural finish, disc. 2010.

| | $600 | $350 - 425 | $200 - 250 | $869 |

EGB2S – jumbo style single cutaway body, solid spruce top, mahogany back and sides, round soundhole, abalone rosette, rosewood fingerboard, TP4T preamp, available in Gloss Black or Gloss Natural finish, mfg. 2010-13.

| | $550 | $325 - 400 | $195 - 235 | $800 |

Also available in left-handed configuration (Model EGB 2S-LH), 2013 only.

TB-240SC – jumbo style single cutaway body, solid cedar top, mahogany back and sides, round soundhole, abalone rosette, rosewood fingerboard, Cool Tube electronics, rosewood bridge, chrome tuners, available in Satin Natural finish, mfg. 2010-12.

| | $2,100 | $1,200 - 1,500 | $725 - 900 | $3,000 |

TB-250SC – jumbo style single cutaway body, solid spruce top, flamed maple back and sides, round soundhole, abalone rosette, rosewood fingerboard, Cool Tube electronics, rosewood bridge, gold tuners, available in Sunburst finish, mfg. 2010-12.

| | $2,600 | $1,500 - 1,850 | $900 - 1,100 | $3,700 |

MSR/NOTES	100%	EXCELLENT	AVERAGE	LAST MSR

TAKU SAKASHTA GUITARS

Instruments previously built in Sebastopol, CA and in Van Nuys, CA between 1994 and early 2010.

CONTACT INFORMATION
TAKU SAKASHTA GUITARS
PO Box 2236
Rohnert Park, CA 94927
Phone No.: 707-623-9917
www.sakashtaguitars.com
info@sakashtaguitars.com

Luthier Taku Sakashta built high quality acoustic archtop and steel string guitars in his California shop. All were offered with custom options per model. Sakashta was murdered outside of his shop on February 12, 2010.

ACOUSTIC: ARCHTOP SERIES

Taku Sakashta guitars were widely available with numerous custom body wood choices, hardware wood choices, and finishes and nearly all guitars were individually quoted and priced by Sakashta. The following information is offered as a guideline to the available models produced by luthier Sakashta. The **Avalon** featured a 17 in. single cutaway body constructed of AAA quarter-sawn Sitka spruce top and AA Eastern rock maple sides and matching back, with a one piece Honduran mahogany neck, an East Indian rosewood fingerboard with pearl inlays, either an ebony or rosewood tailpiece, and a rosewood bridge, pickguard, and headstock overlay. The **Karizma** also featured a 17 in. single cutaway body with a AAA quarter-sawn Englemann spruce top, matching back and sides of AA Eastern rock maple, a one piece Honduran mahogany neck, East Indian rosewood fingerboard with pearl inlays, either an ebony or rosewood tailpiece, rosewood bridge, pickguard, and headstock overlay.

ACOUSTIC: STEEL STRING SERIES

Like the Archtop Series of guitars, the Sakashta's steel string models were also available with numerous custom wood options for tops, backs, and sides. The **Auditorium** model featured a Sitka spruce, Englemann spruce, or Western red cedar top, East Indian rosewood back and matching sides, a bound Honduras mahogany one piece neck with a Gaboon ebony fingerboard with diamond or dot position markers, ebony headstock overlay, Brazilian rosewood bridge, abalone soundhole ring decoration, three-per-side Schaller tuning machines, and a nitrocellulose natural lacquer finish. The **S O** model is similar to the Auditorium model, except the design is slightly modified. The **Dreadnought** model featured the same construction materials, but designed along the lines of a dreadnought style guitar. Though similar, the **S D** model is a modified version of the Dreadnought. The **Jumbo** model featured the same construction materials as well, and is a full sized acoustic guitar design. The modified version **S J** model is similar in base design to the Jumbo.

TAMA

Instruments previously produced in Japan from 1975 through 1979 by Ibanez. Distributed in the U.S. by the Chesbro Music Company of Idaho Falls, ID.

The Tama trademark is better known on the Hoshino-produced quality drum sets. Nevertheless, the Tama trademark was used on two series of acoustic guitars offered during the mid- to late 1970s. The first series introduced was entry level to good quality D-45 shaped acoustics that featured a laminated top. However, the quality level jumped on the second series. The second series featured a solid top, mahogany neck, and East Indian and Brazilian rosewoods, as well as a light oil finish.

One way to determine a solid top acoustic from a ply or laminated top is to check the cross section of the wood on the edge of the soundhole. If the wood seems continuous, it's probably a solid top. If you can see layers, or if the inside of the edge is painted (check the wood inside the top - if it is different in appearance from the outside it's probably laminated), then the top is plywood. No, it's not the sheets that you build houses with! A plywood top is several layers of wood glued and pressed together. However, a solid top guitar will resonate better (because it's one piece of wood) and the tone will get better as the wood ages, (Tama Guitars overview courtesy Michael R. Stanger, Stringed Instrument Division of Missoula, Montana, Model descriptions courtesy Michael Wright, et. al., *Ibanez, The Untold Story*).

ACOUSTIC: 4 DIGIT MODELS

3548 – classical body, solid spruce top, rosewood back and sides, mfg. 1974 only.

N/A	$200 - 250	$100 - 150

3550 – classical body, solid spruce top, jacaranda back and sides, mahogany neck, rosewood fingerboard, rosewood bridge, mfg. 1974 only.

N/A	$200 - 250	$100 - 150

3551 – classical body, solid spruce top, rosewood back and sides, mfg. 1974-76.

N/A	$250 - 300	$125 - 175

3552 – classical body, solid spruce top, rosewood back and sides, deluxe binding, mfg. 1974 only.

N/A	$225 - 275	$125 - 175

3553 – dreadnought body, solid spruce top, rosewood back and sides, mfg. 1974 only.

N/A	$250 - 300	$125 - 175

3554 – grand concert body, solid spruce top, rosewood back and sides, mfg. 1974 only.

N/A	$250 - 300	$125 - 175

MSR/NOTES	100%	EXCELLENT	AVERAGE	LAST MSR

3555 – dreadnought body, solid spruce top, rosewood back and sides, mahogany neck, mfg. 1974-76.

| | N/A | $275 - 350 | $150 - 200 | |

3556 – grand concert body, solid spruce top, jacaranda back and sides, mfg. 1974 only.

| | N/A | $250 - 300 | $125 - 175 | |

3557 – dreadnought body, solid spruce top, jacaranda back and sides, mfg. 1974 only.

| | N/A | $250 - 300 | $125 - 175 | |

* *3557/12* – similar to the 3557, except in 12-string configuration and six-per-side tuners, mfg. 1975-76.

| | N/A | $275 - 325 | $125 - 175 | |

3558 – dreadnought body, solid spruce top, jacaranda back and sides, mahogany neck, ebonized fingerboard, abalone inlays, mfg. 1974-76.

| | N/A | $325 - 400 | $175 - 225 | |

3560 – dreadnought custom body, solid spruce top, rosewood back and sides, mahogany neck, ebonized fingerboard, abalone inlays, mfg. 1974-76.

| | N/A | $375 - 450 | $200 - 250 | |

* *3560/12* – similar to the 3560, except in 12-string configuration and six-per-side tuners, mfg. 1975-76.

| | N/A | $400 - 475 | $225 - 275 | |

3561 – dreadnought body, solid spruce top, rosewood back and sides, wood herringbone binding, mahogany neck, ebonized fingerboard, abalone snowflake inlays, mfg. 1974-76.

| | N/A | $375 - 450 | $200 - 250 | |

3563 – dreadnought Renaissance body, solid spruce top, rosewood back and sides, wood herringbone binding, mahogany neck, ebonized fingerboard, MOP tree-of-life inlays, mfg. 1974-76.

| | N/A | $425 - 500 | $250 - 300 | |

3565 – dreadnought D-35 style body, solid spruce top, three piece jacaranda/rosewood/jacaranda back and sides, mahogany neck, ebonized fingerboard, mfg. 1974-76.

| | N/A | $425 - 500 | $250 - 300 | |

3566 – dreadnought D-41 style body, solid spruce top, rosewood back and sides, mahogany neck, ebonized fingerboard, abalone inlays, mfg. 1974-76.

| | N/A | $425 - 500 | $250 - 300 | |

3568 – dreadnought body, solid spruce top, rosewood back and sides, mahogany neck, ebonized fingerboard, small tree-of-life inlays, mfg. 1974-76.

| | N/A | $450 - 525 | $250 - 300 | |

3570 – dreadnought body, solid spruce top, rosewood back and sides, mahogany neck, ebony fingerboard, cat's eye inlays, mfg. 1975-76.

| | N/A | $375 - 450 | $200 - 250 | |

3571 – dreadnought body, solid spruce top, pearl binding, rosewood back and sides, mahogany neck, ebony fingerboard, cat's eye inlays, mfg. 1975-76.

| | N/A | $400 - 475 | $225 - 275 | |

3575 – dreadnought body with new style bracing, mfg. 1976 only.

| | N/A | $350 - 425 | $200 - 250 | |

3576 – dreadnought body with new style bracing, shaded top finish, mfg. 1976 only.

| | N/A | $350 - 425 | $200 - 250 | |

ACOUSTIC: TC, TG, & TW MODELS

TC-8 – classical body, solid spruce top, solid rosewood back and sides, mfg. 1977-78.

| | N/A | $450 - 525 | $275 - 325 | |

TC-10 – classical body, solid spruce top, solid rosewood back and sides, mfg. 1977-78.

| | N/A | $450 - 525 | $275 - 325 | |

TC-15 – classical body, solid spruce top, solid jacaranda back and sides, mfg. 1977-78.

| | N/A | $450 - 525 | $275 - 325 | |

TG-80 – dreadnought body, solid spruce top, solid mahogany back and sides, mfg. 1977-79.

| | N/A | $450 - 525 | $275 - 325 | |

In 1979, this guitar was renamed the Artwood AW60.

MSR/NOTES	100%	EXCELLENT	AVERAGE	LAST MSR

* *TG-80/12* – similar to the TG-80, except in 12-string configuration and six-per-side tuners, mfg. 1979 only.

	N/A	$450 - 525	$275 - 325	

In late 1979, this guitar was renamed the Artwood AW75.

TG-120 – dreadnought body, solid spruce top, solid rosewood back and sides, mfg. 1977-79.

	N/A	$500 - 600	$300 - 350	

In 1979, this guitar was renamed the Artwood AW90.

* *TG-120-12* – similar to the TG-120, except in 12-string configuration and six-per-side tuners, mfg. 1979 only.

	N/A	$525 - 625	$300 - 350	

In late 1979, this guitar was renamed the Artwood AW95.

TG-135 – dreadnought body, solid spruce top, solid three-piece rosewood back and sides, mfg. 1977-79.

	N/A	$550 - 650	$325 - 400	

In 1979, this guitar was renamed the Artwood AW100.

TG-160 – dreadnought body, solid spruce top, jacaranda back and sides, mfg. 1977-79.

	N/A	$450 - 525	$275 - 325	

TG-190 – dreadnought body, custom hand-made, mfg. 1978 only.

	N/A	$550 - 650	$325 - 400	

TW-07 – dreadnought body, solid spruce top, solid mahogany back and sides, snowflake inlays, mfg. 1977-79.

	N/A	$500 - 600	$300 - 350	

In 1979, this guitar was renamed the Artwood AW20.

TW-09 – dreadnought body, solid spruce top, solid rosewood back and sides, snowflake inlays, mfg. 1977-79.

	N/A	$550 - 650	$325 - 400	

In 1979, this guitar was renamed the Artwood AW30.

TW-10 – dreadnought body, solid spruce top, solid three-piece rosewood back and sides, snowflake inlays, mfg. 1977-79.

	N/A	$600 - 700	$350 - 425	

TANARA

Instruments previously built in Korea and Indonesia during the 1990s and early 2000s. Distributed by the Chesbro Music Company in Idaho Falls, ID.

Chesbro Music imported the Tanara line of guitars that included a range of acoustic and electric guitars designed for the entry level to student guitarist.

ACOUSTIC: ACOUSTIC SERIES

All Tanara guitar models feature a round soundhole, 3-per-side headstock, chrome hardware, and a Natural finish (unless otherwise specified).

SC26 – concert size steel string, pacific spruce top, mahogany back/sides, disc.

	N/A	$90 - 120	$60 - 80	$219

SD24 – dreadnought size, pacific spruce top, mahogany back/sides, available in Natural gloss finish, disc.

	N/A	$90 - 120	$60 - 80	$219

SD26 – dreadnought size, natural spruce top, mahogany back/sides, adjustable neck, three-per-side machine heads, available in Black, Brown Sunburst, and Natural gloss finish, disc.

	N/A	$100 - 130	$70 - 90	$239

SD30 – dreadnought size, spruce top, mahogany back/sides, rosewood fingerboard/bridge, scalloped X-bracing, three-per-side die-cast tuners, available in Natural satin finish, disc.

	N/A	$130 - 170	$90 - 110	$339

SD32 – similar to the SD30, except in 12-string configuration with six-per-side tuners, covered tuning gears, disc.

	N/A	$150 - 200	$110 - 130	$379

ACOUSTIC: CLASSICAL SERIES

TC26 – concert size, spruce top, mahogany back/sides, adjustable neck, three-per-side butterfly knobs, available in Pumpkin Amber finish, disc.

	N/A	$70 - 95	$40 - 60	$189

TC46 – similar to the TC26, except features ovangkol back/sides, multiple binding, available in Pumpkin Amber finish, disc.

	N/A	$110 - 140	$80 - 100	$259

MSR/NOTES	100%	EXCELLENT	AVERAGE	LAST MSR

ACOUSTIC ELECTRIC

TSF1 – grand concert size with single cutaway, spruce top, mahogany back/sides, bound body/headstock, bound rosewood fingerboard with offset pearl position markers, rosewood bridge, three-per-side chrome tuners, piezo pickup, volume/3-band EQ controls, disc.

	N/A	$250 - 300	$150 - 200	$569

TSJ5 – solid spruce top, mahogany back/sides/neck, rosewood fingerboard, three-per-side gold tuners, Fishman pickup, volume/EQ controls, disc.

	N/A	$275 - 325	$175 - 225	$669

ACOUSTIC ELECTRIC BASS

TR720BF – select maple top, maple back/sides/neck, die-cast tuners, available in Natural finish, disc.

	N/A	$350 - 400	$200 - 250	$779

TANGLEWOOD GUITAR COMPANY UK

Instruments currently produced in China. Currently distributed by Musiquip Inc. in Dorval, Quebec Canada. Tanglewood Guitar Co. UK is part produced by the European Music Company (EMC), Ltd. of Kent, England. Tanglewood Guitar Co. UK has been producing guitars since the early 1990s.

The European Music Company, Ltd. offers a wide range of acoustic guitars under the Tanglewood trademark, as well as electric models, classical models, bluegrass and folk instruments, an acoustic amp, and accessories. Currently, the North American line ranges from entry-level instruments to handcrafted, all-solid wood models, and consists of seven series of acoustic guitars: MasterDesign, Heritage, Sundance, Premier, Rosewood Grand Reserve, Evolution, and Roadster. Various body shapes are offered, including Dreadnought, Super Folk, Super Jumbo, Orchestra, Grand Auditorium, Parlor, Traveler, and Acoustic Bass models. Tanglewood Guitar Co. UK instruments are very popular in England and throughout Europe where they have been available since the early 1990s. The brand only appeared in North America in the mid-2000s. For further information regarding model specification and pricing, contact Musiquip Inc.

CONTACT INFORMATION
TANGLEWOOD GUITAR COMPANY UK
Musiquip Inc.
325 Boul Bouchard
Dorval, Quebec H9S 1A9 Canada
Phone No.: 866-832-8679
Fax No.: 800-563-2948
www.tanglewoodguitars.com
sales@tanglewoodguitars.com

TAYLOR

Instruments currently built in El Cajon, CA since 1987 and in Tecate, Mexico since the mid-1990s. Distributed in North America by Taylor Guitars of El Cajon, CA and in Europe by Fender Musical Instrument Corporation (FMIC) located in Scottsdale, AZ. Previously produced in Lemon Grove, CA between 1974 through 1987.

Founding partners Bob Taylor, Steve Schemmer, and Kurt Listug were all working at the American Dream guitar repair shop in Lemon Grove, California, in the early 1970s. In 1974, the trio bought the shop and converted it into a guitar building factory. The company went through early growing pains throughout the late 1970s, but slowly and surely the guitars began catching on. In 1983, Listug and Taylor bought out Schemmer's share of the company, and re-incorporated. Fueled by sales of models such as the **Grand Concert** in 1984, the company expanded into new facilities in Santee, California (near El Cajon) in 1987. In 1989, Taylor bought their first CNC machine. In 2007, Taylor reorganized their guitar line to distinguish their acoustic, acoustic/electric, and electric lines from one another. All cutaway electric models remain in the number series, while acoustic models were renamed and organized according to their body shape. Taylor also has a complete custom shop open. In 2008, Fender began distributing Taylor Guitars in Europe. For a complete history and timeline of Taylor guitars, visit their website. For more information contact Taylor directly.

CONTACT INFORMATION
TAYLOR
1980 Gillespie Way
El Cajon, CA 92020-1096
Phone No.: 619-258-1207
www.taylorguitars.com

TAYLOR MODEL DESIGNATIONS/BODY DIMENSIONS/GENERAL INFORMATION

Taylor Retail list prices do not include a case. Cases carry an additional cost. TC Series hardshell cases retail at $299, and SC Series SKB/Taylor cases retail at $199. Taylor acoustics are available with a wide range of custom options, including Engelmann spruce tops or Fishman transducer systems. There is no charge for a left-handed configuration (not available on all models). Fishman electronics were available until 2004. In 2005, all models 300 and up feature Expression system electronics.

Each Taylor model number also describes the particular guitar in relationship to the overall product line. The first of three numbers denotes the series (Taylor series comprise a specific combination of woods, bindings, inlays, etc.). The second number indicates whether it is a six-string (1), or a 12-string (5). The exception to this rule is the 400 series, which include models 420 and 422. Finally, the third number indicates the body size: Dreadnought (0), Grand Concert (2), Grand Auditorium (4), Jumbo (5), and Grand Symphony (6). The Grand Auditorium size models carry a prefix of **GA**. Any upper case letters that follow the three digit designation may indicate a cutaway (**C**), electronics (**E**) or a left-handed model (**L**).

Dreadnought (DN): Body Width 16 in., Body Length 20 in., Body Depth 4.625 in.

Grand Auditorium (GA): Body Width 16 in., Body Length 20 in., Body Depth 4.625 in.

Grand Concert (GC): Body Width 15 in., Body Length 19.5 in., Body Depth 4.375 in.

Grand Symphony (GS): Body Width 16.25 in., Body Length: 20 in., Body Depth: 4.625 in.

Jumbo (JM): Body Width 17 in., Body Length 21 in., Body Depth 4.625 in.

MSR/NOTES	100%	EXCELLENT	AVERAGE	LAST MSR

Baby: Body Width 12.5 in., Body Length 15.75 in., Body Depth 3.375 in.
Big Baby: Body Width 15 in., Body Length 19.5 in., Body Depth 4 in.
GS Mini: Body Width 14.375 in., Body Length 17.625 in., Body Depth 4.375 in.
T5: Body Width 16 in., Body Length 20 in., Body Depth 2.333 in.
- **Add $200 for Sunburst finish.**

ACOUSTIC: BABY TAYLOR SERIES

Baby Taylor models are entry-level guitars that are produced in Mexico.

An example of a Baby Taylor courtesy Taylor

BABY TAYLOR (BT1) – 3/4 size, dreadnought body, solid Sitka spruce top, round soundhole, laser-etched rosette, mahogany veneer back/sides, mahogany neck, 14/19-fret ebony fingerboard with pearloid dot inlay, Lexan peghead veneer, three-per-side chrome diecast tuners, ebony bridge, available in Natural satin finish, gig bag included, mfg. 1997-present.

MSR $398	$300	$175 - 225	$110 - 140	

* *Baby Taylor (Maple, Bubinga, Koa, & Rosewood)* – similar to the Baby Taylor, except features respective wood type top, available in Natural satin finish, disc. 2003.

	N/A	$200 - 250	$120 - 150	$428

* *Baby Taylor M (Mahogany, BT2)* – similar to the Baby Taylor, except has a solid mahogany top, available in Natural satin finish, current mfg.

MSR $398	$300	$175 - 225	$110 - 140	

BIG BABY (BBT) – similar to the Baby Taylor, except has a 15/16 in. sized body, available in Natural satin finish, current mfg.

MSR $528	$400	$225 - 275	$135 - 170	

ACOUSTIC: 100/200 SERIES

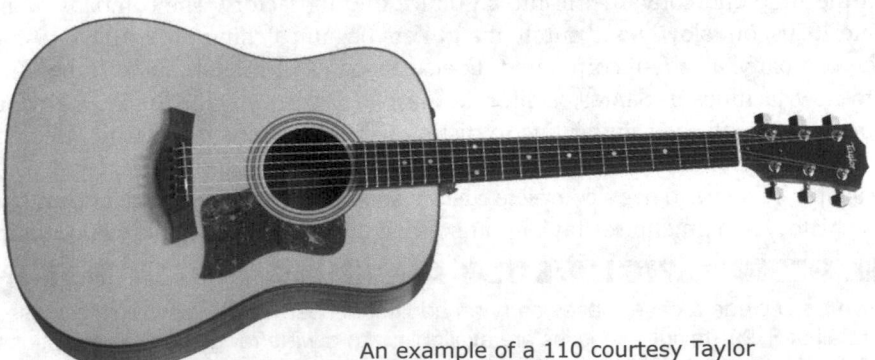

An example of a 110 courtesy Taylor

110 – dreadnought style, Sitka spruce top, sapele laminated back and sides, Tropical American Mahogany neck, 20-fret ebony fingerboard with dot inlay, black plastic binding, chrome hardware, varnish natural finish, mfg. 2004-2013.

	$600	$350 - 425	$200 - 250	$868

* *110CE* – similar to the 110, except has a single cutaway and ES T electronics, mfg. 2008-present.

MSR $1,058	$800	$450 - 525	$300 - 350	

* *110E* – similar to the 110, except has ES Blue (2005-06) or ES T (2007-present) electronics, mfg. 2005-present.

MSR $798	$650	$375 - 450	$200 - 250	

114 – grand auditorium style, Sitka spruce top, sapele laminated back and sides, Tropical American Mahogany neck, 20-fret ebony fingerboard with dot inlay, black plastic binding, chrome hardware, varnish natural finish, mfg. 2007-2013.

	$650	$400 - 475	$225 - 275	$868

MSR/NOTES	100%	EXCELLENT	AVERAGE	LAST MSR
* *114CE* – similar to the 114, except has a single cutaway and ES T electronics, mfg. 2008-present.				
MSR $1,058	$800	$500 - 575	$300 - 350	
* *114E* – similar to the 114, except has ES T electronics, mfg. 2007-present.				
MSR $798	$650	$375 - 450	$200 - 250	
210 – dreadnought style, Sitka spruce top, sapele back and sides, Tropical American Mahogany neck, 20-fret ebony fingerboard with dot inlay, black plastic binding, chrome hardware, varnish natural finish, mfg. 2005-present.				
MSR $1,068	$800	$500 - 575	$300 - 350	
* *210CE* – similar to the 210, except has a single cutaway and ES T electronics, mfg. 2008-present.				
MSR $1,328	$1,000	$575 - 675	$350 - 425	
»*210CE-BLK Black* – similar to the 210CE, except has laminated maple back and sides, an abalone rosette, and an ebony headstock overlay, available in Black finish, mfg. 2013 only.				
	$1,200	$675 - 825	$400 - 500	$1,598
»*210CE-K Koa* – similar to the 210CE, except has laminated koa back and sides, available in Natural finish, mfg. 2013 only.				
	$1,250	$700 - 850	$425 - 525	$1,698
»*210CE-SB Sunburst* – similar to the 210CE, except has laminated rosewood back and sides, an abalone rosette, and an Indian rosewood headstock overlay, available in Sunburst finish, mfg. 2013 only.				
	$1,200	$675 - 825	$400 - 500	$1,598
* *210E* – similar to the 210, except has ES Blue (2005-06) or ES T (2007-present) electronics, mfg. 2005-present.				
MSR $1,198	$900	$525 - 625	$325 - 400	
214 – grand auditorium style, Sitka spruce top, sapele back and sides, Tropical American Mahogany neck, 20-fret ebony fingerboard with dot inlay, black plastic binding, chrome hardware, varnish natural finish, mfg. 2004-present.				
MSR $1,068	$800	$500 - 575	$300 - 350	
* *214CE* – similar to the 214, except has a single cutaway and ES T electronics, mfg. 2008-present.				
MSR $1,328	$1,000	$575 - 675	$350 - 425	
»*214CE-BLK Black* – similar to the 214CE, except has laminated maple back and sides, an abalone rosette, and an ebony headstock overlay, available in Black finish, mfg. 2012-13.				
	$1,200	$675 - 825	$400 - 500	$1,598
»*214CE-K Koa* – similar to the 214CE, except has laminated koa back and sides, available in Natural finish, mfg. 2013 only.				
	$1,250	$700 - 850	$425 - 525	$1,698
»*214CE-SB Sunburst* – similar to the 214CE, except has laminated rosewood back and sides, an abalone rosette, and an Indian rosewood headstock overlay, available in Sunburst finish, mfg. 2012-13.				
	$1,200	$675 - 825	$400 - 500	$1,598
* *214E* – similar to the 214, except has ES Blue (2005-06) or ES T (2007-present) electronics, mfg. 2005-present.				
MSR $1,198	$900	$525 - 600	$325 - 400	
214E-N NYLON – nylon-string configuration, single cutaway Grand Auditorium (GA)-style body, solid Sitka spruce top, laminated Indian rosewood back and sides, nylon bracing, round soundhole with three-ring rosette, white multi-ply body binding, Tropical American Mahogany neck, 14/20-fret ebony fingerboard with dot inlays, slotted headstock with Indian rosewood overlay and logo, three-per-side open-style chrome tuners with pearloid buttons, ebony tied bridge, ES-N electronics, available in Natural finish, 1.875 in. nut width, 25.5 in. scale, hard bag case included, mfg. 2012-13.				
	$900	$525 - 600	$325 - 400	$1,198
* *214CE-N Nylon* – similar to the 214E-N Nylon, except has a single cutaway, mfg. 2012-present.				
MSR $1,328	$1,000	$575 - 675	$350 - 425	

ACOUSTIC: 300 SERIES

The 300 series models each feature a solid Sitka spruce top, sapele mahogany back and sides, three-ply black plastic body binding, plastic ring inlay rosette, mahogany neck, 25.5 in. scale, 20-fret ebony fingerboard with pearl dot inlay, Indian rosewood peghead veneer, ebony bridge, Tusq nut and saddle.

310 – dreadnought body, tortoiseshell pickguard, three-per-side chrome Grover tuners, available in Natural satin finish with gloss top, mfg. 1998-2006, reintroduced 2013-present.

MSR $1,598	$1,250	$650 - 800	$400 - 500	

MSR/NOTES	100%	EXCELLENT	AVERAGE	LAST MSR

310 CE – similar to the 310, except features a single Venetian cutaway dreadnought body, Fishman Prefix electronics, available in Natural satin finish with gloss top, mfg. 1998-present.

| MSR $2,198 | $1,700 | $950 - 1,200 | $575 - 725 | |

312 CE – grand concert body with single Venetian cutaway, tortoiseshell pickguard, three-per-side chrome Grover tuners, Fishman Prefix electronics, available in Natural satin finish with gloss top, mfg. 1998-present.

| MSR $2,198 | $1,700 | $950 - 1,200 | $575 - 725 | |

312 CE-N NYLON – nylon configuration, single cutaway Grand Concert-style (GC) body, Sitka spruce top, Sapele back and sides, round soundhole with multi-ring rosette, black body binding, mahogany neck, 12/17-fret ebony fingerboard with pearl dot inlays, slotted headstock with Indian rosewood overlay and Taylor logo, three-per-side open-style chrome tuners with pearloid buttons, ebony tied bridge, ES-N electronics, available in Natural finish, 1.875 in. nut width, 25.5 in. scale, mfg. 2012-present.

| MSR $2,198 | $1,700 | $950 - 1,200 | $575 - 725 | |

314 – grand auditorium body, tortoiseshell pickguard, three-per-side chrome Grover tuners, available in Natural satin finish with gloss top, mfg. 1998-2006, reintroduced 2013-present.

| MSR $1,598 | $1,250 | $650 - 800 | $400 - 500 | |

314 CE – similar to the 314, except features a single Venetian cutaway dreadnought body, Fishman Prefix electronics, available in Natural satin finish with gloss top, mfg. 2000-present.

| MSR $2,198 | $1,700 | $950 - 1,200 | $575 - 725 | |

314 CE-N NYLON – nylon configuration, single cutaway Grand Auditorium-style (GA) body, Sitka spruce top, Sapele back and sides, round soundhole with multi-ring rosette, black body binding, mahogany neck, 12/17-fret ebony fingerboard with pearl dot inlays, slotted headstock with Indian rosewood overlay and Taylor logo, three-per-side open-style chrome tuners with pearloid buttons, ebony tied bridge, ES-N electronics, available in Natural finish, 1.875 in. nut width, 25.5 in. scale, mfg. 2012-present.

| MSR $2,198 | $1,700 | $950 - 1,200 | $575 - 725 | |

315 – jumbo body, tortoiseshell pickguard, three-per-side chrome Grover tuners, available in Natural satin finish with gloss top, mfg. 2005-06.

| | N/A | $800 - 1,000 | $475 - 600 | $1,538 |

315CE – similar to the 315, except features a single Venetian cutaway dreadnought body, Expression electronics, available in Natural satin finish with gloss top, mfg. 1998-2011.

| | $1,650 | $950 - 1,200 | $575 - 725 | $2,238 |

316 CE – single cutaway Grand Symphony (GS) body style, Sitka spruce top, Sapele back and sides, forward-shifted pattern bracing with relief rout, round soundhole with three-ring rosette, black top and back binding, multi-ply top inlay, Tropical American mahogany neck, 14/20-fret bound ebony fingerboard with small pearl dot inlays, Indian rosewood headstock overlay with pearl logo, three-per-side chrome tuners, ebony bridge, tortoise pickguard, Taylor Expression electronics, available in Natural Gloss finish, 1.75 in. nut width, 25.5 in. scale, hardshell case included, mfg. 2012-present.

| MSR $2,198 | $1,700 | $950 - 1,200 | $575 - 725 | |

354 CE 12-STRING – 12-string configuration, grand auditorium cutaway, six-per-side tuners, Expression system electronics, Natural Satin finish, mfg. 2004-2011.

| | $1,800 | $1,050 - 1,300 | $625 - 775 | $2,438 |

355 12-STRING – 12-string configuration, jumbo cutaway body, tortoiseshell pickguard, six-per-side chrome Grover tuners, available in Natural satin finish with gloss top, mfg. 1998-2006.

| | N/A | $875 - 1,100 | $525 - 650 | $1,738 |

355 CE 12-String – similar to the 355, except has a single cutaway and electronics, mfg. 2000-2011.

| | $1,800 | $1,050 - 1,300 | $625 - 775 | $2,438 |

356 CE – 12-string configuration, single cutaway Grand Symphony (GS) body style, Sitka spruce top, Sapele back and sides, 12-string bracing with relief rout, round soundhole with three-ring rosette, black top and back binding, multi-ply top inlay, Tropical American mahogany neck, 14/20-fret bound ebony fingerboard with small pearl dot inlays, Indian rosewood headstock overlay with pearl logo, six-per-side chrome tuners, ebony bridge, tortoise pickguard, Taylor Expression electronics, available in Natural Gloss finish, 1.875 in. nut width, 25.5 in. scale, hardshell case included, mfg. 2012-present.

| MSR $2,398 | $1,850 | $1,050 - 1,300 | $625 - 775 | |

ACOUSTIC: 400 SERIES

In 1998, Taylor changed the 400 series' mahogany or maple back and sides in favor of solid ovankol (also spelled ovangkol). All six-string models feature scalloped bracing. Earlier acoustic/electric models may be equipped with an optional Acoustic Matrix pickup system.

410 – dreadnought body, solid Sitka spruce top, round soundhole, tortoiseshell pickguard, white plastic body binding, three-ply body, three-ring inlay rosette, solid mahogany back/sides, mahogany neck, 14/20-fret rosewood fingerboard with pearl dot inlay, rosewood bridge, rosewood veneer on peghead, three-per-side chrome Grover tuners, available in Natural satin finish with gloss top, mfg. 1991-2006.

| | N/A | $850 - 1,050 | $525 - 625 | $1,698 |

In 1994, pearl peghead logo inlay was introduced. In 1998, ovangkol back/sides replaced mahogany back/sides; ebony fingerboard replaced the rosewood fingerboard; ebony bridge replaced the rosewood bridge.

MSR/NOTES	100%	EXCELLENT	AVERAGE	LAST MSR

* 410 CE – similar to 410, except has an single Venetian cutaway body, Fishman Prefix system, available in Natural satin finish with gloss top, current mfg.

| MSR $2,658 | $2,000 | $1,125 - 1,400 | $675 - 850 | |

412 – grand concert body, solid spruce top, round soundhole, tortoiseshell pickguard, white plastic body binding, three-ply body, three-ring inlay rosette, solid mahogany back/sides, mahogany neck, 14/20-fret rosewood fingerboard with pearl dot inlay, rosewood bridge, rosewood veneer on peghead, three-per-side chrome Grover tuners, available in Natural satin finish with gloss top, mfg. 1991-98.

| | N/A | $875 - 1,100 | $525 - 650 | $998 |

* 412 CE – similar to the 412, except features single Venetian cutaway body, ovankol back/sides, ebony fingerboard, ebony bridge, Fishman Prefix electronics, available in Natural satin finish with gloss top, mfg. 1998-present.

| MSR $2,658 | $2,000 | $1,125 - 1,400 | $675 - 850 | |

412 CE-N NYLON – nylon configuration, single cutaway Grand Concert-style (GC) body, Sitka spruce top, Ovangkol back and sides, nylon bracing, round soundhole with multi-ring rosette, multi-ply body binding, mahogany neck, 12/17-fret bound ebony fingerboard with progressive dot inlays, slotted headstock with Indian rosewood overlay and Taylor logo, three-per-side open-style chrome tuners with pearloid buttons, ebony tied bridge, ES-N electronics, available in Natural finish, 1.875 in. nut width, 25.5 in. scale, mfg. 2012-present.

| MSR $2,658 | $2,000 | $1,125 - 1,400 | $675 - 850 | |

414 – grand auditorium body, solid Sitka spruce top, round soundhole, tortoiseshell pickguard, white plastic body binding, three-ply body, three-ring inlay rosette, solid ovankol back/sides, mahogany neck, 14/20-fret ebony fingerboard with pearl dot inlay, ebony bridge, rosewood veneer on peghead, three-per-side chrome Grover tuners, available in Natural satin finish with gloss top, mfg. 1998-2006.

| | N/A | $875 - 1,100 | $525 - 650 | $1,868 |

* 414 CE – similar to 414, except has a single Venetian cutaway body, Fishman Prefix system, available in Natural satin finish with gloss top, current mfg.

| MSR $2,658 | $2,000 | $1,125 - 1,400 | $675 - 850 | |

414 CE-N NYLON – nylon configuration, single cutaway Grand Auditorium-style (GA) body, Sitka spruce top, Ovangkol back and sides, nylon bracing, round soundhole with multi-ring rosette, multi-ply body binding, mahogany neck, 14/20-fret bound ebony fingerboard with progressive dot inlays, slotted headstock with Indian rosewood overlay and Taylor logo, three-per-side open-style chrome tuners with pearloid buttons, ebony tied bridge, ES-N electronics, available in Natural finish, 1.875 in. nut width, 25.5 in. scale, mfg. 2012-present.

| MSR $2,658 | $2,000 | $1,125 - 1,400 | $675 - 850 | |

415 – jumbo body, solid Sitka spruce top, round soundhole, tortoiseshell pickguard, white plastic body binding, three-ply body, three-ring inlay rosette, solid ovankol back/sides, mahogany neck, 14/20-fret ebony fingerboard with pearl dot inlay, ebony bridge, rosewood veneer on peghead, three-per-side chrome Grover tuners, available in Natural satin finish with gloss top, mfg. 1998-2006.

| | N/A | $875 - 1,100 | $525 - 650 | $1,868 |

* 415 CE – similar to the 415, except has a single cutaway and Expression system electronics, Natural finish, mfg. 2004-06.

| | N/A | $1,075 - 1,350 | $650 - 800 | $2,468 |

416 CE – single cutaway Grand Symphony (GS) body style, Sitka spruce top, ovangkol back and sides, Standard II (forward shifted pattern) bracing, round soundhole with three-ring rosette, white top and back binding, multi-ply top inlay, Tropical American mahogany neck, 14/20-fret bound ebony fingerboard with large pearl dot inlays, Tropical American mahogany headstock overlay with pearl logo, three-per-side chrome tuners, ebony bridge, tortoise pickguard, Taylor Expression electronics, available in Natural Gloss finish, 25.5 in. scale, hardshell case included, mfg. 2011-present.

| MSR $2,658 | $2,000 | $1,125 - 1,400 | $675 - 850 | |

420 – similar to the 410, except has maple back and sides, available in Natural finish, mfg. 1990-97.

| | N/A | $875 - 1,100 | $525 - 650 | $1,198 |

* 420 PF Limited Edition – similar to 420, except has solid pau ferro back and sides, disc. 1997.

| | N/A | $1,000 - 1,250 | $600 - 750 | $1,400 |

422 – similar to 412, except has maple back and sides, disc. 1998.

| | N/A | $925 - 1,150 | $550 - 700 | $1,198 |

450 – similar to the 410, except in 12-string configuration with six-per-side tuners, mfg. 1996-97.

| | N/A | $875 - 1,100 | $525 - 650 | $1,298 |

454 CE 12-STRING – 12-string configuration, grand auditorium cutaway, six-per-side tuners, Expression system electronics, Natural Satin finish, mfg. 2004-2011.

| | $2,050 | $1,150 - 1,450 | $675 - 850 | $2,768 |

MSR/NOTES	100%	EXCELLENT	AVERAGE	LAST MSR

455 12-STRING – 12-string configuration, jumbo body, solid Sitka spruce top, round soundhole, tortoiseshell pickguard, white plastic body binding, three-ply body, three-ring inlay rosette, solid ovangkol back/sides, mahogany neck, 14/20-fret ebony fingerboard with pearl dot inlay, rosewood veneer on peghead, six-per-side chrome Grover tuners, ebony bridge, available in Natural satin finish with gloss top, mfg. 2000-06.

	N/A	$925 - 1,150	$550 - 700	$2,068

* 455 CE 12-String – similar to the 455, except has a cutaway with electronics, mfg. 2000-2011.

	$2,050	$1,150 - 1,450	$675 - 850	$2,768

456 CE – 12-string configuration, single cutaway Grand Symphony (GS) body style, Sitka spruce top, ovangkol back and sides, 12-string bracing with relief rout, round soundhole with three-ring rosette, white top and back binding, multi-ply top inlay, Tropical American mahogany neck, 14/20-fret bound ebony fingerboard with large pearl dot inlays, Indian rosewood headstock overlay with pearl logo, three-per-side chrome tuners, ebony bridge, tortoise pickguard, Taylor Expression electronics, available in Natural Gloss finish, 1.875 in. nut width, 25.5 in. scale, hardshell case included, mfg. 2012-present.

MSR $2,858	$2,100	$1,200 - 1,500	$725 - 900	

ACOUSTIC: 500 SERIES

The 500 series models feature solid mahogany backs and sides; current fancy appointments include abalone inlay on the soundhole rosettes and pearl diamond inlays on the fingerboard.

An example of a 510 CE courtesy Taylor

510 – dreadnought body, solid Engelmann spruce top, round soundhole, tortoiseshell pickguard, three-stripe bound body/rosette, solid mahogany back/sides/neck, 14/20-fret ebony fingerboard with pearl dot inlay, rosewood veneer on peghead, three-per-side gold tuners, ebony bridge with black pins, available in Natural gloss finish, mfg. 1978-2006.

1978-1989	N/A	$1,200 - 1,500	$725 - 900	
1990-2006	N/A	$1,075 - 1,350	$650 - 800	$2,598

In 1994, pearl peghead logo inlay, abalone rosette, abalone slotted diamond fingerboard inlay, black abalone dot bridgepins replaced original items. In 1998, chrome Grover tuners replaced the gold-plated tuners.

* 510 CE – similar to 510, except has a single Venetian cutaway body, Fishman Onboard Blender system, available in Natural gloss finish, mfg. 1998-present.

MSR $3,198	$2,450	$1,350 - 1,700	$825 - 1,025	

512 – grand concert body, solid Engelmann spruce top, round soundhole, tortoiseshell pickguard, three-stripe bound body/rosette, solid mahogany back/sides/neck, 14/20-fret ebony fingerboard with pearl dot inlay, ebony bridge with black pins, rosewood veneer on peghead, three-per-side gold tuners, available in Natural gloss finish, mfg. 1978-2000.

1978-1989	N/A	$1,200 - 1,500	$725 - 900	
1990-2000	N/A	$1,125 - 1,400	$675 - 850	$2,868

In 1994, pearl peghead logo inlay, abalone rosette, abalone slotted diamond fingerboard inlay, black abalone dot bridgepins replaced original items. In 1998, chrome Grover tuners replaced the gold-plated tuners.

* 512 CE – similar to 512, except has a single Venetian cutaway body, Fishman Onboard Blender system, available in Natural gloss finish, mfg. 2001-present.

MSR $3,198	$2,450	$1,350 - 1,700	$825 - 1,025	

512 CE-N NYLON – nylon configuration, single cutaway Grand Concert-style (GC) body, Western red cedar top, Tropical mahogany back and sides, nylon bracing, round soundhole with three-ring abalone rosette, tortoise body binding, mahogany neck, 12/17-fret tortoise-bound ebony fingerboard with deco diamond inlays, slotted headstock with Indian rosewood overlay and MOP Taylor logo, three-per-side open-style gold tuners with ivory buttons, ebony tied bridge, ES-N electronics, available in Natural finish, 1.875 in. nut width, 25.5 in. scale, deluxe hardshell case included, mfg. 2012-13.

	$2,800	$1,550 - 1,900	$925 - 1,150	$3,718

514 C – grand auditorium body with single Venetian cutaway, solid Western red cedar top, round soundhole, tortoiseshell pickguard, three-stripe bound body/rosette, solid mahogany back/sides/neck, 14/20-fret ebony fingerboard with pearl dot inlay, ebony bridge with black pins, rosewood veneer on peghead, three-per-side gold tuners, available in Natural gloss finish, mfg. 1990-98.

	N/A	$1,275 - 1,600	$750 - 950	$2,198

In 1994, pearl peghead logo inlay, abalone rosette, abalone slotted diamond fingerboard inlay, black abalone dot bridgepins replaced original items. In 1998, chrome Grover tuners replaced the gold-plated tuners.

MSR/NOTES	100%	EXCELLENT	AVERAGE	LAST MSR

514 CE – similar to 514 C, except has a Fishman Onboard Blender system, available in Natural gloss finish, mfg. 1998-present.

| MSR $3,198 | $2,450 | $1,350 - 1,700 | $825 - 1,025 | |

514 CE-N NYLON – nylon configuration, single cutaway Grand Auditorium-style (GA) body, Western red cedar top, Tropical mahogany back and sides, nylon bracing, round soundhole with three-ring abalone rosette, tortoise body binding, mahogany neck, 14/20-fret tortoise-bound ebony fingerboard with deco diamond inlays, slotted headstock with Indian rosewood overlay and MOP Taylor logo, three-per-side open-style gold tuners with ivory buttons, ebony tied bridge, ES-N electronics, available in Natural finish, 1.875 in. nut width, 25.5 in. scale, deluxe hardshell case included, mfg. 2012-present.

| MSR $3,198 | $2,450 | $1,350 - 1,700 | $825 - 1,025 | |

516 CE – single cutaway Grand Symphony (GS) body style, Western red cedar top, Tropical American mahogany back and sides, round soundhole with abalone rosette, Indian rosewood top and back binding, multi-ply top inlay, Tropical American mahogany neck, 14/20-fret ebony fingerboard with small pearl dots, Tropical American mahogany headstock overlay with pearl logo, three-per-side gold tuners, ebony bridge, tortoise pickguard, Taylor Expression electronics, available in Natural Gloss finish, 25.5 in. scale, hardshell case included, mfg. 2008-present.

| MSR $3,198 | $2,450 | $1,350 - 1,700 | $825 - 1,025 | |

554 CE 12-STRING – 12-string configuration, grand auditorium cutaway, six-per-side tuners, Expression system electronics, Natural Satin finish, mfg. 2004-06.

| | N/A | $1,475 - 1,850 | $875 - 1,150 | $3,658 |

555 12-STRING – 12-string configuration, jumbo body, solid Sitka spruce top, round soundhole, tortoiseshell pickguard, three-stripe bound body/rosette, solid mahogany back/sides/neck, 14/20-fret ebony fingerboard with pearl dot inlay, rosewood veneer on peghead, six-per-side gold tuners, ebony bridge with black pins, available in Natural gloss finish, mfg. 1978-2006.

| 1978-1989 | N/A | $1,450 - 1,800 | $875 - 1,100 | |
| 1990-2006 | N/A | $1,350 - 1,700 | $825 - 1,025 | $3,058 |

In 1994, pearl peghead logo inlay, abalone rosette, abalone slotted diamond fingerboard inlay, black abalone dot bridgepins replaced original items. In 1998, chrome Grover tuners replaced the gold-plated tuners.

555 CE 12-String – similar to 555, except has a single cutaway and electronics, available in Natural gloss finish, mfg. 1998-2006.

| | N/A | $1,475 - 1,850 | $875 - 1,100 | $3,658 |

556 CE 12-STRING – 12-string configuration, single cutaway Grand Symphony (GS) body style, Western red cedar top, Tropical American mahogany back and sides, 12-string bracing, round soundhole with abalone rosette, Indian rosewood top and back binding, multi-ply top inlay, Tropical American mahogany neck, 14/20-fret ebony fingerboard with small pearl dots, Tropical American mahogany headstock overlay with pearl logo, three-per-side gold tuners, ebony bridge, tortoise pickguard, Taylor Expression electronics, available in Natural Gloss finish, 25.5 in. scale, hardshell case included, mfg. 2012-present.

| MSR $3,398 | $2,600 | $1,475 - 1,850 | $900 - 1,100 | |

ACOUSTIC: 600 SERIES

The 600 series features curly maple back and side, scalloped bracing (on the six-string models), an abalone soundhole rosette, and pearl "Leaf Pattern" inlays. The models originally featured Amber-stained back and sides and gloss finish. In 1998, when five acoustic/electric models debuted, the stain colors expanded to Amber, Black, Blue, Green, Natural, and Red (and gloss finish).

An example of a 615 CE
courtesy Dave Rogers, Dave's Guitar Shop

610 – dreadnought body, solid spruce top, round soundhole, tortoiseshell pickguard, white plastic body binding, ring design rosette, solid maple back/sides, mahogany neck, 14/20-fret bound rosewood fingerboard with pearl dot inlay, rosewood bridge with black pins, rosewood veneer on peghead, three-per-side gold Grover tuners, available in Amber Stain finish, mfg. 1978-1998.

| 1978-1989 | N/A | $1,400 - 1,750 | $850 - 1,050 | |
| 1990-1998 | N/A | $1,275 - 1,600 | $750 - 950 | $1,898 |

In 1994, the abalone rosette, bound ebony fingerboard with pearl leaf inlay, ebony bridge with black abalone dot bridge pins, ebony peghead veneer with pearl logo inlay replaced original items.

MSR/NOTES	100%	EXCELLENT	AVERAGE	LAST MSR

* 610 CE – similar to 610, except has an single Venetian cutaway body, Sitka spruce top, Big leaf maple back/sides, Fishman Onboard Blender system, available in Amber, Black, Blue, Green, Natural, or Red gloss finish, mfg. 1998-present.

MSR $3,998	$3,000	$1,650 - 2,100	$1,000 - 1,250	

612 – grand concert body, solid spruce top, round soundhole, tortoiseshell pickguard, three-stripe bound body/rosette, solid maple back/sides, mahogany neck, 14/20-fret bound rosewood fingerboard with pearl dot inlay, rosewood bridge with black pins, rosewood veneer on peghead, three-per-side gold tuners, available in Natural finish, mfg. 1984-1992.

	N/A	$1,275 - 1,600	$750 - 950	$1,840

* 612 C – similar to 612, except has single Venetian cutaway body, mfg. 1993-98.

	N/A	$1,325 - 1,650	$800 - 1,000	$2,198

In 1994, single round cutaway, abalone rosette, bound ebony fingerboard with pearl leaf inlay, ebony bridge with black abalone dot bridge pins, ebony peghead veneer with pearl logo inlay replaced original items.

* 612 CE – similar to 612, except has an single Venetian cutaway body, Sitka spruce top, Big leaf maple back/sides, Fishman Onboard Blender system, available in Amber, Black, Blue, Green, Natural, or Red gloss finish, mfg. 1998-present.

MSR $3,998	$3,000	$1,650 - 2,100	$1,000 - 1,250	

612 CE-N NYLON – nylon configuration, single cutaway Grand Concert-style (GC) body, Sitka spruce top, Big Leaf maple back and sides, nylon bracing, round soundhole with three-ring abalone rosette, white body binding, mahogany neck, 12/17-fret white-bound ebony fingerboard with twisted oval inlays, slotted headstock with ebony overlay and MOP Taylor logo, three-per-side open-style gold tuners with ivoroid buttons, ebony tied bridge, ES-N electronics, available in Amber, Black, Brown Sugar, Cherry Black Sunburst, Cherry Sunburst, Green, Honey Sunburst, Koi Blue, Purple, Tobacco Sunburst, Trans. Black, Trans. Blue, Trans. Orange, or Trans. Red finish, 1.875 in. nut width, 25.5 in. scale, deluxe hardshell case included, mfg. 2012-present.

MSR $3,998	$3,000	$1,650 - 2,100	$1,000 - 1,250	

614 C – grand auditorium body, with single Venetian cutaway, solid spruce top, round soundhole, tortoiseshell pickguard, three-stripe bound body/rosette, solid maple back/sides, mahogany neck, 14/20-fret bound rosewood fingerboard with pearl dot inlay, rosewood bridge with black pins, rosewood veneer on peghead, three-per-side gold tuners, available in Natural finish, disc. 1998.

	N/A	$1,525 - 1,900	$925 - 1,150	$2,298

* 614 CE – similar to 614, except has an single Venetian cutaway body, Sitka spruce top, Big leaf maple back/sides, Fishman Onboard Blender system, available in Amber, Black, Blue, Green, Natural, and Red gloss finish, mfg. 1998-present.

MSR $3,998	$3,000	$1,650 - 2,100	$1,000 - 1,250	

614 CE-N NYLON – nylon configuration, single cutaway Grand Auditorium-style (GA) body, Sitka spruce top, Big Leaf maple back and sides, nylon bracing, round soundhole with three-ring abalone rosette, white body binding, mahogany neck, 14/20-fret white-bound ebony fingerboard with twisted oval inlays, slotted headstock with ebony overlay and MOP Taylor logo, three-per-side open-style gold tuners with ivoroid buttons, ebony tied bridge, ES-N electronics, available in Amber, Black, Brown Sugar, Cherry Black Sunburst, Cherry Sunburst, Green, Honey Sunburst, Koi Blue, Purple, Tobacco Sunburst, Trans. Black, Trans. Blue, Trans. Orange, or Trans. Red finish, 1.875 in. nut width, 25.5 in. scale, deluxe hardshell case included, mfg. 2012-present.

MSR $3,998	$3,000	$1,650 - 2,100	$1,000 - 1,250	

615 – jumbo body, solid spruce top, round soundhole, tortoise pickguard, three-stripe bound body/rosette, solid maple back/sides, mahogany neck, 14/20-fret bound rosewood fingerboard with pearl dot inlay, rosewood bridge with black pins, rosewood veneer on peghead, three-per-side gold tuners, available in Natural finish, mfg. 1981-1998.

	N/A	$1,600 - 2,000	$950 - 1,200	$2,198

In 1994, abalone rosette, bound ebony fingerboard with pearl leaf inlay, ebony bridge with black abalone dot bridge pins, ebony peghead veneer with pearl logo inlay replaced original items.

* 615 CE – similar to 615, except has a single Venetian cutaway body, Sitka spruce top, Big leaf maple back/sides, Fishman Onboard Blender system, available in Amber, Black, Blue, Green, Natural, or Red gloss finish, mfg. 1998-2011.

	$2,950	$1,650 - 2,100	$1,000 - 1,250	$3,948

616 CE – single cutaway Grand Symphony (GS) body style, Sitka spruce top, Big Leaf maple back and sides, round soundhole with abalone rosette, white plastic top and back binding, multi-ply top inlay, Hard Rock maple neck, 14/20-fret bound ebony fingerboard with pearl leaf pattern inlays, Indian rosewood bound headstock overlay with pearl logo, three-per-side gold tuners, ebony bridge, tortoise pickguard, Taylor Expression electronics, available in Natural Gloss finish, 25.5 in. scale, hardshell case included, mfg. 2008-present.

MSR $3,998	$3,000	$1,650 - 2,100	$1,000 - 1,250	

654 CE 12-STRING – 12-string configuration, grand auditorium cutaway, six-per-side tuners, Expression system electronics, Natural Satin finish, mfg. 2004-2011.

	$3,100	$1,750 - 2,200	$1,050 - 1,300	$4,148

MSR/NOTES	100%	EXCELLENT	AVERAGE	LAST MSR

655 12-STRING – 12-string configuration, jumbo body, solid spruce top, round soundhole, tortoise pickguard, three-stripe bound body/rosette, solid maple back/sides, mahogany neck, 14/20-fret bound rosewood fingerboard with pearl dot inlay, rosewood veneer on peghead, six-per-side gold tuners, rosewood bridge with black pins, available in Natural finish, mfg. 1978-1998, reintroduced 2001-06.

1978-1998	N/A	$1,600 - 2,000	$950 - 1,200	
2001-2006	N/A	$1,525 - 1,900	$925 - 1,150	$3,448

* **655 CE 12-String** – similar to 655, except has a single Venetian cutaway body, Sitka spruce top, Big leaf maple back/sides, Fishman Onboard Blender system, available in Amber, Black, Blue, Green, Natural, or Red gloss finish, mfg. 1998-2011.

	$3,100	$1,750 - 2,200	$1,050 - 1,300	$4,148

656 CE 12-STRING – similar to the 616 CE, except in 12-string configuration with six-per-side tuners, mfg. 2008-present.

MSR $4,198	$3,150	$1,750 - 2,200	$1,050 - 1,300	

ACOUSTIC: 700 SERIES

The 700 Series models feature Indian rosewood back and sides, abalone soundhole rosette and neck dot inlays. Models prior to 1998 have solid spruce tops; models after 1998 now feature Western red cedar tops.

710 – dreadnought body, solid spruce top, round soundhole, tortoiseshell pickguard, three-stripe bound body/rosette, rosewood back/sides, mahogany neck, 14/20-fret ebony fingerboard with pearl dot inlay, rosewood veneer on peghead, three-per-side gold tuners, ebony bridge with black pins, available in Natural finish, mfg. 1977-2006.

1977-1989	N/A	$1,350 - 1,700	$825 - 1,025	
1990-2006	N/A	$1,275 - 1,600	$750 - 950	$2,798

In 1994, abalone rosette, abalone dot fingerboard inlay, black abalone dot bridge pins, pearl logo peghead inlay replaced original items. In 1998, a Western Red cedar top replaced spruce top.

* **710 CE** – similar to 710, except has a single Venetian cutaway body, Fishman Onboard Blender system, available in Natural gloss finish, mfg. 1998-present.

MSR $3,778	$2,800	$1,600 - 2,000	$950 - 1,200	

712 – grand concert body, solid spruce top, round soundhole, tortoiseshell pickguard, three-stripe bound body and rosette, rosewood back/sides, mahogany neck, 14/20-fret ebony fingerboard with pearl dot inlay, rosewood veneer on peghead, three-per-side gold tuners, ebony bridge with black pins, available in Natural finish, mfg. 1984-2006.

1984-1989	N/A	$1,400 - 1,750	$850 - 1,050	
1990-2006	N/A	$1,325 - 1,650	$800 - 1,000	$2,938

In 1994, abalone rosette, abalone dot fingerboard inlay, black abalone dot bridge pins, pearl logo peghead inlay replaced original items. In 1998, a Western Red cedar top replaced spruce top.

* **712 CE** – similar to 712, except has a single Venetian cutaway body, Fishman Onboard Blender system, available in Natural gloss finish, mfg. 2000-present.

MSR $3,778	$2,800	$1,600 - 2,000	$950 - 1,200	

712 CE-N NYLON – nylon configuration, single cutaway Grand Concert-style (GC) body, Englemann spruce top, Indian rosewood back and sides, nylon bracing, round soundhole with three-ring ivoroid rosette, ivoroid body binding, Tropical mahogany neck, 12/17-fret ivoroid-bound ebony fingerboard with heritage diamond inlays, slotted headstock with Indian rosewood overlay and ivoroid Taylor logo, three-per-side open-style gold tuners with ivoroid buttons, ebony tied bridge, ES-N electronics, available in Natural or Sunburst finish, 1.875 in. nut width, 25.5 in. scale, deluxe hardshell case included, mfg. 2012-13.

	$2,800	$1,600 - 2,000	$950 - 1,200	$3,778

714 – grand auditorium body, solid spruce top, round soundhole, tortoiseshell pickguard, three-stripe bound body and rosette, rosewood back/sides, mahogany neck, 14/20-fret ebony fingerboard with pearl dot inlay, rosewood veneer on peghead, three-per-side gold tuners, ebony bridge with black pins, available in Natural finish, mfg. 1996-2006.

	N/A	$1,400 - 1,750	$850 - 1,050	$3,078

In 1998, a Western Red cedar top replaced spruce top.

* **714 CE** – similar to 714, except has a single Venetian cutaway body, Fishman Onboard Blender system, available in Natural gloss finish, mfg. 1998-present.

MSR $3,778	$2,800	$1,600 - 2,000	$950 - 1,200	

714 CE-N NYLON – nylon configuration, single cutaway Grand Auditorium-style (GA) body, Englemann spruce top, Indian rosewood back and sides, nylon bracing, round soundhole with three-ring ivoroid rosette, ivoroid body binding, Tropical mahogany neck, 14/20-fret ivoroid-bound ebony fingerboard with heritage diamond inlays, slotted headstock with Indian rosewood overlay and ivoroid Taylor logo, three-per-side open-style gold tuners with ivoroid buttons, ebony tied bridge, ES-N electronics, available in Natural or Sunburst finish, 1.875 in. nut width, 25.5 in. scale, deluxe hardshell case included, mfg. 2012-present.

MSR $3,778	$2,800	$1,600 - 2,000	$950 - 1,200	

MSR/NOTES	100%	EXCELLENT	AVERAGE	LAST MSR

716 CE – single cutaway Grand Symphony (GS) body style, Western Red cedar top, Indian rosewood back and sides, round soundhole with abalone rosette, Indian rosewood top and back binding with W/B inlays, Tropical American mahogany neck, 14/20-fret ebony fingerboard with small pearl dot inlays, Indian rosewood headstock overlay with pearl logo, three-per-side gold tuners, ebony bridge, tortoise pickguard, Taylor Expression electronics, available in Natural Gloss finish, 25.5 in. scale, hardshell case included, mfg. 2008-present.

MSR $3,778	$2,800	$1,600 - 2,000	$950 - 1,200	

750 12-STRING – similar to 710, except in 12-string configuration and six-per-side tuners, mfg. 1990-98.

	N/A	$1,475 - 1,850	$875 - 1,100	$1,898

754 12-STRING – 12-string configuration, grand auditorium, and six-per-side tuners, Natural Satin finish, mfg. 2004-06.

	N/A	$1,475 - 1,850	$875 - 1,100	$3,278

*   *754 CE 12-String* – similar to the 754, except has a single cutaway and Expression system electronics, mfg. 2004-06.

	N/A	$1,600 - 2,000	$950 - 1,200	$3,878

756 CE – 12-string configuration, single cutaway Grand Symphony (GS) body style, Western Red cedar top, Indian rosewood back and sides, 12-string bracing with relief rout, round soundhole with three-ring ivoroid rosette, ivoroid binding with W/B inlays, Tropical American mahogany neck, 14/20-fret ivoroid-bound ebony fingerboard with heritage diamond inlays, Indian rosewood headstock overlay with ivoroid logo, three-per-side chrome tuners, ebony bridge, tortoise pickguard, Taylor Expression electronics, available in Natural or Sunburst Gloss finish, 1.875 in. nut width, 25.5 in. scale, hardshell case included, mfg. 2012-present.

MSR $3,978	$3,000	$1,675 - 2,100	$1,000 - 1,250	

ACOUSTIC: 800 SERIES

The Taylor 800 series are referred to as "the descendants of Bob Taylor's original design." These deluxe models feature Indian rosewood back and sides, scalloped bracing (on six-string models), abalone soundhole rosette, and pearl "Progressive Diamond" fretboard inlay.

810 – dreadnought body, solid Sitka spruce top, round soundhole, tortoiseshell pickguard, three-stripe bound body, abalone rosette, Indian rosewood back/sides, mahogany neck, 14/20-fret bound rosewood fingerboard with pearl snowflake inlay, rosewood veneer on bound peghead w/ pearl logo inlay, three-per-side gold tuners, rosewood bridge with black abalone dot pins, available in Natural finish, mfg. 1975-2010.

1977-1989	N/A	$1,350 - 1,700	$825 - 1,025	
1990-2010	$2,350	$1,275 - 1,600	$750 - 950	$3,148

In 1994, pearl progressive diamond fingerboard inlay replaced the snowflake inlay. In 1998, ebony fingerboard replaced rosewood fingerboard; ebony bridge replaced the rosewood bridge.

*   *810 CE* – similar to 810, except has a single Florentine or Venetian cutaway body, Fishman Onboard Blender system, available in Natural gloss finish, mfg. 1998-present.

MSR $4,378	$3,400	$1,800 - 2,250	$1,075 - 1,350	

812 – grand concert body, solid (Sitka) spruce top, round soundhole, tortoiseshell pickguard, three-stripe bound body, abalone rosette, rosewood back/sides, mahogany neck, 14/20-fret bound rosewood fingerboard with pearl snowflake inlay, rosewood bridge with black abalone dot pins, rosewood veneer on bound peghead with pearl logo inlay, three-per-side gold tuners, available in Natural finish, disc. 1992.

	N/A	$1,400 - 1,750	$850 - 1,050	$1,960

*   *812 C* – similar to 812, except has single sharp cutaway, mfg. 1993-98.

	N/A	$1,475 - 1,850	$875 - 1,100	$2,298

In 1994, single round cutaway, pearl progressive diamond fingerboard inlay replaced original items.

*   *812 CE* – similar to 812, except has a single Florentine or Venetian cutaway body, Fishman Onboard Blender system, available in Natural gloss finish, mfg. 1998-present.

MSR $4,378	$3,400	$1,800 - 2,250	$1,075 - 1,350	

812 CE-N NYLON – nylon configuration, single cutaway Grand Concert-style (GC) body, Sitka spruce top, Indian rosewood back and sides, nylon bracing, round soundhole with single-ring abalone rosette, curly maple body binding, W/B top inlay, Tropical mahogany neck, 12/17-fret curly maple-bound ebony fingerboard with progressive diamond inlays, slotted headstock with Indian rosewood overlay and MOP Taylor logo, three-per-side open-style gold tuners with ivoroid buttons, ebony tied bridge, ES-N electronics, available in Honey Sunburst, Natural, or Tobacco Sunburst finish, 1.875 in. nut width, 25.5 in. scale, deluxe hardshell case included, mfg. 2012-present.

MSR $4,378	$3,400	$1,800 - 2,250	$1,075 - 1,350	

814 – grand auditorium body, solid Sitka spruce top, round soundhole, tortoise pickguard, three-stripe bound body, abalone rosette, rosewood back/sides, mahogany neck, 14/20-fret bound rosewood fingerboard with pearl snowflake inlay, rosewood veneer on bound peghead with pearl logo inlay, three-per-side gold tuners, rosewood bridge with black abalone dot pins, mfg. 2005-06.

	N/A	$1,450 - 1,800	$875 - 1,100	$3,358

*   *814C* – similar to the 814, except has a single Florentine or Venetian cutaway, mfg. 1996-97.

	N/A	$1,525 - 1,900	$925 - 1,150	$2,398

MSR/NOTES	100%	EXCELLENT	AVERAGE	LAST MSR

* 814 CE – similar to 814 C, except has electronics, available in Natural gloss finish, mfg. 1998-present.

| MSR $4,378 | $3,400 | $1,800 - 2,250 | $1,075 - 1,350 | |

814 CE-N NYLON – nylon configuration, single cutaway Grand Auditorium-style (GA) body, Sitka spruce top, Indian rosewood back and sides, nylon bracing, round soundhole with single-ring abalone rosette, curly maple body binding, W/B top inlay, Tropical mahogany neck, 14/20-fret curly maple-bound ebony fingerboard with progressive diamond inlays, slotted headstock with Indian rosewood overlay and MOP Taylor logo, three-per-side open-style gold tuners with ivoroid buttons, ebony tied bridge, ES-N electronics, available in Honey Sunburst, Natural, or Tobacco Sunburst finish, 1.875 in. nut width, 25.5 in. scale, deluxe hardshell case included, mfg. 2012-present.

| MSR $4,378 | $3,400 | $1,800 - 2,250 | $1,075 - 1,350 | |

815 – jumbo body, no cutaway, mfg. 2004-06.

| | N/A | $1,600 - 2,000 | $950 - 1,200 | $3,358 |

815 C – jumbo body with single sharp cutaway, solid Sitka spruce top, round soundhole, tortoise pickguard, three-stripe bound body, abalone rosette, rosewood back/sides, mahogany neck, 14/20-fret bound rosewood fingerboard with pearl snowflake inlay, rosewood bridge with black abalone dot pins, rosewood veneer on bound peghead with pearl logo inlay, three-per-side gold tuners, mfg. 1993-98.

| | N/A | $1,675 - 2,100 | $1,000 - 1,250 | $2,398 |

In 1994, pearl progressive diamond fingerboard inlay replaced original item.

* 815 CE – similar to 815 C, except has electronics, available in Natural gloss finish, mfg. 1998-2011.

| | $3,000 | $1,725 - 2,150 | $1,050 - 1,300 | $4,058 |

816 CE – single cutaway Grand Symphony (GS) body style, Sitka spruce top, Indian rosewood back and sides, round soundhole with abalone rosette, maple top and back binding with W/B inlays, Tropical American mahogany neck, 14/20-fret maple-bound ebony fingerboard with Pearl 800 Series inlays, Indian rosewood maple-bound headstock overlay with pearl logo, three-per-side gold tuners, ebony bridge, tortoise pickguard, Taylor Expression electronics, available in Natural Gloss finish, 25.5 in. scale, hardshell case included, mfg. 2008-present.

| MSR $4,378 | $3,400 | $1,800 - 2,250 | $1,075 - 1,350 | |

854 CE 12-STRING – 12-string configuration, grand auditorium cutaway, six-per-side tuners, Expression system electronics, Natural Satin finish, mfg. 2004-2011.

| | $3,150 | $1,800 - 2,250 | $1,075 - 1,300 | $4,258 |

855 12-STRING – 12-string configuration, jumbo body, solid (Sitka) spruce top, round soundhole, tortoiseshell pickguard, three-stripe bound body, abalone rosette, rosewood back/sides, mahogany neck, 14/20-fret bound rosewood fingerboard with pearl snowflake inlay, rosewood veneer on bound peghead with pearl logo inlay, six-per-side gold tuners, rosewood bridge with black abalone dot pins, available in Natural finish, mfg. 1993-2006.

| | N/A | $1,675 - 2,100 | $1,000 - 1,250 | $3,558 |

In 1994, pearl progressive diamond fingerboard inlay replaced original item.

* 855 CE 12-String – similar to 855, except has electronics, available in Natural gloss finish, mfg. 2000-2011.

| | $3,150 | $1,800 - 2,250 | $1,075 - 1,300 | $4,258 |

856 CE 12-STRING – similar to the 816 CE, except in 12-string configuration with six-per-side tuners, mfg. 2008-present.

| MSR $4,578 | $3,500 | $1,850 - 2,300 | $1,100 - 1,325 | |

ACOUSTIC: 900 SERIES

The 900 series models feature Engelmann spruce tops, Indian rosewood back and sides, scalloped bracing (on six-string models), abalone top edging combined with rosewood binding, distinct abalone soundhole rosette, and the abalone and pearl "Cindy" design fingerboard inlays. In 2011, Taylor returned to their elegant appointment package from several years ago with the Cindy fingerboard inlay, rosewood binding, and red purfling.

910 – dreadnought body, solid Engelmann spruce top, round soundhole, tortoiseshell pickguard, abalone edge inlay/rosewood body binding, abalone rosette, maple back and sides (1977-1993) or Indian rosewood back and sides (1986-2010), 14/20-fret ebony fingerboard with abalone stylized inlay, rosewood peghead veneer with abalone stylized T/logo inlay, three-per-side gold tuners, ebony bridge with black abalone dot pins, available in Natural finish, mfg. 1977-2010.

| 1977-1993 Maple | N/A | $2,200 - 2,750 | $1,325 - 1,650 | |
| 1986-2010 Indian Rosewood | $3,300 | $2,000 - 2,500 | $1,200 - 1,500 | $4,398 |

In 1993, rosewood back/sides, mahogany neck were optional. In 1994, abalone purfling, abalone flower fingerboard inlay replaced original items, abalone stylized T peghead inlay was discontinued.

* 910 CE – similar to 910, except has single Florentine or Venetian cutaway body and electronics, available in Natural Gloss finish, mfg. 1998-present.

| MSR $5,858 | $4,500 | $2,400 - 3,000 | $1,450 - 1,800 | |

MSR/NOTES	100%	EXCELLENT	AVERAGE	LAST MSR

912 – grand concert body, solid (Engelmann) spruce top, round soundhole, tortoiseshell pickguard, wood bound body, abalone rosette, maple back/sides/neck, 14/20-fret ebony fingerboard with abalone stylized inlay, ebony bridge with black abalone dot pins, rosewood veneer with abalone stylized T/logo inlay on peghead, three-per-side gold tuners, available in Natural finish, disc. 1992.

	N/A	$2,200 - 2,750	$1,325 - 1,650	$2,715

* *912 CE* – similar to 912, except has single Florentine or Venetian cutaway body, and electronics, mfg. 1993-present.

MSR $5,858	$4,500	$2,400 - 3,000	$1,450 - 1,800	

In 1994, abalone purfling, abalone flower fingerboard inlay replaced original items, abalone stylized T peghead inlay was discontinued.

912 CE-N NYLON – nylon configuration, single cutaway Grand Concert-style (GC) body, Sitka spruce top, Indian rosewood back and sides, nylon bracing, round soundhole with single-ring abalone rosette, Indian rosewood body binding, abalone purfling, Tropical mahogany neck, 12/17-fret Indian rosewood-bound ebony fingerboard with abalone "Cindy" inlays, slotted headstock with ebony overlay and MOP Taylor logo, three-per-side open-style gold tuners with ivoroid buttons, ebony tied bridge, ES-N electronics, available in Honey Sunburst, Natural, or Tobacco Sunburst finish, 1.875 in. nut width, 25.5 in. scale, deluxe hardshell case included, mfg. 2012-present.

MSR $5,858	$4,500	$2,400 - 3,000	$1,450 - 1,800	

914 CE – similar to the 912, except features a grand auditorium body with a single Florentine or Venetian cutaway, and Fishman Onboard Blender system, current mfg.

MSR $5,858	$4,500	$2,400 - 3,000	$1,450 - 1,800	

914 CE-N NYLON – nylon configuration, single cutaway Grand Auditorium-style (GA) body, Sitka spruce top, Indian rosewood back and sides, nylon bracing, round soundhole with single-ring abalone rosette, Indian rosewood body binding, abalone purfling, Tropical mahogany neck, 14/20-fret Indian rosewood-bound ebony fingerboard with abalone "Cindy" inlays, slotted headstock with ebony overlay and MOP Taylor logo, three-per-side open-style gold tuners with ivoroid buttons, ebony tied bridge, ES-N electronics, available in Honey Sunburst, Natural, or Tobacco Sunburst finish, 1.875 in. nut width, 25.5 in. scale, deluxe hardshell case included, mfg. 2012-present.

MSR $5,858	$4,500	$2,400 - 3,000	$1,450 - 1,800	

915 – jumbo body, solid spruce top, round soundhole, tortoise pickguard, wood bound body, abalone rosette, maple back/sides/neck, 14/20-fret ebony fingerboard with abalone stylized inlay, ebony bridge with black abalone dot pins, rosewood veneer with abalone stylized T/logo inlay on peghead, three-per-side gold tuners, available in Natural finish, disc. 1992.

	N/A	$2,200 - 2,750	$1,325 - 1,650	$2,815

* *915 CE* – similar to 915, except has single Florentine or Venetian cutaway body and electronics, mfg. 1998-2006.

	N/A	$2,400 - 3,000	$1,450 - 1,800	$5,328

916 CE – single cutaway Grand Symphony (GS) body style, Sitka spruce top, Indian rosewood back and sides, round soundhole with abalone rosette, ivoroid top and back binding (2008-2010) or rosewood binding (2011-present), abalone pearl purfling, Tropical American mahogany neck, 14/20-fret ivoroid-bound ebony fingerboard with Pearl 900 Series inlays (2008-2010) or Cindy inlays (2011-present), ebony headstock overlay with pearl logo and floral design, three-per-side gold Gotoh 510 tuners, ebony bridge, Taylor Expression electronics, available in Natural Gloss finish, 25.5 in. scale, hardshell case included, mfg. 2008-present.

MSR $5,858	$4,500	$2,400 - 3,000	$1,450 - 1,800	

954 CE 12-STRING – 12-string configuration, single cutaway Grand Auditorium (GA) body style, Sitka spruce top, Indian rosewood back and sides, round soundhole with abalone rosette, ivoroid top and back binding (2004-06) or rosewood binding (2011 only), abalone pearl purfling, Tropical American mahogany neck, 14/20-fret ivoroid-bound ebony fingerboard with Pearl 900 Series inlays (2004-06) or Cindy inlays (2011 only), ebony headstock overlay with pearl logo and floral design, six-per-side gold Gotoh 510 tuners, ebony bridge, Taylor Expression electronics, available in Natural Gloss finish, 25.5 in. scale, hardshell case included, mfg. 2004-06, reintroduced 2011 only.

	$4,400	$2,500 - 3,100	$1,500 - 1,875	$5,858

955 12-STRING – 12-string configuration, jumbo body, solid spruce top, round soundhole, tortoiseshell pickguard, wood bound body, abalone rosette, maple back/sides/neck, 14/20-fret ebony fingerboard with abalone stylized inlay, rosewood veneer with abalone stylized T/logo inlay on peghead, six-per-side gold tuners, ebony bridge with black abalone dot pins, Natural finish, disc. 2006.

	N/A	$2,275 - 2,850	$1,350 - 1,700	$4,928

956 CE 12-STRING – 12-string configuration, single cutaway Grand Symphony (GS) body style, Sitka spruce top, Indian rosewood back and sides, 12-string bracing, round soundhole with abalone rosette, Indian rosewood binding, abalone pearl purfling, Tropical American mahogany neck, 14/20-fret Indian rosewood-bound ebony fingerboard with abalone "Cindy" inlays, ebony headstock overlay with pearl logo and floral design, three-per-side gold Gotoh 510 tuners, ebony bridge, Taylor Expression electronics, available in Natural Gloss finish, 25.5 in. scale, hardshell case included, mfg. 2012-present.

MSR $6,058	$4,650	$2,550 - 3,200	$1,550 - 1,925	

ACOUSTIC: DN SERIES

DN3 – dreadnought style, Sitka spruce top, Sapele back and sides, round soundhole with rings rosette, cream plastic binding, Tropical American mahogany neck, 20-fret bound ebony fingerboard with pearl dot inlays, three-per-side chrome tuners, ebony bridge, tortoise pickguard, 25.5 in. scale, available in Natural finish, mfg. 2007-2012.

	$1,100	$650 - 800	$400 - 500	$1,498

MSR/NOTES	100%	EXCELLENT	AVERAGE	LAST MSR

DN4 – dreadnought style, Sitka spruce top, Ovangkol back and sides, round soundhole with rings rosette, cream plastic binding, Tropical American mahogany neck, 20-fret bound ebony fingerboard with pearl dot inlays, three-per-side chrome tuners, ebony bridge, tortoise pickguard, 25.5 in. scale, available in Natural finish, mfg. 2007-2012.

	$1,350	$750 - 950	$450 - 550	$1,798

DN5 – dreadnought style, Englemann spruce top, Tropical American mahogany back and sides, round soundhole with fancy rosette, ivoroid plastic binding, Tropical American mahogany neck, 20-fret bound ebony fingerboard with abalone dot inlays, three-per-side gold tuners, ebony bridge, 25.5 in. scale, available in Natural finish, mfg. 2007-2012.

	$2,250	$1,250 - 1,575	$750 - 925	$2,998

DN6 – dreadnought style, Sitka spruce top, big leaf maple back and sides, round soundhole with fancy rosette, ivoroid plastic binding, Tropical American mahogany neck, 20-fret bound ebony fingerboard with abalone dot inlays, three-per-side gold tuners, ebony bridge, 25.5 in. scale, available in Natural finish, mfg. 2012 only.

	$2,250	$1,250 - 1,575	$750 - 925	$2,998

DN7 – dreadnought style, Englemann spruce top, Indian rosewood back and sides, round soundhole with fancy rosette, ivoroid plastic binding, Tropical American mahogany neck, 20-fret bound ebony fingerboard with abalone dot inlays, three-per-side gold tuners, ebony bridge, 25.5 in. scale, available in Natural finish, mfg. 2012 only.

	$2,250	$1,250 - 1,575	$750 - 925	$2,998

DN8 – dreadnought style, Sitka spruce top, Indian rosewood back and sides, round soundhole with fancy rosette, ivoroid plastic binding, Tropical American mahogany neck, 20-fret bound ebony fingerboard with abalone dot inlays, three-per-side gold tuners, ebony bridge, 25.5 in. scale, available in Natural finish, mfg. 2007-2012.

	$2,250	$1,250 - 1,575	$750 - 925	$2,998

DN-K – dreadnought style, Sitka spruce top, Hawaiian koa back and sides, round soundhole with abalone rosette, cream plastic binding, abalone pearl purfling, Tropical American mahogany neck, 20-fret bound ebony fingerboard with abalone koa series inlays, three-per-side gold tuners, ebony bridge, 25.5 in. scale, available in Natural finish, hardshell case included, mfg. summer 2007-2012.

	$3,400	$1,875 - 2,350	$1,125 - 1,400	$4,498

ACOUSTIC: GA SERIES

GA3 – grand auditorium style, Sitka spruce top, Sapele back and sides, round soundhole with rings rosette, cream plastic binding, Tropical American mahogany neck, 20-fret bound ebony fingerboard with pearl dot inlays, three-per-side chrome tuners, ebony bridge, tortoise pickguard, 25.5 in. scale, available in Natural finish, mfg. 2007-2012.

	$1,150	$675 - 825	$400 - 500	$1,548

* *GA3-12 12-String* – similar to the GA3, except in 12-string configuration and six-per-side tuners, available in Natural finish, mfg. 2007-2012.

	$1,300	$750 - 925	$450 - 575	$1,748

GA4 – grand auditorium style, Sitka spruce top, Ovangkol back and sides, round soundhole with rings rosette, cream plastic binding, Tropical American mahogany neck, 20-fret bound ebony fingerboard with pearl dot inlays, three-per-side chrome tuners, ebony bridge, tortoise pickguard, 25.5 in. scale, available in Natural finish, mfg. 2007-2012.

	$1,400	$775 - 975	$450 - 575	$1,848

* *GA4-12 12-String* – similar to the GA4, except in 12-string configuration and six-per-side tuners, available in Natural finish, mfg. 2007-2012.

	$1,600	$850 - 1,075	$525 - 650	$2,048

GA5 – grand auditorium style, red cedar top, Tropical American mahogany back and sides, round soundhole with fancy rosette, ivoroid plastic binding, Tropical American mahogany neck, 20-fret bound ebony fingerboard with abalone dot inlays, three-per-side gold tuners, ebony bridge, 25.5 in. scale, available in Natural finish, mfg. 2007-2012.

	$2,250	$1,250 - 1,575	$750 - 925	$2,998

GA6 – grand auditorium style, Sitka spruce top, Big Leaf maple back and sides, round soundhole with fancy rosette, ivoroid plastic binding, Tropical American mahogany neck, 20-fret bound ebony fingerboard with abalone dot inlays, three-per-side gold tuners, ebony bridge, 25.5 in. scale, available in Natural finish, mfg. 2007-2012.

	$2,250	$1,250 - 1,575	$750 - 925	$2,998

* *GA6-12 12-String* – similar to the GA6, except in 12-string configuration and six-per-side tuners, available in Natural finish, mfg. 2007-2011.

	$2,350	$1,300 - 1,625	$775 - 975	$3,098

GA7 – grand auditorium style, red cedar top, Indian rosewood back and sides, round soundhole with fancy rosette, ivoroid plastic binding, Tropical American mahogany neck, 20-fret bound ebony fingerboard with abalone dot inlays, three-per-side gold tuners, ebony bridge, 25.5 in. scale, available in Natural finish, mfg. 2007-2012.

	$2,250	$1,250 - 1,575	$750 - 925	$2,998

MSR/NOTES	100%	EXCELLENT	AVERAGE	LAST MSR

GA8 – grand auditorium style, Sitka spruce top, Indian rosewood back and sides, round soundhole with fancy rosette, ivoroid plastic binding, Tropical American mahogany neck, 20-fret bound ebony fingerboard with abalone dot inlays, three-per-side gold tuners, ebony bridge, 25.5 in. scale, available in Natural finish, mfg. 2007-2012.

	$2,250	$1,250 - 1,575	$750 - 925	$2,998

* **GA8-12 12-String** – similar to the GA8, except in 12-string configuration and six-per-side tuners, available in Natural finish, mfg. 2007-2011.

	$2,350	$1,300 - 1,625	$775 - 975	$3,098

GA-K – Grand Auditorium body style, Sitka spruce top, Hawaiian koa back and sides, round soundhole with abalone rosette, cream plastic binding, abalone pearl purfling, Tropical American mahogany neck, 20-fret bound ebony fingerboard with abalone snowflake inlays, three-per-side gold tuners, ebony bridge, 25.5 in. scale, available in Natural finish, hardshell case included, mfg. summer 2007-2012.

	$3,400	$1,875 - 2,350	$1,125 - 1,400	$4,498

* **GA-K-12 12-String** – similar to the GA-K, except in 12-string configuration with six-per-side tuners, mfg. summer 2007-2011.

	$3,450	$1,950 - 2,425	$1,150 - 1,450	$4,598

ACOUSTIC: GC SERIES

GC3 – grand concert style, Sitka spruce top, Sapele back and sides, round soundhole with rings rosette, cream plastic binding, Tropical American mahogany neck, 20-fret bound ebony fingerboard with pearl dot inlays, three-per-side chrome tuners, ebony bridge, tortoise pickguard, 25.5 in. scale, available in Natural finish, mfg. 2007-2012.

	$1,150	$675 - 825	$400 - 500	$1,548

GC4 – grand concert style, Sitka spruce top, Ovangkol back and sides, round soundhole with rings rosette, cream plastic binding, Tropical American mahogany neck, 20-fret bound ebony fingerboard with pearl dot inlays, three-per-side chrome tuners, ebony bridge, tortoise pickguard, 25.5 in. scale, available in Natural finish, mfg. 2007-2012.

	$1,400	$775 - 975	$450 - 575	$1,848

GC5 – grand concert style, red cedar top, Tropical American mahogany back and sides, round soundhole with fancy rosette, ivoroid plastic binding, Tropical American mahogany neck, 20-fret bound ebony fingerboard with abalone dot inlays, three-per-side gold tuners, ebony bridge, 25.5 in. scale, available in Natural finish, mfg. 2007-2012.

	$2,250	$1,250 - 1,575	$750 - 925	$2,998

GC6 – grand concert style, Sitka spruce top, Big Leaf maple back and sides, round soundhole with fancy rosette, ivoroid plastic binding, Tropical American mahogany neck, 20-fret bound ebony fingerboard with abalone dot inlays, three-per-side gold tuners, ebony bridge, 25.5 in. scale, available in Natural finish, mfg. 2007-2012.

	$2,250	$1,250 - 1,575	$750 - 925	$2,998

GC7 – grand concert style, red cedar top, Indian rosewood back and sides, round soundhole with fancy rosette, ivoroid plastic binding, Tropical American mahogany neck, 20-fret bound ebony fingerboard with abalone dot inlays, three-per-side gold tuners, ebony bridge, 25.5 in. scale, available in Natural finish, mfg. 2007-2012.

	$2,250	$1,250 - 1,575	$750 - 925	$2,998

GC8 – grand concert style, Sitka spruce top, Indian rosewood back and sides, round soundhole with fancy rosette, ivoroid plastic binding, Tropical American mahogany neck, 20-fret bound ebony fingerboard with abalone dot inlays, three-per-side gold tuners, ebony bridge, 25.5 in. scale, available in Natural finish, mfg. 2007-2012.

	$2,250	$1,250 - 1,575	$750 - 925	$2,998

GC-K – Grand Concert body style, Sitka spruce top, Hawaiian koa back and sides, round soundhole with abalone rosette, cream plastic binding, abalone pearl purfling, Tropical American mahogany neck, 20-fret bound ebony fingerboard with abalone koa series inlays, three-per-side gold tuners, ebony bridge, 25.5 in. scale, available in Natural finish, hardshell case included, mfg. summer 2007-2012.

	$3,400	$1,875 - 2,350	$1,125 - 1,400	$4,498

ACOUSTIC: GS SERIES

The GS body shape is an original by Bob Taylor. It is similar to the Grand Auditorium with a wider waste and stretched top-end.

GS5 – GS body style, solid cedar top, solid mahogany back and sides, round soundhole with abalone rosette, ivoroid body and neck binding, 14/20-fret rosewood fingerboard with abalone dot inlays, rosewood headstock veneer with three-per-side gold tuners, ebony bridge, available in Natural finish, mfg. 2006-2012.

	$2,250	$1,250 - 1,575	$750 - 925	$2,998

* **GS5-12 12-String** – similar to the GS5 respectively, except in 12-string configuration with six-per-side tuners, mfg. 2008-2012.

	$2,400	$1,350 - 1,675	$825 - 1,025	$3,198

MSR/NOTES	100%	EXCELLENT	AVERAGE	LAST MSR

GS6 – GS body style, solid cedar top, solid Sitka spruce top, solid maple back and sides, round soundhole with abalone rosette, ivoroid body and neck binding, 14/20-fret rosewood fingerboard with abalone dot inlays, rosewood headstock veneer with three-per-side gold tuners, ebony bridge, available in Natural finish, mfg. 2006-2012.

	$2,250	$1,250 - 1,575	$750 - 925	$2,998

* *GS6-12 12-String* – similar to the GS6, except in 12-string configuration with six-per-side tuners, mfg. 2009-2012.

	$2,400	$1,350 - 1,675	$825 - 1,025	$3,198

GS7 – GS body style, solid cedar top, Indian rosewood back and sides, round soundhole with abalone rosette, ivoroid body and neck binding, 14/20-fret rosewood fingerboard with abalone dot inlays, rosewood headstock veneer with three-per-side gold tuners, ebony bridge, available in Natural finish, mfg. 2006-2012.

	$2,250	$1,250 - 1,575	$750 - 925	$2,998

* *GS7-12 12-String* – similar to the GS7 respectively, except in 12-string configuration with six-per-side tuners, mfg. 2012 only.

	$2,400	$1,350 - 1,675	$825 - 1,025	$3,198

GS8 – GS body style, solid spruce top, solid Indian rosewood back and sides, round soundhole with abalone rosette, ivoroid body and neck binding, 14/20-fret rosewood fingerboard with abalone dot inlays, rosewood headstock veneer with three-per-side gold tuners, ebony bridge, available in Natural finish, mfg. 2006-2012.

	$2,250	$1,250 - 1,575	$750 - 925	$2,998

* *GS8-12 12-String* – similar to the GS8, except in 12-string configuration with six-per-side tuners, mfg. 2008-2012.

	$2,400	$1,350 - 1,675	$825 - 1,025	$3,198

GS-K – Grand Symphony body style, Sitka spruce top, Hawaiian koa back and sides, round soundhole with abalone rosette, cream plastic binding, abalone pearl purfling, Tropical American mahogany neck, 20-fret bound ebony fingerboard with abalone koa series inlays, three-per-side gold tuners, ebony bridge, 25.5 in. scale, available in Natural finish, hardshell case included, mfg. summer 2007-2012.

	$3,400	$1,875 - 2,350	$1,125 - 1,400	$4,498

* *GS-K-12 12-String* – similar to the GS-K, except in 12-string configuration with six-per-side tuners, mfg. 2009-2012.

	$3,550	$1,950 - 2,450	$1,150 - 1,450	$4,698

GS MINI – mini GS-style body, solid Sitka spruce top, laminated Sapele back and sides, three-ring soundhole rosette, B/W/B top purfling, Sapele neck, 14/20-fret ebony fingerboard with pearloid dot inlays, Lexan headstock overlay, three-per-side chrome tuners, ebony bridge, tortoise pickguard, available in Natural satin finish, 23.5 in. scale, GS mini hard bag included, mfg. summer 2010-present.

MSR $678	$500	$300 - 375	$175 - 225	

* *GS Mini Mahogany* – similar to the GS Mini, except has a Tropical mahogany top, available in Natural satin finish, GS mini hard bag included, mfg. 2012-present.

MSR $678	$500	$300 - 375	$175 - 225	

ACOUSTIC: KOA SERIES

Different Koa Series models feature Engelmann spruce, western red cedar, or Hawaiian koa tops. Each model features Hawaiian koa back and sides, tortoiseshell body binding, abalone rosette, mahogany neck, 20-fret ebony fingerboard with a special 1995 Limited Edition pattern, ebony bridge with black bridgepins, ebony peghead veneer, gold plated Grover tuners. In 2000, all models that had cutaways had electronics put in them. The Koa Models were discontinued in 2003 and reintroduced again in 2006.

K 10 – dreadnought body, Engelmann spruce top, three-per-side tuners, available in Natural gloss finish, mfg. 1998-2003, 2006.

	N/A	$1,750 - 2,200	$1,050 - 1,325	$4,098

* *K 10CE* – similar to the K 10, except has a single Venetian cutaway and Taylor Expression electronics, mfg. summer 2007-2012.

	$3,900	$2,200 - 2,750	$1,325 - 1,650	$5,198

K 12 – grand concert body, Engelmann spruce top, three-per-side tuners, available in Natural gloss finish, mfg. 1998-2003, 2006.

	N/A	$1,875 - 2,350	$1,125 - 1,400	$4,308

* *K 12CE* – similar to the K 12, except has a single Venetian cutaway and Taylor Expression electronics, mfg. summer 2007-2012.

	$3,900	$2,200 - 2,750	$1,325 - 1,650	$5,198

K 14 CE – grand auditorium body with single Venetian cutaway, solid Englemann spruce or Sitka spruce top, Fishman Onboard Blender or Expression electronics, available in Natural gloss finish, mfg. 1998-2003, 2006, summer 2007-2012.

	$3,900	$2,200 - 2,750	$1,325 - 1,650	$5,198

K 16CE – single Venetian cutaway Grand Symphony body, Sitka spruce top, Hawaiian Koa back and sides, round soundhole with abalone rosette, maple top and back body binding, Tropical American mahogany neck, 14/20-fret ebony fingerboard with Koa Series outline inlays, ebony headstock overlay, three-per-side gold tuners, ebony bridge, Taylor ES-T electronics, Natural Gloss finish, 25.5 in. scale, hardshell case included, mfg. 2008-2012.

	$3,900	$2,200 - 2,750	$1,325 - 1,650	$5,198

MSR/NOTES	100%	EXCELLENT	AVERAGE	LAST MSR

K 20 – dreadnought body, koa top/back/sides/neck, round soundhole, tortoise pickguard, 3-stripe bound body, abalone rosette, 14/20-fret rosewood fingerboard with pearl diamond inlay, rosewood bridge with black abalone dot pins, ebony veneer with abalone logo inlay on peghead, 3-per-side gold tuners, available in Natural finish, disc. 1992.

	N/A	$1,850 - 2,300	$1,125 - 1,400	$2,115

This model had solid spruce top as an option.

* **K 20 C** – similar to the K 20, except features single Venetian cutaway body, Hawaiian koa top, mahogany neck, ebony fingerboard with 1995 Limited Edition pattern inlay, ebony bridge, tortoise body binding, available in Natural gloss finish, mfg. 1998-2000.

	N/A	$2,000 - 2,500	$1,200 - 1,500	$3,896

* **K 20 CE** – similar to the K 20C, except has Fishman onboard Blender system, mfg. 2001-03, 2006, summer 2007-2012.

	$4,000	$2,275 - 2,850	$1,350 - 1,700	$5,398

K 22 (VERSION I) – grand concert body, koa top/back/sides/neck, round soundhole, tortoise pickguard, 3-stripe bound body, abalone rosette, 14/20-fret rosewood fingerboard with pearl diamond inlay, rosewood bridge with black abalone dot pins, ebony veneer with abalone logo inlay on peghead, 3-per-side gold tuners, available in Natural finish, disc. 1992.

	N/A	$2,000 - 2,500	$1,200 - 1,500	$2,190

K 22 (VERSION II) – similar to the K 22 (Version I), except features a Hawaiian koa top, mahogany neck, tortoise body binding, 14/20-fret ebony fingerboard with the 1995 Limited Edition pattern inlay, ebony bridge, mfg. 1998-2000.

	N/A	$2,000 - 2,500	$1,200 - 1,500	$3,872

* **K 22CE** – similar to the K 22, except has a single cutaway and Fishman onboard Blender or Expression electronics, mfg. 2000-03, 2006, summer 2007-present.

MSR $5,398	$4,000	$2,275 - 2,850	$1,350 - 1,700	

K 24CE – single Venetian cutaway Grand Auditorium body, Hawaiian Koa top, back, and sides, round soundhole with abalone rosette, maple top and back body binding, Tropical American mahogany neck, 14/20-fret bound ebony fingerboard with Koa Series outline inlays, ebony headstock overlay, three-per-side gold tuners, ebony bridge, Taylor Expression electronics, Natural Gloss finish, 25.5 in. scale, hardshell case included, mfg. summer 2007-present.

MSR $5,398	$4,000	$2,275 - 2,850	$1,350 - 1,700	

K 26CE – single Venetian cutaway Grand Symphony body, Hawaiian Koa top, back, and sides, round soundhole with abalone rosette, maple top and back body binding, Tropical American mahogany neck, 14/20-fret ebony fingerboard with Koa Series outline inlays, ebony headstock overlay, three-per-side gold tuners, ebony bridge, Taylor ES-T electronics, Natural Gloss finish, 25.5 in. scale, hardshell case included, mfg. 2008-present.

MSR $5,398	$4,000	$2,275 - 2,850	$1,350 - 1,700	

K 54 CE 12-STRING – 12-string configuration, grand auditorium single cutaway-style body, Expression electronics, six-per-side tuners, available in Natural finish, mfg. 2006, summer 2007-2011.

	$4,000	$2,275 - 2,850	$1,350 - 1,700	$5,398

K 55 12-STRING – 12-string configuration, jumbo koa body, available in Natural finish, mfg. 2000-03, 2006.

	N/A	$2,150 - 2,700	$1,275 - 1,600	$4,708

K 56CE 12-STRING – 12-string configuration, single Venetian cutaway Grand Symphony body, Sitka spruce top, Hawaiian koa back and sides, round soundhole with abalone rosette, maple top and back body binding, Tropical American mahogany neck, 14/20-fret bound ebony fingerboard with Koa Series inlays, ebony headstock overlay, six-per-side gold tuners, ebony bridge, Taylor Expression electronics, Natural Gloss finish, 25.5 in. scale, hardshell case included, mfg. summer 2007-2012.

	$4,000	$2,275 - 2,850	$1,350 - 1,700	$5,398

K 64CE 12-STRING – 12-string configuration, single Venetian cutaway Grand Auditorium body, Hawaiian Koa top, back, and sides, round soundhole with abalone rosette, maple top and back body binding, Tropical American mahogany neck, 14/20-fret bound ebony fingerboard with Koa Series outline inlays, ebony headstock overlay, six-per-side gold tuners, ebony bridge, Taylor Expression electronics, Natural Gloss finish, 25.5 in. scale, hardshell case included, mfg. summer 2007-2011.

	$4,200	$2,350 - 2,950	$1,400 - 1,750	$5,598

K 65 12-STRING – 12-string configuration, jumbo body, Hawaiian koa top, six-per-side tuners, available in Natural gloss finish, mfg. 1998-99.

	N/A	$2,250 - 2,800	$1,350 - 1,700	$4,246

* **K 65CE 12-String** – similar to the K 65, except has a single cutaway and Fishman onboard Blender or Expression electronics, mfg. 2000-03, 2006, summer 2007-2011.

	$4,200	$2,350 - 2,950	$1,400 - 1,750	$5,598

K 66CE 12-STRING – 12-string configuration, single Venetian cutaway Grand Symphony body, Hawaiian Koa top, back, and sides, round soundhole with abalone rosette, maple top and back body binding, Tropical American mahogany neck, 14/20-fret ebony fingerboard with Koa Series outline inlays, ebony headstock overlay, six-per-side gold tuners, ebony bridge, Taylor ES-T electronics, Natural Gloss finish, 25.5 in. scale, hardshell case included, mfg. 2008-present.

MSR $5,598	$4,200	$2,350 - 2,950	$1,400 - 1,750	

MSR/NOTES	100%	EXCELLENT	AVERAGE	LAST MSR

ACOUSTIC: LIMITED EDITIONS 2004-2010

Every year, Taylor releases several limited edition guitars. These guitars are typically based on many existing models with a few tweaks. These guitars are also not factory cataloged or priced. Most of the time these guitars are only available through special or custom orders and many dealers do not stock them. We are slowly putting together individual model listings together on Taylor Limited Editions, but it is difficult to obtain specifications, quantities, and original MSRs. Anyone with documented information on a Taylor Limited Edition is encouraged to send it to Blue Book Publications. Also, if you are looking for a value on a Taylor Limited Edition guitar that is not listed here, please email or call Blue Book Publications and we'll try to provide you with that information. Taylor's website is also a very good resource for past limited editions.

2004 Fall Limited Editions: The 300 Series feature Tasmanian Koa back and sides and were available as the **310-L7** (MSR $1,598), **310CE-L7** (MSR $2,198), **312CE-L7** (MSR $2,268), **314-L7** (MSR $1,738), **314CE-L7** (MSR $2,338), **315-L7** (MSR $1,738), **315CE-L7** (MSR $2,338), **354CE-L7** (MSR $2,538), **355-L7** (MSR $1,938), and the **355CE-L7** (MSR $2,538). The 400 Series feature Indian rosewood back and sides and were available as the **410-L7** (MSR $1,848), **410CE-L7** (MSR $2,448), **412CE-L7** (MSR $2,538), **414-L7** (MSR $2,018), **414CE-L7** (MSR $2,618), **415-L7** (MSR $2,018), **415CE-L7** (MSR $2,618), **454CE-L7** (MSR $2,618), **455-L7** (MSR $2,218), and the **455CE-L7** (MSR $2,818). The 600 Series feature curly maple 3-piece back with koa center wedge, koa binding, & deluxe hardshell case and were available as the **610CE-L7** (MSR $3,848), **612CE-L7** (MSR $3,998), **614CE-L7** (MSR $4,138), **615CE-L7** (MSR $4,138), **654CE-L7** (MSR $4,338), **655-L7** (MSR $3,738), and the **655CE-L7** (MSR $4,338). The 800 Series feature Cocobolo 3-piece back with maple center wedge, concobolo-edged top & deluxe hardshell case and were available as the **810-L7** (MSR $3,398), **810CE-L7** (MSR $3,998), **812CE-L7** (MSR $4,148), **814-L7** (MSR $3,698), **814CE-L7** (MSR $4,298), **815-L7** (MSR $3,698), **815CE-L7** (MSR $4,298), **854CE-L7** (MSR $4,498), **855-L7** (MSR $3,898), and the **855CE-L7** (MSR $4,498). The 900 Series Brazilian rosewood back and sides with "Cindy" inlay & deluxe hardshell case and were available as the **910-L7** (MSR $4,798), **910CE-L7** (MSR $5,398), **912CE-L7** (MSR $5,608), **914CE-L7** (MSR $5,818), **915CE-L7** (MSR $5,818), **954CE-L7** (MSR $6,018), and the **955-L7** (MSR $5,418). The Koa Series feature Hawaiian koa back and sides with "Tropical Vine" inlay & deluxe hardshell case and were available as the **K10-L7** (MSR $4,448), **K12-L7** (MSR $4,648), **K14CE-L7** (MSR $5,438), **K20CE-L7** (MSR $5,248), **K22CE-L7** (MSR $5,448), **K55-L7** (MSR $5,038), **K54CE-L7** (MSR $5,538), and the **K65CE-L7** (MSR $5,838).

2005 Fall Limited Editions: All 2005 LEs feature Expression electronics: **310CE-L10** Hawaiian koa (MSR $2,248), **320CE-L10** Hawaiian koa and koa top (MSR $2,348), **314CE-L10** Hawaiian koa grand auditorium (MSR $2,388), **324CE-L10** Hawaiian koa and koa top grand auditorium (MSR $2,488), **410CE-L10** Indian rosewood dreadnought cutaway (MSR $2,448), **414CE-L10** Indian rosewood grand auditorium (MSR $2,618), **512CE-L10** mahogany grand concert cutaway (MSR $3,378), **514CE-L10** mahogany grand auditorium (MSR $3,498), **810CE-L10** cocobolo dreadnought cutaway (MSR $3,998), and the **814CE-L10** cocobolo grand auditorium cutaway (MSR $4,298).

Taylor also released a 30th Anniversary line of guitars to commemorate their 30th Anniversary as a company.

2007 Limited Editions: 410CE-LTD (MSR $2,498) has a Sitka spruce top and Indian rosewood back and sides, the **814CE-LTD** (MSR $4,998) has a Sitka spruce top and walnut back and sides, the **914CE-LTD** (MSR $7,498) has a Sitka spruce top and Brazilian rosewood back and sides, **GS4E-LTD** (MSR $2,198) has a Sitka spruce top and Tazmanian Blackwood back and sides, and the **T5-LTD** (MSR $3,498) has a flamed maple top and Big Leaf maple back and sides.

For Taylor's 35th Anniversary (2009), they introduced a line of limited edition models called the 35th Anniversary Series. Models included the **9-String** (MSR $4,998), **12-Fret** (MSR $6,998), **Armrest** (MSR $7,498), **Baritone** (MSR $4,998), **Brazilian** (MSR N/A), **Parlor** (MSR $5,998), **Solidbody Koa** (MSR $3,798), **Solidbody Maple** (MSR $3,798), **T3 Cocobolo** (MSR $3,798), and the **T3 Koa** (MSR $3,798).

2009 Fall Limited Editions: include the 400 Indian Rosewood Series with the **410CE-LTD-R** (MSR $2,798), **412CE-LTD-R** (MSR $2,798), **414CE-LTD-R** (MSR $2,798), and the **416CE-LTD-R** (MSR $2,798), the GA/GS Quilted Maple Series with the **GACE-LTD-M** (MSR $4,998) and the **GSCE-LTD-M** (MSR $4,998), and the GA/GS Cocobolo Series with the **GACE-LTD-C** (MSR $4,998) and the **GSCE-LTD-C** (MSR $4,998).

2010 Spring Limited Editions: include the Walnut 400 Series with the **410CE-LTD** (MSR $2,798/100% $2,200), **412CE-LTD** (MSR $2,798/100% $2,200), **414CE-LTD** (MSR $2,798/100% $2,200), and the **416CE-LTD** (MSR $2,798/100% $2,200), the Blackwood 500 Series with the **514CE-LTD** (MSR $3,698/100% $2,900) and the **516CE-LTD** (MSR $3,698/100% $2,900), the Imbuia 700 Series with the **714CE-LTD** (MSR $3,898/100% $3,000) and the **714CE-LTD** (MSR $3,898/100% $3,000), and the **12-Fret-LTD** Hawaiian Koa (MSR $5,198/100% $4,000).

2010 Fall Limited Editions: include the 800 Series with the **810CE-LTD**, **812CE-LTD**, **814CE-LTD**, and the **816CE-LTD**, the Koa 500 Series with the **510CE-LTD**, **512CE-LTD**, **514CE-LTD**, and the **516CE-LTD**, the GS Mahogany Series with the **Mahogany GS-LTD**, and the All-Mahogany Electric Series with the **SB-X LTD** and the **T3-B LTD**.

CUJO GUITAR LIMITED EDITION – Grand Auditorium or Dreadnought-style body, spruce top, walnut back and sides used from the walnut tree in the movie Cujo, round soundhole with red spiny oyster shell rosette, tortoise body binding with multi-ply B/W/Red/W top inlay, mahogany neck, 14/20-fret tortoise-bound ebony fingerboard with elaborate Cujo-themed inlays made of agoya shell, abalone, black oyster shell, mahogany, maple, and Formica, ebony headstock overlay with pearl Taylor logo and red spiny oyster shell "Cujo" inlay, three-per-side gold tuners, ebony bridge, interior label signed by Bob Taylor and Stephen King, available in Natural finish, 25.5 in. scale, limited edition run of 250 instruments (125 in Grand Auditorium body and 125 in Dreadnought body), mfg. 1995 only.

| N/A | $1,600 - 2,000 | $1,050 - 1,300 | |

MSR/NOTES	100%	EXCELLENT	AVERAGE	LAST MSR

LTG LIBERTY TREE GUITAR LIMITED EDITION – Grand Concert-style body, Sitka spruce top, Liberty Tree tulip poplar back and sides, round soundhole with maple, bloodwood, koa, and color core 13-star American Flag themed rosette, ivoroid body binding with abalone top inlay, Tropical American mahogany neck, 14/20-fret bound ebony fingerboard with 12-20 fret laser etched maple, bloodwood, koa, and color core rendition of a rolled Declaration of Independence that extends into the top of the guitar, bound headstock with ebony overlay, Taylor logo, and 13 star bloodwood and dyed maple American Flag inlay, three-per-side gold tuners with ebony buttons, ebony bridge, available in Natural gloss finish, 25.5 in. scale, limited edition run of approximately 400 instruments, mfg. 2002 only.

	N/A	$5,000 - 6,000	$3,000 - 3,750	

The back and sides of this guitar is from the Liberty Tree that originally stood on St. John's College in Annapolis, MD. Hurricane Floyd destroyed the tree in 1999, and Bob Taylor eventually purchased the salvageable wood from the tree.

ACOUSTIC: LIMITED EDITIONS 2011-PRESENT

2011 Spring Limited Editions include the **Macassar Ebony 12-Fret**, the **Macassar Ebony T3/B-LTD**, the Walnut Series with the **W12CE-LTD**, **W14CE-LTD**, and the **W16CE-LTD**, the Walnut 400 Series with the **412CE-LTD**, **414CE-LTD**, and the **416CE-LTD**, and the Mahogany Series with the **MAH DN-LTD**, **MAH GA-LTD**, **MAH GC-LTD**, and the **MAH GS-LTD**.

2012 Spring Limited Editions include the Hawaiian Koa 300 Series with the **310CE-LTD** (MSR $2,898), **312CE-LTD** (MSR $2,898), **312CE-N-LTD** (MSR $2,898), **314CE-LTD** (MSR $2,898), **314CE-N-LTD** (MSR $2,898), and the **316CE-LTD** (MSR $2,898), the **416CE-LTD Baritone** (MSR $2,798), the GS Mini Limited Series with the **GS Mini Blackwood** (MSR $748), **GS Mini Maple** (MSR $748), and the **GS Mini Rosewood** (MSR $748), and the Cocobolo 800 Series with the **814CE-LTD** (MAP $3,599) and the **816CE-LTD** (MAP $3,599).

ACOUSTIC: NYLON SERIES

NS24E – grand auditorium nylon body, Sitka spruce top, laminated Indian rosewood back and sides, Mexican cypress soundhole rosette, black body binding, Tropical American mahogany neck, ebony fingerboard, Indian rosewood headstock overlay, three-per-side open-style chrome tuners with pearl buttons, ebony bridge, ES-N electronics, available in Natural finish, 25.5 in. scale, hardshell case included, mfg. 2010-2011.

	$900	$525 - 600	$325 - 400	$1,198

* **NS24CE** – similar to the NS24E, except has a single smooth cutaway, mfg. 2010-2011.

	$1,000	$600 - 700	$375 - 450	$1,398

NS32CE – deep grand concert nylon body, Sitka spruce top, African mahogany back and sides, ebony fingerboard and bridge, three-per-side open tuners, available in Natural finish, electronics, mfg. 2003-2011.

	$1,450	$850 - 1,000	$525 - 600	$1,968

NS34CE – deep grand auditorium cutaway nylon body, Sitka spruce top, African Mahogany back and sides, ebony fingerboard and bridge, three-per-side open tuners, electronics, available in Natural finish, mfg. 2004-2011.

	$1,500	$900 - 1,050	$550 - 650	$2,038

NS42CE – deep grand concert nylon body, Sitka spruce top, ovangkol back and sides, ebony fingerboard and bridge, three-per-side open tuners, available in Natural finish, electronics, mfg. 2003-06.

	N/A	$950 - 1,150	$625 - 725	$2,188

NS44CE – deep grand auditorium cutaway nylon body, Sitka spruce top, Ovangkol back and sides, ebony fingerboard and bridge, three-per-side open tuners, electronics, available in Natural finish, mfg. 2004-06.

	N/A	$1,000 - 1,200	$625 - 750	$2,268

NS52CE – deep grand concert nylon body, Sitka spruce top, mahogany back and sides, ebony fingerboard and bridge, three-per-side open tuners, available in Natural finish, electronics, mfg. 2003-06.

	N/A	$1,400 - 1,750	$850 - 1,000	$3,228

NS54CE – deep grand auditorium cutaway nylon body, Western Red Cedar top, Tropical African Mahogany back and sides, Indian Rosewood binding, ebony fingerboard and bridge, three-per-side open tuners, electronics, available in Natural Gloss finish, mfg. 2004-06.

	N/A	$1,450 - 1,800	$900 - 1,050	$3,358

NS62CE – deep grand concert nylon body, Sitka spruce top, maple back and sides, ebony fingerboard, cocobolo (disc. mid-2010) or ebony (mid-2010-2011) headstock overlay, three-per-side open tuners, cocobolo (disc. mid-2010) or ebony (mid-2010-2011) bridge, available in Natural finish, electronics, mfg. 2003-2011.

	$2,700	$1,650 - 1,900	$1,100 - 1,250	$3,698

NS64CE – deep grand auditorium cutaway nylon body, Englemann spruce top, Big Leaf maple back and sides, Indian Rosewood binding, cocobolo fingerboard, cocobolo (disc. mid-2010) or ebony (mid-2010-2011) headstock overlay, three-per-side open tuners, cocobolo (disc. mid-2010) or ebony (mid-2010-2011) bridge, electronics, available in Natural Gloss finish, mfg. 2004-2011.

	$2,850	$1,750 - 2,050	$1,150 - 1,350	$3,848

NS72CE – deep grand concert nylon body, Sitka spruce top, rosewood back and sides, ebony fingerboard and bridge, three-per-side open tuners, available in Natural finish, electronics, mfg. 2003-2011.

	$2,650	$1,600 - 1,850	$1,050 - 1,200	$3,538

MSR/NOTES	100%	EXCELLENT	AVERAGE	LAST MSR

NS74CE – deep grand auditorium cutaway nylon body, Western red cedar top, Indian Rosewood back and sides, Indian Rosewood binding, ebony fingerboard and bridge, three-per-side open tuners, electronics, available in Natural Gloss finish, mfg. 2004-2011.

	$2,750	$1,650 - 1,950	$1,100 - 1,250	$3,678

ACOUSTIC: PRESENTATION SERIES

The Taylor **Presentation Series** guitar models each feature a solid Engelmann spruce top, scalloped X-bracing (tapered on the PS 55), ivoroid body binding with abalone edging, solid Hawaiian koa back and sides, abalone soundhole rosette, mahogany neck, 25.5 in. scale, 20-fret ebony fingerboard with "Byzantine" fretboard inlays, ebony bridge, ebony peghead veneer, Tusq nut and saddle, and gold Schaller tuners with ebony buttons.

Between 2007 and 2010, Taylor stopped producing standard Presentation models and shifted the line over to an entire custom process. Models started at $7,498 for six-strings and $7,698 for 12-strings, and are available in dreadnought, grand auditorium, grand concert, grand symphony, and jumbo body sizes. Cocobolo, maple, and walnut body woods are standard with Hawaiian koa, Macassar ebony, and Madagascar rosewood available for an extra $2,500, and Brazilian rosewood for an extra $4,000. Sitka spruce, Western red cedar, and Englemann Spruce tops are standard with Sinker redwood, Adirondack spruce, walnut, and Hawaiian koa are available for an extra $500.

In 2011, Taylor reintroduced their standard production Presentation Series with cocobolo back, sides, and backstrap, an ebony armrest and binding, green heart abalone purfling, and new fingerboard and headstock inlays. New Presentation models include the **PS10CE** (MSR $9,318), **PS12CE** (MSR $9,318), **PS14CE** (MSR $9,318), **PS15CE** (2011 only, last MSR was $7,998), **PS16CE** (MSR $9,318), **PS54CE** (2011 only, last MSR was $8,198), **PS55CE** (2011 only, last MSR was $8,198), and the **PS56CE** (MSR $9,518).

PS 10 – dreadnought body, three-per-side tuners, available in Natural gloss finish, disc. 2006.

	N/A	$4,750 - 5,500	$2,900 - 3,400	$10,498

* *PS 10 CE* – similar to the PS10, except has a single cutaway and Expression electronics, mfg. 2004-06.

	N/A	$5,000 - 5,800	$3,050 - 3,600	$11,098

PS 12 C – grand concert body with single Venetian cutaway, three-per-side tuners, available in Natural gloss finish, disc. 2003.

	N/A	$4,950 - 5,700	$3,000 - 3,500	$10,168

* *PS 12 CE* – similar to the PS12C, except has Expression electronics, mfg. 2004-06.

	N/A	$5,250 - 6,100	$3,200 - 3,700	$11,628

PS 14 C – grand auditorium body with single Venetian cutaway, three-per-side tuners, available in Natural gloss finish, disc. 2003.

	N/A	$5,100 - 5,900	$3,100 - 3,650	$10,648

* *PS 14 CE* – similar to the PS14, except has Expression electronics, mfg. 2004-06.

	N/A	$5,500 - 6,350	$3,350 - 3,950	$12,148

PS 15 – jumbo body, three-per-side tuners, available in Natural gloss finish, disc. 2006.

	N/A	$5,200 - 6,050	$3,200 - 3,750	$11,548

PS 54 CE 12-STRING – 12-string configuration, grand auditorium cutaway, six-per-side tuners, Expression system electronics, Natural Satin finish, mfg. 2004-06.

	N/A	$5,600 - 6,450	$3,400 - 4,000	$12,348

PS 55 12-STRING – 12-string configuration, jumbo body, six-per-side tuners, available in Natural gloss finish, disc. 2006.

	N/A	$5,300 - 6,150	$3,250 - 3,800	$11,748

* *PS 55 CE 12-String* – similar to the PS55, except has a single cutaway and Expression electronics, mfg. 2004-06.

	N/A	$5,600 - 6,450	$3,400 - 4,000	$12,348

ACOUSTIC: SIGNATURE SERIES

DCSM DAN CRARY SIGNATURE – single rounded cutaway dreadnought body, Sitka spruce top, Indian rosewood back and sides, round soundhole with abalone rosette, five-stripe white plastic body binding, mahogany neck, 14/20-fret bound ebony fingerboard with pearl diamond inlay, bound rosewood headstock overlay with pearl logo inlay, three-per-side gold tuners, ebony bridge with black abalone dot pins, tortoise pickguard, available in Natural gloss finish, body width 16 in., body length 20 in., body depth 4.625 in., 25.5 in. scale, disc. 2000.

	N/A	$1,600 - 2,000	$1,050 - 1,300	$2,798

This model was designed in conjunction with guitarist Dan Crary.

DDSM DOYLE DYKES SIGNATURE – single sharp cutaway dreadnought body, Sitka spruce top, big leaf maple back/sides, round soundhole with abalone rosette, five-stripe ivoroid body binding with abalone edging, mahogany (early models) or hard rock maple (later models) neck, 14/20-fret bound ebony fingerboard with offset pearl thumbnail inlays, bound ebony headstock overlay with pearl flower inlay, three-per-side gold tuners with ebony buttons, ebony bridge, Taylor Expression system or L.R. Baggs electronics, available in Black, Brown Sugar, Natural, Orange, or Trans. Black finish, 25.5 in. scale, mfg. 2000-03, reintroduced 2005-2012.

	$3,750	$2,400 - 2,800	$1,600 - 1,850	$4,998

MSR/NOTES	100%	EXCELLENT	AVERAGE	LAST MSR

DMSM DAVE MATTHEWS SIGNATURE – single cutaway Grand Auditorium body, solid Sitka spruce top, solid Indian rosewood back and sides, abalone soundhole rosette, ivoroid binding, abalone purfling, Tropical American mahogany neck, 14/20-fret ivoroid-bound ebony fingerboard with Dave Matthews "Grux" inlays, bound headstock with Dave Matthews signature overlay, three-per-side gold Gotoh tuners, ebony bridge, Taylor Expression electronics, available in Natural finish with an aged toner on the top, 25.5 in. scale, guitar label and certificate of authenticity personally signed by Matthews, deluxe hardshell case included, mfg. spring 2010-12.

	$4,000	$2,550 - 2,950	$1,700 - 1,950	$5,428

The DMSM Dave Matthews Signature Model is inspired by his 914CE and has custom fingerboard inlays from his guitar that pays tribute to the Dave Matthews Band longtime saxaphone player who died in 2008.

DOYLE DELUXE – single smooth cutaway Grand Auditorium-style body, Sitka spruce top, laminated maple back and sides, round soundhole with pearl fishbone rosette, cream body binding, hard rock maple neck, 14/20-fret bound ebony fingerboard with offset pearl thumbnail inlays, ebony headstock overlay with "Doyle Deluxe" signature, three-per-side chrome tuners, ebony bridge, Taylor ES-T electronics, available in Black finish, 25.5 in. scale, hardshell gig bag included, mfg. 2011 only.

	$1,200	$675 - 800	$350 - 425	$1,498

JMSM JASON MRAZ SIGNATURE – nylon-string configuration, single cutaway Grand Concert-style body, western red cedar top, Indian rosewood back and sides, maple body binding, zodiac soundhole rosette with koa, bubinga, and Mexican cypress, Tropical American mahogany neck, 12/18-fret ebony fingerboard with 12th fret Jason Mraz "Be Love" inlay, slotted headstock with Indian rosewood overlay, three-per-side open-style gold Ping classical tuners with ivoroid buttons, ebony bridge, ES-N electronics, available in Natural finish, 25.5 in. scale, hardshell case included, mfg. 2010-present.

MSR $3,798	$2,900	$1,750 - 2,050	$1,150 - 1,300	

LKSM12 LEO KOTTKE SIGNATURE – 12-string configuration, jumbo body, spruce top, American mahogany back/sides, round soundhole, rosewood body binding, mahogany neck, 14/20-fret ebony fingerboard, rosewood headstock overlay with pearl logo inlay, six-per-side gold tuners, ebony bridge with black pins, available in Natural finish, 17 in. body width, 21 in. body length, 4.625 in. body depth, disc. 2003, reintroduced 2005-2012.

	$2,500	$1,550 - 1,800	$1,000 - 1,150	$3,398

In 1994, 12th fret fingerboard inlay was discontinued. This model was designed in conjunction with guitarist Leo Kottke.

* **LKSM-6 Leo Kottke Signature** – similar to the LKSM, except in six-string configuration with three-per-side tuners, available in Natural gloss finish, 17 in. body width, 21 in. body length, 4.625 in. body depth, mfg. 1997-2003, reintroduced 2005-2012.

	$2,350	$1,400 - 1,650	$900 - 1,050	$3,198

SCCSM STEVEN CURTIS CHAPMAN SIGNATURE – Grand Auditorium-style body, western red cedar top, Indian rosewood back and sides, Indian rosewood body binding, three-ring abalone soundhole rosette, Tropical American mahogany neck, 14/20-fret ebony fingerboard with 12th fret Steven Curtis Chapman "SEE" inlay, black headstock overlay with Taylor logo and Steven Curtis Chapman multi-color flower inlays, three-per-side open-style gold tuners, ebony bridge, tortoise pickguard, Taylor Expression system electronics, available in Tobacco Sunburst finish, 25.5 in. scale, hardshell case included, mfg. 2011-12.

	$3,200	$1,925 - 2,250	$1,275 - 1,475	$3,998

STSM-T5 SERJ TANKIAN SIGNATURE – single cutaway thinline hollow Sapele body, maple top, two split unbound f-holes, black body binding, red purfling, Sapele neck, 21-fret red-bound ebony fingerboard with red Serj Tankian energy wheel inlays, red-bound headstock with black overlay and red Serj Tankian energy wheel, three-per-side tuners, ebony bridge, three total pickups: under-fingerboard neck humbucker, visible bridge humbucker, and acoustic body sensor mounted to the inside surface of the top, three knobs, five-way pickup switch, chrome plated hardware, available in Black finish, 24.875 in. scale, hardshell case and certificate of authenticity included, mfg. 2010-2011.

	$2,400	$1,350 - 1,650	$750 - 900	$3,198

TSBT TAYLOR SWIFT SIGNATURE – 3/4-size dreadnought-style body, solid Sitka spruce top, laminated sapele back and sides, round soundhole with screen printed custom artwork rosette, mahogany neck, 14/19-fret ebony fingerboard with pearloid dot inlays, Lexan headstock overlay, three-per-side chrome tuners, ebony bridge, available in Natural satin finish, 22.75 in. scale, gig bag included, mfg. 2010-present.

MSR $398	$300	$175 - 225	$110 - 140	

ACOUSTIC: SPECIALTY SERIES

12-FRET GRAND CONCERT – single cutaway Grand Concert-style body, solid Sitka spruce top, solid Indian rosewood back and sides, 900 Series abalone soundhole rosette, ivoroid binding, Tropical American mahogany neck, 12/18-fret bound ebony fingerboard with micro dot inlays, slotted headstock with Indian rosewood headstock overlay, three-per-side open-style gold tuners with pearloid buttons, ebony bridge, Taylor Expression electronics, available in Natural gloss finish, 24.875 in. scale, deluxe hardshell case included, mfg. 2010-12.

	$2,900	$1,750 - 2,050	$1,150 - 1,300	$3,898

* **12-Fret Grand Concert Mahogany** – similar to the 12-Fret Grand Concert, except has mahogany back and sides, available in Natural gloss finish, deluxe hardshell case included, mfg. 2012 only.

	$2,900	$1,750 - 2,050	$1,150 - 1,300	$3,898

MSR/NOTES	100%	EXCELLENT	AVERAGE	LAST MSR

BARITONE SIX-STRING CE – baritone configuration tuned B to B, single cutaway GS-style body, solid Sitka spruce top, solid Indian rosewood back and sides, abalone soundhole rosette, Indian rosewood binding, Tropical American mahogany neck, 14/19-fret ebony fingerboard with small diamond inlays, Indian rosewood headstock overlay, three-per-side gold tuners, ebony bridge, Taylor Expression electronics, available in Natural gloss finish, 27 in. scale, deluxe hardshell case included, mfg. 2010-13.

	$3,000	$1,850 - 2,150	$1,200 - 1,400	$3,798

* *Baritone Six-String Mahogany CE* – similar to the Baritone Six-String, except has mahogany back and sides, available in Natural gloss finish, deluxe hardshell case included, mfg. 2012-13.

	$3,000	$1,850 - 2,150	$1,200 - 1,400	$3,798

* *Baritone Eight-String CE* – similar to the Baritone Six-String, except in eight-string configuration with two upper octave strings paired with the third and fourth strings, available in Natural gloss finish, mfg. 2010-13.

	$3,200	$1,900 - 2,250	$1,300 - 1,500	$3,998

»*Baritone Eight-String Mahogany CE* – similar to the Baritone Eight-String, except has mahogany back and sides, available in Natural gloss finish, deluxe hardshell case included, mfg. 2012-13.

	$3,200	$1,900 - 2,250	$1,300 - 1,500	$3,998

ACOUSTIC: WALNUT SERIES

Different Walnut Series models feature Sitka spruce, Western red cedar, or Claro walnut tops. Each Walnut Series guitar models feature scalloped X-bracing (tapered on the W 65), ivoroid body binding with abalone edging, solid Claro walnut back and sides, abalone soundhole rosette, mahogany neck, 25.5 in. scale, 20-fret ebony fingerboard with Original 900 Series inlay pattern, ebony bridge, ebony peghead veneer, Tusq nut and saddle, and gold Grover tuners. Taylor's Walnut Series was introduced in 1998, discontinued in 2003 due to lack of supply, and reintroduced again in 2006 for only that year.

W 10 – dreadnought body, Sitka spruce top, three-per-side tuners, available in Natural gloss finish, mfg. 1998-2003, 2006.

	N/A	$1,450 - 1,800	$950 - 1,150	$3,498

* *W 10CE* – similar to the W10, except has a single cutaway and Fishman onboard Blender or Expression electronics, disc. 2003, 2006.

	N/A	$1,650 - 2,100	$1,050 - 1,300	$4,098

W 12 C – grand concert body with single Venetian cutaway, Western red cedar top, three-per-side tuners, available in Natural gloss finish, mfg. 1998-2000.

	N/A	$1,600 - 2,000	$1,050 - 1,275	$4,070

* *W 12CE* – similar to the W12C, except has a single cutaway and Fishman onboard Blender or Expression electronics, mfg. 2000-03, 2006.

	N/A	$1,750 - 2,200	$1,125 - 1,375	$4,278

W 14 C – grand auditorium body with single Venetian cutaway, Western red cedar top, three-per-side tuners, available in Natural gloss finish, mfg. 1998-2000.

	N/A	$1,650 - 2,100	$1,050 - 1,300	$4,256

* *W 14CE* – similar to the W14C, except has a Fishman onboard Blender or Expression electronics, mfg. 2000-03, 2006.

	N/A	$1,825 - 2,300	$1,150 - 1,400	$4,448

W 15 – jumbo body, Sitka spruce top, three-per-side tuners, available in Natural gloss finish, mfg. 1998-2006.

	N/A	$1,550 - 1,950	$1,025 - 1,250	$3,848

W 54 CE 12-STRING – 12-string configuration, grand auditorium single cutaway-style body, Expression electronics, six-per-side tuners, available in Natural finish, mfg. 2006 only.

	N/A	$1,850 - 2,350	$1,150 - 1,400	$4,648

W 55 12-STRING – 12-string configuration, jumbo body, Sitka spruce top, six-per-side tuners, available in Natural gloss finish, mfg. 2000-03, 2006.

	N/A	$1,650 - 2,100	$1,050 - 1,300	$4,048

W 65 12-STRING – 12-string configuration, jumbo body, Claro walnut top, six-per-side tuners, available in Natural gloss finish, disc.

	N/A	$1,750 - 2,200	$1,125 - 1,375	$4,356

* *W 65CE 12-String* – similar to the W65, except has a single cutaway and Fishman onboard Blender or Expression electronics, mfg. 2000-03, 2006.

	N/A	$2,000 - 2,500	$1,300 - 1,600	$4,848

ACOUSTIC: THINLINE SERIES

The Taylor T-5 Thinline is a fine line between an acoustic and electric guitar. It has a full hollow-body, but has an exposed pickup. There are body sensors (not piezo's) inside to amplify sound. The result of all this creates an electric/acoustic instrument with endless tonal possiblities.

MSR/NOTES	100%	EXCELLENT	AVERAGE	LAST MSR

T5 S STANDARD – single cutaway thinline hollow Sapele body, Sitka spruce top, two split f-holes, multi-layer binding, Tropical American mahogany neck, 21-fret bound ebony fingerboard with micro dot inlays, ebony overlaid headstock, three-per-side tuners, ebony bridge, single exposed pickup, body sensors, three knobs, five-way switch, chrome plated hardware, available in Black, Blue Sunburst, Honey Sunburst, Red Edgeburst, Tobacco Sunburst, or Trans. Black Edgeburst, mfg. 2005-present.

| MSR $2,598 | $2,000 | $1,150 - 1,350 | $700 - 825 | |

* *T512 S Standard 12-String* – similar to the T5 S Standard, except in 12-string configuration and six-per-side tuners, mfg. 2007-present.

| MSR $2,798 | $2,100 | $1,300 - 1,500 | $750 - 875 | |

* *T5 S-1 Standard* – similar to the T5 S Standard, except has a flamed maple top, mfg. 2005-present.

| MSR $3,098 | $2,500 | $1,400 - 1,600 | $900 - 1,050 | |

» *T512 S1 Standard 12-String* – similar to the T5 S1 Standard, except in 12-string configuration and six-per-side tuners, mfg. 2007-present.

| MSR $3,298 | $2,500 | $1,500 - 1,750 | $950 - 1,100 | |

T5 CLASSIC – single cutaway thinline hollow Sapele body, Ovangkol top, two split unbound f-holes, Sapele neck, 21-fret ebony fingerboard with small diamond inlays, ebony headstock overlay, three-per-side tuners, ebony bridge, three total pickups: under-fingerboard neck humbucker, visible bridge humbucker, and acoustic body sensor mounted to the inside surface of the top, three knobs, five-way switch, chrome plated hardware, available in Natural finish, 24.875 in. scale, gig bag included, mfg. 2010-present.

| MSR $2,098 | $1,600 | $875 - 1,100 | $525 - 650 | |

* *T5X-12 Classic 12-String* – similar to the T5 Classic, except in 12-string configuration with six-per-side tuners, mfg. 2011-present.

| MSR $2,298 | $1,750 | $950 - 1,200 | $575 - 725 | |

T5 C CUSTOM – similar to the T5 S Standard, execept has Taylor Artist T-5 fingerboard inlays and gold hardware, available in Blue Edgeburst, Cherry Sunburst, Honey Sunburst, Red Edgeburst, Trans. Black Edgeburst, or Tobacco Sunburst finish, mfg. 2005-present.

| MSR $2,998 | $2,300 | $1,350 - 1,550 | $850 - 1,000 | |

* *T512 C Custom 12-String* – similar to the T5 C Custom, except in 12-string configuration and six-per-side tuners, mfg. 2007-present.

| MSR $3,198 | $2,400 | $1,450 - 1,675 | $925 - 1,075 | |

* *T5 C1 Custom* – similar to the T5 C Custom, except has a maple top, mfg. 2005-present.

| MSR $3,498 | $2,700 | $1,600 - 1,850 | $1,050 - 1,200 | |

» *T512 C1 Custom 12-String* – similar to the T5 C1 Custom, except in 12-string configuration and six-per-side tuners, mfg. 2007-present.

| MSR $3,698 | $2,800 | $1,700 - 1,950 | $1,100 - 1,250 | |

* *T5 C2 Custom* – similar to the T5 C Custom, except has a koa top, mfg. 2005-present.

| MSR $3,798 | $2,900 | $1,750 - 2,000 | $1,150 - 1,300 | |

» *T512 C2 Custom 12-String* – similar to the T5 C2 Custom, except in 12-string configuration and six-per-side tuners, mfg. 2007-present.

| MSR $3,998 | $3,000 | $1,800 - 2,100 | $1,200 - 1,400 | |

* *T5 C3 Custom* – similar to the T5 C Custom, except has a cocobolo top, mfg. 2009-present.

| MSR $3,798 | $2,900 | $1,750 - 2,000 | $1,150 - 1,300 | |

» *T512 C3 Custom 12-String* – similar to the T5 C3 Custom, except in 12-string configuration and six-per-side tuners, mfg. 2009-present.

| MSR $3,998 | $3,000 | $1,800 - 2,100 | $1,200 - 1,400 | |

* *T5 C4 Custom* – similar to the T5 C Custom, except has a walnut top, mfg. 2009-present.

| MSR $3,798 | $2,900 | $1,750 - 2,000 | $1,150 - 1,300 | |

» *T512 C4 Custom 12-String* – similar to the T5 C4 Custom, except in 12-string configuration and six-per-side tuners, mfg. 2009-present.

| MSR $3,998 | $3,000 | $1,800 - 2,100 | $1,200 - 1,400 | |

* *T5 C5 Custom* – similar to the T5 C Custom, except has a Macassar ebony top, mfg. 2009-present.

| MSR $4,548 | $3,450 | $1,950 - 2,350 | $1,250 - 1,500 | |

» *T512 C5 Custom 12-String* – similar to the T5 C5 Custom, except in 12-string configuration and six-per-side tuners, mfg. 2009-present.

| MSR $4,748 | $3,600 | $2,150 - 2,500 | $1,350 - 1,650 | |

ACOUSTIC BASS: AB SERIES

Bob Taylor and Steve Klein collaborated on an acoustic bass design in a 34 in. scale with a Fishman pickup system. The rugged padded gig bag for the AB Series basses lists at $155.

AB 1 – single rounded cutaway body, Sitka spruce top, round soundhole offset to the treble bout, tuned Imbuia ring rosette, Imbuia Brazilian Walnut back/sides, mahogany neck/Imbuia peghead, 24-fret ebony fingerboard with pearl Steve Klein signature inlay, ebony bridge, Imbuia peghead veneer, 2-per-side chrome Grover tuners, available in Natural satin finish, disc. 2003.

| | N/A | $1,450 - 1,800 | $950 - 1,150 | $2,750 |

MSR/NOTES	100%	EXCELLENT	AVERAGE	LAST MSR

AB 2 – similar to the AB 1, except features Imbuia top, available in Natural satin finish, disc. 2003.

	N/A	$1,450 - 1,800	$950 - 1,150	$2,850

AB 3 – similar to the AB 1, except features big leaf maple back/sides, tuned ebony ring rosette, maple neck, ebony peghead veneer, white plastic body binding, available in Amber, Black, Blue, Green, Natural, or Red gloss finish, disc. 2003.

	N/A	$1,500 - 1,850	$1,000 - 1,200	$2,950

AB 4 – similar to the AB 3, except features a maple top, available in Amber, Black, Blue, Green, Natural, or Red gloss finish, disc. 2003.

	N/A	$1,550 - 1,900	$1,050 - 1,250	$3,150

TEISCO

See Teisco Del Rey. Instruments previously produced in Japan. Distributed in the U.S. by Westheimer Musical Instruments of Evanston, IL.

One of the original Teisco importers was George Rose of Los Angeles, California. Some instruments may bear the shortened "Teisco" logo, many others were shipped in unlabeled. Please: no jokes about Teisco "no-casters," (source: Michael Wright, *Guitar Stories*, Volume One).

TEISCO DEL REY

Instruments previously produced in Japan from 1956 to 1973. Distributed in the U.S. by Westheimer Musical Instruments of Evanston, IL.

In 1946, Mr. Atswo Kaneko and Mr. Doryu Matsuda founded the Aoi Onpa Kenkyujo company, makers of the guitars bearing the Teisco and other trademarks (the company name roughly translates to the **Hollyhock Soundwave or Electricity Laboratories**). The Teisco name was chosen by Mr. Kaneko, and was used primarily in domestic markets. Early models include lap steel and electric-Spanish guitars. By the 1950s, the company was producing slab-bodied designs with bolt-on necks. In 1956, the company name was changed to the Nippon Onpa Kogyo Co., Ltd. - but the guitars still stayed Teisco!

As the demand for guitars in the U.S. market began to expand, Mr. Jack Westheimer of WMI Corporation of Evanston, Illinois started to import Japanese guitars in the late 1950s, perhaps circa 1958. WMI began importing the Teisco-built Kingston guitars in 1961, and also used the Teisco Del Rey trademark extensively beginning in 1964. Other Teisco-built guitars had different trademarks (a rebranding technique), and the different brand names will generally indicate the U.S. importer/distributor. The Japanese company again changed names, this time to the Teisco Co. Ltd. The Teisco line included all manners of solid body and semi-hollowbody guitars, and their niche in the American guitar market (as entry level or beginner's guitars) assured steady sales.

In 1967, the Kawai Corporation purchased the Teisco company. Not one to ruin a good thing, Kawai continued exporting the Teisco line to the U.S. (although they did change some designs through the years) until 1973. Due to the recent popularity in the Teisco name, Kawai actually produced some limited edition Teisco Spectrum Five models lately in Japan, although they were not made available to the U.S. market (source: Michael Wright, *Vintage Guitar Magazine*).

One dating method for identifying Teisco guitars (serial numbers are non-existent, and some electronic parts may not conform to the U.S. EIA code) is the change in pickguards that occurred in 1965. Pre-1965 pickguards are plastic construction, while 1965 and post-1965 pickguards are striped metal.

Pricing on Teisco Del Rey models and other Teiscos remains a bit strange. Most models that hang on walls are tagged at $99 (and sometimes lower), but clean cool shaped models sometimes command the $200 to $300 range.

TELE-STAR

Instruments previously produced in Japan circa late 1960s to 1983.

The Tele-Star trademark was distributed in the U.S. by the Tele-Star Musical Instrument Corporation of New York, New York. Tele-Star offered a full range of acoustic, thinline acoustic/electric hollow body, and solid body electric guitars and basses. Many were built by Kawai of Japan, and some models feature sparkle finishes (source: Michael Wright, *Vintage Guitar Magazine*).

TERRAPLANE RESONATOR GUITAR CO.

Instruments currently built in Bridgewater, NJ since 2004.

Luthier Mark Simon began building guitars in the 1970s, and he founded Terraplane in 2004 to build metal-bodied resonators. Simon uses brass and nickel-silver metals, National-style or Dobro-style spider cones, and Jason Lollar pickups in his construction. Simon also offers some non-traditional features in his resonators including a single cutaway and a patent-pending string anchoring system with no actual tailpiece. Simon has built instruments for Johnny Winter, Sonny Landreth, Arlen Roth, and Cindy Cashdollar. His resonators start at $7,700. Simon also offers a line of tube amplifiers designed specifically for use with his resonators. For more information, visit Terraplane's website or contact Simon directly.

CONTACT INFORMATION
TERRAPLANE RESONATOR GUITAR CO.
PO Box 6095
Bridgewater, NJ 08807
Phone No.: 908-218-9229
terraplaneguitars.com
info@terraplaneguitars.com

TEXARKANA

Instruments previously built in Korea. Distributed by the V. J. Rendano Music Company, Inc. of Youngstown, OH.

Texarkana offered a number of acoustic guitar models designed for the entry level or beginning guitar student. Suggested new retail prices ranged from $129 (dreadnought style) up to $379 (cutaway dreadnought with piezo pickup system).

THE MUSIC LINK

Distributor/parent company of a variety of brands located in Hayward, CA.

The Music Link is the distributor and parent company of a variety of trademarks including Axl, The Loar, Recording King, Johnson, and VHT amps. The Music Link was founded in 1997 as a distributor/supplier of mainly entry-level guitars that were produced in Asia in company-owned factories. By the mid-2000s, they had added several brands to their catalog and offer a variety of instruments at all pricing levels. In 2009, The Music Link moved from Brisbane, CA to a larger facility in Hayward, CA.

CONTACT INFORMATION
THE MUSIC LINK
31067 San Clemente Street
Hayward, CA 94544
Phone No.: 415-570-0970
Fax No.: 415-570-0651
www.themusiclink.net
info@themusiclink.net

THOMAS

Instruments previously produced in Italy from the late 1960s through the early 1970s.

Thomas semi-hollowbodies are medium quality guitars that feature original designs (source: Tony Bacon and Paul Day, *The Guru's Guitar Guide*).

THOMAS HUMPHREY GUITARS

Instruments previously produced between 1970 and 2008 in Gardiner, NY and New York City, NY.

Luthier Thomas Humphrey (1948-2008) built classical guitars for almost forty years. In 1985, Humphrey startled the lutherie world when he introduced the **Millennium** models, which featured an innovative, tapered body design and elevated fingerboard. This innovation to the classical guitar represented some of the very few alterations to the fundamental design of the traditional Antonio Torres model. Though initially questioned, the new design has since been universally accepted by both players and other guitar makers.

Luthier Humphrey was known for producing primarily spruce top guitars and (almost exclusively) Brazilian rosewood back and sides. Humphrey produced guitars for the first twenty-seven years in New York City; and later moved to the countryside near the village of Gardiner, NY. In 1996, Humphrey contracted a standardized design of his design to the C.F. Martin Guitar company of Nazareth, PA. The Martin-built versions of Humphrey's design, **Model C-TSH** (Standard Series) and **Model C-1R** (1 Series), were available in late 1996/early 1997. The Martin version of the Humphrey design utilizes both spruce and cedar soundboards as well as rosewood and other back and side material in order to reach a wide range of price points. In late 1997, the C.F. Martin company introduced the Sting Signature version of the Humphrey design (**Model C-MSH** Limited Edition). These Martin instruments were produced through mid-2002. On April 16, 2008, Humphrey died of a heart attack. At the time of his death, Humphrey was building an estimated twenty guitars a year and his instruments are still being used in both recording and concert situations by many of the world's leading guitarists. Also, Humphrey was currently building a variety of new Millenium classical guitars at the time of his passing and an early mentor has agreed to finish these instruments.

Humphrey's classical design features primarily spruce tops and (almost exclusively) Brazilian rosewood back and sides. The classical model design has a tapered body and elevated fingerboard.

Since these guitars are highly regarded, pricing them is a delicate process. Every guitar needs to be valued individually according to the configuration and wood. Prices on older models can range from anywhere between $2,000 and $20,000. Brazillian rosewood brings the highest premium. The *Blue Book of Acoustic Guitars* recommends several appraisals when determining value on a Thomas Humphrey instrument.

THOS SHA CZAR

Instruments previously built in Valley Stream, NY circa late 1970s through 1980s.

Luthier/designer Tom Leiberman of "The Woodshop" in Valley Stream, New York built a number of acoustic bowl-back basses for the past number of years. In addition to a custom bass built several years ago for Jack Cassidy (Hot Tuna), Leiberman also built the **Stanley Clarke Bass** back in the 1970s. Leiberman currently focuses his talents on furniture, but may accept custom commissions (preliminary information courtesy Jeff Meyer). In the late 1970s, Leiberman's Thos Sha Czar bowl-backed basses had a list price of $4,000.

THREET GUITARS

Instruments currently built in Calgary (Alberta), Canada since 1990.

Always interested in music, luthier Judy Threet had been playing guitar both semi-professionally and for pleasure for many years. Initially pursuing an academic career, she earned her Ph.D in Philosophy at Stanford (Palo Alto, California) in 1986; she then taught for a few years at the University of Calgary (Alberta, Canada). While teaching in

CONTACT INFORMATION
THREET GUITARS
1215 13th St. S.E. #212
Calgary, Alberta T2G 3J4 Canada
Phone No.: 403-232-8332
www.threetguitars.com
jthreet@threetguitars.com

Calgary, Threet met luthier Michael Heiden (see Heiden Stringed Instruments) and learned the art of inlay ("as a diversion," she claims).

Living in Calgary at the time, Heiden was gaining a reputation as a highly gifted luthier - and as a result was becoming increasingly busy. Heiden needed some help at his shop (especially doing inlay work), and Threet's Fine Arts background from her early university days served her well as she offered to help. Over the next year and a half, Threet spent time away from her teaching career working with Heiden on inlays, and in the process began to learn the rudiments of guitar building.

In 1990, Threet decided to switch careers and become a luthier. She asked Heiden to teach her how to build and repair guitars, and it was agreed that under his careful supervision she would build a guitar from start to finish. When Heiden subsequently moved to British Columbia, Threet opened her own shop in 1991. Initially concentrating on guitar repair, Threet's focus shifted to building acoustic guitars. She designed and completed eight guitars by the end of 1994.

In her current location (a warehouse loft in one of Calgary's oldest areas), Threet individually handcrafts acoustic guitars and often customizes them to her client's wishes. Custom inlays are a specialty and are highly encouraged.

Threet guitars are relatively small-bodied instruments that are lightweight but strong and are especially well-suited to finger style playing. Threet estimates that she produces six to eight instruments per year.

Threet individually handcrafts each guitar, and takes great care in choosing the tonewoods and in voicing the tops. Necks are entirely handcarved and are joined in the traditional dovetail joint. Each instrument is monitored throughout the building process to optimize its tone. Many Custom Options, such as custom neck shapes, nut widths, string spacings, various tonewoods and custom inlays are available; most at an additional cost.

All five Threet models are available either **Deluxe** or **Custom**. The Deluxe configuration includes a Sitka spruce top, back and sides of either Honduran mahogany or Indian rosewood, ebony binding/fingerboard/bridge, abalone rosette, and a nitrocellulose lacquer finish. The Custom configuration, by far the most common, might feature some other combination of tonewoods, a rosette of a different style, a custom inlay, etc. Previously, Threet offered a Standard configuration.

The five Threet models correspond roughly to the traditional sizes of **0, 00, 000, dreadnought**, and **mini-jumbo**. Threet's **Model A** is practically a parlor sized guitar, with dimensions: body length - 18.375 in., width - 13.75 in., and depth - 3.5 in. tapering to 4.25 in.. The **Model B** is a slightly larger parlor sized guitar: body length - 18.875 in., width - 14.125 in., and depth - 3.25 in. tapering to 4.125 in.. The **Model C** is larger still, with dimensions: body length - 19.375 in., width - 14.5 in., and depth - 3.25 in. tapering to 4.125 in.. The **Model D** is a hybrid size best described as a cross between a Model C and a Dreadnought: body length - 20 in., width - 15.25 in., and depth - 3.5 in. tapering to 4.5 in.. Models A, B, and C have a 24 27/32 in. scale, while the Model D has a 25 11/32 in. scale. The **Model E** has a tighter waist and rounder bouts than the Model D: body length - 20 in., width - 15.625 in., and depth - 3.5 in. tapering to 4.5 in.. Models A and B have a 24.9 in. scale. Model D has a 25.4 in. scale. Models C and E are available in either of these scales. The price for a Deluxe guitar (without case) is $6,000.

For further information regarding Custom pricing, inlay work, and additional model specifications, please contact luthier Judy Threet directly.

TILTON

Instruments previously manufactured in Boston, MA from 1865 to the early 1900s.

The Oliver Ditson Company, Inc. was formed in 1835 by music publisher Oliver Ditson (1811-1888). Ditson was a primary force in music merchandising, distribution, and retail sales on the East Coast. He also helped establish two musical instrument manufacturers: The John Church Company of Cincinnati, Ohio, and Lyon & Healy (Washburn) in Chicago, Illinois.

In 1865, Ditson established a manufacturing branch of his company under the supervision of John Haynes, called the John C. Haynes Company. This branch built guitars for a number of trademarks, such as **Bay State**, **Tilton**, and **Haynes Excelsior** (source: Tom Wheeler, *American Guitars*).

TIMELESS INSTRUMENTS

Instruments currently built in Tugaske (Saskatchewan), Canada, since 1980.

Timeless Instruments is owned and operated by David Freeman. Founded in 1980, it has been contributing to lutherie around the world for over 30 years. Timeless Instruments offers training to new and developing Luthiers, supplies for a variety of instrument construction, as well as creating fine custom built instruments.

CONTACT INFORMATION
TIMELESS INSTRUMENTS
PO Box 51
Tugaske, Saskatchewan S0H 4B0
Canada
Phone No.: 1-888-884-2753
www.timelessinstruments.com
david@timelessinstruments.com

As a builder, David is constantly pushing himself in the areas of research, design, and craftsmanship. He draws on his extensive experience of teaching and building since 1980. He builds one instrument at a time, focusing on sound, playability, and aesthetics. He has completed a series of instruments researching off-center (offcet) soundholes. This has allowed him to build guitars featuring 24 frets with a deep cutaway for easy access to the fingerboard, opening up more options for the player. The offset soundhole also increases the ability for the player to hear themselves without compromising projection to the audience. It acts like a side port monitor but keeps the projection straight out to the audience.

After 30 plus years, David has a large inventory selection of aged wood dating as far back as the 1960s to choose from when creating a new instrument. Back and sides can be built of traditional rosewoods, figured maple and mahogany are available, as well as a selection of alternative tonewoods. A sampling includes: Ancient Kauri, Spanish Cedar, American Black Walnut, Cherry, figured Hawaiian Koa, Holly, and Cucumber Magnolia. For tops there are five types of spruce, (Sitka, Italian sp,

German sp, Engelmann, Lutz,) red cedar, and yellow cedar, sub-alpine fir, and Douglas fir. Neck wood can be mahogany, cherry, walnut, and maple for steel strings or Spanish cedar and yellow cedar for flamencos and classicals.

Timeless Instruments has also begun a line of Tenor Ukuleles " The White Tui" model features New Zealand Ancient Kauri for back & sides, with spruce of cedar soundboard.

David also builds wooden body resonators - both round neck and square neck - and harps of various sizes as custom builds. From 22 string lap harps to 36 string floor models the wood used varies with the sound and appearance the customer desires.

In the fall of 2011, Seth Freeman (David's son) began working at Timeless Instruments and works in building and marketing. A new website is launching in December 2014. He is also training to teach lutherie in the future.

SCHOOL OF LUTHERIE

Timeless Instruments began the School of Lutherie in 1986 to provide Canadians with musical instrument construction training. Since then people from over twenty-five different countries have studied here, going on to some form of musical instrument construction.

The school of lutherie consists of a seven-week immersion course. Each student designs and creates an instrument under the guidance of David Freeman. Taking only seven students at a time, David develops an understanding of each student's skill level to optimize the learning experience of each student. He teaches both the theories and methods of Lutherie, explaining the foundational principles of sound, both in the top and back plates as well as the bracing systems. Design of the body shape with the effects it has on the style of instrument being built. Playability is taught for the neck action and feel, with the fit of the body being considered. Overall aesthetic design lines, choice of woods and inlays that will appeal to players. Upon completing the core course, students may choose to take optional modular training, deepening their understanding of guitar construction or branching into other areas of lutherie. These include mandolins, resophonic, archtops, harps, or electrics to name a few. Graduates range from successful custom or production builders, repair technicians, retail operators, and hobbyists.

Timeless Instruments' supplies provide builders with a selection of woods and solutions for their building needs. As a supplier, David has accumulated a variety of traditional and alternative woods. This allows him to provide other builders with exactly what they are looking for. His experience as a luthier helps many new builders to make informed decisions on the supplies they need and ensure they receive high quality products. Recently he has been expanding to provide materials such as mahogany and Pearl shell to Canadians and overseas that has become harder to obtain across USA international borders. This provides individual builders an affordable option for their supplies.

ACOUSTIC: STEEL STRINGS, CLASSICALS, & FLAMENCOS

Steel String Guitars include:

GM-50: This model is a slope shoulder jumbo style with a round lower bout and a tight waist. It works well for dropped tunings and Baritone guitars.

GM-03: Smaller than a dreadnought, larger than a 000 this model that still retains some clarity to the notes but can deliver the bass boominess. With a 15.25 in. lower bout it fits under the strumming arm comfortably.

Monarch: OM sized model with very appealing lines. This is the first original Timeless design!

DVK: small body size. This shape works great for a 14 fret resonator. Add a cutaway for full access. As a small guitar the clarity and response for quick finger-picking is all there.

Dreadnought: David has been known to make these on request, his true love is small body guitars!

Classicals and Flamencos include:

Small Torres copy: This is for the traditionalist.

Fleta copy: This is a larger guitar body for those that desire the extra volume.

"10": This is David Freeman's design culminating from three different influences. It works well as a classical and a flamenco. It is a small body design, with lots of curves!

TIM REEDE CUSTOM GUITARS

Instruments currently built in Minneapolis, MN since 2003.

Luthier Tim Reede has been building guitars professionally since 2003. Reede builds unique, one of a kind acoustic, archtop, and electric instruments, and some are created specifically for an individual. Customers can choose the size and features of their guitar to conform to their playing style and aesthetics. Custom designed pearl inlays, woods, and controls for electrics are also available. For more information, visit Reede's website or contact him directly.

CONTACT INFORMATION
TIM REEDE CUSTOM GUITARS
3302 24th Ave. S.
Minneapolis, MN 55406
Phone No.: 612-721-8032
www.reedeguitars.com
tim@reedeguitars.com

ACOUSTIC/ACOUSTIC ARCHTOP

Prices begin at $3,200 for acoustic flattops and models include the Grand Concert, the 000, the dreadnought, and a classical model. Prices begin at $4,500 for archtop instruments and they include cutaway and non-cutaway models.

TIPPIN GUITAR COMPANY

Instruments currently built in Marblehead, MA, since 1978.

CONTACT INFORMATION
TIPPIN GUITAR COMPANY
3 Beacon Street
Marblehead, MA 01945
Phone No.: 781-631-5749
Fax No.: 781-639-0934
www.tippinguitars.com
bill@tippinguitars.com

With a background in furniture making and boat building, Bill Tippin is well versed in the art of fine craftsmanship and has built his own guitars since 1978. He constructs each guitar with the finest wood available, the finest hardware, and to his exacting standards. For many years Bill stayed with a more traditional style of guitar building; however, in more recent years, he has created four original designs (Staccato, Crescendo, Bravado, and Baritone) that have been well received by those seeking fine hand crafted musical instruments. Bill is eager to explore new ideas for the future of Tippin Guitars. For more information, visit Tippin's website or contact him directly.

Tippin offers several acoustic models including the featured OMT model. This guitar is a choice for finger picking players with a 14-fret neck and 25.4 in. scale. Other models include the 00, 000, Dreadnought D-style, DST-12, and a JT jumbo. Several options are also available.

TIPS MCGEE GUITARWORKS

Instruments previously built Fort Tilden, NY.

Tips McGee Guitarworks produced guitars for a few short years. It is unknown what was produced and how much they are worth.

TOMMYHAWK

Instruments previously built in NJ. Distributed by Tom Barth's Music Box of Succasuanna, NJ.

CONTACT INFORMATION
TOMMYHAWK
www.tombarthsmusicbox.com
custserv@kennysmusicbox.com

Designer Tom Barth offered a 24 in. travel-style guitar that is a one-piece carved mahogany body (back, sides, neck, and bracing). The solid spruce top, bridge, and top bracing are then glued on-forming a solid, tone projecting little guitar! In 1997, the soundhole was redesigned into a more elliptical shape. Barth's full size (25.5 in. scale) electric/acoustic has a double cutaway body, Tele-style neck with a 21-fret rosewood or maple fingerboard, and a Seymour Duncan Duckbucker pickup. Tom passed away on September 1, 2005. It is unknown if the Tommyhawk name will be used on future guitars. For more information refer to the Tommyhawk website.

TONEMASTER

See chapter on House Brands.

This trademark has been identified as a House Brand ascribed to several distributors such as Harris-Teller of Illinois, Schmidt of Minnesota, and Squire of Michigan. While one recognized source has claimed that instruments under this trademark were built by Harmony, author/researcher Willie G. Moseley has also seen this brand on a Valco-made lap steel (source: Willie G. Moseley, *Stellas & Stratocasters*).

TORRES

Instruments previously built in Spain.

Noted luthier Don Antonio de Torres Jurado (1817-1892) has been identified as the leading craftsman of what scholars have termed the "third renaissance" of the guitar, and developed the guitar to its current classical configuration.

Before the early 1800s, the European guitar featured five courses, which could be a single string or a pair of strings. Torres' new design focused on the five individual strings, and also added the low 'E' string for a total of six individual strings. Torres developed a larger bodied guitar design, and fan-bracing to support a thinner, more resonant top. The new design offered a larger tonal range (especially in the bass response), and was widely adopted both in Spain and throughout Europe.

Torres had two workshops during his career. He produced guitars both in Seville (1852-1869), and his place of birth, Almeria (1875-1892). It has been estimated that Torres built about 320 guitars during his two workshop period. Only 66 instruments have been identified as his work. Source: Tony Bacon, *The Ultimate Guitar Book*.

TOYOTA

Instruments previously produced in Japan during the early 1970s.

Toyota guitars were distributed in the U.S. by the Hershman company of New York, New York. The Toyota trademark was applied to a full range of acoustic, thinline acoustic/electric hollowbody, and solid body electric guitars and basses. Source: Michael Wright, *Guitar Stories*, Volume One.

Toyota classical models include the Concert-sized **No. 110** with a light spruce top and mahogany back and sides (Last MSR was $69.50) and the Concert-sized **No. 115** with a light spruce top and rosewood back and sides (Last MSR was $89.50).

Toyota acoustic models include the Grand Concert-sized **No. 605** with a spruce top and brown shina back and sides (Last MSR was $59.50), Grand Concert-sized **No. 610** with a spruce top and mahogany back and sides (Last MSR was $79.50), and the dreadnought **No. 615** with a spruce top and mahogany back and sides (Last MSR was $89.50). Used Toyota acoustic guitars are generally valued between $200 and $300 in excellent condition.

TRAUGOTT, JEFF

Instruments currently built in Santa Cruz, CA since 1991.

Luthier Jeff Traugott builds a line of high-end acoustic steel string guitars and produces twelve guitars a year. He focuses on high-level craftsmanship, as well as a clean, sophisticated sense of design. Jeff Traugott's Guitars have a reputation for excellent projection and clear, bell-like tones up and down the neck. Traugott guitars come in four basic models and a variety of woods but Traugott is especially known for using old growth, high grade Brazilian Rosewood back and sides and German spruce tops. For more information on model specification, pricing, and availability, please contact Jeff Traugott directly.

The **Model BK** has a 25.375 in. scale, the **Model 00** has a 24.9 in. scale, the **Model R** has an 25.375 in. scale, and the **Model RJ** is a 17 in. jumbo with a 25.375 in. Contact Traugott for pricing and for example models in 2004 sold for over $22,000 and orders for 2006 sold for over $26,500.

CONTACT INFORMATION
TRAUGOTT, JEFF
2553 B Mission Street
Santa Cruz, CA 95060
Phone No.: 831-426-2313
www.traugottguitars.com
jeff@traugottguitars.com

TRIBECA

Instruments currently produced overseas. Distributed by HSS, a division of Hohner, Inc.

Tribeca guitars are licensed from Jeff Babicz Design LTD. See Babicz, Jeff for more information on Babicz guitars. The Tribeca line of guitars offer more traditional designs than the Babicz counterpart. Models are offered in dreadnought and orchestra model size with or without a cutaway. These guitars do not feature the sound anchors that the standard Babicz design has. Prices range from $700 to $1,200. Contact Babicz for more information or visit their website.

CONTACT INFORMATION
TRIBECA
Distributed by HSS
1 Civic Center Plaza, Suite 301
Poughkeepsie, NY 12601
Phone No.: 845-790-5250
Phone No.: 877-856-0780
Fax No.: 845-790-5260
www.babiczguitars.com

TRIGGS GUITARS

Instruments currently hand built in the Kansas City area. Previously manufactured in Nashville, TN.

Luthier Jim Triggs has been building instruments since the mid-1970s. While at Gibson between 1986 and 1992, Jim carried several titles, including Artist Relations, Custom Shop Manager, Archtop Guitar Supervisor, Custom Mandolin Builder, and Art Guitar Designer. Jim left Gibson in March of 1992, and has been custom building ever since. Triggs has also built for several famous clients including Alan Jackson, Luke Bryan, Jimmy Buffett, Mac McAnally, and Peter Mayer of the Coral Reefer Band, Steve Miller, Elliot Easton, Pat Martino, Mundell Lowe, Vince Gill, Marty Stuart, Lee Brice, Jerrod Niemann, Easton Corbin, Joe Perry and Brad Whitford of Aerosmith, and S.P. Fjestad (we felt obligated to include Steve on our artist roster although we were a little apprehensive as we've heard rumors that S.P. has never changed a string on his collection of over 100 guitars).

Jim's son Ryan has been working with him in the shop since 2002, and this "team," may be the only father and son duo currently working on archtops together. The Triggs Boys keep busy with a constant back order of acoutics, electrics, archtops, and F-5 style mandolins. Much of Jim's time in the shop is spent on design work for other companies especially with Cort Guitars where several models are currently in their product line. For more information, visit Triggs' website or contact him directly.

Since Triggs builds mainly custom instruments, the sky's the limit when it comes to options and prices. Electrics start at $3,000, acoustics and jazzboxes start at $4,000, and hand-carved archtops 16 in. at $5,000. Their F-style mandolins and 17 in.+ archtop guitars begin at $6,000.

CONTACT INFORMATION
TRIGGS GUITARS
2413 Anderson Road
Lawrence, KS 66046
Phone No.: 785-424-3242
www.triggsguitars.com
jim@triggsguitars.com

TRINITY RIVER

Instruments currently produced in Asia. Distributed by M&M Merchandisers of Ft. Worth, TX.

Since 1976 M&M Merchandisers has been a national wholesaler of musical instruments and consumer electronics. Tiring of quality issues usually associated with the entry level guitars offered to them at the time, M&M decided to make a change to better serve their dealer base. In July of 2001 M&M introduced their Trinity River brand of import acoustic guitars, banjos, mandolins, and resonators (as well as Z.Z. Ryder electric guitars and Kona acoustic guitars) to have better control over the quality and features offered. Most acoustic models retail at $250 and $300. Electronics are available on several models. For more information, contact Trinity River or M&M Merchandisers directly.

CONTACT INFORMATION
TRINITY RIVER
1923 Bomar Ave.
Fort Worth, TX 76103
Phone No.: 800-299-9035
www.trinityriverguitars.com
chuck@mmwholesale.com

U/V SECTIONS
UNICORD

See Univox. Instruments previously produced in Japan.

The Merson Musical Supply Company of Westbury, New York was the primary importer of Univox guitars. Merson evolved into Unicord, and also became a distributor for Westbury brand guitars. Source: Michael Wright, *Guitar Stories*, Volume One.

UNITY

Instruments previously built by the Unity Guitar Company in Vicksburg and Kalamazoo, MI during the mid-1990s.

The Unity Guitar Company was founded by Aaron Cowles and Kevin Moats in 1994. Cowles, a former Gibson employee (from 1961 to 1983) opened his own music and repair shop after the Kalamazoo plant was closed down. Moats, son of Heritage Guitar's J.P. Moats, comes from a family background of musical instrument building.

In 1994, Unity offered a limited edition of the **100th Anniversary Model** arch top guitar, which celebrates the 100 years of musical instrument building in Kalamazoo, MI. The inlay work was done by Maudie Moore (Moore's Engraving), who has over thirty years experience. Unity was scheduled to begin offering their Custom Carved series of archtop guitars in 1995, but it is unknown if these guitars were ever produced.

UNIVERSITY

Instruments previously produced by Regal (original company of Wulschner & Son) during the late 1890s.

Indianapolis retailer/wholesaler Emil Wulschner introduced the Regal line in the 1880s, and in 1896 opened a factory to build guitars and mandolins under the following three trademarks: Regal, 20th Century, and University. After Wulschner's death in 1900, the factory became part of a larger corporation. Source: John Teagle, *Washburn: Over One Hundred Years of Fine Stringed Instruments*.

UNIVOX

Instruments previously built in Japan circa 1969 to 1978, and imported into the U.S. by the Merson Musical Supply Company of Westbury, NY.

Merson Musical Supply later evolved into the Unicord company. The Univox trademark was offered on a full range of acoustic, thinline acoustic/electric hollow body, and solid body electric guitars and basses. The majority of the Univox guitars produced were built by Arai of Japan (See Aria), and are entry level to intermediate quality for players. Source: Michael Wright, *Guitar Stories*, Volume One.

MSR/NOTES	100%	EXCELLENT	AVERAGE	LAST MSR

ACOUSTIC

MISC. ACOUSTICS – various configurations including dreadnoughts, mainly low-end appointments, mfg. 1970s.

	N/A	$200 - 250	$120 - 150	

U.S. MUSIC CORP.

Distributor/parent company of a variety of brands located in Buffalo Grove, IL.

U.S. Music Corp. is the distributor and parent company of a variety of trademarks including Washburn, Parker, Oscar Schmidt, Hagstrom, Jay Turser, Eden Electronics, Randall Amplification, Soundtech, Vinci, and GWL. In August 2009, JAM Industries of Canada aquired U.S. Music Corp.

VAGABOND

Instruments currently produced. Distributed by Vagabond Travel Guitars in Castleton, NY. Vagabond has been producing guitars since 1981.

Luthier Kevin Smith's Vagabond Travel Guitar has been "defining the acoustic travel guitar since 1981." Smith says that his design is the perfect balance of playability, portability, and sound in an attractive shape. Visit the Vagabond website for more information.

The Vagabond Travel Guitar has a solid spruce top, mahogany integral neck, adjustable truss rod, 24.5 in. scale with 21 full frets. The **Standard** model (list $399) has laminated maple back and sides, black and white binding, Gotoh open tuners, and a deluxe travel bag. In 2004, a left-handed model was introduced as well. The **Deluxe** (last MSR was $499) is similar to the Standard, but has purpleheart and herringbone custom bindings, a tortoiseshell pickguard, and Schaller mini tuners. Both models were available with a Fishman transducer (disc.), Fishman Matrix active system (disc.), Martin Thinline ($89) or Martin Thinline Gold ($129).

MSR/NOTES	100%	EXCELLENT	AVERAGE	LAST MSR

VALCO

Instruments previously built in Chicago, IL between 1943 and 1968. See National, Supro, and Airline.

Louis Dopyera bought out the National company, and as he owned more than 50% of the stock in Dobro, "merged" the two companies back together (as National Dobro). In 1936, the decision was made to move the company to Chicago, Illinois. Chicago was a veritable hotbed of mass produced musical instruments during the early 1900s to pre-World War II. Manufacturers like Washburn and Regal had facilities, and major wholesalers and retailers like the Tonk Bros. and Lyon & Healy were based there. Victor Smith, Al Frost, and Louis Dopyera moved their operation to Chicago, and in 1943 formally announced the change to Valco (the initials of their three first names: V-A-L company). Valco worked on war materials during World War II, and returned to instrument production afterwards. Valco produced the National/Supro/Airline fiberglass body guitars in the 1950s and 1960s, as well as wood-bodied models. In the late 1960s, Valco was absorbed by the Kay company (See Kay). In 1968, Kay/Valco Guitars, Inc. went out of business. Both the National and the Supro trademarks were purchased at the 1969 liquidation auction by Chicago's Strum 'N Drum Music Company. Source: Tom Wheeler, *American Guitars*.

VALLEY ARTS

Electric instruments currently produced in Nashville, TN. Acoustic instruments are currently not produced. Trademark currently owned and distributed by Gibson since late 2002. Distributed by Gibson Guitars in Nashville, TN. Instruments previously produced by Samick in City of Industry, CA from 1993 to 2002. and in North Hollywood, CA from 1977 to 1993.

> **CONTACT INFORMATION**
> **VALLEY ARTS**
> *A Division of Gibson*
> 1121 Church Street
> Nashville, TN 37203
> Phone No.: 615-244-0252
> Phone No.: 800-444-2766
> www.gibson.com

Valley Arts originally began as a North Hollywood teaching studio in 1963. The facilities relocated to Studio City, California and through the years became known as a respected retail store that specialized in professional quality music gear. Production moved back to North Hollywood and into larger facilities in 1989, and luthier/co-owner Michael McGuire directed a staff of fifteen employees.

In 1992, the Samick corporation became involved in a joint venture with Valley Arts, and by June of 1993 had acquired full ownership of the company. Samick operated Valley Arts as the custom shop wing for the company, as well as utilizing Valley Arts designs for their Samick production guitars built overseas.

In 2002, Mike McGuire and Al Carness, who both founded Valley Arts in the beginning, became part of the company again when Gibson acquired the company. Al is now the manager of the Valley Arts retail Store and Mike is the operations manager for the Gibson Custom Shop. Valley Arts is currently a custom order only guitar manufacturer. There are online order forms to select what you want. They are also a repair shop for guitars. Visit their website for more information.

ACOUSTIC

VALLEY ARTS GRAND (MODEL VAGD-1) – dreadnought style, solid AAA spruce top, rosewood back and sides, round soundhole, herringbone binding, mahogany neck, ebony fingerboard, three-per-side tuners, ebony bridge, tortoise pickguard, gold hardware, available in Natural finish, 25.5 in. scale, disc. 2002.

	N/A	$725 - 850	$500 - 575	$1,580

* *Valley Arts Grand Electric (Model VAGD-1E)* – similar to the Valley Arts Grand, except has a piezo bridge pickup and volume/3-band active EQ, available in Natural finish, disc 2002.

	N/A	$800 - 925	$525 - 600	$1,720

VALLEY ARTS GRAND CONCERT (MODEL VAGC-1) – 000 Grand Concert-style, solid AAA spruce top, rosewood back and sides, round soundhole, herringbone binding, mahogany neck, three-per-side tuners, ebony fingerboard, tortoise pickguard, ebony bridge, gold hardware, available in Natural finish, 25 in. scale, disc. 2002.

	N/A	$725 - 850	$500 - 575	$1,580

* *Valley Arts Grand Concert Electric (Model VAGD-1E)* – similar to the Valley Arts Grand Concert, except has a piezo bridge pickup and volume/3-band active EQ, available in Natural finish, disc. 2002.

	N/A	$800 - 925	$525 - 600	$1,720

ROBERT JOHNSON ESTATE (MODEL J 1935 N) – jumbo-style body, solid spruce top, maple back and sides, round soundhole, 12/19-fret rosewood fingerboard with pearl dot inlay, engraved plate on headstock, three-per-side deluxe Kluson tuners, rosewood bridge, available in Natural or Vintage Black Burst finish, mfg. 1994-96.

	N/A	N/A	N/A	

Model has not traded sufficiently to quote pricing.

VANTAGE

Instruments previously produced in Japan between 1977 and 1990 and in Korea between 1990 and the mid-1990s. Distributed by Music Industries Corporation in Floral Park, NY.

The Vantage trademark was established in Matsumoto, Japan, around 1977 and guitars were originally manufactured by Matsumoku. When Matsumoku stopped buliding guitars in the late 1980s, production moved to Korea in 1990. The last

MSR/NOTES	100%	EXCELLENT	AVERAGE	LAST MSR

catalog from Vantage was from 1996 and it appears that they stopped building guitars shortly thereafter. Vantage offered a wide range of guitars designed for the beginning student to the intermediate player.

ACOUSTIC: CLASSICAL SERIES

VC-10 – classical style, spruce top, round soundhole, bound body, wooden inlay rosette, nato back/sides/neck, 12/19-fret rosewood fingerboard/ tied bridge, rosewood peghead veneer, three-per-side chrome tuners with plastic buttons, available in Light Pumpkin finish, disc.

	N/A	$80 - 100	$45 - 60	$200

VC-20 – classic style, cedar top, round soundhole, bound body, wooden inlay rosette, ovankol back/sides, nato neck, 12/19-fret rosewood fingerboard/tied bridge, ovankol peghead veneer, three-per-side gold tuners with plastic buttons, available in Natural finish, disc.

	N/A	$135 - 170	$80 - 100	$339

*   *VC-20CE* – similar to VSC-20, except has single round cutaway, piezo bridge pickup, 3-band EQ with volume slide control, disc.

	N/A	$175 - 225	$105 - 130	$439

VSC-30 – similar to VSC-20, except has rosewood back/sides, available in Light Pumpkin finish, disc.

	N/A	$170 - 215	$100 - 125	$429

ACOUSTIC: DREADNOUGHT SERIES

VS-5 – dreadnought style, spruce top, round soundhole, black pickguard, bound body, three-stripe rosette, nato back/sides/neck, 14/20-fret nato fingerboard with white dot inlay, ebonized maple bridge with white black dot pins, three-per-side chrome tuners, available in Natural finish, disc.

	N/A	$130 - 160	$80 - 100	$319

*   **Add $10 for left-handed version (Model VS-5/LH).**

VS-10 – similar to VS-5, except has three-stripe bound body, disc.

	N/A	$135 - 170	$80 - 100	$329

VS-12 – similar to VS-10, except in 12-string configuration with six-per-side tuners, disc.

	N/A	$135 - 170	$80 - 100	$329

*   **Add $10 for Black finish (Model VS-12B).**

VS-15 – dreadnought style, spruce top, round soundhole, black pickguard, three-stripe bound body/rosette, nato back/sides/neck, 14/20-fret rosewood fingerboard with white dot inlay, rosewood bridge with black white dot pins, three-per-side chrome tuners, available in Natural finish, disc.

	N/A	$120 - 150	$70 - 90	$309

VS-20 – dreadnought style, nato top, round soundhole, black pickguard, three-stripe bound body/rosette, nato back/sides/neck, 14/20-fret bound rosewood fingerboard with white dot inlay, rosewood bridge with white black dot pins, bound peghead, three-per-side chrome tuners, available in Black, Natural, or Tobacco Sunburst finish, disc.

	N/A	$150 - 190	$95 - 115	$369

VS-25 – dreadnought style, cedar top, round soundhole, black pickguard, herringbone bound body/rosette, ovankol back/sides, mahogany neck, 14/20-fret rosewood fingerboard with white dot inlay, rosewood bridge with white black dot pins, three-per-side tuners, available in Natural finish, disc.

	N/A	$150 - 190	$95 - 115	$379

*   **Add $50 for a solid cedar top (Model VS-25S).**
*   **Add $60 for left-handed configuration with a solid cedar top (Model VS-25S/LH).**

*   *VS-25SCE* – similar to the VS-25, except has a single sharp cutaway, solid cedar top, and piezo bridge pickup with a 3-band EQ with volume slide control, disc.

	N/A	$175 - 225	$105 - 130	$459

»*VS-25SCE-12* – similar to the VS-25SCE, except in 12-string configuration with six-per-side tuners, disc.

	N/A	$275 - 325	$160 - 200	$629

VS-30 – dreadnought style, maple top, round soundhole, black pickguard, three-stripe bound body/rosette, maple back/sides/neck, 14/20-fret bound rosewood fingerboard w/ white dot inlay, rosewood bridge w/ white black dot pins, bound peghead, three-per-side chrome tuners, available in Natural finish, disc.

	N/A	$150 - 190	$95 - 115	$379

VS-33 – dreadnought style, spruce top, round soundhole, black pickguard, five-stripe bound body/rosette, oak back/sides, mahogany neck, 14/20-fret bound rosewood fingerboard, rosewood bridge with white black dot pins, bound peghead, three-per-side chrome tuners, available in Trans. Black, Trans. Blue, or Trans. Red finish, disc.

	N/A	$160 - 200	$95 - 120	$399

VS-35CE – single sharp cutaway dreadnought style, nato top, oval soundhole, three-stripe bound body/rosette, nato back/sides/neck, 20-fret bound rosewood fingerboard with white dot inlay, rosewood bridge with white black dot pins, bound peghead, three-per-side chrome tuners, piezo bridge pickup, 3-band EQ with volume slide control, available in Black or Tobacco Sunburst finish, disc. 1997.

	N/A	$170 - 215	$100 - 125	$430

*   **Add $10 for left-handed version of this model (Model VS-35CE/LH).**

MSR/NOTES	100%	EXCELLENT	AVERAGE	LAST MSR

VS-50S – dreadnought style, solid spruce top, round soundhole, black pickguard, herringbone bound body/rosette, nato back/sides/neck, 14/20-fret rosewood fingerboard with white dot inlay, rosewood bridge with white black dot pins, bound peghead, three-per-side gold tuners, available in Natural finish, disc.

	N/A	$175 - 225	$105 - 130	$449

- **Add $10 for left-handed version of this model (Model VS-50S/LH).**

ACOUSTIC ELECTRIC

VS-40CE – single sharp cutaway dreadnought style, nato top, oval soundhole, three-stripe bound body/rosette, nato back/sides/neck, 20-fret bound rosewood fingerboard with white dot inlay, rosewood bridge with white black dot pins, bound peghead, three-per-side chrome tuners, piezo bridge pickup, 3-band EQ with volume slide control, available in Black or White finish, disc.

	N/A	$200 - 250	$120 - 150	$499

* *VS-40CE/M* – similar to the VS-40CE, except has maple back/sides, disc.

	N/A	$225 - 275	$135 - 170	$519

- **Add $10 for left-handed configuration (Model VS-40CE/MLH).**
- **Add $10 for 12-string configuration (VS-40CEM-12).**

VST-40SCE – single sharp cutaway dreadnought style, solid spruce top, round soundhole, three-stripe bound body, herringbone rosette, nato back/sides/neck, 20-fret rosewood fingerboard with white dot inlay, rosewood bridge with white black dot pins, bound peghead, three-per-side gold tuners, piezo bridge pickup, 3-band EQ with volume slide control, available in Natural finish, current mfg.

	N/A	$200 - 250	$120 - 150	$500

VANTEK

Instruments previously produced in Korea during the 1990s. Distributed by Music Industries Corp. in Floral Park, NY.

Vantke instruments were built with the entry level player or beginning student in mind by Vantage in Korea. Models included the dreadnought-shaped **VIS-1**, **VIS-1G** (last MSR was $160), **VIS-2G**, **VIS-3G**, and **VIS-4G** and the nylon-stringed classical **VIC-1**, **VIC-1G** (last MSR was $150), **VIC-2G**, and **VIC-4G**. Used values on these instruments typically range between $50 and $150.

VARSITY

See Weymann & Sons.

VEGA

Instruments previously built in Boston, MA between 1881 and 1970, Nazareth, PA between 1971 and the mid-1970s, the Netherlands in the mid- to late 1970s, Japan in the late 1970s, and in Korea between 1979 and the late 1980s.

The predessor company to Vega was founded in 1881 by Swedish immigrant Julius Nelson, C.F. Sunderberg, Mr. Swenson, and several other men. Nelson was the foreman of a 20-odd man workforce (which later rose to 130 employees during the 1920s banjo boom). Nelson, and his brother Carl, gradually bought out the other partners, and incorporated in 1903 as Vega named after a star. In 1904, Vega acquired banjo maker A.C. Fairbanks & Company after Fairbanks suffered a fire, and Fairbank's David L. Day became Vega's general manager.

Vega built banjos under the Bacon trademark, named after popular banjo artist Frederick J. Bacon. Bacon set up his own production facility in Connecticut in 1921, and a year later wooed Day away from Vega to become the vice president in the newly reformed **Bacon & Day** company. While this company marketed several models of guitars, they had no facility for building them. It is speculated that the Bacon & Day guitars were built by the Regal company of Chicago, Illinois.

In the mid-1920s, Vega began marketing a guitar called the **Vegaphone**. By the early 1930s, Vega started concentrating more on guitar production, and less on banjo making. Vega debuted its Electrovox electric guitar and amplifier in 1936, and a electric volume control footpedal in 1937. Vega is reported to have built over 40,000 guitars during the 1930s.

In the 1940s, Vega continued to introduce models such as the Duo-Tron and the Supertron, and by 1949 had become both a guitar producer and a guitar wholesaler as it bought bodies built by Harmony. In 1970, the C.F. Martin company aquired Vega primarily for its banjo operations. Martin soon folded Vega's guitar production, and in 1976, Martin applied the Vega trademark to a line of acoustic guitars that were imported from the Netherlands. These guitars were built very poorly and many of them were unable to be sold because of defects. Martin also offered some Vega-branded guitars in Japan during the late 1970s. In 1979, Martin sold the Vega trademark rights to the Galaxy Trading Company in Santa Fe Springs, CA. In 1989, the Deering Banjo Company in Spring Valley, CA purchased the Vega after Galaxy let the Vega trademark lapse. Deering currently uses Vega on a line of banjos. In 1998, Martin commissioned a Deering-produced Vega banjo as part of their Kingston Trio Limited Edition set.

Sources: *American Guitars* by Tom Wheeler and *Martin Guitars: A History* by Richard Johnston, Dick Boak, and Mike Longworth.

MSR/NOTES	100%	EXCELLENT	AVERAGE	LAST MSR

ACOUSTIC

C-SERIES ARCHTOPS – carved archtops with various appointments, mfg. 1930s-1950s.

1930s	N/A	$800 - 1,000	$475 - 600
1940s	N/A	$650 - 800	$400 - 500
1950s	N/A	$525 - 650	$325 - 400

PROFUNDO ACOUSTIC – dreadnought body style, solid spruce top, mahogany or Brazilian rosewood back and sides, rosewood fingerboard with dot and large diamond inlays, large Vega logo on headstock with three-per-side tuners, rosewood bridge, available in Natural finish, mfg. 1940s-1950s.

Rosewood	N/A	$2,000 - 2,500	$1,200 - 1,500
Mahogany	N/A	$1,400 - 1,750	$850 - 1,050

VEILLETTE GUITARS

Instruments currently built in Woodstock, NY. Distributed by Veillette Guitars. Veillette has been producing guitars since 1991.

Veillette Guitars are individually handmade by well known luthier Joe Veillette. Veillette offers a wide range of quality acoustic electric instruments in various configurations, including the world's first baritone 12-string acoustic electric guitar. Even though Veillette Guitars appear to be acoustic electric instruments, the company refers to them as electric/acoustic, and because of this, these models are included in the *Blue Book of Electric Guitars*. However, Veillette has introduced complete acoustic models. Look for more information in further editions. For more information regarding these instruments, please contact the company directly.

CONTACT INFORMATION
VEILLETTE GUITARS
2628 Route 212
Woodstock, NY 12498
Phone No.: 845-679-6154
www.veilletteguitars.com
joe@veilletteguitars.com

VENSON

Instruments previously produced in Seoul, Korea during the 1990s.

Sungbo Industrial Co., Ltd. offered a wide range of acoustic guitars and acoustic basses under the Venson trademark. The acoustic guitar line contains a number of dreadnought, jumbo, and classical models.

VENTURA

Instruments previously produced in Japan duing the 1970s and in China during the mid-2000s.

Ventura guitars were distributed in the U.S. market by C. Bruno & Company of New York, NY. Ventura models were both full body and thinline hollow body electric archtop guitars, and generally medium to good quality versions of popular American models. The Ventura trademark was later introduced on a line of guitars produced in China during the mid-2000s. Source: Michael Wright, *Guitar Stories*, Volume One, and Sam Maggio.

VERSOUL

Instruments currently built in Helsinki, Finland since 1994.

CONTACT INFORMATION
VERSOUL
Arinatie 8 C
Helsinki, 00370 Finland
Phone No.: +358-9-565 1876
www.versoul.com
kari.nieminen@versoul.com

Founded in 1994, Versoul specializes in the design and construction of high end string instruments for professional musicians. Since the beginning of the company, the product range has broadened from two acoustic models in 1995, to nineteen production models in 2008. Versoul instruments are available internationally through dealers in the US, Europe, and Japan. Each element of the Versoul instruments, from the sound to the materials, technology and finish, is the result of thorough research and development process. Innovation with materials serves many purposes. For example, certain species of rosewood and mahogany, traditionally used extensively in the construction of stringed instruments, are becoming more scarce. Versoul builds instruments using local, ecological wood choices, such as aspen, European alder, and maple from carefully selected sources. Versoul instruments have been used in hundreds of professional recordings and live performances over the years in Europe and in the USA. In addition to professional performing artists, musicians and guitar technicians, customers of Versoul include collectors, investors, and guitar enthusiasts. Versoul artists include Kenny Burrell, Ronnie Wood, Billy F. Gibbons, Dusty Hill, Roger Daltrey, Henry Kaiser, Bernie Leadon, Amancio Prada, John Hanlon, Allan Holdsworth, and Terry Britten.

Although the modern guitar has been constantly developed and redeveloped for centuries, there is always room for improvement. The design of each Versoul model begins with music and the musician in mind - how to refine the sound and improve the instrument for the benefit of both the music and the musician. The development and design of Versoul instruments combines the study of classic instruments with extensive research on materials. This approach - merging respect towards the traditional instrument with the desire to take the guitar further - has lead to such innovative designs as the Buxom Baritone 12 string and the Reso Sun resonator guitars. Versoul designs are first and foremost professional tools in terms of ergonomics, functionality and playability. An equal emphasis is placed on the sound and visual design of each model. This results in instruments, which are practical, esthetically pleasing and most importantly, produce an exceptional sound.

Mr. Kari Nieminen holds an MFA degree in industrial design. He received his degree in 1989 from the University of Art and Design in Helsinki, Finland. As his diploma work, Kari produced an experimental series of six acoustic steel string flat top guitars. In 1998, he was awarded "Industrial Designer of The Year" by the Association of Finnish Industrial Designers. Kari has been building guitars for over thirty years. His experience, together with his formal art education background, has lead to a unique attitude towards making instruments. Through meticulous study of classic builds, Kari has obtained an excellent base of knowledge on sound and construction. While many guitars of today excel in technological design, Kari is convinced that a certain amount of tradition will yield better results in sound. His mission is to complement the centuries of tradition in guitar building with uniquely modern design. For more information, visit Versoul's website or contact Kari directly.

Acoustic models include the **Buxom 6 Acoustic**, **Buxom 6 Baritone**, **Buxom 6 Classical Baritone**, **Buxom 12 Classical Baritone**, **Buxom 12 Acoustic**, **Buxom 12 Baritone**, **Buxom 6 Minor Acoustic**, **Buxom 12 Minor Acoustic**, **Buxom 12 Minor Baritone Acoustic**, **Caspian Acoustic 12-String Sitar Guitar**, **Touco Classical**, **Zoel 6**, **Zoel 12**, **Guitar Banjo 6 String**, and the **Guitar Banjo 12 String**.

VICTOR

See chapter on House Brands.

This trademark has been identified as a House Brand of the RCA Victor Record Stores. Source: Willie G. Moseley, *Stellas & Stratocasters*.

VICTORIA

Instruments previously distributed by Buegeleisen & Jacobson in New York, NY between circa 1902 and 1920.

Victoria was a brand name used by musical instrument distributor Buegeleisen & Jacobson during the 1900s and 1910s. Most Victoria guitars were built by the Oscar Schmidt company in Jersey City, NJ, but it is possible that they were built by other manufacturers as well. Most Victoria guitars are parlor acoustic guitars built in the same style as Oscar Schmidt guitars of the same time period.

VINTAGE

Instruments currently produced in Asia. Distributed in the U.S. by LPD Music in Madison Heights, MI and distributed worldwide by John Hornby Skewes & Co., Ltd. in Garforth (Leeds), England.

CONTACT INFORMATION

VINTAGE

Headquarters/UK Distribution: John Hornby Skewes & Co. Ltd.
Salem House, Parkinson Approach
Garforth, Leeds LS25 2HR United Kingdom
Phone No.: +44 (0) 1132 865 381
Fax No.: +44 (0) 1132 868 515
www.jhs.co.uk
webinfo@jhs.co.uk

U.S. Distributor: LPD Music
32575 Industrial Drive
Madison Heights, MI 48071
Phone No.: 248-585-9630
www.lpdmusic.com

The Vintage trademark is a brand name of UK importer John Hornby Skewes & Co., Ltd. The company was founded in 1965 by its namesake, Mr. John Hornby Skewes. The Vintage line consists of solidly built guitars and basses that feature designs based on popular American favorites. Vintage instruments are generally entry-level to intermediate quality. For more information, visit JHS's website or contact them directly.

Acoustic models are split up into different numbered series. Series/models include the folk-style **V200** (MSR $615), the folk-style with a solid top **V300** (MSR starts at $490), the dreadnought **V400** (MSR starts at $490), the dreadnought-style with a solid spruce top **V800** (MSR $710), the dreadnought-style with a solid spruce top and rosewood back and sides **V900** (MSR $800), the dreadnought-style with a solid spruce top and solid rosewood back and sides **V1100** (MSR $1,045), the folk-style with a solid spruce top **V1300** (MSR $1,045), the dreadnought-style with a solid spruce top, solid mahogany back and sides, and abalone purfling and rosette **V1400** (MSR $1,140), the dreadnought-style with a solid spruce top, solid Indian rosewood back and sides, and abalone purfling and rosette **V1500** (MSR $1,325), the jumbo-style with a solid spruce top and solid Canadian maple back and sides **V1700** (MSR $1,800), and the parlor-style with a solid spruce top, solid rosewood back and sides, and abalone inlays, purfling, and rosette **V1800** (MSR $1,665). Several electric, 12-string, and left-handed configuration versions are available for each model.

VIVI-TONE

Instruments previously built in Kalamazoo, MI between 1933 and circa 1936.

After pioneering such high quality instruments for Gibson in the 1920s (such as the F-5 Mandolin), Designer/engineer/builder Lloyd Loar founded the Vivi-Tone company to continue exploring designs too radical for Gibson. It is rumored that Loar designed a form of stand-up bass that was amplified while at Gibson, but this prototype was never developed into a production model.

Loar, along with partners Lewis A. Williams and Walter Moon started Vivi-Tone in 1933. Loar continued building his pioneering designs, such as an acoustic guitar with sound holes in the rear, but failed to find commercial success. However, it is because of his early successes at Gibson that researchers approach the Vivi-tone designs with some wonderment instead of discounting the radical ideas altogether. Source: Tom Wheeler, *American Guitars*.

VOGEL GUITARS

Fine instruments made in Quito, Ecuador in South America since 1995. Distributed in the U.S. by Vogel Guitars in Walnut, CA.

Vogel Guitars produces electric, electric bass, and acoustic and electro-classic guitars, all made in Ecuador. Bob Vogel was born in Pasadena, CA, and knew the famous Eddie and Alex Van Halen. In 1988, he went to Ecuador for missionary work and ended up marrying a woman he met there. After moving there in 1991, he looked into building guitars, and by 1995, two others and himself had begun building guitars. Vogel guitars are mostly hand-crafted, taking advantage of the inherent skill of Ecuadorian craftsmen and the Spanish guitar heritage latent in the Latin culture. For more information contact Bob Vogel directly.

CONTACT INFORMATION
VOGEL GUITARS
Factory
La Pensa 4316
Quito, Ecuador
Phone No.: 5932-253-5486
Fax No.: 5486-259-8457
www.vogelguitars.com
bob@vogelguitars.com

VOX

Acoustic guitars previously produced in Italy between circa 1965 and 1969. Distributed by the Thomas Organ company.

The Vox company, perhaps better known for its amplifier design, also built fashionable and functional guitars and basses during the 1960s. While the early guitar models produced tended to be entry level instruments based on popular Fender designs, later models expressed an originality that fit in well with the 1960s British "Pop" music explosion. In 1965, the Thomas Organ Company in California began importing a line of acoustic guitars that were built by the EKO company in Italy. Information courtesy: David Peterson and Dick Denney, *The Vox Story*. Model information courtesy: Walter Murray, Frankenstein Fretworks.

ACOUSTIC

COUNTRY WESTERN (MODEL V238) – square-shouldered dreadnought-style body, spruce top, maple back and sides, single bound top, round soundhole with large ornate rosette, 14/20-fret rosewood fingerboard with dot inlays, simple horizontal logo on headstock, three-per-side chrome tuners, reverse belly bridge with adj. saddle, scalloped three-point pickguard, available in Natural finish, mfg. 1966-69.

| | N/A | $400 - 500 | $250 - 300 | |

FOLK XII (MODEL V239) – 12-string configuration, square-shouldered dreadnought-style body, spruce top, maple back and sides, single bound top, round soundhole with large ornate rosette, 14/20-fret rosewood fingerboard with pearl block inlays, simple horizontal logo on headstock, six-per-side chrome tuners, reverse belly bridge with adj. saddle, scalloped three-point pickguard, available in Natural finish, mfg. 1966-69.

| | N/A | $350 - 450 | $200 - 250 | |

* *Folk XII Electro (Model V240)* – similar to the Folk XII (Model V239), except has a pickup mounted in the soundhole directly below the fingerboard and two knobs on the top of the guitar (v, tone), available in Natural finish, mfg. 1966-69.

| | N/A | $400 - 500 | $250 - 300 | |

RIO GRANDE (MODEL V278) – dreadnought style body, round soundhole with large rosette, bound fingerboard with block inlays, horizontal logo with MOP inlays on headstock, three-point pickguard with "Rio Grande", available in Natural finish, mfg. 1966-69.

| | N/A | $400 - 500 | $250 - 300 | |

SERENADER (MODEL V220) – student/beginner style, unbound body, neck joins body between 12th and 13th fret, 19-fret rosewood fingerboard with dot markers, symmetrical headstock with skunk stripe, tear drop pickguard, Natural finish, mfg. 1966-69.

| | N/A | $250 - 300 | $150 - 190 | |

SHENANDOAH (MODEL V279) – 12-string configuration, round-shouldered concert auditorium-style body, round soundhole with large ornate rosette, 14/20-fret rosewood fingerboard with pearl block inlays, pearl horizontal logo with pearl design inlays on headstock, six-per-side chrome tuners, reverse belly bridge with adj. saddle, scalloped three-point pickguard, available in Natural finish, mfg. 1966-69.

| | N/A | $325 - 400 | $200 - 250 | |

* *Silver Sage (Model V280)* – similar to the Shenandoah (Model V279), except has a pickup mounted in the soundhole directly below the fingerboard and two knobs on the top of the guitar (v, tone), available in Natural finish, mfg. 1966-69.

| | N/A | $350 - 450 | $200 - 250 | |

VOYAGE-AIR

Instruments currently produced in China since the mid-2000s.

Luthier Harvey Leach invented the Voyage-Air guitar to offer a full-size, tone-rich, yet portable guitar. All Voyage-Air guitars feature the patented Voyage-Air hinge where the neck meets the body. During transport or storage, the neck of the Voyage-Air folds down toward the bottom of the body and the loose strings are stored inside of the body through the soundhole. Voyage-Air also has a unique gig bag for the guitar when it is folded downward. For more information, visit Voyage-Air's website or contact them directly.

CONTACT INFORMATION
VOYAGE-AIR
6752 Preston Ave., Suite E
Livermore, CA 94551
Phone No.: 800-371-6478
www.voyageairguitar.com
alec@voyageairguitar.com

ACOUSTIC

Voyage-Air offers three different series of travel guitars. The Transit Series are Voyage-Air's most affordable option with the **VAMD-02** (MSR $399) and the **VAOM-02** (MSR $399). The Songwriter Series are Voyage-Air's mid-grade models with the **VAD-04** (MSR $529), **VAD-06** (MSR $599), **VAOM-4** (MSR $529), and the **VAOM-06** (MSR $599). The Premier Series are Voyage-Air's highest-end models with the **VAD-1** (MSR $1,355), **VAD-2** (MSR $1,610), **VAOM-1C** (MSR $1,440), and the **VAOM-2C** (MSR $1,695).

NOTES

W SECTION
WABASH

Instruments previously produced during the 1950s. See chapter on House Brands.

Wabash was a house brand of the David Wexler company during the 1950s. Wabash instruments were likely produced by Kay, but were probably made by other manufacturers as well. They offered acoustic and electric guitars as well as lap steels and amplifiers. Source: Willie G. Moseley, *Stellas & Stratocasters*.

WALDEN

Instruments currently produced in China. Distributed in the U.S. by KHS America in Mount Juliet, TN.

CONTACT INFORMATION
WALDEN
12020 Eastgate Blvd.
Mount Juliet, TN 37122
Phone No.: 888-925-3369
Fax No.: 615-773-9975
www.waldenguitars.com
info-request@waldenguitars.com

Luthier Johathan Lee founded Walden guitars in 1996. Lee, who studied and worked under luthier Charles Fox, leads a group of skilled builders in the small town of Lilan, Norther China. Walden introduced their line of guitars to the U.S. at the Summer NAMM show in 2003. Walden produces a wide variety of guitars in various configurations including Dreadnoughts, Nylon-stringed classicals, and Grand Auditoriums. Prices start at $300 and climb to $1,500 for the top-of-the-line model. For more information, visit Walden's website or contact them directly.

WALKER GUITARS

Instruments currently built in North Stonington, CT since 1984.

CONTACT INFORMATION
WALKER GUITARS
314 Pendleton Hill Road
North Stonington, CT 06359
Phone No.: 860-599-1907
www.walkerguitars.com
kim@walkerguitars.com

Luthier Kim Walker was involved in the musical instrument making business since 1973, and began building F-5 style mandolins in 1982. Walker worked for a number of years at George Gruhn's repair and restoration workshop, where he was able to work in close association with other fine instrument builders such as Mark Lacey, Paul McGill, and Steven Gilchrist. Walker later served as both a prototype builder and R&D/Custom shop supervisor at Guild beginning in 1986. Walker builds archtop and flattop acoustic guitars. As of 2006, Walker is no longer accepting deposits for archtop guitars since the backlog is so long. Flattop guitar orders are still available but the backorder list is over six years long! For more information or how to order, contact Kim Walker directly or visit his website.

Walker offered a variety of archtop models including the **Black Tie**, **Excel**, **Classic**, and **Solo Nova**, which are traditional style archtops with different appointments and body binding styles, and the top-of-the-line **Empress**, which is a limited edition custom model. Walker stopped taking orders for archtops in 2006, and the last offered starting price for archtop guitars was $17,000.

Walker builds flattop acoustic guitars that feature pre-war style scalloped bracing, and are finished in a gloss varnish. Flattop acoustics are available as the **Style A** (prices start at $12,300), Style A Deluxe (prices start at $14,000), **Style A Special** (prices start at $14,000), **Style B Special** (prices start at $12,300), and the **Style C** (prices start at $12,000).

Used values on Walker Guitars often sell for much more than when he built them new. This causes current pricing to be very tough and with a backlog so long it is difficult to offer a "locked" price. Contact Walker for the most current information.

WARRIOR

Instruments currently built in Rossville, GA. Distributed by Warrior. Warrior has been producing guitars since 1995.

CONTACT INFORMATION
WARRIOR
93 Direct Connection Drive
Rossville, GA 30741
Phone No.: 706-891-3009
Fax No.: 706-891-3935
www.warriorinstruments.com
anointed@warriorinstruments.com

Warrior Annointed Hand Made Instruments currently offers high quality custom-built bass models that feature bolt-on and neck-through designs, exotic woods, and an innovative "through-body stringing" that corrects the floppy feeling of the low B-string. Warrior has a full design team to create the guitars. They also do not produce a standard line of guitars. Most models have several options available and many customers do not order their guitars with only standard features. In 2006, Warrior introduced a line of acoustic guitars as well. For more information, contact Warrior directly or visit their website.

WARWICK

Instruments currently produced in Markneukirchen, Germany by Warwick GmbH & Co., Musicequipment KG since 1982. Distributed exclusively in the U.S. by U.S. Music Corp. in Buffalo Grove, IL. Previously distributed by Dana B. Goods in Ventura, CA and Hanser Music Group in Hebron, KY.

CONTACT INFORMATION
WARWICK
U.S. Distribution: U.S. Music Corp.
1000 Corporate Grove Drive
Buffalo Grove, IL 60089
Phone No.: 847-949-0444
Phone No.: 800-877-6863
Fax No.: 847-949-8444
www.usmusiccorp.com
guitar.support@usmusiccorp.com

CONTACT INFORMATION
WARWICK
Factory
Gewerbegebiet Wohlhausen
Markneukirchen, Germany
Phone No.: 0049-037422-555-0
Fax No.: 0049-037422-555-99
www.warwick.de
info@warwick.sh.cn

Hans Peter Wilfer, son of Framus' Frederick Wilfer, established the Warwick trademark in 1982 in Erlangen (Bavaria). Wilfer literally grew up in the Framus factories of his father, and learned all aspects of construction and production right at the source. The high quality of Warwick basses quickly gained notice with bass players worldwide.

MSR/NOTES	100%	EXCELLENT	AVERAGE	LAST MSR

In 1995, Warwick moved to Markneukirchen (in the Saxon Vogtland) to take advantage of the centuries of instrument-making traditions. Construction of the new plant provided the opportunity to install new state-of-the-art machinery to go with the skilled craftsmen. The Warwick company continues to focus on producing high quality bass guitars; and since 1993, Warwick also offers a full range of bass amplification systems and speaker cabinets.

ACOUSTIC BASS

ALIEN – single sharp cutaway concert style, laminated spruce top, laminated ovankol (disc. 1994, 2008-present) or laminated rosewood (2001-05) back/sides, asymmetrical soundhole located in upper bass bout with ovangkol soundhole cap, rosewood thumb rest, wood body binding, two-piece mahogany neck with wenge center strip, 24-fret wenge or fretless ebony fingerboard, ebony headstock overlay with pearl W inlay, two-per-side chrome tuners, wenge or ebony bridge, metal tailpiece, Fishman Prefix Plus piezo pickup and electronics, available in Natural Satin finish, disc. 1994, 2001-05, and 2008-present.

1990-1994	N/A	$1,550 - 1,800	$950 - 1,100
2001-2005	N/A	$800 - 1,000	$500 - 600
2008-Present MSR $2,320	$1,600	$950 - 1,200	$575 - 725

Also available in left-handed configuration.

* **Alien Five-String** – similar to the Alien, except in five-string configuration with 3/2-per-side tuners, available in Natural Satin finish, mfg. 2010-present.

MSR $2,460	$1,700	$1,050 - 1,300	$625 - 775

* **Alien Six-String** – similar to the Alien, except in six-string configuration with three-per-side tuners, available in Natural Satin finish, mfg. 2012-present.

MSR $2,600	$1,800	$1,125 - 1,400	$675 - 850

WASHBURN

Instruments currently produced in suburban Chicago, IL, China, and Korea. Previously produced in Chicago, IL between the 1880s and the 1940s and Japan between the 1960s and 1990s. Washburn is currently a division of and distributed by U.S. Music Corporation in Buffalo Grove, IL.

CONTACT INFORMATION
WASHBURN
1000 Corporate Grove Dr.
Buffalo Grove, IL 60089
Phone No.: 847-949-0444
Phone No.: 800-877-6863
Fax No.: 847-949-8444
www.washburn.com
guitar.support@usmusiccorp.com

The Washburn trademark was originated by the Lyon & Healy company of Chicago, Illinois. George Washburn Lyon and Patrick Joseph Healy were chosen by Oliver Ditson, who had formed the Oliver Ditson Company, Inc. in 1835 as a musical publisher. Ditson was a primary force in music merchandising, distribution, and retail sales on the East Coast. In 1864, the Lyon & Healy music store opened for business. The late 1800s found the company ever expanding from retail, to producer, and finally distributor. The Washburn trademark was formally filed for in 1887, and the name applied to quality stringed instruments produced by a manufacturing department of Lyon & Healy.

Lyon & Healy were part of the Chicago musical instrument production conglomerate that produced musical instruments throughout the early and mid-1900s. As in business, if there is demand, a successful business will supply. Due to their early pioneering of mass production, the Washburn facility averaged up to one hundred instruments a day! Lyon & Healy/Washburn were eventually overtaken by the Tonk Bros. company, and the Washburn trademark was eventually discarded.

When the trademark was revived in 1964, the initial production of acoustic guitars came from Japan. Washburn electric guitars were re-introduced to the American market in 1979, and featured U.S. designs on Japanese-built instruments. Production of the entry level models was switched to Korea during the mid- to late 1980s. As the company gained a larger foothold in the guitar market, American production was reintroduced in the late 1980s as well. Grover Jackson (ex-Jackson/Charvel) was instrumental in introducing new designs for Washburn for the Chicago series in 1993.

In 1998, Washburn adopted the Buzz Feiten Tuning System on the American-produced models. The Buzz Feiten Tuning System is a new tempered tuning system that produces a more "in-tune" guitar.

Early company history courtesy of John Teagle in his book *Washburn: Over One Hundred Years of Fine Stringed Instruments*. The actual history is a lot more involved and convoluted than the above outline suggests, and Teagle's book does a fine job of unravelling the narrative.

ACOUSTIC: PREWAR GUITARS

The first Washburn guitars were produced in the 1880s, however the actual beginning date is a little vague. Washburn dates the beginning of the company to 1883, which is indicated in a 1887 patent application. The first catalog featuring Lyon & Healey guitars was issued in 1885. The first Washburn guitar catalog was produced in 1889.

Like many companies that produced guitars early on, they used a numbering system that indicated the body style, size, and configuration. Washburn utilized a few different numbering schemes over the early years. The earliest guitars used a three-digit numbering system. The first number indicated the size (1 Standard, 2 Concert, 3 Grand Concert, and 4 Auditorium). The second number was always zero. The last number indicated the level of intricacy (ranged 1 through 8). A model 503 Contra Bass Guitar was also produced early on. These early guitars all featured a spruce top, mahogany or spruce necks, Brazilian rosewood back

MSR/NOTES	100%	EXCELLENT	AVERAGE	LAST MSR

and sides, and ebony fingerboard/bridge.

Circa 1892, a fancier style 9 was introduced that featured pearl side stripes, ornate fingerboard inlay, and multi-colored inlays around the edge.

In the mid-1890s, Washburn changed their numbering slightly. The first and last digits stayed the same, but the second number became one less than the last digit. This did not apply to the style 8 or 9 where the second and third numbers were the same. For example, 345, 167, 388, 299. The style 8 and 9 also were overhauled.

1905 signaled a numbering change again, and this one also followed a scheme made popular by many companies. The first number was the size, and the second number was the price of the guitar at the time. The beginner model was the 115 ($15) and the high-end model was the 380 ($380). Models around this time include the **115**, **320**, **125 (122)**, **217**, **227 (225)**, **330 (333)**, **135 (132)**, **237 (235)**, **340**, **150**, **252**, **355**, **388**, **435**, and the **3/4 24**. Many of these models are the same as they never had model names and they were changed between years when the prices on the guitar changed. A model **3150** was introduced in 1912 and cost almost twice the previous high-end model 380.

The **Lakeside Jumbo Size** guitar was also introduced in 1912. The Lakeside Jumbo has measurements of the modern day dreadnought, thus making Washburn the first guitar company to produce a dreadnought (however, there are people that would disagree). Martin's D-1 didn't come out until 1931, and Ditson models weren't released until 1917. This model was produced from 1912 until the mid 1920s.

After WWI, a new line of guitars came out. Washburn realized it was near impossible to keep the price of guitars the same over a number of years so they tried a new way of numbering. The first two digits indicated the size (21 Standard, 22 Concert, 23 Grand Concert, and 24 Auditorium, and the second two indicated the style. Models included the **2123**, **2128**, **2135**, **2146**, **2164**, **2231**, **2238**, **2250**, **2270**, **2333**, **2342**, **2354**, **2375**, **2444**, **3136**, and **3148**. For a brief period in the early 1920s, the guitars were lettered A ($100) through G ($15).

In the mid-1920s, Washburn introduced the numbering system that would take them to the end in the mid-1940s. This system covered all lines of stringed instruments. A four digit number was applied to each instrument and sometimes a name accompanied it. The first two digits indicated the type of instrument: 51 for banjos, 52 for guitars, and 53 for mandolins/ukuleles. The last two numbers indicated the style. Keep in mind that most of these guitars were produced during the depression and many high-end instruments were discontinued and the rest of the line was thinned out immensely. The first guitars were the **5200 Inspiration**, **5201 Classic**, **5202 Aristocrat**, and **5203 Deluxe**. These were all in concert body styles and were available as a grand concert in models **5235**, **5236**, **5237**, and **5238** respectively. The Aristocrat was also offered as an auditorium model **5239**.

Steel string guitars were introduced around 1930. The first guitar was the **5234 Deluxe**. The **5256 Solo** replaced the Aristocrat, and the **5257 Solo** replaced the Deluxe. The **5257 1/2**, which was a fancier version of the 5257, was later changed to the **5249 Solo Deluxe**. Other models include the **5241 Super Auditorium Classic** and the **5244 Extra Super Auditorium Inspiration** (similar to an SJ200).

Archtop models appeared in the early to mid-1930s. Models include the **5250 Archtop Collegian**, **5255 Archtop Superb**, **5258 Archtop Deluxe**, **5259 Archtop Super Deluxe**, **5242 Collegian Super Auditorium**, **5248 Superb Extra Super Auditorium**, and **5243 Aristocrat Super Auditorium**.

Since there are so many models and variations, it does not make sense to list them all individually. Also, there is not much standard pricing on a lot of these instruments. However, prices can generally be found by the model. Generally, the higher the last one or two digits on the guitar, the more features and more ornate the guitar is. Many of these instruments are in very poor condition and they do not have much value to start with anyway. Anyone with pricing information or other model information is encouraged to submit it directly to Blue Book Publications.

ACOUSTIC: 125TH ANNIVERSARY SERIES

R316SKK 125TH ANNIVERSARY – parlor-style body, solid spruce top, solid Trembesi back and sides, round soundhole with three-ring pearl rosette, ivoroid top and back binding, pearl top border, mahogany neck, 12/18-fret bound ebony fingerboard with 11-13th fret "125th Anniversary" inlay, slotted bound headstock with Trembesi overlay and early Washburn design inlays, three-per-side open-style gold tuners, ebony moustache bridge, available in Natural Antiqued finish, case included, mfg. 2008-09.

N/A	$400 - 475	$250 - 300		$1,000

R316SWRK 125TH ANNIVERSARY – parlor-style body, solid spruce top, solid rosewood back and sides, round soundhole with three-ring pearl rosette, ivoroid top and back binding, pearl top border, mahogany neck, 12/18-fret bound ebony fingerboard with 11-13th fret "125th Anniversary" inlay, slotted bound headstock with rosewood overlay and early Washburn design inlays, three-per-side open-style gold tuners, ebony moustache bridge, available in Natural Antiqued finish, case included, mfg. 2008-09.

N/A	$300 - 375	$175 - 225		$830

WSJ125K 125TH ANNIVERSARY – Southern Jumbo-style slope-shouldered dreadnought body, spruce top, Trembesi back and sides, round soundhole with three-ring pearl rosette, ivoroid top and back binding, pearl top border, mahogany neck, 14/20-fret bound ebony fingerboard with "Tree-of-Life" inlay, bound headstock with Trembesi overlay and early Washburn logo, three-per-side gold Grover Sta-tite tuners, ebony butterfly bridge, available in Natural Antiqued finish, case included, mfg. 2008-09.

N/A	$450 - 525	$275 - 325		$1,150

ACOUSTIC: CLASSICAL MODELS (C SERIES)

Student grade models C10, C30, and C50 were produced in the late 1970s and early 1980s, but there is no specific information on these guitars.

MSR/NOTES	100%	EXCELLENT	AVERAGE	LAST MSR

C5 – classical style, spruce top, mahogany (catapla) back and sides, round soundhole with mosaic rosette, black body binding, mahogany neck, 12/19-fret rosewood fingerboard, slotted headstock, three-per-side open-style chrome tuners, tied rosewood bridge, available in Natural finish, 25.5 in. scale, mfg. 2011-present.

MSR $195	$110	$60 - 80	$30 - 45	

* C5CE Cutaway Electric – similar to the C5, except has a single smooth cutaway and EVT electronics with tuner, available in Natural finish, mfg. 2011-present.

MSR $266	$150	$85 - 110	$50 - 65	

C20 – classic style, spruce top, round soundhole, three-stripe bound body, wooden inlay rosette, mahogany back/sides/neck, 12/19-fret rosewood fingerboard, tied rosewood bridge, three-per-side nylon head chrome tuners, available in Natural finish, mfg. 1994 only.

	N/A	$70 - 100	$40 - 60	$180

C40 CADIZ – classic style, spruce top, round soundhole, three-stripe bound body, wooden inlay rosette, mahogany back/sides, mahogany neck, 12/19-fret rosewood fingerboard, tied rosewood bridge, three-per-side nylon head chrome tuners, available in Natural finish, mfg. late 1980s-present.

MSR $230	$140	$80 - 110	$50 - 70	

By 1997, Washburn appeared on the headstock.

C44CE CUTAWAY ELECTRIC – single cutaway classical style, spruce top, mahogany back and sides, round soundhole with mosaic rosette, black body binding, mahogany neck, 12/19-fret rosewood fingerboard, slotted headstock, three-per-side open-style chrome tuners, tied rosewood bridge, EQ4-T electronics with tuner, available in Natural finish, 25.5 in. scale, mfg. 2011-present.

MSR $320	$180	$110 - 140	$65 - 85	

C60 ZARAZOGA – classic style, spruce top, round soundhole, three-stripe bound body, wooden inlay rosette, rosewood back/sides, mahogany neck, 12/19-fret rosewood fingerboard, tied rosewood bridge, rosewood peghead veneer, three-per-side nylon head gold tuners, available in Natural finish, mfg. late 1970s-1993.

	N/A	$140 - 180	$90 - 110	$370

C64 (S)CE – single rounded cutaway classical body, spruce top, round soundhole, bound body, wood marquetry rosette, ovankol back/sides, mahogany neck, 19-fret rosewood fingerboard, tied rosewood bridge, three-per-side gold tuners with nylon buttons, acoustic bridge pickup, volume/tone controls, Equis Standard preamp, available in Natural finish, mfg. 1994-present.

MSR $516	$290	$190 - 240	$115 - 145	

In 2006, a solid spruce top was introduced.

C80 S – classic style, solid spruce/cedar top, round soundhole, three-stripe bound body, wooden inlay rosette, rosewood back/sides, mahogany neck, 12/19-fret rosewood fingerboard, tied rosewood bridge, rosewood peghead veneer, three-per-side nylon head gold tuners, available in Natural finish, mfg. late 1980s-present.

Late 1980s-1994	N/A	$150 - 200	$95 - 125	
MSR $445	$240	$145 - 180	$85 - 110	

In 1995, a solid cedar top replaced the solid spruce top. By 1997, Washburn appeared on the headstock.

C84 (S)CE – single rounded cutaway body, solid spruce top, round soundhole, three-stripe bound body, wood marquetry rosette, rosewood back/sides, mahogany neck, 12/19-fret rosewood fingerboard, tied rosewood bridge, rosewood peghead veneer, three-per-side nylon head gold tuners, acoustic bridge pickup, 4-band EQ, available in Natural finish, mfg. 1992-94.

	N/A	$300 - 350	$175 - 225	$650

C94 SCE – similar to the C84CE, except features solid cedar top, wooden inlay rosette, jacaranda back/sides, 19-fret rosewood fingerboard, volume/tone control, 3-band EQ, available in Natural finish, mfg. 1994-95.

	N/A	$400 - 475	$250 - 300	$900

C100 S CLASSIC – classical design, solid cedar top, rosewood back and sides, mahogany neck, 12/19-fret ebonized rosewood fingerboard, open-style headstock with three-per-side gold tuners, rosewood bridge, Natural finish, mfg. late 1970s-mid 1980s.

	N/A	$150 - 200	$95 - 125	

C100 SW VALENCIA – classic style, solid cedar top, round soundhole, three-stripe bound body, wood marquetry rosette, rosewood back/sides, mahogany neck, 12/19-fret ebony fingerboard, jacaranda bridge with bone saddle, rosewood peghead veneer, three-per-side pearl head gold tuners, available in Natural finish, mfg. late 1980s-1991.

	N/A	$600 - 750	$375 - 450	$1,500

C104 SCE – single rounded cutaway classical body, solid cedar top, round soundhole, bound body, wood marquetry rosette, rosewood back/sides, mahogany neck, 19-fret rosewood fingerboard, tied rosewood bridge, three-per-side gold tuners with nylon buttons, acoustic bridge pickup, Equis Silver/Gold electronics, available in Natural finish, mfg. 1996-present.

MSR $570	$330	$210 - 260	$120 - 150	

In 1998, Equis Silver electronics replaced Equis Gold.

MSR/NOTES	100%	EXCELLENT	AVERAGE	LAST MSR

C111S FLAMENCO – classical Flamenco design, solid spruce top, spruce back and sides, round soundhole with classical rosette, rosewood body binding, mahogany neck, 12/19-fret rosewood fingerboard, slotted headstock with black overlay and Washburn logo, three-per-side open-style gold tuners, rosewood tied bridge, available in Natural finish, case included, mfg. 2008-09.

	N/A	$250 - 300	$135 - 175	$660

C114K – classical style body, cedar top, rosewood back and sides, round soundhole with two-ring abalone rosette, multi-ply cream body binding with rope pattern purfling, set mahogany neck, 12/18-fret bound ebony fingerboard, slotted headstock with rosewood overlay and Washburn logo, three-per-side open-style distressed tuners with pearl buttons, ebony bridge, available in aged Natural finish, disc. 2011.

	$400	$250 - 300	$150 - 190	$640

C120 S FLETA DESIGN – classical style, select solid spruce top, rosewood back and sides, mahogany neck, 12/19-fret ebony fingerboard, open-style headstock, three-per-side gold tuners, ebony bridge, Natural finish, 3.875 in. depth, 25.625 in. scale, mfg. late 1970s-mid 1980s.

	N/A	$250 - 300	$100 - 150	

This model was based on the Spanish designer Ignacio Fleta.

C124SW – classical style, solid cedar top, solid rosewood back and sides, round soundhole with classical-style rosette, mahogany body binding, mahogany neck, 12/19-fret rosewood fingerboard, slotted headstock with black overlay and no logo, three-per-side open-style gold tuners, rosewood tied bridge, wooden arm rest on the lower bass bout, available in Natural finish, case included, mfg. 2008-09.

	N/A	$500 - 575	$300 - 350	$1,160

* **C124SWCE Cutaway Electric** – similar to the C124SW, except has a single cutaway and B-Band A-15 electronics, mfg. 2008-09.

	N/A	$575 - 650	$325 - 400	$1,330

C134 SCE – single rounded cutaway classical body, solid cedar top, round soundhole, abalone body binding, abalone rosette, rosewood back/sides, mahogany neck, 12/19-fret ebony fingerboard, open-style headstock with three-per-side gold tuners, tied ebony bridge, Equis Gold electronics, Fishman Matrix transducer, available in Natural finish, mfg. 1996-97.

	N/A	$550 - 650	$325 - 450	$1,400

C140 S HAUSER DESIGN – classical style, solid aged spruce top, solid rosewood back and sides, mahogany neck, 12/19-fret ebony fingerboard, open-style headstock, three-per-side gold tuners, ebony bridge, Natural finish, 4 in. depth, 25.625 in. scale, mfg. late 1970s-mid 1980s.

	N/A	$350 - 425	$150 - 200	

This model was based on the German designer Hermann Hauser.

C160 SW RAMIREZ DESIGN – classical style, solid aged cedar top, solid aged rosewood back and sides, two-piece rosewood reinforced mahogany neck, 12/19-fret Madagascar ebony fingerboard, open-style headstock, three-per-side gold tuners, ebony bridge, Natural finish, 4.1875 in. depth, 25.625 in. scale, mfg. 1980-mid 1980s.

	N/A	$475 - 550	$250 - 300	

This model was based on the Spanish designer Ramirez.

C200 SW SEVILLA – similar to C100SW, except has ebony reinforcement in the neck, mfg. late 1980s-1991.

	N/A	$650 - 800	$425 - 500	$1,900

CF110 S FLAMENCO – classical Flamenco style, solid cedar top, cypress back and sides, mahogany neck, 12/19-fret ebony fingerboard, three-per-side tuners, ebony bridge, Natural finish, mfg. late 1970s-mid 1980s.

	N/A	$200 - 250	$120 - 150	

EC41 TANGLEWOOD – classical style, spruce top, oval soundhole, 5-stripe bound body/rosette, ovankol back/sides, mahogany neck, 21-fret bound rosewood fingerboard with pearl dot inlay, rosewood bridge, ovangkol veneer on bound peghead, 3-per-side pearl button gold tuners, EQUIS II preamp system, available in Natural finish, mfg. late 1980s-1992.

	N/A	$325 - 375	$200 - 250	$700

WC160SW – classical style, solid cedar top, solid mahogany back and sides, round soundhole with mosaic rosette, rosewood body binding, satin mahogany neck with two-way truss rod, 12/19-fret rosewood fingerboard, slotted headstock, three-per-side open-style gold tuners with ebonite buttons, tied rosewood bridge, available in Natural finish, 25.5 in. scale, mfg. 2011-present.

MSR $891	$500	$300 - 375	$175 - 225	

* **WC160SWCE Cutaway Electric** – similar to the WC160SW, except has a single smooth cutaway, a Sonicore pickup, and Fishman Presys electronics, available in Natural finish, mfg. 2011-present.

MSR $1,159	$650	$375 - 475	$225 - 275	

ACOUSTIC: DREADNOUGHT/SOUTHERN JUMBO MODELS (D SERIES)

Most Dreadnought and Southern Jumbo models are listed here. Models that aren't include the D20, D20 12, D25, and D25 12. These are all laminated guitars that had short runs in the late 1970s and early 1980s.

D6S – dreadnought-style body, solid spruce top, mahogany back and sides, round soundhole with decorative rosette, black body binding, mahogany neck, 14/20-fret rosewood fingerboard with dot inlays, natural headstock overlay with logo, three-per-side tuners, rosewood bridge, black pickguard, available in Natural finish, mfg. 2010 only.

	$180	$110 - 140	$65 - 85	$320

MSR/NOTES	100%	EXCELLENT	AVERAGE	LAST MSR

D8 – dreadnought style, spruce top, round soundhole, black pickguard, bound body, three-stripe purfling/rosette, mahogany back/sides/neck, 14/20-fret rosewood fingerboard with pearl dot inlay, rosewood bridge with black white dot pins, rosewood peghead veneer with screened logo, three-per-side chrome tuners, available in Natural finish, mfg. 1994, 2001-02.

	N/A	$75 - 125	$40 - 60	$250

* **D8 E** – similar to D8, except has electronics, mfg. 2001-02.

	N/A	$120 - 160	$60 - 80	$330

* **D8 M** – similar to D8, except has mahogany top, mfg. 1994 only.

	N/A	$70 - 95	$40 - 60	$190

D9 – dreadnought-style body, spruce top, mahogany back and sides, round soundhole with decorative rosette, multi-ply body binding, mahogany neck, 14/20-fret bound rosewood fingerboard with dot inlays, black headstock overlay with logo, three-per-side tuners with ebonite buttons, rosewood bridge, black pickguard, available in Natural finish, mfg. 2009-2010.

	$250	$145 - 185	$85 - 110	$400

* **D9CE Cutaway Electric** – similar to the D9, except has a single smooth cutaway and WT-92 pickup/electronics with an electronic tuner, available in Natural finish, mfg. 2009-2010.

	$300	$175 - 225	$95 - 120	$480

D10 – dreadnought style, select spruce top, round soundhole, black pickguard, three-stripe bound body and rosette, mahogany back/sides/neck, 14/20-fret rosewood fingerboard with pearl dot inlay, rosewood bridge with pearl dot black pins, three-per-side chrome Grover tuners, available in Black, Blueburst, Natural, Trans. Red, or Sunburst finish, mfg. 1990-2000.

	N/A	$125 - 175	$75 - 100	$350

* **D10 M** – similar to D10, except has mahogany top, available in Caribbean Blue, Mahogany, Trans. Blue, or Trans. Wine Red finish, mfg. 1998-2000.

	N/A	$150 - 190	$80 - 100	$329

* **D10 Q** – similar to D10, except has a quilted maple top, available in Sunburst finish, mfg. 1997-2010.

	$350	$210 - 260	$105 - 140	$560

* **D10 S** – similar to the D10, except has a solid spruce top, available in Black, Natural, Natural Satin (2009-2010), Tobacco Sunburst (2009-2010), or White (2009-2010) finish, mfg. 2001-2010.

	$300	$175 - 225	$100 - 130	$500

»**D10 S 12 12-String** – similar to D10 S, except in 12-string configuration with six-per-side tuners, available in Natural finish, mfg. 2001-2010.

	$390	$250 - 300	$135 - 175	$670

»**D10 S LH Left-Handed** – similar to D10 S, except in left-hand configuration, available in Natural finish, mfg. 2001-2010.

	$360	$225 - 275	$120 - 150	$560

»**D10 S DL Rosewood** – similar to D10 S, except has rosewood back and sides, mfg. 2005-2010.

	$480	$300 - 350	$175 - 225	$800

»**D10 S R Rosewood** – similar to D10 S, except has Natural Rosewood, available in Natural finish, mfg. 2010 only.

	$360	$225 - 275	$120 - 150	$560

D10 E – dreadnought style, select spruce top, round soundhole, black pickguard, three-stripe bound body/rosette, mahogany back/sides/neck, 14/20-fret rosewood fingerboard with pearl dot inlay, rosewood bridge with pearl dot black pins, three-per-side chrome Grover tuners, piezo bridge pickup, volume/tone controls, passive preamp, available in Black or Natural finish, mfg. 1996-2000.

	N/A	$180 - 230	$110 - 140	$420

D10 CE – single rounded cutaway dreadnought style, select spruce top, round soundhole, black pickguard, three-stripe bound body and rosette, mahogany back/sides/neck, 14/20-fret rosewood fingerboard with pearl dot inlay, rosewood bridge with pearl dot black pins, three-per-side chrome Grover tuners, piezo bridge pickup, volume/tone controls, three-band EQ, Equis Standard preamp, available in Black or Natural finish, mfg. 1992-2000.

	N/A	$225 - 275	$125 - 175	$500

* **D10 CE LH Left-Handed** – similar to the D12 CE, except in left-handed configuration, available in Natural finish, mfg. 1996-2000.

	N/A	$250 - 300	$140 - 190	$550

* **D10 CE M Mahogany** – similar to the D10 CE, except features an all mahogany body, available in Caribbean Blue, Mahogany, Trans. Blue, or Trans. Wine Red finish, mfg. 1997-2000.

	N/A	$225 - 275	$125 - 175	$499

In 2000, Trans. Blue replaced Carribean Blue finish.

* **D10 CE Q Quilted Maple** – similar to the D10 CE, except features a quilted maple top, available in Sunburst finish, mfg. 1997-2010.

	$420	$265 - 315	$145 - 190	$720

MSR/NOTES	100%	EXCELLENT	AVERAGE	LAST MSR

* **D10 S CE** – similar to the D10 CE, except has a solid spruce top, available in Black, Natural, or Natural Satin (2009-2010) finish, mfg. 2001-2010.

	$400	$250 - 300	$135 - 175	$670

»**D10 S CE 12 12-String** – similar to D10 SCE, except in 12-string configuration and six-per-side tuners, available in Black or Natural finish, mfg. 2007-2010.

	$470	$300 - 350	$175 - 225	$800

»**D10 S CE LH Left-Handed** – similar to the D10 S CE, except in left-handed configuration, available in Natural finish, mfg. 2001-2010.

	$440	$280 - 330	$160 - 210	$720

»**D10 S CE DL Rosewood** – similar to D10 SCE, except has rosewood back and sides, mfg. 2005-2010.

	$560	$325 - 400	$175 - 225	$880

»**D10 S R CE Rosewood** – similar to the D10 S CE, except has Natural Rosewood, available in Natural finish, mfg. 2010 only.

	$440	$280 - 330	$160 - 210	$720

D11 – similar to D10, except has a mountain ash top, mountain ash back/sides, available in Antique Natural, Brown, Trans. Red, or Trans. Blue finish, mfg. 1996-2004.

	N/A	$150 - 200	$95 - 120	$390

Antique Natural finish introduced in 2000.

D12 – dreadnought style, spruce top, round soundhole, black pickguard, three-stripe bound body and rosette, mahogany back/sides/neck, 14/20-fret rosewood fingerboard with pearl dot inlay, rosewood bridge with pearl dot black pins, three-per-side chrome diecast tuners, available in Black, Brown, Natural, White, Woodstone Blue (1990-91 only), or Woodstone Brown (1990-91 only) finish, mfg. late 1970s-1994.

	N/A	$150 - 200	$80 - 100	$350

* **D12 LH Left-Handed** – similar to D12, except in left-handed configuration, available in Natural finish, mfg. 1992-94.

	N/A	$170 - 220	$90 - 110	$380

* **D12 12 12-String** – similar to D12, except features 12-string configuration, six-per-side chrome diecast tuners, available in Black, Brown, Natural, Tobacco Sunburst, or White finish, mfg. 1980s-1994.

	N/A	$175 - 225	$100 - 130	$400

* **D12 S** – similar to D12, except has a solid spruce top, available in Black or Natural finish, mfg. 1993-2000.

	N/A	$200 - 250	$120 - 160	$449

»**D12 S LH Left-Handed** – similar to D12 S, except in left-handed configuration, available in Natural finish, mfg. 1995-2000.

	N/A	$200 - 250	$120 - 160	$499

»**D12 S 12 12-String** – similar to D12 S, except in 12-string configuration, six-per-side chrome diecast tuners, available in Natural finish, mfg. 1995-2000.

	N/A	$200 - 250	$120 - 160	$499

D12 CE – single rounded cutaway dreadnought style, spruce top, round soundhole, black pickguard, three-stripe bound body and rosette, mahogany back/sides/neck, 14/20-fret rosewood fingerboard with pearl dot inlay/pearl W inlay at 12th fret, rosewood bridge with pearl dot black pins, three-per-side chrome diecast tuners, piezo bridge pickup, volume/tone control, three-band EQ, Equis Standard preamp, available in Black, Natural, Tobacco Sunburst, White, or Woodstone Brown finish, mfg. mid 1980s-1993.

	N/A	$275 - 325	$150 - 200	$600

* **D12 S CE** – similar to the D12 CE, except features a solid spruce top, available in Black or Natural finish, mfg. 1994-2000.

	N/A	$285 - 335	$180 - 230	$629

* **D12 12 CE 12-String Cutaway** – similar to D12 CE, except in 12-string configuration and six-per-side tuners, available in Natural or Tobacco Sunburst finish, mfg. mid 1980s-1993.

	N/A	$320 - 370	$190 - 240	$680

»**D12 12 E 12-String** – similar to D12 12 CE, except has a non-cutaway body, available in Natural finish, mfg. 1994 only.

	N/A	$230 - 280	$130 - 180	$530

D13 – dreadnought style, spruce top, round soundhole, black pickguard, three-stripe bound body and rosette, ovankol back/sides, mahogany neck, 14/20-fret rosewood fingerboard with pearl dot inlay, rosewood bridge w/ white black dot pins, three-per-side chrome diecast tuners, available in Natural finish, mfg. 1988-1994.

	N/A	$170 - 220	$90 - 110	$390

* **D13 12 12-String** – similar to D13, except in 12-string configuration, six-per-side tuners, mfg. 1992-94.

	N/A	$200 - 250	$120 - 160	$450

* **D13 S** – similar to D13, except has a solid spruce top, mfg. 1994-2004.

	N/A	$225 - 275	$130 - 180	$500

MSR/NOTES	100%	EXCELLENT	AVERAGE	LAST MSR

»**D13 S 12 12-String** – similar to D13, except in 12-string configuration, solid spruce top, six-per-side tuners, mfg. 1994 only.

| | N/A | $225 - 275 | $130 - 180 | $500 |

D14 – dreadnought style, spruce top, round soundhole, tortoise pickguard, three-stripe bound body and rosette, rosewood back/sides, mahogany neck, 14/20-fret rosewood fingerboard with pearl dot inlay, rosewood bridge with pearl dot white pins, three-per-side chrome diecast tuners, available in Natural or Tobacco Sunburst finish, mfg. 1980-1992.

| | N/A | $150 - 200 | $80 - 100 | $350 |

* **D14 LH Left-Handed** – similar to the D14, except in left-handed configuration, available in Natural or Tobacco Sunburst finish, mfg. 1980s-1991.

| | N/A | $175 - 225 | $85 - 110 | $400 |

D15 – dreadnought style, select spruce top, unknown back/sides, mfg. late 1970s-early 1980s.

| | N/A | $100 - 150 | $50 - 75 | |

* **D15-12 12-String** – similar to the D15, except in 12-string configuration, mfg. late 1970s-early 1980s.

| | N/A | $125 - 175 | $75 - 95 | |

D15 S – dreadnought style, solid spruce top, mahogany back and sides, mahogany neck, 14/20-fret rosewood fingerboard with pearl dot inlays, 3-per-side tuners, abalone top binding, tortoise pickguard, available in Natural finish, mfg. 1999-2000.

| | N/A | $275 - 325 | $150 - 200 | $600 |

D17 S CE – single rounded cutaway dreadnought style, solid spruce top, round soundhole, black pickguard, three-stripe bound body/rosette, mahogany back/sides/neck, 20-fret bound rosewood fingerboard with pearl diamond inlay, stylized W inlay at 12th fret, rosewood bridge with black white dot pins, pearl diamond inlay on bridge wings, bound peghead, three-per-side gold tuners with pearl buttons, acoustic bridge pickup, volume/tone control, 3-band EQ, 1/4/XLR output jack, available in Black or Natural finish, mfg. 1993-94.

| | N/A | $350 - 425 | $200 - 250 | $800 |

* **D17 CE Flamed Maple** – similar to D17 S CE, except has an all flamed maple body, available in Brown or Wine Red finish, mfg. 1992-97.

| | N/A | $450 - 525 | $250 - 300 | $1,000 |

* **D17 CE 12 Flamed Maple 12-String** – similar to D17 CE Flamed Maple, except in 12-string configuration and six-per-side tuners, mfg. 1992-93.

| | N/A | $375 - 450 | $225 - 275 | $880 |

* **D17 S CE 12 12-String** – similar to D17 SCE , except in 12-string configuration and six-per-side tuners, mfg. 1993-94.

| | N/A | $375 - 450 | $225 - 275 | $850 |

D18 M – dreadnought style, select mahogany top/back/sides, steel reinforced mahogany neck, 14/20-fret rosewood fingerboard with dot inlays, rosewood headstock overlay with three-per-side gold tuners, rosewood bridge, brass nut, saddle, and endpins, Natural finish, mfg. 1980-85.

| | N/A | $150 - 200 | $95 - 120 | |

D20 – dreadnought style, Hawaiian koa top, round soundhole, 3-stripe bound body/rosette, Hawaiian koa back/sides, mahogany neck, 14/20-fret rosewood fingerboard with pearl dot inlay, rosewood bridge with white bridgepins, 3-per-side gold diecast tuners, available in Natural finish, mfg. 1997-98.

| | N/A | $350 - 425 | $200 - 250 | $799 |

D20 S – dreadnought style, solid spruce top, round soundhole, tortoiseshell pickguard, 3-stripe bound body and rosette, flame maple back/sides, mahogany neck, 14/20-fret rosewood fingerboard with pearl diamond/12th fret W inlay, rosewood bridge with pearl dot white pins, rosewood veneer on peghead, 3-per-side chrome diecast tuners, available in Natural finish, mfg. late 1980s-1993.

| | N/A | $240 - 290 | $140 - 190 | $530 |

D21 S – dreadnought style, solid spruce top, round soundhole, tortoiseshell pickguard, three-stripe bound body/rosette, rosewood back/sides, mahogany neck, 14/20-fret rosewood fingerboard with pearl diamond/12th fret W inlay, rosewood bridge with pearl dot white pins, rosewood peghead veneer, three-per-side gold diecast tuners, available in Natural or Tobacco Sunburst finish, mfg. late 1980s-2000.

| | N/A | $275 - 325 | $150 - 200 | $600 |

In 1992, Tobacco Sunburst finish was disc.

* **D21 S LH** – similar to D21S, except is left-handed, available in Natural finish, mfg. late 1980s-1992.

| | N/A | $275 - 325 | $150 - 200 | $550 |

* **D21 SE** – similar to the D21 S, except has an acoustic bridge pickup, volume/tone control and 3-band EQ, available in Natural finish, mfg. late 1980s-1991.

| | N/A | $250 - 300 | $140 - 190 | $570 |

D22 CE VIRGINIAN – dreadnought style, spruce top, unknown back and sides, mahogany neck, 14/20-fret rosewood fingerboard with dot inlay, three-per-side tuners, rosewood bridge, pickguard, Washburn 3200 electronics, Natural finish, mfg. mid 1980s.

| | N/A | $225 - 275 | $120 - 150 | |

MSR/NOTES	100%	EXCELLENT	AVERAGE	LAST MSR

D23 CE MISSOURI – single dreadnought style, spruce top, unknown back and sides, mahogany neck, 14/20-fret rosewood fingerboard with dot inlay, three-per-side tuners, rosewood bridge, pickguard, Washburn 3200 electronics, Natural finish, mfg. mid 1980s-late 1980s.

	N/A	$250 - 300	$140 - 180	

* *D23 CE 12 Missouri 12-String* – similar to the D23 CE Missouri except in 12-string configuration and six-per-side tuners, mfg. mid 1980s-late 1980s.

	N/A	$300 - 350	$175 - 225	

D24 S 12 12-STRING – Southern Jumbo style, solid spruce top, round soundhole, tortoise pickguard, bound body, three-stripe purfling/rosette, mahogany back/sides/neck, 14/20-fret rosewood fingerboard with pearl dot inlay, rosewood bridge with white black dot pins, six-per-side chrome Grover tuners, available in Natural finish, mfg. 1994-99.

	N/A	$350 - 425	$200 - 250	$799

D25 S – Southern Jumbo style, solid spruce/cedar top, round soundhole, tortoise pickguard, bound body three-stripe purfling/rosette, Ovankol mahogany back/sides/neck, 14/20-fret rosewood fingerboard with pearl diamond/12th fret 'W' inlay, rosewood bridge with pearl dot white pins, three-per-side gold diecast tuners, available in Natural or Tobacco Sunburst finish, mfg. 1985-2000.

	N/A	$275 - 325	$150 - 200	$630

In 1994 a solid cedar top replaced solid spruce top, dot inlays replaced the 12th fret inlay, and Tobacco Sunburst finish was introduced. In 1999, Tobacco Sunburst finish was disc.

* *D25 S 12 12-String* – similar to D25 S, except in 12-string configuration, six-per-side tuners, mfg. 1985-1992.

	N/A	$300 - 350	$175 - 225	$500

D26 S – dreadnought style, solid cedar top, mahogany back and sides, mahogany neck, 14/20-fret rosewood fingerboard with dot inlay, three-per-side tuners, rosewood bridge, pickguard, Natural finish, mfg. 1978-mid-1980s.

	N/A	$325 - 375	$175 - 225	

* *D26 S 12 12-String* – similar to the D26 S, except in 12-string configuration and six-per-side tuners, Natural finish, mfg. 1978-mid-1980s.

	N/A	$325 - 400	$175 - 225	

D27 S – Southern Jumbo style, solid spruce top, book matched figure koa back and sides, mahogany neck, 14/20-fret rosewood fingerboard with 12th fret inlay, pearl headstock overlay with three-per-side Nickel Grover tuners, rosewood bridge, tortoise pickguard, Natural finish, mfg. 1995-97.

	N/A	$275 - 325	$150 - 200	$700

D28 S – dreadnought style, solid spruce top, round soundhole, black pickguard, three-stripe bound body and rosette, three-piece rosewood back/sides, mahogany neck, 14/20-fret bound rosewood fingerboard with snowflake inlay, rosewood bridge with pearl dot white pins, bound peghead, three-per-side gold diecast tuners, available in Natural finish, mfg. 1978-early 1980s, late 1980s-1994.

	N/A	$275 - 325	$150 - 200	$600

* *D28 S LH* – similar to D28 S, except in left-handed configuration, mfg. late 1980s-1991.

	N/A	$275 - 325	$150 - 200	$580

* *D28 S 12 12-String* – similar to D28 S, except in 12-string configuration, six-per-side tuners, mfg. 1980s-1993.

	N/A	$300 - 350	$175 - 225	$650

* *D28 12 LH 12-String Left-Handed* – similar to D28 S 12 12-string except is in left-handed configuration, mfg. late 1980s-1991.

	N/A	$300 - 350	$175 - 225	$620

D29 S (FIRST VERSION) – dreadnought style, solid cedar top, round soundhole, tortoiseshell pickguard, three-stripe bound body and rosette, rosewood back/sides, five-piece mahogany/rosewood neck, 14/20-fret rosewood fingerboard with diamond/12th fret W inlay, rosewood bridge with pearl dot white pins, three-per-side gold diecast tuners, available in Natural finish, mfg. 1980-1991.

	N/A	$250 - 300	$150 - 200	$550

* *D29 CE* – similar to the D29 S, except has a single cutaway and Equis II electronics, mfg. mid 1980s-1991.

	N/A	$300 - 350	$175 - 225	$700

D29 S (SECOND VERSION) – dreadnought style, solid spruce top, Jacaranda back and sides, mahogany neck, 14/20-fret rosewood fingerboard with dot inlays, exotic wood headstock overlay with three-per-side chrome Grover tuners, tortoise pickguard, Natural finish, mfg. 1997-99.

	N/A	$400 - 475	$225 - 275	$899

D30 S (FIRST VERSION) – dreadnought style, solid cedar top, round soundhole, bound body, three-stripe purfling, five-stripe rosette, rosewood back/sides, mahogany neck, 14/20-fret rosewood fingerboard with herringbone/snowflake inlay, bound headstock with three-per-side chrome diecast tuners, rosewood bridge with pearl dot white pins and bone saddle, tortoise pickguard, available in Natural finish, mfg. 1978-early 1980s.

	N/A	$375 - 450	$200 - 250	

* *D30 S 12 12-String* – similar to the D30 S, except in 12-string configuration and six-per-side tuners, available in Natural finish, mfg. 1978-early 1980s.

	N/A	$400 - 475	$225 - 275	

MSR/NOTES	100%	EXCELLENT	AVERAGE	LAST MSR

D30 S (SECOND VERSION) – Southern Jumbo style, solid cedar top, round soundhole, tortoise pickguard, bound body, three-stripe purfling, five-stripe rosette, bird's-eye maple back/sides, mahogany neck, 14/20-fret rosewood fingerboard with pearl dot inlay, rosewood bridge with pearl dot white pins and bone saddle, bird's-eye maple peghead veneer, three-per-side chrome diecast tuners, available in Natural finish, mfg. 1985-1994.

	N/A	$350 - 400	$200 - 250	$750

D31 S (FIRST VERSION) – dreadnought style, solid spruce top, round soundhole with several rings, select rosewood back and sides, natural hardwood purfling, mahogany neck, adjustable truss rod, 14/20-fret rosewood fingerboard with brass target inlays, three-per-side gold tuners, rosewood bridge, pickguard, Natural finish, mfg. early 1980s-mid 1980s.

	N/A	$400 - 475	$225 - 275	

D31 S (SECOND VERSION) – dreadnought style, solid spruce top, round soundhole, tortoiseshell pickguard, three-stripe bound body/ rosette, flamed maple back/sides, mahogany neck, 14/20-fret rosewood fingerboard with pearl dot inlay, rosewood bridge with white bridgepins, three-per-side gold diecast tuners, available in Natural finish, mfg. 1998-99.

	N/A	$450 - 525	$275 - 325	$1,000

D32 S – similar to D30S, except has Makassar back/sides, bound fingerboard/headstock, Makassar veneer on peghead, mfg. late 1980s-1994.

	N/A	$350 - 425	$200 - 250	$800

* **D32 S 12 12-String** – similar to D32S, except in 12-string configuration, six-per-side tuners, mfg. late 1980s-1991.

	N/A	$375 - 450	$225 - 275	$780

D33 S – similar to the D31 S, except features rosewood back/sides, available in Natural finish, mfg. 1998-99.

	N/A	$500 - 575	$300 - 350	$1,099

D34 S – Southern Jumbo style, solid spruce top, round soundhole, bound body three-stripe purfling/rosette, mahogany back/sides, mahogany neck, 14/20-fret rosewood fingerboard with pearl dot inlay, rosewood bridge with white bridgepins, three-per-side gold diecast tuners, available in Natural finish, disc. 1995-98.

	N/A	$325 - 375	$175 - 225	$729

D34 S AUGUSTA – dreadnought style, solid spruce top, quilted maple back and sides, maple neck, bound body, rosewood finberboard and butterfly bridge, diamond inlays, three-per-side tuners, crown style headstock, Buzz Feiten Tuning System, available in Natural finish, mfg. 2002-05.

	N/A	$375 - 450	$225 - 275	$850

* **D34 S CE (AUGUSTA)** – similar to the D34 S Augusta, except has a single cutaway and B Band electronics, available in Natural or Tobacco Sunburst finish, mfg. 2002-05.

	N/A	$450 - 525	$275 - 325	$1,000

D36 S TAHOE – dreadnought style, solid spruce top, rosewood back and sides, mahogany neck, bound body, ebony finberboard and butterfly bridge, arrowhead inlays, 3-per-side tuners, crown style headstock, Buzz Feiten Tuning System, available in Natural finish, mfg. 2002-03.

	N/A	$400 - 475	$250 - 300	$900

* **D36 SDL** – similar to the D36S, except has MOP tree of life inlay, mfg. 2002-05.

	N/A	$450 - 525	$275 - 325	$1,000

D42 SW HARVEST – dreadnought style, solid Sitka spruce top, bookmatched mahogany back and sides, mahogany neck, 14/20-fret rosewood fingerboard with 12th fret snowflake inlay, pearl inlayed crown headstock with three-per-side nickel Grover tuners, rosewood Butterfly bridge, tortoise pickguard, Natural finish, mfg. 1995 only.

	N/A	$325 - 400	$175 - 225	$800

D42 S SOUTHWEST – dreadnought style, solid North American spruce top, Honduran mahogany back and sides, mahogany neck, bound top, offset position markers, rosewood fingerboard, 3-per-side tuners, available in Natural finish, mfg. 2000-02.

	N/A	$225 - 275	$130 - 180	$500

* **D42 S CE Southwest** – similar to the D42 S Southwest, except has a single cutaway, and Equis Extra electronics, available in Natural finish, mfg. 2000-02.

	N/A	$325 - 375	$175 - 225	$699

* **D42 S 12 Southwest 12-String** – similar to the D42S, except in 12-string configuration, six-per-side tuners, mfg. 2000-02.

	N/A	$250 - 300	$125 - 175	$570

D44 SW GOLDEN HARVEST – similar to the D42 SW Harvest, dreadnought style, solid Sitka spruce top, bookmatched Indian rosewood back and sides, ivoroid body and neck binding, mahogany neck, 14/20-fret rosewood fingerboard with 12th fret snowflake inlay, pearl inlayed crown headstock with three-per-side nickel Grover tuners, rosewood Butterfly bridge, tortoise pickguard, Natural finish, mfg. 1995 only.

	N/A	$350 - 425	$200 - 250	$870

D46 S CHEYENNE – dreadnought style, solid spruce top, rosewood back and sides, mahogany neck, 14/20-fret rosewood fingerboard with dot inlay, crown headdress inlay and logo with three-per-side chrome tuners, rosewood Butterfly bridge, tortoise pickguard, Natural finish, mfg. 1996 only.

	N/A	$425 - 500	$275 - 325	$1,000

MSR/NOTES	100%	EXCELLENT	AVERAGE	LAST MSR

D46 S SOUTHWEST – dreadnought style, Alaskan close grained spruce top, Macasssar rosewood back and sides, rosewood fingerboard, offset position markers, bound top, three-per-side tuners, available in Natural finish, mfg. 2000-2010.

	$480	$300 - 350	$175 - 225	$800

* **D46 S CE Southwest** – similar to the D46 S, except has a single cutaway and Equis Plus electronics, mfg. 2000-2010.

	$570	$375 - 450	$225 - 275	$960

* **D46 S 12 Southwest 12-String** – similar to the D46S, except in 12-string configuration with six-per-side tuners, mfg. 2002-2010.

	$540	$350 - 425	$200 - 250	$880

»**D46 S CE 12 Southwest 12-String** – similar to Model D46 S 12 except has a single cutaway and electronics, available in Natural finish, mfg. 2000-2010.

	$630	$425 - 500	$275 - 325	$1,040

D46 SP SOUTHWEST – dreadnought style, spalted maple top, back, and sides, round soundhole with Southwest-style rosette, pearloid binding, maple neck, 14/20-fret pearloid-bound rosewood fingerboard with offset position Southwest-style inlays, pearloid-bound spalted maple headstock overlay with large Washburn logo, three-per-side chrome Grover tuners, rosewood butterfly bridge, no pickguard, Buzz Feiten Tuning System, available in Natural finish, case included, mfg. 2008-2010.

	$540	$325 - 400	$200 - 250	$880

* **D46 CESP Southwest Cutaway Electric** – similar to the D46 SP, except has a single smooth cutaway and B-Band A3T electronics, mfg. 2008-2010.

	$600	$400 - 475	$250 - 300	$1,040

D48 S COMANCHE – dreadnought style, solid spruce top, mahogany back and sides, mahogany neck, 14/20-fret rosewood fingerboard with dot inlay, crown headdress inlay and logo with three-per-side chrome tuners, rosewood Butterfly bridge, tortoise pickguard, Natural finish, mfg. 1996 only.

	N/A	$450 - 525	$275 - 325	$1,100

D50 S – dreadnought style, solid spruce top, solid rosewood back and sides, multi-colored marquetry body binding and rosette, mahogany neck, 14/20-fret ebony fingerboard with snowflake inlays, three-per-side tuners, ebony bridge, pickguard, Natural finish, mfg. late 1970s-early 1980s.

	N/A	$425 - 500	$250 - 300	

* **D50 S 12 12-String** – similar to the D50 S, except in 12-string configuration and six-per-side tuners, mfg. late 1970s-early 1980s.

	N/A	$450 - 525	$275 - 325	

D51 SW APACHE (U.S. MFG.) – dreadnought style, solid spruce top, solid bird's-eye maple back and sides, mahogany neck, 14/20-fret rosewood fingerboard with dot inlay, abalone Apache feather headstock logo with three-per-side chrome tuners, rosewood Butterfly bridge, tortoise pickguard, Natural finish, mfg. 1995-96.

	N/A	$1,000 - 1,200	$600 - 700	$2,800

D52 SW TIMBER RIDGE – dreadnought style, solid spruce top, solid mahogany back and sides, round soundhole with rosette, maple body and neck binding, mahogany neck, 14/20-fret rosewood fingerboard with snowflake inlays, three-per-side tuners, rosewood bridge, tortoise pickguard, chrome hardware, Natural Satin finish, mfg. 2005-2010.

	$650	$400 - 500	$250 - 300	$1,120

* **D52 SW CE Timber Ridge** – similar to the D52 SW CE Timber Ridge, except has a single cutaway and B-Band electronics, mfg. 2005-2010.

	$750	$450 - 575	$275 - 350	$1,200

D55 SW CHEROKEE (U.S. MFG.) – dreadnought style, solid spruce top, solid rosewood back and sides, rope-style binding and rosette, mahogany neck, 14/20-fret ebony fingerboard with pearl feather inlay, abalone double Cherokee feather headstock logo with three-per-side chrome tuners, ebony Butterfly bridge, tortoise pickguard, Natural finish, mfg. 1995-96.

	N/A	$1,100 - 1,300	$650 - 750	$2,800

D56 SW PRAIRIE SONG – dreadnought style, solid spruce top, solid rosewood back and sides, round soundhole with rosette, maple body and neck binding, mahogany neck, 14/20-fret rosewood fingerboard with snowflake inlays, three-per-side tuners, rosewood bridge, tortoise pickguard, chrome hardware, Natural finish, mfg. 2005-2010.

	$700	$450 - 550	$250 - 325	$1,200

* **D56 SW CE Prairie Song** – similar to the D56 SW Prairie Song, except has a single cutaway and B-Band electronics, chrome hardware, mfg. 2005-2010.

	$800	$475 - 600	$275 - 350	$1,280

D56 SW SAVANNAH (U.S. MFG.) – Southern Jumbo style, solid Sitka spruce top, solid curly koa back and sides, herringbone rope-style binding and rosette, mahogany neck, 14/20-fret ebony fingerboard with pearl crown inlay, pearl headstock logo with three-per-side chrome tuners, ebony Butterfly bridge, tortoise pickguard, Natural finish, mfg. 1996 only.

	N/A	$1,200 - 1,500	$700 - 850	$3,000

MSR/NOTES	100%	EXCELLENT	AVERAGE	LAST MSR

D60 E – slope-shouldered dreadnought, solid wood construction, mahogany neck, 14/20-fret rosewood fingerboard, three-per-side tuners, rosewood bridge, pickguard, Washburn 3200 electronics, mfg. 1985-late 1980s.

| | N/A | $525 - 600 | $300 - 375 | |

D61 S(W) PRAIRIE SONG – dreadnought style, solid spruce top, round soundhole, rosewood pickguard, three-stripe bound body, five-stripe rosette, rosewood back/sides, mahogany neck, 14/20-fret rosewood fingerboard with pearl dot inlay, rosewood bridge with pearl dot black pins, rosewood veneer on peghead, three-per-side chrome diecast tuners, available in Natural finish, mfg. mid-1980s-1994.

| | N/A | $550 - 650 | $325 - 400 | $1,200 |

* Add $100 for Equis II electronics.

In 1992, the W was dropped from the name. In 1994, ovangkol back/sides replaced rosewood.

* **D61 S(W)CE Prairie Song** – similar to the D61 S, except has a single cutaway and electronics, mfg. late 1980s-1994.

| | N/A | $675 - 800 | $400 - 475 | $1,500 |

In 1992, the W was dropped from the model name and Equis II electronics replaced Washburn electronics. In 1994, Ovangkol back and sides replaced rosewood.

* **D61 SW 12 12-String** – similar to D61 SW, except in 12-string configuration, six-per-side tuners, mfg. mid-1980s-1991.

| | N/A | $600 - 700 | $375 - 450 | $940 |

D64SW THE BLUEGRASS – dreadnought body style, solid spruce top, solid rosewood back and sides, round soundhole with mulit-layer abalone rosette, ivoroid body binding, mahogany neck, 14/20-fret bound ebony fingerboard with diamond inlays, bound rosewood overlay haeadstock, three-per-side chrome Grover tuners, ebony butterfly bridge, leopard print pickguard, available in Natural finish, mfg. 2007-2010.

| $800 | $475 - 600 | $275 - 350 | $1,280 |

D68 S(W) HARVEST – dreadnought style, solid spruce top, round soundhole, rosewood pickguard, maple/rosewood binding and rosette, rosewood back/sides, five-piece mahogany/rosewood neck, 14/20-fret rosewood fingerboard with pearl dot inlay, ebony bridge with pearl dot black pins, rosewood veneered maple bound peghead with abalone Washburn inlay, three-per-side chrome diecast tuners with pearloid buttons, available in Natural finish, mfg. mid-1980s-1993.

| | N/A | $650 - 750 | $375 - 450 | $1,500 |

* Add $100 for Equis II electronics.

In 1992, the W was dropped from the model designation.

* **D68 S(W) CE Harvest** – similar to the D68 S, except has a single cutaway, an acoustic bridge pickup, and a 4-band EQ, available in Natural finish, mfg. 1992-94.

| | N/A | $825 - 950 | $525 - 600 | $1,800 |

D70 S(W) HARVEST DELUXE – dreadnought style, solid spruce top, round soundhole, rosewood pickguard, maple/rosewood bound body, abalone inlay rosette, three-piece rosewood back/sides, five-piece mahogany/rosewood neck, 14/20-fret ebony fingerboard with abalone eye inlay, ebony bridge with abalone box inlay and Washburn inlay, three-per-side chrome diecast tuners with pearloid buttons, available in Natural finish, mfg. mid 1980s-1993.

| | N/A | $950 - 1,100 | $600 - 700 | $2,000 |

* Add $100 for Equis II electronics.

D80 SW HIGHLAND (U.S. MFG.) – dreadnought style, AAA solid spruce top, solid figured maple back and sides, one piece mahogany neck, rosewood fingerboard with small pearl dots, tortoiseshell pickguard, roman style headstock, three-per-side tuners, abalone rosette, Buzz Feiten tuning system, Natural finish, mfg. 2002-06.

| | N/A | $825 - 950 | $525 - 600 | $1,900 |

D82 SW HIGHLAND (U.S. MFG.) – dreadnought style, AAA solid spruce top, solid Indian Rosewood back and sides, one piece mahogany neck, rosewood fingerboard with small pearl dots, tortoiseshell pickguard, roman style headstock, figured maple body binding, three-per-side tuners, abalone rosette, Buzz Feiten tuning system, Natural finish, mfg. 2002-05, 2007-08.

| | N/A | $950 - 1,150 | $600 - 700 | $2,400 |

* **D82 SW CE Highland Cutaway Electric (U.S. Mfg.)** – similar to the D82 SW Highland, except has a single smooth cutaway and Custom Fishman pickup/electronics, mfg. 2007-08.

| | N/A | $1,000 - 1,200 | $625 - 725 | $2,500 |

D84 SW HIGHLAND (U.S. MFG.) – dreadnought style, AAA solid spruce top, solid Hawaiian Koa back and sides, abalone rosette, figured maple body binding, one-piece mahogany neck, rosewood fingerboard with small pearl dots, roman style headstock, three-per-side tuners, tortoiseshell pickguard, Buzz Feiten tuning system, Natural finish, mfg. 2002-05, 2007-08.

| | N/A | $1,050 - 1,250 | $675 - 775 | $2,650 |

D90 S(W) GOLDEN HARVEST – dreadnought style, solid European spruce top, solid Indian rosewood back and sides, maple/rosewood body binding with abalone inlay, abalone rosette, five-piece mahogany/rosewood neck, 14/20-fret ebony fingerboard with tree-of-life inlay, three-per-side gold tuners, ebony bridge with abalone inlay, Brazilian rosewood pickguard, Natural finish, mfg. mid-1980s-1993.

| | N/A | $1,900 - 2,200 | $1,100 - 1,250 | $4,000 |

In 1992, the W was dropped from the model designation.

MSR/NOTES	100%	EXCELLENT	AVERAGE	LAST MSR

D96 SW PARAMOUNT – dreadnought style, solid Englemann spruce top, solid rosewood back and sides, Trilight bracing, abalone and pearl rosette, abalone heart top binding, one-piece mahogany neck, bound 14/22-fret ebony fingerboard, fingerboard and headstock pearl and abalone Ascanthus vine inlay, three-per-side gold tuners with ebony buttons, butterfly ebony bridge, tortoise pickguard, Natural finish, mfg. 1996-97.

	N/A	$4,000 - 5,000	$2,500 - 3,000	$8,000

D200 S(K) – dreadnought style, solid spruce top, round soundhole, tortoiseshell pickguard, bound body, three-stripe rosette, flame maple back/sides, mahogany neck, 14/20-fret bound rosewood fingerboard with pearl dot inlay, rosewood bridge with white bridgepins, three-per-side gold diecast tuners, Buzz Feiten tuning system, available in Natural finish, mfg. summer 1998-99.

	N/A	$825 - 950	$525 - 600	$1,800

D250 S(K) – similar to the D200 S(K), except features rosewood back/sides, mfg. summer 1998-99.

	N/A	$875 - 1,000	$575 - 675	$1,900

ACOUSTIC: DREADNOUGHT MODELS (WD SERIES)

WD7S HARVEST – dreadnought-style body, solid spruce top, mahogany back and sides, round soundhole with custom wood inlay rosette, cream body binding, set satin mahogany neck with two-way truss rod, 14/20-fret rosewood fingerboard with dot inlays, natural headstock overlay, three-per-side chrome tuners, rosewood bridge, available in Matte Cherry Burst, Matte Tobacco Burst, Natural Gloss, or Sunburst Gloss finish, 25.5 in. scale, mfg. 2011-present.

MSR $355	$200	$120 - 150	$70 - 90	

* **WD7SCE Cutaway Electric Harvest** – similar to the WD7S, except has a single smooth cutaway and EQ4-T, available in Matte Cherry Burst, Matte Tobacco Burst, Natural Gloss, or Sunburst Gloss finish, 25.5 in. scale, mfg. 2011-present.

MSR $445	$250	$145 - 180	$90 - 110	

WD10S HERITAGE – dreadnought-style body, solid Sitka spruce top, mahogany back and sides, round soundhole with custom wood inlay rosette, cream multi-ply body binding, set satin mahogany neck with two-way truss rod, 14/20-fret bound rosewood fingerboard with dot inlays, matching finish bound headstock overlay, three-per-side chrome tuners, rosewood bridge, available in Antique Sunburst, Black, or Natural finish, 25.5 in. scale, mfg. 2011-present.

MSR $445	$250	$145 - 180	$90 - 110	

* **WD10S12 12-String Heritage** – similar to the WD10S, except in 12-string configuration with six-per-side tuners, available in Natural finish, mfg. 2011-present.

MSR $534	$300	$175 - 225	$105 - 130	

* **WD10SLH Left-Handed Heritage** – similar to the WD10S, except in left-handed configuration, available in Natural finish, mfg. 2011-present.

MSR $478	$270	$160 - 200	$95 - 120	

* **WD10SCE Cutaway Electric Heritage** – similar to the WD10S, except has a single smooth cutaway and Fishman Isys+ electronics, available in Antique Burst, Black, or Natural finish, mfg. 2011-present.

MSR $534	$300	$175 - 225	$105 - 130	

» **WD10SCE12 Cutaway Electric 12-String Heritage** – similar to the WD10SCE, except in 12-string configuration with six-per-side tuners, available in Natural finish, mfg. 2011-present.

MSR $623	$350	$215 - 265	$130 - 160	

» **WD10SCELH Cutaway Electric Left-Handed Heritage** – similar to the WD10SCE, except in left-handed configuration, available in Natural finish, mfg. 2011-present.

MSR $570	$320	$190 - 240	$115 - 145	

WD11S HERITAGE – dreadnought-style body, solid cedar top, mahogany back and sides, round soundhole with custom wood inlay rosette, cream multi-ply body binding, set satin mahogany neck with two-way truss rod, 14/20-fret bound rosewood fingerboard with dot inlays, matching finish bound headstock overlay, three-per-side chrome tuners, rosewood bridge, available in Natural finish, 25.5 in. scale, mfg. 2011-present.

MSR $445	$250	$145 - 180	$90 - 110	

* **WD11SCE Cutaway Electric Heritage** – similar to the WD11S, except has a single smooth cutaway and Fishman Isys+ electronics, available in Natural finish, mfg. 2011-present.

MSR $534	$300	$175 - 225	$105 - 130	

WD15S HERITAGE DELUXE – dreadnought-style body, solid Sitka spruce top, mahogany back and sides, round soundhole with abalone rosette, maple body binding with abalone purfling, set satin mahogany neck with two-way truss rod, 14/20-fret bound rosewood fingerboard with dot inlays, matching finish bound headstock overlay, three-per-side chrome tuners, rosewood bridge, available in Natural finish, 25.5 in. scale, mfg. 2011-present.

MSR $534	$300	$175 - 225	$105 - 130	

MSR/NOTES	100%	EXCELLENT	AVERAGE	LAST MSR

* **WD15SCE Cutaway Electric Heritage Deluxe** – similar to the WD15S Heritage Deluxe, except has a single smooth cutaway and Fishman Isys+ electronics, available in Natural finish, mfg. 2011-present.

MSR $623	$350	$215 - 265	$130 - 160	

WD20S TAHOE – dreadnought-style body, solid Sitka spruce top, rosewood back and sides, round soundhole with custom wood inlay rosette, cream multi-ply body binding, set satin mahogany neck with two-way truss rod, 14/20-fret bound rosewood fingerboard with dot inlays, bound headstock with rosewood overlay, three-per-side chrome tuners, rosewood bridge, available in Natural finish, 25.5 in. scale, mfg. 2011-present.

MSR $534	$300	$175 - 225	$105 - 130	

* **WD20SCE Cutaway Electric Tahoe** – similar to the WD20S Tahoe, except has a single smooth cutaway and Fishman Isys+ electronics, available in Natural finish, mfg. 2011-present.

MSR $623	$350	$215 - 265	$130 - 160	

WD21S TAHOE – dreadnought-style body, solid cedar top, rosewood back and sides, round soundhole with custom wood inlay rosette, cream multi-ply body binding, set satin mahogany neck with two-way truss rod, 14/20-fret bound rosewood fingerboard with dot inlays, bound headstock with rosewood overlay, three-per-side chrome tuners, rosewood bridge, available in Natural finish, 25.5 in. scale, mfg. 2011-present.

MSR $534	$300	$175 - 225	$105 - 130	

* **WD21SCE Cutaway Electric Tahoe** – similar to the WD21S Tahoe, except has a single smooth cutaway and Fishman Isys+ electronics, available in Natural finish, mfg. 2011-present.

MSR $623	$350	$215 - 265	$130 - 160	

WD25S TAHOE DELUXE – dreadnought-style body, solid Sitka spruce top, rosewood back and sides, round soundhole with abalone rosette, maple body binding with abalone purfling, set satin mahogany neck with two-way truss rod, 14/20-fret bound rosewood fingerboard with dot inlays, matching finish bound headstock overlay, three-per-side chrome tuners, rosewood bridge, available in Natural finish, 25.5 in. scale, mfg. 2011-present.

MSR $623	$350	$215 - 265	$130 - 160	

* **WD25SCE Cutaway Electric Tahoe Deluxe** – similar to the WD25S Tahoe Deluxe, except has a single smooth cutaway and Fishman Isys+ electronics, available in Natural finish, mfg. 2011-present.

MSR $713	$400	$250 - 300	$140 - 180	

WD30S AUGUSTA – dreadnought-style body, solid Sitka spruce top, quilted Tamo ash back and sides, round soundhole with custom wood inlay rosette, cream multi-ply body binding, set satin mahogany neck with two-way truss rod, 14/20-fret bound rosewood fingerboard with dot inlays, bound headstock with rosewood overlay, three-per-side gold tuners, rosewood bridge, available in Natural finish, 25.5 in. scale, mfg. 2011-present.

MSR $623	$350	$215 - 265	$130 - 160	

* **WD30S12 12-String Augusta** – similar to the WD30S Augusta, except in 12-string configuration with six-per-side tuners, available in Natural finish, mfg. 2011-present.

MSR $713	$400	$250 - 300	$140 - 180	

* **WD30SLH Left-Handed Augusta** – similar to the WD30S Augusta, except in left-handed configuration, available in Natural finish, mfg. 2011-present.

MSR $659	$370	$230 - 280	$135 - 170	

* **WD30SCE Cutaway Electric Augusta** – similar to the WD30S Augusta, except has a single smooth cutaway and Fishman Presys+ electronics, available in Natural finish, mfg. 2011-present.

MSR $802	$450	$275 - 350	$160 - 200	

» **WD30SCE12 Cutaway Electric 12-String Augusta** – similar to the WD30SCE Cutaway Electric Augusta, except in 12-string configuration with six-per-side tuners, available in Natural finish, mfg. 2011-present.

MSR $891	$500	$300 - 375	$175 - 225	

» **WD30SCELH Cutaway Electric Left-Handed Augusta** – similar to the WD30SCE Cutaway Electric Augusta, except in left-handed configuration, available in Natural finish, mfg. 2011-present.

MSR $838	$470	$290 - 360	$170 - 215	

WD35S AUGUSTA DELUXE – dreadnought-style body, solid Sitka spruce top, quilted Tamo ash back and sides, round soundhole with abalone rosette, maple/rosewood body binding with abalone purfling, set satin mahogany neck with two-way truss rod, 14/20-fret bound rosewood fingerboard with dot inlays, matching finish bound headstock overlay, three-per-side gold tuners, rosewood bridge, available in Natural finish, 25.5 in. scale, mfg. 2011-present.

MSR $713	$400	$250 - 300	$140 - 180	

* **WD35SCE Cutaway Electric Augusta Deluxe** – similar to the WD35S Augusta Deluxe, except has a single smooth cutaway and Fishman Presys+ electronics, available in Natural finish, mfg. 2011-present.

MSR $891	$500	$300 - 375	$175 - 225	

MSR/NOTES	100%	EXCELLENT	AVERAGE	LAST MSR

WD150SW TIMBER RIDGE – dreadnought-style body, solid Sitka spruce top, solid mahogany back and sides, round soundhole with abalone rosette, mahogany body binding, set satin mahogany neck with two-way truss rod, 14/20-fret rosewood fingerboard with offset dot inlays, rosewood headstock overlay, three-per-side chrome tuners, rosewood bridge, available in Natural finish, 25.5 in. scale, mfg. 2011-present.

| MSR $891 | $500 | $300 - 375 | $175 - 225 | |

* *WD150SWCE Cutaway Electric Timber Ridge* – similar to the WD150SW, except has a single smooth cutaway, Sonicore pickup, and Fishman Presys Blend electronics, available in Natural finish, mfg. 2011-present.

| MSR $1,159 | $650 | $400 - 500 | $250 - 300 | |

WD160SW TIMBER RIDGE – dreadnought-style body, solid cedar top, solid mahogany back and sides, round soundhole with abalone rosette, mahogany body binding, set satin mahogany neck with two-way truss rod, 14/20-fret rosewood fingerboard with offset dot inlays, rosewood headstock overlay, three-per-side chrome tuners, rosewood bridge, available in Natural finish, 25.5 in. scale, mfg. 2011-present.

| MSR $891 | $500 | $300 - 375 | $175 - 225 | |

* *WD160SWCE Cutaway Electric Timber Ridge* – similar to the WD160SW, except has a single smooth cutaway, Sonicore pickup, and Fishman Presys Blend electronics, available in Natural finish, mfg. 2011-present.

| MSR $1,159 | $650 | $400 - 500 | $250 - 300 | |

WD250SW TIMBER RIDGE – dreadnought-style body, solid Sitka spruce top, solid rosewood back and sides, round soundhole with abalone rosette, rosewood body binding, set satin mahogany neck with two-way truss rod, 14/20-fret rosewood fingerboard with offset dot inlays, rosewood headstock overlay, three-per-side chrome tuners, rosewood bridge, available in Natural finish, 25.5 in. scale, mfg. 2011-present.

| MSR $1,070 | $600 | $350 - 450 | $225 - 275 | |

* *WD250SWCE Cutaway Electric Timber Ridge* – similar to the WD250SW, except has a single smooth cutaway, Sonicore pickup, and Fishman Presys Blend electronics, available in Natural finish, mfg. 2011-present.

| MSR $1,338 | $750 | $450 - 575 | $250 - 325 | |

WCD18 COMFORT – dreadnought-style body, contoured select spruce top, contoured mahogany back and sides, round soundhole with multi-ring abalone rosette, multi-ply cream body binding, set satin mahogany neck with two-way truss rod, 14/20-fret bound rosewood fingerboard with dot inlays, bound headstock with black overlay, three-per-side chrome tuners, rosewood bridge, available in Natural finish, 25.5 in. scale, mfg. 2011-present.

| MSR $355 | $200 | $120 - 150 | $70 - 90 | |

* *WCD18CE Cutaway Electric Comfort* – similar to the WCD18 Comfort, except has a single smooth cutaway and Fishman Isys+ electronics, available in Natural finish, mfg. 2011-present.

| MSR $498 | $280 | $170 - 210 | $100 - 125 | |

WDFLB26SCE FORREST LEE BENDER – single cutaway dreadnought-style body, solid cedar top, rosewood back and sides, round soundhole with abalone rosette, maple body binding with abalone purfling, abalone back strip, set mahogany neck with two-way truss rod, 14/20-fret bound rosewood fingerboard with abalone tree-of-life inlays, bound headstock with rosewood overlay with MOP logo/inlay, three-per-side chrome tuners, rosewood bridge with B-Bender string bender, Fishman Isys+ electronics, available in Natural finish, 25.5 in. scale, mfg. 2012-present.

| MSR $1,784 | $1,000 | $600 - 750 | $350 - 450 | |

ACOUSTIC: FOLK MODELS (F/WF SERIES)

In the late 1970s/early 1980s, Washburn offered many folk/auditorium body style counterparts to their Dreadnought series. However information is limited on these guitars. We know that the folk model is typically the same as the Dreadnought counterpart in specs, and prices are a bit lower on the folk models. Models include, but are not limited to, the **F20**, **F25**, and **F27 S**. Any information on these guitars can be submitted directly to Blue Book Publications.

F1 SK (JOEY) – smaller travel guitar, solid spruce top, round soundhole, ovangkol back/sides, mahogany neck, rosewood fingerboard with pearl dot inlay, rosewood bridge with white bridgepins, three-per-side chrome Grover tuners, available in Natural finish, mfg. summer 1998-2000.

| | N/A | $125 - 175 | $70 - 95 | $299 |

F8 – folk style, select spruce top, bound mahogany back and sides, bound 14/20-fret rosewood fingerboard with dot inlay, three-per-side chrome tuners, rosewood bridge, Natural finish, mfg. 2001-02.

| | N/A | $100 - 140 | $50 - 70 | $240 |

F10S – folk style, solid spruce top, mahogany back/sides, mahogany neck, 14/20-fret bound rosewood fingerboard with pearl dot inlay, rosewood bridge with black bridgepins, three-per-side tuners, available in Natural finish, mfg. 2002-2010.

| MSR $500 | $250 | $150 - 190 | $90 - 115 | |

F11 – folk style, mountain ash top, round soundhole, bound body, three-stripe purfling/rosette, mountain ash back/sides, mahogany neck, 14/20-fret bound rosewood fingerboard with pearl dot inlay, rosewood bridge with black bridgepins, three-per-side chrome Grover tuners, available in Antique Natural, Brown, or Natural (1997-99) finish, mfg. 1997-2002.

| | N/A | $170 - 220 | $90 - 110 | $380 |

MSR/NOTES	100%	EXCELLENT	AVERAGE	LAST MSR

F12 – folk style, spruce top, round soundhole, mahogany back/sides/neck, 14/20-fret rosewood fingerboard with dot inlay, rosewood bridge with pearl dot black pins, three-per-side chrome diecast tuners, Natural finish, mfg. 1980-early 1980s.

	N/A	$125 - 175	$70 - 95	

F15 – folk style, select spruce top, unknown back/sides, mfg. late 1970s-early 1980s.

	N/A	$100 - 150	$50 - 75	

F21 S – folk style, solid Sitka spruce top, rosewood back and sides, bound top/back, bound 14/20-fret rosewood fingerboard with dot inlay, three-per-side tuners, rosewood bridge, chrome hardware, Natural finish, mfg. 1996-97.

	N/A	$200 - 250	$120 - 150	$450

F26 S – folk style, solid cedar top, mahogany back and sides, mahogany neck, 14/20-fret rosewood fingerboard with dot inlay, three-per-side tuners, rosewood bridge, pickguard, Natural finish, mfg. 1978-early 1980s.

	N/A	$325 - 375	$175 - 225	

F28 S – folk style, solid spruce top, round soundhole, black pickguard, three-stripe bound body and rosette, three-piece rosewood back/sides, mahogany neck, 14/20-fret bound rosewood fingerboard with snowflake inlay, rosewood bridge with pearl dot white pins, bound peghead, three-per-side gold diecast tuners, available in Natural finish, mfg. 1978-early 1980s.

	N/A	$275 - 325	$150 - 200	$600

F30 S – folk style, solid cedar top, round soundhole, bound body, three-stripe purfling, five-stripe rosette, rosewood back/sides, mahogany neck, 14/20-fret rosewood fingerboard with herringbone/snowflake inlay, bound headstock with three-per-side chrome diecast tuners, rosewood bridge with pearl dot white pins and bone saddle, tortoise pickguard, available in Natural finish, mfg. 1978-early 1980s.

	N/A	$375 - 450	$200 - 250	

F32 SCE – thinline single cutaway style, solid spruce top, solid rosewood back and sides, round soundhole with rosette, maple body and neck binding, mahogany neck, 14/20-fret rosewood fingerboard with dot inlays, three-per-side tuners, rosewood bridge, tortoise pickguard, B-Band electronics, chrome hardware, available in Natural or Sunburst finish, mfg. 2005-06.

	N/A	$300 - 375	$175 - 225	$700

F50 S – folk style, solid spruce top, solid rosewood back and sides, multi-colored marquetry body binding and rosette, mahogany neck, 14/20-fret ebony fingerboard with snowflake inlays, three-per-side tuners, ebony bridge, pickguard, Natural finish, mfg. late 1970s-early 1980s.

	N/A	$425 - 500	$250 - 300	

F52 SWCE TIMBER RIDGE – dreadnought single cutaway style, solid spruce top, solid mahogany back and sides, round soundhole with rosette, maple body and neck binding, mahogany neck, 14/20-fret rosewood fingerboard with snowflake inlays, three-per-side tuners, rosewood bridge, tortoise pickguard, B-Band electronics, chrome hardware, Natural Satin finish, mfg. 2005-2010.

	$700	$450 - 550	$250 - 325	$1,200

WF10S HERITAGE – folk-style body, solid Sitka spruce top, mahogany back and sides, round soundhole with custom wood inlay rosette, cream multi-ply body binding, set satin mahogany neck with two-way truss rod, 14/20-fret bound rosewood fingerboard with dot inlays, bound headstock with rosewood overlay, three-per-side chrome tuners, rosewood bridge, available in Natural finish, 25.5 in. scale, mfg. 2012-present.

MSR $445	$250	$145 - 180	$90 - 110	

* **WF10SCE Cutaway Electric Heritage** – similar to the WF10S, except has a single smooth cutaway and Fishman Isys+ electronics, available in Natural finish, mfg. 2012-present.

MSR $534	$300	$175 - 225	$105 - 130	

WF11S HERITAGE – folk-style body, solid cedar top, mahogany back and sides, round soundhole with custom wood inlay rosette, cream multi-ply body binding, set satin mahogany neck with two-way truss rod, 14/20-fret bound rosewood fingerboard with dot inlays, bound headstock with rosewood overlay, three-per-side chrome tuners, rosewood bridge, available in Natural finish, 25.5 in. scale, mfg. 2012-present.

MSR $445	$250	$145 - 180	$90 - 110	

* **WF11SCE Cutaway Electric Heritage** – similar to the WD11S, except has a single smooth cutaway and Fishman Isys+ electronics, available in Natural finish, mfg. 2012-present.

MSR $534	$300	$175 - 225	$105 - 130	

ACOUSTIC: GRAND AUDITORIUM MODELS (WG SERIES)

WG7S HARVEST – grand auditorium-style body, solid spruce top, mahogany back and sides, round soundhole with custom wood inlay rosette, cream body binding, set satin mahogany neck with two-way truss rod, 14/20-fret rosewood fingerboard with dot inlays, natural headstock overlay, three-per-side chrome tuners, rosewood bridge, available in Natural Gloss finish, 25.5 in. scale, mfg. 2012-present.

MSR $355	$200	$120 - 150	$70 - 90	

* **WG7SCE Harvest Cutaway Electric** – similar to the WG7S Harvest, except has a single smooth cutaway and EQ4-T, available in Natural Gloss finish, 25.5 in. scale, mfg. 2012-present.

MSR $445	$250	$145 - 180	$90 - 110	

MSR/NOTES	100%	EXCELLENT	AVERAGE	LAST MSR

WG10S HERITAGE – grand auditorium-style body, solid Sitka spruce top, mahogany back and sides, round soundhole with custom wood inlay rosette, cream multi-ply body binding, set satin mahogany neck with two-way truss rod, 14/20-fret bound rosewood fingerboard with dot inlays, matching finish bound headstock overlay, three-per-side chrome tuners, rosewood bridge, available in Natural finish, 25.5 in. scale, mfg. 2012-present.

| MSR $445 | $250 | $145 - 180 | $90 - 110 | |

* *WG10SCE Heritage Cutaway Electric* – similar to the WG10S, except has a single smooth cutaway and Fishman Isys+ electronics, available in Natural finish, mfg. 2012-present.

| MSR $534 | $300 | $175 - 225 | $105 - 130 | |

WG16S HERITAGE DELUXE – grand auditorium-style body, solid cedar top, mahogany back and sides, round soundhole with abalone rosette, maple body binding with abalone purfling, set satin mahogany neck with two-way truss rod, 14/20-fret bound rosewood fingerboard with dot inlays, matching finish bound headstock overlay, three-per-side chrome tuners, rosewood bridge, available in Natural finish, 25.5 in. scale, mfg. 2011-present.

| MSR $534 | $300 | $175 - 225 | $105 - 130 | |

* *WG16SCE Heritage Deluxe Cutaway Electric* – similar to the WG16S Heritage Deluxe, except has a single smooth cutaway and Fishman Isys+ electronics, available in Natural finish, mfg. 2011-present.

| MSR $623 | $350 | $215 - 265 | $130 - 160 | |

WG26S TAHOE DELUXE – grand auditorium-style body, solid cedar top, rosewood back and sides, round soundhole with abalone rosette, maple body binding with abalone purfling, set satin mahogany neck with two-way truss rod, 14/20-fret bound rosewood fingerboard with dot inlays, matching finish bound headstock overlay, three-per-side chrome tuners, rosewood bridge, available in Natural finish, 25.5 in. scale, mfg. 2011-present.

| MSR $623 | $350 | $215 - 265 | $130 - 160 | |

* *WG26SE Tahoe Deluxe Electric* – similar to the WG26S Tahoe Deluxe, except has Fishman Isys+ electronics, available in Natural finish, mfg. 2011-present.

| MSR $713 | $400 | $250 - 300 | $140 - 180 | |

* *WG26SCE Tahoe Deluxe Cutaway Electric* – similar to the WG26S Tahoe Deluxe, except has a single smooth cutaway and Fishman Isys+ electronics, available in Natural finish, mfg. 2011-present.

| MSR $713 | $400 | $250 - 300 | $140 - 180 | |

WG016S WOODLINE – grand auditorium-style body, solid cedar top, mahogany back and sides, round soundhole with abalone rosette, set satin mahogany neck with two-way truss rod, 14/20-fret bound rosewood fingerboard with dot inlays, bound headstock with rosewood overlay and MOP logo/"W" inlay, three-per-side chrome tuners, rosewood bridge, available in Natural finish, 25.5 in. scale, mfg. 2011-present.

| MSR $534 | $300 | $175 - 225 | $105 - 130 | |

* *WG016SCE Woodline Cutaway Electric* – similar to the WG016S Woodline, except has a single smooth cutaway and Fishman Isys+ electronics, available in Natural finish, mfg. 2011-present.

| MSR $623 | $350 | $215 - 265 | $130 - 160 | |

WG026S WOODLINE – grand auditorium-style body, solid cedar top, rosewood back and sides, round soundhole with decorative rosette, set satin mahogany neck with two-way truss rod, 14/20-fret bound rosewood fingerboard with dot inlays, bound headstock with rosewood overlay and MOP logo/inlay, three-per-side chrome tuners, rosewood bridge, available in Natural finish, 25.5 in. scale, mfg. 2011-present.

| MSR $623 | $350 | $215 - 265 | $130 - 160 | |

* *WG026SCE Woodline Cutaway Electric* – similar to the WG026S Woodline, except has a single smooth cutaway and Fishman Isys+ electronics, available in Natural finish, mfg. 2011-present.

| MSR $713 | $400 | $250 - 300 | $140 - 180 | |

WCG18CE COMFORT – single smooth cutaway grand auditorium-style body, contoured select spruce top, contoured mahogany back and sides, round soundhole with multi-ring abalone rosette, multi-ply cream body binding, set satin mahogany neck with two-way truss rod, 14/20-fret bound rosewood fingerboard with dot inlays, bound headstock with black overlay, three-per-side chrome tuners, rosewood bridge, Fishman Isys+ electronics, available in Natural finish, 25.5 in. scale, mfg. 2011-present.

| MSR $498 | $280 | $170 - 210 | $100 - 125 | |

ACOUSTIC: JUMBO/BABY JUMBO MODELS (J/WB/WJ SERIES)

J12 S – medium jumbo style, solid spruce top, rosewood back and sides, mahogany neck, 14/21-fret rosewood fingerboard with pearl snowflake inlays, rosewood butterfly bridge, chrome hardware, natural finish, mfg. 2001-04.

| | N/A | $275 - 325 | $150 - 200 | $600 |

J20 S – jumbo style, solid cedar top, oval soundhole, bound body, five-stripe rosette, walnut back/sides, mahogany neck, 21-fret rosewood fingerboard with pearl snowflake inlay at 12th fret, rosewood bridge with pearl dot white pins and bone saddle, walnut veneer on peghead, three-per-side chrome diecast tuners, available in Natural finish, mfg. 1991-93.

| | N/A | $400 - 475 | $250 - 300 | $900 |

MSR/NOTES	100%	EXCELLENT	AVERAGE	LAST MSR

J21 CE – single rounded cutaway jumbo body, spruce top, oval soundhole, bound body, three-stripe purfling, five-stripe rosette, mahogany back/sides/neck, 21-fret bound rosewood fingerboard, pearl diamond inlay at 12th fret, rosewood bridge with white black dot pins, bound rosewood veneered peghead with screened logo, three-per-side chrome tuners, acoustic bridge pickup, 4-band EQ, available in Black, Natural, or Tobacco Sunburst finish, mfg. 1994 only.

	N/A	$300 - 350	$150 - 200	$650

J27 CE CUMBERLAND – single cutaway jumbo style, Java Ebony top, back, and sides, round soundhole with three-ring rosette, multi-ply body binding, mahogany neck, 14/20-fret bound rosewood fingerobard with pearl diamond inlays, bound Java Ebony headstock overlay with large Washburn logo and special inlay, three-per-side gold Grover Exclusive tuners with ebony buttons, rosewood butterfly bridge, tortoiseshell pickguard, B-Band A-15 electronics, Buzz Feiten Tuning System, available in Natural finish, case included, mfg. 2008-2010.

	$720	$475 - 550	$275 - 325	$1,200

J28 SDL CUMBERLAND – jumbo style, AAA solid spruce top, quilted maple back/sides, maple neck with truss-rod, rosewood fingerobard and butterfly bridge, tortoiseshell pickguard, black and white top binding, crown style headstock, three-per-side tuners, available in Natural finish, mfg. 2000-2010.

	$700	$450 - 525	$275 - 325	$1,120

* *J28 S12DL Cumberland 12-String* – similar to the J28SDL, except in 12-string configuration and six-per-side tuners, mfg. 2000-2010.

	$750	$500 - 575	$300 - 350	$1,280

* *J28 SCEDL Cumberland Cutaway Electric* – similar to the J28 SDL, except has a single rounded cutaway and B-Band electronics, available in Natural or Trans. Black finish, mfg. 2001-2010.

	$800	$550 - 625	$325 - 400	$1,280

J28 SCE – single rounded cutaway jumbo body, solid spruce top, round soundhole, bound body, inlaid rosette, mahogany back/sides/neck, 14/20-fret bound rosewood fingerboard with pearl 'crown' inlay, rosewood bridge with white bridgepins, three-per-side chrome Grover tuners, piezo bridge pickup, volume/3-band EQ controls, Equis Gold preamp, available in Tobacco Sunburst or Natural finish, mfg. 1995-2000.

	N/A	$500 - 600	$325 - 375	$1,150

This model is different than the Cumberland model that is similar to the other J28 SDL models. The original J28 SCE has mahogany back and sides.

J30 SCE – single smooth cutaway jumbo style with a slight bass bout cutaway (similar to a Telecaster), solid spruce top, mahogany back and sides, abalone rosette, fully bound body, bound mahogany neck, bound 15/24-fret ebonized rosewood fingerboard with an extended treble section into soundhole, three-per-side gold tuners, ebonized rosewood Butterfly bridge, black pickguard, Buzz Feiten Tuning System, available in Black, Natural, or Trans. Wine Red finish, mfg. summer 1998-99.

	N/A	$850 - 1,000	$550 - 650	$1,850

J32S CE GEORGE LYNCH – single cutaway jumbo style, solid spruce top, mahogany back and sides, round soundhole, multi-ply body binding, mahogany neck, 14/20-fret bound rosewood fingerboard with special pearl diamond inlays, matching finish headstock overlay with large Washburn logo and graphics, three-per-side aged finish Grover Exclusive tuners, rosewood butterfly bridge, B-Band A-15 electronics, Buzz Feiten Tuning System, available in custom outlaw graphic finish, case included, mfg. 2009-2010.

	$700	$500 - 575	$275 - 325	$1,280

J50 S – jumbo style, solid spruce top, bookmatched bird's-eye maple back/sides, fully bound body, 14/21-fret bound rosewood fingerboard with 12th fret pearl snowflake inlay, bird's-eye maple veneer on bound headstock with three-per-side pearl button gold diecast tuners, available in Natural finish, mfg. 1991-93.

	N/A	$525 - 625	$325 - 375	$1,150

J52 SW TIMBER CRAFT – solid spruce top, solid mahogany back and sides, maple binding, round soundhole with abalone rosette, mahogany neck, 14/20-fret rosewood fingerboard with diamond inlays, rosewood headstock veneer with three-per-side chrome Grover tuners, rosewood butterfly bridge, tortoise pickguard, available in Satin Natural finish, mfg. 2006-07.

	N/A	$450 - 575	$275 - 325	$1,250

J56 SW TIMBER CRAFT – solid spruce top, solid rosewood back and sides, maple binding, round soundhole with abalone rosette, mahogany neck, 14/20-fret rosewood fingerboard with diamond inlays, rosewood headstock veneer with three-per-side chrome Grover tuners, rosewood butterfly bridge, tortoise pickguard, available in Satin Gloss finish, mfg. 2006-07.

	N/A	$500 - 625	$300 - 375	$1,450

J58 SW TIMBER CRAFT – solid spruce top, solid flame maple back and sides, maple binding, round soundhole with abalone rosette, mahogany neck, 14/20-fret rosewood fingerboard with diamond inlays, rosewood headstock veneer with three-per-side chrome Grover tuners, rosewood butterfly bridge, tortoise pickguard, available in Gloss Natural finish, mfg. 2006-07.

	N/A	$725 - 900	$450 - 550	$2,000

J61 SCE – similar to J28 S CE, except has flame maple back/sides and Gotoh tuners, available in Natural or Tobacco Sunburst finish, mfg. 1997-99.

	N/A	$850 - 1,000	$550 - 650	$1,849

MSR/NOTES	100%	EXCELLENT	AVERAGE	LAST MSR

SJ45 S – Southern Jumbo style, AAA solid cedar top, Hawaiian Koa back and sides, bound body and neck, abalone rosette and top trim, 14/20-fret ebony fingerboard with pearl diamond and fancy 12th fret inlays, tortoise pickguard, ebony bridge, Buzz Feiten Tuning System, gold hardware, natural finish, mfg. 2004-05.

| | N/A | $350 - 400 | $200 - 250 | $750 |

WB200S – baby jumbo style, solid spruce top, mahogany back and sides, oval soundhole with checkered rosette, multi-ply ivoroid body binding, mahogany neck, 14/20-fret bound rosewood fingerboard with pearl dot inlays, bound headstock with Washburn logo, three-per-side chrome Grover Sta-tite tuners, rosewood butterfly bridge, available in Natural finish, case included, mfg. 2008-2010.

| | $480 | $275 - 350 | $170 - 210 | $800 |

* *WB200S CE Cutaway Electric* – similar to the WB200S, except has a single cutaway and B-Band A15 electronics, mfg. 2008-2010.

| | $580 | $350 - 425 | $210 - 260 | $960 |

» *WB200S CES Cutaway Electric Graphic* – similar to the WB200S CE Cutaway Electric, except has special Stephen Jensen graphics on the top and headstock, a special 12th fret inlay, and Natural finish on the back and sides, mfg. 2009-2010.

| | $900 | $550 - 675 | $300 - 350 | $1,500 |

WB400SW – baby jumbo style, solid cedar top, solid rosewood back and sides, oval soundhole with abalone rosette, multi-ply ivoroid body binding, 14/20-fret ebony fingerboard with pearl oval inlays, bound headstock with rosewood overlay, three-per-side gold tuners, rosewood butterfly bridge, available in Natural finish, mfg. 2007-2010.

| | $920 | $525 - 650 | $325 - 400 | $1,520 |

* *WB400SW CE Cutaway Electric* – similar to the WD400SW, except has a single smooth cutaway, solid spruce top, pearl pyramid fingerboard inlays, and custom Fishman pickup/electronics, available in Natural finish, mfg. 2007-2010.

| | $1,050 | $600 - 750 | $350 - 450 | $1,760 |

WJ40S CUMBERLAND – jumbo-style body, solid Sitka spruce top, flame maple back and sides, round soundhole with custom wood inlay rosette, cream multi-ply body binding, set satin mahogany neck with two-way truss rod, 14/20-fret bound rosewood fingerboard with dot inlays, bound headstock with flame maple overlay, three-per-side gold tuners, rosewood bridge, available in Natural finish, 25.5 in. scale, mfg. 2011-present.

| MSR $713 | $400 | $250 - 300 | $140 - 180 | |

* *WJ40SCE Cumberland Cutaway Electric* – similar to the WJ40S Cumberland, except has a single smooth cutaway and Fishman Presys+ electronics, available in Natural finish, mfg. 2011-present.

| MSR $891 | $500 | $300 - 375 | $175 - 225 | |

WJ45S CUMBERLAND DELUXE – jumbo-style body, solid Sitka spruce top, flame back and sides, round soundhole with abalone rosette, maple/rosewood body binding with abalone purfling, set satin mahogany neck with two-way truss rod, 14/20-fret bound rosewood fingerboard with dot inlays, bound headstock with flame maple overlay, three-per-side gold tuners, rosewood bridge, available in Natural finish, 25.5 in. scale, mfg. 2011-present.

| MSR $802 | $450 | $275 - 350 | $160 - 200 | |

* *WJ45S12 Cumberland Deluxe 12-String* – similar to the WJ45S Cumberland Deluxe, except in 12-string configuration with six-per-side tuners, available in Natural finish, mfg. 2011-present.

| MSR $891 | $500 | $300 - 375 | $175 - 225 | |

* *WJ45SLH Cumberland Deluxe Left-Handed* – similar to the WJ45S Cumberland Deluxe, except in left-handed configuration, available in Natural finish, mfg. 2011-present.

| MSR $838 | $470 | $290 - 360 | $170 - 215 | |

* *WJ45SCE Cumberland Deluxe Cutaway Electric* – similar to the WJ45S Cumberland Deluxe, except has a single smooth cutaway and Fishman Presys+ electronics, available in Natural finish, mfg. 2011-present.

| MSR $980 | $550 | $350 - 425 | $200 - 250 | |

» *WJ45SCE12 Cumberland Deluxe Cutaway Electric 12-String* – similar to the WJ45SCE Cumberland Deluxe Cutaway Electric, except in 12-string configuration with six-per-side tuners, available in Natural finish, mfg. 2011-present.

| MSR $1,070 | $600 | $350 - 450 | $225 - 275 | |

» *WJ45SCELH Cumberland Deluxe Cutaway Electric Left-Handed* – similar to the WJ45SCE Cumberland Deluxe Cutaway Electric, except in left-handed configuration, available in Natural finish, mfg. 2011-present.

| MSR $1,016 | $570 | $350 - 435 | $210 - 260 | |

ACOUSTIC: PAUL STANLEY SERIES

PS9 – dreadnought style, spruce top, select wood body, round soundhole with red ring rosette, red body binding, mahogany neck, 20-fret red bound fingerboard with red dot inlays, white headstock with black star, three-per-side chrome tuners, rosewood bridge, available in Black finish with Paul Stanley graphic, includes Paul Stanley gig bag and carton, mfg. 2007 only.

| | N/A | $140 - 175 | $85 - 105 | $360 |

MSR/NOTES	100%	EXCELLENT	AVERAGE	LAST MSR

PS11E – single sharp cutaway folk style, spruce top, select wood body, round soundhole with red ring rosette, red body binding, mahogany neck, 20-fret red bound fingerboard with red dot inlays, white headstock with black star, three-per-side gold tuners, rosewood bridge, WT92 preamp/ electronics, available in Black finish with Paul Stanley graphic, includes Paul Stanley gig bag and carton, mfg. 2007 only.

	N/A	$225 - 275	$135 - 170	$630

ACOUSTIC: PRAIRIE STATE MODELS (PR SERIES)

The Prairie State series features guitars that have a unique body shape to them. They are based on a type of 1920s body styling where the body looks like it has been squashed on the top to make it wider and shorter. A model **PR300** was built in USA as well.

PR100S – 1920s body style, solid cedar top, mahogany back and sides with inlay strip, rosewood fingerboard with dot inlay, rosewood "bass balanced" bridge, Roman-style headstock, three-per-side tuners, Buzz Feiten tuning system, available in Sunburst finish, mfg. 2002-03.

	N/A	$600 - 700	$375 - 450	$1,400

PR200S – 1920s body style, solid cedar top, rosewood back and sides with inlay strip, rosewood fingerboard with dot inlay, rosewood "bass balanced" bridge, Roman-style headstock, three-per-side tuners, Buzz Feiten tuning system, available in Sunburst finish, mfg. 2002-03.

	N/A	$625 - 750	$400 - 475	$1,500

ACOUSTIC: 1896 REISSUE/VINTAGE SERIES (R SERIES)

R301 – concert style, solid spruce top, round soundhole, bound body, three-stripe purfling/rosette, mahogany back/sides/neck, 12/18-fret rosewood fingerboard with pearl dot inlay, rosewood bridge with black white dot pins, rosewood veneered slotted peghead, three-per-side diecast chrome tuners, available in Natural finish, mfg. 1994 only.

	N/A	$275 - 325	$150 - 200	$600

R305 S – parlor style, solid cedar top, bound rosewood back and sides, 20s style rosette, mahogany neck, bound 12/18-fret rosewood fingerboard with 20s inlay pattern, bound open-style headstock with star and diamond logo and three-per-side chrome tuners with pearl buttons, rosewood bridge, Natural finish, mfg. 2001-03.

	N/A	$325 - 375	$175 - 225	$730

R306 – auditorium style, solid cedar top, rosewood back/sides, mahogany neck, 12/18-fret rosewood fingerboard with pearl multi-symbol inlay, rosewood bridge with carved fans/pearl dot inlay, white abalone dot bridge pins, rosewood veneered slotted peghead with pearl fan/diamond inlay, three-per-side diecast chrome tuners with pearl buttons, available in Natural finish, mfg. 1993-95.

	N/A	$350 - 425	$200 - 250	$800

R310 VICTORIAN – parlor (concert) style, solid spruce top, round soundhole, bound body, three-stripe purfling/rosette, rosewood back/sides, mahogany neck, 12/18-fret rosewood fingerboard with pearl dot inlay, rosewood bridge with black bridgepins, rosewood veneered slotted peghead, three-per-side diecast chrome tuners, available in Natural finish, mfg. 1996-98.

	N/A	$700 - 825	$425 - 500	$1,500

R312 PRESENTATION – parlor (concert) style, solid Englemann spruce top, solid rosewood back/sides, bound body, round soundhole, pearl and abalone floral rosette, mahogany neck, 12/18-fret ebony fingerboard with pearl and abalone Ascanthus vine fingerboard inlay, pearl and abalone inlaid rosewood veneered slotted peghead with three-per-side diecast chrome tuners, carved ebony bridge with black bridgepins, available in Natural finish, mfg. 1995-97.

	N/A	$3,000 - 3,500	N/A	$6,000

R314K – parlor style body, spruce top, Trembesi back and sides, round soundhole with two ring abalone rosette, cream multi-ply body binding with rope pattern purfling, set mahogany V-shaped neck, 12/18-fret bound ebony fingerboard with various pattern dot/diamond/star inlays, bound slotted headstock with decorative inlays, three-per-side open-style distressed tuners with pearl buttons, decorative ebony bridge, available in aged Natural finish, 24.75 in. scale, case included, current mfg.

MSR $713	$400	$250 - 300	$140 - 180	

R315K – parlor style body, spruce top, Trembesi back and sides, round soundhole with two ring abalone rosette, cream multi-ply body binding with rope pattern purfling, set mahogany V-shaped neck, 12/18-fret bound ebony fingerboard with various pattern dot/diamond/star inlays, bound slotted headstock with decorative inlays, three-per-side open-style tuners with pearl buttons, decorative ebony bridge, available in Natural finish, 24.75 in. scale, case included, mfg. 2010-present.

MSR $713	$400	$250 - 300	$140 - 180	

R319SWK – parlor style body, solid spruce top, solid Trembesi back and sides, round soundhole with two ring abalone rosette, cream multi-ply body binding with rope pattern purfling, set mahogany V-shaped neck, 12/18-fret bound ebony fingerboard, bound slotted headstock with decorative inlays, three-per-side open-style distressed tuners with pearl buttons, decorative ebony bridge, available in aged Natural finish, 24.75 in. scale, case included, mfg. summer 2009-present.

MSR $980	$550	$350 - 425	$200 - 250	

R320SWR – parlor style body, solid spruce top, solid rosewood back and sides, round soundhole with two ring abalone rosette, cream multi-ply body binding with rope pattern purfling, set mahogany V-shaped neck, 12/18-fret bound ebony fingerboard with tree of life inlay, bound slotted headstock with decorative inlays, three-per-side open-style distressed tuners with pearl buttons, decorative ebony bridge, available in aged Natural finish, 24.75 in. scale, mfg. 2010-present.

MSR $1,070	$600	$350 - 450	$225 - 275	

MSR/NOTES	100%	EXCELLENT	AVERAGE	LAST MSR

R321SWR – parlor style body, solid spruce top, solid rosewood back and sides, round soundhole with two ring abalone rosette, cream multi-ply body binding with rope pattern purfling, set mahogany V-shaped neck, 12/18-fret bound ebony fingerboard with tree of life inlay, bound slotted headstock with decorative inlays, three-per-side open-style tuners with pearl buttons, decorative ebony bridge, available in Natural finish, 24.75 in. scale, case included, mfg. 2010-present.

MSR $1,070	$600	$350 - 450	$225 - 275	

WSJ124 – slope-shouldered Southern Jumbo-style body, spruce top, Trembesi back and sides, round soundhole with two ring abalone rosette, cream multi-ply body binding with rope pattern purfling, set mahogany V-shaped neck, 14/20-fret bound ebony fingerboard with pearl diamond inlays, bound headstock with mahogany overlay and Washburn logo, three-per-side chrome tuners, butterfly ebony bridge, available in Natural finish, 24.75 in. scale, case included, current mfg.

MSR $802	$450	$275 - 350	$160 - 200	

ACOUSTIC: STEPHEN'S EXTENDED CUTAWAY MODELS (DC SERIES)

This series has a patented neck to body joint called the Stephen's Extended Cutaway (designed by Stephen Davies) that allows full access to all 24 frets.

DC60 LEXINGTON – single round cutaway dreadnought style, solid spruce top, oval soundhole, bound body, three-stripe purfling/rosette, ovankol back/sides, mahogany neck, 24-fret bound rosewood fingerboard with pearl dot inlay, rosewood bridge with black dot pins, three-per-side pearloid chrome diecast tuners, available in Natural finish, mfg. 1987-1991.

	N/A	$350 - 450	$200 - 250	$830

* *DC60 12 12-String Lexington* – similar to the DC60 Lexington, except in 12-string configuration and six-per-side tuners, mfg. 1987-1990.

	N/A	$475 - 600	$275 - 350	

* *DC60 E Lexington* – similar to the DC60 Lexington, except has an acoustic bridge pickup and 4-band EQ electronics, mfg. 1987-1994.

	N/A	$550 - 700	$325 - 400	$1,400

DC80 CHARLESTON – similar to DC60 Lexington, except features a solid cedar top, rosewood back/sides, mahogany neck, 24-fret bound rosewood fingerboard with diamond inlay, rosewood bridge with pearl dot white pins, rosewood veneer on bound peghead, three-per-side pearloid head gold diecast tuners, available in Natural finish, mfg. 1987-1991.

	N/A	$375 - 475	$225 - 275	$900

* *DC80 E Charleston* – similar to DC60 E Charleston, except has an acoustic bridge pickup and 4-band EQ electronics, mfg. 1987-1994.

	N/A	$600 - 750	$350 - 450	$1,500

ACOUSTIC: NATURAL WOOD MODELS (WD SERIES)

The WD Series are made with a "Veil Process" finish that is applied very thin. This process allows the wood to breath and age quicker than a normal finish that leads to a fuller sound of the guitar.

WD 9 SW – dreadnought style, solid sapele top/back/sides, tortoise pickguard, mahogany neck, 14/20-fret ebony fingerboard with dot inlay, ebony bridge, gold hardware, natural finish, 3/4 size of the WD 18 SW, mfg. 2005-06.

	N/A	$250 - 290	$140 - 180	$550

WD18 SW – dreadnought style, solid sapele top/back/sides, tortoise pickguard, sapele neck, 14/20-fret ebony fingerboard with dot inlay, ebony bridge, gold hardware, Natural finish, mfg. 2004-07.

	N/A	$225 - 275	$135 - 170	$600

WD20 S – dreadnought style, solid spruce top, round soundhole, black pickguard, bound body, three-stripe rosette, mahogany back/sides/neck, 14/20-fret rosewood fingerboard with pearl dot inlay, rosewood bridge with black white dot pins, rosewood peghead veneer with screened logo, three-per-side chrome tuners, available in Natural finish, mfg. 1993-98.

	N/A	$275 - 325	$150 - 200	$629

* *WD20 SCE* – similar to the WD20 S, except has a single cutaway, Fishman USA pickup, and Equis II+ electronics, mfg. 1994-95.

	N/A	$325 - 375	$175 - 225	$700

WD32 SW – dreadnought style, solid spruce top, round soundhole, bound body, mahogany back/sides/neck, 14/20-fret rosewood fingerboard with pearl slash inlay, rosewood butterfly bridge with black white dot pins, crown headstock, three-per-side chrome tuners, available in Natural finish, mfg. 2001-07.

	N/A	$250 - 300	$150 - 190	$650

* *WD32 SCE* – similar to the WD32 SW, except has a single cutaway and B-Band pickup and electronics, available in Natural finish, mfg. 2001-03.

	N/A	$300 - 350	$150 - 200	$660

WD40 S – similar to WD20 S, except has a solid cedar top and rosewood back and sides, mfg. 1993-94.

	N/A	$230 - 280	$130 - 180	$530

MSR/NOTES	100%	EXCELLENT	AVERAGE	LAST MSR

WD41 S/WD42 S/WD44 S/WD46 S 120TH ANNIVERSARY RAREWOOD – dreadnought style, bound solid cedar or spruce top, bound Macassar Ebony (WD41), Flamed Olive Ash (WD42), Hawaiian Koa (WD44), or Rosewood (WD46) back and sides, round soundhole with abalone rosette, mahogany neck, bound rosewood fingerboard with MOP diamond inlays, vintage crown headstock with abalone logo and inlay, three-per-side Grover tuners, rosewood butterfly bridge, pickguard, Natural finish, mfg. 2003 only.

WD41/WD42	N/A	$275 - 325	$150 - 200	
WD44/WD46	N/A	$325 - 375	$175 - 225	$600/$700

ACOUSTIC: TRAVEL MODELS

B52 SW – travel guitar, solid Sitka spruce top, solid mahogany back and sides, mahogany body binding, round soundhole with abalone rosette, mahogany neck, 14/19-fret rosewood fingerboard with dot inlay, three-per-side gold tuners with ebonite buttons, rosewood butterfly bridge, available in Natural finish, mfg. 2006-07.

	N/A	$250 - 300	$150 - 190	$760

RO5 ROVER – travel-sized three-string dulcimer guitar, solid spruce top, mahogany back and sides, oval soundhole, five-ply maple/rosewood fingerboard, maple fingerboard with various fret spacings, three-on-one-side tuners, available in Natural finish, instructional handbook included, mfg. 2009-2010.

	$120	$65 - 85	$40 - 50	$200

RO10 ROVER – travel guitar, solid spruce top, mahogany back and sides, oval soundhole, mahogany neck, 14/19-fret rosewood fingerboard with offset dot inlay, three-per-side gold tuners with ebonite buttons, rosewood bridge, available in Black, Camo (2008-2010), Cowboy Graphic (2008-2010), Natural, Trans. Blue, or Trans. Red finish, 24 in. scale, case, CD-ROM, strap and picks included, current mfg.

MSR $284	$150	$85 - 105	$50 - 65	

- Add 10% (Last MSR was $266) for camo finish.
- Add 10% (Last MSR was $266) for Cowboy "Rover" graphic finish.

ACOUSTIC ELECTRIC: ELECTRO-ACOUSTIC MODELS (NV SERIES)

NV100 – adjustable pitch single cutaway style, solid spruce top, 1-piece mahogany back, mahogany neck, roman style headstock, three-per-side tuners, ebony fingerboard and bridge, bound body, B-Band electronics, available in Natural, Black, or Vintage Sunburst finish, mfg. 2002-06.

	N/A	$425 - 500	$250 - 300	$1,200

- Add $75 for padauk back and sides with Padauk Natural Matte finish.

NV100C – classic single cutaway style, solid spruce top, one-piece mahogany back, mahogany neck, roman style headstock, three-per-side tuners, ebony fingerboard and bridge, bound body, B-Band electronics, available in Natural, Black, or Natural Matte finish, mfg. 2002-06.

	N/A	$425 - 500	$275 - 325	$1,100

NV300 – similar to the NV100, except has Fishman piezo and electronics, available in Natural, Vintage Sunburst, Black, or Natural Matte finish, mfg. 2002-06.

	N/A	$475 - 550	$300 - 350	$1,250

- Add $75 for padauk back and sides with Padauk Natural Matte finish.

ACOUSTIC ELECTRIC: FESTIVAL MODELS (EA SERIES)

Washburn's Festival Series models are equipped with Equis preamp systems and Fishman USA pickups. A model **EA50** was produced very briefly in the late 1980s. Very little information is known and any input is appreciated.

EA10 (NEWPORT) – deep single sharp cutaway deep body, spruce top, oval soundhole, bound body, three-stripe purfling/rosette, mahogany back/sides/neck, 21-fret bound rosewood fingerboard with pearl dot inlay, rosewood bridge with white black dot pins, bound peghead with screened logo, three-per-side chrome Grover tuners, acoustic bridge pickup, Equis Standard preamp, available in Black or Natural finish, mfg. 1994-2003.

	N/A	$330 - 380	$175 - 225	$730

In 1995 only, this model was named the Newport. Circa 2000, Buzz Feiten Tuning System was introduced.

EA10 (SECOND VERSION) – single cutaway petitie jumbo-style body, basswood top, back, and sides, round soundhole with abalone rosette, multi-ply body binding, set mahogany neck with two-way truss rod, 12/19-fret bound rosewood fingerboard with pearl dot inlays, bound headstock with matching finish overlay and pearl logo/inlay, three-per-side chrome tuners, rosewood bridge, EQ4-T electronics, available in Black or Red finish, 24 in. scale, mfg. 2010-present.

MSR $355	$200	$120 - 150	$70 - 90	

EA12 – single cutaway mini jumbo-style body, basswood top, back, and sides, round soundhole with abalone rosette, multi-ply body binding, set mahogany neck with two-way truss rod, 14/21-fret bound rosewood fingerboard with pearl dot inlays, bound headstock with matching finish overlay and pearl logo/inlay, three-per-side chrome tuners, rosewood bridge, EQ4-T electronics, available in Black or Red finish, 25.5 in. scale, mfg. 2010-present.

MSR $355	$200	$120 - 150	$70 - 90	

MSR/NOTES	100%	EXCELLENT	AVERAGE	LAST MSR

EA14 – single cutaway mini jumbo-style body, spruce top, catalpa back and sides, round soundhole with abalone rosette, multi-ply body binding, set mahogany neck with two-way truss rod, 14/21-fret bound rosewood fingerboard with pearl dot inlays, bound headstock with matching finish overlay and pearl logo/inlay, three-per-side chrome tuners, rosewood bridge, EQ4-T electronics, available in Tobacco Burst finish, 25.5 in. scale, mfg. 2010-present.

MSR $355	$200	$120 - 150	$70 - 90	

EA15 – single cutaway mini jumbo-style body, flame maple top, catalpa back and sides, round soundhole with abalone rosette, multi-ply body binding, set mahogany neck with two-way truss rod, 14/21-fret bound rosewood fingerboard with pearl dot inlays, bound headstock with matching finish overlay and pearl logo/inlay, three-per-side chrome tuners, rosewood bridge, EQ4-T electronics, available in Tobacco Burst finish, 25.5 in. scale, mfg. 2010-present.

MSR $391	$220	$130 - 165	$75 - 95	

EA16 (FIRST VERSION) – single smooth cutaway thin unbound body, maple top/back/sides, 14/20-fret bound rosewood fingerboard, matching headstock with three-per-side chrome tuners, rosewood Butterfly bridge, B-Band electronics, available in Metallic Blue, Metallic Cherry, Pearl Black, or Pearl White finish, mfg. 2001-04.

	N/A	$275 - 325	$150 - 200	$600

In 2002, Metallic Cherry and Pearl White finish were disc.

EA16 (SECOND VERSION) – single smooth cutaway thin bound body, spruce top mahogany back and sides, mahogany neck, 14/20-fret bound rosewood fingerboard, three-per-side chrome tuners, rosewood Butterfly bridge, B-Band/WT-82 electronics, available in Metallic Blue (2005-08), Natural, Pearl Black, or Tobacco Sunburst finish, mfg. 2005-2010.

	$300	$175 - 225	$105 - 130	$500

EA17 (FIRST VERSION) – deep single sharp cutaway style, solid spruce top, quilt maple back and sides, maple neck, 14/20-fret rosewood fingerboard with offset dot inlays, round soundhole with abalone rosette, rosewood bridge, B-Band microphone and preamp, Buzz Feiten Tuning System, chrome hardware, available in Black or Quilted Trans. Wine Red finish, mfg. 2004 only.

	N/A	$325 - 375	$175 - 225	$700

EA17 (SECOND VERSION) – single sharp cutaway deep body, ash top, quilted ash back and sides, oval soundhole with single ring rosette, multi-ply top and back binding, mahogany neck, 14/22-fret bound rosewood fingerboard with pearl diamond inlays, quilted ash matching finish headstock overlay with small Washburn logo and torch inlay, three-per-side chrome tuners, rosewood bridge, B-Band A15 electronics, available in Natural or Trans. Red finish, case included, mfg. 2008-2010.

	$390	$225 - 275	$135 - 170	$640

EA18 – single smooth cutaway, bound ash top/back/sides, mahogany neck, bound 14/22-fret rosewood fingerboard with diamond inlays, bound matching headstock with pearl sweeping crown logo and three-per-side chrome tuners, rosewood Butterfly bridge, Equis/B-Band electronics, available in Tobacco Sunburst or Trans. Red finish, mfg. 1997-2007.

	N/A	$300 - 375	$175 - 225	$750

In 2000, Equis Extra electronics replaced Equis Standard. In 2001, Equis Plus electronics replaced Equis Extra. In 2002, B-Band Electronics replaced Equis Plus.

EA20 (NEWPORT/WOODSTOCK) – thin single sharp cutaway thin body, select spruce or mahogany top, oval soundhole, bound body, three-stripe rosette, mahogany back/sides/neck, 14/21-fret rosewood fingerboard with pearl dot inlay, matching headstock with three-per-side Grover diecast tuners, rosewood bridge with pearl dot white pins, acoustic bridge pickup, Equis electonics, available in Black, Tobacco Sunburst, White, Woodstone Blue, Woodstone Brown, or Woodstone Silver finish, mfg. mid 1980s-2000.

	N/A	$400 - 475	$250 - 300	$1,000

In 1992, Woodstone finishes were disc. In 1993, Natural finish was introduced. In 1994, a select spruce/mahogany top replaced regular mahogany and White finish was disc. Until 1994, this guitar was referred to as the Newport. In 1995 only, this guitar was called the Woodstock, which is not to be confused with other Woodstock models (EA40). In 1996, Equis Gold electronics replaced Equis II. In 2000, Equis Plus electronics replaced Equis Gold.

* ***EA20 LH Left-Handed*** – similar to the EA20, except in left-handed configuration, available in Black finish, mfg. mid-1990s.

	N/A	$425 - 500	$275 - 325	$990

* ***EA20 SDL*** – similar to the EA20, except has a solid cedar or spruce top, abalone rosette, quilted maple back and sides, maple neck, bound 14/21-fret rosewood fingerboard with dot inlay, Natural wood headstock with three-per-side chrome tuners with ebonite buttons, rosewood bridge, Equis Chorus/B-Band electronics, Buzz Feiten Tuning System, availble in Natural finish, mfg. 2001-2010.

	$750	$450 - 550	$250 - 325	$1,200

In 2002, a solid spruce top replaced the solid cedar and B-Band electronics replaced Equis.

* ***EA20 12 (Newport/Woodstock) 12-String*** – similar to EA20, except in 12 string configuration and six-per-side tuners, available in Black, Natural, or White finish, mfg. mid 1980s-1997.

	N/A	$400 - 475	$250 - 300	$900

In 1993, White finish was disc. and Natural finish was introduced. In 1994, Natural finish was disc. In 1996, Equis Gold electronics replaced Equis II.

MSR/NOTES	100%	EXCELLENT	AVERAGE	LAST MSR

* *EA20 X Melissa Limited Edition* – similar to EA20, except has special Melissa fingerboard inlay, available in Black finish, mfg. 1995 only.

	N/A	$500 - 575	$300 - 350	$949

This model was designed in conjunction with Greg Allman (Allman Brothers). It is estimated that only 500 instruments were built and each one is individually numbered.

EA20 (SECOND VERSION) – single sharp cutaway Festival-style body, spruce top, flame maple back and sides, oval soundhole with abalone rosette, multi-ply body binding, set maple neck with two-way truss rod, 14/21-fret bound rosewood fingerboard with pearl dot inlays, bound headstock with matching finish flame maple overlay and pearl logo/inlay, three-per-side chrome tuners, rosewood bridge, EQ4-T electronics, available in Natural finish, 25.5 in. scale, mfg. 2010-present.

MSR $445	$250	$145 - 180	$90 - 110	

EA21HM – single sharp cutaway thin body, mahogany top, back, and sides, oval soundhole with large abalone pearl rosette, multi-ply top and back binding, abalone pearl top border, mahogany neck, 14/21-fret rosewood fingerboard with pearl star inlays, hockey stick-style headstock with black overlay and Washburn logo, six-on-one-side chrome Grover Exclusive tuners, rosewood bridge, B-Band A15 electronics, Buzz Feiten Tuning System, available in Black, White (2008 only), or Wine Red finish, case included, mfg. 2008-2010.

	$750	$450 - 550	$250 - 325	$1,200

EA22 NUNO BETTENCOURT LIMITED EDITION – single sharp cutaway folk style, spruce top, oval soundhole, bound body, five-stripe purfling, nine-stripe rosette, mahogany back/sides/neck, 21-fret bound rosewood fingerboard with pearl wings inlay, rosewood bridge with white black dot pins, bound blackface peghead with screened signature/logo, three-per-side chrome Grover tuners, acoustic bridge pickup, volume/tone control, 3-band EQ, numbered commemorative metal plate inside body, available in Black finish, mfg. 1992-94.

	N/A	$475 - 550	$300 - 350	$1,000

EA26 CRAIG CHACQUICO SIGNATURE – thin single sharp cutaway jumbo body, select spruce top, oval soundhole, bound body, abalone rosette, mahogany back/sides/neck, 21-fret rosewood fingerboard with special abalone position markers, rosewood bridge with pearl dot white pins, three-per-side Grover diecast tuners, gold hardware, acoustic bridge pickup, volume/tone controls, Equis Gold preamp, available in Black, Natural, or White finish, mfg. 1996-2000.

	N/A	$550 - 650	$350 - 425	$1,200

Black finish discontinued in 1999.

EA27 K – similar to the EA26, except features chrome hardware, Equis Silver preamp, available in Natural finish, mfg. 1997-99.

	N/A	$525 - 600	$325 - 375	$1,159

EA28 S – single sharp cutaway thin body, solid spruce top, oval soundhole, mahogany back and sides, mahogany neck, 14/21-fret rosewood fingerboard with dot inlay, three-per-side chrome tuners, rosewood bridge, Equis Gold electronics, Fishman Matrix transducer, Natural finish, mfg. 1996-97.

	N/A	$525 - 625	$350 - 425	$1,200

EA30 MONTEREY – single sharp cutaway dreadnought style, spruce top, oval soundhole, bound body, three-stripe purfling, five-stripe rosette, flame maple back/sides, mahogany neck, 21-fret rosewood fingerboard, rosewood bridge with white pearl dot pins, three-per-side chrome diecast tuners, acoustic bridge pickup, volume/tone control, 3-band EQ, available in Natural, Trans. Red, Trans. Blue, or Trans. Black finish, late 1980s-1991.

	N/A	$325 - 375	$175 - 225	$730

* *EA30 12 Monterey 12-String* – similar to the EA30, except in 12-string configuration and six-per-side tuners, available in Natural finish, late 1980s-1991.

	N/A	$325 - 400	$175 - 225	$770

* *EA30 LH Monterey Left-Handed* – similar to the EA30, except in left-handed configuration, available in Natural finish, late 1980s-1991.

	N/A	$325 - 400	$175 - 225	$830

EA32 S – single sharp cutaway deep body, solid cedar top, oval soundhole, flamed sycamore back and sides, mahogany neck, 14/21-fret rosewood fingerboard with diamond inlay, three-per-side gold tuners, rosewood bridge, Equis Gold electronics, Fishman Matrix transducer, Natural finish, mfg. 1996-97.

	N/A	$650 - 750	$425 - 500	$1,500

EA33 S K – deep single sharp cutaway jumbo body, solid spruce top, oval soundhole, bound body, three-stripe rosette, flamed maple back/sides, mahogany neck, 21-fret rosewood fingerboard with pearl dot inlay, rosewood bridge with pearl dot white pins, three-per-side Grover diecast tuners, gold hardware, acoustic bridge pickup, volume/tone controls, Equis Gold preamp, Buzz Feiten Tuning System, available in Natural finish, mfg. 1997-99.

	N/A	$775 - 900	$500 - 575	$1,700

EA36/EA46 (MARQUEE) – single sharp cutaway thin body, flame/bird's-eye maple top/back/sides, three-stripe bound body, 6 or 9 diagonal sound channels, mahogany neck, 14/23-fret extended rosewood bound fingerboard with pearl diamond inlay, flame maple or rosewood veneer on bound peghead, three-per-side pearl button gold diecast tuners, rosewood bridge with pearl dot black pins, acoustic bridge pickup, Equis Gold preamp, available in Blue, Natural, Tobacco Sunburst, or Vintage Sunburst finish, mfg. late 1980s-1997.

	N/A	$500 - 600	$275 - 325	$1,000

• Add 25% for Blue finish (special order only).

MSR/NOTES	100%	EXCELLENT	AVERAGE	LAST MSR

In 1992, the Marquee was renumbered the EA36 (previously EA46), flamed maple top/back/sides were changed to birdseye maple, the sound channels were narrowed and more were added to bring the total from six to nine, Tobacco Sunburst was disc., and Vintage Sunburst was introduced. In 1994, Vintage Sunburst was disc. In 1996, Marquee was dropped from the model name, and Equis Gold electronics replaced Equis II.

* *EA36 12 Marquee 12-String* – similar to EA36 Marquee, except in 12-string configuration and six-per-side tuners, available in Natural or Vintage Sunburst finish, mfg. 1992-93.

	N/A	$550 - 650	$350 - 400	$1,050

EA40 WOODSTOCK – single sharp cutaway dreadnought style, mahogany top, oval soundhole, bound body, abalone purfling/rosette, mahogany back/sides/neck, 21-fret bound rosewood fingerboard, rosewood bridge with pearl dot black pins, three-per-side chrome diecast tuners, Washburn 3200/Equis II preamp system, available in Black, Natural, Tobacco Sunburst, White, or Wine Red finish, mfg. 1979-1991.

	N/A	$500 - 575	$325 - 375	$1,000

In the mid-1980s, a spruce top replaced the mahogany top. Circa 1987, EQ300 electronics were introduced (sliders instead of knobs). By 1990, Equis II electronics were being used. This model had birdseye maple back/sides with Natural finish as an option.

* *EA40 12 Woodstock 12-String* – similar to the EA40 Woodstock, except in 12-string configuration and six-per-side tuners, mfg. 1979-1991.

	N/A	$525 - 600	$325 - 375	$1,040

In the mid-1980s, a spruce top replaced the mahogany top. Circa 1987, EQ300 electronics were introduced (sliders instead of knobs). By 1990, Equis II electronics were being used.

EA44 MONTEREY – single sharp cutaway thin style, solid cedar top, oval soundhole, bound body, three-stripe purfling/rosette, rosewood back/sides, mahogany neck, 14/20-fret bound rosewood fingerboard with pearl diamond inlay, rosewood bridge with white black pins, bound peghead with rosewood veneer, three-per-side chrome tuners with pearl buttons, acoustic bridge pickup, Washburn 3200/EQ300/Equis II electronics, available in Black, Natural, or Tobacco Sunburst finish, mfg. 1979-1985, 1987-89, 1992-94.

	N/A	$500 - 575	$325 - 375	$1,100

This model was introduced three separate times, so the description may vary a bit. It is one of the three original Festival guitars and did not have the EA44 designation until the mid-1980s. In 1987, the EQ300 electronic system was introduced with sliders instead of knobs, and the guitar was only known as the EA44. In 1992, the Equis II electronic system was introduced, and the guitar was known as both the Monterey and EA44.

EA45 TANGLEWOOD – similar to EA44 except has a deep body, available in Natural or Tobacco Sunburst finish, mfg. 1979-1985, 1987-89, 1992-94.

	N/A	$525 - 600	$350 - 400	$1,150

This model was introduced three separate times, so the description may vary a bit. It is one of the three original Festival guitars and did not have the EA45 designation until the mid-1980s. In 1987, the EQ300 electronic system was introduced with sliders instead of knobs, and the guitar was only known as the EA45. In 1992, the Equis II electronic system was introduced, and the guitar was known as both the Tanglewood and EA45.

EA45 S – similar to the EA45, single sharp cutaway deep bound body, solid cedar top, abalone rosette, koa back and sides, maple neck, bound 14/21-fret rosewood fingerboard with pearl diamond inlays, matching bound headstock with three-per-side gold tuners with ebonite buttons, rosewood bridge, B Band electronics, Buzz Feiten Tuning System, available in Natural finish, mfg. 2002-03.

	N/A	$450 - 525	$275 - 325	$1,000

EA46 – see the EA36/EA46 Marquee listing.

EA48 – single sharp cutaway thin body, solid cedar top, oval soundhole, abalone body binding and rosette, Jacaranda back and sides, seven-piece rosewood/mahogany neck, 14/21-fret bound rosewood fingerboard with wing fret markers, bound headstock with three-per-side gold tuners with pearl buttons, rosewood bridge, Equis II electronics, available in Black, Natural, or Tobacco Sunburst finish, mfg. 1992 only.

	N/A	$900 - 1,050	$550 - 650	$1,800

EA52 SW – single sharp cutaway, solid spruce top, solid mahogany back and sides, oval soundhole with abalone rosette, 14/20-fret bound rosewood fingerboard with snowflake inlays, rosewood capped headstock with three-per-side chrome Grover tuners, rosewood butterfly bridge, BBand tape mic and preamp, available in Natural finish, mfg. 2006 only.

	N/A	$550 - 650	$325 - 400	$1,400

EA220 DOUBLENECK – deep single sharp cutaway thin body, select spruce top, oval soundhole, bound body, three-stripe rosette, mahogany back/sides/neck, 21-fret rosewood fingerboard with pearl dot inlay, rosewood bridge with pearl dot white pins, 12-string configuration neck (six-per-side Grover diecast tuners), six-string configuration neck (three-per-side Grover diecast tuners), chrome hardware, acoustic bridge pickups, volume/tone controls, neck selector toggle switch, Equis Gold preamp, available in Black or Natural finish, mfg. 1996-2000.

	N/A	$950 - 1,100	$600 - 700	$2,100

In 2000, Equis Plus electronics replaced Equis Gold, and Black finish was disc.

EC41 TANGLEWOOD – single sharp cutaway thin body, nylon string classical style, solid spruce top, oval soundhole, ovangkol back and sides, mahogany neck, 14/21-fret rosewood fingerboard with dot inlay, open-style headstock with three-per-side gold tuners and pearl buttons, rosewood bridge, Equis II electronics, Natural finish, mfg. late 1980s-1992.

	N/A	$375 - 450	$225 - 275	$900

MSR/NOTES	100%	EXCELLENT	AVERAGE	LAST MSR

ACOUSTIC ELECTRIC: MIRAGE/SOLIDBODY MODELS (CB/SBC/SBF SERIES)

The Mirage Series was introduced in 1984 as the original acoustic/electric solidbody line. After a short period, the Mirage Series was changed to the Solid Body Folk (SBF) and Solid Body Classic (SBC) Series. There are no differences in the construction/design of the series. In 1987, a Tele- and Strat-look alike solidbody acoustics were introduced. The **SBS20** looked like a Stratocaster and the **SBT21** look like a Telecaster. They both had pointed headstocks with six-on-one-side tuners. Any information on these guitars can be submitted directly to Blue Book Publications.

CB400 (US MFG.) – solid body acoustic single cutaway, solid spruce/maple top, one-piece mahogany back, mahogany neck, rosewood fingerboard with pearl slash inlays, rosewood bridge, B Band electronics and pickup, three knobs on face of guitar, available in Vintage Sunburst, Quilted Cherry Gloss, or FCRB finish, mfg. 2002-03.

	N/A	$900 - 1,050	$550 - 650	$2,000

SBC20/MIRAGE CLASSIC – single rounded cutaway classic style, spruce top, round soundhole, bound body, wooden inlay rosette, routed out mahogany body, mahogany neck, 14/22-fret rosewood fingerboard with pearl dot inlay, rosewood bridge, open-style headstock with three-per-side chrome diecast tuners, Washburn 3200 Sensor pickup, two knobs, available in Natural or Tobacco Sunburst finish, mfg. 1984-87, 1990-91.

	N/A	$250 - 300	$125 - 175	$550

SBC50/MIRAGE CLASSIC DL – similar to the SBC20/Classic, except has the addition of a mid-range control in the EQ section, available in Natural finish, mfg. 1984-87.

	N/A	$275 - 325	$150 - 200	

SBC70 – single cutaway classic style routed out mahogany body, multi-bound spruce top, mahogany neck, 14/22-fret bound rosewood fingerboard, tied rosewood bridge, rosewood veneered slotted peghead, three-per-side chrome tuners with pearloid buttons, acoustic bridge pickup, volume/tone controls, available in Natural finish, mfg. 1994 only.

	N/A	$300 - 350	$175 - 225	$700

SBF24/MIRAGE STANDARD/DL – single round cutaway dreadnought style, spruce top, round soundhole, bound body, wooden inlay rosette, routed out mahogany body, mahogany neck, 14/22-fret rosewood fingerboard with pearl dot inlay, matching headstock with three-per-side chrome diecast tuners, rosewood bridge with white pearl dot pins, Washburn 3200 Sensor pickup, two knobs (v, tone), active electronics, available in Black, Blue Sun Burst, Natural, Pearl White, or Tobacco Sunburst finish, mfg. 1984-1991.

	N/A	$250 - 300	$125 - 175	$570

* **SBF24 12/Mirage DL 12-String** – similar to the SBF24, except in 12-string configuration and six-per-side tuners, available in Black or Natural finish, mfg. mid 1980s.

	N/A	$275 - 325	$150 - 200	

SBF25/MIRAGE PRO – similar to the SBF24/Mirage Standard/DL, except has an exposed humbucker pickup below the soundhole, a mid-range knob in the EQ section, and two knobs and a three-way switch on the front of the guitar, available in Black, Ivory, Natural, or Tobacco Sunburst finish, mfg. 1984-87.

	N/A	$300 - 350	$175 - 200	

SBF80 – single cutaway dreadnought style routed out mahogany body, multi-bound figured maple top, mahogany neck, 22-fret bound rosewood fingerboard with pearl slotted diamond inlay, rosewood bridge with white abalone dot pins, bound figured maple peghead with screened logo, three-per-side chrome Grover tuners with pearloid buttons, acoustic bridge pickup, three knobs, active electronics, available in Black, Natural, or Cherry Sunburst finish, mfg. 1992-95.

	N/A	$350 - 400	$200 - 250	$750

In 1993, Natural finish was introduced. In 1994, Black and Natural finishes were disc., and the headstock matched the finish (Cherry Sunburst).

* **SBF80 12 12-String** – similar to the SBF80, except in 12-string configuration and six-per-side tuners, available in Black or Cherry Sunburst finish, mfg. 1992 only.

	N/A	$375 - 450	$225 - 275	$800

In 1993, Natural finish was introduced. In 1994, Black and Natural finishes were disc., and the headstock matched the finish (Cherry Sunburst).

ACOUSTIC ELECTRIC: RED ROCKER MODELS (RR SERIES)

These models were designed in conjunction with guitarist Sammy Hagar.

RR100 – single sharp cutaway semi-solid mahogany body, solid spruce top, 22-fret rosewood fingerboard with offset inlay, black headstock with three-per-side chrome Grover tuners, rosewood Butterfly bridge, Duncan Designed Hot Rails exposed pickup, Fishman Matrix Transducer in bridge, active electronics, four knobs, available in Black or Trans. Red finish, mfg. 1996-97.

	N/A	$350 - 425	$200 - 250	$950

RR150 – single sharp cutaway semi-hollow alder body, bound quilted maple top, mahogany neck, 22-fret rosewood fingerboard with pearl dot inlay, blackface peghead, rosewood bridge, 3-per-side Grover tuners, two exposed humbucker pickups, acoustic piezo pickup, three knobs, three-position switch, chrome hardware, available in Black or Trans. Red finish, mfg. 1997-99.

	N/A	$550 - 650	$300 - 375	$1,200

MSR/NOTES	100%	EXCELLENT	AVERAGE	LAST MSR

RR180 – single sharp cutaway solid chambered mahogany body, standard maple top, ivoroid body binding, 22-fret bound rosewood fingerboard with offset inlay, black headstock with three-per-side chrome tuners with pearl buttons, rosewood Butterfly bridge, Duncan Designed Hot Rails exposed pickup, Fishman Matrix Transducer in bridge, active electronics, three knobs, available in Black or Trans. Red finish, mfg. 1996-97.

	N/A	$750 - 900	$425 - 500	$2,000

RR200 – single sharp cutaway solid chambered mahogany body, figured maple top, pearloid body binding, 22-fret bound rosewood fingerboard with "Red Rocker" pearl inlay, bound black headstock with three-per-side chrome tuners with pearl buttons, rosewood Butterfly bridge, Duncan Designed Hot Rails exposed pickup, Fishman Matrix Transducer in bridge, active electronics, three knobs, available in Trans. Red finish, mfg. 1996-97.

	N/A	$850 - 1,000	$475 - 550	$2,200

RR300 (US MFG.) – single sharp cutaway semi-hollow mahogany body, bound spruce top, mahogany neck, 22-fret rosewood fingerboard with pearl dot inlay, black headstock with pearl inlays, three-per-side Schaller Kluson tuners with pearl buttons, rosewood bridge, one P-90 soapbar pickup, acoustic piezo pickup, three knobs, Buzz Feiten Tuning System, chrome hardware, available in Antique Natural, Black, or Trans. Red finish, mfg. 1997-99.

	N/A	$800 - 950	$475 - 550	$2,000

ACOUSTIC ELECTRIC BASS: AB SERIES

AB5 – single smooth cutaway thin jumbo body, spruce top, mahogany back and sides, round soundhole with single ring rosette, multi-ply body binding, set mahogany neck, 15/22-fret rosewood fingerboard with pearl dot inlays, mahogany (Natural finish) or black (Black finish) headstock overlay, two-per-side chrome tuners, rosewood bridge, QPH electronics, available in Black or Natural finish, 32 in. scale, mfg. 2011-present.

MSR $534	$300	$175 - 225	$105 - 130	

AB10 – single sharp cutaway thin jumbo body, select spruce top, diagonal slotted sound channels (soundhole), bound body, mahogany back/sides, maple neck, 23-fret rosewood fingerboard with pearl dot inlay, rosewood bridge with brass insert, two-per-side tuners, chrome hardware, Equis Silver bass preamp system, available in Black, Natural (1994-2003), or Tobacco Sunburst (1994, 2011-present) finish, mfg. 1994-present.

MSR $1,070	$600	$350 - 450	$210 - 260	

In 1999, Equis Standard electronics replaced Equis Silver. In 2000, Equis Extra electronics replaced Equis Standard. In 2004, Equis Crystal electronics replaced Equis Extra.

AB20 – single sharp cutaway thin jumbo body, mahogany top, diagonal sound channels (soundhole), bound body, mahogany back/sides, maple neck, 23-fret rosewood fingerboard with pearl dot inlay, rosewood bridge with brass insert, two-per-side tuners, chrome hardware, Equis Gold bass preamp system, available in Black, Natural, Tobacco Sunburst, Trans. Black, Woodstone Brown, or Woodstone Red finish, mfg. late 1980s-1999.

	N/A	$550 - 650	$350 - 425	$1,200

This model was available with a fretless fingerboard (option disc. in 1996). In 1991, Woodstone finishes were disc. In 1992, Trans. Black was disc. In 1995, Natural finish was disc., reintroduced 1996 only.

AB25 – similar to AB20, except in five-string configuration, 3/2-per-side tuners, available in Black or Tobacco Sunburst finish, mfg. 1992-97.

	N/A	$600 - 700	$375 - 450	$1,050

Black finish was only available in 1995.

AB30 – single sharp cutaway thin body, flamed sycamore top/back/sides, diagonal sound channels (soundhole), 15/23-fret exended rosewood fingerboard with dot inlay, black headstock with two-per-side chrome tuners, rosewood bridge, one bass humbucker pickup, piezo pickup in bridge, four knobs on face of guitar, active electronics, available in Natural or Tobacco Sunburst finish, mfg. 1994-97.

	N/A	$500 - 600	$300 - 350	$1,000

In 1995, Tobacco Sunburst finish was disc.

AB32 – single smooth cutaway deep body, select bound spruce top, oval soundhole, mahogany back and sides, mahogany neck, 17/24-fret rosewood fingerboard with dot inlay, two-per-side chrome tuners, rosewood bridge, Equis Silver electronics, available in Natural or Tobacco Sunburst finish, mfg. 1997-99.

	N/A	$500 - 600	$300 - 350	$1,100

In 1999, Antique Natural replaced Natural finish.

AB34 – single cutaway with "Xtra-cut" jumbo body, select spruce top, round soundhole, mahogany back and sides, mahogany neck, 18/23-fret rosewood fingerboard with 12th fret Washburn inlay, two-per-side tuners, rosewood bridge, Equis Plus electronics, chrome hardware, available in Natural or Tobacco Sunburst finish, mfg. 1999-2003.

	N/A	$500 - 575	$300 - 350	$1,100

In 2002, Tobacco Sunburst finish was disc.

AB35 – similar to the AB34, except in five-string configuration, 3/2-per-side tuners, mfg. 1999-2002.

	N/A	$550 - 650	$325 - 375	$1,200

* **AB35 FL Fretless** – similar to the AB35, except has a fretless fingerboard, available in Tobacco Sunburst finish, mfg. 2000-02.

	N/A	$575 - 675	$325 - 400	$1,300

MSR/NOTES	100%	EXCELLENT	AVERAGE	LAST MSR

AB40 FIRST VERSION – single round cutaway deep body, arched solid spruce top, diagonal sound channels (soundhole), bound body, quilted ash back/sides, multi-layer maple neck, 16/24-fret bound ebony fingerboard with pearl dot inlay, ebonized rosewood bridge with brass insert, bound peghead with pearl Washburn logo and stylized inlay, two-per-side tuners, gold hardware, active electronics, three knobs (v, 2 tone), Equis II bass preamp system, available in Natural or Tobacco Sunburst finish, mfg. late 1980s-1993.

	N/A	$1,050 - 1,200	$675 - 800	$2,250

* *AB40 FL Fretless* – similar to the AB40, except in fretless fingerboard configuration, available in Tobacco Sunburst finish, mfg. late 1980s-1991.

	N/A	$1,000 - 1,150	$650 - 775	$1,750

* *AB40 (Second Version)* – similar to the AB40, except has a select spruce top, maple back and sides, and Washburn electronics, available in Vintage Sunburst finish, mfg. 2004-present.

MSR $1,427	$800	$475 - 600	$275 - 350	

AB40 STU HAMM SIGNATURE – single round cutaway deep acoustic bass body, arched spruce top, arched maple back, maple sides, round soundhole with no rosette, multi-ply body binding, mahogany neck, 16/24 extended-fret bound rosewood fingerboard with custom Stu Hamm yin-yang inlays, bound headstock with black overlay, Washburn logo, and Stu Hamm initial, two-per-side Grover tuners, monorail bridge, custom piezo bridge with three knobs, Buzz Feiten Tuning System, black chrome hardware, available in Black Cherry Burst or Natural finish, mfg. 2009-present.

MSR $1,516	$850	$525 - 650	$325 - 400	

AB42 – similar to AB40, except has an additional humbucker pickup, available in Tobacco Sunburst finish, mfg. 1992-93.

	N/A	$1,100 - 1,250	$700 - 825	$2,500

AB45 – similar to AB40, except in five-string configuration, 3/2-per-side tuners, available in Trans. Black or Vintage Sunburst (2011-present) finish, mfg. late 1980s-1991, reintroduced in 2006 and is currently produced.

1980s-1991	N/A	$1,100 - 1,250	$700 - 825	
2006-Present MSR $1,516	$850	$525 - 650	$325 - 400	

WATERSTONE GUITARS

Instruments currently produced overseas and set up in Nashville, TN, since 2004.

Waterstone Guitars was created by a group of individuals who love guitars and music. Their goal is to bring quality built, exceptional sounding, and reasonably priced guitars to the market place. Guitars are designed and developed in the U.S., produced overseas, and then inspected at their shop in Nashville, TN. For more information contact Waterstone directly.

CONTACT INFORMATION
WATERSTONE GUITARS
1200 Clinton Street, Unit 35
Nashville, TN 37203
Phone No.: 615-750-5649
www.waterstoneguitars.com
info@modguitars.com

WEBBER GUITARS

Instruments currently built in North Vancouver, British Columbia, Canada.

Luthier David Webber and his "small factory" build high quality acoustic guitars. He has currently built more than 1,100 guitars and produces a wide variety of guitar body styles and configurations as well as Irish bouzoukis, octave mandolins, and baritone ukuleles. Prices start at $2,700. For further information contact David Webber directly.

CONTACT INFORMATION
WEBBER GUITARS
262 East Esplanade, Unit #7
North Vancouver, British Columbia V7L
1A3 Canada
Phone No.: 604-980-0315
www.webberguitars.com
davidw@uniserve.com

WEBSTER

Instruments previously produced by Kay in Chicago, IL during the 1940s and 1950s.

Webster was a trademark for an unknown dealer/distributor produced by Kay in Chicago, IL during the 1940s and early 1950s. Webster guitars include acoustic archtops with "Webster" inlaid on the headstock. Any further information on Webster can be submitted directly to the *Blue Book of Acoustic Guitars*.

WECHTER GUITARS

Instruments curently built in Fort Wayne, IN since 2008 and in China. Previously produced in Paw Paw, MI between 1997 and 2008. Distributed by Wechter Guitars in Fort Wayne, IN. Distributed in Japan by Okada International, Inc. of Tokyo, Japan.

Luthier Abraham Wechter began his guitar building career in the early 1970s by making dulcimers and repairing guitars in Seattle, Washington. Shortly thereafter he started looking for a mentor to apprentice with. In December of 1974, he moved to Detroit to begin an apprenticeship with Richard Schneider. He was captivated by Schneider's art, along with the scientific work Schneider was doing with Dr. Kasha.

CONTACT INFORMATION
WECHTER GUITARS
PO Box 8738
Fort Wayne, IN 46898-8738
Phone No.: 260-407-3836
Fax No.: 260-407-3827
www.wechterguitars.com
info@wechterguitars.com

MSR/NOTES	100%	EXCELLENT	AVERAGE	LAST MSR

Wechter worked with Schneider developing prototypes for what later became the "Mark" project at Gibson Guitars. Schneider was working regularly for Gibson developing prototypes, and as a result Wechter started working for Gibson as a model (prototype) builder. Schneider and Wechter moved to Kalamazoo in December 1976. After a few years, Wechter was given the opportunity to work as an independent consultant to Gibson. He continued on until June of 1984, performing prototype work on many of the guitars Gibson produced during that time period.

While at Gibson, Wechter continued his apprenticeship with Schneider, building handmade, world-class guitars. He actually rented space from Schneider during this time and started building his own models. In 1984, when Gibson moved to Nashville, Wechter decided to remain in Michigan. Wechter moved to Paw Paw, Michigan, a rural town about twenty miles west of Kalamazoo, where he set up shop and started designing and building his own guitars.

Wechter built handmade classical, jazz-nylon, bass, and steel-string acoustic guitars. He did a tremendous amount of research into how and why guitars perform. As a result, he became sought after by many high profile people in the industry. Between 1985 and 1995, Wechter designed and hand built guitars for artists like John McLaughlin, Steve Howe, Al DiMeola, Giovanni, John Denver, Earl Klugh, and Jonas Hellborg. During this time period he developed a reputation as one of the world's finest craftsman and guitar designers.

In November of 1994, Wechter built a prototype of an innovative new design, and realized that it would have applications far beyond the high price range he was working in. This was the birth of the Pathmaker guitar. The Pathmaker model is a revolutionary acoustic guitar. The double cutaway construction provides a full nineteen frets clear of the body in a design that is both inherently stable and visually striking.

Wechter then laid out the groundwork for mass production and distribution of the Pathmaker - the first production models were scheduled for January, 1997. A limited number of handmade premier models are being built, along with a small number of classical and jazz-nylon guitars. Wechter has since expanded to offer a full line of Pathmaker-style guitars along with traditional acoustic guitars, resonators, and a budget line known as Maple Lake.

In 2000, Wechter began offering resonator instruments that are designed by Tim Scheerhorn. In 2004, Wechter began importing guitars from Asia and Wechter regularly travels to Asia to oversee production and quality. In 2008, Wechter relocated to Fort Wayne, IN. Wechter is also one of the few guitar manufacturers that owns a Plek Pro that levels the frets on fingerboards for all Wechter instruments. In 2010, Wechter introduced a line of solidbody electric guitars.

For more information on availability and pricing, contact Wechter Guitars directly. Biography courtesy Abraham Wechter and Michael Davidson, August 2, 1996.

ACOUSTIC: MAPLE LAKE SERIES

The Maple Lake logo appears on the headstock even though they are Wechter guitars. This is similar to what Fender has with Squier and Gibson with Epiphone.

1600 TRAVEL GUITAR – single cutaway miniature body, spruce top, maple back and sides, multiple black and white binding, mahogany neck, 14/20-fret rosewood fingerboard with dot inlay, rosewood bridge, black pickguard, electronics, available in Black, Blue Sunburst, Green Sunburst, Lacewood, Ovankol, Red, or Tobacco Sunburst finish, disc. 2005.

	N/A	$120 - 145	$60 - 80	$280

* Add $15 for Lacewood or Ovankol tops.

2200 SERIES – dreadnought or dreadnought 7/8 size, spruce top, agathis back and sides, 14/20-fret rosewood fingerboard with dot inlay, rosewood bridge, black pickguard, Natural finish, disc. 2005.

	N/A	$75 - 90	$40 - 50	$170

* Add $15 for padded gig-bag.
* Add $135 for Wechter 3-pickup system electronics.

2411/2411-78/2412/2413/2414 – dreadnought (2411), dreadnought 7/8 size (2411-78), grand auditorium (2412), jumbo (2414), or parlor (2413) style, spruce top, mahogany back and sides, tortoiseshell binding, 14/20-fret rosewood fingerboard with dot inlay, rosewood bridge, black pickguard, Natural finish, disc. 2008.

	N/A	$130 - 150	$70 - 95	$290

* Add 35% (Last MSR was $390) for regular 3-band electronics.
* Add 60% (Last MSR was $470) for Wechter 3-pickup system electronics.

* *2412C Cutaway* – similar to the 2412 except has a single cutaway style, mfg. 2007-08.

	N/A	$140 - 170	$80 - 110	$310

* Add 32.5% (Last MSR was $410) for regular 3-band electronics.
* Add 60% (Last MSR was $490) for Wechter 3-pickup system electronics.

2611C/2612C CUTAWAY – single cutaway dreadnought (2611C) or grand auditorium (2612C) style, spruce top, lacewood back and sides, tortoiseshell binding, 14/20-fret rosewood fingerboard with dot inlay, rosewood bridge, black pickguard, Natural finish, disc. 2008.

	N/A	$150 - 180	$90 - 120	$340

* Add 30% (Last MSR was $440) for regular 3-band electronics.
* Add 50% (Last MSR was $520) for Wechter 3-pickup system electronics.

MSR/NOTES	100%	EXCELLENT	AVERAGE	LAST MSR

2613/2614 – jumbo (2614) or parlor (2613) style, spruce top, lacewood back and sides, tortoiseshell binding, 14/20-fret rosewood fingerboard with dot inlay, rosewood bridge, black pickguard, Natural finish, disc. 2008.

	N/A	$140 - 170	$80 - 110	$320

- Add 30% (Last MSR was $420) for regular 3-band electronics.
- Add 50% (Last MSR was $500) for Wechter 3-pickup system electronics.

DN-2411CE CUTAWAY ELECTRIC – single cutaway dreadnought body, solid spruce top, laminated mahogany back and sides, round soundhole with abalone rosette, maple binding, set mahogany neck, 14/20-fret rosewood fingerboard with dot inlays, black headstock overlay with "Maple Lake" logo and design inlays, three-per-side chrome tuners, rosewood bridge, tortoise pickguard, AW-1 electronics, available in Hazel Nut Brown or Natural finish, 25.5 in. scale, current mfg.

MSR $449	$300	$200 - 250	$120 - 150	

ACOUSTIC: PATHMAKER SERIES

In November of 1994, Wechter built a prototype of an innovative new design that led to the introduction of the Pathmaker. The unique double cutaway body design features a neck with 19-frets clear of the body.

Earlier model may be equipped with either a Fishman Axis system or Axis+ or Axis-M. The **Pathmaker** "Recessed Tailblock" has a Fishman Matrix transducer mounted on the tailblock of the instrument.

The original **Pathmaker Standard** has a dual cutaway acoustic body, solid Sitka spruce top, solid mahogany back and sides (Last MSR was $1,899) or rosewood back and sides (Last MSR was $2,000), round soundhole, abalone rosette, wood binding, mahogany neck, 19/22-fret rosewood fingerboard with offset abalone dot inlay, three-per-side tuners, rosewood peghead veneer with mother-of-pearl logo inlay, rosewood bridge with white bridgepins, tortoise pickguard, Fishman Prefix + system, and available in Natural gloss finish.

Wechter also offered the **Pathmaker Elite Nylon String**, which was similar to the Pathmaker Standard, except has a nylon string configuration, and was available in mahogany back and sides (Last MSR was $2,049) or rosewood back and sides (Last MSR was $2,149). The **Pathmaker Starburst** is similar to the Pathmaker Standard, except features white ABS body binding, available with mahogany back and sides (Last MSR was $2,099) or rosewood back and sides (Last MSR was $2,199) and available in Tobacco Brown Starburst finish.

PATHMAKER MODEL 3101/3102/3103 – double sharp cutaway, spruce top, maple back and sides, mahogany neck, 19/22-fret rosewood fingerboard with offset dot inlay, tortoise pickguard, rosewood bridge, bound body and neck, chrome hardware, optional electronics (Fishman Aero 501 standard in 2009), available in Jet Black (3101), Trans. Red (3102, disc. 2008), or Trans. Blue (3103, disc. 2008) finish, disc. 2009.

	N/A	$250 - 325	$150 - 190	$600

- Add 10% (Last MSR was $649) for left-handed configuration.
- Subtract 20% for no electronics.

Wechter offered a variety of electronics on their Pathmaker Series, but when the model was discontinued, only one variation was offered only with electronics so the last MSR and subsequent pricing reflects a guitar with electronics. The following is a list of electronics offered by Wechter and their last MSRs. The last MSR on a plain acoustic guitar was $450. Regular 3-band electronics (Last MSR was $570), Wechter 3-pickup system electronics (Last MSR was $630), Artec HT-TBL electronics, Schertler Bluestick system electronics (Last MSR was $750), Fishman Natural I electronics, and Fishman Prefix Plus Electronics.

* Pathmaker Thinline Model 3101T/3101TE – similar to the Pathmaker 3101, except has a thinline body and optional electronics (standard by 2009), available in Black finish, mfg. 2007-present.

MSR $665	$500	$300 - 375	$175 - 225	

- Subtract 20% for no electronics.
- Add 10% (Last MSR was $500) for left-handed configuration (disc. 2008).
- Add 25% (Last MSR was $750) for Schertler Bluestick system electronics (disc. 2008).

* Pathmaker Model 3120/3120E – similar to the Pathmaker Model 3100, except has ovangkol back and sides, optional electronics (Fishman Aero 501 standard in 2009), available in Natural finish, disc. 2009.

	N/A	$300 - 375	$175 - 225	$669

- Add 10% (Last MSR was $550) for left-handed configuration.
- Subtract 20% for no electronics.

Wechter offered a variety of electronics on their Pathmaker Series, but when the model was discontinued, only one variation was offered only with electronics so the last MSR and subsequent pricing reflects a guitar with electronics. The following is a list of electronics offered by Wechter and their last MSRs. The last MSR on a plain acoustic guitar was $450. Regular 3-band electronics (Last MSR was $620), Wechter 3-pickup system electronics (Last MSR was $680), Artec HT-TBL electronics, Schertler Bluestick system electronics (Last MSR was $800), Fishman Natural I electronics, and Fishman Prefix Plus Electronics.

»Pathmaker Thinline Model 3120T/3120TE – similar to the Pathmaker Model 3120, except has a thinline body and optional electronics (standard by 2009), available in Natural finish, mfg. 2007-present.

MSR $699	$525	$325 - 400	$200 - 250	

- Subtract 20% for no electronics.
- Add 10% (Last MSR was $550) for left-handed configuration (disc. 2008).
- Add 25% (Last MSR was $800) for Schertler Bluestick system electronics (disc. 2008).

MSR/NOTES	100%	EXCELLENT	AVERAGE	LAST MSR

* *Pathmaker Model 3135* – similar to the Pathmaker Model 3100, except has lacewood back and sides and tortoiseshell binding, available in Natural finish, disc. 2008.

	N/A	$225 - 275	$130 - 165	$550

- Add 10% (Last MSR was $600) for left-handed configuration.
- Add 22.5% (Last MSR was $670) for regular 3-band electronics.
- Add 35% (Last MSR was $730) for Wechter 3-pickup system electronics.
- Add 40% for Artec HT-TBL system electronics (disc.).
- Add 50% for Fishman Natural I electronics (disc.).
- Add 55% (Last MSR was $850) for Schertler Bluestick electronics.
- Add 95% for Fishman Prefix Plus Electronics (disc.).

* *Pathmaker Deluxe Thinline Mahogany Model 3140TE* – similar to the Pathmaker Model 3101, except has a thinline body and Fishman Presys+ electronics, available in Natural finish, mfg. 2010-present.

MSR $770	$580	$350 - 425	$200 - 250	

PATHMAKER ELITE (MODEL 5730/5730E) – symmetrical double cutaway body, solid spruce top, rosewood back and sides, round soundhole with abalone rosette, ivoroid body binding, set nato neck, 19/22-fret bound rosewood fingerboard with offset mini dot inlays, bound headstock with black or woodgrain overlay and Wechter logo/design inlays, three-per-side tuners, rosewood bridge, Fishman Presys 501 electronics (early models were available with no electronics), available in Natural high-gloss finish, 1.715 in. nut width, 25.5 in. scale, hardshell case included, mfg. 2006-present.

MSR $929	$700	$425 - 500	$225 - 300	

ACOUSTIC: SELECT SERIES

Wechter's Select Series are based on popular Martin designs from the "Golden Era" or production during the 1930s.

DREADNOUGHT SELECT MAHOGANY (MODEL DN-8118) – 14-fret Dreadnought-style body, solid spruce top, solid mahogany back and sides, round soundhole with multi-ring rosette, tortoise binding, mahogany neck, 14/20-fret rosewood fingerboard with dot inlays, black headstock overlay with Wechter logo and design inlay, three-per-side gold tuners, rosewood belly bridge, tortoise pickguard, available in Natural gloss finish, 1.6875 in. nut width, 25.5 in. scale, case included, mfg. 2012-present.

MSR $795	$600	$350 - 425	$200 - 250	

DREADNOUGHT SELECT ROSEWOOD (MODEL DN-8128) – 14-fret Dreadnought-style body, solid spruce top, solid rosewood back and sides, round soundhole with abalone rosette, white binding with herringbone purfling, mahogany neck, 14/20-fret ebony fingerboard with MOP diamond inlays, black headstock overlay with Wechter logo and design inlay, three-per-side gold tuners, ebony belly bridge, tortoise pickguard, available in Natural gloss finish, 1.6875 in. nut width, 25.5 in. scale, case included, mfg. 2012-present.

MSR $1,230	$925	$550 - 675	$325 - 400	

DREADNOUGHT SELECT ROSEWOOD (MODEL DN-8142) – 14-fret Dreadnought-style body, solid spruce top, solid rosewood back and sides, round soundhole with abalone rosette, white binding with abalone purfling, mahogany neck, 14/20-fret ebony fingerboard with MOP snowflake inlays, black headstock overlay with Wechter logo and design inlay, three-per-side gold tuners, ebony belly bridge with MOP snowflake inlays, tortoise pickguard, available in Natural gloss finish, 1.6875 in. nut width, 25.5 in. scale, case included, mfg. 2012-present.

MSR $1,529	$1,150	$700 - 850	$400 - 500	

GRAND AUDITORIUM SELECT ROSEWOOD (MODEL GA-8221CE) – single cutaway 14-fret Grand Auditorium-style body, solid spruce top, solid rosewood back and sides, round soundhole with multi-ring rosette, tortoise binding, mahogany neck, 14/20-fret rosewood fingerboard with dot inlays, black headstock overlay with Wechter logo and design inlay, three-per-side chrome tuners, rosewood belly bridge, tortoise pickguard, L.R. Baggs Stage Pro electronics, available in Natural gloss finish, 1.6875 in. nut width, 25.5 in. scale, case included, mfg. 2012-present.

MSR $1,195	$900	$525 - 650	$300 - 375	

TRIPLE-0 SELECT MAHOGANY (MODEL TO-8418) – 12-fret Grand Auditorium 000-style body, solid spruce top, solid mahogany back and sides, round soundhole with multi-ring rosette, tortoise binding, mahogany neck, 12/20-fret rosewood fingerboard with dot inlays, slotted headstock, three-per-side open-style gold tuners, rosewood pyramid bridge, tortoise pickguard, available in Natural gloss finish, 1.875 in. nut width, 25.5 in. scale, case included, mfg. 2011-present.

MSR $869	$650	$400 - 475	$225 - 275	

TRIPLE-0 SELECT ROSEWOOD (MODEL TO-8428) – 12-fret Grand Auditorium 000-style body, solid spruce top, solid mahogany back and sides, round soundhole with abalone rosette, white binding with herringbone purfling, mahogany neck, 12/20-fret ebony fingerboard with MOP diamond inlays, slotted headstock, three-per-side open-style gold tuners, ebony pyramid bridge, tortoise pickguard, available in Natural gloss finish, 1.875 in. nut width, 25.5 in. scale, case included, mfg. 2011-present.

MSR $1,295	$975	$575 - 700	$350 - 425	

TRIPLE-0 SELECT ROSEWOOD (MODEL TO-8442) – 12-fret Grand Auditorium 000-style body, solid spruce top, solid mahogany back and sides, round soundhole with abalone rosette, white binding with abalone purfling, mahogany neck, 12/20-fret ebony fingerboard with MOP snowflake inlays, slotted headstock, three-per-side open-style gold tuners, ebony pyramid bridge, tortoise pickguard, available in Natural gloss finish, 1.875 in. nut width, 25.5 in. scale, case included, mfg. 2011-present.

MSR $1,595	$1,200	$725 - 875	$425 - 525	

MSR/NOTES	100%	EXCELLENT	AVERAGE	LAST MSR

ACOUSTIC: MISC. MODELS

The Elite 9000 Series were offered as Wechter U.S. models. Prices started at $3,000, and an acoustic bass was also available.

5711/5712C/5713/5714 – dreadnought (Model 5711), grand auditorium cutaway (Model 5712C), jumbo (Model 5714), or parlor (Model 5713), body style, solid spruce top, rosewood back and sides, black and white binding, abalone rosette, nato neck, 14/20-fret rosewood fingerboard with dot inlay, three-per-side chrome tuners, rosewood bridge, available in Natural Open-Pore finish, 25.5 in. scale, mfg. 2006-08.

	N/A	$250 - 300	$125 - 175	$620

- Add 5% (Last MSR was $650) for grand auditorium cutaway (Model 5712C), or jumbo (Model 5714) body styles.
- Add 30% (Last MSR was $800, 830) for Wechter 3-Pickup system electronics.
- Add 50% (Last MSR was $920, 950) for Schertler Bluestick system electronics.

NASHVILLE-TUNED ELITE NV-5413 – parlor-style body, solid cedar top, mahogany back and sides, round soundhole with abalone rosette, nato neck, 14/21-fret bound rosewood fingerboard with dot inlays, bound headstock with black overlay and pearl logo/inlay, three-per-side chrome tuners, rosewood bridge, available in Natural or optional Hazel Nut Brown top toner, 1.687 in. nut width, 25.5 in. scale, mfg. 2008-present.

MSR $625	$470	$275 - 350	$150 - 200	

The Nashville-tuned Elite is designed to sound like a 12-string only utilizing six strings. The high E and B strings are strung regular while the four bottom strings are strung an octave above a regular six-string.

* *Nashville-Tuned Elite Cutaway Electric NV-5413CE* – similar to the Nashville-Tuned Elite NV-5413, except has a smooth cutaway and Fishman Presys 501 electronics, available in Natural or optional Hazel Nut Brown top toner, mfg. 2008-present.

MSR $839	$630	$375 - 450	$225 - 275	

* *Nashville-Tuned Elite Cutaway Electric NV-5513CE* – similar to the Nashville-Tuned Elite NV-5413, except only the bottom two strings are strung up an octave, has a smooth cutaway, solid spruce top, and Fishman Presys 501 electronics, available in Natural finish, mfg. 2008-present.

MSR $839	$630	$375 - 450	$225 - 275	

TRAVEL TV-1710 – travel-sized parlor-style body, solid spruce top, mahogany back and sides, round soundhole with multi-ring rosette, multi-ply white binding, nato neck, 12/18-fret bound rosewood fingerboard with dot inlays, three-per-side tuners, rosewood bridge, available in Natural finish, 23.25 in. scale, mfg. 2006-present.

MSR $385	$290	$175 - 210	$95 - 125	

- Add 25% (Last MSR was $400) for rosewood back and sides (Model 1730).
- Add 25% (Last MSR was $400) for lacewood back and sides (Model 1735).
- Subtract 30% (Last MSR was $225) for small body version (Model 1705, mfg. 2006 only).

* *Travel TV-1710E* – similar to the Travel TV-1710, except has Fishman Isys 601 electronics, available in Natural finish, mfg. 2006-present.

MSR $490	$370	$220 - 270	$125 - 160	

TRAVEL TV-1720 – travel-sized parlor-style body, solid mahogany top, mahogany back and sides, round soundhole with multi-ring rosette, multi-ply white binding, nato neck, 12/18-fret bound rosewood fingerboard with dot inlays, three-per-side tuners, rosewood bridge, available in Natural finish, mfg. 2006-present.

MSR $385	$290	$175 - 210	$95 - 125	

* *Travel TV-1720E* – similar to the Travel TV-1720, except has Fishman Isys 601 electronics, available in Natural finish, mfg. 2006-present.

MSR $490	$370	$220 - 270	$125 - 160	

RESONATORS

SCHEERHORN MODEL 6510-F/6510-R – resonator body, mahogany top, back, and sides, two f-holes (Model 6510-F, disc.) or a round soundhole (Model 6510-R), square neck, 19-fret fingerboard with dot inlays, three-per-side tuners, available in Antique Natural or Tobacco Sunburst finish, current mfg.

MSR $999	$750	$450 - 550	$250 - 325	

- Add 30% (Last MSR was $1,300) for Schertler Basik electronics (disc. 2011).

SCHEERHORN MODEL 6524-F/6524-R – resonator body, curly maple top, back, and sides, two f-holes (Model 6524-F, disc) or round soundhole (Model 6524-R), square style neck, 19-fret fingerboard with dot inlay, three-per-side tuners, available in Almond Sunburst finish, current mfg.

MSR $1,199	$900	$550 - 650	$325 - 400	

- Add 25% (Last MSR was $1,500) for Schertler Basik electronics (disc. 2010).

SCHEERHORN MODEL 6530F – resonator body, spruce top, rosewood back and sides, two f-holes, square style neck, 19-fret fingerboard with dot inlay, three-per-side tuners, available in Antique Natural finish, disc. 2008.

	N/A	$550 - 650	$325 - 400	$1,200

- Add 25% (Last MSR was $1,500) for Schertler Basik electronics.

MSR/NOTES	100%	EXCELLENT	AVERAGE	LAST MSR

SCHEERHORN MODEL 6535-R ROB ICKES MODEL – resonator body, spruce top, rosewood back and sides, two small round soundholes, square style neck, 19-fret fingerboard with dot and Rob Ickes signature inlays, three-per-side tuners, small tortoise pickguard, available Natural finish, mfg. 2006-present.

MSR $1,499	$1,125	$675 - 825	$400 - 500	

* **Add 27.5% (MSR $1,899) for Schertler Basik electronics.**

SCHEERHORN MODEL RS-6610F – resonator body, laminated mahogany top, back, and sides, two f-holes, single-ply body binding, round nato neck, 12/19-fret rosewood fingerboard with dot inlays, black headstock overlay, three-per-side tuners, rosewood bridge, chrome hardware, available in Tobacco Sunburst finish, case included, mfg. 2012-present.

MSR $1,065	$800	$475 - 575	$275 - 350	

* *Scheerhorn Model RS-6610FC Cutaway* – similar to the Scheerhorn Model RS-6610F, except has a single smooth cutaway, available in Tobacco Sunburst finish, case included, mfg. 2012-present.

MSR $1,099	$825	$500 - 600	$275 - 350	

WEISSENBORN

Instruments previously built in CA during the 1920s and early 1930s.

H. Weissenborn instruments were favorites of slide guitar players in Hawaii and the West Coast in the early 1900s. All four models featured koa construction, and different binding packages per model. After the advent of resonator and electric instruments in the thirties, these odd koa instruments were seemingly appreciated only by a handful of players like David Lindley, Ry Cooder and John Fahey. More recently, Weissenborns have been made popular by Ben Harper, and used by steel and resonator-guitar players like Jerry Douglas, Mike Auldridge, Greg Leisz, Sally Van Meter and Cindy Cashdollar.

As prices of Weissenborns have multiplied, new enthusiasts have discovered in these guitars a mysterious sound adaptable to many musical styles and the first instrument specifically made for Hawaiian playing. More than just a Spanish guitar laid flat on the lap, Weissenborns were made with a high nut and inlaid flush fret markers. Credit for the hollow-neck design might belong to Christopher J. Knutsen (also a harp-guitar pioneer), but Weissenborn enjoyed more success, both structurally and commercially.

Weissenborn's guitars also directly influenced the instruments of his undoing - National and Dobro resophonics. Hermann C. Weissenborn (often confused with and likely not related to Herman W. Weissenborn, a mid-1800s partner of Charles Bruno in New York City) was born in Hanover, Germany in 1863. He took up musical instrument-making around 1879, later emigrating to New York City around 1900, moving to Los Angeles around 1910. He emphasized violin building, instrument repair and piano tuning even after the Hawaiian music craze was in full swing. All dates pertaining to Weissenborn instruments are approximate, because his instruments are not dated or serial numbered, but a general range would be 1920 up until his death in 1937. There does seem to be a progression of features that suggest an evolution of these instruments and a means of distinguishing relative age.

Confusion exists as to which instruments are Weissenborn-made and which aren't. It's not precisely true that anything that looks like a Weissenborn (hollow neck, koa wood, rope-marquetry binding) probably was made by him. The most often-encountered Weissenborn-made brand is the Kona Hawaiian guitar, marketed by Los Angeles teacher and publisher C.S. DeLano. Although Konas and Weissenborns initially appear identical (a vintage-instrument calendar made this mistake, despite a visible Kona label), Konas are narrower across the lower bout (13.25 in. vs. 15.25 in.) and deeper (4 in. vs. 3 in.) than most Weissenborns. Konas have solid round necks that join the body at the seventh fret with an angled joint. Konas have wire frets rather than flush markers. The sound of Konas is generally regarded as equivalent to (though deeper than) Weissenborns. The most-often encountered marking is a 1 in. shield enclosing H. WEISSENBORN, LOS ANGELES, CAL and burned into the backstrip inside the soundhole. Some instruments have an additional brand of Henry STADLMAIR, NEW YORK, SOLE EASTERN DISTRIBUTOR.

Brands that, despite appearances, are not Weissenborn-made include Knutsen (see separate entry), Hilo and brands of Los Angelesí Schireson Brothers, including Lyric and Mai Kai. The principal feature that distinguishes Weissenborns from these other brands is Weissenborn's use of X-bracing on the tops. Hilo and the Schireson brands (more similar to each other than to Weissenborns), are ladder-braced. The difference is even more audible than visible. Hilos generally fall far short of Weissenborns in volume and tone. The manufacturer of these instruments was probably one of the large Chicago factories of the period, while some theories say Oscar Schmidt.

MODEL & STYLE INFORMATION

Most Weissenborn Hawaiians are three inches deep, although there are early Examples ranging from 2 to 2.5 in. and some little more than 1 in. deep. In general, Weissenborns were made in four styles:

Additional pearl triangle marker lies with long side flush against nut.

Weissenborn also made Spanish guitars and other instruments, although the Hawaiians seem to be the most numerous extant today. A handful of examples of mandolins, tenor and plectrum guitars have been seen and several uke models appear in Tonk

MSR/NOTES	100%	EXCELLENT	AVERAGE	LAST MSR

Bros. catalogs. The curious paucity of ukuleles encountered so far makes valuation speculative at best.

Note: Konas (because they are less familiar among players, collectors and experts) and Spanish guitars with features equivalent to the Hawaiian models above may bring slightly lower prices.

The publisher wishes to express his thanks to Mr. Ben Elder for the above information.

ACOUSTIC: WEISSENBORN HAWAIIANS

STYLE 1 – no body binding, three light-colored rings around the soundhole, single pearl-dot fret markers. Catalogs mention optional spruce top on Styles 1 and 2, but these are seen more often on early instruments.

	N/A	$2,600 - 3,250	$1,550 - 1,950	

STYLE 2 – black body binding, rope marquetry around soundhole, French curve on end of fingerboard (unique to Style 2), light wood binding on fretboard, fancier fret marker pattern.

	N/A	$3,000 - 3,750	$1,800 - 2,250	

STYLE 3 – rope (alternating angled light and dark wood marquetry) binding around top, soundhole and fretboard. Fretmarkers include double dots at 5 and 9, diamond or parallelogram at 12.

	N/A	$3,600 - 4,500	$2,150 - 2,700	

STYLE 4 – similar to Style 3, but with rope binding around back and headstock.

	N/A	$4,400 - 5,500	$2,650 - 3,300	

ACOUSTIC: KONA HAWAIIANS

Konas seem to follow the general scheme as the Hawaiians, except a Style 2 with black body binding has never been reported. There are Konas with variations on Style 1: some examples have no body binding; others have white plastic binding around the top. Experts including George Gruhn tend to regard these white-bound examples as Style 1 variants rather than as a separate style. Several Style 1 Konas have spruce tops that are both bound and unbound.

STYLE 1 – no body binding, three light-colored rings around the soundhole, single pearl-dot fret markers. Catalogs mention optional spruce top on Styles 1 and 2, but these are seen more often on early instruments.

	N/A	$2,600 - 3,250	$1,550 - 1,950	

STYLE 2 – black body binding, rope marquetry around soundhole, French curve on end of fingerboard (unique to Style 2), light wood binding on fretboard, fancier fret marker pattern.

	N/A	$3,000 - 3,750	$1,800 - 2,250	

STYLE 3 – rope (alternating angled light and dark wood marquetry) binding around top, soundhole and fretboard. Fretmarkers include double dots at 5 and 9, diamond or parallelogram at 12.

	N/A	$3,600 - 4,500	$2,150 - 2,700	

STYLE 4 – similar to Style 3, but with rope binding around back and headstock.

	N/A	$4,400 - 5,500	$2,650 - 3,300	

ACOUSTIC: SPANISH GUITARS

Spanish guitar models (and plectrum instruments; tenor bodies are smaller) are similar in dimension to a 12-fret Martin "0" size. Their bodies are also exactly the same dimensions as Kona Hawaiians, except for the Konasí unique 7th-fret neck joint. Weissenborn Spanish instruments are designated Styles A, B, C, and D, which parallel the Hawaiians 1, 2, 3, and 4. Weissenborn Spanish guitars feature X-bracing, and necks without truss rods. Spanish-neck Weissenborns tend to need neck re-sets (Weissenborn used a dovetail neck joint). Weissenborn Spanish guitars don't sound as distinctively different from other roundnecks as do the Weissenborn Hawaiians from other steels. However, because of their rarity, Weissenborn Spanish guitar prices run close to those of their corresponding Hawaiian models and not much less than the more numerous Martin koa Spanish models like the 0-18K and 0-28K.

STYLE A – no body binding, three light-colored rings around the soundhole, single pearl-dot fret markers. Catalogs mention optional spruce top on Styles 1 and 2, but these are seen more often on early instruments.

	N/A	$2,800 - 3,500	$1,700 - 2,100	

STYLE B – black body binding, rope marquetry around soundhole, French curve on end of fingerboard (unique to Style 2), light wood binding on fretboard, fancier fret marker pattern.

	N/A	$3,200 - 4,000	$1,950 - 2,400	

STYLE C – rope (alternating angled light and dark wood marquetry) binding around top, soundhole and fretboard. Fretmarkers include double dots at 5 and 9, diamond or parallelogram at 12.

	N/A	$3,800 - 4,750	$2,300 - 2,850	

STYLE D – similar to Style 3, but with rope binding around back and headstock.

	N/A	$4,600 - 5,750	$2,750 - 3,450	

WEYMANN & SONS

Instruments previously built in Philadelphia, PA between 1864 and the 1940s. Some models under the Weymann & Son trademark were built by Regal (Chicago, IL), and Vega (Boston, MA).

H.A. Weymann & Son, Incorporated was established in 1864 in Philadelphia. Later, it incorporated as the Weymann Company in 1904, and distributed numerous guitar models that ranged from entry level student up to fine quality. Other trademarks may include Weymann, Keystone State, W & S, and Varsity. Some of the guitars were actually produced by Vega or Regal, and share similarities to the company of origin's production instruments.

WHITEBROOK, MARK

Instruments previously built in CA during the 1970s.

Mark Whitebrook was an apprentice to luthier Roy Noble for a number of years. Whitebrook built high quality acoustic guitars, and was luthier to James Taylor for a number of years. Any information would be appreciated and can be submitted directly to the *Blue Book of Acoustic Guitars*.

WILKANOWSKI

Instruments previously produced in Brooklyn, NY during the late 1930s and early 1940s.

Luthier W. Wilkanowski (his first name is unknown) built a handful of guitars during the late 1930s. Wilkanowski immigrated to the U.S. from Poland in the early 1920s and began building violins for Oliver Ditson. In circa 1938, he moved to New York City and began building violins for Gretsch. Before 1940, he opened his own shop and began building violins and violas under his own name. After establishing his violin business, he built a few guitars based on violin design. The body shape, soundholes, body edge/bindings, and pickguard are all very similar in design to a violin. It is estimated that he built around thirty guitars between the late 1930s and the early 1940s. Source: *20th Century Guitar* magazine.

WINDSOR

Instruments previously produced between circa 1890s and mid-1910s. See chapter on House Brands.

The Windsor trademark was a House Brand for Montgomery Wards around the turn of the century (circa 1890s to mid-1910s). These beginner's grade acoustic flattop guitars and mandolins were built by various American manufacturers such as Lyon & Healy (and possibly Harmony). Source: Michael Wright, *Vintage Guitar Magazine*.

WINSTON

Instruments previously produced in Japan between circa 1963 and 1967. Distributed in the U.S. by Buegeleisen & Jacobson in New York, NY.

The Winston trademark was a brand name used by U.S. importers Buegeleisen & Jacobson in New York, New York. The Winston brand appeared on a full range of acoustic guitars, thinline acoustic/electric archtops, and solidbody electric guitars and basses. Winston instruments are generally the shorter scale beginner's guitar. Although the manufacturers are unknown, some models appear to be built by Guyatone. Source: Michael Wright, *Vintage Guitar Magazine*.

WOOD, RANDY

Instruments currently built in Bloomingdale, GA, since 1978. Previously produced in Savannah, GA.

Luthier Randy Wood was one of three partners who formed GTR, Inc. in Nashville in 1970. Wood left GTR to form the Old Time Picking Parlor in 1972, a combination custom instrument shop and nightclub that featured Bluegrass music. In 1978, he sold the Parlor and moved to Savannah, Georgia to concentrate on instruments building. Since then, he has produced over 1,500 stringed instruments from guitars to mandolins, dobros, violins, and banjos. For more information, refer to their website.

The Randy Wood Cutaway guitar retails for $8,500. Wood has also built archtops and resonators.

Randy Wood serialization is composed of four digits. The first digit indicates what number instrument was made that month. The second digit indicates the month it was made, and the third and fourth digits are the last two years of the year. For example #1805 would be the first instrument made in the month of August in 2005.

WORLAND GUITARS

Instruments currently produced in Rockford, IL since 1997.

Luthier Jim Worland hand-builds acoustic guitars to custom specifications in his Rockford, IL shop. Worland offers several models all of which can be customized by the customer. Prices start at $2,850 for most models with the exception of the Prairie, which starts at $1,450. Current build time for Worland's guitars is nine months. Worland also builds a few electric instruments and unusual instruments such as harp guitars, lutes, bouzoukis, and dulcimers. For more information, visit Worland's website or contact him directly.

W & S

See Weymann & Sons.

WURLITZER

Instruments previously built by C.F. Martin & Co. in Nazareth, PA during the mid-1920s.

Wurlitzer, who produce a variety of electric products including jukeboxes, organs, and pianos, offered a line of guitars during two different eras. Wurlitzer first sold a line of acoustic guitars built by Martin in the mid-1920s. In 1965, they began offering a line of electric guitars built by the Holman-Woodell facility in Neodesha, KS who also built instruments for other trademarks including 21st Century, Alray, Holman, and La Baye. Electric guitar production continued in Kansas until circa 1968, when Wurlitzer decided to begin importing foreign-built guitars as production costs began to rise in the U.S. Wurlitzer began importing guitars built by the Welson company from Italy, and production continued through the late 1960s and early 1970s. For information on electric Wurlitzer guitars, refer to the *Blue Book of Electric Guitars*.

Martin began building specially branded Wurlitzer guitars for the company in 1922. All Wurlitzer guitars were based on regular production Martin instruments including Sizes 0, 00, 000, 1, and 2, but featured a Wurlitzer stamp on the back of the headstock and a single ring soundhole rosette. Wurlitzer utilized a four-digit model number (20XX) that each had a corresponding Martin-style model name/number. Total production was just under 300 instruments when Martin discontinued the Wurlitzer brand name, and Wurlitzer began selling regular Martin-branded instruments in their stores. Early production Wurlitzer guitars do not have a serial number, but on February 28, 1923 they began using Martin's serialization system that lasted until production of Wurlitzer guitars ended on March 22, 1924. Please note that the Wurlitzer stamp along with the Martin trademark appeared on guitars built by Martin after March 22, 1924.

Wurlitzer acoustics are seldom encountered in the used vintage marketplace, and every guitar needs to be evaluated individually. Since each Wurlitzer guitar is based on a corresponding Martin guitar from the same era, the value for said Martin guitar should be close to the value of the Wurlitzer guitar.

X SECTION
XAVIERE

Instruments currently produced in China. Distributed by GuitarFetish.com in Boston, MA.

CONTACT INFORMATION
XAVIERE
45 Hopkinton Rd.
Westborough, MA 01581
www.guitarfetish.com

Jay Abend founded GuitarFetish as an online company that offers several guitar components for those who like to build their own guitars at home. GuitarFetish also offers fully-built guitars under the trademark of Xaviere. These guitars are mainly designed around popular American designs such as the Stratocaster, Telecaster, Jazzmaster, and Les Paul. Guitars are sold direct from their website and prices typically range between $150 and $300. In 2012, they added acoustic guitars to their product line. For more information, visit their website.

Y SECTION
YAMAHA

CONTACT INFORMATION
YAMAHA
Yamaha Corporation of America
6600 Orangethorpe Avenue
Buena Park, CA 90620
Phone No.: 714-522-9011
Phone No.: 800-322-4322
Fax No.: 714-522-9587
www.yamahaguitars.com

Instruments currently produced in the U.S., Japan, Taiwan, Korea, and Indonesia since the mid-1940s. Distributed in the U.S. by the Yamaha Corporation of America, in Buena Park, CA. The Yamaha company headquarters is located in Hamamatsu, Japan.

Yamaha has a tradition of building musical instruments for over one hundred years. The first Yamaha solid body electric guitars were introduced to the American market in 1966. While the first series relied on designs based on classic American favorites, the second series developed more original designs. In the mid-1970s, Yamaha was recognized as the first Oriental brand to emerge as a prominent force equal to the big-name U.S. builders.

Production shifted to Taiwan in the early 1980s as Yamaha built its own facility to maintain quality. In 1990, the Yamaha Corporation of America (located in Buena Park, California) opened the Yamaha Guitar Development (YGD) center in North Hollywood, California. The Yamaha Guitar Development center focuses on design, prototyping, and customizing both current and new models. The YGD also custom-builds and maintains many of the Yamaha artist's instruments. The center's address on Weddington Street probably was the namesake of the Weddington series instruments of the early 1990s.

The Yamaha company produces a full range of musical instruments, including pianos, band instruments, stringed instruments, amplifiers, and sound reinforcement equipment.

ACOUSTIC: CJ/FJ COUNTRY JUMBO SERIES

The CJ and FJ acoustics by Yamaha are similar to Gibson's large J-200/SJ-200 acoustics.

CJ12 – SJ-200 jumbo-style body, spruce top, agathis back and sides, round soundhole with three-stripe rosette, multi-ply body binding, mahogany neck, 14/20-fret bound rosewood fingerboard with pearl pentagon inlays, bound headstock with black overlay and logo/design inlays, three-per-side gold tuners, rosewood moustache-style bridge, tortoise pickguard, available in Violin Sunburst finish, mfg. 1996-2007.

| N/A | $300 - 350 | $175 - 225 | $700 |

* ***CJX12SA Solid Top Electric*** – similar to the CJ12, except has a solid spruce top, abalone rosette, a black pickguard, and System 45 two-way electronics with three-band EQ, volume, mic. volume, phase shift, and AMF slider controls, available in Black finish, mfg. summer 2001-07.

| N/A | $550 - 675 | $350 - 425 | $1,299 |

CJ32 HANDCRAFTED – SJ-200 jumbo-style body, solid spruce top, solid maple back and sides, round soundhole with three-ring abalone pearl rosette, cream body binding with abalone pearl purfling, maple neck, 14/20-fret bound ebony fingerboard with split pearl triangular inlays, bound headstock with matching wood overlay and logo/design inlays, three-per-side gold tuners, ebony moustache-style bridge, tortoise pickguard, available in Antique Brown Sunburst finish, mfg. 2002-08.

| N/A | $1,100 - 1,250 | $700 - 825 | $2,500 |

* ***CJX32 Handcrafted Electric*** – similar to the CJ32, except has System 41 two-way electronics with volume, mic. volume, three-band EQ, mic. tone, AMF, and phase switch controls, available in Antique Brown Sunburst finish, mfg. 2002-08.

| N/A | $1,350 - 1,550 | $725 - 850 | $2,900 |

FJ645A – SJ-200 jumbo-style body, spruce top, agathis back and sides, round soundhole with three-stripe rosette, multi-ply body binding, nato neck, 14/20-fret bound rosewood fingerboard with pearl pentagon inlays, bound headstock with black overlay and logo/design inlays, three-per-side chrome tuners, rosewood bridge, black pickguard, available in Violin Sunburst finish, mfg. 1989-1994.

| N/A | $250 - 300 | $125 - 175 | $549 |

FJ651 – SJ-200 jumbo-style body, spruce top, agathis back and sides, round soundhole with three-stripe rosette, multi-ply body binding, African mahogany neck, 14/20-fret bound rosewood fingerboard with pearl pentagon inlays, bound headstock with black overlay and logo/design inlays, three-per-side gold tuners, rosewood moustache-style bridge, black pickguard, available in Violin Sunburst finish, mfg. 1994-95.

| N/A | $250 - 300 | $125 - 175 | $579 |

FJ661 – SJ-200 jumbo-style body, spruce top, nato back and sides, round soundhole with three-stripe rosette, multi-ply body binding, African mahogany neck, 14/20-fret bound rosewood fingerboard with pearl pentagon inlays, bound headstock with black overlay and logo/design inlays, three-per-side gold tuners, rosewood moustache-style bridge, no pickguard, available in Natural finish, mfg. 1994-95.

| N/A | $275 - 325 | $150 - 200 | $659 |

FJ681 – SJ-200 jumbo-style body, spruce top, agathis back and sides, round soundhole with three-stripe rosette, multi-ply body binding, African mahogany neck, 14/20-fret bound rosewood fingerboard that comes to a point in the soundhole with pearl dot inlays, bound headstock with black overlay and logo, three-per-side black tuners, rosewood bridge, large square black pickguard that surrounds the soundhole, System 26 one-way electronics with pop-up controls, available in Black finish, mfg. 1994-95.

| N/A | $300 - 375 | $175 - 225 | $729 |

This model was inspired (intentionally or not) by the Everly Brothers guitars with the large pickguards.

ACOUSTIC: DREADNOUGHT (DW) SERIES

Yamaha produced the DW Series as an all-dreadnought all solid-top series that was marketed as higher quality than the FG Series. There were three distinct series of these guitars, but the features remained very similar. The first series was produced

MSR/NOTES	100%	EXCELLENT	AVERAGE	LAST MSR

between 1996 and 1998 (DW-4S, DW-5S, DW-103E, and DW-105), the second series was produced between 1999 and 2002 (DW6, DW8, DW10, and DW20), and the third series was produced between 2005 and 2007 (DW7, DW9, and DW15).

DW-4S – dreadnought-style body, solid spruce top, nato back and sides, round soundhole with three-ring rosette, multi-ply body binding, nato neck, 14/20-fret bound rosewood fingerboard with dot inlays, bound headstock with rosewood overlay and logo, three-per-side gold tuners, rosewood bridge, black pickguard, available in Marine Burst, Natural, or Violin Sunburst finish, mfg. 1996-98.

	N/A	$250 - 300	$135 - 175	$599

* **DW-4S-12 12-String** – similar to the DW-4S, except in 12-string configuration with six-per-side tuners, available in Natural finish, mfg. 1996-98.

	N/A	$275 - 325	$150 - 200	$649

* **DW-4SC Cutaway Electric** – similar to the DW-4S, except has a single smooth cutaway and mono one-way electronics with three-band EQ, volume, and AMF controls, available in Marine Burst, Natural, or Violin Sunburst finish, mfg. 1996-98.

	N/A	$375 - 450	$250 - 300	$899

* **DW-4SLE Left-Handed Electric** – similar to the DW-4S, except in left-handed configuration and mono one-way electronics with three-band EQ, volume, and AMF controls, available in Natural finish, mfg. 1996-98.

	N/A	$300 - 350	$175 - 225	$699

DW-5S – dreadnought-style body, solid spruce top, rosewood back and sides, round soundhole with three-ring rosette, multi-ply body binding with abalone purfling, nato neck, 14/20-fret bound rosewood fingerboard with diamond inlays, bound headstock with rosewood overlay and logo, three-per-side gold tuners, rosewood bridge, black (Natural finish) or tortoise (Tobacco Brown Sunburst) pickguard, available in Natural or Tobacco Brown Sunburst finish, mfg. 1996-98.

	N/A	$300 - 350	$150 - 200	$649

DW6 – dreadnought-style body, solid spruce top, nato back and sides, round soundhole with three-ring rosette, black body binding, nato neck, 14/20-fret rosewood fingerboard with dot inlays, black headstock overlay with logo and floral MOP inlays, three-per-side chrome tuners, rosewood bridge, tortoise pickguard, available in Natural finish, 25.0625 in. scale, mfg. 1999-2002.

	N/A	$225 - 275	$120 - 150	$549

DW7 – dreadnought-style body, solid Englemann spruce top, rosewood back and sides, round soundhole with single multi-ring rosette, multi-ply body binding, nato neck, 14/20-fret rosewood fingerboard with dot inlays, black headstock overlay with logo, three-per-side gold tuners, rosewood bridge, tortoise pickguard, available in Natural finish, 25.5625 in. scale, mfg. 2005-07.

	N/A	$175 - 225	$105 - 130	

* **DW7-12 12-String** – similar to the DW7, except in 12-string configuration with six-per-side tuners, available in Natural finish, 25 in. scale, mfg. 2005-07.

	N/A	$200 - 250	$120 - 150	

* **DW7L Left-Handed** – similar to the DW7, except in left-handed configuration, available in Natural finish, mfg. 2005-07.

	N/A	$200 - 250	$120 - 150	

* **DWX7C Cutaway Electric** – similar to the DW7, except has a single smooth cutaway and System 45 two-way piezo/microphone electronics with volume, mic. volume, three-band EQ, AMF, and phase switch controls, available in Antique Brown Sunburst, Azzuro Sunburst, or Tobacco Sunburst finish, mfg. 2005-07.

	N/A	$260 - 325	$160 - 200	

DW8 – dreadnought-style body, solid spruce top, nato back and sides, round soundhole with three-ring rosette, multi-ply body binding, nato neck, 14/20-fret bound rosewood fingerboard with dot inlays, bound headstock with rosewood overlay and logo/floral MOP inlays, three-per-side gold tuners, rosewood bridge, tortoise pickguard, available in Black, Natural, or Vintage Red Sunburst finish, 25.0625 in. scale, mfg. 1999-2002.

	N/A	$250 - 300	$135 - 175	$599

* **DW8-12 12-String** – similar to the DW8, except in 12-string configuration with six-per-side tuners, available in Natural finish, mfg. 1999-2002.

	N/A	$275 - 325	$150 - 200	$649

* **DWX8C Cutaway Electric** – similar to the DW8, except has a single smooth cutaway and System 39 one-way electronics with three-band EQ, AMF, mid-shape, and volume controls, available in Black, Natural, or Oriental Blue Burst finish, mfg. 1999-2002.

	N/A	$350 - 425	$200 - 250	$849

* **DW8L Left-Handed** – similar to the DW8, except in left-handed configuration, available in Natural finish, mfg. 1999-2002.

	N/A	$250 - 300	$135 - 175	$599

DW9 – dreadnought-style body, solid Englemann spruce top, solid rosewood back, rosewood sides, round soundhole with single multi-ring rosette, multi-ply body binding, nato neck, 14/20-fret rosewood fingerboard with dot inlays, black headstock overlay with logo, three-per-side gold tuners, rosewood bridge, tortoise pickguard, available in Natural finish, 25.5625 in. scale, mfg. 2005-07.

	N/A	$250 - 300	$150 - 190	

MSR/NOTES	100%	EXCELLENT	AVERAGE	LAST MSR

DW10 – dreadnought-style body, solid spruce top, rosewood back and sides, round soundhole with three-ring rosette, multi-ply body binding, nato neck, 14/20-fret bound rosewood fingerboard with dot inlays, bound headstock with rosewood overlay and logo/floral MOP inlays, three-per-side gold tuners, rosewood bridge, tortoise pickguard, available in Natural finish, 25.0625 in. scale, mfg. 1999-2002.

	N/A	$275 - 325	$150 - 200	$649

DW15 – dreadnought-style body, solid Englemann spruce top, solid rosewood back and sides, round soundhole with single multi-ring rosette, multi-ply body binding, decorative back stripe, nato neck, 14/20-fret ebony fingerboard with snowflake inlays, black headstock overlay with logo, three-per-side gold tuners, ebony bridge, tortoise pickguard, available in Natural finish, 25.5625 in. scale, mfg. 2005-07.

	N/A	$275 - 350	$165 - 210	$699

DW20 – dreadnought-style body, solid spruce top, rosewood back and sides, round soundhole with three-ring abalone pearl rosette, multi-ply body binding with abalone purfling, nato neck, 14/20-fret bound rosewood fingerboard with snowflake inlays, bound headstock with rosewood overlay and logo/floral MOP inlays, three-per-side gold tuners, rosewood bridge, tortoise pickguard, available in Natural finish, 25.0625 in. scale, mfg. 1999-2002.

	N/A	$375 - 450	$250 - 300	$899

DW-103E – dreadnought-style body, solid spruce top, nato back and sides, round soundhole with single multi-ring rosette, multi-ply top and back binding, nato neck, 14/20-fret rosewood fingerboard with no inlays, rosewood headstock overlay and logo, three-per-side chrome tuners, rosewood bridge, no pickguard, includes an external preamp with volume, three-band EQ, EQ pass, AMF, and mix controls, available in Natural finish, mfg. 1996-98.

	N/A	$375 - 450	$250 - 300	$899

DW-105 – dreadnought-style body, solid spruce top, nato back and sides, round soundhole with single multi-ring rosette, multi-ply top and back binding, nato neck, 14/20-fret rosewood fingerboard with no inlays, rosewood headstock overlay and logo, three-per-side chrome tuners, rosewood bridge, no pickguard, available in Natural Satin finish, mfg. 1997-98.

	N/A	$250 - 300	$135 - 175	$599

* ***DW-105C Cutaway Electric*** – similar to the DW-105, except has a single smooth cutaway and mono one-way electronics with three-band EQ, volume, and AMF controls, available in Natural Satin finish, mfg. 1997-98.

	N/A	$325 - 400	$200 - 250	$799

ACOUSTIC: FG SERIES

The FG Series has been a consistent staple in Yamaha's line up since the late 1960s. Yamaha has also changed the series several times since the original red label guitars were introduced. We were unable to compile any information on the FG Series between approximately the mid-1970s and the late 1980s because there are no catalogs available for that time period. Any catalog or price list information from this era would be greatly appreciated and it will help bridge the gap. A brief overview of the FG Series is compiled here.

The **FG-140**, **FG-180**, and the **FG-300** were the original six-string jumbo guitars introduced in 1969. Also released that year was the 12-string **FG-230**, Spanish **FG-75**, and the folk body **FG-110** and **FG-150** models. Guitars from this era have a red label, and early models have wide heads.

In 1971, some higher end models were introduced with fancier appointments including the **FG-580**, **FG-630**, **FG-700S**, **FG-1000J**, **FG-1200J**, **FG-1500**, **FG-2000**, and the **FG-2500**.

In 1972, the FG-140, FG-300, FG-230, and FG170 were discontinued as a whole new line of models were introduced. In the six string series, the **FG-160**, **FG-210**, **FG-280**, **FG-165S**, and the **FG-295S** were introduced. The 12-String model became the **FG-260**. A 3/4 sized model was introduced as the **FG-45**. The folk series gained the **FG-170**. The first acoustic/electrics debuted this year as well with the **FG-100E** and the **FG-160E**. Guitars now feature a green label, and should all have the narrow headstock.

In 1974, all model numbers were changed to carry an "I" suffix (FG-160-I, FG-180-I, etc.). Exact model specification changes are unknown, but the labels were changed to black and the necks were made out of Toog.

In 1977, an entirely new line of guitars was introduced that started with "3". The only models to survive the switch were the folk acoustic electric models and the high-end models. Eight new models were introduced and they included the **FG-335**, **FG-340**, **FG-345**, **FG-350W**, **FG-365S**, **FG-375S**, **FG-336SG**, and the **FG-351SB**. The first solid top FG models were introduced and they carried an "S" suffix, which previously indicated Sunburst finish (now noted as SB). Three 12-String models were also introduced with the **FG-312**, **FG-412SB**, and the **FG-512**. Other models included the Spanish body **FG-325** and the Folk Guitar series with the **FG-300** and the **FG-331**. These guitars featured orange oval labels and a nato neck.

In 1978, the high-end series of FG models became the L Series. In 1979, a mid-range series was introduced featuring the **FG-750S** and **FG-770S** models. Between 1978 and 1980, a transition of moving the tension rod adjustment from the head to the body occurred. By 1981, the tension rod was in the body.

In 1981, the FG-350W, FG-336SB, and the FG-351SB were all discontinued. In the same series the **FG-340T** and **355SB** were introduced. It appears that this year a prefix was added to all the models, but what happen is unknown. The 12-String series gained the model **FG-612S**. The Folk guitar series became the Semi-Jumbo series and brought in the models **SJ-180** and **SJ-400S**. The acoustic/electric series was overhauled with new models **FG-335E** and **FG-365SE** replacing the old ones. In 1982, the **FG-332** was added to the six-string line. In 1984, the **FG-335SB** and the **FG-346SB** were introduced for one year only into the six-string line. Also in 1984, the first cutaway acoustics were introduced with the models **CW-350E**, **CW-370SE**, and non-electric models **CW-350** and the **CW-370** were introduced.

MSR/NOTES	100%	EXCELLENT	AVERAGE	LAST MSR

In 1985, the entire line of FG acoustic guitars was overhauled. No models retained their same model designation. The six-string jumbo models were now the **FG-400, FG-405, FG-410, FG-420, FG-430, FG-440, FG-450S, FG-460S, FG-470S,** and **FG-480S.** The 12-string models were changed to the **FG-420-12, FG-440-12,** and **FG-460S-12.**

The model lineup remained unchanged until 1989 when all models earned an A suffix. The FG-405, FG-440, and the FG-480 were all discontinued. The FS-350S, and the cutaway FG-420C and FG-450C models were discontinued. 1989 marked the first year for Yamaha left-handed acoustic instruments and these new models included the **FG-420LA** and **FG-450LA** (the L suffix stands for left-hand). The leaf logo was now on the headstock.

In 1995, they discontinued many of the models and changed the last 0 to a 1, so an FG-400A became the FG-401, etc. In 1999 the dropped the 1 in favor of a 2 and introduced some new models. Then in 2001, they dropped the 2 for the 3. In 2005, Yamaha overhauled the entire line with the 700 FG Series, which is currently available.

FG-45 – student Spanish-style body, spruce top, katsura back and sides, round soundhole with single ring rosette, black body binding, nato neck, 12/18-fret rosewood fingerboard with dot inlays, three-per-side nickel-plated tuners with plastic buttons, rosewood bridge, tortoise pickguard, available in Natural finish, 21.5 in. scale, mfg. 1972-73.

| | N/A | $120 - 150 | $70 - 90 | |

FG-75 – Spanish-style body, spruce top, maple or katsura back and sides, round soundhole with two color multi-ring rosette, black body binding, nato neck, 14/20-fret rosewood fingerboard with dot inlays, three-per-side nickel-plated tuners with plastic buttons, rosewood bridge, black or tortoise pickguard, available in Natural finish, 25 in. scale, mfg. 1969-1973.

| | N/A | $250 - 300 | $150 - 190 | |

FG-110 – folk-style body, spruce top, maple or katsura back and sides, round soundhole with multi-ring rosette, black body binding, nato neck, 14/20-fret bubinga fingerboard with dot inlays, three-per-side nickel-plated tuners with plastic buttons, rosewood bridge, black or tortoise pickguard, available in Natural finish, 25 in. scale, mfg. 1969-1973.

| | N/A | $250 - 300 | $150 - 190 | |

* **FG-110E Electric** – similar to the FG-110, except has a single coil pickup mounted near the fingerboard in the soundhole and two knobs mounted on the top (v, tone), available in Natural finish, mfg. 1972-73.

| | N/A | $275 - 350 | $165 - 210 | |

FG-140 – dreadnought-style body, spruce top, mahogany back and sides, round soundhole with multi-ring rosette, black body binding, mahogany neck, 14/20-fret rosewood fingerboard with dot inlays, three-per-side nickel-plated tuners, rosewood bridge, black pickguard, available in Natural finish, mfg. 1969-1971.

| | N/A | $275 - 350 | $165 - 210 | |

FG-150 – folk-style body, spruce top, mahogany back and sides, round soundhole with multi-ring rosette, black body binding, nato neck, 14/20-fret rosewood fingerboard with dot inlays, three-per-side chrome-plated tuners, rosewood bridge, black pickguard, available in Natural finish, mfg. 1969-1971.

| | N/A | $275 - 350 | $165 - 210 | |

FG-160 – dreadnought-style body, spruce top, mahogany back and sides, round soundhole with multi-ring rosette, black body binding, mahogany neck, 14/20-fret rosewood fingerboard with dot inlays, three-per-side nickel-plated tuners, rosewood bridge, tortoise pickguard, available in Natural finish, 25 in. scale, mfg. 1972-73.

| | N/A | $200 - 250 | $120 - 150 | |

* **FG-160E Electric** – similar to the FG-160, except has a single coil pickup mounted near the fingerboard in the soundhole and two knobs mounted on the top (v, tone), available in Natural finish, mfg. 1972-73.

| | N/A | $225 - 275 | $135 - 170 | |

FG-170 – folk-style body, spruce top, mahogany back and sides, round soundhole with multi-ring rosette, black body binding, nato neck, 14/20-fret rosewood fingerboard with dot inlays, three-per-side chrome-plated tuners, rosewood bridge, tortoise pickguard, available in Natural finish, 25 in. scale, mfg. 1972-73.

| | N/A | $250 - 300 | $150 - 190 | |

FG-180 – dreadnought-style body, select spruce top, mahogany back and sides, round soundhole with multi-ring rosette, multi-ply body binding, mahogany neck, 14/20-fret rosewood fingerboard with dot inlays, three-per-side nickel-plated tuners, rosewood bridge, black pickguard, available in Natural finish, mfg. 1969-1971.

| | N/A | $325 - 400 | $200 - 250 | |

FG-200 – dreadnought-style body, solid spruce top, mahogany back and sides, round soundhole with multi-ring rosette, black body binding, mahogany neck, 14/20-fret rosewood fingerboard with dot inlays, three-per-side nickel-plated tuners, rosewood bridge, tortoise pickguard, available in Natural finish, 25 in. scale, mfg. 1972-73.

| | N/A | $250 - 300 | $150 - 190 | |

FG-230 – 12-string configuration, dreadnought-style body, select spruce top, mahogany back and sides, round soundhole with multi-ring rosette, multi-ply body binding, mahogany neck, 14/20-fret rosewood fingerboard with dot inlays, six-per-side chrome-plated tuners, rosewood bridge, tortoise pickguard, available in Natural finish, mfg. 1969-1971.

| | N/A | $350 - 425 | $200 - 250 | |

MSR/NOTES	100%	EXCELLENT	AVERAGE	LAST MSR

FG-260 – 12-string configuration, dreadnought-style body, spruce top, mahogany back and sides, round soundhole with multi-ring rosette, black body binding, mahogany neck, 14/20-fret rosewood fingerboard with dot inlays, slotted headstock with six-per-side open-style nickel-plated tuners and plastic buttons, rosewood bridge, tortoise pickguard, available in Natural finish, 25 in. scale, mfg. 1972-73.

	N/A	$250 - 300	$150 - 190	

FG-300 – dreadnought-style body, select spruce top, rosewood back and sides, round soundhole with multi-ring rosette, multi-ply top and back binding, mahogany neck, 14/20-fret bound rosewood fingerboard with split parallelogram inlays, bound headstock, three-per-side chrome-plated tuners, adj. rosewood bridge with pearl inlays, large three-point tortoise pickguard, available in Natural finish, mfg. 1969-1973.

	N/A	$350 - 450	$200 - 250	

FG300A – dreadnought-style body, spruce top, Indonesia mahogany/jetulong back and sides, round soundhole with multi-stripe rosette, black body binding, nato neck, 14/20-fret Indonesia rosewood/sonokeling fingerboard with pearl dot inlays, reddish/brown headstock overlay with logo and leaf design inlay, three-per-side chrome tuners with plastic buttons, sonokeling bridge, black pickguard, available in Natural finish, mfg. late 1980s-1993.

	N/A	$75 - 100	$50 - 65	$199

FG-360 – dreadnought-style body, select spruce top, rosewood back and sides, round soundhole with multi-ring rosette, multi-ply body binding, mahogany neck, 14/20-fret bound ebony fingerboard with dot inlays, three-per-side nickel-plated tuners, ebony bridge, tortoise pickguard, available in Natural finish, 25 in. scale, mfg. 1972-73.

	N/A	$250 - 300	$135 - 175	

FG400A – dreadnought-style body, spruce top, nato back and sides, round soundhole with multi-ring rosette, black body binding, nato neck, 14/20-fret bubinga fingerboard with pearl dot inlays, nato headstock overlay with logo and leaf design inlay, three-per-side chrome tuners with white plastic buttons, nato bridge, black pickguard, available in Natural finish, mfg. 1989-1994.

	N/A	$100 - 130	$60 - 80	$259

FG401 – dreadnought-style body, spruce top, nato back and sides, round soundhole with multi-ring rosette, black body binding, nato neck, 14/20-fret bubinga or rosewood fingerboard with dot inlays, mahgaony headstock overlay with logo and design inlay, three-per-side chrome tuners, rosewood bridge, black pickguard, available in Natural finish, 25.5625 in. scale, mfg. 1994-97.

	N/A	$120 - 160	$80 - 100	$319

FG402 – dreadnought-style body, spruce top, nato back and sides, round soundhole with multi-ring rosette, black body binding, nato neck, 14/20-fret rosewood fingerboard with dot inlays, mahgaony headstock overlay with logo and design inlay, three-per-side chrome tuners, rosewood bridge, black pickguard, available in Natural finish, 25.5625 in. scale, mfg. 1998-2001.

	N/A	$135 - 175	$85 - 110	$339

* ***FG402MS*** – similar to the FG402 except has a solid spruce top and Matte Natural finish, mfg. 1998-2001.

	N/A	$150 - 200	$95 - 120	$349

FG403S/FG403MS – dreadnought-style body, solid spruce top, nato back and sides, round soundhole with multi-ring rosette, body binding, nato neck, 14/20-fret rosewood fingerboard with dot inlays, mahgaony headstock overlay with logo and design inlay, three-per-side chrome tuners, rosewood bridge, black pickguard, available in Natural (FG403S) or Natural Matte (FG403MS) finish, 25.5625 in. scale, mfg. 2002-04.

	N/A	$120 - 150	$70 - 95	$300

FG410A – dreadnought-style body, spruce top, nato back and sides, round soundhole with multi-ring rosette, black body binding, nato neck, 14/20-fret bubinga fingerboard with pearl dot inlays, nato headstock overlay with logo and leaf design inlay, three-per-side chrome tuners, nato bridge, black pickguard, available in Natural finish, mfg. 1989-1994.

	N/A	$135 - 175	$85 - 110	$329

* ***FG410-12A 12-String*** – similar to the FG410A, except in 12-string configuration with six-per-side tuners, mfg. 1989-1994.

	N/A	$140 - 180	$85 - 110	$359

* ***FG410EA Electric*** – similar to the FG410A, except has a piezo APX pickup with three knobs (volume, two tone), mfg. 1989-1994.

	N/A	$225 - 275	$125 - 175	$519

FG411 – dreadnought-style body, spruce top, nato or agathis back and sides, round soundhole with multi-ring rosette, black or multi-ply (Black finish only) body binding, nato neck, 14/20-fret rosewood fingerboard with dot inlays, matching finish headstock overlay with logo and design inlay, three-per-side chrome tuners, rosewood bridge, black pickguard, available in Black, Natural, or Violin Sunburst finish, 25.5625 in. scale, mfg. 1993-97.

	N/A	$150 - 200	$95 - 120	$399

* ***FG411-12 12-String*** – similar to the FG411, except in 12-string configuration with six-per-side tuners, mfg. 1993-97.

	N/A	$175 - 225	$110 - 140	$449

»***FG411C(E)-12 Cutaway Electric 12-String*** – similar to the FG411-12 12-String, except has a single round cutaway and System 26 one-way electronics with pop out controls (1993-94) or three-band EQ, volume, and AMF controls (1995-97), available in Black, Natural, or Violin Sunburst finish, mfg. 1993-97.

	N/A	$300 - 350	$175 - 225	$679

MSR/NOTES	100%	EXCELLENT	AVERAGE	LAST MSR

* **FG411C(E) Cutaway Electric** – similar to the FG411, except has a single round cutaway and System 26 one-way electronics with pop out controls (1993-94) or three-band EQ, volume, and AMF controls (1995-97), available in Black, Marine Blue, Natural, or Violin Sunburst finish, mfg. 1993-97.

	N/A	$275 - 325	$150 - 200	$649

* **FG411E Electric** – similar to the FG411, except has System 26 one-way electronics with three-band EQ, volume, and AMF controls, available in Natural finish, mfg. 1997 only.

	N/A	$200 - 250	$120 - 150	$499

* **FG411L Left-Handed** – similar to the FG411, except in left-handed configuration, mfg. 1993-97.

	N/A	$165 - 210	$100 - 135	$419

* **FG411S Solid Top** – similar to the FG411, except has a solid spruce top, available in Natural or Violin Sunburst finish, mfg. 1993-97.

	N/A	$175 - 225	$110 - 140	$449

»**FG411S-12 Solid Top 12-String** – similar to the FG411S Solid Top, except in 12-string configuration with six-per-side tuners, mfg. 1993-95.

	N/A	$200 - 250	$120 - 150	$490

»**FG411SC(E) Solid Top Cutaway Electric** – similar to the FG411S, except has a single round cutaway and System 26 one-way electronics with pop out controls (1993-94) or three-band EQ, volume, and AMF controls (1995-97), available in Natural or Tobacco Brown Sunburst finish, mfg. 1993-97.

	N/A	$300 - 350	$150 - 200	$679

»**FG411SL Solid Top Left-Handed** – similar to the FG411S Solid Top, except in left-handed configuration, mfg. 1993-96.

	N/A	$200 - 250	$120 - 150	$479

FG412 – dreadnought-style body, spruce top, nato back and sides, round soundhole with multi-ring rosette, black or multi-ply (Black finish only) body binding, nato neck, 14/20-fret rosewood fingerboard with dot inlays, matching finish headstock overlay with logo and design inlay, three-per-side chrome tuners, rosewood bridge, black pickguard, available in Black, Natural, or Violin Sunburst finish, 25.5625 in. scale, mfg. 1998-2001.

	N/A	$150 - 200	$95 - 120	$399

* **FG412-12 12-String** – similar to the FG412, except in 12-string configuration with six-per-side tuners, available in Natural finish, 25 in. scale, mfg. 1998-2001.

	N/A	$175 - 225	$110 - 140	$449

»**FGX412C-12 Cutaway Electric 12-String** – similar to the FGX412-12 12-String, except has a single round cutaway and System 33 one-way electronics with three-band EQ, volume, and AMF controls, available in Black or Natural finish, mfg. 1998-2001.

	N/A	$300 - 350	$175 - 225	$699

* **FGX412C Cutaway Electric** – similar to the FGX412, except has a single round cutaway and System 33 one-way electronics with three-band EQ, volume, and AMF controls, available in Black, Natural, Marine BlueBurst, or Violin Sunburst finish, mfg. 1998-2001.

	N/A	$275 - 325	$150 - 200	$649

* **FG412L Left-Handed** – similar to the FG412, except in left-handed configuration, available in Natural finish, mfg. 1998-2001.

	N/A	$165 - 210	$100 - 130	$419

* **FG412S Solid Top** – similar to the FG412, except has a solid spruce top, available in Natural finish, mfg. 1998-2001.

	N/A	$175 - 225	$110 - 140	$449

»**FGX412SC Cutaway Electric Solid Top** – similar to the FGX412S Solid top, except has a single rounded cutaway and System 33 one-way electronics with three-band EQ, volume, and AMF controls, available in Natural or Tobacco Sunburst finish, mfg. 1998-2001.

	N/A	$300 - 350	$175 - 225	$699

* **FGX412 Electric** – similar to the FG412, except has System 33 one-way electronics with three-band EQ, volume, and AMF controls available in Natural finish, mfg. 1998-2001.

	N/A	$200 - 250	$120 - 150	$519

FG413S – dreadnought-style body, solid spruce top, nato back and sides, round soundhole with multi-ring rosette, black body binding, nato neck, 14/20-fret rosewood fingerboard with dot inlays, rosewood headstock overlay with logo and design inlay, three-per-side chrome tuners, rosewood bridge, black pickguard, available in Natural or Sand Burst finish, 25.5625 in. scale, mfg. 2002-04.

	N/A	$150 - 200	$95 - 120	$370

* **FG413S-12 12-String** – similar to the FG413S, except in 12-string configuration with six-per-side tuners, available in Natural finish, mfg. 2002-04.

	N/A	$175 - 225	$110 - 140	$450

* **FG413SL Left-Handed** – similar to the FG413S, except in left-handed configuration, available in Natural finish, mfg. 2002-04.

	N/A	$175 - 225	$110 - 140	$450

MSR/NOTES	100%	EXCELLENT	AVERAGE	LAST MSR

* FGX413SC Cutaway Electric – similar to the FG413S, except has a single smooth cutaway and System 46 electronics with three-band EQ, volume, and AMF slider controls, available in Natural finish, mfg. 2002-04.

	N/A	$250 - 300	$135 - 175	$600

»FGX413SC-12 Cutaway Electric 12-String – similar to the FGX413SC Cutaway Electric, except in 12-string configuration with six-per-side tuners, available in Natural finish, mfg. 2002-04.

	N/A	$275 - 325	$150 - 200	$650

FG420A – dreadnought-style body, spruce top, nato back and sides, round soundhole with a multi-ring abalone rosette, multi-ply body binding, nato neck, 14/20-fret bound bubinga fingerboard with pearl dot inlays, nato headstock overlay with logo and leaf design inlay, three-per-side chrome tuners, rosewood bridge, black pickguard, available in Natural finish, mfg. 1989-1994.

	N/A	$150 - 200	$95 - 120	$379

* FG420-12A 12-String – similar to the FG420A, except in 12-string configuration with six-per-side tuners, available in Natural finish, mfg. 1989-1994.

	N/A	$175 - 225	$110 - 140	$419

»FG420E-12A Electric 12-String – similar to the FG420-12A 12-String, except has a piezo APX pickup with three knobs (volume, two tone), mfg. 1989-1994.

	N/A	$225 - 275	$135 - 175	$529

* FG420LA Left-Handed – similar to the FG420A, except in left-handed configuration, available in Natural finish, mfg. 1989-1994.

	N/A	$150 - 200	$95 - 120	$379

FG421 – dreadnought-style body, spruce top, nato back and sides, round soundhole with multi-ring rosette, multi-ply body binding, nato neck, 14/20-fret bound rosewood fingerboard with dot inlays, mahogany headstock overlay with logo and design inlay, three-per-side chrome tuners, rosewood bridge, black pickguard, available in Natural finish, 25.5625 in. scale, mfg. 1994 only.

	N/A	$175 - 225	$110 - 140	$429

FG422 – dreadnought-style body, spruce top, nato back and sides, round soundhole with multi-ring rosette, multi-ply body binding, nato neck, 14/20-fret bound rosewood fingerboard with dot inlays, matching finish headstock overlay with logo and design inlay, three-per-side chrome tuners, rosewood bridge, black pickguard, available in Natural, Oriental Blue Burst, or Tobacco Sunburst finish, 25.5625 in. scale, mfg. 1998-2001.

	N/A	$175 - 225	$110 - 140	$469

FG423S – dreadnought-style body, solid spruce top, nato back and sides, round soundhole with multi-ring rosette, multi-ply body binding, nato neck, 14/20-fret bound rosewood fingerboard with dot inlays, matching finish headstock overlay with logo and design inlay, three-per-side chrome tuners, rosewood bridge, black pickguard, available in Black, Dark Sun Red, Natural, Oriental Blue Burst, or Tobacco Brown finish, 25.5625 in. scale, mfg. 2002-04.

	N/A	$175 - 225	$110 - 140	$450

* FGX423SC Cutaway Electric – similar to the FG423S, except has a single smooth cutaway and System 46 electronics with three-band EQ, volume, and AMF slider controls, available in Black or Marine Blue finish, mfg. 2002-04.

	N/A	$300 - 350	$175 - 225	$680

»FGX423SC-12 Cutaway Electric 12-String – similar to the FGX423SC Cutaway Electric, except in 12-string configuration with six-per-side tuners, available in Black finish, mfg. 2002-04.

	N/A	$300 - 375	$175 - 225	$750

FG430A – dreadnought-style body, spruce top, nato back and sides, round soundhole with a multi-ring abalone rosette, multi-ply body binding, nato neck, 14/20-fret bound rosewood fingerboard with pearl dot inlays, bound headstock with nato overlay and logo/leaf design inlay, three-per-side chrome tuners, rosewood bridge, black pickguard, available in Natural finish, mfg. 1989-1994.

	N/A	$175 - 225	$110 - 140	$429

FG432 – dreadnought-style body, solid Englemann spruce top, nato back and sides, round soundhole with multi-ring rosette, multi-ply body binding, nato neck, 14/20-fret bound rosewood fingerboard with pearl dot inlays, bound headstock with rosewood overlay and logo/design inlay, three-per-side chrome tuners, rosewood bridge, black pickguard, available in Natural finish, 25.5625 in. scale, mfg. 1998-2001.

	N/A	$200 - 250	$120 - 150	$479

* FG432S Solid Top – similar to the FG432, except has a solid spruce top, available in Natural finish, mfg. 1998-2001.

	N/A	$225 - 275	$135 - 175	$549

FG433S – dreadnought-style body, solid Englemann spruce top, nato back and sides, round soundhole with multi-ring abalone pearl rosette, multi-ply body binding, nato neck, 14/20-fret bound rosewood fingerboard with pearl dot inlays, bound headstock with rosewood overlay and logo/design inlay, three-per-side gold tuners, rosewood bridge, black pickguard, available in Natural finish, 25.5625 in. scale, mfg. 2002-04.

	N/A	$225 - 275	$135 - 175	$530

MSR/NOTES	100%	EXCELLENT	AVERAGE	LAST MSR

FG435A – dreadnought-style body, spruce top, agathis back and sides, round soundhole with a multi-ring abalone rosette, multi-ply body binding, nato neck, 14/20-fret bound bubinga fingerboard with pearl dot inlays, nato headstock overlay with logo and leaf design inlay, three-per-side chrome tuners, rosewood bridge, black pickguard, available in Black, Brown Sunburst, Marine Blue, Oriental Blue, or Tinted finish, mfg. 1989-1994.

	N/A	$175 - 225	$100 - 130	$419

FG441 – dreadnought-style body, spruce top, ovangkol or agathis (Black finish only) back and sides, round soundhole with multi-ring abalone rosette, multi-ply body binding, nato neck, 14/20-fret bound rosewood fingerboard with pearl dot inlays, bound headstock with rosewood overlay and logo/design inlay, three-per-side chrome tuners, rosewood bridge, black pickguard, available in Black, Natural, or Tobacco Brown Sunburst finish, 25.5625 in. scale, mfg. 1994-95.

	N/A	$200 - 250	$120 - 150	$479

* **FG441C(E) Cutaway Electric** – similar to the FG441, except has a single round cutaway and System 26 one-way electronics with pop out controls (1994 only) or three-band EQ, volume, and AMF controls (1995-97), available in Black, Marine Burst, Natural, or Tobacco Brown Sunburst finish, mfg. 1994-96.

	N/A	$300 - 375	$175 - 225	$749

* **FG441L Left-Handed** – similar to the FG441, except in left-handed configuration, mfg. 1994-96.

	N/A	$225 - 275	$135 - 175	$549

* **FG441S Solid Top** – similar to the FG441, except has a solid spruce top, available in Natural finish, mfg. 1994-97.

	N/A	$225 - 275	$135 - 175	$529

»**FG441S-12 Solid Top 12-String** – similar to the FG441S Solid Top, except in 12-string configuration with six-per-side tuners, available in Natural finish, mfg. 1994-95.

	N/A	$250 - 300	$135 - 175	$599

FG450SA – dreadnought-style body, solid spruce top, ovangkol back and sides, scalloped bracing, round soundhole with a multi-ring abalone rosette, multi-ply body binding, nato neck, 14/20-fret bound rosewood fingerboard with pearl diamond inlays, bound headstock with rosewood overlay and logo/leaf design inlay, three-per-side chrome tuners, rosewood bridge, black pickguard, available in Natural finish, mfg. 1989-1994.

	N/A	$200 - 250	$120 - 150	$500

* **FG450SLA Left-Handed** – similar to the FG450SA, except in left-handed configuration, available in Natural finish, mfg. 1989-1994.

	N/A	$200 - 250	$120 - 150	$499

FG460SA – dreadnought-style body, solid spruce top, Indian rosewood back and sides, scalloped bracing, round soundhole with a multi-ring abalone rosette, multi-ply body binding with abalone purfling, nato neck, 14/20-fret bound rosewood fingerboard with pearl diamond inlays, bound headstock with rosewood overlay and logo/leaf design inlay, three-per-side gold tuners, rosewood bridge, black pickguard, available in Natural finish, mfg. 1989-1994.

	N/A	$250 - 300	$135 - 175	$589

* **FG460S-12A 12-String** – similar to the FG460SA, except in 12-string configuration with six-per-side tuners, mfg. 1989-1994.

	N/A	$275 - 325	$150 - 200	$619

FG461S – dreadnought-style body, solid spruce top, Indian rosewood back and sides, round soundhole with multi-ring abalone rosette, multi-ply body binding with abalone purfling, nato neck, 14/20-fret bound rosewood fingerboard with pearl diamond inlays, bound headstock with black overlay and logo/design inlay, three-per-side gold tuners, rosewood bridge, black pickguard, available in Natural finish, 25.5625 in. scale, mfg. 1994-97.

	N/A	$300 - 350	$175 - 225	$679

FG470SA – dreadnought-style body, solid spruce top, Indian rosewood back and sides, scalloped bracing, round soundhole with a multi-ring abalone rosette, multi-ply body binding with abalone purfling, nato neck, 14/20-fret bound rosewood fingerboard with pearl diamond inlays, bound headstock with rosewood overlay and logo/leaf design inlay, three-per-side gold tuners, rosewood bridge, black pickguard, available in Natural finish, mfg. 1989-1994.

	N/A	$300 - 350	$175 - 225	$659

FG502 – dreadnought-style body, solid spruce top, solid mahogany back and sides, round soundhole with multi-ring rosette, multi-ply body binding, nato neck, 14/20-fret rosewood fingerboard with pearl dot inlays, mahogany headstock overlay and logo and design inlay, three-per-side chrome Kluson tuners, rosewood bridge, tortoise pickguard, available in Natural Matte finish, 25.5625 in. scale, mfg. 1999-2003.

	N/A	$325 - 400	$200 - 250	$799

* **FG502M** – similar to the FG502 except has a solid mahogany top, available in Natural Matte finish, mfg. 1999-2003.

	N/A	$325 - 400	$200 - 250	$799

FG700S/FG700MS – dreadnought-style body, solid spruce top, nato back and sides, round soundhole with multi-ring rosette, body binding, nato neck, 14/20-fret rosewood fingerboard with dot inlays, rosewood headstock overlay with logo, three-per-side chrome tuners, rosewood bridge, tortoise pickguard, available in Natural (FG700S) or Natural Satin (FG700MS) (mfg. 2005-2010) finish, 25.5625 in. scale, mfg. 2005-present.

MSR $322	$200	$130 - 160	$75 - 100	

MSR/NOTES	100%	EXCELLENT	AVERAGE	LAST MSR

* FGX700SC Cutaway Electric – similar to the the FG700S, except has a single smooth cutaway and System 55 piezo pickup electronics, available in Brown Sunburst or Natural finish, mfg. 2012-present.

MSR $483	$300	$200 - 250	$120 - 150	

FG720S – dreadnought-style body, solid spruce top, nato back and sides, round soundhole with multi-ring rosette, multi-ply body binding, nato neck, 14/20-fret bound rosewood fingerboard with dot inlays, matching finish headstock overlay with logo, and decorative inlay, three-per-side chrome tuners, rosewood bridge, tortoise pickguard, available in Black, Brown Sunburst, Dusk Sun Red, Natural, or Ocean Blueburst/Oriental Blue Burst finish, 25.5625 in. scale, mfg. 2005-present.

MSR $442	$280	$180 - 220	$110 - 140	

* FG720S-12 12-String – similar to the FG720S, except in 12-string configuration with six-per-side tuners, available in Natural finish, 25 in. scale, mfg. 2005-present.

MSR $523	$330	$210 - 260	$130 - 160	

* FG720SL Left-Handed – similar to the FG720S, except in left-handed configuration, available in Natural finish, mfg. 2005-present.

MSR $523	$330	$210 - 260	$130 - 160	

* FGX720SC/FGX720SCA Cutaway Electric – similar to the FG720S, except has a single smooth cutaway and System 55 piezo pickup electronics, available in Black, Brown Sunburst, or Natural finish, mfg. 2005-present.

MSR $675	$420	$270 - 330	$165 - 215	

FG730S – dreadnought-style body, solid spruce top, rosewood back and sides, round soundhole with multi-ring abalone pearl rosette, multi-ply body binding, nato neck, 14/20-fret bound rosewood fingerboard with dot inlays, bound headstock with rosewood overlay and logo/decorative inlays, three-per-side chrome tuners, rosewood bridge, tortoise pickguard, available in Natural, Tobacco Brown Sunburst, or Vintage Cherry Sunburst finish, 25.5625 in. scale, mfg. 2005-present.

MSR $493	$300	$200 - 250	$120 - 150	

* FGX730SC Cutaway Electric – similar to the FG730S, except has a single smooth cutaway and System 56CB one-way piezo pickup electronics, available in Black, Brown Sunburst, or Natural finish, mfg. 2008-present.

MSR $865	$500	$350 - 430	$200 - 250	

FG750S – dreadnought-style body, solid spruce top, sycamore back and sides, round soundhole with multi-ring tortoise rosette, multi-ply body binding, nato neck, 14/20-fret tortoise-bound rosewood fingerboard with dot inlays, tortoise-bound headstock with rosewood overlay and logo/decorative inlays, three-per-side chrome tuners with tortoise buttons, rosewood bridge, tortoise pickguard, available in Natural finish, 25.5625 in. scale, mfg. 2005-2010.

	$425	$275 - 325	$150 - 200	$650

ACOUSTIC: F/FS SERIES

F310/F325 – dreadnought-style body, spruce top, jetulong or meranti back and sides, round soundhole with three-stripe rosette, black body binding, nato neck, 14/20-fret sonokeling or rosewood fingerboard with pearl dot inlays, three-per-side chrome tuners, sonokeling or rosewood bridge, black pickguard, available in Cherry Sunburst (disc.), Natural, or Tobacco Sunburst finish, mfg. 1995-present.

MSR $221	$150	$90 - 110	$50 - 70	

- Add 7.5% for Tobacco Sunburst finish (MSR $241).
- Add 35% for deluxe plush hardshell case (MSR $305).
- Add 40% for Tobacco Sunburst finish with deluxe plush hardshell case (MSR $325).

This model is branded the F325 in the U.S. and F310 in all other countries.

* F310P Pack – similar to the F310/F325, except comes with along a gig bag and various other accessories, available in Natural or Tobacco Brown Sunburst finish, mfg. 1997-present.

	$225	$135 - 175	$85 - 110	$330

This model is still produced by Yamaha, but it is not currently available in the U.S.

* FX310/FX325 Electric – similar to the F310/F325, except has System 42 electronics with volume and tone controls (early models) or System 53 electronics with volume, treble, and bass controls (later models), available in Cherry Sunburst (disc.) or Natural finish, mfg. 1999-present.

MSR $302	$190	$120 - 150	$70 - 95	

- Add 15% for hardshell case (FX325HC MSR $372)

This model is branded the FX325 in the U.S. and FX310 in all other countries.

F335 – dreadnought-style body, spruce top, meranti back and sides, round soundhole with three-stripe rosette, body binding, nato neck, 14/20-fret rosewood fingerboard with pearl dot inlays, black headstock overlay with logo and tree design inlays, three-per-side gold tuners, rosewood bridge, black (Black finish) or tortoise (Natural and Tobacco Brown Sunburst finish) pickguard, available in Black, Natural, or Tobacco Brown Sunburst finish, current mfg.

MSR $350	$150	$90 - 120	$50 - 70	

MSR/NOTES	100%	EXCELLENT	AVERAGE	LAST MSR

* **FX335 Electric** – similar to the F335, except has System 53 electronics with volume, treble, and bass controls, available in Natural finish, disc. 2011.

	$200	$120 - 150	$70 - 95	$300

F340 – dreadnought-style body, spruce top, meranti back and sides, round soundhole with three-ring rosette, black body binding, nato neck, 14/20-fret rosewood fingerboard with dot inlays, meranti headstock overlay with logo and floral design inlays, three-per-side chrome tuners, rosewood bridge, available in Black or Natural finish, 25 in. scale, mfg. 1999-2006.

	N/A	$130 - 170	$80 - 100	$299

F345 – dreadnought-style body, sycamore top, mahogany back and sides, round soundhole with three-stripe rosette, body binding, nato neck, 14/20-fret rosewood fingerboard with pearl dot inlays, black headstock overlay with logo and tree design inlays, three-per-side gold tuners, rosewood bridge, tortoise pickguard, available in Tobacco Brown Sunburst finish, current mfg.

MSR $420	$230	$135 - 175	$85 - 110	

F370 – dreadnought-style body, spruce top, nato back and sides, round soundhole with three-ring rosette, multi-ply body binding, nato neck, 14/20-fret rosewood fingerboard with dot inlays, nato headstock overlay with logo and floral design inlays, three-per-side chrome tuners, rosewood bridge, black pickguard, available in Black, Natural, or Tobacco Sunburst finish, 25 in. scale, mfg. 2006-2010.

	$200	$120 - 150	$70 - 95	

* **FX370C Cutaway Electric** – similar to the F370, except has a single rounded cutaway and System 58 one-way electronics with volume, three-band EQ, and AMF slider controls, available in Black (disc.), Natural, or Tobacco Brown Sunburst (disc.) finish, mfg. 2006-present.

MSR $412	$250	$160 - 210	$100 - 125	

• **Add 20% for hardshell case (FX370C HC MSR $483).**

F380 – dreadnought-style body, spruce top, nato back and sides, round soundhole with three-ring rosette, multi-ply body binding, nato neck, 14/20-fret rosewood fingerboard with dot inlays, nato headstock overlay with logo and floral design inlays, three-per-side gold tuners, rosewood bridge, black pickguard, available in Black, Natural, or Tobacco Sunburst finish, 25 in. scale, mfg. 1999-2007.

	N/A	$140 - 175	$85 - 105	$299

FD01S – dreadnought-style body, solid spruce top, nato back and sides, round soundhole with three-ring rosette, black body binding, nato neck, 14/20-fret rosewood fingerboard with dot inlays, wood grain headstock overlay with logo, three-per-side chrome tuners, rosewood bridge, black pickguard, available in Natural finish, current mfg.

MSR $280	$190	$110 - 140	$70 - 90	

• **Add 22.5% for deluxe plush hardshell case (F1HC MSR $377).**

FS310 A – folk-style body, spruce top, nato back and sides, round soundhole with three-ring rosette, black body binding, nato neck, 14/20-fret bubinga fingerboard with dot inlays, nato headstock overlay with logo and floral design inlays, three-per-side chrome tuners, nato bridge, black pickguard, available in Natural finish, 24.4 in. scale, mfg. 1989-1993.

	N/A	$135 - 175	$85 - 110	$329

FS311 – folk-style body, spruce top, nato back and sides, round soundhole with three-ring rosette, black body binding, nato neck, 14/20-fret rosewood fingerboard with dot inlays, nato headstock overlay with logo and floral design inlays, three-per-side chrome tuners, rosewood bridge, black pickguard, available in Natural finish, 24.4 in. scale, mfg. 1994-2001.

	N/A	$150 - 200	$95 - 120	$399

FS340 – folk-style body, spruce top, meranti back and sides, round soundhole with three-ring rosette, black body binding, nato neck, 14/20-fret rosewood fingerboard with dot inlays, meranti headstock overlay with logo and floral design inlays, three-per-side chrome tuners, rosewood bridge, black pickguard, available in Natural finish, 24.1875 in. scale, mfg. 1999-2004.

	N/A	$130 - 170	$80 - 100	$299

FS413S – folk-style body, solid Sitka spruce top, nato back and sides, round soundhole with three-ring rosette, black body binding, nato neck, 14/20-fret rosewood fingerboard with dot inlays, nato headstock overlay with logo and floral design inlays, three-per-side chrome tuners, rosewood bridge, black pickguard, available in Natural finish, 24.1875 in. scale, mfg. 2002-03.

	N/A	$150 - 200	$95 - 120	$370

FS720S – folk-style body, solid Sitka spruce top, nato back and sides, round soundhole with three-ring rosette, multi-ply body binding, nato neck, 14/20-fret bound rosewood fingerboard with dot inlays, wood headstock overlay with logo and floral design inlays, three-per-side chrome tuners, rosewood bridge, tortoise pickguard, available in Black, Dusk Sun Red, Natural, Tobacco Brown Sunburst, or Tropical Marine Blue/ Cobalt Aqua finish, 25 in. scale, mfg. 2005-present.

MSR $442	$280	$180 - 220	$110 - 140	

JR1 (FG JUNIOR) – 3/4-size dreadnought-style body, spruce top, Indonesian mahogany or meranti back and sides, round soundhole with a single two-ring rosette, black body binding, nato neck, 14/20-fret Javanese rosewood fingerboard with pearl dot inlays, three-per-side chrome tuners, rosewood bridge, tortoise pickguard, available in Natural finish, gig bag included, mfg. 1999-present.

MSR $211	$130	$80 - 105	$50 - 65	

JR2 – 3/4-size dreadnought-style body, spruce top, nato back and sides, round soundhole with a single two-ring rosette, black body binding, nato neck, 14/20-fret rosewood fingerboard with pearl dot inlays, three-per-side chrome tuners, rosewood bridge, tortoise pickguard, available in Natural or Tobacco Sunburst finish, gig bag included, 21.75 in. scale, mfg. 2012-present.

MSR $250	$160	$105 - 130	$65 - 80	

MSR/NOTES	100%	EXCELLENT	AVERAGE	LAST MSR

ACOUSTIC: L SERIES

Yamaha's L Series represent their standard production top-of-the-line models. In 1978, Yamaha introduced their first L Series guitars in response to the popularity of custom guitar designs. By the mid-1980s, the L Series had expanded to several different body shapes including the LA, LL, and LS designs. In the 1990s other body shapes included the LD and LW designs. In 2004, Yamaha reorganized their entire L Series line into three body shapes: LJ, LL, and LS and four distinct trim offerings: 6, 16, 26, and 36.

L-5A – dreadnought-style body, solid spruce top, two-piece solid mahogany back, solid mahogany sides, round soundhole with three-ring rosette, multi-ply body binding, African mahogany neck, 14/20-fret Indian rosewood fingerboard with dot inlays, mahogany headstock overlay with logo, three-per-side chrome tuners, Indian rosewood bridge, black pickguard, available in Natural gloss finish, mfg. 1978-1983.

	N/A	$600 - 750	$375 - 450	

L-10A – dreadnought-style body, solid spruce top, two-piece solid Indian rosewood back, solid Indian rosewood sides, round soundhole with three-ring rosette, multi-ply body binding, African mahogany neck, 14/20-fret Indian rosewood fingerboard with dot inlays, mahogany headstock overlay with logo, three-per-side chrome tuners, Indian rosewood bridge, black pickguard, available in Natural gloss finish, mfg. 1978-1983.

	N/A	$700 - 850	$450 - 525	

L-15A – dreadnought-style body, solid white spruce top, two-piece solid Indian rosewood back, solid Indian rosewood sides, round soundhole with three-ring herringbone rosette, cream body binding with herringbone purfling, herringbone back purfling, African mahogany neck, 14/20-fret ebony fingerboard with pearl diamond inlays, mahogany headstock overlay with logo, three-per-side gold tuners, ebony bridge, black pickguard, available in Natural gloss finish, mfg. 1978-1983.

	N/A	$850 - 1,000	$550 - 650	

L-20A – dreadnought-style body, solid white spruce top, three-piece solid Indian rosewood back with a solid center wedge of Jacaranda, solid Indian rosewood sides, round soundhole with three-ring herringbone rosette, cream body binding with herringbone purfling, back herringbone purfling, African mahogany neck, 14/20-fret bound ebony fingerboard with pearl diamond inlays, bound headstock with mahogany overlay and logo, three-per-side gold tuners, ebony bridge, black pickguard, available in Natural gloss finish, mfg. 1978-1983.

	N/A	$1,050 - 1,250	$725 - 850	

L-25A/L-25AT – dreadnought-style body, solid white spruce top, three-piece solid Jacaranda back and sides, solid Jacaranda sides, round soundhole with three-ring herringbone rosette, cream body binding with herringbone purfling, back herringbone purfling, Honduras mahogany neck, 14/20-fret bound ebony fingerboard with pearl oval inlays, bound headstock with mahogany overlay and logo, three-per-side gold tuners, ebony bridge, black pickguard, available in Natural gloss finish (L-25A) or Natural tinted top with satin back and sides (L-25AT), mfg. 1978-1983.

	N/A	$1,250 - 1,500	$900 - 1,050	

LA-8 – dreadnought-style body, solid spruce top, Indian rosewood back and sides, round soundhole with three stripe abalone rosette, multi-ply body binding, mahogany neck, 14/20-fret bound ebony fingerboard with pearl snowflake/cross inlays, bound rosewood headstock overlay with pearl logo inlay, three-per-side gold tuners, ebony bridge, white bridge pins with pearl dots, available in Natural finish, mfg. 1985-89, 1993-2003.

	N/A	$425 - 500	$250 - 300	$949

LA-18 – dreadnought-style body, solid spruce top, solid mahogany back and sides, round soundhole with three stripe abalone rosette, multi-ply body binding, mahogany neck, 14/20-fret bound ebony fingerboard with pearl dot inlays, bound rosewood headstock overlay with pearl logo and shadowed "L" inlays, three-per-side gold tuners, ebony bridge, white bridge pins with pearl dots, available in Natural finish, mfg. 1990-96.

	N/A	$550 - 625	$325 - 375	$1,159

LA-28 – dreadnought-style body, solid spruce top, solid Indian rosewood back and sides, round soundhole with three stripe abalone rosette, multi-ply body binding, mahogany neck, 14/20-fret bound ebony fingerboard with pearl snowflake/cross inlays, bound rosewood headstock overlay with pearl logo and shadowed "L" inlays, three-per-side gold tuners, ebony bridge, white bridge pins with pearl dots, available in Natural finish, mfg. 1985-1996.

	N/A	$725 - 850	$375 - 450	$1,649

LD-10 – dreadnought-style body, solid white spruce top, Indian rosewood back and sides, round soundhole with three-ring abalone rosette, white body binding with abalone purfling, African mahogany neck, 14/20-fret bound rosewood fingerboard with pearl dot inlays, bound headstock with rosewood overlay, logo, and "LD" inlays, three-per-side gold tuners, rosewood bridge, black bridge pins with pearl dots, black pickguard, available in Natural finish, mfg. 1990-94.

	N/A	$350 - 400	$200 - 250	$759

* **LD-10E** – similar to the LD10, except has a two-way bridge/interal electronics with volume, treble, bass, and mix pop-up controls, mfg. 1990-94.

	N/A	$425 - 500	$250 - 300	$1,049

LJ6 – LJ jumbo-style body, solid Englemann spruce top, rosewood back and sides, round soundhole with three-ring abalone rosette, cream multi-ply body binding, three ply mahogany/rosewood neck, 14/20-fret bound ebony fingerboard with dot inlays, bound headstock with rosewood overlay and logo, three-per-side gold tuners, ebony bridge, black pickguard, available in Natural finish, mfg. 2004-present.

MSR $835	$500	$330 - 415	$215 - 265	

MSR/NOTES	100%	EXCELLENT	AVERAGE	LAST MSR

* **LJX6C/LJX6CA Cutaway Electric** – similar to the LJ-6, except has a single cutaway and System 45 two-way piezo/microphone electronics with volume, three-band EQ, mic. volume, and AMF slider controls (2004-08) or A.R.T. System 57 three-way electronics with master volume, bass volume, treble volume, three-band EQ, and digital tuner controls (mfg. 2009-present), available in Natural finish, mfg. 2004-present.

MSR $1,210	$700	$480 - 600	$300 - 400	

LJ16 – LJ jumbo-style body, solid Englemann spruce top, solid rosewood back and sides, round soundhole with three-ring abalone rosette, cream multi-ply body binding, three ply mahogany/rosewood neck, 14/20-fret bound ebony fingerboard with dot inlays, bound headstock with rosewood overlay and logo, three-per-side gold tuners, ebony bridge, black pickguard, available in Natural finish, mfg. 2004-present.

MSR $1,210	$750	$480 - 600	$325 - 400	

* **LJ16CP Cutaway Piezo** – similar to the LJ16, except has a single cutaway with SRT System 63 piezo/preamp, available in Natural finish, current mfg.

MSR $2,015	$1,100	$800 - 1,000	$725 - 775	

LJ26 – LJ jumbo-style body, solid Englemann spruce top, solid Indian rosewood back and sides, round soundhole with three-ring rosette, maple multi-ply body binding, five-ply mahogany/padauk neck, 14/20-fret ebony fingerboard with diamond inlays, rosewood headstock overlay with logo, three-per-side gold vintage tuners, ebony bridge, tortoise pickguard, available in Natural finish, mfg. 2004-present.

MSR $4,025	$2,300	$1,600 - 2,000	$1,200 - 1,400	

* **LJX26C Cutaway Electric** – similar to the LJ26, except has a single cutaway and System 41 two-way piezo/microphone electronics with volume, mic. volume, mic. tone, three-band EQ, AMF, and phase switch controls (2004-07) or System 60 three-way electronics with Master Volume, bass volume, treble volume, and main volume push-in knobs (2008-2011), mfg. 2005-2011.

	$2,800	$2,000 - 2,400	$1,300 - 1,600	$4,800

»**LJX26CP Cutaway Piezo** – similar to the LJX26C Cutaway Electric, except with an SRT System 63 piezo/preamp, available in Natural finish, current mfg.

MSR $5,825	$3,300	$2,300 - 2,900	$1,500 - 2,000	

LJ36 – LJ jumbo-style body, solid Englemann spruce top, solid Indian rosewood back and sides, round soundhole with three-ring abalone rosette, maple body binding with abalone purfling, maple back purfling, five-ply mahogany/padauk neck, 14/20-fret bound ebony fingerboard with diamond inlays, bound headstock with rosewood overlay and logo, three-per-side gold vintage tuners, ebony bridge, black pickguard, available in Natural finish, mfg. 2004-2011.

	$2,700	$1,900 - 2,400	$1,200 - 1,700	$4,900

* **LJX36C Cutaway Electric** – similar to the LJ36, except has a single cutaway and System 41 two-way piezo/microphone electronics with volume, mic. volume, mic. tone, three-band EQ, AMF, and phase switch controls (2004-07) or System 60 three-way electronics with Master Volume, bass volume, treble volume, and main volume push-in knobs (2008-2011), mfg. 2005-2011.

	$3,200	$2,200 - 2,800	$1,400 - 1,900	$5,600

LL-5 – dreadnought-style body, solid spruce top, African mahogany back and sides, scalloped bracing, round soundhole with three ring rosette, multi-ply body binding, mahogany neck, 14/20-fret Indian rosewood fingerboard with pearl dot inlays, rosewood headstock overlay with logo and shadowed "L" inlays, three-per-side chrome tuners, Indian rosewood bridge, black bridge pins with pearl dots, black pickguard, available in Natural finish, mfg. 1984-89.

	N/A	$425 - 500	$250 - 300	

* **LL-5-12 12-String** – similar to the LL-5, except in 12-string configuration and six-per-side tuners, available in Natural finish, mfg. 1984-89.

	N/A	$475 - 550	$275 - 325	

* **LL-5C Cutaway** – similar to the LL-5, except has a single cutaway, available in Natural finish, mfg. 1984-89.

	N/A	$475 - 550	$275 - 325	

»**LL-5EC Cutaway Electric** – similar to the LL-5C Cutaway, except has electronics, available in Natural finish, mfg. 1984-89.

	N/A	$525 - 600	$300 - 375	

LL6 – LL dreadnought-style body, solid Englemann spruce top, rosewood back and sides, round soundhole with three-ring abalone rosette, cream multi-ply body binding, three ply mahogany/rosewood neck, 14/20-fret bound ebony fingerboard with dot inlays, bound headstock with rosewood overlay and logo, three-per-side gold tuners, ebony bridge, black pickguard, available in Natural, Sunburst, or Tinted Natural finish, mfg. 2004-present.

MSR $835	$500	$325 - 400	$200 - 250	

• **Add 5% (MSR $875) for Sunburst or Tinted Natural finish.**

* **LLX6/LLX6A Electric** – similar to the LL6, except has System 54 one-way direct out electronics (2004-08) or A.R.T. System 57 three-way electronics with master volume, bass volume, treble volume, three-band EQ, and digital tuner controls (2009-2010), available in Black, Brown Sunburst, Natural, or Tobacco Brown Sunburst finish, mfg. 2004-2010.

	$700	$450 - 525	$275 - 325	$1,070

• **Add 5% (Last MSR was $1,130) for Black, Brown Sunburst, or Tobacco Brown Sunburst finish.**

MSR/NOTES	100%	EXCELLENT	AVERAGE	LAST MSR

LLX6 DN DAVE NAVARRO SIGNATURE – LL dreadnought-style body, solid Englemann spruce top, satin sycamore back and sides, round soundhole with simple black two-ring rosette, black body binding, three ply mahogany/rosewood neck, 14/20-fret bound ebony fingerboard with star inlays, black headstock overlay with logo and Dave Navarro design inlays, three-per-side black tuners with pearl buttons, ebony bridge, black pickguard, System 45 two-way piezo/microphone electronics with volume, mic. volume, mic. tone, AMF, three-band EQ, and phase switch controls, available in White finish, 25.5625 in. scale, mfg. 2005-07.

	N/A	$600 - 750	$350 - 450	$1,500

LL-10 – dreadnought-style body, solid spruce top, African mahogany back and sides, scalloped bracing, round soundhole with three ring rosette, multi-ply body binding, mahogany neck, 14/20-fret bound Indian rosewood fingerboard with pearl dot inlays, bound headstock with rosewood overlay, logo, and shadowed "L" inlays, three-per-side chrome tuners, Indian rosewood bridge, black bridge pins with pearl dots, black pickguard, available in Natural finish, mfg. 1984-89.

	N/A	$475 - 550	$275 - 325	

LL-11 – round shoulder dreadnought-style body, solid spruce top, Indian rosewood back and sides, scalloped bracing, round soundhole with three-ring abalone rosette, white body binding with abalone purfling, mahogany neck, 14/20-fret Indian rosewood fingerboard with pearl dot inlays, bound headstock with rosewood overlay, logo, and shadowed "L" inlays, three-per-side gold tuners, Indian rosewood bridge, black pickguard, available in Natural finish, mfg. 1995-2003.

	N/A	$325 - 400	$200 - 250	$759

* **LL-11E Electric** – similar to the LL-11, except has System 38 two-way electronics with an external preamp (volume, three-band EQ, AMF, Mix, and EQ pass controls), available in Natural finish, mfg. 1995-2003.

	N/A	$550 - 650	$325 - 400	$1,199

LL-15 – dreadnought-style body, solid spruce top, solid mahogany back and sides, scalloped bracing, round soundhole with three ring rosette, multi-ply body binding, mahogany neck, 14/20-fret ebony fingerboard with pearl dot inlays, rosewood headstock overlay with logo and shadowed "L" inlays, three-per-side gold tuners, ebony bridge, black bridge pins with pearl dots, black pickguard, available in Natural finish, mfg. 1984-1996.

	N/A	$550 - 625	$325 - 375	$1,199

* **LL-15C Cutaway** – similar to the LL-15, except has a single cutaway, available in Natural finish, mfg. 1984-89.

	N/A	$575 - 650	$325 - 400	

»**LL-15EC Cutaway Electric** – similar to the LL-15C, except has electronics, available in Natural finish, mfg. 1984-89.

	N/A	$600 - 700	$350 - 425	

LL16 – LJ jumbo-style body, solid Englemann spruce top, solid rosewood back and sides, round soundhole with three-ring abalone rosette, cream multi-ply body binding, three ply mahogany/rosewood neck, 14/20-fret bound ebony fingerboard with dot inlays, bound headstock with rosewood overlay and logo, three-per-side gold tuners, ebony bridge, black pickguard, available in Natural finish, mfg. 2004-present.

MSR $1,210	$750	$525 - 600	$325 - 400	

* **LL16-12 12-String** – similar to the LL16, except in 12-string configuration with six-per-side tuners, available in Natural finish, mfg. 2005-present.

MSR $1,310	$800	$575 - 650	$350 - 425	

* **LLX16 Electric** – similar to the LL16, except has System 60 A.R.T. three-way electronics with master volume, bass volume, middle volume, and treble volume pop-up controls, available in Black, Brown Sunburst, Natural, or Tobacco Brown Sunburst finish, mfg. 2009-2010.

	$1,100	$725 - 850	$475 - 550	$1,700

* Add 5% (Last MSR was $1,800) for Black, Brown Sunburst, or Tobacco Brown Sunburst finish.

* **LL16L Left-Handed** – similar to the LL16, except in left-handed configuration, available in Natural finish, mfg. 2005-present.

MSR $1,310	$800	$575 - 650	$350 - 425	

LL26 – LL dreadnought-style body, solid Englemann spruce top, solid Indian rosewood back and sides, round soundhole with three-ring rosette, maple multi-ply body binding, five-ply mahogany/padauk neck, 14/20-fret ebony fingerboard with diamond inlays, rosewood headstock overlay with logo, three-per-side gold vintage tuners, ebony bridge, tortoise pickguard, available in Natural finish, mfg. 2004-present.

MSR $4,025	$2,300	$1,600 - 2,000	$1,000 - 1,400	

* **LLX26C Cutaway Electric** – similar to the LL26, except has a single cutaway and System 41 two-way piezo/microphone electronics with volume, mic. volume, mic. tone, three-band EQ, AMF, and phase switch controls (2004-07) or System 60 three-way electronics with Master Volume, bass volume, treble volume, and main volume push-in knobs (2008-present), mfg. 2004-present.

MSR $4,850	$2,800	$1,900 - 2,400	$1,200 - 1,500	

* **LLX26 Electric** – similar to the LL26, except has System 60 A.R.T. three-way electronics with master volume, bass volume, middle volume, and treble volume pop-up controls, available in Natural finish, mfg. 2009-present.

MSR $4,650	$2,700	$1,800 - 2,300	$1,150 - 1,450	

MSR/NOTES	100%	EXCELLENT	AVERAGE	LAST MSR

LL-35 – dreadnought-style body, solid spruce top, solid Jacaranda back and sides, scalloped bracing, round soundhole with three ring abalone rosette, multi-ply body binding, mahogany neck, 14/20-fret ebony bound fingerboard with pearl snowflake inlays, bound headstock with rosewood overlay, logo, and shadowed "L" inlays, three-per-side gold tuners, ebony bridge, black bridge pins with pearl dots, black pickguard, available in Natural finish, mfg. 1984-1996.

	N/A	$875 - 1,000	$550 - 650	$1,999

LL36 – LL dreadnought-style body, solid Englemann spruce top, solid Indian rosewood back and sides, round soundhole with three-ring abalone rosette, maple body binding with abalone purfling, maple back purfling, five-ply mahogany/padauk neck, 14/20-fret bound ebony fingerboard with diamond inlays, bound headstock with rosewood overlay and logo, three-per-side gold vintage tuners, ebony bridge, black pickguard, available in Natural finish, mfg. 2004-2011.

	$2,700	$1,950 - 2,450	$1,200 - 1,500	$4,900

* **LLX36C Cutaway Electric** – similar to the LL36, except has a single cutaway and System 41 two-way piezo/microphone electronics with volume, mic. volume, mic. tone, three-band EQ, AMF, and phase switch controls (2004-07) or System 60 three-way electronics with Master Volume, bass volume, treble volume, and main volume push-in knobs (2008-2011), mfg. 2004-2011.

	$3,200	$2,250 - 2,800	$1,400 - 1,800	$5,600

LL400 – LL-style body, solid Sitka spruce top, solid mahogany back and sides, round soundhole with three-ring abalone rosette, multi-ply body binding, mahogany neck, 14/20-fret bound rosewood fingerboard with MOP snowflake inlays, bound headstock with rosewood overlay and logo, three-per-side gold tuners, rosewood bridge, black bridge pins with white dots, clear pickguard, available in Natural gloss finish, mfg. 1999-2003.

	N/A	$675 - 800	$400 - 475	$1,499

* **LLX400 Electric** – similar to the LL400, except has System 40G two-way piezo/mic electronics with volume, three-band EQ, blend, AMF, and mid controls, soundhole cover included, available in Natural finish, mfg. 2000-03.

	N/A	$875 - 1,000	$500 - 600	$1,899

LL500 – LL-style body, solid Sitka spruce top, solid rosewood back and sides, round soundhole with three-ring abalone rosette, multi-ply body binding, mahogany neck, 14/20-fret bound rosewood fingerboard with MOP snowflake inlays, bound headstock with rosewood overlay and logo, three-per-side gold tuners, rosewood bridge, black bridge pins with white dots, clear pickguard, available in Natural gloss finish, mfg. 1999-2003.

	N/A	$775 - 900	$500 - 575	$1,799

* **LLX500C Cutaway Electric** – similar to the LL500, except has a single cutaway and System 41 two-way piezo/mic electronics with volume, three-band EQ, mic. volume, mic. tone, AMF, and phase switch controls, soundhole cover included, available in Natural finish, mfg. 2001-03.

	N/A	$1,100 - 1,250	$650 - 750	$2,399

LS6 – LS concert-style body, solid Englemann spruce top, rosewood back and sides, round soundhole with three-ring abalone rosette, cream multi-ply body binding, three ply mahogany/rosewood neck, 14/20-fret bound ebony fingerboard with dot inlays, bound headstock with rosewood overlay and logo, three-per-side gold tuners, ebony bridge, black pickguard, available in Natural or Tobacco Brown Sunburst (LS6 TBS, 2011-present) finish, mfg. 2004-present.

MSR $835	$500	$325 - 400	$200 - 250	

• **Add 5% for Tobacco Brown Sunburst finish (MSR $875).**

LS16 – LS concert-style body, solid Englemann spruce top, solid rosewood back and sides, round soundhole with three-ring abalone rosette, cream multi-ply body binding, three ply mahogany/rosewood neck, 14/20-fret bound ebony fingerboard with dot inlays, bound headstock with rosewood overlay and logo, three-per-side gold tuners, ebony bridge, black pickguard, available in Natural finish, mfg. 2004-present.

MSR $1,210	$750	$525 - 600	$325 - 400	

LS26 – LS concert-style body, solid Englemann spruce top, solid Indian rosewood back and sides, round soundhole with three-ring rosette, maple multi-ply body binding, five-ply mahogany/padauk neck, 14/20-fret ebony fingerboard with diamond inlays, rosewood headstock overlay with logo, three-per-side gold vintage tuners, ebony bridge, tortoise pickguard, available in Natural finish, mfg. 2004-present.

MSR $4,025	$2,300	$1,600 - 2,000	$1,000 - 1,200	

* **LSX26C Cutaway Electric** – similar to the LS26, except has a single cutaway and System 41 two-way piezo/microphone electronics with volume, mic. volume, mic. tone, three-band EQ, AMF, and phase switch controls (2004-07) or System 60 three-way electronics with Master Volume, bass volume, treble volume, and main volume push-in knobs (2008-present), available in Natural finish, mfg. 2005-present.

MSR $4,850	$2,800	$1,900 - 2,400	$1,200 - 1,500	

LS36 – LS concert-style body, solid Englemann spruce top, solid Indian rosewood back and sides, round soundhole with three-ring abalone rosette, maple body binding with abalone purfling, maple back purfling, five-ply mahogany/padauk neck, 14/20-fret bound ebony fingerboard with diamond inlays, bound headstock with rosewood overlay and logo, three-per-side gold vintage tuners, ebony bridge, black pickguard, available in Natural finish, mfg. 2004-2011.

	$2,700	$1,900 - 2,400	$1,200 - 1,500	$4,900

MSR/NOTES	100%	EXCELLENT	AVERAGE	LAST MSR

* LSX36C Cutaway Electric – similar to the LS36, except has a single cutaway and System 41 two-way piezo/microphone electronics with volume, mic. volume, mic. tone, three-band EQ, AMF, and phase switch controls (2004-07) or System 60 three-way electronics with Master Volume, bass volume, treble volume, and main volume push-in knobs (2008-2011), mfg. 2005-2011.

	$4,000	$2,500 - 3,000	N/A	$5,600

LS400 – LS concert-style body, solid Sitka spruce top, solid mahogany back and sides, round soundhole with three-ring abalone rosette, multi-ply ivory cell body binding, mahogany neck, 14/20-fret bound rosewood fingerboard with MOP snowflake inlays, bound headstock with rosewood overlay and logo, three-per-side gold tuners, rosewood bridge, black bridge pins with white dots, clear pickguard, available in Black, Natural, or Vintage Tint finish, mfg. 1999-2003.

	N/A	$675 - 800	$400 - 475	$1,499

* LSX400 Electric – similar to the LS400, except has System 40G two-way piezo/microphone electronics system with three-band EQ, volume, blend, midrange, and AMF controls, soundhole cover included, available in Natural finish, mfg. 2000-03.

	N/A	$875 - 1,000	$500 - 600	$1,899

LS500 – LS concert-style body, solid Sitka spruce top, solid rosewood back and sides, round soundhole with three-ring abalone rosette, multi-ply body binding, mahogany neck, 14/20-fret bound rosewood fingerboard with MOP snowflake inlays, bound headstock with rosewood overlay and logo, three-per-side gold tuners, rosewood bridge, black bridge pins with white dots, clear pickguard, available in Natural gloss finish, mfg. 1999-2003.

	N/A	$775 - 900	$500 - 575	$1,799

* LSX500C Cutaway Electric – similar to the LS500, except has a single cutaway and System 41 two-way piezo/microphone electronics system with three-band EQ, volume, blend, midrange, AMF, and phase switch controls, soundhole cover included, available in Natural finish, mfg. 2001-03.

	N/A	$1,100 - 1,250	$650 - 750	$2,399

LW5 – dreadnought-style body, solid spruce top, mahogany back and sides, scalloped bracing, round soundhole with three-ring rosette, multi-ply body binding, mahogany neck, 14/20-fret rosewood fingerboard, three-per-side chrome tuners, rosewood bridge, black bridge pins with white dots, no pickguard, available in Natural finish, mfg. 1995-96.

	N/A	$250 - 300	$135 - 175	$599

* LW5C Cutaway Electric – similar to the LW5, except has a single smooth cutaway and one-way piezo electronics with volume, three-band EQ, AMF, and EQ pass controls, available in Natural finish, mfg. 1996 only.

	N/A	$325 - 400	$175 - 225	$799

LW15 – dreadnought-style body, solid spruce top, mahogany back and sides, scalloped bracing, round soundhole with three-ring rosette, multi-ply body binding, mahogany neck, 14/20-fret bound rosewood fingerboard with pearl flower inlay, bound headstock with rosewood overlay and pearl logo inlay, three-per-side chrome tuners, rosewood bridge, black bridge pins with white dots, black pickguard, available in Natural finish, mfg. 1994-96.

	N/A	$300 - 375	$175 - 225	$699

* LW15C Cutaway Electric – similar to the LW15, except has a single smooth cutaway and System 28C one-way piezo electronics with volume, three-band EQ, AMF, and EQ pass controls, available in Natural finish, mfg. 1996 only.

	N/A	$425 - 500	$275 - 325	$999

LW25 – dreadnought-style body, solid spruce top, Indian rosewood back and sides, scalloped bracing, round soundhole with three-ring rosette, multi-ply body binding, mahogany neck, 14/20-fret bound ebony fingerboard with pearl flower inlays, bound headstock with rosewood overlay and pearl logo inlay, three-per-side gold tuners, ebony bridge, black bridge pins with white dots, black pickguard, available in Natural finish, mfg. 1994-96.

	N/A	$350 - 425	$200 - 250	$829

ACOUSTIC: PARLOR (CSF) SERIES

CSF35 – small parlor-sized body, solid Sitka spruce top, nato back and sides, round soundhole with single multi-ring rosette, multi-ply body binding, nato neck, 14/20-fret rosewood fingerboard with dots and 12th fret bridge-shaped abalone inlays, bound headstock with nato overlay and logo, three-per-side chrome Kluson-type tuners, rosewood bridge, available in Tobacco Sunburst finish, 25 in. scale, mfg. 2002-05.

	N/A	$200 - 250	$120 - 150	$500

CSF60 – small parlor-sized body, solid Sitka spruce top, solid Sapele back and sides, round soundhole with single multi-ring abalone rosette, multi-ply body binding, nato neck, 14/20-fret rosewood fingerboard with dots and 12th fret bridge-shaped abalone inlays, multi-ply bound headstock with rosewood overlay and logo, three-per-side chrome Kluson-type tuners, rosewood bridge, available in Tobacco Sunburst finish, 25 in. scale, mfg. 2002-05.

	N/A	$325 - 400	$175 - 225	$800

* CSF60C Cutaway Electric – similar to the CSF60, except has an extreme cutaway and System 50 one-way electronics with no controls, available in Tobacco Sunburst finish, mfg. 2003-05.

	N/A	$425 - 500	$275 - 325	$980

MSR/NOTES	100%	EXCELLENT	AVERAGE	LAST MSR

ACOUSTIC ELECTRIC: A SERIES

A1M – single cutaway dreadnought folk-style body, solid Sitka spruce top, mahogany back and sides, round soundhole with multi-ring rosette, mahogany body binding, mahogany neck, 17/20-fret rosewood fingerboard with white dot inlays, headstock with logo, three-per-side chrome tuners, ebony bridge with black pins and white dots, System 66 preamp, SRT pickup, tortoiseshell pickguard, available in Natural finish, 25.5906 in. scale, mfg. 2011-present.

| MSR $955 | $600 | $375 - 475 | $240 - 285 | |

* **AC1M** – similar to the A1M, except with a concert-style body, available in Natural finish, mfg. 2011-present.

| MSR $955 | $600 | $375 - 475 | $240 - 285 | |

A1R – single cutaway dreadnought folk-style body, solid Sitka spruce top, rosewood back and sides, round soundhole with multi-ring rosette, mahogany body binding, mahogany neck, 17/20-fret rosewood fingerboard with white dot inlays, headstock with logo, three-per-side chrome tuners, ebony bridge with black pins and white dots, System 66 preamp, SRT pickup, tortoiseshell pickguard, available in Natural finish, 25.5906 in. scale, mfg. 2011-present.

| MSR $1,055 | $700 | $425 - 525 | $265 - 325 | |

* **AC1R** – similar to the A1R, except with a concert-style body, available in Natural finish, mfg. 2011-present.

| MSR $1,055 | $700 | $425 - 525 | $265 - 325 | |

A3M – single cutaway dreadnought folk-style body, solid Sitka spruce top, solid mahogany back and sides, round soundhole with multi-ring rosewood/mahogany rosette, mahogany body binding, mahogany neck, 17/20-fret ebony fingerboard with white dot inlays, headstock with logo, three-per-side chrome tuners, ebony bridge with black pins and white dots, System 63 SRT pickup and SRT preamp combination, tortoiseshell pickguard, available in Natural finish, 25.5906 in. scale, mfg. 2011-present.

| MSR $1,260 | $800 | $500 - 625 | $300 - 375 | |

* **AC3M** – similar to the A3M, except with a concert-style body, available in Natural finish, mfg. 2011-present.

| MSR $1,260 | $800 | $500 - 625 | $300 - 375 | |

A3R – single cutaway dreadnought folk-style body, solid Sitka spruce top, solid rosewood back and sides, round soundhole with multi-ring rosewood/mahogany rosette, mahogany body binding, mahogany neck, 17/20-fret ebony fingerboard with white dot inlays, headstock with logo, three-per-side chrome tuners, ebony bridge with black pins and white dots, System 63 SRT pickup and SRT preamp combination, tortoiseshell pickguard, available in Natural finish, 25.5906 in. scale, mfg. 2011-present.

| MSR $1,360 | $900 | $550 - 675 | $325 - 400 | |

* **A3RBC** – similar to the A3R, except has a solid Bear Claw Sitka spruce top, available in Natural finish, mfg. 2012-present.

| MSR $1,500 | $1,000 | $600 - 750 | $350 - 450 | |

* **AC3R** – similar to the A3R, except with a concert-style body, available in Natural finish, mfg. 2011-present.

| MSR $1,360 | $900 | $550 - 675 | $325 - 400 | |

»**AC3RBC** – similar to the AC3R, except has a solid Bear Claw Sitka spruce top, available in Natural finish, mfg. 2012-present.

| MSR $1,500 | $1,000 | $600 - 750 | $350 - 450 | |

ACOUSTIC ELECTRIC: APX SERIES

The APX Series of acoustic/electric instruments was introduced in the late 1980s, and they were the first acoustics with cutaways to be offered by Yamaha. They also featured thinner bodies with arched backs, multiple piezo pickups, and several mono and stereo electronic configurations. The APX Series is still available from Yamaha, but the line has undergone several changes throughout the years and most models were changed all at once. The first series of APX guitars was produced until 1993 and they can be distinguished by pop-up control knobs in the side of the body. 1994 was a transition year with the introduction of the C APX Series where all models featured a C suffix. These models have an actual control plate for the electronics, but they only lasted around a year. In 1995, Yamaha introduced the A APX Series that slowly evolved to include all APX models by 1997, when an A suffix was attached to each model. In 2000, the third series of APX models was introduced. In mid-2006, the fourth series of APX models was introduced that featured a three digit number in the model name. Yamaha also offers nylon-string APX models that have overlapped most of the aforementioned series.

APX 3/APX 3M – single smooth cutaway APX-style body, spruce top, nato back and sides, oval soundhole with black/brown custom rosette, top and back black body binding, nato neck, 14/22-fret rosewood fingerboard with dot inlays, nato headstock overlay with logo and custom design inlays, three-per-side chrome tuners, rosewood bridge, white bridge pins with black dots, no pickguard, System 46 one-way electronics, available in Cherry Sunburst, Natural Satin (APX3M), Tinted, or Tobacco Brown Sunburst finish, 25.5625 in. scale, mfg. 2003-06.

| | N/A | $275 - 325 | $150 - 200 | $630 |

APX 4 – single smooth cutaway APX-style body, spruce top, agathis back and sides, oval soundhole with multi-ring rosette, multi-ply top binding, nato neck, 22-fret rosewood fingerboard with dot inlays, black headstock overlay with logo and decorative design, three-per-side chrome tuners, rosewood bridge, no pickguard, one-way Piezo pickup and electronics, available in Black, Natural, or Violin Sunburst finish, 25.625 in. scale, mfg. 1992-94.

| | N/A | $200 - 250 | $120 - 150 | $499 |

MSR/NOTES	100%	EXCELLENT	AVERAGE	LAST MSR

* **APX 4 12-String** – similar to the APX 4, except in 12-string configuration with six-per-side tuners, available in Black or Violin Sunburst finish, mfg. 1994 only.

	N/A	$225 - 275	$135 - 175	

APX 4A – single smooth cutaway APX-style body, spruce top, nato back and sides, oval soundhole with wood pattern rosette, multi-ply body binding, nato neck, 22-fret rosewood fingerboard with pearl dot inlays, black headstock overlay with screened logo and flower design, three-per-side chrome tuners, rosewood bridge, no pickguard, piezo bridge pickup, System 34 one-way electronics with three-band EQ, available in Black, Natural, Trans. Blue Burst, or Violin Sunburst finish, 25.5 in. scale, mfg. 1995-99.

	N/A	$275 - 325	$150 - 200	$649

* **APX 4-12A 12-String** – similar to the APX 4A, except in 12-string configuration with six-per-side tuners, available in Natural or Violin Sunburst finish, mfg. 1995-99.

	N/A	$300 - 350	$175 - 225	$679

* **APX 4ASPL Special** – similar to the APX 4A, except has a flamed sycamore top, available in Marine BlueBurst and Tobacco Brown Sunburst finish, mfg. 1998-99.

	N/A	$300 - 375	$175 - 225	$749

APX 5A – single smooth cutaway APX-style body, spruce top, nato back and sides, oval soundhole with black/brown custom rosette, top and back three-ply body binding, nato neck, 14/22-fret rosewood fingerboard with dot inlays, corresponding finish headstock overlay with logo and custom design inlays, three-per-side chrome tuners, rosewood bridge, white bridge pins with black dots, no pickguard, System 46 one-way electronics, available in Natural, Sand Burst, or Trans. Blue Burst finish, 25.5625 in. scale, mfg. 2000-06.

	N/A	$300 - 375	$175 - 225	$730

* **APX 5A-12A 12-String** – similar to the APX 5A, except in 12-string configuration with six-per-side tuners, available in Black or Sand Burst finish, 25 in. scale, mfg. 2000-06.

	N/A	$325 - 400	$200 - 250	$780

* **APX 5LA Left-Handed** – similar to the APX 5LA, except in left-handed configuration, available in Sand Burst finish, mfg. 2000-06.

	N/A	$325 - 400	$200 - 250	$780

APX 5NA – nylon string configuration, single smooth cutaway APX-style, spruce top, nato back and sides, oval soundhole with decorative rosette, multi-ply top and back body binding, nato neck, 22-fret rosewood fingerboard with no inlays, slotted headstock with wooden overlay, three-per-side open-style banjo gold tuners, rosewood tied bridge, System 46N one-way electronics, available in Natural finish, 25.5625 in. scale, mfg. 2000-2010.

	$650	$425 - 500	$275 - 325	$1,000

APX 6 – single round cutaway APX-style body, spruce top, agathis back and sides, oval soundhole with wood pattern rosette, multi-ply body binding, nato neck, 24-fret extended rosewood fingerboard with pearl dot inlays, black headstock overlay with screened logo/flower design, three-per-sides chrome tuners, rosewood bridge, two-way piezo pickups, pop up volume/treble/bass/mix controls, available in Black, Cherry Sunburst, or Cream White finish, mfg. late 1980s-1993.

	N/A	$300 - 375	$175 - 225	$729

APX 6A – single round cutaway APX-style body, spruce top, nato back and sides, oval soundhole with wood pattern rosette, multi-ply body binding, nato neck, 24-fret extended rosewood fingerboard with pearl dot inlays, black headstock overlay with screened logo/flower design, three-per-sides gold tuners, rosewood bridge, one-way piezo pickup, three-band EQ, available in Brown Sunburst, Natural, Trans. Blue Burst, Trans. Green Burst finish, mfg. late 1995-99.

	N/A	$350 - 425	$200 - 250	$819

* **APX 6LA Left-Handed** – similar to the APX 6A, except in left-handed configuration, available in Brown Sunburst finish, mfg. late 1995-99.

	N/A	$425 - 500	$250 - 300	$999

APX 6C – single round cutaway APX-style body, spruce top, agathis back and sides, oval soundhole with wood pattern rosette, multi-ply body binding, nato neck, 24-fret extended rosewood fingerboard with pearl dot inlays, black headstock overlay with screened logo/flower design, three-per-sides chrome tuners, rosewood bridge, System 28A/28L one-way Piezo pickup, three-band EQ, available in Black, Tobacco Brown Sunburst, or Trans. Blue Burst finish, mfg. 1994 only.

	N/A	$300 - 375	$175 - 225	

* **APX 6CL Left-Handed** – similar to the APX 6C, except in left-handed configuration, available in Black, Tobacco Brown Sunburst, or Trans. Blue Burst finish, mfg. 1994 only.

	N/A	$325 - 400	$200 - 250	

APX 6N – nylon-string configuration, APX non-cutaway body style, spruce top, ovankol back and sides, oval soundhole with wooden inlay rosette, multi-ply body binding, nato neck, 14/22-fret rosewood fingerboard with no inlays, slotted headstock with rosewood overlay and logo, three-per-side open-style gold tuners, rosewood tied bridge, two-way bridge/body piezo pickups, volume/treble/bass/mix controls, available in Natural finish, mfg. late 1980s-1993.

	N/A	$300 - 375	$175 - 225	$729

MSR/NOTES	100%	EXCELLENT	AVERAGE	LAST MSR

APX 6NA – nylon-string configuration, single smooth cutaway APX-style body, spruce top, nato back and sides, oval soundhole with wooden inlay rosette, multi-ply body binding, nato neck, 14/22-fret extended rosewood fingerboard with no inlays, slotted headstock with rosewood overlay and logo, three-per-side open-style gold tuners, rosewood tied bridge, one-way piezo pickups, three-brand EQ, available in Natural Satin finish, mfg. late 1995-99.

	N/A	$325 - 400	$200 - 250	$799

APX 7 – single smooth cutaway APX-style body, spruce top, agathis back and sides, oval soundhole with a wooden inlay rosette cap, multi-ply body binding, African mahogany neck, 24-fret extended bound rosewood fingerboard with pearl dot inlays, bound headstock with black overlay and screened logo/flower design, three-per-side gold tuners, rosewood bridge, two-way bridge/body piezo pickups, pop-up volume/treble/bass/mix controls, available in Black, Blue Burst, or Light Brown Sunburst finish, mfg. late 1980s-1993.

	N/A	$350 - 425	$200 - 250	$849

APX 7A – single smooth cutaway folk-style thin body, solid spruce top, nato back and sides, oval soundhole with a black/abalone custom rosette, top and back five-ply body binding, nato neck, 14/22-fret bound rosewood fingerboard with dot inlays, bound headstock with black overlay with logo and custom design inlays, three-per-side gold tuners, rosewood bridge, white bridge pins with black dots, no pickguard, System 44 one-way electronics, available in Amber, Natural, Oriental Blue Burst, or Trans. Green Burst finish, 25.5625 in. scale, mfg. 2000-06.

	N/A	$400 - 475	$250 - 300	$900

APX 7C – single smooth cutaway APX-style body, spruce top, agathis back and sides, oval soundhole with a wooden inlay rosette cap, multi-ply body binding, African mahogany neck, 24-fret extended bound rosewood fingerboard with pearl dot inlays, bound headstock with black overlay and screened logo/flower design, three-per-side gold tuners, rosewood bridge, System 28A one-way bridge piezo pickup, three-band EQ, available in Black, Brown Sunburst, or Red Blond Burst finish, mfg. 1994 only.

	N/A	$350 - 425	$200 - 250	

* **APX 7CT** – similar to the APX 7C, except has ovangkol back and sides, available in Natural Satin finish, mfg. 1994 only.

	N/A	$350 - 425	$200 - 250	

APX 7CN – nylon string configuration, single round cutaway APX-style body, spruce top, ovangkol back and sides, oval soundhole with rosette decal, multi-ply body binding, nato neck, 24-fret extended rosewood fingerboard with no inlays, slotted headstock with rosewood overlay and screened logo, three-per-side open-style gold tuners with pearloid buttons, rosewood tied bridge, System 28B one-way piezo bridge pickup, three-band EQ, available in Natural Satin finish, mfg. 1994 only.

	N/A	$400 - 475	$250 - 300	$899

APX 8 – single smooth cutaway APX-style body, spruce top, agathis back and sides, oval soundhole with a wooden inlay rosette cap, multi-ply body binding, African mahogany neck, 24-fret extended bound rosewood fingerboard with pearl dot inlays, bound headstock with black overlay and screened logo/flower design, three-per-side gold tuners, rosewood bridge, stereo one-way bridge piezo pickup, pop-up volume/treble/bass/stereo selector controls, available in Gray Burst or Light Brown Sunburst finish, mfg. 1992-93.

	N/A	$400 - 475	$250 - 300	$949

APX 8A – single smooth cutaway APX-style body, spruce top, ovangkol back and sides, oval soundhole with an abalone inlay rosette cap, multi-ply top and back body binding, African mahogany neck, 22-fret bound rosewood fingerboard that follows the contour of the soundhole with pearl dot inlays, bound headstock with black overlay and screened logo/flower design, three-per-side gold tuners, rosewood bridge, System 29 mono two-way bridge/body piezo pickups, three-band EQ, EQ pass, mix, volume, and AMF controls, available in Brown Sunburst or Natural Satin finish, mfg. 1995-99.

	N/A	$475 - 550	$300 - 350	$1,099

* **APX 8-12A 12-String** – similar to the APX 8A, except in 12-string configuration with six-per-side tuners, available in Natural Satin finish, mfg. 1995-99.

	N/A	$500 - 600	$300 - 375	$1,199

APX 8C – single smooth cutaway APX-style body, spruce top, agathis back and sides, oval soundhole with a wooden inlay rosette cap, multi-ply body binding, African mahogany neck, 24-fret extended bound rosewood fingerboard with pearl dot inlays, bound headstock with black overlay and screened logo/flower design, three-per-side gold tuners, rosewood bridge, System 29 mono two-way bridge/body piezo pickups, three-band EQ, EQ pass, mix, and volume controls, available in Black Burst, Brown Sunburst, or Trans. Blue Burst finish, mfg. 1994 only.

	N/A	$475 - 550	$300 - 350	$1,099

* **APX 8C-12 12-String** – similar to the APX 8C, except in 12-string configuration with six-per-side tuners, available in Brown Sunburst or Trans. Green Burst finish, mfg. 1994 only.

	N/A	$500 - 600	$325 - 375	$1,189

APX 8D DEEP BODY – single smooth cutaway APX-style body, solid spruce top, agathis back and sides, oval soundhole with an oblong orbit-style wooden/abalone inlay rosette cap, multi-ply body binding, African mahogany neck, 24-fret extended bound rosewood fingerboard with pearl dot inlays, bound headstock with black overlay and screened logo/flower design, three-per-side gold tuners, rosewood bridge, two-way bridge/body piezo pickups, pop-up volume/treble/bass/mix controls, available in Black Burst or Brown Sunburst finish, 25.625 in. scale, mfg. 1993-94.

	N/A	$500 - 600	$325 - 375	$1,199

MSR/NOTES	100%	EXCELLENT	AVERAGE	LAST MSR

APX 9C – single smooth cutaway folk-style thin body, solid spruce top, sycamore back and sides, oval soundhole with a black/abalone custom rosette, top and back seven-ply body binding, nato neck, 14/22-fret bound ebony fingerboard with dot inlays, bound headstock with black overlay with logo and custom design inlays, three-per-side gold tuners, ebony bridge, white bridge pins with black dots, no pickguard, System 45 two-way electronics with a soundhole cover and microphone capabilities, available in Black Cherry, Dusk Sun Red, or Yellow Natural Satin finish, 25.5625 in. scale, mfg. 2000-06.

	N/A	$550 - 650	$325 - 375	$1,200

APX 9-12 12-STRING – 12-string configuration, single smooth cutaway APX-style body, spruce top, agathis back and sides, oval soundhole with a wooden inlay rosette cap, multi-ply body binding, African mahogany neck, 24-fret extended bound rosewood fingerboard with pearl dot inlays, bound headstock with black overlay and screened logo/flower design, six-per-side chrome tuners, rosewood bridge, stereo two-way bridge/body piezo pickup, pop-up volume/treble/bass/stereo selector controls, available in Black or Light Brown Sunburst finish, mfg. late 1980s-1993.

	N/A	$500 - 600	$300 - 350	$1,149

APX 9NA – nylon string configuration, single smooth cutaway, solid cedar top, rosewood back and sides, oval soundhole with decorative rosette, multi-ply top and back body binding, nato neck, 22-fret ebony fingerboard with no inlays, slotted headstock with wooden overlay, three-per-side open-style banjo gold tuners, ebony tied bridge, System 46N one-way electronics, available in Natural finish, 25.5625 in. scale, mfg. 2000-06.

	N/A	$525 - 600	$300 - 375	$1,200

APX 10 – single smooth cutaway APX-style body, spruce top with scalloped bracing, sycamore back and sides, oval soundhole with abalone inlay rosette cap, multi-ply body binding, African mahogany neck, 24-fret extended bound ebony fingerboard with pearl diamond inlays, bound headstock with black overlay and screened logo/flower design, three-per-side gold tuners, ebony bridge, stereo two-way bridge/body piezo pickups, pop-up volume/treble/bass/stereo selector controls, available in Antique Satin Sunburst or Burgundy Red finish, mfg. late 1980s-1993.

	N/A	$600 - 700	$375 - 450	$1,399

APX 10A – single smooth cutaway APX-style body, solid spruce top, sycamore back and sides, oval soundhole with abalone inlay rosette cap, multi-ply body binding, African mahogany neck, 24-fret extended bound rosewood fingerboard with pearl diamond inlays, bound headstock with black overlay and screened logo/flower design, three-per-side gold tuners, rosewood bridge, System 29 mono two-way bridge/body piezo pickups, three-band EQ, EQ pass, mix, volume, and AMF controls, available in Black Cherry or Yellow Natural Satin finish, 25.625 in. scale, mfg. 1997-99.

	N/A	$625 - 750	$400 - 475	$1,499

* *APX 10LA Left-Handed* – similar to the APX 10A, except in left-handed configuration, available in Black Cherry or Natural Satin finish, mfg. 1997-99.

	N/A	$650 - 775	$425 - 500	$1,559

APX 10C – single smooth cutaway APX-style body, spruce top, sycamore back and sides, oval soundhole with abalone inlay rosette cap, multi-ply body binding, African mahogany neck, 24-fret extended bound rosewood fingerboard with pearl diamond inlays, bound headstock with black overlay and screened logo/flower design, three-per-side gold tuners, rosewood bridge, System 30 stereo two-way bridge/body piezo pickups, three-band EQ, EQ pass, mix, volume, AMF, and stereo switch controls, available in Antique Brown Sunburst, Antique Satin Sunburst, or Black Burst finish, 25.625 in. scale, mfg. 1994-96.

	N/A	$600 - 700	$375 - 450	$1,399

* *APX 10CL Left-Handed* – similar to the APX 10C, except in left-handed configuration, available in Black Burst finish, mfg. 1994-96.

	N/A	$625 - 750	$400 - 475	$1,559

* *APX 10CT* – similar to the APX 10C, except has Indian rosewood back and sides, available in Natural Satin finish, mfg. 1994-96.

	N/A	$600 - 700	$375 - 450	$1,399

APX 10CN – nylon string configuration, single smooth cutaway APX-style body, solid cedar top, Indian rosewood back and sides, oval soundhole with wooden/rope pattern rosette, multi-ply body binding, African mahogany neck, 24-fret extended ebony fingerboard, slotted headstock with rosewood overlay and logo, three-per-side open-style gold tuners with pearloid buttons, Indian rosewood bridge, System 30 stereo two-way bridge/body piezo pickups, three-band EQ, EQ pass, mix, volume, AMF, and stereo switch controls, available in Natural Satin finish, mfg. 1994-96.

	N/A	$600 - 700	$375 - 450	$1,349

APX 10D DEEP BODY – single smooth cutaway APX-style body, solid spruce top, sycamore back and sides, oval soundhole with an oblong orbit-style wooden/abalone inlay rosette cap, multi-ply body binding, African mahogany neck, 24-fret extended bound rosewood fingerboard with pearl diamond inlays, bound headstock with black overlay and screened logo/flower design, three-per-side gold tuners, rosewood bridge, two-way bridge/body piezo pickups, pop-up volume/treble/bass/mix/stereo selector controls, available in Black Burst or Light Brown Sunburst finish, 25.625 in. scale, mfg. 1993-94.

	N/A	$500 - 600	$325 - 375	

APX 10N – nylon string configuration, single smooth cutaway APX-style body, spruce top, Indian rosewood back and sides, oval soundhole with wooden/rope pattern rosette, multi-ply body binding, African mahogany neck, 24-fret extended ebony fingerboard, slotted headstock with rosewood overlay and logo, three-per-side open-style gold tuners with pearloid buttons, Brazilian rosewood bridge, stereo two-way bridge/body piezo pickups, pop-up volume/treble/bass/mix/stereo switch controls, available in Natural finish, mfg. late 1980s-1993.

	N/A	$500 - 600	$300 - 350	$1,199

MSR/NOTES	100%	EXCELLENT	AVERAGE	LAST MSR

APX 10NA – nylon string configuration, single smooth cutaway APX-style body, solid cedar top, rosewood back and sides, oval soundhole with wooden/rope pattern rosette, multi-ply body binding, African mahogany neck, 24-fret extended ebony fingerboard, slotted headstock with rosewood overlay and logo, three-per-side open-style gold tuners with pearloid buttons, Indian rosewood bridge, System 29 two-way bridge/body piezo pickups, three-band EQ, EQ pass, mix, volume, and AMF controls, available in Natural Satin finish, 25.5625 in. scale, mfg. 1997-99.

	N/A	$550 - 650	$350 - 425	$1,299

APX 20 – single smooth cutaway APX-style body, solid spruce top with scalloped bracing, sycamore back and sides, oval soundhole with abalone inlay rosette cap, abalone body binding, African mahogany neck, 24-fret extended bound ebony fingerboard with abalone pearl large triangular inlays, bound headstock with rosewood overlay and screened logo/flower design, three-per-side gold tuners, ebony bridge, stereo two-way bridge/body piezo pickups, pop-up volume/treble/bass/stereo selector controls, available in Cream White or Light Brown Sunburst finish, mfg. late 1980s-1993.

	N/A	$650 - 800	$425 - 500	$1,599

APX 20C – single smooth cutaway APX-style body, solid spruce top, flame maple back and sides, oval soundhole with abalone inlay rosette cap, single-ply binding with abalone purfling, African mahogany neck, 24-fret extended bound ebony fingerboard with abalone pearl large triangular inlays, bound headstock with black overlay and screened logo/flower design, three-per-side gold tuners, ebony bridge, System 30C stereo two-way bridge/body piezo pickups, three-band EQ, EQ pass, mix, volume, mix, and stereo switch controls, available in Antique Brown Sunburst or Yellow Natural Satin finish, mfg. 1994-96.

	N/A	$725 - 850	$475 - 550	$1,699

APX 20D DEEP BODY – single smooth cutaway APX-style body, solid spruce top, sycamore back and sides, oval soundhole with an oblong orbit-style wooden/abalone inlay rosette cap, abalone body binding, African mahogany neck, 24-fret extended bound ebony fingerboard with pearl decorative inlays, bound headstock with black overlay and screened logo/flower design, three-per-side gold tuners, ebony bridge, two-way bridge/body piezo pickups, pop-up volume/treble/bass/mix/stereo selector controls, available in Antique Satin Sunburst or Cream White finish, 25.625 in. scale, mfg. 1993-94.

	N/A	$500 - 600	$325 - 375	

APX 97LTD – single smooth cutaway APX-style body, spruce top, sycamore back and sides, oval soundhole with black/abalone inlay rosette cap, single-ply body binding with abalone purfling, African mahogany neck, 24-fret extended bound rosewood fingerboard with pearl cherry blossom inlays, bound headstock with white overlay and screened logo/colored cherry blossom design, three-per-side gold tuners, rosewood bridge, System 29 mono two-way bridge/body piezo pickups, three-band EQ, EQ pass, mix, volume, and AMF controls, available in Pearl Snow White finish, 25.625 in. scale, mfg. 1997 only.

	N/A	$850 - 1,000	$600 - 700	$1,999

APX500/APX500 II – single smooth cutaway folk-style thin body, spruce top, nato back and sides, oval soundhole with black/white custom rosette, top and back three-ply body binding, nato neck, 14/22-fret bound rosewood fingerboard with dot inlays, matching finish headstock overlay with logo and custom design inlays, three-per-side chrome tuners, rosewood bridge, black bridge pins with white dots, no pickguard, System 55TA or System 65 (2011-present) electronics, available in Black, Dark Red Burst, Natural, Old Violin Sunburst, Oriental Blue Burst, Red Metallic (APX500 II only), or Vintage White (APX500 II only) finish, 25 in. scale, mfg. summer 2006-present.

MSR $463	$300	$175 - 225	$110 - 140	

* **APX500 FM/APX500 FM II** – similar to the APX500/APX500 II, except has a flame maple top, available in Old Violin Sunburst or Oriental Blue Burst (APX500 FM only) finish, mfg. 2009-present.

MSR $564	$350	$225 - 275	$135 - 175	

APX700/APX700 II – single smooth cutaway folk-style thin body, solid spruce top, nato back and sides, oval soundhole with abalone design custom rosette, top and back five-ply body binding, nato neck, 14/22-fret bound rosewood fingerboard with dot inlays, bound headstock with matching finish overlay and logo/custom design inlays, three-per-side chrome tuners, rosewood bridge, black bridge pins with white dots, no pickguard, System 56 or System64 (2011-present) electronics, available in Black, Brown Sunburst (APX700 II only), Cobalt Aqua (APX700 only), Dusk Sun Red (APX700 only), Natural, Sand Burst, Vintage Cherry Sunburst (2011 only, limited edition), or Violin Sunburst (APX700 II only) finish, 25.5625 in. scale, mfg. summer 2006-present.

MSR $805	$500	$325 - 400	$175 - 225	

* **APX700-12/APX700 II-12 12-String** – similar to the APX700/APX700 II, except in 12-string configuration with six-per-side tuners, available in Black (APX700 II-12 only) or Natural finish, 25 in. scale, mfg. summer 2006-present.

MSR $855	$550	$350 - 425	$200 - 250	

* **APX700L/APX700 IIL Left-Handed** – similar to the APX700/APX700 II, except in left-handed configuration, available in Natural finish, mfg. summer 2006-present.

MSR $855	$550	$350 - 425	$200 - 250	

APX900 – single smooth cutaway folk-style thin body, solid spruce top, flame maple back and sides, oval soundhole with abalone design custom rosette, top and back five-ply body binding, nato neck, 14/22-fret bound ebony fingerboard with custom triangular inlays, bound headstock with rosewood overlay and logo/custom design inlays, three-per-side gold tuners, rosewood bridge, black bridge pins with white dots, no pickguard, System 57 electronics, available in Crimson Red Burst, Mocha Black, Natural, or Ultramarine finish, 25.5625 in. scale, mfg. summer 2006-2011.

	$700	$500 - 600	$300 - 350	$1,200

MSR/NOTES	100%	EXCELLENT	AVERAGE	LAST MSR

APX1000 – single smooth cutaway folk-style thin body, solid spruce top, flamed maple back and sides, oval soundhole with mahogany and abalone rosette, vintage creme body binding, nato neck, 19/22-fret bound rosewood fingerboard with MOP inlays, bound headstock with matching finish overlay and logo/custom design inlays, three-per-side gold tuners, rosewood bridge, black bridge pins with white dots, no pickguard, System 63 SRT electronics, available in Crimson Red Burst, Mocha Black, Natural, or Pearl White finish, 25.5906 in. scale, mfg. 2011-present.

| MSR $1,210 | $800 | $500 - 600 | $250 - 325 | |

APX1200 – single smooth cutaway folk-style thin body, solid spruce top, solid rosewood back and sides, oval soundhole with mahogany and abalone rosette, mahogany body binding, nato neck, 19/22-fret bound ebony fingerboard with MOP inlays, bound headstock with matching finish overlay and logo/custom design inlays, three-per-side gold tuners, rosewood bridge, black bridge pins with white dots, no pickguard, System 62 SRT electronics, available in Natural or Trans. Black finish, 25.5906 in. scale, mfg. 2011-present.

| MSR $2,115 | $1,300 | $850 - 1,050 | $500 - 650 | |

APX SPECIAL I – single smooth cutaway APX-style body, sycamore tiger stripe top, agathis back and sides, oval soundhole with multi-ring rosette, multi-ply top binding, nato neck, 22-fret rosewood fingerboard with dot inlays, black headstock overlay with logo and decorative design, three-per-side chrome tuners, rosewood bridge, no pickguard, System 26 mono one-way Piezo bridge pickup, pop-up volume, treble, and bass controls, available in Red Blond or See-Through Blue Burst finish, 25.625 in. scale, mfg. 1992-94.

| | N/A | $250 - 300 | $135 - 175 | $599 |

APX SPECIAL II – single smooth cutaway APX-style body, bird's-eye maple top, agathis back and sides, oval soundhole with multi-ring rosette, multi-ply top binding, nato neck, 22-fret rosewood fingerboard with dot inlays, black headstock overlay with logo and decorative design, three-per-side chrome tuners, rosewood bridge, no pickguard, System 26 mono one-way Piezo bridge pickup, pop-up volume, treble, and bass controls, available in Purple Burst or Trans. Red Burst finish, 25.625 in. scale, mfg. 1992-94.

| | N/A | $250 - 300 | $135 - 175 | $599 |

APX T1 (TRAVEL SERIES) – single rounded cutaway small body, spruce top, agathis/alder back and sides, oval soundhole, with three-stripe rosette, bound body, maple neck, 22-fret rosewood fingerboard with pearl dot inlay, blackface headstock overlay with screened logo and flowers inlays, three-per-side chrome tuners, string-through rosewood bridge, piezo bridge pickup with System 35 one-way electronics, available in BlueBurst or Violin Sunburst finish, 23.625 in. scale, mfg. 1995-2002.

| | N/A | $200 - 250 | $120 - 150 | $469 |

APX T1N (TRAVEL SERIES) – nylon string configuration, single rounded cutaway small body, spruce top, agathis/alder back and sides, oval soundhole, with three-stripe rosette, bound body, maple neck, 22-fret rosewood fingerboard with pearl dot inlay, slotted headstock with blackface overlay and screened logo/flowers inlays, three-per-side chrome tuners, tied rosewood bridge, piezo bridge pickup with System 35 1 way electronics, available in Natural finish, 23.625 in. scale, mfg. 1995-2002.

| | N/A | $200 - 250 | $120 - 150 | $469 |

ACOUSTIC ELECTRIC: COMPASS SERIES

Yamaha introduced their Compass (CPX) Series in 1998. The Compass Series featured a single smooth cutaway body that was a bit smaller than a regular full-sized jumbo acoustic and Yamaha used their two-way piezo/mic pickup electronics. The CPX 15 handcrafted series came in two regular versions (CPX 15/CPX 15A and the CPX 15CM) as well as four guitars named after the four points of the compass. Each direction represented a certain area of the world and each guitar had unique appointments in body woods, rosettes, and fingerboard inlays. In 2006, Yamaha introduced an entirely new line of Compass models that had three digit model numbers. In 2011, Yamaha introduced System 65T electronics on all their CPX models and they became the second series (CPX Series II).

CPX 5 – single smooth cutaway jumbo Compass-style body, spruce top, nato back and sides, round soundhole with multi rings rosette, three-ply body binding, nato neck, 14/20-fret rosewood fingerboard with pearl dot inlays, matching finish headstock overlay with logo and Compass inlays, three-per-side chrome tuners, rosewood bridge, no pickguard, System 39 one-way piezo bridge pickup, three-band EQ, volume, AMF, and mid-shape button controls, available in Black, Yellow Natural, Trans. Blue Burst, or Violin Sunburst finish, 25.625 in. scale, mfg. 1999-2006.

| | N/A | $325 - 375 | $175 - 225 | $700 |

* **CPX 5S** – similar to the CPX 5, except has a solid spruce top, available in Cherry Sunburst or Tropical Marine Blue finish, mfg. 2003-06.

| | N/A | $325 - 400 | $200 - 250 | $800 |

CPX 7 – single smooth cutaway jumbo Compass-style body, spruce top, mahogany back and sides, round soundhole with decorative color rosette, three-ply body binding, mahogany neck, 14/20-fret rosewood fingerboard with pearl dot and 12th fret offset triangle inlays, wood headstock overlay with logo and Compass inlays, three-per-side chrome tuners, rosewood bridge with three pearl dots, clear pickguard, System 39 one-way piezo bridge pickup, three-band EQ, volume, AMF, and mid-shape button controls, available in Natural finish, 25.625 in. scale, mfg. 1998-2000.

| | N/A | $375 - 450 | $225 - 275 | $900 |

CPX 8 – single smooth cutaway jumbo Compass-style body, solid spruce top, rosewood back and sides, round soundhole with decorative pattern rosette, five-ply body binding, nato neck, 14/20-fret bound rosewood fingerboard with pearl dot inlays, bound headstock with rosewood overlay and logo/Compass inlays, three-per-side gold tuners, rosewood bridge, clear pickguard, System 45 two-way piezo bridge/mic pickups, three-band EQ, volume, mic. volume, AMF slider, and phase button controls, available in Natural finish, 25.625 in. scale, mfg. 2000-06.

| | N/A | $525 - 600 | $325 - 400 | $1,200 |

MSR/NOTES	100%	EXCELLENT	AVERAGE	LAST MSR

* **CPX 8M** – similar to the CPX 8, except has a solid cedar top and mahogany back and sides, available in Natural finish, mfg. 2000-06.

	N/A	$525 - 600	$325 - 400	$1,200

* **CPX 8SY** – similar to the CPX 8 except features white sycamore back and sides, a compass-themed rosette, and a wood pattern headstock overlay, available in four ocean colors: Dusk Sun Red, Lagoon Green, Morning Sea Violet, or Tropical Marina Blue finish, mfg. 2001-06.

	N/A	$525 - 600	$325 - 400	$1,200

* **CPX 8-12 12-String** – similar to the CPX 8, except in 12-string configuration with six-per-side tuners, available in Natural finish, mfg. 2000-06.

	N/A	$550 - 650	$350 - 425	$1,300

CPX 10 – single smooth cutaway jumbo Compass-style body, solid spruce top, rosewood back and sides, round soundhole with decorative color rosette, five-ply body binding, mahogany neck, 14/20-fret bound rosewood fingerboard with offset trapezoid thumbnail inlays, bound headstock with wood overlay and logo/Compass inlays, three-per-side gold tuners, ebony bridge with three pearl dots, clear pickguard, System 39 one-way piezo bridge pickup, three-band EQ, volume, AMF, and mid-shape button controls, available in Natural finish, 25.625 in. scale, mfg. 1998-2000.

	N/A	$600 - 700	$375 - 450	$1,400

CPX 15/CPX 15A/CPX 15II – single smooth cutaway jumbo Compass-style body, solid spruce top, rosewood back and sides, round soundhole with nautical flags rosette, soundhole cover included, five-ply body binding, mahogany neck, 14/20-fret bound ebony fingerboard with offset nautical flag inlays, bound headstock with rosewood overlay and logo/Compass inlays, three-per-side gold tuners, ebony bridge, clear pickguard, System 40 (1999-2000), System 41 (2001-07) two-way piezo bridge/mic electronics with three-band EQ, volume, mic. volume, mic. tone, AMF, and phase button controls, or System 59 three-way electronics with master volume, treble volume, main volume, bass volume, and three-band EQ controls (2008-2010), available in Natural finish, 25.625 in. scale, mfg. 1999-2010.

1999-2007	N/A	$850 - 1,000	$550 - 650	
2008-2010	$1,700	$1,100 - 1,300	$750 - 900	$2,600

* **CPX-15AD Art Deco Limited Edition** – similar to the CPX 15/CPX 15A, except has a turquoise Art Deco, and custom turquoise/abalone pearl Art Deco fingerboard inlays, available in Natural finish, mfg. 2002-03.

	N/A	$1,250 - 1,500	$900 - 1,050	$3,000

* **CPX 15CM** – similar to the CPX 15/CPX 15A, except has a solid cedar top, mahogany back and sides, a multi-ring rosette with abalone pearl, and pearl dot fingerboard inlays, available in Natural finish, mfg. 2000-06.

	N/A	$850 - 1,000	$500 - 600	$1,900

* **CPX 15E/CPX 15EA/CPX 15II East** – similar to the CPX 15/CPX 15A/CPX 15II, except has an Egyptian hieroglyphics theme with quilted mahogany back and sides, wood Egyptian symbols rosette, and Egyptian symbols fingerboard inlays, available in Sunburst finish, mfg. 1999-2010.

1999-2007	N/A	$850 - 1,000	$500 - 600	
2008-2010	$1,750	$1,150 - 1,350	$775 - 925	$2,700

* **CPX 15N/CPX 15NA/CPX 15II North** – similar to the CPX 15/CPX 15A/CPX 15II, except has an Arctic theme with satin sycamore back and sides, midnight sun scene rosette, and whale's tail pearl fingerboard inlays, available in Snowburst finish, mfg. 1999-2010.

1999-2007	N/A	$850 - 1,000	$500 - 600	
2008-2010	$1,950	$1,250 - 1,500	$850 - 1,000	$3,000

* **CPX 15S/CPX 15SA/CPX 15II South** – similar to the CPX 15/CPX 15A/CPX 15II, except has a tropical sea theme with white sycamore back and sides, multi-wood palm tree rosette, and MOP porpoises fingerboard inlays, available in Miami Ocean Blue finish, mfg. 1999-2010.

1999-2007	N/A	$850 - 1,000	$500 - 600	
2008-2010	$1,750	$1,150 - 1,350	$775 - 925	$2,700

* **CPX 15W/CPX 15WA/CPX 15II West** – similar to the CPX 15/CPX 15A/CPX 15II, except has an American West theme with walnut back and sides, interlocking longhorn design rosette, and concho belt inlays of pearl and turquoise fingerboard inlays, available in Antique Violin Sunburst finish, mfg. 1999-2010.

1999-2007	N/A	$850 - 1,000	$500 - 600	
2008-2010	$1,750	$1,150 - 1,350	$775 - 925	$2,700

CPX 50 – single smooth cutaway jumbo Compass-style body, solid spruce top, solid rosewood back and sides, round soundhole with nautical flags rosette, soundhole cover included, multi-ply body binding with rope pattern purfling, mahogany neck, 14/20-fret bound ebony fingerboard with offset nautical flag inlays, bound headstock with ebony overlay, rope pattern purfling, and logo/Compass inlays, three-per-side gold tuners, ebony bridge, clear pickguard, System 40 two-way piezo bridge/mic pickups, three-band EQ, volume, mic. volume, mic. tone, AMF, and phase button controls, available in Natural finish, 25.625 in. scale, mfg. 1999-2002.

	N/A	$3,750 - 4,250	$2,300 - 2,700	$7,999

CPX500/CPX500 II – single smooth cutaway jumbo Compass-style body, spruce top, nato or agathis back and sides, round soundhole with abalone rings rosette, three-ply body binding, nato neck, 14/20-fret bound rosewood fingerboard with pearl dot inlays, matching finish headstock overlay with logo and Compass inlays, three-per-side chrome tuners, rosewood bridge, no pickguard, System 55T or System 65T (2011-present) one-way piezo bridge pickup, three-band EQ, volume, AMF, and tuner controls, available in Black, Dark Red Burst, Natural, or Old Violin Sunburst finish, 25.625 in. scale, mfg. 2008-present.

MSR $564	$350	$225 - 275	$135 - 175	

MSR/NOTES	100%	EXCELLENT	AVERAGE	LAST MSR

* *CPX500 FM* – similar to the CPX500, except has a flame maple top, available in Old Violin Sunburst finish, mfg. 2009-2011.

	$400	$250 - 300	$140 - 190	$610

CPX700/CPX700 II – single smooth cutaway jumbo Compass-style body, solid spruce top, nato or agathis back and sides, round soundhole with abalone rings rosette, five-ply body binding, nato neck, 14/20-fret bound rosewood fingerboard with pearl dot inlays, bound matching finish headstock overlay with logo and Compass inlays, three-per-side chrome tuners, rosewood bridge, clear pickguard, System 56T or System 64T (2011-present) one-way piezo bridge pickup, three-band EQ, volume, AMF, and tuner controls, available in Black, Dark Red Burst (Dusk Sun Red), Natural, Oriental Blue Burst (CPX700 only), Sand Burst, or Tinted (CPX700 II only) finish, 25.625 in. scale, mfg. summer 2006-present.

MSR $885	$550	$350 - 450	$225 - 275	

* *CPX700-12/CPX700 II-12 12-String* – similar to the CPX700/CPX700 II, except in 12-string configuration, available in Natural finish, 25 in. scale, mfg. summer 2006-present.

MSR $1,010	$600	$400 - 500	$275 - 325	

CPX900 – single smooth cutaway jumbo Compass-style body, solid spruce top, flame maple back and sides, round soundhole with abalone rings rosette, five-ply body binding, nato neck, 14/20-fret bound ebony fingerboard with pearl diamond inlays, bound matching finish headstock overlay with logo and Compass inlays, three-per-side gold tuners, ebony bridge, clear pickguard, System 57T three-way piezo pickups, three-band EQ, volume, two sub pickup mix knobs, and tuner controls, available in Brown Sunburst, Mocha Black, Natural, or Ultramarine finish, 25.625 in. scale, mfg. summer 2006-2011.

	$750	$525 - 650	$350 - 425	$1,300

CPX1000 – single smooth cutaway jumbo Compass-style body, solid spruce top, flamed maple back and sides, round soundhole with MOP rosette, vintage creme body binding, nato neck, 17/20-fret bound rosewood fingerboard with MOP arrow of compass inlays, bound matching finish headstock overlay with logo and Compass inlays, three-per-side gold tuners, rosewood bridge, clear pickguard, System 63 SRT piezo pickups, available in Brown Sunburst, Natural, Trans. Black, or Ultramarine finish, 25.5906 in. scale, mfg. 2011-present.

MSR $1,310	$850	$525 - 650	$300 - 450	

CPX1200 – single smooth cutaway jumbo Compass-style body, solid spruce top, solid rosewood back and sides, round soundhole with multi-ply binding rosette, mahogany body binding, mahogany neck, 17/20-fret bound rosewood fingerboard with diamond inlays, matching finish headstock overlay with logo and Compass inlays, three-per-side gold tuners, rosewood bridge, clear pickguard, System 62 SRT piezo and preamp pickups, available in Trans. Black or Vintage Sunburst finish, 25.5906 in. scale, mfg. 2011-present.

MSR $2,215	$1,350	$900 - 1,100	$550 - 650	

ACOUSTIC ELECTRIC: FINGERSTYLE SERIES

FPX300 – folk-style body, solid cedar top, ovankol back and sides, oval soundhole with abalone rosette, nato neck, 14/20-fret wide rosewood fingerboard with no inlays, slotted headstock with rosewood overlay and logo, three-per-side open-style tuners, rosewood bridge with pearl dot inlays, System 45 two-way piezo/microphone electronics, with volume, mic. volume, three-band EQ, AMF slider, and phase switch controls, available in Natural finish, mfg. 2001-04.

	N/A	$450 - 525	$275 - 325	$999

FPX300N – nylon-string configuration, folk-style body, solid cedar top, ovankol back and sides, oval soundhole with abalone rosette, nato neck, 14/20-fret wide rosewood fingerboard with no inlays, slotted headstock with rosewood overlay and logo, three-per-side open-style tuners, rosewood tied bridge with pearl dot inlays, System 45N two-way piezo/microphone electronics, with volume, mic. volume, three-band EQ, AMF slider, and phase switch controls, available in Natural finish, mfg. 2001-04.

	N/A	$450 - 525	$275 - 325	$999

ACOUSTIC ELECTRIC: FJX SERIES

FJX720SC – single smooth cutaway medium jumbo-sized body, solid spruce top, nato back and sides, round soundhole with multi-ring rosette, multi-ply binding, nato neck, 14/20-fret bound rosewood fingerboard with dot inlays, matching finish headstock overlay with Yamaha logo and leaf design, three-per-side chrome tuners, rosewood bridge, tortoise pickguard, System 55T one-way electronics with volume, three-band EQ, AMF, and tuner controls, available in Black, Brown Sunburst, or Natural finish, 25.5625 in. scale, mfg. 2009-present.

MSR $795	$470	$325 - 400	$175 - 225	

FJX730SC – single smooth cutaway medium jumbo-sized body, solid spruce top, rosewood back and sides, round soundhole with multi-ring abalone rosette, multi-ply binding, nato neck, 14/20-fret bound rosewood fingerboard with dot inlays, matching finish bound headstock overlay with Yamaha logo and leaf design, three-per-side chrome tuners, rosewood bridge, tortoise pickguard, System 56CB A.R.T. one-way electronics with volume, three-band EQ, AMF, and tuner controls, available in Black, Brown Sunburst, or Natural finish, 25.5625 in. scale, mfg. 2009-present.

MSR $905	$560	$375 - 450	$225 - 275	

ACOUSTIC ELECTRIC: FSX SERIES

FSX720SC – single smooth cutaway small folk-style body, solid Sitka top, mahogany back and sides, round soundhole with multi-ring rosette, multi-ply binding, nato neck, 14/20-fret bound rosewood fingerboard with dot inlays, matching finish headstock overlay with Yamaha logo and leaf design, three-per-side chrome tuners, rosewood bridge, tortoise pickguard, System 55T one-way electronics with volume, three-band EQ, AMF, and tuner controls, available in Black, Brown Sunburst, or Natural finish, 25 in. scale, mfg. 2010-present.

MSR $654	$400	$260 - 325	$160 - 195	

MSR/NOTES	100%	EXCELLENT	AVERAGE	LAST MSR

FSX730SC – single smooth cutaway small folk-style body, solid Sitka top, rosewood back and sides, round soundhole with multi-ring MOP rosette, multi-ply binding, nato neck, 14/20-fret bound rosewood fingerboard with dot inlays, matching finish headstock overlay with Yamaha logo and leaf design, three-per-side chrome tuners, rosewood bridge, tortoise pickguard, System 56CB one-way electronics with volume, three-band EQ, AMF, and tuner controls, available in Black, Brown Sunburst, or Natural finish, 25 in. scale, mfg. 2010-present.

| MSR $805 | $500 | $325 - 400 | $175 - 250 | |

ACOUSTIC ELECTRIC: SILENT GUITAR SERIES

The Silent Guitar by Yamaha is a guitar designed to travel and be a silent instrument that you can plug headphones in directly to hear. There are onboard effects yet the guitar can be plugged in to external equipment to be amplified. The body is also very light with only the outline of the body making up the majority of the guitar.

SLG100N – nylon-string configuration, single cutaway maple body, detachable black frame, mahogany neck, 12/19-fret rosewood fingerboard with no inlays, slotted headstock with rosewood overlay and Yamaha logo, three-per-side open-style gold tuners, rosewood tied bridge, B-Band piezo pickup and electronics with volume, bass, and treble knobs, reverb switch, headphone jack with on/off switch, aux. in line with level control, line out jack, available in Natural finish, gig bag included, mfg. 2002-2010.

| | $650 | $400 - 475 | $250 - 300 | $920 |

SLG100S – single cutaway maple body, detachable black frame, mahogany neck, 12/19-fret rosewood fingerboard with small dot inlays, rosewood headstock overlay with Yamaha logo, three-per-side gold tuners with brown pearl buttons, rosewood bridge, B-Band piezo pickup and electronics with volume, bass, and treble knobs, reverb switch, headphone jack with on/off switch, aux. in line with level control, line out jack, available in Natural finish, gig bag included, mfg. 2003-2010.

| | $650 | $400 - 475 | $250 - 300 | $920 |

SLG110N – nylon-string configuration, single cutaway maple body, detachable black frame, mahogany neck, 17/19-fret rosewood fingerboard with no inlays, slotted headstock with rosewood overlay and tuning fork inlay, three-per-side open-style wood tuners, rosewood tied bridge, electronics with volume, bass, and treble knobs, reverb switch, headphone jack with on/off switch, aux. in line with level control, line out jack, available in Natural or Tobacco Brown Sunburst finish, gig bag and ear buds included, mfg. 2011-present.

| MSR $925 | $560 | $375 - 450 | $230 - 275 | |

SLG110S – steel-string configuration, single cutaway maple body, detachable black frame, mahogany neck, 20/22-fret rosewood fingerboard with white dot inlays, headstock with rosewood overlay and tuning fork inlay, three-per-side wood tuners, rosewood tied bridge, electronics with volume, bass, and treble knobs, reverb switch, headphone jack with on/off switch, aux. in line with level control, line out jack, available in Natural or Tobacco Brown Sunburst finish, gig bag and ear buds included, mfg. 2011-present.

| MSR $920 | $560 | $375 - 450 | $230 - 275 | |

SLG130NW – nylon-string configuration, single cutaway maple body, detachable wooden frame with matching finish overlay, mahogany neck, 17/19-fret ebony fingerboard with no inlays, slotted headstock with tuning fork inlay, three-per-side open-style wooden tuners, rosewood tied bridge, electronics with volume, bass, and treble knobs, reverb switch, headphone jack with on/off switch, aux. in line with level control, line out jack, available in Light Amber Burst finish, gig bag and ear buds included, mfg. 2011-present.

| MSR $1,075 | $660 | $425 - 550 | $270 - 325 | |

CLASSICAL: CONCERT (C/CG) SERIES

Yamaha has produced several standard/concert-grade classical guitars, but unfortunately, we only have documentation on a handful of them. All models since 1990 are listed and a few from the late 1960s and early 1970s appear below as well. However, without any factory catalogs or specifications, we are unable to list all of them. If you have information, catalogs, or specifications on any Yamaha classical guitar that is not listed, please submit directly to Blue Book Publications.

C40/CG40A – classical-style body, spruce top, round soundhole with wood pattern rosette, Jelutong, Indonesian mahogany, or Meranti back and sides, nato neck, 14/19-fret rosewood, Javanese rosewood, or Sonokeling fingerboard, slotted headstock, three-per-side open-style chrome tuners, rosewood, Javanese rosewood, or Sonokeling tied bridge, available in Natural finish, 25.6 in. scale, mfg. 1993-present.

| MSR $221 | $140 | $90 - 110 | $55 - 75 | |

This model was labeled the CG-40A when it was initially released. The C40 is also available as a package (MSR $251) that includes a gig bag, method book, and an instructional DVD.

* CS40 – similar to the C40, except has a 7/8-sized body with 22.8 in. scale, available in Natural finish, mfg. 1999-present.

| MSR $211 | $130 | $85 - 105 | $45 - 60 | |

G-50A – classical-style body, pine or spruce top, Judas wood back and sides, round soundhole with wooden rosette, single-ply binding, nato neck, 12/19-fret bubinga fingerboard, slotted headstock, three-per-side open-style chrome tuners, bubinga tied bridge, Natural finish, 26 in. scale, mfg. 1969-1971.

| | N/A | $90 - 120 | $50 - 75 | |

G-55A – classical-style body, spruce top, Katsura back and sides, round soundhole with wooden rosette, single-ply binding, nato neck, 12/19-fret bubinga fingerboard, slotted headstock, three-per-side open-style chrome tuners, bubinga tied bridge, Natural finish, mfg. 1972-73.

| | N/A | $90 - 120 | $50 - 75 | |

MSR/NOTES	100%	EXCELLENT	AVERAGE	LAST MSR

G-60A – classical-style body, pine or spruce top, maple back and sides, round soundhole with wooden rosette, single-ply binding, nato neck, 12/19-fret bubinga fingerboard, slotted headstock, three-per-side open-style chrome tuners, bubinga tied bridge, Natural finish, 26 in. scale, mfg. 1969-1971.

	N/A	$120 - 150	$70 - 95	

G-65A – classical-style body, spruce top, Katsura back and sides, round soundhole with wooden rosette, single-ply binding, nato neck, 12/19-fret rosewood fingerboard, slotted headstock, three-per-side open-style chrome tuners, rosewood tied bridge, Natural finish, mfg. 1972-73.

	N/A	$120 - 150	$70 - 95	

C80 – classical-style body, spruce top, nato back and sides, round soundhole with wood pattern rosette, black multi-ply binding, nato neck, 14/19-fret rosewood fingerboard, slotted headstock, three-per-side open-style gold tuners, rosewood tied bridge, available in Natural finish, 25.6 in. scale, mfg. 2003-present.

MSR N/A	$190	$110 - 140	$60 - 80	

This model is currently not available in the U.S.

G-85A – classical-style body, two-piece pine or spruce top, nato back and sides, round soundhole with wooden rosette, single-ply binding, nato neck, 12/19-fret rosewood fingerboard, slotted headstock, three-per-side open-style chrome tuners, rosewood tied bridge, Natural finish, 26 in. scale, mfg. 1970-71.

	N/A	$135 - 175	$80 - 110	

G-90A – classical-style body, spruce top, Katsura back and sides, round soundhole with wooden rosette, single-ply binding, nato neck, 12/19-fret rosewood fingerboard, slotted headstock, three-per-side open-style chrome tuners, rosewood tied bridge, Natural finish, mfg. 1972-73.

	N/A	$135 - 175	$80 - 110	

CG-90MA – classical-style body, spruce top, nato back and sides, round soundhole with decorative wood rosette, black body binding, nato neck, 12/19-fret bubinga fingerboard, slotted headstock, three-per-side chrome tuners, rosewood tied bridge, available in Natural Satin finish, mfg. 1995-99.

	N/A	$105 - 135	$65 - 85	$259

* **CG-90SA** – similar to the CG-90MA, except has a solid spruce top, available in Natural satin finish, mfg. 1999 only.

	N/A	$120 - 150	$75 - 95	$299

G-100A – classical-style body, two-piece pine or spruce top, ovangkol back and sides, round soundhole with wooden rosette, single-ply binding, nato neck, 12/19-fret plastic/wood combination fingerboard, slotted headstock, three-per-side open-style chrome tuners, rosewood tied bridge, Natural finish, 26 in. scale, mfg. 1970-71.

	N/A	$135 - 175	$80 - 110	

CG-100A – classical-style body, spruce top, nato back and sides, round soundhole with decorative wood rosette, black body binding, nato neck, 12/19-fret bubinga fingerboard, slotted headstock, three-per-side chrome tuners, rosewood tied bridge, available in Natural finish, mfg. 1989-1999.

	N/A	$120 - 150	$70 - 95	$279

* **CG-100MA** – similar to the CG-100A, except has a Satin Natural finish, mfg. 1992-95.

	N/A	$120 - 150	$70 - 95	$269

* **CG-100SA** – similar to CG-100A, except has a solid spruce top, available in Natural finish, mfg. 1999 only.

	N/A	$130 - 160	$85 - 110	$309

* **CS-100A** – similar to the CG-100A, except has 7/8-size body, 23.6 in. scale, mfg. 1993-99.

	N/A	$120 - 150	$70 - 95	$309

CG101/CG101A – classical-style body, spruce top, nato back and sides, round soundhole with decorative wood rosette, black body binding, nato neck, 12/19-fret rosewood fingerboard, slotted headstock, three-per-side chrome tuners, rosewood tied bridge, available in Natural finish, mfg. 1999-2011.

	$200	$130 - 160	$80 - 100	$310

* **CG101M** – similar to the CG101, except has a Natural Matte finish, mfg. 1999-2005.

	N/A	$125 - 175	$70 - 90	$270

* **CG101MS** – similar to Model CG101M except, has a solid spruce top, available in Natural Matte finish, mfg. 1999-2004.

	N/A	$125 - 175	$70 - 90	$300

* **CGX101/CGX101A Electric** – similar to the CG101, except has System 33 one-way electronics with volume, three-band EQ, AMF, and mute switch controls (1999 only), System 46N electronics (2000-02), or System 48 one-way electronics with volume, three-band EQ, and AMF controls (2003-2011), available in Natural finish, mfg. 1999-2011.

	$380	$230 - 285	$135 - 175	$570

MSR/NOTES	100%	EXCELLENT	AVERAGE	LAST MSR

* **CS101C** – similar to the CG101, except has a 3/4-sized body with a solid cedar top, 23 in. scale, mfg. 1999-2002.

	N/A	$130 - 160	$80 - 100	$319

CGS102/CGS102A – 1/2-sized student classic-style body, spruce top, meranti back and sides, round soundhole with wooden inlay rosette, nato neck, 12/19-fret rosewood fingerboard, slotted headstock, three-per-side chrome tuners, rosewood tied bridge, available in Natural finish, 21 in. scale, mfg. 2002-present.

MSR $191	$120	$75 - 95	$50 - 65	

* **CG102 Pack** – includes CG102 Classical guitar, gig bag, guitar stand, extra set of strings, string winder, and instructional DVD, mfg. 2012-present.

MSR $312	$200	$130 - 160	$80 - 100	

CGS103/CGS103A – 3/4-sized student classic-style body, spruce top, meranti back and sides, round soundhole with wooden inlay rosette, nato neck, 12/19-fret rosewood fingerboard, slotted headstock, three-per-side chrome tuners, rosewood tied bridge, available in Natural finish, 22.8 in. scale, mfg. 2002-present.

MSR $211	$130	$85 - 105	$60 - 75	

CGS104/CGS104A – full-sized student classic-style body, spruce top, meranti back and sides, round soundhole with wooden inlay rosette, nato neck, 12/19-fret rosewood fingerboard, slotted headstock, three-per-side chrome tuners, rosewood tied bridge, available in Natural finish, 25.6 in. scale, mfg. 2002-present.

MSR $221	$140	$90 - 110	$65 - 80	

CG-110A – classical-style body, spruce top, nato back and sides, round soundhole with decorative wood rosette, black body binding, nato neck, 12/19-fret rosewood fingerboard, slotted headstock, three-per-side chrome tuners, rosewood tied bridge, available in Natural finish, mfg. 1989-1999.

	N/A	$120 - 150	$70 - 95	$319

* **CG-110CE Cutaway Electric** – similar to the CG-110A, except has a single cutaway and System 33 one-way electronics with volume, three-band EQ, AMF, and mute switch controls, available in Natural finish, mfg. 1995-99.

	N/A	$275 - 325	$150 - 200	$629

* **CG-110EA Electric** – similar to the CG-110A, except has System 27 one-way electronics with pop-up controls, available in Natural finish, mfg. 1993-94.

	N/A	$200 - 250	$120 - 150	

* **CG-110MA** – similar to the CG-110A, except has a Satin Natural finish, mfg. 1992-96.

	N/A	$120 - 150	$70 - 95	$309

* **CG-110SA** – similar to the CG-110A, except has a solid spruce top, mfg. 1992-99.

	N/A	$150 - 200	$95 - 120	$379

CG111S – classical-style body, solid spruce top, nato back and sides, round soundhole with decorative wood rosette, black body binding, nato neck, 12/19-fret rosewood fingerboard, slotted headstock, three-per-side chrome tuners, rosewood tied bridge, available in Natural finish, mfg. 1999-2011.

	$250	$135 - 175	$80 - 110	$350

* **CG111C Cedar** – similar to the CG111S, except has a solid cedar top, available in Natural finish, mfg. 1999-2011.

	$250	$135 - 175	$80 - 110	$350

* **CGX111SC/CGX111SCA Cutaway Electric** – similar to the CG111S, except has System 42 one-way B-Band electronics with volume, high, and low controls (1999 only) or System 48 electronics with volume, three-band EQ, and AMF controls (2000-present), available in Natural finish, mfg. 1999-2006.

	N/A	$325 - 375	$175 - 225	$700

CG-115E – classical-style body, spruce top, nato back and sides, round soundhole with decorative wood rosette, black body binding, natoneck, 12/19-fret rosewood fingerboard, slotted headstock, three-per-side chrome tuners, rosewood tied bridge, System 33 one-way electronics with volume, three-band EQ, AMF, and mute switch controls, available in Natural finish, mfg. 1996-98.

	N/A	$200 - 250	$120 - 150	

G-120A – classical-style body, spruce top, mahogany back and sides, round soundhole with wooden rosette, single-ply binding, nato neck, 12/19-fret rosewood fingerboard, slotted headstock, three-per-side open-style chrome tuners, rosewood tied bridge, Natural finish, mfg. 1972-73.

	N/A	$135 - 175	$80 - 110	

CG-120A – classical-style body, spruce top, nato back and sides, round soundhole with decorative wood rosette, black body binding, nato neck, 12/19-fret Indian rosewood fingerboard, slotted headstock, three-per-side chrome tuners, Indian rosewood tied bridge, available in Natural finish, mfg. 1989-1999.

	N/A	$135 - 175	$85 - 110	$359

MSR/NOTES	100%	EXCELLENT	AVERAGE	LAST MSR

CG122MC – classical-style body, solid American cedar top, nato back and sides, round soundhole with decorative wood rosette, black and white plastic body binding, nato neck, 12/19-fret rosewood fingerboard, slotted headstock, three-per-side chrome tuners, rosewood tied bridge, available in Matte Natural finish, mfg. 2010-present.

MSR $362	$220	$145 - 180	$90 - 110	

CG122MS – classical-style body, solid Engelmann spruce top, nato back and sides, round soundhole with decorative wood rosette, black and white plastic body binding, nato neck, 12/19-fret rosewood fingerboard, slotted headstock, three-per-side chrome tuners, rosewood tied bridge, available in Matte Natural finish, mfg. 2010-present.

MSR $362	$220	$145 - 180	$90 - 110	

G-130A – classical-style body, two-piece pine or spruce top, zebrawood back and sides, round soundhole with wooden rosette, single-ply binding, nato neck, 12/19-fret wood/plastic combination fingerboard, slotted headstock, three-per-side open-style chrome tuners, rosewood tied bridge, Natural finish, 26 in. scale, mfg. 1969-1971.

	N/A	$150 - 200	$90 - 120	

CG-130A – classical-style body, spruce top, nato back and sides, round soundhole with decorative wood rosette, black body binding, nato neck, 12/19-fret Indian rosewood fingerboard, slotted headstock, three-per-side chrome tuners, Indian rosewood tied bridge, available in Natural finish, mfg. 1989-1996.

	N/A	$150 - 200	$95 - 120	$399

* *CG-130SA* – similar to the CG-130A, except has a solid spruce top, available in Natural finish, mfg. 1998-99.

	N/A	$150 - 200	$95 - 120	$409

CG131S – classical-style body, solid spruce top, nato back and sides, round soundhole with decorative wood rosette, multi-ply black body binding, nato neck, 12/19-fret Indian rosewood fingerboard, slotted headstock, three-per-side chrome tuners, Indian rosewood tied bridge, available in Natural finish, mfg. 1999-2011.

	$300	$175 - 225	$110 - 140	$430

CG142C – classical-style body, solid American cedar top, nato back and sides, round soundhole with decorative wood rosette, black and white plastic body binding, nato neck, 12/19-fret rosewood fingerboard, slotted headstock, three-per-side chrome tuners, rosewood tied bridge, available in Natural finish, mfg. 2010-present.

MSR $433	$280	$175 - 215	$110 - 130	

CG142S – classical-style body, solid Engelmann spruce top, nato back and sides, round soundhole with decorative wood rosette, black and white plastic body binding, nato neck, 12/19-fret rosewood fingerboard, slotted headstock, three-per-side chrome tuners, rosewood tied bridge, available in Natural finish, mfg. 2010-present.

MSR $433	$280	$175 - 215	$110 - 130	

G-150A – classical-style body, spruce top, mahogany back and sides, round soundhole with wooden rosette, single-ply binding, nato neck, 12/19-fret rosewood fingerboard, slotted headstock, three-per-side open-style chrome tuners, rosewood tied bridge, Natural finish, mfg. 1972-73.

	N/A	$150 - 200	$90 - 120	

CG-150SA – classical-style body, solid spruce top, ovnagkol back and sides, round soundhole with decorative wood rosette, multi-ply body binding, nato neck, 12/19-fret Indian rosewood fingerboard, slotted headstock with rosewood overlay, three-per-side gold tuners, Indian rosewood tied bridge, available in Natural finish, mfg. 1989-1999.

	N/A	$200 - 250	$120 - 150	$469

* *CG-150CA Cedar* – similar to the CG-150SA, except has a solid cedar top, available in Natural finish, mfg. 1989-1999.

	N/A	$200 - 250	$120 - 150	$469

»*CG-150CCA Cedar Cutaway Electric* – similar to the CG-150CA, except has a single cutaway and System 27 one-way electronics with pop-up controls, available in Natural finish, mfg. 1993-94.

	N/A	$300 - 375	$175 - 225	

»*CG-150CCE Cedar Cutaway Electric* – similar to the CG-150CA, except has a single cutaway and System 33 one-way electronics with volume, three-band EQ, AMF, and mute switch controls, available in Natural finish, mfg. 1995-98.

	N/A	$300 - 375	$175 - 225	$729

CG151S – classical-style body, solid Sitka spruce top, ovangkol back and sides, round soundhole with decorative wood rosette, multi-ply body binding, nato neck, 12/19-fret ebony fingerboard, slotted headstock with rosewood overlay, three-per-side gold tuners, Indian rosewood tied bridge, available in Natural finish, mfg. 1999-2011.

	$370	$225 - 275	$135 - 175	$520

* *CG151C Cedar* – similar to the CG151S, except has a solid American cedar top, available in Natural finish, mfg. 1999-2011.

	$370	$225 - 275	$135 - 175	$520

MSR/NOTES	100%	EXCELLENT	AVERAGE	LAST MSR

CG162C – classical-style body, solid American cedar top, ovangkol back and sides, round soundhole with decorative wood rosette, brown, black, and white plastic body binding, nato neck, 12/19-fret rosewood fingerboard, slotted headstock, three-per-side gold tuners, rosewood tied bridge, available in Natural finish, mfg. 2010-present.

| MSR $523 | $350 | $210 - 260 | $130 - 155 | |

CG162S – classical-style body, solid Engelmann spruce top, ovangkol back and sides, round soundhole with decorative wood rosette, brown, black, and white plastic body binding, nato neck, 12/19-fret rosewood fingerboard, slotted headstock, three-per-side gold tuners, rosewood tied bridge, available in Natural finish, mfg. 2010-present.

| MSR $523 | $350 | $210 - 260 | $130 - 155 | |

G-170A – classical-style body, two-piece pine or spruce top, rosewood back and sides, round soundhole with wooden rosette, single-ply binding, nato neck, 12/19-fret wood/plastic combination fingerboard, slotted headstock with rosewood overlay, three-per-side open-style chrome tuners, rosewood tied bridge, Natural finish, 26 in. scale, mfg. 1969-1973.

| | N/A | $200 - 250 | $120 - 150 | |

CG-170SA – classical-style body, solid spruce top, Indian rosewood back and sides, round soundhole with decorative wood rosette, multi-ply body binding with wood pattern purfling, nato neck, 12/19-fret Indian rosewood fingerboard, slotted headstock with rosewood overlay, three-per-side gold tuners, Indian rosewood tied bridge, available in Natural finish, mfg. 1989-1999.

| | N/A | $250 - 300 | $150 - 200 | $609 |

* *CG-170CA Cedar* – similar to the CG-170SA, except has a solid cedar top, available in Natural finish, mfg. 1989-1999.

| | N/A | $250 - 300 | $150 - 200 | $609 |

CG171S – classical-style body, solid spruce top, Indian rosewood back and sides, round soundhole with decorative wood rosette, multi-ply body binding with wood pattern purfling, nato neck, 12/19-fret Indian rosewood fingerboard, slotted headstock with rosewood overlay, three-per-side gold tuners, Indian rosewood tied bridge, available in Natural finish, mfg. 1999-2011.

| $470 | $300 - 350 | $175 - 225 | $670 | |

* *CG171C Cedar* – similar to the CG171S, except has a solid American cedar top, available in Natural finish, mfg. 1999-2011.

| $470 | $300 - 350 | $175 - 225 | $670 | |

»*CGX171CC/CGX171CCA Cedar Cutaway Electric* – similar to the CG171C, except has System 43 two-way B-Band piezo/microphone electronics with volume, mic., high, and low controls (1999 only) or System 49 two-way piezo/microphone electronics with volume, mic. volume, three-band EQ, AMF, and phase switch controls (2000-2011), available in Natural finish, mfg. 1999-2011.

| $750 | $475 - 550 | $300 - 350 | $1,100 | |

* *CG171SF Flamenco* – similar to the CG171S, except has cypress back and sides, mfg. 2002-2011.

| $395 | $250 - 300 | $135 - 175 | $560 | |

»*CGX171SCF Flamenco Cutaway Electric* – similar to the CG171SF Flamenco, except has System 49 two-way piezo/microphone electronics with volume, mic. volume, three-band EQ, AMF, and phase switch controls, available in Natural finish, mfg. 2002-2011.

| $640 | $400 - 475 | $250 - 300 | $910 | |

CG172SF FLAMENCO – classical-style flamenco body, solid European spruce top, cypress back and sides, round soundhole with decorative wood rosette, nato neck, 12/19-fret rosewood fingerboard, slotted headstock, three-per-side gold tuners, rosewood tied bridge, available in Natural finish, mfg. 2011-present.

| MSR $503 | $330 | $200 - 250 | $125 - 150 | |

CG-180SA – classical-style body, solid white spruce top, Indian rosewood back and sides, round soundhole with decorative wood rosette, multi-ply body binding with wood pattern purfling, nato neck, 12/19-fret ebony fingerboard, slotted headstock with rosewood overlay, three-per-side gold tuners, Indian rosewood tied bridge, available in Natural finish, mfg. 1989-1999.

| | N/A | $300 - 375 | $175 - 225 | $739 |

CG182C – classical-style body, solid American cedar top, rosewood back and sides, round soundhole with decorative wood rosette, wood inlay body binding, nato neck, 12/19-fret ebony fingerboard, slotted headstock, three-per-side gold tuners, rosewood tied bridge, available in Natural finish, mfg. 2010-present.

| MSR $705 | $450 | $275 - 350 | $175 - 210 | |

CG182S – classical-style body, solid European spruce top, rosewood back and sides, round soundhole with decorative wood rosette, wood inlay body binding, nato neck, 12/19-fret ebony fingerboard, slotted headstock, three-per-side gold tuners, rosewood tied bridge, available in Natural finish, mfg. 2010-present.

| MSR $705 | $450 | $275 - 350 | $175 - 210 | |

CG192C – classical-style body, solid American cedar top, rosewood back and sides, round soundhole with decorative wood rosette, wood inlay body binding, mahogany neck, 12/19-fret ebony fingerboard, slotted headstock, three-per-side gold tuners, rosewood tied bridge, available in Natural finish, mfg. 2010-present.

| MSR $805 | $500 | $325 - 400 | $200 - 240 | |

MSR/NOTES	100%	EXCELLENT	AVERAGE	LAST MSR

CG192S – classical-style body, solid European spruce top, rosewood back and sides, round soundhole with decorative wood rosette, wood inlay body binding, mahogany neck, 12/19-fret ebony fingerboard, slotted headstock, three-per-side gold tuners, rosewood tied bridge, available in Natural finish, mfg. 2010-present.

MSR $805	$500	$325 - 400	$200 - 240	

CG201S – classical-style body, solid European spruce top, solid mahogany back and sides, round soundhole with decorative wood rosette, multi-ply body binding with wood pattern purfling, nato neck, 12/19-fret ebony fingerboard, slotted headstock with rosewood overlay, three-per-side gold tuners, Indian rosewood tied bridge, available in Natural finish, mfg. 1999-2010.

	$600	$375 - 450	$225 - 275	$870

G-220A – classical-style body, spruce top, rosewood back and sides, round soundhole with wooden rosette, multi-ply binding, nato neck, 12/19-fret rosewood combination fingerboard, slotted headstock with rosewood overlay, three-per-side open-style chrome tuners, rosewood tied bridge, Natural finish, mfg. 1972-73.

	N/A	$200 - 250	$120 - 150	

CLASSICAL: HANDCRAFTED/GRAND CONCERT (GC) SERIES

Yamaha's Handcrafted and Grand Concert series of classical guitars represent their top-of-the-line models. Many higher end models (GC60, GC70, GC71, etc.) were only available by special order. Yamaha also offered a 10-string variation of the GC-60, but it is unknown if any were ever sold in the U.S.

GC21 – classic-style body, solid European spruce top, Indian rosewood back and sides, round soundhole with decorative wood inlay rosette, multi-ply body binding, mahogany neck, 12/19-fret ebony fingerboard, slotted headstock with rosewood overlay, three-per-side open-style gold tuners, rosewood tied bridge, available in Natural finish, 25.6 in. scale, mfg. 2000-2011.

	$1,125	$725 - 850	$475 - 550	$1,600

* *GC21C Cedar* – similar to the GC21, except has a solid American cedar top, available in Natural finish, mfg. 2000-2011.

	$1,125	$725 - 850	$475 - 550	$1,600

GC30 – classic-style body, solid white spruce top, solid Indian rosewood back and sides, round soundhole with decorative wood inlay rosette, multi-ply body binding, African mahogany neck, 12/19-fret ebony fingerboard, slotted headstock with rosewood overlay, three-per-side open-style gold tuners, Jacaranda or rosewood tied bridge, available in Natural finish, 25.5625 in. scale, mfg. 1986-1999.

	N/A	$600 - 700	$375 - 450	$1,379

* *GC30C Cedar* – similar to the GC30, except has a solid cedar top, available in Natural finish, mfg. 1986-1999.

	N/A	$600 - 700	$375 - 450	$1,379

GC31 – classic-style body, solid European spruce top, solid Indian rosewood back and sides, round soundhole with decorative wood inlay rosette, multi-ply body binding, mahogany neck, 12/19-fret ebony fingerboard, slotted headstock with rosewood overlay, three-per-side open-style gold tuners, rosewood tied bridge, available in Natural finish, 25.6 in. scale, mfg. 2000-present.

MSR $2,315	$1,300	$950 - 1,150	$600 - 700	

* *GC31C Cedar* – similar to the GC31, except has a solid American cedar top, available in Natural finish, mfg. 2000-present.

MSR $2,315	$1,300	$950 - 1,150	$600 - 700	

* *GCX31C Cutaway Electric* – similar to the GC31, except has a single smooth cutaway and System 49 two-way piezo/microphone electronics with volume, mic. volume, three-band EQ, AMF, and phase switch controls, available in Natural finish, mfg. 2001-present.

MSR $2,915	$1,800	$1,150 - 1,450	$725 - 850	

GC40 – classic-style body, solid white spruce top, solid Jacaranda back and sides, round soundhole with decorative wood inlay rosette, multi-ply body binding with decorative purfling, African mahogany neck, 12/19-fret ebony fingerboard, slotted headstock with rosewood overlay, three-per-side open-style gold tuners, rosewood tied bridge, available in Natural finish, 25.5625 in. scale, mfg. 1986-1995.

	N/A	$950 - 1,100	$600 - 700	$2,099

* *GC40C Cedar* – similar to the GC40, except has a solid cedar top, available in Natural finish, mfg. 1986-1999.

	N/A	$950 - 1,100	$600 - 700	$2,099

GC41 – classic-style body, solid European spruce top, solid Honduras rosewood back and sides, round soundhole with decorative wood inlay rosette, multi-ply body binding with decorative purfling, mahogany neck, 12/19-fret ebony fingerboard, slotted headstock with rosewood overlay, three-per-side open-style gold tuners, rosewood tied bridge, available in Natural finish, 25.6 in. scale, mfg. 2000-present.

MSR $2,615	$1,600	$1,050 - 1,300	$700 - 825	

* *GC41C Cedar* – similar to the GC41, except has a solid American cedar top, available in Natural finish, mfg. 2000-present.

MSR $2,615	$1,600	$1,050 - 1,300	$700 - 825	

MSR/NOTES	100%	EXCELLENT	AVERAGE	LAST MSR

GC50 – classic-style body, solid white spruce (early models) or Rumanian spruce (later models) top, solid Jacaranda (early models) or solid Indian rosewood (later models) back and sides, round soundhole with deocrative wood inlay rosette, multi-ply body binding with decorative purfling, Honduras mahogany neck, 12/19-fret ebony fingerboard, slotted headstock with rosewood overlay, three-per-side open-style gold tuners, Jacaranda (early models) or rosewood (later models) tied bridge, available in Natural finish, 25.6 in. scale, mfg. 1986-2004.

	N/A	$1,650 - 2,000	$1,000 - 1,250	$3,799

* *GC50C Cedar* – similar to the GC50, except has a solid cedar top, available in Natural finish, mfg. 1986-2004.

	N/A	$1,650 - 2,000	$1,000 - 1,250	$3,799

GC60 – classic-style body, solid German spruce (early models) or Rumanian spruce (later models) top, solid Jacaranda (early models) or solid Honduras rosewood (later models) back and sides, round soundhole with decorative wood inlay rosette, multi-ply body binding, Honduras mahogany neck, 12/19-fret ebony fingerboard, slotted headstock with rosewood overlay, three-per-side open-style gold tuners, Jacaranda (early models) or rosewood (later models) tied bridge, available in Natural finish, 25.5625 in. scale, mfg. 1986-2004.

	N/A	$2,250 - 2,750	$1,500 - 1,850	$4,999

* *GC60C Cedar* – similar to the GC60, except has a solid cedar top, available in Natural finish, mfg. 1986-2004.

	N/A	$2,250 - 2,750	$1,500 - 1,850	$4,999

GC70 – classic-style body, solid German spruce (early models) or Rumanian spruce (later models) top, solid Jacaranda (early models), selected solid rosewood (mid models), or solid Brazilian rosewood (later models) back and sides, round soundhole with decorative wood inlay rosette, multi-ply body binding, Honduras mahogany neck, 12/19-fret ebony fingerboard, slotted headstock with rosewood overlay, three-per-side open-style gold tuners, Jacaranda (early models) or selected rosewood (mid models), or solid Brazilian rosewood (later models) tied bridge, available in Natural finish, 25.5625 in. scale, mfg. 1986-2006.

Jacaranda/Selected Rosewood	N/A	$2,500 - 3,000	$1,650 - 2,000	
Brazilian Rosewood	N/A	$6,100 - 7,000	$3,700 - 4,300	$12,000

* *GC70C Cedar* – similar to the GC70, except has a solid cedar top, available in Natural finish, mfg. 1986-2006.

Jacaranda/Selected Rosewood	N/A	$2,500 - 3,000	$1,650 - 2,000	
Brazilian Rosewood	N/A	$6,100 - 7,000	$3,700 - 4,300	$12,000

GC71 – classic-style body, solid German spruce (early models) or Rumanian spruce (later models) top, solid Jacaranda (early models), selected solid rosewood (mid models), or solid Brazilian rosewood (later models) back and sides, round soundhole with decorative wood inlay rosette, multi-ply body binding, Honduras mahogany neck, 12/19-fret ebony fingerboard, slotted headstock with rosewood overlay, three-per-side open-style gold tuners, Jacaranda (early models) or selected rosewood (mid models), or solid Brazilian rosewood (later models) tied bridge, available in Natural finish, 25.5625 in. scale, mfg. 1986-2006.

Jacaranda/Selected Rosewood	N/A	$2,500 - 3,000	$1,650 - 2,000	
Brazilian Rosewood	N/A	$6,100 - 7,000	$3,700 - 4,300	$12,000

The GC71 was developed by Yamaha to meet the high standards set by classical guitarist Andres Segovia.

GD10 – classic-style body, solid white spruce top, Indian rosewood back and sides, round soundhole with decorative wood inlay rosette, multi-ply body binding, African mahogany neck, 12/19-fret ebony fingerboard, slotted headstock with rosewood overlay, three-per-side open-style gold tuners, rosewood tied bridge, available in Natural finish, 25.6 in. scale, mfg. 1986-1999.

	N/A	$375 - 450	$225 - 275	$839

* *GD10C Cedar* – similar to the GD10, except has a solid cedar top, available in Natural finish, mfg. 1986-1999.

	N/A	$375 - 450	$225 - 275	$839

GD20 – classic-style body, solid white spruce top, solid Indian rosewood back and sides, round soundhole with decorative wood inlay rosette, multi-ply body binding, African mahogany neck, 12/19-fret ebony fingerboard, slotted headstock with rosewood overlay, three-per-side open-style gold tuners, rosewood tied bridge, available in Natural finish, 25.6 in. scale, mfg. 1986-1995.

	N/A	$475 - 550	$300 - 350	$1,049

* *GD20C Cedar* – similar to the GD20, except has a solid cedar top, available in Natural finish, mfg. 1986-1995.

	N/A	$475 - 550	$300 - 350	$1,049

CLASSICAL: NX SERIES

This new series, introduced in 2010, features two lines: the NCX Line and the NTX Line. The guitars feature nylon strings and pickup systems to deliver a natural classical guitar sound.

NCX700 – single smooth cutaway classical-style body, solid Sitka spruce top, nato back and sides, round soundhole with decorative wood rosette, nato neck, 12/19-fret rosewood fingerboard, slotted headstock, three-per-side tuners, rosewood tied bridge, System61 ART two-way pickups, three-band EQ with on board tuner, available in Natural finish, mfg. 2011-present.

MSR $865	$500	$350 - 425	$215 - 260	

NCX900FM – single smooth cutaway classical-style body, solid Engelmann spruce top, flamed maple back and sides, round soundhole with decorative wood rosette, nato neck, 12/19-fret rosewood fingerboard, slotted headstock, three-per-side tuners, rosewood tied bridge, System61 ART two-way pickups, three-band EQ with on board tuner, available in Natural finish, mfg. 2010-present.

MSR $1,170	$700	$460 - 575	$290 - 350	

MSR/NOTES	100%	EXCELLENT	AVERAGE	LAST MSR

NCX900R – single smooth cutaway classical-style body, solid Sitka spruce top, rosewood back and sides, round soundhole with decorative wood rosette, nato neck, 12/19-fret rosewood fingerboard, slotted headstock, three-per-side tuners, rosewood tied bridge, System61 ART two-way pickups, three-band EQ with on board tuner, available in Natural finish, mfg. 2010-present.

MSR $1,170	$700	$460 - 575	$290 - 350	

NCX1200R – single smooth cutaway classical-style body, solid Sitka spruce top, solid rosewood back and sides, round soundhole with decorative wood rosette, African mahogany neck, 12/19-fret ebony fingerboard, slotted headstock, three-per-side tuners, rosewood tied bridge, System61 ART two-way pickups, three-band EQ with on board tuner, available in Natural finish, case included, mfg. 2010-present.

MSR $1,710	$1,000	$675 - 850	$425 - 500	

NCX2000FM – single smooth cutaway classical-style body, solid Hokkaido spruce top, solid flamed maple back and sides, round soundhole with decorative wood rosette, African mahogany neck, 12/19-fret ebony fingerboard, slotted headstock, three-per-side tuners, rosewood tied bridge, System61 ART two-way pickups, three-band EQ with on board tuner, available in Natural finish, case included, mfg. 2010-present.

MSR $5,050	$3,000	$2,000 - 2,500	$1,250 - 1,500	

NCX2000R – single smooth cutaway classical-style body, solid Hokkaido spruce top, solid rosewood back and sides, round soundhole with decorative wood rosette, African mahogany neck, 12/19-fret ebony fingerboard, slotted headstock, three-per-side tuners, rosewood tied bridge, System61 ART two-way pickups, three-band EQ with on board tuner, available in Natural finish, case included, mfg. 2010-present.

MSR $5,050	$3,000	$2,000 - 2,500	$1,250 - 1,500	

NTX700 – single smooth cutaway NTX-style thin-line body, solid spruce top, nato back and sides, elliptical soundhole with decorative wood rosette, nato neck, 14/22-fret rosewood fingerboard, slotted headstock, three-per-side tuners, rosewood tied bridge, System61 ART two-way pickups, three-band EQ with on board tuner, available in Black or Natural finish, mfg. 2010-present.

MSR $865	$500	$350 - 425	$215 - 260	

NTX900FM – single smooth cutaway NTX-style thin-line body, solid Engelmann spruce top, flamed maple back and sides, elliptical soundhole with decorative wood rosette, nato neck, 14/22-fret rosewood fingerboard, slotted headstock, three-per-side tuners, rosewood tied bridge, System61 ART two-way pickups, three-band EQ with on board tuner, available in Natural finish, mfg. 2010-present.

MSR $1,170	$700	$460 - 580	$290 - 350	

NTX1200R – single smooth cutaway NTX-style thin-line body, solid Sitka spruce top, solid rosewood back and sides, elliptical soundhole with decorative wood rosette, African Mahogany neck, 14/22-fret ebony fingerboard, slotted headstock, three-per-side tuners, rosewood tied bridge, System61 ART two-way pickups, three-band EQ with on board tuner, available in Natural finish, case included, mfg. 2010-present.

MSR $1,710	$1,000	$680 - 850	$425 - 500	

YAMAKI

See Daion in the D section. Instruments previously produced in Japan during the late 1970s through the 1980s.

YAMAMOTO, TONY

Instruments currently produced in Dublin, CA.

Luthier Tony Yamamoto hand builds custom acoustic guitars one at a time in his Dublin shop that is located in San Francisco near the East Bay. Yamamoto moved to California from Japan in the 1980s where he first worked as an engineer in semiconductors, but after a number of layoffs he decided to pursue guitar building. In 2003, Yamamoto attended one of Harry Fleishman's ten-day guitar building courses, which set him on his way to start building his own guitars. Yamamoto offers a variety of designs, but he has four main models including the OMY, the Talus, a Baritone, and a Multiscale Six-String. Prices start at $3,000 and several options are available. For more information, visit Yamamoto's website or contact him directly.

CONTACT INFORMATION
YAMAMOTO, TONY
7922 Agate Way
Dublin, CA 94568
Phone No.: 925-803 0476
yamamotoguitar.com
tony@yamamotoguitar.com

YAMATO

Instruments previously produced in Japan during the late 1970s and early 1980s.

Yamato guitars are medium quality instruments that feature both original and designs based on classic American favorites. Source: Tony Bacon and Paul Day, *The Guru's Guitar Guide*.

YURIY

Instruments previously built in Wheeling, IL between 1990 and 2002.

Luthier Yuriy Shishkov was born in 1964 in St. Petersburg. As with many other guitar makers, Shishkov began his career from discovering a big personal attraction to music. After spending 10 years playing guitars that he found unsatisfactory, Yuriy attempted to build his own instrument in 1986. The results amazed everyone who played the instrument, including Yuriy himself! From this initial bit of success, Yuriy gained a reputation as a luthier as well as several orders for guitars.

CONTACT INFORMATION
YURIY
www.shishkovguitars.ru

In 1990, Yuriy moved to Chicago, Illinois. A year later, he secured a job at Washburn International, a major guitar company based in Chicago. His experience with personal guitar building lead him to a position of handling the difficult repairs, restorations, intricate inlay work, company prototypes, and the custom-built instruments for the artist endorsees.

Luthier Yuriy Shishkov offered custom designed and construction of instruments from solid body guitars to his passion of archtop acoustics and hollowbody electrics. Yuriy is no longer producing guitars. He is currently the Senior Master builder at the Fender Custom Shop, and for more information on his Fender Custom Shop instruments, refer to his unofficial Russian website.

Yuriy had a number of Jazz-style archtop guitars. Models included the 16 in. **Minuet** (last list price was $3,700) or **Soprano** (last list price was $3,900), 17 in. **Capitol** (last list price was $4,300), **Sunset** (last list price was $4,600), and **Concerto** (last list price was $4,900), and 18 in. **Imperial** (last list price was $5,400) and **Triumph** (last list price was $5,900). Archtop models included features like hand carved spruce tops, figured maple back and sides, rock maple necks, and rosewood fingerboard. Models were finished in Nitrocellulose Lacquer finishes.

Z SECTION
ZEIDLER

Instruments previously built in Philadelphia, PA between 1977 and 2002.

Master luthier John R. Zeidler built quality custom guitars for over twenty-five years between the mid-1970s and 2002. Zeidler's background encompassed woodworking, metal smithing, tool making, and music. Zeidler built high quality archtop and flattop guitars, as well as mandolins and a few electric guitars and pedal steels early on. Zeidler was also commissioned to build one of the blue guitars for the Scott Chinery/Smithsonian Institute display. John passed away from leukemia at the age of forty-four in May, 2002. After Zeidler's death, fourteen master luthiers came together to build the Zeidler Project guitar, which featured several high quality appointments and was offered for sale at $100,000.

ACOUSTIC FLATTOP/ACOUSTIC ARCHTOP

Zeidler built all of his guitars to order one at a time. Zeidler also worked by himself and almost all components on his guitars including hardware were designed and constructed by him. While there were a handful of models with base prices, it is unlikely that he ever produced two guitars that were exactly the same. Zeidler's last price list (1999) lists the following models and prices: **Auditorium** ($4,675, with cutaway $5,175), **Excalibur** ($4,675, with cutaway $5,175), **Archtop** ($8,150), **Jazz** (16 in. and 17 in. body widths $9,200, 18 in. body width $10,200), and the **Jazz Deluxe** (16 in. and 17 in. body widths $11,225, 18 in. body width $12,250).

Used guitar evaluation on a Zeidler needs to be performed on a case by case basis because of the uniqueness of each guitar. Very few guitars come up for sale in the market either, which also makes used guitar evaluation tricky. Basic Zeidler guitars start around $5,000, but most guitars are valued between $7,500 and $15,000. Some of Zeidler's best models could sell for much higher than $15,000.

ZEMAITIS

CONTACT INFORMATION
ZEMAITIS
Zemaitis International
3-4 Kaji-cho Chiyoda-ku
Tokyo, 101-0045 Japan
Phone No.: 81-3-3254-3617
Fax No.: 81-3-3254-3660
www.zemaitis.net
info@zemaitis.net

Zemaitis Guitar Owners Club
Attn: Keith Smart
Addlestone, KT15 3YZ Great Britain
www.zemaitisclub.com
info@zemaitisclub.com

Instruments currently produced in Japan by Kanda since 2004. Previously hand-built in England between 1957 and 2001.

Tony Zemaitis was born Antanus (Anthony) Casimere (Charles) Zemaitis in 1935. While his grandparents were Lithuanian, both Tony and his parents were born in the UK. At age sixteen he left college to be an apprentice at cabinet making. As part of a hobby, he refashioned an old damaged guitar found in the family attic. In 1955, the first turning point to luthiery: Zemaitis built his first half decent guitar, a classical, nylon string with peghead. In the mid to late 1950s, Zemaitis served for two years in Britian's National Service.

Upon his return to civilian life, Zemaitis continued his guitar building hobby, only now a number of the guitars began turning up onto the folk scene. By 1960, he was selling guitars for the price of the materials, and a number of the originals that Zemaitis calls **Oldies** still exist. Early users include Spencer Davis, Long John Baldry, and Jimi Hendrix.

In 1965, Zemaitis' hobby had acquired enough interest that he was able to become self employed. By the late 1960s, the orders were coming in from a number of top players such as Ron Wood, Eric Clapton, and George Harrison. The house and shop all moved lock, stock, and barrel to Kent in 1972. A **Student** model was introduced in 1980, but proved to be too popular and time consuming to produce the number of orders, so it was discontinued.

In 1995, Zemaitis celebrated the 40th Anniversary of the first classical guitar he built in 1955. Guitar production was limited to 10 guitars a year. In 2001, Tony Zemaitis finally decided to retire and enjoy himself.

Sadly, in 2002, Tony passed away. His family and friends commented that despite his retirement, he couldn't stay out of the workshop! Before Tony died, he was in touch with Kanda (Japan) regarding the sale of this name. He felt that if one company owned the Zemaitis name, it would eliminate unathorized copies. His family completed the sale after he died and spent the next two years researching and making prototype Zemaitis instruments. Tony's family had some input in making the guitar and advice on the finishes. In 2004, Kanda started producing Zemaitis guitars again. Many people claim the Japanese Zemaitis models are very close to the original instruments built by Tony.

Several years ago, George Harrison lent three of his Zemaitis acoustic models to an exhibition in the U.K. organized by Viscount Linley (Princess Margaret's son). Source: Tony Zemaitis, March 1996, Keith Smart 2001, Information courtesy Keith Smart, *The Z Gazette*: magazine of the Zemaitis Guitar Owners Club based in England. Visit their website www.zemaitisclub.com for more information.

AUTHENTICITY

In the late 1980s, Zemaitis was surprised to see that his guitars were even more valuable in the secondhand market than originally priced. As his relative output was limited, an alarming trend of forgeries has emerged in England, Japan, and the U.S. Serial number identification and dating on guitars will continue to be unreported in this edition, due to the number of forgeries that keep turning up (and we're not going to add tips to the "help-yourself merchants" as Tony liked to call them). To clarify matters simply: Tony Zemaitis had granted NO ONE permission to build reproductions and NO licensing deals have been made to any company.

POINTS TO CONSIDER WHEN BUYING A ZEMAITIS

Prior to spending a large amount of money on what may very well turn out to be a copy of a Zemaitis, it is always best to ask for advice.

There are German, Japanese, and English copies. At first glance they may look a little like a Zemaitis, but they will not sound like one due to the use of second-rate materials. Because of the mass produced nature of these fakes, the intonation and general finish will be inferior to the genuine article. Even more alarming, what starts out as a cheap copy changes hands once or twice and eventually ends up being advertised as the real thing without proper research.

The more difficult fakes to spot are the genuine Zemaitis guitars that started life as a cheaper version (Student or Test model), and have been unofficially upgraded. In other words, a plain front guitar suddenly becomes a Pearl Front guitar. While parts and pieces will be genuine, the newer finish and general appearance are nothing like the real thing.

Always ask for a receipt, even if you are not buying from a shop. Always check the spelling of "Zemaitis." Look at the engraving, and make sure that it is engraved by hand (not photo etching - it is too clean and has not been worked on by hand, (Reprinted courtesy Keith Smart, The Z Gazette).

The *Blue Book of Acoustic Guitars* strongly recommends two or three written estimates of any Zemaitis instrument from accredited sources. If possible, ask to see the original paperwork. Here are two more serious tips: Usually the person who commissioned the guitar has their initials on the truss rod cover. Additionally, some of Zemaitis' acoustic models do not have truss rods. Also, review the printed label and logo (there's only one correct spelling for Mr. Zemaitis' name - and contrary to word of mouth, he does not intentionally misspell it on his guitars. Prices on models in excellent condition easily start at $10,000 and can go to and above $25,000.

MODEL DESCRIPTIONS

Here is a brief overview of model histories and designations. During the late 1950s, a few basic acoustic models were built to learn about sizes, shapes, wood response, and soundholes. From 1960 to 1964, guitar building was still a hobby, so there was no particular standard; also, the paper labels inside are hand labeled. In 1965, Zemaitis turned pro and introduced the **Standard**, **Superior**, and **Custom** models of acoustic guitars. These terms are relative, not definitive as there is some overlapping from piece to piece. While some soundholes are round, there are a number of acoustic guitars built with the heart-shaped sound hole.

Kanda produced a few acoustic models in 2004. The **Z-JHW/R** is a jumbo body with a spruce top and rosewood back and sides. The **Z-SHD/R** is a small-body guitar with a spruce top and rosewood back and sides. Both models feature the heart-shaped soundhole.

ZIMNICKI

Instruments currently built in Allen Park, MI. Zimnicki has been building guitars since 1978.

Luthier Gary Zimnicki has been developing his guitar building skills since 1978. Currently, he builds classical and steel-string flattop guitars and acoustic and electric archtop guitars, mandolins, and ukuleles. As of mid-2012, Zimnicki had produced over 275 instruments. For more information, visit Zimnicki's website or contact him directly.

CONTACT INFORMATION
ZIMNICKI
15106 Garfield
Allen Park, MI 48101
Phone No.: 313-381-2817
www.zimnicki.com
zimnicki@att.net

ACOUSTIC/ACOUSTIC ELECTRIC

Zimnicki uses aged tonewoods for his carved graduated tops, and wood bindings. Due to the nature of these commissioned pieces, the customer determines the body size, neck scale, types of wood/fingerboard inlays/pickups, and finish. All prices include a hardshell case.

The **Acoustic Archtop** (MSR $7,500) features a single cutaway bound body, carved arched top, two f-holes, ebony tailpiece/full contact bridge/fingerboard, three-per-side Schaller gold tuners, and is available in Natural or Trans. high gloss nitrocellulose lacquer finishes.

The **Classical** (MSR $3,350) features a classical style body, round soundhole with rosette, 14/20-fret unbound fingerboard, three-per-side headstock, and classical style tied bridge.

The **Flattop Steel String** (MSR $2,900) is available in a variety of sizes, and available as a non-cutaway or single rounded cutaway, round soundhole with rosette, 12/20 or 14/20-fret unbound fingerboard, three-per-side headstock, and conventional style bridge.

* **Add $200 for Sunburst finish.**
* **Add $250 for seven string configuration.**

ZWIER, JACK

Instruments currently produced in Netherlands, since 1988.

Luthier Jack Zwier has been building and repairing guitars since 1988. In 1990, he attended the College for Musical Instrument Building in Belgium. He has produced over 150 hand crafted guitars and most of them are one-offs. Prices start at $1,400 for acoustic guitars. For more information contact luthier Zwier directly.

CONTACT INFORMATION
ZWIER, JACK
4381 BW
Vlissingen, The Netherlands
Phone No.: 31 0 118-416668
Fax No.: 31 0 118-414068
www.zwiergitaarbouw.nl
zwier@zeelandnet.nl

HOUSE BRANDS/BUDGET BRANDS

The phenomenon of large production companies producing House Brand instruments dates back to the late 1800s and early 1900s. A House Brand is defined as a trademark used by distributors, wholesalers, and retailers to represent their respective company instead of the manufacturer. These brands are found (for the most part) on budget instruments, although some models are currently sought after by players and collectors on the basis of playability, tone, or relative degree of "coolness" they project.

In the 1800s, many guitar manufacturers were located in New York and Philadelphia; by the early 1900s large guitar factories were centered in Chicago. The "Big Three" that evolved out of the early 1930s were Harmony, Kay, and Valco. Valco, producer of National and Supro instruments, produced the Airline House Brand as well as bodies and resonator parts that were sold to Harmony and Kay. However, the majority of House Brand instruments found today probably originated at either Harmony or Kay. On the East Coast, Danelectro was a large builder/supplier to Sears & Roebuck under Sears' Silvertone label (sometimes up to 85 percent of Danelectro's output).

Prior to World War II, Harmony and Kay sold straight to wholesalers like catalog houses and large distributors. In turn, these wholesalers would send their salesmen and "reps" out on the road to generate sales – no territories, no music store chains – just straight sales. Business was fierce, and companies used their own private labels to denote "their" product. House Brands were typically used as a marketing tool for distributors, wholesalers, and/or retailers to try to eliminate consumer shopping for the best price on popular makes and models of the time. How could you shop a trademark that didn't exist anywhere else? Tom Wheeler, in his book, *American Guitars*, quoted former Harmony president Charles A. Rubovits' recollection that the company built fifty-seven private brands for the wholesalers – and sold over five million guitars.

An informative essay about House Brands and their place in the vintage guitar spectrum can be found in *Stellas & Stratocasters* (Vintage Guitar Books) by Willie G. Moseley, feature writer/columnist for *Vintage Guitar Magazine*. Moseley's commentary includes a listing of thirty-eight brands and their retailers/distributors, brief anecdotes about the major American manufacturers of budget instruments (Harmony, Kay, etc.), and photos of twenty-five American-made House Brand instruments.

Since writing that article, Moseley has advised the *Blue Book of Acoustic Guitars*: "I've come across a couple of other house brands in my travels; one example was a low-end, Stella-type variant with `Superior' sloppily screen-printed on its headstock. It was one of those cheap, beginner's instruments that were and still are at the nadir of American-made guitars, but so far I haven't been able to determine anything about its brand name...not that it matters too much!"

"It's my opinion, and I dare say the opinion of most vintage guitar enthusiasts, that a good rule of thumb concerning the collectibility of House Brands would be something along the lines of 'If it was a budget instrument then, it's proportionally a budget instrument now.' Regrettably, as the interest in vintage guitars continues to grow, some individuals and/or businesses tend to assume that simply because an instrument is 'old' and/or 'discontinued' and/or 'American-made', that automatically makes it a 'collector's item' and/or 'valuable.' That's certainly not the case, especially with House Brands. It's disheartening to walk into a pawn shop and see a Kay-made Silvertone archtop electric from the Sixties labeled as an 'antique' and priced at $499, when the instrument is worth no more than $100 in the vintage guitar market, and such incidents are apparently on the increase. And that's unfortunate for everybody."

The *Blue Book of Acoustic Guitars* is continuing to collect data and evaluate the collectibility and pricing on these House Brand instruments. Condition is a large factor in the pricing, as a thirty-to-forty year old guitar ordered from a catalog may have been used/abused by younger members of a household (to the detriment of the instrument). House Brand guitars may be antiques, they may be somewhat collectible, and they may be "classic pieces of Americana" (as one antique shop's sign declared), but they should still be relatively inexpensive when compared to the rest of the vintage guitar market. We believe Mr. Moseley to be correct in his C-note assessment of this aspect of the vintage market (at average condition); other music markets that service players and students may find pricing at a slightly wider range of $75 to $150 depending on other factors (playability, possessing an adjustable truss rod, appearance/"coolness" factor, a solid wood top versus plywood, veneer sides, additional parts, etc.) This is the bottom line: this book should help identify the brand/original company, give a few hints as to the quality and desirability, and a price range. The rest is up to you! We will continue to survey the market for pricing trends and "hot" models – further information will be included in upcoming editions of the *Blue Book of Acoustic Guitars*.

SERIALIZATION

ADAMAS

For Adamas serialization, please see the Ovation serialization.

AMERICAN ARCHTOP

According to luthier Dale Unger, the digits after the dash in the serial number are the year the guitar was completed.

ALVAREZ YAIRI

Alvarez Yairi guitars can be dated by the number stamped onto the back of the heel. The number is based on the Emperor of Japan at the time the guitar was built. The first two numbers represent the number of years the Emperor of Japan has been in term. The next two numbers indicate the number of the month. The following chart shows what number indicates what year.

NUMBER	YEAR
45	1970
46	1971
47	1972
48	1973
49	1974
50	1975
51	1976
52	1977
53	1978
54	1979
55	1980
56	1981
57	1982
58	1983
59	1984
60	1985
61	1986
62	1987
63	1988
1	1989
2	1990
3	1991
4	1992
5	1993
6	1994
7	1995
8	1996
9	1997
10	1998
11	1999
12	2000

Alvarez Yairi stopped using the emperor code in 2000 (2000 was the last year with #12). New serialization is a two-digit number code that matches the year. 01=2001, 02=2002, etc.

NUMBER	YEAR
01	2001
02	2002
03	2003
04	2004
05	2005
06	2006
07	2007
08	2008
09	2009
10	2010
11	2011
12	2012

ARIA/ARIA PRO II

Aria started using serial numbers in the mid-1970s, and models before this have no serial number. Several different schemes have been used for serialization. Guitars built between 1979 and 1987 may use either one of these formats: YNNNNN or YYNNNNNN. The first one or two digits indicate the year. A 79XXXXX would be a 1979 and a 2XXXXXX would be a 1982. Some models built in Korea may use a year and week code for the first four digits.

Serial numbers after 1987 are unknown at this point. Keep in mind that several variations have been used and anything is quite possible.

Source: Michael Wright, Aria

BENEDETTO

To date, Robert Benedetto has completed over 750 musical instruments. 466 are archtop guitars, with the remainder being compromised of 51 violins, five violas, one classical guitar, two mandolins, eleven semi-hollow electrics, 209 electric solidbody electric guitars and basses, and one cello. The eleven semi-hollow electrics include six unique, carved top, semi-hollow electrics made between 1982 and 1986. The other five include three prototypes for, and two finished examples of, his new "benny" semi-hollow electric line introduced in 1998. The 209 electric solid bodies include 157 electric guitars and 52 electric basses. Benedetto began making them in 1986 with John Buscarino. He stopped making them in the Spring of 1987. The eleven semi-hollow electrics and the one classical guitar are included in the archtop guitar serial numbering system. The two mandolins have no serial numbers. The violins, violas, and cello have their own serial number system (starting with #101) as do the electric solid body guitars and basses (starting with #1001).

Serial Numbers:

All Benedetto archtop guitars (except his first two) are numbered in one series, and electric solidbodies and basses each have their own separate series, as do the violins, violas and cello. Archtop guitars have a four- or five- digit serial number with configuration ##(#)YY. Two (or three) digits ##(#) indicate ranking, beginning with #1 in 1968.

The last two digits (YY) indicate the year.

Example: 43599 was made in 1999 and is the 435th archtop made since 1968.

Note: year listed on the right indicates date shipped, not made:

NUMBER	YEAR
0168 (#1)*	1968
0270 (#2)*	1970
0372	1972
0473	1973
0575-0676	1976
0777-1177	1977
1277-2778	1978
2879-4279	1979
4380-5580	1980
5681-7381	1981
7482-9582	1982
9682-10983	1983
11084-11984	1984
12085-12885	1985
12986-13586	1986
13686-13987-A	1987
14087-16488	1988
16588-19189	1989
19289-22490-A	1990
22591-25091	1991
25192-28092	1992

NUMBER	YEAR
28193-30293	1993
30393-32994	1994
33095-36595	1995
36696-39496	1996
39597-40697	1997
40798-43498	1998
43599-45199	1999
45200-46200	2000
46301-46601	2001

Note: Benedetto models made at the Guild Custom Shop in Nashville had a separate serial number system beginning with the letter N.

*Actual number in log: Benedetto did not adopt his current serial number system until his third guitar, serial #0372.

Seven guitar serial numbers are follwed by the letter "A". Example: archtop guitar #23891 and #23891-A are two separate instruments even though both are numbered the "238th."

From Robert Benedetto's Archtop Guitar Serial Number Logbook. Further information and a full serial number list can be found in Robert Benedetto's book, **Making an Archtop Guitar** *(Center - stream Publishing/Hal Leonard, 1994).*

BREEDLOVE

Breedlove Custom Shop serial numbers can be found on the guitar's label inside the guitar (look through the soundhole). Serial numbers on the Atlas series do not follow this system. Through 1999, a five digit serialization system was used where the first two digits indicate the last two numbers of the year, and the following three digits are sequential numbering. Example: Serial number 96-040 was the 40th guitar built in 1996. In 1999, Breedlove switched to a completely sequential numbering serialization system. The system started at 2000, and remember that the serial number is assigned at the beginning of construction and not the end.

NUMBER	YEAR
2000-2630	1999
2631-3217	2000
3218-4070	2001
4071-5160	2002
5161-6444	2003
6445-7499	2004
7500-8490	2005
8491-9736	2006
9737-	2007

BUSCARINO

Luthier John Buscarino had the priviledge of apprenticing with not one but two Master Builders, Augustino LoPrinzi and Robert Benedetto. Buscarino formed his first company, **Nova U.S.A.** in 1981; he changed the company to **Buscarino Guitars** in 1990.

The last two digits of the Buscarino serial number are the year the guitar was completed.

CARVIN

Originally founded by Lowell C. Kiesel as the pickup-building L. C. Kiesel Company, Carvin has expanded through the years into a full line mail order company that offers guitars, basses, amplifiers, P.A. gear, and replacement parts. The company initially offered kit-built guitars, and, by 1964, completed models.

The 2,000 to 4,000 instruments built between 1964 and 1970 did not have serial numbers. The first serial number issued in 1970 was number 5000, and numbers since then have been sequential. Serial numbers up until the late 1990s were stamped on the jackplate. On models with rounded edges and no jackplates, the serial number was stamped into the end of the fingerboard unless it was maple. In that case, the number may be stamped inside the control cavity cover plate.

Carvin's serialization is sequential, but there appears to be no logical order in the way they are assigned. A TL60 built in 2002 has a serial number of 63663 while a Bolt built in 2000 has a serial number of 82398, and an LB70 bass built in 1998 has a serial number of 63094. The following chart of serial numbers contains several overlaps in numbers. The numbers recorded represent the lowest and highest numbers found for each year. More possibilities exist. Carvin suggests dating your guitar by certain features rather than the serial number. Refer to the Carvin Museum website for more information: www.carvinmuseum.com.

NUMBER	YEAR
1970-1979	5000-10019
1980-1983	10768-15919
1984-1987	13666-25332
1988-1990	22731-25683
1991-1994	25359-42547
1995-1999	45879-81427
2000-Present	56162-approx. 95,000

Source: Carvin Museum.

CHRIS LARKIN CUSTOM GUITARS

Since 1982, a simple six-digit system has been used. The first two digits indicate the year, the next two the month, and the final two the sequence in that month. For example, 970103 was the third instrument in January 1997. Before 1982, the numbers are a bit chaotic! Chris Larkin has full documentation for almost every instrument that he has ever built, so he can supply a history from the serial number in most cases.

COLLINGS

Collings guitar serial numbers are expressed as the date, which is written on the label on the inside of the guitar. However, here is a more expanded view on Collings serialization:

Flattop Serialization

1975-1987: Guitars do not posses a serial number. Most are marked with a handwritten date on the underside of the top. Some guitars from 1987 may have a serial number.

1988 to date: Guitars began a consecutive numbering series that began with number 175. The serial number is stamped on the neck block.

Archtop Serialization

Before 1991: Archtops before 1991 had their own separate serialization.

1991 to date: Archtops are now numbered with a two part serial number. The first number indicates the archtop as part of the general company serialization; and the second number indicates the ranking in the archtop series list.

(Serialization information courtesy Collings Guitars, Inc.)

D'ANGELICO

Master Luthier John D'Angelico (1905-1964) opened his own shop at age 27, and every guitar was hand built - many to the specifications or nuances of the customer commissioning the instrument. In the course of his brief lifetime, he created 1,164 numbered guitars, as well as unnumbered mandolins, novelty instruments, and the necks for the plywood semi-hollowbody electrics. The objective of this list is to help identify the production of numbered guitars.

D'Angelico kept a pair of ledger books and some loose sheets of paper as a log of the guitars created, models, date of completion (or possibly the date of shipment), the person or business to whom the guitar was sold, and the date. The following list is a rough approximation of the ledgers and records.

First *Loose Sheets*

NUMBER	YEAR
1002-1073	1932-1934

Ledger Book One

1169-1456	1936-1939
1457-1831	1940-1949
1832-1849	1950

Ledger Book Two

1850-2098	1950-1959
2099-2122	1960
2123	1961

Second *Loose Sheets*

2124-2164	Dates not recorded

Again, it must be stressed that the above system is a guide only. In 1991, author Paul William Schmidt published a book entitled *Acquired of the Angels: The Lives and Works of Master Guitar Makers John D'Angelico and James L. D'Aquisto* (The Scarecrow Press, Inc.; Metuchen, N.J. & London). In Appendix 1 the entire ledger information is reprinted save information on persons or businesses to whom the guitar was sold. This book is recommended to anyone seeking information on luthiers John D'Angelico and James L. D'Aquisto.

D'AQUISTO

Master luthier James L. D'Aquisto (1935-1995) met John D'Angelico around 1953. At the early age of 17, D'Aquisto became D'Angelico's apprentice, and by 1959 was handling the decorative procedures and other lutherie jobs.

D'Aquisto, like his mentor before him, kept ledger books as a log of the guitars created, models, date of completion (or possibly the date of shipmeng), the person or business to whom the guitar was sold, and the date. The following list is a rough approximation of the ledger. As the original pages contain some idiosyncrasies, the following list will by nature be inaccurate as well, and should only be used as a guide for dating individual instruments. The objective of this list is to help identify the production of numbered guitars.

The D'Aquisto Ledger

NUMBER	YEAR
1001-1035	1965-1969
1036-1084	1970-1974
1085-1133	1975-1979
1134-1175	1980-1984
1176-1228	1985-1990

Beginning in 1988, serialization started with 1230. 1257 was D'Aquisto's last serial number on non-futuristic models.

Other guitars that D'Aquisto built had their own serial numbers. For example, solid body and semi-hollow body guitars from 1976 to 1987 had an *E* before the three-digit number. D'Aquisto also built some classical models, some flat-top acoustics, and some hollowbody electric models (hollowbody guitars run from #1 to #30, 1976 to 1980; and #101 to #118, 1982 to 1988).

In 1991, author Paul William Schmidt published a book entitled *Acquired of the Angels: The Lives and Works of Master Guitar Makers John D'Angelico and James L. D'Aquisto* (The Scarecrow Press, Inc.; Metuchen, N.J. & London). In Appendix 2, the entire ledger information is reprinted up to the year 1988 except for information on persons or businesses to whom the guitar was sold. This book is recommended to anyone seeking information on luthiers John D'Angelico and James L. D'Aquisto.

DOBRO

The convoluted history of the Dopyera brothers (Dobro, National Dobro, Valco, Original Music Instrument Company) has been discussed in a number of wonderful guitar texts. Serialization of Dobro instruments is far less tangled, but there are different forms of the numbers to contend with. Dobro serial numbers should always be used in conjunction with other identifying features for dating purposes.

Dobro was founded in Los Angeles in 1929, and production continued until the outbreak of World War II in 1942 (resonator guitar production ends). The numbers listed by year are the serialization ranges, not production amounts.

NUMBER	YEAR
900-2999	1928-1930
3000-3999	1930-1931

NUMBER	YEAR

Between 1931 and 1932, the *cyclops* models carried a serial number code of B XXX.

5000-5599	1932-1933
5700-7699	1934-1936
8000-9999	1937-1942

In the mid-1950s, Rudy and Ed Dopyera return to building wood-bodied Dobros from pre-war parts under the trademark of **DB Original**. The serialization of these models is still unknown.

In 1961, Louis Dopyera of Valco transfered the **Dobro** trademark to Rudy and Ed. These models are distinguished by a serialization code of D plus three digits.

After Semie Moseley gained the rights to the Dobro trademark, the Original Music Instrument Company was founded in 1967 by Ed, Rudy, and Gabriela Lazar. OMI regained the Dobro name in 1970, and instituted a new coding on the instruments. The code had a prefix of **D** (Wood body) or **B** (Metal body), followed by three or four digits (production ranking) and a single digit to indicate the year, thus:

D XXXX Y   OMI Dobro coding 1970-1979

The code reversed itself in 1980. The single digit prefix indicated the year/decade, then three or four digits (production ranking), another single digit to indicate the year, then the body material designation (D or B), like:

8 XXXX YD   OMI Dobro coding 1980-1987

In 1988, the code became a little more specialized, and shared more information. The prefix consisted of a letter and number that indicated the model style, three or four digits for production ranking, another letter for neck style, two digits for year of production, and the body material designation (D or B):

AX XXXX NYYD   OMI Dobro coding 1988 - 1992

In 1993, Gibson bought OMI/Dobro. Production was maintained at the California location from 1993 to 1996, and the serialization stayed similar to the 1988 - 1992 style coding. In 1997, Gibson moved Dobro to Nashville.

EPIPHONE

1920S-1950: Acoustc guitars were first produced in 1930, and were built in New York City, New York through 1953. However, some various models were built in the late 1920s. Electric models were introduced in 1935. Company manufacturing was moved to Philadelphia due to union harrassment in New York, and Epiphone continued on through 1957. Serial numbers on original Epiphones can be found on a label inside of the guitar.

NUMBER	YEAR
1-999	Late 1920s
1000's	1931
5000's	1932
6000's	1933
7200's	1934
8000's-9000's	1935
10000's	1936
11000's	1937
12000's	1938
13000's-14400's	1939
145000's	1940
16000's-17400's	1941
17500's-18100's	1942
18200's-18900's	1943
19000's-20000's	1944
50000's-52000's	1944
52000's-54000's	1945
54000's-55000's	1946
56000's	1947
57000's	1948
58000's	1949

1950-1957: In 1951, electric instruments were brought under the same numbering system as acoustics, and serial numbers were relocated to a paper label in the instrument's interior. Some transitional instruments bear both impressed numbers and a paper label with differing numbers. The latter are more accurate for use in dating.

NUMBER	YEAR
59000's	1950
60000S-63000's	1951
64000's	1952
64000's-66000's	1953
67000's	1954
68000's	1955
69000's	1957

1958-1961: In May of 1957, Epiphone was purchased by CMI and became a division of Gibson. Gibson-built Epiphone guitars in Kalamazoo from 1958 to 1970. Hollow body guitars had the serial number on the inside label, and were prefixed with "A-", plus four digits for the first three years (note: this is different than the similar Gibson serialization).

A 1000's	1959
A 2000's	1959-1960
A 3000's-A4312	1960-Early 1961

1961-1970: In 1961, the numbering scheme changed as all models had the serial number pressed into the back on the headstock. There were numerous examples of duplication of serial numbers, so when dating a Epiphone from this time period, consideration of parts, configuration and other details is equally important.

NUMBER	YEAR
100-41199	1961
4100-41199	1961
41200-61180	1962
61450-64222	1963
64240-71040	1964
71041-71178	1962, 1964
71180-95846	1962
95849-99999	1963
000001-008009	1967
010000-042899	1967
044000-044100	1967
050000-054400	1967
055000-070909	1967
090000-099999	1967
100000-106099	1963, 1967
106100-108999	1963
109000-109999	1963, 1967
110000-111549	1963
111550-115799	1963, 1967
115800-118299	1963
118300-120999	1963, 1967
121000-139999	1963
140000-140100	1963, 1967
140101-144304	1963
144305-144380	1963, 1964
144381-145000	1963
147001-149891	1963, 1964
149892-152989	1963
152990-174222	1964
174223-179098	1964, 1965
179099-199999	1964
200000-250199	1964
250540-290998	1965
300000-305999	1965
306000-306099	1965, 1967
307000-307984	1965
309653-310999	1965, 1967
311000-320149	1965

NUMBER	YEAR
320150-320699	1967
320700-325999	1965
326000-326999	1965, 1966
327000-329999	1965
330000-330999	1965, 1967, 1968
331000-346119	1965
346120-347099	1965, 1966
348000-349100	1966
349101-368639	1965
370000-370999	1967, 1968
380000-380999	1966, 1967, 1968
381000-385309	1966
390000-390998	1967
400001-400999	1965, 1966, 1967, 1968
401000-408699	1966
408800-409670	1966, 1967, 1968
410000-438922	1966
500000-500999	1965, 1966, 1967, 1968
501009-501600	1965
501601-501702	1968
501703-502706	1965, 1968
503010-503109	1968
503405-515499	1965, 1968
515500-518120	1965, 1966, 1968
518121-520955	1965, 1968
520956-530050	1968
530061-530469	1966
530470-530850	1966, 1968, 1969
530851-530993	1968, 1969
530994-539999	1969
540000-540795	1966, 1969
540796-544095	1969
547001-547499	1968
555000-556909	1966
558012-567800	1969
570099-570643	1966
570645-570755	1966
580000-580999	1966, 1969
600000-600998	1966, 1967, 1968
601000-601090	1969
605901-606090	1969
700000-700799	1966, 1967, 1968
750000-750999	1968, 1969
800000-800999	1966, 1967, 1968, 1969
801000-801999	1966
802000-803999	1966
804000-804999	1966, 1967, 1969
805000-809999	1966, 1969
810000-810999	1966, 1967, 1969
811000-812838	1966, 1969
812900-819999	1969
820000-820999	1966, 1969
821000-823830	1966
824000-828999	1969
829000-829999	1966, 1969
830000-830999	1966, 1967, 1969
831000-837999	1969
840000-847498	1966, 1967, 1969
847499-848999	1966, 1967
849000-849999	1966, 1967, 1968
850000-850999	1966, 1968
851000-858999	1966
859001-891999	1967
892000-892999	1967, 1968
893000-895499	1967
895500-895999	1968

NUMBER	YEAR
896000-896999	1968, 1969
897000-898999	1967
899000-899999	1968
900000-900999	1966, 1967, 1968
901000-902250	1968
903000-920899	1968
940000-942999	1968
945000-956999	1968
959000-960909	1968
970000-982178	1968

1970-Present (Foreign): In 1970, production of Epiphone instruments moved to Japan. Japanese Epiphones were manufactured between 1970 and 1983. According to author/researcher Walter Carter, the serial numbers on these are unreliable as a usable tool for dating models. Comparison to catalogs is one of the few means available for dating these instruments. Earlier Kalamazoo labels were generally orange with black printing and said "Made in Kalamazoo", while the Japanese instruments featured blue labels which read "Epiphone of Kalamazoo, Michigan" (note that it doesn't say "Made in Kalamazoo", nor does it say "Made in Japan"). Research of the model should be more thorough than just glancing at the label. Serial numbers from Japanese-made models are still unknown.

During the early 1980s, the Japanese production costs became pricey due to the changing ratio of the dollar to the yen. Production then moved to Korea where a different serialization system was used.

NUMBER	YEAR	TYPE
1000	1985	Solidbodies
4000000's	1985	Hollowbodies
4100000's	1985	Hollowbodies
5060000's	1985	Solidbodies
5080000's	1985	Solidbodies
5090000's	1985	Hollowbodies
5100000's	1985	Solidbodies

Current Epiphones manufactured overseas typically utilize a seven- or eight-digit serial number, the first digit being the last one or two numbers of the year of manufacture, and the third and fourth digits being the week of manufacture. Many of these instruments have an alphabetical character designating the manufacturing facility:

China

BW	Unknown
DW	DaeWon
EA	Qing Dao
EE	Qing Dao
MC	Muse
SJ	Sae Jung
Z	Zaozhuang Saehan

Czech

B	Bohemia Musico-Delicia

Indonesia

SI	Samick

Japan

F	FujiGen
J/T	Terada

Korea

I	Saein
P/R	Peerless
S	Samick
U	Unsung
K	Korea

Examples: S3061789 refers to an instrument mfg. June, 1993 by Samick, R5068265 indicates an instrument mfg. during 1995 by Aria.

S02104385 indicates a Samick model produced in October, 2002. Models produced in the late 1990s and early 2000s are more likely to have the eight-digit system.

Elite/Elitist Models:

Epiphone Elitist models utilize a different serialization system that consists of one letter and five digits (FYNNNN). F indicates the factory code, which will be either a T or an F as all Elitist models are built in Japan, the Y indicates the last number of the year, and the remaining four digits are sequential numbering. Example: T30765 is a 2003 Elitist built in the Terada factory and was the 765th instrument that year.

1977-Present (U.S.): Some top-of-the-line Epiphones were produced in the U.S. at Gibson's Kalamazoo, Nashville, or Montana facility since the mid 70s. Like Gibson numbers, there are eight digits in the complete number, and follows the code of YDDDYNNN. The YY (first and fifth) indicate the year built. DDD indicates the day of the year (so DDD can't be above 365), and the NNN indicates the instrument's production ranking for that day (NNN = 021 = 21st guitar built). The Nashville facility begins each day at number 501, and the Montana workshop begins at number 001 (as did Kalamazoo). However, in 1994, the Nashville-produced Epiphones were configured as YYNNNNNN: YY = 94 (the year) and NNNNNN is the ranking for the entire year. Example: 82303025 was built on the 230th day of 1983 and was the 25th instrument built at Kalamazoo that day.

Source: Walter Carter, Epiphone The Complete History, Walter Carter and George Gruhn, Gruhn's Guide to Vintage Guitars.

FENDER

Fender acoustics do not correspond to their electric counterparts in serialization. The records are not complete enough to create a rough approximation. However, on Fender's website, they have created a listing of all of their acoustic guitars along with their production years and features. This should help date a guitar within a few years. Visit www.fender.com for more information.

FRAMUS

Framus serial numbers were generally placed on the back of the peghead or on a label inside the body. The main body of the serial number is followed by an additional pair of digits and a letter. This additional pair of numbers indicate the production year.

For example:

51334 63L =	1963
65939 70L =	1970

Serial number information courtesy Tony Bacon and Barry Moorehouse, The Bass Book, GPI Books, 1995

GIBSON

Identifying Gibson instruments by serial number is tricky at best, and downright impossible in some cases. The best method of identifying them is to use a combination of the serial number, the factory order number and any features that are particular to a specific time (i.e. logo design change, headstock volutes, etc).

In addition to the serial number information, Gibson also used Factory Order Numbers (FON) to track batches of instruments being produced at the time. In the earlier years at Gibson, guitars were normally built in batches of forty instruments. Gibson's Factory Order Numbers were an internal coding that followed the group of instruments through the factory. Thus, the older Gibson guitars may have a serial number and a FON. The FON may indicate the year, batch number, and the ranking (order of production within the batch of forty).

This system is useful in helping to date and authenticate instruments. There are three separate groupings of numbers that have been identified and which are used for their accuracy. The numbers are usually stamped or written on the instrument's back and seen through the lower f-hole or round soundhole, or maybe impressed on the back of the headstock.

Code Letter FONs were discontinued after 1941, and any instruments made during or right after World War II do not bear an FON codes. In 1949, a four-digit FON was used, but not in conjunction with any code letter indicating the year.

From 1952-1961, the FON scheme followed the pattern of a letter, the batch number, and an instrument ranking number (when the guitar was built in the run of forty). The FON is the only identification number on Gibson's lower grade models (like the ES-125, ES-140, J-160E, etc.) which do not feature a paper label. Higher grade models (such as the Super 400, L-5, J-200, etc.) feature both a serial number **and** a FON. When both numbers are present on a higher grade model, remember that the FON was assigned at the beginning of the production run, while the serial number was recorded later (before shipping). The serial number would properly indicate the actual date of the guitar.

1902-1947: The first serialization system was started in 1902. The serial numbers started with number 100 for acoustics, around 90000 for electrics and run up to 99999. All numbers are approximates. In most cases, only the upper end instruments were assigned identification numbers. Serial numbers appear ink-stamped on a white paper label.

FONs first became date coded by a letter in 1935. Other FONs may appear that aren't listed here that were produced during WWII. From 1935 to 1937, the letter appeared between the batch and instrument numbers (i.e. 722 A 23, 465 D 58, 863 E 02). The number is ink-stamped inside the guitar on the back. In 1938, the FON was changed to a two- or three-letter prefix before the batch and instrument numbers. The first letter indicates the year, the second indicates the brand (i.e. G for Gibson, K for Kalamazoo), and the third (if applicable) for electric. The FON is either ink-stamped on the label or on the back of the headstock.

Nick Lucas models produced between 1928 and 1933, will all have serial numbers from 1928 or 1929.

SERIAL NUMBERS

APPROX. LAST NUMBER	YEAR
1500	1903
2500	1904
3500	1905
5500	1906
8300	1907
9700	1908
10100	1909
10600	1910
10850	1911
13350	1912
16100	1913
20150	1914
25150	1915
32000	1916
39500	1917
47900	1918
53800	1919
63650	1920
69300	1921
71400	1922
74900	1923
81200	1924
82700	1925
83600	1926
85400	1927
87300	1928
89750	1929
90200	1930
90450	1931
90700	1932
91400	1933
92300	1934
92800	1935

APPROX. LAST NUMBER	YEAR
94100	1936
95200	1937
95750	1938
96050	1939
96600	1940
97400	1941
97700	1942
97850	1943
98250	1944
98650	1945
99300	1946
99999	1947

FACTORY ORDER NUMBERS (FON)

BATCH NUMBERS	YEAR
259	1908
309	1909
545, 927	1910
1260, 1295	1911
1408, 1593	1912
1811, 1902	1913
1936, 2152	1914
2209, 3207	1915
2667, 3508	1916
3246, 11010	1917
9839, 11159	1918
11146, 11212	1919
11329, 11367	1920
11375, 11527	1921
11565, 11729	1922
11973	1923

LETTER	NUMBER
A	1935
B	1936
C	1937
D	1938
DA	1938
E/EA (X, or Other Letters)	1939
E	1941
F	1940

LETTER	NUMBER
FA	1940
G	1941
H	1942

1947-1961: Gibson changed their serialization system once they reached 99999 and decided they did not want to go to a six-digit system. Instead, they added an A prefix followed by a three-, four-, or five-digit number. The new system started on April 28, 1947 with number A 100. The last number was used on February 21, 1961. From 1947 to early 1955, white oval labels were used. In early 1955, the label was changed to an orange oval. Serial numbers are on the label and FONs are ink-stamped on the inside back of the guitar. FONs consisted of a letter, four-digit batch number, and count number (i.e. Y 2230 21, V 4867 8, R 6785 15). FONs were discontinued after Gibson changed to the new serialization system in 1961.

SERIAL NUMBERS

APPROX. LAST NUMBER	YEAR
A 1304	1947
A 2665	1948
A 4413	1949

APPROX. LAST NUMBER	YEAR
A 6597	1950
A 9419	1951
A 12462	1952
A 16101	1953
A 18667	1954
A 21909	1955
A 24755	1956
A 26819	1957
A 28880	1958
A 32284	1959
A 35645	1960
A 36147	1961

FACTORY ORDER NUMBERS (FON)

APPROX. LAST NUMBER	YEAR
Low 100's-Low 2000's	1949
High 2000's-Low 5000's	1950
High 5000's-Low 9000's	1951
High 9000's	1952

FACTORY ORDER NUMBERS (FON)

LETTER/NUMBER	YEAR
Z	1952
Y	1953
X	1954
W	1955
V	1956
U	1957
T	1958
S	1959
R	1960
Q	1961

1961-1970: In 1961, Gibson started a new serial number system that covered all instrument lines. It consisted of numbers that were impressed into the wood. This is generally considered to be the most confusing out of all Gibson's serial number systems used between the years 1961 and 1970. There are several instances where batches of numbers are switched in order and duplicated, not just once, but up to four times, and seem to be randomly assigned throughout the decade.

Note: If "MADE IN USA" is stamped in the back of the headstock near the serial number, the guitar is not from the 1960s, but the 1970s. In this case, please refer to the next section on serialization for 1970-1975 guitars.

NUMBER	YEAR
100-41199	1961
41200-61180	1962
61450-64222	1963
64240-71040	1964
71041-71178	1962, 1964
71180-95846	1962
95849-99999	1963
000001-008009	1967
010000-042899	1967
044000-044100	1967
050000-054400	1967
055000-070909	1967
090000-099999	1967
100000-106099	1963, 1967
106100-108999	1963
109000-109999	1963, 1967
110000-111549	1963
111550-115799	1963, 1967
115800-118299	1963
118300-120999	1963, 1967

NUMBER	YEAR
121000-139999	1963
140000-140100	1963, 1967
140101-144304	1963
144305-144380	1963, 1964
144381-145000	1963
147001-149891	1963, 1964
149892-152989	1963
152990-174222	1964
174223-179098	1964, 1965
179099-199999	1964
200000-250199	1964
250540-290998	1965
300000-305999	1965
306000-306099	1965, 1967
307000-307984	1965
309653-310999	1965, 1967
311000-320149	1965
320150-320699	1967
320700-325999	1965
326000-326999	1965, 1966
327000-329999	1965
330000-330999	1965, 1967, 1968
331000-346119	1965
346120-347099	1965, 1966
348000-349100	1966
349101-368639	1965
370000-370999	1967, 1968
380000-380999	1966, 1967, 1968
381000-385309	1966
390000-390998	1967
400001-400999	1965, 1966, 1967, 1968
401000-408699	1966
408800-409670	1966, 1967, 1968
410000-438922	1966
500000-500999	1965, 1966, 1967, 1968
501009-501600	1965
501601-501702	1968
501703-502706	1965, 1968
503010-503109	1968
503405-515499	1965, 1968
515500-518120	1965, 1966, 1968
518121-520955	1965, 1968
520956-530050	1968
530061-530469	1966
530470-530850	1966, 1968, 1969
530851-530993	1968, 1969
530994-539999	1969
540000-540795	1966, 1969
540796-544095	1969
547001-547499	1968
555000-556909	1966
558012-567800	1969
570099-570643	1966
570645-570755	1966
580000-580999	1966, 1969
600000-600998	1966, 1967, 1968
601000-601090	1969
605901-606090	1969
700000-700799	1966, 1967, 1968
750000-750999	1968, 1969
800000-800999	1966, 1967, 1968, 1969
801000-801999	1966
802000-803999	1966
804000-804999	1966, 1967, 1969
805000-809999	1966, 1969
810000-810999	1966, 1967, 1969
811000-812838	1966, 1969
812900-819999	1969
820000-820999	1966, 1969
821000-823830	1966
824000-828999	1969

NUMBER	YEAR
829000-829999	1966, 1969
830000-830999	1966, 1967, 1969
831000-837999	1969
840000-847498	1966, 1967, 1969
847499-848999	1966, 1967
849000-849999	1966, 1967, 1968
850000-850999	1966, 1968
851000-858999	1966
859001-891999	1967
892000-892999	1967, 1968
893000-895499	1967
895500-895999	1968
896000-896999	1968, 1969
897000-898999	1967
899000-899999	1968
900000-900999	1966, 1967, 1968
901000-902250	1968
903000-920899	1968
940000-942999	1968
945000-956999	1968
959000-960909	1968
970000-982178	1968

1970-1975: From 1970 to 1975 the method of serializing instruments at Gibson became even more random. All numbers were impressed into the wood and a six-digit number was assigned, though no particular order was given and some instruments had a letter prefix. The orange labels inside hollow bodied instruments were discontinued in 1970 and were replaced by white and orange rectangular labels on the acoustics, and small black, purple, and white rectangular labels were placed on electric models.

In 1970, the words **MADE IN USA** were impressed into the back of instrument headstocks (though a few instruments from the 1950s also had this). The difference between a 1960s and a 1970s Gibson model is the "MADE IN USA" stamp on the back of the headstock.

NUMBER	YEAR
000000's	1973
100000's	1970, 1971, 1972, 1973, 1974
200000's	1972, 1973, 1974, 1975
300000's	1974, 1975
400000's	1974, 1975
500000's	1974, 1975
600000's	1970, 1971, 1972, 1974, 1975
700000's	1970, 1971, 1972
800000's	1970, 1973, 1974, 1975
900000's	1970, 1971, 1972, 1973
6 Digits + A	1970

NUMBER	YEAR
A + 6 Digits	1973, 1974, 1975
B + 6 Digits	1974, 1975
C + 6 Digits	1975
D + 6 Digits	1975
E + 6 Digits	1975
F + 6 Digits	1975

When the Nashville Gibson plant was opened in 1974, it was decided that the bulk of the production of products would be run in the South; the Kalamazoo plant would produce the higher end (fancier) models in the North. Of course, many of the older guitar builders and craftsmen were still in Kalamazoo, and if they weren't ready to change how they built guitars, then they may not have been ready to change how they numbered them! Certain guitar models built in the late 1970s can be used to demonstrate the old-style, six-digit serial numbers. It is estimated that Gibson's Kalamazoo plant continued to use the six-digit serial numbers through 1978 and 1979. So double check the serial numbers on those 1970s L-5s, Super 400s, and Super 5 BJBs!

1975-1977: During the period from 1975 to 1977, Gibson used a transfer that had eight-digit numbers. The first two indicate the year (99=1975, 00=1976 and 06=1977), and the following six digits are in the 100000 to 200000 range. *MADE IN USA* was also included on the transfer and some models had *LIMITED EDITION* also applied. A few bolt-on neck instruments had a date ink stamped on the heel area.

NUMBER	YEAR
99XXXXXX	1975
00XXXXXX	1976
06XXXXXX	1977

1977-Present: In 1977, Gibson first introduced the serialization method that is in practice today. This updated system utilizes an impressed, eight-digit numbering scheme that covers both serializing and dating functions. The Custom/Historic/Art divisions do not use this system. Certain models in the Standard series do not follow this, either. Please refer to the end of the section for exceptions. The pattern is as follows:

YDDDYPPP

YY is the production year

DDD is the day of the year

PPP is the plant designation and/or instrument rank.

In 1994, for Gibson's Centennial, they used a special serialization. Every serial number started with 94 followed by six digits, which were the production dates and number (YYNNNNNN).

The three PPP numbers 001-499 indicate Kalamazoo production from 1977 to 1984. The Kalamazoo numbers were discontinued in 1984 when the factory closed. The three PPP numbers 500-999 indicate Nashville production from 1977 to 1989.

All currently manufactured Gibsons (non-custom shop) are stamped with a hand arbor, and start at 300 or 500, and continue until production is finished that day. This hand stamp used to be reset daily at #300 or #500 for all the LP style headstocks. The other shapes (Flying V, T-Bird, Explorer, etc.) were started at 700.

When acoustic production began at the plant in Bozeman, Montana (in 1989), the series' numbers were reorganized. Bozeman instruments began using 001-299 designations and, in 1990, Nashville instruments began using 300-999 designations. It should also be noted that the Nashville plant did not reach the 900's for many years, so these numbers were reserved for prototypes. In July 2005, Gibson added another number to their serialization system, but this only applies to electric models built in Nashville (they were building more guitars than they had numbers for in a day, so they had to add a batch number, which becomes the sixth digit). This only applies to electrics and acoustics still use the old eight-digit serialization system! Also, to celebrate Gibson's 120th Anniversary (1894-2014), they stamped their Gibson USA electric guitars starting with 14XXXXXXX, similar to the "94" they used on all guitars built in 1994, but note, this does not apply to Gibson acoustics! Examples:

70108276 means the instrument was produced on Jan. 10, 1978, in Kalamazoo and was the 276th instrument stamped that day.

82765501 means the instrument was produced on Oct. 3, 1985, in Nashville and was the 1st instrument stamped that day.

03202652 means the instrument was produced in Bozeman on November 16, 2002 and was the 152nd instrument stamped that day (assuming they started at 500).

There are a few exceptions to this system.

Centennial Year/Models: 1994 is the most notable exception, with the first two numbers representing the year, so all models start with 94 and are followed by six digits. The Centennial models produced for the 1994 model year have an inked-on serial number that is six digits long. The serial number appears as YYYYMM. The first four represent the number produced. They all started on 1894, which represents instrument #1, and 1994 would be instrument #101. The last two digits indicate the month of the guitar released. A new model was released each month with a total of fourteen different models that includes two prototypes. The last two numbers will range from one to fourteen.

Dove's In Flight: Gibson uses a SERIAL number consisting of "DF YNNNY" for their Dove's In Flight model. The last two digits of the year are indicated by the first and fifth digits of the serial number.

Montana Gold: Gibson uses a serial number consisting of "MG

YNNNY" for their Montana Gold model. The last two digits of the year are indicated by the first and fifth digits of the serial number.

Special Runs/Limited Editions: Certain special editions in the 1970s and 1980s may feature serial numbers with six digits in the configuration of YY NNNN. The YY indicates the year and the NNNN is the instrument ranking.

CUSTOM SHOP: Most custom shop models use the configuration of Y9NNN or Y9NNNN (if the production run is higher than 1000 units in a year). The Y indicates the last digit of the year the guitar was built. 9 is assigned to every custom shop guitar, and the last three or four digits are production numbers.

Historic ES models use a slightly different system than the Custom Shop. The configuration consists of a letter prefix + MYNNN. The letter, which is usually an A or B, indicates that it is part of the Historic Collection, the M indicates the last year of reissue model, the Y indicates the last number of the year the guitar was built, and the final NNN digits are production numbers.

Custom Shop Signature Models use a serialization system with the artist's initials and the instrument production number.

Other models such as the Gibson Les Paul Classic may use serialization that was used on the models during that time period. These would be six-digit serial numbers.

*Source: **A.R. Duchossoir,** Gibson Electrics, The Classic Years and **Walter Carter and George Gruhn,** Gruhn's Guide to Vintage Guitars.*

GRETSCH

Before World War II, serial and model number replaced the penciled numbers inside the instruments. By 1949, small labels bearing "Fred Gretsch Mfg. Co.," were used. This label was replaced by a different style label, an orange and grey one, sometime in 1957. A few variations of this scheme occurred throughout the company's history, the most common being the use of impressed numbers in the headstock of instruments, beginning about 1949. Serial numbers were also stamped into the headstock nameplate of a few models. The numbers remain consecutive throughout, and the following chart gives approximations of the years they occurred.

1940-1949: Serial numbers were penciled onto labels on the inside backs of Gretsch's higher-end instruments. The number can usually be viewed from the bass side f-hole. Numbers were assigned consecutively, but little is known about year-to-year specifics.

APPROX. NUMBERS	YEARS
001 - 1000	1939-1945
1001 - 2000	1946-1949

1949-1965: The label changed to read: The "Fred Gretsch Mfg. Co." with the company's address in New York. There are two spots where the model is printed and serial number is written in. The serial number should be in red and the model number written in blue or black. The label could be viewed from the f-hole on hollowbody models. On solidbody models, the number was placed inside the electronic compartment either on the wood or on the control plate. Some models produced in the 1960s may have the number impressed into the back of the headstock.

APPROX. NUMBERS	YEAR
2000 - 3000S	1950
3000 - 5000S	1951
5000 - 6000S	1952
6000 - 8000S	1953
8000 - 12000S	1954
12000 - 16000S	1955
16000 - 21000S	1956
21000- 26000S	1957
26000 - 30000S	1958
30000 - 34000S	1959
34000 - 39000S	1960
39000 - 45000S	1961
45000 - 52000S	1962
52000 - 63000S	1963

APPROX. NUMBERS	YEAR
63000 - 77000S	1964
77000 - 85000S	1965

1965-1972: In the latter part of 1965, Gretsch decided to begin using a date coded system of serialization. It consisted of the first digit (sometimes two) which identified the month; the second or third identifying the year, and the remaining digit (or digits) represented the number of the instruments in production for that month. Some examples of this system would be:

997	September, 1969 (7th instrument produced)
11255	November, 1972 (55th instrument produced)
70250	July, 1968 (250th instrument produced)

On solid body instruments, impressed headstock numbers were used. In 1967, *Made in USA* was added. Hollow body instruments still made use of a label placed on the inside back of the instrument.

1973-1981: In 1973, the label style changed once again, becoming a black and white rectangle with *Gretsch Guitars* and the date coded serialization on it. A hyphen was also added between the month and the year to help avoid confusion.

Serialization Examples:

12-4387	December, 1974 (387th Instrument Produced)
3-745	March, 1977 (45th Instrument Produced)
10-056	October, 1980 (56th Instrument Produced)

1989-2002: Gretsch serialization beginning in 1989 utilized a nine digit format (YYMMmmm(m)xxx). YY indicates the last two digits of the year (i.e., 97 = 1997). M or MM indicates the month of the year (1-12). mmm(m) references the model number with either three or four digits (i.e., a 6136 reads 136). x(xx) refers to a one-to- three-digit production count. Examples: A currently manufactured Country Club Model (Model No. 6196) with ser. no. 01319652 indicates it was built in March of 2001, the last three numbers of the model number are next - 196. 52 indicates the production count. A Model No. 6121 Roundup with a ser. no. of 999121447 indicates it was built in Sept. of 1999, 121 represents the last three digits of the model number, and 447 is the production count.

2003-Present: When Fender bought Gretsch in 2003, they also implemented a new serialization system. This new format follows a two letter and eight digit serialization system (JTYYMMNNNN). The first two letters should be JT indicating the Japan Terada factory, the first two numbers indicate the last two digits of the year (03 indicates 2003), the third and fourth digits indicate the month (08 indicates August), and the final four digits are a general numerical sequence that has no specific model numbering.

GUILD

Guild Serialization went through three distinct phases, and can be both a helpful guide as well as a confusing one when trying to determine the manufacturing date of a guitar. The primary fact to keep in mind is that most Guild models use a **separate serial numbering system for each guitar model** - there is no "overall system" to plug a number into! While serial numbers are sometimes a helpful tool, other dating devices like potentiomter codes or dating by hardware may be more exact.

1952-1965: Between the inception of the Guild company in 1952 and 1965, the serialization was sequential for all models.

APPROXIMATE LAST NUMBER	YEAR
350	1952
840	1953
1526	1954
2468	1955
3830	1956
5712	1957
8348	1958
12035	1959
14713	1960

APPROXIMATE LAST NUMBER	YEAR
18419	1961
22722	1962
28943	1963
38636	1964
46606	1965

1966-1969: While some models retained the serialization from the original series, many models were designated with a two-letter prefix and an independent numbering series for each individual model between 1966 and 1969.

Continued Original Serialization Series

APPROXIMATE LAST NUMBER	YEAR
46608	1966
46637	1967
46656	1968
46695	1969

The models that were numbered with the new two-letter prefix started each separate serial number series with 101.

1970-1979: The following chart details the serial numbers as produced through the 1970s. There are no corresponding model names or numbers for this time period.

APPROXIMATE LAST NUMBER	YEAR
50978	1970
61463	1971
75602	1972
95496	1973
112803	1974
130304	1975
149625	1976
169867	1977
190567	1978
211877	1979

1979-1989: In 1979, Guild returned to the separate prefix/serial number system. Serial numbers after the two-letter prefix in each separate system began with 100001 (thus, you would need a serialization table for each model/by year to date by serialization alone). In 1987, a third system was devised. In some cases, the **Model Designation** became the *prefix* for the serial number. For example:

D300041   D-30, #0041 (41st D-30 instrument produced)

With acoustic models, you can cross-reference the model name to the serial number to judge the rest of the serialization; the resulting serial number must still be checked in the serialization table.

1990-2004: Between 1990 and 2004, Guild continued with the separate prefix/serialization system. In 1994, only the model prefix and last serial numbers for each model were recorded; better records continued in 1995.

Guild Custom Shop: The three Guild Custom Shop models (**45th Anniversary, Deco**, and **Finesse**) all used a completely different serial numbering system. Each instrument has a serial number on the back of the headstock that indicates which number it is out of the complete series. Inside the guitar there is a seven-digit code: The first three numbers (starting with 500) indicate the production sequence, while the last four digits indicate the date of production (the fourth and seventh digit in reverse indicate the year, the fifth and sixth digits are the month).

Guild has a series of charts available on their website (www.guildguitars.com) to help date a Guild model during its different manufacturing periods. It is recommended that you refer to this information, as there are many charts needed for the individual model serialization.

Through the years (and different owners of the company), some of the historical documentation has been lost or destroyed. However, these tables are some of the most comprehensive available to the public. They are up to date through December 1997.

2005-Present: In 2005, Fender bought the Tacoma company and moved all Guild acoustic production to their facility in Washington. They also implemented a new serialization system that follows Tacoma's system. This serialization system follows a two letter and six digit format (TYDDDNNN). When Guild production moved to New Hartford, CT in late 2008, they kept using the same serialization system. The first letter is either a T or an N, which inidicates the guitar was built in either the Tacoma (T) or New Hartford (N) factory. The second letter indicates the year and this is based on Tacoma's system that was started in 1998.

LETTER	YEAR
I	2005
J	2006
K	2007
L	2008
M	2009
N	2010
O	2011
P	2012
Q	2013
R	2014

The first three digits indicate the day of the year based on the Julian calendar, and the final three digits are the production number on that day. Example: TJ 289 015 indicates a guitar built at the Tacoma factory on the 289th day (October 16th) in 2006 and was the 15th guitar produced that day.

Serialization reference source: Hans Moust, The Guild Guitar Book; and Jay Pilzer, Guild Authority; additional company information courtesy Bill Acton, Guild Guitars

IBANEZ

Ibanez offers a wide selection of models with a corresponding wide range of features. This means there are a lot of models and, of course, a lot of different model numbers to try and keep track of. Ibanez serial numbers never indicated the model number, and still don't. Most solid body Ibanez guitars and basses didn't feature model numbers until recently, and even then, only on Korean-made instruments. On some semi-hollow models, some model numbers will appear on the label visible through the f-hole.

Here's how the Ibanez model numbers work (of course, there are always exceptions - but for the Ibanez models commonly encountered, this system applies pretty consistently).

SERIES: the first in the model number designate the series: RG550BK, RG Series; SR800BK is a Soundgear, etc. Also, in the Artstar lines, AS indicates (A)rtstar (S)emihollow, AF indicates (A)rtstar (F)ull hollow.

FINISH: the last two letters designate the finish: RG550BK, Black finish; RX240CA, Candy Apple. **Exceptions**: finishes such as Amber Pearl and Stained Oil Finish use three letters: AMP, SOL, etc. (having offered so many finishes, Ibanez is running out of traditional two letter combinations!).

The numbers following the Series letters indicate two items:

1. Point of Manufacture

On solid body guitars and basses, the numbers 500 and above indicate Japanese manufacture: RG550BK, SR800BK, BL850VB, the numbers 400 and below indicate Korean manufacture: SR400BK, RX240MG, etc.

This system doesn't apply to hollow bodies, and many signature guitars. J of White Zombie's signature model, the IJ100WZ is made in Japan, as is the JPM100.

2. Pickup Configuration

On solid body guitars only, the last two numbers indicate pickup configuration:

20= two humbucking pickups with or w/o pickguard (ex: TC420MD)
30 = three single coils with or w/o pickguard (no current models)

40 = sin/sin/hum with a pickguard (ex: TC740MN)
50 = hum/sin/hum with a pickguard (ex: RG550BK)
60 = sin/sin/hum with no pickguard (no current models)
70 = hum/sin/hum with no pickguard (ex: RG570FBL)

Exceptions: Of course! For example, TC825 (which has two humbuckers and a pickguard) and BL1025 (hum/sin/hum with a pickguard), etc.

Author/researcher Michael Wright successfully discussed the Ibanez/Hoshino history in his book, *Guitar Stories,* Volume One (Vintage Guitar Books, 1995). Early serial numbers and foreign-built potentiometer codes on Japanese guitars aren't much help in the way of clues, but Ibanez did institute a meaningful numbering system as part of their warranty program in 1975.

1975-1987: In general, Ibanez serial numbers between 1975 and 1987 had seven digits, arranged **XYYZZZZ**. The letter prefix "X" stands for the month (January = A, February = B, etc. on to L); the next following two digits (YY) are the year. The last four digits indicate the number of instruments built per month through a particular production date.

An outside source indicated that the month/letter code prefix was discontinued in 1988, and the previous dating code was discontinued in 1990. However, in 1987 the **XYYZZZZ** still appeared the same, but the new listing shifted to **XYZZZZZ**.

1987-1997: The opening alphabetical prefix "X" now indicates production **location** instead of month: **F** (Fuji, Japan), or **C** (Cort, Korea). The first digit "Y" indicates the year: As in 198**Y** and 199**Y**. Bright-eyed serialization students will have already noticed that while the year is obtainable, the decade isn't! Because of this, it is good to have a working knowledge of which models were available in approximately which time periods. All following numbers again are the production ranking code (**ZZZZZ**).

1997-Present: In mid-1997, Ibanez changed the format, and the second two digits after the alphabetical prefix indicate the last two digits of the actual year of production (i.e, F0003680 indicates a guitar built in Fuji during 2000).

CE Designation: In late 1996, in addition to the serial number on the back of the headstock, Ibanez electric guitars and basses added the "CE" designation. This indicated that the product met the electronic standards of the European Common Market, similar to our UL approval.

For more information on individual Ibanez guitar models, refer to *Ibanez - The Untold Story*, by Paul Specht, Michael Wright, Jim Donahue, and Pat Lefferts. This book features all of the history about Ibanez and features individual model listings. It may be easier to date the guitar from the production time that it was produced.

Source: Michael Wright, Guitar Stories, Volume One, Jim Donahue, Ibanez Guitars.

MARTIN

The serial numbers listed do not include the Backpacker or Little Martin models.

YEAR	LAST NUMBER
1898	8348
1899	8716
1900	9128
1901	9310
1902	9528
1903	9810
1904	9988
1905	10120
1906	10329
1907	10727
1908	10883
1909	11018
1910	11203
1911	11413
1912	11565
1913	11821
1914	12047
1915	12209

YEAR	LAST NUMBER
1916	12390
1917	12988
1918	13450
1919	14512
1920	15848
1921	16758
1922	17839
1923	19891
1924	22008
1925	24116
1926	28689
1927	34435
1928	37568
1929	40843
1930	45317
1931	49589
1932	52590
1933	55084
1934	58679
1935	61947
1936	65176
1937	68865
1938	71866
1939	74061
1940	76734
1941	80013
1942	83107
1943	86724
1944	90149
1945	93623
1946	98158
1947	103468
1948	108269
1949	112961
1950	117961
1951	122799
1952	128436
1953	134501
1954	141345
1955	147328
1956	152775
1957	159061
1958	165576
1959	171047
1960	175689
1961	181297
1962	187384
1963	193327
1964	199626
1965	207030
1966	217215
1967	230095
1968	241925
1969	256003
1970	271633
1971	294270
1972	313302
1973	333873
1974	353387
1975	371828
1976	388800
1977	399625
1978	407800
1979	419900
1980	430300
1981	436474

YEAR	LAST NUMBER
1982	439627
1983	446101
1984	453300
1985	460575
1986	468175
1987	476216
1988	483952
1989	493279
1990	503309
1991	512487
1992	522655
1993	535223
1994	551696
1995	570434
1996	592930
1997	624799
1998	668796
1999	724077
2000	780500
2001	845644
2002	916759
2003	978706
2004	1042558
2005	1115862
2006	1197799
2007	1268091
2008	1337042
2009	1406715
2010	1473461
2011	1555767
2012	1656742
2013	1755536

Source: Lon Werner, The Martin Guitar Company.

MOONSTONE

The most important factor in determining the year of manufacture for Moonstone instruments is that each model had its own set of serial numbers. There is no grouping of models by year of manufacture.

D-81 Eagle

L001-L004	1981
L005-L011	1982
4809-4816	1981
4017-4031	1981
4032-4052	1982
4053-4064	1983

Moondolins

T001-T002	1981
T003-T006	1983
T007	1984

OVATION

Three-digit numbers (no letter prefix):

NUMBER	YEAR
006-319	1966
320-999	1967 (February - November)

Four-digit numbers (no letter prefix):

1000-	1967 (November) to 1968 (July)

Five-digit numbers (no letter prefix):

10000-	1970 (February) to 1972 (May)

Six-digit numbers (1971 to present, except Adamas models):

000001-007000	1972 (May - December)
007001-020000	1973
020001-039000	1974

NUMBER	YEAR
039001-067000	1975
067001-086000	1976
086001-103000	1977 (January - September)
103001-126000	1977 (September) to 1978 (April)
126001-157000	1978 (April - December)
157001-203000	1979
211011-214933	1980
214934-263633	1981
263634-291456	1982
291457-302669	1983
302670-303319	1984 [Elite models only]
315001-331879	1984 (May - December) [Balladeer models only]
303320-356000	1985 to 1986
357000-367999	1987
368000-382106	1988
382107-392900	1989
403760-420400	1990
421000-430680	1991
402700-406000	1992
446001-457810	1992
457811-470769	1993
470770-484400	1994
484401-501470	1995
501471-518689	1996
518690-528368	1997
528369-536826	1998
536827-545890	1999
545891-555979	2000
555980-564478	2001
564479-571883	2002
571884-579654	2003
579655- 592919	2004
592920-601450	2005
601451-609566	2006
609567-618494	2007
618495-620263	2008
620264-621209	2009
621210-621981	2010
621982-622147	2011
622148-622419	2012
622420-622539	2013
622540-	2014

Adamas Models Serialization:

Serialization for the Adamas models begins with number 0077 on September, 1977.

NUMBER	YEAR
0077-0099	1977
0100-0608	1978
0609-1058	1979
1059-1670	1980
1671-2668	1981
2669-3242	1982
3243-3859	1983
3860-4109	1984
4110-4251	1985
4252-4283	1986
4284-4427	1987
4428-4696	1988
4697-4974	1989

NUMBER	YEAR
4975-5541	1990
5542-6278	1991
6279-7088	1992
7089-8159	1993
8160-9778	1994
9779-11213	1995
11214-12448	1996
12449-13020	1997
13021-14623	1998
14624-16136	1999
16137-17393	2000
17394-18961	2001
18962-20040	2002
20041-20802	2003
20803-21085	2004
21086-21514	2005
21515-22211	2006
22212-22522	2007
22523-22878	2008
22879-23155	2009
23156-23402	2010
23403-23591	2011
23592-23763	2012
23764-23845	2013
23845-	2014

Letter Prefix plus digits:

A + 3 digits	1968 (July - November)
B + 3 digits	1968 (November) to 1969 (February)
B + 5 digits	1974 to 1979 [Magnum solid bodybasses]
C + 3 digits	1969 (February - September)
D + 3 digits	1969 (September) to 1970 (February)
E + 4 digits	1973 (January) to 1975 (February) [solid bodies]
E + 5 digits	1975 (February) to 1980 [solid bodies]
E + 6 digits	1980 (late) to 1981 [UK II guitars]
F Prefix	1968 (July) to 1970 (February)
G Prefix	1968 (July) to 1970 (February)
H Prefix	1970 to 1973 [Electric Storm series]
I Prefix	1970 to 1973 [Electric Storm series]
J Prefix	1970 to 1973 [Electric Storm series]
L Prefix	1970 to 1973 [Electric Storm series]

*Source: Walter Carter, **The History of the Ovation Guitar.** Information collected in Mr. Carter's Ovation Appendices was researched and compiled by Paul Bechtoldt.*

PAUL REED SMITH (PRS)

Paul Reed Smith began building their acoustic series in 2009. All acoustic guitars have serial numbers that begin with "A" followed by a two-digit year prefix:

Prefix/Number	Year
A09	2009
A10	2010
A11	2011

The remaining numbers are the production number for that year beginning with 0001.

NUMBER	YEAR
0001-0190	2009
0191-0517	2010
0518-	2011

PEAVEY

While more musicians may be aware of Peavey through the numerous high quality amplifiers and P.A. systems they build, the company has been producing solidbody guitars and basses since 1978. Peavey serial numbers exist more for the company's warranty program than an actual dating system. According to researcher Michael Wright, the earliest serial numbers had six digits; by 1978, the company switched to eight digits. Peavey can supply the shipping date (which is within a few weeks of actual production) for the more inquisitive.

Replacement manuals are generally available for Peavey products. For further information, contact Peavey Electronics.

*Information courtesy Michael Wright, **Guitar Stories, Volume One.***

RICKENBACKER

Rickenbacker offered a number of guitar models as well as lap steels prior to World War II, such as the **Ken Roberts Spanish** electric f-hole flattop (mid-1930s to 1940) and the **559** model archtop in the early 1940s. The company put production on hold during the war; in 1946, they began producing an **Electric Spanish** archtop. Serialization on early Rickenbacker models from 1931 to 1953 is unreliable, but models may be dated by patent information. This method should be used in conjunction with comparisons of parts, and design changes.

In 1953, Rickenbacker/Electro was purchased by Francis C. Hall. The **Combo 600** and **Combo 800** models debuted in 1954. From 1954 on, the serial number appears on the bridge or jackplate of the instrument. The Rickenbacker serial numbers during the 1950s have four to seven digits. The letter within the code indicates the type of instrument (Combo/guitar, bass, mandolin, etc), and the number after the letter indicates the year of production:

Example: X(X)B7XX (A bass from 1957)

1961-1986: In 1961, the serialization scheme changes. The new code has two-letter prefixes, followed by digits. The first letter prefix indicates the year; the second letter indicates the month of production.

PREFIX	YEAR
A	1961
B	1962
C	1963
D	1964
E	1965
F	1966
G	1967
H	1968
I	1969
J	1970
K	1971
L	1972
M	1973
N	1974
O	1975
P	1976
Q	1977
R	1978
S	1979
T	1980
U	1981
V	1982
W	1983
X	1984
Y	1985
Z	1986

PREFIX	MONTH
A	January
B	February
C	March
D	April
E	May

PREFIX	MONTH
F	June
G	July
H	August
I	September
J	October
K	November
L	December

1987-1998: In 1987, the serialization was revised, again. The updated serial number code has letter prefix (A to L) that still indicates month; the following digit that indicates the year. It is unknown what was used for 1997 and 1998.

DIGIT	YEAR
0	1987
1	1988
2	1989
3	1990
4	1991
5	1992
6	1993
7	1994
8	1995
9	1996

The following digits after the month/year digits are production (for example, *L2XXXX* would be an instrument built in December, 1989).

1999-2006: The numbering/lettering system was replaced by two digits that indicate the last two numbers of the year (99=1999, 02=2002). Rickenbacker has a serial number decoder on their website, and readers are encouraged to use this for more specific identification.

STROMBERG

This Boston-based instrument shop was founded by Charles Stromberg, a Swedish immigrant, in 1906. Stromberg generally concentrated on banjo and drum building, leaving the guitar lutherie to his son Elmer. Elmer joined the family business in 1910, and began building guitars in the late 1920s.

Total production of guitars reached about 640. The labels on the guitars were business cards, so the instruments can be dated (roughly) by the telephone number on the cards.

In the late 1930s, the Blue shipping labels inside the guitar body were either typed or handwritten

LABEL	YEAR
Bowdoin 1228R-1728-M	1920-1927
Bowdoin 1242 W	1927-1929
Bowdoin 1878 R	1929-1932
CA 3174	1932-1945
CA 7-3174	1949-1955

Source: Jim Speros, Stromberg research.

TACOMA

Tacoma first built guitars in 1996 and the serialization system for that year only was a four digit number. By 1997, the four digit system was phased out and a new six-digit system was introduced the followed the format of 97XXXX. 97 indicates 1997 and the last four digits are production numbering. In 1998, Tacoma introduced the serialization system that is still in use today that follows the format of **Y DDD NNN N**. The first letter corresponds to the year the guitar was built. The first three digits indicate the day of the year based on the Julian calendar. The fourth digit will be either a 0 indicating a traditional soundhole or a 5 indicating a wing soundhole. The fifth and sixth digits are the production number of the guitar on that day. The seventh and final digit indicates if the guitar was a factory second. Almost all guitars will have a 0, which means the guitar was of regular production,

first quality. If the guitar was returned to the factory for neck replacement or some other fix, this digit will be a 5. Examples: B 290 011 0 indicates a guitar built on the 290th day (October 17th) in 1998, that it has a traditional soundhole, was the 11th guitar built on that day, and was a regular production instrument. G 213 506 5 indicates a guitar built on the 213th day (June 1st) in 2003, that it has a wing soundhole, was the 6th guitar built on that day, and was a returned to the factory for repair. This chart shows the letter to year correspondence.

LETTER	YEAR
B	1998
C	1999
D	2000
E	2001
F	2002
G	2003
H	2004
I	2005
J	2006
K	2007
L	2008

TAKAMINE

The eight digit serial number on Takamine instruments can be deciphered by breaking down the number into four groups of two digits, thus:

YYMMDDXX = (YY)(MM)(DD)(XX)

The first two digits (YY) indicate the year; the next two digits (MM) indicate the month; the third group of digits (DD) indicates the day of production; and the remaining two digits indicates the ranking in the number of instruments produced that day. If a nine-digit serial number is encountered, assume that the last three digits indicate the production ranking.

Example: 91060979 indicates an instrument manufactured June 9th of 1991, and was the 79th instuments manufactured that day.

TAYLOR

1974-1992: Taylor did not introduce serialization until 1975 and used the first two numbers as the year (10 was 1975, 20 was 1976, and 30 was 1977) and the next three numbers were production numbers. In 1977 they started with a new system that was strictly numeric and ran until 1992.

NUMBER	YEAR
10109-10146	1975
20147-20315	1976
30316 & up 001-450	1977
451-900	1978
901-1300	1979
1301-1400	1980
1401-1670	1981
1671-1951	1982
1952-2445	1983
2446-3206	1984
3207-3888	1985
3889-4778	1986
4779-5981	1987
5982-7831	1988
7832-10070	1989
10071-12497	1990
12498-15249	1991
15250-17947	1992

1993-2009: In 1993, they started a serialization system that can pinpoint when the guitar was made down to the day and month. Between 1993 and 1999 they used a nine-digit number system. The first two digits indicate the year. The next two are the month. The third two indicate the exact day production was started on the guitar, the seventh digit is either a 1 or 0 and 300 and 400 series instruments get the 0 and 500 or higher recieve the 1 designation. The final two digits indicate the production number that day. In 2000, they expanded to an 11-digit system where the only difference is there is now a four-digit year to accomodate to Y2K worries. For example: serial number 980626109 indicates a 500 series or higher guitar built (started) on June 26, 1998 and was the ninth instrument of the day. Another example of the 11-digit system would be 20010402012, indicating a 300 or 400 series built on April 2, 2001 and was the 12th instrument produced that day.

2009-Present: On November 2, 2009, Taylor introduced a new serialization system that was part of a transition to a new inventory software system. This new system is 10-digits and also indicates what factory the guitar was produced at. The first digit indicates the factory (1= El Cajon, 2 = Tecate), the second and seventh digits indicate the last two years of the date, the third and fourth digits indicate the month, the fifth and six digits indicate the day, and the remaining three digits indicate the production for that date. For example, the number 1011029001 indicates a Taylor guitar built at their El Cajon factory (1), it was produced November (11) 2 (02), 2009 (0, 9), and was the first guitar produced that day.

Source: www.taylorguitars.com.

THREET GUITARS

The serial number on Threet acoustic guitars consists of a letter followed by three (sometimes four) numbers. The letter indicates the model:

A	Parlor-size (similar to a traditional Model O)
B	A "large person's" parlor-size (similar to a Model OO)
C	Larger, balanced sound parlor-size (similar to a Model OOO)
D	Cross between a Model C and a dreadrought

The first two numbers indicate the year the guitar was started (and, hopefully, completed). The third (and occasionally fourth) number indicate the guitar's "rank" in that year's production. For example:

C 964 =   Model C built in 1996 4th Guitar Produced

Keep in mind, Threet guitars are offered in both *Standard* and *Deluxe* versions. Review the appointments to determine the level of construction, and watch for *Custom* level inlays as well.

Source: Judy Threet, Threet Guitars.

WASHBURN

The Washburn trademark was introduced by the Lyon & Healy company of Chicago, Illinois in 1864. While this trademark has changed hands a number of times, the historical records have not! Washburn suffered a fire in the 1920s that destoyed all records and paperwork that was on file; in the 1950s, another fire destroyed the accumulated files yet again.

When the trademark was revived yet again in 1964, the first production of Washburn acoustic guitars was in Japan. Washburn electric guitars debuted in 1979, and featured U.S. designs and Japanese production.

Production of Washburn guitars changed to Korea in the mid- to late 1980s; a number of U.S.-produced **Chicago Series** models were introduced in the late 1980s as well. Serial numbers from 1988 on use the first two digits of the instrument's serial number to indicate the year the instrument was produced (19**88** = **88**XXX). This process works for most, but not all, of the instruments since then.

Washburn Limited Editions feature the year in the model name. For example, **D-95 LTD** is a Limited Edition introduced in 1995. No corresponding serialization information is available at this time.

Washburn information courtesy Dr. Duck's AxWax.

YAMAHA

Yamaha instruments were originally produced in Japan; production switched to Taiwan in the early 1980s. Instruments are currently produced in the U.S., Taiwan, and Indonesia. It is important to recognize that Yamaha uses two different serialization systems.

Yamaha electric guitars and basses have a letter/number (two letters followed by five numbers) code that indicates production date. The first two letters of the serial number indicate the year and month of production (the first letter indicates the year, the second letter indicates the month). Yamaha's coding system substitutes a letter for a number indicating year and month, thus:

CODE LETTER	MONTH or YEAR NUMBER
H	1
I	2
J	3
K	4
L	5
M	6
N	7
O	8
P	9
X	10
Y	11
Z	12

For example, an "H" in the first of two letters would be a "1," indicating the last digit of the year (1981 or 1991). An "H" in the second of two letters would also be a "1," indicating the first month (January). Like Hamer, the digits will cycle around every ten years.

After the two-letter prefixes, five digits follow. The first two digits represent the day of the month, and the three digits indicate the production ranking for that day. For example:

NZ19218   December 19, 1987 (or 1997); #218.

The example's code should be properly broken down as N - Z - 27 - 19 - 218. The "N" in the first of the two letters would be a "7," indicating the last digit of the year (1987 or 1997). The "Z" in the second of the two letters would be a "12," indicating the twelfth month (December). The two-digit pair after the letters is the day of the month, the 19th. The final three digits indicate production ranking, therefore this imaginary guitar is the 218th instrument built that day.

Yamaha Acoustics and Acoustic Electrics contain eight-digit serial numbers. In this coding scheme, the first digit represents the last digit of the year (for example, 1987 = 7); the second and third numbers indicate the month (numbers 01 through 12); the fourth and fifth numbers will indicate the day of the month, and the final three digits will indicate the production ranking of the instrument.

This system works for most (but not all) Yamaha products. If a serial number doesn't fit the coding system, Yamaha offers internal research via their website (www.yamahaguitars.com) - just email them your request.

INDEX

A

B

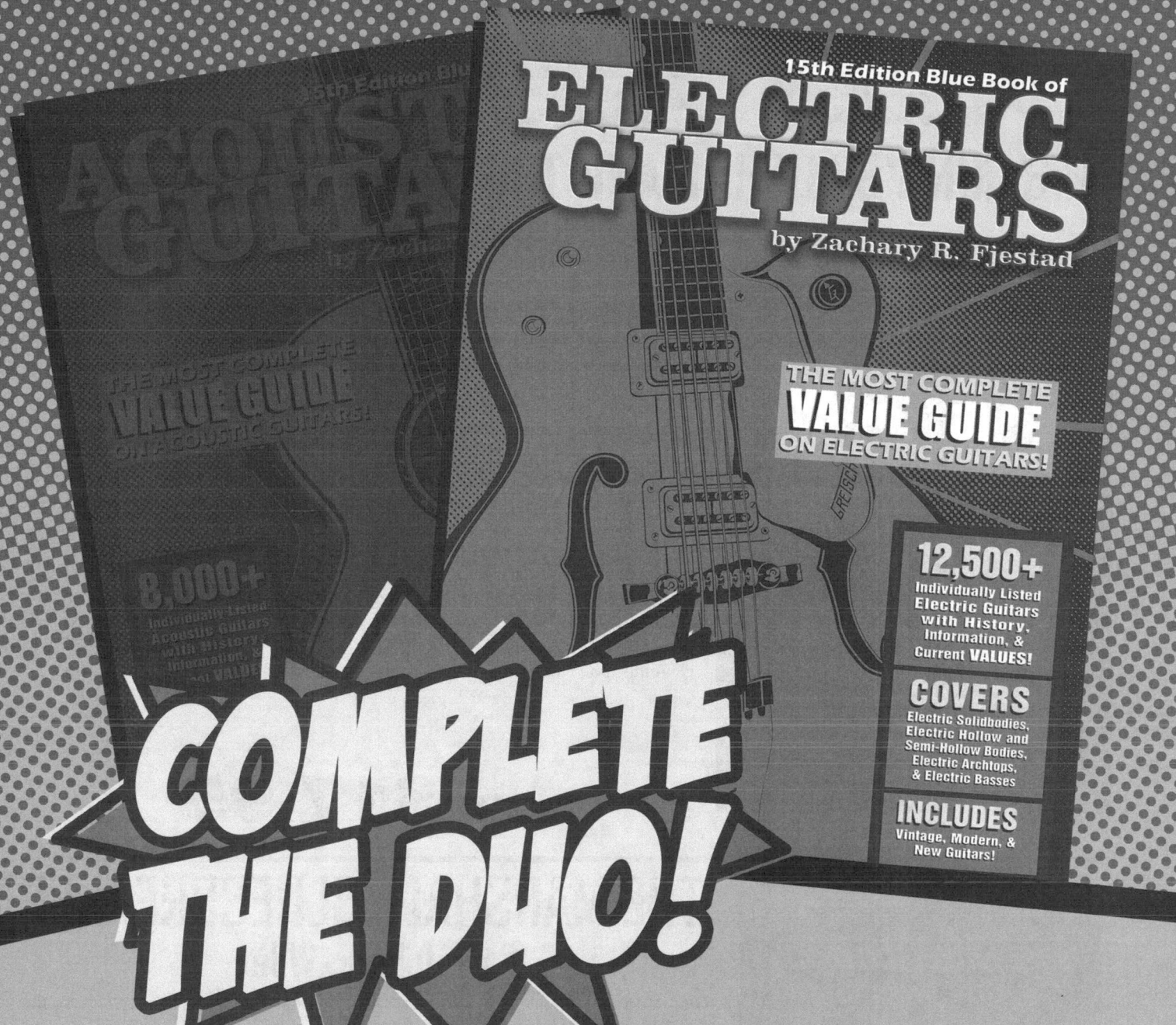

ALSO AVAILABLE!

B.B. KING'S LUCILLE AND THE LOVES BEFORE HER
by Eric E. Dahl

B.B. King is well known as the "King of the Blues," and his beloved Gibson guitar Lucille is his choice instrument for letting the blues come out! *B.B. King's Lucille and the Loves Before Her* explores all the guitars, amplifiers, and other gear the blues legend has used since he began playing in the 1930s, including the behind-the-scenes stories and people along with it.

- Interviews with King's vice president of bookings, rhythm guitarist, and drummer for an inside look at King's gear

- An eight-page color section with detailed pictures of King's guitars and concert images

- Foreword written by B.B. King, and an introduction written by Rick Vito

- Eric Dahl's fascinating story of returning King's stolen guitar

- Complete specifications, serialization, and current values of King's signature models

Don't miss your chance to own the exciting story of King's musical gear over the years and the stories behind the gear. Order today!

MSRP $17.95

THE MARSHALL BLUESBREAKER
by John R. Wiley

For the first time, the complete story of Marshall's first ever combo amplifier, nicknamed the Bluesbreaker, is told here in *The Marshall Bluesbreaker – The Story of Marshall's First Combo.* Highlights include:

- The entire history of the Bluesbreaker including the development of the JTM45 and how Eric Clapton requested the first Marshall combo amplifier

- A complete listing of all the Bluesbreaker components

- A guide section listing year-by-year specifications and changes to the Bluesbreaker including reissues and limited editions

- Listings and specifications on modern builders who offer replica and clone amplifiers based on the Bluesbreaker and Mini Bluesbreaker designs

- A 16-page color section featuring original and reissue Bluesbreakers, Mini Bluesbreakers, and Bluesbreaker components

- A step-by-step guide on converting a stock Marshall Bluesbreaker Reissue into a Clapton-spec Bluesbreaker

- A foreword written by the founder himself, the late Jim Marshall

MSRP $29.95

From the beginning of Marshall amplifiers in the early 1960s to the reissues currently produced today, the story of the Bluesbreaker is told in its entirety for the first time!

In Memorial: Jack Wadsworth Jr., 1949-2013

Part of the Texas Blue Book Crew, Jack never missed a guitar show that Blue Book Publications attended. Jack's love of guitars and music was clearly evident – here he is seen playing a D'Angelico and a Michael Stevens LJ Model.

As Billy Joel sang on his 1977 album, "Only the good die young" could not apply more to Jack Wadsworth - a good friend we lost in December to kidney failure. Blue Book Publications' publisher S.P. Fjestad and I recently made the trip to Fort Worth, Texas to pay our respects. It was unfortunate that it took the death of a good friend to take a non-work related trip to north Texas.

For those of you familiar with the *Blue Book of Guitar Values*, Jack Wadsworth was a fixture at the Blue Book booth during every Dallas Guitar Show and Arlington Guitar Show since the late 1990s. He became what I called a Blue Book ambassador - a title very few people were privileged to possess. Jack was always bringing in pieces of his personal collection for us to photograph when he knew it was missing from the database. Jack was so dedicated to Blue Book that he even worked the one-and-done Texas Guitar and Gun Show where the mythical Chupacabra stole the show!

Jack was one of the nicest guys I ever knew. He never asked for any compensation for helping us at shows. He'd even be at the booth first thing Sunday morning when the rest of us were, er, still recovering from the night before. He'd give S.P. rides to the airport after the show was done in his big Lincoln town car. For many years, art director Clint Schmidt and I would drive the redeye on Interstate 35 back to Minneapolis and he'd always email or call us to make sure we had made it back safe. Jack was a man who truly cared about other people.

When Jill (my wife) and I were preparing for our wedding in 2007, we extended invitations to our "Texas Crew" mainly as a nice gesture. I'd gotten to know Jack, Rick, and Chris quite well over the years and felt like they should be included on our invitation list. I certainly didn't expect anyone to make the trip all the way to Minnesota though. Low and behold, we received Jack and his wife Bobbie's RSVP in the mail and received an email shortly thereafter asking for recommendations on where to say. Sure enough, they flew into Minneapolis, rented a car, and drove the 200 miles to Fergus Falls for our wedding. I certainly can't think of anyone who came farther to watch us take the nuptials.

Jack was a musician and regularly used his large collection of guitars on a regular basis. Clint and I began going to his shows when we were in the Dallas/Fort Worth area and quickly realized how talented he really was. Not only could he play bass, guitar, and sing, but he also busted out his rapping chops with Funky Cold Medina! We celebrated his 60th birthday as he and his band played at a cowboy bar. His entire family was there and we got to spend some time with them. Little did we know that he'd only have four more years on this planet.

Sixty-four is much too young to die, but when it's your time to go, you don't have much choice. A number of ailments plagued Jack, but it all seemed to start with his kidneys. Once he went to the hospital, he never really left. He had good days along with his bad days, but from what I heard during the eulogy, he still had his sense of humor while in a hospital bed. I'm going to miss you, Jack, but at least I got to come see you one last time in Texas. ∎

Zachary R. Fjestad,
Author, *Blue Book of Acoustic Guitars* & *Blue Book of Electric Guitars*